THE ALEXANDER TEXT
OF
WILLIAM SHAKESPEARE
THE COMPLETE WORKS

WILLIAM SHAKESPEARE

THE COMPLETE WORKS

A new edition, edited with an
introduction and glossary by
PETER ALEXANDER
*Late Professor Emeritus of English Language
and Literature, University of Glasgow*

COLLINS
LONDON AND GLASGOW

FIRST PUBLISHED 1951
REPRINTED 1953, 1954, 1956, 1957,
1959, 1960, 1962, 1963, 1964 (twice),
1965, 1966, 1968, 1970, 1971, 1974, 1975,
1978, 1979, 1980, 1983, 1985

Hardback Edition ISBN 0 00 410502 8
Paperback Edition ISBN 0 00 435642 10
Leather Edition ISBN 0 00 435643 8

PRINTED IN GREAT BRITAIN
COLLINS CLEAR-TYPE PRESS: LONDON AND GLASGOW

ACKNOWLEDGMENTS

' All trustworthy restoration of corrupted texts is founded on a study of their history.' This principle, long established in the recension of classical and biblical texts, is implicit in the work of Shakespeare's earlier editors, but its full implications were first made completely explicit in the criticism of A. W. Pollard, R. B. McKerrow and Sir Walter Greg. Their study of Elizabethan books and theatrical documents in the light of collateral evidence hitherto neglected or misinterpreted enabled them to redraw on more probable and intelligible lines the history of the versions in which Shakespeare's work has been transmitted to us. The gap the earlier editors left between Shakespeare and his text, they closed : minutiae—such as the original punctuation—once considered negligible, they have made relevant for the interpretation of the text.

This development in critical method has prompted the present revision of the text of Shakespeare that Messrs. Collins first published nearly ninety years ago. That edition was based on the work of the earlier editors, and their contribution to the elucidation of the text is naturally still invaluable. The lines are now numbered as in the great Cambridge edition of Clark and Wright. They were the first editors to provide so simple but necessary a means of reference; and by this and their authoritative survey of all previous editions, digested in a compendious textual apparatus, they greatly facilitated subsequent work on the text. It is unfortunate that the standard concordance follows the line-numbering of their Globe edition, for there the references no longer always correspond with that of the apparatus, so indispensable to all students of the text, of their major edition.

The range of detail that now confronts a general editor is so extensive that he is necessarily indebted not merely to previous editors but more and more to scholars who have made an intensive study of some aspect or portion of the text. Of the many special contributions that I have found most helpful I must name Dr. Greg's *The Variants in the First Quarto of ' King Lear '*, and its sequel, Professor G. I. Duthie's ' oldspelling ' edition of the play; Professor David Patrick's *The Textual History of ' Richard III '*, a study of a text that shares a peculiar history with *Lear*; Professor J. Dover Wilson's *The Manuscript of ' Hamlet '*, and its sequel, the critical study of the play by Professor Thomas Parrott and Professor Hardin Craig, an edition admirably adapted *editorum in usum*. In the interpretation of the punctuation of the early texts—for to reproduce this punctuation would merely confuse and mislead the general reader—I am indebted to Dr. Percy Simpson's *Shakespearian Punctuation* and to the studies of the late Alfred Thiselton. To the glossaries of Dr. C. J. Onions and R. J. Cunliffe I am conscious of owing much; and I have found helpful matter in the work of Professor M. A. Shaaber and Dr. Richard Flatter.

The complete editions I have consulted with advantage include those by Mr. M. R. Ridley and G. L. Kittredge and that by W. A. Neilson and

ACKNOWLEDGMENTS

Professor C. J. Hill. Lastly I must mention the edition still in progress edited by Professor J. Dover Wilson, although my debt to him is not the least I have to acknowledge; for whenever I have ventured to disagree with him on general principles or their particular application, I have not spared myself the expense of second thoughts.

My personal thanks are due to Mr. George F. Maine, 'the onlie begetter' of this revision, for his constant encouragement and assistance; to Mr. James C. Harrison and the caseroom staff for their courtesy and patience in spite of my many requests; to Mrs. Hilda Bone for all her care and pains in the task; and to Sir Walter Greg and the Syndics of the Cambridge University Press for their generous permission to reproduce the special transcript of Shakespeare's contribution to *Sir Thomas More*.

P. A.

CONTENTS

CONTENTS

INTRODUCTION*

IT is still true in the study of Shakespeare that 'the dispersion of error is the first step in the discovery of truth'. The scholarly criticism of his plays, which found but casual expression in his lifetime and took systematic shape only in the eighteenth century when men of letters and scholars found the editing of his works a source of profit or reputation, began by remarking that he ignored the Rules. These rules or laws of the drama were generalizations from the practice of the Greek dramatists ; and Renaissance critics and their eighteenth century disciples regarded plays that failed to conform to these Laws as deficient in Art. Shakespeare ignored the Rules so constantly that his critics, however much they admired his natural powers, could not accept him as a great Artist. This opinion is still maintained to-day by men of distinction in letters ; but it is an opinion born of a fashion in European thought that has passed away, and it survives only as a prejudice that will no longer bear critical examination.

It is now realised that this demand for the scholarly imitation of the external or accidental features of classical masterpieces is an appeal to the letter not to the spirit of Art. No one to-day will argue that Westminster Abbey is inferior as a work of art to St. Paul's because the Gothic builders were not so familiar as Wren with 'the four regular orders of Greece'. Indeed, the complete revolution wrought by the progress of European criticism is best seen in the attitude of the French, who were the most jealous guardians of what they considered 'classical' form. The French were in this phase of their culture as severe in their

*To spare the reader a succession of footnotes, I mention here some of the studies I should otherwise have to refer him to in passing. J. S. Smart's *Shakespeare: Truth and Tradition*, 'a new landmark in Shakespeare scholarship' is the best introduction to a study of *A Life of Shakespeare* by J. Quincy Adams ; the student will then be in a position to profit by *Shakespeare: A Study of Facts and Problems* by Sir Edmund Chambers. The best idea of the structure of Shakespeare's theatre is given by *The Globe Playhouse* by John C. Adams, of Shakespeare's Audience by Alfred Harbage's *Shakespeare's Audience*. On dramatic questions Granville-Barker's *Prefaces* are most helpful. Bradley's *Shakespearean Tragedy* is still an important guide in interpretation, and those who fancy that recent 'historical or objective' criticism has outmoded his method should read Alfred Harbage's *As They Liked It*. Dr. Tillyard's *Shakespeare's History Plays* is a valuable study of Shakespeare's attitude to his material and of the implications it suggests ; and in Dr. Ivor Brown's *Shakespeare* can be seen the reactions to academic opinion of one familiar with the modern theatre. All Dr. Hotson's works have added valuable touches to the social background of Shakespeare's life and his *Shakespeare's Sonnets Dated* makes further apology for the dates here suggested for Shakespeare's 'First Period' unnecessary. Pollard's *Shakespeare's Fight with the Pirates* is the ideal preparation for Sir Walter Greg's *The Editorial Problem in Shakespeare*, an authoritative review that will enable the reader to study with advantage Professor Dover Wilson's *Introductions* to the Cambridge 'New Shakespeare'. The views summarized in the introduction now before the reader will be found argued in some detail in the writer's *Shakespeare's Life and Art*.

denunciations of their own early architecture as they were of the lawless Shakespeare. Now France is proud to reckon the buildings they once despised as Gothic as their greatest and most original contribution to the art of the world. And for the very same reasons the English may now claim that Shakespeare is the greatest artist to whom their race has so far given birth—a dramatist unsurpassed, as all acknowledge, in the gifts that nature alone can bestow, but as unsurpassed for the judgment that gives to work almost as various as nature itself the unity and commanding power found only in the world's supreme masterpieces.

When Rowe in 1709 and Pope in 1725 ventured on the systematic criticism of Shakespeare, so important did the Rules seem to them and their contemporaries that they deduced from Shakespeare's practice three important conclusions that were long accepted as almost self-evident. First : Shakespeare could not have received any instruction worthy of the name of education, and consequently Stratford where he was born and brought up must have been peopled merely by ignorant and unbookish rustics. Second : the form in which Shakespeare cast his dramas, not being prescribed by the Rules of Art, was dictated by the dramatist's desire to gratify, in his pursuit of gain, an ignorant and untaught audience. Third : so little interest, except financial, did Shakespeare and his even more ignorant fellow-actors take in his works that his plays were transmitted to posterity in so sadly mangled a condition, so full of interpolations from hands other than his own, that it was hardly possible to judge in many instances which were and which were not his writings, or to believe that we had them in a form even approximating to that in which he left them.

On the first and third of these issues modern criticism has shown that in general the truth is the very opposite to what was once so confidently maintained ; on the second the wiser judgments of the great critics of the past are being gradually confirmed and developed.

STRATFORD

IN Elizabethan England every self-respecting community made careful provision for the education of its children. Measured by this standard the inhabitants of Stratford could claim an honourable place amongst their countrymen. Education had in its beginnings in England been the business of the Church, but, like many other functions of the Church, education had in the course of the Middle Ages been transferred to lay administration ; and the school at Stratford had passed from the Church into the keeping of the Guild of the Holy Cross, the organisation in which the social instincts of the locality, according to the fashion of the time, found expression. There has been a long-standing belief that the schools of England were largely the creation of the Reformation, but this serious historical error was exposed by A. F. Leach ; and in his

Social History of England Sir George Trevelyan has summarised the true course of events when he says that it was not the Reformation that made the Schools of England but the schools that made the Reformation. In 1553 the school at Stratford was renamed The King's New School of Stratford-upon-Avon ; but the school owed nothing to Edward VI or his Council, and was not new by some centuries.

This renaming of the school merely marks the change from the old Guild system to a more modern form of administration in which Stratford became by Royal Charter a corporate borough under a Bailiff, Alderman, and Burgesses. The new Common Council, whose original members had all served on the Guild, now paid the Vicar and the Schoolmaster and administered the property and revenues of the Guild. It was during this period of transition that the poet's father, John Shakespeare, came to Stratford.

John Shakespeare must have left his father's home in Snitterfield, some four miles to the north of Stratford—where his father Richard Shakespeare worked as a yeoman farmer—at least seven years before 1552. In that year is found the first mention of him in Stratford records, and he is already in business as a glover in Henley Street ; and to become a member of the Craft of Glovers, Whitetawers and Collar-makers, he must have served a seven year apprenticeship. By 1557 John Shakespeare had so prospered in business that he was able to return to the district of his birth to marry the youngest daughter of Robert Arden, the gentleman from whom his father, Richard Shakespeare, rented his land.

Further than Richard Shakespeare no one has yet traced with any certainty the poet's paternal connections. But on his mother's side he was related to one of the great families of the West Country, for Robert Arden came of a younger branch of the Ardens of Park Hall, a family settled in the Arden district of Warwickshire, from which they took their name, from before the Norman Conquest.

Of the marriage of John Shakespeare and Mary Arden there were eight children—four sons and four daughters. William, the third child and first son, was christened on 26th April 1564. The only member of this group to survive the poet was his younger sister Joan, who is mentioned in his will. The other three girls died in infancy, and though his brothers reached manhood they too predeceased him.

In the year of his marriage John Shakespeare was elected to the Common Council and soon took a leading part in its affairs. He acted as Chamberlain for four years—a term of office without precedent in Stratford—presumably because he was specially qualified for keeping the borough accounts. In 1568 he became Bailiff, and by virtue of his office a gentleman entitled to his coat of arms. In 1577, however, after twenty years of continuous service, he suddenly ceased to attend the Council meetings.

It has been conjectured that in his zeal for public affairs he had neglected his own business ; and he certainly, at this time, was or wished to be taken for a poor man, mortgaging as he did a valuable property inherited by his wife. The authorities however took a different view of his circumstances : in 1580 he was summoned before the Queen's Bench in Westminster and fined £20 for failing to provide security that he would keep the Queen's peace ; and on the same day he was fined another £20, as he had stood surety for another man in the same position as himself. That this was the outcome of the measures of John Whitgift, the new Bishop of Worcester, who had come to Worcester as he was later to go to Canterbury to restore church discipline, there can be little doubt. John Shakespeare's troubles therefore were probably political not financial, and that he was a ' recusant ' there is no doubt, though the grounds of his discontent are unknown.

In 1582 his son William married Ann Hathaway the daughter of an old family friend. The licence was issued in November 1582 ; the first child of the marriage, Susanna, was born in May 1583. All attempts to show from an examination of the Bishop's *Register* and the circumstances of the marriage that it reflects discredit on either party rest on the unhistorical conjecture that the church ceremony was then, as it would be now, the marriage ceremony. The church ceremony, for which the licence was obtained, was in respectable Elizabethan society frequently no more than an after-ceremony to the marriage proper ; the licence is in no respect out of the ordinary. Ann Hathaway may have been eight years older than her husband, but this is not absolutely certain, and even if it were this would be no proof of irregularity. Those who still insist that there was some impropriety in the matter may be asked to produce their evidence. In February 1585, the twins, Hamnet and Judith, were christened at Stratford.

How Shakespeare intended to support a wife and family is a natural question, and fortunately the only tradition about Shakespeare's youth that has any trustworthy pedigree behind it supplies the answer. The group of traditions that gathers round Rowe's account of Shakespeare's deer-stealing and of his prosecution by Sir Thomas Lucy has not only no pedigree but is contradicted by the fact that there was no deer-park at Charlecote at that time, the Lucy family establishing one there only in the next generation. The passage from the first scene of *The Merry Wives of Windsor* that is regularly cited as Shakespeare's reminiscence of this adventure is more probably the origin of the story itself ; and, as Professor Hotson has shown, any personal reference in the lines may be directed towards a man very different in character from Sir Thomas Lucy. This and the other popular stories about Shakespeare's youth are the kind of conjecture commonly drawn in to fill the vacuum that biographers naturally abhor. The story however that the youthful Shakespeare was a country schoolmaster rests on a quite different foundation. The antiquary John Aubrey, who made a valuable series of notes on the men of Shakespeare's generation, was advised to visit

William Beeston, then an old man, but well informed about the history of the stage, for he, like his father, Christopher Beeston, had been an actor and actor-manager. His father, Christopher, had actually been in the same company as Shakespeare for a number of years. That Aubrey discussed with Beeston the observation by Jonson on Shakespeare's ' small Latin and less Greek ' is revealed in Aubrey's note :

' Though as Ben Jonson says of him that he had but little Latin and less Greek, he understood Latin pretty well, for he had been in his younger years a schoolmaster in the country '.

In the margin Aubrey recorded that his authority was Mr. Beeston.

Shakespeare's next step—his departure to London—is a venture that needs no fanciful embroidery to make it intelligible. Conscious, like a later country schoolmaster, of the genius within him, he naturally sought the field where alone his talents could find their full employment.

LONDON

THOSE who think of Shakespeare as an ignorant youth driven by a wrathful landlord from his careless rustic existence have now to explain how he started on his new and very different career in London. It is not surprising that some look elsewhere, to Bacon or to Lord Oxford, for the author of *Hamlet* or the *Sonnets*; for the explanation usually offered is as improbable as the transformation it attempts to account for. Shakespeare began, we are told, by rewriting the plays of others, among them those of Robert Greene. Why the works of a writer who boasted of a degree from both Universities should have been turned over to an illiterate new-comer is hardly to be understood ; and the evidence that was for long advanced by scholars in support of this story is now seen to indicate a different and more natural course of events.

Those, however, who accept Beeston's statement that Shakespeare had been a schoolmaster find no difficulty in understanding his beginnings and progress as a dramatist. No miracle except that of genius, no hidden hand, whether that of Bacon or Lord Oxford, need be invoked. Shakespeare began as any educated young man might have begun by adapting for his purposes the models prescribed by the fashion of his time, the Latin authors familiar to him from his schooling.

Before grouping his plays in the approximate order of their composition one important observation that emerges from such a chronological arrangement as almost self-evident must be considered. Viewed as a whole and as the successive episodes in the life of one creative mind his plays reveal in their creator powers of development and self-criticism found, whether the medium be music, or painting, or literature, only in the greatest masters—those who gave to their art the devotion of a life-time. To suppose that this development could come by chance or from the mere desire to gain the applause or money of the ignorant is to deny the evidence of experience. Shakespeare had of course to make the major contribution to the fortunes of a large and important Company of actors, and at times this part of his task affected his work, but such plays as *Hamlet* and *Othello* are clearly the creations of a man who had thought long and deeply about his art. A later and in its own opinion better instructed generation did not hesitate to deny to Shakespeare even the rudiments of stage craft. The more carefully, however, this side of Shakespeare's work is examined the more clearly it is seen to be skilfully contrived for his own stage ; and, what is more important, the more clearly it is seen that his craft is not an end in itself but the technical mastery inseparable from any powerful manifestation of art.

Beginning then with plays fashioned on the models then approved— plays so little like his masterpieces that they are frequently attributed to other hands—Shakespeare soon developed an original style of his own that commanded the applause of a wide public. In spite, however, of his popularity and success he was not content to repeat himself but from about his thirty-fifth year started on the series of tragic masterpieces, matched, if at all, only by the drama of ancient Athens. Nor do the works of his later years echo in feebler tones these triumphs but bring with their colouring and glow the splendid evening to the noon-day intensity of his genius—a conclusion visionary and apocalyptic.

FIRST PERIOD

From Shakespeare's arrival in London (1584) to his joining the Lord Chamberlain's men (1594)

No definite date can be given for Shakespeare's arrival in London; but by 1594 he had a body of work to his credit that must have occupied a considerable number of years. Naturally no details survive of his London connections when he was still unknown to the world, but what evidence there is indicates that he was for a time at least a member of Lord Pembroke's Company, and that for them he wrote some of his early plays.

Before the end of this period Shakespeare had established himself as a popular dramatist and as a poet of whom much was expected. The first reference to him in print, from the pen of the poet and dramatist Robert Greene, provides, indirectly, evidence of his success. Greene had failed to find in London the reward he expected for his work, and his irregular life was closing in misery and want. He felt with much bitterness that a writer received but a small return for his plays compared with the drawings taken by the performers ; and on his death-bed he wrote for publication a letter to some playwrights with whom he claimed acquaintance, warning them by his own fate against depending on such ungrateful employers as the actors.

APPROXIMATE ORDER OF COMPOSITION OF SHAKESPEARE'S WORKS

PERIOD	COMEDIES	HISTORIES	TRAGEDIES
1584 I 1592	Comedy of Errors Taming of the Shrew Two Gentlemen of Verona	1, 2, 3 Henry VI Richard III King John	Titus Andronicus
1594 II	Love's Labour's Lost Midsummer-Night's Dream Merchant of Venice Merry Wives of Windsor Much Ado About Nothing As You Like It	Venus and Adonis ⎫ poems Rape of Lucrece ⎭ Richard II 1 Henry IV 2 Henry IV Henry V	Romeo and Juliet
1599 III	Twelfth Night Troilus and Cressida Measure for Measure All's Well		Julius Caesar Hamlet Othello Timon of Athens Lear Macbeth Antony and Cleopatra Coriolanus
1608 IV 1613	Pericles Cymbeline Winter's Tale Tempest	Henry VIII	

' Base minded men all three of you, if by my misery you be not warn'd ; for unto none of you (like me) sought those burrs to cleave— those Puppets (I mean) that spake from our mouths, those Anticks garnisht in our colours.'

Greene then, as the allusions indicate, goes on to attack Shakespeare not merely as an actor but also as an actor-dramatist whose success, though undeserved, was making it more difficult for Greene and his friends to gain a living.

' Yes trust them not ; for there is an upstart Crow, beautified with our feathers, that with his *Tiger's heart wrapt in a Player's hide* supposes he is as well able to bombast out a blank verse as the best of you ; and being an absolute *Johannes fac totum* is in his own conceit the only Shake-scene in a country.'

Soon after Greene's death his friend Chettle printed this letter in a pamphlet entitled *Greene's Groatsworth of Wit bought with a Million of Repentance*.

Marlowe, with whom Greene claimed acquaintance, was naturally displeased with the letter, for Greene like many self-confessed sinners found satisfaction in proclaiming the faults of his friends. Shakespeare also was annoyed. Chettle, three months later, in a preface to his own *Kind-Heart's Dream* refused to admit he had wronged Marlowe but made full apology for what he confessed was an unwarranted attack on Shakespeare.

' I am as sorry as if the original fault had been my fault, because myself have seen his demeanour no less civil than he excellent in the quality he professes. Besides, divers of worship have reported his uprightness of dealing, which argues his honesty, and his facetious grace in writing, that approves his Art.'

As Chettle's words indicate, Shakespeare was already highly thought of in courtly circles ; and this is confirmed by the publication of his *Venus and Adonis* in 1593 and the *Rape of Lucrece* in 1594, with dedications to Lord Southampton, whose gracious entertainment of the poet is publicly and warmly acknowledged in the dedicatory epistle to *Lucrece*. Further evidence of Shakespeare's familiarity with courtly and learned circles is found in his *Love's Labour's Lost* with its copious allusion to personalities, events, and fashions, then current topics in such society. Shakespeare's poems were no doubt written during the years 1591-93 when the plague and other troubles had closed the London theatres and the Companies had to tour the provinces for a living. Shakespeare can hardly have been on tour during this period of composition, and it was not till the return to London of the leading companies, and after the extensive regrouping that it made necessary, that he joined the Lord Chamberlain's men.

Venus and Adonis, although Shakespeare's first published work, was that of a writer of recognised reputation. His success had been made on the stage ; but actors were very unwilling to publish their pieces, partly owing to lack of copyright protection, partly owing to their belief that publication would lessen their takings at the theatre. In this policy Shakespeare acquiesced throughout his life-time, never hastening into print with new pieces. The straitened circumstances of the actors however during their enforced absence from London gave the publishers a chance to pick up some of these much desired productions, and versions, good and bad, of certain of Shakespeare's plays now appeared in print.

From this and related evidence one can with some confidence assign to the period before the poems : his first tragedy, *Titus Andronicus* ; his comedies, *The Comedy of Errors, The Taming of the Shrew, The Two Gentlemen of Verona* ; his history plays, *Henry VI* (in three parts), and possibly *Richard III*. The assumption that Shakespeare did not begin his work as a dramatist till 1591 rests on the misinterpretation by Malone of Greene's attack on Shakespeare. Malone interpreted it as a charge of plagiarism. Now that this interpretation is rejected the conclusions drawn from it are unsupported, and indeed contradicted not only by the evidence of Greene and Chettle but by the circumstances in which his Poems and early plays were printed. Shakespeare must have been working as a dramatist for some years before 1590. This period of successful work explains how by 1594 he could take a leading place in the first company of the age.

SECOND PERIOD

From Shakespeare's joining the Lord Chamberlain's men in 1594 to the opening of the Globe Theatre in 1599

THE Company which Shakespeare now joined included Richard Burbage, who was to prove himself in the rôles Shakespeare provided for him the greatest tragic actor of his age, Will Kemp the popular comedian, and John Heminge and Henry Condell, who became the Company's managers and later Shakespeare's first editors. Their headquarters were at The Theatre, the first play-house to be built in England for theatrical performances.

During this period Shakespeare was living, as the subsidy rolls indicate, in easy circumstances in London ; and there still survives a letter to him from a friend of his father, Richard Quiney, who was twice Bailiff of Stratford, that confirms the evidence of the subsidies. In 1596 John Shakespeare obtained from the College of Heralds a grant of arms. He was entitled to this as a former Bailiff of Stratford, but although nearly thirty years before the actual grant he had taken the preliminary steps towards this dignity, he had allowed the matter to lapse. It was no doubt considered proper in view of the poet's position in London to complete the necessary formalities, and the family shield now showed ' in a field of gold upon a bend sable, a spear of the first, the point upward, headed argent ', and above as crest ' a falcon, with his wings displayed, standing on a wreath of his colours, supporting a spear, armed, headed, and steeled silver '. The motto was ' NON SANS DROICT '. In 1597 Shakespeare bought New Place at Stratford.

Whatever his interests at this time in his personal and private affairs, Shakespeare's mind must have been unsparingly given to his work in the theatre. In 1598 Francis Meres in his *Palladis Tamia* describes him as ' the most excellent in both kinds [comedy and tragedy] for the stage ', and adds ' for comedy, witnes his *Gentlemen of Verona*, his *Errors*, his *Love labours lost*, his *Love labours wonne*, his *Midsummer night's dreame*, and his *Merchant of Venice:* for tragedy his *Richard II*, *Richard III*, *Henry IV*, *King John*, *Titus Andronicus*, and his *Romeo and Juliet*.' He also mentions his poems and ' his sugred Sonnets among his private friends'.

The period opens with a group of ' poetical plays ', *Midsummer-Night's Dream*, *Richard II*, and *Romeo and Juliet*. The comedy is perfect in its kind and unsurpassed for the marvellous harmony it establishes among so many apparently discordant elements. The tragedy is another of the early masterpieces and anticipates in its spacious design and intensity of handling the works of Shakespeare's full maturity. But for some years to come comedy and prose were the main interest, and this, in the figure of Falstaff, overwhelms even the historical interest in the two parts of *Henry IV*. With Falstaff gone, there is little left for *Henry V* but pageantry; yet this opportunity for costume effects and patriotic verse may have been not unwelcome to Shakespeare as a suitable opening for the new Globe Theatre in 1599.

THIRD PERIOD

From the opening of the Globe (1599) to the taking over of the Blackfriars Theatre (1608)

THE Globe Theatre was opened about May 1599. With the lease of the ground on which the Theatre stood nearing an end, the Burbages bought the old dining-hall of the Blackfriars and furnished it as a theatre, but an influential circle who lived in the vicinity had this project defeated. The Burbages then acquired ground just over London Bridge on the Bankside. To this side, south of the river, they transferred some of the main timbers from the Theatre ; force was necessary for the landlord hoped to retain their building for his own profit. To meet this additional expense they took into partnership as ' householders ' five of the leading ' sharers ' of the company, of whom Shakespeare was one.

The Blackfriars they leased to the Children of the Queen's Revels. The actors were choir boys and their theatre was described as ' private '

INTRODUCTION

to distinguish it from ordinary theatres where the charges were not beyond the vulgar purse.

Near the beginning of this period Shakespeare's father died, in 1601 ; at the end, his mother, in 1608. His daughter Susanna married the well-known physician John Hall in 1607.

The great public event of the time was the death of Queen Elizabeth and the arrival of James in London in May 1603. The King at once took over the Lord Chamberlain's Company and they were now known as the King's Men. The senior members became Grooms of the Royal Chamber and in that capacity formed part of the entourage of the Spanish Ambassador who came in August 1604, to negotiate a peace between England and Spain.

During part of this period, as Professor Wallace has shown, Shakespeare lodged with a Huguenot family in Silver Street. He was now in a position to make considerable purchases of land at Stratford and investments in the tithes of the parish.

As before, however, Shakespeare must have given unremitting attention to his art, for he was now from his thirty-fifth year to engage in the most sustained and intense effort of his career.

The plays that were to make the name of the Globe for ever famous were very different from *Henry V*. During the next ten years Shakespeare produced there his seven great tragedies : *Julius Cæsar, Hamlet, Othello, Lear, Macbeth, Antony and Cleopatra*, and *Coriolanus*.

Many explanations have been offered for this apparently sudden shift in Shakespeare's interest. Some have blamed the dark lady of the Sonnets and the conduct of the friend for inducing a mood of gloom and misanthropy ; others have dwelt on Shakespeare's connections with Essex and Southampton, and the former's death on the block, as the cause of his disillusionment and pessimism ; others again see in this tragic mood Shakespeare's infection with the spirit of a new age. The accidents of life undoubtedly provide the material on which the imagination operates ; but the relationship between this accidental and the universal element in art is not so simple as cause and effect. The process of transformation is even more complicated and vital than that of digestion. But it is unnecessary to attempt an analysis of this psychological problem here, for the tragedies rightly interpreted do not reveal a spirit of gloom and disillusionment.

Many critics have dwelt on the bitterness and disgust in the works of this period. And it is true that nowhere can one find a fiercer invective and more withering scorn than that poured by these plays on the baser side of our nature. The picture of man dressed in a little brief authority playing his fantastic tricks before high heaven with an effrontery that makes the angels weep has never been drawn with more penetrating irony. And as a background we have the cowardly or malignant complacency in our natures that tolerates such shameless

xix

wickedness. Passage after passage emphasizes the degradation to which men can sink. It is summed up in one terrible line from *King Lear*

A dog's obey'd in office.

King Lear has been described as a tragedy of ingratitude—an ingratitude that divides parent from child and splits the very core of human existence. And the elements seem to take part in the confusion as the old and cast-off father rages on the heath with a fury that out-tongues the elements. But those who find in this fury the climax of the drama have missed half the vision and the half that is greater than the whole. The design on which the drama is constructed is one familiar to great spirits in all ages, and is perhaps exhibited in its simplest elements in the old story of Elijah fleeing from Jezebel's vengeance and how as he stood at the mouth of a cave

' a great and strong wind rent the mountains and brake in pieces the rocks before the Lord; but the Lord was not in the wind; and after the wind an earthquake, but the Lord was not in the earthquake; and after the earthquake a fire, but the Lord was not in the fire; and after the fire a still small voice '.

The heart of Shakespeare's drama is not reached till the storm and tempest are over and we come on the stillness of Lear's reconciliation with Cordelia. Here at last he recognises goodness for what it is in its own right. And the play's real theme is the gratitude of the con-verted heart at such a revelation. To see the virtues struggling in a world where their very virtue is the cause of their undoing is to be aware of tragedy; but—and this is the touch of nature that makes the reader kin with the poet—this makes us love the virtues not less but more. Had Shakespeare not seen so clearly the hollowness of the world he could not have created with such passionate brooding those spirits whom his art has made the dwellers for all time in the imaginations of men. He is not confounded by his terrible visions, for he sees in the midst of them what walks unscathed; and we read his plays because, however unconsciously, we share in that triumph, and have at least a sense, however our intelligence or conduct may later deny it, of what the soul hungers to attain to.

This revelation which is the consummation of his art did not come to Shakespeare suddenly or because a woman was false or a friend disloyal. It is born of the modest and ceaseless years of thought and labour which are not without their intimations of the final triumph of this period. Viewed in retrospect the humour and comedy, which his earlier critics found more natural to his genius, are only another aspect, a partial realisation, of his tragic vision. Philosophers have indeed main-tained that tragedy and comedy have another and finer connection than that of contrast; but, though there have been great tragic artists and great comic artists before and since Shakespeare's time, nowhere are they found united as in his work, and in such a manner that each but adds a new force to its apparent opposite.

Viewed after the event, the tragic period is seen as the natural development of the previous periods and to be explained only in so far as we can explain to ourselves the growth and nature of Shakespeare's art.

FOURTH PERIOD

From the taking over of the Blackfriars (1608) to the burning of the Globe Theatre (1613)

THE manager of the Children at the Blackfriars theatre was foolish enough to allow indiscreet stage allusions to royalty that led to the suppression of his company. The Burbages and a group of actors as ' householders ' that included Shakespeare took over from him his lease, and the King's men now acted at the Blackfriars during the winter months instead of in the open Globe Theatre, to the very substantial increase in their takings. The King's men were now too well established in official favour for the old objections to their presence there to be raised again.

The plays of this period have happy endings ; but to distinguish their peculiar colouring from that of his earlier comedies they have been called Romances.

Once again critics have dwelt on the contrasts between this and the previous period and denied any spiritual continuity between them, or have paradoxically asserted that the Romances are the flight into a world of make-believe that alone could save the poet from the madness in which his tragic thoughts would inevitably have engulfed him. Or again the fashion of the time is thought by some to have directed Shakespeare's interest to this type of play.

But the tragedies are the foundation on which the Romances rest. If Shakespeare had found the heart of man wanting in the fiery trial of the tragedies, what would be the hopes and aspirations in which human nature reclothes itself with every new generation as regularly as the flowers return with the spring—what would these hopes and aspirations be but will-o'-the-wisps to lure mankind to its destruction, or to leave it, should it survive, bogged in disillusion and a dreary materialism ?

If fashion had anything to do with Shakespeare's return to comedy, it was because it gave him an opportunity for the expression of something he had now very much at heart, something that came naturally after the struggle of the tragedies, as naturally as Prospero's sympathies with Miranda's hopes and fears.

There can be little doubt that the *Tempest*, considered in conjunction with what we know of Shakespeare's arrangements at this date for taking over his house in Stratford from his cousin Thomas Greene, the town-clerk, indicates that he intended it to be his farewell to the stage. Persuaded no doubt by the importunity of his old colleagues he returned to take a final bow in *Henry VIII*. During the first performance of the piece, on 29th June 1613, the Globe was burnt to the ground ; and this accident, for lack of more precise knowledge, may be taken as marking the conclusion of Shakespeare's work as an actor and dramatist.

STRATFORD

SHAKESPEARE seems to have passed his last days quietly at Stratford, though there is a record of at least one visit to London.

He made his will in January 1615 or 1616, and revised it on 25th March 1616, after the marriage of his second daughter Judith to Thomas Quiney in February 1616. He remembers amongst other friends his old colleagues, Burbage, Heminge and Condell, the last survivors of the group with which he had acted for some twenty years. He makes provision for Judith and for his sister Joan Hart, but the bulk of his estate is settled on his daughter Susanna and her heirs. His wife was obviously going to live with her daughter, who was, if what she put on her mother's grave gives any echo of truth, devoted to her.

Shakespeare died on St. George's day, 23rd April 1616, and was buried, having this right as a tithe-holder, in the Chancel of the Church at Stratford. The monument on the north wall was erected sometime before 1623. In 1623 his wife was buried beside him, and his daughter Susanna not far away in 1649. She left a daughter Elizabeth Hall who had married Thomas Nash and, on his death, Sir John Bernard, but was to die without issue. Judith Shakespeare had three sons who all died childless before her. From his sister only, and that through her second son Thomas, can those living to-day who are related to Shakespeare claim their descent.

THE FIRST FOLIO

IN 1623, seven years after Shakespeare's death, his old friends and fellow-actors, John Heminge and Henry Condell, gave the world the first collected edition of Shakespeare's plays. This is now known as the First Folio, because of its format and to distinguish it from the Second, Third, and Fourth Folios, issued in 1632, 1663, and 1685 respectively. Each of these later Folios is in turn based on its predecessor. Heminge and Condell attributed thirty-six plays to Shakespeare, all that are included in the present volume except *Pericles*, for *Pericles*, although its omission by Shakespeare's colleagues is good evidence that it is not wholly his, undoubtedly contains scenes from his pen.

Their long friendship with Shakespeare, their admiration for his genius, their position of authority in the company, for they had acted as its managers for many years, made Heminge and Condell in some respects well qualified for their task. They, if anyone did, must have known what was by Shakespeare and what was not; their office in the company had made them familiar with his manuscripts. Yet their edition has presented students with problems for which reasonable solutions have been found only in recent years; problems that may be summarized here in the questions: Why did Shakespeare himself not supervise the printing of his plays; and why, since Heminge and Condell claimed to be Shakespeare's literary executors and to have used his papers, is the First Folio not accepted as the last and final authority for the text of all the plays? Why have there been so many subsequent editors, a line that begins with Rowe in 1709, and includes Pope (1725), Theobald (1733), Johnson (1765), Capell (1768) and Malone (1790), and threatens, like the phantom procession that appalled Macbeth, to stretch out to the crack of doom.

Shakespeare did not print his plays when he produced them because the actors did not favour such a procedure. They feared that publication might affect adversely their takings at the theatre, and the financial return from such publications, at least to the author or actors, was insufficient to overcome this fear. It was not because there was no reading public; publishers were only too ready to print his plays; but there was nothing in the nature of modern copyright to protect the author's interest; and to dispose for a pittance of plays that were drawing good houses did not seem sound policy. Yet in spite of these considerations nineteen of Shakespeare's plays were printed in some form or other during his lifetime, and a twentieth just before 1623.

THE QUARTOS

THE Quartos, so called from their format, contained single plays and sold at sixpence apiece, compared with the pound charged for the First Folio. For their printing the initiative lay with the publishers rather than with the actors. Enterprising if unscrupulous printers were ready to issue even imperfect versions of the plays, whether put together by needy actors who had had parts in them, or vamped up by someone who had carried away from performances the drift of the plot. Seven plays were published in this manner: *The Contention, The True Tragedy* (these were pirated versions of 2 and 3 *Henry VI*), *A Shrew, Romeo and Juliet, Merry Wives of Windsor, Henry V*, and *Hamlet*—and *The Troublesome Reign of King John* may be an eighth. These are now known as the Bad Quartos.

This attack on their property inevitably provoked a reaction in Shakespeare and his company. They published in reply the genuine text of *Romeo and Juliet* and *Hamlet*, and they were not unwilling to print plays that had become well known through frequent performance. In contrast, then, to the seven or eight mutilated or distorted versions stand fourteen authorised or authoritative texts : *Titus Andronicus, Love's Labour's Lost, Romeo and Juliet, Richard II, Richard III,* 1 and 2 *Henry IV, Merchant of Venice, Midsummer-Night's Dream, Much Ado, Hamlet, Troilus and Cressida, King Lear, Othello.* These are the Good Quartos. Even they, however, were treated as in some measure provisional publications. Shakespeare never revised the proofs for any of them, and the printer, although he was in quite a number working from a manuscript in Shakespeare's own hand, found difficulties (*see* p. 1350) he failed to master. The Good Quartos are therefore in places faulty or corrupt, and Shakespeare died before he cared to mend matters.

The actors, when at last they came to their task, had to provide the publisher with copy that extends in print to nearly 900 pages in double column. Their knowledge that many of the Good Quartos were set up from the author's manuscript or an authorised transcript prompted their use of some printed versions as copy for their own text ; they took the precaution, however, of having the printed versions compared with manuscripts in their possession, but too casually to exclude all error. The manuscript copy they had to provide for the other plays was also defective for much the same reasons that the Quarto prints were not faultless : the scribe prepared his draft from material not originally designed for the printer's use, and only careful supervision could have prevented his not infrequent stumblings.

To the printed record of this large body of theatrical copy, often entangled as it were in Quarto and Folio, a modern editor has to address himself in an attempt to remove its corruptions. Heminge and Condell discharged their task honestly and with all the skill that could be expected of them ; posterity can never be too grateful for their care and pains ; but only those who read their Shakespeare regularly in the early versions can know how much the general reader owes to the subsequent editorial labours of those whom Johnson defined as harmless drudges.

PETER ALEXANDER

The Preliminary Matter to the
FIRST FOLIO (1623)

Heminge and Condell, who edited the first collected edition of Shakespeare's plays, arranged their contents in three sections: Comedies, Histories, and Tragedies. That arrangement as well as the order in which they placed the pieces in each section is preserved in this edition.

To their text the editors prefixed the preliminary matter here reproduced. Opposite the engraved portrait of Shakespeare which stood as frontispiece—now known as the Droeshout engraving after the name of the engraver—they placed Ben Jonson's lines *To the Reader*. Then follow their dedicatory epistle and the address to ' the great variety of readers '. They also included Ben Jonson's famous lines to Shakespeare's memory and short tributes from Leonard Digges and John Mabbe, both of Oxford University, and verses from the sister University of Cambridge by Hugh Holland.

Their ' Catalogue ' does not mention *Troilus and Cressida*, for they were able to include this play, in a kind of no man's land, between the Histories and the Tragedies, only at the last moment and after the settlement of a dispute with the publishers who had issued the Quarto version in 1609. Heminge and Condell originally intended to place *Troilus and Cressida* among the Tragedies immediately after *Romeo and Juliet*.

TO THE READER

This Figure, that thou here seest put,
    It was for gentle Shakespeare cut ;
Wherein the Grauer had a strife
    with Nature, to out-doo the life :
O, could he but haue drawne his wit
    As well in brasse, as he hath hit
His face ; the Print would then surpasse
    All, that vvas euer vvrit in brasse.
But, since he cannot, Reader, looke
    Not on his Picture, but his Booke.

                    B. I.

TO THE MOST NOBLE AND INCOMPARABLE PAIRE OF BRETHREN, WILLIAM, EARLE OF PEMBROKE, &c., LORD CHAMBERLAINE TO THE KINGS MOST EXCELLENT MAIESTY, AND PHILIP, EARLE OF MONTGOMERY, &c., GENTLEMAN OF HIS MAIESTIES BED-CHAMBER; BOTH KNIGHTS OF THE MOST NOBLE ORDER OF THE GARTER, AND OUR SINGULAR GOOD LORDS.

Right Honourable,

WHILST we studie to be thankful in our particular, for the many fauors we haue receiued from your L.L. we are falne vpon the ill fortune, to mingle two the most diuerse things that can bee, feare, and rashnesse; rashnesse in the enterprize, and feare of the successe. For, when we valew the places your H.H. sustaine, we cannot but know their dignity greater, then to descend to the reading of these trifles: and, while we name them trifles, we haue depriu'd our selues of the defence of our Dedication. But since your L.L. haue beene pleas'd to thinke these trifles some-thing, heeretofore; and haue prosequuted both them, and their Author liuing, with so much fauour: we hope, that (they out-liuing him, and he not hauing the fate, common with some, to be exequutor to his owne writings) you will vse the like indulgence toward them, you haue done vnto their parent. There is a great differ-ence, whether any Booke choose his Patrones, or finde them: This hath done both. For, so much were your L.L. likings of the seuerall parts, when they were acted, as before they were published, the Volume ask'd to be yours. We haue but collected them, and done an office to the dead, to procure his Orphanes, Guardians; without ambition either of selfe-profit, or fame: onely to keepe the memory of so worthy a Friend, & Fellow aliue, as was our *Shakespeare*, by humble offer of his playes, to your most noble patronage. Wherein, as we haue iustly obserued, no man to come neere your L.L. but with a kind of religious addresse; it hath bin the height of our care, who are the Presenters, to make the present worthy of your H.H. by the perfection. But, there we must also craue our abilities to be considerd, my Lords. We cannot go beyond our owne powers. Country hands reach foorth milke, creame, fruites, or what they haue: and many Nations (we haue heard) that had not gummes & incense, obtained their requests with a leauened Cake. It was no fault to approch their Gods, by what meanes they could: And the most, though meanest, of things are made more precious, when they are dedicated to Temples. In that name therefore, we most humbly consecrate to your H.H. these remaines of your seruant *Shakespeare;* that what delight is in them, may be euer your L.L. the reputation his, & the faults ours, if any be committed, by a payre so carefull to shew their gratitude both to the liuing, and the dead, as is

Your Lordshippes most bounden,

IOHN HEMINGE.
HENRY CONDELL.

TO THE GREAT VARIETY OF READERS

FROM the most able, to him that can but spell : There you are number'd. We had rather you were weighd. Especially, when the fate of all Bookes depends vpon your capacities : and not of your heads alone, but of your purses. Well ! it is now publique, & you wil stand for your priuiledges wee know : to read, and censure. Do so, but buy it first. That doth best commend a Booke, the Stationer saies. Then, how odde soeuer your braines be, or your wisedomes, make your licence the same, and spare not. Iudge your sixe-pen'orth, your shillings worth, your fiue shillings worth at a time, or higher, so you rise to the iust rates, and welcome. But, what euer you do, Buy. Censure will not driue a Trade, or make the Iacke go. And though you be a Magistrate of wit, and sit on the Stage at *Black-Friers*, or the *Cock-pit*, to arraigne Playes dailie, know, these Playes haue had their triall alreadie, and stood out all Appeales ; and do now come forth quitted rather by a Decree of Court, then any purchas'd Letters of commendation.

It had bene a thing, we confesse, worthie to haue bene wished, that the Author himselfe had liu'd to haue set forth, and ouerseen his owne writings ; But since it hath bin ordain'd otherwise, and he by death departed from that right, we pray you do not envie his Friends, the office of their care, and paine, to haue collected & publish'd them ; and so to haue publish'd them, as where (before) you were abus'd with diuerse stolne, and surreptitious copies, maimed, and deformed by the frauds and stealthes of iniurious imposters, that expos'd them : euen those, are now offer'd to your view cur'd, and perfect of their limbes ; and all the rest, absolute in their numbers, as he conceiued them. Who, as he was a happie imitator of Nature, was a most gentle expresser of it. His mind and hand went together : And what he thought, he vttered with that easinesse, that wee haue scarse receiued from him a blot in his papers. But it is not our prouince, who onely gather his works, and giue them you, to praise him. It is yours that reade him. And there we hope, to your diuers capacities, you will finde enough, both to draw, and hold you : for his wit can no more lie hid, then it could be lost. Reade him, therefore ; and againe, and againe : And if then you doe not like him, surely you are in some manifest danger, not to vnderstand him. And so we leaue you to other of his Friends, whom if you need, can bee your guides : if you neede them not, you can leade your selues, and others. And such Readers we wish him.

IOHN HEMINGE.
HENRIE CONDELL.

TO THE MEMORY OF MY BELOUED, THE AVTHOR
MR. WILLIAM SHAKESPEARE:
AND WHAT HE HATH LEFT VS.

To draw no enuy (*Shakespeare*) on thy name,
   Am I thus ample to thy Booke, and Fame :
While I confesse thy writings to be such,
   As neither *Man*, nor *Muse*, can praise too much.
'Tis true, and all mens suffrage. But these wayes
   Were not the paths I meant vnto thy praise :
For seeliest Ignorance on these may light,
   Which, when it sounds at best, but eccho's right ;
Or blinde Affection, which doth ne're aduance
   The truth, but gropes, and vrgeth all by chance ;
Or crafty Malice, might pretend this praise,
   And thinke to ruine, where it seem'd to raise.
These are, as some infamous Baud, or Whore,
   Should praise a Matron. What could hurt her more ?
But thou art proofe against them, and indeed
   Aboue th' ill fortune of them, or the need.
I, therefore will begin. Soule of the Age !
   The applause ! delight ! the wonder of our Stage !
My *Shakespeare*, rise ; I will not lodge thee by
   Chaucer, or *Spenser*, or bid *Beaumont* lye
A little further, to make thee a roome :
   Thou art a Moniment, without a tombe,
And art aliue still, while thy Booke doth liue,
   And we haue wits to read, and praise to giue.
That I not mixe thee so, my braine excuses ;
   I meane with great, but disproportion'd *Muses* :
For, if I thought my judgement were of yeeres,
   I should commit thee surely with thy peeres,
And tell, how farre thou didst our *Lily* out-shine,
   Or sporting *Kid*, or *Marlowes* mighty line.
And though thou hadst small *Latine*, and lesse *Greeke*,
   From thence to honour thee, I would not seeke
For names ; but call forth thund'ring *Æschilus*,
   Euripides, and *Sophocles* to vs,
Paccuuius, *Accius*, him of *Cordoua* dead,
   To life againe, to heare thy Buskin tread,
And shake a Stage : Or, when thy Sockes were on,
   Leaue thee alone, for the comparison
Of all, that insolent *Greece*, or haughtie *Rome*
   sent forth, or since did from their ashes come.
Triũmph, my *Britaine*, thou hast one to showe,
   To whom all Scenes of *Europe* homage owe.
He was not of an age, but for all time !
   And all the *Muses* still were in their prime,

When like *Apollo* he came forth to warme
    Our eares, or like a *Mercury* to charme !
Nature her selfe was proud of his designes,
    And ioy'd to weare the dressing of his lines !
Which were so richly spun, and wouen so fit,
    As, since, she will vouchsafe no other Wit.
The merry *Greeke*, tart *Aristophanes*,
    Neat *Terence*, witty *Plautus*, now not please ;
But antiquated, and deserted lye
    As they were not of Natures family.
Yet must I not giue Nature all : Thy Art,
    My gentle *Shakespeare*, must enioy a part.
For though the *Poets* matter, Nature be,
    His Art doth giue the fashion. And, that he,
Who casts to write a liuing line, must sweat,
    (such as thine are) and strike the second heat
Vpon the *Muses* anuile : turne the same,
    (And himselfe with it) that he thinkes to frame ;
Or for the lawrell, he may gaine a scorne,
    For a good *Poet's* made, as well as borne.
And such wert thou. Looke how the fathers face
    Liues in his issue, euen so, the race
Of *Shakespeares* minde, and manners brightly shines
    In his well torned, and true-filed lines :
In each of which, he seemes to shake a Lance,
    As brandish't at the eyes of Ignorance.
Sweet Swan of *Auon* ! what a sight it were
    To see thee in our waters yet appeare,
And make those flights vpon the bankes of *Thames*,
    That so did take *Eliza*, and our *Iames* !
But stay, I see thee in the *Hemisphere*
    Aduanc'd, and made a Constellation there !
Shine forth, thou Starre of *Poets*, and with rage,
    Or influence, chide, or cheere the drooping Stage ;
Which, since thy flight from hence, hath mourn'd like night,
    And despaires day, but for thy Volumes light.

                             BEN : IONSON.

VPON THE LINES AND LIFE OF THE FAMOUS SCENICKE POET,
MASTER WILLIAM SHAKESPEARE

Those hands, which you so clapt, go now, and wring
You *Britaines* braue ; for done are *Shakespeares* dayes :
His dayes are done, that made the dainty Playes,
Which made the Globe of heau'n and earth to ring.
Dry'de is that veine, dry'd is the *Thespian* Spring,
Turn'd all to teares, and *Phœbus* clouds his rayes :
That corp's, that coffin now besticke those bayes,
Which crown'd him *Poet* first, then *Poets* King.
If *Tragedies* might any *Prologue* haue,
All those he made, would scarse make one to this :
Where *Fame*, now that he gone is to the graue
(Deaths publique tyring-house) the *Nuncius* is.

     For though his line of life went soone about,
     The life yet of his lines shall neuer out.

HVGH HOLLAND.

TO THE MEMORIE OF THE DECEASED AUTHOUR
MAISTER W. SHAKESPEARE.

SHAKE-SPEARE, at length thy pious fellowes giue
  The world thy Workes : thy Workes, by which, out-liue
Thy Tombe, thy name must : when that stone is rent,
And Time dissolues thy *Stratford* Moniment,
Here we aliue shall view thee still. This Booke,
When Brasse and Marble fade, shall make thee looke
Fresh to all Ages : when Posteritie
Shall loath what's new, thinke all is prodegie
That is not *Shake-speares* ; eu'ry Line, each Verse
Here shall reuiue, redeeme thee from thy Herse.
Nor Fire, nor cankring Age, as *Naso* said,
Of his, thy wit-fraught Booke shall once inuade.
Nor shall I e're beleeue, or thinke thee dead
(Though mist) vntill our bankrout Stage be sped
(Impossible) with some new straine t' out-do
Passions of *Iuliet*, and her *Romeo* ;
Or till I heare a Scene more nobly take,
Then when thy half-Sword parlying *Romans* spake.
Till these, till any of thy Volumes rest
Shall with more fire, more feeling be exprest,
Be sure, our *Shake-speare*, thou canst neuer dye,
But crown'd with Lawrell, liue eternally.

L. DIGGES.

M. W. *SHAKE-SPEARE*

WEE wondred (*Shake-speare*) that thou went'st so soone
From the Worlds-Stage, to the Graues-Tyring-roome.
Wee thought thee dead, but this thy printed worth,
Tels thy Spectators, that thou went'st but forth
To enter with applause. An Actors Art,
Can dye, and liue, to acte a second part.
That's but an *Exit* of Mortalitie ;
This, a Re-entrance to a Plaudite.

I. M.

THE WORKES OF WILLIAM SHAKESPEARE,
CONTAINING ALL HIS COMEDIES, HISTORIES, AND TRAGEDIES:
TRUELY SET FORTH, ACCORDING TO THEIR FIRST ORIGINALL.

THE NAMES OF THE PRINCIPALL ACTORS IN ALL THESE PLAYES.

William Shakespeare.
Richard Burbadge.
John Hemmings.
Augustine Phillips.
William Kempt.
Thomas Poope.
George Bryan.
Henry Condell.
William Slye.
Richard Cowly.
John Lowine.
Samuell Crosse.
Alexander Cooke.

Samuel Gilburne.
Robert Armin.
William Ostler.
Nathan Field.
John Underwood.
Nicholas Tooley.
William Ecclestone.
Joseph Taylor.
Robert Benfield.
Robert Goughe.
Richard Robinson.
Iohn Shancke.
Iohn Rice.

A CATALOGVE

OF THE SEUERALL COMEDIES, HISTORIES, AND
TRAGEDIES CONTAINED IN THIS VOLUME.

COMEDIES.

HISTORIES.

TRAGEDIES.

THE TEMPEST

ACT ONE

SCENE I. *On a ship at sea ; a tempestuous noise of thunder and lightning heard.*

Enter a Shipmaster and a Boatswain.

Master. Boatswain !
Boats. Here, master ; what cheer ?
Master. Good ! Speak to th' mariners ; fall to 't yarely, or we run ourselves aground ; bestir, bestir. [*Exit.*

Enter Mariners.

Boats. Heigh, my hearts ! cheerly, cheerly, my hearts ! yare, yare ! Take in the topsail. Tend to th' master's whistle. Blow till thou burst thy wind, if room enough. 7

Enter ALONSO, SEBASTIAN, ANTONIO, FERDINAND, GONZALO, *and* Others.

Alon. Good boatswain, have care. Where's the master ? Play the men.
Boats. I pray now, keep below. 10
Ant. Where is the master, boson ?
Boats. Do you not hear him ? You mar our labour ; keep your cabins ; you do assist the storm.
Gon. Nay, good, be patient. 14
Boats. When the sea is. Hence ! What cares these roarers for the name of king ? To cabin ! silence ! Trouble us not.
Gon. Good, yet remember whom thou hast aboard. 18
Boats. None that I more love than myself. You are a counsellor ; if you can command these elements to silence, and work the peace of the present, we will not hand a rope more. Use your authority ; if you cannot, give thanks you have liv'd so long, and make yourself ready in your cabin for the mischance of the hour, if it so hap.—

Cheerly, good hearts !—Out of our way, I say. [*Exit.*
Gon. I have great comfort from this fellow. Methinks he hath no drowning mark upon him ; his complexion is perfect gallows. Stand fast, good Fate, to his hanging ; make the rope of his destiny our cable, for our own doth little advantage. If he be not born to be hang'd, our case is miserable. [*Exeunt.*

Re-enter Boatswain.

Boats. Down with the topmast. Yare, lower, lower ! Bring her to try wi' th' maincourse. [*A cry within*] A plague upon this howling ! They are louder than the weather or our office. 35

Re-enter SEBASTIAN, ANTONIO, *and* GONZALO.

Yet again ! What do you here ? Shall we give o'er, and drown ? Have you a mind to sink ?
Seb. A pox o' your throat, you bawling, blasphemous, incharitable dog !
Boats. Work you, then. 40
Ant. Hang, cur ; hang, you whoreson, insolent noise-maker ; we are less afraid to be drown'd than thou art.
Gon. I'll warrant him for drowning, though the ship were no stronger than a nutshell, and as leaky as an unstanched wench. 45
Boats. Lay her a-hold, a-hold ; set her two courses ; off to sea again ; lay her off.

Enter Mariners, wet.

Mar. All lost ! to prayers, to prayers ! all lost ! [*Exeunt.*
Boats. What, must our mouths be cold ?
Gon. The King and Prince at prayers ! Let's assist them, 50

1

For our case is as theirs.
Seb.   I am out of patience.   51
Ant. We are merely cheated of our lives
        by drunkards.
This wide-chopp'd rascal—would thou
        mightst lie drowning
The washing of ten tides!
Gon.   He'll be hang'd yet,
Though every drop of water swear against
        it,   55
And gape at wid'st to glut him.
        [*A confused noise within*: Mercy on us!
We split, we split! Farewell, my wife and
        children!
Farewell, brother! We split, we split, we
        split!
Ant. Let's all sink wi' th' King.   60
Seb. Let's take leave of him.
                        [*Exeunt Ant. and Seb.*
Gon. Now would I give a thousand fur-
longs of sea for an acre of barren ground—
long heath, brown furze, any thing. The
wills above be done, but I would fain die a
dry death.   [*Exeunt.*

SCENE II. *The island. Before Prospero's cell.*

Enter PROSPERO *and* MIRANDA.

Mira. If by your art, my dearest father,
        you have
Put the wild waters in this roar, allay them.
The sky, it seems, would pour down stink-
        ing pitch,
But that the sea, mounting to th' welkin's
        cheek,
Dashes the fire out. O, I have suffered   5
With those that I saw suffer! A brave
        vessel,
Who had no doubt some noble creature in
        her,
Dash'd all to pieces! O, the cry did knock
Against my very heart! Poor souls, they
        perish'd.
Had I been any god of power, I would   10
Have sunk the sea within the earth or ere
It should the good ship so have swallow'd
        and
The fraughting souls within her.
Pro.   Be collected;
No more amazement; tell your piteous
        heart
There's no harm done.
Mira.   O, woe the day!
Pro.   No harm.
I have done nothing but in care of thee, 16
Of thee, my dear one, thee, my daughter,
        who
Art ignorant of what thou art, nought
        knowing
Of whence I am, nor that I am more better
Than Prospero, master of a full poor cell,
And thy no greater father.
Mira.   More to know   21
Did never meddle with my thoughts.

Pro.   'Tis time
I should inform thee farther. Lend thy hand,
And pluck my magic garment from me. So,
                        [*Lays down his mantle.*
Lie there my art. Wipe thou thine eyes;
        have comfort.   25
The direful spectacle of the wreck, which
        touch'd
The very virtue of compassion in thee,
I have with such provision in mine art
So safely ordered that there is no soul—
No, not so much perdition as an hair   30
Betid to any creature in the vessel
Which thou heard'st cry, which thou saw'st
        sink. Sit down,
For thou must now know farther.
Mira.   You have often
Begun to tell me what I am; but stopp'd,
And left me to a bootless inquisition,   35
Concluding ' Stay; not yet '.
Pro.   The hour's now come;
The very minute bids thee ope thine ear.
Obey, and be attentive. Canst thou re-
        member
A time before we came unto this cell?
I do not think thou canst; for then thou
                        wast not   40
Out three years old.
Mira.   Certainly, sir, I can.
Pro. By what? By any other house, or
        person?
Of any thing the image, tell me, that   43
Hath kept with thy remembrance?
Mira.   'Tis far off,
And rather like a dream than an assurance
That my remembrance warrants. Had I not
Four, or five, women once, that tended me?
Pro. Thou hadst, and more, Miranda.
        But how is it   48
That this lives in thy mind? What seest
        thou else
In the dark backward and abysm of time?
If thou rememb'rest aught, ere thou cam'st
        here,   51
How thou cam'st here thou mayst.
Mira.   But that I do not.
Pro. Twelve year since, Miranda, twelve
        year since,
Thy father was the Duke of Milan, and
A prince of power.
Mira.   Sir, are not you my father?
Pro. Thy mother was a piece of virtue,
        and   56
She said thou wast my daughter; and thy
        father
Was Duke of Milan, and his only heir
And princess no worse issued.
Mira.   O, the heavens!
What foul play had we that we came from
        thence?   60
Or blessed was't we did?
Pro.   Both, both, my girl.
By foul play, as thou say'st, were we heav'd
        thence;

But blessedly holp hither.
   Mira.   O, my heart bleeds
To think o' th' teen that I have turn'd
    you to,
Which is from my remembrance. Please
    you, farther.   65
   Pro. My brother and thy uncle, call'd
    Antonio—
I pray thee, mark me that a brother should
Be so perfidious. He, whom next thyself
Of all the world I lov'd, and to him put
The manage of my state ; as at that time
Through all the signories it was the first, 71
And Prospero the prime duke, being so
    reputed
In dignity, and for the liberal arts
Without a parallel, those being all my
    study—
The government I cast upon my brother 75
And to my state grew stranger, being trans-
    ported
And rapt in secret studies. Thy false
    uncle—
Dost thou attend me ?
   Mira.   Sir, most heedfully.
   Pro. Being once perfected how to grant
    suits,
How to deny them, who t' advance, and who
To trash for over-topping, new created 81
The creatures that were mine, I say, or
    chang'd 'em,
Or else new form'd 'em ; having both the
    key
Of officer and office, set all hearts i' th' state
To what tune pleas'd his ear ; that now he
    was   85
The ivy which had hid my princely trunk
And suck'd my verdure out on't. Thou
    attend'st not.
   Mira. O, good sir, I do !
   Pros.   I pray thee, mark me.
I thus neglecting worldly ends, all dedicated
To closeness and the bettering of my mind
With that which, but by being so retir'd, 91
O'er-priz'd all popular rate, in my false
    brother
Awak'd an evil nature ; and my trust,
Like a good parent, did beget of him
A falsehood, in its contrary as great   95
As my trust was ; which had indeed no
    limit,
A confidence sans bound. He being thus
    lorded,
Not only with what my revenue yielded,
But what my power might else exact, like
    one
Who having into truth, by telling of it, 100
Made such a sinner of his memory,
To credit his own lie—he did believe
He was indeed the Duke ; out o' th' sub-
    stitution,
And executing th' outward face of royalty
With all prerogative. Hence his ambition
    growing—   105

Dost thou hear ?
   Mira. Your tale, sir, would cure deafness.
   Pro. To have no screen between this part
    he play'd
And him he play'd it for, he needs will be
Absolute Milan. Me, poor man—my library
Was dukedom large enough—of temporal
    royalties   110
He thinks me now incapable ; confederates,
So dry he was for sway, wi' th' King of
    Naples,
To give him annual tribute, do him homage,
Subject his coronet to his crown, and bend
The dukedom, yet unbow'd—alas, poor
    Milan !   115
To most ignoble stooping.
   Mira.   O the heavens !
   Pro. Mark his condition, and th' event,
    then tell me
If this might be a brother.
   Mira.   I should sin
To think but nobly of my grandmother :
Good wombs have borne bad sons.
   Pro.   Now the condition :
This King of Naples, being an enemy 121
To me inveterate, hearkens my brother's
    suit ;
Which was, that he, in lieu o' th' premises,
Of homage, and I know not how much
    tribute,   124
Should presently extirpate me and mine
Out of the dukedom, and confer fair Milan
With all the honours on my brother.
    Whereon,
A treacherous army levied, one midnight
Fated to th' purpose, did Antonio open
The gates of Milan ; and, i' th' dead of
    darkness,   130
The ministers for th' purpose hurried
    thence
Me and thy crying self.
   Mira.   Alack, for pity !
I, not rememb'ring how I cried out then,
Will cry it o'er again ; it is a hint
That wrings mine eyes to't.
   Pro.   Hear a little further,
And then I'll bring thee to the present
    business   136
Which now's upon 's ; without the which
    this story
Were most impertinent.
   Mira.   Wherefore did they not
That hour destroy us ?
   Pro.   Well demanded, wench !
My tale provokes that question. Dear, they
    durst not,   140
So dear the love my people bore me ; nor
    set
A mark so bloody on the business ; but
With colours fairer painted their foul ends.
In few, they hurried us aboard a bark ;
Bore us some leagues to sea, where they
    prepared   145
A rotten carcass of a butt, not rigg'd,

3

Nor tackle, sail, nor mast ; the very rats
Instinctively have quit it.   There they
   hoist us,
To cry to th' sea, that roar'd to us ; to sigh
To th' winds, whose pity, sighing back
   again,   150
Did us but loving wrong.
   Mira.   Alack, what trouble
Was I then to you !
   Pro.   O, a cherubin
Thou wast that did preserve me! Thou didst
   smile,
Infused with a fortitude from heaven,
When I have deck'd the sea with drops
   full salt,   155
Under my burden groan'd ; which rais'd in
   me
An undergoing stomach, to bear up
Against what should ensue.
   Mira.   How came we ashore ?
   Pro. By Providence divine.
Some food we had and some fresh water
   that   160
A noble Neapolitan, Gonzalo,
Out of his charity, who being then ap-
   pointed
Master of this design, did give us, with
Rich garments, linens, stuffs, and neces-
   saries,
Which since have steaded much ; so, of his
   gentleness,   165
Knowing I lov'd my books, he furnish'd me
From mine own library with volumes that
I prize above my dukedom.
   Mira.   Would I might
But ever see that man !
   Pro.   Now I arise.
       [*Puts on his mantle.*
Sit still, and hear the last of our sea-sorrow.
Here in this island we arriv'd ; and here
Have I, thy schoolmaster, made thee more
   profit   172
Than other princess' can, that have more
   time
For vainer hours, and tutors not so careful.
   Mira. Heavens thank you for't! And now,
   I pray you, sir,   175
For still 'tis beating in my mind, your
   reason
For raising this sea-storm ?
   Pro.   Know thus far forth :
By accident most strange, bountiful
   Fortune,
Now my dear lady, hath mine enemies
Brought to this shore ; and by my pre-
   science   180
I find my zenith doth depend upon
A most auspicious star, whose influence
If now I court not, but omit, my fortunes
Will ever after droop. Here cease more
   questions ;
Thou art inclin'd to sleep ; 'tis a good
   dullness,   185

And give it way. I know thou canst not
   choose.
       [*Miranda sleeps.*
Come away, servant ; come ; I am ready
   now.
Approach, my Ariel. Come.

      Enter ARIEL.

   Ari. All hail, great master ! grave sir,
   hail ! I come
To answer thy best pleasure ; be't to fly,
To swim, to dive into the fire, to ride   191
On the curl'd clouds. To thy strong bidding
   task
Ariel and all his quality.
   Pro.   Hast thou, spirit,
Perform'd to point the tempest that I bade
   thee ?
   Ari. To every article.   195
I boarded the King's ship ; now on the beak,
Now in the waist, the deck, in every cabin,
I flam'd amazement. Sometime I'd divide,
And burn in many places ; on the topmast,
The yards, and bowsprit, would I flame
   distinctly,   200
Then meet and join. Jove's lightning, the
   precursors
O' th' dreadful thunder-claps, more mom-
   entary
And sight-outrunning were not ; the fire
   and cracks
Of sulphurous roaring the most mighty
   Neptune
Seem to besiege, and make his bold waves
   tremble,   205
Yea, his dread trident shake.
   Pro.   My brave spirit !
Who was so firm, so constant, that this coil
Would not infect his reason ?
   Ari.   Not a soul
But felt a fever of the mad, and play'd
Some tricks of desperation. All but
   mariners   210
Plung'd in the foaming brine, and quit the
   vessel,
Then all afire with me ; the King's son,
   Ferdinand,
With hair up-staring—then like reeds, not
   hair—
Was the first man that leapt ; cried ' Hell
   is empty,   214
And all the devils are here '.
   Pro.   Why, that's my spirit !
But was not this nigh shore ?
   Ari.   Close by, my master.
   Pro. But are they, Ariel, safe ?
   Ari.   Not a hair perish'd ;
On their sustaining garments not a blemish,
But fresher than before ; and, as thou
   bad'st me,
In troops I have dispers'd them 'bout the
   isle.   220
The King's son have I landed by himself,
Whom I left cooling of the air with sighs

4

In an odd angle of the isle, and sitting,
His arms in this sad knot.
    Pro.   Of the King's ship,
The mariners, say how thou hast dispos'd,
And all the rest o' th' fleet ?
    Ari.   Safely in harbour
Is the King's ship ; in the deep nook, where
    once   227
Thou call'dst me up at midnight to fetch
    dew
From the still-vex'd Bermoothes, there she's
    hid ;
The mariners all under hatches stowed,   230
Who, with a charm join'd to their suff'red
    labour,
I have left asleep ; and for the rest o' th'
    fleet,
Which I dispers'd, they all have met again,
And are upon the Mediterranean flote
Bound sadly home for Naples,   235
Supposing that they saw the King's ship
    wreck'd,
And his great person perish.
    Pro.   Ariel, thy charge
Exactly is perform'd ; but there's more
    work.
What is the time o' th' day ?
    Ari.   Past the mid season.
    Pro. At least two glasses. The time 'twixt
    six and now   240
Must by us both be spent most preciously.
    Ari. Is there more toil ? Since thou dost
    give me pains,
Let me remember thee what thou hast
    promis'd,
Which is not yet perform'd me.
    Pro.   How now, moody ?
What is 't thou canst demand ?
    Ari.   My liberty.
    Pro. Before the time be out ? No more !
    Ari.   I prithee,
Remember I have done thee worthy service,
Told thee no lies, made thee no mistakings,
    serv'd   248
Without or grudge or grumblings. Thou
    didst promise
To bate me a full year.
    Pro.   Dost thou forget
From what a torment I did free thee ?
    Ari.   No.
    Pro. Thou dost ; and think'st it much to
    tread the ooze   252
Of the salt deep,
To run upon the sharp wind of the north,
To do me business in the veins o' th' earth
When it is bak'd with frost.
    Ari.   I do not, sir.
    Pro. Thou liest, malignant thing. Hast
    thou forgot   257
The foul witch Sycorax, who with age and
    envy
Was grown into a hoop ? Hast thou forgot
    her ?
    Ari. No, sir.

    Pro.   Thou hast. Where was she
    born ? Speak ; tell me.   260
    Ari. Sir, in Argier.
    Pro.   O, was she so ? I must
Once in a month recount what thou hast
    been,
Which thou forget'st. This damn'd witch
    Sycorax,
For mischiefs manifold, and sorceries
    terrible
To enter human hearing, from Argier   265
Thou know'st was banish'd ; for one thing
    she did
They would not take her life. Is not this
    true ?
    Ari. Ay, sir.
    Pro. This blue-ey'd hag was hither
    brought with child,
And here was left by th' sailors. Thou, my
    slave,   270
As thou report'st thyself, wast then her
    servant ;
And, for thou wast a spirit too delicate
To act her earthy and abhorr'd commands,
Refusing her grand hests, she did confine
    thee,
By help of her more potent ministers,   275
And in her most unmitigable rage,
Into a cloven pine ; within which rift
Imprison'd thou didst painfully remain
A dozen years ; within which space she
    died,
And left thee there, where thou didst vent
    thy groans   280
As fast as mill-wheels strike. Then was this
    island—
Save for the son that she did litter here,
A freckl'd whelp, hag-born—not honour'd
    with
A human shape.
    Ari.   Yes, Caliban her son.
    Pro. Dull thing, I say so ; he, that Caliban
Whom now I keep in service. Thou best
    know'st   286
What torment I did find thee in ; thy groans
Did make wolves howl, and penetrate the
    breasts
Of ever-angry bears ; it was a torment
To lay upon the damn'd, which Sycorax
Could not again undo. It was mine art,
When I arriv'd and heard thee, that made
    gape   292
The pine, and let thee out.
    Ari.   I thank thee, master.
    Pro. If thou more murmur'st, I will rend
    an oak
And peg thee in his knotty entrails, till 295
Thou hast howl'd away twelve winters.
    Ari.   Pardon, master ;
I will be correspondent to command,
And do my spriting gently.
    Pro.   Do so ; and after two days
I will discharge thee.
    Ari.   That's my noble master !

5

What shall I do ?   Say what.   What shall
  I do ?   300
  Pro. Go make thyself like a nymph o' th'
      sea ; be subject
To no sight but thine and mine, invisible
To every eyeball else. Go take this shape,
And hither come in 't. Go, hence with
      diligence !   [*Exit Ariel.*
Awake, dear heart, awake ; thou hast slept
      well ;   305
Awake.
  Mira. The strangeness of your story put
Heaviness in me.
  Pro.   Shake it off. Come on,
We'll visit Caliban, my slave, who never
Yields us kind answer.
  Mira.   'Tis a villain, sir,
I do not love to look on.
  Pro.   But as 'tis,   310
We cannot miss him : he does make our
      fire,
Fetch in our wood, and serves in offices
That profit us. What ho ! slave ! Caliban !
Thou earth, thou ! Speak.
  Cal. [*Within*] There's wood enough
      within.
  Pro. Come forth, I say ; there's other
      business for thee.   315
Come, thou tortoise ! when ?

        Re-enter ARIEL *like a water-nymph.*

Fine apparition ! My quaint Ariel,
Hark in thine ear.
  Ari.   My lord, it shall be done. [*Exit.*
  Pro. Thou poisonous slave, got by the
      devil himself
Upon thy wicked dam, come forth !   320

                Enter CALIBAN.

  Cal. As wicked dew as e'er my mother
      brush'd
With raven's feather from unwholesome
      fen
Drop on you both ! A south-west blow
      on ye
And blister you all o'er !
  Pro. For this, be sure, to-night thou shalt
      have cramps,   325
Side-stitches that shall pen thy breath up ;
      urchins
Shall, for that vast of night that they may
      work,
All exercise on thee ; thou shalt be pinch'd
As thick as honeycomb, each pinch more
      stinging   329
Than bees that made 'em.
  Cal.   I must eat my dinner.
This island's mine, by Sycorax my mother,
Which thou tak'st from me. When thou
      cam'st first,
Thou strok'st me and made much of me,
      wouldst give me
Water with berries in 't, and teach me how
To name the bigger light, and how the less,

That burn by day and night ; and then I
      lov'd thee,   336
And show'd thee all the qualities o' th' isle,
The fresh springs, brine-pits, barren place
      and fertile.
Curs'd be I that did so ! All the charms
Of Sycorax, toads, beetles, bats, light on
      you !   340
For I am all the subjects that you have,
Which first was mine own king ; and here
      you sty me
In this hard rock, whiles you do keep from
      me
The rest o' th' island.
  Pro.   Thou most lying slave,
Whom stripes may move, not kindness ! I
      have us'd thee,   345
Filth as thou art, with human care, and
      lodg'd thee
In mine own cell, till thou didst seek to
      violate
The honour of my child.
  Cal. O ho, O ho ! Would 't had been done.
Thou didst prevent me ; I had peopl'd else
This isle with Calibans.
  Mira.   Abhorred slave,   351
Which any print of goodness wilt not take,
Being capable of all ill ! I pitied thee,
Took pains to make thee speak, taught
      thee each hour
One thing or other. When thou didst not,
      savage,   355
Know thine own meaning, but wouldst
      gabble like
A thing most brutish, I endow'd thy
      purposes
With words that made them known. But
      thy vile race,
Though thou didst learn, had that in't
      which good natures
Could not abide to be with ; therefore wast
      thou   360
Deservedly confin'd into this rock, who
      hadst
Deserv'd more than a prison.
  Cal. You taught me langauge, and my
      profit on't
Is, I know how to curse. The red plague
      rid you
For learning me your language !
  Pro.   Hag-seed, hence !
Fetch us in fuel. And be quick, thou 'rt
      best,   366
To answer other business. Shrug'st thou,
      malice ?
If thou neglect'st, or dost unwillingly
What I command, I'll rack thee with old
      cramps,
Fill all thy bones with aches, make thee
      roar,   370
That beasts shall tremble at thy din.
  Cal.   No, pray thee.
[*Aside*] I must obey. His art is of such pow'r,
It would control my dam's god, Setebos,

And make a vassal of him.
Pro.   So, slave ; hence !
                                [Exit Caliban.

Re-enter ARIEL invisible, playing and sing-
    ing ; FERDINAND following.

Ariel's Song.

Come unto these yellow sands,   375
    And then take hands ;
Curtsied when you have and kiss'd,
    The wild waves whist,
Foot it featly here and there,   379
And, sweet sprites, the burden bear.
    Hark, hark !
Burden dispersedly. Bow-wow.
    The watch dogs bark.
Burden dispersedly. Bow-wow.
    Hark, hark ! I hear
The strain of strutting chanticleer   385
    Cry, Cock-a-diddle-dow.

Fer. Where should this music be ? I' th'
        air or th' earth ?
It sounds no more ; and sure it waits upon
Some god o' th' island. Sitting on a bank,
Weeping again the King my father's wreck,
This music crept by me upon the waters,
Allaying both their fury and my passion
With its sweet air ; thence I have follow'd
        it,
Or it hath drawn me rather. But 'tis gone.
No, it begins again.

Ariel's Song.

Full fathom five thy father lies ;
    Of his bones are coral made ;
Those are pearls that were his eyes ;
    Nothing of him that doth fade
But doth suffer a sea-change   400
    Into something rich and strange.
Sea-nymphs hourly ring his knell :
                        Burden. Ding-dong.
Hark ! now I hear them—Ding-dong
    bell.

Fer. The ditty does remember my
        drown'd father.   405
This is no mortal business, nor no sound
That the earth owes. I hear it now above
    me.
Pro. The fringed curtains of thine eye
        advance,
And say what thou seest yond.
    Mira.   What is't ? a spirit ?
Lord, how it looks about ! Believe me, sir,
It carries a brave form. But 'tis a spirit.
Pro. No, wench ; it eats and sleeps and
        hath such senses   412
As we have, such. This gallant which thou
        seest
Was in the wreck ; and but he's something
        stain'd

With grief, that's beauty's canker, thou
        mightst call him   415
A goodly person. He hath lost his fellows,
And strays about to find 'em.
    Mira.   I might call him
A thing divine ; for nothing natural
I ever saw so noble.
    Pro. [Aside]   It goes on, I see,
As my soul prompts it. Spirit, fine spirit !
    I'll free thee   420
Within two days for this.
    Fer.   Most sure, the goddess
On whom these airs attend ! Vouchsafe my
        pray'r
May know if you remain upon this island ;
And that you will some good instruction
        give
How I may bear me here. My prime
        request,   425
Which I do last pronounce, is, O you
        wonder !
If you be maid or no ?
    Mira.   No wonder, sir ;
But certainly a maid.
    Fer.   My language ? Heavens !
I am the best of them that speak this speech,
Were I but where 'tis spoken.
    Pro.   How ? the best ?
What wert thou, if the King of Naples
        heard thee ?   431
    Fer. A single thing, as I am now, that
        wonders
To hear thee speak of Naples. He does hear
        me ;
And that he does I weep. Myself am
        Naples,
Who with mine eyes, never since at ebb,
        beheld   435
The King my father wreck'd.
    Mira.   Alack, for mercy !
    Fer. Yes, faith, and all his lords, the
        Duke of Milan
And his brave son being twain.
    Pro. [Aside]   The Duke of Milan
And his more braver daughter could
        control thee,
If now 'twere fit to do't. At the first sight
They have chang'd eyes. Delicate Ariel,
I'll set thee free for this. [To Fer.] A word,
        good sir ;   442
I fear you have done yourself some wrong ;
        a word.
    Mira. Why speaks my father so un-
        gently ? This
Is the third man that e'er I saw ; the first
That e'er I sigh'd for. Pity move my father
To be inclin'd my way !
    Fer.   O, if a virgin,
And your affection not gone forth, I'll make
        you   448
The Queen of Naples.
    Pro.   Soft, sir ! one word more.
[Aside] They are both in either's pow'rs ;
        but this swift business   450

I must uneasy make, lest too light winning
Make the prize light. [*To Fer.*] One word
　　more ; I charge thee
That thou attend me ; thou dost here usurp
The name thou ow'st not ; and hast put
　　thyself
Upon this island as a spy, to win it   455
From me, the lord on't.
　Fer.　　　　　　No, as I am a man.
　Mira. There's nothing ill can dwell in
　　such a temple.
If the ill spirit have so fair a house,
Good things will strive to dwell with't.
　Pro.　　　　　　　Follow me.
Speak not you for him ; he's a traitor.
　　Come ;   460
I'll manacle thy neck and feet together.
Sea-water shalt thou drink ; thy food shall be
The fresh-brook mussels, wither'd roots,
　　and husks
Wherein the acorn cradled. Follow.
　Fer.   No ;
I will resist such entertainment till   465
Mine enemy has more power.
　　　[*He draws, and is charmed from moving.*
　Mira.　　　　　　O dear father,
Make not too rash a trial of him, for
He's gentle, and not fearful.
　Pro.　　　　　　　What, I say,
My foot my tutor ? Put thy sword up,
　　traitor ;
Who mak'st a show but dar'st not strike,
　　thy conscience   470
Is so possess'd with guilt. Come from thy
　　ward ;
For I can here disarm thee with this stick
And make thy weapon drop.
　Mira.　　　　　Beseech you, father !
　Pro. Hence ! Hang not on my garments.
　Mira.　　　　　　Sir, have pity ;
I'll be his surety.
　Pro.　　　　　Silence ! One word more
Shall make me chide thee, if not hate
　　thee. What !   476
An advocate for an impostor ! hush !
Thou think'st there is no more such shapes
　　as he,
Having seen but him and Caliban. Foolish
　　wench !
To th' most of men this is a Caliban,   480
And they to him are angels.
　Mira.　　　　　My affections
Are then most humble ; I have no ambition
To see a goodlier man.
　Pro.　　　　　Come on ; obey.
Thy nerves are in their infancy again,
And have no vigour in them.
　Fer.　　　　　　So they are ;
My spirits, as in a dream, are all bound up.
My father's loss, the weakness which I feel,
The wreck of all my friends, nor this man's
　　threats   488
To whom I am subdu'd, are but light to me,
Might I but through my prison once a day

Behold this maid. All corners else o' th'
　　earth   491
Let liberty make use of ; space enough
Have I in such a prison.
　Pro. [*Aside*] It works. [*To Fer.*] Come
　　on.—
Thou hast done well, fine Ariel ! [*To Fer.*]
　　Follow me.
[*To Ariel*] Hark what thou else shalt do me.
　Mira.　　　　　　Be of comfort ;
My father's of a better nature, sir,   496
Than he appears by speech ; this is un-
　　wonted
Which now came from him.
　Pro. [*To Ariel*] Thou shalt be as free
As mountain winds ; but then exactly do
All points of my command.
　Ari.　　　　　　To th' syllable.
　Pro. [*To Fer.*] Come, follow. [*To Mira.*]
　　Speak not for him.　　　　　[*Exeunt.*

ACT TWO

Scene I. *Another part of the island.*

Enter Alonso, Sebastian, Antonio,
Gonzalo, Adrian, Francisco, *and* Others.

　Gon. Beseech you, sir, be merry ; you
　　have cause,
So have we all, of joy ; for our escape
Is much beyond our loss. Our hint of woe
Is common ; every day, some sailor's wife,
The masters of some merchant, and the
　　merchant,   5
Have just our theme of woe ; but for the
　　miracle,
I mean our preservation, few in millions
Can speak like us. Then wisely, good sir,
　　weigh
Our sorrow with our comfort.
　Alon.　　　　　　Prithee, peace.
　Seb. He receives comfort like cold
porridge.   10
　Ant. The visitor will not give him o'er so.
　Seb. Look, he's winding up the watch of
his wit ; by and by it will strike.
　Gon. Sir—
　Seb. One—Tell.   15
　Gon. When every grief is entertain'd
　　that's offer'd,
Comes to th' entertainer—
　Seb. A dollar.
　Gon. Dolour comes to him, indeed ; you
have spoken truer than you purpos'd.   20
　Seb. You have taken it wiselier than I
meant you should.
　Gon. Therefore, my lord—
　Ant. Fie, what a spendthrift is he of his
　　tongue !
　Alon. I prithee, spare.
　Gon. Well, I have done ; but yet—   25
　Seb. He will be talking.
　Ant. Which, of he or Adrian, for a good
wager, first begins to crow ?

Seb. The old cock.

Ant. The cock'rel.   30

Seb. Done. The wager?

Ant. A laughter.

Seb. A match!

Adr. Though this island seem to be desert—

Ant. Ha, ha, ha!

Seb. So, you're paid.   35

Adr. Uninhabitable, and almost inaccessible—

Seb. Yet—

Adr. Yet—

Ant. He could not miss't.

Adr. It must needs be of subtle, tender, and delicate temperance.   41

Ant. Temperance was a delicate wench.

Seb. Ay, and a subtle; as he most learnedly deliver'd.

Adr. The air breathes upon us here most sweetly.

Seb. As if it had lungs, and rotten ones.

Ant. Or, as 'twere perfum'd by a fen.

Gon. Here is everything advantageous to life.   47

Ant. True; save means to live.

Seb. Of that there's none, or little.

Gon. How lush and lusty the grass looks! how green!   50

Ant. The ground indeed is tawny.

Seb. With an eye of green in't.

Ant. He misses not much.

Seb. No; he doth but mistake the truth totally.

Gon. But the rarity of it is, which is indeed almost beyond credit—   56

Seb. As many vouch'd rarities are.

Gon. That our garments, being, as they were, drench'd in the sea, hold, notwithstanding, their freshness and glosses, being rather new-dy'd, than stain'd with salt water.   60

Ant. If but one of his pockets could speak, would it not say he lies?

Seb. Ay, or very falsely pocket up his report.

Gon. Methinks our garments are now as fresh as when we put them on first in Afric, at the marriage of the King's fair daughter Claribel to the King of Tunis. 66

Seb. 'Twas a sweet marriage, and we prosper well in our return.

Adr. Tunis was never grac'd before with such a paragon to their queen.   70

Gon. Not since widow Dido's time.

Ant. Widow! a pox o' that! How came that 'widow' in? Widow Dido!

Seb. What if he had said 'widower Æneas' too? Good Lord, how you take it!

Adr. 'Widow Dido' said you? You make me study of that. She was of Carthage, not of Tunis.   77

Gon. This Tunis, sir, was Carthage.

Adr. Carthage?

Gon. I assure you, Carthage.   80

Ant. His word is more than the miraculous harp.

Seb. He hath rais'd the wall, and houses too.

Ant. What impossible matter will he make easy next?

Seb. I think he will carry this island home in his pocket, and give it his son for an apple.   85

Ant. And, sowing the kernels of it in the sea, bring forth more islands.

Gon. Ay.

Ant. Why, in good time.   89

Gon. Sir, we were talking that our garments seem now as fresh as when we were at Tunis at the marriage of your daughter, who is now Queen.

Ant. And the rarest that e'er came there.

Seb. Bate, I beseech you, widow Dido.

Ant. O, widow Dido! Ay, widow Dido.

Gon. Is not, sir, my doublet as fresh as the first day I wore it? I mean, in a sort.

Ant. That 'sort' was well fish'd for.   98

Gon. When I wore it at your daughter's marriage?

Alon. You cram these words into mine ears against   100
The stomach of my sense. Would I had never
Married my daughter there; for, coming thence,
My son is lost; and, in my rate, she too, 104
Who is so far from Italy removed
I ne'er again shall see her. O thou mine heir
Of Naples and of Milan, what strange fish
Hath made his meal on thee?

Fran.   Sir, he may live;
I saw him beat the surges under him,
And ride upon their backs; he trod the water,
Whose enmity he flung aside, and breasted
The surge most swoln that met him; his bold head   111
'Bove the contentious waves he kept, and oared
Himself with his good arms in lusty stroke
To th' shore, that o'er his wave-worn basis bowed,
As stooping to relieve him. I not doubt 115
He came alive to land.

Alon.   No, no, he's gone.

Seb. Sir, you may thank yourself for this great loss,
That would not bless our Europe with your daughter,
But rather lose her to an African;
Where she, at least, is banish'd from your eye,   120
Who hath cause to wet the grief on't.

Alon.   Prithee, peace.

Seb. You were kneel'd to, and importun'd otherwise
By all of us; and the fair soul herself

Weigh'd between loathness and obedience at
Which end o' th' beam should bow. We have lost your son, 125
I fear, for ever. Milan and Naples have
Moe widows in them of this business' making,
Than we bring men to comfort them;
The fault's your own.

Alon. So is the dear'st o' th' loss.

Gon. My lord Sebastian, 130
The truth you speak doth lack some gentleness,
And time to speak it in; you rub the sore,
When you should bring the plaster.

Seb. Very well.

Ant. And most chirurgeonly.

Gon. It is foul weather in us all, good sir, When you are cloudy.

Seb. Fowl weather?

Ant. Very foul.

Gon. Had I plantation of this isle, my lord— 137

Ant. He'd sow 't with nettle-seed.

Seb. Or docks, or mallows.

Gon. And were the king on't, what would I do?

Seb. Scape being drunk for want of wine.

Gon. I' th' commonwealth I would by contraries 141
Execute all things; for no kind of traffic
Would I admit; no name of magistrate;
Letters should not be known; riches, poverty,
And use of service, none; contract, succession, 145
Bourn, bound of land, tilth, vineyard, none;
No use of metal, corn, or wine, or oil;
No occupation; all men idle, all;
And women too, but innocent and pure;
No sovereignty—

Seb. Yet he would be king on't.

Ant. The latter end of his commonwealth forgets the beginning. 152

Gon. All things in common nature should produce
Without sweat or endeavour. Treason, felony,
Sword, pike, knife, gun, or need of any engine, 155
Would I not have; but nature should bring forth,
Of it own kind, all foison, all abundance,
To feed my innocent people.

Seb. No marrying 'mong his subjects?

Ant. None, man; all idle; whores and knaves. 160

Gon. I would with such perfection govern, sir,
T' excel the golden age.

Seb. Save his Majesty!

Ant. Long live Gonzalo!

Gon. And—do you mark me, sir?

Alon. Prithee, no more; thou dost talk nothing to me. 164

Gon. I do well believe your Highness; and did it to minister occasion to these gentlemen, who are of such sensible and nimble lungs that they always use to laugh at nothing.

Ant. 'Twas you we laugh'd at.

Gon. Who in this kind of merry fooling am nothing to you; so you may continue, and laugh at nothing still. 170

Ant. What a blow was there given!

Seb. An it had not fall'n flat-long.

Gon. You are gentlemen of brave mettle; you would lift the moon out of her sphere, if she would continue in it five weeks without changing. 175

Enter ARIEL, *invisible, playing solemn music.*

Seb. We would so, and then go a-bat-fowling.

Ant. Nay, good my lord, be not angry.

Gon. No, I warrant you; I will not adventure my discretion so weakly. Will you laugh me asleep, for I am very heavy? 181

Ant. Go sleep, and hear us.
[*All sleep but Alon., Seb. and Ant.*

Alon. What, all so soon asleep! I wish mine eyes
Would, with themselves, shut up my thoughts; I find
They are inclin'd to do so.

Seb. Please you, sir,
Do not omit the heavy offer of it: 185
It seldom visits sorrow; when it doth,
It is a comforter.

Ant. We two, my lord,
Will guard your person while you take your rest,
And watch your safety.

Alon. Thank you—wondrous heavy!
[*Alonso sleeps. Exit Ariel.*

Seb. What a strange drowsiness possesses them! 190

Ant. It is the quality o' th' climate.

Seb. Why
Doth it not then our eyelids sink? I find not
Myself dispos'd to sleep.

Ant. Nor I; my spirits are nimble.
They fell together all, as by consent;
They dropp'd, as by a thunder-stroke. What might, 195
Worthy Sebastian? O, what might! No more!
And yet methinks I see it in thy face,
What thou shouldst be; th' occasion speaks thee; and
My strong imagination sees a crown 199
Dropping upon thy head.

Seb. What, art thou waking?

Ant. Do you not hear me speak?

Seb. I do; and surely
It is a sleepy language, and thou speak'st

Out of thy sleep. What is it thou didst say?
This is a strange repose, to be asleep
With eyes wide open; standing, speaking, 205
    moving,
And yet so fast asleep.
    Ant.   Noble Sebastian,
Thou let'st thy fortune sleep—die rather;
    wink'st
Whiles thou art waking.
    Seb.   Thou dost snore distinctly;
There's meaning in thy snores.
    Ant. I am more serious than my custom; 210
    you
Must be so too, if heed me; which to do
Trebles thee o'er.
    Seb.   Well, I am standing water.
    Ant. I'll teach you how to flow.
    Seb.   Do so: to ebb,
Hereditary sloth instructs me.
    Ant.   O,
If you but knew how you the purpose
    cherish, 215
Whiles thus you mock it! how, in stripping
    it,
You more invest it! Ebbing men indeed,
Most often, do so near the bottom run
By their own fear or sloth.
    Seb.   Prithee say on.
The setting of thine eye and cheek proclaim
A matter from thee; and a birth, indeed,
Which throes thee much to yield.
    Ant.   Thus, sir:
Although this lord of weak remembrance,
    this
Who shall be of as little memory
When he is earth'd, hath here almost
    persuaded— 225
For he's a spirit of persuasion, only
Professes to persuade—the King his son's
    alive,
'Tis as impossible that he's undrown'd
As he that sleeps here swims.
    Seb.   I have no hope
That he's undrown'd.
    Ant.   O, out of that 'no hope'
What great hope have you! No hope that
    way is 231
Another way so high a hope, that even
Ambition cannot pierce a wink beyond,
But doubt discovery there. Will you grant
    with me
That Ferdinand is drown'd?
    Seb.   He's gone.
    Ant.   Then tell me,
Who's the next heir of Naples?
    Seb.   Claribel. 236
    Ant. She that is Queen of Tunis; she
    that dwells
Ten leagues beyond man's life; she that
    from Naples
Can have no note, unless the sun were post,
The Man i' th' Moon's too slow, till new-
    born chins 240
Be rough and razorable; she that from whom

We all were sea-swallow'd, though some
    cast again,
And by that destiny, to perform an act
Whereof what's past is prologue, what to
    come
In yours and my discharge.
    Seb. What stuff is this! How say you?
'Tis true, my brother's daughter's Queen of
    Tunis; 246
So is she heir of Naples; 'twixt which
    regions
There is some space.
    Ant.   A space whose ev'ry cubit
Seems to cry out 'How shall that Claribel
Measure us back to Naples? Keep in Tunis,
And let Sebastian wake'. Say this were
    death 251
That now hath seiz'd them; why, they
    were no worse
Than now they are. There be that can rule
    Naples
As well as he that sleeps; lords that can
    prate
As amply and unnecessarily 255
As this Gonzalo; I myself could make
A chough of as deep chat. O, that you bore
The mind that I do! What a sleep were this
For your advancement! Do you under-
    stand me? 259
    Seb. Methinks I do.
    Ant.   And how does your content
Tender your own good fortune?
    Seb.   I remember
You did supplant your brother Prospero.
    Ant.   True.
And look how well my garments sit upon
    me,
Much feater than before. My brother's
    servants
Were then my fellows; now they are my
    men. 265
    Seb. But, for your conscience—
    Ant. Ay, sir; where lies that? If 'twere
    a kibe,
'Twould put me to my slipper; but I feel
    not
This deity in my bosom; twenty con-
    sciences
That stand 'twixt me and Milan, candied
    be they 270
And melt, ere they molest! Here lies your
    brother,
No better than the earth he lies upon,
If he were that which now he's like—
    that's dead;
Whom I with this obedient steel, three
    inches of it,
Can lay to bed for ever; whiles you, doing
    thus, 275
To the perpetual wink for aye might put
This ancient morsel, this Sir Prudence, who
Should not upbraid our course. For all the
    rest,
They'll take suggestion as a cat laps milk;

They'll tell the clock to any business that
We say befits the hour.

Seb.   Thy case, dear friend,
Shall be my precedent; as thou got'st
Milan,   282
I'll come by Naples. Draw thy sword. One
stroke
Shall free thee from the tribute which thou
payest;
And I the King shall love thee.

Ant.   Draw together;
And when I rear my hand, do you the like,
To fall it on Gonzalo.

Seb.   O, but one word.   287
              [*They talk apart.*

Re-enter ARIEL, *invisible, with music and*
song.

Ari. My master through his art foresees
    the danger
That you, his friend, are in; and sends me
    forth—
For else his project dies—to keep them
    living.   290
           [*Sings in Gonzalo's ear.*

  While you here do snoring lie,
  Open-ey'd conspiracy
    His time doth take.
  If of life you keep a care,
  Shake off slumber, and beware.   295
    Awake, awake!

Ant. Then let us both be sudden.

Gon.   Now, good angels
Preserve the King!   [*They wake.*

Alon. Why, how now?—Ho, awake!—
Why are you drawn?
Wherefore this ghastly looking?

Gon.   What's the matter?

Seb. Whiles we stood here securing your
    repose,   301
Even now, we heard a hollow burst of
    bellowing
Like bulls, or rather lions; did't not wake
    you?
It struck mine ear most terribly.

Alon.   I heard nothing.

Ant. O, 'twas a din to fright a monster's
    ear,   305
To make an earthquake! Sure it was the roar
Of a whole herd of lions.

Alon.   Heard you this, Gonzalo?

Gon. Upon mine honour, sir, I heard a
    humming,
And that a strange one too, which did
    awake me;
I shak'd you, sir, and cried; as mine eyes
    open'd,   310
I saw their weapons drawn—there was a
    noise,
That's verily. 'Tis best we stand upon our
    guard,
Or that we quit this place. Let's draw our
    weapons.

Alon. Lead off this ground; and let's
make further search
For my poor son.

Gon. Heavens keep him from these beasts!
For he is, sure, i' th' island.

Alon.   Lead away.   316

Ari. Prospero my lord shall know what I
    have done;
So, King, go safely on to seek thy son.
             [*Exeunt.*

SCENE II. *Another part of the island.*

Enter CALIBAN, *with a burden of wood.*
A noise of thunder heard.

Cal. All the infections that the sun sucks
    up
From bogs, fens, flats, on Prosper fall, and
    make him
By inch-meal a disease! His spirits hear
    me,
And yet I needs must curse. But they'll
    nor pinch,
Fright me with urchin-shows, pitch me i'
    th' mire,   5
Nor lead me, like a firebrand, in the dark
Out of my way, unless he bid 'em; but
For every trifle are they set upon me;
Sometime like apes that mow and chatter
    at me,
And after bite me; then like hedgehogs
    which   10
Lie tumbling in my barefoot way, and
    mount
Their pricks at my footfall; sometime
    am I
All wound with adders, who with cloven
    tongues
Do hiss me into madness.

Enter TRINCULO.

           Lo, now, lo!
Here comes a spirit of his, and to torment
    me   15
For bringing wood in slowly. I'll fall flat;
Perchance he will not mind me.

Trin. Here's neither bush nor shrub to
bear off any weather at all, and another
storm brewing; I hear it sing i' th' wind.
Yond same black cloud, yond huge one,
looks like a foul bombard that would shed
his liquor. If it should thunder as it did
before, I know not where to hide my head.
Yond same cloud cannot choose but fall by
pailfuls. What have we here? a man or a
fish? dead or alive? A fish: he smells like
a fish; a very ancient and fish-like smell;
a kind of not-of-the-newest Poor-John.
A strange fish! Were I in England now, as
once I was, and had but this fish painted,
not a holiday fool there but would give a
piece of silver. There would this monster
make a man; any strange beast there
makes a man; when they will not give a

doit to relieve a lame beggar, they will lay out ten to see a dead Indian. Legg'd like a man, and his fins like arms! Warm, o' my troth! I do now let loose my opinion; hold it no longer: this is no fish, but an islander, that hath lately suffered by a thunderbolt. [*Thunder*] Alas, the storm is come again! My best way is to creep under his gaberdine; there is no other shelter hereabout. Misery acquaints a man with strange bedfellows. I will here shroud till the dregs of the storm be past.

Enter STEPHANO *singing; a bottle in his hand.*

Ste. I shall no more to sea, to sea,   40
    Here shall I die ashore—

This is a very scurvy tune to sing at a man's funeral; well, here's my comfort. [*Drinks.*

    The master, the swabber, the boat-
        swain, and I,
    The gunner, and his mate,   45
    Lov'd Mall, Meg, and Marian, and
        Margery,
    But none of us car'd for Kate;
    For she had a tongue with a tang,
    Would cry to a sailor 'Go hang!'
    She lov'd not the savour of tar nor
        of pitch,   50
    Yet a tailor might scratch her
        where'er she did itch.
    Then to sea, boys, and let her go
        hang!

This is a scurvy tune too; but here's my comfort.   [*Drinks.*
Cal. Do not torment me. O!   54
Ste. What's the matter? Have we devils here? Do you put tricks upon 's with savages and men of Ind? Ha! I have not scap'd drowning to be afeard now of your four legs; for it hath been said: As proper a man as ever went on four legs cannot make him give ground; and it shall be said so again, while Stephano breathes at nostrils.   60
Cal. The spirit torments me. O!
Ste. This is some monster of the isle with four legs, who hath got, as I take it, an ague. Where the devil should he learn our language? I will give him some relief, if it be but for that. If I can recover him, and keep him tame, and get to Naples with him, he's a present for any emperor that ever trod on neat's leather.
Cal. Do not torment me, prithee; I'll bring my wood home faster.   69
Ste. He's in his fit now, and does not talk after the wisest. He shall taste of my bottle: if he have never drunk wine afore, it will go near to remove his fit. If I can recover him, and keep him tame, I will not take too much for him; he shall pay for

him that hath him, and that soundly.   74
Cal. Thou dost me yet but little hurt; thou wilt anon, I know it by thy trembling; now Prosper works upon thee.   76
Ste. Come on your ways; open your mouth; here is that which will give language to you, cat. Open your mouth; this will shake your shaking, I can tell you, and that soundly; you cannot tell who's your friend. Open your chaps again.   80
Trin. I should know that voice; it should be—but he is drown'd; and these are devils. O, defend me!   82
Ste. Four legs and two voices; a most delicate monster! His forward voice, now, is to speak well of his friend; his backward voice is to utter foul speeches and to detract. If all the wine in my bottle will recover him, I will help his ague. Come—Amen! I will pour some in thy other mouth.
Trin. Stephano!   89
Ste. Doth thy other mouth call me? Mercy, mercy! This is a devil, and no monster; I will leave him; I have no long spoon.
Trin. Stephano! If thou beest Stephano, touch me, and speak to me; for I am Trinculo—be not afeard—thy good friend Trinculo.   95
Ste. If thou beest Trinculo, come forth; I'll pull thee by the lesser legs; if any be Trinculo's legs, these are they. Thou art very Trinculo indeed! How cam'st thou to be the siege of this moon-calf? Can he vent Trinculos?   99
Trin. I took him to be kill'd with a thunderstroke. But art thou not drown'd, Stephano? I hope now thou are not drown'd. Is the storm overblown? I hid me under the dead moon-calf's gaberdine for fear of the storm. And art thou living, Stephano? O Stephano, two Neapolitans scap'd!   105
Ste. Prithee, do not turn me about; my stomach is not constant.
Cal. [*Aside*] These be fine things, an if
      they be not sprites.
That's a brave god, and bears celestial liquor.
I will kneel to him.   110
Ste. How didst thou scape? How cam'st thou hither? Swear by this bottle how thou cam'st hither—I escap'd upon a butt of sack, which the sailors heaved o'erboard—by this bottle, which I made of the bark of a tree, with mine own hands, since I was cast ashore.   115
Cal. I'll swear upon that bottle to be thy true subject, for the liquor is not earthly.
Ste. Here; swear then how thou escap'dst.
Trin. Swum ashore, man, like a duck; I can swim like a duck, I'll be sworn.   120

13

Ste. [*Passing the bottle*] Here, kiss the book. Though thou canst swim like a duck, thou art made like a goose.   122

Trin. O Stephano, hast any more of this?

Ste. The whole butt, man; my cellar is in a rock by th' seaside, where my wine is hid. How now, moon-calf! How does thine ague?   126

Cal. Hast thou not dropp'd from heaven?

Ste. Out o' th' moon, I do assure thee; I was the Man i' th' Moon, when time was.

Cal. I have seen thee in her, and I do adore thee. My mistress show'd me thee, and thy dog and thy bush.   131

Ste. Come, swear to that; kiss the book. I will furnish it anon with new contents. Swear.   [*Caliban drinks.*

Trin. By this good light, this is a very shallow monster! I afeard of him! A very weak monster! The Man i' th' Moon! A most poor credulous monster! Well drawn, monster, in good sooth!   137

Cal. I'll show thee every fertile inch o' th' island; and I will kiss thy foot. I prithee be my god.

Trin. By this light, a most perfidious and drunken monster! When 's god's asleep he'll rob his bottle.   141

Cal. I'll kiss thy foot; I'll swear myself thy subject.

Ste. Come on, then; down, and swear.

Trin. I shall laugh myself to death at this puppy-headed monster. A most scurvy monster! I could find in my heart to beat him—   146

Ste. Come, kiss.

Trin. But that the poor monster's in drink. An abominable monster!

Cal. I'll show thee the best springs; I'll pluck thee berries;   150
I'll fish for thee, and get thee wood enough. A plague upon the tyrant that I serve! I'll bear him no more sticks, but follow thee, Thou wondrous man.

Trin. A most ridiculous monster, to make a wonder of a poor drunkard!   156

Cal. I prithee let me bring thee where crabs grow;
And I with my long nails will dig thee pignuts;
Show thee a jay's nest, and instruct thee how
To snare the nimble marmoset; I'll bring thee   160
To clust'ring filberts, and sometimes I'll get thee
Young scamels from the rock. Wilt thou go with me?

Ste. I prithee now, lead the way without any more talking. Trinculo, the King and all our company else being drown'd, we will inherit here. Here, bear my bottle. Fellow Trinculo, we'll fill him by and by again.   166

Cal. [*Sings drunkenly*] Farewell, master; farewell, farewell!

Trin. A howling monster; a drunken monster!

Cal. No more dams I'll make for fish;
Nor fetch in firing   170
At requiring,
Nor scrape trenchering, nor wash dish.
'Ban 'Ban, Ca—Caliban,
Has a new master—Get a new man.

Freedom, high-day! high-day, freedom! freedom, high-day, freedom!   176

Ste. O brave monster! Lead the way.
[*Exeunt.*

ACT THREE

SCENE I. *Before Prospero's cell.*

Enter FERDINAND, *bearing a log.*

Fer. There be some sports are painful, and their labour
Delight in them sets off; some kinds of baseness
Are nobly undergone, and most poor matters
Point to rich ends. This my mean task
Would be as heavy to me as odious, but
The mistress which I serve quickens what's dead,   6
And makes my labours pleasures. O, she is
Ten times more gentle than her father's crabbed;
And he's compos'd of harshness. I must remove
Some thousands of these logs, and pile them up,   10
Upon a sore injunction; my sweet mistress
Weeps when she sees me work, and says such baseness
Had never like executor. I forget;
But these sweet thoughts do even refresh my labours,
Most busy, least when I do it.

Enter MIRANDA; *and* PROSPERO *at a distance, unseen.*

Mira.   Alas, now; pray you,
Work not so hard; I would the lightning had   16
Burnt up those logs that you are enjoin'd to pile.
Pray, set it down and rest you; when this burns,
'Twill weep for having wearied you. My father
Is hard at study; pray, now, rest yourself;
He's safe for these three hours.

Fer.   O most dear mistress,
The sun will set before I shall discharge
What I must strive to do.

Mira.   If you'll sit down,
I'll bear your logs the while; pray give me that;   21

I'll carry it to the pile.

Fer.   No, precious creature ;
I had rather crack my sinews, break my
  back,   26
Than you should such dishonour undergo,
While I sit lazy by.

Mira.   It would become me
As well as it does you ; and I should do it
With much more ease ; for my good will
  is to it,   30
And yours it is against.

Pro. [*Aside*] Poor worm, thou art infected !
This visitation shows it.

Mira.   You look wearily.

Fer. No, noble mistress ; 'tis fresh morn-
  ing with me
When you are by at night. I do beseech
  you,   34
Chiefly that I might set it in my prayers,
What is your name ?

Mira.   Miranda—O my father,
I have broke your hest to say so !

Fer.   Admir'd Miranda !
Indeed the top of admiration ; worth
What's dearest to the world ! Full many a
  lady
I have ey'd with best regard ; and many a
  time   40
Th' harmony of their tongues hath into
  bondage
Brought my too diligent ear ; for several
  virtues
Have I lik'd several women, never any
With so full soul, but some defect in her
Did quarrel with the noblest grace she
  ow'd,   45
And put it to the foil ; but you, O you,
So perfect and so peerless, are created
Of every creature's best !

Mira.   I do not know
One of my sex ; no woman's face remember,
Save, from my glass, mine own ; nor have
  I seen   50
More that I may call men than you, good
  friend,
And my dear father. How features are
  abroad,
I am skilless of ; but, by my modesty,
The jewel in my dower, I would not wish
Any companion in the world but you ;   55
Nor can imagination form a shape,
Besides yourself, to like of. But I prattle
Something too wildly, and my father's
  precepts
I therein do forget.

Fer.   I am, in my condition,
A prince, Miranda ; I do think, a king—
I would not so !—and would no more endure
This wooden slavery than to suffer   62
The flesh-fly blow my mouth. Hear my
  soul speak :
The very instant that I saw you, did
My heart fly to your service ; there resides

To make me slave to it ; and for your sake
Am I this patient log-man.

Mira.   Do you love me ?

Fer. O heaven, O earth, bear witness to
  this sound,
And crown what I profess with kind event,
If I speak true ! If hollowly, invert   70
What best is boded me to mischief ! I,
Beyond all limit of what else i' th' world,
Do love, prize, honour you.

Mira.   I am a fool
To weep at what I am glad of.

Pro. [*Aside*]   Fair encounter
Of two most rare affections ! Heavens rain
  grace   75
On that which breeds between 'em !

Fer.   Wherefore weep you ?

Mira. At mine unworthiness, that dare
  not offer
What I desire to give, and much less take
What I shall die to want. But this is
  trifling ;
And all the more it seeks to hide itself,   80
The bigger bulk it shows. Hence, bashful
  cunning !
And prompt me plain and holy innocence !
I am your wife, if you will marry me ;
If not, I'll die your maid. To be your fellow
You may deny me ; but I'll be your
  servant,   85
Whether you will or no.

Fer.   My mistress, dearest ;
And I thus humble ever.

Mira.   My husband, then ?

Fer. Ay, with a heart as willing
As bondage e'er of freedom. Here's my
  hand.

Mira. And mine, with my heart in't. And
  now farewell   90
Till half an hour hence.

Fer.   A thousand thousand !
  [*Exeunt Fer. and Mira. severally.*

Pro. So glad of this as they I cannot be,
Who are surpris'd withal ; but my rejoicing
At nothing can be more. I'll to my book ;
For yet ere supper time must I perform   95
Much business appertaining.   [*Exit.*

SCENE II. *Another part of the island.*

Enter CALIBAN, STEPHANO *and* TRINCULO.

Ste. Tell not me—when the butt is out
we will drink water, not a drop before ;
therefore bear up, and board 'em. Servant-
monster, drink to me.

Trin. Servant-monster ! The folly of this
island ! They say there's but five upon this
isle : we are three of them ; if th' other two
be brain'd like us, the state totters.   6

Ste. Drink, servant-monster, when I bid
thee ; thy eyes are almost set in thy head.

Trin. Where should they be set else ?
He were a brave monster indeed, if they
were set in his tail.   10

Ste. My man-monster hath drown'd his
tongue in sack. For my part, the sea cannot
drown me ; I swam, ere I could recover the
shore, five and thirty leagues, off and on.
By this light, thou shalt be my lieutenant,
monster, or my standard.   15

Trin. Your lieutenant, if you list ; he's
no standard.

Ste. We'll not run, Monsieur Monster.

Trin. Nor go neither ; but you'll lie like
dogs, and yet say nothing neither.

Ste. Moon-calf, speak once in thy life, if
thou beest a good moon-calf.   21

Cal. How does thy honour ? Let me lick
thy shoe.
I'll not serve him ; he is not valiant.

Trin. Thou liest, most ignorant monster :
I am in case to justle a constable. Why,
thou debosh'd fish, thou, was there ever
man a coward that hath drunk so much
sack as I to-day ? Wilt thou tell a monstrous lie, being but half a fish and half a
monster ?   28

Cal. Lo, how he mocks me ! Wilt thou
let him, my lord ?

Trin. ' Lord ' quoth he ! That a monster
should be such a natural !   31

Cal. Lo, lo again ! Bite him to death, I
prithee.

Ste. Trinculo, keep a good tongue in your
head ; if you prove a mutineer—the next
tree ! The poor monster's my subject, and
he shall not suffer indignity.   35

Cal. I thank my noble lord. Wilt thou be
pleas'd to hearken once again to the suit I
made to thee ?

Ste. Marry will I ; kneel and repeat it ; I
will stand, and so shall Trinculo.   39

Enter ARIEL, *invisible.*

Cal. As I told thee before, I am subject
to a tyrant, a sorcerer, that by his cunning
hath cheated me of the island.

Ari. Thou liest.

Cal.   Thou liest, thou jesting
                       monkey, thou ;
I would my valiant master would destroy
                       thee.
I do not lie.

Ste. Trinculo, if you trouble him any
more in's tale, by this hand, I will supplant
some of your teeth.   46

Trin. Why, I said nothing.

Ste. Mum, then, and no more. Proceed.

Cal. I say, by sorcery he got this isle ;
From me he got it. If thy greatness will
Revenge it on him—for I know thou dar'st,
But this thing dare not—   52

Ste. That's most certain.

Cal. Thou shalt be lord of it, and I'll
serve thee.

Ste. How now shall this be compass'd ?
Canst thou bring me to the party ?   56

Cal. Yea, yea my lord ; I'll yield him
                       thee asleep,
Where thou mayst knock a nail into his
                       head.

Ari. Thou liest ; thou canst not.

Cal. What a pied ninny's this ! Thou
scurvy patch !   60
I do beseech thy greatness, give him blows,
And take his bottle from him. When that's
                       gone
He shall drink nought but brine ; for I'll
                       not show him
Where the quick freshes are.   64

Ste. Trinculo, run into no further danger ;
interrupt the monster one word further
and, by this hand, I'll turn my mercy out o'
doors, and make a stock-fish of thee.

Trin. Why, what did I ? I did nothing.
I'll go farther off.

Ste. Didst thou not say he lied ?   70

Ari. Thou liest.

Ste. Do I so ? Take thou that. [*Beats
him*] As you like this, give me the lie
another time.   73

Trin. I did not give the lie. Out o' your
wits and hearing too ? A pox o' your bottle !
This can sack and drinking do. A murrain
on your monster, and the devil take your
fingers !   77

Cal. Ha, ha, ha !

Ste. Now, forward with your tale.—
Prithee stand further off.   80

Cal. Beat him enough ; after a little time,
I'll beat him too.

Ste. Stand farther. Come, proceed.

Cal. Why, as I told thee, 'tis a custom
                       with him
I' th' afternoon to sleep ; there thou mayst
                       brain him,
Having first seiz'd his books ; or with a log
Batter his skull, or paunch him with a
                       stake,   86
Or cut his wezand with thy knife. Re-
                       member
First to possess his books ; for without
                       them
He's but a sot, as I am, nor hath not
One spirit to command ; they all do hate
                       him   90
As rootedly as I. Burn but his books.
He has brave utensils—for so he calls
                       them—
Which, when he has a house, he'll deck
                       withal.
And that most deeply to consider is
The beauty of his daughter ; he himself
Calls her a nonpareil. I never saw a woman
But only Sycorax my dam and she ;   97
But she as far surpasseth Sycorax
As great'st does least.

Ste.   Is it so brave a lass ?

Cal. Ay, lord ; she will become thy bed,
                       I warrant,   100
And bring thee forth brave brood.

Ste. Monster, I will kill this man; his daughter and I will be King and Queen—save our Graces!—and Trinculo and thyself shall be viceroys. Dost thou like the plot, Trinculo?   105

Trin. Excellent.

Ste. Give me thy hand; I am sorry I beat thee; but while thou liv'st, keep a good tongue in thy head.

Cal. Within this half hour will he be asleep.
Wilt thou destroy him then?

Ste.   Ay, on mine honour.

Ari. This will I tell my master.   111

Cal. Thou mak'st me merry; I am full of pleasure.
Let us be jocund; will you troll the catch
You taught me but while-ere?

Ste. At thy request, monster, I will do reason, any reason. Come on, Trinculo, let us sing.   [*Sings.*

> Flout 'em and scout 'em,
> And scout 'em and flout 'em;
>   Thought is free.

Cal. That's not the tune.
[*Ariel plays the tune on a tabor and pipe.*
Ste. What is this same?   20
Trin. This is the tune of our catch, play'd by the picture of Nobody.
Ste. If thou beest a man, show thyself in thy likeness; if thou beest a devil, take't as thou list.
Trin. O, forgive me my sins!   125
Ste. He that dies pays all debts. I defy thee. Mercy upon us!
Cal. Art thou afeard?
Ste. No, monster, not I.
Cal. Be not afeard. The isle is full of noises,   130
Sounds, and sweet airs, that give delight, and hurt not.
Sometimes a thousand twangling instruments
Will hum about mine ears; and sometime voices,
That, if I then had wak'd after long sleep,
Will make me sleep again; and then, in dreaming,   135
The clouds methought would open and show riches
Ready to drop upon me, that, when I wak'd,
I cried to dream again.
Ste. This will prove a brave kingdom to me, where I shall have my music for nothing.   140
Cal. When Prospero is destroy'd.
Ste. That shall be by and by; I remember the story.
Trin. The sound is going away; let's follow it, and after do our work.   144
Ste. Lead, monster; we'll follow. I would I could see this taborer; he lays it on.

Trin. Wilt come? I'll follow, Stephano.
                                      [*Exeunt.*

SCENE III.   *Another part of the island.*

Enter ALONSO, SEBASTIAN, ANTONIO,
GONZALO, ADRIAN, FRANCISCO, *and* Others.

Gon. By'r lakin, I can go no further, sir;
My old bones ache. Here's a maze trod, indeed,
Through forth-rights and meanders! By your patience,
I needs must rest me.
Alon.   Old lord, I cannot blame thee,
Who am myself attach'd with weariness   5
To th' dulling of my spirits; sit down and rest.
Even here I will put off my hope, and keep it
No longer for my flatterer; he is drown'd
Whom thus we stray to find, and the sea mocks
Our frustrate search on land. Well, let him go.   10
Ant. [*Aside to Seb.*] I am right glad that he's so out of hope.
Do not, for one repulse, forgo the purpose
That you resolv'd t' effect.
Seb. [*Aside to Ant.*] The next advantage
Will we take throughly.
Ant. [*Aside to Seb.*] Let it be to-night;
For, now they are oppress'd with travel, they   15
Will not, nor cannot, use such vigilance
As when they are fresh.
Seb. [*Aside to Ant.*] I say, to-night; no more.

Solemn and strange music; and PROSPERO
*on the top, invisible. Enter several strange
Shapes, bringing in a banquet; and dance
about it with gentle actions of salutations;
and inviting the King, &c., to eat, they
depart.*

Alon. What harmony is this? My good friends, hark!
Gon. Marvellous sweet music!
Alon. Give us kind keepers, heavens! What were these?   20
Seb. A living drollery. Now I will believe
That there are unicorns; that in Arabia
There is one tree, the phœnix' throne, one phœnix
At this hour reigning there.
Ant.   I'll believe both;
And what does else want credit, come to me,   25
And I'll be sworn 'tis true; travellers ne'er did lie,
Though fools at home condemn 'em.
Gon.   If in Naples
I should report this now, would they believe me?
If I should say, I saw such islanders,   29
For certes these are people of the island,

Who though they are of monstrous shape
    yet, note,   31
Their manners are more gentle-kind than of
Our human generation you shall find
Many, nay, almost any.
  Pro. [*Aside*]   Honest lord,
Thou hast said well ; for some of you there
    present   35
Are worse than devils.
  Alon.   I cannot too much muse
Such shapes, such gesture, and such sound,
    expressing,
Although they want the use of tongue, a kind
Of excellent dumb discourse.
  Pro. [*Aside*]   Praise in departing. 39
  Fran. They vanish'd strangely.
  Seb.   No matter, since
They have left their viands behind ; for we
    have stomachs.
Will't please you taste of what is here ?
  Alon.   Not I.
  Gon. Faith, sir, you need not fear. When
    we were boys,
Who would believe that there were
    mountaineers,
Dewlapp'd like bulls, whose throats had
    hanging at 'em   45
Wallets of flesh ? or that there were such
    men
Whose heads stood in their breasts? which
    now we find
Each putter-out of five for one will bring us
Good warrant of.
  Alon.   I will stand to, and feed,
Although my last ; no matter, since I feel
The best is past. Brother, my lord the
    Duke,   51
Stand to, and do as we.

Thunder and lightning. Enter ARIEL, *like a
harpy ; claps his wings upon the table ;
and, with a quaint device, the banquet
vanishes.*

  Ari. You are three men of sin, whom
    Destiny,
That hath to instrument this lower world
And what is in't, the never-surfeited sea
Hath caus'd to belch up you ; and on this
    island   56
Where man doth not inhabit—you 'mongst
    men
Being most unfit to live. I have made you
    mad ;
And even with such-like valour men hang
    and drown
Their proper selves.
    [*Alon., Seb. &c., draw their swords.*
        You fools ! I and my fellows
Are ministers of Fate ; the elements   61
Of whom your swords are temper'd may as
    well
Wound the loud winds, or with bemock'd-
    at stabs
Kill the still-closing waters, as diminish

One dowle that's in my plume ; my fellow-
    ministers   65
Are like invulnerable. If you could hurt,
Your swords are now too massy for your
    strengths
And will not be uplifted. But remember—
For that's my business to you—that you
    three
From Milan did supplant good Prospero ;
Expos'd unto the sea, which hath requit it,
Him, and his innocent child ; for which
    foul deed   72
The pow'rs, delaying, not forgetting, have
Incens'd the seas and shores, yea, all the
    creatures,
Against your peace. Thee of thy son,
    Alonso,   75
They have bereft ; and do pronounce by me
Ling'ring perdition, worse than any death
Can be at once, shall step by step attend
You and your ways ; whose wraths to
    guard you from—
Which here, in this most desolate isle, else
    falls   80
Upon your heads—is nothing but heart's
    sorrow,
And a clear life ensuing,

*He vanishes in thunder ; then, to soft music,
enter the* Shapes *again, and dance, with
mocks and mows, and carrying out the table.*

  Pro. Bravely the figure of this harpy
    hast thou
Perform'd, my Ariel ; a grace it had,
    devouring.   86
Of my instruction hast thou nothing bated
In what thou hadst to say ; so, with good life
And observation strange, my meaner
    ministers
Their several kinds have done. My high
    charms work,
And these mine enemies are all knit up
In their distractions. They now are in my
    pow'r ;   90
And in these fits I leave them, while I visit
Young Ferdinand, whom they suppose is
    drown'd,
And his and mine lov'd darling.
              [*Exit above.*
  Gon. I' th' name of something holy, sir,
    why stand you
In this strange stare ?
  Alon.   O, it is monstrous, monstrous !
Methought the billows spoke, and told me
    of it ;   96
The winds did sing it to me ; and the
    thunder,
That deep and dreadful organ-pipe, pro-
    nounc'd
The name of Prosper ; it did bass my
    trespass.
Therefore my son i' th' ooze is bedded ; and
I'll seek him deeper than e'er plummet
    sounded,   101

And with him there lie mudded.   [*Exit.*
  Seb.   But one fiend at a time,
I'll fight their legions o'er.
  Ant.   I'll be thy second.
             [*Exeunt Seb. and Ant.*
  Gon. All three of them are desperate ;
    their great guilt,
Like poison given to work a great time
    after,   105
Now gins to bite the spirits. I do beseech
    you,
That are of suppler joints, follow them
    swiftly,
And hinder them from what this ecstasy
May now provoke them to.
  Adr.   Follow, I pray you. [*Exeunt.*

ACT FOUR

Scene I. *Before Prospero's cell.*

Enter Prospero, Ferdinand, *and*
    Miranda.

  Pro. If I have too austerely punish'd you,
Your compensation makes amends ; for I
Have given you here a third of mine own life,
Or that for which I live ; who once again
I tender to thy hand. All thy vexations   5
Were but my trials of thy love, and thou
Hast strangely stood the test ; here, afore
    heaven,
I ratify this my rich gift. O Ferdinand !
Do not smile at me that I boast her off,
For thou shalt find she will outstrip all
    praise,   10
And make it halt behind her.
  Fer.   I do believe it
Against an oracle.
  Pro.   Then, as my gift, and thine own
    acquisition
Worthily purchas'd, take my daughter. But
If thou dost break her virgin-knot before   15
All sanctimonious ceremonies may
With full and holy rite be minist'red,
No sweet aspersion shall the heavens let fall
To make this contract grow ; but barren
    hate,
Sour-ey'd disdain, and discord, shall
    bestrew   20
The union of your bed with weeds so
    loathly
That you shall hate it both. Therefore
    take heed,
As Hymen's lamps shall light you.
  Fer.   As I hope
For quiet days, fair issue, and long life,
With such love as 'tis now, the murkiest
    den,   25
The most opportune place, the strong'st
    suggestion
Our worser genius can, shall never melt
Mine honour into lust, to take away
The edge of that day's celebration,
When I shall think or Phœbus' steeds are
    founder'd   30

Or Night kept chain'd below.
  Pro.   Fairly spoke.
Sit, then, and talk with her ; she is thine
    own.
What, Ariel ! my industrious servant,
    Ariel !

        Enter Ariel.

  Ari. What would my potent master ?
    Here I am.
  Pro. Thou and thy meaner fellows your
    last service   35
Did worthily perform ; and I must use you
In such another trick. Go bring the rabble,
O'er whom I give thee pow'r, here to this
    place.   38
Incite them to quick motion ; for I must
Bestow upon the eyes of this young couple
Some vanity of mine art ; it is my promise,
And they expect it from me.
  Ariel.   Presently ?
  Pro. Ay, with a twink.
  Ari. Before you can say ' come ' and
    ' go ',   44
    And breathe twice, and cry ' so, so ',
    Each one, tripping on his toe,
    Will be here with mop and mow.
    Do you love me, master ? No ?
  Pro. Dearly, my delicate Ariel. Do not
    approach
Till thou dost hear me call.
  Ari.   Well ! I conceive. [*Exit.*
  Pro. Look thou be true ; do not give
    dalliance   51
Too much the rein ; the strongest oaths are
    straw
To th' fire i' th' blood. Be more abstemious,
Or else good night your vow !
  Fer.   I warrant you, sir,
The white cold virgin snow upon my heart
Abates the ardour of my liver.
  Pro.   Well !   56
Now come, my Ariel, bring a corollary,
Rather than want a spirit ; appear, and
    pertly.
No tongue ! All eyes ! Be silent.
                [*Soft music.*

        Enter Iris.

  Iris. Ceres, most bounteous lady, thy
    rich leas   60
Of wheat, rye, barley, vetches, oats, and
    pease ;
Thy turfy mountains, where live nibbling
    sheep,
And flat meads thatch'd with stover, them
    to keep ;
Thy banks with pioned and twilled brims,
Which spongy April at thy hest betrims,
To make cold nymphs chaste crowns ; and
    thy broom groves,   66
Whose shadow the dismissed bachelor loves,
Being lass-lorn ; thy pole-clipt vineyard ;
And thy sea-marge, sterile and rocky-hard,

Where thou thyself dost air—the Queen o'
    th' sky,   70
Whose wat'ry arch and messenger am I,
Bids thee leave these ; and with her
    sovereign grace,
Here on this grass-plot, in this very place,
To come and sport. Her peacocks fly amain.

Juno descends in her car.

Approach, rich Ceres, her to entertain. 75

Enter Ceres.

Cer. Hail, many-coloured messenger, that
    ne'er
Dost disobey the wife of Jupiter ;
Who, with thy saffron wings, upon my flow'rs
Diffusest honey drops, refreshing show'rs ;
And with each end of thy blue bow dost
    crown   80
My bosky acres and my unshrubb'd down,
Rich scarf to my proud earth—why hath
    thy Queen
Summon'd me hither to this short-grass'd
    green ?
Iris. A contract of true love to celebrate,
And some donation freely to estate   85
On the blest lovers.
Cer.   Tell me, heavenly bow,
If Venus or her son, as thou dost know,
Do now attend the Queen ? Since they did
    plot
The means that dusky Dis my daughter got,
Her and her blind boy's scandal'd company
I have forsworn.
Iris.   Of her society   91
Be not afraid. I met her Deity
Cutting the clouds towards Paphos, and
    her son
Dove-drawn with her. Here thought they
    to have done
Some wanton charm upon this man and
    maid,   95
Whose vows are that no bed-rite shall be paid
Till Hymen's torch be lighted ; but in vain.
Mars's hot minion is return'd again ;
Her waspish-headed son has broke his
    arrows,
Swears he will shoot no more, but play with
    sparrows,   100
And be a boy right out.
                     [Juno alights.
Cer.   Highest Queen of state,
Great Juno, comes ; I know her by her gait.
Juno. How does my bounteous sister ? Go
    with me
To bless this twain, that they may prosper-
    ous be,   104
And honour'd in their issue.

They sing.

Juno. Honour, riches, marriage-blessing,
    Long continuance, and increasing,
    Hourly joys be still upon you !
    Juno sings her blessings on you.

Cer. Earth's increase, foison plenty,
    Barns and garners never empty ;
    Vines with clust'ring bunches grow-
      ing,   112
    Plants with goodly burden bowing ;
    Spring come to you at the farthest,
    In the very end of harvest !   115
    Scarcity and want shall shun you,
    Ceres' blessing so is on you.

Fer. This is a most majestic vision, and
Harmonious charmingly. May I be bold
To think these spirits ?
Pro.   Spirits, which by mine art
I have from their confines call'd to enact
My present fancies.
Fer.   Let me live here ever ;
So rare a wond'red father and a wise   123
Makes this place Paradise.
              [Juno and Ceres whisper, and
              send Iris on employment.
Pro.   Sweet now, silence ;
Juno and Ceres whisper seriously.   125
There's something else to do ; hush, and be
    mute,
Or else our spell is marr'd.
Iris. You nymphs, call'd Naiads, of the
    wind'ring brooks,
With your sedg'd crowns and ever harmless
    looks,
Leave your crisp channels, and on this
    green land   130
Answer your summons ; Juno does com-
    mand.
Come, temperate nymphs, and help to
    celebrate
A contract of true love ; be not too late.

Enter certain Nymphs.

You sun-burnt sicklemen, of August
    weary,
Come hither from the furrow, and be merry;
Make holiday ; your rye-straw hats put on,
And these fresh nymphs encounter every
    one   137
In country footing.

Enter certain Reapers, *properly habited ;
they join with the Nymphs in a graceful
dance ; towards the end whereof Prospero
starts suddenly, and speaks ; after which,
to a strange, hollow, and confused noise,
they heavily vanish.*

Pro. [*Aside*] I had forgot that foul con-
    spiracy   139
Of the beast Caliban and his confederates
Against my life ; the minute of their plot
Is almost come. [*To the Spirits*] Well done ;
    avoid ; no more !
Fer. This is strange ; your father's in
    some passion
That works him strongly.
Mira.   Never till this day

Saw I him touch'd with anger so dis-
  temper'd.   145
  Pro. You do look, my son, in a mov'd
    sort,
As if you were dismay'd ; be cheerful, sir.
Our revels now are ended. These our actors,
As I foretold you, were all spirits, and
Are melted into air, into thin air ;   150
And, like the baseless fabric of this vision,
The cloud-capp'd towers, the gorgeous
    palaces,
The solemn temples, the great globe itself,
Yea, all which it inherit, shall dissolve, 154
And, like this insubstantial pageant faded,
Leave not a rack behind. We are such stuff
As dreams are made on ; and our little life
Is rounded with a sleep. Sir, I am vex'd ;
Bear with my weakness ; my old brain is
    troubled ;
Be not disturb'd with my infirmity.   160
If you be pleas'd, retire into my cell
And there repose ; a turn or two I'll walk
To still my beating mind.
  Fer., Mira.   We wish your peace.
                                    [*Exeunt.*
  Pro. Come, with a thought. I thank thee,
    Ariel ; come.

                Enter ARIEL.

  Ari. Thy thoughts I cleave to. What's
    thy pleasure ?
  Pro.   Spirit,   165
We must prepare to meet with Caliban.
  Ari. Ay, my commander. When I pre-
    sented 'Ceres',
I thought to have told thee of it ; but I
    fear'd
Lest I might anger thee.
  Pro. Say again, where didst thou leave
    these varlets ?   170
  Ari. I told you, sir, they were red-hot
    with drinking ;
So full of valour that they smote the air
For breathing in their faces ; beat the
    ground
For kissing of their feet ; yet always
    bending
Towards their project. Then I beat my
    tabor,   175
At which like unback'd colts they prick'd
    their ears,
Advanc'd their eyelids, lifted up their
    noses
As they smelt music ; so I charm'd their
    ears,
That calf-like they my lowing follow'd
    through
Tooth'd briers, sharp furzes, pricking goss,
    and thorns,   180
Which ent'red their frail shins. At last I
    left them
I' th' filthy mantled pool beyond your cell,
There dancing up to th' chins, that the foul
    lake

O'erstunk their feet.
  Pro.   This was well done, my bird.
Thy shape invisible retain thou still.   185
The trumpery in my house, go bring it
    hither
For stale to catch these thieves.
  Ari.   I go, I go. [*Exit.*
  Pro. A devil, a born devil, on whose
    nature
Nurture can never stick ; on whom my
    pains,   189
Humanely taken, all, all lost, quite lost ;
And as with age his body uglier grows,
So his mind cankers. I will plague them all,
Even to roaring.

Re-enter ARIEL, *loaden with glistering
            apparel, &c.*

        Come, hang them on this line.

Prospero and Ariel remain, invisible. Enter
CALIBAN, STEPHANO, *and* TRINCULO,
all wet.

  Cal. Pray you, tread softly, that the
    blind mole may not   194
Hear a foot fall ; we now are near his cell.
  Ste. Monster, your fairy, which you say is
a harmless fairy, has done little better than
play'd the Jack with us.
  Trin. Monster, I do smell all horse-piss at
which my nose is in great indignation. 199
  Ste. So is mine. Do you hear, monster ?
If I should take a displeasure against you,
look you—
  Trin. Thou wert but a lost monster.
  Cal. Good my lord, give me thy favour
    still.
Be patient, for the prize I'll bring thee to
Shall hoodwink this mischance; therefore
    speak softly.   205
All's hush'd as midnight yet.
  Trin. Ay, but to lose our bottles in the
pool !
  Ste. There is not only disgrace and dis-
honour in that, monster, but an infinite loss.
  Trin. That's more to me than my wet-
ting ; yet this is your harmless fairy,
monster.   211
  Ste. I will fetch off my bottle, though I be
o'er ears for my labour.
  Cal. Prithee, my king, be quiet. Seest
    thou here,
This is the mouth o' th' cell ; no noise, and
    enter.   215
Do that good mischief which may make
    this island
Thine own for ever, and I, thy Caliban,
For aye thy foot-licker.
  Ste. Give me thy hand. I do begin to
have bloody thoughts.   220
  Trin. O King Stephano ! O peer ! O
worthy Stephano ! Look what a wardrobe
here is for thee !

                                              21

Cal. Let it alone, thou fool ; it is but
    trash. 223
Trin. O, ho, monster ; we know what
belongs to a frippery. O King Stephano !
Ste. Put off that gown, Trinculo ; by this
hand, I'll have that gown. 227
Trin. Thy Grace shall have it.
Cal. The dropsy drown this fool ! What
    do you mean
To dote thus on such luggage ? Let't
    alone,
And do the murder first. If he awake, 231
From toe to crown he'll fill our skins with
    pinches ;
Make us strange stuff.
Ste. Be you quiet, monster. Mistress line,
is not this my jerkin ? Now is the jerkin
under the line ; now, jerkin, you are like to
lose your hair, and prove a bald jerkin. 237
Trin. Do, do. We steal by line and level,
an't like your Grace.
Ste. I thank thee for that jest ; here's a
garment for't. Wit shall not go unre-
warded while I am king of this country.
' Steal by line and level ' is an excellent
pass of pate ; there's another garment
for't.
Trin. Monster, come, put some lime upon
your fingers, and away with the rest. 245
Cal. I will have none on't. We shall lose
    our time,
And all be turn'd to barnacles, or to apes
With foreheads villainous low.
Ste. Monster, lay-to your fingers ; help to
bear this away where my hogshead of wine
is, or I'll turn you out of my kingdom. Go
to, carry this. 251
Trin. And this.
Ste. Ay, and this.

*A noise of hunters heard.   Enter divers
Spirits, in shape of dogs and hounds,
hunting them about ; Prospero and Ariel
setting them on.*

Pro. Hey, Mountain, hey !
Ari. Silver ! there it goes, Silver ! 255
Pro. Fury, Fury ! There, Tyrant, there !
    Hark, hark !
    [*Cal., Ste., and Trin. are driven out.*
Go charge my goblins that they grind their
    joints
With dry convulsions, shorten up their
    sinews
With aged cramps, and more pinch-
    spotted make them
Than pard or cat o' mountain.
Ari.   Hark, they roar.
Pro. Let them be hunted soundly. At
    this hour 261
Lies at my mercy all mine enemies.
Shortly shall all my labours end, and thou
Shalt have the air at freedom ; for a
    little
Follow, and do me service.   [*Exeunt.*

ACT FIVE

SCENE I.   *Before Prospero's cell.*

Enter PROSPERO *in his magic robes, and*
ARIEL.

Pro. Now does my project gather to a
    head ;
My charms crack not, my spirits obey ; and
    time
Goes upright with his carriage. How's the
    day ?
Ari. On the sixth hour ; at which time,
    my lord,
You said our work should cease.
Pro.   I did say so,
When first I rais'd the tempest. Say, my
    spirit, 6
How fares the King and 's followers ?
Ari.   Confin'd together
In the same fashion as you gave in charge ;
Just as you left them ; all prisoners, sir,
In the line-grove which weather-fends your
    cell ; 10
They cannot budge till your release. The
    King,
His brother, and yours, abide all three
    distracted,
And the remainder mourning over them,
Brim full of sorrow and dismay ; but chiefly
Him you term'd, sir, ' the good old lord,
    Gonzalo ' ; 15
His tears run down his beard, like winter's
    drops
From eaves of reeds. Your charm so
    strongly works 'em
That if you now beheld them your affections
Would become tender.
Pro.   Dost thou think so, spirit ?
Ari. Mine would, sir, were I human.
Pro.   And mine shall.
Hast thou, which art but air, a touch, a
    feeling 21
Of their afflictions, and shall not myself,
One of their kind, that relish all as sharply,
Passion as they, be kindlier mov'd than
    thou art ?
Though with their high wrongs I am struck
    to th' quick, 25
Yet with my nobler reason 'gainst my fury
Do I take part ; the rarer action is
In virtue than in vengeance ; they being
    penitent,
The sole drift of my purpose doth extend
Not a frown further. Go release them,
    Ariel ; 30
My charms I'll break, their senses I'll restore,
And they shall be themselves.
Ari.   I'll fetch them, sir. [*Exit.*
Pro. Ye elves of hills, brooks, standing
    lakes, and groves ;
And ye that on the sands with printless foot
Do chase the ebbing Neptune, and do fly
    him 35

When he comes back ; you demi-puppets
　　that
By moonshine do the green sour ringlets
　　make,
Whereof the ewe not bites ; and you
　　whose pastime
Is to make midnight mushrooms, that
　　rejoice
To hear the solemn curfew ; by whose
　　aid—　　　　　　　　　　　　　　40
Weak masters though ye be—I have be-
　　dimm'd
The noontide sun, call'd forth the mutinous
　　winds,
And 'twixt the green sea and the azur'd
　　vault
Set roaring war. To the dread rattling
　　thunder
Have I given fire, and rifted Jove's stout
　　oak　　　　　　　　　　　　　　45
With his own bolt ; the strong-bas'd
　　promontory
Have I made shake, and by the spurs
　　pluck'd up
The pine and cedar. Graves at my com-
　　mand
Have wak'd their sleepers, op'd, and let 'em
　　forth,　　　　　　　　　　　　　49
By my so potent art. But this rough magic
I here abjure ; and, when I have requir'd
Some heavenly music—which even now I
　　do—
To work mine end upon their senses that
This airy charm is for, I'll break my staff,
Bury it certain fathoms in the earth,　　55
And deeper than did ever plummet sound
I'll drown my book.　　　[Solemn music.

Here enters ARIEL *before ; then* ALONSO,
with a frantic gesture, attended by GON-
ZALO ; SEBASTIAN *and* ANTONIO *in like
manner, attended by* ADRIAN *and* FRAN-
CISCO. *They all enter the circle which
Prospero had made, and there stand
charm'd ; which Prospero observing,
speaks.*

A solemn air, and the best comforter
To an unsettled fancy, cure thy brains,
Now useless, boil'd within thy skull ! There
　　stand,　　　　　　　　　　　　60
For you are spell-stopp'd.
Holy Gonzalo, honourable man,
Mine eyes, ev'n sociable to the show of
　　thine,
Fall fellowly drops. The charm dissolves
　　apace,　　　　　　　　　　　　64
And as the morning steals upon the night,
Melting the darkness, so their rising senses
Begin to chase the ignorant fumes that
　　mantle
Their clearer reason. O good Gonzalo,
My true preserver, and a loyal sir　　69
To him thou follow'st ! I will pay thy graces
Home both in word and deed. Most cruelly

Didst thou, Alonso, use me and my
　　daughter ;
Thy brother was a furtherer in the act.
Thou art pinch'd for 't now, Sebastian.
　　Flesh and blood,
You, brother mine, that entertain'd
　　ambition,　　　　　　　　　　75
Expell'd remorse and nature, who, with
　　Sebastian—
Whose inward pinches therefore are most
　　strong—
Would here have kill'd your king, I do
　　forgive thee,
Unnatural though thou art. Their under-
　　standing
Begins to swell, and the approaching tide
Will shortly fill the reasonable shore　　81
That now lies foul and muddy. Not one of
　　them
That yet looks on me, or would know me.
　　Ariel,
Fetch me the hat and rapier in my cell ;
I will discase me, and myself present　　85
As I was sometime Milan. Quickly, spirit ;
Thou shalt ere long be free.

　　ARIEL, *on returning, sings and helps to
　　　　attire him.*

　　Where the bee sucks, there suck I ;
　　In a cowslip's bell I lie ;
　　There I couch when owls do cry.　90
　　On the bat's back I do fly
　　After summer merrily.
Merrily, merrily shall I live now
Under the blossom that hangs on the
　　bough.

Pro. Why, that's my dainty Ariel ! I
　　shall miss thee ;　　　　　　　95
But yet thou shalt have freedom. So, so, so.
To the King's ship, invisible as thou art ;
There shalt thou find the mariners asleep
Under the hatches ; the master and the
　　boatswain
Being awake, enforce them to this place ;
And presently, I prithee.　　　　　101
　　Ari. I drink the air before me, and return
Or ere your pulse twice beat.　　[Exit.
　　Gon. All torment, trouble, wonder and
　　amazement,
Inhabits here. Some heavenly power guide
　　us　　　　　　　　　　　　　105
Out of this fearful country !
　　Pro.　　　　　　　Behold, Sir King,
The wronged Duke of Milan, Prospero.
For more assurance that a living prince
Does now speak to thee, I embrace thy
　　body ;
And to thee and thy company I bid　　110
A hearty welcome.
　　Alon.　　　　Whe'er thou be'st he or no,
Or some enchanted trifle to abuse me,
As late I have been, I not know. Thy
　　pulse

Beats, as of flesh and blood ; and, since I
    saw thee,
Th' affliction of my mind amends, with
    which,   115
I fear, a madness held me. This must
    crave—
An if this be at all—a most strange story.
Thy dukedom I resign, and do entreat
Thou pardon me my wrongs. But how
    should Prospero
Be living and be here ?
  Pro.   First, noble friend,   120
Let me embrace thine age, whose honour
    cannot
Be measur'd or confin'd.
  Gon.   Whether this be
Or be not, I'll not swear.
  Pro.   You do yet taste
Some subtleties o' th' isle, that will not let
    you
Believe things certain. Welcome, my
    friends all !   125
[*Aside to Seb. and Ant.*] But you, my brace
    of lords, were I so minded,
I here could pluck his Highness' frown upon
    you,
And justify you traitors ; at this time
I will tell no tales.
  Seb. [*Aside*] The devil speaks in him.
  Pro.   No.
For you, most wicked sir, whom to call
    brother   130
Would even infect my mouth, I do forgive
Thy rankest fault—all of them ; and
    require
My dukedom of thee, which perforce I
    know
Thou must restore.
  Alon.   If thou beest Prospero,
Give us particulars of thy preservation ;
How thou hast met us here, whom three
    hours since   136
Were wreck'd upon this shore ; where I
    have lost—
How sharp the point of this remembrance
    is !—
My dear son Ferdinand.
  Pro.   I am woe for't, sir.
  Alon. Irreparable is the loss ; and
    patience   140
Says it is past her cure.
  Pro.   I rather think
You have not sought her help, of whose
    soft grace
For the like loss I have her sovereign aid,
And rest myself content.
  Alon.   You the like loss !
  Pro. As great to me as late ; and,
    supportable   145
To make the dear loss, have I means much
    weaker
Than you may call to comfort you, for I
Have lost my daughter.
  Alon.   A daughter !

O heavens, that they were living both in
    Naples,
The King and Queen there! That they
    were, I wish   150
Myself were mudded in that oozy bed
Where my son lies. When did you lose your
    daughter ?
  Pro. In this last tempest. I perceive
    these lords
At this encounter do so much admire
That they devour their reason, and scarce
    think   155
Their eyes do offices of truth, their words
Are natural breath ; but, howsoe'er you
    have
Been justled from your senses, know for
    certain
That I am Prospero, and that very duke
Which was thrust forth of Milan ; who
    most strangely   160
Upon this shore, where you were wreck'd,
    was landed
To be the lord on't. No more yet of
    this ;
For 'tis a chronicle of day by day,
Not a relation for a breakfast, nor
Befitting this first meeting. Welcome, sir ;
This cell's my court ; here have I few
    attendants,   166
And subjects none abroad; pray you, look in.
My dukedom since you have given me
    again,
I will requite you with as good a thing ;
At least bring forth a wonder, to content ye
As much as me my dukedom.   171

Here Prospero discovers FERDINAND *and*
    MIRANDA *playing at chess.*

  Mira. Sweet lord, you play me false.
  Fer.   No, my dearest love,
I would not for the world.
  Mira. Yes, for a score of kingdoms you
    should wrangle,
And I would call it fair play.
  Alon.   If this prove   175
A vision of the island, one dear son
Shall I twice lose.
  Seb.   A most high miracle !
  Fer. Though the seas threaten, they are
    merciful ;
I have curs'd them without cause. [*Kneels.*
  Alon.   Now all the blessings
Of a glad father compass thee about !   180
Arise, and say how thou cam'st here.
  Mira.   O, wonder !
How many goodly creatures are there here !
How beauteous mankind is ! O brave new
    world
That has such people in't !
  Pro.   'Tis new to thee.
  Alon. What is this maid with whom thou
    wast at play ?   185
Your eld'st acquaintance cannot be three
    hours ;

Is she the goddess that hath sever'd us,
And brought us thus together?
    Fer.   Sir, she is mortal;
But by immortal Providence she's mine.
I chose her when I could not ask my father
For his advice, nor thought I had one. She
Is daughter to this famous Duke of Milan,
Of whom so often I have heard renown
But never saw before; of whom I have
Receiv'd a second life; and second father
This lady makes him to me.
    Alon.   I am hers. 196
But, O, how oddly will it sound that I
Must ask my child forgiveness!
    Pro.   There, sir, stop;
Let us not burden our remembrances with
A heaviness that's gone.
    Gon.   I have inly wept,
Or should have spoke ere this. Look down,
    you gods,   201
And on this couple drop a blessed crown;
For it is you that have chalk'd forth the
    way
Which brought us hither.
    Alon.   I say, Amen, Gonzalo!
    Gon. Was Milan thrust from Milan, that
    his issue   205
Should become Kings of Naples? O, rejoice
Beyond a common joy, and set it down
With gold on lasting pillars: in one voyage
Did Claribel her husband find at Tunis;
And Ferdinand, her brother, found a wife
Where he himself was lost; Prospero his
    dukedom   211
In a poor isle; and all of us ourselves
When no man was his own.
    Alon. [*To Fer. and Mir.*] Give me your
    hands.
Let grief and sorrow still embrace his heart
That doth not wish you joy.
    Gon.   Be it so. Amen! 215

Re-enter ARIEL, *with the* Master *and* Boat-
    swain *amazedly following.*

O look, sir; look, sir! Here is more of us!
I prophesied, if a gallows were on land,
This fellow could not drown. Now,
    blasphemy,
That swear'st grace o'erboard, not an oath
    on shore?
Hast thou no mouth by land? What is the
    news?   220
    Boats. The best news is that we have
    safely found
Our King and company; the next, our
    ship—
Which but three glasses since we gave out
    split—
Is tight and yare, and bravely rigg'd, as
    when
We first put out to sea.
    Ari. [*Aside to Pro.*] Sir, all this service
Have I done since I went.
    Pro. [*Aside to Ari.*] My tricksy spirit!

    Alon. These are not natural events; they
    strengthen   227
From strange to stranger. Say, how came
    you hither?
    Boats. If I did think, sir, I were well
    awake,
I'd strive to tell you. We were dead of
    sleep,   230
And—how, we know not—all clapp'd under
    hatches;
Where, but even now, with strange and
    several noises
Of roaring, shrieking, howling, jingling
    chains,
And moe diversity of sounds, all horrible,
We were awak'd; straightway at liberty;
Where we, in all her trim, freshly beheld
Our royal, good, and gallant ship; our
    master   237
Cap'ring to eye her. On a trice, so please
    you,
Even in a dream, were we divided from
    them,
And were brought moping hither.
    Ari. [*Aside to Pro.*] Was't well done?
    Pro. [*Aside to Ari.*] Bravely, my dili-
    gence. Thou shalt be free.   241
    Alon. This is as strange a maze as e'er
    men trod;
And there is in this business more than
    nature
Was ever conduct of. Some oracle
Must rectify our knowledge.
    Pro.   Sir, my liege,   245
Do not infest your mind with beating on
The strangeness of this business; at pick'd
    leisure,
Which shall be shortly, single I'll resolve
    you,
Which to you shall seem probable, of every
These happen'd accidents; till when, be
    cheerful   250
And think of each thing well. [*Aside to
    Ari.*] Come hither, spirit;
Set Caliban and his companions free;
Untie the spell. [*Exit Ariel*] How fares
    my gracious sir?   253
There are yet missing of your company
Some few odd lads that you remember not.

Re-enter ARIEL, *driving in* CALIBAN,
    STEPHANO, *and* TRINCULO, *in their stolen
    apparel.*

    Ste. Every man shift for all the rest, and
let no man take care for himself; for all is
but fortune. Coragio, bully-monster, coragio!
    Trin. If these be true spies which I wear
in my head, here's a goodly sight.   260
    Cal. O Setebos, these be brave spirits
    indeed!
How fine my master is! I am afraid
He will chastise me.
    Seb. Ha, ha!

What things are these, my lord Antonio ?
Will money buy 'em ?
 Ant.   Very like ; one of them
Is a plain fish, and no doubt marketable.
 Pro. Mark but the badges of these men,
  my lords,   267
Then say if they be true. This mis-shapen
  knave—
His mother was a witch, and one so strong
That could control the moon, make flows
  and ebbs,   270
And deal in her command without her
  power.
These three have robb'd me ; and this
  demi-devil—
For he's a bastard one—had plotted with
  them
To take my life. Two of these fellows you
Must know and own ; this thing of dark-
  ness I   275
Acknowledge mine.
 Cal.   I shall be pinch'd to death.
 Alon. Is not this Stephano, my drunken
  butler ?
 Seb. He is drunk now ; where had he
wine ?
 Alon. And Trinculo is reeling ripe ; where
  should they
Find this grand liquor that hath gilded
  'em ?   280
How cam'st thou in this pickle ?
 Trin. I have been in such a pickle since
I saw you last that, I fear me, will never
out of my bones. I shall not fear fly-
blowing.
 Seb. Why, how now, Stephano ! 285
 Ste. O, touch me not ; I am not Steph-
ano, but a cramp.
 Pro. You'd be king 'o the isle, sirrah ?
 Ste. I should have been a sore one, then.
 Alon. [*Pointing to Caliban*] This is as
  strange a thing as e'er I look'd on.
 Pro. He is as disproportion'd in his
  manners   290
As in his shape. Go, sirrah, to my cell ;
Take with you your companions ; as you
  look
To have my pardon, trim it handsomely.
 Cal. Ay, that I will ; and I'll be wise
  hereafter,
And seek for grace. What a thrice-double
  ass   295
Was I to take this drunkard for a god,
And worship this dull fool !
 Pro.   Go to ; away !

 Alon. Hence, and bestow your luggage
  where you found it.
 Seb. Or stole it, rather.
     [*Exeunt Cal., Ste., and Trin.*
 Pro. Sir, I invite your Highness and your
  train   300
To my poor cell, where you shall take your
  rest
For this one night ; which, part of it, I'll
  waste
With such discourse as, I not doubt, shall
  make it
Go quick away—the story of my life,
And the particular accidents gone by 305
Since I came to this isle. And in the morn
I'll bring you to your ship, and so to Naples,
Where I have hope to see the nuptial
Of these our dear-belov'd solemnized, 309
And thence retire me to my Milan, where
Every third thought shall be my grave.
 Alon.   I long
To hear the story of your life, which must
Take the ear strangely.
 Pro.   I'll deliver all ;
And promise you calm seas, auspicious
  gales,
And sail so expeditious that shall catch 315
Your royal fleet far off. [*Aside to Ari.*] My
     Ariel, chick,
That is thy charge. Then to the elements
Be free, and fare thou well !—Please you,
  draw near.   [*Exeunt.*

EPILOGUE

SPOKEN BY PROSPERO

Now my charms are all o'erthrown,
And what strength I have's mine own,
Which is most faint. Now 'tis true,
I must be here confin'd by you,
Or sent to Naples. Let me not, 5
Since I have my dukedom got,
And pardon'd the deceiver, dwell
In this bare island by your spell ;
But release me from my bands
With the help of your good hands. 10
Gentle breath of yours my sails
Must fill, or else my project fails,
Which was to please. Now I want
Spirits to enforce, art to enchant ;
And my ending is despair 15
Unless I be reliev'd by prayer,
Which pierces so that it assaults
Mercy itself, and frees all faults.
As you from crimes would pardon'd be,
Let your indulgence set me free. 20

THE TWO GENTLEMEN OF VERONA

DRAMATIS PERSONÆ

DUKE OF MILAN, *father to Silvia.*
VALENTINE, } *the two gentlemen.*
PROTEUS,
ANTONIO, *father to Proteus.*
THURIO, *a foolish rival to Valentine.*
EGLAMOUR, *agent for Silvia in her escape.*
SPEED, *a clownish servant to Valentine.*
LAUNCE, *the like to Proteus.*
PANTHINO, *servant to Antonio.*

Host, *where Julia lodges in Milan.*
Outlaws, *with Valentine.*

JULIA, *a lady of Verona, beloved of Proteus.*
SILVIA, *the Duke's daughter, beloved of Valentine.*
LUCETTA, *waiting-woman to Julia.*

Servants.
Musicians.

THE SCENE : *Verona ; Milan ; the frontiers of Mantua.*

ACT ONE

SCENE I. *Verona. An open place.*

Enter VALENTINE *and* PROTEUS.

Val. Cease to persuade, my loving
    Proteus :
Home-keeping youth have ever homely wits.
Were't not affection chains thy tender days
To the sweet glances of thy honour'd love,
I rather would entreat thy company   5
To see the wonders of the world abroad,
Than, living dully sluggardiz'd at home,
Wear out thy youth with shapeless idleness.
But since thou lov'st, love still, and thrive
    therein,
Even as I would, when I to love begin.   10
  Pro. Wilt thou be gone ? Sweet Valen-
    tine, adieu !
Think on thy Proteus, when thou haply
    seest
Some rare noteworthy object in thy travel.
Wish me partaker in thy happiness
When thou dost meet good hap ; and in
    thy danger,   15
If ever danger do environ thee,
Commend thy grievance to my holy
    prayers,
For I will be thy beadsman, Valentine.
  Val. And on a love-book pray for my
    success ?
  Pro. Upon some book I love I'll pray for
    thee.   20
  Val. That's on some shallow story of deep
    love :
How young Leander cross'd the Hellespont.
  Pro. That's a deep story of a deeper love ;
For he was more than over shoes in love.
  Val. 'Tis true ; for you are over boots in
    love,   25
And yet you never swum the Hellespont.
  Pro. Over the boots ! Nay, give me not
    the boots.
  Val. No, I will not, for it boots thee not.
  Pro.   What ?

  Val. To be in love—where scorn is bought
    with groans,
Coy looks with heart-sore sighs, one fad-
    ing moment's mirth   30
With twenty watchful, weary, tedious
    nights ;
If haply won, perhaps a hapless gain ;
If lost, why then a grievous labour won ;
However, but a folly bought with wit,
Or else a wit by folly vanquished.   35
  Pro. So, by your circumstance, you call
    me fool.
  Val. So, by your circumstance, I fear
    you'll prove.
  Pro. 'Tis love you cavil at ; I am not
    Love.
  Val. Love is your master, for he masters
    you ;
And he that is so yoked by a fool,   40
Methinks, should not be chronicled for wise.
  Pro. Yet writers say, as in the sweetest
    bud
The eating canker dwells, so eating love
Inhabits in the finest wits of all.
  Val. And writers say, as the most for-
    ward bud   45
Is eaten by the canker ere it blow,
Even so by love the young and tender wit
Is turn'd to folly, blasting in the bud,
Losing his verdure even in the prime,
And all the fair effects of future hopes. 50
But wherefore waste I time to counsel thee
That art a votary to fond desire ?
Once more adieu. My father at the road
Expects my coming, there to see me shipp'd.
  Pro. And thither will I bring thee,
    Valentine.   55
  Val. Sweet Proteus, no ; now let us take
    our leave.
To Milan let me hear from thee by letters
Of thy success in love, and what news else
Betideth here in absence of thy friend ;
And I likewise will visit thee with mine. 60
  Pro. All happiness bechance to thee in
    Milan !

Val. As much to you at home ; and so
    farewell !   [*Exit Valentine.*
Pro. He after honour hunts, I after love ;
He leaves his friends to dignify them more :
I leave myself, my friends, and all for love.
Thou, Julia, thou hast metamorphis'd me,
Made me neglect my studies, lose my time,
War with good counsel, set the world at
    nought ;
Made wit with musing weak, heart sick with
    thought.   69

Enter SPEED.

Speed. Sir Proteus, save you ! Saw you
    my master ?
Pro. But now he parted hence to embark
    for Milan.
Speed. Twenty to one then he is shipp'd
    already,
And I have play'd the sheep in losing him.
Pro. Indeed a sheep doth very often stray,
An if the shepherd be awhile away.   75
Speed. You conclude that my master is a
    shepherd then, and I a sheep ?
Pro. I do.
Speed. Why then, my horns are his
    horns, whether I wake or sleep.
Pro. A silly answer, and fitting well a
    sheep.
Speed. This proves me still a sheep.   80
Pro. True ; and thy master a shepherd.
Speed. Nay, that I can deny by a circum-
stance.
Pro. It shall go hard but I'll prove it by
another.
Speed. The shepherd seeks the sheep, and
not the sheep the shepherd ; but I seek my
master, and my master seeks not me ;
therefore, I am no sheep.   86
Pro. The sheep for fodder follow the
shepherd ; the shepherd for food follows
not the sheep : thou for wages followest
thy master ; thy master for wages follows
not thee. Therefore, thou art a sheep.   90
Speed. Such another proof will make me
cry ' baa '.
Pro. But dost thou hear ? Gav'st thou
my letter to Julia ?
Speed. Ay, sir ; I, a lost mutton, gave
your letter to her, a lac'd mutton ; and she,
a lac'd mutton, gave me, a lost mutton,
nothing for my labour.   96
Pro. Here's too small a pasture for such
store of muttons.
Speed. If the ground be overcharg'd, you
were best stick her.   99
Pro. Nay, in that you are astray : 'twere
best pound you.
Speed. Nay, sir, less than a pound shall
serve me for carrying your letter.   102
Pro. You mistake ; I mean the pound—
a pinfold.
Speed. From a pound to a pin ? Fold it
    over and over,

'Tis threefold too little for carrying a letter
    to your lover.   105
Pro. But what said she ?
Speed. [*Nodding*] Ay.
Pro. Nod-ay. Why, that's ' noddy '.
Speed. You mistook, sir ; I say she did
nod ; and you ask me if she did nod ; and
I say ' Ay '.   110
Pro. And that set together is ' noddy '.
Speed. Now you have taken the pains to
set it together, take it for your pains.
Pro. No, no ; you shall have it for bear-
ing the letter.
Speed. Well, I perceive I must be fain to
bear with you.   115
Pro. Why, sir, how do you bear with me ?
Speed. Marry, sir, the letter, very orderly;
having nothing but the word 'noddy' for
my pains.
Pro. Beshrew me, but you have a quick
wit.
Speed. And yet it cannot overtake your
slow purse.   120
Pro. Come, come, open the matter ; in
brief, what said she ?
Speed. Open your purse, that the money
and the matter may be both at once
delivered.
Pro. Well, sir, here is for your pains.
What said she ?   125
Speed. Truly, sir, I think you'll hardly
win her.
Pro. Why, couldst thou perceive so much
from her ?
Speed. Sir, I could perceive nothing at all
from her ; no, not so much as a ducat for
delivering your letter ; and being so hard
to me that brought your mind, I fear she'll
prove as hard to you in telling your mind.
Give her no token but stones, for she's as
hard as steel.   132
Pro. What said she ? Nothing ?
Speed. No, not so much as ' Take this for
thy pains '. To testify your bounty, I thank
you, you have testern'd me ; in requital
whereof, henceforth carry your letters yourself ; and so, sir, I'll commend you to my
master.   137
Pro. Go, go, be gone, to save your ship
    from wreck,
Which cannot perish, having thee aboard,
Being destin'd to a drier death on shore.
        [*Exit Speed.*
I must go send some better messenger.   141
I fear my Julia would not deign my lines,
Receiving them from such a worthless post.
        [*Exit.*

SCENE II. *Verona. The garden of
Julia's house.*

Enter JULIA *and* LUCETTA.

Jul. But say, Lucetta, now we are alone,
Wouldst thou then counsel me to fall in love ?

Luc. Ay, madam; so you stumble not
　　unheedfully.
Jul. Of all the fair resort of gentlemen
That every day with parle encounter me,　5
In thy opinion which is worthiest love?
Luc. Please you, repeat their names; I'll
　　show my mind
According to my shallow simple skill.
Jul. What think'st thou of the fair Sir
　　Eglamour?
Luc. As of a knight well-spoken, neat,
　　and fine;　10
But, were I you, he never should be mine.
Jul. What think'st thou of the rich
　　Mercatio?
Luc. Well of his wealth; but of himself,
　　so so.
Jul. What think'st thou of the gentle
　　Proteus?
Luc. Lord, Lord! to see what folly reigns
　　in us!　15
Jul. How now! what means this passion
　　at his name?
Luc. Pardon, dear madam; 'tis a passing
　　shame
That I, unworthy body as I am,
Should censure thus on lovely gentlemen.
Jul. Why not on Proteus, as of all the
　　rest?　20
Luc. Then thus: of many good I think
　　him best.
Jul. Your reason?
Luc. I have no other but a woman's
　　reason:
I think him so, because I think him so.
Jul. And wouldst thou have me cast my
　　love on him?　25
Luc. Ay, if you thought your love not
　　cast away.
Jul. Why, he, of all the rest, hath never
　　mov'd me.
Luc. Yet he, of all the rest, I think, best
　　loves ye.
Jul. His little speaking shows his love but
　　small.
Luc. Fire that 's closest kept burns most
　　of all.　30
Jul. They do not love that do not show
　　their love.
Luc. O, they love least that let men know
　　their love.
Jul. I would I knew his mind.
Luc. Peruse this paper, madam.
Jul. ' To Julia '—Say, from whom?　35
Luc. That the contents will show.
Jul. Say, say, who gave it thee?
Luc. Sir Valentine's page; and sent, I
　　think, from Proteus.
He would have given it you; but I, being
　　in the way,
Did in your name receive it; pardon the
　　fault, I pray..　40
Jul. Now, by my modesty, a goodly
　　broker!

Dare you presume to harbour wanton lines?
To whisper and conspire against my youth?
Now, trust me, 'tis an office of great worth,
And you an officer fit for the place.　45
There, take the paper; see it be return'd;
Or else return no more into my sight.
Luc. To plead for love deserves more fee
　　than hate.
Jul. Will ye be gone?
Luc.　　　That you may ruminate. [*Exit.*
Jul. And yet, I would I had o'erlook'd
　　the letter.　50
It were a shame to call her back again,
And pray her to a fault for which I chid her.
What fool is she, that knows I am a maid
And would not force the letter to my view!
Since maids, in modesty, say ' No ' to that
Which they would have the profferer con-
　　strue ' Ay '.　56
Fie, fie, how wayward is this foolish love,
That like a testy babe will scratch the
　　nurse,
And presently, all humbled, kiss the rod!
How churlishly I chid Lucetta hence,　60
When willingly I would have had her here!
How angerly I taught my brow to frown,
When inward joy enforc'd my heart to
　　smile!
My penance is to call Lucetta back
And ask remission for my folly past.　65
What ho! Lucetta!

Re-enter LUCETTA.

Luc.　　　What would your ladyship?
Jul. Is 't near dinner time?
Luc.　　　　　I would it were,
That you might kill your stomach on your
　　meat
And not upon your maid.
Jul. What is't that you took up so
　　gingerly?　70
Luc. Nothing.
Jul. Why didst thou stoop then?
Luc. To take a paper up that I let fall.
Jul. And is that paper nothing?
Luc. Nothing concerning me.　75
Jul. Then let it lie for those that it
　　concerns.
Luc. Madam, it will not lie where it con-
　　cerns,
Unless it have a false interpreter.
Jul. Some love of yours hath writ to you
　　in rhyme.
Luc. That I might sing it, madam, to a
　　tune.　80
Give me a note; your ladyship can set.
Jul. As little by such toys as may be
　　possible.
Best sing it to the tune of ' Light o' Love '.
Luc. It is too heavy for so light a tune.
Jul. Heavy! belike it hath some burden
　　then.　85
Luc. Ay; and melodious were it, would
　　you sing it.

29

Jul. And why not you ?
Luc.   I cannot reach so high.
Jul. Let's see your song. [*Lucetta with-
holds the letter*] How now, minion !
Luc. Keep tune there still, so you will
     sing it out.   89
And yet methinks I do not like this tune.
Jul. You do not !
Luc.   No, madam ; 'tis too sharp.
Jul. You, minion, are too saucy.
Luc. Nay, now you are too flat
And mar the concord with too harsh a
     descant ;   94
There wanteth but a mean to fill your song.
Jul. The mean is drown'd with your
     unruly bass.
Luc. Indeed, I bid the base for Proteus.
Jul. This babble shall not henceforth
     trouble me.
Here is a coil with protestation !   99
                    [*Tears the letter.*
Go, get you gone ; and let the papers lie.
You would be fing'ring them, to anger me.
Luc. She makes it strange ; but she
     would be best pleas'd
To be so ang'red with another letter. [*Exit.*
Jul. Nay, would I were so ang'red with
     the same !   104
O hateful hands, to tear such loving words !
Injurious wasps, to feed on such sweet
     honey
And kill the bees that yield it with your
     stings !
I'll kiss each several paper for amends.
Look, here is writ ' kind Julia '. Unkind
     Julia,
As in revenge of thy ingratitude,   110
I throw thy name against the bruising
     stones,
Trampling contemptuously on thy disdain.
And here is writ ' love-wounded Proteus '.
Poor wounded name ! my bosom, as a bed,
Shall lodge thee till thy wound be through-
     ly heal'd ;   115
And thus I search it with a sovereign kiss.
But twice or thrice was ' Proteus ' written
     down.
Be calm, good wind, blow not a word away
Till I have found each letter in the letter—
Except mine own name ; that some whirl-
     wind bear   120
Unto a ragged, fearful, hanging rock,
And throw it thence into the raging sea.
Lo, here in one line is his name twice writ :
' Poor forlorn Proteus, passionate Proteus,
To the sweet Julia '. That I'll tear away ;
And yet I will not, sith so prettily   126
He couples it to his complaining names.
Thus will I fold them one upon another ;
Now kiss, embrace, contend, do what you
     will.

          Re-enter LUCETTA.

Luc. Madam,   130

Dinner is ready, and your father stays.
Jul. Well, let us go.
Luc. What, shall these papers lie like
     tell-tales here ?
Jul. If you respect them, best to take
     them up.
Luc. Nay, I was taken up for laying them
     down ;   135
Yet here they shall not lie for catching cold.
Jul. I see you have a month's mind to
     them.
Luc. Ay, madam, you may say what
     sights you see ;   138
I see things too, although you judge I wink.
Jul. Come, come ; will't please you go ?
                                [*Exeunt.*

SCENE III. *Verona. Antonio's house.*

     Enter ANTONIO *and* PANTHINO.

Ant. Tell me, Panthino, what sad talk
     was that
Wherewith my brother held you in the
     cloister ?
Pan. 'Twas of his nephew Proteus, your
     son.
Ant. Why, what of him ?
Pan.   He wond'red that your lordship
Would suffer him to spend his youth at
     home,   5
While other men, of slender reputation,
Put forth their sons to seek preferment out:
Some to the wars, to try their fortune there;
Some to discover islands far away ;
Some to the studious universities.   10
For any, or for all these exercises,
He said that Proteus, your son, was meet ;
And did request me to importune you
To let him spend his time no more at home,
Which would be great impeachment to his
     age,   15
In having known no travel in his youth.
Ant. Nor need'st thou much importune
     me to that
Whereon this month I have been hammer-
     ing.
I have consider'd well his loss of time,
And how he cannot be a perfect man,   20
Not being tried and tutor'd in the world :
Experience is by industry achiev'd,
And perfected by the swift course of time.
Then tell me whither were I best to send
     him.   24
Pan. I think your lordship is not ignorant
How his companion, youthful Valentine,
Attends the Emperor in his royal court.
Ant. I know it well.
Pan. 'Twere good, I think, your lordship
     sent him thither :
There shall he practise tilts and tourna-
     ments,   30
Hear sweet discourse, converse with noble-
     men,
And be in eye of every exercise

Worthy his youth and nobleness of birth.
   Ant. I like thy counsel ; well hast thou
     advis'd ;
And that thou mayst perceive how well I
     like it,   35
The execution of it shall make known :
Even with the speediest expedition
I will dispatch him to the Emperor's court.
   Pan. To-morrow, may it please you, Don
     Alphonso
With other gentlemen of good esteem   40
Are journeying to salute the Emperor,
And to commend their service to his will.
   Ant. Good company ; with them shall
     Proteus go.

         Enter PROTEUS.

And—in good time !—now will we break
     with him.   44
   Pro. Sweet love ! sweet lines ! sweet life !
Here is her hand, the agent of her heart ;
Here is her oath for love, her honour's pawn.
O that our fathers would applaud our loves,
To seal our happiness with their consents !
O heavenly Julia !   50
   Ant. How now ! What letter are you
     reading there ?
   Pro. May't please your lordship, 'tis a
     word or two
Of commendations sent from Valentine,
Deliver'd by a friend that came from him.
   Ant. Lend me the letter ; let me see what
     news.   55
   Pro. There is no news, my lord ; but that
     he writes
How happily he lives, how well-belov'd
And daily graced by the Emperor ;
Wishing me with him, partner of his fortune.
   Ant. And how stand you affected to his
     wish ?   60
   Pro. As one relying on your lordship's
     will,
And not depending on his friendly wish.
   Ant. My will is something sorted with his
     wish.
Muse not that I thus suddenly proceed ;
For what I will, I will, and there an end.   65
I am resolv'd that thou shalt spend some
     time
With Valentinus in the Emperor's court ;
What maintenance he from his friends
     receives,
Like exhibition thou shalt have from me.
To-morrow be in readiness to go—   70
Excuse it not, for I am peremptory.
   Pro. My lord, I cannot be so soon pro-
     vided ;
Please you, deliberate a day or two.
   Ant. Look, what thou want'st shall be
     sent after thee.   74
No more of stay ; to-morrow thou must go.
Come on, Panthino ; you shall be employ'd
To hasten on his expedition.
         [*Exeunt Ant. and Pan.*

   Pro. Thus have I shunn'd the fire for fear
     of burning,
And drench'd me in the sea, where I am
     drown'd.
I fear'd to show my father Julia's letter,   80
Lest he should take exceptions to my love ;
And with the vantage of mine own excuse
Hath he excepted most against my love.
O, how this spring of love resembleth
The uncertain glory of an April day,   85
Which now shows all the beauty of the
     sun,
And by and by a cloud takes all away !

     Re-enter PANTHINO.

   Pan. Sir Proteus, your father calls for
     you ;
He is in haste ; therefore, I pray you, go.
   Pro. Why, this it is : my heart accords
     thereto ;   90
And yet a thousand times it answers ' No '.
         [*Exeunt.*

ACT TWO

SCENE I. *Milan. The Duke's palace.*

Enter VALENTINE *and* SPEED.

Speed. Sir, your glove.
Val.   Not mine : my gloves are on.
Speed. Why, then, this may be yours ;
   for this is but one.
Val. Ha ! let me see ; ay, give it me, it's
   mine ;
Sweet ornament that decks a thing divine !
Ah, Silvia ! Silvia !   5
   Speed. [*Calling*] Madam Silvia ! Madam
Silvia !
   Val. How now, sirrah ?
   Speed. She is not within hearing, sir.
   Val. Why, sir, who bade you call her ?
   Speed. Your worship, sir ; or else I
mistook.   10
   Val. Well, you'll still be too forward.
   Speed. And yet I was last chidden for
being too slow.
   Val. Go to, sir ; tell me, do you know
Madam Silvia ?
   Speed. She that your worship loves ?
   Val. Why, how know you that I am in
love ?   15
   Speed. Marry, by these special marks :
first, you have learn'd, like Sir Proteus, to
wreath your arms like a malcontent ; to
relish a love-song, like a robin redbreast ;
to walk alone, like one that had the pestilence ; to sigh, like a school-boy that had
lost his A B C ; to weep, like a young wench
that had buried her grandam ; to fast, like
one that takes diet ; to watch, like one that
fears robbing ; to speak puling, like a beggar at Hallowmas. You were wont, when
you laughed, to crow like a cock ; when you
walk'd, to walk like one of the lions ; when
you fasted, it was presently after dinner ;

when you look'd sadly, it was for want of
money. And now you are metamorphis'd
with a mistress, that, when I look on you,
I can hardly think you my master.   28
Val. Are all these things perceiv'd in me?
Speed. They are all perceiv'd without ye.
Val. Without me ? They cannot.   31
Speed. Without you ! Nay, that's certain;
for, without you were so simple, none else
would ; but you are so without these follies
that these follies are within you, and shine
through you like the water in an urinal, that
not an eye that sees you but is a physician
to comment on your malady.   36
Val. But tell me, dost thou know my lady
Silvia ?
Speed. She that you gaze on so, as she sits
at supper ?
Val. Hast thou observ'd that ? Even she,
I mean.
Speed. Why, sir, I know her not.   40
Val. Dost thou know her by my gazing
on her, and yet know'st her not ?
Speed. Is she not hard-favour'd, sir ?
Val. Not so fair, boy, as well-favour'd.
Speed. Sir, I know that well enough.   45
Val. What dost thou know ?
Speed. That she is not so fair as, of you,
well favour'd.
Val. I mean that her beauty is exquisite,
but her favour infinite.
Speed. That's because the one is painted,
and the other out of all count.   51
Val. How painted ? and how out of
count ?
Speed. Marry, sir, so painted, to make her
fair, that no man counts of her beauty.
Val. How esteem'st thou me ? I account
of her beauty.   55
Speed. You never saw her since she was
deform'd.
Val. How long hath she been deform'd ?
Speed. Ever since you lov'd her.
Val. I have lov'd her ever since I saw her,
and still I see her beautiful.   60
Speed. If you love her, you cannot see her.
Val. Why ?
Speed. Because Love is blind. O that you
had mine eyes ; or your own eyes had the
lights they were wont to have when you
chid at Sir Proteus for going ungarter'd !   65
Val. What should I see then ?
Speed. Your own present folly and her
passing deformity ; for he, being in love,
could not see to garter his hose ; and you,
being in love, cannot see to put on your
hose.   69
Val. Belike, boy, then you are in love ;
for last morning you could not see to wipe
my shoes.   71
Speed. True, sir ; I was in love with my
bed. I thank you, you swing'd me for my
love, which makes me the bolder to chide
you for yours.

Val. In conclusion, I stand affected to
her.   75
Speed. I would you were set, so your
affection would cease.
Val. Last night she enjoin'd me to write
some lines to one she loves.
Speed. And have you ?   80
Val. I have.
Speed. Are they not lamely writ ?
Val. No, boy, but as well as I can do
them.

Enter SILVIA.

Peace ! here she comes.   84
Speed. [*Aside*] O excellent motion ! O
exceeding puppet ! Now will he interpret
to her.
Val. Madam and mistress, a thousand
good morrows.
Speed. [*Aside*] O, give ye good ev'n !
Here's a million of manners.
Sil. Sir Valentine and servant, to you two
thousand.   90
Speed. [*Aside*] He should give her in-
terest, and she gives it him.
Val. As you enjoin'd me, I have writ
your letter
Unto the secret nameless friend of yours ;
Which I was much unwilling to proceed in,
But for my duty to your ladyship.   96
Sil. I thank you, gentle servant. 'Tis
very clerkly done.
Val. Now trust me, madam, it came
hardly off ;
For, being ignorant to whom it goes,
I writ at random, very doubtfully.   100
Sil. Perchance you think too much of so
much pains ?
Val. No, madam ; so it stead you, I will
write,
Please you command, a thousand times as
much ;
And yet—
Sil. A pretty period ! Well, I guess the
sequel ;   105
And yet I will not name it—and yet I care
not.
And yet take this again—and yet I thank
you—
Meaning henceforth to trouble you no
more.
Speed. [*Aside*] And yet you will ; and yet
another ' yet '.
Val. What means your ladyship ? Do you
not like it ?   110
Sil. Yes, yes ; the lines are very quaintly
writ ;
But, since unwillingly, take them again.
Nay, take them.   [*Gives back the letter.*
Val. Madam, they are for you.
Sil. Ay, ay, you writ them, sir, at my
request ;   115
But I will none of them ; they are for you :
I would have had them writ more movingly.

Val. Please you, I'll write your ladyship
  another.
Sil. And when it's writ, for my sake read
  it over ;
And if it please you, so : if not, why, so. 120
Val. If it please me, madam, what then ?
Sil. Why, if it please you, take it for your
  labour.
And so good morrow, servant. [*Exit Silvia.*
Speed. O jest unseen, inscrutable, in-
  visible,
As a nose on a man's face, or a weather-
  cock on a steeple !   125
My master sues to her ; and she hath taught
He being her pupil, to become her tutor.
O excellent device! Was there ever heard a
  better,
That my master, being scribe, to himself
  should write the letter ?   129
Val. How now, sir ! What are you
reasoning with yourself ?
Speed. Nay, I was rhyming : 'tis you
that have the reason.
Val. To do what ?
Speed. To be a spokesman from Madam
Silvia ?   135
Val. To whom ?
Speed. To yourself ; why, she woos you
by a figure.
Val. What figure ?
Speed. By a letter, I should say.
Val. Why, she hath not writ to me.   140
Speed. What need she, when she hath
made you write to yourself ? Why, do you
not perceive the jest ?
Val. No, believe me.
Speed. No believing you indeed, sir. But
did you perceive her earnest ?   145
Val. She gave me none except an angry
word.
Speed. Why, she hath given you a letter.
Val. That's the letter I writ to her friend.
Speed. And that letter hath she deliver'd,
and there an end.   150
Val. I would it were no worse.
Speed. I'll warrant you 'tis as well.
' For often have you writ to her ; and she,
  in modesty,
Or else for want of idle time, could not
  again reply ;
Or fearing else some messenger that might
  her mind discover,   155
Herself hath taught her love himself to
  write unto her lover.'
All this I speak in print, for in print I
found it. Why muse you, sir ? 'Tis dinner
time.
Val. I have din'd.   159
Speed. Ay, but hearken, sir ; though the
chameleon Love can feed on the air, I am
one that am nourish'd by my victuals, and
would fain have meat. O, be not like your
mistress ! Be moved, be moved. [*Exeunt.*

SCENE II. *Verona. Julia's house.*

Enter PROTEUS *and* JULIA.

Pro. Have patience, gentle Julia.
Jul. I must, where is no remedy.
Pro. When possibly I can, I will return.
Jul. If you turn not, you will return the
  sooner.
Keep this remembrance for thy Julia's
  sake.   [*Giving a ring.*
Pro. Why, then, we'll make exchange.
  Here, take you this.   6
Jul. And seal the bargain with a holy kiss.
Pro. Here is my hand for my true con-
  stancy ;
And when that hour o'erslips me in the day
Wherein I sigh not, Julia, for thy sake, 10
The next ensuing hour some foul mischance
Torment me for my love's forgetfulness !
My father stays my coming ; answer not ;
The tide is now—nay, not thy tide of tears :
That tide will stay me longer than I should.
Julia, farewell !   [*Exit Julia.*
    What, gone without a word ?
Ay, so true love should do : it cannot speak;
For truth hath better deeds than words to
  grace it.   18

Enter PANTHINO.

Pan. Sir Proteus, you are stay'd for.
Pro. Go ; I come, I come.   20
Alas ! this parting strikes poor lovers dumb.
    [*Exeunt.*

SCENE III. *Verona. A street.*

Enter LAUNCE, *leading a dog.*

Laun. Nay, 'twill be this hour ere I have
done weeping ; all the kind of the Launces
have this very fault. I have receiv'd my
proportion, like the Prodigious Son, and am
going with Sir Proteus to the Imperial's
court. I think Crab my dog be the sourest-
natured dog that lives : my mother weeping, my father wailing, my sister crying,
our maid howling, our cat wringing her
hands, and all our house in a great perplexity ; yet did not this cruel-hearted cur
shed one tear. He is a stone, a very pebble
stone, and has no more pity in him than
a dog. A Jew would have wept to have
seen our parting ; why, my grandam having no eyes, look you, wept herself blind at
my parting. Nay, I'll show you the manner
of it. This shoe is my father ; no, this left
shoe is my father ; no, no, this left shoe is
my mother ; nay, that cannot be so neither;
yes, it is so, it is so, it hath the worser sole.
This shoe with the hole in it is my mother,
and this my father. A vengeance on 't !
There 'tis. Now, sir, this staff is my sister,
for, look you, she is as white as a lily and
as small as a wand ; this hat is Nan our

maid; I am the dog; no, the dog is himself, and I am the dog—O, the dog is me,
and I am myself; ay, so, so. Now come I
to my father: 'Father, your blessing'.
Now should not the shoe speak a word for
weeping; now should I kiss my father;
well, he weeps on. Now come I to my
mother. O that she could speak now like
a wood woman! Well, I kiss her—why there
'tis; here's my mother's breath up and
down. Now come I to my sister; mark the
moan she makes. Now the dog all this while
sheds not a tear, nor speaks a word; but
see how I lay the dust with my tears.   29

Enter PANTHINO.

Pan. Launce, away, away aboard! Thy
master is shipp'd, and thou art to post
after with oars. What's the matter? Why
weep'st thou, man? Away, ass! You'll
lose the tide if you tarry any longer.   33
Laun. It is no matter if the tied were lost;
for it is the unkindest tied that ever any
man tied.   35
Pan. What's the unkindest tide?
Laun. Why, he that's tied here, Crab, my
dog.
Pan. Tut, man, I mean thou'lt lose the
flood, and, in losing the flood, lose thy
voyage, and, in losing thy voyage, lose thy
master, and, in losing thy master, lose thy
service, and, in losing thy service—Why
dost thou stop my mouth?   41
Laun. For fear thou shouldst lose thy
tongue.
Pan. Where should I lose my tongue?
Laun. In thy tale.
Pan. In thy tail!   45
Laun. Lose the tide, and the voyage, and
the master, and the service, and the tied!
Why, man, if the river were dry, I am able
to fill it with my tears; if the wind were
down, I could drive the boat with my sighs.
Pan. Come, come away, man; I was
sent to call thee.   50
Laun. Sir, call me what thou dar'st.
Pan. Wilt thou go?
Laun. Well, I will go.   [*Exeunt.*

SCENE IV. *Milan. The Duke's palace.*

Enter SILVIA, VALENTINE, THURIO, *and*
SPEED.

Sil. Servant!
Val. Mistress?
Speed. Master, Sir Thurio frowns on you.
Val. Ay, boy, it's for love.
Speed. Not of you.   5
Val. Of my mistress, then.
Speed. 'Twere good you knock'd him.
    [*Exit.*
Sil. Servant, you are sad.
Val. Indeed, madam, I seem so.
Thu. Seem you that you are not?   10

Val. Haply I do.
Thu. So do counterfeits.
Val. So do you.
Thu. What seem I that I am not?
Val. Wise.   15
Thu. What instance of the contrary?
Val. Your folly.
Thu. And how quote you my folly?
Val. I quote it in your jerkin.
Thu. My jerkin is a doublet.   20
Val. Well, then, I'll double your folly.
Thu. How?
Sil. What, angry, Sir Thurio! Do you
change colour?
Val. Give him leave, madam; he is a
kind of chameleon.
Thu. That hath more mind to feed on
your blood than live in your air.   26
Val. You have said, sir.
Thu. Ay, sir, and done too, for this time.
Val. I know it well, sir; you always end
ere you begin.
Sil. A fine volley of words, gentlemen,
and quickly shot off.   31
Val. 'Tis indeed, madam; we thank the
giver.
Sil. Who is that, servant?
Val. Yourself, sweet lady; for you gave
the fire. Sir Thurio borrows his wit from
your ladyship's looks, and spends what he
borrows kindly in your company.   36
Thu. Sir, if you spend word for word with
me, I shall make your wit bankrupt.
Val. I know it well, sir; you have an
exchequer of words, and, I think, no other
treasure to give your followers; for it
appears by their bare liveries that they live
by your bare words.   42

Enter DUKE.

Sil. No more, gentlemen, no more. Here
comes my father.
Duke. Now, daughter Silvia, you are
    hard beset.   45
Sir Valentine, your father is in good health.
What say you to a letter from your friends
Of much good news?
Val.   My lord, I will be thankful
To any happy messenger from thence.
Duke. Know ye Don Antonio, your
    countryman?   50
Val. Ay, my good lord, I know the
    gentleman
To be of worth and worthy estimation,
And not without desert so well reputed.
Duke. Hath he not a son?
Val. Ay, my good lord; a son that well
    deserves   55
The honour and regard of such a father.
Duke. You know him well?
Val. I knew him as myself; for from our
    infancy
We have convers'd and spent our hours
    together;

And though myself have been an idle
   truant,   60
Omitting the sweet benefit of time
To clothe mine age with angel-like per-
   fection,
Yet hath Sir Proteus, for that's his name,
Made use and fair advantage of his days :
His years but young, but his experience old;
His head unmellowed, but his judgment
   ripe ;   66
And, in a word, for far behind his worth
Comes all the praises that I now bestow,
He is complete in feature and in mind,
With all good grace to grace a gentleman.
   Duke. Beshrew me, sir, but if he make
    this good,   71
He is as worthy for an empress' love
As meet to be an emperor's counsellor.
Well, sir, this gentleman is come to me
With commendation from great potentates,
And here he means to spend his time
   awhile.   76
I think 'tis no unwelcome news to you.
   Val. Should I have wish'd a thing, it had
    been he.
   Duke. Welcome him, then, according to
    his worth—
Silvia, I speak to you, and you, Sir
   Thurio ;   80
For Valentine, I need not cite him to it.
I will send him hither to you presently.
          [*Exit Duke.*
   Val. This is the gentleman I told your
    ladyship
Had come along with me but that his
   mistress   84
Did hold his eyes lock'd in her crystal
   looks.
   Sil. Belike that now she hath enfran-
    chis'd them
Upon some other pawn for fealty.
   Val. Nay, sure, I think she holds them
    prisoners still.
   Sil. Nay, then, he should be blind ; and,
    being blind,
How could he see his way to seek out you ?
   Val. Why, lady, Love hath twenty pair
    of eyes.   91
   Thu. They say that Love hath not an eye
    at all.
   Val. To see such lovers, Thurio, as
    yourself ;
Upon a homely object Love can wink.
          [*Exit Thurio.*

   Enter PROTEUS.

   Sil. Have done, have done ; here comes
    the gentleman.   95
   Val. Welcome, dear Proteus ! Mistress,
    I beseech you
Confirm his welcome with some special
   favour.
   Sil. His worth is warrant for his welcome
   hither,

If this be he you oft have wish'd to hear
   from.
   Val. Mistress, it is ; sweet lady, entertain
    him   100
To be my fellow-servant to your ladyship.
   Sil. Too low a mistress for so high a
    servant.
   Pro. Not so, sweet lady ; but too mean a
    servant   103
To have a look of such a worthy mistress.
   Val. Leave off discourse of disability ;
Sweet lady, entertain him for your servant.
   Pro. My duty will I boast of, nothing else.
   Sil. And duty never yet did want his
    meed.
Servant, you are welcome to a worthless
   mistress.
   Pro. I'll die on him that says so but
    yourself.   110
   Sil. That you are welcome ?
   Pro.   That you are worthless.

   Re-enter THURIO.

   Thu. Madam, my lord your father would
    speak with you.
   Sil. I wait upon his pleasure. Come, Sir
    Thurio,
Go with me. Once more, new servant,
   welcome.   114
I'll leave you to confer of home affairs ;
When you have done we look to hear from
   you.
   Pro. We'll both attend upon your lady-
    ship. [*Exeunt Silvia and Thurio.*
   Val. Now, tell me, how do all from
    whence you came ?
   Pro. Your friends are well, and have them
    much commended.   119
   Val. And how do yours ?
   Pro.   I left them all in health.
   Val. How does your lady, and how
    thrives your love ?
   Pro. My tales of love were wont to weary
    you ;
I know you joy not in a love-discourse.
   Val. Ay, Proteus, but that life is alter'd
    now ;
I have done penance for contemning
   Love,   125
Whose high imperious thoughts have
   punish'd me
With bitter fasts, with penitential groans,
With nightly tears, and daily heart-sore
   sighs ;
For, in revenge of my contempt of love,
Love hath chas'd sleep from my enthralled
   eyes   130
And made them watchers of mine own
   heart's sorrow.
O gentle Proteus, Love's a mighty lord,
And hath so humbled me as I confess
There is no woe to his correction,   134
Nor to his service no such joy on earth.
Now no discourse, except it be of love ;

Now can I break my fast, dine, sup, and
   sleep,
Upon the very naked name of love.
  Pro. Enough ; I read your fortune in
   your eye.   139
Was this the idol that you worship so ?
  Val. Even she ; and is she not a heavenly
   saint ?
  Pro. No ; but she is an earthly paragon.
  Val. Call her divine.
  Pro.   I will not flatter her.
  Val. O, flatter me ; for love delights in
   praises !
  Pro. When I was sick you gave me bitter
   pills,   145
And I must minister the like to you.
  Val. Then speak the truth by her ; if not
   divine,
Yet let her be a principality,
Sovereign to all the creatures on the earth.
  Pro. Except my mistress.
  Val.   Sweet, except not any ; 150
Except thou wilt except against my love.
  Pro. Have I not reason to prefer mine
   own ?
  Val. And I will help thee to prefer her
   too :
She shall be dignified with this high
   honour—   154
To bear my lady's train, lest the base earth
Should from her vesture chance to steal a
   kiss
And, of so great a favour growing proud,
Disdain to root the summer-swelling
   flow'r
And make rough winter everlastingly.
  Pro. Why, Valentine, what braggardism
   is this ?   160
  Val. Pardon me, Proteus ; all I can is
   nothing
To her, whose worth makes other worthies
   nothing ;
She is alone.
  Pro.   Then let her alone.
  Val. Not for the world ! Why, man, she is
   mine own ;
And I as rich in having such a jewel 165
As twenty seas, if all their sand were pearl,
The water nectar, and the rocks pure gold.
Forgive me that I do not dream on thee,
Because thou seest me dote upon my love.
My foolish rival, that her father likes 170
Only for his possessions are so huge,
Is gone with her along ; and I must after,
For love, thou know'st, is full of jealousy.
  Pro. But she loves you ?
  Val. Ay, and we are betroth'd ; nay
   more, our marriage-hour, 175
With all the cunning manner of our flight,
Determin'd of—how I must climb her
   window,   177
The ladder made of cords, and all the means
Plotted and 'greed on for my happiness.
Good Proteus, go with me to my chamber,

In these affairs to aid me with thy counsel.
  Pro. Go on before ; I shall enquire you
   forth ;
I must unto the road to disembark
Some necessaries that I needs must use ;
And then I'll presently attend you. 185
  Val. Will you make haste ?
  Pro. I will.   [*Exit Valentine.*
Even as one heat another heat expels
Or as one nail by strength drives out an-
   other,
So the remembrance of my former love 190
Is by a newer object quite forgotten.
Is it my mind, or Valentinus' praise,
Her true perfection, or my false trans-
   gression,   193
That makes me reasonless to reason thus ?
She is fair ; and so is Julia that I love—
That I did love, for now my love is thaw'd ;
Which like a waxen image 'gainst a fire
Bears no impression of the thing it was.
Methinks my zeal to Valentine is cold,
And that I love him not as I was wont. 200
O ! but I love his lady too too much,
And that's the reason I love him so little.
How shall I dote on her with more advice
That thus without advice begin to love her !
'Tis but her picture I have yet beheld, 205
And that hath dazzled my reason's light ;
But when I look on her perfections,
There is no reason but I shall be blind.
If I can check my erring love, I will ;
If not, to compass her I'll use my skill. 210
                     [*Exit.*

SCENE V. *Milan. A street.*

Enter SPEED *and* LAUNCE *severally.*

  Speed. Launce ! by mine honesty,
welcome to Padua.
  Laun. Forswear not thyself, sweet youth,
for I am not welcome. I reckon this always,
that a man is never undone till he be
hang'd, nor never welcome to a place till
some certain shot be paid, and the hostess
say ' Welcome ! '   5
  Speed. Come on, you madcap ; I'll to the
alehouse with you presently ; where, for
one shot of five pence, thou shalt have five
thousand welcomes. But, sirrah, how did
thy master part with Madam Julia ?
  Laun. Marry, after they clos'd in earnest,
they parted very fairly in jest. 11
  Speed. But shall she marry him ?
  Laun. No.
  Speed. How then ? Shall he marry her ?
  Laun. No, neither.   15
  Speed. What, are they broken ?
  Laun. No, they are both as whole as a
fish.
  Speed. Why then, how stands the matter
with them ?
  Laun. Marry, thus : when it stands well
with him, it stands well with her. 20

Speed. What an ass art thou! I understand thee not.

Laun. What a block art thou that thou canst not! My staff understands me.

Speed. What thou say'st? 24

Laun. Ay, and what I do too; look thee, I'll but lean, and my staff understands me.

Speed. It stands under thee, indeed. 27

Laun. Why, stand-under and understand is all one.

Speed. But tell me true, will't be a match?

Laun. Ask my dog. If he say ay, it will; if he say no, it will; if he shake his tail and say nothing, it will. 31

Speed. The conclusion is, then, that it will.

Laun. Thou shalt never get such a secret from me but by a parable. 34

Speed. 'Tis well that I get it so. But, Launce, how say'st thou that my master is become a notable lover?

Laun. I never knew him otherwise. 37

Speed. Than how?

Laun. A notable lubber, as thou reportest him to be.

Speed. Why, thou whoreson ass, thou mistak'st me. 40

Laun. Why, fool, I meant not thee, I meant thy master.

Speed. I tell thee my master is become a hot lover.

Laun. Why, I tell thee I care not though he burn himself in love. If thou wilt, go with me to the alehouse; if not, thou art an Hebrew, a Jew, and not worth the name of a Christian. 46

Speed. Why?

Laun. Because thou hast not so much charity in thee as to go to the ale with a Christian. Wilt thou go? 49

Speed. At thy service. [*Exeunt.*

SCENE VI. *Milan. The Duke's palace.*

Enter PROTEUS.

Pro. To leave my Julia, shall I be forsworn;
To love fair Silvia, shall I be forsworn;
To wrong my friend, I shall be much forsworn;
And ev'n that pow'r which gave me first my oath
Provokes me to this threefold perjury: 5
Love bade me swear, and Love bids me forswear.
O sweet-suggesting Love, if thou hast sinn'd,
Teach me, thy tempted subject, to excuse it!
At first I did adore a twinkling star,
But now I worship a celestial sun. 10
Unheedful vows may heedfully be broken;
And he wants wit that wants resolved will
To learn his wit t' exchange the bad for better.

Fie, fie, unreverend tongue, to call her bad
Whose sovereignty so oft thou hast preferr'd
With twenty thousand soul-confirming oaths! 16
I cannot leave to love, and yet I do;
But there I leave to love where I should love.
Julia I lose, and Valentine I lose;
If I keep them, I needs must lose myself;
If I lose them, thus find I by their loss: 21
For Valentine, myself; for Julia, Silvia.
I to myself am dearer than a friend;
For love is still most precious in itself;
And Silvia—witness heaven, that made her fair!— 25
Shows Julia but a swarthy Ethiope.
I will forget that Julia is alive,
Remem'bring that my love to her is dead;
And Valentine I'll hold an enemy,
Aiming at Silvia as a sweeter friend. 30
I cannot now prove constant to myself
Without some treachery us'd to Valentine.
This night he meaneth with a corded ladder
To climb celestial Silvia's chamber window,
Myself in counsel, his competitor. 35
Now presently I'll give her father notice
Of their disguising and pretended flight,
Who, all enrag'd, will banish Valentine,
For Thurio, he intends, shall wed his daughter;
But, Valentine being gone, I'll quickly cross 40
By some sly trick blunt Thurio's dull proceeding.
Love, lend me wings to make my purpose swift,
As thou hast lent me wit to plot this drift.
[*Exit.*

SCENE VII. *Verona. Julia's house.*

Enter JULIA *and* LUCETTA.

Jul. Counsel, Lucetta; gentle girl, assist me;
And, ev'n in kind love, I do conjure thee,
Who art the table wherein all my thoughts
Are visibly character'd and engrav'd,
To lesson me and tell me some good mean
How, with my honour, I may undertake
A journey to my loving Proteus. 7

Luc. Alas, the way is wearisome and long!

Jul. A true-devoted pilgrim is not weary
To measure kingdoms with his feeble steps;
Much less shall she that hath Love's wings to fly, 11
And when the flight is made to one so dear,
Of such divine perfection, as Sir Proteus.

Luc. Better forbear till Proteus make return.

Jul. O, know'st thou not his looks are my soul's food? 15
Pity the dearth that I have pined in
By longing for that food so long a time.
Didst thou but know the inly touch of love,

Thou wouldst as soon go kindle fire with
    snow
As seek to quench the fire of love with
    words.   20
  Luc. I do not seek to quench your love's
    hot fire,
But qualify the fire's extreme rage,
Lest it should burn above the bounds of
    reason.
  Jul. The more thou dam'st it up, the
    more it burns.
The current that with gentle murmur
    glides,   25
Thou know'st, being stopp'd, impatiently
    doth rage ;
But when his fair course is not hindered,
He makes sweet music with th' enamell'd
    stones,
Giving a gentle kiss to every sedge
He overtaketh in his pilgrimage ;   30
And so by many winding nooks he strays,
With willing sport, to the wild ocean.
Then let me go, and hinder not my course.
I'll be as patient as a gentle stream,
And make a pastime of each weary step, 35
Till the last step have brought me to my
    love ;
And there I'll rest as, after much turmoil,
A blessed soul doth in Elysium.
  Luc. But in what habit will you go along?
  Jul. Not like a woman, for I would
    prevent   40
The loose encounters of lascivious men ;
Gentle Lucetta, fit me with such weeds
As may beseem some well-reputed page.
  Luc. Why then, your ladyship must cut
    your hair.
  Jul. No, girl ; I'll knit it up in silken
    strings   45
With   twenty   odd-conceited   true-love
    knots—
To be fantastic may become a youth
Of greater time than I shall show to be.
  Luc. What fashion, madam, shall I make
    your breeches ?
  Jul. That fits as well as ' Tell me, good
    my lord,   50
What compass will you wear your farth-
    ingale '.
Why ev'n what fashion thou best likes,
    Lucetta.
  Luc. You must needs have them with a
    codpiece, madam.
  Jul. Out, out, Lucetta, that will be ill-
    favour'd.
  Luc. A round hose, madam, now's not
    worth a pin,   55
Unless you have a codpiece to stick pins on.
  Jul. Lucetta, as thou lov'st me, let me
    have
What thou think'st meet, and is most
    mannerly.
But tell me, wench, how will the world
    repute me

For undertaking so unstaid a journey ? 60
I fear me it will make me scandaliz'd.
  Luc. If you think so, then stay at home
    and go not.
  Jul. Nay, that I will not.
  Luc. Then never dream on infamy, but
    go.
If Proteus like your journey when you
    come,   65
No matter who's displeas'd when you are
    gone.
I fear me he will scarce be pleas'd withal.
  Jul. That is the least, Lucetta, of my fear:
A thousand oaths, an ocean of his tears,
And instances of infinite of love,   70
Warrant me welcome to my Proteus.
  Luc. All these are servants to deceitful
    men.
  Jul. Base men that use them to so base
    effect !
But truer stars did govern Proteus' birth :
His words are bonds, his oaths are oracles,
His love sincere, his thoughts immaculate,
His tears pure messengers sent from his
    heart,   77
His heart as far from fraud as heaven from
    earth.
  Luc. Pray heav'n he prove so when you
    come to him.
  Jul. Now, as thou lov'st me, do him not
    that wrong   80
To bear a hard opinion of his truth ;
Only deserve my love by loving him.
And presently go with me to my chamber,
To take a note of what I stand in need of
To furnish me upon my longing journey. 85
All that is mine I leave at thy dispose,
My goods, my lands, my reputation ;
Only, in lieu thereof, dispatch me hence.
Come, answer not, but to it presently ; 89
I am impatient of my tarriance. [*Exeunt.*

ACT THREE

SCENE I. *Milan. The Duke's palace.*

Enter DUKE, THURIO, *and* PROTEUS.

  Duke. Sir Thurio, give us leave, I pray,
    awhile ;
We have some secrets to confer about.
                   [*Exit Thurio.*
Now tell me, Proteus, what's your will
    with me ?
  Pro. My gracious lord, that which I would
    discover
The law of friendship bids me to conceal ; 5
But, when I call to mind your gracious
    favours
Done to me, undeserving as I am,
My duty pricks me on to utter that
Which else no worldly good should draw
    from me.
Know, worthy prince, Sir Valentine, my
    friend,

This night intends to steal away your
  daughter;
Myself am one made privy to the plot.
I know you have determin'd to bestow her
On Thurio, whom your gentle daughter
  hates;
And should she thus be stol'n away from
  you,   15
It would be much vexation to your age.
Thus, for my duty's sake, I rather chose
To cross my friend in his intended drift
Than, by concealing it, heap on your
  head
A pack of sorrows which would press you
  down,   20
Being unprevented, to your timeless grave.
  Duke. Proteus, I thank thee for thine
    honest care,
Which to requite, command me while I live.
This love of theirs myself have often seen,
Haply when they have judg'd me fast
  asleep,   25
And oftentimes have purpos'd to forbid
Sir Valentine her company and my court;
But, fearing lest my jealous aim might err
And so, unworthily, disgrace the man,
A rashness that I ever yet have shunn'd, 30
I gave him gentle looks, thereby to find
That which thyself hast now disclos'd to me.
And, that thou mayst perceive my fear of
  this,
Knowing that tender youth is soon
  suggested,
I nightly lodge her in an upper tow'r,   35
The key whereof myself have ever kept;
And thence she cannot be convey'd away.
  Pro. Know, noble lord, they have devis'd
    a mean   38
How he her chamber window will ascend
And with a corded ladder fetch her down;
For which the youthful lover now is gone,
And this way comes he with it presently;
Where, if it please you, you may intercept
  him.
But, good my lord, do it so cunningly
That my discovery be not aimed at;   45
For love of you, not hate unto my friend,
Hath made me publisher of this pretence.
  Duke. Upon mine honour, he shall never
    know
That I had any light from thee of this.   49
  Pro. Adieu, my lord; Sir Valentine is
    coming.   [*Exit.*

Enter VALENTINE.

  Duke. Sir Valentine, whither away so
    fast?
  Val. Please it your Grace, there is a
    messenger
That stays to bear my letters to my friends,
And I am going to deliver them.
  Duke. Be they of much import?   55
  Val. The tenour of them doth but signify
My health and happy being at your court.

  Duke. Nay then, no matter; stay with
    me awhile;
I am to break with thee of some affairs
That touch me near, wherein thou must be
  secret.   60
'Tis not unknown to thee that I have sought
To match my friend Sir Thurio to my
  daughter.
  Val. I know it well, my lord; and, sure,
    the match
Were rich and honourable; besides, the
  gentleman
Is full of virtue, bounty, worth, and
  qualities   65
Beseeming such a wife as your fair daughter.
Cannot your Grace win her to fancy him?
  Duke. No, trust me; she is peevish,
    sullen, froward,
Proud, disobedient, stubborn, lacking duty;
Neither regarding that she is my child   70
Nor fearing me as if I were her father;
And, may I say to thee, this pride of hers,
Upon advice, hath drawn my love from her;
And, where I thought the remnant of mine
  age
Should have been cherish'd by her child-
  like duty,   75
I now am full resolv'd to take a wife
And turn her out to who will take her in.
Then let her beauty be her wedding-dow'r;
For me and my possessions she esteems not.
  Val. What would your Grace have me to
    do in this?   80
  Duke. There is a lady, in Verona here,
Whom I affect; but she is nice, and coy,
And nought esteems my aged eloquence.
Now, therefore, would I have thee to my
  tutor—
For long agone I have forgot to court;   85
Besides, the fashion of the time is chang'd—
How and which way I may bestow myself
To be regarded in her sun-bright eye.
  Val. Win her with gifts, if she respect
    not words:
Dumb jewels often in their silent kind   90
More than quick words do move a woman's
  mind.
  Duke. But she did scorn a present that I
    sent her.
  Val. A woman sometime scorns what
    best contents her.
Send her another; never give her o'er,
For scorn at first makes after-love the more.
If she do frown, 'tis not in hate of you, 96
But rather to beget more love in you;
If she do chide, 'tis not to have you gone,
For why the fools are mad if left alone.
Take no repulse, whatever she doth say;
For 'Get you gone' she doth not mean
  'Away!'   101
Flatter and praise, commend, extol their
  graces;
Though ne'er so black, say they have angels'
  faces.

That man that hath a tongue, I say, is no man,
If with his tongue he cannot win a woman.
Duke. But she I mean is promis'd by her friends 106
Unto a youthful gentleman of worth;
And kept severely from resort of men,
That no man hath access by day to her.
Val. Why then I would resort to her by night. 110
Duke. Ay, but the doors be lock'd and keys kept safe,
That no man hath recourse to her by night.
Val. What lets but one may enter at her window?
Duke. Her chamber is aloft, far from the ground,
And built so shelving that one cannot climb it 115
Without apparent hazard of his life.
Val. Why then a ladder, quaintly made of cords,
To cast up with a pair of anchoring hooks,
Would serve to scale another Hero's tow'r,
So bold Leander would adventure it. 120
Duke. Now, as thou art a gentleman of blood,
Advise me where I may have such a ladder.
Val. When would you use it? Pray, sir, tell me that.
Duke. This very night; for Love is like a child,
That longs for everything that he can come by. 125
Val. By seven o'clock I'll get you such a ladder.
Duke. But, hark thee; I will go to her alone;
How shall I best convey the ladder thither?
Val. It will be light, my lord, that you may bear it
Under a cloak that is of any length. 130
Duke. A cloak as long as thine will serve the turn?
Val. Ay, my good lord.
Duke. Then let me see thy cloak.
I'll get me one of such another length.
Val. Why, any cloak will serve the turn, my lord.
Duke. How shall I fashion me to wear a cloak? 135
I pray thee, let me feel thy cloak upon me.
What letter is this same? What's here?
   ' To Silvia '!
And here an engine fit for my proceeding!
I'll be so bold to break the seal for once.
                                              [*Reads.*

' My thoughts do harbour with my Silvia nightly, 140
   And slaves they are to me, that send them flying.
O, could their master come and go as lightly,

Himself would lodge where, senseless, they are lying!
My herald thoughts in thy pure bosom rest them,
   While I, their king, that thither them importune, 145
Do curse the grace that with such grace hath blest them,
   Because myself do want my servants' fortune.
I curse myself, for they are sent by me,
That they should harbour where their lord should be.'

What's here? 150
' Silvia, this night I will enfranchise thee.'
'Tis so; and here's the ladder for the purpose.
Why, Phaethon—for thou art Merops' son—
Wilt thou aspire to guide the heavenly car,
And with thy daring folly burn the world?
Wilt thou reach stars because they shine on thee? 156
Go, base intruder, over-weening slave,
Bestow thy fawning smiles on equal mates;
And think my patience, more than thy desert,
Is privilege for thy departure hence. 160
Thank me for this more than for all the favours
Which, all too much, I have bestow'd on thee.
But if thou linger in my territories
Longer than swiftest expedition
Will give thee time to leave our royal court, 165
By heaven! my wrath shall far exceed the love
I ever bore my daughter or thyself.
Be gone; I will not hear thy vain excuse,
But, as thou lov'st thy life, make speed from hence. [*Exit Duke.*
   Val. And why not death rather than living torment? 170
To die is to be banish'd from myself,
And Silvia is myself; banish'd from her
Is self from self, a deadly banishment.
What light is light, if Silvia be not seen?
What joy is joy, if Silvia be not by? 175
Unless it be to think that she is by,
And feed upon the shadow of perfection.
Except I be by Silvia in the night,
There is no music in the nightingale;
Unless I look on Silvia in the day, 180
There is no day for me to look upon.
She is my essence, and I leave to be
If I be not by her fair influence
Foster'd, illumin'd, cherish'd, kept alive.
I fly not death, to fly his deadly doom: 185
Tarry I here, I but attend on death;
But fly I hence, I fly away from life.

Enter PROTEUS *and* LAUNCE.

Pro. Run, boy, run, run, and seek him out.

Laun. So-ho, so-ho !

Pro. What seest thou ?   190

Laun. Him we go to find : there's not a hair on 's head but 'tis a Valentine.

Pro. Valentine ?

Val. No.

Pro. Who then ? his spirit ?   195

Val. Neither.

Pro. What then ?

Val. Nothing.

Laun. Can nothing speak ? Master, shall I strike ?

Pro. Who wouldst thou strike ?   200

Laun. Nothing.

Pro. Villain, forbear.

Laun. Why, sir, I'll strike nothing. I pray you—

Pro. Sirrah, I say, forbear. Friend Valentine, a word.

Val. My ears are stopp'd and cannot hear good news,   205

So much of bad already hath possess'd them.

Pro. Then in dumb silence will I bury mine,

For they are harsh, untuneable, and bad.

Val. Is Silvia dead ?

Pro. No, Valentine.   210

Val. No Valentine, indeed, for sacred Silvia.

Hath she forsworn me ?

Pro. No, Valentine.

Val. No Valentine, if Silvia have forsworn me.

What is your news ?   215

Laun. Sir, there is a proclamation that you are vanished.

Pro. That thou art banished—O, that's the news !—

From hence, from Silvia, and from me thy friend.

Val. O, I have fed upon this woe already, And now excess of it will make me surfeit. Doth Silvia know that I am banished ?

Pro. Ay, ay ; and she hath offered to the doom—   222

Which, unrevers'd, stands in effectual force—

A sea of melting pearl, which some call tears ;

Those at her father's churlish feet she tender'd ;   225

With them, upon her knees, her humble self, Wringing her hands, whose whiteness so became them

As if but now they waxed pale for woe.

But neither bended knees, pure hands held up,

Sad sighs, deep groans, nor silver-shedding tears,   230

Could penetrate her uncompassionate sire—

But Valentine, if he be ta'en, must die.

Besides, her intercession chaf'd him so,

When she for thy repeal was suppliant,

That to close prison he commanded her,   235

With many bitter threats of biding there.

Val. No more ; unless the next word that thou speak'st

Have some malignant power upon my life ;

If so, I pray thee breathe it in mine ear,

As ending anthem of my endless dolour.   240

Pro. Cease to lament for that thou canst not help,

And study help for that which thou lament'st.

Time is the nurse and breeder of all good.

Here if thou stay thou canst not see thy love ;

Besides, thy staying will abridge thy life.

Hope is a lover's staff ; walk hence with that,   246

And manage it against despairing thoughts.

Thy letters may be here, though thou art hence,

Which, being writ to me, shall be deliver'd

Even in the milk-white bosom of thy love.

The time now serves not to expostulate.

Come, I'll convey thee through the city gate ;   252

And, ere I part with thee, confer at large

Of all that may concern thy love affairs.

As thou lov'st Silvia, though not for thyself,

Regard thy danger, and along with me.

Val. I pray thee, Launce, an if thou seest my boy,   257

Bid him make haste and meet me at the Northgate.

Pro. Go, sirrah, find him out. Come, Valentine.   259

Val. O my dear Silvia ! Hapless Valentine !

[*Exeunt Valentine and Proteus.*

Laun. I am but a fool, look you, and yet I have the wit to think my master is a kind of a knave ; but that's all one if he be but one knave. He lives not now that knows me to be in love ; yet I am in love ; but a team of horse shall not pluck that from me ; nor who 'tis I love ; and yet 'tis a woman ; but what woman I will not tell myself ; and yet 'tis a milkmaid ; yet 'tis not a maid, for she hath had gossips ; yet 'tis a maid, for she is her master's maid and serves for wages. She hath more qualities than a water-spaniel—which is much in a bare Christian. Here is the cate-log [*Pulling out a paper*] of her condition. 'Inprimis: She can fetch and carry.' Why, a horse can do no more ; nay, a horse cannot fetch, but only carry ; therefore is she better than a jade. ' Item : She can milk.' Look you, a sweet virtue in a maid with clean hands.   275

Enter SPEED.

Speed. How now, Signior Launce ! What news with your mastership ?

Laun. With my master's ship? Why, it is at sea.

Speed. Well, your old vice still: mistake the word. What news, then, in your paper? 280

Laun. The black'st news that ever thou heard'st.

Speed. Why, man? how black?

Laun. Why, as black as ink.

Speed. Let me read them.

Laun. Fie on thee, jolt-head; thou canst not read. 285

Speed. Thou liest; I can.

Laun. I will try thee. Tell me this: Who begot thee?

Speed. Marry, the son of my grandfather.

Laun. O illiterate loiterer. It was the son of thy grandmother. This proves that thou canst not read. 290

Speed. Come, fool, come; try me in thy paper.

Laun. [*Handing over the paper*] There; and Saint Nicholas be thy speed.

Speed. [*Reads*] 'Inprimis: She can milk.'

Laun. Ay, that she can.

Speed. 'Item: She brews good ale.' 295

Laun. And thereof comes the proverb: Blessing of your heart, you brew good ale.

Speed. 'Item: She can sew.'

Laun. That's as much as to say 'Can she so?'

Speed. 'Item: She can knit.' 300

Laun. What need a man care for a stock with a wench, when she can knit him a stock.

Speed. 'Item: She can wash and scour.'

Laun. A special virtue; for then she need not be wash'd and scour'd. 305

Speed. 'Item: She can spin.'

Laun. Then may I set the world on wheels, when she can spin for her living.

Speed. 'Item: She hath many nameless virtues.' 309

Laun. That's as much as to say 'bastard virtues'; that indeed know not their fathers, and therefore have no names. 312

Speed. 'Here follow her vices.'

Laun. Close at the heels of her virtues.

Speed. 'Item: She is not to be kiss'd fasting, in respect of her breath.' 316

Laun. Well, that fault may be mended with a breakfast. Read on.

Speed. 'Item: She hath a sweet mouth.'

Laun. That makes amends for her sour breath. 320

Speed. 'Item: She doth talk in her sleep.'

Laun. It's no matter for that, so she sleep not in her talk. 323

Speed. 'Item: She is slow in words.'

Laun. O villain, that set this down among her vices! To be slow in words is a woman's only virtue. I pray thee, out with't; and place it for her chief virtue.

Speed. 'Item: She is proud.'

Laun. Out with that too; it was Eve's legacy, and cannot be ta'en from her. 330

Speed. 'Item: She hath no teeth.'

Laun. I care not for that neither, because I love crusts.

Speed. 'Item: She is curst.'

Laun. Well, the best is, she hath no teeth to bite. 335

Speed. 'Item: She will often praise her liquor.'

Laun. If her liquor be good, she shall; if she will not, I will; for good things should be praised.

Speed. 'Item: She is too liberal.' 339

Laun. Of her tongue she cannot, for that's writ down she is slow of; of her purse she shall not, for that I'll keep shut. Now of another thing she may, and that cannot I help. Well, proceed. 343

Speed. 'Item: She hath more hair than wit, and more faults than hairs, and more wealth than faults.' 345

Laun. Stop there; I'll have her; she was mine, and not mine, twice or thrice in that last article. Rehearse that once more.

Speed. 'Item: She hath more hair than wit'— 349

Laun. More hair than wit. It may be; I'll prove it: the cover of the salt hides the salt, and therefore it is more than the salt; the hair that covers the wit is more than the wit, for the greater hides the less. What's next? 353

Speed. 'And more faults than hairs'—

Laun. That's monstrous. O that that were out! 355

Speed. 'And more wealth than faults.'

Laun. Why, that word makes the faults gracious. Well, I'll have her; an if it be a match, as nothing is impossible—

Speed. What then? 360

Laun. Why, then will I tell thee—that thy master stays for thee at the Northgate.

Speed. For me?

Laun. For thee! ay, who art thou? He hath stay'd for a better man than thee.

Speed. And must I go to him? 366

Laun. Thou must run to him, for thou hast stay'd so long that going will scarce serve the turn. 368

Speed. Why didst not tell me sooner? Pox of your love letters! [*Exit.*

Laun. Now will he be swing'd for reading my letter. An unmannerly slave that will thrust himself into secrets! I'll after, to rejoice in the boy's correction. [*Exit.*

SCENE II. *Milan. The Duke's palace.*

Enter DUKE *and* THURIO.

Duke. Sir Thurio, fear not but that she
    will love you
Now Valentine is banish'd from her sight.

Thu. Since his exile she hath despis'd me
    most,
Forsworn my company and rail'd at me,
That I am desperate of obtaining her.   5
  Duke. This weak impress of love is as a
    figure
Trenched in ice, which with an hour's heat
Dissolves to water and doth lose his form.
A little time will melt her frozen thoughts,
And worthless Valentine shall be forgot.   10

Enter PROTEUS.

How now, Sir Proteus! Is your country-
    man,
According to our proclamation, gone?
  Pro. Gone, my good lord.
  Duke. My daughter takes his going
    grievously.
  Pro. A little time, my lord, will kill that
    grief.   15
  Duke. So I believe; but Thurio thinks
    not so.
Proteus, the good conceit I hold of thee—
For thou hast shown some sign of good
    desert—
Makes me the better to confer with thee.
  Pro. Longer than I prove loyal to your
    Grace   20
Let me not live to look upon your Grace.
  Duke. Thou know'st how willingly I
    would effect
The match between Sir Thurio and my
    daughter.
  Pro. I do, my lord.
  Duke. And also, I think, thou art not
    ignorant   25
How she opposes her against my will.
  Pro. She did, my lord, when Valentine
    was here.
  Duke. Ay, and perversely she persevers
    so.
What might we do to make the girl forget
The love of Valentine, and love Sir Thurio?
  Pro. The best way is to slander Valentine
With falsehood, cowardice, and poor
    descent—   32
Three things that women highly hold in
    hate.
  Duke. Ay, but she'll think that it is spoke
    in hate.
  Pro. Ay, if his enemy deliver it;   35
Therefore it must with circumstance be
    spoken
By one whom she esteemeth as his friend.
  Duke. Then you must undertake to
    slander him.
  Pro. And that, my lord, I shall be loath
    to do:
'Tis an ill office for a gentleman,   40
Especially against his very friend.
  Duke. Where your good word cannot
    advantage him,
Your slander never can endamage him;
Therefore the office is indifferent,

Being entreated to it by your friend.   45
  Pro. You have prevail'd, my lord; if I
    can do it
By aught that I can speak in his dispraise,
She shall not long continue love to him.
But say this weed her love from Valentine,
It follows not that she will love Sir Thurio.
  Thu. Therefore, as you unwind her love
    from him,   51
Lest it should ravel and be good to none,
You must provide to bottom it on me;
Which must be done by praising me as
    much
As you in worth dispraise Sir Valentine.   55
  Duke. And, Proteus, we dare trust you in
    this kind,
Because we know, on Valentine's report,
You are already Love's firm votary
And cannot soon revolt and change your
    mind.   59
Upon this warrant shall you have access
Where you with Silvia may confer at large—
For she is lumpish, heavy, melancholy,
And, for your friend's sake, will be glad of
    you—
Where you may temper her by your
    persuasion
To hate young Valentine and love my
    friend.   65
  Pro. As much as I can do I will effect.
But you, Sir Thurio, are not sharp enough;
You must lay lime to tangle her desires
By wailful sonnets, whose composed
    rhymes
Should be full-fraught with serviceable
    vows.   70
  Duke. Ay,
Much is the force of heaven-bred poesy.
  Pro. Say that upon the altar of her
    beauty
You sacrifice your tears, your sighs, your
    heart;
Write till your ink be dry, and with your
    tears   75
Moist it again, and frame some feeling
    line
That may discover such integrity;
For Orpheus' lute was strung with poets'
    sinews,
Whose golden touch could soften steel and
    stones,
Make tigers tame, and huge leviathans   80
Forsake unsounded deeps to dance on sands.
After your dire-lamenting elegies,
Visit by night your lady's chamber window
With some sweet consort; to their instru-
    ments
Tune a deploring dump—the night's dead
    silence   85
Will well become such sweet-complaining
    grievance.
This, or else nothing, will inherit her.
  Duke. This discipline shows thou hast
    been in love.

43

Thu. And thy advice this night I'll put in
    practice;
Therefore, sweet Proteus, my direction-
    giver,   90
Let us into the city presently
To sort some gentlemen well skill'd in
    music.
I have a sonnet that will serve the turn
To give the onset to thy good advice.
   Duke. About it, gentlemen!   95
   Pro. We'll wait upon your Grace till after
    supper,
And afterward determine our proceedings.
   Duke. Even now about it! I will pardon
    you.   [*Exeunt.*

ACT FOUR

SCENE I. *The frontiers of Mantua. A forest.*

Enter certain Outlaws.

   1 *Out.* Fellows, stand fast; I see a
    passenger.
   2 *Out.* If there be ten, shrink not, but
    down with 'em.

Enter VALENTINE *and* SPEED.

   3 *Out.* Stand, sir, and throw us that you
    have about ye;
If not, we'll make you sit, and rifle you.
   Speed. Sir, we are undone; these are the
    villains   5
That all the travellers do fear so much.
   Val. My friends,—
   1 *Out.* That's not so, sir; we are your
    enemies.
   2 *Out.* Peace! we'll hear him.
   3 *Out.* Ay, by my beard, will we; for he
is a proper man.   10
   Val. Then know that I have little wealth
    to lose;
A man I am cross'd with adversity;
My riches are these poor habiliments,
Of which if you should here disfurnish me,
You take the sum and substance that I
    have.   15
   2 *Out.* Whither travel you?
   Val. To Verona.
   1 *Out.* Whence came you?
   Val. From Milan.   19
   3 *Out.* Have you long sojourn'd there?
   Val. Some sixteen months, and longer
    might have stay'd,
If crooked fortune had not thwarted me.
   1 *Out.* What, were you banish'd thence?
   Val. I was.
   2 *Out.* For what offence?   25
   Val. For that which now torments me to
    rehearse:
I kill'd a man, whose death I much repent;
But yet I slew him manfully in fight,
Without false vantage or base treachery.
   1 *Out.* Why, ne'er repent it, if it were
    done so.   30

But were you banish'd for so small a fault?
   Val. I was, and held me glad of such a
    doom.'
   2 *Out.* Have you the tongues?
   Val. My youthful travel therein made me
    happy,
Or else I often had been miserable.   35
   3 *Out.* By the bare scalp of Robin Hood's
    fat friar,
This fellow were a king for our wild faction!
   1 *Out.* We'll have him. Sirs, a word.
   Speed. Master, be one of them; it 's an
honourable kind of thievery.   40
   Val. Peace, villain!
   2 *Out.* Tell us this: have you anything
to take to?
   Val. Nothing but my fortune.
   3 *Out.* Know, then, that some of us are
    gentlemen,
Such as the fury of ungovern'd youth   45
Thrust from the company of awful men;
Myself was from Verona banished
For practising to steal away a lady,
An heir, and near allied unto the Duke.
   2 *Out.* And I from Mantua, for a gentle-
    man   50
Who, in my mood, I stabb'd unto the heart.
   1 *Out.* And I for such-like petty crimes
    as these.
But to the purpose—for we cite our faults
That they may hold excus'd our lawless
    lives;
And, partly, seeing you are beautified   55
With goodly shape, and by your own report
A linguist, and a man of such perfection
As we do in our quality much want—
   2 *Out.* Indeed, because you are a banish'd
    man,
Therefore, above the rest, we parley to
    you.
Are you content to be our general—   61
To make a virtue of necessity,
And live as we do in this wilderness?
   3 *Out.* What say'st thou? Wilt thou be
    of our consort?
Say 'ay' and be the captain of us all.   65
We'll do thee homage, and be rul'd by
    thee,
Love thee as our commander and our king.
   1 *Out.* But if thou scorn our courtesy
    thou diest.
   2 *Out.* Thou shalt not live to brag what
    we have offer'd.
   Val. I take your offer, and will live with
    you,   70
Provided that you do no outrages
On silly women or poor passengers.
   3 *Out.* No, we detest such vile base
    practices.
Come, go with us; we'll bring thee to our
    crews,   74
And show thee all the treasure we have got;
Which, with ourselves, all rest at thy
    dispose.   [*Exeunt.*

SCENE II. *Milan. Outside the Duke's palace, under Silvia's window.*

Enter PROTEUS.

Pro. Already have I been false to Valentine,
And now I must be as unjust to Thurio.
Under the colour of commending him
I have access my own love to prefer;
But Silvia is too fair, too true, too holy, 5
To be corrupted with my worthless gifts.
When I protest true loyalty to her,
She twits me with my falsehood to my
　　friend;
When to her beauty I commend my vows,
She bids me think how I have been forsworn
In breaking faith with Julia whom I lov'd;
And notwithstanding all her sudden quips,
The least whereof would quell a lover's
　　hope,
Yet, spaniel-like, the more she spurns my
　　love 14
The more it grows and fawneth on her still.

Enter THURIO *and* Musicians.

But here comes Thurio. Now must we to
　　her window,
And give some evening music to her ear.
　　Thu. How now, Sir Proteus, are you crept
　　　　before us?
　　Pro. Ay, gentle Thurio; for you know
　　　　that love
Will creep in service where it cannot go. 20
　　Thu. Ay, but I hope, sir, that you love
　　　　not here.
　　Pro. Sir, but I do; or else I would be
　　　　hence.
　　Thu. Who? Silvia?
　　Pro.　　　　　　Ay, Silvia—for your sake.
　　Thu. I thank you for your own. Now,
　　　　gentlemen,
Let's tune, and to it lustily awhile. 25

Enter at a distance, Host, *and* JULIA *in boy's clothes.*

　　Host. Now, my young guest, methinks
you're allycholly; I pray you, why is it?
　　Jul. Marry, mine host, because I cannot
be merry.
　　Host. Come, we'll have you merry; I'll
bring you where you shall hear music, and
see the gentleman that you ask'd for. 31
　　Jul. But shall I hear him speak?
　　Host. Ay, that you shall. [*Music plays.*
　　Jul. That will be music.
　　Host. Hark, hark! 35
　　Jul. Is he among these?
　　Host. Ay; but peace! let's hear 'em.

Song.

Who is Silvia? What is she,
　　That all our swains commend her?

Holy, fair, and wise is she; 40
　　The heaven such grace did lend
　　　her,
That she might admired be.

Is she kind as she is fair?
　　For beauty lives with kindness.
Love doth to her eyes repair, 45
　　To help him of his blindness;
And, being help'd, inhabits there.

Then to Silvia let us sing
　　That Silvia is excelling;
She excels each mortal thing 50
　　Upon the dull earth dwelling.
To her let us garlands bring.

　　Host. How now, are you sadder than you
were before? How do you, man? The
music likes you not.
　　Jul. You mistake; the musician likes me
not. 55
　　Host. Why, my pretty youth?
　　Jul. He plays false, father.
　　Host. How, out of tune on the strings?
　　Jul. Not so; but yet so false that he
grieves my very heart-strings. 60
　　Host. You have a quick ear.
　　Jul. Ay, I would I were deaf; it makes
me have a slow heart.
　　Host. I perceive you delight not in music.
　　Jul. Not a whit, when it jars so. 65
　　Host. Hark, what fine change is in the
music!
　　Jul. Ay, that change is the spite.
　　Host. You would have them always play
but one thing?
　　Jul. I would always have one play but
　　　　one thing.
But, Host, doth this Sir Proteus, that we
　　talk on, 70
Often resort unto this gentlewoman?
　　Host. I tell you what Launce, his man,
told me: he lov'd her out of all nick.
　　Jul. Where is Launce? 74
　　Host. Gone to seek his dog, which to-
morrow, by his master's command, he must
carry for a present to his lady.
　　Jul. Peace, stand aside; the company
parts.
　　Pro. Sir Thurio, fear not you; I will so
plead 78
That you shall say my cunning drift excels.
　　Thu. Where meet we?
　　Pro.　　　　　　At Saint Gregory's well.
　　Thu.　　　　　　　　　　　　Farewell.
　　　　[*Exeunt Thurio and Musicians.*

Enter SILVIA *above, at her window.*

　　Pro. Madam, good ev'n to your ladyship.
　　Sil. I thank you for your music, gentle-
men.
Who is that that spake?
　　Pro. One, lady, if you knew his pure
　　　　heart's truth,

You would quickly learn to know him by
   his voice.   85
  Sil. Sir Proteus, as I take it.
  Pro. Sir Proteus, gentle lady, and your
   servant.
  Sil. What's your will ?
  Pro.   That I may compass yours.
  Sil. You have your wish ; my will is even
   this,
That presently you hie you home to bed. 90
Thou subtle, perjur'd, false, disloyal man,
Think'st thou I am so shallow, so con-
   ceitless,
To be seduced by thy flattery   93
That hast deceiv'd so many with thy vows ?
Return, return, and make thy love amends.
For me, by this pale queen of night I swear,
I am so far from granting thy request
That I despise thee for thy wrongful suit,
And by and by intend to chide myself
Even for this time I spend in talking to
   thee.   100
  Pro. I grant, sweet love, that I did love a
   lady ;
But she is dead.
  Jul. [*Aside*] 'Twere false, if I should
   speak it ;
For I am sure she is not buried.
  Sil. Say that she be ; yet Valentine, thy
   friend,
Survives, to whom, thyself art witness, 105
I am betroth'd ; and art thou not asham'd
To wrong him with thy importunacy ?
  Pro. I likewise hear that Valentine is
   dead.
  Sil. And so suppose am I ; for in his grave
Assure thyself my love is buried.   110
  Pro. Sweet lady, let me rake it from the
   earth.
  Sil. Go to thy lady's grave, and call hers
   thence ;
Or, at the least, in hers sepulchre thine.
  Jul. [*Aside*] He heard not that.   114
  Pro. Madam, if your heart be so obdurate,
Vouchsafe me yet your picture for my love,
The picture that is hanging in your
   chamber ;
To that I'll speak, to that I'll sigh and weep ;
For, since the substance of your perfect self
Is else devoted, I am but a shadow ;   120
And to your shadow will I make true love.
  Jul. [*Aside*] If 'twere a substance, you
   would, sure, deceive it
And make it but a shadow, as I am.
  Sil. I am very loath to be your idol, sir ;
But since your falsehood shall become you
   well   125
To worship shadows and adore false shapes,
Send to me in the morning, and I'll send it ;
And so, good rest.
  Pro.   As wretches have o'ernight
That wait for execution in the morn.
          [*Exeunt Proteus and Silvia.*
  Jul. Host, will you go ?   130

  Host. By my halidom, I was fast asleep.
  Jul. Pray you, where lies Sir Proteus ?
  Host. Marry, at my house. Trust me, I
think 'tis almost day.
  Jul. Not so ; but it hath been the longest
   night   135
That e'er I watch'd, and the most heaviest.
                  [*Exeunt.*

SCENE III.   *Under Silvia's window.*

Enter EGLAMOUR.

  Egl. This is the hour that Madam Silvia
Entreated me to call and know her mind ;
There's some great matter she'd employ me
   in.
Madam, madam !

Enter SILVIA *above, at her window.*

  Sil.   Who calls ?
  Egl.   Your servant and your friend ;
One that attends your ladyship's command.
  Sil. Sir Eglamour, a thousand times good
   morrow !   6
  Egl. As many, worthy lady, to yourself !
According to your ladyship's impose,
I am thus early come to know what service
It is your pleasure to command me in.   10
  Sil. O Eglamour, thou art a gentleman—
Think not I flatter, for I swear I do not—
Valiant, wise, remorseful, well accomplish'd.
Thou art not ignorant what dear good will
I bear unto the banish'd Valentine ;   15
Nor how my father would enforce me marry
Vain Thurio, whom my very soul abhors.
Thyself hast lov'd ; and I have heard thee say
No grief did ever come so near thy heart
As when thy lady and thy true love died, 20
Upon whose grave thou vow'dst pure
   chastity.
Sir Eglamour, I would to Valentine,
To Mantua, where I hear he makes abode ;
And, for the ways are dangerous to pass,
I do desire thy worthy company,   25
Upon whose faith and honour I repose.
Urge not my father's anger, Eglamour,
But think upon my grief, a lady's grief,
And on the justice of my flying hence
To keep me from a most unholy match,
Which heaven and fortune still rewards
   with plagues.   31
I do desire thee, even from a heart
As full of sorrows as the sea of sands,
To bear me company and go with me ;
If not, to hide what I have said to thee, 35
That I may venture to depart alone.
  Egl. Madam, I pity much your griev-
   ances ;
Which since I know they virtuously are
   plac'd,
I give consent to go along with you,
Recking as little what betideth me   40
As much I wish all good befortune you.
When will you go ?

Sil.   This evening coming.

Egl. Where shall I meet you ?

Sil.   At Friar Patrick's cell,
Where I intend holy confession.

Egl. I will not fail your ladyship. Good
morrow, gentle lady.   46

Sil. Good morrow, kind Sir Eglamour.
                              [*Exeunt.*

SCENE IV. *Under Silvia's window.*

Enter LAUNCE, *with his dog.*

Laun. When a man's servant shall play
the cur with him, look you, it goes hard—
one that I brought up of a puppy ; one
that I sav'd from drowning, when three or
four of his blind brothers and sisters went
to it. I have taught him, even as one would
say precisely ' Thus I would teach a dog '.
I was sent to deliver him as a present to
Mistress Silvia from my master ; and I
came no sooner into the dining-chamber,
but he steps me to her trencher and steals
her capon's leg. O, 'tis a foul thing when a
cur cannot keep himself in all companies !
I would have, as one should say, one that
takes upon him to be a dog indeed, to be,
as it were, a dog at all things. If I had not
had more wit than he, to take a fault upon
me that he did, I think verily he had been
hang'd for't ; sure as I live, he had suffer'd
for't. You shall judge. He thrusts me
himself into the company of three or four
gentleman-like dogs under the Duke's table ;
he had not been there, bless the mark, a
pissing while but all the chamber smelt
him. ' Out with the dog ' says one ; ' What
cur is that ? ' says another ; ' Whip him
out ' says the third ; ' Hang him up ' says
the Duke. I, having been acquainted with
the smell before, knew it was Crab, and
goes me to the fellow that whips the dogs.
' Friend,' quoth I ' you mean to whip the
dog.' ' Ay, marry do I ' quoth he. ' You do
him the more wrong ; ' quoth I ' 'twas I
did the thing you wot of.' He makes me
no more ado, but whips me out of the
chamber. How many masters would do
this for his servant ? Nay, I'll be sworn,
I have sat in the stocks for puddings he
hath stol'n, otherwise he had been executed ;
I have stood on the pillory for geese he hath
kill'd, otherwise he had suffer'd for't. Thou
think'st not of this now. Nay, I remember
the trick you serv'd me when I took my
leave of Madam Silvia. Did not I bid thee
still mark me and do as I do ? When didst
thou see me heave up my leg and make
water against a gentlewoman's farthingale ?
Didst thou ever see me do such a trick ? 36

Enter PROTEUS *and* JULIA *in boy's clothes.*

Pro. Sebastian is thy name ? I like thee
well,

And will employ thee in some service
    presently.

Jul. In what you please ; I'll do what I
    can.

Pro. I hope thou wilt. [*To Launce*] How
    now, you whoreson peasant !   40
Where have you been these two days
    loitering ?

Laun. Marry, sir, I carried Mistress Silvia
the dog you bade me.

Pro. And what says she to my little
jewel ?   44

Laun. Marry, she says your dog was a
cur, and tells you currish thanks is good
enough for such a present.

Pro. But she receiv'd my dog ?

Laun. No, indeed, did she not ; here have
I brought him back again.

Pro. What, didst thou offer her this from
me ?   50

Laun. Ay, sir ; the other squirrel was
stol'n from me by the hangman's boys in
the market-place ; and then I offer'd her
mine own, who is a dog as big as ten of
yours, and therefore the gift the greater.

Pro. Go, get thee hence and find my dog
again,   55
Or ne'er return again into my sight.
Away, I say. Stayest thou to vex me here ?
                        [*Exit Launce.*
A slave that still an end turns me to shame !
Sebastian, I have entertained thee,
Partly that I have need of such a youth 60
That can with some discretion do my
    business,
For 'tis no trusting to yond foolish lout,
But chiefly for thy face and thy behaviour,
Which, if my augury deceive me not,
Witness good bringing up, fortune, and
    truth ;   65
Therefore, know thou, for this I entertain
    thee.
Go presently, and take this ring with thee,
Deliver it to Madam Silvia—
She lov'd me well deliver'd it to me.

Jul. It seems you lov'd not her, to leave
    her token.   70
She is dead, belike ?

Pro.   Not so ; I think she lives.

Jul. Alas !

Pro. Why dost thou cry ' Alas ' ?

Jul.   I cannot choose
But pity her.

Pro. Wherefore shouldst thou pity her ?

Jul. Because methinks that she lov'd
you as well   75
As you do love your lady Silvia.
She dreams on him that has forgot her love ;
You dote on her that cares nor for your
    love.
'Tis pity love should be so contrary ;
And thinking on it makes me cry ' Alas ! '

Pro. Well, give her that ring, and there-
    withal   81

This letter. That's her chamber. Tell my
    lady
I claim the promise for her heavenly
    picture.
Your message done, hie home unto my
    chamber,   84
Where thou shalt find me sad and solitary.
               [*Exit Proteus.*
  Jul. How many women would do such a
    message ?
Alas, poor Proteus, thou hast entertain'd
A fox to be the shepherd of thy lambs.
Alas, poor fool, why do I pity him
That with his very heart despiseth me ? 90
Because he loves her, he despiseth me ;
Because I love him, I must pity him.
This ring I gave him, when he parted from
    me,
To bind him to remember my good will ;
And now am I, unhappy messenger, 95
To plead for that which I would not
    obtain,
To carry that which I would have refus'd,
To praise his faith, which I would have
    dispais'd.
I am my master's true confirmed love,
But cannot be true servant to my master
Unless I prove false traitor to myself. 101
Yet will I woo for him, but yet so coldly
As, heaven it knows, I would not have him
    speed.

      Enter SILVIA, *attended.*

Gentlewoman, good day ! I pray you be
    my mean
To bring me where to speak with Madam
    Silvia. 105
  Sil. What would you with her, if that I
    be she ?
  Jul. If you be she, I do entreat your
    patience
To hear me speak the message I am sent on.
  Sil. From whom ?
  Jul. From my master, Sir Proteus,
madam. 110
  Sil. O, he sends you for a picture ?
  Jul. Ay, madam.
  Sil. Ursula, bring my picture there.
Go, give your master this. Tell him from
    me,
One Julia, that his changing thoughts
    forget, 115
Would better fit his chamber than this
    shadow.
  Jul. Madam, please you peruse this letter.
Pardon me, madam ; I have unadvis'd
Deliver'd you a paper that I should not.
This is the letter to your ladyship. 120
  Sil. I pray thee let me look on that again.
  Jul. It may not be ; good madam, par-
    don me.
  Sil. There, hold !
I will not look upon your master's lines.
I know they are stuff'd with protestations,

And full of new-found oaths, which he will
    break 126
As easily as I do tear his paper.
  Jul. Madam, he sends your ladyship this
    ring.
  Sil. The more shame for him that he
    sends it me ;
For I have heard him say a thousand times
His Julia gave it him at his departure. 131
Though his false finger have profan'd the
    ring,
Mine shall not do his Julia so much wrong.
  Jul. She thanks you.
  Sil. What say'st thou ? 135
  Jul. I thank you, madam, that you tender
    her.
Poor gentlewoman, my master wrongs her
    much.
  Sil. Dost thou know her ?
  Jul. Almost as well as I do know myself.
To think upon her woes, I do protest 140
That I have wept a hundred several times.
  Sil. Belike she thinks that Proteus hath
    forsook her.
  Jul. I think she doth, and that's her
    cause of sorrow.
  Sil. Is she not passing fair ?
  Jul. She hath been fairer, madam, than
    she is. 145
When she did think my master lov'd her
    well,
She, in my judgment, was as fair as you ;
But since she did neglect her looking-glass
And threw her sun-expelling mask away,
The air hath starv'd the roses in her cheeks
And pinch'd the lily-tincture of her face,
That now she is become as black as I. 152
  Sil. How tall was she ?
  Jul. About my stature ; for at Pentecost,
When all our pageants of delight were
    play'd, 155
Our youth got me to play the woman's
    part,
And I was trimm'd in Madam Julia's gown ;
Which served me as fit, by all men's judg-
    ments,
As if the garment had been made for me ;
Therefore I know she is about my height.
And at that time I made her weep agood,
For I did play a lamentable part. 162
Madam, 'twas Ariadne passioning
For Theseus' perjury and unjust flight ;
Which I so lively acted with my tears
That my poor mistress, moved therewithal,
Wept bitterly ; and would I might be dead
If I in thought felt not her very sorrow.
  Sil. She is beholding to thee, gentle
    youth.
Alas, poor lady, desolate and left ! 170
I weep myself, to think upon thy words.
Here, youth, there is my purse ; I give thee
    this
For thy sweet mistress' sake, because thou
    lov'st her.

Farewell.   [*Exit Silvia with attendants.*
  Jul. And she shall thank you for't, if e'er
    you know her.   175
A virtuous gentlewoman, mild and beauti-
    ful!
I hope my master's suit will be but cold,
Since she respects my mistress' love so
    much.
Alas, how love can trifle with itself!
Here is her picture; let me see. I think,
If I had such a tire, this face of mine   181
Were full as lovely as is this of hers;
And yet the painter flatter'd her a little,
Unless I flatter with myself too much.
Her hair is auburn, mine is perfect yellow;
If that be all the difference in his love,   186
I'll get me such a colour'd periwig.
Her eyes are grey as glass, and so are
    mine;
Ay, but her forehead's low, and mine's as
    high.   189
What should it be that he respects in her
But I can make respective in myself,
If this fond Love were not a blinded
    god?
Come, shadow, come, and take this shadow
    up,
For 'tis thy rival. O thou senseless form,
Thou shalt be worshipp'd, kiss'd, lov'd, and
    ador'd!   195
And were there sense in his idolatry
My substance should be statue in thy
    stead.
I'll use thee kindly for thy mistress' sake,
That us'd me so; or else, by Jove I vow,
I should have scratch'd out your unseeing
    eyes,   200
To make my master out of love with thee.
                     [*Exit.*

ACT FIVE

Scene I.   *Milan.   An abbey.*

Enter EGLAMOUR.

  Egl. The sun begins to gild the western
    sky,
And now it is about the very hour
That Silvia at Friar Patrick's cell should
    meet me.
She will not fail, for lovers break not hours
Unless it be to come before their time,   5
So much they spur their expedition.

Enter SILVIA.

See where she comes.   Lady, a happy
    evening!
  Sil. Amen, amen! Go on, good Egla-
    mour,
Out at the postern by the abbey wall;
I fear I am attended by some spies.   10
  Egl. Fear not. The forest is not three
    leagues off;
If we recover that, we are sure enough.
                    [*Exeunt.*

Scene II.   *Milan.   The Duke's palace.*

Enter THURIO, PROTEUS, *and* JULIA *as
Sebastian.*

  Thu. Sir Proteus, what says Silvia to my
    suit?
  Pro. O, sir, I find her milder than she was;
And yet she takes exceptions at your per-
    son.
  Thu. What, that my leg is too long?
  Pro. No; that it is too little.   5
  Thu. I'll wear a boot to make it some-
    what rounder.
  Jul. [*Aside*] But love will not be spurr'd
    to what it loathes.
  Thu. What says she to my face?
  Pro. She says it is a fair one.
  Thu. Nay, then, the wanton lies; my
    face is black.   10
  Pro. But pearls are fair; and the old
    saying is:
Black men are pearls in beauteous ladies'
    eyes.
  Jul. [*Aside*] 'Tis true, such pearls as put
    out ladies' eyes;
For I had rather wink than look on them.
  Thu. How likes she my discourse?   15
  Pro. Ill, when you talk of war.
  Thu. But well when I discourse of love
    and peace?
  Jul. [*Aside*] But better, indeed, when you
    hold your peace.
  Thu. What says she to my valour?   19
  Pro. O, sir, she makes no doubt of that.
  Jul. [*Aside*] She needs not, when she
    knows it cowardice.
  Thu. What says she to my birth?
  Pro. That you are well deriv'd.
  Jul. [*Aside*] True; from a gentleman to
  a fool.
  Thu. Considers she my possessions?   25
  Pro. O, ay; and pities them.
  Thu. Wherefore?
  Jul. [*Aside*] That such an ass should owe
  them.
  Pro. That they are out by lease.
  Jul. Here comes the Duke.   30

Enter DUKE.

  Duke. How now, Sir Proteus! how now,
    Thurio!
Which of you saw Sir Eglamour of late?
  Thu. Not I.
  Pro.   Nor I.
  Duke.   Saw you my daughter?
  Pro.   Neither.
  Duke. Why then,
She's fled unto that peasant Valentine;
And Eglamour is in her company.   36
'Tis true; for Friar Lawrence met them
    both
As he in penance wander'd through the
    forest;

49

Him he knew well, and guess'd that it was
   she,
But, being mask'd, he was not sure of it ;
Besides, she did intend confession   41
At Patrick's cell this even ; and there she
   was not.
These likelihoods confirm her flight from
   hence ;
Therefore, I pray you, stand not to dis-
   course,
But mount you presently, and meet with
   me   45
Upon the rising of the mountain foot
That leads toward Mantua, whither they
   are fled.
Dispatch, sweet gentlemen, and follow me.
                  [*Exit.*
  Thu. Why, this it is to be a peevish girl
That flies her fortune when it follows her.
I'll after, more to be reveng'd on Eglamour
Than for the love of reckless Silvia. [*Exit.*
  Pro. And I will follow, more for Silvia's
   love
Than hate of Eglamour, that goes with her.
                  [*Exit.*
  Jul. And I will follow, more to cross that
   love   55
Than hate for Silvia, that is gone for love.
                  [*Exit.*

SCENE III.   *The frontiers of Mantua.*
           The forest.

    Enter Outlaws *with* SILVIA.

1 *Out.* Come, come,
Be patient ; we must bring you to our
   captain.
  Sil. A thousand more mischances than
   this one
Have learn'd me how to brook this
   patiently.
2 *Out.* Come, bring her away.   5
1 *Out.* Where is the gentleman that was
   with her ?
2 *Out.* Being nimble-footed, he hath outrun us,
But Moyses and Valerius follow him.
Go thou with her to the west end of the
   wood ;
There is our captain ; we'll follow him
   that's fled.   10
The thicket is beset ; he cannot 'scape.
1 *Out.* Come, I must bring you to our
   captain's cave ;
Fear not ; he bears an honourable mind,
And will not use a woman lawlessly.   14
  Sil. O Valentine, this I endure for thee !
                  [*Exeunt.*

SCENE IV.   *Another part of the forest.*

      Enter VALENTINE.

  Val. How use doth breed a habit in a
   man !

This shadowy desert, unfrequented woods,
I better brook than flourishing peopled
   towns.
Here can I sit alone, unseen of any,   4
And to the nightingale's complaining notes
Tune my distresses and record my woes.
O thou that dost inhabit in my breast,
Leave not the mansion so long tenantless,
Lest, growing ruinous, the building fall
And leave no memory of what it was !   10
Repair me with thy presence, Silvia ;
Thou gentle nymph, cherish thy forlorn
   swain.
What halloing and what stir is this to-day ?
These are my mates, that make their wills
   their law,
Have some unhappy passenger in chase.   15
They love me well ; yet I have much to do
To keep them from uncivil outrages.
Withdraw thee, Valentine.   Who's this
   comes here ?   [*Steps aside.*

   Enter PROTEUS, SILVIA, *and* JULIA
          as Sebastian.

  Pro. Madam, this service I have done for
   you,
Though you respect not aught your servant
   doth,   20
To hazard life, and rescue you from him
That would have forc'd your honour and
   your love.
Vouchsafe me, for my meed, but one fair
   look ;
A smaller boon than this I cannot beg,
And less than this, I am sure, you cannot
   give.   25
  Val. [*Aside*] How like a dream is this I
   see and hear !
Love, lend me patience to forbear awhile.
  Sil. O miserable, unhappy that I am !
  Pro. Unhappy were you, madam, ere I
   came ;
But by my coming I have made you happy.
  Sil. By thy approach thou mak'st me
   most unhappy.   31
  Jul. [*Aside*] And me, when he approach-
   eth to your presence.
  Sil. Had I been seized by a hungry lion,
I would have been a breakfast to the beast
Rather than have false Proteus rescue me.
O, heaven be judge how I love Valentine,
Whose life's as tender to me as my soul !
And full as much, for more there cannot be,
I do detest false, perjur'd Proteus.
Therefore be gone ; solicit me no more.   40
  Pro. What dangerous action, stood it next
   to death,
Would I not undergo for one calm look ?
O, 'tis the curse in love, and still approv'd,
When women cannot love where they're
   belov'd !
  Sil. When Proteus cannot love where he's
   belov'd !   45
Read over Julia's heart, thy first best love,

For whose dear sake thou didst then rend
    thy faith
Into a thousand oaths ; and all those oaths
Descended into perjury, to love me.
Thou hast no faith left now, unless thou'dst
    two,   50
And that's far worse than none ; better
    have none
Than plural faith, which is too much by
    one.
Thou counterfeit to thy true friend !
    Pro.   In love,
Who respects friend ?
    Sil.   All men but Proteus.
    Pro. Nay, if the gentle spirit of moving
    words   55
Can no way change you to a milder form,
I'll woo you like a soldier, at arms' end,
And love you 'gainst the nature of love—
    force ye.
    Sil. O heaven !
    Pro.   I'll force thee yield to my desire.
    Val. Ruffian ! let go that rude uncivil
    touch ;   60
Thou friend of an ill fashion !
    Pro.   Valentine !
    Val. Thou common friend, that's without
    faith or love—
For such is a friend now ; treacherous man,
Thou hast beguil'd my hopes ; nought but
    mine eye
Could have persuaded me. Now I dare not
    say   65
I have one friend alive : thou wouldst
    disprove me.
Who should be trusted, when one's own
    right hand
Is perjured to the bosom ? Proteus,
I am sorry I must never trust thee more,
But count the world a stranger for thy sake.
The private wound is deepest. O time
    most accurst !   71
'Mongst all foes that a friend should be the
    worst !
    Pro. My shame and guilt confounds me.
Forgive me, Valentine ; if hearty sorrow
Be a sufficient ransom for offence,   75
I tender 't here ; I do as truly suffer
As e'er I did commit.
    Val.   Then I am paid ;
And once again I do receive thee honest.
Who by repentance is not satisfied
Is nor of heaven nor of earth, for these are
    pleas'd ;   80
By penitence th' Eternal's wrath's ap-
    peas'd.
And, that my love may appear plain and
    free,
All that was mine in Silvia I give thee.
    Jul. O me unhappy !   [*Swoons.*
    Pro. Look to the boy.   85
    Val. Why, boy ! why, wag ! how now !
What's the matter ? Look up ; speak.
    Jul. O good sir, my master charg'd me

to deliver a ring to Madam Silvia, which,
out of my neglect, was never done.   90
    Pro. Where is that ring, boy ?
    Jul. Here 'tis ; this is it.
    Pro. How ! let me see. Why, this is the
ring I gave to Julia.
    Jul. O, cry you mercy, sir, I have mis-
took ;
This is the ring you sent to Silvia.   95
    Pro. But how cam'st thou by this ring ?
At my depart I gave this unto Julia.
    Jul. And Julia herself did give it me ;
And Julia herself have brought it hither.
    Pro. How ! Julia !   100
    Jul. Behold her that gave aim to all thy
    oaths,
And entertain'd 'em deeply in her heart.
How oft hast thou with perjury cleft the
    root !   103
O Proteus, let this habit make thee blush !
Be thou asham'd that I have took upon
    me
Such an immodest raiment—if shame live
In a disguise of love.
It is the lesser blot, modesty finds,
Women to change their shapes than men
    their minds.
    Pro. Than men their minds ! 'tis true. O
    heaven, were man   110
But constant, he were perfect ! That one
    error
Fills him with faults ; makes him run
    through all th' sins :
Inconstancy falls off ere it begins.
What is in Silvia's face but I may spy   114
More fresh in Julia's with a constant eye ?
    Val. Come, come, a hand from either.
Let me be blest to make this happy close ;
'Twere pity two such friends should be long
    foes.
    Pro. Bear witness, heaven, I have my
    wish for ever.
    Jul. And I mine.   120

    Enter Outlaws, *with* DUKE *and*
           THURIO.

    Out. A prize, a prize, a prize !
    Val. Forbear, forbear, I say ; it is my
    lord the Duke.
Your Grace is welcome to a man disgrac'd,
Banished Valentine.
    Duke.   Sir Valentine !   124
    Thu. Yonder is Silvia ; and Silvia's mine.
    Val. Thurio, give back, or else embrace
    thy death ;
Come not within the measure of my wrath ;
Do not name Silvia thine ; if once again,
Verona shall not hold thee. Here she stands
Take but possession of her with a touch—
I dare thee but to breathe upon my love.
    Thu. Sir Valentine, I care not for her, I ;
I hold him but a fool that will endanger
His body for a girl that loves him not.   134
I claim her not, and therefore she is thine.

Duke. The more degenerate and base art
    thou   136
To make such means for her as thou hast
    done
And leave her on such slight conditions.
Now, by the honour of my ancestry,
I do applaud thy spirit, Valentine,   140
And think thee worthy of an empress'
    love.
Know then, I here forget all former griefs,
Cancel all grudge, repeal thee home again,
Plead a new state in thy unrivall'd merit,
To which I thus subscribe : Sir Valentine,
Thou art a gentleman, and well deriv'd ;
Take thou thy Silvia, for thou hast deserv'd
    her   147
    Val. I thank your Grace ; the gift hath
    made me happy.
I now beseech you, for your daughter's sake,
To grant one boon that I shall ask of you.
    Duke. I grant it for thine own, whate'er
    it be.   151
    Val. These banish'd men, that I have
    kept withal,
Are men endu'd with worthy qualities ;
Forgive them what they have committed
    here,
And let them be recall'd from their exile :

They are reformed, civil, full of good, 156
And fit for great employment, worthy lord.
    Duke. Thou hast prevail'd ; I pardon
    them and thee ;
Dispose of them as thou know'st their
    deserts.
Come, let us go ; we will include all jars 160
With triumphs, mirth, and rare solemnity.
    Val. And, as we walk along, I dare be
    bold
With our discourse to make your Grace to
    smile.
What think you of this page, my lord ?
    Duke. I think the boy hath grace in him ;
    he blushes.   165
    Val. I warrant you, my lord—more grace
    than boy.
    Duke. What mean you by that saying ?
    Val. Please you, I'll tell you as we pass
    along,
That you will wonder what hath fortuned.
Come, Proteus, 'tis your penance but to
    hear,   170
The story of your loves discovered.
That done, our day of marriage shall be
    yours ;
One feast, one house, one mutual happiness!
                          [Exeunt.

THE MERRY WIVES OF WINDSOR

DRAMATIS PERSONÆ

SIR JOHN FALSTAFF.
FENTON, *a young gentleman.*
SHALLOW, *a country justice.*
SLENDER, *cousin to Shallow.*
FORD, } *gentlemen of Windsor.*
PAGE, }
WILLIAM PAGE, *a boy, son to Page.*
SIR HUGH EVANS, *a Welsh parson.*
DOCTOR CAIUS, *a French physician.*
Host *of the Garter Inn.*
BARDOLPH, }
PISTOL, } *followers of Falstaff.*
NYM, }

ROBIN, *page to Falstaff.*
SIMPLE, *servant to Slender.*
RUGBY, *servant to Doctor Caius.*

MISTRESS FORD.
MISTRESS PAGE.
MISTRESS ANNE PAGE, *her daughter.*
MISTRESS QUICKLY, *servant to Doctor Caius.*

Servants *to Page, Ford, &c.*

THE SCENE: *Windsor, and the neighbourhood.*

ACT ONE

SCENE I. *Windsor. Before Page's house.*

Enter JUSTICE SHALLOW, SLENDER *and* SIR HUGH EVANS.

Shal. Sir Hugh, persuade me not; I will make a Star Chamber matter of it; if he were twenty Sir John Falstaffs, he shall not abuse Robert Shallow, esquire.

Slen. In the county of Gloucester, Justice of Peace, and Coram. 5

Shal. Ay, cousin Slender, and Custalorum.

Slen. Ay, and Ratolorum too; and a gentleman born, Master Parson, who writes himself 'Armigero' in any bill, warrant, quittance, or obligation—'Armigero'. 9

Shal. Ay, that I do; and have done any time these three hundred years.

Slen. All his successors, gone before him, hath done't; and all his ancestors, that come after him, may: they may give the dozen white luces in their coat.

Shal. It is an old coat. 15

Evans. The dozen white louses do become an old coat well; it agrees well, passant; it is a familiar beast to man, and signifies love.

Shal. The luce is the fresh fish; the salt fish is an old coat. 20

Slen. I may quarter, coz.

Shal. You may, by marrying.

Evans. It is marring indeed, if he quarter it.

Shal. Not a whit. 24

Evans. Yes, py'r lady! If he has a quarter of your coat, there is but three skirts for yourself, in my simple conjectures; but that is all one. If Sir John Falstaff have committed disparagements unto you, I am of the church, and will be glad to do my benevolence, to make atonements and compremises between you. 30

Shal. The Council shall hear it; it is a riot.

Evans. It is not meet the Council hear a riot; there is no fear of Got in a riot; the Council, look you, shall desire to hear the fear of Got, and not to hear a riot; take your vizaments in that. 35

Shal. Ha! o' my life, if I were young again, the sword should end it.

Evans. It is petter that friends is the sword and end it; and there is also another device in my prain, which peradventure prings goot discretions with it. There is Anne Page, which is daughter to Master George Page, which is pretty virginity. 42

Slen. Mistress Anne Page? She has brown hair, and speaks small like a woman.

Evans. It is that fery person for all the orld, as just as you will desire; and seven hundred pounds of moneys, and gold, and silver, is her grandsire upon his death's-bed —Got deliver to a joyful resurrections!— give, when she is able to overtake seventeen years old. It were a goot motion if we leave our pribbles and prabbles, and desire a marriage between Master Abraham and Mistress Anne Page. 51

Shal. Did her grandsire leave her seven hundred pound?

Evans. Ay, and her father is make her a petter penny.

Shal. I know the young gentlewoman; she has good gifts. 55

Evans. Seven hundred pounds, and possibilities, is goot gifts.

Shal. Well, let us see honest Master Page. Is Falstaff there? 59

53

Evans. Shall I tell you a lie ? I do despise a liar as I do despise one that is false ; or as I despise one that is not true. The knight Sir John is there ; and, I beseech you, be ruled by your well-willers. I will peat the door for Master Page. [*Knocks*] What, hoa ! Got pless your house here !

Page. [*Within*] Who's there ?   65

Enter PAGE.

Evans. Here is Got's plessing, and your friend, and Justice Shallow ; and here young Master Slender, that peradventures shall tell you another tale, if matters grow to your likings.   69

Page. I am glad to see your worships well. I thank you for my venison, Master Shallow.

Shal. Master Page, I am glad to see you ; much good do it your good heart ! I wish'd your venison better ; it was ill kill'd. How doth good Mistress Page ?—and I thank you always with my heart, la ! with my heart.   75

Page. Sir, I thank you.

Shal. Sir, I thank you ; by yea and no, I do.

Page. I am glad to see you, good Master Slender.

Slen. How does your fallow greyhound, sir ? I heard say he was outrun on Cotsall.

Page. It could not be judg'd, sir.   81

Slen. You'll not confess, you'll not confess.

Shal. That he will not. 'Tis your fault ; 'tis your fault ; 'tis a good dog.

Page. A cur, sir.   85

Shal. Sir, he's a good dog, and a fair dog. Can there be more said ? He is good, and fair. Is Sir John Falstaff here ?

Page. Sir, he is within ; and I would I could do a good office between you.

Evans. It is spoke as a Christians ought to speak.   90

Shal. He hath wrong'd me, Master Page.

Page. Sir, he doth in some sort confess it.

Shal. If it be confessed, it is not redressed ; is not that so, Master Page ? He hath wrong'd me ; indeed he hath ; at a word, he hath, believe me ; Robert Shallow, esquire, saith he is wronged.   96

Page. Here comes Sir John.

Enter SIR JOHN FALSTAFF, BARDOLPH, NYM *and* PISTOL.

Fal. Now, Master Shallow, you'll complain of me to the King ?   99

Shal. Knight, you have beaten my men, kill'd my deer, and broke open my lodge.

Fal. But not kiss'd your keeper's daughter.

Shal. Tut, a pin ! this shall be answer'd.

Fal. I will answer it straight : I have done all this. That is now answer'd.   105

Shal. The Council shall know this.

Fal. 'Twere better for you if it were known in counsel : you'll be laugh'd at.

Evans. Pauca verba, Sir John ; goot worts.

Fal. Good worts ! good cabbage ! Slender, I broke your head ; what matter have you against me ?   111

Slen. Marry, sir, I have matter in my head against you ; and against your conycatching rascals, Bardolph, Nym, and Pistol. They carried me to the tavern, and made me drunk, and afterward pick'd my pocket.

Bard. You Banbury cheese !   115

Slen. Ay, it is no matter.

Pist. How now, Mephostophilus !

Slen. Ay, it is no matter.

Nym. Slice, I say ! pauca, pauca ; slice ! That's my humour.   120

Slen. Where's Simple, my man ? Can you tell, cousin ?

Evans. Peace, I pray you. Now let us understand. There is three umpires in this matter, as I understand : that is, Master Page, fidelicet Master Page ; and there is myself, fidelicet myself ; and the three party is, lastly and finally, mine host of the Garter.   127

Page. We three to hear it and end it between them.

Evans. Fery goot. I will make a prief of it in my note-book ; and we will afterwards ork upon the cause with as great discreetly as we can.   131

Fal. Pistol !

Pist. He hears with ears.

Evans. The tevil and his tam ! What phrase is this, ' He hears with ear ' ? Why, it is affectations.   135

Fal. Pistol, did you pick Master Slender's purse ?

Slen. Ay, by these gloves, did he—or I would I might never come in mine own great chamber again else !—of seven groats in mill-sixpences, and two Edward shovelboards that cost me two shilling and two pence apiece of Yead Miller, by these gloves.   141

Fal. Is this true, Pistol ?

Evans. No, it is false, if it is a pick-purse.

Pist. Ha, thou mountain-foreigner ! Sir John, and master mine,   145
I combat challenge of this latten bilbo.
Word of denial in thy labras here !
Word of denial ! Froth and scum, thou liest.

Slen. By these gloves, then, 'twas he. 149

Nym. Be avis'd, sir, and pass good humours ; I will say ' marry trap ' with you, if you run the nuthook's humour on me ; that is the very note of it.   152

Slen. By this hat, then, he in the red face had it ; for though I cannot remember what I did when you made me drunk, yet I am not altogether an ass.   155

Fal. What say you, Scarlet and John ?

Bard. Why, sir, for my part, I say the gentleman had drunk himself out of his five sentences.

Evans. It is his five senses ; fie, what the ignorance is !

Bard. And being fap, sir, was, as they say, cashier'd ; and so conclusions pass'd the careers.   161

Slen. Ay, you spake in Latin then too ; but 'tis no matter ; I'll ne'er be drunk whilst I live again, but in honest, civil, godly company, for this trick. If I be drunk, I'll be drunk with those that have the fear of God, and not with drunken knaves.   166

Evans. So Got udge me, that is a virtuous mind.

Fal. You hear all these matters deni'd, gentlemen ; you hear it.   169

Enter MISTRESS ANNE PAGE *with wine ;* MISTRESS FORD *and* MISTRESS PAGE, *following.*

Page. Nay, daughter, carry the wine in ; we'll drink within.   [*Exit Anne Page.*

Slen. O heaven! this is Mistress Anne Page.

Page. How now, Mistress Ford !   173

Fal. Mistress Ford, by my troth, you are very well met ; by your leave, good mistress.   [*Kisses her.*

Page. Wife, bid these gentlemen welcome. Come, we have a hot venison pasty to dinner ; come, gentlemen, I hope we shall drink down all unkindness.   178

[*Exeunt all but Shallow, Slender, and Evans.*

Slen. I had rather than forty shillings I had my Book of Songs and Sonnets here.

Enter SIMPLE.

How now, Simple ! Where have you been ? I must wait on myself, must I ? You have not the Book of Riddles about you, have you ?   183

Sim. Book of Riddles ! Why, did you not lend it to Alice Shortcake upon Allhallowmas last, a fortnight afore Michaelmas ?   186

Shal. Come, coz ; come, coz ; we stay for you. A word with you, coz ; marry, this, coz : there is, as 'twere, a tender, a kind of tender, made afar off by Sir Hugh here. Do you understand me ?   190

Slen. Ay, sir, you shall find me reasonable ; if it be so, I shall do that that is reason.

Shal. Nay, but understand me.

Slen. So I do, sir.   194

Evans. Give ear to his motions : Master Slender, I will description the matter to you, if you be capacity of it.   196

Slen. Nay, I will do as my cousin Shallow says ; I pray you pardon me ; he's a justice of peace in his country, simple though I stand here.   199

Evans. But that is not the question. The question is concerning your marriage.   201

Shal. Ay, there's the point, sir.

Evans. Marry is it ; the very point of it ; to Mistress Anne Page.

Slen. Why, if it be so, I will marry her upon any reasonable demands.   206

Evans. But can you affection the oman ? Let us command to know that of your mouth or of your lips ; for divers philosophers hold that the lips is parcel of the mouth. Therefore, precisely, can you carry your good will to the maid ?   211

Shal. Cousin Abraham Slender, can you love her ?

Slen. I hope, sir, I will do as it shall become one that would do reason.

Evans. Nay, Got's lords and his ladies ! you must speak possitable, if you can carry her your desires towards her.   217

Shal. That you must. Will you, upon good dowry, marry her ?

Slen. I will do a greater thing than that upon your request, cousin, in any reason.

Shal. Nay, conceive me, conceive me, sweet coz ; what I do is to pleasure you, coz. Can you love the maid ?   223

Slen. I will marry her, sir, at your request ; but if there be no great love in the beginning, yet heaven may decrease it upon better acquaintance, when we are married and have more occasion to know one another. I hope upon familiarity will grow more contempt. But if you say ' marry her ', I will marry her ; that I am freely dissolved, and dissolutely.   229

Evans. It is a fery discretion answer, save the fall is in the ord ' dissolutely ': the ort is, according to our meaning, ' resolutely ' ; his meaning is good.

Shal. Ay, I think my cousin meant well.

Slen. Ay, or else I would I might be hang'd, la !   234

Re-enter ANNE PAGE.

Shal. Here comes fair Mistress Anne. Would I were young for your sake, Mistress Anne !   236

Anne. The dinner is on the table ; my father desires your worships' company.

Shal. I will wait on him, fair Mistress Anne !

Evans. Od's plessed will ! I will not be absence at the grace.   241

[*Exeunt Shallow and Evans.*

Anne. Will't please your worship to come in, sir ?

Slen. No, I thank you, forsooth, heartily ; I am very well.

Anne. The dinner attends you, sir.   245

Slen. I am not a-hungry, I thank you, forsooth. Go, sirrah, for all you are my

man, go wait upon my cousin Shallow.
[*Exit Simple*] A justice of peace sometime
may be beholding to his friend for a man.
I keep but three men and a boy yet, till my
mother be dead. But what though ? Yet
I live like a poor gentleman born.   251
Anne. I may not go in without your
worship ; they will not sit till you come.
Slen. I' faith, I'll eat nothing ; I thank
you as much as though I did.   255
Anne. I pray you, sir, walk in.
Slen. I had rather walk here, I thank you.
I bruis'd my shin th' other day with playing
at sword and dagger with a master of fence
—three veneys for a dish of stew'd prunes—
and, I with my ward defending my head, he
hot my shin, and, by my troth, I cannot
abide the smell of hot meat since. Why do
your dogs bark so ? Be there bears i' th'
town ?   262
Anne. I think there are, sir ; I heard
them talk'd of.
Slen. I love the sport well ; but I shall as
soon quarrel at it as any man in England.
You are afraid, if you see the bear loose, are
you not ?
Anne. Ay, indeed, sir.   267
Slen. That's meat and drink to me now.
I have seen Sackerson loose twenty times,
and have taken him by the chain ; but, I
warrant you, the women have so cried and
shriek'd at it that it pass'd ; but women,
indeed, cannot abide 'em ; they are very
ill-favour'd rough things.   272

Re-enter PAGE.

Page. Come, gentle Master Slender, come ;
we stay for you.
Slen. I'll eat nothing, I thank you, sir.   275
Page. By cock and pie, you shall not
choose, sir ! Come, come.
Slen. Nay, pray you lead the way.
Page. Come on, sir.
Slen. Mistress Anne, yourself shall go
first.   280
Anne. Not I, sir ; pray you keep on.
Slen. Truly, I will not go first ; truly, la !
I will not do you that wrong.
Anne. I pray you, sir.   284
Slen. I'll rather be unmannerly than
troublesome. You' do yourself wrong in-
deed, la !   [*Exeunt.*

SCENE II. *Before Page's house.*

Enter SIR HUGH EVANS *and* SIMPLE.

Evans. Go your ways, and ask of Doctor
Caius' house which is the way ; and there
dwells one Mistress Quickly, which is in the
manner of his nurse, or his dry nurse, or his
cook, or his laundry, his washer, and his
wringer.
Sim. Well, sir.   5
Evans. Nay, it is petter yet. Give her this
letter ; for it is a oman that altogether 's
acquaintance with Mistress Anne Page ;
and the letter is to desire and require her
to solicit your master's desires to Mistress
Anne Page. I pray you be gone. I will
make an end of my dinner ; there's pippins
and cheese to come.   [*Exeunt.*

SCENE III. *The Garter Inn.*

Enter FALSTAFF, HOST, BARDOLPH, NYM,
PISTOL *and* ROBIN.

Fal. Mine host of the Garter !
Host. What says my bully rook ? Speak
scholarly and wisely.
Fal. Truly, mine host, I must turn away
some of my followers.   5
Host. Discard, bully Hercules ; cashier ;
let them wag ; trot, trot.
Fal. I sit at ten pounds a week.
Host. Thou'rt an emperor—Cæsar, Keiser,
and Pheazar. I will entertain Bardolph ; he
shall draw, he shall tap ; said I well, bully
Hector ?   11
Fal. Do so, good mine host.
Host. I have spoke ; let him follow. [*To
Bardolph*] Let me see thee froth and lime.
I am at a word ; follow.   [*Exit Host.*
Fal. Bardolph, follow him. A tapster is
a good trade ; an old cloak makes a new
jerkin ; a wither'd serving-man a fresh
tapster. Go ; adieu.   17
Bard. It is a life that I have desir'd ; I
will thrive.
Pist. O base Hungarian wight ! Wilt thou
the spigot wield ?   [*Exit Bardolph.*
Nym. He was gotten in drink. Is not the
humour conceited ?   22
Fal. I am glad I am so acquit of this
tinder-box : his thefts were too open ; his
filching was like an unskilful singer—he
kept not time.   25
Nym. The good humour is to steal at a
minute's rest.
Pist. ' Convey ' the wise it call. ' Steal '
foh ! A fico for the phrase !
Fal. Well, sirs, I am almost out at heels.
Pist. Why, then, let kibes ensue.   30
Fal. There is no remedy ; I must cony-
catch ; I must shift.
Pist. Young ravens must have food.
Fal. Which of you know Ford of this
town ?
Pist. I ken the wight ; he is of substance
good.   35
Fal. My honest lads, I will tell you what
I am about.
Pist. Two yards, and more.   37
Fal. No quips now, Pistol. Indeed, I am
in the waist two yards about ; but I am
now about no waste ; I am about thrift.
Briefly, I do mean to make love to Ford's
wife ; I spy entertainment in her ; she
discourses, she carves, she gives the leer of

invitation; I can construe the action of her familiar style; and the hardest voice of her behaviour, to be English'd rightly, is ' I am Sir John Falstaff's '. 45

Pist. He hath studied her well, and translated her will out of honesty into English.

Nym. The anchor is deep; will that humour pass? 48

Fal. Now, the report goes she has all the rule of her husband's purse; he hath a legion of angels. 50

Pist. As many devils entertain; and ' To her, boy ' say I.

Nym. The humour rises; it is good; humour me the angels. 54

Fal. I have writ me here a letter to her; and here another to Page's wife, who even now gave me good eyes too, examin'd my parts with most judicious œillades; sometimes the beam of her view gilded my foot, sometimes my portly belly. 59

Pist. Then did the sun on dunghill shine.

Nym. I thank thee for that humour. 61

Fal. O, she did so course o'er my exteriors with such a greedy intention that the appetite of her eye did seem to scorch me up like a burning-glass! Here's another letter to her. She bears the purse too; she is a region in Guiana, all gold and bounty. I will be cheaters to them both, and they shall be exchequers to me; they shall be my East and West Indies, and I will trade to them both. Go, bear thou this letter to Mistress Page; and thou this to Mistress Ford. We will thrive, lads, we will thrive.

Pist. Shall I Sir Pandarus of Troy become, 72
And by my side wear steel? Then Lucifer take all!

Nym. I will run no base humour. Here, take the humour-letter; I will keep the haviour of reputation. 75

Fal. [*To Robin*] Hold, sirrah; bear you these letters tightly;
Sail like my pinnace to these golden shores.
Rogues, hence, avaunt! vanish like hail-stones, go;
Trudge, plod away i' th' hoof; seek shelter, pack! 79
Falstaff will learn the humour of the age;
French thrift, you rogues; myself, and skirted page.
[*Exeunt Falstaff and Robin.*

Pist. Let vultures gripe thy guts! for gourd and fullam holds,
And high and low beguiles the rich and poor;
Tester I'll have in pouch when thou shalt lack,
Base Phrygian Turk! 85

Nym. I have operations in my head which be humours of revenge.

Pist. Wilt thou revenge?

Nym. By welkin and her star!

Pist. With wit or steel?

Nym. With both the humours, I. 90
I will discuss the humour of this love to Page.

Pist. And I to Ford shall eke unfold
How Falstaff, varlet vile,
His dove will prove, his gold will hold,
And his soft couch defile. 95

Nym. My humour shall not cool; I will incense Page to deal with poison; I will possess him with yellowness; for the revolt of mine is dangerous. That is my true humour.. 98

Pist. Thou art the Mars of malcontents; I second thee; troop on. [*Exeunt*

SCENE IV. *Doctor Caius's house.*

Enter MISTRESS QUICKLY, SIMPLE *and* RUGBY.

Quick. What, John Rugby! I pray thee go to the casement and see if you can see my master, Master Doctor Caius, coming. If he do, i' faith, and find anybody in the house, here will be an old abusing of God's patience and the King's English. 5

Rug. I'll go watch.

Quick. Go; and we'll have a posset for't soon at night, in faith, at the latter end of a sea-coal fire. [*Exit Rugby*] An honest, willing, kind fellow, as ever servant shall come in house withal; and, I warrant you, no tell-tale nor no breed-bate; his worst fault is that he is given to prayer; he is something peevish that way; but nobody but has his fault; but let that pass. Peter Simple you say your name is?

Sim. Ay, for fault of a better. 15

Quick. And Master Slender's your master?

Sim. Ay, forsooth.

Quick. Does he not wear a great round beard, like a glover's paring-knife?

Sim. No, forsooth; he hath but a little whey face, with a little yellow beard, a Cain-colour'd beard. 21

Quick. A softly-sprighted man, is he not?

Sim. Ay, forsooth; but he is as tall a man of his hands as any is between this and his head; he hath fought with a warrener. 25

Quick. How say you? O, I should remember him. Does he not hold up his head, as it were, and strut in his gait?

Sim. Yes, indeed, does he. 28

Quick. Well, heaven send Anne Page no worse fortune! Tell Master Parson Evans I will do what I can for your master. Anne is a good girl, and I wish— 31

Re-enter RUGBY.

Rug. Out, alas! here comes my master.

Quick. We shall all be shent. Run in here, good young man; go into this closet.
[*Shuts Simple in the closet*] He will not

stay long. What, John Rugby! John! what John, I say! Go, John, go inquire for my master; I doubt he be not well that he comes not home. [Singing.

And down, down, adown-a, etc. 38

Enter DOCTOR CAIUS.

Caius. Vat is you sing? I do not like des toys. Pray you, go and vetch me in my closet un boitier vert—a box, a green-a box. Do intend vat I speak? A green-a box.

Quick. Ay, forsooth, I'll fetch it you. [*Aside*] I am glad he went not in himself; if he had found the young man, he would have been horn-mad. 44

Caius. Fe, fe, fe, fe! ma foi, il fait fort chaud. Je m'en vais à la cour—la grande affaire. 46

Quick. Is it this, sir?

Caius. Oui; mette le au mon pocket: dépêche, quickly. Vere is dat knave, Rugby?

Quick. What, John Rugby! John! 50

Rug. Here, sir.

Caius. You are John Rugby, and you are Jack Rugby. Come, take-a your rapier, and come after my heel to the court.

Rug. 'Tis ready, sir, here in the porch. 55

Caius. By my trot, I tarry too long. Od's me! Qu'ai j' oublié? Dere is some simples in my closet dat I vill not for the varld I shall leave behind.

Quick. Ay me, he'll find the young man there, and be mad! 60

Caius. O diable, diable! vat is in my closet? Villainy! larron! [*Pulling Simple out*] Rugby, my rapier!

Quick. Good master, be content. 63

Caius. Wherefore shall I be content-a?

Quick. The young man is an honest man.

Caius. What shall de honest man do in my closet? Dere is no honest man dat shall come in my closet. 67

Quick. I beseech you, be not so phlegmatic; hear the truth of it. He came of an errand to me from Parson Hugh.

Caius. Vell? 70

Sim. Ay, forsooth, to desire her to—

Quick. Peace, I pray you.

Caius. Peace-a your tongue. Speak-a your tale. 73

Sim. To desire this honest gentlewoman, your maid, to speak a good word to Mistress Anne Page for my master, in the way of marriage. 76

Quick. This is all, indeed, la! but I'll ne'er put my finger in the fire, and need not.

Caius. Sir Hugh send-a you? Rugby, baillez me some paper. Tarry you a little-a-while. [*Writes.*

Quick. [*Aside to Simple*] I am glad he is so quiet; if he had been throughly moved, you should have heard him so loud and so

melancholy. But notwithstanding, man, I'll do you your master what good I can; and the very yea and the no is, the French doctor, my master—I may call him my master, look you, for I keep his house; and I wash, wring, brew, bake, scour, dress meat and drink, make the beds, and do all myself— 88

Sim. [*Aside to Quickly*] 'Tis a great charge to come under one body's hand. 90

Quick. [*Aside to Simple*] Are you avis'd o' that? You shall find it a great charge; and to be up early and down late; but notwithstanding—to tell you in your ear, in my master himself is in love with Mistress Anne Page; but notwithstanding that, I know Anne's mind—that's neither here nor there. 96

Caius. You jack'nape; give-a this letter to Sir Hugh; by gar, it is a shallenge; I will cut his troat in de park; and I will teach a scurvy jack-a-nape priest to meddle or make. You may be gone; it is not good you tarry here. By gar, I will cut all his two stones; by gar, he shall not have a stone to throw at his dog. [*Exit Simple.*

Quick. Alas, he speaks but for his friend.

Caius. It is no matter-a ver dat. Do not you tell-a me dat I shall have Anne Page for myself? By gar, I vill kill de Jack priest; and I have appointed mine host of de Jarteer to measure our weapon. By gar, I will myself have Anne Page. 108

Quick. Sir, the maid loves you, and all shall be well. We must give folks leave to prate. What the good-year! 110

Caius. Rugby, come to the court with me. By gar, if I have not Anne Page, I shall turn your head out of my door. Follow my heels, Rugby. 113

[*Exeunt Caius and Rugby.*

Quick. You shall have—An fool's-head of your own. No, I know Anne's mind for that; never a woman in Windsor knows more of Anne's mind than I do; nor can do more than I do with her, I thank heaven.

Fent. [*Within*] Who's within there? ho!

Quick. Who's there, I trow? Come near the house, I pray you. 120

Enter FENTON.

Fent. How now, good woman, how dost thou?

Quick. The better that it pleases your good worship to ask.

Fent. What news? How does pretty Mistress Anne? 124

Quick. In truth, sir, and she is pretty, and honest, and gentle; and one that is your friend, I can tell you that by the way; I praise heaven for it.

Fent. Shall I do any good, think'st thou? Shall I not lose my suit? 129

Quick. Troth, sir, all is in His hands

above; but notwithstanding, Master Fenton, I'll be sworn on a book she loves you. Have not your worship a wart above your eye ?   132

Fent. Yes, marry, have I; what of that ?

Quick. Well, thereby hangs a tale; good faith, it is such another Nan; but, I detest, an honest maid as ever broke bread. We had an hour's talk of that wart; I shall never laugh but in that maid's company! But, indeed, she is given too much to allicholy and musing; but for you—well, go to.   139

Fent. Well, I shall see her to-day. Hold, there's money for thee; let me have thy voice in my behalf. If thou seest her before me, commend me.   142

Quick. Will I? I'faith, that we will; and I will tell your worship more of the wart the next time we have confidence; and of other wooers.   145

Fent. Well, farewell; I am in great haste now.

Quick. Farewell to your worship. [*Exit Fenton*] Truly, an honest gentleman; but Anne loves him not; for I know Anne's mind as well as another does. Out upon 't, what have I forgot ?   [*Exit.*

ACT TWO

SCENE I. *Before Page's house.*

Enter MISTRESS PAGE, *with a letter.*

Mrs. Page. What! have I scap'd love-letters in the holiday-time of my beauty, and am I now a subject for them ? Let me see.   [*Reads.*

' Ask me no reason why I love you; for though Love use Reason for his precisian, he admits him not for his counsellor. You are not young, no more am I; go to, then, there's sympathy. You are merry, so am I; ha! ha! then there's more sympathy. You love sack, and so do I; would you desire better sympathy ? Let it suffice thee, Mistress Page—at the least, if the love of soldier can suffice—that I love thee. I will not say, Pity me: 'tis not a soldier-like phrase; but I say, Love me. By me,

> Thine own true knight,
> By day or night,
> Or any kind of light,
> With all his might,
> For thee to fight,
>   JOHN FALSTAFF.'   15

What a Herod of Jewry is this! O wicked, wicked world! One that is well-nigh worn to pieces with age to show himself a young gallant! What an unweighed behaviour hath this Flemish drunkard pick'd—with the devil's name!—out of my conversation, that he dares in this manner assay me ? Why, he hath not been thrice in my company! What should I say to him ? I was then frugal of my mirth. Heaven forgive me! Why, I'll exhibit a bill in the parliament for the putting down of men. How shall I be reveng'd on him ? for reveng'd I will be, as sure as his guts are made of puddings.   26

Enter MISTRESS FORD.

Mrs. Ford. Mistress Page! trust me, I was going to your house.

Mrs. Page. And, trust me, I was coming to you. You look very ill.   30

Mrs. Ford. Nay, I'll ne'er believe that; I have to show to the contrary.

Mrs. Page. Faith, but you do, in my mind.

Mrs. Ford. Well, I do, then; yet, I say, I could show you to the contrary. O Mistress Page, give me some counsel.   36

Mrs. Page. What's the matter, woman ?

Mrs. Ford. O woman, if it were not for one trifling respect, I could come to such honour!

Mrs. Page. Hang the trifle, woman; take the honour. What is it ? Dispense with trifles; what is it ?

Mrs. Ford. If I would but go to hell for an eternal moment or so, I could be knighted.

Mrs. Page. What ? Thou liest. Sir Alice Ford! These knights will hack; and so thou shouldst not alter the article of thy gentry.   46

Mrs. Ford. We burn daylight. Here, read, read; perceive how I might be knighted. I shall think the worse of fat men as long as I have an eye to make difference of men's liking. And yet he would not swear; prais'd women's modesty, and gave such orderly and well-behaved reproof to all uncomeliness that I would have sworn his disposition would have gone to the truth of his words; but they do no more adhere and keep place together than the Hundredth Psalm to the tune of ' Greensleeves '. What tempest, I trow, threw this whale, with so many tuns of oil in his belly, ashore at Windsor ? How shall I be revenged on him ? I think the best way were to entertain him with hope, till the wicked fire of lust have melted him in his own grease. Did you ever hear the like ?   60

Mrs. Page. Letter for letter, but that the name of Page and Ford differs. To thy great comfort in this mystery of ill opinions, here's the twin-brother of thy letter; but let thine inherit first, for, I protest, mine never shall. I warrant he hath a thousand of these letters, writ with blank space for different names—sure, more!—and these are of the second edition. He will print them, out of doubt; for he cares not what he puts into the press when he would put us two. I had rather be a giantess and lie under Mount Pelion. Well, I will find you twenty lascivious turtles ere one chaste man.   71

Mrs. Ford. Why, this is the very same; the very hand, the very words. What doth he think of us?   73

Mrs. Page. Nay, I know not; it makes me almost ready to wrangle with mine own honesty. I'll entertain myself like one that I am not acquainted withal; for, sure, unless he know some strain in me that I know not myself, he would never have boarded me in this fury.   78

Mrs. Ford. ' Boarding ' call you it? I'll be sure to keep him above deck.   80

Mrs. Page. So will I; if he come under my hatches, I'll never to sea again. Let's be reveng'd on him; let's appoint him a meeting, give him a show of comfort in his suit, and lead him on with a fine-baited delay, till he hath pawn'd his horses to mine host of the Garter.   85

Mrs. Ford. Nay, I will consent to act any villainy against him that may not sully the chariness of our honesty. O that my husband saw this letter! It would give eternal food to his jealousy.   89

Mrs. Page. Why, look where he comes; and my good man too; he's as far from jealousy as I am from giving him cause; and that, I hope, is an unmeasurable distance.   93

Mrs. Ford. You are the happier woman.

Mrs. Page. Let's consult together against this greasy knight. Come hither.   96

[*They retire.*

Enter FORD *with* PISTOL, *and* PAGE *with* NYM.

Ford. Well, I hope it be not so.

Pist. Hope is a curtal dog in some affairs.

Sir John affects thy wife.   99

Ford. Why, sir, my wife is not young.

Pist. He woos both high and low, both rich and poor,

Both young and old, one with another, Ford;

He loves the gallimaufry. Ford, perpend.

Ford. Love my wife!

Pist. With liver burning hot. Prevent, or go thou,   105

Like Sir Actæon he, with Ringwood at thy heels.

O, odious is the name!

Ford. What name, sir?

Pist. The horn, I say. Farewell.

Take heed, have open eye, for thieves do foot by night;   110

Take heed, ere summer comes, or cuckoo birds do sing.

Away, Sir Corporal Nym.

Believe it, Page; he speaks sense.

[*Exit Pistol.*

Ford. [*Aside*] I will be patient; I will find out this.   114

Nym. [*To Page*] And this is true; I like not the humour of lying. He hath wronged me in some humours; I should have borne the humour'd letter to her; but I have a sword, and it shall bite upon my necessity. He loves your wife; there's the short and the long.

My name is Corporal Nym; I speak, and I avouch;   120

'Tis true. My name is Nym, and Falstaff loves your wife.

Adieu! I love not the humour of bread and cheese; and there's the humour of it. Adieu.   [*Exit Nym.*

Page. ' The humour of it ' quoth 'a! Here's a fellow frights English out of his wits.   125

Ford. I will seek out Falstaff.

Page. I never heard such a drawling, affecting rogue.

Ford. If I do find it—well.

Page. I will not believe such a Cataian though the priest o' th' town commended him for a true man.   130

Ford. 'Twas a good sensible fellow. Well.

[*Mistress Page and Mistress Ford come forward.*

Page. How now, Meg!

Mrs. Page. Whither go you, George? Hark you.

Mrs. Ford. How now, sweet Frank, why art thou melancholy?   135

Ford. I melancholy! I am not melancholy. Get you home; go.

Mrs. Ford. Faith, thou hast some crotchets in thy head now. Will you go, Mistress Page?   139

Enter MISTRESS QUICKLY.

Mrs. Page. Have with you. You'll come to dinner, George? [*Aside to Mrs. Ford*] Look who comes yonder; she shall be our messenger to this paltry knight.   142

Mrs. Ford. [*Aside to Mrs. Page*] Trust me, I thought on her; she'll fit it.

Mrs. Page. You are come to see my daughter Anne?   145

Quick. Ay, forsooth; and, I pray, how does good Mistress Anne?

Mrs. Page. Go in with us and see; we have an hour's talk with you.

[*Exeunt Mistress Page, Mistress Ford, and Mistress Quickly.*

Page. How now, Master Ford!   150

Ford. You heard what this knave told me, did you not?

Page. Yes; and you heard what the other told me?

Ford. Do you think there is truth in them?   153

Page. Hang 'em, slaves ! I do not think the knight would offer it ; but these that accuse him in his intent towards our wives are a yoke of his discarded men ; very rogues, now they be out of service.   157

Ford. Were they his men ?

Page. Marry, were they.

Ford. I like it never the better for that. Does he lie at the Garter ?   161

Page. Ay, marry, does he. If he should intend this voyage toward my wife, I would turn her loose to him ; and what he gets more of her than sharp words, let it lie on my head.   165

Ford. I do not misdoubt my wife ; but I would be loath to turn them together. A man may be too confident. I would have nothing lie on my head. I cannot be thus satisfied.   169

Enter HOST.

Page. Look where my ranting host of the Garter comes. There is either liquor in his pate or money in his purse when he looks so merrily. How now, mine host !

Host. How now, bully rook ! Thou'rt a gentleman. [*To Shallow following*] Cavaleiro Justice, I say.   175

Enter SHALLOW.

Shal. I follow, mine host, I follow. Good even and twenty, good Master Page ! Master Page, will you go with us ? We have sport in hand.   178

Host. Tell him, Cavaleiro Justice ; tell him, bully rook.

Shal. Sir, there is a fray to be fought between Sir Hugh the Welsh priest and Caius the French doctor.   181

Ford. Good mine host o' th' Garter, a word with you.

Host. What say'st thou, my bully rook ?
[*They go aside.*]

Shal. [*To Page*] Will you go with us to behold it ? My merry host hath had the measuring of their weapons ; and, I think, hath appointed them contrary places ; for, believe me, I hear the parson is no jester. Hark, I will tell you what our sport shall be.   [*They converse apart.*]

Host. Hast thou no suit against my knight, my guest-cavaleiro ?   190

Ford. None, I protest ; but I'll give you a pottle of burnt sack to give me recourse to him, and tell him my name is Brook—only for a jest.   193

Host. My hand, bully ; thou shalt have egress and regress—said I well ?—and thy name shall be Brook. It is a merry knight. Will you go, Mynheers ?   196

Shal. Have with you, mine host.

Page. I have heard the Frenchman hath good skill in his rapier.   199

Shal. Tut, sir, I could have told you more. In these times you stand on distance, your passes, stoccadoes, and I know not what. 'Tis the heart, Master Page ; 'tis here, 'tis here. I have seen the time with my long sword I would have made you four tall fellows skip like rats.   204

Host. Here, boys, here, here ! Shall we wag ?

Page. Have with you. I had rather hear them scold than fight.   207
[*Exeunt all but Ford.*]

Ford. Though Page be a secure fool, and stands so firmly on his wife's frailty, yet I cannot put off my opinion so easily. She was in his company at Page's house, and what they made there I know not. Well, I will look further into 't, and I have a disguise to sound Falstaff. If I find her honest, I lose not my labour ; if she be otherwise, 'tis labour well bestowed. [*Exit.*]

SCENE II. *A room in the Garter Inn.*

Enter FALSTAFF *and* PISTOL.

Fal. I will not lend thee a penny.

Pist. I will retort the sum in equipage.

Fal. Not a penny.

Pist. Why, then the world's mine oyster, Which I with sword will open.

Fal. Not a penny. I have been content, sir, you should lay my countenance to pawn. I have grated upon my good friends for three reprieves for you and your coach-fellow, Nym ; or else you had look'd through the grate, like a geminy of baboons. I am damn'd in hell for swearing to gentlemen my friends you were good soldiers and tall fellows ; and when Mistress Bridget lost the handle of her fan, I took 't upon mine honour thou hadst it not.   10

Pist. Didst not thou share ? Hadst thou not fifteen pence ?

Fal. Reason, you rogue, reason. Think'st thou I'll endanger my soul gratis ? At a word, hang no more about me, I am no gibbet for you. Go—a short knife and a throng !—to your manor of Pickt-hatch ; go. You'll not bear a letter for me, you rogue ! You stand upon your honour ! Why, thou unconfinable baseness, it is as much as I can do to keep the terms of my honour precise. I, I, I myself sometimes, leaving the fear of God on the left hand, and hiding mine honour in my necessity, am fain to shuffle, to hedge, and to lurch ; and yet you, rogue, will ensconce your rags, your cat-a-mountain looks, your red-lattice phrases, and your bold-beating oaths, under the shelter of your honour ! You will not do it, you !   25

Pist. I do relent ; what would thou more of man ?

Enter ROBIN.

Rob. Sir, here's a woman would speak with you.

Fal. Let her approach.

Enter MISTRESS QUICKLY.

Quick. Give your worship good morrow.

Fal. Good morrow, good wife.   30

Quick. Not so, an't please your worship.

Fal. Good maid, then.

Quick. I'll be sworn;
As my mother was, the first hour I was born.

Fal. I do believe the swearer. What with me ?   35

Quick. Shall I vouchsafe your worship a word or two ?

Fal. Two thousand, fair woman; and I'll vouchsafe thee the hearing.

Quick. There is one Mistress Ford, sir— I pray, come a little nearer this ways. I myself dwell with Master Doctor Caius.   41

Fal. Well, on : Mistress Ford, you say—

Quick. Your worship says very true. I pray your worship come a little nearer this ways.

Fal. I warrant thee nobody hears— mine own people, mine own people.   46

Quick. Are they so ? God bless them, and make them his servants !

Fal. Well ; Mistress Ford, what of her ?

Quick. Why, sir, she's a good creature. Lord, Lord, your worship's a wanton ! Well, heaven forgive you, and all of us, I pray.   52

Fal. Mistress Ford ; come, Mistress Ford—

Quick. Marry, this is the short and the long of it : you have brought her into such a canaries as 'tis wonderful. The best courtier of them all, when the court lay at Windsor, could never have brought her to such a canary. Yet there has been knights, and lords, and gentlemen, with their coaches ; I warrant you, coach after coach, letter after letter, gift after gift ; smelling so sweetly, all musk, and so rushling, I warrant you, in silk and gold ; and in such alligant terms ; and in such wine and sugar of the best and the fairest, that would have won any woman's heart ; and, I warrant you, they could never get an eye-wink of her. I had myself twenty angels given me this morning ; but I defy all angels, in any such sort, as they say, but in the way of honesty ; and, I warrant you, they could never get her so much as sip on a cup with the proudest of them all ; and yet there has been earls, nay, which is more, pensioners ; but, I warrant you, all is one with her.   70

Fal. But what says she to me ? Be brief, my good she-Mercury.

Quick. Marry, she hath receiv'd your letter ; for the which she thanks you a thousand times ; and she gives you to notify that her husband will be absence from his house between ten and eleven.   76

Fal. Ten and eleven ?

Quick. Ay, forsooth ; and then you may come and see the picture, she says, that you wot of. Master Ford, her husband, will be from home. Alas, the sweet woman leads an ill life with him ! He's a very jealousy man ; she leads a very frampold life with him, good heart.   82

Fal. Ten and eleven. Woman, commend me to her ; I will not fail her.   84

Quick. Why, you say well. But I have another messenger to your worship. Mistress Page hath her hearty commendations to you too ; and let me tell you in your ear, she's as fartuous a civil modest wife, and one, I tell you, that will not miss you morning nor evening prayer, as any is in Windsor, whoe'er be the other ; and she bade me tell your worship that her husband is seldom from home, but she hopes there will come a time. I never knew a woman so dote upon a man ; surely I think you have charms, la ! Yes, in truth.   94

Fal. Not I, I assure thee ; setting the attraction of my good parts aside, I have no other charms.   96

Quick. Blessing on your heart for 't !

Fal. But, I pray thee, tell me this : has Ford's wife and Page's wife acquainted each other how they love me ?   99

Quick. That were a jest indeed ! They have not so little grace, I hope—that were a trick indeed ! But Mistress Page would desire you to send her your little page of all loves. Her husband has a marvellous infection to the little page ; and truly Master Page is an honest man. Never a wife in Windsor leads a better life than she does ; do what she will, say what she will, take all, pay all, go to bed when she list, rise when she list, all is as she will ; and truly she deserves it ; for if there be a kind woman in Windsor, she is one. You must send her your page ; no remedy.   110

Fal. Why, I will.

Quick. Nay, but do so then ; and, look you, he may come and go between you both ; and in any case have a nay-word, that you may know one another's mind, and the boy never need to understand any thing ; for 'tis not good that children should know any wickedness. Old folks, you know, have discretion, as they say, and know the world.   117

Fal. Fare thee well ; commend me to them both. There's my purse ; I am yet thy debtor. Boy, go along with this woman. [*Exeunt Quickly and Robin*] This news distracts me.   121

Pist. [*Aside*] This punk is one of Cupid's carriers;
Clap on more sails; pursue; up with your fights;
Give fire; she is my prize, or ocean whelm them all!   [*Exit Pistol.*

Fal. Say'st thou so, old Jack; go thy ways; I'll make more of thy old body than I have done. Will they yet look after thee? Wilt thou, after the expense of so much money, be now a gainer? Good body, I thank thee. Let them say 'tis grossly done; so it be fairly done, no matter.   129

Enter BARDOLPH.

Bard. Sir John, there's one Master Brook below would fain speak with you, and be acquainted with you; and hath sent your worship a morning's draught of sack.

Fal. Brook is his name?

Bard. Ay, sir.   134

Fal. Call him in. [*Exit Bardolph*] Such Brooks are welcome to me, that o'erflows such liquor. Ah, ha! Mistress Ford and Mistress Page, have I encompass'd you? Go to; via!   137

Re-enter BARDOLPH, *with* FORD *disguised.*

Ford. Bless you, sir!

Fal. And you, sir! Would you speak with me?

Ford. I make bold to press with so little preparation upon you.   141

Fal. You're welcome. What's your will? Give us leave, drawer.   [*Exit Bardolph.*

Ford. Sir, I am a gentleman that have spent much; my name is Brook.   145

Fal. Good Master Brook, I desire more acquaintance of you.

Ford. Good Sir John, I sue for yours—not to charge you; for I must let you understand I think myself in better plight for a lender than you are; the which hath something embold'ned me to this unseason'd intrusion; for they say, if money go before, all ways do lie open.   152

Fal. Money is a good soldier, sir, and will on.

Ford. Troth, and I have a bag of money here troubles me; if you will help to bear it, Sir John, take all, or half, for easing me of the carriage.   156

Fal. Sir, I know not how I may deserve to be your porter.

Ford. I will tell you, sir, if you will give me the hearing.

Fal. Speak, good Master Brook; I shall be glad to be your servant.   161

Ford. Sir, I hear you are a scholar—I will be brief with you—and you have been a man long known to me, though I had never so good means as desire to make myself acquainted with you. I shall discover a thing to you, wherein I must very much lay open mine own imperfection; but, good Sir John, as you have one eye upon my follies, as you hear them unfolded, turn another into the register of your own, that I may pass with a reproof the easier, sith you yourself know how easy is it to be such an offender.   170

Fal. Very well, sir; proceed.

Ford. There is a gentlewoman in this town, her husband's name is Ford.

Fal. Well, sir.   174

Ford. I have long lov'd her, and, I protest to you, bestowed much on her; followed her with a doting observance; engross'd opportunities to meet her; fee'd every slight occasion that could but niggardly give me sight of her; not only bought many presents to give her, but have given largely to many to know what she would have given; briefly, I have pursu'd her as love hath pursued me; which hath been on the wing of all occasions. But whatsoever I have merited, either in my mind or in my means, meed, I am sure, I have received none, unless experience be a jewel; that I have purchased at an infinite rate, and that hath taught me to say this: 'Love like a shadow flies when substance love pursues;   187
Pursuing that that flies, and flying what pursues'.

Fal. Have you receiv'd no promise of satisfaction at her hands?   190

Ford. Never.

Fal. Have you importun'd her to such a purpose?

Ford. Never.

Fal. Of what quality was your love, then?   194

Ford. Like a fair house built on another man's ground; so that I have lost my edifice by mistaking the place where I erected it.

Fal. To what purpose have you unfolded this to me?   198

Ford. When I have told you that, I have told you all. Some say that though she appear honest to me, yet in other places she enlargeth her mirth so far that there is shrewd construction made of her. Now, Sir John, here is the heart of my purpose: you are a gentleman of excellent breeding, admirable discourse, of great admittance, authentic in your place and person, generally allow'd for your many war-like, court-like, and learned preparations.   206

Fal. O, sir!

Ford. Believe it, for you know it. There is money; spend it, spend it; spend more; spend all I have; only give me so much of your time in exchange of it as to lay an amiable siege to the honesty of this Ford's wife; use your art of wooing, win her to

63

consent to you; if any man may, you may
as soon as any.   213

Fal. Would it apply well to the vehemency of your affection, that I should win
what you would enjoy? Methinks you
prescribe to yourself very preposterously.

Ford. O, understand my drift. She
dwells so securely on the excellency of her
honour that the folly of my soul dares not
present itself; she is too bright to be
look'd against. Now, could I come to her
with any detection in my hand, my desires
had instance and argument to commend
themselves; I could drive her then from
the ward of her purity, her reputation, her
marriage vow, and a thousand other her
defences, which now are too too strongly
embattl'd against me. What say you to 't,
Sir John?   225

Fal. Master Brook, I will first make bold
with your money; next, give me your
hand; and last, as I am a gentleman, you
shall, if you will, enjoy Ford's wife.

Ford. O good sir!

Fal. I say you shall.   230

Ford. Want no money, Sir John; you
shall want none.

Fal. Want no Mistress Ford, Master
Brook; you shall want none. I shall be
with her, I may tell you, by her own
appointment; even as you came in to me
her assistant, or go-between, parted from
me; I say I shall be with her between ten
and eleven; for at that time the jealous
rascally knave, her husband, will be forth.
Come you to me at night; you shall know
how I speed.   238

Ford. I am blest in your acquaintance.
Do you know Ford, sir?   240

Fal. Hang him, poor cuckoldly knave! I
know him not; yet I wrong him to call
him poor; they say the jealous wittolly
knave hath masses of money; for the
which his wife seems to me well-favour'd.
I will use her as the key of the cuckoldl
rogue's coffer; and there's my harvest-
home.   245

Ford. I would you knew Ford, sir, that
you might avoid him if you saw him.   247

Fal. Hang him, mechanical salt-butter
rogue! I will stare him out of his wits; I
will awe him with my cudgel; it shall hang
like a meteor o'er the cuckold's horns.
Master Brook, thou shalt know I will predominate over the peasant, and thou shalt
lie with his wife. Come to me soon at
night. Ford's a knave, and I will aggravate
his style; thou, Master Brook, shalt know
him for knave and cuckold. Come to me
soon at night.   [*Exit.* 255

Ford. What a damn'd Epicurean rascal is
this! My heart is ready to crack with
impatience. Who says this is improvident
jealousy? My wife hath sent to him; the
hour is fix'd; the match is made. Would
any man have thought this? See the hell
of having a false woman! My bed shall be
abus'd, my coffers ransack'd, my reputation gnawn at; and I shall not only
receive this villainous wrong, but stand
under the adoption of abominable terms,
and by him that does me this wrong.
Terms! names! Amaimon sounds well;
Lucifer, well; Barbason, well; yet they
are devils' additions, the names of fiends.
But cuckold! Wittol! Cuckold! the devil
himself hath not such a name. Page is an
ass, a secure ass; he will trust his wife;
he will not be jealous; I will rather trust
a Fleming with my butter, Parson Hugh
the Welshman with my cheese, an Irishman with my aqua-vitæ bottle, or a thief
to walk my ambling gelding, than my wife
with herself. Then she plots, then she
ruminates, then she devises; and what
they think in their hearts they may effect,
they will break their hearts but they will
effect. God be prais'd for my jealousy!
Eleven o'clock the hour. I will prevent
this, detect my wife, be reveng'd on Falstaff, and laugh at Page. I will about it;
better three hours too soon than a minute
too late. Fie, fie, fie! cuckold! cuckold!
cuckold!   [*Exit.* 279

SCENE III. *A field near Windsor.*

Enter CAIUS *and* RUGBY.

Caius. Jack Rugby!

Rug. Sir?

Caius. Vat is de clock, Jack?

Rug. 'Tis past the hour, sir, that Sir
Hugh promis'd to meet.   5

Caius. By gar, he has save his soul dat
he is no come; he has pray his Pible well
dat he is no come; by gar, Jack Rugby, he
is dead already, if he be come.

Rug. He is wise, sir; he knew your
worship would kill him if he came.   10

Caius. By gar, de herring is no dead so as
I vill kill him. Take your rapier, Jack; I
vill tell you how I vill kill him.

Rug. Alas, sir, I cannot fence!

Caius. Villainy, take your rapier.   15

Rug. Forbear; here's company.

Enter HOST, SHALLOW, SLENDER *and* PAGE.

Host. Bless thee, bully doctor!

Shal. Save you, Master Doctor Caius!

Page. Now, good Master Doctor!

Slen. Give you good morrow, sir.   20

Caius. Vat be all you, one, two, tree,
four, come for?

Host. To see thee fight, to see thee foin,
to see thee traverse; to see thee here, to
see thee there; to see thee pass thy punto,
thy stock, thy reverse, thy distance, thy
montant. Is he dead, my Ethiopian? Is he

dead, my Francisco? Ha, bully! What says my Æsculapius? my Galen? my heart of elder? Ha! is he dead, bully stale? Is he dead? 27

Caius. By gar, he is de coward Jack priest of de vorld; he is not show his face.

Host. Thou art a Castalion-King-Urinal. Hector of Greece, my boy! 31

Caius. I pray you, bear witness that me have stay six or seven, two tree hours for him, and he is no come.

Shal. He is the wiser man, Master Doctor: he is a curer of souls, and you a curer of bodies; if you should fight, you go against the hair of your professions. Is it not true, Master Page? 37

Page. Master Shallow, you have yourself been a great fighter, though now a man of peace. 39

Shal. Bodykins, Master Page, though I now be old, and of the peace, if I see a sword out, my finger itches to make one. Though we are justices, and doctors, and churchmen, Master Page, we have some salt of our youth in us; we are the sons of women, Master Page.

Page. 'Tis true, Master Shallow. 45

Shal. It will be found so, Master Page. Master Doctor Caius, I am come to fetch you home. I am sworn of the peace; you have show'd yourself a wise physician, and Sir Hugh hath shown himself a wise and patient churchman. You must go with me, Master Doctor. 50

Host. Pardon, Guest Justice. A word, Mounseur Mockwater.

Caius. Mock-vater! Vat is dat?

Host. Mockwater, in our English tongue, is valour, bully. 55

Caius. By gar, then I have as much mockvater as de Englishman. Scurvy jack-dog priest! By gar, me vill cut his ears.

Host. He will clapper-claw thee tightly, bully.

Caius. Clapper-de-claw! Vat is dat? 60

Host. That is, he will make thee amends.

Caius. By gar, me do look he shall clapper-de-claw me; for, by gar, me vill have it.

Host. And I will provoke him to 't, or let him wag.

Caius. Me tank you for dat. 65

Host. And, moreover, bully—but first: [*Aside to the others*] Master Guest, and Master Page, and eke Cavaleiro Slender, go you through the town to Frogmore. 68

Page. [*Aside*] Sir Hugh is there, is he?

Host. [*Aside*] He is there. See what humour he is in; and I will bring the doctor about by the fields. Will it do well?

Shal. [*Aside*] We will do it. 73

Page, Shal., and Slen. Adieu, good Master Doctor. [*Exeunt Page, Shallow, and Slender.*

Caius. By gar, me vill kill de priest; for

he speak for a jack-an-ape to Anne Page.

Host. Let him die. Sheathe thy impatience; throw cold water on thy choler; go about the fields with me through Frogmore; I will bring thee where Mistress Anne Page is, at a farm-house, a-feasting; and thou shalt woo her. Cried game! Said I well? 81

Caius. By gar, me dank you vor dat; by gar, I love you; and I shall procure-a you de good guest, de earl, de knight, de lords, de gentlemen, my patients. 84

Host. For the which I will be thy adversary toward Anne Page. Said I well?

Caius. By gar, 'tis good; vell said.

Host. Let us wag, then. 88

Caius. Come at my heels, Jack Rugby. [*Exeunt.*

ACT THREE

SCENE I. *A field near Frogmore.*

Enter SIR HUGH EVANS *and* SIMPLE.

Evans. I pray you now, good Master Slender's serving-man, and friend Simple by your name, which way have you look'd for Master Caius, that calls himself Doctor of Physic? 4

Sim. Marry, sir, the pittie-ward, the park-ward; every way; old Windsor way, and every way but the towL way.

Evans. I most fehemently desire you you will also look that way. 8

Sim. I will, sir. [*Exit.*

Evans. Pless my soul, how full of chollors I am, and trempling of mind! I shall be glad if he have deceived me. How melancholies I am! I will knog his urinals about his knave's costard when I have good opportunities for the ork. Pless my soul! [*Sings.*

To shallow rivers, to whose falls 15
Melodious birds sings madrigals;
There will we make our peds of roses,
And a thousand fragrant posies.
To shallow—

Mercy on me! I have a great dispositions to cry. [*Sings.*

Melodious birds sing madrigals—
Whenas I sat in Pabylon—
And a thousand vagram posies.
To shallow, etc.

Re-enter SIMPLE.

Sim. Yonder he is, coming this way, Sir Hugh. 25

Evans. He's welcome. [*Sings.*

To shallow rivers, to whose falls—

Heaven prosper the right! What weapons is he?

Sim. No weapons, sir. There comes my master, Master Shallow, and another gentleman, from Frogmore, over the stile, this way.   31

Evans. Pray you give me my gown ; or else keep it in your arms. [*Takes out a book.*

Enter PAGE, SHALLOW, *and* SLENDER.

Shal. How now, Master Parson ! Good morrow, good Sir Hugh. Keep a gamester from the dice, and a good student from his book, and it is wonderful.   36

Slen. [*Aside*] Ah, sweet Anne Page !

Page. Save you, good Sir Hugh !

Evans. Pless you from his mercy sake, all of you !   39

Shal. What, the sword and the word ! Do you study them both, Master Parson ?

Page. And youthful still, in your doublet and hose, this raw rheumatic day !   43

Evans. There is reasons and causes for it.

Page. We are come to you to do a good office, Master Parson.   46

Evans. Fery well ; what is it ?

Page. Yonder is a most reverend gentleman, who, belike having received wrong by some person, is at most odds with his own gravity and patience that ever you saw. 50

Shal. I have lived fourscore years and upward ; I never heard a man of his place, gravity, and learning, so wide of his own respect.

Evans. What is he ?   54

Page. I think you know him : Master Doctor Caius, the renowned French physician.

Evans. Got's will and his passion of my heart ! I had as lief you would tell me of a mess of porridge.

Page. Why ?   59

Evans. He has no more knowledge in Hibocrates and Galen, and he is a knave besides—a cowardly knave as you would desires to be acquainted withal.   62

Page. I warrant you, he's the man should fight with him.

Slen. [*Aside*] O sweet Anne Page !   65

Shal. It appears so, by his weapons. Keep them asunder ; here comes Doctor Caius.

Enter HOST, CAIUS, *and* RUGBY.

Page. Nay, good Master Parson, keep in your weapon.

Shal. So do you, good Master Doctor. 69

Host. Disarm them, and let them question ; let them keep their limbs whole and hack our English.   71

Caius. I pray you, let-a me speak a word with your ear. Verefore vill you not meet-a me ?

Evans. [*Aside to Caius*] Pray you use your patience ; in good time.   75

Caius. By gar, you are de coward, de Jack dog, John ape.

Evans. [*Aside to Caius*] Pray you, let us

not be laughing-stocks to other men's humours ; I desire you in friendship, and I will one way or other make you amends. [*Aloud*] I will knog your urinals about your knave's cogscomb for missing your meetings and appointments.   82

Caius. Diable ! Jack Rugby—mine Host de Jarteer—have I not stay for him to kill him ? Have I not, at de place I did appoint ?   85

Evans. As I am a Christians soul, now, look you, this is the place appointed. I'll be judgment by mine host of the Garter.

Host. Peace, I say, Gallia and Gaul, French and Welsh, soul-curer and body-curer.   90

Caius. Ay, dat is very good ! excellent !

Host. Peace, I say. Hear mine host of the Garter. Am I politic ? am I subtle ? am I a Machiavel ? Shall I lose my doctor ? No ; he gives me the potions and the motions. Shall I lose my parson, my priest, my Sir Hugh ? No ; he gives me the proverbs and the noverbs. Give me thy hand, terrestrial ; so. Give me thy hand, celestial ; so. Boys of art, I have deceiv'd you both ; I have directed you to wrong places ; your hearts are mighty, your skins are whole, and let burnt sack be the issue. Come, lay their swords to pawn. Follow me, lads of peace ; follow, follow, follow.   102

Shal. Trust me, a mad host. Follow, gentlemen, follow.

Slen. [*Aside*] O sweet Anne Page !   105

[*Exeunt all but Caius and Evans.*

Caius. Ha, do I perceive dat ? Have you make-a de sot of us, ha, ha ?

Evans. This is well ; he has made us his vlouting-stog. I desire you that we may be friends ; and let us knog our prains together to be revenge on this same scall, scurvy, cogging companion, the host of the Garter.

Caius. By gar, with all my heart. He promise to bring me where is Anne Page ; by gar, he deceive me too.   113

Evans. Well, I will smite his noddles. Pray you follow.   [*Exeunt.*

SCENE II. *The street in Windsor.*

Enter MISTRESS PAGE *and* ROBIN.

Mrs. Page. Nay, keep your way, little gallant ; you were wont to be a follower, but now you are a leader. Whether had you rather lead mine eyes, or eye your master's heels ?

Rob. I had rather, forsooth, go before you like a man than follow him like a dwarf.   5

Mrs. Page. O, you are a flattering boy ; now I see you'll be a courtier.

Enter FORD.

Ford. Well met, Mistress Page. Whither go you ?

Mrs. Page. Truly, sir, to see your wife. Is she at home ? 9

Ford. Ay ; and as idle as she may hang together, for want of company. I think, if your husbands were dead, you two would marry. 12

Mrs. Page. Be sure of that—two other husbands.

Ford. Where had you this pretty weathercock ?

Mrs. Page. I cannot tell what the dickens his name is my husband had him of. What do you call your knight's name, sirrah ?

Rob. Sir John Falstaff.

Ford. Sir John Falstaff ! 19

Mrs. Page. He, he ; I can never hit on 's name. There is such a league between my good man and he ! Is your wife at home indeed ?

Ford. Indeed she is. 23

Mrs. Page. By your leave, sir. I am sick till I see her. [*Exeunt Mrs. Page and Robin.*

Ford. Has Page any brains ? Hath he any eyes ? Hath he any thinking ? Sure, they sleep ; he hath no use of them. Why, this boy will carry a letter twenty mile as easy as a cannon will shoot pointblank twelve score. He pieces out his wife's inclination ; he gives her folly motion and advantage ; and now she's going to my wife, and Falstaff's boy with her. A man may hear this show'r sing in the wind. And Falstaff's boy with her! Good plots ! They are laid ; and our revolted wives share damnation together. Well ; I will take him, then torture my wife, pluck the borrowed veil of modesty from the so seeming Mistress Page, divulge Page himself for a secure and wilful Actæon ; and to these violent proceedings all my neighbours shall cry aim. [*Clock strikes*] The clock gives me my cue, and my assurance bids me search ; there I shall find Falstaff. I shall be rather prais'd for this than mock'd ; for it is as positive as the earth is firm that Falstaff is there. I will go. 41

Enter PAGE, SHALLOW, SLENDER, HOST, SIR HUGH EVANS, CAIUS, *and* RUGBY.

Shal., Page, &c. Well met, Master Ford.

Ford. Trust me, a good knot ; I have good cheer at home, and I pray you all go with me. 44

Shal. I must excuse myself, Master Ford.

Slen. And so must I, sir ; we have appointed to dine with Mistress Anne, and I would not break with her for more money than I'll speak of.

Shal. We have linger'd about a match between Anne Page and my cousin Slender, and this day we shall have our answer. 51

Slen. I hope I have your good will, father Page.

Page. You have, Master Slender ; I stand wholly for you. But my wife, Master Doctor, is for you altogether.

Caius. Ay, be-gar ; and de maid is love-a me ; my nursh-a Quickly tell me so mush. 56

Host. What say you to young Master Fenton ? He capers, he dances, he has eyes of youth, he writes verses, he speaks holiday, he smells April and May ; he will carry 't, he will carry 't ; 'tis in his buttons ; he will carry 't. 60

Page. Not by my consent, I promise you. The gentleman is of no having : he kept company with the wild Prince and Poins ; he is of too high a region, he knows too much. No, he shall not knit a knot in his fortunes with the finger of my substance ; if he take her, let him take her simply ; the wealth I have waits on my consent, and my consent goes not that way. 67

Ford. I beseech you, heartily, some of you go home with me to dinner : besides your cheer, you shall have sport ; I will show you a monster. Master Doctor, you shall go ; so shall you, Master Page ; and you, Sir Hugh. 71

Shal. Well, fare you well ; we shall have the freer wooing at Master Page's.

[*Exeunt Shallow and Slender.*

Caius. Go home, John Rugby ; I come anon. [*Exit Rugby.*

Host. Farewell, my hearts ; I will to my honest knight Falstaff, and drink canary with him. [*Exit Host.*

Ford. [*Aside*] I think I shall drink in pipe-wine first with him ; I'll make him dance. Will you go, gentles ? 78

All. Have with you to see this monster.

[*Exeunt.*

SCENE III. *Ford's house.*

Enter MISTRESS FORD *and* MISTRESS PAGE.

Mrs. Ford. What, John ! what, Robert !

Mrs. Page. Quickly, quickly ! Is the buck-basket—

Mrs. Ford. I warrant. What, Robin, I say !

Enter Servants with a basket.

Mrs. Page. Come, come, come.

Mrs. Ford. Here, set it down.

Mrs. Page. Give your men the charge ; we must be brief.

Mrs. Ford. Marry, as I told you before, John and Robert, be ready here hard by in the brew-house ; and when I suddenly call you, come forth, and, without any pause or staggering, take this basket on your shoulders. That done, trudge with it in all haste, and carry it among the whitsters in Datchet Mead, and there empty it in the muddy ditch close by the Thames side. 13

Mrs. Page. You will do it?

Mrs. Ford. I ha' told them over and over; they lack no direction. Be gone, and come when you are call'd. 16

[*Exeunt Servants.*

Mrs. Page. Here comes little Robin.

Enter ROBIN.

Mrs. Ford. How now, my eyas-musket, what news with you? 19

Rob. My master Sir John is come in at your back-door, Mistress Ford, and requests your company.

Mrs. Page. You little Jack-a-Lent, have you been true to us? 23

Rob. Ay, I'll be sworn. My master knows not of your being here, and hath threat'ned to put me into everlasting liberty, if I tell you of it; for he swears he'll turn me away.

Mrs. Page. Thou 'rt a good boy; this secrecy of thine shall be a tailor to thee, and shall make thee a new doublet and hose. I'll go hide me. 29

Mrs. Ford. Do so. Go tell thy master I am alone. [*Exit Robin*] Mistress Page, remember you your cue. 31

Mrs. Page. I warrant thee; if I do not act it, hiss me. [*Exit Mrs. Page.*

Mrs. Ford. Go to, then; we'll use this unwholesome humidity, this gross wat'ry pumpion; we'll teach him to know turtles from jays. 35

Enter FALSTAFF.

Fal. Have I caught thee, my heavenly jewel?

Why, now let me die, for I have liv'd long enough; this is the period of my ambition. O this blessed hour!

Mrs. Ford. O sweet Sir John! 39

Fal. Mistress Ford, I cannot cog, I cannot prate, Mistress Ford. Now shall I sin in my wish; I would thy husband were dead; I'll speak it before the best lord, I would make thee my lady.

Mrs. Ford. I your lady, Sir John? Alas, I should be a pitiful lady. 45

Fal. Let the court of France show me such another. I see how thine eye would emulate the diamond; thou hast the right arched beauty of the brow that becomes the ship-tire, the tire-valiant, or any tire of Venetian admittance. 49

Mrs. Ford. A plain kerchief, Sir John; my brows become nothing else, nor that well neither. 51

Fal. By the Lord, thou art a tyrant to say so; thou wouldst make an absolute courtier, and the firm fixture of thy foot would give an excellent motion to thy gait in a semi-circled farthingale. I see what thou wert, if Fortune thy foe were, not Nature, thy friend. Come, thou canst not hide it. 56

Mrs. Ford. Believe me, there's no such thing in me.

Fal. What made me love thee? Let that persuade thee there's something extra-ordinary in thee. Come, I cannot cog, and say thou art this and that, like a many of these lisping hawthorn-buds that come like women in men's apparel, and smell like Bucklersbury in simple time; I cannot; but I love thee, none but thee; and thou deserv'st it. 63

Mrs. Ford. Do not betray me, sir; I fear you love Mistress Page. 65

Fal. Thou mightst as well say I love to walk by the Counter-gate, which is as hateful to me as the reek of a lime-kiln.

Mrs. Ford. Well, heaven knows how I love you; and you shall one day find it. 70

Fal. Keep in that mind; I'll deserve it.

Mrs. Ford. Nay, I must tell you, so you do; or else I could not be in that mind. 73

Rob. [*Within*] Mistress Ford, Mistress Ford! here's Mistress Page at the door, sweating and blowing and looking wildly, and would needs speak with you presently.

Fal. She shall not see me; I will ensconce me behind the arras. 78

Mrs. Ford. Pray you, do so; she's a very tattling woman. [*Falstaff hides himself.*

Re-enter MISTRESS PAGE *and* ROBIN.

What's the matter? How now! 81

Mrs. Page. O Mistress Ford, what have you done? You're sham'd, y'are over-thrown, y'are undone for ever.

Mrs. Ford. What's the matter, good Mistress Page? 84

Mrs. Page. O well-a-day, Mistress Ford, having an honest man to your husband, to give him such cause of suspicion! 87

Mrs. Ford. What cause of suspicion?

Mrs. Page. What cause of suspicion? Out upon you, how am I mistook in you!

Mrs. Ford. Why, alas, what's the matter?

Mrs. Page. Your husband's coming hither, woman, with all the officers in Windsor, to search for a gentleman that he says is here now in the house, by your consent, to take an ill advantage of his absence. You are undone. 95

Mrs. Ford. 'Tis not so, I hope.

Mrs. Page. Pray heaven it be not so that you have such a man here; but 'tis most certain your husband 's coming, with half Windsor at his heels, to search for such a one. I come before to tell you. If you know yourself clear, why, I am glad of it; but if you have a friend here, convey, convey him out. Be not amaz'd; call all your senses to you; defend your reputa-tion, or bid farewell to your good life for ever. 104

Mrs. Ford. What shall I do? There is a gentleman, my dear friend; and I fear not mine own shame so much as his peril. I had rather than a thousand pound he were out of the house. 108

Mrs. Page. For shame, never stand ' you had rather ' and ' you had rather ' ! Your husband's here at hand ; bethink you of some conveyance ; in the house you cannot hide him. O, how have you deceiv'd me ! Look, here is a basket ; if he be of any reasonable stature, he may creep in here ; and throw foul linen upon him, as if it were going to bucking, or—it is whiting-time—send him by your two men to Datchet Mead. 116

Mrs. Ford. He's too big to go in there. What shall I do ?

Fal. [*Coming forward*] Let me see 't, let me see 't. O, let me see 't ! I'll in, I'll in ; follow your friend's counsel ; I'll in. 121

Mrs. Page. What, Sir John Falstaff ! [*Aside to Falstaff*] Are these your letters, knight ?

Fal. [*Aside to Mrs. Page*] I love thee and none but thee ; help me away.—Let me creep in here ; I'll never— 125
[*Gets into the basket ; they cover him with foul linen.*

Mrs. Page. Help to cover your master, boy. Call your men, Mistress Ford. You dissembling knight !

Mrs. Ford. What, John ! Robert ! John !
[*Exit Robin.*

Re-enter Servants.

Go, take up these clothes here, quickly ; where's the cowl-staff ? Look how you drumble. Carry them to the laundress in Datchet Mead ; quickly, come. 131

Enter FORD, PAGE, CAIUS, *and* SIR HUGH EVANS.

Ford. Pray you come near. If I suspect without cause, why then make sport at me, then let me be your jest ; I deserve it. How now, whither bear you this ?

Serv. To the laundress, forsooth. 135

Mrs. Ford. Why, what have you to do whither they bear it ? You were best meddle with buck-washing. 137

Ford. Buck ? I would I could wash my-self of the buck ! Buck, buck, buck ! ay, buck ! I warrant you, buck ; and of the season too, it shall appear. [*Exeunt Servants with the basket*] Gentlemen, I have dream'd to-night ; I'll tell you my dream. Here, here, here be my keys ; ascend my chambers, search, seek, find out. I'll warrant we'll unkennel the fox. Let me stop this way first. [*Locking the door*] So, now uncape. 145

Page. Good Master Ford, be contented ; you wrong yourself too much.

Ford. True, Master Page. Up, gentle-men, you shall see sport anon ; follow me, gentlemen. [*Exit.*

Evans. This is fery fantastical humours and jealousies. 150

Caius. By gar, 'tis no the fashion of France ; it is not jealous in France.

Page. Nay, follow him, gentlemen ; see the issue of his search.
[*Exeunt Evans, Page, and Caius.*

Mrs. Page. Is there not a double excel-lency in this ? 155

Mrs. Ford. I know not which pleases me better, that my husband is deceived, or Sir John. 157

Mrs. Page. What a taking was he in when your husband ask'd who was in the basket !

Mrs. Ford. I am half afraid he will have need of washing ; so throwing him into the water will do him a benefit. 161

Mrs. Page. Hang him, dishonest rascal ! I would all of the same strain were in the same distress.

Mrs. Ford. I think my husband hath some special suspicion of Falstaff's being here, for I never saw him so gross in his jealousy till now. 166

Mrs. Page. I will lay a plot to try that, and we will yet have more tricks with Falstaff. His dissolute disease will scarce obey this medicine. 169

Mrs. Ford. Shall we send that foolish carrion, Mistress Quickly, to him, and excuse his throwing into the water, and give him another hope, to betray him to another punishment ? 173

Mrs. Page. We will do it ; let him be sent for to-morrow eight o'clock, to have amends. 175

Re-enter FORD, PAGE, CAIUS, *and* SIR HUGH EVANS.

Ford. I cannot find him ; may be the knave bragg'd of that he could not compass.

Mrs. Page. [*Aside to Mrs. Ford*] Heard you that ? 178

Mrs. Ford. You use me well, Master Ford, do you ?

Ford. Ay, I do so. 180

Mrs. Ford. Heaven make you better than your thoughts !

Ford. Amen.

Mrs. Page. You do yourself mighty wrong, Master Ford.

Ford. Ay, ay ; I must bear it. 185

Evans. If there be any pody in the house, and in the chambers, and in the coffers, and in the presses, heaven forgive my sins at the day of judgment !

Caius. Be gar, nor I too ; there is no bodies. 189

Page. Fie, fie, Master Ford, are you not asham'd ? What spirit, what devil suggests this imagination ? I would not ha' your

69

distemper in this kind for the wealth of Windsor Castle.

Ford. 'Tis my fault, Master Page; I suffer for it. 194

Evans. You suffer for a pad conscience. Your wife is as honest a omans as I will desires among five thousand, and five hundred too.

Caius. By gar, I see 'tis an honest woman. 198

Ford. Well, I promis'd you a dinner. Come, come, walk in the Park. I pray you pardon me; I will hereafter make known to you why I have done this. Come, wife, come, Mistress Page; I pray you pardon me; pray heartily, pardon me. 203

Page. Let's go in, gentlemen; but, trust me, we'll mock him. I do invite you to-morrow morning to my house to breakfast; after, we'll a-birding together; I have a fine hawk for the bush. Shall it be so? 207

Ford. Any thing.

Evans. If there is one, I shall make two in the company. 210

Caius. If there be one or two, I shall make-a the turd.

Ford. Pray you go, Master Page.

Evans. I pray you now, remembrance to-morrow on the lousy knave, mine host.

Caius. Dat is good; by gar, with all my heart. 215

Evans. A lousy knave, to have his gibes and his mockeries! [*Exeunt.*

SCENE IV. *Before Page's house.*

Enter FENTON *and* ANNE PAGE.

Fent. I see I cannot get thy father's love; Therefore no more turn me to him, sweet Nan.

Anne. Alas, how then?

Fent. Why, thou must be thyself. He doth object I am too great of birth; And that, my state being gall'd with my expense, 5
I seek to heal it only by his wealth. Besides these, other bars he lays before me, My riots past, my wild societies; And tells me 'tis a thing impossible I should love thee but as a property. 10

Anne. May be he tells you true.

Fent. No, heaven so speed me in my time to come! Albeit I will confess thy father's wealth Was the first motive that I woo'd thee, Anne; Yet, wooing thee, I found thee of more value 15
Than stamps in gold, or sums in sealed bags; And 'tis the very riches of thyself That now I aim at.

Anne. Gentle Master Fenton, Yet seek my father's love; still seek it, sir. If opportunity and humblest suit 20

Cannot attain it, why then—hark you hither. [*They converse apart.*

Enter SHALLOW, SLENDER, *and* MISTRESS QUICKLY.

Shal. Break their talk, Mistress Quickly; my kinsman shall speak for himself.

Slen. I'll make a shaft or a bolt on 't; 'slid, 'tis but venturing. 25

Shal. Be not dismay'd.

Slen. No, she shall not dismay me. I care not for that, but that I am afeard.

Quick. Hark ye, Master Slender would speak a word with you. 30

Anne. I come to him. [*Aside*] This is my father's choice.
O, what a world of vile ill-favour'd faults Looks handsome in three hundred pounds a year!

Quick. And how does good Master Fenton? Pray you, a word with you. 35

Shal. She's coming; to her, coz. O boy, thou hadst a father!

Slen. I had a father, Mistress Anne; my uncle can tell you good jests of him. Pray you, uncle, tell Mistress Anne the jest how my father stole two geese out of a pen, good uncle.

Shal. Mistress Anne, my cousin loves you. 41

Slen. Ay, that I do; as well as I love any woman in Gloucestershire.

Shal. He will maintain you like a gentle-woman.

Slen. Ay, that I will come cut and long-tail, under the degree of a squire. 45

Shal. He will make you a hundred and fifty pounds jointure.

Anne. Good Master Shallow, let him woo for himself.

Shal. Marry, I thank you for it; I thank you for that good comfort. She calls you, coz; I'll leave you. 50

Anne. Now, Master Slender—

Slen. Now, good Mistress Anne—

Anne. What is your will? 55

Slen. My will! 'Od's heartlings, that's a pretty jest indeed! I ne'er made my will yet, I thank heaven; I am not such a sickly creature, I give heaven praise.

Anne. I mean, Master Slender, what would you with me? 60

Slen. Truly, for mine own part I would little or nothing with you. Your father and my uncle hath made motions; if it be my luck, so; if not, happy man be his dole! They can tell you how things go better than I can. You may ask your father; here he comes. 65

Enter PAGE *and* MISTRESS PAGE.

Page. Now, Master Slender! Love him, daughter Anne— Why, how now, what does Master Fenton here?

You wrong me, sir, thus still to haunt my
    house.
I told you, sir, my daughter is dispos'd of.
    Fent. Nay, Master Page, be not im-
    patient.   70
    Mrs. Page. Good Master Fenton, come
    not to my child.
    Page. She is no match for you.
    Fent. Sir, will you hear me ?
    Page.   No, good Master Fenton.
Come, Master Shallow ; come, son Slender ;
    in.
Knowing my mind, you wrong me, Master
    Fenton.   75
        [*Exeunt Page, Shallow, and Slender.*
    Quick. Speak to Mistress Page.
    Fent. Good Mistress Page, for that I love
    your daughter
In such a righteous fashion as I do,
Perforce, against all checks, rebukes, and
    manners,
I must advance the colours of my love,   80
And not retire. Let me have your good will.
    Anne. Good mother, do not marry me to
    yond fool.
    Mrs. Page. I mean it not ; I seek you a
    better husband.
    Quick. That's my master, Master Doctor.
    Anne. Alas, I had rather be set quick i'
    th' earth,   85
And bowl'd to death with turnips.
    Mrs. Page. Come, trouble not yourself.
    Good Master Fenton,
I will not be your friend, nor enemy ;
My daughter will I question how she loves
    you,
And as I find her, so am I affected ;   90
Till then, farewell, sir ; she must needs
    go in ;
Her father will be angry.
    Fent. Farewell, gentle mistress ; fare-
    well, Nan.
            [*Exeunt Mrs. Page and Anne.*
    Quick. This is my doing now : ' Nay,'
said I ' will you cast away your child on a
fool, and a physician ? Look on Master
Fenton '. This is my doing.   96
    Fent. I thank thee ; and I pray thee,
    once to-night
Give my sweet Nan this ring. There's for
    thy pains.   98
    Quick. Now Heaven send thee good
fortune ! [*Exit Fenton*] A kind heart he
hath ; a woman would run through fire and
water for such a kind heart. But yet I
would my master had Mistress Anne ; or I
would Master Slender had her ; or, in
sooth, I would Master Fenton had her ; I
will do what I can for them all three, for so
I have promis'd, and I'll be as good as my
word ; but speciously for Master Fenton.
Well, I must of another errand to Sir John
Falstaff from my two mistresses. What a
beast am I to slack it !   [*Exit.*

SCENE V. *The Garter Inn.*

Enter FALSTAFF *and* BARDOLPH.

    Fal. Bardolph, I say !
    Bard. Here, sir.
    Fal. Go fetch me a quart of sack ; put a
toast in 't. [*Exit Bard.*] Have I liv'd to be
carried in a basket, like a barrow of
butcher's offal, and to be thrown in the
Thames ? Well, if I be serv'd such another
trick, I'll have my brains ta'en out and
butter'd, and give them to a dog for a new-
year's gift. The rogues slighted me into the
river with as little remorse as they would
have drown'd a blind bitch's puppies,
fifteen i' th' litter ; and you may know by
my size that I have a kind of alacrity in
sinking ; if the bottom were as deep as hell
I should down. I had been drown'd but
that the shore was shelvy and shallow—a
death that I abhor ; for the water swells a
man ; and what a thing should I have been
when I had been swell'd ! I should have
been a mountain of mummy.   16

Re-enter BARDOLPH, *with sack.*

    Bard. Here's Mistress Quickly, sir, to
speak with you.
    Fal. Come, let me pour in some sack to
the Thames water ; for my belly's as cold
as if I had swallow'd snow-balls for pills to
cool the reins. Call her in.   20
    Bard. Come in, woman.

Enter MISTRESS QUICKLY.

    Quick. By your leave ; I cry you mercy.
Give your worship good morrow.
    Fal. Take away these chalices. Go, brew
me a pottle of sack finely.   25
    Bard. With eggs, sir ?
    Fal. Simple of itself ; I'll no pullet-sperm
in my brewage. [*Exit Bardolph*] How now !
    Quick. Marry, sir, I come to your worship
from Mistress Ford.   30
    Fal. Mistress Ford ! I have had ford
enough ; I was thrown into the ford ; I
have my belly full of ford.
    Quick. Alas the day, good heart, that
was not her fault ! She does so take on with
her men ; they mistook their erection. 35
    Fal. So did I mine, to build upon a
foolish woman's promise.
    Quick. Well, she laments, sir, for it, that
it would yearn your heart to see it. Her
husband goes this morning a-birding ; she
desires you once more to come to her
between eight and nine ; I must carry her
word quickly. She'll make you amends, I
warrant you.   42
    Fal. Well, I will visit her. Tell her so ;
and bid her think what a man is. Let her
consider his frailty, and then judge of my
merit.   45
    Quick. I will tell her.

Fal. Do so. Between nine and ten, say'st thou ?

Quick. Eight and nine, sir.

Fal. Well, be gone ; I will not miss her.

Quick. Peace be with you, sir.   [*Exit.*

Fal. I marvel I hear not of Master Brook ; he sent me word to stay within. I like his money well. O, here he comes.

Enter FORD *disguised.*

Ford. Bless you, sir !   54

Fal. Now, Master Brook, you come to know what hath pass'd between me and Ford's wife ?   56

Ford. That, indeed, Sir John, is my business.

Fal. Master Brook, I will not lie to you : I was at her house the hour she appointed me.

Ford. And sped you, sir ?   60

Fal. Very ill-favouredly, Master Brook.

Ford. How so, sir ; did she change her determination ?   62

Fal. No, Master Brook ; but the peaking cornuto her husband, Master Brook, dwelling in a continual 'larum of jealousy, comes me in the instant of our encounter, after we had embrac'd, kiss'd, protested, and, as it were, spoke the prologue of our comedy ; and at his heels a rabble of his companions, thither provoked and instigated by his distemper, and, forsooth, to search his house for his wife's love.   70

Ford. What, while you were there ?

Fal. While I was there.

Ford. And did he search for you, and could not find you ?   74

Fal. You shall hear. As good luck would have it, comes in one Mistress Page, gives intelligence of Ford's approach ; and, in her invention and Ford's wife's distraction, they convey'd me into a buck-basket.

Ford. A buck-basket !   79

Fal. By the Lord, a buck-basket ! Ramm'd me in with foul shirts and smocks, socks, foul stockings, greasy napkins, that, Master Brook, there was the rankest compound of villainous smell that ever offended nostril.

Ford. And how long lay you there ?   84

Fal. Nay, you shall hear, Master Brook, what I have suffer'd to bring this woman to evil for your good. Being thus cramm'd in the basket, a couple of Ford's knaves, his hinds, were call'd forth by their mistress to carry me in the name of foul clothes to Datchet Lane ; they took me on their shoulders ; met the jealous knave their master in the door ; who ask'd them once or twice what they had in their basket. I quak'd for fear lest the lunatic knave would have search'd it ; but Fate, ordaining he should be a cuckold, held his hand. Well, on went he for a search, and away went I

for foul clothes. But mark the sequel, Master Brook—I suffered the pangs of three several deaths : first, an intolerable fright to be detected with a jealous rotten bell-wether ; next, to be compass'd like a good bilbo in the circumference of a peck, hilt to point, heel to head ; and then, to be stopp'd in, like a strong distillation, with stinking clothes that fretted in their own grease. Think of that—a man of my kidney. Think of that—that am as subject to heat as butter ; a man of continual dissolution and thaw. It was a miracle to scape suffocation. And in the height of this bath, when I was more than half-stew'd in grease, like a Dutch dish, to be thrown into the Thames, and cool'd, glowing hot, in that surge, like a horse-shoe ; think of that—hissing hot. Think of that, Master Brook.   108

Ford. In good sadness, sir, I am sorry that for my sake you have suffer'd all this. My suit, then, is desperate ; you'll undertake her no more.   111

Fal. Master Brook, I will be thrown into Etna, as I have been into Thames, ere I will leave her thus. Her husband is this morning gone a-birding ; I have received from her another embassy of meeting ; 'twixt eight and nine is the hour, Master Brook.

Ford. 'Tis past eight already, sir.   117

Fal. Is it ? I will then address me to my appointment. Come to me at your convenient leisure, and you shall know how I speed ; and the conclusion shall be crowned with your enjoying her. Adieu. You shall have her, Master Brook ; Master Brook, you shall cuckold Ford. [*Exit.*   122

Ford. Hum ! ha ! Is this a vision ? Is this a dream ? Do I sleep ? Master Ford, awake ; awake, Master Ford. There's a hole made in your best coat, Master Ford. This 'tis to be married ; this 'tis to have linen and buck-baskets ! Well, I will proclaim myself what I am ; I will now take the lecher ; he is at my house. He cannot scape me ; 'tis impossible he should ; he cannot creep into a halfpenny purse nor into a pepper box. But, lest the devil that guides him should aid him, I will search impossible places. Though what I am I cannot avoid, yet to be what I would not shall not make me tame. If I have horns to make one mad, let the proverb go with me—I'll be horn mad.   [*Exit.*   134

ACT FOUR

SCENE I. *Windsor. A street.*

Enter MISTRESS PAGE, MISTRESS QUICKLY, *and* WILLIAM.

Mrs. Page. Is he at Master Ford's already, think'st thou ?

Quick. Sure he is by this ; or will be

presently ; but truly he is very courageous mad about his throwing into the water. Mistress Ford desires you to come suddenly.

Mrs. Page. I'll be with her by and by ; I'll but bring my young man here to school. Look where his master comes ; 'tis a playing day, I see.   8

Enter SIR HUGH EVANS.

How now, Sir Hugh, no school to-day ?

Evans. No ; Master Slender is let the boys leave to play.

Quick. Blessing of his heart !   12

Mrs. Page. Sir Hugh, my husband says my son profits nothing in the world at his book ; I pray you ask him some questions in his accidence.   15

Evans. Come hither, William ; hold up your head ; come.

Mrs. Page. Come on, sirrah ; hold up your head ; answer your master ; be not afraid.

Evans. William, how many numbers is in nouns ?

Will. Two.   20

Quick. Truly, I thought there had been one number more, because they say ' Od's nouns '.

Evans. Peace your tattlings. What is ' fair ', William ?

Will. Pulcher.

Quick. Polecats ! There are fairer things than polecats, sure.   26

Evans. You are a very simplicity oman ; I pray you, peace. What is ' lapis ', William ?

Will. A stone.

Evans. And what is ' a stone ', William ?

Will. A pebble.   31

Evans. No, it is ' lapis ' ; I pray you remember in your prain.

Will. Lapis.

Evans. That is a good William. What is he, William, that does lend articles ?   36

Will. Articles are borrowed of the pronoun, and be thus declined : Singulariter, nominativo ; hic, hæc, hoc.

Evans. Nominativo, hig, hag, hog ; pray you, mark : genitivo, hujus. Well, what is your accusative case ?   40

Will. Accusativo, hinc.

Evans. I pray you, have your remembrance, child. Accusativo, hung, hang, hog.

Quick. ' Hang-hog ' is Latin for bacon, I warrant you.

Evans. Leave your prabbles, oman. What is the focative case, William ?   46

Will. O—vocativo, O.

Evans. Remember, William : focative is caret.

Quick. And that's a good root.

Evans. Oman, forbear.   50

Mrs. Page. Peace.

Evans. What is your genitive case plural, William ?

Will. Genitive case ?

Evans. Ay.

Will. Genitive : horum, harum, horum.   55

Quick. Vengeance of Jenny's case ; fie on her ! Never name her, child, if she be a whore.

Evans. For shame, oman.   58

Quick. You do ill to teach the child such words. He teaches him to hick and to hack, which they'll do fast enough of themselves ; and to call ' horum ' ; fie upon you !   62

Evans. Oman, art thou lunatics ? Hast thou no understandings for thy cases, and the numbers of the genders ? Thou art as foolish Christian creatures as I would desires.   65

Mrs. Page. Prithee hold thy peace.

Evans. Show me now, William, some declensions of your pronouns.

Will. Forsooth, I have forgot.   69

Evans. It is qui, quæ, quod ; if you forget your qui's, your quæ's, and your quod's, you must be preeches. Go your ways and play ; go.   72

Mrs. Page. He is a better scholar than I thought he was.

Evans. He is a good sprag memory. Farewell, Mistress Page.   76

Mrs. Page. Adieu, good Sir Hugh. [*Exit Sir Hugh*] Get you home, boy. Come, we stay too long.   [*Exeunt.*

SCENE II. *Ford's house.*

Enter FALSTAFF *and* MISTRESS FORD.

Fal. Mistress Ford, your sorrow hath eaten up my sufferance. I see you are obsequious in your love, and I profess requital to a hair's breadth ; not only, Mistress Ford, in the simple office of love, but in all the accoutrement, complement, and ceremony of it. But are you sure of your husband now ?   6

Mrs. Ford. He's a-birding, sweet Sir John.

Mrs. Page. [*Within*] What hoa, gossip Ford, what hoa !

Mrs. Ford. Step into th' chamber, Sir John.   [*Exit Falstaff.*

Enter MISTRESS PAGE.

Mrs. Page. How now, sweetheart, who's at home besides yourself ?   11

Mrs. Ford. Why, none but mine own people.

Mrs. Page. Indeed ?

Mrs. Ford. No, certainly. [*Aside to her*] Speak louder.

Mrs. Page. Truly, I am so glad you have nobody here.   15

Mrs. Ford. Why ?

Mrs. Page. Why, woman, your husband

is in his old lunes again. He so takes on
yonder with my husband ; so rails against
all married mankind ; so curses all Eve's
daughters, of what complexion soever ; and
so buffets himself on the forehead, crying
' Peer-out, peer-out ! ' that any madness I
ever yet beheld seem'd but tameness,
civility, and patience, to this his distemper
he is in now. I am glad the fat knight is
not here.

Mrs. Ford. Why, does he talk of him ? 25

Mrs. Page. Of none but him ; and swears
he was carried out, the last time he search'd
for him, in a basket ; protests to my
husband he is now here ; and hath drawn
him and the rest of their company from
their sport, to make another experiment of
his suspicion. But I am glad the knight is
not here ; now he shall see his own foolery.

Mrs. Ford. How near is he, Mistress
Page ?   32

Mrs. Page. Hard by, at street end ; he
will be here anon.

Mrs. Ford. I am undone : the knight is
here.   34

Mrs. Page. Why, then, you are utterly
sham'd, and he's but a dead man. What a
woman are you ! Away with him, away
with him ; better shame than murder. 37

Mrs. Ford. Which way should he go ?
How should I bestow him ? Shall I put him
into the basket again ?

Re-enter FALSTAFF.

Fal. No, I'll come no more i' th' basket.
May I not go out ere he come ?   41

Mrs. Page. Alas, three of Master Ford's
brothers watch the door with pistols, that
none shall issue out ; otherwise you might
slip away ere he came. But what make you
here ?   45

Fal. What shall I do ? I'll creep up into
the chimney.

Mrs. Ford. There they always use to
discharge their birding-pieces.

Mrs. Page. Creep into the kiln-hole.

Fal. Where is it ?   49

Mrs. Ford. He will seek there, on my
word. Neither press, coffer, chest, trunk,
well, vault, but he hath an abstract for the
remembrance of such places, and goes to
them by his note. There is no hiding you
in the house.

Fal. I'll go out then.   54

Mrs. Page. If you go out in your own
semblance, you die, Sir John. Unless you
go out disguis'd.

Mrs. Ford. How might we disguise him ?

Mrs. Page. Alas the day, I know not !
There is no woman's gown big enough for
him ; otherwise he might put on a hat, a
muffler, and a kerchief, and so escape. 60

Fal. Good hearts, devise something ; any
extremity rather than a mischief.

Mrs. Ford. My maid's aunt, the fat
woman of Brainford, has a gown above. 64

Mrs. Page. On my word, it will serve
him ; she's as big as he is ; and there's her
thrumm'd hat, and her muffler too. Run
up, Sir John.

Mrs. Ford. Go, go, sweet Sir John.
Mistress Page and I will look some linen for
your head.   69

Mrs. Page. Quick, quick ; we'll come
dress you straight. Put on the gown the
while.   [*Exit Falstaff.*

Mrs. Ford. I would my husband would
meet him in this shape ; he cannot abide
the old woman of Brainford ; he swears
she's a witch, forbade her my house, and
hath threat'ned to beat her.   75

Mrs. Page. Heaven guide him to thy
husband's cudgel ; and the devil guide his
cudgel afterwards !

Mrs. Ford. But is my husband coming ?

Mrs. Page. Ay, in good sadness is he ;
and talks of the basket too, howsoever he
hath had intelligence.   80

Mrs. Ford. We'll try that ; for I'll
appoint my men to carry the basket again,
to meet him at the door with it as they did
last time.

Mrs. Page. Nay, but he'll be here presently ; let's go dress him like the witch
of Brainford.   85

Mrs. Ford. I'll first direct my men what
they shall do with the basket. Go up ; I'll
bring linen for him straight.   [*Exit.*

Mrs. Page. Hang him, dishonest varlet !
we cannot misuse him enough.

We'll leave a proof, by that which we will
do,   90
Wives may be merry and yet honest too.
We do not act that often jest and laugh ;
'Tis old but true : Still swine eats all the
draff.   [*Exit.*

Re-enter MISTRESS FORD, *with two* Servants.

Mrs. Ford. Go, sirs, take the basket again
on your shoulders ; your master is hard at
door ; if he bid you set it down, obey him ;
quickly, dispatch.   [*Exit.*

1 Serv. Come, come, take it up.   97

2 Serv. Pray heaven it be not full of
knight again.

1 Serv. I hope not ; I had lief as bear so
much lead.

Enter FORD, PAGE, SHALLOW, CAIUS, *and*
SIR HUGH EVANS.

Ford. Ay, but if it prove true, Master
Page, have you any way then to unfool me
again ? Set down the basket, villain !
Somebody call my wife. Youth in a basket !
O you panderly rascals, there's a knot, a
ging, a pack, a conspiracy against me. Now
shall the devil be sham'd. What, wife, I
say ! Come, come forth ; behold what

honest clothes you send forth to bleaching.   106

Page. Why, this passes, Master Ford;
you are not to go loose any longer; you
must be pinion'd.

Evans. Why, this is lunatics. This is mad
as a mad dog.   110

Shal. Indeed, Master Ford, this is not
well, indeed.

Ford. So say I too, sir.

Re-enter MISTRESS FORD.

Come hither, Mistress Ford; Mistress Ford,
the honest woman, the modest wife, the
virtuous creature, that hath the jealous
fool to her husband! I suspect without
cause, mistress, do I?   116

Mrs. Ford. Heaven be my witness, you
do, if you suspect me in any dishonesty.

Ford. Well said, brazen-face; hold it out.
Come forth, sirrah.   120

[*Pulling clothes out of the basket.*]
Page. This passes!

Mrs. Ford. Are you not asham'd? Let
the clothes alone.

Ford. I shall find you anon.

Evans. 'Tis unreasonable. Will you take
up your wife's clothes? Come away. 125

Ford. Empty the basket, I say.

Mrs. Ford. Why, man, why?

Ford. Master Page, as I am a man, there
was one convey'd out of my house yesterday
in this basket. Why may not he be there
again? In my house I am sure he is; my
intelligence is true; my jealousy is reasonable. Pluck me out all the linen. 132

Mrs. Ford. If you find a man there, he
shall die a flea's death.

Page. Here 's no man.   135

Shal. By my fidelity, this is not well,
Master Ford; this wrongs you.

Evans. Master Ford, you must pray, and
not follow the imaginations of your own
heart; this is jealousies.

Ford. Well, he's not here I seek for. 140

Page. No, nor nowhere else but in your
brain.

Ford. Help to search my house this one
time. If I find not what I seek, show no
colour for my extremity; let me for ever be
your table sport; let them say of me 'As
jealous as Ford, that search'd a hollow
walnut for his wife's leman'. Satisfy me
once more; once more search with me.

Mrs. Ford. What, hoa, Mistress Page!
Come you and the old woman down; my
husband will come into the chamber. 148

Ford. Old woman? What old woman's
that?

Mrs. Ford. Why, it is my maid's aunt of
Brainford.   150

Ford. A witch, a quean, an old cozening
quean! Have I not forbid her my house?
She comes of errands, does she? We are

simple men; we do not know what's
brought to pass under the profession of
fortune-telling. She works by charms, by
spells, by th' figure, and such daub'ry as
this is, beyond our element. We know
nothing. Come down, you witch, you hag
you; come down, I say.   157

Mrs. Ford. Nay, good sweet husband!
Good gentlemen, let him not strike the old
woman.

Re-enter FALSTAFF *in woman's clothes, and*
MISTRESS PAGE.

Mrs. Page. Come, Mother Prat; come,
give me your hand.   161

Ford. I'll prat her. [*Beating him*] Out of
my door, you witch, you hag, you baggage,
you polecat, you ronyon! Out, out! I'll
conjure you, I'll fortune-tell you.

[*Exit Falstaff.*

Mrs. Page. Are you not asham'd? I
think you have kill'd the poor woman. 166

Mrs. Ford. Nay, he will do it. 'Tis a
goodly credit for you.

Ford. Hang her, witch!

Evans. By yea and no, I think the oman
is a witch indeed; I like not when a oman
has a great peard; I spy a great peard
under his muffler.   172

Ford. Will you follow, gentlemen? I
beseech you follow; see but the issue of my
jealousy; if I cry out thus upon no trail,
never trust me when I open again. 175

Page. Let's obey his humour a little
further. Come, gentlemen.

[*Exeunt all but Mrs. Ford and*
Mrs. Page.

Mrs. Page. Trust me, he beat him most
pitifully.

Mrs. Ford. Nay, by th' mass, that he did
not; he beat him most unpitifully methought.   180

Mrs. Page. I 'll have the cudgel hallow'd
and hung o'er the altar; it hath done
meritorious service.

Mrs. Ford. What think you? May we,
with the warrant of womanhood and the
witness of a good conscience, pursue him
with any further revenge?   185

Mrs. Page. The spirit of wantonness is
sure scar'd out of him; if the devil have
him not in fee-simple, with fine and
recovery, he will never, I think, in the way
of waste, attempt us again.   189

Mrs. Ford. Shall we tell our husbands
how we have serv'd him?   191

Mrs. Page. Yes, by all means; if it be but
to scrape the figures out of your husband's
brains. If they can find in their hearts the
poor unvirtuous fat knight shall be any
further afflicted, we two will still be the
ministers.   195

Mrs. Ford. I 'll warrant they'll have him
publicly sham'd; and methinks there

would be no period to the jest, should he
not be publicly sham'd.   198

Mrs. Page. Come, to the forge with it
then; shape it. I would not have things
cool.   [*Exeunt.*

SCENE III. *The Garter Inn.*

Enter HOST *and* BARDOLPH.

Bard. Sir, the Germans desire to have
three of your horses; the Duke himself
will be to-morrow at court, and they are
going to meet him.

Host. What duke should that be comes so
secretly? I hear not of him in the court.
Let me speak with the gentlemen; they
speak English?   6

Bard. Ay, sir; I'll call them to you.

Host. They shall have my horses, but I'll
make them pay; I'll sauce them; they
have had my house a week at command;
I have turn'd away my other guests. They
must come off; I'll sauce them. Come. 11
                                        [*Exeunt.*

SCENE IV. *Ford's house.*

Enter PAGE, FORD, MISTRESS PAGE,
MISTRESS FORD, *and* SIR HUGH EVANS.

Evans. 'Tis one of the best discretions of
a oman as ever I did look upon.

Page. And did he send you both these
letters at an instant?   4

Mrs. Page. Within a quarter of an hour.

Ford. Pardon me, wife. Henceforth, do
   what thou wilt;
I rather will suspect the sun with cold
Than thee with wantonness. Now doth thy
   honour stand,
In him that was of late an heretic,   9
As firm as faith.

Page.   'Tis well, 'tis well; no more.
Be not as extreme in submission as in
   offence:
But let our plot go forward. Let our wives
Yet once again, to make us public sport,
Appoint a meeting with this old fat fellow,
Where we may take him and disgrace him
   for it.   16

Ford. There is no better way than that
   they spoke of.

Page. How? To send him word they'll
meet him in the Park at midnight? Fie,
fie! he'll never come!   19

Evans. You say he has been thrown in
the rivers; and has been grievously peaten
as an old oman; methinks there should be
terrors in him, that he should not come;
methinks his flesh is punish'd; he shall have
no desires.

Page. So think I too.

Mrs. Ford. Devise but how you'll use
   him when he comes,   25
And let us two devise to bring him thither.

Mrs. Page. There is an old tale goes that
   Herne the Hunter,
Sometime a keeper here in Windsor Forest,
Doth all the winter-time, at still midnight,
Walk round about an oak, with great
   ragg'd horns;   30
And there he blasts the tree, and takes the
   cattle,
And makes milch-kine yield blood, and
   shakes a chain
In a most hideous and dreadful manner.
You have heard of such a spirit, and well
   you know
The superstitious idle-headed eld   35
Receiv'd, and did deliver to our age,
This tale of Herne the Hunter for a truth.

Page. Why yet there want not many
   that do fear
In deep of night to walk by this Herne's
   oak.   39
But what of this?

Mrs. Ford.   Marry, this is our device—
That Falstaff at that oak shall meet with us,
Disguis'd, like Herne, with huge horns on
   his head.

Page. Well, let it not be doubted but he'll
   come,
And in this shape. When you have brought
   him thither,
What shall be done with him? What is
   your plot?

Mrs. Page. That likewise have we
   thought upon, and thus: 45
Nan Page my daughter, and my little son,
And three or four more of their growth,
   we'll dress
Like urchins, ouphes, and fairies, green and
   white,
With rounds of waxen tapers on their heads,
And rattles in their hands; upon a sudden,
As Falstaff, she, and I, are newly met,   51
Let them from forth a sawpit rush at once
With some diffused song; upon their sight
We two in great amazedness will fly.
Then let them all encircle him about,   55
And fairy-like, to pinch the unclean knight;
And ask him why, that hour of fairy revel,
In their so sacred paths he dares to tread
In shape profane.

Mrs. Ford.   And till he tell the truth,
Let the supposed fairies pinch him sound,
And burn him with their tapers.

Mrs. Page.   The truth being known,
We'll all present ourselves; dis-horn the
   spirit,
And mock him home to Windsor.

Ford.   The children must
Be practis'd well to this or they'll nev'r
   do 't.   64

Evans. I will teach the children their
behaviours; and I will be like a jack-an-
apes also, to burn the knight with my taber.

Ford. That will be excellent. I'll go buy
them vizards.   69

Mrs. Page. My Nan shall be the Queen of
all the Fairies.
Finely attired in a robe of white.

Page. That silk will I go buy. [*Aside*] And
in that time
Shall Master Slender steal my Nan away,
And marry her at Eton.—Go, send to
Falstaff straight.

Ford. Nay, I'll to him again, in name of
Brook ;   75
He'll tell me all his purpose. Sure, he'll
come.

Mrs. Page. Fear not you that. Go get us
properties
And tricking for our fairies.

Evans. Let us about it. It is admirable
pleasures, and fery honest knaveries.
          [*Exeunt Page, Ford, and Evans.*

Mrs. Page. Go, Mistress Ford,   81
Send Quickly to Sir John to know his mind.
          [*Exit Mrs. Ford.*
I'll to the Doctor ; he hath my good will,
And none but he, to marry with Nan Page.
That Slender, though well landed, is an
idiot ;   85
And he my husband best of all affects.
The Doctor is well money'd, and his friends
Potent at court ; he, none but he, shall
have her,
Though twenty thousand worthier come to
crave her.   [*Exit.*

SCENE V. *The Garter Inn.*

Enter HOST *and* SIMPLE.

Host. What wouldst thou have, boor ?
What, thick-skin ? Speak, breathe, discuss ;
brief, short, quick, snap.

Sim. Marry, sir, I come to speak with Sir
John Falstaff from Master Slender.   4

Host. There's his chamber, his house, his
castle, his standing-bed and truckle-bed ;
'tis painted about with the story of the
Prodigal, fresh and new. Go, knock and
call ; he'll speak like an Anthropophaginian unto thee. Knock, I say.   9

Sim. There's an old woman, a fat woman,
gone up into his chamber ; I'll be so bold
as stay, sir, till she come down ; I come to
speak with her, indeed.   12

Host. Ha ! a fat woman ? The knight may
be robb'd. I'll call. Bully knight ! Bully
Sir John ! Speak from thy lungs military.
Art thou there ? It is thine host, thine
Ephesian, calls.   16

Fal. [*Above*] How now, mine host ?

Host. Here's a Bohemian-Tartar tarries
the coming down of thy fat woman. Let
her descend, bully, let her descend ; my
chambers are honourable. Fie, privacy, fie !

Enter FALSTAFF.

Fal. There was, mine host, an old fat
woman even now with me ; but she's gone.

Sim. Pray you, sir, was't not the wise
woman of Brainford ?

Fal. Ay, marry was it, mussel-shell.
What would you with her ?   26

Sim. My master, sir, my Master Slender,
sent to her, seeing her go thorough the
streets, to know, sir, whether one Nym, sir,
that beguil'd him of a chain, had the chain
or no.   29

Fal. I spake with the old woman about it.

Sim. And what says she, I pray, sir ? 31

Fal. Marry, she says that the very same
man that beguil'd Master Slender of his
chain cozen'd him of it.   33

Sim. I would I could have spoken with
the woman herself ; I had other things to
have spoken with her too, from him.   36

Fal. What are they ? Let us know.

Host. Ay, come ; quick.

Sim. I may not conceal them, sir.

Fal. Conceal them, or thou diest.   40

Sim. Why, sir, they were nothing but
about Mistress Anne Page : to know if it
were my master's fortune to have her
or no.

Fal. 'Tis, 'tis his fortune.

Sim. What, sir ?   45

Fal. To have her, or no. Go ; say the
woman told me so.

Sim. May I be bold to say so, sir ?

Fal. Ay, sir ; like who more bold ?

Sim. I thank your worship ; I shall make
my master glad with these tidings.   51
          [*Exit Simple.*

Host. Thou art clerkly, thou art clerkly,
Sir John. Was there a wise woman with
thee ?

Fal. Ay, that there was, mine host ; one
that hath taught me more wit than ever I
learn'd before in my life ; and I paid
nothing for it neither, but was paid for my
learning.   57

Enter BARDOLPH.

Bard. Out, alas, sir, cozenage, mere
cozenage !

Host. Where be my horses ? Speak well
of them, varletto.   60

Bard. Run away with the cozeners ; for
so soon as I came beyond Eton, they threw
me off from behind one of them, in a slough
of mire ; and set spurs and away, like
three German devils, three Doctor
Faustuses.   64

Host. They are gone but to meet the
Duke, villain ; do not say they be fled.
Germans are honest men.

Enter SIR HUGH EVANS.

Evans. Where is mine host ?

Host. What is the matter, sir ?

Evans. Have a care of your entertain-
ments. There is a friend of mine come to
town tells me there is three cozen-germans

that has cozen'd all the hosts of Readins, of Maidenhead, of Colebrook, of horses and money. I tell you for good will, look you; you are wise, and full of gibes and vlouting-stogs, and 'tis not convenient you should be cozened. Fare you well. [*Exit.*

Enter DOCTOR CAIUS.

Caius. Vere is mine host de Jarteer?
Host. Here, Master Doctor, in perplexity and doubtful dilemma. 78
Caius. I cannot tell vat is dat; but it is tell-a me dat you make grand preparation for a Duke de Jamany. By my trot, dere is no duke that the court is know to come; I tell you for good will. Adieu. [*Exit.*
Host. Hue and cry, villain, go! Assist me, knight; I am undone. Fly, run, hue and cry, villain; I am undone. 85
[*Exeunt Host and Bardolph.*
Fal. I would all the world might be cozen'd, for I have been cozen'd and beaten too. If it should come to the ear of the court how I have been transformed, and how my transformation hath been wash'd and cudgell'd, they would melt me out of my fat, drop by drop, and liquor fishermen's boots with me; I warrant they would whip me with their fine wits till I were as crest-fall'n as a dried pear. I never prosper'd since I forswore myself at primero. Well, if my wind were but long enough to say my prayers, I would repent. 95

Enter MISTRESS QUICKLY.

Now! whence come you?
Quick. From the two parties, forsooth.
Fal. The devil take one party and his dam the other! And so they shall be both bestowed. I have suffer'd more for their sakes, more than the villainous inconstancy of man's disposition is able to bear. 101
Quick. And have not they suffer'd? Yes, I warrant; speciously one of them; Mistress Ford, good heart, is beaten black and blue, that you cannot see a white spot about her. 105
Fal. What tell'st thou me of black and blue? I was beaten myself into all the colours of the rainbow; and I was like to be apprehended for the witch of Brainford. But that my admirable dexterity of wit, my counterfeiting the action of an old woman, deliver'd me, the knave constable had set me i' th' stocks, i' th' common stocks, for a witch. 112
Quick. Sir, let me speak with you in your chamber; you shall hear how things go, and, I warrant, to your content. Here is a letter will say somewhat. Good hearts, what ado here is to bring you together! Sure, one of you does not serve heaven well, that you are so cross'd. 117
Fal. Come up into my chamber. [*Exeunt.*

SCENE VI. *The Garter Inn.*

Enter FENTON *and* HOST.

Host. Master Fenton, talk not to me; my mind is heavy; I will give over all.
Fent. Yet hear me speak. Assist me in my purpose,
And, as I am a gentleman, I'll give thee
A hundred pound in gold more than your loss. 5
Host. I will hear you, Master Fenton; and I will, at the least, keep your counsel.
Fent. From time to time I have ac-quainted you 8
With the dear love I bear to fair Anne Page;
Who, mutually, hath answer'd my affection,
So far forth as herself might be her chooser,
Even to my wish. I have a letter from her
Of such contents as you will wonder at;
The mirth whereof so larded with my matter
That neither, singly, can be manifested 15
Without the show of both. Fat Falstaff
Hath a great scene. The image of the jest
I'll show you here at large. Hark, good mine host:
To-night at Herne's oak, just 'twixt twelve and one,
Must my sweet Nan present the Fairy Queen— 20
The purpose why is here—in which dis-guise,
While other jests are something rank on foot,
Her father hath commanded her to slip
Away with Slender, and with him at Eton
Immediately to marry; she hath con-sented. 25
Now, sir,
Her mother, even strong against that match
And firm for Doctor Caius, hath appointed
That he shall likewise shuffle her away
While other sports are tasking of their minds, 30
And at the dean'ry, where a priest attends,
Straight marry her. To this her mother's plot
She seemingly obedient likewise hath
Made promise to the doctor. Now thus it rests:
Her father means she shall be all in white;
And in that habit, when Slender sees his time 36
To take her by the hand and bid her go,
She shall go with him; her mother hath intended,
The better to denote her to the doctor—
For they must all be mask'd and vizarded—
That quaint in green she shall be loose enrob'd, 41
With ribands pendent, flaring 'bout her head;
And when the doctor spies his vantage ripe,

To pinch her by the hand, and, on that
token,
The maid hath given consent to go with
him.   45
 Host. Which means she to deceive,
father or mother ?
 Fent. Both, my good host, to go along
with me.
And here it rests—that you'll procure the
vicar
To stay for me at church, 'twixt twelve and
one,
And in the lawful name of marrying, 50
To give our hearts united ceremony.
 Host. Well, husband your device ; I'll to
the vicar.
Bring you the maid, you shall not lack a
priest.
 Fent. So shall I evermore be bound to
thee ;
Besides, I'll make a present recompense. 55
          [*Exeunt.*

ACT FIVE

Scene I. *The Garter Inn.*

Enter FALSTAFF *and* MISTRESS QUICKLY.

 Fal. Prithee, no more prattling ; go.
I'll hold. This is the third time ; I hope
good luck lies in odd numbers. Away, go ;
they say there is divinity in odd numbers,
either in nativity, chance, or death. Away.
 Quick. I'll provide you a chain, and I'll
do what I can to get you a pair of horns. 6
 Fal. Away, I say ; time wears ; hold up
your head, and mince. [*Exit Mrs. Quickly.*

Enter FORD, *disguised.*

How now, Master Brook ! Master Brook,
the matter will be known to-night or never.
Be you in the Park about midnight, at
Herne's oak, and you shall see wonders.
 Ford. Went you not to her yesterday, sir,
as you told me you had appointed ? 13
 Fal. I went to her, Master Brook, as you
see, like a poor old man ; but I came from
her, Master Brook, like a poor old woman.
That same knave Ford, her husband, hath
the finest mad devil of jealousy in him,
Master Brook, that ever govern'd frenzy.
I will tell you—he beat me grievously in
the shape of a woman ; for in the shape of
man, Master Brook, I fear not Goliath with
a weaver's beam ; because I know also life
is a shuttle. I am in haste ; go along with
me ; I'll tell you all, Master Brook. Since
I pluck'd geese, play'd truant, and whipp'd
top, I knew not what 'twas to be beaten
till lately. Follow me. I'll tell you strange
things of this knave Ford, on whom to-
night I will be revenged, and I will deliver
his wife into your hand. Follow. Strange
things in hand, Master Brook ! Follow. 28
          [*Exeunt.*

Scene II. *Windsor Park.*

Enter PAGE, SHALLOW, *and* SLENDER.

 Page. Come, come ; we'll couch i' th'
Castle ditch till we see the light of our
fairies. Remember, son Slender, my
daughter. 3
 Slen. Ay, forsooth ; I have spoke with
her, and we have a nay-word how to know
one another. I come to her in white and
cry ' mum ' ; she cries ' budget ' ; and by
that we know one another. 7
 Shal. That's good too ; but what needs
either your mum or her budget ? The white
will decipher her well enough. It hath
struck ten o'clock. 10
 Page. The night is dark ; light and spirits
will become it well. Heaven prosper our
sport ! No man means evil but the devil,
and we shall know him by his horns. Let's
away ; follow me. [*Exeunt.*

Scene III. *A street leading to the Park.*

Enter MISTRESS PAGE, MISTRESS FORD, *and*
DOCTOR CAIUS.

 Mrs. Page. Master Doctor, my daughter
is in green ; when you see your time, take
her by the hand, away with her to the
deanery, and dispatch it quickly. Go before
into the Park ; we two must go together.
 Caius. I know vat I have to do ; adieu. 5
 Mrs. Page. Fare you well, sir. [*Exit
Caius*] My husband will not rejoice so much
at the abuse of Falstaff as he will chafe at
the doctor's marrying my daughter ; but
'tis no matter ; better a little chiding than
a great deal of heart-break. 10
 Mrs. Ford. Where is Nan now, and her
troop of fairies, and the Welsh devil, Hugh ?
 Mrs. Page. They are all couch'd in a pit
hard by Herne's oak, with obscur'd lights ;
which, at the very instant of Falstaff's and
our meeting, they will at once display to
the night. 16
 Mrs. Ford. That cannot choose but
amaze him.
 Mrs. Page. If he be not amaz'd, he will be
mock'd ; if he be amaz'd, he will every way
be mock'd.
 Mrs. Ford. We'll betray him finely. 20
 Mrs. Page. Against such lewdsters and
their lechery,
Those that betray them do no treachery.
 Mrs. Ford. The hour draws on. To the
oak, to the oak ! [*Exeunt.*

Scene IV. *Windsor Park.*

Enter SIR HUGH EVANS *like a satyr, with
Others as fairies.*

 Evans. Trib, trib, fairies ; come ; and
remember your parts. Be pold, I pray you ;
follow me into the pit ; and when I give

79

the watch-ords, do as I pid you. Come,
come ; trib, trib.   [*Exeunt.*

SCENE V. *Another part of the Park.*

Enter FALSTAFF *disguised as Herne.*

Fal. The Windsor bell hath struck
twelve ; the minute draws on. Now the
hot-blooded gods assist me! Remember,
Jove, thou wast a bull for thy Europa ;
love set on thy horns. O powerful love !
that in some respects makes a beast a man ;
in some other a man a beast. You were
also, Jupiter, a swan, for the love of Leda.
O omnipotent love! how near the god drew
to the complexion of a goose ! A fault done
first in the form of a beast—O Jove, a
beastly fault !—and then another fault in
the semblance of a fowl—think on't, Jove,
a foul fault ! When gods have hot backs
what shall poor men do ? For me, I am
here a Windsor stag ; and the fattest, I
think, i' th' forest. Send me a cool rut-
time, Jove, or who can blame me to piss my
tallow ? Who comes here ? my doe ?   14

Enter MISTRESS FORD *and* MISTRESS PAGE.

Mrs. Ford. Sir John ! Art thou there, my
deer, my male deer.   16

Fal. My doe with the black scut ! Let
the sky rain potatoes ; let it thunder to the
tune of Greensleeves, hail kissing-comfits,
and snow eringoes ; let there come a
tempest of provocation, I will shelter me
here.   [*Embracing her.*

Mrs. Ford. Mistress Page is come with
me, sweetheart.   21

Fal. Divide me like a brib'd buck, each a
haunch ; I will keep my sides to myself, my
shoulders for the fellow of this walk, and
my horns I bequeath your husbands. Am I
a woodman, ha ? Speak I like Herne the
Hunter ? Why, now is Cupid a child of
conscience ; he makes restitution. As I am
a true spirit, welcome ! [*A noise of horns.*

Mrs. Page. Alas ! what noise ?
Mrs. Ford. Heaven forgive our sins !
Fal. What should this be ?   30
Mrs. Ford. }
Mrs. Page. } Away, away. [*They run off.*

Fal. I think the devil will not have me
damn'd, lest the oil that's in me should set
hell on fire ; he would never else cross me
thus.   34

Enter SIR HUGH EVANS *like a satyr,* ANNE
PAGE *as a fairy, and* Others *as the Fairy
Queen, fairies, and Hobgoblin* ; *all with
tapers.*

Fairy Queen. Fairies, black, grey, green,
and white,   35
You moonshine revellers, and shades of
night,
You orphan heirs of fixed destiny,

Attend your office and your quality.
Crier Hobgoblin, make the fairy oyes.
Puck. Elves, list your names ; silence,
you airy toys.   40
Cricket, to Windsor chimneys shalt thou
leap ;
Where fires thou find'st unrak'd, and
hearths unswept,
There pinch the maids as blue as bilberry ;
Our radiant Queen hates sluts and sluttery.
Fal. They are fairies ; he that speaks to
them shall die.   45
I'll wink and couch ; no man their works
must eye. [*Lies down upon his face.*
Evans. Where's Pede ? Go you, and
where you find a maid
That, ere she sleep, has thrice her prayers
said,
Raise up the organs of her fantasy,
Sleep she as sound as careless infancy ;   50
But those as sleep and think not on their
sins,
Pinch them, arms, legs, backs, shoulders,
sides, and shins.
Fairy Queen. About, about ;
Search Windsor castle, elves, within and
out ;
Strew good luck, ouphes, on every sacred
room,   55
That it may stand till the perpetual doom
In state as wholesome as in state 'tis fit,
Worthy the owner and the owner it.
The several chairs of order look you scour
With juice of balm and every precious
flower ;   60
Each fair instalment, coat, and sev'ral
crest,
With loyal blazon, evermore be blest !
And nightly, meadow-fairies, look you sing,
Like to the Garter's compass, in a ring ;
Th' expressure that it bears, green let it be,
More fertile-fresh than all the field to see ;
And ' Honi soit qui mal y pense' write 67
In em'rald tufts, flow'rs purple, blue and
white ;
Like sapphire, pearl, and rich embroidery,
Buckled below fair knighthood's bending
knee.   70
Fairies use flow'rs for their charactery.
Away, disperse ; but till 'tis one o'clock,
Our dance of custom round about the oak
Of Herne the Hunter let us not forget.
Evans. Pray you, lock hand in hand ;
yourselves in order set ;   75
And twenty glow-worms shall our lanterns
be,
To guide our measure round about the
tree.
But, stay. I smell a man of middle earth.
Fal. Heavens defend me from that Welsh
fairy, lest he transform me to a piece of
cheese !   80
Puck. Vile worm, thou wast o'erlook'd
even in thy birth.

Fairy Queen. With trial-fire touch me
    his finger-end ;
If he be chaste, the flame will back descend,
And turn him to no pain ; but if he start,
It is the flesh of a corrupted heart.   85
    Puck. A trial, come.
    Evans. Come, will this wood take fire ?
        [*They put the tapers to his fingers,*
           and he starts.
    Fal. Oh, oh, oh !
    Fairy Queen. Corrupt, corrupt, and
    tainted in desire !
About him, fairies ; sing a scornful rhyme ;
And, as you trip, still pinch him to your
    time.   90

      The Song.

Fie on sinful fantasy !
Fie on lust and luxury !
Lust is but a bloody fire,
Kindled with unchaste desire,
Fed in heart, whose flames aspire,   95
As thoughts do blow them, higher and
    higher.
Pinch him, fairies, mutually ;
Pinch him for his villainy ;
Pinch him and burn him and turn him
    about,
Till candles and star-light and moonshine
    be out.   100

During this song they pinch Falstaff.
    DOCTOR CAIUS *comes one way, and steals
    away a fairy in green ;* SLENDER *another
    way, and takes off a fairy in white ; and*
    FENTON *steals away Anne Page. A
    noise of hunting is heard within. All
    the fairies run away. Falstaff pulls off
    his buck's head, and rises.*

    Enter PAGE, FORD, MISTRESS PAGE,
MISTRESS FORD, *and* SIR HUGH EVANS.

    Page. Nay, do not fly ; I think we have
    watch'd you now.
Will none but Herne the Hunter serve your
    turn ?
    Mrs. Page. I pray you, come, hold up the
jest no higher.
Now, good Sir John, how like you Windsor
    wives ?
See you these, husband ? Do not these fair
    yokes   105
Become the forest better than the town ?
    Ford. Now, sir, who's a cuckold now ?
Master Page, Falstaff's a knave, a
cuckoldly knave ; here are his horns,
Master Page ; and, Master Page, he hath
enjoyed nothing of Ford's but his buck-
basket, his cudgel, and twenty pounds of
money, which must be paid to Master
Brook ; his horses are arrested for it,
Master Brook.   112
    Mrs. Ford. Sir John, we have had ill luck ;
we could never meet. I will never take you

for my love again ; but I will always count
you my deer.   115
    Fal. I do begin to perceive that I am
made an ass.
    Ford. Ay, and an ox too ; both the proofs
are extant.
    Fal. And these are not fairies ? I was
three or four times in the thought they were
not fairies ; and yet the guiltiness of my
mind, the sudden surprise of my powers,
drove the grossness of the foppery into a
receiv'd belief, in despite of the teeth of all
rhyme and reason, that they were fair es.
See now how wit may be made a Jack-a-
Lent when 'tis upon ill employment.   124
    Evans. Sir John Falstaff, serve Got, and
leave your desires, and fairies will not pinse
you.
    Ford. Well said, fairy Hugh.
    Evans. And leave you your jealousies
too, I pray you.   128
    Ford. I will never mistrust my wife again,
till thou art able to woo her in good English.
    Fal. Have I laid my brain in the sun, and
dried it, that it wants matter to prevent so
gross o'er-reaching as this ? Am I ridden
with a Welsh goat too ? Shall I have a coxcomb of frieze ? 'Tis time I were chok'd
with a piece of toasted cheese.   135
    Evans. Seese is not good to give putter ;
your belly is all putter.
    Fal. ' Seese ' and ' putter ' ! Have I liv'd
to stand at the taunt of one that makes
fritters of English ? This is enough to be
the decay of lust and late-walking through
the realm.   140
    Mrs. Page. Why, Sir John, do you think,
though we would have thrust virtue out of
our hearts by the head and shoulders, and
have given ourselves without scruple to
hell, that ever the devil could have made
you our delight ?
    Ford. What, a hodge-pudding ? a bag of
flax ?   145
    Mrs. Page. A puff'd man ?
    Page. Old, cold, wither'd, and of intoler-
able entrails ?
    Ford. And one that is as slanderous as
Satan ?
    Page. And as poor as Job ?
    Ford. And as wicked as his wife ?   150
    Evans. And given to fornications, and to
taverns, and sack, and wine, and methe-
glins, and to drinkings, and swearings, and
starings, pribbles and prabbles ?   153
    Fal. Well, I am your theme ; you have
the start of me ; I am dejected ; I am not
able to answer the Welsh flannel ; ignorance itself is a plummet o'er me ; use me
as you will.   157
    Ford. Marry, sir, we'll bring you to
Windsor, to one Master Brook, that you
have cozen'd of money, to whom you
should have been a pander. Over and

above that you have suffer'd, I think to repay that money will be a biting affliction.

Page. Yet be cheerful, knight ; thou shalt eat a posset to-night at my house, where I will desire thee to laugh at my wife, that now laughs at thee. Tell her Master Slender hath married her daughter.

Mrs. Page. [*Aside*] Doctors doubt that ; if Anne Page be my daughter, she is, by this, Doctor Caius' wife. 168

Enter SLENDER.

Slen. Whoa, ho, ho, father Page !

Page. Son, how now ! how now, son ! Have you dispatch'd ? 171

Slen. Dispatch'd ! I'll make the best in Gloucestershire know on't ; would I were hang'd, la, else !

Page. Of what, son ? 174

Slen. I came yonder at Eton to marry Mistress Anne Page, and she's a great lubberly boy. If it had not been i' th' church, I would have swing'd him, or he should have swing'd me. If I did not think it had been Anne Page, would I might never stir !—and 'tis a postmaster's boy.

Page. Upon my life, then, you took the wrong. 180

Slen. What need you tell me that ? I think so, when I took a boy for a girl. If I had been married to him, for all he was in woman's apparel, I would not have had him. 183

Page. Why, this is your own folly. Did not I tell you how you should know my daughter by her garments ? 185

Slen. I went to her in white and cried ' mum ' and she cried ' budget ' as Anne and I had appointed ; and yet it was not Anne, but a postmaster's boy. 188

Mrs. Page. Good George, be not angry. I knew of your purpose ; turn'd my daughter into green ; and, indeed, she is now with the Doctor at the dean'ry, and there married. 192

Enter CAIUS.

Caius. Vere is Mistress Page ? By gar, I am cozened ; I ha' married un garçon, a boy ; un paysan, by gar, a boy ; it is not Anne Page ; by gar, I am cozened. 195

Mrs. Page. Why, did you take her in green ?

Caius. Ay, be gar, and 'tis a boy ; be gar, I'll raise all Windsor. [*Exit Caius.*

Ford. This is strange. Who hath got the right Anne ?

Page. My heart misgives me ; here comes Master Fenton. 201

Enter FENTON *and* ANNE PAGE.

How now, Master Fenton !

Anne. Pardon, good father. Good my mother, pardon.

Page. Now, Mistress, how chance you went not with Master Slender ? 205

Mrs. Page. Why went you not with Master Doctor, maid ?

Fent. You do amaze her. Hear the truth of it.
You would have married her most shamefully,
Where there was no proportion held in love.
The truth is, she and I, long since contracted, 210
Are now so sure that nothing can dissolve us.
Th' offence is holy that she hath committed;
And this deceit loses the name of craft,
Of disobedience, or unduteous title,
Since therein she doth evitate and shun 215
A thousand irreligious cursed hours,
Which forced marriage would have brought upon her.

Ford. Stand not amaz'd ; here is no remedy.
In love, the heavens themselves do guide the state ;
Money buys lands, and wives are sold by fate. 220

Fal. I am glad, though you have ta'en a special stand to strike at me, that your arrow hath glanc'd.

Page. Well, what remedy ? Fenton, heaven give thee joy !
What cannot be eschew'd must be embrac'd.

Fal. When night-dogs run, all sorts of deer are chas'd. 225

Mrs. Page. Well, I will muse no further. Master Fenton,
Heaven give you many, many merry days !
Good husband, let us every one go home,
And laugh this sport o'er by a country fire ;
Sir John and all.

Ford.   Let it be so. Sir John, 230
To Master Brook you yet shall hold your word ;
For he, to-night, shall lie with Mistress Ford. [*Exeunt.*

MEASURE FOR MEASURE

DRAMATIS PERSONÆ

VINCENTIO, *the Duke.*
ANGELO, *the Deputy.*
ESCALUS, *an ancient Lord.*
CLAUDIO, *a young gentleman.*
LUCIO, *a fantastic.*
Two other like gentlemen.
VARRIUS, *a gentleman, servant to the Duke.*
PROVOST.
THOMAS, } *two friars.*
PETER,
A JUSTICE.
ELBOW, *a simple constable.*
FROTH, *a foolish gentleman.*

POMPEY, *a clown and servant to Mistress Overdone.*
ABHORSON, *an executioner.*
BARNARDINE, *a dissolute prisoner.*

ISABELLA, *sister to Claudio.*
MARIANA, *betrothed to Angelo.*
JULIET, *beloved of Claudio.*
FRANCISCA, *a nun.*
MISTRESS OVERDONE, *a bawd.*

Lords, Officers, Citizens, Boy, *and* Attendants.

THE SCENE : *Vienna.*

ACT ONE

SCENE I. *The Duke's palace.*

Enter DUKE, ESCALUS, Lords, *and Attendants.*

Duke. Escalus!
Escal. My lord.
Duke. Of government the properties to unfold
Would seem in me t' affect speech and discourse,
Since I am put to know that your own science   5
Exceeds, in that, the lists of all advice
My strength can give you ; then no more remains
But that to your sufficiency—as your worth is able—
And let them work. The nature of our people,   10
Our city's institutions, and the terms
For common justice, y'are as pregnant in
As art and practice hath enriched any
That we remember. There is our commission,
From which we would not have you warp.
Call hither,   15
I say, bid come before us Angelo.
    [Exit an Attendant.
What figure of us think you he will bear ?
For you must know we have with special soul
Elected him our absence to supply ;
Lent him our terror, dress'd him with our love,   20
And given his deputation all the organs
Of our own power. What think you of it ?
Escal. If any in Vienna be of worth
To undergo such ample grace and honour,
It is Lord Angelo.

Enter ANGELO.

Duke.   Look where he comes.   25
Ang. Always obedient to your Grace's will,
I come to know your pleasure.
Duke.   Angelo,
There is a kind of character in thy life
That to th' observer doth thy history
Fully unfold. Thyself and thy belongings
Are not thine own so proper as to waste   31
Thyself upon thy virtues, they on thee.
Heaven doth with us as we with torches do,
Not light them for themselves ; for if our virtues
Did not go forth of us, 'twere all alike   35
As if we had them not. Spirits are not finely touch'd
But to fine issues ; nor Nature never lends
The smallest scruple of her excellence
But, like a thrifty goddess, she determines
Herself the glory of a creditor,   40
Both thanks and use. But I do bend my speech
To one that can my part in him advertise.
Hold, therefore, Angelo—
In our remove be thou at full ourself ;
Mortaity and mercy in Vienna   45
Live in thy tongue and heart. Old Escalus,
Though first in question, is thy secondary.
Take thy commission.
Ang.   Now, good my lord,
Let there be some more test made of my metal,
Before so noble and so great a figure   50
Be stamp'd upon it.
Duke.   No more evasion !
We have with a leaven'd and prepared choice
Proceeded to you ; therefore take your honours.

Our haste from hence is of so quick
    condition
That t prefers itself, and leaves un-
    question'd   55
Matters of needful value. We shall write
    to you,
As time and our concernings shall im-
    portune,
How it goes with us, and do look to know
What doth befall you here. So, fare you
    well.
To th' hopeful execution do I leave you 60
Of your commissions.
    Ang.   Yet give leave, my lord,
That we may bring you something on the
    way.
    Duke. My haste may not admit it ;
Nor need you, on mine honour, have to do
With any scruple : your scope is as mine
    own,   65
So to enforce or qualify the laws
As to your soul seems good. Give me your
    hand ;
I'll privily away I love the people,
But do not like to stage me to their eyes ;
Though it do well, I do not relish well 70
Their loud applause and Aves vehement ;
Nor do I think he man of safe discretion
That does affect it. Once more, fare you
    well.
    Ang. The heavens give safety to your
    purposes !
    Escal. Lead forth and bring you back in
    happiness !   75
    Duke. I thank you. Fare you well. [*Exit.*
    Escal. I shall desire you, sir, to give me
    leave
To have free speech with you ; and it con-
    cerns me
To look into the bottom of my place :
A pow'r I have, but of what strength and
    nature   80
I am not yet instructed.
    Ang. 'Tis so with me. Let us withdraw
    together,
And we may soon our satisfaction have
Touching that point.
    Escal.   I'll wait upon your honour.
    [*Exeunt.*

SCENE II. *A street.*

Enter LUCIO *and two other* Gentlemen.

Lucio. If the Duke, with the other dukes,
come not to composition with the King of
Hungary, why then all the dukes fall upon
the King.
    1 *Gent.* Heaven grant us its peace, but
not the King of Hungary's !   5
    2 *Gent.* Amen.
    Lucio. Thou conclud'st like the sancti-
monious pirate that went to sea with the
Ten Commandments, but scrap'd one out
of the table.

    2 *Gent.* 'Thou shalt not steal'?   10
    Lucio. Ay, that he raz'd.
    1 *Gent.* Why, 'twas a commandment to
command the captain and all the rest from
their functions : they put forth to steal.
There's not a soldier of us all that, in the
thanksgiving before meat, do relish the
petition well that prays for peace.   16
    2 *Gent.* I never heard any soldier dislike it.
    Lucio. I believe thee ; for I think thou
never wast where grace was said.
    2 *Gent.* No ? A dozen times at least. 20
    1 *Gent.* What, in metre ?
    Lucio. In any proportion or in any
language.
    1 *Gent.* I think, or in any religion.
    Lucio. Ay, why not ? Grace is grace,
despite of all controversy ; as, for example,
thou thyself art a wicked villain, despite of
all grace.   26
    1 *Gent.* Well, there went but a pair of
shears between us.
    Lucio. I grant ; as there may between
the lists and the velvet. Thou art the list.
    1 *Gent.* And thou the velvet ; thou art
good velvet ; thou 'rt a three-pil'd piece,
I warrant thee. I had as lief be a list of an
English kersey as be pil'd, as thou art pil'd,
for a French velvet. Do I speak feelingly
now ?   34
    Lucio. I think thou dost ; and, indeed,
with most painful feeling of thy speech. I
will, out of thine own confession, learn to
begin thy health ; but, whilst I live, forget
to drink after thee.
    1 *Gent.* I think I have done myself wrong,
have I not ?   40
    2 *Gent.* Yes, that thou hast, whether thou
art tainted or free.

Enter MISTRESS OVERDONE.

    Lucio. Behold, behold, where Madam
Mitigation comes ! I have purchas'd as
many diseases under her roof as come to—
    2 *Gent.* To what, I pray ?   46
    1 *Gent.* Judge.
    2 *Gent.* To three thousand dolours a year.
    1 *Gent.* Ay, and more.
    Lucio. A French crown more.   50
    1 *Gent.* Thou art always figuring diseases
in me, but thou art full of error ; I am
sound.
    Lucio. Nay, not, as one would say,
healthy ; but so sound as things that are
hollow : thy bones are hollow ; impiety
has made a feast of thee.   55
    1 *Gent.* How now ! which of your hips has
the most profound sciatica ?
    Mrs. Ov. Well, well ! there's one yonder
arrested and carried to prison was worth
five thousand of you all.
    1 *Gent.* Who's that, I pray thee ?   60
    Mrs. Ov. Marry, sir, that's Claudio,
Signior Claudio.

1 Gent. Claudio to prison ? 'Tis not so.

Mrs. Ov. Nay, but I know 'tis so : I saw him arrested   saw him carried away ; and, which is more, within these three days his head to be chopp'd off.   65

Lucio. But, after all this fooling, I would not have it so.   Art thou sure of this ?

Mrs. Ov. I am too sure of it ; and it is for getting Madam Julietta with child.   69

Lucio. Believe me, th s may be ; he promis'd to meet me two hours since, and he was ever precise in promise-keeping.   72

2 Gent. Besides, you know, it draws something near to the speech we had to such a purpose.

1 Gent. But most of all agreeing with the proclamat.on.   76

Lucio. Away ; let's go learn the truth of it.   [*Exeunt Lucio and Gentlemen.*

Mrs. Ov. Thus, what with the war, what with the sweat, what with the gallows, and what with poverty, I am custom-shrunk.

Enter POMPEY.

How now ! what's the news with you ?   81

Pom. Yonder man is carried to prison.

Mrs. Ov. Well, what has he done ?

Pom. A woman.

Mrs. Ov. But what's his offence ?   85

Pom. Groping for trouts in a peculiar river.

Mrs. Ov. What ! is there a maid w th child by him ?

Pom. No ; but there's a woman with maid by him.   You have not heard of the proclamation, have you ?

Mrs. Ov. What proclamation, man ?   90

Pom. All houses in the suburbs of Vienna must be pluck'd down.

Mrs. Ov. And what shall become of those in the city ?

Pom. They shall stand for seed ; they had gone down too, but that a wise burgher put in for them.   95

Mrs. Ov. But shall all our houses of resort in the suburbs be pull'd down ?

Pom. To the ground, mistress.

Mrs. Ov. Why, here's a change indeed in the commonwealth ! What shall become of me ?   100

Pom. Come, fear not you : good counsellors lack no clients.   Though you change your place you need not change your trade ; I'll be your tapster still.   Courage, there will be pity taken on you ; you that have worn your eyes almost out in the service, you will be considered.   105

Mrs. Ov. What's to do here, Thomas Tapster ? Let's withdraw.

Pom. Here comes Signior Claudio, led by the provost to prison ; and there's Madam Juliet.   [*Exeunt.*

Enter PROVOST, CLAUDIO, JULIET, *and*
Officers ; LUCIO *following.*

Claud. Fellow, why dost thou show me thus to th' world ?   110
Bear me to prison, where I am committed.

Prov. I do it not in evil disposition,
But from Lord Angelo by special charge.

Claud. Thus can the demigod Authority
Make us pay down for our offence by weight
The words of heaven : on whom it w ll, it will ;   116
On whom it will not, so ; yet still 'tis just.

Lucio. Why, how now, Claudio, whence comes this restraint ?

Claud. From too much liberty, my Lucio, liberty ;
As surfeit is the father of much fast,   120
So every scope by the immoderate use
Turns to restraint.   Our natures do pursue,
Like rats that ravin down their proper bane,
A thirsty evil ; and when we drink we die.

Lucio. If I could speak so wisely under an arrest, I would send for certain of my creditors ; and yet, to say the truth, I had as lief have the foppery of freedom as the morality of imprisonment.   What's thy offence, Claudio ?

Claud. What but to speak of would offend again.

Lucio. What, is't murder ?   130

Claud. No.

Lucio. Lechery ?

Claud. Call it so.

Prov. Away, sir ; you must go.

Claud. One word, good friend.   Lucio, a word with you.   135

Lucio. A hundred, if they'll do you any good.   Is lechery so look'd after ?

Claud. Thus stands it with me : upon a true contract
I got possession of Julietta's bed.   139
You know the lady   she is fast my wife,
Save that we do the denunciation lack
Of outward order ; this we came not to,
Only for propagation of a dow'r
Remaining in the coffer of her friends.
From whom we thought it meet to hide our love   145
Till time had made them for us.   But it chances
The stealth of our most mutual entertainment,
With character too gross, is writ on Juliet.

Lucio. With child, perhaps ?

Claud. Unhappily, even so.   149
And the new deputy now for the Duke—
Whether it be the fault and glimpse of newness,
Or whether that the body public be
A horse whereon the governor doth ride,
Who, newly in the seat, that it may know
He can command, lets it straight feel the spur ;   155

Whether the tyranny be in his place,
Or in his eminence that fills it up,
I stagger in. But this new governor
Awakes me all the enrolled penalties
Which have, like unscour'd armour, hung
        by th' wall   160
So long that nineteen zodiacs have gone
        round
And none of them been worn ; and, for a
        name,
Now puts the drowsy and neglected act
Freshly on me. 'Tis surely for a name. 164
    Lucio. I warrant it is ; and thy head
stands so tickle on thy shoulders that a
milkmaid, if she be in love, may sigh it off.
Send after the Duke, and appeal to him.
    Claud. I have done so, but he's not to be
        found.   168
I prithee, Lucio, do me this kind service :
This day my sister should the cloister enter,
And there receive her approbation ;
Acquaint her with the danger of my state ;
Implore her, in my voice, that she make
        friends
To the strict deputy ; bid herself assay him.
I have great hope in that ; for in her
        youth
There is a prone and speechless dialect 176
Such as move men ; beside, she hath
        prosperous art
When she will play with reason and dis-
        course,
And well she can persuade.   179
    Lucio. I pray she may ; as well for the
encouragement of the like, which else would
stand under grievous imposition, as for the
enjoying of thy life, who I would be sorry
should be thus foolishly lost at a game of
tick-tack. I'll to her.
    Claud. I thank you, good friend Lucio.
    Lucio. Within two hours.   186
    Claud. Come, officer, away. [*Exeunt.*

SCENE III. *A monastery.*

Enter DUKE *and* FRIAR THOMAS.

    Duke. No, holy father ; throw away that
        thought ;
Believe not that the dribbling dart of love
Can pierce a complete bosom. Why I desire
        thee
To give me secret harbour hath a purpose
More grave and wrinkled than the aims and
        ends   5
Of burning youth.
    Fri.   May your Grace speak of it ?
    Duke. My holy sir, none better knows
        than you
How I have ever lov'd the life removed,
And held in idle price to haunt assemblies
Where youth, and cost, a witless bravery
        keeps.   10
I have deliver'd to Lord Angelo,
A man of stricture and firm abstinence,

My absolute power and place here in
        Vienna,
And he supposes me travell'd to Poland ;
For so I have strew'd it in the common
        ear,
And so it is receiv'd. Now, pious sir,   16
You will demand of me why I do this.
    Fri. Gladly, my lord.
    Duke. We have strict statutes and most
        biting laws,
The needful bits and curbs to headstrong
        steeds,   20
Which for this fourteen years we have let
        slip ;
Even like an o'ergrown lion in a cave,
That goes not out to prey. Now, as fond
        fathers,
Having bound up the threat'ning twigs of
        birch,
Only to stick it in their children's sight 25
For terror, not to use, in time the rod
Becomes more mock'd than fear'd ; so our
        decrees,
Dead to infliction, to themselves are dead ;
And liberty plucks justice by the nose ;
The baby beats the nurse, and quite
        athwart   30
Goes all decorum.
    Fri.   It rested in your Grace
To unloose this tied-up justice when you
        pleas'd ;
And it in you more dreadful would have
        seem'd
Than in Lord Angelo.
    Duke.   I do fear, too dreadful.
Sith 'twas my fault to give the people scope,
'Twould be my tyranny to strike and gall
        them   36
For what I bid them do ; for we bid this
        be done,
When evil deeds have their permissive pass
And not the punishment. Therefore, in-
        deed, my father,
I have on Angelo impos'd the office ;   40
Who may, in th' ambush of my name, strike
        home,
And yet my nature never in the fight
To do in slander. And to behold his sway,
I will, as 'twere a brother of your order,
Visit both prince and people. Therefore, I
        prithee,   45
Supply me with the habit, and instruct me
How I may formally in person bear me
Like a true friar. Moe reasons for this
        action
At our more leisure shall I render you.
Only, this one : Lord Angelo is precise ; 50
Stands at a guard with envy ; scarce
        confesses
That his blood flows, or that his appetite
Is more to bread than stone. Hence shall
        we see,
If power change purpose, what our seemers
        be.   [*Exeunt.*

86

SCENE IV. *A nunnery.*

Enter ISABELLA *and* FRANCISCA.

Isab. And have you nuns no farther privileges ?

Fran. Are not these large enough ?

Isab. Yes, truly I speak not as desiring more,
But rather wishing a more strict restraint
Upon the sisterhood, the votarists of Saint
Clare.   5

Lucio. [*Within*] Ho ! Peace be in this
place !

Isab.   Who's that which calls ?

Fran. It is a man's voice. Gentle Isabella,
Turn you the key, and know his business
of him ;
You may, I may not ; you are yet un-
sworn ;
When you have vow'd, you must not speak
with men   10
But in the presence of the prioress ;
Then, if you speak, you must not show your
face,
Or, if you show your face, you must not
speak.
He calls again ; I pray you answer him.
                       [*Exit Francisca.*

Isab. Peace and prosperity ! Who is't
that calls ?   15

Enter LUCIO.

Lucio. Hail, virgin, if you be, as those
cheek-roses
Proclaim you are no less. Can you so stead
me
As bring me to the sight of Isabella,
A novice of this place, and the fair sister
To her unhappy brother Claudio ?   20

Isab. Why her 'unhappy brother'? Let
me ask
The rather, for I now must make you know
I am that Isabella, and his sister.

Lucio. Gentle and fair, your brother
kindly greets you.
Not to be weary with you, he's in prison. 25

Isab. Woe me ! For what ?

Lucio. For that which, if myself might be
his judge,
He should receive his punishment in thanks:
He hath got his friend with child.

Isab. Sir, make me not your story.

Lucio.   It is true.
I would not—though 'tis my familiar sin 31
With maids to seem the lapwing, and to
jest,
Tongue far from heart—play with all
virgins so :
I hold you as a thing enskied and sainted,
By your renouncement an immortal spirit,
And to be talk'd with in sincerity,   36
As with a saint.

Isab. You do blaspheme the good in
mocking me.

Lucio. Do not believe it. Fewness and
truth, 'tis thus :
Your brother and his lover have embrac'd ;
As those that feed grow full, as blossoming
time   41
That from the seedness the bare fallow
brings
To teeming foison, even so her plenteous
womb
Expresseth his full tilth and husbandry.

Isab. Some one with child by him ? My
cousin Juliet ?   45

Lucio. Is she your cousin ?

Isab. Adoptedly, as school-maids change
their names
By vain though apt affection.

Lucio.   She it is.

Isab. O, let him marry her !

Lucio.   This is the point.
The Duke is very strangely gone from
hence ;   50
Bore many gentlemen, myself being one,
In hand, and hope of action ; but we do
learn,
By those that know the very nerves of
state,
His givings-out were of an infinite dis-
tance
From his true-meant design. Upon his
place,   55
And with full line of his authority,
Governs Lord Angelo, a man whose blood
Is very snow-broth, one who never feels
The wanton stings and motions of the sense,
But doth rebate and blunt his natural edge
With profits of the mind, study and fast. 61
He—to give fear to use and liberty,
Which have for long run by the hideous
law,
As mice by lions—hath pick'd out an act
Under whose heavy sense your brother's
life   65
Falls into forfeit ; he arrests him on it,
And follows close the rigour of the statute
To make him an example. All hope is gone,
Unless you have the grace by your fair
prayer
To soften Angelo. And that's my pith of
business   70
'Twixt you and your poor brother.

Isab. Doth he so seek his life ?

Lucio.   Has censur'd him
Already, and, as I hear, the Provost hath
A warrant for his execution.

Isab. Alas ! what poor ability's in me 75
To do him good ?

Lucio.   Assay the pow'r you have.

Isab. My power, alas, I doubt !

Lucio.   Our doubts are traitors,
And make us lose the good we oft might
win
By fearing to attempt. Go to Lord Angelo,
And let him learn to know, when maidens
sue,   80

Men give like gods ; but when they weep
    and kneel,
All their petitions are as freely theirs
As they themselves would owe them.
   Isab. I'll see what I can do.
   Lucio.   But speedily.
   Isab. I will about it straight ;   85
No longer staying but to give the Mother
Notice of my affair. I humbly thank you.
Commend me to my brother ; soon at night
I'll send him certain word of my success.
   Lucio. I take my leave of you.
   Isab.   Good sir, adieu. 90
                   [*Exeunt.*

ACT TWO

SCENE I. *A hall in Angelo's house.*

Enter ANGELO, ESCALUS, *a* JUSTICE, PRO-
VOST, Officers, *and other* Attendants.

   Ang. We must not make a scarecrow of
    the law,
Setting it up to fear the birds of prey,
And let it keep one shape till custom
    make it
Their perch, and not their terror.
   Escal.   Ay, but yet
Let us be keen, and rather cut a little   5
Than fall and bruise to death. Alas ! this
    gentleman,
Whom I would save, had a most noble
    father.
Let but your honour know,
Whom I believe to be most strait in virtue,
That, in the working of your own affections,
Had time coher'd with place, or place with
    wishing,   11
Or that the resolute acting of our blood
Could have attain'd th' effect of your own
    purpose,
Whether you had not sometime in your
    life
Err'd in this point which now you censure
    him,   15
And pull'd the law upon you.
   Ang. 'Tis one thing to be tempted,
    Escalus,
Another thing to fall. I not deny
The jury, passing on the prisoner's life,
May in the sworn twelve have a thief or
    two   20
Guiltier than him they try. What's open
    made to justice,
That justice seizes. What knows the laws
That thieves do pass on thieves ? 'Tis very
    pregnant,
The jewel that we find, we stoop and take 't,
Because we see it ; but what we do not see
We tread upon, and never think of it. 26
You may not so extenuate his offence
For I have had such faults ; but rather tell
    me,
When I, that censure him, do so offend,

Let mine own judgment pattern out my
    death,   30
And nothing come in partial. Sir, he must
    die.
   Escal. Be it as your wisdom will.
   Ang.   Where is the Provost ?
   Prov. Here, if it like your honour.
   Ang.   See that Claudio
Be executed by nine to-morrow morning ;
Bring him his confessor ; let him be
    prepar'd ;   35
For that's the utmost of his pilgrimage.
                  [*Exit Provost.*
   Escal. [*Aside*] Well, heaven forgive him !
    and forgive us all !
Some rise by sin, and some by virtue fall ;
Some run from breaks of ice, and answer
    none,
And some condemned for a fault alone. 40

Enter ELBOW *and* Officers *with* FROTH
and POMPEY.

   Elb. Come, bring them away ; if these be
good people in a commonweal that do
nothing but use their abuses in common
houses, I know no law ; bring them
away.
   Ang. How now, sir ! What's your name,
and what's the matter ?   45
   Elb. If it please your honour, I am the
poor Duke's constable, and my name is
Elbow ; I do lean upon justice, sir, and do
bring in here before your good honour two
notorious benefactors.
   Ang. Benefactors ! Well—what benefactors are they ? Are they not malefactors ?   51
   Elb. If it please your honour, I know not
well what they are ; but precise villains
they are, that I am sure of, and void of all
profanation in the world that good Christians ought to have.   55
   Escal. This comes off well ; here's a wise
officer.
   Ang. Go to ; what quality are they of ?
Elbow is your name ? Why dost thou not
speak, Elbow ?
   Pom. He cannot, sir ; he's out at elbow.
   Ang. What are you, sir ?   60
   Elb. He, sir ? A tapster, sir ; parcel-
bawd ; one that serves a bad woman ;
whose house, sir, was, as they say, pluck'd
down in the suburbs ; and now she professes a hot-house, which, I think, is a very
ill house too.
   Escal. How know you that ?   65
   Elb. My wife, sir, whom I detest before
heaven and your honour—
   Escal. How ! thy wife !
   Elb. Ay, sir ; whom, I thank heaven, is
an honest woman—   70
   Escal. Dost thou detest her therefore ?
   Elb. I say, sir, I will detest myself also,
as well as she, that this house, if it be not

a bawd's house, it is pity of her life, for it
is a naughty house.

Escal. How dost thou know that,
constable ?   75

Elb. Marry, sir, by my wife ; who, if she
had been a woman cardinally given, might
have been accus'd in fornication, adultery,
and all uncleanliness there.

Escal. By the woman's means ?

Elb. Ay, sir, by Mistress Overdone's
means ; but as she spit in his face, so she
defied him.   81

Pom. Sir, if it please your honour, this is
not so.

Elb. Prove it before these varlets here,
thou honourable man, prove it.

Escal. Do you hear how he misplaces ? 85

Pom. Sir, she came in great with child ;
and longing, saving your honour's reverence, for stew'd prunes. Sir, we had but
two in the house, which at that very distant
time stood, as it were, in a fruit dish, a dish
of some three pence ; your honours have
seen such dishes ; they are not China dishes,
but very good dishes.   91

Escal. Go to, go to ; no matter for the
dish, sir.

Pom. No, indeed, sir, not of a pin ; you
are therein in the right ; but to the point.
As I say, this Mistress Elbow, being, as I
say, with child, and being great-bellied, and
longing, as I said, for prunes ; and having
but two in the dish, as I said, Master Froth
here, this very man, having eaten the rest,
as I said, and, as I say, paying for them
very honestly ; for, as you know, Master
Froth, I could not give you three pence
again—   100

Froth. No, indeed.

Pom. Very well ; you being then, if you
be remem'bred, cracking the stones of the
foresaid prunes—

Froth. Ay, so I did indeed.   104

Pom. Why, very well ; I telling you then,
if you be remem'bred, that such a one and
such a one were past cure of the thing you
wot of, unless they kept very good diet, as
I told you—

Froth. All this is true.

Pom. Why, very well then—   110

Escal. Come, you are a tedious fool. To
the purpose : what was done to Elbow's
wife that he hath cause to complain of ?
Come me to what was done to her.

Pom. Sir, your honour cannot come to
that yet.

Escal. No, sir, nor I mean it not.   115

Pom. Sir, but you shall come to it, by
your honour's leave. And, I beseech you,
look into Master Froth here, sir, a man of
fourscore pound a year ; whose father died
at Hallowmas—was't not at Hallowmas,
Master Froth ?

Froth. All-hallond eve.   120

Pom. Why, very well ; I hope here be
truths. He, sir, sitting, as I say, in a lower
chair, sir ; 'twas in the Bunch of Grapes,
where, indeed, you have a delight to sit,
have you not ?   124

Froth. I have so ; because it is an open
room, and good for winter.   126

Pom. Why, very well then ; I hope here
be truths.

Ang. This will last out a night in Russia,
When nights are longest there ; I'll take
        my leave,
And leave you to the hearing of the cause,
Hoping you'll find good cause to whip them
        all.   131

Escal. I think no less. Good morrow to
        your lordship.   [*Exit Angelo.*
Now, sir, come on ; what was done to
Elbow's wife, once more ?   134

Pom. Once ?—sir. There was nothing
done to her once.

Elb. I beseech you, sir, ask him what this
man did to my wife.

Pom. I beseech your honour, ask me.   137

Escal. Well, sir, what did this gentleman
to her ?

Pom. I beseech you, sir, look in this
gentleman's face. Good Master Froth, look
upon his honour ; 'tis for a good purpose.
Doth your honour mark his face ?   142

Escal. Ay, sir, very well.

Pom. Nay, I beseech you, mark it well.

Escal. Well, I do so.   145

Pom. Doth your honour see any harm in
his face ?

Escal. Why, no.

Pom. I'll be suppos'd upon a book his
face is the worst thing about him. Good
then ; if his face be the worst thing about
him, how could Master Froth do the constable's wife any harm ? I would know
that of your honour.   152

Escal. He's in the right, constable ; what
say you to it ?

Elb. First, an it like you, the house is a
respected house ; next, this is a respected
fellow ; and his mistress is a respected
woman.   156

Pom. By this hand, sir, his wife is a more
respected person than any of us all.

Elb. Varlet, thou liest ; thou liest,
wicked varlet ; the time is yet to come that
she was ever respected with man, woman,
or child.   161

Pom. Sir, she was respected with him
before he married with her.

Escal. Which is the wiser here, Justice or
Iniquity ? Is this true ?   165

Elb. O thou caitiff ! O thou varlet ! O
thou wicked Hannibal ! I respected with
her before I was married to her ! If ever I
was respected with her, or she with me, let
not your worship think me the poor Duke's
officer. Prove this, thou wicked Hannibal,

or I'll have mine action of batt'ry on thee.

Escal. If he took you a box o' th' ear, you might have your action of slander too. 173

Elb. Marry, I thank your good worship for it. What is't your worship's pleasure I shall do with this wicked caitiff ? 176

Escal. Truly, officer, because he hath some offences in him that thou wouldst discover if thou couldst, let him continue in his courses till thou know'st what they are. 179

Elb. Marry, I thank your worship for it. Thou seest, thou wicked varlet, now, what's come upon thee : thou art to continue now, thou varlet ; thou art to continue.

Escal. Where were you born, friend ?

Froth. Here in Vienna, sir.

Escal. Are you of fourscore pounds a year ? 185

Froth. Yes, an't please you, sir.

Escal. So. What trade are you of, sir ?

Pom. A tapster, a poor widow's tapster.

Escal. Your mistress' name ?

Pom. Mistress Overdone. 190

Escal. Hath she had any more than one husband ?

Pom. Nine, sir ; Overdone by the last.

Escal. Nine ! Come hither to me, Master Froth. Master Froth, I would not have you acquainted with tapsters : they will draw you, Master Froth, and you will hang them. Get you gone, and let me hear no more of you. 196

Froth. I thank your worship. For mine own part, I never come into any room in a taphouse but I am drawn in. 199

Escal. Well, no more of it, Master Froth ; farewell. [*Exit Froth*] Come you hither to me, Master Tapster ; what's your name, Master Tapster ?

Pom. Pompey.

Escal. What else ?

Pom. Bum, sir. 205

Escal. Troth, and your bum is the greatest thing about you ; so that, in the beastliest sense, you are Pompey the Great. Pompey, you are partly a bawd, Pompey, howsoever you colour it in being a tapster. Are you not ? Come, tell me true ; it shall be the better for you. 210

Pom. Truly, sir, I am a poor fellow that would live.

Escal. How would you live, Pompey—by being a bawd ? What do you think of the trade, Pompey ? Is it a lawful trade ?

Pom. If the law would allow it, sir. 215

Escal. But the law will not allow it, Pompey ; nor it shall not be allowed in Vienna.

Pom. Does your worship mean to geld and splay all the youth of the city ?

Escal. No, Pompey. 220

Pom. Truly, sir, in my poor opinion, they will to't then. If your worship will take order for the drabs and the knaves, you need not to fear the bawds.

Escal. There is pretty orders beginning, I can tell you : it is but heading and hanging. 225

Pom. If you head and hang all that offend that way but for ten year together, you'll be glad to give out a commission for more heads ; if this law hold in Vienna ten year, I'll rent the fairest house in it, after three-pence a bay. If you live to see this come to pass, say Pompey told you so. 231

Escal. Thank you, good Pompey ; and, in requital of your prophecy, hark you : I advise you, let me not find you before me again upon any complaint whatsoever—no, not for dwelling where you do ; if I do, Pompey, I shall beat you to your tent, and prove a shrewd Cæsar to you ; in plain dealing, Pompey, I shall have you whipt. So for this time, Pompey, fare you well. 238

Pom. I thank your worship for your good counsel ; [*Aside*] but I shall follow it as the flesh and fortune shall better determine. 241

Whip me ? No, no ; let carman whip his
  jade ;

The valiant heart's not whipt out of his
  trade.   [*Exit.*

Escal. Come hither to me, Master Elbow ; come hither, Master Constable. How long have you been in this place of constable ?

Elb. Seven year and a half, sir. 247

Escal. I thought, by the readiness in the office, you had continued in it some time. You say seven years together ? 250

Elb. And a half, sir.

Escal. Alas, it hath been great pains to you ! They do you wrong to put you so oft upon't. Are there not men in your ward sufficient to serve it ? 254

Elb. Faith, sir, few of any wit in such matters ; as they are chosen, they are glad to choose me for them ; I do it for some piece of money, and go through with all.

Escal. Look you, bring me in the names of some six or seven, the most sufficient of your parish.

Elb. To your worship's house, sir ? 260

Escal. To my house. Fare you well.
[*Exit Elbow*] What's o'clock, think you ?

Just. Eleven sir.

Escal. I pray you home to dinner with me.

Just. I humbly thank you. 265

Escal. It grieves me for the death of
  Claudio ;
But there's no remedy.

Just. Lord Angelo is severe.

Escal.   It is but needful :
Mercy is not itself that oft looks so ;
Pardon is still the nurse of second woe. 270
But yet, poor Claudio ! There is no remedy.
Come, sir.   [*Exeunt.*

SCENE II. *Another room in Angelo's house.*

Enter PROVOST *and a* Servant.

Serv. He's hearing of a cause; he will
    come straight.
I'll tell him of you.
Prov.   Pray you do. [*Exit Servant*]
           I'll know
His pleasure; may be he will relent. Alas,
He hath but as offended in a dream!
All sects, all ages, smack of this vice; and he
To die for 't!

Enter ANGELO.

Ang.   Now, what's the matter,
    Provost?   7
Prov. Is 't your will Claudio shall die
    to-morrow?
Ang. Did not I tell thee yea? Hadst
    thou not order?
Why dost thou ask again?
Prov.   Lest I might be too rash;   10
Under your good correction, I have seen
When, after execution, judgment hath
Repented o'er his doom.
Ang.   Go to; let that be mine.
Do you your office, or give up your
    place,
And you shall well be spar'd.
Prov.   I crave your honour's pardon.
What shall be done, sir, with the groaning
    Juliet?   15
She's very near her hour.
Ang.   Dispose of her
To some more fitter place, and that with
    speed.

Re-enter Servant.

Serv. Here is the sister of the man con-
    demn'd
Desires access to you.
Ang.   Hath he a sister?
Prov. Ay, my good lord; a very virtuous
    maid,   20
And to be shortly of a sisterhood,
If not already.
Ang.   Well, let her be admitted.
                    [*Exit Servant.*
See you the fornicatress be remov'd;
Let her have needful but not lavish means;
There shall be order for't.

Enter LUCIO *and* ISABELLA.

Prov. [*Going*]   Save your honour! 25
Ang. Stay a little while. [*To Isabella*]
    Y'are welcome; what's your will?
Isab. I am a woeful suitor to your honour,
Please but your honour hear me.
Ang.   Well; what's your suit?
Isab. There is a vice that most I do abhor,
And most desire should meet the blow of
    justice;   30
For which I would not plead, but that I
    must;

For which I must not plead, but that I am
At war 'twixt will and will not.
Ang.   Well; the matter?
Isab. I have a brother is condemn'd to
    die;
I do beseech you, let it be his fault,   35
And not my brother.
Prov. [*Aside*] Heaven give thee moving
    graces!
Ang. Condemn the fault and not the
    actor of it!
Why, every fault 's condemn'd ere it be
    done;
Mine were the very cipher of a function,
To fine the faults whose fine stands in
    record,   40
And let go by the actor.
Isab.   O just but severe law!
I had a brother, then. Heaven keep your
    honour!
Lucio. [*To Isabella*] Give't not o'er so; to
    him again, entreat him,
Kneel down before him, hang upon his
    gown;   44
You are too cold: if you should need a pin,
You could not with more tame a tongue
    desire it.
To him, I say.
Isab. Must he needs die?
Ang.   Maiden, no remedy.
Isab. Yes; I do think that you might
    pardon him,
And neither heaven nor man grieve at the
    mercy.   50
Ang. I will not do't.
Isab.   But can you, if you would?
Ang. Look, what I will not, that I cannot
    do.
Isab. But might you do't, and do the
    world no wrong,
If so your heart were touch'd with that
    remorse
As mine is to him?
Ang.   He's sentenc'd; 'tis too late.
Lucio. [*To Isabella*] You are too cold. 56
Isab. Too late? Why, no; I, that do
    speak a word,
May call it back again. Well, believe this:
No ceremony that to great ones longs,
Not the king's crown nor the deputed
    sword,   60
The marshal's truncheon nor the judge's
    robe,
Become them with one half so good a grace
As mercy does.
If he had been as you, and you as he,
You would have slipp'd like him; but he,
    like you,   65
Would not have been so stern.
Ang.   Pray you be gone.
Isab. I would to heaven I had your
    potency,
And you were Isabel! Should it then be
    thus?

No ; I would tell what 'twere to be a judge
And what a prisoner.
   Lucio. [*To Isabella*] Ay, touch him ;
     there's the vein.   70
   Ang. Your brother is a forfeit of the law,
And you but waste your words.
   Isab.   Alas ! alas !
Why, all the souls that were were forfeit
     once ;
And He that might the vantage best have
     took   74
Found out the remedy. How would you be
If He, which is the top of judgment, should
But judge you as you are ? O, think on
     that ;   77
And mercy then will breathe within your
     lips,
Like man new made.
   Ang.   Be you content, fair maid.
It is the law, not I condemn your brother.
Were he my kinsman, brother, or my son,
It should be thus with him. He must die
     to-morrow.   82
   Isab. To-morrow ! O, that's sudden !
     Spare him, spare him.
He's not prepar'd for death. Even for our
     kitchens
We kill the fowl of season ; shall we serve
     heaven   85
With less respect than we do minister
To our gross selves ? Good, good my lord,
     bethink you.
Who is it that hath died for this offence ?
There's many have committed it.
   Lucio. [*Aside*]   Ay, well said.
   Ang. The law hath not been dead, though
     it hath slept.   90
Those many had not dar'd to do that evil
If the first that did th' edict infringe
Had answer'd for his deed. Now 'tis awake,
Takes note of what is done, and, like a
     prophet,
Looks in a glass that shows what future
     evils—   95
Either now or by remissness new conceiv'd,
And so in progress to be hatch'd and
     born—
Are now to have no successive degrees,
But here they live to end.
   Isab.   Yet show some pity.
   Ang. I show it most of all when I show
     justice ;   100
For then I pity those I do not know,
Which a dismiss'd offence would after gall,
And do him right that, answering one foul
     wrong,
Lives not to act another. Be satisfied ;   104
Your brother dies to-morrow ; be content.
   Isab. So you must be the first that gives
     this sentence,
And he that suffers. O, it is excellent
To have a giant's strength ! But it is
     tyrannous
To use it like a giant.

   Lucio. [*To Isabella*] That's well said.
   Isab. Could great men thunder   110
As Jove himself does, Jove would never be
     quiet,
For every pelting petty officer
Would use his heaven for thunder,
Nothing but thunder. Merciful Heaven,
Thou rather, with thy sharp and sulphurous
     bolt,   115
Splits the unwedgeable and gnarled oak
Than the soft myrtle. But man, proud
     man,
Dress'd in a little brief authority,
Most ignorant of what he's most assur'd,
His glassy essence, like an angry ape,   120
Plays such fantastic tricks before high
     heaven
As makes the angels weep ; who, with our
     spleens,
Would all themselves laugh mortal.
   Lucio. [*To Isabella*] O, to him, to him,
     wench ! He will relent ;   124
He's coming ; I perceive 't.
   Prov. [*Aside*] Pray heaven she win him.
   Isab. We cannot weigh our brother with
     ourself.
Great men may jest with saints : 'tis wit
     in them ;
But in the less foul profanation.
   Lucio. [*To Isabella*] Thou'rt i' th' right,
     girl ; more o' that.
   Isab. That in the captain's but a choleric
     word   130
Which in the soldier is flat blasphemy.
   Lucio. [*To Isabella*] Art avis'd o' that ?
     More on't.
   Ang. Why do you put these sayings upon
     me ?
   Isab. Because authority, though it err
     like others,
Hath yet a kind of medicine in itself
That skins the vice o' th' top. Go to your
     bosom,   136
Knock there, and ask your heart what it
     doth know
That's like my brother's fault. If it con-
     fess
A natural guiltiness such as is his,
Let it not sound a thought upon your
     tongue   140
Against my brother's life.
   Ang. [*Aside*]   She speaks, and 'tis
Such sense that my sense breeds with it.—
     Fare you well.
   Isab. Gentle my lord, turn back.
   Ang. I will bethink me. Come again
     to-morrow.
   Isab. Hark how I'll bribe you ; good, my
     lord, turn back.
   Ang. How, bribe me ?   146
   Isab. Ay, with such gifts that heaven shall
     share with you.
   Lucio. [*To Isabella*] You had marr'd all
     else.

Isab. Not with fond sicles of the tested
  gold,
Or stones, whose rate are either rich or
  poor
As fancy values them ; but with true
  prayers   151
That shall be up at heaven and enter
  there
Ere sun-rise, prayers from preserved souls,
From fasting maids, whose minds are
  dedicate
To nothing temporal.
 Ang. Well ; come to me to-morrow.
 Lucio. [*To Isabella*] Go to ; 'tis well ;
away.   156
 Isab. Heaven keep your honour safe!
 Ang.   [*Aside*] Amen ; for I
Am that way going to temptation
Where prayers cross.
 Isab.   At what hour to-morrow
Shall I attend your lordship ?
 Ang.   At any time 'fore noon.
 Isab. Save your honour !
    [*Exeunt all but Angelo.*
 Ang. From thee ; even from thy
  virtue !   161
What's this, what's this ? Is this her fault
  or mine ?
The tempter or the tempted, who sins
  most ?
Ha !
Not she ; nor doth she tempt ; but it is I
That, lying by the violet in the sun, 166
Do as the carrion does, not as the flow'r,
Corrupt with virtuous season. Can it be
That modesty may more betray our sense
Than woman's lightness ? Having waste
  ground enough,   170
Shall we desire to raze the sanctuary,
And pitch our evils there ? O, fie, fie, fie !
What dost thou, or what art thou, Angelo ?
Dost thou desire her foully for those
  things
That make her good ? O, let her brother
  live !   175
Thieves for their robbery have authority
When judges steal themselves. What, do I
  love her,
That I desire to hear her speak again,
And feast upon her eyes ? What is't I
  dream on ?
O cunning enemy, that, to catch a saint, 180
With saints dost bait thy hook ! Most
  dangerous
Is that temptation that doth goad us on
To sin in loving virtue. Never could the
  strumpet,
With all her double vigour, art and
  nature,
Once stir my temper ; but this virtuous
  maid   185
Subdues me quite. Ever till now,
When men were fond, I smil'd and wond'red
    [*Exit.*

SCENE III. *A prison.*

Enter, severally, DUKE, *disguised as a Friar,
and* PROVOST.

 Duke. Hail to you, Provost ! so I think
  you are.
 Prov. I am the Provost. What's your
  will, good friar ?
 Duke. Bound by my charity and my
  blest order,
I come to visit the afflicted spirits
Here in the prison. Do me the common
  right   5
To let me see them, and to make me know
The nature of their crimes, that I may
  minister
To them accordingly.
 Prov. I would do more than that, if more
  were needful.

    Enter JULIET.

Look, here comes one ; a gentlewoman of
  mine,   10
Who, falling in the flaws of her own youth,
Hath blister'd her report. She is with
  child ;
And he that got it, sentenc'd—a young
  man
More fit to do another such offence
Than die for this.   15
 Duke. When must he die ?
 Prov. As I do think, to-morrow.
[*To Juliet*] I have provided for you ; stay
  awhile
And you shall be conducted.
 Duke. Repent you, fair one, of the sin
  you carry ?
 Juliet. I do ; and bear the shame most
  patiently.   20
 Duke. I'll teach you how you shall
  arraign your conscience,
And try your penitence, if it be sound
Or hollowly put on.
 Juliet. I'll gladly learn.
 Duke. Love you the man that wrong'd
  you ?
 Juliet. Yes, as I love the woman that
  wrong'd him.   25
 Duke. So then, it seems, your most
  offenceful act
Was mutually committed.
 Juliet. Mutually.
 Duke. Then was your sin of heavier kind
  than his.
 Juliet. I do confess it, and repent it,
  father.
 Duke. 'Tis meet so, daughter ; but lest
  you do repent   30
As that the sin hath brought you to this
  shame,
Which sorrow is always toward ourselves,
  not heaven,
Showing we would not spare heaven as we
  love it,

But as we stand in fear—
  Juliet. I do repent me as it is an evil, 35
And take the shame with joy.
  Duke.   There rest.
Your partner, as I hear, must die to-
    morrow,
And I am going with instruction to him.
Grace go with you! Benedicite!   [*Exit.*
  Juliet. Must die to-morrow! O, in-
    jurious law,
That respites me a life whose very comfort 40
Is still a dying horror!
  Prov.   'Tis pity of him. [*Exeunt.*

SCENE IV. *Angelo's house.*

Enter ANGELO.

  Ang. When I would pray and think, I
    think and pray
To several subjects.   Heaven hath my
    empty words,
Whilst my invention, hearing not my
    tongue,
Anchors on Isabel.   Heaven in my mouth,
As if I did but only chew his name,   5
And in my heart the strong and swelling
    evil
Of my conception.   The state whereon I
    studied
Is, like a good thing being often read,
Grown sere and tedious; yea, my
    gravity,
Where n—let no man hear me—I take
    pride,   10
Could I with boot change for an idle plume
Which the air beats for vain. O place, O
    form,
How often dost thou with thy case, thy
    habit,
Wrench awe from fools, and tie the wiser
    souls
To thy false seeming! Blood, thou art
    blood.   15
Let's write 'good angel' on the devil's horn;
'Tis not the devil's crest.

Enter Servant.

          How now, who's there?
  Serv. One Isabel, a sister, desires access
    to you.
  Ang. Teach her the way. [*Exit Servant*]
    O heavens!
Why does my blood thus muster to my
    heart,   20
Making both it unable for itself
And dispossessing all my other parts
Of necessary fitness?
So play the foolish throngs with one that
    swoons;
Come all to help him, and so stop the air 25
By which he should revive; and even so
The general subject to a well-wish'd king
Quit their own part, and in obsequious
    fondness

Crowd to his presence, where their untaught
    love
Must needs appear offence.

Enter ISABELLA.

          How now, fair maid?   30
  Isab. I am come to know your pleasure.
  Ang. That you might know it would
    much better please me
Than to demand what 'tis. Your brother
    cannot live.
  Isab. Even so! Heaven keep your
    honour!
  Ang. Yet may he live awhile, and, it may
    be,   35
As long as you or I; yet he must die.
  Isab. Under your sentence?
  Ang. Yea.
  Isab. When? I beseech you; that in his
    reprieve,
Longer or shorter, he may be so fitted   40
That his soul sicken not.
  Ang. Ha! Fie, these filthy vices! It
    were as good
To pardon him that hath from nature stol'n
A man already made, as to remit
Their saucy sweetness that do coin heaven's
    image
In stamps that are forbid; 'tis all as easy 45
Falsely to take away a life true made
As to put metal in restrained means
To make a false one.
  Isab. 'Tis set down so in heaven, but not
    in earth.   50
  Ang. Say you so? Then I shall pose you
    quickly.
Which had you rather—that the most just
    law
Now took your brother's life; or, to redeem
    him,
Give up your body to such sweet unclean-
    ness
As she that he hath stain'd?
  Isab.   Sir, believe this: 55
I had rather give my body than my soul.
  Ang. I talk not of your soul; our com-
    pell'd sins
Stand more for number than for accompt.
  Isab.   How say you?
  Ang. Nay, I'll not warrant that; for I
    can speak
Against the thing I say. Answer to this:
I, now the voice of the recorded law,   61
Pronounce a sentence on your brother's
    life;
Might there not be a charity in sin
To save this brother's life?
  Isab.   Please you to do't,
I'll take it as a peril to my soul   65
It is no sin at all, but charity.
  Ang. Pleas'd you to do't at peril of your
    soul,
Were equal poise of sin and charity.
  Isab. That I do beg his life, if it be sin,

Heaven let me bear it ! You granting of my
    suit,   70
If that be sin, I'll make it my morn prayer
To have it added to the faults of mine,
And nothing of your answer.
    Ang.   Nay, but hear me ;
Your sense pursues not mine ; either you
    are ignorant
Or seem so, craftily ; and that's not good.
    Isab. Let me be ignorant, and in nothing
    good   76
But graciously to know I am no better.
    Ang. Thus wisdom wishes to appear most
    bright
When it doth tax itself ; as these black
    masks
Proclaim an enshielded beauty ten times
    louder   80
Than beauty could, display'd. But mark
    me :
To be received plain, I'll speak more
    gross—
Your brother is to die.
    Isab. So.   84
    Ang. And his offence is so, as it appears,
Accountant to the law upon that pain.
    Isab. True.
    Ang. Admit no other way to save his life,
As I subscribe not that, nor any other,
But, in the loss of question, that you, his
    sister,   90
Finding yourself desir'd of such a person
Whose credit with the judge, or own great
    place,
Could fetch your brother from the manacles
Of the all-binding law ; and that there were
No earthly mean to save him but that either
You must lay down the treasures of your
    body   96
To this supposed, or else to let him suffer—
What would you do ?
    Isab. As much for my poor brother as
    myself ;
That is, were I under the terms of death,
Th' impression of keen whips I'd wear as
    rubies,   101
And strip myself to death as to a bed
That longing have been sick for, ere I'd
    yield
My body up to shame.
    Ang.   Then must your brother die.
    Isab. And 'twere the cheaper way : 105
Better it were a brother died at once
Than that a sister, by redeeming him,
Should die for ever.
    Ang. Were not you, then, as cruel as the
    sentence
That you have slander'd so ?   110
    Isab. Ignominy in ransom and free
    pardon
Are of two houses : lawful mercy
Is nothing kin to foul redemption.
    Ang. You seem'd of late to make the law
    a tyrant ;

And rather prov'd the sliding of your
    brother   115
A merriment than a vice.
    Isab. O, pardon me, my lord ! It oft falls
    out,
To have what we would have, we speak not
    what we mean :
I something do excuse the thing I hate
For his advantage that I dearly love. 120
    Ang. We are all frail.
    Isab.   Else let my brother die,
If not a fedary but only he
Owe and succeed thy weakness.
    Ang. Nay, women are frail too.
    Isab. Ay, as the glasses where they view
    themselves,   125
Which are as easy broke as they make
    forms.
Women, help heaven ! Men their creation
    mar
In profiting by them. Nay, call us ten
    times frail ;
For we are soft as our complexions are,
And credulous to false prints.
    Ang.   I think it well ; 130
And from this testimony of your own
    sex,
Since I suppose we are made to be no
    stronger
Than faults may shake our frames, let me
    be bold.
I do arrest your words. Be that you are,
That is, a woman ; if you be more, you're
    none ;   135
If you be one, as you are well express'd
By all external warrants, show it now
By putting on the destin'd livery.
    Isab. I have no tongue but one ; gentle,
    my lord,
Let me intreat you speak the former
    language.   140
    Ang. Plainly conceive, I love you.
    Isab. My brother did love Juliet,
And you tell me that he shall die for't.
    Ang. He shall not, Isabel, if you give me
    love.
    Isab. I know your virtue hath a license
    in't,   145
Which seems a little fouler than it is,
To pluck on others.
    Ang.   Believe me, on mine honour,
My words express my purpose.
    Isab. Ha ! little honour to be much
    believ'd,
And most pernicious purpose ! Seeming,
    seeming !   150
I will proclaim thee, Angelo, look for't.
Sign me a present pardon for my brother
Or, with an outstretch'd throat, I'll tell the
    world aloud
What man thou art.
    Ang.   Who will believe thee, Isabel ?
My unsoil'd name, th' austereness of my
    life,   155

My vouch against you, and my place i' th'
    state,
Will so your accusation overweigh
That you shall stifle in your own report,
And smell of calumny. I have begun,
And now I give my sensual race the rein :
Fit thy consent to my sharp appetite ;   161
Lay by all nicety and prolixious blushes
That banish what they sue for ; redeem thy
    brother
By yielding up thy body to my will ;
Or else he must not only die the death,   165
But thy unkindness shall his death draw
    out
To ling'ring sufferance. Answer me to-
    morrow,
Or, by the affection that now guides me
    most,
I'll prove a tyrant to him. As for you,
Say what you can : my false o'erweighs
    your true.   [*Exit.*

   Isab. To whom should I complain ? Did
    I tell this,   171
Who would believe me ?   O perilous
    mouths
That bear in them one and the self-same
    tongue
Either of condemnation or approof,
Bidding the law make curtsy to their will ;
Hooking both right and wrong to th'
    appetite,   176
To follow as it draws ! I'll to my brother.
Though he hath fall'n by prompture of the
    blood,
Yet hath he in him such a mind of honour
That, had he twenty heads to tender down
On twenty bloody blocks, he'd yield them
    up   181
Before his sister should her body stoop
To such abhorr'd pollution.
Then, Isabel, live chaste, and, brother, die :
More than our brother is our chastity.   185
I'll tell him yet of Angelo's request,
And fit his mind to death, for his soul's rest.
                            [*Exit.*

ACT THREE.

SCENE I. *The prison.*

Enter DUKE, *disguised as before,* CLAUDIO,
    and PROVOST.

   Duke. So, then you hope of pardon from
    Lord Angelo ?
   Claud. The miserable have no other
    medicine
But only hope :
I have hope to live, and am prepar'd to die.
   Duke. Be absolute for death ; either
    death or life
Shall thereby be the sweeter. Reason thus   5
    with life.
If I do lose thee, I do lose a thing
That none but fools would keep. A breath
    thou art,

Servile to all the skyey influences,
That dost this habitation where thou
    keep'st   10
Hourly afflict. Merely, thou art Death's
    fool ;
For him thou labour'st by thy flight to
    shun
And yet run'st toward him still. Thou art
    not noble ;
For all th' accommodations that thou
    bear'st
Are nurs'd by baseness. Thou 'rt by no
    means valiant ;   15
For thou dost fear the soft and tender fork
Of a poor worm. Thy best of rest is sleep,
And that thou oft provok'st ; yet grossly
    fear'st
Thy death, which is no more. Thou art
    not thyself ;
For thou exists on many a thousand
    grains   20
That issue out of dust. Happy thou art
    not ;
For what thou hast not, still thou striv'st
    to get,
And what thou hast, forget'st. Thou art
    not certain ;
For thy complexion shifts to strange effects,
After the moon. If thou art rich, thou'rt
    poor ;   25
For, like an ass whose back with ingots
    bows,
Thou bear'st thy heavy riches but a
    journey,
And Death unloads thee. Friend hast thou
    none ;
For thine own bowels which do call thee
    sire,
The mere effusion of thy proper loins,   30
Do curse the gout, serpigo, and the rheum,
For ending thee no sooner. Thou hast nor
    youth nor age,
But, as it were, an after-dinner's sleep,
Dreaming on both ; for all thy blessed
    youth
Becomes as aged, and doth beg the alms   35
Of palsied eld ; and when thou art old and
    rich,
Thou hast neither heat, affection, limb, nor
    beauty,
To make thy riches pleasant. What's yet
    in this
That bears the name of life ? Yet in this life
Lie hid moe thousand deaths ; yet death
    we fear,   40
That makes these odds all even.
   Claud.   I humbly thank you.
To sue to live, I find I seek to die ;
And, seeking death, find life. Let it come
    on.
   Isab. [*Within*] What, ho ! Peace here ;
    grace and good company !
   Prov. Who's there ? Come in ; the wish
    deserves a welcome.   45

Duke. Dear sir, ere long I'll visit you
again.

Claud. Most holy sir, I thank you.

Enter ISABELLA.

Isab. My business is a word or two with
Claudio.

Prov. And very welcome. Look, signior,
here's your sister.   50

Duke. Provost, a word with you.

Prov. As many as you please.

Duke. Bring me to hear them speak,
where I may be conceal'd.

[*Exeunt Duke and Provost.*

Claud. Now, sister, what's the comfort?

Isab. Why,   56
As all comforts are; most good, most
good, indeed.
Lord Angelo, having affairs to heaven,
Intends you for his swift ambassador,
Where you shall be an everlasting leiger. 60
Therefore, your best appointment make
with speed;
To-morrow you set on.

Claud.   Is there no remedy?

Isab. None, but such remedy as, to save
a head,
To cleave a heart in twain.

Claud.   But is there any?

Isab. Yes, brother, you may live: 65
There is a devilish mercy in the judge,
If you'll implore it, that will free your
life,
But fetter you till death.

Claud.   Perpetual durance?

Isab. Ay, just; perpetual durance, a
restraint,   69
Though all the world's vastidity you had,
To a determin'd scope.

Claud.   But in what nature?

Isab. In such a one as, you consenting
to't,
Would bark your honour from that trunk
you bear,
And leave you naked.

Claud.   Let me know the point.

Isab. O, I do fear thee, Claudio; and I
quake,   75
Lest thou a feverous life shouldst entertain,
And six or seven winters more respect
Than a perpetual honour. Dar'st thou die?
The sense of death is most in apprehension;
And the poor beetle that we tread upon 80
In corporal sufferance finds a pang as great
As when a giant dies.

Claud.   Why give you me this shame?
Think you I can a resolution fetch
From flow'ry tenderness? If I must die,
I will encounter darkness as a bride   85
And hug it in mine arms.

Isab. There spake my brother; there
my father's grave
Did utter forth a voice. Yes, thou must die:
Thou art too noble to conserve a life

In base appliances. This outward-sainted
deputy,   90
Whose settled visage and deliberate word
Nips youth i' th' head, and follies doth
enew
As falcon doth the fowl, is yet a devil;
His filth within being cast, he would appear
A pond as deep as hell.

Claud.   The precise Angelo!

Isab. O, 'tis the cunning livery of hell 96
The damned'st body to invest and cover
In prenz: guards! Dost thou think,
Claudio,
If I would yield him my virginity
Thou mightst be freed?

Claud.   O heavens! it cannot be.

Isab. Yes, he would give't thee, from this
rank offence,   101
So to offend him still. This night's the time
That I should do what I abhor to name,
Or else thou diest to-morrow.

Claud.   Thou shalt not do't.

Isab. O, were it but my life!   105
I'd throw it down for your deliverance
As frankly as a pin.

Claud.   Thanks, dear Isabel.

Isab. Be ready, Claudio, for your death
to-morrow.

Claud. Yes. Has he affections in him
That thus can make him bite the law by th'
nose   110
When he would force it? Sure it is no sin;
Or of the deadly seven it is the least.

Isab. Which is the least?

Claud. If it were damnable, he being so
wise,
Why would he for the momentary trick 115
Be perdurably fin'd?—O Isabel!

Isab. What says my brother?

Claud.   Death is a fearful thing.

Isab. And shamed life a hateful.

Claud. Ay, but to die, and go we know
not where;
To lie in cold obstruction, and to rot;   120
This sensible warm motion to become
A kneaded clod; and the delighted spirit
To bathe in fiery floods or to reside
In thrilling region of thick-ribbed ice;
To be imprison'd in the viewless winds, 125
And blown with restless violence round
about
The pendent world; or to be worse than
worst
Of those that lawless and incertain thought
Imagine howling—'tis too horrible.   129
The weariest and most loathed worldly life
That age, ache, penury, and imprisonment,
Can lay on nature is a paradise
To what we fear of death.

Isab. Alas, alas!

Claud.   Sweet sister, let me live.
What sin you do to save a brother's life,
Nature dispenses with the deed so far   136
That it becomes a virtue.

Isab.   O you beast!
O faithless coward! O dishonest wretch!
Wilt thou be made a man out of my vice?
Is't not a kind of incest to take life   140
From thine own sister's shame? What
        should I think?
Heaven shield my mother play'd my father
        fair!
For such a warped slip of wilderness
Ne'er issu'd from his blood. Take my
        defiance;   144
Die; perish. Might but my bending down
Reprieve thee from thy fate, it should
        proceed.
I'll pray a thousand prayers for thy death,
No word to save thee.
  Claud. Nay, hear me, Isabel.
  Isab.   O fie, fie, fie!
Thy sin's not accidental, but a trade.   150
Mercy to thee would prove itself a bawd;
'Tis best that thou diest quickly.
  Claud.   O, hear me, Isabella.

Re-enter DUKE.

  Duke. Vouchsafe a word, young sister,
but one word.
  Isab. What is your will?   154
  Duke. Might you dispense with your
leisure, I would by and by have some
speech with you; the satisfaction I would
require is likewise your own benefit. 157
  Isab. I have no superfluous leisure; my
stay must be stolen out of other affairs;
but I will attend you awhile. [*Walks apart.*
  Duke. Son, I have overheard what hath
pass'd between you and your sister. Angelo
had never the purpose to corrupt her; only
he hath made an assay of her virtue to
practise his judgment with the disposition
of natures. She, having the truth of honour
in her, hath made him that gracious denial
which he is most glad to receive. I am
confessor to Angelo, and I know this to be
true; therefore prepare yourself to death.
Do not satisfy your resolution with hopes
that are fallible; to-morrow you must die;
go to your knees and made ready.   169
  Claud. Let me ask my sister pardon. I
am so out of love with life that I will sue
to be rid of it.
  Duke. Hold you there. Farewell. [*Exit
Claudio*] Provost, a word with you.

Re-enter PROVOST.

  Pro. What's your will, father?   174
  Duke. That, now you are come, you will
be gone. Leave me a while with the maid;
my mind promises with my habit no loss
shall touch her by my company.   177
  Prov. In good time.   [*Exit Provost.*
  Duke. The hand that hath made you fair
hath made you good; the goodness that is
cheap in beauty makes beauty brief in goodness; but grace, being the soul of your

complexion, shall keep the body of it ever
fair. The assault that Angelo hath made to
you, fortune hath convey'd to my understanding; and, but that frailty hath examples for his falling, I should wonder at
Angelo. How will you do to content this
substitute, and to save your brother? 186
  Isab. I am now going to resolve him; I
had rather my brother die by the law than
my son should be unlawfully born. But, O,
how much is the good Duke deceiv'd in
Angelo! If ever he return, and I can speak
to him, I will open my lips in vain, or
discover his government.   191
  Duke. That shall not be much amiss;
yet, as the matter now stands, he will avoid
your accusation: he made trial of you only.
Therefore fasten your ear on my advisings;
to the love I have in doing good a remedy
presents itself. I do make myself believe
that you may most uprighteously do a poor
wronged lady a merited benefit; redeem
your brother from the angry law; do no
stain to your own gracious person; and
much please the absent Duke, if peradventure he shall ever return to have hearing
of this business.   200
  Isab. Let me hear you speak farther; I
have spirit to do anything that appears not
foul in the truth of my spirit.
  Duke. Virtue is bold, and goodness never
fearful. Have you not heard speak of
Mariana, the sister of Frederick, the great
soldier who miscarried at sea?   205
  Isab. I have heard of the lady, and good
words went with her name.
  Duke. She should this Angelo have
married; was affianced to her by oath, and
the nuptial appointed; between which
time of the contract and limit of the
solemnity her brother Frederick was
wreck'd at sea, having in that perished
vessel the dowry of his sister. But mark
how heavily this befell to the poor gentlewoman: there she lost a noble and renowned brother, in his love toward her ever
most kind and natural; with him the
portion and sinew of her fortune, her
marriage-dowry; with both, her combinate
husband, this well-seeming Angelo.   217
  Isab. Can this be so? Did Angelo so
leave her?
  Duke. Left her in her tears, and dried not
one of them with his comfort; swallowed
his vows whole, pretending in her discoveries of dishonour; in few, bestow'd her
on her own lamentation, which she yet
wears for his sake; and he, a marble to her
tears, is washed with them, but relents not.
  Isab. What a merit were it in death to
take this poor maid from the world! What
corruption in this life that it will let this
man live! But how out of this can she
avail?   226

Duke. It is a rupture that you may easily heal ; and the cure of it not only saves your brother, but keeps you from dishonour in doing it.

Isab. Show me how, good father.   230

Duke. This forenamed maid hath yet in her the continuance of her first affection ; his unjust unkindness, that in all reason should have quenched her love, hath, like an impediment in the current, made it more violent and unruly. Go you to Angelo ; answer his requiring with a plausible obedience ; agree with his demands to the point ; only refer yourself to this advantage : first, that your stay with him may not be long ; that the time may have all shadow and silence in it ; and the place answer to convenience. This being granted in course— and now follows all : we shall advise this wronged maid to stead up your appointment, go in your place. If the encounter acknowledge itself hereafter, it may compel him to her recompense ; and here, by this, is your brother saved, your honour untainted, the poor Mariana advantaged, and the corrupt deputy scaled. The maid will I frame and make fit for his attempt. If you think well to carry this as you may, the doubleness of the benefit defends the deceit from reproof. What think you of it ?   249

Isab. The image of it gives me content already ; and I trust it will grow to a most prosperous perfection.   251

Duke. It lies much in your holding up. Haste you speedily to Angelo ; if for this night he entreat you to his bed, give him promise of satisfaction. I will presently to Saint Luke's ; there, at the moated grange, resides this dejected Mariana. At that place call upon me ; and dispatch with Angelo, that it may be quickly.   257

Isab. I thank you for this comfort. Fare you well, good father.   [*Exeunt severally.*

SCENE II. *The street before the prison.*

Enter, on one side, DUKE *disguised as before ; on the other,* ELBOW, *and* Officers *with* POMPEY.

Elb. Nay, if there be no remedy for it, but that you will needs buy and sell men and women like beasts, we shall have all the world drink brown and white bastard.

Duke. O heavens ! what stuff is here ?   4

Pom. 'Twas never merry world since, of two usuries, the merriest was put down, and the worser allow'd by order of law a furr'd gown to keep him warm ; and furr'd with fox on lamb-skins too, to signify that craft, being richer than innocency, stands for the facing.   9

Elb. Come your way, sir. Bless you, good father friar.

Duke. And you, good brother father.

What offence hath this man made you, sir ?

Elb. Marry, sir, he hath offended the law ; and, sir, we take him to be a thief too, sir, for we have found upon him, sir, a strange picklock, which we have sent to the deputy.   15

Duke. Fie, sirrah, a bawd, a wicked bawd !
The evil that thou causest to be done,
That is thy means to live. Do thou but think
What 'tis to cram a maw or clothe a back   20
From such a filthy vice ; say to thyself
' From their abominable and beastly touches
I drink, I eat, array myself, and live '.
Canst thou believe thy living is a life,
So stinkingly depending ? Go mend, go mend.   24

Pom. Indeed, it does stink in some sort, sir ; but yet, sir, I would prove—

Duke. Nay, if the devil have given thee proofs for sin,
Thou wilt prove his. Take him to prison, officer ;
Correction and instruction must both work
Ere this rude beast will profit.   30

Elb. He must before the deputy, sir ; he has given him warning. The deputy cannot abide a whoremaster ; if he be a whoremonger, and comes before him, he were as good go a mile on his errand.

Duke. That we were all, as some would seem to be,   35
From our faults, as his faults from seeming, free.

Elb. His neck will come to your waist—a cord, sir.

Enter LUCIO.

Pom. I spy comfort ; I cry bail. Here's a gentleman, and a friend of mine.   39

Lucio. How now, noble Pompey ! What, at the wheels of Cæsar ? Art thou led in triumph ? What, is there none of Pygmalion's images, newly made woman, to be had now for putting the hand in the pocket and extracting it clutch'd ? What reply, ha ? What say'st thou to this tune, matter, and method ? Is't not drown'd i' th' last rain, ha ? What say'st thou, trot ? Is the world as it was, man ? Which is the way ? Is it sad, and few words ? or how ? The trick of it ?   48

Duke. Still thus, and thus ; still worse !

Lucio. How doth my dear morsel, thy mistress ? Procures she still, ha ?   51

Pom. Troth, sir, she hath eaten up all her beef, and she is herself in the tub.

Lucio. Why, 'tis good ; it is the right of it ; it must be so ; ever your fresh whore and your powder'd bawd—an unshunn'd consequence ; it must be so. Art going to prison, Pompey ?   57

Pom. Yes, faith, sir.

Lucio. Why, 'tis not amiss, Pompey. Farewell; go, say I sent thee thither. For debt, Pompey—or how? 60

Elb. For being a bawd, for being a bawd.

Lucio. Well, then, imprison him. If imprisonment be the due of a bawd, why, 'tis his right. Bawd is he doubtless, and of antiquity, too; bawd-born. Farewell, good Pompey. Commend me to the prison, Pompey. You will turn good husband now, Pompey; you will keep the house. 66

Pom. I hope, sir, your good worship will be my bail.

Lucio. No, indeed, will I not, Pompey; it is not the wear. I will pray, Pompey, to increase your bondage. If you take it not patiently, why, your mettle is the more. Adieu, trusty Pompey. Bless you, friar.

Duke. And you. 72

Lucio. Does Bridget paint still, Pompey, ha?

Elb. Come your ways, sir; come.

Pom. You will not bail me then, sir? 75

Lucio. Then, Pompey, nor now. What news abroad, friar? what news?

Elb. Come your ways, sir; come.

Lucio. Go to kennel, Pompey, go.

[*Exeunt Elbow, Pompey and Officers.*
What news, friar, of the Duke? 80

Duke. I know none. Can you tell me of any?

Lucio. Some say he is with the Emperor of Russia; other some, he is in Rome; but where is he, think you?

Duke. I know not where; but wheresoever, I wish him well. 85

Lucio. It was a mad fantastical trick of him to steal from the state and usurp the beggary he was never born to. Lord Angelo dukes it well in his absence; he puts transgression to't.

Duke. He does well in't. 90

Lucio. A little more lenity to lechery would do no harm in him. Something too crabbed that way, friar.

Duke. It is too general a vice, and severity must cure it. 93

Lucio. Yes, in good sooth, the vice is of a great kindred; it is well allied; but it is impossible to extirp it quite, friar, till eating and drinking be put down. They say this Angelo was not made by man and woman after this downright way of creation. Is it true, think you?

Duke. How should he be made, then? 99

Lucio. Some report a sea-maid spawn'd him; some, that he was begot between two stock-fishes. But it is certain that when he makes water his urine is congeal'd ice; that I know to be true. And he is a motion generative; that's infallible. 104

Duke. You are pleasant, sir, and speak apace.

Lucio. Why, what a ruthless thing is this in him, for the rebellion of a codpiece to take away the life of a man! Would the Duke that is absent have done this? Ere he would have hang'd a man for the getting a hundred bastards, he would have paid for the nursing a thousand. He had some feeling of the sport; he knew the service, and that instructed him to mercy. 112

Duke. I never heard the absent Duke much detected for women; he was not inclin'd that way.

Lucio. O, sir, you are deceiv'd. 115

Duke. 'Tis not possible.

Lucio. Who—not the Duke? Yes, your beggar of fifty; and his use was to put a ducat in her clack-dish. The Duke had crotchets in him. He would be drunk too; that let me inform you. 120

Duke. You do him wrong, surely.

Lucio. Sir, I was an inward of his. A shy fellow was the Duke; and I believe I know the cause of his withdrawing.

Duke. What, I prithee, might be the cause? 125

Lucio. No, pardon; 'tis a secret must be lock'd within the teeth and the lips; but this I can let you understand: the greater file of the subject held the Duke to be wise.

Duke. Wise? Why, no question but he was.

Lucio. A very superficial, ignorant, unweighing fellow. 130

Duke. Either this is envy in you, folly, or mistaking; the very stream of his life, and the business he hath helmed, must, upon a warranted need, give him a better proclamation. Let him be but testimonied in his own bringings-forth, and he shall appear to the envious a scholar, a statesman, and a soldier. Therefore you speak unskilfully; or, if your knowledge be more, it is much dark'ned in your malice. 138

Lucio. Sir, I know him, and I love him.

Duke. Love talks with better knowledge, and knowledge with dearer love. 141

Lucio. Come, sir, I know what I know.

Duke. I can hardly believe that, since you know not what you speak. But, if ever the Duke return, as our prayers are he may, let me desire you to make your answer before him. If it be honest you have spoke, you have courage to maintain it; I am bound to call upon you; and I pray you your name?

Lucio. Sir, my name is Lucio, well known to the Duke. 150

Duke. He shall know you better, sir, if I may live to report you.

Lucio. I fear you not.

Duke. O, you hope the Duke will return no more; or you imagine me too unhurtful an opposite. But, indeed, I can do you little harm: you'll forswear this again. 156

Lucio. I'll be hang'd first. Thou art

deceiv'd in me, friar. But no more of this.
Canst thou tell if Claudio die to-morrow or
no ?

Duke. Why should he die, sir ?   160

Lucio. Why ? For filling a bottle with a
tun-dish. I would the Duke we talk of were
return'd again. This ungenitur'd agent will
unpeople the province with continency ;
sparrows must not build in his house-eaves
because they are lecherous. The Duke yet
would have dark deeds darkly answered ;
he would never bring them to light. Would
he were return'd ! Marry, this Claudio is
condemned for untrussing. Farewell, good
friar ; I prithee pray for me. The Duke,
I say to thee again, would eat mutton on
Fridays. He's not past it yet ; and, I say
to thee, he would mouth with a beggar
though she smelt brown bread and garlic.
Say that I said so. Farewell.   [*Exit.*

Duke. No might nor greatness in mortality
Can censure scape ; back-wounding calumny
The whitest virtue strikes. What king so
strong   175
Can tie the gall up in the slanderous
tongue ?
But who comes here ?   177

Enter ESCALUS, PROVOST, *and* OFFICERS
with MISTRESS OVERDONE.

Escal. Go, away with her to prison.

Mrs. Ov. Good my lord, be good to me ;
your honour is accounted a merciful man ;
good my lord.   180

Escal. Double and treble admonition, and
still forfeit in the same kind ! This would
make mercy swear and play the tyrant.

Prov. A bawd of eleven years' continuance, may it please your honour.   185

Mrs. Ov. My lord, this is one Lucio's
information against me. Mistress Kate
Keepdown was with child by him in the
Duke's time ; he promis'd her marriage.
His child is a year and a quarter old come
Philip and Jacob ; I have kept it myself ;
and see how he goes about to abuse me.   191

Escal. That fellow is a fellow of much
license. Let him be call'd before us. Away
with her to prison. Go to ; no more words.
[*Exeunt Officers with Mistress Overdone*]
Provost, my brother Angelo will not be
alter'd : Claudio must die to-morrow. Let
him be furnish'd with divines, and have all
charitable preparation. If my brother
wrought by my pity, it should not be so
with him.   198

Prov. So please you, this friar hath been
with him, and advis'd him for th' entertainment of death.   200

Escal. Good even, good father.

Duke. Bliss and goodness on you !

Escal. Of whence are you ?

Duke. Not of this country, though my
chance is now
To use it for my time. I am a brother   205
Of gracious order, late come from the See
In special business from his Holiness.

Escal. What news abroad i' th' world ?

Duke. None, but that there is so great a
fever on goodness that the dissolution of
it must cure it. Novelty is only in request ;
and, as it is, as dangerous to be aged in any
kind of course as it is virtuous to be constant in any undertaking. There is scarce
truth enough alive to make societies secure ;
but security enough to make fellowships
accurst. Much upon this riddle runs the
wisdom of the world. This news is old
enough, yet it is every day's news. I pray
you, sir, of what disposition was the Duke ?

Escal. One that, above all other strifes,
contended especially to know himself.   219

Duke. What pleasure was he given to ?

Escal. Rather rejoicing to see another
merry than merry at anything which profess'd to make him rejoice ; a gentleman
of all temperance. But leave we him to his
events, with a prayer they may prove
prosperous ; and let me desire to know
how you find Claudio prepar'd. I am made
to understand that you have lent him
visitation.   226

Duke. He professes to have received no
sinister measure from his judge, but most
willingly humbles himself to the determination of justice. Yet had he framed to himself, by the instruction of his frailty, many
deceiving promises of life ; which I, by my
good leisure, have discredited to him, and
now is he resolv'd to die.   232

Escal. You have paid the heavens your
function, and the prisoner the very debt of
your calling. I have labour'd for the poor
gentleman to the extremest shore of my
modesty ; but my brother justice have I
found so severe that he hath forc'd me to
tell him he is indeed Justice.   237

Duke. If his own life answer the strait-
ness of his proceeding, it shall become him
well ; wherein if he chance to fail, he hath
sentenc'd himself.   240

Escal. I am going to visit the prisoner.
Fare you well.

Duke. Peace be with you !
             [*Exeunt Escalus and Provost.*
He who the sword of heaven will bear
Should be as holy as severe ;
Pattern in himself to know,   245
Grace to stand, and virtue go ;
More nor less to others paying
Than by self-offences weighing.
Shame to him whose cruel striking
Kills for faults of his own liking !   250
Twice treble shame on Angelo,
To weed my vice and let his grow !
O, what may man within him hide,

Though angel on the outward side !
How may likeness, made in crimes,   255
Make a practice on the times,
To draw with idle spiders' strings
Most ponderous and substantial things !
Craft against vice I must apply.
With Angelo to-night shall lie   260
His old betrothed but despised ;
So disguise shall, by th' disguised,
Pay with falsehood false exacting,
And perform an old contracting.   [*Exit.*

ACT FOUR

SCENE I. *The moated grange at Saint Luke's.*

Enter MARIANA ; *and* Boy *singing.*

Song

Take, O, take those lips away,
  That so sweetly were forsworn ;
And those eyes, the break of day,
  Lights that do mislead the morn ;
But my kisses bring again, bring again ; 5
Seals of love, but seal'd in vain, seal'd in
    vain.

Enter DUKE, *disguised as before.*

Mari. Break off thy song, and haste thee
    quick away ;
Here comes a man of comfort, whose advice
Hath often still'd my brawling discontent.
                              [*Exit Boy.*
I cry you mercy, sir, and well could wish
You had not found me here so musical.   11
Let me excuse me, and believe me so,
My mirth it much displeas'd, but pleas'd
    my woe.
Duke. 'Tis good ; though music oft hath
    such a charm
To make bad good and good provoke to
    harm.   15
I pray you tell me hath anybody inquir'd
for me here to-day. Much upon this time
have I promis'd here to meet.
Mari. You have not been inquir'd after ;
I have sat here all day.   19

Enter ISABELLA.

Duke. I do constantly believe you. The
time is come even now. I shall crave your
forbearance a little. May be I will call
upon you anon, for some advantage to
yourself.
Mari. I am always bound to you. [*Exit.*
Duke. Very well met, and well come. 24
What is the news from this good deputy ?
Isab. He hath a garden circummur'd
with brick,
Whose western side is with a vineyard
    back'd ;
And to that vineyard is a planched gate
That makes his opening with this bigger
    key ;

This other doth command a little door   30
Which from the vineyard to the garden
    leads.
There have I made my promise
Upon the heavy middle of the night
To call upon him.
  Duke. But shall you on your knowledge
    find this way ?   35
  Isab. I have ta'en a due and wary note
    upon't ;
With whispering and most guilty diligence,
In action all of precept, he did show me
The way twice o'er.
  Duke.   Are there no other tokens
Between you 'greed concerning her observ-
    ance ?   40
  Isab. No, none, but only a repair i' th'
    dark ;
And that I have possess'd him my most stay
Can be but brief ; for I have made him
    know
I have a servant comes with me along,   44
That stays upon me ; whose persuasion is
I come about my brother.
  Duke.   'Tis well borne up.
I have not yet made known to Mariana
A word of this. What ho, within ! come
    forth.

Re-enter MARIANA.

I pray you be acquainted with this maid ;
She comes to do you good.
  Isab.   I do desire the like.
  Duke. Do you persuade yourself that I
    respect you ?   51
  Mari. Good friar, I know you do, and
    have found it.
  Duke. Take, then, this your companion
    by the hand,
Who hath a story ready for your ear.   54
I shall attend your leisure ; but make haste ;
The vaporous night approaches.
  Mari. Will't please you walk aside ?
                  [*Exeunt Mariana and Isabella.*
  Duke. O place and greatness ! Millions
    of false eyes
Are stuck upon thee. Volumes of report
Run with these false, and most contrarious
    quest   60
Upon thy doings. Thousand escapes of wit
Make thee the father of their idle dream,
And rack thee in their fancies.

Re-enter MARIANA *and* ISABELLA.

                      Welcome, how agreed ?
  Isab. She'll take the enterprise upon her,
    father,
If you advise it.
  Duke.   It is not my consent,   65
But my entreaty too.
  Isab.   Little have you to say,
When you depart from him, but, soft and
    low,
' Remember now my brother '.

Mari.   Fear me not.
Duke. Nor, gentle daughter, fear you not
        at all.
He is your husband on a pre-contract. 70
To bring you thus together 'tis no sin,
Sith that the justice of your title to him
Doth flourish the deceit. Come, let us go ;
Our corn's to reap, for yet our tithe's to sow.
                                        [*Exeunt.*

SCENE II. *The prison.*

Enter PROVOST *and* POMPEY.

Prov. Come hither, sirrah. Can you cut
off a man's head ?
Pom. If the man be a bachelor, sir, I can ;
but if he be a married man, he's his wife's
head, and I can never cut off a woman's
head.   4
Prov. Come, sir, leave me your snatches
and yield me a direct answer. To-morrow
morning are to die Claudio and Barnardine.
Here is in our prison a common executioner,
who in his office lacks a helper ; if you will
take it on you to assist him, it shall redeem
you from your gyves ; if not, you shall have
your full time of imprisonment, and your
deliverance with an unpitied whipping, for
you have been a notorious bawd.   12
Pom. Sir, I have been an unlawful bawd
time out of mind ; but yet I will be content
to be a lawful hangman. I would be glad
to receive some instruction from my fellow
partner.   16
Prov. What ho, Abhorson ! Where's
Abhorson there ?

Enter ABHORSON.

Abhor. Do you call, sir ?
Prov. Sirrah, here's a fellow will help you
to-morrow in your execution. If you think
it meet, compound with him by the year,
and let him abide here with you ; if not,
use him for the present, and dismiss him.
He cannot plead his estimation with you ;
he hath been a bawd.
Abhor. A bawd, sir ? Fie upon him ! He
will discredit our mystery.   25
Prov. Go to, sir ; you weigh equally ; a
feather will turn the scale.   [*Exit.*
Pom. Pray, sir, by your good favour—
for surely, sir, a good favour you have but
that you have a hanging look—do you call,
sir, your occupation a mystery ?   30
Abhor. Ay, sir ; a mystery.
Pom. Painting, sir, I have heard say, is a
mystery ; and your whores, sir, being
members of my occupation, using painting,
do prove my occupation a mystery ; but
what mystery there should be in hanging,
if I should be hang'd, I cannot imagine. 36
Abhor. Sir, it is a mystery.
Pom. Proof ?
Abhor. Every true man's apparel fits
your thief : if it be too little for your thief,

your true man thinks it big enough ; if it
be too big for your thief, your thief thinks
it little enough ; so every true man's
apparel fits your thief.   42

Re-enter PROVOST.

Prov. Are you agreed ?
Pom. Sir, I will serve him ; for I do find
your hangman is a more penitent trade than
your bawd ; he doth oftener ask forgiveness.   46
Prov. You, sirrah, provide your block and
your axe to-morrow four o'clock.
Abhor. Come on, bawd ; I will instruct
thee in my trade ; follow.   50
Pom. I do desire to learn, sir ; and I hope,
if you have occasion to use me for your own
turn, you shall find me yare ; for truly, sir,
for your kindness I owe you a good turn. 54
Prov. Call hither Barnardine and Claudio.
                [*Exeunt Abhorson and Pompey.*
Th' one has my pity ; not a jot the other,
Being a murderer, though he were my
        brother.   57

Enter CLAUDIO.

Look, here's the warrant, Claudio, for thy
        death :
'Tis now dead midnight, and by eight to-
        morrow
Thou must be made immortal. Where's
        Barnardine ?   60
Claud. As fast lock'd up in sleep as
        guiltless labour
When it lies starkly in the traveller's bones.
He will not wake.
Prov.   Who can do good on him ?
Well, go, prepare yourself.   [*Knocking
        within*] But hark, what noise ?   64
Heaven give your spirits comfort !
                              [*Exit Claudio.*
        [*Knocking continues*] By and by.
I hope it is some pardon or reprieve
For the most gentle Claudio.

Enter DUKE, *disguised as before.*

                    Welcome, father.
Duke. The best and wholesom'st spirits
        of the night
Envelop you, good Provost ! Who call'd
        here of late ?
Prov. None, since the curfew rung.   70
Duke. Not Isabel ?
Prov. No.
Duke. They will then, ere't be long.
Prov. What comfort is for Claudio ?
Duke. There's some in hope.
Prov. It is a bitter deputy.   74
Duke. Not so, not so ; his life is parallel'd
Even with the stroke and line of his great
        justice ;
He doth with holy abstinence subdue
That in himself which he spurs on his pow'r
To qualify in others. Were he meal'd with
        that

Which he corrects, then were he tyran-
    nous ;   80
But this being so, he's just. [*Knocking
    within*] Now are they come.
                        [*Exit Provost.*
This is a gentle provost ; seldom when
The steeled gaoler is the friend of men.
                   [*Knocking within.*
How now, what noise ! That spirit's
    possess'd with haste
That wounds th' unsisting postern with
    these strokes.   85

       Re-enter PROVOST.

Prov. There he must stay until the officer
Arise to let him in ; he is call'd up.
Duke. Have you no countermand for
    Claudio yet
But he must die to-morrow ?
Prov.   None, sir, none.
Duke. As near the dawning, Provost, as
    it is,   90
You shall hear more ere morning.
Prov.   Happily
You something know ; yet I believe there
    comes
No countermand ; no such example have
    we.
Besides, upon the very siege of justice,
Lord Angelo hath to the public ear   95
Profess'd the contrary.

      Enter a Messenger.

          This is his lordship's man.
Duke. And here comes Claudio's pardon.
Mess. My lord hath sent you this note ;
and by me this further charge, that you
swerve not from the smallest article of it,
neither in time, matter, or other circum-
stance. Good morrow ; for as I take it, it
is almost day.   101
Prov. I shall obey him. [*Exit Messenger.*
Duke. [*Aside*] This is his pardon,
    purchas'd by such sin
For which the pardoner himself is in ;
Hence hath offence his quick celerity,   105
When it is borne in high authority.
When vice makes mercy, mercy's so ex-
    tended
That for the fault's love is th' offender
    friended.
Now, sir, what news ?   109
Prov. I told you : Lord Angelo, belike
thinking me remiss in mine office, awakens
me with this unwonted putting-on ; me-
thinks strangely, for he hath not us'd it
before.
Duke. Pray you, let's hear.   113
Prov. [*Reads*] ' Whatsoever you may hear
to the contrary, let Claudio be executed by
four of the clock, and, in the afternoon,
Barnardine. For my better satisfaction, let
me have Claudio's head sent me by five.
Let this be duly performed, with a thought

that more depends on it than we must yet
deliver. Thus fail not to do your office, as
you will answer it at your peril.'
What say you to this, sir ?   120
  Duke. What is that Barnardine who is to
be executed in th' afternoon ?
  Prov. A Bohemian born ; but here nurs'd
up and bred. One that is a prisoner nine
years old.   124
  Duke. How came it that the absent Duke
had not either deliver'd him to his liberty
or executed him ? I have heard it was ever
his manner to do so.   127
  Prov. His friends still wrought reprieves
for him ; and, indeed, his fact, till now in
the government of Lord Angelo, came not
to an undoubtful proof.   130
  Duke. It is now apparent ?
  Prov. Most manifest, and not denied by
himself.
  Duke. Hath he borne himself penitently
in prison ? How seems he to be touch'd ?
  Prov. A man that apprehends death no
more dreadfully but as a drunken sleep ;
careless, reckless, and fearless, of what's
past, present, or to come ; insensible of
mortality and desperately mortal.   138
  Duke. He wants advice.
  Prov. He will hear none. He hath evermore had the liberty of the prison ; give
him leave to escape hence, he would not ;
drunk many times a day, if not many days
entirely drunk. We have very oft awak'd
him, as if to carry him to execution, and
show'd him a seeming warrant for it ; it
hath not moved him at all.   145
  Duke. More of him anon. There is written
in your brow, Provost, honesty and constancy. If I read it not truly, my ancient
skill beguiles me ; but in the boldness of my
cunning I will lay myself in hazard. Claudio,
whom here you have warrant to execute, is
no greater forfeit to the law than Angelo
who hath sentenc'd him. To make you
understand this in a manifested effect, I
crave but four days' respite ; for the which
you are to do me both a present and a
dangerous courtesy.
  Prov. Pray, sir, in what ?   155
  Duke. In the delaying death.
  Prov. Alack ! How may I do it, having
the hour limited, and an express command,
under penalty, to deliver his head in the
view of Angelo ? I may make my case as
Claudio's, to cross this in the smallest. 160
  Duke. By the vow of mine order, I
warrant you, if my instructions may be
your guide. Let this Barnardine be this
morning executed, and his head borne to
Angelo.
  Prov. Angelo hath seen them both, and
will discover the favour.   165
  Duke. O, death's a great disguiser ; and

you may add to it. Shave the head and tie the beard; and say it was the desire of the penitent to be so bar'd before his death. You know the course is common. If anything fall to you upon this more than thanks and good fortune, by the saint whom I profess, I will plead against it with my life.

Prov. Pardon me, good father; it is against my oath.   172

Duke. Were you sworn to the Duke, or to the deputy?

Prov. To him and to his substitutes.

Duke. You will think you have made no offence if the Duke avouch the justice of your dealing?   176

Prov. But what likelihood is in that?

Duke. Not a resemblance, but a certainty. Yet since I see you fearful, that neither my coat, integrity, nor persuasion, can with ease attempt you, I will go further than I meant, to pluck all fears out of you. Look you, sir, here is the hand and seal of the Duke. You know the character, I doubt not; and the signet is not strange to you.

Prov. I know them both.   184

Duke. The contents of this is the return of the Duke; you shall anon over-read it at your pleasure, where you shall find within these two days he will be here. This is a thing that Angelo knows not; for he this very day receives letters of strange tenour, perchance of the Duke's death, perchance entering into some monastery; but, by chance, nothing of what is writ. Look, th' unfolding star calls up the shepherd. Put not yourself into amazement how these things should be: all difficulties are but easy when they are known. Call your executioner, and off with Barnardine's head. I will give him a present shrift, and advise him for a better place. Yet you are amaz'd, but this shall absolutely resolve you. Come away; it is almost clear dawn. [*Exeunt.*

Scene III. *The prison.*

Enter POMPEY.

Pom. I am as well acquainted here as I was in our house of profession; one would think it were Mistress Overdone's own house, for here be many of her old customers. First, here's young Master Rash; he's in for a commodity of brown paper and old ginger, nine score and seventeen pounds, of which he made five marks ready money. Marry, then ginger was not much in request, for the old women were all dead. Then is there here one Master Caper, at the suit of Master Threepile the mercer, for some four suits of peach-colour'd satin, which now peaches him a beggar. Then have we here young Dizy, and young Master Deepvow, and Master Copperspur, and Master Starvelackey, the

rapier and dagger man, and young Dropheir that kill'd lusty Pudding, and Master Forthlight the tilter, and brave Master Shootie the great traveller, and wild Halfcan that stabb'd Pots, and I think, forty more—all great doers in our trade, and are now ' for the Lord's sake '.   18

Enter ABHORSON.

Abhor. Sirrah, bring Barnardine hither.

Pom. Master Barnardine! You must rise and be hang'd, Master Barnardine!   21

Abhor. What ho, Barnardine!

Barnar. [*Within*] A pox o' your throats! Who makes that noise there? What are you?

Pom. Your friends, sir; the hangman. You must be so good, sir, to rise and be put to death.   26

Barnar. [*Within*] Away, you rogue, away; I am sleepy.

Abhor. Tell him he must awake, and that quickly too.

Pom. Pray, Master Barnardine, awake till you are executed, and sleep afterwards.   30

Abhor. Go in to him, and fetch him out.

Pom. He is coming, sir, he is coming; I hear his straw rustle.

Enter BARNARDINE.

Abhor. Is the axe upon the block, sirrah?

Pom. Very ready, sir.   35

Barnar. How now, Abhorson, what's the news with you?

Abhor. Truly, sir, I would desire you to clap into your prayers; for, look you, the warrant's come.

Barnar. You rogue, I have been drinking all night; I am not fitted for't.   40

Pom. O, the better, sir! For he that drinks all night and is hanged betimes in the morning may sleep the sounder all the next day.   43

Enter DUKE, *disguised as before.*

Abhor. Look you, sir, here comes your ghostly father. Do we jest now, think you?

Duke. Sir, induced by my charity, and hearing how hastily you are to depart, I am come to advise you, comfort you, and pray with you.   48

Barnar. Friar, not I; I have been drinking hard all night, and I will have more time to prepare me, or they shall beat out my brains with billets. I will not consent to die this day, that's certain.   52

Duke. O, sir, you must; and therefore I beseech you
Look forward on the journey you shall go.

Barnar. I swear I will not die to-day for any man's persuasion.   56

Duke. But hear you—

Barnar. Not a word; if you have any-

thing to say to me, come to my ward ; for
thence will not I to-day.   [*Exit.*
  Duke. Unfit to live or die. O gravel
    heart !   60
After him, fellows ; bring him to the block.
    [*Exeunt Abhorson and Pompey.*

        Enter PROVOST.

  Prov. Now, sir, how do you find the
    prisoner ?
  Duke. A creature unprepar'd, unmeet for
    death ;
And to transport him in the mind he is 64
Were damnable.
  Prov.   Here in the prison, father,
There died this morning of a cruel fever
One Ragozine, a most notorious pirate,
A man of Claudio's years ; his beard and
    head
Just of his colour. What if we do omit 69
This reprobate till he were well inclin'd,
And satisfy the deputy with the visage
Of Ragozine, more like to Claudio ?
  Duke. O, 'tis an accident that heaven
    provides !
Dispatch it presently ; the hour draws on
Prefix'd by Angelo. See this be done,   75
And sent according to command ; whiles I
Persuade this rude wretch willingly to die.
  Prov. This shall be done, good father,
    presently.
But Barnardine must die this afternoon ;
And how shall we continue Claudio,   80
To save me from the danger that might
    come
If he were known alive ?
  Duke.   Let this be done :
Put them in secret holds, both Barnardine
    and Claudio.
Ere twice the sun hath made his journal
    greeting
To the under generation, you shall find 85
Your safety manifested.
  Prov. I am your free dependant.
  Duke. Quick, dispatch, and send the head
    to Angelo.   [*Exit Provost.*
Now will I write letters to Angelo—
The Provost, he shall bear them—whose
    contents   90
Shall witness to him I am near at home,
And that, by great injunctions, I am bound
To enter publicly. Him I'll desire
To meet me at the consecrated fount,   94
A league below the city ; and from thence,
By cold gradation and well-balanc'd form,
We shall proceed with Angelo.

       Re-enter PROVOST.

  Prov. Here is the head ; I'll carry it
    myself.
  Duke. Convenient is it. Make a swift
    return ;
For I would commune with you of such
    things   100

That want no ear but yours.
  Prov.   I'll make all speed. [*Exit.*
  Isab. [*Within*] Peace, ho, be here !
  Duke. The tongue of Isabel. She's come
    to know
If yet her brother's pardon be come hither ;
But I will keep her ignorant of her good, 105
To make her heavenly comforts of despair
When it is least expected.

       Enter ISABELLA.

  Isab.   Ho, by your leave !
  Duke. Good morning to you, fair and
    gracious daughter.
  Isab. The better, given me by so holy a
    man.
Hath yet the deputy sent my brother's
    pardon ?   110
  Duke. He hath releas'd him, Isabel, from
    the world.
His head is off and sent to Angelo.
  Isab. Nay, but it is not so.
  Duke.   It is no other.
Show your wisdom, daughter, in your close
    patience.   115
  Isab. O, I will to him and pluck out his
    eyes !
  Duke. You shall not be admitted to his
    sight.
  Isab.   Unhappy Claudio ! Wretched
    Isabel !
Injurious world ! Most damned Angelo !
  Duke. This nor hurts him nor profits you
    a jot ;   120
Forbear it, therefore ; give your cause to
    heaven.
Mark what I say, which you shall find
By every syllable a faithful verity.
The Duke comes home to-morrow. Nay,
    dry your eyes.
One of our covent, and his confessor,   125
Gives me this instance. Already he hath
    carried
Notice to Escalus and Angelo,
Who do prepare to meet him at the
    gates,
There to give up their pow'r. If you can,
    pace your wisdom   129
In that good path that I would wish it go,
And you shall have your bosom on this
    wretch,
Grace of the Duke, revenges to your heart,
And general honour.
  Isab.   I am directed by you.
  Duke. This letter, then, to Friar Peter
    give ;   134
'Tis that he sent me of the Duke's return.
Say, by this token, I desire his company
At Mariana's house to-night. Her cause
    and yours
I'll perfect him withal ; and he shall bring
    you
Before the Duke ; and to the head of
    Angelo

Accuse him home and home. For my poor
  self,   140
I am combined by a sacred vow,
And shall be absent. Wend you with this
  letter.
Command these fretting waters from your
  eyes
With a light heart; trust not my holy
  order,
If I pervert your course. Who's here? 145

Enter Lucio.

  Lucio. Good even. Friar, where's the
Provost?
  Duke. Not within, sir.   147
  Lucio. O pretty Isabella, I am pale at
mine heart to see thine eyes so red. Thou
must be patient. I am fain to dine and sup
with water and bran; I dare not for my
head fill my belly; one fruitful meal would
set me to't. But they say the Duke will be
here to-morrow. By my troth, Isabel, I
lov'd thy brother. If the old fantastical
Duke of dark corners had been at home, he
had lived.   [*Exit Isabella.*
  Duke. Sir, the Duke is marvellous little
beholding to your reports; but the best is,
he lives not in them.   156
  Lucio. Friar, thou knowest not the Duke
so well as I do; he's a better woodman than
thou tak'st him for.
  Duke. Well, you'll answer this one day.
Fare ye well.
  Lucio. Nay, tarry; I'll go along with
thee; I can tell thee pretty tales of the
Duke.   161
  Duke. You have told me too many of him
already, sir, if they be true; if not true,
none were enough.
  Lucio. I was once before him for getting
a wench with child.   165
  Duke. Did you such a thing?
  Lucio. Yes, marry, did I; but I was fain
to forswear it: they would else have
married me to the rotten medlar.
  Duke. Sir, your company is fairer than
honest. Rest you well.   170
  Lucio. By my troth, I'll go with thee to
the lane's end. If bawdy talk offend you,
we'll have very little of it. Nay, friar, I am
a kind of burr; I shall stick.   [*Exeunt.*

SCENE IV. *Angelo's house.*

Enter ANGELO *and* ESCALUS.

  Escal. Every letter he hath writ hath
disvouch'd other.
  Ang. In most uneven and distracted
manner. His actions show much like to
madness; pray heaven his wisdom be not
tainted! And why meet him at the gates,
and redeliver our authorities there?   5
  Escal. I guess not.
  Ang. And why should we proclaim it in

an hour before his ent'ring that, if any
crave redress of injustice, they should exhibit their petitions in the street?   9
  Escal. He shows his reason for that: to
have a dispatch of complaints; and to
deliver us from devices hereafter, which
shall then have no power to stand against
us.   12
  Ang. Well, I beseech you, let it be pro-
  claim'd;
Betimes i' th' morn I'll call you at your
  house;
Give notice to such men of sort and suit
As are to meet him.   15
  Escal. I shall, sir; fare you well.
  Ang. Good night.   [*Exit Escalus.*
This deed unshapes me quite, makes me
  unpregnant
And dull to all proceedings. A deflow'red
  maid!
And by an eminent body that enforc'd 20
The law against it! But that her tender
  shame
Will not proclaim against her maiden loss,
How might she tongue me! Yet reason
  dares her no;
For my authority bears a so credent bulk 24
That no particular scandal once can touch
But it confounds the breather. He should
  have liv'd,
Save that his riotous youth, with dangerous
  sense,
Might in the times to come have ta'en
  revenge,
By so receiving a dishonour'd life
With ransom of such shame. Would yet he
  had liv'd!   30
Alack, when once our grace we have forgot,
Nothing goes right; we would, and we
  would not.   [*Exit.*

SCENE V. *Fields without the town.*

Enter DUKE *in his own habit, and* FRIAR
PETER.

  Duke. These letters at fit time deliver me.
                 [*Giving letters.*
The Provost knows our purpose and our
  plot.
The matter being afoot, keep your in-
  struction
And hold you ever to our special drift;
Though sometimes you do blench from this
  to that   5
As cause doth minister. Go, call at Flavius'
  house,
And tell him where I stay; give the like
  notice
To Valentinus, Rowland, and to Crassus,
And bid them bring the trumpets to the
  gate;   9
But send me Flavius first.
  F. Peter.   It shall be speeded well.
                     [*Exit Friar.*

Enter VARRIUS.

Duke. I thank thee, Varrius; thou hast
    made good haste.
Come, we will walk. There's other of our
    friends
Will greet us here anon. My gentle Varrius!
                                          [*Exeunt.*

SCENE VI. *A street near the city gate.*

Enter ISABELLA *and* MARIANA.

Isab. To speak so indirectly I am loath;
I would say the truth; but to accuse him so,
That is your part. Yet I am advis'd to
    do it;
He says, to veil full purpose.
    Mari.   Be rul'd by him.
    Isab. Besides, he tells me that, if perad-
    venture   5
He speak against me on the adverse side,
I should not think it strange; for 'tis a
    physic
That's bitter to sweet end.
    Mari. I would friar Peter—

Enter FRIAR PETER.

Isab.   O, peace! the friar is come.
F. Peter. Come, I have found you out a
    stand most fit,   10
Where you may have such vantage on the
    Duke
He shall not pass you. Twice have the
    trumpets sounded;
The generous and gravest citizens
Have hent the gates, and very near upon
The Duke is ent'ring; therefore, hence,
    away.   [*Exeunt.*

ACT FIVE

SCENE I. *The city gate.*

Enter at several doors DUKE, VARRIUS,
    Lords; ANGELO, ESCALUS, LUCIO,
    PROVOST, *Officers, and* Citizens.

Duke. My very worthy cousin, fairly met!
Our old and faithful friend, we are glad to
    see you.
    Ang. } Happy return be to your royal
    Escal. }   Grace!
Duke. Many and hearty thankings to you
    both.   4
We have made inquiry of you, and we hear
Such goodness of your justice that our soul
Cannot but yield you forth to public
    thanks,
Forerunning more requital.
    Ang. You make my bonds still greater.
Duke. O, your desert speaks loud; and I
    should wrong it   10
To lock it in the wards of covert bosom,
When it deserves, with characters of brass,
A forted residence 'gainst the tooth of time
And razure of oblivion. Give me your hand,

And let the subject see, to make them know
That outward courtesies would fain pro-
    claim   15
Favours that keep within. Come, Escalus,
You must walk by us on our other hand;
And good supporters are you.

Enter FRIAR PETER *and* ISABELLA.

F. Peter. Now is your time; speak loud,
    and kneel before him.
    Isab. Justice, O royal Duke! Vail your
    regard   20
Upon a wrong'd—I would fain have said
    a maid!
O worthy Prince, dishonour not your eye
By throwing it on any other object
Till you have heard me in my true com-
    plaint,
And given me justice, justice, justice,
    justice.   25
    Duke. Relate your wrongs. In what?
    By whom? Be brief.
Here is Lord Angelo shall give you justice;
Reveal yourself to him.
    Isab.   O worthy Duke,
You bid me seek redemption of the devil!
Hear me yourself; for that which I must
    speak   30
Must either punish me, not being believ'd,
Or wring redress from you. Hear me, O,
    hear me, here!
    Ang. My lord, her wits, I fear me, are not
    firm;
She hath been a suitor to me for her
    brother,   34
Cut off by course of justice.—
    Isab.   By course of justice!
    Ang. And she will speak most bitterly
    and strange.
    Isab. Most strange, but yet most truly,
    will I speak.
That Angelo's forsworn, is it not strange?
That Angelo's a murderer, is't not strange?
That Angelo is an adulterous thief,   40
An hypocrite, a virgin-violator,
Is it not strange and strange?
    Duke.   Nay, it is ten times strange.
    Isab. It is not truer he is Angelo
Than this is all as true as it is strange; 44
Nay, it is ten times true; for truth is truth
To th' end of reck'ning.
    Duke.   Away with her. Poor soul,
She speaks this in th' infirmity of sense.
    Isab. O Prince! I conjure thee, as thou
    believ'st
There is another comfort than this world,
That thou neglect me not with that opinion
That I am touch'd with madness. Make
    not impossible   51
That which but seems unlike: 'tis not
    impossible
But one, the wicked'st caitiff on the ground,
May seem as shy, as grave, as just, as
    absolute,

As Angelo; even so may Angelo,   55
In all his dressings, characts, titles, forms,
Be an arch-villain. Believe it, royal Prince,
If he be less, he's nothing; but he's
 more,
Had I more name for badness.
 Duke.   By mine honesty,
If she be mad, as I believe no other, 60
Her madness hath the oddest frame of
 sense,
Such a dependency of thing on thing,
As e'er I heard in madness.
 Isab.   O gracious Duke,
Harp not on that; nor do not banish
 reason   64
For inequality; but let your reason serve
To make the truth appear where it seems
 hid,
And hide the false seems true.
 Duke.   Many that are not mad
Have, sure, more lack of reason. What
 would you say?
 Isab. I am the sister of one Claudio,
Condemn'd upon the act of fornication 70
To lose his head; condemn'd by Angelo.
I, in probation of a sisterhood,
Was sent to by my brother; one Lucio
As then the messenger—
 Lucio.   That's I, an't like your Grace.
I came to her from Claudio, and desir'd her
To try her gracious fortune with Lord
 Angelo   76
For her poor brother's pardon.
 Isab.   That's he, indeed.
 Duke. You were not bid to speak.
 Lucio.   No, my good lord;
Nor wish'd to hold my peace.
 Duke.   I wish you now, then;
Pray you take note of it; and when you
 have   80
A business for yourself, pray heaven you
 then
Be perfect.
 Lucio. I warrant your honour.
 Duke. The warrant's for yourself; take
 heed to't.
 Isab. This gentleman told somewhat of
 my tale.
 Lucio. Right.   85
 Duke. It may be right; but you are i' the
 wrong
To speak before your time. Proceed.
 Isab.   I went
To this pernicious caitiff deputy.
 Duke. That's somewhat madly spoken.
 Isab.   Pardon it;
The phrase is to the matter.   90
 Duke. Mended again. The matter—
 proceed.
 Isab. In brief—to set the needless process
 by,
How I persuaded, how I pray'd, and
 kneel'd,
How he refell'd me, and how I replied,

For this was of much length—the vile con-
 clusion   95
I now begin with grief and shame to utter:
He would not, but by gift of my chaste
 body
To his concupiscible intemperate lust,
Release my brother; and, after much de-
 batement,   99
My sisterly remorse confutes mine honour,
And I did yield to him. But the next morn
 betimes,
His purpose surfeiting, he sends a warrant
For my poor brother's head.
 Duke.   This is most likely!
 Isab. O that it were as like as it is true!
 Duke. By heaven, fond wretch, thou
 know'st not what thou speak'st,
Or else thou art suborn'd against his honour
In hateful practice. First, his integrity 107
Stands without blemish; next, it imports
 no reason
That with such vehemency he should
 pursue
Faults proper to himself. If he had so
 offended,   110
He would have weigh'd thy brother by
 himself,
And not have cut him off. Some one hath
 set you on;
Confess the truth, and say by whose advice
Thou cam'st here to complain.
 Isab.   And is this all?
Then, O you blessed ministers above, 115
Keep me in patience; and, with ripened
 time,
Unfold the evil which is here wrapt up
In countenance! Heaven shield your Grace
 from woe,
As I, thus wrong'd, hence unbelieved go!
 Duke. I know you'd fain be gone. An
 officer!   120
To prison with her! Shall we thus permit
A blasting and a scandalous breath to fall
On him so near us? This needs must be a
 practice.
Who knew of your intent and coming
 hither?
 Isab. One that I would were here, friar
 Lodowick.   125
 Duke. A ghostly father, belike. Who
 knows that Lodowick?
 Lucio. My lord, I know him; 'tis a
 meddling friar.
I do not like the man; had he been lay,
 my lord,
For certain words he spake against your
 Grace
In your retirement, I had swing'd him
 soundly.   130
 Duke. Words against me? This 's a good
 friar, belike!
And to set on this wretched woman here
Against our substitute! Let this friar be
 found.

Lucio. But yesternight, my lord, she and
    that friar,
I saw them at the prison ; a saucy friar, 136
A very scurvy fellow.
    F. Peter. Blessed be your royal Grace !
I have stood by, my lord, and I have heard
Your royal ear abus'd. First, hath this
    woman 139
Most wrongfully accus'd your substitute ;
Who is as free from touch or soil with her
As she from one ungot.
    Duke.   We did believe no less.
Know you that friar Lodowick that she
    speaks of ?
    F. Peter. I know him for a man divine and
    holy ;
Not scurvy, nor a temporary meddler, 145
As he's reported by this gentleman ;
And, on my trust, a man that never yet
Did, as he vouches, misreport your Grace.
    Lucio. My lord, most villainously ;
    believe it.
    F. Peter. Well, he in time may come to
    clear himself ; 150
But at this instant he is sick, my lord,
Of a strange fever. Upon his mere request—
Being come to knowledge that there was
    complaint
Intended 'gainst Lord Angelo—came I
    hither
To speak, as from his mouth, what he doth
    know 155
Is true and false ; and what he, with his
    oath
And all probation, will make up full clear,
Whensoever he's convented. First, for this
    woman—
To justify this worthy nobleman,
So vulgarly and personally accus'd— 160
Her shall you hear disproved to her eyes,
Till she herself confess it.
    Duke.   Good friar, let's hear it.
                 [*Exit Isabella guarded.*
Do you not smile at this, Lord Angelo ?
O heaven, the vanity of wretched fools !
Give us some seats. Come, cousin Angelo ;
In this I'll be impartial ; be you judge 166
Of your own cause.

    Enter MARIANA *veiled.*

           Is this the witness friar ?
First let her show her face, and after speak.
    Mari. Pardon, my lord ; I will not show
    my face
Until my husband bid me. 170
    Duke. What, are you married?
    Mari. No, my lord.
    Duke. Are you a maid ?
    Mari. No, my lord.
    Duke. A widow, then ? 175
    Mari. Neither, my lord.
    Duke. Why, you are nothing then ;
neither maid, widow, nor wife.
    Lucio. My lord, she may be a punk ; for

many of them are neither maid, widow, nor
wife. 180
    Duke. Silence that fellow. I would he had
    some cause
To prattle for himself.
    Lucio. Well, my lord.
    Mari. My lord, I do confess I ne'er was
    married,
And I confess, besides, I am no maid. 185
I have known my husband ; yet my
    husband
Knows not that ever he knew me.
    Lucio. He was drunk, then, my lord ; it
can be no better.
    Duke. For the benefit of silence, would
thou wert so too !
    Lucio. Well, my lord. 190
    Duke. This is no witness for Lord Angelo.
    Mari. Now I come to't, my lord :
She that accuses him of fornication,
In self-same manner doth accuse my
    husband ; 194
And charges him, my lord, with such a time
When I'll depose I had him in mine arms,
With all th' effect of love.
    Ang. Charges she moe than me ?
    Mari.   Not that I know.
    Duke. No ? You say your husband.
    Mari. Why, just, my lord, and that is
    Angelo, 200
Who thinks he knows that he ne'er knew
    my body,
But knows he thinks that he knows Isabel's.
    Ang. This is a strange abuse. Let's see
    thy face.
    Mari. My husband bids me ; now I will
    unmask. [*Unveiling.*
This is that face, thou cruel Angelo, 205
Which once thou swor'st was worth the
    looking on ;
This is the hand which, with a vow'd
    contract,
Was fast belock'd in thine ; this is the body
That took away the match from Isabel, 209
And did supply thee at thy garden-house
In her imagin'd person.
    Duke.   Know you this woman ?
    Lucio. Carnally, she says.
    Duke.   Sirrah, no more.
    Lucio. Enough, my lord.
    Ang. My lord, I must confess I know this
    woman ;
And five years since there was some speech
    of marriage 215
Betwixt myself and her ; which was broke
    off,
Partly for that her promised proportions
Came short of composition ; but in chief
For that her reputation was disvalued 219
In levity. Since which time of five years
I never spake with her, saw her, nor heard
    from her,
Upon my faith and honour.
    Mari.   Noble Prince,

As there comes light from heaven and
    words from breath,
As there is sense in truth and truth in
    virtue,   224
I am affianc'd this man's wife as strongly
As words could make up vows. And, my
    good lord,
But Tuesday night last gone, in's garden-
    house,
He knew me as a wife. As this is true,
Let me in safety raise me from my knees,
Or else for ever be confixed here,   230
A marble monument !

    Ang.   I did but smile till now.
Now, good my lord, give me the scope of
    justice ;
My patience here is touch'd. I do perceive
These poor informal women are no more
But instruments of some more mightier
    member   235
That sets them on. Let me have way,
    my lord,
To find this practice out.

    Duke.   Ay, with my heart ;
And punish them to your height of pleas-
    ure.
Thou foolish friar, and thou pernicious
    woman,
Compact with her that's gone, think'st thou
    thy oaths,   240
Though they would swear down each
    particular saint,
Were testimonies against his worth and
    credit,
That's seal'd in approbation ? You, Lord
    Escalus,
Sit with my cousin ; lend him your kind
    pains   244
To find out this abuse, whence 'tis deriv'd.
There is another friar that set them on ;
Let him be sent for.

    F. Peter. Would he were here, my lord !
    For he indeed
Hath set the women on to this complaint.
Your provost knows the place where he
    abides,   250
And he may fetch him.

    Duke.   Go, do it instantly.
                    [*Exit Provost.*
And you, my noble and well-warranted
    cousin,
Whom it concerns to hear this matter forth,
Do with your injuries as seems you best
In any chastisement. I for a while will
    leave you ;   255
But stir not you till you have well de-
    termin'd
Upon these slanderers.

    Escal.   My lord, we'll do it throughly.
                    [*Exit Duke.*
Signior Lucio, did not you say you knew
that friar Lodowick to be a dishonest
person ?   260
    Lucio. ' Cucullus non facit monachum ' :

honest in nothing but in his clothes ; and
one that hath spoke most villainous speeches
of the Duke.
    Escal. We shall entreat you to abide here
till he come, and enforce them against him.
We shall find this friar a notable fellow.   266
    Lucio. As any in Vienna, on my word.
    Escal. Call that same Isabel here once
again ; I would speak with her. [*Exit an
Attendant*] Pray you, my lord, give me leave
to question ; you shall see how I'll handle
her.   271
    Lucio. Not better than he, by her own
report.
    Escal. Say you ?
    Lucio. Marry, sir, I think, if you handled
her privately, she would sooner confess ;
perchance, publicly, she'll be asham'd.   276

    Re-enter Officers *with* ISABELLA ; *and*
PROVOST *with the* DUKE *in his friar's habit.*

    Escal. I will go darkly to work with her.
    Lucio. That's the way ; for women are
light at midnight.
    Escal. Come on, mistress ; here's a gentle-
woman denies all that you have said.   280
    Lucio. My lord, here comes the rascal I
spoke of, here with the Provost.
    Escal. In very good time. Speak not you
to him till we call upon you.
    Lucio. Mum.   285
    Escal. Come, sir ; did you set these
women on to slander Lord Angelo ? They
have confess'd you did.
    Duke. 'Tis false.
    Escal. How ! Know you where you are ?
    Duke. Respect to your great place ! and
    let the devil   290
Be sometime honour'd for his burning
    throne !
Where is the Duke ? 'Tis he should hear me
    speak.
    Escal. The Duke's in us ; and we will
    hear you speak ;
Look you speak justly.
    Duke. Boldly, at least. But, O, poor
    souls,   295
Come you to seek the lamb here of the fox,
Good night to your redress ! Is the Duke
    gone ?
Then is your cause gone too. The Duke's
    unjust
Thus to retort your manifest appeal,
And put your trial in the villain's mouth
Which here you come to accuse.   301
    Lucio. This is the rascal ; this is he I
    spoke of.
    Escal. Why, thou unreverend and un-
hallowed friar,
Is't not enough thou hast suborn'd these
    women
To accuse this worthy man, but, in foul
    mouth,   305
And in the witness of his proper ear,

III

To call him villain; and then to glance
from him
To th' Duke himself, to tax him with
injustice?
Take him hence; to th' rack with him!
We'll touze you
Joint by joint, but we will know his pur-
pose.   310
What, 'unjust'!
    Duke.   Be not so hot; the Duke
Dare no more stretch this finger of mine
than he
Dare rack his own; his subject am I not,
Nor here provincial. My business in this
state
Made me a looker-on here in Vienna, 315
Where I have seen corruption boil and
bubble
Till it o'errun the stew: laws for all faults,
But faults so countenanc'd that the strong
statutes
Stand like the forfeits in a barber's shop,
As much in mock as mark.   320
    Escal. Slander to th' state! Away with
him to prison!
    Ang. What can you vouch against him,
Signior Lucio?   322
Is this the man that you did tell us of?
    Lucio. 'Tis he, my lord. Come hither,
good-man bald-pate. Do you know me?
    Duke. I remember you, sir, by the sound
of your voice. I met you at the prison, in
the absence of the Duke.   327
    Lucio. O did you so? And do you re-
member what you said of the Duke?
    Duke. Most notedly, sir.   330
    Lucio. Do you so, sir? And was the Duke
a fleshmonger, a fool, and a coward, as you
then reported him to be?   333
    Duke. You must, sir, change persons with
me ere you make that my report; you,
indeed, spoke so of him; and much more,
much worse.   336
    Lucio. O thou damnable fellow! Did not
I pluck thee by the nose for thy speeches?
    Duke. I protest I love the Duke as I love
myself.
    Ang. Hark how the villain would close
now, after his treasonable abuses!   341
    Escal. Such a fellow is not to be talk'd
withal. Away with him to prison! Where
is the Provost? Away with him to prison!
Lay bolts enough upon him; let him speak
no more. Away with those giglets too, and
with the other confederate companion! 346
    [*The Provost lays hands on the Duke.*
    Duke. Stay, sir; stay awhile.
    Ang. What, resists he? Help him, Lucio.
    Lucio. Come, sir; come, sir; come, sir;
foh, sir! Why, you bald-pated lying rascal,
you must be hooded, must you? Show
your knave's visage, with a pox to you!
show your sheep-biting face, and be hang'd
an hour! Will't not off?   353

    [*Pulls off the friar's hood, and
                discovers the Duke.*
    Duke. Thou art the first knave that e'er
mad'st a duke.
First, Provost, let me bail these gentle
three.   355
[*To Lucio*] Sneak not away, sir, for the
friar and you
Must have a word anon. Lay hold on him.
    Lucio. This may prove worse than
hanging.
    Duke. [*To Escalus*] What you have spoke
I pardon; sit you down.
We'll borrow place of him. [*To Angelo*] Sir,
by your leave.   360
Hast thou or word, or wit, or impudence,
That yet can do thee office? If thou hast,
Rely upon it till my tale be heard,
And hold no longer out.
    Ang.   O my dread lord,
I should be guiltier than my guiltiness, 365
To think I can be undiscernible,
When I perceive your Grace, like pow'r
divine,
Hath look'd upon my passes. Then, good
Prince,   368
No longer session hold upon my shame,
But let my trial be mine own confession;
Immediate sentence then, and sequent
death,
Is all the grace I beg.
    Duke.   Come hither, Mariana.
Say, wast thou e'er contracted to this
woman?
    Ang. I was, my lord.
    Duke. Go, take her hence and marry her
instantly.   375
Do you the office, friar; which consum-
mate,
Return him here again. Go with him,
Provost.
    [*Exeunt Angelo, Mariana, Friar
              Peter, and Provost.*
    Escal. My lord, I am more amaz'd at his
dishonour
Than at the strangeness of it.
    Duke.   Come hither, Isabel.
Your friar is now your prince. As I was
then   380
Advertising and holy to your business,
Not changing heart with habit, I am still
Attorney'd at your service.
    Isab.   O, give me pardon,
That I, your vassal, have employ'd and
pain'd   384
Your unknown sovereignty.
    Duke.   You are pardon'd Isabel.
And now, dear maid, be you as free to us.
Your brother's death, I know, sits at your
heart;
And you may marvel why I obscur'd
myself,
Labouring to save his life, and would not
rather

Make rash remonstrance of my hidden
       pow'r   390
Than let him so be lost. O most kind maid,
It was the swift celerity of his death,
Which I did think with slower foot came on,
That brain'd my purpose. But peace be
       with him !   394
That life is better life, past fearing death,
Than that which lives to fear. Make it
       your comfort,
So happy is your brother.
    Isab.   I do, my lord.

Re-enter ANGELO, MARIANA, FRIAR
     PETER, *and* PROVOST.

    Duke. For this new-married man ap-
       proaching here,
Whose salt imagination yet hath wrong'd
Your well-defended honour, you must
       pardon   400
For Mariana's sake ; but as he adjudg'd
       your brother—
Being criminal in double violation
Of sacred chastity and of promise-breach,
Thereon dependent, for your brother's
       life—
The very mercy of the law cries out   405
Most audible, even from his proper tongue,
' An Angelo for Claudio, death for death ! '
Haste still pays haste, and leisure answers
       leisure ;
Like doth quit like, and Measure still for
       Measure.   409
Then, Angelo, thy fault's thus manifested,
Which, though thou wouldst deny, denies
       thee vantage.
We do condemn thee to the very block
Where Claudio stoop'd to death, and with
       like haste.
Away with him !
    Mari.   O my most gracious lord,
I hope you will not mock me with a
       husband.   415
    Duke. It is your husband mock'd you with
       a husband.
Consenting to the safeguard of your honour,
I thought your marriage fit ; else imputa-
       tion,
For that he knew you, might reproach your
       life,
And choke your good to come. For his
       possessions,   420
Although by confiscation they are ours,
We do instate and widow you withal,
To buy you a better husband.
    Mari.   O my dear lord,
I crave no other, nor no better man.   424
    Duke. Never crave him ; we are definitive.
    Mari. Gentle, my liege—   [*Kneeling.*
    Duke.   You do but lose your labour.
Away with him to death ! [*To Lucio*] Now,
       sir, to you.
    Mari. O my good lord ! Sweet Isabel,
       take my part ;   428

Lend me your knees, and all my life to
       come
I'll lend you all my life to do you service.
    Duke. Against all sense you do importune
       her.
Should she kneel down in mercy of this fact,
Her brother's ghost his paved bed would
       break,   433
And take her hence in horror.
    Mari.   Isabel,
Sweet Isabel, do yet but kneel by me ;   435
Hold up your hands, say nothing ; I'll
       speak all.
They say best men are moulded out of
       faults ;
And, for the most, become much more the
       better
For being a little bad ; so may my husband.
O Isabel, will you not lend a knee ?   440
    Duke. He dies for Claudio's death.
    Isab.   [*Kneeling*] Most bounteous sir,
Look, if it please you, on this man con-
       demn'd,
As if my brother liv'd. I partly think
A due sincerity govern'd his deeds
Till he did look on me ; since it is so,   445
Let him not die. My brother had but
       justice,
In that he did the thing for which he died ;
For Angelo,
His act did not o'ertake his bad intent,
And must be buried but as an intent   450
That perish'd by the way. Thoughts are no
       subjects ;
Intents but merely thoughts.
    Mari.   Merely, my lord.
    Duke. Your suit's unprofitable ; stand
       up, I say.
I have bethought me of another fault.   454
Provost, how came it Claudio was beheaded
At an unusual hour ?
    Prov.   It was commanded so.
    Duke. Had you a special warrant for the
       deed ?
    Prov. No, my good lord ; it was by
       private message.
    Duke. For which I do discharge you of
       your office ;   459
Give up your keys.
    Prov.   Pardon me, noble lord ;
I thought it was a fault, but knew it not ;
Yet did repent me, after more advice ;
For testimony whereof, one in the prison,
That should by private order else have died,
I have reserv'd alive.
    Duke.   What's he ?
    Prov.   His name is Barnardine.
    Duke. I would thou hadst done so by
       Claudio.   466
Go fetch him hither ; let me look upon him.
       [*Exit Provost.*
    Escal. I am sorry one so learned and so
       wise
As you, Lord Angelo, have still appear'd,

Should slip so grossly, both in the heat of
blood   470
And lack of temper'd judgment afterward.

Ang. I am sorry that such sorrow I
procure ;
And so deep sticks it in my penitent heart
That I crave death more willingly than
mercy ;
'Tis my deserving, and I do entreat it.   475

Re-enter PROVOST, *with* BARNARDINE,
CLAUDIO (*muffled*), *and* JULIET.

Duke. Which is that Barnardine ?
Prov.   This, my lord.
Duke. There was a friar told me of this
man.
Sirrah, thou art said to have a stubborn
soul,
That apprehends no further than this
world,
And squar'st thy life according. Thou'rt
condemn'd ;   480
But, for those earthly faults, I quit them
all,
And pray thee take this mercy to provide
For better times to come. Friar, advise
him ;
I leave him to your hand. What muffl'd
fellow's that ?
Prov. This is another prisoner that I
sav'd,   485
Who should have died when Claudio lost
his head ;
As like almost to Claudio as himself.
                              [*Unmuffles Claudio.*
Duke. [*To Isabella*] If he be like your
brother, for his sake
Is he pardon'd ; and for your lovely sake,
Give me your hand and say you will be
mine,   490
He is my brother too. But fitter time for
that.
By this Lord Angelo perceives he's safe ;
Methinks I see a quick'ning in his eye.
Well, Angelo, your evil quits you well.
Look that you love your wife ; her worth
worth yours.   495
I find an apt remission in myself ;
And yet here's one in place I cannot pardon.
[*To Lucio*] You, sirrah, that knew me for a
fool, a coward,
One all of luxury, an ass, a madman !

Wherein have I so deserv'd of you   500
That you extol me thus ?
Lucio. Faith, my lord, I spoke it but
according to the trick. If you will hang me
for it, you may ; but I had rather it would
please you I might be whipt.
Duke. Whipt first, sir, and hang'd
after.   505
Proclaim it, Provost, round about the city,
If any woman wrong'd by this lewd
fellow—
As I have heard him swear himself there's
one
Whom he begot with child, let her appear,
And he shall marry her. The nuptial
finish'd,   510
Let him be whipt and hang'd.
Lucio. I beseech your Highness, do not
marry me to a whore. Your Highness said
even now I made you a duke ; good my
lord, do not recompense me in making me a
cuckold.   515
Duke. Upon mine honour, thou shalt
marry her.
Thy slanders I forgive ; and therewithal
Remit thy other forfeits. Take him to
prison ;
And see our pleasure herein executed.
Lucio. Marrying a punk, my lord, is
pressing to death, whipping, and hanging.
Duke. Slandering a prince deserves it.   522
                          [*Exeunt Officers with Lucio.*
She, Claudio, that you wrong'd, look you
restore.
Joy to you, Mariana ! Love her, Angelo ;
I have confess'd her, and I know her virtue.
Thanks, good friend Escalus, for thy much
goodness ;   526
There's more behind that is more gratulate.
Thanks, Provost, for thy care and secrecy ;
We shall employ thee in a worthier place.
Forgive him, Angelo, that brought you
home   530
The head of Ragozine for Claudio's ;
Th' offence pardons itself. Dear Isabel,
I have a motion much imports your good ;
Whereto if you'll a willing ear incline,
What's mine is yours, and what is yours is
mine.   535
So, bring us to our palace, where we'll show
What's yet behind that's meet you all
should know.   [*Exeunt.*

THE COMEDY OF ERRORS

DRAMATIS PERSONÆ

SOLINUS, *Duke of Ephesus.*
ÆGEON, *a merchant of Syracuse.*
ANTIPHOLUS of
    Ephesus, } *twin brothers, and sons to*
ANTIPHOLUS of } *Ægeon and Æmilia.*
    Syracuse,)
DROMIO of Ephesus, } *twin brothers, and*
DROMIO of Syracuse, } *attendants on the two Antipholuses.*
BALTHAZAR, *a merchant.*
ANGELO, *a goldsmith.*
First Merchant, *friend to Antipholus of Syracuse.*

Second Merchant, *to whom Angelo is a debtor.*
PINCH, *a schoolmaster.*

ÆMILIA, *wife to Ægeon ; an abbess at Ephesus.*
ADRIANA, *wife to Antipholus of Ephesus.*
LUCIANA, *her sister.*
LUCE, *servant to Adriana.*
A Courtezan.

Gaoler, Officers, Attendants.

THE SCENE : *Ephesus.*

ACT ONE

SCENE I. *A hall in the Duke's palace.*

Enter the DUKE OF EPHESUS, ÆGEON, *the Merchant of Syracusa, Gaoler, Officers, and other* Attendants.

Æge. Proceed, Solinus, to procure my fall,
And by the doom of death end woes and all.
  Duke. Merchant of Syracusa, plead no more ;
I am not partial to infringe our laws.
The enmity and discord which of late   5
Sprung from the rancorous outrage of your duke
To merchants, our well-dealing countrymen,
Who, wanting guilders to redeem their lives,
Have seal'd his rigorous statutes with their bloods,
Excludes all pity from our threat'ning looks.   10
For, since the mortal and intestine jars
'Twixt thy seditious countrymen and us,
It hath in solemn synods been decreed,
Both by the Syracusians and ourselves,
To admit no traffic to our adverse towns ;
Nay, more : if any born at Ephesus   16
Be seen at any Syracusian marts and fairs ;
Again, if any Syracusian born
Come to the bay of Ephesus—he dies,   20
His goods confiscate to the Duke's dispose,
Unless a thousand marks be levied,
To quit the penalty and to ransom him.
Thy substance, valued at the highest rate,
Cannot amount unto a hundred marks ;   25
Therefore by law thou art condemn'd to die.
  Æge. Yet this my comfort : when your words are done,
My woes end likewise with the evening sun.

  Duke. Well, Syracusian, say in brief the cause
Why thou departed'st from thy native home,   30
And for what cause thou cam'st to Ephesus.
  Æge. A heavier task could not have been impos'd
Than I to speak my griefs unspeakable ;
Yet, that the world may witness that my end   34
Was wrought by nature, not by vile offence,
I'll utter what my sorrow gives me leave.
In Syracusa was I born, and wed
Unto a woman, happy but for me,
And by me, had not our hap been bad.
With her I liv'd in joy ; our wealth increas'd   40
By prosperous voyages I often made
To Epidamnum ; till my factor's death,
And the great care of goods at random left,
Drew me from kind embracements of my spouse ;
From whom my absence was not six months old,   45
Before herself, almost at fainting under
The pleasing punishment that women bear,
Had made provision for her following me,
And soon and safe arrived where I was.
There had she not been long but she became
A joyful mother of two goodly sons ;   51
And, which was strange, the one so like the other
As could not be distinguish'd but by names.
That very hour, and in the self-same inn,
A mean woman was delivered   55
Of such a burden, male twins, both alike.
Those, for their parents were exceeding poor,
I bought, and brought up to attend my sons.
My wife, not meanly proud of two such boys,   59

115

Made daily motions for our home return ;
Unwilling I agreed. Alas ! too soon
We came aboard.
A league from Epidamnum had we sail'd
Before the always-wind-obeying deep
Gave any tragic instance of our harm ; 65
But longer did we not retain much hope,
For what obscured light the heavens did
    grant
Did but convey unto our fearful minds
A doubtful warrant of immediate death ;
Which though myself would gladly have
    embrac'd,   70
Yet the incessant weepings of my wife,
Weeping before for what she saw must
    come,
And piteous plainings of the pretty babes,
That mourn'd for fashion, ignorant what to
    fear,   74
Forc'd me to seek delays for them and me.
And this it was, for other means was none :
The sailors sought for safety by our boat,
And left the ship, then sinking-ripe, to us ;
My wife, more careful for the latter-born,
Had fast'ned him unto a small spare mast,
Such as sea-faring men provide for storms ;
To him one of the other twins was bound,
Whilst I had been like heedful of the other.
The children thus dispos'd, my wife and I,
Fixing our eyes on whom our care was fix'd,
Fast'ned ourselves at either end the mast,
And, floating straight, obedient to the
    stream,   87
Was carried towards Corinth, as we thought.
At length the sun, gazing upon the earth,
Dispers'd those vapours that offended us ;
And, by the benefit of his wished light, 91
The seas wax'd calm, and we discovered
Two ships from far making amain to us—
Of Corinth that, of Epidaurus this.
But ere they came—O, let me say no
    more !   95
Gather the sequel by that went before.
    Duke. Nay, forward, old man, do not
        break off so ;
For we may pity, though not pardon thee.
    Æge. O, had the gods done so, I had not
        now
Worthily term'd them merciless to us ! 100
For, ere the ships could meet by twice five
    leagues,
We were encount'red by a mighty rock,
Which being violently borne upon,
Our helpful ship was splitted in the midst ;
So that, in this unjust divorce of us, 105
Fortune had left to both of us alike
What to delight in, what to sorrow for.
Her part, poor soul, seeming as burdened
With lesser weight, but not with lesser woe,
Was carried with more speed before the
    wind ;   110
And in our sight they three were taken up
By fishermen of Corinth, as we thought.
At length another ship had seiz'd on us ;

And, knowing whom it was their hap to
    save,
Gave healthful welcome to their ship-
    wreck'd guests,   115
And would have reft the fishers of their
    prey,
Had not their bark been very slow of sail ;
And therefore homeward did they bend
    their course.
Thus have you heard me sever'd from my
    bliss,   119
That by misfortunes was my life prolong'd,
To tell sad stories of my own mishaps.
    Duke. And, for the sake of them thou
        sorrowest for,
Do me the favour to dilate at full
What have befall'n of them and thee till
    now.
    Æge. My youngest boy, and yet my
        eldest care,   125
At eighteen years became inquisitive
After his brother, and importun'd me
That his attendant—so his case was like,
Reft of his brother, but retain'd his name—
Might bear him company in the quest of
    him ;   130
Whom whilst I laboured of a love to see,
I hazarded the loss of whom I lov'd.
Five summers have I spent in farthest
    Greece,
Roaming clean through the bounds of
    Asia,   134
And, coasting homeward, came to Ephesus;
Hopeless to find, yet loath to leave un-
    sought
Or that or any place that harbours men.
But here must end the story of my life ;
And happy were I in my timely death, 139
Could all my travels warrant me they live.
    Duke. Hapless Ægeon, whom the fates
        have mark'd
To bear the extremity of dire mishap !
Now, trust me, were it not against our
    laws,
Against my crown, my oath, my dignity,
Which princes, would they, may not dis-
    annul,   145
My soul should sue as advocate for thee.
But though thou art adjudged to the death,
And passed sentence may not be recall'd
But to our honour's great disparagement,
Yet will I favour thee in what I can. 150
Therefore, merchant, I'll limit thee this day
To seek thy help by beneficial hap.
Try all the friends thou hast in Ephesus ;
Beg thou, or borrow, to make up the sum,
And live ; if no, then thou art doom'd to
    die.   155
Gaoler, take him to thy custody.
    Gaol. I will, my lord.
    Æge. Hopeless and helpless doth Ægeon
        wend,
But to procrastinate his lifeless end.
                            [*Exeunt.*

SCENE II. *The mart.*

Enter ANTIPHOLUS of Syracuse, DROMIO of Syracuse, *and* First Merchant.

First Mer. Therefore, give out you are of
　　　Epidamnum,
Lest that your goods too soon be confiscate.
This very day a Syracusian merchant
Is apprehended for arrival here ;
And, not being able to buy out his life,　5
According to the statute of the town,
Dies ere the weary sun set in the west.
There is your money that I had to keep.
　　Ant. S. Go bear it to the Centaur, where
　　　we host.　　9
And stay there, Dromio, till I come to thee.
Within this hour it will be dinner-time ;
Till that, I'll view the manners of the town,
Peruse the traders, gaze upon the buildings,
And then return and sleep within mine inn ;
For with long travel I am stiff and weary.
Get thee away.　　16
　　Dro. S. Many a man would take you at
　　　your word,
And go indeed, having so good a mean.
　　　　　　　　　[*Exit Dromio S.*
　　Ant. S. A trusty villain, sir, that very oft,
When I am dull with care and melancholy,
Lightens my humour with his merry jests.
What, will you walk with me about the
　　　town,
And then go to my inn and dine with me ?
　　First Mer. I am invited, sir, to certain
　　　merchants,
Of whom I hope to make much benefit ;　25
I crave your pardon. Soon at five o'clock,
Please you, I'll meet with you upon the
　　　mart,
And afterward consort you till bed time.
My present business calls me from you now.
　　Ant. S. Farewell till then. I will go lose
　　　myself,　　30
And wander up and down to view the city.
　　First Mer. Sir, I commend you to your
　　　own content. [*Exit First Merchant.*
　　Ant. S. He that commends me to mine
　　　own content
Commends me to the thing I cannot get.
I to the world am like a drop of water　35
That in the ocean seeks another drop,
Who, falling there to find his fellow forth,
Unseen, inquisitive, confounds himself.
So I, to find a mother and a brother,
In quest of them, unhappy, lose myself.　40

Enter DROMIO of Ephesus.

Here comes the almanac of my true date.
What now ? How chance thou art return'd
　　　so soon ?
　　Dro. E. Return'd so soon ! rather
　　　approach'd too late.
The capon burns, the pig falls from the spit;
The clock hath strucken twelve upon the
　　　bell—　　45
My mistress made it one upon my cheek ;
She is so hot because the meat is cold,
The meat is cold because you come not
　　　home,
You come not home because you have no
　　　stomach,
You have no stomach, having broke your
　　　fast ;　　50
But we, that know what 'tis to fast and
　　　pray,
Are penitent for your default to-day.
　　Ant. S. Stop in your wind, sir ; tell me
　　　this, I pray :
Where have you left the money that I gave
　　　you ?
　　Dro. E. O—sixpence that I had a
　　　Wednesday last　　55
To pay the saddler for my mistress'
　　　crupper ?
The saddler had it, sir ; I kept it not.
　　Ant. S. I am not in a sportive humour
　　　now ;
Tell me, and dally not, where is the money?
We being strangers here, how dar'st thou
　　　trust　　60
So great a charge from thine own custody ?
　　Dro. E. I pray you jest, sir, as you sit
　　　at dinner.
I from my mistress come to you in post ;
If I return, I shall be post indeed,　64
For she will score your fault upon my pate.
Methinks your maw, like mine, should be
　　　your clock,
And strike you home without a messenger.
　　Ant. S. Come, Dromio, come, these jests
　　　are out of season ;　　68
Reserve them till a merrier hour than this.
Where is the gold I gave in charge to thee ?
　　Dro. E. To me, sir ? Why, you gave no
　　　gold to me.
　　Ant. S. Come on, sir knave, have done
　　　your foolishness,
And tell me how thou hast dispos'd thy
　　　charge.
　　Dro. E. My charge was but to fetch you
　　　from the mart
Home to your house, the Phœnix, sir, to
　　　dinner.　　75
My mistress and her sister stays for you.
　　Ant. S. Now, as I am a Christian, answer
　　　me
In what safe place you have bestow'd my
　　　money,
Or I shall break that merry sconce of yours,
That stands on tricks when I am un-
　　　dispos'd.　　80
Where is the thousand marks thou hadst
　　　of me ?
　　Dro. E. I have some marks of yours upon
　　　my pate,
Some of my mistress' marks upon my
　　　shoulders,
But not a thousand marks between you
　　　both.　　84

117

If I should pay your worship those again,
Perchance you will not bear them patiently.
   Ant. S. Thy mistress' marks! What
    mistress, slave, hast thou?
   Dro. E. Your worship's wife, my mistress
    at the Phœnix;
She that doth fast till you come home to
   dinner,
And prays that you will hie you home to
   dinner.   90
   Ant. S. What, wilt thou flout me thus
    unto my face,
Being forbid? There, take you that, sir
   knave.   [*Beats him.*
   Dro. E. What mean you, sir? For God's
    sake hold your hands!
Nay, an you will not, sir, I'll take my heels.
              [*Exit Dromio E.*
   Ant. S. Upon my life, by some device or
    other   95
The villain is o'erraught of all my money.
They say this town is full of cozenage;
As, nimble jugglers that deceive the eye,
Dark-working sorcerers that change the
   mind,   99
Soul-killing witches that deform the body,
Disguised cheaters, prating mountebanks,
And many such-like liberties of sin;
If it prove so, I will be gone the sooner.
I'll to the Centaur to go seek this slave.
I greatly fear my money is not safe. [*Exit.*

ACT TWO

SCENE I. *The house of Antipholus of
Ephesus.*

Enter ADRIANA, *wife to Antipholus of
Ephesus, with* LUCIANA, *her sister.*

   Adr. Neither my husband nor the slave
    return'd
That in such haste I sent to seek his master!
Sure, Luciana, it is two o'clock.
   Luc. Perhaps some merchant hath in-
    vited him,
And from the mart he's somewhere gone to
   dinner;   5
Good sister, let us dine, and never fret.
A man is master of his liberty;
Time is their master, and when they see
   time,
They'll go or come. If so, be patient, sister.
   Adr. Why should their liberty than ours
    be more?   10
   Luc. Because their business still lies out
    o' door.
   Adr. Look, when I serve him so, he takes
    it ill.
   Luc. O, know he is the bridle of your will.
   Adr. There's none but asses will be
    bridled so.
   Luc. Why, headstrong liberty is lash'd
    with woe.   15
There's nothing situate under heaven's eye

But hath his bound, in earth, in sea, in sky.
The beasts, the fishes, and the winged fowls,
Are their males' subjects, and at their
   controls.   19
Man, more divine, the master of all these,
Lord of the wide world and wild wat'ry
   seas,
Indu'd with intellectual sense and souls,
Of more pre-eminence than fish and fowls,
Are masters to their females, and their
   lords;   24
Then let your will attend on their accords.
   Adr. This servitude makes you to keep
    unwed.
   Luc. Not this, but troubles of the
    marriage-bed.
   Adr. But, were you wedded, you would
    bear some sway.
   Luc. Ere I learn love, I'll practise to obey.
   Adr. How if your husband start some
    other where?   30
   Luc. Till he come home again, I would
    forbear.
   Adr. Patience unmov'd! no marvel
    though she pause:
They can be meek that have no other cause.
A wretched soul, bruis'd with adversity,
We bid be quiet when we hear it cry;   35
But were we burd'ned with like weight of
   pain,
As much, or more, we should ourselves
   complain.
So thou, that hast no unkind mate to grieve
   thee,
With urging helpless patience would relieve
   me;
But if thou live to see like right bereft,   40
This fool-begg'd patience in thee will be left.
   Luc. Well, I will marry one day, but to
    try.
Here comes your man, now is your husband
   nigh.

Enter DROMIO *of Ephesus.*

   Adr. Say, is your tardy master now at
    hand?
   Dro. E. Nay, he's at two hands with me,
and that my two ears can witness.   46
   Adr. Say, didst thou speak with him?
    Know'st thou his mind?
   Dro. E. Ay, ay, he told his mind upon
    mine ear.
Beshrew his hand, I scarce could under-
stand it.
   Luc. Spake he so doubtfully thou couldst
not feel his meaning?   51
   Dro. E. Nay, he struck so plainly I could
too well feel his blows; and withal so
doubtfully that I could scarce understand
them.
   Adr. But say, I prithee, is he coming
    home?   55
It seems he hath great care to please his
   wife.

Dro. E. Why, mistress, sure my master is
 horn-mad.

Adr. Horn-mad, thou villain!

Dro. E.   I mean not cuckold-mad;
But, sure, he is stark mad.
When I desir'd him to come home to
 dinner, 60
He ask'd me for a thousand marks in gold.
' 'Tis dinner time' quoth I; ' My gold!'
 quoth he.
' Your meat doth burn' quoth I; ' My
 gold!' quoth he.
' Will you come home?' quoth I; ' My
 gold!' quoth he
' Where is the thousand marks I gave thee,
 villain?' 65
'The pig' quoth I 'is burn'd'; ' My gold!'
 quoth he.
' My mistress, sir' quoth I; ' Hang up thy
 mistress;
I know not thy mistress; out on thy
 mistress.'

Luc. Quoth who?

Dro. E. Quoth my master. 70
' I know' quoth he ' no house, no wife,
 no mistress.'
So that my errand, due unto my tongue,
I thank him, I bare home upon my
 shoulders;
For, in conclusion, he did beat me there.

Adr. Go back again, thou slave, and fetch
 him home. 75

Dro. E. Go back again, and be new beaten
 home?
For God's sake, send some other messenger.

Adr. Back, slave, or I will break thy pate
 across.

Dro. E. And he will bless that cross with
 other beating;
Between you I shall have a holy head. 80

Adr. Hence, prating peasant! Fetch thy
 master home.

Dro. E. Am I so round with you, as you
 with me,
That like a football you do spurn me thus?
You spurn me hence, and he will spurn me
 hither; 84
If I last in this service, you must case me
 in leather. [*Exit.*

Luc. Fie, how impatience loureth in your
 face!

Adr. His company must do his minions
 grace,
Whilst I at home starve for a merry look.
Hath homely age th' alluring beauty took
From my poor cheek? Then he hath wasted
 it. 90
Are my discourses dull? Barren my wit?
If voluble and sharp discourse be marr'd,
Unkindness blunts it more than marble
 hard.
Do their gay vestments his affections bait?
That's not my fault; he's master of my
 state. 95

What ruins are in me that can be found
By him not ruin'd? Then is he the ground
Of my defeatures. My decayed fair
A sunny look of his would soon repair.
But, too unruly deer, he breaks the pale, 100
And feeds from home; poor I am but his
 stale.

Luc. Self-harming jealousy! fie, beat it
 hence.

Adr. Unfeeling fools can with such
 wrongs dispense. 103
I know his eye doth homage otherwhere;
Or else what lets it but he would be here?
Sister, you know he promis'd me a chain;
Would that alone a love he would detain,
So he would keep fair quarter with his bed!
I see the jewel best enamelled
Will lose his beauty; yet the gold bides
 still 110
That others touch and, often touching, will
Where gold; and no man that hath a
 name
By falsehood and corruption doth it shame.
Since that my beauty cannot please his eye,
I'll weep what's left away, and weeping die.

Luc. How many fond fools serve mad
 jealousy! [*Exeunt.*

SCENE II. *The mart.*

Enter ANTIPHOLUS *of Syracuse.*

Ant. S. The gold I gave to Dromio is laid
 up
Safe at the Centaur, and the heedful slave
Is wand'red forth in care to seek me out.
By computation and mine host's report
I could not speak with Dromio since at first
I sent him from the mart. See, here he
 comes. 6

Enter DROMIO *of Syracuse.*

How now, sir, is your merry humour
 alter'd?
As you love strokes, so jest with me again.
You know no Centaur! You receiv'd no
 gold!
Your mistress sent to have me home to
 dinner! 10
My house was at the Phœnix! Wast thou
 mad,
That thus so madly thou didst answer me?

Dro. S. What answer, sir? When spake
 I such a word?

Ant. S. Even now, even here, not half an
 hour since.

Dro. S. I did not see you since you sent
 me hence, 15
Home to the Centaur, with the gold you
 gave me.

Ant. S. Villain, thou didst deny the gold's
 receipt,
And told'st me of a mistress and a dinner;
For which, I hope, thou felt'st I was
 displeas'd.

Dro. S. I am glad to see you in this merry
vein.   20
What means this jest ? I pray you, master,
tell me.
   Ant. S. Yea, dost thou jeer and flout me
in the teeth ?
Think'st thou I jest ? Hold, take thou that,
and that.   [*Beating him.*
   Dro. S. Hold, sir, for God's sake ! Now
your jest is earnest.
Upon what bargain do you give it me ? 25
   Ant. S. Because that I familiarly some-
times
Do use you for my fool and chat with you,
Your sauciness will jest upon my love,
And make a common of my serious hours.
When the sun shines let foolish gnats make
sport,   30
But creep in crannies when he hides his
beams.
If you will jest with me, know my aspect,
And fashion your demeanour to my looks,
Or I will beat this method in your sconce.
   Dro. S. Sconce, call you it ? So you
would leave battering, I had rather have it
a head. An you use these blows long, I
must get a sconce for my head, and
insconce it too ; or else I shall seek my
wit in my shoulders. But I pray, sir, why
am I beaten ?
   Ant. S. Dost thou not know ?   40
   Dro. S. Nothing, sir, but that I am
beaten.
   Ant. S. Shall I tell you why ?
   Dro. S. Ay, sir, and wherefore ; for they
say every why hath a wherefore.
   Ant S. Why, first for flouting me ; and
then wherefore,   45
For urging it the second time to me.
   Dro. S. Was there ever any man thus
beaten out of season,
When in the why and the wherefore is
neither rhyme nor reason ?
Well, sir, I thank you.
   Ant. S. Thank me, sir ! for what ?   50
   Dro. S. Marry, sir, for this something
that you gave me for nothing.
   Ant S. I'll make you amends next, to give
you nothing for something. But say, sir,
is it dinner-time ?
   Dro. S. No, sir ; I think the meat wants
that I have.   55
   Ant. S. In good time, sir, what's that ?
   Dro. S. Basting.
   Ant. S. Well, sir, then 'twill be dry.
   Dro. S. If it be, sir, I pray you eat none
of it.
   Ant. S. Your reason ?   60
   Dro. S. Lest it make you choleric, and
purchase me another dry basting.
   Ant. S. Well, sir, learn to jest in good
time ; there's a time for all things.
   Dro. S. I durst have denied that, before
you were so choleric.   66

   Ant. S. By what rule, sir ?
   Dro. S. Marry, sir, by a rule as plain as
the plain bald pate of Father Time himself.
   Ant. S. Let's hear it.   70
   Dro. S. There's no time for a man to
recover his hair that grows bald by nature.
   Ant. S. May he not do it by fine and
recovery ?
   Dro. S. Yes, to pay a fine for a periwig,
and recover the lost hair of another man. 75
   Ant. S. Why is Time such a niggard of
hair, being, as it is, so plentiful an excrement ?
   Dro. S. Because it is a blessing that he
bestows on beasts, and what he hath
scanted men in hair he hath given them
in wit.   80
   Ant S. Why, but there's many a man
hath more hair than wit.
   Dro. S. Not a man of those but he hath
the wit to lose his hair.
   Ant. S. Why, thou didst conclude hairy
men plain dealers without wit.   86
   Dro. S. The plainer dealer, the sooner lost;
yet he loseth it in a kind of jollity.
   Ant. S. For what reason ?
   Dro. S. For two ; and sound ones too. 90
   Ant. S. Nay, not sound I pray you.
   Dro. S. Sure ones, then.
   Ant. S. Nay, not sure, in a thing falsing.
   Dro. S. Certain ones, then.
   Ant. S. Name them.   95
   Dro. S. The one, to save the money that
he spends in tiring ; the other, that at
dinner they should not drop in his porridge.
   Ant. S. You would all this time have
prov'd there is no time for all things.   100
   Dro. S. Marry, and did, sir ; namely, no
time to recover hair lost by nature.
   Ant. S. But your reason was not sub-
stantial, why there is no time to recover.
   Dro. S. Thus I mend it : Time himself is
bald, and therefore to the world's end will
have bald followers.   106
   Ant. S. I knew 'twould be a bald conclusion. But, soft, who wafts us yonder ?

Enter ADRIANA *and* LUCIANA.

   Adr. Ay, ay, Antipholus, look strange and
frown.   109
Some other mistress hath thy sweet aspects;
I am not Adriana, nor thy wife.
The time was once when thou unurg'd
wouldst vow
That never words were music to thine ear,
That never object pleasing in thine eye,   114
That never touch well welcome to thy hand,
That never meat sweet-savour'd in thy
taste,
Unless I spake, or look'd, or touch'd, or
carv'd to thee.
How comes it now, my husband, O, how
comes it,
That thou art then estranged from thyself ?

Thyself I call it, being strange to me,   120
That, undividable, incorporate,
Am better than thy dear self's better part.
Ah, do not tear away thyself from me ;
For know, my love, as easy mayst thou fall
A drop of water in the breaking gulf,   125
And take unmingled thence that drop again
Without addition or diminishing,
As take from me thyself, and not me too.
How dearly would it touch thee to the
    quick,   129
Shouldst thou but hear I were licentious,
And that this body, consecrate to thee,
By ruffian lust should be contaminate !
Wouldst thou not spit at me and spurn
    at me,
And hurl the name of husband in my face,
And tear the stain'd skin off my harlot-
    brow,   135
And from my false hand cut the wedding-
    ring,
And break it with a deep-divorcing vow ?
I know thou canst, and therefore see thou
    do it.
I am possess'd with an adulterate blot ;   139
My blood is mingled with the crime of lust ;
For if we two be one, and thou play false,
I do digest the poison of thy flesh,
Being strumpeted by thy contagion.
Keep then fair league and truce with thy
    true bed ;
I live dis-tain'd, thou undishonoured.   145
    Ant. S. Plead you to me, fair dame ? I
    know you not :
In Ephesus I am but two hours old,
As strange unto your town as to your talk,
Who, every word by all my wit being
    scann'd,   149
Wants wit in all one word to understand.
    Luc. Fie, brother, how the world is
    chang'd with you !
When were you wont to use my sister thus ?
She sent for you by Dromio home to dinner.
    Ant. S. By Dromio ?
    Dro. S. By me ?   155
    Adr. By thee ; and this thou didst return
    from him—
That he did buffet thee, and in his blows
Denied my house for his, me for his wife.
    Ant. S. Did you converse, sir, with this
    gentlewoman ?
What is the course and drift of your com-
    pact ?   160
    Dro. S. I, sir ? I never saw her till this
    time.
    Ant. S. Villain, thou liest ; for even her
    very words
Didst thou deliver to me on the mart.
    Dro. S. I never spake with her in all my
    life.
    Ant. S. How can she thus, then, call us by
    our names,   165
Unless it be by inspiration ?
    Adr. How ill agrees it with your gravity

To counterfeit thus grossly with your slave,
Abetting him to thwart me in my mood !
Be it my wrong you are from me exempt,
But wrong not that wrong with a more
    contempt.   171
Come, I will fasten on this sleeve of thine ;
Thou art an elm, my husband, I a vine,
Whose weakness, married to thy stronger
    state,
Makes me with thy strength to communi-
    cate.   175
If aught possess thee from me, it is dross,
Usurping ivy, brier, or idle moss ;
Who all, for want of pruning, with in-
    trusion
Infect thy sap, and live on thy confusion.
    Ant. S. To me she speaks ; she moves me
    for her theme.   180
What, was I married to her in my dream ?
Or sleep I now, and think I hear all this ?
What error drives our eyes and ears amiss ?
Until I know this sure uncertainty,
I'll entertain the offer'd fallacy.   185
    Luc. Dromio, go bid the servants spread
    for dinner.
    Dro. S. O, for my beads ! I cross me for a
    sinner.
This is the fairy land. O spite of spites !
We talk with goblins, owls, and sprites.
If we obey them not, this will ensue :   190
They'll suck our breath, or pinch us black
    and blue.
    Luc. Why prat'st thou to thyself, and
    answer'st not ?
Dromio, thou drone, thou snail, thou slug,
    thou sot !
    Dro. S. I am transformed, master, am
    not I ?
    Ant. S. I think thou art in mind, and so
    am I.   195
    Dro. S. Nay, master, both in mind and in
    my shape.
    Ant. S. Thou hast thine own form.
    Dro. S.   No, I am an ape.
    Luc. If thou art chang'd to aught, 'tis to
    an ass.
    Dro. S. 'Tis true ; she rides me, and I long
    for grass.   199
'Tis so, I am an ass ; else it could never be
But I should know her as well as she knows
    me.
    Adr. Come, come, no longer will I be a
    fool,
To put the finger in the eye and weep,
Whilst man and master laughs my woes to
    scorn.
Come, sir, to dinner. Dromio, keep the
    gate.   205
Husband, I'll dine above with you to-day,
And shrive you of a thousand idle pranks.
Sirrah, if any ask you for your master,
Say he dines forth, and let no creature
    enter.   209
Come, sister. Dromio, play the porter well.

Ant. S. Am I in earth, in heaven, or in
    hell ?
Sleeping or waking, mad or well-advis'd ?
Known unto these, and to myself disguis'd !
I'll say as they say, and persever so,
And in this mist at all adventures go.   215
    Dro. S. Master, shall I be porter at the
        gate ?
    Adr. Ay ; and let none enter, lest I break
        your pate.
    Luc. Come, come, Antipholus, we dine
        too late.   [*Exeunt.*

ACT THREE

SCENE I. *Before the house of Antipholus of*
            Ephesus.

Enter ANTIPHOLUS *of* Ephesus, DROMIO *of*
    Ephesus, ANGELO, *and* BALTHAZAR.

    Ant. E. Good Signior Angelo, you must
        excuse us all ;
My wife is shrewish when I keep not hours.
Say that I linger'd with you at your shop
To see the making of her carcanet,   4
And that to-morrow you will bring it home.
But here's a villain that would face me
    down
He met me on the mart, and that I beat
    him,
And charg'd him with a thousand marks in
    gold,
And that I did deny my wife and house.
Thou drunkard, thou, what didst thou mean
    by this ?   10
    Dro. E. Say what you will, sir, but I know
        what I know.
That you beat me at the mart I have your
    hand to show ;
If the skin were parchment, and the blows
    you gave were ink,
Your own handwriting would tell you what
    I think.
    Ant E. I think thou art an ass.
    Dro. E.   Marry, so it doth appear
By the wrongs I suffer and the blows I bear.
I should kick, being kick'd ; and being at
    that pass,   17
You would keep from my heels, and beware
    of an ass.
    Ant. E. Y'are sad, Signior Balthazar ;
        pray God our cheer
May answer my good will and your good
    welcome here.   20
    Bal. I hold your dainties cheap, sir, and
        your welcome dear.
    Ant. E. O, Signior Balthazar, either at
        flesh or fish,
A table full of welcome makes scarce one
    dainty dish.
    Bal. Good meat, sir, is common ; that
        every churl affords.
    Ant. E. And welcome more common ; for
        that's nothing but words.   25

    Bal. Small cheer and great welcome
        makes a merry feast.
    Ant. E. Ay, to a niggardly host and more
        sparing guest.
But though my cates be mean, take them
    in good part ;
Better cheer may you have, but not with
    better heart.
But, soft, my door is lock'd ; go bid them
    let us in.   30
    Dro. E. Maud, Bridget, Marian, Cicely,
        Gillian, Ginn !
    Dro. S. [*Within*] Mome, malt-horse,
        capon, coxcomb, idiot, patch !
Either get thee from the door, or sit down
    at the hatch.
Dost thou conjure for wenches, that thou
    call'st for such store,
When one is one too many ? Go get thee
    from the door.   35
    Dro. E. What patch is made our porter ?
        My master stays in the street.
    Dro. S. [*Within*] Let him walk from
        whence he came, lest he catch cold
        on 's feet.
    Ant E. Who talks within there ? Ho, open
        the door !
    Dro. S. [*Within*] Right, sir ; I'll tell you
        when, an you'll tell me where-
        fore.
    Ant E. Wherefore ? For my dinner ; I
        have not din'd to-day.   40
    Dro. S. [*Within*] Nor to-day here you
        must not ; come again when you
        may.
    Ant. E. What art thou that keep'st me
        out from the house I owe ?
    Dro. S. [*Within*] The porter for this time,
        sir, and my name is Dromio.
    Dro. E. O villain, thou hast stol'n both
        mine office and my name !
The one ne'er got me credit, the other
    mickle blame.   45
If thou hadst been Dromio to-day in my
    place,
Thou wouldst have chang'd thy face for a
    name, or thy name for an ass.

            Enter LUCE, *within.*

    Luce. [*Within*] What a coil is there,
        Dromio ? Who are those at the
        gate ?
    Dro. E. Let my master in, Luce.
    Luce. [*Within*] Faith, no, he comes too
        late ;
And so tell your master.
    Dro. E.   O Lord, I must laugh !
Have at you with a proverb : Shall I set in
    my staff ?   51
    Luce. [*Within*] Have at you with another :
        that's—when ? can you tell ?
    Dro. S. [*Within*] If thy name be called
        Luce—Luce, thou hast answer'd
        him well.

Ant E. Do you hear, you minion ? You'll
let us in, I hope ?

Luce. [*Within*] I thought to have ask'd
you.

Dro. S. [*Within*] And you said no.

Dro. E. So, come, help ; well struck !
there was blow for blow.   56

Ant E. Thou baggage, let me in.

Luce. [*Within*] Can you tell for whose
sake ?

Dro. E. Master, knock the door hard.

Luce. [*Within*] Let him knock till it ache.

Ant. E. You'll cry for this, minion, if I
beat the door down.

Luce. [*Within*] What needs all that, and a
pair of stocks in the town ?   60

Enter ADRIANA, *within.*

Adr. [*Within*] Who is that at the door,
that keeps all this noise ?

Dro. S. [*Within*] By my troth, your town
is troubled with unruly boys.

Ant. E. Are you there, wife ? You might
have come before.

Adr. [*Within*] Your wife, sir knave ! Go
get you from the door.

Dro. E. If you went in pain, master, this
' knave ' would go sore.   65

Ang. Here is neither cheer, sir, nor
welcome ; we would fain have
either.

Bal. In debating which was best, we shall
part with neither.

Dro. E. They stand at the door, master ;
bid them welcome hither.

Ant. E. There is something in the wind,
that we cannot get in.

Dro. E. You would say so, master, if your
garments were thin.   70

Your cake here is warm within ; you stand
here in the cold ;

It would make a man mad as a buck to be
so bought and sold.

Ant. E. Go fetch me something ; I'll
break ope the gate.

Dro. S. [*Within*] Break any breaking
here, and I'll break your knave's
pate.

Dro. E. A man may break a word with
you, sir ; and words are but wind ;

Ay, and break it in your face, so he break it
not behind.   76

Dro. S. [*Within*] It seems thou want'st
breaking ; out upon thee, hind !

Dro. E. Here's too much ' out upon thee ! '
I pray thee let me in.

Dro. S. [*Within*] Ay, when fowls have no
feathers and fish have no fin.

Ant. E. Well, I'll break in ; go borrow me
a crow.   80

Dro. E. A crow without feather ? Master,
mean you so ?

For a fish without a fin, there's a fowl without a feather ;

If a crow help us in, sirrah, we'll pluck a
crow together.

Ant. E. Go get thee gone ; fetch me an
iron crow.   84

Bal. Have patience, sir ; O, let it not be so !

Herein you war against your reputation,

And draw within the compass of suspect

Th' unviolated honour of your wife.

Once this—your long experience of her
wisdom,

Her sober virtue, years, and modesty,   90

Plead on her part some cause to you unknown ;

And doubt not, sir, but she will well excuse

Why at this time the doors are made
against you.

Be rul'd by me : depart in patience,

And let us to the Tiger all to dinner ;   95

And, about evening, come yourself alone

To know the reason of this strange restraint.

If by strong hand you offer to break in

Now in the stirring passage of the day,

A vulgar comment will be made of it,   100

And that supposed by the common rout

Against your yet ungalled estimation

That may with foul intrusion enter in

And dwell upon your grave when you are
dead ;

For slander lives upon succession,   105

For ever hous'd where it gets possession.

Ant. E. You have prevail'd. I will depart
in quiet,

And in despite of mirth mean to be merry.

I know a wench of excellent discourse,

Pretty and witty ; wild, and yet, too,
gentle ;   110

There will we dine. This woman that I mean,

My wife—but, I protest, without desert—

Hath oftentimes upbraided me withal ;

To her will we to dinner. [*To Angelo*] Get
you home

And fetch the chain ; by this I know 'tis
made.   115

Bring it, I pray you, to the Porpentine ;

For there's the house. That chain will I
bestow—

Be it for nothing but to spite my wife—

Upon mine hostess there ; good sir, make
haste.   119

Since mine own doors refuse to entertain me,

I'll knock elsewhere, to see if they'll disdain
me.

Ang. I'll meet you at that place some
hour hence.

Ant. E. Do so ; this jest shall cost me
some expense.   [*Exeunt.*

SCENE II.   *Before the house of Antipholus
of Ephesus.*

Enter LUCIANA *with* ANTIPHOLUS *of
Syracuse.*

Luc. And may it be that you have quite
forgot

A husband's office ? Shall, Antipholus,
Even in the spring of love, thy love-springs
    rot ?
Shall love, in building, grow so ruinous ?
If you did wed my sister for her wealth, 5
Then for her wealth's sake use her with
    more kindness ;
Or, if you like elsewhere, do it by stealth ;
Muffle your false love with some show of
    blindness ;
Let not my sister read it in your eye ;
Be not thy tongue thy own shame's
    orator ; 10
Look sweet, speak fair, become disloyalty ;
Apparel vice like virtue's harbinger ;
Bear a fair presence, though your heart be
    tainted ;
Teach sin the carriage of a holy saint ;
Be secret-false. What need she be ac-
    quainted ? 15
What simple thief brags of his own
    attaint ?
'Tis double wrong to truant with your bed
And let her read it in thy looks at board ;
Shame hath a bastard fame, well managed ;
Ill deeds is doubled with an evil word. 20
Alas, poor women ! make us but believe,
Being compact of credit, that you love
    us ;
Though others have the arm, show us the
    sleeve ;
We in your motion turn, and you may
    move us.
Then, gentle brother, get you in again ; 25
Comfort my sister, cheer her, call her
    wife.
'Tis holy sport to be a little vain
When the sweet breath of flattery con-
    quers strife.
    Ant. S. Sweet mistress—what your name
    is else, I know not,
Nor by what wonder you do hit of mine—
Less in your knowledge and your grace you
    show not 31
Than our earth's wonder—more than
    earth, divine.
Teach me, dear creature, how to think and
    speak ;
Lay open to my earthy-gross conceit, 34
Smoth'red in errors, feeble, shallow, weak,
The folded meaning of your words' deceit.
Against my soul's pure truth why labour
    you
To make it wander in an unknown field ? .
Are you a god ? Would you create me new ?
Transform me, then, and to your pow'r
    I'll yield. 40
But if that I am I, then well I know
Your weeping sister is no wife of mine,
Nor to her bed no homage do I owe ;
Far more, far more, to you do I decline.
O, train me not, sweet mermaid, with thy
    note, 45
To drown me in thy sister's flood of tears.

Sing, siren, for thyself, and I will dote ;
Spread o'er the silver waves thy golden
    hairs,
And as a bed I'll take them, and there lie ;
And in that glorious supposition think 50
He gains by death that hath such means
    to die.
Let Love, being light, be drowned if she
    sink.
    Luc. What, are you mad, that you do
    reason so ?
    Ant. S. Not mad, but mated ; how, I do
    not know.
    Luc. It is a fault that springeth from
    your eye. 55
    Ant. S. For gazing on your beams, fair
    sun, being by.
    Luc. Gaze where you should, and that
    will clear your sight.
    Ant. S. As good to wink, sweet love, as
    look on night.
    Luc. Why call you me love ? Call my
    sister so. 59
    Ant. S. Thy sister's sister.
    Luc.   That's my sister.
    Ant. S.   No ;
It is thyself, mine own self's better part ;
Mine eye's clear eye, my dear heart's dearer
    heart,
My food, my fortune, and my sweet hope's
    aim,
My sole earth's heaven, and my heaven's
    claim.
    Luc. All this my sister is, or else should
    be. 65
    Ant. S. Call thyself sister, sweet, for I
    am thee ;
Thee will I love, and with thee lead my life ;
Thou hast no husband yet, nor I no wife.
Give me thy hand.
    Luc.   O, soft, sir, hold you still ;
I'll fetch my sister to get her good will. 70
                   [*Exit Luciana.*

        Enter Dromio *of Syracuse.*

    Ant. S. Why, how now, Dromio ! Where
run'st thou so fast ?
    Dro. S. Do you know me, sir ? Am I
Dromio ? Am I your man ? Am I myself ?
    Ant. S. Thou art Dromio, thou art my
man, thou art thyself. 76
    Dro. S. I am an ass, I am a woman's
man, and besides myself.
    Ant. S. What woman's man, and how
besides thyself ?
    Dro. S. Marry, sir, besides myself, I am
due to a woman—one that claims me, one
that haunts me, one that will have me.
    Ant. S. What claim lays she to thee ? 83
    Dro. S. Marry, sir, such claim as you
would lay to your horse : and she would
have me as a beast : not that, I being a
beast, she would have me ; but that she,

being a very beastly creature, lays claim
to me.   87

Ant. S. What is she?

Dro. S. A very reverent body; ay, such
a one as a man may not speak of without
he say 'Sir-reverence'. I have but lean
luck in the match, and yet is she a wondrous fat marriage.   92

Ant. S. How dost thou mean a fat
marriage?

Dro. S. Marry, sir, she's the kitchen-
wench, and all grease; and I know not
what use to put her to but to make a lamp
of her and run from her by her own light.
I warrant, her rags and the tallow in them
will burn a Poland winter. If she lives
till doomsday, she'll burn a week longer
than the whole world.

Ant. S. What complexion is she of?   100

Dro. S. Swart, like my shoe; but her face
nothing like so clean kept; for why she
sweats, a man may go over shoes in the
grime of it.

Ant. S. That's a fault that water will
mend.

Dro. S. No, sir, 'tis in grain; Noah's
flood could not do it.   106

Ant. S. What's her name?

Dro. S. Nell, sir; but her name and
three quarters, that's an ell and three
quarters, will not measure her from hip to
hip.   110

Ant. S. Then she bears some breadth?

Dro. S. No longer from head to foot than
from hip to hip: she is spherical, like a
globe; I could find out countries in her.

Ant. S. In what part of her body stands
Ireland?   115

Dro. S. Marry, sir, in her buttocks; I
found it out by the bogs.

Ant. S. Where Scotland?

Dro. S. I found it by the barrenness, hard
in the palm of the hand.   120

Ant. S. Where France?

Dro. S. In her forehead, arm'd and re-
verted, making war against her heir.

Ant. S. Where England?   124

Dro. S. I look'd for the chalky cliffs, but
I could find no whiteness in them; but I
guess it stood in her chin, by the salt rheum
that ran between France and it.

Ant. S. Where Spain?

Dro. S. Faith, I saw it not, but I felt it
hot in her breath.   130

Ant. S. Where America, the Indies?

Dro. S. O, sir, upon her nose, all o'er
embellished with rubies, carbuncles, sap-
phires, declining their rich aspect to the hot
breath of Spain; who sent whole armadoes
of caracks to be ballast at her nose.   135

Ant. S. Where stood Belgia, the Nether-
lands?

Dro. S. O, sir, I did not look so low. To
conclude: this drudge or diviner laid claim

to me; call'd me Dromio; swore I was
assur'd to her; told me what privy marks
I had about me, as, the mark of my shoulder,
the mole in my neck, the great wart on my
left arm, that I, amaz'd, ran from her as a
witch.   142

And, I think, if my breast had not been
      made of faith, and my heart of steel,
She had transform'd me to a curtal dog,
      and made me turn i' th' wheel.

Ant. S. Go hie thee presently post to the
      road;   145
An if the wind blow any way from shore,
I will not harbour in this town to-night.
If any bark put forth, come to the mart,
Where I will walk till thou return to me.
If every one knows us, and we know
      none,   150
'Tis time, I think, to trudge, pack, and be
      gone.

Dro. S. As from a bear a man would run
      for life,
So fly I from her that would be my wife.
                       [*Exit.*

Ant. S. There's none but witches do
      inhabit here,
And therefore 'tis high time that I were
      hence.   155
She that doth call me husband, even my
      soul
Doth for a wife abhor. But her fair sister,
Possess'd with such a gentle sovereign
      grace,   158
Of such enchanting presence and discourse,
Hath almost made me traitor to myself;
But, lest myself be guilty to self-wrong,
I'll stop mine ears against the mermaid's
      song.   162

Enter ANGELO *with the chain.*

Ang. Master Antipholus!

Ant. S.   Ay, that's my name.

Ang. I know it well, sir. Lo, here is the
      chain.
I thought to have ta'en you at the Por-
      pentine;   165
The chain unfinish'd made me stay thus
      long.

Ant. S. What is your will that I shall do
      with this?

Ang. What please yourself, sir; I have
      made it for you.

Ant. S. Made it for me, sir! I bespoke it
      not.

Ang. Not once nor twice, but twenty
      times you have.   170
Go home with it, and please your wife
      withal;
And soon at supper-time I'll visit you,
And then receive my money for the chain.

Ant. S. I pray you, sir, receive the money
      now,
For fear you ne'er see chain nor money
      more.   175

Ang. You are a merry man, sir; fare you
    well.   [*Exit.*

Ant. S. What I should think of this I
    cannot tell ;

But this I think, there's no man is so vain
That would refuse so fair an offer'd chain.
I see a man here needs not live by shifts,
When in the streets he meets such golden
    gifts.   181
I'll to the mart, and there for Dromio stay ;
If any ship put out, then straight away.
                              [*Exit.*

ACT FOUR

Scene I. *A public place.*

Enter Second Merchant, ANGELO, *and an*
Officer.

Sec. Mer. You know since Pentecost the
    sum is due,

And since I have not much importun'd you;
Nor now I had not, but that I am bound
To Persia, and want guilders for my voyage;
Therefore make present satisfaction,   5
Or I'll attach you by this officer.

Ang. Even just the sum that I do owe
    to you

Is growing to me by Antipholus ;
And in the instant that I met with you
He had of me a chain ; at five o'clock   10
I shall receive the money for the same.
Pleaseth you walk with me down to his
    house,

I will discharge my bond, and thank you
    too.

Enter ANTIPHOLUS of Ephesus, *and*
DROMIO of Ephesus, *from the courtezan's.*

Off. That labour may you save ; see
    where he comes.

Ant. E. While I go to the goldsmith's
    house, go thou   15
And buy a rope's end ; that will I bestow
Among my wife and her confederates,
For locking me out of my doors by day.
But, soft, I see the goldsmith. Get thee
    gone ;   19
Buy thou a rope, and bring it home to me.

Dro. E. I buy a thousand pound a year ;
    I buy a rope.   [*Exit Dromio.*

Ant. E. A man is well holp up that trusts
    to you !

I promised your presence and the chain ;
But neither chain nor goldsmith came to
    me.

Belike you thought our love would last too
    long,   25
If it were chain'd together, and therefore
    came not.

Ang. Saving your merry humour, here's
    the note

How much your chain weighs to the utmost
    carat,
The fineness of the gold, and chargeful
    fashion,

Which doth amount to three odd ducats
    more   30
Than I stand debted to this gentleman.
I pray you see him presently discharg'd,
For he is bound to sea, and stays but for it.

Ant. E. I am not furnish'd with the
    present money ;   34
Besides, I have some business in the town.
Good signior, take the stranger to my house,
And with you take the chain, and bid my
    wife
Disburse the sum on the receipt thereof.
Perchance I will be there as soon as you.

Ang. Then you will bring the chain to her
    yourself ?   40

Ant. E. No ; bear it with you, lest I come
    not time enough.

Ang. Well, sir, I will. Have you the
    chain about you ?

Ant. E. An if I have not, sir, I hope you
    have ;

Or else you may return without your
    money.

Ang. Nay, come, I pray you, sir, give me
    the chain ;   45
Both wind and tide stays for this gentle-
    man,
And I, to blame, have held him here too
    long.

Ant. E. Good Lord ! you use this dalliance
    to excuse   48
Your breach of promise to the Porpentine ;
I should have chid you for not bringing it,
But, like a shrew, you first begin to brawl.

Sec. Mer. The hour steals on ; I pray you,
    sir, dispatch.

Ang. You hear how he importunes me—
    the chain !

Ant. E. Why, give it to my wife, and
    fetch your money.

Ang. Come, come, you know I gave it
    you even now.   55
Either send the chain or send by me some
    token.

Ant. E. Fie, now you run this humour
    out of breath !
Come, where's the chain ? I pray you let
    me see it.

Sec. Mer. My business cannot brook this
    dalliance.
Good sir, say whe'r you'll answer me or no ;
If not, I'll leave him to the officer.   61

Ant. E. I answer you ! What should I
    answer you ?

Ang. The money that you owe me for the
    chain.

Ant. E. I owe you none till I receive the
    chain.

Ang. You know I gave it you half an
    hour since.   65

Ant. E. You gave me none ; you wrong
    me much to say so.

Ang. You wrong me more, sir, in denying
    it.

Consider how it stands upon my credit.

Sec. Mer. Well, officer, arrest him at my
　　suit.

Off. I do ; and charge you in the Duke's
　　name to obey me.　　　　　　　　71

Ang. This touches me in reputation.
Either consent to pay this sum for me,
Or I attach you by this officer.

Ant. E. Consent to pay thee that I never
　　had !　　　　　　　　　　　　　75
Arrest me, foolish fellow, if thou dar'st.

Ang. Here is thy fee ; arrest him, officer.
I would not spare my brother in this case,
If he should scorn me so apparently.　79

Off. I do arrest you, sir ; you hear the suit.

Ant. E. I do obey thee till I give thee bail.
But, sirrah, you shall buy this sport as dear
As all the metal in your shop will answer.

Ang. Sir, sir, I shall have law in Ephesus,
To your notorious shame, I doubt it not.　85

Enter DROMIO *of Syracuse, from the bay.*

Dro. S. Master, there's a bark of Epidam-
　　num
That stays but till her owner comes aboard,
And then, sir, she bears away. Our fraught-
　　age, sir,
I have convey'd aboard ; and I have bought
The oil, the balsamum, and aqua-vitæ.　90
The ship is in her trim ; the merry wind
Blows fair from land ; they stay for nought
　　at all
But for their owner, master, and yourself.

Ant. E. How now ! a madman ? Why,
　　thou peevish sheep,
What ship of Epidamnum stays for me ?　95

Dro. S. A ship you sent me to, to hire
　　waftage.

Ant. E. Thou drunken slave, I sent thee
　　for a rope ;
And told thee to what purpose and what
　　end.

Dro. S. You sent me for a rope's end as
　　soon—
You sent me to the bay, sir, for a bark.　100

Ant. E. I will debate this matter at more
　　leisure,
And teach your ears to list me with more
　　heed.
To Adriana, villain, hie thee straight ;
Give her this key, and tell her in the desk
That's cover'd o'er with Turkish tapestry
There is a purse of ducats ; let her send it.
Tell her I am arrested in the street,　　107
And that shall bail me ; hie thee, slave, be
　　gone.
On, officer, to prison till it come.
　　　　　　　　　[*Exeunt all but Dromio.*

Dro. S. To Adriana ! that is where we
　　din'd,　　　　　　　　　　　　110
Where Dowsabel did claim me for her
　　husband.
She is too big, I hope, for me to compass.
Thither I must, although against my will,

For servants must their masters' minds
　　fulfil.　　　　　　　　　　[*Exit.*

SCENE II.　*The house of Antipholus of
　　　　　　　　　　Ephesus.*

Enter ADRIANA *and* LUCIANA.

Adr. Ah, Luciana, did he tempt thee so ?
Mightst thou perceive austerely in his eye
That he did plead in earnest ? Yea or no ?
Look'd he or red or pale, or sad or
　　merrily ?　　　　　　　　　　　4
What observation mad'st thou in this case
Of his heart's meteors tilting in his face ?

Luc. First he denied you had in him no
　　right.

Adr. He meant he did me none—the
　　more my spite.

Luc. Then swore he that he was a stranger
　　here.

Adr. And true he swore, though yet
　　forsworn he were.　　　　　　　10

Luc. Then pleaded I for you.

Adr. 　　　　　　　And what said he ?

Luc. That love I begg'd for you he begg'd
　　of me.

Adr. With what persuasion did he tempt
　　thy love ?

Luc. With words that in an honest suit
　　might move.
First he did praise my beauty, then my
　　speech.　　　　　　　　　　15

Adr. Didst speak him fair ?

Luc. 　　　　　　Have patience, I beseech.

Adr. I cannot, nor I will not hold me still ;
My tongue, though not my heart, shall have
　　his will.
He is deformed, crooked, old, and sere,
Ill-fac'd, worse bodied, shapeless every-
　　where ;　　　　　　　　　　20
Vicious, ungentle, foolish, blunt, unkind ;
Stigmatical in making, worse in mind.

Luc. Who would be jealous then of such
　　a one ?
No evil lost is wail'd when it is gone.

Adr. Ah, but I think him better than I
　　say,　　　　　　　　　　　25
And yet would herein others' eyes were
　　worse.
Far from her nest the lapwing cries away ;
My heart prays for him, though my tongue
　　do curse.

Enter DROMIO *of Syracuse.*

Dro. S. Here go—the desk, the purse.
Sweet now, make haste.

Luc. How hast thou lost thy breath ?

Dro. S. 　　　　　　　By running fast.

Adr. Where is thy master, Dromio ? Is
　　he well ?　　　　　　　　　　31

Dro. S. No, he's in Tartar limbo, worse
　　than hell.
A devil in an everlasting garment hath him ;
One whose hard heart is button'd up with
　　steel ;

A fiend, a fairy, pitiless and rough ;   35
A wolf, nay worse, a fellow all in buff ;
A back-friend, a shoulder-clapper, one that
    countermands
The passages of alleys, creeks, and narrow
    lands ;
A hound that runs counter, and yet draws
    dry-foot well ;
One that, before the Judgment, carries poor
    souls to hell.   40
  Adr. Why, man, what is the matter ?
  Dro. S. I do not know the matter ; he is
'rested on the case.
  Adr. What, is he arrested ? Tell me, at
whose suit ?
  Dro. S. I know not at whose suit he is
arrested well ;
But he's in a suit of buff which 'rested him,
    that can I tell.   45
Will you send him, mistress, redemption,
    the money in his desk ?
  Adr. Go fetch it, sister. [*Exit Luciana*]
    This I wonder at :
Thus he unknown to me should be in debt.
Tell me, was he arrested on a band ?
  Dro. S. Not on a band, but on a stronger
    thing,   50
A chain, a chain. Do you not hear it ring ?
  Adr. What, the chain ?
  Dro. S. No, no, the bell ; 'tis time that
    I were gone.
It was two ere I left him, and now the
    clock strikes one.
  Adr. The hours come back ! That did I
    never hear.   55
  Dro. S. O yes. If any hour meet a
sergeant, 'a turns back for very fear.
  Adr. As if Time were in debt ! How
fondly dost thou reason !
  Dro. S. Time is a very bankrupt, and owes
more than he's worth to season.
Nay, he's a thief too : have you not heard
    men say
That Time comes stealing on by night and
    day ?   60
If 'a be in debt and theft, and a sergeant in
    the way,
Hath he not reason to turn back an hour
    in a day ?

     Re-enter LUCIANA *with a purse.*

  Adr. Go, Dromio, there's the money ;
    bear it straight,
And bring thy master home immediately.
Come, sister ; I am press'd down with
    conceit—   65
Conceit, my comfort and my injury.
             [*Exeunt.*

    SCENE III. *The mart.*

    Enter ANTIPHOLUS *of* Syracuse.

  Ant. S. There's not a man I meet but
    doth salute me
As if I were their well-acquainted friend ;

And every one doth call me by my name.
Some tender money to me, some invite me,
Some other give me thanks for kindnesses,
Some offer me commodities to buy ;   6
Even now a tailor call'd me in his shop,
And show'd me silks that he had bought for
    me,
And therewithal took measure of my body.
Sure, these are but imaginary wiles,   10
And Lapland sorcerers inhabit here.

    Enter DROMIO *of* Syracuse.

  Dro. S. Master, here's the gold you sent
me for. What, have you got the picture of
old Adam new-apparell'd ?
  Ant. S. What gold is this ? What Adam
dost thou mean ?   14
  Dro. S. Not that Adam that kept the
Paradise, but that Adam that keeps the
prison ; he that goes in the calf's skin that
was kill'd for the Prodigal ; he that came
behind you, sir, like an evil angel, and bid
you forsake your liberty.
  Ant. S. I understand thee not.   19
  Dro. S. No ? Why, 'tis a plain case : he
that went, like a bass-viol, in a case of
leather ; the man, sir, that, when gentlemen are tired, gives them a sob, and rests
them ; he, sir, that takes pity on decayed
men, and gives them suits of durance ; he
that sets up his rest to do more exploits
with his mace than a morris-pike.   25
  Ant. S. What, thou mean'st an officer ?
  Dro. S. Ay, sir, the sergeant of the band ;
he that brings any man to answer it that
breaks his band ; one that thinks a man
always going to bed, and says ' God give
you good rest ! '   30
  Ant. S. Well, sir, there rest in your
foolery. Is there any ship puts forth to-
night ? May we be gone ?
  Dro. S. Why, sir, I brought you word an
hour since that the bark Expedition put
forth to-night ; and then were you
hind'red by the sergeant, to tarry for the
hoy Delay. Here are the angels that you
sent for to deliver you.   36
  Ant. S. The fellow is distract, and so am I ;
And here we wander in illusions.
Some blessed power deliver us from hence !

    Enter a Courtezan.

  Cour. Well met, well met, Master
    Antipholus.   40
I see, sir, you have found the goldsmith now.
Is that the chain you promis'd me to-day ?
  Ant. S. Satan, avoid ! I charge thee,
    tempt me not.
  Dro. S. Master, is this Mistress Satan ?
  Ant. S. It is the devil.   45
  Dro. S. Nay, she is worse, she is the
devil's dam, and here she comes in the habit
of a light wench ; and thereof comes that
the wenches say ' God damn me ! ' That's

as much to say 'God make me a light
wench!' It is written they appear to men
like angels of light; light is an effect of fire,
and fire will burn; ergo, light wenches will
burn. Come not near her.   52
    Cour. Your man and you are marvellous
merry, sir.
Will you go with me? We'll mend our
    dinner here.
    Dro. S. Master, if you do, expect spoon-
meat, or bespeak a long spoon.   56
    Ant. S. Why, Dromio?
    Dro. S. Marry, he must have a long spoon
that must eat with the devil.
    Ant. S. Avoid then, fiend! What tell'st
    thou me of supping?   60
Thou art, as you are all, a sorceress;
I conjure thee to leave me and be gone.
    Cour. Give me the ring of mine you had
    at dinner,
Or, for my diamond, the chain you
    promis'd,
And I'll be gone, sir, and not trouble you.
    Dro. S. Some devils ask but the parings
    of one's nail,   66
A rush, a hair, a drop of blood, a pin,
A nut, a cherry-stone;
But she, more covetous, would have a chain.
Master, be wise; an if you give it her, 70
The devil will shake her chain, and fright
    us with it.
    Cour. I pray you, sir, my ring, or else the
    chain;
I hope you do not mean to cheat me so.
    Ant. S. Avaunt, thou witch! Come,
    Dromio, let us go.
    Dro. 'Fly pride' says the peacock.
    Mistress, that you know.   75
         [*Exeunt Ant. S. and Dro. S.*
    Cour. Now, out of doubt, Antipholus is
    mad,
Else would he never so demean himself.
A ring he hath of mine worth forty ducats,
And for the same he promis'd me a chain;
Both one and other he denies me now. 80
The reason that I gather he is mad,
Besides this present instance of his rage,
Is a mad tale he told to-day at dinner
Of his own doors being shut against his
    entrance.
Belike his wife, acquainted with his fits, 85
On purpose shut the doors against his way.
My way is now to hie home to his house,
And tell his wife that, being lunatic,
He rush'd into my house and took perforce
My ring away. This course I fittest choose,
For forty ducats is too much to lose. [*Exit.*

         SCENE IV. *A street.*

    Enter ANTIPHOLUS *of Ephesus with
         the Officer.*

    Ant. E. Fear me not, man; I will not
    break away.

I'll give thee, ere I leave thee, so much
    money,
To warrant thee, as I am 'rested for.
My wife is in a wayward mood to-day,
And will not lightly trust the messenger. 5
That I should be attach'd in Ephesus,
I tell you 'twill sound harshly in her ears.

    Enter DROMIO *of Ephesus, with a
         rope's-end.*

Here comes my man; I think he brings the
    money.
How now, sir! Have you that I sent you
    for?
    Dro. E. Here's that, I warrant you, will
    pay them all.   10
    Ant. E. But where's the money?
    Dro. E. Why, sir, I gave the money for
    the rope.
    Ant. E. Five hundred ducats, villain, for
    a rope?
    Dro. E. I'll serve you, sir, five hundred at
    the rate.
    Ant. E. To what end did I bid thee hie
    thee home?   15
    Dro. E. To a rope's-end, sir; and to that
    end am I return'd.
    Ant. E. And to that end, sir, I will
    welcome you.   [*Beating him.*
    Off. Good sir, be patient.
    Dro. E. Nay, 'tis for me to be patient;
I am in adversity.   20
    Off. Good now, hold thy tongue.
    Dro. E. Nay, rather persuade him to hold
his hands.
    Ant. E. Thou whoreson, senseless villain!
    Dro. E. I would I were senseless, sir, that
I might not feel your blows.   25
    Ant. E. Thou art sensible in nothing but
blows, and so is an ass.
    Dro. E. I am an ass indeed; you may
prove it by my long 'ears. I have served
him from the hour of my nativity to this
instant, and have nothing at his hands for
my service but blows. When I am cold he
heats me with beating; when I am warm
he cools me with beating. I am wak'd with
it when I sleep; rais'd with it when I sit;
driven out of doors with it when I go from
home; welcom'd home with it when I
return; nay, I bear it on my shoulders as
a beggar wont her brat; and I think, when
he hath lam'd me, I shall beg with it from
door to door.   37

    Enter ADRIANA, LUCIANA, *the* Courtezan,
         and a Schoolmaster *call'd* PINCH.

    Ant. E. Come, go along; my wife is
    coming yonder.
    Dro. E. Mistress, 'respice finem', respect
your end; or rather, to prophesy like the
parrot, 'Beware the rope's-end'.   40
    Ant. E. Wilt thou still talk? [*Beating him.*

                                    129

Cour. How say you now ? Is not your
    husband mad ?

Adr. His incivility confirms no less.

Good Doctor Pinch, you are a conjurer :

Establish him in his true sense again,   45

And I will please you what you will demand.

Luc. Alas, how fiery and how sharp he
    looks !

Cour. Mark how he trembles in his
    ecstasy.

Pinch. Give me your hand, and let me
    feel your pulse.   49

Ant. E. There is my hand, and let it feel
    your ear.   [*Striking him.*

Pinch. I charge thee, Satan, hous'd
    within this man,

To yield possession to my holy prayers,

And to thy state of darkness hie thee
    straight.

I conjure thee by all the saints in heaven.

Ant. E. Peace, doting wizard, peace ! I
    am not mad.   55

Adr. O, that thou wert not, poor dis-
    tressed soul !

Ant. E. You minion, you, are these your
    customers ?

Did this companion with the saffron face

Revel and feast it at my house to-day,

Whilst upon me the guilty doors were shut,

And I denied to enter in my house ?   61

Adr. O husband, God doth know you
    din'd at home,

Where would you had remain'd until this
    time,

Free from these slanders and this open
    shame !

Ant. E. Din'd at home ! Thou villain,
    what sayest thou ?   65

Dro. E. Sir, sooth to say, you did not
    dine at home.

Ant. E. Were not my doors lock'd up and
    I shut out ?

Dro. E. Perdie, your doors were lock'd
    and you shut out.

Ant. E. And did not she herself revile me
    there ?

Dro. E. Sans fable, she herself revil'd you
    there.   70

Ant. E. Did not her kitchen-maid rail,
    taunt, and scorn me ?

Dro. E. Certes, she did ; the kitchen-
    vestal scorn'd you.

Ant. E. And did not I in rage depart from
    thence ?

Dro. E. In verity, you did. My bones
    bear witness,   74

That since have felt the vigour of his
    rage.

Adr. Is't good to soothe him in these
    contraries ?

Pinch. It is no shame ; the fellow finds
    his vein,

And, yielding to him, humours well his
    frenzy.

Ant. E. Thou hast suborn'd the gold-
    smith to arrest me.

Adr. Alas, I sent you money to redeem
    you,   80

By Dromio here, who came in haste for it.

Dro. E. Money by me ! Heart and good-
    will you might,

But surely, master, not a rag of money.

Ant. E. Went'st not thou to her for a
    purse of ducats ?   84

Adr. He came to me, and I deliver'd it.

Luc. And I am witness with her that she
    did.

Dro. E. God and the rope-maker bear me
    witness

That I was sent for nothing but a rope !

Pinch. Mistress, both man and master is
    possess'd ;

I know it by their pale and deadly looks.   90

They must be bound, and laid in some dark
    room.

Ant. E. Say, wherefore didst thou lock
    me forth to-day ?

And why dost thou deny the bag of gold ?

Adr. I did not, gentle husband, lock thee
    forth.

Dro. E. And, gentle master, I receiv'd no
    gold ;   95

But I confess, sir, that we were lock'd
    out.

Adr. Dissembling villain, thou speak'st
    false in both.

Ant. E. Dissembling harlot, thou art
    false in all,

And art confederate with a damned pack

To make a loathsome abject scorn of me ;

But with these nails I'll pluck out these
    false eyes   101

That would behold in me this shameful
    sport.

Adr. O, bind him, bind him ; let him not
    come near me.

Pinch. More company ! The fiend is
    strong within him.

*Enter three or four, and offer to bind him.
He strives.*

Luc. Ay me, poor man, how pale and
    wan he looks !   105

Ant. E. What, will you murder me ?
    Thou gaoler, thou,

I am thy prisoner. Wilt thou suffer them

To make a rescue ?

Off.   Masters, let him go ;

He is my prisoner, and you shall not have
    him.

Pinch. Go bind this man, for he is frantic
    too.   [*They bind Dromio.*

Adr. What wilt thou do, thou peevish
    officer ?   111

Hast thou delight to see a wretched man

Do outrage and displeasure to himself ?

Off. He is my prisoner ; if I let him go,

The debt he owes will be requir'd of me.

Adr. I will discharge thee ere I go from
thee ;   116
Bear me forthwith unto his creditor,
And, knowing how the debt grows, I will
     pay it.
Good Master Doctor, see him safe convey'd
Home to my house. O most unhappy day !
     Ant. E. O most unhappy strumpet ! 121
     Dro. E. Master, I am here ent'red in bond
     for you.
     Ant. E. Out on thee, villain ! Wherefore
     dost thou mad me ?
     Dro. E. Will you be bound for nothing ?
Be mad, good master ; cry ' The devil ! '
     Luc. God help, poor souls, how idly do
     they talk !   126
     Adr. Go bear him hence. Sister, go you
     with me.
         [*Exeunt all but Adriana, Luciana,*
         Officer, and Courtezan.
Say now, whose suit is he arrested at ?
     Off. One Angelo, a goldsmith ; do you
     know him ?
     Adr. I know the man. What is the sum
     he owes ?   130
     Off. Two hundred ducats.
     Adr.   Say, how grows it due ?
     Off. Due for a chain your husband had of
     him.
     Adr. He did bespeak a chain for me, but
     had it not.
     Cour. When as your husband, all in rage,
     to-day
Came to my house, and took away my
     ring—   135
The ring I saw upon his finger now—
Straight after did I meet him with a chain.
     Adr. It may be so, but I did never see it.
Come, gaoler, bring me where the gold-
     smith is ;
I long to know the truth hereof at large. 140

Enter ANTIPHOLUS *of Syracuse, with his*
rapier drawn, and DROMIO *of Syracuse.*

     Luc. God, for thy mercy ! they are loose
     again.
     Adr. And come with naked swords.
Let's call more help to have them bound
     again.
     Off. Away, they'll kill us !
         [*Exeunt all but Ant. S. and Dro. S.*
         as fast as may be, frighted.
     Ant. S. I see these witches are afraid of
     swords.   145
     Dro. S. She that would be your wife now
     ran from you.
     Ant. S. Come to the Centaur ; fetch our
     stuff from thence.
I long that we were safe and sound aboard.
     Dro. S. Faith, stay here this night ; they
will surely do us no harm ; you saw they
speak us fair, give us gold ; methinks they
are such a gentle nation that, but for the
mountain of mad flesh that claims marriage

of me, I could find in my heart to stay here
still and turn witch.
     Ant. S. I will not stay to-night for all the
     town ;   154
Therefore away, to get our stuff aboard.
         [*Exeunt.*

ACT FIVE

SCENE I. *A street before a priory.*

Enter Second Merchant *and* ANGELO.

     Ang. I am sorry, sir, that I have hind'red
     you ;
But I protest he had the chain of me,
Though most dishonestly he doth deny it.
     Sec. Mer. How is the man esteem'd here
     in the city ?
     Ang. Of very reverent reputation, sir, 5
Of credit infinite, highly belov'd,
Second to none that lives here in the
     city ;
His word might bear my wealth at any
     time.
     Sec. Mer. Speak softly ; yonder, as I
     think, he walks.

Enter ANTIPHOLUS *of Syracuse and* DROMIO
     of Syracuse.

     Ang. 'Tis so ; and that self chain about
     his neck   10
Which he forswore most monstrously to
     have.
Good sir, draw near to me, I'll speak to him.
Signior Antipholus, I wonder much
That you would put me to this shame and
     trouble ;   14
And, not without some scandal to yourself,
With circumstance and oaths so to deny
This chain, which now you wear so openly.
Beside the charge, the shame, imprison-
     ment,
You have done wrong to this my honest
     friend ;   19
Who, but for staying on our controversy,
Had hoisted sail and put to sea to-day.
This chain you had of me ; can you deny
     it ?
     Ant. S. I think I had ; I never did
     deny it.
     Sec. Mer. Yes, that you did, sir, and
     forswore it too.
     Ant. S. Who heard me to deny it or
     forswear it ?   25
     Sec. Mer. These ears of mine, thou
     know'st, did hear thee.
Fie on thee, wretch ! 'tis pity that thou
     liv'st
To walk where any honest men resort.
     Ant. S. Thou art a villain to impeach
     me thus ;   29
I'll prove mine honour and mine honesty
Against thee presently, if thou dar'st stand.
     Sec. Mer. I dare, and do defy thee for a
     villain.   [*They draw.*

Enter ADRIANA, LUCIANA, *the* Courtezan, *and* Others.

Adr. Hold, hurt him not, for God's sake!
     He is mad.
Some get within him, take his sword away;
Bind Dromio too, and bear them to my
     house.   35
     Dro. S. Run, master, run; for God's sake
     take a house.
This is some priory. In, or we are spoil'd.
     [*Exeunt Ant. S. and Dro. S. to the priory.*

Enter the Lady Abbess.

Abb. Be quiet, people. Wherefore throng
     you hither?
Adr. To fetch my poor distracted hus-
     band hence.   40
Let us come in, that we may bind him
     fast,
And bear him home for his recovery.
     Ang. I knew he was not in his perfect
     wits.
     Sec. Mer. I am sorry now that I did draw
     on him.
     Abb. How long hath this possession held
     the man?
Adr. This week he hath been heavy, sour,
     sad,   45
And much different from the man he was;
But till this afternoon his passion
Ne'er brake into extremity of rage.
     Abb. Hath he not lost much wealth by
     wre_k of sea?
Buried some dear friend? Hath not else
     his eye   50
Stray'd his affection in unlawful love?
A sin prevailing much in youthful men
Who give their eyes the liberty of gazing.
Which of these sorrows is he subject to?
     Adr. To none of these, except it be the
     last;   55
Namely, some love that drew him oft from
     home.
     Abb. You should for that have repre-
     hended him.
Adr. Why, so I did.
Abb.   Ay, but not rough enough.
Adr. As roughly as my modesty would
     let me.   59
Abb. Haply in private.
Adr.   And in assemblies too.
Abb. Ay, but not enough.
Adr. It was the copy of our conference.
In bed, he slept not for my urging it;
At board, he fed not for my urging it;
Alone, it was the subject of my theme; 65
In company, I often glanced it;
Still did I tell him it was vile and bad.
     Abb. And thereof came it that the man
     was mad.
The venom clamours of a jealous woman
Poisons more deadly than a mad dog's
     tooth.   70

It seems his sleeps were hind'red by thy
     railing,
And thereof comes it that his head is
     light.
Thou say'st his meat was sauc'd with thy
     unbraidings:
Unquiet meals make ill digestions;
Thereof the raging fire of fever bred;   75
And what's a fever but a fit of madness?
Thou say'st his sports were hind'red by thy
     brawls.
Sweet recreation barr'd, what doth ensue
But moody and dull melancholy,
Kinsman to grim and comfortless despair,
And at her heels a huge infectious troop 81
Of pale distemperatures and foes to life?
In food, in sport, and life-preserving rest,
To be disturb'd would mad or man or
     beast.
The consequence is, then, thy jealous fits
Hath scar'd thy husband from the use of
     wits.   86
     Luc. She never reprehended him but
     mildly,
When he demean'd himself rough, rude,
     and wildly.
Why bear you these rebukes, and answer
     not?
     Adr. She did betray me to my own
     reproof.   90
Good people, enter, and lay hold on him.
     Abb. No, not a creature enters in my
     house.
     Adr. Then let your servants bring my
     husband forth.
     Abb. Neither; he took this place for
     sanctuary,   94
And it shall privilege him from your hands
Till I have brought him to his wits again,
Or lose my labour in assaying it.
     Adr. I will attend my husband, be his
     nurse,
Diet his sickness, for it is my office,
And will have no attorney but myself; 100
And therefore let me have him home with
     me.
     Abb. Be patient; for I will not let him
     stir
Till I have us'd the approved means I have,
With wholesome syrups, drugs, and holy
     prayers,
To make of him a formal man again.   105
It is a branch and parcel of mine oath,
A charitable duty of my order;
Therefore depart, and leave him here with
     me.
     Adr. I will not hence and leave my
     husband here;
And ill it doth beseem your holiness   110
To separate the husband and the wife.
     Abb. Be quiet, and depart; thou shalt
     not have him.   [*Exit Abbess.*
     Luc. Complain unto the Duke of this
     indignity.

Adr. Come, go ; I will fall prostrate at
his feet, 114
And never rise until my tears and prayers
Have won his Grace to come in person
hither
And take perforce my husband from the
Abbess.
Sec. Mer. By this, I think, the dial points
at five ;
Anon, I'm sure, the Duke himself in person
Comes this way to the melancholy vale, 120
The place of death and sorry execution,
Behind the ditches of the abbey here.
Ang. Upon what cause ?
Sec. Mer. To see a reverend Syracusian
merchant,
Who put unluckily into this bay 125
Against the laws and statutes of this town,
Beheaded publicly for his offence.
Ang. See where they come ; we will
behold his death.
Luc. Kneel to the Duke before he pass
the abbey.

Enter the DUKE, *attended ;* ÆGEON, *bare-
headed ; with the* Headsman *and
other* Officers.

Duke. Yet once again proclaim it publicly,
If any friend will pay the sum for him, 131
He shall not die ; so much we tender him.
Adr. Justice, most sacred Duke, against
the Abbess !
Duke. She is a virtuous and a reverend
lady ; 134
It cannot be that she hath done thee wrong.
Adr. May it please your Grace, Anti-
pholus, my husband,
Who I made lord of me and all I had
At your important letters—this ill day
A most outrageous fit of madness took him,
That desp'rately he hurried through the
street, 140
With him his bondman all as mad as he,
Doing displeasure to the citizens
By rushing in their houses, bearing thence
Rings, jewels, anything his rage did like.
Once did I get him bound and sent him
home, 145
Whilst to take order for the wrongs I went,
That here and there his fury had com-
mitted.
Anon, I wot not by what strong escape,
He broke from those that had the guard
of him, 149
And with his mad attendant and himself,
Each one with ireful passion, with drawn
swords,
Met us again and, madly bent on us,
Chas'd us away ; till, raising of more aid,
We came again to bind them. Then they
fled 154
Into this abbey, whither we pursu'd them ;
And here the Abbess shuts the gates on us,
And will not suffer us to fetch him out,

Nor send him forth that we may bear him
hence.
Therefore, most gracious Duke, with thy
command
Let him be brought forth and borne hence
for help. 160
Duke. Long since thy husband serv'd me
in my wars,
And I to thee engag'd a prince's word,
When thou didst make him master of thy
bed,
To do him all the grace and good I could.
Go, some of you, knock at the abbey gate,
And bid the Lady Abbess come to me. 166
I will determine this before I stir.

Enter a Messenger.

Mess. O mistress, mistress, shift and save
yourself !
My master and his man are both broke
loose,
Beaten the maids a-row and bound the
doctor, 170
Whose beard they have sing'd off with
brands of fire ;
And ever, as it blaz'd, they threw on him
Great pails of puddled mire to quench the
hair.
My master preaches patience to him, and
the while
His man with scissors nicks him like a fool ;
And sure, unless you send some present
help, 176
Between them they will kill the conjurer.
Adr. Peace, fool ! thy master and his man
are here,
And that is false thou dost report to us.
Mess. Mistress, upon my life, I tell you
true ; 180
I have not breath'd almost since I did see it.
He cries for you, and vows, if he can take
you,
To scorch your face, and to disfigure you.
[*Cry within.*
Hark, hark, I hear him, mistress ; fly, be
gone !
Duke. Come, stand by me ; fear nothing.
Guard with halberds. 185
Adr. Ay me, it is my husband ! Witness
you
That he is borne about invisible.
Even now we hous'd him in the abbey here,
And now he's there, past thought of human
reason.

Enter ANTIPHOLUS *of Ephesus and*
DROMIO *of Ephesus.*

Ant. E. Justice, most gracious Duke ; O,
grant me justice ! 190
Even for the service that long since I did
thee,
When I bestrid thee in the wars, and took
Deep scars to save thy life ; even for the
blood

That then I lost for thee, now grant me
  justice.
Æge. Unless the fear of death doth make
  me dote,   195
I see my son Antipholus, and Dromio.
  Ant. E. Justice, sweet Prince, against
    that woman there!
She whom thou gav'st to me to be my wife,
That hath abused and dishonoured me
Even in the strength and height of injury.
Beyond imagination is the wrong   201
That she this day hath shameless thrown
  on me.
  Duke. Discover how, and thou shalt find
    me just.
  Ant. E. This day, great Duke, she shut
    the doors upon me,
While she with harlots feasted in my house.
  Duke. A grievous fault. Say, woman,
    didst thou so?   206
  Adr. No, my good lord. Myself, he, and
    my sister,
To-day did dine together. So befall my soul
As this is false he burdens me withal!
  Luc. Ne'er may I look on day nor sleep
    on night   210
But she tells to your Highness simple truth!
  Ang. O perjur'd woman! They are both
    forsworn.
In this the madman justly chargeth them.
  Ant. E. My liege, I am advised what I
    say;   214
Neither disturbed with the effect of wine,
Nor heady-rash, provok'd with raging ire,
Albeit my wrongs might make one wiser
  mad.
This woman lock'd me out this day from
  dinner;
That goldsmith there, were he not pack'd
  with her,   219
Could witness it, for he was with me then;
Who parted with me to go fetch a chain,
Promising to bring it to the Porpentine,
Where Balthazar and I did dine together.
Our dinner done, and he not coming thither,
I went to seek him. In the street I met him,
And in his company that gentleman.   226
There did this perjur'd goldsmith swear me
  down
That I this day of him receiv'd the chain,
Which, God he knows, I saw not; for the
  which
He did arrest me with an officer.   230
I did obey, and sent my peasant home
For certain ducats; he with none return'd.
Then fairly I bespoke the officer
To go in person with me to my house.
By th' way we met my wife, her sister, and
  a rabble more   235
Of vile confederates. Along with them
They brought one Pinch, a hungry lean-
  fac'd villain,
A mere anatomy, a mountebank,
A threadbare juggler, and a fortune-teller,

A needy, hollow-ey'd, sharp-looking wretch,
A living dead man. This pernicious slave,
Forsooth, took on him as a conjurer,   242
And gazing in mine eyes, feeling my pulse,
And with no face, as 'twere, outfacing me,
Cries out I was possess'd. Then all to-
  gether   245
They fell upon me, bound me, bore me
  thence,
And in a dark and dankish vault at home
There left me and my man, both bound
  together;
Till, gnawing with my teeth my bonds in
  sunder,
I gain'd my freedom, and immediately   250
Ran hither to your Grace; whom I be-
  seech
To give me ample satisfaction
For these deep shames and great indignities.
  Ang. My lord, in truth, thus far I witness
    with him,
That he din'd not at home, but was lock'd
    out.   255
  Duke. But had he such a chain of thee,
    or no?
  Ang. He had, my lord, and when he ran
    in here,
These people saw the chain about his neck.
  Sec. Mer. Besides, I will be sworn these
    ears of mine
Heard you confess you had the chain of
  him,   260
After you first forswore it on the mart;
And thereupon I drew my sword on you,
And then you fled into this abbey here,
From whence, I think, you are come by
  miracle.
  Ant. E. I never came within these abbey
    walls,   265
Nor ever didst thou draw thy sword on me;
I never saw the chain, so help me Heaven!
And this is false you burden me withal.
  Duke. Why, what an intricate impeach
    is this!   269
I think you all have drunk of Circe's cup.
If here you hous'd him, here he would have
  been;
If he were mad, he would not plead so
  coldly.
You say he din'd at home: the goldsmith
  here
Denies that saying. Sirrah, what say you?
  Dro. E. Sir, he din'd with her there, at
    the Porpentine.   275
  Cour. He did; and from my finger
    snatch'd that ring.
  Ant. E. 'Tis true, my liege; this ring I
    had of her.
  Duke. Saw'st thou him enter at the abbey
    here?
  Cour. As sure, my liege, as I do see your
    Grace.
  Duke. Why, this is strange. Go call the
    Abbess hither.

I think you are all mated or stark mad.
[*Exit one to the Abbess.*

Æge. Most mighty Duke, vouchsafe me
    speak a word :
Haply I see a friend will save my life
And pay the sum that may deliver me.
    Duke. Speak freely, Syracusian, what
    thou wilt.   285
    Æge. Is not your name, sir, call'd
Antipholus ?
And is not that your bondman Dromio ?
    Dro. E. Within this hour I was his bond-
    man, sir,
But he, I thank him, gnaw'd in two my
    cords ;   289
Now am I Dromio and his man unbound.
    Æge. I am sure you both of you remember
    me.
    Dro. E. Ourselves we do remember, sir,
    by you ;
For lately we were bound as you are now.
You are not Pinch's patient, are you, sir ?
    Æge. Why look you strange on me ? You
    know me well.   295
    Ant. E. I never saw you in my life till
now.
    Æge. O! grief hath chang'd me since
    you saw me last ;
And careful hours with time's deformed
    hand
Have written strange defeatures in my face.
But tell me yet, dost thou not know my
    voice ?   300
    Ant. E. Neither.
    Æge. Dromio, nor thou ?
    Dro. E.   No, trust me, sir, nor I.
    Æge. I am sure thou dost.
    Dro. E. Ay, sir, but I am sure I do not ;
and whatsoever a man denies, you are now
bound to believe him.   305
    Æge. Not know my voice ! O time's
    extremity,
Hast thou so crack'd and splitted my poor
    tongue
In seven short years that here my only son
Knows not my feeble key of untun'd cares ?
Though now this grained face of mine be
    hid   310
In sap-consuming winter's drizzled snow,
And all the conduits of my blood froze up,
Yet hath my night of life some memory,
My wasting lamps some fading glimmer
    left,
My dull deaf ears a little use to hear ;   315
All these old witnesses—I cannot err—
Tell me thou art my son Antipholus.
    Ant. E. I never saw my father in my life.
    Æge. But seven years since, in Syracusa,
    boy,
Thou know'st we parted ; but perhaps, my
    son,   320
Thou sham'st to acknowledge me in misery.
    Ant. E. The Duke and all that know me
    in the city

Can witness with me that it is not so :
I ne'er saw Syracusa in my life.
    Duke. I tell thee, Syracusian, twenty
    years   325
Have I been patron to Antipholus,
During which time he ne'er saw Syracusa.
I see thy age and dangers make thee dote.

Re-enter the Abbess, *with* ANTIPHOLUS *of*
Syracuse *and* DROMIO *of Syracuse.*

    Abb. Most mighty Duke, behold a man
    much wrong'd.
[*All gather to see them.*
    Adr. I see two husbands, or mine eyes
    deceive me.   330
    Duke. One of these men is genius to the
    other ;
And so of these. Which is the natural man,
And which the spirit ? Who deciphers
    them ?
    Dro. S. I, sir, am Dromio ; command
    him away.
    Dro. E. I, sir, am Dromio ; pray let me
    stay.   335
    Ant. S. Ægeon, art thou not ? or else his
    ghost ?
    Dro. S. O, my old master ! who hath
    bound him here ?
    Abb. Whoever bound him, I will loose
    his bonds,
And gain a husband by his liberty.
Speak, old Ægeon, if thou be'st the man
That hadst a wife once call'd Æmilia,   341
That bore thee at a burden two fair sons,
O, if thou be'st the same Ægeon, speak,
And speak unto the same Æmilia !
    Æge. If I dream not, thou art Æmilia.
If thou art she, tell me where is that son
That floated with thee on the fatal raft ?
    Abb. By men of Epidamnum he and I
And the twin Dromio, all were taken up ;
But by and by rude fishermen of Corinth
By force took Dromio and my son from
    them,   351
And me they left with those of Epidam-
    num.
What then became of them I cannot tell ;
I to this fortune that you see me in.
    Duke. Why, here begins his morning
    story right.   355
These two Antipholus', these two so like,
And these two Dromios, one in semblance—
Besides her urging of her wreck at sea—
These are the parents to these children,
Which accidentally are met together.   360
Antipholus, thou cam'st from Corinth
    first ?
    Ant. S. No, sir, not I ; I came from
    Syracuse.
    Duke. Stay, stand apart ; I know not
    which is which.
    Ant. E. I came from Corinth, my most
    gracious lord.
    Dro. E. And I with him.   365

Ant. E. Brought to this town by that most famous warrior,
Duke Menaphon, your most renowned uncle.

Adr. Which of you two did dine with me to-day ?

Ant. S. I, gentle mistress.

Adr.   And are not you my husband ?

Ant. E. No ; I say nay to that. 370

Ant. S. And so do I, yet did she call me so ;
And this fair gentlewoman, her sister here,
Did call me brother. [*To Luciana*] What I told you then,
I hope I shall have leisure to make good ;
If this be not a dream I see and hear. 375

Ang. That is the chain, sir, which you had of me.

Ant. S. I think it be, sir ; I deny it not.

Ant. E. And you, sir, for this chain arrested me.

Ang. I think I did, sir ; I deny it not.

Adr. I sent you money, sir, to be your bail, 380
By Dromio ; but I think he brought it not.

Dro. E. No, none by me.

Ant. S. This purse of ducats I receiv'd from you,
And Dromio my man did bring them me.
I see we still did meet each other's man, 385
And I was ta'en for him, and he for me,
And thereupon these ERRORS are arose.

Ant. E. These ducats pawn I for my father here.

Duke. It shall not need ; thy father hath his life.

Cour. Sir, I must have that diamond from you. 390

Ant. E. There, take it ; and much thanks for my good cheer.

Abb. Renowned Duke, vouchsafe to take the pains
To go with us into the abbey here,
And hear at large discoursed all our fortunes ;

And all that are assembled in this place 395
That by this sympathized one day's error
Have suffer'd wrong, go keep us company,
And we shall make full satisfaction.
Thirty-three years have I but gone in travail 399
Of you, my sons ; and till this present hour
My heavy burden ne'er delivered.
The Duke, my husband, and my children both,
And you the calendars of their nativity,
Go to a gossips' feast, and go with me ;
After so long grief, such nativity ! 405

Duke. With all my heart, I'll gossip at this feast. [*Exeunt all but Ant. S., Ant. E., Dro. S., and Dro. E.*

Dro. S. Master, shall I fetch your stuff from shipboard ?

Ant. E. Dromio, what stuff of mine hast thou embark'd ?

Dro. S. Your goods that lay at host, sir, in the Centaur.

Ant. S. He speaks to me. I am your master, Dromio. 410
Come, go with us ; we'll look to that anon.
Embrace thy brother there ; rejoice with him.   [*Exeunt Ant. S. and Ant. E.*

Dro. S. There is a fat friend at your master's house,
That kitchen'd me for you to-day at dinner;
She now shall be my sister, not my wife. 415

Dro. E. Methinks you are my glass, and not my brother;
I see by you I am a sweet-fac'd youth.
Will you walk in to see their gossiping ?

Dro. S. Not I, sir ; you are my elder.

Dro. E. That's a question ; how shall we try it ? 420

Dro. S. We'll draw cuts for the senior ;
till then, lead thou first.

Dro. E. Nay, then, thus :
We came into the world like brother and brother,
And now let's go hand in hand, not one before another.   [*Exeunt.*

MUCH ADO ABOUT NOTHING

DRAMATIS PERSONÆ

DON PEDRO, *Prince of Arragon*.
DON JOHN, *his bastard brother*.
CLAUDIO, *a young lord of Florence*.
BENEDICK, *a young lord of Padua*.
LEONATO, *Governor of Messina*.
ANTONIO, *his brother*.
BALTHASAR, *attendant on Don Pedro*.
BORACHIO, }
CONRADE, } *followers of Don John*.
FRIAR FRANCIS.

DOGBERRY, *a constable*.
VERGES, *a headborough*.
A Sexton.
A Boy.

HERO, *daughter to Leonato*.
BEATRICE, *niece to Leonato*.
MARGARET, } *gentlewomen attending on*
URSULA, } *Hero*.

Messengers, Watch, Attendants.

THE SCENE : *Messina*.

ACT ONE

SCENE I. *Before Leonato's house.*

Enter LEONATO, HERO, *and* BEATRICE, *with a* Messenger.

Leon. I learn in this letter that Don Pedro of Arragon comes this night to Messina.

Mess. He is very near by this ; he was not three leagues off when I left him.

Leon. How many gentlemen have you lost in this action ? 5

Mess. But few of any sort, and none of name.

Leon. A victory is twice itself when the achiever brings home full numbers. I find here that Don Pedro hath bestowed much honour on a young Florentine called Claudio. 9

Mess. Much deserv'd on his part, and equally rememb'red by Don Pedro. He hath borne himself beyond the promise of his age, doing, in the figure of a lamb, the feats of a lion ; he hath, indeed, better bett'red expectation than you must expect of me to tell you how. 14

Leon. He hath an uncle here in Messina will be very much glad of it.

Mess. I have already delivered him letters, and there appears much joy in him ; even so much that joy could not show itself modest enough without a badge of bitterness.

Leon. Did he break out into tears ? 20

Mess. In great measure.

Leon. A kind overflow of kindness. There are no faces truer than those that are so wash'd. How much better is it to weep at joy than to joy at weeping !

Beat. I pray you, is Signior Mountanto return'd from the wars or no ? 26

Mess. I know none of that name, lady ; there was none such in the army of any sort.

Leon. What is he that you ask for, niece ?

Hero. My cousin means Signior Benedick of Padua. 30

Mess. O, he's return'd, and as pleasant as ever he was.

Beat. He set up his bills here in Messina, and challeng'd Cupid at the flight ; and my uncle's fool, reading the challenge, subscrib'd for Cupid, and challeng'd him at the bird-bolt. I pray you, how many hath he kill'd and eaten in these wars ? But how many hath he kill'd ? For, indeed, I promised to eat all of his killing. 37

Leon. Faith, niece, you tax Signior Benedick too much ; but he'll be meet with you, I doubt it not.

Mess. He hath done good service, lady, in these wars. 40

Beat. You had musty victual, and he hath holp to eat it ; he is a very valiant trencherman ; he hath an excellent stomach.

Mess. And a good soldier too, lady.

Beat. And a good soldier to a lady ; but what is he to a lord ? 46

Mess. A lord to a lord, a man to a man ; stuff'd with all honourable virtues.

Beat. It is so, indeed ; he is no less than a stuff'd man ; but for the stuffing—well, we are all mortal. 50

Leon. You must not, sir, mistake my niece : there is a kind of merry war betwixt Signior Benedick and her ; they never meet but there's a skirmish of wit between them. 53

Beat. Alas, he gets nothing by that. In our last conflict four of his five wits went halting off, and now is the whole man govern'd with one ; so that if he have wit enough to keep himself warm, let him bear it for a difference between himself and his horse ; for it is all the wealth that he hath left, to be known a reasonable creature. Who is his companion now ? He hath every month a new sworn brother. 60

Mess. Is't possible?

Beat. Very easily possible: he wears his faith but as the fashion of his hat; it ever changes with the next block.

Mess. I see, lady, the gentleman is not in your books. 64

Beat. No; an he were, I would burn my study. But, I pray you, who is his companion? Is there no young squarer now that will make a voyage with him to the devil?

Mess. He is most in the company of the right noble Claudio. 69

Beat. O Lord! he will hang upon him like a disease; he is sooner caught than the pestilence, and the taker runs presently mad. God help the noble Claudio! If he have caught the Benedick, it will cost him a thousand pound ere 'a be cured. 74

Mess. I will hold friends with you, lady.

Beat. Do, good friend.

Leon. You will never run mad, niece.

Beat. No, not till a hot January.

Mess. Don Pedro is approach'd. 79

Enter DON PEDRO, CLAUDIO, BENEDICK, BALTHASAR, *and* JOHN *the Bastard.*

D. Pedro. Good Signior Leonato, are you come to meet your trouble? The fashion of the world is to avoid cost, and you encounter it. 82

Leon. Never came trouble to my house in the likeness of your Grace; for trouble being gone comfort should remain; but when you depart from me sorrow abides, and happiness takes his leave. 86

D. Pedro. You embrace your charge too willingly. I think this is your daughter.

Leon. Her mother hath many times told me so.

Bene. Were you in doubt, sir, that you ask'd her? 90

Leon. Signior Benedick, no; for then were you a child.

D. Pedro. You have it full, Benedick; we may guess by this what you are, being a man. Truly, the lady fathers herself. Be happy, lady, for you are like an honourable father. 95

Bene. If Signior Leonato be her father, she would not have his head on her shoulders for all Messina, as like him as she is.

Beat. I wonder that you will still be talking, Signior Benedick; nobody marks you. 100

Bene. What, my dear Lady Disdain! Are you yet living?

Beat. Is it possible disdain should die while she hath such meet food to feed it as Signior Benedick? Courtesy itself must convert to disdain if you come in her presence. 104

Bene. Then is courtesy a turncoat. But it is certain I am loved of all ladies, only

you excepted; and I would I could find in my heart that I had not a hard heart, for, truly, I love none. 108

Beat. A dear happiness to women! They would else have been troubled with a pernicious suitor. I thank God, and my cold blood, I am of your humour for that: I had rather hear my dog bark at a crow than a man swear he loves me. 112

Bene. God keep your ladyship still in that mind! So some gentleman or other shall scape a predestinate scratch'd face.

Beat. Scratching could not make it worse, an 'twere such a face as yours were. 116

Bene. Well, you are a rare parrot-teacher.

Beat. A bird of my tongue is better than a beast of yours. 119

Bene. I would my horse had the speed of your tongue, and so good a continuer. But keep your way a God's name, I have done.

Beat. You always end with a jade's trick; I know you of old. 124

D. Pedro. That is the sum of all, Leonato. Signior Claudio and Signior Benedick, my dear friend Leonato hath invited you all. I tell him we shall stay here at the least a month; and he heartily prays some occasion may detain us longer. I dare swear he is no hypocrite, but prays from his heart. 130

Leon. If you swear, my lord, you shall not be forsworn. [*To Don John*] Let me bid you welcome, my lord—being reconciled to the Prince your brother, I owe you all duty.

D. John. I thank you; I am not of many words, but I thank you. 135

Leon. Please it your Grace lead on?

D. Pedro. Your hand, Leonato; we will go together.

[*Exeunt all but Benedick and Claudio.*

Claud. Benedick, didst thou note the daughter of Signior Leonato? 139

Bene. I noted her not, but I look'd on her.

Claud. Is she not a modest young lady?

Bene. Do you question me, as an honest man should do, for my simple true judgment; or would you have me speak after my custom, as being a professed tyrant to their sex? 145

Claud. No, I pray thee speak in sober judgment.

Bene. Why, i' faith, methinks she's too low for a high praise, too brown for a fair praise, and too little for a great praise; only this commendation I can afford her, that were she other than she is, she were unhandsome, and being no other but as she is, I do not like her. 151

Claud. Thou thinkest I am in sport; I pray thee tell me truly how thou lik'st her.

Bene. Would you buy her, that you inquire after her? 154

Claud. Can the world buy such a jewel?

Bene. Yea, and a case to put it into. But speak you this with a sad brow, or do you play the flouting Jack, to tell us Cupid is a good hare-finder, and Vulcan a rare carpenter? Come, in what key shall a man take you to go in the song?   160

Claud. In mine eye she is the sweetest lady that ever I look'd on.

Bene. I can see yet without spectacles, and I see no such matter; there's her cousin, an she were not possess'd with a fury, exceeds her as much in beauty as the first of May doth the last of December. But I hope you have no intent to turn husband, have you?   167

Claud. I would scarce trust myself, though I had sworn the contrary, if Hero would be my wife.   169

Bene. Is't come to this? In faith, hath not the world one man but he will wear his cap with suspicion? Shall I never see a bachelor of threescore again? Go to, i' faith; an thou wilt needs thrust thy neck into a yoke, wear the print of it, and sigh away Sundays. Look, Don Pedro is returned to seek you.   175

Re-enter DON PEDRO.

D. Pedro. What secret hath held you here, that you followed not to Leonato's?

Bene. I would your Grace would constrain me to tell.   178

D. Pedro. I charge thee on thy allegiance.

Bene. You hear, Count Claudio; I can be secret as a dumb man, I would have you think so; but on my allegiance, mark you this, on my allegiance—he is in love. With who? now that is your Grace's part. Mark how short his answer is: with Hero, Leonato's short daughter.   184

Claud. If this were so, so were it utt'red.

Bene. Like the old tale, my lord: 'It is not so, nor 'twas not so; but, indeed, God forbid it should be so!'   187

Claud. If my passion change not shortly, God forbid it should be otherwise!

D. Pedro. Amen, if you love her; for the lady is very well worthy.   191

Claud. You speak this to fetch me in, my lord?

D. Pedro. By my troth, I speak my thought.

Claud. And, in faith, my lord, I spoke mine.

Bene. And, by my two faiths and troths, my lord, I spoke mine.   196

Claud. That I love her, I feel.

D. Pedro. That she is worthy, I know.

Bene. That I neither feel how she should be loved, nor know how she should be worthy, is the opinion that fire cannot melt out of me; I will die in it at the stake.   201

D. Pedro. Thou wast ever an obstinate heretic in the despite of beauty.

Claud. And never could maintain his part but in the force of his will.   205

Bene. That a woman conceived me, I thank her; that she brought me up, I likewise give her most humble thanks; but that I will have a recheat winded in my forehead, or hang my bugle in an invisible baldrick, all women shall pardon me. Because I will not do them the wrong to mistrust any, I will do myself the right to trust none; and the fine is, for the which I may go the finer, I will live a bachelor.

D. Pedro. I shall see thee, ere I die, look pale with love.   214

Bene. With anger, with sickness, or with hunger, my lord; not with love. Prove that ever I lose more blood with love than I will get again with drinking, pick out mine eyes with a ballad-maker's pen, and hang me up at the door of a brothel-house for the sign of blind Cupid.   219

D. Pedro. Well, if ever thou dost fall from this faith, thou wilt prove a notable argument.

Bene. If I do, hang me in a bottle like a cat, and shoot at me; and he that hits me, let him be clapp'd on the shoulder and call'd Adam.

D. Pedro. Well, as time shall try.   225
'In time the savage bull doth bear the yoke.'

Bene. The savage bull may; but if ever the sensible Benedick bear it, pluck off the bull's horns and set them in my forehead, and let me be vilely painted; and in such great letters as they write 'Here is good horse to hire' let them signify under my sign 'Here you may see Benedick the married man'.   232

Claud. If this should ever happen, thou wouldst be horn-mad.

D. Pedro. Nay, if Cupid have not spent all his quiver in Venice, thou wilt quake for this shortly.   236

Bene. I look for an earthquake too, then.

D. Pedro. Well, you will temporize with the hours. In the meantime, good Signior Benedick, repair to Leonato's; commend me to him, and tell him I will not fail him at supper; for, indeed, he hath made great preparation.   241

Bene. I have almost matter enough in me for such an embassage; and so I commit you—

Claud. To the tuition of God. From my house—if I had it—   245

D. Pedro. The sixth of July. Your loving friend, Benedick.

Bene. Nay, mock not, mock not. The body of your discourse is sometime guarded with fragments, and the guards are but slightly basted on neither; ere you flout old ends any further, examine your conscience; and so I leave you. [*Exit Benedick.*

Claud. My liege, your Highness now may
    do me good.
D. Pedro. My love is thine to teach ;
    teach it but how,   253
And thou shalt see how apt it is to learn
Any hard lesson that may do thee good.
Claud. Hath Leonato any son, my lord ?
D. Pedro. No child but Hero ; she's his
    only heir.   257
Dost thou affect her, Claudio ?
Claud.   O, my lord,
When you went onward on this ended
    action,
I look'd upon her with a soldier's eye,   260
That lik'd, but had a rougher task in hand
Than to drive liking to the name of love ;
But now I am return'd, and that war-
    thoughts   263
Have left their places vacant, in their rooms
Come thronging soft and delicate desires,
All prompting me how fair young Hero is,
Saying I lik'd her ere I went to wars.
D. Pedro. Thou wilt be like a lover
    presently,
And tire the hearer with a book of words.
If thou dost love fair Hero, cherish it ; 270
And I will break with her, and with her
    father,
And thou shalt have her. Was't not to this
    end
That thou began'st to twist so fine a story ?
Claud. How sweetly you do minister to
    love,   274
That know love's grief by his complexion !
But lest my liking might too sudden seem,
I would have salv'd it with a longer
    treatise.   277
D. Pedro. What need the bridge much
    broader than the flood ?
The fairest grant is the necessity.
Look what will serve is fit. 'Tis once, thou
    lovest ;   280
And I will fit thee with the remedy.
I know we shall have revelling to-night ;
I will assume thy part in some disguise,
And tell fair Hero I am Claudio ;   284
And in her bosom I'll unclasp my heart,
And take her hearing prisoner with the force
And strong encounter of my amorous tale.
Then, after, to her father will I break ; 288
And the conclusion is she shall be thine.
In practice let us put it presently. [*Exeunt.*

SCENE II. *Leonato's house.*

Enter, severally, LEONATO *and* ANTONIO.

Leon. How now, brother ! Where is my
cousin, your son ? Hath he provided this
music ?
Ant. He is very busy about it. But,
brother, I can tell you strange news that
you yet dreamt not of.
Leon. Are they good ?   5
Ant. As the event stamps them ; but

they have a good cover ; they show well
outward. The Prince and Count Claudio,
walking in a thick-pleached alley in mine
orchard, were thus much overheard by a
man of mine : the Prince discovered to
Claudio that he loved my niece your
daughter, and meant to acknowledge it this
night in a dance ; and, if he found her
accordant, he meant to take the present
time by the top, and instantly break with
you of it.   13
Leon. Hath the fellow any wit that told
you this ?
Ant. A good sharp fellow ; I will send for
him, and question him yourself.   16
Leon. No, no ; we will hold it as a dream,
till it appear itself ; but I will acquaint my
daughter withal, that she may be the better
prepared for an answer, if peradventure
this be true. Go you and tell her of it.
[*Several persons cross the stage*] Cousins, you
know what you have to do. O, I cry you
mercy, friend ; go with me, and I will use
your skill. Good cousin, have a care this
busy time.   [*Exeunt.*

SCENE III. *Leonato's house.*

Enter DON JOHN *and* CONRADE.

Con. What the good-year, my lord ! Why
are you thus out of measure sad ?
D. John. There is no measure in the
occasion that breeds ; therefore the sadness
is without limit.
Con. You should hear reason.   5
D. John. And when I have heard it, what
blessing brings it ?
Con. If not a present remedy, at least a
patient sufferance.
D. John. I wonder that thou, being, as
thou say'st thou art, born under Saturn,
goest about to apply a moral medicine to a
mortifying mischief. I cannot hide what I
am ; I must be sad when I have cause, and
smile at no man's jests ; eat when I have
stomach, and wait for no man's leisure ;
sleep when I am drowsy, and tend on no
man's business ; laugh when I am merry,
and claw no man in his humour.   15
Con. Yea, but you must not make the
full show of this till you may do it without
controlment. You have of late stood out
against your brother, and he hath ta'en you
newly into his grace ; where it is impossible
you should take true root but by the fair
weather that you make yourself ; it is needful that you frame the season for your own
harvest.   21
D. John. I had rather be a canker in a
hedge than a rose in his grace ; and it
better fits my blood to be disdain'd of all
than to fashion a carriage to rob love from
any. In this, though I cannot be said to be
a flattering honest man, it must not be

denied but I am a plain-dealing villain. I am trusted with a muzzle and enfranchis'd with a clog; therefore I have decreed not to sing in my cage. If I had my mouth, I would bite; if I had my liberty, I would do my liking; in the meantime let me be that I am, and seek not to alter me.   31

Con. Can you make no use of your discontent?

D. John. I make all use of it, for I use it only. Who comes here?

Enter BORACHIO.

What news, Borachio?   35

Bora. I came yonder from a great supper. The Prince, your brother, is royally entertain'd by Leonato; and I can give you intelligence of an intended marriage.

D. John. Will it serve for any model to build mischief on? What is he for a fool that betroths himself to unquietness?   41

Bora. Marry, it is your brother's right hand.

D. John. Who? The most exquisite Claudio?

Bora. Even he.

D. John. A proper squire! And who, and who? Which way looks he?   46

Bora. Marry, on Hero, the daughter and heir of Leonato.

D. John. A very forward March-chick! How came you to this?   49

Bora. Being entertain'd for a perfumer, as I was smoking a musty room, comes me the Prince and Claudio hand in hand, in sad conference. I whipt me behind the arras, and there heard it agreed upon that the Prince should woo Hero for himself, and, having obtain'd her, give her to Count Claudio.   55

D. John. Come, come, let us thither; this may prove food to my displeasure; that young start-up hath all the glory of my overthrow. If I can cross him any way, I bless myself every way. You are both sure, and will assist me?

Con. To the death, my lord.   60

D. John. Let us to the great supper; their cheer is the greater that I am subdued. Would the cook were o' my mind! Shall we go prove what's to be done?

Bora. We'll wait upon your lordship.

                   [*Exeunt.*

ACT TWO

SCENE I. *A hall in Leonato's house.*

Enter LEONATO, ANTONIO, HERO, BEATRICE, MARGARET, URSULA, *and* Others.

Leon. Was not Count John here at supper?

Ant. I saw him not.

Beat. How tartly that gentleman looks! I never can see him but I am heart-burn'd an hour after.

Hero. He is of a very melancholy disposition.   5

Beat. He were an excellent man that were made just in the mid-way between him and Benedick: the one is too like an image and says nothing, and the other too like my lady's eldest son, evermore tattling.   9

Leon. Then half Signior Benedick's tongue in Count John's mouth, and half Count John's melancholy in Signior Benedick's face—   12

Beat. With a good leg and a good foot, uncle, and money enough in his purse, such a man would win any woman in the world, if 'a could get her good-will.   15

Leon. By my troth, niece, thou wilt never get thee a husband if thou be so shrewd of thy tongue.

Ant. In faith, she's too curst.   18

Beat. Too curst is more than curst. I shall lessen God's sending that way; for it is said ' God sends a curst cow short horns'; but to a cow too curst he sends none.   21

Leon. So, by being too curst, God will send you no horns.

Beat. Just, if he send me no husband; for the which blessing I am at him upon my knees every morning and evening. Lord! I could not endure a husband with a beard on his face; I had rather lie in the woollen.   26

Leon. You may light on a husband that hath no beard.

Beat. What should I do with him? Dress him in my apparel, and make him my waiting gentlewoman? He that hath a beard is more than a youth, and he that hath no beard is less than a man; and he that is more than a youth is not for me, and he that is less than a man I am not for him; therefore I will even take sixpence in earnest of the berrord, and lead his apes into hell.

Leon. Well then, go you into hell?   35

Beat. No; but to the gate, and there will the devil meet me, like an old cuckold, with horns on his head, and say ' Get you to heaven, Beatrice, get you to heaven; here's no place for you maids'. So deliver I up my apes and away to Saint Peter for the heavens; he shows me where the bachelors sit, and there live we as merry as the day is long.   41

Ant. [*To Hero*] Well, niece, I trust you will be rul'd by your father.

Beat. Yes, faith; it is my cousin's duty to make curtsy, and say ' Father, as it please you'. But yet for all that, cousin, let him be a handsome fellow, or else make another curtsy and say ' Father, as it please me'.   47

Leon. Well, niece, I hope to see you one day fitted with a husband.

Beat. Not till God make men of some

other metal than earth. Would it not
grieve a woman to be over-master'd with a
piece of valiant dust, to make an account
of her life to a clod of wayward marl? No,
uncle, I'll none: Adam's sons are my
brethren; and, truly, I hold it a sin to
match in my kindred.   55

Leon. Daughter, remember what I told
you: if the Prince do solicit you in that
kind, you know your answer.   57

Beat. The fault will be in the music,
cousin, if you be not wooed in good time.
If the Prince be too important, tell him
there is measure in every thing, and so
dance out the answer. For, hear me, Hero:
wooing, wedding, and repenting, is as a
Scotch jig, a measure, and a cinquepace;
the first suit is hot and hasty, like a Scotch
jig, and full as fantastical; the wedding,
mannerly modest, as a measure, full of
state and ancientry; and then comes
repentance, and, with his bad legs, falls
into the cinquepace faster and faster, till
he sink into his grave.   67

Leon. Cousin, you apprehend passing
shrewdly.

Beat. I have a good eye, uncle; I can see
a church by daylight.   70

Leon. The revellers are ent'ring, brother;
make good room.   [*Antonio masks.*

Enter DON PEDRO, CLAUDIO, BENEDICK,
BALTHASAR, DON JOHN, *and* BORACHIO,
as maskers, with a drum.

D. Pedro. Lady, will you walk about
with your friend?   73

Hero. So you walk softly, and look
sweetly, and say nothing, I am yours for the
walk; and, especially, when I walk away.

D. Pedro. With me in your company?

Hero. I may say so, when I please.   78

D. Pedro. And when please you to say so?

Hero. When I like your favour; for God
defend the lute should be like the case!   81

D. Pedro. My visor is Philemon's roof;
within the house is Jove.

Hero. Why, then, your visor should be
thatch'd.

D. Pedro. Speak low, if you speak love.
                           [*Takes her aside.*

Balth. Well, I would you did like me.   86

Marg. So would not I, for your own sake;
for I have many ill qualities.

Balth. Which is one?

Marg. I say my prayers aloud.   90

Balth. I love you the better; the hearers
may cry Amen.

Marg. God match me with a good dancer!

Balth. Amen.

Marg. And God keep him out of my
sight when the dance is done! Answer,
clerk.   95

Balth. No more words; the clerk is
answered.

Urs. I know you well enough; you are
Signior Antonio.

Ant. At a word, I am not.

Urs. I know you by the waggling of your
head.   99

Ant. To tell you true, I counterfeit him.

Urs. You could never do him so ill-well
unless you were the very man. Here's his
dry hand up and down; you are he, you
are he.

Ant. At a word, I am not.   104

Urs. Come, come; do you think I do not
know you by your excellent wit? Can
virtue hide itself? Go to; mum; you are
he; graces will appear, and there's an end.

Beat. Will you not tell me who told you
so?

Bene. No, you shall pardon me.   109

Beat. Nor will you not tell me who you
are?

Bene. Not now.

Beat. That I was disdainful, and that I
had my good wit out of the 'Hundred
Merry Tales'—well, this was Signior
Benedick that said so.

Bene. What's he?   115

Beat. I am sure you know him well
enough.

Bene. Not I, believe me.

Beat. Did he never make you laugh?

Bene. I pray you, what is he?   119

Beat. Why, he is the Prince's jester, a
very dull fool; only his gift is in devising
impossible slanders; none but libertines
delight in him, and the commendation is
not in his wit but in his villainy; for he
both pleases men and angers them, and
then they laugh at him and beat him. I am
sure he is in the fleet; I would he had
boarded me.   125

Bene. When I know the gentleman, I'll
tell him what you say.

Beat. Do, do; he'll but break a comparison or two on me; which, peradventure, not mark'd, or not laugh'd at, strikes
him into melancholy; and then there's a
partridge wing saved, for the fool will eat
no supper that night. [*Music*] We must
follow the leaders.   132

Bene. In every good thing.

Beat. Nay, if they lead to any ill, I will
leave them at the next turning.   135

      [*Dance. Then exeunt all but Don John,
                          Borachio, and Claudio.*

D. John. Sure, my brother is amorous on
Hero, and hath withdrawn her father to
break with him about it. The ladies follow
her, and but one visor remains.   138

Bora. And that is Claudio; I know him
by his bearing.

D. John. Are not you Signior Benedick?

Claud. You know me well; I am he. 141

D. John. Signior, you are very near my
brother in his love; he is enamour'd on

Hero; I pray you dissuade him from her; she is no equal for his birth. You may do the part of an honest man in it.　145

Claud. How know you he loves her?

D. John. I heard him swear his affection.

Bora. So did I too; and he swore he would marry her to-night.

D. John. Come, let us to the banquet.　150
　　　　　[*Exeunt Don John and Borachio.*

Claud. Thus answer I in name of Benedick,

But hear these ill news with the ears of Claudio.

'Tis certain so: the Prince woos for himself.

Friendship is constant in all other things

Save in the office and affairs of love;　155

Therefore all hearts in love use their own tongues.

Let every eye negotiate for itself,

And trust no agent; for beauty is a witch

Against whose charms faith melteth into blood.

This is an accident of hourly proof,　160

Which I mistrusted not. Farewell, therefore, Hero.

Re-enter BENEDICK.

Bene. Count Claudio?

Claud. Yea, the same.

Bene. Come, will you go with me?

Claud. Whither?　165

Bene. Even to the next willow, about your own business, County. What fashion will you wear the garland of? About your neck, like an usurer's chain, or under your arm, like a lieutenant's scarf? You must wear it one way, for the Prince hath got your Hero.　170

Claud. I wish him joy of her.

Bene. Why, that's spoken like an honest drovier; so they sell bullocks. But did you think the Prince would have served you thus?

Claud. I pray you leave me.　175

Bene. Ho! now you strike like the blind man; 'twas the boy that stole your meat, and you'll beat the post.

Claud. If it will not be, I'll leave you.
　　　　　[*Exit.*

Bene. Alas, poor hurt fowl! Now will he creep into sedges. But that my Lady Beatrice should know me, and not know me! The Prince's fool! Ha! It may be I go under that title because I am merry. Yea, but so I am apt to do myself wrong; I am not so reputed; it is the base, though bitter, disposition of Beatrice that puts the world into her person, and so gives me out. Well, I'll be revenged as I may.　186

Re-enter DON PEDRO.

D. Pedro. Now, signior, where's the Count? Did you see him?

Bene. Troth, my lord, I have played the part of Lady Fame. I found him here as melancholy as a lodge in a warren; I told him, and I think I told him true, that your Grace had got the good will of this young lady; and I off'red him my company to a willow tree, either to make him a garland, as being forsaken, or to bind him up a rod, as being worthy to be whipt.　195

D. Pedro. To be whipt! What's his fault?

Bene. The flat transgression of a schoolboy, who, being overjoyed with finding a bird's nest, shows it his companion, and he steals it.

D. Pedro. Wilt thou make a trust a transgression? The transgression is in the stealer.　201

Bene. Yet it had not been amiss the rod had been made, and the garland too; for the garland he might have worn himself, and the rod he might have bestowed on you, who, as I take it, have stol'n his bird's nest.

D. Pedro. I will but teach them to sing, and restore them to the owner.　207

Bene. If their singing answer your saying, by my faith, you say honestly.

D. Pedro. The Lady Beatrice hath a quarrel to you; the gentleman that danc'd with her told her she is much wrong'd by you.　212

Bene. O, she misus'd me past the endurance of a block; an oak but with one green leaf on it would have answered her; my very visor began to assume life and scold with her. She told me, not thinking I had been myself, that I was the Prince's jester, that I was duller than a great thaw; huddling jest upon jest with such impossible conveyance upon me that I stood like a man at a mark, with a whole army shooting at me. She speaks poniards, and every word stabs; if her breath were as terrible as her terminations, there were no living near her; she would infect to the north star. I would not marry her though she were endowed with all that Adam had left him before he transgress'd; she would have made Hercules have turn'd spit, yea, and have cleft his club to make the fire too. Come, talk not of her; you shall find her the infernal Ate in good apparel. I would to God some scholar would conjure her; for certainly, while she is here, a man may live as quiet in hell as in a sanctuary; and people sin upon purpose, because they would go thither; so, indeed, all disquiet, horror, and perturbation, follows her.　232

Re-enter CLAUDIO *and* BEATRICE, LEONATO *and* HERO.

D. Pedro. Look, here she comes.

Bene. Will your Grace command me any service to the world's end? I will go on the slightest errand now to the Antipodes that you can devise to send me on ; I will fetch you a toothpicker now from the furthest inch of Asia ; bring you the length of Prester John's foot ; fetch you a hair off the great Cham's beard ; do you any embassage to the Pigmies—rather than hold three words' conference with this harpy. You have no employment for me ?

D. Pedro. None, but to desire your good company.   243

Bene. O God, sir, here's a dish I love not ; I cannot endure my Lady Tongue. [*Exit.*

D. Pedro. Come, lady, come ; you have lost the heart of Signior Benedick.   247

Beat. Indeed, my lord, he lent it me awhile ; and I gave him use for it, a double heart for his single one ; marry, once before he won it of me with false dice, therefore your Grace may well say I have lost it. 251

D. Pedro. You have put him down, lady, you have put him down.

Beat. So I would not he should do me, my lord, lest I should prove the mother of fools. I have brought Count Claudio, whom you sent me to seek.   256

D. Pedro. Why, how now, Count ! Wherefore are you sad ?

Claud. Not sad, my lord.

D. Pedro. How then, sick ?   260

Claud. Neither, my lord.

Beat. The Count is neither sad, nor sick, nor merry, nor well ; but civil count—civil as an orange, and something of that jealous complexion.   264

D. Pedro. I' faith, lady, I think your blazon to be true, though I'll be sworn, if he be so, his conceit is false. Here, Claudio, I have wooed in thy name, and fair Hero is won. I have broke with her father, and his good will obtained. Name the day of marriage, and God give thee joy !   270

Leon. Count, take of me my daughter, and with her my fortunes ; his Grace hath made the match, and all grace say Amen to it !

Beat. Speak, Count, 'tis your cue.   274

Claud. Silence is the perfectest herald of joy : I were but little happy if I could say how much. Lady, as you are mine, I am yours ; I give away myself for you, and dote upon the exchange.   278

Beat. Speak, cousin ; or, if you cannot, stop his mouth with a kiss, and let not him speak neither.   280

D. Pedro. In faith, lady, you have a merry heart.

Beat. Yea, my lord ; I thank it, poor fool, it keeps on the windy side of care. My cousin tells him in his ear that he is in her heart.

Claud. And so she doth, cousin.   285

Beat. Good Lord, for alliance ! Thus goes every one to the world but I, and I am

sunburnt ; I may sit in a corner and cry ' Heigh-ho for a husband ! '   288

D. Pedro. Lady Beatrice, I will get you one.

Beat. I would rather have one of your father's getting. Hath your Grace ne'er a brother like you ? Your father got excellent husbands, if a maid could come by them.   292

D. Pedro. Will you have me, lady ?

Beat. No, my lord, unless I might have another for working-days ; your Grace is too costly to wear every day. But, I beseech your Grace, pardon me ; I was born to speak all mirth and no matter. 297

D. Pedro. Your silence most offends me, and to be merry best becomes you ; for, out o' question, you were born in a merry hour.   300

Beat. No, sure, my lord, my mother cried ; but then there was a star danc'd, and under that was I born. Cousins, God give you joy !

Leon. Niece, you will look to those things I told you of ?   305

Beat. I cry your mercy, uncle. By your Grace's pardon.   [*Exit Beatrice.*

D. Pedro. By my troth, a pleasant-spirited lady.   308

Leon. There's little of the melancholy element in her, my lord ; she is never sad but when she sleeps, and not ever sad then ; for I have heard my daughter say she hath often dreamt of unhappiness, and wak'd herself with laughing.   313

D. Pedro. She cannot endure to hear tell of a husband.

Leon. O, by no means ; she mocks all her wooers out of suit.

D. Pedro. She were an excellent wife for Benedick.   316

Leon. O Lord, my lord, if they were but a week married, they would talk themselves mad.

D. Pedro. County Claudio, when mean you to go to church ?   321

Claud. To-morrow, my lord. Time goes on crutches till love have all his rites.

Leon. Not till Monday, my dear son, which is hence a just seven-night ; and a time too brief, too, to have all things answer my mind.   326

D. Pedro. Come, you shake the head at so long a breathing ; but I warrant thee, Claudio, the time shall not go dully by us. I will in the interim undertake one of Hercules' labours ; which is, to bring Signior Benedick and the Lady Beatrice into a mountain of affection th' one with th' other. I would fain have it a match ; and I doubt not but to fashion it if you three will but minister such assistance as I shall give you direction.   334

Leon. My lord, I am for you, though it cost me ten nights' watchings.

Claud. And I, my lord.   337
D. Pedro. And you too, gentle Hero ?
Hero. I will do any modest office, my lord, to help my cousin to a good husband.
D. Pedro. And Benedick is not the unhopefullest husband that I know. Thus far can I praise him : he is of a noble strain, of approved valour, and confirm'd honesty. I will teach you how to humour your cousin that she shall fall in love with Benedick ; and I, with your two helps, will so practise on Benedick that, in despite of his quick wit and his queasy stomach, he shall fall in love with Beatrice. If we can do this, Cupid is no longer an archer ; his glory shall be ours, for we are the only love-gods. Go in with me, and I will tell you my drift.
[*Exeunt.*

SCENE II. *Leonato's house.*

Enter DON JOHN *and* BORACHIO.

D. John. It is so : the Count Claudio shall marry the daughter of Leonato.
Bora. Yea, my lord, but I can cross it. 3
D. John. Any bar, any cross, any impediment, will be med'cinable to me. I am sick in displeasure to him ; and whatsoever comes athwart his affection ranges evenly with mine. How canst thou cross this marriage ?   7
Bora. Not honestly, my lord ; but so covertly that no dishonesty shall appear in me.
D. John. Show me briefly how.   10
Bora. I think I told your lordship a year since how much I am in the favour of Margaret, the waiting gentlewoman to Hero.
D. John. I remember.   14
Bora. I can at any unseasonable instant of the night appoint her to look out at her lady's chamber window.
D. John. What life is in that, to be the death of this marriage ?   18
Bora. The poison of that lies in you to temper. Go you to the Prince your brother ; spare not to tell him that he hath wronged his honour in marrying the renowned Claudio—whose estimation do you mightily hold up—to a contaminated stale, such a one as Hero.   23
D. John. What proof shall I make of that ?
Bora. Proof enough to misuse the Prince, to vex Claudio, to undo Hero, and kill Leonato. Look you for any other issue ?
D. John. Only to despite them I will endeavour anything.   29
Bora. Go, then ; find me a meet hour to draw Don Pedro and the Count Claudio alone ; tell them that you know that Hero loves me ; intend a kind of zeal both to the Prince and Claudio—as in love of your brother's honour, who hath made this match, and his friend's reputation, who is thus like to be cozen'd with the semblance of a maid—that you have discover'd thus. They will scarcely believe this without trial ; offer them instances ; which shall bear no less likelihood than to see me at her chamber window ; hear me call Margaret Hero ; hear Margaret term me Borachio ; and bring them to see this the very night before the intended wedding—for in the meantime I will so fashion the matter that Hero shall be absent—and there shall appear such seeming truth of Hero's disloyalty that jealousy shall be call'd assurance, and all the preparation overthrown.
D. John. Grow this to what adverse issue it can, I will put it in practice. Be cunning in the working this, and thy fee is a thousand ducats.   48
Bora. Be you constant in the accusation, and my cunning shall not shame me.   50
D. John. I will presently go learn their day of marriage.   [*Exeunt.*

SCENE III. *Leonato's orchard.*

Enter BENEDICK, *alone.*

Bene. Boy !
Boy. [*Within*] Signior ?
Bene. In my chamber-window lies a book ; bring it hither to me in the orchard.
Boy. [*Above, at chamber window*] I am here already, sir.   5
Bene. I know that ; but I would have thee hence and here again. [*Boy brings book ; Exit*] I do much wonder that one man, seeing how much another man is a fool when he dedicates his behaviours to love, will, after he hath laugh'd at such shallow follies in others, become the argument of his own scorn by falling in love ; and such a man is Claudio. I have known when there was no music with him but the drum and the fife, and now had he rather hear the tabor and the pipe ; I have known when he would have walk'd ten mile afoot to see a good armour, and now will he lie ten nights awake carving the fashion of a new doublet. He was wont to speak plain and to the purpose, like an honest man and a soldier, and now is he turn'd orthography ; his words are a very fantastical banquet, just so many strange dishes. May I be so converted, and see with these eyes ? I cannot tell ; I think not. I will not be sworn but love may transform me to an oyster ; but I'll take my oath on it, till he have made an oyster of me he shall never make me such a fool. One woman is fair, yet I am well ; another is wise, yet I am well ; another virtuous, yet I am well ; but till all graces be in one woman, one woman shall not come in my grace. Rich she shall be, that's

145

certain; wise, or I'll none; virtuous, or I'll never cheapen her; fair, or I'll never look on her; mild, or come not near me; noble, or not I for an angel; of good discourse, an excellent musician, and her hair shall be of what colour it please God. Ha! the Prince and Monsieur Love! I will hide me in the arbour. [*Withdraws.*

Enter DON PEDRO, LEONATO, *and* CLAUDIO.

D. Pedro. Come, shall we hear this music?
Claud. Yea, my good lord. How still the evening is, 34
As hush'd on purpose to grace harmony!
D. Pedro. See you where Benedick hath hid himself?
Claud. O, very well, my lord; the music ended,
We'll fit the kid-fox with a pennyworth. 38

Enter BALTHASAR, *with music.*

D. Pedro. Come, Balthasar, we'll hear that song again.
Balth. O, good my lord, tax not so bad a voice 40
To slander music any more than once.
D. Pedro. It is the witness still of excellency
To put a strange face on his own perfection.
I pray thee sing, and let me woo no more.
Balth. Because you talk of wooing, I will sing, 45
Since many a wooer doth commence his suit
To her he thinks not worthy; yet he woos;
Yet will he swear he loves.
D. Pedro. Nay, pray thee, come;
Or if thou wilt hold longer argument,
Do it in notes.
Balth. Note this before my notes:
There's not a note of mine that's worth the noting. 51
D. Pedro. Why, these are very crotchets that he speaks;
Note notes, forsooth, and nothing! [*Music.*
Bene. Now, divine air! now is his soul ravish'd. Is it not strange that sheeps' guts should hale souls out of men's bodies? Well, a horn for my money, when all's done.

Balthasar sings.

Sigh no more, ladies, sigh no more,
  Men were deceivers ever,
One foot in sea and one on shore,
  To one thing constant never. 60
Then sigh not so, but let them go,
  And be you blithe and bonny;
Converting all your sounds of woe
  Into Hey nonny nonny.

Sing no more ditties, sing no moe 65
  Of dumps so dull and heavy;
The fraud of men was ever so,
  Since summer first was leavy.
  Then sigh not so, &c.

D. Pedro. By my troth, a good song. 70
Balth. And an ill singer, my lord.
Claud. Ha, no; no, faith; thou sing'st well enough for a shift. 73
Bene. An he had been a dog that should have howl'd thus, they would have hang'd him; and I pray God his bad voice bode no mischief. I had as lief have heard the night-raven, come what plague could have come after it. 77
D. Pedro. Yea, marry; dost thou hear, Balthasar? I pray thee get us some excellent music; for to-morrow night we would have it at the Lady Hero's chamber window. 80
Balth. The best I can, my lord.
D. Pedro. Do so; farewell. [*Exit Balthasar*] Come hither, Leonato. What was it you told me of to-day—that your niece Beatrice was in love with Signior Benedick?
Claud. O ay; stalk on, stalk on; the fowl sits. I did never think that lady would have loved any man. 87
Leon. No, nor I neither; but most wonderful that she should so dote on Signior Benedick, whom she hath in all outward behaviours seem'd ever to abhor.
Bene. Is't possible? Sits the wind in that corner? 91
Leon. By my troth, my lord, I cannot tell what to think of it; but that she loves him with an enraged affection—it is past the infinite of thought.
D. Pedro. May be she doth but counterfeit. 95
Claud. Faith, like enough.
Leon. O God, counterfeit! There was never counterfeit of passion came so near the life of passion as she discovers it.
D. Pedro. Why, what effects of passion shows she?
Claud. Bait the hook well; this fish will bite. 100
Leon. What effects, my lord? She will sit you—you heard my daughter tell you how.
Claud. She did, indeed. 103
D. Pedro. How, how, I pray you? You amaze me; I would have thought her spirit had been invincible against all assaults of affection. 106
Leon. I would have sworn it had, my lord; especially against Benedick.
Bene. I should think this a gull, but that the white-bearded fellow speaks it; knavery cannot, sure, hide himself in such reverence. 111
Claud. He hath ta'en th' infection; hold it up.
D. Pedro. Hath she made her affection known to Benedick?
Leon. No; and swears she never will; that's her torment. 116
Claud. 'Tis true, indeed; so your

daughter says. ' Shall I,' says she ' that have so oft encount'red him with scorn, write to him that I love him ? '   119

Leon. This says she now, when she is beginning to write to him ; for she'll be up twenty times a night ; and there will she sit in her smock till she have writ a sheet of paper. My daughter tells us all.   123

Claud. Now you talk of a sheet of paper, I remember a pretty jest your daughter told us of.   125

Leon. O, when she had writ it, and was reading it over, she found ' Benedick ' and ' Beatrice ' between the sheet !

Claud. That.   128

Leon. O, she tore the letter into a thousand halfpence ; rail'd at herself that she should be so immodest to write to one that she knew would flout her. ' I measure him ' says she ' by my own spirit ; for I should flout him if he writ to me ; yea, though I love him, I should.'   133

Claud. Then down upon her knees she falls, weeps, sobs, beats her heart, tears her hair, prays, curses—' O sweet Benedick ! God give me patience ! '   136

Leon. She doth indeed ; my daughter says so ; and the ecstasy hath so much overborne her that my daughter is sometime afeard she will do a desperate outrage to herself. It is very true.   140

D. Pedro. It were good that Benedick knew of it by some other, if she will not discover it.

Claud. To what end ? He would make but a sport of it, and torment the poor lady worse.   144

D. Pedro. An he should, it were an alms to hang him. She's an excellent sweet lady, and, out of all suspicion, she is virtuous.

Claud. And she is exceeding wise.

D. Pedro. In everything but in loving Benedick.   149

Leon. O my lord, wisdom and blood combating in so tender a body, we have ten proofs to one that blood hath the victory. I am sorry for her, as I have just cause, being her uncle and her guardian.   153

D. Pedro. I would she had bestowed this dotage on me ; I would have daff'd all other respects and made her half myself. I pray you, tell Benedick of it, and hear what 'a will say.   157

Leon. Were it good, think you ?

Claud. Hero thinks surely she will die ; for she says she will die if he love her not ; and she will die ere she make her love known ; and she will die if he woo her, rather than she will bate one breath of her accustomed crossness.   163

D. Pedro. She doth well ; if she should make tender of her love, 'tis very possible he'll scorn it ; for the man, as you know all, hath a contemptible spirit.   166

Claud. He is a very proper man.

D. Pedro. He hath, indeed, a good outward happiness.

Claud. Before God, and in my mind, very wise !

D. Pedro. He doth, indeed, show some sparks that are like wit.   171

Leon. And I take him to be valiant.

D. Pedro. As Hector, I assure you ; and in the managing of quarrels you may say he is wise, for either he avoids them with great discretion, or undertakes them with a most Christian-like fear.   176

Leon. If he do fear God, 'a must necessarily keep peace ; if he break the peace, he ought to enter into a quarrel with fear and trembling.   179

D. Pedro. And so will he do ; for the man doth fear God, howsoever it seems not in him by some large jests he will make. Well, I am sorry for your niece. Shall we go seek Benedick, and tell him of her love ?

Claud. Never tell him, my lord ; let her wear it out with good counsel.   185

Leon. Nay, that's impossible ; she may wear her heart out first.

D. Pedro. Well, we will hear further of it by your daughter ; let it cool the while. I love Benedick well ; and I could wish he would modestly examine himself, to see how much he is unworthy so good a lady.

Leon. My lord, will you walk ? Dinner is ready.   192

Claud. If he do not dote on her upon this, I will never trust my expectation.   194

D. Pedro. Let there be the same net spread for her ; and that must your daughter and her gentlewomen carry. The sport will be when they hold one an opinion of another's dotage, and no such matter ; that's the scene that I would see, which will be merely a dumb show. Let us send her to call him in to dinner.   200

[*Exeunt Don Pedro, Claudio, and Leonato.*

Bene. [*Coming forward*] This can be no trick : the conference was sadly borne ; they have the truth of this from Hero ; they seem to pity the lady ; it seems her affections have their full bent. Love me ! Why, it must be requited. I hear how I am censur'd : they say I will bear myself proudly if I perceive the love come from her ; they say, too, that she will rather die than give any sign of affection. I did never think to marry. I must not seem proud ; happy are they that hear their detractions and can put them to mending. They say the lady is fair ; 'tis a truth, I can bear them witness ; and virtuous ; 'tis so, I cannot reprove it ; and wise, but for loving me. By my troth, it is no addition to her wit ; nor no great argument of her folly, for I will be horribly in love with her. I may chance have some odd quirks and remnants of wit broken on me because I have railed so long against marriage ; but doth not the appetite alter ? A man loves the meat in his youth that he cannot endure in his age. Shall quips, and sentences, and these paper bullets of the brain, awe a man from the career of his humour ? No ; the world must be peopled. When I said I would die a bachelor, I did not think I should live till I were married. Here comes Beatrice. By this day, she's a fair lady ; I do spy some marks of love in her.   223

Enter BEATRICE.

Beat. Against my will I am sent to bid you come in to dinner.   225

Bene. Fair Beatrice, I thank you for your pains.

Beat. I took no more pains for those thanks than you take pains to thank me ; if it had been painful, I would not have come.

Bene. You take pleasure, then, in the message ?   230

Beat. Yea, just so much as you may take upon a knife's point, and choke a daw withal. You have no stomach, signior ; fare you well.   [*Exit.*

Bene. Ha ! ' Against my will I am sent to bid you come in to dinner '—there's a double meaning in that. ' I took no more pains for those thanks than you took pains to thank me '—that's as much as to say ' Any pains that I take for you is as easy as thanks '. If I do not take pity of her, I am a villain ; if I do not love her, I am a Jew. I will go get her picture.   [*Exit.*

ACT THREE

SCENE I. *Leonato's orchard.*

Enter HERO, MARGARET, *and* URSULA.

Hero. Good Margaret, run thee to the parlour ;
There shalt thou find my cousin Beatrice
Proposing with the Prince and Claudio.
Whisper her ear, and tell her I and Ursula
Walk in the orchard, and our whole discourse   5
Is all of her ; say that thou overheard'st us ;
And bid her steal into the pleached bower,
Where honeysuckles, ripened by the sun,
Forbid the sun to enter—like favourites,
Made proud by princes, that advance their pride   10
Against that power that bred it. There will she hide her
To listen our propose. This is thy office ;
Bear thee well in it, and leave us alone.

Marg. I'll make her come, I warrant you, presently.   [*Exit.*

Hero. Now, Ursula, when Beatrice doth come,   15

As we do trace this alley up and down,
Our talk must only be of Benedick.
When I do name him, let it be thy part
To praise him more than ever man did merit ;
My talk to thee must be how Benedick   20
Is sick in love with Beatrice. Of this matter
Is little Cupid's crafty arrow made,
That only wounds by hearsay. Now begin ;

Enter BEATRICE, *behind.*

For look where Beatrice, like a lapwing, runs   24
Close by the ground, to hear our conference.

Urs. The pleasant'st angling is to see the fish
Cut with her golden oars the silver stream,
And greedily devour the treacherous bait.
So angle we for Beatrice ; who even now
Is couched in the woodbine coverture.   30
Fear you not my part of the dialogue.

Hero. Then go we near her, that her ear lose nothing
Of the false sweet bait that we lay for it.
     [*They advance to the bower.*
No, truly, Ursula, she is too disdainful ;
I know her spirits are as coy and wild   35
As haggards of the rock.

Urs.   But are you sure
That Benedick loves Beatrice so entirely ?

Hero. So says the Prince and my new-trothed lord.

Urs. And did they bid you tell her of it, madam ?

Hero. They did entreat me to acquaint her of it ;   40
But I persuaded them, if they lov'd Benedick,
To wish him wrestle with affection,
And never to let Beatrice know of it.

Urs. Why did you so ? Doth not the gentleman
Deserve as full as fortunate a bed   45
As ever Beatrice shall couch upon ?

Hero. O god of love ! I know he doth deserve
As much as may be yielded to a man ;
But nature never fram'd a woman's heart
Of prouder stuff than that of Beatrice.   50
Disdain and scorn ride sparkling in her eyes,
Misprising what they look on ; and her wit
Values itself so highly that to her
All matter else seems weak. She cannot love,
Nor take no shape nor project of affection,
She is so self-endeared.

Urs.   Sure, I think so ;   56
And therefore, certainly, it were not good
She knew his love, lest she'll make sport at it.

Hero. Why, you speak truth. I never yet saw man,
How wise, how noble, young, how rarely featur'd,   60

But she would spell him backward. If fair-
  fac'd,
She would swear the gentleman should be
  her sister ;
If black, why, Nature, drawing of an antic,
Made a foul blot ; if tall, a lance ill-headed ;
If low, an agate very vilely cut ;   65
If speaking, why, a vane blown with all
  winds ;
If silent, why, a block moved with none.
So turns she every man the wrong side out,
And never gives to truth and virtue that
Which simpleness and merit purchaseth. 70
  Urs. Sure, sure, such carping is not com-
  mendable.
  Hero. No ; not to be so odd and from all
  fashions,
As Beatrice is, cannot be commendable ;
But who dare tell her so ? If I should
  speak,
She would mock me into air ; O, she would
  laugh me   75
Out of myself, press me to death with wit !
Therefore let Benedick, like cover'd fire,
Consume away in sighs, waste inwardly.
It were a better death than die with mocks,
Which is as bad as die with tickling.   80
  Urs. Yet tell her of it ; hear what she
  will say.
  Hero. No ; rather I will go to Benedick
And counsel him to fight against his passion ;
And, truly, I'll devise some honest slanders
To stain my cousin with. One doth not
  know   85
How much an ill word may empoison liking.
  Urs. O, do not do your cousin such a
  wrong !
She cannot be so much without true judg-
  ment—
Having so swift and excellent a wit
As she is priz'd to have—as to refuse   90
So rare a gentleman as Signior Benedick.
  Hero. He is the only man of Italy,
Always excepted my dear Claudio.
  Urs. I pray you be not angry with me,
  madam,
Speaking my fancy : Signior Benedick, 95
For shape, for bearing, argument, and
  valour,
Goes foremost in report through Italy.
  Hero. Indeed, he hath an excellent good
  name.
  Urs. His excellence did earn it ere he had
  it.
When are you married, madam ?   100
  Hero. Why, every day—to-morrow.
  Come, go in ;
I'll show thee some attires, and have thy
  counsel
Which is the best to furnish me to-morrow.
  Urs. She's lim'd, I warrant you ; we
  have caught her, madam.
  Hero. If it prove so, then loving goes by
  haps :   105

Some Cupid kills with arrows, some with
  traps.   [*Exeunt Hero and Ursula.*
  Beat. [*Coming forward*] What fire is in
  mine ears ? Can this be true ?
Stand I condemn'd for pride and scorn
  so much ?
Contempt, farewell ! and maiden pride,
  adieu !
No glory lives behind the back of such. 110
And, Benedick, love on ; I will requite
  thee,
Taming my wild heart to thy loving
  hand ;
If thou dost love, my kindness shall incite
  thee
To bind our loves up in a holy band ;
For others say thou dost deserve, and I 115
Believe it better than reportingly.   [*Exit.*

SCENE II. *Leonato's house.*

Enter DON PEDRO, CLAUDIO, BENEDICK,
  and LEONATO.

  D. Pedro. I do but stay till your marriage
be consummate, and then go I toward
Arragon.
  Claud. I'll bring you thither, my lord, if
you'll vouchsafe me.   4
  D. Pedro. Nay, that would be as great a
soil in the new gloss of your marriage as to
show a child his new coat, and forbid him
to wear it. I will only be bold with Benedick for his company ; for, from the crown
of his head to the sole of his foot, he is all
mirth ; he hath twice or thrice cut Cupid's
bow-string, and the little hangman dare not
shoot at him ; he hath a heart as sound as
a bell, and his tongue is the clapper ; for
what his heart thinks, his tongue speaks.   12
  Bene. Gallants, I am not as I have been.
  Leon. So say I ; methinks you are sadder.
  Claud. I hope he be in love.   15
  D. Pedro. Hang him, truant ! There's no
true drop of blood in him to be truly
touch'd with love ; if he be sad, he wants
money.
  Bene. I have the toothache.
  D. Pedro. Draw it.   20
  Bene. Hang it !
  Claud. You must hang it first and draw
it afterwards.
  D. Pedro. What ! sigh for the toothache ?
  Leon. Where is but a humour or a worm.
  Bene. Well, every one can master a grief
but he that has it.   26
  Claud. Yet, say I, he is in love.
  D. Pedro. There is no appearance of fancy
in him, unless it be a fancy that he hath to
strange disguises ; as to be a Dutchman to-
day, a Frenchman to-morrow ; or in the
shape of two countries at once, as a German
from the waist downward, all slops, and a
Spaniard from the hip upward, no doublet.
Unless he have a fancy to this foolery, as it

appears he hath, he is no fool for fancy, as
you would have it appear he is.   35
  Claud. If he be not in love with some
woman, there is no believing old signs : 'a
brushes his hat o' mornings ; what should
that bode ?   38
  D. Pedro. Hath any man seen him at the
barber's ?
  Claud. No, but the barber's man hath
been seen with him ; and the old ornament
of his cheek hath already stuff'd tennis-
balls.   42
  Leon. Indeed, he looks younger than he
did, by the loss of a beard.
  D. Pedro. Nay, 'a rubs himself with civet.
Can you smell him out by that ?   46
  Claud. That's as much as to say the
sweet youth's in love.
  D. Pedro. The greatest note of it is his
melancholy.
  Claud. And when was he wont to wash
his face ?   50
  D. Pedro. Yea, or to paint himself ? For
the which I hear what they say of him.
  Claud. Nay, but his jesting spirit, which
is now crept into a lute-string, and now
govern'd by stops.
  D. Pedro. Indeed, that tells a heavy tale
for him ; conclude, conclude, he is in
love.   56
  Claud. Nay, but I know who loves him.
  D. Pedro. That would I know too ; I
warrant, one that knows him not.
  Claud. Yes, and his ill conditions ; and,
in despite of all, dies for him.   61
  D. Pedro. She shall be buried with her
face upwards.
  Bene. Yet is this no charm for the toothache. Old signior, walk aside with me ; I
have studied eight or nine wise words to
speak to you, which these hobby-horses
must not hear.   66
            [*Exeunt Benedick and Leonato.*
  D. Pedro. For my life, to break with him
about Beatrice.
  Claud. 'Tis even so. Hero and Margaret
have by this played their parts with
Beatrice ; and then the two bears will not
bite one another when they meet.   70

                  Enter DON JOHN

  D. John. My lord and brother, God save
you !
  D. Pedro. Good den, brother.
  D. John. If your leisure serv'd, I would
speak with you.
  D. Pedro. In private ?
  D. John. If it please you ; yet Count
Claudio may hear, for what I would speak
of concerns him.   76
  D. Pedro. What's the matter ?
  D. John. [*To Claudio*] Means your lord-
ship to be married to-morrow ?
  D. Pedro. You know he does.   80

  D. John. I know not that, when he knows
what I know.
  Claud. If there be any impediment, I
pray you discover it.   83
  D. John. You may think I love you not ;
let that appear hereafter, and aim better at
me by that I now will manifest. For my
brother, I think he holds you well, and in
dearness of heart hath holp to effect your
ensuing marriage—surely suit ill spent, and
labour ill bestowed.
  D. Pedro. Why, what's the matter ?   89
  D. John. I came hither to tell you ; and,
circumstances short'ned, for she has been
too long a talking of, the lady is disloyal.
  Claud. Who ? Hero ?   93
  D. John. Even she—Leonato's Hero,
your Hero, every man's Hero.
  Claud. Disloyal ?   96
  D. John. The word is too good to paint
out her wickedness ; I could say she were
worse ; think you of a worse title, and I will
fit her to it. Wonder not till further
warrant ; go but with me to-night, you
shall see her chamber window ent'red, even
the night before her wedding-day. If you
love her then, to-morrow wed her ; but it
would better fit your honour to change your
mind.   103
  Claud. May this be so ?
  D. Pedro. I will not think it.   105
  D. John. If you dare not trust that you
see, confess not that you know. If you will
follow me, I will show you enough ; and
when you have seen more, and heard more,
proceed accordingly.   109
  Claud. If I see anything to-night why I
should not marry her, to-morrow in the
congregation where I should wed, there
will I shame her.   112
  D. Pedro. And, as I wooed for thee to
obtain her, I will join with thee to disgrace
her.   114
  D. John. I will disparage her no farther
till you are my witnesses ; bear it coldly
but till midnight, and let the issue show
itself.   117
  D. Pedro. O day untowardly turned !
  Claud. O mischief strangely thwarting !
  D. John. O plague right well prevented !
So will you say when you have seen the
sequel.   [*Exeunt.*

            SCENE III. *A street.*

Enter DOGBERRY *and his compartner*
        VERGES, *with the* Watch.

  Dogb. Are you good men and true ?
  Verg. Yea, or else it were pity but they
should suffer salvation, body and soul.
  Dogb. Nay, that were a punishment too
good for them, if they should have any
allegiance in them, being chosen for the
Prince's watch.   6

Verg. Well, give them their charge, neighbour Dogberry.

Dogb. First, who think you the most desartless man to be constable ?

1 Watch. Hugh Oatcake, sir, or George Seacoal ; for they can write and read.   11

Dogb. Come hither, neighbour Seacoal. God hath bless'd you with a good name. To be a well-favoured man is the gift of fortune ; but to write and read comes by nature.   14

2 Watch. Both which, Master Constable—

Dogb. You have ; I knew it would be your answer. Well, for your favour, sir, why, give God thanks, and make no boast of it ; and for your writing and reading, let that appear when there is no need of such vanity. You are thought here to be the most senseless and fit man for the constable of the watch ; therefore bear you the lantern. This is your charge : you shall comprehend all vagrom men ; you are to bid any man stand, in the Prince's name.

2 Watch. How if 'a will not stand ?   24

Dogb. Why, then, take no note of him, but let him go ; and presently call the rest of the watch together, and thank God you are rid of a knave.   27

Verg. If he will not stand when he is bidden, he is none of the Prince's subjects.

Dogb. True, and they are to meddle with none but the Prince's subjects. You shall also make no noise in the streets ; for for the watch to babble and to talk is most tolerable and not to be endured.

2 Watch. We will rather sleep than talk ; we know what belongs to a watch.   35

Dogb. Why, you speak like an ancient and most quiet watchman, for I cannot see how sleeping should offend ; only, have a care that your bills be not stol'n. Well, you are to call at all the ale-houses, and bid those that are drunk get them to bed.

2 Watch. How if they will not ?   41

Dogb. Why, then, let them alone till they are sober ; if they make you not then the better answer, you may say they are not the men you took them for.

2 Watch. Well, sir.   45

Dogb. If you meet a thief, you may suspect him, by virtue of your office, to be no true man ; and, for such kind of men, the less you meddle or make with them, why, the more is for your honesty.   49

2 Watch. If we know him to be a thief, shall we not lay hands on him ?   51

Dogb. Truly, by your office you may, but I think they that touch pitch will be defil'd ; the most peaceable way for you, if you do take a thief, is to let him show himself what he is, and steal out of your company.   55

Verg. You have been always called a merciful man, partner.

Dogb. Truly, I would not hang a dog by my will, much more a man who hath any honesty in him.

Verg. If you hear a child cry in the night, you must call to the nurse and bid her still it.   61

2 Watch. How if the nurse be asleep and will not hear us ?

Dogb. Why, then, depart in peace, and let the child wake her with crying ; for the ewe that will not hear her lamb when it baes will never answer a calf when he bleats.   66

Verg. 'Tis very true.

Dogb. This is the end of the charge : you, constable, are to present the Prince's own person ; if you meet the Prince in the night, you may stay him.   70

Verg. Nay, by'r lady, that I think 'a cannot.

Dogb. Five shillings to one on't, with any man that knows the statues, he may stay him ; marry, not without the Prince be willing ; for, indeed, the watch ought to offend no man, and it is an offence to stay a man against his will.   75

Verg. By'r lady, I think it be so.

Dogb. Ha, ah, ha ! Well, masters, good night ; an there be any matter of weight chances, call up me ; keep your fellows' counsels and your own, and good night. Come, neighbour.   80

2 Watch. Well, masters, we hear our charge ; let us go sit here upon the church bench till two, and then all to bed.   83

Dogb. One word more, honest neighbours : I pray you watch about Signior Leonato's door ; for the wedding being there to-morrow, there is a great coil to-night. Adieu ; be vigitant, I beseech you.

      [*Exeunt Dogberry and Verges.*

     Enter BORACHIO *and* CONRADE.

Bora. What, Conrade !

2 Watch [*Aside*] Peace, stir not.

Bora. Conrade, I say !   90

Con. Here, man, I am at thy elbow.

Bora. Mass, and my elbow itch'd ; I thought there would a scab follow.

Con. I will owe thee an answer for that ; and now forward with thy tale.   95

Bora. Stand thee close then under this penthouse, for it drizzles rain ; and I will, like a true drunkard, utter all to thee.   98

2 Watch. [*Aside*] Some treason, masters ; yet stand close.

Bora. Therefore know I have earned of Don John a thousand ducats.   101

Con. Is it possible that any villainy should be so dear ?

Bora. Thou shouldst rather ask if it were possible any villainy should be so rich ; for when rich villains have need of poor ones, poor ones may make what price they will.

Con. I wonder at it.   106

Bora. That shows thou art unconfirm'd. Thou knowest that the fashion of a doublet, or a hat, or a cloak, is nothing to a man.

Con. Yes, it is apparel.   110

Bora. I mean the fashion.

Con. Yes, the fashion is the fashion.

Bora. Tush! I may as well say the fool's the fool. But seest thou not what a deformed thief this fashion is?   114

2 Watch. [*Aside*] I know that Deformed; 'a has been a vile thief this seven year; 'a goes up and down like a gentleman; I remember his name.   117

Bora. Didst thou not hear somebody?

Con. No; 'twas the vane on the house.

Bora. Seest thou not, I say, what a deformed thief this fashion is, how giddily 'a turns about all the hot bloods between fourteen and five and thirty, sometimes fashioning them like Pharaoh's soldiers in the reechy painting, sometime like god Bel's priests in the old church-window, sometime like the shaven Hercules in the smirch'd worm-eaten tapestry, where his codpiece seems as massy as his club?   126

Con. All this I see; and I see that the fashion wears out more apparel than the man. But art not thou thyself giddy with the fashion too, that thou hast shifted out of thy tale into telling me of the fashion?

Bora. Not so neither; but know that I have to-night wooed Margaret, the Lady Hero's gentlewoman, by the name of Hero; she leans me out at her mistress' chamber-window, bids me a thousand times good night—I tell this tale vilely. I should first tell thee how the Prince, Claudio, and my master, planted and placed and possessed by my master Don John, saw afar off in the orchard this amiable encounter.   138

Con. And thought they Margaret was Hero?

Bora. Two of them did, the Prince and Claudio; but the devil my master knew she was Margaret; and partly by his oaths, which first possess'd them, partly by the dark night, which did deceive them, but chiefly by my villainy, which did confirm any slander that Don John had made, away went Claudio enrag'd; swore he would meet her, as he was appointed, next morning at the temple, and there, before the whole congregation, shame her with what he saw o'er night, and send her home again without a husband.   148

2 Watch. We charge you in the Prince's name, stand.   150

1 Watch. Call up the right Master Constable; we have here recover'd the most dangerous piece of lechery that ever was known in the commonwealth.

2 Watch. And one Deformed is one of them; I know him, 'a wears a lock.   155

Con. Masters, masters!

2 Watch. You'll be made bring Deformed forth, I warrant you.

Con. Masters—

1 Watch. Never speak, we charge you; let us obey you to go with us.   161

Bora. We are like to prove a goodly commodity, being taken up of these men's bills.

Con. A commodity in question, I warrant you. Come, we'll obey you.   [*Exeunt.*

SCENE IV. *Hero's apartment.*

Enter HERO, MARGARET, *and* URSULA.

Hero. Good Ursula, wake my cousin Beatrice, and desire her to rise.

Urs. I will, lady.

Hero. And bid her come hither.   4

Urs. Well.   [*Exit Ursula.*

Marg. Troth, I think your other rabato were better.

Hero. No, pray thee, good Meg, I'll wear this.

Marg. By my troth's not so good; and I warrant your cousin will say so.

Hero. My cousin's a fool, and thou art another; I'll wear none but this.   11

Marg. I like the new tire within excellently, if the hair were a thought browner; and your gown's a most rare fashion, i' faith. I saw the Duchess of Milan's gown that they praise so.   15

Hero. O, that exceeds, they say.

Marg. By my troth's but a night-gown in respect of yours—cloth o' gold, and cuts, and lac'd with silver, set with pearls, down sleeves, side sleeves, and skirts, round underborne with a bluish tinsel; but for a fine, quaint, graceful, and excellent fashion, yours is worth ten on't.   21

Hero. God give me joy to wear it, for my heart is exceeding heavy.

Marg. 'Twill be heavier soon, by the weight of a man.   24

Hero. Fie upon thee! art not ashamed?

Marg. Of what, lady, of speaking honourably? Is not marriage honourable in a beggar? Is not your lord honourable without marriage? I think you would have me say 'saving your reverence, a husband'; an bad thinking do not wrest true speaking I'll offend nobody. Is there any harm in 'the heavier for a husband'? None, I think, an it be the right husband and the right wife; otherwise 'tis light, and not heavy. Ask my Lady Beatrice else; here she comes.

Enter BEATRICE.

Hero. Good morrow, coz.

Beat. Good morrow, sweet Hero.   35

Hero. Why, how now! do you speak in the sick tune?

Beat. I am out of all other tune, methinks.

Marg. Clap's into ' Light o' love '; that goes without a burden. Do you sing it, and I'll dance it.   39

Beat. Ye light o' love with your heels! Then if your husband have stables enough, you'll see he shall lack no barnes.   42

Marg. O illegitimate construction! I scorn that with my heels.

Beat. 'Tis almost five o'clock, cousin; 'tis time you were ready. By my troth, I am exceeding ill. Heigh-ho!   46

Marg. For a hawk, a horse, or a husband?

Beat. For the letter that begins them all—H.

Marg. Well, an you be not turn'd Turk, there's no more sailing by the star.   50

Beat. What means the fool, trow?

Marg. Nothing I; but God send every one their heart's desire!

Hero. These gloves the Count sent me; they are an excellent perfume.   55

Beat. I am stuff'd, cousin, I cannot smell.

Marg. A maid and stuff'd! There's goodly catching of cold.   58

Beat. O, God help me! God help me! How long have you profess'd apprehension?

Marg. Ever since you left it. Doth not my wit become me rarely?   62

Beat. It is not seen enough; you should wear it in your cap. By my troth, I am sick.

Marg. Get you some of this distill'd Carduus Benedictus, and lay it to your heart; it is the only thing for a qualm.

Hero. There thou prick'st her with a thistle.   68

Beat. Benedictus! why Benedictus? You have some moral in this ' Benedictus '.   70

Marg. Moral? No, by my troth, I have no moral meaning; I meant plain holy-thistle. You may think, perchance, that I think you are in love. Nay, by'r lady, I am not such a fool to think what I list; nor I list not to think what I can; nor, indeed, I cannot think, if I would think my heart out of thinking, that you are in love, or that you will be in love, or that you can be in love. Yet Benedick was such another, and now is he become a man; he swore he would never marry, and yet now, in despite of his heart, he eats his meat without grudging. And how you may be converted I know not; but methinks you look with your eyes as other women do.   82

Beat. What pace is this that thy tongue keeps?

Marg. Not a false gallop.

Re-enter URSULA.

Urs. Madam, withdraw; the Prince, the Count, Signior Benedick, Don John, and all the gallants of the town, are come to fetch you to church.   87

Hero. Help to dress me, good coz, good Meg, good Ursula.   [*Exeunt.*

SCENE V.   *Leonato's house.*

Enter LEONATO, *with* DOGBERRY *and* VERGES.

Leon. What would you with me, honest neighbour?

Dogb. Marry, sir, I would have some confidence with you that decerns you nearly.

Leon. Brief, I pray you; for you see it is a busy time with me.   5

Dogb. Marry, this it is, sir.

Verg. Yes, in truth it is, sir.

Leon. What is it, my good friends?   8

Dogb. Goodman Verges, sir, speaks a little off the matter—an old man, sir, and his wits are not so blunt as, God help, I would desire they were; but, in faith, honest as the skin between his brows.   12

Verg. Yes, I thank God I am as honest as any man living that is an old man and no honester than I.

Dogb. Comparisons are odorous; palabras, neighbour Verges.   16

Leon. Neighbours, you are tedious.

Dogb. It pleases your worship to say so, but we are the poor Duke's officers; but, truly, for mine own part, if I were as tedious as a king, I could find in my heart to bestow it all of your worship.   21

Leon. All thy tediousness on me, ah?

Dogb. Yea, an 'twere a thousand pound more than 'tis; for I hear as good exclamation on your worship as of any man in the city; and though I be but a poor man, I am glad to hear it.   26

Verg. And so am I.

Leon. I would fain know what you have to say.

Verg. Marry, sir, our watch to-night, excepting your worship's presence, ha' ta'en a couple of as arrant knaves as any in Messina.   31

Dogb. A good old man, sir, he will be talking; as they say ' When the age is in the wit is out'. God help us, it is a world to see! Well said, i' faith, neighbour Verges; well, God's a good man; an two men ride of a horse, one must ride behind. An honest soul, i' faith, sir, by my troth he is, as ever broke bread; but God is to be worshipp'd; all men are not alike; alas, good neighbour!   38

Leon. Indeed, neighbour, he comes too short of you.

Dogb. Gifts that God gives.   40

Leon. I must leave you.

Dogb. One word, sir: our watch, sir, have indeed comprehended two aspicious persons, and we would have them this morning examined before your worship.

Leon. Take their examination yourself, and bring it me; I am now in great haste, as it may appear unto you.   46

153

Dogb. It shall be suffigance.

Leon. Drink some wine ere you go ; fare you well.

Enter a Messenger.

Mess. My lord, they stay for you to give your daughter to her husband.   50

Leon. I'll wait upon them ; I am ready.
                              [*Exeunt Leonato and Messenger.*

Dogb. Go, good partner, go, get you to Francis Seacoal ; bid him bring his pen and inkhorn to the gaol ; we are now to examination these men.

Verg. And we must do it wisely.   55

Dogb. We will spare for no wit, I warrant you ; here's that shall drive some of them to a non-come ; only get the learned writer to set down our excommunication, and meet me at the gaol.   [*Exeunt.*

ACT FOUR

SCENE I. *A church.*

Enter DON PEDRO, DON JOHN, LEONATO, FRIAR FRANCIS, CLAUDIO, BENEDICK, HERO, BEATRICE, *and* Attendants.

Leon. Come, Friar Francis, be brief ; only to the plain form of marriage, and you shall recount their particular duties afterwards.

Friar. You come hither, my lord, to marry this lady ?

Claud. No.   5

Leon. To be married to her, friar! You come to marry her.

Friar. Lady, you come hither to be married to this count ?

Hero. I do.   10

Friar. If either of you know any inward impediment why you should not be conjoined, I charge you, on your souls, to utter it.

Claud. Know you any, Hero ?

Hero. None, my lord.   15

Friar. Know you any, Count ?

Leon. I dare make his answer, None.

Claud. O, what men dare do ! What men may do ! What men daily do, not knowing what they do !   19

Bene. How now ! Interjections ? Why, then, some be of laughing, as, ah, ha, he !

Claud. Stand thee by, friar. Father, by your leave :

Will you with free and unconstrained soul
Give me this maid, your daughter ?

Leon. As freely, son, as God did give her me.   25

Claud. And what have I to give you back whose worth

May counterpoise this rich and precious gift ?

D. Pedro. Nothing, unless you render her again.

Claud. Sweet Prince, you learn me noble thankfulness.

There, Leonato, take her back again ;   30
Give not this rotten orange to your friend ;
She's but the sign and semblance of her honour.
Behold how like a maid she blushes here.
O, what authority and show of truth
Can cunning sin cover itself withal !   35
Comes not that blood as modest evidence
To witness simple virtue ? Would you not swear,
All you that see her, that she were a maid
By these exterior shows ? But she is none :
She knows the heat of a luxurious bed ;   40
Her blush is guiltiness, not modesty.

Leon. What do you mean, my lord ?

Claud.   Not to be married,
Not to knit my soul to an approved wanton.

Leon. Dear, my lord, if you, in your own proof,
Have vanquish'd the resistance of her youth,   45
And made defeat of her virginity—

Claud. I know what you would say. If I have known her,
You will say she did embrace me as a husband,
And so extenuate the 'forehand sin.
No, Leonato,   50
I never tempted her with word too large
But, as a brother to his sister, show'd
Bashful sincerity and comely love.

Hero. And seem'd I ever otherwise to you ?

Claud. Out on thee! Seeming! I will write against it.   55
You seem to me as Dian in her orb,
As chaste as is the bud ere it be blown ;
But you are more intemperate in your blood
Than Venus, or those pamp'red animals
That rage in savage sensuality.   60

Hero. Is my lord well, that he doth speak so wide ?

Leon. Sweet Prince, why speak not you ?

D. Pedro.   What should I speak ?
I stand dishonour'd that have gone about
To link my dear friend to a common stale.

Leon. Are these things spoken, or do I but dream ?   65

D. John. Sir, they are spoken, and these things are true.

Bene. This looks not like a nuptial.

Hero.   True ! O God !

Claud. Leonato, stand I here ?
Is this the Prince ? Is this the Prince's brother ?   69
Is this face Hero's ? Are our eyes our own ?

Leon. All this is so ; but what of this, my lord ?

Claud. Let me but move one question to your daughter ;
And, by that fatherly and kindly power
That you have in her, bid her answer truly.

Leon. I charge thee do so, as thou art my child.

Hero. O, God defend me! how am I beset!
What kind of catechising call you this?
   Claud. To make you answer truly to your
      name.
   Hero. Is it not Hero? Who can blot that
      name   79
With any just reproach?
   Claud.   Marry, that can Hero;
Hero itself can blot out Hero's virtue.
What man was he talk'd with you yester-
      night
Out at your window, betwixt twelve and
      one?
Now, if you are a maid, answer to this.
   Hero. I talk'd with no man at that hour,
      my lord.   85
   D. Pedro. Why, then are you no maiden.
      Leonato,
I am sorry you must hear: upon mine
      honour,
Myself, my brother, and this grieved Count,
Did see her, hear her, at that hour last
      night,   89
Talk with a ruffian at her chamber window;
Who hath, indeed, most like a liberal
      villain,
Confess'd the vile encounters they have had
A thousand times in secret.
   D. John. Fie, fie! they are not to be
      nam'd, my lord,
Not to be spoke of;   95
There is not chastity enough in language
Without offence to utter them.   Thus,
      pretty lady,
I am sorry for thy much misgovernment.
   Claud. O Hero, what a Hero hadst thou
      been,   99
If half thy outward graces had been placed
About thy thoughts and counsels of thy
      heart!
But fare thee well, most foul, most fair!
      Farewell,   102
Thou pure impiety and impious purity!
For thee I'll lock up all the gates of love,
And on my eyelids shall conjecture hang,
To turn all beauty into thoughts of harm,
And never shall it more be gracious.   107
   Leon. Hath no man's dagger here a point
      for me?   [*Hero swoons.*
   Beat. Why, how now, cousin! Where-
      fore sink you down?
   D. John. Come, let us go. These things,
      come thus to light,   110
Smother her spirits up.
[*Exeunt Don Pedro, Don John, and Claudio.*
   Bene. How doth the lady?
   Beat.   Dead, I think. Help, uncle!
Hero! why, Hero! Uncle! Signior Bene-
      dick! Friar!
   Leon. O Fate, take not away thy heavy
      hand!   114
Death is the fairest cover for her shame
That may be wish'd for.
   Beat.   How now, cousin Hero!

   Friar. Have comfort, lady.
   Leon. Dost thou look up?
   Friar. Yea; wherefore should she not?
   Leon. Wherefore! Why, doth not every
      earthly thing   120
Cry shame upon her? Could she here
      deny
The story that is printed in her blood?
Do not live, Hero; do not ope thine eyes;
For, did I think thou wouldst not quickly
      die,
Thought I thy spirits were stronger than
      thy shames,   125
Myself would, on the rearward of re-
      proaches,
Strike at thy life. Griev'd I I had but one?
Chid I for that at frugal nature's frame?
O, one too much by thee! Why had I one?
Why ever wast thou lovely in my eyes?   130
Why had I not, with charitable hand,
Took up a beggar's issue at my gates,
Who smirched thus and mir'd with infamy,
I might have said ' No part of it is mine;
This shame derives itself from unknown
      loins '?   135
But mine, and mine I lov'd, and mine I
      prais'd,
And mine that I was proud on; mine so
      much
That I myself was to myself not mine,
Valuing of her—why, she, O, she is fall'n
Into a pit of ink, that the wide sea   140
Hath drops too few to wash her clean again,
And salt too little which may season give
To her foul tainted flesh!
   Bene.   Sir, sir, be patient.
For my part, I am so attir'd in wonder,
I know not what to say.   145
   Beat. O, on my soul, my cousin is belied!
   Bene. Lady, were you her bedfellow last
      night?
   Beat. No, truly not; although, until last
      night,
I have this twelvemonth been her bed-
      fellow.
   Leon. Confirm'd, confirm'd! O, that is
      stronger made   150
Which was before barr'd up with ribs of
      iron!
Would the two princes lie; and Claudio lie,
Who lov'd her so, that, speaking of her
      foulness,
Wash'd it with tears? Hence from her!
      let her die.
   Friar. Hear me a little;   155
For I have only been silent so long,
And given way unto this course of fortune,
By noting of the lady: I have mark'd
A thousand blushing apparitions
To start into her face, a thousand innocent
      shames   160
In angel whiteness beat away those
      blushes;
And in her eye there hath appear'd a fire

To burn the errors that these princes hold
Against her maiden truth. Call me a fool;
Trust not my reading nor my observations,
Which with experimental seal doth warrant
The tenour of my book; trust not my age,
My reverence, calling, nor divinity,   168
If this sweet lady lie not guiltless here
Under some biting error.
 Leon.   Friar, it cannot be.   170
Thou seest that all the grace that she hath
 left
Is that she will not add to her damnation
A sin of perjury; she not denies it.
Why seek'st thou then to cover with excuse
That which appears in proper nakedness?
 Friar. Lady, what man is he you are
 accus'd of?   176
 Hero. They know that do accuse me; I
 know none.
If I know more of any man alive
Than that which maiden modesty doth
 warrant,   179
Let all my sins lack mercy! O my father,
Prove you that any man with me convers'd
At hours unmeet, or that I yesternight
Maintain'd the change of words with any
 creature,   183
Refuse me, hate me, torture me to death.
 Friar. There is some strange misprision
 in the princes.
 Bene. Two of them have the very bent of
 honour;   186
And if their wisdoms be misled in this,
The practice of it lives in John the bastard,
Whose spirits toil in frame of villainies.
 Leon. I know not. If they speak but
 truth of her,   190
These hands shall tear her; if they wrong
 her honour,
The proudest of them shall well hear of it.
Time hath not yet so dried this blood of
 mine,
Nor age so eat up my invention,   194
Nor fortune made such havoc of my means,
Nor my bad life reft me so much of
 friends,
But they shall find awak'd in such a kind
Both strength of limb and policy of mind,
Ability in means and choice of friends,   199
To quit me of them throughly.
 Friar.   Pause awhile,
And let my counsel sway you in this case.
Your daughter here the princes left for
 dead;
Let her awhile be secretly kept in,
And publish it that she is dead indeed;
Maintain a mourning ostentation,   205
And on your family's old monument
Hang mournful epitaphs, and do all rites
That appertain unto a burial.
 Leon. What shall become of this? What
 will this do?
 Friar. Marry, this, well carried, shall on
 her behalf   210

Change slander to remorse; that is some
 good.
But not for that dream I on this strange
 course,
But on this travail look for greater birth.
She dying, as it must be so maintain'd,
Upon the instant that she was accus'd,   215
Shall be lamented, pitied, and excus'd,
Of every hearer; for it so falls out
That what we have we prize not to the
 worth
Whiles we enjoy it, but being lack'd and
 lost,   219
Why, then we rack the value, then we find
The virtue that possession would not show
 us
Whiles it was ours. So will it fare with
 Claudio.
When he shall hear she died upon his
 words,
Th' idea of her life shall sweetly creep
Into his study of imagination,   225
And every lovely organ of her life
Shall come apparell'd in more precious
 habit,
More moving, delicate, and full of life,
Into the eye and prospect of his soul,
Than when she liv'd indeed. Then shall he
 mourn,   230
If ever love had interest in his liver,
And wish he had not so accused her—
No, though he thought his accusation true.
Let this be so, and doubt not but success
Will fashion the event in better shape   235
Than I can lay it down in likelihood.
But if all aim but this be levell'd false,
The supposition of the lady's death
Will quench the wonder of her infamy.
And if it sort not well, you may conceal
 her,   240
As best befits her wounded reputation,
In some reclusive and religious life,
Out of all eyes, tongues, minds, and
 injuries.
 Bene. Signior Leonato, let the friar advise
 you;
And though you know my inwardness and
 love   245
Is very much unto the Prince and Claudio,
Yet, by mine honour, I will deal in this
As secretly and justly as your soul
Should with your body.
 Leon.   Being that I flow in grief
The smallest twine may lead me.   250
 Friar. 'Tis well consented. Presently
 away;
For to strange sores strangely they strain
 the cure.
Come, lady, die to live; this wedding day
Perhaps is but prolong'd; have patience
 and endure.
   [*Exeunt all but Benedick and Beatrice.*
 Bene. Lady Beatrice, have you wept all
this while?   255

Beat. Yea, and I will weep a while longer.

Bene. I will not desire that.

Beat. You have no reason; I do it freely.

Bene. Surely I do believe your fair cousin is wronged.

Beat. Ah, how much might the man deserve of me that would right her! 261

Bene. Is there any way to show such friendship?

Beat. A very even way, but no such friend.

Bene. May a man do it? 264

Beat. It is a man's office, but not yours.

Bene. I do love nothing in the world so well as you. Is not that strange? 267

Beat. As strange as the thing I know not. It were as possible for me to say I lov'd nothing so well as you; but believe me not, and yet I lie not; I confess nothing, nor I deny nothing. I am sorry for my cousin. 271

Bene. By my sword, Beatrice, thou lovest me.

Beat. Do not swear, and eat it.

Bene. I will swear by it that you love me; and I will make him eat it that says I love you not. 275

Beat. Will you not eat your word?

Bene. With no sauce that can be devised to it; I protest I love thee.

Beat. Why, then, God forgive me!

Bene. What offence, sweet Beatrice? 280

Beat. You have stayed me in a happy hour; I was about to protest I loved you.

Bene. And do it with all thy heart?

Beat. I love you with so much of my heart that none is left to protest. 285

Bene. Come, bid me do anything for thee.

Beat. Kill Claudio.

Bene. Ha! not for the wide world.

Beat. You kill me to deny it. Farewell.

Bene. Tarry, sweet Beatrice. 290

Beat. I am gone though I am here; there is no love in you; nay, I pray you, let me go.

Bene. Beatrice—

Beat. In faith, I will go.

Bene. We'll be friends first. 295

Beat. You dare easier be friends with me than fight with mine enemy.

Bene. Is Claudio thine enemy? 298

Beat. Is 'a not approved in the height a villain that hath slandered, scorned, dishonoured, my kinswoman? O that I were a man! What! bear her in hand until they come to take hands, and then with public accusation, uncover'd slander, unmitigated rancour—O God, that I were a man! I would eat his heart in the market-place.

Bene. Hear me, Beatrice. 305

Beat. Talk with a man out at a window! A proper saying!

Bene. Nay, but, Beatrice—

Beat. Sweet Hero! She is wrong'd, she is sland'red, she is undone. 310

Bene. Beat—

Beat. Princes and Counties! Surely, a princely testimony, a goodly count, Count Comfect; a sweet gallant, surely! O that I were a man for his sake! or that I had any friend would be a man for my sake! But manhood is melted into curtsies, valour into compliment, and men are only turn'd into tongue, and trim ones too. He is now as valiant as Hercules that only tells a lie and swears it. I cannot be a man with wishing, therefore I will die a woman with grieving. 320

Bene. Tarry, good Beatrice. By this hand, I love thee.

Beat. Use it for my love some other way than swearing by it.

Bene. Think you in your soul the Count Claudio hath wrong'd Hero? 325

Beat. Yea, as sure as I have a thought or a soul.

Bene. Enough, I am engag'd; I will challenge him; I will kiss your hand, and so I leave you. By this hand, Claudio shall render me a dear account. As you hear of me, so think of me. Go comfort your cousin; I must say she is dead; and so, farewell. [*Exeunt.*

SCENE II. *A prison.*

Enter DOGBERRY, VERGES, *and* Sexton, *in gowns; and the* Watch, *with* CONRADE *and* BORACHIO.

Dogb. Is our whole dissembly appear'd?

Verg. O, a stool and a cushion for the sexton!

Sexton. Which be the malefactors?

Dogb. Marry, that am I and my partner.

Verg. Nay, that's certain; we have the exhibition to examine. 6

Sexton. But which are the offenders that are to be examin d? Let them come before Master Constable.

Dogb. Yea, marry, let them come before me. What is your name, friend? 10

Bora. Borachio.

Dogb. Pray write down Borachio. Yours, sirrah?

Con. I am a gentleman, sir, and my name is Conrade.

Dogb. Write down Master Gentleman Conrade. Masters, do you serve God? 15

Con.
Bora. }Yea, sir, we hope.

Dogb. Write down that they hope they serve God; and write God first; for God defend but God should go before such villains! Masters, it is proved already that you are little better than false knaves, and it will go near to be thought so shortly. How answer you for yourselves? 21

Con. Marry, sir, we say we are none.

Dogb. A marvellous witty fellow, I assure you ; but I will go about with him. Come you hither, sirrah ; a word in your ear : sir, I say to you it is thought you are false knaves. 26

Bora. Sir, I say to you we are none.

Dogb. Well, stand aside. Fore God, they are both in a tale. Have you writ down that they are none ? 29

Sexton. Master Constable, you go not the way to examine ; you must call forth the watch that are their accusers. 31

Dogb. Yea, marry, that's the eftest way. Let the watch come forth. Masters, I charge you in the Prince's name, accuse these men. 34

1 Watch. This man said, sir, that Don John, the Prince's brother, was a villain.

Dogb. Write down Prince John a villain. Why, this is flat perjury, to call a prince's brother villain. 38

Bora. Master Constable—

Dogb. Pray thee, fellow, peace ; I do not like thy look, I promise thee. 41

Sexton. What heard you him say else ?

2 Watch. Marry, that he had received a thousand ducats of Don John for accusing the Lady Hero wrongfully. 45

Dogb. Flat burglary as ever was committed.

Verg. Yea, by mass, that it is.

Sexton. What else, fellow ?

1 Watch. And that Count Claudio did mean, upon his words, to disgrace Hero before the whole assembly, and not marry her. 51

Dogb. O villain ! thou wilt be condemn'd into everlasting redemption for this.

Sexton. What else ?

2 Watch. This is all. 55

Sexton. And this is more, masters, than you can deny. Prince John is this morning secretly stol'n away ; Hero was in this manner accus'd, in this very manner refus'd, and upon the grief of this suddenly died. Master Constable, let these men be bound and brought to Leonato's ; I will go before and show him their examination. 61

[*Exit.*

Dogb. Come, let them be opinion'd.

Verg. Let them be in the hands.

Con. Off, coxcomb.

Dogb. God's my life, where's the sexton ? Let him write down the Prince's officer coxcomb. Come, bind them. Thou naughty varlet ! 67

Con. Away ! you are an ass, you are an ass.

Dogb. Dost thou not suspect my place ? Dost thou not suspect my years ? O that he were here to write me down an ass ! But, masters, remember that I am an ass ; though it be not written down, yet forget not that I am an ass. No, thou villain, thou

art full of piety, as shall be prov'd upon thee by good witness. I am a wise fellow ; and, which is more, an officer ; and, which is more, a householder ; and, which is more, as pretty a piece of flesh as any is in Messina ; and one that knows the law, go to ; and a rich fellow enough, go to ; and a fellow that hath had losses ; and one that hath two gowns, and everything handsome about him. Bring him away. O that I had been writ down an ass ! [*Exeunt.*

ACT FIVE

Scene I. *Before Leonato's house.*

Enter Leonato *and* Antonio.

Ant. If you go on thus, you will kill yourself,
And 'tis not wisdom thus to second grief
Against yourself.

Leon. I pray thee cease thy counsel,
Which falls into mine ears as profitless 4
As water in a sieve. Give not me counsel ;
Nor let no comforter delight mine ear
But such a one whose wrongs do suit with mine.
Bring me a father that so lov'd his child,
Whose joy of her is overwhelm'd like mine,
And bid him speak of patience ; 10
Measure his woe the length and breadth of mine,
And let it answer every strain for strain ;
As thus for thus, and such a grief for such,
In every lineament, branch, shape, and form.
If such a one will smile and stroke his beard, 15
And sorrow wag, cry 'hem !' when he should groan,
Patch grief with proverbs, make misfortune drunk
With candle-wasters—bring him yet to me,
And I of him will gather patience.
But there is no such man ; for, brother, men 20
Can counsel and speak comfort to that grief
Which they themselves not feel ; but, tasting it,
Their counsel turns to passion, which before
Would give preceptial medicine to rage, 24
Fetter strong madness in a silken thread,
Charm ache with air and agony with words.
No, no ; 'tis all men's office to speak patience
To those that wring under the load of sorrow,
But no man's virtue nor sufficiency
To be so moral when he shall endure 30
The like himself. Therefore, give me no counsel ;
My griefs cry louder than advertisement.

Ant. Therein do men from children
    nothing differ.
Leon. I pray thee peace ; I will be flesh
    and blood ;
For there was never yet philosopher   35
That could endure the toothache patiently,
However they have writ the style of gods,
And made a push at chance and sufferance.
Ant. Yet bend not all the harm upon
    yourself ;
Make those that do offend you suffer too. 40
Leon. There thou speak'st reason ; nay,
    I will do so.
My soul doth tell me Hero is belied ;
And that shall Claudio know ; so shall the
    Prince,
And all of them that thus dishonour her.
Ant. Here comes the Prince and Claudio
    hastily.   45

Enter DON PEDRO *and* CLAUDIO.

D. Pedro. Good den, good den.
Claud.   Good day to both of you.
Leon. Hear you, my lords !
D. Pedro. We have some haste, Leonato.
Leon. Some haste, my lord ! Well, fare
    you well, my lord.
Are you so hasty now ? Well, all is one.
D. Pedro. Nay, do not quarrel with
    us, good old man.   50
Ant. If he could right himself with
    quarrelling,
Some of us would lie low.
Claud.   Who wrongs him ?
Leon. Marry, thou dost wrong me ; thou
    dissembler, thou !   53
Nay, never lay thy hand upon thy sword ;
I fear thee not.
Claud.   Marry, beshrew my hand
If it should give your age such cause of fear !
In faith, my hand meant nothing to my
    sword.
Leon. Tush, tush, man ; never fleer and
    jest at me ;
I speak not like a dotard nor a fool,
As under privilege of age to brag   60
What I have done being young, or what
    would do
Were I not old. Know, Claudio, to thy
    head,
Thou hast so wrong'd mine innocent child
    and me
That I am forc'd to lay my reverence by,
And with grey hairs and bruise of many
    days   65
Do challenge thee to trial of a man.
I say thou hast belied mine innocent child ;
Thy slander hath gone through and
    through her heart,
And she lies buried with her ancestors—
O ! in a tomb where never scandal slept,   70
Save this of hers, fram'd by thy villainy.
Claud. My villainy !
Leon.   Thine, Claudio ; thine, I say.

D. Pedro. You say not right, old man.
Leon.   My lord, my lord,
I'll prove it on his body if he dare,
Despite his nice fence and his active
    practice,   75
His May of youth and bloom of lustihood.
Claud. Away ! I will not have to do with
    you.
Leon. Canst thou so daff me ? Thou hast
    kill'd my child ;
If thou kill'st me, boy, thou shalt kill a
    man.
Ant. He shall kill two of us, and men
    indeed ;   80
But that's no matter ; let him kill one first.
Win me and wear me ; let him answer me.
Come, follow me, boy ; come, sir boy, come
    follow me ;
Sir boy, I'll whip you from your foining
    fence ;
Nay, as I am a gentleman, I will.   85
Leon. Brother—
Ant. Content yourself.   God knows I
    lov'd my niece ;
And she is dead, slander'd to death by
    villains,
That dare as well answer a man indeed
As I dare take a serpent by the tongue.   90
Boys, apes, braggarts, Jacks, milksops !
Leon.   Brother Antony—
Ant. Hold you content. What, man ! I
    know them, yea,
And what they weigh, even to the utmost
    scruple—
Scambling, out-facing, fashion-monging
    boys,
That lie and cog and flout, deprave and
    slander,   95
Go anticly, and show outward hideousness,
And speak off half a dozen dang'rous words,
How they might hurt their enemies, if they
    durst ;
And this is all.   99
Leon. But, brother Antony—
Ant.   Come, 'tis no matter ;
Do not you meddle ; let me deal in this.
D. Pedro. Gentlemen both, we will not
    wake your patience.
My heart is sorry for your daughter's death;
But, on my honour, she was charg'd with
    nothing   104
But what was true, and very full of proof.
Leon. My lord, my lord—
D. Pedro.   I will not hear you.
Leon.   No ?
Come, brother, away. I will be heard.
Ant. And shall, or some of us will smart
    for it. [*Exeunt Leonato and Antonio.*
D. Pedro. See, see ; here comes the man
    we went to seek.   110

Enter BENEDICK.

Claud. Now, signior, what news ?
Bene. Good day, my lord.

D. Pedro. Welcome, signior; you are almost come to part almost a fray.

Claud. We had lik'd to have had our two noses snapp'd off with two old men without teeth. 116

D. Pedro. Leonato and his brother. What think'st thou? Had we fought, I doubt we should have been too young for them.

Bene. In a false quarrel there is no true valour. I came to seek you both. 121

Claud. We have been up and down to seek thee; for we are high-proof melancholy, and would fain have it beaten away. Wilt thou use thy wit?

Bene. It is in my scabbard; shall I draw it? 125

D. Pedro. Dost thou wear thy wit by thy side?

Claud. Never any did so, though very many have been beside their wit. I will bid thee draw, as we do the minstrels—draw to pleasure us.

D. Pedro. As I am an honest man, he looks pale. Art thou sick or angry? 131

Claud. What, courage, man! What though care kill'd a cat, thou hast mettle enough in thee to kill care.

Bene. Sir, I shall meet your wit in the career, an you charge it against me. I pray you choose another subject. 135

Claud. Nay, then, give him another staff; this last was broke cross.

D. Pedro. By this light, he changes more and more; I think he be angry indeed.

Claud. If he be, he knows how to turn his girdle. 140

Bene. Shall I speak a word in your ear?

Claud. God bless me from a challenge!

Bene. [*Aside to Claudio*] You are a villain; I jest not; I will make it good how you dare, with what you dare, and when you dare. Do me right, or I will protest your cowardice. You have kill'd a sweet lady, and her death shall fall heavy on you. Let me hear from you. 147

Claud. Well, I will meet you, so I may have good cheer.

D. Pedro. What, a feast? a feast? 149

Claud. I' faith, I thank him; he hath bid me to a calf's head and a capon, the which if I do not carve most curiously, say my knife's naught. Shall I not find a woodcock too?

Bene. Sir, your wit ambles well; it goes easily. 154

D. Pedro. I'll tell thee how Beatrice prais'd thy wit the other day. I said thou hadst a fine wit. 'True,' said she 'a fine little one.' 'No,' said I 'a great wit.' 'Right,' says she 'a great gross one.' 'Nay,' said I 'a good wit.' 'Just,' said she 'it hurts nobody.' 'Nay,' said I 'the gentleman is wise.' 'Certain,' said she 'a wise gentleman.' 'Nay,' said I 'he hath the tongues.' 'That I believe,' said she 'for he swore a thing to me on Monday night, which he forswore on Tuesday morning. There's a double tongue; there's two tongues.' Thus did she, an hour together, trans-shape thy particular virtues; yet, at last, she concluded, with a sigh, thou wast the proper'st man in Italy.

Claud. For the which she wept heartily, and said she cared not. 168

D. Pedro. Yea, that she did; but yet, for all that, an if she did not hate him deadly, she would love him dearly. The old man's daughter told us all. 171

Claud. All, all; and, moreover, 'God saw him when he was hid in the garden'.

D. Pedro. But when shall we set the savage bull's horns on the sensible Benedick's head? 175

Claud. Yea, and text underneath, 'Here dwells Benedick the married man'? 177

Bene. Fare you well, boy; you know my mind. I will leave you now to your gossiplike humour; you break jests as braggarts do their blades, which, God be thanked, hurt not. My lord, for your many courtesies I thank you. I must discontinue your company. Your brother the bastard is fled from Messina. You have among you kill'd a sweet and innocent lady. For my Lord Lackbeard there, he and I shall meet; and till then, peace be with him. 185

[*Exit Benedick.*]

D. Pedro. He is in earnest.

Claud. In most profound earnest; and I'll warrant you for the love of Beatrice.

D. Pedro. And hath challeng'd thee?

Claud. Most sincerely. 190

D. Pedro. What a pretty thing man is when he goes in his doublet and hose and leaves off his wit!

Claud. He is then a giant to an ape; but then is an ape a doctor to such a man.

D. Pedro. But, soft you, let me be; pluck up, my heart, and be sad. Did he not say my brother was fled? 196

Enter DOGBERRY, VERGES, *and the* Watch, *with* CONRADE *and* BORACHIO.

Dogb. Come, you, sir; if justice cannot tame you, she shall ne'er weigh more reasons in her balance; nay, an you be a cursing hypocrite once, you must be look'd to. 199

D. Pedro. How now! two of my brother's men bound—Borachio one.

Claud. Hearken after their offence, my lord.

D. Pedro. Officers, what offence have these men done? 203

Dogb. Marry, sir, they have committed false report; moreover, they have spoken untruths; secondarily, they are slanders; sixth and lastly, they have belied a lady;

thirdly, they have verified unjust things;
and to conclude, they are lying knaves. 208

D. Pedro. First, I ask thee what they
have done; thirdly, I ask thee what's
their offence; sixth and lastly, why they
are committed; and to conclude, what
you lay to their charge. 212

Claud. Rightly reasoned, and in his own
division; and, by my troth, there's one
meaning well suited.

D. Pedro. Who have you offended,
masters, that you are thus bound to your
answer? This learned constable is too
cunning to be understood. What's your
offence? 217

Bora. Sweet Prince, let me go no farther
to mine answer; do you hear me, and let
this Count kill me. I have deceived even
your very eyes. What your wisdoms could
not discover, these shallow fools have
brought to light; who, in the night, overheard me confessing to this man how Don
John your brother incensed me to slander
the Lady Hero; how you were brought
into the orchard, and saw me court
Margaret in Hero's garments; how you
disgrac'd her, when you should marry her.
My villainy they have upon record; which
I had rather seal with my death than repeat
over to my shame. The lady is dead upon
mine and my master's false accusation;
and, briefly, I desire nothing but the reward of a villain. 230

D. Pedro. Runs not this speech like iron
through your blood?

Claud. I have drunk poison whiles he
utter'd it.

D. Pedro. But did my brother set thee on
to this?

Bora. Yea, and paid me richly for the
practice of it.

D. Pedro. He is compos'd and fram'd of
treachery,
And fled he is upon this villainy. 236

Claud. Sweet Hero, now thy image doth
appear
In the rare semblance that I lov'd it first.

Dogb. Come, bring away the plaintiffs;
by this time our sexton hath reformed
Signior Leonato of the matter. And,
masters, do not forget to specify, when
time and place shall serve, that I am
an ass. 242

Verg. Here, here comes Master Signior
Leonato and the sexton too.

Re-enter LEONATO *and* ANTONIO, *with the*
Sexton.

Leon. Which is the villain? Let me see
his eyes, 245
That when I note another man like him
I may avoid him. Which of these is he?

Bora. If you would know your wronger,
look on me.

Leon. Art thou the slave that with thy
breath hast kill'd
Mine innocent child?

Bora.   Yea, even I alone. 250

Leon. No, not so, villain; thou beliest
thyself;
Here stand a pair of honourable men,
A third is fled, that had a hand in it.
I thank you, princes, for my daughter's
death; 254
Record it with your high and worthy deeds;
'Twas bravely done, if you bethink you
of it.

Claud. I know not how to pray your
patience,
Yet I must speak. Choose your revenge
yourself;
Impose me to what penance your invention
Can lay upon my sin; yet sinn'd I not 260
But in mistaking.

D. Pedro.   By my soul, nor I;
And yet, to satisfy this good old man,
I would bend under any heavy weight
That he'll enjoin me to.

Leon. I cannot bid you bid my daughter
live— 265
That were impossible; but, I pray you
both,
Possess the people in Messina here
How innocent she died; and, if your love
Can labour aught in sad invention,
Hang her an epitaph upon her tomb, 270
And sing it to her bones; sing it to-night.
To-morrow morning come you to my house;
And since you could not be my son-in-law,
Be yet my nephew. My brother hath a
daughter, 274
Almost the copy of my child that's dead;
And she alone is heir to both of us.
Give her the right you should have giv'n
her cousin,
And so dies my revenge.

Claud.   O noble sir!
Your over-kindness doth wring tears from
me.
I do embrace your offer; and dispose 280
For henceforth of poor Claudio.

Leon. To-morrow, then, I will expect
your coming;
To-night I take my leave. This naughty
man 283
Shall face to face be brought to Margaret,
Who, I believe, was pack'd in all this wrong,
Hir'd to it by your brother.

Bora.   No, by my soul, she was not;
Nor knew not what she did when she spoke
to me;
But always hath been just and virtuous
In anything that I do know by her. 289

Dogb. Moreover, sir, which indeed is not
under white and black, this plaintiff here,
the offender, did call me ass; I beseech
you, let it be remember'd in his punishment. And also, the watch heard them talk

of one Deformed; they say he wears a key in his ear and a lock hanging by it, and borrows money in God's name; the which he hath us'd so long, and never paid, that now men grow hard-hearted, and will lend nothing for God's sake. Pray you examine him upon that point. 298

Leon. I thank thee for thy care and honest pains.

Dogb. Your worship speaks like a most thankful and reverend youth, and I praise God for you. 301

Leon. There's for thy pains.

Dogb. God save the foundation!

Leon. Go; I discharge thee of thy prisoner, and I thank thee. 305

Dogb. I leave an arrant knave with your worship; which I beseech your worship to correct yourself, for the example of others. God keep your worship! I wish your worship well; God restore you to health! I humbly give you leave to depart; and if a merry meeting may be wish'd, God prohibit it! Come, neighbour. 311

[*Exeunt Dogberry and Verges.*

Leon. Until to-morrow morning, lords, farewell.

Ant. Farewell, my lords; we look for you to-morrow.

D. Pedro. We will not fail.

Claud. To-night I'll mourn with Hero.

[*Exeunt Don Pedro and Claudio.*

Leon. [*To the Watch*] Bring you these fellows on. We'll talk with Margaret 315 How her acquaintance grew with this lewd fellow. [*Exeunt severally.*

SCENE II. *Leonato's orchard.*

Enter BENEDICK *and* MARGARET, *meeting.*

Bene. Pray thee, sweet Mistress Margaret, deserve well at my hands by helping me to the speech of Beatrice.

Marg. Will you then write me a sonnet in praise of my beauty? 4

Bene. In so high a style, Margaret, that no man living shall come over it; for, in most comely truth, thou deservest it. 7

Marg. To have no man come over me! Why, shall I always keep below stairs?

Bene. Thy wit is as quick as the greyhound's mouth; it catches. 11

Marg. And yours as blunt as the fencer's foils, which hit, but hurt not.

Bene. A most manly wit, Margaret; it will not hurt a woman; and so, I pray thee, call Beatrice. I give thee the bucklers. 16

Marg. Give us the swords; we have bucklers of our own.

Bene. If you use them, Margaret, you must put in the pikes with a vice; and they are dangerous weapons for maids. 19

Marg. Well, I will call Beatrice to you, who, I think, hath legs. [*Exit Margaret.*

Bene. And therefore will come. 22

[*Sings*] The god of love,
That sits above,
And knows me, and knows me, 25
How pitiful I deserve—

I mean in singing; but in loving—Leander the good swimmer, Troilus the first employer of panders, and a whole bookful of these quondam carpet-mongers, whose names yet run smoothly in the even road of a blank verse, why, they were never so truly turn'd over and over as my poor self in love. Marry, I cannot show it in rhyme; I have tried; I can find out no rhyme to 'lady' but 'baby'—an innocent rhyme; for 'scorn', 'horn'—a hard rhyme; for 'school', 'fool'—a babbling rhyme; very ominous endings. No, I was not born under a rhyming planet, nor I cannot woo in festival terms. 37

Enter BEATRICE.

Sweet Beatrice, wouldst thou come when I call'd thee?

Beat. Yea, signior, and depart when you bid me.

Bene. O, stay but till then! 40

Beat. 'Then' is spoken; fare you well now. And yet, ere I go, let me go with that I came, which is, with knowing what hath pass'd between you and Claudio.

Bene. Only foul words; and thereupon I will kiss thee. 44

Beat. Foul words is but foul wind, and foul wind is but foul breath, and foul breath is noisome; therefore I will depart unkiss'd. 47

Bene. Thou hast frighted the word out of his right sense, so forcible is thy wit. But, I must tell thee plainly, Claudio undergoes my challenge; and either I must shortly hear from him, or I will subscribe him a coward. And, I pray thee now, tell me for which of my bad parts didst thou first fall in love with me? 53

Beat. For them all together; which maintain'd so politic a state of evil that they will not admit any good part to intermingle with them. But for which of my good parts did you first suffer love for me? 57

Bene. Suffer love—a good epithet! I do suffer love indeed, for I love thee against my will.

Beat. In spite of your heart, I think; alas, poor heart! If you spite it for my sake, I will spite it for yours; for I will never love that which my friend hates. 62

Bene. Thou and I are too wise to woo peaceably.

Beat. It appears not in this confession: there's not one wise man among twenty that will praise himself. 65

Bene. An old, an old instance, Beatrice, that liv'd in the time of good neighbours ; if a man do not erect in this age his own tomb ere he dies, he shall live no longer in monument than the bell rings and the widow weeps.   69

Beat. And how long is that, think you ?

Bene. Question : why, an hour in clamour, and a quarter in rheum. Therefore is it most expedient for the wise, if Don Worm, his conscience, find no impediment to the contrary, to be the trumpet of his own virtues, as I am to myself. So much for praising myself, who, I myself will bear witness, is praiseworthy. And now tell me, how doth your cousin ?   76

Beat. Very ill.

Bene. And how do you ?

Beat. Very ill too.

Bene. Serve God, love me, and mend ; there will I leave you too, for here comes one in haste.   81

Enter URSULA.

Urs. Madam, you must come to your uncle. Yonder's old coil at home. It is proved my Lady Hero hath been falsely accus'd, the Prince and Claudio mightily abus'd ; and Don John is the author of all, who is fled and gone. Will you come presently ?   86

Beat. Will you go hear this news, signior ?

Bene. I will live in thy heart, die in thy lap, and be buried in thy eyes ; and, moreover, I will go with thee to thy uncle's. 90
                                      [*Exeunt.*

SCENE III. *A churchyard.*

Enter DON PEDRO, CLAUDIO, *and* three *or* four *with tapers.*

Claud. Is this the monument of Leonato ?

A Lord. It is, my lord.

Claud. [*Reads from a scroll*]

Epitaph.

'Done to death by slanderous tongues
    Was the Hero that here lies ;
Death, in guerdon of her wrongs,   5
    Gives her fame which never dies.
So the life that died with shame
Lives in death with glorious fame.'

Hang thou there upon the tomb,
    Praising her when I am dumb.   10
Now, music, sound, and sing your solemn
    hymn.

Song.

Pardon, goddess of the night,
    Those that slew thy virgin knight ;
For the which, with songs of woe,
    Round about her tomb they go.   15
Midnight, assist our moan ;

    Help us to sigh and groan,
        Heavily, heavily.
Graves, yawn, and yield your dead,
Till death be uttered,   20
    Heavily, heavily.

Claud. Now, unto thy bones good night.
    Yearly will I do this rite.

D. Pedro. Good morrow, masters ; put
    your torches out ;
The wolves have prey'd ; and look, the
    gentle day,   25
Before the wheels of Phœbus, round about
Dapples the drowsy east with spots of grey.
Thanks to you all, and leave us. Fare you
    well.

Claud. Good morrow, masters ; each his
    several way.

D. Pedro. Come, let us hence, and put on
    other weeds ;   30
And then to Leonato's we will go.

Claud. And Hymen now with luckier
    issue speed's
Than this for whom we rend'red up this
    woe.   [*Exeunt.*

SCENE IV. *Leonato's house.*

Enter LEONATO, ANTONIO, BENEDICK, BEATRICE, MARGARET, URSULA, FRIAR FRANCIS, *and* HERO.

Friar. Did I not tell you she was inno-
    cent ?

Leon. So are the Prince and Claudio, who
    accus'd her
Upon the error that you heard debated.
But Margaret was in some fault for this,
Although against her will, as it appears 5
In the true course of all the question.

Ant. Well, I am glad that all things sorts
    so well.

Bene. And so am I, being else by faith
    enforc'd
To call young Claudio to a reckoning for it.

Leon. Well, daughter, and you gentle-
    women all,   10
Withdraw into a chamber by yourselves ;
And when I send for you, come hither
    mask'd.
The Prince and Claudio promis'd by this
    hour
To visit me. You know your office, brother:
You must be father to your brother's
    daughter,   15
And give her to young Claudio.
                          [*Exeunt Ladies.*

Ant. Which I will do with confirm'd
    countenance.

Bene. Friar, I must entreat your pains, I
    think.

Friar. To do what, signior ?

Bene. To bind me, or undo me—one of
    them.   20
Signior Leonato, truth it is, good signior,

Your niece regards me with an eye of
    favour.
Leon. That eye my daughter lent her.
    'Tis most true.
Bene. And I do with an eye of love requite
    her.
Leon. The sight whereof, I think, you had
    from me,   25
From Claudio, and the Prince. But what's
    your will ?
Bene. Your answer, sir, is enigmatical.
But, for my will, my will is your good will
May stand with ours, this day to be con-
    join'd
In the state of honourable marriage ;   30
In which, good friar, I shall desire your
    help.
Leon. My heart is with your liking.
Friar.   And my help.
Here comes the Prince and Claudio.

Enter DON PEDRO *and* CLAUDIO, *with*
    Attendants.

D. Pedro. Good morrow to this fair
    assembly.
Leon. Good morrow, Prince ; good
    morrow, Claudio ;   35
We here attend you. Are you yet deter-
    min'd
To-day to marry with my brother's
    daughter ?
Claud. I'll hold my mind were she an
    Ethiope.
Leon. Call her forth, brother ; here's the
    friar ready.   [*Exit Antonio.*
D. Pedro. Good morrow, Benedick. Why,
    what's the matter   40
That you have such a February face,
So full of frost, of storm, and cloudiness ?
Claud. I think he thinks upon the savage
    bull.
Tush, fear not, man ; we'll tip thy horns
    with gold,
And all Europa shall rejoice at thee,   45
As once Europa did at lusty Jove,
When he would play the noble beast in love.
Bene. Bull Jove, sir, had an amiable low ;
And some such strange bull leap'd your
    father's cow,
And got a calf in that same noble feat   50
Much like to you, for you have just his
    bleat.

Re-enter ANTONIO, *with the* Ladies *masked.*

Claud. For this I owe you. Here comes
    other reck'nings.
Which is the lady I must seize upon ?
Ant. This same is she, and I do give you
    her.
Claud. Why, then she's mine. Sweet, let
    me see your face.   55
Leon. No, that you shall not, till you take
    her hand
Before this friar, and swear to marry her.

Claud. Give me your hand ; before this
    holy friar
I am your husband, if you like of me.   59
Hero. And when I liv'd I was your other
    wife ;   [*Unmasking* ;
And when you lov'd you were my other
    husband.
Claud. Another Hero !
Hero.   Nothing certainer.
One Hero died defil'd ; but I do live,
And, surely as I live, I am a maid.
D. Pedro. The former Hero ! Hero that is
    dead !   65
Leon. She died, my lord, but whiles her
    slander liv'd.
Friar. All this amazement can I qualify,
When, after that the holy rites are ended,
I'll tell you largely of fair Hero's death.
Meantime let wonder seem familiar,   70
And to the chapel let us presently.
Bene. Soft and fair, friar. Which is
    Beatrice ?
Beat. I answer to that name. [*Unmasking*]
    What is your will ?
Bene. Do not you love me ?
Beat.   Why no, no more than reason.
Bene. Why, then your uncle, and the
    Pr nce, and Claudio,   75
Have been deceived : they swore you
    did.
Beat. Do not you love me ?
Bene.   Troth no, no more than reason.
Beat. Why, then my cousin, Margaret,
    and Ursula,
Are much deceiv'd ; for they did swear you
    did.
Bene. They swore that you were almost
    sick for me.   80
Beat. They swore that you were well-nigh
    dead for me.
Bene. 'Tis no such matter. Then you do
    not love me ?
Beat. No, truly, but in friendly recom-
    pense.
Leon. Come, cousin, I am sure you love
    the gentleman.
Claud. And I'll be sworn upon't that he
    loves her ;   85
For here's a paper written in his hand,
A halting sonnet of his own pure brain,
Fashion'd to Beatrice.
Hero.   And here's another,
Writ in my cousin's hand, stol'n from her
    pocket,
Containing her affection unto Benedick.   90
Bene. A miracle ! here's our own hands
against our hearts. Come, I will have thee ;
but, by this light, I take thee for pity.   93
Beat. I would not deny you ; but, by this
good day, I yield upon great persuasion ;
and partly to save your life, for I was told
you were in a consumption.   96
Bene. Peace ; I will stop your mouth.
                 [*Kissing her.*

D. Pedro. How dost thou, Benedick the
    married man ?   98

Bene. I'll tell thee what, Prince : a college
of wit-crackers cannot flout me out of my
humour.   Dost thou think I care for a
satire or an epigram ?   No.   If a man will
be beaten with brains, 'a shall wear nothing
handsome about him.   In brief, since I do
purpose to marry, I will think nothing to
any purpose that the world can say against
it ;   and therefore never flout at me for
what I have said against it ;   for man is
a giddy thing, and this is my conclusion.
For thy part, Claudio, I did think to have
beaten thee ;   but in that thou art like to
be my kinsman, live unbruis'd, and love
my cousin.   108

Claud. I had well hop'd thou wouldst
have denied Beatrice, that I might have
cudgell'd thee out of thy single life, to make
thee a double dealer ; which out of question
thou wilt be, if my cousin do not look
exceeding narrowly to thee.   112

Bene. Come, come, we are friends.   Let's
have a dance ere we are married, that we
may lighten our own hearts and our wives'
heels.   115

Leon. We'll have dancing afterward.

Bene. First, of my word ; therefore play,
music.   Prince, thou art sad ; get thee a
wife, get thee a wife.   There is no staff more
reverend than one tipp'd with horn.

Enter a Messenger.

Mess. My lord, your brother John is ta'en
    in flight,   120
And brought with armed men back to
    Messina.

Bene. Think not on him till to-morrow.
I'll devise thee brave punishments for him.
Strike up, pipers.   *[Dance. Exeunt.*

LOVE'S LABOUR'S LOST

DRAMATIS PERSONÆ

FERDINAND, *King of Navarre.*
BEROWNE,
LONGAVILLE, } *lords attending on the King.*
DUMAIN,
BOYET, } *lords attending on the Princess*
MARCADE, } *of France.*
DON ADRIANO DE ARMADO, *a fantastical Spaniard.*
SIR NATHANIEL, *a curate.*
HOLOFERNES, *a schoolmaster.*
DULL, *a constable.*

COSTARD, *a clown.*
MOTH, *page to Armado.*
A Forester.

THE PRINCESS OF FRANCE.
ROSALINE,
MARIA, } *ladies attending on the*
KATHARINE, } *Princess.*
JAQUENETTA, *a country wench.*

Lords, Attendants, etc.

THE SCENE: *Navarre.*

ACT ONE

SCENE I. Navarre. The King's park.

Enter the KING, BEROWNE, LONGAVILLE, *and* DUMAIN.

King. Let fame, that all hunt after in their lives,
Live regist'red upon our brazen tombs,
And then grace us in the disgrace of death;
When, spite of cormorant devouring Time,
Th' endeavour of this present breath may buy 5
That honour which shall bate his scythe's keen edge,
And make us heirs of all eternity.
Therefore, brave conquerors—for so you are
That war against your own affections 9
And the huge army of the world's desires—
Our late edict shall strongly stand in force:
Navarre shall be the wonder of the world;
Our court shall be a little Academe,
Still and contemplative in living art.
You three, Berowne, Dumain, and Longaville, 15
Have sworn for three years' term to live with me
My fellow-scholars, and to keep those statutes
That are recorded in this schedule here.
Your oaths are pass'd; and now subscribe your names,
That his own hand may strike his honour down 20
That violates the smallest branch herein.
If you are arm'd to do as sworn to do,
Subscribe to your deep oaths, and keep it too.

Long. I am resolv'd; 'tis but a three years' fast.
The mind shall banquet, though the body pine. 25

Fat paunches have lean pates; and dainty bits
Make rich the ribs, but bankrupt quite the wits.

Dum. My loving lord, Dumain is mortified.
The grosser manner of these world's delights
He throws upon the gross world's baser slaves; 30
To love, to wealth, to pomp, I pine and die,
With all these living in philosophy.

Ber. I can but say their protestation over;
So much, dear liege, I have already sworn,
That is, to live and study here three years. 35
But there are other strict observances,
As: not to see a woman in that term,
Which I hope well is not enrolled there;
And one day in a week to touch no food,
And but one meal on every day beside, 40
The which I hope is not enrolled there;
And then to sleep but three hours in the night
And not be seen to wink of all the day—
When I was wont to think no harm all night,
And make a dark night too of half the day— 45
Which I hope well is not enrolled there.
O, these are barren tasks, too hard to keep,
Not to see ladies, study, fast, not sleep!

King. Your oath is pass'd to pass away from these.

Ber. Let me say no, my liege, an if you please: 50
I only swore to study with your Grace,
And stay here in your court for three years' space.

Long. You swore to that, Berowne, and to the rest.

166

Ber. By yea and nay, sir, then I swore
 in jest.

What is the end of study, let me know. 55

 King. Why, that to know which else we
 should not know.

 Ber. Things hid and barr'd, you mean,
 from common sense ?

 King. Ay, that is study's god-like recompense.

 Ber. Come on, then ; I will swear to study

To know the thing I am forbid to know, 60

As thus : to study where I well may dine,

When I to feast expressly am forbid ;

Or study where to meet some mistress fine,

When mistresses from common sense are
 hid ; 64

Or, having sworn too hard-a-keeping oath,

Study to break it, and not break my troth.

If study's gain be thus, and this be so,

Study knows that which yet it doth not
 know.

Swear me to this, and I will ne'er say no.

 King. These be the stops that hinder
 study quite, 70

And train our intellects to vain delight.

 Ber. Why, all delights are vain ; but
 that most vain

Which, with pain purchas'd, doth inherit
 pain,

As painfully to pore upon a book

To seek the light of truth ; while truth the
 while 75

Doth falsely blind the eyesight of his look.

Light, seeking light, doth light of light
 beguile ;

So, ere you find where light in darkness lies,

Your light grows dark by losing of your
 eyes.

Study me how to please the eye indeed, 80

By fixing it upon a fairer eye ;

Who dazzling so, that eye shall be his heed,

And give him light that it was blinded by.

Study is like the heaven's glorious sun,

That will not be deep-search'd with saucy
 looks ; 85

Small have continual plodders ever won,

Save base authority from others' books.

These earthly godfathers of heaven's lights

That give a name to every fixed star 89

Have no more profit of their shining nights

Than those that walk and wot not what
 they are.

Too much to know is to know nought but
 fame ;

And every godfather can give a name.

 King. How well he's read, to reason
 against reading !

 Dum. Proceeded well, to stop all good
 proceeding ! 95

 Long. He weeds the corn, and still lets
 grow the weeding.

 Ber. The spring is near, when green geese
 are a-breeding.

 Dum. How follows that ?

 Ber.   Fit in his place and time.

 Dum. In reason nothing.

 Ber.   Something then in rhyme.

 Long. Berowne is like an envious sneaping frost 100

That bites the first-born infants of the
 spring.

 Ber. Well, say I am ; why should proud
 summer boast

Before the birds have any cause to sing ?

Why should I joy in any abortive birth ?

At Christmas I no more desire a rose 105

Than wish a snow in May's new-fangled
 shows ;

But like of each thing that in season grows ;

So you, to study now it is too late,

Climb o'er the house to unlock the little
 gate.

 King. Well, sit you out ; go home,
 Berowne ; adieu. 110

 Ber. No, my good lord ; I have sworn to
 stay with you ;

And though I have for barbarism spoke
 more

Than for that angel knowledge you can say,

Yet confident I'll keep what I have swore,

And bide the penance of each three years'
 day. 115

Give me the paper ; let me read the same ;

And to the strictest decrees I'll write my
 name.

 King. How well this yielding rescues thee
 from shame !

 Ber. [*Reads*] ' Item. That no woman
shall come within a mile of my court '—

Hath this been proclaimed ? 120

 Long. Four days ago.

 Ber. Let's see the penalty. [*Reads*] ' —on
pain of losing her tongue.' Who devis'd
this penalty ?

 Long. Marry, that did I.

 Ber. Sweet lord, and why ? 125

 Long. To fright them hence with that
 dread penalty.

 Ber. A dangerous law against gentility.

[*Reads*] ' Item. If any man be seen to
talk with a woman within the term of three
years, he shall endure such public shame as
the rest of the court can possibly devise.'

This article, my liege, yourself must break ;

For well you know here comes in embassy

The French king's daughter, with yourself
 to speak—

A maid of grace and complete majesty—

About surrender up of Aquitaine 135

To her decrepit, sick, and bedrid father ;

Therefore this article is made in vain,

Or vainly comes th' admired princess
 hither.

 King. What say you, lords ? Why, this
 was quite forgot.

 Ber. So study evermore is over-shot. 140

While it doth study to have what it would,

It doth forget to do the thing it should ;
And when it hath the thing it hunteth most,
'Tis won as towns with fire—so won, so lost.
 King. We must of force dispense with
  this decree ;   145
She must lie here on mere necessity.
 Ber. Necessity will make us all forsworn
Three thousand times within this three
 years' space ;
For every man with his affects is born,
Not by might mast'red, but by special
 grace.   150
If I break faith, this word shall speak for
 me :
I am forsworn on mere necessity.
So to the laws at large I write my name ;
      [*Subscribes.*
And he that breaks them in the least degree
Stands in attainder of eternal shame. 155
Suggestions are to other as to me ;
But I believe, although I seem so loath,
I am the last that will last keep his oath.
But is there no quick recreation granted ?
 King. Ay, that there is. Our court, you
  know, is haunted   160
With a refined traveller of Spain,
A man in all the world's new fashion
 planted,
That hath a mint of phrases in his brain ;
One who the music of his own vain tongue
Doth ravish like enchanting harmony ; 165
A man of complements, whom right and
 wrong
Have chose as umpire of their mutiny.
This child of fancy, that Armado hight,
For interim to our studies shall relate,
In high-born words, the worth of many a
 knight   170
From tawny Spain lost in the world's
 debate.
How you delight, my lords, I know not, I ;
But I protest I love to hear him lie,
And I will use him for my minstrelsy. 174
 Ber. Armado is a most illustrious wight,
A man of fire-new words, fashion's own
 knight.
 Long. Costard the swain and he shall be
  our sport ;
And so to study three years is but short.

 Enter DULL, *a constable, with a letter,
  and* COSTARD.

 Dull. Which is the Duke's own person ?
 Ber. This, fellow. What wouldst ? 180
 Dull. I myself reprehend his own person,
for I am his Grace's farborough ; but I
would see his own person in flesh and
blood.
 Ber. This is he.   184
 Dull. Signior Arme—Arme—commends
you. There's villainy abroad ; this letter
will tell you more.
 Cost. Sir, the contempts thereof are as
touching me.   187

 King. A letter from the magnificent
Armado.
 Ber. How low soever the matter, I hope
in God for high words. 190
 Long. A high hope for a low heaven. God
grant us patience !
 Ber. To hear, or forbear hearing ?
 Long. To hear meekly, sir, and to laugh
moderately ; or, to forbear both. 195
 Ber. Well, sir, be it as the style shall give
us cause to climb in the merriness.
 Cost. The matter is to me, sir, as concerning Jaquenetta. The manner of it is, I
was taken with the manner.
 Ber. In what manner ? 200
 Cost. In manner and form following, sir ;
all those three : I was seen with her in the
manor-house, sitting with her upon the
form, and taken following her into the
park ; which, put together, is in manner
and form following. Now, sir, for the
manner—it is the manner of a man to
speak to a woman. For the form—in some
form.   206
 Ber. For the following, sir ?
 Cost. As it shall follow in my correction ;
and God defend the right !
 King. Will you hear this letter with
attention ?   210
 Ber. As we would hear an oracle.
 Cost. Such is the simplicity of man to
hearken after the flesh.
 King. [*Reads*] ' Great deputy, the
welkin's vicegerent and sole dominator of
Navarre, my soul's earth's god and body's
fost'ring patron '— 216
 Cost. Not a word of Costard yet.
 King. [*Reads*] ' So it is '—
 Cost. It may be so ; but if he say it is so,
he is, in telling true, but so. 220
 King. Peace !
 Cost. Be to me, and every man that
dares not fight !
 King. No words !
 Cost. Of other men's secrets, I beseech
you.   224
 King. [*Reads*] ' So it is, besieged with
sable-coloured melancholy, I did commend
the black oppressing humour to the most
wholesome physic of thy health-giving air ;
and, as I am a gentleman, betook myself
to walk. The time When ? About the sixth
hour ; when beasts most graze, birds best
peck, and men sit down to that nourishment which is called supper. So much for
the time When. Now for the ground Which ?
which, I mean, I walk'd upon ; it is ycleped
thy park. Then for the place Where ?
where, I mean, I did encounter that obscene and most prepost'rous event that
draweth from my snow-white pen the ebon-
coloured ink which here thou viewest,
beholdest, surveyest, or seest. But to the
place Where ? It standeth north-north-east

and by east from the west corner of thy
curious-knotted garden. There did I see
that low-spirited swain, that base minnow
of thy mirth,' 237
  Cost. Me ?
  King. 'that unlettered small-knowing
     soul,'
  Cost. Me ? 240
  King. 'that shallow vassal,'
  Cost. Still me ?
  King. 'which, as I remember, hight
Costard,'
  Cost. O, me ! 244
  King. 'sorted and consorted, contrary to
thy established proclaimed edict and con-
tinent canon; which, with, O, with—but with
this I passion to say wherewith—'
  Cost. With a wench. 248
  King. 'with a child of our grandmother
Eve, a female ; or, for thy more sweet
understanding, a woman. Him I, as my
ever-esteemed duty pricks me on, have
sent to thee, to receive the meed of punishment, by thy sweet Grace's officer, Antony
Dull, a man of good repute, carriage,
bearing, and estimation.' 253
  Dull. Me, an't shall please you ; I am
Antony Dull.
  King. 'For Jaquenetta—so is the
weaker vessel called, which I apprehended with the aforesaid swain—I keep
her as a vessel of thy law's fury ; and shall,
at the least of thy sweet notice, bring her
to trial. Thine, in all compliments of
devoted and heart-burning heat of duty,
     DON ADRIANO DE ARMADO.'

  Ber. This is not so well as I look'd for,
but the best that ever I heard. 261
  King. Ay, the best for the worst. But,
sirrah, what say you to this ?
  Cost. Sir, I confess the wench.
  King. Did you hear the proclamation ?
  Cost. I do confess much of the hearing it,
but little of the marking of it. 267
  King. It was proclaimed a year's im-
prisonment to be taken with a wench.
  Cost. I was taken with none, sir ; I was
taken with a damsel. 271
  King. Well, it was proclaimed damsel.
  Cost. This was no damsel neither, sir ;
she was a virgin.
  King. It is so varied too, for it was
proclaimed virgin.
  Cost. If it were, I deny her virginity ; I
was taken with a maid. 276
  King. This 'maid' will not serve your
turn, sir.
  Cost. This maid will serve my turn, sir.
  King. Sir, I will pronounce your sentence : you shall fast a week with bran and
water.
  Cost. I had rather pray a month with
mutton and porridge. 282

  King. And Don Armado shall be your
keeper.
My Lord Berowne, see him delivered o'er ;
And go we, lords, to put in practice that
Which each to other hath so strongly
    sworn.
    [*Exeunt King, Longaville, and Dumain.*
  Ber. I'll lay my head to any good man's
    hat 287
These oaths and laws will prove an idle
    scorn.
Sirrah, come on.
  Cost. I suffer for the truth, sir ; for true
it is I was taken with Jaquenetta, and
Jaquenetta is a true girl ; and therefore
welcome the sour cup of prosperity !
Affliction may one day smile again ; and
till then, sit thee down, sorrow. [*Exeunt.*

SCENE II. *The park.*

Enter ARMADO *and* MOTH, *his page.*

  Arm. Boy, what sign is it when a man of
great spirit grows melancholy ?
  Moth. A great sign, sir, that he will look
sad.
  Arm. Why, sadness is one and the self-
same thing, dear imp. 5
  Moth. No, no ; O Lord, sir, no !
  Arm. How canst thou part sadness and
melancholy, my tender juvenal ?
  Moth. By a familiar demonstration of the
working, my tough signior. 10
  Arm. Why tough signior ? Why tough
signior ?
  Moth. Why tender juvenal ? Why tender
juvenal ?
  Arm. I spoke it, tender juvenal, as a con-
gruent epitheton appertaining to thy young
days, which we may nominate tender. 15
  Moth. And I, tough signior, as an apper-
tinent title to your old time, which we may
name tough.
  Arm. Pretty and apt.
  Moth. How mean you, sir ? I pretty, and
my saying apt ? or I apt, and my saying
pretty ? 20
  Arm. Thou pretty, because little.
  Moth. Little pretty, because little.
Wherefore apt ?
  Arm. And therefore apt, because quick.
  Moth. Speak you this in my praise,
master ?
  Arm. In thy condign praise. 25
  Moth. I will praise an eel with the same
praise.
  Arm. What, that an eel is ingenious ?
  Moth. That an eel is quick.
  Arm. I do say thou art quick in answers ;
thou heat'st my blood. 30
  Moth. I am answer'd, sir.
  Arm. I love not to be cross'd.
  Moth. [*Aside*] He speaks the mere con-
trary : crosses love not him.

Arm. I have promised to study three years with the Duke.   36

Moth. You may do it in an hour, sir.

Arm. Impossible.

Moth. How many is one thrice told?

Arm. I am ill at reck'ning; it fitteth the spirit of a tapster.   41

Moth. You are a gentleman and a gamester, sir.

Arm. I confess both; they are both the varnish of a complete man.

Moth. Then I am sure you know how much the gross sum of deuce-ace amounts to.   46

Arm. It doth amount to one more than two.

Moth. Which the base vulgar do call three.

Arm. True.   49

Moth. Why, sir, is this such a piece of study? Now here is three studied ere ye'll thrice wink; and how easy it is to put 'years' to the word 'three', and study three years in two words, the dancing horse will tell you.

Arm. A most fine figure!

Moth. [*Aside*] To prove you a cipher.   55

Arm. I will hereupon confess I am in love. And as it is base for a soldier to love, so am I in love with a base wench. If drawing my sword against the humour of affection would deliver me from the reprobate thought of it, I would take Desire prisoner, and ransom him to any French courtier for a new-devis'd curtsy. I think scorn to sigh; methinks I should out-swear Cupid. Comfort me, boy; what great men have been in love?   63

Moth. Hercules, master.

Arm. Most sweet Hercules! More authority, dear boy, name more; and, sweet my child, let them be men of good repute and carriage.   67

Moth. Samson, master; he was a man of good carriage, great carriage, for he carried the town gates on his back like a porter; and he was in love.   70

Arm. O well-knit Samson! strong-jointed Samson! I do excel thee in my rapier as much as thou didst me in carrying gates. I am in love too. Who was Samson's love, my dear Moth?

Moth. A woman, master.   75

Arm. Of what complexion?

Moth. Of all the four, or the three, or the two, or one of the four.

Arm. Tell me precisely of what complexion.

Moth. Of the sea-water green, sir.   80

Arm. Is that one of the four complexions?

Moth. As I have read, sir; and the best of them too.

Arm. Green, indeed, is the colour of lovers; but to have a love of that colour, methinks Samson had small reason for it. He surely affected her for her wit.   85

Moth. It was so, sir; for she had a green wit.

Arm. My love is most immaculate white and red.

Moth. Most maculate thoughts, master, are mask'd under such colours.

Arm. Define, define, well-educated infant.   90

Moth. My father's wit and my mother's tongue assist me!

Arm. Sweet invocation of a child; most pretty, and pathetical!

Moth. If she be made of white and red,   95
    Her faults will ne'er be known;
For blushing cheeks by faults are bred,
    And fears by pale white shown.
Then if she fear, or be to blame,
    By this you shall not know;   100
For still her cheeks possess the same
    Which native she doth owe.
A dangerous rhyme, master, against the reason of white and red.

Arm. Is there not a ballad, boy, of the King and the Beggar?   106

Moth. The world was very guilty of such a ballad some three ages since; but I think now 'tis not to be found; or if it were, it would neither serve for the writing nor the tune.   110

Arm. I will have that subject newly writ o'er, that I may example my digression by some mighty precedent. Boy, I do love that country girl that I took in the park with the rational hind Costard; she deserves well.   114

Moth. [*Aside*] To be whipt; and yet a better love than my master.

Arm. Sing, boy; my spirit grows heavy in love.

Moth. And that's great marvel, loving a light wench.

Arm. I say, sing.   119

Moth. Forbear till this company be past.

Enter DULL, COSTARD, *and* JAQUENETTA.

Dull. Sir, the Duke's pleasure is that you keep Costard safe; and you must suffer him to take no delight nor no penance; but 'a must fast three days a week. For this damsel, I must keep her at the park; she is allow'd for the day-woman. Fare you well.   125

Arm. I do betray myself with blushing. Maid!

Jaq. Man!

Arm. I will visit thee at the lodge.

Jaq. That's hereby.

Arm. I know where it is situate.

Jaq. Lord, how wise you are!

Arm. I will tell thee wonders.

Jaq. With that face?

Arm. I love thee.

Jaq. So I heard you say.   135
Arm. And so, farewell.
Jaq. Fair weather after you!
Dull. Come, Jaquenetta, away.
　　　　[*Exeunt Dull and Jaquenetta.*
Arm. Villain, thou shalt fast for thy
offences ere thou be pardoned.   140
Cost. Well, sir, I hope when I do it I
shall do it on a full stomach.
Arm. Thou shalt be heavily punished.
Cost. I am more bound to you than your
fellows, for they are but lightly rewarded.
Arm. Take away this villain; shut him
up.   146
Moth. Come, you transgressing slave,
away.
Cost. Let me not be pent up, sir; I will
fast, being loose.
Moth. No, sir; that were fast and loose.
Thou shalt to prison.   150
Cost. Well, if ever I do see the merry days
of desolation that I have seen, some shall
see.
Moth. What shall some see?   153
Cost. Nay, nothing, Master Moth, but
what they look upon. It is not for prisoners
to be too silent in their words, and therefore I will say nothing. I thank God I have
as little patience as another man, and
therefore I can be quiet.   157
　　　　[*Exeunt Moth and Costard.*
Arm. I do affect the very ground, which
is base, where her shoe, which is baser,
guided by her foot, which is basest, doth
tread. I shall be forsworn—which is a great
argument of falsehood—if I love. And how
can that be true love which is falsely
attempted? Love is a familiar; Love is a
devil. There is no evil angel but Love. Yet
was Samson so tempted, and he had an
excellent strength; yet was Solomon so
seduced, and he had a very good wit.
Cupid's butt-shaft is too hard for Hercules'
club, and therefore too much odds for a
Spaniard's rapier. The first and second
cause will not serve my turn; the passado
he respects not, the duello he regards not;
his disgrace is to be called boy, but his
glory is to subdue men. Adieu, valour;
rust, rapier; be still, drum; for your
manager is in love; yea, he loveth. Assist
me, some extemporal god of rhyme, for I
am sure I shall turn sonnet. Devise, wit;
write, pen; for I am for whole volumes
in folio.   [*Exit.*

ACT TWO

SCENE I. *The park.*

Enter the PRINCESS OF FRANCE, *with three*
attending ladies, ROSALINE, MARIA,
KATHARINE, BOYET, *and two other Lords.*

Boyet. Now, madam, summon up your
　　　dearest spirits.

Consider who the King your father sends,
To whom he sends, and what's his embassy:
Yourself, held precious in the world's
　　　esteem,
To parley with the sole inheritor   5
Of all perfections that a man may owe,
Matchless Navarre; the plea of no less
　　　weight
Than Aquitaine, a dowry for a queen.
Be now as prodigal of all dear grace
As Nature was in making graces dear,   10
When she did starve the general world
　　　beside
And prodigally gave them all to you.
　Prin. Good Lord Boyet, my beauty,
　　　though but mean,
Needs not the painted flourish of your
　　　praise.   14
Beauty is bought by judgment of the eye,
Not utt'red by base sale of chapmen's
　　　tongues;
I am less proud to hear you tell my
　　　worth
Than you much willing to be counted wise
In spending your wit in the praise of mine.
But now to task the tasker: good Boyet,   20
You are not ignorant all-telling fame
Doth noise abroad Navarre hath made a
　　　vow,
Till painful study shall outwear three years,
No woman may approach his silent court.
Therefore to's seemeth it a needful course,
Before we enter his forbidden gates,   26
To know his pleasure; and in that behalf,
Bold of your worthiness, we single you
As our best-moving fair solicitor.
Tell him the daughter of the King of
　　　France,   30
On serious business, craving quick dispatch,
Importunes personal conference with his
　　　Grace.
Haste, signify so much; while we attend,
Like humble-visag'd suitors, his high will.
　Boyet. Proud of employment, willingly
　　　I go.   35
　Prin. All pride is willing pride, and yours
　　　is so.   [*Exit Boyet.*
Who are the votaries, my loving lords,
That are vow-fellows with this virtuous
　　　duke?
　1 Lord. Lord Longaville is one.
　Prin.　　　　　Know you the man?
　Mar. I know him, madam; at a marriage
　　　feast,   40
Between Lord Perigort and the beauteous
　　　heir
Of Jaques Falconbridge, solemnized
In Normandy, saw I this Longaville.
A man of sovereign parts, peerless esteem'd,
Well fitted in arts, glorious in arms;   45
Nothing becomes him ill that he would
　　　well.
The only soil of his fair virtue's gloss,
If virtue's gloss will stain with any soil,

Is a sharp wit match'd with too blunt a will,
Whose edge hath power to cut, whose will
  still wills   50
It should none spare that come within his
  power.
  Prin. Some merry mocking lord, belike ;
  is't so ?
  Mar. They say so most that most his
  humours know.
  Prin. Such short-liv'd wits do wither as
  they grow.
Who are the rest ?   55
  Kath. The young Dumain, a well-
  accomplish'd youth,
Of all that virtue love for virtue loved ;
Most power to do most harm, least knowing
  ill ;
For he hath wit to make an ill shape good,
And shape to win grace though he had no
  wit.   60
I saw him at the Duke Alençon's once ;
And much too little of that good I saw
Is my report to his great worthiness.
  Ros. Another of these students at that
  time
Was there with him, if I have heard a
  truth.   65
Berowne they call him ; but a merrier man,
Within the limit of becoming mirth,
I never spent an hour's talk withal.
His eye begets occasion for his wit,
For every object that the one doth catch   70
The other turns to a mirth-moving jest,
Which his fair tongue, conceit's expositor,
Delivers in such apt and gracious words
That aged ears play truant at his tales,
And younger hearings are quite ravished ;
So sweet and voluble is his discourse.   76
  Prin. God bless my ladies ! Are they all
  in love,
That every one her own hath garnished
With such bedecking ornaments of praise ?
  1 Lord. Here comes Boyet.

        Re-enter BOYET.

  Prin.   Now, what admittance, lord ?
  Boyet. Navarre had notice of your fair
  approach,   81
And he and his competitors in oath
Were all address'd to meet you, gentle lady,
Before I came. Marry, thus much I have
  learnt :
He rather means to lodge you in the field,
Like one that comes here to besiege his
  court,   86
Than seek a dispensation for his oath,
To let you enter his unpeopled house.
        [*The ladies-in-waiting mask.*

  Enter KING, LONGAVILLE, DUMAIN,
    BEROWNE, *and* Attendants.

Here comes Navarre.
  King. Fair Princess, welcome to the
  court of Navarre.   90

  Prin. ' Fair ' I give you back again ; and
' welcome ' I have not yet. The roof of this
court is too high to be yours, and welcome
to the wide fields too base to be mine.
  King. You shall be welcome, madam, to
  my court.
  Prin. I will be welcome then ; conduct
  me thither.   95
  King. Hear me, dear lady : I have sworn
  an oath—
  Prin. Our Lady help my lord ! He'll be
  forsworn.
  King. Not for the world, fair madam, by
  my will.
  Prin. Why, will shall break it ; will, and
  nothing else.
  King. Your ladyship is ignorant what
  it is.   100
  Prin. Were my lord so, his ignorance
  were wise,
Where now his knowledge must prove
  ignorance.
I hear your Grace hath sworn out house-
  keeping.
'Tis deadly sin to keep that oath, my lord,
And sin to break it.   105
But pardon me, I am too sudden bold ;
To teach a teacher ill beseemeth me.
Vouchsafe to read the purpose of my
  coming,
And suddenly resolve me in my suit.
        [*Giving a paper.*
  King. Madam, I will, if suddenly I may.
  Prin. You will the sooner that I were
  away,   111
For you'll prove perjur'd if you make me
  stay.
  Ber. Did not I dance with you in
  Brabant once ?
  Kath. Did not I dance with you in
  Brabant once ?   114
  Ber. I know you did.
  Kath. How needless was it then to ask
  the question !
  Ber. You must not be so quick.
  Kath. 'Tis long of you, that spur me with
  such questions.
  Ber. Your wit 's too hot, it speeds too
  fast, 'twill tire.
  Kath. Not till it leave the rider in the
  mire.   120
  Ber. What time o' day ?
  Kath. The hour that fools should ask.
  Ber. Now fair befall your mask !
  Kath. Fair fall the face it covers !
  Ber. And send you many lovers !   125
  Kath. Amen, so you be none.
  Ber. Nay, then will I be gone.
  King. Madam, your father here doth
  intimate
The payment of a hundred thousand
  crowns ;
Being but the one half of an entire sum   130
Disbursed by my father in his wars.

But say that he or we, as neither have,
Receiv'd that sum, yet there remains
    unpaid
A hundred thousand more, in surety of the
    which,
One part of Aquitaine is bound to us, 135
Although not valued to the money's worth.
If then the King your father will restore
But that one half which is unsatisfied,
We will give up our right in Aquitaine,
And hold fair friendship with his Majesty.
But that, it seems, he little purposeth, 141
For here he doth demand to have repaid
A hundred thousand crowns; and not
    demands,
On payment of a hundred thousand crowns,
To have his title live in Aquitaine; 145
Which we much rather had depart withal,
And have the money by our father lent,
Than Aquitaine so gelded as it is.
Dear Princess, were not his requests so far
From reason's yielding, your fair self should
    make 150
A yielding 'gainst some reason in my breast,
And go well satisfied to France again.
    Prin. You do the King my father too
    much wrong,
And wrong the reputation of your name,
In so unseeming to confess receipt 155
Of that which hath so faithfully been paid.
    King. I do protest I never heard of it;
And, if you prove it, I'll repay it back
Or yield up Aquitaine.
    Prin.   We arrest your word.
Boyet, you can produce acquittances 160
For such a sum from special officers
Of Charles his father.
    King.   Satisfy me so.
    Boyet. So please your Grace, the packet
    is not come, 163
Where that and other specialties are bound;
To-morrow you shall have a sight of them.
    King. It shall suffice me; at which
    interview
All liberal reason I will yield unto.
Meantime receive such welcome at my hand
As honour, without breach of honour, may
Make tender of to thy true worthiness. 170
You may not come, fair Princess, within
    my gates;
But here without you shall be so receiv'd
As you shall deem yourself lodg'd in my
    heart,
Though so denied fair harbour in my house.
Your own good thoughts excuse me, and
    farewell. 175
To-morrow shall we visit you again.
    Prin. Sweet health and fair desires con-
    sort your Grace!
    King. Thy own wish wish I thee in every
    place.   [*Exit with attendants.*
    Ber. Lady, I will commend you to mine
own heart.
    Ros. Pray you, do my commendations;

I would be glad to see it.   181
    Ber. I would you heard it groan.
    Ros. Is the fool sick?
    Ber. Sick at the heart.
    Ros. Alack, let it blood.   185
    Ber. Would that do it good?
    Ros. My physic says 'ay'.
    Ber. Will you prick't with your eye?
    Ros. No point, with my knife.
    Ber. Now, God save thy life!   190
    Ros. And yours from long living!
    Ber. I cannot stay thanksgiving.
                [*Retiring.*
    Dum. Sir, I pray you, a word: what lady
    is that same?
    Boyet. The heir of Alençon, Katharine
    her name.   194
    Dum. A gallant lady! Monsieur, fare you
    well.   [*Exit.*
    Long. I beseech you a word: what is she
    in the white?
    Boyet. A woman sometimes, an you saw
    her in the light.
    Long. Perchance light in the light. I desire
    her name.
    Boyet. She hath but one for herself; to
    desire that were a shame.
    Long. Pray you, sir, whose daughter? 200
    Boyet. Her mother's, I have heard.
    Long. God's blessing on your beard!
    Boyet. Good sir, be not offended;
She is an heir of Falconbridge.
    Long. Nay, my choler is ended.   205
She is a most sweet lady.
    Boyet. Not unlike, sir; that may be.
             [*Exit Longaville.*
    Ber. What's her name in the cap?
    Boyet. Rosaline, by good hap.
    Ber. Is she wedded or no?   210
    Boyet. To her will, sir, or so.
    Ber. You are welcome, sir; adieu!
    Boyet. Farewell to me, sir, and welcome
    to you.
        [*Exit Berowne. Ladies unmask.*
    Mar. That last is Berowne, the merry
    mad-cap lord;   214
Not a word with him but a jest.
    Boyet.   And every jest but a word.
    Prin. It was well done of you to take him
    at his word.
    Boyet. I was as willing to grapple as he
    was to board.
    Kath. Two hot sheeps, marry!
    Boyet.   And wherefore not ships?
No sheep, sweet lamb, unless we feed on
    your lips.
    Kath. You sheep and I pasture—shall
    that finish the jest?   220
    Boyet. So you grant pasture for me.
             [*Offering to kiss her.*
    Kath.   Not so, gentle beast;
My lips are no common, though several
    they be.
    Boyet. Belonging to whom?

Kath.   To my fortunes and me.
Prin. Good wits will be jangling ; but,
        gentles, agree ;
This civil war of wits were much better
        used   225
On Navarre and his book-men, for here 'tis
        abused.
Boyet. If my observation, which very
        seldom lies,
By the heart's still rhetoric disclosed with
        eyes,
Deceive me not now, Navarre is infected.
Prin. With what ?   230
Boyet. With that which we lovers entitle
        ' affected '.
Prin. Your reason ?
Boyet. Why, all his behaviours did make
        their retire
To the court of his eye, peeping thorough
        desire.
His heart, like an agate, with your print
        impressed,   235
Proud with his form, in his eye pride
        expressed ;
His tongue, all impatient to speak and not
        see,
Did stumble with haste in his eyesight to
        be ;
All senses to that sense did make their
        repair,
To feel only looking on fairest of fair.   240
Methought all his senses were lock'd in his
        eye,
As jewels in crystal for some prince to buy ;
Who, tend'ring their own worth from where
        they were glass'd,
Did point you to buy them, along as you
        pass'd.
His face's own margent did quote such
        amazes   245
That all eyes saw his eyes enchanted with
        gazes.
I'll give you Aquitaine and all that is his,
An you give him for my sake but one
        loving kiss.
Prin. Come, to our pavilion. Boyet is
        dispos'd.
Boyet. But to speak that in words which
        his eye hath disclos'd ;   250
I only have made a mouth of his eye,
By adding a tongue which I know will not
        lie.
Mar. Thou art an old love-monger, and
        speakest skilfully.
Kath. He is Cupid's grandfather, and
        learns news of him.
Ros. Then was Venus like her mother ;
        for her father is but grim.   255
Boyet. Do you hear, my mad wenches ?
Mar. No.
Boyet.   What, then ; do you see ?
Mar. Ay, our way to be gone.
Boyet.   You are too hard for me.
                                  [*Exeunt.*

ACT THREE

Scene I. *The park.*

Enter ARMADO *and* MOTH.

Arm. Warble, child ; make passionate
my sense of hearing.
              [*Moth sings* Concolinel.
Arm. Sweet air ! Go, tenderness of years,
take this key, give enlargement to the
swain, bring him festinately hither ; I must
employ him in a letter to my love.   6
Moth. Master, will you win your love
with a French brawl ?
Arm. How meanest thou ? Brawling in
French ?   9
Moth. No, my complete master ; but to
jig off a tune at the tongue's end, canary
to it with your feet, humour it with turning
up your eyelids, sigh a note and sing a note,
sometime through the throat, as if you
swallowed love with singing love, sometime
through the nose, as if you snuff'd up love
by smelling love, with your hat penthouse-
like o'er the shop of your eyes, with your
arms cross'd on your thin-belly doublet,
like a rabbit on a spit, or your hands in
your pocket, like a man after the old
painting ; and keep not too long in one
tune, but a snip and away. These are
complements, these are humours ; these
betray nice wenches, that would be betrayed
without these ; and make them men of
note—do you note me ?—that most are
affected to these.   22
Arm. How hast thou purchased this
experience ?
Moth. By my penny of observation.
Arm. But O—but O—   25
Moth. The hobby-horse is forgot.
Arm. Call'st thou my love ' hobby-
horse ' ?
Moth. No, master ; the hobby-horse is
but a colt, and your love perhaps a hackney.
But have you forgot your love ?   30
Arm. Almost I had.
Moth. Negligent student ! learn her by
heart.
Arm. By heart and in heart, boy.
Moth. And out of heart, master ; all
those three I will prove.   35
Arm. What wilt thou prove ?
Moth. A man, if I live ; and this, by, in,
and without, upon the instant. By heart
you love her, because your heart cannot
come by her ; in heart you love her, because
your heart is in love with her ; and out of
heart you love her, being out of heart that
you cannot enjoy her.   41
Arm. I am all these three.
Moth. And three times as much more, and
yet nothing at all.
Arm. Fetch hither the swain ; he must
carry me a letter.   45

Moth. A message well sympathiz'd—a
horse to be ambassador for an ass?

Arm. Ha, ha, what sayest thou?

Moth. Marry, sir, you must send the ass
upon the horse, for he is very slow-gaited.
But I go.   50

Arm. The way is but short; away.

Moth. As swift as lead, sir.

Arm. The meaning, pretty ingenious?
Is not lead a metal heavy, dull, and slow?

Moth. Minime, honest master; or rather,
master, no.   55

Arm. I say lead is slow.

Moth. You are too swift, sir, to say so:
Is that lead slow which is fir'd from a
gun?

Arm. Sweet smoke of rhetoric!
He reputes me a cannon; and the bullet,
that's he;   59
I shoot thee at the swain.

Moth. Thump, then, and I flee. [*Exit.*

Arm. A most acute juvenal; volable and
free of grace!   61
By thy favour, sweet welkin, I must sigh
in thy face;
Most rude melancholy, valour gives thee
place.
My herald is return'd.

Re-enter MOTH *with* COSTARD.

Moth. A wonder, master! here's a
costard broken in a shin.   65

Arm. Some enigma, some riddle; come,
thy l'envoy; begin.

Cost. No egma, no riddle, no l'envoy; no
salve in the mail, sir. O, sir, plantain, a
plain plantain; no l'envoy, no l'envoy; no
salve, sir, but a plantain!   69

Arm. By virtue thou enforcest laughter;
thy silly thought, my spleen; the heaving
of my lungs provokes me to ridiculous
smiling. O, pardon me, my stars! Doth the
inconsiderate take salve for l'envoy, and
the word 'l'envoy' for a salve?   74

Moth. Do the wise think them other? Is
not l'envoy a salve?

Arm. No, page; it is an epilogue or
discourse to make plain
Some obscure precedence that hath tofore
been sain.
I will example it:
    The fox, the ape, and the humble-
    bee,   79
    Were still at odds, being but three.
There's the moral. Now the l'envoy.

Moth. I will add the l'envoy. Say the
moral again.

Arm. The fox, the ape, and the humble-
    bee,   83
    Were still at odds, being but three.

Moth. Until the goose came out of door,
    And stay'd the odds by adding four.
Now will I begin your moral, and do you
follow with my l'envoy.   88

    The fox, the ape, and the humble-
    bee,
    Were still at odds, being but three.

Arm. Until the goose came out of door,
    Staying the odds by adding four.

Moth. A good l'envoy, ending in the
goose; would you desire more?

Cost. The boy hath sold him a bargain,
    a goose, that's flat.   95
Sir, your pennyworth is good, an your
goose be fat.
To sell a bargain well is as cunning as fast
    and loose;
Let me see: a fat l'envoy; ay, that's a fat
goose.

Arm. Come hither, come hither. How
    did this argument begin?

Moth. By saying that a costard was
    broken in a shin.   100
Then call'd you for the l'envoy.

Cost. True, and I for a plantain. Thus
    came your argument in;
Then the boy's fat l'envoy, the goose that
    you bought;
And he ended the market.

Arm. But tell me: how was there a
costard broken in a shin?   106

Moth. I will tell you sensibly.

Cost. Thou hast no feeling of it, Moth; I
will speak that l'envoy.
I, Costard, running out, that was safely
    within,   110
Fell over the threshold and broke my shin.

Arm. We will talk no more of this matter.

Cost. Till there be more matter in the
shin.

Arm. Sirrah Costard, I will enfranchise
thee.   114

Cost. O, marry me to one Frances! I
smell some l'envoy, some goose, in this.

Arm. By my sweet soul, I mean setting
thee at liberty, enfreedoming thy person;
thou wert immured, restrained, captivated,
bound.

Cost. True, true; and now you will be
my purgation, and let me loose.   121

Arm. I give thee thy liberty, set thee
from durance; and, in lieu thereof, impose
on thee nothing but this: bear this
significant [*giving a letter*] to the country
maid Jaquenetta; there is remuneration,
for the best ward of mine honour is reward-
ing my dependents. Moth, follow. [*Exit.*

Moth. Like the sequel, I. Signior
    Costard, adieu.   127

Cost. My sweet ounce of man's flesh, my
    incony Jew!   [*Exit Moth.*
Now will I look to his remuneration.
Remuneration! O, that's the Latin word
for three farthings. Three farthings—
remuneration. 'What's the price of this
inkle?'—'One penny.'—'No, I'll give you
a remuneration.' Why, it carries it. Remuneration! **Why, it is a fairer name**

175

than French crown. I will never buy and
sell out of this word.   134

Enter BEROWNE.

Ber. My good knave Costard, exceed-
ingly well met !   135
Cost. Pray you, sir, how much carnation
ribbon may a man buy for a remuneration ?
Ber. What is a remuneration ?
Cost. Marry, sir, halfpenny farthing.
Ber. Why, then, three-farthing worth of
silk.   140
Cost. I thank your worship. God be wi'
you !
Ber. Stay, slave ; I must employ thee.
As thou wilt win my favour, good my knave,
Do one thing for me that I shall entreat.
Cost. When would you have it done, sir ?
Ber. This afternoon.   146
Cost. Well, I will do it, sir ; fare you well.
Ber. Thou knowest not what it is.
Cost. I shall know, sir, when I have
done it.
Ber. Why, villain, thou must know first.
Cost. I will come to your worship to-
morrow morning.   151
Ber. It must be done this afternoon.
Hark, slave, it is but this :
The Princess comes to hunt here in the
park,
And in her train there is a gentle lady ; 155
When tongues speak sweetly, then they
name her name,
And Rosaline they call her. Ask for her,
And to her white hand see thou do com-
mend
This seal'd-up counsel. There's thy
guerdon ; go. [*Giving him a shilling.*
Cost. Gardon, O sweet gardon ! better
than remuneration ; a 'leven-pence farthing
better ; most sweet gardon ! I will do it,
sir, in print. Gardon—remuneration ! [*Exit.*
Ber. And I, forsooth, in love ; I, that
have been love's whip ;
A very beadle to a humorous sigh ;   165
A critic, nay, a night-watch constable ;
A domineering pedant o'er the boy,
Than whom no mortal so magnificent !
This wimpled, whining, purblind, wayward
boy,
This sen or-junior, giant-dwarf, Dan
Cupid ;   170
Regent of love-rhymes, lord of folded arms,
Th' anointed sovereign of sighs and groans,
Liege of all loiterers and malcontents,
Dread prince of plackets, king of codpieces,
Sole imperator, and great general   175
Of trotting paritors. O my little heart !
And I to be a corporal of his field,
And wear his colours like a tumbler's hoop !
What ! I love, I sue, I seek a wife—
A woman, that is like a German clock,   180
Still a-repairing, ever out of frame,
And never going aright, being a watch,

But being watch'd that it may still go
right !
Nay, to be perjur'd, which is worst of all ;
And, among three, to love the worst of all,
A whitely wanton with a velvet brow,   186
With two pitch balls stuck in her face for
eyes ;
Ay, and, by heaven, one that will do the
deed,
Though Argus were her eunuch and her
guard.
And I to sigh for her ! to watch for her ! 190
To pray for her ! Go to ; it is a plague
That Cupid will impose for my neglect
Of his almighty dreadful little might.
Well, I will love, write, sigh, pray, sue, and
groan :   194
Some men must love my lady, and some
Joan.   [*Exit.*

ACT FOUR

SCENE I. *The park.*

Enter the PRINCESS, ROSALINE, MARIA,
KATHARINE, BOYET, Lords, Attendants,
and a Forester.

Prin. Was that the King that spurr'd his
horse so hard
Against the steep-up rising of the hill ?
Boyet. I know not ; but I think it was
not he.
Prin. Whoe'er 'a was, 'a show'd a
mounting mind.
Well, lords, to-day we shall have our
dispatch ;   5
On Saturday we will return to France.
Then, forester, my friend, where is the bush
That we must stand and play the murderer
in ?
For. Hereby, upon the edge of yonder
coppice ;
A stand where you may make the fairest
shoot.   10
Prin. I thank my beauty I am fair that
shoot,
And thereupon thou speak'st the fairest
shoot.
For. Pardon me, madam, for I meant
not so.
Prin. What, what ? First praise me, and
again say no ?
O short-liv'd pride ! Not fair ? Alack for
woe !   15
For. Yes, madam, fair.
Prin.   Nay, never paint me now ;
Where fair is not, praise cannot mend the
brow.
Here, good my glass, take this for telling
true :   [*Giving him money.*
Fair payment for foul words is more than
due.
For. Nothing but fair is that which you
inherit.   20

Prin. See, see, my beauty will be sav'd
by merit.
O heresy in fair, fit for these days!
A giving hand, though foul, shall have fair
praise.
But come, the bow. Now mercy goes to kill,
And shooting well is then accounted ill ;   25
Thus will I save my credit in the shoot :
Not wounding, pity would not let me do't ;
If wounding, then it was to show my skill,
That more for praise than purpose meant
to kill.
And, out of question, so it is sometimes :   30
Glory grows guilty of detested crimes,
When, for fame's sake, for praise, an out-
ward part,
We bend to that the working of the heart ;
As I for praise alone now seek to spill
The poor deer's blood that my heart means
no ill.   35

Boyet. Do not curst wives hold that self-
sovereignty
Only for praise sake, when they strive to be
Lords o'er their lords ?

Prin. Only for praise ; and praise we may
afford
To any lady that subdues a lord.   40

Enter COSTARD.

Boyet. Here comes a member of the
commonwealth.

Cost. God dig-you-den all ! Pray you,
which is the head lady ?

Prin. Thou shalt know her, fellow, by the
rest that have no heads.   45

Cost. Which is the greatest lady, the
highest ?

Prin. The thickest and the tallest.

Cost. The thickest and the tallest ! It is
so ; truth is truth.
An your waist, mistress, were as slender as
my wit,
One o' these maids' girdles for your waist
should be fit.   50
Are not you the chief woman ? You are the
thickest here.

Prin. What's your will, sir ? What's
your will ?

Cost. I have a letter from Monsieur
Berowne to one Lady Rosaline.

Prin. O, thy letter, thy letter ! He's a
good friend of mine.
Stand aside, good bearer. Boyet, you can
carve.   55
Break up this capon.

Boyet.   I am bound to serve.
This letter is mistook ; it importeth none
here.
It is writ to Jaquenetta.

Prin.   We will read it, I swear.
Break the neck of the wax, and every one
give ear.   59

Boyet. [*Reads*] ' By heaven, that thou art
fair is most infallible ; true that thou art
beauteous ; truth itself that thou art
lovely. More fairer than fair, beautiful than
beauteous, truer than truth itself, have
commiseration on thy heroical vassal. The
magnanimous and most illustrate king
Cophetua set eye upon the pernicious and
indubitate beggar Zenelophon ; and he it
was that might rightly say, ' Veni, vidi,
vici ' ; which to annothanize in the vulgar,
—O base and obscure vulgar !—videlicet,
He came, saw, and overcame. He came, one ;
saw, two ; overcame, three. Who came ?—
the king. Why did he come ?—to see. Why
did he see ?—to overcome. To whom came
he ?—to the beggar. What saw he ?—the
beggar. Who overcame he ?—the beggar.
The conclusion is victory ; on whose side ?—
the king's. The captive is enrich'd ; on whose
side ?—the beggar's. The catastrophe
is a nuptial ; on whose side ?—the king's.
No, on both in one, or one in both. I am
the king, for so stands the comparison ;
thou the beggar, for so witnesseth thy
lowliness. Shall I command thy love ? I
may. Shall I enforce thy love ? I could.
Shall I entreat thy love ? I will. What
shalt thou exchange for rags ?—robes, for
tittles ?—titles, for thyself ?—me. Thus
expecting thy reply, I profane my lips on
thy foot, my eyes on thy picture, and
my heart on thy every part.

Thine in the dearest design of industry,
DON ADRIANO DE ARMADO.'   80

' Thus dost thou hear the Nemean lion roar
'Gainst thee, thou lamb, that standest as
his prey ;
Submissive fall his princely feet before,
And he from forage will incline to play.
But if thou strive, poor soul, what art thou
then ?   85
Food for his rage, repasture for his den.'

Prin. What plume of feathers is he that
indited this letter ?
What vane ? What weathercock ? Did
you ever hear better ?

Boyet. I am much deceived but I remember the style.

Prin. Else your memory is bad, going
o'er it erewhile.   90

Boyet. This Armado is a Spaniard, that
keeps here in court ;
A phantasime, a Monarcho, and one that
makes sport
To the Prince and his book-mates.

Prin.   Thou fellow, a word.
Who gave thee this letter ?

Cost.   I told you : my lord.

Prin. To whom shouldst thou give it ?

Cost.   From my lord to my lady.

Prin. From which lord to which lady ?

Cost. From my Lord Berowne, a good
master of mine,   97
To a lady of France that he call'd Rosaline.

Prin. Thou hast mistaken his letter.
  Come, lords, away.

[*To Rosaline*] Here, sweet, put up this;
  'twill be thine another day.   100

  [*Exeunt Princess and Train.*

Boyet. Who is the shooter? who is the
  shooter?

Ros.   Shall I teach you to know?

Boyet. Ay, my continent of beauty.

Ros.   Why, she that bears the bow.

Finely put off!

Boyet. My lady goes to kill horns; but,
  if thou marry,

Hang me by the neck, if horns that year
  miscarry.   105

Finely put on!

Ros. Well then, I am the shooter.

Boyet.   And who is your deer?

Ros. If we choose by the horns, yourself
  come not near.

Finely put on indeed!

Mar. You still wrangle with her, Boyet,
  and she strikes at the brow.   110

Boyet. But she herself is hit lower. Have
  I hit her now?

Ros. Shall I come upon thee with an old
saying, that was a man when King Pepin
of France was a little boy, as touching the
hit it?   114

Boyet. So I may answer thee with one as
old, that was a woman when Queen
Guinever of Britain was a little wench, as
touching the hit it.

Ros. [*Singing*]

  Thou canst not hit it, hit it, hit it,
  Thou canst not hit it, my good man.

Boyet. An I cannot, cannot, cannot,   120
  An I cannot, another can.

  [*Exeunt Rosaline and Katharine*

Cost. By my troth, most pleasant! How
  both did fit it!

Mar. A mark marvellous well shot; for
  they both did hit it.

Boyet. A mark! O, mark but that mark!
  A mark, says my lady!

Let the mark have a prick in't, to mete at,
  if it may be.   125

Mar. Wide o' the bow-hand! I' faith,
  your hand is out.

Cost. Indeed, 'a must shoot nearer, or
  he'll ne'er hit the clout.

Boyet. An if my hand be out, then belike
  your hand is in.

Cost. Then will she get the upshoot by
  cleaving the pin.

Mar. Come, come, you talk greasily; your
  lips grow foul.   130

Cost. She's too hard for you at pricks,
  sir; challenge her to bowl.

Boyet. I fear too much rubbing; good-
  night, my good owl.

  [*Exeunt Boyet and Maria.*

Cost. By my soul, a swain, a most simple
  clown!

Lord, Lord! how the ladies and I have put
  him down!

O' my troth, most sweet jests, most incony
  vulgar wit!   135

When it comes so smoothly off, so obscenely, as it were, so fit.

Armado a th' t'one side—O, a most dainty
  man!

To see him walk before a lady and to bear
  her fan!

To see him kiss his hand, and how most
  sweetly 'a will swear!

And his page a t' other side, that handful
  of wit!   140

Ah, heavens, it is a most pathetical nit!

Sola, sola!   [*Exit Costard.*

SCENE II. *The park.*

From the shooting within, enter HOLOFERNES,
  SIR NATHANIEL, *and* DULL.

Nath. Very reverent sport, truly; and
done in the testimony of a good conscience.

Hol. The deer was, as you know, sanguis,
in blood; ripe as the pomewater, who now
hangeth like a jewel in the ear of caelo,
the sky, the welkin, the heaven; and anon
falleth like a crab on the face of terra, the
soil, the land, the earth.   6

Nath. Truly, Master Holofernes, the
epithets are sweetly varied, like a scholar
at the least; but, sir, I assure ye it was a
buck of the first head.

Hol. Sir Nathaniel, haud credo.   10

Dull. 'Twas not a haud credo; 'twas a
pricket.

Hol. Most barbarous intimation! yet a
kind of insinuation, as it were, in via, in
way, of explication; facere, as it were,
replication, or rather, ostentare, to show,
as it were, his inclination, after his un-
dressed, unpolished, uneducated, unpruned,
untrained, or rather unlettered, or ratherest
unconfirmed fashion, to insert again my
haud credo for a deer.   17

Dull. I said the deer was not a haud
credo; 'twas a pricket.

Hol. Twice-sod simplicity, bis coctus!
O thou monster Ignorance, how deformed
  dost thou look!   21

Nath. Sir, he hath never fed of the
  dainties that are bred in a book;

He hath not eat paper, as it were; he hath
not drunk ink; his intellect is not replenished; he is only an animal, only
sensible in the duller parts;   25

And such barren plants are set before us
  that we thankful should be—

Which we of taste and feeling are—for
  those parts that do fructify in us
  more than he.

For as it would ill become me to be vain,
  indiscreet, or a fool,

So, were there a patch set on learning, to
　　see him in a school.
But, omne bene, say I, being of an old
　　father's mind :　　　　　　　　　　　30
Many can brook the weather that love not
　　the wind.
　　Dull. You two are book-men : can you
tell me by your wit
What was a month old at Cain's birth
　　that's not five weeks old as yet ?
　　Hol. Dictynna, goodman Dull ; Dic-
tynna, goodman Dull.
　　Dull. What is Dictynna ?　　　　　35
　　Nath. A title to Phœbe, to Luna, to the
　　moon.
　　Hol. The moon was a month old when
　　Adam was no more,
And raught not to five weeks when he came
　　to five-score.
Th' allusion holds in the exchange.
　　Dull. 'Tis true, indeed ; the collusion
holds in the exchange.　　　　　　　　41
　　Hol. God comfort thy capacity ! I say
th' allusion holds in the exchange.
　　Dull. And I say the polusion holds in the
exchange ; for the moon is never but a
month old ; and I say, beside, that 'twas a
pricket that the Princess kill'd.　　　46
　　Hol. Sir Nathaniel, will you hear an
extempore epitaph on the death of the
deer ? And, to humour the ignorant, call
the deer the Princess kill'd a pricket.
　　Nath. Perge, good Master Holofernes,
perge, so it shall please you to abrogate
scurrility.　　　　　　　　　　　　　51
　　Hol. I will something affect the letter, for
it argues facility.

The preyful Princess pierc'd and prick'd
　　a pretty pleasing pricket.
Some say a sore ; but not a sore
　　till now made sore with shooting.　　55
The dogs did yell ; put el to sore,
　　then sorel jumps from thicket—
Or pricket sore, or else sorel ;
　　the people fall a-hooting.
If sore be sore, then L to sore
　　makes fifty sores o' sorel.
Of one sore I an hundred make
　　by adding but one more L.

　　Nath. A rare talent !　　　　　　　60
　　Dull [Aside] If a talent be a claw, look
how he claws him with a talent.
　　Hol. This is a gift that I have, simple,
simple ; a foolish extravagant spirit, full
of forms, figures, shapes, objects, ideas,
apprehensions, motions, revolutions. These
are begot in the ventricle of memory,
nourish'd in the womb of pia mater, and
delivered upon the mellowing of occasion.
But the gift is good in those in whom it is
acute, and I am thankful for it.　　　69
　　Nath. Sir, I praise the Lord for you, and
so may my parishioners ; for their sons

are well tutor'd by you, and their daughters
profit very greatly under you. You are a
good member of the commonwealth.　　73
　　Hol. Mehercle, if their sons be ingenious,
they shall want no instruction ; if their
daughters be capable, I will put it to them ;
but, vir sapit qui pauca loquitur. A soul
feminine saluteth us.　　　　　　　　77

　　Enter JAQUENETTA *and* COSTARD.

　　Jaq. God give you good morrow, Master
Person.
　　Hol. Master Person, quasi pers-one. And
if one should be pierc'd, which is the
one ?
　　Cost. Marry, Master Schoolmaster, he
that is likest to a hogshead.　　　　　82
　　Hol. Piercing a hogshead ! A good
lustre of conceit in a turf of earth ; fire
enough for a flint, pearl enough for a swine ;
'tis pretty ; it is well.　　　　　　　85
　　Jaq. Good Master Parson, be so good as
read me this letter ; it was given me by
Costard, and sent me from Don Armado. I
beseech you read it.　　　　　　　　88
　　Hol. Fauste, precor gelida quando pecus
　　omne sub umbra
Ruminat—
and so forth. Ah, good old Mantuan ! I
may speak of thee as the traveller doth of
Venice :　　　　　　　　　　　　　91
　　　　Venetia, Venetia,
　　　　Chi non ti vede, non ti pretia.
Old Mantuan, old Mantuan ! Who under-
standeth thee not, loves thee not—
　　　　Ut, re, sol, la, mi, fa.
Under pardon, sir, what are the contents ?
or rather as Horace says in his—What, my
soul, verses ?
　　Nath. Ay, sir, and very learned.
　　Hol. Let me hear a staff, a stanze, a verse ;
Lege, domine.
　　Nath. [Reads] ' If love make me forsworn,
　　　　how shall I swear to love ?　　　100
Ah, never faith could hold, if not to
　　beauty vowed !
Though to myself forsworn, to thee I'll
　　faithful prove ;
Those thoughts to me were oaks, to thee
　　like osiers bowed ;
Study his bias leaves, and makes his book
　　thine eyes,
Where all those pleasures live that art
　　would comprehend.　　　　　　105
If knowledge be the mark, to know thee
　　shall suffice ;
Well learned is that tongue that well
　　can thee commend ;
All ignorant that soul that sees thee
　　without wonder ;
Which is to me some praise that I thy
　　parts admire.
Thy eye Jove's lightning bears, thy voice
　　his dreadful thunder,　　　　　110

Which, not to anger bent, is music and
    sweet fire.
Celestial as thou art, O, pardon love this
    wrong,
That singes heaven's praise with such an
    earthly tongue.'

Hol. You find not the apostrophas, and so
miss the accent : let me supervise the
canzonet. Here are only numbers ratified ;
but, for the elegancy, facility, and golden
cadence of poesy, caret. Ovidius Naso was
the man. And why, indeed, ' Naso ' but for
smelling out the odoriferous flowers of
fancy, the jerks of invention ? Imitari is
nothing : so doth the hound his master,
the ape his keeper, the tired horse his rider.
But, damosella virgin, was this directed to
you ?   122

Jaq. Ay, sir, from one Monsieur Berowne,
one of the strange queen's lords.   124

Hol. I will overglance the superscript :
' To the snow-white hand of the most
beauteous Lady Rosaline'. I will look
again on the intellect of the letter, for the
nomination of the party writing to the
person written unto : ' Your Ladyship's in
all desired employment, Berowne'. Sir
Nathaniel, this Berowne is one of the
votaries with the King ; and here he hath
framed a letter to a sequent of the stranger
queen's which accidentally, or by the way
of progression, hath miscarried. Trip and
go, my sweet ; deliver this paper into the
royal hand of the King ; it may concern
much. Stay not thy compliment ; I forgive
thy duty. Adieu.   135

Jaq. Good Costard, go with me. Sir, God
save your life !

Cost. Have with thee, my girl.
    [*Exeunt Costard and Jaquenetta.*

Nath. Sir, you have done this in the fear
of God, very religiously ; and, as a certain
father saith——   139

Hol. Sir, tell not me of the father ; I do
fear colourable colours. But to return to
the verses : did they please you, Sir
Nathaniel ?

Nath. Marvellous well for the pen.   143

Hol. I do dine to-day at the father's of a
certain pupil of mine ; where, if, before
repast, it shall please you to gratify the
table with a grace, I will, on my privilege
I have with the parents of the foresaid
child or pupil, undertake your ben venuto ;
where I will prove those verses to be very
unlearned, neither savouring of poetry,
wit, nor invention. I beseech your
society.   150

Nath. And thank you too ; for society,
saith the text, is the happiness of life.

Hol. And certes, the text most infallibly
concludes it. [*To Dull*] Sir, I do invite you
too ; you shall not say me nay : pauca
verba. Away ; the gentles are at their

game, and we will to our recreation.   156
    [*Exeunt.*

SCENE III. *The park.*

Enter BEROWNE, *with a paper in his hand,
alone.*

Ber. The King he is hunting the deer : I
am coursing myself. They have pitch'd a
toil : I am toiling in a pitch—pitch that
defiles. Defile ! a foul word. Well, ' set
thee down, sorrow ! ' for so they say the
fool said, and so say I, and I am the fool.
Well proved, wit. By the Lord, this love
is as mad as Ajax : it kills sheep ; it kills
me—I a sheep. Well proved again o' my
side. I will not love ; if I do, hang me. I'
faith, I will not. O, but her eye ! By this
light, but for her eye, I would not love her
—yes for her two eyes. Well, I do nothing
in the world but lie, and lie in my throat.
By heaven, I do love ; and it hath taught
me to rhyme, and to be melancholy ; and
here is part of my rhyme, and here my
melancholy. Well, she hath one o' my
sonnets already ; the clown bore it, the
fool sent it, and the lady hath it : sweet
clown, sweeter fool, sweetest lady ! By the
world, I would not care a pin if the other
three were in. Here comes one with a
paper ; God give him grace to groan !   17
    [*Climbs into a tree.*

Enter the KING, *with a paper.*

King. Ay me !

Ber. Shot, by heaven ! Proceed, sweet
Cupid ; thou hast thump'd him with
thy bird-bolt under the left pap. In faith,
secrets !   21

King. [*Reads*]
' So sweet a kiss the golden sun gives not
To those fresh morning drops upon the
    rose,
As thy eye-beams, when their fresh rays
    have smote
The night of dew that on my cheeks down
    flows ;   25
Nor shines the silver moon one half so
    bright
Through the transparent bosom of the deep,
As doth thy face through tears of mine give
    light.
Thou shin'st in every tear that I do weep ;
No drop but as a coach doth carry thee ;   30
So ridest thou triumphing in my woe.
Do but behold the tears that swell in me,
And they thy glory through my grief will
    show.
But do not love thyself ; then thou wilt
    keep
My tears for glasses, and still make me
    weep.   35
O queen of queens ! how far dost thou excel
No thought can think nor tongue of mortal
    tell.'

How shall she know my griefs ? I'll drop
　　the paper—
Sweet leaves, shade folly. Who is he comes
　　here ?　　　　　　　　　　[*Steps aside.*

Enter LONGAVILLE, *with a paper.*

What, Longaville, and reading ! Listen, ear.
　　Ber. Now, in thy likeness, one more fool
　　　　appear !　　　　　　　　　　　41
　　Long. Ay me, I am forsworn !
　　Ber. Why, he comes in like a perjure,
wearing papers.
　　King. In love, I hope ; sweet fellowship
　　　　in shame !　　　　　　　　　　45
　　Ber. One drunkard loves another of the
　　　　name.
　　Long. Am I the first that have been
　　　　perjur'd so ?
　　Ber. I could put thee in comfort : not
　　　　by two that I know ;
Thou makest the triumviry, the corner-cap
　　of society,
The shape of Love's Tyburn that hangs up
　　simplicity.　　　　　　　　　　　50
　　Long. I fear these stubborn lines lack
　　　　power to move.
O sweet Maria, empress of my love !
These numbers will I tear, and write in
　　prose.
　　Ber. O, rhymes are guards on wanton
　　　　Cupid's hose :
Disfigure not his slop.
　　Long.　　　　　　This same shall go.　55
　　　　　　　　　　　[*He reads the sonnet.*
' Did not the heavenly rhetoric of thine eye,
'Gainst whom the world cannot hold argu-
　　ment,
Persuade my heart to this false perjury ?
Vows for thee broke deserve not punish-
　　ment.
A woman I forswore ; but I will prove,　60
Thou being a goddess, I forswore not thee :
My vow was earthly, thou a heavenly love ;
Thy grace being gain'd cures all disgrace
　　in me.
Vows are but breath, and breath a vapour
　　is ;
Then thou, fair sun, which on my earth
　　dost shine,　　　　　　　　　　　65
Exhal'st this vapour-vow ; in thee it is.
If broken, then it is no fault of mine ;
　　If by me broke, what fool is not so
　　　　wise
　　To lose an oath to win a paradise ? '
　　Ber. This is the liver-vein, which makes
　　　　flesh a deity,　　　　　　　　70
A green goose a goddess—pure, pure
　　idolatry.
God amend us, God amend ! We are much
　　out o' th' way.

Enter DUMAIN, *with a paper.*

　　Long. By whom shall I send this ?—
　　　　Company ! Stay.　　　[*Steps aside.*

　　Ber. ' All hid, all hid '—an old infant
　　　　play.
Like a demigod here sit I in the sky,　75
And wretched fools' secrets heedfully
　　o'er-eye.
More sacks to the mill ! O heavens, I have
　　my wish !
Dumain transformed ! Four woodcocks in
　　a dish !
　　Dum. O most divine Kate !
　　Ber. O most profane coxcomb !　80
　　Dum. By heaven, the wonder in a mortal
　　　　eye !
　　Ber. By earth, she is not, corporal ; there
　　　　you lie.
　　Dum. Her amber hairs for foul hath
　　　　amber quoted.
　　Ber. An amber-colour'd raven was well
　　　　noted.
　　Dum. As upright as the cedar.
　　Ber.　　　　　　Stoop, I say ;　85
Her shoulder is with child.
　　Dum.　　　　　　As fair as day.
　　Ber. Ay, as some days ; but then no sun
　　　　must shine.
　　Dum. O that I had my wish !
　　Long.　　　　　And I had mine !
　　King. And I mine too, good Lord !
　　Ber. Amen, so I had mine ! Is not that a
　　　　good word ?　　　　　　　　90
　　Dum. I would forget her ; but a fever
　　　　she
Reigns in my blood, and will rememb'red
　　be.
　　Ber. A fever in your blood ? Why, then
　　　　incision
Would let her out in saucers. Sweet mis-
　　prision !
　　Dum. Once more I'll read the ode that I
　　　　have writ.　　　　　　　　　95
　　Ber. Once more I'll mark how love can
　　　　vary wit.
　　Dum. [*Reads*]
　　　　' On a day—alack the day !—
　　　　Love, whose month is ever May,
　　　　Spied a blossom passing fair
　　　　Playing in the wanton air.　100
　　　　Through the velvet leaves the wind,
　　　　All unseen, can passage find ;
　　　　That the lover, sick to death,
　　　　Wish'd himself the heaven's breath.
　　　　"Air," quoth he "thy cheeks may
　　　　　blow ;　　　　　　　　　105
　　　　Air, would I might triumph so !
　　　　But, alack, my hand is sworn
　　　　Ne'er to pluck thee from thy thorn ;
　　　　Vow, alack, for youth unmeet,
　　　　Youth so apt to pluck a sweet.　110
　　　　Do not call it sin in me
　　　　That I am forsworn for thee ;
　　　　Thou for whom Jove would swear
　　　　Juno but an Ethiope were ;
　　　　And deny himself for Jove,　115
　　　　Turning mortal for thy love." '

This will I send; and something else more plain
That shall express my true love's fasting pain.
O, would the King, Berowne and Longaville,
Were lovers too! Ill, to example ill, 120
Would from my forehead wipe a perjur'd note;
For none offend where all alike do dote.

Long. [*Advancing*] Dumain, thy love is far from charity,
That in love's grief desir'st society;
You may look pale, but I should blush, I know, 125
To be o'erheard and taken napping so.

King. [*Advancing*] Come, sir, you blush; as his, your case is such.
You chide at him, offending twice as much:
You do not love Maria! Longaville
Did never sonnet for her sake compile; 130
Nor never lay his wreathed arms athwart
His loving bosom, to keep down his heart.
I have been closely shrouded in this bush,
And mark'd you both, and for you both did blush.
I heard your guilty rhymes, observ'd your fashion, 135
Saw sighs reek from you, noted well your passion.
' Ay me!' says one. ' O Jove!' the other cries.
One, her hairs were gold; crystal the other's eyes.
[*To Long.*] You would for paradise break faith and troth;
[*To Dum.*] And Jove for your love would infringe an oath. 140
What will Berowne say when that he shall hear
Faith infringed which such zeal did swear?
How will he scorn, how will he spend his wit!
How will he triumph, leap, and laugh at it!
For all the wealth that ever I did see, 145
I would not have him know so much by me.

Ber. [*Descending*] Now step I forth to whip hypocrisy.
Ah, good my liege, I pray thee pardon me.
Good heart, what grace hast thou thus to reprove
These worms for loving, that art most in love? 150
Your eyes do make no coaches; in your tears
There is no certain princess that appears;
You'll not be perjur'd; 'tis a hateful thing;
Tush, none but minstrels like of sonneting.
But are you not ashamed? Nay, are you not, 155
All three of you, to be thus much o'ershot?
You found his mote; the King your mote did see;
But I a beam do find in each of three.
O, what a scene of fool'ry have I seen, 159

Of sighs, of groans, of sorrow, and of teen!
O me, with what strict patience have I sat,
To see a king transformed to a gnat!
To see great Hercules whipping a gig,
And profound Solomon to tune a jig,
And Nestor play at push-pin with the boys,
And critic Timon laugh at idle toys! 166
Where lies thy grief, O, tell me, good Dumain?
And, gentle Longaville, where lies thy pain?
And where my liege's? All about the breast.
A caudle, ho!

King. Too bitter is thy jest. 170
Are we betrayed thus to thy over-view?

Ber. Not you by me, but I betrayed to you.
I that am honest, I that hold it sin
To break the vow I am engaged in;
I am betrayed by keeping company 175
With men like you, men of inconstancy.
When shall you see me write a thing in rhyme?
Or groan for Joan? or spend a minute's time
In pruning me? When shall you hear that I 179
Will praise a hand, a foot, a face, an eye,
A gait, a state, a brow, a breast, a waist,
A leg, a limb—

King. Soft! whither away so fast?
A true man or a thief that gallops so?

Ber. I post from love; good lover, let me go. 184

Enter JAQUENETTA *and* COSTARD.

Jaq. God bless the King!

King. What present hast thou there?

Cost. Some certain treason.

King. What makes treason here?

Cost. Nay, it makes nothing, sir.

King. If it mar nothing neither,
The treason and you go in peace away together.

Jaq. I beseech your Grace, let this letter be read;
Our person misdoubts it; 'twas treason he said. 190

King. Berowne, read it over.
[*Berowne reads the letter.*
Where hadst thou it?

Jaq. Of Costard.

King. Where hadst thou it? 194

Cost. Of Dun Adramadio, Dun Adramadio. [*Berowne tears the letter.*

King. How now! What is in you? Why dost thou tear it? 196

Ber. A toy, my liege, a toy! Your Grace needs not fear it.

Long. It did move him to passion, and therefore let's hear it.

Dum. It is Berowne's writing, and here is his name. [*Gathering up the pieces.*

Ber. [*To Costard*] Ah, you whoreson
loggerhead, you were born to do
me shame.   200
Guilty, my lord, guilty! I confess, I
confess.

King. What?

Ber. That you three fools lack'd me fool
to make up the mess;
He, he, and you—and you, my liege!—
and I
Are pick-purses in love, and we deserve
to die.   205
O, dismiss this audience, and I shall tell
you more.

Dum. Now the number is even.

Ber.   True, true, we are four.
Will these turtles be gone?

King.   Hence, sirs, away.

Cost. Walk aside the true folk, and let the
traitors stay.
                    [*Exeunt Costard and Jaquenetta.*

Ber. Sweet lords, sweet lovers, O, let us
embrace!   210
As true we are as flesh and blood can be.
The sea will ebb and flow, heaven show his
face;
Young blood doth not obey an old decree.
We cannot cross the cause why we were
born,   214
Therefore of all hands must we be forsworn.

King. What, did these rent lines show
some love of thine?

Ber. 'Did they?' quoth you. Who sees
the heavenly Rosaline
That, like a rude and savage man of Inde
At the first op'ning of the gorgeous east,
Bows not his vassal head and, strucken
blind,   220
Kisses the base ground with obedient
breast?
What peremptory eagle-sighted eye
Dares look upon the heaven of her brow
That is not blinded by her majesty?

King. What zeal, what fury hath in-
spir'd thee now?   225
My love, her mistress, is a gracious moon;
She, an attending star, scarce seen a light.

Ber. My eyes are then no eyes, nor I
Berowne.
O, but for my love, day would turn to
night!   229
Of all complexions the cull'd sovereignty
Do meet, as at a fair, in her fair cheek,
Where several worthies make one dignity,
Where nothing wants that want itself doth
seek.   233
Lend me the flourish of all gentle tongues—
Fie, painted rhetoric! O, she needs it not!
To things of sale a seller's praise belongs:
She passes praise; then praise too short
doth blot.   237
A wither'd hermit, five-score winters worn,
Might shake off fifty, looking in her eye.
Beauty doth varnish age, as if new-born,

And gives the crutch the cradle's infancy.
O, 'tis the sun that maketh all things shine!

King. By heaven, thy love is black as
ebony.

Ber. Is ebony like her? O wood divine!
A wife of such wood were felicity.   245
O, who can give an oath? Where is a book?
That I may swear beauty doth beauty lack,
If that she learn not of her eye to look.
No face is fair that is not full so black.

King. O paradox! Black is the badge of
hell,   250
The hue of dungeons, and the school of
night;
And beauty's crest becomes the heavens
well.

Ber. Devils soonest tempt, resembling
spirits of light.   253
O, if in black my lady's brows be deckt,
It mourns that painting and usurping
hair
Should ravish doters with a false aspect;
And therefore is she born to make black
fair.
Her favour turns the fashion of the days;
For native blood is counted painting now;
And therefore red that would avoid
disprise   260
Paints itself black, to imitate her brow.

Dum. To look like her are chimney-
sweepers black.

Long. And since her time are colliers
counted bright.

King. And Ethiopes of their sweet complexion crack.

Dum. Dark needs no candles now, for
dark is light.   265

Ber. Your mistresses dare never come in
rain
For fear their colours should be wash'd
away.

King. 'Twere good yours did; for, sir, to
tell you plain,
I'll find a fairer face not wash'd to-day.

Ber. I'll prove her fair, or talk till dooms-
day here.   270

King. No devil will fright thee then so
much as she.

Dum. I never knew man hold vile stuff
so dear.

Long. Look, here's thy love: my foot
and her face see. [*Showing his shoe.*

Ber. O, if the streets were paved with
thine eyes,
Her feet were much too dainty for such
tread!   275

Dum. O vile! Then, as she goes, what
upward lies
The street should see as she walk'd overhead.

King. But what of this? Are we not all
in love?

Ber. Nothing so sure; and thereby all
forsworn.

King. Then leave this chat ; and, good
 Berowne, now prove 280
Our loving lawful, and our faith not torn.
 Dum. Ay, marry, there ; some flattery
 for this evil.
 Long. O, some authority how to proceed ;
Some tricks, some quillets, how to cheat
 the devil !
 Dum. Some salve for perjury.
 Ber. 'Tis more than need. 285
Have at you, then, affection's men-at-arms.
Consider what you first did swear unto :
To fast, to study, and to see no woman—
Flat treason 'gainst the kingly state of
 youth.
Say, can you fast ? Your stomachs are too
 young, 290
And abstinence engenders maladies.
And where that you have vow'd to study, lords,
In that each of you have forsworn his book,
Can you still dream, and pore, and thereon
 look ?
For when would you, my lord, or you, or you,
Have found the ground of study's excellence
Without the beauty of a woman's face ? 297
From women's eyes this doctrine I derive :
They are the ground, the books, the academes,
From whence doth spring the true Promethean
 fire. 300
Why, universal plodding poisons up
The nimble spirits in the arteries,
As motion and long-during action tires
The sinewy vigour of the traveller.
Now, for not looking on a woman's face, 305
You have in that forsworn the use of eyes,
And study too, the causer of your vow ;
For where is any author in the world
Teaches such beauty as a woman's eye ?
Learning is but an adjunct to ourself, 310
And where we are our learning likewise is ;
Then when ourselves we see in ladies' eyes,
With ourselves,
Do we not likewise see our learning there ?
O, we have made a vow to study, lords,
And in that vow we have forsworn our
 books. 315
For when would you, my liege, or you, or
 you,
In leaden contemplation have found out
Such fiery numbers as the prompting eyes
Of beauty's tutors have enrich'd you with ?
Other slow arts entirely keep the brain ; 320
And therefore, finding barren practisers,
Scarce show a harvest of their heavy
 toil ;
But love, first learned in a lady's eyes,
Lives not alone immured in the brain,
But with the motion of all elements 325
Courses as swift as thought in every power,
And gives to every power a double power,
Above their functions and their offices.
It adds a precious seeing to the eye :
A lover's eyes will gaze an eagle blind. 330
A lover's ear will hear the lowest sound,

When the suspicious head of theft is
 stopp'd.
Love's feeling is more soft and sensible
Than are the tender horns of cockled snails ;
Love's tongue proves dainty Bacchus gross
 in taste. 335
For valour, is not Love a Hercules,
Still climbing trees in the Hesperides ?
Subtle as Sphinx ; as sweet and musical
As bright Apollo's lute, strung with his
 hair.
And when Love speaks, the voice of all the
 gods 340
Make heaven drowsy with the harmony.
Never durst poet touch a pen to write
Until his ink were temp'red with Love's
 sighs ;
O, then his lines would ravish savage ears,
And plant in tyrants mild humility. 345
From women's eyes this doctrine I derive.
They sparkle still the right Promethean fire;
They are the books, the arts, the academes,
That show, contain, and nourish, all the
 world, 349
Else none at all in aught proves excellent.
Then fools you were these women to
 forswear ;
Or, keeping what is sworn, you will prove
 fools.
For wisdom's sake, a word that all men
 love ;
Or for Love's sake, a word that loves all
 men ;
Or for men's sake, the authors of these
 women ;
Or women's sake, by whom we men are 355
 men—
Let us once lose our oaths to find ourselves,
Or else we lose ourselves to keep our oaths.
It is religion to be thus forsworn ;
For charity itself fulfils the law,
And who can sever love from charity ? 360
 King. Saint Cupid, then ! and, soldiers,
 to the field !
 Ber. Advance your standards, and upon
 them, lords ;
Pell-mell, down with them ! But be first
 advis'd,
In conflict, that you get the sun of them. 364
 Long. Now to plain-dealing ; lay these
 glozes by.
Shall we resolve to woo these girls of
 France ?
 King. And win them too ; therefore let
 us devise
Some entertainment for them in their tents.
 Ber. First, from the park let us conduct
 them thither ;
Then homeward every man attach the hand 370
Of his fair mistress. In the afternoon
We will with some strange pastime solace
 them,
Such as the shortness of the time can shape;
For revels, dances, masks, and merry hours,

Forerun fair Love, strewing her way with
   flowers.   376
  King. Away, away ! No time shall be
   omitted
That will betime, and may by us be fitted.
  Ber. Allons ! allons ! Sow'd cockle reap'd
   no corn,
And justice always whirls in equal measure.
Light wenches may prove plagues to men
   forsworn ;   381
If so, our copper buys no better treasure.
                    [*Exeunt.*

ACT FIVE

Scene I. *The park.*

Enter Holofernes, Sir Nathaniel, *and*
Dull.

  Hol. Satis quod sufficit.
  Nath. I praise God for you, sir. Your
reasons at dinner have been sharp and
sententious ; pleasant without scurrility,
witty without affection, audacious without
impudency, learned without opinion, and
strange without heresy. I did converse this
quondam day with a companion of the
King's, who is intituled, nominated, or
called, Don Adriano de Armado.   7
  Hol. Novi hominem tanquam te. His
humour is lofty, his discourse peremptory,
his tongue filed, his eye ambitious, his gait
majestical, and his general behaviour vain,
ridiculous, and thrasonical. He is too
picked, too spruce, too affected, too odd,
as it were, too peregrinate, as I may call it.
  Nath. A most singular and choice epithet.
              [*Draws out his table-book.*
  Hol. He draweth out the thread of his
verbosity finer than the staple of his argument. I abhor such fanatical phantasimes,
such insociable and point-devise companions ; such rackers of orthography, as
to speak ' dout ' fine, when he should say
' doubt ' ; ' det ' when he should pronounce
' debt '—d, e, b, t, not d, e, t. He clepeth
a calf ' cauf ', half ' hauf '; neighbour
vocatur ' nebour '; ' neigh ' abbreviated
' ne '. This is abhominable—which he
would call ' abbominable '. It insinuateth
me of insanie : ne intelligis, domine ? to
make frantic, lunatic.   23
  Nath. Laus Deo, bone intelligo.
  Hol. ' Bone ' ?—' bone ' for ' bene '.
Priscian a little scratch'd ; 'twill serve. 26

Enter Armado, Moth, *and* Costard.

  Nath. Videsne quis venit ?
  Hol. Video, et gaudeo.
  Arm. [*To Moth*] Chirrah !
  Hol. Quare ' chirrah ', not ' sirrah ' ? 30
  Arm. Men of peace, well encount'red.
  Hol. Most military sir, salutation.
  Moth. [*Aside to Costard*] They have been
at a great feast of languages and stol'n the
scraps.   34
  Cost. O, they have liv'd long on the alms-
basket of words. I marvel thy master hath
not eaten thee for a word, for thou are not
so long by the head as honorificabili-
tudinitatibus ; thou art easier swallowed
than a flap-dragon.
  Moth. Peace ! the peal begins.
  Arm. [*To Hol.*] Monsieur, are you not
lett'red ?   40
  Moth. Yes, yes ; he teaches boys the
hornbook. What is a, b, spelt backward
with the horn on his head ?
  Hol. Ba, pueritia, with a horn added.
  Moth. Ba, most silly sheep with a horn.
You hear his learning.   45
  Hol. Quis, quis, thou consonant ?
  Moth. The third of the five vowels, if You
repeat them ; or the fifth, if I.
  Hol. I will repeat them : a, e, I—
  Moth. The sheep ; the other two con-
cludes it : o, U.   50
  Arm. Now, by the salt wave of the
Mediterraneum, a sweet touch, a quick
venue of wit—snip, snap, quick and home.
It rejoiceth my intellect. True wit !
  Moth. Offer'd by a child to an old man ;
which is wit-old.
  Hol. What is the figure ? What is the
figure ?   55
  Moth. Horns.
  Hol. Thou disputes like an infant ; go
whip thy gig.
  Moth. Lend me your horn to make one,
and I will whip about your infamy circum
circa—a gig of a cuckold's horn.   59
  Cost. An I had but one penny in the
world, thou shouldst have it to buy ginger-
bread. Hold, there is the very remuneration I had of thy master, thou halfpenny
purse of wit, thou pigeon-egg of discretion.
O, an the heavens were so pleased that
thou wert but my bastard, what a joyful
father wouldest thou make me ! Go to ;
thou hast it ad dunghill, at the fingers'
ends, as they say.   66
  Hol. O, I smell false Latin ; ' dunghill '
for unguem.
  Arm. Arts-man, preambulate ; we will be
singuled from the barbarous. Do you not
educate youth at the charge-house on the
top of the mountain ?   70
  Hol. Or mons, the hill.
  Arm. At your sweet pleasure, for the
mountain.
  Hol. I do, sans question.
  Arm. Sir, it is the King's most sweet
pleasure and affection to congratulate the
Princess at her pavilion, in the posteriors
of this day ; which the rude multitude call
the afternoon.   77
  Hol. The posterior of the day, most
generous sir, is liable, congruent, and

measurable, for the afternoon. The word is well cull'd, chose, sweet, and apt, I do assure you, sir, I do assure. 81

Arm. Sir, the King is a noble gentleman, and my familiar, I do assure ye, very good friend. For what is inward between us, let it pass. I do beseech thee, remember thy courtesy. I beseech thee, apparel thy head. And among other importunate and most serious designs, and of great import indeed, too—but let that pass; for I must tell thee it will please his Grace, by the world, sometime to lean upon my poor shoulder, and with his royal finger thus dally with my excrement, with my mustachio; but, sweet heart, let that pass. By the world, I recount no fable: some certain special honours it pleaseth his greatness to impart to Armado, a soldier, a man of travel, that hath seen the world; but let that pass. The very all of all is—but, sweet heart, I do implore secrecy—that the King would have me present the Princess, sweet chuck, with some delightful ostentation, or show, or pageant, or antic, or firework. Now, understanding that the curate and your sweet self are good at such eruptions and sudden breaking-out of mirth, as it were, I have acquainted you withal, to the end to crave your assistance. 101

Hol. Sir, you shall present before her the Nine Worthies. Sir Nathaniel, as concerning some entertainment of time, some show in the posterior of this day, to be rend'red by our assistance, the King's command, and this most gallant, illustrate, and learned gentleman, before the Princess—I say none so fit as to present the Nine Worthies. 107

Nath. Where will you find men worthy enought to present them? 109

Hol. Joshua, yourself; myself, Alexander; this gallant gentleman, Judas Maccabæus; this swain, because of his great limb or joint, shall pass Pompey the Great; the page, Hercules. 112

Arm. Pardon, sir; error: he is not quantity enough for that Worthy's thumb; he is not so big as the end of his club.

Hol. Shall I have audience? He shall present Hercules in minority: his enter and exit shall be strangling a snake; and I will have an apology for that purpose. 117

Moth. An excellent device! So, if any of the audience hiss, you may cry 'Well done, Hercules; now thou crushest the snake!' That is the way to make an offence gracious, though few have the grace to do it. 121

Arm. For the rest of the Worthies?

Hol. I will play three myself.

Moth. Thrice-worthy gentleman!

Arm. Shall I tell you a thing? 125

Hol. We attend.

Arm. We will have, if this fadge not, an antic. I beseech you, follow.

Hol. Via, goodman Dull! Thou hast spoken no word all this while. 130

Dull. Nor understood none neither, sir.

Hol. Allons! we will employ thee.

Dull. I'll make one in a dance, or so; or I will play
On the tabor to the Worthies, and let them dance the hay.

Hol. Most dull, honest Dull! To our sport, away. [*Exeunt.*

SCENE II. *The park.*

Enter the PRINCESS, MARIA, KATHARINE, *and* ROSALINE.

Prin. Sweet hearts, we shall be rich ere we depart,
If fairings come thus plentifully in.
A lady wall'd about with diamonds!
Look you what I have from the loving King.

Ros. Madam, came nothing else along with that? 5

Prin. Nothing but this! Yes, as much love in rhyme
As would be cramm'd up in a sheet of paper
Writ o' both sides the leaf, margent and all,
That he was fain to seal on Cupid's name.

Ros. That was the way to make his godhead wax; 10
For he hath been five thousand year a boy.

Kath. Ay, and a shrewd unhappy gallows too.

Ros. You'll ne'er be friends with him: 'a kill'd your sister.

Kath. He made her melancholy, sad, and heavy;
And so she died. Had she been light, like you, 15
Of such a merry, nimble, stirring spirit,
She might 'a been a grandam ere she died.
And so may you; for a light heart lives long.

Ros. What's your dark meaning, mouse, of this light word? 19

Kath. A light condition in a beauty dark.

Ros. We need more light to find your meaning out.

Kath. You'll mar the light by taking it in snuff;
Therefore I'll darkly end the argument.

Ros. Look what you do, you do it still i' th' dark.

Kath. So do not you; for you are a light wench. 25

Ros. Indeed, I weigh not you; and therefore light.

Kath. You weigh me not? O, that's you care not for me.

Ros. Great reason; for 'past cure is still past care'.

Prin. Well bandied both; a set of wit
    well play'd.
But, Rosaline, you have a favour too?   30
Who sent it? and what is it?
  Ros.   I would you knew.
An if my face were but as fair as yours,
My favour were as great: be witness this.
Nay, I have verses too, I thank Berowne;
The numbers true, and, were the numb'ring
    too,   35
I were the fairest goddess on the ground.
I am compar'd to twenty thousand fairs.
O, he hath drawn my picture in his letter!
  Prin. Anything like?
  Ros. Much in the letters; nothing in the
    praise.   40
  Prin. Beauteous as ink—a good con-
    clusion.
  Kath. Fair as a text B in a copy-book.
  Ros. Ware pencils, ho! Let me not die
    your debtor,
My red dominical, my golden letter:
O that your face were not so full of O's! 45
  Kath. A pox of that jest! and I beshrew
    all shrows!
  Prin. But, Katharine, what was sent to
    you from fair Dumain?
  Kath. Madam, this glove.
  Prin.   Did he not send you twain?
  Kath. Yes, madam; and, moreover, 49
Some thousand verses of a faithful lover;
A huge translation of hypocrisy,
Vilely compil'd, profound simplicity.
  Mar. This, and these pearl, to me sent
    Longaville;
The letter is too long by half a mile.
  Prin. I think no less. Dost thou not wish
    in heart   55
The chain were longer and the letter short?
  Mar. Ay, or I would these hands might
    never part.
  Prin. We are wise girls to mock our
    lovers so.
  Ros. They are worse fools to purchase
    mocking so.
That same Berowne I'll torture ere I go. 60
O that I knew he were but in by th' week!
How I would make him fawn, and beg, and
    seek,
And wait the season, and observe the times,
And spend his prodigal wits in bootless
    rhymes,
And shape his service wholly to my hests,
And make him proud to make me proud
    that jests! 66
So pertaunt-like would I o'ersway his state
That he should be my fool, and I his fate.
  Prin. None are so surely caught, when
    they are catch'd,
As wit turn'd fool; folly, in wisdom
    hatch'd,   70
Hath wisdom's warrant and the help of
    school,
And wit's own grace to grace a learned fool.

  Ros. The blood of youth burns not with
    such excess
As gravity's revolt to wantonness.
  Mar. Folly in fools bears not so strong a
    note   75
As fool'ry in the wise when wit doth dote,
Since all the power thereof it doth apply
To prove, by wit, worth in simplicity.

Enter BOYET.

  Prin. Here comes Boyet, and mirth is in
    his face.
  Boyet. O, I am stabb'd with laughter!
    Where's her Grace?   80
  Prin. Thy news, Boyet?
  Boyet.   Prepare, madam, prepare!
Arm, wenches, arm! Encounters mounted
    are
Against your peace. Love doth approach
    disguis'd,
Armed in arguments; you'll be surpris'd.
Muster your wits; stand in your own
    defence;   85
Or hide your heads like cowards, and fly
    hence.
  Prin. Saint Dennis to Saint Cupid! What
    are they
That charge their breath against us? Say,
    scout, say.
  Boyet. Under the cool shade of a syca-
    more
I thought to close mine eyes some half an
    hour;   90
When, lo! to interrupt my purpos'd rest,
Toward that shade I might behold addrest
The King and his companions; warily
I stole into a neighbour thicket by,
And overheard what you shall overhear— 95
That, by and by, disguis'd they will be here.
Their herald is a pretty knavish page,
That well by heart hath conn'd his em-
    bassage.
Action and accent did they teach him there:
'Thus must thou speak' and 'thus thy
    body bear',   100
And ever and anon they made a doubt
Presence majestical would put him out;
'For' quoth the King 'an angel shalt thou
    see;
Yet fear not thou, but speak audaciously'.
The boy replied 'An angel is not evil;
I should have fear'd her had she been a
    devil'.   106
With that all laugh'd, and clapp'd him on
    the shoulder,
Making the bold wag by their praises bolder.
One rubb'd his elbow, thus, and fleer'd, and
    swore
A better speech was never spoke before.
Another with his finger and his thumb 111
Cried 'Via! we will do't, come what will
    come'.
The third he caper'd, and cried 'All goes
    well'.

The fourth turn'd on the toe, and down he
    fell.
With that they all did tumble on the
    ground,   115
With such a zealous laughter, so profound,
That in this spleen ridiculous appears,
To check their folly, passion's solemn tears.
    Prin. But what, but what, come they to
      visit us ?
    Boyet. They do, they do ; and are
      apparell'd thus,   120
Like Muscovites or Russians, as I guess.
Their purpose is to parley, court, and dance ;
And every one his love-feat will advance
Unto his several mistress ; which they'll
    know
By favours several which they did bestow.
    Prin. And will they so ? The gallants
      shall be task'd,   126
For, ladies, we will every one be mask'd ;
And not a man of them shall have the
    grace,
Despite of suit, to see a lady's face.   129
Hold, Rosaline, this favour thou shalt wear,
And then the King will court thee for his
    dear ;
Hold, take thou this, my sweet, and give me
    thine,
So shall Berowne take me for Rosaline.
And change you favours too ; so shall your
    loves   134
Woo contrary, deceiv'd by these removes.
    Ros. Come on, then, wear the favours
      most in sight.
    Kath. But, in this changing, what is your
      intent ?
    Prin. The effect of my intent is to cross
      theirs.
They do it but in mocking merriment,
And mock for mock is only my intent.   140
Their several counsels they unbosom shall
To loves mistook, and so be mock'd withal
Upon the next occasion that we meet
With visages display'd to talk and greet.
    Ros. But shall we dance, if they desire us
      to't ?   145
    Prin. No, to the death, we will not move
      a foot,
Nor to their penn'd speech render we no
    grace ;
But while 'tis spoke each turn away her
    face.
    Boyet. Why, that contempt will kill the
      speaker's heart,
And quite divorce his memory from his
    part.   150
    Prin. Therefore I do it ; and I make no
      doubt
The rest will ne'er come in, if he be out.
There's no such sport as sport by sport
    o'erthrown,
To make theirs ours, and ours none but our
    own ;   154
So shall we stay, mocking intended game,

And they well mock'd depart away with
    shame.   [*Trumpet sounds within.*
    Boyet. The trumpet sounds ; be mask'd ;
      the maskers come.
                [*The Ladies mask.*

Enter Blackamoors *with music,* MOTH
    as Prologue, the KING *and his* Lords *as*
    maskers, in the guise of Russians.

    Moth. All hail, the richest beauties on the
      earth !
    Boyet. Beauties no richer than rich
      taffeta.   159
    Moth. A holy parcel of the fairest dames
        [*The Ladies turn their backs to him.*
That ever turn'd their—backs—to mortal
    views !
    Ber. Their eyes, villain, their eyes.
    Moth. That ever turn'd their eyes to
      mortal views !
Out—
    Boyet. True ; *out* indeed.
    Moth. Out of your favours, heavenly
      spirits, vouchsafe   165
Not to behold—
    Ber. Once to behold, rogue.
    Moth. Once to behold with your sun-
      beamed eyes—with your sun-beamed
      eyes—
    Boyet. They will not answer to that
      epithet ;   170
You were best call it ' daughter-beamed
    eyes '.
    Moth. They do not mark me, and that
      brings me out.
    Ber. Is this your perfectness ? Be gone,
      you rogue.   [*Exit Moth.*
    Ros. What would these strangers ? Know
      their minds, Boyet.   174
If they do speak our language, 'tis our will
That some plain man recount their pur-
    poses.
Know what they would.
    Boyet.   What would you with the
      Princess ?
    Ber. Nothing but peace and gentle
      visitation.
    Ros. What would they, say they ?   180
    Boyet. Nothing but peace and gentle
      visitation.
    Ros. Why, that they have ; and bid them
      so be gone.
    Boyet. She says you have it, and you may
      be gone.
    King. Say to her we have measur'd many
      miles   184
To tread a measure with her on this grass.
    Boyet. They say that they have measur'd
      many a mile
To tread a measure with you on this grass.
    Ros. It is not so. Ask them how many
      inches
Is in one mile ? If they have measured
    many,

The measure, then, of one is eas'ly told. 190
  Boyet. If to come hither you have
    measur'd miles,
And many miles, the Princess bids you tell
How many inches doth fill up one mile.
  Ber. Tell her we measure them by weary
    steps.
  Boyet. She hears herself.
  Ros.   How many weary steps 195
Of many weary miles you have o'ergone
Are numb'red in the travel of one mile ?
  Ber. We number nothing that we spend
    for you ;
Our duty is so rich, so infinite, 199
That we may do it still without accompt.
Vouchsafe to show the sunshine of your
    face,
That we, like savages, may worship it.
  Ros. My face is but a moon, and clouded
    too.
  King. Blessed are clouds, to do as such
    clouds do.
Vouchsafe, bright moon, and these thy
    stars, to shine, 205
Those clouds removed, upon our watery
    eyne.
  Ros. O vain petitioner ! beg a greater
    matter ;
Thou now requests but moonshine in the
    water.
  King. Then in our measure do but
    vouchsafe one change.
Thou bid'st me beg ; this begging is not
    strange. 210
  Ros. Play, music, then. Nay, you must
    do it soon.
Not yet ? No dance ! Thus change I like
    the moon.
  King. Will you not dance ? How come
    you thus estranged ?
  Ros. You took the moon at full ; but
    now she's changed.
  King. Yet still she is the Moon, and I the
    Man. 215
The music plays ; vouchsafe some motion
    to it.
  Ros. Our ears vouchsafe it.
  King.   But your legs should do it.
  Ros. Since you are strangers, and come
    here by chance,
We'll not be nice ; take hands. We will
    not dance.
  King. Why take we hands then ?
  Ros.   Only to part friends.
Curtsy, sweet hearts ; and so the measure
    ends. 221
  King. More measure of this measure ; be
    not nice.
  Ros. We can afford no more at such a
    price.
  King. Price you yourselves. What buys
    your company ?
  Ros. Your absence only.
  King.   That can never be. 225

  Ros. Then cannot we be bought ; and so
    adieu—
Twice to your visor and half once to you.
  King. If you deny to dance, let's hold
    more chat.
  Ros. In private then.
  King.   I am best pleas'd with that.
                [*They converse apart.*
  Ber. White-handed mistress, one sweet
    word with thee. 230
  Prin. Honey, and milk, and sugar ; there
    is three.
  Ber. Nay, then, two treys, an if you
    grow so nice,
Metheglin, wort, and malmsey ; well run,
    dice !
There's half a dozen sweets.
  Prin.   Seventh sweet, adieu !
Since you can cog, I'll play no more with
    you. 235
  Ber. One word in secret.
  Prin.   Let it not be sweet.
  Ber. Thou grievest my gall.
  Prin.   Gall ! bitter.
  Ber.   Therefore meet.
                 [*They converse apart.*
  Dum. Will you vouchsafe with me to
    change a word ?
  Mar. Name it.
  Dum.   Fair lady—
  Mar.   Say you so ? Fair lord—
Take that for your fair lady.
  Dum.   Please it you, 240
As much in private, and I'll bid adieu.
                 [*They converse apart.*
  Kath. What, was your vizard made with-
    out a tongue ?
  Long. I know the reason, lady, why you
    ask.
  Kath. O for your reason ! Quickly, sir ;
    I long.
  Long. You have a double tongue within
    your mask, 245
And would afford my speechless vizard
    half.
  Kath. ' Veal ' quoth the Dutchman. Is
    not ' veal ' a calf ?
  Long. A calf, fair lady !
  Kath.   No, a fair lord calf.
  Long. Let's part the word.
  Kath.   No, I'll not be your half.
Take all and wean it ; it may prove an ox.
  Long. Look how you butt yourself in
    these sharp mocks ! 251
Will you give horns, chaste lady ? Do not
    so.
  Kath. Then die a calf, before your horns
    do grow.
  Long. One word in private with you ere
    I die.
  Kath. Bleat softly, then ; the butcher
    hears you cry. [*They converse apart.*
  Boyet. The tongues of mocking wenches
    are as keen 256

As is the razor's edge invisible,
Cutting a smaller hair than may be seen,
Above the sense of sense ; so sensible
Seemeth their conference ; their conceits
    have wings,   260
Fleeter than arrows, bullets, wind, thought,
    swifter things.

Ros. Not one word more, my maids ;
    break off, break off.

Ber. By heaven, all dry-beaten with pure
    scoff !

King. Farewell, mad wenches ; you have
    simple wits.

    [*Exeunt King, Lords, and Blackamoors.*

Prin. Twenty adieus, my frozen Musco-
    vits.   265
Are these the breed of wits so wondered at ?

Boyet. Tapers they are, with your sweet
    breaths puff'd out.

Ros. Well-liking wits they have ; gross,
    gross ; fat, fat.

Prin. O poverty in wit, kingly-poor flout !
Will they not, think you, hang themselves
    to-night ?   270
Or ever but in vizards show their faces ?
This pert Berowne was out of count'nance
    quite.

Ros. They were all in lamentable cases !
The King was weeping-ripe for a good
    word.

Prin. Berowne did swear himself out of
    all suit.   275

Mar. Dumain was at my service, and his
    sword.
' No point ' quoth I ; my servant straight
    was mute.

Kath. Lord Longaville said I came o'er
    his heart ;
And trow you what he call'd me ?

Prin.   Qualm, perhaps.

Kath. Yes, in good faith.

Prin.   Go, sickness as thou art !   280

Ros. Well, better wits have worn plain
    statute-caps.
But will you hear ? The King is my love
    sworn.

Prin. And quick Berowne hath plighted
    faith to me.

Kath. And Longaville was for my service
    born.

Mar. Dumain is mine, as sure as bark on
    tree.   285

Boyet. Madam, and pretty mistresses,
    give ear :
Immediately they will again be here
In their own shapes ; for it can never be
They will digest this harsh indignity.   289

Prin. Will they return ?

Boyet. They will, they will, God knows,
And leap for joy, though they are lame with
    blows :
Therefore, change favours ; and, when they
    repair,
Blow like sweet roses in this summer air.

Prin. How blow ? how blow ? Speak to
    be understood.

Boyet. Fair ladies mask'd are roses in
    their bud :   295
Dismask'd, their damask sweet commixture
    shown,
Are angels vailing clouds, or roses blown.

Prin. Avaunt, perplexity ! What shall
    we do
If they return in their own shapes to woo ?

Ros. Good madam, if by me you'll be
    advis'd,   300
Let's mock them still, as well known as
    disguis'd.
Let us complain to them what fools were
    here,
Disguis'd like Muscovites, in shapeless gear;
And wonder what they were, and to what
    end
Their shallow shows and prologue vilely
    penn'd,   305
And their rough carriage so ridiculous,
Should be presented at our tent to us.

Boyet. Ladies, withdraw ; the gallants
    are at hand.

Prin. Whip to our tents, as roes run o'er
    land. [*Exeunt Princess, Rosaline,*
                    Katharine, and Maria.

Re-enter the KING, BEROWNE, LONGAVILLE,
    and DUMAIN, *in their proper habits.*

King. Fair sir, God save you ! Where's
    the Princess ?   310

Boyet. Gone to her tent. Please it your
    Majesty
Command me any service to her thither ?

King. That she vouchsafe me audience
    for one word.

Boyet. I will ; and so will she, I know,
    my lord.   [*Exit.*

Ber. This fellow pecks up wit as pigeons
    pease,   315
And utters it again when God doth please.
He is wit's pedlar, and retails his wares
At wakes, and wassails, meetings, markets,
    fairs ;
And we that sell by gross, the Lord doth
    know,
Have not the grace to grace it with such
    show.   320
This gallant pins the wenches on his sleeve ;
Had he been Adam, he had tempted Eve.
'A can carve too, and lisp ; why this is he
That kiss'd his hand away in courtesy ;
This is the ape of form, Monsieur the
    Nice,
That, when he plays at tables, chides the
    dice   326
In honourable terms ; nay, he can sing
A mean most meanly ; and in ushering,
Mend him who can. The ladies call him
    sweet ;
The stairs, as he treads on them, kiss his
    feet.   330

This is the flow'r that smiles on every one,
To show his teeth as white as whales-bone ;
And consciences that will not die in debt
Pay him the due of 'honey-tongued
    Boyet'.
  King. A blister on his sweet tongue, with
    my heart,   335
That put Armado's page out of his part !

Re-enter the PRINCESS, *ushered by* BOYET ;
  ROSALINE, MARIA, *and* KATHARINE.

  Ber. See where it comes ! Behaviour,
    what wert thou
Till this man show'd thee ? And what art
    thou now ?
  King. All hail, sweet madam, and fair
    time of day !
  Prin. 'Fair' in 'all hail' is foul, as I
    conceive.   340
  King. Construe my speeches better, if you
    may.
  Prin. Then wish me better ; I will give
    you leave.
  King. We came to visit you, and purpose
    now
To lead you to our court ; vouchsafe it
    then.
  Prin. This field shall hold me, and so
    hold your vow :   345
Nor God, nor I, delights in perjur'd men.
  King. Rebuke me not for that which you
    provoke.
The virtue of your eye must break my oath.
  Prin. You nickname virtue : vice you
    should have spoke ;
For virtue's office never breaks men's
    troth.   350
Now by my maiden honour, yet as pure
As the unsullied lily, I protest,
A world of torments though I should
    endure,
I would not yield to be your house's guest ;
So much I hate a breaking cause to be   355
Of heavenly oaths, vowed with integrity.
  King. O, you have liv'd in desolation
    here,
Unseen, unvisited, much to our shame.
  Prin. Not so, my lord ; it is not so, I
    swear ;
We have had pastimes here, and pleasant
    game ;   360
A mess of Russians left us but of late.
  King. How, madam ! Russians !
  Prin.   Ay, in truth, my lord ;
Trim gallants, full of courtship and of state.
  Ros. Madam, speak true. It is not so, my
    lord.
My lady, to the manner of the days,   365
In courtesy gives undeserving praise.
We four indeed confronted were with four
In Russian habit ; here they stayed an
    hour
And talk'd apace ; and in that hour, my
    lord,   369

They did not bless us with one happy word.
I dare not call them fools ; but this I think,
When they are thirsty, fools would fain
    have drink.
  Ber. This jest is dry to me. Fair gentle
    sweet,
Your wit makes wise things foolish ; when
    we greet,
With eyes best seeing, heaven's fiery eye, 375
By light we lose light ; your capacity
Is of that nature that to your huge store
Wise things seem foolish and rich things
    but poor.
  Ros. This proves you wise and rich, for in
    my eye—
  Ber. I am a fool, and full of poverty.   380
  Ros. But that you take what doth to you
    belong,
It were a fault to snatch words from my
    tongue.
  Ber. O, I am yours, and all that I possess.
  Ros. All the fool mine ?
  Ber.   I cannot give you less.
  Ros. Which of the vizards was it that you
    wore ?   385
  Ber. Where ? when ? what vizard ? Why
    demand you this ?
  Ros. There, then, that vizard ; that
    superfluous case
That hid the worse and show'd the better
    face.
  King. We were descried ; they'll mock
    us now downright.   389
  Dum. Let us confess, and turn it to a jest.
  Prin. Amaz'd, my lord ? Why looks
    your Highness sad ?
  Ros. Help, hold his brows ! he'll swoon !
    Why look you pale ?
Sea-sick, I think, coming from Muscovy.
  Ber. Thus pour the stars down plagues
    for perjury.
Can any face of brass hold longer out ?   395
Here stand I, lady—dart thy skill at me,
Bruise me with scorn, confound me with a
    flout,
Thrust thy sharp wit quite through my
    ignorance,
Cut me to pieces with thy keen conceit ;
And I will wish thee never more to dance,
Nor never more in Russian habit wait.   401
O, never will I trust to speeches penn'd,
Nor to the motion of a school-boy's tongue,
Nor never come in vizard to my friend,
Nor woo in rhyme, like a blind harper's
    song.   405
Taffeta phrases, silken terms precise,
Three-pil'd hyperboles, spruce affectation,
Figures pedantical—these summer-flies
Have blown me full of maggot ostentation.
I do forswear them ; and I here protest,   410
By this white glove—how white the hand,
    God knows !—
Henceforth my wooing mind shall be
    express'd

In russet yeas, and honest kersey noes.
And, to begin, wench—so God help me,
  law!—   414
My love to thee is sound, sans crack or flaw.
  Ros. Sans 'sans', I pray you.
  Ber.   Yet I have a trick
Of the old rage ; bear with me, I am sick ;
I'll leave it by degrees. Soft, let us see—
Write ' Lord have mercy on us ' on those
  three ;   419
They are infected ; in their hearts it lies ;
They have the plague, and caught it of
  your eyes.
These lords are visited ; you are not free,
For the Lord's tokens on you do I see.
  Prin. No, they are free that gave these
    tokens to us.
  Ber. Our states are forfeit ; seek not to
    undo us.   425
  Ros. It is not so ; for how can this be
    true,
That you stand forfeit, being those that
  sue ?
  Ber. Peace ; for I will not have to do
    with you.
  Ros. Nor shall not, if I do as I intend.
  Ber. Speak for yourselves ; my wit is at
    an end.   430
  King. Teach us, sweet madam, for our
    rude transgression
Some fair excuse.
  Prin.   The fairest is confession.
Were not you here but even now, disguis'd?
  King. Madam, I was.
  Prin.   And were you well advis'd ?
  King. I was, fair madam.
  Prin.   When you then were here,   435
What did you whisper in your lady's
  ear ?
  King. That more than all the world I did
    respect her.
  Prin. When she shall challenge this, you
    will reject her.
  King. Upon mine honour, no.
  Prin.   Peace, peace, forbear ;
Your oath once broke, you force not to
  forswear.   440
  King. Despise me when I break this oath
    of mine.
  Prin. I will ; and therefore keep it.
    Rosaline,
What did the Russian whisper in your ear ?
  Ros. Madam, he swore that he did hold
    me dear
As precious eyesight, and did value me   445
Above this world ; adding thereto, more-
  over,
That he would wed me, or else die my lover.
  Prin. God give thee joy of him ! The
    noble lord
Most honourably doth uphold his word.
  King. What mean you, madam ? By my
    life, my troth,   450
I never swore this lady such an oath.

  Ros. By heaven, you did ; and, to con-
    firm it plain,
You gave me this ; but take it, sir, again.
  King. My faith and this the Princess I
    did give ;   454
I knew her by this jewel on her sleeve.
  Prin. Pardon me, sir, this jewel did she
    wear ;
And Lord Berowne, I thank him, is my
    dear.
What, will you have me, or your pearl
    again ?
  Ber. Neither of either ; I remit both
    twain.
I see the trick on't : here was a consent,   460
Knowing aforehand of our merriment,
To dash it like a Christmas comedy.
Some carry-tale, some please-man, some
    slight zany,
Some mumble-news, some trencher-knight,
    some Dick,
That smiles his cheek in years and knows
    the trick   465
To make my lady laugh when she's dispos'd,
Told our intents before ; which once
    disclos'd,
The ladies did change favours ; and then
    we,
Following the signs, woo'd but the sign of
    she.
Now, to our perjury to add more terror,   470
We are again forsworn in will and error.
Much upon this it is ; [*To Boyet*] and
    might not you
Forestall our sport, to make us thus untrue?
Do not you know my lady's foot by th'
    squier,
And laugh upon the apple of her eye ?   475
And stand between her back, sir, and the
    fire,
Holding a trencher, jesting merrily ?
You put our page out. Go, you are allow'd ;
Die when you will, a smock shall be your
    shroud.   479
You leer upon me, do you ? There's an eye
Wounds like a leaden sword.
  Boyet.   Full merrily
Hath this brave manage, this career, been
    run.
  Ber. Lo, he is tilting straight ! Peace ; I
    have done.

Enter COSTARD.

Welcome, pure wit ! Thou part'st a fair
    fray.
  Cost. O Lord, sir, they would know   485
Whether the three Worthies shall come in
    or no ?
  Ber. What, are there but three ?
  Cost.   No, sir ; but it is vara fine,
For every one pursents three.
  Ber.   And three times thrice is nine.
  Cost. Not so, sir ; under correction, sir,
    I hope it is not so.

You cannot beg us, sir, I can assure you,
    sir ; we know what we know ;   490
I hope, sir, three times thrice, sir—
  Ber. Is not nine.
  Cost. Under correction, sir, we know
whereuntil it doth amount.
  Ber. By Jove, I always took three threes
for nine.   495
  Cost. O Lord, sir, it were pity you should
get your living by reck'ning, sir.
  Ber. How much is it ?
  Cost. O Lord, sir, the parties themselves,
the actors, sir, will show whereuntil it doth
amount. For mine own part, I am, as they
say, but to parfect one man in one poor
man, Pompion the Great, sir.   502
  Ber. Art thou one of the Worthies ?
  Cost. It pleased them to think me worthy
of Pompey the Great ; for mine own part,
I know not the degree of the Worthy ; but
I am to stand for him.   506
  Ber. Go, bid them prepare.
  Cost. We will turn it finely off, sir ; we
will take some care. [*Exit Costard.*
  King. Berowne, they will shame us ; let
them not approach.
  Ber. We are shame-proof, my lord, and
'tis some policy   510
To have one show worse than the King's
and his company.
  King. I say they shall not come.
  Prin. Nay, my good lord, let me o'errule
you now.
That sport best pleases that doth least
    know how ;
Where zeal strives to content, and the
    contents   515
Dies in the zeal of that which it presents.
Their form confounded makes most form
    in mirth,
When great things labouring perish in their
    birth.
  Ber. A right description of our sport, my
lord.

Enter ARMADO.

  Arm. Anointed, I implore so much expense of thy royal sweet breath as will
utter a brace of words.   521
    [*Converses apart with the King, and
           delivers a paper.*
  Prin. Doth this man serve God ?
  Ber. Why ask you ?
  Prin. 'A speaks not like a man of God
his making.   524
  Arm. That is all one, my fair, sweet,
honey monarch ; for, I protest, the schoolmaster is exceeding fantastical ; too too
vain, too too vain ; but we will put it, as
they say, to fortuna de la guerra. I wish
you the peace of mind, most royal couplement !   [*Exit Armado.*
  King. Here is like to be a good presence
of Worthies. He presents Hector of Troy ;

the swain, Pompey the Great ; the parish
curate, Alexander ; Armado's page, Her-
cules ; the pedant, Judas Maccabæus.
And if these four Worthies in their first
    show thrive,
These four will change habits and present
    the other five.   535
  Ber. There is five in the first show.
  King. You are deceived, 'tis not so.
  Ber. The pedant, the braggart, the hedge-
priest, the fool, and the boy ;
Abate throw at novum, and the whole
    world again   540
Cannot pick out five such, take each one
    in his vein.
  King. The ship is under sail, and here she
    comes amain.

Enter COSTARD, *armed for* Pompey.

  Cost. I Pompey am—
  Ber.   You lie, you are not he.
  Cost. I Pompey am—
  Boyet.   With libbard's head on knee.
  Ber. Well said, old mocker ; I must
    needs be friends with thee.   545
  *Cost. I Pompey am, Pompey surnam'd the
    Big—*
  Dum. The Great.
  Cost. It is *Great,* sir.
    Pompey surnam'd the Great,
*That oft in field, with targe and shield, did
    make my foe to sweat ;*
*And travelling along this coast, I here am
    come by chance,*   550
*And lay my arms before the legs of this sweet
    lass of France.*
If your ladyship would say ' Thanks,
Pompey ', I had done.
  Prin. Great thanks, great Pompey.
  Cost. 'Tis not so much worth ; but I hope
I was perfect. I made a little fault in
Great.
  Ber. My hat to a halfpenny, Pompey
proves the best Worthy.   557

Enter SIR NATHANIEL, *for* Alexander.

  *Nath. When in the world I liv'd, I was the
    world's commander ;*
*By east, west, north, and south, I spread my
    conquering might.*
*My scutcheon plain declares that I am
    Alisander—*   560
  Boyet. Your nose says, no, you are not ;
    for it stands too right.
  Ber. Your nose smells ' no ' in this, most
    tender-smelling knight.
  Prin. The conqueror is dismay'd. Pro-
ceed, good Alexander.
  *Nath. When in the world I liv'd, I was the
    world's commander—*
  Boyet. Most true, 'tis right, you were so,
    Alisander.   565
  Ber. Pompey the Great !
  Cost. Your servant, and Costard.

Ber. Take away the conqueror, take away Alisander.   568

Cost. [*To Sir Nath.*] O, sir, you have overthrown Alisander the conqueror ! You will be scrap'd out of the painted cloth for this. Your lion, that holds his poleaxe sitting on a close-stool, will be given to Ajax. He will be the ninth Worthy. A conqueror and afeard to speak ! Run away for shame, Alisander. [*Sir Nath. retires*] There, an't shall please you, a foolish mild man ; an honest man, look you, and soon dash'd. He is a marvellous good neighbour, faith, and a very good bowler ; but for Alisander—alas ! you see how 'tis—a little o'erparted. But there are Worthies a-coming will speak their mind in some other sort.

Prin. Stand aside, good Pompey.   580

Enter HOLOFERNES, *for* Judas ; *and* MOTH, *for* Hercules.

Hol. Great Hercules is presented by this imp,
Whose club kill'd Cerberus, that three-headed canus ;
And when he was a babe, a child, a shrimp,
Thus did he strangle serpents in his manus.
Quoniam he seemeth in minority,   585
Ergo I come with this apology.

Keep some state in thy exit, and vanish.
                    [*Moth retires.*
Judas I am—
   Dum. A Judas !
   Hol. Not Iscariot, sir.   590
Judas I am, ycliped Maccabæus.
   Dum. Judas Maccabæus clipt is plain Judas.
   Ber. A kissing traitor. How art thou prov'd Judas ?
   Hol. Judas I am—
   Dum. The more shame for you, Judas !
   Hol. What mean you, sir ?   596
   Boyet. To make Judas hang himself.
   Hol. Begin, sir ; you are my elder.
   Ber. Well followed : Judas was hanged on an elder.
   Hol. I will not be put out of countenance.
   Ber. Because thou hast no face.   601
   Hol. What is this ?
   Boyet. A cittern-head.
   Dum. The head of a bodkin.
   Ber. A death's face in a ring.   605
   Long. The face of an old Roman coin, scarce seen.
   Boyet. The pommel of Cæsar's falchion.
   Dum. The carv'd-bone face on a flask.
   Ber. Saint George's half-cheek in a brooch.
   Dum. Ay, and in a brooch of lead.   610
   Ber. Ay, and worn in the cap of a tooth-drawer. And now, forward ; for we have put thee in countenance.

Hol. You have put me out of countenance
   Ber. False : we have given thee faces.
   Hol. But you have outfac'd them all.   615
   Ber. An thou wert a lion we would do so.
   Boyet. Therefore, as he is an ass, let him go.
And so adieu, sweet Jude ! Nay, why dost thou stay ?
   Dum. For the latter end of his name.
   Ber. For the ass to the Jude ; give it him—Jud-as, away.   620
   Hol. This is not generous, not gentle, not humble.
   Boyet. A light for Monsieur Judas ! It grows dark, he may stumble.
                    [*Holofernes retires.*
Prin. Alas, poor Maccabæus, how hath he been baited !

Enter ARMADO, *for* Hector.

   Ber. Hide thy head, Achilles ; here comes Hector in arms.   625
   Dum. Though my mocks come home by me, I will now be merry.
   King. Hector was but a Troyan in respect of this.
   Boyet. But is this Hector ?
   Dum. I think Hector was not so clean-timber'd.   630
   Long. His leg is too big for Hector's.
   Dum. More calf, certain.
   Boyet. No ; he is best indued in the small.
   Ber. This cannot be Hector.
   Dum. He's a god or a painter, for he makes faces.   635
   Arm. The armipotent Mars, of lances the almighty,
Gave Hector a gift—
   Dum. A gilt nutmeg.
   Ber. A lemon.
   Long. Stuck with cloves.   640
   Dum. No, cloven.
   Arm. Peace !
The armipotent Mars, of lances the almighty,
Gave Hector a gift, the heir of Ilion ;
A man so breathed that certain he would fight ye,   645
From morn till night out of his pavilion.
I am that flower—
   Dum.   That mint.
   Long.   That columbine.
   Arm. Sweet Lord Longaville, rein thy tongue.
   Long. I must rather give it the rein, for it runs against Hector.   650
   Dum. Ay, and Hector's a greyhound.
   Arm. The sweet war-man is dead and rotten ; sweet chucks, beat not the bones of the buried ; when he breathed, he was a man. But I will forward with my device. [*To the Princess*] Sweet royalty, bestow on me the sense of hearing.   655
[*Berowne steps forth, and speaks to Costard.*

Prin. Speak, brave Hector ; we are much
   delighted.
Arm. I do adore thy sweet Grace's
slipper.
Boyet. [*Aside to Dumain*] Loves her by
the foot.
Dum. [*Aside to Boyet*] He may not by
the yard.
Arm. This Hector far surmounted Han-
   nibal—   660
Cost. The party is gone, fellow Hector,
she is gone ; she is two months on her
way.
Arm. What meanest thou ?
Cost. Faith, unless you play the honest
Troyan, the poor wench is cast away. She's
quick ; the child brags in her belly already ;
'tis yours.   666
Arm. Dost thou infamonize me among
potentates ? Thou shalt die.
Cost. Then shall Hector be whipt for
Jaquenetta that is quick by him, and
hang'd for Pompey that is dead by him. 670
Dum. Most rare Pompey !
Boyet. Renowned Pompey !
Ber. Greater than Great ! Great, great,
great Pompey ! Pompey the Huge !
Dum. Hector trembles.   675
Ber. Pompey is moved. More Ates, more
Ates ! Stir them on ! stir them on !
Dum. Hector will challenge him.
Ber. Ay, if 'a have no more man's blood
in his belly than will sup a flea.   680
Arm. By the North Pole, I do challenge
thee.
Cost. I will not fight with a pole, like a
Northren man ; I'll slash ; I'll do it by the
sword. I bepray you, let me borrow my
arms again.
Dum. Room for the incensed Worthies !
Cost. I'll do it in my shirt.   686
Dum. Most resolute Pompey !
Moth. Master, let me take you a button-
hole lower. Do you not see Pompey is un-
casing for the combat ? What mean you ?
You will lose your reputation.   690
Arm. Gentlemen and soldiers, pardon
me ; I will not combat in my shirt.
Dum. You may not deny it : Pompey
hath made the challenge.
Arm. Sweet bloods, I both may and will.
Ber. What reason have you for 't ? 696
Arm. The naked truth of it is : I have no
shirt ; I go woolward for penance.
Boyet. True, and it was enjoined him in
Rome for want of linen ; since when, I'll
be sworn, he wore none but a dish-clout of
Jaquenetta's, and that 'a wears next his
heart for a favour.   702

Enter as messenger, MONSIEUR MARCADE.

Mar. God save you, madam !
Prin.   Welcome, Marcade ;
But that thou interruptest our merriment.

Mar. I am sorry, madam ; for the news I
   bring   706
Is heavy in my tongue. The King your
   father—
Prin. Dead, for my life !
Mar.   Even so ; my tale is told.
Ber. Worthies, away ; the scene begins
   to cloud.   710
Arm. For mine own part, I breathe free
breath. I have seen the day of wrong
through the little hole of discretion, and I
will right myself like a soldier.
                 [*Exeunt Worthies.*
King. How fares your Majesty ?
Prin. Boyet, prepare ; I will away to-
   night.   715
King. Madam, not so ; I do beseech you
   stay.
Prin. Prepare, I say. I thank you,
   gracious lords,
For all your fair endeavours, and entreat,
Out of a new-sad soul, that you vouchsafe
In your rich wisdom to excuse or hide   720
The liberal opposition of our spirits,
If over-boldly we have borne ourselves
In the converse of breath—your gentleness
Was guilty of it. Farewell, worthy lord.
A heavy heart bears not a nimble tongue.
Excuse me so, coming too short of thanks
For my great suit so easily obtain'd.
   King. The extreme parts of time ex-
   tremely forms
All causes to the purpose of his speed ;
And often at his very loose decides   730
That which long process could not arbi-
   trate.
And though the mourning brow of progeny
Forbid the smiling courtesy of love
The holy suit which fain it would convince,
Yet, since love's argument was first on foot,
Let not the cloud of sorrow justle it   736
From what it purpos'd ; since to wail
   friends lost
Is not by much so wholesome-profitable
As to rejoice at friends but newly found.
   Prin. I understand you not ; my griefs
   are double.   740
   Ber. Honest plain words best pierce the
   ear of grief ;
And by these badges understand the King.
For your fair sakes have we neglected time,
Play'd foul play with our oaths ; your
   beauty, ladies,
Hath much deformed us, fashioning our
   humours   745
Even to the opposed end of our intents ;
And what in us hath seem'd ridiculous,
As love is full of unbefitting strains,
All wanton as a child, skipping and vain ;
Form'd by the eye and therefore, like the
   eye,   750
Full of strange shapes, of habits, and of
   forms,
Varying in subjects as the eye doth roll

To every varied object in his glance ;
Which parti-coated presence of loose love
Put on by us, if in your heavenly eyes 755
Have misbecom'd our oaths and gravities,
Those heavenly eyes that look into these
    faults
Suggested us to make. Therefore, ladies,
Our love being yours, the error that love
    makes
Is likewise yours. We to ourselves prove
    false,   760
By being once false for ever to be true
To those that make us both—fair ladies,
    you ;
And even that falsehood, in itself a sin,
Thus purifies itself and turns to grace.
    Prin. We have receiv'd your letters, full
        of love ;   765
Your favours, the ambassadors of love ;
And, in our maiden council, rated them
At courtship, pleasant jest, and courtesy,
As bombast and as lining to the time ;
But more devout than this in our respects
Have we not been ; and therefore met your
    loves   771
In their own fashion, like a merriment.
    Dum. Our letters, madam, show'd much
        more than jest.
    Long. So did our looks.
    Ros.   We did not quote them so.
    King. Now, at the latest minute of the
        hour,   775
Grant us your loves.
    Prin.   A time, methinks, too short
To make a world-without-end bargain in.
No, no, my lord, your Grace is perjur'd
    much,   778
Full of dear guiltiness ; and therefore this,
If for my love, as there is no such cause,
You will do aught—this shall you do for
    me :
Your oath I will not trust ; but go with
    speed   782
To some forlorn and naked hermitage,
Remote from all the pleasures of the world ;
There stay until the twelve celestial signs
Have brought about the annual reckoning.
If this austere insociable life
Change not your offer made in heat of
    blood,
If frosts and fasts, hard lodging and thin
    weeds,   789
Nip not the gaudy blossoms of your love,
But that it bear this trial, and last love,
Then, at the expiration of the year,
Come, challenge me, challenge me by these
    deserts ;   793
And, by this virgin palm now kissing thine,
I will be thine ; and, till that instant, shut
My woeful self up in a mournful house,
Raining the tears of lamentation
For the remembrance of my father's death.
If this thou do deny, let our hands part,
Neither intitled in the other's heart.   800

    King. If this, or more than this, I would
        deny,
To flatter up these powers of mine with
    rest,
The sudden hand of death close up mine
    eye !
Hence hermit then, my heart is in thy breast.
    Ber. And what to me, my love ? and what
        to me ?   805
    Ros. You must be purged too, your sins are
        rack'd ;
You are attaint with faults and perjury ;
Therefore, if you my favour mean to get,
A twelvemonth shall you spend, and never
    rest,
But seek the weary beds of people sick.   810
    Dum. But what to me, my love ? but
        what to me ?
A wife ?
    Kath. A beard, fair health, and honesty ;
With threefold love I wish you all these
    three.
    Dum. O, shall I say I thank you, gentle
        wife ?
    Kath. Not so, my lord ; a twelvemonth
        and a day   815
I'll mark no words that smooth-fac'd
    wooers say.
Come when the King doth to my lady come ;
Then, if I have much love, I'll give you
    some.
    Dum. I'll serve thee true and faithfully
        till then.
    Kath. Yet swear not, lest ye be forsworn
        again.   820
    Long. What says Maria ?
    Mar.   At the twelvemonth's end
I'll change my black gown for a faithful
    friend.
    Long. I'll stay with patience ; but the
        time is long.
    Mar. The liker you ; few taller are so
        young.
    Ber. Studies my lady ? Mistress, look on
        me ;   825
Behold the window of my heart, mine eye,
What humble suit attends thy answer there.
Impose some service on me for thy love.
    Ros. Oft have I heard of you, my Lord
        Berowne,
Before I saw you ; and the world's large
    tongue   830
Proclaims you for a man replete with
    mocks,
Full of comparisons and wounding flouts,
Which you on all estates will execute
That lie within the mercy of your wit.
To weed this wormwood from your fruitful
    brain,   835
And therewithal to win me, if you please,
Without the which I am not to be won,
You shall this twelvemonth term from day
    to day
Visit the speechless sick, and still converse

With groaning wretches; and your task
   shall be,   840
With all the fierce endeavour of your wit,
To enforce the pained impotent to smile.
 Ber. To move wild laughter in the throat
   of death?
It cannot be; it is impossible;
Mirth cannot move a soul in agony. 845
 Ros. Why, that's the way to choke a
   gibing spirit,
Whose influence is begot of that loose grace
Which shallow laughing hearers give to
   fools.
A jest's prosperity lies in the ear 849
Of him that hears it, never in the tongue
Of him that makes it; then, if sickly ears,
Deaf'd with the clamours of their own dear
   groans, 852
Will hear your idle scorns, continue then,
And I will have you and that fault withal.
But if they will not, throw away that spirit,
And I shall find you empty of that fault,
Right joyful of your reformation. 857
 Ber. A twelvemonth? Well, befall what
   will befall,
I'll jest a twelvemonth in an hospital.
 Prin. [*To the King*] Ay, sweet my lord,
   and so I take my leave. 860
 King. No, madam; we will bring you on
   your way.
 Ber. Our wooing doth not end like an old
   play;
Jack hath not Jill. These ladies' courtesy
Might well have made our sport a comedy.
 King. Come, sir, it wants a twelvemonth
   an' a day, 865
And then 'twill end.
 Ber.   That's too long for a play.

   Re-enter ARMADO.

 Arm. Sweet Majesty, vouchsafe me—
 Prin. Was not that Hector?
 Dum. The worthy knight of Troy. 869
 Arm. I will kiss thy royal finger, and take
leave. I am a votary: I have vow'd to
Jaquenetta to hold the plough for her sweet
love three year. But, most esteemed greatness, will you hear the dialogue that the two
learned men have compiled in praise of the
Owl and the Cuckoo? It should have
followed in the end of our show. 875
 King. Call them forth quickly; we will
do so.

 Arm. Holla! approach.

   Enter All.

This side is Hiems, Winter; this Ver, the
Spring—the one maintained by the Owl, th'
other by the Cuckoo. Ver, begin. 880

   Spring.

When daisies pied and violets blue
And lady-smocks all silver-white
And cuckoo-buds of yellow hue
Do paint the meadows with delight,
The cuckoo then on every tree 885
Mocks married men, for thus sings he:
' Cuckoo;
Cuckoo, cuckoo '—O word of fear,
Unpleasing to a married ear!

When shepherds pipe on oaten straws, 890
And merry larks are ploughmen's clocks;
When turtles tread, and rooks and daws,
And maidens bleach their summer smocks;
The cuckoo then on every tree
Mocks married men, for thus sings he: 895
' Cuckoo;
Cuckoo, cuckoo '—O word of fear,
Unpleasing to a married ear!

   Winter.

When icicles hang by the wall,
And Dick the shepherd blows his nail, 900
And Tom bears logs into the hall,
And milk comes frozen home in pail,
When blood is nipp'd, and ways be foul,
Then nightly sings the staring owl:
' Tu-who; 905
Tu-whit, Tu-who '—A merry note,
While greasy Joan doth keel the pot.

When all aloud the wind doth blow,
And coughing drowns the parson's saw,
And birds sit brooding in the snow, 910
And Marian's nose looks red and raw,
When roasted crabs hiss in the bowl,
Then nightly sings the staring owl:
' Tu-who;
Tu-whit, To-who '—A merry note, 915
While greasy Joan doth keel the pot.

 Arm. The words of Mercury are harsh
after the songs of Apollo. You that way:
we this way.   [*Exeunt.*

A MIDSUMMER NIGHT'S DREAM

DRAMATIS PERSONÆ

THESEUS, *Duke of Athens.*
EGEUS, *father to Hermia.*
LYSANDER, ⎱ *in love with Hermia.*
DEMETRIUS, ⎰
PHILOSTRATE, *Master of the Revels to Theseus.*
QUINCE, *a carpenter.*
SNUG, *a joiner.*
BOTTOM, *a weaver.*
FLUTE, *a bellows-mender.*
SNOUT, *a tinker.*
STARVELING, *a tailor.*

HIPPOLYTA, *Queen of the Amazons, betrothed to Theseus.*
HERMIA, *daughter to Egeus, in love with Lysander.*
HELENA, *in love with Demetrius.*

OBERON, *King of the Fairies.*
TITANIA, *Queen of the Fairies.*
PUCK, *or* ROBIN GOODFELLOW.
PEASEBLOSSOM, ⎫
COBWEB, ⎬ *fairies.*
MOTH, ⎪
MUSTARDSEED, ⎭

PROLOGUE, ⎫   QUINCE.
PYRAMUS, ⎪   BOTTOM.
THISBY, ⎬ *presented* FLUTE.
WALL, ⎪   *by*   SNOUT.
MOONSHINE, ⎪   STARVELING.
LION, ⎭   SNUG.

Other Fairies *attending their King and Queen.*
Attendants *on Theseus and Hippolyta.*

THE SCENE : *Athens and a wood near it.*

ACT ONE

SCENE I. *Athens. The palace of Theseus.*

Enter THESEUS, HIPPOLYTA, PHILOSTRATE, *and* Attendants.

The. Now, fair Hippolyta, our nuptial hour
Draws on apace ; four happy days bring in
Another moon ; but, O, methinks, how slow
This old moon wanes ! She lingers my desires,
Like to a step-dame or a dowager,   5
Long withering out a young man's revenue.
Hip. Four days will quickly steep themselves in night ;
Four nights will quickly dream away the time ;
And then the moon, like to a silver bow
New-bent in heaven, shall behold the night
Of our solemnities.
The.   Go, Philostrate,   11
Stir up the Athenian youth to merriments ;
Awake the pert and nimble spirit of mirth ;
Turn melancholy forth to funerals ;
The pale companion is not for our pomp.   15
              [*Exit Philostrate.*
Hippolyta, I woo'd thee with my sword,
And won thy love doing thee injuries ;
But I will wed thee in another key,
With pomp, with triumph, and with revelling.

Enter EGEUS, *and his daughter* HERMIA, LYSANDER, *and* DEMETRIUS.

Ege. Happy be Theseus, our renowned Duke !   20

The. Thanks, good Egeus ; what's the news with thee ?
Ege. Full of vexation come I, with complaint
Against my child, my daughter Hermia.
Stand forth, Demetrius. My noble lord,
This man hath my consent to marry her. 25
Stand forth, Lysander. And, my gracious Duke,
This man hath bewitch'd the bosom of my child.
Thou, thou, Lysander, thou hast given her rhymes,
And interchang'd love-tokens with my child ;
Thou hast by moonlight at her window sung,   30
With feigning voice, verses of feigning love,
And stol'n the impression of her fantasy
With bracelets of thy hair, rings, gawds, conceits,
Knacks, trifles, nosegays, sweetmeats—messengers
Of strong prevailment in unhardened youth ;   35
With cunning hast thou filch'd my daughter's heart ;
Turn'd her obedience, which is due to me,
To stubborn harshness. And, my gracious Duke,
Be it so she will not here before your Grace
Consent to marry with Demetrius,   40
I beg the ancient privilege of Athens :
As she is mine I may dispose of her ;
Which shall be either to this gentleman
Or to her death, according to our law
Immediately provided in that case.   45

198

The. What say you, Hermia? Be
  advis'd, fair maid.
To you your father should be as a god;
One that compos'd your beauties; yea,
  and one
To whom you are but as a form in wax,
By him imprinted, and within his power 50
To leave the figure, or disfigure it.
Demetrius is a worthy gentleman.
  Her. So is Lysander.
  The.   In himself he is;
But, in this kind, wanting your father's
  voice,
The other must be held the worthier. 55
  Her. I would my father look'd but with
  my eyes.
  The. Rather your eyes must with his
  judgment look.
  Her. I do entreat your Grace to pardon
  me.
I know not by what power I am made bold,
Nor how it may concern my modesty 60
In such a presence here to plead my
  thoughts;
But I beseech your Grace that I may know
The worst that may befall me in this case,
If I refuse to wed Demetrius. 64
  The. Either to die the death, or to abjure
For ever the society of men.
Therefore, fair Hermia, question your
  desires,
Know of your youth, examine well your
  blood,
Whether, if you yield not to your father's
  choice,
You can endure the livery of a nun, 70
For aye to be in shady cloister mew'd,
To live a barren sister all your life,
Chanting faint hymns to the cold fruitless
  moon.
Thrice-blessed they that master so their
  blood
To undergo such maiden pilgrimage; 75
But earthlier happy is the rose distill'd
Than that which withering on the virgin
  thorn
Grows, lives, and dies, in single blessedness.
  Her. So will I grow, so live, so die, my
  lord,
Ere I will yield my virgin patent up 80
Unto his lordship, whose unwished yoke
My soul consents not to give sovereignty.
  The. Take time to pause; and by the
  next new moon—
The sealing-day betwixt my love and me
For everlasting bond of fellowship— 85
Upon that day either prepare to die
For disobedience to your father's will,
Or else to wed Demetrius, as he would,
Or on Diana's altar to protest
For aye austerity and single life. 90
  Dem. Relent, sweet Hermia; and,
  Lysander, yield
Thy crazed title to my certain right.

  Lys. You have her father's love,
  Demetrius;
Let me have Hermia's; do you marry him.
  Ege. Scornful Lysander, true, he hath
  my love; 95
And what is mine my love shall render
  him;
And she is mine; and all my right of her
I do estate unto Demetrius.
  Lys. I am, my lord, as well deriv'd as he,
As well possess'd; my love is more than
  his; 100
My fortunes every way as fairly rank'd,
If not with vantage, as Demetrius';
And, which is more than all these boasts
  can be,
I am belov'd of beauteous Hermia. 104
Why should not I then prosecute my right?
Demetrius, I'll avouch it to his head,
Made love to Nedar's daughter, Helena,
And won her soul; and she, sweet lady,
  dotes,
Devoutly dotes, dotes in idolatry,
Upon this spotted and inconstant man. 110
  The. I must confess that I have heard so
  much,
And with Demetrius thought to have spoke
  thereof;
But, being over-full of self-affairs, 113
My mind did lose it. But, Demetrius, come;
And come, Egeus; you shall go with me;
I have some private schooling for you both.
For you, fair Hermia, look you arm yourself
To fit your fancies to your father's will,
Or else the law of Athens yields you up—
Which by no means we may extenuate—
To death, or to a vow of single life. 121
Come, my Hippolyta; what cheer, my
  love?
Demetrius, and Egeus, go along;
I must employ you in some business
Against our nuptial, and confer with you
Of something nearly that concerns your-
  selves. 126
  Ege. With duty and desire we follow you.
    [*Exeunt all but Lysander and Hermia.*
  Lys. How now, my love! Why is your
  cheek so pale?
How chance the roses there do fade so fast?
  Her. Belike for want of rain, which I
  could well 130
Beteem them from the tempest of my eyes.
  Lys. Ay me! for aught that I could ever
  read,
Could ever hear by tale or history,
The course of true love never did run
  smooth;
But either it was different in blood——
  Her. O cross! too high to be enthrall'd
  to low. 136
  Lys. Or else misgraffed in respect of
  years—
  Her. O spite! too old to be engag'd to
  young.

Lys. Or else it stood upon the choice of
friends—

Her. O hell ! to choose love by another's
eyes. 140

Lys. Or, if there were a sympathy in
choice,
War, death, or sickness, did lay siege to it,
Making it momentary as a sound,
Swift as a shadow, short as any dream,
Brief as the lightning in the collied night 145
That, in a spleen, unfolds both heaven and
earth,
And ere a man hath power to say 'Behold !'
The jaws of darkness do devour it up ;
So quick bright things come to confusion.

Her. If then true lovers have been ever
cross'd, 150
It stands as an edict in destiny.
Then let us teach our trial patience,
Because it is a customary cross,
As due to love as thoughts and dreams and
sighs, 154
Wishes and tears, poor Fancy's followers.

Lys. A good persuasion ; therefore, hear
me, Hermia :
I have a widow aunt, a dowager
Of great revenue, and she hath no child—
From Athens is her house remote seven
leagues—
And she respects me as her only son. 160
There, gentle Hermia, may I marry thee ;
And to that place the sharp Athenian law
Cannot pursue us. If thou lovest me then,
Steal forth thy father's house to-morrow
night ;
And in the wood, a league without the
town, 165
Where I did meet thee once with Helena
To do observance to a morn of May,
There will I stay for thee.

Her. My good Lysander !
I swear to thee by Cupid's strongest bow,
By his best arrow, with the golden head, 170
By the simplicity of Venus' doves,
By that which knitteth souls and prospers
loves,
And by that fire which burn'd the Carthage
Queen, 173
When the false Troyan under sail was seen,
By all the vows that ever men have broke,
In number more than ever women spoke,
In that same place thou hast appointed me,
To-morrow truly will I meet with thee.

Lys. Keep promise, love. Look, here
comes Helena.

Enter HELENA.

Her. God speed fair Helena ! Whither
away ? 180

Hel. Call you me fair ? That fair again
unsay.
Demetrius loves your fair. O happy fair !
Your eyes are lode-stars and your
tongue's sweet air

More tuneable than lark to shepherd's ear,
When wheat is green, when hawthorn buds
appear. 185
Sickness is catching ; O, were favour so,
Yours would I catch, fair Hermia, ere I go !
My ear should catch your voice, my eye
your eye,
My tongue should catch your tongue's
sweet melody.
Were the world mine, Demetrius being
bated, 190
The rest I'd give to be to you translated.
O, teach me how you look, and with what
art
You sway the motion of Demetrius' heart !

Her. I frown upon him, yet he loves me
still.

Hel. O that your frowns would teach my
smiles such skill ! 195

Her. I give him curses, yet he gives me
love.

Hel. O that my prayers could such
affection move !

Her. The more I hate, the more he follows
me.

Hel. The more I love, the more he hateth
me.

Her. His folly, Helena, is no fault of
mine. 200

Hel. None, but your beauty ; would that
fault were mine !

Her. Take comfort : he no more shall see
my face ;
Lysander and myself will fly this place.
Before the time I did Lysander see,
Seem'd Athens as a paradise to me. 205
O, then, what graces in my love do dwell,
That he hath turn'd a heaven unto a
hell !

Lys. Helen, to you our minds we will
unfold :
To-morrow night, when Phœbe doth behold
Her silver visage in the wat'ry glass, 210
Decking with liquid pearl the bladed grass,
A time that lovers' flights doth still conceal,
Through Athens' gates have we devis'd to
steal.

Her. And in the wood where often you
and I 214
Upon faint primrose beds were wont to lie,
Emptying our bosoms of their counsel
sweet,
There my Lysander and myself shall meet ;
And thence from Athens turn away our
eyes,
To seek new friends and stranger com-
panies.
Farewell, sweet playfellow ; pray thou for
us, 220
And good luck grant thee thy Demetrius !
Keep word, Lysander ; we must starve our
sight
From lovers' food till morrow deep
midnight.

Lys. I will, my Hermia. [*Exit Hermia.*
Helena adieu;
As you on him, Demetrius dote on you! 225
[*Exit Lysander.*

Hel. How happy some o'er other some
can be!
Through Athens I am thought as fair as she.
But what of that? Demetrius thinks not so;
He will not know what all but he do know.
And as he errs, doting on Hermia's eyes, 230
So I, admiring of his qualities.
Things base and vile, holding no quantity,
Love can transpose to form and dignity.
Love looks not with the eyes, but with the
mind;
And therefore is wing'd Cupid painted
blind. 235
Nor hath Love's mind of any judgment
taste;
Wings and no eyes figure unheedy haste;
And therefore is Love said to be a child,
Because in choice he is so oft beguil'd.
As waggish boys in game themselves for-
swear, 240
So the boy Love is perjur'd everywhere;
For ere Demetrius look'd on Hermia's eyne,
He hail'd down oaths that he was only
mine;
And when this hail some heat from Hermia
felt,
So he dissolv'd, and show'rs of oaths did
melt. 245
I will go tell him of fair Hermia's flight;
Then to the wood will he to-morrow night
Pursue her; and for this intelligence
If I have thanks, it is a dear expense.
But herein mean I to enrich my pain, 250
To have his sight thither and back again.
[*Exit.*

SCENE II. *Athens. Quince's house.*

Enter QUINCE, SNUG, BOTTOM, FLUTE,
SNOUT *and* STARVELING.

Quin. Is all our company here?
Bot. You were best to call them generally,
man by man, according to the scrip.
Quin. Here is the scroll of every man's
name which is thought fit, through all
Athens, to play in our interlude before the
Duke and the Duchess on his wedding-day
at night. 6
Bot. First, good Peter Quince, say what
the play treats on; then read the names
of the actors; and so grow to a point. 9
Quin. Marry, our play is 'The most
Lamentable Comedy and most Cruel Death
of Pyramus and Thisby'.
Bot. A very good piece of work, I assure
you, and a merry. Now, good Peter Quince,
call forth your actors by the scroll. Masters,
spread yourselves. 14
Quin. Answer, as I call you. Nick
Bottom, the weaver.

Bot. Ready. Name what part I am for,
and proceed.
Quin. You, Nick Bottom, are set down
for Pyramus.
Bot. What is Pyramus? A lover, or a
tyrant?
Quin. A lover, that kills himself most
gallant for love. 19
Bot. That will ask some tears in the true
performing of it. If I do it, let the audience
look to their eyes; I will move storms; I
will condole in some measure. To the rest—
yet my chief humour is for a tyrant. I
could play Ercles rarely, or a part to tear
a cat in, to make all split.

'The raging rocks 25
And shivering shocks
Shall break the locks
Of prison gates;
And Phibbus' car
Shall shine from far, 30
And make and mar
The foolish Fates.'

This was lofty. Now name the rest of the
players. This is Ercles' vein, a tyrant's
vein: a lover is more condoling. 34
Quin. Francis Flute, the bellows-mender.
Flu. Here, Peter Quince.
Quin. Flute, you must take Thisby on
you.
Flu. What is Thisby? A wand'ring
knight?
Quin. It is the lady that Pyramus must
love. 39
Flu. Nay, faith, let not me play a woman;
I have a beard coming.
Quin. That's all one; you shall play it
in a mask, and you may speak as small as
you will. 43
Bot. An I may hide my face, let me play
Thisby too. I'll speak in a monstrous little
voice: 'Thisne, Thisne!' [*Then speaking
small*] 'Ah Pyramus, my lover dear! Thy
Thisby dear, and lady dear!' 46
Quin. No, no, you must play Pyramus;
and, Flute, you Thisby.
Bot. Well, proceed.
Quin. Robin Starveling, the tailor. 50
Star. Here, Peter Quince.
Quin. Robin Starveling, you must play
Thisby's mother. Tom Snout, the tinker.
Snout. Here, Peter Quince. 54
Quin. You, Pyramus' father; myself,
Thisby's father; Snug, the joiner, you, the
lion's part. And, I hope, here is a play
fitted. 57
Snug. Have you the lion's part written?
Pray you, if it be, give it me, for I am slow
of study.
Quin. You may do it extempore, for it is
nothing but roaring. 61
Bot. Let me play the lion too. I will roar
that I will do any man's heart good to hear

me; I will roar that I will make the Duke
say 'Let him roar again, let him roar
again'.   65

Quin. An you should do it too terribly,
you would fright the Duchess and the
ladies, that they would shriek; and that
were enough to hang us all.

All. That would hang us, every mother's
son.   69

Bot. I grant you, friends, if you should
fright the ladies out of their wits, they
would have no more discretion but to hang
us; but I will aggravate my voice so, that
I will roar you as gently as any sucking
dove; I will roar you an 'twere any
nightingale.   74

Quin. You can play no part but Pyramus;
for Pyramus is a sweet-fac'd man; a
proper man, as one shall see in a summer's
day; a most lovely gentleman-like man;
therefore you must needs play Pyramus.

Bot. Well, I will undertake it. What
beard were I best to play it in?   80

Quin. Why, what you will.

Bot. I will discharge it in either your
straw-colour beard, your orange-tawny
beard, your purple-in-grain beard, or your
French-crown-colour beard, your perfect
yellow.   85

Quin. Some of your French crowns have
no hair at all, and then you will play bare-
fac'd. But, masters, here are your parts;
and I am to entreat you, request you, and
desire you, to con them by to-morrow
night; and meet me in the palace wood,
a mile without the town, by moonlight;
there will we rehearse; for if we meet in
the city, we shall be dogg'd with company,
and our devices known. In the meantime
I will draw a bill of properties, such as our
play wants. I pray you, fail me not.   94

Bot. We will meet; and there we may
rehearse most obscenely and courageously.
Take pains; be perfect; adieu.

Quin. At the Duke's oak we meet.   97

Bot. Enough; hold, or cut bow-strings.
                                            [*Exeunt.*

ACT TWO

SCENE I. *A wood near Athens.*

Enter a Fairy *at one door, and* PUCK *at another.*

Puck. How now, spirit! whither wander
    you?

Fai. Over hill, over dale,
    Thorough bush, thorough brier,
Over park, over pale,
    Thorough flood, thorough fire,   5
I do wander every where,
Swifter than the moon's sphere;
And I serve the Fairy Queen,
To dew her orbs upon the green.   9

The cowslips tall her pensioners be;
In their gold coats spots you see;
Those be rubies, fairy favours,
    In those freckles live their savours.
I must go seek some dewdrops here,
And hang a pearl in every cowslip's ear.   15
Farewell, thou lob of spirits; I'll be gone.
Our Queen and all her elves come here anon.

Puck. The King doth keep his revels here
    to-night;
Take heed the Queen come not within his
    sight;
For Oberon is passing fell and wrath,   20
Because that she as her attendant hath
A lovely boy, stolen from an Indian king.
She never had so sweet a changeling;
And jealous Oberon would have the child
Knight of his train, to trace the forests wild;
But she perforce withholds the loved boy,
Crowns him with flowers, and makes him
    all her joy.   27
And now they never meet in grove or green,
By fountain clear, or spangled starlight
    sheen,
But they do square, that all their elves for
    fear   30
Creep into acorn cups and hide them there.

Fai. Either I mistake your shape and
    making quite,
Or else you are that shrewd and knavish
    sprite
Call'd Robin Goodfellow. Are not you he
That frights the maidens of the villagery,
Skim milk, and sometimes labour in the
    quern,   36
And bootless make the breathless housewife
    churn,
And sometime make the drink to bear no
    barm,
Mislead night-wanderers, laughing at their
    harm?
Those that Hobgoblin call you, and sweet
    Puck,   40
You do their work, and they shall have
    good luck.
Are not you he?

Puck.   Thou speakest aright:
I am that merry wanderer of the night.
I jest to Oberon, and make him smile
When I a fat and bean-fed horse beguile,   45
Neighing in likeness of a filly foal;
And sometime lurk I in a gossip's bowl
In very likeness of a roasted crab,
And, when she drinks, against her lips
    I bob,   49
And on her withered dewlap pour the ale.
The wisest aunt, telling the saddest tale,
Sometime for three-foot stool mistaketh
    me;
Then slip I from her bum, down topples
    she,
And 'tailor' cries, and falls into a cough;
And then the whole quire hold their hips
    and laugh,   55

And waxen in their mirth, and neeze, and
    swear
A merrier hour was never wasted there.
But room, fairy, here comes Oberon.
   Fai. And here my mistress. Would that
he were gone !

Enter OBERON *at one door, with his* Train,
and TITANIA, *at another, with hers.*

   Obe. Ill met by moonlight, proud Titania.
   Tita. What, jealous Oberon ! Fairies,
    skip hence ;   61
I have forsworn his bed and company.
   Obe. Tarry, rash wanton ; am not I thy
    lord ?
   Tita. Then I must be thy lady ; but I
    know
When thou hast stolen away from fairy
    land,   65
And in the shape of Corin sat all day,
Playing on pipes of corn, and versing love
To amorous Phillida. Why art thou here,
Come from the farthest steep of India,
But that, forsooth, the bouncing Amazon,
Your buskin'd mistress and your warrior
    love,   71
To Theseus must be wedded, and you
    come
To give their bed joy and prosperity ?
   Obe. How canst thou thus, for shame,
    Titania,
Glance at my credit with Hippolyta,   75
Knowing I know thy love to Theseus ?
Didst not thou lead him through the
    glimmering night
From Perigouna, whom he ravished ?
And make him with fair Ægles break his
    faith,
With Ariadne and Antiopa ?   80
   Tita. These are the forgeries of jealousy ;
And never, since the middle summer's
    spring,
Met we on hill, in dale, forest, or mead,
By paved fountain, or by rushy brook,
Or in the beached margent of the sea, 85
To dance our ringlets to the whistling wind,
But with thy brawls thou hast disturb'd
    our sport.
Therefore the winds, piping to us in vain,
As in revenge, have suck'd up from the sea
Contagious fogs ; which, falling in the land,
Hath every pelting river made so proud 91
That they have overborne their continents.
The ox hath therefore stretch'd his yoke in
    vain,
The ploughman lost his sweat, and the
    green corn   94
Hath rotted ere his youth attain'd a beard ;
The fold stands empty in the drowned field,
And crows are fatted with the murrion
    flock ;
The nine men's morris is fill'd up with mud,
And the quaint mazes in the wanton green,
For lack of tread, are undistinguishable. 100

The human mortals want their winter
    here ;
No night is now with hymn or carol blest ;
Therefore the moon, the governess of floods,
Pale in her anger, washes all the air,
That rheumatic diseases do abound.   105
And thorough this distemperature we see
The seasons alter : hoary-headed frosts
Fall in the fresh lap of the crimson rose ;
And on old Hiems' thin and icy crown 109
An odorous chaplet of sweet summer buds
Is, as in mockery, set. The spring, the
    summer,
The childing autumn, angry winter, change
Their wonted liveries ; and the mazed
    world,
By their increase, now knows not which is
    which.
And this same progeny of evils comes 115
From our debate, from our dissension ;
We are their parents and original.
   Obe. Do you amend it, then ; it lies in
    you.
Why should Titania cross her Oberon ?
I do but beg a little changeling boy 120
To be my henchman.
   Tita.   Set your heart at rest ;
The fairy land buys not the child of me.
His mother was a vot'ress of my order ;
And, in the spiced Indian air, by night,
Full often hath she gossip'd by my side ; 125
And sat with me on Neptune's yellow sands,
Marking th' embarked traders on the flood ;
When we have laugh'd to see the sails
    conceive,
And grow big-bellied with the wanton wind ;
Which she, with pretty and with swimming
    gait   130
Following—her womb then rich with my
    young squire—
Would imitate, and sail upon the land,
To fetch me trifles, and return again,
As from a voyage, rich with merchandise.
But she, being mortal, of that boy did
    die ;
And for her sake do I rear up her boy ; 136
And for her sake I will not part with him.
   Obe. How long within this wood intend
    you stay ?
   Tita. Perchance till after Theseus' wed-
    ding-day.
If you will patiently dance in our round, 140
And see our moonlight revels, go with us ;
If not, shun me, and I will spare your
    haunts.
   Obe. Give me that boy and I will go with
    thee.
   Tita. Not for thy fairy kingdom. Fairies,
    away.   144
We shall chide downright if I longer stay.
              [*Exit Titania with her Train.*
   Obe. Well, go thy way ; thou shalt not
    from this grove
Till I torment thee for this injury.

My gentle Puck, come hither. Thou re-
  memb'rest
Since once I sat upon a promontory,   149
And heard a mermaid on a dolphin's back
Uttering such dulcet and harmonious
  breath
That the rude sea grew civil at her song,
And certain stars shot madly from their
  spheres
To hear the sea-maid's music.
    Puck.   I remember.
    Obe. That very time I saw, but thou
    couldst not,   155
Flying between the cold moon and the
  earth
Cupid, all arm'd; a certain aim he took
At a fair vestal, throned by the west,
And loos'd his love-shaft smartly from his
  bow,
As it should pierce a hundred thousand
  hearts;   160
But I might see young Cupid's fiery shaft
Quench'd in the chaste beams of the wat'ry
  moon;
And the imperial vot'ress passed on,
In maiden meditation, fancy-free.
Yet mark'd I where the bolt of Cupid fell.
It fell upon a little western flower,   166
Before milk-white, now purple with love's
  wound,
And maidens call it Love-in-idleness.
Fetch me that flow'r, the herb I showed
  thee once.
The juice of it on sleeping eyelids laid   170
Will make or man or woman madly dote
Upon the next live creature that it sees.
Fetch me this herb, and be thou here again
Ere the leviathan can swim a league.
    Puck. I'll put a girdle round about the
    earth   175
In forty minutes.   *[Exit Puck.*
    Obe.   Having once this juice,
I'll watch Titania when she is asleep,
And drop the liquor of it in her eyes;
The next thing then she waking looks upon,
Be it on lion, bear, or wolf, or bull,   180
On meddling monkey, or on busy ape,
She shall pursue it with the soul of love.
And ere I take this charm from off her
  sight,
As I can take it with another herb,
I'll make her render up her page to me.   185
But who comes here? I am invisible;
And I will overhear their conference.

Enter DEMETRIUS, HELENA *following him.*

    Dem. I love thee not, therefore pursue
    me not.
Where is Lysander and fair Hermia?
The one I'll slay, the other slayeth me.   190
Thou told'st me they were stol'n unto this
  wood,
And here am I, and wood within this wood,
Because I cannot meet my Hermia.

Hence, get thee gone, and follow me no
  more.
    Hel. You draw me, you hard-hearted
    adamant;   195
But yet you draw not iron, for my heart
Is true as steel. Leave you your power to
  draw,
And I shall have no power to follow you.
    Dem. Do I entice you? Do I speak you
    fair?
Or, rather, do I not in plainest truth   200
Tell you I do not nor I cannot love you?
    Hel. And even for that do I love you the
    more.
I am your spaniel; and, Demetrius,
The more you beat me, I will fawn on you.
Use me but as your spaniel, spurn me, strike
  me,   205
Neglect me, lose me; only give me leave,
Unworthy as I am, to follow you.
What worser place can I beg in your love,
And yet a place of high respect with me,
Than to be used as you use your dog?   210
    Dem. Tempt not too much the hatred of
    my spirit;
For I am sick when I do look on thee.
    Hel. And I am sick when I look not on
    you.
    Dem. You do impeach your modesty too
    much
To leave the city and commit yourself   215
Into the hands of one that loves you not;
To trust the opportunity of night,
And the ill counsel of a desert place,
With the rich worth of your virginity.
    Hel. Your virtue is my privilege for
    that: 220
It is not night when I do see your face,
Therefore I think I am not in the night;
Nor doth this wood lack worlds of com-
  pany,
For you, in my respect, are all the world.
Then how can it be said I am alone   225
When all the world is here to look on me?
    Dem. I'll run from thee and hide me in
    the brakes,
And leave thee to the mercy of wild beasts.
    Hel. The wildest hath not such a heart as
    you.
Run when you will; the story shall be
  chang'd: 230
Apollo flies, and Daphne holds the chase;
The dove pursues the griffin; the mild
  hind
Makes speed to catch the tiger—bootless
  speed,
When cowardice pursues and valour flies.
    Dem. I will not stay thy questions; let
    me go;   235
Or, if thou follow me, do not believe
But I shall do thee mischief in the wood.
    Hel. Ay, in the temple, in the town, the
    field,
You do me mischief. Fie, Demetrius!

Your wrongs do set a scandal on my sex. 240
We cannot fight for love as men may do ;
We should be woo'd, and were not made
　　to woo.　　　　[*Exit Demetrius.*
I'll follow thee, and make a heaven of hell,
To die upon the hand I love so well.
　　　　　　　　　[*Exit Helena.*
　Obe. Fare thee well, nymph ; ere he do
　　leave this grove,　　　　245
Thou shalt fly him, and he shall seek thy
　　love.

　　　　Re-enter PUCK.

Hast thou the flower there ?　Welcome,
　　wanderer.
　Puck. Ay, there it is.
　Obe.　　　　I pray thee give it me.
I know a bank where the wild thyme blows,
Where oxlips and the nodding violet grows,
Quite over-canopied with luscious wood-
　　bine,　　　　　251
With sweet musk-roses, and with eglantine ;
There sleeps Titania sometime of the night,
Lull'd in these flowers with dances and
　　delight ;
And there the snake throws her enamell'd
　　skin,　　　　255
Weed wide enough to wrap a fairy in ;
And with the juice of this I'll streak her
　　eyes,
And make her full of hateful fantasies.
Take thou some of it, and seek through this
　　grove :
A sweet Athenian lady is in love　　260
With a disdainful youth ; anoint his eyes ;
But do it when the next thing he espies
May be the lady.　Thou shalt know the man
By the Athenian garments he hath on.
Effect it with some care, that he may prove
More fond on her than she upon her love.
And look thou meet me ere the first cock
　　crow.　　　　267
　Puck. Fear not, my lord ; your servant
　　shall do so.　　　　[*Exeunt.*

　SCENE II.　*Another part of the wood.*

　　Enter TITANIA, *with her* Train.

　Tita. Come now, a roundel and a fairy
　　song ;
Then, for the third part of a minute, hence :
Some to kill cankers in the musk-rose buds ;
Some war with rere-mice for their leathern
　　wings,
To make my small elves coats ; and some
　　keep back　　　　5
The clamorous owl that nightly hoots and
　　wonders
At our quaint spirits.　Sing me now asleep ;
Then to your offices, and let me rest.

　　　　The Fairies sing.

1 Fairy. You spotted snakes with double
　　tongue,

Thorny hedgehogs, be not seen ; 10
Newts and blind-worms, do no
　　wrong,
Come not near our fairy Queen.

Chorus.　　Philomel with melody
　　　　Sing in our sweet lullaby.
　　　　Lulla, lulla, lullaby ; lulla, lulla,
　　　　　lullaby.　　　　15
　　　　Never harm
　　　　Nor spell nor charm
　　　　Come our lovely lady nigh.
　　　　So good night, with lullaby. 19

2 Fairy. Weaving spiders, come not here ;
　　　　Hence, you long-legg'd spinners,
　　　　　hence.
　　　　Beetles black, approach not near ;
　　　　Worm nor snail do no offence.

Chorus.　　Philomel with melody, etc.
　　　　　　　　[*Titania sleeps.*

1 Fairy. Hence away ; now all is well. 25
　　　　One aloof stand sentinel.
　　　　　　　　[*Exeunt Fairies.*

Enter OBERON *and squeezes the flower on
　　Titania's eyelids.*

　Obe. What thou seest when thou dost
　　wake,
Do it for thy true-love take ;
Love and languish for his sake.
Be it ounce, or cat, or bear,
Pard, or boar with bristled hair,
In thy eye that shall appear
When thou wak'st, it is thy dear.
Wake when some vile thing is near. [*Exit.*

　　Enter LYSANDER *and* HERMIA.

　Lys. Fair love, you faint with wand'ring
　　in the wood ;　　　　35
And, to speak troth, I have forgot our
　　way ;
We'll rest us, Hermia, if you think it good,
And tarry for the comfort of the day.
　Her. Be it so, Lysander : find you out a
　　bed,
For I upon this bank will rest my head. 40
　Lys. One turf shall serve as pillow for us
　　both ;
One heart, one bed, two bosoms, and one
　　troth.
　Her. Nay, good Lysander ; for my sake,
　　my dear,
Lie further off yet ; do not lie so near.
　Lys. O, take the sense, sweet, of my
　　innocence !　　　　45
Love takes the meaning in love's confer-
　　ence.
I mean that my heart unto yours is knit,
So that but one heart we can make of it ;
Two bosoms interchained with an oath,
So then two bosoms and a single troth. 50
Then by your side no bed-room me deny,
For lying so, Hermia, I do not lie.

Her. Lysander riddles very prettily.
Now much beshrew my manners and my
    pride,
If Hermia meant to say Lysander lied ! 55
But, gentle friend, for love and courtesy
Lie further off, in human modesty ;
Such separation as may well be said
Becomes a virtuous bachelor and a maid,
So far be distant ; and good night, sweet
    friend.   60
Thy love ne'er alter till thy sweet life end !
Lys. Amen, amen, to that fair prayer
    say I ;
And then end life when I end loyalty !
Here is my bed ; sleep give thee all his rest !
Her. With half that wish the wisher's
    eyes be press'd !   [*They sleep.*

Enter PUCK.

Puck. Through the forest have I gone,
    But Athenian found I none   67
    On whose eyes I might approve
    This flower's force in stirring love.
    Night and silence—Who is here ?
    Weeds of Athens he doth wear :
    This is he, my master said,   72
    Despised the Athenian maid ;
    And here the maiden, sleeping
        sound,
    On the dank and dirty ground. 75
    Pretty soul ! she durst not lie
    Near this lack-love, this kill-
        courtesy.
    Churl, upon thy eyes I throw
    All the power this charm doth
        owe :   79
    When thou wak'st let love forbid
    Sleep his seat on thy eyelid.
    So awake when I am gone ;
    For I must now to Oberon. [*Exit.*

Enter DEMETRIUS *and* HELENA, *running.*

Hel. Stay, though thou kill me, sweet
    Demetrius.
Dem. I charge thee, hence, and do not
    haunt me thus.   85
Hel. O, wilt thou darkling leave me ? Do
    not so.
Dem. Stay on thy peril ; I alone will go.
                            [*Exit Demetrius.*
Hel. O, I am out of breath in this fond
    chase !
The more my prayer, the lesser is my
    grace.
Happy is Hermia, wheresoe'er she lies, 90
For she hath blessed and attractive eyes.
How came her eyes so bright ? Not with
    salt tears ;
If so, my eyes are oft'ner wash'd than hers.
No, no, I am as ugly as a bear,
For beasts that meet me run away for fear ;
Therefore no marvel though Demetrius 96
Do, as a monster, fly my presence thus.
What wicked and dissembling glass of mine

Made me compare with Hermia's sphery
    eyne ?
But who is here ?   Lysander ! on the
    ground !   100
Dead, or asleep ?   I see no blood, no
    wound.
Lysander, if you live, good sir, awake.
Lys. [*Waking*] And run through fire I will
    for thy sweet sake.
Transparent Helena ! Nature shows art,
That through thy bosom makes me see thy
    heart.   105
Where is Demetrius ? O, how fit a word
Is that vile name to perish on my sword !
Hel. Do not say so, Lysander ; say not so.
What though he love your Hermia ? Lord,
    what though ?
Yet Hermia still loves you ; then be
    content.   110
Lys. Content with Hermia ! No ; I do
    repent
The tedious minutes I with her have spent.
Not Hermia but Helena I love :
Who will not change a raven for a dove ?
The will of man is by his reason sway'd ; 115
And reason says you are the worthier maid.
Things growing are not ripe until their
    season ;
So I, being young, till now ripe not to
    reason ;
And touching now the point of human
    skill,
Reason becomes the marshal to my will, 120
And leads me to your eyes, where I o'erlook
Love's stories, written in Love's richest
    book.
Hel. Wherefore was I to this keen
    mockery born ?
When at your hands did I deserve this
    scorn ?
Is't not enough, is't not enough, young
    man,   125
That I did never, no, nor never can,
Deserve a sweet look from Demetrius' eye,
But you must flout my insufficiency ?
Good troth, you do me wrong, good sooth,
    you do,
In such disdainful manner me to woo. 130
But fare you well ; perforce I must confess
I thought you lord of more true gentleness.
O, that a lady of one man refus'd
Should of another therefore be abus'd !
                                    [*Exit.*
Lys. She sees not Hermia. Hermia, sleep
    thou there ;   135
And never mayst thou come Lysander near !
For, as a surfeit of the sweetest things
The deepest loathing to the stomach brings,
Or as the heresies that men do leave
Are hated most of those they did deceive,
So thou, my surfeit and my heresy, 141
Of all be hated, but the most of me !
And, all my powers, address your love and
    might

To honour Helen, and to be her knight!
　　　　　　　　　　　　　　[*Exit.*
　Her. [*Starting*] Help me, Lysander, help
　　me; do thy best　　　　　　　145
To pluck this crawling serpent from my
　　breast.
Ay me, for pity! What a dream was here!
Lysander, look how I do quake with fear.
Methought a serpent eat my heart away,
And you sat smiling at his cruel prey.　150
Lysander! What, remov'd? Lysander!
　　lord!
What, out of hearing gone? No sound, no
　　word?
Alack, where are you? Speak, an if you
　　hear;
Speak, of all loves! I swoon almost with
　　fear.　　　　　　　　　　　154
No? Then I well perceive you are not nigh.
Either death or you I'll find immediately.
　　　　　　　　　　　　　　[*Exit.*

ACT THREE

SCENE I. *The wood. Titania lying asleep.*

Enter QUINCE, SNUG, BOTTOM, FLUTE,
　SNOUT, *and* STARVELING.

　Bot. Are we all met?
　Quin. Pat, pat; and here's a marvellous
convenient place for our rehearsal. This
green plot shall be our stage, this hawthorn
brake our tiring-house; and we will do it
in action, as we will do it before the Duke.
　Bot. Peter Quince!　　　　　　6
　Quin. What sayest thou, bully Bottom?
　Bot. There are things in this comedy of
Pyramus and Thisby that will never please.
First, Pyramus must draw a sword to kill
himself; which the ladies cannot abide.
How answer you that?　　　　　11
　Snout. By'r lakin, a parlous fear.
　Star. I believe we must leave the killing
out, when all is done.　　　　　14
　Bot. Not a whit; I have a device to make
all well. Write me a prologue; and let the
prologue seem to say we will do no harm
with our swords, and that Pyramus is not
kill'd indeed; and for the more better
assurance, tell them that I Pyramus am not
Pyramus but Bottom the weaver. This will
put them out of fear.　　　　　20
　Quin. Well, we will have such a prologue;
and it shall be written in eight and six.
　Bot. No, make it two more; let it be
written in eight and eight.
　Snout. Will not the ladies be afeard of the
lion?　　　　　　　　　　25
　Star. I fear it, I promise you.
　Bot. Masters, you ought to consider with
yourself to bring in—God shield us!—a
lion among ladies is a most dreadful thing;
for there is not a more fearful wild-fowl
than your lion living; and we ought to
look to't.　　　　　　　　　30

　Snout. Therefore another prologue must
tell he is not a lion.
　Bot. Nay, you must name his name, and
half his face must be seen through the lion's
neck; and he himself must speak through,
saying thus, or to the same defect: 'Ladies,'
or 'Fair ladies, I would wish you' or 'I
would request you' or 'I would entreat
you not to fear, not to tremble. My life for
yours! If you think I come hither as a
lion, it were pity of my life. No, I am no
such thing; I am a man as other men are'.
And there, indeed, let him name his name,
and tell them plainly he is Snug the joiner.
　Quin. Well, it shall be so. But there is
two hard things—that is, to bring the
moonlight into a chamber; for, you know,
Pyramus and Thisby meet by moonlight.
　Snout. Doth the moon shine that night
we play our play?　　　　　　45
　Bot. A calendar, a calendar! Look in
the almanack; find out moonshine, find
out moonshine.
　Quin. Yes, it doth shine that night.
　Bot. Why, then may you leave a casement of the great chamber window, where
we play, open; and the moon may shine
in at the casement.　　　　　51
　Quin. Ay; or else one must come in with
a bush of thorns and a lantern, and say he
comes to disfigure or to present the person
of Moonshine. Then there is another thing:
we must have a wall in the great chamber;
for Pyramus and Thisby, says the story,
did talk through the chink of a wall.　57
　Snout. You can never bring in a wall.
What say you, Bottom?
　Bot. Some man or other must present
Wall; and let him have some plaster, or
some loam, or some rough-cast about him,
to signify wall; and let him hold his fingers
thus, and through that cranny shall
Pyramus and Thisby whisper.　　63
　Quin. If that may be, then all is well.
Come, sit down, every mother's son, and
rehearse your parts. Pyramus, you begin;
when you have spoken your speech, enter
into that brake; and so every one according to his cue.　　　　　　67

Enter PUCK *behind.*

　Puck. What hempen homespuns have we
　　swagg'ring here,
So near the cradle of the Fairy Queen?
What, a play toward! I'll be an auditor;
An actor too perhaps, if I see cause.　71
　Quin. Speak, Pyramus. Thisby, stand
forth.
　Bot. Thisby, the flowers of odious savours
　　sweet
　Quin. 'Odious'—odorous!
　Bot.——*odours savours sweet;*　　75
So hath thy breath, my dearest Thisby dear.
But hark, a voice! Stay thou but here awhile,

And by and by I will to thee appear.   [*Exit.*
    Puck. A stranger Pyramus than e'er
        played here !   [*Exit.*
    Flu. Must I speak now ?   80
    Quin. Ay, marry, must you ; for you
must understand he goes but to see a noise
that he heard, and is to come again.
    Flu. Most radiant Pyramus, most lily-
        white of hue,
*Of colour like the red rose on triumphant
    brier,*
*Most brisky juvenal, and eke most lovely
    Jew,*   85
*As true as truest horse, that yet would never
    tire,*
I'll meet thee, Pyramus, at Ninny's tomb.
    Quin. 'Ninus' tomb', man ! Why, you
must not speak that yet ; that you answer
to Pyramus. You speak all your part at
once, cues and all. Pyramus enter : your
cue is past ; it is 'never tire'.   91
    Flu. O—*As true as truest horse, that yet
        would never tire.*

Re-enter PUCK, *and* BOTTOM *with an ass's
        head.*

    Bot. *If I were fair, Thisby, I were only
        thine.*
    Quin. O monstrous ! O strange ! We are
haunted. Pray masters ! fly, masters !
Help !   95
        [*Exeunt all but Bottom and Puck.*
    Puck. I'll follow you ; I'll lead you about
        a round,
Through bog, through bush, through
        brake, through brier ;
Sometime a horse I'll be, sometime a hound,
A hog, a headless bear, sometime a fire ;
And neigh, and bark, and grunt, and roar,
        and burn,   100
Like horse, hound, hog, bear, fire, at every
        turn.   [*Exit.*
    Bot. Why do they run away ? This is a
knavery of them to make me afeard.

Re-enter SNOUT.

    Snout. O Bottom, thou art chang'd !
What do I see on thee ?   105
    Bot. What do you see ? You see an ass-
head of your own, do you ?   [*Exit Snout.*

Re-enter QUINCE.

    Quin. Bless thee, Bottom, bless thee !
Thou art translated.   [*Exit.* 109
    Bot. I see their knavery : this is to make
an ass of me ; to fright me, if they could.
But I will not stir from this place, do what
they can ; I will walk up and down here,
and I will sing, that they shall hear I am
not afraid.   [*Sings.*

    The ousel cock, so black of hue,
        With orange-tawny bill,   115
    The throstle with his note so true,
        The wren with little quill.

    Tita. What angel wakes me from my
        flow'ry bed ?
    Bot. [*Sings*]
    The finch, the sparrow, and the lark,
        The plain-song cuckoo grey,   120
    Whose note full many a man doth
        mark,
        And dares not answer nay—
for, indeed, who would set his wit to so
foolish a bird ? Who would give a bird the
lie, though he cry ' cuckoo ' never so ? 124
    Tita. I pray thee, gentle mortal, sing
        again.
Mine ear is much enamoured of thy note ;
So is mine eye enthralled to thy shape ;
And thy fair virtue's force perforce doth
        move me,
On the first view, to say, to swear, I love
        thee.   129
    Bot. Methinks, mistress, you should have
little reason for that. And yet, to say the
truth, reason and love keep little company
together now-a-days. The more the pity
that some honest neighbours will not make
them friends. Nay, I can gleek upon
occasion.   134
    Tita. Thou art as wise as thou art
        beautiful.
    Bot. Not so, neither ; but if I had wit
enough to get out of this wood, I have
enough to serve mine own turn.
    Tita. Out of this wood do not desire to go ;
Thou shalt remain here whether thou wilt
        or no.
I am a spirit of no common rate ;   140
The summer still doth tend upon my state ;
And I do love thee ; therefore, go with
        me.
I'll give thee fairies to attend on thee ;
And they shall fetch thee jewels from the
        deep,
And sing, while thou on pressed flowers dost
        sleep ;   145
And I will purge thy mortal grossness
That thou shalt like an airy spirit go.
Peaseblossom ! Cobweb ! Moth ! and Mus-
        tardseed !

Enter PEASEBLOSSOM, COBWEB, MOTH, *and*
        MUSTARDSEED.

    Peas. Ready.
    Cob.   And I.
    Moth.   And I.
    Mus.   And I.
    All.   Where shall we go ?
    Tita. Be kind and courteous to this
        gentleman ;   150
Hop in his walks and gambol in his eyes ;
Feed him with apricocks and dewberries,
With purple grapes, green figs, and mul-
        berries ;
The honey bags steal from the humble-bees,
And for night-tapers crop their waxen
        thighs,   155

And light them at the fiery glow-worm's
　　eyes,
To have my love to bed and to arise ;
And pluck the wings from painted butter-
　　flies,
To fan the moonbeams from his sleeping
　　eyes.
Nod to him, elves, and do him courtesies.
　　Peas. Hail, mortal !　　　　　　　　161
　　Cob. Hail !
　　Moth. Hail !
　　Mus. Hail !
　　Bot. I cry your worships mercy, heartily ;
I beseech your worship's name.　　　166
　　Cob. Cobweb.
　　Bot. I shall desire you of more acquaint-
ance, good Master Cobweb. If I cut my
finger, I shall make bold with you. Your
name, honest gentleman ?　　　　170
　　Peas. Peaseblossom.
　　Bot. I pray you, commend me to Mistress
Squash, your mother, and to Master Peas-
cod, your father. Good Master Pease-
blossom, I shall desire you of more
acquaintance too. Your name, I beseech
you, sir ?　　　　　　　　　175
　　Mus. Mustardseed.
　　Bot. Good Master Mustardseed, I know
your patience well. That same cowardly
giant-like ox-beef hath devour'd many a
gentleman of your house. I promise you
your kindred hath made my eyes water ere
now. I desire you of more acquaintance,
good Master Mustardseed.　　　181
　　Tita. Come, wait upon him ; lead him to
my bower.
The moon, methinks, looks with a wat'ry
　　eye ;
And when she weeps, weeps every little
　　flower,
Lamenting some enforced chastity.　185
Tie up my love's tongue, bring him
　　silently.　　　　　　　　[*Exeunt.*

SCENE II. *Another part of the wood.*

Enter OBERON.

Obe. I wonder if Titania be awak'd ;
Then, what it was that next came in her eye,
Which she must dote on in extremity.

Enter PUCK.

Here comes my messenger. How now, mad
　　spirit !
What night-rule now about this haunted
　　grove ?　　　　　　　　5
　　Puck. My mistress with a monster is in
love.
Near to her close and consecrated bower,
While she was in her dull and sleeping hour,
A crew of patches, rude mechanicals,　9
That work for bread upon Athenian stalls,
Were met together to rehearse a play
Intended for great Theseus' nuptial day.

The shallowest thickskin of that barren sort,
Who Pyramus presented, in their sport
Forsook his scene and ent'red in a brake ;
When I did him at this advantage take,　16
An ass's nole I fixed on his head.
Anon his Thisby must be answered,
And forth my mimic comes. When they
　　him spy,
As wild geese that the creeping fowler eye,
Or russet-pated choughs, many in sort,　21
Rising and cawing at the gun's report,
Sever themselves and madly sweep the sky,
So at his sight away his fellows fly ;
And at our stamp here, o'er and o'er one
　　falls ;　　　　　　　　25
He murder cries, and help from Athens
　　calls.
Their sense thus weak, lost with their fears
　　thus strong,
Made senseless things begin to do them
　　wrong,
For briers and thorns at their apparel
　　snatch ;
Some sleeves, some hats, from yielders all
　　things catch.　　　　　　　30
I led them on in this distracted fear,
And left sweet Pyramus translated there ;
When in that moment, so it came to pass,
Titania wak'd, and straightway lov'd an
　　ass.
　　Obe. This falls out better than I could
　　devise.　　　　　　　　35
But hast thou yet latch'd the Athenian's eyes
With the love-juice, as I did bid thee do ?
　　Puck. I took him sleeping—that is
　　finish'd too—
And the Athenian woman by his side ;
That, when he wak'd, of force she must be
　　ey'd.　　　　　　　　40

Enter DEMETRIUS *and* HERMIA.

　　Obe. Stand close ; this is the same
　　Athenian.
　　Puck. This is the woman, but not this the
　　man.
　　Dem. O, why rebuke you him that loves
　　you so ?
Lay breath so bitter on your bitter foe.
　　Her. Now I but chide, but I should use
　　thee worse,　　　　　　　45
For thou, I fear, hast given me cause to
　　curse.
If thou hast slain Lysander in his sleep,
Being o'er shoes in blood, plunge in the
　　deep,
And kill me too.
The sun was not so true unto the day　50
As he to me. Would he have stolen away
From sleeping Hermia ? I'll believe as soon
This whole earth may be bor'd, and that
　　the moon
May through the centre creep and so
　　displease　　　　　　　54
Her brother's noontide with th' Antipodes.

It cannot be but thou hast murd'red him ;
So should a murderer look—so dead, so grim.
   Dem. So should the murdered look ; and so should I,
Pierc'd through the heart with your stern cruelty ;
Yet you, the murderer, look as bright, as clear, 60
As yonder Venus in her glimmering sphere.
   Her. What's this to my Lysander ? Where is he ?
Ah, good Demetrius, wilt thou give him me?
   Dem. I had rather give his carcass to my hounds.
   Her. Out, dog ! out, cur ! Thou driv'st me past the bounds 65
Of maiden's patience. Hast thou slain him, then ?
Henceforth be never numb'red among men !
O, once tell true ; tell true, even for my sake !
Durst thou have look'd upon him being awake,
And hast thou kill'd him sleeping ? O brave touch ! 70
Could not a worm, an adder, do so much ?
An adder did it ; for with doubler tongue
Than thine, thou serpent, never adder stung.
   Dem. You spend your passion on a mis-pris'd mood :
I am not guilty of Lysander's blood ; 75
Nor is he dead, for aught that I can tell.
   Her. I pray thee, tell me then that he is well.
   Dem. An if I could, what should I get therefore ?
   Her. A privilege never to see me more.
And from thy hated presence part I so ; 80
See me no more whether he be dead or no.
                [Exit.
   Dem. There is no following her in this fierce vein ;
Here, therefore, for a while I will remain.
So sorrow's heaviness doth heavier grow
For debt that bankrupt sleep doth sorrow owe ; 85
Which now in some slight measure it will pay,
If for his tender here I make some stay.
                [Lies down.
   Obe. What hast thou done ? Thou hast mistaken quite,
And laid the love-juice on some true-love's sight.
Of thy misprision must perforce ensue 90
Some true love turn'd, and not a false turn'd true.
   Puck. Then fate o'er-rules that, one man holding troth,
A million fail, confounding oath on oath.
   Obe. About the wood go swifter than the wind,

And Helena of Athens look thou find ; 95
All fancy-sick she is and pale of cheer,
With sighs of love that costs the fresh blood dear.
By some illusion see thou bring her here ;
I'll charm his eyes against she do appear.
   Puck. I go, I go ; look how I go, 100
Swifter than arrow from the Tartar's bow.
                [Exit.
   Obe. Flower of this purple dye,
Hit with Cupid's archery,
Sink in apple of his eye.
When his love he doth espy, 105
Let her shine as gloriously
As the Venus of the sky.
When thou wak'st, if she be by,
Beg of her for remedy.

Re-enter PUCK.

   Puck. Captain of our fairy band, 110
Helena is here at hand,
And the youth mistook by me
Pleading for a lover's fee ;
Shall we their fond pageant see ?
Lord, what fools these mortals be ! 115
   Obe. Stand aside. The noise they make
Will cause Demetrius to awake.
   Puck. Then will two at once woo one.
That must needs be sport alone ;
And those things do best please me
That befall prepost'rously. 121

Enter LYSANDER *and* HELENA.

   Lys. Why should you think that I should woo in scorn ?
Scorn and derision never come in tears.
Look when I vow, I weep ; and vows so born,
In their nativity all truth appears. 125
How can these things in me seem scorn to you,
Bearing the badge of faith, to prove them true ?
   Hel. You do advance your cunning more and more.
When truth kills truth, O devilish-holy fray !
These vows are Hermia's. Will you give her o'er ? 130
Weigh oath with oath, and you will nothing weigh :
Your vows to her and me, put in two scales,
Will even weigh ; and both as light as tales.
   Lys. I had no judgment when to her I swore.
   Hel. Nor none, in my mind, now you give her o'er. 135
   Lys. Demetrius loves her, and he loves not you.
   Dem. [*Awaking*] O Helen, goddess, nymph, perfect, divine !
To what, my love, shall I compare thine eyne ?
Crystal is muddy. O, how ripe in show

Thy lips, those kissing cherries, tempting
    grow !   140
That pure congeal'd white, high Taurus'
    snow,
Fann'd with the eastern wind, turns to a
    crow
When thou hold'st up thy hand. O, let me
    kiss
This princess of pure white, this seal of
    bliss !
    Hel. O spite ! O hell ! I see you all are
    bent   145
To set against me for your merriment.
If you were civil and knew courtesy,
You would not do me thus much injury.
Can you not hate me, as I know you do,
But you must join in souls to mock me
    too ?
If you were men, as men you are in show,
You would not use a gentle lady so :   152
To vow, and swear, and superpraise my
    parts,
When I am sure you hate me with your
    hearts.
You both are rivals, and love Hermia ; 155
And now both rivals, to mock Helena.
A trim exploit, a manly enterprise,
To conjure tears up in a poor maid's eyes
With your derision ! None of noble sort
Would so offend a virgin, and extort   160
A poor soul's patience, all to make you
    sport.
    Lys. You are unkind, Demetrius ; be not
    so ;
For you love Hermia. This you know I
    know ;
And here, with all good will, with all my
    heart,
In Hermia's love I yield you up my part ;
And yours of Helena to me bequeath, 166
Whom I do love and will do till my death.
    Hel. Never did mockers waste more idle
    breath.
    Dem. Lysander, keep thy Hermia ; I will
    none.
If e'er I lov'd her, all that love is gone. 170
My heart to her but as guest-wise sojourn'd,
And now to Helen is it home return'd,
There to remain.
    Lys.   Helen, it is not so.
    Dem. Disparage not the faith thou dost
    not know,
Lest, to thy peril, thou aby it dear.   175
Look where thy love comes ; yonder is thy
    dear.

          Enter HERMIA.

    Her. Dark night, that from the eye his
    function takes,
The ear more quick of apprehension makes ;
Wherein it doth impair the seeing sense,
It pays the hearing double recompense. 180
Thou art not by mine eye, Lysander,
    found ;

Mine ear, I thank it, brought me to thy
    sound.
But why unkindly didst thou leave me so ?
    Lys. Why should he stay whom love doth
    press to go ?
    Her. What love could press Lysander
    from my side ?   185
    Lys. Lysander's love, that would not let
    him bide—
Fair Helena, who more engilds the night
Than all yon fiery oes and eyes of light.
Why seek'st thou me ? Could not this make
    thee know   189
The hate I bare thee made me leave thee so?
    Her. You speak not as you think ; it
    cannot be.
    Hel. Lo, she is one of this confederacy !
Now I perceive they have conjoin'd all three
To fashion this false sport in spite of me.
Injurious Hermia ! most ungrateful maid !
Have you conspir'd, have you with these
    contriv'd,   196
To bait me with this foul derision ?
Is all the counsel that we two have shar'd,
The sisters' vows, the hours that we have
    spent,   199
When we have chid the hasty-footed time
For parting us—O, is all forgot ?
All   school-days'   friendship,   childhood
    innocence ?
We, Hermia, like two artificial gods,
Have with our needles created both one
    flower,
Both on one sampler, sitting on one
    cushion,   205
Both warbling of one song, both in one
    key ;
As if our hands, our sides, voices, and minds,
Had been incorporate. So we grew together,
Like to a double cherry, seeming parted,
But yet an union in partition,   210
Two lovely berries moulded on one stem ;
So, with two seeming bodies, but one heart ;
Two of the first, like coats in heraldry,
Due but to one, and crowned with one
    crest.
And will you rent our ancient love asunder,
To join with men in scorning your poor
    friend ?   216
It is not friendly, 'tis not maidenly ;
Our sex, as well as I, may chide you for it,
Though I alone do feel the injury.
    Her. I am amazed at your passionate
    words ;   220
I scorn you not ; it seems that you scorn
    me.
    Hel. Have you not set Lysander, as in
    scorn,
To follow me and praise my eyes and face ?
And made your other love, Demetrius,
Who even but now did spurn me with his
    foot,   225
To call me goddess, nymph, divine, and
    rare,

Precious, celestial ? Wherefore speaks he this
To her he hates ? And wherefore doth Lysander
Deny your love, so rich within his soul,
And tender me, forsooth, affection,   230
But by your setting on, by your consent ?
What though I be not so in grace as you,
So hung upon with love, so fortunate,
But miserable most, to love unlov'd ?   234
This you should pity rather than despise.
Her. I understand not what you mean by this.
Hel. Ay, do—persever, counterfeit sad looks,
Make mouths upon me when I turn my back,   238
Wink each at other ; hold the sweet jest up ;
This sport, well carried, shall be chronicled.
If you have any pity, grace, or manners,
You would not make me such an argument.
But fare ye well ; 'tis partly my own fault,
Which death, or absence, soon shall remedy.
Lys. Stay, gentle Helena ; hear my excuse ;   245
My love, my life, my soul, fair Helena !
Hel. O excellent !
Her.   Sweet, do not scorn her so.
Dem. If she cannot entreat, I can compel.
Lys. Thou canst compel no more than she entreat ;
Thy threats have no more strength than her weak prayers.
Helen, I love thee, by my life I do ;   251
I swear by that which I will lose for thee
To prove him false that says I love thee not.
Dem. I say I love thee more than he can do.
Lys. If thou say so, withdraw, and prove it too.   255
Dem. Quick, come.
Her.   Lysander, whereto tends all this ?
Lys. Away, you Ethiope !
Dem.   No, no, he will
Seem to break loose—take on as you would follow,
But yet come not. You are a tame man ; go !
Lys. Hang off, thou cat, thou burr ; vile thing, let loose,   260
Or I will shake thee from me like a serpent.
Her. Why are you grown so rude ? What change is this,
Sweet love ?
Lys.   Thy love ! Out, tawny Tartar, out !
Out, loathed med'cine ! O hated potion, hence !
Her. Do you not jest ?
Hel.   Yes, sooth ; and so do you. 265
Lys. Demetrius, I will keep my word with thee.
Dem. I would I had your bond ; for I perceive

A weak bond holds you ; I'll not trust your word.
Lys. What, should I hurt her, strike her, kill her dead ?
Although I hate her, I'll not harm her so. 270
Her. What ! Can you do me greater harm than hate ?
Hate me ! wherefore ? O me ! what news, my love ?
Am not I Hermia ? Are not you Lysander ?
I am as fair now as I was erewhile.
Since night you lov'd me ; yet since night you left me.
Why then, you left me—O, the gods forbid !—   276
In earnest, shall I say ?
Lys.   Ay, by my life !
And never did desire to see thee more.
Therefore be out of hope, of question, of doubt ;
Be certain, nothing truer ; 'tis no jest   280
That I do hate thee and love Helena.
Her. O me ! you juggler ! you canker-blossom !
You thief of love ! What ! Have you come by night,
And stol'n my love's heart from him ?
Hel.   Fine, i' faith !
Have you no modesty, no maiden shame,
No touch of bashfulness ? What ! Will you tear   286
Impatient answers from my gentle tongue ?
Fie, fie ! you counterfeit, you puppet you !
Her. ' Puppet ! ' why so ? Ay, that way goes the game.
Now I perceive that she hath made compare   290
Between our statures ; she hath urg'd her height ;
And with her personage, her tall personage,
Her height, forsooth, she hath prevail'd with him.
And are you grown so high in his esteem
Because I am so dwarfish and so low ? 295
How low am I, thou painted maypole ? Speak.
How low am I ? I am not yet so low
But that my nails can reach unto thine eyes.
Hel. I pray you, though you mock me, gentlemen,
Let her not hurt me. I was never curst ; 300
I have no gift at all in shrewishness ;
I am a right maid for my cowardice ;
Let her not strike me. You perhaps may think,
Because she is something lower than myself,
That I can match her.
Her.   ' Lower ' hark, again. 305
Hel. Good Hermia, do not be so bitter with me.
I evermore did love you, Hermia,
Did ever keep your counsels, never wrong'd you ;
Save that, in love unto Demetrius,   309

I told him of your stealth unto this wood.
He followed you ; for love I followed him ;
But he hath chid me hence, and threat'ned
 me
To strike me, spurn me, nay, to kill me too ;
And now, so you will let me quiet go,
To Athens will I bear my folly back, 315
And follow you no further. Let me go.
You see how simple and how fond I am.

Her. Why, get you gone ! Who is't that
 hinders you ?

Hel. A foolish heart that I leave here
 behind.

Her. What ! with Lysander ?

Hel.   With Demetrius. 320

Lys. Be not afraid ; she shall not harm
 thee, Helena.

Dem. No, sir, she shall not, though you
 take her part.

Hel. O, when she is angry, she is keen and
 shrewd ;
She was a vixen when she went to school ;
And, though she be but little, she is fierce.

Her. ' Little ' again ! Nothing but ' low '
 and ' little ' ! 326
Why will you suffer her to flout me thus ?
Let me come to her.

Lys.   Get you gone, you dwarf ;
You minimus, of hind'ring knot-grass
 made ;
You bead, you acorn.

Dem.   You are too officious 330
In her behalf that scorns your services.
Let her alone ; speak not of Helena ;
Take not her part ; for if thou dost intend
Never so little show of love to her,
Thou shalt aby it.

Lys.   Now she holds me not. 335
Now follow, if thou dar'st, to try whose
 right,
Of thine or mine, is most in Helena.

Dem. Follow ! Nay, I'll go with thee,
 cheek by jowl.

   [*Exeunt Lysander and Demetrius.*

Her. You, mistress, all this coil is long
 of you.
Nay, go not back.

Hel.   I will not trust you, I ; 340
Nor longer stay in your curst company.
Your hands than mine are quicker for a
 fray ;
My legs are longer though, to run away.
          [*Exit.*

Her. I am amaz'd, and know not what
 to say.   [*Exit.*

Obe. This is thy negligence. Still thou
 mistak'st, 345
Or else committ'st thy knaveries wilfully.

Puck. Believe me, king of shadows, I
 mistook.
Did not you tell me I should know the man
By the Athenian garments he had on ?
And so far blameless proves my enterprise
That I have 'nointed an Athenian's eyes ;

And so far am I glad it so did sort, 352
As this their jangling I esteem a sport.

Obe. Thou seest these lovers seek a place
 to fight.
Hie therefore, Robin, overcast the night ;
The starry welkin cover thou anon 356
With drooping fog as black as Acheron,
And lead these testy rivals so astray
As one come not within another's way.
Like to Lysander sometime frame thy
 tongue, 360
Then stir Demetrius up with bitter wrong ;
And sometime rail thou like Demetrius ;
And from each other look thou lead them
 thus,
Till o'er their brows death-counterfeiting
 sleep
With leaden legs and batty wings doth
 creep. 365
Then crush this herb into Lysander's eye ;
Whose liquor hath this virtuous property,
To take from thence all error with his might
And make his eyeballs roll with wonted
 sight.
When they next wake, all this derision 370
Shall seem a dream and fruitless vision ;
And back to Athens shall the lovers wend
With league whose date till death shall
 never end.
Whiles I in this affair do thee employ, 374
I'll to my queen, and beg her Indian
 boy ;
And then I will her charmed eye release
From monster's view, and all things shall
 be peace.

Puck. My fairy lord, this must be done
 with haste,
For night's swift dragons cut the clouds full
 fast ;
And yonder shines Aurora's harbinger, 380
At whose approach ghosts, wand'ring here
 and there,
Troop home to churchyards. Damned
 spirits all,
That in cross-ways and floods have burial,
Already to their wormy beds are gone,
For fear lest day should look their shames
 upon ; 385
They wilfully themselves exil'd from light,
And must for aye consort with black-
 brow'd night.

Obe. But we are spirits of another sort :
I with the Morning's love have oft made
 sport ; 389
And, like a forester, the groves may tread
Even till the eastern gate, all fiery red,
Opening on Neptune with fair blessed
 beams,
Turns into yellow gold his salt green
 streams.
But, notwithstanding, haste, make no
 delay ;
We may effect this business yet ere day. 395
          [*Exit Oberon.*

Puck. Up and down, up and down,
 I will lead them up and down.
 I am fear'd in field and town.
 Goblin, lead them up and down.

Here comes one.   400

Enter LYSANDER.

Lys. Where art thou, proud Demetrius ?
 Speak thou now.
Puck. Here, villain, drawn and ready.
 Where art thou ?
Lys. I will be with thee straight.
Puck.   Follow me, then,
To plainer ground. [*Exit Lysander as follow-
       ing the voice.*

Enter DEMETRIUS.

Dem.   Lysander, speak again.
Thou runaway, thou coward, art thou fled ?
Speak ! In some bush ? Where dost thou
 hide thy head ?   406
Puck. Thou coward, art thou bragging to
 the stars,
Telling the bushes that thou look'st for
 wars,
And wilt not come ? Come, recreant, come,
 thou child ;
I'll whip thee with a rod. He is defil'd   410
That draws a sword on thee.
 Dem.   Yea, art thou there ?
Puck. Follow my voice ; we'll try no
 manhood here.   [*Exeunt.*

Re-enter LYSANDER.

Lys. He goes before me, and still dares
 me on ;   413
When I come where he calls, then he is gone.
The villain is much lighter heel'd than I.
I followed fast, but faster he did fly,
That fallen am I in dark uneven way,
And here will rest me. [*Lies down*] Come,
 thou gentle day.
For if but once thou show me thy grey
 light,   419
I'll find Demetrius, and revenge this spite.
        [*Sleeps.*

Re-enter PUCK *and* DEMETRIUS.

Puck. Ho, ho, ho ! Coward, why com'st
 thou not ?
Dem. Abide me, if thou dar'st ; for well I
 wot
Thou run'st before me, shifting every
 place,
And dar'st not stand, nor look me in the
 face.
Where art thou now ?
 Puck.   Come hither ; I am here. 425
Dem. Nay, then, thou mock'st me. Thou
 shalt buy this dear,
If ever I thy face by daylight see ;
Now, go thy way. Faintness constraineth
 me
To measure out my length on this cold bed.

By day's approach look to be visited.   430
      [*Lies down and sleeps.*

Enter HELENA.

Hel. O weary night, O long and tedious
 night,
Abate thy hours ! Shine comforts from the
 east,
That I may back to Athens by daylight,
From these that my poor company detest.
And sleep, that sometimes shuts up
 sorrow's eye,   435
Steal me awhile from mine own company.
        [*Sleeps.*
Puck. Yet but three ? Come one more ;
 Two of both kinds makes up four.
 Here she comes, curst and sad.
 Cupid is a knavish lad,   440
 Thus to make poor females mad.

Enter HERMIA.

Her. Never so weary, never so in woe,
Bedabbled with the dew, and torn with
 briers,
I can no further crawl, no further go ;   444
My legs can keep no pace with my desires.
Here will I rest me till the break of day.
Heavens shield Lysander, if they mean a
 fray !   [*Lies down and sleeps.*
Puck.   On the ground
    Sleep sound ;
    I'll apply   450
    To your eye,
 Gentle lover, remedy.
 [*Squeezing the juice on Lysander's eyes.*
    When thou wak'st,
    Thou tak'st
    True delight   455
    In the sight
 Of thy former lady's eye ;
 And the country proverb known,
 That every man should take his
  own,
 In your waking shall be shown.
    Jack shall have Jill ;   461
    Nought shall go ill ;
The man shall have this mare again, and all
 shall be well.   [*Exit.*

ACT FOUR

SCENE I. *The wood. Lysander, Demetrius,
Helena, and Hermia, lying asleep.*

Enter TITANIA *and* BOTTOM ; PEASE-
BLOSSOM, COBWEB, MOTH, MUSTARDSEED
and other Fairies *attending ;* OBERON
behind, unseen.

Tita. Come, sit thee down upon this
 flow'ry bed,
While I thy amiable cheeks do coy,
And stick musk-roses in thy sleek smooth
 head,
And kiss thy fair large ears, my gentle joy.

Bot. Where's Peaseblossom ?   5

Peas. Ready.

Bot. Scratch my head, Peaseblossom.
Where's Mounsieur Cobweb ?

Cob. Ready.   9

Bot. Mounsieur Cobweb; good mounsieur,
get you your weapons in your hand and kill
me a red-hipp'd humble-bee on the top of a
thistle ; and, good mounsieur, bring me the
honey-bag. Do not fret yourself too much
in the action, mounsieur ; and, good
mounsieur, have a care the honey-bag
break not ; I would be loath to have you
overflowen with a honey-bag, signior.
Where's Mounsieur Mustardseed ?   16

Must. Ready.

Bot. Give me your neaf, Mounsieur
Mustardseed. Pray you, leave your
curtsy, good mounsieur.

Must. What's your will ?   20

Bot. Nothing, good mounsieur, but to
help Cavalery Cobweb to scratch. I must
to the barber's, mounsieur ; for methinks
I am marvellous hairy about the face ; and
I am such a tender ass, if my hair do but
tickle me I must scratch.   24

Tita. What, wilt thou hear some music,
my sweet love ?

Bot. I have a reasonable good ear in
music. Let's have the tongs and the
bones.

Tita. Or say, sweet love, what thou
desirest to eat.   28

Bot. Truly, a peck of provender ; I could
munch your good dry oats. Methinks I have
a great desire to a bottle of hay. Good hay,
sweet hay, hath no fellow.   31

Tita. I have a venturous fairy that shall
seek
The squirrel's hoard, and fetch thee new
nuts.

Bot. I had rather have a handful or two
of dried peas. But, I pray you, let none of
your people stir me ; I have an exposition
of sleep come upon me.   36

Tita. Sleep thou, and I will wind thee in
my arms.
Fairies, be gone, and be all ways away.
    [*Exeunt Fairies.*
So doth the woodbine the sweet honey-
suckle
Gently entwist ; the female ivy so   40
Enrings the barky fingers of the elm.
O, how I love thee ! how I dote on thee !
    [*They sleep.*

Enter PUCK.

Obe. [*Advancing*] Welcome, good Robin.
Seest thou this sweet sight ?
Her dotage now I do begin to pity ;   44
For, meeting her of late behind the wood,
Seeking sweet favours for this hateful fool,
I did upbraid her and fall out with her.
For she his hairy temples then had rounded

With coronet of fresh and fragrant flowers ;
And that same dew which sometime on the
buds   50
Was wont to swell like round and orient
pearls
Stood now within the pretty flowerets' eyes,
Like tears that did their own disgrace
bewail.   53
When I had at my pleasure taunted her,
And she in mild terms begg'd my patience,
I then did ask of her her changeling child ;
Which straight she gave me, and her fairy
sent
To bear him to my bower in fairy land.
And now I have the boy, I will undo
This hateful imperfection of her eyes.   60
And, gentle Puck, take this transformed
scalp
From off the head of this Athenian swain,
That he awaking when the other do
May all to Athens back again repair,   64
And think no more of this night's accidents
But as the fierce vexation of a dream.
But first I will release the Fairy Queen.
    [*Touching her eyes.*
Be as thou wast wont to be ;
See as thou was wont to see.
Dian's bud o'er Cupid's flower   70
Hath such force and blessed power.
Now, my Titania ; wake you, my sweet
queen.

Tita. My Oberon ! What visions have I
seen !
Methought I was enamour'd of an ass.   74

Obe. There lies your love.

Tita. How came these things to pass ?
O, how mine eyes do loathe his visage now !

Obe. Silence awhile. Robin, take off this
head.
Titania, music call ; and strike more dead
Than common sleep of all these five the
sense.

Tita. Music, ho, music, such as charmeth
sleep !   80

Puck. Now when thou wak'st with thine
own fool's eyes peep.

Obe. Sound, music. Come, my Queen,
take hands with me,   [*Music.*
And rock the ground whereon these sleepers
be.
Now thou and I are new in amity,
And will to-morrow midnight solemnly   85
Dance in Duke Theseus' house triumph-
antly,
And bless it to all fair prosperity.
There shall the pairs of faithful lovers be
Wedded, with Theseus, all in jollity.

Puck. Fairy King, attend and mark ;   90
I do hear the morning lark.

Obe. Then, my Queen, in silence sad,
Trip we after night's shade.
We the globe can compass soon,
Swifter than the wand'ring moon.

Tita. Come, my lord ; and in our flight,

Tell me how it came this night 97
That I sleeping here was found
With these mortals on the ground.
[*Exeunt.*

To the winding of horns, enter THESEUS,
HIPPOLYTA, EGEUS, *and* Train.

The. Go, one of you, find out the forester ;
For now our observation is perform'd, 101
And since we have the vaward of the day,
My love shall hear the music of my hounds.
Uncouple in the western valley ; let them
go.
Dispatch, I say, and find the forester. 105
[*Exit an attendant.*
We will, fair Queen, up to the mountain's
top,
And mark the musical confusion
Of hounds and echo in conjunction.
Hip. I was with Hercules and Cadmus
once
When in a wood of Crete they bay'd the
bear 110
With hounds of Sparta ; never did I hear
Such gallant chiding, for, besides the groves,
The skies, the fountains, every region near,
Seem'd all one mutual cry. I never heard
So musical a discord, such sweet thunder.
The. My hounds are bred out of the
Spartan kind, 116
So flew'd, so sanded ; and their heads are
hung
With ears that sweep away the morning
dew ;
Crook-knee'd and dew-lapp'd like Thes-
salian bulls ;
Slow in pursuit, but match'd in mouth like
bells, 120
Each under each. A cry more tuneable
Was never holla'd to, nor cheer'd with horn,
In Crete, in Sparta, nor in Thessaly.
Judge when you hear. But, soft, what
nymphs are these ?
Ege. My lord, this is my daughter here
asleep ; 125
And this Lysander, this Demetrius is,
This Helena, old Nedar's Helena.
I wonder of their being here together.
The. No doubt they rose up early to
observe 129
The rite of May ; and, hearing our intent,
Came here in grace of our solemnity.
But speak, Egeus ; is not this the day
That Hermia should give answer of her
choice ?
Ege. It is, my lord.
The. Go, bid the huntsmen wake them
with their horns. 135
[*Horns and shout within. The
sleepers awake and kneel to Theseus.*
Good-morrow, friends. Saint Valentine
is past ;
Begin these wood-birds but to couple now ?
Lys. Pardon, my lord.

The. I pray you all, stand up.
I know you two are rival enemies ;
How comes this gentle concord in the
world 140
That hatred is so far from jealousy
To sleep by hate, and fear no enmity ?
Lys. My lord, I shall reply amazedly,
Half sleep, half waking ; but as yet, I
swear,
I cannot truly say how I came here, 145
But, as I think—for truly would I speak,
And now I do bethink me, so it is—
I came with Hermia hither. Our intent
Was to be gone from Athens, where we
might,
Without the peril of the Athenian law— 150
Ege. Enough, enough, my Lord ; you
have enough ;
I beg the law, the law upon his head.
They would have stol'n away, they would,
Demetrius,
Thereby to have defeated you and me :
You of your wife, and me of my consent,
Of my consent that she should be your wife.
Dem. My lord, fair Helen told me of their
stealth,
Of this their purpose hither to this wood ;
And I in fury hither followed them,
Fair Helena in fancy following me. 160
But, my good lord, I wot not by what
power—
But by some power it is—my love to
Hermia,
Melted as the snow, seems to me now
As the remembrance of an idle gaud 164
Which in my childhood I did dote upon ;
And all the faith, the virtue of my heart,
The object and the pleasure of mine eye,
Is only Helena. To her, my lord, 168
Was I betroth'd ere I saw Hermia.
But, like a sickness, did I loathe this food ;
But, as in health, come to my natural taste,
Now I do wish it, love it, long for it, 172
And will for evermore be true to it.
The. Fair lovers, you are fortunately met ;
Of this discourse we more will hear anon.
Egeus, I will overbear your will ; 176
For in the temple, by and by, with us
These couples shall eternally be knit.
And, for the morning now is something
worn,
Our purpos'd hunting shall be set aside.
Away with us to Athens, three and three ;
We'll hold a feast in great solemnity. 182
Come, Hippolyta. [*Exeunt Theseus, Hip-
polyta, Egeus and Train.*
Dem. These things seem small and un-
distinguishable, 184
Like far-off mountains turned into clouds.
Her. Methinks I see these things with
parted eye,
When every thing seems double.
Hel. So methinks ;
And I have found Demetrius like a jewel,

Mine own, and not mine own.

Dem.   Are you sure
That we are awake? It seems to me   190
That yet we sleep, we dream. Do not you
    think
The Duke was here, and bid us follow him?

Her. Yea, and my father.

Hel.   And Hippolyta.

Lys. And he did bid us follow to the
    temple.

Dem. Why, then, we are awake; let's
    follow him;   195
And by the way let us recount our dreams.
                              [*Exeunt.*

Bot. [*Awaking*] When my cue comes, call
me, and I will answer. My next is 'Most
fair Pyramus'. Heigh-ho! Peter Quince!
Flute, the bellows-mender! Snout, the
tinker! Starveling! God's my life, stol'n
hence, and left me asleep! I have had
a most rare vision. I have had a dream,
past the wit of man to say what dream
it was. Man is but an ass if he go
about to expound this dream. Methought
I was—there is no man can tell what.
Methought I was, and methought I had,
but man is but a patch'd fool, if he will
offer to say what methought I had. The
eye of man hath not heard, the ear of man
hath not seen, man's hand is not able to
taste, his tongue to conceive, nor his heart
to report, what my dream was. I will get
Peter Quince to write a ballad of this
dream. It shall be call'd 'Bottom's Dream',
because it hath no bottom; and I will sing
it in the latter end of a play, before the
Duke. Peradventure, to make it the more
gracious, I shall sing it at her death. [*Exit.*

SCENE II. *Athens. Quince's house.*

Enter QUINCE, FLUTE, SNOUT, *and*
STARVELING.

Quin. Have you sent to Bottom's house?
Is he come home yet?

Star. He cannot be heard of. Out of
doubt he is transported.

Flu. If he come not, then the play is
marr'd; it goes not forward, doth it?   6

Quin. It is not possible. You have not
a man in all Athens able to discharge
Pyramus but he.

Flu. No; he hath simply the best wit of
any handicraft man in Athens.   10

Quin. Yea, and the best person too; and
he is a very paramour for a sweet voice.

Flu. You must say 'paragon'. A paramour is—God bless us!—a thing of
naught.   14

Enter SNUG.

Snug. Masters, the Duke is coming from
the temple; and there is two or three lords

and ladies more married. If our sport had
gone forward, we had all been made men.   17

Flu. O sweet bully Bottom! Thus hath
he lost sixpence a day during his life; he
could not have scaped sixpence a day. An
the Duke had not given him sixpence a day
for playing Pyramus, I'll be hanged. He
would have deserved it: sixpence a day in
Pyramus, or nothing.   22

Enter BOTTOM.

Bot. Where are these lads? Where are
these hearts?

Quin. Bottom! O most courageous day!
O most happy hour!   25

Bot. Masters, I am to discourse wonders;
but ask me not what; for if I tell you, I am
not true Athenian. I will tell you everything, right as it fell out.

Quin. Let us hear, sweet Bottom.   29

Bot. Not a word of me. All that I will
tell you is, that the Duke hath dined. Get
your apparel together; good strings to
your beards, new ribbons to your pumps;
meet presently at the palace; every man
look o'er his part; for the short and the
long is, our play is preferr'd. In any case,
let Thisby have clean linen; and let not
him that plays the lion pare his nails, for
they shall hang out for the lion's claws.
And, most dear actors, eat no onions nor
garlic, for we are to utter sweet breath;
and I do not doubt but to hear them say
it is a sweet comedy. No more words.
Away, go, away!   [*Exeunt.*

ACT FIVE

SCENE I. *Athens. The palace of Theseus.*

Enter THESEUS, HIPPOLYTA, PHILOSTRATE,
    Lords *and* Attendants.

Hip. 'Tis strange, my Theseus, that these
    lovers speak of.

The. More strange than true. I never may
    believe
These antique fables, nor these fairy toys.
Lovers and madmen have such seething
    brains,
Such shaping fantasies, that apprehend   5
More than cool reason ever comprehends.
The lunatic, the lover, and the poet,
Are of imagination all compact.
One sees more devils than vast hell can
    hold:
That is the madman. The lover, all as
    frantic,   10
Sees Helen's beauty in a brow of Egypt.
The poet's eye, in a fine frenzy rolling,
Doth glance from heaven to earth, from
    earth to heaven;
And as imagination bodies forth
The forms of things unknown, the poet's
    pen   15

Turns them to shapes, and gives to airy
    nothing
A local habitation and a name.
Such tricks hath strong imagination
That, if it would but apprehend some joy,
It comprehends some bringer of that joy ;
Or in the night, imagining some fear,   21
How easy is a bush suppos'd a bear ?
  Hip. But all the story of the night told
    over,
And all their minds transfigur'd so together,
More witnesseth than fancy's images,   25
And grows to something of great constancy,
But howsoever strange and admirable.

Enter LYSANDER, DEMETRIUS, HERMIA,
  and HELENA.

  The. Here come the lovers, full of joy and
    mirth.
Joy, gentle friends, joy and fresh days of
    love
Accompany your hearts !
  Lys.   More than to us   30
Wait in your royal walks, your board, your
    bed !
  The. Come now ; what masques, what
    dances shall we have,
To wear away this long age of three hours
Between our after-supper and bed-time ?
Where is our usual manager of mirth ?   35
What revels are in hand ? Is there no play
To ease the anguish of a torturing hour ?
Call Philostrate.
  Phil.   Here, mighty Theseus.
  The. Say, what abridgment have you for
    this evening ?
What masque ? what music ? How shall we
    beguile   40
The lazy time, if not with some delight ?
  Phil. There is a brief how many sports
    are ripe ;
Make choice of which your Highness will
    see first.   [*Giving a paper.*
  The. ' The battle with the Centaurs,
    to be sung
By an Athenian eunuch to the harp.'   45
We'll none of that : that have I told my
    love,
In glory of my kinsman Hercules.
' The riot of the tipsy Bacchanals,
Tearing the Thracian singer in their rage.'
That is an old device, and it was play'd 50
When I from Thebes came last a conqueror.
' The thrice three Muses mourning for the
    death
Of Learning, late deceas'd in beggary.'
That is some satire, keen and critical,   55
Not sorting with a nuptial ceremony.
' A tedious brief scene of young Pyramus
And his love Thisby ; very tragical mirth.'
Merry and tragical ! tedious and brief !
That is hot ice and wondrous strange snow.
How shall we find the concord of this dis-
    cord ?   60

  Phil. A play there is, my lord, some ten
    words long,
Which is as brief as I have known a play ;
But by ten words, my lord, it is too long,
Which makes it tedious ; for in all the
    play
There is not one word apt, one player fitted.
And tragical, my noble lord, it is ;   66
For Pyramus therein doth kill himself.
Which when I saw rehears'd, I must confess,
Made mine eyes water ; but more merry
    tears
The passion of loud laughter never shed. 70
  The. What are they that do play it ?
  Phil. Hard-handed men that work in
    Athens here,
Which never labour'd in their minds till
    now ;
And now have toil'd their unbreathed
    memories   74
With this same play against your nuptial.
  The. And we will hear it.
  Phil.   No, my noble lord,
It is not for you. I have heard it over,
And it is nothing, nothing in the world ;
Unless you can find sport in their intents,
Extremely stretch'd and conn'd with cruel
    pain,   80
To do you service.
  The.   I will hear that play ;
For never anything can be amiss
When simpleness and duty tender it.
Go, bring them in ; and take your places,
    ladies.   [*Exit Philostrate.*
  Hip. I love not to see wretchedness o'er-
    charged,   85
And duty in his service perishing.
  The. Why, gentle sweet, you shall see no
    such thing.
  Hip. He says they can do nothing in this
    kind.
  The. The kinder we, to give them thanks
    for nothing.
Our sport shall be to take what they
    mistake ;   90
And what poor duty cannot do, noble
    respect
Takes it in might, not merit.
Where I have come, great clerks have
    purposed
To greet me with premeditated welcomes ;
Where I have seen them shiver and look
    pale,   95
Make periods in the midst of sentences,
Throttle their practis'd accent in their fears,
And, in conclusion, dumbly have broke off,
Not paying me a welcome.   Trust me,
    sweet,   99
Out of this silence yet I pick'd a welcome ;
And in the modesty of fearful duty
I read as much as from the rattling tongue
Of saucy and audacious eloquence.
Love, therefore, and tongue-tied simplicity
In least speak most to my capacity.   105

Re-enter PHILOSTRATE.

Phil. So please your Grace, the Prologue
is address'd.
The. Let him approach.

[*Flourish of trumpets.*

Enter QUINCE *as the* PROLOGUE.

Prol. If we offend, it is with our good will.
That you should think, we come not to offend,
But with good will. To show our simple skill,
That is the true beginning of our end.   111
Consider then, we come but in despite.
We do not come, as minding to content you,
Our true intent is. All for your delight
We are not here. That you should here repent
    you,   115
The actors are at hand ; and, by their show,
You shall know all, that you are like to know.
The. This fellow doth not stand upon
points.
Lys. He hath rid his prologue like a rough
colt ; he knows not the stop. A good moral
my lord : it is not enough to speak, but to
speak true.   121
Hip. Indeed he hath play'd on this
prologue like a child on a recorder—a
sound, but not in government.
The. His speech was like a tangled chain ;
nothing impaired, but all disordered. Who
is next ?   125

Enter, with a Trumpet before them, as in
dumb show, PYRAMUS *and* THISBY, WALL,
MOONSHINE, *and* LION.

Prol. Gentles, perchance you wonder at
    this show ;
But wonder on, till truth make all things
    plain.
This man is Pyramus, if you would know ;
This beauteous lady Thisby is certain.
This man, with lime and rough-cast, doth
    present   130
Wall, that vile Wall which did these lovers
    sunder ;
And through Wall's chink, poor souls, they
    are content
To whisper. At the which let no man wonder.
This man, with lanthorn, dog, and bush of
    thorn,   134
Presenteth Moonshine ; for, if you will know,
By moonshine did these lovers think no scorn
To meet at Ninus' tomb, there, there to woo.
This grisly beast, which Lion hight by name,
The trusty Thisby, coming first by night,
Did scare away, or rather did affright ;   140
And as she fled, her mantle she did fall ;
Which Lion vile with bloody mouth did stain.
Anon comes Pyramus, sweet youth and tall,
And finds his trusty Thisby's mantle slain ;
Whereat with blade, with bloody blameful
    blade,   145
He bravely broach'd his boiling bloody breast ;
And Thisby, tarrying in mulberry shade,

His dagger drew, and died. For all the rest,
Let Lion, Moonshine, Wall, and lovers twain,
At large discourse while here they do remain.

[*Exeunt Prologue, Pyramus, Thisby,*
        Lion, and Moonshine.

The. I wonder if the lion be to speak.
Dem. No wonder, my lord : one lion may,
when many asses do.   153
Wall. In this same interlude it doth befall
That I, one Snout by name, present a wall ;
And such a wall as I would have you think
That had in it a crannied hole or chink,   157
Through which the lovers, Pyramus and
    Thisby,
Did whisper often very secretly.
This loam, this rough-cast, and this stone,
    doth show   160
That I am that same wall ; the truth is so ;
And this the cranny is, right and sinister,
Through which the fearful lovers are to
    whisper.
The. Would you desire lime and hair to
speak better ?
Dem. It is the wittiest partition that ever
I heard discourse, my lord.   166

Enter PYRAMUS.

The. Pyramus draws near the wall ;
silence.
Pyr. O grim-look'd night ! O night with
    hue so black !
O night, which ever art when day is not !
O night, O night, alack, alack, alack,   170
I fear my Thisby's promise is forgot !
And thou, O wall, O sweet, O lovely wall,
That stand'st between her father's ground and
    mine ;
Thou wall, O wall, O sweet and lovely wall,
Show me thy chink, to blink through with
    mine eyne.   175

[*Wall holds up his fingers.*

Thanks, courteous wall. Jove shield thee well
    for this !
But what see I ? No Thisby do I see.
O wicked wall, through whom I see no bliss ;
Curs'd be thy stones for thus deceiving me !
The. The wall, methinks, being sensible,
should curse again.   181
Pyr. No, in truth, sir, he should not.
Deceiving me is Thisby's cue. She is to
enter now, and I am to spy her through the
wall. You shall see it will fall pat as I told
you ; yonder she comes.   185

Enter THISBY.

This. O wall, full often hast thou heard my
    moans,
For parting my fair Pyramus and me !
My cherry lips have often kiss'd thy stones,
Thy stones with lime and hair knit up in thee.
Pyr. I see a voice ; now will I to the chink,
To spy an I can hear my Thisby's face.   191
Thisby !
This. My love ! thou art my love, I think.

Pyr. Think what thou wilt, I am thy lover's
    grace ;
And like Limander am I trusty still.   195
  This. And I like Helen, till the Fates me
    kill.
Pyr. Not Shafalus to Procrus was so true.
This. As Shafalus to Procrus, I to you.
Pyr. O, kiss me through the hole of this
    vile wall.
This. I kiss the wall's hole, not your lips
    at all.   200
Pyr. Wilt thou at Ninny's tomb meet me
    straightway ?
This. Tide life, tide death, I come without
    delay.
            [*Exeunt Pyramus and Thisby.*
Wall. Thus have I, Wall, my part dis-
    charged so ;
And, being done, thus Wall away doth go.
                    [*Exit Wall.*
The. Now is the moon used between the
two neighbours.   206
Dem. No remedy, my lord, when walls
are so wilful to hear without warning.
Hip. This is the silliest stuff that ever I
heard.
The. The best in this kind are but
shadows ; and the worst are no worse, if
imagination amend them.   211
Hip. It must be your imagination then,
and not theirs.
The. If we imagine no worse of them than
they of themselves, they may pass for excellent men. Here come two noble beasts
in, a man and a lion.   215

      Enter LION *and* MOONSHINE.

Lion. You, ladies, you, whose gentle hearts
    do fear
The smallest monstrous mouse that creeps on
    floor,
May now, perchance, both quake and
    tremble here,
When lion rough in wildest rage doth
    roar.
Then know that I as Snug the joiner am   220
A lion fell, nor else no lion's dam ;
For, if I should as lion come in strife
Into this place, 'twere pity on my life.
The. A very gentle beast, and of a good
conscience.
Dem. The very best at a beast, my lord,
that e'er I saw.   225
Lys. This lion is a very fox for his valour.
The. True ; and a goose for his discretion.
Dem. Not so, my lord ; for his valour
cannot carry his discretion, and the fox
carries the goose.
The. His discretion, I am sure, cannot
carry his valour ; for the goose carries not
the fox. It is well. Leave it to his discretion,
and let us listen to the Moon.   232
Moon. This lanthorn doth the horned moon
    present—

Dem. He should have worn the horns on
his head.
The. He is no crescent, and his horns are
invisible within the circumference.   236
Moon. This lanthorn doth the horned moon
    present ;
Myself the Man i' th' Moon do seem to be.
The. This is the greatest error of all the
rest ; the man should be put into the
lantern. How is it else the man i' th' moon ?
Dem. He dares not come there for the
candle ; for, you see, it is already in snuff.
Hip. I am aweary of this moon. Would
he would change !   245
The. It appears, by his small light of
discretion, that he is in the wane ; but yet,
in courtesy, in all reason, we must stay the
time.
Lys. Proceed, Moon.   249
Moon. All that I have to say is to tell
you that the lanthorn is the moon ; I, the
Man i' th' Moon ; this thorn-bush, my
thorn-bush ; and this dog, my dog.
Dem. Why, all these should be in the
lantern ; for all these are in the moon. But
silence ; here comes Thisby.

          Re-enter THISBY.

This. This is old Ninny's tomb. Where is
    my love ?   255
Lion. [*Roaring*] O—   [*Thisby runs off.*
Dem. Well roar'd, Lion.
The. Well run, Thisby.
Hip. Well shone, Moon. Truly, the moon
shines with a good grace.   260
     [*The Lion tears Thisby's mantle, and exit.*
The. Well mous'd, Lion.

          Re-enter PYRAMUS.

Dem. And then came Pyramus.
Lys. And so the lion vanish'd.
Pyr. Sweet Moon, I thank thee for thy
    sunny beams ;
I thank thee, Moon, for shining now so
    bright ;   265
For, by thy gracious, golden, glittering gleams,
I trust to take of truest Thisby sight.
        But stay, O spite !
        But mark, poor knight,
    What dreadful dole is here !   270
        Eyes, do you see ?
        How can it be ?
    O dainty duck ! O dear !
        Thy mantle good,
        What ! stain'd with blood ?   275
    Approach, ye Furies fell.
        O Fates ! come, come ;
        Cut thread and thrum ;
    Quail, crush, conclude, and quell.
The. This passion, and the death of a
dear friend, would go near to make a man
look sad.   281
Hip. Beshrew my heart, but I pity the
man.

Pyr. O wherefore, Nature, didst thou lions
    frame ?
Since lion vile hath here deflower'd my dear ;
Which is—no, no—which was the fairest
    dame	285
That liv'd, that lov'd, that lik'd, that look'd
    with cheer.
    Come, tears, confound ;
    Out, sword, and wound
The pap of Pyramus ;
    Ay, that left pap,	290
    Where heart doth hop.
                        [*Stabs himself.*
Thus die I, thus, thus, thus.
    Now am I dead,
    Now am I fled ;
My soul is in the sky.	295
    Tongue, lose thy light ;
    Moon, take thy flight.
                        [*Exit Moonshine.*
Now die, die, die, die, die.   [*Dies.*
    Dem. No die, but an ace, for him ; for he
is but one.	299
    Lys. Less than an ace, man ; for he is
dead ; he is nothing.
    The. With the help of a surgeon he might
yet recover and yet prove an ass.
    Hip. How chance Moonshine is gone
before Thisby comes back and finds her
lover ?	305

                Re-enter THISBY.

    The. She will find him by starlight. Here
she comes ; and her passion ends the play.
    Hip. Methinks she should not use a long
one for such a Pyramus ; I hope she will be
brief.	309
    Dem. A mote will turn the balance, which
Pyramus, which Thisby, is the better—he
for a man, God warrant us : she for a
woman, God bless us !
    Lys. She hath spied him already with
those sweet eyes.
    Dem. And thus she moans, videlicet :—
    This. *Asleep, my love ?*	315
        What, dead, my dove ?
    O Pyramus, arise,
        Speak, speak. Quite dumb ?
        Dead, dead ? A tomb
    Must cover thy sweet eyes.	320
        These lily lips,
        This cherry nose,
    These yellow cowslip cheeks,
        Are gone, are gone ;
        Lovers, make moan ;	325
    His eyes were green as leeks.
        O Sisters Three,
        Come, come to me,
    With hands as pale as milk ;
        Lay them in gore,	330
        Since you have shore
    With shears his thread of silk.
        Tongue, not a word.
        Come, trusty sword ;

    Come, blade, my breast imbrue.	335
                        [*Stabs herself.*
        And farewell, friends ;
        Thus Thisby ends ;
    Adieu, adieu, adieu.   [*Dies.*
    The. Moonshine and Lion are left to bury
the dead.
    Dem. Ay, and Wall too.	340
    Bot. [*Starting up*] No, I assure you ; the
wall is down that parted their fathers. Will
it please you to see the Epilogue, or to hear
a Bergomask dance between two of our
company ?	344
    The. No epilogue, I pray you ; for your
play needs no excuse. Never excuse ; for
when the players are all dead there need
none to be blamed. Marry, if he that writ
it had played Pyramus, and hang'd himself
in Thisby's garter, it would have been a
fine tragedy. And so it is, truly ; and very
notably discharg'd. But come, your Bergomask ; let your epilogue alone. [*A dance.*
The iron tongue of midnight hath told
    twelve.	352
Lovers, to bed ; 'tis almost fairy time.
I fear we shall out-sleep the coming morn,
As much as we this night have overwatch'd.
This palpable-gross play hath well beguil'd
The heavy gait of night. Sweet friends, to
    bed.	357
A fortnight hold we this solemnity,
In nightly revels and new jollity. [*Exeunt.*

            Enter PUCK *with a broom.*

Puck. Now the hungry lion roars,	360
    And the wolf behowls the moon ;
    Whilst the heavy ploughman snores,
    All with weary task fordone.
    Now the wasted brands do glow,
    Whilst the screech-owl, screeching loud,
    Puts the wretch that lies in woe	366
    In remembrance of a shroud.
    Now it is the time of night
    That the graves, all gaping wide,
    Every one lets forth his sprite,	370
    In the church-way paths to glide.
    And we fairies, that do run
    By the triple Hecate's team
    From the presence of the sun,
    Following darkness like a dream,	375
    Now are frolic. Not a mouse
    Shall disturb this hallowed house.
    I am sent with broom before,
    To sweep the dust behind the door.

Enter OBERON *and* TITANIA, *with all their*
            Train.

Obe. Through the house give glimmering
    light,	380
    By the dead and drowsy fire ;
    Every elf and fairy sprite
    Hop as light as bird from brier ;
    And this ditty, after me,
    Sing and dance it trippingly.	385

Tita. First, rehearse your song by rote,
  To each word a warbling note ;
  Hand in hand, with fairy grace,
  Will we sing, and bless this place.

Oberon leading, the Fairies sing and dance.

Obe. Now, until the break of day,   390
  Through this house each fairy stray.
  To the best bride-bed will we,
  Which by us shall blessed be ;
  And the issue there create
  Ever shall be fortunate.   395
  So shall all the couples three
  Ever true in loving be ;
  And the blots of Nature's hand
  Shall not in their issue stand ;
  Never mole, hare-lip, nor scar,   400
  Nor mark prodigious, such as are
  Despised in nativity,
  Shall upon their children be.
  With this field-dew consecrate,
  Every fairy take his gait,   405
  And each several chamber bless,

  Through this palace, with sweet peace ;
  And the owner of it blest
  Ever shall in safety rest.
  Trip away ; make no stay ;   410
  Meet me all by break of day.
        [Exeunt all but Puck.

Puck. If we shadows have offended,
  Think but this, and all is mended,
  That you have but slumb'red here
  While these visions did appear.   415
  And this weak and idle theme,
  No more yielding but a dream,
  Gentles, do not reprehend.
  If you pardon, we will mend.
  And, as I am an honest Puck,   420
  If we have unearned luck
  Now to scape the serpent's tongue,
  We will make amends ere long ;
  Else the Puck a liar call.
  So, good night unto you all.   425
  Give me your hands, if we be friends,
  And Robin shall restore amends.
        [Exit.

THE MERCHANT OF VENICE

DRAMATIS PERSONÆ

THE DUKE OF VENICE.

THE PRINCE OF MOROCCO, } suitors to
THE PRINCE OF ARRAGON, } *Portia.*

ANTONIO, *a merchant of Venice.*

BASSANIO, *his friend, suitor to Portia.*

SOLANIO, }
SALERIO, } *friends to Antonio and*
GRATIANO, } *Bassanio.*

LORENZO, *in love with Jessica.*

SHYLOCK, *a rich Jew.*

TUBAL, *a Jew, his friend.*

LAUNCELOT GOBBO, *a clown, servant to Shylock.*

OLD GOBBO, *father to Launcelot.*

LEONARDO, *servant to Bassanio.*

BALTHASAR, } *servants to Portia.*
STEPHANO, }

PORTIA, *a rich heiress.*

NERISSA, *her waiting-maid.*

JESSICA, *daughter to Shylock.*

Magnificoes of Venice, Officers of the Court of Justice, Gaoler, Servants, *and other* Attendants.

THE SCENE : *Venice, and Portia's house at Belmont.*

ACT ONE

SCENE I. *Venice. A street.*

Enter ANTONIO, SALERIO, *and* SOLANIO.

Ant. In sooth, I know not why I am so sad.
It wearies me ; you say it wearies you ;
But how I caught it, found it, or came by it,
What stuff 'tis made of, whereof it is born,
I am to learn ;   5
And such a want-wit sadness makes of me
That I have much ado to know myself.
Saler. Your mind is tossing on the ocean ;
There where your argosies, with portly sail—   9
Like signiors and rich burghers on the flood,
Or as it were the pageants of the sea—
Do overpeer the petty traffickers,
That curtsy to them, do them reverence,
As they fly by them with their woven wings.
Solan. Believe me, sir, had I such venture forth,   15
The better part of my affections would
Be with my hopes abroad. I should be still
Plucking the grass to know where sits the wind,
Peering in maps for ports, and piers, and roads;   19
And every object that might make me fear
Misfortune to my ventures, out of doubt,
Would make me sad.
Saler.   My wind, cooling my broth,
Would blow me to an ague when I thought
What harm a wind too great might do at sea.   24
I should not see the sandy hour-glass run
But I should think of shallows and of flats,
And see my wealthy Andrew dock'd in sand,
Vailing her high top lower than her ribs
To kiss her burial. Should I go to church
And see the holy edifice of stone,   30
And not bethink me straight of dangerous rocks,
Which, touching but my gentle vessel's side,
Would scatter all her spices on the stream,
Enrobe the roaring waters with my silks,
And, in a word, but even now worth this,
And now worth nothing ? Shall I have the thought   35
To think on this, and shall I lack the thought
That such a thing bechanc'd would make me sad ?
But tell not me ; I know Antonio
Is sad to think upon his merchandise.   40
Ant. Believe me, no ; I thank my fortune for it,
My ventures are not in one bottom trusted,
Nor to one place ; nor is my whole estate
Upon the fortune of this present year ;
Therefore my merchandise makes me not sad.   45
Solan. Why then you are in love.
Ant.   Fie, fie !
Solan. Not in love neither ? Then let us say you are sad
Because you are not merry ; and 'twere as easy
For you to laugh and leap and say you are merry,
Because you are not sad. Now, by two-headed Janus,   50
Nature hath fram'd strange fellows in her time :
Some that will evermore peep through their eyes,
And laugh like parrots at a bag-piper ;
And other of such vinegar aspect

That they'll not show their teeth in way of smile 55
Though Nestor swear the jest be laughable.

Enter BASSANIO, LORENZO, *and* GRATIANO.

Here comes Bassanio, your most noble kinsman,
Gratiano and Lorenzo. Fare ye well;
We leave you now with better company.
 Saler. I would have stay'd till I had made you merry, 60
If worthier friends had not prevented me.
 Ant. Your worth is very dear in my regard.
I take it your own business calls on you,
And you embrace th' occasion to depart.
 Saler. Good morrow, my good lords. 65
 Bass. Good signiors both, when shall we laugh? Say when.
You grow exceeding strange; must it be so?
 Saler. We'll make our leisures to attend on yours.
                    [*Exeunt Salerio and Solanio.*
 Lor. My Lord Bassanio, since you have found Antonio, 69
We two will leave you; but at dinner-time,
I pray you, have in mind where we must meet.
 Bass. I will not fail you.
 Gra. You look not well, Signior Antonio;
You have too much respect upon the world;
They lose it that do buy it with much care. 75
Believe me, you are marvellously chang'd.
 Ant. I hold the world but as the world, Gratiano—
A stage, where every man must play a part,
And mine a sad one.
 Gra.   Let me play the fool.
With mirth and laughter let old wrinkles come; 80
And let my liver rather heat with wine
Than my heart cool with mortifying groans.
Why should a man whose blood is warm within
Sit like his grandsire cut in alabaster,
Sleep when he wakes, and creep into the jaundice 85
By being peevish? I tell thee what, Antonio—
I love thee, and 'tis my love that speaks—
There are a sort of men whose visages
Do cream and mantle like a standing pond,
And do a wilful stillness entertain, 90
With purpose to be dress'd in an opinion
Of wisdom, gravity, profound conceit;
As who should say 'I am Sir Oracle,
And when I ope my lips let no dog bark'.
O my Antonio, I do know of these 95
That therefore only are reputed wise
For saying nothing; when, I am very sure,
If they should speak, would almost damn those ears

Which, hearing them, would call their brothers fools.
I'll tell thee more of this another time. 100
But fish not with this melancholy bait
For this fool gudgeon, this opinion.
Come, good Lorenzo. Fare ye well awhile;
I'll end my exhortation after dinner.
 Lor. Well, we will leave you then till dinner-time. 105
I must be one of these same dumb wise men,
For Gratiano never lets me speak.
 Gra. Well, keep me company but two years moe,
Thou shalt not know the sound of thine own tongue.
 Ant. Fare you well; I'll grow a talker for this gear. 110
 Gra. Thanks, i' faith, for silence is only commendable
In a neat's tongue dried, and a maid not vendible.
                 [*Exeunt Gratiano and Lorenzo.*
 Ant. Is that anything now? 113
 Bass. Gratiano speaks an infinite deal of nothing, more than any man in all Venice. His reasons are as two grains of wheat hid in two bushels of chaff: you shall seek all day ere you find them, and when you have them they are not worth the search. 118
 Ant. Well; tell me now what lady is the same
To whom you swore a secret pilgrimage, 120
That you to-day promis'd to tell me of?
 Bass. 'Tis not unknown to you, Antonio,
How much I have disabled mine estate
By something showing a more swelling port
Than my faint means would grant continuance; 125
Nor do I now make moan to be abridg'd
From such a noble rate; but my chief care
Is to come fairly off from the great debts
Wherein my time, something too prodigal,
Hath left me gag'd. To you, Antonio, 130
I owe the most, in money and in love;
And from your love I have a warranty
To unburden all my plots and purposes
How to get clear of all the debts I owe.
 Ant. I pray you, good Bassanio, let me know it; 135
And if it stand, as you yourself still do,
Within the eye of honour, be assur'd
My purse, my person, my extremest means,
Lie all unlock'd to your occasions.
 Bass. In my school-days, when I had lost one shaft, 140
I shot his fellow of the self-same flight
The self-same way, with more advised watch,
To find the other forth; and by adventuring both
I oft found both. I urge this childhood proof,
Because what follows is pure innocence. 145

I owe you much ; and, like a wilful youth,
That which I owe is lost ; but if you please
To shoot another arrow that self way
Which you did shoot the first, I do not
    doubt,
As I will watch the aim, or to find both, 150
Or bring your latter hazard back again
And thankfully rest debtor for the first.

Ant. You know me well, and herein spend
    but time
To wind about my love with circumstance ;
And out of doubt you do me now more
    wrong   155
In making question of my uttermost
Than if you had made waste of all I have.
Then do but say to me what I should do
That in your knowledge may by me be
    done,   159
And I am prest unto it ; therefore, speak.

Bass. In Belmont is a lady richly left,
And she is fair and, fairer than that
    word,
Of wondrous virtues. Sometimes from her
    eyes
I did receive fair speechless messages. 164
Her name is Portia—nothing undervalu'd
To Cato's daughter, Brutus' Portia.
Nor is the wide world ignorant of her
    worth ;
For the four winds blow in from every coast
Renowned suitors, and her sunny locks
Hang on her temples like a golden fleece,
Which makes her seat of Belmont Colchos'
    strond,   171
And many Jasons come in quest of her.
O my Antonio, had I but the means
To hold a rival place with one of them,
I have a mind presages me such thrift 175
That I should questionless be fortunate.

Ant. Thou know'st that all my fortunes
    are at sea ;
Neither have I money nor commodity
To raise a present sum ; therefore go forth,
Try what my credit can in Venice do ; 180
That shall be rack'd, even to the uttermost,
To furnish thee to Belmont to fair Portia.
Go presently inquire, and so will I,
Where money is ; and I no question make
To have it of my trust or for my sake. 185
                                [Exeunt.

SCENE II. *Belmont. Portia's house.*

Enter PORTIA *with her waiting-woman,*
NERISSA.

Por. By my troth, Nerissa, my little body
is aweary of this great world.

Ner. You would be, sweet madam, if
your miseries were in the same abundance
as your good fortunes are ; and yet, for
aught I see, they are as sick that surfeit
with too much as they that starve with
nothing. It is no mean happiness, therefore, to be seated in the mean : superfluity

comes sooner by white hairs, but competency lives longer.

Por. Good sentences, and well pronounc'd.

Ner. They would be better, if well 10
followed.

Por. If to do were as easy as to know
what were good to do, chapels had been
churches, and poor men's cottages princes'
palaces. It is a good divine that follows his
own instructions ; I can easier teach
twenty what were good to be done than
to be one of the twenty to follow mine own
teaching. The brain may devise laws for
the blood, but a hot temper leaps o'er a
cold decree ; such a hare is madness the
youth, to skip o'er the meshes of good
counsel the cripple. But this reasoning is
not in the fashion to choose me a husband.
O me, the word ' choose '! I may neither
choose who I would nor refuse who I
dislike ; so is the will of a living daughter
curb'd by the will of a dead father. Is it
not hard, Nerissa, that I cannot choose one,
nor refuse none ?   23

Ner. Your father was ever virtuous, and
holy men at their death have good inspira-
tions ; therefore the lott'ry that he hath
devised in these three chests, of gold, silver,
and lead—whereof who chooses his meaning chooses you—will no doubt never be
chosen by any rightly but one who you
shall rightly love. But what warmth is
there in your affection towards any of these
princely suitors that are already come ? 31

Por. I pray thee over-name them ; and
as thou namest them, I will describe them ;
and according to my description, level at my
affection.   34

Ner. First, there is the Neapolitan prince.

Por. Ay, that's a colt indeed, for he doth
nothing but talk of his horse ; and he
makes it a great appropriation to his own
good parts that he can shoe him himself ;
I am much afear'd my lady his mother
play'd false with a smith.   39

Ner. Then is there the County Palatine.

Por. He doth nothing but frown, as who
should say 'An you will not have me,
choose '. He hears merry tales and smiles
not. I fear he will prove the weeping
philosopher when he grows old, being so
full of unmannerly sadness in his youth.
I had rather be married to a death's-head
with a bone in his mouth than to either of
these. God defend me from these two !

Ner. How say you by the French lord,
Monsieur Le Bon ?   49

Por. God made him, and therefore let
him pass for a man. In truth, I know it is
a sin to be a mocker, but he—why, he hath
a horse better than the Neapolitan's, a
better bad habit of frowning than the
Count Palatine ; he is every man in no

man. If a throstle sing he falls straight a-
cap'ring; he will fence with his own
shadow; if I should marry him, I should
marry twenty husbands. If he would
despise me, I would forgive him; for if
he love me to madness, I shall never requite
him.

Ner. What say you then to Falconbridge,
the young baron of England? 60

Por. You know I say nothing to him, for
he understands not me, nor I him: he
hath neither Latin, French, nor Italian,
and you will come into the court and swear
that I have a poor pennyworth in the
English. He is a proper man's picture;
but, alas, who can converse with a dumb-
show? How oddly he is suited! I think
he bought his doublet in Italy, his round
hose in France, his bonnet in Germany, and
his behaviour everywhere. 68

Ner. What think you of the Scottish lord,
his neighbour?

Por. That he hath a neighbourly charity
in him, for he borrowed a box of the ear of
the Englishman, and swore he would pay
him again when he was able; I think the
Frenchman became his surety, and seal'd
under for another.

Ner. How like you the young German,
the Duke of Saxony's nephew? 75

Por. Very vilely in the morning when he
is sober; and most vilely in the afternoon
when he is drunk. When he is best, he is a
little worse than a man, and when he is
worst, he is little better than a beast. An
the worst fall that ever fell, I hope I shall
make shift to go without him. 80

Ner. If he should offer to choose, and
choose the right casket, you should refuse
to perform your father's will, if you should
refuse to accept him. 83

Por. Therefore, for fear of the worst, I
pray thee set a deep glass of Rhenish wine
on the contrary casket; for if the devil be
within and that temptation without, I
know he will choose it. I will do anything,
Nerissa, ere I will be married to a sponge.

Ner. You need not fear, lady, the having
any of these lords; they have acquainted
me with their determinations, which is
indeed to return to their home, and to
trouble you with no more suit, unless you
may be won by some other sort than your
father's imposition, depending on the
caskets. 94

Por. If I live to be as old as Sibylla, I
will die as chaste as Diana, unless I be
obtained by the manner of my father's will.
I am glad this parcel of wooers are so
reasonable; for there is not one among
them but I dote on his very absence, and
I pray God grant them a fair departure. 99

Ner. Do you not remember, lady, in your
father's time, a Venetian, a scholar and a
soldier, that came hither in company of the
Marquis of Montferrat?

Por. Yes, yes, it was Bassanio; as I
think, so was he call'd. 104

Ner. True, madam; he, of all the men
that ever my foolish eyes look'd upon, was
the best deserving a fair lady.

Por. I remember him well, and I remember him worthy of thy praise.

Enter a Servingman.

How now! what news? 109

Serv. The four strangers seek for you,
madam, to take their leave; and there is
a forerunner come from a fifth, the Prince
of Morocco, who brings word the Prince
his master will be here to-night. 113

Por. If I could bid the fifth welcome with
so good heart as I can bid the other four
farewell, I should be glad of his approach;
if he have the condition of a saint and the
complexion of a devil, I had rather he
should shrive me than wive me. 118
Come, Nerissa. Sirrah, go before.
Whiles we shut the gate upon one wooer,
    another knocks at the door. [*Exeunt.*

SCENE III. *Venice. A public place.*

Enter BASSANIO *with* SHYLOCK *the Jew.*

Shy. Three thousand ducats—well.

Bass. Ay, sir, for three months.

Shy. For three months—well.

Bass. For the which, as I told you,
Antonio shall be bound. 5

Shy. Antonio shall become bound—well.

Bass. May you stead me? Will you
pleasure me? Shall I know your answer?

Shy. Three thousand ducats for three
months, and Antonio bound. 10

Bass. Your answer to that.

Shy. Antonio is a good man.

Bass. Have you heard any imputation to
the contrary?

Shy. Ho, no, no, no, no; my meaning
in saying he is a good man is to have you
understand me that he is sufficient; yet
his means are in supposition: he hath an
argosy bound to Tripolis, another to the
Indies; I understand, moreover, upon the
Rialto, he hath a third at Mexico, a fourth
for England—and other ventures he hath,
squand'red abroad. But ships are but
boards, sailors but men; there be land-
rats and water-rats, water-thieves and land-
thieves—I mean pirates; and then there
is the peril of waters, winds, and rocks.
The man is, notwithstanding, sufficient.
Three thousand ducats—I think I may
take his bond.

Bass. Be assur'd you may. 25

Shy. I will be assur'd I may; and, that
I may be assured, I will bethink me. May
I speak with Antonio?

Bass. If it please you to dine with us.

Shy. Yes, to smell pork, to eat of the habitation which your prophet, the Nazarite, conjured the devil into! I will buy with you, sell with you, talk with you, walk with you, and so following; but I will not eat with you, drink with you, nor pray with you. What news on the Rialto? Who is he comes here?

Enter ANTONIO.

Bass. This is Signior Antonio.   35

Shy. [*Aside*] How like a fawning publican he looks!
I hate him for he is a Christian;
But more for that in low simplicity
He lends out money gratis, and brings down   39
The rate of usance here with us in Venice.
If I can catch him once upon the hip,
I will feed fat the ancient grudge I bear him.
He hates our sacred nation; and he rails,
Even there where merchants most do congregate,
On me, my bargains, and my well-won thrift,   45
Which he calls interest. Cursed be my tribe
If I forgive him!

Bass.   Shylock, do you hear?

Shy. I am debating of my present store,
And, by the near guess of my memory,
I cannot instantly raise up the gross   50
Of full three thousand ducats. What of that?
Tubal, a wealthy Hebrew of my tribe,
Will furnish me. But soft! how many months
Do you desire? [*To Antonio*] Rest you fair, good signior?
Your worship was the last man in our mouths.   55

Ant. Shylock, albeit I neither lend nor borrow
By taking nor by giving of excess,
Yet, to supply the ripe wants of my friend,
I'll break a custom. [*To Bassanio*] Is he yet possess'd   59
How much ye would?

Shy.   Ay, ay, three thousand ducats.

Ant. And for three months.

Shy. I had forgot—three months; you told me so.
Well then, your bond; and, let me see—but hear you,
Methoughts you said you neither lend nor borrow
Upon advantage.

Ant.   I do never use it.   65

Shy. When Jacob graz'd his uncle Laban's sheep—
This Jacob from our holy Abram was,
As his wise mother wrought in his behalf,
The third possessor; ay, he was the third—

Ant. And what of him? Did he take interest?   70

Shy. No, not take interest; not, as you would say,
Directly int'rest; mark what Jacob did:
When Laban and himself were compromis'd
That all the eanlings which were streak'd and pied
Should fall as Jacob's hire, the ewes, being rank,   75
In end of autumn turned to the rams;
And when the work of generation was
Between these woolly breeders in the act,
The skilful shepherd pill'd me certain wands,
And, in the doing of the deed of kind,   80
He stuck them up before the fulsome ewes,
Who, then conceiving, did in eaning time
Fall parti-colour'd lambs, and those were Jacob's.
This was a way to thrive, and he was blest;
And thrift is blessing, if men steal it not. 85

Ant. This was a venture, sir, that Jacob serv'd for;
A thing not in his power to bring to pass,
But sway'd and fashion'd by the hand of heaven.
Was this inserted to make interest good?
Or is your gold and silver ewes and rams?

Shy. I cannot tell; I make it breed as fast.   91
But note me, signior.

Ant. [*Aside*]   Mark you this, Bassanio,
The devil can cite Scripture for his purpose.
An evil soul producing holy witness
Is like a villain with a smiling cheek,   95
A goodly apple rotten at the heart.
O, what a goodly outside falsehood hath!

Shy. Three thousand ducats—'tis a good round sum.
Three months from twelve; then let me see, the rate—

Ant. Well, Shylock, shall we be beholding to you?   100

Shy. Signior Antonio, many a time and oft
In the Rialto you have rated me
About my moneys and my usances;
Still have I borne it with a patient shrug,
For suff'rance is the badge of all our tribe;
You call me misbeliever, cut-throat dog,
And spit upon my Jewish gaberdine,
And all for use of that which is mine own.
Well then, it now appears you need my help;   109
Go to, then; you come to me, and you say
'Shylock, we would have moneys'. You say so—
You that did void your rheum upon my beard
And foot me as you spurn a stranger cur
Over your threshold; moneys is your suit.

What should I say to you ? Should I not
   say   115
'Hath a dog money ? Is it possible
A cur can lend three thousand ducats ? ' Or
Shall I bend low and, in a bondman's key,
With bated breath and whisp'ring humble-
   ness,
Say this :   120
' Fair sir, you spit on me on Wednesday last,
You spurn'd me such a day ; another time
You call'd me dog ; and for these courtesies
I'll lend you thus much moneys ' ?
   Ant. I am as like to call thee so again, 125
To spit on thee again, to spurn thee too.
If thou wilt lend this money, lend it not
As to thy friends—for when did friendship
   take
A breed for barren metal of his friend ?—
But lend it rather to thine enemy,   130
Who if he break thou mayst with better
   face
Exact the penalty.
   Shy. Why, look you, how you storm !
I would be friends with you, and have your
   love,
Forget the shames that you have stain'd me
   with,
Supply your present wants, and take no
   doit   135
Of usance for my moneys, and you'll not
   hear me.
This is kind I offer.
   Bass. This were kindness.
   Shy.   This kindness will I show.
Go with me to a notary, seal me there
Your single bond, and, in a merry sport, 140
If you repay me not on such a day,
In such a place, such sum or sums as are
Express'd in the condition, let the forfeit
Be nominated for an equal pound   144
Of your fair flesh, to be cut off and taken
In what part of your body pleaseth me.
   Ant. Content, in faith ; I'll seal to such
   a bond,
And say there is much kindness in the Jew.
   Bass. You shall not seal to such a bond
   for me ;
I'll rather dwell in my necessity.   150
   Ant. Why, fear not, man; I will not
   forfeit it ;
Within these two months—that's a month
   before
This bond expires—I do expect return
Of thrice three times the value of this bond.
   Shy. O father Abram, what these
   Christians are,   155
Whose own hard dealings teaches them
   suspect
The thoughts of others ! Pray you, tell me
   this :
If he should break his day, what should I
   gain
By the exaction of the forfeiture ?
A pound of man's flesh taken from a man

Is not so estimable, profitable neither, 161
As flesh of muttons, beefs, or goats. I say,
To buy his favour, I extend this friendship ;
If he will take it, so ; if not, adieu ;
And, for my love, I pray you wrong me not.
   Ant. Yes, Shylock, I will seal unto this
   bond.   166
   Shy. Then meet me forthwith at the
   notary's ;
Give him direction for this merry bond,
And I will go and purse the ducats straight,
See to my house, left in the fearful guard
Of an unthrifty knave, and presently   171
I'll be with you.
   Ant.   Hie thee, gentle Jew.
                [*Exit Shylock.*
The Hebrew will turn Christian : he grows
   kind.
   Bass. I like not fair terms and a villain's
   mind.
   Ant. Come on ; in this there can be no
   dismay ;   175
My ships come home a month before the
   day.   [*Exeunt.*

ACT TWO

SCENE I. *Belmont. Portia's house.*

Flourish of cornets. Enter the PRINCE OF
MOROCCO, *a tawny Moor all in white, and
three or four* Followers *accordingly, with*
PORTIA, NERISSA, *and* Train.

   Mor. Mislike me not for my complexion,
The shadowed livery of the burnish'd sun,
To whom I am a neighbour, and near bred.
Bring me the fairest creature northward
   born,
Where Phœbus' fire scarce thaws the icicles,
And let us make incision for your love   6
To prove whose blood is reddest, his or
   mine.
I tell thee, lady, this aspect of mine
Hath fear'd the valiant ; by my love, I
   swear
The best-regarded virgins of our clime   10
Have lov'd it too. I would not change this
   hue,
Except to steal your thoughts, my gentle
   queen.
   Por. In terms of choice I am not solely led
By nice direction of a maiden's eyes ;
Besides, the lott'ry of my destiny   15
Bars me the right of voluntary choosing.
But, if my father had not scanted me,
And hedg'd me by his wit to yield myself
His wife who wins me by that means I told
   you,
Yourself, renowned Prince, then stood as
   fair   20
As any comer I have look'd on yet
For my affection.
   Mor.   Even for that I thank you.
Therefore, I pray you, lead me to the
   caskets

To try my fortune. By this scimitar, 24
That slew the Sophy and a Persian prince,
That won three fields of Sultan Solyman,
I would o'erstare the sternest eyes that
    look,
Outbrave the heart most daring on the
    earth,
Pluck the young sucking cubs from the
    she-bear, 29
Yea, mock the lion when 'a roars for
    prey,
To win thee, lady. But, alas the while!
If Hercules and Lichas play at dice
Which is the better man, the greater throw
May turn by fortune from the weaker hand.
So is Alcides beaten by his page; 35
And so may I, blind Fortune leading me,
Miss that which one unworthier may attain,
And die with grieving.
  Por.   You must take your chance,
And either not attempt to choose at all,
Or swear before you choose, if you choose
    wrong, 40
Never to speak to lady afterward
In way of marriage; therefore be advis'd.
  Mor. Nor will not; come, bring me unto
my chance.
  Por. First, forward to the temple. After
dinner 44
Your hazard shall be made.
  Mor.   Good fortune then,
To make me blest or cursed'st among men!
      [*Cornets, and exeunt.*

SCENE II. *Venice. A street.*

Enter LAUNCELOT GOBBO.

  Laun. Certainly my conscience will serve
me to run from this Jew my master. The
fiend is at mine elbow and tempts me,
saying to me 'Gobbo, Launcelot Gobbo,
good Launcelot' or 'good Gobbo' or 'good
Launcelot Gobbo, use your legs, take the
start, run away'. My conscience says 'No;
take heed, honest Launcelot, take heed,
honest Gobbo' or, as aforesaid, 'honest
Launcelot Gobbo, do not run; scorn
running with thy heels'. Well, the most
courageous fiend bids me pack. 'Via!'
says the fiend; 'away!' says the fiend.
'For the heavens, rouse up a brave mind'
says the fiend 'and run.' Well, my conscience, hanging about the neck of my
heart, says very wisely to me 'My
honest friend Launcelot, being an honest
man's son' or rather 'an honest woman's
son'; for indeed my father did something
smack, something grow to, he had a
kind of taste—well, my conscience says
'Launcelot, budge not'. 'Budge' says the
fiend. 'Budge not' says my conscience.
'Conscience,' say I 'you counsel well.'
'Fiend,' say I 'you counsel well.' To be
rul'd by my conscience, I should stay with

the Jew my master, who—God bless the
mark!—is a kind of devil; and, to run
away from the Jew, I should be ruled by
the fiend, who—saving your reverence!—
is the devil himself. Certainly the Jew is
the very devil incarnation; and, in my
conscience, my conscience is but a kind of
hard conscience to offer to counsel me to
stay with the Jew. The fiend gives the
more friendly counsel. I will run, fiend; my
heels are at your commandment; I will run.

Enter Old GOBBO, *with a basket.*

  Gob. Master young man, you, I pray you,
which is the way to master Jew's? 29
  Laun. [*Aside*] O heavens! This is my
true-begotten father, who, being more than
sand-blind, high-gravel blind, knows me
not. I will try confusions with him.
  Gob. Master young gentleman, I pray
you, which is the way to master Jew's? 34
  Laun. Turn up on your right hand at the
next turning, but, at the next turning of
all, on your left; marry, at the very next
turning, turn of no hand, but turn down
indirectly to the Jew's house. 38
  Gob. Be God's sonties, 'twill be a hard
way to hit! Can you tell me whether one
Launcelot, that dwells with him, dwell with
him or no? 41
  Laun. Talk you of young Master
Launcelot? [*Aside*] Mark me now; now
will I raise the waters.—Talk you of young
Master Launcelot? 44
  Gob. No master, sir, but a poor man's son;
his father, though I say't, is an honest
exceeding poor man, and, God be thanked,
well to live. 47
  Laun. Well, let his father be what 'a will,
we talk of young Master Launcelot.
  Gob. Your worship's friend, and Launcelot, sir. 50
  Laun. But I pray you, ergo, old man,
ergo, I beseech you, talk you of young
Master Launcelot?
  Gob. Of Launcelot, an't please your
mastership. 53
  Laun. Ergo, Master Launcelot. Talk not
of Master Launcelot, father; for the young
gentleman, according to Fates and Destinies
and such odd sayings, the Sisters Three and
such branches of learning, is indeed
deceased; or, as you would say in plain
terms, gone to heaven.
  Gob. Marry, God forbid! The boy was
the very staff of my age, my very prop. 60
  Laun. Do I look like a cudgel or a hovel-
post, a staff or a prop? Do you know me,
father?
  Gob. Alack the day, I know you not,
young gentleman; but I pray you tell me,
is my boy—God rest his soul!—alive or
dead? 65
  Laun. Do you not know me, father?

Gob. Alack, sir, I am sand-blind; I know you not.

Laun. Nay, indeed, if you had your eyes, you might fail of the knowing me: it is a wise father that knows his own child. Well, old man, I will tell you news of your son. Give me your blessing; truth will come to light; murder cannot be hid long; a man's son may, but in the end truth will out.

Gob. Pray you, sir, stand up; I am sure you are not Launcelot my boy.   75

Laun. Pray you, let's have no more fooling about it, but give me your blessing; I am Launcelot, your boy that was, your son that is, your child that shall be.

Gob. I cannot think you are my son.   79

Laun. I know not what I shall think of that; but I am Launcelot, the Jew's man, and I am sure Margery your wife is my mother.   8

Gob. Her name is Margery, indeed. I'll be sworn, if thou be Launcelot, thou art mine own flesh and blood. Lord worshipp'd might he be, what a beard hast thou got! Thou hast got more hair on thy chin than Dobbin my fill-horse has on his tail.   87

Laun. It should seem, then, that Dobbin's tail grows backward; I am sure he had more hair of his tail than I have of my face when I last saw him.   90

Gob. Lord, how art thou chang'd! How dost thou and thy master agree? I have brought him a present. How 'gree you now?   93

Laun. Well, well; but, for mine own part, as I have set up my rest to run away, so I will not rest till I have run some ground. My master's a very Jew. Give him a present! Give him a halter. I am famish'd in his service; you may tell every finger I have with my ribs. Father, I am glad you are come; give me your present to one Master Bassanio, who indeed gives rare new liveries; if I serve not him, I will run as far as God has any ground. O rare fortune! Here comes the man. To him, father, for I am a Jew, if I serve the Jew any longer.

Enter BASSANIO, *with* LEONARDO, *with a* Follower *or two.*

Bass. You may do so; but let it be so hasted that supper be ready at the farthest by five of the clock. See these letters delivered, put the liveries to making, and desire Gratiano to come anon to my lodging.   [*Exit a servant.*

Laun. To him, father.

Gob. God bless your worship!

Bass. Gramercy; wouldst thou aught with me?   110

Gob. Here's my son, sir, a poor boy—

Laun. Not a poor boy, sir, but the rich Jew's man, that would, sir, as my father shall specify—

Gob. He hath a great infection, sir, as one would say, to serve—   115

Laun. Indeed, the short and the long is, I serve the Jew, and have a desire, as my father shall specify—

Gob. His master and he, saving your worship's reverence, are scarce cater-cousins—   119

Laun. To be brief, the very truth is that the Jew, having done me wrong, doth cause me, as my father, being I hope an old man, shall frutify unto you—

Gob. I have here a dish of doves that I would bestow upon your worship; and my suit is—   124

Laun. In very brief, the suit is impertinent to myself, as your worship shall know by this honest old man; and, though I say it, though old man, yet poor man, my father.

Bass. One speak for both. What would you?

Laun. Serve you, sir.

Gob. That is the very defect of the matter, sir.   130

Bass. I know thee well; thou hast obtain'd thy suit.

Shylock thy master spoke with me this day,
And hath preferr'd thee, if it be preferment
To leave a rich Jew's service to become
The follower of so poor a gentleman.   135

Laun. The old proverb is very well parted between my master Shylock and you, sir: you have the grace of God, sir, and he hath enough.

Bass. Thou speak'st it well. Go, father, with thy son.

Take leave of thy old master, and inquire
My lodging out. [*To a servant*] Give him a livery   141
More guarded than his fellows'; see it done.

Laun. Father, in. I cannot get a service, no! I have ne'er a tongue in my head! [*Looking on his palm*] Well; if any man in Italy have a fairer table which doth offer to swear upon a book—I shall have good fortune. Go to, here's a simple line of life; here's a small trifle of wives; alas, fifteen wives is nothing; a'leven widows and nine maids is a simple coming-in for one man. And then to scape drowning thrice, and to be in peril of my life with the edge of a feather-bed—here are simple scapes. Well, if Fortune be a woman, she's a good wench for this gear. Father, come; I'll take my leave of the Jew in the twinkling.   153

[*Exeunt Launcelot and Old Gobbo.*

Bass. I pray thee, good Leonardo, think on this.

These things being bought and orderly bestowed,   155
Return in haste, for I do feast to-night
My best esteem'd acquaintance; hie thee, go.

Leon. My best endeavours shall be done
    herein.

       Enter GRATIANO.

Gra. Where's your master ?
Leon.   Yonder, sir, he walks. [*Exit.*
Gra. Signior Bassanio !   160
Bass. Gratiano !
Gra. I have suit to you.
Bass.   You have obtain'd it.
Gra. You must not deny me : I must go
with you to Belmont.
  Bass. Why, then you must.   But hear
    thee, Gratiano :   165
Thou art too wild, too rude, and bold of
  voice—
Parts that become thee happily enough,
And in such eyes as ours appear not faults ;
But where thou art not known, why there
  they show   169
Something too liberal. Pray thee, take pain
To allay with some cold drops of modesty
Thy skipping spirit ; lest through thy wild
  behaviour
I be misconstr'red in the place I go to
And lose my hopes.
  Gra.   Signior Bassanio, hear me :
If I do not put on a sober habit,   175
Talk with respect, and swear but now and
  then,
Wear prayer-books in my pocket, look
  demurely,
Nay more, while grace is saying hood mine
  eyes
Thus with my hat, and sigh, and say amen,
Use all the observance of civility   180
Like one well studied in a sad ostent
To please his grandam, never trust me more.
  Bass. Well, we shall see your bearing.
  Gra. Nay, but I bar to-night ; you shall
    not gauge me   184
By what we do to-night.
  Bass.   No, that were pity ;
I would entreat you rather to put on
Your boldest suit of mirth, for we have
  friends
That purpose merriment.   But fare you
  well ;
I have some business.
  Gra. And I must to Lorenzo and the rest ;
But we will visit you at supper-time.   191
          [*Exeunt.*

  SCENE III.   *Venice.   Shylock's house.*

    Enter JESSICA *and* LAUNCELOT.

  Jes. I am sorry thou wilt leave my father
    so.
Our house is hell ; and thou, a merry devil,
Didst rob it of some taste of tediousness.
But fare thee well ; there is a ducat for
  thee ;
And, Launcelot, soon at supper shalt thou
  see   5

Lorenzo, who is thy new master's guest.
Give him this letter ; do it secretly.
And so farewell.   I would not have my
  father
See me in talk with thee.   9
  Laun. Adieu ! tears exhibit my tongue.
Most beautiful pagan, most sweet Jew ! If
a Christian do not play the knave and get
thee, I am much deceived.   But, adieu !
these foolish drops do something drown my
manly spirit ; adieu !   14
  Jes. Farewell, good Launcelot.   [*Exit.*
Alack, what heinous sin is it in me
To be asham'd to be my father's child !
But though I am a daughter to his blood,
I am not to his manners. O Lorenzo,   19
If thou keep promise, I shall end this strife,
Become a Christian and thy loving wife.
          [*Exit.*

  SCENE IV.   *Venice.   A street.*

Enter GRATIANO, LORENZO, SALERIO, *and*
        SOLANIO.

  Lor. Nay, we will slink away in supper-
    time,
Disguise us at my lodging, and return
All in an hour.
  Gra. We have not made good preparation.
  Saler. We have not spoke us yet of
    torch-bearers.   5
  Solan. 'Tis vile, unless it may be quaintly
    ordered ;
And better in my mind not undertook.
  Lor. 'Tis now but four o'clock ; we have
    two hours
To furnish us.

    Enter LAUNCELOT, *with a letter.*

    Friend Launcelot, what's the news ?
  Laun. An it shall please you to break up
this, it shall seem to signify.   11
  Lor. I know the hand ; in faith, 'tis a
    fair hand,
And whiter than the paper it writ on
Is the fair hand that writ.
  Gra.   Love-news, in faith !
  Laun. By your leave, sir.   15
  Lor. Whither goest thou ?
  Laun. Marry, sir, to bid my old master,
the Jew, to sup to-night with my new
master, the Christian.
  Lor. Hold, here, take this.   Tell gentle
    Jessica
I will not fail her ; speak it privately.   20
Go, gentlemen,   [*Exit Launcelot.*
Will you prepare you for this masque to-
  night ?
I am provided of a torch-bearer.
  Saler. Ay, marry, I'll be gone about it
    straight.
  Solan. And so will I.
  Lor.   Meet me and Gratiano 25
At Gratiano's lodging some hour hence.

Saler. 'Tis good we do so.

          [*Exeunt Salerio and Solanio.*

Gra. Was not that letter from fair Jessica?

Lor. I must needs tell thee all. She hath directed
How I shall take her from her father's house;   30
What gold and jewels she is furnish'd with;
What page's suit she hath in readiness.
If e'er the Jew her father come to heaven,
It will be for his gentle daughter's sake;
And never dare misfortune cross her foot,
Unless she do it under this excuse,   36
That she is issue to a faithless Jew.
Come, go with me, peruse this as thou goest;
Fair Jessica shall be my torch-bearer.

          [*Exeunt.*

SCENE V. *Venice. Before Shylock's house.*

    Enter SHYLOCK *and* LAUNCELOT.

Shy. Well, thou shalt see; thy eyes shall be thy judge,
The difference of old Shylock and Bassanio.—
What, Jessica!—Thou shalt not gormandize
As thou hast done with me—What, Jessica!—   4
And sleep and snore, and rend apparel out—
Why, Jessica, I say!

Laun.   Why, Jessica!

Shy. Who bids thee call? I do not bid thee call.

Laun. Your worship was wont to tell me I could do nothing without bidding.

    Enter JESSICA.

Jes. Call you? What is your will?   10

Shy. I am bid forth to supper, Jessica;
There are my keys. But wherefore should I go?
I am not bid for love; they flatter me;
But yet I'll go in hate, to feed upon
The prodigal Christian. Jessica, my girl, 15
Look to my house. I am right loath to go;
There is some ill a-brewing towards my rest,
For I did dream of money-bags to-night.

Laun. I beseech you, sir, go; my young master doth expect your reproach.   20

Shy. So do I his.

Laun. And they have conspired together; I will not say you shall see a masque, but if you do, then it was not for nothing that my nose fell a-bleeding on Black Monday last at six o'clock i' th' morning, falling out that year on Ash Wednesday was four year, in th' afternoon.   26

Shy. What, are there masques? Hear you me, Jessica:
Lock up my doors, and when you hear the drum,

And the vile squealing of the wry-neck'd fife,   29
Clamber not you up to the casements then,
Nor thrust your head into the public street
To gaze on Christian fools with varnish'd faces;
But stop my house's ears—I mean my casements;   33
Let not the sound of shallow fopp'ry enter
My sober house. By Jacob's staff, I swear
I have no mind of feasting forth to-night;
But I will go. Go you before me, sirrah;
Say I will come.

Laun. I will go before, sir. Mistress, look out at window for all this.   40
    There will come a Christian by
    Will be worth a Jewess' eye. [*Exit.*

Shy. What says that fool of Hagar's offspring, ha?

Jes. His words were 'Farewell, mistress'; nothing else.

Shy. The patch is kind enough, but a huge feeder,   45
Snail-slow in profit, and he sleeps by day
More than the wild-cat; drones hive not with me,
Therefore I part with him; and part with him
To one that I would have him help to waste
His borrowed purse. Well, Jessica, go in;
Perhaps I will return immediately.   51
Do as I bid you, shut doors after you.
Fast bind, fast find—
A proverb never stale in thrifty mind.

          [*Exit.*

Jes. Farewell; and if my fortune be not crost,   55
I have a father, you a daughter, lost. [*Exit.*

SCENE VI. *Venice. Before Shylock's house.*

Enter the maskers, GRATIANO *and* SALERIO.

Gra. This is the pent-house under which Lorenzo
Desired us to make stand.

Saler.   His hour is almost past.

Gra. And it is marvel he out-dwells his hour,
For lovers ever run before the clock.

Saler. O, ten times faster Venus' pigeons fly   5
To seal love's bonds new made than they are wont
To keep obliged faith unforfeited!

Gra. That ever holds: who riseth from a feast   8
With that keen appetite that he sits down?
Where is the horse that doth untread again
His tedious measures with the unbated fire
That he did pace them first? All things that are
Are with more spirit chased than enjoy'd.
How like a younker or a prodigal   14

The scarfed bark puts from her native bay,
Hugg'd and embraced by the strumpet
    wind ;
How like the prodigal doth she return,
With over-weather'd ribs and ragged sails,
Lean, rent, and beggar'd by the strumpet
    wind !

Enter LORENZO.

Saler. Here comes Lorenzo ; more of
    this hereafter.   20
Lor. Sweet friends, your patience for my
    long abode !
Not I, but my affairs, have made you wait.
When you shall please to play the thieves
    for wives,
I'll watch as long for you then. Approach ;
Here dwells my father Jew. Ho ! who's
    within ?   25

Enter JESSICA, *above, in boy's clothes.*

Jes. Who are you ? Tell me, for more
    certainty,
Albeit I'll swear that I do know your
    tongue.
Lor. Lorenzo, and thy love.
Jes. Lorenzo, certain ; and my love
    indeed ;
For who love I so much ? And now who
    knows   30
But you, Lorenzo, whether I am yours ?
Lor. Heaven and thy thoughts are witness
    that thou art.
Jes. Here, catch this casket ; it is worth
    the pains.
I am glad 'tis night, you do not look on me,
For I am much asham'd of my exchange ;
But love is blind, and lovers cannot see 36
The pretty follies that themselves commit,
For, if they could, Cupid himself would
    blush
To see me thus transformed to a boy.
Lor. Descend, for you must be my torch-
    bearer.   40
Jes. What ! must I hold a candle to my
    shames ?
They in themselves, good sooth, are too
    too light.
Why, 'tis an office of discovery, love,
And I should be obscur'd.
Lor.   So are you, sweet,
Even in the lovely garnish of a boy.   45
But come at once,
For the close night doth play the runaway,
And we are stay'd for at Bassanio's feast.
Jes. I will make fast the doors, and gild
    myself   49
With some moe ducats, and be with you
    straight.   [*Exit above.*
Gra. Now, by my hood, a gentle, and no
    Jew.
Lor. Beshrew me, but I love her heartily,
For she is wise, if I can judge of her,
And fair she is, if that mine eyes be true,

And true she is, as she hath prov'd herself ;
And therefore, like herself, wise, fair, and
    true,   56
Shall she be placed in my constant soul.

Enter JESSICA, *below.*

What, art thou come ? On, gentlemen,
    away ;
Our masquing mates by this time for us
    stay. [*Exit with Jessica and Salerio.*

Enter ANTONIO.

Ant. Who's there ?   60
Gra. Signior Antonio ?
Ant. Fie, fie, Gratiano, where are all the
    rest ?
'Tis nine o'clock ; our friends all stay for
    you ;
No masque to-night ; the wind is come
    about ;
Bassanio presently will go aboard ;   65
I have sent twenty out to seek for you.
Gra. I am glad on't ; I desire no more
    delight
Than to be under sail and gone to-night.
                      [*Exeunt.*

SCENE VII. *Belmont. Portia's house.*

Flourish of Cornets. Enter PORTIA, *with the*
PRINCE OF MOROCCO, *and their* Trains.

Por. Go draw aside the curtains and
    discover
The several caskets to this noble Prince.
Now make your choice.
Mor. The first, of gold, who this inscrip-
    tion bears :
'Who chooseth me shall gain what many
    men desire'.   5
The second, silver, which this promise
    carries :
'Who chooseth me shall get as much as he
    deserves '.
This third, dull lead, with warning all as
    blunt :
'Who chooseth me must give and hazard
    all he hath '.   9
How shall I know if I do choose the right ?
Por. The one of them contains my
    picture, Prince ;
If you choose that, then I am yours withal.
Mor. Some god direct my judgment !
    Let me see ;
I will survey th' inscriptions back again.
What says this leaden casket ?   15
'Who chooseth me must give and hazard
    all he hath.'
Must give—for what ? For lead ? Hazard
    for lead !
This casket threatens ; men that hazard all
Do it in hope of fair advantages.   19
A golden mind stoops not to shows of dross ;
I'll then nor give nor hazard aught for lead.
What says the silver with her virgin hue ?

'Who chooseth me shall get as much as he
    deserves.'
As much as he deserves!   Pause there,
    Morocco,
And weigh thy value with an even hand.   25
If thou beest rated by thy estimation,
Thou dost deserve enough, and yet enough
May not extend so far as to the lady ;
And yet to be afeard of my deserving
Were but a weak disabling of myself.   30
As much as I deserve ?   Why, that's the
    lady !
I do in birth deserve her, and in fortunes,
In graces, and in qualities of breeding ;
But more than these, in love I do deserve.
What if I stray'd no farther, but chose
    here ?   35
Let's see once more this saying grav'd in
    gold :
'Who chooseth me shall gain what many
    men desire'.
Why, that's the lady !   All the world
    desires her,
From the four corners of the earth they
    come
To kiss this shrine, this mortal-breathing
    saint.   40
The Hyrcanian deserts and the vasty wilds
Of wide Arabia are as throughfares now
For princes to come view fair Portia.
The watery kingdom, whose ambitious head
Spits in the face of heaven, is no bar   45
To stop the foreign spirits, but they come
As o'er a brook to see fair Portia.
One of these three contains her heavenly
    picture.
Is't like that lead contains her ?   'Twere
    damnation
To think so base a thought ; it were too
    gross   50
To rib her cerecloth in the obscure grave.
Or shall I think in silver she's immur'd,
Being ten times undervalued to tried gold ?
O sinful thought !   Never so rich a gem
Was set in worse than gold.   They have in
    England   55
A coin that bears the figure of an angel
Stamp'd in gold ; but that's insculp'd
    upon.
But here an angel in a golden bed
Lies all within.   Deliver me the key ;
Here do I choose, and thrive I as I may !   60
  Por. There, take it, Prince, and if my
    form lie there,
Then I am yours.
           [*He opens the golden casket.*
  Mor.   O hell ! what have we here ?
A carrion Death, within whose empty eye
There is a written scroll !   I'll read the
    writing.

' All that glisters is not gold,   65
  Often have you heard that told ;
Many a man his life hath sold

But my outside to behold.
Gilded tombs do worms infold.
Had you been as wise as bold,   70
Young in limbs, in judgment old,
Your answer had not been inscroll'd.
Fare you well, your suit is cold.'

Cold indeed, and labour lost,   74
Then farewell, heat, and welcome, frost.
Portia, adieu !   I have too griev'd a heart
To take a tedious leave ; thus losers part.
    [*Exit with his train.   Flourish of cornets.*
  Portia. A gentle riddance.   Draw the
    curtains, go.
Let all of his complexion choose me so.
                       [*Exeunt.*

SCENE VIII.   *Venice.   A street.*

Enter SALERIO *and* SOLANIO.

  Saler. Why, man, I saw Bassanio under
    sail ;
With him is Gratiano gone along ;
And in their ship I am sure Lorenzo is not.
  Solan. The villain Jew with outcries
    rais'd the Duke,
Who went with him to search Bassanio's
    ship.   5
  Saler. He came too late, the ship was
    under sail ;
But there the Duke was given to under-
    stand
That in a gondola were seen together
Lorenzo and his amorous Jessica ;
Besides, Antonio certified the Duke   10
They were not with Bassanio in his ship.
  Solan. I never heard a passion so con-
    fus'd,
So strange, outrageous, and so variable,
As the dog Jew did utter in the streets.
' My daughter !   O my ducats !   O my
    daughter !   15
Fled with a Christian !   O my Christian
    ducats !
Justice !   the law !   My ducats and my
    daughter !
A sealed bag, two sealed bags of ducats,
Of double ducats, stol'n from me by my
    daughter !
And jewels—two stones, two rich and
    precious stones,   20
Stol'n by my daughter !   Justice !   Find the
    girl ;
She hath the stones upon her and the
    ducats.'
  Saler. Why all the boys in Venice follow
    him,
Crying, his stones, his daughter, and his
    ducats.
  Solan. Let good Antonio look he keep
    his day,   25
Or he shall pay for this.
  Saler.   Marry, well rememb'red ;
I reason'd with a Frenchman yesterday,

Who told me, in the narrow seas that part
The French and English, there miscarried
A vessel of our country richly fraught. 　30
I thought upon Antonio when he told me,
And wish'd in silence that it were not his.
  Solan. You were best to tell Antonio
    what you hear ;
Yet do not suddenly, for it may grieve him.
  Saler. A kinder gentleman treads not the
    earth. 　35
I saw Bassanio and Antonio part.
Bassanio told him he would make some speed
Of his return.　He answered ' Do not so ;
Slubber not business for my sake, Bassanio,
But stay the very riping of the time ; 　40
And for the Jew's bond which he hath of me,
Let it not enter in your mind of love ;
Be merry, and employ your chiefest thoughts
To courtship, and such fair ostents of love
As shall conveniently become you there '. 45
And even there, his eye being big with tears,
Turning his face, he put his hand behind him,
And with affection wondrous sensible
He wrung Bassanio's hand ; and so they parted.
  Solan. I think he only loves the world for
    him. 　50
I pray thee, let us go and find him out,
And quicken his embraced heaviness
With some delight or other.
  Saler.　　　　　Do we so. 　[*Exeunt.*

Scene IX.　*Belmont.　Portia's house.*

Enter Nerissa, *and a* Servitor.

  Ner. Quick, quick, I pray thee, draw the
    curtain straight ;
The Prince of Arragon hath ta'en his oath,
And comes to his election presently.

Flourish of Cornets.　Enter the Prince of
Arragon, Portia, *and their* Trains.

  Por. Behold, there stand the caskets,
    noble Prince.
If you choose that wherein I am contain'd,
Straight shall our nuptial rites be
    solemniz'd ; 　6
But if you fail, without more speech, my lord,
You must be gone from hence immediately.
  Ar. I am enjoin'd by oath to observe
    three things :
First, never to unfold to any one 　10
Which casket 'twas I chose ; next, if I fail
Of the right casket, never in my life
To woo a maid in way of marriage ;
Lastly,
If I do fail in fortune of my choice, 　15
Immediately to leave you and be gone.

  Por. To these injunctions every one doth
    swear
That comes to hazard for my worthless self.
  Ar. And so have I address'd me.　For-
    tune now
To my heart's hope ! Gold, silver, and base
    lead. 　20
'Who chooseth me must give and hazard
    all he hath.'
You shall look fairer ere I give or hazard.
What says the golden chest ? Ha ! let me
    see :
'Who chooseth me shall gain what many
    men desire '.
What many men desire—that ' many ' may
    be meant 　25
By the fool multitude, that choose by show,
Not learning more than the fond eye doth
    teach ;
Which pries not to th' interior, but, like
    the martlet,
Builds in the weather on the outward wall,
Even in the force and road of casualty. 　30
I will not choose what many men desire,
Because I will not jump with common
    spirits
And rank me with the barbarous multi-
    tudes.
Why, then to thee, thou silver treasure-
    house !
Tell me once more what title thou dost
    bear. 　35
'Who chooseth me shall get as much as he
    deserves.'
And well said too ; for who shall go about
To cozen fortune, and be honourable
Without the stamp of merit ? Let none
    presume
To wear an undeserved dignity. 　40
O that estates, degrees, and offices,
Were not deriv'd corruptly, and that clear
    honour
Were purchas'd by the merit of the wearer !
How many then should cover that stand
    bare ! 　44
How many be commanded that command !
How much low peasantry would then be
    gleaned
From the true seed of honour ! and how
    much honour
Pick'd from the chaff and ruin of the times,
To be new varnish'd ! Well, but to my
    choice.
'Who chooseth me shall get as much as he
    deserves.' 　50
I will assume desert. Give me a key for
    this,
And instantly unlock my fortunes here.
        [*He opens the silver casket.*
  Por. [*Aside*] Too long a pause for that
    which you find there.
  Ar. What's here ?　The portrait of a
    blinking idiot

235

Presenting me a schedule ! I will read it. 55
How much unlike art thou to Portia !
How much unlike my hopes and my
      deservings !
' Who chooseth me shall have as much as
      he deserves.'
Did I deserve no more than a fool's head ?
Is that my prize ? Are my deserts no
      better ?   60
   Por. To offend and judge are distinct
      offices
And of opposed natures.
   Ar.   What is here ? [*Reads.*
' The fire seven times tried this ;
   Seven times tried that judgment is
   That did never choose amiss.   65
   Some there be that shadows kiss,
   Such have but a shadow's bliss.
   There be fools alive iwis
   Silver'd o'er, and so was this.
   Take what wife you will to bed,   70
   I will ever be your head.
   So be gone ; you are sped.'

Still more fool I shall appear
By the time I linger here.
With one fool's head I came to woo,   75
But I go away with two.
Sweet, adieu ! I'll keep my oath,
Patiently to bear my wroth.
                    [*Exit with his Train.*
   Por. Thus hath the candle sing'd the
      moth.
O, these deliberate fools ! When they do
      choose,   80
They have the wisdom by their wit to lose.
   Ner. The ancient saying is no heresy :
Hanging and wiving goes by destiny.
   Por. Come, draw the curtain, Nerissa.

Enter a Servant.

   Serv. Where is my lady ?
   Por.   Here ; what would my lord ? 85
   Serv. Madam, there is alighted at your
      gate
A young Venetian, one that comes before
To signify th' approaching of his lord,
From whom he bringeth sensible regreets ;
To wit, besides commends and courteous
      breath,   90
Gifts of rich value. Yet I have not seen
So likely an ambassador of love.
A day in April never came so sweet
To show how costly summer was at hand
As this fore-spurrer comes before his lord.
   Por. No more, I pray thee ; I am half
      afeard   96
Thou wilt say anon he is some kin to thee,
Thou spend'st such high-day wit in praising
      him.
Come, come, Nerissa, for I long to see 99
Quick Cupid's post that comes so mannerly.
   Ner. Bassanio, Lord Love, if thy will it
      be !   [*Exeunt.*

ACT THREE

SCENE I. *Venice. A street.*

Enter SOLANIO *and* SALERIO.

   Solan. Now, what news on the Rialto ?
   Saler. Why, yet it lives there uncheck'd
that Antonio hath a ship of rich lading
wreck'd on the narrow seas ; the Goodwins
I think they call the place, a very dangerous
flat and fatal, where the carcases of many
a tall ship lie buried, as they say, if my
gossip Report be an honest woman of her
word.   7
   Solan. I would she were as lying a gossip
in that as ever knapp'd ginger or made her
neighbours believe she wept for the death
of a third husband. But it is true, without
any slips of prolixity or crossing the plain
highway of talk, that the good Antonio,
the honest Antonio——O that I had a
title good enough to keep his name company !——   13
   Saler. Come, the full stop.
   Solan. Ha ! What sayest thou ? Why,
the end is, he hath lost a ship.
   Saler. I would it might prove the end of
his losses.   17
   Solan. Let me say amen betimes, lest the
devil cross my prayer, for here he comes in
the likeness of a Jew.

Enter SHYLOCK.

How now, Shylock ? What news among
the merchants ?   20
   Shy. You knew, none so well, none so
well as you, of my daughter's flight.
   Saler. That's certain ; I, for my part,
knew the tailor that made the wings she
flew withal.   24
   Solan. And Shylock, for his own part,
knew the bird was flidge ; and then it is
the complexion of them all to leave the
dam.   27
   Shy. She is damn'd for it.
   Saler. That's certain, if the devil may be
her judge.
   Shy. My own flesh and blood to rebel ! 30
   Solan. Out upon it, old carrion ! Rebels
it at these years ?
   Shy. I say my daughter is my flesh and
my blood.   32
   Saler. There is more difference between
thy flesh and hers than between jet and
ivory ; more between your bloods than
there is between red wine and Rhenish. But
tell us, do you hear whether Antonio have
had any loss at sea or no ?   36
   Shy. There I have another bad match : a
bankrupt, a prodigal, who dare scarce show
his head on the Rialto ; a beggar, that was
us'd to come so smug upon the mart. Let
him look to his bond. He was wont to call

me usurer; let him look to his bond. He was wont to lend money for a Christian courtesy; let him look to his bond.   42

Saler. Why, I am sure, if he forfeit, thou wilt not take his flesh. What's that good for?   44

Shy. To bait fish withal. If it will feed nothing else, it will feed my revenge. He hath disgrac'd me and hind'red me half a million; laugh'd at my losses, mock'd at my gains, scorned my nation, thwarted my bargains, cooled my friends, heated mine enemies. And what's his reason? I am a Jew. Hath not a Jew eyes? Hath not a Jew hands, organs, dimensions, senses, affections, passions, fed with the same food, hurt with the same weapons, subject to the same diseases, healed by the same means, warmed and cooled by the same winter and summer, as a Christian is? If you prick us, do we not bleed? If you tickle us, do we not laugh? If you poison us, do we not die? And if you wrong us, shall we not revenge? If we are like you in the rest, we will resemble you in that. If a Jew wrong a Christian, what is his humility? Revenge. If a Christian wrong a Jew, what should his sufferance be by Christian example? Why, revenge. The villainy you teach me I will execute; and it shall go hard but I will better the instruction.   62

Enter a Man *from Antonio.*

Man. Gentlemen, my master Antonio is at his house, and desires to speak with you both.

Saler. We have been up and down to seek him.   65

Enter TUBAL.

Solan. Here comes another of the tribe; a third cannot be match'd, unless the devil himself turn Jew.   67

[*Exeunt Solanio, Salerio, and Man.*

Shy. How now, Tubal, what news from Genoa? Hast thou found my daughter?

Tub. I often came where I did hear of her, but cannot find her.   71

Shy. Why there, there, there, there! A diamond gone, cost me two thousand ducats in Frankfort! The curse never fell upon our nation till now; I never felt it till now. Two thousand ducats in that, and other precious, precious jewels. I would my daughter were dead at my foot, and the jewels in her ear! would she were hears'd at my foot, and the ducats in her coffin! No news of them? Why, so—and I know not what's spent in the search. Why, thou—loss upon loss! The thief gone with so much, and so much to find the thief; and no satisfaction, no revenge; nor no ill luck stirring but what lights o' my shoulders;

no sighs but o' my breathing; no tears but o' my shedding!

Tub. Yes, other men have ill luck too: Antonio, as I heard in Genoa—   85

Shy. What, what, what? Ill luck, ill luck?

Tub. Hath an argosy cast away coming from Tripolis.

Shy. I thank God, I thank God. Is it true, is it true?

Tub. I spoke with some of the sailors that escaped the wreck.   90

Shy. I thank thee, good Tubal. Good news, good news—ha, ha!—heard in Genoa.

Tub. Your daughter spent in Genoa, as I heard, one night, fourscore ducats.   94

Shy. Thou stick'st a dagger in me—I shall never see my gold again. Fourscore ducats at a sitting! Fourscore ducats!   97

Tub. There came divers of Antonio's creditors in my company to Venice that swear he cannot choose but break.

Shy. I am very glad of it; I'll plague him, I'll torture him; I am glad of it.   101

Tub. One of them showed me a ring that he had of your daughter for a monkey.

Shy. Out upon her! Thou torturest me, Tubal. It was my turquoise; I had it of Leah when I was a bachelor; I would not have given it for a wilderness of monkeys.

Tub. But Antonio is certainly undone.

Shy. Nay, that's true; that's very true. Go, Tubal, fee me an officer; bespeak him a fortnight before. I will have the heart of him, if he forfeit; for, were he out of Venice, I can make what merchandise I will. Go, Tubal, and meet me at our synagogue; go, good Tubal; at our synagogue, Tubal.   [*Exeunt.*

SCENE II. *Belmont. Portia's house.*

Enter BASSANIO, PORTIA, GRATIANO, NERISSA, *and all their* Trains.

Por. I pray you tarry; pause a day or two
Before you hazard; for, in choosing wrong,
I lose your company; therefore forbear a awhile.
There's something tells me—but it is not love—
I would not lose you; and you know yourself   5
Hate counsels not in such a quality.
But lest you should not understand me well—
And yet a maiden hath no tongue but thought—
I would detain you here some month or two
Before you venture for me. I could teach you   10

237

How to choose right, but then I am
    forsworn ;
So will I never be ; so may you miss me ;
But if you do, you'll make me wish a sin,
That I had been forsworn. Beshrew your
    eyes !   14
They have o'erlook'd me and divided me ;
One half of me is yours, the other half
    yours—
Mine own, I would say ; but if mine, then
    yours,
And so all yours. O ! these naughty times
Puts bars between the owners and their
    rights ;
And so, though yours, not yours. Prove
    it so,   20
Let fortune go to hell for it, not I.
I speak too long, but 'tis to peize the time,
To eke it, and to draw it out in length,
To stay you from election.
    Bass.   Let me choose ;
For as I am, I live upon the rack.   25
    Por. Upon the rack, Bassanio ? Then
    confess
What treason there is mingled with your
    love.
    Bass. None but that ugly treason of
    mistrust,
Which makes me fear th' enjoying of my
    love ;
There may as well be amity and life   30
'Tween snow and fire as treason and my
    love.
    Por. Ay, but I fear you speak upon the
    rack,
Where men enforced do speak anything.
    Bass. Promise me life, and I'll confess the
    truth.
    Por. Well then, confess and live.
    Bass.   ' Confess ' and ' love '   35
Had been the very sum of my confession.
O happy torment, when my torturer
Doth teach me answers for deliverance !
But let me to my fortune and the caskets.
    Por. Away, then ; I am lock'd in one of
    them.   40
If you do love me, you will find me out.
Nerissa and the rest, stand all aloof ;
Let music sound while he doth make his
    choice ;
Then, if he lose, he makes a swan-like end,
Fading in music. That the comparison
May stand more proper, my eye shall be
    the stream   46
And wat'ry death-bed for him. He may
    win ;
And what is music then ? Then music is
Even as the flourish when true subjects
    bow
To a new-crowned monarch ; such it is 50
As are those dulcet sounds in break of day
That creep into the dreaming bridegroom's
    ear
And summon him to marriage. Now he goes,

With no less presence, but with much more
    love,
Than young Alcides when he did redeem 55
The virgin tribute paid by howling Troy
To the sea-monster. I stand for sacrifice ;
The rest aloof are the Dardanian wives,
With bleared visages come forth to view
The issue of th' exploit. Go, Hercules ! 60
Live thou, I live. With much much more
    dismay
I view the fight than thou that mak'st the
    fray.

A Song, the whilst Bassanio comments on the
    caskets to himself.

       Tell me where is fancy bred,
       Or in the heart or in the head,
       How begot, how nourished ?   65
       Reply, reply.
       It is engend'red in the eyes,
       With gazing fed ; and fancy dies
       In the cradle where it lies.
       Let us all ring fancy's knell :   70
       I'll begin it—Ding, dong, bell.
    All.   Ding, dong—bell.

    Bass. So may the outward shows be least
    themselves ;
The world is still deceiv'd with ornament.
In law, what plea so tainted and corrupt 75
But, being season'd with a gracious voice,
Obscures the show of evil ? In religion,
What damned error but some sober brow
Will bless it, and approve it with a text,
Hiding the grossness with fair ornament ?
There is no vice so simple but assumes   81
Some mark of virtue on his outward parts.
How many cowards, whose hearts are all
    as false
As stairs of sand, wear yet upon their chins
The beards of Hercules and frowning Mars ;
Who, inward search'd, have livers white as
    milk !   86
And these assume but valour's excrement
To render them redoubted. Look on beauty
And you shall see 'tis purchas'd by the
    weight,
Which therein works a miracle in nature, 90
Making them lightest that wear most of it ;
So are those crisped snaky golden locks
Which make such wanton gambols with the
    wind
Upon supposed fairness often known
To be the dowry of a second head—   95
The skull that bred them in the sepulchre.
Thus ornament is but the guiled shore
To a most dangerous sea ; the beauteous
    scarf
Veiling an Indian beauty ; in a word,
The seeming truth which cunning times
    put on   100
To entrap the wisest. Therefore, thou
    gaudy gold,
Hard food for Midas, I will none of thee ;

Nor none of thee, thou pale and common
 drudge
'Tween man and man; but thou, thou
 meagre lead,
Which rather threaten'st than dost promise
 aught,   105
Thy plainness moves me more than elo-
 quence,
And here choose I. Joy be the consequence!
 Por. [*Aside*] How all the other passions
 fleet to air,
As doubtful thoughts, and rash-embrac'd
 despair,
And shudd'ring fear, and green-ey'd
 jealousy!   110
O love, be moderate, allay thy ecstasy,
In measure rain thy joy, scant this excess!
I feel too much thy blessing. Make it less,
For fear I surfeit.
 Bass. [*Opening the leaden casket*] What
 find I here?   114
Fair Portia's counterfeit! What demi-god
Hath come so near creation? Move these
 eyes?
Or whether riding on the balls of mine
Seem they in motion? Here are sever'd
 lips,
Parted with sugar breath; so sweet a bar
Should sunder such sweet friends. Here in
 her hairs   120
The painter plays the spider, and hath
 woven
A golden mesh t' entrap the hearts of men
Faster than gnats in cobwebs. But her
 eyes—
How could he see to do them? Having
 made one,
Methinks it should have power to steal
 both his,   125
And leave itself unfurnish'd. Yet look how
 far
The substance of my praise doth wrong this
 shadow
In underprizing it, so far this shadow
Doth limp behind the substance. Here's
 the scroll,   129
The continent and summary of my fortune.

 ' You that choose not by the view,
  Chance as fair and choose as true!
  Since this fortune falls to you,
  Be content and seek no new.
  If you be well pleas'd with this,   135
  And hold your fortune for your bliss,
  Turn you where your lady is
  And claim her with a loving kiss.'

A gentle scroll. Fair lady, by your leave;
I come by note, to give and to receive.   140
Like one of two contending in a prize,
That thinks he hath done well in people's
 eyes,
Hearing applause and universal shout,
Giddy in spirit, still gazing in a doubt   144
Whether those peals of praise be his or no;

So, thrice-fair lady, stand I even so,
As doubtful whether what I see be true,
Until confirm'd, sign'd, ratified by you.
 Por. You see me, Lord Bassanio, where I
 stand,
Such as I am. Though for myself alone   150
I would not be ambitious in my wish
To wish myself much better, yet for you
I would be trebled twenty times myself,
A thousand times more fair, ten thousand
 times more rich,   155
That only to stand high in your account
I might in virtues, beauties, livings, friends,
Exceed account. But the full sum of me
Is sum of something which, to term in gross,
Is an unlesson'd girl, unschool'd, un-
 practis'd;   160
Happy in this, she is not yet so old
But she may learn; happier than this,
She is not bred so dull but she can learn;
Happiest of all is that her gentle spirit
Commits itself to yours to be directed,   165
As from her lord, her governor, her king.
Myself and what is mine to you and yours
Is now converted. But now I was the lord
Of this fair mansion, master of my servants,
Queen o'er myself; and even now, but now,
This house, these servants, and this same
 myself,   171
Are yours—my lord's. I give them with
 this ring,
Which when you part from, lose, or give
 away,
Let it presage the ruin of your love,
And be my vantage to exclaim on you.   175
 Bass. Madam, you have bereft me of all
 words;
Only my blood speaks to you in my veins;
And there is such confusion in my powers
As, after some oration fairly spoke
By a beloved prince, there doth appear   180
Among the buzzing pleased multitude,
Where every something, being blent to-
 gether,
Turns to a wild of nothing, save of joy
Express'd and not express'd. But when
 this ring
Parts from this finger, then parts life
 from hence;   185
O, then be bold to say Bassanio's dead!
 Ner. My lord and lady, it is now our time
That have stood by and seen our wishes
 prosper
To cry ' Good joy '. Good joy, my lord and
 lady!
 Gra. My Lord Bassanio, and my gentle
 lady,   190
I wish you all the joy that you can wish,
For I am sure you can wish none from me;
And, when your honours mean to solemnize
The bargain of your faith, I do beseech you
Even at that time I may be married too.
 Bass. With all my heart, so thou canst
 get a wife.   196

Gra. I thank your lordship you have got me one.

My eyes, my lord, can look as swift as yours:
You saw the mistress, I beheld the maid;
You lov'd, I lov'd; for intermission   200
No more pertains to me, my lord, than you.
Your fortune stood upon the caskets there,
And so did mine too, as the matter falls;
For wooing here until I sweat again,
And swearing till my very roof was dry   205
With oaths of love, at last—if promise last—
I got a promise of this fair one here
To have her love, provided that your fortune
Achiev'd her mistress.

Por.   Is this true, Nerissa?

Ner. Madam, it is, so you stand pleas'd withal.   210

Bass. And do you, Gratiano, mean good faith?

Gra. Yes, faith, my lord.

Bass. Our feast shall be much honoured in your marriage.

Gra. We'll play with them: the first boy for a thousand ducats.   216

Ner. What, and stake down?

Gra. No; we shall ne'er win at that sport, and stake down—
But who comes here? Lorenzo and his infidel?   220
What, and my old Venetian friend, Salerio!

Enter LORENZO, JESSICA, *and* SALERIO, *a messenger from Venice.*

Bass. Lorenzo and Salerio, welcome hither,
If that the youth of my new int'rest here
Have power to bid you welcome. By your leave,
I bid my very friends and countrymen,   225
Sweet Portia, welcome.

Por.   So do I, my lord;
They are entirely welcome.

Lor. I thank your honour. For my part, my lord,
My purpose was not to have seen you here;
But meeting with Salerio by the way,   230
He did entreat me, past all saying nay,
To come with him along.

Saler.   I did, my lord,
And I have reason for it. Signior Antonio
Commends him to you.
                        [*Gives Bassanio a letter.*

Bass.   Ere I ope his letter,
I pray you tell me how my good friend doth.   235

Saler. Not sick, my lord, unless it be in mind;
Nor well, unless in mind; his letter there
Will show you his estate.
                        [*Bassanio opens the letter.*

Gra. Nerissa, cheer yond stranger; bid her welcome.
Your hand, Salerio. What's the news from Venice?   240
How doth that royal merchant, good Antonio?
I know he will be glad of our success:
We are the Jasons, we have won the fleece.

Saler. I would you had won the fleece that he hath lost.

Por. There are some shrewd contents in yond same paper   245
That steals the colour from Bassanio's cheek:
Some dear friend dead, else nothing in the world
Could turn so much the constitution
Of any constant man. What, worse and worse!   249
With leave, Bassanio: I am half yourself,
And I must freely have the half of anything
That this same paper brings you.

Bass.   O sweet Portia,
Here are a few of the unpleasant'st words
That ever blotted paper! Gentle lady,
When I did first impart my love to you,   255
I freely told you all the wealth I had
Ran in my veins—I was a gentleman;
And then I told you true. And yet, dear lady,
Rating myself at nothing, you shall see
How much I was a braggart. When I told you   260
My state was nothing, I should then have told you
That I was worse than nothing; for indeed
I have engag'd myself to a dear friend,
Engag'd my friend to his mere enemy,
To feed my means. Here is a letter, lady,
The paper as the body of my friend,   266
And every word in it a gaping wound
Issuing life-blood. But is it true, Salerio?
Hath all his ventures fail'd? What, not one hit?
From Tripolis, from Mexico, and England,
From Lisbon, Barbary, and India,   271
And not one vessel scape the dreadful touch
Of merchant-marring rocks?

Saler.   Not one, my lord.
Besides, it should appear that, if he had
The present money to discharge the Jew,
He would not take it. Never did I know   276
A creature that did bear the shape of man
So keen and greedy to confound a man.
He plies the Duke at morning and at night,
And doth impeach the freedom of the state,
If they deny him justice. Twenty merchants,   281
The Duke himself, and the magnificoes
Of greatest port, have all persuaded with him;
But none can drive him from the envious plea
Of forfeiture, of justice, and his bond.   285

Jes. When I was with him, I have heard
　　him swear
To Tubal and to Chus, his countrymen,
That he would rather have Antonio's flesh
Than twenty times the value of the sum
That he did owe him; and I know, my
　　lord,　　　　　　　　　　　290
If law, authority, and power, deny not,
It will go hard with poor Antonio.

　Por. Is it your dear friend that is thus
　　in trouble?

　Bass. The dearest friend to me, the
　　kindest man,　　　　　　294
The best condition'd and unwearied spirit
In doing courtesies; and one in whom
The ancient Roman honour more appears
Than any that draws breath in Italy.

　Por. What sum owes he the Jew?　299

　Bass. For me, three thousand ducats.

　Por.　　　　　　　　What! no more?
Pay him six thousand, and deface the bond;
Double six thousand, and then treble that,　303
Before a friend of this description
Shall lose a hair through Bassanio's fault.
First go with me to church and call me wife,
And then away to Venice to your friend;　307
For never shall you lie by Portia's side
With an unquiet soul. You shall have gold
To pay the petty debt twenty times over.
When it is paid, bring your true friend along.
My maid Nerissa and myself meantime
Will live as maids and widows. Come,
　　away;　　　　　　　　　312
For you shall hence upon your wedding-
　　day.
Bid your friends welcome, show a merry
　　cheer;
Since you are dear bought, I will love you
　　dear.　　　　　　　　　315
But let me hear the letter of your friend.

　Bass [*Reads*] ' Sweet Bassanio, my ships
have all miscarried, my creditors grow
cruel, my estate is very low, my bond to the
Jew is forfeit; and since, in paying it, it
is impossible I should live, all debts are
clear'd between you and I, if I might but
see you at my death. Notwithstanding,
use your pleasure; if your love do not
persuade you to come, let not my letter.'

　Por. O love, dispatch all business and be
　　gone!

　Bass. Since I have your good'leave to go
　　away,　　　　　　　　　325
I will make haste; but, till I come again,
No bed shall e'er be guilty of my stay,
Nor rest be interposer 'twixt us twain.
　　　　　　　　　　　　[*Exeunt.*

SCENE III. *Venice. A street.*

Enter SHYLOCK, SOLANIO, ANTONIO, *and*
　　Gaoler.

　Shy. Gaoler, look to him. Tell not me of
　　mercy—

This is the fool that lent out money gratis.
Gaoler, look to him.

　Ant.　　　　　Hear me yet, good Shylock.

　Shy. I'll have my bond; speak not
　　against my bond.
I have sworn an oath that I will have my
　　bond.　　　　　　　　　5
Thou call'dst me dog before thou hadst a
　　cause,
But, since I am a dog, beware my fangs;
The Duke shall grant me justice. I do
　　wonder,
Thou naughty gaoler, that thou art so fond
To come abroad with him at his request.　10

　Ant. I pray thee hear me speak.

　Shy. I'll have my bond. I will not hear
　　thee speak;
I'll have my bond; and therefore speak no
　　more.
I'll not be made a soft and dull-ey'd fool,
To shake the head, relent, and sigh, and
　　yield,　　　　　　　　　15
To Christian intercessors. Follow not;
I'll have no speaking; I will have my bond.
　　　　　　　　　　　　[*Exit.*

　Solan. It is the most impenetrable cur
That ever kept with men.

　Ant.　　　　　　Let him alone;
I'll follow him no more with bootless
　　prayers.　　　　　　　　20
He seeks my life; his reason well I know:
I oft deliver'd from his forfeitures
Many that at times made moan to me;
Therefore he hates me.

　Solan.　　　　I am sure the Duke
Will never grant this forfeiture to hold.　25

　Ant. The Duke cannot deny the course
　　of law;
For the commodity that strangers have
With us in Venice, if it be denied,　　28
Will much impeach the justice of the state,
Since that the trade and profit of the city
Consisteth of all nations. Therefore, go;
These griefs and losses have so bated me
That I shall hardly spare a pound of flesh
To-morrow to my bloody creditor.　　34
Well, gaoler, on; pray God Bassanio come
To see me pay his debt, and then I care not.
　　　　　　　　　　　　[*Exeunt.*

SCENE IV. *Belmont. Portia's house.*

Enter PORTIA, NERISSA, LORENZO, JESSICA,
　　and BALTHASAR.

　Lor. Madam, although I speak it in your
　　presence,
You have a noble and a true conceit
Of godlike amity, which appears most
　　strongly
In bearing thus the absence of your lord.
But if you knew to whom you show this
　　honour,　　　　　　　　5
How true a gentleman you send relief,
How dear a lover of my lord your husband,

I know you would be prouder of the work
Than customary bounty can enforce you.

Por. I never did repent for doing good,
Nor shall not now; for in companions 11
That do converse and waste the time to-
gether,
Whose souls do bear an equal yoke of love,
There must be needs a like proportion
Of lineaments, of manners, and of spirit, 15
Which makes me think that this Antonio,
Being the bosom lover of my lord,
Must needs be like my lord. If it be so,
How little is the cost I have bestowed
In purchasing the semblance of my soul 20
From out the state of hellish cruelty!
This comes too near the praising of myself;
Therefore, no more of it; hear other things.
Lorenzo, I commit into your hands
The husbandry and manage of my house 25
Until my lord's return; for mine own part,
I have toward heaven breath'd a secret
vow
To live in prayer and contemplation,
Only attended by Nerissa here,
Until her husband and my lord's return. 30
There is a monastery two miles off,
And there we will abide. I do desire you
Not to deny this imposition,
The which my love and some necessity
Now lays upon you.

Lor. Madam, with all my heart
I shall obey you in all fair commands. 36

Por. My people do already know my
mind,
And will acknowledge you and Jessica
In place of Lord Bassanio and myself.
So fare you well till we shall meet again. 40

Lor. Fair thoughts and happy hours
attend on you!

Jes. I wish your ladyship all heart's
content.

Por. I thank you for your wish, and am
well pleas'd
To wish it back on you. Fare you well,
Jessica.
[*Exeunt Jessica and Lorenzo.*
Now, Balthasar, 45
As I have ever found thee honest-true,
So let me find thee still. Take this same
letter,
And use thou all th' endeavour of a man
In speed to Padua; see thou render this
Into my cousin's hands, Doctor Bellario;
And look what notes and garments he doth
give thee, 51
Bring them, I pray thee, with imagin'd
speed
Unto the traject, to the common ferry
Which trades to Venice. Waste no time in
words,
But get thee gone; I shall be there before
thee. 55

Balth. Madam, I go with all convenient
speed. [*Exit.*

Por. Come on, Nerissa, I have work in
hand
That you yet know not of; we'll see our
husbands
Before they think of us.

Ner. Shall they see us?

Por. They shall, Nerissa; but in such a
habit 60
That they shall think we are accomplished
With that we lack. I'll hold thee any
wager,
When we are both accoutred like young
men,
I'll prove the prettier fellow of the two, 64
And wear my dagger with the braver grace,
And speak between the change of man and
boy
With a reed voice; and turn two mincing
steps
Into a manly stride; and speak of frays
Like a fine bragging youth; and tell quaint
lies,
How honourable ladies sought my love, 70
Which I denying, they fell sick and died—
I could not do withal. Then I'll repent,
And wish, for all that, that I had not kill'd
them.
And twenty of these puny lies I'll tell,
That men shall swear I have discontinued
school 75
Above a twelvemonth. I have within my
mind
A thousand raw tricks of these bragging
Jacks,
Which I will practise.

Ner. Why, shall we turn to men?

Por. Fie, what a question's that,
If thou wert near a lewd interpreter! 80
But come, I'll tell thee all my whole device
When I am in my coach, which stays for us
At the park gate; and therefore haste
away,
For we must measure twenty miles to-day.
[*Exeunt.*

SCENE V. *Belmont. The garden.*

Enter LAUNCELOT *and* JESSICA.

Laun. Yes, truly; for, look you, the sins
of the father are to be laid upon the
children; therefore, I promise you, I fear
you. I was always plain with you, and so
now I speak my agitation of the matter;
therefore be o' good cheer, for truly I think
you are damn'd. There is but one hope
in it that can do you any good, and that
is but a kind of bastard hope neither. 7

Jes. And what hope is that, I pray thee?

Laun. Marry, you may partly hope that
your father got you not—that you are not
the Jew's daughter. 10

Jes. That were a kind of bastard hope
indeed; so the sins of my mother should
be visited upon me.

Laun. Truly then I fear you are damn'd both by father and mother; thus when I shun Scylla, your father, I fall into Charybdis, your mother; well, you are gone both ways.   15

Jes. I shall be sav'd by my husband; he hath made me a Christian.

Laun. Truly, the more to blame he; we were Christians enow before, e'en as many as could well live one by another. This making of Christians will raise the price of hogs; if we grow all to be pork-eaters, we shall not shortly have a rasher on the coals for money.   22

Enter LORENZO.

Jes. I'll tell my husband, Launcelot, what you say; here he comes.

Lor. I shall grow jealous of you shortly, Launcelot, if you thus get my wife into corners.   26

Jes. Nay, you need nor fear us, Lorenzo; Launcelot and I are out; he tells me flatly there's no mercy for me in heaven, because I am a Jew's daughter; and he says you are no good member of the commonwealth, for in converting Jews to Christians you raise the price of pork.   31

Lor. I shall answer that better to the commonwealth than you can the getting up of the negro's belly; the Moor is with child by you, Launcelot.   34

Laun. It is much that the Moor should be more than reason; but if she be less than an honest woman, she is indeed more than I took her for.   37

Lor. How every fool can play upon the word! I think the best grace of wit will shortly turn into silence, and discourse grow commendable in none only but parrots. Go in, sirrah; bid them prepare for dinner.   41

Laun. That is done, sir; they have all stomachs.

Lor. Goodly Lord, what a wit-snapper are you! Then bid them prepare dinner.

Laun. That is done too, sir, only 'cover' is the word.   45

Lor. Will you cover, then, sir?

Laun. Not so, sir, neither; I know my duty.

Lor. Yet more quarrelling with occasion! Wilt thou show the whole wealth of thy wit in an instant? I pray thee understand a plain man in his plain meaning: go to thy fellows, bid them cover the table, serve in the meat, and we will come in to dinner. 52

Laun. For the table, sir, it shall be serv'd in; for the meat, sir, it shall be cover'd; for your coming in to dinner, sir, why, let it be as humours and conceits shall govern.   [*Exit.*

Lor. O dear discretion, how his words are suited!

The fool hath planted in his memory
An army of good words; and I do know
A many fools that stand in better place, 59
Garnish'd like him, that for a tricksy word
Defy the matter.   How cheer'st thou,
            Jessica?
And now, good sweet, say thy opinion,
How dost thou like the Lord Bassanio's
            wife?

Jes. Past all expressing. It is very meet
The Lord Bassanio live an upright life, 65
For, having such a blessing in his lady,
He finds the joys of heaven here on earth;
And if on earth he do not merit it,
In reason he should never come to heaven.
Why, if two gods should play some heaven-
            ly match,   70
And on the wager lay two earthly women,
And Portia one, there must be something
            else
Pawn'd with the other; for the poor rude
            world
Hath not her fellow.

Lor.   Even such a husband
Hast thou of me as she is for a wife.   75

Jes. Nay, but ask my opinion too of
            that.

Lor. I will anon; first let us go to dinner.

Jes. Nay, let me praise you while I have
            a stomach.

Lor. No, pray thee, let it serve for table-
            talk;
Then howsome'er thou speak'st, 'mong
            other things   80
I shall digest it.

Jes.   Well, I'll set you forth. [*Exeunt.*

ACT FOUR

SCENE I. *Venice. The court of justice.*

Enter the DUKE, *the* MAGNIFICOES, ANTONIO,
BASSANIO, GRATIANO, SALERIO, *and* Others.

Duke. What, is Antonio here?

Ant. Ready, so please your Grace.

Duke. I am sorry for thee; thou art
            come to answer
A stony adversary, an inhuman wretch,
Uncapable of pity, void and empty   5
From any dram of mercy.

Ant.   I have heard
Your Grace hath ta'en great pains to
            qualify
His rigorous course; but since he stands
            obdurate,
And that no lawful means can carry me
Out of his envy's reach, I do oppose   10
My patience to his fury, and am arm'd
To suffer with a quietness of spirit
The very tyranny and rage of his.

Duke. Go one, and call the Jew into the
            court.

Saler. He is ready at the door; he comes,
            my lord.   15

243

Enter SHYLOCK.

Duke. Make room, and let him stand
    before our face.
Shylock, the world thinks, and I think so
    too,
That thou but leadest this fashion of thy
    malice
To the last hour of act; and then, 'tis
    thought,
Thou'lt show thy mercy and remorse, more
    strange   20
Than is thy strange apparent cruelty;
And where thou now exacts the penalty,
Which is a pound of this poor merchant's
    flesh,
Thou wilt not only loose the forfeiture,
But, touch'd with human gentleness and
    love,   25
Forgive a moiety of the principal,
Glancing an eye of pity on his losses,
That have of late so huddled on his back—
Enow to press a royal merchant down,
And pluck commiseration of his state   30
From brassy bosoms and rough hearts of
    flint,
From stubborn Turks and Tartars, never
    train'd
To offices of tender courtesy.
We all expect a gentle answer, Jew.
    Shy. I have possess'd your Grace of what
        I purpose,   35
And by our holy Sabbath have I sworn
To have the due and forfeit of my bond.
If you deny it, let the danger light
Upon your charter and your city's freedom.
You'll ask me why I rather choose to have
A weight of carrion flesh than to receive 41
Three thousand ducats. I'll not answer
    that,
But say it is my humour—is it answer'd?
What if my house be troubled with a rat,
And I be pleas'd to give ten thousand
    ducats   45
To have it ban'd? What, are you answer'd
    yet?
Some men there are love not a gaping pig;
Some that are mad if they behold a cat;
And others, when the bagpipe sings i' th'
    nose,   49
Cannot contain their urine; for affection,
Mistress of passion, sways it to the mood
Of what it likes or loathes. Now, for your
    answer:
As there is no firm reason to be rend'red
Why he cannot abide a gaping pig;
Why he, a harmless necessary cat;   55
Why he, a woollen bagpipe, but of force
Must yield to such inevitable shame
As to offend, himself being offended;
So can I give no reason, nor I will not,
More than a lodg'd hate and a certain
    loathing   60
I bear Antonio, that I follow thus

A losing suit against him. Are you
    answered?
    Bass. This is no answer, thou unfeeling
        man,
To excuse the current of thy cruelty.
    Shy. I am not bound to please thee with
        my answers.   65
    Bass. Do all men kill the things they do
        not love?
    Shy. Hates any man the thing he would
        not kill?
    Bass. Every offence is not a hate at first.
    Shy. What, wouldst thou have a serpent
        sting thee twice?
    Ant. I pray you, think you question with
        the Jew.   70
You may as well go stand upon the beach
And bid the main flood bate his usual
    height;
You may as well use question with the wolf,
Why he hath made the ewe bleat for the
    lamb;   74
You may as well forbid the mountain pines
To wag their high tops and to make no
    noise
When they are fretten with the gusts of
    heaven;
You may as well do any thing most hard
As seek to soften that—than which what's
    harder?—
His Jewish heart. Therefore, I do beseech
    you,   80
Make no moe offers, use no farther means,
But with all brief and plain conveniency
Let me have judgment, and the Jew his
    will.
    Bass. For thy three thousand ducats here
        is six.
    Shy. If every ducat in six thousand
        ducats   85
Were in six parts, and every part a ducat,
I would not draw them; I would have my
    bond.
    Duke. How shalt thou hope for mercy,
        rend'ring none?
    Shy What judgment shall I dread, doing
        no wrong?
You have among you many a purchas'd
    slave,   90
Which, like your asses and your dogs and
    mules,
You use in abject and in slavish parts,
Because you bought them; shall I say to
    you
' Let them be free, marry them to your
    heirs—
Why sweat they under burdens?—let their
    beds   95
Be made as soft as yours, and let their
    palates
Be season'd with such viands'? You will
    answer
' The slaves are ours'. So do I answer you:
The pound of flesh which I demand of him

Is dearly bought, 'tis mine, and I will
   have it.   100
If you deny me, fie upon your law !
There is no force in the decrees of Venice.
I stand for judgment ; answer ; shall I
   have it ?
   Duke. Upon my power I may dismiss this
     court,
Unless Bellario, a learned doctor,   105
Whom I have sent for to determine this,
Come here to-day.
   Saler.   My lord, here stays without
A messenger with letters from the doctor,
New come from Padua.
   Duke. Bring us the letters ; call the
     messenger.   110
   Bass. Good cheer, Antonio ! What, man,
     courage yet !
The Jew shall have my flesh, blood, bones,
   and all,
Ere thou shalt lose for me one drop of
   blood.
   Ant. I am a tainted wether of the flock,
Meetest for death ; the weakest kind of
   fruit   115
Drops earliest to the ground, and so let me.
You cannot better be employ'd, Bassanio,
Than to live still, and write mine epitaph.

Enter NERISSA, *dressed like a lawyer's clerk.*

   Duke. Came you from Padua, from
     Bellario ?   119
   Ner. From both, my lord. Bellario greets
     your Grace.   [*Presents a letter.*
   Bass. Why dost thou whet thy knife so
     earnestly ?
   Shy. To cut the forfeiture from that
     bankrupt there.
   Gra. Not on thy sole, but on thy soul,
     harsh Jew,
Thou mak'st thy knife keen ; but no metal
   can,
No, not the hangman's axe, bear half the
   keenness   125
Of thy sharp envy. Can no prayers pierce
   thee ?
   Shy. No, none that thou hast wit enough
     to make.
   Gra. O, be thou damn'd, inexecrable dog !
And for thy life let justice be accus'd.   129
Thou almost mak'st me waver in my faith,
To hold opinion with Pythagoras
That souls of animals infuse themselves
Into the trunks of men. Thy currish spirit
Govern'd a wolf who, hang'd for human
   slaughter,   134
Even from the gallows did his fell soul
   fleet,
And, whilst thou layest in thy unhallowed
   dam,
Infus'd itself in thee ; for thy desires
Are wolfish, bloody, starv'd, and ravenous.
   Shy. Till thou canst rail the seal from off
     my bond,

Thou but offend'st thy lungs to speak so
   loud ;   140
Repair thy wit, good youth, or it will fall
To cureless ruin. I stand here for law.
   Duke. This letter from Bellario doth
     commend
A young and learned doctor to our court.
Where is he ?
   Ner.   He attendeth here hard by   145
To know your answer, whether you'll admit
   him.
   Duke. With all my heart. Some three or
     four of you
Go give him courteous conduct to this place.
Meantime, the court shall hear Bellario's
   letter.   149
   Clerk. [*Reads*] ' Your Grace shall understand that at the receipt of your letter I
am very sick ; but in the instant that your
messenger came, in loving visitation was
with me a young doctor of Rome—his name
is Balthazar. I acquainted him with the
cause in controversy between the Jew and
Antonio the merchant ; we turn'd o'er
many books together ; he is furnished with
my opinion which, bettered with his own
learning—the greatness whereof I cannot
enough commend—comes with him at my
importunity to fill up your Grace's request
in my stead. I beseech you let his lack of
years be no impediment to let him lack a
reverend estimation, for I never knew so
young a body with so old a head. I leave
him to your gracious acceptance, whose
trial shall better publish his commendation.'

Enter PORTIA *for* BALTHAZAR, *dressed like
a Doctor of Laws.*

   Duke. You hear the learn'd Bellario,
     what he writes ;
And here, I take it, is the doctor come.   163
Give me your hand ; come you from old
   Bellario ?
   Por. I did, my lord.
   Duke.   You are welcome ; take your
     place.
Are you acquainted with the difference
That holds this present question in the
   court ?
   Por. I am informed throughly of the
     cause.
Which is the merchant here, and which the
   Jew ?
   Duke. Antonio and old Shylock, both
     stand forth.   170
   Por. Is your name Shylock ?
   Shy.   Shylock is my name.
   Por. Of a strange nature is the suit you
     follow ;
Yet in such rule that the Venetian law   173
Cannot impugn you as you do proceed.
You stand within his danger, do you not ?
   Ant. Ay, so he says.
   Por.   Do you confess the bond ?

Ant. I do.

Por.   Then must the Jew be merciful.

Shy. On what compulsion must I ? Tell
me that.   178

Por. The quality of mercy is not strain'd ;
It droppeth as the gentle rain from heaven
Upon the place beneath. It is twice blest :
It blesseth him that gives and him that
takes.   182
'Tis mightiest in the mightiest ; it becomes
The throned monarch better than his crown;
His sceptre shows the force of temporal
power,   185
The attribute to awe and majesty,
Wherein doth sit the dread and fear of
kings ;
But mercy is above this sceptred sway,
It is enthroned in the hearts of kings,
It is an attribute to God himself ;   190
And earthly power doth then show likest
God's
When mercy seasons justice. Therefore,
Jew,
Though justice be thy plea, consider this—
That in the course of justice none of us
Should see salvation ; we do pray for
mercy,   195
And that same prayer doth teach us all to
render
The deeds of mercy. I have spoke thus
much
To mitigate the justice of thy plea,
Which if thou follow, this strict court of
Venice
Must needs give sentence 'gainst the
merchant there.   200

Shy. My deeds upon my head ! I crave
the law,
The penalty and forfeit of my bond.

Por. Is he not able to discharge the
money ?

Bass. Yes ; here I tender it for him in
the court ;   204
Yea, twice the sum ; if that will not suffice,
I will be bound to pay it ten times o'er
On forfeit of my hands, my head, my
heart ;
If this will not suffice, it must appear
That malice bears down truth. And, I
beseech you,
Wrest once the law to your authority ;   210
To do a great right do a little wrong,
And curb this cruel devil of his will.

Por. It must not be ; there is no power
in Venice
Can alter a decree established ;
'Twill be recorded for a precedent,   215
And many an error, by the same example,
Will rush into the state ; it cannot be.

Shy. A Daniel come to judgment ! Yea,
a Daniel !
O wise young judge, how I do honour thee !

Por. I pray you, let me look upon the
bond.   220

Shy. Here 'tis, most reverend Doctor ;
here it is.

Por. Shylock, there's thrice thy money
off'red thee.

Shy. An oath, an oath ! I have an oath
in heaven.
Shall I lay perjury upon my soul ?
No, not for Venice.

Por.   Why, this bond is forfeit ; 225
And lawfully by this the Jew may claim
A pound of flesh, to be by him cut off
Nearest the merchant's heart. Be merciful.
Take thrice thy money ; bid me tear the
bond.

Shy. When it is paid according to the
tenour.   230
It doth appear you are a worthy judge ;
You know the law ; your exposition
Hath been most sound ; I charge you by
the law,
Whereof you are a well-deserving pillar,
Proceed to judgment. By my soul I swear
There is no power in the tongue of man
To alter me. I stay here on my bond. 237

Ant. Most heartily I do beseech the court
To give the judgment.

Por.   Why then, thus it is :
You must prepare your bosom for his knife.

Shy. O noble judge ! O excellent young
man !   241

Por. For the intent and purpose of the
law
Hath full relation to the penalty,
Which here appeareth due upon the bond.

Shy. 'Tis very true. O wise and upright
judge,   245
How much more elder art thou than thy
looks !

Por. Therefore, lay bare your bosom.

Shy.   Ay, his breast—
So says the bond ; doth it not, noble
judge ?
'Nearest his heart', those are the very
words.

Por. It is so. Are there balance here to
weigh   250
The flesh ?

Shy.   I have them ready.

Por. Have by some surgeon, Shylock, on
your charge,
To stop his wounds, lest he do bleed to
death.

Shy. Is it so nominated in the bond ?

Por. It is not so express'd, but what of
that ?   255
'Twere good you do so much for charity.

Shy. I cannot find it ; 'tis not in the
bond.

Por. You, merchant, have you anything
to say ?

Ant. But little : I am arm'd and well
prepar'd.   259
Give me your hand Bassanio ; fare you well.
Grieve not that I am fall'n to this for you,

For herein Fortune shows herself more
    kind
Than is her custom. It is still her use
To let the wretched man outlive his wealth,
To view with hollow eye and wrinkled
    brow   265
An age of poverty; from which ling'ring
    penance
Of such misery doth she cut me off.
Commend me to your honourable wife;
Tell her the process of Antonio's end;
Say how I lov'd you; speak me fair in
    death;   270
And, when the tale is told, bid her be judge
Whether Bassanio had not once a love.
Repent but you that you shall lose your
    friend,
And he repents not that he pays your debt;
For if the Jew do cut but deep enough,   275
I'll pay it instantly with all my heart.

    Bass. Antonio, I am married to a wife
Which is as dear to me as life itself;
But life itself, my wife, and all the world,
Are not with me esteem'd above thy life;
I would lose all, ay, sacrifice them all   281
Here to this devil, to deliver you.

    Por. Your wife would give you little
    thanks for that,
If she were by to hear you make the offer,

    Gra. I have a wife who I protest I love;
I would she were in heaven, so she could
Entreat some power to change this currish
    Jew.   287

    Ner. 'Tis well you offer it behind her
    back;
The wish would make else an unquiet house.

    Shy. [*Aside*] These be the Christian
    husbands! I have a daughter—
Would any of the stock of Barrabas   291
Had been her husband, rather than a
    Christian!—
We trifle time; I pray thee pursue
    sentence.

    Por. A pound of that same merchant's
    flesh is thine.
The court awards it and the law doth
    give it.   295

    Shy. Most rightful judge!

    Por. And you must cut this flesh from off
    his breast.
The law allows it and the court awards it.

    Shy. Most learned judge! A sentence!
    Come, prepare.

    Por. Tarry a little; there is something
    else.   300
This bond doth give thee here no jot of
    blood:
The words expressly are ' a pound of flesh '.
Take then thy bond, take thou thy pound
    of flesh;
But, in the cutting it, if thou dost shed
One drop of Christian blood, thy lands and
    goods   305
Are, by the laws of Venice, confiscate

Unto the state of Venice.

    Gra. O upright judge!   Mark, Jew.   O
    learned judge!

    Shy. Is that the law?

    Por.   Thyself shalt see the act;
For, as thou urgest justice, be assur'd   310
Thou shalt have justice, more than thou
    desir'st.

    Gra. O learned judge!   Mark, Jew.   A
    learned judge!

    Shy. I take this offer then: pay the
    bond thrice,
And let the Christian go.

    Bass.   Here is the money.

    Por. Soft!   315
The Jew shall have all justice. Soft! No
    haste.
He shall have nothing but the penalty.

    Gra. O Jew! an upright judge, a learned
    judge!

    Por. Therefore, prepare thee to cut off
    the flesh.
Shed thou no blood, nor cut thou less nor
    more   320
But just a pound of flesh; if thou tak'st
    more
Or less than a just pound—be it but so
    much
As makes it light or heavy in the substance,
Or the divison of the twentieth part
Of one poor scruple; nay, if the scale do
    turn   325
But in the estimation of a hair—
Thou diest, and all thy goods are confiscate.

    Gra. A second Daniel, a Daniel, Jew!
Now, infidel, I have you on the hip.

    Por. Why doth the Jew pause?   Take
    thy forfeiture.   330

    Shy. Give me my principal, and let me go.

    Bass. I have it ready for thee; here it is.

    Por. He hath refus'd it in the open court;
He shall have merely justice, and his bond.

    Gra. A Daniel still say I, a second
    Daniel!   335
I thank thee, Jew, for teaching me that
    word.

    Shy. Shall I not have barely my
    principal?

    Por. Thou shalt have nothing but the
    forfeiture
To be so taken at thy peril, Jew.

    Shy. Why, then the devil give him good
    of it!   340
I'll stay no longer question.

    Por.   Tarry, Jew.
The law hath yet another hold on you.
It is enacted in the laws of Venice,
If it be prov'd against an alien
That by direct or indirect attempts   345
He seek the life of any citizen,
The party 'gainst the which he doth
    contrive
Shall seize one half his goods; the other
    half

Comes to the privy coffer of the state ;
And the offender's life lies in the mercy 350
Of the Duke only, 'gainst all other voice.
In which predicament, I say, thou stand'st ;
For it appears by manifest proceeding
That indirectly, and directly too, 354
Thou hast contrived against the very life
Of the defendant ; and thou hast incurr'd
The danger formerly by me rehears'd.
Down, therefore, and beg mercy of the
     Duke.
  Gra. Beg that thou mayst have leave to
     hang thyself ;
And yet, thy wealth being forfeit to the
     state, 360
Thou hast not left the value of a cord ;
Therefore thou must be hang'd at the
     state's charge.
  Duke. That thou shalt see the difference
     of our spirit,
I pardon thee thy life before thou ask it.
For half thy wealth, it is Antonio's ; 365
The other half comes to the general state,
Which humbleness may drive unto a
     fine.
  Por. Ay, for the state ; not for Antonio.
  Shy. Nay, take my life and all, pardon
     not that.
You take my house when you do take the
     prop 370
That doth sustain my house ; you take my
     life
When you do take the means whereby I
     live.
  Por. What mercy can you render him,
     Antonio ?
  Gra. A halter gratis ; nothing else, for
     God's sake !
  Ant. So please my lord the Duke and
     all the court 375
To quit the fine for one half of his goods ;
I am content, so he will let me have
The other half in use, to render it
Upon his death unto the gentleman
That lately stole his daughter— 380
Two things provided more : that, for this
     favour,
He presently become a Christian ;
The other, that he do record a gift,
Here in the court, of all he dies possess'd
Unto his son Lorenzo and his daughter. 385
  Duke. He shall do this, or else I do recant
The pardon that I late pronounced here.
  Por. Art thou contented, Jew ? What
     dost thou say ?
  Shy. I am content.
  Por.   Clerk, draw a deed of gift.
  Shy. I pray you, give me leave to go
     from hence ; 390
I am not well ; send the deed after me
And I will sign it.
  Duke.   Get thee gone, but do it.
  Gra. In christ'ning shalt thou have two
     god-fathers ;

Had I been judge, thou shouldst have had
     ten more,
To bring thee to the gallows, not to the
     font.   [*Exit Shylock.*
  Duke. Sir, I entreat you home with me
     to dinner. 396
  Por. I humbly do desire your Grace of
     pardon ;
I must away this night toward Padua,
And it is meet I presently set forth.
  Duke. I am sorry that your leisure serves
     you not. 400
Antonio, gratify this gentleman,
For in my mind you are much bound to
     him.
     [*Exeunt Duke, Magnificoes, and Train.*
  Bass. Most worthy gentleman, I and my
     friend
Have by your wisdom been this day
     acquitted
Of grievous penalties ; in lieu whereof 405
Three thousand ducats, due unto the Jew,
We freely cope your courteous pains
     withal.
  Ant. And stand indebted, over and
     above,
In love and service to you evermore.
  Por. He is well paid that is well satisfied,
And I, delivering you, am satisfied, 411
And therein do account myself well paid.
My mind was never yet more mercenary.
I pray you, know me when we meet again ;
I wish you well, and so I take my leave. 415
  Bass. Dear sir, of force I must attempt
     you further ;
Take some remembrance of us, as a tribute,
Not as fee. Grant me two things, I pray
     you,
Not to deny me, and to pardon me.
  Por. You press me far, and therefore I
     will yield. 420
[*To Antonio*] Give me your gloves, I'll
     wear them for your sake.
[*To Bassanio*] And, for your love, I'll take
     this ring from you.
Do not draw back your hand : I'll take no
     more,
And you in love shall not deny me this.
  Bass. This ring, good sir—alas, it is a
     trifle ; 425
I will not shame myself to give you this.
  Por. I will have nothing else but only
     this ;
And now, methinks, I have a mind to it.
  Bass. There's more depends on this than
     on the value.
The dearest ring in Venice will I give you,
And find it out by proclamation ; 431
Only for this, I pray you, pardon me.
  Por. I see, sir, you are liberal in offers ;
You taught me first to beg, and now, me-
     thinks,
You teach me how a beggar should be
     answer'd. 435

Bass. Good sir, this ring was given me by
     my wife ;
And, when she put it on, she made me vow
That I should neither sell, nor give, nor
     lose it.
     Por. That 'scuse serves many men to
     save their gifts.
An if your wife be not a mad woman,   440
And know how well I have deserv'd this
     ring,
She would not hold out enemy for ever
For giving it to me. Well, peace be with
     you ! [*Exeunt Portia and Nerissa.*
     Ant. My Lord Bassanio, let him have
     the ring.
Let his deservings, and my love withal,   445
Be valued 'gainst your wife's command-
     ment.
     Bass. Go, Gratiano, run and overtake
     him ;
Give him the ring, and bring him, if thou
     canst,
Unto Antonio's house. Away, make haste.
                        [*Exit Gratiano.*
Come, you and I will thither presently ;   450
And in the morning early will we both
Fly toward Belmont. Come, Antonio.
                             [*Exeunt.*

Scene II. *Venice. A street.*

Enter PORTIA and NERISSA.

     Por. Inquire the Jew's house out, give
     him this deed,
And let him sign it ; we'll away to-night,
And be a day before our husbands home.
This deed will be well welcome to Lorenzo.

Enter GRATIANO.

     Gra. Fair sir, you are well o'erta'en.   5
My Lord Bassanio, upon more advice,
Hath sent you here this ring, and doth
     entreat
Your company at dinner.
     Por.   That cannot be.
His ring I do accept most thankfully,
And so, I pray you, tell him. Furthermore,
I pray you show my youth old Shylock's
     house.   11
     Gra. That will I do.
     Ner.   Sir, I would speak with you.
[*Aside to Portia*] I'll see if I can get my
     husband's ring,
Which I did make him swear to keep for
     ever.
     Por. [*To Nerissa*] Thou mayst, I warrant.
     We shall have old swearing   15
That they did give the rings away to men ;
But we'll outface them, and outswear them
     too.
[*Aloud*] Away, make haste, thou know'st
     where I will tarry.
     Ner. Come, good sir, will you show me to
     this house ?   [*Exeunt.*

ACT FIVE

SCENE I.   *Belmont.*   *The garden before
             Portia's house.*

Enter LORENZO and JESSICA.

     Lor. The moon shines bright. In such a
     night as this,
When the sweet wind did gently kiss the
     trees,
And they did make no noise—in such a
     night,
Troilus methinks mounted the Troyan
     walls,
And sigh'd his soul toward the Grecian
     tents,   5
Where Cressid lay that night.
     Jes.   In such a night
Did Thisby fearfully o'ertrip the dew,
And saw the lion's shadow ere himself,
And ran dismayed away.
     Lor.   In such a night
Stood Dido with a willow in her hand   10
Upon the wild sea-banks, and waft her love
To come again to Carthage.
     Jes.   In such a night
Medea gathered the enchanted herbs
That did renew old Æson.
     Lor.   In such a night
Did Jessica steal from the wealthy Jew,   15
And with an unthrift love did run from
     Venice
As far as Belmont.
     Jes.   In such a night
Did young Lorenzo swear he lov'd her well,
Stealing her soul with many vows of faith,
And ne'er a true one.
     Lor.   In such a night   20
Did pretty Jessica, like a little shrew,
Slander her love, and he forgave it her.
     Jes. I would out-night you, did no body
     come ;
But, hark, I hear the footing of a man.

Enter STEPHANO.

     Lor. Who comes so fast in silence of the
     night ?   25
     Steph. A friend.
     Lor. A friend ! What friend ? Your
     name, I pray you, friend ?
     Steph. Stephano is my name, and I bring
     word
My mistress will before the break of day   29
Be here at Belmont ; she doth stray about
By holy crosses, where she kneels and prays
For happy wedlock hours.
     Lor.   Who comes with her ?
     Steph. None but a holy hermit and her
     maid.
I pray you, is my master yet return'd ?
     Lor. He is not, nor we have not heard
     from him.   35
But go we in, I pray thee, Jessica,

And ceremoniously let us prepare
Some welcome for the mistress of the house.

Enter LAUNCELOT.

Laun. Sola, sola! wo ha, ho! sola, sola!
Lor. Who calls?   40
Laun. Sola! Did you see Master Lorenzo?
Master Lorenzo! Sola, sola!
  Lor. Leave holloaing, man. Here!
  Laun. Sola! Where, where?
  Lor. Here!   45
  Laun. Tell him there's a post come from
my master with his horn full of good news;
my master will be here ere morning. [*Exit.*
  Lor. Sweet soul, let's in, and there expect
their coming.   49
And yet no matter—why should we go in?
My friend Stephano, signify, I pray you,
Within the house, your mistress is at
hand;
And bring your music forth into the air.
                      [*Exit Stephano.*
How sweet the moonlight sleeps upon this
bank!   54
Here will we sit and let the sounds of music
Creep in our ears; soft stillness and the
night
Become the touches of sweet harmony.
Sit, Jessica. Look how the floor of heaven
Is thick inlaid with patines of bright gold;
There's not the smallest orb which thou
behold'st   60
But in his motion like an angel sings,
Still quiring to the young-ey'd cherubins;
Such harmony is in immortal souls,
But whilst this muddy vesture of decay 64
Doth grossly close it in, we cannot hear it.

Enter Musicians.

Come, ho, and wake Diana with a hymn;
With sweetest touches pierce your mistress'
ear,
And draw her home with music. [*Music.*
  Jes. I am never merry when I hear sweet
music.
  Lor. The reason is your spirits are
attentive;   70
For do but note a wild and wanton herd,
Or race of youthful and unhandled colts,
Fetching mad bounds, bellowing and
neighing loud,
Which is the hot condition of their blood—
If they but hear perchance a trumpet
sound,   75
Or any air of music touch their ears,
You shall perceive them make a mutual
stand,
Their savage eyes turn'd to a modest gaze
By the sweet power of music. Therefore
the poet
Did feign that Orpheus drew trees, stones,
and floods;   80
Since nought so stockish, hard, and full of
rage,

But music for the time doth change his
nature.
The man that hath no music in himself,
Nor is not mov'd with concord of sweet
sounds,   84
Is fit for treasons, stratagems, and spoils;
The motions of his spirit are dull as night,
And his affections dark as Erebus.
Let no such man be trusted. Mark the
music.

Enter PORTIA *and* NERISSA.

  Por. That light we see is burning in my
hall.   89
How far that little candle throws his beams!
So shines a good deed in a naughty world.
  Ner. When the moon shone, we did not
see the candle.
  Por. So doth the greater glory dim the
less:
A substitute shines brightly as a king
Until a king be by, and then his state 95
Empties itself, as doth an inland brook
Into the main of waters. Music! hark!
  Ner. It is your music, madam, of the
house.
  Por. Nothing is good, I see, without
respect;
Methinks it sounds much sweeter than by
day.   100
  Ner. Silence bestows that virtue on it,
madam.
  Por. The crow doth sing as sweetly as
the lark
When neither is attended; and I think
The nightingale, if she should sing by
day,
When every goose is cackling, would be
thought   105
No better a musician than the wren.
How many things by season season'd are
To their right praise and true perfection!
Peace, ho! The moon sleeps with Endy-
mion,
And would not be awak'd. [*Music ceases.*
  Lor.   That is the voice, 110
Or I am much deceiv'd, of Portia.
  Por. He knows me as the blind man
knows the cuckoo,
By the bad voice.
  Lor.   Dear lady, welcome home.
  Por. We have been praying for our
husbands' welfare,
Which speed, we hope, the better for our
words.   115
Are they return'd?
  Lor.   Madam, they are not yet;
But there is come a messenger before,
To signify their coming.
  Por.   Go in, Nerissa;
Give order to my servants that they take
No note at all of our being absent hence;
Nor you, Lorenzo; Jessica, nor you. 121
                      [*A tucket sounds.*

Ner. Ay, and I'll give them him without
    a fee.   290
There do I give to you and Jessica,
From the rich Jew, a special deed of gift,
After his death, of all he dies possess'd of.
    Lor. Fair ladies, you drop manna in the
    way
Of starved people.
    Por.   It is almost morning,   295
And yet I am sure you are not satisfied
Of these events at full. Let us go in,
And charge us there upon inter'gatories,
And we will answer all things faithfully.

    Gra. Let it be so. The first inter'gatory
That my Nerissa shall be sworn on is,   301
Whether till the next night she had rather
    stay,
Or go to bed now, being two hours to
    day.
But were the day come, I should wish it
    dark,
Till I were couching with the doctor's
    clerk.   305
Well, while I live, I'll fear no other thing
So sore as keeping safe Nerissa's ring.
                               [Exeunt.

AS YOU LIKE IT

DRAMATIS PERSONÆ

DUKE, *living in exile.*
FREDERICK, *his brother, and usurper of his dominions.*
AMIENS, } *lords attending on the banished*
JAQUES, } *Duke.*
LE BEAU, *a courtier attending upon Frederick.*
CHARLES, *wrestler to Frederick.*
OLIVER, }
JAQUES, } *sons of Sir Rowland de Boys.*
ORLANDO, }
ADAM,   } *servants to Oliver.*
DENNIS, }

TOUCHSTONE, *the court jester.*
SIR OLIVER MARTEXT, *a vicar.*
CORIN,   } *shepherds.*
SILVIUS, }
WILLIAM, *a country fellow, in love with Audrey.*
A person representing HYMEN.

ROSALIND, *daughter to the banished Duke.*
CELIA, *daughter to Frederick.*
PHEBE, *a shepherdess.*
AUDREY, *a country wench.*

Lords, Pages, Foresters, and Attendants.

THE SCENE: *Oliver's house; Frederick's court; and the Forest of Arden.*

ACT ONE

SCENE I. *Orchard of Oliver's house.*

Enter ORLANDO *and* ADAM.

Orl. As I remember, Adam, it was upon this fashion bequeathed me by will but poor a thousand crowns, and, as thou say'st, charged my brother, on his blessing, to breed me well; and there begins my sadness. My brother Jaques he keeps at school, and report speaks goldenly of his profit. For my part, he keeps me rustically at home, or, to speak more properly, stays me here at home unkept; for call you that keeping for a gentleman of my birth that differs not from the stalling of an ox? His horses are bred better; for, besides that they are fair with their feeding, they are taught their manage, and to that end riders dearly hir'd; but I, his brother, gain nothing under him but growth; for the which his animals on his dunghills are as much bound to him as I. Besides this nothing that he so plentifully gives me, the something that nature gave me his countenance seems to take from me. He lets me feed with his hinds, bars me the place of a brother, and as much as in him lies, mines my gentility with my education. This is it, Adam, that grieves me; and the spirit of my father, which I think is within me, begins to mutiny against this servitude. I will no longer endure it, though yet I know no wise remedy how to avoid it. 22

Enter OLIVER.

Adam. Yonder comes my master, your brother.

Orl. Go apart, Adam, and thou shalt hear how he will shake me up. [*Adam retires.*

Oli. Now, sir! what make you here? 26

Orl. Nothing; I am not taught to make any thing.

Oli. What mar you then, sir?

Orl. Marry, sir, I am helping you to mar that which God made, a poor unworthy brother of yours, with idleness. 30

Oli. Marry, sir, be better employed, and be nought awhile.

Orl. Shall I keep your hogs, and eat husks with them? What prodigal portion have I spent that I should come to such penury? 35

Oli. Know you where you are, sir?

Orl. O, sir, very well; here in your orchard.

Oli. Know you before whom, sir? 38

Orl. Ay, better than him I am before knows me. I know you are my eldest brother; and, in the gentle condition of blood, you should so know me. The courtesy of nations allows you my better in that you are the first-born; but the same tradition takes not away my blood, were there twenty brothers betwixt us. I have as much of my father in me as you, albeit I confess your coming before me is nearer to his reverence. 46

Oli. What, boy! [*Strikes him.*

Orl. Come, come, elder brother, you are too young in this. 49

Oli. Wilt thou lay hands on me, villain?

Orl. I am no villain; I am the youngest son of Sir Rowland de Boys. He was my father; and he is thrice a villain that says such a father begot villains. Wert thou not my brother, I would not take this hand from thy throat till this other had pull'd out thy tongue for saying so. Thou has rail'd on thyself.   56

Adam. [*Coming forward*] Sweet masters, be patient; for your father's remembrance, be at accord.

Oli. Let me go, I say.   59

Orl. I will not, till I please; you shall hear me. My father charg'd you in his will to give me good education: you have train'd me like a peasant, obscuring and hiding from me all gentleman-like qualities. The spirit of my father grows strong in me, and I will no longer endure it; therefore allow me such exercises as may become a gentleman, or give me the poor allottery my father left me by testament; with that I will go buy my fortunes.   67

Oli. And what wilt thou do? Beg, when that is spent? Well, sir, get you in. I will not long be troubled with you; you shall have some part of your will. I pray you leave me.   70

Orl. I will no further offend you than becomes me for my good.

Oli. Get you with him, you old dog.   73

Adam. Is 'old dog' my reward? Most true, I have lost my teeth in your service. God be with my old master! He would not have spoke such a word.   76

[*Exeunt Orlando and Adam.*

Oli. Is it even so? Begin you to grow upon me? I will physic your rankness, and yet give no thousand crowns neither. Holla, Dennis!

Enter DENNIS.

Den. Calls your worship?   80

Oli. Was not Charles, the Duke's wrestler, here to speak with me?

Den. So please you, he is here at the door and importunes access to you.   84

Oli. Call him in. [*Exit Dennis*] 'Twill be a good way; and to-morrow the wrestling is.

Enter CHARLES.

Cha. Good morrow to your worship.

Oli. Good Monsieur Charles! What's the new news at the new court?   89

Cha. There's no news at the court, sir, but the old news; that is, the old Duke is banished by his younger brother the new Duke; and three or four loving lords have put themselves into voluntary exile with him, whose lands and revenues enrich the new Duke; therefore he gives them good leave to wander.   95

Oli. Can you tell if Rosalind, the Duke's daughter, be banished with her father?   97

Cha. O, no; for the Duke's daughter, her cousin, so loves her, being ever from their cradles bred together, that she would have followed her exile, or have died to stay behind her. She is at the court, and no less

beloved of her uncle than his own daughter; and never two ladies loved as they do. 103

Oli. Where will the old Duke live?

Cha. They say he is already in the Forest of Arden, and a many merry men with him; and there they live like the old Robin Hood of England. They say many young gentlemen flock to him every day, and fleet the time carelessly, as they did in the golden world.   109

Oli. What, you wrestle to-morrow before the new Duke?

Cha. Marry, do I, sir; and I came to acquaint you with a matter. I am given, sir, secretly to understand that your younger brother, Orlando, hath a disposition to come in disguis'd against me to try a fall. To-morrow, sir, I wrestle for my credit; and he that escapes me without some broken limb shall acquit him well. Your brother is but young and tender; and, for your love, I would be loath to foil him, as I must, for my own honour, if he come in; therefore, out of my love to you, I came hither to acquaint you withal, that either you might stay him from his intendment, or brook such disgrace well as he shall run into, in that it is a thing of his own search and altogether against my will. 122

Oli. Charles, I thank thee for thy love to me, which thou shalt find I will most kindly requite. I had myself notice of my brother's purpose herein, and have by underhand means laboured to dissuade him from it; but he is resolute. I'll tell thee, Charles, it is the stubbornest young fellow of France; full of ambition, an envious emulator of every man's good parts, a secret and villainous contriver against me his natural brother. Therefore use thy discretion: I had as lief thou didst break his neck as his finger. And thou wert best look to't; for if thou dost him any slight disgrace, or if he do not mightily grace himself on thee, he will practise against thee by poison, entrap thee by some treacherous device, and never leave thee till he hath ta'en thy life by some indirect means or other; for, I assure thee, and almost with tears I speak it, there is not one so young and so villainous this day living. I speak but brotherly of him; but should I anatomize him to thee as he is, I must blush and weep, and thou must look pale and wonder.   140

Cha. I am heartily glad I came hither to you. If he come to-morrow I'll give him his payment. If ever he go alone again, I'll never wrestle for prize more. And so, God keep your worship!   [*Exit.*

Oli. Farewell, good Charles. Now will I stir this gamester. I hope I shall see an end of him; for my soul, yet I know not why, hates nothing more than he. Yet he's gentle; never school'd and yet learned;

full of noble device; of all sorts enchantingly beloved; and, indeed, so much in the heart of the world, and especially of my own people, who best know him, that I am altogether misprised. But it shall not be so long; this wrestler shall clear all. Nothing remains but that I kindle the boy thither, which now I'll go about.   [*Exit*.

SCENE II. *A lawn before the Duke's palace.*

Enter ROSALIND *and* CELIA.

Cel. I pray thee, Rosalind, sweet my coz, be merry.

Ros. Dear Celia, I show more mirth than I am mistress of; and would you yet I were merrier? Unless you could teach me to forget a banished father, you must not learn me how to remember any extraordinary pleasure.   5

Cel. Herein I see thou lov'st me not with the full weight that I love thee. If my uncle, thy banished father, had banished thy uncle, the Duke my father, so thou hadst been still with me, I could have taught my love to take thy father for mine; so wouldst thou, if the truth of thy love to me were so righteously temper'd as mine is to thee.   11

Ros. Well, I will forget the condition of my estate, to rejoice in yours.

Cel. You know my father hath no child but I, nor none is like to have; and, truly, when he dies thou shalt be his heir; for what he hath taken away from thy father perforce, I will render thee again in affection. By mine honour, I will; and when I break that oath, let me turn monster; therefore, my sweet Rose, my dear Rose, be merry.   20

Ros. From henceforth I will, coz, and devise sports. Let me see; what think you of falling in love?

Cel. Marry, I prithee, do, to make sport withal; but love no man in good earnest, nor no further in sport neither than with safety of a pure blush thou mayst in honour come off again.   26

Ros. What shall be our sport, then?

Cel. Let us sit and mock the good housewife Fortune from her wheel, that her gifts may henceforth be bestowed equally.   30

Ros. I would we' could do so; for her benefits are mightily misplaced; and the bountiful blind woman doth most mistake in her gifts to women.   33

Cel. 'Tis true; for those that she makes fair she scarce makes honest; and those that she makes honest she makes very ill-favouredly.   36

Ros. Nay; now thou goest from Fortune's office to Nature's: Fortune reigns in gifts of the world, not in the lineaments of Nature.   39

Enter TOUCHSTONE.

Cel. No; when Nature hath made a fair creature, may she not by Fortune fall into the fire? Though Nature hath given us wit to flout at Fortune, hath not Fortune sent in this fool to cut off the argument?   43

Ros. Indeed, there is Fortune too hard for Nature, when Fortune makes Nature's natural the cutter-off of Nature's wit.   46

Cel. Peradventure this is not Fortune's work neither, but Nature's, who perceiveth our natural wits too dull to reason of such goddesses, and hath sent this natural for our whetstone; for always the dullness of the fool is the whetstone of the wits. How now, wit! Whither wander you?   51

Touch. Mistress, you must come away to your father.

Cel. Were you made the messenger?

Touch. No, by mine honour; but I was bid to come for you.   55

Ros. Where learned you that oath, fool?

Touch. Of a certain knight that swore by his honour they were good pancakes, and swore by his honour the mustard was naught. Now I'll stand to it, the pancakes were naught and the mustard was good, and yet was not the knight forsworn.   61

Cel. How prove you that, in the great heap of your knowledge?

Ros. Ay, marry, now unmuzzle your wisdom.

Touch. Stand you both forth now: stroke your chins, and swear by your beards that I am a knave.   66

Cel. By our beards, if we had them, thou art.

Touch. By my knavery, if I had it, then I were. But if you swear by that that is not, you are not forsworn; no more was this knight, swearing by his honour, for he never had any; or if he had, he had sworn it away before ever he saw those pancakes or that mustard.   72

Cel. Prithee, who is't that thou mean'st?

Touch. One that old Frederick, your father, loves.   74

Cel. My father's love is enough to honour him. Enough, speak no more of him; you'll be whipt for taxation one of these days.

Touch. The more pity that fools may not speak wisely what wise men do foolishly.   79

Cel. By my troth, thou sayest true; for since the little wit that fools have was silenced, the little foolery that wise men have makes a great show. Here comes Monsieur Le Beau.   83

Enter LE BEAU.

Ros. With his mouth full of news.

Cel. Which he will put on us as pigeons feed their young.

Ros. Then shall we be news-cramm'd.   86

Cel. All the better ; we shall be the more marketable. Bon jour, Monsieur Le Beau. What's the news ?

Le Beau. Fair Princess, you have lost much good sport.

Cel. Sport ! of what colour ?   90

Le Beau. What colour, madam ? How shall I answer you ?

Ros. As wit and fortune will.

Touch. Or as the Destinies decrees.

Cel. Well said ; that was laid on with a trowel.

Touch. Nay, if I keep not my rank—   95

Ros. Thou losest thy old smell.

Le Beau. You amaze me, ladies. I would have told you of good wrestling, which you have lost the sight of.

Ros. Yet tell us the manner of the wrestling.   99

Le Beau. I will tell you the beginning, and, if it please your ladyships, you may see the end ; for the best is yet to do ; and here, where you are, they are coming to perform it.   10

Cel. Well, the beginning that is dead and buried.

Le Beau. There comes an old man and his three sons—

Cel. I could match this beginning with an old tale.   105

Le Beau. Three proper young men, of excellent growth and presence.

Ros. With bills on their necks : ' Be it known unto all men by these presents'—   109

Le Beau. The eldest of the three wrestled with Charles, the Duke's wrestler ; which Charles in a moment threw him, and broke three of his ribs, that there is little hope of life in him. So he serv'd the second, and so the third. Yonder they lie ; the poor old man, their father, making such pitiful dole over them that all the beholders take his part with weeping.   116

Ros. Alas !

Touch. But what is the sport, monsieur, that the ladies have lost ?   119

Le Beau. Why, this that I speak of.

Touch. Thus men may grow wiser every day. It is the first time that ever I heard breaking of ribs was sport for ladies.

Cel. Or I, I promise thee.   124

Ros. But is there any else longs to see this broken music in his sides ? Is there yet another dotes upon rib-breaking ? Shall we see this wrestling, cousin ?

Le Beau. You must, if you stay here ; for here is the place appointed for the wrestling, and they are ready to perform it.   130

Cel. Yonder, sure, they are coming. Let us now stay and see it.

Flourish. Enter DUKE FREDERICK, *Lords,* ORLANDO, CHARLES, *and Attendants.*

Duke F. Come on ; since the youth will not be entreated, his own peril on his forwardness.

Ros. Is yonder the man ?   135

Le Beau. Even he, madam.

Cel. Alas, he is too young ; yet he looks successfully.

Duke F. How now, daughter and cousin ! Are you crept hither to see the wrestling ?

Ros. Ay, my liege ; so please you give us leave.   140

Duke F. You will take little delight in it, I can tell you, there is such odds in the man. In pity of the challenger's youth I would fain dissuade him, but he will not be entreated.   Speak to him, ladies ; see if you can move him.

Cel. Call him hither, good Monsieur Le Beau.   145

Duke F. Do so ; I'll not be by.

[*Duke Frederick goes apart.*

Le Beau. Monsieur the Challenger, the Princess calls for you.

Orl. I attend them with all respect and duty.

Ros. Young man, have you challeng'd Charles the wrestler ?   151

Orl. No, fair Princess ; he is the general challenger.   I come but in, as others do, to try with him the strength of my youth.   154

Cel. Young gentleman, your spirits are too bold for your years.   You have seen cruel proof of this man's strength ; if you saw yourself with your eyes, or knew yourself with your judgment, the fear of your adventure would counsel you to a more equal enterprise.   We pray you, for your own sake, to embrace your own safety and give over this attempt.   160

Ros. Do, young sir ; your reputation shall not therefore be misprised : we will make it our suit to the Duke that the wrestling might not go forward.   163

Orl. I beseech you, punish me not with your hard thoughts, wherein I confess me much guilty to deny so fair and excellent ladies any thing.   But let your fair eyes and gentle wishes go with me to my trial ; wherein if I be foil'd, there is but one sham'd that was never gracious ; if kill'd, but one dead that is willing to be so.   I shall do my friends no wrong, for I have none to lament me ; the world no injury, for in it I have nothing ; only in the world I fill up a place, which may be better supplied when I have made it empty.   173

Ros. The little strength that I have, I would it were with you.   175

Cel. And mine to eke out hers.

Ros. Fare you well.   Pray heaven I be deceiv'd in you !

Cel. Your heart's desires be with you !

Cha. Come, where is this young gallant that is so desirous to lie with his mother earth ?   180

257

Orl. Ready, sir ; but his will hath in it a
more modest working.

Duke F. You shall try but one fall.

Cha. No, I warrant your Grace, you
shall not entreat him to a second, that have
so mightily persuaded him from a first. 186

Orl. You mean to mock me after ; you
should not have mock'd me before ; but
come your ways.

Ros. Now, Hercules be thy speed, young
man ! 189

Cel. I would I were invisible, to catch the
strong fellow by the leg. [*They wrestle.*

Ros. O excellent young man ! 192

Cel. If I had a thunderbolt in mine eye,
I can tell who should down.

           [*Charles is thrown. Shout.*

Duke F. No more, no more. 195

Orl. Yes, I beseech your Grace ; I am
not yet well breath'd.

Duke F. How dost thou, Charles ?

Le Beau. He cannot speak, my lord.

Duke F. Bear him away. What is thy
name, young man ? 200

Orl. Orlando, my liege ; the youngest son
of Sir Rowland de Boys.

Duke F. I would thou hadst been son to
    some man else.
The world esteem'd thy father honourable,
But I did find him still mine enemy. 205
Thou shouldst have better pleas'd me with
    this deed,
Hadst thou descended from another house.
But fare thee well ; thou art a gallant
    youth ;
I would thou hadst told me of another
    father.
    [*Exeunt Duke, Train, and Le Beau.*

Cel. Were I my father, coz, would I do
this ? 210

Orl. I am more proud to be Sir Rowland's
    son,
His youngest son—and would not change
    that calling
To be adopted heir to Frederick.

Ros. My father lov'd Sir Rowland as his
    soul, 214
And all the world was of my father's mind ;
Had I before known this young man his
    son,
I should have given him tears unto en-
    treaties 217
Ere he should thus have ventur'd.

Cel.   Gentle cousin,
Let us go thank him, and encourage him ;
My father's rough and envious disposition
Sticks me at heart. Sir, you have well
    deserv'd ; 221
If you do keep your promises in love
But justly as you have exceeded all
    promise,
Your mistress shall be happy.

Ros.   Gentleman, 224
    [*Giving him a chain from her neck.*

Wear this for me ; one out of suits with
    fortune, 225
That could give more, but that her hand
    lacks means.
Shall we go, coz ?

Cel.   Ay. Fare you well, fair gentleman.

Orl. Can I not say 'I thank you' ? My
    better parts
Are all thrown down ; and that which here
    stands up
Is but a quintain, a mere lifeless block. 230

Ros. He calls us back. My pride fell with
    my fortunes ;
I'll ask him what he would. Did you call,
    sir ?
Sir, you have wrestled well, and overthrown
More than your enemies.

Cel.   Will you go, coz ?

Ros. Have with you. Fare you well. 235
    [*Exeunt Rosalind and Celia.*

Orl. What passion hangs these weights
    upon my tongue ?
I cannot speak to her, yet she urg'd con-
    ference.
O poor Orlando, thou art overthrown !
Or Charles or something weaker masters
    thee.

        Re-enter LE BEAU.

Le Beau. Good sir, I do in friendship
    counsel you 240
To leave this place. Albeit you have
    deserv'd
High commendation, true applause, and
    love,
Yet such is now the Duke's condition
That he misconstrues all that you have
    done. 244
The Duke is humorous ; what he is, indeed,
More suits you to conceive than I to speak
    of.

Orl. I thank you, sir ; and pray you tell
    me this :
Which of the two was daughter of the Duke
That here was at the wrestling ?

Le Beau. Neither his daughter, if we
    judge by manners ; 250
But yet, indeed, the smaller is his daughter ;
The other is daughter to the banish'd Duke,
And here detain'd by her usurping uncle,
To keep his daughter company ; whose
    loves 254
Are dearer than the natural bond of sisters.
But I can tell you that of late this Duke
Hath ta'en displeasure 'gainst his gentle
    niece,
Grounded upon no other argument
But that the people praise her for her
    virtues
And pity her for her good father's sake ; 260
And, on my life, his malice 'gainst the
    lady
Will suddenly break forth. Sir, fare you
    well.

Hereafter, in a better world than this,
I shall desire more love and knowledge of
    you.
    Orl. I rest much bounden to you ; fare
    you well.   [*Exit Le Beau.*
Thus must I from the smoke into the
    smother ;   266
From tyrant Duke unto a tyrant brother.
But heavenly Rosalind !   [*Exit.*

SCENE III.   *The Duke's palace.*

Enter CELIA *and* ROSALIND.

    Cel. Why, cousin ! why, Rosalind ! Cupid
have mercy ! Not a word ?
    Ros. Not one to throw at a dog.
    Cel. No, thy words are too precious to be
cast away upon curs ; throw some of them
at me ; come, lame me with reasons.   6
    Ros. Then there were two cousins laid up,
when the one should be lam'd with reasons
and the other mad without any.
    Cel. But is all this for your father ?   10
    Ros. No, some of it is for my child's
father. O, how full of briers is this working-
day world !
    Cel. They are but burs, cousin, thrown
upon thee in holiday foolery ; if we walk
not in the trodden paths, our very petticoats will catch them.   15
    Ros. I could shake them off my coat :
these burs are in my heart.
    Cel. Hem them away.
    Ros. I would try, if I could cry 'hem' and
have him.
    Cel. Come, come, wrestle with thy
affections.   20
    Ros. O, they take the part of a better
wrestler than myself.
    Cel. O, a good wish upon you ! You will
try in time, in despite of a fall. But, turning
these jests out of service, let us talk in good
earnest. Is it possible, on such a sudden,
you should fall into so strong a liking with
old Sir Rowland's youngest son ?   27
    Ros. The Duke my father lov'd his father
dearly.
    Cel. Doth it therefore ensue that you
should love his son dearly ? By this kind
of chase I should hate him, for my father
hated his father dearly ; yet I hate not
Orlando.   31
    Ros. No, faith, hate him not, for my sake.
    Cel. Why should I not ? Doth he not
deserve well ?

Enter DUKE FREDERICK, *with* Lords.

    Ros. Let me love him for that ; and do
you love him because I do. Look, here
comes the Duke.   35
    Cel. With his eyes full of anger.
    Duke F. Mistress, dispatch you with your
    safest haste,
And get you from our court.

    Ros.   Me, uncle ?
    Duke F.   You, cousin.
Within these ten days if that thou beest
    found   39
So near our public court as twenty miles,
Thou diest for it.
    Ros.   I do beseech your Grace,
Let me the knowledge of my fault bear with
    me.
If with myself I hold intelligence,
Or have acquaintance with mine own
    desires ;   44
If that I do not dream, or be not frantic—
As I do trust I am not—then, dear uncle,
Never so much as in a thought unborn
Did I offend your Highness.
    Duke F.   Thus do all traitors ;
If their purgation did consist in words,
They are as innocent as grace itself.   50
Let it suffice thee that I trust thee not.
    Ros. Yet your mistrust cannot make me
    a traitor.
Tell me whereon the likelihood depends.
    Duke F. Thou art thy father's daughter ;
    there's enough.
    Ros. So was I when your Highness took
    his dukedom ;   55
So was I when your Highness banish'd him.
Treason is not inherited, my lord ;
Or, if we did derive it from our friends,
What's that to me ? My father was no
    traitor.
Then, good my liege, mistake me not so
    much   60
To think my poverty is treacherous.
    Cel. Dear sovereign, hear me speak.
    Duke F. Ay, Celia ; we stay'd her for
    your sake,
Else had she with her father rang'd along.
    Cel. I did not then entreat to have her
    stay ;   65
It was your pleasure, and your own
    remorse ;
I was too young that time to value her,
But now I know her. If she be a traitor,
Why so am I : we still have slept together,
Rose at an instant, learn'd, play'd, eat
    together ;   70
And wheresoe'er we went, like Juno's
    swans,
Still we went coupled and inseparable.
    Duke F. She is too subtle for thee ; and
    her smoothness,
Her very silence and her patience,
Speak to the people, and they pity her.   75
Thou art a fool. She robs thee of thy name ;
And thou wilt show more bright and seem
    more virtuous
When she is gone. Then open not thy lips.
Firm and irrevocable is my doom
Which I have pass'd upon her ; she is
    banish'd.   80
    Cel. Pronounce that sentence, then, on
    me, my liege ;

I cannot live out of her company.

Duke F. You are a fool. You, niece,
provide yourself. 83
If you outstay the time, upon mine honour,
And in the greatness of my word, you die.
[*Exeunt Duke and Lords.*

Cel. O my poor Rosalind! Whither wilt
thou go? 86
Wilt thou change fathers? I will give thee
mine.
I charge thee be not thou more griev'd than
I am.

Ros. I have more cause.

Cel.   Thou hast not, cousin.
Prithee be cheerful. Know'st thou not the
Duke 90
Hath banish'd me, his daughter?

Ros.   That he hath not.

Cel. No, hath not? Rosalind lacks, then,
the love
Which teacheth thee that thou and I am
one.
Shall we be sund'red? Shall we part, sweet
girl?
No; let my father seek another heir. 95
Therefore devise with me how we may fly,
Whither to go, and what to bear with us;
And do not seek to take your charge upon
you,
To bear your griefs yourself, and leave me
out;
For, by this heaven, now at our sorrows
pale, 100
Say what thou canst, I'll go along with thee.

Ros. Why, whither shall we go?

Cel. To seek my uncle in the Forest of
Arden.

Ros. Alas, what danger will it be to us,
Maids as we are, to travel forth so far! 105
Beauty provoketh thieves sooner than gold.

Cel. I'll put myself in poor and mean
attire,
And with a kind of umber smirch my
face;
The like do you; so shall we pass along, 109
And never stir assailants.

Ros.   Were it not better,
Because that I am more than common tall,
That I did suit me all points like a man?
A gallant curtle-axe upon my thigh,
A boar spear in my hand; and—in my
heart
Lie there what hidden woman's fear there
will— 115
We'll have a swashing and a martial out-
side,
As many other mannish cowards have
That do outface it with their semblances.

Cel. What shall I call thee when thou art
a man?

Ros. I'll have no worse a name than
Jove's own page, 120
And therefore look you call me Ganymede.
But what will you be call'd?

Cel. Something that hath a reference to
my state:
No longer Celia, but Aliena.

Ros. But, cousin, what if we assay'd to
steal 125
The clownish fool out of your father's court?
Would he not be a comfort to our travel?

Cel. He'll go along o'er the wide world
with me;
Leave me alone to woo him. Let's away,
And get our jewels and our wealth together;
Devise the fittest time and safest way 131
To hide us from pursuit that will be made
After my flight. Now go we in content
To liberty, and not to banishment. [*Exeunt.*

ACT TWO

SCENE I. *The Forest of Arden.*

Enter DUKE SENIOR, AMIENS, *and two or
three* LORDS, *like foresters.*

Duke S. Now, my co-mates and brothers
in exile,
Hath not old custom made this life more
sweet
Than that of painted pomp? Are not these
woods
More free from peril than the envious court?
Here feel we not the penalty of Adam, 5
The seasons' difference; as the icy fang
And churlish chiding of the winter's wind,
Which when it bites and blows upon my
body, 8
Even till I shrink with cold, I smile and say
'This is no flattery; these are counsellors
That feelingly persuade me what I am'.
Sweet are the uses of adversity;
Which, like the toad, ugly and venomous,
Wears yet a precious jewel in his head; 14
And this our life, exempt from public haunt,
Finds tongues in trees, books in the running
brooks,
Sermons in stones, and good in everything.
I would not change it.

Ami.   Happy is your Grace,
That can translate the stubbornness of
fortune
Into so quiet and so sweet a style. 20

Duke S. Come, shall we go and kill us
venison?
And yet it irks me the poor dappled fools,
Being native burghers of this desert city,
Should, in their own confines, with forked
heads 24
Have their round haunches gor'd.

1 Lord.   Indeed, my lord,
The melancholy Jaques grieves at that;
And, in that kind, swears you do more
usurp
Than doth your brother that hath banish'd
you.
To-day my Lord of Amiens and myself
Did steal behind him as he lay along 30

Under an oak whose antique root peeps
    out
Upon the brook that brawls along this
    wood !
To the which place a poor sequest'red
    stag,
That from the hunter's aim had ta'en a
    hurt,
Did come to languish ; and, indeed, my
    lord,   35
The wretched animal heav'd forth such
    groans
That their discharge did stretch his leathern
    coat
Almost to bursting ; and the big round
    tears
Cours'd one another down his innocent
    nose   39
In piteous chase ; and thus the hairy fool,
Much marked of the melancholy Jaques,
Stood on th' extremest verge of the swift
    brook,
Augmenting it with tears.
    Duke S.   But what said Jaques ?
Did he not moralize this spectacle ?   44
    1 Lord. O, yes, into a thousand similes.
First, for his weeping into the needless
    stream :
' Poor deer,' quoth he ' thou mak'st a testa-
    ment
As worldlings do, giving thy sum of more
To that which had too much '. Then, being
    there alone,   49
Left and abandoned of his velvet friends :
' 'Tis right ; ' quoth he ' thus misery doth
    part
The flux of company '.   Anon, a careless
    herd,
Full of the pasture, jumps along by him
And never stays to greet him. ' Ay,' quoth
    Jaques
' Sweep on, you fat and greasy citizens ; 55
'Tis just the fashion.   Wherefore do you
    look
Upon that poor and broken bankrupt
    there ? '
Thus most invectively he pierceth through
The body of the country, city, court,   59
Yea, and of this our life ; swearing that
    we
Are mere usurpers, tyrants, and what's
    worse,
To fright the animals, and to kill them up
In their assign'd and native dwelling-place.
    Duke S. And did you leave him in this
    contemplation ?
    2 Lord. We did, my lord, weeping and
    commenting   65
Upon the sobbing deer.
    Duke S.   Show me the place ;
I love to cope him in these sullen fits,
For then he's full of matter.
    1 Lord. I'll bring you to him straight. 69
                          [Exeunt.

SCENE II.   *The Duke's palace.*

Enter DUKE FREDERICK, *with* Lords.

Duke F. Can it be possible that no man saw
    them ?
It cannot be ; some villains of my court
Are of consent and sufferance in this.
    1 Lord. I cannot hear of any that did see
    her.   4
The ladies, her attendants of her chamber,
Saw her abed, and in the morning early
They found the bed untreasur'd of their
    mistress.
    2 Lord. My lord, the roynish clown, at
    whom so oft
Your Grace was wont to laugh, is also
    missing.
Hisperia, the Princess' gentlewoman,   10
Confesses that she secretly o'erheard
Your daughter and her cousin much com-
    mend
The parts and graces of the wrestler
That did but lately foil the sinewy Charles;
And she believes, wherever they are gone,
That youth is surely in their company. 16
    Duke F. Send to his brother ; fetch that
    gallant hither.
If he be absent, bring his brother to me ;
I'll make him find him.   Do this suddenly ;
And let not search and inquisition quail 20
To bring again these foolish runaways.
                          [Exeunt.

SCENE III.   *Before Oliver's house.*

Enter ORLANDO *and* ADAM, *meeting.*

    Orl. Who's there ?
    Adam. What, my young master ?   O my
    gentle master !
O my sweet master !   O you memory
Of old Sir Rowland !   Why, what make you
    here ?
Why are you virtuous ?   Why do people
    love you ?   5
And wherefore are you gentle, strong, and
    valiant ?
Why would you be so fond to overcome
The bonny prizer of the humorous Duke ?
Your praise is come too swiftly home before
    you.
Know you not, master, to some kind of
    men   10
Their graces serve them but as enemies ?
No more do yours.   Your virtues, gentle
    master,
Are sanctified and holy traitors to you.
O, what a world is this, when what is
    comely
Envenoms him that bears it !   15
    Orl. Why, what's the matter ?
    Adam.   O unhappy youth !
Come not within these doors ; within this
    roof
The enemy of all your graces lives.

Your brother—no, no brother; yet the
   son—
Yet not the son; I will not call him son 20
Of him I was about to call his father—
Hath heard your praises; and this night he
   means
To burn the lodging where you use to lie,
And you within it. If he fail of that,
He will have other means to cut you off;
I overheard him and his practices. 26
This is no place; this house is but a
   butchery;
Abhor it, fear it, do not enter it.
  Orl. Why, whither, Adam, wouldst thou
    have me go?
  Adam. No matter whither, so you come
    not here. 30
  Orl. What, wouldst thou have me go and
    beg my food,
Or with a base and boist'rous sword enforce
A thievish living on the common road?
This I must do, or know not what to do;
Yet this I will not do, do how I can. 35
I rather will subject me to the malice
Of a diverted blood and bloody brother.
  Adam. But do not so. I have five
    hundred crowns,
The thrifty hire I sav'd under your father,
Which I did store to be my foster-nurse, 40
When service should in my old limbs lie
   lame,
And unregarded age in corners thrown.
Take that, and He that doth the ravens
   feed,
Yea, providently caters for the sparrow,
Be comfort to my age! Here is the gold; 45
All this I give you. Let me be your
   servant;
Though I look old, yet I am strong and
   lusty;
For in my youth I never did apply
Hot and rebellious liquors in my blood,
Nor did not with unbashful forehead woo
The means of weakness and debility; 51
Therefore my age is as a lusty winter,
Frosty, but kindly. Let me go with you;
I'll do the service of a younger man
In all your business and necessities. 55
  Orl. O good old man, how well in thee
    appears
The constant service of the antique world,
When service sweat for duty, not for meed!
Thou art not for the fashion of these times,
Where none will sweat but for promotion,
And having that do choke their service up
Even with the having; it is not so with
   thee. 62
But, poor old man, thou prun'st a rotten
   tree
That cannot so much as a blossom yield
In lieu of all thy pains and husbandry. 65
But come thy ways, we'll go along together,
And ere we have thy youthful wages spent
We'll light upon some settled low content.

  Adam. Master, go on; and I will follow
    thee
To the last gasp, with truth and loyalty. 70
From seventeen years till now almost four-
   score
Here lived I, but now live here no more.
At seventeen years many their fortunes
   seek,
But at fourscore it is too late a week; 74
Yet fortune cannot recompense me better
Than to die well and not my master's
   debtor.   [*Exeunt.*

SCENE IV. *The Forest of Arden.*

Enter ROSALIND *for* GANYMEDE, CELIA *for*
ALIENA, *and* Clown *alias* TOUCHSTONE.

  Ros. O Jupiter, how weary are my spirits!
  Touch. I care not for my spirits, if my
legs were not weary. 3
  Ros. I could find in my heart to disgrace
my man's apparel, and to cry like a woman;
but I must comfort the weaker vessel, as
doublet and hose ought to show itself
courageous to petticoat; therefore, courage, good Aliena. 7
  Cel. I pray you bear with me; I cannot
go no further.
  Touch. For my part, I had rather bear
with you than bear you; yet I should bear
no cross if I did bear you; for I think you
have no money in your purse. 11
  Ros. Well, this is the Forest of Arden.
  Touch. Ay, now am I in Arden; the
more fool I; when I was at home I was in
a better place; but travellers must be
content. 15

Enter CORIN *and* SILVIUS.

  Ros. Ay, be so, good Touchstone. Look
you, who comes here, a young man and
an old in solemn talk.
  Cor. That is the way to make her scorn
    you still.
  Sil. O Corin, that thou knew'st how I do
    love her! 20
  Cor. I partly guess; for I have lov'd ere
    now.
  Sil. No, Corin, being old, thou canst not
    guess,
Though in thy youth thou wast as true a
   lover
As ever sigh'd upon a midnight pillow.
But if thy love were ever like to mine, 25
As sure I think did never man love so,
How many actions most ridiculous
Hast thou been drawn to by thy fantasy?
  Cor. Into a thousand that I have for-
    gotten.
  Sil. O, thou didst then never love so
    heartily! 30
If thou rememb'rest not the slightest folly
That ever love did make thee run into,
Thou hast not lov'd;

Or if thou hast not sat as I do now,   34
Wearing thy hearer in thy mistress' praise,
Thou hast not lov'd;
Or if thou hast not broke from company
Abruptly, as my passion now makes me,
Thou hast not lov'd.   39
O Phebe, Phebe, Phebe!   [*Exit Silvius.*
  Ros. Alas, poor shepherd! searching of
    thy wound,   41
I have by hard adventure found mine own.
  Touch. And I mine. I remember, when I
was in love, I broke my sword upon a stone,
and bid him take that for coming a-night
to Jane Smile; and I remember the kissing
of her batler, and the cow's dugs that her
pretty chopt hands had milk'd; and I
remember the wooing of a peascod instead
of her; from whom I took two cods, and,
giving her them again, said with weeping
tears ' Wear these for my sake'. We that
are true lovers run into strange capers; but
as all is mortal in nature, so is all nature in
love mortal in folly.   52
  Ros. Thou speak'st wiser than thou art
ware of.
  Touch. Nay, I shall ne'er be ware of mine
own wit till I break my shins against it. 55
  Ros. Jove, Jove! this shepherd's passion
    Is much upon my fashion.
  Touch. And mine; but it grows some-
thing stale with me.
  Cel. I pray you, one of you question yond
man
If he for gold will give us any food;   60
I faint almost to death.
  Touch. Holla, you clown!
  Ros. Peace, fool; he's not thy kinsman.
  Cor. Who calls?
  Touch. Your betters, sir.
  Cor.   Else are they very wretched.
  Ros. Peace, I say. Good even to you,
friend.
  Cor. And to you, gentle sir, and to you
all.   65
  Ros. I prithee, shepherd, if that love or
gold
Can in this desert place buy entertainment,
Bring us where we may rest ourselves and
feed.
Here's a young maid with travel much
    oppress'd,   69
And faints for succour.
  Cor.   Fair sir, I pity her,
And wish, for her sake more than for mine
    own,
My fortunes were more able to relieve her;
But I am shepherd to another man,
And do not shear the fleeces that I graze.
My master is of churlish disposition,   75
And little recks to find the way to heaven
By doing deeds of hospitality.
Besides, his cote, his flocks, and bounds of
    feed,   78
Are now on sale; and at our sheepcote now,

By reason of his absence, there is nothing
That you will feed on; but what is, come
    see,
And in my voice most welcome shall you be.
  Ros. What is he that shall buy his flock
    and pasture?
  Cor. That young swain that you saw
    here but erewhile,
That little cares for buying any thing.   85
  Ros. I pray thee, if it stand with honesty,
Buy thou the cottage, pasture, and the
    flock,
And thou shalt have to pay for it of us.
  Cel. And we will mend thy wages. I like
this place,
And willingly could waste my time in it. 90
  Cor. Assuredly the thing is to be sold.
Go with me; if you like upon report
The soil, the profit, and this kind of life,
I will your very faithful feeder be,   94
And buy it with your gold right suddenly.
                      [*Exeunt.*

SCENE V. *Another part of the Forest.*

Enter AMIENS, JAQUES, *and* Others.

Song.

Ami. Under the greenwood tree
    Who loves to lie with me,
    And turn his merry note
    Unto the sweet bird's throat,
Come hither, come hither, come hither.   5
    Here shall he see
    No enemy
But winter and rough weather.

  Jaq. More, more, I prithee, more.
  Ami. It will make you melancholy,
Monsieur Jaques.   10
  Jaq. I thank it. More, I prithee, more.
I can suck melancholy out of a song, as a
weasel sucks eggs. More, I prithee, more.
  Ami. My voice is ragged; I know I
cannot please you.   14
  Jaq. I do not desire you to please me; I
do desire you to sing. Come, more; another stanzo. Call you 'em stanzos?
  Ami. What you will, Monsieur Jaques.
  Jaq. Nay, I care not for their names;
they owe me nothing. Will you sing?
  Ami. More at your request than to please
myself.   20
  Jaq. Well then, if ever I thank any man,
I'll thank you; but that they call compliment is like th' encounter of two dog-apes;
and when a man thanks me heartily, methinks I have given him a penny, and he
renders me the beggarly thanks. Come,
sing; and you that will not, hold your
tongues.   26
  Ami. Well, I'll end the song. Sirs, cover
the while; the Duke will drink under this
tree. He hath been all this day to look you.

Jaq. And I have been all this day to
avoid him. He is too disputable for my
company. I think of as many matters as
he; but I give heaven thanks, and make
no boast of them. Come, warble, come. 33

Song.

All together here.

Who doth ambition shun,
And loves to live i' th' sun, 35
Seeking the food he eats,
And pleas'd with what he gets,
Come hither, come hither, come hither.
Here shall he see
No enemy 40
But winter and rough weather.

Jaq. I'll give you a verse to this note
that I made yesterday in despite of my
invention.
Ami. And I'll sing it.
Jaq. Thus it goes : 45

If it do come to pass
That any man turn ass,
Leaving his wealth and ease
A stubborn will to please,
Ducdame, ducdame, ducdame; 50
Here shall he see
Gross fools as he,
An if he will come to me.

Ami. What's that ' ducdame ' ? 54
Jaq. 'Tis a Greek invocation, to call fools
into a circle. I'll go sleep, if I can; if I
cannot, I'll rail against all the first-born of
Egypt.
Ami. And I'll go seek the Duke; his
banquet is prepar'd. [*Exeunt severally.*

Scene VI. *The forest.*

Enter ORLANDO *and* ADAM.

Adam. Dear master, I can go no further.
O, I die for food ! Here lie I down, and
measure out my grave. Farewell, kind
master. 3
Orl. Why, how now, Adam ! No greater
heart in thee ? Live a little; comfort a
little; cheer thyself a little. If this uncouth forest yield anything savage, I will
either be food for it or bring it for food to
thee. Thy conceit is nearer death than thy
powers. For my sake be comfortable; hold
death awhile at the arm's end. I will here
be with thee presently; and if I bring
thee not something to eat, I will give thee
leave to die; but if thou diest before I
come, thou art a mocker of my labour.
Well said ! thou look'st cheerly; and I'll
be with thee quickly. Yet thou liest in the
bleak air. Come, I will bear thee to some
shelter; and thou shalt not die for lack of
a dinner, if there live any thing in this
desert. Cheerly, good Adam ! [*Exeunt.*

Scene VII. *The forest.*

A table set out. Enter DUKE SENIOR, AMIENS,
and Lords, *like outlaws.*

Duke S. I think he be transform'd into a
beast ;
For I can nowhere find him like a man.
1 *Lord.* My lord, he is but even now gone
hence ;
Here was he merry, hearing of a song.
Duke S. If he, compact of jars, grow
musical, 5
We shall have shortly discord in the
spheres.
Go seek him ; tell him I would speak with
him.

Enter JAQUES.

1 *Lord.* He saves my labour by his own
approach.
Duke S. Why, how now, monsieur ! what
a life is this,
That your poor friends must woo your com-
pany ? 10
What, you look merrily !
Jaq. A fool, a fool ! I met a fool i' th'
forest,
A motley fool. A miserable world !
As I do live by food, I met a fool,
Who laid him down and bask'd him in the
sun, 15
And rail'd on Lady Fortune in good terms,
In good set terms—and yet a motley fool.
' Good morrow, fool ' quoth I ; ' No, sir,'
quoth he
' Call me not fool till heaven hath sent me
fortune.'
And then he drew a dial from his poke, 20
And, looking on it with lack-lustre eye,
Says very wisely ' It is ten o'clock ;
Thus we may see ' quoth he ' how the
world wags ;
'Tis but an hour ago since it was nine ; 24
And after one hour more 'twill be eleven ;
And so, from hour to hour, we ripe and ripe,
And then, from hour to hour, we rot and rot ;
And thereby hangs a tale '. When I did hear
The motley fool thus moral on the time,
My lungs began to crow like chanticleer 30
That fools should be so deep contemplative;
And I did laugh sans intermission
An hour by his dial. O noble fool !
A worthy fool ! Motley's the only wear.
Duke S. What fool is this ? 35
Jaq. O worthy fool ! One that hath been
a courtier,
And says, if ladies be but young and fair,
They have the gift to know it ; and in his
brain,
Which is as dry as the remainder biscuit
After a voyage, he hath strange places
cramm'd 40
With observation, the which he vents
In mangled forms. O that I were a fool !

I am ambitious for a motley coat.
   Duke S. Thou shalt have one.
   Jaq.   It is my only suit,
Provided that you weed your better judg-
    ments   45
Of all opinion that grows rank in them
That I am wise. I must have liberty
Withal, as large a charter as the wind,
To blow on whom I please, for so fools have;
And they that are most galled with my
    folly,   50
They most must laugh. And why, sir, must
    they so ?
The why is plain as way to parish church :
He that a fool doth very wisely hit
Doth very foolishly, although he smart,
Not to seem senseless of the bob ; if not, 55
The wise man's folly is anatomiz'd
Even by the squand'ring glances of the fool.
Invest me in my motley ; give me leave
To speak my mind, and I will through and
    through   59
Cleanse the foul body of th' infected world,
If they will patiently receive my medicine.
   Duke S. Fie on thee ! I can tell what thou
    wouldst do.
   Jaq. What, for a counter, would I do but
    good ?
   Duke S. Most mischievous foul sin, in
    chiding sin ;
For thou thyself hast been a libertine, 65
As sensual as the brutish sting itself ;
And all th' embossed sores and headed
    evils
That thou with licence of free foot hast
    caught
Wouldst thou disgorge into the general
    world.
   Jaq. Why, who cries out on pride 70
That can therein tax any private party ?
Doth it not flow as hugely as the sea,
Till that the wearer's very means do ebb ?
What woman in the city do I name
When that I say the city-woman bears 75
The cost of princes on unworthy shoulders ?
Who can come in and say that I mean her,
When such a one as she such is her neigh-
    bour ?
Or what is he of basest function
That says his bravery is not on my cost, 80
Thinking that I mean him, but therein suits
His folly to the mettle of my speech ?
There then ! how then ? what then ? Let
    me see wherein
My tongue hath wrong'd him : if it do him
    right,
Then he hath wrong'd himself ; if he be
    free,   85
Why then my taxing like a wild-goose flies,
Unclaim'd of any man. But who comes
    here ?

   Enter ORLANDO, *with his sword drawn.*

   Orl. Forbear, and eat no more.

   Jaq.   Why, I have eat none yet.
   Orl. Nor shalt not, till necessity be serv'd.
   Jaq. Of what kind should this cock come
    of ?   90
   Duke S. Art thou thus bolden'd, man, by
    thy distress ?
Or else a rude despiser of good manners,
That in civility thou seem'st so empty ?
   Orl. You touch'd my vein at first : the
    thorny point
Of bare distress hath ta'en from me the
    show   95
Of smooth civility ; yet am I inland bred,
And know some nurture. But forbear, I
    say ;
He dies that touches any of this fruit
Till I and my affairs are answered.
   Jaq. An you will not be answer'd with
reason, I must die.   101
   Duke S. What would you have ? Your
    gentleness shall force
More than your force move us to gentleness.
   Orl. I almost die for food, and let me
    have it.
   Duke S. Sit down and feed, and welcome
    to our table.   105
   Orl. Speak you so gently ? Pardon me, I
    pray you ;
I thought that all things had been savage
    here,
And therefore put I on the countenance
Of stern commandment. But whate'er you
    are
That in this desert inaccessible, 110
Under the shade of melancholy boughs,
Lose and neglect the creeping hours of
    time ;
If ever you have look'd on better days,
If ever been where bells have knoll'd to
    church,
If ever sat at any good man's feast, 115
If ever from your eyelids wip'd a tear,
And know what 'tis to pity and be pitied,
Let gentleness my strong enforcement be ;
In the which hope I blush, and hide my
    sword.
   Duke S. True is it that we have seen
    better days,   120
And have with holy bell been knoll'd to
    church,
And sat at good men's feasts, and wip'd our
    eyes
Of drops that sacred pity hath engend'red ;
And therefore sit you down in gentleness,
And take upon command what help we
    have   125
That to your wanting may be minist'red.
   Orl. Then but forbear your food a little
    while,
Whiles, like a doe, I go to find my fawn,
And give it food. There is an old poor
    man
Who after me hath many a weary step 130
Limp'd in pure love ; till he be first suffic'd,

Oppress'd with two weak evils, age and
    hunger,
I will not touch a bit.
    Duke S.   Go find him out.
And we will nothing waste till you return.
    Orl. I thank ye ; and be blest for your
        good comfort !   [*Exit.*
    Duke S. Thou seest we are not all alone
        unhappy :   136
This wide and universal theatre
Presents more woeful pageants than the
    scene   138
Wherein we play in.
    Jaq.   All the world's a stage,
And all the men and women merely players;
They have their exits and their entrances ;
And one man in his time plays many parts,
His acts being seven ages. At first the
    infant,
Mewling and puking in the nurse's arms ;
Then the whining school-boy, with his
    satchel   145
And shining morning face, creeping like
    snail
Unwillingly to school. And then the lover,
Sighing like furnace, with a woeful ballad
Made to his mistress' eyebrow. Then a
    soldier,
Full of strange oaths, and bearded like the
    pard,   150
Jealous in honour, sudden and quick in
    quarrel,
Seeking the bubble reputation
Even in the cannon's mouth. And then the
    justice,
In fair round belly with good capon lin'd,
With eyes severe and beard of formal cut,
Full of wise saws and modern instances ; 156
And so he plays his part. The sixth age shifts
Into the lean and slipper'd pantaloon,
With spectacles on nose and pouch on side,
His youthful hose, well sav'd, a world too
    wide   160
For his shrunk shank ; and his big manly
    voice,
Turning again toward childish treble, pipes
And whistles in his sound. Last scene of all,
That ends this strange eventful history,
Is second childishness and mere oblivion ;
Sans teeth, sans eyes, sans taste, sans every
    thing.   166

Re-enter ORLANDO *with* ADAM.

    Duke S. Welcome. Set down your
        venerable burden.
And let him feed.
    Orl. I thank you most for him.
    Adam.   So had you need ;
I scarce can speak to thank you for myself.
    Duke S. Welcome ; fall to. I will not
        trouble you   171
As yet to question you about your fortunes.
Give us some music ; and, good cousin,
    sing.

Song.

Blow, blow, thou winter wind,
Thou art not so unkind   175
    As man's ingratitude ;
Thy tooth is not so keen,
Because thou art not seen,
    Although thy breath be rude.
Heigh-ho ! sing heigh-ho ! unto the green
    holly.   180
Most friendship is feigning, most loving
    mere folly.
    Then, heigh-ho, the holly !
        This life is most jolly.

Freeze, freeze, thou bitter sky,
That dost not bite so nigh   185
    As benefits forgot ;
Though thou the waters warp,
Thy sting is not so sharp
    As friend rememb'red not.
Heigh-ho ! sing, &c.   190

    Duke S. If that you were the good Sir
        Rowland's son,
As you have whisper'd faithfully you were,
And as mine eye doth his effigies witness
Most truly limn'd and living in your face,
Be truly welcome hither. I am the Duke
That lov'd your father. The residue of your
    fortune,   196
Go to my cave and tell me. Good old man,
Thou art right welcome as thy master is.
Support him by the arm. Give me your
    hand,   199
And let me all your fortunes understand.
                                    [*Exeunt.*

ACT THREE

SCENE I. *The palace.*

Enter DUKE FREDERICK, OLIVER, *and*
    Lords.

    Duke F. Not see him since ! Sir, sir, that
        cannot be.
But were I not the better part made mercy,
I should not seek an absent argument
Of my revenge, thou present. But look
    to it :
Find out thy brother wheresoe'er he is ; 5
Seek him with candle ; bring him dead or
    living
Within this twelvemonth, or turn thou no
    more
To seek a living in our territory.
Thy lands and all things that thou dost call
    thine   9
Worth seizure do we seize into our hands,
Till thou canst quit thee by thy brother's
    mouth
Of what we think against thee.
    Oli. O that your Highness knew my heart
        in this !
I never lov'd my brother in my life.
    Duke F. More villain thou. Well, push
        him out of doors ;   15

And let my officers of such a nature
Make an extent upon his house and
  lands.
Do this expediently, and turn him going.
                                    [*Exeunt.*

SCENE II. *The forest.*

Enter ORLANDO, *with a paper.*

Orl. Hang there, my verse, in witness of
  my love ;
And thou, thrice-crowned Queen of Night,
  survey
With thy chaste eye, from thy pale sphere
  above,
Thy huntress' name that my full life doth
  sway.   4
O Rosalind ! these trees shall be my books,
And in their barks my thoughts I'll
  character,
That every eye which in this forest looks
Shall see thy virtue witness'd every
  where.
Run, run, Orlando ; carve on every tree, 9
The fair, the chaste, and unexpressive she.
                                    [*Exit.*

Enter CORIN *and* TOUCHSTONE.

Cor. And how like you this shepherd's
life, Master Touchstone ?   12
Touch. Truly, shepherd, in respect of
itself, it is a good life; but in respect that it
is a shepherd's life, it is nought. In respect
that it is solitary, I like it very well ; but in
respect that it is private, it is a very vile
life. Now in respect it is in the fields, it
pleaseth me well ; but in respect it is not
in the court, it is tedious. As it is a spare
life, look you, it fits my humour well ; but
as there is no more plenty in it, it goes
much against my stomach. Hast any
philosophy in thee, shepherd ?   21
Cor. No more but that I know the more
one sickens the worse at ease he is ; and
that he that wants money, means, and content, is without three good friends ; that
the property of rain is to wet, and fire to
burn ; that good pasture makes fat sheep ;
and that a great cause of the night is lack
of the sun ; that he that hath learned no
wit by nature nor art may complain of good
breeding, or comes of a very dull kindred.
Touch. Such a one is a natural philosopher. Wast ever in court, shepherd ?   30
Cor. No, truly.
Touch. Then thou art damn'd.
Cor. Nay, I hope.
Touch. Truly, thou art damn'd, like an
ill-roasted egg, all on one side.   35
Cor. For not being at court ? Your
reason.
Touch. Why, if thou never wast at court
thou never saw'st good manners ; if thou
never saw'st good manners, then thy manners must be wicked ; and wickedness is

sin, and sin is damnation. Thou art in a
parlous state, shepherd.   40
Cor. Not a whit, Touchstone. Those that
are good manners at the court are as
ridiculous in the country as the behaviour
of the country is most mockable at the
court. You told me you salute not at the
court, but you kiss your hands ; that
courtesy would be uncleanly if courtiers
were shepherds.   45
Touch. Instance, briefly ; come, instance.
Cor. Why, we are still handling our ewes;
and their fells, you know, are greasy.
Touch. Why, do not your courtier's hands
sweat ? And is not the grease of a mutton
as wholesome as the sweat of a man ?
Shallow, shallow. A better instance, I say ;
come.   51
Cor. Besides, our hands are hard.
Touch. Your lips will feel them the
sooner. Shallow again. A more sounder
instance ; come.   54
Cor. And they are often tarr'd over with
the surgery of our sheep ; and would you
have us kiss tar ? The courtier's hands are
perfum'd with civet.   57
Touch. Most shallow man ! thou worm's
meat in respect of a good piece of flesh
indeed ! Learn of the wise, and perpend :
civet is of a baser birth than tar—the very
uncleanly flux of a cat. Mend the instance,
shepherd.   61
Cor. You have too courtly a wit for me ;
I'll rest.
Touch. Wilt thou rest damn'd ? God help
thee, shallow man ! God make incision in
thee ! thou art raw.   64
Cor. Sir, I am a true labourer : I earn
that I eat, get that I wear ; owe no man
hate, envy no man's happiness ; glad of
other men's good, content with my harm ;
and the greatest of my pride is to see my
ewes graze and my lambs suck.   68
Touch. That is another simple sin in you :
to bring the ewes and the rams together,
and to offer to get your living by the
copulation of cattle ; to be bawd to a
bell-wether, and to betray a she-lamb of
a twelvemonth to a crooked-pated, old,
cuckoldly ram, out of all reasonable match.
If thou beest not damn'd for this, the devil
himself will have no shepherds ; I cannot
see else how thou shouldst scape.   75
Cor. Here comes young Master Ganymede, my new mistress's brother.

Enter ROSALIND, *reading a paper.*

Ros. 'From the east to western Inde,
      No jewel is like Rosalinde.
      Her worth, being mounted on the
        wind,   80
      Through all the world bears
        Rosalinde.
      All the pictures fairest lin'd

Are but black to Rosalinde.
Let no face be kept in mind
But the fair of Rosalinde.'   85

Touch. I'll rhyme you so eight years together, dinners, and suppers, and sleeping
hours, excepted.   It is the right butter-
women's rank to market.
Ros. Out, fool !
Touch. For a taste :   90

If a hart do lack a hind,
Let him seek out Rosalinde.
If the cat will after kind,
So be sure will Rosalinde.
Winter garments must be lin'd,   95
So must slender Rosalinde.
They that reap must sheaf and bind,
Then to cart with Rosalinde.
Sweetest nut hath sourest rind,
Such a nut is Rosalinde.   100
He that sweetest rose will find
Must find love's prick and Rosalinde.

This is the very false gallop of verses ; why
do you infect yourself with them ?
Ros. Peace, you dull fool ! I found them
on a tree.   105
Touch. Truly, the tree yields bad fruit.
Ros. I'll graff it with you, and then I
shall graff it with a medlar.   Then it will
be the earliest fruit i' th' country ; for you'll
be rotten ere you be half ripe, and that's the
right virtue of the medlar.   110
Touch. You have said ; but whether
wisely or no, let the forest judge.

Enter CELIA, *with a writing.*

Ros. Peace !
Here comes my sister, reading ; stand
aside.
Cel. 'Why should this a desert be ?   115
For it is unpeopled ? No ;
Tongues I'll hang on every tree
That shall civil sayings show.
Some, how brief the life of man
Runs his erring pilgrimage,   120
That the stretching of a span
Buckles in his sum of age ;
Some, of violated vows
'Twixt the souls of friend and
friend ;
But upon the fairest boughs,   125
Or at every sentence end,
Will I Rosalinda write,
Teaching all that read to know
The quintessence of every sprite
Heaven would in little show.   130
Therefore heaven Nature charg'd
That one body should be fill'd
With all graces wide-enlarg'd.
Nature presently distill'd
Helen's cheek, but not her heart, 135
Cleopatra's majesty,

Atalanta's better part,
Sad Lucretia's modesty.
Thus Rosalinde of many parts   139
By heavenly synod was devis'd,
Of many faces, eyes, and hearts,
To have the touches dearest priz'd.
Heaven would that she these gifts
should have,
And I to live and die her slave.'   144

Ros. O most gentle pulpiter !   What
tedious homily of love have you wearied
your parishioners withal, and never cried
' Have patience, good people '.
Cel. How now ! Back, friends ; shepherd,
go off a little ; go with him, sirrah.   149
Touch. Come, shepherd, let us make an
honourable retreat ; though not with bag
and baggage, yet with scrip and scrippage.
                    [*Exeunt Corin and Touchstone.*
Cel. Didst thou hear these verses ?   153
Ros. O, yes, I heard them all, and more
too ; for some of them had in them more
feet than the verses would bear.   155
Cel. That's no matter ; the feet might
bear the verses.
Ros. Ay, but the feet were lame, and
could not bear themselves without the
verse, and therefore stood lamely in the
verse.   159
Cel. But didst thou hear without wonder-
ing how thy name should be hang'd and
carved upon these trees ?   161
Ros. I was seven of the nine days out of
the wonder before you came ; for look here
what I found on a palm-tree.   I was never
so berhym'd since Pythagoras' time that I
was an Irish rat, which I can hardly
remember.   165
Cel. Trow you who hath done this ?
Ros. Is it a man ?
Cel. And a chain, that you once wore,
about his neck.   Change you colour ?
Ros. I prithee, who ?   170
Cel. O Lord, Lord ! it is a hard matter
for friends to meet ; but mountains may
be remov'd with earthquakes, and so
encounter.
Ros. Nay, but who is it ?
Cel. Is it possible ?   175
Ros. Nay, I prithee now, with most
petitionary vehemence, tell me who it is.
Cel. O wonderful, wonderful, and most
wonderful wonderful, and yet again wonderful, and after that, out of all whooping !
Ros. Good my complexion ! dost thou
think, though I am caparison'd like a man,
I have a doublet and hose in my disposition?
One inch of delay more is a South Sea of
discovery.   I prithee tell me who is it
quickly, and speak apace.   I would thou
couldst stammer, that thou mightst pour
this conceal'd man out of thy mouth, as
wine comes out of a narrow-mouth'd

bottle—either too much at once or none at all. I prithee take the cork out of thy mouth that I may drink thy tidings. 189

Cel. So you may put a man in your belly.

Ros. Is he of God's making? What manner of man? Is his head worth a hat or his chin worth a beard?

Cel. Nay, he hath but a little beard. 193

Ros. Why, God will send more if the man will be thankful. Let me stay the growth of his beard, if thou delay me not the knowledge of his chin. 196

Cel. It is young Orlando, that tripp'd up the wrestler's heels and your heart both in an instant.

Ros. Nay, but the devil take mocking! Speak sad brow and true maid. 200

Cel. I' faith, coz, 'tis he.

Ros. Orlando?

Cel. Orlando. 203

Ros. Alas the day! what shall I do with my doublet and hose? What did he when thou saw'st him? What said he? How look'd he? Wherein went he? What makes he here? Did he ask for me? Where remains he? How parted he with thee? And when shalt thou see him again? Answer me in one word. 209

Cel. You must borrow me Gargantua's mouth first; 'tis a word too great for any mouth of this age's size. To say ay and no to these particulars is more than to answer in a catechism. 213

Ros. But doth he know that I am in this forest, and in man's apparel? Looks he as freshly as he did the day he wrestled? 216

Cel. It is as easy to count atomies as to resolve the propositions of a lover; but take a taste of my finding him, and relish it with good observance. I found him under a tree, like a dropp'd acorn. 220

Ros. It may well be call'd Jove's tree, when it drops forth such fruit.

Cel. Give me audience, good madam.

Ros. Proceed.

Cel. There lay he, stretch'd along like a wounded knight. 226

Ros. Though it be pity to see such a sight, it well becomes the ground.

Cel. Cry ' Holla ' to thy tongue, I prithee; it curvets unseasonably. He was furnish'd like a hunter. 230

Ros. O, ominous! he comes to kill my heart.

Cel. I would sing my song without a burden; thou bring'st me out of tune.

Ros. Do you not know I am a woman? When I think, I must speak. Sweet, say on.

Cel. You bring me out. Soft! comes he not here? 236

Enter ORLANDO *and* JAQUES.

Ros. 'Tis he; slink by, and note him.

Jaq. I thank you for your company; but,

good faith, I had as lief have been myself alone.

Orl. And so had I; but yet, for fashion sake, I thank you too for your society. 241

Jaq. God buy you; let's meet as little as we can.

Orl. I do desire we may be better strangers.

Jaq. I pray you mar no more trees with writing love songs in their barks. 245

Orl. I pray you mar no moe of my verses with reading them ill-favouredly.

Jaq. Rosalind is your love's name?

Orl. Yes, just.

Jaq. I do not like her name. 250

Orl. There was no thought of pleasing you when she was christen'd.

Jaq. What stature is she of?

Orl. Just as high as my heart. 254

Jaq. You are full of pretty answers. Have you not been acquainted with goldsmiths' wives, and conn'd them out of rings? 257

Orl. Not so; but I answer you right painted cloth, from whence you have studied your questions. 259

Jaq. You have a nimble wit; I think 'twas made of Atalanta's heels. Will you sit down with me? and we two will rail against our mistress the world, and all our misery. 262

Orl. I will chide no breather in the world but myself, against whom I know most faults.

Jaq. The worst fault you have is to be in love. 265

Orl. 'Tis a fault I will not change for your best virtue. I am weary of you.

Jaq. By my troth, I was seeking for a fool when I found you.

Orl. He is drown'd in the brook; look but in, and you shall see him. 271

Jaq. There I shall see mine own figure.

Orl. Which I take to be either a fool or a cipher.

Jaq. I'll tarry no longer with you; farewell, good Signior Love. 275

Orl. I am glad of your departure; adieu, good Monsieur Melancholy.

[*Exit Jaques.*

Ros. [*Aside to Celia*] I will speak to him like a saucy lackey, and under that habit play the knave with him.—Do you hear, forester? 280

Orl. Very well; what would you?

Ros. I pray you, what is't o'clock?

Orl. You should ask me what time o' day; there's no clock in the forest. 284

Ros. Then there is no true lover in the forest, else sighing every minute and groaning every hour would detect the lazy foot of Time as well as a clock.

Orl. And why not the swift foot of Time? Had not that been as proper? 289

Ros. By no means, sir. Time travels in divers paces with divers persons. I'll tell you who Time ambles withal, who Time trots withal, who Time gallops withal, and who he stands still withal. 293

Orl. I prithee, who doth he trot withal?

Ros. Marry, he trots hard with a young maid between the contract of her marriage and the day it is solemniz'd; if the interim be but a se'nnight, Time's pace is so hard that it seems the length of seven year.

Orl. Who ambles Time withal? 299

Ros. With a priest that lacks Latin and a rich man that hath not the gout; for the one sleeps easily because he cannot study, and the other lives merrily because he feels no pain; the one lacking the burden of lean and wasteful learning, the other knowing no burden of heavy tedious penury. These Time ambles withal. 305

Orl. Who doth he gallop withal?

Ros. With a thief to the gallows; for though he go as softly as foot can fall, he thinks himself too soon there.

Orl. Who stays it still withal? 309

Ros. With lawyers in the vacation; for they sleep between term and term, and then they perceive not how Time moves.

Orl. Where dwell you, pretty youth?

Ros. With this shepherdess, my sister; here in the skirts of the forest, like fringe upon a petticoat. 315

Orl. Are you native of this place?

Ros. As the coney that you see dwell where she is kindled. 317

Orl. Your accent is something finer than you could purchase in so removed a dwelling.

Ros. I have been told so of many; but indeed an old religious uncle of mine taught me to speak, who was in his youth an inland man; one that knew courtship too well, for there he fell in love. I have heard him read many lectures against it; and I thank God I am not a woman, to be touch'd with so many giddy offences as he hath generally tax'd their whole sex withal. 326

Orl. Can you remember any of the principal evils that he laid to the charge of women?

Ros. There were none principal; they were all like one another as halfpence are; every one fault seeming monstrous till his fellow-fault came to match it. 331

Orl. I prithee recount some of them.

Ros. No; I will not cast away my physic but on those that are sick. There is a man haunts the forest that abuses our young plants with carving 'Rosalind' on their barks; hangs odes upon hawthorns and elegies on brambles; all, forsooth, deifying the name of Rosalind. If I could meet that fancy-monger, I would give him some good counsel, for he seems to have the quotidian of love upon him. 339

Orl. I am he that is so love-shak'd; I pray you tell me your remedy. 341

Ros. There is none of my uncle's marks upon you; he taught me how to know a man in love; in which cage of rushes I am sure you are not prisoner.

Orl. What were his marks? 345

Ros. A lean cheek, which you have not; a blue eye and sunken, which you have not; an unquestionable spirit, which you have not; a beard neglected, which you have not; but I pardon you for that, for simply your having in beard is a younger brother's revenue. Then your hose should be ungarter'd, your bonnet unbanded, your sleeve unbutton'd, your shoe untied, and every thing about you demonstrating a careless desolation. But you are no such man; you are rather point-device in your accoutrements, as loving yourself than seeming the lover of any other. 355

Orl. Fair youth, I would I could make thee believe I love.

Ros. Me believe it! You may as soon make her that you love believe it; which, I warrant, she is apter to do than to confess she does. That is one of the points in the which women still give the lie to their consciences. But, in good sooth, are you he that hangs the verses on the trees where-in Rosalind is so admired? 363

Orl. I swear to thee, youth, by the white hand of Rosalind, I am that he, that unfortunate he. 365

Ros. But are you so much in love as your rhymes speak?

Orl. Neither rhyme nor reason can express how much.

Ros. Love is merely a madness; and, I tell you, deserves as well a dark house and a whip as madmen do; and the reason why they are not so punish'd and cured is that the lunacy is so ordinary that the whippers are in love too. Yet I profess curing it by counsel. 372

Orl. Did you ever cure any so?

Ros. Yes, one; and in this manner. He was to imagine me his love, his mistress; and I set him every day to woo me; at which time would I, being but a moonish youth, grieve, be effeminate, changeable, longing and liking, proud, fantastical, apish, shallow, inconstant, full of tears, full of smiles; for every passion something and for no passion truly anything, as boys and women are for the most part cattle of this colour; would now like him, now loathe him; then entertain him, then forswear him; now weep for him, then spit at him; that I drave my suitor from his mad humour of love to a living humour of madness; which was, to forswear the full stream of the world and to live in a nook merely monastic. And thus I cur'd him; and this

way will I take upon me to wash your liver
as clean as a sound sheep's heart, that there
shall not be one spot of love in 't.

Orl. I would not be cured, youth.   389

Ros. I would cure you, if you would but
call me Rosalind, and come every day to
my cote and woo me.

Orl. Now, by the faith of my love, I will.
Tell me where it is.   393

Ros. Go with me to it, and I'll show it
you ; and, by the way, you shall tell me
where in the forest you live. Will you go ?

Orl. With all my heart, good youth.   397

Ros. Nay, you must call me Rosalind.
Come, sister, will you go ?   [*Exeunt.*

SCENE III. *The forest.*

Enter TOUCHSTONE *and* AUDREY ; JAQUES
behind.

Touch. Come apace, good Audrey ; I
will fetch up your goats, Audrey. And how,
Audrey, am I the man yet ? Doth my
simple feature content you ?   3

Aud. Your features ! Lord warrant us !
What features ?

Touch. I am here with thee and thy goats,
as the most capricious poet, honest Ovid,
was among the Goths.   6

Jaq. [*Aside*] O knowledge ill-inhabited,
worse than Jove in a thatch'd house !

Touch. When a man's verses cannot be
understood, nor a man's good wit seconded
with the forward child understanding, it
strikes a man more dead than a great
reckoning in a little room. Truly, I would
the gods had made thee poetical.   13

Aud. I do not know what ' poetical ' is.
Is it honest in deed and word ? Is it a true
thing ?   15

Touch. No, truly ; for the truest poetry
is the most feigning, and lovers are given
to poetry ; and what they swear in poetry
may be said as lovers they do feign.

Aud. Do you wish, then, that the gods
had made me poetical ?   20

Touch. I do, truly, for thou swear'st to
me thou art honest ; now, if thou wert a
poet, I might have some hope thou didst
feign.   23

Aud. Would you not have me honest ?

Touch. No, truly, unless thou wert hard-
favour'd ; for honesty coupled to beauty
is to have honey a sauce to sugar.

Jaq. [*Aside*] A material fool !

Aud. Well, I am not fair ; and therefore
I pray the gods make me honest.   30

Touch. Truly, and to cast away honesty
upon a foul slut were to put good meat into
an unclean dish.

Aud. I am not a slut, though I thank the
gods I am foul.   34

Touch. Well, praised be the gods for thy
foulness ; sluttishness may come hereafter.

But be it as it may be, I will marry thee ;
and to that end I have been with Sir Oliver
Martext, the vicar of the next village, who
hath promis'd to meet me in this place of
the forest, and to couple us.   39

Jaq. [*Aside*] I would fain see this meeting.

Aud. Well, the gods give us joy !

Touch. Amen. A man may, if he were of
a fearful heart, stagger in this attempt ; for
here we have no temple but the wood, no
assembly but horn-beasts.   But what
though ?   Courage !   As horns are odious,
they are necessary.   It is said : ' Many a
man knows no end of his goods '.   Right !
Many a man has good horns and knows no
end of them.   Well, that is the dowry of
his wife ; 'tis none of his own getting.
Horns ?   Even so.   Poor men alone ?   No,
no ;   the noblest deer hath them as huge
as the rascal.   Is the single man therefore
blessed ?   No ; as a wall'd town is more
worthier than a village, so is the forehead
of a married man more honourable than the
bare brow of a bachelor ; and by how much
defence is better than no skill, by so much
is a horn more precious than to want.   Here
comes Sir Oliver.   55

Enter SIR OLIVER MARTEXT.

Sir Oliver Martext, you are well met. Will
you dispatch us here under this tree, or
shall we go with you to your chapel ?

Sir Oli. Is there none here to give the
woman ?

Touch. I will not take her on gift of any
man.   60

Sir Oli. Truly, she must be given, or the
marriage is not lawful.

Jaq. [*Discovering himself*] Proceed, proceed ; I'll give her.

Touch. Good even, good Master What-ye-
call't ; how do you, sir ? You are very well
met. Goddild you for your last company. I
am very glad to see you. Even a toy in
hand here, sir. Nay ; pray be cover'd.   67

Jaq. Will you be married, motley ?

Touch. As the ox hath his bow, sir, the
horse his curb, and the falcon her bells, so
man hath his desires ; and as pigeons bill,
so wedlock would be nibbling.   71

Jaq. And will you, being a man of your
breeding, be married under a bush, like a
beggar ?   Get you to church and have a
good priest that can tell you what marriage
is ; this fellow will but join you together
as they join wainscot ; then one of you will
prove a shrunk panel, and like green timber
warp, warp.   77

Touch. [*Aside*] I am not in the mind but
I were better to be married of him than of
another ; for he is not like to marry me
well ; and not being well married, it will
be a good excuse for me hereafter to leave
my wife.   81

Jaq. Go thou with me, and let me counsel thee.

Touch. Come, sweet Audrey;
We must be married or we must live in bawdry.
Farewell, good Master Oliver. Not— 85

> O sweet Oliver,
> O brave Oliver,
> Leave me not behind thee.

But—

> Wind away, 90
> Begone, I say,
> I will not to wedding witn thee.

[Exeunt Jaques, Touchstone, and Audrey.
Sir Oli. 'Tis no matter; ne'er a fantastical knave of them all shall flout me out of my calling.   [*Exit.*

SCENE IV. *The forest.*

Enter ROSALIND *and* CELIA.

Ros. Never talk to me; I will weep.

Cel. Do, I prithee; but yet have the grace to consider that tears do not become a man.

Ros. But have I not cause to weep?

Cel. As good cause as one would desire; therefore weep. 5

Ros. His very hair is of the dissembling colour.

Cel. Something browner than Judas's. Marry, his kisses are Judas's own children.

Ros. I'faith, his hair is of a good colour.

Cel. An excellent colour: your chestnut was ever the only colour. 11

Ros. And his kissing is as full of sanctity as the touch of holy bread.

Cel. He hath bought a pair of cast lips of Diana. A nun of winter's sisterhood kisses not more religiously; the very ice of chastity is in them. 16

Ros. But why did he swear he would come this morning, and comes not?

Cel. Nay, certainly, there is no truth in him.

Ros. Do you think so? 20

Cel. Yes; I think he is not a pick-purse nor a horse-stealer; but for his verity in love, I do think him as concave as a covered goblet or a worm-eaten nut.

Ros. Not true in love?

Cel. Yes, when is he in; but I think he is not in. 25

Ros. You have heard him swear downright he was.

Cel. ' Was ' is not ' is '; besides, the oath of a lover is no stronger than the word of a tapster; they are both the confirmer of false reckonings. He attends here in the forest on the Duke, your father. 30

Ros. I met the Duke yesterday, and had much question with him. He asked me of

what parentage I was; I told him, of as good as he; so he laugh'd and let me go. But what talk we of fathers when there is such a man as Orlando? 35

Cel. O, that's a brave man! He writes brave verses, speaks brave words, swears brave oaths, and breaks them bravely, quite traverse, athwart the heart of his lover; as a puny tilter, that spurs his horse but on one side, breaks his staff like a noble goose. But all's brave that youth mounts and folly guides. Who comes here? 41

Enter CORIN.

Cor. Mistress and master, you have oft enquired
After the shepherd that complain'd of love,
Who you saw sitting by me on the turf,
Praising the proud disdainful shepherdess
That was his mistress.

Cel.   Well, and what of him?

Cor. If you will see a pageant truly play'd 47
Between the pale complexion of true love
And the red glow of scorn and proud disdain,
Go hence a little, and I shall conduct you,
If you will mark it.

Ros.   O, come, let us remove!
The sight of lovers feedeth those in love.
Bring us to this sight, and you shall say
I'll prove a busy actor in their play. 54

[Exeunt.

SCENE V. *Another part of the forest.*

Enter SILVIUS *and* PHEBE.

Sil. Sweet Phebe, do not scorn me; do not, Phebe.
Say that you love me not; but say not so
In bitterness. The common executioner,
Whose heart th' accustom'd sight of death makes hard,
Falls not the axe upon the humbled neck 5
But first begs pardon. Will you sterner be
Than he that dies and lives by bloody drops?

Enter ROSALIND, CELIA, *and* CORIN, *at a distance.*

Phe. I would not be thy executioner;
I fly thee, for I would not injure thee.
Thou tell'st me there is murder in mine eye.
'Tis pretty, sure, and very probable, 11
That eyes, that are the frail'st and softest things,
Who shut their coward gates on atomies,
Should be call'd tyrants, butchers, murderers! 14
Now I do frown on thee with all my heart;
And if mine eyes can wound, now let them kill thee.
Now counterfeit to swoon; why, now fall down;

Or, if thou canst not, O, for shame, for
    shame,
Lie not, to say mine eyes are murderers.
Now show the wound mine eye hath made
    in thee.   20
Scratch thee but with a pin, and there
    remains
Some scar of it ; lean upon a rush,
The cicatrice and capable impressure
Thy palm some moment keeps ; but now
    mine eyes,   24
Which I have darted at thee, hurt thee
    not;
Nor, I am sure, there is not force in eyes
That can do hurt.
    Sil.   O dear Phebe,
If ever—as that ever may be near—
You meet in some fresh cheek the power of
    fancy,   29
Then shall you know the wounds invisible
That love's keen arrows make.
    Phe.   But till that time
Come not thou near me ; and when that
    time comes,
Afflict me with thy mocks, pity me not ;
As till that time I shall not pity thee.
    Ros. [*Advancing*] And why, I pray you ?
    Who might be your mother,   35
That you insult, exult, and all at once,
Over the wretched ?   What though you
    have no beauty—
As, by my faith, I see no more in you
Than without candle may go dark to bed—
Must you be therefore proud and pitiless ?
Why, what means this ? Why do you look
    on me ?   41
I see no more in you than in the ordinary
Of nature's sale-work. 'Od's my little life,
I think she means to tangle my eyes too !
No, faith, proud mistress, hope not after it;
'Tis not your inky brows, your black silk
    hair,   46
Your bugle eyeballs, nor your cheek of
    cream,
That can entame my spirits to your
    worship.
You foolish shepherd, wherefore do you
    follow her,
Like foggy south, puffing with wind and
    rain ?   50
You are a thousand times a properer man
Than she a woman. 'Tis such fools as you
That makes the world full of ill-favour'd
    children.   53
'Tis not her glass, but you, that flatters her;
And out of you she sees herself more proper
Than any of her lineaments can show her.
But, mistress, know yourself.   Down on
    your knees,   57
And thank heaven, fasting, for a good man's
    love ;
For I must tell you friendly in your ear :
Sell when you can ; you are not for all
    markets.   60

Cry the man mercy, love him, take his
    offer ;
Foul is most foul, being foul to be a scoffer.
So take her to thee, shepherd.   Fare you
    well.
    Phe. Sweet youth, I pray you chide a
    year together ;
I had rather hear you chide than this man
    woo.   65
    Ros. He's fall'n in love with your foul-
ness, and she'll fall in love with my anger.
If it be so, as fast as she answers thee with
frowning looks, I'll sauce her with bitter
words. Why look you so upon me ?
    Phe. For no ill will I bear you.   70
    Ros. I pray you do not fall in love with
    me,
For I am falser than vows made in wine ;
Besides, I like you not. If you will know
    my house,
'Tis at the tuft of olives here hard by.
Will you go, sister ?   Shepherd, ply her
    hard.   75
Come, sister.   Shepherdess, look on him
    better,
And be not proud ; though all the world
    could see,
None could be so abus'd in sight as he.
Come, to our flock.
        [*Exeunt Rosalind, Celia, and Corin.*
    Phe. Dead shepherd, now I find thy saw
    of might :   80
' Who ever lov'd that lov'd not at first
    sight ? '
    Sil. Sweet Phebe.
    Phe.   Ha ! what say'st thou, Silvius ?
    Sil. Sweet Phebe, pity me.
    Phe. Why, I am sorry for thee, gentle
    Silvius.   84
    Sil. Wherever sorrow is, relief would be.
If you do sorrow at my grief in love,
By giving love, your sorrow and my grief
Were both extermin'd.
    Phe. Thou hast my love ; is not that
    neighbourly ?   89
    Sil. I would have you.
    Phe.   Why, that were covetousness.
Silvius, the time was that I hated thee ;
And yet it is not that I bear thee love ;
But since that thou canst talk of love so
    well,
Thy company, which erst was irksome to
    me,
I will endure ; and I'll employ thee too.
But do not look for further recompense 96
Than thine own gladness that thou art
    employ'd.
    Sil. So holy and so perfect is my love,
And I in such a poverty of grace,
That I shall think it a most plenteous crop
To glean the broken ears after the man
That the main harvest reaps ; loose now and
    then   102
A scatt'red smile, and that I'll live upon.

Phe. Know'st thou the youth that spoke
    to me erewhile ?
Sil. Not very well ; but I have met him
    oft ;   105
And he hath bought the cottage and the
    bounds
That the old carlot once was master of.
   Phe. Think not I love him, though I ask
    for him ;
'Tis but a peevish boy ; yet he talks well.
But what care I for words ? Yet words do
    well   110
When he that speaks them pleases those
    that hear.
It is a pretty youth—not very pretty ;
But, sure, he's proud ; and yet his pride
    becomes him.
He'll make a proper man. The best thing
    in him
Is his complexion ; and faster than his
    tongue   115
Did make offence, his eye did heal it up.
He is not very tall ; yet for his years he's
    tall ;
His leg is but so-so ; and yet 'tis well.
There was a pretty redness in his lip,
A little riper and more lusty red   120
Than that mix'd in his cheek ; 'twas just
    the difference
Betwixt the constant red and mingled
    damask.
There be some women, Silvius, had they
    mark'd him   123
In parcels as I did, would have gone near
To fall in love with him ; but, for my part,
I love him not, nor hate him not ; and yet
I have more cause to hate him than to love
    him ;   127
For what had he to do to chide at me ?
He said mine eyes were black, and my hair
    black,
And, now I am rememb'red, scorn'd at me.
I marvel why I answer'd not again ;   131
But that's all one : omittance is no
    quittance.
I'll write to him a very taunting letter,
And thou shalt bear it ; wilt thou, Silvius ?
   Sil. Phebe, with all my heart.
   Phe.   I'll write it straight ;
The matter's in my head and in my heart ;
I will be bitter with him and passing short.
Go with me, Silvius.   [*Exeunt.*

ACT FOUR

Scene I. *The forest.*

Enter Rosalind, Celia, *and* Jaques.

   Jaq. I prithee, pretty youth, let me be
better acquainted with thee.
   Ros. They say you are a melancholy
fellow.
   Jaq. I am so ; I do love it better than
laughing.   4

   Ros. Those that are in extremity of either
are abominable fellows, and betray themselves to every modern censure worse than
drunkards.
   Jaq. Why, 'tis good to be sad and say
nothing.
   Ros. Why then, 'tis good to be a post.   9
   Jaq. I have neither the scholar's melancholy, which is emulation ; nor the
musician's, which is fantastical ; nor the
courtier's, which is proud ; nor the soldier's,
which is ambitious ; nor the lawyer's,
which is politic ; nor the lady's, which is
nice ; nor the lover's, which is all these ;
but it is a melancholy of mine own, compounded of many simples, extracted from
many objects, and, indeed, the sundry
contemplation of my travels ; in which my
often rumination wraps me in a most
humorous sadness.   18
   Ros. A traveller ! By my faith, you have
great reason to be sad. I fear you have sold
your own lands to see other men's ; then
to have seen much and to have nothing is
to have rich eyes and poor hands.   22
   Jaq. Yes, I have gain'd my experience.

Enter Orlando.

   Ros. And your experience makes you sad.
I had rather have a fool to make me merry
than experience to make me sad—and to
travel for it too.   26
   Orl. Good day, and happiness, dear
Rosalind !
   Jaq. Nay, then, God buy you, an you
talk in blank verse.   29
   Ros. Farewell, Monsieur Traveller ; look
you lisp and wear strange suits, disable
all the benefits of your own country, be
out of love with your nativity, and almost
chide God for making you that countenance
you are ; or I will scarce think you have
swam in a gondola. [*Exit Jaques*] Why,
how now, Orlando ! where have you been
all this while ? You a lover ! An you serve
me such another trick, never come in my
sight more.
   Orl. My fair Rosalind, I come within an
hour of my promise.   39
   Ros. Break an hour's promise in love !
He that will divide a minute into a thousand
parts, and break but a part of the thousand
part of a minute in the affairs of love, it may
be said of him that Cupid hath clapp'd him
o' th' shoulder, but I'll warrant him heart-
whole.
   Orl. Pardon me, dear Rosalind.   45
   Ros. Nay, an you be so tardy, come no
more in my sight. I had as lief be woo'd
of a snail.
   Orl. Of a snail !   48
   Ros. Ay, of a snail ; for though he comes
slowly, he carries his house on his head—a
better jointure, I think, than you make a

woman; besides, he brings his destiny
with him.   51

Orl. What's that?

Ros. Why, horns; which such as you are
fain to be beholding to your wives for; but
he comes armed in his fortune, and prevents
the slander of his wife.   55

Orl. Virtue is no horn-maker; and my
Rosalind is virtuous.

Ros. And I am your Rosalind.   58

Cel. It pleases him to call you so; but he
hath a Rosalind of a better leer than you.

Ros. Come, woo me, woo me; for now I
am in a holiday humour, and like enough
to consent. What would you say to me
now, an I were your very very Rosalind?

Orl. I would kiss before I spoke.   64

Ros. Nay, you were better speak first;
and when you were gravell'd for lack of
matter, you might take occasion to kiss.
Very good orators, when they are out, they
will spit; and for lovers lacking—God
warn us!—matter, the cleanliest shift is to
kiss.

Orl. How if the kiss be denied?   70

Ros. Then she puts you to entreaty, and
there begins new matter.

Orl. Who could be out, being before his
beloved mistress?

Ros. Marry, that should you, if I were
your mistress; or I should think my
honesty ranker than my wit.   75

Orl. What, of my suit?

Ros. Not out of your apparel, and yet out
of your suit. Am not I your Rosalind?

Orl. I take some joy to say you are,
because I would be talking of her.   80

Ros. Well, in her person, I say I will not
have you.

Orl. Then, in mine own person, I die.   8

Ros. No, faith, die by attorney. The poor
world is almost six thousand years old, and
in all this time there was not any man died
in his own person, videlicet, in a love-cause.
Troilus had his brains dash'd out with a
Grecian club; yet he did what he could to
die before, and he is one of the patterns
of love. Leander, he would have liv'd many
a fair year, though Hero had turn'd nun,
if it had not been for a hot midsummer-
night; for, good youth, he went but forth
to wash him in the Hellespont, and, being
taken with the cramp, was drown'd; and
the foolish chroniclers of that age found it
was—Hero of Sestos. But these are all lies:
men have died from time to time, and
worms have eaten them, but not for love.

Orl. I would not have my right Rosalind
of this mind; for, I protest, her frown
might kill me.   97

Ros. By this hand, it will not kill a fly.
But come, now I will be your Rosalind in
a more coming-on disposition; and ask me
what you will, I will grant it.   100

Orl. Then love me, Rosalind.

Ros. Yes, faith, will I, Fridays and
Saturdays, and all.

Orl. And wilt thou have me?

Ros. Ay, and twenty such.

Orl. What sayest thou?   105

Ros. Are you not good?

Orl. I hope so.

Ros. Why then, can one desire too much
of a good thing? Come, sister, you shall be
the priest, and marry us. Give me your
hand, Orlando. What do you say, sister?

Orl. Pray thee, marry us.   111

Cel. I cannot say the words.

Ros. You must begin 'Will you,
Orlando'—

Cel. Go to. Will you, Orlando, have to
wife this Rosalind?   115

Orl. I will.

Ros. Ay, but when?

Orl. Why, now; as fast as she can marry
us.

Ros. Then you must say 'I take thee,
Rosalind, for wife'.   120

Orl. I take thee, Rosalind, for wife.

Ros. I might ask you for your commission; but—I do take thee, Orlando, for my
husband. There's a girl goes before the
priest; and, certainly, a woman's thought
runs before her actions.   125

Orl. So do all thoughts; they are wing'd.

Ros. Now tell me how long you would
have her, after you have possess'd her.

Orl. For ever and a day.   129

Ros. Say 'a day' without the 'ever'.
No, no, Orlando; men are April when they
woo, December when they wed: maids are
May when they are maids, but the sky
changes when they are wives. I will be
more jealous of thee than a Barbary cock-
pigeon over his hen, more clamorous
than a parrot against rain, more new-
fangled than an ape, more giddy in my
desires than a monkey. I will weep for
nothing, like Diana in the fountain, and I
will do that when you are dispos'd to be
merry; I will laugh like a hyen, and that
when thou art inclin'd to sleep.

Orl. But will my Rosalind do so?   140

Ros. By my life, she will do as I do.

Orl. O, but she is wise.

Ros. Or else she could not have the wit to
do this. The wiser, the waywarder. Make
the doors upon a woman's wit, and it will
out at the casement; shut that, and 'twill
out at the key-hole; stop that, 'twill fly
with the smoke out at the chimney.   147

Orl. A man that had a wife with such a
wit, he might say 'Wit, whither wilt?'

Ros. Nay, you might keep that check for
it, till you met your wife's wit going to your
neighbour's bed.   151

Orl. And what wit could wit have to
excuse that?

275

Ros. Marry, to say she came to seek you there. You shall never take her without her answer, unless you take her without her tongue. O, that woman that cannot make her fault her husband's occasion, let her never nurse her child herself, for she will breed it like a fool!   157

Orl. For these two hours, Rosalind, I will leave thee.

Ros. Alas, dear love, I cannot lack thee two hours!   159

Orl. I must attend the Duke at dinner; by two o'clock I will be with thee again.

Ros. Ay, go your ways, go your ways. I knew what you would prove; my friends told me as much, and I thought no less. That flattering tongue of yours won me. 'Tis but one cast away, and so, come death! Two o'clock is your hour?   166

Orl. Ay, sweet Rosalind.

Ros. By my troth, and in good earnest, and so God mend me, and by all pretty oaths that are not dangerous, if you break one jot of your promise, or come one minute behind your hour, I will think you the most pathetical break-promise, and the most hollow lover, and the most unworthy of her you call Rosalind, that may be chosen out of the gross band of the unfaithful. Therefore beware my censure, and keep your promise.   175

Orl. With no less religion than if thou wert indeed my Rosalind; so, adieu.

Ros. Well, Time is the old justice that examines all such offenders, and let Time try. Adieu.   [*Exit Orlando.*

Cel. You have simply misus'd our sex in your love-prate. We must have your doublet and hose pluck'd over your head, and show the world what the bird hath done to her own nest.   183

Ros. O coz, coz, coz, my pretty little coz, that thou didst know how many fathom deep I am in love! But it cannot be sounded; my affection hath an unknown bottom, like the Bay of Portugal.

Cel. Or rather, bottomless; that as fast as you pour affection in, it runs out.   189

Ros. No; that same wicked bastard of Venus, that was begot of thought, conceiv'd of spleen, and born of madness; that blind rascally boy, that abuses every one's eyes, because his own are out—let him be judge how deep I am in love. I'll tell thee, Aliena, I cannot be out of the sight of Orlando. I'll go find a shadow, and sigh till he come.   195

Cel. And I'll sleep.   [*Exeunt.*

SCENE II. *The forest.*

Enter JAQUES *and Lords, in the habit of foresters.*

Jaq. Which is he that killed the deer?

Lord. Sir, it was I.

Jaq. Let's present him to the Duke, like a Roman conqueror; and it would do well to set the deer's horns upon his head for a branch of victory. Have you no song, forester, for this purpose?   6

Lord. Yes, sir.

Jaq. Sing it; 'tis no matter how it be in tune, so it make noise enough.

Song.

What shall he have that kill'd the deer?   10
His leather skin and horns to wear.
        [*The rest shall bear this burden*:
Then sing him home.

Take thou no scorn to wear the horn;
It was a crest ere thou wast born.
    Thy father's father wore it;   15
    And thy father bore it.
The horn, the horn, the lusty horn,
Is not a thing to laugh to scorn.
                                    [*Exeunt.*

SCENE III. *The forest.*

Enter ROSALIND *and* CELIA.

Ros. How say you now? Is it not past two o'clock? And here much Orlando!

Cel. I warrant you, with pure love and troubled brain, he hath ta'en his bow and arrows, and is gone forth—to sleep. Look, who comes here.   5

Enter SILVIUS.

Sil. My errand is to you, fair youth;
My gentle Phebe did bid me give you this.
I know not the contents; but, as I guess
By the stern brow and waspish action
Which she did use as she was writing of it,
It bears an angry tenour. Pardon me,   11
I am but as a guiltless messenger.

Ros. Patience herself would startle at
    this letter,
And play the swaggerer. Bear this, bear all.
She says I am not fair, that I lack manners;
She calls me proud, and that she could not
        love me,   16
Were man as rare as Phœnix. 'Od's my
        will!
Her love is not the hare that I do hunt;
Why writes she so to me? Well, shepherd,
        well,
This is a letter of your own device.   20

Sil. No, I protest, I know not the contents;
Phebe did write it.

Ros.   Come, come, you are a fool,
And turn'd into the extremity of love.
I saw her hand; she has a leathern hand,
A freestone-colour'd hand; I verily did
        think   25
That her old gloves were on, but 'twas her
        hands;

She has a huswife's hand—but that's no
     matter.
I say she never did invent this letter :
This is a man's invention, and his hand.

Sil. Sure, it is hers.   30

Ros. Why, 'tis a boisterous and a cruel
     style ;
A style for challengers. Why, she defies me,
Like Turk to Christian. Women's gentle
     brain
Could not drop forth such giant-rude in-
     vention,   34
Such Ethiope words, blacker in their effect
Than in their countenance. Will you hear
     the letter ?

Sil. So please you, for I never heard it
     yet ;
Yet heard too much of Phebe's cruelty.

Ros. She Phebes me : mark how the
     tyrant writes.   [*Reads.*

          ' Art thou god to shepherd turn'd, 40
            That a maiden's heart hath
               burn'd ? '

Can a woman rail thus ?

Sil. Call you this railing ?

Ros. ' Why, thy godhead laid apart, 44
            War'st thou with a woman's
               heart ? '

Did you ever hear such railing ?

          ' Whiles the eye of man did woo me,
            That could do no vengeance to me.'

Meaning me a beast.

          ' If the scorn of your bright eyne 50
            Have power to raise such love in
               mine,
            Alack, in me what strange effect
            Would they work in mild aspect !
            Whiles you chid me, I did love ;
            How then might your prayers
               move !   55
            He that brings this love to thee
            Little knows this love in me ;
            And by him seal up thy mind,
            Whether that thy youth and kind
            Will the faithful offer take   60
            Of me and all that I can make ;
            Or else by him my love deny,
            And then I'll study how to die.'

Sil. Call you this chiding ?

Cel. Alas, poor shepherd !   65

Ros. Do you pity him ? No, he deserves
no pity. Wilt thou love such a woman ?
What, to make thee an instrument, and
play false strains upon thee ! Not to be
endur'd ! Well, go your way to her, for I
see love hath made thee a tame snake, and
say this to her—that if she love me, I
charge her to love thee ; if she will not, I
will never have her unless thou entreat for
her. If you be a true lover, hence, and not

a word ; for here comes more company. 73
                              [*Exit Silvius.*

Enter OLIVER.

Oli. Good morrow, fair ones ; pray you,
     if you know,   74
Where in the purlieus of this forest stands
A sheep-cote fenc'd about with olive trees ?

Cel. West of this place, down in the
     neighbour bottom.
The rank of osiers by the murmuring
     stream
Left on your right hand brings you to the
     place.   79
But at this hour the house doth keep itself ;
There's none within.

Oli. If that an eye may profit by a
     tongue,
Then should I know you by description—
Such garments, and such years : 'The boy
     is fair,
Of female favour, and bestows himself 85
Like a ripe sister ; the woman low,
And browner than her brother '. Are not
     you
The owner of the house I did inquire for ?

Cel. It is no boast, being ask'd, to say
     we are.

Oli. Orlando doth commend him to you
     both ;   90
And to that youth he calls his Rosalind
He sends this bloody napkin. Are you he ?

Ros. I am. What must we understand by
     this ?

Oli. Some of my shame ; if you will know
     of me
What man I am, and how, and why, and
     where,   95
This handkercher was stain'd.

Cel.   I pray you, tell it.

Oli. When last the young Orlando parted
     from you,
He left a promise to return again
Within an hour ; and, pacing through the
     forest,   99
Chewing the food of sweet and bitter fancy,
Lo, what befell ! He threw his eye aside,
And mark what object did present itself.
Under an oak, whose boughs were moss'd
     with age,
And high top bald with dry antiquity,
A wretched ragged man, o'ergrown with
     hair,   105
Lay sleeping on his back. About his
     neck
A green and gilded snake had wreath'd
     itself,
Who with her head nimble in threats
     approach'd
The opening of his mouth ; but suddenly,
Seeing Orlando, it unlink'd itself,   110
And with indented glides did slip away
Into a bush ; under which bush's shade
A lioness, with udders all drawn dry,

Lay couching, head on ground, with cat-
    like watch,
When that the sleeping man should stir;
    for 'tis   115
The royal disposition of that beast
To prey on nothing that doth seem as dead.
This seen, Orlando did approach the man,
And found it was his brother, his elder
    brother.
   Cel. O, I have heard him speak of that
    same brother;   120
And he did render him the most unnatural
That liv'd amongst men.
   Oli.   And well he might so do,
For well I know he was unnatural.
   Ros. But, to Orlando: did he leave him
    there,   124
Food to the suck'd and hungry lioness?
   Oli. Twice did he turn his back, and
    purpos'd so;
But kindness, nobler ever than revenge,
And nature, stronger than his just occasion,
Made him give battle to the lioness,
Who quickly fell before him; in which
    hurtling   130
From miserable slumber I awak'd.
   Cel. Are you his brother?
   Ros.   Was't you he rescu'd?
   Cel. Was't you that did so oft contrive to
    kill him?
   Oli. 'Twas I; but 'tis not I. I do not
    shame
To tell you what I was, since my con-
    version   135
So sweetly tastes, being the thing I am.
   Ros. But for the bloody napkin?
   Oli.   By and by.
When from the first to last, betwixt us two,
Tears our recountments had most kindly
    bath'd,
As how I came into that desert place— 140
In brief, he led me to the gentle Duke,
Who gave me fresh array and entertain-
    ment,
Committing me unto my brother's love;
Who led me instantly unto his cave,
There stripp'd himself, and here upon his
    arm   145
The lioness had torn some flesh away,
Which all this while had bled; and now he
    fainted,
And cried, in fainting, upon Rosalind.
Brief, I recover'd him, bound up his wound,
And, after some small space, being strong
    at heart,   150
He sent me hither, stranger as I am,
To tell this story, that you might excuse
His broken promise, and to give this
    napkin,   153
Dy'd in his blood, unto the shepherd youth
That he in sport doth call his Rosalind.
              [*Rosalind swoons.*
   Cel. Why, how now, Ganymede! sweet
    Ganymede!

   Oli. Many will swoon when they do look
    on blood.   157
   Cel. There is more in it. Cousin Gany-
    mede!
   Oli. Look, he recovers.
   Ros. I would I were at home.
   Cel.   We'll lead you thither.   160
I pray you, will you take him by the arm?
   Oli. Be of good cheer, youth. You a man!
You lack a man's heart.
   Ros. I do so, I confess it. Ah, sirrah, a
body would think this was well counter-
feited. I pray you tell your brother how
well I counterfeited. Heigh-ho!   166
   Oli. This was not counterfeit; there is
too great testimony in your complexion
that it was a passion of earnest.
   Ros. Counterfeit, I assure you.
   Oli. Well then, take a good heart and
counterfeit to be a man.   171
   Ros. So I do; but, i' faith, I should have
been a woman by right.
   Cel. Come, you look paler and paler;
pray you draw homewards. Good sir, go
with us.   175
   Oli. That will I, for I must bear answer
back
How you excuse my brother, Rosalind.
   Ros. I shall devise something; but, I
pray you, commend my counterfeiting to
him. Will you go?   [*Exeunt.*

ACT FIVE

Scene I. *The forest.*

Enter Touchstone *and* Audrey.

   Touch. We shall find a time, Audrey;
patience, gentle Audrey.
   Aud. Faith, the priest was good enough,
for all the old gentleman's saying.   4
   Touch. A most wicked Sir Oliver, Audrey,
a most vile Martext. But, Audrey, there is
a youth here in the forest lays claim to you.
   Aud. Ay, I know who 'tis; he hath no
interest in me in the world; here comes the
man you mean.   9

Enter William.

   Touch. It is meat and drink to me to see
a clown. By my troth, we that have good
wits have much to answer for: we shall be
flouting; we cannot hold.   12
   Will. Good ev'n, Audrey.
   Aud. God ye good ev'n, William.
   Will. And good ev'n to you, sir.   15
   Touch. Good ev'n, gentle friend. Cover
thy head, cover thy head; nay, prithee be
cover'd. How old are you, friend?
   Will. Five and twenty, sir.
   Touch. A ripe age. Is thy name William?
   Will. William, sir.   20
   Touch. A fair name. Wast born i' th'
forest here?

Will. Ay, sir, I thank God.

Touch. 'Thank God.' A good answer. Art rich?

Will. Faith, sir, so so.

Touch. 'So so' is good, very good, very excellent good; and yet it is not; it is but so so. Art thou wise?   26

Will. Ay, sir, I have a pretty wit.

Touch. Why, thou say'st well. I do now remember a saying: 'The fool doth think he is wise, but the wise man knows himself to be a fool'. The heathen philosopher, when he had a desire to eat a grape, would open his lips when he put it into his mouth; meaning thereby that grapes were made to eat and lips to open. You do love this maid?   33

Will. I do, sir.

Touch. Give me your hand. Art thou learned?

Will. No, sir.   36

Touch. Then learn this of me: to have is to have; for it is a figure in rhetoric that drink, being pour'd out of a cup into a glass, by filling the one doth empty the other; for all your writers do consent that ipse is he; now, you are not ipse, for I am he.   41

Will. Which he, sir?

Touch. He, sir, that must marry this woman. Therefore, you clown, abandon—which is in the vulgar leave—the society—which in the boorish is company—of this female—which in the common is woman—which together is: abandon the society of this female; or, clown, thou perishest; or, to thy better understanding, diest; or, to wit, I kill thee, make thee away, translate thy life into death, thy liberty into bondage. I will deal in poison with thee, or in bastinado, or in steel; I will bandy with thee in faction; I will o'er-run thee with policy; I will kill thee a hundred and fifty ways; therefore tremble, and depart.

Aud. Do, good William.   54

Will. God rest you merry, sir.   [*Exit.*

Enter CORIN.

Cor. Our master and mistress seeks you; come away, away.   57

Touch. Trip, Audrey, trip, Audrey. I attend, I attend.   [*Exeunt.*

SCENE II. *The forest.*

Enter ORLANDO and OLIVER.

Orl. Is't possible that on so little acquaintance you should like her? that but seeing you should love her? and loving woo? and, wooing, she should grant? and will you persever to enjoy her?   4

Oli. Neither call the giddiness of it in question, the poverty of her, the small acquaintance, my sudden wooing, nor her sudden consenting; but say with me, I love Aliena; say with her that she loves me; consent with both that we may enjoy each other. It shall be to your good; for my father's house and all the revenue that was old Sir Rowland's will I estate upon you, and here live and die a shepherd.   11

Orl. You have my consent. Let your wedding be to-morrow. Thither will I invite the Duke and all's contented followers. Go you and prepare Aliena; for, look you, here comes my Rosalind.   15

Enter ROSALIND.

Ros. God save you, brother.

Oli. And you, fair sister.   [*Exit.*

Ros. O, my dear Orlando, how it grieves me to see thee wear thy heart in a scarf!

Orl. It is my arm.   20

Ros. I thought thy heart had been wounded with the claws of a lion.

Orl. Wounded it is, but with the eyes of a lady.

Ros. Did your brother tell you how I counterfeited to swoon when he show'd me your handkercher?   25

Orl. Ay, and greater wonders than that.

Ros. O, I know where you are. Nay, 'tis true. There was never any thing so sudden but the fight of two rams and Cæsar's thrasonical brag of 'I came, saw, and overcame'. For your brother and my sister no sooner met but they look'd; no sooner look'd but they lov'd; no sooner lov'd but they sigh'd; no sooner sigh'd but they ask'd one another the reason; no sooner knew the reason but they sought the remedy—and in these degrees have they made a pair of stairs to marriage, which they will climb incontinent, or else be incontinent before marriage. They are in the very wrath of love, and they will together. Clubs cannot part them.   38

Orl. They shall be married to-morrow; and I will bid the Duke to the nuptial. But, O, how bitter a thing it is to look into happiness through another man's eyes! By so much the more shall I to-morrow be at the height of heart-heaviness, by how much I shall think my brother happy in having what he wishes for.

Ros. Why, then, to-morrow I cannot serve your turn for Rosalind?   46

Orl. I can live no longer by thinking.

Ros. I will weary you, then, no longer with idle talking. Know of me then—for now I speak to some purpose—that I know you are a gentleman of good conceit. I speak not this that you should bear a good opinion of my knowledge, insomuch I say I know you are; neither do I labour for a greater esteem than may in some little measure draw a belief from you, to do yourself good, and not to grace me. Believe then, if you please, that I can do strange things. I have, since I was three year old, convers'd with a magician, most profound in his art and yet not damnable. If you do love Rosalind so near the heart as your gesture cries it out, when your brother marries Aliena shall you marry her. I know into what straits of fortune she is driven; and it is not impossible to me, if it appear not inconvenient to you, to set her before your eyes to-morrow, human as she is, and without any danger.

Orl. Speak'st thou in sober meanings? 64

Ros. By my life, I do; which I tender dearly, though I say I am a magician. Therefore put you in your best array, bid your friends; for if you will be married to-morrow, you shall; and to Rosalind, if you will. 68

Enter SILVIUS *and* PHEBE.

Look, here comes a lover of mine, and a lover of hers.

Phe. Youth, you have done me much ungentleness 70
To show the letter that I writ to you.

Ros. I care not if I have. It is my study
To seem despiteful and ungentle to you.
You are there follow'd by a faithful shepherd;
Look upon him, love him; he worships you. 75

Phe. Good shepherd, tell this youth what 'tis to love.

Sil. It is to be all made of sighs and tears;
And so am I for Phebe.

Phe. And I for Ganymede.

Orl. And I for Rosalind. 80

Ros. And I for no woman.

Sil. It is to be all made of faith and service;
And so am I for Phebe.

Phe. And I for Ganymede.

Orl. And I for Rosalind. 85

Ros. And I for no woman.

Sil. It is to be all made of fantasy,
All made of passion, and all made of wishes;
All adoration, duty, and observance,
All humbleness, all patience, and all impatience, 90
All purity, all trial, all obedience;
And so am I for Phebe.

Phe. And so am I for Ganymede.

Orl. And so am I for Rosalind.

Ros. And so am I for no woman. 95

Phe. If this be so, why blame you me to love you?

Sil. If this be so, why blame you me to love you?

Orl. If this be so, why blame you me to love you?

Ros. Why do you speak too 'Why blame you me to love you?' 100

Orl. To her that is not here, nor doth not hear.

Ros. Pray you, no more of this; 'tis like the howling of Irish wolves against the moon. [*To Silvius*] I will help you if I can. [*To Phebe*] I would love you if I could.— To-morrow meet me all together. [*To Phebe*] I will marry you if ever I marry woman, and I'll be married to-morrow. [*To Orlando*] I will satisfy you if ever I satisfied man, and you shall be married to-morrow. [*To Silvius*] I will content you if what pleases you contents you, and you shall be married to-morrow. [*To Orlando*] As you love Rosalind, meet. [*To Silvius*] As you love Phebe, meet;—and as I love no woman, I'll meet. So, fare you well; I have left you commands. 112

Sil. I'll not fail, if I live.

Phe. Nor I.

Orl. Nor I.   [*Exeunt.*

SCENE III. *The forest.*

Enter TOUCHSTONE *and* AUDREY.

Touch. To-morrow is the joyful day, Audrey; to-morrow will we be married.

Aud. I do desire it with all my heart; and I hope it is no dishonest desire to desire to be a woman of the world. Here come two of the banish'd Duke's pages. 5

Enter two Pages.

1 Page. Well met, honest gentleman.

Touch. By my troth, well met. Come sit, sit, and a song.

2 Page. We are for you; sit i' th' middle.

1 Page. Shall we clap into't roundly, without hawking, or spitting, or saying we are hoarse, which are the only prologues to a bad voice? 11

2 Page. I'faith, i'faith; and both in a tune, like two gipsies on a horse.

Song.

It was a lover and his lass,
  With a hey, and a ho, and a hey nonino,
That o'er the green corn-field did pass 16
  In the spring time, the only pretty ring time,
When birds do sing, hey ding a ding, ding.
Sweet lovers love the spring.

Between the acres of the rye, 20
  With a hey, and a ho, and a hey nonino,
These pretty country folks would lie,
  In the spring time, &c.

This carol they began that hour,
  With a hey, and a ho, and a hey nonino,
How that a life was but a flower, 26
  In the spring time, &c.

And therefore take the present time,
  With a hey, and a ho, and a hey nonino,

For love is crowned with the prime,   30
  In the spring time, &c.

Touch. Truly, young gentlemen, though there was no great matter in the ditty, yet the note was very untuneable.

1 *Page.* You are deceiv'd, sir ; we kept time, we lost not our time.   35

Touch. By my troth, yes; I count it but time lost to hear such a foolish song. God buy you ; and God mend your voices. Come, Audrey.   [*Exeunt.*

SCENE IV. *The forest.*

Enter DUKE SENIOR, AMIENS, JAQUES, ORLANDO, OLIVER, *and* CELIA.

Duke S. Dost thou believe, Orlando, that the boy
Can do all this that he hath promised ?

Orl. I sometimes do believe and sometimes do not ;
As those that fear they hope, and know they fear.

Enter ROSALIND, SILVIUS, *and* PHEBE.

Ros. Patience once more, whiles our com-
  pact is urg'd :
You say, if I bring in your Rosalind,   6
You will bestow her on Orlando here ?

Duke S. That would I, had I kingdoms to give with her.

Ros. And you say you will have her when I bring her ?

Orl. That would I, were I of all kingdoms king.   10

Ros. You say you'll marry me, if I be willing ?

Phe. That will I, should I die the hour after.

Ros. But if you do refuse to marry me,
You'll give yourself to this most faithful shepherd ?

Phe. So is the bargain.   15

Ros. You say that you'll have Phebe, if she will ?

Sil. Though to have her and death were both one thing.

Ros. I have promis'd to make all this matter even.
Keep you your word, O Duke, to give your daughter ;
You yours, Orlando, to receive his daughter ;   20
Keep your word, Phebe, that you'll marry me,
Or else, refusing me, to wed this shepherd ;
Keep your word, Silvius, that you'll marry her
If she refuse me ; and from hence I go,
To make these doubts all even.   25
    [*Exeunt Rosalind and Celia.*

Duke S. I do remember in this shepherd boy

Some lively touches of my daughter's favour.

Orl. My lord, the first time that I ever saw him
Methought he was a brother to your daughter.   29
But, my good lord, this boy is forest-born,
And hath been tutor'd in the rudiments
Of many desperate studies by his uncle,
Whom he reports to be a great magician,
Obscured in the circle of this forest.   34

Enter TOUCHSTONE *and* AUDREY.

Jaq. There is, sure, another flood toward, and these couples are coming to the ark. Here comes a pair of very strange beasts which in all tongues are call'd fools.   37

Touch. Salutation and greeting to you all !

Jaq. Good my lord, bid him welcome. This is the motley-minded gentleman that I have so often met in the forest. He hath been a courtier, he swears.   41

Touch. If any man doubt that, let him put me to my purgation. I have trod a measure ; I have flatt'red a lady ; I have been politic with my friend, smooth with mine enemy ; I have undone three tailors; I have had four quarrels, and like to have fought one.   46

Jaq. And how was that ta'en up ?

Touch. Faith, we met, and found the quarrel was upon the seventh cause.

Jaq. How seventh cause ? Good my lord, like this fellow.   51

Duke S. I like him very well.

Touch. God 'ild you, sir ; I desire you of the like. I press in here, sir, amongst the rest of the country copulatives, to swear and to forswear, according as marriage binds and blood breaks. A poor virgin, sir, an ill-favour'd thing, sir, but mine own ; a poor humour of mine, sir, to take that that no man else will. Rich honesty dwells like a miser, sir, in a poor house ; as your pearl in your foul oyster.   59

Duke S. By my faith, he is very swift and sententious.

Touch. According to the fool's bolt, sir, and such dulcet diseases.

Jaq. But, for the seventh cause : how did you find the quarrel on the seventh cause ?   64

Touch. Upon a lie seven times removed—bear your body more seeming, Audrey—as thus, sir. I did dislike the cut of a certain courtier's beard ; he sent me word, if I said his beard was not cut well, he was in the mind it was. This is call'd the Retort Courteous. If I sent him word again it was not well cut, he would send me word he cut it to please himself. This is call'd the Quip Modest. If again it was not well cut, he disabled my judgment. This is call'd

the Reply Churlish. If again it was not
well cut, he would answer I spake not
true. This is call'd the Reproof Valiant.
If again it was not well cut, he would
say I lie. This is call'd the Countercheck
Quarrelsome. And so to Lie Circumstantial
and the Lie Direct.   77

Jaq. And how oft did you say his beard
was not well cut?

Touch. I durst go no further than the
Lie Circumstantial, nor he durst not give
me the Lie Direct; and so we measur'd
swords and parted.

Jaq. Can you nominate in order now the
degrees of the lie?   84

Touch. O, sir, we quarrel in print by the
book, as you have books for good manners.
I will name you the degrees. The first, the
Retort Courteous; the second, the Quip
Modest; the third, the Reply Churlish;
the fourth, the Reproof Valiant; the fifth,
the Countercheck Quarrelsome; the sixth,
the Lie with Circumstance; the seventh,
the Lie Direct. All these you may avoid
but the Lie Direct; and you may avoid
that too with an If. I knew when seven
justices could not take up a quarrel; but
when the parties were met themselves, one
of them thought but of an If, as: 'If you
said so, then I said so'. And they shook
hands, and swore brothers. Your If is the
only peace-maker; much virtue in If.   97

Jaq. Is not this a rare fellow, my lord?
He's as good at any thing, and yet a fool.

Duke S. He uses his folly like a stalking-
horse, and under the presentation of that
he shoots his wit.   101

Enter HYMEN, ROSALIND, *and* CELIA. *Still
music.*

Hym. Then is there mirth in heaven,
    When earthly things made even
        Atone together.   104
    Good Duke, receive thy daughter;
    Hymen from heaven brought her,
        Yea, brought her hither,
    That thou mightst join her hand
        with his,
    Whose heart within his bosom is.

Ros. [*To Duke*] To you I give myself, for
    I am yours.   110
[*To Orlando*] To you I give myself, for I
    am yours.

Duke S. If there be truth in sight, you
    are my daughter.

Orl. If there be truth in sight, you are my
    Rosalind.

Phe. If sight and shape be true,
    Why then, my love adieu!   115

Ros. I'll have no father, if you be not
    he;
I'll have no husband, if you be not he;
Nor ne'er wed woman, if you be not she.

Hym. Peace, ho! I bar confusion;
    'Tis I must make conclusion   120
    Of these most strange events.
    Here's eight that must take hands
    To join in Hymen's bands,
        If truth holds true contents.   124
    You and you no cross shall part;
    You and you are heart in heart;
    You to his love must accord,   127
    Or have a woman to your lord;
    You and you are sure together,
    As the winter to foul weather.
    Whiles a wedlock-hymn we sing,
    Feed yourselves with questioning,
    That reason wonder may diminish,
    How thus we met, and these things
        finish.

Song.

Wedding is great Juno's crown;   135
    O blessed bond of board and bed!
'Tis Hymen peoples every town;
    High wedlock then be honoured.
Honour, high honour, and renown,
To Hymen, god of every town!   140

Duke S. O my dear niece, welcome thou
    art to me!
Even daughter, welcome in no less degree.

Phe. I will not eat my word, now thou
    art mine;
Thy faith my fancy to thee doth combine.

Enter JAQUES DE BOYS.

Jaq. de B. Let me have audience for a
    word or two.   145
I am the second son of old Sir Rowland,
That bring these tidings to this fair
    assembly.
Duke Frederick, hearing how that every
    day
Men of great worth resorted to this forest,
Address'd a mighty power; which were on
    foot,   150
In his own conduct, purposely to take
His brother here, and put him to the sword;
And to the skirts of this wild wood he came,
Where, meeting with an old religious
    man,
After some question with him, was con-
    verted   155
Both from his enterprise and from the
    world;
His crown bequeathing to his banish'd
    brother,
And all their lands restor'd to them again
That were with him exil'd. This to be true
I do engage my life.
Duke S.   Welcome, young man.
Thou offer'st fairly to thy brothers' wed-
    ding: 161
To one, his lands withheld; and to the
    other,
A land itself at large, a potent dukedom.

First, in this forest let us do those ends
That here were well begun and well begot ;
And after, every of this happy number,
That have endur'd shrewd days and nights
    with us,   167
Shall share the good of our returned for-
    tune,
According to the measure of their states.
Meantime, forget this new-fall'n dignity,
And fall into our rustic revelry.   171
Play, music ; and you brides and bride-
    grooms all,
With measure heap'd in joy, to th' measures
    fall.
  Jaq. Sir, by your patience. If I heard you
    rightly,
The Duke hath put on a religious life,   175
And thrown into neglect the pompous
    court.
  Jaq de B. He hath.
  Jaq. To him will I. Out of these con-
    vertites
There is much matter to be heard and
    learn'd.
[*To Duke*] You to your former honour I
    bequeath ;   180
Your patience and your virtue well deserves
    it.
[*To Orlando*] You to a love that your true
    faith doth merit ;
[*To Oliver*] You to your land, and love,
    and great allies ;
[*To Silvius*] You to a long and well-deserved
    bed ;
[*To Touchstone*] And you to wrangling ; for
    thy loving voyage   185
Is but for two months victuall'd.—So to
    your pleasures ;
I am for other than for dancing measures.

  Duke S. Stay, Jaques, stay.
  Jaq. To see no pastime I.   What you
    would have   189
I'll stay to know at your abandon'd cave.
                       [*Exit.*
  Duke S. Proceed, proceed. We will begin
    these rites,
As we do trust they'll end, in true delights.
             [*A dance. Exeunt.*

EPILOGUE

  Ros. It is not the fashion to see the lady
the epilogue ; but it is no more unhandsome than to see the lord the prologue. If
it be true that good wine needs no bush,
'tis true that a good play needs no epilogue.
Yet to good wine they do use good bushes ;
and good plays prove the better by the help
of good epilogues. What a case am I in
then, that am neither a good epilogue, nor
cannot insinuate with you in the behalf of
a good play ! I am not furnish'd like a
beggar ; therefore to beg will not become
me. My way is to conjure you ; and I'll
begin with the women. I charge you, O
women, for the love you bear to men, to
like as much of this play as please you ;
and I charge you, O men, for the love you
bear to women—as I perceive by your
simp'ring none of you hates them—that
between you and the women the play may
please. If I were a woman, I would kiss as
many of you as had beards that pleas'd me,
complexions that lik'd me, and breaths
that I defied not ; and, I am sure, as many
as have good beards, or good faces, or sweet
breaths, will, for my kind offer, when I
make curtsy, bid me farewell.   20

THE TAMING OF THE SHREW

DRAMATIS PERSONÆ

A Lord,
CHRISTOPHER SLY, *a tinker,*
Hostess, Page, Players, Hunts-
men, Servants,
} *Persons in the Induction.*

BAPTISTA MINOLA, *a gentleman of Padua.*
VINCENTIO, *a merchant of Pisa.*
LUCENTIO, *son to Vincentio, in love with Bianca.*
PETRUCHIO, *a gentleman of Verona, a suitor to Katherina.*
GREMIO,
HORTENSIO,
} *suitors to Bianca.*

TRANIO,
BIONDELLO,
} *servants to Lucentio.*
GRUMIO,
CURTIS,
} *servants to Petruchio.*
A Pedant.

KATHERINA, *the shrew,*
BIANCA,
} *daughters to Baptista.*
A Widow.

Tailor, Haberdasher, *and* Servants *attending on Baptista and Petruchio.*

THE SCENE : *Padua, and Petruchio's house in the country.*

INDUCTION

SCENE I. *Before an alehouse on a heath.*

Enter Hostess *and* SLY.

Sly. I'll pheeze you, in faith.
Host. A pair of stocks, you rogue!
Sly. Y'are a baggage ; the Slys are no rogues. Look in the chronicles : we came in with Richard Conqueror. Therefore, paucas pallabris ; let the world slide. Sessa! 5
Host. You will not pay for the glasses you have burst ?
Sly. No, not a denier. Go by, Saint Jeronimy, go to thy cold bed and warm thee. 8
Host. I know my remedy ; I must go fetch the thirdborough. [*Exit.*
Sly. Third, or fourth, or fifth borough, I'll answer him by law. I'll not budge an inch, boy ; let him come, and kindly.
[*Falls asleep.*

Wind horns. Enter a Lord *from hunting, with his* Train.

Lord. Huntsman, I charge thee, tender well my hounds ; 14
Brach Merriman, the poor cur, is emboss'd ;
And couple Clowder with the deep-mouth'd brach.
Saw'st thou not, boy, how Silver made it good
At the hedge corner, in the coldest fault ?
I would not lose the dog for twenty pound.
1 Hun. Why, Belman is as good as he, my lord ; 20
He cried upon it at the merest loss,
And twice to-day pick'd out the dullest scent ;
Trust me, I take him for the better dog.

Lord. Thou art a fool ; if Echo were as fleet,
I would esteem him worth a dozen such. 25
But sup them well, and look unto them all ;
To-morrow I intend to hunt again.
1 Hun. I will, my lord.
Lord. What's here ? One dead, or drunk?
See, doth he breathe ?
2 Hun. He breathes, my lord. Were he not warm'd with ale, 30
This were a bed but cold to sleep so soundly.
Lord. O monstrous beast, how like a swine he lies !
Grim death, how foul and loathsome is thine image !
Sirs, I will practise on this drunken man.
What think you, if he were convey'd to bed,
Wrapp'd in sweet clothes, rings put upon his fingers,
A most delicious banquet by his bed, 37
And brave attendants near him when he wakes,
Would not the beggar then forget himself ?
1 Hun. Believe me, lord, I think he cannot choose. 40
2 Hun. It would seem strange unto him when he wak'd.
Lord. Even as a flatt'ring dream or worthless fancy.
Then take him up, and manage well the jest :
Carry him gently to my fairest chamber,
And hang it round with all my wanton pictures ; 45
Balm his foul head in warm distilled waters,
And burn sweet wood to make the lodging sweet ;
Procure me music ready when he wakes,
To make a dulcet and a heavenly sound ;
And if he chance to speak, be ready straight,
And with a low submissive reverence 51

284

Say ' What is it your honour will com-
        mand ? '
Let one attend him with a silver basin
Full of rose-water and bestrew'd with
        flowers ;   54
Another bear the ewer, the third a diaper,
And say ' Will't please your lordship cool
        your hands ? '
Some one be ready with a costly suit,
And ask him what apparel he will wear ;
Another tell him of his hounds and horse,
And that his lady mourns at his disease ; 60
Persuade him that he hath been lunatic,
And, when he says he is, say that he
        dreams,
For he is nothing but a mighty lord.
This do, and do it kindly, gentle sirs ;
It will be pastime passing excellent,   65
If it be husbanded with modesty.
    1 *Hun.* My lord, I warrant you we will
        play our part
As he shall think by our true diligence
He is no less than what we say he is.
    Lord. Take him up gently, and to bed
        with him ;   70
And each one to his office when he wakes.
        [*Sly is carried out.   A trumpet sounds.*
Sirrah, go see what trumpet 'tis that
        sounds—   [*Exit Servant.*
Belike some noble gentleman that means,
Travelling some journey, to repose him
        here.

            Re-enter a Servingman.

How now ! who is it ?
    Serv. An't please your honour, players
That offer service to your lordship.   76
    Lord. Bid them come near.

            Enter Players.

        Now, fellows, you are welcome.
    Players. We thank your honour.
    Lord. Do you intend to stay with me
        to-night ?
    Player. So please your lordship to accept
        our duty.   80
    Lord. With all my heart. This fellow I
        remember
Since once he play'd a farmer's eldest son ;
'Twas where you woo'd the gentlewoman so
        well.
I have forgot your name ; but, sure, that
        part   84
Was aptly fitted and naturally perform'd.
    Player. I think 'twas Soto that your
        honour means.
    Lord. 'Tis very true ; thou didst it
        excellent.
Well, you are come to me in happy time, 88
The rather for I have some sport in hand
Wherein your cunning can assist me much.
There is a lord will hear you play to-night ;
But I am doubtful of your modesties,
Lest, over-eying of his odd behaviour,

For yet his honour never heard a play,
You break into some merry passion   95
And so offend him ; for I tell you, sirs,
If you should smile, he grows impatient.
    Player. Fear not, my lord ; we can con-
        tain ourselves,
Were he the veriest antic in the world.
    Lord. Go, sirrah, take them to the
        buttery,   100
And give them friendly welcome every one ;
Let them want nothing that my house
        affords. [*Exit one with the Players.*
Sirrah, go you to Barthol'mew my page,
And see him dress'd in all suits like a lady ;
That done, conduct him to the drunkard's
        chamber,   105
And call him ' madam', do him obeisance.
Tell him from me—as he will win my love—
He bear himself with honourable action,
Such as he hath observ'd in noble ladies
Unto their lords, by them accomplished ;
Such duty to the drunkard let him do, 111
With soft low tongue and lowly courtesy,
And say ' What is't your honour will com-
        mand,
Wherein your lady and your humble wife
May show her duty and make known her
        love ? '   115
And then with kind embracements, tempt-
        ing kisses,
And with declining head into his bosom,
Bid him shed tears, as being overjoyed
To see her noble lord restor'd to health,
Who for this seven years hath esteemed
        him
No better than a poor and loathsome
        beggar.   121
And if the boy have not a woman's gift
To rain a shower of commanded tears,
An onion will do well for such a shift,
Which, in a napkin being close convey'd,
Shall in despite enforce a watery eye. 126
See this dispatch'd with all the haste thou
        canst ;
Anon I'll give thee more instructions.
                    [*Exit a Servingman.*
I know the boy will well usurp the grace,
Voice, gait, and action, of a gentlewoman ;
I long to hear him call the drunkard
        ' husband ' ;   131
And how my men will stay themselves
        from laughter
When they do homage to this simple
        peasant.
I'll in to counsel them ; haply my presence
May well abate the over-merry spleen, 135
Which otherwise would grow into extremes.
                                    [*Exeunt.*

SCENE II.   *A bedchamber in the Lord's
                house.*

Enter aloft SLY, *with* Attendants ; *some
with apparel, basin and ewer, and other
appurtenances ; and* Lord.

Sly. For God's sake, a pot of small ale.

1 *Serv.* Will't please your lordship drink a cup of sack ?

2 *Serv.* Will't please your honour taste of these conserves ?

3 *Serv.* What raiment will your honour wear to-day ?   4

Sly. I am Christophero Sly ; call not me 'honour' nor 'lordship'. I ne'er drank sack in my life ; and if you give me any conserves, give me conserves of beef. Ne'er ask me what raiment I'll wear, for I have no more doublets than backs, no more stockings than legs, nor no more shoes than feet—nay, sometime more feet than shoes, or such shoes as my toes look through the overleather.   11

Lord. Heaven cease this idle humour in your honour !

O, that a mighty man of such descent, Of such possessions, and so high esteem, Should be infused with so foul a spirit ! 15

Sly. What, would you make me mad? Am not I Christopher Sly, old Sly's son of Burton Heath ; by birth a pedlar, by education a cardmaker, by transmutation a bearherd, and now by present profession a tinker ? Ask Marian Hacket, the fat alewife of Wincot, if she know me not ; if she say I am not fourteen pence on the score for sheer ale, score me up for the lying'st knave in Christendom. What ! I am not bestraught. [*Taking a pot of ale*] Here's—

3 *Serv.* O, this it is that makes your lady mourn !   24

2 *Serv.* O, this is it that makes your servants droop !

Lord. Hence comes it that your kindred shuns your house,

As beaten hence by your strange lunacy. O noble lord, bethink thee of thy birth ! Call home thy ancient thoughts from banishment, And banish hence these abject lowly dreams.   30

Look how thy servants do attend on thee, Each in his office ready at thy beck. Wilt thou have music ? Hark ! Apollo plays,   [*Music.*

And twenty caged nightingales do sing. Or wilt thou sleep ? We'll have thee to a couch   35

Softer and sweeter than the lustful bed On purpose trimm'd up for Semiramis.

Say thou wilt walk : we will bestrew the ground.

Or wilt thou ride ? Thy horses shall be trapp'd,

Their harness studded all with gold and pearl.   40

Dost thou love hawking ? Thou hast hawks will soar

Above the morning lark. Or wilt thou hunt ?

Thy hounds shall make the welkin answer them

And fetch shrill echoes from the hollow earth.

1 *Serv.* Say thou wilt course ; thy greyhounds are as swift   45

As breathed stags ; ay, fleeter than the roe.

2 *Serv.* Dost thou love pictures ? We will fetch thee straight

Adonis painted by a running brook, And Cytherea all in sedges hid, Which seem to move and wanton with her breath   50

Even as the waving sedges play wi' th' wind.

Lord. We'll show thee Io as she was a maid

And how she was beguiled and surpris'd, As lively painted as the deed was done.

3 *Serv.* Or Daphne roaming through a thorny wood,   55

Scratching her legs, that one shall swear she bleeds ;

And at that sight shall sad Apollo weep, So workmanly the blood and tears are drawn.

Lord. Thou art a lord, and nothing but a lord.

Thou hast a lady far more beautiful   60

Than any woman in this waning age.

1 *Serv.* And, till the tears that she hath shed for thee

Like envious floods o'er-run her lovely face, She was the fairest creature in the world ; And yet she is inferior to none.   65

Sly. Am I a lord and have I such a lady ? Or do I dream ? Or have I dream'd till now ?

I do not sleep : I see, I hear, I speak ; I smell sweet savours, and I feel soft things.

Upon my life, I am a lord indeed,   70

And not a tinker, nor Christopher Sly. Well, bring our lady hither to our sight ; And once again, a pot o' th' smallest ale.

2 *Serv.* Will't please your Mightiness to wash your hands ?

O, how we joy to see your wit restor'd ! 75

O, that once more you knew but what you are !

These fifteen years you have been in a dream ;

Or, when you wak'd, so wak'd as if you slept.

Sly. These fifteen years ! by my fay, a goodly nap.   79

But did I never speak of all that time ?

1 *Serv.* O, yes, my lord, but very idle words ;

For though you lay here in this goodly chamber,

Yet would you say ye were beaten out of door ;

And rail upon the hostess of the house,   84

And say you would present her at the leet,
Because she brought stone jugs and no
    seal'd quarts.
Sometimes you would call out for Cicely
    Hacket.
   Sly. Ay, the woman's maid of the house.
   3 Serv. Why, sir, you know no house nor
    no such maid,   89
Nor no such men as you have reckon'd
    up,
As Stephen Sly, and old John Naps of
    Greece,
And Peter Turph, and Henry Pimpernell ;
And twenty more such names and men as
    these,
Which never were, nor no man ever saw.
   Sly. Now, Lord be thanked for my good
    amends !   95
   All. Amen.

Enter the Page *as a lady, with* Attendants.

   Sly. I thank thee ; thou shalt not lose
    by it.
   Page. How fares my noble lord ?
   Sly. Marry, I fare well ; for here is cheer
enough.
Where is my wife ?   100
   Page. Here, noble lord ; what is thy will
    with her ?
   Sly. Are you my wife, and will not call
    me husband ?
My men should call me ' lord ' ; I am your
    goodman.
   Page. My husband and my lord, my lord
    and husband ;
I am your wife in all obedience.   105
   Sly. I know it well. What must I call
    her ?
   Lord.   Madam.
   Sly. Al'ce madam, or Joan madam ?
   Lord. Madam, and nothing else ; so lords
    call ladies.
   Sly. Madam wife, they say that I have
    dream'd   110
And slept above some fifteen year or more.
   Page. Ay, and the time seems thirty unto
    me,
Being all this time abandon'd from your
    bed.
   Sly. 'Tis much. Servants, leave me and
    her alone.   [*Exeunt Servants.*
Madam, undress you, and come now to bed.
   Page. Thrice noble lord, let me entreat
    of you   116
To pardon me yet for a night or two ;
Or, if not so, until the sun be set.
For your physicians have expressly charg'd,
In peril to incur your former malady,   120
That I should yet absent me from your bed.
I hope this reason stands for my excuse.
   Sly. Ay, it stands so that I may hardly
tarry so long. But I would be loath to fall
into my dreams again. I will therefore
tarry in despite of the flesh and the blood.

Enter a Messenger.

   Mess. You honour's players, hearing your
    amendment,   126
Are come to play a pleasant comedy ;
For so your doctors hold it very meet,
Seeing too much sadness hath congeal'd
    your blood,
And melancholy is the nurse of frenzy. 130
Therefore they thought it good you hear a
    play
And frame your mind to mirth and merri-
    ment,
Which bars a thousand harms and length-
    ens life.
   Sly. Marry, I will ; let them play it. Is
not a comonty a Christmas gambold or a
tumbling-trick ?   135
   Page. No, my good lord, it is more
    pleasing stuff.
   Sly. What, household stuff ?
   Page. It is a kind of history.   138
   Sly. Well, we'll see't. Come, madam wife,
sit by my side and let the world slip ; we
shall ne'er be younger.   [*They sit down.*

A flourish of trumpets announces the play.

ACT ONE

SCENE I. *Padua. A public place.*

Enter LUCENTIO *and his man* TRANIO.

   Luc. Tranio, since for the great desire
    I had
To see fair Padua, nursery of arts,
I am arriv'd for fruitful Lombardy,
The pleasant garden of great Italy,
And by my father's love and leave am
    arm'd   5
With his good will and thy good company,
My trusty servant well approv'd in all,
Here let us breathe, and haply institute
A course of learning and ingenious studies.
Pisa, renowned for grave citizens,   10
Gave me my being and my father first,
A merchant of great traffic through the
    world,
Vincentio, come of the Bentivolii ;
Vincentio's son, brought up in Florence, 14
It shall become to serve all hopes conceiv'd,
To deck his fortune with his virtuous deeds.
And therefore, Tranio, for the time I study,
Virtue and that part of philosophy
Will I apply that treats of happiness
By virtue specially to be achiev'd.   20
Tell me thy mind ; for I have Pisa left
And am to Padua come as he that leaves
A shallow plash to plunge him in the deep,
And with satiety seeks to quench his thirst.
   Tra. Mi perdonato, gentle master mine ;
I am in all affected as yourself ;   26
Glad that you thus continue your resolve
To suck the sweets of sweet philosophy.
Only, good master, while we do admire

This virtue and this moral discipline,   30
Let's be no Stoics nor no stocks, I pray,
Or so devote to Aristotle's checks
As Ovid be an outcast quite abjur'd.
Balk logic with acquaintance that you have,
And practise rhetoric in your common talk ;
Music and poesy use to quicken you ;   36
The mathematics and the metaphysics,
Fall to them as you find your stomach
   serves you.
No profit grows where is no pleasure ta'en ;
In brief, sir, study what you most affect. 40
   Luc. Gramercies, Tranio, well dost thou
     advise.
If, Biondello, thou wert come ashore,
We could at once put us in readiness,
And take a lodging fit to entertain   44
Such friends as time in Padua shall beget.

Enter BAPTISTA *with his two daughters,*
KATHERINA *and* BIANCA ; GREMIO, *a
pantaloon,* HORTENSIO, *suitor to Bianca.
Lucentio and Tranio stand by.*

But stay awhile ; what company is this ?
   Tra. Master, some show to welcome us to
     town.
   Bap. Gentlemen, importune me no
     farther,
For how I firmly am resolv'd you know ;
That is, not to bestow my youngest
   daughter   50
Before I have a husband for the elder.
If either of you both love Katherina,
Because I know you well and love you well,
Leave shall you have to court her at your
   pleasure.
   Gre. To cart her rather. She's too rough
     for me.   55
There, there, Hortensio, will you any wife ?
   Kath. [*To Baptista*] I pray you, sir, is it
     your will
To make a stale of me amongst these
   mates ?
   Hor. Mates, maid ! How mean you that ?
     No mates for you,   59
Unless you were of gentler, milder mould.
   Kath. I' faith, sir, you shall never need
     to fear ;
Iwis it is not halfway to her heart ;
But if it were, doubt not her care should be
To comb your noddle with a three-legg'd
   stool,
And paint your face, and use you like a
   fool.   65
   Hor. From all such devils, good Lord
     deliver us !
   Gre. And me, too, good Lord !
   Tra. Husht, master ! Here's some good
     pastime toward ;
That wench is stark mad or wonderful
   froward.
   Luc. But in the other's silence do I see 70
Maid's mild behaviour and sobriety.
Peace, Tranio !

   Tra. Well said, master ; mum ! and gaze
     your fill.
   Bap. Gentlemen, that I may soon make
     good
What I have said—Bianca, get you in ;   75
And let it not displease thee, good Bianca,
For I will love thee ne'er the less, my girl.
   Kath. A pretty peat ! it is best
Put finger in the eye, an she knew why.
   Bian. Sister, content you in my discon-
     tent.   80
Sir, to your pleasure humbly I subscribe ;
My books and instruments shall be my
   company,
On them to look, and practise by myself.
   Luc. Hark, Tranio, thou mayst hear
     Minerva speak !
   Hor. Signior Baptista, will you be so
     strange ?   85
Sorry am I that our good will effects
Bianca's grief.
   Gre.   Why will you mew her up,
Signior Baptista, for this fiend of hell,
And make her bear the penance of her
   tongue ?
   Bap. Gentlemen, content ye ; I am
     resolv'd.   90
Go in, Bianca.   [*Exit Bianca.*
And for I know she taketh most delight
In music, instruments, and poetry,
Schoolmasters will I keep within my house
Fit to instruct her youth. If you, Hor-
   tensio,   95
Or, Signior Gremio, you, know any such,
Prefer them hither ; for to cunning men
I will be very kind, and liberal   98
To mine own children in good bringing-up ;
And so, farewell. Katherina, you may stay ;
For I have more to commune with Bianca.
                   [*Exit.*
   Kath. Why, and I trust I may go too,
     may I not ?   102
What ! shall I be appointed hours, as
   though, belike,
I knew not what to take and what to
     leave ? Ha !   [*Exit.*
   Gre. You may go to the devil's dam ;
your gifts are so good here's none will hold
you. There ! Love is not so great, Hortensio,
but we may blow our nails together, and
fast it fairly out ; our cake's dough on both
sides. Farewell ; yet, for the love I bear
my sweet Bianca, if I can by any means
light on a fit man to teach her that wherein
she delights, I will wish him to her father.
   Hor. So will I, Signior Gremio ; but a
word, I pray. Though the nature of our
quarrel yet never brook'd parle, know now,
upon advice, it toucheth us both—that we
may yet again have access to our fair
mistress, and be happy rivals in Bianca's
love—to labour and effect one thing
specially.   116
   Gre. What's that, I pray ?

Hor. Marry, sir, to get a husband for her sister.

Gre. A husband ? a devil.

Hor. I say a husband.   120

Gre. I say a devil. Think'st thou, Hortensio, though her father be very rich, any man is so very a fool to be married to hell ?   123

Hor. Tush, Gremio ! Though it pass your patience and mine to endure her loud alarums, why, man, there be good fellows in the world, an a man could light on them, would take her with all faults, and money enough.

Gre. I cannot tell ; but I had as lief take her dowry with this condition—to be whipp'd at the high cross every morning.

Hor. Faith, as you say, there's small choice in rotten apples. But, come ; since this bar in law makes us friends, it shall be so far forth friendly maintain'd till by helping Baptista's eldest daughter to a husband we set his youngest free for a husband, and then have to't afresh. Sweet Bianca ! Happy man be his dole ! He that runs fastest gets the ring. How say you, Signior Gremio ?   136

Gre. I am agreed ; and would I had given him the best horse in Padua to begin his wooing that would thoroughly woo her, wed her, and bed her, and rid the house of her ! Come on.   140

[*Exeunt Gremio and Hortensio.*

Tra. I pray, sir, tell me, is it possible That love should of a sudden take such hold ?

Luc. O Tranio, till I found it to be true, I never thought it possible or likely.
But see ! while idly I stood looking on, 145
I found the effect of love in idleness ;
And now in plainness do confess to thee,
That art to me as secret and as dear
As Anna to the Queen of Carthage was—
Tranio, I burn, I pine, I perish, Tranio, 150
If I achieve not this young modest girl.
Counsel me, Tranio, for I know thou canst ;
Assist me, Tranio, for I know thou wilt.

Tra. Master, it is no time to chide you now ;
Affection is not rated from the heart ; 155
If love have touch'd you, nought remains but so :
' Redime te captum quam queas minimo'.

Luc. Gramercies, lad. Go forward ; this contents ;
The rest will comfort, for thy counsel's sound.

Tra. Master, you look'd so longly on the maid,   160
Perhaps you mark'd not what's the pith of all,

Luc. O, yes, I saw sweet beauty in her face,
Such as the daughter of Agenor had,

That made great Jove to humble him to her hand,
When with his knees he kiss'd the Cretan strand.   165

Tra. Saw you no more ? Mark'd you not how her sister
Began to scold and raise up such a storm
That mortal ears might hardly endure the din ?

Luc. Tranio, I saw her coral lips to move,
And with her breath she did perfume the air ;   170
Sacred and sweet was all I saw in her.

Tra. Nay, then 'tis time to stir him from his trance.
I pray, awake, sir. If you love the maid,
Bend thoughts and wits to achieve her.
Thus it stands :
Her elder sister is so curst and shrewd 175
That, till the father rid his hands of her,
Master, your love must live a maid at home ;
And therefore has he closely mew'd her up,
Because she will not be annoy'd with suitors.

Luc. Ah, Tranio, what a cruel father's he !   180
But art thou not advis'd he took some care
To get her cunning schoolmasters to instruct her ?

Tra. Ay, marry, am I, sir, and now 'tis plotted.

Luc. I have it, Tranio.

Tra.   Master, for my hand,
Both our inventions meet and jump in one.

Luc. Tell me thine first.

Tra.   You will be schoolmaster,
And undertake the teaching of the maid—
That's your device.

Luc.   It is. May it be done ?

Tra. Not possible ; for who shall bear your part
And be in Padua here Vincentio's son ; 190
Keep house and ply his book, welcome his friends,
Visit his countrymen, and banquet them ?

Luc. Basta, content thee, for I have it full.   193
We have not yet been seen in any house,
Nor can we be distinguish'd by our faces
For man or master. Then it follows thus :
Thou shalt be master, Tranio, in my stead,
Keep house and port and servants, as I should ;
I will some other be—some Florentine,
Some Neapolitan, or meaner man of Pisa.
'Tis hatch'd, and shall be so. Tranio, at once   201
Uncase thee ; take my colour'd hat and cloak.
When Biondello comes, he waits on thee ;
But I will charm him first to keep his tongue.

s.—6

Tra. So had you need.   205
                              [*They exchange habits.*
In brief, sir, sith it your pleasure is,
And I am tied to be obedient—
For so your father charg'd me at our
    parting :
' Be serviceable to my son' quoth he,   209
Although I think 'twas in another sense—
I am content to be Lucentio,
Because so well I love Lucentio.

Luc. Tranio, be so because Lucentio
    loves ;
And let me be a slave t' achieve that maid
Whose sudden sight hath thrall'd my
    wounded eye.   215

Enter BIONDELLO.

Here comes the rogue. Sirrah, where have
    you been ?

Bio. Where have I been !   Nay, how
    now !   where are you ?
Master, has my fellow Tranio stol'n your
    clothes ?
Or you stol'n his ? or both ? Pray, what's
    the news ?

Luc. Sirrah, come hither ; 'tis no time
    to jest,   220
And therefore frame your manners to the
    time.
Your fellow Tranio here, to save my life,
Puts my apparel and my count'nance on,
And I for my escape have put on his ;
For in a quarrel since I came ashore   225
I kill'd a man, and fear I was descried.
Wait you on him, I charge you, as becomes,
While I make way from hence to save my
    life.
You understand me ?

Bion.   I, sir ? Ne'er a whit.

Luc. And not a jot of Tranio in your
    mouth :   230
Tranio is chang'd into Lucentio.

Bion. The better for him ; would I were
    so too !

Tra. So could I, faith, boy, to have the
    next wish after,
That Lucentio indeed had Baptista's
    youngest daughter.
But, sirrah, not for my sake but your
    master's, I advise   235
You use your manners discreetly in all kind
    of companies.
When I am alone, why, then I am Tranio ;
But in all places else your master Lucentio.

Luc. Tranio, let's go.
One thing more rests, that thyself execute—
To make one among these wooers. If thou
    ask me why—   240
Sufficeth, my reasons are both good and
    weighty.   [*Exeunt.*

The Presenters above speak.

1 Serv. My lord, you nod ; you do not
    mind the play.

Sly. Yes, by Saint Anne do I.   A good
matter, surely ; comes there any more of
it ?

Page. My lord, 'tis but begun.   245

Sly. 'Tis a very excellent piece of work,
madam lady.   Would 'twere done !
                              [*They sit and mark.*

SCENE II. *Padua. Before Hortensio's house.*

Enter PETRUCHIO *and his man* GRUMIO.

Pet. Verona, for a while I take my leave,
To see my friends in Padua ; but of all
My best beloved and approved friend,
Hortensio ; and I trow this is his house.
Here, sirrah Grumio, knock, I say.   5

Gru. Knock, sir ! Whom should I knock ?
Is there any man has rebus'd your
worship ?

Pet. Villain, I say, knock me here
soundly.

Gru. Knock you here, sir ? Why, sir,
what am I, sir, that I should knock you
here, sir ?   10

Pet. Villain, I say, knock me at this gate,
And rap me well, or I'll knock your knave's
    pate.

Gru. My master is grown quarrelsome. I
    should knock you first,
And then I know after who comes by the
    worst.

Pet. Will it not be ?   15
Faith, sirrah, an you'll not knock I'll
    ring it ;
I'll try how you can sol-fa, and sing it.
                       [*He wrings him by the ears.*

Gru. Help, masters, help ! My master is
mad.

Pet. Now knock when I bid you, sirrah
villain !

Enter HORTENSIO.

Hor. How now ! what's the matter ? My
old friend Grumio and my good friend
Petruchio ! How do you all at Verona ?   22

Pet. Signior Hortensio, come you to part
the fray ?
' Con tutto il cuore ben trovato' may I say.

Hor. Alla nostra casa ben venuto,
        Molto honorato signor mio Pet-
        rucio.   26
Rise, Grumio, rise ; we will compound this
    quarrel.

Gru. Nay, 'tis no matter, sir, what he
'leges in Latin. If this be not a lawful
cause for me to leave his service—look you,
sir : he bid me knock him and rap him
soundly, sir. Well, was it fit for a servant
to use his master so ; being, perhaps, for
aught I see, two and thirty, a pip out ? 32
Whom would to God I had well knock'd at
    first,
Then had not Grumio come by the worst.

Pet. A senseless villain ! Good Hortensio,
I bade the rascal knock upon your gate, 36
And could not get him for my heart to do it.
Gru. Knock at the gate ? O heavens !
Spake you not these words plain : ' Sirrah
knock me here, rap me here, knock me well,
and knock me soundly ' ? And come you
now with ' knocking at the gate ' ?   41
Pet. Sirrah, be gone, or talk not, I advise
you.
Hor. Petruchio, patience ; I am Grumio's
pledge ;
Why, this's a heavy chance 'twixt him and
you,
Your ancient, trusty, pleasant servant
Grumio.   45
And tell me now, sweet friend, what happy
gale
Blows you to Padua here from old Verona ?
Pet. Such wind as scatters young men
through the world
To seek their fortunes farther than at home,
Where small experience grows.   But in a
few,   50
Signior Hortensio, thus it stands with me :
Antonio, my father, is deceas'd,
And I have thrust myself into this maze,
Haply to wive and thrive as best I may ;
Crowns in my purse I have, and goods at
home,   55
And so am come abroad to see the world.
Hor. Petruchio, shall I then come
roundly to thee
And wish thee to a shrewd ill-favour'd
wife ?
Thou'dst thank me but a little for my
counsel,
And yet I'll promise thee she shall be rich,
And very rich ; but th'art too much my
friend,   61
And I'll not wish thee to her.
Pet. Signior Hortensio, 'twixt such friends
as we
Few words suffice ; and therefore, if thou
know
One rich enough to be Petruchio's wife, 65
As wealth is burden of my wooing dance,
Be she as foul as was Florentius' love,
As old as Sibyl, and as curst and shrewd
As Socrates' Xanthippe or a worse—
She moves me not, or not removes, at
least,   70
Affection's edge in me, were she as rough
As are the swelling Adriatic seas.
I come to wive it wealthily in Padua ;
If wealthily, then happily in Padua.   74
Gru. Nay, look you, sir, he tells you flatly
what his mind is.   Why, give him gold
enough and marry him to a puppet or an
aglet-baby, or an old trot with ne'er a
tooth in her head, though she have as many
diseases as two and fifty horses.   Why,
nothing comes amiss, so money comes
withal.   80

Hor. Petruchio, since we are stepp'd thus
far in,
I will continue that I broach'd in jest.
I can, Petruchio, help thee to a wife
With wealth enough, and young and
beauteous ;
Brought up as best becomes a gentle-
woman ;   85
Her only fault, and that is faults enough,
Is—that she is intolerable curst,
And shrewd and froward so beyond all
measure
That, were my state far worser than it is,
I would not wed her for a mine of gold. 90
Pet. Hortensio, peace ! thou know'st not
gold's effect.
Tell me her father's name, and 'tis enough ;
For I will board her though she chide as
loud
As thunder when the clouds in autumn
crack.
Hor. Her father is Baptista Minola,   95
An affable and courteous gentleman ;
Her name is Katherina Minola,
Renown'd in Padua for her scolding
tongue.
Pet. I know her father, though I know
not her ;
And he knew my deceased father well. 100
I will not sleep, Hortensio, till I see her ;
And therefore let me be thus bold with you
To give you over at this first encounter,
Unless you will accompany me thither. 104
Gru. I pray you, sir, let him go while the
humour lasts.   O' my word, an she knew
him as well as I do, she would think scolding would do little good upon him.   She
may perhaps call him half a score knaves
or so.   Why, that's nothing ; an he begin
once, he'll rail in his rope-tricks.   I'll tell
you what, sir : an she stand him but a
little, he will throw a figure in her face, and
so disfigure her with it that she shall have
no more eyes to see withal than a cat.   You
know him not, sir.   113
Hor. Tarry, Petruchio, I must go with
thee,
For in Baptista's keep my treasure is. 115
He hath the jewel of my life in hold,
His youngest daughter, beautiful Bianca ;
And her withholds from me, and other
more,
Suitors to her and rivals in my love ;
Supposing it a thing impossible—   120
For those defects I have before rehears'd—
That ever Katherina will be woo'd.
Therefore this order hath Baptista ta'en,
That none shall have access unto Bianca
Till Katherine the curst have got a husband.
Gru. Katherine the curst !   126
A title for a maid of all titles the worst.
Hor. Now shall my friend Petruchio do
me grace,
And offer me disguis'd in sober robes

To old Baptista as a schoolmaster   130
Well seen in music, to instruct Bianca ;
That so I may by this device at least
Have leave and leisure to make love to her,
And unsuspected court her by herself.

Enter GREMIO *with* LUCENTIO *disguised as
Cambio.*

Gru. Here's no knavery ! See, to beguile
the old folks, how the young folks lay their
heads together ! Master, master, look
about you. Who goes there, ha ?   137
Hor. Peace, Grumio ! It is the rival of my
love. Petruchio, stand by awhile.
Gru. A proper stripling, and an amorous !
[*They stand aside.*
Gre. O, very well ; I have perus'd the
note.   141
Hark you, sir ; I'll have them very fairly
bound—
All books of love, see that at any hand ;
And see you read no other lectures to her.
You understand me—over and beside   145
Signior Baptista's liberality,
I'll mend it with a largess.   Take your
paper too,
And let me have them very well perfum'd,
For she is sweeter than perfume itself
To whom they go to.   What will you read
to her ?   150
Luc. Whate'er I read to her, I'll plead for
you
As for my patron, stand you so assur'd,
As firmly as yourself were still in place ;
Yea, and perhaps with more successful
words   154
Than you, unless you were a scholar, sir.
Gre. O this learning, what a thing it is !
Gru. O this woodcock, what an ass it is !
Pet. Peace, sirrah !
Hor. Grumio, mum ! [*Coming forward*]
God save you, Signior Gremio !
Gre. And you are well met, Signior
Hortensio.   160
Trow you whither I am going ?   To Baptista
Minola.
I promis'd to enquire carefully
About a schoolmaster for the fair Bianca ;
And by good fortune I have lighted well
On this young man ;   for learning and
behaviour   165
Fit for her turn, well read in poetry
And other books—good ones, I warrant ye.
Hor. 'Tis well ;   and I have met a gentle-
man
Hath promis'd me to help me to another,
A fine musician to instruct our mistress ;   170
So shall I no whit be behind in duty
To fair Bianca, so beloved of me.
Gre. Beloved of me—and that my deeds
shall prove.
Gru. And that his bags shall prove.
Hor. Gremio, 'tis now no time to vent
our love.   175

Listen to me, and if you speak me fair
I'll tell you news indifferent good for either.
Here is a gentleman whom by chance I met,
Upon agreement from us to his liking,
Will undertake to woo curst Katherine ;
Yea, and to marry her, if her dowry please.
Gre. So said, so done, is well.   182
Hortensio, have you told him all her faults?
Pet. I know she is an irksome brawling
scold ;
If that be all, masters, I hear no harm.   185
Gre. No, say'st me so, friend ?   What
countryman ?
Pet. Born in Verona, old Antonio's son.
My father dead, my fortune lives for me ;
And I do hope good days and long to see.
Gre. O sir, such a life with such a wife
were strange !   190
But if you have a stomach, to't a God's
name ;
You shall have me assisting you in all.
But will you woo this wild-cat ?
Pet.   Will I live ?
Gru. Will he woo her ?   Ay, or I'll hang
her.
Pet. Why came I hither but to that
intent ?   195
Think you a little din can daunt mine ears ?
Have I not in my time heard lions roar ?
Have I not heard the sea, puff'd up with
winds,
Rage like an angry boar chafed with sweat ?
Have I not heard great ordnance in the
field,   200
And heaven's artillery thunder in the skies?
Have I not in a pitched battle heard
Loud 'larums, neighing steeds, and trum-
pets' clang ?
And do you tell me of a woman's tongue,
That gives not half so great a blow to hear
As will a chestnut in a farmer's fire ?   206
Tush ! tush ! fear boys with bugs.
Gru.   For he fears none.
Gre. Hortensio, hark :
This gentleman is happily arriv'd,
My mind presumes, for his own good and
ours.   210
Hor. I promis'd we would be contributors
And bear his charge of wooing, whatsoe'er.
Gre. And so we will—provided that he
win her.
Gru. I would I were as sure of a good
dinner.

Enter TRANIO, *bravely apparelled as
Lucentio, and* BIONDELLO.

Tra. Gentlemen, God save you !   If I may
be bold,   215
Tell me, I beseech you, which is the readiest
way
To the house of Signior Baptista Minola ?
Bion. He that has the two fair daughters ;
is't he you mean ?
Tra. Even he, Biondello.   220

Gre. Hark you, sir, you mean not her to—

Tra. Perhaps him and her, sir ; what have you to do ?

Pet. Not her that chides, sir, at any hand, I pray.

Tra. I love no chiders, sir. Biondello, let's away.

Luc. [*Aside*] Well begun, Tranio.

Hor.   Sir, a word ere you go.
Are you a suitor to the maid you talk of, yea or no ?   226

Tra. And if I be, sir, is it any offence ?

Gre. No ; if without more words you will get you hence.

Tra. Why, sir, I pray, are not the streets as free
For me as for you ?

Gre.   But so is not she.   230

Tra. For what reason, I beseech you ?

Gre.   For this reason, if you'll know,
That she's the choice love of Signior Gremio.

Hor. That she's the chosen of Signior Hortensio.

Tra. Softly, my masters ! If you be gentlemen,   234
Do me this right—hear me with patience.
Baptista is a noble gentleman,
To whom my father is not all unknown,
And, were his daughter fairer than she is,
She may more suitors have, and me for one.
Fair Leda's daughter had a thousand wooers ;   240
Then well one more may fair Bianca have ;
And so she shall : Lucentio shall make one,
Though Paris came in hope to speed alone.

Gre. What, this gentleman will out-talk us all !

Luc. Sir, give him head ; I know he'll prove a jade.   245

Pet. Hortensio, to what end are all these words ?

Hor. Sir, let me be so bold as ask you,
Did you yet ever see Baptista's daughter ?

Tra. No, sir, but hear I do that he hath two :   249
The one as famous for a scolding tongue
As is the other for beauteous modesty.

Pet. Sir, sir, the first's for me ; let her go by.

Gre. Yea, leave that labour to great Hercules,
And let it be more than Alcides' twelve.

Pet. Sir, understand you this of me, in sooth :   255
The youngest daughter, whom you hearken for,
Her father keeps from all access of suitors,
And will not promise her to any man
Until the elder sister first be wed.   259
The younger then is free, and not before.

Tra. If it be so, sir, that you are the man
Must stead us all, and me amongst the rest ;
And if you break the ice, and do this feat,

Achieve the elder, set the younger free
For our access—whose hap shall be to have her   265
Will not so graceless be to be ingrate.

Hor. Sir, you say well, and well you do conceive ;
And since you do profess to be a suitor,
You must, as we do, gratify this gentleman,
To whom we all rest generally beholding.

Tra. Sir, I shall not be slack ; in sign whereof,   271
Please ye we may contrive this afternoon,
And quaff carouses to our mistress' health ;
And do as adversaries do in law—
Strive mightily, but eat and drink as friends.   275

Gru., Bion. O excellent motion ! Fellows, let's be gone.

Hor. The motion's good indeed, and be it so.
Petruchio, I shall be your ben venuto.
                                        [*Exeunt.*

ACT TWO

Scene I. *Padua. Baptista's house.*

Enter KATHERINA *and* BIANCA.

Bian. Good sister, wrong me not, nor wrong yourself,
To make a bondmaid and a slave of me ;
That I disdain ; but for these other gawds,
Unbind my hands, I'll pull them off myself,
Yea, all my raiment, to my petticoat ;   5
Or what you will command me will I do,
So well I know my duty to my elders.

Kath. Of all thy suitors here I charge thee tell
Whom thou lov'st best. See thou dissemble not.

Bian. Believe me, sister, of all the men alive   10
I never yet beheld that special face
Which I could fancy more than any other.

Kath. Minion, thou liest. Is't not Hortensio ?

Bian. If you affect him, sister, here I swear
I'll plead for you myself but you shall have him.   15

Kath. O then, belike, you fancy riches more :
You will have Gremio to keep you fair.

Bian. Is it for him you do envy me so ?
Nay, then you jest ; and now I well perceive
You have but jested with me all this while.
I prithee, sister Kate, untie my hands.   21

Kath. [*Strikes her*] If that be jest, then all the rest was so.

Enter BAPTISTA.

Bap. Why, how now, dame ! Whence grows this insolence ?

Bianca, stand aside—poor girl! she weeps.
[*He unbinds her.*
Go ply thy needle ; meddle not with her.
For shame, thou hilding of a devilish spirit,
Why dost thou wrong her that did ne'er
wrong thee ?   27
When did she cross thee with a bitter word?
    Kath. Her silence flouts me, and I'll be
reveng'd.   [*Flies after Bianca.*
    Bap. What, in my sight ? Bianca, get
thee in.   [*Exit Bianca.*
    Kath. What, will you not suffer me ?
Nay, now I see   31
She is your treasure, she must have a
husband,
I must dance bare-foot on her wedding-
day,
And for your love to her lead apes in hell.
Talk not to me ; I will go sit and weep, 35
Till I can find occasion of revenge.
                    [*Exit Katherina.*
    Bap. Was ever gentleman thus griev'd
as I ?
But who comes here ?

Enter GREMIO, *with* LUCENTIO *in the habit of
a mean man ;* PETRUCHIO, *with* HOR-
TENSIO *as a musician ; and* TRANIO, *as
Lucentio, with his boy,* BIONDELLO,
bearing a lute and books.

    Gre. Good morrow, neighbour Baptista.
    Bap. Good morrow, neighbour Gremio.
God save you, gentlemen !   41
    Pet. And you, good sir ! Pray, have you
not a daughter
Call'd Katherina, fair and virtuous ?
    Bap. I have a daughter, sir, call'd
Katherina.   44
    Gre. You are too blunt ; go to it orderly.
    Pet. You wrong me, Signior Gremio ; give
me leave.
I am a gentleman of Verona, sir,
That, hearing of her beauty and her wit,
Her affability and bashful modesty,   49
Her wondrous qualities and mild behaviour,
Am bold to show myself a forward guest
Within your house, to make mine eye the
witness
Of that report which I so oft have heard.
And, for an entrance to my entertainment,
I do present you with a man of mine, 55
                    [*Presenting Hortensio.*
Cunning in music and the mathematics,
To instruct her fully in those sciences,
Whereof I know she is not ignorant.
Accept of him, or else you do me wrong—
His name is Licio, born in Mantua.   60
    Bap. Y'are welcome, sir, and he for
your good sake ;
But for my daughter Katherine, this I
know,
She is not for your turn, the more my grief.
    Pet. I see you do not mean to part with
her ;

Or else you like not of my company.   65
    Bap. Mistake me not ; I speak but as I
find.
Whence are you, sir ? What may I call
your name ?
    Pet. Petruchio is my name, Antonio's son,
A man well known throughout all Italy.
    Bap. I know him well ; you are welcome
for his sake.   70
    Gre. Saving your tale, Petruchio, I pray,
Let us that are poor petitioners speak too.
Bacare ! you are marvellous forward.
    Pet. O, pardon me, Signior Gremio ! I
would fain be doing.
    Gre. I doubt it not, sir ; but you will
curse your wooing.   75
Neighbour, this is a gift very grateful, I am
sure of it. To express the like kindness,
myself, that have been more kindly beholding to you than any, freely give unto you
this young scholar [*presenting Lucentio*]
that hath been long studying at Rheims ;
as cunning in Greek, Latin, and other
languages, as the other in music and mathematics. His name is Cambio. Pray accept
his service.   82
    Bap. A thousand thanks, Signior Gremio.
Welcome, good Cambio. [*To Tranio*] But,
gentle sir, methinks you walk like a
stranger. May I be so bold to know the
cause of your coming ?   86
    Tra. Pardon me, sir, the boldness is mine
own
That, being a stranger in this city here,
Do make myself a suitor to your daughter,
Unto Bianca, fair and virtuous.   90
Nor is your firm resolve unknown to me
In the preferment of the eldest sister.
This liberty is all that I request—
That, upon knowledge of my parentage,
I may have welcome 'mongst the rest that
woo,   95
And free access and favour as the rest.
And toward the education of your
daughters
I here bestow a simple instrument,
And this small packet of Greek and Latin
books.
If you accept them, then their worth is
great.   100
    Bap. Lucentio is your name ? Of whence,
I pray ?
    Tra. Of Pisa, sir ; son to Vincentio.
    Bap. A mighty man of Pisa. By report
I know him well. You are very welcome,
sir.
Take you the lute, and you the set of
books ;   105
You shall go see your pupils presently.
Holla, within !

Enter a Servant.

            Sirrah, lead these gentlemen
To my daughters ; and tell them both

294

These are their tutors. Bid them use them
    well.   [*Exit Servant leading Hor-*
    tensio carrying the lute and
    Lucentio with the books.
We will go walk a little in the orchard, 110
And then to dinner.   You are passing
    welcome,
And so I pray you all to think yourselves.
    Pet. Signior Baptista, my business asketh
    haste,
And every day I cannot come to woo. 114
You knew my father well, and in him me,
Left solely heir to all his lands and goods,
Which I have bettered rather than de-
    creas'd.
Then tell me, if I get your daughter's love,
What dowry shall I have with her to wife ?
    Bap. After my death, the one half of my
    lands   120
And, in possession, twenty thousand
    crowns.
    Pet. And for that dowry, I'll assure her of
Her widowhood, be it that she survive me,
In all my lands and leases whatsoever.
Let specialties be therefore drawn between
    us,   125
That covenants may be kept on either hand.
    Bap. Ay, when the special thing is well
    obtain'd,
That is, her love ; for that is all in all.
    Pet. Why, that is nothing ; for I tell you,
    father,   129
I am as peremptory as she proud-minded ;
And where two raging fires meet together,
They do consume the thing that feeds their
    fury.
Though little fire grows great with little
    wind,
Yet extreme gusts will blow out fire and all.
So I to her, and so she yields to me ; 135
For I am rough, and woo not like a babe.
    Bap. Well mayst thou woo, and happy be
    thy speed !
But be thou arm'd for some unhappy
    words.
    Pet. Ay, to the proof, as mountains are
    for winds,
That shake not though they blow per-
    petually.   140

Re-enter HORTENSIO, *with his head broke.*

    Bap. How now, my friend ! Why dost
    thou look so pale ?
    Hor. For fear, I promise you, if I look
    pale.
    Bap. What, will my daughter prove a
    good musician ?
    Hor. I think she'll sooner prove a soldier :
Iron may hold with her, but never lutes. 145
    Bap. Why, then thou canst not break her
    to the lute ?
    Hor. Why, no ; for she hath broke the
    lute to me.
I did but tell her she mistook her frets,

And bow'd her hand to teach her fingering,
When, with a most impatient devilish
    spirit,   150
' Frets, call you these ? ' quoth she ' I'll
    fume with them '.
And with that word she struck me on the
    head,
And through the instrument my pate made
    way ;
And there I stood amazed for a while, 154
As on a pillory, looking through the lute,
While she did call me rascal fiddler
And twangling Jack, with twenty such vile
    terms,
As had she studied to misuse me so.
    Pet. Now, by the world, it is a lusty
    wench ;   159
I love her ten times more than e'er I did.
O, how I long to have some chat with her !
    Bap. Well, go with me, and be not so
    discomfited ;
Proceed in practice with my younger
    daughter ;
She's apt to learn, and thankful for good
    turns.
Signior Petruchio, will you go with us, 165
Or shall I send my daughter Kate to you ?
    Pet. I pray you do.
             [*Exeunt all but Petruchio.*
               I'll attend her here,
And woo her with some spirit when she
    comes.
Say that she rail ; why, then I'll tell her
    plain
She sings as sweetly as a nightingale. 170
Say that she frown ; I'll say she looks as
    clear
As morning roses newly wash'd with dew.
Say she be mute, and will not speak a word;
Then I'll commend her volubility, 174
And say she uttereth piercing eloquence.
If she do bid me pack, I'll give her thanks,
As though she bid me stay by her a week ;
If she deny to wed, I'll crave the day
When I shall ask the banns, and when be
    married.
But here she comes ; and now, Petruchio,
    speak.   180

    Enter KATHERINA.

Good morrow, Kate—for that's your name,
    I hear.
    Kath. Well have you heard, but some-
    thing hard of hearing :
They call me Katherine that do talk of me.
    Pet. You lie, in faith, for you are call'd
    plain Kate,
And bonny Kate, and sometimes Kate the
    curst ;   185
But, Kate, the prettiest Kate in Christen-
    dom,
Kate of Kate Hall, my super-dainty Kate,
For dainties are all Kates, and therefore,
    Kate,

Take this of me, Kate of my consolation—
Hearing thy mildness prais'd in every town,
Thy virtues spoke of, and thy beauty
   sounded,   191
Yet not so deeply as to thee belongs,
Myself am mov'd to woo thee for my wife.
  Kath. Mov'd! in good time! Let him
   that mov'd you hither   194
Remove you hence. I knew you at the
   first
You were a moveable.
  Pet.   Why, what's a moveable?
  Kath. A join'd-stool.
  Pet.   Thou hast hit it. Come, sit on me.
  Kath. Asses are made to bear, and so are
   you.
  Pet. Women are made to bear, and so are
   you.
  Kath. No such jade as you, if me you
   mean.   200
  Pet. Alas, good Kate, I will not burden
   thee!
For, knowing thee to be but young and
   light—
  Kath. Too light for such a swain as you
   to catch;
And yet as heavy as my weight should be.
  Pet. Should be! should—buzz!
  Kath.   Well ta'en, and like a buzzard.
  Pet. O, slow-wing'd turtle, shall a buz-
   zard take thee?   206
  Kath. Ay, for a turtle, as he takes a
   buzzard.
  Pet. Come, come, you wasp; i' faith, you
   are too angry.
  Kath. If I be waspish, best beware my
   sting.   209
  Pet. My remedy is then to pluck it out.
  Kath. Ay, if the fool could find it where
   it lies.
  Pet. Who knows not where a wasp does
   wear his sting?
In his tail.
  Kath. In his tongue.
  Pet. Whose tongue?
  Kath. Yours, if you talk of tales; and so
   farewell.
  Pet. What, with my tongue in your tail?
   Nay, come again,   215
Good Kate; I am a gentleman.
  Kath.   That I'll try.
         [*She strikes him.*
  Pet. I swear I'll cuff you, if you strike
   again.
  Kath. So may you lose your arms.
If you strike me, you are no gentleman;
And if no gentleman, why then no arms.
  Pet. A herald, Kate? O, put me in thy
   books!   221
  Kath. What is your crest—a coxcomb?
  Pet. A combless cock, so Kate will be my
   hen.
  Kath. No cock of mine: you crow too
   like a craven.

  Pet. Nay, come, Kate, come; you must
   not look so sour.   225
  Kath. It is my fashion, when I see a crab.
  Pet. Why, here's no crab; and therefore
   look not sour.
  Kath. There is, there is.
  Pet. Then show it me.
  Kath.   Had I a glass I would.
  Pet. What, you mean my face?
  Kath.   Well aim'd of such a young one.
  Pet. Now, by Saint George, I am too
   young for you.   231
  Kath. Yet you are wither'd.
  Pet.   'Tis with cares.
  Kath.   I care not.
  Pet. Nay, hear you, Kate—in sooth, you
   scape not so.
  Kath. I chafe you, if I tarry; let me go.
  Pet. No, not a whit; I find you passing
   gentle.   235
'Twas told me you were rough, and coy,
   and sullen,
And now I find report a very liar;
For thou art pleasant, gamesome, passing
   courteous,
But slow in speech, yet sweet as spring-
   time flowers.
Thou canst not frown, thou canst not look
   askance,   240
Nor bite the lip, as angry wenches will,
Nor hast thou pleasure to be cross in talk;
But thou with mildness entertain'st thy
   wooers;
With gentle conference, soft and affable.
Why does the world report that Kate doth
   limp?   245
O sland'rous world! Kate like the hazel-
   twig
Is straight and slender, and as brown in hue
As hazel-nuts, and sweeter than the kernels.
O, let me see thee walk. Thou dost not halt.
  Kath. Go, fool, and whom thou keep'st
   command.   250
  Pet. Did ever Dian so become a grove
As Kate this chamber with her princely
   gait?
O, be thou Dian, and let her be Kate;
And then let Kate be chaste, and Dian
   sportful!
  Kath. Where did you study all this
   goodly speech?   255
  Pet. It is extempore, from my mother wit.
  Kath. A witty mother! witless else her
   son.
  Pet. Am I not wise?
  Kath. Yes, keep you warm.
  Pet. Marry, so I mean, sweet Katherine,
   in thy bed.   259
And therefore, setting all this chat aside,
Thus in plain terms: your father hath
   consented
That you shall be my wife; your dowry
   'greed on;   262
And will you, nill you, I will marry you.

Now, Kate, I am a husband for your turn;
For, by this light, whereby I see thy beauty,
Thy beauty that doth make me like thee
    well,
Thou must be married to no man but me;
For I am he am born to tame you, Kate,
And bring you from a wild Kate to a Kate
Conformable as other household Kates. 270

Re-enter BAPTISTA, GREMIO, *and* TRANIO.

Here comes your father.   Never make
    denial;
I must and will have Katherine to my wife.
    Bap. Now, Signior Petruchio, how speed
      you with my daughter?
    Pet. How but well, sir? how but well?
It were impossible I should speed amiss.
    Bap. Why, how now, daughter Katherine,
      in your dumps? 276
    Kath. Call you me daughter? Now I
      promise you
You have show'd a tender fatherly regard
To wish me wed to one half lunatic,
A mad-cap ruffian and a swearing Jack, 280
That thinks with oaths to face the matter
    out.
    Pet. Father, 'tis thus: yourself and all
      the world
That talk'd of her have talk'd amiss of her.
If she be curst, it is for policy,
For she's not froward, but modest as the
    dove; 285
She is not hot, but temperate as the morn;
For patience she will prove a second Grissel,
And Roman Lucrece for her chastity.
And, to conclude, we have 'greed so well
    together
That upon Sunday is the wedding-day. 290
    Kath. I'll see thee hang'd on Sunday first.
    Gre. Hark, Petruchio; she says she'll see
      thee hang'd first.
    Tra. Is this your speeding? Nay, then
      good-night our part!
    Pet. Be patient, gentlemen; I choose her
      for myself; 294
If she and I be pleas'd, what's that to you?
'Tis bargain'd 'twixt us twain, being alone,
That she shall still be curst in company.
I tell you 'tis incredible to believe
How much she loves me—O, the kindest
    Kate! 299
She hung about my neck, and kiss on kiss
She vied so fast, protesting oath on oath,
That in a twink she won me to her love.
O, you are novices! 'Tis a world to see
How tame, when men and women are
    alone,
A meacock wretch can make the curstest
    shrew. 305
Give me thy hand, Kate; I will unto
    Venice,
To buy apparel 'gainst the wedding-day.
Provide the feast, father, and bid the
    guests;

I will be sure my Katherine shall be fine.
    Bap. I know not what to say; but give
      me your hands. 310
God send you joy, Petruchio! 'Tis a match.
    Gre., Tra. Amen, say we; we will be
      witnesses.
    Pet. Father, and wife, and gentlemen,
      adieu.
I will to Venice; Sunday comes apace;
We will have rings and things, and fine
    array; 315
And kiss me, Kate; we will be married a
    Sunday.
    [*Exeunt Petruchio and Katherina severally.*
    Gre. Was ever match clapp'd up so
      suddenly?
    Bap. Faith, gentlemen, now I play a
      merchant's part,
And venture madly on a desperate mart.
    Tra. 'Twas a commodity lay fretting by
      you; 320
'Twill bring you gain, or perish on the seas.
    Bap. The gain I seek is quiet in the match.
    Gre. No doubt but he hath got a quiet
      catch.
But now, Baptista, to your younger
    daughter: 324
Now is the day we long have looked for;
I am your neighbour, and was suitor first.
    Tra. And I am one that love Bianca more
Than words can witness or your thoughts
    can guess.
    Gre. Youngling, thou canst not love so
      dear as I.
    Tra. Greybeard, thy love doth freeze.
    Gre.   But thine doth fry.
Skipper, stand back; 'tis age that nour-
    isheth. 331
    Tra. But youth in ladies' eyes that flour-
    isheth.
    Bap. Content you, gentlemen; I will
      compound this strife.
'Tis deeds must win the prize, and he of
    both
That can assure my daughter greatest
    dower 335
Shall have my Bianca's love.
Say, Signior Gremio, what can you assure
    her?
    Gre. First, as you know, my house within
      the city
Is richly furnished with plate and gold,
Basins and ewers to lave her dainty hands;
My hangings all of Tyrian tapestry; 341
In ivory coffers I have stuff'd my crowns;
In cypress chests my arras counterpoints,
Costly apparel, tents, and canopies,
Fine linen, Turkey cushions boss'd with
    pearl, 345
Valance of Venice gold in needle-work;
Pewter and brass, and all things that
    belongs
To house or housekeeping. Then at my
    farm

I have a hundred milch-kine to the pail,
Six score fat oxen standing in my stalls, 350
And all things answerable to this portion.
Myself am struck in years, I must confess ;
And if I die to-morrow this is hers,
If whilst I live she will be only mine.

Tra. That ' only ' came well in. Sir, list
    to me : 355
I am my father's heir and only son ;
If I may have your daughter to my wife,
I'll leave her houses three or four as good
Within rich Pisa's walls as any one
Old Signior Gremio has in Padua ; 360
Besides two thousand ducats by the year
Of fruitful land, all which shall be her
    jointure.
What, have I pinch'd you, Signior Gremio ?

Gre. Two thousand ducats by the year of
    land !

[*Aside*] My land amounts not to so much
    in all.— 365
That she shall have, besides an argosy
That now is lying in Marseilles road.
What, have I chok'd you with an argosy ?

Tra. Gremio, 'tis known my father hath
    no less
Than three great argosies, besides two
    galliasses, 370
And twelve tight galleys. These I will
    assure her,
And twice as much whate'er thou off'rest
    next.

Gre. Nay, I have off'red all ; I have no
    more ; 373
And she can have no more than all I have ;
If you like me, she shall have me and mine.

Tra. Why, then the maid is mine from
    all the world 376
By your firm promise ; Gremio is out-vied.

Bap. I must confess your offer is the best;
And let your father make her the assurance,
She is your own. Else, you must pardon me;
If you should die before him, where's her
    dower ? 381

Tra. That's but a cavil ; he is old, I
    young.

Gre. And may not young men die as well
    as old ?

Bap. Well, gentlemen,
I am thus resolv'd : on Sunday next you
    know 385
My daughter Katherine is to be married ;
Now, on the Sunday following shall Bianca
Be bride to you, if you make this assurance;
If not, to Signior Gremio.
And so I take my leave, and thank you
    both. 390

Gre. Adieu, good neighbour.

             [*Exit Baptista.*
          Now, I fear thee not.
Sirrah young gamester, your father were a
    fool
To give thee all, and in his waning age
Set foot under thy table. Tut, a toy !

An old Italian fox is not so kind, my boy.
                      [*Exit.*

Tra. A vengeance on your crafty withered
    hide ! 396
Yet I have fac'd it with a card of ten.
'Tis in my head to do my master good :
I see no reason but suppos'd Lucentio
Must get a father, call'd suppos'd Vin-
    centio ; 400
And that's a wonder—fathers commonly
Do get their children ; but in this case of
    wooing
A child shall get a sire, if I fail not of my
    cunning.   [*Exit.*

ACT THREE

SCENE I. *Padua. Baptista's house.*

Enter LUCENTIO *as Cambio,* HORTENSIO *as*
    Licio, and BIANCA.

Luc. Fiddler, forbear ; you grow too
    forward, sir.
Have you so soon forgot the entertainment
Her sister Katherine welcom'd you withal ?

Hor. But, wrangling pedant, this is
The patroness of heavenly harmony. 5
Then give me leave to have prerogative ;
And when in music we have spent an hour,
Your lecture shall have leisure for as much.

Luc. Preposterous ass, that never read so
    far 9
To know the cause why music was ordain'd !
Was it not to refresh the mind of man
After his studies or his usual pain ?
Then give me leave to read philosophy,
And while I pause serve in your harmony.

Hor. Sirrah, I will not bear these braves
    of thine. 15

Bian. Why, gentlemen, you do me double
    wrong
To strive for that which resteth in my
    choice.
I am no breeching scholar in the schools,
I'll not be tied to hours nor 'pointed times,
But learn my lessons as I please myself. 20
And to cut off all strife : here sit we down ;
Take you your instrument, play you the
    whiles ;
His lecture will be done ere you have tun'd.

Hor. You'll leave his lecture when I am
    in tune ?

Luc. That will be never—tune your in-
    strument. 25

Bian. Where left we last ?

Luc. Here, madam :
' Hic ibat Simois, hic est Sigeia tellus,
Hic steterat Priami regia celsa senis '.

Bian. Construe them. 30

Luc. ' Hic ibat ' as I told you before—
' Simois ' I am Lucentio—' hic est ' son
unto Vincentio of Pisa—' Sigeia tellus '
disguised thus to get your love—' Hic
steterat ' and that Lucentio that comes

a-wooing—'Priami' is my man Tranio—
'regia' bearing my port—'celsa senis' that
we might beguile the old pantaloon.   36
  Hor. Madam, my instrument's in tune.
  Bian. Let's hear. O fie! the treble jars.
  Luc. Spit in the hole, man, and tune
again.   39
  Bian. Now let me see if I can construe
it: 'Hic ibat Simois' I know you not—
'hic est Sigeia tellus' I trust you not—
'Hic steterat Priami' take heed he hear us
not—'regia' presume not—'celsa senis'
despair not.   43
  Hor. Madam, 'tis now in tune.
  Luc.   All but the bass.
  Hor. The bass is right; 'tis the base
knave that jars.
  [*Aside*] How fiery and forward our pedant
is!   46
Now, for my life, the knave doth court my
love.
Pedascule, I'll watch you better yet.
  Bian. In time I may believe, yet I
mistrust.   49
  Luc. Mistrust it not—for, sure, Æacides
Was Ajax, call'd so from his grandfather.
  Bian. I must believe my master; else, I
promise you,
I should be arguing still upon that doubt;
But let it rest. Now, Licio, to you.
Good master, take it not unkindly, pray,   55
That I have been thus pleasant with you
both.
  Hor. [*To Lucentio*] You may go walk and
give me leave awhile;
My lessons make no music in three parts.
  Luc. Are you so formal, sir? Well, I
must wait,
  [*Aside*] And watch withal; for, but I be
deceiv'd,   60
Our fine musician groweth amorous.
  Hor. Madam, before you touch the in-
strument
To learn the order of my fingering,
I must begin with rudiments of art,
To teach you gamut in a briefer sort,   65
More pleasant, pithy, and effectual,
Than hath been taught by any of my
trade;
And there it is in writing fairly drawn.
  Bian. Why, I am past my gamut long
ago.
  Hor. Yet read the gamut of Hortensio.   70
  Bian. [*Reads*]
'"Gamut" I am, the ground of all accord—
"A re" to plead Hortensio's passion—
"B mi" Bianca, take him for thy lord—
"C fa ut" that loves with all affection—
"D sol re" one clef, two notes have I—
"E la mi" show pity or I die.'   76
Call you this gamut? Tut, I like it not!
Old fashions please me best; I am not so
nice
To change true rules for odd inventions.

Enter a Servant.

  Serv. Mistress, your father prays you
leave your books   80
And help to dress your sister's chamber up.
You know to-morrow is the wedding-day.
  Bian. Farewell, sweet masters, both; I
must be gone.
             [*Exeunt Bianca and Servant.*
  Luc. Faith, mistress, then I have no
cause to stay.   [*Exit.*
  Hor. But I have cause to pry into this
pedant;   85
Methinks he looks as though he were in
love.
Yet if thy thoughts, Bianca, be so humble
To cast thy wand'ring eyes on every stale—
Seize thee that list. If once I find thee
ranging,
Hortensio will be quit with thee by chang-
ing.   [*Exit.*

Scene II. *Padua. Before Baptista's house.*

Enter Baptista, Gremio, Tranio *as*
Lucentio, Katherina, Bianca, Lucentio *as Cambio, and* Attendants.

  Bap. [*To Tranio*] Signior Lucentio, this is
the 'pointed day
That Katherine and Petruchio should be
married,
And yet we hear not of our son-in-law.
What will be said? What mockery will
it be
To want the bridegroom when the priest
attends   5
To speak the ceremonial rites of marriage!
What says Lucentio to this shame of ours?
  Kath. No shame but mine; I must,
forsooth, be forc'd
To give my hand, oppos'd against my
heart,   9
Unto a mad-brain rudesby, full of spleen,
Who woo'd in haste and means to wed at
leisure.
I told you, I, he was a frantic fool,
Hiding his bitter jests in blunt behaviour;
And, to be noted for a merry man,
He'll woo a thousand, 'point the day of
marriage,   15
Make friends invited, and proclaim the
banns;
Yet never means to wed where he hath
woo'd.
Now must the world point at poor
Katherine,
And say 'Lo, there is mad Petruchio's wife,
If it would please him come and marry her!'
  Tra. Patience, good Katherine, and
Baptista too.   21
Upon my life, Petruchio means but well,
Whatever fortune stays him from his word.
Though he be blunt, I know him passing
wise;

Though he be merry, yet withal he's honest.
  Kath. Would Katherine had never seen
      him though !   26
[*Exit, weeping, followed by Bianca and others.*
  Bap. Go, girl, I cannot blame thee now
      to weep,
For such an injury would vex a very
    saint ;
Much more a shrew of thy impatient
    humour.

Enter BIONDELLO.

  Bion. Master, master ! News, and such
old news as you never heard of !   31
  Bap. Is it new and old too ? How may
that be ?
  Bion. Why, is it not news to hear of
Petruchio's coming ?
  Bap. Is he come ?
  Bion. Why, no, sir.   35
  Bap. What then ?
  Bion. He is coming.
  Bap. When will he be here ?
  Bion. When he stands where I am and
sees you there.   39
  Tra. But, say, what to thine old news ?
  Bian. Why, Petruchio is coming—in a
new hat and an old jerkin ; a pair of old
breeches thrice turn'd ; a pair of boots that
have been candle-cases, one buckled, another lac'd ; an old rusty sword ta'en out
of the town armoury, with a broken hilt,
and chapeless ; with two broken points ;
his horse hipp'd, with an old mothy saddle
and stirrups of no kindred ; besides,
possess'd with the glanders and like to
mose in the chine, troubled with the lampass, infected with the fashions, full of
windgalls, sped with spavins, rayed with
the yellows, past cure of the fives, stark
spoil'd with the staggers, begnawn with the
bots, sway'd in the back and shoulder-
shotten, near-legg'd before, and with a
half-cheek'd bit, and a head-stall of sheep's
leather which, being restrain'd to keep
him from stumbling, hath been often burst,
and now repaired with knots ; one girth
six times piec'd, and a woman's crupper of
velure, which hath two letters for her name
fairly set down in studs, and here and there
piec'd with pack-thread.
  Bap. Who comes with him ?   60
  Bion. O, sir, his lackey, for all the world
caparison'd like the horse—with a linen
stock on one leg and a kersey boot-hose on
the other, gart'red with a red and blue list ;
an old hat, and the humour of forty
fancies prick'd in't for a feather ; a
monster, a very monster in apparel, and
not like a Christian footboy or a gentleman's
lackey.   67
  Tra. 'Tis some odd humour pricks him
    to this fashion ;
Yet oftentimes he goes but mean-apparell'd.

  Bap. I am glad he's come, howsoe'er he
comes.   70
  Bion. Why, sir, he comes not.
  Bap. Didst thou not say he comes ?
  Bion. Who ? that Petruchio came ?
  Bap. Ay, that Petruchio came.
  Bion. No, sir ; I say his horse comes with
him on his back.   76
  Bap. Why, that's all one.
  Bion. Nay, by Saint Jamy,
    I hold you a penny,
    A horse and a man   80
    Is more than one,
    And yet not many.

Enter PETRUCHIO *and* GRUMIO.

  Pet. Come, where be these gallants ?
Who's at home ?
  Bap. You are welcome, sir.
  Pet.   And yet I come not vell.
  Bap. And yet you halt not.
  Tra.   Not so well apparell'd
As I wish you were.   86
  Pet. Were it better, I should rush in thus.
But where is Kate ? Where is my lovely
    bride ?
How does my father ? Gentles, methinks
    you frown ;   89
And wherefore gaze this goodly company
As if they saw some wondrous monument,
Some comet or unusual prodigy ?
  Bap. Why, sir, you know this is your
    wedding-day.
First were we sad, fearing you would not
    come ;   94
Now sadder, that you come so unprovided.
Fie, doff this habit, shame to your estate,
An eye-sore to our solemn festival !
  Tra. And tell us what occasion of import
Hath all so long detain'd you from your
    wife,
And sent you hither so unlike yourself ? 100
  Pet. Tedious it were to tell, and harsh to
    hear ;
Sufficeth I am come to keep my word,
Though in some part enforced to digress,
Which at more leisure I will so excuse
As you shall well be satisfied withal.   105
But where is Kate ? I stay too long from
    her ;
The morning wears, 'tis time we were at
    church.
  Tra. See not your bride in these un-
    reverent robes ;
Go to my chamber, put on clothes of mine.
  Pet. Not I, believe me ; thus I'll visit her.
  Bap. But thus, I trust, you will not marry
    her.   111
  Pet. Good sooth, even thus ; therefore
    ha' done with words ;
To me she's married, not unto my clothes.
Could I repair what she will wear in me
As I can change these poor accoutrements,
'Twere well for Kate and better for myself.

But what a fool am I to chat with you,
When I should bid good morrow to my
    bride
And seal the title with a lovely kiss !
        [*Exeunt Petruchio and Grumio.*

  Tra. He hath some meaning in his mad
    attire.   120
We will persuade him, be it possible,
To put on better ere he go to church.

  Bap. I'll after him and see the event of
    this.
      [*Exeunt Baptista, Gremio, Biondello,
        and Attendants.*

  Tra. But to her love concerneth us to
    add   124
Her father's liking ; which to bring to pass,
As I before imparted to your worship,
I am to get a man—whate'er he be
It skills not much ; we'll fit him to our
    turn—
And he shall be Vincentio of Pisa,
And make assurance here in Padua   130
Of greater sums than I have promised.
So shall you quietly enjoy your hope
And marry sweet Bianca with consent.

  Luc. Were it not that my fellow school-
    master
Doth watch Bianca's steps so narrowly, 135
'Twere good, methinks, to steal our
    marriage ;
Which once perform'd, let all the world say
    no,
I'll keep mine own despite of all the world.

  Tra. That by degrees we mean to look
    into   139
And watch our vantage in this business ;
We'll over-reach the greybeard, Gremio,
The narrow-prying father, Minola,
The quaint musician, amorous Licio—
All for my master's sake, Lucentio.

        Re-enter GREMIO.

Signior Gremio, came you from the
    church ?   145

  Gre. As willingly as e'er I came from
    school.

  Tra. And is the bride and bridegroom
    coming home ?

  Gre. A bridegroom, say you ? 'Tis a
    groom indeed,
A grumbling groom, and, that the girl shall
    find.

  Tra. Curster than she ? Why, 'tis im-
    possible.   150

  Gre. Why, he's a devil, a devil, a very
    fiend.

  Tra. Why, she's a devil, a devil, the
    devil's dam.

  Gre. Tut, she's a lamb, a dove, a fool, to
    him !
I'll tell you, Sir Lucentio : when the priest
Should ask if Katherine should be his wife,
' Ay, by gogs-wouns ' quoth he, and swore
    so loud   156

That, all amaz'd, the priest let fall the
    book ;
And as he stoop'd again to take it up,
This mad-brain'd bridegroom took him
    such a cuff
That down fell priest and book, and book
    and priest.   160
' Now take them up,' quoth he ' if any
    list.'

  Tra. What said the wench, when he rose
    again ?

  Gre. Trembled and shook, for why he
    stamp'd and swore
As if the vicar meant to cozen him.
But after many ceremonies done   165
He calls for wine : ' A health ! ' quoth he,
    as if
He had been abroad, carousing to his mates
After a storm ; quaff'd off the muscadel,
And threw the sops all in the sexton's face,
Having no other reason   170
But that his beard grew thin and hungerly
And seem'd to ask him sops as he was
    drinking.
This done, he took the bride about the neck,
And kiss'd her lips with such a clamorous
    smack   174
That at the parting all the church did echo.
And I, seeing this, came thence for very
    shame ;
And after me, I know, the rout is coming.
Such a mad marriage never was before.
Hark, hark ! I hear the minstrels play.
             [*Music plays.*

Enter PETRUCHIO, KATHERINA, BIANCA,
BAPTISTA, HORTENSIO, GRUMIO, *and*
Train.

  Pet. Gentlemen and friends, I thank you
    for your pains.   180
I know you think to dine with me to-day,
And have prepar'd great store of wedding
    cheer ;
But so it is—my haste doth call me hence,
And therefore here I mean to take my
    leave.

  Bap. Is't possible you will away to-
    night ?   185

  Pet. I must away to-day before night
    come.
Make it no wonder ; if you knew my
    business,
You would entreat me rather go than stay.
And, honest company, I thank you all
That have beheld me give away myself 190
To this most patient, sweet, and virtuous
    wife.
Dine with my father, drink a health to me,
For I must hence ; and farewell to you all.

  Tra. Let us entreat you stay till after
    dinner.   194

  Pet. It may not be.

  Gre.   Let me entreat you.

  Pet. It cannot be.

Kath.   Let me entreat you.
Pet. I am content.
Kath.   Are you content to stay ?
Pet. I am content you shall entreat me
stay ;
But yet not stay, entreat me how you can.
Kath. Now, if you love me, stay.
Pet.   Grumio, my horse.
Gru. Ay, sir, they are ready ; the oats
have eaten the horses.   202
Kath. Nay, then,
Do what thou canst, I will not go to-day ;
No, nor to-morrow, not till I please myself.
The door is open, sir ; there lies your way ;
You may be jogging whiles your boots are
green ;   207
For me, I'll not be gone till I please myself.
'Tis like you'll prove a jolly surly groom
That take it on you at the first so roundly.
Pet. O Kate, content thee ; prithee be
not angry.   211
Kath. I will be angry ; what hast thou
to do ?
Father, be quiet ; he shall stay my leisure.
Gre. Ay, marry, sir, now it begins to
work.
Kath. Gentlemen, forward to the bridal
dinner.   215
I see a woman may be made a fool
If she had not a spirit to resist.
Pet. They shall go forward, Kate, at thy
command.
Obey the bride, you that attend on her ;
Go to the feast, revel and domineer,   220
Carouse full measure to her maidenhead ;
Be mad and merry, or go hang yourselves.
But for my bonny Kate, she must with
me.
Nay, look not big, nor stamp, nor stare, nor
fret ;
I will be master of what is mine own—   225
She is my goods, my chattels, she is my
house,
My household stuff, my field, my barn,
My horse, my ox, my ass, my any thing,
And here she stands ; touch her whoever
dare ;   229
I'll bring mine action on the proudest
That stops my way in Padua. Grumio,
Draw forth thy weapon ; we are beset with
thieves ;
Rescue thy mistress, if thou be a man.
Fear not, sweet wench ; they shall not touch
thee, Kate ;
I'll buckler thee against a million.   235
[*Exeunt Petruchio, Katherina, and Grumio.*
Bap. Nay, let them go, a couple of quiet
ones.
Gre. Went they not quickly, I should die
with laughing.
Tra. Of all mad matches, never was the
like.
Luc. Mistress, what's your opinion of
your sister ?

Bian. That, being mad herself, she's
madly mated.   240
Gre. I warrant him, Petruchio is Kated.
Bap. Neighbours and friends, though
bride and bridegroom wants
For to supply the places at the table,
You know there wants no junkets at the
feast.
Lucentio, you shall supply the bride-
groom's place ;   245
And let Bianca take her sister's room.
Tra. Shall sweet Bianca practise how to
bride it ?
Bap. She shall, Lucentio. Come, gentle-
men, let's go.   [*Exeunt.*

ACT FOUR

SCENE I. *Petruchio's country house.*

Enter GRUMIO.

Gru. Fie, fie on all tired jades, on all mad
masters, and all foul ways ! Was ever man
so beaten ? Was ever man so ray'd ? Was
ever man so weary ? I am sent before to
make a fire, and they are coming after to
warm them. Now were not I a little pot
and soon hot, my very lips might freeze to
my teeth, my tongue to the roof of my
mouth, my heart in my belly, ere I should
come by a fire to thaw me. But I with
blowing the fire shall warm myself ; for,
considering the weather, a taller man than
I will take cold. Holla, ho ! Curtis !   10

Enter CURTIS.

Curt. Who is that calls so coldly ?
Gru. A piece of ice. If thou doubt it,
thou mayst slide from my shoulder to my
heel with no greater a run but my head and
my neck. A fire, good Curtis.
Curt. Is my master and his wife coming,
Grumio ?   15
Gru. O, ay, Curtis, ay ; and therefore
fire, fire ; cast on no water.
Curt. Is she so hot a shrew as she's
reported ?
Gru. She was, good Curtis, before this
frost ; but thou know'st winter tames man,
woman, and beast ; for it hath tam'd my
old master, and my new mistress, and
myself, fellow Curtis.   22
Curt. Away, you three-inch fool ! I am
no beast.
Gru. Am I but three inches ? Why, thy
horn is a foot, and so long am I at the least.
But wilt thou make a fire, or shall I complain on thee to our mistress, whose hand
—she being now at hand—thou shalt soon
feel, to thy cold comfort, for being slow in
thy hot office ?
Curt. I prithee, good Grumio, tell me
how goes the world ?   30
Gru. A cold world, Curtis, in every office

but thine ; and therefore fire. Do thy duty,
and have thy duty, for my master and
mistress are almost frozen to death.

Curt. There's fire ready ; and therefore,
good Grumio, the news ?   35

Gru. Why, ' Jack boy ! ho, boy ! ' and as
much news as wilt thou.

Curt. Come, you are so full of conycatching !   38

Gru. Why, therefore, fire ; for I have
caught extreme cold. Where's the cook ?
Is supper ready, the house trimm'd, rushes
strew'd, cobwebs swept, the serving-men in
their new fustian, their white stockings, and
every officer his wedding-garment on ? Be
the jacks fair within, the jills fair without,
the carpets laid, and everything in order ?

Curt. All ready ; and therefore, I pray
thee, news.   45

Gru. First know my horse is tired ; my
master and mistress fall'n out.

Curt. How ?

Gru. Out of their saddles into the dirt ;
and thereby hangs a tale.   50

Curt. Let's ha't, good Grumio.

Gru. Lend thine ear.

Curt. Here.

Gru. There.   [*Striking him.*

Curt. This 'tis to feel a tale, not to hear
a tale.   55

Gru. And therefore 'tis call'd a sensible
tale ; and this cuff was but to knock at
your ear and beseech list'ning. Now I
begin : Imprimis, we came down a foul
hill, my master riding behind my mistress—

Curt. Both of one horse ?   60

Gru. What's that to thee ?

Curt. Why, a horse.

Gru. Tell thou the tale. But hadst thou
not cross'd me, thou shouldst have heard
how her horse fell and she under her horse ;
thou shouldst have heard in how miry a
place, how she was bemoil'd, how he left
her with the horse upon her, how he beat
me because her horse stumbled, how she
waded through the dirt to pluck him off
me, how he swore, how she pray'd that
never pray'd before, how I cried, how the
horses ran away, how her bridle was burst,
how I lost my crupper—with many things
of worthy memory, which now shall die in
oblivion, and thou return unexperienc'd to
thy grave.   73

Curt. By this reck'ning he is more shrew
than she.

Gru. Ay, and that thou and the proudest
of you all shall find when he comes home.
But what talk I of this ? Call forth
Nathaniel, Joseph, Nicholas, Philip, Walter,
Sugarsop, and the rest ; let their heads be
sleekly comb'd, their blue coats brush'd and
their garters of an indifferent knit ; let
them curtsy with their left legs, and not
presume to touch a hair of my master's

horse-tail till they kiss their hands. Are
they all ready ?   82

Curt. They are.

Gru. Call them forth.

Curt. Do you hear, ho ? You must meet
my master, to countenance my mistress.   86

Gru. Why, she hath a face of her own.

Curt. Who knows not that ?

Gru. Thou, it seems, that calls for company to countenance her.   90

Curt. I call them forth to credit her.

Gru. Why, she comes to borrow nothing
of them.

Enter four or five Servingmen.

Nath. Welcome home, Grumio !

Phil. How now, Grumio !

Jos. What, Grumio !   95

Nich. Fellow Grumio !

Nath. How now, old lad !

Gru. Welcome, you !—how now, you !—
what, you !—fellow, you !—and thus much
for greeting. Now, my spruce companions,
is all ready, and all things neat ?   100

Nath. All things is ready. How near is
our master ?

Gru. E'en at hand, alighted by this ; and
therefore be not—Cock's passion, silence !
I hear my master.

Enter PETRUCHIO *and* KATHERINA.

Pet. Where be these knaves ? What, no
        man at door   104
To hold my stirrup nor to take my horse !
Where is Nathaniel, Gregory, Philip ?

All Serv. Here, here, sir ; here, sir.

Pet. Here, sir ! here, sir ! here, sir ! here,
        sir !   108
You logger-headed and unpolish'd grooms !
What, no attendance ? no regard ? no duty ?
Where is the foolish knave I sent before ?

Gru. Here, sir ; as foolish as I was before.

Pet. You peasant swain ! you whoreson
        malt-horse drudge !
Did I not bid thee meet me in the park
And bring along these rascal knaves with
        thee ?   115

Gru. Nathaniel's coat, sir, was not fully
        made,
And Gabriel's pumps were all unpink'd i'
        th' heel ;
There was no link to colour Peter's hat,
And Walter's dagger was not come from
        sheathing ;
There were none fine but Adam, Ralph, and
        Gregory ;   120
The rest were ragged, old, and beggarly ;
Yet, as they are, here are they come to
        meet you.

Pet. Go, rascals, go and fetch my supper
        in.   [*Exeunt some of the Servingmen.*

[*Sings*] Where is the life that late I led ?
        Where are those—

Sit down, Kate, and welcome. Soud, soud,
soud, soud !   126

Re-enter Servants *with supper.*

Why, when, I say ? Nay, good sweet Kate,
be merry.
Off with my boots, you rogues ! you villains,
when ?   128

[*Sings*] It was the friar of orders grey,
    As he forth walked on his way—

Out, you rogue ! you pluck my foot awry ;
Take that, and mend the plucking off the
    other.   [*Strikes him.*
Be merry, Kate. Some water, here, what,
    ho !   133

Enter One *with water.*

Where's my spaniel Troilus ? Sirrah, get
    you hence,
And bid my cousin Ferdinand come hither :
        [*Exit Servingman.*
One, Kate, that you must kiss and be
    acquainted with.   136
Where are my slippers ? Shall I have some
    water ?
Come, Kate, and wash, and welcome
    heartily.
You whoreson villain ! will you let it fall ?
        [*Strikes him.*
  Kath. Patience, I pray you ; 'twas a
    fault unwilling.   140
  Pet. A whoreson, beetle-headed, flap-
    ear'd knave !
Come, Kate, sit down ; I know you have
    a stomach.
Will you give thanks, sweet Kate, or else
    shall I ?
What's this ? Mutton ?
  1 Serv.   Ay.
  Pet.   Who brought it ?
  Peter.   I.
  Pet. 'Tis burnt ; and so is all the meat.
What dogs are these ? Where is the rascal
    cook ?   146
How durst you villains bring it from the
    dresser
And serve it thus to me that love it not ?
There, take it to you, trenchers, cups, and
    all ;
        [*Throws the meat, &c., at them.*
You heedless joltheads and unmanner'd
    slaves !   150
What, do you grumble ? I'll be with you
    straight.   [*Exeunt Servants.*
  Kath. I pray you, husband, be not so
    disquiet ;
The meat was well, if you were so contented.
  Pet. I tell thee, Kate, 'twas burnt and
    dried away,
And I expressly am forbid to touch it ; 155
For it engenders choler, planteth anger ;
And better 'twere that both of us did fast,
Since, of ourselves, ourselves are choleric,

Than feed it with such over-roasted flesh.
Be patient ; to-morrow 't shall be mended,
And for this night we'll fast for company.
Come, I will bring thee to thy bridal
    chamber.   [*Exeunt.*

Re-enter Servants *severally.*

  Nath. Peter, didst ever see the like ?
  Peter. He kills her in her own humour.

Re-enter CURTIS.

  Gru. Where is he ?   165
  Curt. In her chamber. Making a sermon
of continency to her,
And rails, and swears, and rates, that she,
    poor soul,
Knows not which way to stand, to look, to
    speak,
And sits as one new risen from a dream. 170
Away, away ! for he is coming hither.
               [*Exeunt.*

Re-enter PETRUCHIO.

  Pet. Thus have I politicly begun my
    reign,
And 'tis my hope to end successfully.
My falcon now is sharp and passing empty,
And till she stoop she must not be full-
    gorg'd,   175
For then she never looks upon her lure.
Another way I have to man my haggard,
To make her come, and know her keeper's
    call,
That is, to watch her, as we watch these
    kites
That bate and beat, and will not be
    obedient.   180
She eat no meat to-day, nor none shall eat ;
Last night she slept not, nor to-night she
    shall not ;
As with the meat, some undeserved fault
I'll find about the making of the bed ;
And here I'll fling the pillow, there the
    bolster,   185
This way the coverlet, another way the
    sheets ;
Ay, and amid this hurly I intend
That all is done in reverend care of her—
And, in conclusion, she shall watch all night;
And if she chance to nod I'll rail and brawl
And with the clamour keep her still awake.
This is a way to kill a wife with kindness,
And thus I'll curb her mad and headstrong
    humour.   193
He that knows better how to tame a shrew,
Now let him speak ; 'tis charity to show.
               [*Exit.*

SCENE II. *Padua. Before Baptista's house.*

Enter TRANIO *as Lucentio, and* HORTENSIO
as Licio.

  Tra. Is't possible, friend Licio, that
    Mistress Bianca

Doth fancy any other but Lucentio ?
I tell you, sir, she bears me fair in hand.

 Hor. Sir, to satisfy you in what I have said, 4
Stand by and mark the manner of his
  teaching. [*They stand aside.*

Enter BIANCA *and* LUCENTIO *as Cambio.*

 Luc. Now, mistress, profit you in what
  you read ?
 Bian. What, master, read you ? First
  resolve me that.
 Luc. I read that I profess, ' The Art to
  Love '.
 Bian. And may you prove, sir, master of
  your art !
 Luc. While you, sweet dear, prove
  mistress of my heart. 10
        [*They retire.*
 Hor. Quick proceeders, marry ! Now tell
  me, I pray,
You that durst swear that your Mistress
  Bianca
Lov'd none in the world so well as Lucentio.

 Tra. O despiteful love ! unconstant
  womankind !
I tell thee, Licio, this is wonderful. 15

 Hor. Mistake no more ; I am not Licio,
Nor a musician as I seem to be ;
But one that scorn to live in this disguise
For such a one as leaves a gentleman
And makes a god of such a cullion. 20
Know, sir, that I am call'd Hortensio.

 Tra. Signior Hortensio, I have often
  heard
Of your entire affection to Bianca ;
And since mine eyes are witness of her
  lightness,
I will with you, if you be so contented, 25
Forswear Bianca and her love for ever.

 Hor. See, how they kiss and court !
  Signior Lucentio,
Here is my hand, and here I firmly vow
Never to woo her more, but do forswear her,
As one unworthy all the former favours 30
That I have fondly flatter'd her withal.

 Tra. And here I take the like unfeigned
  oath,
Never to marry with her though she would
  entreat ;
Fie on her ! See how beastly she doth court
  him !

 Hor. Would all the world but he had
  quite forsworn ! 35
For me, that I may surely keep mine oath,
I will be married to a wealthy widow
Ere three days pass, which hath as long
  lov'd me
As I have lov'd this proud disdainful
  haggard.
And so farewell, Signior Lucentio. 40
Kindness in women, not their beauteous
  looks,
Shall win my love ; and so I take my leave,

In resolution as I swore before. [*Exit.*

 Tra. Mistress Bianca, bless you with such
  grace
As 'longeth to a lover's blessed case ! 45
Nay, I have ta'en you napping, gentle love,
And have forsworn you with Hortensio.

 Bian. Tranio, you jest ; but have you
  both forsworn me ?
 Tra. Mistress, we have.
 Luc.   Then we are rid of Licio.
 Tra. I' faith, he'll have a lusty widow
  now, 50
That shall be woo'd and wedded in a day.
 Bian. God give him joy !
 Tra. Ay, and he'll tame her.
 Bian.   He says so, Tranio.
 Tra. Faith, he is gone unto the taming-
  school.
 Bian. The taming-school ! What, is there
  such a place ? 55
 Tra. Ay, mistress ; and Petruchio is the
  master,
That teacheth tricks eleven and twenty
  long,
To tame a shrew and charm her chattering
  tongue.

Enter BIONDELLO.

 Bion. O master, master, I have watch'd
  so long 59
That I am dog-weary ; but at last I spied
An ancient angel coming down the hill
Will serve the turn.
 Tra.   What is he, Biondello ?
 Bion. Master, a mercatante or a pedant,
I know not what ; but formal in apparel,
In gait and countenance surely like a
  father. 65
 Luc. And what of him, Tranio ?
 Tra. If he be credulous and trust my tale,
I'll make him glad to seem Vincentio,
And give assurance to Baptista Minola
As if he were the right Vincentio. 70
Take in your love, and then let me alone.
    [*Exeunt Lucentio and Bianca.*

Enter a Pedant.

 Ped. God save you, sir !
 Tra.   And you, sir ; you are welcome.
Travel you far on, or are you at the
  farthest ?
 Ped. Sir, at the farthest for a week or
  two ; 74
But then up farther, and as far as Rome ;
And so to Tripoli, if God lend me life.
 Tra. What countryman, I pray ?
 Ped.   Of Mantua.
 Tra. Of Mantua, sir ? Marry, God forbid,
And come to Padua, careless of your life !
 Ped. My life, sir ! How, I pray ? For
  that goes hard. 80
 Tra. 'Tis death for any one in Mantua
To come to Padua. Know you not the
  cause ?

Your ships are stay'd at Venice; and the
 Duke,
For private quarrel 'twixt your Duke and
 him, 84
Hath publish'd and proclaim'd it openly.
'Tis marvel—but that you are but newly
 come,
You might have heard it else proclaim'd
 about.
 Ped. Alas, sir, it is worse for me than so!
For I have bills for money by exchange
From Florence, and must here deliver them.
 Tra. Well, sir, to do you courtesy, 91
This will I do, and this I will advise you—
First, tell me, have you ever been at Pisa?
 Ped. Ay, sir, in Pisa have I often been,
Pisa renowned for grave citizens. 95
 Tra. Among them know you one Vin-
 centio?
 Ped. I know him not, but I have heard
 of him,
A merchant of incomparable wealth.
 Tra. He is my father, sir; and, sooth to
 say,
In count'nance somewhat doth resemble
 you. 100
 Bion. [*Aside*] As much as an apple doth
an oyster, and all one.
 Tra. To save your life in this extremity,
This favour will I do you for his sake;
And think it not the worst of all your
 fortunes
That you are like to Sir Vincentio. 105
His name and credit shall you undertake,
And in my house you shall be friendly
 lodg'd;
Look what you take upon you as you should.
You understand me, sir. So shall you stay
Till you have done your business in the
 city. 110
If this be court'sy, sir, accept of it.
 Ped. O, sir, I do; and will repute you
 ever
The patron of my life and liberty.
 Tra. Then go with me to make the
 matter good.
This, by the way, I let you understand: 115
My father is here look'd for every day
To pass assurance of a dow'r in marriage
'Twixt me and one Baptista's daughter
 here.
In all these circumstances I'll instruct you.
Go with me to clothe you as becomes you.
         [*Exeunt.*

SCENE III. *Petruchio's house.*

Enter KATHERINA *and* GRUMIO.

 Gru. No, no, forsooth; I dare not for my
 life.
 Kath. The more my wrong, the more his
 spite appears.
What, did he marry me to famish me?
Beggars that come unto my father's door

Upon entreaty have a present alms; 5
If not, elsewhere they meet with charity;
But I, who never knew how to entreat,
Nor never needed that I should entreat,
Am starv'd for meat, giddy for lack of
 sleep;
With oaths kept waking, and with brawling
 fed; 10
And that which spites me more than all
 these wants—
He does it under name of perfect love;
As who should say, if I should sleep or
 eat,
'Twere deadly sickness or else present
 death.
I prithee go and get me some repast; 15
I care not what, so it be wholesome food.
 Gru. What say you to a neat's foot?
 Kath. 'Tis passing good; I prithee let me
 have it.
 Gru. I fear it is too choleric a meat.
How say you to a fat tripe finely broil'd?
 Kath. I like it well; good Grumio, fetch
 it me. 21
 Gru. I cannot tell; I fear 'tis choleric.
What say you to a piece of beef and
 mustard?
 Kath. A dish that I do love to feed upon.
 Gru. Ay, but the mustard is too hot a
 little. 25
 Kath. Why then the beef, and let the
 mustard rest.
 Gru. Nay, then I will not; you shall
 have the mustard,
Or else you get no beef of Grumio.
 Kath. Then both, or one, or anything
 thou wilt.
 Gru. Why then the mustard without the
 beef. 30
 Kath. Go, get thee gone, thou false
 deluding slave, [*Beats him.*
That feed'st me with the very name of
 meat.
Sorrow on thee and all the pack of you
That triumph thus upon my misery!
Go, get thee gone, I say. 35

Enter PETRUCHIO, *and* HORTENSIO *with
meat.*

 Pet. How fares my Kate? What, sweet-
 ing, all amort?
 Hor. Mistress, what cheer?
 Kath.   Faith, as cold as can be.
 Pet. Pluck up thy spirits, look cheerfully
 upon me.
Here, love, thou seest how diligent I am,
To dress thy meat myself, and bring it thee.
I am sure, s*w*eet Kate, this kindness merits
 thanks. 41
What, not a word? Nay, then thou lov'st
 it not,
And all my pains is sorted to no proof.
Here, take away this dish.
 Kath.   I pray you, let it stand.

Pet. The poorest service is repaid with
  thanks ;   45
And so shall mine, before you touch the
  meat.
  Kath. I thank you, sir.
  Hor. Signior Petruchio, fie ! you are to
  blame.
Come, Mistress Kate, I'll bear you company.
  Pet. [*Aside*] Eat it up all, Hortensio, if
  thou lovest me.—   50
Much good do it unto thy gentle heart !
Kate, eat apace. And now, my honey love,
Will we return unto thy father's house
And revel it as bravely as the best,
With silken coats and caps, and golden
  rings,   55
With ruffs and cuffs and farthingales and
  things,
With scarfs and fans and double change of
  brav'ry,
With amber bracelets, beads, and all this
  knav'ry.
What, hast thou din'd ? The tailor stays
  thy leisure,   59
To deck thy body with his ruffling treasure.

                  Enter Tailor.

Come, tailor, let us see these ornaments ;
Lay forth the gown.

              Enter Haberdasher.

              What news with you, sir ?
  Hab. Here is the cap your worship did
  bespeak.
  Pet. Why, this was moulded on a
  porringer ;
A velvet dish. Fie, fie ! 'tis lewd and filthy ;
Why, 'tis a cockle or a walnut-shell,   66
A knack, a toy, a trick, a baby's cap.
Away with it. Come, let me have a bigger.
  Kath. I'll have no bigger ; this doth fit
  the time,
And gentlewomen wear such caps as these.
  Pet. When you are gentle, you shall have
  one too,   71
And not till then.
  Hor. [*Aside*] That will not be in haste.
  Kath. Why, sir, I trust I may have leave
  to speak ;   73
And speak I will. I am no child, no babe.
Your betters have endur'd me say my mind,
And if you cannot, best you stop your ears.
My tongue will tell the anger of my heart,
Or else my heart, concealing it, will break ;
And rather than it shall, I will be free   79
Even to the uttermost, as I please, in words.
  Pet. Why, thou say'st true ; it is a paltry
  cap,
A custard-coffin, a bauble, a silken pie ;
I love thee well in that thou lik'st it not.
  Kath. Love me or love me not, I like the
  cap ;
And it I will have, or I will have none.   85
                        [*Exit Haberdasher.*

Pet. Thy gown ? Why, ay. Come, tailor,
  let us see't.
O mercy, God ! what masquing stuff is
  here ?
What's this ? A sleeve ? 'Tis like a demi-
  cannon.
What, up and down, carv'd like an apple-
  tart ?
Here's snip and nip and cut and slish and
  slash,   90
Like to a censer in a barber's shop.
Why, what a devil's name, tailor, call'st
  thou this ?
  Hor. [*Aside*] I see she's like to have
  neither cap nor gown.
  Tai. You bid me make it orderly and
  well,
According to the fashion and the time.   95
  Pet. Marry, and did ; but if you be
  rememb'red,
I did not bid you mar it to the time.
Go, hop me over every kennel home,
For you shall hop without my custom, sir.
I'll none of it ; hence ! make your best
  of it.   100
  Kath. I never saw a better fashion'd
  gown,
More quaint, more pleasing, nor more com-
  mendable ;
Belike you mean to make a puppet of me.
  Pet. Why, true ; he means to make a
  puppet of thee.
  Tai. She says your worship means to
  make a puppet of her.   105
  Pet. O monstrous arrogance ! Thou liest,
  thou thread, thou thimble,
Thou yard, three-quarters, half-yard,
  quarter, nail,
Thou flea, thou nit, thou winter-cricket
  thou—
Brav'd in mine own house with a skein of
  thread !   110
Away, thou rag, thou quantity, thou
  remnant ;
Or I shall so bemete thee with thy yard
As thou shalt think on prating whilst thou
  liv'st !
I tell thee, I, that thou hast marr'd her
  gown.
  Tai. Your worship is deceiv'd ; the gown
  is made   115
Just as my master had direction.
Grumio gave order how it should be done.
  Gru. I gave him no order ; I gave him
  the stuff.
  Tai. But how did you desire it should be
  made ?   119
  Gru. Marry, sir, with needle and thread.
  Tai. But did you not request to have it
  cut ?
  Gru. Thou hast fac'd many things.
  Tai. I have.
  Gru. Face not me. Thou hast brav'd
many men ; brave not me. I will neither

be fac'd nor brav'd. I say unto thee, I bid thy master cut out the gown; but I did not bid him cut it to pieces. Ergo, thou liest.   127

Tai. Why, here is the note of the fashion to testify.

Pet. Read it.

Gru. The note lies in's throat, if he say I said so.   130

Tai. [*Reads*] ' Imprimis, a loose-bodied gown '—

Gru. Master, if ever I said loose-bodied gown, sew me in the skirts of it and beat me to death with a bottom of brown bread; I said a gown.

Pet. Proceed.   135

Tai. [*Reads*] ' With a small compass'd cape '—

Gru. I confess the cape.

Tai. [*Reads*] ' With a trunk sleeve '—

Gru. I confess two sleeves.   139

Tai. [*Reads*] ' The sleeves curiously cut.'

Pet. Ay, there's the villainy.

Gru. Error i' th' bill, sir; error i' th' bill! I commanded the sleeves should be cut out, and sew'd up again; and that I'll prove upon thee, though thy little finger be armed in a thimble.   145

Tai. This is true that I say; an I had thee in place where, thou shouldst know it.

Gru. I am for thee straight; take thou the bill, give me thy mete-yard, and spare not me.

Hor. God-a-mercy, Grumio! Then he shall have no odds.

Pet. Well, sir, in brief, the gown is not for me.   151

Gru. You are i' th' right, sir; 'tis for my mistress.

Pet. Go, take it up unto thy master's use.

Gru. Villain, not for thy life! Take up my mistress' gown for thy master's use!

Pet. Why, sir, what's your conceit in that?   156

Gru. O, sir, the conceit is deeper than you think for.

Take up my mistress' gown to his master's use!

O fie, fie, fie!

Pet. [*Aside*] Hortensio, say thou wilt see the tailor paid.—

Go take it hence; be gone, and say no more.   161

Hor. Tailor, I'll pay thee for thy gown to-morrow;

Take no unkindness of his hasty words.

Away, I say; commend me to thy master.
                                      [*Exit Tailor.*

Pet. Well, come, my Kate; we will unto your father's   165

Even in these honest mean habiliments;

Our purses shall be proud, our garments poor;

For 'tis the mind that makes the body rich;

And as the sun breaks through the darkest clouds,

So honour peereth in the meanest habit. 170

What, is the jay more precious than the lark

Because his feathers are more beautiful?

Or is the adder better than the eel

Because his painted skin contents the eye?

O no, good Kate; neither art thou the worse   175

For this poor furniture and mean array.

If thou account'st it shame, lay it on me;

And therefore frolic; we will hence forthwith

To feast and sport us at thy father's house.

Go call our men, and let us straight to him;

And bring our horses unto Long-lane end;

There will we mount, and thither walk on foot.   182

Let's see; I think 'tis now some seven o'clock,

And well we may come there by dinnertime.

Kath. I dare assure you, sir, 'tis almost two,   185

And 'twill be supper-time ere you come there.

Pet. It shall be seven ere I go to horse.

Look what I speak, or do, or think to do,

You are still crossing it. Sirs, let't alone;

I will not go to-day; and ere I do,   190

It shall be what o'clock I say it is.

Hor. Why, so this gallant will command the sun.   [*Exeunt.*

SCENE IV. *Padua. Before Baptista's house.*

Enter TRANIO *as Lucentio, and the* Pedant *dress'd like Vincentio.*

Tra. Sir, this is the house; please it you that I call?

Ped. Ay, what else? And, but I be deceived,

Signior Baptista may remember me

Near twenty years ago in Genoa,

Where we were lodgers at the Pegasus.   5

Tra. 'Tis well; and hold your own, in any case,

With such austerity as longeth to a father.

Enter BIONDELLO.

Ped. I warrant you. But, sir, here comes your boy;

'Twere good he were school'd.   9

Tra. Fear you not him. Sirrah Biondello,

Now do your duty throughly, I advise you.

Imagine 'twere the right Vincentio.

Bion. Tut, fear not me.

Tra. But hast thou done thy errand to Baptista?

Bion. I told him that your father was at Venice,   15

And that you look'd for him this day in Padua.

Tra. Th'art a tall fellow; hold thee
    that to drink.
Here comes Baptista.   Set your counten-
    ance, sir.

Enter BAPTISTA, *and* LUCENTIO *as Cambio.*

Signior Baptista, you are happily met.
[*To the Pedant*] Sir, this is the gentleman
    I told you of;   20
I pray you stand good father to me now;
Give me Bianca for my patrimony.
  Ped. Soft, son!
Sir, by your leave: having come to Padua
To gather in some debts, my son Lucentio
Made me acquainted with a weighty cause
Of love between your daughter and himself;
And—for the good report I hear of you,
And for the love he beareth to your
    daughter,   29
And she to him—to stay him not too long,
I am content, in a good father's care,
To have him match'd; and, if you please
    to like
No worse than I, upon some agreement
Me shall you find ready and willing   34
With one consent to have her so bestow'd;
For curious I cannot be with you,
Signior Baptista, of whom I hear so well.
  Bap. Sir, pardon me in what I have to
    say.
Your plainness and your shortness please
    me well.
Right true it is your son Lucentio here 40
Doth love my daughter, and she loveth
    him,
Or both dissemble deeply their affections;
And therefore, if you say no more than
    this,
That like a father you will deal with him,
And pass my daughter a sufficient dower,
The match is made, and all is done—   46
Your son shall have my daughter with
    consent.
  Tra. I thank you, sir.   Where then do you
    know best
We be affied, and such assurance ta'en
As shall with either part's agreement stand?
  Bap. Not in my house, Lucentio, for you
    know   51
Pitchers have ears, and I have many
    servants;
Besides, old Gremio is heark'ning still,
And happily we might be interrupted.
  Tra. Then at my lodging, an it like you.
There doth my father lie; and there this
    night   56
We'll pass the business privately and well.
Send for your daughter by your servant
    here;
My boy shall fetch the scrivener presently.
The worst is this, that at so slender
    warning   60
You are like to have a thin and slender
    pittance.

  Bap. It likes me well.   Cambio, hie you
    home,
And bid Bianca make her ready straight;
And, if you will, tell what hath happened—
Lucentio's father is arriv'd in Padua,   65
And how she's like to be Lucentio's wife.
                  [*Exit Lucentio.*
  Bion. I pray the gods she may, with all
    my heart.
  Tra. Dally not with the gods, but get
    thee gone.   [*Exit Biondello.*
Signior Baptista, shall I lead the way?
Welcome! One mess is like to be your
    cheer;   70
Come, sir; we will better it in Pisa.
  Bap. I follow you.   [*Exeunt.*

Re-enter LUCENTIO *as Cambio, and*
    BIONDELLO.

  Bion. Cambio.
  Luc. What say'st thou, Biondello?
  Bion. You saw my master wink and
laugh upon you?   75
  Luc. Biondello, what of that?
  Bion. Faith, nothing; but has left me
here behind to expound the meaning or
moral of his signs and tokens.
  Luc. I pray thee moralize them.
  Bion. Then thus: Baptista is safe, talking with the deceiving father of a deceitful
son.   81
  Luc. And what of him?
  Bion. His daughter is to be brought by
you to the supper.
  Luc. And then?
  Bion. The old priest at Saint Luke's
church is at your command at all hours. 86
  Luc. And what of all this?
  Bion. I cannot tell, except they are
busied about a counterfeit assurance.   Take
your assurance of her, *cum privilegio ad
imprimendum solum*; to th' church take
the priest, clerk, and some sufficient honest
witnesses.   91
If this be not that you look for, I have no
    more to say,
But bid Bianca farewell for ever and a
    day.
  Luc. Hear'st thou, Biondello?   94
  Bion. I cannot tarry.   I knew a wench
married in an afternoon as she went to the
garden for parsley to stuff a rabbit; and so
may you, sir; and so adieu, sir.   My master
hath appointed me to go to Saint Luke's to
bid the priest be ready to come against you
come with your appendix.   [*Exit.*
  Luc. I may and will, if she be so con-
    tented.   100
She will be pleas'd; then wherefore should
    I doubt?
Hap what hap may, I'll roundly go about
    her;
It shall go hard if Cambio go without her.
                      [*Exit.*

SCENE V. *A public road.*

Enter PETRUCHIO, KATHERINA, HORTENSIO, *and* Servants.

Pet. Come on, a God's name ; once more
    toward our father's.
Good Lord, how bright and goodly shines
    the moon !
Kath. The moon ? The sun ! It is not
    moonlight now.
Pet. I say it is the moon that shines so
    bright.
Kath. I know it is the sun that shines so
    bright.   5
Pet. Now by my mother's son, and that's
    myself,
It shall be moon, or star, or what I list,
Or ere I journey to your father's house.
Go on and fetch our horses back again.
Evermore cross'd and cross'd ; nothing but
    cross'd !   10
Hor. Say as he says, or we shall never go.
Kath. Forward, I pray, since we have
    come so far,
And be it moon, or sun, or what you please;
And if you please to call it a rush-candle,
Henceforth I vow it shall be so for me.   15
Pet. I say it is the moon.
Kath.   I know it is the moon.
Pet. Nay, then you lie ; it is the blessed
    sun.
Kath. Then, God be bless'd, it is the
    blessed sun ;
But sun it is not, when you say it is not ;
And the moon changes even as your mind.
What you will have it nam'd, even that it is,
And so it shall be so for Katherine.   22
Hor. Petruchio, go thy ways, the field is
    won.
Pet. Well, forward, forward ! thus the
    bowl should run,
And not unluckily against the bias.   25
But, soft ! Company is coming here.

Enter VINCENTIO.

[*To Vincentio*] Good-morrow, gentle mis-
    tress ; where away ?—
Tell me, sweet Kate, and tell me truly too,
Hast thou beheld a fresher gentlewoman ?
Such war of white and red within her
    cheeks !   30
What stars do spangle heaven with such
    beauty
As those two eyes become that heavenly
    face ?
Fair lovely maid, once more good day to
    thee.
Sweet Kate, embrace her for her beauty's
    sake.
Hor. 'A will make the man mad, to make
a woman of him.   35
Kath. Young budding virgin, fair and
    fresh and sweet,

Whither away, or where is thy abode ?
Happy the parents of so fair a child ;
Happier the man whom favourable stars
Allots thee for his lovely bed-fellow.   40
Pet. Why, how now, Kate, I hope thou
    art not mad !
This is a man, old, wrinkled, faded, with-
    ered,
And not a maiden, as thou sayst he is.
Kath. Pardon, old father, my mistaking
    eyes,   44
That have been so bedazzled with the sun
That everything I look on seemeth green ;
Now I perceive thou art a reverend father.
Pardon, I pray thee, for my mad mistaking.
Pet. Do, good old grandsire, and withal
    make known
Which way thou travellest—if along with
    us,   50
We shall be joyful of thy company.
Vin. Fair sir, and you my merry mistress,
That with your strange encounter much
    amaz'd me,
My name is call'd Vincentio, my dwelling
    Pisa,
And bound I am to Padua, there to visit   55
A son of mine, which long I have not seen.
Pet. What is his name ?
Vin.   Lucentio, gentle sir.
Pet. Happily met ; the happier for thy
    son.
And now by law, as well as reverend age,
I may entitle thee my loving father :   60
The sister to my wife, this gentlewoman,
Thy son by this hath married. Wonder not,
Nor be not grieved—she is of good esteem,
Her dowry wealthy, and of worthy birth ;
Beside, so qualified as may beseem   65
The spouse of any noble gentleman.
Let me embrace with old Vincentio ;
And wander we to see thy honest son,
Who will of thy arrival be full joyous.
Vin. But is this true ; or is it else your
    pleasure,   70
Like pleasant travellers, to break a jest
Upon the company you overtake ?
Hor. I do assure thee, father, so it is.
Pet. Come, go along, and see the truth
    hereof ;
For our first merriment hath made thee
    jealous.   75
                 [*Exeunt all but Hortensio.*
Hor. Well, Petruchio, this has put me in
    heart.
Have to my widow ; and if she be froward,
Then hast thou taught Hortensio to be
    untoward.   [*Exit.*

ACT FIVE

SCENE I. *Padua.   Before Lucentio's house.*

Enter BIONDELLO, LUCENTIO, *and* BIANCA ;
    GREMIO *is out before.*

Bion. Softly and swiftly, sir, for the priest is ready.

Luc. I fly, Biondello; but they may chance to need thee at home, therefore leave us.

Bion. Nay, faith, I'll see the church a your back, and then come back to my master's as soon as I can.   5

[*Exeunt Lucentio, Bianca, and Biondello.*

Gre. I marvel Cambio comes not all this while.

Enter PETRUCHIO, KATHERINA, VINCENTIO, GRUMIO, *and* Attendants.

Pet. Sir, here's the door; this is Lucentio's house;
My father's bears more toward the market-place;
Thither must I, and here I leave you, sir.

Vin. You shall not choose but drink before you go;   10
I think I shall command your welcome here,
And by all likelihood some cheer is toward.

[*Knocks.*

Gre. They're busy within; you were best knock louder.

Pedant looks out of the window.

Ped. What's he that knocks as he would beat down the gate?   15

Vin. Is Signior Lucentio within, sir?

Ped. He's within, sir, but not to be spoken withal.

Vin. What if a man bring him a hundred pound or two to make merry withal?   19

Ped. Keep your hundred pounds to yourself; he shall need none so long as I live.

Pet. Nay, I told you your son was well beloved in Padua. Do you hear, sir? To leave frivolous circumstances, I pray you tell Signior Lucentio that his father is come from Pisa, and is here at the door to speak with him.   25

Ped. Thou liest: his father is come from Padua, and here looking out at the window.

Vin. Art thou his father?

Ped. Ay, sir; so his mother says, if I may believe her.

Pet. [*To Vincentio*] Why, how now, gentleman! Why, this is flat knavery to take upon you another man's name.   31

Ped. Lay hands on the villain; I believe 'a means to cozen somebody in this city under my countenance.

Re-enter BIONDELLO.

Bion. I have seen them in the church together. God send 'em good shipping! But who is here? Mine old master, Vincentio! Now we are undone and brought to nothing.   37

Vin. [*Seeing Biondello*] Come hither, crack-hemp.

Bion. I hope I may choose, sir.

Vin. Come hither, you rogue. What, have you forgot me?   41

Bion. Forgot you! No, sir. I could not forget you, for I never saw you before in all my life.

Vin. What, you notorious villain, didst thou never see thy master's father, Vincentio?   45

Bion. What, my old worshipful old master? Yes, marry, sir; see where he looks out of the window.

Vin. Is't so, indeed? [*He beats Biondello.*

Bion. Help, help, help! Here's a madman will murder me.   [*Exit.*

Ped. Help, son! help, Signior Baptista!

[*Exit from above.*

Pet. Prithee, Kate, let's stand aside and see the end of this controversy.

[*They stand aside.*

Re-enter Pedant *below*; BAPTISTA, TRANIO, *and* Servants.

Tra. Sir, what are you that offer to beat my servant?   54

Vin. What am I, sir? Nay, what are you, sir? O immortal gods! O fine villain! A silken doublet, a velvet hose, a scarlet cloak, and a copatain hat! O, I am undone! I am undone! While I play the good husband at home, my son and my servant spend all at the university.

Tra. How now! what's the matter?   60

Bap. What, is the man lunatic?

Tra. Sir, you seem a sober ancient gentleman by your habit, but your words show you a madman. Why, sir, what 'cerns it you if I wear pearl and gold? I thank my good father, I am able to maintain it.   65

Vin. Thy father! O villain! he is a sailmaker in Bergamo.

Bap. You mistake, sir; you mistake, sir. Pray, what do you think is his name?   69

Vin. His name! As if I knew not his name! I have brought him up ever since he was three years old, and his name is Tranio.   72

Ped. Away, away, mad ass! His name is Lucentio; and he is mine only son, and heir to the lands of me, Signior Vincentio.

Vin. Lucentio! O, he hath murd'red his master! Lay hold on him, I charge you, in the Duke's name. O, my son, my son! Tell me, thou villain, where is my son, Lucentio?

Tra. Call forth an officer.   80

Enter One *with an* Officer.

Carry this mad knave to the gaol. Father Baptista, I charge you see that he be forthcoming.

Vin. Carry me to the gaol!

Gre. Stay, Officer; he shall not go to prison.

Bap. Talk not, Signior Gremio; I say
he shall go to prison.   86
Gre. Take heed, Signior Baptista, lest you
be cony-catch'd in this business; I dare
swear this is the right Vincentio.
Ped. Swear if thou dar'st.   90
Gre. Nay, I dare not swear it.
Tra. Then thou wert best say that I am
not Lucentio.
Gre. Yes, I know thee to be Signior
Lucentio.
Bap. Away with the dotard; to the gaol
with him!
Vin. Thus strangers may be hal'd and
abus'd. O monstrous villain!   96

Re-enter BIONDELLO, *with* LUCENTIO *and*
BIANCA.

Bion. O, we are spoil'd; and yonder he
is! Deny him, forswear him, or else we are
all undone. [*Exeunt Biondello, Tranio, and*
Pedant, as fast as may be.
Luc. [*Kneeling*] Pardon, sweet father.
Vin.   Lives my sweet son?
Bian. Pardon, dear father.
Bap.   How hast thou offended?
Where is Lucentio?
Luc.   Here's Lucentio,   101
Right son to the right Vincentio,
That have by marriage made thy daughter
      mine,
While counterfeit supposes blear'd thine
      eyne.
Gre. Here's packing, with a witness, to
deceive us all!
Vin. Where is that damned villain,
      Tranio,   106
That fac'd and brav'd me in this matter so?
Bap. Why, tell me, is not this my
      Cambio?
Bian. Cambio is chang'd into Lucentio.
Luc. Love wrought these miracles.
      Bianca's love   110
Made me exchange my state with Tranio,
While he did bear my countenance in the
      town;
And happily I have arrived at the last
Unto the wished haven of my bliss.   114
What Tranio did, myself enforc'd him to;
Then pardon him, sweet father, for my sake.
Vin. I'll slit the villain's nose that would
have sent me to the gaol.
Bap. [*To Lucentio*] But do you hear, sir?
Have you married my daughter without
asking my good will?   120
Vin. Fear not, Baptista; we will content
you, go to; but I will in to be revenged
for this villainy.   [*Exit.*
Bap. And I to sound the depth of this
knavery.   [*Exit.*
Luc. Look not pale, Bianca; thy father
will not frown. [*Exeunt Lucentio and Bianca.*
Gre. My cake is dough, but I'll in among
      the rest;   125

Out of hope of all but my share of the feast.
                                   [*Exit.*
Kath. Husband, let's follow to see the
      end of this ado.
Pet. First kiss me, Kate, and we will.
Kath. What, in the midst of the street?
Pet. What, art thou asham'd of me? 130
Kath. No, sir; God forbid; but asham'd
      to kiss.
Pet. Why, then, let's home again. Come,
      sirrah, let's away.
Kath. Nay, I will give thee a kiss; now
      pray thee, love, stay.
Pet. Is not this well? Come, my sweet
      Kate: 134
Better once than never, for never too late.
                                   [*Exeunt.*

SCENE II. *Lucentio's house.*

Enter BAPTISTA, VINCENTIO, GREMIO, *the*
Pedant, LUCENTIO, BIANCA, PETRU-
CHIO, KATHERINA, HORTENSIO, *and*
Widow. *The* Servingmen *with* TRANIO,
BIONDELLO, *and* GRUMIO, *bringing in a*
banquet.

Luc. At last, though long, our jarring
      notes agree;
And time it is when raging war is done
To smile at scapes and perils overblown.
My fair Bianca, bid my father welcome,
While I with self-same kindness welcome
      thine.   5
Brother Petruchio, sister Katherina,
And thou, Hortensio, with thy loving
      widow,
Feast with the best, and welcome to my
      house.
My banquet is to close our stomachs up
After our great good cheer. Pray you, sit
      down;   10
For now we sit to chat as well as eat.
                                   [*They sit.*
Pet. Nothing but sit and sit, and eat and
      eat!
Bap. Padua affords this kindness, son
      Petruchio.
Pet. Padua affords nothing but what is
      kind.
Hor. For both our sakes I would that
      word were true.   15
Pet. Now, for my life, Hortensio fears his
      widow.
Wid. Then never trust me if I be afeard.
Pet. You are very sensible, and yet you
      miss my sense:
I mean Hortensio is afeard of you.
Wid. He that is giddy thinks the world
      turns round.   20
Pet. Roundly replied.
Kath.   Mistress, how mean you that?
Wid. Thus I conceive by him.
Pet. Conceives by me! How likes
      Hortensio that?

Hor. My widow says thus she conceives
   her tale.
Pet. Very well mended. Kiss him for
   that, good widow.   25
Kath. ' He that is giddy thinks the world
   turns round.'
I pray you tell me what you meant by that.
Wid. Your husband, being troubled with
   a shrew,
Measures my husband's sorrow by his woe ;
And now you know my meaning.   30
Kath. A very mean meaning.
Wid.   Right, I mean you.
Kath. And I am mean, indeed, respecting
   you.
Pet. To her, Kate !
Hor. To her, widow !
Pet. A hundred marks, my Kate does put
   her down.   35
Hor. That's my office.
Pet. Spoke like an officer—ha' to thee,
   lad.   [*Drinks to Hortensio.*
Bap. How likes Gremio these quick-
   witted folks ?
Gre. Believe me, sir, they butt together
   well.
Bian. Head and butt ! An hasty-witted
   body   40
Would say your head and butt were head
   and horn.
Vin. Ay, mistress bride, hath that
   awakened you ?
Bian. Ay, but not frighted me ; therefore
   I'll sleep again.
Pet. Nay, that you shall not ; since you
   have begun,
Have at you for a bitter jest or two.   45
Bian. Am I your bird ? I mean to shift
   my bush,
And then pursue me as you draw your bow.
You are welcome all.
   [*Exeunt Bianca, Katherina, and Widow.*
Pet. She hath prevented me. Here,
   Signior Tranio,
This bird you aim'd at, though you hit her
   not ;   50
Therefore a health to all that shot and
   miss'd.
Tra. O, sir, Lucentio slipp'd me like his
   greyhound,
Which runs himself, and catches for his
   master.
Pet. A good swift simile, but something
   currish.
Tra. 'Tis well, sir, that you hunted for
   yourself ;   55
Tis thought your deer does hold you at a
   bay.
Bap. O, O, Petruchio ! Tranio hits you
   now.
Luc. I thank thee for that gird, good
   Tranio.
Hor. Confess, confess ; hath he not hit
   you here ?   59

Pet. 'A has a little gall'd me, I confess ;
And, as the jest did glance away from me,
'Tis ten to one it maim'd you two outright.
Bap. Now, in good sadness, son Petruchio,
I think thou hast the veriest shrew of all.
Pet. Well, I say no ; and therefore, for
   assurance,   65
Let's each one send unto his wife,
And he whose wife is most obedient,
To come at first when he doth send for her,
Shall win the wager which we will propose.
Hor. Content. What's the wager ?
Luc.   Twenty crowns.
Pet. Twenty crowns !   71
I'll venture so much of my hawk or hound,
But twenty times so much upon my wife.
Luc. A hundred then.
Hor.   Content.
Pet.   A match ! 'tis done.
Hor. Who shall begin ?
Luc.   That will I.   75
Go, Biondello, bid your mistress come to
   me.
Bion. I go.   [*Exit.*
Bap. Son, I'll be your half Bianca comes.
Luc. I'll have no halves ; I'll bear it all
   myself.   79

    Re-enter BIONDELLO.

How now ! what news ?
Bion.   Sir, my mistress sends you word
That she is busy and she cannot come.
Pet. How ! She's busy, and she cannot
   come !
Is that an answer ?
Gre.   Ay, and a kind one too.
Pray God, sir, your wife send you not a
   worse.
Pet. I hope better.   85
Hor. Sirrah Biondello, go and entreat my
   wife
To come to me forthwith. [*Exit Biondello.*
Pet.   O, ho ! entreat her !
Nay, then she must needs come.
Hor.   I am afraid, sir,
Do what you can, yours will not be
   entreated.

    Re-enter BIONDELLO.

Now, where's my wife ?   90
Bion. She says you have some goodly jest
   in hand :
She will not come ; she bids you come to
   her.
Pet. Worse and worse ; she will not
   come ! O vile,
Intolerable, not to be endur'd !
Sirrah Grumio, go to your mistress ;   95
Say I command her come to me.
                  [*Exit Grumio.*
Hor. I know her answer.
Pet.   What ?
Hor.   She will not.

Pet. The fouler fortune mine, and there
an end.

Re-enter KATHERINA.

Bap. Now, by my holidame, here comes
Katherina !
Kath. What is your will, sir, that you
send for me ? 100
Pet. Where is your sister, and Hortensio's
wife ?
Kath. They sit conferring by the parlour
fire.
Pet. Go, fetch them hither ; if they deny
to come,
Swinge me them soundly forth unto their
husbands.
Away, I, say, and bring them hither
straight. [*Exit Katherina.*
Luc. Here is a wonder, if you talk of a
wonder. 106
Hor. And so it is. I wonder what it bodes.
Pet. Marry, peace it bodes, and love, and
quiet life,
An awful rule, and right supremacy ;
And, to be short, what not that's sweet and
happy. 110
Bap. Now fair befall thee, good Petruchio!
The wager thou hast won ; and I will add
Unto their losses twenty thousand crowns ;
Another dowry to another daughter, 114
For she is chang'd, as she had never been.
Pet. Nay, I will win my wager better yet,
And show more sign of her obedience,
Her new-built virtue and obedience.

Re-enter KATHERINA *with* BIANCA
and WIDOW.

See where she comes, and brings your
froward wives
As prisoners to her womanly persuasion. 120
Katherine, that cap of yours becomes you
not :
Off with that bauble, throw it underfoot.
[*Katherina complies.*
Wid. Lord, let me never have a cause to
sigh
Till I be brought to such a silly pass !
Bian. Fie ! what a foolish duty call you
this ? 125
Luc. I would your duty were as foolish
too ;
The wisdom of your duty, fair Bianca,
Hath cost me a hundred crowns since
supper-time !
Bian. The more fool you for laying on my
duty.
Pet. Katherine, I charge thee, tell these
headstrong women 130
What duty they do owe their lords and
husbands.
Wid. Come, come, you're mocking ; we
will have no telling.
Pet. Come on, I say ; and first begin
with her.

Wid. She shall not.
Pet. I say she shall. And first begin with
her. 135
Kath. Fie, fie ! unknit that threatening
unkind brow,
And dart not scornful glances from those
eyes
To wound thy lord, thy king, thy governor.
It blots thy beauty as frosts do bite the
meads,
Confounds thy fame as whirlwinds shake
fair buds, 140
And in no sense is meet or amiable.
A woman mov'd is like a fountain troub-
led—
Muddy, ill-seeming, thick, bereft of beauty ;
And while it is so, none so dry or thirsty
Will deign to sip or touch one drop of it. 145
Thy husband is thy lord, thy life, thy
keeper,
Thy head, thy sovereign ; one that cares
for thee,
And for thy maintenance commits his body
To painful labour both by sea and land,
To watch the night in storms, the day in
cold, 150
Whilst thou liest warm at home, secure and
safe ;
And craves no other tribute at thy hands
But love, fair looks, and true obedience—
Too little payment for so great a debt.
Such duty as the subject owes the prince,
Even such a woman oweth to her husband ;
And when she is froward, peevish, sullen,
sour, 157
And not obedient to his honest will,
What is she but a foul contending rebel
And graceless traitor to her loving lord ?
I am asham'd that women are so simple
To offer war where they should kneel for
peace ;
Or seek for rule, supremacy, and sway,
When they are bound to serve, love, and
obey.
Why are our bodies soft and weak and
smooth, 165
Unapt to toil and trouble in the world,
But that our soft conditions and our hearts
Should well agree with our external parts ?
Come, come, you froward and unable
worms ! 169
My mind hath been as big as one of yours,
My heart as great, my reason haply more,
To bandy word for word and frown for
frown ;
But now I see our lances are but straws,
Our strength as weak, our weakness past
compare,
That seeming to be most which we indeed
least are. 175
Then vail your stomachs, for it is no boot,
And place your hands below your husband's
foot ;
In token of which duty, if he please,

My hand is ready, may it do him ease.

Pet. Why, there's a wench! Come on, and kiss me, Kate.   180

Luc. Well, go thy ways, old lad, for thou shalt ha't.

Vin. 'Tis a good hearing when children are toward.

Luc. But a harsh hearing when women are froward.

Pet. Come, Kate, we'll to bed.   184

We three are married, but you two are sped. [*To Lucentio*] 'Twas I won the wager, though you hit the white ;
And being a winner, God give you good night !
                [*Exeunt Petruchio and Katherina.*

Hor. Now go thy ways ; thou hast tam'd a curst shrow.

Luc. 'Tis a wonder, by your leave, she will be tam'd so.   [*Exeunt.*

ALL'S WELL THAT ENDS WELL

DRAMATIS PERSONÆ

THE KING OF FRANCE.
THE DUKE OF FLORENCE.
BERTRAM, *Count of Rousillon.*
LAFEU, *an old lord.*
PAROLLES, *a follower of Bertram.*
Two French Lords, *serving with Bertram.*
Steward,
LAVACHE, *a clown,* } *servants to the Countess of Rousillon.*
A Page,

COUNTESS OF ROUSILLON, *mother to Bertram.*
HELENA, *a gentlewoman protected by the Countess.*
A Widow of Florence.
DIANA, *daughter to the Widow.*
VIOLENTA, } *neighbours and friends to the*
MARIANA, } *Widow.*
Lords, Officers, Soldiers, etc., French and Florentine.

THE SCENE : *Rousillon ; Paris ; Florence ; Marseilles.*

ACT ONE

SCENE I. *Rousillon. The Count's palace.*

Enter BERTRAM, *the* COUNTESS OF ROUSILLON, HELENA, *and* LAFEU, *all in black.*

Count. In delivering my son from me, I bury a second husband.

Ber. And I in going, madam, weep o'er my father's death anew ; but I must attend his Majesty's command, to whom I am now in ward, evermore in subjection. 5

Laf. You shall find of the King a husband, madam ; you, sir, a father. He that so generally is at all times good must of necessity hold his virtue to you, whose worthiness would stir it up where it wanted, rather than lack it where there is such abundance. 10

Count. What hope is there of his Majesty's amendment ?

Laf. He hath abandon'd his physicians, madam ; under whose practices he hath persecuted time with hope, and finds no other advantage in the process but only the losing of hope by time. 15

Count. This young gentlewoman had a father—O, that ' had ', how sad a passage 'tis !—whose skill was almost as great as his honesty ; had it stretch'd so far, would have made nature immortal, and death should have play for lack of work. Would, for the King's sake, he were living ! I think it would be the death of the King's disease.

Laf. How call'd you the man you speak of, madam ? 22

Count. He was famous, sir, in his profession, and it was his great right to be so— Gerard de Narbon. 24

Laf. He was excellent indeed, madam ; the King very lately spoke of him admiringly and mourningly ; he was skilful enough to have liv'd still, if knowledge could be set up against mortality.

Ber. What is it, my good lord, the King languishes of ?

Laf. A fistula, my lord. 30

Ber. I heard not of it before.

Laf. I would it were not notorious. Was this gentlewoman the daughter of Gerard de Narbon ?

Count. His sole child, my lord, and bequeathed to my overlooking. I have those hopes of her good that her education promises ; her dispositions she inherits, which makes fair gifts fairer ; for where an unclean mind carries virtuous qualities, there commendations go with pity—they are virtues and traitors too. In her they are the better for their simpleness ; she derives her honesty, and achieves her goodness. 40

Laf. Your commendations, madam, get from her tears.

Count. 'Tis the best brine a maiden can season her praise in. The remembrance of her father never approaches her heart but the tyranny of her sorrows takes all livelihood from her cheek. No more of this, Helena ; go to, no more, lest it be rather thought you affect a sorrow than to have—

Hel. I do affect a sorrow indeed, but I have it too. 47

Laf. Moderate lamentation is the right of the dead : excessive grief the enemy to the living.

Count. If the living be enemy to the grief, the excess makes it soon mortal. 51

Ber. Madam, I desire your holy wishes.

Laf. How understand we that ?

Count. Be thou blest, Bertram, and succeed thy father
In manners, as in shape! Thy blood and virtue 55
Contend for empire in thee, and thy goodness
Share with thy birthright! Love all, trust a few,

Do wrong to none ; be able for thine enemy
Rather in power than use, and keep thy
    friend
Under thy own life's key ; be check'd for
    silence,   60
But never tax'd for speech. What heaven
    more will,
That thee may furnish, and my prayers
    pluck down,
Fall on thy head ! Farewell. My lord,
'Tis an unseason'd courtier ; good my lord,
Advise him.
    Laf.   He cannot want the best   65
That shall attend his love.
    Count. Heaven bless him ! Farewell,
    Bertram.   *[Exit Countess.*
    Ber. The best wishes that can be forg'd in
your thoughts be servants to you ! [*To
Helena*] Be comfortable to my mother,
your mistress, and make much of her.   70
    Laf. Farewell, pretty lady ; you must
hold the credit of your father.
          [Exeunt Bertram and Lafeu.
    Hel. O, were that all ! I think not on my
    father ;
And these great tears grace his remem-
    brance more
Than those I shed for him. What was he
    like ?   75
I have forgot him ; my imagination
Carries no favour in't but Bertram's.
I am undone ; there is no living, none,
If Bertram be away. 'Twere all one   79
That I should love a bright particular star
And think to wed it, he is so above me.
In his bright radiance and collateral light
Must I be comforted, not in his sphere.
Th' ambition in my love thus plagues itself :
The hind that would be mated by the lion
Must die for love. 'Twas pretty, though a
    plague,   86
To see him every hour ; to sit and draw
His arched brows, his hawking eye, his curls,
In our heart's table—heart too capable   89
Of every line and trick of his sweet favour.
But now he's gone, and my idolatrous fancy
Must sanctify his relics. Who comes here ?

    Enter PAROLLES.

[*Aside*] One that goes with him. I love him
    for his sake ;
And yet I know him a notorious liar,
Think him a great way fool, solely a
    coward ;   95
Yet these fix'd evils sit so fit in him
That they take place when virtue's steely
    bones
Looks bleak i' th' cold wind ; withal, full
    oft we see
Cold wisdom waiting on superfluous folly.
    Par. Save you, fair queen !   100
    Hel. And you, monarch !
    Par. No.
    Hel. And no.

    Par. Are you meditating on virginity ?
    Hel. Ay. You have some stain of soldier
in you ; let me ask you a question. Man
is enemy to virginity ; how may we
barricado it against him ?   107
    Par. Keep him out.
    Hel. But he assails ; and our virginity,
though valiant in the defence, yet is weak.
Unfold to us some warlike resistance.   111
    Par. There is none. Man, setting down
before you, will undermine you and blow
you up.
    Hel. Bless our poor virginity from under-
miners and blowers-up ! Is there no
military policy how virgins might blow up
men ?   116
    Par. Virginity being blown down, man
will quicklier be blown up ; marry, in
blowing him down again, with the breach
yourselves made, you lose your city. It is
not politic in the commonwealth of nature
to preserve virginity. Loss of virginity is
rational increase ; and there was never
virgin got till virginity was first lost. That
you were made of is metal to make virgins.
Virginity by being once lost may be ten
times found ; by being ever kept, it is ever
lost. 'Tis too cold a companion ; away
with't.   125
    Hel. I will stand for 't a little, though
therefore I die a virgin.
    Par. There's little can be said in't ; 'tis
against the rule of nature. To speak on the
part of virginity is to accuse your mothers ;
which is most infallible disobedience. He
that hangs himself is a virgin ; virginity
murders itself, and should be buried in
highways, out of all sanctified limit, as a
desperate offendress against nature. Virginity breeds mites, much like a cheese ;
consumes itself to the very paring, and so
dies with feeding his own stomach. Besides,
virginity is peevish, proud, idle, made of
self-love, which is the most inhibited sin in
the canon. Keep it not ; you cannot choose
but lose by't. Out with't. Within ten
year it will make itself ten, which is a
goodly increase ; and the principal itself
not much the worse. Away with't.   140
    Hel. How might one do, sir, to lose it to
her own liking ?
    Par. Let me see. Marry, ill to like him
that ne'er it likes. 'Tis a commodity will
lose the gloss with lying ; the longer kept,
the less worth. Off with't while 'tis vendible ; answer the time of request. Virginity,
like an old courtier, wears her cap out of
fashion, richly suited but unsuitable ; just
like the brooch and the toothpick, which
wear not now. Your date is better in your
pie and your porridge than in your cheek.
And your virginity, your old virginity, is
like one of our French wither'd pears : it
looks ill, it eats drily ; marry, 'tis a

wither'd pear; it was formerly better;
marry, yet 'tis a wither'd pear. Will you
anything with it?   152
   Hel. Not my virginity yet.
There shall your master have a thousand
   loves,
A mother, and a mistress, and a friend,   155
A phœnix, captain, and an enemy,
A guide, a goddess, and a sovereign,
A counsellor, a traitress, and a dear;
His humble ambition, proud humility,   159
His jarring concord, and his discord dulcet,
His faith, his sweet disaster; with a world
Of pretty, fond, adoptious christendoms
That blinking Cupid gossips. Now shall
   he—
I know not what he shall. God send him
   well!
The court's a learning-place, and he is
   one—   165
   Par. What one, i' faith?
   Hel. That I wish well. 'Tis pity—
   Par. What's pity?
   Hel. That wishing well had not a body
in't
Which might be felt; that we, the poorer
   born,   170
Whose baser stars do shut us up in wishes,
Might with effects of them follow our
   friends
And show what we alone must think, which
   never
Returns us thanks.   174

                Enter Page.

   Page. Monsieur Parolles, my lord calls
for you.   [*Exit Page.*
   Par. Little Helen, farewell; if I can
remember thee, I will think of thee at
court.
   Hel. Monsieur Parolles, you were born
under a charitable star.
   Par. Under Mars, I.   180
   Hel. I especially think, under Mars.
   Par. Why under Mars?
   Hel. The wars hath so kept you under
that you must needs be born under Mars.
   Par. When he was predominant.   185
   Hel. When he was retrograde, I think,
rather.
   Par. Why think you so?
   Hel. You go so much backward when
you fight.
   Par. That's for advantage.   189
   Hel. So is running away, when fear pro-
poses the safety; but the composition that
your valour and fear makes in you is a
virtue of a good wing, and I like the wear
well.   192
   Par. I am so full of businesses I cannot
answer thee acutely. I will return perfect
courtier; in the which my instruction
shall serve to naturalize thee, so thou wilt
be capable of a courtier's counsel, and

understand what advice shall thrust upon
thee; else thou diest in thine unthankfulness, and thine ignorance makes thee away.
Farewell. When thou hast leisure, say thy
prayers; when thou hast none, remember
thy friends. Get thee a good husband, and
use him as he uses thee. So, farewell.   201
                                         [*Exit.*
   Hel. Our remedies oft in ourselves do lie,
Which we ascribe to heaven. The fated
   sky
Gives us free scope; only doth backward
   pull
Our slow designs when we ourselves are
   dull.   205
What power is it which mounts my love so
   high,
That makes me see, and cannot feed mine
   eye?
The mightiest space in fortune nature
   brings
To join like likes, and kiss like native
   things.
Impossible be strange attempts to those   210
That weigh their pains in sense, and do
   suppose
What hath been cannot be. Who ever
   strove
To show her merit that did miss her love?
The King's disease—my project may
   deceive me,   214
But my intents are fix'd, and will not leave
   me.   [*Exit.*

SCENE II.   *Paris.   The King's palace.*

Flourish of cornets.   Enter the KING OF
FRANCE, *with letters, and divers* Attendants.

   King. The Florentines and Senoys are by
   th' ears;
Have fought with equal fortune, and con-
   tinue
A braving war.
   1 Lord.   So 'tis reported, sir.
   King. Nay, 'tis most credible. We here
   receive it,
A certainty, vouch'd from our cousin
   Austria,   5
With caution, that the Florentine will move
   us
For speedy aid; wherein our dearest friend
Prejudicates the business, and would seem
To have us make denial.
   1 Lord.   His love and wisdom,
Approv'd so to your Majesty, may plead 10
For amplest credence.
   King.   He hath arm'd our answer,
And Florence is denied before he comes;
Yet, for our gentlemen that mean to see
The Tuscan service, freely have they leave
To stand on either part.
   2 Lord.   It well may serve 15
A nursery to our gentry, who are sick

For breathing and exploit.
   King.   What's he comes here ?

Enter BERTRAM, LAFEU, *and* PAROLLES.

  1 Lord. It is the Count Rousillon, my
     good lord,
Young Bertram.
   King.   Youth, thou bear'st thy father's
     face ;   19
Frank nature, rather curious than in haste,
Hath well compos'd thee. Thy father's
     moral parts
Mayst thou inherit too! Welcome to Paris.
   Ber. My thanks and duty are your
     Majesty's.
   King. I would I had that corporal sound-
     ness now,
As when thy father and myself in friend-
     ship   25
First tried our soldiership. He did look far
Into the service of the time, and was
Discipled of the bravest. He lasted long ;
But on us both did haggish age steal on, 29
And wore us out of act. It much repairs me
To talk of your good father. In his youth
He had the wit which I can well observe
To-day in our young lords ; but they may
     jest
Till their own scorn return to them un-
     noted
Ere they can hide their levity in honour.   35
So like a courtier, contempt nor bitterness
Were in his pride or sharpness ; if they
     were,
His equal had awak'd them ; and his
     honour,   38
Clock to itself, knew the true minute when
Exception bid him speak, and at this time
His tongue obey'd his hand. Who were
     below him
He us'd as creatures of another place ;
And bow'd his eminent top to their low
     ranks,
Making them proud of his humility
In their poor praise he humbled. Such a
     man   45
Might be a copy to these younger times ;
Which, followed well, would demonstrate
     them now
But goers backward.
   Ber.   His good remembrance, sir,
Lies richer in your thoughts than on his
     tomb ;
So in approof lives not his epitaph   50
As in your royal speech.
   King. Would I were with him ! He would
     always say—
Methinks I hear him now ; his plausive
     words
He scatter'd not in ears, but grafted them
To grow there, and to bear—' Let me not
     live '—   55
This his good melancholy oft began,
On the catastrophe and heel of pastime,

When it was out—' Let me not live ' quoth he
' After my flame lacks oil, to be the snuff
Of younger spirits, whose apprehensive
     senses   60
All but new things disdain ; whose judg-
     ments are
Mere fathers of their garments ; whose
     constancies
Expire before their fashions '. This he
     wish'd.
I, after him, do after him wish too,
Since I nor wax nor honey can bring home,
I quickly were dissolved from my hive, 66
To give some labourers room.
   2 Lord.   You're loved, sir ;
They that least lend it you shall lack you
     first.
   King. I fill a place, I know't. How long
     is't, Count,   69
Since the physician at your father's died ?
He was much fam'd.
   Ber.   Some six months since, my lord.
   King. If he were living, I would try him
     yet—
Lend me an arm—the rest have worn me
     out
With several applications. Nature and sick-
     ness   74
Debate it at their leisure. Welcome, Count;
My son's no dearer.
   Ber.   Thank your Majesty.
                       [Exeunt. Flourish.

SCENE III. *Rousillon. The Count's palace.*

Enter COUNTESS, Steward, *and* Clown.

   Count. I will now hear ; what say you of
this gentlewoman ?
   Stew. Madam, the care I have had to even
your content I wish might be found in the
calendar of my past endeavours ; for then
we wound our modesty, and make foul the
clearness of our deservings, when of ourselves we publish them.   7
   Count. What does this knave here ? Get
you gone, sirrah. The complaints I have
heard of you I do not all believe ; 'tis my
slowness that I do not, for I know you lack
not folly to commit them and have ability
enough to make such knaveries yours.   12
   Clo. 'Tis not unknown to you, madam, I
am a poor fellow.
   Count. Well, sir.   15
   Clo. No, madam, 'tis not so well that I
am poor, though many of the rich are
damn'd ; but if I may have your ladyship's
good will to go to the world, Isbel the
woman and I will do as we may.
   Count. Wilt thou needs be a beggar ? 20
   Clo. I do beg your good will in this case.
   Count. In what case ?
   Clo. In Isbel's case and mine own.
Service is no heritage ; and I think I shall
never have the blessing of God till I have

issue o' my body; for they say barnes are blessings.   26

Count. Tell me thy reason why thou wilt marry.

Clo. My poor body, madam, requires it. I am driven on by the flesh; and he must needs go that the devil drives.   29

Count. Is this all your worship's reason?

Clo. Faith, madam, I have other holy reasons, such as they are.   32

Count. May the world know them?

Clo. I have been, madam, a wicked creature, as you and all flesh and blood are; and, indeed, I do marry that I may repent.

Count. Thy marriage, sooner than thy wickedness.   37

Clo. I am out o' friends, madam, and I hope to have friends for my wife's sake.

Count. Such friends are thine enemies, knave.   40

Clo. Y'are shallow, madam—in great friends; for the knaves come to do that for me which I am aweary of. He that ears my land spares my team, and gives me leave to in the crop. If I be his cuckold, he's my drudge. He that comforts my wife is the cherisher of my flesh and blood; he that cherishes my flesh and blood loves my flesh and blood; he that loves my flesh and blood is my friend; ergo, he that kisses my wife is my friend. If men could be contented to be what they are, there were no fear in marriage; for young Charbon the puritan and old Poysam the papist, howsome'er their hearts are sever'd in religion, their heads are both one: they may jowl horns together like any deer i' th' herd.   52

Count. Wilt thou ever be a foul-mouth'd and calumnious knave?

Clo. A prophet I, madam; and I speak the truth the next way: 56

For I the ballad will repeat,
  Which men full true shall find:
Your marriage comes by destiny,
  Your cuckoo sings by kind.   60

Count. Get you gone, sir; I'll talk with you more anon.

Stew. May it please you, madam, that he bid Helen come to you. Of her I am to speak.

Count. Sirrah, tell my gentlewoman I would speak with her; Helen I mean.   65

Clo. [*Sings*]
' Was this fair face the cause' quoth she
' Why the Grecians sacked Troy?
Fond done, done fond,
  Was this King Priam's joy?'
With that she sighed as she stood,   70
With that she sighed as she stood,
  And gave this sentence then:
' Among nine bad if one be good,
Among nine bad if one be good,
  There's yet one good in ten'.   75

Count. What, one good in ten? You corrupt the song, sirrah.

Clo. One good woman in ten, madam, which is a purifying o' th' song. Would God would serve the world so all the year! We'd find no fault with the tithe-woman, if I were the parson. One in ten, quoth 'a! An we might have a good woman born before every blazing star, or at an earthquake, 'twould mend the lottery well: a man may draw his heart out ere 'a pluck one.

Count. You'll be gone, sir knave, and do as I command you.   86

Clo. That man should be at woman's command, and yet no hurt done! Though honesty be no puritan, yet it will do no hurt; it will wear the surplice of humility over the black gown of a big heart. I am going, forsooth. The business is for Helen to come hither.   [*Exit.*

Count. Well, now.

Stew. I know, madam, you love your gentlewoman entirely.   94

Count. Faith, I do. Her father bequeath'd her to me; and she herself, without other advantage, may lawfully make title to as much love as she finds. There is more owing her than is paid; and more shall be paid her than she'll demand.

Stew. Madam, I was very late more near her than I think she wish'd me. Alone she was, and did communicate to herself her own words to her own ears; she thought, I dare vow for her, they touch'd not any stranger sense. Her matter was, she loved your son. Fortune, she said, was no goddess, that had put such difference betwixt their two estates; Love no god, that would not extend his might only where qualities were level; Diana no queen of virgins, that would suffer her poor knight surpris'd without rescue in the first assault, or ransom afterward. This she deliver'd in the most bitter touch of sorrow that e'er I heard virgin exclaim in; which I held my duty speedily to acquaint you withal: sithence, in the loss that may happen, it concerns you something to know it.   112

Count. You have discharg'd this honestly; keep it to yourself. Many likelihoods inform'd me of this before, which hung so tott'ring in the balance that I could neither believe nor misdoubt. Pray you leave me. Stall this in your bosom; and I thank you for your honest care. I will speak with you further anon.   [*Exit Steward.*

Enter HELENA.

Even so it was with me when I was young.
If ever we are nature's, these are ours; this thorn   120
Doth to our rose of youth rightly belong;
Our blood to us, this to our blood is born.

It is the show and seal of nature's truth,
Where love's strong passion is impress'd in youth. 124
By our remembrances of days foregone,
Such were our faults, or then we thought them none.
Her eye is sick on't; I observe her now.
　　Hel. What is your pleasure, madam?
　　Count.　　　　　　　You know, Helen,
I am a mother to you.
　　Hel. Mine honourable mistress.
　　Count.　　　　　　Nay, a mother. 130
Why not a mother? When I said 'a mother',
Methought you saw a serpent. What's in ' mother '
That you start at it? I say I am your mother,
And put you in the catalogue of those
That were enwombed mine. 'Tis often seen
Adoption strives with nature, and choice breeds 136
A native slip to us from foreign seeds.
You ne'er oppress'd me with a mother's groan,
Yet I express to you a mother's care.
God's mercy, maiden! does it curd thy blood 140
To say I am thy mother? What's the matter,
That this distempered messenger of wet,
The many-colour'd Iris, rounds thine eye?
Why, that you are my daughter?
　　Hel.　　　　　　　That I am not.
　　Count. I say I am your mother.
　　Hel.　　　　　　Pardon, madam. 145
The Count Rousillon cannot be my brother:
I am from humble, he from honoured name;
No note upon my parents, his all noble.
My master, my dear lord he is; and I
His servant live, and will his vassal die. 150
He must not be my brother.
　　Count.　　　　　Nor I your mother?
　　Hel. You are my mother, madam; would you were—
So that my lord your son were not my brother—
Indeed my mother! Or were you both our mothers,
I care no more for than I do for heaven, 155
So I were not his sister. Can't no other,
But, I your daughter, he must be my brother?
　　Count. Yes, Helen, you might be my daughter-in-law.
God shield you mean it not! ' daughter ' and ' mother '
So strive upon your pulse. What! pale again? 160
My fear hath catch'd your fondness. Now I see
The myst'ry of your loneliness, and find
Your salt tears' head. Now to all sense 'tis gross
You love my son; invention is asham'd,

Against the proclamation of thy passion,
To say thou dost not. Therefore tell me true; 166
But tell me then, 'tis so; for, look, thy cheeks
Confess it, th' one to th' other; and thine eyes
See it so grossly shown in thy behaviours
That in their kind they speak it; only sin
And hellish obstinacy tie thy tongue, 171
That truth should be suspected. Speak, is't so?
If it be so, you have wound a goodly clew;
If it be not, forswear't; howe'er, I charge thee, 174
As heaven shall work in me for thine avail,
To tell me truly.
　　Hel.　　　　　Good madam, pardon me.
　　Count. Do you love my son?
　　Hel.　　　　　Your pardon, noble mistress.
　　Count. Love you my son?
　　Hel.　　　Do not you love him, madam?
　　Count. Go not about; my love hath in't a bond
Whereof the world takes note. Come, come, disclose 180
The state of your affection; for your passions
Have to the full appeach'd.
　　Hel.　　　　　Then I confess,
Here on my knee, before high heaven and you,
That before you, and next unto high heaven,
I love your son. 185
My friends were poor, but honest; so's my love.
Be not offended, for it hurts not him
That he is lov'd of me; I follow him not
By any token of presumptuous suit,
Nor would I have him till I do deserve him; 190
Yet never know how that desert should be.
I know I love in vain, strive against hope;
Yet in this captious and intenible sieve
I still pour in the waters of my love,
And lack not to lose still. Thus, Indian-like, 195
Religious in mine error, I adore
The sun that looks upon his worshipper
But knows of him no more. My dearest madam,
Let not your hate encounter with my love,
For loving where you do; but if yourself,
Whose aged honour cites a virtuous youth,
Did ever in so true a flame of liking 202
Wish chastely and love dearly that your Dian
Was both herself and Love; O, then, give pity
To her whose state is such that cannot choose 205
But lend and give where she is sure to lose;

That seeks not to find that her search
    implies,
But, riddle-like, lives sweetly where she
    dies!
  Count. Had you not lately an intent—
    speak truly—
To go to Paris?
  Hel. Madam, I had.
  Count. Wherefore? Tell true. 210
  Hel. I will tell truth; by grace itself I
    swear.
You know my father left me some pre-
    scriptions
Of rare and prov'd effects, such as his
    reading
And manifest experience had collected
For general sovereignty; and that he
    will'd me 215
In heedfull'st reservation to bestow them,
As notes whose faculties inclusive were
More than they were in note. Amongst the
    rest
There is a remedy, approv'd, set down, 219
To cure the desperate languishings whereof
The King is render'd lost.
  Count. This was your motive
For Paris, was it? Speak.
  Hel. My lord your son made me to think
    of this, 223
Else Paris, and the medicine, and the King,
Had from the conversation of my thoughts
Haply been absent then.
  Count. But think you, Helen,
If you should tender your supposed aid,
He would receive it? He and his physicians
Are of a mind: he, that they cannot help
    him;
They, that they cannot help. How shall
    they credit 230
A poor unlearned virgin, when the schools,
Embowell'd of their doctrine, have left off
The danger to itself?
  Hel. There's something in't
More than my father's skill, which was the
    great'st
Of his profession, that his good receipt 235
Shall for my legacy be sanctified
By th' luckiest stars in heaven; and, would
    your honour
But give me leave to try success, I'd
    venture
The well-lost life of mine on his Grace's
    cure
By such a day and hour.
  Count. Dost thou believe't? 240
  Hel. Ay, madam, knowingly.
  Count. Why, Helen, thou shalt have my
    leave and love,
Means and attendants, and my loving
    greetings
To those of mine in court. I'll stay at
    home, 244
And pray God's blessing into thy attempt.
Be gone to-morrow; and be sure of this,

What I can help thee to thou shalt not miss.
    [*Exeunt.*

ACT TWO

Scene I. *Paris. The King's palace.*

Flourish of cornets. Enter the King *with
    divers young* Lords *taking leave for the
    Florentine war;* Bertram *and* Parolles;
    Attendants.

  King. Farewell, young lords; these war-
    like principles
Do not throw from you. And you, my lords,
    farewell;
Share the advice betwixt you; if both
    gain all,
The gift doth stretch itself as 'tis receiv'd,
And is enough for both.
  1 Lord. 'Tis our hope, sir, 5
After well-ent'red soldiers, to return
And find your Grace in health.
  King. No, no, it cannot be; and yet my
    heart
Will not confess he owes the malady
That doth my life besiege. Farewell, young
    lords; 10
Whether I live or die, be you the sons
Of worthy Frenchmen; let higher Italy—
Those bated that inherit but the fall
Of the last monarchy—see that you come
Not to woo honour, but to wed it; when 15
The bravest questant shrinks, find what
    you seek,
That fame may cry you loud. I say fare-
    well.
  2 Lord. Health, at your bidding, serve
    your Majesty!
  King. Those girls of Italy, take heed of
    them; 19
They say our French lack language to
    deny,
If they demand; beware of being capt ves
Before you serve.
  Both. Our hearts receive your warnings.
  King. Farewell. [*To Attendants*] Come
    hither to me.
    [*The King retires attended.*
  1 Lord. O my sweet lord, that you will
    stay behind us!
  Par. 'Tis not his fault, the spark.
  2 Lord. O, 'tis brave wars!
  Par. Most admirable! I have seen those
    wars. 26
  Ber. I am commanded here and kept a
    coil with
' Too young ' and ' The next year ' and
  ' 'Tis too early '.
  Par. An thy mind stand to 't, boy, steal
    away bravely.
  Ber. I shall stay here the forehorse to a
    smock, 30
Creaking my shoes on the plain masonry,
Till honour be bought up, and no sword
    worn

But one to dance with. By heaven, I'll
    steal away.
1 Lord. There's honour in the theft.
Par.   Comm.t it, Count.
2 Lord. I am your accessary; and so
    farewell.   35
Ber. I grow to you, and our parting is a
tortur'd body.
1 Lord. Farewell, Captain.
2 Lord. Sweet Monsieur Parolles!   38
Par. Noble heroes, my sword and yours
are kin. Good sparks and lustrous, a word,
good metals : you shall find in the regiment
of the Spinii one Captain Spurio, with his
cicatrice, an emblem of war, here on his
sinister cheek; it was this very sword
entrench'd it. Say to him I live; and
observe his reports for me.
1 Lord. We shall, noble Captain.   45
Par. Mars dote on you for his novices!
[*Exeunt Lords*] What will ye do?

Re-enter the KING.

Ber. Stay; the King!
Par. Use a more spacious ceremony to the
noble lords; you have restrain'd yourself
within the list of too cold an adieu. Be
more expressive to them; for they wear
themselves in the cap of the time; there do
muster true gait; eat, speak, and move,
under the influence of the most receiv'd
star; and though the devil lead the
measure, such are to be followed. After
them, and take a more dilated farewell. 55
Ber. And I will do so.
Par. Worthy fellows; and like to prove
most sinewy sword-men.

[*Exeunt Bertram and Parolles.*

Enter LAFEU.

Laf. [*Kneeling*] Pardon, my lord, for me
    and for my tidings.
King. I'll fee thee to stand up.   60
Laf. Then here's a man stands that has
    brought his pardon.
I would you had kneel'd, my lord, to ask
    me mercy;
And that at my bidding you could so stand
    up.
King. I would I had; so I had broke thy
    pate,   64
And ask'd thee mercy for't.
Laf.   Good faith, across!
But, my good lord, 'tis thus : will you be
    cur'd
Of your infirmity?
King.   No.
Laf.   O, will you eat
No grapes, my royal fox? Yes, but you
    will
My noble grapes, an if my royal fox   70
Could reach them : I have seen a medicine
That's able to breathe life into a stone,
Quicken a rock, and make you dance canary

With spritely fire and motion; whose
    simple touch
Is powerful to araise King Pepin, nay,   75
To give great Charlemain a pen in's hand
And write to her a love-line.
King.   What her is this?
Laf. Why, Doctor She! My lord, there's
    one arriv'd,
If you will see her. Now, by my faith and
    honour,
If seriously I may convey my thoughts 80
In this my light deliverance, I have spoke
With one that in her sex, her years, pro-
    fession,
Wisdom, and constancy, hath amaz'd me
    more
Than I dare blame my weakness. Will you
    see her,
For that is her demand, and know her
    business?   85
That done, laugh well at me.
King.   Now, good Lafeu,
Bring in the admiration, that we with thee
May spend our wonder too, or take off
    thine
By wond'ring how thou took'st it.
Laf.   Nay, I'll fit you,
And not be all day neither. [*Exit Lafeu.*
King. Thus he his special nothing ever
    prologues.   91

Re-enter LAFEU *with* HELENA.

Laf. Nay, come your ways.
King.   This haste hath wings indeed.
Laf. Nay, come your ways;
This is his Majesty; say your mind to him.
A traitor you do look like; but such
    traitors   95
His Majesty seldom fears. I am Cressid's
    uncle,
That dare leave two together. Fare you
    well.   [*Exit.*
King. Now, fair one, does your business
    follow us?
Hel. Ay, my good lord.
Gerard de Narbon was my father,   100
In what he did profess, well found.
King.   I knew him.
Hel. The rather will I spare my praises
    towards him;
Knowing him is enough. On's bed of death
Many receipts he gave me; chiefly one,
Which, as the dearest issue of his practice,
And of his old experience th' only darling,
He bade me store up as a triple eye,   107
Safer than mine own two, more dear. I
    have so
And, hearing your high Majesty is touch'd
With that malignant cause wherein the
    honour   110
Of my dear father's gift stands chief in
    power,
I come to tender it, and my appliance,
With all bound humbleness.

King.   We thank you, maiden ;
But may not be so credulous of cure,
When our most learned doctors leave us,
  and   115
The congregated college have concluded
That labouring art can never ransom nature
From her inaidable estate—I say we must
  not
So stain our judgment, or corrupt our hope,
To prostitute our past-cure malady   120
To empirics ; or to dissever so
Our great self and our credit to esteem
A senseless help, when help past sense we
  deem.
  Hel. My duty then shall pay me for my
    pains.   124
I will no more enforce mine office on you ;
Humbly entreating from your royal
  thoughts
A modest one to bear me back again.
  King. I cannot give thee less, to be call'd
    grateful.
Thou thought'st to help me ; and such
  thanks I give
As one near death to those that wish him
  live.   130
But what at full I know, thou know'st no
  part ;
I knowing all my peril, thou no art.
  Hel. What I can do can do no hurt to try,
Since you set up your rest 'gainst remedy.
He that of greatest works is finisher   135
Oft does them by the weakest minister.
So holy writ in babes hath judgment shown,
When judges have been babes.   Great
  floods have flown
From simple sources, and great seas have
  dried
When miracles have by the greatest been
  denied.   140
Oft expectation fails, and most oft there
Where most it promises ; and oft it hits
Where hope is coldest, and despair most
  fits.
  King. I must not hear thee. Fare thee
    well, kind maid ;
Thy pains, not us'd, must by thyself be
  paid ;   145
Proffers not took reap thanks for their
  reward.
  Hel. Inspired merit so by breath is
    barr'd.
It is not so with Him that all things knows,
As 'tis with us that square our guess by
  shows ;
But most it is presumption in us when 150
The help of heaven we count the act of men.
Dear sir, to my endeavours give consent ;
Of heaven, not me, make an experiment.
I am not an impostor, that proclaim
Myself against the level of mine aim ;   155
But know I think, and think I know most
  sure,
My art is not past power nor you past cure.

  King. Art thou so confident ? Within
    what space
Hop'st thou my cure ?
  Hel.   The greatest Grace lending grace,
Ere twice the horses of the sun shall bring
Their fiery torcher his diurnal ring,   161
Ere twice in murk and occidental damp
Moist Hesperus hath quench'd his sleepy
  lamp,
Or four and twenty times the pilot's glass
Hath told the thievish minutes how they
  pass,   165
What is infirm from your sound parts shall
  fly,
Health shall live free, and sickness freely
  die.
  King. Upon thy certainty and confidence
What dar'st thou venture ?
  Hel.   Tax of impudence,
A strumpet's boldness, a divulged shame,
Traduc'd by odious ballads ; my maiden's
  name   171
Sear'd otherwise ; ne worse of worst—
  extended
With vilest torture let my life be ended.
  King. Methinks in thee some blessed
    spirit doth speak
His powerful sound within an organ weak ;
And what impossibility would slay   176
In common sense, sense saves another
  way.
Thy life is dear ; for all that life can rate
Worth name of life in thee hath estimate :
Youth, beauty, wisdom, courage, all   180
That happiness and prime can happy call.
Thou this to hazard needs must intimate
Skill infinite or monstrous desperate.
Sweet practiser, thy physic I will try,
That ministers thine own death if I die. 185
  Hel. If I break time, or flinch in property
Of what I spoke, unpitied let me die ;
And well deserv'd. Not helping, death's my
  fee ;   188
But, if I help, what do you promise me ?
  King. Make thy demand.
  Hel.   But will you make it even ?
  King. Ay, by my sceptre and my hopes
    of heaven.
  Hel. Then shalt thou give me with thy
    kingly hand
What husband in thy power I will com-
  mand.
Exempted be from me the arrogance
To choose from forth the royal blood of
  France,   195
My low and humble name to propagate
With any branch or image of thy state ;
But such a one, thy vassal, whom I know
Is free for me to ask, thee to bestow.
  King. Here is my hand ; the premises
    observ'd,   200
Thy will by my performance shall be serv'd.
So make the choice of thy own time, for I,
Thy resolv'd patient, on thee still rely.

More should I question thee, and more I
　　must,
Though more to know could not be more to
　　trust,　　　　　　　　　　　　　205
From whence thou cam'st, how tended on.
　　But rest
Unquestion'd welcome and undoubted
　　blest.
Give me some help here, ho! If thou
　　proceed
As high as word, my deed shall match thy
　　deed.　　　　　　　[*Flourish. Exeunt.*

SCENE II. *Rousillon. The Count's palace.*

Enter COUNTESS *and* Clown.

Count. Come on, sir; I shall now put you
to the height of your breeding.

Clo. I will show myself highly fed and
lowly taught. I know my business is but to
the court.　　　　　　　　　　　　4

Count. To the court! Why, what place
make you special, when you put off that
with such contempt? But to the court!　7

Clo. Truly, madam, if God have lent a
man any manners, he may easily put it off
at court. He that cannot make a leg, put
off's cap, kiss his hand, and say nothing,
has neither leg, hands, lip, nor cap; and
indeed such a fellow, to say precisely, were
not for the court; but for me, I have an
answer will serve all men.

Count. Marry, that's a bountiful answer
that fits all questions.　　　　　　15

Clo. It is like a barber's chair, that fits
all buttocks—the pin buttock, the quatch
buttock, the brawn buttock, or any
buttock.

Count. Will your answer serve fit to all
questions?　　　　　　　　　　19

Clo. As fit as ten groats is for the hand
of an attorney, as your French crown for
your taffety punk, as Tib's rush for Tom's
forefinger, as a pancake for Shrove
Tuesday, a morris for Mayday, as the nail
to his hole, the cuckold to his horn, as a
scolding quean to a wrangling knave, as
the nun's lip to the friar's mouth; nay, as
the pudding to his skin.　　　　　　26

Count. Have you, I say, an answer of
such fitness for all questions?

Clo. From below your duke to beneath
your constable, it will fit any question.　30

Count. It must be an answer of most
monstrous size that must fit all demands.

Clo. But a trifle neither, in good faith, if
the learned should speak truth of it. Here
it is, and all that belongs to't. Ask me if
I am a courtier: it shall do you no harm
to learn.　　　　　　　　　　　36

Count. To be young again, if we could, I
will be a fool in question, hoping to be the
wiser by your answer. I pray you, sir, are
you a courtier?

Clo. O Lord, sir!—There's a simple
putting off. More, more, a hundred of them.

Count. Sir, I am a poor friend of yours,
that loves you.　　　　　　　　　42

Clo. O Lord, sir!—Thick thick; spare
not me.

Count. I think, sir, you can eat none of
this homely meat.

Clo. O Lord, sir!—Nay, put me to't, I
warrant you.

Count. You were lately whipp'd, sir, as I
think.　　　　　　　　　　　　46

Clo. O Lord, sir!—Spare not me.

Count. Do you cry 'O Lord, sir!' at
your whipping, and 'spare not me'?
Indeed your 'O Lord, sir!' is very sequent
to your whipping. You would answer very
well to a whipping, if you were but bound
to't.　　　　　　　　　　　　51

Clo. I ne'er had worse luck in my life in
my 'O Lord, sir!' I see things may serve
long, but not serve ever.

Count. I play the noble housewife with
　　the time,
To entertain it so merrily with a fool.　55

Clo. O Lord, sir!—Why, there't serves
well again.

Count. An end, sir! To your business:
　　give Helen this,
And urge her to a present answer back;
Commend me to my kinsmen and my son.
This is not much.　　　　　　　　60

Clo. Not much commendation to them?

Count. Not much employment for you.
You understand me?

Clo. Most fruitfully; I am there before
my legs.

Count. Haste you again.　　[*Exeunt.*

SCENE III. *Paris. The King's palace.*

Enter BERTRAM, LAFEU, *and* PAROLLES.

Laf. They say miracles are past; and we
have our philosophical persons to make
modern and familiar things supernatural
and causeless. Hence is it that we make
trifles of terrors, ensconcing ourselves into
seeming knowledge when we should submit
ourselves to an unknown fear.　　　6

Par. Why, 'tis the rarest argument of
wonder that hath shot out in our latter
times.

Ber. And so 'tis.

Laf. To be relinquish'd of the artists—

Par. So I say—both of Galen and Paracelsus.　　　　　　　　　　　11

Laf. Of all the learned and authentic
fellows—

Par. Right; so I say.

Laf. That gave him out incurable—

Par. Why, there 'tis; so say I too.　15

Laf. Not to be help'd—

Par. Right; as 'twere a man assur'd
of a—

Laf. Uncertain life and sure death.

Par. Just; you say well; so would I have said.

Laf. I may truly say it is a novelty to the world.

Par. It is indeed. If you will have it in showing, you shall read it in what-do-ye-call't here.   22

Laf. [*Reading the ballad title*] ' A Showing of a Heavenly Effect in an Earthly Actor.'

Par. That's it; I would have said the very same.

Laf. Why, your dolphin is not lustier. Fore me, I speak in respect—   26

Par. Nay, 'tis strange, 'tis very strange; that is the brief and the tedious of it; and he's of a most facinerious spirit that will not acknowledge it to be the—

Laf. Very hand of heaven.   30

Par. Ay; so I say.

Laf. In a most weak—

Par. And debile minister, great power, great transcendence; which should, indeed, give us a further use to be made than alone the recov'ry of the King, as to be—   35

Laf. Generally thankful.

Enter KING, HELENA, *and* Attendants.

Par. I would have said it; you say well. Here comes the King.

Laf. Lustig, as the Dutchman says. I'll like a maid the better, whilst I have a tooth in my head. Why, he's able to lead her a coranto.   41

Par. Mort du vinaigre! Is not this Helen?

Laf. Fore God, I think so.

King. Go, call before me all the lords in court.   [*Exit an Attendant.*

Sit, my preserver, by thy patient's side; 45
And with this healthful hand, whose banish'd sense
Thou hast repeal'd, a second time receive
The confirmation of my promis'd gift,
Which but attends thy naming.

Enter three or four Lords.

Fair maid, send forth thine eye. This youthful parcel   50
Of noble bachelors stand at my bestowing,
O'er whom both sovereign power and father's voice
I have to use. Thy frank election make;
Thou hast power to choose, and they none to forsake.

Hel. To each of you one fair and virtuous mistress   55
Fall, when you please. Marry, to each but one!

Laf. I'd give bay Curtal and his furniture
My mouth no more were broken than these boys',
And writ as little beard.

326

King.   Peruse them well.
Not one of those but had a noble father. 60

Hel. Gentlemen,
Heaven hath through me restor'd the King to health.

All. We understand it, and thank heaven for you.

Hel. I am a simple maid, and therein wealthiest
That I protest I simply am a maid.   65
Please it your Majesty, I have done already.
The blushes in my cheeks thus whisper me:
' We blush that thou shouldst choose; but, be refused,
Let the white death sit on thy cheek for ever,   69
We'll ne'er come there again '.

King.   Make choice and see:
Who shuns thy love shuns all his love in me.

Hel. Now, Dian, from thy altar do I fly,
And to imperial Love, that god most high,
Do my sighs stream. Sir, will you hear my suit?   74

1 Lord. And grant it.

Hel. Thanks, sir; all the rest is mute.

Laf. I had rather be in this choice than throw ames-ace for my life.

Hel. The honour, sir, that flames in your fair eyes,
Before I speak, too threat'ningly replies.
Love make your fortunes twenty times above   80
Her that so wishes, and her humble love!

2 Lord. No better, if you please.

Hel.   My wish receive,
Which great Love grant; and so I take my leave.

Laf. Do all they deny her? An they were sons of mine I'd have them whipt; or I would send them to th' Turk to make eunuchs of.   86

Hel. Be not afraid that I your hand should take;
I'll never do you wrong for your own sake.
Blessing upon your vows; and in your bed
Find fairer fortune, if you ever wed!   90

Laf. These boys are boys of ice; they'll none have her. Sure, they are bastards to the English; the French ne'er got 'em.

Hel. You are too young, too happy, and too good,
To make yourself a son out of my blood. 95

4 Lord. Fair one, I think not so.

Laf. There's one grape yet; I am sure thy father drunk wine—but if thou be'st not an ass, I am a youth of fourteen; I have known thee already.

Hel. [*To Bertram*] I dare not say I take you; but I give
Me and my service, ever whilst I live,   101
Into your guiding power. This is the man.

King. Why, then, young Bertram, take her; she's thy wife.

Ber. My wife, my liege ! I shall beseech your Highness,
In such a business give me leave to use 105
The help of mine own eyes.

King.   Know'st thou not, Bertram,
What she has done for me ?

Ber.   Yes, my good lord ;
But never hope to know why I should marry her.

King. Thou know'st she has rais'd me from my sickly bed.

Ber. But follows it, my lord, to bring me down 110
Must answer for your raising ? I know her well :
She had her breeding at my father's charge.
A poor physician's daughter my wife ! Disdain
Rather corrupt me ever !

King. 'Tis only title thou disdain'st in her, the which 115
I can build up. Strange is it that our bloods,
Of colour, weight, and heat, pour'd all together,
Would quite confound distinction, yet stand off
In differences so mighty. If she be
All that is virtuous—save what thou dislik'st, 120
A poor physician's daughter—thou dislik'st
Of virtue for the name ; but do not so.
From lowest place when virtuous things proceed,
The place is dignified by th' doer's deed ;
Where great additions swell 's, and virtue none, 125
It is a dropsied honour. Good alone
Is good without a name. Vileness is so :
The property by what it is should go,
Not by the title. She is young, wise, fair ;
In these to nature she's immediate heir ;
And these breed honour. That is honour's scorn 131
Which challenges itself as honour's born
And is not like the sire. Honours thrive
When rather from our acts we them derive
Than our fore-goers. The mere word's a slave, 135
Debauch'd on every tomb, on every grave
A lying trophy ; and as oft is dumb
Where dust and damn'd oblivion is the tomb
Of honour'd bones indeed. What should be said ?
If thou canst like this creature as a maid,
I can create the rest. Virtue and she 141
Is her own dower ; honour and wealth from me.

Ber. I cannot love her, nor will strive to do't.

King. Thou wrong'st thyself, if thou shouldst strive to choose.

Hel. That you are well restor'd, my lord, I'm glad.
Let the rest go. 146

King. My honour's at the stake ; which to defeat,
I must produce my power. Here, take her hand,
Proud scornful boy, unworthy this good gift,
That dost in vile misprision shackle up 150
My love and her desert ; that canst not dream
We, poising us in her defective scale,
Shall weigh thee to the beam ; that wilt not know
It is in us to plant thine honour where
We please to have it grow. Check thy contempt ; 155
Obey our will, which travails in thy good ;
Believe not thy disdain, but presently
Do thine own fortunes that obedient right
Which both thy duty owes and our power claims ;
Or I will throw thee from my care for ever
Into the staggers and the careless lapse 161
Of youth and ignorance ; both my revenge and hate
Loosing upon thee in the name of justice,
Without all terms of pity. Speak ; thine answer.

Ber. Pardon, my gracious lord ; for I submit 165
My fancy to your eyes. When I consider
What great creation and what dole of honour
Flies where you bid it, I find that she which late
Was in my nobler thoughts most base is now 169
The praised of the King ; who, so ennobled,
Is as 'twere born so.

King.   Take her by the hand,
And tell her she is thine ; to whom I promise
A counterpoise, if not to thy estate
A balance more replete.

Ber.   I take her hand.

King. Good fortune and the favour of the King 175
Smile upon this contract ; whose ceremony
Shall seem expedient on the now-born brief,
And be perform'd to-night. The solemn feast
Shall more attend upon the coming space,
Expecting absent friends. As thou lov'st her, 180
Thy love's to me religious ; else, does err.

[*Exeunt all but Lafeu and Parolles
who stay behind, commenting of
this wedding.*

Laf. Do you hear, monsieur ? A word with you.

Par. Your pleasure, sir ?

Laf. Your lord and master did well to make his recantation. 185

Par. Recantation! My Lord! my master!

Laf. Ay ; is it not a language I speak ?

Par. A most harsh one, and not to be understood without bloody succeeding. My master !

Laf. Are you companion to the Count Rousillon ? 190

Par. To any count ; to all counts ; to what is man.

Laf. To what is count's man : count's master is of another style.

Par. You are too old, sir ; let it satisfy you, you are too old. 195

Laf. I must tell thee, sirrah, I write man ; to which title age cannot bring thee.

Par. What I dare too well do, I dare not do. 198

Laf. I did think thee, for two ordinaries, to be a pretty wise fellow ; thou didst make tolerable vent of thy travel ; it might pass. Yet the scarfs and the bannerets about thee did manifoldly dissuade me from believing thee a vessel of too great a burden. I have now found thee ; when I lose thee again I care not ; yet art thou good for nothing but taking up ; and that thou'rt scarce worth. 205

Par. Hadst thou not the privilege of antiquity upon thee—

Laf. Do not plunge thyself too far in anger, lest thou hasten thy trial ; which if —Lord have mercy on thee for a hen ! So, my good window of lattice, fare thee well ; thy casement I need not open, for I look through thee. Give me thy hand. 212

Par. My lord, you give me most egregious indignity.

Laf. Ay, with all my heart ; and thou art worthy of it.

Par. I have not, my lord, deserv'd it. 215

Laf. Yes, good faith, ev'ry dram of it ; and I will not bate thee a scruple.

Par. Well, I shall be wiser. 218

Laf. Ev'n as soon as thou canst, for thou hast to pull at a smack o' th' contrary. If ever thou be'st bound in thy scarf and beaten, thou shalt find what it is to be proud of thy bondage. I have a desire to hold my acquaintance with thee, or rather my knowledge, that I may say in the default ' He is a man I know '. 224

Par. My lord, you do me most insupportable vexation.

Laf. I would it were hell pains for thy sake, and my poor doing eternal ; for doing I am past, as I will by thee, in what motion age will give me leave. [*Exit.*

Par. Well, thou hast a son shall take this disgrace off me ; scurvy, old, filthy, scurvy lord ! Well, I must be patient ; there is no fettering of authority. I'll beat him, by my life, if I can meet him with any convenience, an he were double and double a lord. I'll have no more pity of his age than I would have of — I'll beat him, an if I could but meet him again. 235

Re-enter LAFEU.

Laf. Sirrah, your lord and master's married ; there's news for you ; you have a new mistress.

Par. I most unfeignedly beseech your lordship to make some reservation of your wrongs. He is my good lord : whom I serve above is my master. 240

Laf. Who ? God ?

Par. Ay, sir.

Laf. The devil it is that's thy master. Why dost thou garter up thy arms o' this fashion ? Dost make hose of thy sleeves ? Do other servants so ? Thou wert best set thy lower part where thy nose stands. By mine honour, if I were but two hours younger, I'd beat thee. Methink'st thou art a general offence, and every man should beat thee. I think thou wast created for men to breathe themselves upon thee. 250

Par. This is hard and undeserved measure, my lord.

Laf. Go to, sir ; you were beaten in Italy for picking a kernel out of a pomegranate ; you are a vagabond, and no true traveller ; you are more saucy with lords and honourable personages than the commission of your birth and virtue gives you heraldry. You are not worth another word, else I'd call you knave. I leave you. [*Exit.*

Enter BERTRAM.

Par. Good, very good, it is so then. Good, very good ; let it be conceal'd awhile.

Ber. Undone, and forfeited to cares for ever ! 260

Par. What's the matter, sweetheart ?

Ber. Although before the solemn priest I have sworn,
I will not bed her.

Par. What, what, sweetheart ?

Ber. O my Parolles, they have married me ! 265
I'll to the Tuscan wars, and never bed her.

Par. France is a dog-hole, and it no more merits
The tread of a man's foot. To th' wars !

Ber. There's letters from my mother ; what th' import is
I know not yet. 270

Par. Ay, that would be known. To th' wars, my boy, to th' wars !
He wears his honour in a box unseen
That hugs his kicky-wicky here at home,
Spending his manly marrow in her arms,
Which should sustain the bound and high curvet 275

Of Mars's fiery steed. To other regions !
France is a stable ; we that dwell in't
    jades ;
Therefore, to th' war !
   Ber. It shall be so ; I'll send her to my
    house,   279
Acquaint my mother with my hate to
    her,
And wherefore I am fled ; write to the
    King
That which I durst not speak. His present
    gift
Shall furnish me to those Italian fields
Where noble fellows strike. War is no
    strife
To the dark house and the detested wife.
   Par. Will this capriccio hold in thee, art
    sure ?   286
   Ber. Go with me to my chamber and
    advise me.
I'll send her straight away. To-morrow
I'll to the wars, she to her single sorrow.
   Par. Why, these balls bound ; there's
    noise in it. 'Tis hard :   290
A young man married is a man that's
    marr'd.
Therefore away, and leave her bravely ; go.
The King has done you wrong ; but, hush,
    'tis so.   [*Exeunt.*

SCENE IV. *Paris. The King's palace.*

Enter HELENA *and* Clown.

   Hel. My mother greets me kindly ; is she
well ?
   Clo. She is not well, but yet she has her
health ; she's very merry, but yet she is
not well. But thanks be given, she's very
well, and wants nothing i' th' world ; but
yet she is not well.   5
   Hel. If she be very well, what does she
ail that she's not very well ?
   Clo. Truly, she's very well indeed, but
for two things.
   Hel. What two things ?
   Clo. One, that she's not in heaven,
whither God send her quickly ! The other,
that she's in earth, from whence God send
her quickly !   12

Enter PAROLLES.

   Par. Bless you, my fortunate lady !
   Hel. I hope, sir, I have your good will to
have mine own good fortunes.   15
   Par. You had my prayers to lead them
on ; and to keep them on, have them still.
O, my knave, how does my old lady ?
   Clo. So that you had her wrinkles and I
her money, I would she did as you say.   20
   Par. Why, I say nothing.
   Clo. Marry, you are the wiser man ; for
many a man's tongue shakes out his
master's undoing. To say nothing, to do
nothing, to know nothing, and to have

nothing, is to be a great part of your title,
which is within a very little of nothing. 26
   Par. Away ! th'art a knave.
   Clo. You should have said, sir, ' Before
a knave th'art a knave' ; that's ' Before
me th'art a knave'. This had been truth,
sir.   30
   Par. Go to, thou art a witty fool ; I have
found thee.
   Clo. Did you find me in yourself, sir,
or were you taught to find me ? The search,
sir, was profitable ; and much fool may
you find in you, even to the world's
pleasure and the increase of laughter. 35
   Par. A good knave, i' faith, and well fed.
Madam, my lord will go away to-night :
A very serious business calls on him.
The great prerogative and rite of love,
Which, as your due, time claims, he does
    acknowledge ;
But puts it off to a compell'd restraint ; 41
Whose want, and whose delay, is strew'd
    with sweets,
Which they distil now in the curbed time,
To make the coming hour o'erflow with
    joy
And pleasure drown the brim.
   Hel.   What's his will else ? 45
   Par. That you will take your instant
    leave o' th' King,
And make this haste as your own good
    proceeding,
Strength'ned with what apology you think
May make it probable need.
   Hel.   What more commands he ?
   Par. That, having this obtain'd, you
    presently   50
Attend his further pleasure.
   Hel. In everything I wait upon his will.
   Par. I shall report it so.
   Hel. I pray you. [*Exit Parolles*] Come,
    sirrah.   [*Exeunt.*

SCENE V. *Paris. The King's palace.*

Enter LAFEU *and* BERTRAM.

   Laf. But I hope your lordship thinks not
him a soldier.
   Ber. Yes, my lord, and of very valiant
approof.
   Laf. You have it from his own deliverance.
   Ber. And by other warranted testimony.
   Laf. Then my dial goes not true ; I took
this lark for a bunting.   6
   Ber. I do assure you, my lord, he is very
great in knowledge, and accordingly
valiant.
   Laf. I have then sinn'd against his experience and transgress'd against his
valour ; and my state that way is dangerous, since I cannot yet find in my heart to
repent. Here he comes ; I pray you make
us friends ; I will pursue the amity.   13

Enter PAROLLES.

Par. [*To Bertram*] These things shall be done, sir.

Laf. Pray you, sir, who's his tailor ?   15

Par. Sir !

Laf. O, I know him well. Ay, sir; he, sir, 's a good workman, a very good tailor.

Ber. [*Aside to Parolles*] Is she gone to the King ?

Par. She is.   20

Ber. Will she away to-night ?

Par. As you'll have her.

Ber. I have writ my letters, casketed my treasure,
Given order for our horses ; and to-night,
When I should take possession of the bride,
End ere I do begin.   26

Laf. A good traveller is something at the latter end of a dinner ; but one that lies three-thirds and uses a known truth to pass a thousand nothings with, should be once heard and thrice beaten. God save you, Captain.   30

Ber. Is there any unkindness between my lord and you, monsieur ?

Par. I know not how I have deserved to run into my lord's displeasure.   34

Laf. You have made shift to run into 't, boots and spurs and all, like him that leapt into the custard ; and out of it you'll run again, rather than suffer question for your residence.

Ber. It may be you have mistaken him, my lord.   39

Laf. And shall do so ever, though I took him at's prayers. Fare you well, my lord ; and believe this of me : there can be no kernel in this light nut ; the soul of this man is his clothes ; trust him not in matter of heavy consequence ; I have kept of them tame, and know their natures. Farewell, monsieur ; I have spoken better of you than you have or will to deserve at my hand ; but we must do good against evil.
[*Exit.*

Par. An idle lord, I swear.

Ber. I think so.

Par. Why, do you not know him ?   50

Ber. Yes, I do know him well ; and common speech
Gives him a worthy pass. Here comes my clog.

Enter HELENA.

Hel. I have, sir, as I was commanded from you,
Spoke with the King, and have procur'd his leave
For present parting ; only he desires   55
Some private speech with you.

Ber.   I shall obey his will.
You must not marvel, Helen, at my course,
Which holds not colour with the time, nor does
The ministration and required office
On my particular. Prepar'd I was not   60
For such a business ; therefore am I found
So much unsettled. This drives me to entreat you
That presently you take your way for home,
And rather muse than ask why I entreat you ;   64
For my respects are better than they seem,
And my appointments have in them a need
Greater than shows itself at the first view
To you that know them not. This to my mother.   [*Giving a letter.*
'Twill be two days ere I shall see you ; so
I leave you to your wisdom.

Hel.   Sir, I can nothing say   70
But that I am your most obedient servant.

Ber. Come, come, no more of that.

Hel.   And ever shall
With true observance seek to eke out that
Wherein toward me my homely stars have fail'd
To equal my great fortune.

Ber.   Let that go.   75
My haste is very great. Farewell ; hie home.

Hel. Pray, sir, your pardon.

Ber.   Well, what would you say ?

Hel. I am not worthy of the wealth I owe,
Nor dare I say 'tis mine, and yet it is ;
But, like a timorous thief, most fain would steal   80
What law does vouch mine own.

Ber.   What would you have ?

Hel. Something ; and scarce so much ; nothing, indeed.
I would not tell you what I would, my lord.
Faith, yes ;
Strangers and foes do sunder and not kiss.

Ber. I pray you, stay not, but in haste to horse.   85

Hel. I shall not break your bidding, good my lord.

Ber. Where are my other men, monsieur ? Farewell !   [*Exit Helena.*
Go thou toward home, where I will never come
Whilst I can shake my sword or hear the drum.   89
Away, and for our flight.

Par.   Bravely, coragio !   [*Exeunt.*

ACT THREE

SCENE I.   *Florence.   The Duke's palace.*

Flourish.   Enter the DUKE OF FLORENCE, *attended ; two French Lords, with a* Troop of Soldiers.

Duke. So that, from point to point, now have you heard
The fundamental reasons of this war ;

Whose great decision hath much blood let
forth   3
And more thirsts after.

1 Lord.   Holy seems the quarrel
Upon your Grace's part; black and fearful
On the opposer.

Duke. Therefore we marvel much our
cousin France
Would in so just a business shut his bosom
Against our borrowing prayers.

2 Lord.   Good my lord,
The reasons of our state I cannot yield, 10
But like a common and an outward man
That the great figure of a council frames
By self-unable motion; therefore dare not
Say what I think of it, since I have found
Myself in my incertain grounds to fail 15
As often as I guess'd.

Duke.   Be it his pleasure.

1 Lord. But I am sure the younger of our
nature,
That surfeit on their ease, will day by day
Come here for physic.

Duke.   Welcome shall they be;
And all the honours that can fly from us 20
Shall on them settle. You know your places
well;
When better fall, for your avails they fell.
To-morrow to th' field. [*Flourish. Exeunt.*

SCENE II. *Rousillon. The Count's palace.*

Enter COUNTESS *and* Clown.

Count. It hath happen'd all as I would
have had it, save that he comes not along
with her.

Clo. By my troth, I take my young lord
to be a very melancholy man.   4

Count. By what observance, I pray you?

Clo. Why, he will look upon his boot and
sing; mend the ruff and sing; ask questions and sing; pick his teeth and sing. I
know a man that had this trick of melancholy sold a goodly manor for a song.   9

Count. Let me see what he writes, and
when he means to come. [*Opening a letter.*

Clo. I have no mind to Isbel since I was
at court. Our old ling and our Isbels o' th'
country are nothing like your old ling and
your Isbels o' th' court. The brains of my
Cupid's knock'd out; and I begin to love, as
an old man loves money, with no stomach.

Count. What have we here?   17

Clo. E'en that you have there. [*Exit.*

Count. [*Reads*] 'I have sent you a
daughter-in-law; she hath recovered the
King and undone me. I have wedded her,
not bedded her; and sworn to make the
" not " eternal. You shall hear I am run
away; know it before the report come. If
there be breadth enough in the world, I will
hold a long distance. My duty to you.

                Your unfortunate son,
                        BERTRAM.'   25

This is not well, rash and unbridled boy,
To fly the favours of so good a king,
To pluck his indignation on thy head
By the misprizing of a maid too virtuous
For the contempt of empire.   30

Re-enter Clown.

Clo. O madam, yonder is heavy news
within between two soldiers and my young
lady.

Count. What is the matter?

Clo. Nay, there is some comfort in the
news, some comfort; your son will not be
kill'd so soon as I thought he would.   36

Count. Why should he be kill'd?

Clo. So say I, madam, if he run away, as
I hear he does; the danger is in standing
to 't; that's the loss of men, though it be
the getting of children. Here they come
will tell you more. For my part, I only hear
your son was run away.   [*Exit.*

Enter HELENA *and the two* French
Gentlemen.

2 Gent. Save you, good madam.

Hel. Madam, my lord is gone, for ever
gone.

1 Gent. Do not say so.   45

Count. Think upon patience. Pray you,
gentlemen—
I have felt so many quirks of joy and
grief
That the first face of neither, on the start,
Can woman me unto 't. Where is my son,
I pray you.

1 Gent. Madam, he's gone to serve the
Duke of Florence.   50
We met him thitherward; for thence we
came,
And, after some dispatch in hand at court,
Thither we bend again.

Hel. Look on this letter, madam; here's
my passport.
[*Reads*] ' When thou canst get the ring upon
my finger, which never shall come off, and
show me a child begotten of thy body that
I am father to, then call me husband; but
in such a " then " I write a " never ".'   58
This is a dreadful sentence.

Count. Brought you this letter, gentlemen?

1 Gent.   Ay, madam;
And for the contents' sake are sorry for our
pains.   61

Count. I prithee, lady, have a better
cheer;
If thou engrossest all the griefs are thine,
Thou robb'st me of a moiety. He was my
son;
But I do wash his name out of my blood, 65
And thou art all my child. Towards
Florence is he?

1 Gent. Ay, madam.

Count.   And to be a soldier?

1 Gent. Such is his noble purpose ; and,
      believe 't,
The Duke will lay upon him all the honour
That good convenience claims.
      Count.   Return you thither ? 70
      2 Gent. Ay, madam, with the swiftest
            wing of speed.
Hel. [*Reads*] ' Till I have no wife, I have
nothing in France.'
'Tis bitter.
      Count. Find you that there ?
      Hel.   Ay, madam.
      2 Gent. 'Tis but the boldness of his hand
haply, which his heart was not consenting
to.   76
      Count. Nothing in France until he have
            no wife !
There's nothing here that is too good for
      him
But only she ; and she deserves a lord
That twenty such rude boys might tend
      upon,   80
And call her hourly mistress. Who was
      with him ?
      2 Gent. A servant only, and a gentleman
Which I have sometime known.
      Count.   Parolles, was it not ?
      2 Gent. Ay, my good lady, he.
      Count. A very tainted fellow, and full of
            wickedness.
My son corrupts a well-derived nature 86
With his inducement.
      2 Gent.   Indeed, good lady,
The fellow has a deal of that too much
Which holds him much to have.
      Count.   Y'are welcome, gentlemen. 90
I will entreat you, when you see my son,
To tell him that his sword can never win
The honour that he loses. More I'll entreat
      you
Written to bear along.
      1 Gent.   We serve you, madam,
In that and all your worthiest affairs.   95
      Count. Not so, but as we change our
            courtesies.
Will you draw near ?
            [*Exeunt Countess and Gentlemen.*
      Hel. ' Till I have no wife, I have nothing
in France.'
Nothing in France until he has no wife !
Thou shalt have none, Rousillon, none in
      France ;   100
Then hast thou all again. Poor lord !
      is't I
That chase thee from thy country, and
      expose
Those tender limbs of thine to the event
Of the none-sparing war ? And is it I
That drive thee from the sportive court,
      where thou   105
Wast shot at with fair eyes, to be the mark
Of smoky muskets ? O you leaden mes-
      sengers,
That ride upon the violent speed of fire,

Fly with false aim ; move the still-piecing
      air,
That sings with piercing ; do not touch my
      lord.   110
Whoever shoots at him, I set him there ;
Whoever charges on his forward breast,
I am the caitiff that do hold him to't ;
And though I kill him not, I am the cause
His death was so effected. Better 'twere
I met the ravin lion when he roar'd   116
With sharp constraint of hunger ; better
      'twere
That all the miseries which nature owes
Were mine at once. No ; come thou home,
      Rousillon,
Whence honour but of danger wins a scar,
As oft it loses all. I will be gone.   121
My being here it is that holds thee hence.
Shall I stay here to do't ? No, no, although
The air of paradise did fan the house,
And angels offic'd all. I will be gone, 125
That pitiful rumour may report my flight
To consolate thine ear. Come, night ; end,
      day.
For with the dark, poor thief, I'll steal
      away.   [*Exit.*

SCENE III.   *Florence.   Before the Duke's
            palace.*

Flourish.   Enter the DUKE OF FLORENCE,
      BERTRAM, PAROLLES, *Soldiers, drum and
      trumpets.*

      Duke. The General of our Horse thou art ;
            and we,
Great in our hope, lay our best love and
      credence
Upon thy promising fortune.
      Ber.   Sir, it is
A charge too heavy for my strength ; but
      yet   4
We'll strive to bear it for your worthy sake
To th' extreme edge of hazard.
      Duke.   Then go thou forth ;
And Fortune play upon thy prosperous
      helm,
As thy auspicious mistress !
      Ber.   This very day,
Great Mars, I put myself into thy file ;
Make me but like my thoughts, and I shall
      prove   10
A lover of thy drum, hater of love. [*Exeunt.*

SCENE IV.   *Rousillon.   The Count's palace.*

      Enter COUNTESS *and* Steward.

      Count. Alas ! and would you take the
            letter of her ?
Might you not know she would do as she
      has done
By sending me a letter ? Read it again.
      Stew. [*Reads*] ' I am Saint Jaques'
            pilgrim, thither gone.
Ambitious love hath so in me offended   5

That barefoot plod I the cold ground upon,
With sainted vow my faults to have
    amended.
Write, write, that from the bloody course
    of war
My dearest master, your dear son, may hie.
Bless him at home in peace, whilst I from
    far   10
His name with zealous fervour sanctify.
His taken labours bid him me forgive;
I, his despiteful Juno, sent him forth
From courtly friends, with camping foes to
    live,
Where death and danger dogs the heels of
    worth.   15
He is too good and fair for death and me;
Whom I myself embrace to set him free.'
   Count. Ah, what sharp stings are in her
    mildest words!
Rinaldo, you did never lack advice so much
As letting her pass so; had I spoke with
   her,   20
I could have well diverted her intents,
Which thus she hath prevented.
   Stew.   Pardon me, madam;
If I had given you this at over-night,
She might have been o'erta'en; and yet
    she writes
Pursuit would be but vain.
   Count.   What angel shall   25
Bless this unworthy husband? He cannot
    thrive,
Unless her prayers, whom heaven delights
    to hear
And loves to grant, reprieve him from the
    wrath
Of greatest justice. Write, write, Rinaldo,
To this unworthy husband of his wife;   30
Let every word weigh heavy of her worth
That he does weigh too light. My greatest
    grief,
Though little he do feel it, set down sharply.
Dispatch the most convenient messenger.
When haply he shall hear that she is gone
He will return; and hope I may that she,
Hearing so much, will speed her foot again,
Led hither by pure love. Which of them
    both
Is dearest to me I have no skill in sense
To make distinction. Provide this messen-
    ger.   40
My heart is heavy, and mine age is weak;
Grief would have tears, and sorrow bids me
    speak.   [*Exeunt.*

SCENE V. *Without the walls of Florence.*

A tucket afar off. Enter an old Widow *of
    Florence, her daughter* DIANA, VIOLENTA,
    and MARIANA, *with other* Citizens.

   Wid. Nay, come; for if they do approach the city we shall lose all the sight.
   Dia. They say the French count has done
most honourable service.   4

   Wid. It is reported that he has taken
their great'st commander; and that with
his own hand he slew the Duke's brother.
[*Tucket*] We have lost our labour; they are
gone a contrary way. Hark! you may
know by their trumpets.   8
   Mar. Come, let's return again, and
suffice ourselves with the report of it. Well,
Diana, take heed of this French earl; the
honour of a maid is her name, and no
legacy is so rich as honesty.   12
   Wid. I have told my neighbour how you
have been solicited by a gentleman his
companion.
   Mar. I know that knave, hang him!
one Parolles; a filthy officer he is in those
suggestions for the young earl. Beware of
them, Diana: their promises, enticements,
oaths, tokens, and all these engines of lust,
are not the things they go under; many a
maid hath been seduced by them; and the
misery is, example, that so terrible shows
in the wreck of maidenhood, cannot for all
that dissuade succession, but that they are
limed with the twigs that threatens them.
I hope I need not to advise you further;
but I hope your own grace will keep you
where you are, though there were no further
danger known but the modesty which is so
lost.   25
   Dia. You shall not need to fear me.

Enter HELENA *in the dress of a pilgrim.*

   Wid. I hope so. Look, here comes a
pilgrim. I know she will lie at my house:
thither they send one another. I'll question
her. God save you, pilgrim! Whither are
bound?   30
   Hel. To Saint Jaques le Grand.
Where do the palmers lodge, I do beseech
    you?
   Wid. At the Saint Francis here, beside
    the port.
   Hel. Is this the way?   [*A march afar.*
   Wid. Ay, marry, is't. Hark you! They
    come this way.   35
If you will tarry, holy pilgrim,
But till the troops come by,
I will conduct you where you shall be
    lodg'd;
The rather for I think I know your hostess
As ample as myself.
   Hel.   Is it yourself?   40
   Wid. If you shall please so, pilgrim.
   Hel. I thank you, and will stay upon your
    leisure.
   Wid. You came, I think, from France?
   Hel.   I did so.
   Wid. Here you shall see a countryman of
    yours
That has done worthy service.
   Hel.   His name, I pray you.   45
   Dia. The Count Rousillon. Know you
    such a one?

Hel. But by the ear, that hears most
    nobly of him ;
His face I know not.
Dia.   Whatsome'er he is,
He's bravely taken here. He stole from
    France,
As 'tis reported, for the King had married
    him   50
Against his liking. Think you it is so ?
Hel. Ay, surely, mere the truth ; I know
    his face.
Dia. There is a gentleman that serves the
    Count
Reports but coarsely of her.
Hel.   What's his name ?
Dia. Monsieur Parolles.
Hel.   O, I believe with him, 55
In argument of praise, or to the worth
Of the great Count himself, she is too mean
To have her name repeated ; all her
    deserving
Is a reserved honesty, and that
I have not heard examin'd.
Dia.   Alas, poor lady ! 60
'Tis a hard bondage to become the wife
Of a detesting lord.
Wid. I weet, good creature, wheresoe'er
    she is
Her heart weighs sadly. This young maid
    might do her
A shrewd turn, if she pleas'd.
Hel.   How do you mean ? 65
May be the amorous Count solicits her
In the unlawful purpose.
Wid.   He does, indeed ;
And brokes with all that can in such a suit
Corrupt the tender honour of a maid ;
But she is arm'd for him, and keeps her
    guard   70
In honestest defence.

Enter, with drum and colours, BERTRAM,
PAROLLES, *and the whole* Army.

Mar.   The gods forbid else !
Wid. So, now they come.
That is Antonio, the Duke's eldest son ;
That, Escalus.
Hel.   Which is the Frenchman ?
Dia.   He—
That with the plume ; 'tis a most gallant
    fellow.   75
I would he lov'd his wife ; if he were
    honester
He were much goodlier. Is't not a hand-
    some gentleman ?
Hel. I like him well.
Dia. 'Tis pity he is not honest. Yond's
    that same knave
That leads him to these places ; were I his
    lady   80
I would poison that vile rascal.
Hel.   Which is he ?
Dia. That jack-an-apes with scarfs. Why
is he melancholy ?

Hel. Perchance he's hurt i' th' battle.
Par. Lose our drum ! well.   85
Mar. He's shrewdly vex'd at something.
Look, he has spied us.
Wid. Marry, hang you !
Mar. And your courtesy, for a ring-
carrier !
    [*Exeunt Bertram, Parolles, and army.*
Wid. The troop is past. Come, pilgrim,
    I will bring you   90
Where you shall host. Of enjoin'd peni-
    tents
There's four or five, to great Saint Jacques
    bound,
Already at my house.
Hel.   I humbly thank you.
Please it this matron and this gentle maid
To eat with us to-night ; the charge and
    thanking   95
Shall be for me, and, to requite you
    further,
I will bestow some precepts of this virgin,
Worthy the note.
Both.   We'll take your offer kindly.
    [*Exeunt.*

SCENE VI. *Camp before Florence.*

Enter BERTRAM, *and the two* French Lords.

2 Lord. Nay, good my lord, put him to't ;
let him have his way.
1 Lord. If your lordship find him not a
hilding, hold me no more in your respect.
2 Lord. On my life, my lord, a bubble. 5
Ber. Do you think I am so far deceived
in him ?
2 Lord. Believe it, my lord, in mine own
direct knowledge, without any malice, but
to speak of him as my kinsman, he's a most
notable coward, an infinite and endless liar,
an hourly promise-breaker, the owner of no
one good quality worthy your lordship's
entertainment.   11
1 Lord. It were fit you knew him ; lest,
reposing too far in his virtue, which he hath
not, he might at some great and trusty
business in a main danger fail you.   14
Ber. I would I knew in what particular
action to try him.
1 Lord. None better than to let him fetch
off his drum, which you hear him so confidently undertake to do.   17
2 Lord. I with a troop of Florentines will
suddenly surprise him ; such I will have
whom I am sure he knows not from the
enemy. We will bind and hoodwink him so
that he shall suppose no other but that he
is carried into the leaguer of the adversaries
when we bring him to our own tents. Be
but your lordship present at his examination ; if he do not, for the promise of his
life and in the highest compulsion of base
fear, offer to betray you and deliver all the
intelligence in his power against you, and

would serve the turn, or the breaking of my
Spanish sword.

2 Lord. We cannot afford you so.   45

Par. Or the baring of my beard ; and to
say it was in stratagem.

2 Lord. 'Twould not do.

Par. Or to drown my clothes, and say I
was stripp'd.

2 Lord. Hardly serve.   50

Par. Though I swore I leap'd from the
window of the citadel—

2 Lord. How deep ?

Par. Thirty fathom.

2 Lord. Three great oaths would scarce
make that be believed.   56

Par. I would I had any drum of the
enemy's ; I would swear I recover'd it.

2 Lord. You shall hear one anon.
                 [*Alarum within.*

Par. A drum now of the enemy's !   60

2 Lord. Throca movousus, cargo, cargo,
cargo.

All. Cargo, cargo, cargo, villianda par
corbo, cargo.

Par. O, ransom, ransom ! Do not hide
mine eyes.   [*They blindfold him.*

1 Sold. Boskos thromuldo boskos.

Par. I know you are the Muskos' regiment,   65

And I shall lose my life for want of
language.

If there be here German, or Dane, Low
Dutch,

Italian, or French, let him speak to me ;

I'll discover that which shall undo the
Florentine.   69

1 Sold. Boskos vauvado. I understand
thee, and can speak thy tongue. Kerely-
bonto, sir, betake thee to thy faith, for
seventeen poniards are at thy bosom.

Par. O !

1 Sold.   O, pray, pray, pray ! Manka
revania dulche.   75

2 Lord. Oscorbidulchos volivorco.

1 Sold. The General is content to spare
thee yet ;

And, hoodwink'd as thou art, will lead thee
on

To gather from thee. Haply thou mayst
inform

Something to save thy life.

Par.   O, let me live,   80

And all the secrets of our camp I'll show,

Their force, their purposes. Nay, I'll speak
that

Which you will wonder at.

1 Sold.   But wilt thou faithfully ?

Par. If I do not, damn me.

1 Sold. Acordo linta.   85

Come on ; thou art granted space.
            [*Exit, with Parolles guarded.*
               A short alarum within.

2 Lord. Go, tell the Count Rousillon and
my brother

We have caught the woodcock, and will
keep him muffled

Till we do hear from them.

2 Sold.   Captain, I will.

2 Lord. 'A will betray us all unto ourselves—   90

Inform on that.

2 Sold. So I will, sir.

2 Lord. Till then I'll keep him dark and
safely lock'd.   [*Exeunt.*

SCENE II. *Florence. The Widow's house.*

Enter BERTRAM *and* DIANA.

Ber. They told me that your name was
Fontibell.

Dia. No, my good lord, Diana.

Ber.   Titled goddess ;

And worth it, with addition ! But, fair soul,

In your fine frame hath love no quality ?

If the quick fire of youth light not your
mind,   5

You are no maiden, but a monument ;

When you are dead, you should be such a
one

As you are now, for you are cold and stern ;

And now you should be as your mother was

When your sweet self was got.   10

Dia. She then was honest.

Ber.   So should you be.

Dia.   No.

My mother did but duty ; such, my lord,

As you owe to your wife.

Ber.   No more o' that !

I prithee do not strive against my vows.

I was compell'd to her ; but I love thee   15

By love's own sweet constraint, and will for
ever

Do thee all rights of service.

Dia.   Ay, so you serve us

Till we serve you ; but when you have our
roses

You barely leave our thorns to prick
ourselves,

And mock us with our bareness.

Ber.   How have I sworn !   20

Dia. 'Tis not the many oaths that makes
the truth,

But the plain single vow that is vow'd true.

What is not holy, that we swear not by,

But take the High'st to witness. Then,
pray you, tell me :   24

If I should swear by Jove's great attributes

I lov'd you dearly, would you believe my
oaths

When I did love you ill ? This has no
holding,

To swear by him whom I protest to love

That I will work against him. Therefore
your oaths

Are words and poor conditions, but unseal'd—   30

At least in my opinion.

Ber.   Change it, change it ;

Be not so holy-cruel. Love is holy ;
And my integrity ne'er knew the crafts
That you do charge men with. Stand no
     more off,
But give thyself unto my sick desires, 35
Who then recovers. Say thou art mine, and
     ever
My love as it begins shall so persever.
  Dia. I see that men make ropes in such
     a scarre
That we'll forsake ourselves. Give me that
     ring.
  Ber. I'll lend it thee, my dear, but have
     no power   40
To give it from me.
  Dia.   Will you not, my lord ?
  Ber. It is an honour 'longing to our
     house,
Bequeathed down from many ancestors ;
Which were the greatest obloquy i' th'
     world
In me to lose.
  Dia.   Mine honour's such a ring : 45
My chastity's the jewel of our house,
Bequeathed down from many ancestors ;
Which were the greatest obloquy i' th'
     world
In me to lose.   Thus your own proper
     wisdom   49
Brings in the champion Honour on my part
Against your vain assault.
  Ber.   Here, take my ring ;
My house, mine honour, yea, my life, be
     thine,
And I'll be bid by thee.
  Dia. When midnight comes, knock at my
     chamber window ;
I'll order take my mother shall not hear. 55
Now will I charge you in the band of truth,
When you have conquer'd my yet maiden
     bed,
Remain there but an hour, nor speak to me:
My reasons are most strong ; and you shall
     know them
When back again this ring shall be
     deliver'd.   60
And on your finger in the night I'll put
Another ring, that what in time proceeds
May token to the future our past deeds.
Adieu till then ; then fail not. You have
     won
A wife of me, though there my hope be
     done.   65
  Ber. A heaven on earth I have won by
     wooing thee.   [*Exit.*
  Dia. For which live long to thank both
     heaven and me !
You may so in the end.
My mother told me just how he would woo,
As if she sat in's heart ; she says all men 70
Have the like oaths. He had sworn to
     marry me
When his wife's dead ; therefore I'll lie
     with him

When I am buried. Since Frenchmen are so
     braid,
Marry that will, I live and die a maid.
Only, in this disguise, I think't no sin 75
To cozen him that would unjustly win.
                                        [*Exit.*

           SCENE III. *The Florentine camp.*

Enter the two French Lords, *and two or three*
                    Soldiers.

  2 Lord. You have not given him his
mother's letter ?
  1 Lord. I have deliv'red it an hour since.
There is something in't that stings his
nature ; for on the reading it he chang'd
almost into another man.
  2 Lord. He has much worthy blame laid
upon him for shaking off so good a wife and
so sweet a lady.   6
  1 Lord. Especially he hath incurred the
everlasting displeasure of the King, who
had even tun'd his bounty to sing happiness
to him. I will tell you a thing, but you
shall let it dwell darkly with you.   10
  2 Lord. When you have spoken it, 'tis
dead, and I am the grave of it.
  1 Lord. He hath perverted a young
gentlewoman here in Florence, of a most
chaste renown ; and this night he fleshes
his will in the spoil of her honour. He hath
given her his monumental ring, and thinks
himself made in the unchaste composition.
  2 Lord. Now, God delay our rebellion ! As
we are ourselves, what things are we !   19
  1 Lord. Merely our own traitors. And as
in the common course of all treasons we
still see them reveal themselves till they
attain to their abhorr'd ends ; so he that
in this action contrives against his own
nobility, in his proper stream, o'erflows
himself.   24
  2 Lord. Is it not meant damnable in us to
be trumpeters of our unlawful intents ? We
shall not then have his company to-night ?
  1 Lord. Not till after midnight ; for he is
dieted to his hour.   29
  2 Lord. That approaches apace. I would
gladly have him see his company anatomiz'd, that he might take a measure of
his own judgments, wherein so curiously
he had set this counterfeit.
  1 Lord. We will not meddle with him till
he come ; for his presence must be the whip
of the other.   35
  2 Lord. In the meantime, what hear you
of these wars ?
  1 Lord. I hear there is an overture of
peace.
  2 Lord. Nay, I assure you, a peace concluded.
  1 Lord. What will Count Rousillon do
then ? Will he travel higher, or return
again into France ?   41

2 Lord. I perceive, by this demand, you are not altogether of his counsel.

1 Lord. Let it be forbid, sir! So should I be a great deal of his act.   45

2 Lord. Sir, his wife, some two months since, fled from his house. Her pretence is a pilgrimage to Saint Jaques le Grand; which holy undertaking with most austere sanctimony she accomplish'd; and, there residing, the tenderness of her nature became as a prey to her grief; in fine, made a groan of her last breath, and now she sings in heaven.

1 Lord. How is this justified?   52

2 Lord. The stronger part of it by her own letters, which makes her story true even to the point of her death. Her death itself, which could not be her office to say is come, was faithfully confirm'd by the rector of the place.   56

1 Lord. Hath the Count all this intelligence?

2 Lord. Ay, and the particular confirmations, point from point, to the full arming of the verity.

1 Lord. I am heartily sorry that he'll be glad of this.

2 Lord. How mightily sometimes we make us comforts of our losses!   62

1 Lord. And how mightily some other times we drown our gain in tears! The great dignity that his valour hath here acquir'd for him at home be encount'red with a shame as ample.   66

2 Lord. The web of our life is of a mingled yarn, good and ill together. Our virtues would be proud if our faults whipt them not; and our crimes would despair if they were not cherish'd by our virtues.   70

Enter a Messenger.

How now? Where's your master?

Serv. He met the Duke in the street, sir; of whom he hath taken a solemn leave. His lordship will next morning for France. The Duke hath offered him letters of commendations to the King.   75

2 Lord. They shall be no more than needful there, if they were more than they can commend.

1 Lord. They cannot be too sweet for the King's tartness. Here's his lordship now.

Enter BERTRAM.

How now, my lord, is't not after midnight?   80

Ber. I have to-night dispatch'd sixteen businesses, a month's length apiece: by an abstract of success: I have congied with the Duke, done my adieu with his nearest; buried a wife, mourn'd for her; writ to my lady mother I am returning; entertain'd my convoy; and between these main parcels of dispatch effected many nicer needs. The last was the greatest, but that I have not ended yet.   87

2 Lord. If the business be of any difficulty and this morning your departure hence, it requires haste of your lordship.   90

Ber. I mean the business is not ended, as fearing to hear of it hereafter. But shall we have this dialogue between the Fool and the Soldier? Come, bring forth this counterfeit module has deceiv'd me like a double-meaning prophesier.   95

2 Lord. Bring him forth. [*Exeunt Soldiers*] Has sat i' th' stocks all night, poor gallant knave.

Ber. No matter; his heels have deserv'd it, in usurping his spurs so long. How does he carry himself?   99

2 Lord. I have told your lordship already the stocks carry him. But to answer you as you would be understood: he weeps like a wench that had shed her milk; he hath confess'd himself to Morgan, whom he supposes to be a friar, from the time of his remembrance to this very instant disaster of his setting i' th' stocks. And what think you he hath confess'd?   106

Ber. Nothing of me, has 'a?

2 Lord. His confession is taken, and it shall be read to his face; if your lordship be in't, as I believe you are, you must have the patience to hear it.   110

Enter PAROLLES *guarded, and* First Soldier *as interpreter.*

Ber. A plague upon him! muffled! He can say nothing of me.

2 Lord. Hush, hush! Hoodman comes. Portotartarossa.

1 Sold. He calls for the tortures. What will you say without 'em?   115

Par. I will confess what I know without constraint; if ye pinch me like a pasty, I can say no more.

1 Sold. Bosko chimurcho.

2 Lord. Boblibindo chicurmurco.

1 Sold. You are a merciful general. Our General bids you answer to what I shall ask you out of a note.

Par. And truly, as I hope to live.   122

1 Sold. ' First demand of him how many horse the Duke is strong.' What say you to that?

Par. Five or six thousand; but very weak and unserviceable. The troops are all scattered, and the commanders very poor rogues, upon my reputation and credit, and as I hope to live.   128

1 Sold. Shall I set down your answer so?

Par. Do; I'll take the sacrament on't, how and which way you will.

Ber. All's one to him. What a past-saving slave is this!   132

2 Lord. Y'are deceiv'd, my lord; this is Monsieur Parolles, the gallant militarist—

that was his own phrase—that had the whole theoric of war in the knot of his scarf, and the practice in the chape of his dagger.   136

1 Lord. I will never trust a man again for keeping his sword clean ; nor believe he can have everything in him by wearing his apparel neatly.   140

1 Sold. Well, that's set down.

Par. ' Five or six thousand horse ' I said —I will say true—' or thereabouts ' set down, for I'll speak truth.

2 Lord. He's very near the truth in this.

Ber. But I con him no thanks for't in the nature he delivers it.   145

Par. ' Poor rogues ' I pray you say.

1 Sold. Well, that's set down.

Par. I humbly thank you, sir. A truth's a truth—the rogues are marvellous poor.

1 Sold. ' Demand of him of what strength they are a-foot.' What say you to that ?

Par. By my troth, sir, if I were to live this present hour, I will tell true. Let me see : Spurio, a hundred and fifty ; Sebastian, so many ; Corambus, so many ; Jaques, so many ; Guiltian, Cosmo, Lodowick, and Gratii, two hundred fifty each ; mine own company, Chitopher, Vaumond, Bentii, two hundred fifty each ; so that the muster-file, rotten and sound, upon my life, amounts not to fifteen thousand poll ; half of the which dare not shake the snow from off their cassocks lest they shake themselves to pieces.   160

Ber. What shall be done to him ?

2 Lord. Nothing, but let him have thanks. Demand of him my condition, and what credit I have with the Duke.   163

1 Sold. Well, that's set down. ' You shall demand of him whether one Captain Dumain be i' th' camp, a Frenchman ; what his reputation is with the Duke, what his valour, honesty, expertness in wars ; or whether he thinks it were not possible, with well-weighing sums of gold, to corrupt him to a revolt.' What say you to this ? What do you know of it ?   169

Par. I beseech you, let me answer to the particular of the inter'gatories. Demand them singly.   171

1 Sold. Do you know this Captain Dumain ?

Par. I know him : 'a was a botcher's prentice in Paris, from whence he was whipt for getting the shrieve's fool with child—a dumb innocent that could not say him nay.   175

Ber. Nay, by your leave, hold your hands ; though I know his brains are forfeit to the next tile that falls.

1 Sold. Well, is this captain in the Duke of Florence's camp ?   179

Par. Upon my knowledge, he is, and lousy.

2 Lord. Nay, look not so upon me ; we shall hear of your lordship anon.

1 Sold. What is his reputation with the Duke ?   183

Par. The Duke knows him for no other but a poor officer of mine ; and writ to me this other day to turn him out o' th' band. I think I have his letter in my pocket.

1 Sold. Marry, we'll search.   187

Par. In good sadness, I do not know ; either it is there or it is upon a file with the Duke's other letters in my tent.

1 Sold. Here 'tis ; here's a paper. Shall I read it to you ?   191

Par. I do not know if it be it or no.

Ber. Our interpreter does it well.

2 Lord. Excellently.   194

1 Sold. [*Reads*] ' Dian, the Count's a fool, and full of gold.'

Par. That is not the Duke's letter, sir ; that is an advertisement to a proper maid in Florence, one Diana, to take heed of the allurement of one Count Rousillon, a foolish idle boy, but for all that very ruttish. I pray you, sir, put it up again.

1 Sold. Nay, I'll read it first by your favour.   201

Par. My meaning in't, I protest, was very honest in the behalf of the maid ; for I knew the young Count to be a dangerous and lascivious boy, who is a whale to virginity, and devours up all the fry it finds.   205

Ber. Damnable both-sides rogue !

1 Sold. [*Reads*].

' When he swears oaths, bid him drop gold,
      and take it ;
After he scores, he never pays the score.
Half won is match well made ; match, and
      well make it ;   209
He ne'er pays after-debts, take it before.
And say a soldier, Dian, told thee this :
Men are to mell with, boys are not to
      kiss ;
For count of this, the Count's a fool, I
      know it,
Who pays before, but not when he does
      owe it.   214

Thine, as he vow'd to thee in thine ear,
                                  PAROLLES.'

Ber. He shall be whipt through the army with this rhyme in's forehead.

1 Lord. This is your devoted friend, sir, the manifold linguist, and the armipotent soldier.   220

Ber. I could endure anything before but a cat, and now he's a cat to me.

1 Sold. I perceive, sir, by our General's looks we shall be fain to hang you. 224

Par. My life, sir, in any case ! Not that I am afraid to die, but that, my offences being many, I would repent out the remainder of nature. Let me live, sir, in

a dungeon, i' th' stocks, or anywhere, so I
may live.   228
1 *Sold.* We'll see what may be done, so
you confess freely ; therefore, once more to
this Captain Dumain : you have answer'd
to his reputation with the Duke, and to his
valour ; what is his honesty ?   232
Par. He will steal, sir, an egg out of a
cloister ; for rapes and ravishments he
parallels Nessus. He professes not keeping
of oaths ; in breaking 'em he is stronger
than Hercules. He will lie, sir, with such
volubility that you would think truth were
a fool. Drunkenness is his best virtue, for
he will be swine-drunk ; and in his sleep
he does little harm, save to his bedclothes
about him ; but they know his conditions
and lay him in straw. I have but little
more to say, sir, of his honesty. He has
everything that an honest man should not
have ; what an honest man should have he
has nothing.   243
2 *Lord.* I begin to love him for this.
Ber. For this description of thine honesty ? A pox upon him ! For me, he's more
and more a cat.   246
1 *Sold.* What say you to his expertness
in war ?
Par. Faith, sir, has led the drum before
the English tragedians—to belie him I will
not—and more of his soldiership I know
not, except in that country he had the honour to be the officer at a place there called
Mile-end to instruct for the doubling of
files—I would do the man what honour I
can—but of this I am not certain.
2 *Lord.* He hath out-villain'd villainy so
far that the rarity redeems him.   255
Ber. A pox on him ! he's a cat still.
1 *Sold.* His qualities being at this poor
price, I need not to ask you if gold will
corrupt him to revolt.
Par. Sir, for a cardecue he will sell the
fee-simple of his salvation, the inheritance
of it ; and cut th' entail from all remainders
and a perpetual succession for it perpetually.   261
1 *Sold.* What's his brother, the other
Captain Dumain ?
1 *Lord.* Why does he ask him of me ?
1 *Sold.* What's he ?   265
Par. E'en a crow o' th' same nest ; not
altogether so great as the first in goodness,
but greater a great deal in evil. He excels
his brother for a coward ; yet his brother
is reputed one of the best that is. In a
retreat he outruns any lackey : marry, in
coming on he has the cramp.   270
1 *Sold.* If your life be saved, will you
undertake to betray the Florentine ?
Par. Ay, and the Captain of his Horse,
Count Rousillon.
1 *Sold.* I'll whisper with the General, and
know his pleasure.   275

Par. [*Aside*] I'll no more drumming. A
plague of all drums ! Only to seem to
deserve well, and to beguile the supposition
of that lascivious young boy the Count,
have I run into this danger. Yet who
would have suspected an ambush where I
was taken ?   280
1 *Sold.* There is no remedy, sir, but you
must die. The General says you that have
so traitorously discover'd the secrets of
your army, and made such pestiferous
reports of men very nobly held, can serve
the world for no honest use ; therefore you
must die. Come, headsman, off with his
head.   286
Par. O Lord, sir, let me live, or let me
see my death !
1 *Sold.* That shall you, and take your
leave of all your friends. [*Unmuffling him.*
So look about you ; know you any here ?
Ber. Good morrow, noble Captain.   291
1 *Lord.* God bless you, Captain Parolles.
2 *Lord.* God save you, noble Captain.
1 *Lord.* Captain, what greeting will you
to my Lord Lafeu ? I am for France.   295
2 *Lord.* Good Captain, will you give me a
copy of the sonnet you writ to Diana in
behalf of the Count Rousillon ? An I were
not a very coward I'd compel it of you ; but
fare you well. [*Exeunt Bertram and Lords.*
1 *Sold.* You are undone, Captain, all but
your scarf ; that has a knot on't yet.   301
Par. Who cannot be crush'd with a plot ?
1 *Sold.* If you could find out a country
where but women were that had received
so much shame, you might begin an
impudent nation. Fare ye well, sir ; I am
for France too ; we shall speak of you
there.   [*Exit with Soldiers.*
Par. Yet am I thankful. If my heart
were great,   307
'Twould burst at this. Captain I'll be no
more ;
But I will eat, and drink, and sleep as soft
As captain shall. Simply the thing I am   310
Shall make me live. Who knows himself a
braggart,
Let him fear this ; for it will come to pass
That every braggart shall be found an
ass.
Rust, sword ; cool, blushes ; and, Parolles,
live
Safest in shame. Being fool'd, by fool'ry
thrive.   315
There's place and means for every man
alive.
I'll after them.   [*Exit.*

SCENE IV. *Florence. The Widow's house.*

Enter HELENA, Widow, *and* DIANA.

Hel. That you may well perceive I have
not wrong'd you,
One of the greatest in the Christian world

341

Shall be my surety ; fore whose throne 'tis
　　needful,
Ere I can perfect mine intents, to kneel.
Time was I did him a desired office,   5
Dear almost as his life ; which gratitude
Through flinty Tartar's bosom would peep
　　forth,
And answer 'Thanks'. I duly am inform'd
His Grace is at Marseilles, to which place
We have convenient convoy. You must
　　know   10
I am supposed dead. The army breaking,
My husband hies him home ; where,
　　heaven aiding,
And by the leave of my good lord the King,
We'll be before our welcome.
　　Wid.   Gentle madam,
You never had a servant to whose trust   15
Your business was more welcome.
　　Hel.   Nor you, mistress.
Ever a friend whose thoughts more truly
　　labour
To recompense your love. Doubt not but
　　heaven
Hath brought me up to be your daughter's
　　dower,
As it hath fated her to be my motive   20
And helper to a husband. But, O strange
　　men !
That can such sweet use make of what they
　　hate,
When saucy trusting of the cozen'd
　　thoughts   23
Defiles the pitchy night. So lust doth play
With what it loathes, for that which is away.
But more of this hereafter. You, Diana,
Under my poor instructions yet must suffer
Something in my behalf.
　　Dia.   Let death and honesty
Go with your impositions, I am yours
Upon your will to suffer.
　　Hel.   Yet, I pray you :   30
But with the word the time will bring on
　　summer,
When briers shall have leaves as well as
　　thorns
And be as sweet as sharp. We must away ;
Our waggon is prepar'd, and time revives us.
All's Well That Ends Well. Still the fine's
　　the crown.   35
Whate'er the course, the end is the renown.
　　　　　　　　　　　　　　　　　[Exeunt.

Scene V. *Rousillon. The Count's palace.*

Enter Countess, Lafeu, *and* Clown.

　　Laf. No, no, no, your son was misled
with a snipt-taffeta fellow there, whose
villainous saffron would have made all the
unbak'd and doughy youth of a nation in
his colour. Your daughter-in-law had been
alive at this hour, and your son here at
home, more advanc'd by the King than by
that red-tail'd humble-bee I speak of.   6

　　Count. I would I had not known him. It
was the death of the most virtuous gentlewoman that ever nature had praise for
creating. If she had partaken of my flesh,
and cost me the dearest groans of a mother,
I could not have owed her a more rooted
love.   11
　　Laf. 'Twas a good lady, 'twas a good
lady. We may pick a thousand sallets ere
we light on such another herb.
　　Clo. Indeed, sir, she was the sweet-
marjoram of the sallet, or, rather, the herb
of grace.   15
　　Laf. They are not sallet-herbs, you
knave ; they are nose-herbs.
　　Clo. I am no great Nebuchadnezzar, sir ;
I have not much skill in grass.   19
　　Laf. Whether dost thou profess thyself—a
knave or a fool ?
　　Clo. A fool, sir, at a woman's service, and
a knave at a man's.
　　Laf. Your distinction ?
　　Clo. I would cozen the man of his wife,
and do his service.
　　Laf. So you were a knave at his service,
indeed.   25
　　Clo. And I would give his wife my
bauble, sir, to do her service.
　　Laf. I will subscribe for thee ; thou art
both knave and fool.
　　Clo. At your service.   30
　　Laf. No, no, no.
　　Clo. Why, sir, if I cannot serve you, I can
serve as great a prince as you are.
　　Laf. Who's that ? A Frenchman ?   34
　　Clo. Faith, sir, 'a has an English name ;
but his fisnomy is more hotter in France
than there.
　　Laf. What prince is that ?
　　Clo. The Black Prince, sir ; alias, the
Prince of Darkness ; alias, the devil.   39
　　Laf. Hold thee, there's my purse. I give
thee not this to suggest thee from thy
master thou talk'st of ; serve him still.
　　Clo. I am a woodland fellow, sir, that
always loved a great fire ; and the master
I speak of ever keeps a good fire. But, sure,
he is the prince of the world ; let his
nobility remain in's court. I am for the
house with the narrow gate, which I take
to be too little for pomp to enter. Some
that humble themselves may ; but the
many will be too chill and tender ; and
they'll be for the flow'ry way that leads
to the broad gate and the great fire.   49
　　Laf. Go thy ways, I begin to be aweary
of thee ; and I tell thee so before, because
I would not fall out with thee. Go thy
ways ; let my horses be well look'd to,
without any tricks.   53
　　Clo. If I put any tricks upon 'em, sir,
they shall be jades' tricks, which are their
own right by the law of nature.   *[Exit.*
　　Laf. A shrewd knave, and an unhappy.

Count. So 'a is. My lord that's gone made
himself much sport out of him. By his
authority he remains here, which he thinks
is a patent for his sauciness ; and indeed he
has no pace, but runs where he will.   60

Laf. I like him well ; 'tis not amiss. And
I was about to tell you, since I heard of the
good lady's death, and that my lord your
son was upon his return home, I moved the
King my master to speak in the behalf of
my daughter ; which, in the minority of
them both, his Majesty out of a self-
gracious remembrance did first propose.
His Highness hath promis'd me to do it ;
and, to stop up the displeasure he hath
conceived against your son, there is no
fitter matter. How does your ladyship
like it ?   69

Count. With very much content, my lord ;
and I wish it happily effected.

Laf. His Highness comes post from
Marseilles, of as able body as when he
number'd thirty ; 'a will be here to-morrow,
or I am deceiv'd by him that in such
intelligence hath seldom fail'd.   75

Count. It rejoices me that I hope I shall
see him ere I die. I have letters that my
son will be here to-night. I shall beseech
your lordship to remain with me till they
meet together.

Laf. Madam, I was thinking with what
manners I might safely be admitted.   81

Count. You need but plead your honourable privilege.

Laf. Lady, of that I have made a bold
charter ; but, I thank my God, it holds yet.

Re-enter Clown.

Clo. O madam, yonder's my lord your
son with a patch of velvet on's face ;
whether there be a scar under 't or no, the
velvet knows ; but 'tis a goodly patch of
velvet. His left cheek is a cheek of two
pile and a half, but his right cheek is worn
bare.   89

Laf. A scar nobly got, or a noble scar, is
a good liv'ry of honour ; so belike is that.

Clo. But it is your carbonado'd face. 92

Laf. Let us go see your son, I pray you ;
I long to talk with the young noble soldier.

Clo. Faith, there's a dozen of 'em, with
delicate fine hats, and most courteous
feathers, which bow the head and nod at
every man.   [*Exeunt.*

ACT FIVE

SCENE I. *Marseilles. A street.*

Enter HELENA, Widow, *and* DIANA, *with
two* Attendants.

Hel. But this exceeding posting day and
        night
Must wear your spirits low ; we cannot
        help it.

But since you have made the days and
        nights as one,
To wear your gentle limbs in my affairs,
Be bold you do so grow in my requital 5
As nothing can unroot you.

Enter a Gentleman.

                        In happy time !
This man may help me to his Majesty's ear,
If he would spend his power. God save you,
        sir.

Gent. And you.

Hel. Sir, I have seen you in the court of
        France.   10

Gent. I have been sometimes there.

Hel. I do presume, sir, that you are not
        fall'n
From the report that goes upon your
        goodness ;
And therefore, goaded with most sharp
        occasions,
Which lay nice manners by, I put you to 15
The use of your own virtues, for the which
I shall continue thankful.

Gent.   What's your will ?

Hel. That it will please you
To give this poor petition to the King ;
And aid me with that store of power you
        have   20
To come into his presence.

Gent. The King's not here.

Hel.   Not here, sir ?

Gent.   Not indeed.
He hence remov'd last night, and with
        more haste
Than is his use.

Wid.   Lord, how we lose our pains !

Hel. All's Well That Ends Well yet, 25
Though time seem so adverse and means
        unfit.
I do beseech you, whither is he gone ?

Gent. Marry, as I take it, to Rousillon ;
Whither I am going.

Hel.   I do beseech you, sir,
Since you are like to see the King before me,
Commend the paper to his gracious hand ;
Which I presume shall render you no
        blame,   32
But rather make you thank your pains
        for it.
I will come after you with what good speed
Our means will make us means.

Gent.   This I'll do for you. 35

Hel. And you shall find yourself to be
        well thank'd,
Whate'er falls more. We must to horse
        again ;
Go, go, provide.   [*Exeunt.*

SCENE II. *Rousillon. The inner court of
the Count's palace.*

Enter Clown *and* PAROLLES.

Par. Good Monsieur Lavache, give my
Lord Lafeu this letter. I have ere now, sir,

been better known to you, when I have held familiarity with fresher clothes; but I am now, sir, muddied in Fortune's mood, and smell somewhat strong of her strong displeasure.   5

Clo. Truly, Fortune's displeasure is but sluttish, if it smell so strongly as thou speak'st of. I will henceforth eat no fish of Fortune's butt'ring. Prithee, allow the wind.

Par. Nay, you need not to stop your nose, sir; I spake but by a metaphor.   10

Clo. Indeed, sir, if your metaphor stink, I will stop my nose; or against any man's metaphor. Prithee, get thee further.   13

Par. Pray you, sir, deliver me this paper.

Clo. Foh! prithee stand away. A paper from Fortune's close-stool to give to a nobleman! Look here he comes himself.

Enter LAFEU.

Here is a pur of Fortune's, sir, or of Fortune's cat, but not a musk-cat, that has fall'n into the unclean fishpond of her displeasure, and, as he says, is muddied withal. Pray you, sir, use the carp as you may; for he looks like a poor, decayed, ingenious, foolish, rascally knave. I do pity his distress in my similes of comfort, and leave him to your lordship.   [*Exit.*

Par. My lord, I am a man whom Fortune hath cruelly scratch'd.   26

Laf. And what would you have me to do? 'Tis too late to pare her nails now. Wherein have you played the knave with Fortune, that she should scratch you, who of herself is a good lady and would not have knaves thrive long under her? There's a cardecue for you. Let the justices make you and Fortune friends; I am for other business.

Par. I beseech your honour to hear me one single word.   35

Laf. You beg a single penny more; come, you shall ha't; save your word.

Par. My name, my good lord, is Parolles.

Laf. You beg more than word then. Cox my passion! give me your hand. How does your drum?   40

Par. O my good lord, you were the first that found me.

Laf. Was I, in sooth? And I was the first that lost thee.

Par. It lies in you, my lord, to bring me in some grace, for you did bring me out. 45

Laf. Out upon thee, knave! Dost thou put upon me at once both the office of God and the devil? One brings thee in grace, and the other brings thee out. [*Trumpets sound*] The King's coming; I know by his trumpets. Sirrah, inquire further after me; I had talk of you last night. Though you are a fool and a knave, you shall eat. Go to; follow.   51

Par. I praise God for you.   [*Exeunt.*

SCENE III. *Rousillon. The Count's palace.*

Flourish. Enter KING, COUNTESS, LAFEU, *the two* French Lords, *with* Attendants.

King. We lost a jewel of her, and our
       esteem
Was made much poorer by it; but your
       son,
As mad in folly, lack'd the sense to know
Her estimation home.

Count.   'Tis past, my liege;
And I beseech your Majesty to make it   5
Natural rebellion, done i' th' blaze of youth,
When oil and fire, too strong for reason's
       force,
O'erbears it and burns on.

King.   My honour'd lady,
I have forgiven and forgotten all;
Though my revenges were high bent upon
       him   10
And watch'd the time to shoot.

Laf.   This I must say—
But first, I beg my pardon: the young lord
Did to his Majesty, his mother, and his
       lady,
Offence of mighty note; but to himself
The greatest wrong of all. He lost a wife 15
Whose beauty did astonish the survey
Of richest eyes; whose words all ears took
       captive;
Whose dear perfection hearts that scorn'd
       to serve
Humbly call'd mistress.

King.   Praising what is lost
Makes the remembrance dear. Well, call
       him hither;   20
We are reconcil'd, and the first view shall
       kill
All repetition. Let him not ask our pardon;
The nature of his great offence is dead,
And deeper than oblivion do we bury   24
Th' incensing relics of it; let him approach,
A stranger, no offender; and inform him
So 'tis our will he should.

Gent.   I shall, my liege.
                      [*Exit Gentleman.*

King. What says he to your daughter?
       Have you spoke?

Laf. All that he is hath reference to your
       Highness.

King. Then shall we have a match. I
       have letters sent me   30
That sets him high in fame.

Enter BERTRAM.

Laf.   He looks well on't.

King. I am not a day of season,
For thou mayst see a sunshine and a hail
In me at once. But to the brightest beams
Distracted clouds give way; so stand thou
       forth;   35
The time is fair again.

Ber.   My high-repented blames,
Dear sovereign, pardon to me.

King.　　　　　　　All is whole;
Not one word more of the consumed time.
Let's take the instant by the forward top;
For we are old, and on our quick'st decrees
Th' inaudible and noiseless foot of Time　41
Steals ere we can effect them.　You re-
　　member
The daughter of this lord?
　Ber. Admiringly, my liege.　At first
I stuck my choice upon her, ere my heart
Durst make too bold a herald of my
　　tongue;　　　　　　　　　　46
Where the impression of mine eye infixing,
Contempt his scornful perspective did lend
　　me,
Which warp'd the line of every other
　　favour,　　　　　　　　　　49
Scorn'd a fair colour or express'd it stol'n,
Extended or contracted all proportions
To a most hideous object.　Thence it came
That she whom all men prais'd, and whom
　　myself,
Since I have lost, have lov'd, was in mine
　　eye
The dust that did offend it.
　King.　　　　　　Well excus'd.　55
That thou didst love her, strikes some
　　scores away
From the great compt; but love that comes
　　too late,
Like a remorseful pardon slowly carried,
To the great sender turns a sour offence,
Crying 'That's good that's gone'.　Our
　　rash faults　　　　　　　　60
Make trivial price of serious things we have,
Not knowing them until we know their
　　grave.
Oft our displeasures, to ourselves unjust,
Destroy our friends, and after weep their
　　dust;
Our own love waking cries to see what's
　　done,　　　　　　　　　　65
While shameful hate sleeps out the after-
　　noon.
Be this sweet Helen's knell.　And now for-
　　get her.
Send forth your amorous token for fair
　　Maudlin.
The main consents are had; and here we'll
　　stay　　　　　　　　　　69
To see our widower's second marriage-day.
　Count. Which better than the first, O dear
　　heaven, bless!
Or, ere they meet, in me, O nature, cesse!
　Laf. Come on, my son, in whom my
　　house's name
Must be digested; give a favour from you,
To sparkle in the spirits of my daughter,　75
That she may quickly come.
　　　　　　[*Bertram gives a ring.*
　　　　　　By my old beard,
And ev'ry hair that's on't, Helen, that's
　　dead,
Was a sweet creature; such a ring as this,

The last that e'er I took her leave at court,
I saw upon her finger.
　Ber.　　　　　　Hers it was not.　80
　King. Now, pray you, let me see it; for
　　mine eye,
While I was speaking, oft was fasten'd to't.
This ring was mine; and when I gave it
　　Helen
I bade her, if her fortunes ever stood
Necessitied to help, that by this token　85
I would relieve her.　Had you that craft to
　　reave her
Of what should stead her most?
　Ber.　　　　　　My gracious sovereign,
Howe'er it pleases you to take it so,
The ring was never hers.
　Count.　　　　　Son, on my life,
I have seen her wear it; and she reckon'd it
At her life's rate.
　Laf.　　　I am sure I saw her wear it.
　Ber. You are deceiv'd, my lord; she
　　never saw it.　　　　　　　92
In Florence was it from a casement thrown
　　me,
Wrapp'd in a paper, which contain'd the
　　name
Of her that threw it.　Noble she was, and
　　thought　　　　　　　　95
I stood engag'd; but when I had subscrib'd
To mine own fortune, and inform'd her
　　fully
I could not answer in that course of honour
As she had made the overture, she ceas'd,
In heavy satisfaction, and would never　100
Receive the ring again.
　King.　　　　　Plutus himself,
That knows the tinct and multiplying
　　med'cine,
Hath not in nature's mystery more science
Than I have in this ring.　'Twas mine, 'twas
　　Helen's,　　　　　　　　104
Whoever gave it you.　Then, if you know
That you are well acquainted with yourself,
Confess 'twas hers, and by what rough
　　enforcement
You got it from her.　She call'd the saints
　　to surety
That she would never put it from her finger
Unless she gave it to yourself in bed—　110
Where you have never come—or sent it us
Upon her great disaster.
　Ber.　　　　　She never saw it.
　King. Thou speak'st it falsely, as I love
　　mine honour;
And mak'st conjectural fears to come into
　　me
Which I would fain shut out.　If it should
　　prove　　　　　　　　　115
That thou art so inhuman—'twill not
　　prove so.
And yet I know not—thou didst hate her
　　deadly,
And she is dead; which nothing, but to
　　close　　　　　　　　　118

345

Her eyes myself, could win me to believe
More than to see this ring. Take him away.
                    [*Guards seize Bertram.*
My fore-past proofs, howe'er the matter
    fall,
Shall tax my fears of little vanity,
Having vainly fear'd too little. Away with
    him.   123
We'll sift this matter further.
    Ber.   If you shall prove
This ring was ever hers, you shall as easy
Prove that I husbanded her bed in Flor-
    ence,   126
Where she yet never was. [*Exit, guarded.*
    King. I am wrapp'd in dismal thinkings.

            Enter a Gentleman.

    Gent.   Gracious sovereign,
Whether I have been to blame or no, I
    know not :
Here's a petition from a Florentine,   130
Who hath, for four or five removes, come
    short
To tender it herself. I undertook it,
Vanquish'd thereto by the fair grace and
    speech
Of the poor suppliant, who by this, I know,
Is here attending ; her business looks in her
With an importing visage ; and she told me
In a sweet verbal brief it did concern
Your Highness with herself.   138
    King. [*Reads the letter*] ' Upon his many
protestations to marry me when his wife
was dead, I blush to say it, he won me.
Now is the Count Rousillon a widower ;
his vows are forfeited to me, and my
honour's paid to him. He stole from
Florence, taking no leave, and I follow him
to his country for justice. Grant it me, O
King ! in you it best lies ; otherwise a
seducer flourishes, and a poor maid is
undone.   144
                  DIANA CAPILET.'
    Laf. I will buy me a son-in-law in a fair,
and toll for this. I'll none of him.
    King. The heavens have thought well on
    thee, Lafeu,
To bring forth this discov'ry. Seek these
    suitors.
Go speedily, and bring again the Count. 150
                 [*Exeunt Attendants.*
I am afeard the life of Helen, lady,
Was foully snatch'd.
    Count.   Now, justice on the doers !

        Enter BERTRAM, *guarded.*

    King. I wonder, sir, sith wives are
    monsters to you,
And that you fly them as you swear them
    lordship,   154
Yet you desire to marry.

     Enter Widow *and* DIANA.

               What woman's that ?

    Dia. I am, my lord, a wretched Floren-
    tine,
Derived from the ancient Capilet.
My suit, as I do understand, you know,
And therefore know how far I may be
    pitied.
    Wid. I am her mother, sir, whose age and
    honour   160
Both suffer under this complaint we bring,
And both shall cease, without your remedy.
    King. Come hither, Count ; do you know
    these women ?
    Ber. My lord, I neither can nor will deny
But that I know them. Do they charge me
    further ?   165
    Dia. Why do you look so strange upon
    your wife.
    Ber. She's none of mine, my lord.
    Dia.   If you shall marry,
You give away this hand, and that is mine ;
You give away heaven's vows, and those
    are mine ;
You give away myself, which is known
    mine ;   170
For I by vow am so embodied yours
That she which marries you must marry me,
Either both or none.
    Laf. [*To Bertram*] Your reputation comes
too short for my daughter ; you are no
husband for her.   175
    Ber. My lord, this is a fond and desp'rate
    creature
Whom sometime I have laugh'd with. Let
    your Highness
Lay a more noble thought upon mine
    honour
Than for to think that I would sink it here.
    King. Sir, for my thoughts, you have
    them ill to friend
Till your deeds gain them. Fairer prove
    your honour   181
Than in my thought it lies !
    Dia.   Good my lord,
Ask him upon his oath if he does think
He had not my virginity.   184
    King. What say'st thou to her ?
    Ber.   She's impudent, my lord,
And was a common gamester to the camp.
    Dia. He does me wrong, my lord ; if I
    were so
He might have bought me at a common
    price.
Do not believe him. O, behold this ring,
Whose high respect and rich validity   190
Did lack a parallel ; yet, for all that,
He gave it to a commoner o' th' camp,
If I be one.
    Count.   He blushes, and 'tis it.
Of six preceding ancestors, that gem   194
Conferr'd by testament to th' sequent issue,
Hath it been ow'd and worn. This is his
    wife :
That ring's a thousand proofs.
    King.   Methought you said

You saw one here in court could witness it.
  Dia. I did, my lord, but loath am to
    produce   199
So bad an instrument ; his name's Parolles.
  Laf. I saw the man to-day, if man he be.
  King. Find him, and bring him hither.
               [*Exit an Attendant.*
  Ber.   What of him ?
He's quoted for a most perfidious slave,
With all the spots o' th' world tax'd and
    debauch'd,   204
Whose nature sickens but to speak a truth.
Am I or that or this for what he'll utter
That will speak anything ?
  King.   She hath that ring of yours.
  Ber. I think she has. Certain it is I lik'd
    her,
And boarded her i' th' wanton way of
    youth.
She knew her distance, and did angle for
    me,   210
Madding my eagerness with her restraint,
As all impediments in fancy's course
Are motives of more fancy ; and, in fine,
Her infinite cunning with her modern grace
Subdu'd me to her rate. She got the ring ;
And I had that which any inferior might 216
At market-price have bought.
  Dia.   I must be patient.
You that have turn'd off a first so noble
    wife
May justly diet me. I pray you yet—
Since you lack virtue, I will lose a hus-
    band—
Send for your ring, I will return it home,
And give me mine again.
  Ber.   I have it not. 222
  King. What ring was yours, I pray you ?
  Dia.   Sir, much like
The same upon your finger.
  King. Know you this ring ? This ring
    was his of late.
  Dia. And this was it I gave him, being
    abed.   226
  King. The story, then, goes false you
    threw it him
Out of a casement.
  Dia.   I have spoke the truth.

       Enter PAROLLES.

  Ber. My lord, I do confess the ring was
    hers.
  King. You boggle shrewdly ; every
    feather starts you.
Is this the man you speak of ?
  Dia.   Ay, my lord. 231
  King. Tell me, sirrah—but tell me true I
    charge you,
Not fearing the displeasure of your master,
Which, on your just proceeding, I'll keep
    off—
By him and by this woman here what know
    you ?   235
  Par. So please your Majesty, my master

hath been an honourable gentleman ; tricks
he hath had in him, which gentlemen have.
  King. Come, come, to th' purpose. Did
he love this woman ?   240
  Par. Faith, sir, he did love her ; but
how ?
  King. How, I pray you ?
  Par. He did love her, sir, as a gentleman
loves a woman.
  King. How is that ?
  Par. He lov'd her, sir, and lov'd her
not.   245
  King. As thou art a knave and no knave.
What an equivocal companion is this !
  Par. I am a poor man, and at your
Majesty's command.
  Laf. He's a good drum, my lord, but a
naughty orator.
  Dia. Do you know he promis'd me
marriage ?   250
  Par. Faith, I know more than I'll speak.
  King. But wilt thou not speak all thou
know'st ?
  Par. Yes, so please your Majesty. I did
go between them, as I said ; but more
than that, he loved her—for indeed he was
mad for her, and talk'd of Satan, and of
Limbo, and of Furies, and I know not
what. Yet I was in that credit with them
at that time that I knew of their going to
bed ; and of other motions, as promising
her marriage, and things which would
derive me ill will to speak of ; therefore
I will not speak what I know. 260
  King. Thou hast spoken all already,
unless thou canst say they are married ;
but thou art too fine in thy evidence ;
therefore stand aside.
This ring, you say, was yours ?
  Dia.   Ay, my good lord.
  King. Where did you buy it ? Or who
    gave it you ?
  Dia. It was not given me, nor I did not
    buy it.   266
  King. Who lent it you ?
  Dia.   It was not lent me neither.
  King. Where did you find it then ?
  Dia.   I found it not.
  King. If it were yours by none of all
    these ways,
How could you give it him ?
  Dia.   I never gave it him.
  Laf. This woman's an easy glove, my
lord ; she goes off and on at pleasure. 272
  King. This ring was mine, I gave it his
    first wife.
  Dia. It might be yours or hers, for aught
    I know.
  King. Take her away, I do not like her
    now ;   275
To prison with her. And away with him.
Unless thou tell'st me where thou hadst
    this ring,
Thou diest within this hour.

Dia.   I'll never tell you.
King. Take her away.
Dia.   I'll put in bail, my liege.
King. I think thee now some common
    customer.   280
Dia. By Jove, if ever I knew man, 'twas
    you.
King. Wherefore hast thou accus'd him
    all this while ?
Dia. Because he's guilty, and he is not
    guilty.
He knows I am no maid, and he'll swear
    to't :   284
I'll swear I am a maid, and he knows not.
Great King, I am no strumpet, by my
    life ;
I am either maid, or else this old man's
    wife.   [*Pointing to Lafeu.*
King. She does abuse our ears ; to prison
    with her.   288
Dia. Good mother, fetch my bail. Stay,
    royal sir ;   [*Exit Widow.*
The jeweller that owes the ring is sent
    for,
And he shall surety me. But for this lord
Who hath abus'd me as he knows himself,
Though yet he never harm'd me, here I
    quit him.   293
He knows himself my bed he hath defil'd ;
And at that time he got his wife with child.
Dead though she be, she feels her young one
    kick :
So there's my riddle : one that's dead is
    quick—   297
And now behold the meaning.

Re-enter Widow *with* HELENA.

King.   Is there no exorcist
Beguiles the truer office of mine eyes ?
Is't real that I see ?
Hel.   No, my good lord ;   300
'Tis but the shadow of a wife you see,
The name and not the thing.
Ber.   Both, both ; O, pardon !
Hel. O, my good lord, when I was like
    this maid,

I found you wondrous kind. There is your
    ring,
And, look you, here's your letter. This it
    says :   305
' When from my finger you can get this ring,
And are by me with child,' &c. This is done.
Will you be mine now you are doubly won ?
Ber. If she, my liege, can make me know
    this clearly,
I'll love her dearly, ever, ever dearly.   310
Hel. If it appear not plain, and prove
    untrue,
Deadly divorce step between me and you !
O my dear mother, do I see you living ?
Laf. Mine eyes smell onions ; I shall weep
anon. [*To Parolles*] Good Tom Drum, lend
me a handkercher. So, I thank thee. Wait
on me home, I'll make sport with thee ;
let thy curtsies alone, they are scurvy ones.
King. Let us from point to point this
    story know,
To make the even truth in pleasure flow.
[*To Diana*] If thou beest yet a fresh un-
    cropped flower,   320
Choose thou thy husband, and I'll pay thy
    dower ;
For I can guess that by thy honest aid
Thou kept'st a wife herself, thyself a
    maid.—
Of that and all the progress, more and less,
Resolvedly more leisure shall express.   325
All yet seems well ; and if it end so meet,
The bitter past, more welcome is the sweet.
                    [*Flourish.*

EPILOGUE

The King's a beggar, now the play is done.
All is well ended if this suit be won,
That you express content ; which we will
    pay
With strife to please you, day exceeding
    day.
Ours be your patience then, and yours our
    parts ;   5
Your gentle hands lend us, and take our
    hearts.   [*Exeunt omnes.*

TWELFTH NIGHT

DRAMATIS PERSONÆ

ORSINO, *Duke of Illyria.*
SEBASTIAN, *brother of Viola.*
ANTONIO, *a sea captain, friend of Sebastian.*
A Sea Captain, *friend of Viola.*
VALENTINE, } *gentlemen attending on the*
CURIO, } *Duke.*
SIR TOBY BELCH, *uncle of Olivia.*
SIR ANDREW AGUECHEEK.
MALVOLIO, *steward to Olivia.*

FABIAN, } *servants to Olivia.*
FESTE, *a clown,* }
OLIVIA, *a rich countess.*
VIOLA, *sister of Sebastian.*
MARIA, *Olivia's waiting woman.*

Lords, Priest, Sailors, Officers, Musicians,
and Attendants.

THE SCENE: *A city in Illyria; and the sea-coast near it.*

ACT ONE

SCENE I. *The Duke's palace.*

Enter ORSINO, *Duke of Illyria,* CURIO, *and other Lords;* Musicians *attending.*

Duke. If music be the food of love, play on,
Give me excess of it, that, surfeiting,
The appetite may sicken and so die.
That strain again! It had a dying fall;
O, it came o'er my ear like the sweet sound
That breathes upon a bank of violets, 6
Stealing and giving odour! Enough, no more;
'Tis not so sweet now as it was before.
O spirit of love, how quick and fresh art thou!
That, notwithstanding thy capacity 10
Receiveth as the sea, nought enters there,
Of what validity and pitch soe'er,
But falls into abatement and low price
Even in a minute. So full of shapes is fancy,
That it alone is high fantastical. 15
Cur. Will you go hunt, my lord?
Duke.   What, Curio?
Cur. The hart.
Duke. Why so I do, the noblest that I have.
O, when mine eyes did see Olivia first, 19
Methought she purg'd the air of pestilence!
That instant was I turn'd into a hart,
And my desires, like fell and cruel hounds,
E'er since pursue me.

Enter VALENTINE.

            How now! what news from her?
Val. So please my lord, I might not be admitted,
But from her handmaid do return this answer 25
The element itself, till seven years' heat,
Shall not behold her face at ample view;
But like a cloistress she will veiled walk,
And water once a day her chamber round

With eye-offending brine; all this to season 30
A brother's dead love, which she would keep fresh
And lasting in her sad remembrance.
Duke. O, she that hath a heart of that fine frame
To pay this debt of love but to a brother,
How will she love when the rich golden shaft 35
Hath kill'd the flock of all affections else
That live in her; when liver, brain, and heart,
These sovereign thrones, are all supplied and fill'd, 38
Her sweet perfections, with one self king!
Away before me to sweet beds of flow'rs:
Love-thoughts lie rich when canopied with bow'rs. [*Exeunt.*

SCENE II. *The sea-coast.*

Enter VIOLA, *a* Captain, *and* Sailors.

Vio. What country, friends, is this?
Cap. This is Illyria, lady.
Vio. And what should I do in Illyria?
My brother he is in Elysium.
Perchance he is not drown'd—what think you, sailors? 5
Cap. It is perchance that you yourself were saved.
Vio. O my poor brother! and so perchance may he be.
Cap. True, madam, and, to comfort you with chance,
Assure yourself, after our ship did split,
When you, and those poor number saved with you, 10
Hung on our driving boat, I saw your brother,
Most provident in peril, bind himself—
Courage and hope both teaching him the practice—
To a strong mast that liv'd upon the sea;
Where, like Arion on the dolphin's back, 15

349

I saw him hold acquaintance with the waves
So long as I could see.
    Vio. For saying so, there's gold.
Mine own escape unfoldeth to my hope,
Whereto thy speech serves for authority,   20
The like of him.   Know'st thou this country ?
    Cap. Ay, madam, well ; for I was bred and born
Not three hours' travel from this very place.
    Vio. Who governs here ?   24
    Cap. A noble duke, in nature as in name.
    Vio. What is his name ?
    Cap. Orsino.
    Vio. Orsino ! I have heard my father name him.
He was a bachelor then.   29
    Cap. And so is now, or was so very late ;
For but a month ago I went from hence,
And then 'twas fresh in murmur—as, you know,
What great ones do the less will prattle of—
That he did seek the love of fair Olivia.
    Vio. What's she ?   35
    Cap. A virtuous maid, the daughter of a count
That died some twelvemonth since, then leaving her
In the protection of his son, her brother,
Who shortly also died ; for whose dear love,
They say, she hath abjur'd the company   40
And sight of men.
    Vio.   O that I serv'd that lady,
And might not be delivered to the world,
Till I had made mine own occasion mellow,
What my estate is !
    Cap.   That were hard to compass,
Because she will admit no kind of suit—   45
No, not the Duke's.
    Vio. There is a fair behaviour in thee, Captain ;
And though that nature with a beauteous wall
Doth oft close in pollution, yet of thee
I will believe thou hast a mind that suits   50
With this thy fair and outward character.
I prithee, and I'll pay thee bounteously,
Conceal me what I am, and be my aid   53
For such disguise as haply shall become
The form of my intent. I'll serve this duke :
Thou shalt present me as an eunuch to him ;
It may be worth thy pains, for I can sing
And speak to him in many sorts of music,
That will allow me very worth his service.
What else may hap to time I will commit ;
Only shape thou thy silence to my wit.   61
    Cap. Be you his eunuch and your mute I'll be ;
When my tongue blabs, then let mine eyes not see.
    Vio. I thank thee. Lead me on. [*Exeunt.*

SCENE III. *Olivia's house.*

Enter SIR TOBY BELCH *and* MARIA.

    Sir To. What a plague means my niece to take the death of her brother thus ? I am sure care's an enemy to life.
    Mar. By my troth, Sir Toby, you must come in earlier o' nights ; your cousin, my lady, takes great exceptions to your ill hours.   5
    Sir To. Why, let her except before excepted.
    Mar. Ay, but you must confine yourself within the modest limits of order.   8
    Sir To. Confine ! I'll confine myself no finer than I am. These clothes are good enough to drink in, and so be these boots too ; an they be not, let them hang themselves in their own straps.   12
    Mar. That quaffing and drinking will undo you ; I heard my lady talk of it yesterday, and of a foolish knight that you brought in one night here to be her wooer.
    Sir To. Who ? Sir Andrew Aguecheek ?
    Mar. Ay, he.   17
    Sir To. He's as tall a man as any's in Illyria.
    Mar. What's that to th' purpose ?
    Sir To. Why, he has three thousand ducats a year.   20
    Mar. Ay, but he'll have but a year in all these ducats ; he's a very fool and a prodigal.   22
    Sir To. Fie that you'll say so ! He plays o' th' viol-de-gamboys, and speaks three or four languages word for word without book, and hath all the good gifts of nature.
    Mar. He hath indeed, almost natural ; for, besides that he's a fool, he's a great quarreller ; and but that he hath the gift of a coward to allay the gust he hath in quarrelling, 'tis thought among the prudent he would quickly have the gift of a grave.
    Sir To. By this hand, they are scoundrels and substractors that say so of him. Who are they ?   32
    Mar. They that add, moreover, he's drunk nightly in your company.   34
    Sir To. With drinking healths to my niece ; I'll drink to her as long as there is a passage in my throat and drink in Illyria. He's a coward and a coystrill that will not drink to my niece till his brains turn o' th' toe like a parish-top. What, wench ! Castiliano vulgo ! for here comes Sir Andrew Agueface.   40

Enter SIR ANDREW AGUECHEEK.

    Sir And. Sir Toby Belch ! How now, Sir Toby Belch !
    Sir To. Sweet Sir Andrew !
    Sir And. Bless you, fair shrew.

Mar. And you too, sir.

Sir To. Accost, Sir Andrew, accost.　45

Sir And. What's that?

Sir To. My niece's chambermaid.

Sir And. Good Mistress Accost, I desire better acquaintance.

Mar. My name is Mary, sir.　50

Sir And. Good Mistress Mary Accost—

Sir To. You mistake, knight. 'Accost' is front her, board her, woo her, assail her.

Sir And. By my troth, I would not undertake her in this company. Is that the meaning of 'accost'?　55

Mar. Fare you well, gentlemen.

Sir To. An thou let part so, Sir Andrew, would thou mightst never draw sword again!

Sir And. An you part so, mistress, I would I might never draw sword again. Fair lady, do you think you have fools in hand?　61

Mar. Sir, I have not you by th' hand.

Sir And. Marry, but you shall have; and here's my hand.

Mar. Now, sir, thought is free. I pray you, bring your hand to th' butt'ry-bar and let it drink.　66

Sir And. Wherefore, sweetheart? What's your metaphor?

Mar. It's dry, sir.

Sir And. Why, I think so; I am not such an ass but I can keep my hand dry. But what's your jest?　71

Mar. A dry jest, sir.

Sir And. Are you full of them?

Mar. Ay, sir, I have them at my fingers' ends; marry, now I let go your hand, I am barren. [*Exit Maria.*

Sir To. O knight, thou lack'st a cup of canary! When did I see thee so put down?

Sir And. Never in your life, I think; unless you see canary put me down. Methinks sometimes I have no more wit than a Christian or an ordinary man has; but I am a great eater of beef, and I believe that does harm to my wit.　81

Sir To. No question.

Sir And. An I thought that, I'd forswear it. I'll ride home to-morrow, Sir Toby.

Sir To. Pourquoi, my dear knight?　85

Sir And. What is 'pourquoi'—do or not do? I would I had bestowed that time in the tongues that I have in fencing, dancing, and bear-baiting. O, had I but followed the arts!

Sir To. Then hadst thou had an excellent head of hair.　91

Sir And. Why, would that have mended my hair?

Sir To. Past question; for thou seest it will not curl by nature.

Sir And. But it becomes me well enough, does't not?　95

Sir To. Excellent; it hangs like flax on a distaff, and I hope to see a huswife take thee between her legs and spin it off.　98

Sir And. Faith, I'll home to-morrow, Sir Toby. Your niece will not be seen, or if she be, it's four to one she'll none of me; the Count himself here hard by woos her.

Sir To. She'll none o' th' Count; she'll not match above her degree, neither in estate, years, nor wit; I have heard her swear't. Tut, there's life in't, man.　104

Sir And. I'll stay a month longer. I am a fellow o' th' strangest mind i' th' world; I delight in masques and revels sometimes altogether.

Sir To. Art thou good at these kick-shawses, knight?　108

Sir And. As any man in Illyria, whatsoever he be, under the degree of my betters; and yet I will not compare with an old man.　111

Sir To. What is thy excellence in a galliard, knight?

Sir And. Faith, I can cut a caper.

Sir To. And I can cut the mutton to't.

Sir And. And I think I have the back-trick simply as strong as any man in Illyria.　116

Sir To. Wherefore are these things hid? Wherefore have these gifts a curtain before 'em? Are they like to take dust, like Mistress Mall's picture? Why dost thou not go to church in a galliard and come home in a coranto? My very walk should be a jig; I would not so much as make water but in a sink-a-pace. What dost thou mean? Is it a world to hide virtues in? I did think, by the excellent constitution of thy leg, it was form'd under the star of a galliard.　125

Sir And. Ay, 'tis strong, and it does indifferent well in a flame-colour'd stock. Shall we set about some revels?

Sir To. What shall we do else? Were we not born under Taurus?

Sir And. Taurus? That's sides and heart.　130

Sir To. No, sir; it is legs and thighs. Let me see thee caper. Ha, higher! Ha, ha, excellent!　[*Exeunt.*

SCENE IV. *The Duke's palace.*

Enter VALENTINE, *and* VIOLA *in man's attire.*

Val. If the Duke continue these favours towards you, Cesario, you are like to be much advanc'd; he hath known you but three days, and already you are no stranger.

Vio. You either fear his humour or my negligence, that you call in question the continuance of his love. Is he inconstant, sir, in his favours?　6

Val. No, believe me.

Enter DUKE, CURIO, *and* Attendants.

Vio. I thank you. Here comes the Count.
Duke. Who saw Cesario, ho ?
Vio. On your attendance, my lord, here.
Duke. Stand you awhile aloof. Cesario,
Thou know'st no less but all ; I have un-
clasp'd 12
To thee the book even of my secret soul.
Therefore, good youth, address thy gait
unto her ;
Be not denied access, stand at her doors, 15
And tell them there thy fixed foot shall
grow
Till thou have audience.
Vio. Sure, my noble lord,
If she be so abandon'd to her sorrow
As it is spoke, she never will admit me.
Duke. Be clamorous and leap all civil
bounds, 20
Rather than make unprofited return.
Vio. Say I do speak with her, my lord,
what then ?
Duke. O, then unfold the passion of my
love,
Surprise her with discourse of my dear
faith ! 24
It shall become thee well to act my woes :
She will attend it better in thy youth
Than in a nuncio's of more grave aspect.
Vio. I think not so, my lord.
Duke. Dear lad, believe it,
For they shall yet belie thy happy years
That say thou art a man : Diana's lip 30
Is not more smooth and rubious ; thy small
pipe
Is as the maiden's organ, shrill and sound,
And all is semblative a woman's part.
I know thy constellation is right apt
For this affair. Some four or five attend
him— 35
All, if you will, for I myself am best
When least in company. Prosper well in
this,
And thou shalt live as freely as thy lord
To call his fortunes thine.
Vio. I'll do my best
To woo your lady. [*Aside*] Yet, a barful
strife ! 40
Whoe'er I woo, myself would be his wife.

SCENE V. *Olivia's house.*

Enter MARIA *and* Clown.

Mar. Nay, either tell me where thou hast
been, or I will not open my lips so wide as
a bristle may enter in way of thy excuse ;
my lady will hang thee for thy absence.
Clo. Let her hang me. He that is well
hang'd in this world needs to fear no
colours. 5
Mar. Make that good.
Clo. He shall see none to fear.

Mar. A good lenten answer. I can tell
thee where that saying was born, of ' I fear
no colours'.
Clo. Where, good Mistress Mary ? 10
Mar. In the wars ; and that may you be
bold to say in your foolery.
Clo. Well, God give them wisdom that
have it ; and those that are fools, let them
use their talents. 14
Mar. Yet you will be hang'd for being so
long absent ; or to be turn'd away—is not
that as good as a hanging to you ?
Clo. Many a good hanging prevents a bad
marriage ; and for turning away, let
summer bear it out.
Mar. You are resolute, then ? 20
Clo. Not so, neither ; but I am resolv'd
on two points.
Mar. That if one break, the other will
hold ; or if both break, your gaskins fall.
Clo. Apt, in good faith, very apt ! Well,
go thy way ; if Sir Toby would leave
drinking, thou wert as witty a piece of
Eve's flesh as any in Illyria. 26
Mar. Peace, you rogue, no more o' that.
Here comes my lady. Make your excuse
wisely, you were best. [*Exit.*

Enter OLIVIA *and* MALVOLIO.

Clo. Wit, an't be thy will, put me into
good fooling ! Those wits that think they
have thee do very oft prove fools ; and I
that am sure I lack thee may pass for a
wise man. For what says Quinapalus ?
' Better a witty fool than a foolish wit.'
God bless thee, lady !
Oli. Take the fool away. 35
Clo. Do you not hear, fellows ? Take
away the lady.
Oli. Go to, y'are a dry fool ; I'll no
more of you. Besides, you grow dishonest.
Clo. Two faults, madonna, that drink
and good counsel will amend ; for give the
dry fool drink, then is the fool not dry.
Bid the dishonest man mend himself : if
he mend, he is no longer dishonest ; if he
cannot, let the botcher mend him. Anything
that's mended is but patch'd ; virtue that
transgresses is but patch'd with sin, and sin
that amends is but patch'd with virtue.
If that this simple syllogism will serve, so ;
if it will not, what remedy ? As there is
no true cuckold but calamity, so beauty's
a flower. The lady bade take away the fool ;
therefore, I say again, take her away.
Oli. Sir, I bade them take away you. 49
Clo. Misprision in the highest degree !
Lady, ' Cucullus non facit monachum ' ;
that's as much to say as I wear not motley
in my brain. Good madonna, give me
leave to prove you a fool.
Oli. Can you do it ?
Clo. Dexteriously, good madonna. 55
Oli. Make your proof.

Clo. I must catechize you for it, madonna. Good my mouse of virtue, answer me.

Oli. Well, sir, for want of other idleness, I'll bide your proof.   60

Clo. Good madonna, why mourn'st thou?

Oli. Good fool, for my brother's death.

Clo. I think his soul is in hell, madonna.

Oli. I know his soul is in heaven, fool. 64

Clo. The more fool, madonna, to mourn for your brother's soul being in heaven. Take away the fool, gentlemen.

Oli. What think you of this fool, Malvolio? Doth he not mend?   69

Mal. Yes, and shall do, till the pangs of death shake him. Infirmity, that decays the wise, doth ever make the better fool.

Clo. God send you, sir, a speedy infirmity, for the better increasing your folly! Sir Toby will be sworn that I am no fox; but he will not pass his word for twopence that you are no fool.   76

Oli. How say you to that, Malvolio?

Mal. I marvel your ladyship takes delight in such a barren rascal; I saw him put down the other day with an ordinary fool that has no more brain than a stone. Look you now, he's out of his guard already; unless you laugh and minister occasion to him, he is gagg'd. I protest I take these wise men that crow so at these set kind of fools no better than the fools' zanies.   84

Oli. O, you are sick of self-love, Malvolio, and taste with a distemper'd appetite. To be generous, guiltless, and of free disposition, is to take those things for bird-bolts that you deem cannon bullets. There is no slander in an allow'd fool, though he do nothing but rail; nor no railing in a known discreet man, though he do nothing but reprove.   90

Clo. Now Mercury endue thee with leasing, for thou speak'st well of fools!

Re-enter MARIA.

Mar. Madam, there is at the gate a young gentleman much desires to speak with you.

Oli. From the Count Orsino, is it?   95

Mar. I know not, madam; 'tis a fair young man, and well attended.

Oli. Who of my people hold him in delay?

Mar. Sir Toby, madam, your kinsman.

Oli. Fetch him off, I pray you; he speaks nothing but madman. Fie on him! [*Exit Maria*] Go you, Malvolio: if it be a suit from the Count, I am sick, or not at home—what you will to dismiss it. [*Exit Malvolio*] Now you see, sir, how your fooling grows old, and people dislike it. 104

Clo. Thou hast spoke for us, madonna, as if thy eldest son should be a fool; whose skull Jove cram with brains! For—

here he comes—one of thy kin has a most weak pia mater.

Enter SIR TOBY.

Oli. By mine honour, half drunk! What is he at the gate, cousin?   110

Sir To. A gentleman.

Oli. A gentleman! What gentleman?

Sir To. 'Tis a gentleman here. [*Hiccups*] A plague o' these pickle-herring! How now, sot!

Clo. Good Sir Toby!   115

Oli. Cousin, cousin, how have you come so early by this lethargy?

Sir To. Lechery! I defy lechery. There's one at the gate.

Oli. Ay, marry; what is he?   119

Sir To. Let him be the devil an he will, I care not; give me faith, say I. Well, it's all one.   [*Exit.*

Oli. What's a drunken man like, fool?

Clo. Like a drown'd man, a fool, and a madman: one draught above heat makes him a fool; the second mads him; and a third drowns him.   125

Oli. Go thou and seek the crowner, and let him sit o' my coz; for he's in the third degree of drink, he's drown'd; go look after him.   128

Clo. He is but mad yet, madonna, and the fool shall look to the madman. [*Exit.*

Re-enter MALVOLIO.

Mal. Madam, yond young fellow swears he will speak with you. I told him you were sick; he takes on him to understand so much, and therefore comes to speak with you. I told him you were asleep; he seems to have a foreknowledge of that too, and therefore comes to speak with you. What is to be said to him, lady? He's fortified against any denial.   137

Oli. Tell him he shall not speak with me.

Mal. Has been told so; and he says he'll stand at your door like a sheriff's post, and be the supporter to a bench, but he'll speak with you.   141

Oli. What kind o' man is he?

Mal. Why, of mankind.

Oli. What manner of man?

Mal. Of very ill manner; he'll speak with you, will you or no.   146

Oli. Of what personage and years is he?

Mal. Not yet old enough for a man, nor young enough for a boy; as a squash is before 'tis a peascod, or a codling when 'tis almost an apple; 'tis with him in standing water, between boy and man. He is very well-favour'd, and he speaks very shrewishly; one would think his mother's milk were scarce out of him.

Oli. Let him approach. Call in my gentlewoman.   154

Mal. Gentlewoman, my lady calls. [*Exit.*

S.—7

353

Re-enter MARIA.

Oli. Give me my veil ; come, throw it
  o'er my face ;
We'll once more hear Orsino's embassy.

Enter VIOLA.

Vio. The honourable lady of the house,
which is she ?
Oli. Speak to me ; I shall answer for her.
Your will ?   159
Vio. Most radiant, exquisite, and unmatchable beauty—I pray you tell me if
this be the lady of the house, for I never
saw her. I would be loath to cast away my
speech ; for, besides that it is excellently
well penn'd, I have taken great pains to
con it. Good beauties, let me sustain no
scorn ; I am very comptible, even to the
least sinister usage.
Oli. Whence came you, sir ?   166
Vio. I can say little more than I have
studied, and that question's out of my
part. Good gentle one, give me modest
assurance if you be the lady of the house,
that I may proceed in my speech.   170
Oli. Are you a comedian ?
Vio. No, my profound heart ; and yet,
by the very fangs of malice I swear, I am
not that I play. Are you the lady of the
house ?
Oli. If I do not usurp myself, I am. 175
Vio. Most certain, if you are she, you do
usurp yourself ; for what is yours to bestow
is not yours to reserve. But this is from
my commission. I will on with my speech
in your praise, and then show you the heart
of my message.
Oli. Come to what is important in't. I
forgive you the praise.   181
Vio. Alas, I took great pains to study it,
and 'tis poetical.
Oli. It is the more like to be feigned ; I
pray you keep it in. I heard you were saucy
at my gates, and allow'd your approach
rather to wonder at you than to hear you.
If you be not mad, be gone ; if you have
reason, be brief ; 'tis not that time of
moon with me to make one in so skipping a
dialogue.
Mar. Will you hoist sail, sir ? Here lies
your way.   190
Vio. No, good swabber, I am to hull
here a little longer. Some mollification for
your giant, sweet lady.
Oli. Tell me your mind.
Vio. I am a messenger.
Oli. Sure, you have some hideous matter
to deliver, when the courtesy of it is so
fearful. Speak your office.   195
Vio. It alone concerns your ear. I bring
no overture of war, no taxation of homage :
I hold the olive in my hand ; my words are
as full of peace as matter.

Oli. Yet you began rudely. What are
you ? What would you ?   200
Vio. The rudeness that hath appear'd in
me have I learn'd from my entertainment.
What I am and what I would are as secret
as maidenhead—to your ears, divinity ; to
any other's, profanation.   204
Oli. Give us the place alone ; we will
hear this divinity. [*Exeunt Maria and
Attendants*] Now, sir, what is your text ?
Vio. Most sweet lady—
Oli. A comfortable doctrine, and much
may be said of it. Where lies your text ?
Vio. In Orsino's bosom.   210
Oli. In his bosom ! In what chapter of
his bosom ?
Vio. To answer by the method : in the
first of his heart.
Oli. O, I have read it ; it is heresy. Have
you no more to say ?   214
Vio. Good madam, let me see your face.
Oli. Have you any commission from your
lord to negotiate with my face ? You are
now out of your text ; but we will draw
the curtain and show you the picture.
[*Unveiling*] Look you, sir, such a one I was
this present. Is't not well done ?   220
Vio. Excellently done, if God did all.
Oli. 'Tis in grain, sir ; 'twill endure wind
and weather.
Vio. 'Tis beauty truly blent, whose red
        and white
Nature's own sweet and cunning hand laid
        on.
Lady, you are the cruell'st she alive, 225
If you will lead these graces to the grave,
And leave the world no copy.
Oli. O, sir, I will not be so hard-hearted ;
I will give out divers schedules of my
beauty. It shall be inventoried, and every
particle and utensil labell'd to my will :
as—item, two lips indifferent red ; item,
two grey eyes with lids to them ; item, one
neck, one chin, and so forth. Were you
sent hither to praise me ?
Vio. I see you what you are : you are
        too proud ;
But, if you were the devil, you are fair. 235
My lord and master loves you—O, such love
Could be but recompens'd though you were
        crown'd
The nonpareil of beauty !
Oli. How does he love me ?
Vio. With adorations, fertile tears,
With groans that thunder love, with sighs
        of fire.   240
Oli. Your lord does know my mind ; I
cannot love him.
Yet I suppose him virtuous, know him
        noble,
Of great estate, of fresh and stainless youth;
In voices well divulg'd, free, learn'd, and
        valiant,   244
And in dimension and the shape of nature

A gracious person ; but yet I cannot love
    him.
He might have took his answer long ago.
    Vio. If I did love you in my master's
    flame,
With such a suff'ring, such a deadly life,
In your denial I would find no sense ; 250
I would not understand it.
    Oli.   Why, what would you ?
    Vio. Make me a willow cabin at your
    gate,
And call upon my soul within the house ;
Write loyal cantons of contemned love
And sing them loud even in the dead of
    night ; 255
Halloo your name to the reverberate hills,
And make the babbling gossip of the air
Cry out ' Olivia ! ' O, you should not rest
Between the elements of air and earth
But you should pity me !
    Oli.   You might do much.
What is your parentage ? 261
    Vio. Above my fortunes, yet my state is
    well :
I am a gentleman.
    Oli.   Get you to your lord.
I cannot love him ; let him send no more—
Unless perchance you come to me again 265
To tell me how he takes it. Fare you well.
I thank you for your pains ; spend this
    for me.
    Vio. I am no fee'd post, lady ; keep your
    purse ;
My master, not myself, lacks recompense.
Love make his heart of flint that you shall
    love ; 270
And let your fervour, like my master's, be
Plac'd in contempt ! Farewell, fair cruelty.
                           [*Exit.*

    Oli. ' What is your parentage ? '
' Above my fortunes, yet my state is well :
I am a gentleman.' I'll be sworn thou
    art ;
Thy tongue, thy face, thy limbs, actions,
    and spirit, 276
Do give thee five-fold blazon. Not too fast !
    Soft, soft !
Unless the master were the man. How now !
Even so quickly may one catch the plague ?
Methinks I feel this youth's perfections 280
With an invisible and subtle stealth
To creep in at mine eyes. Well, let it be.
What ho, Malvolio !

           Re-enter MALVOLIO.

    Mal.   Here, madam, at your service.
    Oli. Run after that same peevish
    messenger,
The County's man. He left this ring behind
    him, 285
Would I or not. Tell him I'll none of it.
Desire him not to flatter with his lord,
Nor hold him up with hopes ; I am not for
    him.

If that the youth will come this way to-
    morrow,
I'll give him reasons for't.   Hie thee,
    Malvolio. 290
    Mal. Madam, I will.   [*Exit.*
    Oli. I do I know not what, and fear to find
Mine eye too great a flatterer for my mind.
Fate, show thy force : ourselves we do not
    owe ;
What is decreed must be ; and be this so !
                            [*Exit.*

ACT TWO

Scene I. *The sea-coast.*

Enter ANTONIO *and* SEBASTIAN.

    Ant. Will you stay no longer ; nor will
you not that I go with you ?
    Seb. By your patience, no. My stars
shine darkly over me ; the malignancy of
my fate might perhaps distemper yours ;
therefore I shall crave of you your leave
that I may bear my evils alone. It were a
bad recompense for your love to lay any
of them on you. 7
    Ant. Let me yet know of you whither you
are bound.
    Seb. No, sooth, sir ; my determinate
voyage is mere extravagancy. But I
perceive in you so excellent a touch of
modesty that you will not extort from me
what I am willing to keep in ; therefore it
charges me in manners the rather to express
myself.   You must know of me then,
Antonio, my name is Sebastian, which I
call'd Roderigo ; my father was that
Sebastian of Messaline whom I know you
have heard of. He left behind him myself
and a sister, both born in an hour ; if the
heavens had been pleas'd, would we had so
ended ! But you, sir, alter'd that ; for
some hour before you took me from the
breach of the sea was my sister drown'd. 20
    Ant. Alas the day !
    Seb. A lady, sir, though it was said she
much resembled me, was yet of many
accounted beautiful ; but though I could
not with such estimable wonder overfar
believe that, yet thus far I will boldly
publish her : she bore a mind that envy
could not but call fair. She is drown'd
already, sir, with salt water, though I seem
to drown her remembrance again with
more. 28
    Ant. Pardon me, sir, your bad entertain-
ment.
    Seb. O good Antonio, forgive me your
trouble. 30
    Ant. If you will not murder me for my
love, let me be your servant.
    Seb. If you will not undo what you have
done—that is, kill him whom you have
recover'd—desire it not. Fare ye well at
once ; my bosom is full of kindness, and I

am yet so near the manners of my mother that, upon the least occasion more, mine eyes will tell tales of me. I am bound to the Count Orsino's court. Farewell. [*Exit.*

Ant. The gentleness of all the gods go with thee !
I have many enemies in Orsino's court,   40
Else would I very shortly see thee there.
But come what may, I do adore thee so
That danger shall seem sport, and I will go.
[*Exit.*

SCENE II. *A street.*

Enter VIOLA *and* MALVOLIO *at several doors.*

Mal. Were you not ev'n now with the Countess Olivia ?

Vio. Even now, sir ; on a moderate pace I have since arriv'd but hither.   3

Mal. She returns this ring to you, sir ; you might have saved me my pains, to have taken it away yourself. She adds, moreover, that you should put your lord into a desperate assurance she will none of him. And one thing more : that you be never so hardy to come again in his affairs, unless it be to report your lord's taking of this. Receive it so.   10

Vio. She took the ring of me ; I'll none of it.

Mal. Come, sir, you peevishly threw it to her ; and her will is it should be so return'd. If it be worth stooping for, there it lies in your eye; if not, be it his that finds it.   [*Exit.*

Vio. I left no ring with her ; what means this lady ?   15
Fortune forbid my outside have not charm'd her !
She made good view of me ; indeed, so much
That methought her eyes had lost her tongue,
For she did speak in starts distractedly.
She loves me, sure: the cunning of her passion   20
Invites me in this churlish messenger.
None of my lord's ring ! Why, he sent her none.
I am the man. If it be so—as 'tis—
Poor lady, she were better love a dream.
Disguise, I see thou art a wickedness   25
Wherein the pregnant enemy does much.
How easy is it for the proper-false
In women's waxen hearts to set their forms !
Alas, our frailty is the cause, not we !
For such as we are made of, such we be.   30
How will this fadge ? My master loves her dearly,
And I, poor monster, fond as much on him ;
And she, mistaken, seems to dote on me.
What will become of this ? As I am man,
My state is desperate for my master's love ;
As I am woman—now alas the day !—

What thriftless sighs shall poor Olivia breathe !   37
O Time, thou must untangle this, not I ;
It is too hard a knot for me t' untie !
[*Exit.*

SCENE III. *Olivia's house.*

Enter SIR TOBY *and* SIR ANDREW.

Sir To. Approach, Sir Andrew. Not to be abed after midnight is to be up betimes ; and ' diluculo surgere ' thou know'st—

Sir And. Nay, by my troth, I know not ; but I know to be up late is to be up late.   5

Sir To. A false conclusion ! I hate it as an unfill'd can. To be up after midnight and to go to bed then is early ; so that to go to bed after midnight is to go to bed betimes. Does not our lives consist of the four elements ?   9

Sir And. Faith, so they say ; but I think it rather consists of eating and drinking.

Sir To. Th'art a scholar ; let us therefore eat and drink. Marian, I say ! a stoup of wine.

Enter Clown.

Sir And. Here comes the fool, i' faith.

Clo. How now, my hearts ! Did you never see the picture of ' we three ' ?   16

Sir To. Welcome, ass. Now let's have a catch.

Sir And. By my troth, the fool has an excellent breast. I had rather than forty shillings I had such a leg, and so sweet a breath to sing, as the fool has. In sooth, thou wast in very gracious fooling last night, when thou spok'st of Pigrogromitus, of the Vapians passing the equinoctial of Queubus ; 'twas very good, i' faith. I sent thee sixpence for thy leman ; hadst it ?   24

Clo. I did impeticos thy gratillity ; for Malvolio's nose is no whipstock. My lady has a white hand, and the Myrmidons are no bottle-ale houses.   27

Sir And. Excellent ! Why, this is the best fooling, when all is done. Now, a song.

Sir To. Come on, there is sixpence for you. Let's have a song.   31

Sir And. There's a testril of me too ; if one knight give a—

Clo. Would you have a love-song, or a song of good life ?   35

Sir To. A love-song, a love-song.

Sir And. Ay, ay ; I care not for good life.

Clown sings.

O mistress mine, where are you roaming ?
O, stay and hear ; your true love's coming,
    That can sing both high and low.
Trip no further, pretty sweeting ;
Journeys end in lovers meeting,
    Every wise man's son doth know.

Sir And. Excellent good, i' faith !
Sir To. Good, good !

Clown sings.

What is love ? 'Tis not hereafter ;
Present mirth hath present laughter ;
　What's to come is still unsure.
In delay there lies no plenty,
Then come kiss me, sweet and twenty ;　50
　Youth's a stuff will not endure.

Sir And. A mellifluous voice, as I am
true knight.

Sir To. A contagious breath.

Sir And. Very sweet and contagious, i'
faith.　　　　　　　　　　　　　　　54

Sir To. To hear by the nose, it is dulcet
in contagion. But shall we make the
welkin dance indeed ? Shall we rouse the
night-owl in a catch that will draw three
souls out of one weaver ? Shall we do that ?

Sir And. An you love me, let's do't. I am
dog at a catch.　　　　　　　　　　　60

Clo. By'r lady, sir, and some dogs will
catch well.

Sir And. Most certain. Let our catch be
' Thou knave '.

Clo. 'Hold thy peace, thou knave'
knight ? I shall be constrain'd in't to call
thee knave, knight.　　　　　　　　　65

Sir And. 'Tis not the first time I have
constrained one to call me knave. Begin,
fool : it begins ' Hold thy peace '.

Clo. I shall never begin if I hold my
peace.

Sir And. Good, i' faith ! Come, begin. 69
　　　　　　　　　　　　　　　[*Catch sung.*

Enter MARIA.

Mar. What a caterwauling do you keep
here ! If my lady have not call'd up her
steward Malvolio, and bid him turn you
out of doors, never trust me.　　　　　72

Sir To. My lady's a Cataian, we are
politicians, Malvolio's a Peg-a-Ramsey,
and [*Sings*]
　Three merry men be we.
Am not I consanguineous ? Am I not of
her blood ? Tilly-vally, lady. [*Sings*]
　There dwelt a man in Babylon,
　　Lady, lady.　　　　　　　　　　76

Clo. Beshrew me, the knight's in admirable fooling.

Sir And. Ay, he does well enough if he
be dispos'd, and so do I too ; he does it
with a better grace, but I do it more
natural.　　　　　　　　　　　　　80

Sir To. [*Sings*] O' the twelfth day of
December—

Mar. For the love o' God, peace !

Enter MALVOLIO.

Mal. My masters, are you mad ? Or what
are you ? Have you no wit, manners, nor
honesty, but to gabble like tinkers at this
time of night ? Do ye make an ale-house
of my lady's house, that ye squeak out
your coziers' catches without any mitigation or remorse of voice ? Is there no
respect of place, persons, nor time, in you ?

Sir To. We did keep time, sir, in our
catches. Sneck up !　　　　　　　　90

Mal. Sir Toby, I must be round with you.
My lady bade me tell you that, though she
harbours you as her kinsman, she's nothing
allied to your disorders. If you can separate
yourself and your misdemeanours, you are
welcome to the house ; if not, and it would
please you to take leave of her, she is very
willing to bid you farewell.　　　　　96

Sir To. [*Sings*] Farewell, dear heart, since
　I must needs be gone.

Mar. Nay, good Sir Toby.

Clo. [*Sings*] His eyes do show his days are
　almost done.

Mal. Is't even so ?　　　　　　　　100

Sir To. [*Sings*] But I will never die.
　　　　　　　　　　　　　　　[*Falls down.*

Clo. [*Sings*] Sir Toby, there you lie.

Mal. This is much credit to you.

Sir To. [*Sings*] Shall I bid him go ?

Clo. [*Sings*] What an if you do ?　　105

Sir To. [*Sings*] Shall I bid him go, and
　spare not ?

Clo. [*Sings*] O, no, no, no, no, you dare
　not.

Sir To. [*Rising*] Out o' tune, sir ! Ye lie.
Art any more than a steward ? Dost thou
think, because thou art virtuous, there
shall be no more cakes and ale ?　　110

Clo. Yes, by Saint Anne ; and ginger
shall be hot i' th' mouth too.

Sir To. Th'art i' th' right. Go, sir, rub
your chain with crumbs. A stoup of wine,
Maria !　　　　　　　　　　　　114

Mal. Mistress Mary, if you priz'd my
lady's favour at anything more than contempt, you would not give means for this
uncivil rule ; she shall know of it, by this
hand.　　　　　　　　　　　　[*Exit.*

Mar. Go shake your ears.

Sir And. 'Twere as good a deed as to
drink when a man's ahungry, to challenge
him the field, and then to break promise
with him and make a fool of him.　　121

Sir To. Do't, knight. I'll write thee a
challenge ; or I'll deliver thy indignation
to him by word of mouth.

Mar. Sweet Sir Toby, be patient for tonight ; since the youth of the Count's was
to-day with my lady, she is much out of
quiet. For Monsieur Malvolio, let me alone
with him ; if I do not gull him into a naycord, and make him a common recreation,
do not think I have wit enough to lie
straight in my bed. I know I can do it. 129

Sir To. Possess us, possess us ; tell us
something of him.

Mar. Marry, sir, sometimes he is a kind
of Puritan.

357

Sir And. O, if I thought that, I'd beat him like a dog.

Sir To. What, for being a Puritan ? Thy exquisite reason, dear knight ?   134

Sir And. I have no exquisite reason for't, but I have reason good enough.

Mar. The devil a Puritan that he is, or anything constantly but a time-pleaser ; an affection'd ass that cons state without book and utters it by great swarths ; the best persuaded of himself, so cramm'd, as he thinks, with excellencies that it is his grounds of faith that all that look on him love him ; and on that vice in him will my revenge find notable cause to work.

Sir To. What wilt thou do ?   144

Mar. I will drop in his way some obscure epistles of love ; wherein, by the colour of his beard, the shape of his leg, the manner of his gait, the expressure of his eye, forehead, and complexion, he shall find himself most feelingly personated. I can write very like my lady, your niece ; on a forgotten matter we can hardly make distinction of our hands.   151

Sir To. Excellent ! I smell a device.

Sir And. I have't in my nose too.

Sir To. He shall think, by the letters that thou wilt drop, that they come from my niece, and that she's in love with him.

Mar. My purpose is, indeed, a horse of that colour.   157

Sir And. And your horse now would make him an ass.

Mar. Ass, I doubt not.

Sir And. O, 'twill be admirable !   160

Mar. Sport royal, I warrant you. I know my physic will work with him. I will plant you two, and let the fool make a third, where he shall find the letter ; observe his construction of it. For this night, to bed, and dream on the event. Farewell. [*Exit.*

Sir To. Good night, Penthesilea.   166

Sir And. Before me, she's a good wench.

Sir To. She's a beagle true-bred, and one that adores me. What o' that ?

Sir And. I was ador'd once too.   170

Sir To. Let's to bed, knight. Thou hadst need send for more money.

Sir And. If I cannot recover your niece, I am a foul way out.

Sir To. Send for money, knight ; if thou hast her not i' th' end, call me Cut.   176

Sir And. If I do not, never trust me ; take it how you will.

Sir To. Come, come, I'll go burn some sack ; 'tis too late to go to bed now. Come, knight ; come, knight.   [*Exeunt.*

SCENE IV. *The Duke's palace.*

Enter DUKE, VIOLA, CURIO, *and* Others.

Duke. Give me some music. Now, good morrow, friends.

Now, good Cesario, but that piece of song, That old and antique song we heard last night ;

Methought it did relieve my passion much, More than light airs and recollected terms 5 Of these most brisk and giddy-paced times. Come, but one verse.

Cur. He is not here, so please your lordship, that should sing it.

Duke. Who was it ?   10

Cur. Feste, the jester, my lord ; a fool that the Lady Olivia's father took much delight in. He is about the house.

Duke. Seek him out, and play the tune the while.   [*Exit Curio. Music plays.*

Come hither, boy. If ever thou shalt love, In the sweet pangs of it remember me ;   15 For such as I am all true lovers are, Unstaid and skittish in all motions else Save in the constant image of the creature That is belov'd. How dost thou like this tune ?

Vio. It gives a very echo to the seat   20 Where Love is thron'd.

Duke.   Thou dost speak masterly. My life upon't, young though thou art, thine eye

Hath stay'd upon some favour that it loves ; Hath it not, boy ?

Vio.   A little, by your favour.   24

Duke. What kind of woman is't ?

Vio.   Of your complexion.

Duke. She is not worth thee, then. What years, i' faith ?

Vio. About your years, my lord.

Duke. Too old, by heaven ! Let still the woman take   28 An elder than herself ; so wears she to him, So sways she level in her husband's heart. For, boy, however we do praise ourselves, Our fancies are more giddy and unfirm, 32 More longing, wavering, sooner lost and won,

Than women's are.

Vio.   I think it well, my lord.

Duke. Then let thy love be younger than thyself,   35 Or thy affection cannot hold the bent ; For women are as roses, whose fair flow'r Being once display'd doth fall that very hour.

Vio. And so they are ; alas, that they are so !   39 To die, even when they to perfection grow !

Re-enter CURIO *and* Clown.

Duke. O, fellow, come, the song we had last night.

Mark it, Cesario ; it is old and plain ; The spinsters and the knitters in the sun, And the free maids that weave their thread with bones,

Do use to chant it ; it is silly sooth,   45 And dallies with the innocence of love,

Like the old age.

  Clo. Are you ready, sir ?

  Duke. Ay ; prithee, sing.   [*Music.*

Feste's Song.

Come away, come away, death ;   50
And in sad cypress let me be laid ;
  Fly away, fly away, breath,
I am slain by a fair cruel maid.
My shroud of white, stuck all with yew,
      O, prepare it !   55
My part of death no one so true
      Did share it.

Not a flower, not a flower sweet,
On my black coffin let there be strown ;
  Not a friend, not a friend greet   60
My poor corpse where my bones shall be
    thrown ;
A thousand thousand sighs to save,
      Lay me, O, where
Sad true lover never find my grave,
      To weep there !   65

  Duke. There's for thy pains.

  Clo. No pains, sir ; I take pleasure in
singing, sir.

  Duke. I'll pay thy pleasure, then.

  Clo. Truly, sir, and pleasure will be paid
one time or another.   70

  Duke. Give me now leave to leave thee.

  Clo. Now the melancholy god protect
thee ; and the tailor make thy doublet of
changeable taffeta, for thy mind is a very
opal. I would have men of such constancy
put to sea, that their business might be
everything, and their intent everywhere ;
for that's it that always makes a good
voyage of nothing. Farewell. [*Exit Clown.*

  Duke. Let all the rest give place.
        [*Exeunt Curio and Attendants.*
                Once more, Cesario,
Get thee to yond same sovereign cruelty.
Tell her my love, more noble than the
    world,   80
Prizes not quantity of dirty lands ;
The parts that fortune hath bestow'd upon
    her,
Tell her I hold as giddily as Fortune ;
But 'tis that miracle and queen of gems
That Nature pranks her in attracts my
    soul.   85

  Vio. But if she cannot love you, sir ?

  Duke. I cannot be so answer'd.

  Vio.   Sooth, but you must.
Say that some lady, as perhaps there is,
Hath for your love as great a pang of heart
As you have for Olivia. You cannot love
    her ;   90
You tell her so. Must she not then be
    answer'd ?

  Duke. There is no woman's sides
Can bide the beating of so strong a passion
As love doth give my heart ; no woman's
    heart   94

So big to hold so much ; they lack retention.
Alas, their love may be call'd appetite—
No motion of the liver, but the palate—
That suffer surfeit, cloyment, and revolt ;
But mine is all as hungry as the sea,   99
And can digest as much. Make no compare
Between that love a woman can bear me
And that I owe Olivia.

  Vio.   Ay, but I know—

  Duke. What dost thou know ?

  Vio. Too well what love women to men
    may owe.
In faith, they are as true of heart as we. 105
My father had a daughter lov'd a man,
As it might be perhaps, were I a woman,
I should your lordship.

  Duke.   And what's her history ?

  Vio. A blank, my lord. She never told
    her love,   109
But let concealment, like a worm i' th' bud,
Feed on her damask cheek. She pin'd in
    thought ;
And with a green and yellow melancholy
She sat like Patience on a monument,
Smiling at grief. Was not this love indeed?
We men may say more, swear more, but
    indeed   115
Our shows are more than will ; for still we
    prove
Much in our vows, but little in our love.

  Duke. But died thy sister of her love, my
    boy ?

  Vio. I am all the daughters of my father's
    house,
And all the brothers too—and yet I know
    not.   120
Sir, shall I to this lady ?

  Duke.   Ay, that's the theme.
To her in haste. Give her this jewel ; say
My love can give no place, bide no denay.
                [*Exeunt.*

Scene V. *Olivia's garden.*

Enter Sir Toby, Sir Andrew, *and*
Fabian.

  Sir To. Come thy ways, Signior Fabian.

  Fab. Nay, I'll come ; if I lose a scruple
of this sport let me be boil'd to death with
melancholy.

  Sir To. Wouldst thou not be glad to have
the niggardly rascally sheep-biter come by
some notable shame ?   5

  Fab. I would exult, man ; you know he
brought me out o' favour with my lady
about a bear-baiting here.

  Sir To. To anger him we'll have the bear
again ; and we will fool him black and blue
—shall we not, Sir Andrew ?

  Sir And. An we do not, it is pity of our
lives.   10

Enter Maria.

  Sir To. Here comes the little villain.
How now, my metal of India !

Mar. Get ye all three into the box-tree. Malvolio's coming down this walk. He has been yonder i' the sun practising behaviour to his own shadow this half hour. Observe him, for the love of mockery, for I know this letter will make a contemplative idiot of him. Close, in the name of jesting ! [*As the men hide she drops a letter*] Lie thou there ; for here comes the trout that must be caught with tickling.   [*Exit.* 20

Enter MALVOLIO.

Mal. 'Tis but fortune ; all is fortune. Maria once told me she did affect me ; and I have heard herself come thus near, that, should she fancy, it should be one of my complexion. Besides, she uses me with a more exalted respect than any one else that follows her. What should I think on't ? 26

Sir To. Here's an overweening rogue !

Fab. O, peace ! Contemplation makes a rare turkey-cock of him ; how he jets under his advanc'd plumes !

Sir And. 'Slight, I could so beat the rogue—   30

Sir To. Peace, I say.

Mal. To be Count Malvolio !

Sir To. Ah, rogue !

Sir And. Pistol him, pistol him.

Sir To. Peace, peace !   35

Mal. There is example for't: the Lady of the Strachy married the yeoman of the wardrobe.

Sir And. Fie on him, Jezebel !

Fab. O, peace ! Now he's deeply in ; look how imagination blows him.   40

Mal. Having been three months married to her, sitting in my state—

Sir To. O, for a stone-bow to hit him in the eye !

Mal. Calling my officers about me, in my branch'd velvet gown, having come from a day-bed—where I have left Olivia sleeping—   46

Sir To. Fire and brimstone !

Fab. O, peace, peace !

Mal. And then to have the humour of state ; and after a demure travel of regard, telling them I know my place as I would they should do theirs, to ask for my kinsman Toby—

Sir To. Bolts and shackles !   52

Fab. O, peace, peace, peace ! Now, now.

Mal. Seven of my people, with an obedient start, make out for him. I frown the while, and perchance wind up my watch, or play with my—some rich jewel. Toby approaches ; curtsies there to me—

Sir To. Shall this fellow live ?

Fab. Though our silence be drawn from us with cars, yet peace.   60

Mal. I extend my hand to him thus, quenching my familiar smile with an austere regard of control—

Sir To. And does not Toby take you a blow o' the lips then ?   64

Mal. Saying ' Cousin Toby, my fortunes having cast me on your niece give me this prerogative of speech '—

Sir To. What, what ?

Mal. 'You must amend your drunkenness '—

Sir To. Out, scab !   69

Fab. Nay, patience, or we break the sinews of our plot.

Mal. ' Besides, you waste the treasure of your time with a foolish knight '—

Sir And. That's me, I warrant you.

Mal. ' One Sir Andrew.'

Sir And. I knew 'twas I ; for many do call me fool.   75

Mal. What employment have we here ?
                [*Taking up the letter.*

Fab. Now is the woodcock near the gin.

Sir To. O, peace ! And the spirit of humours intimate reading aloud to him !

Mal. By my life, this is my lady's hand : these be her very C's, her U's, and her T's ; and thus makes she her great P's. It is, in contempt of question, her hand.   82

Sir And. Her C's, her U's, and her T's. Why that ?

Mal. [*Reads*] ' To the unknown belov'd, this, and my good wishes.' Her very phrases ! By your leave, wax. Soft ! And the impressure her Lucrece with which she uses to seal ; 'tis my lady. To whom should this be ?

Fab. This wins him, liver and all.

Mal. [*Reads*] ' Jove knows I love,
        But who ?   90
                Lips, do not move ;
                No man must know.'

' No man must know.' What follows ? The numbers alter'd ! ' No man must know.' If this should be thee, Malvolio ?

Sir To. Marry, hang thee, brock !   95

Mal. [*Reads*]
' I may command where I adore ;
        But silence, like a Lucrece knife,
        With bloodless stroke my heart doth gore ;
        M. O. A. I. doth sway my life.'

Fab. A fustian riddle !   100

Sir To. Excellent wench, say I.

Mal. ' M. O. A. I. doth sway my life.' Nay, but first let me see, let me see, let me see.

Fab. What dish o' poison has she dress'd him !   104

Sir To. And with what wing the staniel checks at it !

Mal. ' I may command where I adore.' Why, she may command me : I serve her ; she is my lady. Why, this is evident to any formal capacity ; there is no obstruction in this. And the end—what should that alphabetical position portend ? If I could make that resemble something in me. Softly ! M. O. A. I.—   111

Sir To. O, ay, make up that ! He is now at a cold scent.

Fab. Sowter will cry upon't for all this, though it be as rank as a fox.   114

Mal. M—Malvolio ; M—why, that begins my name.

Fab. Did not I say he would work it out ? The cur is excellent at faults.

Mal. M—But then there is no consonancy in the sequel ; that suffers under probation : A should follow, but O does.

Fab. And O shall end, I hope.   120

Sir To. Ay, or I'll cudgel him, and make him cry ' O ! '

Mal. And then I comes behind.

Fab. Ay, an you had any eye behind you, you might see more detraction at your heels than fortunes before you.   124

Mal. M. O. A. I. This simulation is not as the former ; and yet, to crush this a little, it would bow to me, for every one of these letters are in my name. Soft ! here follows prose.

[*Reads*] ' If this fall into thy hand, revolve. In my stars I am above thee ; but be not afraid of greatness. Some are born great, some achieve greatness, and some have greatness thrust upon 'em. Thy Fates open their hands ; let thy blood and spirit embrace them ; and, to inure thyself to what thou art like to be, cast thy humble slough and appear fresh. Be opposite with a kinsman, surly with servants ; let thy tongue tang arguments of state ; put thyself into the trick of singularity. She thus advises thee that sighs for thee. Remember who commended thy yellow stockings, and wish'd to see thee ever cross-garter'd. I say, remember. Go to, thou art made, if thou desir'st to be so ; if not, let me see thee a steward still, the fellow of servants, and not worthy to touch Fortune's fingers. Farewell. She that would alter services with thee,   140
        THE FORTUNATE-UNHAPPY.'

Daylight and champain discovers not more. This is open. I will be proud, I will read politic authors, I will baffle Sir Toby, I will wash off gross acquaintance, I will be point-devise the very man. I do not now fool myself to let imagination jade me ; for every reason excites to this, that my lady loves me. She did commend my yellow stockings of late, she did praise my leg being cross-garter'd ; and in this she manifests herself to my love, and with a kind of injunction drives me to these habits of her liking. I thank my stars I am happy. I will be strange, stout, in yellow stockings, and cross-garter'd, even with the swiftness

of putting on. Jove and my stars be praised ! Here is yet a postscript.

[*Reads*] ' Thou canst not choose but know who I am. If thou entertain'st my love, let it appear in thy smiling ; thy smiles become thee well. Therefore in my presence still smile, dear my sweet, I prithee.'

Jove, I thank thee. I will smile ; I will do everything that thou wilt have me.   [*Exit.*

Fab. I will not give my part of this sport for a pension of thousands to be paid from the Sophy.   161

Sir To. I could marry this wench for this device.

Sir And. So could I too.

Sir To. And ask no other dowry with her but such another jest.   165

           Enter MARIA.

Sir And. Nor I neither.

Fab. Here comes my noble gull-catcher.

Sir To. Wilt thou set thy foot o' my neck ?

Sir And. Or o' mine either ?

Sir To. Shall I play my freedom at tray-trip, and become thy bond-slave ?   171

Sir And. I' faith, or I either ?

Sir To. Why, thou hast put him in such a dream that when the image of it leaves him he must run mad.

Mar. Nay, but say true ; does it work upon him ?   175

Sir To. Like aqua-vitæ with a midwife.

Mar. If you will then see the fruits of the sport, mark his first approach before my lady. He will come to her in yellow stockings, and 'tis a colour she abhors, and cross-garter'd, a fashion she detests ; and he will smile upon her, which will now be so unsuitable to her disposition, being addicted to a melancholy as she is, that it cannot but turn him into a notable contempt. If you will see it, follow me.

Sir To. To the gates of Tartar, thou most excellent devil of wit !   185

Sir And. I'll make one too.   [*Exeunt.*

ACT THREE

SCENE I. *Olivia's garden.*

Enter VIOLA, *and* Clown *with a tabor.*

Vio. Save thee, friend, and thy music ! Dost thou live by thy tabor ?

Clo. No, sir, I live by the church.

Vio. Art thou a churchman ?   4

Clo. No such matter, sir : I do live by the church ; for I do live at my house, and my house doth stand by the church.

Vio. So thou mayst say the king lies by a beggar, if a beggar dwell near him ; or the church stands by thy tabor, if thy tabor stand by the church.   9

Clo. You have said, sir. To see this age ! A sentence is but a chev'ril glove to a good wit. How quickly the wrong side may be turn'd outward !   12

Vio. Nay, that's certain ; they that dally nicely with words may quickly make them wanton.

Clo. I would, therefore, my sister had had no name, sir.

Vio. Why, man ?   16

Clo. Why, sir, her name's a word ; and to dally with that word might make my sister wanton. But indeed words are very rascals since bonds disgrac'd them.

Vio. Thy reason, man ?   20

Clo. Troth, sir, I can yield you none without words, and words are grown so false I am loath to prove reason with them.

Vio. I warrant thou art a merry fellow and car'st for nothing.   25

Clo. Not so, sir ; I do care for something ; but in my conscience, sir, I do not care for you. If that be to care for nothing, sir, I would it would make you invisible.   28

Vio. Art not thou the Lady Olivia's fool ?

Clo. No, indeed, sir ; the Lady Olivia has no folly ; she will keep no fool, sir, till she be married ; and fools are as like husbands as pilchers are to herrings—the husband's the bigger. I am indeed not her fool, but her corrupter of words.

Vio. I saw thee late at the Count Orsino's.   35

Clo. Foolery, sir, does walk about the orb like the sun—it shines everywhere. I would be sorry, sir, but the fool should be as oft with your master as with my mistress : I think I saw your wisdom there.   39

Vio. Nay, an thou pass upon me, I'll no more with thee. Hold, there's expenses for thee.   [*Giving a coin.*

Clo. Now Jove, in his next commodity of hair, send thee a beard !

Vio. By my troth, I'll tell thee, I am almost sick for one ; [*Aside*] though I would not have it grow on my chin.—Is thy lady within ?   46

Clo. Would not a pair of these have bred, sir ?

Vio. Yes, being kept together and put to use.

Clo. I would play Lord Pandarus of Phrygia, sir, to bring a Cressida to this Troilus.   50

Vio. I understand you, sir ; 'tis well begg'd.   [*Giving another coin.*

Clo. The matter, I hope, is not great, sir, begging but a beggar : Cressida was a beggar. My lady is within, sir. I will construe to them whence you come ; who you are and what you would are out of my

welkin—I might say ' element ' but the word is overworn.   [*Exit.*

Vio. This fellow is wise enough to play the fool ;   57
And to do that well craves a kind of wit.
He must observe their mood on whom he jests,
The quality of persons, and the time ;   60
And, like the haggard, check at every feather
That comes before his eye.   This is a practice
As full of labour as a wise man's art ;
For folly that he wisely shows is fit ;
But wise men, folly-fall'n, quite taint their wit.   65

Enter SIR TOBY *and* SIR ANDREW.

Sir To. Save you, gentleman !
Vio. And you, sir.
Sir And. Dieu vous garde, monsieur.
Vio. Et vous aussi ; votre serviteur.
Sir And. I hope, sir, you are ; and I am yours.   70
Sir To. Will you encounter the house ? My niece is desirous you should enter, if your trade be to her.
Vio. I am bound to your niece, sir ; I mean, she is the list of my voyage.
Sir To. Taste your legs, sir ; put them to motion.   75
Vio. My legs do better understand me, sir, than I understand what you mean by bidding me taste my legs.
Sir To. I mean, to go, sir, to enter.
Vio. I will answer you with gait and entrance.   But we are prevented.   80

Enter OLIVIA *and* MARIA.

Most excellent accomplish'd lady, the heavens rain odours on you !
Sir And. That youth's a rare courtier— ' Rain odours ' well !
Vio. My matter hath no voice, lady, but to your own most pregnant and vouchsafed ear.   86
Sir And. ' Odours ', ' pregnant ', and ' vouchsafed '—I'll get 'em all three all ready.   88
Oli. Let the garden door be shut, and leave me to my hearing. [*Exeunt all but Olivia and Viola*] Give me your hand, sir.
Vio. My duty, madam, and most humble service.   92
Oli. What is your name ?
Vio. Cesario is your servant's name, fair Princess.
Oli. My servant, sir ! 'Twas never merry world   95
Since lowly feigning was call'd compliment.
Y'are servant to the Count Orsino, youth.
Vio. And he is yours, and his must needs be yours :

Your servant's servant is your servant,
    madam.
  Oli. For him, I think not on him; for
    his thoughts,   100
Would they were blanks rather than fill'd
    with me!
  Vio. Madam, I come to whet your gentle
    thoughts
On his behalf.
  Oli.   O, by your leave, I pray you:
I bade you never speak again of him;
But, would you undertake another suit, 105
I had rather hear you to solicit that
Than music from the spheres.
  Vio.   Dear lady—
  Oli. Give me leave, beseech you. I did
    send,
After the last enchantment you did here,
A ring in chase of you; so did I abuse 110
Myself, my servant, and, I fear me, you.
Under your hard construction must I sit,
To force that on you in a shameful cunning
Which you knew none of yours. What
    might you think?   114
Have you not set mine honour at the stake,
And baited it with all th' unmuzzled
    thoughts
That tyrannous heart can think? To one of
    your receiving
Enough is shown: a cypress, not a bosom,
Hides my heart. So, let me hear you speak.
  Vio. I pity you.
  Oli.   That's a degree to love.
  Vio. No, not a grize; for 'tis a vulgar
    proof   121
That very oft we pity enemies.
  Oli. Why, then, methinks 'tis time to
    smile again.
O world, how apt the poor are to be proud!
If one should be a prey, how much the
    better   125
To fall before the lion than the wolf!
                            [*Clock strikes.*
The clock upbraids me with the waste of
    time.
Be not afraid, good youth; I will not have
    you;
And yet, when wit and youth is come to
    harvest,
Your wife is like to reap a proper man. 130
There lies your way, due west.
  Vio.   Then westward-ho!
Grace and good disposition attend your
    ladyship!
You'll nothing, madam, to my lord by me?
  Oli. Stay.   134
I prithee tell me what thou think'st of me.
  Vio. That you do think you are not what
    you are.
  Oli. If I think so, I think the same of you.
  Vio. Then think you right: I am not
    what I am.
  Oli. I would you were as I would have
    you be!

  Vio. Would it be better, madam, than
    I am?   140
I wish it might, for now I am your fool.
  Oli. O, what a deal of scorn looks
    beautiful
In the contempt and anger of his lip!
A murd'rous guilt shows not itself more
    soon
Than love that would seem hid: love's
    night is noon.
Cesario, by the roses of the spring,   146
By maidhood, honour, truth, and every
    thing,
I love thee so that, maugre all thy pride,
Nor wit nor reason can my passion hide.
Do not extort thy reasons from this clause,
For that I woo, thou therefore hast no
    cause;
But rather reason thus with reason fetter:
Love sought is good, but given unsought is
    better.
  Vio. By innocence I swear, and by my
    youth,   154
I have one heart, one bosom, and one truth,
And that no woman has; nor never none
Shall mistress be of it, save I alone.
And so adieu, good madam; never more
Will I my master's tears to you deplore.
  Oli. Yet come again; for thou perhaps
    mayst move   160
That heart which now abhors to like his
    love.   [*Exeunt.*

SCENE II. *Olivia's house.*

Enter SIR TOBY, SIR ANDREW, *and* FABIAN.

  Sir And. No, faith, I'll not stay a jot
longer.
  Sir To. Thy reason, dear venom, give thy
reason.
  Fab. You must needs yield your reason,
Sir Andrew.
  Sir And. Marry, I saw your niece do
more favours to the Count's servingman
than ever she bestow'd upon me; I saw't
i' th' orchard.   6
  Sir To. Did she see thee the while, old
boy? Tell me that.
  Sir And. As plain as I see you now.   9
  Fab. This was a great argument of love
in her toward you.
  Sir And. 'Slight! will you make an ass
o' me?
  Fab. I will prove it legitimate, sir, upon
the oaths of judgment and reason.
  Sir To. And they have been grand-
jurymen since before Noah was a sailor. 16
  Fab. She did show favour to the youth in
your sight only to exasperate you, to awake
your dormouse valour, to put fire in your
heart and brimstone in your liver. You
should then have accosted her; and with
some excellent jests, fire-new from the
mint, you should have bang'd the youth

into dumbness. This was look'd for at your hand, and this was baulk'd. The double gilt of this opportunity you let time wash off, and you are now sail'd into the north of my lady's opinion ; where you will hang like an icicle on a Dutchman's beard, unless you do redeem it by some laudable attempt either of valour or policy.   27

Sir And. An't be any way, it must be with valour, for policy I hate ; I had as lief be a Brownist as a politician.

Sir To. Why, then, build me thy fortunes upon the basis of valour. Challenge me the Count's youth to fight with him ; hurt him in eleven places. My niece shall take note of it ; and assure thyself there is no love-broker in the world can more prevail in man's commendation with woman than report of valour.   35

Fab. There is no way but this, Sir Andrew.

Sir And. Will either of you bear me a challenge to him ?   38

Sir To. Go, write it in a martial hand ; be curst and brief ; it is no matter how witty, so it be eloquent and full of invention. Taunt him with the license of ink ; if thou thou'st him some thrice, it shall not be amiss ; and as many lies as will lie in thy sheet of paper, although the sheet were big enough for the bed of Ware in England, set 'em down ; go about it. Let there be gall enough in thy ink, though thou write with a goose-pen, no matter. About it.   47

Sir And. Where shall I find you ?

Sir To. We'll call thee at the *cubiculo*. Go.   [*Exit Sir Andrew.*

Fab. This is a dear manakin to you, Sir Toby.   50

Sir To. I have been dear to him, lad—some two thousand strong, or so.

Fab. We shall have a rare letter from him ; but you'll not deliver't ?   54

Sir To. Never trust me then ; and by all means stir on the youth to an answer. I think oxen and wainropes cannot hale them together. For Andrew, if he were open'd and you find so much blood in his liver as will clog the foot of a flea, I'll eat the rest of th' anatomy.

Fab. And his opposite, the youth, bears in his visage no great presage of cruelty.   61

Enter MARIA.

Sir To. Look where the youngest wren of nine comes.

Mar. If you desire the spleen, and will laugh yourselves into stitches, follow me. Yond gull Malvolio is turned heathen, a very renegado ; for there is no Christian that means to be saved by believing rightly can ever believe such impossible passages of grossness. He's in yellow stockings.

Sir To. And cross-garter'd ?   69

Mar. Most villainously ; like a pedant that keeps a school i' th' church. I have dogg'd him like his murderer. He does obey every point of the letter that I dropp'd to betray him. He does smile his face into more lines than is in the new map with the augmentation of the Indies. You have not seen such a thing as 'tis ; I can hardly forbear hurling things at him. I know my lady will strike him ; if she do, he'll smile and take't for a great favour.   77

Sir To. Come, bring us, bring us where he is.   [*Exeunt.*

SCENE III. *A street.*

Enter SEBASTIAN *and* ANTONIO.

Seb. I would not by my will have
    troubled you ;
But since you make your pleasure of your
    pains,
I will no further chide you.
    Ant. I could not stay behind you : my
    desire,
More sharp than filed steel, did spur me
    forth ;   5
And not all love to see you—though so
    much
As might have drawn one to a longer
    voyage—
But jealousy what might befall your travel,
Being skilless in these parts ; which to a
    stranger,
Unguided and unfriended, often prove   10
Rough and unhospitable. My willing love,
The rather by these arguments of fear,
Set forth in your pursuit.
    Seb.   My kind Antonio,
I can no other answer make but thanks,
And thanks, and ever thanks ; and oft
    good turns   15
Are shuffl'd off with such uncurrent pay ;
But were my worth as is my conscience
    firm,
You should find better dealing. What's to
    do ?
Shall we go see the reliques of this
    town ?
    Ant. To-morrow, sir ; best first go see
    your lodging.
    Seb. I am not weary, and 'tis long to
    night ;   21
I pray you, let us satisfy our eyes
With the memorials and the things of fame
That do renown this city.
    Ant.   Would you'd pardon me.
I do not without danger walk these streets :
Once in a sea-fight 'gainst the Count his
    galleys   26
I did some service ; of such note, indeed,
That, were I ta'en here, it would scarce be
    answer'd.
    Seb. Belike you slew great number of his
    people.

Ant. Th' offence is not of such a bloody
     nature ;   30
Albeit the quality of the time and quarrel
Might well have given us bloody argument.
It might have since been answer'd in
     repaying
What we took from them ; which, for
     traffic's sake,
Most of our city did. Only myself stood out;
For which, if I be lapsed in this place,   36
I shall pay dear.
     Seb.   Do not then walk too open.
     Ant. It doth not fit me. Hold, sir, here's
     my purse ;
In the south suburbs, at the Elephant,
Is best to lodge. I will bespeak our diet,   40
Whiles you beguile the time and feed your
     knowledge
With viewing of the town ; there shall you
     have me.
     Seb. Why I your purse ?
     Ant. Haply your eye shall light upon
     some toy
You have desire to purchase ; and your
     store,   45
I think, is not for idle markets, sir.
     Seb. I'll be your purse-bearer, and leave
     you for
An hour.
     Ant.   To th' Elephant.
     Seb.   I do remember.
                                           [*Exeunt.*

SCENE IV. *Olivia's garden.*

Enter OLIVIA *and* MARIA.

     Oli. I have sent after him ; he says he'll
     come.
How shall I feast him ? What bestow of
     him ?
For youth is bought more oft than begg'd
     or borrow'd.
I speak too loud.
Where's Malvolio ? He is sad and civil,   5
And suits well for a servant with my
     fortunes.
Where is Malvolio ?
     Mar. He's coming, madam ; but in very
strange manner. He is sure possess'd,
madam.
     Oli. Why, what's the matter ? Does he
rave ?   10
     Mar. No, madam, he does nothing but
smile. Your ladyship were best to have
some guard about you if he come ; for
sure the man is tainted in's wits.
     Oli. Go call him hither.   [*Exit Maria.*
                    I am as mad as he,
If sad and merry madness equal be.   15

Re-enter MARIA *with* MALVOLIO.

How now, Malvolio !
     Mal. Sweet lady, ho, ho.
     Oli. Smil'st thou ?

I sent for thee upon a sad occasion.   19
     Mal. Sad, lady ? I could be sad. This
does make some obstruction in the blood,
this cross-gartering ; but what of that ?
If it please the eye of one, it is with me
as the very true sonnet is : ' Please one and
please all '.
     Oli. Why, how dost thou, man ? What
is the matter with thee ?   25
     Mal. Not black in my mind, though
yellow in my legs. It did come to his
hands, and commands shall be executed. I
think we do know the sweet Roman hand.
     Oli. Wilt thou go to bed, Malvolio ?   29
     Mal. To bed ? Ay, sweetheart, and I'll
come to thee.
     Oli. God comfort thee ! Why dost thou
smile so, and kiss thy hand so oft ?
     Mar. How do you, Malvolio ?
     Mal. At your request ? Yes, nightingales
answer daws !
     Mar. Why appear you with this ridicu-
lous boldness before my lady ?   36
     Mal. ' Be not afraid of greatness.' 'Twas
well writ.
     Oli. What mean'st thou by that,
Malvolio ?
     Mal. ' Some are born great,'—
     Oli. Ha ?   40
     Mal. ' Some achieve greatness,'—
     Oli. What say'st thou ?
     Mal. ' And some have greatness thrust
upon thee.'
     Oli. Heaven restore thee !
     Mal. ' Remember who commended thy
yellow stockings,'—   46
     Oli. ' Thy yellow stockings ' ?
     Mal. ' And wish'd to see thee cross-
garter'd.'
     Oli. ' Cross-garter'd ' ?
     Mal. ' Go to, thou art made, if thou
desir'st to be so ; '—
     Oli. Am I made ?   51
     Mal. ' If not, let me see thee a servant
still.'
     Oli. Why, this is very midsummer mad-
ness.

Enter Servant.

     Ser. Madam, the young gentleman of the
Count Orsino's is return'd ; I could hardly
entreat him back ; he attends your ladyship's pleasure.   56
     Oli. I'll come to him. [*Exit Servant*]
Good Maria, let this fellow be look'd to.
Where's my cousin Toby ? Let some of my
people have a special care of him ; I would
not have him miscarry for the half of my
dowry.   [*Exeunt Olivia and Maria.*
     Mal. O, ho ! do you come near me now ?
No worse man than Sir Toby to look to me !
This concurs directly with the letter : she
sends him on purpose, that I may appear
stubborn to him ; for she incites me to
that in the letter. ' Cast thy humble

slough' says she. 'Be opposite with a kinsman, surly with servants; let thy tongue tang with arguments of state; put thyself into the trick of singularity' and consequently sets down the manner how, as: a sad face, a reverend carriage, a slow tongue, in the habit of some sir of note, and so forth. I have lim'd her; but it is Jove's doing, and Jove make me thankful! And when she went away now—' Let this fellow be look'd to'. 'Fellow' not 'Malvolio' nor after my degree, but 'fellow'. Why, everything adheres together, that no dram of a scruple, no scruple of a scruple, no obstacle, no incredulous or unsafe circumstance—what can be said? Nothing that can be can come between me and the full prospect of my hopes. Well, Jove, not I, is the doer of this, and he is to be thanked.   78

Re-enter MARIA, *with* SIR TOBY *and* FABIAN.

Sir To. Which way is he, in the name of sanctity? If all the devils of hell be drawn in little, and Legion himself possess'd him, yet I'll speak to him.   81
Fab. Here he is, here he is. How is't with you, sir?
Sir To. How is't with you, man?
Mal. Go off; I discard you. Let me enjoy my private; go off.   85
Mar. Lo, how hollow the fiend speaks within him! Did not I tell you? Sir Toby, my lady prays you to have a care of him.
Mal. Ah, ha! does she so?   89
Sir To. Go to, go to; peace, peace; we must deal gently with him. Let me alone. How do you, Malvolio? How is't with you? What, man, defy the devil; consider, he's an enemy to mankind.   93
Mal. Do you know what you say?
Mar. La you, an you speak ill of the devil, how he takes it at heart! Pray God he be not bewitch'd.   96
Fab. Carry his water to th' wise woman.
Mar. Marry, and it shall be done tomorrow morning, if I live. My lady would not lose him for more than I'll say.   100
Mal. How now, mistress!
Mar. O Lord!
Sir To. Prithee hold thy peace; this is not the way. Do you not see you move him? Let me alone with him.
Fab. No way but gentleness—gently, gently. The fiend is rough, and will not be roughly us'd.   106
Sir To. Why, how now, my bawcock! How dost thou, chuck?
Mal. Sir!   109
Sir To. Ay, Biddy, come with me. What, man, 'tis not for gravity to play at cherrypit with Satan. Hang him, foul collier!
Mar. Get him to say his prayers, good Sir Toby, get him to pray.

Mal. My prayers, minx!   115
Mar. No, I warrant you, he will not hear of godliness.
Mal. Go, hang yourselves all! You are idle shallow things; I am not of your element; you shall know more hereafter. [*Exit.*
Sir To. Is't possible?   120
Fab. If this were play'd upon a stage now, I could condemn it as an improbable fiction.
Sir To. His very genius hath taken the infection of the device, man.
Mar. Nay, pursue him now, lest the device take air and taint.   126
Fab. Why, we shall make him mad indeed.
Mar. The house will be the quieter.
Sir To. Come, we'll have him in a dark room and bound. My niece is already in the belief that he's mad. We may carry it thus, for our pleasure and his penance, till our very pastime, tired out of breath, prompt us to have mercy on him; at which time we will bring the device to the bar and crown thee for a finder of madmen. But see, but see.   135

Enter SIR ANDREW.

Fab. More matter for a May morning.
Sir And. Here's the challenge; read it. I warrant there's vinegar and pepper in't.
Fab. Is't so saucy?
Sir And. Ay, is't, I warrant him; do but read.   140
Sir To. Give me. [*Reads*] ' Youth, whatsoever thou art, thou art but a scurvy fellow.'
Fab. Good and valiant.
Sir To. [*Reads*] ' Wonder not, nor admire not in thy mind, why I do call thee so, for I will show thee no reason for't.'   145
Fab. A good note; that keeps you from the blow of the law.
Sir To. [*Reads*] ' Thou com'st to the Lady Olivia, and in my sight she uses thee kindly; but thou liest in thy throat; that is not the matter I challenge thee for.' 150
Fab. Very brief, and to exceeding good sense—less.
Sir To. [*Reads*] ' I will waylay thee going home; where if it be thy chance to kill me '—
Fab. Good.
Sir To. ' Thou kill'st me like a rogue and a villain.'   155
Fab. Still you keep o' th' windy side of the law. Good!
Sir To. [*Reads*] ' Fare thee well; and God have mercy upon one of our souls! He may have mercy upon mine; but my hope is better, and so look to thyself. Thy friend, as thou usest him, and thy sworn enemy,   ANDREW AGUECHEEK.'

If this letter move him not, his legs cannot. I'll give't him. 163

Mar. You may have very fit occasion for't ; he is now in some commerce with my lady, and will by and by depart. 166

Sir To. Go, Sir Andrew ; scout me for him at the corner of the orchard, like a bum-baily ; so soon as ever thou seest him, draw ; and as thou draw'st, swear horrible ; for it comes to pass oft that a terrible oath, with a swaggering accent sharply twang'd off, gives manhood more approbation than ever proof itself would have earn'd him. Away. 173

Sir And. Nay, let me alone for swearing.
                                             [*Exit.*

Sir To. Now will not I deliver his letter ; for the behaviour of the young gentleman gives him out to be of good capacity and breeding ; his employment between his lord and my niece confirms no less. Therefore this letter, being so excellently ignorant, will breed no terror in the youth : he will find it comes from a clodpole. But, sir, I will deliver his challenge by word of mouth, set upon Aguecheek a notable report of valour, and drive the gentleman —as I know his youth will aptly receive it—into a most hideous opinion of his rage, skill, fury, and impetuosity. This will so fright them both that they will kill one another by the look, like cockatrices. 186

Re-enter OLIVIA, *with* VIOLA.

Fab. Here he comes with your niece ; give them way till he take leave, and presently after him.

Sir To. I will meditate the while upon some horrid message for a challenge. 190
   [*Exeunt Sir Toby, Fabian, and Maria.*

Oli. I have said too much unto a heart of stone,
And laid mine honour too unchary out ;
There's something in me that reproves my fault ;
But such a headstrong potent fault it is
That it but mocks reproof. 195

Vio. With the same haviour that your passion bears
Goes on my master's griefs ;

Oli. Here, wear this jewel for me ; 'tis my picture.
Refuse it not ; it hath no tongue to vex you.
And I beseech you come again to-morrow.
What shall you ask of me that I'll deny, 201
That honour sav'd may upon asking give ?

Vio. Nothing but this—your true love for my master.

Oli. How with mine honour may I give him that
Which I have given to you ?

Vio.   I will acquit you. 205

Oli. Well, come again to-morrow. Fare thee well ;

A fiend like thee might bear my soul to hell.   [*Exit.*

Re-enter SIR TOBY *and* FABIAN.

Sir To. Gentleman, God save thee.

Vio. And you, sir. 209

Sir To. That defence thou hast, betake thee to't. Of what nature the wrongs are thou hast done him, I know not ; but thy intercepter, full of despite, bloody as the hunter, attends thee at the orchard end. Dismount thy tuck, be yare in thy preparation, for thy assailant is quick, skilful, and deadly. 215

Vio. You mistake, sir ; I am sure no man hath any quarrel to me ; my remembrance is very free and clear from any image of offence done to any man. 218

Sir To. You'll find it otherwise, I assure you ; therefore, if you hold your life at any price, betake you to your guard ; for your opposite hath in him what youth, strength, skill, and wrath, can furnish man withal. 222

Vio. I pray you, sir, what is he ?

Sir To. He is knight, dubb'd with unhatch'd rapier and on carpet consideration ; but he is a devil in private brawl. Souls and bodies hath he divorc'd three ; and his incensement at this moment is so implacable that satisfaction can be none but by pangs of death and sepulchre. Hobnob is his word—give't or take't. 229

Vio. I will return again into the house and desire some conduct of the lady. I am no fighter. I have heard of some kind of men that put quarrels purposely on others to taste their valour ; belike this is a man of that quirk. 233

Sir To. Sir, no ; his indignation derives itself out of a very competent injury ; therefore, get you on and give him his desire. Back you shall not to the house, unless you undertake that with me which with as much safety you might answer him ; therefore on, or strip your sword stark naked ; for meddle you must, that's certain, or forswear to wear iron about you.

Vio. This is as uncivil as strange. I beseech you do me this courteous office as to know of the knight what my offence to him is : it is something of my negligence, nothing of my purpose. 244

Sir To. I will do so. Signior Fabian, stay you by this gentleman till my return.
                            [*Exit Sir Toby.*

Vio. Pray you, sir, do you know of this matter ?

Fab. I know the knight is incens'd against you, even to a mortal arbitrement ; but nothing of the circumstance more. 250

Vio. I beseech you, what manner of man is he ?

Fab. Nothing of that wonderful promise,

to read him by his form, as you are like to find him in the proof of his valour. He is indeed, sir, the most skilful, bloody, and fatal opposite that you could possibly have found in any part of Illyria. Will you walk towards him ? I will make your peace with him if I can.   257

Vio. I shall be much bound to you for't. I am one that would rather go with sir priest than sir knight. I care not who knows so much of my mettle.   [*Exeunt.*

Re-enter SIR TOBY *with* SIR ANDREW.

Sir To. Why, man, he's a very devil ; I have not seen such a firago. I had a pass with him, rapier, scabbard, and all, and he gives me the stuck in with such a mortal motion that it is inevitable ; and on the answer, he pays you as surely as your feet hit the ground they step on. They say he has been fencer to the Sophy.   266

Sir And. Pox on't, I'll not meddle with him.

Sir To. Ay, but he will not now be pacified ; Fabian can scarce hold him yonder.   269

Sir And. Plague on't ; an I thought he had been valiant, and so cunning in fence, I'd have seen him damn'd ere I'd have challeng'd him. Let him let the matter slip, and I'll give him my horse, grey Capilet.   273

Sir To. I'll make the motion. Stand here, make a good show on't ; this shall end without the perdition of souls. [*Aside*] Marry, I'll ride your horse as well as I ride you.   276

Re-enter FABIAN *and* VIOLA.

[*To Fabian*] I have his horse to take up the quarrel ; I have persuaded him the youth's a devil.

Fab. [*To Sir Toby*] He is as horribly conceited of him ; and pants and looks pale, as if a bear were at his heels.   280

Sir To. [*To Viola*] There's no remedy, sir : he will fight with you for's oath sake. Marry, he hath better bethought him of his quarrel, and he finds that now scarce to be worth talking of. Therefore draw for the supportance of his vow ; he protests he will not hurt you.   285

Vio. [*Aside*] Pray God defend me ! A little thing would make me tell them how much I lack of a man.   287

Fab. Give ground if you see him furious.

Sir To. Come, Sir Andrew, there's no remedy ; the gentleman will, for his honour's sake, have one bout with you ; he cannot by the duello avoid it ; but he has promis'd me, as he is a gentleman and a soldier, he will not hurt you. Come on ; to't.

Sir And. Pray God he keep his oath !
                                          [*They draw.*

Enter ANTONIO.

Vio. I do assure you 'tis against my will.

Ant. Put up your sword. If this young gentleman   296
Have done offence, I take the fault on me :
If you offend him, I for him defy you.

Sir To. You, sir ! Why, what are you ?

Ant. One, sir, that for his love dares yet do more
Than you have heard him brag to you he will.   301

Sir To. Nay, if you be an undertaker, I am for you.   [*They draw.*

Enter Officers.

Fab. O good Sir Toby, hold ! Here come the officers.

Sir To. [*To Antonio*] I'll be with you anon.

Vio. Pray, sir, put your sword up, if you please.   305

Sir And. Marry, will I, sir ; and for that I promis'd you, I'll be as good as my word. He will bear you easily and reins well.

1 Off. This is the man ; do thy office.

2 Off. Antonio, I arrest thee at the suit Of Count Orsino.   311

Ant.   You do mistake me, sir.

1 Off. No, sir, no jot ; I know your favour well,
Though now you have no sea-cap on your head.   314
Take him away ; he knows I know him well.

Ant. I must obey. [*To Viola*] This comes with seeking you ;
But there's no remedy ; I shall answer it.
What will you do, now my necessity
Makes me to ask you for my purse ? It grieves me
Much more for what I cannot do for you 320
Than what befalls myself. You stand amaz'd ;
But be of comfort.

2 Off. Come, sir, away.

Ant. I must entreat of you some of that money.

Vio. What money, sir ?   325
For the fair kindness you have show'd me here,
And part being prompted by your present trouble,
Out of my lean and low ability
I'll lend you something. My having is not much ;   329
I'll make division of my present with you ;
Hold, there's half my coffer.

Ant.   Will you deny me now ?
Is't possible that my deserts to you
Can lack persuasion ? Do not tempt my misery,
Lest that it make me so unsound a man
As to upbraid you with those kindnesses
That I have done for you.

Vio.   I know of none,
Nor know I you by voice or any feature.
I hate ingratitude more in a man   338
Than lying, vainness, babbling drunken-
      ness,
Or any taint of vice whose strong corrup-
      tion   340
Inhabits our frail blood.
      Ant.   O heavens themselves !
2 *Off.* Come, sir, I pray you go.
      Ant. Let me speak a little. This youth
      that you see here
I snatch'd one half out of the jaws of
      death,
Reliev'd him with such sanctity of love, 345
And to his image, which methought did
      promise
Most venerable worth, did I devotion,
1 *Off.* What's that to us ? The time goes
      by ; away.
      Ant. But, O, how vile an idol proves this
      god !
Thou hast, Sebastian, done good feature
      shame.   350
In nature there's no blemish but the mind :
None can be call'd deform'd but the un-
      kind.
Virtue is beauty ; but the beauteous evil
Are empty trunks, o'erflourish'd by the
      devil.
1 *Off.* The man grows mad. Away with
      him. Come, come, sir.   355
      Ant. Lead me on.   [*Exit with Officers.*
      Vio. Methinks his words do from such
      passion fly
That he believes himself ; so do not I. 358
Prove true, imagination, O, prove true,
That I, dear brother, be now ta'en for you !
      Sir To. Come hither, knight ; come
      hither, Fabian ; we'll whisper o'er a couplet
      or two of most sage saws.
      Vio. He nam'd Sebastian. I my brother
      know
Yet living in my glass ; even such and so
In favour was my brother ; and he went 365
Still in this fashion, colour, ornament,
For him I imitate. O, if it prove,
Tempests are kind, and salt waves fresh in
      love !   [*Exit.*
      Sir To. A very dishonest paltry boy, and
more a coward than a hare. His dishonesty
appears in leaving his friend here in
necessity and denying him ; and for his
cowardship, ask Fabian.   372
      Fab. A coward, a most devout coward,
religious in it.
      Sir And. 'Slid, I'll after him again and
beat him.
      Sir To. Do ; cuff him soundly, but never
draw thy sword.   376
      Sir And. An I do not—   [*Exit.*
      Fab. Come, let's see the event.
      Sir To. I dare lay any money 'twill be
nothing yet.   [*Exeunt.*

ACT FOUR

SCENE I. *Before Olivia's house.*

Enter SEBASTIAN *and* Clown.

Clo. Will you make me believe that I am
not sent for you ?
      Seb. Go to, go to, thou art a foolish
fellow ; let me be clear of thee.   4
      Clo. Well held out, i' faith ! No, I do not
know you ; nor I am not sent to you by
my lady, to bid you come speak with her ;
nor your name is not Master Cesario ; nor
this is not my nose neither. Nothing that
is so is so.
      Seb. I prithee vent thy folly somewhere
      else.
Thou know'st not me.   10
      Clo. Vent my folly ! He has heard that
word of some great man, and now applies
it to a fool. Vent my folly ! I am afraid
this great lubber, the world, will prove a
cockney. I prithee now, ungird thy strangeness, and tell me what I shall vent to my
lady. Shall I vent to her that thou art
coming ?   16
      Seb. I prithee, foolish Greek, depart from
      me ;
There's money for thee; if you tarry
      longer
I shall give worse payment.   19
      Clo. By my troth, thou hast an open
hand.   These wise men that give fools
money get themselves a good report—
after fourteen years' purchase.

Enter SIR ANDREW, SIR TOBY, *and* FABIAN.

Sir And. Now, sir, have I met you again ?
[*Striking Sebastian*] There's for you.
      Seb. Why, there's for thee, and there,
      and there.   25
Are all the people mad ?
      Sir To. Hold, sir, or I'll throw your
dagger o'er the house. [*Holding Sebastian.*
      Clo. This will I tell my lady straight. I
would not be in some of your coats for
two-pence.   [*Exit.* 30
      Sir To. Come on, sir ; hold.
      Sir And. Nay, let him alone. I'll go
another way to work with him ; I'll have
an action of battery against him, if there
be any law in Illyria ; though I struck him
first, yet it's no matter for that.   35
      Seb. Let go thy hand.
      Sir To. Come, sir, I will not let you go.
Come, my young soldier, put up your iron ;
you are well flesh'd. Come on.   39
      Seb. I will be free from thee. What
wouldst thou now ?
If thou dar'st tempt me further, draw thy
      sword.   [*Draws.*
      Sir To. What, what ? Nay, then I must
have an ounce or two of this malapert
blood from you.   [*Draws.*

Enter OLIVIA.

Oli. Hold, Toby; on thy life, I charge
thee hold.

Sir To. Madam! 45

Oli. Will it be ever thus? Ungracious
wretch,
Fit for the mountains and the barbarous
caves,
Where manners ne'er were preach'd! Out
of my sight!
Be not offended, dear Cesario— 49
Rudesby, be gone!
[*Exeunt* Sir Toby, Sir Andrew, *and* Fabian.
                    I prithee, gentle friend,
Let thy fair wisdom, not thy passion, sway
In this uncivil and unjust extent
Against thy peace. Go with me to my
house,
And hear thou there how many fruitless
pranks
This ruffian hath botch'd up, that thou
thereby 55
Mayst smile at this. Thou shalt not choose
but go;
Do not deny. Beshrew his soul for me!
He started one poor heart of mine in thee.

Seb. What relish is in this? How runs
the stream?
Or I am mad, or else this is a dream. 60
Let fancy still my sense in Lethe steep;
If it be thus to dream, still let me sleep!

Oli. Nay, come, I prithee. Would
thou'dst be rul'd by me!

Seb. Madam, I will.

Oli.   O, say so, and so be!
                                    [*Exeunt.*

SCENE II. *Olivia's house.*

Enter MARIA *and* Clown.

Mar. Nay, I prithee, put on this gown
and this beard; make him believe thou art
Sir Topas the curate; do it quickly. I'll
call Sir Toby the whilst. [*Exit.*

Clo. Well, I'll put it on, and I will
dissemble myself in't; and I would I were
the first that ever dissembled in such a
gown. I am not tall enough to become the
function well nor lean enough to be
thought a good student; but to be said
an honest man and a good housekeeper
goes as fairly as to say a careful man and
a great scholar. The competitors enter. 10

Enter SIR TOBY *and* MARIA.

Sir To. Jove bless thee, Master Parson.

Clo. Bonos dies, Sir Toby; for as the old
hermit of Prague, that never saw pen and
ink, very wittily said to a niece of King
Gorboduc 'That that is is'; so I, being
Master Parson, am Master Parson; for
what is 'that' but that, and 'is' but is?

Sir To. To him, Sir Topas. 17

Clo. What ho, I say! Peace in this
prison!

Sir To. The knave counterfeits well; a
good knave.

Mal. [*Within*] Who calls there? 20

Clo. Sir Topas the curate, who comes to
visit Malvolio the lunatic.

Mal. Sir Topas, Sir Topas, good Sir
Topas, go to my lady.

Clo. Out, hyperbolical fiend! How
vexest thou this man! Talkest thou nothing
but of ladies? 26

Sir To. Well said, Master Parson.

Mal. Sir Topas, never was man thus
wronged. Good Sir Topas, do not think I
am mad; they have laid me here in hideous
darkness. 30

Clo. Fie, thou dishonest Satan! I call
thee by the most modest terms, for I am
one of those gentle ones that will use the
devil himself with courtesy. Say'st thou
that house is dark?

Mal. As hell, Sir Topas. 35

Clo. Why, it hath bay windows transparent as barricadoes, and the clerestories
toward the south north are as lustrous as
ebony; and yet complainest thou of
obstruction?

Mal. I am not mad, Sir Topas. I say to
you this house is dark. 40

Clo. Madman, thou errest. I say there is
no darkness but ignorance; in which thou
art more puzzled than the Egyptians in
their fog. 43

Mal. I say this house is as dark as
ignorance, though ignorance were as dark
as hell; and I say there was never man
thus abus'd. I am no more mad than you
are; make the trial of it in any constant
question.

Clo. What is the opinion of Pythagoras
concerning wild fowl? 49

Mal. That the soul of our grandam
might haply inhabit a bird.

Clo. What think'st thou of his opinion?

Mal. I think nobly of the soul, and no
way approve his opinion. 54

Clo. Fare thee well. Remain thou still
in darkness: thou shalt hold th' opinion
of Pythagoras ere I will allow of thy wits;
and fear to kill a woodcock, lest thou
dispossess the soul of thy grandam. Fare
thee well.

Mal. Sir Topas, Sir Topas!

Sir To. My most exquisite Sir Topas! 60

Clo. Nay, I am for all waters.

Mar. Thou mightst have done this
without thy beard and gown: he sees thee
not. 63

Sir To. To him in thine own voice, and
bring me word how thou find'st him. I
would we were well rid of this knavery.
If he may be conveniently deliver'd, I
would he were; for I am now so far in

offence with my niece that I cannot pursue
with any safety this sport to the upshot.
Come by and by to my chamber. 69
    [*Exeunt Sir Toby and Maria.*
Clo. [*Sings*] Hey, Robin, jolly Robin,
      Tell me how thy lady does.
Mal. Fool!
Clo. [*Sings*] My lady is unkind, perdy.
Mal. Fool!
Clo. [*Sings*] Alas, why is she so? 75
Mal. Fool I say!
Clo. [*Sings*] She loves another—Who
calls, ha?
Mal. Good fool, as ever thou wilt deserve
well at my hand, help me to a candle, and
pen, ink, and paper; as I am a gentleman,
I will live to be thankful to thee for't. 80
Clo. Master Malvolio?
Mal. Ay, good fool.
Clo. Alas, sir, how fell you besides your
five wits?
Mal. Fool, there was never man so
notoriously abus'd; I am as well in my
wits, fool, as thou art. 85
Clo. But as well? Then you are mad
indeed, if you be no better in your wits
than a fool.
Mal. They have here propertied me;
keep me in darkness, send ministers to me,
asses, and do all they can to face me out
of my wits. 90
Clo. Advise you what you say; the
minister is here. [*Speaking as Sir Topas*]
Malvolio, Malvolio, thy wits the heavens
restore! Endeavour thyself to sleep, and
leave thy vain bibble-babble.
Mal. Sir Topas! 94
Clo. Maintain no words with him, good
fellow.—Who, I, sir? Not I, sir. God buy
you, good Sir Topas.—Marry, amen.—I
will, sir, I will.
Mal. Fool, fool, fool, I say!
Clo. Alas, sir, be patient. What say you,
sir? I am shent for speaking to you. 100
Mal. Good fool, help me to some light
and some paper. I tell thee I am as well in
my wits as any man in Illyria.
Clo. Well-a-day that you were, sir! 104
Mal. By this hand, I am. Good fool,
some ink, paper, and light; and convey
what I will set down to my lady. It shall
advantage thee more than ever the bearing
of letter did.
Clo. I will help you to't. But tell me
true, are you not mad indeed, or do you
but counterfeit? 110
Mal. Believe me, I am not; I tell thee
true.
Clo. Nay, I'll ne'er believe a madman till
I see his brains. I will fetch you light and
paper and ink.
Mal. Fool, I'll requite it in the highest
degree; I prithee be gone. 115

Clo. [*Singing*]
    I am gone, sir,
    And anon, sir,
  I'll be with you again,
    In a trice,
  Like to the old Vice, 120
  Your need to sustain;
  Who with dagger of lath,
  In his rage and his wrath,
    Cries, Ah, ha! to the devil;
  Like a mad lad, 125
  Pare thy nails, dad.
    Adieu, goodman devil.
        [*Exit.*

  Scene III. *Olivia's garden.*

    Enter Sebastian.

Seb. This is the air; that is the glorious
    sun;
This pearl she gave me, I do feel't and see't;
And though 'tis wonder that enwraps me
    thus,
Yet 'tis not madness. Where's Antonio,
    then?
I could not find him at the Elephant; 5
Yet there he was; and there I found this
    credit,
That he did range the town to seek me out.
His counsel now might do me golden service;
For though my soul disputes well with my
    sense
That this may be some error, but no
    madness, 10
Yet doth this accident and flood of fortune
So far exceed all instance, all discourse,
That I am ready to distrust mine eyes
And wrangle with my reason, that persuades
    me
To any other trust but that I am mad, 15
Or else the lady's mad; yet if 'twere so,
She could not sway her house, command
    her followers,
Take and give back affairs and their
    dispatch
With such a smooth, discreet, and stable
    bearing,
As I perceive she does. There's something
    in't 20
That is deceivable. But here the lady
    comes.

    Enter Olivia *and* Priest.

Oli. Blame not this haste of mine. If you
    mean well,
Now go with me and with this holy man
Into the chantry by; there, before him
And underneath that consecrated roof, 25
Plight me the full assurance of your faith,
That my most jealous and too doubtful soul
May live at peace. He shall conceal it
Whiles you are willing it shall come to note,
What time we will our celebration keep 30
According to my birth. What do you say?

Seb. I'll follow this good man, and go
　　　with you ;
And, having sworn truth, ever will be true.
Oli. Then lead the way, good father ; and
　　　heavens so shine　　　　　　　34
That they may fairly note this act of mine !
　　　　　　　　　　　　　　　　[*Exeunt.*

ACT FIVE.

Scene I. *Before Olivia's house.*

Enter Clown *and* Fabian.

Fab. Now, as thou lov'st me, let me see
his letter.
Clo. Good Master Fabian, grant me
another request.
Fab. Anything.
Clo. Do not desire to see this letter.
Fab. This is to give a dog, and in recom-
pense desire my dog again.　　　　　6

Enter Duke, Viola, Curio *and* Lords.

Duke. Belong you to the Lady Olivia,
friends ?
Clo. Ay, sir, we are some of her trappings.
Duke. I know thee well. How dost thou,
my good fellow ?
Clo. Truly, sir, the better for my foes
and the worse for my friends.　　　11
Duke. Just the contrary : the better for
thy friends.
Clo. No, sir, the worse.
Duke. How can that be ?　　　　14
Clo. Marry, sir, they praise me and make
an ass of me. Now my foes tell me plainly
I am an ass ; so that by my foes, sir, I
profit in the knowledge of myself, and by
my friends I am abused ; so that, conclusions to be as kisses, if your four
negatives make your two affirmatives, why
then, the worse for my friends and the
better for my foes.　　　　　　　20
Duke. Why, this is excellent.
Clo. By my troth, sir, no ; though it
please you to be one of my friends.
Duke. Thou shalt not be the worse for
me. There's gold.
Clo. But that it would be double-dealing,
sir, I would you could make it another.　26
Duke. O, you give me ill counsel.
Clo. Put your grace in your pocket, sir,
for this once, and let your flesh and blood
obey it.
Duke. Well, I will be so much a sinner to
be a double-dealer. There's another.　31
Clo. Primo, secundo, tertio, is a good
play ; and the old saying is ' The third
pays for all '. The triplex, sir, is a good
tripping measure ; or the bells of Saint
Bennet, sir, may put you in mind—one,
two, three.　　　　　　　　　35
Duke. You can fool no more money out
of me at this throw ; if you will let your

lady know I am here to speak with her,
and bring her along with you, it may
awake my bounty further.　　　　39
Clo. Marry, sir, lullaby to your bounty
till I come again. I go, sir ; but I would
not have you to think that my desire of
having is the sin of covetousness. But, as
you say, sir, let your bounty take a nap ;
I will awake it anon.　　　　　[*Exit.*

Enter Antonio *and* Officers.

Vio. Here comes the man, sir, that did
　　　rescue me.
Duke. That face of his I do remember
　　　well ;　　　　　　　　　45
Yet when I saw it last it was besmear'd
As black as Vulcan in the smoke of war.
A baubling vessel was he captain of,
For shallow draught and bulk unprizable,
With which such scathful grapple did he
　　　make　　　　　　　　　50
With the most noble bottom of our fleet
That very envy and the tongue of loss
Cried fame and honour on him. What's the
　　　matter ?
1 Off. Orsino, this is that Antonio
That took the Phœnix and her fraught from
　　　Candy ;　　　　　　　　55
And this is he that did the Tiger board
When your young nephew Titus lost his
　　　leg.
Here in the streets, desperate of shame and
　　　state,
In private brabble did we apprehend him.
Vio. He did me kindness, sir ; drew on
　　　my side ;　　　　　　　　60
But in conclusion put strange speech upon
　　　me.
I know not what 'twas but distraction.
Duke. Notable pirate, thou salt-water
　　　thief !
What foolish boldness brought thee to their
　　　mercies
Whom thou, in terms so bloody and so dear,
Hast made thine enemies ?
Ant.　　　　　Orsino, noble sir, 66
Be pleas'd that I shake off these names you
　　　give me :
Antonio never yet was thief or pirate,
Though I confess, on base and ground
　　　enough,
Orsino's enemy. A witchcraft drew me
　　　hither :　　　　　　　　70
That most ingrateful boy there by your
　　　side
From the rude sea's enrag'd and foamy
　　　mouth
Did I redeem ; a wreck past hope he was.
His life I gave him, and did thereto add
My love without retention or restraint, 75
All his in dedication ; for his sake,
Did I expose myself, pure for his love,
Into the danger of this adverse town ;
Drew to defend him when he was beset ;

Where being apprehended, his false
 cunning,   80
Not meaning to partake with me in danger,
Taught him to face me out of his acquaint-
 ance,
And grew a twenty years removed thing
While one would wink; denied me mine
 own purse,
Which I had recommended to his use 85
Not half an hour before.
 Vio.   How can this be?
 Duke. When came he to this town?
 Ant. To-day, my lord; and for three
  months before,
No int'rim, not a minute's vacancy, 89
Both day and night did we keep company.

 Enter OLIVIA *and* Attendants.

 Duke. Here comes the Countess; now
  heaven walks on earth.
But for thee, fellow—fellow, thy words are
  madness.
Three months this youth hath tended upon
  me—
But more of that anon. Take him aside.
 Oli. What would my lord, but that he
  may not have,
Wherein Olivia may seem serviceable? 96
Cesario, you do not keep promise with me.
 Vio. Madam?
 Duke. Gracious Olivia—
 Oli. What do you say, Cesario? Good
  my lord—
 Vio. My lord would speak; my duty
  hushes me.   101
 Oli. If it be aught to the old tune, my
  lord,
It is as fat and fulsome to mine ear
As howling after music.
 Duke.   Still so cruel?
 Oli. Still so constant, lord. 105
 Duke. What, to perverseness? You un-
  civil lady,
To whose ingrate and unauspicious altars
My soul the faithfull'st off'rings hath
  breath'd out
That e'er devotion tender'd! What shall
  I do?
 Oli. Even what it please my lord, that
  shall become him.   110
 Duke. Why should I not, had I the heart
  to do it,
Like to the Egyptian thief at point of
  death,
Kill what I love?—a savage jealousy
That sometime savours nobly. But hear
  me this: 114
Since you to non-regardance cast my faith,
And that I partly know the instrument
That screws me from my true place in your
  favour,
Live you the marble-breasted tyrant still;
But this your minion, whom I know you
  love,

And whom, by heaven I swear, I tender
  dearly,   120
Him will I tear out of that cruel eye
Where he sits crowned in his master's spite.
Come, boy, with me; my thoughts are ripe
  in mischief:
I'll sacrifice the lamb that I do love
To spite a raven's heart within a dove. 125
 Vio. And I, most jocund, apt, and will-
  ingly,
To do you rest, a thousand deaths would die.
 Oli. Where goes Cesario?
 Vio.   After him I love
More than I love these eyes, more than
  my life,
More, by all mores, than e'er I shall love
  wife.   130
If I do feign, you witnesses above
Punish my life for tainting of my love!
 Oli. Ay me, detested! How am I
  beguil'd!
 Vio. Who does beguile you? Who does
  do you wrong?
 Oli. Hast thou forgot thyself? Is it so
  long?   135
Call forth the holy father.
      [*Exit an Attendant.*
 Duke.   Come, away!
 Oli. Whither, my lord? Cesario, husband,
  stay.
 Duke. Husband?
 Oli. Ay, husband; can he that deny?
 Duke. Her husband, sirrah?
 Vio.   No, my lord, not I.
 Oli. Alas, it is the baseness of thy fear 140
That makes thee strangle thy propriety.
Fear not, Cesario, take thy fortunes up;
Be that thou know'st thou art, and then
  thou art
As great as that thou fear'st.

    Enter Priest.

     O, welcome, father!
Father, I charge thee, by thy reverence, 145
Here to unfold—though lately we intended
To keep in darkness what occasion now
Reveals before 'tis ripe—what thou dost
  know
Hath newly pass'd between this youth and
  me.   149
 Priest. A contract of eternal bond of love,
Confirm'd by mutual joinder of your hands,
Attested by the holy close of lips,
Strength'ned by interchangement of your
  rings;
And all the ceremony of this compact 154
Seal'd in my function, by my testimony;
Since when, my watch hath told me, toward
  my grave,
I have travell'd but two hours.
 Duke. O thou dissembling cub! What
  wilt thou be,   158
When time hath sow'd a grizzle on thy case?
Or will not else thy craft so quickly grow

That thine own trip shall be thine over-
throw ?
Farewell, and take her ; but direct thy feet
Where thou and I henceforth may never
meet.
   Vio. My lord, I do protest—
   Oli.   O, do not swear !
Hold little faith, though thou has too much
fear.   165

Enter Sir Andrew.

   Sir And. For the love of God, a surgeon !
Send one presently to Sir Toby.
   Oli. What's the matter ?
   Sir And. Has broke my head across, and
has given Sir Toby a bloody coxcomb too.
For the love of God, your help ! I had
rather than forty pound I were at home. 171
   Oli. Who has done this, Sir Andrew ?
   Sir And. The Count's gentleman, one
Cesario. We took him for a coward, but he's
the very devil incardinate.
   Duke. My gentleman, Cesario ?   175
   Sir And. Od's lifelings, here he is ! You
broke my head for nothing ; and that that
I did, I was set on to do't by Sir Toby.
   Vio. Why do you speak to me ? I never
hurt you.
You drew your sword upon me without
cause ;   180
But I bespake you fair and hurt you not.

Enter Sir Toby *and* Clown.

   Sir And. If a bloody coxcomb be a hurt,
you have hurt me ; I think you set
nothing by a bloody coxcomb. Here comes
Sir Toby halting ; you shall hear more ;
but if he had not been in drink, he would
have tickl'd you othergates than he did. 186
   Duke. How now, gentleman ? How is't
with you ?
   Sir To. That's all one ; has hurt me, and
there's th' end on't. Sot, didst see Dick
Surgeon, sot ?
   Clo. O, he's drunk, Sir Toby, an hour
agone ; his eyes were set at eight i' th'
morning.   191
   Sir To. Then he's a rogue and a passy
measures pavin. I hate a drunken rogue.
   Oli. Away with him. Who hath made
this havoc with them ?   195
   Sir And. I'll help you, Sir Toby, because
we'll be dress'd together.
   Sir To. Will you help—an ass-head and
a coxcomb and a knave, a thin fac'd knave,
a gull ?
   Oli. Get him to bed, and let his hurt be
look'd to.   200
   [*Exeunt Clown, Fabian, Sir Toby,
and Sir Andrew*

Enter Sebastian.

   Seb. I am sorry, madam, I have hurt
your kinsman ;

But, had it been the brother of my blood,
I must have done no less with wit and
safety.
You throw a strange regard upon me, and
by that
I do perceive it hath offended you.   205
Pardon me, sweet one, even for the vows
We made each other but so late ago.
   Duke. One face, one voice, one habit, and
two persons !
A natural perspective, that is and is not.
   Seb. Antonio, O my dear Antonio !   210
How have the hours rack'd and tortur'd me
Since I have lost thee !
   Ant. Sebastian are you ?
   Seb.   Fear'st thou that, Antonio ?
   Ant. How have you made division of
yourself ?
An apple cleft in two is not more twin   215
Than these two creatures. Which is
Sebastian ?
   Oli. Most wonderful !
   Seb. Do I stand there ? I never had a
brother ;
Nor can there be that deity in my nature
Of here and everywhere. I had a sister   220
Whom the blind waves and surges have
devour'd.
Of charity, what kin are you to me ?
What countryman, what name, what
parentage ?
   Vio. Of Messaline ; Sebastian was my
father.
Such a Sebastian was my brother too ;   225
So went he suited to his watery tomb ;
If spirits can assume both form and suit,
You come to fright us.
   Seb.   A spirit I am indeed,
But am in that dimension grossly clad
Which from the womb I did participate. 230
Were you a woman, as the rest goes even,
I should my tears let fall upon your cheek,
And say ' Thrice welcome, drowned Viola ! '
   Vio. My father had a mole upon his brow.
   Seb. And so had mine.   235
   Vio. And died that day when Viola from
her birth
Had numb'red thirteen years.
   Seb. O, that record is lively in my soul !
He finished indeed his mortal act
That day that made my sister thirteen
years.   240
   Vio. If nothing lets to make us happy
both
But this my masculine usurp'd attire,
Do not embrace me till each circumstance
Of place, time, fortune, do cohere and
jump
That I am Viola ; which to confirm,   245
I'll bring you to a captain in this town,
Where lie my maiden weeds ; by whose
gentle help
I was preserv'd to serve this noble Count.
All the occurrence of my fortune since

Hath been between this lady and this lord.
  Seb. [*To Olivia*] So comes it, lady, you
have been mistook ;   251
But nature to her bias drew in that.
You would have been contracted to a maid ;
Nor are you therein, by my life, deceiv'd ;
You are betroth'd both to a maid and man.
  Duke. Be not amaz'd ; right noble is his
    blood.   256
If this be so, as yet the glass seems true,
I shall have share in this most happy
    wreck.
[*To Viola*] Boy, thou hast said to me a
    thousand times
Thou never shouldst love woman like to me.
  Vio. And all those sayings will I over-
    swear ;   261
And all those swearings keep as true in soul
As doth that orbed continent the fire
That severs day from night.
  Duke.   Give me thy hand ;
And let me see thee in thy woman's weeds.
  Vio. The captain that did bring me first
    on shore   266
Hath my maid's garments. He, upon some
    action,
Is now in durance, at Malvolio's suit,
A gentleman and follower of my lady's.
  Oli. He shall enlarge him. Fetch
    Malvolio hither ;   270
And yet, alas, now I remember me,
They say, poor gentleman, he's much
    distract.

Re-enter Clown, *with a letter, and* FABIAN.

A most extracting frenzy of mine own
From my remembrance clearly banish'd
    his.
How does he, sirrah ?   275
  Clo. Truly, madam, he holds Belzebub
at the stave's end as well as a man in his
case may do. Has here writ a letter to you ;
I should have given 't you to-day morning,
but as a madman's epistles are no gospels,
so it skills not much when they are
deliver'd.   280
  Oli. Open't, and read it.
  Clo. Look then to be well edified when
the fool delivers the madman. [*Reads
madly*] ' By the Lord, madam— '
  Oli. How now ! Art thou mad ?   284
  Clo. No, madam, I do but read madness.
An your ladyship will have it as it ought
to be, you must allow vox.
  Oli. Prithee read i' thy right wits.
  Clo. So I do, madonna ; but to read his
right wits is to read thus ; therefore perpend, my Princess, and give ear.
  Oli. [*To Fabian*] Read it you, sirrah.   290
  Fab. [*Reads*] ' By the Lord, madam, you
wrong me, and the world shall know it.
Though you have put me into darkness and
given your drunken cousin rule over me,
yet have I the benefit of my senses as well

as your ladyship. I have your own letter
that induced me to the semblance I put
on, with the which I doubt not but to do
myself much right or you much shame.
Think of me as you please. I leave my
duty a little unthought of, and speak out
of my injury.
           THE MADLY-US'D MALVOLIO.'
  Oli. Did he write this ?
  Clo. Ay, Madam.   300
  Duke. This savours not much of distrac-
    tion.
  Oli. See him deliver'd, Fabian ; bring
    him hither.   [*Exit Fabian.*
My lord, so please you, these things further
    thought on,
To think me as well a sister as a wife,
One day shall crown th' alliance on't, so
    please you,   305
Here at my house, and at my proper cost.
  Duke. Madam, I am most apt t' embrace
    your offer.
[*To Viola*] Your master quits you ; and,
    for your service done him,
So much against the mettle of your sex,
So far beneath your soft and tender
    breeding,   310
And since you call'd me master for so long,
Here is my hand ; you shall from this
    time be
Your master's mistress.
  Oli.   A sister ! You are she.

Re-enter FABIAN, *with* MALVOLIO.

  Duke. Is this the madman ?
  Oli.   Ay, my lord, this same.
How now, Malvolio !
  Mal. Madam, you have done me wrong,
Notorious wrong.
  Oli.   Have I, Malvolio ? No.
  Mal. Lady, you have. Pray you peruse
    that letter.   317
You must not now deny it is your hand ;
Write from it if you can, in hand or phrase ;
Or say 'tis not your seal, not your in-
    vention ;   320
You can say none of this. Well, grant it
    then,
And tell me, in the modesty of honour,
Why you have given me such clear lights
    of favour,
Bade me come smiling and cross-garter'd
    to you,   324
To put on yellow stockings, and to frown
Upon Sir Toby and the lighter people ;
And, acting this in an obedient hope,
Why have you suffer'd me to be imprison'd,
Kept in a dark house, visited by the priest,
And made the most notorious geck and gull
That e'er invention play'd on ? Tell me
    why.   331
  Oli. Alas, Malvolio, this is not my writing,
Though, I confess, much like the character ;
But out of question 'tis Maria's hand.

And now I do bethink me, it was she 335
First told me thou wast mad ; then cam'st
    in smiling,
And in such forms which here were pre-
    suppos'd
Upon thee in the letter. Prithee, be con-
    tent ;
This practice hath most shrewdly pass'd
    upon thee,
But, when we know the grounds and
    authors of it, 340
Thou shalt be both the plaintiff and the
    judge
Of thine own cause.
    Fab.   Good madam, hear me speak,
And let no quarrel nor no brawl to come
Taint the condition of this present hour,
Which I have wond'red at. In hope it shall
    not, 345
Most freely I confess myself and Toby
Set this device against Malvolio here,
Upon some stubborn and uncourteous parts
We had conceiv'd against him. Maria writ
The letter, at Sir Toby's great importance,
In recompense whereof he hath married her.
How with a sportful malice it was follow'd
May rather pluck on laughter than revenge,
If that the injuries be justly weigh'd
That have on both sides pass'd. 355
    Oli. Alas, poor fool, how have they
    baffl'd thee !
    Clo. Why, ' Some are born great, some
achieve greatness, and some have greatness
thrown upon them '. I was one, sir, in
this interlude—one Sir Topas, sir ; but
that's all one. ' By the Lord, fool, I am
not mad ! ' But do you remember—
' Madam, why laugh you at such a barren
rascal ? An you smile not, he's gagg'd ' ?
And thus the whirligig of time brings in
his revenges. 363
    Mal. I'll be reveng'd on the whole pack
of you.   *[Exit.*

    Oli. He hath been most notoriously
    abus'd. 365
    Duke. Pursue him, and entreat him to a
    peace ;
He hath not told us of the captain yet.
When that is known, and golden time
    convents,
A solemn combination shall be made 369
Of our dear souls. Meantime, sweet sister,
We will not part from hence. Cesario,
    come;
For so you shall be while you are a
    man ;
But when in other habits you are seen,
Orsino's mistress, and his fancy's queen.
          [Exeunt all but the Clown.

        Clown sings.

When that I was and a little tiny boy, 375
  With hey, ho, the wind and the rain,
A foolish thing was but a toy,
  For the rain it raineth every day.

But when I came to man's estate,
  With hey, ho, the wind and the rain, 380
'Gainst knaves and thieves men shut their
    gate,
  For the rain it raineth every day.

But when I came, alas ! to wive,
  With hey, ho, the wind and the rain,
By swaggering could I never thrive, 385
  For the rain it raineth every day.

But when I came unto my beds,
  With hey, ho, the wind and the rain,
With toss-pots still had drunken heads,
  For the rain it raineth every day. 390

A great while ago the world begun,
  With hey, ho, the wind and the rain,
But that's all one, our play is done,
  And we'll strive to please you every day.
                    [Exit.

THE WINTER'S TALE

DRAMATIS PERSONÆ

LEONTES, *King of Sicilia.*
MAMILLIUS, *his son, the young Prince of Sicilia.*
CAMILLO,
ANTIGONUS, } *lords of Sicilia.*
CLEOMENES,
DION,
POLIXENES, *King of Bohemia.*
FLORIZEL, *his son, Prince of Bohemia.*
ARCHIDAMUS, *a lord of Bohemia.*
Old Shepherd, *reputed father of Perdita.*
Clown, *his son.*
AUTOLYCUS, *a rogue.*

A Mariner.
A Gaoler.
TIME, *as Chorus.*

HERMIONE, *Queen to Leontes.*
PERDITA, *daughter to Leontes and Hermione.*
PAULINA, *wife to Antigonus.*
EMILIA, *a lady attending on the Queen.*
MOPSA,
DORCAS, } *shepherdesses.*

Other Lords, Gentlemen, Ladies, Officers, Servants, Shepherds, Shepherdesses.

THE SCENE : *Sicilia and Bohemia.*

ACT ONE

SCENE I. *Sicilia. The palace of Leontes.*

Enter CAMILLO *and* ARCHIDAMUS.

Arch. If you shall chance, Camillo, to visit Bohemia, on the like occasion whereon my services are now on foot, you shall see, as I have said, great difference betwixt our Bohemia and your Sicilia. 4

Cam. I think this coming summer the King of Sicilia means to pay Bohemia the visitation which he justly owes him.

Arch. Wherein our entertainment shall shame us we will be justified in our loves ; for indeed—

Cam. Beseech you— 10

Arch. Verily, I speak it in the freedom of my knowledge : we cannot with such magnificence, in so rare—I know not what to say. We will give you sleepy drinks, that your senses, unintelligent of our insufficiency, may, though they cannot praise us, as little accuse us. 15

Cam. You pay a great deal too dear for what's given freely.

Arch. Believe me, I speak as my understanding instructs me and as mine honesty puts it to utterance. 19

Cam. Sicilia cannot show himself overkind to Bohemia. They were train'd together in their childhoods ; and there rooted betwixt them then such an affection which cannot choose but branch now. Since their more mature dignities and royal necessities made separation of their society, their encounters, though not personal, have been royally attorneyed with interchange of gifts, letters, loving embassies ; that they have seem'd to be together, though absent ; shook hands, as over a vast ; and embrac'd as it were from the ends of opposed winds. The heavens continue their loves ! 30

Arch. I think there is not in the world either malice or matter to alter it. You have an unspeakable comfort of your young Prince Mamillius ; it is a gentleman of the greatest promise that ever came into my note. 34

Cam. I very well agree with you in the hopes of him. It is a gallant child ; one that indeed physics the subject, makes old hearts fresh ; they that went on crutches ere he was born desire yet their life to see him a man. 38

Arch. Would they else be content to die ?

Cam. Yes ; if there were no other excuse why they should desire to live. 41

Arch. If the King had no son, they would desire to live on crutches till he had one.

[*Exeunt.*

SCENE II. *Sicilia. The palace of Leontes.*

Enter LEONTES, POLIXENES, HERMIONE, MAMILLIUS, CAMILLO, *and* Attendants.

Pol. Nine changes of the wat'ry star hath been
The shepherd's note since we have left our throne
Without a burden. Time as long again
Would be fill'd up, my brother, with our thanks ;
And yet we should for perpetuity 5
Go hence in debt. And therefore, like a cipher,
Yet standing in rich place, I multiply
With one ' We thank you ' many thousands moe
That go before it.

Leon. Stay your thanks a while,

And pay them when you part.
 Pol.   Sir, that's to-morrow. 10
I am question'd by my fears of what may
  chance
Or breed upon our absence, that may blow
No sneaping winds at home, to make us say
' This is put forth too truly'. Besides, I
  have stay'd
To tire your royalty.
 Leon. We are tougher, brother, 15
Than you can put us to't.
 Pol.   No longer stay.
 Leon. One sev'night longer.
 Pol.   Very sooth, to-morrow.
 Leon. We'll part the time between's then ;
  and in that
I'll no gainsaying.
 Pol. Press me not, beseech you, so.
There is no tongue that moves, none, none
  i' th' world, 20
So soon as yours could win me. So it should
  now,
Were there necessity in your request,
  although
'Twere needful I denied it. My affairs
Do even drag me homeward ; which to
  hinder 24
Were in your love a whip to me ; my stay
To you a charge and trouble. To save both,
Farewell, our brother.
 Leon. Tongue-tied, our Queen ? Speak
  you.
 Her. I had thought, sir, to have held my
  peace until
You had drawn oaths from him not to stay.
  You, sir,
Charge him too coldly. Tell him you are
  sure 30
All in Bohemia's well—this satisfaction
The by-gone day proclaim'd. Say this to
  him,
He's beat from his best ward.
 Leon.   Well said, Hermione.
 Her. To tell he longs to see his son were
  strong ;
But let him say so then, and let him go ; 35
But let him swear so, and he shall not
  stay ;
We'll thwack him hence with distaffs.
[*To Polixenes*] Yet of your royal presence
  I'll adventure
The borrow of a week. When at Bohemia
You take my lord, I'll give him my com-
  mission 40
To let him there a month behind the gest
Prefix'd for's parting.—Yet, good deed,
  Leontes,
I love thee not a jar o' th' clock behind
What lady she her lord.—You'll stay ?
 Pol.   No, madam.
 Her. Nay, but you will ?
 Pol. I may not, verily. 45
 Her. Verily !
You put me off with limber vows ; but I,

Though you would seek t' unsphere the
  stars with oaths,
Should yet say ' Sir, no going '. Verily,
You shall not go ; a lady's ' verily ' is 50
As potent as a lord's. Will you go yet ?
Force me to keep you as a prisoner,
Not like a guest ; so you shall pay your fees
When you depart, and save your thanks.
  How say you ?
My prisoner or my guest ? By your dread
  ' verily ', 55
One of them you shall be.
 Pol. Your guest, then, madam :
To be your prisoner should import offend-
  ing ;
Which is for me less easy to commit
Than you to punish.
 Her. Not your gaoler then,
But your kind hostess. Come, I'll question
  you 60
Of my lord's tricks and yours when you
  were boys.
You were pretty lordings then !
 Pol.   We were, fair Queen,
Two lads that thought there was no more
  behind
But such a day to-morrow as to-day,
And to be boy eternal.
 Her. Was not my lord 65
The verier wag o' th' two ?
 Pol. We were as twinn'd lambs that did
  frisk i' th' sun
And bleat the one at th' other. What we
  chang'd
Was innocence for innocence ; we knew not
The doctrine of ill-doing, nor dream'd 70
That any did. Had we pursu'd that life,
And our weak spirits ne'er been higher
  rear'd
With stronger blood, we should have
  answer'd heaven
Boldly ' Not guilty ', the imposition clear'd
Hereditary ours.
 Her. By this we gather 75
You have tripp'd since.
 Pol. O my most sacred lady,
Temptations have since then been born
  to 's, for
In those unfledg'd days was my wife a girl ;
Your precious self had then not cross'd the
  eyes
Of my young playfellow.
 Her.   Grace to boot ! 80
Of this make no conclusion, lest you say
Your queen and I are devils. Yet, go on ;
Th' offences we have made you do we'll
  answer,
If you first sinn'd with us, and that with us
You did continue fault, and that you slipp'd
  not 85
With any but with us.
 Leon. Is he won yet ?
 Her. He'll stay, my lord.
 Leon. At my request he would not.

Hermione, my dearest, thou never spok'st
To better purpose.
   Her.   Never ?
   Leon.   Never but once.
   Her. What ! Have I twice said well ?
    When was't before ?   90
I prithee tell me ; cram's with praise, and
   make's
As fat as tame things. One good deed dying
   tongueless
Slaughters a thousand waiting upon that.
Our praises are our wages ; you may ride's
With one soft kiss a thousand furlongs ere
With spur we heat an acre. But to th' goal :
My last good deed was to entreat his stay ;
What was my first ? It has an elder sister,
Or I mistake you. O, would her name were
   Grace !
But once before I spoke to th' purpose—
   When ?   100
Nay, let me have 't ; I long.
   Leon.   Why, that was when
Three crabbed months had sour'd them-
   selves to death,
Ere I could make thee open thy white hand
And clap thyself my love ; then didst thou
   utter
' I am yours for ever '.
   Her.   'Tis Grace indeed. 105
Why, lo you now, I have spoke to th'
   purpose twice :
The one for ever earn'd a royal husband ;
Th' other for some while a friend.
           [Giving her hand to Polixenes.
   Leon. [*Aside*]   Too hot, too hot !
To mingle friendship far is mingling bloods.
I have tremor cordis on me ; my heart
   dances,   110
But not for joy, not joy. This entertain-
   ment
May a free face put on ; derive a liberty
From heartiness, from bounty, fertile
   bosom,
And well become the agent. 'T may, I
   grant ;
But to be paddling palms and pinching
   fingers,   115
As now they are, and making practis'd
   smiles
As in a looking-glass ; and then to sigh, as
   'twere
The mort o' th' deer. O, that is entertain-
   ment
My bosom likes not, nor my brows !
   Mamillius,   119
Art thou my boy ?
   Mam.   Ay, my good lord.
   Leon.   I' fecks !
Why, that's my bawcock. What ! hast
   smutch'd thy nose ?   121
They say it is a copy out of mine. Come,
   Captain,
We must be neat—not neat, but cleanly,
   Captain.

And yet the steer, the heifer, and the calf,
Are all call'd neat.—Still virginalling 125
Upon his palm ?—How now, you wanton
   calf,
Art thou my calf ?
   Mam.   Yes, if you will, my lord.
   Leon. Thou want'st a rough pash and the
   shoots that I have,
To be full like me ; yet they say we are
Almost as like as eggs. Women say so, 130
That will say any thing. But were they false
As o'er-dy'd blacks, as wind, as waters—
   false
As dice are to be wish'd by one that fixes
No bourn 'twixt his and mine ; yet were
   it true
To say this boy were like me. Come, sir
   page,   135
Look on me with your welkin eye. Sweet
   villain !
Most dear'st ! my collop ! Can thy dam ?—
   may't be ?
Affection ! thy intention stabs the centre.
Thou dost make possible things not so held,
Communicat'st with dreams—how can
   this be ?—   140
With what's unreal thou coactive art,
And fellow'st nothing. Then 'tis very
   credent
Thou mayst co-join with something ; and
   thou dost—
And that beyond commission ; and I find
   it,
And that to the infection of my brains 145
And hard'ning of my brows.
   Pol.   What means Sicilia ?
   Her. He something seems unsettled.
   Pol.   How, my lord !
What cheer ? How is't with you, best
   brother ?
   Her.   You look
As if you held a brow of much distraction.
Are you mov'd, my lord ?
   Leon.   No, in good earnest. 150
How sometimes nature will betray its folly,
Its tenderness, and make itself a pastime
To harder bosoms ! Looking on the lines
Of my boy's face, methoughts I did recoil
Twenty-three years ; and saw myself un-
   breech'd,   155
In my green velvet coat ; my dagger
   muzzl'd,
Lest it should bite its master and so prove,
As ornaments oft do, too dangerous.
How like, methought, I then was to this
   kernel,
This squash, this gentleman. Mine honest
   friend,   160
Will you take eggs for money ?
   Mam. No, my lord, I'll fight.
   Leon. You will ? Why, happy man be's
   dole ! My brother,
Are you so fond of your young prince as we
Do seem to be of ours ?

Pol.   If at home, sir, 165
He's all my exercise, my mirth, my matter ;
Now my sworn friend, and then mine
    enemy ;
My parasite, my soldier, statesman, all.
He makes a July's day short as December,
And with his varying childness cures in
    me   170
Thoughts that would thick my blood.
    Leon.   So stands this squire
Offic'd with me. We two will walk, my lord,
And leave you to your graver steps.
    Hermione,
How thou lov'st us show in our brother's
    welcome ;
Let what is dear in Sicily be cheap ;   175
Next to thyself and my young rover, he's
Apparent to my heart.
    Her.   If you would seek us,
We are yours i' th' garden. Shall's attend
    you there ?
    Leon. To your own bents dispose you ;
    you'll be found,
Be you beneath the sky. [*Aside*] I am
    angling now,   180
Though you perceive me not how I give line.
Go to, go to !
How she holds up the neb, the bill to him !
And arms her with the boldness of a wife
To her allowing husband ! [*Exeunt Polix-
    enes, Hermione, and Attendants.*
    Gone already ! 185
Inch-thick, knee-deep, o'er head and ears
    a fork'd one !
Go, play, boy, play ; thy mother plays,
    and I
Play too ; but so disgrac'd a part, whose
    issue
Will hiss me to my grave. Contempt and
    clamour
Will be my knell. Go, play, boy, play.
    There have been,   190
Or I am much deceiv'd, cuckolds ere now ;
And many a man there is, even at this
    present,
Now while I speak this, holds his wife by
    th' arm
That little thinks she has been sluic'd in's
    absence,
And his pond fish'd by his next neighbour,
    by   195
Sir Smile, his neighbour. Nay, there's
    comfort in't,
Whiles other men have gates and those
    gates open'd,
As mine, against their will. Should all
    despair
That have revolted wives, the tenth of
    mankind
Would hang themselves. Physic for't
    there's none ;   200
It is a bawdy planet, that will strike
Where 'tis predominant ; and 'tis pow'rful,
    think it,

From east, west, north, and south. Be it
    concluded,
No barricado for a belly. Know't,
It will let in and out the enemy   205
With bag and baggage. Many thousand
    on's
Have the disease, and feel't not. How now,
    boy !
    Mam. I am like you, they say.
    Leon.   Why, that's some comfort.
What ! Camillo there ?
    Cam. Ay, my good lord.   210
    Leon. Go play, Mamillius ; thou'rt an
        honest man.   [*Exit Mamillius.*
Camillo, this great sir will yet stay longer.
    Cam. You had much ado to make his
        anchor hold ;
When you cast out, it still came home.
    Leon.   Didst note it ?
    Cam. He would not stay at your peti-
        tions ; made   215
His business more material.
    Leon.   Didst perceive it ?
[*Aside*] They're here with me already ;
    whisp'ring, rounding,
' Sicilia is a so-forth '. 'Tis far gone
When I shall gust it last.—How came't,
    Camillo,
That he did stay ?
    Cam.   At the good Queen's entreaty.
    Leon. ' At the Queen's ' be't. ' Good '
        should be pertinent ;   221
But so it is, it is not. Was this taken
By any understanding pate but thine ?
For thy conceit is soaking, will draw in
More than the common blocks. Not noted,
    is't,   225
But of the finer natures, by some severals
Of head-piece extraordinary ? Lower
    messes
Perchance are to this business purblind ?
    Say.
    Cam. Business, my lord ? I think most
        understand   229
Bohemia stays here longer.
    Leon.   Ha ?
    Cam.   Stays here longer.
    Leon. Ay, but why ?
    Cam. To satisfy your Highness, and the
        entreaties
Of our most gracious mistress.
    Leo.   Satisfy !
Th' entreaties of your mistress ! Satisfy !
Let that suffice. I have trusted thee,
    Camillo,   235
With all the nearest things to my heart, as
    well
My chamber-councils, wherein, priest-like,
    thou
Hast cleans'd my bosom—I from thee
    departed
Thy penitent reform'd ; but we have been
Deceiv'd in thy integrity, deceiv'd   240
In that which seems so.

Cam.　　　　　　Be it forbid, my lord !
Leon. To bide upon't : thou art not
　honest ; or,
If thou inclin'st that way, thou art a
　coward,
Which hoxes honesty behind, restraining
From course requir'd ; or else thou must
　be counted　　　　245
A servant grafted in my serious trust,
And therein negligent ; or else a fool
That seest a game play'd home, the rich
　stake drawn,
And tak'st it all for jest.
Cam.　　　　　My gracious lord,
I may be negligent, foolish, and fearful : 250
In every one of these no man is free
But that his negligence, his folly, fear,
Among the infinite doings of the world,
Sometime puts forth. In your affairs, my
　lord,
If ever I were wilful-negligent,　　255
It was my folly ; if industriously
I play'd the fool, it was my negligence,
Not weighing well the end ; if ever fearful
To do a thing where I the issue doubted,
Whereof the execution did cry out　　260
Against the non-performance, 'twas a fear
Which oft infects the wisest. These, my
　lord,
Are such allow'd infirmities that honesty
Is never free of. But, beseech your Grace,
Be plainer with me ; let me know my
　trespass　　　　265
By its own visage ; if I then deny it,
'Tis none of mine.
Leon.　　　　Ha' not you seen, Camillo—
But that's past doubt ; you have, or your
　eye-glass
Is thicker than a cockold's horn—or
　heard—
For to a vision so apparent rumour　270
Cannot be mute—or thought—for cogi-
　tation
Resides not in that man that does not
　think—
My wife is slippery ? If thou wilt confess—
Or else be impudently negative,
To have nor eyes nor ears nor thought—
　then say　　　275
My wife's a hobby-horse, deserves a name
As rank as any flax-wench that puts to
Before her troth-plight. Say't and justify't.
Cam. I would not be a stander-by to hear
My sovereign mistress clouded so, without
My present vengeance taken. Shrew my
　heart !　　　281
You never spoke what did become you less
Than this ; which to reiterate were sin
As deep as that, though true.
Leon.　　　Is whispering nothing ?
Is leaning cheek to cheek ? Is meeting
　noses ?　　　285
Kissing with inside lip ? Stopping the
　career

Of laughter with a sigh ?—a note infallible
Of breaking honesty. Horsing foot on foot?
Skulking in corners ? Wishing clocks more
　swift ;
Hours, minutes ; noon, midnight ? And all
　eyes　　　290
Blind with the pin and web but theirs,
　theirs only,
That would unseen be wicked—is this
　nothing ?
Why, then the world and all that's in't is
　nothing ;
The covering sky is nothing ; Bohemia
　nothing ;
My wife is nothing ; nor nothing have these
　nothings,　　　295
If this be nothing.
Cam.　　　　Good my lord, be cur'd
Of this diseas'd opinion, and betimes ;
For 'tis most dangerous.
Leon.　　　　Say it be, 'tis true.
Cam. No, no, my lord.
Leon.　　　　It is ; you lie, you lie.
I say thou liest, Camillo, and I hate thee ;
Pronounce thee a gross lout, a mindless
　slave,　　　301
Or else a hovering temporizer that
Canst with thine eyes at once see good and
　evil,
Inclining to them both. Were my wife's
　liver
Infected as her life, she would not live　305
The running of one glass.
Cam.　　　　Who does infect her ?
Leon. Why, he that wears her like her
　medal, hanging
About her neck, Bohemia ; who—if I
Had servants true about me that bare eyes 310
To see alike mine honour as their profits,
Their own particular thrifts, they would do
　that
Which should undo more doing. Ay, and
　thou,
His cupbearer—whom I from meaner form
Have bench'd and rear'd to worship ; who
　mayst see,
Plainly as heaven sees earth and earth sees
　heaven,　　　315
How I am gall'd—mightst bespice a cup
To give mine enemy a lasting wink ;
Which draught to me were cordial.
Cam.　　　　Sir, my lord,
I could do this ; and that with no rash
　potion,
But with a ling'ring dram that should not
　work　　　320
Maliciously like poison. But I cannot
Believe this crack to be in my dread
　mistress,
So sovereignly being honourable.
I have lov'd thee—
Leon. Make that thy question, and go
　rot !
Dost think I am so muddy, so unsettled, 325

To appoint myself in this vexation ; sully
The purity and whiteness of my sheets—
Which to preserve is sleep, which being
    spotted
Is goads, thorns, nettles, tails of wasps ;
Give scandal to the blood o' th' Prince, my
    son—   330
Who I do think is mine, and love as mine—
Without ripe moving to 't ?   Would I do
    this ?
Could man so blench ?
    Cam.   I must believe you, sir.
I do ; and will fetch off Bohemia for't ;
Provided that, when he's remov'd, your
    Highness   335
Will take again your queen as yours at first,
Even for your son's sake ; and thereby for
    sealing
The injury of tongues in courts and king-
    doms
Known and allied to yours.
    Leon.   Thou dost advise me
Even so as I mine own course have set
    down.   340
I'll give no blemish to her honour, none.
    Cam. My lord,
Go then ; and with a countenance as clear
As friendship wears at feasts, keep with
    Bohemia   344
And with your queen.   I am his cupbearer ;
If from me he have wholesome beverage,
Account me not your servant.
    Leon.   This is all :
Do't, and thou hast the one half of my
    heart ;
Do't not, thou split'st thine own.
    Cam.   I'll do't, my lord. 349
    Leon. I will seem friendly, as thou hast
    advis'd me.   [*Exit.*
    Cam. O miserable lady !   But, for me,
What case stand I in ?   I must be the
    poisoner
Of good Polixenes ; and my ground to do't
Is the obedience to a master ; one   354
Who, in rebellion with himself, will have
All that are his so too.   To do this deed,
Promotion follows.   If I could find example
Of thousands that had struck anointed
    kings
And flourish'd after, I'd not do't ; but
    since
Nor brass, nor stone, nor parchment, bears
    not one,   360
Let villainy itself forswear't.   I must
Forsake the court.   To do't, or no, is certain
To me a break-neck.   Happy star reign now !
Here comes Bohemia.

Enter POLIXENES.

    Pol.   This is strange.   Methinks
My favour here begins to warp.   Not speak ?
Good day, Camillo.
    Cam.   Hail, most royal sir !
    Pol. What is the news i' th' court ?

    Cam.   None rare, my lord.
    Pol. The King hath on him such a
    countenance
As he had lost some province, and a region
Lov'd as he loves himself ; even now I met
    him   370
With customary compliment, when he,
Wafting his eyes to th' contrary and falling
A lip of much contempt, speeds from me ;
    and
So leaves me to consider what is breeding
That changes thus his manners.   375
    Cam. I dare not know, my lord.
    Pol. How, dare not ! Do not.   Do you
    know, and dare not
Be intelligent to me ?   'Tis thereabouts ;
For, to yourself, what you do know, you
    must,
And cannot say you dare not.   Good
    Camillo,   380
Your chang'd complexions are to me a
    mirror
Which shows me mine chang'd too ; for I
    must be
A party in this alteration, finding
Myself thus alter'd with't.
    Cam.   There is a sickness
Which puts some of us in distemper ; but
I cannot name the disease ; and it is caught
Of you that yet are well.
    Pol.   How ! caught of me ?
Make me not sighted like the basilisk ;
I have look'd on thousands who have sped
    the better   389
By my regard, but kill'd none so.   Camillo—
As you are certainly a gentleman ; thereto
Clerk-like experienc'd, which no less adorns
Our gentry than our parents' noble names,
In whose success we are gentle—I beseech
    you,
If you know aught which does behove my
    knowledge   395
Thereof to be inform'd, imprison't not
In ignorant concealment.
    Cam.   I may not answer.
    Pol. A sickness caught of me, and yet I
    well ?
I must be answer'd.   Dost thou hear,
    Camillo ?
I conjure thee, by all the parts of man 400
Which honour does acknowledge, whereof
    the least
Is not this suit of mine, that thou declare
What incidency thou dost guess of harm
Is creeping toward me ; how far off, how
    near ;
Which way to be prevented, if to be ; 405
If not, how best to bear it.
    Cam.   Sir, I will tell you ;
Since I am charg'd in honour, and by
    him
That I think honourable.   Therefore mark
    my counsel,
Which must be ev'n as swiftly followed as

I mean to utter it, or both yourself and me
Cry lost, and so goodnight.
  Pol.   On, good Camillo.
  Cam. I am appointed him to murder you.
  Pol. By whom, Camillo ?
  Cam.   By the King.
  Pol.   For what ?
  Cam. He thinks, nay, with all confidence
    he swears,
As he had seen 't or been an instrument 415
To vice you to't, that you have touch'd his
    queen
Forbiddenly.
  Pol.   O, then my best blood turn
To an infected jelly, and my name
Be yok'd with his that did betray the Best !
Turn then my freshest reputation to   420
A savour that may strike the dullest nostril
Where I arrive, and my approach be
    shunn'd,
Nay, hated too, worse than the great'st
    infection
That e'er was heard or read !
  Cam.   Swear his thought over
By each particular star in heaven and   425
By all their influences, you may as well
Forbid the sea for to obey the moon
As or by oath remove or counsel shake
The fabric of his folly, whose foundation
Is pil'd upon his faith and will continue 430
The standing of his body.
  Pol.   How should this grow ?
  Cam. I know not ; but I am sure 'tis
    safer to
Avoid what's grown than question how 'tis
    born.   433
If therefore you dare trust my honesty,
That lies enclosed in this trunk which you
Shall bear along impawn'd, away to-night.
Your followers I will whisper to the busi-
    ness ;
And will, by twos and threes, at several
    posterns, 438
Clear them o' th' city. For myself, I'll put
My fortunes to your service, which are here
By this discovery lost. Be not uncertain,
For, by the honour of my parents, I
Have utt'red truth ; which if you seek to
    prove,
I dare not stand by ; nor shall you be safer
Than one condemn'd by the King's own
    mouth, thereon 445
His execution sworn.
  Pol.   I do believe thee :
I saw his heart in's face. Give me thy
    hand ;
Be pilot to me, and thy places shall
Still neighbour mine. My ships are ready,
    and
My people did expect my hence departure
Two days ago. This jealousy   451
Is for a precious creature ; as she's rare,
Must it be great ; and, as his person's
    mighty,

Must it be violent ; and as he does conceive
He is dishonour'd by a man which ever 455
Profess'd to him, why, his revenges must
In that be made more bitter. Fear o'er-
    shades me.
Good expedition be my friend, and comfort
The gracious Queen, part of his theme, but
    nothing
Of his ill-ta'en suspicion ! Come, Camillo ;
I will respect thee as a father, if   461
Thou bear'st my life off hence. Let us
    avoid.
  Cam. It is in mine authority to command
The keys of all the posterns. Please your
    Highness 464
To take the urgent hour. Come, sir, away.
                      [*Exeunt.*

ACT TWO

Scene I. *Sicilia. The palace of Leontes.*

Enter Hermione, Mamillius, *and* Ladies.

  Her. Take the boy to you ; he so troubles
    me,
'Tis past enduring.
  1 Lady.   Come, my gracious lord,
Shall I be your playfellow ?
  Mam.   No, I'll none of you.
  1 Lady. Why, my sweet lord ?
  Mam. You'll kiss me hard, and speak to
    me as if   5
I were a baby still. I love you better.
  2 Lady. And why so, my lord ?
  Mam.   Not for because
Your brows are blacker ; yet black brows,
    they say,
Become some women best ; so that there
    be not
Too much hair there, but in a semicircle 10
Or a half-moon made with a pen.
  2 Lady.   Who taught't this ?
  Mam. I learn'd it out of women's faces.
    Pray now,
What colour are your eyebrows ?
  1 Lady.   Blue, my lord.
  Mam. Nay, that's a mock. I have seen
    a lady's nose
That has been blue, but not her eyebrows.
  1 Lady.   Hark ye : 15
The Queen your mother rounds apace. We
    shall
Present our services to a fine new prince
One of these days ; and then you'd wanton
    with us,
If we would have you.
  2 Lady.   She is spread of late
Into a goodly bulk. Good time encounter
    her ! 20
  Her. What wisdom stirs amongst you ?
    Come, sir, now
I am for you again. Pray you sit by us,
And tell's a tale.
  Mam.   Merry or sad shall't be ?
  Her. As merry as you will.

Mam. A sad tale's best for winter. I have
    one   25
Of sprites and goblins.
Her.   Let's have that, good sir.
Come on, sit down; come on, and do your
    best
To fright me with your sprites; you're
    pow'rful at it.
Mam. There was a man—
Her.   Nay, come, sit down; then on.
Mam. Dwelt by a churchyard—I will
    tell it softly;   30
Yond crickets shall not hear it.
Her.   Come on then,
And give't me in mine ear.

Enter LEONTES, ANTIGONUS, Lords *and*
    Others.

Leon. Was he met there? his train?
    Camillo with him?
1 *Lord.* Behind the tuft of pines I met
    them; never
Saw I men scour so on their way. I ey'd
    them   35
Even to their ships.
Leon.   How blest am I
In my just censure, in my true opinion!
Alack, for lesser knowledge! How accurs'd
In being so blest! There may be in the
    cup
A spider steep'd, and one may drink, de-
    part,   40
And yet partake no venom, for his know-
    ledge
Is not infected; but if one present
Th' abhorr'd ingredient to his eye, make
    known
How he hath drunk, he cracks his gorge,
    his sides,
With violent hefts. I have drunk, and seen
    the spider.   45
Camillo was his help in this, his pander.
There is a plot against my life, my crown;
All's true that is mistrusted. That false
    villain
Whom I employ'd was pre-employ'd by
    him;
He has discover'd my design, and I   50
Remain a pinch'd thing; yea, a very trick
For them to play at will. How came the
    posterns
So easily open?
1 *Lord.* By his great authority;
Which often hath no less prevail'd than so
On your command.
Leon.   I know't too well.   55
Give me the boy. I am glad you did not
    nurse him;
Though he does bear some signs of me, yet
    you
Have too much blood in him.
Her.   What is this? Sport?
Leon. Bear the boy hence; he shall not
    come about her;   59

Away with him; and let her sport herself
    [*Mamillius is led out.*
With that she's big with—for 'tis Poli-
    xenes
Has made thee swell thus.
Her.   But I'd say he had not,
And I'll be sworn you would believe my
    saying,
Howe'er you lean to th' nayward.
Leon.   You, my lords,
Look on her, mark her well; be but about
To say ' She is a goodly lady ' and   66
The justice of your hearts will thereto add
' 'Tis pity she's not honest—honourable '.
Praise her but for this her without-door
    form,
Which on my faith deserves high speech,
    and straight   70
The shrug, the hum or ha, these petty
    brands
That calumny doth use—O, I am out!—
That mercy does, for calumny will sear
Virtue itself—these shrugs, these hum's
    and ha's,
When you have said she's goodly, come
    between,   75
Ere you can say she's honest. But be't
    known,
From him that has most cause to grieve it
    should be,
She's an adultress.
Her.   Should a villain say so,
The most replenish'd villain in the world,
He were as much more villain: you, my
    lord,   80
Do but mistake.
Leon.   You have mistook, my lady,
Polixenes for Leontes. O thou thing!
Which I'll not call a creature of thy place,
Lest barbarism, making me the precedent,
Should a like language use to all degrees   85
And mannerly distinguishment leave out
Betwixt the prince and beggar. I have said
She's an adultress; I have said with whom.
More, she's a traitor; and Camillo is
A federary with her, and one that knows   90
What she should shame to know herself
But with her most vile principal—that she's
A bed-swerver, even as bad as those
That vulgars give bold'st titles; ay, and
    privy
To this their late escape.
Her.   No, by my life,   95
Privy to none of this. How will this grieve
    you,
When you shall come to clearer knowledge,
    that
You thus have publish'd me! Gentle my
    lord,
You scarce can right me throughly then to
    say
You did mistake.
Leon.   No; if I mistake   100
In those foundations which I build upon,

The centre is not big enough to bear
A school-boy's top. Away with her to
    prison.
He who shall speak for her is afar off guilty
But that he speaks.
    Her.   There's some ill planet reigns.
I must be patient till the heavens look 106
With an aspect more favourable. Good my
    lords,
I am not prone to weeping, as our sex
Commonly are—the want of which vain dew
Perchance shall dry your pities—but I have
That honourable grief lodg'd here which
    burns   111
Worse than tears drown. Beseech you all,
    my lords,
With thoughts so qualified as your charities
Shall best instruct you, measure me ;
    and so
The King's will be perform'd !
    Leon. [*To the Guard*] Shall I be heard ?
    Her. Who is't that goes with me ?
    Beseech your Highness   116
My women may be with me, for you see
My plight requires it. Do not weep, good
    fools ;
There is no cause ; when you shall know
    your mistress   119
Has deserv'd prison, then abound in tears
As I come out : this action I now go on
Is for my better grace. Adieu, my lord.
I never wish'd to see you sorry ; now
I trust I shall. My women, come ; you have
    leave.
    Leon. Go, do our bidding ; hence ! 125
    [*Exeunt Hermione, guarded, and ladies.*
    1 Lord. Beseech your Highness, call the
    Queen again.
    Ant. Be certain what you do, sir, lest
    your justice
Prove violence, in the which three great
    ones suffer,
Yourself, your queen, your son.
    1 Lord.   For her, my lord,
I dare my life lay down—and will do't, sir,
Please you t' accept it—that the Queen is
    spotless   131
I' th' eyes of heaven and to you—I mean
In this which you accuse her.
    Ant.   If it prove
She's otherwise, I'll keep my stables where
I lodge my wife ; I'll go in couples with her;
Than when I feel and see her no farther
    trust her ;   136
For every inch of woman in the world,
Ay, every dram of woman's flesh is false,
If she be.
    Leon. Hold your peaces.
    1 Lord.   Good my lord—
    Ant. It is for you we speak, not for
    ourselves.   140
You are abus'd, and by some putter-on
That will be damn'd for't. Would I knew
    the villain !

I would land-damn him. Be she honour-
    flaw'd—
I have three daughters : the eldest is
    eleven ;
The second and the third, nine and some
    five ;   145
If this prove true, they'll pay for't. By
    mine honour,
I'll geld 'em all ; fourteen they shall not see
To bring false generations. They are co-
    heirs ;
And I had rather glib myself than they
Should not produce fair issue.
    Leon.   Cease ; no more. 150
You smell this business with a sense as cold
As is a dead man's nose ; but I do see't and
    feel't
As you feel doing thus ; and see withal
The instruments that feel.
    Ant.   If it be so,
We need no grave to bury honesty ;   155
There's not a grain of it the face to sweeten
Of the whole dungy earth.
    Leon.   What ! Lack I credit ?
    1 Lord. I had rather you did lack than I,
    my lord,
Upon this ground ; and more it would
    content me
To have her honour true than your
    suspicion,   160
Be blam'd for't how you might.
    Leon.   Why, what need we
Commune with you of this, but rather
    follow
Our forceful instigation ? Our prerogative
Calls not your counsels ; but our natural
    goodness   164
Imparts this ; which, if you—or stupefied
Or seeming so in skill—cannot or will not
Relish a truth like us, inform yourselves
We need no more of your advice. The
    matter,
The loss, the gain, the ord'ring on't, is all
Properly ours.
    Ant.   And I wish, my liege, 170
You had only in your silent judgment tried
    it,
Without more overture.
    Leon.   How could that be ?
Either thou art most ignorant by age,
Or thou wert born a fool. Camillo's flight,
Added to their familiarity—   175
Which was as gross as ever touch'd con-
    jecture,
That lack'd sight only, nought for appro-
    bation
But only seeing, all other circumstances
Made up to th' deed—doth push on this
    proceeding.
Yet, for a greater confirmation—   180
For, in an act of this importance, 'twere
Most piteous to be wild—I have dispatch'd
    in post
To sacred Delphos, to Apollo's temple,

385

Cleomenes and Dion, whom you know
Of stuff'd sufficiency. Now, from the oracle
They will bring all, whose spiritual counsel
        had,   186
Shall stop or spur me. Have I done well ?
1 *Lord.* Well done, my lord.
    Leon. Though I am satisfied, and need no
        more
Than what I know, yet shall the oracle 190
Give rest to th' minds of others such as he
Whose ignorant credulity will not
Come up to th' truth. So have we thought
        it good
From our free person she should be confin'd,
Lest that the treachery of the two fled
        hence   195
Be left her to perform. Come, follow us ;
We are to speak in public ; for this business
Will raise us all.
    Ant. [*Aside*] To laughter, as I take it,
If the good truth were known.   [*Exeunt.*

SCENE II. *Sicilia. A prison.*

Enter PAULINA, *a* Gentleman, *and*
Attendants.

    Paul. The keeper of the prison—call to
        him ;
Let him have knowledge who I am.
                        [*Exit Gentleman.*
                            Good lady !
No court in Europe is too good for thee ;
What dost thou then in prison ?

Re-enter Gentleman *with the* Gaoler.

                        Now, good sir,
You know me, do you not ?
    Gaol.   For a worthy lady, 5
And one who much I honour.
    Paul.   Pray you, then,
Conduct me to the Queen.
    Gaol.   I may not, madam ;
To the contrary I have express command-
        ment.
    Paul. Here's ado, to lock up honesty and
        honour from   10
Th' access of gentle visitors ! Is't lawful,
        pray you,
To see her women—any of them ? Emilia ?
    Gaol. So please you, madam,
To put apart these your attendants, I
Shall bring Emilia forth.
    Paul.   I pray now, call her. 15
Withdraw yourselves. [*Exeunt Attendants.*
    Gaol.   And, madam,
I must be present at your conference.
    Paul. Well, be't so, prithee. [*Exit Gaoler.*
Here's such ado to make no stain a stain
As passes colouring.

Re-enter Gaoler, *with* EMILIA.

                    Dear gentlewoman,   20
How fares our gracious lady ?

    Emil. As well as one so great and so
        forlorn
May hold together. On her frights and
        griefs,
Which never tender lady hath borne greater,
She is, something before her time, deliver'd.
    Paul. A boy ?
    Emil.   A daughter, and a goodly babe,
Lusty, and like to live. The Queen receives
Much comfort in't ; says ' My poor
        prisoner,
I am as innocent as you '.
    Paul.   I dare be sworn.
These dangerous unsafe lunes i' th' King,
        beshrew them !   30
He must be told on't, and he shall. The
        office
Becomes a woman best ; I'll take't upon
        me ;
If I prove honey-mouth'd, let my tongue
        blister,
And never to my red-look'd anger be   34
The trumpet any more. Pray you, Emilia,
Commend my best obedience to the Queen ;
If she dares trust me with her little babe,
I'll show't the King, and undertake to be
Her advocate to th' loud'st. We do not
        know   39
How he may soften at the sight o' th' child :
The silence often of pure innocence
Persuades when speaking fails.
    Emil.   Most worthy madam,
Your honour and your goodness is so
        evident
That your free undertaking cannot miss
A thriving issue ; there is no lady living 45
So meet for this great errand. Please your
        ladyship
To visit the next room, I'll presently
Acquaint the Queen of your most noble
        offer ;
Who but to-day hammer'd of this design,
But durst not tempt a minister of honour,
Lest she should be denied.
    Paul.   Tell her, Emilia,
I'll use that tongue I have ; if wit flow
        from't   52
As boldness from my bosom, let't not be
        doubted
I shall do good.
    Emil.   Now be you blest for it !
I'll to the Queen. Please you come some-
        thing nearer.   55
    Gaol. Madam, if't please the Queen to
        send the babe,
I know not what I shall incur to pass it,
Having no warrant.
    Paul.   You need not fear it, sir.
This child was prisoner to the womb, and is
By law and process of great Nature thence
Freed and enfranchis'd—not a party to   61
The anger of the King, nor guilty of,
If any be, the trespass of the Queen.
    Gaol. I do believe it.

Paul. Do not you fear.   Upon mine
    honour, I   65
Will stand betwixt you and danger.
                    [*Exeunt.*

SCENE III. *Sicilia.   The palace of Leontes.*

Enter LEONTES, ANTIGONUS, *Lords, and*
          Servants.

  Leon. Nor night nor day no rest ! It is
    but weakness
To bear the matter thus—mere weakness. If
The cause were not in being—part o' th'
    cause,
She, th' adultress ; for the harlot king   4
Is quite beyond mine arm, out of the blank
And level of my brain, plot-proof ; but she
I can hook to me—say that she were gone,
Given to the fire, a moiety of my rest
Might come to me again. Who's there ?
  1 Serv.   My lord ?
  Leon. How does the boy ?
  1 Serv.   He took good rest to-night ;
'Tis hop'd his sickness is discharg'd.   11
  Leon. To see his nobleness !
Conceiving the dishonour of his mother,
He straight declin'd, droop'd, took it
    deeply,
Fasten'd and fix'd the shame on't in
    himself,   15
Threw off his spirit, his appetite, his sleep,
And downright languish'd. Leave me solely.
    Go,
See how he fares. [*Exit Servant*] Fie, fie ! no
    thought of him !
The very thought of my revenges that way
Recoil upon me—in himself too mighty,   20
And in his parties, his alliance. Let him be,
Until a time may serve ; for present
    vengeance,
Take it on her. Camillo and Polixenes
Laugh at me, make their pastime at my
    sorrow.
They should not laugh if I could reach
    them ; nor   25
Shall she, within my pow'r.

    Enter PAULINA, *with a* Child.

  1 Lord.   You must not enter.
  Paul. Nay, rather, good my lords, be
    second to me.
Fear you his tyrannous passion more, alas,
Than the Queen's life ? A gracious innocent
    soul,   29
More free than he is jealous.
  Ant.   That's enough.
  2 Serv. Madam, he hath not slept to-
    night ; commanded
None should come at him.
  Paul.   Not so hot, good sir ;
I come to bring him sleep. 'Tis such as you,
That creep like shadows by him, and do
    sigh   34
At each his needless heavings—such as you

Nourish the cause of his awaking : I
Do come with words as medicinal as true,
Honest as either, to purge him of that
    humour
That presses him from sleep.
  Leon.   What noise there, ho ?
  Paul. No noise, my lord ; but needful
    conference   40
About some gossips for your Highness.
  Leon.   How !
Away with that audacious lady ! Antigonus,
I charg'd thee that she should not come
    about me ;
I knew she would.
  Ant.   I told her so, my lord,
On your displeasure's peril, and on mine,   45
She should not visit you.
  Leon.   What, canst not rule her ?
  Paul. From all dishonesty he can : in
    this,
Unless he take the course that you have
    done—
Commit me for committing honour—trust
    it,
He shall not rule me.
  Ant.   La you now, you hear !   50
When she will take the rein, I let her run ;
But she'll not stumble.
  Paul.   Good my liege, I come—
And I beseech you hear me, who professes
Myself your loyal servant, your physician,
Your most obedient counsellor ; yet that
    dares   55
Less appear so, in comforting your evils,
Than such as most seem yours—I say I
    come
From your good Queen.
  Leon. Good Queen !
  Paul. Good Queen, my lord, good Queen
    —I say good Queen ;
And would by combat make her good, so
    were I   60
A man, the worst about you.
  Leon.   Force her hence.
  Paul. Let him that makes but trifles of
    his eyes
First hand me. On mine own accord I'll off ;
But first I'll do my errand.   The good
    Queen,
For she is good, hath brought you forth a
    daughter ;   65
Here 'tis ; commends it to your blessing.
            [*Laying down the child.*
  Leon.   Out !
A mankind witch ! Hence with her, out o'
    door !
A most intelligencing bawd !
  Paul.   Not so.
I am as ignorant in that as you
In so entitling me ; and no less honest   70
Than you are mad ; which is enough, I'll
    warrant,
As this world goes, to pass for honest.
  Leon.   Traitors !

Will you not push her out ? Give her the
    bastard.
[*To Antigonus*] Thou dotard, thou art
    woman-tir'd, unroosted
By thy Dame Partlet here. Take up the
    bastard ;   75
Take't up, I say ; give't to thy crone.
    Paul.   For ever
Unvenerable be thy hands, if thou
Tak'st up the Princess by that forced
    baseness
Which he has put upon't !
    Leon.   He dreads his wife.
    Paul. So I would you did ; then 'twere
        past all doubt   80
You'd call your children yours.
    Leon.   A nest of traitors !
    Ant. I am none, by this good light.
    Paul.   Nor I ; nor any
But one that's here ; and that's himself ;
    for he
The sacred honour of himself, his Queen's,
His hopeful son's, his babe's, betrays to
    slander,   85
Whose sting is sharper than the sword's ;
    and will not—
For, as the case now stands, it is a curse
He cannot be compell'd to 't—once remove
The root of his opinion, which is rotten
As ever oak or stone was sound.
    Leon.   A callat 90
Of boundless tongue, who late hath beat
    her husband,
And now baits me ! This brat is none of
    mine ;
It is the issue of Polixenes.
Hence with it, and together with the dam
Commit them to the fire.
    Paul.   It is yours. 95
And, might we lay th' old proverb to your
    charge,
So like you 'tis the worse. Behold, my
    lords,
Although the print be little, the whole
    matter
And copy of the father—eye, nose, lip,
The trick of's frown, his forehead ; nay,
    the valley,   100
The pretty dimples of his chin and cheek ;
    his smiles ;
The very mould and frame of hand, nail,
    finger.
And thou, good goddess Nature, which hast
    made it
So like to him that got it, if thou hast
The ordering of the mind too, 'mongst all
    colours   105
No yellow in't, lest she suspect, as he
    does,
Her children not her husband's !
    Leon.   A gross hag !
And, lozel, thou art worthy to be hang'd
That wilt not stay her tongue.
    Ant.   Hang all the husbands

That cannot do that feat, you'll leave
    yourself   110
Hardly one subject.
    Leon.   Once more, take her hence.
    Paul. A most unworthy and unnatural
        lord
Can do no more.
    Leon.   I'll ha' thee burnt.
    Paul.   I care not.
It is an heretic that makes the fire,
Not she which burns in't. I'll not call you
    tyrant ;   115
But this most cruel usage of your Queen—
Not able to produce more accusation
Than your own weak-hing'd fancy—some-
    thing savours
Of tyranny, and will ignoble make you,
Yea, scandalous to the world.
    Leon.   On your allegiance, 120
Out of the chamber with her ! Were I a
    tyrant,
Where were her life ? She durst not call
    me so,
If she did know me one. Away with her !
    Paul. I pray you, do not push me ; I'll
        be gone.
Look to your babe, my lord ; 'tis yours.
Jove send her   125
A better guiding spirit ! What needs these
    hands ?
You that are thus so tender o'er his follies
Will never do him good, not one of you.
So, so. Farewell ; we are gone.   [*Exit.*
    Leon. Thou, traitor, hast set on thy wife
        to this.   130
My child ! Away with't. Even thou, that
    hast
A heart so tender o'er it, take it hence,
And see it instantly consum'd with fire ;
Even thou, and none but thou. Take it up
    straight.   134
Within this hour bring me word 'tis done,
And by good testimony, or I'll seize thy
    life,
With what thou else call'st thine. If thou
    refuse,
And wilt encounter with my wrath, say so ;
The bastard brains with these my proper
    hands
Shall I dash out. Go, take it to the fire ; 140
For thou set'st on thy wife.
    Ant.   I did not, sir.
These lords, my noble fellows, if they please,
Can clear me in't.
    Lords.   We can. My royal liege,
He is not guilty of her coming hither.
    Leon. You're liars all.   145
    1 Lord. Beseech your Highness, give us
        better credit.
We have always truly serv'd you ; and
    beseech
So to esteem of us ; and on our knees we
    beg,
As recompense of our dear services

Past and to come, that you do change this
　　purpose,   150
Which being so horrible, so bloody, must
Lead on to some foul issue. We all kneel.
　　Leon. I am a feather for each wind that
　　　　blows.
Shall I live on to see this bastard kneel
And call me father ? Better burn it now 155
Than curse it then. But be it ; let it
　　live.
It shall not neither. [*To Antigonus*] You,
　　sir, come you hither.
You that have been so tenderly officious
With Lady Margery, your midwife there,
To save this bastard's life—for 'tis a
　　bastard,   160
So sure as this beard's grey—what will you
　　adventure
To save this brat's life ?
　　Ant.   Anything, my lord,
That my ability may undergo,
And nobleness impose. At least, thus
　　much :   164
I'll pawn the little blood which I have left
To save the innocent—anything possible.
　　Leon. It shall be possible. Swear by this
　　　　sword
Thou wilt perform my bidding.
　　Ant.   I will, my lord.
　　Leon. Mark, and perform it—seest thou ?
　　　　For the fail
Of any point in't shall not only be   170
Death to thyself, but to thy lewd-tongu'd
　　wife,
Whom for this time we pardon. We enjoin
　　thee,
As thou art liegeman to us, that thou carry
This female bastard hence ; and that thou
　　bear it   174
To some remote and desert place, quite out
Of our dominions ; and that there thou
　　leave it,
Without more mercy, to it own protection
And favour of the climate. As by strange
　　fortune
It came to us, I do in justice charge thee,
On thy soul's peril and thy body's torture,
That thou commend it strangely to some
　　place   181
Where chance may nurse or end it. Take
　　it up.
　　Ant. I swear to do this, though a present
　　　　death
Had been more merciful. Come on, poor
　　babe.
Some powerful spirit instruct the kites and
　　ravens   185
To be thy nurses ! Wolves and bears, they
　　say,
Casting their savageness aside, have done
Like offices of pity. Sir, be prosperous
In more than this deed does require ! And
　　blessing
Against this cruelty fight on thy side,   190

Poor thing, condemn'd to loss !
　　　　　　　　　　　[*Exit with the child.*
　　Leon.   No, I'll not rear
Another's issue.

　　　　　　Enter a Servant.

　　Serv.   Please your Highness, posts
From those you sent to th' oracle are
　　come
An hour since. Cleomenes and Dion,
Being well arriv'd from Delphos, are both
　　landed,   195
Hasting to th' court.
　　1 *Lord.*   So please you, sir, their speed
Hath been beyond account.
　　Leon.   Twenty-three days
They have been absent ; 'tis good speed ;
　　foretells
The great Apollo suddenly will have
The truth of this appear. Prepare you,
　　lords ;   200
Summon a session, that we may arraign
Our most disloyal lady ; for, as she hath
Been publicly accus'd, so shall she have
A just and open trial. While she lives,
My heart will be a burden to me. Leave
　　me ;   205
And think upon my bidding.   [*Exeunt.*

ACT THREE

SCENE I. *Sicilia. On the road to the Capital.*

　　　Enter CLEOMENES *and* DION.

　　Cleo. The climate's delicate, the air most
　　　　sweet,
Fertile the isle, the temple much surpassing
The common praise it bears.
　　Dio.   I shall report,
For most it caught me, the celestial habits—
Methinks I so should term them—and the
　　reverence   5
Of the grave wearers. O, the sacrifice !
How ceremonious, solemn, and unearthly,
It was i' th' off'ring !
　　Cleo.   But of all, the burst
And the ear-deaf'ning voice o' th' oracle,
Kin to Jove's thunder, so surpris'd my
　　sense   10
That I was nothing.
　　Dion.   If th' event o' th' journey
Prove as successful to the Queen—O, be't
　　so !—
As it hath been to us rare, pleasant, speedy,
The time is worth the use on't.
　　Cleo.   Great Apollo
Turn all to th' best ! These proclamations,
So forcing faults upon Hermione,   16
I little like.
　　Dion. The violent carriage of it
Will clear or end the business. When the
　　oracle—
Thus by Apollo's great divine seal'd up—
Shall the contents discover, something rare

Even then will rush to knowledge.   Go;
   fresh horses.   21
And gracious be the issue!   [*Exeunt.*

SCENE II. *Sicilia. A court of justice.*

   Enter LEONTES, Lords, *and* Officers.

  Leon. This sessions, to our great grief we
   pronounce,
Even pushes 'gainst our heart—the party
   tried,
The daughter of a king, our wife, and one
Of us too much belov'd. Let us be clear'd
Of being tyrannous, since we so openly 5
Proceed in justice, which shall have due
   course,
Even to the guilt or the purgation.
Produce the prisoner.
  Offi. It is his Highness' pleasure that the
   Queen
Appear in person here in court.

   Enter HERMIONE, *as to her trial,* PAULINA,
    and Ladies.

              Silence! 10
  Leon. Read the indictment.
  Offi. [*Reads*] ' Hermione, Queen to the
worthy Leontes, King of Sicilia, thou art
here accused and arraigned of high treason,
in committing adultery with Polixenes,
King of Bohemia; and conspiring with
Camillo to take away the life of our
sovereign lord the King, thy royal husband:
the pretence whereof being by circumstances partly laid open, thou, Hermione,
contrary to the faith and allegiance of a true
subject, didst counsel and aid them, for
their better safety, to fly away by night.'
  Her. Since what I am to say must be
   but that   20
Which contradicts my accusation, and
The testimony on my part no other
But what comes from myself, it shall scarce
   boot me
To say ' Not guilty '. Mine integrity
Being counted falsehood shall, as I express
   it,   25
Be so receiv'd. But thus—if pow'rs divine
Behold our human actions, as they do,
I doubt not then but innocence shall make
False accusation blush, and tyranny
Tremble at patience. You, my lord, best
   know—   30
Who least will seem to do so—my past life
Hath been as continent, as chaste, as true,
As I am now unhappy; which is more
Than history can pattern, though devis'd
And play'd to take spectators; for behold
   me—   35
A fellow of the royal bed, which owe
A moiety of the throne, a great king's
   daughter,
The mother to a hopeful prince—here
   standing

To prate and talk for life and honour fore
Who please to come and hear. For life, I
   prize it   40
As I weigh grief, which I would spare; for
   honour,
'Tis a derivative from me to mine,
And only that I stand for. I appeal
To your own conscience, sir, before
   Polixenes
Came to your court, how I was in your
   grace,   45
How merited to be so; since he came,
With what encounter so uncurrent I
Have strain'd t' appear thus; if one jot
   beyond
The bound of honour, or in act or will   49
That way inclining, hard'ned be the hearts
Of all that hear me, and my near'st of kin
Cry fie upon my grave!
  Leon.   I ne'er heard yet
That any of these bolder vices wanted
Less impudence to gainsay what they did
Than to perform it first.
  Her.   That's true enough; 55
Though 'tis a saying, sir, not due to me.
  Leon. You will not own it.
  Her.   More than mistress of
Which comes to me in name of fault, I
   must not
At all acknowledge. For Polixenes,
With whom I am accus'd, I do confess 60
I lov'd him as in honour he requir'd;
With such a kind of love as might become
A lady like me; with a love even such,
So and no other, as yourself commanded;
Which not to have done, I think had been
   in me   65
Both disobedience and ingratitude
To you and toward your friend; whose love
   had spoke,
Even since it could speak, from an infant,
   freely,
That it was yours. Now for conspiracy:
I know not how it tastes, though it be
   dish'd   70
For me to try how; all I know of it
Is that Camillo was an honest man;
And why he left your court, the gods
   themselves,
Wotting no more than I, are ignorant.
  Leon. You knew of his departure, as you
   know   75
What you have underta'en to do in's
   absence.
  Her. Sir,
You speak a language that I understand
   not.
My life stands in the level of your dreams,
Which I'll lay down.
  Leon.   Your actions are my dreams.
You had a bastard by Polixenes,   81
And I but dream'd it. As you were past
   all shame—
Those of your fact are so—so past all truth;

Which to deny concerns more than avails;
    for as
Thy brat hath been cast out, like to itself,
No father owning it—which is indeed   86
More criminal in thee than it—so thou
Shalt feel our justice; in whose easiest
    passage
Look for no less than death.
  Her.   Sir, spare your threats.
The bug which you would fright me with
    I seek.
To me can life be no commodity.   90
The crown and comfort of my life, your
    favour,
I do give lost, for I do feel it gone,
But know not how it went; my second
    joy
And first fruits of my body, from his
    presence   95
I am barr'd, like one infectious; my third
    comfort,
Starr'd most unluckily, is from my breast—
The innocent milk in it most innocent
    mouth—
Hal'd out to murder; myself on every post
Proclaim'd a strumpet; with immodest
    hatred   100
The child-bed privilege denied, which 'longs
To women of all fashion; lastly, hurried
Here to this place, i' th' open air, before
I have got strength of limit. Now, my
    liege,
Tell me what blessings I have here alive 105
That I should fear to die. Therefore
    proceed.
But yet hear this—mistake me not: no
    life,
I prize it not a straw, but for mine honour
Which I would free—if I shall be con-
    demn'd
Upon surmises, all proofs sleeping else 110
But what your jealousies awake, I tell you
'Tis rigour, and not law. Your honours all,
I do refer me to the oracle:
Apollo be my judge!
  1 Lord.   This your request   114
Is altogether just. Therefore, bring forth,
And in Apollo's name, his oracle.
             [*Exeunt certain Officers.*
  Her. The Emperor of Russia was my
    father;
O that he were alive, and here beholding
His daughter's trial! that he did but see
The flatness of my misery; yet with eyes
Of pity, not revenge!   121

Re-enter Officers, *with* CLEOMENES *and*
    DION.

  Offi. You here shall swear upon this
    sword of justice
That you, Cleomenes and Dion, have
Been both at Delphos, and from thence
    have brought   124
This seal'd-up oracle, by the hand deliver'd

Of great Apollo's priest; and that since
    then
You have not dar'd to break the holy seal
Nor read the secrets in't.
  Cleo., Dion.   All this we swear.
  Leon. Break up the seals and read. 129
  Offi. [*Reads*] 'Hermione is chaste;
Polixenes blameless; Camillo a true
subject; Leontes a jealous tyrant; his
innocent babe truly begotten; and the
King shall live without an heir, if that
which is lost be not found.'
  Lords. Now blessed be the great Apollo!
  Her.   Praised!
  Leon. Hast thou read truth?
  Offi.   Ay, my lord; even so
As it is here set down.   136
  Leon. There is no truth at all i' th'
    oracle.
The sessions shall proceed. This is mere
    falsehood.

Enter a Servant.

  Serv. My lord the King, the King!
  Leon.   What is the business?
  Serv. O sir, I shall be hated to report it:
The Prince your son, with mere conceit and
    fear   141
Of the Queen's speed, is gone.
  Leon.   How! Gone?
  Serv.   Is dead.
  Leon. Apollo's angry; and the heavens
    themselves
Do strike at my injustice.
               [*Hermione swoons.*
             How now, there!
  Paul. This news is mortal to the Queen.
    Look down   145
And see what death is doing.
  Leon.   Take her hence.
Her heart is but o'ercharg'd; she will
    recover.
I have too much believ'd mine own
    suspicion.
Beseech you tenderly apply to her
Some remedies for life. [*Exeunt Paulina
            and Ladies with Hermione.*
             Apollo, pardon   150
My great profaneness 'gainst thine oracle.
I'll reconcile me to Polixenes,
New woo my queen, recall the good
    Camillo—
Whom I proclaim a man of truth, of mercy.
For, being transported by my jealousies 155
To bloody thoughts and to revenge, I chose
Camillo for the minister to poison
My friend Polixenes; which had been done
But that the good mind of Camillo tardied
My swift command, though I with death
    and with   160
Reward did threaten and encourage him,
Not doing it and being done. He, most
    humane
And fill'd with honour, to my kingly guest

Unclasp'd my practice, quit his fortunes
        here,
Which you knew great, and to the certain
        hazard   165
Of all incertainties himself commended,
No richer than his honour. How he glisters
Thorough my rust ! And how his piety
Does my deeds make the blacker !

Re-enter PAULINA.

  Paul.   Woe the while !
O, cut my lace, lest my heart, cracking it,
Break too !
  1 *Lord.*   What fit is this, good lady ?
  Paul.   What studied torments, tyrant,
        hast for me ?   172
What wheels, racks, fires ? what flaying,
        boiling
In leads or oils ? What old or newer torture
Must I receive, whose every word deserves
To taste of thy most worst ? Thy tyranny
Together working with thy jealousies,   177
Fancies too weak for boys, too green and
        idle
For girls of nine—O, think what they have
        done,
And then run mad indeed, stark mad ;
        for all   180
Thy by-gone fooleries were but spices of it.
That thou betray'dst Polixenes, 'twas
        nothing ;
That did but show thee, of a fool, incon-
        stant,
And damnable ingrateful. Nor was't much
Thou wouldst have poison'd good Camillo's
        honour,   185
To have him kill a king—poor trespasses,
More monstrous standing by ; whereof I
        reckon
The casting forth to crows thy baby
        daughter
To be or none or little, though a devil
Would have shed water out of fire ere
        done't ;
Nor is't directly laid to thee, the death   191
Of the young Prince, whose honourable
        thoughts—
Thoughts high for one so tender—cleft the
        heart
That could conceive a gross and foolish sire
Blemish'd his gracious dam. This is not, no,
Laid to thy answer ; but the last—O lords,
When I have said, cry ' Woe ! '—the
        Queen, the Queen,   197
The sweet'st, dear'st creature's dead ; and
        vengeance for't
Not dropp'd down yet.
  1 *Lord.*   The higher pow'rs forbid !
  Paul. I say she's dead ; I'll swear't. If
        word nor oath   200
Prevail not, go and see. If you can bring
Tincture or lustre in her lip, her eye,
Heat outwardly or breath within, I'll serve
        you

As I would do the gods.   But, O thou
        tyrant !
Do not repent these things, for they are
        heavier   205
Than all thy woes can stir ; therefore be-
        take thee
To nothing but despair. A thousand knees
Ten thousand years together, naked,
        fasting,
Upon a barren mountain, and still winter
In storm perpetual, could not move the
        gods   210
To look that way thou wert.
  Leon.   Go on, go on.
Thou canst not speak too much ; I have
        deserv'd
All tongues to talk their bitt'rest.
  1 *Lord.*   Say no more ;
Howe'er the business goes, you have made
        fault
I' th' boldness of your speech.
  Paul.   I am sorry for't. 215
All faults I make, when I shall come to
        know them,
I do repent. Alas, I have show'd too much
The rashness of a woman ! He is touch'd
To th' noble heart. What's gone and what's
        past help
Should be past grief.   Do not receive
        affliction   220
At my petition ; I beseech you, rather
Let me be punish'd that have minded you
Of what you should forget. Now, good my
        liege,
Sir, royal sir, forgive a foolish woman. 224
The love I bore your queen—lo, fool again !
I'll speak of her no more, nor of your
        children ;
I'll not remember you of my own lord,
Who is lost too. Take your patience to you,
And I'll say nothing.
  Leon.   Thou didst speak but well
When most the truth ; which I receive
        much better   230
Than to be pitied of thee. Prithee, bring
        me
To the dead bodies of my queen and son.
One grave shall be for both. Upon them
        shall
The causes of their death appear, unto
Our shame perpetual. Once a day I'll visit
The chapel where they lie ; and tears shed
        there   236
Shall be my recreation. So long as nature
Will bear up with this exercise, so long
I daily vow to use it. Come, and lead me
To these sorrows.   [*Exeunt.*

SCENE III. *Bohemia.   The sea-coast.*

Enter ANTIGONUS *with the* Child, *and a*
        Mariner.

  Ant. Thou art perfect then our ship hath
        touch'd upon

The deserts of Bohemia ?

   Mar.   Ay, my lord, and fear
We have landed in ill time ; the skies look
     grimly
And threaten present blusters.   In my
     conscience,
The heavens with that we have in hand are
     angry   5
And frown upon 's.

   Ant. Their sacred wills be done ! Go, get
     aboard ;
Look to thy bark. I'll not be long before
I call upon thee.

   Mar.   Make your best haste ; and go not
Too far i' th' land ; 'tis like to be loud
     weather ;   11
Besides, this place is famous for the
     creatures
Of prey that keep upon't.

   Ant.   Go thou away ;
I'll follow instantly.

   Mar.   I am glad at heart
To be so rid o' th' business.   [*Exit.*

   Ant.   Come, poor babe. 15
I have heard, but not believ'd, the spirits
     o' th' dead
May walk again. If such thing be, thy
     mother
Appear'd to me last night ; for ne'er was
     dream
So like a waking. To me comes a creature,
Sometimes her head on one side some
     another—   20
I never saw a vessel of like sorrow,
So fill'd and so becoming ; in pure white
     robes,
Like very sanctity, she did approach
My cabin where I lay ; thrice bow'd before
     me ;   24
And, gasping to begin some speech, her eyes
Became two spouts ; the fury spent, anon
Did this break from her : ' Good Antigonus,
Since fate, against thy better disposition,
Hath made thy person for the thrower-
     out
Of my poor babe, according to thine oath,
Places remote enough are in Bohemia, 31
There weep, and leave it crying ; and, for
     the babe
Is counted lost for ever, Perdita
I prithee call't. For this ungentle business,
Put on thee by my lord, thou ne'er shalt see
Thy wife Paulina more'. And so, with
     shrieks,   36
She melted into air. Affrighted much,
I did in time collect myself, and thought
This was so and no slumber. Dreams are
     toys ;
Yet, for this once, yea, superstitiously, 40
I will be squar'd by this. I do believe
Hermione hath suffer'd death, and that
Apollo would, this being indeed the issue
Of King Polixenes, it should here be laid,
Either for life or death, upon the earth 45

Of its right father. Blossom, speed thee
     well !   [*Laying down the child.*
There lie, and there thy character ; there
     these   [*Laying down a bundle.*
Which may, if fortune please, both breed
     thee, pretty,
And still rest thine.   The storm begins.
     Poor wretch,   49
That for thy mother's fault art thus expos'd
To loss and what may follow ! Weep I
     cannot,
But my heart bleeds ; and most accurs'd
     am I
To be by oath enjoin'd to this. Farewell !
The day frowns more and more. Thou'rt
     like to have
A lullaby too rough ; I never saw   55
The heavens so dim by day. [*Noise of
     hunt within*] A savage clamour !
Well may I get aboard !   This is the chase ;
I am gone for ever.   [*Exit, pursued by a bear.*

Enter an old Shepherd.

   Shep. I would there were no age between
ten and three and twenty, or that youth
would sleep out the rest ; for there is
nothing in the between but getting wenches
with child, wronging the ancientry, stealing,
fighting—[*Horns*] Hark you now ! Would
any but these boil'd brains of nineteen and
two and twenty hunt this weather ? They
have scar'd away two of my best sheep,
which I fear the wolf will sooner find than
the master. If any where I have them, 'tis
by the sea-side, browsing of ivy. Good
luck, an't be thy will ! What have we here ?
[*Taking up the child*] Mercy on's, a barne !
A very pretty barne. A boy or a child, I
wonder ? A pretty one ; a very pretty
one—sure, some scape. Though I am not
bookish, yet I can read waiting-gentlewoman in the scape. This has been some
stair-work, some trunk-work, some behind-
door-work ; they were warmer that got
this than the poor thing is here. I'll take
it up for pity ; yet I'll tarry till my son
come ; he halloo'd but even now. Whoa-
ho-hoa !   76

Enter Clown.

   Clo. Hilloa, loa !
   Shep. What, art so near ? If thou'lt see
a thing to talk on when thou art dead and
rotten, come hither. What ail'st thou,
man ?   80
   Clo. I have seen two such sights, by sea
and by land ! But I am not to say it is a
sea, for it is now the sky ; betwixt the
firmament and it you cannot thrust a
bodkin's point.
   Shep. Why, boy, how is it ?   85
   Clo. I would you did but see how it
chafes, how it rages, how it takes up the
shore ! But that's not to the point. O, the

most piteous cry of the poor souls! Sometimes to see 'em, and not to see 'em; now the ship boring the moon with her mainmast, and anon swallowed with yeast and froth, as you'd thrust a cork into a hogshead. And then for the land service—to see how the bear tore out his shoulder-bone; how he cried to me for help, and said his name was Antigonus, a nobleman! But to make an end of the ship—to see how the sea flap-dragon'd it; but first, how the poor souls roared, and the sea mock'd them; and how the poor gentleman roared, and the bear mock'd him, both roaring louder than the sea or weather.

Shep. Name of mercy, when was this, boy?   100

Clo. Now, now; I have not wink'd since I saw these sights; the men are not yet cold under water, nor the bear half din'd on the gentleman; he's at it now.

Shep. Would I had been by to have help'd the old man!   105

Clo. I would you had been by the ship-side, to have help'd her; there your charity would have lack'd footing.

Shep. Heavy matters, heavy matters! But look thee here, boy. Now bless thyself; thou met'st with things dying, I with things new-born. Here's a sight for thee; look thee, a bearing-cloth for a squire's child! Look thee here; take up, take up, boy; open't. So, let's see—it was told me I should be rich by the fairies. This is some changeling. Open't. What's within, boy?   114

Clo. You're a made old man; if the sins of your youth are forgiven you, you're well to live. Gold! all gold!

Shep. This is fairy gold, boy, and 'twill prove so. Up with't, keep it close. Home, home, the next way! We are lucky, boy; and to be so still requires nothing but secrecy. Let my sheep go. Come, good boy, the next way home.   121

Clo. Go you the next way with your findings. I'll go see if the bear be gone from the gentleman, and how much he hath eaten. They are never curst but when they are hungry. If there be any of him left, I'll bury it.   125

Shep. That's a good deed. If thou mayest discern by that which is left of him what he is, fetch me to th' sight of him.

Clo. Marry, will I; and you shall help to put him i' th' ground.   130

Shep. 'Tis a lucky day, boy; and we'll do good deeds on't.   [*Exeunt.*

ACT FOUR

Scene I.

Enter Time, *the* Chorus.

Time. I, that please some, try all, both joy and terror

Of good and bad, that makes and unfolds error,
Now take upon me, in the name of Time,
To use my wings. Impute it not a crime
To me or my swift passage that I slide   5
O'er sixteen years, and leave the growth untried
Of that wide gap, since it is in my pow'r
To o'erthrow law, and in one self-born hour
To plant and o'erwhelm custom. Let me pass
The same I am, ere ancient'st order was   10
Or what is now receiv'd. I witness to
The times that brought them in; so shall I do
To th' freshest things now reigning, and make stale
The glistering of this present, as my tale
Now seems to it. Your patience this allowing,   15
I turn my glass, and give my scene such growing
As you had slept between. Leontes leaving—
Th' effects of his fond jealousies so grieving
That he shuts up himself—imagine me,
Gentle spectators, that I now may be   20
In fair Bohemia; and remember well
I mention'd a son o' th' King's, which Florizel
I now name to you; and with speed so pace
To speak of Perdita, now grown in grace   24
Equal with wond'ring. What of her ensues
I list not prophesy; but let Time's news
Be known when 'tis brought forth. A shepherd's daughter,
And what to her adheres, which follows after,
Is th' argument of Time. Of this allow,   29
If ever you have spent time worse ere now;
If never, yet that Time himself doth say
He wishes earnestly you never may. [*Exit.*

Scene II. *Bohemia. The palace of Polixenes.*

Enter Polixenes *and* Camillo.

Pol. I pray thee, good Camillo, be no more importunate: 'tis a sickness denying thee anything; a death to grant this.

Cam. It is fifteen years since I saw my country; though I have for the most part been aired abroad, I desire to lay my bones there. Besides, the penitent King, my master, hath sent for me; to whose feeling sorrows I might be some allay, or I o'erween to think so, which is another spur to my departure.   9

Pol. As thou lov'st me, Camillo, wipe not out the rest of thy services by leaving me now. The need I have of thee thine own goodness hath made. Better not to have had thee than thus to want thee; thou, having made me businesses which none without thee can sufficiently manage, must either stay to execute them thyself, or take away with thee the very services thou hast done; which if I have not enough considered—as too much I cannot—to be more thankful to thee shall be my study; and my profit therein the heaping friendships. Of that fatal country Sicilia, prithee, speak no more; whose very naming punishes me with the remembrance of that penitent, as thou call'st him, and reconciled king, my brother; whose loss of his most precious queen and children are even now to be afresh lamented. Say to me, when saw'st thou the Prince Florizel, my son? Kings are no less unhappy, their issue not being gracious, than they are in losing them when they have approved their virtues.   27

Cam. Sir, it is three days since I saw the Prince. What his happier affairs may be are to me unknown; but I have missingly noted he is of late much retired from court, and is less frequent to his princely exercises than formerly he hath appeared.   32

Pol. I have considered so much, Camillo, and with some care, so far that I have eyes under my service which look upon his removedness; from whom I have this intelligence, that he is seldom from the house of a most homely shepherd—a man, they say, that from very nothing, and beyond the imagination of his neighbours, is grown into an unspeakable estate.   39

Cam. I have heard, sir, of such a man, who hath a daughter of most rare note. The report of her is extended more than can be thought to begin from such a cottage.   42

Pol. That's likewise part of my intelligence; but, I fear, the angle that plucks our son thither. Thou shalt accompany us to the place; where we will, not appearing what we are, have some question with the shepherd; from whose simplicity I think it not uneasy to get the cause of my son's resort thither. Prithee be my present partner in this business, and lay aside the thoughts of Sicilia.

Cam. I willingly obey your command. 50

Pol. My best Camillo! We must disguise ourselves.   [*Exeunt.*

SCENE III. *Bohemia. A road near the shepherd's cottage.*

Enter AUTOLYCUS, *singing.*

When daffodils begin to peer,
  With heigh! the doxy over the dale,
Why, then comes in the sweet o' the
    year,
  For the red blood reigns in the winter's
    pale.

The white sheet bleaching on the hedge, 5
  With heigh! the sweet birds, O, how
    they sing!
Doth set my pugging tooth on edge,
  For a quart of ale is a dish for a king.

The lark, that tirra-lirra chants,
  With heigh! with heigh! the thrush and
    the jay,   10
Are summer songs for me and my aunts,
  While we lie tumbling in the hay.

I have serv'd Prince Florizel, and in my time wore three-pile; but now I am out of service.

But shall I go mourn for that, my dear? 15
  The pale moon shines by night;
And when I wander here and there,
  I then do most go right.

If tinkers may have leave to live,
  And bear the sow-skin budget,   20
Then my account I well may give
  And in the stocks avouch it.

My traffic is sheets; when the kite builds, look to lesser linen. My father nam'd me Autolycus; who, being, as I am, litter'd under Mercury, was likewise a snapper-up of unconsidered trifles. With die and drab I purchas'd this caparison; and my revenue is the silly-cheat. Gallows and knock are too powerful on the highway; beating and hanging are terrors to me; for the life to come, I sleep out the thought of it. A prize! a prize!   30

Enter Clown.

Clo. Let me see: every 'leven wether tods; every tod yields pound and odd shilling; fifteen hundred shorn, what comes the wool to?

Aut. [*Aside*] If the springe hold, the cock's mine.   34

Clo. I cannot do 't without counters. Let me see: what am I to buy for our sheep-shearing feast? Three pound of sugar, five pound of currants, rice—what will this sister of mine do with rice? But my father hath made her mistress of the feast, and she lays it on. She hath made me four and twenty nosegays for the shearers—three-man song-men all, and very good ones; but they are most of them means and bases; but one Puritan amongst them, and he sings psalms to hornpipes. I must have saffron to colour the warden pies; mace; dates—none, that's out of my note; nutmegs, seven; a race or two of ginger, but that I may beg; four pound of prunes, and as many of raisins o' th' sun.   46

Aut. [*Grovelling on the ground*] O that ever I was born!

Clo. I' th' name of me!

Aut. O, help me, help me ! Pluck but off these rags ; and then, death, death !   50

Clo. Alack, poor soul ! thou hast need of more rags to lay on thee, rather than have these off.

Aut. O sir, the loathsomeness of them offend me more than the stripes I have received, which are mighty ones and millions.   55

Clo. Alas, poor man ! a million of beating may come to a great matter.

Aut. I am robb'd, sir, and beaten ; my money and apparel ta'en from me, and these detestable things put upon me.   60

Clo. What, by a horseman or a footman ?

Aut. A footman, sweet sir, a footman.

Clo. Indeed, he should be a footman, by the garments he has left with thee ; if this be a horseman's coat, it hath seen very hot service. Lend me thy hand, I'll help thee. Come, lend me thy hand.   66

[*Helping him up.*

Aut. O, good sir, tenderly, O !

Clo. Alas, poor soul !

Aut. O, good sir, softly, good sir ; I fear, sir, my shoulder blade is out.   70

Clo. How now ! Canst stand ?

Aut. Softly, dear sir [*Picks his pocket*] ; good sir, softly. You ha' done me a charitable office.

Clo. Dost lack any money ? I have a little money for thee.   75

Aut. No, good sweet sir ; no, I beseech you, sir. I have a kinsman not past three quarters of a mile hence, unto whom I was going ; I shall there have money or any-thing I want. Offer me no money, I pray you ; that kills my heart.   80

Clo. What manner of fellow was he that robb'd you ?

Aut. A fellow, sir, that I have known to go about with troll-my-dames ; I knew him once a servant of the Prince. I cannot tell, good sir, for which of his virtues it was, but he was certainly whipt out of the court.   85

Clo. His vices, you would say ; there's no virtue whipt out of the court. They cherish it to make it stay there ; and yet it will no more but abide.   88

Aut. Vices, I would say, sir. I know this man well ; he hath been since an ape-bearer ; then a process-server, a bailiff ; then he compass'd a motion of the Prodigal Son, and married a tinker's wife within a mile where my land and living lies ; and, having flown over many knavish profes-sions, he settled only in rogue. Some call him Autolycus.   95

Clo. Out upon him ! prig, for my life, prig ! He haunts wakes, fairs, and bear-baitings.

Aut. Very true, sir ; he, sir, he ; that's the rogue that put me into this apparel.   99

Clo. Not a more cowardly rogue in all Bohemia ; if you had but look'd big and spit at him, he'd have run.

Aut. I must confess to you, sir, I am no fighter ; I am false of heart that way ; and that he knew, I warrant him.

Clo. How do you now ?   105

Aut. Sweet sir, much better than I was ; I can stand and walk. I will even take my leave of you, and pace softly towards my kinsman's.

Clo. Shall I bring thee on the way ?   109

Aut. No, good-fac'd sir ; no, sweet sir.

Clo. Then fare thee well. I must go buy spices for our sheep-shearing.

Aut. Prosper you, sweet sir ! [*Exit Clown.* Your purse is not hot enough to purchase your spice. I'll be with you at your sheep-shearing too. If I make not this cheat bring out another, and the shearers prove sheep, let me be unroll'd, and my name put in the book of virtue !   [*Sings.*

> Jog on, jog on, the footpath way,
>   And merrily hent the stile-a ;
> A merry heart goes all the day,   120
>   Your sad tires in a mile-a.   [*Exit.*

SCENE IV. *Bohemia. The shepherd's cottage.*

Enter FLORIZEL *and* PERDITA.

Flo. These your unusual weeds to each part of you
Do give a life—no shepherdess, but Flora
Peering in April's front. This your sheep-shearing
Is as a meeting of the petty gods,
And you the Queen on't.

Per.   Sir, my gracious lord,   5
To chide at your extremes it not becomes me—
O, pardon that I name them ! Your high self,
The gracious mark o' th' land, you have obscur'd
With a swain's wearing ; and me, poor lowly maid,
Most goddess-like prank'd up. But that our feasts   10
In every mess have folly, and the feeders
Digest it with a custom, I should blush
To see you so attir'd ; swoon, I think,
To show myself a glass.

Flo.   I bless the time   14
When my good falcon made her flight across
Thy father's ground.

Per.   Now Jove afford you cause !
To me the difference forges dread ; your greatness
Hath not been us'd to fear. Even now I tremble
To think your father, by some accident,
Should pass this way, as you did. O, the Fates !   20

How would he look to see his work, so
    noble,
Vilely bound up ? What would he say ? Or
    how
Should I, in these my borrowed flaunts,
    behold
The sternness of his presence ?
    Flo.   Apprehend   24
Nothing but jollity. The gods themselves,
Humbling their deities to love, have taken
The shapes of beasts upon them : Jupiter
Became a bull and bellow'd ; the green
    Neptune
A ram and bleated ; and the fire-rob'd
    god,
Golden Apollo, a poor humble swain,   30
As I seem now. Their transformations
Were never for a piece of beauty rarer,
Nor in a way so chaste, since my desires
Run not before mine honour, nor my lusts
Burn hotter than my faith.
    Per.   O, but, sir,   35
Your resolution cannot hold when 'tis
Oppos'd, as it must be, by th' pow'r of the
    King.
One of these two must be necessities,
Which then will speak, that you must
    change this purpose,
Or I my life.
    Flo.   Thou dearest Perdita,   40
With these forc'd thoughts, I prithee,
    darken not
The mirth o' th' feast. Or I'll be thine, my
    fair,
Or not my father's ; for I cannot be
Mine own, nor anything to any, if   44
I be not thine. To this I am most constant,
Though destiny say no. Be merry, gentle ;
Strangle such thoughts as these with
    any thing
That you behold the while. Your guests are
    coming.
Lift up your countenance, as it were the day
Of celebration of that nuptial which   50
We two have sworn shall come.
    Per.   O Lady Fortune,
Stand you auspicious !
    Flo.   See, your guests approach.
Address yourself to entertain them
    sprightly,
And let's be red with mirth.

Enter Shepherd, *with* POLIXENES *and* CAM-
ILLO, *disguised* ; Clown, MOPSA, DORCAS,
with Others.

    Shep. Fie, daughter ! When my old wife
    liv'd, upon   55
This day she was both pantler, butler, cook;
Both dame and servant ; welcom'd all ;
    serv'd all ;
Would sing her song and dance her turn ;
    now here
At upper end o' th' table, now i' th' middle ;
On his shoulder, and his ; her face o' fire   60

With labour, and the thing she took to
    quench it
She would to each one sip. You are retired,
As if you were a feasted one, and not
The hostess of the meeting. Pray you bid
These unknown friends to's welcome, for
    it is   65
A way to make us better friends, more
    known.
Come, quench your blushes, and present
    yourself
That which you are, Mistress o' th' Feast.
    Come on,
And bid us welcome to your sheep-
    shearing,
As your good flock shall prosper.
    Per. [*To Polixenes*]   Sir, welcome.   70
It is my father's will I should take on me
The hostess-ship o' th' day. [*To Camillo*]
    You're welcome, sir.
Give me those flow'rs there, Dorcas.
    Reverend sirs,
For you there's rosemary and rue ; these
    keep
Seeming and savour all the winter long.   75
Grace and remembrance be to you both !
And welcome to our shearing.
    Pol.   Shepherdess—
A fair one are you—well you fit our ages
With flow'rs of winter.
    Per.   Sir, the year growing ancient,
Not yet on summer's death nor on the birth
Of trembling winter, the fairest flow'rs o'
    th' season   81
Are our carnations and streak'd gillyvors,
Which some call nature's bastards. Of that
    kind
Our rustic garden's barren ; and I care not
To get slips of them.
    Pol.   Wherefore, gentle maiden,   85
Do you neglect them ?
    Per.   For I have heard it said
There is an art which in their piedness
    shares
With great creating nature.
    Pol.   Say there be ;
Yet nature is made better by no mean
But nature makes that mean ; so over
    that art,   90
Which you say adds to nature, is an art
That nature makes. You see, sweet maid,
    we marry
A gentler scion to the wildest stock,
And make conceive a bark of baser kind
By bud of nobler race. This is an art   95
Which does mend nature—change it
    rather ; but
The art itself is nature.
    Per.   So it is.
    Pol. Then make your garden rich in
    gillyvors,   98
And do not call them bastards.
    Per.   I'll not put
The dibble in earth to set one slip of them ;

No more than were I painted I would wish
This youth should say 'twere well, and only
therefore   102
Desire to breed by me. Here's flow'rs for
you :
Hot lavender, mints, savory, marjoram ;
The marigold, that goes to bed wi' th' sun,
And with him rises weeping ; these are
flow'rs   106
Of middle summer, and I think they are
given
To men of middle age. Y'are very
welcome.
   Cam. I should leave grazing, were I of
your flock,
And only live by gazing.
   Per.   Out, alas !   110
You'd be so lean that blasts of January
Would blow you through and through.
Now, my fair'st friend,
I would I had some flow'rs o' th' spring
that might
Become your time of day—and yours, and
yours,   114
That wear upon your virgin branches yet
Your maidenheads growing. O Proserpina,
For the flowers now that, frighted, thou
let'st fall
From Dis's waggon !—daffodils,
That come before the swallow dares, and
take
The winds of March with beauty ; violets,
dim   120
But sweeter than the lids of Juno's eyes
Or Cytherea's breath ; pale primroses,
That die unmarried ere they can behold
Bright Phœbus in his strength—a malady
Most incident to maids ; bold oxlips, and
The crown-imperial ; lilies of all kinds,   126
The flow'r-de-luce being one. O, these I
lack
To make you garlands of, and my sweet
friend
To strew him o'er and o'er !
   Flo.   What, like a corse ?
   Per. No ; like a bank for love to lie and
play on ;   130
Not like a corse ; or if—not to be buried,
But quick, and in mine arms. Come, take
your flow'rs.
Methinks I play as I have seen them do
In Whitsun pastorals. Sure, this robe of
mine   134
Does change my disposition.
   Flo.   What you do
Still betters what is done. When you speak,
sweet,
I'd have you do it ever. When you sing,
I'd have you buy and sell so ; so give alms ;
Pray so ; and, for the ord'ring your affairs,
To sing them too. When you do dance, I
wish you   140
A wave o' th' sea, that you might ever do
Nothing but that ; move still, still so,

And own no other function. Each your
doing,
So singular in each particular,
Crowns what you are doing in the present
deeds,   145
That all your acts are queens.
   Per.   O Doricles,
Your praises are too large. But that your
youth,
And the true blood which peeps fairly
through't,
Do plainly give you out an unstain'd
shepherd,
With wisdom I might fear, my Doricles, 150
You woo'd me the false way.
   Flo.   I think you have
As little skill to fear as I have purpose
To put you to't. But, come ; our dance,
I pray,
Your hand, my Perdita ; so turtles pair
That never mean to part.
   Per.   I'll swear for 'em. 155
   Pol. This is the prettiest low-born lass
that ever
Ran on the green-sward ; nothing she does
or seems
But smacks of something greater than
herself,
Too noble for this place.
   Cam.   He tells her something
That makes her blood look out. Good
sooth, she is   160
The queen of curds and cream.
   Clo.   Come on, strike up.
   Dor. Mopsa must be your mistress ;
marry, garlic,
To mend her kissing with !
   Mop.   Now, in good time !
   Clo. Not a word, a word ; we stand upon
our manners.   164
Come, strike up.   [*Music.*

Here a dance of Shepherds and Shepherdesses.

   Pol. Pray, good shepherd, what fair
swain is this
Which dances with your daughter ?
   Shep. They call him Doricles, and boasts
himself
To have a worthy feeding ; but I have it
Upon his own report, and I believe it : 170
He looks like sooth. He says he loves my
daughter ;
I think so too ; for never gaz'd the moon
Upon the water as he'll stand and read,
As 'twere, my daughter's eyes ; and, to be
plain,
I think there is not half a kiss to choose 175
Who loves another best.
   Pol.   She dances featly.
   Shep. So she does any thing ; though I
report it
That should be silent. If young Doricles
Do light upon her, she shall bring him that
Which he not dreams of.   180

Enter a Servant.

Serv. O master, if you did but hear the pedlar at the door, you would never dance again after a tabor and pipe; no, the bagpipe could not move you. He sings several tunes faster than you'll tell money; he utters them as he had eaten ballads, and all men's ears grew to his tunes.   185

Clo. He could never come better; he shall come in. I love a ballad but even too well, if it be doleful matter merrily set down, or a very pleasant thing indeed and sung lamentably.   189

Serv. He hath songs for man or woman of all sizes; no milliner can so fit his customers with gloves. He has the prettiest love-songs for maids; so without bawdry, which is strange; with such delicate burdens of dildos and fadings, 'jump her and thump her'; and where some stretch-mouth'd rascal would, as it were, mean mischief, and break a foul gap into the matter, he makes the maid to answer 'Whoop, do me no harm, good man'—puts him off, slights him, with 'Whoop, do me no harm, good man'.   198

Pol. This is a brave fellow.

Clo. Believe me, thou talkest of an admirable conceited fellow. Has he any unbraided wares?   201

Serv. He hath ribbons of all the colours i' th' rainbow; points, more than all the lawyers in Bohemia can learnedly handle, though they come to him by th' gross; inkles, caddisses, cambrics, lawns. Why he sings 'em over as they were gods or goddesses; you would think a smock were a she-angel, he so chants to the sleeve-hand and the work about the square on't.

Clo. Prithee bring him in; and let him approach singing.   209

Per. Forewarn him that he use no scurrilous words in's tunes. [*Exit Servant.*

Clo. You have of these pedlars that have more in them than you'd think, sister.   213

Per. Ay, good brother, or go about to think.

Enter AUTOLYCUS, *singing*:

Lawn as white as driven snow;   215
Cypress black as e'er was crow;
Gloves as sweet as damask roses;
Masks for faces and for noses;
Bugle bracelet, necklace amber,
Perfume for a lady's chamber;   220
Golden quoifs and stomachers,
For my lads to give their dears;
Pins and poking-sticks of steel—
What maids lack from head to heel.
Come, buy of me, come; come buy, come
      buy;   225
Buy, lads, or else your lasses cry.
Come, buy.

Clo. If I were not in love with Mopsa, thou shouldst take no money of me; but being enthrall'd as I am, it will also be the bondage of certain ribbons and gloves.   230

Mop. I was promis'd them against the feast; but they come not too late now.

Dor. He hath promis'd you more than that, or there be liars.

Mop. He hath paid you all he promis'd you. May be he has paid you more, which will shame you to give him again.   237

Clo. Is there no manners left among maids? Will they wear their plackets where they should bear their faces? Is there not milking-time, when you are going to bed, or kiln-hole, to whistle off these secrets, but you must be tittle-tattling before all our guests? 'Tis well they are whisp'ring. Clammer your tongues, and not a word more.   243

Mop. I have done. Come, you promis'd me a tawdry-lace, and a pair of sweet gloves.

Clo. Have I not told thee how I was cozen'd by the way, and lost all my money?

Aut. And indeed, sir, there are cozeners abroad; therefore it behoves men to be wary.   249

Clo. Fear not thou, man; thou shalt lose nothing here.

Aut. I hope so, sir; for I have about me many parcels of charge.

Clo. What hast here? Ballads?

Mop. Pray now, buy some. I love a ballad in print a-life, for then we are sure they are true.   255

Aut. Here's one to a very doleful tune: how a usurer's wife was brought to bed of twenty money-bags at a burden, and how she long'd to eat adders' heads and toads carbonado'd.

Mop. Is it true, think you?   260

Aut. Very true, and but a month old.

Dor. Bless me from marrying a usurer!

Aut. Here's the midwife's name to't, one Mistress Taleporter, and five or six honest wives that were present. Why should I carry lies abroad?   265

Mop. Pray now, buy it.

Clo. Come on, lay it by; and let's first see moe ballads; we'll buy the other things anon.   268

Aut. Here's another ballad, of a fish that appeared upon the coast on Wednesday the fourscore of April, forty thousand fathom above water, and sung this ballad against the hard hearts of maids. It was thought she was a woman, and was turn'd into a cold fish for she would not exchange flesh with one that lov'd her. The ballad is very pitiful, and as true.   275

Dor. Is it true too, think you?

Aut. Five justices' hands at it ; and witnesses more than my pack will hold.

Clo. Lay it by too. Another.

Aut. This is a merry ballad, but a very pretty one.

Mop. Let's have some merry ones.   281

Aut. Why, this is a passing merry one, and goes to the tune of ' Two maids wooing a man '. There's scarce a maid westward but she sings it ; 'tis in request, I can tell you.   285

Mop. We can both sing it. If thou'lt bear a part, thou shalt hear ; 'tis in three parts.

Dor. We had the tune on't a month ago.

Aut. I can bear my part ; you must know 'tis my occupation. Have at it with you.   290

Song.

Aut. Get you hence, for I must go
      Where it fits not you to know.
Dor. Whither ?
Mop.   O, whither ?
Dor.   Whither ?
Mop. It becomes thy oath full well
      Thou to me thy secrets tell.   295
Dor. Me too ! Let me go thither.
Mop. Or thou goest to th' grange or mill.
Dor. If to either, thou dost ill.
Aut. Neither.
Dor.   What, neither ?
Aut.   Neither.
Dor. Thou hast sworn my love to be.   300
Mop. Thou hast sworn it more to me.
      Then whither goest ? Say, whither ?

Clo. We'll have this song out anon by ourselves ; my father and the gentlemen are in sad talk, and we'll not trouble them. Come, bring away thy pack after me. Wenches, I'll buy for you both. Pedlar, let's have the first choice. Follow me, girls.
                [*Exit with Dorcas and Mopsa.*

Aut. And you shall pay well for 'em.
                [*Exit Autolycus, singing* :

      Will you buy any tape,
        Or lace for your cape,   310
      My dainty duck, my dear-a ?
      Any silk, any thread,
      Any toys for your head,
      Of the new'st and fin'st, fin'st wear-a ?
        Come to the pedlar ;   315
        Money's a meddler
      That doth utter all men's ware-a.

Re-enter Servant.

Serv. Master, there is three carters, three shepherds, three neat-herds, three swine-herds, that have made themselves all men of hair ; they call themselves Saltiers, and they have a dance which the wenches say is a gallimaufry of gambols, because they are not in't ; but they themselves are o'

th' mind, if it be not too rough for some that know little but bowling, it will please plentifully.   324

Shep. Away ! We'll none on't ; here has been too much homely foolery already. I know, sir, we weary you.

Pol. You weary those that refresh us. Pray, let's see these four threes of herds-men.   328

Serv. One three of them, by their own report, sir, hath danc'd before the King ; and not the worst of the three but jumps twelve foot and a half by th' squier.   331

Shep. Leave your prating ; since these good men are pleas'd, let them come in ; but quickly now.

Serv. Why, they stay at door, sir. [*Exit.*

Here a Dance of twelve Satyrs.

Pol. [*To Shepherd*] O, father, you'll know
      more of that hereafter.
[*To Camillo*] Is it not too far gone ? 'Tis
      time to part them.
He's simple and tells much. [*To Florizel*]
      How now, fair shepherd !
Your heart is full of something that does
      take
Your mind from feasting. Sooth, when I
      was young
And handed love as you do, I was wont   340
To load my she with knacks ; I would have
      ransack'd
The pedlar's silken treasury and have
      pour'd it
To her acceptance : you have let him go
And nothing marted with him. If your lass
Interpretation should abuse and call this   345
Your lack of love or bounty, you were
      straited
For a reply, at least if you make a care
Of happy holding her.
Flo.   Old sir, I know
She prizes not such trifles as these are.
The gifts she looks from me are pack'd and
      lock'd   350
Up in my heart, which I have given already,
But not deliver'd. O, hear me breathe my
      life
Before this ancient sir, whom, it should
      seem,
Hath sometime lov'd. I take thy hand—
      this hand,   354
As soft as dove's down and as white as it,
Or Ethiopian's tooth, or the fann'd snow
      that's bolted
By th' northern blasts twice o'er.
Pol.   What follows this ?
How prettily the young swain seems to
      wash
The hand was fair before ! I have put
      you out.
But to your protestation ; let me hear   360
What you profess.
Flo.   Do, and be witness to't.

Pol. And this my neighbour too ?
Flo.   And he, and more
Than he, and men—the earth, the heavens,
     and all :
That, were I crown'd the most imperial
     monarch,
Thereof most worthy, were I the fairest
     youth   365
That ever made eye swerve, had force and
     knowledge
More than was ever man's, I would not
     prize them
Without her love ; for her employ them all;
Commend them and condemn them to her
     service
Or to their own perdition.
Pol.   Fairly offer'd.   370
Cam. This shows a sound affection.
Shep.   But, my daughter,
Say you the like to him ?
Per.   I cannot speak
So well, nothing so well ; no, nor mean
     better.
By th' pattern of mine own thoughts I
     cut out
The purity of his.
Shep.   Take hands, a bargain !   375
And, friends unknown, you shall bear
     witness to't :
I give my daughter to him, and will make
Her portion equal his.
Flo.   O, that must be
I' th' virtue of your daughter. One being
     dead,
I shall have more than you can dream
     of yet ;   380
Enough then for your wonder. But come
     on,
Contract us fore these witnesses.
Shep.   Come, your hand ;
And, daughter, yours.
Pol. Soft, swain, awhile, beseech you ;
Have you a father ?
Flo.   I have, but what of him ?
Pol. Knows he of this ?
Flo.   He neither does nor shall.   385
Pol. Methinks a father
Is at the nuptial of his son a guest
That best becomes the table. Pray you,
     once more,
Is not your father grown incapable
Of reasonable affairs ? Is he not stupid   390
With age and alt'ring rheums ? Can he
     speak, hear,
Know man from man, dispute his own
     estate ?
Lies he not bed-rid, and again does nothing
But what he did being childish ?
Flo.   No, good sir ;
He has his health, and ampler strength
     indeed   395
Than most have of his age.
Pol.   By my white beard,
You offer him, if this be so, a wrong

Something unfilial. Reason my son
Should choose himself a wife ; but as good
     reason   399
The father—all whose joy is nothing else
But fair posterity—should hold some
     counsel
In such a business.
Flo.   I yield all this ;
But, for some other reasons, my grave sir,
Which 'tis not fit you know, I not acquaint
My father of this business.
Pol.   Let him know't.   405
Flo. He shall not.
Pol.   Prithee let him.
Flo.   No, he must not.
Shep. Let him, my son ; he shall not
     need to grieve
At knowing of thy choice.
Flo.   Come, come, he must not.
Mark our contract.
Pol. [*Discovering himself*] Mark your
     divorce, young sir,
Whom son I dare not call ; thou art too
     base   410
To be acknowledg'd—thou a sceptre's heir,
That thus affects a sheep-hook ! Thou, old
     traitor,
I am sorry that by hanging thee I can but
Shorten thy life one week. And thou,
     fresh piece
Of excellent witchcraft, who of force must
     know   415
The royal fool thou cop'st with—
Shep.   O, my heart !
Pol. I'll have thy beauty scratch'd with
     briers and made
More homely than thy state. For thee, fond
     boy,
If I may ever know thou dost but sigh
That thou no more shalt see this knack—
     as never   420
I mean thou shalt—we'll bar thee from
     succession ;
Not hold thee of our blood, no, not our
     kin,
Farre than Deucalion off. Mark thou my
     words.
Follow us to the court. Thou churl, for
     this time,
Though full of our displeasure, yet we free
     thee   425
From the dead blow of it. And you,
     enchantment,
Worthy enough a herdsman—yea, him too
That makes himself, but for our honour
     therein,
Unworthy thee—if ever henceforth thou
These rural latches to his entrance open,   430
Or hoop his body more with thy embraces,
I will devise a death as cruel for thee
As thou art tender to't.   [*Exit.*
Per.   Even here undone !
I was not much afeard ; for once or twice
I was about to speak and tell him plainly

The self-same sun that shines upon his
    court   436
Hides not his visage from our cottage, but
Looks on alike. [*To Florizel*] Will't please
    you, sir, be gone ?
I told you what would come of this.
    Beseech you,
Of your own state take care. This dream
    of mine—   440
Being now awake, I'll queen it no inch
    farther,
But milk my ewes and weep.
    Cam.   Why, how now, father !
Speak ere thou diest.
    Shep.   I cannot speak nor think,
Nor dare to know that which I know. [*To
    Florizel*] O sir,   444
You have undone a man of fourscore-three
That thought to fill his grave in quiet, yea,
To die upon the bed my father died,
To lie close by his honest bones ; but now
Some hangman must put on my shroud and
    lay me
Where no priest shovels in dust. [*To
    Perdita*] O cursed wretch,   450
That knew'st this was the Prince, and
    wouldst adventure
To mingle faith with him !—Undone,
    undone !
If I might die within this hour, I have liv'd
To die when I desire.   [*Exit.*
    Flo.   Why look you so upon me ?
I am but sorry, not afeard ; delay'd,   455
But nothing alt'red. What I was, I am :
More straining on for plucking back ; not
    following
My leash unwillingly.
    Cam.   Gracious, my lord,
You know your father's temper. At this
    time   459
He will allow no speech—which I do guess
You do not purpose to him—and as hardly
Will he endure your sight as yet, I fear ;
Then, till the fury of his Highness settle,
Come not before him.
    Flo.   I not purpose it.
I think Camillo ?
    Cam.   Even he, my lord.   465
    Per. How often have I told you 'twould
    be thus !
How often said my dignity would last
But till 'twere known !
    Flo.   It cannot fail but by
The violation of my faith ; and then
Let nature crush the sides o' th' earth
    together   470
And mar the seeds within ! Lift up thy
    looks.
From my succession wipe me, father ; I
Am heir to my affection.
    Cam.   Be advis'd.
    Flo. I am—and by my fancy ; if my
    reason   474
Will thereto be obedient, I have reason ;

If not, my senses, better pleas'd with
    madness,
Do bid it welcome.
    Cam.   This is desperate, sir.
    Flo. So call it ; but it does fulfil my vow :
I needs must think it honesty. Camillo,   479
Not for Bohemia, nor the pomp that may
Be thereat glean'd, for all the sun sees or
The close earth wombs, or the profound
    seas hides
In unknown fathoms, will I break my oath
To this my fair belov'd. Therefore, I pray
    you,
As you have ever been my father's honour'd
    friend,   485
When he shall miss me—as, in faith, I
    mean not
To see him any more—cast your good
    counsels
Upon his passion. Let myself and Fortune
Tug for the time to come. This you may
    know,
And so deliver : I am put to sea   490
With her who here I cannot hold on shore.
And most opportune to her need I have
A vessel rides fast by, but not prepar'd
For this design. What course I mean to
    hold   494
Shall nothing benefit your knowledge, nor
Concern me the reporting.
    Cam.   O my lord,
I would your spirit were easier for advice,
Or stronger for your need.
    Flo.   Hark, Perdita.   498
    [*Takes her aside.*
[*To Camillo*] I'll hear you by and by.
    Cam.   He's irremovable,
Resolv'd for flight. Now were I happy if
His going I could frame to serve my turn,
Save him from danger, do him love and
    honour,
Purchase the sight again of dear Sicilia
And that unhappy king, my master, whom
I so much thirst to see.
    Flo.   Now, good Camillo,   505
I am so fraught with curious business that
I leave out ceremony.
    Cam.   Sir, I think
You have heard of my poor services i' th'
    love
That I have borne your father ?
    Flo.   Very nobly
Have you deserv'd. It is my father's music
To speak your deeds ; not little of his
    care   511
To have them recompens'd as thought on.
    Cam.   Well, my lord,
If you may please to think I love the King,
And through him what's nearest to him,
    which is
Your gracious self, embrace but my
    direction.   515
If your more ponderous and settled project
May suffer alteration, on mine honour,

I'll point you where you shall have such
    receiving
As shall become your Highness; where you
    may
Enjoy your mistress, from the whom,
    I see,   520
There's no disjunction to be made but by,
As heavens forfend! your ruin—marry
    her;
And with my best endeavours in your
    absence
Your discontenting father strive to qualify,
And bring him up to liking.

    Flo.   How, Camillo, 525
May this, almost a miracle, be done?
That I may call thee something more than
    man,
And after that trust to thee.

    Cam.   Have you thought on
A place whereto you'll go?

    Flo.   Not any yet;
But as th' unthought-on accident is guilty
To what we wildly do, so we profess 531
Ourselves to be the slaves of chance and
    flies
Of every wind that blows.

    Cam.   Then list to me.
This follows, if you will not change your
    purpose 534
But undergo this flight: make for Sicilia,
And there present yourself and your fair
    princess—
For so, I see, she must be—fore Leontes.
She shall be habited as it becomes
The partner of your bed. Methinks I see
Leontes opening his free arms and weeping
His welcomes forth; asks thee there ' Son,
    forgiveness!' 541
As 'twere i' th' father's person; kisses the
    hands
Of your fresh princess; o'er and o'er
    divides him
'Twixt his unkindness and his kindness—
    th'one 544
He chides to hell, and bids the other grow
Faster than thought or time.

    Flo.   Worthy Camillo,
What colour for my visitation shall I
Hold up before him?

    Cam.   Sent by the King your father
To greet him and to give him comforts. Sir,
The manner of your bearing towards him,
    with 550
What you as from your father shall deliver,
Things known betwixt us three, I'll write
    you down;
The which shall point you forth at every
    sitting
What you must say, that he shall not
    perceive
But that you have your father's bosom
    there 555
And speak his very heart.

    Flo.   I am bound to you.

There is some sap in this.

    Cam.   A course more promising
Than a wild dedication of yourselves
To unpath'd waters, undream'd shores,
    most certain 559
To miseries enough; no hope to help you,
But as you shake off one to take another;
Nothing so certain as your anchors, who
Do their best office if they can but stay you
Where you'll be loath to be. Besides, you
    know
Prosperity's the very bond of love, 565
Whose fresh complexion and whose heart
    together
Affliction alters.

    Per.   One of these is true:
I think affliction may subdue the cheek,
But not take in the mind.

    Cam.   Yea, say you so?
There shall not at your father's house these
    seven years
Be born another such.

    Flo.   My good Camillo, 571
She is as forward of her breeding as
She is i' th' rear o' our birth.

    Cam.   I cannot say 'tis pity
She lacks instructions, for she seems a
    mistress
To most that teach.

    Per.   Your pardon, sir; for this
I'll blush you thanks.

    Flo.   My prettiest Perdita! 576
But, O, the thorns we stand upon!
    Cam'llo—
Preserver of my father, now of me;
The medicine of our house—how shall we
    do?
We are not furnish'd like Bohemia's son;
Nor shall appear in Sicilia.

    Cam.   My lord, 581
Fear none of this. I think you know my
    fortunes
Do all lie there. It shall be so my care
To have you royally appointed as if
The scene you play were mine. For
    instance, sir, 585
That you may know you shall not want—
    one word.   [*They talk aside.*

    Re-enter AUTOLYCUS.

    Aut. Ha, ha! what a fool Honesty is!
and Trust, his sworn brother, a very simple
gentleman! I have sold all my trumpery;
not a counterfeit stone, not a ribbon, glass,
pomander, brooch, table-book, ballad,
knife, tape, glove, shoe-tie, bracelet, horn-
ring, to keep my pack from fasting. They
throng who should buy first, as if my
trinkets had been hallowed and brought a
benediction to the buyer; by which means
I saw whose purse was best in picture; and
what I saw, to my good use I rememb'red.
My clown, who wants but something to be
a reasonable man, grew so in love with the

wenches' song that he would not stir his
pettitoes till he had both tune and words,
which so drew the rest of the herd to me
that all their other senses stuck in ears.
You might have pinch'd a placket, it was
senseless ; 'twas nothing to geld a codpiece
of a purse ; I would have fil'd keys off
that hung in chains. No hearing, no feeling,
but my sir's song, and admiring the
nothing of it. So that in this time of
lethargy I pick'd and cut most of their
festival purses ; and had not the old man
come in with a whoobub against his daughter
and the King's son and scar'd my choughs
from the chaff, I had not left a purse alive
in the whole army. [_Camillo, Florizel, and
                        Perdita, come forward._

Cam. Nay, but my letters, by this means
                being there   610
So soon as you arrive, shall clear that
        doubt.
Flo. And those that you'll procure from
        King Leontes ?
Cam. Shall satisfy your father.
Per.   Happy be you !
All that you speak shows fair.
Cam. [_Seeing Autolycus_] Who have we
        here ?
We'll make an instrument of this ; omit 615
Nothing may give us aid.
Aut. [_Aside_] If they have overheard me
now—why, hanging.
Cam. How now, good fellow ! Why
shak'st thou so ? Fear not, man ; here's
no harm intended to thee.
Aut. I am a poor fellow, sir.   620
Cam. Why, be so still ; here's nobody
will steal that from thee. Yet for the
outside of thy poverty we must make an
exchange ; therefore discase thee instantly
—thou must think there's a necessity in't
—and change garments with this gentleman. Though the pennyworth on his side
be the worst, yet hold thee, there's some
boot.   [_Giving money._ 627
Aut. I am a poor fellow, sir. [_Aside_] I
know ye well enough.
Cam. Nay, prithee dispatch. The gentleman is half flay'd already.   631
Aut. Are you in earnest, sir ? [_Aside_] I
smell the trick on't.
Flo. Dispatch, I prithee.
Aut. Indeed, I have had earnest ; but I
cannot with conscience take it.   636
Cam. Unbuckle, unbuckle. [_Florizel and
                Autolycus exchange garments._
Fortunate mistress—let my prophecy
Come home to ye !—you must retire
        yourself
Into some covert ; take your sweetheart's
        hat   640
And pluck it o'er your brows, muffle your
        face,
Dismantle you, and, as you can, disliken

The truth of your own seeming, that you
        may—
For I do fear eyes over—to shipboard
Get undescried.
Per.   I see the play so lies 645
That I must bear a part.
Cam.   No remedy.
Have you done there ?
Flo.   Should I now meet my father,
He would not call me son.
Cam.   Nay, you shall have no hat.
                        [_Giving it to Perdita._
Come, lady, come. Farewell, my friend.
Aut.   Adieu, sir.
Flo. O Perdita, what have we twain
        forgot !   650
Pray you a word.   [_They converse apart._
Cam. [_Aside_] What I do next shall be to
        tell the King
Of this escape, and whither they are bound ;
Wherein my hope is I shall so prevail
To force him after ; in whose company 655
I shall re-view Sicilia, for whose sight
I have a woman's longing.
Flo.   Fortune speed us !
Thus we set on, Camillo, to th' sea-side.
Cam. The swifter speed the better.   659
        [_Exeunt Florizel, Perdita, and Camillo._
Aut. I understand the business, I hear
it. To have an open ear, a quick eye, and
a nimble hand, is necessary for a cutpurse ; a good nose is requisite also, to
smell out work for th' other senses. I see
this is the time that the unjust man doth
thrive. What an exchange had this been
without boot ! What a boot is here with
this exchange ! Sure, the gods do this year
connive at us, and we may do anyth'ng
extempore. The Prince himself is about a
piece of iniquity—stealing away from his
father with his clog at his heels. If I
thought it were a piece of honesty to
acquaint the King withal, I would not do't.
I hold it the more knavery to conceal it ;
and therein am I constant to my profession.

Re-enter Clown _and_ Shepherd.

Aside, aside—here is more matter for a hot
brain. Every lane's end, every shop,
church, session, hanging, yields a careful
man work.   675
Clo. See, see ; what a man you are now !
There is no other way but to tell the King
she's a changeling and none of your flesh
and blood.
Shep. Nay, but hear me.
Clo. Nay—but hear me.   680
Shep. Go to, then.
Clo. She being none of your flesh and
blood, your flesh and blood has not
offended the King ; and so your flesh and
blood is not to be punish'd by him. Show
those things you found about her, those
secret things—all but what she has with

her. This being done, let the law go
whistle; I warrant you.　　　　　　687

Shep. I will tell the King all, every word
—yea, and his son's pranks too; who, I
may say, is no honest man, neither to his
father nor to me, to go about to make me
the King's brother-in-law.　　　　691

Clo. Indeed, brother-in-law was the
farthest off you could have been to him;
and then your blood had been the dearer by
I know how much an ounce.

Aut. [*Aside*] Very wisely, puppies!　695

Shep. Well, let us to the King. There is
that in this fardel will make him scratch his
beard.

Aut. [*Aside*] I know not what impediment this complaint may be to the flight
of my master.

Clo. Pray heartily he be at palace.　700

Aut. [*Aside*] Though I am not naturally
honest, I am so sometimes by chance. Let
me pocket up my pedlar's excrement.
[*Takes off his false beard*] How now, rustics!
Whither are you bound?

Shep. To th' palace, an it like your
worship.　　　　　　　　　　705

Aut. Your affairs there, what, with
whom, the condition of that fardel, the
place of your dwelling, your names, your
ages, of what having, breeding, and anything that is fitting to be known—discover.

Clo. We are but plain fellows, sir.　710

Aut. A lie: you are rough and hairy.
Let me have no lying; it becomes none
but tradesmen, and they often give us
soldiers the lie; but we pay them for it
with stamped coin, not stabbing steel;
therefore they do not give us the lie.　715

Clo. Your worship had like to have given
us one, if you had not taken yourself with
the manner.

Shep. Are you a courtier, an't like you,
sir?　　　　　　　　　　　718

Aut. Whether it like me or no, I am a
courtier. Seest thou not the air of the
court in these enfoldings? Hath not my
gait in it the measure of the court?
Receives not thy nose court-odour from
me? Reflect I not on thy baseness court-
contempt? Think'st thou, for that I
insinuate, that toaze from thee thy business,
I am therefore no courtier? I am courtier
cap-a-pe, and one that will either push
on or pluck back thy business there;
whereupon I command thee to open thy
affair.　　　　　　　　　　727

Shep. My business, sir, is to the King.

Aut. What advocate hast thou to him?

Shep. I know not, an't like you.　730

Clo. Advocate's the court-word for a
pheasant; say you have none.

Shep. None, sir; I have no pheasant,
cock nor hen.

Aut. How blessed are we that are not
simple men!
Yet nature might have made me as these
are,　　　　　　　　　　　735
Therefore I will not disdain.

Clo. This cannot be but a great courtier.

Shep. His garments are rich, but he wears
them not handsomely.　　　　　739

Clo. He seems to be the more noble in
being fantastical. A great man, I'll warrant;
I know by the picking on's teeth.

Aut. The fardel there? What's i' th'
fardel? Wherefore that box?　744

Shep. Sir, there lies such secrets in this
fardel and box which none must know but
the King; and which he shall know within
this hour, if I may come to th' speech of
him.

Aut. Age, thou hast lost thy labour.

Shep. Why, sir?　　　　　　750

Aut. The King is not at the palace; he
is gone aboard a new ship to purge melancholy and air himself; for, if thou be'st
capable of things serious, thou must know
the King is full of grief.　　　　754

Shep. So 'tis said, sir—about his son,
that should have married a shepherd's
daughter.

Aut. If that shepherd be not in hand-
fast, let him fly; the curses he shall have,
the tortures he shall feel, will break the
back of man, the heart of monster.

Clo. Think you so, sir?　　　　760

Aut. Not he alone shall suffer what wit
can make heavy and vengeance bitter; but
those that are germane to him, though
remov'd fifty times, shall all come under
the hangman—which, though it be great
pity, yet it is necessary. An old sheep-
whistling rogue, a ram-tender, to offer to
have his daughter come into grace! Some
say he shall be ston'd; but that death is
too soft for him, say I. Draw our throne
into a sheep-cote!—all deaths are too few,
the sharpest too easy.　　　　770

Clo. Has the old man e'er a son, sir, do
you hear, an't like you, sir?

Aut. He has a son—who shall be flay'd
alive; then 'nointed over with honey, set
on the head of a wasp's nest; then stand
till he be three quarters and a dram dead;
then recover'd again with aqua-vitæ or
some other hot infusion; then, raw as he
is, and in the hottest day prognostication
proclaims, shall he be set against a brick
wall, the sun looking with a southward eye
upon him, where he is to behold him with
flies blown to death. But what talk we of
these traitorly rascals, whose miseries are
to be smil'd at, their offences being so
capital? Tell me, for you seem to be
honest plain men, what you have to the
King. Being something gently consider'd,
I'll bring you where he is aboard, tender

your persons to his presence, whisper him
in your behalfs; and if it be in man besides
the King to effect your suits, here is man
shall do it. 788

Clo. He seems to be of great authority.
Close with him, give him gold; and though
authority be a stubborn bear, yet he is oft
led by the nose with gold. Show the inside
of your purse to the outside of his hand,
and no more ado. Remember—ston'd and
flay'd alive. 793

Shep. An't please you, sir, to undertake
the business for us, here is that gold I have.
I'll make it as much more, and leave this
young man in pawn till I bring it you. 797

Aut. After I have done what I promised?

Shep. Ay, sir.

Aut. Well, give me the moiety. Are you
a party in this business? 801

Clo. In some sort, sir; but though my
case be a pitiful one, I hope I shall not be
flay'd out of it. 803

Aut. O, that's the case of the shepherd's
son! Hang him, he'll be made an example.

Clo. Comfort, good comfort! We must
to the King and show our strange sights.
He must know 'tis none of your daughter
nor my sister; we are gone else. Sir, I will
give you as much as this old man does, when
the business is performed; and remain, as
he says, your pawn till it be brought you.

Aut. I will trust you. Walk before toward
the sea-side; go on the right-hand; I will
but look upon the hedge, and follow you. 814

Clo. We are blest in this man, as I may
say, even blest.

Shep. Let's before, as he bids us. He was
provided to do us good. 817

[*Exeunt Shepherd and Clown.*

Aut. If I had a mind to be honest, I see
Fortune would not suffer me: she drops
booties in my mouth. I am courted now
with a double occasion—gold, and a means
to do the Prince my master good; which
who knows how that may turn back to my
advancement? I will bring these two moles,
these blind ones, aboard him. If he think
it fit to shore them again, and that the
complaint they have to the King concerns
him nothing, let him call me rogue for being
so far officious; for I am proof against that
title, and what shame else belongs to't. To
him will I present them. There may be
matter in it. [*Exit.* 829

ACT FIVE

SCENE I. *Sicilia. The palace of Leontes.*

Enter LEONTES, CLEOMENES, DION,
PAULINA, *and* Others.

Cleo. Sir, you have done enough, and
have perform'd
A saint-like sorrow. No fault could you
make

Which you have not redeem'd; indeed,
paid down
More penitence than done trespass. At the
last,
Do as the heavens have done: forget your
evil; 5
With them forgive yourself.

Leon. Whilst I remember
Her and her virtues, I cannot forget
My blemishes in them, and so still think of
The wrong I did myself; which was so
much
That heirless it hath made my kingdom, and 10
Destroy'd the sweet'st companion that e'er
man
Bred his hopes out of.

Paul. True, too true, my lord.
If, one by one, you wedded all the world,
Or from the all that are took something
good
To make a perfect woman, she you kill'd 15
Would be unparallel'd.

Leon. I think so. Kill'd!
She I kill'd! I did so; but thou strik'st me
Sorely, to say I did. It is as bitter
Upon thy tongue as in my thought. Now,
good now,
Say so but seldom.

Cleo. Not at all, good lady. 20
You might have spoken a thousand things
that would
Have done the time more benefit, and
grac'd
Your kindness better.

Paul. You are one of those
Would have him wed again.

Dion. If you would not so,
You pity not the state, nor the remem-
brance 25
Of his most sovereign name; consider little
What dangers, by his Highness' fail of issue,
May drop upon his kingdom and devour
Incertain lookers-on. What were more holy
Than to rejoice the former queen is well?
What holier than, for royalty's repair, 31
For present comfort, and for future good,
To bless the bed of majesty again
With a sweet fellow to't?

Paul. There is none worthy,
Respecting her that's gone. Besides, the
gods 35
Will have fulfill'd their secret purposes;
For has not the divine Apollo said,
Is't not the tenour of his oracle,
That King Leontes shall not have an heir
Till his lost child be found? Which that
it shall, 40
Is all as monstrous to our human reason
As my Antigonus to break his grave
And come again to me; who, on my life,
Did perish with the infant. 'Tis your
counsel 44
My lord should to the heavens be contrary,

Oppose against their wills. [*To Leontes*]
       Care not for issue ;
The crown will find an heir. Great Alex-
       ander
Left his to th' worthiest ; so his successor
Was like to be the best.
     Leon.   Good Paulina,
Who hast the memory of Hermione,   50
I know, in honour, O that ever I
Had squar'd me to thy counsel ! Then,
       even now,
I might have look'd upon my queen's full
       eyes,
Have taken treasure from her lips—
     Paul.   And left them
More rich for what they yielded.
     Leon.   Thou speak'st truth.   55
No more such wives ; therefore, no wife.
     One worse,
And better us'd, would make her sainted
       spirit
Again possess her corpse, and on this stage,
Where we offend her now, appear soul-
       vex'd,
And begin ' Why to me '—
     Paul.   Had she such power,   60
She had just cause.
     Leon.   She had ; and would incense me
To murder her I married.
     Paul.   I should so.
Were I the ghost that walk'd, I'd bid you
       mark
Her eye, and tell me for what dull part
       in't
You chose her ; then I'd shriek, that even
       your ears   65
Should rift to hear me ; and the words that
       follow'd
Should be ' Remember mine '.
     Leon.   Stars, stars,
And all eyes else dead coals ! Fear thou no
       wife ;
I'll have no wife, Paulina.
     Paul.   Will you swear
Never to marry but by my free leave ?   70
     Leon.   Never, Paulina ; so be blest my
       spirit !
     Paul. Then, good my lords, bear witness
       to his oath.
     Cleo. You tempt him over-much.
     Paul.   Unless another,
As like Hermione as is her picture,
Affront his eye.
     Cleo.   Good madam—
     Paul.   I have done.   75
Yet, if my lord will marry—if you will, sir,
No remedy but you will—give me the office
To choose you a queen. She shall not be so
       young
As was your former ; but she shall be such
As, walk'd your first queen's ghost, it
       should take joy   80
To see her in your arms.
     Leon.   My true Paulina,

We shall not marry till thou bid'st us.
     Paul.   That
Shall be when your first queen's again in
       breath ;
Never till then.

         Enter a Gentleman.

     Gent. One that gives out himself Prince
       Florizel,   85
Son of Polixenes, with his princess—she
The fairest I have yet beheld—desires
       access
To your high presence.
     Leon.   What with him ? He comes not
Like to his father's greatness. His approach,
So out of circumstance and sudden, tells us
'Tis not a visitation fram'd, but forc'd   91
By need and accident. What train ?
     Gent.   But few,
And those but mean.
     Leon.   His princess, say you, with him ?
     Gent. Ay ; the most peerless piece of
       earth, I think,   94
That e'er the sun shone bright on.
     Paul.   O Hermione,
As every present time doth boast itself
Above a better gone, so must thy grave
Give way to what's seen now ! Sir, you
       yourself
Have said and writ so, but your writing now
Is colder than that theme : ' She had not
       been,   100
Nor was not to be equall'd '. Thus your verse
Flow'd with her beauty once ; 'tis shrewdly
       ebb'd,
To say you have seen a better.
     Gent.   Pardon, madam.
The one I have almost forgot—your pardon ;
The other, when she has obtain'd your eye,
Will have your tongue too. This is a
       creature,   106
Would she begin a sect, might quench the
       zeal
Of all professors else, make proselytes
Of who she but bid follow.
     Paul.   How ! not women ?
     Gent. Women will love her that she is a
       woman   110
More worth than any man ; men, that she is
The rarest of all women.
     Leon.   Go, Cleomenes ;
Yourself, assisted with your honour'd
       friends,
Bring them to our embracement. [*Exeunt*]
       Still, 'tis strange
He thus should steal upon us.
     Paul.   Had our prince,   115
Jewel of children, seen this hour, he had
       pair'd
Well with this lord ; there was not full a
       month
Between their births.
     Leon. Prithee no more ; cease. Thou
       know'st   119

He dies to me again when talk'd of. Sure,
When I shall see this gentleman, thy
   speeches
Will bring me to consider that which may
Unfurnish me of reason.

    Re-enter CLEOMENES, *with* FLORIZEL,
        PERDITA, *and* Attendants.

               They are come.
Your mother was most true to wedlock,
   Prince ;
For she did print your royal father off, 125
Conceiving you. Were I but twenty-one,
Your father's image is so hit in you,
His very air, that I should call you brother,
As I did him, and speak of something wildly
By us perform'd before.   Most dearly
   welcome !   130
And your fair princess—goddess ! O, alas !
I lost a couple that 'twixt heaven and
   earth
Might thus have stood begetting wonder as
You, gracious couple, do. And then I lost—
All mine own folly—the society,   135
Amity too, of your brave father, whom,
Though bearing misery, I desire my life
Once more to look on him.
   Flo.   By his command
Have I here touch'd Sicilia, and from him
Give you all greetings that a king, at friend,
Can send his brother ; and, but infirmity,
Which waits upon worn times, hath some-
   thing seiz'd   142
His wish'd ability, he had himself
The lands and waters 'twixt your throne
   and his
Measur'd, to look upon you ; whom he
   loves,   145
He bade me say so, more than all the
   sceptres
And those that bear them living.
   Leon.   O my brother—
Good gentleman !—the wrongs I have done
   thee stir
Afresh within me ; and these thy offices,
So rarely kind, are as interpreters   150
Of my behind-hand slackness ! Welcome
   hither,
As is the spring to th' earth. And hath he
   too
Expos'd this paragon to th' fearful usage,
At least ungentle, of the dreadful Neptune,
To greet a man not worth her pains, much
   less   155
Th' adventure of her person ?
   Flo.   Good, my lord,
She came from Libya.
   Leon.   Where the warlike Smalus,
That noble honour'd lord, is fear'd and
   lov'd ?
   Flo. Most royal sir, from thence ; from
   him whose daughter
His tears proclaim'd his, parting with her ;
   thence,   160

A prosperous south-wind friendly, we have
   cross'd,
To execute the charge my father gave me
For visiting your Highness. My best train
I have from your Sicilian shores dismiss'd ;
Who for Bohemia bend, to signify   165
Not only my success in Libya, sir,
But my arrival and my wife's in safety
Here where we are.
   Leon.   The blessed gods
Purge all infection from our air whilst you
Do climate here ! You have a holy father,
A graceful gentleman, against whose person,
So sacred as it is, I have done sin,   172
For which the heavens, taking angry note,
Have left me issueless ; and your father's
   blest,
As he from heaven merits it, with you, 175
Worthy his goodness. What might I have
   been,
Might I a son and daughter now have look'd
   on,
Such goodly things as you !

            Enter a Lord.

   Lord.   Most noble sir,
That which I shall report will bear no credit,
Were not the proof so nigh. Please you,
   great sir,   180
Bohemia greets you from himself by me ;
Desires you to attach his son, who has—
His dignity and duty both cast off—
Fled from his father, from his hopes, and
   with
A shepherd's daughter.
   Leon.   Where's Bohemia ? Speak. 185
   Lord. Here in your city ; I now came
   from him.
I speak amazedly ; and it becomes
My marvel and my message. To your court
Whiles he was hast'ning—in the chase, it
   seems,
Of this fair couple—meets he on the way 190
The father of this seeming lady and
Her brother, having both their country
   quitted
With this young prince.
   Flo.   Camillo has betray'd me ;
Whose honour and whose honesty till now
Endur'd all weathers.
   Lord.   Lay't so to his charge ;
He's with the King your father.
   Leon.   Who ? Camillo ?
   Lord. Camillo, sir ; I spake with him ;
   who now
Has these poor men in question. Never
   saw I
Wretches so quake. They kneel, they kiss
   the earth ;   199
Forswear themselves as often as they speak.
Bohemia stops his ears, and threatens them
With divers deaths in death.
   Per.   O my poor father !
The heaven sets spies upon us, will not have

Our contract celebrated.
   Leon.   You are married ?
   Flo. We are not, sir, nor are we like to be;
The stars, I see, will kiss the valleys first.
The odds for high and low's alike.
   Leon.   My lord,
Is this the daughter of a king ?
   Flo.   She is,
When once she is my wife.
   Leon. That ' once ', I see by your good
      father's speed, 210
Will come on very slowly. I am sorry,
Most sorry, you have broken from his liking
Where you were tied in duty ; and as sorry
Your choice is not so rich in worth as
      beauty,
That you might well enjoy her.
   Flo.   Dear, look up. 215
Though Fortune, visible an enemy,
Should chase us with my father, pow'r no
      jot
Hath she to change our loves. Beseech you,
      sir,
Remember since you ow'd no more to time
Than I do now. With thought of such
      affections, 220
Step forth mine advocate ; at your request
My father will grant precious things as
      trifles.
   Leon. Would he do so, I'd beg your
      precious mistress,
Which he counts but a trifle.
   Paul.   Sir, my liege,
Your eye hath too much youth in't. Not a
      month 225
Fore your queen died, she was more worth
      such gazes
Than what you look on now.
   Leon.   I thought of her
Even in these looks I made. [*To Florizel*]
      But your petition
Is yet unanswer'd. I will to your father.
Your honour not o'erthrown by your
      desires, 230
I am friend to them and you. Upon which
      errand
I now go toward him ; therefore, follow me,
And mark what way I make. Come, good
      my lord.   [*Exeunt.*

SCENE II. *Sicilia. Before the palace of
Leontes.*

Enter AUTOLYCUS *and a* Gentleman.

   Aut. Beseech you, sir, were you present
at this relation ?
   1 Gent. I was by at the opening of the
fardel, heard the old shepherd deliver the
manner how he found it ; whereupon, after
a little amazedness, we were all commanded
out of the chamber ; only this, methought
I heard the shepherd say he found the child.
   Aut. I would most gladly know the issue
of it.   8

   1 Gent. I make a broken delivery of the
business ; but the changes I perceived in
the King and Camillo were very notes of
admiration.   They seem'd almost, with
staring on one another, to tear the cases of
their eyes ; there was speech in their
dumbness, language in their very gesture ;
they look'd as they had heard of a world
ransom'd, or one destroyed. A notable
passion of wonder appeared in them ; but
the wisest beholder that knew no more but
seeing could not say if th' importance were
joy or sorrow—but in the extremity of the
one it must needs be.   19

Enter another Gentleman.

Here comes a gentleman that happily
knows more. The news, Rogero ?
   2 Gent. Nothing but bonfires. The oracle
is fulfill'd : the King's daughter is found.
Such a deal of wonder is broken out within
this hour that ballad-makers cannot be
able to express it.   25

Enter another Gentleman.

Here comes the Lady Paulina's steward ;
he can deliver you more. How goes it now,
sir ? This news, which is call'd true, is so
like an old tale that the verity of it is in
strong suspicion. Has the King found his
heir ?   29
   3 Gent. Most true, if ever truth were
pregnant by circumstance. That which you
hear you'll swear you see, there is such
unity in the proofs. The mantle of Queen
Hermione's ; her jewel about the neck of
it ; the letters of Antigonus found with it,
which they know to be his character ; the
majesty of the creature in resemblance of
the mother ; the affection of nobleness
which nature shows above her breeding ;
and many other evidences—proclaim her
with all certainty to be the King's daughter.
Did you see the meeting of the two kings ?
   2 Gent. No.   40
   3 Gent. Then have you lost a sight which
was to be seen, cannot be spoken of. There
might you have beheld one joy crown another, so and in such manner that it seem'd
sorrow wept to take leave of them ; for
their joy waded in tears. There was casting
up of eyes, holding up of hands, with
countenance of such distraction that they
were to be known by garment, not by
favour. Our king, being ready to leap out
of himself for joy of his found daughter, as
if that joy were now become a loss, cries
' O, thy mother, thy mother ! ' then asks
Bohemia forgiveness ; then embraces his
son-in-law ; then again worries he his
daughter with clipping her. Now he thanks
the old shepherd, which stands by like a
weather-bitten conduit of many kings'
reigns. I never heard of such another

encounter, which lames report to follow it and undoes description to do it.   56

2 *Gent.* What, pray you, became of Antigonus, that carried hence the child?

3 *Gent.* Like an old tale still, which will have matter to rehearse, though credit be asleep and not an ear open: he was torn to pieces with a bear. This avouches the shepherd's son, who has not only his innocence, which seems much, to justify him, but a handkerchief and rings of his that Paulina knows.

1 *Gent.* What became of his bark and his followers?   66

3 *Gent.* Wreck'd the same instant of their master's death, and in the view of the shepherd; so that all the instruments which aided to expose the child were even then lost when it was found. But, O, the noble combat that 'twixt joy and sorrow was fought in Paulina! She had one eye declin'd for the loss of her husband, another elevated that the oracle was fulfill'd. She lifted the Princess from the earth, and so locks her in embracing as if she would pin her to her heart, that she might no more be in danger of losing.   76

1 *Gent.* The dignity of this act was worth the audience of kings and princes; for by such was it acted.

3 *Gent.* One of the prettiest touches of all, and that which angl'd for mine eyes— caught the water, though not the fish— was, when at the relation of the Queen's death, with the manner how she came to't bravely confess'd and lamented by the King, how attentiveness wounded his daughter; till, from one sign of dolour to another, she did with an ' Alas! '—I would fain say—bleed tears; for I am sure my heart wept blood. Who was most marble there changed colour; some swooned, all sorrowed. If all the world could have seen't, the woe had been universal.   89

1 *Gent.* Are they returned to the court?

3 *Gent.* No. The Princess hearing of her mother's statue, which is in the keeping of Paulina—a piece many years in doing and now newly perform'd by that rare Italian master, Julio Romano, who, had he himself eternity and could put breath into his work, would beguile nature of her custom, so perfectly he is her ape. He so near to Hermione hath done Hermione that they say one would speak to her and stand in hope of answer—thither with all greediness of affection are they gone, and there they intend to sup.   100

2 *Gent.* I thought she had some great matter there in hand; for she hath privately twice or thrice a day, ever since the death of Hermione, visited that removed house. Shall we thither, and with our company piece the rejoicing?   105

1 *Gent.* Who would be thence that has the benefit of access? Every wink of an eye some new grace will be born. Our absence makes us unthrifty to our knowledge. Let's along. [*Exeunt Gentlemen.* 109

Aut. Now, had I not the dash of my former life in me, would preferment drop on my head. I brought the old man and his son aboard the Prince; told him I heard them talk of a fardel and I know not what; but he at that time over-fond of the shepherd's daughter—so he then took her to be—who began to be much sea-sick, and himself little better, extremity of weather continuing, this mystery remained undiscover'd. But 'tis all one to me; for had I been the finder-out of this secret, it would not have relish'd among my other discredits.   119

Enter Shepherd *and* Clown.

Here come those I have done good to against my will, and already appearing in the blossoms of their fortune.

Shep. Come, boy; I am past moe children, but thy sons and daughters will be all gentlemen born.   123

Clo. You are well met, sir. You denied to fight with me this other day, because I was no gentleman born. See you these clothes? Say you see them not and think me still no gentleman born. You were best say these robes are not gentlemen born. Give me the lie, do; and try whether I am not now a gentleman born.

Aut. I know you are now, sir, a gentleman born.   130

Clo. Ay, and have been so any time these four hours.

Shep. And so have I, boy.

Clo. So you have; but I was a gentleman born before my father; for the King's son took me by the hand and call'd me brother; and then the two kings call'd my father brother; and then the Prince, my brother, and the Princess, my sister, call'd my father father. And so we wept; and there was the first gentleman-like tears that ever we shed.

Shep. We may live, son, to shed many more.   140

Clo. Ay; or else 'twere hard luck, being in so preposterous estate as we are.

Aut. I humbly beseech you, sir, to pardon me all the faults I have committed to your worship, and to give me your good report to the Prince my master.   145

Shep. Prithee, son, do; for we must be gentle, now we are gentlemen.

Clo. Thou wilt amend thy life?

Aut. Ay, an it like your good worship.

Clo. Give me thy hand. I will swear to the Prince thou art as honest a true fellow as any is in Bohemia.   151

Shep. You may say it, but not swear it.

Clo. Not swear it, now I am a gentleman?
Let boors and franklins say it : I'll swear it.
  Shep. How if it be false, son ?   155
  Clo. If it be ne'er so false, a true gentleman may swear it in the behalf of his
friend. And I'll swear to the Prince thou
art a tall fellow of thy hands and that thou
wilt not be drunk ; but I know thou art
no tall fellow of thy hands and that thou
wilt be drunk. But I'll swear it ; and I
would thou wouldst be a tall fellow of thy
hands.
  Aut. I will prove so, sir, to my power. 162
  Clo. Ay, by any means, prove a tall
fellow. If I do not wonder how thou dar'st
venture to be drunk not being a tall fellow,
trust me not. Hark ! the kings and the
princes, our kindred, are going to see the
Queen's picture. Come, follow us ; we'll
be thy good masters.   *[Exeunt.*

SCENE III. *Sicilia. A chapel in Paulina's
house.*

Enter LEONTES, POLIXENES, FLORIZEL,
PERDITA, CAMILLO, PAULINA, *Lords,
and* Attendants.

  Leon. O grave and good Paulina, the
    great comfort
That I have had of thee !
  Paul.   What, sovereign sir,
I did not well, I meant well. All my services
You have paid home ; but that you have
    vouchsaf'd,
With your crown'd brother and these your
    contracted   5
Heirs of your kingdoms, my poor house to
    visit,
It is a surplus of your grace, which never
My life may last to answer.
  Leon.   O Paulina,
We honour you with trouble ; but we came
To see the statue of our queen. Your gallery
Have we pass'd through, not without much
    content   11
In many singularities ; but we saw not
That which my daughter came to look
    The statue of her mother.
  Paul.   As she liv'd peerless,
So her dead likeness, I do well believe,   15
Excels whatever yet you look'd upon
Or hand of man hath done ; therefore I
    keep it
Lonely, apart. But here it is. Prepare
To see the life as lively mock'd as ever   19
Still sleep mock'd death. Behold ; and say
    'tis well. *[Pauline draws a curtain,
    and discovers Hermione standing
    like a statue.*
I like your silence ; it the more shows off
Your wonder ; but yet speak. First, you,
    my liege.
Comes it not something near ?

  Leon.   Her natural posture !
Chide me, dear stone, that I may say indeed
Thou art Hermione ; or rather, thou art she
In thy not chiding ; for she was as tender
As infancy and grace. But yet, Paulina, 27
Hermione was not so much wrinkled,
    nothing
So aged as this seems.
  Pol.   O, not by much !
  Paul. So much the more our carver's
    excellence,   30
Which lets go by some sixteen years and
    makes her
As she liv'd now.
  Leon.   As now she might have done,
So much to my good comfort as it is
Now piercing to my soul. O, thus she
    stood,
Even with such life of majesty—warm life,
As now it coldly stands—when first I woo'd
    her !   36
I am asham'd. Does not the stone rebuke
    me
For being more stone than it ? O royal
    piece,
There's magic in thy majesty, which has
My evils conjur'd to remembrance, and 40
From thy admiring daughter took the
    spirits,
Standing like stone with thee !
  Per.   And give me leave,
And do not say 'tis superstition that
I kneel, and then implore her blessing.
    Lady,   44
Dear queen, that ended when I but began,
Give me that hand of yours to kiss.
  Paul.   O, patience !
The statue is but newly fix'd, the colour's
Not dry.
  Cam. My lord, your sorrow was too sore
    laid on,
Which sixteen winters cannot blow away,
So many summers dry. Scarce any joy 51
Did ever so long live ; no sorrow
But kill'd itself much sooner.
  Pol.   Dear my brother,
Let him that was the cause of this have
    pow'r
To take off so much grief from you as he 55
Will piece up in himself.
  Paul.   Indeed, my lord,
If I had thought the sight of my poor image
Would thus have wrought you—for the
    stone is mine—
I'd not have show'd it.
  Leon.   Do not draw the curtain.
  Paul. No longer shall you gaze on't, lest
    your fancy
May think anon it moves.
  Leon.   Let be, let be. 61
Would I were dead, but that methinks
    already—
What was he that did make it ? See, my
    lord,

Would you not deem it breath'd, and that
    those veins
Did verily bear blood ?
  Pol.   Masterly done ! 65
The very life seems warm upon her lip.
  Leon. The fixure of her eye has motion
    in't,
As we are mock'd with art.
  Paul.   I'll draw the curtain.
My lord's almost so far transported that
He'll think anon it lives.
  Leon.   O sweet Paulina, 70
Make me to think so twenty years together!
No settled senses of the world can match
The pleasure of that madness. Let't alone.
  Paul. I am sorry, sir, I have thus far
    stirr'd you ; but
I could afflict you farther.
  Leon.   Do, Paulina ; 75
For this affliction has a taste as sweet
As any cordial comfort. Still, methinks,
There is an air comes from her. What fine
    chisel
Could ever yet cut breath ? Let no man
    mock me,
For I will kiss her.
  Paul.   Good my lord, forbear. 80
The ruddiness upon her lip is wet ;
You'll mar it if you kiss it ; stain your
    own
With oily painting. Shall I draw the
    curtain ?
  Leon. No, not these twenty years.
  Per.   So long could I
Stand by, a looker-on.
  Paul.   Either forbear, 85
Quit presently the chapel, or resolve you
For more amazement. If you can behold
    it,
I'll make the statue move indeed, descend,
And take you by the hand, but then you'll
    think—
Which I protest against—I am assisted 90
By wicked powers.
  Leon.   What you can make her do
I am content to look on ; what to speak
I am content to hear ; for 'tis as easy
To make her speak as move.
  Paul.   It is requir'd
You do awake your faith. Then all stand
    still ; 95
Or those that think it is unlawful business
I am about, let them depart.
  Leon.   Proceed.
No foot shall stir.
  Paul. Music, awake her : strike. [*Music.*
'Tis time ; descend ; be stone no more ;
    approach ;
Strike all that look upon with marvel.
    Come ; 100
I'll fill your grave up. Stir ; nay, come
    away.
Bequeath to death your numbness, for
    from him

Dear life redeems you. You perceive she
    stirs. [*Hermione comes down from
                   the pedestal.*
Start not ; her actions shall be holy as
You hear my spell is lawful. Do not shun
    her 105
Until you see her die again ; for then
You kill her double. Nay, present your
    hand.
When she was young you woo'd her ; now
    in age
Is she become the suitor ?
  Leon.   O, she's warm !
If this be magic, let it be an art 110
Lawful as eating.
  Pol.   She embraces him.
  Cam. She hangs about his neck.
If she pertain to life, let her speak too.
  Pol. Ay, and make it manifest where she
    has liv'd,
Or how stol'n from the dead.
  Paul.   That she is living, 115
Were it but told you, should be hooted at
Like an old tale ; but it appears she lives
Though yet she speak not. Mark a little
    while.
Please you to interpose, fair madam. Kneel,
And pray your mother's blessing. Turn,
    good lady ; 120
Our Perdita is found.
  Her.   You gods, look down,
And from your sacred vials pour your
    graces
Upon my daughter's head ! Tell me, mine
    own,
Where hast thou been preserv'd ? Where
    liv'd ? How found
Thy father's court ? For thou shalt hear
    that I, 125
Knowing by Paulina that the oracle
Gave hope thou wast in being, have pre-
    serv'd
Myself to see the issue.
  Paul.   There's time enough for that,
Lest they desire upon this push to trouble
Your joys with like relation. Go together,
You precious winners all ; your exultation
Partake to every one. I, an old turtle, 132
Will wing me to some wither'd bough, and
    there
My mate, that's never to be found again,
Lament till I am lost.
  Leon.   O peace, Paulina ! 135
Thou shouldst a husband take by my
    consent,
As I by thine a wife. This is a match,
And made between's by vows. Thou hast
    found mine ;
But how, is to be question'd ; for I saw her,
As I thought, dead ; and have, in vain,
    said many 140
A prayer upon her grave. I'll not seek far—
For him, I partly know his mind—to find
    thee

An honourable husband. Come, Camillo,
And take her by the hand whose worth and
    honesty
Is richly noted, and here justified   145
By us, a pair of kings. Let's from this
    place.
What ! look upon my brother. Both your
That e'er I put between your holy looks
My ill suspicion. This your son-in-law,

And son unto the King, whom heavens
    directing,   150
Is troth-plight to your daughter. Good
    Paulina,
Lead us from hence where we may leisurely
Each one demand and answer to his part
Perform'd in this wide gap of time since
    first
We were dissever'd. Hastily lead away.   155
                             [*Exeunt.*

KING JOHN

DRAMATIS PERSONÆ

KING JOHN.
PRINCE HENRY, *his son.*
ARTHUR, DUKE OF BRITAINE, *son of Geffrey, late Duke of Britaine, the elder brother of King John.*
Earl of PEMBROKE.
Earl of ESSEX.
Earl of SALISBURY.
Lord BIGOT.
HUBERT DE BURGH.
ROBERT FAULCONBRIDGE, *son to Sir Robert Faulconbridge.*
PHILIP THE BASTARD, *his half-brother.*
JAMES GURNEY, *servant to Lady Faulconbridge.*
PETER of Pomfret, *a prophet.*
KING PHILIP OF FRANCE.

LEWIS, *the Dauphin.*
LYMOGES, *Duke of Austria.*
CARDINAL PANDULPH, *the Pope's legate.*
MELUN, *a French lord.*
CHATILLON, *ambassador from France to King John.*
QUEEN ELINOR, *widow of King Henry II and mother to King John.*
CONSTANCE, *mother to Arthur.*
BLANCH of Spain, *daughter to the King of Castile and niece to King John.*
LADY FAULCONBRIDGE, *widow of Sir Robert Faulconbridge.*
Lords, Citizens of Angiers, Sheriff, Heralds, Officers, Soldiers, Executioners, Messengers, Attendants.

THE SCENE : *England and France.*

ACT ONE

SCENE I. *King John's palace.*

Enter KING JOHN, QUEEN ELINOR, PEMBROKE, ESSEX, SALISBURY, *and* Others, *with* CHATILLON.

K. John. Now, say, Chatillon, what would France with us ?
Chat. Thus, after greeting, speaks the King of France
In my behaviour to the majesty,
The borrowed majesty, of England here.
   Eli. A strange beginning—' borrowed majesty ' ! 5
   K. John. Silence, good mother ; hear the embassy.
   Chat. Philip of France, in right and true behalf
Of thy deceased brother Geffrey's son,
Arthur Plantagenet, lays most lawful claim
To this fair island and the territories, 10
To Ireland, Poictiers, Anjou, Touraine, Maine,
Desiring thee to lay aside the sword
Which sways usurpingly these several titles,
And put the same into young Arthur's hand,
Thy nephew and right royal sovereign. 15
   K. John. What follows if we disallow of this ?
   Chat. The proud control of fierce and bloody war,
To enforce these rights so forcibly withheld.
   K. John. Here have we war for war, and blood for blood,
Controlment for controlment—so answer France. 20
   Chat. Then take my king's defiance from my mouth—
The farthest limit of my embassy.
   K. John. Bear mine to him, and so depart in peace ;
Be thou as lightning in the eyes of France ;
For ere thou canst report I will be there, 25
The thunder of my cannon shall be heard.
So hence ! Be thou the trumpet of our wrath
And sullen presage of your own decay.
An honourable conduct let him have—
Pembroke, look to 't. Farewell, Chatillon. 30
           [*Exeunt Chatillon and Pembroke.*
   Eli. What now, my son ! Have I not ever said
How that ambitious Constance would not cease
Till she had kindled France and all the world
Upon the right and party of her son ?
This might have been prevented and made whole 35
With very easy arguments of love,
Which now the manage of two kingdoms must
With fearful bloody issue arbitrate.
   K. John. Our strong possession and our right for us !
   Eli. Your strong possession much more than your right, 40
Or else it must go wrong with you and me ;
So much my conscience whispers in your ear,
Which none but heaven and you and I shall hear.

Enter a Sheriff.

Essex. My liege, here is the strangest
    controversy   44
Come from the country to be judg'd by you
That e'er I heard. Shall I produce the men?
    K. John. Let them approach.
                    [Exit Sheriff.
Our abbeys and our priories shall pay
This expedition's charge.

Enter ROBERT FAULCONBRIDGE *and*
    PHILIP, *his bastard brother.*

             What men are you ?
    Bast. Your faithful subject I, a gentle-
    man   50
Born in Northamptonshire, and eldest son,
As I suppose, to Robert Faulconbridge—
A soldier by the honour-giving hand
Of Cœur-de-lion knighted in the field.
    K. John. What art thou ?   55
    Rob. The son and heir to that same
    Faulconbridge.
    K. John. Is that the elder, and art thou
    the heir ?
You came not of one mother then, it seems.
    Bast. Most certain of one mother, mighty
    king—
That is well known—and, as I think, one
    father ;   60
But for the certain knowledge of that truth
I put you o'er to heaven and to my mother.
Of that I doubt, as all men's children may.
    Eli. Out on thee, rude man ! Thou dost
    shame thy mother,   64
And wound her honour with this diffidence.
    Bast. I, madam ? No, I have no reason
    for it—
That is my brother's plea, and none of
    mine ;
The which if he can prove, 'a pops me out
At least from fair five hundred pound a
    year.
Heaven guard my mother's honour and my
    land !   70
    K. John. A good blunt fellow. Why,
    being younger born,
Doth he lay claim to thine inheritance ?
    Bast. I know not why, except to get the
    land.
But once he slander'd me with bastardy ;
But whe'er I be as true begot or no,   75
That still I lay upon my mother's head ;
But that I am as well begot, my liege—
Fair fall the bones that took the pains for
    me !—
Compare our faces and be judge yourself.
If old Sir Robert did beget us both   80
And were our father, and this son like
    him—
O old Sir Robert, father, on my knee
I give heaven thanks I was not like to thee !
    K. John. Why, what a madcap hath
    heaven lent us here !

    Eli. He hath a trick of Cœur-de-lion's
    face ;   85
The accent of his tongue affecteth him.
Do you not read some tokens of my son
In the large composition of this man ?
    K. John. Mine eye hath well examined
    his parts
And finds them perfect Richard. Sirrah,
    speak,   90
What doth move you to claim your
    brother's land ?
    Bast. Because he hath a half-face, like
    my father.
With half that face would he have all my
    land :
A half-fac'd groat five hundred pound a
    year !
    Rob. My gracious liege, when that my
    father liv'd,   95
Your brother did employ my father
    much—
    Bast. Well, sir, by this you cannot get
    my land :
Your tale must be how he employ'd my
    mother.
    Rob. And once dispatch'd him in an
    embassy
To Germany, there with the Emperor 100
To treat of high affairs touching that time.
Th' advantage of his absence took the King,
And in the meantime sojourn'd at my
    father's ;
Where how he did prevail I shame to
    speak—
But truth is truth : large lengths of seas
    and shores   105
Between my father and my mother lay,
As I have heard my father speak himself,
When this same lusty gentleman was got.
Upon his death-bed he by will bequeath'd
His lands to me, and took it on his death 110
That this my mother's son was ..one of
    his ;
And if he were, he came into the world
Full fourteen weeks before the course of
    time.
Then, good my liege, let me have what is
    mine,   114
My father's land, as was my father's will.
    K. John. Sirrah, your brother is legiti-
    mate :
Your father's wife did after wedlock bear
    him,
And if she did play false, the fault was hers ;
Which fault lies on the hazards of all
    husbands
That marry wives. Tell me, how if my
    brother,   120
Who, as you say, took pains to get this son,
Had of your father claim'd this son for his ?
In sooth, good friend, your father might
    have kept
This calf, bred from his cow, from all the
    world ;

In sooth, he might ; then, if he were my
    brother's,   125
My brother might not claim him ; nor your
    father,
Being none of his, refuse him. This con-
    cludes :
My mother's son did get your father's heir ;
Your father's heir must have your father's
    land.
  Rob. Shall then my father's will be of no
    force   130
To dispossess that child which is not his ?
  Bast. Of no more force to dispossess me,
    sir,
Than was his will to get me, as I think.
  Eli. Whether hadst thou rather be a
    Faulconbridge,
And like thy brother, to enjoy thy land, 135
Or the reputed son of Cœur-de-lion,
Lord of thy presence and no land beside ?
  Bast. Madam, an if my brother had my
    shape
And I had his, Sir Robert's his, like him ;
And if my legs were two such riding-rods,
My arms such eel-skins stuff'd, my face so
    thin   141
That in mine ear I durst not stick a rose
Lest men should say ' Look where three-
    farthings goes ! '
And, to his shape, were heir to all this
    land—
Would I might never stir from off this
    place,   145
I would give it every foot to have this face !
I would not be Sir Nob in any case.
  Eli. I like thee well. Wilt thou forsake
    thy fortune,
Bequeath thy land to him and follow me ?
I am a soldier and now bound to France.
  Bast. Brother, take you my land, I'll
    take my chance.   151
Your face hath got five hundred pound a
    year,
Yet sell your face for fivepence and 'tis
    dear.
Madam, I'll follow you unto the death.
  Eli. Nay, I would have you go before me
    thither.   155
  Bast. Our country manners give our
    betters way.
  K. John. What is thy name ?
  Bast. Philip, my liege, so is my name
    begun :
Philip, good old Sir Robert's wife's eldest
    son.
  K. John. From henceforth bear his name
    whose form thou bearest :   160
Kneel thou down Philip, but rise more
    great—
Arise Sir Richard and Plantagenet.
  Bast. Brother by th' mother's side, give
    me your hand ;
My father gave me honour, yours gave land.
Now blessed be the hour, by night or day,

When I was got, Sir Robert was away !
  Eli. The very spirit of Plantagenet !
I am thy grandam, Richard : call me so.
  Bast. Madam, by chance, but not by
    truth ; what though ?
Something about, a little from the right, 170
In at the window, or else o'er the hatch ;
Who dares not stir by day must walk by
    night ;
And have is have, however men do catch.
Near or far off, well won is still well shot ;
And I am I, howe'er I was begot.   175
  K. John. Go, Faulconbridge ; now hast
    thou thy desire :
A landless knight makes thee a landed
    squire.
Come, madam, and come, Richard, we
    must speed
For France, for France, for it is more than
    need.
  Bast. Brother, adieu. Good fortune come
    to thee !   180
For thou wast got i' th' way of honesty.
              [Exeunt all but the Bastard.
A foot of honour better than I was ;
But many a many foot of land the worse.
Well, now can I make any Joan a lady.
' Good den, Sir Richard ! '—' God-a-mercy,
    fellow ! '   185
And if his name be George, I'll call him
    Peter ;
For new-made honour doth forget men's
    names :
'Tis too respective and too sociable
For your conversion. Now your traveller,
He and his toothpick at my worship's
    mess—   190
And when my knightly stomach is suffic'd,
Why then I suck my teeth and catechize
My picked man of countries : ' My dear sir,'
Thus leaning on mine elbow I begin
' I shall beseech you '— That is question
    now ;   195
And then comes answer like an Absey
    book :
' O sir,' says answer ' at your best com-
    mand,
At your employment, at your service, sir ! '
' No, sir,' says question ' I, sweet sir, at
    yours.'
And so, ere answer knows what question
    would,   200
Saving in dialogue of compliment,
And talking of the Alps and Apennines,
The Pyrenean and the river Po—
It draws toward supper in conclusion so.
But this is worshipful society,   205
And fits the mounting spirit like myself ;
For he is but a bastard to the time
That doth not smack of observation—
And so am I, whether I smack or no ;
And not alone in habit and device,   210
Exterior form, outward accoutrement,
But from the inward motion to deliver

Sweet, sweet, sweet poison for the age's
    tooth ;
Which, though I will not practise to
    deceive,
Yet, to avoid deceit, I mean to learn ; 215
For it shall strew the footsteps of my
    rising.
But who comes in such haste in riding-
    robes ?
What woman-post is this ? Hath she no
    husband
That will take pains to blow a horn before
    her ?

Enter LADY FAULCONBRIDGE, *and* JAMES
                GURNEY.

O me, 'tis my mother ! How now, good
    lady !   220
What brings you here to court so hastily ?
    Lady F. Where is that slave, thy brother?
        Where is he
That holds in chase mine honour up and
    down ?
    Bast. My brother Robert, old Sir
        Robert's son ?   224
Colbrand the giant, that same mighty man?
Is it Sir Robert's son that you seek so ?
    Lady F. Sir Robert's son ! Ay, thou un-
        reverend boy,
Sir Robert's son ! Why scorn'st thou at Sir
    Robert ?
He is Sir Robert's son, and so art thou.
    Bast. James Gurney, wilt thou give us
        leave awhile ?   230
    Gur. Good leave, good Philip.
    Bast.   Philip—Sparrow ! James,
There's toys abroad—anon I'll tell thee
    more.   [*Exit Gurney.*
Madam, I was not old Sir Robert's son ;
Sir Robert might have eat his part in me
Upon Good Friday, and ne'er broke his
    fast.   235
Sir Robert could do : well—marry, to con-
    fess—
Could he get me ? Sir Robert could not do it:
We know his handiwork. Therefore, good
    mother,
To whom am I beholding for these limbs ?
Sir Robert never holp to make this leg. 240
    Lady F. Hast thou conspired with thy
        brother too,
That for thine own gain shouldst defend
    mine honour ?
What means this scorn, thou most un-
    toward knave ?
    Bast. Knight, knight, good mother,
        Basilisco-like.
What ! I am dubb'd ; I have it on my
    shoulder.   245
But, mother, I am not Sir Robert's son ;
I have disclaim'd Sir Robert and my land ;
Legitimation, name, and all is gone.
Then, good my mother, let me know my
    father—

Some proper man, I hope. Who was it,
    mother ?   250
    Lady F. Hast thou denied thyself a
        Faulconbridge ?
    Bast. As faithfully as I deny the devil.
    Lady F. King Richard Cœur-de-lion was
        thy father.
By long and vehement suit I was seduc'd
To make room for him in my husband's
    bed.   255
Heaven lay not my transgression to my
    charge !
Thou art the issue of my dear offence,
Which was so strongly urg'd past my
    defence.
    Bast. Now, by this light, were I to get
        again,   259
Madam, I would not wish a better father.
Some sins do bear their privilege on earth,
And so doth yours : your fault was not
    your folly ;
Needs must you lay your heart at his
    dispose,
Subjected tribute to commanding love,
Against whose fury and unmatched force
The aweless lion could not wage the fight
Nor keep his princely heart from Richard's
    hand.
He that perforce robs lions of their hearts
May easily win a woman's. Ay, my mother,
With all my heart I thank thee for my
    father !   270
Who lives and dares but say thou didst not
    well
When I was got, I'll send his soul to hell.
Come, lady, I will show thee to my kin ;
And they shall say when Richard me begot,
If thou hadst said him nay, it had been sin.
Who says it was, he lies ; I say 'twas not.
                                       [*Exeunt.*

ACT TWO

SCENE I. *France. Before Angiers.*

Enter, on one side, AUSTRIA *and* Forces ; *on
the other,* KING PHILIP OF FRANCE, LEWIS
the Dauphin, CONSTANCE, ARTHUR, *and*
Forces.

    K. Phi. Before Angiers well met, brave
        Austria.
Arthur, that great forerunner of thy blood,
Richard, that robb'd the lion of his heart
And fought the holy wars in Palestine,   4
By this brave duke came early to his grave ;
And for amends to his posterity,
At our importance hither is he come
To spread his colours, boy, in thy behalf ;
And to rebuke the usurpation
Of thy unnatural uncle, English John.   10
Embrace him, love him, give him welcome
    hither.
    Arth. God shall forgive you Cœur-de-
        lion's death

S.—8

The rather that you give his offspring life,
Shadowing their right under your wings of
  war, 14
I give you welcome with a powerless hand,
But with a heart full of unstained love ;
Welcome before the gates of Angiers, Duke.
  K. Phi. A noble boy ! Who would not do
    thee right ?
  Aust. Upon thy cheek lay I this zealous
    kiss
As seal to this indenture of my love : 20
That to my home I will no more return
Till Angiers and the right thou hast in
  France,
Together with that pale, that white-fac'd
  shore,
Whose foot spurns back the ocean's roaring
  tides
And coops from other lands her islanders—
Even till that England, hedg'd in with the
  main, 26
That water-walled bulwark, still secure
And confident from foreign purposes—
Even till that utmost corner of the west
Salute thee for her king. Till then, fair boy,
Will I not think of home, but follow arms.
  Const. O, take his mother's thanks, a
    widow's thanks, 32
Till your strong hand shall help to give him
  strength
To make a more requital to your love !
  Aust. The peace of heaven is theirs that
    lift their swords 35
In such a just and charitable war.
  K. Phi. Well then, to work ! Our cannon
    shall be bent
Against the brows of this resisting town ;
Call for our chiefest men of discipline,
To cull the plots of best advantages. 40
We'll lay before this town our royal bones,
Wade to the market-place in Frenchmen's
  blood,
But we will make it subject to this boy.
  Const. Stay for an answer to your em-
    bassy,
Lest unadvis'd you stain your swords with
  blood ; 45
My Lord Chatillon may from England
  bring
That right in peace which here we urge in
  war,
And then we shall repent each drop of
  blood
That hot rash haste so indirectly shed.

Enter CHATILLON.

  K. Phi. A wonder, lady ! Lo, upon thy
    wish, 50
Our messenger Chatillon is arriv'd.
What England says, say briefly, gentle lord;
We coldly pause for thee. Chatillon, speak.
  Chat. Then turn your forces from this
    paltry siege 54
And stir them up against a mightier task.

England, impatient of your just demands,
Hath put himself in arms. The adverse
  winds,
Whose leisure I have stay'd, have given him
  time
To land his legions all as soon as I ;
His marches are expedient to this town, 60
His forces strong, his soldiers confident.
With him along is come the mother-queen,
An Ate, stirring him to blood and strife ;
With her her niece, the Lady Blanch of
  Spain ; 64
With them a bastard of the king's deceas'd;
And all th' unsettled humours of the land—
Rash, inconsiderate, fiery voluntaries,
With ladies' faces and fierce dragons'
  spleens—
Have sold their fortunes at their native
  homes,
Bearing their birthrights proudly on their
  backs, 70
To make a hazard of new fortunes here.
In brief, a braver choice of dauntless spirits
Than now the English bottoms have waft
  o'er
Did never float upon the swelling tide 74
To do offence and scathe in Christendom.
                                    [Drum beats.
The interruption of their churlish drums
Cuts off more circumstance : they are at
  hand ;
To parley or to fight, therefore prepare.
  K. Phi. How much unlook'd for is this
    expedition !
  Aust. By how much unexpected, by so
    much 80
We must awake endeavour for defence,
For courage mounteth with occasion.
Let them be welcome then ; we are pre-
  par'd.

Enter KING JOHN, ELINOR, BLANCH, the
  BASTARD, PEMBROKE, and Others.

  K. John. Peace be to France, if France in
    peace permit
Our just and lineal entrance to our own ! 85
If not, bleed France, and peace ascend to
  heaven,
Whiles we, God's wrathful agent, do correct
Their proud contempt that beats His peace
  to heaven !
  K. Phi. Peace be to England, if that war
    return
From France to England, there to live in
  peace ! 90
England we love, and for that England's
  sake
With burden of our armour here we sweat.
This toil of ours should be a work of thine ;
But thou from loving England art so far
That thou hast under-wrought his lawful
  king, 95
Cut off the sequence of posterity,
Outfaced infant state, and done a rape

Upon the maiden virtue of the crown.
Look here upon thy brother Geffrey's face :
These eyes, these brows, were moulded out
    of his ;   100
This little abstract doth contain that large
Which died in Geffrey, and the hand of
    time
Shall draw this brief into as huge a volume.
That Geffrey was thy elder brother born,
And this his son ; England was Geffrey's
    right,   105
And this is Geffrey's. In the name of God,
How comes it then that thou art call'd a
    king,
When living blood doth in these temples
    beat
Which owe the crown that thou o'er-
    masterest ?
    K. John. From whom hast thou this
        great commission, France,   110
To draw my answer from thy articles ?
    K. Phi. From that supernal judge that
        stirs good thoughts
In any breast of strong authority
To look into the blots and stains of right.
That judge hath made me guardian to this
    boy,   115
Under whose warrant I impeach thy wrong,
And by whose help I mean to chastise it.
    K. John. Alack, thou dost usurp
        authority.
    K. Phi. Excuse it is to beat usurping
        down.
    Eli. Who is it thou dost call usurper,
        France ?   120
    Const. Let me make answer : thy usurp-
        ing son.
    Eli. Out, insolent ! Thy bastard shall be
        king,
That thou mayst be a queen and check the
    world !
    Const. My bed was ever to thy son as
        true
As thine was to thy husband ; and this boy
Liker in feature to his father Geffrey   126
Than thou and John in manners—being as
    like
As rain to water, or devil to his dam.
My boy a bastard ! By my soul, I think
His father never was so true begot ;   130
It cannot be, an if thou wert his mother.
    Eli. There's a good mother, boy, that
        blots thy father.
    Const. There's a good grandam, boy, that
        would blot thee.
    Aust. Peace !
    Bast.   Hear the crier.
    Aust.   What the devil art thou ?
    Bast. One that will play the devil, sir,
        with you,   135
An 'a may catch your hide and you alone.
You are the hare of whom the proverb goes,
Whose valour plucks dead lions by the
    beard ;

I'll smoke your skin-coat an I catch you
    right ;
Sirrah, look to 't ; i' faith I will, i' faith. 140
    Blanch. O, well did he become that lion's
        robe
That did disrobe the lion of that robe !
    Bast. It lies as sightly on the back of him
As great Alcides' shows upon an ass ;
But, ass, I'll take that burden from your
    back,   145
Or lay on that shall make your shoulders
    crack.
    Aust. What cracker is this same that
        deafs our ears
With this abundance of superfluous breath?
King Philip, determine what we shall do
    straight.
    K. Phi. Women and fools, break off your
        conference.   150
King John, this is the very sum of all :
England and Ireland, Anjou, Touraine,
    Maine,
In right of Arthur, do I claim of thee ;
Wilt thou resign them and lay down thy
    arms ?
    K. John. My life as soon. I do defy thee,
        France.   155
Arthur of Britaine, yield thee to my hand,
And out of my dear love I'll give thee more
Than e'er the coward hand of France can
    win.
Submit thee, boy.
    Eli.   Come to thy grandam, child.
    Const. Do, child, go to it grandam, child ;
Give grandam kingdom, and it grandam
    will   161
Give it a plum, a cherry, and a fig.
There's a good grandam !
    Arth.   Good my mother, peace !
I would that I were low laid in my grave :
I am not worth this coil that's made for me.
    Eli. His mother shames him so, poor boy,
        he weeps.   166
    Const. Now shame upon you, whe'er she
        does or no !
His grandam's wrongs, and not his mother's
    shames,
Draws those heaven-moving pearls from his
    poor eyes,
Which heaven shall take in nature of a fee ;
Ay, with these crystal beads heaven shall
    be brib'd   171
To do him justice and revenge on you.
    Eli. Thou monstrous slanderer of heaven
        and earth !
    Const. Thou monstrous injurer of heaven
        and earth,
Call not me slanderer ! Thou and thine
    usurp   175
The dominations, royalties, and rights,
Of this oppressed boy ; this is thy eldest
    son's son,
Infortunate in nothing but in thee.
Thy sins are visited in this poor child ;

The canon of the law is laid on him,   180
Being but the second generation
Removed from thy sin-conceiving womb.
  K. John. Bedlam, have done.
  Const.   I have but this to say—
That he is not only plagued for her sin,
But God hath made her sin and her the
        plague   185
On this removed issue, plagued for her
And with her plague; her sin his injury,
Her injury the beadle to her sin;
All punish'd in the person of this child,
And all for her—a plague upon her!   190
  Eli. Thou unadvised scold, I can produce
A will that bars the title of thy son.
  Const. Ay, who doubts that? A will, a
        wicked will;
A woman's will; a cank'red grandam's will!
  K. Phi. Peace, lady! pause, or be more
        temperate.   195
It ill beseems this presence to cry aim
To these ill-tuned repetitions.
Some trumpet summon hither to the walls
These men of Angiers; let us hear them
        speak   199
Whose title they admit, Arthur's or John's.

Trumpet sounds.   Enter Citizens *upon the
        walls.*

  Cit. Who is it that hath warn'd us to the
        walls?
  K. Phi. 'Tis France, for England.
  K. John.   England for itself.
You men of Angiers, and my loving
        subjects—
  K. Phi. You loving men of Angiers,
        Arthur's subjects,
Our trumpet call'd you to this gentle
        parle—   205
  K. John. For our advantage; therefore
        hear us first.
These flags of France, that are advanced
        here
Before the eye and prospect of your town,
Have hither march'd to your endamage-
        ment;
The cannons have their bowels full of
        wrath,   210
And ready mounted are they to spit forth
Their iron indignation 'gainst your walls;
All preparation for a bloody siege
And merciless proceeding by these French
Confront your city's eyes, your winking
        gates;   215
And but for our approach those sleeping
        stones
That as a waist doth girdle you about
By the compulsion of their ordinance
By this time from their fixed beds of
        lime   219
Had been dishabited, and wide havoc made
For bloody power to rush upon your peace.
But on the sight of us your lawful king,
Who painfully with much expedient march

Have brought a countercheck before your
        gates,
To save unscratch'd your city's threat'ned
        cheeks—   225
Behold, the French amaz'd vouchsafe a
        parle;
And now, instead of bullets wrapp'd in fire,
To make a shaking fever in your walls,
They shoot but calm words folded up in
        smoke,
To make a faithless error in your ears;   230
Which trust accordingly, kind citizens,
And let us in—your King, whose labour'd
        spirits,
Forwearied in this action of swift speed,
Craves harbourage within your city walls.
  K. Phi. When I have said, make answer
        to us both.   235
Lo, in this right hand, whose protection
Is most divinely vow'd upon the right
Of him it holds, stands young Plantagenet,
Son to the elder brother of this man,   239
And king o'er him and all that he enjoys;
For this down-trodden equity we tread
In warlike march these greens before your
        town,
Being no further enemy to you
Than the constraint of hospitable zeal
In the relief of this oppressed child   245
Religiously provokes. Be pleased then
To pay that duty which you truly owe
To him that owes it, namely, this young
        prince;
And then our arms, like to a muzzled bear,
Save in aspect, hath all offence seal'd up;
Our cannons' malice vainly shall be spent
Against th' invulnerable clouds of heaven;
And with a blessed and unvex'd retire,
With unhack'd swords and helmets all un-
        bruis'd,   254
We will bear home that lusty blood again
Which here we came to spout against your
        town,
And leave your children, wives, and you, in
        peace.
But if you fondly pass our proffer'd offer,
'Tis not the roundure of your old-fac'd
        walls
Can hide you from our messengers of war,
Though all these English and their
        discipline   261
Were harbour'd in their rude circumference.
Then tell us, shall your city call us lord
In that behalf which we have challeng'd it;
Or shall we give the signal to our rage,   265
And stalk in blood to our possession?
  Cit. In brief: we are the King of
        England's subjects;
For him, and in his right, we hold this town.
  K. John. Acknowledge then the King,
        and let me in.
  Cit. That can we not; but he that proves
        the King,   270
To him will we prove loyal. Till that time

Have we ramm'd up our gates against the
    world.
    K. John. Doth not the crown of England
        prove the King ?
And if not that, I bring you witnesses :
Twice fifteen thousand hearts of England's
    breed—   275
    Bast. Bastards and else.
    K. John. To verify our title with their
        lives.
    K. Phi. As many and as well-born bloods
        as those—
    Bast. Some bastards too.
    K. Phi. Stand in his face to contradict his
        claim.   280
    Cit. Till you compound whose right is
        worthiest,
We for the worthiest hold the right from
    both.
    K. John. Then God forgive the sin of all
        those souls   284
That to their everlasting residence,
Before the dew of evening fall, shall fleet
In dreadful trial of our kingdom's king !
    K. Phi. Amen, Amen ! Mount, chevaliers ;
        to arms !
    Bast. Saint George, that swing'd the
        dragon, and e'er since
Sits on's horse back at mine hostess' door,
Teach us some fence ! [*to Austria*] Sirrah,
    were I at home,   290
At your den, sirrah, with your lioness,
I would set an ox-head to your lion's hide,
And make a monster of you.
    Aust.   Peace ! no more.
    Bast. O, tremble, for you hear the lion
        roar !
    K. John. Up higher to the plain, where
        we'll set forth   295
In best appointment all our regiments.
    Bast. Speed then to take advantage of the
        field.
    K. Phi. It shall be so ; and at the other
        hill
Command the rest to stand. God and our
    right !   [*Exeunt.*

Here, after excursions, enter the Herald *of*
    France, *with trumpets, to the gates.*

    F. Her. You men of Angiers, open wide
        your gates   300
And let young Arthur, Duke of Britaine,
    in,
Who by the hand of France this day hath
    made
Much work for tears in many an English
    mother,
Whose sons lie scattered on the bleeding
    ground ;
Many a widow's husband grovelling lies, 305
Coldly embracing the discoloured earth ;
And victory with little loss doth play
Upon the dancing banners of the French,
Who are at hand, triumphantly displayed,

To enter conquerors, and to proclaim   310
Arthur of Britaine England's King and
    yours.

    Enter English Herald, *with trumpet.*

    E. Her. Rejoice, you men of Angiers, ring
        your bells !
King John, your king and England's, doth
    approach,
Commander of this hot malicious day.
Their armours that march'd hence so silver-
    bright   315
Hither return all gilt with Frenchmen's
    blood.
There stuck no plume in any English crest
That is removed by a staff of France ;
Our colours do return in those same hands
That did display them when we first
    march'd forth ;   320
And like a jolly troop of huntsmen come
Our lusty English, all with purpled hands,
Dy'd in the dying slaughter of their foes,
Open your gates and give the victors way.
    Cit. Heralds, from off our tow'rs we
        might behold   325
From first to last the onset and retire
Of both your armies, whose equality
By our best eyes cannot be censured.
Blood hath bought blood, and blows have
    answer'd blows ;
Strength match'd with strength, and power
    confronted power ;   330
Both are alike, and both alike we like.
One must prove greatest. While they weigh
    so even,
We hold our town for neither, yet for both.

Enter the two KINGS, *with their* Powers, *at*
    several doors.

    K. John. France, hast thou yet more
        blood to cast away ?
Say, shall the current of our right run on ?
Whose passage, vex'd with thy impedi-
    ment,   336
Shall leave his native channel and o'erswell
With course disturb'd even thy confining
    shores,
Unless thou let his silver water keep
A peaceful progress to the ocean.   340
    K. Phi. England, thou hast not sav'd one
        drop of blood
In this hot trial more than we of France ;
Rather, lost more. And by this hand I
    swear,
That sways the earth this climate overlooks,
Before we will lay down our just-borne
    arms,   345
We'll put thee down, 'gainst whom these
    arms we bear,
Or add a royal number to the dead,
Gracing the scroll that tells of this war's
    loss
With slaughter coupled to the name of
    kings.

Bast. Ha, majesty! how high thy glory
 tow'rs   350
When the rich blood of kings is set on fire!
O, now doth Death line his dead chaps with
 steel;
The swords of soldiers are his teeth, his
 fangs;
And now he feasts, mousing the flesh of
 men,
In undetermin'd differences of kings. 355
Why stand these royal fronts amazed thus?
Cry 'havoc!' kings; back to the stained
 field,
You equal potents, fiery kindled spirits!
Then let confusion of one part confirm
The other's peace. Till then, blows, blood,
 and death!   360
 K. John. Whose party do the townsmen
  yet admit?
 K. Phi. Speak, citizens, for England;
  who's your king?
 Cit. The King of England, when we know
  the King.
 K. Phi. Know him in us that here hold up
  his right.
 K. John. In us that are our own great
  deputy   365
And bear possession of our person here,
Lord of our presence, Angiers, and of you.
 Cit. A greater pow'r than we denies all
  this;
And till it be undoubted, we do lock
Our former scruple in our strong-barr'd
 gates;   370
King'd of our fears, until our fears, resolv'd,
Be by some certain king purg'd and depos'd.
 Bast. By heaven, these scroyles of
  Angiers flout you, kings,
And stand securely on their battlements
As in a theatre, whence they gape and point
At your industrious scenes and acts of
 death.   376
Your royal presences be rul'd by me:
Do like the mutines of Jerusalem,
Be friends awhile, and both conjointly bend
Your sharpest deeds of malice on this town.
By east and west let France and England
 mount   381
Their battering cannon, charged to the
 mouths,
Till their soul-fearing clamours have
 brawl'd down
The flinty ribs of this contemptuous city.
I'd play incessantly upon these jades, 385
Even till unfenced desolation
Leave them as naked as the vulgar air.
That done, dissever your united strengths
And part your mingled colours once again,
Turn face to face and bloody point to
 point;   390
Then in a moment Fortune shall cull forth
Out of one side her happy minion,
To whom in favour she shall give the day,
And kiss him with a glorious victory.

How like you this wild counsel, mighty
 states?   395
Smacks it not something of the policy?
 K. John. Now, by the sky that hangs
  above our heads,
I like it well. France, shall we knit our
 pow'rs
And lay this Angiers even with the ground;
Then after fight who shall be king of it? 400
 Bast. An if thou hast the mettle of a king,
Being wrong'd as we are by this peevish
 town,
Turn thou the mouth of thy artillery,
As we will ours, against these saucy walls;
And when that we have dash'd them to the
 ground,   405
Why then defy each other, and pell-mell
Make work upon ourselves, for heaven or
 hell.
 K. Phi. Let it be so. Say, where will you
  assault?
 K. John. We from the west will send
  destruction
Into this city's bosom.   410
 Aust. I from the north.
 K. Phi. Our thunder from the south
Shall rain their drift of bullets on this town.
 Bast. [*Aside*] O prudent discipline! From
  north to south,
Austria and France shoot in each other's
 mouth.   414
I'll stir them to it.—Come, away, away!
 Cit. Hear us, great kings: vouchsafe
  awhile to stay,
And I shall show you peace and fair-fac'd
 league;
Win you this city without stroke or wound;
Rescue those breathing lives to die in beds
That here come sacrifices for the field. 420
Persever not, but hear me, mighty kings.
 K. John. Speak on with favour; we are
  bent to hear.
 Cit. That daughter there of Spain, the
  Lady Blanch,
Is niece to England; look upon the years
Of Lewis the Dauphin and that lovely maid.
If lusty love should go in quest of beauty,
Where should he find it fairer than in
 Blanch?   427
If zealous love should go in search of virtue,
Where should he find it purer than in
 Blanch?
If love ambitious sought a match of birth,
Whose veins bound richer blood than Lady
 Blanch?   431
Such as she is, in beauty, virtue, birth,
Is the young Dauphin every way com-
 plete—
If not complete of, say he is not she;
And she again wants nothing, to name want,
If want it be not that she is not he. 436
He is the half part of a blessed man,
Left to be finished by such as she;
And she a fair divided excellence,

Whose fulness of perfection lies in him. 440
O, two such silver currents, when they
    join,
Do glorify the banks that bound them in ;
And two such shores to two such streams
    made one,
Two such controlling bounds, shall you be,
    Kings,
To these two princes, if you marry them. 445
This union shall do more than battery can
To our fast-closed gates ; for at this match
With swifter spleen than powder can
    enforce,
The mouth of passage shall we fling wide
    ope
And give you entrance ; but without this
    match,   450
The sea enraged is not half so deaf,
Lions more confident, mountains and rocks
More free from motion—no, not Death
    himself
In mortal fury half so peremptory
As we to keep this city.
    Bast.   Here's a stay 455
That shakes the rotten carcass of old Death
Out of his rags ! Here's a large mouth,
    indeed,
That spits forth death and mountains, rocks
    and seas ;
Talks as familiarly of roaring lions
As maids of thirteen do of puppy-dogs ! 460
What cannoneer begot this lusty blood ?
He speaks plain cannon-fire, and smoke and
    bounce ;
He gives the bastinado with his tongue ;
Our ears are cudgell'd ; not a word of his
But buffets better than a fist of France. 465
Zounds! I was never so bethump'd with
    words
Since I first call'd my brother's father dad.
    Eli. Son, list to this conjunction, make
    this match ;
Give with our niece a dowry large enough ;
For by this knot thou shalt so surely tie 470
Thy now unsur'd assurance to the crown
That yon green boy shall have no sun to
    ripe
The bloom that promiseth a mighty fruit.
I see a yielding in the looks of France ;
Mark how they whisper. Urge them while
    their souls   475
Are capable of this ambition,
Lest zeal, now melted by the windy breath
Of soft petitions, pity, and remorse,
Cool and congeal again to what it was.
    Cit. Why answer not the double majesties
This friendly treaty of our threat'ned town?
    K. Phi. Speak England first, that hath
    been forward first   482
To speak unto this city : what say you ?
    K. John. If that the Dauphin there, thy
    princely son,
Can in this book of beauty read ' I love ', 485
Her dowry shall weigh equal with a queen ;

For Anjou, and fair Touraine, Maine,
    Poictiers,
And all that we upon this side the sea—
Except this city now by us besieg'd—
Find liable to our crown and dignity,   490
Shall gild her bridal bed, and make her rich
In titles, honours, and promotions,
As she in beauty, education, blood,
Holds hand with any princess of the world.
    K. Phi. What say'st thou, boy ? Look in
    the lady's face.   495
    Lew. I do, my lord, and in her eye I find
A wonder, or a wondrous miracle,
The shadow of myself form'd in her eye ;
Which, being but the shadow of your son,
Becomes a sun, and makes your son a
    shadow.   500
I do protest I never lov'd myself
Till now infixed I beheld myself
Drawn in the flattering table of her eye.
               [*Whispers with Blanch.*
    Bast. [*Aside*] Drawn in the flattering
    table of her eye,   504
Hang'd in the frowning wrinkle of her brow,
And quarter'd in her heart—he doth espy
Himself love's traitor. This is pity now,
That hang'd and drawn and quarter'd there
    should be
In such a love so vile a lout as he.
    Blanch. My uncle's will in this respect is
    mine.   510
If he see aught in you that makes him like,
That any thing he sees which moves his
    liking
I can with ease translate it to my will ;
Or if you will, to speak more properly,
I will enforce it eas'ly to my love.   515
Further I will not flatter you, my lord,
That all I see in you is worthy love,
Than this : that nothing do I see in you—
Though churlish thoughts themselves
    should be your judge—
That I can find should merit any hate. 520
    K. John. What say these young ones ?
    What say you, my niece ?
    Blanch. That she is bound in honour still
    to do
What you in wisdom still vouchsafe to say.
    K. John. Speak then, Prince Dauphin ;
    can you love this lady ?
    Lew. Nay, ask me if I can refrain from
    love ;   525
For I do love her most unfeignedly.
    K. John. Then do I give Volquessen,
    Touraine, Maine,
Poictiers, and Anjou, these five provinces,
With her to thee ; and this addition more,
Full thirty thousand marks of English
    coin.   530
Philip of France, if thou be pleas'd withal,
Command thy son and daughter to join
    hands.
    K. Phi. It likes us well ; young princes,
    close your hands.

Aust. And your lips too ; for I am well assur'd

That I did so when I was first assur'd. 535

K. Phi. Now, citizens of Angiers, ope your gates,

Let in that amity which you have made ;

For at Saint Mary's chapel presently

The rites of marriage shall be solemniz'd.

Is not the Lady Constance in this troop? 540

I know she is not ; for this match made up

Her presence would have interrupted much.

Where is she and her son ? Tell me, who knows.

Lew. She is sad and passionate at your Highness' tent.

K. Phi. And, by my faith, this league that we have made 545

Will give her sadness very little cure.

Brother of England, how may we content

This widow lady ? In her right we came ;

Which we, God knows, have turn'd another way,

To our own vantage.

K. John.   We will heal up all, 550

For we'll create young Arthur Duke of Britaine,

And Earl of Richmond ; and this rich fair town

We make him lord of. Call the Lady Constance ;

Some speedy messenger bid her repair

To our solemnity. I trust we shall, 555

If not fill up the measure of her will,

Yet in some measure satisfy her so

That we shall stop her exclamation.

Go we as well as haste will suffer us

To this unlook'd-for, unprepared pomp. 560

[*Exeunt all but the Bastard.*

Bast. Mad world ! mad kings ! mad composition !

John, to stop Arthur's title in the whole,

Hath willingly departed with a part ;

And France, whose armour conscience buckled on,

Whom zeal and charity brought to the field 565

As God's own soldier, rounded in the ear

With that same purpose-changer, that sly devil,

That broker that still breaks the pate of faith,

That daily break-vow, he that wins of all,

Of kings, of beggars, old men, young men, maids, 570

Who having no external thing to lose

But the word ' maid ', cheats the poor maid of that ;

That smooth-fac'd gentleman, tickling commodity,

Commodity, the bias of the world—

The world, who of itself is peised well, 575

Made to run even upon even ground,

Till this advantage, this vile-drawing bias,

This sway of motion, this commodity,

Makes it take head from all indifference,

From all direction, purpose, course, intent— 580

And this same bias, this commodity,

This bawd, this broker, this all-changing word,

Clapp'd on the outward eye of fickle France,

Hath drawn him from his own determin'd aid,

From a resolv'd and honourable war, 585

To a most base and vile-concluded peace.

And why rail I on this commodity ?

But for because he hath not woo'd me yet ;

Not that I have the power to clutch my hand 589

When his fair angels would salute my palm,

But for my hand, as unattempted yet,

Like a poor beggar raileth on the rich.

Well, whiles I am a beggar, I will rail

And say there is no sin but to be rich ;

And being rich, my virtue then shall be 595

To say there is no vice but beggary.

Since kings break faith upon commodity,

Gain, be my lord, for I will worship thee.

[*Exit.*

ACT THREE

SCENE I. *France. The French King's camp.*

Enter CONSTANCE, ARTHUR, *and* SALISBURY.

Const. Gone to be married ! Gone to swear a peace !

False blood to false blood join'd ! Gone to be friends !

Shall Lewis have Blanch, and Blanch those provinces ?

It is not so ; thou hast misspoke, misheard ;

Be well advis'd, tell o'er thy tale again. 5

It cannot be ; thou dost but say 'tis so ;

I trust I may not trust thee, for thy word

Is but the vain breath of a common man :

Believe me I do not believe thee, man ;

I have a king's oath to the contrary. 10

Thou shalt be punish'd for thus frighting me,

For I am sick and capable of fears,

Oppress'd with wrongs, and therefore full of fears ;

A widow, husbandless, subject to fears ;

A woman, naturally born to fears ; 15

And though thou now confess thou didst but jest,

With my vex'd spirits I cannot take a truce,

But they will quake and tremble all this day.

What dost thou mean by shaking of thy head ?

Why dost thou look so sadly on my son ? 20

What means that hand upon that breast of thine ?

Why holds thine eye that lamentable rheum,

Like a proud river peering o'er his bounds ?

Be these sad signs confirmers of thy words ?

Then speak again—not all thy former tale,
But this one word, whether thy tale be true.

Sal. As true as I believe you think them
false   27
That give you cause to prove my saying
true.

Const. O, if thou teach me to believe this
sorrow,
Teach thou this sorrow how to make me
die ;   30
And let belief and life encounter so
As doth the fury of two desperate men
Which in the very meeting fall and die !
Lewis marry Blanch ! O boy, then where
art thou ?
France friend with England ; what becomes
of me ?   35
Fellow, be gone : I cannot brook thy sight ;
This news hath made thee a most ugly man.

Sal. What other harm have I, good lady,
done
But spoke the harm that is by others done ?

Const. Which harm within itself so
heinous is   40
As it makes harmful all that speak of it.

Arth. I do beseech you, madam, be
content.

Const. If thou that bid'st me be content
wert grim,
Ugly, and sland'rous to thy mother's
womb,   44
Full of unpleasing blots and sightless stains,
Lame, foolish, crooked, swart, prodigious,
Patch'd with foul moles and eye-offending
marks,
I would not care, I then would be content ;
For then I should not love thee ; no, nor
thou
Become thy great birth, nor deserve a
crown.   50
But thou art fair, and at thy birth, dear
boy,
Nature and Fortune join'd to make thee
great :
Of Nature's gifts thou mayst with lilies
boast,
And with the half-blown rose ; but
Fortune, O !
She is corrupted, chang'd, and won from
thee ;   55
Sh' adulterates hourly with thine uncle
John,
And with her golden hand hath pluck'd on
France
To tread down fair respect of sovereignty,
And made his majesty the bawd to theirs.
France is a bawd to Fortune and King
John—   60
That strumpet Fortune, that usurping
John !
Tell me, thou fellow, is not France for-
sworn ?
Envenom him with words, or get thee gone
And leave those woes alone which I alone

Am bound to under-bear.

Sal.   Pardon me, madam,   65
I may not go without you to the kings.

Const. Thou mayst, thou shalt ; I will
not go with thee ;
I will instruct my sorrows to be proud,
For grief is proud, and makes his owner
stoop,
To me, and to the state of my great grief, 70
Let kings assemble ; for my grief's so great
That no supporter but the huge firm earth
Can hold it up. [*Seats herself on the ground.*
                    Here I and sorrows sit ;
Here is my throne, bid kings come bow
to it.

Enter KING JOHN, KING PHILIP, LEWIS,
BLANCH, ELINOR, *the* BASTARD, AUSTRIA,
and Attendants.

K. Phi. 'Tis true, fair daughter, and this
blessed day   75
Ever in France shall be kept festival.
To solemnize this day the glorious sun
Stays in his course and plays the alchemist,
Turning with splendour of his precious eye
The meagre cloddy earth to glittering gold.
The yearly course that brings this day
about   81
Shall never see it but a holiday.

Const. [*Rising*] A wicked day, and not a
holy day !
What hath this day deserv'd ? what hath
it done
That it in golden letters should be set   85
Among the high tides in the calendar ?
Nay, rather turn this day out of the week,
This day of shame, oppression, perjury ;
Or, if it must stand still, let wives with
child
Pray that their burdens may not fall this
day,   90
Lest that their hopes prodigiously be
cross'd ;
But on this day let seamen fear no wreck ;
No bargains break that are not this day
made ;
This day, all things begun come to ill end,
Yea, faith itself to hollow falsehood change!

K. Phi. By heaven, lady, you shall have
no cause   96
To curse the fair proceedings of this day.
Have I not pawn'd to you my majesty ?

Const. You have beguil'd me with a
counterfeit
Resembling majesty, which, being touch'd
and tried,   100
Proves valueless ; you are forsworn,
forsworn ;
You came in arms to spill mine enemies'
blood,
But now in arms you strengthen it with
yours.
The grappling vigour and rough frown of
war

Is cold in amity and painted peace,   105
And our oppression hath made up this
   league.
Arm, arm, you heavens, against these
   perjur'd kings !
A widow cries : Be husband to me,
   heavens !
Let not the hours of this ungodly day
Wear out the day in peace ; but, ere sunset,
Set armed discord 'twixt these perjur'd
   kings !   111
Hear me, O, hear me !
  Aust.   Lady Constance, peace !
  Const. War ! war ! no peace ! Peace is
   to me a war.
O Lymoges ! O Austria ! thou dost shame
That bloody spoil.   Thou slave, thou
   wretch, thou coward !   115
Thou little valiant, great in villainy !
Thou ever strong upon the stronger side !
Thou Fortune's champion that dost never
   fight
But when her humorous ladyship is by
To teach thee safety ! Thou art perjur'd
   too,   120
And sooth'st up greatness. What a fool art
   thou,
A ramping fool, to brag and stamp and
   swear
Upon my party ! Thou cold-blooded slave,
Hast thou not spoke like thunder on my
   side,   124
Been sworn my soldier, bidding me depend
Upon thy stars, thy fortune, and thy
   strength,
And dost thou now fall over to my foes ?
Thou wear a lion's hide ! Doff it for shame,
And hang a calf's-skin on those recreant
   limbs.
  Aust. O that a man should speak those
   words to me !   130
  Bast. And hang a calf's-skin on those
   recreant limbs.
  Aust. Thou dar'st not say so, villain, for
   thy life.
  Bast. And hang a calf's-skin on those
   recreant limbs.
  K. John. We like not this : thou dost
   forget thyself.

       Enter PANDULPH.

  K. Phi. Here comes the holy legate of
   the Pope.   135
  Pand. Hail, you anointed deputies of
   heaven !
To thee, King John, my holy errand is.
I Pandulph, of fair Milan cardinal,
And from Pope Innocent the legate here,
Do in his name religiously demand   140
Why thou against the church, our holy
   mother,
So wilfully dost spurn ; and force perforce
Keep Stephen Langton, chosen Archbishop
Of Canterbury, from that holy see ?

This, in our foresaid holy father's name,   145
Pope Innocent, I do demand of thee.
  K. John. What earthly name to interroga-
   tories
Can task the free breath of a sacred king ?
Thou canst not, Cardinal, devise a name
So slight, unworthy, and ridiculous,   150
To charge me to an answer, as the Pope.
Tell him this tale, and from the mouth of
   England
Add thus much more, that no Italian priest
Shall tithe or toll in our dominions ; 154
But as we under heaven are supreme head,
So, under Him that great supremacy,
Where we do reign we will alone uphold,
Without th' assistance of a mortal hand.
So tell the Pope, all reverence set apart
To him and his usurp'd authority.   160
  K. Phi. Brother of England, you blas-
   pheme in this.
  K. John. Though you and all the kings
   of Christendom
Are led so grossly by this meddling priest,
Dreading the curse that money may buy
   out,
And by the merit of vile gold, dross, dust,
Purchase corrupted pardon of a man,   166
Who in that sale sells pardon from himself—
Though you and all the rest, so grossly led,
This juggling witchcraft with revenue
   cherish ;
Yet I alone, alone do me oppose   170
Against the Pope, and count his friends
   my foes.
  Pand. Then by the lawful power that I
   have
Thou shalt stand curs'd and excommuni-
   cate ;
And blessed shall he be that doth revolt
From his allegiance to an heretic ;   175
And meritorious shall that hand be call'd,
Canonized, and worshipp'd as a saint,
That takes away by any secret course
Thy hateful life.
  Const.   O, lawful let it be
That I have room with Rome to curse
   awhile !   180
Good father Cardinal, cry thou ' amen '
To my keen curses ; for without my wrong
There is no tongue hath power to curse him
   right.
  Pand. There's law and warrant, lady, for
   my curse.
  Const. And for mine too : when law can
   do no right,   185
Let it be lawful that law bar no wrong ;
Law cannot give my child his kingdom
   here,
For he that holds his kingdom holds the
   law ;
Therefore, since law itself is perfect wrong,
How can the law forbid my tongue to curse?
  Pand. Philip of France, on peril of a
   curse,   191

Let go the hand of that arch-heretic,
And raise the power of France upon his
   head,
Unless he do submit himself to Rome.
   Eli. Look'st thou pale, France ? Do not
    let go thy hand.   195
   Const. Look to that, devil, lest that
   France repent
And by disjoining hands hell lose a soul.
   Aust. King Philip, listen to the Cardinal.
   Bast. And hang a calf's-skin on his
   recreant limbs.
   Aust. Well, ruffian, I must pocket up
    these wrongs,   200
Because—
   Bast. Your breeches best may carry them.
   K. John. Philip, what say'st thou to the
   Cardinal ?
   Const. What should he say, but as the
   Cardinal ?
   Lew. Bethink you, father ; for the differ-
   ence
Is purchase of a heavy curse from Rome 205
Or the light loss of England for a friend.
Forgo the easier.
   Blanch.   That's the curse of Rome.
   Const. O Lewis, stand fast ! The devil
   tempts thee here
In likeness of a new untrimmed bride.
   Blanch. The Lady Constance speaks not
   from her faith,   210
But from her need.
   Const.   O, if thou grant my need,
Which only lives but by the death of
   faith,
That need must needs infer this principle—
That faith would live again by death of
   need.
O then, tread down my need, and faith
   mounts up :   215
Keep my need up, and faith is trodden
   down !
   K. John. The King is mov'd, and
   answers not to this.
   Const. O, be remov'd from him, and
   answer well !
   Aust. Do so, King Philip ; hang no more
   in doubt.
   Bast. Hang nothing but a calf's-skin,
   most sweet lout.   220
   K. Phi. I am perplex'd and know not
   what to say.
   Pand. What canst thou say but will
   perplex thee more,
If thou stand excommunicate and curs'd ?
   K. Phi. Good reverend father, make my
   person yours,
And tell me how you would bestow your-
   self.   225
This royal hand and mine are newly knit,
And the conjunction of our inward souls
Married in league, coupled and link'd to-
   gether
With all religious strength of sacred vows ;

The latest breath that gave the sound of
   words   230
Was deep-sworn faith, peace, amity, true
   love,
Between our kingdoms and our royal selves;
And even before this truce, but new before,
No longer than we well could wash our
   hands,
To clap this royal bargain up of peace, 235
Heaven knows, they were besmear'd and
   overstain'd
With slaughter's pencil, where revenge did
   paint
The fearful difference of incensed kings.
And shall these hands, so lately purg'd of
   blood,   239
So newly join'd in love, so strong in both,
Unyoke this seizure and this kind regreet ?
Play fast and loose with faith ? so jest
   with heaven,
Make such unconstant children of ourselves,
As now again to snatch our palm from palm,
Unswear faith sworn, and on the marriage-
   bed   245
Of smiling peace to march a bloody host,
And make a riot on the gentle brow
Of true sincerity ? O, holy sir,
My reverend father, let it not be so ! 249
Out of your grace, devise, ordain, impose,
Some gentle order ; and then we shall be
   blest
To do your pleasure, and continue friends.
   Pand. All form is formless, order order-
   less,
Save what is opposite to England's love.
Therefore, to arms ! be champion of our
   church,   255
Or let the church, our mother, breathe her
   curse—
A mother's curse—on her revolting son.
France, thou mayst hold a serpent by the
   tongue,
A chafed lion by the mortal paw,
A fasting tiger safer by the tooth,   260
Than keep in peace that hand which thou
   dost hold.
   K. Phi. I may disjoin my hand, but not
   my faith.
   Pand. So mak'st thou faith an enemy to
   faith ;
And like a civil war set'st oath to oath,
Thy tongue against thy tongue. O, let thy
   vow   265
First made to heaven, first be to heaven
   perform'd,
That is, to be the champion of our church.
What since thou swor'st is sworn against
   thyself
And may not be performed by thyself,
For that which thou hast sworn to do 270
Is not amiss when it is truly done ;
And being not done, where doing tends
   to ill,

The truth is then most done not doing it ;
The better act of purposes mistook
Is to mistake again ; though indirect,   275
Yet indirection thereby grows direct,
And falsehood falsehood cures, as fire cools fire
Within the scorched veins of one new-burn'd.
It is religion that doth make vows kept ;
But thou hast sworn against religion   280
By what thou swear'st against the thing thou swear'st,
And mak'st an oath the surety for thy truth
Against an oath ; the truth thou art unsure
To swear swears only not to be forsworn ;
Else what a mockery should it be to swear !
But thou dost swear only to be forsworn ;
And most forsworn to keep what thou dost swear.
Therefore thy later vows against thy first
Is in thyself rebellion to thyself ;   289
And better conquest never canst thou make
Than arm thy constant and thy nobler parts
Against these giddy loose suggestions ;
Upon which better part our pray'rs come in,
If thou vouchsafe them. But if not, then know
The peril of our curses light on thee   295
So heavy as thou shalt not shake them off,
But in despair die under their black weight.
   Aust. Rebellion, flat rebellion !
   Bast.   Will't not be ?
Will not a calf's-skin stop that mouth of thine ?
   Lew. Father, to arms !
   Blanch.   Upon thy wedding-day ?   300
Against the blood that thou hast married ?
What, shall our feast be kept with slaughtered men ?
Shall braying trumpets and loud churlish drums,
Clamours of hell, be measures to our pomp ?
O husband, hear me ! ay, alack, how new
Is ' husband ' in my mouth !—even for that name,   306
Which till this time my tongue did ne'er pronounce,
Upon my knee I beg, go not to arms
Against mine uncle.
   Const.   O, upon my knee,
Made hard with kneeling, I do pray to thee,
Thou virtuous Dauphin, alter not the doom
Forethought by heaven !   312
   Blanch. Now shall I see thy love. What motive may
Be stronger with thee than the name of wife ?
   Const. That which upholdeth him that thee upholds,
His honour. O, thine honour, Lewis, thine honour !   316

   Lew. I muse your Majesty doth seem so cold,
When such profound respects do pull you on.
   Pand. I will denounce a curse upon his head.
   K. Phi. Thou shalt not need. England, I will fall from thee.   320
   Const. O fair return of banish'd majesty !
   Eli. O foul revolt of French inconstancy !
   K. John. France, thou shalt rue this hour within this hour.
   Bast. Old Time the clock-setter, that bald sexton Time,
Is it as he will ? Well then, France shall rue.   325
   Blanch. The sun's o'ercast with blood. Fair day, adieu !
Which is the side that I must go withal ?
I am with both : each army hath a hand ;
And in their rage, I having hold of both,
They whirl asunder and dismember me.   330
Husband, I cannot pray that thou mayst win ;
Uncle, I needs must pray that thou mayst lose ;
Father, I may not wish the fortune thine ;
Grandam, I will not wish thy wishes thrive.
Whoever wins, on that side shall I lose :   335
Assured loss before the match be play'd.
   Lew. Lady, with me, with me thy fortune lies.
   Blanch. There where my fortune lives, there my life dies.
   K. John. Cousin, go draw our puissance together.   [*Exit Bastard.*
France, I am burn'd up with inflaming wrath,   340
A rage whose heat hath this condition
That nothing can allay, nothing but blood,
The blood, and dearest-valu'd blood, of France.
   K. Phi. Thy rage shall burn thee up, and thou shalt turn
To ashes, ere our blood shall quench that fire.   345
Look to thyself, thou art in jeopardy.
   K. John. No more than he that threats. To arms let's hie !   [*Exeunt severally.*

SCENE II. *France. Plains near Angiers.*

Alarums, excursions.   Enter the BASTARD *with Austria's head.*

   Bast. Now, by my life, this day grows wondrous hot ;
Some airy devil hovers in the sky
And pours down mischief. Austria's head lie there,
While Philip breathes.

Enter KING JOHN, ARTHUR, *and* HUBERT.

   K. John. Hubert, keep this boy. Philip, make up :   5

My mother is assailed in our tent,
And ta'en, I fear.
 Bast.   My lord, I rescued her ;
Her Highness is in safety, fear you not ;
But on, my liege, for very little pains
Will bring this labour to an happy end. 10
         [*Exeunt.*

SCENE III. *France. Plains near Angiers.*

Alarums, excursions, retreat. Enter KING
 JOHN, ELINOR, ARTHUR, *the* BASTARD,
 HUBERT, *and* Lords.

 K. John [*To Elinor*] So shall it be ; your
  Grace shall stay behind,
So strongly guarded. [*To Arthur*] Cousin,
 look not sad ;
Thy grandam loves thee, and thy uncle will
As dear be to thee as thy father was.
 Arth. O, this will make my mother die
  with grief !   5
 K. John. [*To the Bastard*] Cousin, away
  for England ! haste before,
And, ere our coming, see thou shake the bags
Of hoarding abbots ; imprisoned angels
Set at liberty ; the fat ribs of peace
Must by the hungry now be fed upon. 10
Use our commission in his utmost force.
 Bast. Bell, book, and candle, shall not
  drive me back,
When gold and silver becks me to come on.
I leave your Highness. Grandam, I will
 pray,
If ever I remember to be holy, 15
For your fair safety. So, I kiss your hand.
 Eli. Farewell, gentle cousin.
 K. John. Coz, farewell. [*Exit Bastard.*
 Eli. Come hither, little kinsman ; hark,
 a word.
 K. John. Come hither, Hubert. O my
 gentle Hubert,
We owe thee much ! Within this wall of
 flesh   20
There is a soul counts thee her creditor,
And with advantage means to pay thy love;
And, my good friend, thy voluntary oath
Lives in this bosom, dearly cherished.
Give me thy hand. I had a thing to say—
But I will fit it with some better time. 26
By heaven, Hubert, I am almost asham'd
To say what good respect I have of thee.
 Hub. I am much bounden to your
  Majesty.
 K. John. Good friend, thou hast no cause
  to say so yet,   30
But thou shalt have ; and creep time ne'er
 so slow,
Yet it shall come for me to do thee good.
I had a thing to say—but let it go :
The sun is in the heaven, and the proud day,
Attended with the pleasures of the world, 35
Is all too wanton and too full of gawds
To give me audience. If the midnight bell
Did with his iron tongue and brazen mouth
Sound on into the drowsy race of night ;

If this same were a churchyard where we
 stand,   40
And thou possessed with a thousand
 wrongs ;
Or if that surly spirit, melancholy,
Had bak'd thy blood and made it heavy-
 thick,
Which else runs tickling up and down the
 veins,
Making that idiot, laughter, keep men's
 eyes   45
And strain their cheeks to idle merriment,
A passion hateful to my purposes ;
Or if that thou couldst see me without eyes,
Hear me without thine ears, and make
 reply
Without a tongue, using conceit alone, 50
Without eyes, ears, and harmful sound of
 words—
Then, in despite of brooded watchful day,
I would into thy bosom pour my thoughts.
But, ah, I will not ! Yet I love thee well ;
And, by my troth, I think thou lov'st me
 well.   55
 Hub. So well that what you bid me
  undertake,
Though that my death were adjunct to my
 act,
By heaven, I would do it.
 K. John. Do not I know thou wouldst ?
Good Hubert, Hubert, Hubert, throw thine
 eye
On yon young boy. I'll tell thee what, my
 friend,   60
He is a very serpent in my way ;
And wheresoe'er this foot of mine doth
 tread,
He lies before me. Dost thou understand
 me ?
Thou art his keeper.
 Hub.   And I'll keep him so
That he shall not offend your Majesty.
 K. John. Death.   65
 Hub. My lord ?
 K. John. A grave.
 Hub. He shall not live.
 K. John. Enough !
I could be merry now. Hubert, I love thee.
Well, I'll not say what I intend for thee.
Remember. Madam, fare you well ;
I'll send those powers o'er to your Majesty.
 Eli. My blessing go with thee !
 K. John. [*To Arthur*] For England,
  cousin, go ;   71
Hubert shall be your man, attend on you
With all true duty. On toward Calais, ho !
         [*Exeunt.*

SCENE IV. *France. The French King's
    camp.*

Enter KING PHILIP, LEWIS, PANDULPH, *and*
    Attendants.

 K. Phi. So by a roaring tempest on the
  flood

A whole armado of convicted sail
Is scattered and disjoin'd from fellowship.
  Pand. Courage and comfort! All shall
    yet go well. 5
  K. Phi. What can go well, when we have
    run so ill.
Are we not beaten? Is not Angiers lost?
Arthur ta'en prisoner? Divers dear friends
    slain?
And bloody England into England gone,
O'erbearing interruption, spite of France?
  Lew. What he hath won, that hath he
    fortified; 10
So hot a speed with such advice dispos'd,
Such temperate order in so fierce a cause,
Doth want example; who hath read or
    heard
Of any kindred action like to this?
  K. Phi. Well could I bear that England
    had this praise, 15
So we could find some pattern of our shame.

     Enter CONSTANCE.

Look who comes here! a grave unto a
    soul;
Holding th' eternal spirit, against her will,
In the vile prison of afflicted breath.
I prithee, lady, go away with me. 20
  Const. Lo now! now see the issue of your
    peace!
  K. Phi. Patience, good lady! Comfort,
    gentle Constance!
  Const. No, I defy all counsel, all redress,
But that which ends all counsel, true
    redress—
Death, death; O amiable lovely death! 25
Thou odoriferous stench! sound rottenness!
Arise forth from the couch of lasting night,
Thou hate and terror to prosperity,
And I will kiss thy detestable bones, 29
And put my eyeballs in thy vaulty brows,
And ring these fingers with thy household
    worms,
And stop this gap of breath with fulsome
    dust,
And be a carrion monster like thyself.
Come, grin on me, and I will think thou
    smil'st,
And buss thee as thy wife. Misery's love,
O, come to me!
  K. Phi.   O fair affliction, peace! 36
  Const. No, no, I will not, having breath
    to cry.
O that my tongue were in the thunder's
    mouth!
Then with a passion would I shake the
    world,
And rouse from sleep that fell anatomy 40
Which cannot hear a lady's feeble voice,
Which scorns a modern invocation.
  Pand. Lady, you utter madness and not
    sorrow.
  Const. Thou art not holy to belie me so.
I am not mad: this hair I tear is mine; 45

My name is Constance; I was Geffrey's
    wife;
Young Arthur is my son, and he is lost.
I am not mad—I would to heaven I were!
For then 'tis like I should forget myself.
O, if I could, what grief should I forget! 50
Preach some philosophy to make me mad,
And thou shalt be canoniz'd, Cardinal;
For, being not mad, but sensible of grief,
My reasonable part produces reason
How I may be deliver'd of these woes, 55
And teaches me to kill or hang myself.
If I were mad I should forget my son,
Or madly think a babe of clouts were he.
I am not mad; too well, too well I feel
The different plague of each calamity. 60
  K. Phi. Bind up those tresses. O, what
    love I note
In the fair multitude of those her hairs!
Where but by a chance a silver drop hath
    fall'n,
Even to that drop ten thousand wiry friends
Do glue themselves in sociable grief, 65
Like true, inseparable, faithful loves,
Sticking together in calamity.
  Const. To England, if you will.
  K. Phi.   Bind up your hairs.
  Const. Yes, that I will; and wherefore
    will I do it?
I tore them from their bonds, and cried
    aloud 70
'O that these hands could so redeem my
    son,
As they have given these hairs their
    liberty!'
But now I envy at their liberty,
And will again commit them to their bonds,
Because my poor child is a prisoner. 75
And, father Cardinal, I have heard you say
That we shall see and know our friends in
    heaven;
If that be true, I shall see my boy again;
For since the birth of Cain, the first male
    child,
To him that did but yesterday suspire, 80
There was not such a gracious creature
    born.
But now will canker sorrow eat my bud
And chase the native beauty from his cheek,
And he will look as hollow as a ghost,
As dim and meagre as an ague's fit; 85
And so he'll die; and, rising so again,
When I shall meet him in the court of
    heaven
I shall not know him. Therefore never,
    never
Must I behold my pretty Arthur more.
  Pand. You hold too heinous a respect of
    grief. 90
  Const. He talks to me that never had a son.
  K. Phi. You are as fond of grief as of
    your child.
  Const. Grief fills the room up of my
    absent child,

Lies in his bed, walks up and down with me,
Puts on his pretty looks, repeats his words,
Remembers me of all his gracious parts,
Stuffs out his vacant garments with his
    form ;
Then have I reason to be fond of grief.
Fare you well ; had you such a loss as I,
I could give better comfort than you do. 100
I will not keep this form upon my head,
                    [*Tearing her hair.*
When there is such disorder in my wit.
O Lord ! my boy, my Arthur, my fair son !
My life, my joy, my food, my all the world !
My widow-comfort, and my sorrows' cure !
                                    [*Exit.*
    K. Phi. I fear some outrage, and I'll
        follow her.   [*Exit.*
    Lew. There's nothing in this world can
        make me joy.   107
Life is as tedious as a twice-told tale
Vexing the dull ear of a drowsy man ;
And bitter shame hath spoil'd the sweet
    world's taste,
That it yields nought but shame and bitter-
    ness.   111
    Pand. Before the curing of a strong
        disease,
Even in the instant of repair and health,
The fit is strongest ; evils that take leave
On their departure most of all show evil ;
What have you lost by losing of this day ?
    Lew. All days of glory, joy, and happi-
        ness.   117
    Pand. If you had won it, certainly you
        had.
No, no ; when Fortune means to men most
    good,
She looks upon them with a threat'ning
    eye.   120
'Tis strange to think how much King John
    hath lost
In this which he accounts so clearly won.
Are not you griev'd that Arthur is his
    prisoner ?
    Lew. As heartily as he is glad he hath
        him.
    Pand. Your mind is all as youthful as
        your blood.   125
Now hear me speak with a prophetic spirit ;
For even the breath of what I mean to speak
Shall blow each dust, each straw, each little
    rub,
Out of the path which shall directly lead
Thy foot to England's throne. And there-
    fore mark :   130
John hath seiz'd Arthur ; and it cannot be
That, whiles warm life plays in that infant's
    veins,
The misplac'd John should entertain an
    hour,
One minute, nay, one quiet breath of rest.
A sceptre snatch'd with an unruly hand 135
Must be as boisterously maintain'd as
    gain'd,

And he that stands upon a slipp'ry place
Makes nice of no vile hold to stay him up ;
That John may stand then, Arthur needs
    must fall ;
So be it, for it cannot be but so.   140
    Lew. But what shall I gain by young
        Arthur's fall ?
    Pand. You, in the right of Lady Blanch
        your wife,
May then make all the claim that Arthur
        did.
    Lew. And lose it, life and all, as Arthur
        did.
    Pand. How green you are and fresh in
        this old world !   145
John lays you plots ; the times conspire
    with you ;
For he that steeps his safety in true blood
Shall find but bloody safety and untrue.
This act, so evilly borne, shall cool the
    hearts
Of all his people and freeze up their zeal, 150
That none so small advantage shall step
    forth
To check his reign but they will cherish it ;
No natural exhalation in the sky,
No scope of nature, no distemper'd day,
No common wind, no customed event,   155
But they will pluck away his natural cause
And call them meteors, prodigies, and signs,
Abortives, presages, and tongues of heaven,
Plainly denouncing vengeance upon John.
    Lew. May be he will not touch young
        Arthur's life,   160
But hold himself safe in his prisonment.
    Pand. O, sir, when he shall hear of your
        approach,
If that young Arthur be not gone already,
Even at that news he dies ; and then the
    hearts
Of all his people shall revolt from him, 165
And kiss the lips of unacquainted change,
And pick strong matter of revolt and wrath
Out of the bloody fingers' ends of John.
Methinks I see this hurly all on foot ;
And, O, what better matter breeds for you
Than I have nam'd ! The bastard Faulcon-
    bridge   171
Is now in England ransacking the Church,
Offending charity ; if but a dozen French
Were there in arms, they would be as a call
To train ten thousand English to their side ;
Or as a little snow, tumbled about,   176
Anon becomes a mountain.   O noble
    Dauphin,
Go with me to the King. 'Tis wonderful
What may be wrought out of their discon-
    tent,
Now that their souls are topful of offence.
For England go ; I will whet on the King.
    Lew. Strong reasons makes strong actions.
        Let us go ;   182
If you say ay, the King will not say no.
                            [*Exeunt.*

ACT FOUR

SCENE I. *England. A castle.*

Enter HUBERT *and* Executioners.

Hub. Heat me these irons hot ; and look
    thou stand
Within the arras. When I strike my foot
Upon the bosom of the ground, rush forth
And bind the boy which you shall find with
    me
Fast to the chair. Be heedful ; hence, and
    watch.   5
1 Exec. I hope your warrant will bear
    out the deed.
Hub. Uncleanly scruples ! Fear not you.
    Look to't.   [*Exeunt Executioners.*
Young lad, come forth ; I have to say with
    you.

Enter ARTHUR.

Arth. Good morrow, Hubert.
Hub.   Good morrow, little Prince.
Arth. As little prince, having so great a
    title   10
To be more prince, as may be. You are sad.
Hub. Indeed, I have been merrier.
Arth.   Mercy on me !
Methinks no body should be sad but I ;
Yet, I remember, when I was in France, 14
Young gentlemen would be as sad as night,
Only for wantonness. By my christendom,
So I were out of prison and kept sheep,
I should be as merry as the day is long ;
And so I would be here but that I doubt
My uncle practises more harm to me ;   20
He is afraid of me, and I of him.
Is it my fault that I was Geffrey's son ?
No, indeed, is't not ; and I would to
    heaven
I were your son, so you would love me,
    Hubert.
Hub. [*Aside*] If I talk to him, with his
    innocent prate   25
He will awake my mercy, which lies dead ;
Therefore I will be sudden and dispatch.
Arth. Are you sick, Hubert ? You look
    pale to-day ;
In sooth, I would you were a little sick,
That I might sit all night and watch with
    you.   30
I warrant I love you more than you do me.
Hub. [*Aside*] His words do take possession
    of my bosom.—
Read here, young Arthur. [*Showing a paper.*
    [*Aside*] How now, foolish rheum !
Turning dispiteous torture out of door !
I must be brief, lest resolution drop   35
Out at mine eyes in tender womanish
    tears.—
Can you not read it ? Is it not fair writ ?
Arth. Too fairly, Hubert, for so foul effect.
Must you with hot irons burn out both mine
    eyes ?

Hub. Young boy, I must.
Arth.   And will you ?
Hub.   And I will.
Arth. Have you the heart ? When your
    head did but ache,   41
I knit my handkerchief about your brows—
The best I had, a princess wrought it me—
And I did never ask it you again ;
And with my hand at midnight held your
    head ;   45
And, like the watchful minutes to the hour,
Still and anon cheer'd up the heavy time,
Saying ' What lack you ? ' and ' Where lies
    your grief ? '
Or ' What good love may I perform for
    you ? '
Many a poor man's son would have lyen
    still,   50
And ne'er have spoke a loving word to you ;
But you at your sick service had a prince.
Nay, you may think my love was crafty
    love,
And call it cunning. Do, an if you will.
If heaven be pleas'd that you must use
    me ill,   55
Why, then you must. Will you put out
    mine eyes,
These eyes that never did nor never shall
So much as frown on you ?
Hub.   I have sworn to do it ;
And with hot irons must I burn them out.
Arth. Ah, none but in this iron age would
    do it !   60
The iron of itself, though heat red-hot,
Approaching near these eyes would drink
    my tears,
And quench his fiery indignation
Even in the matter of mine innocence ;
Nay, after that, consume away in rust   65
But for containing fire to harm mine eye.
Are you more stubborn-hard than ham-
    mer'd iron ?
An if an angel should have come to me
And told me Hubert should put out mine
    eyes,
I would not have believ'd him—no tongue
    but Hubert's.
Hub. [*Stamps*] Come forth.   71

Re-enter Executioners, *with cord, irons, etc.*

Do as I bid you do.
Arth. O, save me, Hubert, save me ! My
    eyes are out
Even with the fierce looks of these bloody
    men.
Hub. Give me the iron, I say, and bind
    him here.   75
Arth. Alas, what need you be so
    boist'rous rough ?
I will not struggle, I will stand stone-still.
For heaven sake, Hubert, let me not be
    bound !
Nay, hear me, Hubert ! Drive these men
    away,

And I will sit as quiet as a lamb;   80
I will not stir, nor wince, nor speak a word,
Nor look upon the iron angrily;
Thrust but these men away, and I'll forgive
    you,
Whatever torment you do put me to.
    Hub. Go, stand within; let me alone
        with him.   85
    1 *Exec.* I am best pleas'd to be from such
        a deed.   [*Exeunt Executioners.*
    Arth. Alas, I then have chid away my
        friend!
He hath a stern look but a gentle heart.
Let him come back, that his compassion
    may
Give life to yours.
    Hub. Come, boy, prepare yourself. 90
    Arth. Is there no remedy?
    Hub.   None, but to lose your eyes.
    Arth. O heaven, that there were but a
        mote in yours,
A grain, a dust, a gnat, a wandering hair,
Any annoyance in that precious sense!
Then, feeling what small things are
    boisterous there,   95
Your vile intent must needs seem horrible.
    Hub. Is this your promise? Go to, hold
        your tongue.
    Arth. Hubert, the utterance of a brace of
        tongues
Must needs want pleading for a pair of eyes.
Let me not hold my tongue, let me not,
    Hubert;   100
Or, Hubert, if you will, cut out my tongue,
So I may keep mine eyes. O, spare mine
    eyes,
Though to no use but still to look on
    you!
Lo, by my troth, the instrument is cold
And would not harm me.
    Hub.   I can heat it, boy. 105
    Arth. No, in good sooth; the fire is dead
        with grief,
Being create for comfort, to be us'd
In undeserved extremes. See else yourself:
There is no malice in this burning coal;
The breath of heaven hath blown his spirit
    out,   110
And strew'd repentant ashes on his head.
    Hub. But with my breath I can revive it,
        boy.
    Arth. An if you do, you will but make it
        blush
And glow with shame of your proceedings,
    Hubert.   114
Nay, it perchance will sparkle in your eyes,
And, like a dog that is compell'd to fight,
Snatch at his master that doth tarre him on.
All things that you should use to do me
    wrong
Deny their office; only you do lack
That mercy which fierce fire and iron ex-
    tends,   120
Creatures of note for mercy-lacking uses.

    Hub. Well, see to live; I will not touch
        thine eye
For all the treasure that thine uncle owes.
Yet am I sworn, and I did purpose, boy,
With this same very iron to burn them out.
    Arth. O, now you look like Hubert! All
        this while   126
You were disguis'd.
    Hub.   Peace; no more. Adieu.
Your uncle must not know but you are
    dead:
I'll fill these dogged spies with false reports;
And, pretty child, sleep doubtless and
    secure   130
That Hubert, for the wealth of all the
    world,
Will not offend thee.
    Arth. O heaven! I thank you, Hubert.
    Hub. Silence; no more. Go closely in
        with me.
Much danger do I undergo for thee.
                                     [*Exeunt.*

SCENE II. *England. King John's palace.*

Enter KING JOHN, PEMBROKE, SALISBURY,
        and other Lords.

    K. John. Here once again we sit, once
        again crown'd,
And look'd upon, I hope, with cheerful eyes.
    Pem. This once again, but that your
        Highness pleas'd,
Was once superfluous: you were crown'd
    before,
And that high royalty was ne'er pluck'd
    off,   5
The faiths of men ne'er stained with revolt;
Fresh expectation troubled not the land
With any long'd-for change or better state.
    Sal. Therefore, to be possess'd with
        double pomp,
To guard a title that was rich before,   10
To gild refined gold, to paint the lily,
To throw a perfume on the violet,
To smooth the ice, or add another hue
Unto the rainbow, or with taper-light
To seek the beauteous eye of heaven to
    garnish,   15
Is wasteful and ridiculous excess.
    Pem. But that your royal pleasure must
        be done,
This act is as an ancient tale new told
And, in the last repeating, troublesome,
Being urged at a time unseasonable.   20
    Sal. In this the antique and well-noted
        face
Of plain old form is much disfigured;
And like a shifted wind unto a sail
It makes the course of thoughts to fetch
    about,
Startles and frights consideration,   25
Makes sound opinion sick, and truth
    suspected,
For putting on so new a fashion'd robe.

Pem. When workmen strive to do better
    than well,
They do confound their skill in covetous-
    ness ;
And oftentimes excusing of a fault   30
Doth make the fault the worse by th'
    excuse,
As patches set upon a little breach
Discredit more in hiding of the fault
Than did the fault before it was so patch'd.
    Sal. To this effect, before you were new-
    crown'd,   35
We breath'd our counsel ; but it pleas'd
    your Highness
To overbear it ; and we are all well pleas'd,
Since all and every part of what we would
Doth make a stand at what your Highness
    will.
    K. John. Some reasons of this double
    coronation   40
I have possess'd you with, and think them
    strong ;
And more, more strong, when lesser is my
    fear,
I shall indue you with. Meantime but ask
What you would have reform'd that is not
    well,
And well shall you perceive how willingly 45
I will both hear and grant you your
    requests.
    Pem. Then I, as one that am the tongue
    of these,
To sound the purposes of all their hearts,
Both for myself and them—but, chief of
    all,
Your safety, for the which myself and them
Bend their best studies—heartily request
Th' enfranchisement of Arthur, whose
    restraint   52
Doth move the murmuring lips of discon-
    tent
To break into this dangerous argument :
If what in rest you have in right you hold,
Why then your fears—which, as they say,
    attend   56
The steps of wrong—should move you to
    mew up
Your tender kinsman, and to choke his days
With barbarous ignorance, and deny his
    youth
The rich advantage of good exercise ?   60
That the time's enemies may not have this
To grace occasions, let it be our suit
That you have bid us ask his liberty ;
Which for our goods we do no further ask
Than whereupon our weal, on you de-
    pending,   65
Counts it your weal he have his liberty.
    K. John. Let it be so. I do commit his
    youth
To your direction.

    Enter HUBERT.

    [*Aside*] Hubert, what news with you ?

    Pem. This is the man should do the
    bloody deed :
He show'd his warrant to a friend of mine ;
The image of a wicked heinous fault   71
Lives in his eye ; that close aspect of his
Doth show the mood of a much troubled
    breast,
And I do fearfully believe 'tis done
What we so fear'd he had a charge to do. 75
    Sal. The colour of the King doth come
    and go
Between his purpose and his conscience,
Like heralds 'twixt two dreadful battles set.
His passion is so ripe it needs must break.
    Pem. And when it breaks, I fear will
    issue thence   80
The foul corruption of a sweet child's death.
    K. John. We cannot hold mortality's
    strong hand.
Good lords, although my will to give is
    living,
The suit which you demand is gone and
    dead :
He tells us Arthur is deceas'd to-night. 85
    Sal. Indeed, we fear'd his sickness was
    past cure.
    Pem. Indeed, we heard how near his
    death he was,
Before the child himself felt he was sick.
This must be answer'd either here or hence.
    K. John. Why do you bend such solemn
    brows on me ?   90
Think you I bear the shears of destiny ?
Have I commandment on the pulse of life ?
    Sal. It is apparent foul-play ; and 'tis
    shame
That greatness should so grossly offer it.
So thrive it in your game ! and so, farewell.
    Pem. Stay yet, Lord Salisbury, I'll go
    with thee   96
And find th' inheritance of this poor child,
His little kingdom of a forced grave.
That blood which ow'd the breadth of all
    this isle
Three foot of it doth hold—bad world the
    while !   100
This must not be thus borne : this will
    break out
To all our sorrows, and ere long I doubt.
                  [*Exeunt Lords.*
    K. John. They burn in indignation. I
    repent.
There is no sure foundation set on blood,
No certain life achiev'd by others' death. 105

    Enter a Messenger.

A fearful eye thou hast ; where is that
    blood
That I have seen inhabit in those cheeks ?
So foul a sky clears not without a storm.
Pour down thy weather—how goes all in
    France ?
    Mess. From France to England. Never
    such a pow'r   110

For any foreign preparation
Was levied in the body of a land.
The copy of your speed is learn'd by them,
For when you should be told they do
    prepare,
The tidings comes that they are all arriv'd.
   K. John. O, where hath our intelligence
    been drunk ?   116
Where hath it slept ?   Where is my
    mother's care,
That such an army could be drawn in
    France,
And she not hear of it ?
   Mess.   My liege, her ear
Is stopp'd with dust : the first of April
    died   120
Your noble mother ; and as I hear, my
    lord,
The Lady Constance in a frenzy died
Three days before ; but this from rumour's
    tongue
I idly heard—if true or false I know not.
   K. John. Withhold thy speed, dreadful
    occasion !   125
O, make a league with me, till I have
    pleas'd
My discontented peers !   What ! mother
    dead !
How wildly then walks my estate in
    France !
Under whose conduct came those pow'rs of
    France
That thou for truth giv'st out are landed
    here ?   130
   Mess. Under the Dauphin.
   K. John.   Thou hast made me giddy
With these ill tidings.

Enter the BASTARD *and* PETER *of Pomfret.*

            Now ! What says the world
To your proceedings ? Do not seek to stuff
My head with more ill news, for it is full.
   Bast. But if you be afear'd to hear the
    worst,   135
Then let the worst, unheard, fall on your
    head.
   K. John. Bear with me, cousin, for I was
    amaz'd
Under the tide ; but now I breathe again
Aloft the flood, and can give audience
To any tongue, speak it of what it will. 140
   Bast. How I have sped among the clergy-
    men
The sums I have collected shall express.
But as I travell'd hither through the land,
I find the people strangely fantasied ;
Possess'd with rumours, full of idle dreams,
Not knowing what they fear, but full of
    fear ;   146
And here's a prophet that I brought with
    me
From forth the streets of Pomfret, whom I
    found
With many hundreds treading on his heels ;

To whom he sung, in rude harsh-sounding
    rhymes,   150
That, ere the next Ascension-day at noon,
Your Highness should deliver up your
    crown.
   K. John. Thou idle dreamer, wherefore
    didst thou so ?
   Peter. Foreknowing that the truth will
    fall out so.
   K. John. Hubert, away with him ; im-
    prison him ;   155
And on that day at noon whereon he
    says
I shall yield up my crown let him be hang'd.
Deliver him to safety ; and return,
For I must use thee.
             [*Exit Hubert with Peter.*
              O my gentle cousin,
Hear'st thou the news abroad, who are
    arriv'd ?   160
   Bast. The French, my lord ; men's
    mouths are full of it ;
Besides, I met Lord Bigot and Lord
    Salisbury,
With eyes as red as new-enkindled fire,
And others more, going to seek the grave
Of Arthur, whom they say is kill'd to-night
On your suggestion.
   K. John.   Gentle kinsman, go
And thrust thyself into their companies.
I have a way to win their loves again ;
Bring them before me.
   Bast.   I will seek them out.
   K. John. Nay, but make haste ; the
    better foot before.   170
O, let me have no subject enemies
When adverse foreigners affright my towns
With dreadful pomp of stout invasion !
Be Mercury, set feathers to thy heels,
And fly like thought from them to me
    again.   175
   Bast. The spirit of the time shall teach
    me speed.
   K. John. Spoke like a sprightful noble
    gentleman.   [*Exit Bastard.*
Go after him ; for he perhaps shall need
Some messenger betwixt me and the peers ;
And be thou he.
   Mess. With all my heart, my liege. [*Exit.*
   K. John. My mother dead !   181

Re-enter HUBERT.

   Hub. My lord, they say five moons were
    seen to-night ;
Four fixed, and the fifth did whirl about
The other four in wondrous motion.
   K. John. Five moons !
   Hub. Old men and beldams in the streets
Do prophesy upon it dangerously ;   186
Young Arthur's death is common in their
    mouths ;
And when they talk of him, they shake
    their heads,
And whisper one another in the ear ;

And he that speaks doth gripe the hearer's
    wrist,   190
Whilst he that hears makes fearful action
With wrinkled brows, with nods, with roll-
    ing eyes.
I saw a smith stand with his hammer, thus,
The whilst his iron did on the anvil cool,
With open mouth swallowing a tailor's
    news ;   195
Who, with his shears and measure in his
    hand,
Standing on slippers, which his nimble
    haste
Had falsely thrust upon contrary feet,
Told of a many thousand warlike French
That were embattailed and rank'd in Kent.
Another lean unwash'd artificer   201
Cuts off his tale, and talks of Arthur's death.
    K. John. Why seek'st thou to possess me
      with these fears ?
Why urgest thou so oft young Arthur's
    death ?
Thy hand hath murd'red him. I had a
    mighty cause   205
To wish him dead, but thou hadst none to
    kill him.
    Hub. No had, my lord ! Why, did you
      not provoke me ?
    K. John. It is the curse of kings to be
      attended
By slaves that take their humours for a
    warrant
To break within the bloody house of life, 210
And on the winking of authority
To understand a law ; to know the meaning
Of dangerous majesty, when perchance it
    frowns
More upon humour than advis'd respect.
    Hub. Here is your hand and seal for what
      I did.   215
    K. John. O, when the last account 'twixt
      heaven and earth
Is to be made, then shall this hand and seal
Witness against us to damnation !
How oft the sight of means to do ill deeds
Make deeds ill done ! Hadst not thou been
    by,   220
A fellow by the hand of nature mark'd,
Quoted and sign'd to do a deed of shame,
This murder had not come into my mind ;
But, taking note of thy abhorr'd aspect,
Finding thee fit for bloody villainy,   225
Apt, liable to be employ'd in danger,
I faintly broke with thee of Arthur's death ;
And thou, to be endeared to a king,
Made it no conscience to destroy a prince.
    Hub. My lord—   230
    K. John. Hadst thou but shook thy head
      or made a pause,
When I spake darkly what I purposed,
Or turn'd an eye of doubt upon my face,
As bid me tell my tale in express words,
Deep shame had struck me dumb, made me
    break off,   235

And those thy fears might have wrought
    fears in me.
But thou didst understand me by my signs,
And didst in signs again parley with sin ;
Yea, without stop, didst let thy heart
    consent,
And consequently thy rude hand to act   240
The deed which both our tongues held vile
    to name.
Out of my sight, and never see me more !
My nobles leave me ; and my state is
    braved,
Even at my gates, with ranks of foreign
    pow'rs ;
Nay, in the body of this fleshly land,   245
This kingdom, this confine of blood and
    breath,
Hostility and civil tumult reigns
Between my conscience and my cousin's
    death.
    Hub. Arm you against your other
      enemies,
I'll make a peace between your soul and
    you.   250
Young Arthur is alive. This hand of mine
Is yet a maiden and an innocent hand,
Not painted with the crimson spots of
    blood.
Within this bosom never ent'red yet
The dreadful motion of a murderous
    thought ;   255
And you have slander'd nature in my form,
Which, howsoever rude exteriorly,
Is yet the cover of a fairer mind
Than to be butcher of an innocent child.
    K. John. Doth Arthur live ? O, haste
      thee to the peers,   260
Throw this report on their incensed rage
And make them tame to their obedience !
Forgive the comment that my passion
    made
Upon thy feature ; for my rage was blind,
And foul imaginary eyes of blood   265
Presented thee more hideous than thou art.
O, answer not ; but to my closet bring
The angry lords with all expedient haste.
I conjure thee but slowly ; run more fast.
                          [Exeunt.

SCENE III. *England. Before the castle.*

Enter ARTHUR, *on the walls.*

    Arth. The wall is high, and yet will I leap
      down.
Good ground, be pitiful and hurt me not !
There's few or none do know me ; if they
    did,
This ship-boy's semblance hath disguis'd
    me quite.
I am afraid ; and yet I'll venture it.   5
If I get down and do not break my limbs,
I'll find a thousand shifts to get away.
As good to die and go, as die and stay.
                      [Leaps down.

O me! my uncle's spirit is in these stones.
Heaven take my soul, and England keep
  my bones!   [*Dies.*

Enter PEMBROKE, SALISBURY, *and* BIGOT.

  Sal. Lords, I will meet him at Saint
    Edmundsbury;
It is our safety, and we must embrace
This gentle offer of the perilous time.
  Pem. Who brought that letter from the
    Cardinal?
  Sal. The Count Melun, a noble lord of
    France,   15
Whose private with me of the Dauphin's
  love
Is much more general than these lines
  import.
  Big. To-morrow morning let us meet him
    then.
  Sal. Or rather then set forward; for
    'twill be
Two long days' journey, lords, or ere we
  meet.   20

Enter the BASTARD.

  Bast. Once more to-day well met,
    distemper'd lords!
The King by me requests your presence
  straight.
  Sal. The King hath dispossess'd himself
    of us.
We will not line his thin bestained cloak
With our pure honours, nor attend the foot
That leaves the print of blood where'er it
  walks.   26
Return and tell him so. We know the
  worst.
  Bast. Whate'er you think, good words, I
    think, were best.
  Sal. Our griefs, and not our manners,
    reason now.
  Bast. But there is little reason in your
    grief;   30
Therefore 'twere reason you had manners
  now.
  Pem. Sir, sir, impatience hath his
    privilege.
  Bast. 'Tis true—to hurt his master, no
    man else.
  Sal. This is the prison. What is he lies
    here?
  Pem. O death, made proud with pure and
    princely beauty!   35
The earth had not a hole to hide this deed.
  Sal. Murder, as hating what himself hath
    done,
Doth lay it open to urge on revenge.
  Big. Or, when he doom'd this beauty to
    a grave,
Found it too precious-princely for a grave.
  Sal. Sir Richard, what think you? Have
    you beheld,   41
Or have you read or heard, or could you
  think?

Or do you almost think, although you see,
That you do see? Could thought, without
  this object,
Form such another? This is the very top,
The height, the crest, or crest unto the
  crest,   46
Of murder's arms; this is the bloodiest
  shame,
The wildest savagery, the vilest stroke,
That ever wall-ey'd wrath or staring rage
Presented to the tears of soft remorse. 50
  Pem. All murders past do stand excus'd
    in this;
And this, so sole and so unmatchable,
Shall give a holiness, a purity,
To the yet unbegotten sin of times,
And prove a deadly bloodshed but a jest, 55
Exampled by this heinous spectacle.
  Bast. It is a damned and a bloody work;
The graceless action of a heavy hand,
If that it be the work of any hand.
  Sal. If that it be the work of any hand! 60
We had a kind of light what would ensue.
It is the shameful work of Hubert's hand;
The practice and the purpose of the King;
From whose obedience I forbid my soul,
Kneeling before this ruin of sweet life, 65
And breathing to his breathless excellence
The incense of a vow, a holy vow,
Never to taste the pleasures of the world,
Never to be infected with delight,
Nor conversant with ease and idleness, 70
Till I have set a glory to this hand
By giving it the worship of revenge.
  Pem. ⎫ Our souls religiously confirm thy
  Big. ⎭ words.

Enter HUBERT.

  Hub. Lords, I am hot with haste in
    seeking you.
Arthur doth live; the King hath sent for
  you.   75
  Sal. O, he is bold, and blushes not at
    death!
Avaunt, thou hateful villain, get thee gone!
  Hub. I am no villain.
  Sal.   Must I rob the law?
              [*Drawing his sword.*
  Bast. Your sword is bright, sir; put it up
    again.
  Sal. Not till I sheathe it in a murderer's
    skin.   80
  Hub. Stand back, Lord Salisbury, stand
    back, I say;
By heaven, I think my sword's as sharp as
  yours.
I would not have you, lord, forget yourself,
Nor tempt the danger of my true defence;
Lest I, by marking of your rage, forget 85
Your worth, your greatness, and nobility.
  Big. Out, dunghill! Dar'st thou brave a
    nobleman?
  Hub. Not for my life; but yet I dare
    defend

My innocent life against an emperor.
  Sal. Thou art a murderer.
  Hub.   Do not prove me so.
Yet I am none. Whose tongue soe'er speaks
    false,   91
Not truly speaks ; who speaks not truly,
    lies.
  Pem. Cut him to pieces.
  Bast.   Keep the peace, I say.
  Sal. Stand by, or I shall gall you,
    Faulconbridge.
  Bast. Thou wert better gall the devil,
    Salisbury.   95
If thou but frown on me, or stir thy foot,
Or teach thy hasty spleen to do me shame,
I'll strike thee dead. Put up thy sword
    betime ;
Or I'll so maul you and your toasting-iron
That you shall think the devil is come from
    hell.   100
  Big. What wilt thou do, renowned
    Faulconbridge ?
Second a villain and a murderer ?
  Hub. Lord Bigot, I am none.
  Big.   Who kill'd this prince ?
  Hub. 'Tis not an hour since I left him
    well.   104
I honour'd him, I lov'd him, and will weep
My date of life out for his sweet life's loss.
  Sal. Trust not those cunning waters of
    his eyes,
For villainy is not without such rheum ;
And he, long traded in it, makes it seem
Like rivers of remorse and innocency.   110
Away with me, all you whose souls abhor
Th' uncleanly savours of a slaughter-house;
For I am stifled with this smell of sin.
  Big. Away toward Bury, to the Dauphin
    there !   114
  Pem. There tell the King he may inquire
    us out.   [*Exeunt Lords.*
  Bast. Here's a good world ! Knew you
    of this fair work ?
Beyond the infinite and boundless reach
Of mercy, if thou didst this deed of death,
Art thou damn'd, Hubert.
  Hub.   Do but hear me, sir.
  Bast. Ha ! I'll tell thee what :   120
Thou'rt damn'd as black—nay, nothing is
    so black—
Thou art more deep damn'd than Prince
    Lucifer ;
There is not yet so ugly a fiend of hell
As thou shalt be, if thou didst kill this child.
  Hub. Upon my soul—
  Bast.   If thou didst but consent 125
To this most cruel act, do but despair ;
And if thou want'st a cord, the smallest
    thread
That ever spider twisted from her womb
Will serve to strangle thee ; a rush will be
    a beam
To hang thee on ; or wouldst thou drown
    thyself,   130

Put but a little water in a spoon
And it shall be as all the ocean,
Enough to stifle such a villain up.
I do suspect thee very grievously.
  Hub. If I in act, consent, or sin of
    thought,   135
Be guilty of the stealing that sweet breath
Which was embounded in this beauteous
    clay,
Let hell want pains enough to torture me !
I left him well.
  Bast.   Go, bear him in thine arms.
I am amaz'd, methinks, and lose my way
Among the thorns and dangers of this
    world.   141
How easy dost thou take all England up !
From forth this morsel of dead royalty
The life, the right, and truth of all this
    realm
Is fled to heaven ; and England now is left
To tug and scamble, and to part by th'
    teeth   146
The unowed interest of proud-swelling
    state.
Now for the bare-pick'd bone of majesty
Doth dogged war bristle his angry crest
And snarleth in the gentle eyes of peace ; 150
Now powers from home and discontents at
    home
Meet in one line ; and vast confusion waits,
As doth a raven on a sick-fall'n beast,
The imminent decay of wrested pomp.
Now happy he whose cloak and cincture can
Hold out this tempest. Bear away that
    child,   156
And follow me with speed. I'll to the King ;
A thousand businesses are brief in hand,
And heaven itself doth frown upon the land.
                  [*Exeunt.*

ACT FIVE

SCENE I. *England. King John's palace.*

Enter KING JOHN, PANDULPH, *and*
    Attendants.

  K. John. Thus have I yielded up into
    your hand
The circle of my glory.
  Pand. [*Gives back the crown*] Take again
From this my hand, as holding of the Pope,
Your sovereign greatness and authority.
  K. John. Now keep your holy word ; go
    meet the French ;   5
And from his Holiness use all your power
To stop their marches fore we are inflam'd.
Our discontented counties do revolt ;
Our people quarrel with obedience,
Swearing allegiance and the love of soul 10
To stranger blood, to foreign royalty.
This inundation of mistemp'red humour
Rests by you only to be qualified.
Then pause not ; for the present time's so
    sick

That present med'cine must be minist'red
Or overthrow incurable ensues.   16
   Pand. It was my breath that blew this
     tempest up,
Upon your stubborn usage of the Pope ;
But since you are a gentle convertite,
My tongue shall hush again this storm of
     war   20
And make fair weather in your blust'ring
     land.
On this Ascension-day, remember well,
Upon your oath of service to the Pope,
Go I to make the French lay down their
     arms.   [*Exit.*
   K. John. Is this Ascension-day ? Did not
     the prophet   25
Say that before Ascension-day at noon
My crown I should give off ? Even so I
     have.
I did suppose it should be on constraint ;
But, heaven be thank'd, it is but voluntary.

     Enter the BASTARD.

   Bast. All Kent hath yielded ; nothing
     there holds out   30
But Dover Castle. London hath receiv'd,
Like a kind host, the Dauphin and his
     powers.
Your nobles will not hear you, but are gone
To offer service to your enemy ;   34
And wild amazement hurries up and down
The little number of your doubtful friends.
   K. John. Would not my lords return to
     me again
After they heard young Arthur was alive ?
   Bast. They found him dead, and cast into
     the streets,
An empty casket, where the jewel of life   40
By some damn'd hand was robb'd and ta'en
     away.
   K. John. That villain Hubert told me he
     did live.
   Bast. So, on my soul, he did, for aught
     he knew.
But wherefore do you droop ? Why look
     you sad ?
Be great 'n act, as you have been in
     thought ;   45
Let not the world see fear and sad distrust
Govern the motion of a kingly eye.
Be stirring as the time ; be fire with fire ;
Threaten the threat'ner, and outface the
     brow   49
Of bragging horror ; so shall inferior eyes,
That borrow their behaviours from the
     great,
Grow great by your example and put on
The dauntless spirit of resolution.
Away, and glister like the god of war
When he intendeth to become the field ;   55
Show boldness and aspiring confidence.
What, shall they seek the lion in his den,
And fright him there, and make him
     tremble there ?

O, let it not be said ! Forage, and run   59
To meet displeasure farther from the doors
And grapple with him ere he come so nigh.
   K. John. The legate of the Pope hath
     been with me,
And I have made a happy peace with him ;
And he hath promis'd to dismiss the powers
Led by the Dauphin.
   Bast.   O inglorious league !   65
Shall we, upon the footing of our land,
Send fair-play orders, and make com-
     promise,
Insinuation, parley, and base truce,
To arms invasive ? Shall a beardless boy,
A cock'red silken wanton, brave our fields
And flesh his spirit in a warlike soil,   71
Mocking the air with colours idly spread,
And find no check ? Let us, my liege, to
     arms.
Perchance the Cardinal cannot make your
     peace ;
Or, if he do, let it at least be said   75
They saw we had a purpose of defence.
   K. John. Have thou the ordering of this
     present time.
   Bast. Away, then, with good courage !
     Yet, I know
Our party may well meet a prouder foe.
                   [*Exeunt.*

SCENE II. *England. The Dauphin's camp
    at Saint Edmundsbury.*

Enter, in arms, LEWIS, SALISBURY, MELUN,
   PEMBROKE, BIGOT, *and* Soldiers.

   Lew. My Lord Melun, let this be copied
     out
And keep it safe for our remembrance ;
Return the precedent to these lords again,
That, having our fair order written down,
Both they and we, perusing o'er these
     notes,   5
May know wherefore we took the sacra-
     ment,
And keep our faiths firm and inviolable.
   Sal. Upon our sides it never shall be
     broken.
And, noble Dauphin, albeit we swear
A voluntary zeal and an unurg'd faith   10
To your proceedings ; yet, believe me,
     Prince,
I am not glad that such a sore of time
Should seek a plaster by contemn'd revolt,
And heal the inveterate canker of one
     wound
By making many. O, it grieves my soul   15
That I must draw this metal from my side
To be a widow-maker ! O, and there
Where honourable rescue and defence
Cries out upon the name of Salisbury !
But such is the infection of the time   20
That, for the health and physic of our right,
We cannot deal but with the very hand
Of stern injustice and confused wrong.

And is't not pity, O my grieved friends!
That we, the sons and children of this isle, 25
Were born to see so sad an hour as this;
Wherein we step after a stranger-march
Upon her gentle bosom, and fill up
Her enemies' ranks—I must withdraw and
    weep
Upon the spot of this enforced cause— 30
To grace the gentry of a land remote
And follow unacquainted colours here?
What, here? O nation, that thou couldst
    remove!
That Neptune's arms, who clippeth thee
    about,
Would bear thee from the knowledge of
    thyself   35
And grapple thee unto a pagan shore,
Where these two Christian armies might
    combine
The blood of malice in a vein of league,
And not to spend it so unneighbourly!
    Lew. A noble temper dost thou show in
    this;   40
And great affections wrestling in thy bosom
Doth make an earthquake of nobility.
O, what a noble combat hast thou fought
Between compulsion and a brave respect!
Let me wipe off this honourable dew 45
That silverly doth progress on thy cheeks.
My heart hath melted at a lady's tears,
Being an ordinary inundation;
But this effusion of such manly drops,
This show'r, blown up by tempest of the
    soul,   50
Startles mine eyes and makes me more
    amaz'd
Than had I seen the vaulty top of heaven
Figur'd quite o'er with burning meteors.
Lift up thy brow, renowned Salisbury,
And with a great heart heave away this
    storm;   55
Commend these waters to those baby eyes
That never saw the giant world enrag'd,
Nor met with fortune other than at feasts,
Full of warm blood, of mirth, of gossiping.
Come, come; for thou shalt thrust thy
    hand as deep   60
Into the purse of rich prosperity
As Lewis himself. So, nobles, shall you all,
That knit your sinews to the strength of
    mine.

Enter PANDULPH.

And even there, methinks, an angel spake:
Look where the holy legate comes apace, 65
To give us warrant from the hand of
    heaven
And on our actions set the name of right
With holy breath.
    Pand. Hail, noble prince of France!
The next is this: King John hath reconcil'd
Himself to Rome; his spirit is come in, 70
That so stood out against the holy church,
The great metropolis and see of Rome.

Therefore thy threat'ning colours now
    wind up
And tame the savage spirit of wild war,
That, like a lion fostered up at hand, 75
It may lie gently at the foot of peace
And be no further harmful than in show.
    Lew. Your Grace shall pardon me, I will
    not back:
I am too high-born to be propertied,
To be a secondary at control,   80
Or useful serving-man and instrument
To any sovereign state throughout the
    world.
Your breath first kindled the dead coal of
    wars
Between this chastis'd kingdom and myself
And brought in matter that should feed this
    fire;   85
And now 'tis far too huge to be blown out
With that same weak wind which en-
    kindled it.
You taught me how to know the face of
    right,
Acquainted me with interest to this land,
Yea, thrust this enterprise into my heart;
And come ye now to tell me John hath
    made   91
His peace with Rome? What is that peace
    to me?
I, by the honour of my marriage-bed,
After young Arthur, claim this land for mine;
And, now it is half-conquer'd, must I back
Because that John hath made his peace
    with Rome?   96
Am I Rome's slave? What penny hath
    Rome borne,
What men provided, what munition sent,
To underprop this action? Is't not I
That undergo this charge? Who else but I,
And such as to my claim are liable,   101
Sweat in this business and maintain this
    war?
Have I not heard these islanders shout out
'Vive le roi!' as I have bank'd their
    towns?
Have I not here the best cards for the game
To win this easy match, play'd for a crown?
And shall I now give o'er the yielded set?
No, no, on my soul, it never shall be said.
    Pand. You look but on the outside of this
    work.   109
    Lew. Outside or inside, I will not return
Till my attempt so much be glorified
As to my ample hope was promised
Before I drew this gallant head of war,
And cull'd these fiery spirits from the world
To outlook conquest, and to win renown 115
Even in the jaws of danger and of death.
                                    [*Trumpet sounds.*
What lusty trumpet thus doth summon us?

Enter the BASTARD, *attended.*

    Bast. According to the fair play of the
    world,

Let me have audience : I am sent to speak.
My holy lord of Milan, from the King   120
I come, to learn how you have dealt for
    him ;
And, as you answer, I do know the scope
And warrant limited unto my tongue.
  Pand. The Dauphin is too wilful-
    opposite,   124
And will not temporize with my entreaties ;
He flatly says he'll not lay down his
    arms.
  Bast. By all the blood that ever fury
    breath'd,
The youth says well. Now hear our English
    King ;
For thus his royalty doth speak in me.
He is prepar'd, and reason too he should. 130
This apish and unmannerly approach,
This harness'd masque and unadvised revel,
This unhair'd sauciness and boyish troops,
The King doth smile at ; and is well
    prepar'd
To whip this dwarfish war, these pigmy
    arms,   135
From out the circle of his territories.
That hand which had the strength, even at
    your door,
To cudgel you and make you take the hatch,
To dive like buckets in concealed wells,
To crouch in litter of your stable planks, 140
To lie like pawns lock'd up in chests and
    trunks,
To hug with swine, to seek sweet safety
    out
In vaults and prisons, and to thrill and
    shake
Even at the crying of your nation's crow,
Thinking this voice an armed Englishman—
Shall that victorious hand be feebled here
That in your chambers gave you chastise-
    ment ?   147
No. Know the gallant monarch is in arms
And like an eagle o'er his aery tow'rs
To souse annoyance that comes near his
    nest.   150
And you degenerate, you ingrate revolts,
You bloody Neroes, ripping up the womb
Of your dear mother England, blush for
    shame ;
For your own ladies and pale-visag'd maids,
Like Amazons, come tripping after drums,
Their thimbles into armed gauntlets change,
Their needles to lances, and their gentle
    hearts   157
To fierce and bloody inclination.
  Lew. There end thy brave, and turn thy
    face in peace ;
We grant thou canst outscold us. Fare thee
    well ;   160
We hold our time too precious to be spent
With such a brabbler.
  Pand.   Give me leave to speak.
  Bast. No, I will speak.
  Lew.   We will attend to neither.

Strike up the drums ; and let the tongue
    of war,
Plead for our interest and our being here.
  Bast. Indeed, your drums, being beaten,
    will cry out ;   166
And so shall you, being beaten. Do but
    start
An echo with the clamour of thy drum,
And even at hand a drum is ready
    brac'd
That shall reverberate all as loud as thine :
Sound but another, and another shall, 171
As loud as thine, rattle the welkin's ear
And mock the deep-mouth'd thunder ; for
    at hand—
Not trusting to this halting legate here,
Whom he hath us'd rather for sport than
    need—   175
Is warlike John ; and in his forehead sits
A bare-ribb'd death, whose office is this
    day
To feast upon whole thousands of the
    French.
  Lew. Strike up our drums to find this
    danger out.   179
  Bast. And thou shalt find it, Dauphin, do
    not doubt.   [*Exeunt.*

SCENE III.   *England. The field of battle.*

Alarums. Enter KING JOHN *and* HUBERT.

  K. John. How goes the day with us ? O,
    tell me, Hubert.
  Hub. Badly, I fear. How fares your
    Majesty ?
  K. John. This fever that hath troubled me
    so long
Lies heavy on me. O, my heart is sick !

Enter a Messenger.

  Mess. My lord, your valiant kinsman,
    Faulconbridge,   5
Desires your Majesty to leave the field
And send him word by me which way you
    go.
  K. John. Tell him, toward Swinstead, to
    the abbey there.
  Mess. Be of good comfort ; for the great
    supply
That was expected by the Dauphin here 10
Are wreck'd three nights ago on Goodwin
    Sands ;
This news was brought to Richard but even
    now.
The French fight coldly, and retire them-
    selves.
  K. John. Ay me, this tyrant fever burns
    me up
And will not let me welcome this good
    news.   15
Set on toward Swinstead ; to my litter
    straight ;
Weakness possesseth me, and I am faint.
                  [*Exeunt.*

SCENE IV. *England. Another part of the battlefield.*

Enter SALISBURY, PEMBROKE, *and* BIGOT.

Sal. I did not think the King so stor'd with friends.

Pem. Up once again; put spirit in the French;
If they miscarry, we miscarry too.

Sal. That misbegotten devil, Faulconbridge,
In spite of spite, alone upholds the day.   5

Pem. They say King John, sore sick, hath left the field.

Enter MELUN *wounded.*

Mel. Lead me to the revolts of England here.

Sal. When we were happy we had other names.

Pem. It is the Count Melun.

Sal.   Wounded to death.

Mel. Fly, noble English, you are bought and sold;   10
Unthread the rude eye of rebellion,
And welcome home again discarded faith.
Seek out King John, and fall before his feet;
For if the French be lords of this loud day,
He means to recompense the pains you take
By cutting off your heads. Thus hath he sworn,   16
And I with him, and many moe with me,
Upon the altar at Saint Edmundsbury;
Even on that altar where we swore to you
Dear amity and everlasting love.   20

Sal. May this be possible? May this be true?

Mel. Have I not hideous death within my view,
Retaining but a quantity of life,
Which bleeds away even as a form of wax
Resolveth from his figure 'gainst the fire?
What in the world should make me now deceive,   26
Since I must lose the use of all deceit?
Why should I then be false, since it is true
That I must die here, and live hence by truth?
I say again, if Lewis do win the day,   30
He is forsworn if e'er those eyes of yours
Behold another day break in the east;
But even this night, whose black contagious breath
Already smokes about the burning crest
Of the old, feeble, and day-wearied sun,   35
Even this ill night, your breathing shall expire,
Paying the fine of rated treachery
Even with a treacherous fine of all your lives,
If Lewis by your assistance win the day.
Commend me to one Hubert, with your king;   40

The love of him—and this respect besides,
For that my grandsire was an Englishman—
Awakes my conscience to confess all this.
In lieu whereof, I pray you, bear me hence
From forth the noise and rumour of the field,   45
Where I may think the remnant of my thoughts
In peace, and part this body and my soul
With contemplation and devout desires.

Sal. We do believe thee; and beshrew my soul
But I do love the favour and the form   50
Of this most fair occasion, by the which
We will untread the steps of damned flight,
And like a bated and retired flood,
Leaving our rankness and irregular course,
Stoop low within those bounds we have o'erlook'd,   55
And calmly run on in obedience
Even to our ocean, to our great King John.
My arm shall give thee help to bear thee hence;
For I do see the cruel pangs of death
Right in thine eye. Away, my friends!
New flight,   60
And happy newness, that intends old right.
                        [*Exeunt, leading off* Melun.

SCENE V. *England. The French camp.*

Enter LEWIS *and his* Train.

Lew. The sun of heaven, methought, was loath to set,
But stay'd and made the western welkin blush,
When English measure backward their own ground
In faint retire. O, bravely came we off,
When with a volley of our needless shot,   5
After such bloody toil, we bid good night;
And wound our tott'ring colours clearly up,
Last in the field and almost lords of it!

Enter a Messenger.

Mess. Where is my prince, the Dauphin?

Lew.   Here; what news?

Mess. The Count Melun is slain; the English lords   10
By his persuasion are again fall'n off,
And your supply, which you have wish'd so long,
Are cast away and sunk on Goodwin Sands.

Lew. Ah, foul shrewd news! Beshrew thy very heart!
I did not think to be so sad to-night   15
As this hath made me. Who was he that said
King John did fly an hour or two before
The stumbling night did part our weary pow'rs?

Mess. Whoever spoke it, it is true, my lord.

Bast. O, let us pay the time but needful woe,   110
Since it hath been beforehand with our griefs.
This England never did, nor never shall,
Lie at the proud foot of a conqueror,
But when it first did help to wound itself.
Now these her princes are come home again,   115
Come the three corners of the world in arms,
And we shall shock them. Nought shall make us rue,
If England to itself do rest but true.

[Exeunt.

KING RICHARD THE SECOND

DRAMATIS PERSONÆ

KING RICHARD THE SECOND.
JOHN OF GAUNT, *Duke of* Lancaster,
EDMUND OF LANGLEY, *Duke of York.* } *uncles to the King.*
HENRY, *surnamed* BOLINGBROKE, *Duke of Hereford, son of John of Gaunt, afterwards King Henry IV.*
DUKE OF AUMERLE, *son of the Duke of York.*
THOMAS MOWBRAY, *Duke of Norfolk.*
DUKE OF SURREY.
EARL OF SALISBURY.
EARL BERKELEY.
BUSHY,
BAGOT, } *favourites of King Richard.*
GREEN,
EARL OF NORTHUMBERLAND.
HENRY PERCY, *surnamed* HOTSPUR, *his son.*

LORD ROSS.
LORD WILLOUGHBY.
LORD FITZWATER.
BISHOP OF CARLISLE.
ABBOT OF WESTMINSTER.
LORD MARSHAL.
SIR STEPHEN SCROOP.
SIR PIERCE OF EXTON.
Captain *of a band of Welshmen.*
Two Gardeners.

QUEEN *to King Richard.*
DUCHESS OF YORK.
DUCHESS OF GLOUCESTER, *widow of Thomas of Woodstock, Duke of Gloucester.*
Lady *attending on the Queen.*

Lords, Heralds, Officers, Soldiers, Keeper, Messenger, Groom, *and other* Attendants.

THE SCENE : *England and Wales.*

ACT ONE

SCENE I. *London. The palace.*

Enter KING RICHARD, JOHN OF GAUNT, *with other* Nobles *and* Attendants.

K. Rich. Old John of Gaunt, time-honoured Lancaster,
Hast thou, according to thy oath and band,
Brought hither Henry Hereford, thy bold son,
Here to make good the boist'rous late appeal,
Which then our leisure would not let us hear, 5
Against the Duke of Norfolk, Thomas Mowbray ?
Gaunt. I have, my liege.
K. Rich. Tell me, moreover, hast thou sounded him
If he appeal the Duke on ancient malice,
Or worthily, as a good subject should, 10
On some known ground of treachery in him ?
Gaunt. As near as I could sift him on that argument,
On some apparent danger seen in him
Aim'd at your Highness—no inveterate malice.
K. Rich. Then call them to our presence : face to face 15
And frowning brow to brow, ourselves will hear
The accuser and the accused freely speak.
High-stomach'd are they both and full of ire,
In rage, deaf as the sea, hasty as fire.

Enter BOLINGBROKE *and* MOWBRAY.

Boling. Many years of happy days befall
My gracious sovereign, my most loving liege ! 21
Mow. Each day still better other's happiness
Until the heavens, envying earth's good hap,
Add an immortal title to your crown !
K. Rich. We thank you both ; yet one but flatters us, 25
As well appeareth by the cause you come ;
Namely, to appeal each other of high treason.
Cousin of Hereford, what dost thou object
Against the Duke of Norfolk, Thomas Mowbray ?
Boling. First—heaven be the record to my speech ! 30
In the devotion of a subject's love,
Tend'ring the precious safety of my prince,
And free from other misbegotten hate,
Come I appellant to this princely presence.
Now, Thomas Mowbray, do I turn to thee,
And mark my greeting well ; for what I speak 36
My body shall make good upon this earth,
Or my divine soul answer it in heaven—
Thou art a traitor and a miscreant,
Too good to be so, and too bad to live, 40
Since the more fair and crystal is the sky,
The uglier seem the clouds that in it fly.
Once more, the more to aggravate the note,

With a foul traitor's name stuff I thy
    throat ;
And wish—so please my sovereign—ere I
    move,   45
What my tongue speaks, my right drawn
    sword may prove.
   Mow. Let not my cold words here accuse
    my zeal.
'Tis not the trial of a woman's war,
The bitter clamour of two eager tongues,
Can arbitrate this cause betwixt us twain ;
The blood is hot that must be cool'd for
    this.   51
Yet can I not of such tame patience boast
As to be hush'd and nought at all to say.
First, the fair reverence of your Highness
    curbs me
From giving reins and spurs to my free
    speech ;   55
Which else would post until it had return'd
These terms of treason doubled down his
    throat.
Setting aside his high blood's royalty,
And let him be no kinsman to my liege,
I do defy him, and I spit at him,   60
Call him a slanderous coward and a villain ;
Which to maintain, I would allow him odds
And meet him, were I tied to run afoot
Even to the frozen ridges of the Alps,
Or any other ground inhabitable   65
Where ever Englishman durst set his foot.
Meantime let this defend my loyalty—
By all my hopes, most falsely doth he lie.
   Boling. Pale trembling coward, there I
    throw my gage,
Disclaiming here the kindred of the King ;
And lay aside my high blood's royalty,   71
Which fear, not reverence, makes thee to
    except.
If guilty dread have left thee so much
    strength
As to take up mine honour's pawn, then
    stoop.
By that and all the rites of knighthood else
Will I make good against thee, arm to
    arm,   76
What I have spoke or thou canst worse
    devise.
   Mow. I take it up ; and by that sword I
    swear
Which gently laid my knighthood on my
    shoulder
I'll answer thee in any fair degree   80
Or chivalrous design of knightly trial ;
And when I mount, alive may I not light
If I be traitor or unjustly fight !
   K. Rich. What doth our cousin lay to
    Mowbray's charge ?
It must be great that can inherit us   85
So much as of a thought of ill in him.
   Boling. Look what I speak, my life shall
    prove it true—
That Mowbray hath receiv'd eight thousand
    nobles

In name of lendings for your Highness'
    soldiers,
The which he hath detain'd for lewd em-
    ployments   90
Like a false traitor and injurious villain.
Besides, I say and will in battle prove—
Or here, or elsewhere to the furthest verge
That ever was survey'd by English eye—
That all the treasons for these eighteen
    years   95
Complotted and contrived in this land
Fetch from false Mowbray their first head
    and spring.
Further I say, and further will maintain
Upon his bad life to make all this good,
That he did plot the Duke of Gloucester's
    death,   100
Suggest his soon-believing adversaries,
And consequently, like a traitor coward,
Sluic'd out his innocent soul through
    streams of blood ;
Which blood, like sacrificing Abel's, cries,
Even from the tongueless caverns of the
    earth,   105
To me for justice and rough chastisement ;
And, by the glorious worth of my descent,
This arm shall do it, or this life be spent.
   K. Rich. How high a pitch his resolution
    soars !
Thomas of Norfolk, what say'st thou to
    this ?   110
   Mow. O, let my sovereign turn away his
    face
And bid his ears a little while be deaf,
Till I have told this slander of his blood
How God and good men hate so foul a liar.
   K. Rich. Mowbray, impartial are our eyes
    and ears.   115
Were he my brother, nay, my kingdom's
    heir,
As he is but my father's brother's son,
Now by my sceptre's awe I make a vow,
Such neighbour nearness to our sacred
    blood   119
Should nothing privilege him nor partialize
The unstooping firmness of my upright soul.
He is our subject, Mowbray ; so art thou :
Free speech and fearless I to thee allow.
   Mow. Then, Bolingbroke, as low as to
    thy heart,
Through the false passage of thy throat,
    thou liest.   125
Three parts of that receipt I had for Calais
Disburs'd I duly to his Highness' soldiers ;
The other part reserv'd I by consent,
For that my sovereign liege was in my debt
Upon remainder of a dear account   130
Since last I went to France to fetch his
    queen :
Now swallow down that lie. For Glou-
    cester's death—
I slew him not, but to my own disgrace
Neglected my sworn duty in that case.
For you, my noble Lord of Lancaster,   135

The honourable father to my foe,
Once did I lay an ambush for your life,
A trespass that doth vex my grieved soul ;
But ere I last receiv'd the sacrament
I did confess it, and exactly begg'd   140
Your Grace's pardon ; and I hope I had it.
This is my fault. As for the rest appeal'd,
It issues from the rancour of a villain,
A recreant and most degenerate traitor ;
Which in myself I boldly will defend,   145
And interchangeably hurl down my gage
Upon this overweening traitor's foot
To prove myself a loyal gentleman
Even in the best blood chamber'd in his
    bosom.
In haste whereof, most heartily I pray   150
Your Highness to assign our trial day.
    K. Rich. Wrath-kindled gentlemen, be
        rul'd by me ;
Let's purge this choler without letting
        blood—
This we prescribe, though no physician ;
Deep malice makes too deep incision.   155
Forget, forgive ; conclude and be agreed :
Our doctors say this is no month to bleed.
Good uncle, let this end where it begun ;
We'll calm the Duke of Norfolk, you your
        son.
    Gaunt. To be a make-peace shall become
        my age.   160
Throw down, my son, the Duke of Norfolk's
        gage.
    K. Rich. And, Norfolk, throw down his.
    Gaunt.   When, Harry, when ?
Obedience bids I should not bid again.
    K. Rich. Norfolk, throw down ; we bid.
        There is no boot.
    Mow. Myself I throw, dread sovereign, at
        thy foot ;   165
My life thou shalt command, but not my
        shame :
The one my duty owes ; but my fair name,
Despite of death, that lives upon my grave
To dark dishonour's use thou shalt not
        have.
I am disgrac'd, impeach'd, and baffl'd here ;
Pierc'd to the soul with slander's venom'd
        spear,   171
The which no balm can cure but his heart-
        blood
Which breath'd this poison.
    K. Rich.   Rage must be withstood :
Give me his gage—lions make leopards
        tame.
    Mow. Yea, but not change his spots.
        Take but my shame,   175
And I resign my gage. My dear dear lord,
The purest treasure mortal times afford
Is spotless reputation ; that away,
Men are but gilded loam or painted clay.
A jewel in a ten-times barr'd-up chest   180
Is a bold spirit in a loyal breast.
Mine honour is my life ; both grow in one ;
Take honour from me, and my life is done :

Then, dear my liege, mine honour let me
    try ;
In that I live, and for that will I die.   185
    K. Rich. Cousin, throw up your gage ; do
        you begin.
    Boling. O, God defend my soul from such
        deep sin !
Shall I seem crest-fallen in my father's
    sight ?
Or with pale beggar-fear impeach my
    height
Before this outdar'd dastard ? Ere my
    tongue   190
Shall wound my honour with such feeble
    wrong
Or sound so base a parle, my teeth shall
    tear
The slavish motive of recanting fear,
And spit it bleeding in his high disgrace,
Where shame doth harbour, even in Mow-
    bray's face.   [*Exit Gaunt.*
    K. Rich. We were not born to sue, but to
        command ;   196
Which since we cannot do to make you
    friends,
Be ready, as your lives shall answer it,
At Coventry, upon Saint Lambert's day.
There shall your swords and lances
    arbitrate   200
The swelling difference of your settled
    hate ;
Since we can not atone you, we shall see
Justice design the victor's chivalry.
Lord Marshal, command our officers-at-
    arms
Be ready to direct these home alarms.   205
                              [*Exeunt.*

SCENE II. *London. The Duke of Lancaster's
    palace.*

Enter JOHN OF GAUNT *with the* DUCHESS OF
    GLOUCESTER.

    Gaunt. Alas, the part I had in Wood-
        stock's blood
Doth more solicit me than your exclaims
To stir against the butchers of his life !
But since correction lieth in those hands
Which made the fault that we cannot
    correct,   5
Put we our quarrel to the will of heaven ;
Who, when they see the hours ripe on
    earth,
Will rain hot vengeance on offenders' heads.
    Duch. Finds brotherhood in thee no
        sharper spur ?
Hath love in thy old blood no living fire ?
Edward's seven sons, whereof thyself art
    one,   11
Were as seven vials of his sacred blood,
Or seven fair branches springing from one
    root.
Some of those seven are dried by nature's
    course,

Some of those branches by the Destinies
 cut ; 15
But Thomas, my dear lord, my life, my
 Gloucester,
One vial full of Edward's sacred blood,
One flourishing branch of his most royal
 root,
Is crack'd, and all the precious liquor spilt ;
Is hack'd down, and all his summer leaves all
 faded, 20
By envy's hand and murder's bloody axe.
Ah, Gaunt, his blood was thine ! That bed,
 that womb,
That mettle, that self mould, that fashion'd
 thee,
Made him a man ; and though thou livest
 and breathest,
Yet art thou slain in him. Thou dost
 consent 25
In some large measure to thy father's death
In that thou seest thy wretched brother
 die,
Who was the model of thy father's life.
Call it not patience, Gaunt—it is despair ;
In suff'ring thus thy brother to be
 slaught'red, 30
Thou showest the naked pathway to thy
 life,
Teaching stern murder how to butcher thee.
That which in mean men we entitle
 patience
Is pale cold cowardice in noble breasts.
What shall I say ? To safeguard thine own
 life 35
The best way is to venge my Gloucester's
 death.
 Gaunt. God's is the quarrel ; for God's
 substitute,
His deputy anointed in His sight,
Hath caus'd his death ; the which if
 wrongfully,
Let heaven revenge ; for I may never lift 40
An angry arm against His minister.
 Duch. Where then, alas, may I complain
 myself ?
 Gaunt. To God, the widow's champion
 and defence.
 Duch. Why then, I will. Farewell, old
 Gaunt.
Thou goest to Coventry, there to behold 45
Our cousin Hereford and fell Mowbray
 fight.
O, sit my husband's wrongs on Hereford's
 spear,
That it may enter butcher Mowbray's
 breast !
Or, if misfortune miss the first career,
Be Mowbray's sins so heavy in his bosom 50
That they may break his foaming courser's
 back
And throw the rider headlong in the lists,
A caitiff recreant to my cousin Hereford !
Farewell, old Gaunt ; thy sometimes
 brother's wife,

With her companion, Grief, must end her
 life. 55
 Gaunt. Sister, farewell ; I must to
 Coventry.
As much good stay with thee as go with me !
 Duch. Yet one word more—grief boun-
 deth where it falls,
Not with the empty hollowness, but weight.
I take my leave before I have begun, 60
For sorrow ends not when it seemeth done.
Commend me to thy brother, Edmund
 York.
Lo, this is all—nay, yet depart not so ;
Though this be all, do not so quickly go ;
I shall remember more. Bid him—ah,
 what ?— 65
With all good speed at Plashy visit me.
Alack, and what shall good old York there
 see
But empty lodgings and unfurnish'd walls,
Unpeopled offices, untrodden stones ?
And what hear there for welcome but my
 groans ? 70
Therefore commend me ; let him not come
 there
To seek out sorrow that dwells every where.
Desolate, desolate, will I hence and die ;
The last leave of thee takes my weeping
 eye. [*Exeunt.*

SCENE III. *The lists at Coventry.*

Enter the LORD MARSHAL *and the* DUKE
OF AUMERLE.

 Mar. My Lord Aumerle, is Harry Hereford arm'd ?
 Aum. Yea, at all points ; and longs to
 enter in.
 Mar. The Duke of Norfolk, sprightfully
 and bold,
Stays but the summons of the appellant's
 trumpet.
 Aum. Why then, the champions are
 prepar'd, and stay 5
For nothing but his Majesty's approach.

The trumpets sound, and the KING *enters
with his nobles,* GAUNT, BUSHY, BAGOT,
GREEN, *and Others.* *When they are set,
enter* MOWBRAY, DUKE OF NORFOLK, *in
arms, defendant, and a Herald.*

 K. Rich. Marshal, demand of yonder
 champion
The cause of his arrival here in arms ;
Ask him his name ; and orderly proceed
To swear him in the justice of his cause. 10
 Mar. In God's name and the King's, say
 who thou art,
And why thou comest thus knightly clad
 in arms,
Against what man thou com'st, and what
 thy quarrel.
Speak truly on thy knighthood and thy
 oath ;

As so defend thee heaven and thy valour !
Mow. My name is Thomas Mowbray,
    Duke of Norfolk;   16
Who hither come engaged by my oath—
Which God defend a knight should vio-
    late !—
Both to defend my loyalty and truth
To God, my King, and my succeeding issue,
Against the Duke of Hereford that appeals
    me;   21
And, by the grace of God and this mine
    arm,
To prove him, in defending of myself,
A traitor to my God, my King, and me.
And as I truly fight, defend me heaven ! 25

The trumpets sound. Enter BOLINGBROKE,
    DUKE OF HEREFORD, *appellant, in
    armour, and a* Herald.

  K. Rich. Marshal, ask yonder knight in
    arms,
Both who he is and why he cometh hither
Thus plated in habiliments of war;
And formally, according to our law,
Depose him in the justice of his cause.   30
  Mar. What is thy name? and wherefore
    com'st thou hither
Before King Richard in his royal lists?
Against whom comest thou? and what's
    thy quarrel?
Speak like a true knight, so defend thee
    heaven !
  Boling. Harry of Hereford, Lancaster,
    and Derby,   35
Am I; who ready here do stand in arms
To prove, by God's grace and my body's
    valour,
In lists on Thomas Mowbray, Duke of
    Norfolk,
That he is a traitor, foul and dangerous,
To God of heaven, King Richard, and to
    me.   40
And as I truly fight, defend me heaven !
  Mar. On pain of death, no person be so
    bold
Or daring-hardy as to touch the lists,
Except the Marshal and such officers
Appointed to direct these fair designs.   45
  Boling. Lord Marshal, let me kiss my
    sovereign's hand,
And bow my knee before his Majesty;
For Mowbray and myself are like two
    men
That vow a long and weary pilgrimage.
Then let us take a ceremonious leave   50
And loving farewell of our several friends.
  Mar. The appellant in all duty greets
    your Highness,
And craves to kiss your hand and take his
    leave.
  K. Rich. We will descend and fold him
    in our arms.
Cousin of Hereford, as thy cause is right, 55
So be thy fortune in this royal fight !

Farewell, my blood; which if to-day thou
    shed,
Lament we may, but not revenge thee
    dead.
  Boling. O, let no noble eye profane a tear
For me, if I be gor'd with Mowbray's spear.
As confident as is the falcon's flight   61
Against a bird, do I with Mowbray fight.
My loving lord, I take my leave of you;
Of you, my noble cousin, Lord Aumerle;
Not sick, although I have to do with death,
But lusty, young, and cheerly drawing
    breath.   66
Lo, as at English feasts, so I regreet
The daintiest last, to make the end most
    sweet.
O thou, the earthly author of my blood,
Whose youthful spirit, in me regenerate, 70
Doth with a twofold vigour lift me up
To reach at victory above my head,
Add proof unto mine armour with thy
    prayers,
And with thy blessings steel my lance's
    point,
That it may enter Mowbray's waxen coat 75
And furbish new the name of John o'
    Gaunt,
Even in the lusty haviour of his son.
  Gaunt. God in thy good cause make thee
    prosperous !
Be swift like lightning in the execution,
And let thy blows, doubly redoubled,   80
Fall like amazing thunder on the casque
Of thy adverse pernicious enemy.
Rouse up thy youthful blood, be valiant,
    and live.
  Boling. Mine innocence and Saint George
    to thrive !
  Mow. However God or fortune cast my
    lot,   85
There lives or dies, true to King Richard's
    throne,
A loyal, just, and upright gentleman.
Never did captive with a freer heart
Cast off his chains of bondage, and embrace
His golden uncontroll'd enfranchisement, 90
More than my dancing soul doth celebrate
This feast of battle with mine adversary.
Most mighty liege, and my companion
    peers,
Take from my mouth the wish of happy
    years.
As gentle and as jocund as to jest   95
Go I to fight: truth hath a quiet breast.
  K. Rich. Farewell, my lord, securely I
    espy
Virtue with valour couched in thine eye.
Order the trial, Marshal, and begin.
  Mar. Harry of Hereford, Lancaster, and
    Derby,   100
Receive thy lance; and God defend the
    right !
  Boling. Strong as a tower in hope, I cry
    amen.

Mar. [*To an Officer*] Go bear this lance to
　　Thomas, Duke of Norfolk.
1 *Her.* Harry of Hereford, Lancaster, and
　　Derby,
Stands here for God, his sovereign, and
　　himself,　　　　　　　　　　105
On pain to be found false and recreant,
To prove the Duke of Norfolk, Thomas
　　Mowbray,
A traitor to his God, his King, and him;
And dares him to set forward to the fight.
2 *Her.* Here standeth Thomas Mowbray,
　　Duke of Norfolk,　　　　　110
On pain to be found false and recreant,
Both to defend himself, and to approve
Henry of Hereford, Lancaster, and Derby,
To God, his sovereign, and to him dis-
　　loyal,
Courageously and with a free desire　　115
Attending but the signal to begin.
Mar. Sound trumpets; and set forward,
　　combatants.　　　[*A charge sounded.*
Stay, the King hath thrown his warder
　　down.
K. Rich. Let them lay by their helmets
　　and their spears,
And both return back to their chairs again.
Withdraw with us; and let the trumpets
　　sound　　　　　　　　　121
While we return these dukes what we
　　decree.

*A long flourish, while the King consults
　　his Council.*

Draw near,
And list what with our council we have
　　done.
For that our kingdom's earth should not be
　　soil'd　　　　　　　　　125
With that dear blood which it hath fostered;
And for our eyes do hate the dire aspect
Of civil wounds plough'd up with neigh-
　　bours' sword;
And for we think the eagle-winged pride
Of sky-aspiring and ambitious thoughts,
With rival-hating envy, set on you　　131
To wake our peace, which in our country's
　　cradle
Draws the sweet infant breath of gentle
　　sleep;
Which so rous'd up with boist'rous un-
　　tun'd drums,
With harsh-resounding trumpets' dreadful
　　bray,　　　　　　　　　135
And grating shock of wrathful iron arms,
Might from our quiet confines fright fair
　　peace
And make us wade even in our kindred's
　　blood—
Therefore we banish you our territories.
You, cousin Hereford, upon pain of life,　140
Till twice five summers have enrich'd our
　　fields
Shall not regreet our fair dominions,

But tread the stranger paths of banish-
　　ment.
Boling. Your will be done. This must my
　　comfort be—
That sun that warms you here shall shine
　　on me,　　　　　　　　　145
And those his golden beams to you here lent
Shall point on me and gild my banishment.
K. Rich. Norfolk, for thee remains a
　　heavier doom,
Which I with some unwillingness pro-
　　nounce:
The sly slow hours shall not determinate　150
The dateless limit of thy dear exile;
The hopeless word of ' never to return '
Breathe I against thee, upon pain of life.
Mow. A heavy sentence, my most
　　sovereign liege,
And all unlook'd for from your Highness'
　　mouth.　　　　　　　　155
A dearer merit, not so deep a maim
As to be cast forth in the common air,
Have I deserved at your Highness' hands.
The language I have learnt these forty
　　years,
My native English, now I must forgo;　160
And now my tongue's use is to me no more
Than an unstringed viol or a harp;
Or like a cunning instrument cas'd up
Or, being open, put into his hands　164
That knows no touch to tune the harmony.
Within my mouth you have engaol'd my
　　tongue,
Doubly portcullis'd with my teeth and lips;
And dull, unfeeling, barren ignorance
Is made my gaoler to attend on me.
I am too old to fawn upon a nurse,　　170
Too far in years to be a pupil now.
What is thy sentence, then, but speechless
　　death,
Which robs my tongue from breathing
　　native breath?
K. Rich. It boots thee not to be com-
　　passionate;　　　　　　　174
After our sentence plaining comes too late.
Mow. Then thus I turn me from my
　　country's light,
To dwell in solemn shades of endless night.
K. Rich. Return again, and take an oath
　　with thee.
Lay on our royal sword your banish'd
　　hands;
Swear by the duty that you owe to God,　180
Our part therein we banish with yourselves,
To keep the oath that we administer:
You never shall, so help you truth and
　　God,
Embrace each other's love in banishment;
Nor never look upon each other's face;　185
Nor never write, regreet, nor reconcile
This louring tempest of your home-bred
　　hate;
Nor never by advised purpose meet
To plot, contrive, or complot any ill,

'Gainst us, our state, our subjects, or our
   land.   190
  Boling. I swear.
  Mow. And I, to keep all this.
  Boling. Norfolk, so far as to mine enemy :
By this time, had the King permitted us,
One of our souls had wand'red in the air,
Banish'd this frail sepulchre of our flesh,
As now our flesh is banish'd from this
   land—
Confess thy treasons ere thou fly the realm ;
Since thou hast far to go, bear not along
The clogging burden of a guilty soul.   200
  Mow. No, Bolingbroke ; if ever I were
   traitor,
My name be blotted from the book of life,
And I from heaven banish'd as from hence !
But what thou art, God, thou, and I, do
   know ?   204
And all too soon, I fear, the King shall rue.
Farewell, my liege. Now no way can I stray :
Save back to England, all the world's my
   way.   [*Exit.*
  K. Rich. Uncle, even in the glasses of
   thine eyes
I see thy grieved heart. Thy sad aspect
Hath from the number of his banish'd years
Pluck'd four away. [*To Bolingbroke*] Six
   frozen winters spent,   211
Return with welcome home from banish-
   ment.
  Boling. How long a time lies in one little
   word !
Four lagging winters and four wanton
   springs
End in a word : such is the breath of Kings.
  Gaunt. I thank my liege that in regard
   of me   216
He shortens four years of my son's exile ;
But little vantage shall I reap thereby,
For ere the six years that he hath to
   spend
Can change their moons and bring their
   times about,   220
My oil-dried lamp and time-bewasted light
Shall be extinct with age and endless night ;
My inch of taper will be burnt and done,
And blindfold death not let me see my son.
  K. Rich. Why, uncle, thou hast many
   years to live.   225
  Gaunt. But not a minute, King, that
   thou canst give :
Shorten my days thou canst with sullen
   sorrow
And pluck nights from me, but not lend a
   morrow ;
Thou canst help time to furrow me with age,
But stop no wrinkle in his pilgrimage ;   230
Thy word is current with him for my death,
But dead, thy kingdom cannot buy my
   breath.
  K. Rich. Thy son is banish'd upon good
   advice,
Whereto thy tongue a party-verdict gave.

Why at our justice seem'st thou then to
   lour ?   235
  Gaunt. Things sweet to taste prove in
   digestion sour.
You urg'd me as a judge ; but I had rather
You would have bid me argue like a father.
O, had it been a stranger, not my child,
To smooth his fault I should have been
   more mild.   240
A partial slander sought I to avoid,
And in the sentence my own life destroy'd.
Alas, I look'd when some of you should say
I was too strict to make mine own away ;
But you gave leave to my unwilling
   tongue   245
Against my will to do myself this wrong.
  K. Rich. Cousin, farewell ; and, uncle,
   bid him so.
Six years we banish him, and he shall go.
     [*Flourish. Exit King with train.*
  Aum. Cousin, farewell ; what presence
   must not know,
From where you do remain let paper show.
  Mar. My lord, no leave take I, for I will
   ride   251
As far as land will let me by your side.
  Gaunt. O, to what purpose dost thou
   hoard thy words,
That thou returnest no greeting to thy
   friends ?
  Boling. I have too few to take my leave
   of you,   255
When the tongue's office should be prodigal
To breathe the abundant dolour of the
   heart.
  Gaunt. Thy grief is but thy absence for a
   time.
  Boling. Joy absent, grief is present for
   that time.
  Gaunt. What is six winters ? They are
   quickly gone.   260
  Boling. To men in joy ; but grief makes
   one hour ten.
  Gaunt. Call it a travel that thou tak'st for
   pleasure.
  Boling. My heart will sigh when I miscall
   it so,
Which finds it an enforced pilgrimage.
  Gaunt. The sullen passage of thy weary
   steps   265
Esteem as foil wherein thou art to set
The precious jewel of thy home return.
  Boling. Nay, rather, every tedious stride
   I make
Will but remember me what a deal of world
I wander from the jewels that I love.   270
Must I not serve a long apprenticehood
To foreign passages ; and in the end,
Having my freedom, boast of nothing else
But that I was a journeyman to grief ?
  Gaunt. All places that the eye of heaven
   visits   275
Are to a wise man ports and happy havens.
Teach thy necessity to reason thus :

There is no virtue like necessity.
Think not the King did banish thee,
But thou the King. Woe doth the heavier
    sit   280
Where it perceives it is but faintly borne.
Go, say I sent thee forth to purchase
    honour,
And not the King exil'd thee ; or suppose
Devouring pestilence hangs in our air
And thou art flying to a fresher clime. 285
Look what thy soul holds dear, imagine it
To lie that way thou goest, not whence
    thou com'st.
Suppose the singing birds musicians,
The grass whereon thou tread'st the pres-
    ence strew'd,
The flowers fair ladies, and thy steps no
    more   290
Than a delightful measure or a dance ;
For gnarling sorrow hath less power to bite
The man that mocks at it and sets it light.
  Boling. O, who can hold a fire in his hand
By thinking on the frosty Caucasus ? 295
Or cloy the hungry edge of appetite
By bare imagination of a feast ?
Or wallow naked in December snow
By thinking on fantastic summer's heat?
O, no ! the apprehension of the good 300
Gives but the greater feeling to the worse.
Fell sorrow's tooth doth never rankle more
Than when he bites, but lanceth not the
    sore.
  Gaunt. Come, come, my son, I'll bring
    thee on thy way.
Had I thy youth and cause, I would not
    stay.   305
  Boling. Then, England's ground, fare-
    well ; sweet soil, adieu ;
My mother, and my nurse, that bears me
    yet !
Where'er I wander, boast of this I can :
Though banish'd, yet a trueborn English
    man.   [*Exeunt.*

    SCENE IV. *London. The court.*

Enter the KING, *with* BAGOT *and* GREEN,
at one door ; and the DUKE OF AUMERLE
at another.

  K. Rich. We did observe.   Cousin
    Aumerle,
How far brought you high Hereford on his
    way ?
  Aum. I brought high Hereford, if you
    call him so,
But to the next high way, and there I left
    him.
  K. Rich. And say, what store of parting
    tears were shed ?   5
  Aum. Faith, none for me ; except the
    north-east wind,
Which then blew bitterly against our faces,
Awak'd the sleeping rheum, and so by
    chance

Did grace our hollow parting with a tear.
  K. Rich. What said our cousin when you
    parted with him ?   10
  Aum. ' Farewell.'
And, for my heart disdained that my tongue
Should so profane the word, that taught me
    craft
To counterfeit oppression of such grief
That words seem'd buried in my sorrow's
    grave.   15
Marry, would the word ' farewell ' have
    length'ned hours
And added years to his short banishment,
He should have had a volume of farewells ;
But since it would not, he had none of me.
  K. Rich. He is our cousin, cousin ; but
    'tis doubt,   20
When time shall call him home from
    banishment,
Whether our kinsman come to see his
    friends.
Ourself, and Bushy, Bagot here, and Green,
Observ'd his courtship to the common
    people ;   24
How he did seem to dive into their hearts
With humble and familiar courtesy ;
What reverence he did throw away on
    slaves,
Wooing poor craftsmen with the craft of
    smiles   28
And patient underbearing of his fortune,
As 'twere to banish their affects with him.
Off goes his bonnet to an oyster-wench ;
A brace of draymen bid God speed him well
And had the tribute of his supple knee,
With ' Thanks, my countrymen, my loving
    friends ' ;
As were our England in reversion his, 35
And he our subjects' next degree in hope.
  Green. Well, he is gone ; and with him go
    these thoughts !
Now for the rebels which stand out in
    Ireland,
Expedient manage must be made, my liege,
Ere further leisure yield them further
    means   40
For their advantage and your Highness'
    loss.
  K. Rich. We will ourself in person to this
    war ;
And, for our coffers, with too great a court
And liberal largess, are grown somewhat
    light,
We are enforc'd to farm our royal realm ; 45
The revenue whereof shall furnish us
For our affairs in hand. If that come short,
Our substitutes at home shall have blank
    charters ;
Whereto, when they shall know what men
    are rich,
They shall subscribe them for large sums
    of gold,   50
And send them after to supply our wants ;
For we will make for Ireland presently.

Enter BUSHY.

Bushy, what news ?
  Bushy. Old John of Gaunt is grievous
    sick, my lord,
Suddenly taken ; and hath sent post-haste
To entreat your Majesty to visit him.   56
  K. Rich. Where lies he ?
  Bushy. At Ely House.
  K. Rich. Now put it, God, in the
physician's mind
To help him to his grave immediately ! 60
The lining of his coffers shall make coats
To deck our soldiers for these Irish wars.
Come, gentlemen, let's all go visit him.
Pray God we may make haste, and come
    too late !   64
  All. Amen.   [*Exeunt.*

ACT TWO

SCENE I. *London.* *Ely House.*

Enter JOHN OF GAUNT, *sick, with the* DUKE
OF YORK, *etc.*

  Gaunt. Will the King come, that I may
    breathe my last
In wholesome counsel to his unstaid youth?
  York. Vex not yourself, nor strive not
    with your breath ;
For all in vain comes counsel to his ear.
  Gaunt. O, but they say the tongues of
    dying men   5
Enforce attention like deep harmony.
Where words are scarce, they are seldom
    spent in vain ;
For they breathe truth that breathe their
    words in pain.
He that no more must say is listen'd more
Than they whom youth and ease have
    taught to glose ;   10
More are men's ends mark'd than their lives
    before.
The setting sun, and music at the close,
As the last taste of sweets, is sweetest last,
Writ in remembrance more than things long
    past.
Though Richard my life's counsel would
    not hear,   15
My death's sad tale may yet undeaf his ear.
  York. No ; it is stopp'd with other
    flattering sounds,
As praises, of whose taste the wise are fond,
Lascivious metres, to whose venom sound
The open ear of youth doth always listen ;
Report of fashions in proud Italy,   21
Whose manners still our tardy apish nation
Limps after in base imitation.
Where doth the world thrust forth a
    vanity—
So it be new, there's no respect how vile—
That is not quickly buzz'd into his ears ?
Then all too late comes counsel to be heard
Where will doth mutiny with wit's regard.

Direct not him whose way himself will
    choose.
'Tis breath thou lack'st, and that breath
    wilt thou lose.   30
  Gaunt. Methinks I am a prophet new
    inspir'd,
And thus expiring do foretell of him :
His rash fierce blaze of riot cannot last,
For violent fires soon burn out themselves ;
Small showers last long, but sudden storms
    are short ;   35
He tires betimes that spurs too fast be-
    times ;
With eager feeding food doth choke the
    feeder ;
Light vanity, insatiate cormorant,
Consuming means, soon preys upon itself.
This royal throne of kings, this scept'red
    isle,   40
This earth of majesty, this seat of Mars,
This other Eden, demi-paradise,
This fortress built by Nature for herself
Against infection and the hand of war,
This happy breed of men, this little world,
This precious stone set in the silver sea, 46
Which serves it in the office of a wall,
Or as a moat defensive to a house,
Against the envy of less happier lands ;
This blessed plot, this earth, this realm,
    this England,   50
This nurse, this teeming womb of royal
    kings,
Fear'd by their breed, and famous by their
    birth,
Renowned for their deeds as far from home,
For Christian service and true chivalry,
As is the sepulchre in stubborn Jewry   55
Of the world's ransom, blessed Mary's Son ;
This land of such dear souls, this dear dear
    land,
Dear for her reputation through the world,
Is now leas'd out—I die pronouncing it—
Like to a tenement or pelting farm.   60
England, bound in with the triumphant
    sea,
Whose rocky shore beats back the envious
    siege
Of wat'ry Neptune, is now bound in with
    shame,
With inky blots and rotten parchment
    bonds ;
That England, that was wont to conquer
    others,   65
Hath made a shameful conquest of itself.
Ah, would the scandal vanish with my life,
How happy then were my ensuing death !

Enter KING *and* QUEEN, AUMERLE,
BUSHY, GREEN, BAGOT, ROSS, *and*
WILLOUGHBY.

  York. The King is come ; deal mildly
    with his youth,
For young hot colts being rag'd do rage
    the more.   70

Queen. How fares our noble uncle
    Lancaster ?

K. Rich. What comfort, man ? How is't
    with aged Gaunt ?

Gaunt. O, how that name befits my com-
    position !

Old Gaunt, indeed ; and gaunt in being old.

Within me grief hath kept a tedious fast ; 75

And who abstains from meat that is not
    gaunt ?

For sleeping England long time have I
    watch'd ;

Watching breeds leanness, leanness is all
    gaunt.

The pleasure that some fathers feeds upon

Is my strict fast—I mean my children's
    looks ;   80

And therein fasting, hast thou made me
    gaunt.

Gaunt am I for the grave, gaunt as a grave,

Whose hollow womb inherits nought but
    bones.

    K. Rich. Can sick men play so nicely with
    their names ?

    Gaunt. No, misery makes sport to mock
    itself ;   85

Since thou dost seek to kill my name in me,

I mock my name, great king, to flatter thee.

    K. Rich. Should dying men flatter with
    those that live ?

    Gaunt. No, no ; men living flatter those
    that die.

    K. Rich. Thou, now a-dying, sayest thou
    flatterest me.   90

    Gaunt. O, no ! thou diest, though I the
    sicker be.

    K. Rich. I am in health, I breathe, and
    see thee ill.

    Gaunt. Now He that made me knows I
    see thee ill ;

Ill in myself to see, and in thee seeing ill.

Thy death-bed is no lesser than thy land 95

Wherein thou liest in reputation sick ;

And thou, too careless patient as thou art,

Commit'st thy anointed body to the cure

Of those physicians that first wounded thee:

A thousand flatterers sit within thy crown,

Whose compass is no bigger than thy head ;

And yet, incaged in so small a verge,

The waste is no whit lesser than thy land.

O, had thy grandsire with a prophet's eye

Seen how his son's son should destroy his
    sons,   105

From forth thy reach he would have laid
    thy shame,

Deposing thee before thou wert possess'd,

Which art possess'd now to depose thyself.

Why, cousin, wert thou regent of the world,

It were a shame to let this land by lease ; 110

But for thy world enjoying but this land,

Is it not more than shame to shame it so ?

Landlord of England art thou now, not
    King.

Thy state of law is bondslave to the law ;

And thou—

    K. Rich. A lunatic lean-witted fool, 115

Presuming on an ague's privilege,

Darest with thy frozen admonition

Make pale our cheek, chasing the royal
    blood

With fury from his native residence.

Now by my seat's right royal majesty, 120

Wert thou not brother to great Edward's
    son,

This tongue that runs so roundly in thy
    head

Should run thy head from thy unreverent
    shoulders.

    Gaunt. O, spare me not, my brother
    Edward's son,

For that I was his father Edward's son ;

That blood already, like the pelican, 126

Hast thou tapp'd out, and drunkenly
    carous'd.

My brother Gloucester, plain well-meaning
    soul—

Whom fair befall in heaven 'mongst happy
    souls !—

May be a precedent and witness good 130

That thou respect'st not spilling Edward's
    blood.

Join with the present sickness that I have ;

And thy unkindness be like crooked age,

To crop at once a too long withered flower.

Live in thy shame, but die not shame with
    thee !   135

These words hereafter thy tormentors be !

Convey me to my bed, then to my grave.

Love they to live that love and honour
    have.

        [*Exit, borne out by his Attendants.*

    K. Rich. And let them die that age and
    sullens have ;

For both hast thou, and both become the
    grave.   140

    York. I do beseech your Majesty impute
    his words

To wayward sickliness and age in him.

He loves you, on my life, and holds you
    dear

As Harry Duke of Hereford, were he here.

    K. Rich. Right, you say true : as Here-
    ford's love, so his ;   145

As theirs, so mine ; and all be as it is.

        Enter NORTHUMBERLAND.

    North. My liege, old Gaunt commends
    him to your Majesty.

    K. Rich. What says he ?

    North.   Nay, nothing ; all is said.

His tongue is now a stringless instrument ;

Words, life, and all, old Lancaster hath
    spent.   150

    York. Be York the next that must be
    bankrupt so !

Though death be poor, it ends a mortal woe.

    K. Rich. The ripest fruit first falls, and
    so doth he ;

His time is spent, our pilgrimage must be.
So much for that. Now for our Irish wars.
We must supplant those rough rug-headed
    kerns,   156
Which live like venom where no venom else
But only they have privilege to live.
And for these great affairs do ask some
    charge,
Towards our assistance we do seize to us 160
The plate, coin, revenues, and moveables,
Whereof our uncle Gaunt did stand
    possess'd.
    York. How long shall I be patient ? Ah,
    how long
Shall tender duty make me suffer wrong ?
Not Gloucester's death, nor Hereford's
    banishment,   165
Nor Gaunt's rebukes, nor England's private
    wrongs,
Nor the prevention of poor Bolingbroke
About his marriage, nor my own disgrace,
Have ever made me sour my patient cheek
Or bend one wrinkle on my sovereign's face.
I am the last of noble Edward's sons, 171
Of whom thy father, Prince of Wales, was
    first.
In war was never lion rag'd more fierce,
In peace was never gentle lamb more mild,
Than was that young and princely gentle-
    man.   175
His face thou hast, for even so look'd he,
Accomplish'd with the number of thy hours;
But when he frown'd, it was against the
    French
And not against his friends. His noble hand
Did win what he did spend, and spent not
    that   180
Which his triumphant father's hand had
    won.
His hands were guilty of no kindred blood,
But bloody with the enemies of his kin.
O Richard ! York is too far gone with grief,
Or else he never would compare between—
    K. Rich. Why, uncle, what's the matter ?
    York.   O my liege,
Pardon me, if you please ; if not, I, pleas'd
Not to be pardoned, am content withal.
Seek you to seize and gripe into your hands
The royalties and rights of banish'd Here-
    ford ?   190
Is not Gaunt dead ? and doth not Hereford
    live ?
Was not Gaunt just ? and is not Harry true?
Did not the one deserve to have an heir ?
Is not his heir a well-deserving son ?
Take Hereford's rights away, and take
    from Time   195
His charters and his customary rights ;
Let not to-morrow then ensue to-day ;
Be not thyself—for how art thou a king
But by fair sequence and succession ? 199
Now, afore God—God forbid I say true !—
If you do wrongfully seize Hereford's rights,
Call in the letters patents that he hath

By his attorneys-general to sue
His livery, and deny his off'red homage,
You pluck a thousand dangers on your
    head,   205
You lose a thousand well-disposed hearts,
And prick my tender patience to those
    thoughts
Which honour and allegiance cannot think.
    K. Rich. Think what you will, we seize
    into our hands
His plate, his goods, his money, and his
    lands.   210
    York. I'll not be by the while. My liege,
    farewell.
What will ensue hereof there's none can
    tell ;
But by bad courses may be understood
That their events can never fall out good.
                    [*Exit.*
    K. Rich. Go, Bushy, to the Earl of
    Wiltshire straight ;   215
Bid him repair to us to Ely House
To see this business. To-morrow next
We will for Ireland ; and 'tis time, I
    trow.
And we create, in absence of ourself, 219
Our Uncle York Lord Governor of England;
For he is just, and always lov'd us well.
Come on, our queen ; to-morrow must we
    part ;
Be merry, for our time of stay is short.
    [*Flourish. Exeunt King, Queen, Bushy,*
        Aumerle, Green, and Bagot.
    North. Well, lords, the Duke of Lancaster
    is dead.
    Ross. And living too ; for now his son is
    Duke.   225
    Willo. Barely in title, not in revenues.
    North. Richly in both, if justice had her
    right.
    Ross. My heart is great ; but it must
    break with silence,
Ere't be disburdened with a liberal tongue.
    North. Nay, speak thy mind ; and let him
    ne'er speak more   230
That speaks thy words again to do thee
    harm !
    Willo. Tends that thou wouldst speak to
    the Duke of Hereford ?
If it be so, out with it boldly, man ;
Quick is mine ear to hear of good towards
    him.
    Ross. No good at all that I can do for
    him ;   235
Unless you call it good to pity him,
Bereft and gelded of his patrimony.
    North. Now, afore God, 'tis shame such
    wrongs are borne
In him, a royal prince, and many moe 240
Of noble blood in this declining land.
The King is not himself, but basely led
By flatterers ; and what they will inform,
Merely in hate, 'gainst any of us all,
That will the King severely prosecute

'Gainst us, our lives, our children, and our
 heirs.   245
 Ross. The commons hath he pill'd with
  grievous taxes ;
And quite lost their hearts ; the nobles hath
 he fin'd
For ancient quarrels and quite lost their
 hearts.
 Willo. And daily new exactions are
  devis'd,
As blanks, benevolences, and I wot not
 what ;   250
But what, a God's name, doth become of
 this ?
 North. Wars hath not wasted it, for
  warr'd he hath not,
But basely yielded upon compromise
That which his noble ancestors achiev'd
 with blows.
More hath he spent in peace than they in
 wars.   255
 Ross. The Earl of Wiltshire hath the
  realm in farm.
 Willo. The King's grown bankrupt like
  a broken man.
 North. Reproach and dissolution hangeth
  over him.
 Ross. He hath not money for these Irish
  wars,   259
His burdenous taxations notwithstanding,
But by the robbing of the banish'd Duke.
 North. His noble kinsman—most de-
  generate king !
But, lords, we hear this fearful tempest sing,
Yet seek no shelter to avoid the storm ;
We see the wind sit sore upon our sails, 265
And yet we strike not, but securely perish.
 Ross. We see the very wreck that we
  must suffer ;
And unavoided is the danger now
For suffering so the causes of our wreck.
 North. Not so ; even through the hollow
  eyes of death   270
I spy life peering ; but I dare not say
How near the tidings of our comfort is.
 Willo. Nay, let us share thy thoughts as
  thou dost ours.
 Ross. Be confident to speak, Northumber-
  land.
We three are but thyself, and, speaking so,
Thy words are but as thoughts ; therefore
 be bold.   276
 North. Then thus : I have from Le Port
  Blanc, a bay
In Brittany, receiv'd intelligence
That Harry Duke of Hereford, Rainold
 Lord Cobham,   279
That late broke from the Duke of Exeter,
His brother, Archbishop late of Canterbury,
Sir Thomas Erpingham, Sir John Ramston,
Sir John Norbery, Sir Robert Waterton,
 and Francis Quoint—
All these, well furnish'd by the Duke of
 Britaine,   285

With eight tall ships, three thousand men
 of war,
Are making hither with all due expedience,
And shortly mean to touch our northern
 shore.
Perhaps they had ere this, but that they
 stay   289
The first departing of the King for Ireland.
If then we shall shake off our slavish yoke,
Imp out our drooping country's broken
 wing,
Redeem from broking pawn the blemish'd
 crown,
Wipe off the dust that hides our sceptre's
 gilt,
And make high majesty look like itself, 295
Away with me in post to Ravenspurgh ;
But if you faint, as fearing to do so,
Stay and be secret, and myself will go.
 Ross. To horse, to horse ! Urge doubts
  to them that fear.
 Willo. Hold out my horse, and I will first
  be there.   [*Exeunt.*

   SCENE II. *Windsor Castle.*

  Enter QUEEN, BUSHY, *and* BAGOT.

 Bushy. Madam, your Majesty is too much
  sad.
You promis'd, when you parted with the
 King,
To lay aside life-harming heaviness
And entertain a cheerful disposition.
 Queen. To please the King, I did ; to
  please myself   5
I cannot do it ; yet I know no cause
Why I should welcome such a guest as grief,
Save bidding farewell to so sweet a guest
As my sweet Richard. Yet again methinks
Some unborn sorrow, ripe in fortune's
 womb,   10
Is coming towards me, and my inward soul
With nothing trembles. At some thing it
 grieves
More than with parting from my lord the
 King.
 Bushy. Each substance of a grief hath
  twenty shadows,   14
Which shows like grief itself, but is not so ;
For sorrow's eye, glazed with blinding tears,
Divides one thing entire to many objects,
Like perspectives which, rightly gaz'd upon,
Show nothing but confusion—ey'd awry,
Distinguish form. So your sweet Majesty,
Looking awry upon your lord's departure,
Find shapes of grief more than himself to
 wail ;
Which, look'd on as it is, is nought but
 shadows
Of what it is not. Then, thrice-gracious
 Queen,
More than your lord's departure weep not
 —more is not seen ;   25
Or if it be, 'tis with false sorrow's eye,

Which for things true weeps things
imaginary.

Queen. It may be so ; but yet my inward
soul
Persuades me it is otherwise. Howe'er it be,
I cannot but be sad ; so heavy sad   30
As—though, on thinking, on no thought I
think—
Makes me with heavy nothing faint and
shrink.

Bushy. 'Tis nothing but conceit, my
gracious lady.

Queen. 'Tis nothing less : conceit is still
deriv'd
From some forefather grief ; mine is not so,
For nothing hath begot my something
grief,   36
Or something hath the nothing that I
grieve ;
'Tis in reversion that I do possess—
But what it is that is not yet known what,
I cannot name ; 'tis nameless woe, I wot.

Enter GREEN.

Green. God save your Majesty ! and well
met, gentlemen.   41
I hope the King is not yet shipp'd for
Ireland.

Queen. Why hopest thou so ? 'Tis better
hope he is ;
For his designs crave haste, his haste good
hope.
Then wherefore dost thou hope he is not
shipp'd ?   45

Green. That he, our hope, might have
retir'd his power
And driven into despair an enemy's hope
Who strongly hath set footing in this
land.
The banish'd Bolingbroke repeals himself,
And with uplifted arms is safe arriv'd   50
At Ravenspurgh.

Queen.   Now God in heaven forbid !

Green. Ah, madam, 'tis too true ; and
that is worse,
The Lord Northumberland, his son young
Henry Percy,
The Lords of Ross, Beaumond, and
Willoughby,
With all their powerful friends, are fled to
him.   55

Bushy. Why have you not proclaim'd
Northumberland
And all the rest revolted faction traitors ?

Green. We have ; whereupon the Earl of
Worcester
Hath broken his staff, resign'd his steward-
ship,
And all the household servants fled with
him   60
To Bolingbroke.

Queen. So, Green, thou art the midwife to
my woe,
And Bolingbroke my sorrow's dismal heir.

Now hath my soul brought forth her
prodigy ;
And I, a gasping new-deliver'd mother,   65
Have woe to woe, sorrow to sorrow join'd.

Bushy. Despair not, madam.

Queen.   Who shall hinder me ?
I will despair, and be at enmity
With cozening hope—he is a flatterer,
A parasite, a keeper-back of death,   70
Who gently would dissolve the bands of
life,
Which false hope lingers in extremity.

Enter YORK.

Green. Here comes the Duke of York.

Queen. With signs of war about his aged
neck.
O, full of careful business are his looks !   75
Uncle, for God's sake, speak comfortable
words.

York. Should I do so, I should belie my
thoughts.
Comfort's in heaven ; and we are on the
earth,
Where nothing lives but crosses, cares, and
grief.
Your husband, he is gone to save far off,   80
Whilst others come to make him lose at
home.
Here am I left to underprop his land,
Who, weak with age, cannot support my-
self.
Now comes the sick hour that his surfeit
made ;
Now shall he try his friends that flatter'd
him.   85

Enter a Servingman.

Serv. My lord, your son was gone before
I came.

York. He was—why so go all which way
it will !
The nobles they are fled, the commons they
are cold
And will, I fear, revolt on Hereford's side.
Sirrah, get thee to Plashy, to my sister
Gloucester ;   90
Bid her send me presently a thousand
pound.
Hold, take my ring.

Serv. My lord, I had forgot to tell your
lordship,
To-day, as I came by, I called there—
But I shall grieve you to report the rest. 95

York. What is't, knave ?

Serv. An hour before I came, the Duchess
died.

York. God for his mercy ! what a tide of
woes
Comes rushing on this woeful land at once !
I know not what to do. I would to God,   100
So my untruth had not provok'd him to it,
The King had cut off my head with my
brother's.

What, are there no posts dispatch'd for
    Ireland ?
How shall we do for money for these wars ?
Come, sister—cousin, I would say—pray,
    pardon me.   105
Go, fellow, get thee home, provide some
    carts,
And bring away the armour that is there.
                [Exit Servingman.
Gentlemen, will you go muster men ?
If I know how or which way to order these
    affairs
Thus disorderly thrust into my hands,   110
Never believe me. Both are my kinsmen.
T'one is my sovereign, whom both my
    oath
And duty bids defend ; t'other again
Is my kinsman, whom the King hath
    wrong'd,
Whom conscience and my kindred bids to
    right.   115
Well, somewhat we must do.—Come,
    cousin,
I'll dispose of you. Gentlemen, go muster
    up your men,
And meet me presently at Berkeley.
I should to Plashy too,   120
But time will not permit. All is uneven,
And everything is left at six and seven.
             [Exeunt York and Queen.
  Bushy. The wind sits fair for news to go
    to Ireland.
But none returns. For us to levy power
Proportionable to the enemy   125
Is all unpossible.
  Green. Besides, our nearness to the King
    in love
Is near the hate of those love not the King.
  Bagot. And that is the wavering com-
    mons ; for their love
Lies in their purses ; and whoso empties
    them,   130
By so much fills their hearts with deadly
    hate.
  Bushy. Wherein the King stands gener-
    ally condemn'd.
  Bagot. If judgment lie in them, then so
    do we,
Because we ever have been near the King.
  Green. Well, I will for refuge straight to
    Bristow Castle.   135
The Earl of Wiltshire is already there.
  Bushy. Thither will I with you ; for
    little office
Will the hateful commons perform for us,
Except like curs to tear us all to pieces.
Will you go along with us ?   140
  Bagot. No ; I will to Ireland to his
    Majesty.
Farewell. If heart's presages be not vain,
We three here part that ne'er shall meet
    again.
  Bushy. That's as York thrives to beat
    back Bolingbroke.

  Green. Alas, poor Duke! the task he
    undertakes   145
Is numb'ring sands and drinking oceans
    dry.
Where one on his side fights, thousands
    will fly.
Farewell at once—for once, for all, and
    ever.
  Bushy. Well, we may meet again.
  Bagot.   I fear me, never. [*Exeunt.*

      SCENE III. *Gloucestershire.*

Enter BOLINGBROKE *and* NORTHUMBER-
    LAND, *with* FORCES.

  Boling. How far is it, my lord, to
    Berkeley now ?
  North. Believe me, noble lord,
I am a stranger here in Gloucestershire.
These high wild hills and rough uneven
    ways
Draws out our miles, and makes them
    wearisome ;   5
And yet your fair discourse hath been as
    sugar,
Making the hard way sweet and delectable.
But I bethink me what a weary way
From Ravenspurgh to Cotswold will be
    found
In Ross and Willoughby, wanting your
    company,   10
Which, I protest, hath very much beguil'd
The tediousness and process of my travel.
But theirs is sweet'ned with the hope to
    have
The present benefit which I possess ;
And hope to joy is little less in joy   15
Than hope enjoy'd. By this the weary lords
Shall make their way seem short, as mine
    hath done
By sight of what I have, your noble com-
    pany.
  Boling. Of much less value is my com-
    pany
Than your good words. But who comes
    here ?   20

      Enter HARRY PERCY.

  North. It is my son, young Harry Percy,
Sent from my brother Worcester, whence-
    soever.
Harry, how fares your uncle ?
  Percy. I had thought, my lord, to have
    learn'd his health of you.
  North. Why, is he not with the Queen ? 25
  Percy. No, my good lord ; he hath
    forsook the court,
Broken his staff of office, and dispers'd
The household of the King.
  North.   What was his reason ?
He was not so resolv'd when last we spake
    together.
  Percy. Because your lordship was pro-
    claimed traitor.   30

But he, my lord, is gone to Ravenspurgh,
To offer service to the Duke of Hereford ;
And sent me over by Berkeley, to discover
What power the Duke of York had levied
      there ;
Then with directions to repair to Ravens-
      purgh.   35
    North. Have you forgot the Duke of
      Hereford, boy ?
    Percy. No, my good lord ; for that is not
      forgot
Which ne'er I did remember ; to my
      knowledge,
I never in my life did look on him.
    North. Then learn to know him now ;
      this is the Duke.   40
    Percy. My gracious lord, I tender you my
      service,
Such as it is, being tender, raw, and young ;
Which elder days shall ripen, and confirm
To more approved service and desert.
    Boling. I thank thee, gentle Percy ; and
      be sure   45
I count myself in nothing else so happy
As in a soul rememb'ring my good friends ;
And as my fortune ripens with thy love,
It shall be still thy true love's recompense.
My heart this covenant makes, my hand
      thus seals it.   50
    North. How far is it to Berkeley ? And
      what stir
Keeps good old York there with his men of
      war ?
    Percy. There stands the castle, by yon
      tuft of trees,
Mann'd with three hundred men, as I have
      heard ;
And in it are the Lords of York, Berkeley,
      and Seymour—   55
None else of name and noble estimate.

Enter ROSS *and* WILLOUGHBY.

    North. Here come the Lords of Ross and
      Willoughby,
Bloody with spurring, fiery-red with haste.
    Boling. Welcome, my lords. I wot your
      love pursues
A banish'd traitor. All my treasury   60
Is yet but unfelt thanks, which, more
      enrich'd,
Shall be your love and labour's recompense.
    Ross. Your presence makes us rich, most
      noble lord.
    Willo. And far surmounts our labour to
      attain it.
    Boling. Evermore thanks, the exchequer
      of the poor ;   65
Which, till my infant fortune comes to
      years,
Stands for my bounty. But who comes here ?

Enter BERKELEY.

    North. It is my Lord of Berkeley, as I
      guess.

    Berk. My Lord of Hereford, my message
      is to you.
    Boling. My lord, my answer is—' to
      Lancaster ' ;   70
And I am come to seek that name in
      England ;
And I must find that title in your tongue
Before I make reply to aught you say.
    Berk. Mistake me not, my lord ; 'tis not
      my meaning
To raze one title of your honour out.   75
To you, my lord, I come—what lord you
      will—
From the most gracious regent of this land,
The Duke of York, to know what pricks
      you on
To take advantage of the absent time,
And fright our native peace with self-borne
      arms.   80

Enter YORK, *attended.*

    Boling. I shall not need transport my
      words by you ;
Here comes his Grace in person. My noble
      uncle !   [*Kneels.*
    York. Show me thy humble heart, and
      not thy knee,
Whose duty is deceivable and false.
    Boling. My gracious uncle !—   85
    York. Tut, tut !
Grace me no grace, nor uncle me no uncle.
I am no traitor's uncle ; and that word
      ' grace '
In an ungracious mouth is but profane.
Why have those banish'd and forbidden
      legs   90
Dar'd once to touch a dust of England's
      ground ?
But then more ' why ? '—why have they
      dar'd to march
So many miles upon her peaceful bosom,
Frighting her pale-fac'd villages with war
And ostentation of despised arms ?   95
Com'st thou because the anointed King is
      hence ?
Why, foolish boy, the King is left behind,
And in my loyal bosom lies his power.
Were I but now lord of such hot youth
As when brave Gaunt, thy father, and
      myself   100
Rescued the Black Prince, that young Mars
      of men,
From forth the ranks of many thousand
      French,
O, then how quickly should this arm of
      mine,
Now prisoner to the palsy, chastise thee
And minister correction to thy fault ! 105
    Boling. My gracious uncle, let me know
      my fault ;
On what condition stands it and wherein ?
    York. Even in condition of the worst
      degree—
In gross rebellion and detested treason.

Thou art a banish'd man, and here art
  come   110
Before the expiration of thy time,
In braving arms against thy sovereign.
  Boling. As I was banish'd, I was banish'd
    Hereford ;
But as I come, I come for Lancaster.
And, noble uncle, I beseech your Grace 115
Look on my wrongs with an indifferent eye.
You are my father, for methinks in you
I see old Gaunt alive. O, then, my father,
Will you permit that I shall stand con-
    demn'd
A wandering vagabond ; my rights and
    royalties   120
Pluck'd from my arms perforce, and given
    away
To upstart unthrifts ?   Wherefore was I
    born ?
If that my cousin king be King in England,
It must be granted I am Duke of Lancaster.
You have a son, Aumerle, my noble cousin ;
Had you first died, and he been thus trod
    down,   126
He should have found his uncle Gaunt a
    father
To rouse his wrongs and chase them to the
    bay.
I am denied to sue my livery here,
And yet my letters patents give me leave.
My father's goods are all distrain'd and
    sold ;   131
And these and all are all amiss employ'd.
What would you have me do ?   I am a
    subject,
And I challenge law—attorneys are denied
    me ;
And therefore personally I lay my claim
To my inheritance of free descent.   136
  North. The noble Duke hath been too
    much abused.
  Ross. It stands your Grace upon to do
    him right.
  Willo. Base men by his endowments are
    made great.
  York. My lords of England, let me tell
    you this :   140
I have had feeling of my cousin's wrongs,
And labour'd all I could to do him right ;
But in this kind to come, in braving arms,
Be his own carver and cut out his way,
To find out right with wrong—it may not
    be ;   145
And you that do abet him in this kind
Cherish rebellion, and are rebels all.
  North. The noble Duke hath sworn his
    coming is
But for his own ; and for the right of that
We all have strongly sworn to give him aid ;
And let him never see joy that breaks that
    oath !   151
  York. Well, well, I see the issue of these
    arms.
I cannot mend it, I must needs confess,

Because my power is weak and all ill left ;
But if I could, by Him that gave me life, 155
I would attach you all and make you stoop
Unto the sovereign mercy of the King ;
But since I cannot, be it known unto you
I do remain as neuter. So, fare you well ;
Unless you please to enter in the castle, 160
And there repose you for this night.
  Boling. An offer, uncle, that we will
    accept.
But we must win your Grace to go with us
To Bristow Castle, which they say is held
By Bushy, Bagot, and their complices, 165
The caterpillars of the commonwealth,
Which I have sworn to weed and pluck
    away.
  York. It may be I will go with you ; but
    yet I'll pause,
For I am loath to break our country's laws.
Nor friends nor foes, to me welcome you are.
Things past redress are now with me past
    care.   [*Exeunt.*

SCENE IV. *A camp in Wales.*

Enter EARL OF SALISBURY *and a* Welsh
        Captain.

  Cap. My Lord of Salisbury, we have
    stay'd ten days
And hardly kept our countrymen together,
And yet we hear no tidings from the King ;
Therefore we will disperse ourselves.
    Farewell.
  Sal. Stay yet another day, thou trusty
    Welshman ;   5
The king reposeth all his confidence in thee.
  Cap. 'Tis thought the King is dead ; we
    will not stay.
The bay trees in our country are all
    wither'd,
And meteors fright the fixed stars of heaven ;
The pale-fac'd moon looks bloody on the
    earth,   10
And lean-look'd prophets whisper fearful
    change ;
Rich men look sad, and ruffians dance and
    leap—
The one in fear to lose what they enjoy,
The other to enjoy by rage and war.
These signs forerun the death or fall of
    kings.   15
Farewell. Our countrymen are gone and fled,
As well assur'd Richard their King is dead.
                                     [*Exit.*
  Sal. Ah, Richard, with the eyes of heavy
    mind,
I see thy glory like a shooting star
Fall to the base earth from the firmament !
The sun sets weeping in the lowly west,
Witnessing storms to come, woe, and
    unrest ;   22
Thy friends are fled, to wait upon thy foes ;
And crossly to thy good all fortune goes.
                                     [*Exit.*

461

ACT THREE

SCENE I. *Bolingbroke's camp at Bristol.*

Enter BOLINGBROKE, YORK, NORTHUMBER-
LAND, PERCY, ROSS, WILLOUGHBY, *with*
BUSHY *and* GREEN, *prisoners.*

Boling. Bring forth these men.
Bushy and Green, I will not vex your
    souls—
Since presently your souls must part your
    bodies—
With too much urging your pernicious lives,
For 'twere no charity ; yet, to wash your
    blood   5
From off my hands, here in the view of men
I will unfold some causes of your deaths :
You have misled a prince, a royal king,
A happy gentleman in blood and linea-
    ments,
By you unhappied and disfigured clean ; 10
You have in manner with your sinful hours
Made a divorce betwixt his queen and him ;
Broke the possession of a royal bed,
And stain'd the beauty of a fair queen's
    cheeks
With tears drawn from her eyes by your
    foul wrongs ;   15
Myself—a prince by fortune of my birth,
Near to the King in blood, and near in
    love
Till you did make him misinterpret me—
Have stoop'd my neck under your injuries
And sigh'd my English breath in foreign
    clouds,   20
Eating the bitter bread of banishment,
Whilst you have fed upon my signories,
Dispark'd my parks and fell'd my forest
    woods,
From my own windows torn my household
    coat,   24
Raz'd out my imprese, leaving me no sign
Save men's opinions and my living blood
To show the world I am a gentleman.
This and much more, much more than
    twice all this,
Condemns you to the death. See them
    delivered over
To execution and the hand of death.   30
    Bushy. More welcome is the stroke of
        death to me
Than Bolingbroke to England. Lords, fare-
    well.
    Green. My comfort is that heaven will
        take our souls,
And plague injustice with the pains of hell.
    Boling. My Lord Northumberland, see
        them dispatch'd.   35
        [*Exeunt Northumberland, and others,
            with the prisoners.*
Uncle, you say the Queen is at your house ;
For God's sake, fairly let her be entreated.
Tell her I send to her my kind commends ;
Take special care my greetings be delivered.

York. A gentleman of mine I have dis-
    patch'd   40
With letters of your love to her at large.
    Boling. Thanks, gentle uncle. Come,
        lords, away,
To fight with Glendower and his complices.
Awhile to work, and after holiday.
                                        [*Exeunt.*

SCENE II. *The coast of Wales. A castle in
    view.*

*Drums. Flourish and colours. Enter the
    KING, the BISHOP OF CARLISLE, AUMERLE
    and Soldiers.*

    K. Rich. Barkloughly Castle call they
        this at hand ?
    Aum. Yea, my lord. How brooks your
        Grace the air
After your late tossing on the breaking
    seas ?
    K. Rich. Needs must I like it well. I weep
        for joy
To stand upon my kingdom once again.   5
Dear earth, I do salute thee with my hand,
Though rebels wound thee with their
    horses' hoofs.
As a long-parted mother with her child
Plays fondly with her tears and smiles in
    meeting,   9
So weeping-smiling greet I thee, my earth,
And do thee favours with my royal hands.
Feed not thy sovereign's foe, my gentle
    earth,
Nor with thy sweets comfort his ravenous
    sense ;
But let thy spiders, that suck up thy venom,
And heavy-gaited toads, lie in their way, 15
Doing annoyance to the treacherous feet
Which with usurping steps do trample
    thee ;
Yield stinging nettles to mine enemies ;
And when they from thy bosom pluck a
    flower,
Guard it, I pray thee, with a lurking adder,
Whose double tongue may with a mortal
    touch   21
Throw death upon thy sovereign's enemies.
Mock not my senseless conjuration, lords.
This earth shall have a feeling, and these
    stones
Prove armed soldiers, ere her native King
Shall falter under foul rebellion's arms. 26
    Car. Fear not, my lord ; that Power that
        made you king
Hath power to keep you king in spite of all.
The means that heaven yields must be
    embrac'd   29
And not neglected ; else, if heaven would,
And we will not, heaven's offer we refuse,
The proffered means of succour and redress.
    Aum. He means, my lord, that we are too
        remiss ;
Whilst Bolingbroke, through our security,

Grows strong and great in substance and in
    power.   35
  K. Rich. Discomfortable cousin ! know'st
    thou not
That when the searching eye of heaven is
    hid,
Behind the globe, that lights the lower world,
Then thieves and robbers range abroad
    unseen   39
In murders and in outrage boldly here ;
But when from under this terrestrial ball
He fires the proud tops of the eastern pines
And darts his light through every guilty
    hole,
Then murders, treasons, and detested sins,
The cloak of night being pluck'd from off
    their backs,   45
Stand bare and naked, trembling at them-
    selves ?
So when this thief, this traitor, Boling-
    broke,
Who all this while hath revell'd in the night,
Whilst we were wand'ring with the
    Antipodes,   49
Shall see us rising in our throne, the east,
His treasons will sit blushing in his face,
Not able to endure the sight of day,
But self-affrighted tremble at his sin.
Not all the water in the rough rude sea
Can wash the balm off from an anointed
    king ;   55
The breath of worldly men cannot depose
The deputy elected by the Lord.
For every man that Bolingbroke hath
    press'd
To lift shrewd steel against our golden
    crown,
God for his Richard hath in heavenly pay
A glorious angel. Then, if angels fight, 61
Weak men must fall ; for heaven still
    guards the right.

       Enter SALISBURY.

Welcome, my lord. How far off lies your
    power ?
  Sal. Nor near nor farther off, my gracious
    lord,
Than this weak arm. Discomfort guides my
    tongue,   65
And bids me speak of nothing but despair.
One day too late, I fear me, noble lord,
Hath clouded all thy happy days on earth.
O, call back yesterday, bid time return,
And thou shalt have twelve thousand
    fighting men !   70
To-day, to-day, unhappy day, too late,
O'erthrows thy joys, friends, fortune, and
    thy state ;
For all the Welshmen, hearing thou wert
    dead,
Are gone to Bolingbroke, dispers'd, and
    fled.
  Aum. Comfort, my liege, why looks your
    Grace so pale ?   75

  K. Rich. But now the blood of twenty
    thousand men
Did triumph in my face, and they are fled ;
And, till so much blood thither come again,
Have I not reason to look pale and dead ?
All souls that will be safe, fly from my side ;
For time hath set a blot upon my pride.
  Aum. Comfort, my liege ; remember who
    you are.   82
  K. Rich. I had forgot myself ; am I not
    King ?
Awake, thou coward majesty ! thou
    sleepest.
Is not the King's name twenty thousand
    names ?   85
Arm, arm, my name ! a puny subject strikes
At thy great glory. Look not to the ground,
Ye favourites of a king ; are we not high ?
High be our thoughts. I know my uncle
    York
Hath power enough to serve our turn. But
    who comes here ?   90

       Enter SCROOP.

  Scroop. More health and happiness betide
    my liege
Than can my care-tun'd tongue deliver
    him.
  K. Rich. Mine ear is open and my heart
    prepar'd.
The worst is worldly loss thou canst unfold.
Say, is my kingdom lost ? Why, 'twas my
    care ;   95
And what loss is it to be rid of care ?
Strives Bolingbroke to be as great as we ?
Greater he shall not be ; if he serve God,
We'll serve him too, and be his fellow so.
Revolt our subjects ? That we cannot
    mend ;   100
They break their faith to God as well as us.
Cry woe, destruction, ruin, and decay—
The worst is death, and death will have his
    day.
  Scroop. Glad am I that your Highness is
    so arm'd
To bear the tidings of calamity.   105
Like an unseasonable stormy day
Which makes the silver rivers drown their
    shores,
As if the world were all dissolv'd to tears,
So high above his limits swells the rage
Of Bolingbroke, covering your fearful land
With hard bright steel and hearts harder
    than steel.   111
White-beards have arm'd their thin and
    hairless scalps
Against thy majesty ; boys, with women's
    voices,
Strive to speak big, and clap their female
    joints
In stiff unwieldy arms against thy crown ;
Thy very beadsmen learn to bend their
    bows   116
Of double-fatal yew against thy state ;

Yea, distaff-women manage rusty bills
Against thy seat: both young and old
   rebel,
And all goes worse than I have power to
   tell.   120
   K. Rich. Too well, too well thou tell'st a
   tale so ill.
Where is the Earl of Wiltshire? Where is
   Bagot?
What is become of Bushy? Where is
   Green?
That they have let the dangerous enemy
Measure our confines with such peaceful
   steps?   125
If we prevail, their heads shall pay for it.
I warrant they have made peace with
   Bolingbroke.
   Scroop. Peace have they made with him
   indeed, my lord.
   K. Rich. O villains, vipers, damn'd with-
   out redemption!
Dogs, easily won to fawn on any man! 130
Snakes, in my heart-blood warm'd, that
   sting my heart!
Three Judases, each one thrice worse than
   Judas!
Would they make peace? Terrible hell
   make war
Upon their spotted souls for this offence!
   Scroop. Sweet love, I see, changing their
   property,   135
Turns to the sourest and most deadly hate.
Again uncurse their souls; their peace is
   made
With heads, and not with hands; those
   whom you curse
Have felt the worst of death's destroying
   wound
And lie full low, grav'd in the hollow ground.
   Aum. Is Bushy, Green, and the Earl of
   Wiltshire dead?   141
   Scroop. Ay, all of them at Bristow lost
   their heads.
   Aum. Where is the Duke my father with
   his power?
   K. Rich. No matter where—of comfort
   no man speak.
Let's talk of graves, of worms, and epitaphs;
Make dust our paper, and with rainy
   eyes   146
Write sorrow on the bosom of the earth.
Let's choose executors and talk of wills;
And yet not so—for what can we bequeath
Save our deposed bodies to the ground? 150
Our lands, our lives, and all, are Boling-
   broke's.
And nothing can we call our own but death
And that small model of the barren earth
Which serves as paste and cover to our
   bones.   154
For God's sake let us sit upon the ground
And tell sad stories of the death of kings:
How some have been depos'd, some slain
   in war,

Some haunted by the ghosts they have
   depos'd,
Some poison'd by their wives, some sleep-
   ing kill'd,   159
All murder'd—for within the hollow crown
That rounds the mortal temples of a king
Keeps Death his court; and there the antic
   sits,
Scoffing his state and grinning at his pomp;
Allowing him a breath, a little scene,
To monarchize, be fear'd, and kill with
   looks;   165
Infusing him with self and vain conceit,
As if this flesh which walls about our life
Were brass impregnable; and, humour'd
   thus,
Comes at the last, and with a little pin
Bores through his castle wall, and farewell,
   king!   170
Cover your heads, and mock not flesh and
   blood
With solemn reverence; throw away
   respect,
Tradition, form, and ceremonious duty;
For you have but mistook me all this while.
I live with bread like you, feel want, 175
Taste grief, need friends; subjected thus,
How can you say to me I am a king?
   Car. My lord, wise men ne'er sit and wail
   their woes,
But presently prevent the ways to wail.
To fear the foe, since fear oppresseth
   strength,   180
Gives, in your weakness, strength unto your
   foe,
And so your follies fight against yourself.
Fear and be slain—no worse can come to
   fight;
And fight and die is death destroying death,
Where fearing dying pays death servile
   breath.   185
   Aum. My father hath a power; inquire
   of him,
And learn to make a body of a limb.
   K. Rich. Thou chid'st me well. Proud
   Bolingbroke, I come
To change blows with thee for our day of
   doom.
This ague fit of fear is over-blown;   190
An easy task it is to win our own.
Say, Scroop, where lies our uncle with his
   power?
Speak sweetly, man, although thy looks be
   sour.
   Scroop. Men judge by the complexion of
   the sky
The state and inclination of the day; 195
So may you by my dull and heavy eye,
My tongue hath but a heavier tale to say.
I play the torturer, by small and small
To lengthen out the worst that must be
   spoken: 199
Your uncle York is join'd with Bolingbroke;
And all your northern castles yielded up,

And all your southern gentlemen in arms
Upon his party.
    K. Rich.   Thou hast said enough.
[*To Aumerle*] Beshrew thee, cousin, which
    didst lead me forth
Of that sweet way I was in to despair!   205
What say you now? What comfort have
    we now?
By heaven, I'll hate him everlastingly
That bids me be of comfort any more.
Go to Flint Castle; there I'll pine away;
A king, woe's slave, shall kingly woe obey.
That power I have, discharge; and let
    them go   211
To ear the land that hath some hope to
    grow,
For I have none. Let no man speak again
To alter this, for counsel is but vain.
    Aum. My liege, one word.
    K. Rich.   He does me double wrong
That wounds me with the flatteries of his
    tongue.   216
Discharge my followers; let them hence
    away,
From Richard's night to Bolingbroke's fair
    day.   [*Exeunt.*

SCENE III. *Wales. Before Flint Castle.*

Enter, with drum and colours, BOLING-
    BROKE, YORK, NORTHUMBERLAND, *and*
    Forces.

    Boling. So that by this intelligence we
    learn
The Welshmen are dispers'd; and Salis-
    bury
Is gone to meet the King, who lately landed
With some few private friends upon this
    coast.
    North. The news is very fair and good,
    my lord.   5
Richard not far from hence hath hid his
    head.
    York. It would beseem the Lord North-
    umberland
To say ' King Richard'. Alack the heavy
    day
When such a sacred king should hide his
    head!
    North. Your Grace mistakes; only to be
    brief,   10
Left I his title out.
    York.   The time hath been,
Would you have been so brief with him, he
    would
Have been so brief with you, to shorten you,
For taking so the head, your whole head's
    length.
    Boling. Mistake not, uncle, further than
    you should.   15
    York. Take not, good cousin, further than
    you should,
Lest you mistake. The heavens are over
    our heads.

    Boling. I know it, uncle; and oppose not
    myself
Against their will. But who comes here?

             Enter PERCY.

Welcome, Harry. What, will not this castle
    yield?   20
    Percy. The castle royally is mann'd, my
    lord,
Against thy entrance.
    Boling. Royally!
Why, it contains no king?
    Percy.   Yes, my good lord,
It doth contain a king; King Richard lies
Within the limits of yon lime and stone;
And with him are the Lord Aumerle, Lord
    Salisbury,
Sir Stephen Scroop, besides a clergyman
Of holy reverence; who, I cannot learn.
    North. O, belike it is the Bishop of
    Carlisle.   30
    Boling. [*To Northumberland*] Noble lord,
Go to the rude ribs of that ancient castle;
Through brazen trumpet send the breath
    of parley
Into his ruin'd ears, and thus deliver:
Henry Bolingbroke   35
On both his knees doth kiss King Richard's
    hand,
And sends allegiance and true faith of heart
To his most royal person; hither come
Even at his feet to lay my arms and power,
Provided that my banishment repeal'd   40
And lands restor'd again be freely granted;
If not, I'll use the advantage of my power
And lay the summer's dust with showers of
    blood
Rain'd from the wounds of slaughtered
    Englishmen;
The which how far off from the mind of
    Bolingbroke   45
It is such crimson tempest should bedrench
The fresh green lap of fair King Richard's
    land,
My stooping duty tenderly shall show.
Go, signify as much, while here we march
Upon the grassy carpet of this plain.   50
      [*Northumberland advances to the
        Castle, with a trumpet.*
Let's march without the noise of threat'n-
    ing drum,
That from this castle's tottered battlements
Our fair appointments may be well perus'd.
Methinks King Richard and myself should
    meet
With no less terror than the elements   55
Of fire and water, when their thund'ring
    shock
At meeting tears the cloudy cheeks of
    heaven.
Be he the fire, I'll be the yielding water;
The rage be his, whilst on the earth I
    rain   59
My waters—on the earth, and not on him.

March on, and mark King Richard how he
   looks.

*Parle without, and answer within ; then a
   flourish. Enter on the walls, the* KING,
   the BISHOP OF CARLISLE, AUMERLE,
   SCROOP *and* SALISBURY.

See, see, King Richard doth himself appear,
As doth the blushing discontented sun
From out the fiery portal of the east,
When he perceives the envious clouds are
   bent   65
To dim his glory and to stain the track
Of his bright passage to the occident.
   York. Yet looks he like a king. Behold,
   his eye,
As bright as is the eagle's, lightens forth
Controlling majesty. Alack, alack, for woe,
That any harm should stain so fair a show !
   K. Rich. [*To Northumberland*] We are
   amaz'd ; and thus long have we
   stood
To watch the fearful bending of thy knee,
Because we thought ourself thy lawful king ;
And if we be, how dare thy joints forget 75
To pay their awful duty to our presence ?
If we be not, show us the hand of God
That hath dismiss'd us from our steward-
   ship ;
For well we know no hand of blood and
   bone
Can gripe the sacred handle of our sceptre,
Unless he do profane, steal, or usurp.   81
And though you think that all, as you have
   done,
Have torn their souls by turning them from
   us,
And we are barren and bereft of friends,
Yet know—my master, God omnipotent,   85
Is mustering in his clouds on our behalf
Armies of pestilence ; and they shall strike
Your children yet unborn and unbegot,
That lift your vassal hands against my head
And threat the glory of my precious crown.
Tell Bolingbroke, for yon methinks he
   stands,   91
That every stride he makes upon my land
Is dangerous treason ; he is come to open
The purple testament of bleeding war ;
But ere the crown he looks for live in peace,
Ten thousand bloody crowns of mothers'
   sons   96
Shall ill become the flower of England's face,
Change the complexion of her maid-pale
   peace
To scarlet indignation, and bedew
Her pastures' grass with faithful English
   blood.   100
   North. The King of Heaven forbid our
   lord the King
Should so with civil and uncivil arms
Be rush'd upon ! Thy thrice noble cousin,
Harry Bolingbroke, doth humbly kiss thy
   hand ;

And by the honourable tomb he swears   105
That stands upon your royal grandsire's
   bones,
And by the royalties of both your bloods,
Currents that spring from one most
   gracious head,
And by the buried hand of warlike Gaunt,
And by the worth and honour of himself,
Comprising all that may be sworn or said,
His coming hither hath no further scope
Than for his lineal royalties, and to beg
Enfranchisement immediate on his knees ;
Which on thy royal party granted once, 115
His glittering arms he will commend to rust,
His barbed steeds to stables, and his heart
To faithful service of your Majesty.
This swears he, as he is a prince, is just ;
And as I am a gentleman I credit him.   120
   K. Rich. Northumberland, say thus the
   King returns :
His noble cousin is right welcome hither ;
And all the number of his fair demands
Shall be accomplish'd without contradic-
   tion.   124
With all the gracious utterance thou hast
Speak to his gentle hearing kind commends.
[*To Aumerle*] We do debase ourselves,
   cousin, do we not,
To look so poorly and to speak so fair ?
Shall we call back Northumberland, and
   send
Defiance to the traitor, and so die ?   130
   Aum. No, good my lord ; let's fight with
   gentle words
Till time lend friends, and friends their
   helpful swords.
   K. Rich. O God, O God ! that e'er this
   tongue of mine
That laid the sentence of dread banishment
On yon proud man should take it off again
With words of sooth ! O that I were as
   great   136
As is my grief, or lesser than my name !
Or that I could forget what I have been !
Or not remember what I must be now !
Swell'st thou, proud heart ? I'll give thee
   scope to beat,   140
Since foes have scope to beat both thee
   and me.
   Aum. Northumberland comes back from
   Bolingbroke.
   K. Rich. What must the King do now ?
   Must he submit ?   143
The King shall do it. Must he be depos'd ?
The King shall be contented. Must he lose
The name of king ? A God's name, let it go.
I'll give my jewels for a set of beads,
My gorgeous palace for a hermitage,
My gay apparel for an almsman's gown,
My figur'd goblets for a dish of wood,   150
My sceptre for a palmer's walking staff,
My subjects for a pair of carved saints,
And my large kingdom for a little grave,
A little little grave, an obscure grave—

Or I'll be buried in the king's high way, 155
Some way of common trade, where sub-
    jects' feet
May hourly trample on their sovereign's
    head ;
For on my heart they tread now whilst
    I live,
And buried once, why not upon my head ?
Aumerle, thou weep'st, my tender-hearted
    cousin !   160
We'll make foul weather with despised
    tears ;
Our sighs and they shall lodge the summer
    corn
And make a dearth in this revolting land.
Or shall we play the wantons with our woes
And make some pretty match with shed-
    ding tears ?   165
As thus : to drop them still upon one place
Till they have fretted us a pair of graves
Within the earth ; and, therein laid—there
    lies
Two kinsmen digg'd their graves with weep-
    ing eyes.
Would not this ill do well ? Well, well, I
    see   170
I talk but idly, and you laugh at me.
Most mighty prince, my Lord Northumber-
    land,
What says King Bolingbroke ? Will his
    Majesty
Give Richard leave to live till Richard die ?
You make a leg, and Bolingbroke says ay.
    North. My lord, in the base court he doth
    attend   176
To speak with you ; may it please you to
    come down ?
    K. Rich. Down, down I come, like
    glist'ring Phaethon,
Wanting the manage of unruly jades.
In the base court ? Base court, where kings
    grow base,   185
To come at traitors' calls, and do them
    grace.
In the base court ? Come down ? Down,
    court ! down, king !
For night-owls shriek where mounting larks
    should sing.   [*Exeunt from above.*
    Boling. What says his Majesty ?
    North.   Sorrow and grief of heart
Makes him speak fondly, like a frantic man;
Yet he is come.   186

Enter the King, *and his* Attendants, *below.*

    Boling. Stand all apart,
And show fair duty to his Majesty.
                       [*He kneels down.*
My gracious lord—
    K. Rich. Fair cousin, you debase your
    princely knee   190
To make the base earth proud with kissing
    it.
Me rather had my heart might feel your love
Than my unpleas'd eye may see your courtesy.

Up, cousin, up ; your heart is up, I know,
[*Touching his own head*] Thus high at least,
    although your knee be low.   195
    Boling. My gracious lord, I come but for
    mine own.
    K. Rich. Your own is yours, and I am
    yours, and all.
    Boling. So far be mine, my most re-
    doubted lord,
As my true service shall deserve your love.
    K. Rich. Well you deserve. They well
    deserve to have   200
That know the strong'st and surest way to
    get.
Uncle, give me your hands ; nay, dry your
    eyes :
Tears show their love, but want their
    remedies.
Cousin, I am too young to be your father,
Though you are old enough to be my heir.
What you will have, I'll give, and willing
    too ;   206
For do we must what force will have us do.
Set on towards London. Cousin, is it so ?
    Boling. Yea, my good lord.
    K. Rich.   Then I must not say no.
                       [*Flourish. Exeunt.*

Scene IV.   *The Duke of York's garden.*

Enter the Queen *and two* Ladies.

    Queen. What sport shall we devise here
    in this garden
To drive away the heavy thought of care ?
    Lady. Madam, we'll play at bowls.
    Queen. 'Twill make me think the world
    is full of rubs
And that my fortune runs against the bias.
    Lady. Madam, we'll dance.   6
    Queen. My legs can keep no measure in
    delight,
When my poor heart no measure keeps in
    grief ;
Therefore no dancing, girl ; some other
    sport.
    Lady. Madam, we'll tell tales.   10
    Queen. Of sorrow or of joy ?
    Lady.   Of either, madam.
    Queen. Of neither, girl :
For if of joy, being altogether wanting,
It doth remember me the more of sorrow ;
Or if of grief, being altogether had,   15
It adds more sorrow to my want of joy ;
For what I have I need not to repeat,
And what I want it boots not to complain.
    Lady. Madam, I'll sing.
    Queen. 'Tis well that thou hast cause ;
But thou shouldst please me better wouldst
    thou weep.   20
    Lady. I could weep, madam, would it do
    you good.
    Queen. And I could sing, would weeping
    do me good,
And never borrow any tear of thee.

467

Enter a Gardener *and two* Servants.

But stay, here come the gardeners.
Let's step into the shadow of these trees.　25
My wretchedness unto a row of pins,
They will talk of state, for every one doth so
Against a change : woe is forerun with woe.
　　　　　[*Queen and Ladies retire.*
　Gard. Go, bind thou up yon dangling
　　　　apricocks,
Which, like unruly children, make their sire
Stoop with oppression of their prodigal
　　　　weight ;　　　　　　　　　　31
Give some supportance to the bending
　　　　twigs.
Go thou, and like an executioner
Cut off the heads of too fast growing sprays
That look too lofty in our commonwealth :
All must be even in our government.　　36
You thus employ'd, I will go root away
The noisome weeds which without profit
　　　　suck
The soil's fertility from wholesome flowers.
　Serv. Why should we, in the compass of a
　　　　pale,　　　　　　　　　　　40
Keep law and form and due proportion,
Showing, as in a model, our firm estate,
When our sea-walled garden, the whole
　　　　land,
Is full of weeds ; her fairest flowers chok'd up,
Her fruit trees all unprun'd, her hedges
　　　　ruin'd,　　　　　　　　　　45
Her knots disordered, and her wholesome
　　　　herbs
Swarming with caterpillars ?
　Gard.　　　　　　　Hold thy peace.
He that hath suffer'd this disorder'd spring
Hath now himself met with the fall of leaf ;
The weeds which his broad-spreading leaves
　　　　did shelter,　　　　　　　　50
That seem'd in eating him to hold him up,
Are pluck'd up root and all by Boling-
　　　　broke—
I mean the Earl of Wiltshire, Bushy, Green.
　Serv. What, are they dead ?
　Gard.　　　　　They are ; and Bolingbroke
Hath seiz'd the wasteful king. O, what pity
　　　　is it　　　　　　　　　　　55
That he had not so trimm'd and dress'd his
　　　　land
As we this garden ! We at time of year
Do wound the bark, the skin of our
　　　　fruit trees,
Lest, being over-proud in sap and blood,
With too much riches it confound itself ;　60
Had he done so to great and growing men,
They might have liv'd to bear, and he to
　　　　taste
Their fruits of duty. Superfluous branches
We lop away, that bearing boughs may live ;
Had he done so, himself had borne the
　　　　crown,　　　　　　　　　　65
Which waste of idle hours hath quite
　　　　thrown down.

　Serv. What, think you the King shall be
　　　　deposed ?
　Gard. Depress'd he is already, and de-
　　　　pos'd
'Tis doubt he will be.　Letters came last
　　　　night
To a dear friend of the good Duke of York's
That tell black tidings.　　　　　　71
　Queen. O, I am press'd to death through
　　　　want of speaking !
　　　　　　　　　　[*Coming forward.*
Thou, old Adam's likeness, set to dress this
　　　　garden,
How dares thy harsh rude tongue sound
　　　　this unpleasing news ?
What Eve, what serpent, hath suggested
　　　　thee　　　　　　　　　　　75
To make a second fall of cursed man ?
Why dost thou say King Richard is depos'd?
Dar'st thou, thou little better thing than
　　　　earth,
Divine his downfall ?　Say, where, when,
　　　　and how,
Cam'st thou by this ill tidings ?　Speak,
　　　　thou wretch.　　　　　　　　80
　Gard. Pardon me, madam ; little joy
　　　　have I
To breathe this news ; yet what I say is
　　　　true.
King Richard, he is in the mighty hold
Of Bolingbroke.　Their fortunes both are
　　　　weigh'd.　　　　　　　　　　84
In your lord's scale is nothing but himself,
And some few vanities that make him light ;
But in the balance of great Bolingbroke,
Besides himself, are all the English peers,
And with that odds he weighs King Richard
　　　　down.　　　　　　　　　　89
Post you to London, and you will find it so ;
I speak no more than every one doth know.
　Queen. Nimble mischance, that art so
　　　　light of foot,
Doth not thy embassage belong to me,
And am I last that knows it ?　O, thou
　　　　thinkest　　　　　　　　　94
To serve me last, that I may longest keep
Thy sorrow in my breast.　Come, ladies, go
To meet at London London's king in woe.
What, was I born to this, that my sad look
Should grace the triumph of great Boling-
　　　　broke ?
Gard'ner, for telling me these news of woe,
Pray God the plants thou graft'st may
　　　　never grow !　　　　　　　101
　　　　　　　[*Exeunt Queen and Ladies.*
　Gard. Poor Queen, so that thy state
　　　　might be no worse,
I would my skill were subject to thy curse.
Here did she fall a tear ; here in this place
I'll set a bank of rue, sour herb of grace.　105
Rue, even for ruth, here shortly shall be
　　　　seen,
In the remembrance of a weeping queen.
　　　　　　　　　　　　[*Exeunt.*

ACT FOUR

SCENE I. *Westminster Hall.*

Enter, as to the Parliament, BOLINGBROKE, AUMERLE, NORTHUMBERLAND, PERCY, FITZWATER, SURREY, *the* BISHOP OF CARLISLE, *the* ABBOT OF WESTMINSTER, *and* Others; Herald, Officers, *and* BAGOT.

Boling. Call forth Bagot.
Now, Bagot, freely speak thy mind—
What thou dost know of noble Gloucester's death;
Who wrought it with the King, and who perform'd
The bloody office of his timeless end.   5
    Bagot. Then set before my face the Lord Aumerle.
    Boling. Cousin, stand forth, and look upon that man.
    Bagot. My Lord Aumerle, I know your daring tongue
Scorns to unsay what once it hath deliver'd.
In that dead time when Gloucester's death was plotted   10
I heard you say ' Is not my arm of length,
That reacheth from the restful English Court
As far as Calais, to mine uncle's head ? '
Amongst much other talk that very time   14
I heard you say that you had rather refuse
The offer of an hundred thousand crowns
Than Bolingbroke's return to England ;
Adding withal, how blest this land would be
In this your cousin's death.
    Aum. Princes, and noble lords,
What answer shall I make to this base man?
Shall I so much dishonour my fair stars   21
On equal terms to give him chastisement ?
Either I must, or have mine honour soil'd
With the attainder of his slanderous lips.
There is my gage, the manual seal of death
That marks thee out for hell. I say thou liest,   26
And will maintain what thou hast said is false
In thy heart-blood, though being all too base
To stain the temper of my knightly sword.
    Boling. Bagot, forbear ; thou shalt not take it up.   30
    Aum. Excepting one, I would he were the best
In all this presence that hath mov'd me so.
    Fitz. If that thy valour stand on sympathy,
There is my gage, Aumerle, in gage to thine.
By that fair sun which shows me where thou stand'st,   35
I heard thee say, and vauntingly thou spak'st it,
That thou wert cause of noble Gloucester's death.
If thou deniest it twenty times, thou liest ;

And I will turn thy falsehood to thy heart,
Where it was forged, with my rapier's point.
    Aum. Thou dar'st not, coward, live to see that day.   41
    Fitz. Now, by my soul, I would it were this hour.
    Aum. Fitzwater, thou art damn'd to hell for this.
    Percy. Aumerle, thou liest ; his honour is as true
In this appeal as thou art all unjust ;   45
And that thou art so, there I throw my gage,
To prove it on thee to the extremest point
Of mortal breathing. Seize it, if thou dar'st.
    Aum. An if I do not, may my hands rot off
And never brandish more revengeful steel
Over the glittering helmet of my foe !   51
    Another Lord. I task the earth to the like, forsworn Aumerle ;
And spur thee on with full as many lies
As may be holloa'd in thy treacherous ear
From sun to sun. There is my honour's pawn ;   55
Engage it to the trial, if thou darest.
    Aum. Who sets me else ? By heaven, I'll throw at all !
I have a thousand spirits in one breast
To answer twenty thousand such as you.
    Surrey. My Lord Fitzwater, I do remember well   60
The very time Aumerle and you did talk.
    Fitz. 'Tis very true ; you were in presence then,
And you can witness with me this is true.
    Surrey. As false, by heaven, as heaven itself is true.
    Fitz. Surrey, thou liest.
    Surrey.   Dishonourable boy !   65
That lie shall lie so heavy on my sword
That it shall render vengeance and revenge
Till thou the lie-giver and that lie do lie
In earth as quiet as thy father's skull.
In proof whereof, there is my honour's pawn ;   70
Engage it to the trial, if thou dar'st.
    Fitz. How fondly dost thou spur a forward horse !
If I dare eat, or drink, or breathe, or live,
I dare meet Surrey in a wilderness,
And spit upon him whilst I say he lies,   75
And lies, and lies. There is my bond of faith,
To tie thee to my strong correction.
As I intend to thrive in this new world,
Aumerle is guilty of my true appeal.
Besides, I heard the banish'd Norfolk say
That thou, Aumerle, didst send two of thy men   81
To execute the noble Duke at Calais.
    Aum. Some honest Christian trust me with a gage

That Norfolk lies. Here do I throw down
   this,
If he may be repeal'd to try his honour. 85
   Boling. These differences shall all rest
   under gage
Till Norfolk be repeal'd—repeal'd he shall
   be
And, though mine enemy, restor'd again
To all his lands and signories. When he
   is return'd,
Against Aumerle we will enforce his trial.
   Car. That honourable day shall never be
   seen.   91
Many a time hath banish'd Norfolk fought
For Jesu Christ in glorious Christian field,
Streaming the ensign of the Christian cross
Against black pagans, Turks, and Saracens;
And, toil'd with works of war, retir'd
   himself   96
To Italy; and there, at Venice, gave
His body to that pleasant country's earth,
And his pure soul unto his captain, Christ,
Under whose colours he had fought so long.
   Boling. Why, Bishop, is Norfolk dead?
   Car. As surely as I live, my lord.
   Boling. Sweet peace conduct his sweet
   soul to the bosom
Of good old Abraham! Lords appellants,
Your differences shall all rest under gage 105
Till we assign you to your days of trial.

     Enter YORK, *attended.*

   York. Great Duke of Lancaster, I come
   to thee
From plume-pluck'd Richard, who with
   willing soul
Adopts thee heir, and his high sceptre yields
To the possession of thy royal hand. 110
Ascend his throne, descending now from
   him—
And long live Henry, fourth of that name!
   Boling. In God's name, I'll ascend the
   regal throne.
   Car. Marry, God forbid!   114
Worst in this royal presence may I speak,
Yet best beseeming me to speak the truth.
Would God that any in this noble presence
Were enough noble to be upright judge
Of noble Richard!   Then true noblesse
   would   119
Learn him forbearance from so foul a wrong.
What subject can give sentence on his king?
And who sits here that is not Richard's
   subject?
Thieves are not judg'd but they are by to
   hear,
Although apparent guilt be seen in them;
And shall the figure of God's majesty, 125
His captain, steward, deputy elect,
Anointed, crowned, planted many years,
Be judg'd by subject and inferior breath,
And he himself not present? O, forfend
   it, God,
That in a Christian climate souls refin'd 130

Should show so heinous, black, obscene a
   deed!
I speak to subjects, and a subject speaks,
Stirr'd up by God, thus boldly for his
   king.
My Lord of Hereford here, whom you call
   king,   134
Is a foul traitor to proud Hereford's king;
And if you crown him, let me prophesy—
The blood of English shall manure the
   ground,
And future ages groan for this foul act;
Peace shall go sleep with Turks and infidels,
And in this seat of peace tumultuous wars
Shall kin with kin and kind with kind
   confound;   141
Disorder, horror, fear, and mutiny,
Shall here inhabit, and this land be call'd
The field of Golgotha and dead men's skulls.
O, if you raise this house against this house,
It will the woefullest division prove   146
That ever fell upon this cursed earth.
Prevent it, resist it, let it not be so,
Lest child, child's children, cry against you
   woe.
   North. Well have you argued, sir; and,
   for your pains,   150
Of capital treason we arrest you here.
My Lord of Westminster, be it your charge
To keep him safely till his day of trial.
May it please you, lords, to grant the
   commons' suit?
   Boling. Fetch hither Richard, that in
   common view   155
He may surrender; so we shall proceed
Without suspicion.
   York.   I will be his conduct. [*Exit.*
   Boling. Lords, you that here are under
   our arrest,
Procure your sureties for your days of
   answer.
Little are we beholding to your love,   160
And little look'd for at your helping hands.

Re-enter YORK, *with* KING RICHARD, *and*
   Officers *bearing the regalia.*

   K. Rich. Alack, why am I sent for to a
   king,
Before I have shook off the regal thoughts
Wherewith I reign'd? I hardly yet have
   learn'd
To insinuate, flatter, bow, and bend my
   knee.   165
Give sorrow leave awhile to tutor me
To this submission. Yet I well remember
The favours of these men. Were they not
   mine?
Did they not sometime cry 'All hail!' to
   me?
So Judas did to Christ; but he, in twelve,
Found truth in all but one; I, in twelve
   thousand, none.   171
God save the King! Will no man say
   amen?

Am I both priest and clerk ?   Well then,
     amen.   173
God save the King ! although I be not he ;
And yet, amen, if heaven do think him me.
To do what service am I sent for hither ?
     York. To do that office of thine own
       good will
Which tired majesty did make thee offer—
The resignation of thy state and crown
To Henry Bolingbroke.   180
     K. Rich. Give me the crown.   Here,
       cousin, seize the crown.
Here, cousin,
On this side my hand, and on that side
     thine.
Now is this golden crown like a deep well
That owes two buckets, filling one another ;
The emptier ever dancing in the air,   186
The other down, unseen, and full of water.
That bucket down and full of tears am I,
Drinking my griefs, whilst you mount up
     on high.
     Boling. I thought you had been willing
       to resign.   190
     K. Rich. My crown I am ; but still my
       griefs are mine.
You may my glories and my state depose,
But not my griefs ; still am I king of those.
     Boling. Part of your cares you give me
       with your crown.
     K. Rich. Your cares set up do not pluck
       my cares down.   195
My care is loss of care, by old care done ;
Your care is gain of care, by new care won.
The cares I give I have, though given away;
They tend the crown, yet still with me they
     stay.
     Boling. Are you contented to resign the
       crown ?   200
     K. Rich. Ay, no ; no, ay ; for I must
       nothing be ;
Therefore no no, for I resign to thee.
Now mark me how I will undo myself :
I give this heavy weight from off my head,
And this unwieldy sceptre from my hand,
The pride of kingly sway from out my
     heart ;   206
With mine own tears I wash away my balm,
With mine own hands I give away my
     crown,
With mine own tongue deny my sacred
     state,
With mine own breath release all duteous
     oaths ;   210
All pomp and majesty I do forswear ;
My manors, rents, revenues, I forgo ;
My acts, decrees, and statutes, I deny.
God pardon all oaths that are broke to me !
God keep all vows unbroke are made to
     thee !   215
Make me, that nothing have, with nothing
     griev'd,
And thou with all pleas'd, that hast all
     achiev'd.

Long mayst thou live in Richard's seat
     to sit,
And soon lie Richard in an earthy pit.
God save King Henry, unking'd Richard
     says,   220
And send him many years of sunshine days!
What more remains ?
     North.   No more ; but that you read
These accusations, and these grievous
     crimes
Committed by your person and your
     followers   224
Against the state and profit of this land ;
That, by confessing them, the souls of men
May deem that you are worthily depos'd.
     K. Rich. Must I do so ?   And must I
       ravel out
My weav'd-up follies ? Gentle Northumber-
     land,
If thy offences were upon record,   230
Would it not shame thee in so fair a troop
To read a lecture of them ? If thou wouldst,
There shouldst thou find one heinous
     article,
Containing the deposing of a king
And cracking the strong warrant of an oath,
Mark'd with a blot, damn'd in the book of
     heaven.   236
Nay, all of you that stand and look upon
     me
Whilst that my wretchedness doth bait
     myself,
Though some of you, with Pilate, wash your
     hands,   239
Showing an outward pity—yet you Pilates
Have here deliver'd me to my sour cross,
And water cannot wash away your sin.
     North. My lord, dispatch ; read o'er these
       articles.
     K. Rich. Mine eyes are full of tears ; I
       cannot see.
And yet salt water blinds them not so
     much   245
But they can see a sort of traitors here.
Nay, if I turn mine eyes upon myself,
I find myself a traitor with the rest ;
For I have given here my soul's consent
T' undeck the pompous body of a king ;   250
Made glory base, and sovereignty a slave,
Proud majesty a subject, state a peasant.
     North. My lord—
     K. Rich. No lord of thine, thou haught
       insulting man,
Nor no man's lord ; I have no name, no
     title—   255
No, not that name was given me at the
     font—
But 'tis usurp'd.   Alack the heavy day,
That I have worn so many winters out,
And know not now what name to call
     myself !
O that I were a mockery king of snow,   260
Standing before the sun of Bolingbroke
To melt myself away in water drops !

Good king, great king, and yet not greatly
    good,
An if my word be sterling yet in England,
Let it command a mirror hither straight,
That it may show me what a face I have
Since it is bankrupt of his majesty.   267
    Boling. Go some of you and fetch a
      looking-glass. [*Exit an Attendant.*
    North. Read o'er this paper while the
      glass doth come.
    K. Rich. Fiend, thou torments me ere I
      come to hell.   270
    Boling. Urge it no more, my Lord North-
      umberland.
    North. The commons will not, then, be
      satisfied.
    K. Rich. They shall be satisfied. I'll read
      enough,
When I do see the very book indeed
Where all my sins are writ, and that's
    myself.   275

    Re-enter Attendant *with a glass.*

Give me that glass, and therein will I read.
No deeper wrinkles yet ?   Hath sorrow
    struck
So many blows upon this face of mine
And made no deeper wounds ? O flatt'ring
    glass,
Like to my followers in prosperity,   280
Thou dost beguile me ! Was this face the
    face
That every day under his household roof
Did keep ten thousand men ? Was this the
    face
That like the sun did make beholders wink?
Is this the face which fac'd so many follies
That was at last out-fac'd by Bolingbroke ?
A brittle glory shineth in this face ;   287
As brittle as the glory is the face ;
    [*Dashes the glass against the ground.*
For there it is, crack'd in a hundred shivers.
Mark, silent king, the moral of this sport—
How soon my sorrow hath destroy'd my
    face.   291
    Boling. The shadow of your sorrow hath
    destroy'd
The shadow of your face.
    K. Rich.   Say that again.
The shadow of my sorrow ? Ha ! let's see.
'Tis very true : my grief lies all within ;   295
And these external manner of laments
Are merely shadows to the unseen grief
That swells with silence in the tortur'd soul.
There lies the substance ; and I thank thee,
    king,   299
For thy great bounty, that not only giv'st
Me cause to wail, but teachest me the way
How to lament the cause. I'll beg one boon,
And then be gone and trouble you no more.
Shall I obtain it ?
    Boling.   Name it, fair cousin.
    K. Rich. Fair cousin ! I am greater than
      a king ;   305

For when I was a king, my flatterers
Were then but subjects ; being now a
    subject,
I have a king here to my flatterer.
Being so great, I have no need to beg.
    Boling. Yet ask.   310
    K. Rich. And shall I have ?
    Boling. You shall.
    K. Rich. Then give me leave to go.
    Boling. Whither ?
    K. Rich. Whither you will, so I were from
      your sights.   315
    Boling. Go, some of you convey him to
      the Tower.
    K. Rich. O, good ! Convey ! Conveyers
      are you all,
That rise thus nimbly by a true king's fall.
    [*Exeunt King Richard, some Lords,*
        and a Guard.
    Boling. On Wednesday next we solemnly
    set down   319
Our coronation. Lords, prepare yourselves.
    [*Exeunt all but the Abbot of West-*
      minster, the Bishop of Carlisle,
      and Aumerle.
    Abbot. A woeful pageant have we here
      beheld.
    Car. The woe's to come ; the children yet
      unborn
Shall feel this day as sharp to them as
    thorn.
    Aum. You holy clergymen, is there no
      plot
To rid the realm of this pernicious blot ?   325
    Abbot. My lord,
Before I freely speak my mind herein,
You shall not only take the sacrament
To bury mine intents, but also to effect
Whatever I shall happen to devise.   330
I see your brows are full of discontent,
Your hearts of sorrow, and your eyes of
    tears.
Come home with me to supper ; I will
    lay
A plot shall show us all a merry day.
    [*Exeunt.*

ACT FIVE

SCENE I. *London. A street leading to the
    Tower.*

Enter the QUEEN, *with her* Attendants.

    Queen. This way the King will come ;
      this is the way
To Julius Cæsar's ill-erected tower,
To whose flint bosom my condemned lord
Is doom'd a prisoner by proud Bolingbroke.
Here let us rest, if this rebellious earth   5
Have any resting for her true king's queen.

    Enter KING RICHARD *and* Guard.

But soft, but see, or rather do not see,
My fair rose wither. Yet look up, behold,
That you in pity may dissolve to dew,

And wash him fresh again with true-love
    tears.   10
Ah, thou, the model where old Troy did
    stand ;
Thou map of honour, thou King Richard's
    tomb,
And not King Richard; thou most
    beauteous inn,
Why should hard-favour'd grief be lodg'd
    in thee,
When triumph is become an alehouse guest?
    K. Rich. Join not with grief, fair woman,
    do not so,   16
To make my end too sudden. Learn, good
    soul,
To think our former state a happy dream ;
From which awak'd, the truth of what we
    are
Shows us but this : I am sworn brother,
    sweet,   20
To grim Necessity ; and he and I
Will keep a league till death. Hie thee to
    France,
And cloister thee in some religious house.
Our holy lives must win a new world's
    crown,
Which our profane hours here have thrown
    down.   25
    Queen. What, is my Richard both in
    shape and mind
Transform'd and weak'ned ? Hath Boling-
    broke depos'd
Thine intellect ? Hath he been in thy
    heart ?
The lion dying thrusteth forth his paw
And wounds the earth, if nothing else, with
    rage   30
To be o'erpow'r'd ; and wilt thou, pupil-
    like,
Take the correction mildly, kiss the rod,
And fawn on rage with base humility,
Which art a lion and the king of beasts ?
    K. Rich. A king of beasts, indeed ! If
    aught but beasts,   35
I had been still a happy king of men.
Good sometimes queen, prepare thee hence
    for France.
Think I am dead, and that even here thou
    takest,
As from my death-bed, thy last living
    leave.
In winter's tedious nights sit by the fire   40
With good old folks, and let them tell thee
    tales
Of woeful ages long ago betid ;
And ere thou bid good night, to quit their
    griefs
Tell thou the lamentable tale of me,
And send the hearers weeping to their
    beds;   45
For why the senseless brands will sym-
    pathize
The heavy accent of thy moving tongue,
And in compassion weep the fire out ;

And some will mourn in ashes, some coal-
    black,
For the deposing of a rightful king.   50
    Enter NORTHUMBERLAND *attended.*
    North. My lord, the mind of Bolingbroke
    is chang'd ;
You must to Pomfret, not unto the Tower.
And, madam, there is order ta'en for you :
With all swift speed you must away to
    France.
    K. Rich. Northumberland, thou ladder
    wherewithal   55
The mounting Bolingbroke ascends my
    throne,
The time shall not be many hours of age
More than it is, ere foul sin gathering head
Shall break into corruption. Thou shalt
    think
Though he divide the realm and give thee
    half   60
It is too little, helping him to all ;
And he shall think that thou, which
    knowest the way
To plant unrightful kings, wilt know again,
Being ne'er so little urg'd, another way
To pluck him headlong from the usurped
    throne.   65
The love of wicked men converts to fear ;
That fear to hate ; and hate turns one or
    both
To worthy danger and deserved death.
    North. My guilt be on my head, and there
    an end.
Take leave, and part ; for you must part
    forthwith.   70
    K. Rich. Doubly divorc'd ! Bad men, you
    violate
A twofold marriage—'twixt my crown and
    me,
And then betwixt me and my married wife.
Let me unkiss the oath 'twixt thee and me ;
And yet not so, for with a kiss 'twas made.
Part us, Northumberland ; I towards the
    north,   76
Where shivering cold and sickness pines the
    clime ;
My wife to France, from whence set forth
    in pomp,
She came adorned hither like sweet May,
Sent back like Hallowmas or short'st of day.
    Queen. And must we be divided ? Must
    we part ?   81
    K. Rich. Ay, hand from hand, my love,
    and heart from heart.
    Queen. Banish us both, and send the King
    with me.
    North. That were some love, but little
    policy.
    Queen. Then whither he goes thither let
    me go.   85
    K. Rich. So two, together weeping, make
    one woe.
Weep thou for me in France, I for thee here;

Better far off than near, be ne'er the near.
Go, count thy way with sighs ; I mine
  with groans.
   Queen. So longest way shall have the
    longest moans.   90
   K. Rich. Twice for one step I'll groan,
    the way being short,
And piece the way out with a heavy heart.
Come, come, in wooing sorrow let's be brief,
Since, wedding it, there is such length in
  grief.
One kiss shall stop our mouths, and dumbly
  part ;   95
Thus give I mine, and thus take I thy heart.
   Queen. Give me mine own again ; 'twere
    no good part
To take on me to keep and kill thy heart.
So, now I have mine own again, be gone,
That I may strive to kill it with a groan. 100
   K. Rich. We make woe wanton with this
    fond delay.
Once more, adieu ; the rest let sorrow say.
                  [*Exeunt.*

SCENE II. *The Duke of York's palace.*

Enter the DUKE OF YORK *and the* DUCHESS.

   Duch. My lord, you told me you would
    tell the rest,
When weeping made you break the story off,
Of our two cousins' coming into London.
   York. Where did I leave ?
   Duch.   At that sad stop, my lord,
Where rude misgoverned hands from
  windows' tops   5
Threw dust and rubbish on King Richard's
  head.
   York. Then, as I said, the Duke, great
    Bolingbroke,
Mounted upon a hot and fiery steed
Which his aspiring rider seem'd to know,
With slow but stately pace kept on his
  course,   10
Whilst all tongues cried ' God save thee,
  Bolingbroke ! '
You would have thought the very windows
  spake,
So many greedy looks of young and old
Through casements darted their desiring
  eyes
Upon his visage ; and that all the walls 15
With painted imagery had said at once
' Jesu preserve thee ! Welcome, Boling-
  broke ! '
Whilst he, from the one side to the other
  turning,
Bareheaded, lower than his proud steed's
  neck,
Bespake them thus, ' I thank you, country-
  men '.   20
And thus still doing, thus he pass'd along.
   Duch. Alack, poor Richard ! where rode
    he the whilst ?
   York. As in a theatre the eyes of men

After a well-grac'd actor leaves the stage
Are idly bent on him that enters next,   25
Thinking his prattle to be tedious ;
Even so, or with much more contempt,
  men's eyes
Did scowl on gentle Richard ; no man cried
  ' God save him ! '
No joyful tongue gave him his welcome
  home ;   29
But dust was thrown upon his sacred head ;
Which with such gentle sorrow he shook off,
His face still combating with tears and
  smiles,
The badges of his grief and patience,
That had not God, for some strong purpose,
  steel'd
The hearts of men, they must perforce have
  melted,   35
And barbarism itself have pitied him.
But heaven hath a hand in these events,
To whose high will we bound our calm
  contents.
To Bolingbroke are we sworn subjects now,
Whose state and honour I for aye allow.   40
   Duch. Here comes my son Aumerle.
   York.   Aumerle that was ;
But that is lost for being Richard's friend,
And, madam, you must call him Rutland
  now.
I am in Parliament pledge for his truth
And lasting fealty to the new-made king. 45

Enter AUMERLE.

   Duch. Welcome, my son. Who are the
    violets now
That strew the green lap of the new come
  spring ?
   Aum. Madam, I know not, nor I greatly
    care not.
God knows I had as lief be none as one.
   York. Well, bear you well in this new
    spring of time,   50
Lest you be cropp'd before you come to
  prime.
What news from Oxford ? Do these justs
  and triumphs hold ?
   Aum. For aught I know, my lord, they
    do.
   York. You will be there, I know.   54
   Aum. If God prevent not, I purpose so.
   York. What seal is that that hangs with-
    out thy bosom ?
Yea, look'st thou pale ? Let me see the
  writing.
   Aum. My lord, 'tis nothing.
   York.   No matter, then, who see it.
I will be satisfied ; let me see the writing.
   Aum. I do beseech your Grace to pardon
    me ;   60
It is a matter of small consequence
Which for some reasons I would not have
  seen.
   York. Which for some reasons, sir, I
    mean to see.

I fear, I fear—
    Duch.   What should you fear ?
'Tis nothing but some bond that he is
    ent'red into   65
For gay apparel 'gainst the triumph-day.
    York. Bound to himself ! What doth he
        with a bond
That he is bound to ? Wife, thou art a fool.
Boy, let me see the writing.
    Aum. I do beseech you, pardon me ; I
        may not show it.   70
    York. I will be satisfied ; let me see it,
        I say. [*He plucks it out of his bosom,
                        and reads it.*
Treason, foul treason ! Villain ! traitor !
    slave !
    Duch. What is the matter, my lord ?
    York. Ho ! who is within there ?

            Enter a Servant.

                          Saddle my horse.
God for his mercy, what treachery is here !
    Duch. Why, what is it, my lord ?
    York. Give me my boots, I say ; saddle
        my horse.   [*Exit Servant.*
Now, by mine honour, by my life, my
    troth,
I will appeach the villain.
    Duch.   What is the matter ?
    York. Peace, foolish woman.   80
    Duch. I will not peace. What is the
        matter, Aumerle ?
    Aum. Good mother, be content ; it is no
        more
Than my poor life must answer.
    Duch.   Thy life answer !
    York. Bring me my boots. I will unto
        the King.

    His Man *enters with his boots.*

    Duch. Strike him, Aumerle. Poor boy,
        thou art amaz'd.   85
Hence, villain ! never more come in my
    sight.
    York. Give me my boots, I say.
    Duch. Why, York, what wilt thou do ?
Wilt thou not hide the trespass of thine
    own ?
Have we more sons ? or are we like to have ?
Is not my teeming date drunk up with
    time ?   91
And wilt thou pluck my fair son from mine
    age
And rob me of a happy mother's name ?
Is he not like thee ? Is he not thine own ?
    York. Thou fond mad woman,   95
Wilt thou conceal this dark conspiracy ?
A dozen of them here have ta'en the sacra-
    ment,
And interchangeably set down their hands
To kill the King at Oxford.
    Duch.   He shall be none ;
We'll keep him here. Then what is that to
    him ?   100

    York. Away fond woman ! were he
        twenty times my son
I would appeach him.
    Duch.   Hadst thou groan'd for him
As I have done, thou wouldst be more
    pitiful.
But now I know thy mind : thou dost
    suspect
That I have been disloyal to thy bed   105
And that he is a bastard, not thy son.
Sweet York, sweet husband, be not of that
    mind.
He is as like thee as a man may be,
Not like to me, or any of my kin,
And yet I love him.
    York.   Make way, unruly woman ! 110
                                        [*Exit.*
    Duch. After, Aumerle ! Mount thee upon
        his horse ;
Spur post, and get before him to the King,
And beg thy pardon ere he do accuse thee.
I'll not be long behind ; though I be old,
I doubt not but to ride as fast as York ; 115
And never will I rise up from the ground
Till Bolingbroke have pardon'd thee.
    Away, be gone.   [*Exeunt.*

        SCENE III. *Windsor Castle.*

Enter BOLINGBROKE *as King,* PERCY, *and
            other* Lords.

    Boling. Can no man tell me of my
        unthrifty son ?
'Tis full three months since I did see him
    last.
If any plague hang over us, 'tis he.
I would to God, my lords, he might be
    found.
Inquire at London, 'mongst the taverns
    there,   5
For there, they say, he daily doth frequent
With unrestrained loose companions,
Even such, they say, as stand in narrow
    lanes
And beat our watch and rob our passengers,
Which he, young wanton and effeminate
    boy,   10
Takes on the point of honour to support
So dissolute a crew.
    Percy. My lord, some two days since I saw
        the Prince,
And told him of those triumphs held at
    Oxford.
    Boling. And what said the gallant ? 15
    Percy. His answer was, he would unto the
        stews,
And from the common'st creature pluck a
    glove
And wear it as a favour ; and with that
He would unhorse the lustiest challenger.
    Boling. As dissolute as desperate ; yet
        through both   20
I see some sparks of better hope, which elder
    years

May happily bring forth. But who comes
here ?

Enter AUMERLE *amazed.*

Aum. Where is the King ?
Boling. What means our cousin that he
stares and looks
So wildly ?   25
Aum. God save your Grace ! I do beseech
your Majesty,
To have some conference with your Grace
alone.
Boling. Withdraw yourselves, and leave
us here alone.
[*Exeunt Percy and Lords.*
What is the matter with our cousin now ?
Aum. For ever may my knees grow to the
earth,   [*Kneels.*
My tongue cleave to my roof within my
mouth,   31
Unless a pardon ere I rise or speak.
Boling. Intended or committed was this
fault ?
If on the first, how heinous e'er it be,
To win thy after-love I pardon thee.   35
Aum. Then give me leave that I may
turn the key,
That no man enter till my tale be done.
Boling. Have thy desire. [*The Duke of
York knocks at the door and crieth.*
York. [*Within*] My liege, beware ; look
to thyself ;
Thou hast a traitor in thy presence there.
Boling. [*Drawing*] Villain, I'll make thee
safe.   41
Aum. Stay thy revengeful hand ; thou
hast no cause to fear.
York. [*Within*] Open the door, secure,
foolhardy King.
Shall I, for love, speak treason to thy face ?
Open the door, or I will break it open.   45

Enter YORK.

Boling. What is the matter, uncle ?
Speak ;
Recover breath ; tell us how near is danger,
That we may arm us to encounter it.
York. Peruse this writing here, and thou
shalt know
The treason that my haste forbids me show.
Aum. Remember, as thou read'st, thy
promise pass'd.   51
I do repent me ; read not my name there ;
My heart is not confederate with my hand.
York. It was, villain, ere thy hand did set
it down.
I tore it from the traitor's bosom, King ;   55
Fear, and not love, begets his penitence.
Forget to pity him, lest thy pity prove
A serpent that will sting thee to the heart.
Boling. O heinous, strong, and bold con-
spiracy !
O loyal father of a treacherous son !   60
Thou sheer, immaculate, and silver fountain,

From whence this stream through muddy
passages
Hath held his current and defil'd himself !
Thy overflow of good converts to bad ;
And thy abundant goodness shall excuse 65
This deadly blot in thy digressing son.
York. So shall my virtue be his vice's
bawd ;
And he shall spend mine honour with his
shame,
As thriftless sons their scraping fathers'
gold.
Mine honour lives when his dishonour dies,
Or my sham'd life in his dishonour lies. 71
Thou kill'st me in his life ; giving him
breath,
The traitor lives, the true man's put to
death.
Duch. [*Within*] What ho, my liege, for
God's sake, let me in.
Boling. What   shrill-voic'd   suppliant
makes this eager cry ?   75
Duch. [*Within*] A woman, and thine aunt,
great King ; 'tis I.
Speak with me, pity me, open the door.
A beggar begs that never begg'd before.
Boling. Our scene is alt'red from a serious
thing,
And now chang'd to ' The Beggar and the
King '.   80
My dangerous cousin, let your mother in.
I know she is come to pray for your foul sin.
York. If thou do pardon whosoever pray,
More sins for this forgiveness prosper may.
This fest'red joint cut off, the rest rest
sound ;   85
This let alone will all the rest confound.

Enter DUCHESS.

Duch. O King, believe not this hard-
hearted man !
Love loving not itself, none other can.
York. Thou frantic woman, what dost
thou make here ?   89
Shall thy old dugs once more a traitor rear ?
Duch. Sweet York, be patient. Hear me,
gentle liege.   [*Kneels.*
Boling. Rise up, good aunt.
Duch.   Not yet, I thee beseech.
For ever will I walk upon my knees,
And never see day that the happy sees
Till thou give joy ; until thou bid me joy 95
By pardoning Rutland, my transgressing
boy.
Aum. Unto my mother's prayers I bend
my knee.   [*Kneels.*
York. Against them both, my true joints
bended be.   [*Kneels.*
Ill mayst thou thrive, if thou grant any
grace !
Duch. Pleads he in earnest ? Look upon
his face ;   100
His eyes do drop no tears, his prayers are
in jest ;

His words come from his mouth, ours from
　　our breast.
He prays but faintly and would be denied ;
We pray with heart and soul, and all beside.
His weary joints would gladly rise, I know ;
Our knees still kneel till to the ground they
　　grow.   106
His prayers are full of false hypocrisy ;
Ours of true zeal and deep integrity.
Our prayers do out-pray his ; then let them
　　have
That mercy which true prayer ought to
　　have.   110
　　Boling. Good aunt, stand up.
　　Duch.   Nay, do not say ' stand up ' ;
Say ' pardon ' first, and afterwards ' stand
　　up '.
An if I were thy nurse, thy tongue to teach,
' Pardon ' should be the first word of thy
　　speech.
I never long'd to hear a word till now ;   115
Say ' pardon ' King ; let pity teach thee
　　how.
The word is short, but not so short as sweet ;
No word like ' pardon ' for kings' mouths so
　　meet.
　　York. Speak it in French, King, say
　　' pardonne moy '.
　　Duch. Dost thou teach pardon pardon to
　　destroy ?   120
Ah, my sour husband, my hard-hearted
　　lord,
That sets the word itself against the word !
Speak ' pardon ' as 'tis current in our land ;
The chopping French we do not understand.
Thine eye begins to speak, set thy tongue
　　there ;   125
Or in thy piteous heart plant thou thine ear,
That hearing how our plaints and prayers
　　do pierce,
Pity may move thee ' pardon ' to rehearse.
　　Boling. Good aunt, stand up.
　　Duch.   I do not sue to stand ;
Pardon is all the suit I have in hand.   130
　　Boling. I pardon him, as God shall pardon
　　me.
　　Duch. O happy vantage of a kneeling
　　knee !
Yet am I sick for fear. Speak it again.
Twice saying ' pardon ' doth not pardon
　　twain,   134
But makes one pardon strong.
　　Boling.   With all my heart
I pardon him.
　　Duch.   A god on earth thou art.
　　Boling. But for our trusty brother-in-law
　　and the Abbot,
With all the rest of that consorted crew,
Destruction straight shall dog them at the
　　heels.   139
Good uncle, help to order several powers
To Oxford, or where'er these traitors are.
They shall not live within this world, I
　　swear,

But I will have them, if I once know where.
Uncle, farewell ; and, cousin, adieu ;
Your mother well hath pray'd, and prove
　　you true.   145
　　Duch. Come, my old son ; I pray God
　　make thee new.   [*Exeunt.*

SCENE IV. *Windsor Castle.*

Enter SIR PIERCE OF EXTON *and a* Servant.

　　Exton. Didst thou not mark the King,
　　what words he spake ?
' Have I no friend will rid me of this living
　　fear ? '
Was it not so ?
　　Serv.   These were his very words.
　　Exton. ' Have I no friend ? ' quoth he.
　　He spake it twice,
And urg'd it twice together, did he not ?   5
　　Serv. He did.
　　Exton. And, speaking it, he wishtly look'd
　　on me,
As who should say ' I would thou wert the
　　man
That would divorce this terror from my
　　heart ' ;
Meaning the king at Pomfret. Come, let's
　　go.   10
I am the King's friend, and will rid his foe.
　　　　　　　　　　　　　　　　　　[*Exeunt.*

SCENE V. *Pomfret Castle. The dungeon of
　　the Castle.*

Enter KING RICHARD.

　　K. Rich. I have been studying how I may
　　compare
This prison where I live unto the world ;
And, for because the world is populous
And here is not a creature but myself,
I cannot do it. Yet I'll hammer it out.   5
My brain I'll prove the female to my soul,
My soul the father ; and these two beget
A generation of still-breeding thoughts,
And these same thoughts people this little
　　world,   9
In humours like the people of this world,
For no thought is contented. The better
　　sort,
As thoughts of things divine, are inter-
　　mix'd
With scruples, and do set the word itself
Against the word,
As thus : ' Come, little ones ' ; and then
　　again,   15
' It is as hard to come as for a camel
To thread the postern of a small needle's
　　eye '.
Thoughts tending to ambition, they do plot
Unlikely wonders : how these vain weak
　　nails   19
May tear a passage through the flinty ribs
Of this hard world, my ragged prison walls ;
And, for they cannot, die in their own pride.

Thoughts tending to content flatter them-
    selves
That they are not the first of fortune's
    slaves,   24
Nor shall not be the last ; like silly beggars
Who, sitting in the stocks, refuge their
    shame,
That many have and others must sit there ;
And in this thought they find a kind of ease,
Bearing their own misfortunes on the back
Of such as have before endur'd the like. 30
Thus play I in one person many people,
And none contented. Sometimes am I king;
Then treasons make me wish myself a
    beggar,
And so I am. Then crushing penury
Persuades me I was better when a king ; 35
Then am I king'd again ; and by and by
Think that I am unking'd by Bolingbroke,
And straight am nothing. But whate'er
    I be,
Nor I, nor any man that but man is,
With nothing shall be pleas'd till he be
    eas'd   40
With being nothing.

The music plays.

                Music do I hear ?
Ha, ha ! keep time. How sour sweet music
    is
When time is broke and no proportion kept!
So is it in the music of men's lives.
And here have I the daintiness of ear 45
To check time broke in a disorder'd string ;
But, for the concord of my state and time,
Had not an ear to hear my true time broke.
I wasted time, and now doth time waste
    me ;
For now hath time made me his numb'ring
    clock :   50
My thoughts are minutes ; and with sighs
    they jar
Their watches on unto mine eyes, the out-
    ward watch,
Whereto my finger, like a dial's point,
Is pointing still, in cleansing them from
    tears.
Now, sir, the sound that tells what hour
    it is   55
Are clamorous groans which strike upon my
    heart,
Which is the bell. So sighs, and tears, and
    groans,
Show minutes, times, and hours ; but my
    time
Runs posting on in Bolingbroke's proud joy,
While I stand fooling here, his Jack of the
    clock.   60
This music mads me. Let it sound no more;
For though it have holp madmen to their
    wits,
In me it seems it will make wise men mad.
Yet blessing on his heart that gives it me !
For 'tis a sign of love ; and love to Richard

Is a strange brooch in this all-hating world.

Enter a Groom *of the stable.*

Groom. Hail, royal Prince !
K. Rich.   Thanks, noble peer !
The cheapest of us is ten groats too dear.
What art thou ? and how comest thou
    hither,
Where no man never comes but that sad
    dog   70
That brings me food to make misfortune
    live ?
Groom. I was a poor groom of thy stable,
    King,
When thou wert king ; who, travelling
    towards York,
With much ado at length have gotten leave
To look upon my sometimes royal master's
    face.   75
O, how it ern'd my heart, when I beheld,
In London streets, that coronation-day,
When Bolingbroke rode on roan Barbary—
That horse that thou so often hast bestrid,
That horse that I so carefully have dress'd !
K. Rich. Rode he on Barbary ? Tell me,
    gentle friend,   81
How went he under him ?
Groom. So proudly as if he disdain'd the
    ground.
K. Rich. So proud that Bolingbroke was
    on his back !
That jade hath eat bread from my royal
    hand ;   85
This hand hath made him proud with clap-
    ping him.
Would he not stumble ? would he not fall
    down,
Since pride must have a fall, and break the
    neck   88
Of that proud man that did usurp his back ?
Forgiveness, horse ! Why do I rail on thee,
Since thou, created to be aw'd by man,
Wast born to bear ? I was not made a
    horse ;   92
And yet I bear a burden like an ass,
Spurr'd, gall'd, and tir'd, by jauncing
    Bolingbroke.

Enter Keeper *with meat.*

Keep. Fellow, give place ; here is no
    longer stay.   95
K. Rich. If thou love me, 'tis time thou
    wert away.
Groom. What my tongue dares not, that
    my heart shall say.   [*Exit.*
Keep. My lord, will't please you to fall to?
K. Rich. Taste of it first as thou art wont
    to do.
Keep. My lord, I dare not. Sir Pierce of
    Exton,
Who lately came from the King, commands
    the contrary.   101
K. Rich. The devil take Henry of Lan-
    caster and thee !

Patience is stale, and I am weary of it.
               [Beats the Keeper.
  Keep. Help, help, help!

The murderers, EXTON *and Servants, rush
in, armed.*

  K. Rich. How now! What means death
    in this rude assault?   105
Villain, thy own hand yields thy death's
instrument.
    [Snatching a weapon and killing one.
Go thou and fill another room in hell.
    *[He kills another, then Exton strikes
        him down.*
That hand shall burn in never-quenching
fire
That staggers thus my person. Exton, thy
fierce hand
Hath with the King's blood stain'd the
King's own land.   110
Mount, mount, my soul! thy seat is up on
high;
Whilst my gross flesh sinks downward, here
to die.   *[Dies.*
  Exton. As full of valour as of royal blood.
Both have I spill'd. O, would the deed
were good!   114
For now the devil, that told me I did well,
Says that this deed is chronicled in hell.
This dead king to the living king I'll bear.
Take hence the rest, and give them burial
here.   *[Exeunt.*

    SCENE VI. *Windsor Castle.*

Flourish. Enter BOLINGBROKE, *the* DUKE
OF YORK, *with other* Lords *and* Attendants.

  Boling. Kind uncle York, the latest news
we hear
Is that the rebels have consum'd with fire
Our town of Ciceter in Gloucestershire;
But whether they be ta'en or slain we
hear not.

    Enter NORTHUMBERLAND.

Welcome, my lord. What is the news? 5
  North. First, to thy sacred state wish I all
happiness.
The next news is, I have to London sent
The heads of Salisbury, Spencer, Blunt, and
Kent.
The manner of their taking may appear
At large discoursed in this paper here. 10
  Boling. We thank thee, gentle Percy, for
thy pains;
And to thy worth will add right worthy
gains.

    Enter FITZWATER.

  Fitz. My lord, I have from Oxford sent
to London

The heads of Brocas and Sir Bennet Seely;
Two of the dangerous consorted traitors 15
That sought at Oxford thy dire overthrow.
  Boling. Thy pains, Fitzwater, shall not be
forgot;
Right noble is thy merit, well I wot.

Enter PERCY, *with the* BISHOP OF CARLISLE.

  Percy. The grand conspirator, Abbot of
Westminster,
With clog of conscience and sour melan-
choly, 20
Hath yielded up his body to the grave;
But here is Carlisle living, to abide
Thy kingly doom, and sentence of his pride.
  Boling. Carlisle, this is your doom:
Choose out some secret place, some
reverend room, 25
More than thou hast, and with it joy thy
life;
So as thou liv'st in peace, die free from
strife;
For though mine enemy thou hast ever
been,
High sparks of honour in thee have I seen.

Enter EXTON, *with Attendants, bearing a
coffin.*

  Exton. Great King, within this coffin I
present 30
Thy buried fear. Herein all breathless lies
The mightiest of thy greatest enemies,
Richard of Bordeaux, by me hither brought.
  Boling. Exton, I thank thee not; for
thou hast wrought
A deed of slander with thy fatal hand 35
Upon my head and all this famous land.
  Exton. From your own mouth, my lord,
did I this deed.
  Boling. They love not poison that do
poison need,
Nor do I thee. Though I did wish him
dead,
I hate the murderer, love him murdered. 40
The guilt of conscience take thou for thy
labour,
But neither my good word nor princely
favour;
With Cain go wander thorough shades of
night,
And never show thy head by day nor light.
Lords, I protest my soul is full of woe 45
That blood should sprinkle me to make me
grow.
Come, mourn with me for what I do lament,
And put on sullen black incontinent.
I'll make a voyage to the Holy Land,
To wash this blood off from my guilty hand.
March sadly after; grace my mournings
here 51
In weeping after this untimely bier.
        [Exeunt.

THE FIRST PART OF
KING HENRY THE FOURTH

DRAMATIS PERSONÆ

KING HENRY THE FOURTH.
HENRY, PRINCE OF WALES, } sons of
PRINCE JOHN OF LANCASTER, } Henry IV.
EARL OF WESTMORELAND, } friends of the
SIR WALTER BLUNT, } King.
THOMAS PERCY, EARL OF WORCESTER.
HENRY PERCY, EARL OF NORTHUMBER-
LAND.
HENRY PERCY, surnamed HOTSPUR, his son.
EDMUND MORTIMER, EARL OF MARCH.
ARCHIBALD, EARL OF DOUGLAS.
SCROOP, ARCHBISHOP OF YORK.
SIR MICHAEL, friend of the Archbishop.
OWEN GLENDOWER.
SIR RICHARD VERNON.

SIR JOHN FALSTAFF, }
POINS, }
BARDOLPH, } irregular
PETO, } humorists.
GADSHILL, }

LADY PERCY, wife of Hotspur and sister of
Mortimer.
LADY MORTIMER, wife of Mortimer and
daughter of Glendower.
HOSTESS QUICKLY, of the Boar's Head,
Eastcheap.

Lords, Officers, Attendants, Sheriff, Vintner, Chamberlain, Drawers, Carriers,
Travellers.

THE SCENE : *England and Wales.*

ACT ONE

SCENE I. *London. The palace.*

Enter the KING, LORD JOHN OF LANCASTER,
EARL OF WESTMORELAND, SIR WALTER
BLUNT, *and Others.*

King. So shaken as we are, so wan with
care,
Find we a time for frighted peace to pant
And breathe short-winded accents of new
broils
To be commenc'd in strands afar remote.
No more the thirsty entrance of this soil 5
Shall daub her lips with her own children's
blood ;
No more shall trenching war channel her
fields,
Nor bruise her flow'rets with the armed
hoofs
Of hostile paces. Those opposed eyes
Which, like the meteors of a troubled
heaven, 10
All of one nature, of one substance bred,
Did lately meet in the intestine shock
And furious close of civil butchery,
Shall now in mutual well-beseeming ranks
March all one way, and be no more oppos'd
Against acquaintance, kindred, and allies.
The edge of war, like an ill-sheathed knife,
No more shall cut his master. Therefore,
friends,
As far as to the sepulchre of Christ—
Whose soldier now, under whose blessed
cross 20
We are impressed and engag'd to fight—
Forthwith a power of English shall we levy,

Whose arms were moulded in their mothers'
womb
To chase these pagans in those holy fields
Over whose acres walk'd those blessed feet
Which fourteen hundred years ago were
nail'd 26
For our advantage on the bitter cross.
But this our purpose now is twelvemonth
old,
And bootless 'tis to tell you we will go ;
Therefore we meet not now. Then let me
hear 30
Of you, my gentle cousin Westmoreland,
What yesternight our Council did decree
In forwarding this dear expedience.
West. My liege, this haste was hot in
question
And many limits of the charge set down 35
But yesternight, when all athwart there
came
A post from Wales loaden with heavy news;
Whose worst was that the noble Mortimer,
Leading the men of Herefordshire to fight
Against the irregular and wild Glendower,
Was by the rude hands of that Welshman
taken, 41
A thousand of his people butchered ;
Upon whose dead corpse there was such
misuse,
Such beastly shameless transformation,
By those Welshwomen done, as may not be
Without much shame re-told or spoken of.
King. It seems then that the tidings of
this broil 47
Brake off our business for the Holy Land.
West. This match'd with other did, my
gracious Lord ;

For more uneven and unwelcome news 50
Came from the north, and thus it did
    import :
On Holy-rood day, the gallant Hotspur
    there,
Young Harry Percy, and brave Archibald,
That ever-valiant and approved Scot,
At Holmedon met,   55
Where they did spend a sad and bloody
    hour ;
As by discharge of their artillery
And shape of likelihood the news was told ;
For he that brought them, in the very
    heat
And pride of their contention did take
    horse,   60
Uncertain of the issue any way.
    King. Here is a dear, a true industrious
    friend,
Sir Walter Blunt, new lighted from his
    horse,
Stain'd with the variation of each soil
Betwixt that Holmedon and this seat of
    ours ;   65
And he hath brought us smooth and
    welcome news.
The Earl of Douglas is discomfited :
Ten thousand bold Scots, two and twenty
    knights,
Balk'd in their own blood, did Sir Walter
    see
On Holmedon's plains ; of prisoners,
    Hotspur took   70
Mordake, Earl of Fife and eldest son
To beaten Douglas ; and the Earl of
    Athol,
Of Murray, Angus, and Menteith.
And is not this an honourable spoil ?
A gallant prize ? Ha, cousin, is it not ? 75
    West. In faith,
It is a conquest for a prince to boast of.
    King. Yea, there thou mak'st me sad and
    mak'st me sin
In envy that my Lord Northumberland
Should be the father to so blest a son— 80
A son who is the theme of honour's tongue ;
Amongst a grove, the very straightest
    plant ;
Who is sweet Fortune's minion and her
    pride ;
Whilst I, by looking on the praise of him,
See riot and dishonour stain the brow 85
Of my young Harry. O that it could be
    prov'd
That some night-tripping fairy had ex-
    chang'd
In cradle-clothes our children where they
    lay,
And call'd mine Percy, his Plantagenet !
Then would I have his Harry, and he mine.
But let him from my thoughts. What think
    you, coz,   91
Of this young Percy's pride ? The prisoners
Which he in this adventure hath surpris'd

To his own use he keeps ; and sends me
    word,
I shall have none but Mordake Earl of Fife.
    West. This is his uncle's teaching, this is
    Worcester,   96
Malevolent to you in all aspects ;
Which makes him prune himself, and bristle
    up
The crest of youth against your dignity.
    King. But I have sent for him to answer
    this ;   100
And for this cause awhile we must neglect
Our holy purpose to Jerusalem.
Cousin, on Wednesday next our council we
Will hold at Windsor—so inform the lords ;
But come yourself with speed to us again,
For more is to be said and to be done 106
Than out of anger can be uttered.
    West. I will, my liege.   [*Exeunt.*

SCENE II. *London. The Prince's lodging.*

Enter the PRINCE OF WALES *and* SIR JOHN
    FALSTAFF.

Fal. Now, Hal, what time of day is it,
lad ?
    Prince. Thou art so fat-witted with
drinking of old sack, and unbuttoning thee
after supper, and sleeping upon benches
after noon, that thou hast forgotten to
demand that truly which thou wouldest
truly know. What a devil hast thou to do
with the time of the day ? Unless hours
were cups of sack, and minutes capons, and
clocks the tongues of bawds, and dials the
signs of leaping-houses, and the blessed sun
himself a fair hot wench in flame-coloured
taffeta, I see no reason why thou shouldst
be so superfluous to demand the time of the
day.   11
    Fal. Indeed, you come near me now, Hal ;
for we that take purses go by the moon and
the seven stars, and not by Phœbus, he
' that wand'ring knight so fair '. And, I
prithee, sweet wag, when thou art a king,
as, God save thy Grace—Majesty, I should
say ; for grace thou wilt have none— 17
    Prince. What, none ?
    Fal. No, by my troth ; not so much as
will serve to be prologue to an egg and
butter.   20
    Prince. Well, how then ? Come, roundly,
roundly.
    Fal. Marry, then, sweet wag, when thou
art king, let not us that are squires of the
night's body be called thieves of the day's
beauty ; let us be Diana's foresters, gentlemen of the shade, minions of the moon ;
and let men say we be men of good government, being governed, as the sea is, by our
noble and chaste mistress the moon, under
whose countenance we steal.   28
    Prince. Thou sayest well, and it holds
well too ; for the fortune of us that are the

moon's men doth ebb and flow like the sea, being governed, as the sea is, by the moon. As, for proof, now: a purse of gold most resolutely snatch'd on Monday night, and most dissolutely spent on Tuesday morning; got with swearing ' Lay by ' and spent with crying ' Bring in ' ; now in as low an ebb as the foot of the ladder, and by and by in as high a flow as the ridge of the gallows.

Fal. By the Lord, thou say'st true, lad. And is not my hostess of the tavern a most sweet wench?   39

Prince. As the honey of Hybla, my old lad of the castle. And is not a buff jerkin a most sweet robe of durance?

Fal. How now, how now, mad wag! What, in thy quips and thy quiddities? What a plague have I to do with a buff jerkin?   45

Prince. Why, what a pox have I to do with my hostess of the tavern?

Fal. Well, thou hast call'd her to a reckoning many a time and oft.

Prince. Did I ever call for thee to pay thy part?   50

Fal. No; I'll give thee thy due, thou hast paid all there.

Prince. Yea, and elsewhere, so far as my coin would stretch; and where it would not, I have used my credit.   54

Fal. Yea, and so us'd it that, were it not here apparent that thou art heir apparent —but, I prithee, sweet wag, shall there be gallows standing in England when thou art king, and resolution thus fubb'd as it is with the rusty curb of old father antic the law? Do not thou, when thou art king, hang a thief.   60

Prince. No; thou shalt.

Fal. Shall I? O rare! By the Lord, I'll be a brave judge!

Prince. Thou judgest false already: I mean thou shalt have the hanging of the thieves, and so become a rare hangman.   66

Fal. Well, Hal, well; and in some sort it jumps with my humour as well as waiting in the court, I can tell you.

Prince. For obtaining of suits?

Fal. Yea, for obtaining of suits, whereof the hangman hath no lean wardrobe. 'Sblood, I am as melancholy as a gib cat or a lugg'd bear.   72

Prince. Or an old lion, or a lover's lute.

Fal. Yea, or the drone of a Lincolnshire bagpipe.

Prince. What sayest thou to a hare, or the melancholy of Moor Ditch?   76

Fal. Thou hast the most unsavoury similes, and art indeed the most comparative, rascalliest, sweet young prince. But, Hal, I prithee, trouble me no more with vanity. I would to God thou and I knew where a commodity of good names were to be bought. An old lord of the Council

rated me the other day in the street about you, sir, but I mark'd him not; and yet he talk'd very wisely, but I regarded him not; and yet he talk'd wisely, and in the street too.   85

Prince. Thou didst well; for wisdom cries out in the streets, and no man regards it.

Fal. O, thou hast damnable iteration, and art indeed able to corrupt a saint. Thou hast done much harm upon me, Hal— God forgive thee for it! Before I knew thee, Hal, I knew nothing; and now am I, if a man should speak truly, little better than one of the wicked. I must give over this life, and I will give it over. By the Lord, an I do not I am a villain! I'll be damn'd for never a king's son in Christendom.   95

Prince. Where shall we take a purse to-morrow, Jack?

Fal. Zounds, where thou wilt, lad: I'll make one. An I do not, call me villain and baffle me.

Prince. I see a good amendment of life in thee—from praying to purse-taking.   100

Fal. Why, Hal, 'tis my vocation, Hal; 'tis no sin for a man to labour in his vocation.

Enter POINS.

Poins!—Now shall we know if Gadshill have set a match. O, if men were to be saved by merit, what hole in hell were hot enough for him? This is the most omnipotent villain that ever cried 'Stand' to a true man.   106

Prince. Good morrow, Ned.

Poins. Good morrow, sweet Hal. What says Monsieur Remorse? What says Sir John Sack and Sugar? Jack, how agrees the devil and thee about thy soul, that thou soldest him on Good Friday last for a cup of Madeira and a cold capon's leg?   112

Prince. Sir John stands to his word—the devil shall have his bargain; for he was never yet a breaker of proverbs; he will give the devil his due.   115

Poins. Then art thou damn'd for keeping thy word with the devil.

Prince. Else he had been damn'd for cozening the devil.   119

Poins. But, my lads, my lads, to-morrow morning, by four o'clock early, at Gadshill! There are pilgrims going to Canterbury with rich offerings, and traders riding to London with fat purses. I have vizards for you all; you have horses for yourselves. Gadshill lies to-night in Rochester. I have bespoke supper to-morrow night in Eastcheap. We may do it as secure as sleep. If you will go, I will stuff your purses full of crowns; if you will not, tarry at home and be hang'd.   128

Fal. Hear ye, Yedward: if I tarry at home and go not, I'll hang you for going.

Poins. You will, chops?   131

Fal. Hal, wilt thou make one?

Prince. Who?—I rob, I a thief? Not I, by my faith.

Fal. There's neither honesty, manhood, nor good fellowship in thee, nor thou cam'st not of the blood royal, if thou darest not stand for ten shillings.   136

Prince. Well then, once in my days I'll be a madcap.

Fal. Why, that's well said.

Prince. Well, come what will, I'll tarry at home.

Fal. By the lord, I'll be a traitor then, when thou art king.   141

Prince. I care not.

Poins. Sir John, I prithee, leave the Prince and me alone: I will lay him down such reasons for this adventure that he shall go.   145

Fal. Well, God give thee the spirit of persuasion, and him the ears of profiting, that what thou speakest may move, and what he hears may be believed; that the true prince may, for recreation sake, prove a false thief; for the poor abuses of the time want countenance.   Farewell; you shall find me in Eastcheap.   151

Prince. Farewell, thou latter spring! Farewell, All-hallown summer!

[*Exit Falstaff.*

Poins. Now, my good sweet honey lord, ride with us to-morrow. I have a jest to execute that I cannot manage alone. Falstaff, Bardolph, Peto, and Gadshill, shall rob those men that we have already waylaid; yourself and I will not be there; and when they have the booty, if you and I do not rob them, cut this head off from my shoulders.   160

Prince. How shall we part with them in setting forth?

Poins. Why, we will set forth before or after them, and appoint them a place of meeting, wherein it is at our pleasure to fail; and then will they adventure upon the exploit themselves; which they shall have no sooner achieved but we'll set upon them.   167

Prince. Yea, but 'tis like that they will know us by our horses, by our habits, and by every other appointment, to be our-selves.   170

Poins. Tut! our horses they shall not see—I'll tie them in the wood; our vizards we will change after we leave them; and, sirrah, I have cases of buckram for the nonce, to immask our noted outward garments.   174

Prince. Yea, but I doubt they will be too hard for us.

Poins. Well, for two of them, I know

them to be as true-bred cowards as ever turn'd back; and for the third, if he fight longer than he sees reason, I'll forswear arms. The virtue of this jest will be the incomprehensible lies that this same fat rogue will tell us when we meet at supper: how thirty, at least, he fought with; what wards, what blows, what extremities he endured; and in the reproof of this lives the jest.   183

Prince. Well, I'll go with thee. Provide us all things necessary, and meet me to-morrow night in Eastcheap; there I'll sup. Farewell.   186

Poins. Farewell, my lord. [*Exit Poins.*

Prince. I know you all, and will awhile uphold

The unyok'd humour of your idleness;

Yet herein will I imitate the sun,   190

Who doth permit the base contagious clouds

To smother up his beauty from the world,

That, when he please again to be himself,

Being wanted, he may be more wond'red at

By breaking through the foul and ugly mists   195

Of vapours that did seem to strangle him.

If all the year were playing holidays,

To sport would be as tedious as to work;

But when they seldom come, they wish'd-for come,   199

And nothing pleaseth but rare accidents.

So, when this loose behaviour I throw off

And pay the debt I never promised,

By how much better than my word I am,

By so much shall I falsify men's hopes; 204

And, like bright metal on a sullen ground,

My reformation, glitt'ring o'er my fault,

Shall show more goodly and attract more eyes

Than that which hath no foil to set it off.

I'll so offend to make offence a skill,   209

Redeeming time when men think least I will.   [*Exit.*

SCENE III. *London. The palace.*

Enter the KING, NORTHUMBERLAND, WOR-CESTER, HOTSPUR, SIR WALTER BLUNT, *with* Others.

King. My blood hath been too cold and temperate,

Unapt to stir at these indignities,

And you have found me; for accordingly

You tread upon my patience. But be sure

I will from henceforth rather be myself, 5

Mighty and to be fear'd, than my condition,

Which hath been smooth as oil, soft as young down,

And therefore lost that title of respect

Which the proud soul ne'er pays but to the proud.

Wor. Our house, my sovereign liege, little deserves   10

The scourge of greatness to be us'd on it—

483

And that same greatness too which our own
    hands
Have holp to make so portly.
  North. My lord—
  King. Worcester, get thee gone ; for I
    do see   15
Danger and disobedience in thine eye.
O, sir, your presence is too bold and
  peremptory,
And majesty might never yet endure
The moody frontier of a servant brow.
You have good leave to leave us ; when we
  need   20
Your use and counsel, we shall send for you.
               [*Exit Worcester.*
You were about to speak.
  North.   Yea, my good lord.
Those prisoners in your Highness' name
  demanded,
Which Harry Percy here at Holmedon took,
Were, as he says, not with such strength
  denied   25
As is delivered to your Majesty.
Either envy, therefore, or misprision
Is guilty of this fault, and not my son.
  Hot. My liege, I did deny no prisoners.
But I remember when the fight was done,
When I was dry with rage and extreme
  toil,   31
Breathless and faint, leaning upon my
  sword,
Came there a certain lord, neat, and trimly
  dress'd,
Fresh as a bridegroom, and his chin new
  reap'd
Show'd like a stubble-land at harvest-
  home.   35
He was perfumed like a milliner,
And 'twixt his finger and his thumb he held
A pouncet-box, which ever and anon
He gave his nose and took't away again ;
Who therewith angry, when it next came
  there,   40
Took it in snuff—and still he smil'd and
  talk'd—
And as the soldiers bore dead bodies by,
He call'd them untaught knaves, un-
  mannerly,
To bring a slovenly unhandsome corse
Betwixt the wind and his nobility.   45
With many holiday and lady terms
He questioned me : amongst the rest,
  demanded
My prisoners in your Majesty's behalf.
I then, all smarting with my wounds being
  cold,
To be so pest'red with a popinjay,   50
Out of my grief and my impatience
Answer'd neglectingly I know not what—
He should, or he should not—for he made
  me mad
To see him shine so brisk, and smell so
  sweet,
And talk so like a waiting-gentlewoman 55

Of guns, and drums, and wounds—God
  save the mark !—
And telling me the sovereignest thing on
  earth
Was parmaceti for an inward bruise ;
And that it was great pity, so it was,
This villainous saltpetre should be digg'd 60
Out of the bowels of the harmless earth,
Which many a good tall fellow had
  destroy'd
So cowardly ; and but for these vile guns
He would himself have been a soldier.
This bald unjointed chat of his, my lord, 65
I answered indirectly, as I said ;
And I beseech you, let not his report
Come current for an accusation
Betwixt my love and your high Majesty.
  Blunt. The circumstance considered, good
  my lord,   70
Whate'er Lord Harry Percy then had said
To such a person, and in such a place,
At such a time, with all the rest re-told,
May reasonably die, and never rise
To do him wrong, or any way impeach 75
What then he said, so he unsay it now.
  King. Why, yet he doth deny his
  prisoners,
But with proviso and exception—
That we at our own charge shall ransom
  straight   79
His brother-in-law, the foolish Mortimer ;
Who, on my soul, hath wilfully betray'd
The lives of those that he did lead to fight
Against that great magician, damn'd
  Glendower,
Whose daughter, as we hear, that Earl of
  March
Hath lately married. Shall our coffers,
  then,   85
Be emptied to redeem a traitor home ?
Shall we buy treason, and indent with fears,
When they have lost and forfeited them-
  selves ?
No, on the barren mountains let him starve;
For I shall never hold that man my friend
Whose tongue shall ask me for one penny
  cost   91
To ransom home revolted Mortimer.
  Hot. Revolted Mortimer !
He never did fall off, my sovereign liege,
But by the chance of war ; to prove that
  true,   95
Needs no more but one tongue for all those
  wounds,
Those mouthed wounds, which valiantly he
  took
When on the gentle Severn's sedgy bank,
In single opposition hand to hand,
He did confound the best part of an hour 100
In changing hardiment with great Glen-
  dower.
Three times they breath'd, and three times
  did they drink,
Upon agreement, of swift Severn's flood ;

Who then, affrighted with their bloody looks,
Ran fearfully among the trembling reeds 105
And hid his crisp head in the hollow bank
Bloodstained with these valiant combatants.
Never did base and rotten policy
Colour her working with such deadly wounds ;
Nor never could the noble Mortimer 110
Receive so many, and all willingly.
Then let him not be slandered with revolt.
    King. Thou dost belie him, Percy, thou dost belie him ;
He never did encounter with Glendower.
I tell thee 115
He durst as well have met the devil alone
As Owen Glendower for an enemy.
Art thou not asham'd ? But, sirrah, henceforth
Let me not hear you speak of Mortimer ;
Send me your prisoners with the speediest means, 120
Or you shall hear in such a kind from me
As will displease you. My Lord Northumberland,
We license your departure with your son.
Send us your prisoners, or you will hear of it.
    [*Exeunt King Henry, Blunt, and Train.*
    Hot. An if the devil come and roar for them, 125
I will not send them. I will after straight
And tell him so ; for I will ease my heart,
Albeit I make a hazard of my head.
    North. What, drunk with choler ? Stay and pause awhile.
Here comes your uncle.

        Re-enter WORCESTER.

    Hot.   Speak of Mortimer ! 130
Zounds, I will speak of him ; and let my soul
Want mercy if I do not join with him.
Yea, on his part I'll empty all these veins
And shed my dear blood drop by drop in the dust,
But I will lift the down-trod Mortimer 135
As high in the air as this unthankful king,
As this ingrate and cank'red Bolingbroke.
    North. Brother, the King hath made your nephew mad.
    Wor. Who struck this heat up after I was gone ?
    Hot. He will, forsooth, have all my prisoners ; 140
And when I urg'd the ransom once again
Of my wife's brother, then his cheek look'd pale,
And on my face he turn'd an eye of death,
Trembling even at the name of Mortimer.
    Wor. I cannot blame him : was not he proclaim'd 145
By Richard that dead is the next of blood ?

    North. He was : I heard the proclamation ;
And then it was when the unhappy King—
Whose wrongs in us God pardon !—did set forth
Upon his Irish expedition ;   150
From whence he intercepted did return
To be depos'd, and shortly murdered.
    Wor. And for whose death we in the world's wide mouth
Live scandaliz'd and foully spoken of.
    Hot. But soft, I pray you : did King Richard then 155
Proclaim my brother, Edmund Mortimer,
Heir to the crown ?
    North.   He did : myself did hear it.
    Hot. Nay, then I cannot blame his cousin king,
That wish'd him on the barren mountains starve.
But shall it be that you that set the crown
Upon the head of this forgetful man, 161
And for his sake wear the detested blot
Of murderous subornation—shall it be
That you a world of curses undergo,
Being the agents or base second means, 165
The cords, the ladder, or the hangman rather ?
O, pardon me that I descend so low
To show the line and the predicament
Wherein you range under this subtle king !
Shall it, for shame, be spoken in these days
Or fill up chronicles in time to come, 171
That men of your nobility and power
Did gage them both in an unjust behalf—
As both of you, God pardon it ! have done—
To put down Richard, that sweet lovely rose, 175
And plant this thorn, this canker, Bolingbroke ?
And shall it, in more shame, be further spoken
That you are fool'd, discarded, and shook off,
By him for whom these shames ye underwent ?
No ; yet time serves wherein you may redeem 180
Your banish'd honours, and restore yourselves
Into the good thoughts of the world again ;
Revenge the jeering and disdain'd contempt
Of this proud king, who studies day and night
To answer all the debt he owes to you 185
Even with the bloody payment of your deaths.
Therefore I say—
    Wor.   Peace, cousin, say no more.
And now I will unclasp a secret book,
And to your quick-conceiving discontents
I'll read you matter deep and dangerous,
As full of peril and adventurous spirit 191

As to o'er-walk a current roaring loud
On the unsteadfast footing of a spear.
  Hot. If he fall in, good night, or sink or
    swim.
Send danger from the east unto the west,
So honour cross it from the north to south,
And let them grapple. O, the blood more
    stirs   197
To rouse a lion than to start a hare !
  North. Imagination of some great exploit
Drives him beyond the bounds of patience.
  Hot. By heaven, methinks it were an easy
    leap   201
To pluck bright honour from the pale-fac'd
    moon ;
Or dive into the bottom of the deep,
Where fathom-line could never touch the
    ground,
And pluck up drowned honour by the locks;
So he that doth redeem her thence might
    wear   206
Without corrival all her dignities.
But out upon this half-fac'd fellowship !
  Wor. He apprehends a world of figures
    here,   209
But not the form of what he should attend.
Good cousin, give me audience for a while.
  Hot. I cry you mercy.
  Wor.   Those same noble Scots
That are your prisoners—
  Hot.   I'll keep them all ;
By God, he shall not have a Scot of them ;
No, if a Scot would save his soul, he shall
    not.   215
I'll keep them, by this hand.
  Wor.   You start away,
And lend no ear unto my purposes.
Those prisoners you shall keep.
  Hot.   Nay, I will ; that's flat.
He said he would not ransom Mortimer ;
Forbad my tongue to speak of Mortimer ;
But I will find him when he lies asleep, 221
And in his ear I'll holla ' Mortimer ! '
Nay,
I'll have a starling shall be taught to speak
Nothing but ' Mortimer ', and give it him
To keep his anger still in motion.   226
  Wor. Hear you, cousin ; a word.
  Hot. All studies here I solemnly defy,
Save how to gall and pinch this Boling-
    broke.
And that same sword-and-buckler Prince
    of Wales—   230
But that I think his father loves him not
And would be glad he met with some
    mischance—
I would have him poison'd with a pot of ale.
  Wor. Farewell, kinsman : I'll talk to you
When you are better temper'd to attend. 235
  North. Why, what a wasp-stung and
    impatient fool
Art thou to break into this woman's mood,
Tying thine ear to no tongue but thine
    own!

  Hot. Why, look you, I am whipt and
    scourg'd with rods,
Nettled, and stung with pismires, when I
    hear   240
Of this vile politician, Bolingbroke.
In Richard's time—what do you call the
    place ?—
A plague upon it, it is in Gloucestershire—
'Twas where the madcap duke his uncle
    kept—
His uncle York—where I first bow'd my
    knee   245
Unto this king of smiles, this Bolingbroke—
'Sblood !
When you and he came back from Ravens-
    purgh—
  North. At Berkeley Castle.
  Hot. You say true.   250
Why, what a candy deal of courtesy
This fawning greyhound then did proffer
    me !
' Look when his infant fortune came to
    age '
And ' gentle Harry Percy ' and ' kind
    cousin '—
O, the devil take such cozeners !   God
    forgive me !   255
Good uncle, tell your tale—I have done.
  Wor. Nay, if you have not, to it again ;
We will stay your leisure.
  Hot.   I have done, i' faith.
  Wor. Then once more to your Scottish
    prisoners :
Deliver them up without their ransom
    straight,   260
And make the Douglas' son your only mean
For powers in Scotland ; which, for divers
    reasons
Which I shall send you written, be assur'd
Will easily be granted. [*To North*] You, my
    lord,   264
Your son in Scotland being thus employ'd,
Shall secretly into the bosom creep
Of that same noble prelate, well belov'd,
The Archbishop.
  Hot. Of York, is it not ?
  Wor. True ; who bears hard   270
His brother's death at Bristow, the Lord
    Scroop.
I speak not this in estimation,
As what I think might be, but what I know
Is ruminated, plotted, and set down,
And only stays but to behold the face 275
Of that occasion that shall bring it on.
  Hot. I smell it.   Upon my life, it will do
    well.
  North. Before the game is afoot thou
    still let'st slip.
  Hot. Why, it cannot choose but be a
    noble plot.
And then the power of Scotland and of
    York   280
To join with Mortimer, ha ?
  Wor.   And so they shall.

Hot. In faith, it is exceedingly well aim'd.

Wor. And 'tis no little reason bids us
speed,
To save our heads by raising of a head ;
For, bear ourselves as even as we can, 285
The King will always think him in our
debt,
And think we think ourselves unsatisfied,
Till he hath found a time to pay us home.
And see already how he doth begin
To make us strangers to his looks of love.

Hot. He does, he does. We'll be reveng'd
on him. 291

Wor. Cousin, farewell. No further go in
this
Than I by letters shall direct your course.
When time is ripe, which will be suddenly,
I'll steal to Glendower and Lord Mortimer ;
Where you and Douglas and our pow'rs at
once, 296
As I will fashion it, shall happily meet,
To bear our fortunes in our own strong
arms,
Which now we hold at much uncertainty.

North. Farewell, good brother. We shall
thrive, I trust.

Hot. Uncle, adieu. O, let the hours be
short 301
Till fields and blows and groans applaud
our sport !   [*Exeunt.*

ACT TWO

SCENE I. *Rochester. An inn yard.*

Enter a Carrier *with a lantern in his hand.*

First Carrier. Heigh-ho ! an it be not four
by the day, I'll be hang'd ; Charles' wain
is over the new chimney, and yet our horse
not pack'd. What, ostler !

Ost. [*Within*] Anon, anon.   4

First Car. I prithee, Tom, beat Cut's
saddle ; put a few flocks in the point ; poor
jade is wrung in the withers out of all cess.

Enter another Carrier.

Sec. Car. Peas and beans are as dank here
as a dog, and that is the next way to give
poor jades the bots ; this house is turned
upside down since Robin Ostler died.   10

First Car. Poor fellow never joyed since
the price of oats rose ; it was the death of
him.

Sec. Car. I think this be the most
villainous house in all London road for
fleas ; I am stung like a tench.   14

First Car. Like a tench ! By the mass,
there is ne'er a king christen could be
better bit than I have been since the first
cock.

Sec. Car. Why, they will allow us ne'er a
jordan ; and then we leak in your chimney ;
and your chamber-lye breeds fleas like a
loach.   20

First Car. What, ostler ! come away, and
be hang'd ; come away.

Sec. Car. I have a gammon of bacon and
two razes of ginger, to be delivered as far as
Charing Cross.   24

First Car. God's body ! the turkeys in my
pannier are quite starved. What, ostler ! A
plague on thee ! hast thou never an eye in
thy head ? Canst not hear ? An 'twere not
as good deed as drink to break the pate on
thee, I am a very villain. Come, and be
hang'd ! Hast no faith in thee ?   30

Enter GADSHILL.

Gads. Good morrow, carriers. What's
o'clock ?

First Car. I think it be two o'clock.

Gads. I prithee lend me thy lantern to
see my gelding in the stable.

First Car. Nay, by God ! Soft ! I know
a trick worth two of that, i' faith.   36

Gads. I prithee lend me thine.

Sec. Car. Ay, when, canst tell ? Lend me
thy lantern, quoth 'a ? Marry, I'll see thee
hang'd first.

Gads. Sirrah carrier, what time do you
mean to come to London ?   41

Sec. Car. Time enough to go to bed with
a candle, I warrant thee. Come, neighbour
Mugs, we'll call up the gentlemen ; they
will along with company, for they have
great charge.   [*Exeunt Carriers.*

Gads. What, ho ! chamberlain !   46

Cham. [*Within*] At hand, quoth pick-
purse.

Gads. That's even as fair as—at hand,
quoth the chamberlain ; for thou variest
no more from picking of purses than giving
direction doth from labouring ; thou layest
the plot how.   51

Enter Chamberlain.

Cham. Good morrow, Master Gadshill.
It holds current that I told you yesternight :
there's a franklin in the Wild of Kent hath
brought three hundred marks with him in
gold ; I heard him tell it to one of his company last night at supper, a kind of auditor ;
one that hath abundance of charge too—
God knows what. They are up already and
call for eggs and butter ; they will away
presently.

Gads. Sirrah, if they meet not with Saint
Nicholas' clerks, I'll give thee this neck.   60

Cham. No, I'll none of it ; I pray thee
keep that for the hangman ; for I know
thou worshippest Saint Nicholas as truly
as a man of falsehood may.   63

Gads. What talkest thou to me of the
hangman ? If I hang, I'll make a fat pair
of gallows ; for if I hang, old Sir John
hangs with me ; and thou knowest he is
no starveling.   Tut ! there are other
Troyans that thou dream'st not of, the

which for sport sake are content to do the profession some grace; that would, if matters should be look'd into, for their own credit sake, make all whole. I am joined with no foot landrakers, no long-staff six-penny strikers, none of these mad mustachio purple-hu'd malt-worms; but with nobility and tranquillity, burgomasters and great oneyers, such as can hold in, such as will strike sooner than speak, and speak sooner than drink, and drink sooner than pray. And yet, zounds, I lie; for they pray continually to their saint, the commonwealth; or, rather, not pray to her, but prey on her; for they ride up and down on her, and make her their boots.   79

Cham. What, the commonwealth their boots? Will she hold out water in foul way?

Gads. She will, she will; justice hath liquor'd her. We steal as in a castle, cock-sure; we have the receipt of fern-seed, we walk invisible.   84

Cham. Nay, by my faith, I think you are more beholding to the night than to fern-seed for your walking invisible.

Gads. Give me thy hand: thou shalt have a share in our purchase, as I am a true man.

Cham. Nay, rather let me have it, as you are a false thief.   91

Gads. Go to; 'homo' is a common name to all men. Bid the ostler bring my gelding out of the stable. Farewell, you muddy knave.   [*Exeunt.*

SCENE II. *The highway, near Gadshill.*

Enter the PRINCE OF WALES *and* POINS.

Poins. Come, shelter, shelter; I have remov'd Falstaff's horse, and he frets like a gumm'd velvet.

Prince. Stand close.

Enter FALSTAFF.

Fal. Poins! Poins! And be hang'd! Poins!

Prince. Peace, ye fat-kidney'd rascal; what a brawling dost thou keep!   6

Fal. Where's Poins, Hal?

Prince. He is walk'd up to the top of the hill; I'll go seek him.   9

Fal. I am accurs'd to rob in that thief's company; the rascal hath removed my horse, and tied him I know not where. If I travel but four foot by the squier further afoot, I shall break my wind. Well, I doubt not but to die a fair death for all this, if I scape hanging for killing that rogue. I have forsworn his company hourly any time this two and twenty years, and yet I am bewitch'd with the rogue's company. If the rascal have not given me medicines to make me love him, I'll be hang'd. It could not be else: I have drunk medicines.

Poins! Hal! A plague upon you both! Bardolph! Peto! I'll starve ere I'll rob a foot further. An 'twere not as good a deed as drink to turn true man, and to leave these rogues, I am the veriest varlet that ever chewed with a tooth. Eight yards of uneven ground is three-score and ten miles afoot with me; and the stony-hearted villains know it well enough. A plague upon it, when thieves cannot be true one to another! [*They whistle*] Whew! A plague upon you all! Give me my horse, you rogues; give me my horse, and be hang'd.   29

Prince. Peace, ye fat-guts! lie down; lay thine ear close to the ground, and list if thou canst hear the tread of travellers. 32

Fal. Have you any levers to lift me up again, being down? 'Sblood, I'll not bear mine own flesh so far afoot again for all the coin in thy father's exchequer. What a plague mean ye to colt me thus?   36

Prince. Thou liest: thou art not colted, thou art uncolted.

Fal. I prithee, good Prince Hal, help me to my horse, good king's son.   40

Prince. Out, ye rogue! shall I be your ostler?

Fal. Hang thyself in thine own heir-apparent garters. If I be ta'en, I'll peach for this. An I have not ballads made on you all, and sung to filthy tunes, let a cup of sack be my poison. When a jest is so forward, and afoot too!—I hate it.   46

Enter GADSHILL, BARDOLPH *and* PETO *with him.*

Gads. Stand!

Fal. So I do, against my will.

Poins. O, 'tis our setter: I know his voice. Bardolph, what news?   50

Bard. Case ye, case ye; on with your vizards: there's money of the King's coming down the hill; 'tis going to the King's exchequer.

Fal. You lie, ye rogue; 'tis going to the King's tavern.

Gads. There's enough to make us all. 55

Fal. To be hang'd.

Prince. Sirs, you four shall front them in the narrow lane; Ned Poins and I will walk lower; if they scape from your encounter, then they light on us.

Peto. How many be there of them?   60

Gads. Some eight or ten.

Fal. Zounds, will they not rob us?

Prince. What, a coward, Sir John Paunch?

Fal. Indeed, I am not John of Gaunt, your grandfather; but yet no coward, Hal.   65

Prince. Well, we leave that to the proof.

Poins. Sirrah Jack, thy horse stands behind the hedge: when thou need'st him,

there thou shalt find him. Farewell, and
stand fast. 69

Fal. Now cannot I strike him, if I should
be hang'd.

Prince. [*Aside to Poins*] Ned, where are
our disguises ? 71

Poins. [*Aside*] Here, hard by ; stand close.
[*Exeunt the Prince and Poins.*

Fal. Now, my masters, happy man be
his dole, say I ; every man to his business.

Enter the Travellers.

First Trav. Come, neighbour ; the boy
shall lead our horses down the hill ; we'll
walk afoot awhile, and ease our legs.

Thieves. Stand !

Travellers. Jesus bless us ! 79

Fal. Strike ; down with them ; cut the
villains' throats. Ah, whoreson caterpillars ! bacon-fed knaves ! They hate us
youth. Down with them ; fleece them.

Trav. O, we are undone, both we and
ours for ever ! 84

Fal. Hang ye, gorbellied knaves, are ye
undone ? No, ye fat chuffs ; I would your
store were here. On, bacons, on ! What, ye
knaves ! young men must live. You are
grand-jurors, are ye ? we'll jure ye, faith.
[*Here they rob them and bind
them. Exeunt.*

Re-enter the Prince *and* Poins
in buckram.

Prince. The thieves have bound the true
men. Now, could thou and I rob the
thieves and go merrily to London, it would
be argument for a week, laughter for a
month, and a good jest for ever. 92

Poins. Stand close ; I hear them coming.

Enter the Thieves *again.*

Fal. Come, my masters, let us share, and
then to horse before day. An the Prince
and Poins be not two arrant cowards,
there's no equity stirring. There's no
more valour in that Poins than in a wild
duck. 97
[*As they are sharing, the Prince and
Poins set upon them.*

Prince. Your money !

Poins. Villains !
[*They all run away, and Falstaff, after
a blow or two, runs away too, leaving
the booty behind them.*

Prince. Got with much ease. Now merrily
to horse.
The thieves are all scattered, and possess'd
with fear 101
So strongly that they dare not meet each
other ;
Each takes his fellow for an officer.
Away, good Ned. Falstaff sweats to death
And lards the lean earth as he walks along.
Were't not for laughing, I should pity him.

Poins. How the fat rogue roar'd ! [*Exeunt.*

SCENE III. *Warkworth Castle.*

Enter Hotspur *solus, reading a letter.*

Hot. ' But, for mine own part, my lord,
I could be well contented to be there, in
respect of the love I bear your house.' He
could be contented—why is he not, then ?
In respect of the love he bears our house—
he shows in this he loves his own barn
better than he loves our house. Let me
see some more. ' The purpose you undertake is dangerous '—why, that's certain :
'tis dangerous to take a cold, to sleep, to
drink ; but I tell you, my lord fool, out of
this nettle, danger, we pluck this flower,
safety. ' The purpose you undertake is
dangerous ; the friends you have named
uncertain ; the time itself unsorted ; and
your whole plot too light for the counterpoise of so great an opposition.' Say you
so, say you so ? I say unto you again, you
are a shallow, cowardly hind, and you lie.
What a lack-brain is this ! By the Lord,
our plot is a good plot as ever was laid ;
our friends true and constant—a good
plot, good friends, and full of expectation ;
an excellent plot, very good friends. What
a frosty-spirited rogue is this ! Why, my
Lord of York commends the plot and the
general course of the action. Zounds, an I
were now by this rascal, I could brain him
with his lady's fan. Is there not my father,
my uncle, and myself ; Lord Edmund
Mortimer, my Lord of York, and Owen
Glendower ? Is there not, besides, the
Douglas ? Have I not all their letters to
meet me in arms by the ninth of the next
month, and are they not some of them set
forward already ? What a pagan rascal is
this ! an infidel ! Ha ! you shall see now,
in very sincerity of fear and cold heart,
will he to the King and lay open all our
proceedings. O, I could divide myself and
go to buffets for moving such a dish of
skim milk with so honourable an action !
Hang him ; let him tell the King : we are
prepared. I will set forward to-night. 32

Enter Lady Percy.

How now, Kate ! I must leave you within
these two hours.

Lady. O my good lord, why are you thus
alone ?
For what offence have I this fortnight been
A banish'd woman from my Harry's bed ?
Tell me, sweet lord, what is't that takes
from thee 37
Thy stomach, pleasure, and thy golden
sleep ?
Why dost thou bend thine eyes upon the
earth,
And start so often when thou sit'st alone ?
Why hast thou lost the fresh blood in thy
cheeks, 41

And given my treasures and my rights of
thee 42
To thick-ey'd musing and curs'd melan-
choly ?
In thy faint slumbers I by thee have
watch'd,
And heard thee murmur tales of iron wars ;
Speak terms of manage to thy bounding
steed ; 46
Cry ' Courage ! To the field ! ' And thou
hast talk'd
Of sallies and retires, of trenches, tents,
Of palisadoes, frontiers, parapets,
Of basilisks, of cannon, culverin, 50
Of prisoners' ransom, and of soldiers slain,
And all the currents of a heady fight.
Thy spirit within thee hath been so at war,
And thus hath so bestirr'd thee in thy sleep,
That beads of sweat have stood upon thy
brow 55
Like bubbles in a late disturbed stream ;
And in thy face strange motions have
appear'd,
Such as we see when men restrain their
breath
On some great sudden hest. O, what
portents are these ? 59
Some heavy business hath my lord in hand,
And I must know it, else he loves me not.
  Hot. What, ho !

Enter a Servant.

  Is Gilliams with the packet gone ?
Serv. He is, my lord, an hour ago.
Hot. Hath Butler brought those horses
from the sheriff ?
Serv. One horse, my lord, he brought
even now. 65
Hot. What horse ? A roan, a crop-ear, is
it not ?
Serv. It is, my lord.
Hot. That roan shall be my throne.
Well, I will back him straight. O esperance!
Bid Butler lead him forth into the park.
  [*Exit Servant.*
Lady. But hear you, my lord. 70
Hot. What say'st thou, my lady ?
Lady. What is it carries you away ?
Hot. Why, my horse, my love, my horse.
Lady. Out, you mad-headed ape !
A weasel hath not such a deal of spleen 75
As you are toss'd with. In faith,
I'll know your business, Harry, that I will.
I fear my brother Mortimer doth stir
About his title and hath sent for you 79
To line his enterprise ; but if you go—
  Hot. So far afoot, I shall be weary, love.
Lady. Come, come, you paraquito,
answer me
Directly unto this question that I ask.
In faith, I'll break thy little finger, Harry,
An if thou wilt not tell me all things true.
  Hot. Away. 86
Away, you trifler ! Love, I love thee not,

I care not for thee, Kate ; this is no world
To play with mammets and to tilt with lips :
We must have bloody noses and crack'd
crowns, 90
And pass them current too. God's me, my
horse !
What say'st thou, Kate ? what wouldst
thou have with me ?
  Lady. Do you not love me ? Do you not,
indeed ?
Well, do not, then ; for since you love me
not, 94
I will not love myself. Do you not love me?
Nay, tell me if you speak in jest or no.
  Hot. Come, wilt thou see me ride ?
And when I am o' horseback, I will swear
I love thee infinitely. But hark you, Kate :
I must not have you henceforth question
me 100
Whither I go, nor reason whereabout.
Whither I must, I must ; and, to conclude,
This evening must I leave you, gentle Kate.
I know you wise, but yet no farther wise
Than Harry Percy's wife ; constant you
are, 105
But yet a woman ; and for secrecy,
No lady closer : for I well believe
Thou wilt not utter what thou dost not
know,
And so far will I trust thee, gentle Kate.
  Lady. How, so far ? 110
  Hot. Not an inch further. But hark you,
Kate :
Whither I go, thither shall you go too ;
To-day will I set forth, to-morrow you.
Will this content you, Kate ?
  Lady. It must, of force. [*Exeunt.*

SCENE IV. *Eastcheap. The Boar's Head
Tavern.*

Enter the PRINCE, *and* POINS.

  Prince. Ned, prithee, come out of that
fat room and lend me thy hand to laugh
a little.
  Poins. Where hast been, Hal ?
  Prince. With three or four loggerheads
amongst three or fourscore hogsheads. I
have sounded the very base-string of
humility. Sirrah, I am sworn brother to a
leash of drawers and can call them all by
their christen names, as Tom, Dick, and
Francis. They take it already upon their
salvation that though I be but Prince of
Wales yet I am the king of courtesy ; and
tell me flatly I am no proud Jack, like
Falstaff, but a Corinthian, a lad of mettle,
a good boy—by the Lord, so they call me—
and when I am King of England I shall
command all the good lads in Eastcheap.
They call drinking deep, dyeing scarlet ;
and when you breathe in your watering,
they cry ' hem ! ' and bid you play it off.
To conclude, I am so good a proficient in

one quarter of an hour that I can drink with any tinker in his own language during my life. I tell thee, Ned, thou hast lost much honour that thou wert not with me in this action. But, sweet Ned—to sweeten which name of Ned, I give thee this pennyworth of sugar, clapp'd even now into my hand by an under-skinker, one that never spake other English in his life than ' Eight shillings and sixpence ' and ' You are welcome ' with this shrill addition, ' Anon, anon, sir ! Score a pint of bastard in the Half-moon ' or so. But, Ned, to drive away the time till Falstaff come, I prithee, do thou stand in some by-room, while I question my puny drawer to what end he gave me the sugar ; and do thou never leave calling ' Francis ! ' that his tale to me may be nothing but ' Anon '. Step aside, and I'll show thee a precedent. [*Exit Poins.*

Poins. [*Within*] Francis !   32
Prince. Thou are perfect.
Poins. [*Within*] Francis !

Enter FRANCIS.

Fran. Anon, anon, sir. Look down into the Pomgarnet, Ralph.   36
Prince. Come hither, Francis.
Fran. My lord ?
Prince. How long has thou to serve, Francis ?
Fran. Forsooth, five years, and as much as to—   40
Poins. [*Within*] Francis !
Fran. Anon, anon, sir.
Prince. Five year ! by'r lady, a long lease for the clinking of pewter. But, Francis, darest thou be so valiant as to play the coward with thy indenture and show it a fair pair of heels and run from it ?
Fran. O Lord, sir, I'll be sworn upon all the books in England, I could find in my heart—
Poins. [*Within*] Francis !
Fran. Anon, sir.   50
Prince. How old art thou, Francis ?
Fran. Let me see, about Michaelmas next I shall be—
Poins. [*Within*] Francis !
Fran. Anon, sir. Pray stay a little, my lord.
Prince. Nay, but hark you, Francis : for the sugar thou gavest me—'twas a pennyworth, was't not ?   56
Fran. O Lord, I would it had been two !
Prince. I will give thee for it a thousand pound ; ask me when thou wilt, and thou shalt have it.
Poins. [*Within*] Francis !   60
Fran. Anon, anon.
Prince. Anon, Francis ? No, Francis ; but to-morrow, Francis ; or, Francis, o' Thursday ; or indeed, Francis, when thou wilt. But, Francis—

Fran. My lord ?   65
Prince. Wilt thou rob this leathern jerkin, crystal-button, knot-pated, agatering, puke-stocking, caddis-garter, smoothtongue, Spanish-pouch—
Fran. O Lord, sir, who do you mean ? 69
Prince. Why, then, your brown bastard is your only drink ; for, look you, Francis, your white canvas doublet will sully. In Barbary, sir, it cannot come to so much.
Fran. What, sir ?
Poins. [*Within*] Francis !   74
Prince. Away, you rogue ! Dost thou not hear them call ?

[*Here they both call him ; Francis stands amazed, not knowing which way to go.*

Enter Vintner.

Vint. What, stand'st thou still, and hear'st such a calling ? Look to the guests within. [*Exit Francis*] My lord, old Sir John, with half-a-dozen more, are at the door. Shall I let them in ?   80
Prince. Let them alone awhile, and then open the door. [*Exit Vintner*] Poins !

Re-enter POINS.

Poins. Anon, anon, sir.
Prince. Sirrah, Falstaff and the rest of the thieves are at the door. Shall we be merry ?   85
Poins. As merry as crickets, my lad. But hark ye : what cunning match have you made with this jest of the drawer ? Come, what's the issue ?   88
Prince. I am now of all humours that have showed themselves humours since the old days of goodman Adam to the pupil-age of this present twelve o'clock at midnight.

Re-enter FRANCIS.

What's o'clock, Francis ?   93
Fran. Anon, anon, sir.   [*Exit.*
Prince. That ever this fellow should have fewer words than a parrot, and yet the son of a woman ! His industry is upstairs and downstairs ; his eloquence the parcel of a reckoning. I am not yet of Percy's mind, the Hotspur of the north ; he that kills me some six or seven dozen of Scots at a breakfast, washes his hands, and says to his wife ' Fie upon this quiet life ! I want work '. ' O my sweet Harry,' says she ' how many hast thou kill'd to-day ? ' ' Give my roan horse a drench ' says he ; and answers ' Some fourteen,' an hour after, ' a trifle, a trifle '. I prithee call in Falstaff ; I'll play Percy, and that damn'd brawn shall play Dame Mortimer his wife. ' Rivo ! ' says the drunkard. Call in ribs, call in tallow.

Enter FALSTAFF, GADSHILL, BARDOLPH, *and* PETO ; *followed by* FRANCIS *with wine.*

Poins. Welcome, Jack. Where hast thou been ?   108

Fal. A plague of all cowards, I say, and a vengeance too! Marry and amen! Give me a cup of sack, boy. Ere I lead this life long, I'll sew nether-stocks, and mend them and foot them too. A plague of all cowards! Give me a cup of sack, rogue. Is there no virtue extant?   [*He drinks.* 113

Prince. Didst thou never see Titan kiss a dish of butter, pitiful-hearted Titan, that melted at the sweet tale of the sun's? If thou didst, then behold that compound. 116

Fal. You rogue, here's lime in this sack too! There is nothing but roguery to be found in villainous man; yet a coward is worse than a cup of sack with lime in it. A villainous coward! Go thy ways, old Jack; die when thou wilt; if manhood, good manhood, be not forgot upon the face of the earth, then am I a shotten herring. There lives not three good men unhang'd in England, and one of them is fat and grows old. God help the while! A bad world, I say. I would I were a weaver; I could sing psalms or anything. A plague of all cowards, I say still.   127

Prince. How now, woolsack! What mutter you?

Fal. A king's son! If I do not beat thee out of thy kingdom with a dagger of lath, and drive all thy subjects afore thee like a flock of wild geese, I'll never wear hair on my face more. You Prince of Wales! 132

Prince. Why, you whoreson round man, what's the matter?

Fal. Are not you a coward? Answer me to that—and Poins there? 136

Poins. Zounds, ye fat paunch, an ye call me coward, by the Lord, I'll stab thee.

Fal. I call thee coward! I'll see thee damn'd ere I call thee coward; but I would give a thousand pound I could run as fast as thou canst. You are straight enough in the shoulders—you care not who sees your back. Call you that backing of your friends? A plague upon such backing! Give me them that will face me. Give me a cup of sack; I am a rogue if I drunk to-day.   145

Prince. O villain! thy lips are scarce wip'd since thou drunk'st last.

Fal. All is one for that. [*He drinks*] A plague of all cowards, still say I.

Prince. What's the matter? 150

Fal. What's the matter! There be four of us here have ta'en a thousand pound this day morning.

Prince. Where is it, Jack? Where is it?

Fal. Where is it! taken from us it is: a hundred upon poor four of us. 155

Prince. What, a hundred, man?

Fal. I am a rogue if I were not at half-sword with a dozen of them two hours together. I have scap'd by miracle. I am eight times thrust through the doublet, four through the hose; my buckler cut through and through; my sword hack'd like a hand-saw—ecce signum! I never dealt better since I was a man—all would not do. A plague of all cowards! Let them speak; if they speak more or less than truth, they are villains and the sons of darkness.   165

Prince. Speak, sirs; how was it?

Gads. We four set upon some dozen—

Fal. Sixteen at least, my lord.

Gads. And bound them.

Peto. No, no, they were not bound. 170

Fal. You rogue, they were bound, every man of them; or I am a Jew else, an Ebrew Jew.

Gads. As we were sharing, some six or seven fresh men set upon us—

Fal. And unbound the rest, and then come in the other. 176

Prince. What, fought you with them all?

Fal. All! I know not what you call all, but if I fought not with fifty of them, I am a bunch of radish. If there were not two or three and fifty upon poor old Jack, then am I no two-legg'd creature. 181

Prince. Pray God you have not murd'red some of them.

Fal. Nay, that's past praying for: I have pepper'd two of them; two I am sure I have paid—two rogues in buckram suits. I tell thee what, Hal, if I tell thee a lie, spit in my face, call me horse. Thou knowest my old ward: here I lay, and thus I bore my point. Four rogues in buckram let drive at me— 189

Prince. What, four? Thou saidst but two even now.

Fal. Four, Hal; I told thee four.

Poins. Ay, ay, he said four.

Fal. These four came all afront, and mainly thrust at me. I made me no more ado but took all their seven points in my target, thus.   195

Prince. Seven? Why, there were but four even now.

Fal. In buckram.

Poins. Ay, four, in buckram suits.

Fal. Seven, by these hilts, or I am a villain else.

Prince. [*Aside to Poins*] Prithee, let him alone; we shall have more anon. 201

Fal. Dost thou hear me, Hal?

Prince. Ay, and mark thee too, Jack.

Fal. Do so, for it is worth the list'ning to. These nine in buckram that I told thee of— 205

Prince. So, two more already.

Fal. Their points being broken—

Poins. Down fell their hose.

Fal. Began to give me ground; but I followed me close, came in foot and hand, and with a thought seven of the eleven I paid.   211

Prince. O monstrous! eleven buckram men grown out of two!

Fal. But, as the devil would have it, three misbegotten knaves in Kendal green came at my back and let drive at me—for it was so dark, Hal, that thou couldest not see thy hand. 217

Prince. These lies are like their father that begets them—gross as a mountain, open, palpable. Why, thou clay-brain'd guts, thou knotty-pated fool, thou whoreson, obscene, greasy tallow-catch— 221

Fal. What, art thou mad? art thou mad? Is not the truth the truth?

Prince. Why, how couldst thou know these men in Kendal green, when it was so dark thou couldst not see thy hand? Come, tell us your reason; what sayest thou to this? 227

Poins. Come, your reason, Jack, your reason.

Fal. What, upon compulsion? Zounds, an I were at the strappado, or all the racks in the world, I would not tell you on compulsion. Give you a reason on compulsion! If reasons were as plentiful as blackberries, I would give no man a reason upon compulsion, I. 233

Prince. I'll be no longer guilty of this sin; this sanguine coward, this bed-presser, this horse-back-breaker, this huge hill of flesh— 236

Fal. 'Sblood, you starveling, you eel-skin, you dried neat's-tongue, you bull's pizzle, you stock-fish—O for breath to utter what is like thee!—you tailor's yard, you sheath, you bow-case, you vile standing tuck! 240

Prince. Well, breathe awhile, and then to it again; and when thou hast tired thyself in base comparisons, hear me speak but this.

Poins. Mark, Jack. 244

Prince. We two saw you four set on four, and bound them and were masters of their wealth. Mark now, how a plain tale shall put you down. Then did we two set on you four; and, with a word, out-fac'd you from your prize, and have it; yea, and can show it you here in the house. And, Falstaff, you carried your guts away as nimbly, with as quick dexterity, and roar'd for mercy, and still run and roar'd, as ever I heard bull-calf. What a slave art thou to hack thy sword as thou hast done, and then say it was in fight! What trick, what device, what starting-hole, canst thou now find out to hide thee from this open and apparent shame? 256

Poins. Come, let's hear, Jack; what trick hast thou now?

Fal. By the Lord, I knew ye as well as he that made ye. Why, hear you, my masters: was it for me to kill the heir-apparent? Should I turn upon the true prince? Why, thou knowest I am as valiant as Hercules; but beware instinct—the lion will not touch the true prince. Instinct is a great matter: I was now a coward on instinct. I shall think the better of myself and thee during my life—I for a valiant lion, and thou for a true prince. But, by the Lord, lads, I am glad you have the money. Hostess, clap to the doors. Watch to-night, pray to-morrow. Gallants, lads, boys, hearts of gold, all the titles of good fellowship come to you! What, shall we be merry? Shall we have a play extempore? 271

Prince. Content—and the argument shall be thy running away.

Fal. Ah, no more of that, Hal, an thou lovest me!

Enter Hostess.

Host. O Jesu, my lord the Prince! 275

Prince. How now, my lady the hostess! What say'st thou to me?

Host. Marry, my lord, there is a nobleman of the court at door would speak with you; he says he comes from your father.

Prince. Give him as much as will make him a royal man, and send him back again to my mother.

Fal. What manner of man is he?

Host. An old man.

Fal. What doth gravity out of his bed at midnight? Shall I give him his answer? 286

Prince. Prithee do, Jack.

Fal. Faith, and I'll send him packing.

[*Exit.*

Prince. Now, sirs: by'r lady, you fought fair; so did you, Peto; so did you, Bardolph. You are lions too: you ran away upon instinct; you will not touch the true prince; no, fie! 292

Bard. Faith, I ran when I saw others run.

Prince. Faith, tell me now in earnest, how came Falstaff's sword so hack'd? 295

Peto. Why, he hack'd it with his dagger, and said he would swear truth out of England but he would make you believe it was done in fight; and persuaded us to do the like. 299

Bard. Yea, and to tickle our noses with spear-grass to make them bleed, and then to beslubber our garments with it, and swear it was the blood of true men. I did that I did not this seven year before—I blush'd to hear his monstrous devices. 304

Prince. O villain! Thou stolest a cup of sack eighteen years ago, and wert taken with the manner, and ever since thou hast blush'd extempore. Thou hadst fire and sword on thy side, and yet thou ran'st away; what instinct hadst thou for it? 309

Bard. My lord, do you see these meteors? do you behold these exhalations?

Prince. I do.

Bard. What think you they portend ?

Prince. Hot livers and cold purses.

Bard. Choler, my lord, if rightly taken.

Prince. No, if rightly taken, halter. 316

Re-enter FALSTAFF.

Here comes lean Jack, here comes bare-bone. How now, my sweet creature of bombast ! How long is't ago, Jack, since thou sawest thine own knee ? 319

Fal. My own knee ! When I was about thy years, Hal, I was not an eagle's talon in the waist : I could have crept into any alderman's thumb-ring. A plague of sighing and grief ! it blows a man up like a bladder. There's villainous news abroad. Here was Sir John Bracy from your father : you must to the court in the morning. That same mad fellow of the north, Percy, and he of Wales that gave Amaimon the bastinado, and made Lucifer cuckold, and swore the devil his true liegeman upon the cross of a Welsh hook—what a plague call you him ?

Poins. O, Glendower. 330

Fal. Owen, Owen—the same ; and his son-in-law Mortimer, and old Northumberland, and that sprightly Scot of Scots, Douglas, that runs o' horseback up a hill perpendicular— 334

Prince. He that rides at high speed and with his pistol kills a sparrow flying ?

Fal. You have hit it.

Prince. So did he never the sparrow.

Fal. Well, that rascal hath good mettle in him ; he will not run. 340

Prince. Why, what a rascal art thou, then, to praise him so for running !

Fal. O' horseback, ye cuckoo ; but afoot he will not budge a foot.

Prince. Yes, Jack, upon instinct. 345

Fal. I grant ye, upon instinct. Well, he is there too, and one Mordake, and a thousand blue-caps more. Worcester is stol'n away to-night ; thy father's beard is turn'd white with the news ; you may buy land now as cheap as stinking mack'rel. 350

Prince. Why, then, it is like, if there come a hot June, and this civil buffeting hold, we shall buy maidenheads as they buy hob-nails, by the hundreds. 353

Fal. By the mass, lad, thou sayest true : it is like we shall have good trading that way. But tell me, Hal, art not thou horrible afeard ? Thou being heir-apparent, could the world pick thee out three such enemies again as that fiend Douglas, that spirit Percy, and that devil Glendower ? Art thou not horribly afraid ? Doth not thy blood thrill at it ? 360

Prince. Not a whit, i 'faith ; I lack some of thy instinct.

Fal. Well, thou wilt be horribly chid to-morrow when thou comest to thy father. If thou love me, practise an answer. 346

Prince. Do thou stand for my father, and examine me upon the particulars of my life.

Fal. Shall I ? Content ! This chair shall be my state, this dagger my sceptre, and this cushion my crown.

Prince. Thy state is taken for a join'd-stool, thy golden sceptre for a leaden dagger, and thy precious rich crown for a pitiful bald crown ! 371

Fal. Well, an the fire of grace be not quite out of thee, now shalt thou be moved. Give me a cup of sack to make my eyes look red, that it may be thought I have wept ; for I must speak in passion, and I will do it in King Cambyses' vein. 376

Prince. Well, here is my leg.

Fal. And here is my speech. Stand aside, nobility.

Host. O Jesu, this is excellent sport, i' faith !

Fal. Weep not, sweet queen, for trickling tears are vain. 380

Host. O, the father, how he holds his countenance !

Fal. For God's sake, lords, convey my tristful queen ;

For tears do stop the floodgates of her eyes.

Host. O Jesu, he doth it as like one of these harlotry players as ever I see ! 385

Fal. Peace, good pint-pot ; peace, good tickle-brain.—Harry, I do not only marvel where thou spendest thy time, but also how thou art accompanied ; for though the camomile, the more it is trodden on the faster it grows, yet youth, the more it is wasted the sooner it wears. That thou art my son I have partly thy mother's word, partly my own opinion, but chiefly a villainous trick of thine eye, and a foolish hanging of thy nether lip, that doth warrant me. If then thou be son to me, here lies the point : why, being son to me, art thou so pointed at ? Shall the blessed sun of heaven prove a micher and eat black-berries ? A question not to be ask'd. Shall the son of England prove a thief and take purses ? A question to be ask'd. There is a thing, Harry, which thou hast often heard of, and it is known to many in our land by the name of pitch. This pitch, as ancient writers do report, doth defile ; so doth the company thou keepest ; for, Harry, now I do not speak to thee in drink, but in tears ; not in pleasure, but in passion ; not in words only, but in woes also. And yet there is a virtuous man whom I have often noted in thy company, but I know not his name. 406

Prince. What manner of man, an it like your Majesty ?

Fal. A goodly portly man, i' faith, and a corpulent ; of a cheerful look, a pleasing eye, and a most noble carriage ; and, as I think, his age some fifty, or, by 'r lady, inclining to three-score. And now I remember me, his name is Falstaff. If that man should be lewdly given, he deceiveth me ; for, Harry, I see virtue in his looks. If then the tree may be known by the fruit, as the fruit by the tree, then, peremptorily I speak it, there is virtue in that Falstaff : him keep with, the rest banish. And tell me now, thou naughty varlet, tell me, where hast thou been this month ?   417

Prince. Dost thou speak like a king ? Do thou stand for me, and I'll play my father.

Fal. Depose me ? If thou dost it half so gravely, so majestically, both in word and matter, hang me up by the heels for a rabbit-sucker or a poulter's hare.   422

Prince. Well, here I am set.

Fal. And here I stand. Judge, my masters.

Prince. Now, Harry, whence come you ?

Fal. My noble lord, from Eastcheap.

Prince. The complaints I hear of thee are grievous.

Fal. 'Sblood, my lord, they are false. Nay, I'll tickle ye for a young prince, i' faith.   429

Prince. Swearest thou, ungracious boy ? Henceforth ne'er look on me. Thou art violently carried away from grace ; there is a devil haunts thee in the likeness of an old fat man ; a tun of man is thy companion. Why dost thou converse with that trunk of humours, that bolting-hutch of beastliness, that swoll'n parcel of dropsies, that huge bombard of sack, that stuff'd cloak-bag of guts, that roasted Manningtree ox with the pudding in his belly, that reverend vice, that grey iniquity, that father ruffian, that vanity in years ? Wherein is he good, but to taste sack and drink it ? wherein neat and cleanly, but to carve a capon and eat it ? wherein cunning, but in craft ? wherein crafty, but in villainy ? wherein villainous, but in all things ? wherein worthy, but in nothing ?

Fal. I would your Grace would take me with you ; whom means your Grace ?   445

Prince. That villainous abominable misleader of youth, Falstaff, that old white-bearded Satan.

Fal. My lord, the man I know.

Prince. I know thou dost.   449

Fal. But to say I know more harm in him than in myself were to say more than I know. That he is old—the more the pity—his white hairs do witness it ; but that he is—saving your reverence—a whoremaster, that I utterly deny. If sack and sugar be a fault, God help the wicked ! If to be old and merry be a sin, then many an old host that I know is damn'd ; if to be fat be to be hated, then Pharaoh's lean kine are to

be loved. No, my good lord : banish Peto, banish Bardolph, banish Poins ; but, for sweet Jack Falstaff, kind Jack Falstaff, true Jack Falstaff, valiant Jack Falstaff—and therefore more valiant, being, as he is, old Jack Falstaff—banish not him thy Harry's company, banish not him Harry's company. Banish plump Jack, and banish all the world.   463

Prince. I do, I will.   [*A knocking heard.*
[*Exeunt Hostess, Francis, and Bardolph.*

Re-enter BARDOLPH, *running.*

Bard. O, my lord, my lord! the sheriff with a most monstrous watch is at the door.

Fal. Out, ye rogue ! Play out the play : I have much to say in the behalf of that Falstaff.

Re-enter the Hostess.

Host. O Jesu, my lord, my lord !   469

Prince. Heigh, heigh ! the devil rides upon a fiddle-stick ; what's the matter ?

Host. The sheriff and all the watch are at the door ; they are come to search the house. Shall I let them in ?

Fal. Dost thou hear, Hal ? Never call a true piece of gold a counterfeit. Thou art essentially made, without seeming so.   476

Prince. And thou a natural coward, without instinct.

Fal. I deny your major. If you will deny the sheriff, so ; if not, let him enter. If I become not a cart as well as another man, a plague on my bringing up ! I hope I shall as soon be strangled with a halter as another.   481

Prince. Go, hide thee behind the arras ; the rest walk up above. Now, my masters, for a true face and good conscience.

Fal. Both which I have had ; but their date is out, and therefore I'll hide me.   486
[*Exeunt all but the Prince and Peto.*

Prince. Call in the sheriff.

Enter Sheriff *and the* Carrier.

Now, master sheriff, what is your will with me ?

Sher. First, pardon me, my lord. A hue and cry
Hath followed certain men unto this house.

Prince. What men ?   491

Sher. One of them is well known, my gracious lord—
A gross fat man.

Car. As fat as butter.

Prince. The man, I do assure you, is not here,
For I myself at this time have employ'd him.   495
And, sheriff, I will engage my word to thee
That I will, by to-morrow dinner-time,
Send him to answer thee, or any man,

For any thing he shall be charg'd withal;
And so let me entreat you leave the house.

Sher. I will, my lord. There are two
    gentlemen   501
Have in this robbery lost three hundred
    marks.

Prince. It may be so; if he have robb'd
    these men
He shall be answerable; and so, farewell.

Sher. Good night, my noble lord.   505

Prince. I think it is good morrow, is it
    not?

Sher. Indeed, my lord, I think it be two
    o'clock. [*Exeunt Sheriff and Carrier.*

Prince. This oily rascal is known as well
as Paul's. Go, call him forth.   509

Peto. Falstaff! Fast asleep behind the
arras, and snorting like a horse.

Prince. Hark how hard he fetches breath.
Search his pockets. [*He searcheth his pocket,
and findeth certain papers*] What hast thou
found?

Peto. Nothing but papers, my lord.   515

Prince. Let's see what they be: read
them.

Peto. [*Reads*]

Item, A capon - - -	2s.	2d.
Item, Sauce - - - -		4d.
Item, Sack, two gallons -	5s.	8d.
Item, Anchovies and sack after		
supper - - - -	2s.	6d.
Item, Bread - - - -		ob.

Prince. O monstrous! but one halfpenny-
worth of bread to this intolerable deal of
sack! What there is else, keep close; we'll
read it at more advantage. There let him
sleep till day. I'll to the court in the
morning. We must all to the wars, and thy
place shall be honourable. I'll procure this
fat rogue a charge of foot; and I know his
death will be a march of twelve-score. The
money shall be paid back again with advantage. Be with me betimes in the morning; and so, good morrow, Peto.   530

Peto. Good morrow, good my lord.

                  [*Exeunt.*

ACT THREE

SCENE I. *Wales. Glendower's castle.*

Enter HOTSPUR, WORCESTER, MORTIMER,
    and GLENDOWER.

Mort. These promises are fair, the parties
    sure,
And our induction full of prosperous hope.

Hot. Lord Mortimer, and cousin Glen-
    dower,
Will you sit down?
And uncle Worcester—a plague upon it!   5
I have forgot the map.

Glend.   No, here it is.
Sit, cousin Percy; sit, good cousin Hot-
    spur,
For by that name as oft as Lancaster

Doth speak of you, his cheek looks pale, and
    with
A rising sigh he wisheth you in heaven.   10

Hot. And you in hell, as oft as he hears
Owen Glendower spoke of.

Glend. I cannot blame him: at my
    nativity
The front of heaven was full of fiery shapes,
Of burning cressets; and at my birth   15
The frame and huge foundation of the earth
Shaked like a coward.

Hot.   Why, so it would have done
at the same season if your mother's cat had
but kitten'd, though yourself had never
been born.   20

Glend. I say the earth did shake when I
    was born.

Hot. And I say the earth was not of my
    mind,
If you suppose as fearing you it shook.

Glend. The heavens were all on fire, the
    earth did tremble.

Hot. O, then the earth shook to see the
    heavens on fire,   25
And not in fear of your nativity.
Diseased nature oftentimes breaks forth
In strange eruptions; oft the teeming earth
Is with a kind of colic pinch'd and vex'd
By the imprisoning of unruly wind   30
Within her womb; which, for enlargement
    striving,
Shakes the old beldam earth, and topples
    down
Steeples and moss-grown towers. At your
    birth,
Our grandam earth, having this distemp'ra-
    ture,
In passion shook.

Glend.   Cousin, of many men   35
I do not bear these crossings. Give me
    leave
To tell you once again that at my birth
The front of heaven was full of fiery shapes,
The goats ran from the mountains, and the
    herds
Were strangely clamorous to the frighted
    fields.   40
These signs have mark'd me extraordinary;
And all the courses of my life do show
I am not in the roll of common men.
Where is he living, clipp'd in with the sea
That chides the banks of England, Scot-
    land, Wales,   45
Which calls me pupil or hath read to me?
And bring him out that is but woman's son
Can trace me in the tedious ways of art
And hold me pace in deep experiments.

Hot. I think there's no man speaks better
Welsh. I'll to dinner.   51

Mort. Peace, cousin Percy; you will
    make him mad.

Glend. I can call spirits from the vasty
    deep.

Hot. Why, so can I, or so can any man;

But will they come when you do call for
 them ?   55
  Glend. Why, I can teach you, cousin, to
    command
The devil.
  Hot. And I can teach thee, coz, to shame
    the devil
By telling truth : tell truth, and shame the
    devil.
If thou have power to raise him, bring him
    hither,   60
And I'll be sworn I have power to shame
    him hence.
O, while you live, tell truth, and shame the
    devil !
  Mort. Come, come, no more of this un-
    profitable chat.
  Glend. Three times hath Henry Boling-
    broke made head
Against my power ; thrice from the banks
    of Wye   65
And sandy-bottom'd Severn have I sent
    him
Bootless home and weather-beaten back.
  Hot. Home without boots, and in foul
    weather too !
How scapes he agues, in the devil's name ?
  Glend. Come, here is the map ; shall we
    divide our right   70
According to our threefold order ta'en ?
  Mort. The Archdeacon hath divided it
Into three limits very equally :
England, from Trent and Severn hitherto,
By south and east is to my part assign'd ;
All westward, Wales beyond the Severn
    shore,   76
And all the fertile land within that bound,
To Owen Glendower ; and, dear coz, to
    you
The remnant northward lying off from
    Trent.
And our indentures tripartite are drawn ; 80
Which being sealed interchangeably,
A business that this night may execute,
To-morrow, cousin Percy, you and I
And my good Lord of Worcester will set
    forth
To meet your father and the Scottish
    power,   85
As is appointed us, at Shrewsbury.
My father Glendower is not ready yet,
Nor shall we need his help these fourteen
    days.
[*To Glendower*] Within that space you may
    have drawn together
Your tenants, friends, and neighbouring
    gentlemen.   90
  Glend. A shorter time shall send me to
    you, lords ;
And in my conduct shall your ladies come,
From whom you now must steal and take
    no leave ;
For there will be a world of water shed
Upon the parting of your wives and you. 95

  Hot. Methinks my moiety, north from
    Burton here,
In quantity equals not one of yours.
See how this river comes me cranking in,
And cuts me from the best of all my land
A huge half-moon, a monstrous cantle out.
I'll have the current in this place damm'd
    up,   101
And here the smug and silver Trent shall
    run
In a new channel, fair and evenly ;
It shall not wind with such a deep indent
To rob me of so rich a bottom here.   105
  Glend. Not wind ! It shall, it must ; you
    see it doth.
  Mort.   Yea, but
Mark how he bears his course and runs me
    up
With like advantage on the other side,
Gelding the opposed continent as much   110
As on the other side it takes from you.
  Wor. Yea, but a little charge will trench
    him here,
And on this north side win this cape of land,
And then he runs straight and even.
  Hot. I'll have it so ; a little charge will
    do it.   115
  Glend. I'll not have it alt'red.
  Hot.   Will not you ?
  Glend. No, nor you shall not.
  Hot.   Who shall say me nay ?
  Glend. Why, that will I.
  Hot. Let me not understand you, then ;
speak it in Welsh.   120
  Glend. I can speak English, lord, as well
    as you,
For I was train'd up in the English court ;
Where, being but young, I framed to the
    harp
Many an English ditty lovely well,
And gave the tongue a helpful ornament—
A virtue that was never seen in you.   126
  Hot. Marry,
And I am glad of it with all my heart !
I had rather be a kitten and cry mew
Than one of these same metre ballad-
    mongers ;   130
I had rather hear a brazen canstick turn'd,
Or a dry wheel grate on the axle-tree ;
And that would set my teeth nothing on
    edge,
Nothing so much as mincing poetry.
'Tis like the forc'd gait of a shuffling nag. 135
  Glend. Come, you shall have Trent turn'd.
  Hot. I do not care ; I'll give thrice so
    much land
To any well-deserving friend ;
But in the way of bargain, mark ye me,
I'll cavil on the ninth part of a hair.   140
Are the indentures drawn ? Shall we be
    gone ?
  Glend. The moon shines fair ; you may
    away by night ;
I'll haste the writer, and withal

Break with your wives of your departure
   hence.
I am afraid my daughter will run mad, 145
So much she doteth on her Mortimer. [*Exit.*
  Mort. Fie, cousin Percy ! how you cross
    my father !
  Hot. I cannot choose. Sometime he
    angers me
With telling me of the moldwarp and the
   ant,
Of the dreamer Merlin and his prophecies,
And of a dragon and a finless fish, 151
A clip-wing'd griffin and a moulten raven,
A couching lion and a ramping cat,
And such a deal of skimble-skamble stuff
As puts me from my faith. I tell you what :
He held me last night at least nine hours
In reckoning up the several devils' names
That were his lackeys. I cried ' hum ' and
   ' well, go to '
But mark'd him not a word. O, he is as
  tedious
As a tired horse, a railing wife ; 160
Worse than a smoky house ; I had rather
  live
With cheese and garlic in a windmill, far,
Than feed on cates and have him talk to me
In any summer house in Christendom.
  Mort. In faith, he is a worthy gentleman,
Exceedingly well read, and profited 166
In strange concealments ; valiant as a
  lion,
And wondrous affable ; and as bountiful
As mines of India. Shall I tell you, cousin ?
He holds your temper in a high respect, 170
And curbs himself even of his natural scope
When you come 'cross his humour ; faith,
  he does.
I warrant you that man is not alive
Might so have tempted him as you have
  done 174
Without the taste of danger and reproof ;
But do not use it oft, let me entreat you.
  Wor. In faith, my lord, you are too wilful-
   blame ;
And since your coming hither have done
  enough
To put him quite besides his patience.
You must needs learn, lord, to amend this
  fault ; 180
Though sometimes it show greatness,
  courage, blood—
And that's the dearest grace it renders
  you—
Yet oftentimes it doth present harsh rage,
Defect of manners, want of government,
Pride, haughtiness, opinion, and disdain ;
The least of which, haunting a nobleman,
Loseth men's hearts, and leaves behind a
  stain
Upon the beauty of all parts besides,
Beguiling them of commendation. 189
  Hot. Well, I am school'd : good manners
   be your speed !

Here come our wives, and let us take our
  leave.

Re-enter GLENDOWER, *with* LADY MORTIMER
     and LADY PERCY.

  Mort. This is the deadly spite that angers
   me :
My wife can speak no English, I no Welsh.
  Glend. My daughter weeps : she'll not
   part with you ; 194
She'll be a soldier too, she'll to the wars.
  Mort. Good father, tell her that she and
   my aunt Percy
Shall follow in your conduct speedily.
    [*Glendower speaks to her in Welsh, and*
     she answers him in the same.
  Glend. She is desperate here ; a peevish,
self-will'd harlotry, one that no persuasion
can do good upon.
       [*The Lady speaks in Welsh.*
  Mort. I understand thy looks : that
   pretty Welsh 200
Which thou pourest down from these
  swelling heavens
I am too perfect in ; and, but for shame,
In such a parley should I answer thee.
     [*The Lady speaks again in Welsh.*
I understand thy kisses, and thou mine,
And that's a feeling disputation ; 205
But I will never be a truant, love,
Till I have learnt thy language ; for thy
  tongue
Makes Welsh as sweet as ditties highly
  penn'd,
Sung by a fair queen in a summer's bow'r,
With ravishing division, to her lute. 210
  Glend. Nay, if you melt, then will she
  run mad.
     [*The Lady speaks again in Welsh.*
  Mort. O, I am ignorance itself in this !
  Glend. She bids you on the wanton
  rushes lay you down,
And rest your gentle head upon her lap,
And she will sing the song that pleaseth
  you, 215
And on your eyelids crown the god of sleep,
Charming your blood with pleasing heavi-
  ness,
Making such difference 'twixt wake and
  sleep
As is the difference betwixt day and night
The hour before the heavenly-harness'd
  team 220
Begins his golden progress in the east.
  Mort. With all my heart I'll sit and hear
  her sing ;
By that time will our book, I think, be
  drawn.
  Glend. Do so ;
And those musicians that shall play to you
Hang in the air a thousand leagues from
  hence, 226
And straight they shall be here ; sit, and
  attend.

Hot. Come, Kate, thou art perfect in lying down. Come, quick, quick, that I may lay my head in thy lap.

Lady P. Go, ye giddy goose. 230
  [*The music plays.*

Hot. Now I perceive the devil understands Welsh ;
And 'tis no marvel he is so humorous.
By'r lady, he is a good musician.

Lady P. Then should you be nothing but musical, for you are altogether govern'd by humours. Lie still, ye thief, and hear the lady sing in Welsh. 236

Hot. I had rather hear Lady, my brach, howl in Irish.

Lady P. Wouldst thou have thy head broken ?

Hot. No.

Lady P. Then be still. 240

Hot. Neither ; 'tis a woman's fault.

Lady P. Now God help thee !

Hot. To the Welsh lady's bed.

Lady P. What's that ?

Hot. Peace ! she sings. 245
  [*Here the Lady sings a Welsh song.*

Hot. Come, Kate, I'll have your song too.

Lady P. Not mine, in good sooth.

Hot. Not yours, in good sooth ! Heart ! you swear like a comfit-maker's wife. ' Not you, in good sooth ' and ' As true as I live ' and ' As God shall mend me ' and ' As sure as day '. 251
And givest such sarcenet surety for thy oaths
As if thou never walk'st further than Finsbury.
Swear me, Kate, like a lady as thou art,
A good mouth-filling oath ; and leave ' in sooth ' 255
And such protest of pepper-gingerbread
To velvet-guards and Sunday-citizens.
Come, sing.

Lady P. I will not sing. 259

Hot. 'Tis the next way to turn tailor, or be redbreast teacher. An the indentures be drawn, I'll away within these two hours ; and so come in when ye will. [*Exit.*

Glend. Come, come, Lord Mortimer ; you are as slow
As hot Lord Percy is on fire to go. 264
By this our book is drawn ; we'll but seal,
And then to horse immediately.

Mort. With all my heart.
  [*Exeunt.*

SCENE II. *London. The palace.*

Enter the KING, *the* PRINCE OF WALES, *and* Lords.

King. Lords, give us leave ; the Prince of Wales and I
Must have some private conference ; but be near at hand,
For we shall presently have need of you.
  [*Exeunt Lords.*

I know not whether God will have it so,
For some displeasing service I have done, 5
That, in his secret doom, out of my blood
He'll breed revengement and a scourge for me ;
But thou dost in thy passages of life
Make me believe that thou art only mark'd
For the hot vengeance and the rod of heaven 10
To punish my mistreadings. Tell me else,
Could such inordinate and low desires,
Such poor, such bare, such lewd, such mean attempts,
Such barren pleasures, rude society,
As thou art match'd withal and grafted to,
Accompany the greatness of thy blood 16
And hold their level with thy princely heart ?

Prince. So please your Majesty, I would I could
Quit all offences with as clear excuse,
As well as I am doubtless I can purge 20
Myself of many I am charg'd withal ;
Yet such extenuation let me beg,
As, in reproof of many tales devis'd,
Which oft the ear of greatness needs must hear,
By smiling pick-thanks and base newsmongers, 25
I may, for some things true, wherein my youth
Hath faulty wand'red and irregular,
Find pardon on my true submission.

King. God pardon thee ! Yet let me wonder, Harry,
At thy affections, which do hold a wing 30
Quite from the flight of all thy ancestors.
Thy place in council thou hast rudely lost,
Which by thy younger brother is supplied,
And art almost an alien to the hearts
Of all the court and princes of my blood. 35
The hope and expectation of thy time
Is ruin'd, and the soul of every man
Prophetically do forethink thy fall.
Had I so lavish of my presence been,
So common-hackney'd in the eyes of men, 40
So stale and cheap to vulgar company,
Opinion, that did help me to the crown,
Had still kept loyal to possession
And left me in reputeless banishment
A fellow of no mark nor likelihood. 45
By being seldom seen, I could not stir
But, like a comet, I was wond'red at ;
That men would tell their children ' This is he ' ;
Others would say ' Where, which is Bolingbroke ? '
And then I stole all courtesy from heaven,
And dress'd myself in such humility 51
That I did pluck allegiance from men's hearts,
Loud shouts and salutations from their mouths,
Even in the presence of the crowned King.

Thus did I keep my person fresh and new,
My presence, like a robe pontifical, 56
Ne'er seen but wond'red at, and so my state,
Seldom but sumptuous, show'd like a feast
And won by rareness such solemnity.
The skipping King, he ambled up and down
With shallow jesters and rash bavin wits,
Soon kindled and soon burnt; carded his state,
Mingled his royalty with cap'ring fools;
Had his great name profaned with their scorns,
And gave his countenance, against his name, 65
To laugh at gibing boys and stand the push
Of every beardless vain comparative;
Grew a companion to the common streets,
Enfeoff'd himself to popularity;
That, being daily swallowed by men's eyes, 70
They surfeited with honey and began
To loathe the taste of sweetness, whereof a little
More than a little is by much too much.
So, when he had occasion to be seen,
He was but as the cuckoo is in June, 75
Heard, not regarded, seen, but with such eyes
As, sick and blunted with community,
Afford no extraordinary gaze,
Such as is bent on sun-like majesty
When it shines seldom in admiring eyes; 80
But rather drowz'd and hung their eyelids down,
Slept in his face, and rend'red such aspect
As cloudy men use to their adversaries,
Being with his presence glutted, gorg'd, and full. 84
And in that very line, Harry, standest thou;
For thou hast lost thy princely privilege
With vile participation. Not an eye
But is aweary of thy common sight,
Save mine, which hath desir'd to see thee more;
Which now doth that I would not have it do— 90
Make blind itself with foolish tenderness.
    Prince. I shall hereafter, my thrice-gracious lord,
Be more myself.
    King.   For all the world
As thou art to this hour was Richard then
When I from France set foot at Ravenspurgh; 95
And even as I was then is Percy now.
Now, by my sceptre and my soul to boot,
He hath more worthy interest to the state
Than thou the shadow of succession;
For of no right, nor colour like to right, 100
He doth fill fields with harness in the realm;
Turns head against the lion's armed jaws;
And, being no more in debt to years than thou,

Leads ancient lords and reverend bishops on
To bloody battles and to bruising arms. 105
What never-dying honour hath he got
Against renowned Douglas! whose high deeds,
Whose hot incursions, and great name in arms,
Holds from all soldiers chief majority
And military title capital 110
Through all the kingdoms that acknowledge Christ.
Thrice hath this Hotspur, Mars in swathling clothes,
This infant warrior, in his enterprises
Discomfited great Douglas; ta'en him once,
Enlarged him and made a friend of him, 115
To fill the mouth of deep defiance up
And shake the peace and safety of our throne.
And what say you to this? Percy, Northumberland,
The Archbishop's Grace of York, Douglas, Mortimer,
Capitulate against us and are up. 120
But wherefore do I tell these news to thee?
Why, Harry, do I tell thee of my foes,
Which art my nearest and dearest enemy?
Thou that art like enough, through vassal fear,
Base inclination, and the start of spleen, 125
To fight against me under Percy's pay,
To dog his heels, and curtsy at his frowns,
To show how much thou art degenerate.
    Prince. Do not think so; you shall not find it so;
And God forgive them that so much have sway'd 130
Your Majesty's good thoughts away from me!
I will redeem all this on Percy's head,
And in the closing of some glorious day
Be bold to tell you that I am your son,
When I will wear a garment all of blood, 135
And stain my favours in a bloody mask,
Which, wash'd away, shall scour my shame with it;
And that shall be the day, whene'er it lights,
That this same child of honour and renown,
This gallant Hotspur, this all-praised knight, 140
And your unthought-of Harry chance to meet.
For every honour sitting on his helm,
Would they were multitudes, and on my head
My shames redoubled! For the time will come
That I shall make this northern youth exchange 145
His glorious deeds for my indignities.
Percy is but my factor, good my lord,

To engross up glorious deeds on my behalf ;
And I will call him to so strict account
That he shall render every glory up,   150
Yea, even the slightest worship of his time,
Or I will tear the reckoning from his heart.
This, in the name of God, I promise here ;
The which if He be pleas'd I shall perform,
I do beseech your Majesty may salve   155
The long-grown wounds of my intemper-
    ature.
If not, the end of life cancels all bands ;
And I will die a hundred thousand deaths
Ere break the smallest parcel of this vow.
    King. A hundred thousand rebels die in
        this :   160
Thou shalt have charge and sovereign trust
    herein.

Enter SIR WALTER BLUNT.

How now, good Blunt ! Thy looks are full
    of speed.
    Blunt. So hath the business that I come
        to speak of.
Lord Mortimer of Scotland hath sent word
That Douglas and the English rebels met
The eleventh of this month at Shrewsbury.
A mighty and a fearful head they are,   167
If promises be kept on every hand,
As ever off'red foul play in a state.
    King. The Earl of Westmoreland set
        forth to-day,
With him my son, Lord John of Lancaster ;
For this advertisement is five days old.
On Wednesday next, Harry, you shall set
    forward ;   173
On Thursday we ourselves will march. Our
    meeting
Is Bridgenorth. And, Harry, you shall march
Through Gloucestershire ; by which ac-
    count,
Our business valued, some twelve days
    hence
Our general forces at Bridgenorth shall
    meet.   179
Our hands are full of business. Let's away.
Advantage feeds him fat while men delay.
                                [*Exeunt.*

SCENE III.   *Eastcheap.*   *The Boar's Head
    Tavern.*

Enter FALSTAFF *and* BARDOLPH.

    Fal. Bardolph, am I not fall'n away
vilely since this last action ? Do I not
bate ? Do I not dwindle ? Why, my skin
hangs about me like an old lady's loose
gown ; I am withered like an old apple-
john. Well, I'll repent, and that suddenly,
while I am in some liking ; I shall be out
of heart shortly, and then I shall have no
strength to repent. An I have not forgotten
what the inside of a church is made of, I
am a peppercorn, a brewer's horse. The

inside of a church ! Company, villainous
company, hath been the spoil of me.   10
    Bard. Sir John, you are so fretful you
cannot live long.
    Fal. Why, there is it ; come, sing me a
bawdy song, make me merry. I was as
virtuously given as a gentleman need to be ;
virtuous enough : swore little, dic'd not
above seven times a week, went to a bawdy-
house not above once in a quarter—of an
hour, paid money that I borrowed—three
or four times, lived well, and in good compass ; and now I live out of all order, out
of all compass.   20
    Bard. Why, you are so fat, Sir John, that
you must needs be out of all compass—out
of all reasonable compass, Sir John.
    Fal. Do thou amend thy face, and I'll
amend my life. Thou art our admiral, thou
bearest the lantern in the poop, but 'tis in
the nose of thee ; thou art the Knight of
the Burning Lamp.   27
    Bard. Why, Sir John, my face does you
no harm.
    Fal. No, I'll be sworn ; I make as good
use of it as many a man doth of a death's
head or a memento mori : I never see thy
face but I think upon hell-fire, and Dives
that lived in purple ; for there he is in his
robes, burning, burning. If thou wert any
way given to virtue, I would swear by thy
face : my oath should be ' By this fire,
that's God's angel '. But thou art altogether given over, and wert indeed, but for
the light in thy face, the son of utter
darkness. When thou ran'st up Gadshill
in the night to catch my horse, if I did not
think thou hadst been an ignis fatuus or a
ball of wildfire, there's no purchase in
money. O, thou art a perpetual triumph,
an everlasting bonfire light ! Thou hast
saved me a thousand marks in links and
torches, walking with thee in the night
betwixt tavern and tavern ; but the sack
that thou hast drunk me would have
bought me lights as good cheap at the
dearest chandler's in Europe. I have maintained that salamander of yours with fire
any time this two and thirty years ; God
reward me for it !   47
    Bard. 'Sblood, I would my face were in
your belly !
    Fal. God-a-mercy ! so should I be sure
to be heart-burnt.   50

Enter HOSTESS.

How now, Dame Partlet the hen ! Have
you inquir'd yet who pick'd my pocket ?
    Host. Why, Sir John, what do you think,
Sir John ? Do you think I keep thieves in
my house ? I have search'd, I have in-
quired, so has my husband, man by man,
boy by boy, servant by servant. The tithe
of a hair was never lost in my house before.

Fal. Ye lie, hostess : Bardolph was shav'd and lost many a hair, and I'll be sworn my pocket was pick'd. Go to, you are a woman, go.   60

Host. Who, I ? No, I defy thee. God's light, I was never call'd so in mine own house before.

Fal. Go to, I know you well enough.   63

Host. No, Sir John, you do not know me, Sir John. I know you, Sir John : you owe me money, Sir John ; and now you pick a quarrel to beguile me of it. I bought you a dozen of shirts to your back.   67

Fal. Dowlas, filthy dowlas ! I have given them away to bakers' wives ; they have made bolters of them.

Host. Now, as I am a true woman, holland of eight shillings an ell. You owe money here besides, Sir John, for your diet and by-drinkings, and money lent you, four and twenty pound.

Fal. He had his part of it ; let him pay.

Host. He ? Alas, he is poor ; he hath nothing.   75

Fal. How ! poor ? Look upon his face : what call you rich ? Let them coin his nose, let them coin his cheeks. I'll not pay a denier. What, will you make a younker of me ? Shall I not take mine ease in mine inn but I shall have my pocket pick'd ? I have lost a seal-ring of my grandfather's worth forty mark.   81

Host. O Jesu, I have heard the Prince tell him, I know not how oft, that that ring was copper !

Fal. How ! the Prince is a Jack, a sneak-cup. 'Sblood, an he were here, I would cudgel him like a dog if he would say so.   86

Enter the PRINCE *marching, with* PETO ; *and Falstaff meets him, playing upon his truncheon like a fife.*

Fal. How now, lad ! Is the wind in that door, i' faith ? Must we all march ?

Bard. Yea, two and two, Newgate fashion.

Host. My lord, I pray you hear me.   90

Prince. What say'st thou, Mistress Quickly ? How doth thy husband ? I love him well ; he is an honest man.

Host. Good my lord, hear me.

Fal. Prithee, let her alone, and list to me.

Prince. What say'st thou, Jack ?   96

Fal. The other night I fell asleep here behind the arras and had my pocket pick'd ; this house is turn'd bawdy-house ; they pick pockets.

Prince. What didst thou lose, Jack ? 100

Fal. Wilt thou believe me, Hal ? Three or four bonds of forty pound a-piece and a seal-ring of my grandfather's.

Prince. A trifle, some eight-penny matter.

Host. So I told him, my lord ; and I said I heard your Grace say so ; and, my lord, he speaks most vilely of you, like a foul-mouth'd man as he is, and said he would cudgel you.

Prince. What ! he did not ?

Host. There's neither faith, truth, nor womanhood, in me else.   111

Fal. There's no more faith in thee than in a stewed prune ; nor no more truth in thee than in a drawn fox ; and for woman-hood, Maid Marian may be the deputy's wife of the ward to thee. Go, you thing, go. 115

Host. Say, what thing ? what thing ?

Fal. What thing ! Why, a thing to thank God on.

Host. I am no thing to thank God on, I would thou shouldst know it ; I am an honest man's wife ; and setting thy knighthood aside, thou art a knave to call me so.   121

Fal. Setting thy womanhood aside, thou art a beast to say otherwise.

Host. Say, what beast, thou knave, thou ?

Fal. What beast ! Why, an otter.   125

Prince. An otter, Sir John ! Why an otter ?

Fal. Why, she's neither fish nor flesh : a man knows not where to have her.   128

Host. Thou art an unjust man in saying so : thou or any man knows where to have me, thou knave, thou !

Prince. Thou say'st true, hostess ; and he slanders thee most grossly.

Host. So he doth you, my lord ; and said this other day you ought him a thousand pound.   134

Prince. Sirrah, do I owe you a thousand pound ?

Fal. A thousand pound, Hal ! A million. Thy love is worth a million : thou owest me thy love.

Host. Nay, my lord, he call'd you Jack, and said he would cudgel you.

Fal. Did I, Bardolph ?   140

Bard. Indeed, Sir John, you said so.

Fal. Yea, if he said my ring was copper.

Prince. I say 'tis copper. Darest thou be as good as thy word now ?   144

Fal. Why, Hal, thou knowest, as thou art but man, I dare ; but as thou art prince, I fear thee as I fear the roaring of the lion's whelp.

Prince. And why not as the lion ?

Fal. The King himself is to be feared as the lion. Dost thou think I'll fear thee as I fear thy father ? Nay, an I do, I pray God my girdle break.   151

Prince. O, if it should, how would thy guts fall about thy knees ! But, sirrah, there's no room for faith, truth, nor honesty, in this bosom of thine—it is all fill'd up with guts and midriff. Charge an honest woman with picking thy pocket ! Why, thou whoreson, impudent, emboss'd rascal, if there were anything in thy pocket but tavern-reckonings, memorandums of bawdy-houses, and one poor penny-worth of sugar-candy to make thee long-winded— if thy pocket were enrich'd with any other injuries but these, I am a villain. And yet you will stand to it, you will not pocket-up wrong. Art thou not ashamed ? 163

Fal. Dost thou hear, Hal ? Thou knowest in the state of innocency Adam fell ; and what should poor Jack Falstaff do in the days of villainy ? Thou seest I have more flesh than another man, and therefore more frailty. You confess, then, you pick'd my pocket ?

Prince. It appears so by the story. 169

Fal. Hostess, I forgive thee. Go make ready breakfast, love thy husband, look to thy servants, cherish thy guests. Thou shalt find me tractable to any honest reason. Thou seest I am pacified still. Nay, prithee, be gone. [*Exit Hostess*] Now, Hal, to the news at court : for the robbery, lad, how is that answered ? 175

Prince. O, my sweet beef, I must still be good angel to thee : the money is paid back again.

Fal. O, I do not like that paying back ; 'tis a double labour. 179

Prince. I am good friends with my father, and may do anything.

Fal. Rob me the exchequer the first thing thou doest, and do it with unwash'd hands too.

Bard. Do, my lord. 184

Prince. I have procured thee, Jack, a charge of foot.

Fal. I would it had been of horse. Where shall I find one that can steal well ? O for a fine thief, of the age of two and twenty or thereabouts ! I am heinously unprovided. Well, God be thanked for these rebels— they offend none but the virtuous ; I laud them, I praise them. 191

Prince. Bardolph !

Bard. My lord ?

Prince. Go bear this letter to Lord John of Lancaster,

To my brother John ; this to my Lord of Westmoreland. [*Exit Bardolph.*

Go, Peto, to horse, to horse ; for thou and I Have thirty miles to ride yet ere dinner-time. [*Exit Peto.*

Jack, meet me to-morrow in the Temple Hall

At two o'clock in the afternoon ; 199

There shalt thou know thy charge, and there receive

Money and order for their furniture.

The land is burning ; Percy stands on high ; And either we or they must lower lie.

[*Exit.*

Fal. Rare words ! brave world ! Hostess, my breakfast, come ! 204

O, I could wish this tavern were my drum !

[*Exit.*

ACT FOUR

SCENE I. *The rebel camp near Shrewsbury.*

Enter HOTSPUR, WORCESTER, *and* DOUGLAS.

Hot. Well said, my noble Scot. If speaking truth

In this fine age were not thought flattery,

Such attribution should the Douglas have

As not a soldier of this season's stamp

Should go so general current through the world. 5

By God, I cannot flatter ; I do defy

The tongues of soothers ; but a braver place

In my heart's love hath no man than yourself.

Nay, task me to my word ; approve me, lord.

Doug. Thou art the king of honour : 10

No man so potent breathes upon the ground

But I will beard him.

Hot.   Do so, and 'tis well.

Enter a Messenger *with letters.*

What letters hast thou there ?—I can but thank you.

Mess. These letters come from your father.

Hot. Letters from him ! Why comes he not himself ? 15

Mess. He cannot come, my lord, he is grievous sick.

Hot. Zounds ! how has he the leisure to be sick

In such a justling time ? Who leads his power ?

Under whose government come they along ?

Mess. His letters bears his mind, not I, my lord. 20

Wor. I prithee tell me, doth he keep his bed ?

Mess. He did, my lord, four days ere I set forth ;

And at the time of my departure thence

He was much fear'd by his physicians.

Wor. I would the state of time had first been whole 25

Ere he by sickness had been visited :

His health was never better worth than now.

Hot. Sick now ! droop now ! This sickness doth infect

The very life-blood of our enterprise ;

'Tis catching hither, even to our camp. 30

He writes me here that inward sickness—

And that his friends by deputation could not

So soon be drawn ; nor did he think it meet

To lay so dangerous and dear a trust

On any soul remov'd, but on his own. 35

Yet doth he give us bold advertisement

That with our small conjunction we should
   on,
To see how fortune is dispos'd to us ;
For, as he writes, there is no quailing now,
Because the King is certainly possess'd 40
Of all our purposes. What say you to it ?
  Wor. Your father's sickness is a maim
   to us.
  Hot. A perilous gash, a very limb lopp'd
   off.
And yet, in faith, it is not. His present want
Seems more than we shall find it. Were it
   good 45
To set the exact wealth of all our states
All at one cast ? To set so rich a main
On the nice hazard of one doubtful hour ?
It were not good ; for therein should we
   read
The very bottom and the soul of hope, 50
The very list, the very utmost bound
Of all our fortunes.
  Doug.   Faith, and so we should ;
Where now remains a sweet reversion.
We may boldly spend upon the hope of
   what
Is to come in. 55
A comfort of retirement lives in this.
  Hot. A rendezvous, a home to fly unto,
If that the devil and mischance look big
Upon the maidenhead of our affairs.
  Wor. But yet I would your father had
   been here. 60
The quality and hair of our attempt
Brooks no division. It will be thought
By some, that know not why he is away,
That wisdom, loyalty, and mere dislike
Of our proceedings, kept the earl from
   hence ; 65
And think how such an apprehension
May turn the tide of fearful faction
And breed a kind of question in our cause ;
For well you know we of the off'ring side
Must keep aloof from strict arbitrement, 70
And stop all sight-holes, every loop from
   whence
The eye of reason may pry in upon us.
This absence of your father's draws a
   curtain
That shows the ignorant a kind of fear
Before not dreamt of.
  Hot.   You strain too far. 75
I rather of his absence make this use :
It lends a lustre and more great opinion,
A larger dare to our great enterprise,
Than if the earl were here ; for men must
   think,
If we, without his help, can make a head 80
To push against a kingdom, with his help
We shall o'erturn it topsy-turvy down.
Yet all goes well, yet all our joints are
   whole.
  Doug. As heart can think ; there is not
   such a word
Spoke of in Scotland as this term of fear. 85

Enter Sir Richard Vernon.

  Hot. My cousin Vernon ! welcome, by my
   soul.
  Ver. Pray God my news be worth a
   welcome, lord.
The Earl of Westmoreland, seven thousand
   strong,
Is marching hitherwards ; with him Prince
   John. 89
  Hot. No harm ; what more ?
  Ver.   And further, I have learn'd
The King himself in person is set forth,
Or hitherwards intended speedily,
With strong and mighty preparation.
  Hot. He shall be welcome too. Where is
   his son, 94
The nimble-footed madcap Prince of Wales,
And his comrades that daff'd the world aside
And bid it pass ?
  Ver.   All furnish'd, all in arms ;
All plum'd like estridges, that with the
   wind
Bated like eagles having lately bath'd ;
Glittering in golden coats, like images ; 100
As full of spirit as the month of May
And gorgeous as the sun at midsummer ;
Wanton as youthful goats, wild as young
   bulls.
I saw young Harry with his beaver on,
His cushes on his thighs, gallantly arm'd,
Rise from the ground like feathered
   Mercury, 106
And vaulted with such ease into his seat
As if an angel dropp'd down from the clouds
To turn and wind a fiery Pegasus,
And witch the world with noble horseman-
   ship. 110
  Hot. No more, no more ; worse than the
   sun in March,
This praise doth nourish agues. Let them
   come.
They come like sacrifices in their trim,
And to the fire-ey'd maid of smoky war
All hot and bleeding will we offer them. 115
The mailed Mars shall on his altar sit
Up to the ears in blood. I am on fire
To hear this rich reprisal is so nigh
And yet not ours. Come, let me taste my
   horse,
Who is to bear me like a thunderbolt 120
Against the bosom of the Prince of Wales.
Harry to Harry shall, hot horse to horse,
Meet, and ne'er part till one drop down a
   corse.
O that Glendower were come !
  Ver.   There is more news.
I learn'd in Worcester, as I rode along, 125
He cannot draw his power this fourteen
   days.
  Doug. That's the worst tidings that I
   hear of yet.
  Wor. Ay, by my faith, that bears a frosty
   sound.

Hot. What may the King's whole battle
    reach unto ?
Ver. To thirty thousand.
Hot.   Forty let it be : 130
My father and Glendower being both away,
The powers of us may serve so great a day.
Come, let us take a muster speedily.
Doomsday is near ; die all, die merrily.
  Doug. Talk not of dying ; I am out of
    fear 135
Of death or death's hand for this one
    half year.   *[Exeunt.*

Scene II. *A public road near Coventry.*

Enter Falstaff *and* Bardolph.

  Fal. Bardolph, get thee before to
Coventry ; fill me a bottle of sack. Our
soldiers shall march through ; we'll to
Sutton Co'fil' to-night.
  Bard. Will you give me money, Captain ?
  Fal. Lay out, lay out. 5
  Bard. This bottle makes an angel.
  Fal. An if it do, take it for thy labour ;
and if it make twenty, take them all ; I'll
answer the coinage. Bid my lieutenant
Peto meet me at town's end. 9
  Bard. I will, Captain ; farewell. *[Exit.*
  Fal. If I be not ashamed of my soldiers,
I am a sous'd gurnet. I have misused the
King's press damnably. I have got, in
exhange of a hundred and fifty soldiers,
three hundred and odd pounds. I press me
none but good householders, yeomen's sons;
inquire me out contracted bachelors, such
as had been ask'd twice on the banns ; such
a commodity of warm slaves as had as lief
hear the devil as a drum ; such as fear the
report of a caliver worse than a struck fowl
or a hurt wild-duck. I press'd me none but
such toasts-and-butter, with hearts in their
bellies no bigger than pins' heads, and they
have bought out their services ; and now
my whole charge consists of ancients,
corporals, lieutenants, gentlemen of companies—slaves as ragged as Lazarus in the
painted cloth, where the Glutton's dogs
licked his sores ; and such as indeed were
never soldiers, but discarded unjust servingmen, younger sons to younger brothers,
revolted tapsters, and ostlers trade-fall'n ;
the cankers of a calm world and a long
peace ; ten times more dishonourable
ragged than an old-fac'd ancient. And such
have I, to fill up the rooms of them as
have bought out their services, that you
would think that I had a hundred and fifty
tattered Prodigals lately come from swine-
keeping, from eating draff and husks. A
mad fellow met me on the way, and told
me I had unloaded all the gibbets and
press'd the dead bodies. No eye hath seen
such scarecrows. I'll not march through
Coventry with them, that's flat. Nay, and

the villains march wide betwixt the legs, as
if they had gyves on ; for indeed I had the
most of them out of prison. There's not a
shirt and a half in all my company ; and
the half shirt is two napkins tack'd together
and thrown over the shoulders like a
herald's coat without sleeves ; and the
shirt, to say the truth, stol'n from my host
at Saint Albans, or the red-nose innkeeper
of Daventry. But that's all one ; they'll
find linen enough on every hedge.

Enter the Prince of Wales *and*
Westmoreland.

  Prince. How now, blown Jack ! how
now, quilt ! 47
  Fal. What, Hal ! how now, mad wag !
What a devil dost thou in Warwickshire ?
My good Lord of Westmoreland, I cry you
mercy ; I thought your honour had already
been at Shrewsbury. 51
  West. Faith, Sir John, 'tis more than
time that I were there, and you too ; but
my powers are there already. The King,
I can tell you, looks for us all ; we must
away all night. 55
  Fal. Tut, never fear me ; I am as vigilant
as a cat to steal cream.
  Prince. I think, to steal cream indeed ;
for thy theft hath already made thee butter.
But tell me, Jack, whose fellows are these
that come after ? 60
  Fal. Mine, Hal, mine.
  Prince. I did never see such pitiful
rascals.
  Fal. Tut, tut ; good enough to toss ;
food for powder, food for powder ; they'll
fill a pit as well as better : tush, man,
mortal men, mortal men. 65
  West. Ay, but, Sir John, methinks they
are exceeding poor and bare—too beggarly.
  Fal. Faith, for their poverty, I know not
where they had that ; and for their bareness, I am sure they never learn'd that of
me. 70
  Prince. No, I'll be sworn ; unless you
call three fingers in the ribs bare. But,
sirrah, make haste ; Percy is already in
the field.   *[Exit.*
  Fal. What, is the King encamp'd ?
  West. He is, Sir John : I fear we shall
stay too long.   *[Exit.*
  Fal. Well, 76
To the latter end of a fray and the begin-
    ning of a feast
Fits a dull fighter and a keen guest. *[Exit.*

Scene III. *The rebel camp near Shrewsbury.*

Enter Hotspur, Worcester, Douglas,
and Vernon.

  Hot. We'll fight with him to-night.
  Wor.   It may not be.

Doug. You give him, then, advantage.
Ver.   Not a whit.
Hot. Why say you so ? looks he not for
    supply ?
Ver. So do we.
Hot.   His is certain, ours is doubtful.
Wor. Good cousin, be advis'd, stir not
    to-night.   5
Ver. Do not, my lord.
Doug.   You do not counsel well ;
You speak it out of fear and cold heart.
    Ver. Do me no slander, Douglas ; by my
    life,
And I dare well maintain it with my life,
If well-respected honour bid me on,   10
I hold as little counsel with weak fear
As you, my lord, or any Scot that this day
lives ;
Let it be seen to-morrow in the battle
Which of us fears.
    Doug.   Yea, or to-night.
    Ver.   Content.
Hot. To-night, say I.   15
    Ver. Come, come, it may not be.   I
wonder much,
Being men of such great leading as you
    are,
That you foresee not what impediments
Drag back our expedition : certain horse
Of my cousin Vernon's are not yet come up ;
Your uncle Worcester's horse came but to-
    day ;   21
And now their pride and mettle is asleep,
Their courage with hard labour tame and
    dull,
That not a horse is half the half of himself.
    Hot. So are the horses of the enemy   25
In general, journey-bated and brought low ;
The better part of ours are full of rest.
    Wor. The number of the King exceedeth
ours.
For God's sake, cousin, stay till all come in.
    [*The trumpet sounds a parley.*

    Enter SIR WALTER BLUNT.

    Blunt. I come with gracious offers from
    the King,   30
If you vouchsafe me hearing and respect.
    Hot. Welcome, Sir Walter Blunt ; and
    would to God
You were of our determination !
Some of us love you well ; and even those
    some
Envy your great deservings and good name,
Because you are not of our quality,   36
But stand against us like an enemy.
    Blunt. And God defend but still I should
    stand so,
So long as out of limit and true rule
You stand against anointed majesty !   40
But, to my charge.   The King hath sent to
    know
The nature of your griefs ; and whereupon
You conjure from the breast of civil peace

Such bold hostility, teaching his duteous
    land
Audacious cruelty.   If that the King   45
Have any way your good deserts forgot,
Which he confesseth to be manifold,
He bids you name your griefs, and with all
    speed
You shall have your desires with interest,
And pardon absolute for yourself and these
Herein misled by your suggestion.   51
    Hot. The King is kind ; and well we know
    the King
Knows at what time to promise, when to
    pay.
My father and my uncle and myself
Did give him that same royalty he wears ;
And when he was not six and twenty
    strong,   56
Sick in the world's regard, wretched and
    low,
A poor unminded outlaw sneaking home,
My father gave him welcome to the shore ;
And when he heard him swear and vow to
    God   60
He came but to be Duke of Lancaster,
To sue his livery and beg his peace,
With tears of innocency and terms of zeal,
My father, in kind heart and pity mov'd,
Swore him assistance, and perform'd it too.
Now when the lords and barons of the realm
Perceiv'd Northumberland did lean to him,
The more and less came in with cap and
    knee ;
Met him in boroughs, cities, villages ;   69
Attended him on bridges, stood in lanes,
Laid gifts before him, proffer'd him their
    oaths,
Gave him their heirs as pages, followed
    him
Even at the heels in golden multitudes.
He presently—as greatness knows itself—
Steps me a little higher than his vow   75
Made to my father, while his blood was
    poor,
Upon the naked shore at Ravenspurgh ;
And now, forsooth, takes on him to reform
Some certain edicts, and some strait
    decrees
That lie too heavy on the commonwealth ;
Cries out upon abuses, seems to weep   81
Over his country's wrongs ; and by this
    face,
This seeming brow of justice, did he win
The hearts of all that he did angle for ;
Proceeded further : cut me off the heads 85
Of all the favourites that the absent King
In deputation left behind him here,
When he was personal in the Irish war.
    Blunt. Tut, I came not to hear this.
    Hot.   Then to the point.
In short time after, he depos'd the King ;
Soon after that depriv'd him of his life ;
And in the neck of that, task'd the whole
    state ;   92

To make that worse, suff'red his kinsman
    March—
Who is, if every owner were well plac'd,
Indeed his king—to be engag'd in Wales, 95
There without ransom to lie forfeited ;
Disgrac'd me in my happy victories ;
Sought to entrap me by intelligence ;
Rated mine uncle from the council-board ;
In rage dismiss'd my father from the court ;
Broke oath on oath, committed wrong on
    wrong ;   101
And in conclusion drove us to seek out
This head of safety, and withal to pry
Into his title, the which we find
Too indirect for long continuance.   105

Blunt. Shall I return this answer to the
    King ?

Hot. Not so, Sir Walter ; we'll withdraw
    awhile.
Go to the King ; and let there be impawn'd
Some surety for a safe return again,   109
And in the morning early shall mine uncle
Bring him our purposes. And so, farewell.

Blunt. I would you would accept of grace
    and love.

Hot. And may be so we shall.

Blunt.   Pray God you do.
                                    [*Exeunt.*

SCENE IV. *York. The Archbishop's palace.*

Enter the ARCHBISHOP OF YORK, *and* SIR
    MICHAEL.

Arch. Hie, good Sir Michael ; bear this
    sealed brief
With winged haste to the Lord Marshal ;
This to my cousin Scroop ; and all the rest
To whom they are directed. If you knew
How much they do import, you would make
    haste.   5

Sir M. My good lord,
I guess their tenour.

Arch.   Like enough you do.
To-morrow, good Sir Michael, is a day
Wherein the fortune of ten thousand men
Must bide the touch ; for, sir, at Shrews-
    bury,   10
As I am truly given to understand,
The King with mighty and quick-raised
    power
Meets with Lord Harry ; and I fear, Sir
    Michael,
What with the sickness of Northumberland,
Whose power was in the first proportion, 15
And what with Owen Glendower's absence
    thence,
Who with them was a rated sinew too
And comes not in, o'errul'd by prophecies,
I fear the power of Percy is too weak
To wage an instant trial with the King.   20

Sir M. Why, my good lord, you need not
    fear ;
There is Douglas and Lord Mortimer.

Arch. No, Mortimer is not there.

Sir M. But there is Mordake, Vernon,
    Lord Harry Percy,
And there is my Lord of Worcester, and a
    head   25
Of gallant warriors, noble gentlemen.

Arch. And so there is ; but yet the King
    hath drawn
The special head of all the land together :
The Prince of Wales, Lord John of Lan-
    caster,
The noble Westmoreland, and warlike
    Blunt ;   30
And many moe corrivals and dear men
Of estimation and command in arms.

Sir M. Doubt not, my lord, they shall be
    well oppos'd.

Arch. I hope no less, yet needful 'tis to
    fear ;
And, to prevent the worst, Sir Michael,
    speed ;   35
For if Lord Percy thrive not, ere the King
Dismiss his power, he means to visit us—
For he hath heard of our confederacy—
And 'tis but wisdom to make strong against
    him ;
Therefore make haste. I must go write
    again   40
To other friends ; and so farewell, Sir
    Michael.   [*Exeunt severally.*

ACT FIVE

SCENE I. *The King's camp near Shrewsbury.*

Enter the KING, *the* PRINCE OF WALES,
    PRINCE JOHN OF LANCASTER, SIR WALTER
    BLUNT, *and* SIR JOHN FALSTAFF.

King. How bloodily the sun begins to
    peer
Above yon busky hill ! The day looks pale
At his distemp'rature.

Prince.   The southern wind
Doth play the trumpet to his purposes,
And by his hollow whistling in the leaves   5
Foretells a tempest and a blust'ring day.

King. Then with the losers let it sym-
    pathize,
For nothing can seem foul to those that win.
                            [*The trumpet sounds.*

Enter WORCESTER *and* VERNON.

How now, my Lord of Worcester ! 'Tis not
    well
That you and I should meet upon such
    terms   10
As now we meet. You have deceiv'd our
    trust,
And made us doff our easy robes of peace
To crush our old limbs in ungentle steel ;
This is not well, my lord, this is not well.
What say you to it ? Will you again unknit
This churlish knot of all-abhorred war,   16
And move in that obedient orb again
Where you did give a fair and natural light,

And be no more an exhal'd meteor,
A prodigy of fear, and a portent   20
Of broached mischief to the unborn times ?
  Wor. Hear me, my liege :
For mine own part, I could be well content
To entertain the lag-end of my life
With quiet hours ; for I protest   25
I have not sought the day of this dislike.
  King. You have not sought it ! How
    comes it then ?
  Fal. Rebellion lay in his way, and he
found it.
  Prince. Peace, chewet, peace !
  Wor. It pleas'd your Majesty to turn
    your looks   30
Of favour from myself and all our house ;
And yet I must remember you, my lord,
We were the first and dearest of your
    friends.
For you my staff of office did I break
In Richard's time, and posted day and
    night   35
To meet you on the way and kiss your hand,
When yet you were in place and in account
Nothing so strong and fortunate as I.
It was myself, my brother, and his son,
That brought you home, and boldly did
    outdare   40
The dangers of the time. You swore to us—
And you did swear that oath at Doncaster—
That you did nothing purpose 'gainst the
    state,
Nor claim no further than your new-fall'n
    right,   44
The seat of Gaunt, dukedom of Lancaster ;
To this we swore our aid. But in short
    space
It rain'd down fortune show'ring on your
    head ;
And such a flood of greatness fell on you,
What with our help, what with the absent
    King,
What with the injuries of a wanton time, 50
The seeming sufferances that you had borne,
And the contrarious winds that held the
    King
So long in his unlucky Irish wars
That all in England did repute him dead ;
And from this swarm of fair advantages 55
You took occasion to be quickly woo'd
To gripe the general sway into your hand ;
Forgot your oath to us at Doncaster ;
And being fed by us you us'd us so
As that ungentle gull, the cuckoo's bird, 60
Useth the sparrow—did oppress our nest,
Grew by our feeding to so great a bulk
That even our love durst not come near
    your sight
For fear of swallowing ; but with nimble
    wing
We were enforc'd, for safety sake, to fly 65
Out of your sight, and raise this present
    head ;
Whereby we stand opposed by such means

As you yourself have forg'd against your-
    self,
By unkind usage, dangerous countenance,
And violation of all faith and troth   70
Sworn to us in your younger enterprise.
  King. These things, indeed, you have
    articulate,
Proclaim'd at market-crosses, read in
    churches,
To face the garment of rebellion
With some fine colour that may please the
    eye   75
Of fickle changelings and poor discontents,
Which gape and rub the elbow at the news
Of hurlyburly innovation ;
And never yet did insurrection want
Such water-colours to impaint his cause, 80
Nor moody beggars, starving for a time
Of pellmell havoc and confusion.
  Prince. In both your armies there is many
    a soul
Shall pay full dearly for this encounter,
If once they join in trial. Tell your nephew
The Prince of Wales doth join with all the
    world   86
In praise of Henry Percy. By my hopes,
This present enterprise set off his head,
I do not think a braver gentleman,
More active-valiant or more valiant-young,
More daring or more bold, is now alive 91
To grace this latter age with noble deeds.
For my part, I may speak it to my shame,
I have a truant been to chivalry ;
And so I hear he doth account me too. 95
Yet this before my father's majesty—
I am content that he shall take the odds
Of his great name and estimation,
And will, to save the blood on either side,
Try fortune with him in a single fight. 100
  King. And, Prince of Wales, so dare we
    venture thee,
Albeit considerations infinite
Do make against it. No, good Worcester,
    no,
We love our people well ; even those we
    love   104
That are misled upon your cousin's part ;
And will they take the offer of our grace,
Both he and they and you, yea, every man
Shall be my friend again, and I'll be his.
So tell your cousin, and bring me word 109
What he will do. But if he will not yield,
Rebuke and dread correction wait on us,
And they shall do their office. So, be gone ;
We will not now be troubled with reply.
We offer fair ; take it advisedly.
          [*Exeunt Worcester and Vernon.*
  Prince. It will not be accepted, on my
    life :   115
The Douglas and the Hotspur both together
Are confident against the world in arms.
  King. Hence, therefore, every leader to
    his charge ;
For, on their answer, will we set on them ;

And God befriend us, as our cause is just !

[*Exeunt all but the Prince and Falstaff.*

Fal. Hal, if thou see me down in the battle, and bestride me, so ; 'tis a point of friendship.   122

Prince. Nothing but a colossus can do thee that friendship. Say thy prayers, and farewell.

Fal. I would 'twere bed-time, Hal, and all well.   125

Prince. Why, thou owest God a death.

[*Exit.*

Fal. 'Tis not due yet ; I would be loath to pay him before his day. What need I be so forward with him that calls not on me ? Well, 'tis no matter ; honour pricks me on. Yea, but how if honour prick me off when I come on ? How then ? Can honour set to a leg ? No. Or an arm ? No. Or take away the grief of a wound ? No. Honour hath no skill in surgery, then ? No. What is honour ? A word. What is in that word ? Honour. What is that honour ? Air. A trim reckoning ! Who hath it ? He that died o' Wednesday. Doth he feel it ? No. Doth he hear it ? No. 'Tis insensible, then ? Yea, to the dead. But will it not live with the living ? No. Why ? Detraction will not suffer it. Therefore I'll none of it. Honour is a mere scutcheon. And so ends my catechism.   [*Exit.* 140

SCENE II.   *The rebel camp.*

Enter WORCESTER *and* VERNON.

Wor. O, no, my nephew must not know, Sir Richard,
The liberal and kind offer of the King.

Ver. 'Twere best he did.

Wor.   Then are we all undone.
It is not possible, it cannot be,   4
The King should keep his word in loving us ;
He will suspect us still, and find a time
To punish this offence in other faults ;
Supposition all our lives shall be stuck full of eyes,
For treason is but trusted like the fox,
Who, never so tame, so cherish'd, and lock'd up,   10
Will have a wild trick of his ancestors.
Look how we can, or sad or merrily,
Interpretation will misquote our looks,
And we shall feed like oxen at a stall,   14
The better cherish'd still the nearer death.
My nephew's trespass may be well forgot ;
It hath the excuse of youth and heat of blood,
And an adopted name of privilege—
A hare-brain'd Hotspur, govern'd by a spleen.
All his offences live upon my head   20
And on his father's : we did train him on ;
And, his corruption being ta'en from us,
We, as the spring of all, shall pay for all.

Therefore, good cousin, let not Harry know,
In any case, the offer of the King.   25

Ver. Deliver what you will, I'll say 'tis so.
Here comes your cousin.

Enter HOTSPUR *and* DOUGLAS.

Hot.   My uncle is return'd :
Deliver up my Lord of Westmoreland.
Uncle, what news ?   30

Wor. The King will bid you battle presently.

Doug. Defy him by the Lord of Westmoreland.

Hot. Lord Douglas, go you and tell him so.

Doug. Marry, and shall, and very willingly.   [*Exit.*

Wor. There is no seeming mercy in the King.   35

Hot. Did you beg any ? God forbid !

Wor. I told him gently of our grievances,
Of his oath-breaking ; which he mended thus,
By now forswearing that he is forsworn. 39
He calls us rebels, traitors, and will scourge
With haughty arms this hateful name in us.

Re-enter DOUGLAS.

Doug. Arm, gentlemen, to arms ! for I have thrown
A brave defiance in King Henry's teeth—
And Westmoreland, that was engag'd, did bear it—
Which cannot choose but bring him quickly on.   45

Wor. The Prince of Wales stepp'd forth before the King,
And, nephew, challeng'd you to single fight.

Hot. O, would the quarrel lay upon our heads ;
And that no man might draw short breath to-day
But I and Harry Monmouth ! Tell me, tell me,   50
How show'd his tasking ? Seem'd it in contempt ?

Ver. No, by my soul, I never in my life
Did hear a challenge urg'd more modestly,
Unless a brother should a brother dare
To gentle exercise and proof of arms.   55
He gave you all the duties of a man ;
Trimm'd up your praises with a princely tongue ;
Spoke your deservings like a chronicle ;
Making you ever better than his praise,
By still dispraising praise valued with you ;
And, which became him like a prince indeed,
He made a blushing cital of himself,   62
And chid his truant youth with such a grace
As if he mast'red there a double spirit,
Of teaching and of learning instantly.
There did he pause ; but let me tell the world—

If he outlive the envy of this day,   67
England did never owe so sweet a hope,
So much misconstrued in his wantonness.
  Hot. Cousin, I think thou art enamoured
On his follies. Never did I hear   71
Of any prince so wild a liberty.
But be he as he will, yet once ere night
I will embrace him with a soldier's arm,
That he shall shrink under my courtesy.   75
Arm, arm with speed! and, fellows,
          soldiers, friends,
Better consider what you have to do
Than I, that have not well the gift of
          tongue,
Can lift your blood up with persuasion.

Enter a Messenger.

  Mess. My lord, here are letters for you. 80
  Hot. I cannot read them now.
O gentlemen, the time of life is short!
To spend that shortness basely were too
          long,
If life did ride upon a dial's point,
Still ending at the arrival of an hour.   85
An if we live, we live to tread on kings;
If die, brave death, when princes die with
          us!
Now, for our consciences, the arms are fair,
When the intent of bearing them is just.

Enter another Messenger.

  Mess. My lord, prepare; the King comes
          on apace.   90
  Hot. I thank him that he cuts me from
          my tale,
For I profess not talking; only this—
Let each man do his best. And here draw I
A sword, whose temper I intend to stain
With the best blood that I can meet withal
In the adventure of this perilous day.   96
Now, Esperance! Percy! and set on.
Sound all the lofty instruments of war,
And by that music let us all embrace;
For, heaven to earth, some of us never shall
A second time do such a courtesy.   101
          [*They embrace. The trumpets sound.
          Exeunt.*

SCENE III. *A plain between the camps.*

The KING *passes across with his power.
Alarum to the battle. Then enter* DOUGLAS
and SIR WALTER BLUNT.

  Blunt. What is thy name, that in battle
          thus
Thou crossest me? What honour dost thou
          seek
Upon my head?
  Doug. Know, then, my name is Douglas;
And I do haunt thee in the battle thus
Because some tell me that thou art a king.
  Blunt. They tell thee true.   6
  Doug. The Lord of Stafford dear to-day
          hath bought

Thy likeness; for instead of thee, King
          Harry,
This sword hath ended him. So shall it
          thee,
Unless thou yield thee as my prisoner.   10
  Blunt. I was not born a yielder, thou
          proud Scot;
And thou shalt find a king that will revenge
Lord Stafford's death.
          [*They fight. Douglas kills Blunt.*

Enter HOTSPUR.

  Hot. O Douglas, hadst thou fought at
          Holmedon thus,
I never had triumph'd upon a Scot.   15
  Doug. All's done, all's won; here breath-
          less lies the King.
  Hot. Where?
  Doug. Here.
  Hot. This, Douglas? No: I know this
          face full well;
A gallant knight he was, his name was
          Blunt;   20
Semblably furnish'd like the King himself.
  Doug. A fool go with thy soul whither
          it goes!
A borrowed title hast thou bought too dear;
Why didst thou tell me that thou wert a
          king?
  Hot. The King hath many marching in
          his coats.
  Doug. Now, by my sword, I will kill all
          his coats;   25
I'll murder all his wardrobe, piece by piece,
Until I meet the King.
  Hot.   Up, and away!
Our soldiers stand full fairly for the day.
          [*Exeunt.*

Alarum. Enter FALSTAFF, *solus.*

  Fal. Though I could scape shot-free at
London, I fear the shot here: here's no
scoring but upon the pate. Soft! who are
you? Sir Walter Blunt. There's honour for
you! Here's no vanity! I am as hot as
molten lead, and as heavy too. God keep
lead out of me! I need no more weight
than mine own bowels. I have led my
ragamuffins where they are pepper'd;
there's not three of my hundred and fifty
left alive, and they are for the town's end,
to beg during life. But who comes here?

Enter the PRINCE OF WALES.

  Prince. What, stand'st thou idle here?
          Lend me thy sword.
Many a nobleman lies stark and stiff   40
Under the hoofs of vaunting enemies,
Whose deaths are yet unreveng'd. I
prithee lend me thy sword.
  Fal. O Hal, I prithee give me leave to
breathe awhile. Turk Gregory never did
such deeds in arms as I have done this day.
I have paid Percy, I have made him sure.

Prince. He is, indeed, and living to kill
thee. I prithee lend me thy sword.   47
    Fal. Nay, before God, Hal, if Percy be
alive, thou get'st not my sword ; but take
my pistol, if thou wilt.
    Prince. Give it me.   What, is it in the
case ?   50
    Fal. Ay, Hal ; 'tis hot, 'tis hot ; there's
that will sack a city. [*The Prince draws it
        out, and finds it to be a bottle of sack.*
    Prince. What, is it a time to jest and dally
now ?   [*He throws the bottle at him. Exit.*
    Fal. Well, if Percy be alive, I'll pierce
him. If he do come in my way, so ; if he
do not, if I come in his willingly, let him
make a carbonado of me. I like not such
grinning honour as Sir Walter hath. Give
me life, which if I can save, so ; if not,
honour comes unlook'd for, and there's an
end.   [*Exit.*

SCENE IV. *Another part of the field.*

Alarums. Excursions. Enter the KING, *the*
PRINCE OF WALES, PRINCE JOHN OF
LANCASTER, *and* WESTMORELAND.

King. I prithee,
Harry, withdraw thyself ; thou bleedest
        too much ;
Lord John of Lancaster, go you with him.
    P. John. Not I, my lord, unless I did
        bleed too.
    Prince. I beseech your Majesty, make
        up,   5
Lest your retirement do amaze your friends.
    King. I will do so.
My Lord of Westmoreland, lead him to his
        tent.
    West. Come, my lord, I'll lead you to
        your tent.
    Prince. Lead me, my lord ? I do not need
        your help ;   10
And God forbid a shallow scratch should
        drive
The Prince of Wales from such a field as
        this,
Where stain'd nobility lies trodden on,
And rebels' arms triumph in massacres !
    P. John. We breathe too long.   Come,
        cousin Westmoreland,   15
Our duty this way lies ; for God's sake,
        come.
    [*Exeunt Prince John and Westmoreland.*
    Prince. By God, thou hast deceiv'd me,
        Lancaster !
I did not think thee lord of such a spirit ;
Before, I lov'd thee as a brother, John,
But now I do respect thee as my soul.   20
    King. I saw him hold Lord Percy at the
        point
With lustier maintenance than I did look for
Of such an ungrown warrior.
    Prince.   O, this boy
Lends mettle to us all !   [*Exit.*

Enter DOUGLAS.

    Doug. Another king !   They grow like
        Hydra's heads.   25
I am the Douglas, fatal to all those
That wear those colours on them. What art
        thou,
That counterfeit'st the person of a king ?
    King. The King himself, who, Douglas,
        grieves at heart
So many of his shadows thou hast met,   30
And not the very King. I have two boys
Seek Percy and thyself about the field ;
But, seeing thou fall'st on me so luckily,
I will assay thee ; so, defend thyself.
    Doug. I fear thou art another counter-
        feit ;   35
And yet, in faith, thou bearest thee like a
        king ;
But mine I am sure thou art, who'er thou
        be,
And thus I win thee.
    [*They fight, the King being in danger.*

Re-enter the PRINCE.

    Prince. Hold up thy head, vile Scot, or
        thou art like
Never to hold it up again.   The spirits   40
Of valiant Shirley, Stafford, Blunt, are in
        my arms ;
It is the Prince of Wales that threatens thee,
Who never promiseth but he means to pay.
                        [*They fight ; Douglas flies.*
Cheerly, my lord : how fares your Grace ?
Sir Nicholas Gawsey hath for succour sent,
And so hath Clifton. I'll to Clifton straight.
    King. Stay, and breathe awhile.   47
Thou hast redeem'd thy lost opinion ;
And show'd thou mak'st some tender of my
        life,
In this fair rescue thou hast brought to me.
    Prince. O God, they did me too much
        injury
That ever said I heark'ned for your death !
If it were so, I might have let alone
The insulting hand of Douglas over you,
Which would have been as speedy in your
        end   55
As all the poisonous potions in the world,
And sav'd the treacherous labour of your
        son.
    King. Make up to Clifton, I'll to Sir
        Nicholas Gawsey.   [*Exit.*

Enter HOTSPUR.

    Hot. If I mistake not, thou art Harry
        Monmouth.
    Prince. Thou speak'st as if I would deny
        my name.   60
    Hot. My name is Harry Percy.
    Prince.   Why, then I see
A very valiant rebel of the name.
I am the Prince of Wales ; and think not,
        Percy,

To share with me in glory any more.
Two stars keep not their motion in one
    sphere,   65
Nor can one England brook a double reign
Of Harry Percy and the Prince of Wales.
    Hot. Nor shall it, Harry, for the hour is
        come
To end the one of us ; and would to God
Thy name in arms were now as great as
    mine !   70
    Prince. I'll make it greater ere I part
        from thee,
And all the budding honours on thy crest
I'll crop to make a garland for my head.
    Hot. I can no longer brook thy vanities.
                                [*They fight.*

Enter FALSTAFF.

    Fal. Well said, Hal ! to it, Hal ! Nay, you
shall find no boy's play here, I can tell you.

Re-enter DOUGLAS ; *he fights with Falstaff,
who falls down as if he were dead ; Douglas
withdraws. Hotspur is wounded, and falls.*

    Hot. O, Harry, thou hast robb'd me of
        my youth !   77
I better brook the loss of brittle life
Than those proud titles thou hast won of
    me :
They wound my thoughts worse than thy
    sword my flesh ;
But thoughts, the slaves of life, and life,
    time's fool,   81
And time, that takes survey of all the world,
Must have a stop. O, I could prophesy,
But that the earthy and cold hand of death
Lies on my tongue. No, Percy, thou art
    dust   85
And food for—   [*Dies.*
    Prince. For worms, brave Percy. Fare
    thee well, great heart !
Ill-weav'd ambition, how much art thou
    shrunk !
When that this body did contain a spirit,
A kingdom for it was too small a bound ; 90
But now two paces of the vilest earth
Is room enough. This earth that bears thee
    dead
Bears not alive so stout a gentleman.
If thou wert sensible of courtesy,   94
I should not make so dear a show of zeal ;
But let my favours hide thy mangled face,
And, even in thy behalf, I'll thank myself
For doing these fair rites of tenderness.
Adieu, and take thy praise with thee to
    heaven !
Thy ignominy sleep with thee in the grave,
But not rememb'red in thy epitaph !   101
        [*He spieth Falstaff on the ground.*
What, old acquaintance ! Could not all this
    flesh
Keep in a little life ? Poor Jack, farewell !
I could have better spar'd a better man.
O, I should have a heavy miss of thee, 105

If I were much in love with vanity !
Death hath not struck so fat a deer to-day,
Though many dearer, in this bloody fray.
Embowell'd will I see thee by and by ; 109
Till then in blood by noble Percy lie. [*Exit.*
    Fal. [*Rising up*] Embowell'd ! If thou
embowel me to-day, I'll give you leave to
powder me and eat me too to-morrow.
'Sblood, 'twas time to counterfeit, or that
hot termagant Scot had paid me scot and
lot too. Counterfeit ? I lie, I am no
counterfeit : to die is to be a counterfeit ;
for he is but the counterfeit of a man who
hath not the life of a man ; but to counterfeit dying, when a man thereby liveth, is to
be no counterfeit, but the true and perfect
image of life indeed. The better part of
valour is discretion ; in the which better
part I have saved my life. Zounds, I am
afraid of this gunpowder Percy, though he
be dead ; how if he should counterfeit too,
and rise ? By my faith, I am afraid he
would prove the better counterfeit. Therefore I'll make him sure ; yea, and I'll swear
I kill'd him. Why may not he rise as well
as I ? Nothing confutes me but eyes, and
nobody sees me. Therefore, sirrah [*stabbing
him*], with a new wound in your thigh,
come you along with me.   128
                [*He takes up Hotspur on his back.*

Re-enter the PRINCE OF WALES *and* PRINCE
    JOHN OF LANCASTER.

    Prince. Come, brother John, full bravely
        hast thou flesh'd
Thy maiden sword.
    P. John. But, soft ! whom have we here ?
Did you not tell me this fat man was dead ?
    Prince. I did ; I saw him dead,
Breathless and bleeding on the ground. Art
    thou alive ?
Or is it fantasy that plays upon our eye-
    sight ?   134
I prithee speak ; we will not trust our eyes
Without our ears : thou art not what thou
    seem'st.
    Fal. No, that's certain : I am not a
double man ; but if I be not Jack Falstaff,
then am I a Jack. There is Percy [*throwing
the body down*] ; if your father will do me
any honour, so ; if not, let him kill the
next Percy himself. I look to be either earl
or duke, I can assure you.   141
    Prince. Why, Percy I kill'd myself, and
saw thee dead.
    Fal. Didst thou ? Lord, Lord, how this
world is given to lying ! I grant you I was
down and out of breath, and so was he ;
but we rose both at an instant, and fought
a long hour by Shrewsbury clock. If I may
be believ'd, so ; if not, let them that should
reward valour bear the sin upon their own
heads. I'll take it upon my death, I gave
him this wound in the thigh ; if the man

were alive, and would deny it, zounds,
I would make him eat a piece of my
sword.
  P. John. This is the strangest tale that
    ever I heard.
  Prince. This is the strangest fellow,
brother John.
Come, bring your luggage nobly on your
  back.   155
For my part, if a lie may do thee grace,
I'll gild it with the happiest terms I have.
           [*A retreat is sounded.*
The trumpet sounds retreat; the day is
  ours.
Come, brother, let us to the highest of the
  field,   159
To see what friends are living, who are dead.
    [*Exeunt the Prince and Prince
        John of Lancaster.*
  Fal. I'll follow, as they say, for reward.
He that rewards me, God reward him! If
I do grow great, I'll grow less; for I'll
purge, and leave sack, and live cleanly, as
a nobleman should do.   [*Exit.*

SCENE V. *Another part of the field.*

The Trumpets sound. Enter the KING, *the*
PRINCE OF WALES, PRINCE JOHN OF
LANCASTER, WESTMORELAND, *with* WOR-
CESTER *and* VERNON *prisoners.*

  King. Thus ever did rebellion find rebuke.
Ill-spirited Worcester! did not we send
  grace,
Pardon and terms of love to all of you?
And wouldst thou turn our offers contrary?
Misuse the tenour of thy kinsman's trust?
Three knights upon our party slain to-day,
A noble earl, and many a creature else,
Had been alive this hour,
If like a Christian thou hadst truly borne
Betwixt our armies true intelligence.   10
  Wor. What I have done my safety urg'd
  me to;
And I embrace this fortune patiently,
Since not to be avoided it falls on me.

  King. Bear Worcester to the death, and
  Vernon too;
Other offenders we will pause upon.   15
    [*Exeunt Worcester and Vernon guarded.*
How goes the field?
  Prince. The noble Scot, Lord Douglas,
  when he saw
The fortune of the day quite turn'd from
  him,
The noble Percy slain, and all his men
Upon the foot of fear, fled with the rest; 20
And falling from a hill, he was so bruis'd
That the pursuers took him. At my tent
The Douglas is; and I beseech your Grace
I may dispose of him.
  King.   With all my heart.
  Prince. Then, brother John of Lancaster,
  to you   25
This honourable bounty shall belong:
Go to the Douglas, and deliver him
Up to his pleasure, ransomless and free;
His valours shown upon our crests to-day
Have taught us how to cherish such high
  deeds   30
Even in the bosom of our adversaries.
  P. John. I thank your Grace for this
  high courtesy,
Which I shall give away immediately.
  King. Then this remains—that we divide
  our power.
You, son John, and my cousin Westmore-
  land,   35
Towards York shall bend you with your
  dearest speed
To meet Northumberland and the prelate
  Scroop,
Who, as we hear, are busily in arms.
Myself, and you, son Harry, will towards
  Wales
To fight with Glendower and the Earl of
  March.   40
Rebellion in this land shall lose his sway,
Meeting the check of such another day;
And since this business so fair is done,
Let us not leave till all our own be won.
         [*Exeunt.*

THE SECOND PART OF
KING HENRY THE FOURTH

DRAMATIS PERSONÆ

RUMOUR, *the Presenter.*
KING HENRY THE FOURTH.
HENRY, PRINCE OF WALES, *afterwards Henry V,*
PRINCE JOHN OF LANCASTER, } *sons of Henry IV.*
PRINCE HUMPHREY OF GLOUCESTER,
THOMAS, DUKE OF CLARENCE,

EARL OF NORTHUMBERLAND,
SCROOP, ARCHBISHOP OF YORK,
LORD MOWBRAY,
LORD HASTINGS, } *opposites against King Henry IV.*
LORD BARDOLPH,
SIR JOHN COLVILLE,
TRAVERS, } *retainers of*
MORTON, } *Northumberland,*

EARL OF WARWICK,
EARL OF WESTMORELAND,
EARL OF SURREY,
EARL OF KENT, } *of the King's party.*
GOWER,
HARCOURT,
BLUNT,
LORD CHIEF JUSTICE.
Servant, *to Lord Chief Justice.*

SIR JOHN FALSTAFF,
EDWARD POINS,
BARDOLPH, } *irregular Humourists.*
PISTOL,
PETO,
Page, *to Falstaff.*
ROBERT SHALLOW, } *country Justices.*
SILENCE,
DAVY, *servant to Shallow.*
FANG, } *Sheriff's officers.*
SNARE,
RALPH MOULDY,
SIMON SHADOW,
THOMAS WART, } *country soldiers.*
FRANCIS FEEBLE,
PETER BULLCALF,
FRANCIS, *a drawer.*

LADY NORTHUMBERLAND.
LADY PERCY, *Percy's widow.*
HOSTESS QUICKLY, *of the Boar's Head, Eastcheap.*
DOLL TEARSHEET.

Lords, Attendants, Porter, Drawers, Beadles, Grooms, Servants.

THE SCENE : *England.*

INDUCTION

Warkworth. Before Northumberland's castle.

Enter RUMOUR, *painted full of tongues.*

  Rum. Open your ears ; for which of you will stop
The vent of hearing when loud Rumour speaks ?
I, from the orient to the drooping west,
Making the wind my post-horse, still unfold
The acts commenced on this ball of earth. 5
Upon my tongues continual slanders ride,
The which in every language I pronounce,
Stuffing the ears of men with false reports.
I speak of peace while covert enmity,
Under the smile of safety, wounds the world ; 10
And who but Rumour, who but only I,
Make fearful musters and prepar'd defence,
Whiles the big year, swoln with some other grief,
Is thought with child by the stern tyrant war,
And no such matter ? Rumour is a pipe 15

Blown by surmises, jealousies, conjectures,
And of so easy and so plain a stop
That the blunt monster with uncounted heads,
The still-discordant wav'ring multitude,
Can play upon it. But what need I thus 20
My well-known body to anatomize
Among my household ? Why is Rumour here ?
I run before King Harry's victory,
Who, in a bloody field by Shrewsbury,
Hath beaten down young Hotspur and his troops, 25
Quenching the flame of bold rebellion
Even with the rebels' blood. But what mean I
To speak so true at first ? My office is 28
To noise abroad that Harry Monmouth fell
Under the wrath of noble Hotspur's sword,
And that the King before the Douglas' rage
Stoop'd his anointed head as low as death.
This have I rumour'd through the peasant towns
Between that royal field of Shrewsbury 34
And this worm-eaten hold of ragged stone,

Where Hotspur's father, old Northumber-
   land,
Lies crafty-sick. The posts come tiring on,
And not a man of them brings other news
Than they have learnt of me.   From
   Rumour's tongues   39
They bring smooth comforts false, worse
   than true wrongs.   [*Exit.*

ACT ONE

SCENE I. *Warkworth. Before Northumberland's castle.*

Enter LORD BARDOLPH.

L. Bard. Who keeps the gate here, ho ?

    The Porter *opens the gate.*

                    Where is the Earl ?
Port. What shall I say you are ?
L. Bard.   Tell thou the Earl
That the Lord Bardolph doth attend him
   here.
Port. His lordship is walk'd forth into the
   orchard.
Please it your honour knock but at the
   gate,   5
And he himself will answer.

Enter NORTHUMBERLAND.

L. Bard.   Here comes the Earl.
                     [*Exit Porter.*
North. What news, Lord Bardolph ?
   Every minute now
Should be the father of some stratagem.
The times are wild ; contention, like a
   horse
Full of high feeding, madly hath broke
   loose   10
And bears down all before him.
L. Bard.   Noble Earl,
I bring you certain news from Shrewsbury.
North. Good, an God will !
L. Bard. As good as heart can wish.
The King is almost wounded to the death ;   15
And, in the fortune of my lord your son,
Prince Harry slain outright ; and both the
   Blunts
Kill'd by the hand of Douglas ; young
   Prince John,
And Westmoreland, and Stafford, fled the
   field ;
And Harry Monmouth's brawn, the hulk
   Sir John,
Is prisoner to your son. O, such a day,   20
So fought, so followed, and so fairly
   won,
Came not till now to dignify the times,
Since Cæsar's fortunes !
North.   How is this deriv'd ?
Saw you the field ?   Came you from
   Shrewsbury ?
   L. Bard. I spake with one, my lord, that
      came from thence ;   25

A gentleman well bred and of good name,
That freely rend'red me these news for true.

Enter TRAVERS.

North. Here comes my servant Travers,
   whom I sent
On Tuesday last to listen after news.
L. Bard. My lord, I over-rode him on the
   way ;   30
And he is furnish'd with no certainties
More than he haply may retail from me.
   North. Now, Travers, what good tidings
      comes with you ?
   Tra. My lord, Sir John Umfrevile turn'd
      me back
With joyful tidings ; and, being better
   hors'd,   35
Out-rode me.   After him came spurring
   hard
A gentleman, almost forspent with speed,
That stopp'd by me to breathe his bloodied
   horse.
He ask'd the way to Chester ; and of him
I did demand what news from Shrewsbury.
He told me that rebellion had bad luck,   41
And that young Harry Percy's spur was
   cold.
With that he gave his able horse the head
And, bending forward, struck his armed
   heels
Against the panting sides of his poor jade
Up to the rowel-head ; and starting so,   46
He seem'd in running to devour the way,
Staying no longer question.
   North.   Ha ! Again :
Said he young Harry Percy's spur was
   cold ?
Of Hotspur, Coldspur ? that rebellion   50
Had met ill luck ?
   L. Bard.   My lord, I'll tell you what :
If my young lord your son have not the
   day,
Upon mine honour, for a silken point
I'll give my barony. Never talk of it.
   North. Why should that gentleman that
      rode by Travers   55
Give then such instances of loss ?
   L. Bard.   Who—he ?
He was some hilding fellow that had stol'n
The horse he rode on and, upon my life,
Spoke at a venture. Look, here comes
   more news.

Enter MORTON.

   North. Yea, this man's brow, like to a
      title-leaf,   60
Foretells the nature of a tragic volume.
So looks the strand whereon the imperious
   flood
Hath left a witness'd usurpation.
Say, Morton, didst thou come from
   Shrewsbury ?
   Mor. I ran from Shrewsbury, my noble
      lord ;   65

Where hateful death put on his ugliest
   mask
To fright our party.
  North. How doth my son and brother?
Thou tremblest; and the whiteness in thy
   cheek
Is apter than thy tongue to tell thy errand.
Even such a man, so faint, so spiritless, 70
So dull, so dead in look, so woe-begone,
Drew Priam's curtain in the dead of night
And would have told him half his Troy was
   burnt;
But Priam found the fire ere he his tongue,
And I my Percy's death ere thou report'st
   it.   75
This thou wouldst say: ' Your son did
   thus and thus;
Your brother thus; so fought the noble
   Douglas '—
Stopping my greedy ear with their bold
   deeds;
But in the end, to stop my ear indeed,
Thou hast a sigh to blow away this praise,
Ending with ' Brother, son, and all, are
   dead '.   81
  Mor. Douglas is living, and your brother,
   yet;
But for my lord your son—
  North.   Why, he is dead.
See what a ready tongue suspicion hath!
He that but fears the thing he would not
   know   85
Hath by instinct knowledge from others'
   eyes
That what he fear'd is chanced. Yet
   speak, Morton;
Tell thou an earl his divination lies,
And I will take it as a sweet disgrace
And make thee rich for doing me such
   wrong.   90
  Mor. You are too great to be by me
   gainsaid;
Your spirit is too true, your fears too
   certain.
  North. Yet, for all this, say not that
   Percy's dead.
I see a strange confession in thine eye;
Thou shak'st thy head, and hold'st it fear
   or sin   95
To speak a truth. If he be slain, say so:
The tongue offends not that reports his
   death;
And he doth sin that doth belie the dead,
Not he which says the dead is not alive.
Yet the first bringer of unwelcome news 100
Hath but a losing office, and his tongue
Sounds ever after as a sullen bell,
Remember'd tolling a departing friend.
  L. Bard. I cannot think, my lord, your
   son is dead.
  Mor. I am sorry I should force you to
   believe   105
That which I would to God I had not
   seen;

But these mine eyes saw him in bloody
   state,
Rend'ring faint quittance, wearied and out-
   breath'd,
To Harry Monmouth, whose swift wrath
   beat down
The never-daunted Percy to the earth, 110
From whence with life he never more
   sprung up.
In few, his death—whose spirit lent a fire
Even to the dullest peasant in his camp—
Being bruited once, took fire and heat
   away
From the best-temper'd courage in his
   troops;   115
For from his metal was his party steeled;
Which once in him abated, all the rest
Turn'd on themselves, like dull and heavy
   lead.
And as the thing that's heavy in itself 119
Upon enforcement flies with greatest speed,
So did our men, heavy in Hotspur's loss,
Lend to this weight such lightness with
   their fear
That arrows fled not swifter toward their
   aim
Than did our soldiers, aiming at their
   safety,
Fly from the field. Then was that noble
   Worcester   125
Too soon ta'en prisoner; and that furious
   Scot,
The bloody Douglas, whose well-labouring
   sword
Had three times slain th' appearance of the
   King,
Gan vail his stomach and did grace the
   shame
Of those that turn'd their backs, and in
   his flight,   130
Stumbling in fear, was took. The sum of all
Is that the King hath won, and hath sent
   out
A speedy power to encounter you, my lord,
Under the conduct of young Lancaster
And Westmoreland. This is the news at
   full.   135
  North. For this I shall have time enough
   to mourn.
In poison there is physic; and these news,
Having been well, that would have made
   me sick,
Being sick, have in some measure made me
   well;
And as the wretch whose fever-weak'ned
   joints,   140
Like strengthless hinges, buckle under life,
Impatient of his fit, breaks like a fire
Out of his keeper's arms, even so my limbs,
Weak'ned with grief, being now enrag'd
   with grief,
Are thrice themselves. Hence, therefore,
   thou nice crutch!   145
A scaly gauntlet now with joints of steel

Must glove this hand; and hence, thou
    sickly coif!
Thou art a guard too wanton for the head
Which princes, flesh'd with conquest, aim
    to hit.
Now bind my brows with iron; and
    approach   150
The ragged'st hour that time and spite dare
    bring
To frown upon th' enrag'd Northumber-
    land!
Let heaven kiss earth!   Now let not
    Nature's hand
Keep the wild flood confin'd!   Let order
    die!
And let this world no longer be a stage   155
To feed contention in a ling'ring act;
But let one spirit of the first-born Cain
Reign in all bosoms, that, each heart being
    set
On bloody courses, the rude scene may end
And darkness be the burier of the dead!   160
    L. Bard. This strained passion doth you
      wrong, my lord.
    Mor. Sweet Earl, divorce not wisdom
      from your honour.
The lives of all your loving complices
Lean on your health; the which, if you
    give o'er
To stormy passion, must perforce decay.   165
You cast th' event of war, my noble lord,
And summ'd the account of chance before
    you said
'Let us make head'.   It was your pre-
    surmise
That in the dole of blows your son might
    drop.
You knew he walk'd o'er perils on an
    edge,   170
More likely to fall in than to get o'er;
You were advis'd his flesh was capable
Of wounds and scars, and that his forward
    spirit
Would lift him where most trade of danger
    rang'd;
Yet did you say 'Go forth'; and none
    of this,   175
Though strongly apprehended, could re-
    strain
The stiff-borne action.   What hath then
    befall'n,
Or what hath this bold enterprise brought
    forth
More than that being which was like to be?
    L. Bard. We all that are engaged to this
      loss   180
Knew that we ventured on such dangerous
    seas
That if we wrought out life 'twas ten to
    one;
And yet we ventur'd, for the gain propos'd
Chok'd the respect of likely peril fear'd;
And since we are o'erset, venture again.   185
Come, we will all put forth, body and goods.

    Mor. 'Tis more than time. And, my most
      noble lord,
I hear for certain, and dare speak the truth:
The gentle Archbishop of York is up
With well-appointed pow'rs. He is a man
Who with a double surety binds his
    followers.   191
My lord your son had only but the corpse,
But shadows and the shows of men, to fight;
For that same word 'rebellion' did divide
The action of their bodies from their souls;
And they did fight with queasiness, con-
    strain'd,   196
As men drink potions; that their weapons
    only
Seem'd on our side, but for their spirits and
    souls
This word 'rebellion'—it had froze them
    up,
As fish are in a pond. But now the Bishop
Turns insurrection to religion.   201
Suppos'd sincere and holy in his thoughts,
He's follow'd both with body and with
    mind;
And doth enlarge his rising with the blood
Of fair King Richard, scrap'd from Pomfret
    stones;   205
Derives from heaven his quarrel and his
    cause;
Tells them he doth bestride a bleeding land,
Gasping for life under great Bolingbroke;
And more and less do flock to follow him.
    North. I knew of this before; but, to
      speak truth,   210
This present grief had wip'd it from my
    mind.
Go in with me; and counsel every man
The aptest way for safety and revenge.
Get posts and letters, and make friends
    with speed;
Never so few, and never yet more need.   215
                  [*Exeunt.*

SCENE II. *London. A street.*

Enter SIR JOHN FALSTAFF, *with his* Page
bearing his sword and buckler.

    Fal. Sirrah, you giant, what says the
doctor to my water?
    Page. He said, sir, the water itself was a
good healthy water; but for the party
that owed it, he might have moe diseases
than he knew for.   5
    Fal. Men of all sorts take a pride to gird
at me.   The brain of this foolish-com-
pounded clay, man, is not able to invent
anything that intends to laughter, more
than I invent or is invented on me. I am
not only witty in myself, but the cause
that wit is in other men. I do here walk
before thee like a sow that hath overwhelm'd all her litter but one. If the Prince
put thee into my service for any other
reason than to set me off, why then I have

no judgment. Thou whoreson mandrake, thou art fitter to be worn in my cap than to wait at my heels. I was never mann'd with an agate till now; but I will inset you neither in gold nor silver, but in vile apparel, and send you back again to your master, for a jewel—the juvenal, the Prince your master, whose chin is not yet fledge. I will sooner have a beard grow in the palm of my hand than he shall get one off his cheek; and yet he will not stick to say his face is a face-royal. God may finish it when he will, 'tis not a hair amiss yet. He may keep it still at a face-royal, for a barber shall never earn sixpence out of it; and yet he'll be crowing as if he had writ man ever since his father was a bachelor. He may keep his own grace, but he's almost out of mine, I can assure him. What said Master Dommelton about the satin for my short cloak and my slops? 28

Page. He said, sir, you should procure him better assurance than Bardolph. He would not take his band and yours; he liked not the security. 31

Fal. Let him be damn'd, like the Glutton; pray God his tongue be hotter! A whoreson Achitophel! A rascal-yea-forsooth knave, to bear a gentleman in hand, and then stand upon security! The whoreson smooth-pates do now wear nothing but high shoes, and bunches of keys at their girdles; and if a man is through with them in honest taking-up, then they must stand upon security. I had as lief they would put ratsbane in my mouth as offer to stop it with security. I look'd 'a should have sent me two and twenty yards of satin, as I am a true knight, and he sends me security. Well, he may sleep in security; for he hath the horn of abundance, and the lightness of his wife shines through it; and yet cannot he see, though he have his own lanthorn to light him. Where's Bardolph? 45

Page. He's gone into Smithfield to buy your worship a horse.

Fal. I bought him in Paul's, and he'll buy me a horse in Smithfield. An I could get me but a wife in the stews, I were mann'd, hors'd, and wiv'd. 50

Enter the LORD CHIEF JUSTICE *and* Servant.

Page. Sir, here comes the nobleman that committed the Prince for striking him about Bardolph.

Fal. Wait close; I will not see him.

Ch. Justice. What's he that goes there?

Serv. Falstaff, an't please your lordship.

Ch. Just. He that was in question for the robb'ry? 56

Serv. He, my lord; but he hath since done good service at Shrewsbury, and, as I hear, is now going with some charge to the Lord John of Lancaster.

Ch. Just. What, to York? Call him back again. 60

Serv. Sir John Falstaff!

Fal. Boy, tell him I am deaf.

Page. You must speak louder; my master is deaf.

Ch. Just. I am sure he is, to the hearing of anything good. Go, pluck him by the elbow; I must speak with him. 66

Serv. Sir John!

Fal. What! a young knave, and begging! Is there not wars? Is there not employment? Doth not the King lack subjects? Do not the rebels need soldiers? Though it be a shame to be on any side but one, it is worse shame to beg than to be on the worst side, were it worse than the name of rebellion can tell how to make it.

Serv. You mistake me, sir. 74

Fal. Why, sir, did I say you were an honest man? Setting my knighthood and my soldiership aside, I had lied in my throat if I had said so. 77

Serv. I pray you, sir, then set your knighthood and your soldiership aside; and give me leave to tell you you lie in your throat, if you say I am any other than an honest man. 81

Fal. I give thee leave to tell me so! I lay aside that which grows to me! If thou get'st any leave of me, hang me; if thou tak'st leave, thou wert better be hang'd. You hunt counter. Hence! Avaunt! 85

Serv. Sir, my lord would speak with you.

Ch. Just. Sir John Falstaff, a word with you.

Fal. My good lord! God give your lordship good time of day. I am glad to see your lordship abroad. I heard say your lordship was sick; I hope your lordship goes abroad by advice. Your lordship, though not clean past your youth, hath yet some smack of age in you, some relish of the saltness of time; and I most humbly beseech your lordship to have a reverend care of your health.

Ch. Just. Sir John, I sent for you before your expedition to Shrewsbury. 96

Fal. An't please your lordship, I hear his Majesty is return'd with some discomfort from Wales.

Ch. Just. I talk not of his Majesty. You would not come when I sent for you. 100

Fal. And I hear, moreover, his Highness is fall'n into this same whoreson apoplexy.

Ch. Just. Well, God mend him! I pray you let me speak with you. 104

Fal. This apoplexy, as I take it, is a kind of lethargy, an't please your lordship, a kind of sleeping in the blood, a whoreson tingling. 107

Ch. Just. What tell you me of it? Be it as it is.

Fal. It hath it original from much grief,

from study, and perturbation of the brain.
I have read the cause of his effects in
Galen; it is a kind of deafness. 111

Ch. Just. I think you are fall'n into the
disease, for you hear not what I say to you.

Fal. Very well, my lord, very well.
Rather an't please you, it is the disease of
not listening, the malady of not marking,
that I am troubled withal. 116

Ch. Just. To punish you by the heels
would amend the attention of your ears;
and I care not if I do become your physician.

Fal. I am as poor as Job, my lord, but
not so patient. Your lordship may minister
the potion of imprisonment to me in respect
of poverty; but how I should be your
patient to follow your prescriptions, the
wise may make some dram of a scruple, or
indeed a scruple itself. 124

Ch. Just. I sent for you, when there were
matters against you for your life, to come
speak with me.

Fal. As I was then advis'd by my learned
counsel in the laws of this land-service, I
did not come.

Ch. Just. Well, the truth is, Sir John, you
live in great infamy. 130

Fal. He that buckles himself in my belt
cannot live in less.

Ch. Just. Your means are very slender,
and your waste is great.

Fal. I would it were otherwise; I would
my means were greater and my waist
slenderer. 135

Ch. Just. You have misled the youthful
Prince.

Fal. The young Prince hath misled me.
I am the fellow with the great belly, and
he my dog. 138

Ch. Just. Well, I am loath to gall a new-
heal'd wound. Your day's service at
Shrewsbury hath a little gilded over your
night's exploit on Gadshill. You may thank
th' unquiet time for your quiet o'erposting
that action. 142

Fal. My lord—

Ch. Just. But since all is well, keep it so:
wake not a sleeping wolf. 145

Fal. To wake a wolf is as bad as smell a
fox.

Ch. Just. What! you are as a candle, the
better part burnt out.

Fal. A wassail candle, my lord—all
tallow; if I did say of wax, my growth
would approve the truth. 150

Ch. Just. There is not a white hair in
your face but should have his effect of
gravity.

Fal. His effect of gravy, gravy, gravy.

Ch. Just. You follow the young Prince up
and down, like his ill angel. 155

Fal. Not so, my lord. Your ill angel is
light; but I hope he that looks upon me

will take me without weighing. And yet in
some respects, I grant, I cannot go—I
cannot tell. Virtue is of so little regard in
these costermongers' times that true valour
is turn'd berod; pregnancy is made a
tapster, and his quick wit wasted in giving
reckonings; all the other gifts appertinent
to man, as the malice of this age shapes
them, are not worth a gooseberry. You
that are old consider not the capacities of
us that are young; you do measure the
heat of our livers with the bitterness of
your galls; and we that are in the vaward
of our youth, I must confess, are wags too.

Ch. Just. Do you set down your name in
the scroll of youth, that are written down
old with all the characters of age? Have
you not a moist eye, a dry hand, a yellow
cheek, a white beard, a decreasing leg, an
increasing belly? Is not your voice broken,
your wind short, your chin double, your wit
single, and every part about you blasted
with antiquity? And will you yet call
yourself young? Fie, fie, fie, Sir John! 175

Fal. My lord, I was born about three of
the clock in the afternoon, with a white
head and something a round belly. For my
voice—I have lost it with hallooing and
singing of anthems. To approve my youth
further, I will not. The truth is, I am only
old in judgement and understanding; and
he that will caper with me for a thousand
marks, let him lend me the money, and
have at him. For the box of the ear that
the Prince gave you—he gave it like a rude
prince, and you took it like a sensible lord.
I have check'd him for it; and the young
lion repents—marry, not in ashes and sackcloth, but in new silk and old sack. 186

Ch. Just. Well, God send the Prince a
better companion!

Fal. God send the companion a better
prince! I cannot rid my hands of him. 190

Ch. Just. Well, the King hath sever'd
you. I hear you are going with Lord John
of Lancaster against the Archbishop and
the Earl of Northumberland.

Fal. Yea; I thank your pretty sweet wit
for it. But look you pray, all you that kiss
my Lady Peace at home, that our armies
join not in a hot day; for, by the Lord, I
take but two shirts out with me, and I mean
not to sweat extraordinarily. If it be a hot
day, and I brandish anything but a bottle,
I would I might never spit white again.
There is not a dangerous action can peep
out his head but I am thrust upon it. Well,
I cannot last ever; but it was alway yet
the trick of our English nation, if they have
a good thing, to make it too common. If
ye will needs say I am an old man, you
should give me rest. I would to God my
name were not so terrible to the enemy as
it is. I were better to be eaten to death

with a rust than to be scoured to nothing with perpetual motion. 207

Ch. Just. Well, be honest, be honest; and God bless your expedition!

Fal. Will your lordship lend me a thousand pound to furnish me forth? 211

Ch. Just. Not a penny, not a penny; you are too impatient to bear crosses. Fare you well. Commend me to my cousin Westmoreland. [*Exeunt Chief Justice and Servant.*

Fal. If I do, fillip me with a three-man beetle. A man can no more separate age and covetousness than 'a can part young limbs and lechery; but the gout galls the one, and the pox pinches the other; and so both the degrees prevent my curses. Boy!

Page. Sir? 220

Fal. What money is in my purse?

Page. Seven groats and two pence.

Fal. I can get no remedy against this consumption of the purse; borrowing only lingers and lingers it out, but the disease is incurable. Go bear this letter to my Lord of Lancaster; this to the Prince; this to the Earl of Westmoreland; and this to old Mistress Ursula, whom I have weekly sworn to marry since I perceiv'd the first white hair of my chin. About it; you know where to find me. [*Exit Page*] A pox of this gout! or, a gout of this pox! for the one or the other plays the rogue with my great toe. 'Tis no matter if I do halt; I have the wars for my colour, and my pension shall seem the more reasonable. A good wit will make use of anything. I will turn diseases to commodity. [*Exit.*

SCENE III. *York. The Archbishop's palace.*

Enter the ARCHBISHOP, THOMAS MOWBRAY *the Earl Marshal,* LORD HASTINGS *and* LORD BARDOLPH.

Arch. Thus have you heard our cause and known our means;
And, my most noble friends, I pray you all
Speak plainly your opinions of our hopes—
And first, Lord Marshal, what say you to it?

Mowb. I well allow the occasion of our arms; 5
But gladly would be better satisfied
How, in our means, we should advance ourselves
To look with forehead bold and big enough
Upon the power and puissance of the King.

Hast. Our present musters grow upon the file 10
To five and twenty thousand men of choice;
And our supplies live largely in the hope
Of great Northumberland, whose bosom burns
With an incensed fire of injuries.

L. Bard. The question then, Lord Hastings, standeth thus: 15

Whether our present five and twenty thousand
May hold up head without Northumberland?

Hast. With him, we may.

L. Bard. Yea, marry, there's the point;
But if without him we be thought too feeble,
My judgment is we should not step too far 20
Till we had his assistance by the hand;
For, in a theme so bloody-fac'd as this,
Conjecture, expectation, and surmise
Of aids incertain, should not be admitted.

Arch. 'Tis very true, Lord Bardolph; for indeed 25
It was young Hotspur's case at Shrewsbury.

L. Bard. It was, my lord; who lin'd himself with hope,
Eating the air and promise of supply,
Flatt'ring himself in project of a power
Much smaller than the smallest of his thoughts; 30
And so, with great imagination
Proper to madmen, led his powers to death,
And, winking, leapt into destruction.

Hast. But, by your leave, it never yet did hurt
To lay down likelihoods and forms of hope.

L. Bard. Yes, if this present quality of war— 36
Indeed the instant action, a cause on foot—
Lives so in hope, as in an early spring
We see th' appearing buds; which to prove fruit
Hope gives not so much warrant, as despair
That frosts will bite them. When we mean to build, 41
We first survey the plot, then draw the model;
And when we see the figure of the house,
Then must we rate the cost of the erection;
Which if we find outweighs ability, 45
What do we then but draw anew the model
In fewer offices, or at least desist
To build at all? Much more, in this great work—
Which is almost to pluck a kingdom down
And set another up—should we survey 50
The plot of situation and the model,
Consent upon a sure foundation,
Question surveyors, know our own estate
How able such a work to undergo—
To weigh against his opposite; or else 55
We fortify in paper and in figures,
Using the names of men instead of men;
Like one that draws the model of a house
Beyond his power to build it; who, half through, 59
Gives o'er and leaves his part-created cost
A naked subject to the weeping clouds
And waste for churlish winter's tyranny.

Hast. Grant that our hopes—yet likely of fair birth—

Should be still-born, and that we now
   possess'd
The utmost man of expectation,   65
I think we are so a body strong enough,
Even as we are, to equal with the King.
   L. Bard. What, is the King but five and
    twenty thousand ?
   Hast. To us no more ; nay, not so much,
    Lord Bardolph ;
For his divisions, as the times do brawl, 70
Are in three heads : one power against the
   French,
And one against Glendower ; perforce a
   third
Must take up us. So is the unfirm King
In three divided ; and his coffers sound
With hollow poverty and emptiness.   75
   Arch. That he should draw his several
    strengths together
And come against us in full puissance
Need not be dreaded.
   Hast.   If he should do so,
He leaves his back unarm'd, the French and
   Welsh   79
Baying him at the heels. Never fear that.
   L. Bard. Who is it like should lead his
    forces hither ?
   Hast. The Duke of Lancaster and West-
    moreland ;
Against the Welsh, himself and Harry
   Monmouth ;
But who is substituted against the French
I have no certain notice.
   Arch.   Let us on,   85
And publish the occasion of our arms.
The commonwealth is sick of their own
   choice ;
Their over-greedy love hath surfeited.
An habitation giddy and unsure   89
Hath he that buildeth on the vulgar heart.
O thou fond many, with what loud applause
Didst thou beat heaven with blessing
   Bolingbroke
Before he was what thou wouldst have him
   be !
And being now trimm'd in thine own
   desires,
Thou, beastly feeder, art so full of him 95
That thou provok'st thyself to cast him
   up.
So, so, thou common dog, didst thou
   disgorge
Thy glutton bosom of the royal Richard ;
And now thou wouldst eat thy dead vomit
   up,
And howl'st to find it. What trust is in
   these times ?   100
They that, when Richard liv'd, would have
   him die
Are now become enamour'd on his grave.
Thou that threw'st dust upon his goodly
   head,
When through proud London he came
   sighing on

After th' admired heels of Bolingbroke, 105
Criest now ' O earth, yield us that king
   again,
And take thou this ! ' O thoughts of men
   accurs'd !
Past and to come seems best ; things
   present, worst.
   Mowb. Shall we go draw our numbers,
    and set on ?
   Hast. We are time's subjects, and time
    bids be gone.   [*Exeunt.*

ACT TWO

Scene I. *London. A street.*

Enter Hostess *with two officers,* Fang *and*
Snare.

   Host. Master Fang, have you ent'red the
action ?
   Fang. It is ent'red.
   Host. Where's your yeoman ? Is't a
lusty yeoman ? Will 'a stand to't ?
   Fang. Sirrah, where's Snare ?   5
   Host. O Lord, ay ! good Master Snare.
   Snare. Here, here.
   Fang. Snare, we must arrest Sir John
Falstaff.
   Host. Yea, good Master Snare ; I have
ent'red him and all.   10
   Snare. It may chance cost some of us our
lives, for he will stab.
   Host. Alas the day ! take heed of him ;
he stabb'd me in mine own house, and that
most beastly. In good faith, 'a cares not
what mischief he does, if his weapon be
out ; he will foin like any devil ; he will
spare neither man, woman, nor child. 17
   Fang. If I can close with him, I care not
for his thrust.
   Host. No, nor I neither ; I'll be at your
elbow.
   Fang. An I but fist him once ; an 'a
come but within my vice !   21
   Host. I am undone by his going ; I
warrant you, he's an infinitive thing upon
my score. Good Master Fang, hold him
sure. Good Master Snare, let him not
scape. 'A comes continuantly to Pie-
corner—saving your manhoods—to buy a
saddle ; and he is indited to dinner to the
Lubber's Head in Lumbert Street, to
Master Smooth's the silkman. I pray you,
since my exion is ent'red, and my case so
openly known to the world, let him be
brought in to his answer. A hundred mark
is a long one for a poor lone woman to bear ;
and I have borne, and borne, and borne ;
and have been fubb'd off, and fubb'd off,
and fubb'd off, from this day to that day,
that it is a shame to be thought on. There
is no honesty in such dealing ; unless a
woman should be made an ass and a beast,
to bear every knave's wrong.   36

Enter SIR JOHN FALSTAFF, *Page, and*
BARDOLPH.

Yonder he comes; and that arrant malmsey-
nose knave, Bardolph, with him. Do your
offices, do your offices, Master Fang and
Master Snare; do me, do me, do me your
offices.   39
Fal. How now! whose mare's dead?
What's the matter?
Fang. Sir John, I arrest you at the suit
of Mistress Quickly.
Fal. Away, varlets! Draw, Bardolph.
Cut me off the villain's head. Throw the
quean in the channel.   45
Host. Throw me in the channel! I'll
throw thee in the channel. Wilt thou?
wilt thou? thou bastardly rogue! Murder,
murder! Ah, thou honeysuckle villain!
wilt thou kill God's officers and the King's?
Ah, thou honey-seed rogue! thou art a
honey-seed; a man-queller and a woman-
queller.   51
Fal. Keep them off, Bardolph.
Fang. A rescue! a rescue!
Host. Good people, bring a rescue or two.
Thou wot, wot thou! thou wot, wot ta?
Do, do, thou rogue! do, thou hemp-seed!
Page. Away, you scullion! you rampallian! you fustilarian! I'll tickle your
catastrophe.   58

Enter the LORD CHIEF JUSTICE *and his* Men.

Ch. Just. What is the matter? Keep the
peace here, ho!
Host. Good my lord, be good to me. I
beseech you, stand to me.   61
Ch. Just. How now, Sir John! what, are
  you brawling here?
Doth this become your place, your time,
  and business?
You should have been well on your way to
  York.
Stand from him, fellow; wherefore hang'st
  thou upon him?   65
Host. O my most worshipful lord, an't
please your Grace, I am a poor widow of
Eastcheap, and he is arrested at my suit.
Ch. Just. For what sum?   69
Host. It is more than for some, my lord;
it is for all—all I have. He hath eaten me
out of house and home; he hath put all
my substance into that fat belly of his.
But I will have some of it out again, or I
will ride thee a nights like the mare.   74
Fal. I think I am as like to ride the mare,
if I have any vantage of ground to get up.
Ch. Just. How comes this, Sir John? Fie!
Fie! What man of good temper would
endure this tempest of exclamation? Are
you not ashamed to enforce a poor widow
to so rough a course to come by her own?
Fal. What is the gross sum that I owe
thee?   81

Host. Marry, if thou wert an honest man,
thyself and the money too. Thou didst
swear to me upon a parcel-gilt goblet,
sitting in my Dolphin chamber, at the
round table, by a sea-coal fire, upon
Wednesday in Wheeson week, when the
Prince broke thy head for liking his father
to a singing-man of Windsor—thou didst
swear to me then, as I was washing thy
wound, to marry me and make me my lady
thy wife. Canst thou deny it? Did not
goodwife Keech, the butcher's wife, come
in then and call me gossip Quickly?
Coming in to borrow a mess of vinegar,
telling us she had a good dish of prawns,
whereby thou didst desire to eat some,
whereby I told thee they were ill for a
green wound? And didst thou not, when
she was gone down stairs, desire me to be
no more so familiarity with such poor
people, saying that ere long they should
call me madam? And didst thou not kiss
me, and bid me fetch thee thirty shillings?
I put thee now to thy book-oath. Deny it,
if thou canst.   99
Fal. My lord, this is a poor mad soul,
and she says up and down the town that
her eldest son is like you. She hath been
in good case, and, the truth is, poverty
hath distracted her. But for these foolish
officers, I beseech you I may have redress
against them.   104
Ch. Just. Sir John, Sir John, I am well
acquainted with your manner of wrenching
the true cause the false way. It is not a
confident brow, nor the throng of words
that come with such more than impudent
sauciness from you, can thrust me from a
level consideration. You have, as it appears
to me, practis'd upon the easy yielding
spirit of this woman, and made her serve
your uses both in purse and in person.   112
Host. Yea, in truth, my lord.
Ch. Just. Pray thee, peace. Pay her the
debt you owe her, and unpay the villainy
you have done with her; the one you may
do with sterling money, and the other with
current repentance.   117
Fal. My lord, I will not undergo this
sneap without reply. You call honourable
boldness impudent sauciness; if a man
will make curtsy and say nothing, he is
virtuous. No, my lord, my humble duty
rememb'red, I will not be your suitor. I
say to you I do desire deliverance from
these officers, being upon hasty employment in the King's affairs.   124
Ch. Just. You speak as having power to
do wrong; but answer in th' effect of your
reputation, and satisfy the poor woman.
Fal. Come hither hostess.   128

Enter GOWER.

Ch. Just. Now, Master Gower, what news?

Gow. The King, my lord, and Harry
    Prince of Wales   130
Are near at hand. The rest the paper tells.
                                    [*Gives a letter.*
Fal. As I am a gentleman !
Host. Faith, you said so before.
Fal. As I am a gentleman ! Come, no
more words of it.   135
Host. By this heavenly ground I tread on,
I must be fain to pawn both my plate and
the tapestry of my dining-chambers. 138
Fal. Glasses, glasses, is the only drinking;
and for thy walls, a pretty slight drollery,
or the story of the Prodigal, or the German
hunting, in water-work, is worth a thousand
of these bed-hangers and these fly-bitten
tapestries. Let it be ten pound, if thou
canst. Come, an 'twere not for thy
humours, there's not a better wench in
England. Go, wash thy face, and draw the
action. Come, thou must not be in this
humour with me ; dost not know me ?
Come, come, I know thou wast set on to
this.   147
Host. Pray thee, Sir John, let it be but
twenty nobles ; i' faith, I am loath to pawn
my plate, so God save me, la !
Fal. Let it alone ; I'll make other shift.
You'll be a fool still.   151
Host. Well, you shall have it, though I
pawn my gown. I hope you'll come to
supper. You'll pay me all together ?
Fal. Will I live ? [*To Bardolph*] Go, with
her, with her ; hook on, hook on. 156
Host. Will you have Doll Tearsheet meet
you at supper ?
Fal. No more words ; let's have her.
    [*Exeunt Hostess, Bardolph, and Officers.*
Ch. Just. I have heard better news. 160
Fal. What's the news, my lord ?
Ch. Just. Where lay the King to-night ?
Gow. At Basingstoke, my lord.
Fal. I hope, my lord, all's well. What is
the news, my lord ?   165
Ch. Just. Come all his forces back ?
Gow. No ; fifteen hundred foot, five
    hundred horse,
Are march'd up to my Lord of Lancas-
    ter,
Against Northumberland and the Arch-
    bishop.
Fal. Comes the King back from Wales,
my noble lord ?   170
Ch. Just. You shall have letters of me
    presently.
Come, go along with me, good Master
    Gower.
Fal. My lord !
Ch. Just. What's the matter ?
Fal. Master Gower, shall I entreat you
with me to dinner ?   176
Gow. I must wait upon my good lord
here, I thank you, good Sir John.
Ch. Just. Sir John, you loiter here too

long, being you are to take soldiers up in
counties as you go.   180
Fal. Will you sup with me, Master
Gower ?
Ch. Just. What foolish master taught you
these manners, Sir John ?
Fal. Master Gower, if they become me
not, he was a fool that taught them me.
This is the right fencing grace, my lord :
tap for tap, and so part fair.   186
Ch. Just. Now, the Lord lighten thee !
Thou art a great fool.   [*Exeunt.*

SCENE II. *London. Another street.*

Enter PRINCE HENRY *and* POINS.

Prince. Before God, I am exceeding
weary.
Poins. Is't come to that ? I had thought
weariness durst not have attach'd one of so
high blood.
Prince. Faith, it does me ; though it
discolours the complexion of my greatness
to acknowledge it. Doth it not show vilely
in me to desire small beer ?   6
Poins. Why, a prince should not be so
loosely studied as to remember so weak a
composition.
Prince. Belike then my appetite was not
princely got ; for, by my troth, I do now
remember the poor creature, small beer.
But indeed these humble considerations
make me out of love with my greatness.
What a disgrace is it to me to remember
thy name, or to know thy face to-morrow,
or to take note how many pair of silk
stockings thou hast —viz., these, and those
that were thy peach-colour'd ones—or to
bear the inventory of thy shirts—as, one for
superfluity, and another for use ! But that
the tennis-court-keeper knows better than
I ; for it is a low ebb of linen with thee
when thou keepest not racket there ; as
thou hast not done a great while, because
the rest of thy low countries have made a
shift to eat up thy holland. And God knows
whether those that bawl out the ruins of
thy linen shall inherit his kingdom ; but
the midwives say the children are not in
the fault ; whereupon the world increases,
and kindreds are mightily strengthened. 26
Poins. How ill it follows, after you have
laboured so hard, you should talk so idly !
Tell me, how many good young princes
would do so, their fathers being so sick as
yours at this time is ?   30
Prince. Shall I tell thee one thing, Poins ?
Poins. Yes, faith ; and let it be an
excellent good thing.
Prince. It shall serve among wits of no
higher breeding than thine.
Poins. Go to ; I stand the push of your
one thing that you will tell.   36
Prince. Marry, I tell thee it is not meet

that I should be sad, now my father is sick ; albeit I could tell to thee—as to one it pleases me, for fault of a better, to call my friend—I could be sad and sad indeed too.

Poins. Very hardly upon such a subject.

Prince. By this hand, thou thinkest me as far in the devil's book as thou and Falstaff for obduracy and persistency : let the end try the man. But I tell thee my heart bleeds inwardly that my father is so sick ; and keeping such vile company as thou art hath in reason taken from me all ostentation of sorrow.   47

Poins. The reason ?

Prince. What wouldst thou think of me if I should weep ?   50

Poins. I would think thee a most princely hypocrite.

Prince. It would be every man's thought ; and thou art a blessed fellow to think as every man thinks. Never a man's thought in the world keeps the road-way better than thine. Every man would think me an hypocrite indeed. And what accites your most worshipful thought to think so ?   57

Poins. Why, because you have been so lewd and so much engraffed to Falstaff.

Prince. And to thee.   60

Poins. By this light, I am well spoke on ; I can hear it with mine own ears. The worst that they can say of me is that I am a second brother and that I am a proper fellow of my hands ; and those two things, I confess, I cannot help. By the mass, here comes Bardolph.   66

Enter BARDOLPH *and* Page.

Prince. And the boy that I gave Falstaff. 'A had him from me Christian ; and look if the fat villain have not transform'd him ape.

Bard. God save your Grace !   70

Prince. And yours, most noble Bardolph!

Poins. Come, you virtuous ass, you bashful fool, must you be blushing ? Wherefore blush you now ? What a maidenly man-at-arms are you become ! Is't such a matter to get a pottle-pot's maidenhead ?   75

Page. 'A calls me e'en now, my lord, through a red lattice, and I could discern no part of his face from the window. At last I spied his eyes ; and methought he had made two holes in the alewife's new petticoat, and so peep'd through.   80

Prince. Has not the boy profited ?

Bard. Away, you whoreson upright rabbit, away !

Page. Away, you rascally Althæa's dream, away !

Prince. Instruct us, boy ; what dream, boy ?   84

Page. Marry, my lord, Althæa dreamt she was delivered of a fire-brand ; and therefore I call him her dream.   87

Prince. A crown's worth of good interpretation. There 'tis, boy. [*Giving a crown.*

Poins. O that this blossom could be kept from cankers ! Well, there is sixpence to preserve thee.

Bard. An you do not make him be hang'd among you, the gallows shall have wrong.

Prince. And how doth thy master, Bardolph ?   94

Bard. Well, my lord. He heard of your Grace's coming to town. There's a letter for you.

Poins. Deliver'd with good respect. And how doth the martlemas, your master ?

Bard. In bodily health, sir.   99

Poins. Marry, the immortal part needs a physician ; but that moves not him. Though that be sick, it dies not.

Prince. I do allow this wen to be as familiar with me as my dog ; and he holds his place, for look you how he writes.   104

Poins. [*Reads*] ' John Falstaff, knight '—Every man must know that as oft as he has occasion to name himself, even like those that are kin to the King ; for they never prick their finger but they say ' There's some of the King's blood spilt '. ' How comes that ? ' says he that takes upon him not to conceive. The answer is as ready as a borrower's cap : ' I am the King's poor cousin, sir '.   111

Prince. Nay, they will be kin to us, or they will fetch it from Japhet. But the letter : [*Reads*] ' Sir John Falstaff, knight, to the son of the King nearest his father, Harry Prince of Wales, greeting '.

Poins. Why, this is a certificate.   116

Prince. Peace ! [*Reads*] ' I will imitate the honourable Romans in brevity.'—

Poins. He sure means brevity in breath, short-winded.

Prince. [*Reads*] ' I commend me to thee, I commend thee, and I leave thee. Be not too familiar with Poins ; for he misuses thy favours so much that he swears thou art to marry his sister Nell. Repent at idle times as thou mayst, and so farewell.   123

Thine, by yea and no—which is as much as to say as thou usest him—JACK FALSTAFF with my familiars, JOHN with my brothers and sisters, and SIR JOHN with all Europe.'

Poins. My lord, I'll steep this letter in sack and make him eat it.   129

Prince. That's to make him eat twenty o. his words. But do you use me thus, Ned ? Must I marry your sister ?

Poins. God send the wench no worse fortune . But I never said so.   134

Prince. Well, thus we play the fools with th. time, and the spirits of the wise sit in the clouds and mock us. Is your master here in London ?

Bard. Yea, my lord.

Prince. Where sups he ? Doth the old boar feed in the old frank ?   140

Bard. At the old place, my lord, in Eastcheap.

Prince. What company ?

Page. Ephesians, my lord, of the old church.

Prince. Sup any women with him ?   144

Page. None, my lord, but old Mistress Quickly and Mistress Doll Tearsheet.

Prince. What pagan may that be ?

Page. A proper gentlewoman, sir, and a kinswoman of my master's.   149

Prince. Even such kin as the parish heifers are to the town bull. Shall we steal upon them, Ned, at supper ?

Poins. I am your shadow, my lord ; I'll follow you.

Prince. Sirrah, you boy, and Bardolph, no word to your master that I am yet come to town. There's for your silence.   156

Bard. I have no tongue, sir.

Page. And for mine, sir, I will govern it.

Prince. Fare you well ; go. [*Exeunt Bardolph and Page*] This Doll Tearsheet should be some road.   160

Poins. I warrant you, as common as the way between Saint Albans and London.

Prince. How might we see Falstaff bestow himself to-night in his true colours, and not ourselves be seen ?

Poins. Put on two leathern jerkins and aprons, and wait upon him at his table as drawers.   166

Prince. From a god to a bull ? A heavy descension ! It was Jove's case. From a prince to a prentice ? A low transformation ! That shall be mine ; for in everything the purpose must weigh with the folly. Follow me, Ned.   [*Exeunt.*

SCENE III. *Warkworth. Before the castle.*

Enter NORTHUMBERLAND, LADY NORTH-
UMBERLAND, *and* LADY PERCY.

North. I pray thee, loving wife, and gentle daughter,
Give even way unto my rough affairs ;
Put not you on the visage of the times
And be, like them, to Percy troublesome.

Lady N. I have given over, I will speak no more.   5
Do what you will ; your wisdom be your guide.

North. Alas, sweet wife, my honour is at pawn ;
And but my going nothing can redeem it.

Lady P. O, yet, for God's sake, go not to these wars !
The time was, father, that you broke your word,   10
When you were more endear'd to it than now ;

When your own Percy, when my heart's dear Harry,
Threw many a northward look to see his father
Bring up his powers ; but he did long in vain.
Who then persuaded you to stay at home ?
There were two honours lost, yours and your son's.   16
For yours, the God of heaven brighten it !
For his, it stuck upon him as the sun
In the grey vault of heaven ; and by his light
Did all the chivalry of England move   20
To do brave acts. He was indeed the glass
Wherein the noble youth did dress themselves.
He had no legs that practis'd not his gait ;
And speaking thick, which nature made his blemish,
Became the accents of the valiant ;   25
For those that could speak low and tardily
Would turn their own perfection to abuse
To seem like him : so that in speech, in gait,
In diet, in affections of delight,
In military rules, humours of blood,   30
He was the mark and glass, copy and book,
That fashion'd others. And him—O wondrous him !
O miracle of men !—him did you leave—
Second to none, unseconded by you—
To look upon the hideous god of war   35
In disadvantage, to abide a field
Where nothing but the sound of Hotspur's name
Did seem defensible. So you left him.
Never, O never, do his ghost the wrong
To hold your honour more precise and nice
With others than with him ! Let them alone.   41
The Marshal and the Archbishop are strong.
Had my sweet Harry had but half their numbers,
To-day might I, hanging on Hotspur's neck,
Have talk'd of Monmouth's grave.

North.   Beshrew your heart,   45
Fair daughter, you do draw my spirits from me
With new lamenting ancient oversights.
But I must go and meet with danger there,
Or it will seek me in another place,
And find me worse provided.

Lady N.   O, fly to Scotland   50
Till that the nobles and the armed commons
Have of their puissance made a little taste.

Lady P. If they get ground and vantage of the King,
Then join you with them, like a rib of steel,
To make strength stronger ; but, for all our loves,   55
First let them try themselves. So did your son ;

He was so suff'red; so came I a widow;
And never shall have length of life enough
To rain upon remembrance with mine eyes,
That it may grow and sprout as high as
    heaven,   60
For recordation to my noble husband.
   North. Come, come, go in with me. 'Tis
    with my mind
As with the tide swell'd up unto his height,
That makes a still-stand, running neither
    way.
Fain would I go to meet the Archbishop, 65
But many thousand reasons hold me back.
I will resolve for Scotland. There am I,
Till time and vantage crave my company.
                  [Exeunt.

SCENE IV. *London. The Boar's Head
    Tavern in Eastcheap.*

Enter FRANCIS *and* another Drawer.

   Francis. What the devil hast thou brought
there—apple-johns? Thou knowest Sir
John cannot endure an apple-john.   3
   2 Draw. Mass, thou say'st true. The
Prince once set a dish of apple-johns before
him, and told him there were five more
Sir Johns; and, putting off his hat, said
' I will now take my leave of these six dry,
round, old, withered knights'. It ang'red
him to the heart; but he hath forgot that.
   Francis. Why, then, cover and set them
down; and see if thou canst find out
Sneak's noise; Mistress Tearsheet would
fain hear some music.

Enter third Drawer.

   3 Draw. Dispatch! The room where
they supp'd is too hot; they'll come in
straight.   14
   Francis. Sirrah, here will be the Prince
and Master Poins anon; and they will put
on two of our jerkins and aprons; and Sir
John must not know of it. Bardolph hath
brought word.
   3 Draw. By the mass, here will be old
utis; it will be an excellent stratagem. 20
   2 Draw. I'll see if I can find out Sneak.
        [Exeunt second and third Drawers.

Enter Hostess *and* DOLL TEARSHEET.

   Host. I'faith, sweetheart, methinks now
you are in an excellent good temperality.
Your pulsidge beats as extraordinarily as
heart would desire; and your colour, I
warrant you, is as red as any rose, in good
truth, la! But, i' faith, you have drunk
too much canaries; and that's a marvellous searching wine, and it perfumes the
blood ere one can say 'What's this?'
How do you now?
   Doll. Better than I was—hem.   30
   Host. Why, that's well said; a good heart's
worth gold. Lo, here comes Sir John.

Enter FALSTAFF.

   Fal. [*Singing*] ' When Arthur first in
court '—Empty the jordan. [*Exit Francis*]
—[*Singing*] ' And was a worthy king'—
How now, Mistress Doll!   35
   Host. Sick of a calm; yea, good faith.
   Fal. So is all her sect; an they be once
in a calm, they are sick.
   Doll. A pox damn you, you muddy rascal!
Is that all the comfort you give me?   40
   Fal. You make fat rascals, Mistress Doll.
   Doll. I make them! Gluttony and
diseases make them: I make them not.
   Fal. If the cook help to make the
gluttony, you help to make the diseases,
Doll. We catch of you, Doll, we catch of
you; grant that, my poor virtue, grant
that.   46
   Doll. Yea, joy, our chains and our
jewels.
   Fal. ' Your brooches, pearls, and ouches.'
For to serve bravely is to come halting off;
you know, to come off the breach with his
pike bent bravely, and to surgery bravely;
to venture upon the charg'd chambers
bravely—   51
   Doll. Hang yourself, you muddy conger,
hang yourself!
   Host. By my troth, this is the old fashion;
you two never meet but you fall to some
discord. You are both, i' good truth, as
rheumatic as two dry toasts; you cannot
one bear with another's confirmities. What
the good-year! one must bear, and that
must be you. You are the weaker vessel, as
they say, the emptier vessel.   58
   Doll. Can a weak empty vessel bear such
a huge full hogshead? There's a whole
merchant's venture of Bourdeaux stuff in
him; you have not seen a hulk better
stuff'd in the hold. Come, I'll be friends
with thee, Jack.. Thou art going to the
wars; and whether I shall ever see thee
again or no, there is nobody cares.   64

Re-enter FRANCIS.

   Francis. Sir, Ancient Pistol's below and
would speak with you.
   Doll. Hang him, swaggering rascal! Let
him not come hither; it is the foul-
mouth'dst rogue in England.   68
   Host. If he swagger, let him not come
here. No, by my faith! I must live among
my neighbours; I'll no swaggerers. I am
in good name and fame with the very best.
Shut the door. There comes no swaggerers
here; I have not liv'd all this while to
have swaggering now. Shut the door, I
pray you.
   Fal. Dost thou hear, hostess?   75
   Host. Pray ye, pacify yourself, Sir John;
there comes no swaggerers here.
   Fal. Dost thou hear? It is mine ancient.

Host. Tilly-fally, Sir John, ne'er tell me ; and your ancient swagg'rer comes not in my doors. I was before Master Tisick, the debuty, t' other day ; and, as he said to me—'twas no longer ago than Wednesday last, 'i good faith !—' Neighbour Quickly,' says he—Master Dumbe, our minister, was by then—' Neighbour Quickly,' says he ' receive those that are civil, for' said he ' you are in an ill name.' Now 'a said so, I can tell whereupon. ' For' says he ' you are an honest woman and well thought on, therefore take heed what guests you receive. Receive' says he ' no swaggering companions.' There comes none here. You would bless you to hear what he said. No, I'll no swagg'rers.   91

Fal. He's no swagg'rer, hostess ; a tame cheater, i' faith ; you may stroke him as gently as a puppy greyhound. He'll not swagger with a Barbary hen, if her feathers turn back in any show of resistance. Call him up, drawer.   [*Exit Francis.*

Host. Cheater, call you him ? I will bar no honest man my house, nor no cheater ; but I do not love swaggering, by my troth. I am the worse when one says ' swagger '. Feel, masters, how I shake ; look you, I warrant you.   100

Doll. So you do, hostess.

Host. Do I ? Yea, in very truth, do I, an 'twere an aspen leaf. I cannot abide swagg'rers.

Enter PISTOL, BARDOLPH, *and* PAGE.

Pist. God save you, Sir John !   104

Fal. Welcome, Ancient Pistol. Here, Pistol, I charge you with a cup of sack ; do you discharge upon mine hostess.

Pist. I will discharge upon her, Sir John, with two bullets.   109

Fal. She is pistol-proof, sir ; you shall not hardly offend her.

Host. Come, I'll drink no proofs nor no bullets. I'll drink no more than will do me good, for no man's pleasure, I.   113

Pist. Then to you, Mistress Dorothy ; I will charge you.

Doll. Charge me ! I scorn you, scurvy companion. What ! you poor, base, rascally, cheating, lack-linen mate ! Away, you mouldy rogue, away ! I am meat for your master.

Pist. I know you, Mistress Dorothy.   119

Doll. Away, you cut-purse rascal ! you filthy bung, away ! By this wine, I'll thrust my knife in your mouldy chaps, an you play the saucy cuttle with me. Away, you bottle-ale rascal ! you basket-hilt stale juggler, you ! Since when, I pray you, sir ? God's light, with two points on your shoulder ? Much !   125

Pist. God let me not live but I will murder your ruff for this.

Fal. No more, Pistol ; I would not have you go off here. Discharge yourself of our company, Pistol.   129

Host. No, good Captain Pistol ; not here, sweet captain.

Doll. Captain ! Thou abominable damn'd cheater, art thou not ashamed to be called captain ? An captains were of my mind, they would truncheon you out, for taking their names upon you before you have earn'd them. You a captain ! you slave, for what ? For tearing a poor whore's ruff in a bawdy-house ? He a captain ! hang him, rogue ! He lives upon mouldy stew'd prunes and dried cakes. A captain ! God's light, these villains will make the word as odious as the word ' occupy ' ; which was an excellent good word before it was ill sorted. Therefore captains had need look to't.   141

Bard. Pray thee go down, good ancient.

Fal. Hark thee hither, Mistress Doll.

Pist. Not I ! I tell thee what, Corporal Bardolph, I could tear her ; I'll be reveng'd of her.   145

Page. Pray thee go down.

Pist. I'll see her damn'd first ; to Pluto's damn'd lake, by this hand, to th' infernal deep, with Erebus and tortures vile also. Hold hook and line, say I. Down, down, dogs ! down, faitors ! Have we not Hiren here ?   151

Host. Good Captain Peesel, be quiet ; 'tis very late, i' faith ; I beseek you now, aggravate your choler.

Pist. These be good humours, indeed ! Shall packhorses,
And hollow pamper'd jades of Asia,   155
Which cannot go but thirty mile a day,
Compare with Cæsars, and with Cannibals,
And Troiant Greeks ? Nay, rather damn them with
King Cerberus ; and let the welkin roar.
Shall we fall foul for toys ?   160

Host. By my troth, Captain, these are very bitter words.

Bard. Be gone, good ancient ; this will grow to a brawl anon.

Pist. Die men like dogs ! Give crowns like pins ! Have we not Hiren here ?   165

Host. O' my word, Captain, there's none such here. What the good-year ! do you think I would deny her ? For God's sake, be quiet.

Pist. Then feed and be fat, my fair Calipolis.
Come, give's some sack.   170
' Si fortune me tormente sperato me contento.'
Fear we broadsides ? No, let the fiend give fire.
Give me some sack ; and, sweetheart, lie thou there. [*Laying down his sword.*

Come we to full points here, and are etceteras nothings ?

Fal. Pistol, I would be quiet.   175

Pist. Sweet knight, I kiss thy neaf. What! we have seen the seven stars.

Doll. For God's sake thrust him down stairs ; I cannot endure such a fustian rascal.

Pist. Thrust him down stairs ! Know we not Galloway nags ?   181

Fal. Quoit him down, Bardolph, like a shove-groat shilling. Nay, an 'a do nothing but speak nothing, 'a shall be nothing here.

Bard. Come, get you down stairs.   185

Pist. What ! shall we have incision ? Shall we imbrue ?

[*Snatching up his sword.*

Then death rock me asleep, abridge my doleful days !

Why, then, let grievous, ghastly, gaping wounds

Untwine the Sisters Three ! Come, Atropos, I say !

Host. Here's goodly stuff toward !   190

Fal. Give me my rapier, boy.

Doll. I pray thee, Jack, I pray thee, do not draw.

Fal. Get you down stairs.

[*Drawing and driving Pistol out.*

Host. Here's a goodly tumult ! I'll forswear keeping house afore I'll be in these tirrits and frights. So ; murder, I warrant now. Alas, alas ! put up your naked weapons, put up your naked weapons.   197

[*Exeunt Pistol and Bardolph.*

Doll. I pray thee, Jack, be quiet ; the rascal's gone. Ah, you whoreson little valiant villain, you !

Host. Are you not hurt i' th' groin ? Methought 'a made a shrewd thrust at your belly.   201

Re-enter BARDOLPH.

Fal. Have you turn'd him out a doors ?

Bard. Yea, sir. The rascal's drunk. You have hurt him, sir, i' th' shoulder.

Fal. A rascal ! to brave me !   205

Doll. Ah, you sweet little rogue, you ! Alas, poor ape, how thou sweat'st ! Come, let me wipe thy face. Come on, you whoreson chops. Ah, rogue ! i' faith, I love thee. Thou art as valorous as Hector of Troy, worth five of Agamemnon, and ten times better than the Nine Worthies. Ah, villain !   211

Fal. A rascally slave ! I will toss the rogue in a blanket.

Doll. Do, an thou dar'st for thy heart. An thou dost, I'll canvass thee between a pair of sheets.   215

Enter Musicians.

Page. The music is come, sir.

Fal. Let them play. Play, sirs. Sit on

my knee, Doll. A rascal bragging slave ! The rogue fled from me like quicksilver. 219

Doll. I'faith, and thou follow'dst him like a church. Thou whoreson little tidy Bartholomew boar-pig, when wilt thou leave fighting a days and foining a nights, and begin to patch up thine old body for heaven ?   223

Enter, behind, PRINCE HENRY *and* POINS *disguised as drawers.*

Fal. Peace, good Doll ! Do not speak like a death's-head ; do not bid me remember mine end.

Doll. Sirrah, what humour 's the Prince of ?

Fal. A good shallow young fellow. 'A would have made a good pantler ; 'a would ha' chipp'd bread well.

Doll. They say Poins has a good wit.   229

Fal. He a good wit ! hang him, baboon ! His wit's as thick as Tewksbury mustard ; there's no more conceit in him than is in a mallet.

Doll. Why does the Prince love him so, then ?   233

Fal. Because their legs are both of a bigness, and 'a plays at quoits well, and eats conger and fennel, and drinks off candles' ends for flap-dragons, and rides the wild mare with the boys, and jumps upon join'd-stools, and swears with a good grace, and wears his boots very smooth, like unto the sign of the Leg, and breeds no bate with telling of discreet stories ; and such other gambol faculties 'a has, that show a weak mind and an able body, for the which the Prince admits him. For the Prince himself is such another ; the weight of a hair will turn the scales between their avoirdupois.   244

Prince. Would not this nave of a wheel have his ears cut off ?

Poins. Let's beat him before his whore.

Prince. Look whe'er the wither'd elder hath not his poll claw'd like a parrot.   249

Poins. Is it not strange that desire should so many years outlive performance ?

Fal. Kiss me, Doll.

Prince. Saturn and Venus this year in conjunction ! What says th' almanac to that ?   254

Poins. And look whether the fiery Trigon, his man, be not lisping to his master's old tables, his note-book, his counsel-keeper.   257

Fal. Thou dost give me flattering busses.

Doll. By my troth, I kiss thee with a most constant heart.   260

Fal. I am old, I am old.

Doll. I love thee better than I love e'er a scurvy young boy of them all.

Fal. What stuff wilt have a kirtle of ? I shall receive money a Thursday. Shalt have a cap to-morrow. A merry song, come. 'A grows late; we'll to bed. Thou't forget me when I am gone.   267

Doll. By my troth, thou't set me a-weeping, an thou say'st so. Prove that ever I dress myself handsome till thy return. Well, hearken a' th' end.   270

Fal. Some sack, Francis.

Prince. ⎱
Poins. ⎰ Anon, anon, sir. [*Advancing.*

Fal. Ha! a bastard son of the King's? And art thou not Poins his brother?

Prince. Why, thou globe of sinful continents, what a life dost thou lead!   276

Fal. A better than thou. I am a gentleman: thou art a drawer.

Prince. Very true, sir, and I come to draw you out by the ears.   280

Host. O, the Lord preserve thy Grace! By my troth, welcome to London. How the Lord bless that sweet face of thine! O Jesu, are you come from Wales?

Fal. Thou whoreson mad compound of majesty, by this light flesh and corrupt blood, thou art welcome.   285
                [*Leaning his hand upon Doll.*

Doll. How, you fat fool! I scorn you.

Poins. My lord, he will drive you out of your revenge and turn all to a merriment, if you take not the heat.

Prince. You whoreson candle-mine, you, how vilely did you speak of me even now before this honest, virtuous, civil gentlewoman!   291

Host. God's blessing of your good heart! and so she is, by my troth.

Fal. Didst thou hear me?

Prince. Yea; and you knew me, as you did when you ran away by Gadshill. You knew I was at your back, and spoke it on purpose to try my patience.   297

Fal. No, no, no; not so; I did not think thou wast within hearing.

Prince. I shall drive you then to confess the wilful abuse, and then I know how to handle you.   301

Fal. No abuse, Hal, o' mine honour; no abuse.

Prince. Not—to dispraise me, and call me pantler, and bread-chipper, and I know not what!

Fal. No abuse, Hal.   305

Poins. No abuse!

Fal. No abuse, Ned, i' th' world; honest Ned, none. I disprais'd him before the wicked—that the wicked might not fall in love with thee; in which doing, I have done the part of a careful friend and a true subject; and thy father is to give me thanks for it. No abuse, Hal; none, Ned, none; no, faith, boys, none.   312

Prince. See now, whether pure fear and entire cowardice doth not make thee wrong this virtuous gentlewoman to close with us?

Is she of the wicked? Is thine hostess here of the wicked? Or is thy boy of the wicked? Or honest Bardolph, whose zeal burns in his nose, of the wicked?   318

Poins. Answer, thou dead elm, answer.

Fal. The fiend hath prick'd down Bardolph irrecoverable; and his face is Lucifer's privy-kitchen, where he doth nothing but roast malt-worms. For the boy—there is a good angel about him; but the devil outbids him too.

Prince. For the women?   325

Fal. For one of them—she's in hell already, and burns poor souls. For th' other —I owe her money; and whether she be damn'd for that, I know not.

Host. No, I warrant you.   329

Fal. No, I think thou art not; I think thou art quit for that. Marry, there is another indictment upon thee for suffering flesh to be eaten in thy house, contrary to the law; for the which I think thou wilt howl.

Host. All vict'lers do so. What's a joint of mutton or two in a whole Lent?   335

Prince. You, gentlewoman —

Doll. What says your Grace?

Fal. His Grace says that which his flesh rebels against.   [*Knocking within.*

Host. Who knocks so loud at door? Look to th' door there, Francis.   340

Enter PETO.

Prince. Peto, how now! What news?

Pet. The King your father is at Westminster;
And there are twenty weak and wearied posts
Come from the north; and as I came along
I met and overtook a dozen captains,   345
Bare-headed, sweating, knocking at the taverns,
And asking every one for Sir John Falstaff.

Prince. By heaven, Poins, I feel me much to blame
So idly to profane the precious time,
When tempest of commotion, like the south,   350
Borne with black vapour, doth begin to melt
And drop upon our bare unarmed heads.
Give me my sword and cloak. Falstaff, good night.
     [*Exeunt Prince, Poins, Peto, and Bardolph.*

Fal. Now comes in the sweetest morsel of the night, and we must hence, and leave it unpick'd. [*Knocking within*] More knocking at the door!   356

Re-enter BARDOLPH.

How now! What's the matter?

Bard. You must away to court, sir, presently;

A dozen captains stay at door for you. 359
Fal. [*To the Page*] Pay the musicians,
sirrah.—Farewell, hostess; farewell, Doll.
You see, my good wenches, how men of
merit are sought after; the undeserver
may sleep, when the man of action is call'd
on. Farewell, good wenches. If I be not
sent away post, I will see you again ere
I go. 365
Doll. I cannot speak. If my heart be not
ready to burst! Well, sweet Jack, have a
care of thyself.
Fal. Farewell, farewell.
[*Exeunt Falstaff and Bardolph.*
Host. Well, fare thee well. I have known
thee these twenty-nine years, come peascod-
time; but an honester and truer-hearted
man—well, fare thee well. 371
Bard. [*Within*] Mistress Tearsheet!
Host. What's the matter?
Bard. [*Within*] Bid Mistress Tearsheet
come to my master. 375
Host. O, run Doll, run, run, good Doll.
Come. [*To Bardolph*] She comes blubber'd.—
Yea, will you come, Doll? [*Exeunt.*

ACT THREE

SCENE I. *Westminster. The palace.*

Enter the KING *in his nightgown, with a
Page.*

King. Go call the Earls of Surrey and of
Warwick;
But, ere they come, bid them o'er-read
these letters
And well consider of them. Make good
speed. [*Exit Page.*
How many thousand of my poorest subjects
Are at this hour asleep! O sleep, O gentle
sleep, 5
Nature's soft nurse, how have I frighted
thee,
That thou no more wilt weigh my eyelids
down,
And steep my senses in forgetfulness?
Why rather, sleep, liest thou in smoky
cribs,
Upon uneasy pallets stretching thee, 10
And hush'd with buzzing night-flies to thy
slumber,
Than in the perfum'd chambers of the
great,
Under the canopies of costly state,
And lull'd with sound of sweetest melody?
O thou dull god, why liest thou with the
vile 15
In loathsome beds, and leav'st the kingly
couch
A watch-case or a common 'larum-bell?
Wilt thou upon the high and giddy mast
Seal up the ship-boy's eyes, and rock his
brains
In cradle of the rude imperious surge, 20
And in the visitation of the winds,
Who take the ruffian billows by the top,
Curling their monstrous heads, and hanging
them
With deafing clamour in the slippery
clouds,
That with the hurly death itself awakes? 25
Canst thou, O partial sleep, give thy repose
To the wet sea-boy in an hour so rude;
And in the calmest and most stillest night,
With all appliances and means to boot,
Deny it to a king? Then, happy low, lie
down! 30
Uneasy lies the head that wears a crown.

Enter WARWICK *and* SURREY.

War. Many good morrows to your
Majesty!
King. Is it good morrow, lords?
War. 'Tis one o'clock, and past.
King. Why then, good morrow to you
all, my lords. 35
Have you read o'er the letters that I sent
you?
War. We have, my liege.
King. Then you perceive the body of our
kingdom
How foul it is; what rank diseases grow,
And with what danger, near the heart of it.
War. It is but as a body yet distemper'd;
Which to his former strength may be
restored
With good advice and little medicine.
My Lord Northumberland will soon be
cool'd.
King. O God! that one might read the
book of fate, 45
And see the revolution of the times
Make mountains level, and the continent,
Weary of solid firmness, melt itself
Into the sea; and other times to see
The beachy girdle of the ocean 50
Too wide for Neptune's hips; how chances
mock,
And changes fill the cup of alteration
With divers liquors! O, if this were seen,
The happiest youth, viewing his progress
through,
What perils past, what crosses to ensue, 55
Would shut the book and sit him down and
die.
'Tis not ten years gone
Since Richard and Northumberland, great
friends,
Did feast together, and in two years after
Were they at wars. It is but eight years
since 60
This Percy was the man nearest my soul;
Who like a brother toil'd in my affairs
And laid his love and life under my foot;
Yea, for my sake, even to the eyes of
Richard
Gave him defiance. But which of you was
by— 65

[*To Warwick*] You, cousin Nevil, as I may
    remember—
When Richard, with his eye brim full of
    tears,
Then check'd and rated by Northumber-
    land,
Did speak these words, now prov'd a
    prophecy ?
' Northumberland, thou ladder by the
    which   70
My cousin Bolingbroke ascends my
    throne '—
Though then, God knows, I had no such
    intent
But that necessity so bow'd the state
That I and greatness were compell'd to
    kiss—
' The time shall come '—thus did he follow
    it—   75
' The time will come that foul sin, gathering
    head,
Shall break into corruption ' so went on,
Foretelling this same time's condition
And the divison of our amity.   79
War. There is a history in all men's lives,
Figuring the natures of the times deceas'd ;
The which observ'd, a man may prophesy,
With a near aim, of the main chance of
    things
As yet not come to life, who in their seeds
And weak beginning lie intreasured.   85
Such things become the hatch and brood of
    time ;
And, by the necessary form of this,
King Richard might create a perfect guess
That great Northumberland, then false to
    him,
Would of that seed grow to a greater false-
    ness ;   90
Which should not find a ground to root
    upon
Unless on you.
    King. Are these things then necessities ?
Then let us meet them like necessities ;
And that same word even now cries out
    on us.
They say the Bishop and Northumberland
Are fifty thousand strong.
    War.   It cannot be, my lord.
Rumour doth double, like the voice and
    echo,   97
The numbers of the feared. Please it your
    Grace
To go to bed. Upon my soul, my lord,
The powers that you already have sent
    forth   100
Shall bring this prize in very easily.
To comfort you the more, I have receiv'd
A certain instance that Glendower is dead.
Your Majesty hath been this fortnight ill ;
And these unseasoned hours perforce must
    add   105
Unto your sickness.
    King.   I will take your counsel.

And, were these inward wars once out of
    hand,
We would, dear lords, unto the Holy Land.
        [*Exeunt.*

SCENE II. *Gloucestershire. Before Justice
    Shallow's house.*

Enter SHALLOW *and* SILENCE, *meeting ;*
    MOULDY, SHADOW, WART, FEEBLE,
    BULLCALF, *and* Servants, *behind.*

Shal. Come on, come on, come on ; give
me your hand, sir ; give me your hand, sir.
An early stirrer, by the rood ! And how
doth my good cousin Silence ?
    Sil. Good morrow, good cousin Shallow. 4
    Shal. And how doth my cousin, your bed-
fellow ? and your fairest daughter and
mine, my god-daughter Ellen ?
    Sil. Alas, a black ousel, cousin Shallow !
    Shal. By yea and no, sir. I dare say my
cousin William is become a good scholar ;
he is at Oxford still, is he not ?   10
    Sil. Indeed, sir, to my cost.
    Shal. 'A must, then, to the Inns o' Court
shortly. I was once of Clement's Inn ;
where I think they will talk of mad Shallow
yet.
    Sil. You were call'd ' lusty Shallow ' then,
cousin.   15
    Shal. By the mass, I was call'd anything ;
and I would have done anything indeed
too, and roundly too. There was I, and
little John Doit of Staffordshire, and black
George Barnes, and Francis Pickbone, and
Will Squele a Cotsole man—you had not
four such swinge-bucklers in all the Inns
o' Court again. And I may say to you
we knew where the bona-robas were, and
had the best of them all at commandment.
Then was Jack Falstaff, now Sir John, a
boy, and page to Thomas Mowbray, Duke
of Norfolk.   25
    Sil. This Sir John, cousin, that comes
hither anon about soldiers ?
    Shal. The same Sir John, the very same.
I see him break Scoggin's head at the court
gate, when 'a was a crack not thus high ;
and the very same day did I fight with
one Sampson Stockfish, a fruiterer, behind
Gray's Inn. Jesu, Jesu, the mad days that
I have spent ! and to see how many of my
old acquaintance are dead !
    Sil. We shall all follow, cousin.   34
    Shal. Certain, 'tis certain ; very sure,
very sure. Death, as the Psalmist saith, is
certain to all ; all shall die. How a good
yoke of bullocks at Stamford fair ?
    Sil. By my troth, I was not there.
    Shal. Death is certain. Is old Double of
your town living yet ?   40
    Sil. Dead, sir.
    Shal. Jesu, Jesu, dead ! 'A drew a good
bow ; and dead ! 'A shot a fine shoot.

John a Gaunt loved him well, and betted much money on his head. Dead! 'A would have clapp'd i' th' clout at twelve score, and carried you a forehand shaft a fourteen and fourteen and a half, that it would have done a man's heart good to see. How a score of ewes now?

Sil. Thereafter as they be—a score of good ewes may be worth ten pounds.   50

Shal. And is old Double dead?

Enter BARDOLPH *and* One *with him.*

Sil. Here come two of Sir John Falstaff's men, as I think.

Shal. Good morrow, honest gentlemen.

Bard. I beseech you, which is Justice Shallow?   55

Shal. I am Robert Shallow, sir, a poor esquire of this county, and one of the King's justices of the peace. What is your good pleasure with me?

Bard. My captain, sir, commends him to you; my captain, Sir John Falstaff—a tall gentleman, by heaven, and a most gallant leader.   61

Shal. He greets me well, sir; I knew him a good backsword man. How doth the good knight? May I ask how my lady his wife doth?

Bard. Sir, pardon; a soldier is better accommodated than with a wife.   66

Shal. It is well said, in faith, sir; and it is well said indeed too. 'Better accommodated'! It is good; yea, indeed, is it. Good phrases are surely, and ever were, very commendable. 'Accommodated'! It comes of accommodo. Very good; a good phrase.   71

Bard. Pardon, sir; I have heard the word. 'Phrase' call you it? By this day, I know not the phrase; but I will maintain the word with my sword to be a soldier-like word, and a word of exceeding good command, by heaven. Accommodated: that is, when a man is, as they say, accommodated; or, when a man is being—whereby 'a may be thought to be accommodated; which is an excellent thing.   79

Enter FALSTAFF.

Shal. It is very just. Look, here comes good Sir John. Give me your good hand, give me your worship's good hand. By my troth, you like well and bear your years very well. Welcome, good Sir John.   84

Fal. I am glad to see you well, good Master Robert Shallow. Master Surecard, as I think?

Shal. No, Sir John; it is my cousin Silence, in commission with me.

Fal. Good Master Silence, it well befits you should be of the peace.   90

Sil. Your good worship is welcome.

Fal. Fie! this is hot weather. Gentle-

men, have you provided me here half a dozen sufficient men?

Shal. Marry, have we, sir. Will you sit?

Fal. Let me see them, I beseech you.   95

Shal. Where's the roll? Where's the roll? Where's the roll? Let me see, let me see, let me see. So, so, so, so—so, so—yea, marry, sir. Rafe Mouldy! Let them appear as I call; let them do so, let them do so. Let me see; where is Mouldy?

Moul. Here, an't please you.   101

Shal. What think you, Sir John? A good limb'd fellow; young, strong, and of good friends.

Fal. Is thy name Mouldy?

Moul. Yea, an't please you.   105

Fal. 'Tis the more time thou wert us'd.

Shal. Ha, ha, ha! most excellent, i' faith! Things that are mouldy lack use. Very singular good! In faith, well said, Sir John; very well said.

Fal. Prick him.   110

Moul. I was prick'd well enough before, an you could have let me alone. My old dame will be undone now for one to do her husbandry and her drudgery. You need not to have prick'd me; there are other men fitter to go out than I.   115

Fal. Go to; peace, Mouldy; you shall go. Mouldy, it is time you were spent.

Moul. Spent!

Shal. Peace, fellow, peace; stand aside; know you where you are? For th' other, Sir John—let me see. Simon Shadow!   121

Fal. Yea, marry, let me have him to sit under. He's like to be a cold soldier.

Shal. Where's Shadow?

Shad. Here, sir.   125

Fal. Shadow, whose son art thou?

Shad. My mother's son, sir.

Fal. Thy mother's son! Like enough; and thy father's shadow. So the son of the female is the shadow of the male. It is often so indeed; but much of the father's substance!   131

Shal. Do you like him, Sir John?

Fal. Shadow will serve for summer. Prick him; for we have a number of shadows fill up the muster-book.

Shal. Thomas Wart!   135

Fal. Where's he?

Wart. Here, sir.

Fal. Is thy name Wart?

Wart. Yea, sir.

Fal. Thou art a very ragged wart.   140

Shal. Shall I prick him, Sir John?

Fal. It were superfluous; for his apparel is built upon his back, and the whole frame stands upon pins. Prick him no more.

Shal. Ha, ha, ha! You can do it, sir; you can do it. I commend you well. Francis Feeble!   146

Fee. Here, sir.

Fal. What trade art thou, Feeble?

Fee. A woman's tailor, sir.

Shal. Shall I prick him, sir ?   150

Fal. You may ; but if he had been a man's tailor, he'd ha' prick'd you. Wilt thou make as many holes in an enemy's battle as thou hast done in a woman's petticoat ?   154

Fee. I will do my good will, sir ; you can have no more.

Fal. Well said, good woman's tailor ! well said, courageous Feeble ! Thou wilt be as valiant as the wrathful dove or most magnanimous mouse. Prick the woman's tailor—well, Master Shallow, deep, Master Shallow.   159

Fee. I would Wart might have gone, sir.

Fal. I would thou wert a man's tailor, that thou mightst mend him and make him fit to go. I cannot put him to a private soldier, that is the leader of so many thousands. Let that suffice, most forcible Feeble.

Fee. It shall suffice, sir.   165

Fal. I am bound to thee, reverend Feeble. Who is next ?

Shal. Peter Bullcalf o' th' green !

Fal. Yea, marry, let's see Bullcalf.

Bull. Here, sir.   170

Fal. Fore God, a likely fellow ! Come, prick me Bullcalf till he roar again.

Bull. O Lord ! good my lord captain—

Fal. What, dost thou roar before thou art prick'd ?   174

Bull. O Lord, sir ! I am a diseased man.

Fal. What disease hast thou ?

Bull. A whoreson cold, sir, a cough, sir, which I caught with ringing in the King's affairs upon his coronation day, sir.   179

Fal. Come, thou shalt go to the wars in a gown. We will have away thy cold ; and I will take such order that thy friends shall ring for thee. Is here all ?   182

Shal. Here is two more call'd than your number. You must have but four here, sir ; and so, I pray you, go in with me to dinner.

Fal. Come, I will go drink with you, but I cannot tarry dinner. I am glad to see you, by my troth, Master Shallow.

Shal. O, Sir John, do you remember since we lay all night in the windmill in Saint George's Field ?   190

Fal. No more of that, Master Shallow, no more of that.

Shal. Ha, 'twas a merry night. And is Jane Nightwork alive ?

Fal. She lives, Master Shallow.   195

Shal. She never could away with me.

Fal. Never, never ; she would always say she could not abide Master Shallow.

Shal. By the mass, I could anger her to th' heart. She was then a bona-roba. Doth she hold her own well ?

Fal. Old, old, Master Shallow.   201

Shal. Nay, she must be old ; she cannot choose but be old ; certain she's old ; and had Robin Nightwork, by old Nightwork, before I came to Clement's Inn.

Sil. That's fifty-five year ago.   205

Shal. Ha, cousin Silence, that thou hadst seen that that this knight and I have seen ! Ha, Sir John, said I well ?

Fal. We have heard the chimes at midnight, Master Shallow.   210

Shal. That we have, that we have, that we have ; in faith, Sir John, we have. Our watchword was ' Hem, boys ! ' Come, let's to dinner ; come, let's to dinner. Jesus, the days that we have seen ! Come, come.

[*Exeunt Falstaff and the Justices.*

Bull. Good Master Corporate Bardolph, stand my friend ; and here's four Harry ten shillings in French crowns for you. In very truth, sir, I had as lief be hang'd, sir, as go. And yet, for mine own part, sir, I do not care ; but rather because I am unwilling and, for mine own part, have a desire to stay with my friends ; else, sir, I did not care for mine own part so much.

Bard. Go to ; stand aside.   222

Moul. And, good Master Corporal Captain, for my old dame's sake, stand my friend. She has nobody to do anything about her when I am gone ; and she is old, and cannot help herself. You shall have forty, sir.   226

Bard. Go to ; stand aside.

Fee. By my troth, I care not ; a man can die but once ; we owe God a death. I'll ne'er bear a base mind. An't be my destiny, so ; an't be not, so. No man's too good to serve's Prince ; and, let it go which way it will, he that dies this year is quit for the next.   232

Bard. Well said ; th'art a good fellow.

Fee. Faith, I'll bear no base mind.

Re-enter FALSTAFF *and the* Justices.

Fal. Come, sir, which men shall I have ?

Shal. Four of which you please.   236

Bard. Sir, a word with you. I have three pound to free Mouldy and Bullcalf.

Fal. Go to ; well.

Shal. Come, Sir John, which four will you have ?   240

Fal. Do you choose for me.

Shall. Marry, then—Mouldy, Bullcalf, Feeble, and Shadow.

Fal. Mouldy and Bullcalf : for you, Mouldy, stay at home till you are past service ; and for your part, Bullcalf, grow till you come unto it. I will none of you.   246

Shal. Sir John, Sir John, do not yourself wrong. They are your likeliest men, and I would have you serv'd with the best.   249

Fal. Will you tell me, Master Shallow, how to choose a man ? Care I for the limb, the thews, the stature, bulk, and big assemblance of a man ! Give me the spirit,

Master Shallow. Here's Wart; you see what a ragged appearance it is. 'A shall charge you and discharge you with the motion of a pewterer's hammer, come off and on swifter than he that gibbets on the brewer's bucket. And this same half-fac'd fellow, Shadow—give me this man. He presents no mark to the enemy; the foeman may with as great aim level at the edge of a penknife. And, for a retreat—how swiftly will this Feeble, the woman's tailor, run off! O, give me the spare men, and spare me the great ones. Put me a caliver into Wart's hand, Bardolph.   263

Bard. Hold, Wart. Traverse—thus, thus, thus.

Fal. Come, manage me your caliver. So —very well. Go to; very good; exceeding good. O, give me always a little, lean, old, chopt, bald shot. Well said, i' faith, Wart; th'art a good scab. Hold, there's a tester for thee.   269

Shal. He is not his craft's master, he doth not do it right. I remember at Mile-end Green, when I lay at Clement's Inn—I was then Sir Dagonet in Arthur's show—there was a little quiver fellow, and 'a would manage you his piece thus; and 'a would about and about, and come you in and come you in. 'Rah, tah, tah!' would 'a say; 'Bounce!' would 'a say; and away again would 'a go, and again would 'a come. I shall ne'er see such a fellow.   278

Fal. These fellows will do well. Master Shallow, God keep you! Master Silence, I will not use many words with you: Fare you well! Gentlemen both, I thank you. I must a dozen mile to-night. Bardolph, give the soldiers coats.   283

Shal. Sir John, the Lord bless you; God prosper your affairs; God send us peace! At your return, visit our house; let our old acquaintance be renewed. Peradventure I will with ye to the court.   287

Fal. Fore God, would you would.

Shal. Go to; I have spoke at a word. God keep you.   290

Fal. Fare you well, gentle gentlemen. [*Exeunt Justices*] On, Bardolph; lead the men away. [*Exeunt all but Falstaff*] As I return, I will fetch off these justices. I do see the bottom of Justice Shallow. Lord, Lord, how subject we old men are to this vice of lying! This same starv'd justice hath done nothing but prate to me of the wildness of his youth and the feats he hath done about Turnbull Street; and every third word a lie, duer paid to the hearer than the Turk's tribute. I do remember him at Clement's Inn, like a man made after supper of a cheese-paring. When 'a was naked, he was for all the world like a fork'd radish, with a head fantastically carved upon it with a knife. 'A was so forlorn that his dimensions to any thick sight were invisible. 'A was the very genius of famine; yet lecherous as a monkey, and the whores call'd him mandrake. 'A came ever in the rearward of the fashion, and sung those tunes to the overscutch'd huswifes that he heard the carmen whistle, and sware they were his fancies or his good-nights. And now is this Vice's dagger become a squire, and talks as familiarly of John a Gaunt as if he had been sworn brother to him; and I'll be sworn 'a ne'er saw him but once in the Tilt-yard; and then he burst his head for crowding among the marshal's men. I saw it, and told John a Gaunt he beat his own name; for you might have thrust him and all his apparel into an eel-skin; the case of a treble hautboy was a mansion for him, a court—and now has he land and beeves. Well, I'll be acquainted with him if I return; and't shall go hard but I'll make him a philosopher's two stones to me. If the young dace be a bait for the old pike, I see no reason in the law of nature but I may snap at him. Let time shape, and there an end.   [*Exit.*

ACT FOUR

SCENE I. *Yorkshire. Within the Forest of Gaultree.*

Enter the ARCHBISHOP OF YORK, MOWBRAY, HASTINGS, *and Others.*

Arch. What is this forest call'd?

Hast. 'Tis Gaultree Forest, an't shall please your Grace.

Arch. Here stand, my lords, and send discoverers forth
To know the numbers of our enemies.   4

Hast. We have sent forth already.

Arch.   'Tis well done.
My friends and brethren in these great affairs,
I must acquaint you that I have receiv'd
New-dated letters from Northumberland;
Their cold intent, tenour, and substance, thus:
Here doth he wish his person, with such powers   10
As might hold sortance with his quality,
The which he could not levy; where-upon
He is retir'd, to ripe his growing fortunes,
To Scotland; and concludes in hearty prayers
That your attempts may overlive the hazard   15
And fearful meeting of their opposite.

Mowb. Thus do the hopes we have in him touch ground
And dash themselves to pieces.

Enter a Messenger.

Hast.   Now, what news ?
Mess. West of this forest, scarcely off a
  mile,
In goodly form comes on the enemy ;   20
And, by the ground they hide, I judge their
  number
Upon or near the rate of thirty thousand.
  Mowb. The just proportion that we gave
  them out.
Let us sway on and face them in the field.

Enter WESTMORELAND.

  Arch. What well-appointed leader fronts
    us here ?   25
  Mowb. I think it is my Lord of West-
    moreland.
West. Health and fair greeting from our
  general,
The Prince, Lord John and Duke of
  Lancaster.
  Arch. Say on, my Lord of Westmoreland,
    in peace,
What doth concern your coming.
  West.   Then, my lord,
Unto your Grace do I in chief address   31
The substance of my speech.   If that
  rebellion
Came like itself, in base and abject routs,
Led on by bloody youth, guarded with rags,
And countenanc'd by boys and beggary—
I say, if damn'd commotion so appear'd
In his true, native, and most proper shape,
You, reverend father, and these noble lords,
Had not been here to dress the ugly form
Of base and bloody insurrection   40
With your fair honours. You, Lord Arch-
  bishop,
Whose see is by a civil peace maintain'd,
Whose beard the silver hand of peace hath
  touch'd,
Whose learning and good letters peace hath
  tutor'd,   44
Whose white investments figure innocence,
The dove, and very blessed spirit of peace—
Wherefore do you so ill translate yourself
Out of the speech of peace, that bears such
  grace,
Into the harsh and boist'rous tongue of
  war ;
Turning your books to graves, your ink to
  blood,   50
Your pens to lances, and your tongue divine
To a loud trumpet and a point of war ?
  Arch. Wherefore do I this ?   So the
    question stands.
Briefly to this end : we are all diseas'd
And with our surfeiting and wanton hours
Have brought ourselves into a burning
  fever,   56
And we must bleed for it ; of which disease
Our late King, Richard, being infected,
  died.

But, my most noble Lord of Westmoreland,
I take not on me here as a physician ;   60
Nor do I as an enemy to peace
Troop in the throngs of military men ;
But rather show awhile like fearful war
To diet rank minds sick of happiness,
And purge th' obstructions which begin to
  stop   65
Our very veins of life.   Hear me more
  plainly.
I have in equal balance justly weigh'd
What wrongs our arms may do, what
  wrongs we suffer,
And find our griefs heavier than our
  offences.
We see which way the stream of time doth
  run   70
And are enforc'd from our most quiet there
By the rough torrent of occasion ;
And have the summary of all our griefs,
When time shall serve, to show in articles ;
Which long ere this we offer'd to the King,
And might by no suit gain our audience :
When we are wrong'd, and would unfold
  our griefs,
We are denied access unto his person,
Even by those men that most have done us
  wrong.
The dangers of the days but newly gone,   80
Whose memory is written on the earth
With yet appearing blood, and the ex-
  amples
Of every minute's instance, present now,
Hath put us in these ill-beseeming arms ;   85
Not to break peace, or any branch of it,
But to establish here a peace indeed,
Concurring both in name and quality.
  West. When ever yet was your appeal
    denied ;
Wherein have you been galled by the King ;
What peer hath been suborn'd to grate on
  you   90
That you should seal this lawless bloody
  book
Of forg'd rebellion with a seal divine,
And consecrate commotion's bitter edge ?
  Arch. My brother general, the common-
    wealth,
To brother born an household cruelty,   95
I make my quarrel in particular.
  West. There is no need of any such
    redress ;
Or if there were, it not belongs to you.
  Mowb. Why not to him in part, and to us
    all
That feel the bruises of the days before,   100
And suffer the condition of these times
To lay a heavy and unequal hand
Upon our honours ?
  West.   O my good Lord Mowbray,
Construe the times to their necessities,
And you shall say, indeed, it is the time,   105
And not the King, that doth you injuries.
Yet, for your part, it not appears to me,

Either from the King or in the present time,
That you should have an inch of any ground
To build a grief on. Were you not restor'd
To all the Duke of Norfolk's signiories, 111
Your noble and right well-rememb'red
   father's ?
  Mowb. What thing, in honour, had my
   father lost
That need to be reviv'd and breath'd in me?
The King that lov'd him, as the state stood
  then, 115
Was force perforce compell'd to banish him,
And then that Henry Bolingbroke and he,
Being mounted and both roused in their
  seats,
Their neighing coursers daring of the spur,
Their armed staves in charge, their beavers
  down, 120
Their eyes of fire sparkling through sights
  of steel,
And the loud trumpet blowing them to-
  gether—
Then, then, when there was nothing could
  have stay'd
My father from the breast of Bolingbroke,
O, when the King did throw his warder
  down— 125
His own life hung upon the staff he threw—
Then threw he down himself, and all their
  lives
That by indictment and by dint of sword
Have since miscarried under Bolingbroke.
  West. You speak, Lord Mowbray, now
   you know not what. 130
The Earl of Hereford was reputed then
In England the most valiant gentleman.
Who knows on whom fortune would then
  have smil'd ?
But if your father had been victor there,
He ne'er had borne it out of Coventry ; 135
For all the country, in a general voice,
Cried hate upon him ; and all their prayers
  and love
Were set on Hereford, whom they doted on,
And bless'd and grac'd indeed more than
  the King.
But this is mere digression from my
  purpose. 140
Here come I from our princely general
To know your griefs ; to tell you from his
  Grace
That he will give you audience ; and
  wherein
It shall appear that your demands are just,
You shall enjoy them, everything set off. 145
That might so much as think you enemies.
  Mowb. But he hath forc'd us to compel
   this offer ;
And it proceeds from policy, not love.
  West. Mowbray, you overween to take
   it so. 149
This offer comes from mercy, not from fear ;
For, lo ! within a ken our army lies—
Upon mine honour, all too confident

To give admittance to a thought of fear.
Our battle is more full of names than yours,
Our men more perfect in the use of arms, 155
Our armour all as strong, our cause the
  best ;
Then reason will our hearts should be as
  good.
Say you not, then, our offer is compell'd.
  Mowb. Well, by my will we shall admit
   no parley.
  West. That argues but the shame of your
   offence : 160
A rotten case abides no handling.
  Hast. Hath the Prince John a full com-
   mission,
In very ample virtue of his father,
To hear and absolutely to determine
Of what conditions we shall stand upon ?
  West. That is intended in the general's
   name. 166
I muse you make so slight a question.
  Arch. Then take, my Lord of Westmore-
   land, this schedule,
For this contains our general grievances.
Each several article herein redress'd, 170
All members of our cause, both here and
  hence,
That are insinewed to this action,
Acquitted by a true substantial form,
And present execution of our wills
To us and to our purposes confin'd— 175
We come within our awful banks again,
And knit our powers to the arm of peace.
  West. This will I show the general. Please
   you, lords,
In sight of both our battles we may meet ;
And either end in peace —which God so
   frame !— 180
Or to the place of diff'rence call the swords
Which must decide it.
  Arch.   My lord, we will do so.
             [*Exit Westmoreland.*
  Mowb. There is a thing within my bosom
   tells me
That no conditions of our peace can stand.
  Hast. Fear you not that : if we can make
   our peace 185
Upon such large terms and so absolute
As our conditions shall consist upon,
Our peace shall stand as firm as rocky
  mountains.
  Mowb. Yea, but our valuation shall be
   such 189
That every slight and false-derived cause,
Yea, every idle, nice, and wanton reason,
Shall to the King taste of this action ;
That, were our royal faiths martyrs in love,
We shall be winnow'd with so rough a wind
That even our corn shall seem as light as
  chaff, 195
And good from bad find no partition.
  Arch. No, no, my lord. Note this : the
   King is weary
Of dainty and such picking grievances ;

For he hath found to end one doubt by
    death
Revives two greater in the heirs of life ; 200
And therefore will he wipe his tables clean,
And keep no tell-tale to his memory
That may repeat and history his loss
To new remembrance. For full well he
    knows
He cannot so precisely weed this land   205
As his misdoubts present occasion :
His foes are so enrooted with his friends
That, plucking to unfix an enemy,
He doth unfasten so and shake a friend.
So that this land, like an offensive wife 210
That hath enrag'd him on to offer strokes,
As he is striking, holds his infant up,
And hangs resolv'd correction in the arm
That was uprear'd to execution.

    Hast. Besides, the King hath wasted all
      his rods   215
On late offenders, that he now doth lack
The very instruments of chastisement ;
So that his power, like to a fangless lion,
May offer, but not hold.

    Arch.   'Tis very true ;
And therefore be assur'd, my good Lord
    Marshal,   220
If we do now make our atonement well,
Our peace will, like a broken limb united,
Grow stronger for the breaking.

    Mowb.   Be it so.
Here is return'd my Lord of Westmoreland.

       Re-enter WESTMORELAND.

    West. The Prince is here at hand.
    Pleaseth your lordship   225
To meet his Grace just distance 'tween our
    armies ?
    Mowb. Your Grace of York, in God's
name then, set forward.
    Arch. Before, and greet his Grace. My
    lord, we come.   [*Exeunt.*

    SCENE II. *Another part of the forest.*

Enter, from one side, MOWBRAY, *attended ;
afterwards, the* ARCHBISHOP, HASTINGS,
and Others : *from the other side,* PRINCE
JOHN OF LANCASTER, WESTMORELAND,
Officers *and* Others.

    P. John. You are well encount'red here,
    my cousin Mowbray.
Good day to you, gentle Lord Archbishop ;
And so to you, Lord Hastings, and to all.
My Lord of York, it better show'd with
    you
When that your flock, assembled by the
    bell,   5
Encircled you to hear with reverence
Your exposition on the holy text
Than now to see you here an iron man,
Cheering a rout of rebels with your drum,
Turning the word to sword, and life to
    death.   10

That man that sits within a monarch's
    heart
And ripens in the sunshine of his favour,
Would he abuse the countenance of the
    king,
Alack, what mischiefs might be set abroach
In shadow of such greatness ! With you,
    Lord Bishop,   15
It is even so. Who hath not heard it spoken
How deep you were within the books of
    God ?
To us the speaker in His parliament,
To us th' imagin'd voice of God himself,
The very opener and intelligencer   20
Between the grace, the sanctities of heaven,
And our dull workings. O, who shall believe
But you misuse the reverence of your place,
Employ the countenance and grace of
    heav'n
As a false favourite doth his prince's name,
In deeds dishonourable ? You have ta'en
    up,   26
Under the counterfeited zeal of God,
The subjects of His substitute, my father,
And both against the peace of heaven and
    him   29
Have here up-swarm'd them.

    Arch.   Good my Lord of Lancaster,
I am not here against your father's peace ;
But, as I told my Lord of Westmoreland,
The time misord'red doth, in common
    sense,
Crowd us and crush us to this monstrous
    form
To hold our safety up. I sent your Grace 35
The parcels and particulars of our grief,
The which hath been with scorn shov'd
    from the court,
Whereon this hydra son of war is born ;
Whose dangerous eyes may well be
    charm'd asleep
With grant of our most just and right
    desires ;   40
And true obedience, of this madness cur'd,
Stoop tamely to the foot of majesty.

    Mowb. If not, we ready are to try our
    fortunes
To the last man.

    Hast.   And though we here fall down,
We have supplies to second our attempt. 45
If they miscarry, theirs shall second them ;
And so success of mischief shall be born,
And heir from heir shall hold this quarrel up
Whiles England shall have generation.

    P. John. You are too shallow, Hastings,
    much too shallow,   50
To sound the bottom of the after-times.

    West. Pleaseth your Grace to answer
    them directly
How far forth you do like their articles.

    P. John. I like them all and do allow
    them well ;   54
And swear here, by the honour of my blood,
My father's purposes have been mistook ;

And some about him have too lavishly
Wrested his meaning and authority.
My lord, these griefs shall be with speed
    redress'd ;
Upon my soul, they shall. If this may please
    you,   60
Discharge your powers unto their several
    counties,
As we will ours ; and here, between the
    armies,
Let's drink together friendly and embrace,
That all their eyes may bear those tokens
    home
Of our restored love and amity.   65
    Arch. I take your princely word for these
      redresses.
    P. John. I give it you, and will maintain
      my word ;
And thereupon I drink unto your Grace.
    Hast. Go, Captain, and deliver to the
      army
This news of peace. Let them have pay,
    and part.   70
I know it will well please them. Hie thee,
    Captain.   [*Exit Officer.*
    Arch. To you, my noble Lord of West-
      moreland.
    West. I pledge your Grace ; and if you
      knew what pains
I have bestow'd to breed this present
    peace,
You would drink freely ; but my love to ye
Shall show itself more openly hereafter. 76
    Arch. I do not doubt you.
    West.   I am glad of it.
Health to my lord and gentle cousin,
    Mowbray.
    Mowb. You wish me health in very happy
      season,
For I am on the sudden something ill.   80
    Arch. Against ill chances men are ever
      merry ;
But heaviness foreruns the good event.
    West. Therefore be merry, coz ; since
      sudden sorrow
Serves to say thus, ' Some good thing comes
    to-morrow '.
    Arch. Believe me, I am passing light in
      spirit.   85
    Mowb. So much the worse, if your own
      rule be true.   [*Shouts within.*
    P. John. The word of peace is rend'red.
    Hark, how they shout !
    Mowb. This had been cheerful after
      victory.
    Arch. A peace is of the nature of a
      conquest ;
For then both parties nobly are subdu'd, 90
And neither party loser.
    P. John.   Go, my lord,
And let our army be discharged too.
            [*Exit Westmoreland.*
And, good my lord, so please you let our
    trains

March by us, that we may peruse the men
We should have cop'd withal.
    Arch.   Go, good Lord Hastings,
And, ere they be dismiss'd, let them march
    by.   [*Exit Hastings.*
    P. John. I trust, lords, we shall lie to-
    night together.

        Re-enter WESTMORELAND.

Now, cousin, wherefore stands our army
    still ?
    West. The leaders, having charge from
      you to stand,   99
Will not go off until they hear you speak.
    P. John. They know their duties.

        Re-enter HASTINGS.

    Hast. My lord, our army is dispers'd
      already.
Like youthful steers unyok'd, they take
    their courses
East, west, north, south ; or like a school
    broke up,
Each hurries toward his home and sport-
    ing-place.   105
    West. Good tidings, my Lord Hastings ;
      for the which
I do arrest thee, traitor, of high treason ;
And you, Lord Archbishop, and you, Lord
    Mowbray,
Of capital treason I attach you both.
    Mowb. Is this proceeding just and honour-
      able ?   110
    West. Is your assembly so ?
    Arch. Will you thus break your faith ?
    P. John.   I pawn'd thee none :
I promis'd you redress of these same
    grievances
Whereof you did complain ; which, by
    mine honour,   114
I will perform with a most Christian care.
But for you, rebels—look to taste the due
Meet for rebellion and such acts as yours.
Most shallowly did you these arms com-
    mence,
Fondly brought here, and foolishly sent
    hence.
Strike up our drums, pursue the scatt'red
    stray.   120
God, and not we, hath safely fought to-day.
Some guard these traitors to the block of
    death,
Treason's true bed and yielder-up of breath.
            [*Exeunt.*

SCENE III. *Another part of the forest.*

Alarum ; excursions. Enter FALSTAFF *and*
    COLVILLE, *meeting.*

    Fal. What's your name, sir ? Of what
condition are you, and of what place, I
pray ?
    Col. I am a knight sir ; and my name
is Colville of the Dale.   4

Fal. Well then, Colville is your name, a knight is your degree, and your place the Dale. Colville shall be still your name, a traitor your degree, and the dungeon your place—a place deep enough ; so shall you be still Colville of the Dale.

Col. Are not you Sir John Falstaff ?   10

Fal. As good a man as he, sir, whoe'er I am. Do ye yield, sir, or shall I sweat for you ? If I do sweat, they are the drops of thy lovers, and they weep for thy death ; therefore rouse up fear and trembling, and do observance to my mercy.   15

Col. I think you are Sir John Falstaff, and in that thought yield me.

Fal. I have a whole school of tongues in this belly of mine ; and not a tongue of them all speaks any other word but my name. An I had but a belly of any indifferency, I were simply the most active fellow in Europe. My womb, my womb, my womb undoes me. Here comes our general.   23

Enter PRINCE JOHN OF LANCASTER, WEST-MORELAND, BLUNT, *and* Others.

P. John. The heat is past ; follow no
   further now.
Call in the powers, good cousin Westmore-
   land.   [*Exit Westmoreland.*
Now, Falstaff, where have you been all this
   while ?
When everything is ended, then you come.
These tardy tricks of yours will, on my life,
One time or other break some gallows' back.

Fal. I would be sorry, my lord, but it should be thus : I never knew yet but rebuke and check was the reward of valour. Do you think me a swallow, an arrow, or a bullet ? Have I, in my poor and old motion, the expedition of thought ? I have speeded hither with the very extremest inch of possibility ; I have found'red nine score and odd posts ; and here, travel tainted as I am, have, in my pure and immaculate valour, taken Sir John Colville of the Dale, a most furious knight and valorous enemy. But what of that ? He saw me, and yielded ; that I may justly say with the hook-nos'd fellow of Rome—I came, saw, and overcame.   41

P. John. It was more of his courtesy than your deserving.

Fal. I know not. Here he is, and here I yield him ; and I beseech your Grace, let it be book'd with the rest of this day's deeds ; or, by the Lord, I will have it in a particular ballad else, with mine own picture on the top on't, Colville kissing my foot ; to the which course if I be enforc'd, if you do not all show like gilt twopences to me, and I, in the clear sky of fame, o'ershine you as much as the full moon doth the cinders of the element, which show like pins' heads to her, believe not the word

of the noble. Therefore let me have right, and let desert mount.

P. John. Thine's too heavy to mount.   55

Fal. Let it shine, then.

P. John. Thine's too thick to shine.

Fal. Let it do something, my good lord, that may do me good, and call it what you will.

P. John. Is thy name Colville ?   60

Col. It is, my lord.

P. John. A famous rebel art thou, Colville.

Fal. And a famous true subject took him.

Col. I am, my lord, but as my betters are
That led me hither. Had they been rul'd
   by me,   65
You should have won them dearer than you
   have.

Fal. I know not how they sold themselves ; but thou, like a kind fellow, gavest thyself away gratis ; and I thank thee for thee.

Re-enter WESTMORELAND.

P. John. Now, have you left pursuit ?   70

West. Retreat is made, and execution
   stay'd.

P. John. Send Colville, with his con-
   federates,
To York, to present execution.
Blunt, lead him hence ; and see you guard
   him sure. [*Exeunt Blunt and others.*
And now dispatch we toward the court, my
   lords.   75
I hear the King my father is sore sick.
Our news shall go before us to his Majesty,
Which, cousin, you shall bear to comfort
   him ;
And we with sober speed will follow you.   79

Fal. My lord, I beseech you, give me leave to go through Gloucestershire ; and, when you come to court, stand my good lord, pray, in your good report.

P. John. Fare you well, Falstaff. I, in
   my condition,   83
Shall better speak of you than you deserve.
   [*Exeunt all but Falstaff.*

Fal. I would you had but the wit ; 'twere better than your dukedom. Good faith, this same young sober-blooded boy doth not love me ; nor a man cannot make him laugh—but that's no marvel ; he drinks no wine. There's never none of these demure boys come to any proof ; for thin drink doth so over-cool their blood, and making many fish-meals, that they fall into a kind of male green-sickness ; and then, when they marry, they get wenches. They are generally fools and cowards—which some of us should be too, but for inflammation. A good sherris-sack hath a twofold opera-tion in it. It ascends me into the brain ; dries me there all the foolish and dull and crudy vapours which environ it ; makes it apprehensive, quick, forgetive, full of

nimble, fiery, and delectable shapes; which
delivered o'er to the voice, the tongue,
which is the birth, becomes excellent wit.
The second property of your excellent
sherris is the warming of the blood; which
before, cold and settled, left the liver white
and pale, which is the badge of pusillanimity
and cowardice; but the sherris warms it,
and makes it course from the inwards to
the parts extremes. It illumineth the face,
which, as a beacon, gives warning to all the
rest of this little kingdom, man, to arm;
and then the vital commoners and inland
petty spirits muster me all to their captain,
the heart, who, great and puff'd up with
this retinue, doth any deed of courage—and
this valour comes of sherris. So that skill
in the weapon is nothing without sack, for
that sets it a-work; and learning, a mere
hoard of gold kept by a devil till sack com-
mences it and sets it in act and use. Hereof
comes it that Prince Harry is valiant; for
the cold blood he did naturally inherit of
his father, he hath, like lean, sterile, and
bare land, manured, husbanded, and till'd,
with excellent endeavour of drinking good
and good store of fertile sherris, that he is
become very hot and valiant. If I had a
thousand sons, the first humane principle
I would teach them should be to forswear
thin potations, and to addict themselves
to sack.   122

Enter BARDOLPH.

How now, Bardolph!
    Bard. The army is discharged all and
gone.
    Fal. Let them go. I'll through Glou-
cestershire, and there will I visit Master
Robert Shallow, Esquire. I have him
already temp'ring between my finger and
my thumb, and shortly will I seal with
him. Come away.   [*Exeunt.*

SCENE IV. *Westminster. The Jerusalem
        Chamber.*

Enter the KING, PRINCE THOMAS OF CLAR-
ENCE, PRINCE HUMPHREY OF GLOUCES-
TER, WARWICK, *and* Others.

    King. Now, lords, if God doth give
        successful end
To this debate that bleedeth at our doors,
We will our youth lead on to higher fields,
And draw no swords but what are sanctified.
Our navy is address'd, our power collected,
Our substitutes in absence well invested,   6
And everything lies level to our wish.
Only we want a little personal strength;
And pause us till these rebels, now afoot,
Come underneath the yoke of government.
    War. Both which we doubt not but your
        Majesty   11
Shall soon enjoy.

    King. Humphrey, my son of Gloucester,
Where is the Prince your brother?
    P. Humph. I think he's gone to hunt, my
        lord, at Windsor.
    King. And how accompanied?
    P. Humph.   I do not know, my lord.
    King. Is not his brother, Thomas of
        Clarence, with him?   16
    P. Humph. No, my good lord, he is in
        presence here.
    Cla. What would my lord and father?
    King. Nothing but well to thee, Thomas
        of Clarence.
How chance thou art not with the Prince
        thy brother?   20
He loves thee, and thou dost neglect him,
        Thomas,
Thou hast a better place in his affection
Than all thy brothers; cherish it, my boy,
And noble offices thou mayst effect
Of mediation, after I am dead,   25
Between his greatness and thy other
        brethren.
Therefore omit him not; blunt not his love,
Nor lose the good advantage of his grace
By seeming cold or careless of his will;
For he is gracious if he be observ'd.   30
He hath a tear for pity and a hand
Open as day for melting charity;
Yet notwithstanding, being incens'd, he is
        flint;
As humorous as winter, and as sudden
As flaws congealed in the spring of day.   35
His temper, therefore, must be well ob-
        serv'd.
Chide him for faults, and do it reverently,
When you perceive his blood inclin'd to
        mirth;
But, being moody, give him line and scope
Till that his passions, like a whale on
        ground,   40
Confound themselves with working. Learn
        this, Thomas,
And thou shalt prove a shelter to thy
        friends,
A hoop of gold to bind thy brothers in,
That the united vessel of their blood,
Mingled with venom of suggestion—   45
As, force perforce, the age will pour it in—
Shall never leak, though it do work as strong
As aconitum or rash gunpowder.
    Cla. I shall observe him with all care and
        love.
    King. Why art thou not at Windsor with
        him, Thomas?   50
    Cla. He is not there to-day; he dines in
        London.
    King. And how accompanied? Canst
        thou tell that?
    Cla. With Poins, and other his continual
        followers.
    King. Most subject is the fattest soil to
        weeds;
And he, the noble image of my youth,   55

Is overspread with them; therefore my
        grief
Stretches itself beyond the hour of death.
The blood weeps from my heart when I do
        shape,
In forms imaginary, th' unguided days   59
And rotten times that you shall look upon
When I am sleeping with my ancestors.
For when his headstrong riot hath no curb,
When rage and hot blood are his coun-
        sellors,
When means and lavish manners meet
        together,
O, with what wings shall his affections fly 65
Towards fronting peril and oppos'd decay!
    Wor. My gracious lord, you look beyond
        him quite.
The Prince but studies his companions
Like a strange tongue, wherein, to gain the
        language,
'Tis needful that the most immodest word
Be look'd upon and learnt; which once
        attain'd,   71
Your Highness knows, comes to no further
        use
But to be known and hated. So, like gross
        terms,
The Prince will, in the perfectness of time,
Cast off his followers; and their memory 75
Shall as a pattern or a measure live
By which his Grace must mete the lives of
        other,
Turning past evils to advantages.
    King. 'Tis seldom when the bee doth
        leave her comb
In the dead carrion.

            Enter WESTMORELAND.

            Who's here? Westmoreland?
    West. Health to my sovereign, and new
        happiness   81
Added to that that I am to deliver!
Prince John, your son, doth kiss your
        Grace's hand.
Mowbray, the Bishop Scroop, Hastings, and
        all,
Are brought to the correction of your law.
There is not now a rebel's sword un-
        sheath'd,   86
But Peace puts forth her olive everywhere.
The manner how this action hath been
        borne
Here at more leisure may your Highness
        read,
With every course in his particular.   90
    King. O Westmoreland, thou art a sum-
        mer bird,
Which ever in the haunch of winter sings
The lifting up of day.

            Enter HARCOURT.

            Look here's more news.
    Har. From enemies heaven keep your
        Majesty;

And, when they stand against you, may
        they fall   95
As those that I am come to tell you of!
The Earl Northumberland and the Lord
        Bardolph,
With a great power of English and of
        Scots,
Are by the shrieve of Yorkshire overthrown.
The manner and true order of the fight 100
This packet, please it you, contains at
        large.
    King. And wherefore should these good
        news make me sick?
Will Fortune never come with both hands
        full,
But write her fair words still in foulest
        letters?   104
She either gives a stomach and no food—
Such are the poor, in health—or else a
        feast,
And takes away the stomach—such are the
        rich
That have abundance and enjoy it not.
I should rejoice now at this happy news;
And now my sight fails, and my brain is
        giddy.   110
O me! come near me now I am much ill.
    P. Humph. Comfort, your Majesty!
    Cla.   O my royal father!
    West. My sovereign lord, cheer up
        yourself, look up.
    War. Be patient, Princes; you do know
        these fits
Are with his Highness very ordinary.   115
Stand from him, give him air; he'll straight
        be well.
    Cla. No, no; he cannot long hold out
        these pangs.
Th' incessant care and labour of his mind
Hath wrought the mure that should confine
        it in
So thin that life looks through, and will
        break out.   120
    P. Humph. The people fear me; for they
        do observe
Unfather'd heirs and loathly births of
        nature.
The seasons change their manners, as the
        year
Had found some months asleep, and leapt
        them over.
    Cla. The river hath thrice flow'd, no ebb
        between;   125
And the old folk, Time's doting chronicles,
Say it did so a little time before
That our great grandsire, Edward, sick'd
        and died.
    War. Speak lower, Princes, for the King
        recovers.
    P. Humph. This apoplexy will certain be
        his end.   130
    King. I pray you take me up, and bear
        me hence
Into some other chamber. Softly, pray.

SCENE V. *Westminster. Another chamber.*

The KING *lying on a bed;* CLARENCE, GLOUCESTER, WARWICK, *and* Others *in attendance.*

King. Let there be no noise made, my
    gentle friends ;
Unless some dull and favourable hand
Will whisper music to my weary spirit.
War. Call for the music in the other room.
King. Set me the crown upon my pillow
    here.   5
Cla. His eye is hollow, and he changes
    much.
War. Less noise, less noise !

       Enter PRINCE HENRY.

Prince. Who saw the Duke of Clarence ?
Cla. I am here, brother, full of heaviness.
Prince. How now ! Rain within doors,
    and none abroad !
How doth the King ?   10
P. Humph. Exceeding ill.
Prince.   Heard he the good news yet ?
Tell it him.
P. Humph. He alt'red much upon the
    hearing it.
Prince. If he be sick with joy, he'll
recover without physic.   15
War. Not so much noise, my lords.
    Sweet Prince, speak low ;
The King your father is dispos'd to sleep.
Cla. Let us withdraw into the other room.
War. Will't please your Grace to go
    along with us ?
Prince. No ; I will sit and watch here by
    the King.
            [Exeunt all but the Prince.
Why doth the crown lie there upon his
    pillow,   21
Being so troublesome a bedfellow ?
O polish'd perturbation ! golden care !
That keep'st the ports of slumber open wide
To many a watchful night ! Sleep with it
    now !   25
Yet not so sound and half so deeply sweet
As he whose brow with homely biggen
    bound
Snores out the watch of night. O majesty !
When thou dost pinch thy bearer, thou
    dost sit
Like a rich armour worn in heat of day   30
That scald'st with safety. By his gates of
    breath
There lies a downy feather which stirs not.
Did he suspire, that light and weightless
    down
Perforce must move. My gracious lord !
    my father !   34
This sleep is sound indeed ; this is a sleep
That from this golden rigol hath divorc'd
So many English kings. Thy due from me
Is tears and heavy sorrows of the blood

Which nature, love, and filial tenderness,
Shall, O dear father, pay thee plenteously.
My due from thee is this imperial crown, 41
Which, as immediate from thy place and
    blood,
Derives itself to me. [*Putting on the crown*]
    Lo where it sits—
Which God shall guard ; and put the
    world's whole strength
Into one giant arm, it shall not force   45
This lineal honour from me. This from thee
Will I to mine leave as 'tis left to me.
                     [Exit.

King. Warwick ! Gloucester ! Clarence !

    Re-enter WARWICK, GLOUCESTER,
            CLARENCE.

Cla. Doth the King call ?
War. What would your Majesty ? How
    fares your Grace ?   50
King. Why did you leave me here alone,
    my lords ?
Cla. We left the Prince my brother here,
    my liege,
Who undertook to sit and watch by you.
King. The Prince of Wales ! Where is he?
    Let me see him.
He is not here.   55
War. This door is open ; he is gone this
    way.
P. Humph. He came not through the
    chamber where we stay'd.
King. Where is the crown ? Who took
    it from my pillow ?
War. When we withdrew, my liege, we
    left it here.
King. The Prince hath ta'en it hence.
    Go, seek him out.   60
Is he so hasty that he doth suppose
My sleep my death ?
Find him, my Lord of Warwick ; chide him
    hither.   [*Exit Warwick.*
This part of his conjoins with my disease
And helps to end me. See, sons, what
    things you are !   65
How quickly nature falls into revolt
When gold becomes her object !
For this the foolish over-careful fathers
Have broke their sleep with thoughts,
Their brains with care, their bones with
    industry ;   70
For this they have engrossed and pil'd up
The cank'red heaps of strange-achieved
    gold ;
For this they have been thoughtful to invest
Their sons with arts and martial exercises ;
When, like the bee, tolling from every
    flower   75
The virtuous sweets,
Our thighs with wax, our mouths with
    honey pack'd,
We bring it to the hive, and, like the bees,
Are murd'red for our pains. This bitter
    taste

Yields his engrossments to the ending
father.　　　　　　　　　　　　　80

Re-enter WARWICK.

Now where is he that will not stay so long
Till his friend sickness hath determin'd me?
　War. My lord, I found the Prince in the
　　next room,
Washing with kindly tears his gentle cheeks,
With such a deep demeanour in great
　　sorrow,　　　　　　　　　　　85
That tyranny, which never quaff'd but
　　blood,
Would, by beholding him, have wash'd his
　　knife
With gentle eye-drops.　He ~~is~~ coming
　　hither.
　King. But wherefore did he take away
　　the crown ?

Re-enter PRINCE HENRY.

Lo where he comes.　Come hither to me,
　　Harry.　　　　　　　　　　　　90
Depart the chamber, leave us here alone.
　　　　[*Exeunt all but the King and the
　　　　　　Prince.*
　Prince. I never thought to hear you speak
　　again.
　King. Thy wish was father, Harry, to
　　that thought.
I stay too long by thee, I weary thee.
Dost thou so hunger for mine empty chair
That thou wilt needs invest thee with my
　　honours　　　　　　　　　　96
Before thy hour be ripe ?　O foolish youth !
Thou seek'st the greatness that will over-
　　whelm thee.
Stay but a little, for my cloud of dignity
Is held from falling with so weak a wind
That it will quickly drop ; my day is dim.
Thou hast stol'n that which, after some
　　few hours,　　　　　　　　　102
Were thine without offence ; and at my
　　death
Thou hast seal'd up my expectation.
Thy life did manifest thou lov'dst me not,
And thou wilt have me die assur'd of it.
Thou hid'st a thousand daggers in thy
　　thoughts,　　　　　　　　　107
Which thou hast whetted on thy stony
　　heart,
To stab at half an hour of my life.
What, canst thou not forbear me half an
　　hour ?　　　　　　　　　　　110
Then get thee gone, and dig my grave
　　thyself ;
And bid the merry bells ring to thine ear
That thou art crowned, not that I am dead.
Let all the tears that should bedew my
　　hearse
Be drops of balm to sanctify thy head ; 115
Only compound me with forgotten dust ;
Give that which gave thee life unto the
　　worms.

Pluck down my officers, break my decrees ;
For now a time is come to mock at form—
Harry the Fifth is crown'd.　Up, vanity : 120
Down, royal state.　All you sage coun-
　　sellors, hence.
And to the English court assemble now,
From every region, apes of idleness.
Now, neighbour confines, purge you of your
　　scum.
Have you a ruffian that will swear, drink,
　　dance,　　　　　　　　　　　125
Revel the night, rob, murder, and commit
The oldest sins the newest kind of ways ?
Be happy, he will trouble you no more.
England shall double gild his treble guilt ;
England shall give him office, honour,
　　might ;　　　　　　　　　　130
For the fifth Harry from curb'd license
　　plucks
The muzzle of restraint, and the wild dog
Shall flesh his tooth on every innocent.
O my poor kingdom, sick with civil blows !
When that my care could not withhold thy
　　riots,　　　　　　　　　　　135
What wilt thou do when riot is thy care ?
O, thou wilt be a wilderness again,
Peopled with wolves, thy old inhabitants !
　Prince. O, pardon me, my liege !　But for
　　my tears,
The moist impediments unto my speech, 140
I had forestall'd this dear and deep rebuke
Ere you with grief had spoke and I had
　　heard
The course of it so far.　There is your
　　crown,
And He that wears the crown immortally
Long guard it yours ! [*Kneeling*] If I affect
　　it more　　　　　　　　　　145
Than as your honour and as your renown,
Let me no more from this obedience rise,
Which my most inward true and duteous
　　spirit
Teacheth this prostrate and exterior bend-
　　ing !　　　　　　　　　　　149
God witness with me, when I here came in
And found no course of breath within your
　　Majesty,
How cold it struck my heart !　If I do feign,
O, let me in my present wildness die,
And never live to show th' incredulous
　　world
The noble change that I have purposed ! 155
Coming to look on you, thinking you
　　dead—
And dead almost, my liege, to think you
　　were—
I spake unto this crown as having sense,
And thus upbraided it : ' The care on thee
　　depending
Hath fed upon the body of my father ; 160
Therefore thou best of gold art worst of
　　gold.
Other, less fine in carat, is more precious,
Preserving life in med'cine potable ;

But thou, most fine, most honour'd, most renown'd,
Hast eat thy bearer up'. Thus, my most royal liege,
Accusing it, I put it on my head,   166
To try with it—as with an enemy
That had before my face murd'red my father—
The quarrel of a true inheritor.
But if it did infect my blood with joy,   170
Or swell my thoughts to any strain of pride ;
If any rebel or vain spirit of mine
Did with the least affection of a welcome
Give entertainment to the might of it,
Let God for ever keep it from my head,   175
And make me as the poorest vassal is,
That doth with awe and terror kneel to it !
  King. O my son,
God put it in thy mind to take it hence,
That thou mightst win the more thy father's love,   180
Pleading so wisely in excuse of it !
Come hither, Harry ; sit thou by my bed,
And hear, I think, the very latest counsel
That ever I shall breathe. God knows, my son,
By what by-paths and indirect crook'd ways   185
I met this crown ; and I myself know well
How troublesome it sat upon my head :
To thee it shall descend with better quiet,
Better opinion, better confirmation ;
For all the soil of the achievement goes   190
With me into the earth. It seem'd in me
But as an honour snatch'd with boist'rous hand ;
And I had many living to upbraid
My gain of it by their assistances ;
Which daily grew to quarrel and to bloodshed,   195
Wounding supposed peace. All these bold fears
Thou seest with peril I have answered ;
For all my reign hath been but as a scene
Acting that argument. And now my death
Changes the mood ; for what in me was purchas'd   200
Falls upon thee in a more fairer sort ;
So thou the garland wear'st successively.
Yet, though thou stand'st more sure than I could do,
Thou art not firm enough, since griefs are green ;
And all my friends, which thou must make thy friends, 205
Have but their stings and teeth newly ta'en out ;
By whose fell working I was first advanc'd,
And by whose power I well might lodge a fear
To be again displac'd ; which to avoid,
I cut them off ; and had a purpose now   210
To lead out many to the Holy Land,

Lest rest and lying still might make them look
Too near unto my state. Therefore, my Harry,
Be it thy course to busy giddy minds
With foreign quarrels, that action, hence borne out,   215
May waste the memory of the former days.
More would I, but my lungs are wasted so
That strength of speech is utterly denied me.
How I came by the crown, O God, forgive ;
And grant it may with thee in true peace live !   220
  Prince. My gracious liege,
You won it, wore it, kept it, gave it me ;
Then plain and right must my possession be ;
Which I with more than with a common pain
'Gainst all the world will rightfully maintain.   225

Enter PRINCE JOHN OF LANCASTER, WARWICK, _Lords, and_ Others.

  King. Look, look, here comes my John of Lancaster.
  P. John. Health, peace, and happiness, to my royal father !
  King. Thou bring'st me happiness and peace, son John ;
But health, alack, with youthful wings is flown
From this bare wither'd trunk. Upon thy sight   230
My worldly business makes a period.
Where is my Lord of Warwick ?
  Prince.   My Lord of Warwick !
  King. Doth any name particular belong
Unto the lodging where I first did swoon ?
  War. 'Tis call'd Jerusalem, my noble lord.   235
  King. Laud be to God ! Even there my life must end.
It hath been prophesied to me many years,
I should not die but in Jerusalem ;
Which vainly I suppos'd the Holy Land.
But bear me to that chamber ; there I'll lie ;   240
In that Jerusalem shall Harry die. [_Exeunt._

ACT FIVE

SCENE I. _Gloucestershire._ _Shallow's house._

Enter SHALLOW, FALSTAFF, BARDOLPH, _and_ Page.

  Shal. By cock and pie, sir, you shall not away to-night. What, Davy, I say !
  Fal. You must excuse me, Master Robert Shallow.
  Shal. I will not excuse you ; you shall not be excus'd ; excuses shall not be admitted ; there is no excuse shall serve ; you shall not be excus'd. Why, Davy !   6

Enter DAVY.

Davy. Here, sir.

Shal. Davy, Davy, Davy, Davy; let me see, Davy; let me see, Davy; let me see—yea, marry, William cook, bid him come hither. Sir John, you shall not be excus'd.

Davy. Marry, sir, thus : those precepts cannot be served ; and, again, sir—shall we sow the headland with wheat ?   14

Shal. With red wheat, Davy. But for William cook—are there no young pigeons ?

Davy. Yes, sir. Here is now the smith's note for shoeing and plough-irons.

Shal. Let it be cast, and paid. Sir John, you shall not be excused.   20

Davy. Now, sir, a new link to the bucket must needs be had ; and, sir, do you mean to stop any of William's wages about the sack he lost the other day at Hinckley fair ?

Shal. 'A shall answer it. Some pigeons, Davy, a couple of short-legg'd hens, a joint of mutton, and any pretty little tiny kickshaws, tell William cook.

Davy. Doth the man of war stay all night, sir ?   28

Shal. Yea, Davy ; I will use him well. A friend i' th' court is better than a penny in purse. Use his men well, Davy ; for they are arrant knaves and will backbite.

Davy. No worse than they are backbitten, sir ; for they have marvellous foul linen.   34

Shal. Well conceited, Davy—about thy business, Davy.

Davy. I beseech you, sir, to countenance William Visor of Woncot against Clement Perkes o' th' hill.

Shal. There is many complaints, Davy, against that Visor. That Visor is an arrant knave, on my knowledge.   39

Davy. I grant your worship that he is a knave, sir ; but yet God forbid, sir, but a knave should have some countenance at his friend's request. An honest man, sir, is able to speak for himself, when a knave is not. I have serv'd your worship truly, sir, this eight years ; an I cannot once or twice in a quarter bear out a knave against an honest man, I have but a very little credit with your worship. The knave is mine honest friend, sir ; therefore, I beseech you, let him be countenanc'd.   49

Shal. Go to ; I say he shall have no wrong. Look about, Davy. [*Exit Davy*] Where are you, Sir John ? Come, come, come, off with your boots. Give me your hand, Master Bardolph.

Bard. I am glad to see your worship. 54

Shal. I thank thee with all my heart, kind Master Bardolph. [*To the Page*] And welcome, my tall fellow. Come, Sir John.

Fal. I'll follow you, good Master Robert Shallow. [*Exit Shallow*] Bardolph, look to our horses. [*Exeunt Bardolph and Page*] If I were sawed into quantities, I should make four dozen of such bearded hermits' staves as Master Shallow. It is a wonderful thing to see the semblable coherence of his men's spirits and his. They, by observing of him, do bear themselves like foolish justices : he, by conversing with them, is turned into a justice-like serving-man. Their spirits are so married in conjunction with the participation of society that they flock together in consent, like so many wild geese. If I had a suit to Master Shallow, I would humour his men with the imputation of being near their master ; if to his men, I would curry with Master Shallow that no man could better command his servants. It is certain that either wise bearing or ignorant carriage is caught, as men take diseases, one of another ; therefore let men take heed of their company. I will devise matter enough out of this Shallow to keep Prince Harry in continual laughter the wearing out of six fashions, which is four terms, or two actions ; and 'a shall laugh without intervallums. O, it is much that a lie with a slight oath, and a jest with a sad brow, will do with a fellow that never had the ache in his shoulders ! O, you shall see him laugh till his face be like a wet cloak ill laid up !   82

Shal. [*Within*] Sir John !

Fal. I come, Master Shallow ; I come, Master Shallow.   [*Exit.*

SCENE II. *Westminster. The palace.*

Enter, severally, WARWICK *and the* LORD CHIEF JUSTICE.

War. How now, my Lord Chief Justice ; whither away ?

Ch. Just. How doth the King ?

War. Exceeding well ; his cares are now all ended.

Ch. Just. I hope, not dead.

War. He's walk'd the way of nature ; And to our purposes he lives no more.   5

Ch. Just. I would his Majesty had call'd me with him. The service that I truly did his life Hath left me open to all injuries.

War. Indeed I think the young King loves you not.

Ch. Just. I know he doth not, and do arm myself To welcome the condition of the time,   11 Which cannot look more hideously upon me Than I have drawn it in my fantasy.

Enter LANCASTER, CLARENCE, GLOUCESTER, WESTMORELAND, *and* Others.

War. Here come the heavy issue of dead Harry. O that the living Harry had the temper   15

Of he, the worst of these three gentlemen !
How many nobles then should hold their places
That must strike sail to spirits of vile sort !

Ch. Just. O God, I fear all will be over-turn'd.

P. John. Good morrow, cousin Warwick, good morrow. 20

Glou. ⎱
Clar. ⎰ Good morrow, cousin.

P. John. We meet like men that had forgot to speak.

War. We do remember ; but our argument
Is all too heavy to admit much talk.

P. John. Well, peace be with him that hath made us heavy ! 25

Ch. Just. Peace be with us, lest we be heavier !

P. Humph. O, good my lord, you have lost a friend indeed ;
And I dare swear you borrow not that face
Of seeming sorrow—it is sure your own.

P. John. Though no man be assur'd what grace to find, 30
You stand in coldest expectation.
I am the sorrier ; would 'twere otherwise.

Cla. Well, you must now speak Sir John Falstaff fair ;
Which swims against your stream of quality.

Ch. Just. Sweet Princes, what I did, I did in honour, 35
Led by th' impartial conduct of my soul ;
And never shall you see that I will beg
A ragged and forestall'd remission.
If truth and upright innocency fail me,
I'll to the King my master that is dead, 40
And tell him who hath sent me after him.

War. Here comes the Prince.

Enter KING HENRY THE FIFTH, *attended.*

Ch. Just. Good morrow, and God save your Majesty !

King. This new and gorgeous garment, majesty,
Sits not so easy on me as you think. 45
Brothers, you mix your sadness with some fear.
This is the English, not the Turkish court ;
Not Amurath an Amurath succeeds,
But Harry Harry. Yet be sad, good brothers,
For, by my faith, it very well becomes you.
Sorrow so royally in you appears 51
That I will deeply put the fashion on,
And wear it in my heart. Why, then, be sad ;
But entertain no more of it, good brothers,
Than a joint burden laid upon us all. 55
For me, by heaven, I bid you be assur'd,
I'll be your father and your brother too ;
Let me but bear your love, I'll bear your cares.

Yet weep that Harry's dead, and so will I ;
But Harry lives that shall convert those tears 60
By number into hours of happiness.

Brothers. We hope no otherwise from your Majesty.

King. You all look strangely on me ; and you most.
You are, I think, assur'd I love you not.

Ch. Just. I am assur'd, if I be measur'd rightly, 65
Your Majesty hath no just cause to hate me.

King. No ?
How might a prince of my great hopes forget
So great indignities you laid upon me ?
What, rate, rebuke, and roughly send to prison, 70
Th' immediate heir of England ! Was this easy ?
May this be wash'd in Lethe and forgotten ?

Ch. Just. I then did use the person of your father ;
The image of his power lay then in me ;
And in th' administration of his law, 75
Whiles I was busy for the commonwealth,
Your Highness pleased to forget my place,
The majesty and power of law and justice,
The image of the King whom I presented,
And struck me in my very seat of judgment ; 80
Whereon, as an offender to your father,
I gave bold way to my authority
And did commit you. If the deed were ill,
Be you contented, wearing now the garland,
To have a son set your decrees at nought, 85
To pluck down justice from your awful bench,
To trip the course of law, and blunt the sword
That guards the peace and safety of your person ;
Nay, more, to spurn at your most royal image,
And mock your workings in a second body.
Question your royal thoughts, make the case yours ; 91
Be now the father, and propose a son ;
Hear your own dignity so much profan'd,
See your most dreadful laws so loosely slighted,
Behold yourself so by a son disdain'd ; 95
And then imagine me taking your part
And, in your power, soft silencing your son.
After this cold considerance, sentence me ;
And, as you are a king, speak in your state
What I have done that misbecame my place, 100
My person, or my liege's sovereignty.

King. You are right, Justice, and you weigh this well ;
Therefore still bear the balance and the sword ;
And I do wish your honours may increase

Till you do live to see a son of mine   105
Offend you, and obey you, as I did.
So shall I live to speak my father's words :
' Happy am I that have a man so bold
That dares do justice on my proper son ;
And not less happy, having such a son   110
That would deliver up his greatness so
Into the hands of justice '. You did commit
    me ;
For which I do commit into your hand
Th' unstained sword that you have us'd to
    bear ;
With this remembrance—that you use the
    same   115
With the like bold, just, and impartial
    spirit
As you have done 'gainst me. There is my
    hand.
You shall be as a father to my youth ;
My voice shall sound as you do prompt
    mine ear ;
And I will stoop and humble my intents   120
To your well-practis'd wise directions.
And, Princes all, believe me, I beseech you,
My father is gone wild into his grave,
For in his tomb lie my affections ;
And with his spirits sadly I survive,   125
To mock the expectation of the world,
To frustrate prophecies, and to raze out
Rotten opinion, who hath writ me down
After my seeming. The tide of blood in me
Hath proudly flow'd in vanity till now.   130
Now doth it turn and ebb back to the sea,
Where it shall mingle with the state of
    floods,
And flow henceforth in formal majesty.
Now call we our high court of parliament ;
And let us choose such limbs of noble
    counsel,   135
That the great body of our state may go
In equal rank with the best govern'd
    nation ;
That war, or peace, or both at once, may be
As things acquainted and familiar to us ;
In which you, father, shall have foremost
    hand.   140
Our coronation done, we will accite,
As I before rememb'red, all our state ;
And—God consigning to my good intents—
No prince nor peer shall have just cause to
    say,   144
God shorten Harry's happy life one day.
               [Exeunt.

SCENE III.   *Gloucestershire. Shallow's
orchard.*

Enter FALSTAFF, SHALLOW, SILENCE, BAR-
DOLPH, *the* Page, *and* DAVY.

    Shal. Nay, you shall see my orchard,
where, in an arbour, we will eat a last
year's pippin of mine own graffing, with a
dish of caraways, and so forth. Come,
cousin Silence. And then to bed.

    Fal. Fore God, you have here a goodly
dwelling and rich.   6
    Shal. Barren, barren, barren ; beggars
all, beggars all, Sir John—marry, good air.
Spread, Davy, spread, Davy ; well said,
Davy.   9
    Fal. This Davy serves you for good uses ;
he is your serving-man and your husband.
    Shal. A good varlet, a good varlet, a very
good varlet, Sir John. By the mass, I have
drunk too much sack at supper. A good
varlet. Now sit down, now sit down ; come,
cousin.   15
    Sil. Ah, sirrah ! quoth-a—we shall
                   [*Singing.*
Do nothing but eat and make good cheer,
And praise God for the merry year ;
When flesh is cheap and females dear,
And lusty lads roam here and there,   20
    So merrily,
And ever among so merrily.
    Fal. There's a merry heart !   Good
Master Silence, I'll give you a health for
that anon.
    Shal. Give Master Bardolph some wine,
Davy.   25
    Davy. Sweet sir, sit ; I'll be with you
anon ; most sweet sir, sit. Master Page,
good Master Page, sit. Proface ! What you
want in meat, we'll have in drink. But you
must bear ; the heart's all.   [*Exit.*
    Shal. Be merry, Master Bardolph ; and,
my little soldier there, be merry.   31
    Sil. [*Singing*]
Be merry, be merry, my wife has all ;
For women are shrews, both short and tall ;
'Tis merry in hall when beards wag all ;
    And welcome merry Shrove-tide.   35
Be merry, be merry.
    Fal. I did not think Master Silence had
been a man of this mettle.
    Sil. Who, I ? I have been merry twice
and once ere now.   40

            Re-enter DAVY.

    Davy. [*To Bardolph*] There's a dish of
leather-coats for you.
    Shal. Davy !
    Davy. Your worship ! I'll be with you
straight. [*To Bardolph*] A cup of wine, sir ?
    Sil. [*Singing*]
A cup of wine that's brisk and fine,   45
And drink unto the leman mine ;
    And a merry heart lives long-a.
    Fal. Well said, Master Silence.
    Sil. An we shall be merry, now comes in
the sweet o' th' night.   50
    Fal. Health and long life to you, Master
Silence !
    Sil. [*Singing*]
Fill the cup, and let it come,
I'll pledge you a mile to th' bottom.
    Shal. Honest Bardolph, welcome ; if
thou want'st anything and wilt not call,

beshrew thy heart. Welcome, my little tiny thief and welcome indeed too. I'll drink to Master Bardolph, and to all the cabileros about London.   58

Davy. I hope to see London once ere I die.

Bard. An I might see you there, Davy!

Shal. By the mass, you'll crack a quart together—ha! will you not, Master Bardolph?

Bard. Yea, sir, in a pottle-pot.

Shal. By God's liggens, I thank thee. The knave will stick by thee, I can assure thee that. 'A will not out, 'a; 'tis true bred.

Bard. And I'll stick by him, sir.   67

Shal. Why, there spoke a king. Lack nothing; be merry. [*One knocks at door*] Look who's at door there, ho! Who knocks?   [*Exit Davy.*

Fal. [*To Silence, who has drunk a bumper*] Why, now you have done me right.

Sil. [*Singing*] Do me right,
                And dub me knight.
                        Samingo.

Is't not so?   75

Fal. 'Tis so.

Sil. Is't so? Why then, say an old man can do somewhat.

Re-enter DAVY.

Davy. An't please your worship, there's one Pistol come from the court with news.

Fal. From the court? Let him come in.

Enter PISTOL.

How now, Pistol?

Pist. Sir John, God save you!   83

Fal. What wind blew you hither, Pistol?

Pist. Not the ill wind which blows no man to good. Sweet knight, thou art now one of the greatest men in this realm.

Sil. By'r lady, I think 'a be, but goodman Puff of Barson.

Pist. Puff!   90

Puff in thy teeth, most recreant coward base!

Sir John, I am thy Pistol and thy friend,
And helter-skelter have I rode to thee;
And tidings do I bring, and lucky joys, 94
And golden times, and happy news of price.

Fal. I pray thee now, deliver them like a man of this world.

Pist. A foutra for the world and worldlings base!

I speak of Africa and golden joys.

Fal. O base Assyrian knight, what is thy news?   100

Let King Cophetua know the truth thereof.

Sil. [*Singing*] And Robin Hood, Scarlet, and John.

Pist. Shall dunghill curs confront the Helicons?

And shall good news be baffled?

Then, Pistol, lay thy head in Furies' lap. 105

Shal. Honest gentleman, I know not your breeding.

Pist. Why, then, lament therefore.

Shal. Give me pardon, sir. If, sir, you come with news from the court, I take it there's but two ways—either to utter them or conceal them. I am, sir, under the King, in some authority.   111

Pist. Under which king, Bezonian? Speak, or die.

Shal. Under King Harry.

Pist.   Harry the Fourth—or Fifth?

Shal. Harry the Fourth.

Pist.   A foutra for thine office!

Sir John, thy tender lambkin now is King;
Harry the Fifth's the man. I speak the truth.   116

When Pistol lies, do this; and fig me, like
The bragging Spaniard.

Fal. What, is the old king dead?

Pist. As nail in door. The things I speak are just.   120

Fal. Away, Bardolph! saddle my horse. Master Robert Shallow, choose what office thou wilt in the land, 'tis thine. Pistol, I will double-charge thee with dignities.

Bard. O joyful day!   125

I would not take a knighthood for my fortune.

Pist. What, I do bring good news?

Fal. Carry Master Silence to bed. Master Shallow, my Lord Shallow, be what thou wilt—I am Fortune's steward. Get on thy boots; we'll ride all night. O sweet Pistol! Away, Bardolph! [*Exit Bardolph*] Come, Pistol, utter more to me; and withal devise something to do thyself good. Boot, boot, Master Shallow! I know the young King is sick for me. Let us take any man's horses: the laws of England are at my commandment. Blessed are they that have been my friends; and woe to my Lord Chief Justice!   137

Pist. Let vultures vile seize on his lungs also!

'Where is the life that late I led?' say they.

Why, here it is; welcome these pleasant days!   [*Exeunt.*

SCENE IV. *London. A street.*

Enter Beadles, *dragging in* HOSTESS QUICKLY *and* DOLL TEARSHEET.

Host. No, thou arrant knave; I would to God that I might die, that I might have thee hang'd. Thou hast drawn my shoulder out of joint.

1 Bead. The constables have delivered her over to me; and she shall have whipping-cheer enough, I warrant her. There hath been a man or two lately kill'd about her.   7

Doll. Nut-hook, nut-hook, you lie. Come

on ; I'll tell thee what, thou damn'd tripe-
visag'd rascal, an the child I now go with
do miscarry, thou wert better thou hadst
struck thy mother, thou paper-fac'd
villain.

Host. O the Lord, that Sir John were
come ! He would make this a bloody day to
somebody. But I pray God the fruit of her
womb miscarry ! 14

1 Bead. If it do, you shall have a dozen
of cushions again ; you have but eleven
now. Come, I charge you both go with me ;
for the man is dead that you and Pistol
beat amongst you. 18

Doll. I'll tell you what, you thin man in
a censer, I will have you as soundly swing'd
for this—you lue-bottle rogue, you filthy
famish'd correctioner, if you be not
swing'd, I'll forswear half-kirtles.

1 Bead. Come, come, you she knight-
errant, come.

Host. O God, that right should thus overcome might ! Well, of sufferance comes
ease. 25

Doll. Come, you rogue, come ; bring me
to a justice.

Host. Ay, come, you starv'd bloodhound.

Doll. Goodman death, goodman bones !

Host. Thou atomy, thou !

Doll. Come, you thin thing ! come, you
rascal ! 30

1 Bead. Very well. [*Exeunt.*

SCENE V. *Westminster. Near the Abbey.*

Enter Grooms, *strewing rushes.*

1 Groom. More rushes, more rushes !

2 Groom. The trumpets have sounded
twice.

3 Groom. 'Twill be two o'clock ere they
come from the coronation. Dispatch,
dispatch. [*Exeunt.*

Trumpets sound, and the KING *and his* Train
pass over the stage. After them enter
FALSTAFF, SHALLOW, PISTOL, BARDOLPH,
and Page.

Fal. Stand here by me, Master Robert
Shallow ; I will make the King do you
grace. I will leer upon him, as 'a comes by ;
and do but mark the countenance that he
will give me.

Pist. God bless thy lungs, good knight ! 9

Fal. Come here, Pistol ; stand behind
me. [*To Shallow*] O, if I had had time to
have made new liveries, I would have
bestowed the thousand pound I borrowed
of you. But 'tis no matter ; this poor show
doth better ; this doth infer the zeal I had
to see him.

Shal. It doth so. 15

Fal. It shows my earnestness of affection—

Shal. It doth so.

Fal. My devotion—

Shal. It doth, it doth, it doth. 19

Fal. As it were, to ride day and night ;
and not to deliberate, not to remember, not
to have patience to shift me—

Shal. It is best, certain. 23

Fal. But to stand stained with travel,
and sweating with desire to see him ;
thinking of nothing else, putting all affairs
else in oblivion, as if there were nothing
else to be done but to see him.

Pist. 'Tis ' semper idem ' for ' obsque hoc
nihil est '. 'Tis all in every part.

Shal. 'Tis so, indeed. 30

Pist. My knight, I will inflame thy noble
    liver
And make thee rage.
Thy Doll, and Helen of thy noble thoughts,
Is in base durance and contagious prison ;
Hal'd thither 35
By most mechanical and dirty hand.
Rouse up revenge from ebon den with fell
    Alecto's snake,
For Doll is in. Pistol speaks nought but
    truth.

Fal. I will deliver her. 39
  [*Shouts within, and the trumpets sound.*

Pist. There roar'd the sea, and trumpet-
    clangor sounds.

Enter the KING *and his Train, the* LORD
    CHIEF JUSTICE *among them.*

Fal. God save thy Grace, King Hal ; my
    royal Hal !

Pist. The heavens thee guard and keep,
most royal imp of fame !

Fal. God save thee, my sweet boy ! 44

King. My Lord Chief Justice, speak to
    that vain man.

Ch. Just. Have you your wits ? Know
    you what 'tis you speak ?

Fal. My king ! my Jove ! I speak to thee,
    my heart !

King. I know thee not, old man. Fall to
    thy prayers. 48
How ill white hairs become a fool and jester!
I have long dreamt of such a kind of man,
So surfeit-swell'd, so old, and so profane ;
But, being awak'd, I do despise my dream.
Make less thy body hence, and more thy
    grace ;
Leave gormandizing ; know the grave doth
    gape 54
For thee thrice wider than for other men—
Reply not to me with a fool-born jest ;
Presume not that I am the thing I was,
For God doth know, so shall the world
    perceive,
That I have turn'd away my former self ;
So will I those that kept me company. 60
When thou dost hear I am as I have been,
Approach me, and thou shalt be as thou
    wast,
The tutor and the feeder of my riots.

Till then I banish thee, on pain of death, 64
As I have done the rest of my misleaders,
Not to come near our person by ten mile.
For competence of life I will allow you,
That lack of means enforce you not to
  evils ;
And, as we hear you do reform yourselves,
We will, according to your strengths and
  qualities, 70
Give you advancement. Be it your charge,
  my lord,
To see perform'd the tenour of our word.
Set on. [*Exeunt the King and his train.*
  Fal. Master Shallow, I owe you a
thousand pound. 74
  Shal. Yea, marry, Sir John ; which I
beseech you to let me have home with me.
  Fal. That can hardly be, Master Shallow.
Do not you grieve at this ; I shall be sent
for in private to him. Look you, he must
seem thus to the world. Fear not your
advancements ; I will be the man yet that
shall make you great. 81
  Shal. I cannot perceive how, unless
you give me your doublet, and stuff me
out with straw. I beseech you, good Sir
John, let me have five hundred of my
thousand. 85
  Fal. Sir, I will be as good as my word.
This that you heard was but a colour.
  Shal. A colour that I fear you will die in,
Sir John.
  Fal. Fear no colours ; go with me to
dinner. Come, Lieutenant Pistol ; come,
Bardolph. I shall be sent for soon at night.

Re-enter PRINCE JOHN, *the* LORD CHIEF
  JUSTICE, *with* Officers.

  Ch. Just. Go, carry Sir John Falstaff to
the Fleet ; 92
Take all his company along with him.
  Fal. My lord, my lord—
  Ch. Just. I cannot now speak. I will hear
you soon.
Take them away. 96
  Pist. Si fortuna me tormenta, spero me
contenta.
        [*Exeunt all but Prince John and
          the Lord Chief Justice.*
  P. John. I like this fair proceeding of the
King's.
He hath intent his wonted followers
Shall all be very well provided for ; 100
But all are banish'd till their conversations
Appear more wise and modest to the world.
  Ch. Just. And so they are.

  P. John. The King hath call'd his parlia-
ment, my lord.
  Ch. Just. He hath. 105
  P. John. I will lay odds that, ere this
year expire,
We bear our civil swords and native fire
As far as France. I heard a bird so sing,
Whose music, to my thinking, pleas'd the
King.
Come, will you hence ? [*Exeunt.*

EPILOGUE

First my fear, then my curtsy, last my
speech. My fear, is your displeasure ; my
curtsy, my duty ; and my speech, to beg
your pardons. If you look for a good speech
now, you undo me ; for what I have to say
is of mine own making ; and what, indeed,
I should say will, I doubt, prove mine own
marring. But to the purpose, and so to the
venture. Be it known to you, as it is very
well, I was lately here in the end of a
displeasing play, to pray your patience for
it and to promise you a better. I meant,
indeed, to pay you with this ; which if
like an ill venture it come unluckily home,
I break, and you, my gentle creditors, lose.
Here I promis'd you I would be, and here
I commit my body to your mercies. Bate
me some, and I will pay you some, and, as
most debtors do, promise you infinitely ;
and so I kneel down before you—but,
indeed, to pray for the Queen. 16

If my tongue cannot entreat you to
acquit me, will you command me to use my
legs ? And yet that were but light payment
—to dance out of your debt. But a good
conscience will make any possible satisfaction, and so would I. All the gentlewomen
here have forgiven me. If the gentlemen
will not, then the gentlemen do not agree
with the gentlewomen, which was never
seen before in such an assembly. 24

One word more, I beseech you. If you
be not too much cloy'd with fat meat, our
humble author will continue the story,
with Sir John in it, and make you merry
with fair Katharine of France ; where, for
anything I know, Falstaff shall die of a
sweat, unless already 'a be kill'd with your
hard opinions ; for Oldcastle died a
martyr and this is not the man. My
tongue is weary ; when my legs are too, I
will bid you good night. 33

KING HENRY THE FIFTH

DRAMATIS PERSONÆ

CHORUS.
KING HENRY THE FIFTH.
DUKE OF GLOUCESTER, } brothers to the
DUKE OF BEDFORD, } King.
DUKE OF EXETER, uncle to the King.
DUKE OF YORK, cousin to the King.
EARL OF SALISBURY.
EARL OF WESTMORELAND.
EARL OF WARWICK.
ARCHBISHOP OF CANTERBURY.
BISHOP OF ELY.
EARL OF CAMBRIDGE, } conspirators against
LORD SCROOP, } the King.
SIR THOMAS GREY, }
SIR THOMAS ERPINGHAM,
GOWER,
FLUELLEN, } officers in the
MACMORRIS, } King's army.
JAMY,
BATES,
COURT,
WILLIAMS, } soldiers in the
NYM, } King's army.
BARDOLPH,
PISTOL,

Boy.
A Herald.
CHARLES THE SIXTH, King of France.
LEWIS, the Dauphin.
DUKE OF BURGUNDY.
DUKE OF ORLEANS.
DUKE OF BRITAINE.
DUKE OF BOURBON.
The Constable of France.
RAMBURES, } French lords.
GRANDPRÉ, }
Governor of Harfleur.
MONTJOY, a French herald.
Ambassadors to the King of England.

ISABEL, Queen of France.
KATHERINE, daughter to Charles and Isabel.
ALICE, a lady attending her.
HOSTESS of the Boar's Head, Eastcheap ;
formerly Mrs. Quickly, now married
to Pistol.
Lords, Ladies, Officers, Soldiers, Messengers,
Attendants.

THE SCENE : England and France.

PROLOGUE

Enter CHORUS.

Chor. O for a Muse of fire, that would
ascend
The brightest heaven of invention,
A kingdom for a stage, princes to act,
And monarchs to behold the swelling scene!
Then should the warlike Harry, like him-
self, 5
Assume the port of Mars ; and at his heels,
Leash'd in like hounds, should famine,
sword, and fire,
Crouch for employment.   But pardon,
gentles all,
The flat unraised spirits that hath dar'd
On this unworthy scaffold to bring forth 10
So great an object. Can this cockpit hold
The vasty fields of France ? Or may we
cram
Within this wooden O the very casques
That did affright the air at Agincourt ?
O, pardon ! since a crooked figure may 15
Attest in little place a million ;
And let us, ciphers to this great accompt,
On your imaginary forces work.
Suppose within the girdle of these walls 19
Are now confin'd two mighty monarchies,
Whose high upreared and abutting fronts

The perilous narrow ocean parts asunder.
Piece out our imperfections with your
thoughts :
Into a thousand parts divide one man,
And make imaginary puissance ;   25
Think, when we talk of horses, that you see
them
Printing their proud hoofs i' th' receiving
earth ;
For 'tis your thoughts that now must deck
our kings,
Carry them here and there, jumping o'er
times,   29
Turning th' accomplishment of many years
Into an hour-glass ; for the which supply,
Admit me Chorus to this history ;
Who, prologue-like, your humble patience
pray
Gently to hear, kindly to judge, our play.
[*Exit.*

ACT ONE

SCENE I. London. An ante-chamber in the
King's palace.

*Enter the ARCHBISHOP OF CANTERBURY and
the BISHOP OF ELY.*

Cant. My lord, I'll tell you : that self
bill is urg'd

Which in th' eleventh year of the last king's reign
Was like, and had indeed against us pass'd
But that the scambling and unquiet time
Did push it out of farther question.   5
   Ely. But how, my lord, shall we resist it now ?
   Cant. It must be thought on. If it pass against us,
We lose the better half of our possession ;
For all the temporal lands which men devout
By testament have given to the church   10
Would they strip from us ; being valu'd thus—
As much as would maintain, to the King's honour,
Full fifteen earls and fifteen hundred knights,
Six thousand and two hundred good esquires ;
And, to relief of lazars and weak age,   15
Of indigent faint souls, past corporal toil,
A hundred alms-houses right well supplied ;
And to the coffers of the King, beside,
A thousand pounds by th' year : thus runs the bill.
   Ely. This would drink deep.
   Cant.   'Twould drink the cup and all.
   Ely. But what prevention ?   21
   Cant. The King is full of grace and fair regard.
   Ely. And a true lover of the holy Church.
   Cant. The courses of his youth promis'd it not.
The breath no sooner left his father's body
But that his wildness, mortified in him,   26
Seem'd to die too ; yea, at that very moment,
Consideration like an angel came
And whipp'd th' offending Adam out of him,
Leaving his body as a paradise   30
T' envelop and contain celestial spirits.
Never was such a sudden scholar made ;
Never came reformation in a flood,
With such a heady currance, scouring faults ;
Nor never Hydra-headed wilfulness   35
So soon did lose his seat, and all at once,
As in this king.
   Ely.   We are blessed in the change.
   Cant. Hear him but reason in divinity,
And, all-admiring, with an inward wish
You would desire the King were made a prelate ;   40
Hear him debate of commonwealth affairs,
You would say it hath been all in all his study ;
List his discourse of war, and you shall hear
A fearful battle rend'red you in music.
Turn him to any cause of policy,   45
The Gordian knot of it he will unloose,

Familiar as his garter ; that, when he speaks,
The air, a charter'd libertine, is still,
And the mute wonder lurketh in men's ears
To steal his sweet and honey'd sentences ;
So that the art and practic part of life   51
Must be the mistress to this theoric ;
Which is a wonder how his Grace should glean it,
Since his addiction was to courses vain,
His companies unletter'd, rude, and shallow,
His hours fill'd up with riots, banquets, sports ;   56
And never noted in him any study,
Any retirement, any sequestration
From open haunts and popularity.
   Ely. The strawberry grows underneath the nettle,   60
And wholesome berries thrive and ripen best
Neighbour'd by fruit of baser quality ;
And so the Prince obscur'd his contemplation
Under the veil of wildness ; which, no doubt,
Grew like the summer grass, fastest by night,   65
Unseen, yet crescive in his faculty.
   Cant. It must be so ; for miracles are ceas'd ;
And therefore we must needs admit the means
How things are perfected.
   Ely.   But, my good lord,
How now for mitigation of this bill   70
Urg'd by the Commons ? Doth his Majesty
Incline to it, or no ?
   Cant.   He seems indifferent ;
Or rather swaying more upon our part
Than cherishing th' exhibiters against us ;
For I have made an offer to his Majesty—
Upon our spiritual convocation   76
And in regard of causes now in hand,
Which I have open'd to his Grace at large,
As touching France—to give a greater sum
Than ever at one time the clergy yet   80
Did to his predecessors part withal.
   Ely. How did this offer seem receiv'd, my lord ?
   Cant. With good acceptance of his Majesty ;
Save that there was not time enough to hear,
As I perceiv'd his Grace would fain have done,   85
The severals and unhidden passages
Of his true titles to some certain dukedoms,
And generally to the crown and seat of France,
Deriv'd from Edward, his great-grandfather.
   Ely. What was th' impediment that broke this off ?   90

Cant. The French ambassador upon that
    instant
Crav'd audience; and the hour, I think,
    is come
To give him hearing: is it four o'clock?
    Ely. It is.
    Cant. Then go we in, to know his
        embassy;   95
Which I could with a ready guess declare,
Before the Frenchman speak a word of it.
    Ely. I'll wait upon you, and I long to
        hear it.   [Exeunt.

SCENE II. London. The Presence Chamber
    in the King's palace.

Enter the KING, GLOUCESTER, BEDFORD,
    EXETER, WARWICK, WESTMORELAND,
    and Attendants.

    King. Where is my gracious Lord of
        Canterbury?
    Exe. Not here in presence.
    King.   Send for him, good uncle.
    West. Shall we call in th' ambassador,
        my liege?
    King. Not yet, my cousin; we would be
        resolv'd,
Before we hear him, of some things of
    weight   5
That task our thoughts, concerning us and
    France.

Enter the ARCHBISHOP OF CANTERBURY and
    the BISHOP OF ELY.

    Cant. God and his angels guard your
        sacred throne,
And make you long become it!
    King.   Sure, we thank you.
My learned lord, we pray you to proceed,
And justly and religiously unfold   10
Why the law Salique, that they have in
    France,
Or should or should not bar us in our claim;
And God forbid, my dear and faithful lord,
That you should fashion, wrest, or bow
    your reading,
Or nicely charge your understanding soul 15
With opening titles miscreate whose right
Suits not in native colours with the truth;
For God doth know how many, now in
    health,
Shall drop their blood in approbation
Of what your reverence shall incite us to. 20
Therefore take heed how you impawn our
    person,
How you awake our sleeping sword of war—
We charge you, in the name of God, take
    heed;
For never two such kingdoms did contend
Without much fall of blood; whose guilt-
    less drops   25
Are every one a woe, a sore complaint,
'Gainst him whose wrongs gives edge unto
    the swords

That makes such waste in brief mortality.
Under this conjuration speak, my lord;
For we will hear, note, and believe in heart,
That what you speak is in your conscience
    wash'd   31
As pure as sin with baptism.
    Cant. Then hear me, gracious sovereign,
        and you peers,
That owe yourselves, your lives, and
    services,
To this imperial throne. There is no bar 35
To make against your Highness' claim to
    France
But this, which they produce from Phara-
    mond:
'In terram Salicam mulieres ne succed-
    ant'—
'No woman shall succeed in Salique land';
Which Salique land the French unjustly
    gloze   40
To be the realm of France, and Pharamond
The founder of this law and female bar.
Yet their own authors faithfully affirm
That the land Salique is in Germany,
Between the floods of Sala and of Elbe;   45
Where Charles the Great, having subdu'd
    the Saxons,
There left behind and settled certain
    French;
Who, holding in disdain the German
    women
For some dishonest manners of their life,
Establish'd then this law: to wit, no
    female   50
Should be inheritrix in Salique land;
Which Salique, as I said, 'twixt Elbe and
    Sala,
Is at this day in Germany call'd Meisen.
Then doth it well appear the Salique law
Was not devised for the realm of France; 55
Nor did the French possess the Salique land
Until four hundred one and twenty years
After defunction of King Pharamond,
Idly suppos'd the founder of this law;
Who died within the year of our redemption
Four hundred twenty-six; and Charles the
    Great   61
Subdu'd the Saxons, and did seat the
    French
Beyond the river Sala, in the year
Eight hundred five. Besides, their writers
    say,
King Pepin, which deposed Childeric,   65
Did, as heir general, being descended
Of Blithild, which was daughter to King
    Clothair,
Make claim and title to the crown of
    France.
Hugh Capet also, who usurp'd the crown
Of Charles the Duke of Lorraine, sole heir
    male   70
Of the true line and stock of Charles the
    Great,
To find his title with some shows of truth—

Though in pure truth it was corrupt and
   naught—
Convey'd himself as th' heir to th' Lady
   Lingare,   74
Daughter to Charlemain, who was the son
To Lewis the Emperor, and Lewis the son
Of Charles the Great. Also King Lewis the
   Tenth,
Who was sole heir to the usurper Capet,
Could not keep quiet in his conscience, 79
Wearing the crown of France, till satisfied
That fair Queen Isabel, his grandmother,
Was lineal of the Lady Ermengare,
Daughter to Charles the foresaid Duke of
   Lorraine,
By the which marriage the line of Charles
   the Great
Was re-united to the Crown of France. 85
So that, as clear as is the summer's sun,
King Pepin's title, and Hugh Capet's claim,
King Lewis his satisfaction, all appear
To hold in right and title of the female;
So do the kings of France unto this day, 90
Howbeit they would hold up this Salique
   law
To bar your Highness claiming from the
   female;
And rather choose to hide them in a net
Than amply to imbar their crooked titles
Usurp'd from you and your progenitors. 95
   King. May I with right and conscience
     make this claim?
   Cant. The sin upon my head, dread
     sovereign!
For in the book of Numbers is it writ,
When the man dies, let the inheritance
Descend unto the daughter. Gracious lord,
Stand for your own, unwind your bloody
   flag,   101
Look back into your mighty ancestors.
Go, my dread lord, to your great-grand-
   sire's tomb,
From whom you claim; invoke his warlike
   spirit,
And your great-uncle's, Edward the Black
   Prince,   105
Who on the French ground play'd a
   tragedy,
Making defeat on the full power of France,
Whiles his most mighty father on a hill
Stood smiling to behold his lion's whelp
Forage in blood of French nobility. 110
O noble English, that could entertain
With half their forces the full pride of
   France,
And let another half stand laughing by,
All out of work and cold for action!
   Ely. Awake remembrance of these
     valiant dead,   115
And with your puissant arm renew their
   feats.
You are their heir; you sit upon their
   throne;
The blood and courage that renowned them

Runs in your veins; and my thrice-
   puissant liege
Is in the very May-morn of his youth, 120
Ripe for exploits and mighty enterprises.
   Exe. Your brother kings and monarchs
     of the earth
Do all expect that you should rouse
   yourself,
As did the former lions of your blood.
   West. They know your Grace hath cause
     and means and might—   125
So hath your Highness; never King of
   England
Had nobles richer and more loyal subjects,
Whose hearts have left their bodies here in
   England
And lie pavilion'd in the fields of France.
   Cant. O, let their bodies follow, my dear
     liege,   130
With blood and sword and fire to win your
   right!
In aid whereof we of the spirituality
Will raise your Highness such a mighty
   sum
As never did the clergy at one time
Bring in to any of your ancestors. 135
   King. We must not only arm t' invade
     the French,
But lay down our proportions to defend
Against the Scot, who will make road upon
   us
With all advantages.
   Cant. They of those marches, gracious
     sovereign,   140
Shall be a wall sufficient to defend
Our inland from the pilfering borderers.
   King. We do not mean the coursing
     snatchers only,
But fear the main intendment of the Scot,
Who hath been still a giddy neighbour to
   us;   145
For you shall read that my great-grand-
   father
Never went with his forces into France
But that the Scot on his unfurnish'd
   kingdom
Came pouring, like the tide into a breach,
With ample and brim fulness of his
   force,   150
Galling the gleaned land with hot assays,
Girding with grievous siege castles and
   towns;
That England, being empty of defence,
Hath shook and trembled at th' ill neigh-
   bourhood.
   Cant. She hath been then more fear'd
     than harm'd, my liege;   155
For hear her but exampled by herself:
When all her chivalry hath been in France,
And she a mourning widow of her nobles,
She hath herself not only well defended
But taken and impounded as a stray 160
The King of Scots; whom she did send to
   France,

To fill King Edward's fame with prisoner
    kings,
And make her chronicle as rich with praise
As is the ooze and bottom of the sea   164
With sunken wreck and sumless treasuries.
   West. But there's a saying, very old and
    true :
     ' If that you will France win,
      Then with Scotland first begin '.
For once the eagle England being in prey,
To her unguarded nest the weasel Scot 170
Comes sneaking, and so sucks her princely
    eggs,
Playing the mouse in absence of the cat,
To tear and havoc more than she can eat.
   Exe. It follows, then, the cat must stay
    at home ;
Yet that is but a crush'd necessity,   175
Since we have locks to safeguard necessaries
And pretty traps to catch the petty thieves.
While that the armed hand doth fight
    abroad,
Th' advised head defends itself at home ;
For government, though high, and low, and
    lower,   180
Put into parts, doth keep in one consent,
Congreeing in a full and natural close,
Like music.
   Cant. Therefore doth heaven divide
The state of man in divers functions,
Setting endeavour in continual motion ; 185
To which is fixed as an aim or butt
Obedience ; for so work the honey bees,
Creatures that by a rule in nature teach
The act of order to a peopled kingdom.
They have a king, and officers of sorts, 190
Where some like magistrates correct at
    home ;
Others like merchants venture trade
    abroad ;
Others like soldiers, armed in their stings,
Make boot upon the summer's velvet buds,
Which pillage they with merry march 195
bring home
To the tent-royal of their emperor ;
Who, busied in his majesty, surveys
The singing masons building roofs of gold,
The civil citizens kneading up the honey,
The poor mechanic porters crowding in 200
Their heavy burdens at his narrow gate,
The sad-ey'd justice, with his surly hum,
Delivering o'er to executors pale
The lazy yawning drone. I this infer,
That many things, having full reference 205
To one consent, may work contrariously ;
As many arrows loosed several ways
Come to one mark, as many ways meet in
    one town,
As many fresh streams meet in one salt sea,
As many lines close in the dial's centre ; 210
So many a thousand actions, once afoot,
End in one purpose, and be all well borne
Without defeat. Therefore to France, my
    liege.

Divide your happy England into four ; 214
Whereof take you one quarter into France,
And you withal shall make all Gallia shake.
If we, with thrice such powers left at
    home,
Cannot defend our own doors from the dog,
Let us be worried, and our nation lose
The name of hardiness and policy.   220
   King. Call in the messengers sent from
    the Dauphin.
              [*Exeunt some Attendants.*
Now are we well resolv'd ; and, by God's
    help
And yours, the noble sinews of our power,
France being ours, we'll bend it to our awe,
Or break it all to pieces ; or there we'll sit,
Ruling in large and ample empery   226
O'er France and all her almost kingly
    dukedoms,
Or lay these bones in an unworthy urn,
Tombless, with no remembrance over them.
Either our history shall with full mouth
Speak freely of our acts, or else our grave,
Like Turkish mute, shall have a tongueless
    mouth,   232
Not worshipp'd with a waxen epitaph.

     Enter Ambassadors *of France.*

Now are we well prepar'd to know the
    pleasure
Of our fair cousin Dauphin ; for we hear 235
Your greeting is from him, not from the
    King.
   1 *Amb.* May't please your Majesty to
    give us leave
Freely to render what we have in charge ;
Or shall we sparingly show you far off 239
The Dauphin's meaning and our embassy ?
   King. We are no tyrant, but a Christian
    king,
Unto whose grace our passion is as subject
As are our wretches fett'red in our prisons ;
Therefore with frank and with uncurbed
    plainness
Tell us the Dauphin's mind.
   1 *Amb.*   Thus then, in few. 245
Your Highness, lately sending into France,
Did claim some certain dukedoms in the
    right
Of your great predecessor, King Edward
    the Third.
In answer of which claim, the Prince our
    master
Says that you savour too much of your
    youth,   250
And bids you be advis'd there's nought in
    France
That can be with a nimble galliard won ;
You cannot revel into dukedoms there.
He therefore sends you, meeter for your
    spirit,   254
This tun of treasure ; and, in lieu of this,
Desires you let the dukedoms that you
    claim

Hear no more of you. This the Dauphin
    speaks.
  King. What treasure, uncle ?
  Exe.   Tennis-balls, my liege.
  King. We are glad the Dauphin is so
    pleasant with us ;
His present and your pains we thank you
    for.   260
When we have match'd our rackets to these
    balls,
We will in France, by God's grace, play a
    set
Shall strike his father's crown into the
    hazard.
Tell him he hath made a match with such a
    wrangler
That all the courts of France will be
    disturb'd   265
With chaces. And we understand him well,
How he comes o'er us with our wilder days,
Not measuring what use we made of them.
We never valu'd this poor seat of England ;
And therefore, living hence, did give ourself
To barbarous licence ; as 'tis ever common
That men are merriest when they are from
    home.
But tell the Dauphin I will keep my state,
Be like a king, and show my sail of great-
    ness,
When I do rouse me in my throne of
    France ;   275
For that I have laid by my majesty
And plodded like a man for working-days ;
But I will rise there with so full a glory
That I will dazzle all the eyes of France,
Yea, strike the Dauphin blind to look on us.
And tell the pleasant Prince this mock
    of his   281
Hath turn'd his balls to gun-stones, and
    his soul
Shall stand sore charged for the wasteful
    vengeance
That shall fly with them ; for many a
    thousand widows
Shall this his mock mock out of their dear
    husbands ;   285
Mock mothers from their sons, mock castles
    down ;
And some are yet ungotten and unborn
That shall have cause to curse the Dauphin's
    scorn.
But this lies all within the will of God, 289
To whom I do appeal ; and in whose name,
Tell you the Dauphin, I am coming on,
To venge me as I may and to put forth
My rightful hand in a well-hallow'd cause.
So get you hence in peace ; and tell the
    Dauphin
His jest will savour but of shallow wit, 295
When thousands weep more than did laugh
    at it.
Convey them with safe conduct. Fare you
    well.   [*Exeunt Ambassadors.*
  Exe. This was a merry message.

  King. We hope to make the sender blush
    at it.
Therefore, my lords, omit no happy hour 300
That may give furth'rance to our expedi-
    tion ;
For we have now no thought in us but
    France,
Save those to God, that run before our
    business.
Therefore let our proportions for these wars
Be soon collected, and all things thought
    upon   305
That may with reasonable swiftness add
More feathers to our wings ; for, God before,
We'll chide this Dauphin at his father's
    door.
Therefore let every man now task his
    thought   309
That this fair action may on foot be
    brought.   [*Exeunt.*

ACT TWO

PROLOGUE

Flourish. Enter CHORUS.

  Chor. Now all the youth of England are
    on fire,
And silken dalliance in the wardrobe lies ;
Now thrive the armourers, and honour's
    thought
Reigns solely in the breast of every man ;
They sell the pasture now to buy the horse,
Following the mirror of all Christian kings
With winged heels, as English Mercuries. 7
For now sits Expectation in the air,
And hides a sword from hilts unto the point
With crowns imperial, crowns, and coronets,
Promis'd to Harry and his followers.   11
The French, advis'd by good intelligence
Of this most dreadful preparation,
Shake in their fear and with pale policy
Seek to divert the English purposes.   15
O England ! model to thy inward greatness,
Like little body with a mighty heart,
What mightst thou do that honour would
    thee do,
Were all thy children kind and natural !
But see thy fault ! France hath in thee
    found out   20
A nest of hollow bosoms, which he fills
With treacherous crowns ; and three
    corrupted men—
One, Richard Earl of Cambridge, and the
    second,
Henry Lord Scroop of Masham, and the
    third,
Sir Thomas Grey, knight, of Northumber-
    land,   25
Have, for the gilt of France—O guilt
    indeed !—
Confirm'd conspiracy with fearful France ;
And by their hands this grace of kings must
    die—

If hell and treason hold their promises,
Ere he take ship for France—and in South-
    ampton.   30
Linger your patience on, and we'll digest
Th' abuse of distance, force a play.
The sum is paid, the traitors are agreed,
The King is set from London, and the
    scene
Is now transported, gentles, to South-
    ampton ;   35
There is the play-house now, there must
    you sit,
And thence to France shall we convey you
    safe
And bring you back, charming the narrow
    seas
To give you gentle pass ; for, if we may,
We'll not offend one stomach with our play.
But, till the King come forth, and not till
    then,   41
Unto Southampton do we shift our scene.
                                 [*Exit.*

Scene I. *London. Before the Boar's Head
    Tavern, Eastcheap.*

Enter Corporal Nym *and* Lieutenant
    Bardolph.

Bard. Well met, Corporal Nym.
Nym. Good morrow, Lieutenant Bardolph.
Bard. What, are Ancient Pistol and you
friends yet ?
Nym. For my part, I care not ; I say
little, but when time shall serve, there shall
be smiles—but that shall be as it may. I
dare not fight ; but I will wink and hold
out mine iron. It is a simple one ; but
what though ? It will toast cheese, and it
will endure cold as another man's sword
will ; and there's an end.   9
Bard. I will bestow a breakfast to make
you friends ; and we'll be all three sworn
brothers to France. Let't be so, good
Corporal Nym.   12
Nym. Faith, I will live so long as I may,
that's the certain of it ; and when I cannot
live any longer, I will do as I may. That
is my rest, that is the rendezvous of it. 16
Bard. It is certain, Corporal, that he is
married to Nell Quickly ; and certainly
she did you wrong, for you were troth-
plight to her.   19
Nym. I cannot tell ; things must be as
they may. Men may sleep, and they may
have their throats about them at that time ;
and some say knives have edges. It must
be as it may ; though patience be a tired
mare, yet she will plod. There must be
conclusions. Well, I cannot tell. 25

Enter Pistol *and* Hostess.

Bard. Here comes Ancient Pistol and his
wife. Good Corporal, be patient here.

Nym. How now, mine host Pistol !
Pist. Base tike, call'st thou me host ?
Now, by this hand, I swear I scorn the
    term ;
Nor shall my Nell keep lodgers.   30
Host. No, by my troth, not long ; for we
cannot lodge and board a dozen or fourteen
gentlewomen that live honestly by the
prick of their needles, but it will be
thought we keep a bawdy-house straight.
[*Nym draws*] O well-a-day, Lady, if he be
not drawn ! Now we shall see wilful
adultery and murder committed.   36
Bard. Good Lieutenant, good Corporal,
offer nothing here.
Nym. Pish !
Pist. Pish for thee, Iceland dog ! thou
    prick-ear'd cur of Iceland !   40
Host. Good Corporal Nym, show thy
valour, and put up your sword.
Nym. Will you shog off ? I would have
you solus.
Pist. ' Solus ' egregious dog ? O viper
    vile !   44
The ' solus ' in thy most mervailous face ;
The ' solus ' in thy teeth, and in thy throat,
And in thy hateful lungs, yea, in thy maw,
    perdy ;
And, which is worse, within thy nasty
    mouth !
I do retort the ' solus ' in thy bowels ;
For I can take, and Pistol's cock is up, 50
And flashing fire will follow.
Nym. I am not Barbason : you cannot
conjure me. I have an humour to knock
you indifferently well. If you grow foul
with me, Pistol, I will scour you with my
rapier, as I may, in fair terms ; if you
would walk off I would prick your guts a
little, in good terms, as I may, and that's
the humour of it.
Pist. O braggart vile and damned furious
    wight !
The grave doth gape and doting death is
    near ;   59
Therefore exhale.   [*Pistol draws.*
Bard. Hear me, hear me what I say : he
that strikes the first stroke I'll run him up
to the hilts, as I am a soldier.   [*Draws.*
Pist. An oath of mickle might ; and fury
    shall abate.   64
    [*Pistol and Nym sheathe their swords.*
Give me thy fist, thy fore-foot to me give ;
Thy spirits are most tall.
Nym. I will cut thy throat one time or
other, in fair terms ; that is the humour
of it.
Pist. ' Couple a gorge ! '
That is the word. I thee defy again. 70
O hound of Crete, think'st thou my spouse
    to get ?
No ; to the spital go,
And from the powd'ring tub of infamy
Fetch forth the lazar kite of Cressid's kind,

Doll Tearsheet she by name, and her
  espouse.   75
I have, and I will hold, the quondam
  Quickly
For the only she; and—pauca, there's
  enough.
Go to.

Enter the Boy.

Boy. Mine host Pistol, you must come to
my master; and your hostess—he is very
sick, and would to bed. Good Bardolph,
put thy face between his sheets, and do the
office of a warming-pan. Faith, he's very ill.
  Bard. Away, you rogue.   83
  Host. By my troth, he'll yield the crow
a pudding one of these days: the King
has kill'd his heart. Good husband, come
home presently. [*Exeunt Hostess and Boy.*
  Bard. Come, shall I make you two
friends? We must to France together;
why the devil should we keep knives to cut
one another's throats?   89
  Pist. Let floods o'erswell, and fiends for
  food howl on!
  Nym. You'll pay me the eight shillings I
won of you at betting?
  Pist. Base is the slave that pays.
  Nym. That now I will have; that's the
humour of it.   94
  Pist. As manhood shall compound: push
  home.   [*Pistol and Nym draw.*
  Bard. By this sword, he that makes the
first thrust I'll kill him; by this sword, I
will.
  Pist. Sword is an oath, and oaths must
  have their course.
            [*Sheathes his sword.*
  Bard. Corporal Nym, an thou wilt be
friends, be friends; an thou wilt not, why
then be enemies with me too. Prithee
put up.   101
  Nym. I shall have my eight shillings I
won of you at betting?
  Pist. A noble shalt thou have, and
present pay;
And liquor likewise will I give to thee, 105
And friendship shall combine, and brother-
hood.
I'll live by Nym and Nym shall live by
  me.
Is not this just? For I shall sutler be
Unto the camp, and profits will accrue.
Give me thy hand.   110
  Nym. [*Sheathing his sword*] I shall have
my noble?
  Pist. In cash most justly paid.
  Nym. [*Shaking hands*] Well, then, that's
the humour of't.   113

Re-enter Hostess.

  Host. As ever you come of women, come
in quickly to Sir John. Ah, poor heart!
he is so shak'd of a burning quotidian

tertian that it is most lamentable to behold.
Sweet men, come to him.
  Nym. The King hath run bad humours
on the knight; that's the even of it.
  Pist. Nym, thou hast spoke the right; 120
His heart is fracted and corroborate.
  Nym. The King is a good king, but it
must be as it may; he passes some
humours and careers.
  Pist. Let us condole the knight; for,
lambkins, we will live.   [*Exeunt.*

SCENE II. *Southampton. A council-*
              chamber.

Enter EXETER, BEDFORD, *and* WESTMORE-
              LAND.

  Bed. Fore God, his Grace is bold, to trust
    these traitors.
  Exe. They shall be apprehended by and
    by.
  West. How smooth and even they do
    bear themselves,
As if allegiance in their bosoms sat,
Crowned with faith and constant loyalty! 5
  Bed. The King hath note of all that they
    intend,
By interception which they dream not of.
  Exe. Nay, but the man that was his
    bedfellow,
Whom he hath dull'd and cloy'd with
    gracious favours—   9
That he should, for a foreign purse, so sell
His sovereign's life to death and treachery!

Trumpets sound. Enter the KING, SCROOP,
CAMBRIDGE, GREY, *and* Attendants.

  King. Now sits the wind fair, and we will
    aboard.
My Lord of Cambridge, and my kind Lord
    of Masham,
And you, my gentle knight, give me your
    thoughts.
Think you not that the pow'rs we bear with
    us   15
Will cut their passage through the force of
    France,
Doing the execution and the act
For which we have in head assembled them?
  Scroop. No doubt, my liege, if each man
    do his best.
  King. I doubt not that, since we are well
    persuaded   20
We carry not a heart with us from hence
That grows not in a fair consent with ours;
Nor leave not one behind that doth not
    wish
Success and conquest to attend on us.
  Cam. Never was monarch better fear'd
    and lov'd   25
Than is your Majesty. There's not, I think,
    a subject
That sits in heart-grief and uneasiness
Under the sweet shade of your government.

Grey. True: those that were your
　father's enemies
Have steep'd their galls in honey, and do
　serve you　　　　　　　　　　　30
With hearts create of duty and of zeal.
　King. We therefore have great cause of
　　thankfulness,
And shall forget the office of our hand
Sooner than quittance of desert and merit
According to the weight and worthiness. 35
　Scroop. So service shall with steeled
　　sinews toil,
And labour shall refresh itself with hope,
To do your Grace incessant services.
　King. We judge no less. Uncle of Exeter,
Enlarge the man committed yesterday　40
That rail'd against our person. We consider
It was excess of wine that set him on;
And on his more advice we pardon him.
　Scroop. That's mercy, but too much
　　security.
Let him be punish'd, sovereign, lest ex-
　ample　　　　　　　　　　　　45
Breed, by his sufferance, more of such a
　kind.
　King. O, let us yet be merciful!
　Cam. So may your Highness, and yet
　　punish too.
　Grey. Sir,　　　　　　　　　49
You show great mercy if you give him life,
After the taste of much correction.
　King. Alas, your too much love and care
　of me
Are heavy orisons 'gainst this poor wretch!
If little faults proceeding on distemper
Shall not be wink'd at, how shall we stretch
　our eye　　　　　　　　　　　55
When capital crimes, chew'd, swallow'd,
　and digested,
Appear before us? We'll yet enlarge that
　man,
Though Cambridge, Scroop, and Grey, in
　their dear care
And tender preservation of our person,
Would have him punish'd. And now to our
　French causes:　　　　　　　　60
Who are the late commissioners?
　Cam. I one, my lord.
Your Highness bade me ask for it to-day.
　Scroop. So did you me, my liege.
　Grey. And I, my royal sovereign.　65
　King. Then, Richard Earl of Cambridge,
　　there is yours;
There yours, Lord Scroop of Masham; and,
　Sir Knight,
Grey of Northumberland, this same is
　yours.
Read them, and know I know your worthi-
　ness.
My Lord of Westmoreland, and uncle
　Exeter,　　　　　　　　　　　70
We will aboard to-night. Why, how now,
　gentlemen?
What see you in those papers, that you lose

So much complexion? Look ye how they
　change!
Their cheeks are paper. Why, what read
　you there
That have so cowarded and chas'd your
　blood　　　　　　　　　　　75
Out of appearance?
　Cam.　　　　　I do confess my fault,
And do submit me to your Highness' mercy.
　Grey, Scroop. To which we all appeal.
　King. The mercy that was quick in us
　　but late
By your own counsel is suppress'd and
　kill'd.　　　　　　　　　　　80
You must not dare, for shame, to talk of
　mercy;
For your own reasons turn into your
　bosoms
As dogs upon their masters, worrying you.
See you, my princes and my noble peers,
These English monsters! My Lord of
　Cambridge here—　　　　　　85
You know how apt our love was to accord
To furnish him with all appertinents
Belonging to his honour; and this man
Hath, for a few light crowns, lightly
　conspir'd,
And sworn unto the practices of France　90
To kill us here in Hampton; to the which
This knight, no less for bounty bound to us
Than Cambridge is, hath likewise sworn.
But, O,
What shall I say to thee, Lord Scroop, thou
　cruel,
Ingrateful, savage, and inhuman creature?
Thou that didst bear the key of all my
　counsels,　　　　　　　　　　96
That knew'st the very bottom of my soul,
That almost mightst have coin'd me into
　gold,
Wouldst thou have practis'd on me for thy
　use—
May it be possible that foreign hire　100
Could out of thee extract one spark of
　evil
That might annoy my finger? 'Tis so
　strange
That, though the truth of it stands off as
　gross
As black and white, my eye will scarcely
　see it.
Treason and murder ever kept together, 105
As two yoke-devils sworn to either's
　purpose,
Working so grossly in a natural cause
That admiration did not whoop at them;
But thou, 'gainst all proportion, didst
　bring in　　　　　　　　　　109
Wonder to wait on treason and on murder;
And whatsoever cunning fiend it was
That wrought upon thee so preposterously
Hath got the voice in hell for excellence;
And other devils that suggest by treasons
Do botch and bungle up damnation　115

With patches, colours, and with forms,
    being fetch'd
From glist'ring semblances of piety;
But he that temper'd thee bade thee stand
    up,
Gave thee no instance why thou shouldst
    do treason,
Unless to dub thee with the name of
    traitor.   120
If that same demon that hath gull'd thee
    thus
Should with his lion gait walk the whole
    world,
He might return to vasty Tartar back,
And tell the legions ' I can never win
A soul so easy as that Englishman's '.   125
O, how hast thou with jealousy infected
The sweetness of affiance! Show men
    dutiful?
Why, so didst thou. Seem they grave and
    learned?
Why, so didst thou. Come they of noble
    family?
Why, so didst thou. Seem they religious?
Why, so didst thou. Or are they spare
    in diet,   131
Free from gross passion or of mirth or
    anger,
Constant in spirit, not swerving with the
    blood,
Garnish'd and deck'd in modest comple-
    ment,
Not working with the eye without the ear,
And but in purged judgment trusting
    neither?   136
Such and so finely bolted didst thou seem;
And thus thy fall hath left a kind of blot
To mark the full-fraught man and best
    indued   139
With some suspicion. I will weep for thee;
For this revolt of thine, methinks, is like
Another fall of man. Their faults are open.
Arrest them to the answer of the law;
And God acquit them of their practices!
    Exe. I arrest thee of high treason, by the
name of Richard Earl of Cambridge.   146
I arrest thee of high treason, by the name of
Henry Lord Scroop of Masham.
I arrest thee of high treason, by the name of
Thomas Grey, knight, of Northumberland.
    Scroop. Our purposes God justly hath
    discover'd,   151
And I repent my fault more than my death;
Which I beseech your Highness to forgive,
Although my body pay the price of it.
    Cam. For me, the gold of France did not
    seduce,   155
Although I did admit it as a motive
The sooner to effect what I intended;
But God be thanked for prevention,
Which I in sufferance heartily will rejoice,
Beseeching God and you to pardon me. 160
    Grey. Never did faithful subject more
    rejoice

At the discovery of most dangerous treason
Than I do at this hour joy o'er myself,
Prevented from a damned enterprise.
My fault, but not my body, pardon,
    sovereign.   165
    King. God quit you in his mercy! Hear
    your sentence.
You have conspir'd against our royal
    person,
Join'd with an enemy proclaim'd, and from
    his coffers
Receiv'd the golden earnest of our death;
Wherein you would have sold your king to
    slaughter,   170
His princes and his peers to servitude,
His subjects to oppression and contempt,
And his whole kingdom into desolation.
Touching our person seek we no revenge;
But we our kingdom's safety must so
    tender,   175
Whose ruin you have sought, that to her
    laws
We do deliver you. Get you therefore
    hence,
Poor miserable wretches, to your death;
The taste whereof God of his mercy give
You patience to endure, and true repent-
    ance   180
Of all your dear offences. Bear them hence.
        [*Exeunt Cambridge, Scroop, and
                Grey, guarded.*
Now, lords, for France; the enterprise
    whereof
Shall be to you as us like glorious.
We doubt not of a fair and lucky war,
Since God so graciously hath brought to
    light   185
This dangerous treason, lurking in our way
To hinder our beginnings; we doubt not
    now
But every rub is smoothed on our way.
Then, forth, dear countrymen; let us
    deliver
Our puissance into the hand of God,   190
Putting it straight in expedition.
Cheerly to sea; the signs of war advance;
No king of England, if not king of France!
        [*Flourish. Exeunt.*

SCENE III. *Eastcheap. Before the Boar's
            Head tavern.*

Enter PISTOL, Hostess, NYM, BARDOLPH,
            and Boy.

    Host. Prithee, honey-sweet husband, let
me bring thee to Staines.
    Pist. No; for my manly heart doth earn.
Bardolph, be blithe; Nym, rouse thy
            vaunting veins;
Boy, bristle thy courage up. For Falstaff
            he is dead,   5
And we must earn therefore.
    Bard. Would I were with him, where-
some'er he is, either in heaven or in hell! 8

Host. Nay, sure, he's not in hell : he's in Arthur's bosom, if ever man went to Arthur's bosom. 'A made a finer end, and went away an it had been any christom child ; 'a parted ev'n just between twelve and one, ev'n at the turning o' th' tide ; for after I saw him fumble with the sheets, and play with flowers, and smile upon his fingers' end, I knew there was but one way ; for his nose was as sharp as a pen, and 'a babbl'd of green fields. ' How now, Sir John ! ' quoth I ' What, man, be o' good cheer.' So 'a cried out ' God, God, God ! ' three or four times. Now I, to comfort him, bid him 'a should not think of God ; I hop'd there was no need to trouble himself with any such thoughts yet. So 'a bade me lay more clothes on his feet ; I put my hand into the bed and felt them, and they were as cold as any stone ; then I felt to his knees, and so upward and upward, and all was as cold as any stone.   26

Nym. They say he cried out of sack.

Host. Ay, that 'a did.

Bard. And of women.

Host. Nay, that 'a did not.   30

Boy. Yes, that 'a did, and said they were devils incarnate.

Host. 'A could never abide carnation ; 'twas a colour he never lik'd.   34

Boy. 'A said once the devil would have him about women.

Host. 'A did in some sort, indeed, handle women ; but then he was rheumatic, and talk'd of the Whore of Babylon.   39

Boy. Do you not remember 'a saw a flea stick upon Bardolph's nose, and 'a said it was a black soul burning in hell ?

Bard. Well, the fuel is gone that maintain'd that fire : that's all the riches I got in his service.

Nym. Shall we shog ? The King will be gone from Southampton.   46

Pist. Come, let's away. My love, give me thy lips.

Look to my chattels and my moveables ; Let senses rule. The word is ' Pitch and Pay '.

Trust none ;   50

For oaths are straws, men's faiths are wafer-cakes,

And Holdfast is the only dog, my duck.

Therefore, Caveto be thy counsellor.

Go, clear thy crystals. Yoke-fellows in arms,

Let us to France, like horse-leeches, my boys,   55

To suck, to suck, the very blood to suck.

Boy. And that's but unwholesome food, they say.

Pist. Touch her soft mouth and march.

Bard. Farewell, hostess.   [*Kissing her.*

Nym. I cannot kiss, that is the humour of it ; but, adieu.   61

Pist. Let housewifery appear ; keep close, I thee command.

Host. Farewell ; adieu.   [*Exeunt.*

SCENE IV. *France. The King's palace.*

Flourish.   *Enter the* FRENCH KING, *the* DAUPHIN, *the* DUKES OF BERRI *and* BRITAINE, *the* CONSTABLE, *and* Others.

Fr. King. Thus comes the English with full power upon us ;
And more than carefully it us concerns
To answer royally in our defences.
Therefore the Dukes of Berri and of Britaine,
Of Brabant and of Orleans, shall make forth,   5
And you, Prince Dauphin, with all swift dispatch,
To line and new repair our towns of war
With men of courage and with means defendant ;
For England his approaches makes as fierce
As waters to the sucking of a gulf.   10
It fits us, then, to be as provident
As fear may teach us, out of late examples
Left by the fatal and neglected English
Upon our fields.

Dau.   My most redoubted father,
It is most meet we arm us 'gainst the foe ;
For peace itself should not so dull a kingdom,   16
Though war nor no known quarrel were in question,
But that defences, musters, preparations,
Should be maintain'd, assembled, and collected,
As were a war in expectation.   20
Therefore, I say, 'tis meet we all go forth
To view the sick and feeble parts of France;
And let us do it with no show of fear—
No, with no more than if we heard that England   24
Were busied with a Whitsun morris-dance ;
For, my good liege, she is so idly king'd,
Her sceptre so fantastically borne
By a vain, giddy, shallow, humorous youth,
That fear attends her not.

Con.   O peace, Prince Dauphin !
You are too much mistaken in this king.   30
Question your Grace the late ambassadors
With what great state he heard their embassy,
How well supplied with noble counsellors,
How modest in exception, and withal
How terrible in constant resolution,   35
And you shall find his vanities forespent
Were but the outside of the Roman Brutus,
Covering discretion with a coat of folly ;
As gardeners do with ordure hide those roots
That shall first spring and be most delicate.

Dau. Well, 'tis not so, my Lord High Constable ;   41

But though we think it so, it is no matter.
In cases of defence 'tis best to weigh
The enemy more mighty than he seems ;
So the proportions of defence are fill'd ; 45
Which of a weak and niggardly projection
Doth like a miser spoil his coat with scant-
ing
A little cloth.

   Fr. King. Think we King Harry strong ;
And, Princes, look you strongly arm to
meet him.
The kindred of him hath been flesh'd upon
us ; 50
And he is bred out of that bloody strain
That haunted us in our familiar paths.
Witness our too much memorable shame
When Cressy battle fatally was struck,
And all our princes captiv'd by the hand 55
Of that black name, Edward, Black Prince
of Wales ;
Whiles that his mountain sire—on moun-
tain standing,
Up in the air, crown'd with the golden
sun—
Saw his heroical seed, and smil'd to see him, 60
Mangle the work of nature, and deface
The patterns that by God and by French
fathers
Had twenty years been made. This is a
stem
Of that victorious stock ; and let us fear
The native mightiness and fate of him.

        Enter a Messenger.

   Mess. Ambassadors from Harry King of
England 65
Do crave admittance to your Majesty.
   Fr. King. We'll give them present
    audience. Go and bring them.
      [*Exeunt Messenger and certain Lords.*
You see this chase is hotly followed,
friends.
   Dau. Turn head and stop pursuit ; for
coward dogs
Most spend their mouths when what they
seem to threaten 70
Runs far before them. Good my sovereign,
Take up the English short, and let them
know
Of what a monarchy you are the head.
Self-love, my liege, is not so vile a sin
As self-neglecting.

   Re-enter Lords, *with* EXETER *and* Train.

   Fr. King. From our brother of England ?
   Exe. From him, and thus he greets your
    Majesty : 76
He wills you, in the name of God Almighty,
That you divest yourself, and lay apart
The borrowed glories that by gift of
heaven,
By law of nature and of nations, 'longs 80
To him and to his heirs—namely, the
crown,

And all wide-stretched honours that
pertain,
By custom and the ordinance of times,
Unto the crown of France. That you may
know
'Tis no sinister nor no awkward claim, 85
Pick'd from the worm-holes of long-
vanish'd days,
Nor from the dust of old oblivion rak'd,
He sends you this most memorable line,
                [*Gives a paper.*
In every branch truly demonstrative ;
Willing you overlook this pedigree ; 90
And when you find him evenly deriv'd
From his most fam'd of famous ancestors,
Edward the Third, he bids you then resign
Your crown and kingdom, indirectly held
From him, the native and true challenger.
   Fr. King. Or else what follows ? 96
   Exe. Bloody constraint ; for if you hide
    the crown
Even in your hearts, there will he rake
for it.
Therefore in fierce tempest is he coming,
In thunder and in earthquake, like a Jove,
That if requiring fail, he will compel ; 101
And bids you, in the bowels of the Lord,
Deliver up the crown ; and to take mercy
On the poor souls for whom this hungry war
Opens his vasty jaws ; and on your head
Turning the widows' tears, the orphans'
cries, 106
The dead men's blood, the privy maidens'
groans,
For husbands, fathers, and betrothed
lovers,
That shall be swallowed in this controversy.
This is his claim, his threat'ning, and my
message ; 110
Unless the Dauphin be in presence here,
To whom expressly I bring greeting too.
   Fr. King. For us, we will consider of this
further ;
To-morrow shall you bear our full intent
Back to our brother of England.
   Dau.   For the Dauphin : 115
I stand here for him. What to him from
England ?
   Exe. Scorn and defiance, slight regard,
contempt,
And anything that may not misbecome
The mighty sender, doth he prize you at.
Thus says my king : an if your father's
Highness 120
Do not, in grant of all demands at large,
Sweeten the bitter mock you sent his
Majesty,
He'll call you to so hot an answer of it
That caves and womby vaultages of France
Shall chide your trespass and return your
mock 125
In second accent of his ordinance.
   Dau. Say, if my father render fair
return,

It is against my will ; for I desire
Nothing but odds with England. To that
    end,
As matching to his youth and vanity, 130
I did present him with the Paris balls.
    Exe. He'll make your Paris Louvre shake
        for it,
Were it the mistress court of mighty
    Europe ;
And be assur'd you'll find a difference, 134
As we his subjects have in wonder found,
Between the promise of his greener days
And these he masters now. Now he weighs
    time
Even to the utmost grain ; that you shall
    read
In your own losses, if he stay in France.
    Fr. King. To-morrow shall you know our
        mind at full.   140
    Exe. Dispatch us with all speed, lest that
        our king
Come here himself to question our delay ;
For he is footed in this land already.
    Fr. King. You shall be soon dispatch'd
        with fair conditions.   144
A night is but small breath and little pause
To answer matters of this consequence.
                        [*Flourish. Exeunt.*

ACT THREE

PROLOGUE

Flourish. Enter CHORUS.

    Chor. Thus with imagin'd wing our swift
        scene flies,
In motion of no less celerity
Than that of thought.   Suppose that you
    have seen
The well-appointed King at Hampton pier
Embark his royalty ; and his brave fleet 5
With silken streamers the young Phœbus
    fanning.
Play with your fancies ; and in them behold
Upon the hempen tackle ship-boys climb-
    ing ;
Hear the shrill whistle which doth order
    give
To sounds confus'd ; behold the threaden
    sails,   10
Borne with th' invisible and creeping wind,
Draw the huge bottoms through the
    furrowed sea,
Breasting the lofty surge. O, do but think
You stand upon the rivage and behold
A city on th' inconstant billows dancing ; 15
For so appears this fleet majestical,
Holding due course to Harfleur. Follow,
    follow !
Grapple your minds to sternage of this navy
And leave your England as dead midnight
    still,
Guarded with grandsires, babies, and old
    women,   20

Either past or not arriv'd to pith and
    puissance ;
For who is he whose chin is but enrich'd
With one appearing hair that will not follow
These cull'd and choice-drawn cavaliers to
    France ?
Work, work your thoughts, and therein see
    a siege ;   25
Behold the ordnance on their carriages,
With fatal mouths gaping on girded
    Harfleur.
Suppose th' ambassador from the French
    comes back ;
Tells Harry that the King doth offer him
Katharine his daughter, and with her to
    dowry   30
Some petty and unprofitable dukedoms.
The offer likes not ; and the nimble gunner
With linstock now the devilish cannon
    touches,
                [*Alarum, and chambers go off.*
And down goes all before them. Still be
    kind,   34
And eke out our performance with your
    mind.   [*Exit.*

SCENE I. *France. Before Harfleur.*

Alarum.   Enter the KING, EXETER,
    BEDFORD, GLOUCESTER, *and* Soldiers
    with scaling-ladders.

    King. Once more unto the breach, dear
        friends, once more ;
Or close the wall up with our English dead.
In peace there's nothing so becomes a man
As modest stillness and humility ;   4
But when the blast of war blows in our ears,
Then imitate the action of the tiger :
Stiffen the sinews, summon up the blood,
Disguise fair nature with hard-favour'd
    rage ;
Then lend the eye a terrible aspect ;
Let it pry through the portage of the head
Like the brass cannon ; let the brow
    o'erwhelm it   11
As fearfully as doth a galled rock
O'erhang and jutty his confounded base,
Swill'd with the wild and wasteful ocean.
Now set the teeth and stretch the nostril
    wide ;   15
Hold hard the breath, and bend up every
    spirit
To his full height. On, on, you noblest
    English,
Whose blood is fet from fathers of war-
    proof—
Fathers that like so many Alexanders
Have in these parts from morn till even
    fought,   20
And sheath'd their swords for lack of
    argument.
Dishonour not your mothers ; now attest
That those whom you call'd fathers did
    beget you.

Be copy now to men of grosser blood,
And teach them how to war. And you,
    good yeomen,   25
Whose limbs were made in England, show
    us here
The mettle of your pasture ; let us swear
That you are worth your breeding—which
    I doubt not ;
For there is none of you so mean and base
That hath not noble lustre in your eyes. 30
I see you stand like greyhounds in the slips,
Straining upon the start. The game's afoot :
Follow your spirit ; and upon this charge
Cry ' God for Harry, England, and Saint
    George ! '
    [*Exeunt. Alarum, and chambers go off.*

SCENE II. *Before Harfleur.*

Enter NYM, BARDOLPH, PISTOL, *and* Boy.

Bard. On, on, on, on, on ! to the breach,
to the breach !
Nym. Pray thee, Corporal, stay ; the
knocks are too hot, and for mine own part
I have not a case of lives. The humour of
it is too hot ; that is the very plain-song
of it.   5
Pist. The plain-song is most just ; for
    humours do abound.
Knocks go and come ; God's vassals drop
        and die ;
    And sword and shield
    In bloody field
Doth win immortal fame.   10
Boy. Would I were in an alehouse in
London ! I would give all my fame for a
pot of ale and safety.
Pist. And I :
    If wishes would prevail with me,
    My purpose should not fail with me, 15
    But thither would I hie.
Boy. As duly, but not as truly,
    As bird doth sing on bough.

Enter FLUELLEN.

Flu. Up to the breach, you dogs !
Avaunt, you cullions !   20
            [*Driving them forward.*
Pist. Be merciful, great duke, to men of
    mould.
Abate thy rage, abate thy manly rage ;
Abate thy rage, great duke.
Good bawcock, bate thy rage. Use lenity,
    sweet chuck.
Nym. These be good humours. Your
honour wins bad humours.   26
            [*Exeunt all but Boy.*
Boy. As young as I am, I have observ'd
these three swashers. I am boy to them
all three ; but all they three, though they
would serve me, could not be man to me ;
for indeed three such antics do not amount
to a man. For Bardolph, he is white-
liver'd and red-fac'd ; by the means

whereof 'a faces it out, but fights not. For
Pistol, he hath a killing tongue and a
quiet sword ; by the means whereof 'a
breaks words and keeps whole weapons.
For Nym, he hath heard that men of few
words are the best men, and therefore he
scorns to say his prayers lest 'a should be
thought a coward ; but his few bad words
are match'd with as few good deeds ; for 'a
never broke any man's head but his own,
and that was against a post when he was
drunk. They will steal anything, and call
it purchase. Bardolph stole a lute-case,
bore it twelve leagues, and sold it for three
halfpence. Nym and Bardolph are sworn
brothers in filching, and in Calais they stole
a fire-shovel ; I knew by that piece of
service the men would carry coals. They
would have me as familiar with men's
pockets as their gloves or their hand-
kerchers ; which makes much against my
manhood, if I should take from another's
pocket to put into mine ; for it is plain
pocketing up of wrongs. I must leave them
and seek some better service ; their villainy
goes against my weak stomach, and therefore I must cast it up.   [*Exit.*

Re-enter FLUELLEN, GOWER *following.*

Gow. Captain Fluellen, you must come
presently to the mines ; the Duke of
Gloucester would speak with you.   53
Flu. To the mines ! Tell you the Duke
it is not so good to come to the mines ; for,
look you, the mines is not according to the
disciplines of the war ; the concavities of
it is not sufficient. For, look you, th'
athversary—you may discuss unto the
Duke, look you—is digt himself four yard
under the countermines ; by Cheshu, I
think 'a will plow up all, if there is not
better directions.   60
Gow. The Duke of Gloucester, to whom
the order of the siege is given, is altogether
directed by an Irishman—a very valiant
gentleman, i' faith.
Flu. It is Captain Macmorris, is it not ?
Gow. I think it be.   65
Flu. By Cheshu, he is an ass, as in the
world : I will verify as much in his beard ;
he has no more directions in the true
disciplines of the wars, look you, of the
Roman disciplines, than is a puppy-dog.

Enter MACMORRIS *and* Captain JAMY.

Gow. Here 'a comes ; and the Scots
captain, Captain Jamy, with him.   71
Flu. Captain Jamy is a marvellous
falorous gentleman, that is certain, and of
great expedition and knowledge in th'
aunchiant wars, upon my particular
knowledge of his directions. By Cheshu,
he will maintain his argument as well as
any military man in the world, in the

564

disciplines of the pristine wars of the Romans.   77

Jamy. I say gud day, Captain Fluellen.

Flu. God-den to your worship, good Captain James.

Gow. How now, Captain Macmorris! Have you quit the mines? Have the pioneers given o'er?   81

Mac. By Chrish, la, tish ill done! The work ish give over, the trompet sound the retreat. By my hand, I swear, and my father's soul, the work ish ill done; it ish give over; I would have blowed up the town, so Chrish save me, la, in an hour. O, tish ill done, tish ill done; by my hand, tish ill done!   87

Flu. Captain Macmorris, I beseech you now, will you voutsafe me, look you, a few disputations with you, as partly touching or concerning the disciplines of the war, the Roman wars, in the way of argument, look you, and friendly communication; partly to satisfy my opinion, and partly for the satisfaction, look you, of my mind, as touching the direction of the military discipline, that is the point.   95

Jamy. It sall be vary gud, gud feith, gud captains bath; and I sall quit you with gud leve, as I may pick occasion; that sall I, marry.   98

Mac. It is no time to discourse, so Chrish save me. The day is hot, and the weather, and the wars, and the King, and the Dukes; it is no time to discourse. The town is beseech'd, and the trumpet call us to the breach; and we talk and, be Chrish, do nothing. 'Tis shame for us all, so God sa' me, 'tis shame to stand still; it is shame, by my hand; and there is throats to be cut, and works to be done; and there ish nothing done, so Chrish sa' me, la.   107

Jamy. By the mess, ere theise eyes of mine take themselves to slomber, ay'll de gud service, or I'll lig i' th' grund for it; ay, or go to death. And I'll pay't as valorously as I may, that sall I suerly do, that is the breff and the long. Marry, I wad full fain heard some question 'tween you tway.

Flu. Captain Macmorris, I think, look you, under your correction, there is not many of your nation—   115

Mac. Of my nation? What ish my nation? Ish a villain, and a bastard, and a knave, and a rascal. What ish my nation? Who talks of my nation?   118

Flu. Look you, if you take the matter otherwise than is meant, Captain Macmorris, peradventure I shall think you do not use me with that affability as in discretion you ought to use me, look you; being as good a man as yourself, both in the disciplines of war and in the derivation of my birth, and in other particularities. 124

Mac. I do not know you so good a man as myself; so Chrish save me, I will cut off your head.

Gow. Gentlemen both, you will mistake each other.

Jamy. Ah! that's a foul fault.

                         [*A parley sounded.*

Gow. The town sounds a parley.   129

Flu. Captain Macmorris, when there is more better opportunity to be required, look you, I will be so bold as to tell you I know the disciplines of war; and there is an end.   [*Exeunt.*

SCENE III.   *Before the gates of Harfleur.*

Enter the Governor *and some* Citizens *on the walls. Enter the* KING *and all his* Train *before the gates.*

King. How yet resolves the Governor of
    the town?
This is the latest parle we will admit;
Therefore to our best mercy give your-
    selves
Or, like to men proud of destruction,
Defy us to our worst; for, as I am a
    soldier,   5
A name that in my thoughts becomes me
    best,
If I begin the batt'ry once again,
I will not leave the half-achieved Harfleur
Till in her ashes she lie buried.
The gates of mercy shall be all shut up, 10
And the flesh'd soldier, rough and hard of
    heart,
In liberty of bloody hand shall range
With conscience wide as hell, mowing like
    grass
Your fresh fair virgins and your flow'ring
    infants.
What is it then to me if impious war,   15
Array'd in flames, like to the prince of
    fiends,
Do, with his smirch'd complexion, all fell
    feats
Enlink'd to waste and desolation?
What is't to me when you yourselves are
    cause,
If your pure maidens fall into the hand 20
Of hot and forcing violation?
What rein can hold licentious wickedness
When down the hill he holds his fierce
    career?
We may as bootless spend our vain com-
    mand
Upon th' enraged soldiers in their spoil, 25
As send precepts to the Leviathan
To come ashore. Therefore, you men of
    Harfleur,
Take pity of your town and of your people
Whiles yet my soldiers are in my command;
Whiles yet the cool and temperate wind of
    grace   30
O'erblows the filthy and contagious clouds

Of heady murder, spoil, and villainy.
If not—why, in a moment look to see
The blind and bloody soldier with foul hand
Defile the locks of your shrill-shrieking
    daughters ;   35
Your fathers taken by the silver beards,
And their most reverend heads dash'd to
    the walls ;
Your naked infants spitted upon pikes,
Whiles the mad mothers with their howls
    confus'd
Do break the clouds, as did the wives of
    Jewry   40
At Herod's bloody-hunting slaughtermen.
What say you ? Will you yield, and this
    avoid ?
Or, guilty in defence, be thus destroy'd ?
    Gov. Our expectation hath this day an
    end :
The Dauphin, whom of succours we en-
    treated,   45
Returns us that his powers are yet not
    ready
To raise so great a siege. Therefore, great
    King,
We yield our town and lives to thy soft
    mercy.
Enter our gates ; dispose of us and ours ;
For we no longer are defensible.   50
    King. Open your gates. [*Exit Governor.*
Come, uncle Exeter,
Go you and enter Harfleur ; there remain,
And fortify it strongly 'gainst the French ;
Use mercy to them all. For us, dear uncle,
The winter coming on, and sickness growing
Upon our soldiers, we will retire to Calais.
To-night in Harfleur will we be your guest ;
To-morrow for the march are we addrest.
    [*Flourish. The King and his train
    enter the town.*

SCENE IV.   *Rouen. The French King's
palace.*

Enter KATHERINE *and* ALICE.

Kath. Alice, tu as été en Angleterre, et tu
parles bien le langage.
    Alice. Un peu, madame.
    Kath. Je te prie, m'enseignez ; il faut que
j'apprenne à parler. Comment appelez-
vous la main en Anglais ?   5
    Alice. La main ? Elle est appelée de hand.
    Kath. De hand. Et les doigts ?
    Alice. Les doigts ? Ma foi, j'oublie les
doigts ; mais je me souviendrai. Les
doigts ? Je pense qu'ils sont appelés de
fingres ; oui, de fingres.   10
    Kath. La main, de hand ; les doigts,
de fingres. Je pense que je suis le bon
écolier ; j'ai gagné deux mots d'Anglais
vîtement. Comment appelez-vous les
ongles ?
    Alice. Les ongles ? Nous les appelons de
nails.

    Kath. De nails. Ecoutez ; dites-moi si
je parle bien : de hand, de fingres, et
de nails.   16
    Alice. C'est bien dit, madame ; il est fort
bon Anglais.
    Kath. Dites-moi l'Anglais pour le
bras.
    Alice. De arm, madame.
    Kath. Et le coude ?   20
    Alice. D'elbow.
    Kath. D'elbow. Je m'en fais la répétition
de tous les mots que vous m'avez appris
dès à présent.
    Alice. Il est trop difficile, madame,
comme je pense.
    Kath. Excusez-moi, Alice ; écoutez :
d'hand, de fingre, de nails, d'arma, de
bilbow.   26
    Alice, D'elbow, madame.
    Kath. O Seigneur Dieu, je m'en oublie !
D'elbow. Comment appelez-vous le col ?
    Alice. De nick, madame.   30
    Kath. De nick. Et le menton ?
    Alice. De chin.
    Kath. De sin. Le col, de nick ; le
menton, de sin.
    Alice. Oui. Sauf votre honneur, en
vérité, vous prononcez les mots aussi droit
que les natifs d'Angleterre.
    Kath. Je ne doute point d'apprendre, par
la grace de Dieu, et en peu de temps.   37
    Kath. N'avez-vous pas déjà oublié ce que
je vous ai enseigné ?
    Kath. Non, je reciterai à vous prompte-
ment : d'hand, de fingre, de mails—
    Alice. De nails, madame.   42
    Alice. Sauf votre honneur, d'elbow.
    Kath. Ainsi dis-je ; d'elbow, de nick,
et de sin. Comment appelez-vous le pied
et la robe ?   46
    Alice. Le foot, madame ; et le count.
    Kath. Le foot et le count. O Seigneur
Dieu ! ils sont mots de son mauvais,
corruptible, gros, et impudique, et non
pour les dames d'honneur d'user : je ne
voudrais prononcer ces mots devant les
seigneurs de France pour tout le monde.
Foh ! le foot et le count ! Néanmoins,
je reciterai une autre fois ma leçon en-
semble : d'hand, de fingre, de nails,
d'arm, d'elbow, de nick, de sin, de
foot, le count.   55
    Alice. Excellent, madame !
    Kath. C'est assez pour une fois : allons-
nous à dîner.   [*Exeunt.*

SCENE V. *The French King's palace.*

Enter the KING OF FRANCE, *the* DAUPHIN,
DUKE OF BRITAINE, *the* CONSTABLE OF
FRANCE, *and* Others.

    Fr. King. 'Tis certain he hath pass'd the
    river Somme.

Con. And if he be not fought withal, my
    lord,
Let us not live in France; let us quit all,
And give our vineyards to a barbarous
    people.
    Dau. O Dieu vivant! Shall a few sprays
    of us,   5
The emptying of our fathers' luxury,
Our scions, put in wild and savage stock,
Spirt up so suddenly into the clouds,
And overlook their grafters?
    Brit. Normans, but bastard Normans,
    Norman bastards!   10
Mort Dieu, ma vie! if they march along
Unfought withal, but I will sell my duke-
    dom
To buy a slobb'ry and a dirty farm
In that nook-shotten isle of Albion.
    Con. Dieu de batailles! where have they
    this mettle?   15
Is not their climate foggy, raw, and dull;
On whom, as in despite, the sun looks pale,
Killing their fruit with frowns? Can sodden
    water,
A drench for sur-rein'd jades, their barley-
    broth,
Decoct their cold blood to such valiant
    heat?   20
And shall our quick blood, spirited with
    wine,
Seem frosty? O, for honour of our land,
Let us not hang like roping icicles
Upon our houses' thatch, whiles a more
    frosty people
Sweat drops of gallant youth in our rich
    fields—   25
Poor we call them in their native lords!
    Dau. By faith and honour,
Our madams mock at us and plainly say
Our mettle is bred out, and they will give
Their bodies to the lust of English youth   30
To new-store France with bastard warriors.
    Brit. They bid us to the English dancing-
    schools
And teach lavoltas high and swift corantos,
Saying our grace is only in our heels
And that we are most lofty runaways.   35
    Fr. King. Where is Montjoy the herald?
    Speed him hence;
Let him greet England with our sharp
    defiance.
Up, Princes, and, with spirit of honour
    edged
More sharper than your swords, hie to the
    field:
Charles Delabreth, High Constable of
    France;   40
You Dukes of Orleans, Bourbon, and of
    Berri,
Alençon, Brabant, Bar, and Burgundy;
Jaques Chatillon, Rambures, Vaudemont,
Beaumont, Grandpré, Roussi, and Faucon-
    bridge,
Foix, Lestrake, Bouciqualt, and Charolois;

High dukes, great princes, barons, lords,
    and knights,   46
For your great seats now quit you of great
    shames.
Bar Harry England, that sweeps through
    our land
With pennons painted in the blood of
    Harfleur.
Rush on his host as doth the melted snow   50
Upon the valleys, whose low vassal seat
The Alps doth spit and void his rheum
    upon;
Go down upon him, you have power
    enough,
And in a captive chariot into Rouen
Bring him our prisoner.
    Con.   This becomes the great.   55
Sorry am I his numbers are so few,
His soldiers sick and famish'd in their
    march;
For I am sure, when he shall see our army,
He'll drop his heart into the sink of fear,
And for achievement offer us his ransom.   60
    Fr. King. Therefore, Lord Constable,
    haste on Montjoy,
And let him say to England that we send
To know what willing ransom he will give.
Prince Dauphin, you shall stay with us in
    Rouen.
    Dau. Not so, I do beseech your Majesty.
    Fr. King. Be patient, for you shall
    remain with us.   66
Now forth, Lord Constable and Princes all,
And quickly bring us word of England's
    fall.   [*Exeunt.*

SCENE VI. *The English camp in Picardy.*

Enter Captains, *English and Welsh,* GOWER
    and FLUELLEN.

    Gow. How now, Captain Fluellen! Come
you from the bridge?
    Flu. I assure you there is very excellent
services committed at the bridge.
    Gow. Is the Duke of Exeter safe?   5
    Flu. The Duke of Exeter is as magnani-
mous as Agamemnon; and a man that I
love and honour with my soul, and my
heart, and my duty, and my live, and my
living, and my uttermost power. He is not
—God be praised and blessed!—any hurt
in the world, but keeps the bridge most
valiantly, with excellent discipline. There
is an aunchient Lieutenant there at the
bridge—I think in my very conscience he
is as valiant a man as Mark Antony; and
he is a man of no estimation in the world;
but I did see him do as gallant service.   15
    Gow. What do you call him?
    Flu. He is call'd Aunchient Pistol.
    Gow. I know him not.

            Enter PISTOL.

    Flu. Here is the man.

Pist. Captain, I thee beseech to do me
favours.   20
The Duke of Exeter doth love thee
well.
Flu. Ay, I praise God ; and I have
merited some love at his hands.
Pist. Bardolph, a soldier, firm and sound
of heart,   24
And of buxom valour, hath by cruel fate
And giddy Fortune's furious fickle wheel,
That goddess blind,
That stands upon the rolling restless
stone—
Flu. By your patience, Aunchient Pistol.
Fortune is painted blind, with a muffler
afore her eyes, to signify to you that
Fortune is blind ; and she is painted also
with a wheel, to signify to you, which is the
moral of it, that she is turning, and inconstant, and mutability, and variation ; and
her foot, look you, is fixed upon a spherical
stone, which rolls, and rolls, and rolls. In
good truth, the poet makes a most excellent
description of it : Fortune is an excellent
moral.   37
Pist. Fortune is Bardolph's foe, and
frowns on him ;
For he hath stol'n a pax, and hanged must
'a be—
A damned death !   40
Let gallows gape for dog ; let man go free,
And let not hemp his windpipe suffocate.
But Exeter hath given the doom of death
For pax of little price.
Therefore, go speak—the Duke will hear
thy voice ;   45
And let not Bardolph's vital thread be cut
With edge of penny cord and vile reproach.
Speak, Captain, for his life, and I will thee
requite.
Flu. Aunchient Pistol, I do partly under-
stand your meaning.   50
Pist. Why then, rejoice therefore.
Flu. Certainly, Aunchient, it is not a
thing to rejoice at ; for if, look you, he
were my brother, I would desire the Duke
to use his good pleasure, and put him to
execution ; for discipline ought to be used.
Pist. Die and be damn'd ! and figo for
thy friendship !   56
Flu. It is well.
Pist. The fig of Spain !   [*Exit.*
Flu. Very good.
Gow. Why, this is an arrant counterfeit
rascal ; I remember him now—a bawd, a
cutpurse.   61
Flu. I'll assure you, 'a utt'red as prave
words at the pridge as you shall see in a
summer's day. But it is very well ; what
he has spoke to me, that is well, I warrant
you, when time is serve.   65
Gow. Why, 'tis a gull, a fool, a rogue, that
now and then goes to the wars to grace
himself, at his return into London, under

the form of a soldier. And such fellows are
perfect in the great commanders' names ;
and they will learn you by rote where
services were done—at such and such a
sconce, at such a breach, at such a convoy ;
who came off bravely, who was shot, who
disgrac'd, what terms the enemy stood on ;
and this they con perfectly in the phrase of
war, which they trick up with new-tuned
oaths ; and what a beard of the General's
cut and a horrid suit of the camp will do
among foaming bottles and ale-wash'd
wits is wonderful to be thought on. But
you must learn to know such slanders of
the age, or else you may be marvellously
mistook.   79
Flu. I tell you what, Captain Gower, I
do perceive he is not the man that he would
gladly make show to the world he is ; if I
find a hole in his coat I will tell him my
mind. [*Drum within*] Hark you, the King
is coming ; and I must speak with him
from the pridge.

Drum and colours. Enter the KING *and his
poor* Soldiers, *and* GLOUCESTER.

God pless your Majesty !   85
  King. How now, Fluellen ! Cam'st thou
from the bridge ?
  Flu. Ay, so please your Majesty. The
Duke of Exeter has very gallantly maintain'd the pridge ; the French is gone off,
look you, and there is gallant and most
prave passages. Marry, th' athversary was
have possession of the pridge ; but he is
enforced to retire, and the Duke of Exeter
is master of the pridge ; I can tell your
Majesty the Duke is a prave man.   93
  King. What men have you lost, Fluellen?
  Flu. The perdition of th' athversary hath
been very great, reasonable great ; marry,
for my part, I think the Duke hath lost
never a man, but one that is like to be
executed for robbing a church—one
Bardolph, if your Majesty know the man ;
his face is all bubukles, and whelks, and
knobs, and flames o' fire ; and his lips
blows at his nose, and it is like a coal of
fire, sometimes plue and sometimes red ;
but his nose is executed and his fire's out.
  King. We would have all such offenders
so cut off. And we give express charge
that in our marches through the country
there be nothing compell'd from the
villages, nothing taken but paid for, none
of the French upbraided or abused in
disdainful language ; for when lenity and
cruelty play for a kingdom the gentler
gamester is the soonest winner.

Tucket. Enter MONTJOY.

  Mont. You know me by my habit. 110
  King. Well then, I know thee ; what
shall I know of thee ?

Mont. My master's mind.

King. Unfold it.   113

Mont. Thus says my king. Say thou to Harry of England : Though we seem'd dead we did but sleep ; advantage is a better soldier than rashness. Tell him we could have rebuk'd him at Harfleur, but that we thought not good to bruise an injury till it were full ripe. Now we speak upon our cue, and our voice is imperial : England shall repent his folly, see his weakness, and admire our sufferance. Bid him therefore consider of his ransom, which must proportion the losses we have borne, the subjects we have lost, the disgrace we have digested; which, in weight to re-answer, his pettiness would bow under. For our losses his exchequer is too poor ; for th' effusion of our blood, the muster of his kingdom too faint a number ; and for our disgrace, his own person kneeling at our feet but a weak and worthless satisfaction. To this add defiance ; and tell him, for conclusion, he hath betrayed his followers, whose condemnation is pronounc'd. So far my king and master ; so much my office.   131

King. What is thy name ? I know thy quality.

Mont. Montjoy.

King. Thou dost thy office fairly. Turn thee back,   134

And tell thy king I do not seek him now,
But could be willing to march on to Calais
Without impeachment ; for, to say the sooth—
Though 'tis no wisdom to confess so much
Unto an enemy of craft and vantage—
My people are with sickness much enfeebled ;   140
My numbers lessen'd ; and those few I have
Almost no better than so many French ;
Who when they were in health, I tell thee, herald,
I thought upon one pair of English legs
Did march three Frenchmen. Yet forgive me, God,   145
That I do brag thus ; this your air of France
Hath blown that vice in me ; I must repent.
Go, therefore, tell thy master here I am ;
My ransom is this frail and worthless trunk ;
My army but a weak and sickly guard ;   150
Yet, God before, tell him we will come on,
Though France himself and such another neighbour
Stand in our way. There's for thy labour, Montjoy.
Go, bid thy master well advise himself.
If we may pass, we will ; if we be hind'red,
We shall your tawny ground with your red blood   156
Discolour ; and so, Montjoy, fare you well.
The sum of all our answer is but this :

We would not seek a battle as we are ;
Nor as we are, we say, we will not shun it.
So tell your master.   161

Mont. I shall deliver so. Thanks to your Highness.   [*Exit.*

Glo. I hope they will not come upon us now.

King. We are in God's hand, brother, not in theirs.
March to the bridge, it now draws toward night ;   165
Beyond the river we'll encamp ourselves,
And on to-morrow bid them march away.
[*Exeunt.*

SCENE VII. *The French camp near Agincourt.*

Enter the CONSTABLE OF FRANCE, *the* LORD RAMBURES, *the* DUKE OF ORLEANS, *the* DAUPHIN, *with* Others.

Con. Tut ! I have the best armour of the world. Would it were day !

Orl. You have an excellent armour ; but let my horse have his due.

Con. It is the best horse of Europe.   5

Orl. Will it never be morning ?

Dau. My Lord of Orleans and my Lord High Constable, you talk of horse and armour ?

Orl. You are as well provided of both as any prince in the world.   10

Dau. What a long night is this ! I will not change my horse with any that treads but on four pasterns. Ça, ha ! he bounds from the earth as if his entrails were hairs ; le cheval volant, the Pegasus, chez les narines de feu ! When I bestride him I soar, I am a hawk. He trots the air ; the earth sings when he touches it ; the basest horn of his hoof is more musical than the pipe of Hermes.

Orl. He's of the colour of the nutmeg.   19

Dau. And of the heat of the ginger. It is a beast for Perseus : he is pure air and fire ; and the dull elements of earth and water never appear in him, but only in patient stillness while his rider mounts him ; he is indeed a horse, and all other jades you may call beasts.

Con. Indeed, my lord, it is a most absolute and excellent horse.   26

Dau. It is the prince of palfreys ; his neigh is like the bidding of a monarch, and his countenance enforces homage.

Orl. No more, cousin.   30

Dau. Nay, the man hath no wit that cannot, from the rising of the lark to the lodging of the lamb, vary deserved praise on my palfrey. It is a theme as fluent as the sea : turn the sands into eloquent tongues, and my horse is argument for them all ; 'tis a subject for a sovereign to reason

on, and for a sovereign's sovereign to ride
on ; and for the world—familiar to us and
unknown—to lay apart their particular
functions and wonder at him. I once writ
a sonnet in his praise and began thus:
' Wonder of nature '—   40
Orl. I have heard a sonnet begin so to
one's mistress.
Dau. Then did they imitate that which I
compos'd to my courser ; for my horse is
my mistress.
Orl. Your mistress bears well.
Dau. Me well ; which is the prescript
praise and perfection of a good and
particular mistress.   46
Con. Nay, for methought yesterday your
mistress shrewdly shook your back.
Dau. So perhaps did yours.
Con. Mine was not bridled.   50
Dau. O, then belike she was old and
gentle ; and you rode like a kern of Ireland,
your French hose off and in your strait
strossers.
Con. You have good judgment in horse-
manship.   54
Dau. Be warn'd by me, then : they that
ride so, and ride not warily, fall into foul
bogs. I had rather have my horse to my
mistress.
Con. I had as lief have my mistress a
jade.
Dau. I tell thee, Constable, my mistress
wears his own hair.   60
Con. I could make as true a boast as that,
if I had a sow to my mistress.
Dau. ' Le chien est retourné à son propre
vomissement, et la truie lavée au bourbier.'
Thou mak'st use of anything.   65
Con. Yet do I not use my horse for my
mistress, or any such proverb so little kin
to the purpose.
Ram. My Lord Constable, the armour
that I saw in your tent to-night—are those
stars or suns upon it ?
Con. Stars, my lord.   70
Dau. Some of them will fall to-morrow,
I hope.
Con. And yet my sky shall not want.
Dau. That may be, for you bear a many
superfluously, and 'twere more honour some
were away.
Con. Ev'n as your horse bears your
praises, who would trot as well were some
of your brags dismounted.   76
Dau. Would I were able to load him with
his desert ! Will it never be day ? I will
trot to-morrow a mile, and my way shall
be paved with English faces.   79
Con. I will not say so, for fear I should
be fac'd out of my way ; but I would it
were morning, for I would fain be about the
ears of the English.
Ram. Who will go to hazard with me for
twenty prisoners ?

Con. You must first go yourself to hazard
ere you have them.   86
Dau. 'Tis midnight ; I'll go arm myself.
                                              [*Exit.*
Orl. The Dauphin longs for morning.
Ram. He longs to eat the English.
Con. I think he will eat all he kills.   90
Orl. By the white hand of my lady, he's
a gallant prince.
Con. Swear by her foot, that she may
tread out the oath.
Orl. He is simply the most active gentle-
man of France.   95
Con. Doing is activity, and he will still
be doing.
Orl. He never did harm that I heard of.
Con. Nor will do none to-morrow : he
will keep that good name still.
Orl. I know him to be valiant.   100
Con. I was told that by one that knows
him better than you.
Orl. What's he ?
Con. Marry, he told me so himself ; and
he said he car'd not who knew it.   105
Orl. He needs not ; it is no hidden virtue
in him.
Con. By my faith, sir, but it is ; never
anybody saw it but his lackey. 'Tis a
hooded valour, and when it appears it will
bate.
Orl. Ill-will never said well.   110
Con. I will cap that proverb with ' There
is flattery in friendship '.
Orl. And I will take up that with ' Give
the devil his due '.   114
Con. Well plac'd ! There stands your
friend for the devil ; have at the very eye
of that proverb with ' A pox of the devil ! '
Orl. You are the better at proverbs by
how much ' A fool's bolt is soon shot '.
Con. You have shot over.   120
Orl. 'Tis not the first time you were
overshot.

Enter a Messenger.

Mess. My Lord High Constable, the
English lie within fifteen hundred paces of
your tents.
Con. Who hath measur'd the ground ?
Mess. The Lord Grandpré.   125
Con. A valiant and most expert gentleman. Would it were day ! Alas, poor
Harry of England ! he longs not for the
dawning as we do.
Orl. What a wretched and peevish fellow
is this King of England, to mope with his
fat-brain'd followers so far out of his
knowledge !   131
Con. If the English had any apprehension,
they would run away.
Orl. That they lack ; for if their heads
had any intellectual armour, they could
never wear such heavy head-pieces.   136
Ram. That island of England breeds very

valiant creatures ; their mastiffs are of unmatchable courage.

Orl. Foolish curs, that run winking into the mouth of a Russian bear, and have their heads crush'd like rotten apples ! You may as well say that's a valiant flea that dare eat his breakfast on the lip of a lion.

Con. Just, just ! and the men do sympathise with the mastiffs in robustious and rough coming on, leaving their wits with their wives ; and then give them great meals of beef and iron and steel ; they will eat like wolves and fight like devils.　147

Orl. Ay, but these English are shrewdly out of beef.

Con. Then shall we find to-morrow they have only stomachs to eat, and none to fight. Now is it time to arm. Come, shall we about it ?　151

Orl. It is now two o'clock ; but let me see—by ten
We shall have each a hundred Englishmen.
[*Exeunt.*

ACT FOUR

PROLOGUE

Enter CHORUS.

Chor. Now entertain conjecture of a time
When creeping murmur and the poring dark
Fills the wide vessel of the universe.
From camp to camp, through the foul womb of night,
The hum of either army stilly sounds,　5
That the fix'd sentinels almost receive
The secret whispers of each other's watch.
Fire answers fire, and through their paly flames
Each battle sees the other's umber'd face ;
Steed threatens steed, in high and boastful neighs　10
Piercing the night's dull ear ; and from the tents
The armourers accomplishing the knights,
With busy hammers closing rivets up,
Give dreadful note of preparation.
The country cocks do crow, the clocks do toll,　15
And the third hour of drowsy morning name.
Proud of their numbers and secure in soul,
The confident and over-lusty French
Do the low-rated English play at dice ;
And chide the cripple tardy-gaited night　20
Who like a foul and ugly witch doth limp
So tediously away.　The poor condemned English,
Like sacrifices, by their watchful fires
Sit patiently and inly ruminate
The morning's danger ; and their gesture sad　25
Investing lank-lean cheeks and war-worn coats

Presenteth them unto the gazing moon
So many horrid ghosts.　O, now, who will behold
The royal captain of this ruin'd band
Walking from watch to watch, from tent to tent,　30
Let him cry ' Praise and glory on his head ! '
For forth he goes and visits all his host ;
Bids them good morrow with a modest smile,
And calls them brothers, friends, and countrymen.
Upon his royal face there is no note　35
How dread an army hath enrounded him ;
Nor doth he dedicate one jot of colour
Unto the weary and all-watched night ;
But freshly looks, and over-bears attaint
With cheerful semblance and sweet majesty ;　40
That every wretch, pining and pale before,
Beholding him, plucks comfort from his looks ;
A largess universal, like the sun,
His liberal eye doth give to every one,
Thawing cold fear, that mean and gentle all
Behold, as may unworthiness define,　46
A little touch of Harry in the night.
And so our scene must to the battle fly ;
Where—O for pity !—we shall much disgrace
With four or five most vile and ragged foils,
Right ill-dispos'd in brawl ridiculous,　51
The name of Agincourt.　Yet sit and see,
Minding true things by what their mock'ries be.　[*Exit.*

SCENE I.　*France.　The English camp at Agincourt.*

Enter the KING, BEDFORD, *and* GLOUCESTER.

King. Gloucester, 'tis true that we are in great danger ;
The greater therefore should our courage be.
Good morrow, brother Bedford.　God Almighty !
There is some soul of goodness in things evil,
Would men observingly distil it out ;　5
For our bad neighbour makes us early stirrers,
Which is both healthful and good husbandry.
Besides, they are our outward consciences
And preachers to us all, admonishing　9
That we should dress us fairly for our end.
Thus may we gather honey from the weed,
And make a moral of the devil himself.

Enter ERPINGHAM.

Good morrow, old Sir Thomas Erpingham :
A good soft pillow for that good white head
Were better than a churlish turf of France.

Erp. Not so, my liege ; this lodging likes
    me better,   16
Since I may say ' Now lie I like a king '.
    King. 'Tis good for men to love their
        present pains
Upon example ; so the spirit is eased ;
And when the mind is quick'ned, out of
    doubt   20
The organs, though defunct and dead
    'before,
Break up their drowsy grave and newly
    move
With casted slough and fresh legerity.
Lend me thy cloak, Sir Thomas. Brothers
    both,   24
Commend me to the princes in our camp ;
Do my good morrow to them, and anon
Desire them all to my pavilion.
    Glo. We shall, my liege.
    Erp. Shall I attend your Grace ?
    King.   No, my good knight :
Go with my brothers to my lords of
    England ;   30
I and my bosom must debate awhile,
And then I would no other company.
    Erp. The Lord in heaven bless thee, noble
        Harry !   [*Exeunt all but the King.*
    King. God-a-mercy, old heart ! thou
        speak'st cheerfully.

Enter PISTOL.

    Pist. Qui va là ?   35
    King. A friend.
    Pist. Discuss unto me : art thou officer,
Or art thou base, common, and popular ?
    King. I am a gentleman of a company.
    Pist. Trail'st thou the puissant pike ? 40
    King. Even so. What are you ?
    Pist. As good a gentleman as the
Emperor.
    King. Then you are a better than the
King.
    Pist. The King's a bawcock and a heart
        of gold,
A lad of life, an imp of fame ;   45
Of parents good, of fist most valiant.
I kiss his dirty shoe, and from heart-string
I love the lovely bully. What is thy name ?
    King. Harry le Roy.
    Pist. Le Roy ! a Cornish name ; art thou
        of Cornish crew ?   50
    King. No, I am a Welshman.
    Pist. Know'st thou Fluellen ?
    King. Yes.
    Pist. Tell him I'll knock his leek about
        his pate
Upon Saint Davy's day.   55
    King. Do not you wear your dagger in
your cap that day, lest he knock that about
yours.
    Pist. Art thou his friend ?
    King. And his kinsman too.
    Pist. The figo for thee, then !   60
    King. I thank you ; God be with you !

    Pist. My name is Pistol call'd.   [*Exit.*
    King. It sorts well with your fierceness.

Enter FLUELLEN *and* GOWER.

    Gow. Captain Fluellen !
    Flu. So ! in the name of Jesu Christ,
speak fewer. It is the greatest admiration
in the universal world, when the true and
aunchient prerogatifes and laws of the wars
is not kept ; if you would take the pains
but to examine the wars of Pompey the
Great, you shall find, I warrant you, that
there is no tiddle-taddle nor pibble-pabble
in Pompey's camp ; I warrant you, you
shall find the ceremonies of the wars, and
the cares of it, and the forms of it, and the
sobriety of it, and the modesty of it, to be
otherwise.   74
    Gow. Why, the enemy is loud ; you hear
him all night.
    Flu. If the enemy is an ass, and a fool,
and a prating coxcomb, is it meet, think
you, that we should also, look you, be an
ass, and a fool, and a prating coxcomb ? In
your own conscience, now ?   80
    Gow. I will speak lower.
    Flu. I pray you and beseech you that you
will.   [*Exeunt Gower and Fluellen.*
    King. Though it appear a little out of
        fashion,
There is much care and valour in this
        Welshman.

Enter three soldiers : JOHN BATES, ALEX-
ANDER COURT, *and* MICHAEL WILLIAMS.

    Court. Brother John Bates, is not that
the morning which breaks yonder ?   86
    Bates. I think it be ; but we have no
great cause to desire the approach of day.
    Will. We see yonder the beginning of the
day, but I think we shall never see the end
of it. Who goes there ?   91
    King. A friend.
    Will. Under what captain serve you ?
    King. Under Sir Thomas Erpingham.
    Will. A good old commander and a most
kind gentleman. I pray you, what thinks
he of our estate ?   96
    King. Even as men wreck'd upon a sand,
that look to be wash'd off the next tide.
    Bates. He hath not told his thought to
the King ?
    King. No ; nor it is not meet he should.
For though I speak it to you, I think the
King is but a man as I am : the violet
smells to him as it doth to me ; the element
shows to him as it doth to me ; all his
senses have but human conditions ; his
ceremonies laid by, in his nakedness he
appears but a man ; and though his
affections are higher mounted than ours,
yet, when they stoop, they stoop with the
like wing. Therefore, when he sees reason
of fears, as we do, his fears, out of doubt,

be of the same relish as ours are ; yet, in reason, no man should possess him with any appearance of fear, lest he, by showing it, should dishearten his army.   111

Bates. He may show what outward courage he will ; but I believe, as cold a night as 'tis, he could wish himself in Thames up to the neck ; and so I would he were, and I by him, at all adventures, so we were quit here.   116

King. By my troth, I will speak my con-science of the King : I think he would not wish himself anywhere but where he is.

Bates. Then I would he were here alone ; so should he be sure to be ransomed, and a many poor men's lives saved.   122

King. I dare say you love him not so ill to wish him here alone, howsoever you speak this, to feel other men's minds ; methinks I could not die anywhere so con-tented as in the King's company, his cause being just and his quarrel honourable.   127

Will. That's more than we know.

Bates. Ay, or more than we should seek after ; for we know enough if we know we are the King's subjects. If his cause be wrong, our obedience to the King wipes the crime of it out of us.   132

Will. But if the cause be not good, the King himself hath a heavy reckoning to make when all those legs and arms and heads, chopp'd off in a battle, shall join together at the latter day and cry all ' We died at such a place '—some swearing, some crying for a surgeon, some upon their wives left poor behind them, some upon the debts they owe, some upon their children rawly left. I am afeard there are few die well that die in a battle ; for how can they charitably dispose of anything when blood is their argument ? Now, if these men do not die well, it will be a black matter for the King that led them to it ; who to disobey were against all proportion of subjection.   145

King. So, if a son that is by his father sent about merchandise do sinfully mis-carry upon the sea, the imputation of his wickedness, by your rule, should be im-posed upon his father that sent him ; or if a servant, under his master's command transporting a sum of money, be assailed by robbers and die in many irreconcil'd iniquities, you may call the business of the master the author of the servant's damna-tion. But this is not so : the King is not bound to answer the particular endings of his soldiers, the father of his son, nor the master of his servant ; for they purpose not their death when they purpose their services. Besides, there is no king, be his cause never so spotless, if it come to the arbitrement of swords, can try it out with all unspotted soldiers : some peradventure

have on them the guilt of premeditated and contrived murder ; some, of beguiling virgins with the broken seals of perjury ; some, making the wars their bulwark, that have before gored the gentle bosom of peace with pillage and robbery. Now, if these men have defeated the law and outrun native punishment, though they can out-strip men they have no wings to fly from God : war is His beadle, war is His vengeance; so that here men are punish'd for before-breach of the King's laws in now the King's quarrel. Where they feared the death they have borne life away ; and where they would be safe they perish. Then if they die unprovided, no more is the King guilty of their damnation than he was before guilty of those impieties for the which they are now visited. Every subject's duty is the King's ; but every subject's soul is his own. Therefore should every soldier in the wars do as every sick man in his bed—wash every mote out of his conscience ; and dying so, death is to him advantage ; or not dying, the time was blessedly lost wherein such preparation was gained ; and in him that escapes it were not sin to think that, making God so free an offer, He let him outlive that day to see His greatness, and to teach others how they should prepare.   183

Will. 'Tis certain, every man that dies ill, the ill upon his own head—the King is not to answer for it.

Bates. I do not desire he should answer for me, and yet I determine to fight lustily for him.

King. I myself heard the King say he would not be ransom'd.   189

Will. Ay, he said so, to make us fight cheerfully ; but when our throats are cut he may be ransom'd, and we ne'er the wiser.

King. If I live to see it, I will never trust his word after.   194

Will. You pay him then! That's a perilous shot out of an elder-gun, that a poor and a private displeasure can do against a monarch! You may as well go about to turn the sun to ice with fanning in his face with a peacock's feather. You'll never trust his word after! Come, 'tis a foolish saying.   200

King. Your reproof is something too round ; I should be angry with you, if the time were convenient.

Will. Let it be a quarrel between us if you live.

King. I embrace it.

Will. How shall I know thee again ? 205

King. Give me any gage of thine, and I will wear it in my bonnet ; then if ever thou dar'st acknowledge it, I will make it my quarrel.

Will. Here's my glove ; give me another of thine.

King. There.   210

Will. This will I also wear in my cap ; if ever thou come to me and say, after to-morrow, ' This is my glove ', by this hand I will take thee a box on the ear.

King. If ever I live to see it, I will challenge it.

Will. Thou dar'st as well be hang'd.   215

King. Well, I will do it, though I take thee in the King's company.

Will. Keep thy word. Fare thee well.

Bates. Be friends, you English fools, be friends ; we have French quarrels enow, if you could tell how to reckon.   221

King. Indeed, the French may lay twenty French crowns to one they will beat us, for they bear them on their shoulders ; but it is no English treason to cut French crowns, and to-morrow the King himself will be a clipper.   [*Exeunt Soldiers.*
Upon the King ! Let us our lives, our souls,
Our debts, our careful wives,   227
Our children, and our sins, lay on the King !
We must bear all. O hard condition,
Twin-born with greatness, subject to the breath
Of every fool, whose sense no more can feel
But his own wringing ! What infinite heart's ease
Must kings neglect that private men enjoy !
And what have kings that privates have not too,   234
Save ceremony—save general ceremony ?
And what art thou, thou idol Ceremony ?
What kind of god art thou, that suffer'st more
Of mortal griefs than do thy worshippers ?
What are thy rents ? What are thy com-ings-in ?
O Ceremony, show me but thy worth !   240
What is thy soul of adoration ?
Art thou aught else but place, degree, and form,
Creating awe and fear in other men ?
Wherein thou art less happy being fear'd
Than they in fearing.   245
What drink'st thou oft, instead of homage sweet,
But poison'd flattery ? O, be sick, great greatness,
And bid thy ceremony give thee cure !
Thinks thou the fiery fever will go out
With titles blown from adulation ?   250
Will it give place to flexure and low bending ?
Canst thou, when thou command'st the beggar's knee,
Command the health of it ? No, thou proud dream,
That play'st so subtly with a king's repose.
I am a king that find thee ; and I know   255
'Tis not the balm, the sceptre, and the ball,

The sword, the mace, the crown imperial,
The intertissued robe of gold and pearl,
The farced title running fore the king,
The throne he sits on, nor the tide of pomp
That beats upon the high shore of this world—   261
No, not all these, thrice gorgeous ceremony,
Not all these, laid in bed majestical,
Can sleep so soundly as the wretched slave
Who, with a body fill'd and vacant mind,
Gets him to rest, cramm'd with distressful bread ;   266
Never sees horrid night, the child of hell ;
But, like a lackey, from the rise to set
Sweats in the eye of Phœbus, and all night
Sleeps in Elysium ; next day, after dawn,
Doth rise and help Hyperion to his horse ;
And follows so the ever-running year   272
With profitable labour, to his grave.
And but for ceremony, such a wretch,
Winding up days with toil and nights with sleep,   275
Had the fore-hand and vantage of a king.
The slave, a member of the country's peace,
Enjoys it ; but in gross brain little wots
What watch the king keeps to maintain the peace   279
Whose hours the peasant best advantages.

Enter ERPINGHAM.

Erp. My lord, your nobles, jealous of your absence,
Seek through your camp to find you.
King.   Good old knight,
Collect them all together at my tent ;
I'll be before thee.
Erp.   I shall do't, my lord.   [*Exit.*
King. O God of battles, steel my soldiers' hearts,
Possess them not with fear ! Take from them now   286
The sense of reck'ning, if th' opposed numbers
Pluck their hearts from them ! Not to-day, O Lord,
O, not to-day, think not upon the fault
My father made in compassing the crown !
I Richard's body have interred new,   291
And on it have bestowed more contrite tears
Than from it issued forced drops of blood ;
Five hundred poor I have in yearly pay,
Who twice a day their wither'd hands hold up   295
Toward heaven, to pardon blood ; and I have built
Two chantries, where the sad and solemn priests
Sing still for Richard's soul. More will I do ;
Though all that I can do is nothing worth,
Since that my penitence comes after all,   300
Imploring pardon.

Enter GLOUCESTER.

574

Glo. My liege !

King. My brother Gloucester's voice ?
     Ay ;
I know thy errand, I will go with thee ;
The day, my friends, and all things, stay for
     me.   [*Exeunt.*

SCENE II.   *The French camp.*

Enter the DAUPHIN, ORLEANS, RAMBURES,
       and Others.

Orl. The sun doth gild our armour ; up,
     my lords !

Dau. Montez à cheval !   My horse !
     Varlet, laquais !   Ha !

Orl. O brave spirit !

Dau. Via !   Les eaux et la terre—

Orl. Rien puis ?   L'air et le feu—   5

Dau. Ciel ! cousin Orleans.

Enter CONSTABLE.

Now, my Lord Constable !

Con. Hark how our steeds for present
     service neigh !

Dau. Mount them, and make incision in
     their hides,
That their hot blood may spin in English
     eyes,   10
And dout them with superfluous courage,
     ha !

Ram. What, will you have them weep
     our horses' blood ?
How shall we then behold their natural
     tears ?

Enter a Messenger.

Mess. The English are embattl'd, you
     French peers.

Con. To horse, you gallant Princes !
     straight to horse !   15
Do but behold yon poor and starved band,
And your fair show shall suck away their
     souls,
Leaving them but the shales and husks of
     men.
There is not work enough for all our hands ;
Scarce blood enough in all their sickly veins
To give each naked curtle-axe a stain   21
That our French gallants shall to-day draw
     out,
And sheathe for lack of sport. Let us but
     blow on them,
The vapour of our valour will o'erturn them.
'Tis positive 'gainst all exceptions, lords,   25
That our superfluous lackeys and our
     peasants—
Who in unnecessary action swarm
About our squares of battle—were enow
To purge this field of such a hilding foe ;
Though we upon this mountain's basis by   30
Took stand for idle speculation—
But that our honours must not. What's to
     say ?
A very little little let us do,

And all is done.   Then let the trumpets
     sound
The tucket sonance and the note to mount ;
For our approach shall so much dare the
     field   36
That England shall couch down in fear and
     yield.

Enter GRANDPRÉ.

Grand. Why do you stay so long, my
     lords of France ?
Yond island carrions, desperate of their
     bones,
Ill-favouredly become the morning field ;   40
Their ragged curtains poorly are let loose,
And our air shakes them passing scornfully ;
Big Mars seems bankrupt in their beggar'd
     host,
And faintly through a rusty beaver peeps.
The horsemen sit like fixed candlesticks   45
With torch-staves in their hand ; and their
     poor jades
Lob down their heads, dropping the hides
     and hips,
The gum down-roping from their pale-dead
     eyes,
And in their pale dull mouths the gimmal'd
     bit
Lies foul with chaw'd grass, still and
     motionless ;   50
And their executors, the knavish crows,
Fly o'er them, all impatient for their hour.
Description cannot suit itself in words
To demonstrate the life of such a battle
In life so lifeless as it shows itself.   55

Con. They have said their prayers and
     they stay for death.

Dau. Shall we go send them dinners and
     fresh suits,
And give their fasting horses provender,
And after fight with them ?

Con. I stay but for my guidon. To the
     field !   60
I will the banner from a trumpet take,
And use it for my haste. Come, come,
     away !
The sun is high, and we outwear the day.
                 [*Exeunt.*

SCENE III.   *The English camp.*

Enter GLOUCESTER, BEDFORD, EXETER,
ERPINGHAM, *with all his* Host; SALISBURY
and WESTMORELAND.

Glo. Where is the King ?

Bed. The King himself is rode to view
     their battle.

West. Of fighting men they have full
     three-score thousand.

Exe. There's five to one ; besides, they
     all are fresh.

Sal. God's arm strike with us ! 'tis a
     fearful odds.   5
God bye you, Princes all ; I'll to my charge.

If we no more meet till we meet in heaven,
Then joyfully, my noble Lord of Bedford,
My dear Lord Gloucester, and my good
    Lord Exeter,   9
And my kind kinsman—warriors all, adieu!
  Bed. Farewell, good Salisbury ; and good
    luck go with thee !
  Exe. Farewell, kind lord. Fight valiantly
    to-day ;
And yet I do thee wrong to mind thee of it,
For thou art fram'd of the firm truth of
    valour.   [*Exit Salisbury.*
  Bed. He is as full of valour as of kindness;
Princely in both.

Enter the KING.

  West.   O that we now had here
But one ten thousand of those men in
    England   17
That do no work to-day !
  King.   What's he that wishes so ?
My cousin Westmoreland ? No, my fair
    cousin ;
If we are mark'd to die, we are enow   20
To do our country loss ; and if to live,
The fewer men, the greater share of honour.
God's will ! I pray thee, wish not one man
    more.
By Jove, I am not covetous for gold,
Nor care I who doth feed upon my cost ;   25
It yearns me not if men my garments wear ;
Such outward things dwell not in my
    desires.
But if it be a sin to covet honour,
I am the most offending soul alive.
No, faith, my coz, wish not a man from
    England.   30
God's peace ! I would not lose so great an
    honour
As one man more methinks would share
    from me
For the best hope I have. O, do not wish
    one more !
Rather proclaim it, Westmoreland, through
    my host,
That he which hath no stomach to this
    fight,   35
Let him depart ; his passport shall be made,
And crowns for convoy put into his purse ;
We would not die in that man's company
That fears his fellowship to die with us.
This day is call'd the feast of Crispian.   40
He that outlives this day, and comes safe
    home,
Will stand a tip-toe when this day is nam'd,
And rouse him at the name of Crispian.
He that shall live this day, and see old age,
Will yearly on the vigil feast his neighbours,
And say ' To-morrow is Saint Crispian '.   46
Then will he strip his sleeve and show his
    scars,
And say ' These wounds I had on Crispian's
    day '.
Old men forget ; yet all shall be forgot,

But he'll remember, with advantages,   50
What feats he did that day. Then shall our
    names,
Familiar in his mouth as household words—
Harry the King, Bedford and Exeter,
Warwick and Talbot, Salisbury and
    Gloucester—
Be in their flowing cups freshly remem-
    b'red.   55
This story shall the good man teach his son;
And Crispin Crispian shall ne'er go by,
From this day to the ending of the world,
But we in it shall be remembered—
We few, we happy few, we band of
    brothers ;   60
For he to-day that sheds his blood with me
Shall be my brother ; be he ne'er so vile,
This day shall gentle his condition ;
And gentlemen in England now a-bed
Shall think themselves accurs'd they were
    not here,   65
And hold their manhoods cheap whiles any
    speaks
That fought with us upon Saint Crispin's
    day.

Re-enter SALISBURY.

  Sal. My sovereign lord, bestow yourself
    with speed :
The French are bravely in their battles set,
And will with all expedience charge on us.
  King. All things are ready, if our minds
    be so.   71
  West. Perish the man whose mind is
    backward now !
  King. Thou dost not wish more help
    from England, coz ?
  West. God's will, my liege ! would you
    and I alone,
Without more help, could fight this royal
    battle !   75
  King. Why, now thou hast unwish'd five
    thousand men ;
Which likes me better than to wish us one.
You know your places. God be with you all !

Tucket. Enter MONTJOY.

  Mont. Once more I come to know of thee,
    King Harry,
If for thy ransom thou wilt now compound,
Before thy most assured overthrow ;   81
For certainly thou art so near the gulf
Thou needs must be englutted. Besides, in
    mercy,
The Constable desires thee thou wilt mind
Thy followers of repentance, that their souls
May make a peaceful and a sweet retire   86
From off these fields, where, wretches, their
    poor bodies
Must lie and fester.
  King.   Who hath sent thee now ?
  Mont. The Constable of France.
  King. I pray thee bear my former answer
    back :

Bid them achieve me, and then sell my
    bones.   91
Good God ! why should they mock poor
    fellows thus ?
The man that once did sell the lion's skin
While the beast liv'd was kill'd with hunt-
    ing him.
A many of our bodies shall no doubt   95
Find native graves ; upon the which, I
    trust,
Shall witness live in brass of this day's
    work.
And those that leave their valiant bones in
    France,
Dying like men, though buried in your
    dunghills,
They shall be fam'd ; for there the sun shall
    greet them
And draw their honours reeking up to
    heaven,   101
Leaving their earthly parts to choke your
    clime,
The smell whereof shall breed a plague in
    France.
Mark then abounding valour in our English,
That, being dead, like to the bullet's
    grazing   105
Break out into a second course of mischief,
Killing in relapse of mortality.
Let me speak proudly : tell the Constable
We are but warriors for the working-day ;
Our gayness and our gilt are all besmirch'd
With rainy marching in the painful field ;
There's not a piece of feather in our host—
Good argument, I hope, we will not fly—
And time hath worn us into slovenry.
But, by the mass, our hearts are in the
    trim ;   115
And my poor soldiers tell me yet ere night
They'll be in fresher robes, or they will pluck
The gay new coats o'er the French soldiers'
    heads
And turn them out of service. If they do
    this—
As, if God please, they shall—my ransom
    then   120
Will soon be levied. Herald, save thou thy
    labour ;
Come thou no more for ransom, gentle
    herald ;
They shall have none, I swear, but these my
    joints ;
Which if they have, as I will leave 'em them,
Shall yield them little, tell the Constable.
Mont. I shall, King Harry. And so fare
    thee well :   126
Thou never shalt hear herald any more.
                   [*Exit.*

  King. I fear thou wilt once more come
again for a ransom.

      Enter the DUKE OF YORK.

  York. My lord, most humbly on my knee
    I beg

The leading of the vaward.   130
  King. Take it, brave York.   Now,
    soldiers, march away ;
And how thou pleasest, God, dispose the
    day !   [*Exeunt.*

    SCENE IV. *The field of battle.*

Alarum. Excursions. Enter French Soldier,
        PISTOL, *and* Boy.

  Pist. Yield, cur !
  Fr. Sol. Je pense que vous êtes le gentil-
homme de bonne qualité.
  Pist. Cality ! Calen o custure me ! Art
thou a gentleman ? What is thy name ?
Discuss.   5
  Fr. Sol. O Seigneur Dieu !
  Pist. O, Signieur Dew should be a gentle-
man.
Perpend my words, O Signieur Dew, and
    mark :
O Signieur Dew, thou diest on point of fox,
Except, O Signieur, thou do give to me   10
Egregious ransom.
  Fr. Sol. O, prennez miséricorde ; ayez
pitié de moi !
  Pist. Moy shall not serve ; I will have
    forty moys ;
Or I will fetch thy rim out at thy throat
In drops of crimson blood.   15
  Fr. Sol. Est-il impossible d' échapper la
force de ton bras ?
  Pist. Brass, cur !
Thou damned and luxurious mountain-
    goat,
Offer'st me brass ?   20
  Fr. Sol. O, pardonnez-moi !
  Pist. Say'st thou me so ? Is that a ton
    of moys ?
Come hither, boy ; ask me this slave in
    French
What is his name.
  Boy. Ecoutez :   comment êtes-vous
    appelé ?   25
  Fr. Sol. Monsieur le Fer.
  Boy. He says his name is Master Fer.
  Pist. Master Fer ! I'll fer him, and firk
him, and ferret him—discuss the same in
French unto him.
  Boy. I do not know the French for fer,
and ferret, and firk.   31
  Pist. Bid him prepare ; for I will cut his
throat.
  Fr. Sol. Que dit-il, monsieur ?
  Boy. Il me commande à vous dire que
vous faites vous prêt ; car ce soldat ici est
disposé tout à cette heure de couper votre
gorge.   36
  Pist. Owy, cuppele gorge, permafoy !
Peasant, unless thou give me crowns, brave
    crowns ;
Or mangled shalt thou be by this my sword.
  Fr. Sol. O, je vous supplie, pour l'amour
de Dieu, me pardonner ! Je suis gentil-

homme de bonne maison. Gardez ma vie, et je vous donnerai deux cents écus. 42

Pist. What are his words ?

Boy. He prays you to save his life ; he is a gentleman of a good house, and for his ransom he will give you two hundred crowns. 46

Pist. Tell him my fury shall abate, and I The crowns will take.

Fr. Sol. Petit monsieur, que dit-il ? 49

Boy. Encore qu'il est contre son jurement de pardonner aucun prisonnier, néanmoins, pour les écus que vous l'avez promis, il est content à vous donner la liberté, le franchisement. 53

Fr. Sol. Sur mes genoux je vous donne mille remercîmens ; et je m'estime heureux que je suis tombé entre les mains d'un chevalier, je pense, le plus brave, vaillant, et très distingué seigneur d'Angleterre.

Pist. Expound unto me, boy. 58

Boy. He gives you, upon his knees, a thousand thanks ; and he esteems himself happy that he hath fall'n into the hands of one—as he thinks—the most brave, valorous, and thrice-worthy signieur of England.

Pist. As I suck blood, I will some mercy show. 63

Follow me. [*Exit.*

Boy. Suivez-vous le grand capitaine. [*Exit French Soldier*] I did never know so full a voice issue from so empty a heart ; but the saying is true—the empty vessel makes the greatest sound. Bardolph and Nym had ten times more valour than this roaring devil i' th' old play, that every one may pare his nails with a wooden dagger ; and they are both hang'd ; and so would this be, if he durst steal anything adventurously. I must stay with the lackeys, with the luggage of our camp. The French might have a good prey of us, if he knew of it ; for there is none to guard it but boys. [*Exit.*

SCENE V. *Another part of the field of battle.*

Enter CONSTABLE, ORLEANS, BOURBON, DAUPHIN, *and* RAMBURES.

Con. O diable !

Orl. O Seigneur ! le jour est perdu, tout est perdu !

Dau. Mort Dieu, ma vie ! all is confounded, all !

Reproach and everlasting shame Sits mocking in our plumes.

[*A short alarum.*

O méchante fortune ! Do not run away. 5

Con. Why, all our ranks are broke.

Dau. O perdurable shame ! Let's stab ourselves.

Be these the wretches that we play'd at dice for ?

Orl. Is this the king we sent to for his ransom ?

Bour. Shame, and eternal shame, nothing but shame ! 10

Let us die in honour : once more back again ;

And he that will not follow Bourbon now, Let him go hence and, with his cap in hand Like a base pander, hold the chamber-door Whilst by a slave, no gentler than my dog, His fairest daughter is contaminated. 16

Con. Disorder, that hath spoil'd us, friend us now !

Let us on heaps go offer up our lives.

Orl. We are enow yet living in the field To smother up the English in our throngs, If any order might be thought upon. 21

Bour. The devil take order now ! I'll to the throng.

Let life be short, else shame will be too long.

[*Exeunt.*

SCENE VI. *Another part of the field.*

Alarum. Enter the KING *and his* Train, *with* Prisoners ; EXETER, *and* Others.

King. Well have we done, thrice-valiant countrymen ;

But all's not done—yet keep the French the field.

Exe. The Duke of York commends him to your Majesty.

King. Lives he, good uncle ? Thrice within this hour

I saw him down ; thrice up again, and fighting ; 5

From helmet to the spur all blood he was.

Exe. In which array, brave soldier, doth he lie

Larding the plain ; and by his bloody side, Yoke-fellow to his honour-owing wounds, The noble Earl of Suffolk also lies. 10

Suffolk first died ; and York, all haggled over,

Comes to him, where in gore he lay insteeped,

And takes him by the beard, kisses the gashes

That bloodily did yawn upon his face,

He cries aloud ' Tarry, my cousin Suffolk.

My soul shall thine keep company to heaven ; 16

Tarry, sweet soul, for mine, then fly abreast ;

As in this glorious and well-foughten field We kept together in our chivalry '.

Upon these words I came and cheer'd him up ; 20

He smil'd me in the face, raught me his hand,

And, with a feeble grip, says ' Dear my lord,

Commend my service to my sovereign '.

So did he turn, and over Suffolk's neck

He threw his wounded arm and kiss'd his
   lips ;   25
And so, espous'd to death, with blood he
   seal'd
A testament of noble-ending love.
The pretty and sweet manner of it forc'd
Those waters from me which I would have
   stopp'd ;
But I had not so much of man in me,   30
And all my mother came into mine eyes
And gave me up to tears.
King.   I blame you not ;
For, hearing this, I must perforce compound
With mistful eyes, or they will issue too.
                            [*Alarum.*
But, hark ! what new alarum is this same ?
The French have reinforc'd their scatter'd
   men.   36
Then every soldier kill his prisoners ;
Give the word through.   [*Exeunt.*

SCENE VII.   *Another part of the field.*

Enter FLUELLEN *and* GOWER.

Flu. Kill the poys and the luggage ! 'Tis
expressly against the law of arms ; 'tis as
arrant a piece of knavery, mark you now,
as can be offert ; in your conscience, now,
is it not ?   4
Gow. 'Tis certain there's not a boy left
alive ; and the cowardly rascals that ran
from the battle ha' done this slaughter ;
besides, they have burned and carried away
all that was in the King's tent ; wherefore
the King most worthily hath caus'd every
soldier to cut his prisoner's throat. O, 'tis
a gallant King !   10
Flu. Ay, he was porn at Monmouth,
Captain Gower. What call you the town's
name where Alexander the Pig was born ?
Gow. Alexander the Great.   14
Flu. Why, I pray you, is not ' pig ' great ?
The pig, or the great, or the mighty, or the
huge, or the magnanimous, are all one
reckonings, save the phrase is a little
variations.   18
Gow. I think Alexander the Great was
born in Macedon ; his father was called
Philip of Macedon, as I take it.
Flu. I think it is in Macedon where Alexander is porn. I tell you, Captain, if you
look in the maps of the 'orld, I warrant you
sall find, in the comparisons between
Macedon and Monmouth, that the situa-
tions, look you, is both alike. There is a
river in Macedon ; and there is also moreover a river at Monmouth ; it is call'd Wye
at Monmouth, but it is out of my prains
what is the name of the other river ; but
'tis all one, 'tis alike as my fingers is to my
fingers, and there is salmons in both. If you
mark Alexander's life well, Harry of Monmouth's life is come after it indifferent well;
for there is figures in all things. Alexander

—God knows, and you know—in his rages,
and his furies, and his wraths, and his
cholers, and his moods, and his displeasures,
and his indignations, and also being a little
intoxicates in his prains, did, in his ales
and his angers, look you, kill his best
friend, Cleitus.
Gow. Our king is not like him in that :
he never kill'd any of his friends.   39
Flu. It is not well done, mark you now,
to take the tales out of my mouth ere it is
made and finished. I speak but in the
figures and comparisons of it ; as Alexander kill'd his friend Cleitus, being in his
ales and his cups, so also Harry Monmouth,
being in his right wits and his good judgments, turn'd away the fat knight with the
great belly doublet ; he was full of jests,
and gipes, and knaveries, and mocks ; I
have forgot his name.
Gow. Sir John Falstaff.
Flu. That is he. I'll tell you there is good
men porn at Monmouth.   50
Gow. Here comes his Majesty.

Alarum.   Enter the KING, WARWICK,
   GLOUCESTER, EXETER, *and* Others, *with*
   Prisoners. *Flourish.*

King. I was not angry since I came to
   France
Until this instant. Take a trumpet, herald ;
Ride thou unto the horsemen on yond
   hill ;
If they will fight with us, bid them come
   down   55
Or void the field ; they do offend our sight.
If they'll do neither, we will come to them
And make them skirr away as swift as
   stones
Enforced from the old Assyrian slings ;
Besides, we'll cut the throats of those we
   have,   60
And not a man of them that we shall take
Shall taste our mercy. Go and tell them so.

Enter MONTJOY.

Exe. Here comes the herald of the French,
   my liege.
Glo. His eyes are humbler than they us'd
   to be.
King. How now ! What means this,
   herald ? know'st thou not   65
That I have fin'd these bones of mine for
   ransom ?
Com'st thou again for ransom ?
Mont.   No, great King ;
I come to thee for charitable licence,   68
That we may wander o'er this bloody field
To book our dead, and then to bury them ;
To sort our nobles from our common men ;
For many of our princes—woe the while !—
Lie drown'd and soak'd in mercenary
   blood ;
So do our vulgar drench their peasant limbs

In blood of princes; and their wounded
    steeds   75
Fret fetlock deep in gore, and with wild rage
Yerk out their armed heels at their dead
    masters,
Killing them twice. O, give us leave, great
    King,
To view the field in safety, and dispose
Of their dead bodies!
    King.   I tell thee truly, herald, 80
I know not if the day be ours or no;
For yet a many of your horsemen peer
And gallop o'er the field.
    Mont.   The day is yours.
    King. Praised be God, and not our
    strength, for it!
What is this castle call'd that stands hard
    by?   85
    Mont. They call it Agincourt.
    King. Then call we this the field of
    Agincourt,
Fought on the day of Crispin Crispianus.
    Flu. Your grandfather of famous mem-
ory, an't please your Majesty, and your
great-uncle Edward the Plack Prince of
Wales, as I have read in the chronicles,
fought a most prave pattle here in France.
    King. They did, Fluellen.   93
    Flu. Your Majesty says very true; if
your Majesties be rememb'red of it, the
Welshmen did good service in a garden
where leeks did grow, wearing leeks in their
Monmouth caps; which your Majesty
know to this hour is an honourable badge
of the service; and I do believe your
Majesty takes no scorn to wear the leek
upon Saint Tavy's day.   100
    King. I wear it for a memorable honour;
For I am Welsh, you know, good country-
    man.
    Flu. All the water in Wye cannot wash
your Majesty's Welsh plood out of your
pody, I can tell you that. Got pless it and
preserve it as long as it pleases his Grace
and his Majesty too!   106
    King. Thanks, good my countryman.
    Flu. By Jeshu, I am your Majesty's
countryman, I care not who know it; I
will confess it to all the 'orld: I need not
be asham'd of your Majesty, praised be
Got, so long as your Majesty is an honest
man.   111

    Enter WILLIAMS.

    King. God keep me so! Our heralds go
    with him:
Bring me just notice of the numbers dead
On both our parts. Call yonder fellow
    hither.
           [*Exeunt Heralds with Montjoy.*
    Exe. Soldier, you must come to the King.
    King. Soldier, why wear'st thou that
glove in thy cap?   117
    Will. An't please your Majesty, 'tis the

gage of one that I should fight withal, if he
be alive.
    King. An Englishman?   120
    Will. An't please your Majesty, a rascal
that swagger'd with me last night; who, if
'a live and ever dare to challenge this glove,
I have sworn to take him a box o' th' ear;
or if I can see my glove in his cap—which
he swore, as he was a soldier, he would
wear if alive—I will strike it out soundly.
    King. What think you, Captain Fluellen,
is it fit this soldier keep his oath?   128
    Flu. He is a craven and a villain else,
an't please your Majesty, in my conscience.
    King. It may be his enemy is a gentle-
man of great sort, quite from the answer of
his degree.   132
    Flu. Though he be as good a gentleman
as the Devil is, as Lucifer and Belzebub
himself, it is necessary, look your Grace,
that he keep his vow and his oath; if he
be perjur'd, see you now, his reputation is
as arrant a villain and a Jacksauce as ever
his black shoe trod upon God's ground and
his earth, in my conscience, la.
    King. Then keep thy vow, sirrah, when
thou meet'st the fellow.   140
    Will. So I will, my liege, as I live.
    King. Who serv'st thou under?
    Will. Under Captain Gower, my liege.
    Flu. Gower is a good captain, and is
good knowledge and literatured in the wars.
    King. Call him hither to me, soldier.   146
    Will. I will, my liege.   [*Exit.*
    King. Here, Fluellen; wear thou this
favour for me, and stick it in thy cap;
when Alençon and myself were down together, I pluck'd this glove from his helm.
If any man challenge this, he is a friend
to Alençon and an enemy to our person;
if thou encounter any such, apprehend him,
an thou dost me love.   153
    Flu. Your Grace does me as great
honours as can be desir'd in the hearts of
his subjects. I would fain see the man that
has but two legs that shall find himself
aggrief'd at this glove, that is all; but I
would fain see it once, an please God of
his grace that I might see.
    King. Know'st thou Gower?   160
    Flu. He is my dear friend, an please you.
    King. Pray thee, go seek him, and bring
him to my tent.
    Flu. I will fetch him.   [*Exit.*
    King. My Lord of Warwick and my
    brother Gloucester,   165
Follow Fluellen closely at the heels;
The glove which I have given him for a
    favour
May haply purchase him a box o' th' ear.
It is the soldier's: I, by bargain, should
Wear it myself. Follow, good cousin
    Warwick;   170
If that the soldier strike him, as I judge

By his blunt bearing he will keep his word,
Some sudden mischief may arise of it;
For I do know Fluellen valiant,
And touch'd with choler, hot as gunpowder,
And quickly will return an injury;   176
Follow, and see there be no harm between
    them.
Go you with me, uncle of Exeter. [*Exeunt.*

SCENE VIII. *Before King Henry's pavilion.*

Enter GOWER *and* WILLIAMS.

Will. I warrant it is to knight you,
Captain.

Enter FLUELLEN.

Flu. God's will and his pleasure, Captain,
I beseech you now, come apace to the
King: there is more good toward you
peradventure than is in your knowledge to
dream of.
Will. Sir, know you this glove?   5
Flu. Know the glove? I know the glove
is a glove.
Will. I know this; and thus I challenge
it.   [*Strikes him.*
Flu. 'Sblood, an arrant traitor as any's
in the universal world, or in France, or in
England!
Gow. How now, sir! you villain!   10
Will. Do you think I'll be forsworn?
Flu. Stand away, Captain Gower; I will
give treason his payment into plows, I
warrant you.
Will. I am no traitor.   14
Flu. That's a lie in thy throat. I charge
you in his Majesty's name, apprehend him:
he's a friend of the Duke Alençon's.

Enter WARWICK *and* GLOUCESTER.

War. How now, how now! what's the
matter?
Flu. My Lord of Warwick, here is—
praised be God for it!—a most contagious
treason come to light, look you, as you
shall desire in a summer's day. Here is his
Majesty.   22

Enter the KING *and* EXETER.

King. How now! what's the matter?
Flu. My liege, here is a villain and a
traitor, that, look your Grace, has struck
the glove which your Majesty is take out
of the helmet of Alençon.   26
Will. My liege, this was my glove: here
is the fellow of it; and he that I gave it
to in change promis'd to wear it in his cap;
I promis'd to strike him if he did; I met
this man with my glove in his cap, and I
have been as good as my word.   31
Flu. Your Majesty hear now, saving your
Majesty's manhood, what an arrant,
rascally, beggarly, lousy knave it is; I
hope your Majesty is pear me testimony

and witness, and will avouchment, that
this is the glove of Alençon that your
Majesty is give me; in your conscience,
now.
King. Give me thy glove, soldier; look,
here is the fellow of it.   39
'Twas I, indeed, thou promised'st to strike,
And thou hast given me most bitter terms.
Flu. An please your Majesty, let his neck
answer for it, if there is any martial law in
the world.
King. How canst thou make me satisfac-
    tion?   44
Will. All offences, my lord, come from
the heart: never came any from mine that
might offend your Majesty.
King. It was ourself thou didst abuse. 48
Will. Your Majesty came not like yourself: you appear'd to me but as a common
man; witness the night, your garments,
your lowliness; and what your Highness
suffer'd under that shape I beseech you
take it for your own fault, and not mine;
for had you been as I took you for, I made
no offence; therefore, I beseech your
Highness pardon me.   55
King. Here, uncle Exeter, fill this glove
    with crowns,
And give it to this fellow. Keep it,
    fellow;
And wear it for an honour in thy cap
Till I do challenge it. Give him the crowns;
And, Captain, you must needs be friends
    with him.   60
Flu. By this day and this light, the
fellow has mettle enough in his belly:
hold, there is twelve pence for you; and
I pray you to serve God, and keep you out
of prawls, and prabbles, and quarrels, and
dissensions, and, I warrant you, it is the
better for you.   65
Will. I will none of your money.
Flu. It is with a good will; I can tell
you it will serve you to mend your shoes.
Come, wherefore should you be so pashful?
your shoes is not so good, 'tis a good
silling, I warrant you, or I will change it. 70

Enter an English Herald.

King. Now, herald, are the dead num-
    b'red?
Her. Here is the number of the
    slaught'red French. [*Gives a paper.*
King. What prisoners of good sort are
    taken, uncle?
Exe. Charles Duke of Orleans, nephew to
    the King;
John Duke of Bourbon, and Lord Bouci-
    qualt;   75
Of other lords and barons, knights and
    squires,
Full fifteen hundred, besides common men.
King. This note doth tell me of ten
    thousand French

That in the field lie slain; of princes, in
   this number,   79
And nobles bearing banners, there lie dead
One hundred twenty-six; added to these,
Of knights, esquires, and gallant gentle-
   men,
Eight thousand and four hundred; of the
   which
Five hundred were but yesterday dubb'd
   knights.
So that, in these ten thousand they have
   lost,   85
There are but sixteen hundred mercenaries;
The rest are princes, barons, lords, knights,
   squires,
And gentlemen of blood and quality.
The names of those their nobles that lie
   dead :
Charles Delabreth, High Constable of
   France ;   90
Jaques of Chatillon, Admiral of France ;
The master of the cross-bows, Lord
   Rambures ;
Great Master of France, the brave Sir
   Guichard Dolphin ;
John Duke of Alençon ; Antony Duke of
   Brabant,
The brother to the Duke of Burgundy ; 95
And Edward Duke of Bar. Of lusty earls,
Grandpré and Roussi, Fauconbridge and
   Foix,
Beaumont and Marle, Vaudemont and
   Lestrake.
Here was a royal fellowship of death ! 99
Where is the number of our English dead ?
   [*Herald presents another paper.*
Edward the Duke of York, the Earl of
   Suffolk,
Sir Richard Kikely, Davy Gam, Esquire ;
None else of name ; and of all other men
But five and twenty. O God, thy arm was
   here !
And not to us, but to thy arm alone, 105
Ascribe we all. When, without stratagem,
But in plain shock and even play of battle,
Was ever known so great and little loss
On one part and on th' other ? Take it,
   God,
For it is none but thine.
   Exe.   'Tis wonderful ! 110
   King. Come, go we in procession to the
   village ;
And be it death proclaimed through our
   host
To boast of this or take that praise from
   God
Which is his only.
   Flu. Is it not lawful, an please your
Majesty, to tell how many is kill'd ? 116
   King. Yes, Captain ; but with this
   acknowledgment,
That God fought for us.
   Flu. Yes, my conscience, he did us great
good.

   King. Do we all holy rites : 120
Let there be sung ' Non nobis ' and ' Te
   Deum ' ;
The dead with charity enclos'd in clay—
And then to Calais ; and to England then ;
Where ne'er from France arriv'd more
   happy men.   [*Exeunt.*

ACT FIVE

PROLOGUE

Enter CHORUS.

   Chor. Vouchsafe to those that have not
   read the story
That I may prompt them ; and of such as
   have,
I humbly pray them to admit th' excuse
Of time, of numbers, and due course of
   things,
Which cannot in their huge and proper
   life   5
Be here presented. Now we bear the King
Toward Calais. Grant him there. There
   seen,
Heave him away upon your winged
   thoughts
Athwart the sea. Behold, the English
   beach
Pales in the flood with men, with wives,
   and boys,   ·10
Whose shouts and claps out-voice the deep-
   mouth'd sea,
Which, like a mighty whiffler, fore the
   King
Seems to prepare his way. So let him land,
And solemnly see him set on to London.
So swift a pace hath thought that even now
You may imagine him upon Blackheath ;
Where that his lords desire him to have
   borne
His bruised helmet and his bended sword
Before him through the city. He forbids it,
Being free from vainness and self-glorious
   pride ;   20
Giving full trophy, signal, and ostent,
Quite from himself to God. But now behold
In the quick forge and working-house of
   thought,
How London doth pour out her citizens !
The mayor and all his brethren in best
   sort—   25
Like to the senators of th' antique Rome,
With the plebeians swarming at their
   heels—
Go forth and fetch their conqu'ring
   Cæsar in ;
As, by a lower but loving likelihood,
Were now the General of our gracious
   Empress—   30
As in good time he may—from Ireland
   coming,
Bringing rebellion broached on his sword,
How many would the peaceful city quit

To welcome him! Much more, and much
    more cause,
Did they this Harry. Now in London place
    him—   35
As yet the lamentation of the French
Invites the King of England's stay at home;
The Emperor's coming in behalf of France
To order peace between them; and omit
All the occurrences, whatever chanc'd,   40
Till Harry's back-return again to France.
There must we bring him; and myself
    have play'd
The interim, by remem'bring you 'tis past.
Then brook abridgment; and your eyes
    advance,   44
After your thoughts, straight back again to
    France.   [*Exit.*

SCENE I. *France. The English camp.*

Enter FLUELLEN *and* GOWER.

Gow. Nay, that's right; but why wear
you your leek to-day? Saint Davy's day
is past.

Flu. There is occasions and causes why
and wherefore in all things. I will tell you,
ass my friend, Captain Gower: the rascally,
scald, beggarly, lousy, pragging knave,
Pistol—which you and yourself and all
the world know to be no petter than a
fellow, look you now, of no merits—he is
come to me, and prings me pread and salt
yesterday, look you, and bid me eat my
leek; it was in a place where I could not
breed no contention with him; but I will
be so bold as to wear it in my cap till I see
him once again, and then I will tell him
a little piece of my desires.   13

Enter PISTOL.

Gow. Why, here he comes, swelling like
a turkey-cock.

Flu. 'Tis no matter for his swellings nor
his turkey-cocks. God pless you, Aunchient
Pistol! you scurvy, lousy knave, God pless
you!

Pist. Ha! art thou bedlam? Dost thou
thirst, base Trojan,
To have me fold up Parca's fatal web? 19
Hence! I am qualmish at the smell of leek.

Flu. I peseech you heartily, scurvy,
lousy knave, at my desires, and my
requests, and my petitions, to eat, look you,
this leek; because, look you, you do not
love it, nor your affections, and your
appetites, and your digestions, does not
agree with it, I would desire you to eat it.

Pist. Not for Cadwallader and all his
goats.   26

Flu. There is one goat for you. [*Strikes
him*] Will you be so good, scald knave, as
eat it?

Pist. Base Trojan, thou shalt die.

Flu. You say very true, scald knave—

when God's will is. I will desire you to
live in the meantime, and eat your victuals;
come, there is sauce for it. [*Striking him
again*] You call'd me yesterday mountain-
squire; but I will make you to-day a squire
of low degree. I pray you fall to; if you
can mock a leek, you can eat a leek. 35

Gow. Enough, Captain, you have astonish'd him.

Flu. I say I will make him eat some part
of my leek, or I will peat his pate four days.
Bite, I pray you, it is good for your green
wound and your ploody coxcomb.

Pist. Must I bite?   40

Flu. Yes, certainly, and out of doubt,
and out of question too, and ambiguities.

Pist. By this leek, I will most horribly
revenge—I eat and eat, I swear—

Flu. Eat, I pray you; will you have
some more sauce to your leek? There is
not enough leek to swear by.   46

Pist. Quiet thy cudgel: thou dost see I
eat.

Flu. Much good do you, scald knave,
heartily. Nay, pray you throw none away;
the skin is good for your broken coxcomb.
When you take occasions to see leeks
hereafter, I pray you mock at 'em; that
is all.   51

Pist. Good.

Flu. Ay, leeks is good. Hold you, there
is a groat to heal your pate.

Pist. Me a groat!   55

Flu. Yes, verily and in truth, you shall
take it; or I have another leek in my
pocket which you shall eat.

Pist. I take thy groat in earnest of
revenge.

Flu. If I owe you anything I will pay you
in cudgels; you shall be a woodmonger,
and buy nothing of me but cudgels. God
bye you, and keep you, and heal your
pate.   [*Exit.*

Pist. All hell shall stir for this.   63

Gow. Go, go; you are a counterfeit
cowardly knave. Will you mock at an
ancient tradition, begun upon an honourable respect, and worn as a memorable
trophy of predeceased valour, and dare not
avouch in your deeds any of your words?
I have seen you gleeking and galling at this
gentleman twice or thrice. You thought,
because he could not speak English in the
native garb, he could not therefore handle
an English cudgel; you find it otherwise,
and henceforth let a Welsh correction teach
you a good English condition. Fare ye
well.   [*Exit.*

Pist. Doth Fortune play the huswife
    with me now?
News have I that my Nell is dead i' th'
    spital   75
Of malady of France;
And there my rendezvous is quite cut off.

Old I do wax ; and from my weary limbs
Honour is cudgell'd. Well, bawd I'll turn,
And something lean to cutpurse of quick
   hand.   80
To England will I steal, and there I'll steal ;
And patches will I get unto these cudgell'd
   scars,
And swear I got them in the Gallia wars.
                         [*Exit.*

SCENE II.   *France.   The French King's
         palace.*

Enter at one door, KING HENRY, EXETER,
  BEDFORD,   GLOUCESTER,   WARWICK,
  WESTMORELAND, *and other* Lords ; *at
  another, the* FRENCH KING, QUEEN
  ISABEL, *the* PRINCESS KATHERINE,
  ALICE, *and other* Ladies ; *the* DUKE OF
  BURGUNDY, *and his* Train.

  King. Peace to this meeting, wherefore
  we are met !
Unto our brother France, and to our sister,
Health and fair time of day ; joy and good
  wishes
To our most fair and princely cousin
  Katherine.
And, as a branch and member of this
  royalty,   5
By whom this great assembly is contriv'd,
We do salute you, Duke of Burgundy.
And, princes French, and peers, health to
  you all !
  Fr. King. Right joyous are we to behold
  your face,
Most worthy brother England ; fairly met !
So are you, princes English, every one.   11
  Q. Isa. So happy be the issue, brother
  England,
Of this good day and of this gracious
  meeting
As we are now glad to behold your eyes—
Your eyes, which hitherto have borne in
  them,   15
Against the French that met them in their
  bent,
The fatal balls of murdering basilisks ;
The venom of such looks, we fairly hope,
Have lost their quality ; and that this day
Shall change all griefs and quarrels into
  love.   20
  King. To cry amen to that, thus we
  appear.
  Q. Isa. You English princes all, I do
  salute you.
  Bur. My duty to you both, on equal love,
Great Kings of France and England ! That
  I have labour'd
With all my wits, my pains, and strong
  endeavours,   25
To bring your most imperial Majesties
Unto this bar and royal interview,
Your mightiness on both parts best can
  witness.

Since then my office hath so far prevail'd
That face to face and royal eye to eye   30
You have congreeted, let it not disgrace me
If I demand, before this royal view,
What rub or what impediment there is
Why that the naked, poor, and mangled
  Peace,
Dear nurse of arts, plenties, and joyful
  births,   35
Should not in this best garden of the world,
Our fertile France, put up her lovely visage?
Alas, she hath from France too long been
  chas'd !
And all her husbandry doth lie on heaps,
Corrupting in it own fertility.   40
Her vine, the merry cheerer of the heart,
Unpruned dies ; her hedges even-pleach'd,
Like prisoners wildly overgrown with hair,
Put forth disorder'd twigs ; her fallow leas
The darnel, hemlock, and rank fumitory, 45
Doth root upon, while that the coulter
  rusts
That should deracinate such savagery ;
The even mead, that erst brought sweetly
  forth
The freckled cowslip, burnet, and green
  clover,   49
Wanting the scythe, all uncorrected, rank,
Conceives by idleness, and nothing teems
But hateful docks, rough thistles, kecksies,
  burs,
Losing both beauty and utility.
And as our vineyards, fallows, meads, and
  hedges,   54
Defective in their natures, grow to wildness;
Even so our houses and ourselves and
  children
Have lost, or do not learn for want of time,
The sciences that should become our
  country ;
But grow, like savages—as soldiers will, 60
That nothing do but meditate on blood—
To swearing and stern looks, diffus'd attire,
And everything that seems unnatural.
Which to reduce into our former favour
You are assembled ; and my speech
  entreats
That I may know the let why gentle Peace
Should not expel these inconveniences 66
And bless us with her former qualities.
  King. If, Duke of Burgundy, you would
  the peace
Whose want gives growth to th' imperfec-
  tions
Which you have cited, you must buy that
  peace   70
With full accord to all our just demands ;
Whose tenours and particular effects
You have, enschedul'd briefly, in your
  hands.
  Bur. The King hath heard them ; to the
  which as yet
There is no answer made.
  King.   Well then, the peace, 75

Which you before so urg'd, lies in his
    answer.
    Fr. King. I have but with a cursorary eye
O'erglanced the articles ; pleaseth your
    Grace
To appoint some of your council presently
To sit with us once more, with better heed
To re-survey them, we will suddenly   81
Pass our accept and peremptory answer.
    King. Brother, we shall. Go, uncle
    Exeter,
And brother Clarence, and you, brother
    Gloucester,
Warwick, and Huntington, go with the
    King ;   85
And take with you free power to ratify,
Augment, or alter, as your wisdoms best
Shall see advantageable for our dignity,
Any thing in or out of our demands ;
And we'll consign thereto. Will you, fair
    sister,   90
Go with the princes or stay here with us ?
    Q. Isa. Our gracious brother, I will go
    with them ;
Haply a woman's voice may do some good,
When articles too nicely urg'd be stood on.
    King. Yet leave our cousin Katherine
    here with us ;
She is our capital demand, compris'd   96
Within the fore-rank of our articles.
    Q. Isa. She hath good leave.
        [*Exeunt all but the King, Katherine,
                    and Alice.*
    King.   Fair Katherine, and most fair,
Will you vouchsafe to teach a soldier terms
Such as will enter at a lady's ear,   100
And plead thy love-suit to her gentle heart ?
    Kath. Your Majesty shall mock at me ;
I cannot speak your England.
    King. O fair Katherine, if you will love
me soundly with your French heart, I will
be glad to hear you confess it brokenly
with your English tongue. Do you like me,
Kate ?
    Kath. Pardonnez-moi, I cannot tell vat
is like me.
    King. An angel is like you, Kate, and
you are like an angel.   110
    Kath. Que dit-il ? que je suis semblable
à les anges ?
    Alice. Oui, vraiment, sauf votre grace,
ainsi dit-il.
    King. I said so, dear Katherine, and I
must not blush to affirm it.
    Kath. O bon Dieu ! les langues des
hommes sont pleines de tromperies.   116
    King. What says she, fair one ? that the
tongues of men are full of deceits ?
    Alice. Oui, dat de tongues of de mans is
be full of deceits—dat is de Princess.   120
    King. The Princess is the better English-
woman. I'faith, Kate, my wooing is fit for
thy understanding : I am glad thou canst
speak no better English ; for if thou

couldst, thou wouldst find me such a plain
king that thou wouldst think I had sold
my farm to buy my crown. I know no ways
to mince it in love, but directly to say ' I
love you '. Then, if you urge me farther
than to say ' Do you in faith ? ' I wear out
my suit. Give me your answer ; i'faith, do ;
and so clap hands and a bargain. How say
you, lady ?   130
    Kath. Sauf votre honneur, me understand
well.
    King. Marry, if you would put me to
verses or to dance for your sake, Kate,
why you undid me ; for the one I have
neither words nor measure, and for the
other I have no strength in measure, yet a
reasonable measure in strength. If I could
win a lady at leap-frog, or by vaulting into
my saddle with my armour on my back,
under the correction of bragging be it
spoken, I should quickly leap into a wife.
Or if I might buffet for my love, or bound
my horse for her favours, I could lay on
like a butcher, and sit like a jack-an-apes,
never off. But, before God, Kate, I cannot
look greenly, nor gasp out my eloquence,
nor I have no cunning in protestation ; only
downright oaths, which I never use till
urg'd, nor never break for urging. If thou
canst love a fellow of this temper, Kate,
whose face is not worth sun-burning, that
never looks in his glass for love of anything
he sees there, let thine eye be thy cook. I
speak to thee plain soldier. If thou canst
love me for this, take me ; if not, to say
to thee that I shall die is true—but for thy
love, by the Lord, no ; yet I love thee too.
And while thou liv'st, dear Kate, take a
fellow of plain and uncoined constancy ;
for he perforce must do thee right, because
he hath not the gift to woo in other places ;
for these fellows of infinite tongue, that can
rhyme themselves into ladies' favours, they
do always reason themselves out again.
What ! a speaker is but a prater : a rhyme
is but a ballad. A good leg will fall ; a
straight back will stoop ; a black beard will
turn white ; a curl'd pate will grow bald ;
a fair face will wither ; a full eye will wax
hollow. But a good heart, Kate, is the sun
and the moon ; or, rather, the sun, and not
the moon—for it shines bright and never
changes, but keeps his course truly. If thou
would have such a one, take me ; and take
me, take a soldier ; take a soldier, take a
king. And what say'st thou, then, to my
love ? Speak, my fair, and fairly, I pray
thee.   167
    Kath. Is it possible dat I sould love de
enemy of France ?
    King. No, it is not possible you should
love the enemy of France, Kate, but in
loving me you should love the friend of
France ; for I love France so well that I

will not part with a village of it; I will
have it all mine. And, Kate, when France
is mine and I am yours, then yours is
France and you are mine.   175
Kath. I cannot tell vat is dat.

King. No, Kate? I will tell thee in
French, which I am sure will hang upon
my tongue like a new-married wife about
her husband's neck, hardly to be shook off.
Je quand sur le possession de France, et
quand vous avez le possession de moi—let
me see, what then? Saint Denis be my
speed!—donc votre est France et vous
êtes mienne. It is as easy for me, Kate, to
conquer the kingdom as to speak so much
more French: I shall never move thee in
French, unless it be to laugh at me.   186
Kath. Sauf votre honneur, le Français
que vous parlez, il est meilleur que l'Anglais
lequel je parle.

King. No, faith, is't not, Kate; but thy
speaking of my tongue, and I thine, most
truly falsely, must needs be granted to be
much at one. But, Kate, dost thou understand thus much English—Canst thou love
me?
Kath. I cannot tell.   193

King. Can any of your neighbours tell,
Kate? I'll ask them. Come, I know thou
lovest me; and at night, when you come
into your closet, you'll question this gentlewoman about me; and I know, Kate, you
will to her dispraise those parts in me that
you love with your heart. But, good Kate,
mock me mercifully; the rather, gentle
Princess, because I love thee cruelly. If
ever thou beest mine, Kate, as I have a
saving faith within me tells me thou shalt,
I get thee with scambling, and thou must
therefore needs prove a good soldier-
breeder. Shall not thou and I, between
Saint Denis and Saint George, compound a
boy, half French, half English, that shall
go to Constantinople and take the Turk
by the beard? Shall we not? What say'st
thou, my fair flower-de-luce?
Kath. I do not know dat.   209

King. No: 'tis hereafter to know, but
now to promise; do but now promise,
Kate, you will endeavour for your French
part of such a boy; and for my English
moiety take the word of a king and a
bachelor. How answer you, la plus belle
Katherine du monde, mon tres chèr et
divin déesse?   215
Kath. Your Majestee ave fausse French
enough to deceive de most sage damoiselle
dat is en France.

King. Now, fie upon my false French!
By mine honour, in true English, I love
thee, Kate; by which honour I dare not
swear thou lovest me; yet my blood begins
to flatter me that thou dost, notwithstanding the poor and untempering effect of my

visage. Now beshrew my father's ambition!
He was thinking of civil wars when he got
me; therefore was I created with a
stubborn outside, with an aspect of iron,
that when I come to woo ladies I fright
them. But, in faith, Kate, the elder I wax,
the better I shall appear: my comfort is,
that old age, that ill layer-up of beauty,
can do no more spoil upon my face; thou
hast me, if thou hast me, at the worst; and
thou shalt wear me, if thou wear me, better
and better. And therefore tell me, most
fair Katherine, will you have me? Put off
your maiden blushes; avouch the thoughts
of your heart with the looks of an empress;
take me by the hand and say 'Harry of
England, I am thine'. Which word thou
shalt no sooner bless mine ear withal but
I will tell thee aloud 'England is thine,
Ireland is thine, France is thine, and Henry
Plantagenet is thine'; who, though I speak
it before his face, if he be not fellow with
the best king, thou shalt find the best king
of good fellows. Come, your answer in
broken music—for thy voice is music and
thy English broken; therefore, Queen of
all, Katherine, break thy mind to me in
broken English, wilt thou have me?   243
Kath. Dat is as it shall please de roi mon
père.

King. Nay, it will please him well, Kate
—it shall please him, Kate.
Kath. Den it sall also content me.

King. Upon that I kiss your hand, and
I call you my queen.   249
Kath. Laissez, mon seigneur, laissez,
laissez! Ma foi, je ne veux point que vous
abaissiez votre grandeur en baisant la main
d'une, notre seigneur, indigne serviteur;
excusez-moi, je vous supplie, mon très
puissant seigneur.

King. Then I will kiss your lips, Kate. 255
Kath. Les dames et demoiselles pour être
baisées devant leur noces, il n'est pas la
coutume de France.

King. Madam my interpreter, what says
she?
Alice. Dat it is not be de fashion pour le
ladies of France—I cannot tell vat is
baiser en Anglish.   260

King. To kiss.
Alice. Your Majestee entendre bettre que
moi.

King. It is not a fashion for the maids
in France to kiss before they are married,
would she say?
Alice. Oui, vraiment.   265

King. O Kate, nice customs curtsy to
great kings. Dear Kate, you and I cannot
be confin'd within the weak list of a
country's fashion: we are the makers of
manners, Kate; and the liberty that
follows our places stops the mouth of all
find-faults—as I will do yours for upholding

the nice fashion of your country in denying me a kiss ; therefore, patiently and yielding. [*Kissing her*] You have witchcraft in your lips, Kate : there is more eloquence in a sugar touch of them than in the tongues of the French council ; and they should sooner persuade Henry of England than a general petition of monarchs. Here comes your father.   277

Enter the FRENCH POWER *and the* ENGLISH LORDS.

Bur. God save your Majesty ! My royal cousin,
Teach you our princess English ?
King. I would have her learn, my fair cousin, how perfectly I love her ; and that is good English.   281
Bur. Is she not apt ?
King. Our tongue is rough, coz, and my condition is not smooth ; so that, having neither the voice nor the heart of flattery about me, I cannot so conjure up the spirit of love in her that he will appear in his true likeness.   286
Bur. Pardon the frankness of my mirth, if I answer you for that. If you would conjure in her, you must make a circle ; if conjure up love in her in his true likeness, he must appear naked and blind. Can you blame her, then, being a maid yet ros'd over with the virgin crimson of modesty, if she deny the appearance of a naked blind boy in her naked seeing self ? It were, my lord, a hard condition for a maid to consign to.   294
King. Yet they do wink and yield, as love is blind and enforces.
Bur. They are then excus'd, my lord, when they see not what they do.
King. Then, good my lord, teach your cousin to consent winking.   300
Bur. I will wink on her to consent, my lord, if you will teach her to know my meaning ; for maids well summer'd and warm kept are like flies at Bartholomew-tide, blind, though they have their eyes ; and then they will endure handling, which before would not abide looking on.   306
King. This moral ties me over to time and a hot summer ; and so I shall catch the fly, your cousin, in the latter end, and she must be blind too.   309
Bur. As love is, my lord, before it loves.
King. It is so ; and you may, some of you, thank love for my blindness, who cannot see many a fair French city for one fair French maid that stands in my way.
Fr. King. Yes, my lord, you see them perspectively, the cities turned into a maid; for they are all girdled with maiden walls that war hath never ent'red.   316
King. Shall Kate be my wife ?

Fr. King. So please you.
King. I am content, so the maiden cities you talk of may wait on her ; so the maid that stood in the way for my wish shall show me the way to my will.   321
Fr. King. We have consented to all terms of reason.
King. Is't so, my lords of England ?
West. The king hath granted every article :
His daughter first ; and then in sequel, all, 325
According to their firm proposed natures.
Exe. Only he hath not yet subscribed this :
Where your Majesty demands that the King of France, having any occasion to write for matter of grant, shall name your Highness in this form and with this addition, in French, Notre très cher fils Henri, Roi d'Angleterre, Héritier de France; and thus in Latin, Præclarissimus filius noster Henricus, Rex Angliæ et Hæres Franciæ.   333
Fr. King. Nor this I have not, brother, so denied
But your request shall make me let it pass.
King. I pray you, then, in love and dear alliance,
Let that one article rank with the rest ;
And thereupon give me your daughter.
Fr. King. Take her, fair son, and from her blood raise up
Issue to me ; that the contending kingdoms   340
Of France and England, whose very shores look pale
With envy of each other's happiness,
May cease their hatred ; and this dear conjunction
Plant neighbourhood and Christian-like accord
In their sweet bosoms, that never war advance   345
His bleeding sword 'twixt England and fair France.
Lords. Amen !
King. Now, welcome, Kate ; and bear me witness all,
That here I kiss her as my sovereign queen.
[*Flourish.*
Q. Isa. God, the best maker of all marriages,   350
Combine your hearts in one, your realms in one !
As man and wife, being two, are one in love,
So be there 'twixt your kingdoms such a spousal
That never may ill office or fell jealousy,
Which troubles oft the bed of blessed marriage,   355
Thrust in between the paction of these kingdoms,
To make divorce of their incorporate league ;

That English may as French, French
  Englishmen,
Receive each other. God speak this Amen!
All. Amen!   360
  King. Prepare we for our marriage; on
    which day,
My Lord of Burgundy, we'll take your
  oath,
And all the peers', for surety of our leagues.
Then shall I swear to Kate, and you to
  me,   364
And may our oaths well kept and pros-
  p'rous be!   [*Sennet. Exeunt.*

Enter CHORUS.

  Chor. Thus far, with rough and all-unable
    pen,
Our bending author hath pursu'd the
  story,
In little room confining mighty men,

Mangling by starts the full course of their
  glory.
Small time, but, in that small, most greatly
  lived   5
This star of England. Fortune made his
  sword;
By which the world's best garden he
  achieved,
And of it left his son imperial lord.
Henry the Sixth, in infant bands crown'd
  king
Of France and England, did this king
  succeed;   10
Whose state so many had the managing
That they lost France and made his
  England bleed;
Which oft our stage hath shown; and, for
  their sake,
In your fair minds let this acceptance take.
                                          [*Exit.*

THE FIRST PART OF
KING HENRY THE SIXTH

DRAMATIS PERSONÆ

KING HENRY THE SIXTH.

DUKE OF GLOUCESTER, *uncle to the King, and Protector.*

DUKE OF BEDFORD, *uncle to the King, and Regent of France.*

THOMAS BEAUFORT, DUKE OF EXETER, *great-uncle to the King.*

HENRY BEAUFORT, *great-uncle to the King,* BISHOP OF WINCHESTER, *and afterwards* CARDINAL.

JOHN BEAUFORT, EARL OF SOMERSET, *afterwards Duke.*

RICHARD PLANTAGENET, *son of Richard late Earl of Cambridge, afterwards* DUKE OF YORK.

EARL OF WARWICK.

EARL OF SALISBURY.

EARL OF SUFFOLK.

LORD TALBOT, *afterwards* EARL OF SHREWSBURY.

JOHN TALBOT, *his son.*

EDMUND MORTIMER, EARL OF MARCH.

SIR JOHN FASTOLFE.

SIR WILLIAM LUCY.

SIR WILLIAM GLANSDALE.

SIR THOMAS GARGRAVE.

Mayor of London.

WOODVILLE, *Lieutenant of the Tower.*

VERNON, *of the White Rose or York faction.*

BASSET, *of the Red Rose or Lancaster faction.*

A Lawyer.

Gaolers, *to Mortimer.*

CHARLES, *Dauphin, and afterwards King of France.*

REIGNIER, DUKE OF ANJOU, *and titular King of Naples.*

DUKE OF BURGUNDY.

DUKE OF ALENÇON.

BASTARD OF ORLEANS.

Governor of Paris.

Master-Gunner of Orleans, *and his* Son.

General of the French Forces *in Bordeaux.*

A French Sergeant.

A Porter.

An old Shepherd, *father to Joan la Pucelle.*

MARGARET, *daughter to Reignier, afterwards married to King Henry.*

COUNTESS OF AUVERGNE.

JOAN LA PUCELLE, *commonly called* JOAN OF ARC.

Lords, Warders of the Tower, Heralds, Officers, Soldiers, Messengers, English and French Attendants. Fiends *appearing to La Pucelle.*

THE SCENE : *England and France.*

ACT ONE

SCENE I. *Westminster Abbey.*

Dead March. Enter the funeral of King Henry the Fifth, attended on by the DUKE OF BEDFORD, *Regent of France, the* DUKE OF GLOUCESTER, *Protector, the* DUKE OF EXETER, *the* EARL OF WARWICK, *the* BISHOP OF WINCHESTER.

Bed. Hung be the heavens with black, yield day to night !
Comets, importing change of times and states,
Brandish your crystal tresses in the sky
And with them scourge the bad revolting stars
That have consented unto Henry's death !
King Henry the Fifth, too famous to live long !   6
England ne'er lost a king of so much worth.
Glo. England ne'er had a king until his time.
Virtue he had, deserving to command ;
His brandish'd sword did blind men with his beams ;   10
His arms spread wider than a dragon's wings ;
His sparkling eyes, replete with wrathful fire,
More dazzled and drove back his enemies
Than mid-day sun fierce bent against their faces.
What should I say ? His deeds exceed all speech :   15
He ne'er lift up his hand but conquered.
Exe. We mourn in black ; why mourn we not in blood ?
Henry is dead and never shall revive.
Upon a wooden coffin we attend ;
And death's dishonourable victory   20
We with our stately presence glorify,
Like captives bound to a triumphant car.
What ! shall we curse the planets of mishap
That plotted thus our glory's overthrow ?
Or shall we think the subtle-witted French
Conjurers and sorcerers, that, afraid of him,
By magic verses have contriv'd his end ?

589

Win. He was a king bless'd of the King
of kings ;
Unto the French the dreadful judgment-
day
So dreadful will not be as was his sight. 30
The battles of the Lord of Hosts he fought ;
The Church's prayers made him so pros-
perous.
Glo. The Church ! Where is it ? Had not
churchmen pray'd,
His thread of life had not so soon decay'd.
None do you like but an effeminate prince,
Whom like a school-boy you may overawe.
Win. Gloucester, whate'er we like, thou
art Protector 37
And lookest to command the Prince and
realm.
Thy wife is proud ; she holdeth thee in awe
More than God or religious churchmen may.
Glo. Name not religion, for thou lov'st
the flesh ; 41
And ne'er throughout the year to church
thou go'st,
Except it be to pray against thy foes.
Bed. Cease, cease these jars and rest your
minds in peace ;
Let's to the altar. Heralds, wait on us. 45
Instead of gold, we'll offer up our arms,
Since arms avail not, now that Henry's
dead.
Posterity, await for wretched years,
When at their mothers' moist'ned eyes
babes shall suck,
Our isle be made a nourish of salt tears, 50
And none but women left to wail the dead.
Henry the Fifth, thy ghost I invocate :
Prosper this realm, keep it from civil broils,
Combat with adverse planets in the
heavens.
A far more glorious star thy soul will make
Than Julius Cæsar or bright— 56

Enter a Messenger.

Mess. My honourable lords, health to you
all !
Sad tidings bring I to you out of France,
Of loss, of slaughter, and discomfiture :
Guienne, Champagne, Rheims, Orleans, 60
Paris, Guysors, Poictiers, are all quite lost.
Bed. What say'st thou, man, before dead
Henry's corse ?
Speak softly, or the loss of those great
towns
Will make him burst his lead and rise from
death.
Glo. Is Paris lost ? Is Rouen yielded up ?
If Henry were recall'd to life again, 66
These news would cause him once more
yield the ghost.
Exe. How were they lost ? What treach-
ery was us'd ?
Mess. No treachery, but want of men and
money.
Amongst the soldiers this is muttered— 70

That here you maintain several factions ;
And whilst a field should be dispatch'd and
fought,
You are disputing of your generals :
One would have ling'ring wars, with little
cost ;
Another would fly swift, but wanteth wings;
A third thinks, without expense at all, 76
By guileful fair words peace may be
obtain'd.
Awake, awake, English nobility !
Let not sloth dim your honours, new-begot.
Cropp'd are the flower-de-luces in your
arms ; 80
Of England's coat one half is cut away.
Exe. Were our tears wanting to this
funeral,
These tidings would call forth their flowing
tides.
Bed. Me they concern ; Regent I am of
France.
Give me my steeled coat ; I'll fight for
France. 85
Away with these disgraceful wailing robes !
Wounds will I lend the French instead of
eyes,
To weep their intermissive miseries.

Enter a second Messenger.

2 Mess. Lords, view these letters full of
bad mischance.
France is revolted from the English quite,
Except some petty towns of no import. 91
The Dauphin Charles is crowned king in
Rheims ;
The Bastard of Orleans with him is join'd ;
Reignier, Duke of Anjou, doth take his
part ;
The Duke of Alençon flieth to his side. 95
Exe. The Dauphin crowned king ! all fly
to him !
O, whither shall we fly from this reproach ?
Glo. We will not fly but to our enemies'
throats.
Bedford, if thou be slack I'll fight it out.
Bed. Gloucester, why doubt'st thou of
my forwardness ? 100
An army have I muster'd in my thoughts,
Wherewith already France is overrun.

Enter a third Messenger.

3 Mess. My gracious lords, to add to your
laments,
Wherewith you now bedew King Henry's
hearse,
I must inform you of a dismal fight 105
Betwixt the stout Lord Talbot and the
French.
Win. What ! Wherein Talbot overcame ?
Is't so ?
3 Mess. O, no ; wherein Lord Talbot was
o'erthrown.
The circumstance I'll tell you more at large.
The tenth of August last this dreadful lord,

Retiring from the siege of Orleans,　　111
Having full scarce six thousand in his troop,
By three and twenty thousand of the
　　French
Was round encompassed and set upon.
No leisure had he to enrank his men ;　115
He wanted pikes to set before his archers ;
Instead whereof sharp stakes pluck'd out
　　of hedges
They pitched in the ground confusedly
To keep the horsemen off from breaking in.
More than three hours the fight continued ;
Where valiant Talbot, above human
　　thought,
Enacted wonders with his sword and lance :
Hundreds he sent to hell, and none durst
　　stand him ;
Here, there, and everywhere, enrag'd he
　　slew—
The French exclaim'd the devil was in
　　arms ;　　　　　　　　　　　　　　125
All the whole army stood agaz'd on him.
His soldiers, spying his undaunted spirit,
' A Talbot ! a Talbot ! ' cried out amain,
And rush'd into the bowels of the battle.
Here had the conquest fully been seal'd up
If Sir John Fastolfe had not play'd the
　　coward.　　　　　　　　　　　　　131
He, being in the vaward—plac'd behind
With purpose to relieve and follow them—
Cowardly fled, not having struck one
　　stroke ;
Hence grew the general wreck and massacre.
Enclosed were they with their enemies.　136
A base Walloon, to win the Dauphin's
　　grace,
Thrust Talbot with a spear into the back ;
Whom all France, with their chief assem-
　　bled strength,　　　　　　　　　　139
Durst not presume to look once in the
　　face.
　　Bed. Is Talbot slain ? Then I will slay
　　myself,
For living idly here in pomp and ease,
Whilst such a worthy leader, wanting aid,
Unto his dastard foemen is betray'd.
　　3 Mess. O no, he lives, but is took
　　prisoner,　　　　　　　　　　　　145
And Lord Scales with him, and Lord
　　Hungerford ;
Most of the rest slaughter'd or took like-
　　wise.
　　Bed. His ransom there is none but I shall
　　pay.
I'll hale the Dauphin headlong from his
　　throne ;　　　　　　　　　　　　149
His crown shall be the ransom of my friend;
Four of their lords I'll change for one of
　　ours.
Farewell, my masters ; to my task will I ;
Bonfires in France forthwith I am to make
To keep our great Saint George's feast
　　withal.　　　　　　　　　　　　154
Ten thousand soldiers with me I will take,

Whose bloody deeds shall make all Europe
　　quake.
　　3 Mess. So you had need ; for Orleans is
　　besieg'd ;
The English army is grown weak and faint ;
The Earl of Salisbury craveth supply
And hardly keeps his men from mutiny, 160
Since they, so few, watch such a multitude.
　　Exe. Remember, lords, your oaths to
　　Henry sworn,
Either to quell the Dauphin utterly,
Or bring him in obedience to your yoke.
　　Bed. I do remember it, and here take my
　　leave　　　　　　　　　　　　　　165
To go about my preparation.　　　　[*Exit.*
　　Glo. I'll to the Tower with all the haste
　　I can
To view th' artillery and munition ;
And then I will proclaim young Henry king.
　　　　　　　　　　　　　　　　[*Exit.*
　　Exe. To Eltham will I, where the young
　　King is,　　　　　　　　　　　　170
Being ordain'd his special governor ;
And for his safety there I'll best devise.
　　　　　　　　　　　　　　　　[*Exit.*
　　Win. [*Aside*] Each hath his place and
　　function to attend :
I am left out ; for me nothing remains.
But long I will not be Jack out of office. 175
The King from Eltham I intend to steal,
And sit at chiefest stern of public weal.
　　　　　　　　　　　　　　　　[*Exeunt.*

SCENE II.　*France. Before Orleans.*

Sound a flourish.　　Enter CHARLES THE
　DAUPHIN, ALENÇON, *and* REIGNIER,
　marching with drum and Soldiers.

　　Char. Mars his true moving, even as in
　　the heavens
So in the earth, to this day is not known.
Late did he shine upon the English side ;
Now we are victors, upon us he smiles.
What towns of any moment but we have ? 5
At pleasure here we lie near Orleans ;
Otherwhiles the famish'd English, like pale
　　ghosts,
Faintly besiege us one hour in a month.
　　Alen. They want their porridge and their
　　fat bull-beeves.
Either they must be dieted like mules　　10
And have their provender tied to their
　　mouths,
Or piteous they will look, like drowned
　　mice.
　　Reig. Let's raise the siege. Why live we
　　idly here ?
Talbot is taken, whom we wont to fear ;
Remaineth none but mad-brain'd Salis-
　　bury,　　　　　　　　　　　　　15
And he may well in fretting spend his gall—
Nor men nor money hath he to make war.
　　Char. Sound, sound alarum ; we will rush
　　on them.

Now for the honour of the forlorn French !
Him I forgive my death that killeth me, 20
When he sees me go back one foot or flee.
                                        [Exeunt.

*Here alarum. They are beaten back by
the English, with great loss. Re-enter
CHARLES, ALENÇON, and REIGNIER.*

 Char. Who ever saw the like ? What men
    have I !
Dogs ! cowards ! dastards ! I would ne'er
    have fled
But that they left me midst my enemies.
 Reig. Salisbury is a desperate homicide ;
He fighteth as one weary of his life. 26
The other lords, like lions wanting food,
Do rush upon us as their hungry prey.
 Alen. Froissart, a countryman of ours,
    records
England all Olivers and Rowlands bred 30
During the time Edward the Third did
    reign.
More truly now may this be verified ;
For none but Samsons and Goliases
It sendeth forth to skirmish. One to
    ten !
Lean raw-bon'd rascals ! Who would e'er
    suppose 35
They had such courage and audacity ?
 Char. Let's leave this town ; for they are
    hare-brain'd slaves,
And hunger will enforce them to be more
    eager.
Of old I know them ; rather with their
    teeth
The walls they'll tear down than forsake
    the siege. 40
 Reig. I think by some odd gimmers or
    device
Their arms are set, like clocks, still to strike
    on ;
Else ne'er could they hold out so as they do.
By my consent, we'll even let them alone.
 Alen. Be it so. 45

 Enter the BASTARD OF ORLEANS.

 Bast. Where's the Prince Dauphin ? I
    have news for him.
 Char. Bastard of Orleans, thrice welcome
    to us.
 Bast. Methinks your looks are sad, your
    cheer appall'd.
Hath the late overthrow wrought this
    offence ?
Be not dismay'd, for succour is at hand. 50
A holy maid hither with me I bring,
Which, by a vision sent to her from heaven,
Ordained is to raise this tedious siege
And drive the English forth the bounds of
    France.
The spirit of deep prophecy she hath, 55
Exceeding the nine sibyls of old Rome :
What's past and what's to come she can
    descry.

Speak, shall I call her in ? Believe my
    words,
For they are certain and unfallible.
 Char. Go, call her in. [*Exit Bastard*] But
    first, to try her skill, 60
Reignier, stand thou as Dauphin in my
    place ;
Question her proudly ; let thy looks be
    stern ;
By this means shall we sound what skill she
    hath.

*Re-enter the BASTARD OF ORLEANS, with
JOAN LA PUCELLE.*

 Reig. Fair maid, is 't thou wilt do these
    wondrous feats ?
 Puc. Reignier, is 't thou that thinkest to
    beguile me ? 65
Where is the Dauphin ? Come, come from
    behind ;
I know thee well, though never seen before.
Be not amaz'd, there's nothing hid from me.
In private will I talk with thee apart.
Stand back, you lords, and give us leave
    awhile. 70
 Reig. She takes upon her bravely at first
    dash.
 Puc. Dauphin, I am by birth a shepherd's
    daughter,
My wit untrain'd in any kind of art.
Heaven and our Lady gracious hath it
    pleas'd
To shine on my contemptible estate. 75
Lo, whilst I waited on my tender lambs
And to sun's parching heat display'd my
    cheeks,
God's Mother deigned to appear to me,
And in a vision full of majesty
Will'd me to leave my base vocation 80
And free my country from calamity—
Her aid she promis'd and assur'd success.
In complete glory she reveal'd herself ;
And whereas I was black and swart before,
With those clear rays which she infus'd on
    me 85
That beauty am I bless'd with which you
    may see.
Ask me what question thou canst possible,
And I will answer unpremeditated.
My courage try by combat if thou dar'st,
And thou shalt find that I exceed my sex. 90
Resolve on this : thou shalt be fortunate
If thou receive me for thy warlike mate.
 Char. Thou hast astonish'd me with thy
    high terms.
Only this proof I'll of thy valour make—
In single combat thou shalt buckle with me;
And if thou vanquishest, thy words are
    true ; 96
Otherwise I renounce all confidence.
 Puc. I am prepar'd ; here is my keen-
    edg'd sword,
Deck'd with five flower-de-luces on each
    side,

The which at Touraine, in Saint Katherine's
　　churchyard,　　　　　　　　　　　100
Out of a great deal of old iron I chose forth.
　Char. Then come, o' God's name; I fear
　　no woman.
　Puc. And while I live I'll ne'er fly from
　　a man.　　[*Here they fight and Joan
　　　　　　la Pucelle overcomes.*
　Char. Stay, stay thy hands; thou art an
　　Amazon,　　　　　　　　　　　104
And fightest with the sword of Deborah.
　Puc. Christ's Mother helps me, else I
　　were too weak.
　Char. Whoe'er helps thee, 'tis thou that
　　must help me.
Impatiently I burn with thy desire;
My heart and hands thou hast at once
　　subdu'd.
Excellent Pucelle, if thy name be so,　110
Let me thy servant and not sovereign be.
'Tis the French Dauphin sueth to thee thus.
　Puc. I must not yield to any rites of love,
For my profession's sacred from above.
When I have chased all thy foes from hence,
Then will I think upon a recompense.　116
　Char. Meantime look gracious on thy
　　prostrate thrall.
　Reig. My lord, methinks, is very long in
　　talk.
　Alen. Doubtless he shrives this woman to
　　her smock;
Else ne'er could he so long protract his
　　speech.　　　　　　　　　　　120
　Reig. Shall we disturb him, since he keeps
　　no mean?
　Alen. He may mean more than we poor
　　men do know;
These women are shrewd tempters with
　　their tongues.
　Reig. My lord, where are you? What
　　devise you on?
Shall we give o'er Orleans, or no?　125
　Puc. Why, no, I say; distrustful re-
　　creants!
Fight till the last gasp; I will be your
　　guard.
　Char. What she says I'll confirm; we'll
　　fight it out.
　Puc. Assign'd am I to be the English
　　scourge.
This night the siege assuredly I'll raise.　130
Expect Saint Martin's summer, halcyon
　　days,
Since I have entered into these wars.
Glory is like a circle in the water,
Which never ceaseth to enlarge itself
Till by broad spreading it disperse to
　　nought.　　　　　　　　　　　135
With Henry's death the English circle ends;
Dispersed are the glories it included.
Now am I like that proud insulting ship
Which Cæsar and his fortune bare at once.
　Char. Was Mahomet inspired with a
　　dove?　　　　　　　　　　　　140

Thou with an eagle art inspired then.
Helen, the mother of great Constantine,
Nor yet Saint Philip's daughters were like
　　thee.
Bright star of Venus, fall'n down on the
　　earth,
How may I reverently worship thee
　　enough?　　　　　　　　　　　145
　Alen. Leave off delays, and let us raise
　　the siege.
　Reig. Woman, do what thou canst to
　　save our honours;
Drive them from Orleans, and be im-
　　mortaliz'd.
　Char. Presently we'll try. Come, let's
　　away about it.
No prophet will I trust if she prove false.　150
　　　　　　　　　　　　　[*Exeunt.*

SCENE III.　*London.　Before the Tower gates.*

Enter the DUKE OF GLOUCESTER, *with his
　　Serving-men in blue coats.*

　Glo. I am come to survey the Tower this
　　day;
Since Henry's death, I fear, there is convey-
　　ance.
Where be these warders that they wait not
　　here?
Open the gates; 'tis Gloucester that calls.
　1 *Ward.* [*Within*] Who's there that
　　knocks so imperiously?　　　　　5
　1 *Serv.* It is the noble Duke of Gloucester.
　2 *Ward.* [*Within*] Whoe'er he be, you
　　may not be let in.
　1 *Serv.* Villains, answer you so the Lord
　　Protector?
　1 *Ward.* [*Within*] The Lord protect him!
　　so we answer him.
We do no otherwise than we are will'd.　10
　Glo. Who willed you, or whose will stands
　　but mine?
There's none Protector of the realm but I.
Break up the gates, I'll be your warrantize.
Shall I be flouted thus by dunghill grooms?
　　　[*Gloucester's men rush at the Tower
　　　gates, and Woodville the Lieu-
　　　tenant speaks within.*
　Wood. [*Within*] What noise is this?
　　What traitors have we here?　　　15
　Glo. Lieutenant, is it you whose voice I
　　hear?
Open the gates; here's Gloucester that
　　would enter.
　Wood. [*Within*] Have patience, noble
　　Duke, I may not open;
The Cardinal of Winchester forbids.
From him I have express commandment　20
That thou none of thine shall be let in.
　Glo.　Faint-hearted Woodville, prizest
　　him fore me?
Arrogant Winchester, that haughty prelate
Whom Henry, our late sovereign, ne'er
　　could brook!

593

Thou art no friend to God or to the King. 25
Open the gates, or I'll shut thee out shortly.
    Serving-men. Open the gates unto the
        Lord Protector,
Or we'll burst them open, if that you come
    not quickly.

Enter to the Protector at the Tower gates
WINCHESTER *and his Men in tawny coats.*

    Win. How now, ambitious Humphry!
        What means this?
    Glo. Peel'd priest, dost thou command me
        to be shut out?   30
    Win. I do, thou most usurping proditor,
And not Protector of the King or realm.
    Glo. Stand back, thou manifest con-
        spirator,
Thou that contrived'st to murder our dead
    lord;   34
Thou that giv'st whores indulgences to sin.
I'll canvass thee in thy broad cardinal's hat,
If thou proceed in this thy insolence.
    Win. Nay, stand thou back; I will not
        budge a foot.
This be Damascus; be thou cursed Cain,
To slay thy brother Abel, if thou wilt.   40
    Glo. I will not slay thee, but I'll drive
        thee back.
Thy scarlet robes as a child's bearing-cloth
I'll use to carry thee out of this place.
    Win. Do what thou dar'st; I beard thee
        to thy face.
    Glo. What! am I dar'd and bearded to
        my face?   45
Draw, men, for all this privileged place—
Blue-coats to tawny-coats. Priest, beware
    your beard;
I mean to tug it, and to cuff you soundly;
Under my feet I stamp thy cardinal's hat;
In spite of Pope or dignities of church,   50
Here by the cheeks I'll drag thee up and
    down.
    Win. Gloucester, thou wilt answer this
        before the Pope.
    Glo. Winchester goose! I cry 'A rope, a
        rope!'
Now beat them hence; why do you let
    them stay?
Thee I'll chase hence, thou wolf in sheep's
    array.   55
Out, tawny-coats! Out, scarlet hypocrite!

*Here Gloucester's men beat out the Cardinal's
men; and enter in the hurly-burly the*
MAYOR *of London, and his Officers.*

    May. Fie, lords! that you, being
        supreme magistrates,
Thus contumeliously should break the
    peace!
    Glo. Peace, Mayor! thou know'st little of
        my wrongs:
Here's Beaufort, that regards nor God nor
    King,   60
Hath here distrain'd the Tower to his use.

    Win. Here's Gloucester, a foe to citizens;
One that still motions war and never peace,
O'ercharging your free purses with large
    fines;
That seeks to overthrow religion,   65
Because he is Protector of the realm,
And would have armour here out of the
    Tower,
To crown himself King and suppress the
    Prince.
    Glo. I will not answer thee with words,
        but blows.
                    [*Here they skirmish again.*
    May. Nought rests for me in this tumul-
        tuous strife   70
But to make open proclamation. ⸱
Come, officer, as loud as e'er thou canst,
Cry.
    Off. [*Cries*] All manner of men assembled
here in arms this day against God's peace
and the King's, we charge and command
you, in his Highness' name, to repair to
your several dwelling-places; and not to
wear, handle, or use, any sword, weapon,
or dagger, henceforward, upon pain of
death.
    Glo. Cardinal, I'll be no breaker of the
        law;
But we shall meet and break our minds at
    large.   80
    Win. Gloucester, we'll meet to thy cost,
        be sure;
Thy heart-blood I will have for this day's
    work.
    May. I'll call for clubs if you will not
        away.
This Cardinal's more haughty than the
    devil.
    Glo. Mayor, farewell; thou dost but what
        thou mayst.   85
    Win. Abominable Gloucester, guard thy
        head,
For I intend to have it ere long.
            [*Exeunt, severally, Gloucester and
                Winchester with their Servants.*
    May. See the coast clear'd, and then we
        will depart.
Good God, these nobles should such
    stomachs bear!   89
I myself fight not once in forty year.
                                    [*Exeunt.*

SCENE IV. *France. Before Orleans.*

Enter, on the walls, the Master-Gunner of
    Orleans *and his Boy.*

    M. Gun. Sirrah, thou know'st how Orleans
        is besieg'd,
And how the English have the suburbs won.
    Boy. Father, I know; and oft have shot
        at them,
Howe'er unfortunate I miss'd my aim.
    M. Gun. But now thou shalt not. Be
        thou rul'd by me.   5

Chief master-gunner am I of this town;
Something I must do to procure me grace.
The Prince's espials have informed me
How the English, in the suburbs close
    intrench'd,
Wont, through a secret grate of iron bars 10
In yonder tower, to overpeer the city,
And thence discover how with most
    advantage
They may vex us with shot or with assault.
To intercept this inconvenience, 14
A piece of ordnance 'gainst it I have plac'd;
And even these three days have I watch'd
If I could see them. Now do thou watch,
For I can stay no longer.
If thou spy'st any, run and bring me word;
And thou shalt find me at the Governor's. 20
                [Exit.

Boy. Father, I warrant you; take you
    no care;
I'll never trouble you, if I may spy them.
                [Exit.

Enter SALISBURY and TALBOT on the
turrets, with SIR WILLIAM GLANDSDALE,
SIR THOMAS GARGRAVE, and Others.

Sal. Talbot, my life, my joy, again
    return'd!
How wert thou handled being prisoner?
Or by what means got'st thou to be
    releas'd? 25
Discourse, I prithee, on this turret's top.

Tal. The Earl of Bedford had a prisoner
Call'd the brave Lord Ponton de Santrailles;
For him was I exchang'd and ransomed.
But with a baser man of arms by far 30
Once, in contempt, they would have
    barter'd me;
Which I disdaining scorn'd, and craved
    death
Rather than I would be so vile esteem'd.
In fine, redeem'd I was as I desir'd.
But, O! the treacherous Fastolfe wounds
    my heart; 35
Whom with my bare fists I would execute,
If I now had him brought into my power.

Sal. Yet tell'st thou not how thou wert
    entertain'd.

Tal. With scoffs, and scorns, and con-
    tumelious taunts.
In open market-place produc'd they me 40
To be a public spectacle to all;
Here, said they, is the terror of the French,
The scarecrow that affrights our children so.
Then broke I from the officers that led me,
And with my nails digg'd stones out of the
    ground 45
To hurl at the beholders of my shame;
My grisly countenance made others fly;
None durst come near for fear of sudden
    death.
In iron walls they deem'd me not secure;
So great fear of my name 'mongst them was
    spread 50

That they suppos'd I could rend bars of
    steel
And spurn in pieces posts of adamant;
Wherefore a guard of chosen shot I had
That walk'd about me every minute-while;
And if I did but stir out of my bed, 55
Ready they were to shoot me to the heart.

Enter the Boy with a linstock.

Sal. I grieve to hear what torments you
    endur'd;
But we will be reveng'd sufficiently.
Now it is supper-time in Orleans: 59
Here, through this grate, I count each one
And view the Frenchmen how they fortify.
Let us look in; the sight will much delight
    thee.
Sir Thomas Gargrave and Sir William
    Glansdale,
Let me have your express opinions
Where is best place to make our batt'ry
    next. 65

Gar. I think at the North Gate; for there
    stand lords.

Glan. And I here, at the bulwark of the
    bridge.

Tal. For aught I see, this city must be
    famish'd,
Or with light skirmishes enfeebled.
        [Here they shoot and Salisbury
            and Gargrave fall down.

Sal. O Lord, have mercy on us, wretched
    sinners! 70

Gar. O Lord, have mercy on me, woeful
    man!

Tal. What chance is this that suddenly
    hath cross'd us?
Speak, Salisbury; at least, if thou canst
    speak.
How far'st thou, mirror of all martial men?
One of thy eyes and thy cheek's side struck
    off! 75
Accursed tower! accursed fatal hand
That hath contriv'd this woeful tragedy!
In thirteen battles Salisbury o'ercame;
Henry the Fifth he first train'd to the wars;
Whilst any trump did sound or drum struck
    up, 80
His sword did ne'er leave striking in the
    field.
Yet liv'st thou, Salisbury? Though thy
    speech doth fail,
One eye thou hast to look to heaven for
    grace;
The sun with one eye vieweth all the world.
Heaven, be thou gracious to none alive 85
If Salisbury wants mercy at thy hands!
Bear hence his body; I will help to bury it.
Sir Thomas Gargrave, hast thou any life?
Speak unto Talbot; nay, look up to him.
Salisbury, cheer thy spirit with this
    comfort, 90
Thou shalt not die whiles—
He beckons with his hand and smiles on me,

As who should say ' When I am dead and
    gone,
Remember to avenge me on the French '.
Plantagenet, I will ; and like thee, Nero, 95
Play on the lute, beholding the towns burn.
Wretched shall France be only in my name.
        [Here an alarum, and it thunders
                    and lightens.
What stir is this ?   What tumult's in the
    heavens ?
Whence cometh this alarum and the noise ?

        Enter a Messenger.

Mess. My lord, my lord, the French have
    gather'd head.   100
The Dauphin, with one Joan la Pucelle
    join'd,
A holy prophetess new risen up,
Is come with a great power to raise the
    siege. [Here Salisbury lifteth him-
            self up and groans.
Tal. Hear, hear how dying Salisbury
    doth groan.
It irks his heart he cannot be reveng'd. 105
Frenchmen, I'll be a Salisbury to you.
Pucelle or puzzel, dolphin or dogfish,
Your hearts I'll stamp out with my horse's
    heels
And make a quagmire of your mingled
    brains.
Convey me Salisbury into his tent,   110
And then we'll try what these dastard
    Frenchmen dare. [Alarum. Exeunt.

        SCENE V. Before Orleans.

Here an alarum again, and TALBOT pursueth
the DAUPHIN and driveth him. Then enter
JOAN LA PUCELLE driving Englishmen
before her. Then enter TALBOT.

Tal. Where is my strength, my valour,
    and my force ?
Our English troops retire, I cannot stay
    them ;
A woman clad in armour chaseth them.

        Enter LA PUCELLE.

Here, here she comes. I'll have a bout with
    thee.
Devil or devil's dam, I'll conjure thee ; 5
Blood will I draw on thee—thou art a
    witch—
And straightway give thy soul to him thou
    serv'st.
Puc. Come, come, 'tis only I that must
    disgrace thee.   [Here they fight.
Tal. Heavens, can you suffer hell so to
    prevail ?
My breast I'll burst with straining of my
    courage,   10
And from my shoulders crack my arms
    asunder,
But I will chastise this high-minded
    strumpet.   [They fight again.

Puc. Talbot, farewell ; thy hour is not
    yet come.
I must go victual Orleans forthwith.
        [A short alarum ; then enter the
                    town with soldiers.
O'ertake me if thou canst ; I scorn thy
    strength.   15
Go, go, cheer up thy hungry starved
    men ;
Help Salisbury to make his testament.
This day is ours, as many more shall be.
                                [Exit.
Tal. My thoughts are whirled like a
    potter's wheel ;
I know not where I am nor what I do. 20
A witch by fear, not force, like Hannibal,
Drives back our troops and conquers as she
    lists.
So bees with smoke and doves with noisome
    stench
Are from their hives and houses driven
    away.
They call'd us, for our fierceness, English
    dogs ;   25
Now like to whelps we crying run away.
                    [A short alarum.
Hark, countrymen ! Either renew the fight
Or tear the lions out of England's coat ;
Renounce your soil, give sheep in lions'
    stead :
Sheep run not half so treacherous from the
    wolf,   30
Or horse or oxen from the leopard,
As you fly from your oft-subdued slaves.
        [Alarum. Here another skirmish.
It will not be—retire into your trenches.
You all consented unto Salisbury's death,
For none would strike a stroke in his
    revenge.   35
Pucelle is ent'red into Orleans
In spite of us or aught that we could do.
O, would I were to die with Salisbury !
The shame hereof will make me hide my
    head. [Exit Talbot. Alarum ; retreat.

        SCENE VI. Orleans.

Flourish. Enter on the walls, LA PUCELLE,
    CHARLES, REIGNIER, ALENÇON, and
    Soldiers.

Puc. Advance our waving colours on the
    walls ;
Rescu'd is Orleans from the English.
Thus Joan la Pucelle hath perform'd her
    word.
Char. Divinest creature, Astræa's
    daughter,
How shall I honour thee for this success ? 5
Thy promises are like Adonis' gardens,
That one day bloom'd and fruitful were the
    next.
France, triumph in thy glorious prophetess.
Recover'd is the town of Orleans.
More blessed hap did ne'er befall our state.

Reig. Why ring not out the bells aloud
    throughout the town ?   11
Dauphin, command the citizens make
    bonfires
And feast and banquet in the open streets
To celebrate the joy that God hath given us.
    Alen. All France will be replete with
      mirth and joy   15
When they shall hear how we have play'd
    the men.
    Char. 'Tis Joan, not we, by whom the day
      is won ;
For which I will divide my crown with her ;
And all the priests and friars in my realm
Shall in procession sing her endless praise.
A statelier pyramis to her I'll rear   21
Than Rhodope's of Memphis ever was.
In memory of her, when she is dead,
Her ashes, in an urn more precious
Than the rich jewell'd coffer of Darius,   25
Transported shall be at high festivals
Before the kings and queens of France.
No longer on Saint Denis will we cry,
But Joan la Pucelle shall be France's saint.
Come in, and let us banquet royally   30
After this golden day of victory.
               [Flourish. Exeunt.

ACT TWO

SCENE I. *Before Orleans.*

Enter a French Sergeant *and two* Sentinels.

    Sergt. Sirs, take your places and be
      vigilant.
If any noise or soldier you perceive
Near to the walls, by some apparent sign
Let us have knowledge at the court of
    guard.
    1 *Sent.* Sergeant, you shall. *[Exit Sergt.]*
Thus are poor servitors,   5
When others sleep upon their quiet beds,
Constrain'd to watch in darkness, rain, and
    cold.

Enter TALBOT, BEDFORD, BURGUNDY, *and*
Forces, *with scaling-ladders ; their drums
beating a dead march.*

    Tal. Lord Regent, and redoubted Bur-
      gundy,
By whose approach the regions of Artois,
Wallon, and Picardy, are friends to us,   10
This happy night the Frenchmen are secure,
Having all day carous'd and banqueted ;
Embrace we then this opportunity,
As fitting best to quittance their deceit,
Contriv'd by art and baleful sorcery.   15
    Bed. Coward of France, how much he
      wrongs his fame,
Despairing of his own arm's fortitude,
To join with witches and the help of hell !
    Bur. Traitors have never other company.
But what's that Pucelle whom they term so
    pure ?   20

    Tal. A maid, they say.
    Bed.   A maid ! and be so martial !
    Bur. Pray God she prove not masculine
      ere long,
If underneath the standard of the French
She carry armour as she hath begun.
    Tal. Well, let them practise and converse
      with spirits :   25
God is our fortress, in whose conquering
    name
Let us resolve to scale their flinty bulwarks.
    Bed. Ascend, brave Talbot ; we will
      follow thee.
    Tal. Not all together ; better far, I guess,
That we do make our entrance several ways;
That if it chance the one of us do fail   31
The other yet may rise against their force.
    Bed. Agreed ; I'll to yond corner.
    Bur.   And I to this.
    Tal. And here will Talbot mount or make
      his grave.   34
Now, Salisbury, for thee, and for the right
Of English Henry, shall this night appear
How much in duty I am bound to both.
      *[The English scale the walls and
        cry ' Saint George ! a Talbot ! '*
    Sent. Arm ! arm ! The enemy doth make
      assault.

*The French leap o'er the walls in their shirts.
Enter, several ways,* BASTARD, ALENÇON,
REIGNIER, *half ready and half unready.*

    Alen. How now, my lords ? What, all
      unready so ?
    Bast. Unready ! Ay, and glad we 'scap'd
      so well.   40
    Reig. 'Twas time, I trow, to wake and
      leave our beds,
Hearing alarums at our chamber doors.
    Alen. Of all exploits since first I follow'd
      arms
Ne'er heard I of a warlike enterprise
More venturous or desperate than this.   45
    Bast. I think this Talbot be a fiend of
      hell.
    Reig. If not of hell, the heavens, sure,
      favour him.
    Alen. Here cometh Charles ; I marvel
      how he sped.

Enter CHARLES *and* LA PUCELLE.

    Bast. Tut ! holy Joan was his defensive
      guard.
    Char. Is this thy cunning, thou deceitful
      dame ?   50
Didst thou at first, to flatter us withal,
Make us partakers of a little gain
That now our loss might be ten times so
    much ?
    Puc. Wherefore is Charles impatient with
      his friend ?   54
At all times will you have my power alike ?
Sleeping or waking, must I still prevail,
Or will you blame and lay the fault on me ?

Improvident soldiers! Had your watch
been good
This sudden mischief never could have
fall'n.
 Char. Duke of Alençon, this was your
default   60
That, being captain of the watch to-night,
Did look no better to that weighty charge.
 Alen. Had all your quarters been as safely
kept
As that whereof I had the government,   64
We had not been thus shamefully surpris'd.
 Bast. Mine was secure.
 Reig.   And so was mine, my lord.
 Char. And, for myself, most part of all
this night,
Within her quarter and mine own precinct
I was employ'd in passing to and fro
About relieving of the sentinels.   70
Then how or which way should they first
break in ?
 Puc. Question, my lords, no further of
the case,
How or which way; 'tis sure they found
some place
But weakly guarded, where the breach was
made.
And now there rests no other shift but
this—   75
To gather our soldiers, scatter'd and
dispers'd,
And lay new platforms to endamage them.

Alarum. Enter an English Soldier, *crying
' A Talbot ! A Talbot ! ' They fly, leaving
their clothes behind.*

 Sold. I'll be so bold to take what they
have left.
The cry of Talbot serves me for a sword;
For I have loaden me with many spoils,   80
Using no other weapon but his name.
                                       [*Exit.*

SCENE II. *Orleans. Within the town.*

Enter TALBOT, BEDFORD, BURGUNDY, *a*
Captain, *and* Others.

 Bed. The day begins to break, and night
is fled
Whose pitchy mantle over-veil'd the earth.
Here sound retreat and cease our hot
pursuit.   [*Retreat sounded.*
 Tal. Bring forth the body of old Salisbury
And here advance it in the market-place, 5
The middle centre of this cursed town.
Now have I paid my vow unto his soul;
For every drop of blood was drawn from
him
There hath at least five Frenchmen died
to-night.
And that hereafter ages may behold   10
What ruin happened in revenge of him,
Within their chiefest temple I'll erect
A tomb, wherein his corpse shall be interr'd;

Upon the which, that every one may read,
Shall be engrav'd the sack of Orleans,   15
The treacherous manner of his mournful
death,
And what a terror he had been to France.
But, lords, in all our bloody massacre,
I muse we met not with the Dauphin's
grace,
His new-come champion, virtuous Joan of
Arc,   20
Nor any of his false confederates.
 Bed. 'Tis thought, Lord Talbot, when the
fight began,
Rous'd on the sudden from their drowsy
beds,
They did amongst the troops of armed men
Leap o'er the walls for refuge in the field. 25
 Bur. Myself, as far as I could well discern
For smoke and dusky vapours of the night,
Am sure I scar'd the Dauphin and his trull,
When arm in arm they both came swiftly
running,
Like to a pair of loving turtle-doves   30
That could not live asunder day or night.
After that things are set in order here,
We'll follow them with all the power we
have.

Enter a Messenger.

 Mess. All hail, my lords! Which of this
princely train
Call ye the warlike Talbot, for his acts 35
So much applauded through the realm of
France ?
 Tal. Here is the Talbot; who would
speak with him ?
 Mess. The virtuous lady, Countess of
Auvergne,
With modesty admiring thy renown,
By me entreats, great lord, thou wouldst
vouchsafe   40
To visit her poor castle where she lies,
That she may boast she hath beheld the
man
Whose glory fills the world with loud report.
 Bur. Is it even so ? Nay, then I see our
wars
Will turn unto a peaceful comic sport,   45
When ladies crave to be encount'red with.
You may not, my lord, despise her gentle
suit.
 Tal. Ne'er trust me then; for when a
world of men
Could not prevail with all their oratory,
Yet hath a woman's kindness overrul'd;   50
And therefore tell her I return great thanks
And in submission will attend on her.
Will not your honours bear me company ?
 Bed. No, truly; 'tis more than manners
will;   54
And I have heard it said unbidden guests
Are often welcomest when they are gone.
 Tal. Well then, alone, since there's no
remedy,

I mean to prove this lady's courtesy.
Come hither, Captain. [*Whispers*] You per-
　　ceive my mind ?　　　　　　　　59
　　Capt. I do, my lord, and mean accord-
　　　ingly.　　　　　　　　　[*Exeunt.*

SCENE III. *Auvergne. The castle.*

Enter the COUNTESS *and her* Porter.

Count. Porter, remember what I gave in
　　charge ;
And when you have done so, bring the keys
　　to me.
　　Port. Madam, I will.　　　　　[*Exit.*
　　Count. The plot is laid ; if all things fall
　　　out right,
I shall as famous be by this exploit　　5
As Scythian Tomyris by Cyrus' death.
Great is the rumour of this dreadful knight,
And his achievements of no less account.
Fain would mine eyes be witness with mine
　　ears　　　　　　　　　　　　　9
To give their censure of these rare reports.

Enter Messenger *and* TALBOT.

　　Mess. Madam, according as you ladyship
　　　desir'd,
By message crav'd, so is Lord Talbot
　　come.
　　Count. And he is welcome. What ! is this
　　　the man ?
　　Mess. Madam, it is.
　　Count. Is this the scourge of France ?　15
Is this the Talbot, so much fear'd abroad
That with his name the mothers still their
　　babes ?
I see report is fabulous and false.
I thought I should have seen some Hercules,
A second Hector, for his grim aspect　　20
And large proportion of his strong-knit
　　limbs.
Alas, this is a child, a silly dwarf !
It cannot be this weak and writhled shrimp
Should strike such terror to his enemies.
　　Tal. Madam, I have been bold to trouble
　　　you ;　　　　　　　　　　　25
But since your ladyship is not at leisure,
I'll sort some other time to visit you.
　　　　　　　　　　　　　[*Going.*
　　Count. What means he now ? Go ask him
　　　whither he goes.
　　Mess. Stay, my Lord Talbot ; for my
　　　lady craves
To know the cause of your abrupt de-
　　parture.　　　　　　　　　　30
　　Tal. Marry, for that she's in a wrong
　　　belief,
I go to certify her Talbot's here.

Re-enter Porter *with keys.*

　　Count. If thou be he, then art thou
　　　prisoner.
　　Tal. Prisoner ! To whom ?
　　Count.　　　To me, blood-thirsty lord ;

And for that cause I train'd thee to my
　　house.　　　　　　　　　　　35
Long time thy shadow hath been thrall to
　　me,
For in my gallery thy picture hangs ;
But now the substance shall endure the like
And I will chain these legs and arms
　　of thine
That hast by tyranny these many years　40
Wasted our country, slain our citizens,
And sent our sons and husbands captivate.
　　Tal. Ha, ha, ha !
　　Count. Laughest thou, wretch ?　Thy
　　　mirth shall turn to moan.　　　44
　　Tal. I laugh to see your ladyship so fond
To think that you have aught but Talbot's
　　shadow
Whereon to practise your severity.
　　Count. Why, art not thou the man ?
　　Tal.　　　　　　　I am indeed.
　　Count. Then have I substance too.　　49
　　Tal. No, no, I am but shadow of myself.
You are deceiv'd, my substance is not
　　here ;
For what you see is but the smallest part
And least proportion of humanity.
I tell you, madam, were the whole frame
　　here,
It is of such a spacious lofty pitch　　55
Your roof were not sufficient to contain 't.
　　Count. This is a riddling merchant for the
　　　nonce ;
He will be here, and yet he is not here.
How can these contrarieties agree ?
　　Tal. That will I show you presently.　60

*Winds his horn ; drums strike up ; a peal
　　of ordnance. Enter* Soldiers.

How say you, madam ?　Are you now
　　persuaded
That Talbot is but shadow of himself ?
These are his substance, sinews, arms, and
　　strength,
With which he yoketh your rebellious necks,
Razeth your cities, and subverts your
　　towns,　　　　　　　　　　65
And in a moment makes them desolate.
　　Count. Victorious Talbot ! pardon my
　　　abuse.
I find thou art no less than fame hath
　　bruited,
And more than may be gathered by thy
　　shape.
Let my presumption not provoke thy
　　wrath,　　　　　　　　　　70
For I am sorry that with reverence
I did not entertain thee as thou art.
　　Tal. Be not dismay'd, fair lady ; nor
　　　misconster
The mind of Talbot as you did mistake
The outward composition of his body.　75
What you have done hath not offended me.
Nor other satisfaction do I crave
But only, with your patience, that we may

599

Taste of your wine and see what cates you
    have,
For soldiers' stomachs always serve them
    well.   80
  Count. With all my heart, and think me
    honoured
To feast so great a warrior in my house.
                          [Exeunt.

SCENE IV. *London. The Temple garden.*

Enter the EARLS OF SOMERSET, SUFFOLK,
and WARWICK ; RICHARD PLANTAGENET,
VERNON, *and another* Lawyer.

  Plan. Great lords and gentlemen, what
    means this silence ?
Dare no man answer in a case of truth ?
  Suf. Within the Temple Hall we were too
    loud ;
The garden here is more convenient.
  Plan. Then say at once if I maintain'd
    the truth ;   5
Or else was wrangling Somerset in th' error?
  Suf. Faith, I have been a truant in the
    law
And never yet could frame my will to it ;
And therefore frame the law unto my will.
  Som. Judge you, my Lord of Warwick,
    then, between us.   10
  War. Between two hawks, which flies the
    higher pitch ;
Between two dogs, which hath the deeper
    mouth ;
Between two blades, which bears the better
    temper ;
Between two horses, which doth bear him
    best ;
Between two girls, which hath the merriest
    eye—   15
I have perhaps some shallow spirit of
    judgment ;
But in these nice sharp quillets of the law,
Good faith, I am no wiser than a daw.
  Plan. Tut, tut, here is a mannerly
    forbearance :
The truth appears so naked on my side 20
That any purblind eye may find it out.
  Som. And on my side it is so well
    apparell'd,
So clear, so shining, and so evident,
That it will glimmer through a blind man's
    eye.
  Plan. Since you are tongue-tied and so
    loath to speak,   25
In dumb significants proclaim your
    thoughts.
Let him that is a true-born gentleman
And stands upon the honour of his birth,
If he suppose that I have pleaded truth,
From off this brier pluck a white rose with
    me.   30
  Som. Let him that is no coward nor no
    flatterer,
But dare maintain the party of the truth,

Pluck a red rose from off this thorn with
    me.
  War. I love no colours ; and, without all
    colour
Of base insinuating flattery,   35
I pluck this white rose with Plantagenet.
  Suf. I pluck this red rose with young
    Somerset,
And say withal I think he held the right.
  Ver. Stay, lords and gentlemen, and
    pluck no more   39
Till you conclude that he upon whose side
The fewest roses are cropp'd from the
    tree
Shall yield the other in the right opinion.
  Som. Good Master Vernon, it is well
    objected ;
If I have fewest, I subscribe in silence.
  Plan. And I.   45
  Ver. Then, for the truth and plainness of
    the case,
I pluck this pale and maiden blossom here,
Giving my verdict on the white rose side.
  Som. Prick not your finger as you pluck
    it off,
Lest, bleeding, you do paint the white rose
    red,   50
And fall on my side so, against your will.
  Ver. If I, my lord, for my opinion bleed,
Opinion shall be surgeon to my hurt
And keep me on the side where still I am.
  Som. Well, well, come on ; who else ? 55
  Law. [*To Somerset*] Unless my study and
    my books be false,
The argument you held was wrong in you ;
In sign whereof I pluck a white rose too.
  Plan. Now, Somerset, where is your
    argument ?
  Som. Here in my scabbard, meditating
    that   60
Shall dye your white rose in a bloody red.
  Plan. Meantime your cheeks do counter-
    feit our roses ;
For pale they look with fear, as witnessing
The truth on our side.
  Som.   No, Plantagenet,
'Tis not for fear but anger that thy cheeks
Blush for pure shame to counterfeit our
    roses,   66
And yet thy tongue will not confess thy
    error.
  Plan. Hath not thy rose a canker,
    Somerset ?
  Som. Hath not thy rose a thorn, Planta-
    genet ?
  Plan. Ay, sharp and piercing, to main-
    tain his truth ;   70
Whiles thy consuming canker eats his
    falsehood.
  Som. Well, I'll find friends to wear my
    bleeding roses,
That shall maintain what I have said is
    true,
Where false Plantagenet dare not be seen.

Plan. Now, by this maiden blossom in my
hand, 75
I scorn thee and thy fashion, peevish boy.
Suf. Turn not thy scorns this way,
Plantagenet.
Plan. Proud Pole, I will, and scorn both
him and thee.
Suf. I'll turn my part thereof into thy
throat.
Som. Away, away, good William de la
Pole ! 80
We grace the yeoman by conversing with
him.
War. Now, by God's will, thou wrong'st
him, Somerset ;
His grandfather was Lionel Duke of
Clarence,
Third son to the third Edward, King of
England.
Spring crestless yeomen from so deep a
root ? 85
Plan. He bears him on the place's
privilege,
Or durst not for his craven heart say thus.
Som. By Him that made me, I'll maintain
my words
On any plot of ground in Christendom.
Was not thy father, Richard Earl of
Cambridge, 90
For treason executed in our late king's
days ?
And by his treason stand'st not thou
attainted,
Corrupted, and exempt from ancient
gentry ?
His trespass yet lives guilty in thy blood ;
And till thou be restor'd thou art a yeoman.
Plan. My father was attached, not
attainted ; 96
Condemn'd to die for treason, but no
traitor ;
And that I'll prove on better men than
Somerset,
Were growing time once ripened to my will.
For your partaker Pole, and you yourself,
I'll note you in my book of memory 101
To scourge you for this apprehension.
Look to it well, and say you are well
warn'd.
Som. Ay, thou shalt find us ready for
thee still ;
And know us by these colours for thy foes—
For these my friends in spite of thee shall
wear. 106
Plan. And, by my soul, this pale and
angry rose,
As cognizance of my blood-drinking hate,
Will I for ever, and my faction, wear,
Until it wither with me to my grave, 110
Or flourish to the height of my degree.
Suf. Go forward, and be chok'd with thy
ambition !
And so farewell until I meet thee next. 		[*Exit.*

Som. Have with thee, Pole. Farewell,
ambitious Richard. 		[*Exit.*
Plan. How I am brav'd, and must per-
force endure it ! 115
War. This blot that they object against
your house
Shall be wip'd out in the next Parliament,
Call'd for the truce of Winchester and
Gloucester ;
And if thou be not then created York,
I will not live to be accounted Warwick. 120
Meantime, in signal of my love to thee,
Against proud Somerset and William Pole,
Will I upon thy party wear this rose ;
And here I prophesy : this brawl to-day,
Grown to this faction in the Temple
Garden, 125
Shall send between the Red Rose and the
White
A thousand souls to death and deadly
night.
Plan. Good Master Vernon, I am bound
to you
That you on my behalf would pluck a
flower.
Ver. In your behalf still will I wear the
same. 130
Law. And so will I.
Plan. Thanks, gentle sir.
Come, let us four to dinner. I dare say
This quarrel will drink blood another day.
		[*Exeunt.*

SCENE V. *The Tower of London.*

Enter MORTIMER, *brought in a chair, and*
Gaolers.

Mor. Kind keepers of my weak decaying
age,
Let dying Mortimer here rest himself.
Even like a man new haled from the rack,
So fare my limbs with long imprisonment ;
And these grey locks, the pursuivants of
death, 5
Nestor-like aged in an age of care,
Argue the end of Edmund Mortimer.
These eyes, like lamps whose wasting oil is
spent,
Wax dim, as drawing to their exigent ;
Weak shoulders, overborne with burdening
grief, 10
And pithless arms, like to a withered vine
That droops his sapless branches to the
ground.
Yet are these feet, whose strengthless stay
is numb,
Unable to support this lump of clay,
Swift-winged with desire to get a grave, 15
As witting I no other comfort have.
But tell me, keeper, will my nephew come ?
1 Keep. Richard Plantagenet, my lord,
will come.
We sent unto the Temple, unto his
chamber ; 19

And answer was return'd that he will come.
Mor. Enough; my soul shall then be
    satisfied.
Poor gentleman! his wrong doth equal
    mine.
Since Henry Monmouth first began to
    reign,
Before whose glory I was great in arms,
This loathsome sequestration have I had;
And even since then hath Richard been
    obscur'd,   26
Depriv'd of honour and inheritance.
But now the arbitrator of despairs,
Just Death, kind umpire of men's miseries,
With sweet enlargement doth dismiss me
    hence.   30
I would his troubles likewise were expir'd,
That so he might recover what was lost.

     Enter RICHARD PLANTAGENET.

1 *Keep.* My lord, your loving nephew now
    is come.
Mor. Richard Plantagenet, my friend, is
    he come?   34
Plan. Ay, noble uncle, thus ignobly us'd,
Your nephew, late despised Richard, comes.
Mor. Direct mine arms I may embrace
    his neck
And in his bosom spend my latter gasp.
O, tell me when my lips do touch his cheeks,
That I may kindly give one fainting kiss. 40
And now declare, sweet stem from York's
    great stock,
Why didst thou say of late thou wert
    despis'd?
Plan. First, lean thine aged back against
    mine arm;
And, in that ease, I'll tell thee my disease.
This day, in argument upon a case,   45
Some words there grew 'twixt Somerset and
    me;
Among which terms he us'd his lavish
    tongue
And did upbraid me with my father's death;
Which obloquy set bars before my tongue,
Else with the like I had requited him.   50
Therefore, good uncle, for my father's sake,
In honour of a true Plantagenet,
And for alliance sake, declare the cause
My father, Earl of Cambridge, lost his head.
Mor. That cause, fair nephew, that im-
    prison'd me   55
And hath detain'd me all my flow'ring
    youth
Within a loathsome dungeon, there to pine,
Was cursed instrument of his decease.
Plan. Discover more at large what cause
    that was,
For I am ignorant and cannot guess.   60
Mor. I will, if that my fading breath
    permit
And death approach not ere my tale be
    done.
Henry the Fourth, grandfather to this king,

Depos'd his nephew Richard, Edward's son,
The first-begotten and the lawful heir 65
Of Edward king, the third of that descent;
During whose reign the Percies of the
    north,
Finding his usurpation most unjust,
Endeavour'd my advancement to the
    throne.
The reason mov'd these warlike lords to
    this   70
Was, for that—young Richard thus
    remov'd,
Leaving no heir begotten of his body—
I was the next by birth and parentage;
For by my mother I derived am
From Lionel Duke of Clarence, third son 75
To King Edward the Third; whereas he
From John of Gaunt doth bring his pedi-
    gree,
Being but fourth of that heroic line.
But mark: as in this haughty great
    attempt
They laboured to plant the rightful heir, 80
I lost my liberty, and they their lives.
Long after this, when Henry the Fifth,
Succeeding his father Bolingbroke, did
    reign,
Thy father, Earl of Cambridge, then
    deriv'd
From famous Edmund Langley, Duke of
    York,   85
Marrying my sister, that thy mother was,
Again, in pity of my hard distress,
Levied an army, weening to redeem
And have install'd me in the diadem;
But, as the rest, so fell that noble earl, 90
And was beheaded. Thus the Mortimers,
In whom the title rested, were suppress'd.
Plan. Of which, my lord, your honour is
    the last.
Mor. True; and thou seest that I no
    issue have,
And that my fainting words do warrant
    death.   95
Thou art my heir; the rest I wish thee
    gather;
But yet be wary in thy studious care.
Plan. Thy grave admonishments prevail
    with me.
But yet methinks my father's execution
Was nothing less than bloody tyranny. 100
Mor. With silence, nephew, be thou
    politic;
Strong fixed is the house of Lancaster
And like a mountain not to be remov'd.
But now thy uncle is removing hence,
As princes do their courts when they are
    cloy'd   105
With long continuance in a settled place.
Plan. O uncle, would some part of my
    young years
Might but redeem the passage of your age!
Mor. Thou dost then wrong me, as that
    slaughterer doth

Which giveth many wounds when one will
    kill.   110
Mourn not, except thou sorrow for my good;
Only give order for my funeral.
And so, farewell ; and fair be all thy hopes,
And prosperous be thy life in peace and
    war !   [*Dies.*
   Plan. And peace, no war, befall thy
    parting soul !   115
In prison hast thou spent a pilgrimage,
And like a hermit overpass'd thy days.
Well, I will lock his counsel in my breast ;
And what I do imagine, let that rest.   119
Keepers, convey him hence ; and I myself
Will see his burial better than his life.
         [*Exeunt Gaolers, bearing out the*
              body of Mortimer.
Here dies the dusky torch of Mortimer,
Chok'd with ambition of the meaner sort ;
And for those wrongs, those bitter injuries,
Which Somerset hath offer'd to my house,
I doubt not but with honour to redress ;
And therefore haste I to the Parliament,
Either to be restored to my blood,   128
Or make my ill th' advantage of my good.
                         [*Exit.*

ACT THREE

SCENE I. *London. The Parliament House.*

Flourish.   *Enter the* KING, EXETER,
GLOUCESTER, WARWICK, SOMERSET, *and*
SUFFOLK ; *the* BISHOP OF WINCHESTER,
RICHARD PLANTAGENET, *and* Others.
*Gloucester offers to put up a bill ; Win-
chester snatches it, and tears it.*

   Win. Com'st thou with deep premedi-
    tated lines,
With written pamphlets studiously devis'd?
Humphrey of Gloucester, if thou canst
    accuse
Or aught intend'st to lay unto my charge,
Do it without invention, suddenly ;   5
As I with sudden and extemporal speech
Purpose to answer what thou canst object.
   Glo. Presumptuous priest, this place com-
    mands my patience,
Or thou shouldst find thou hast dishonour'd
    me.   9
Think not, although in writing I preferr'd
The manner of thy vile outrageous crimes,
That therefore I have forg'd, or am not able
Verbatim to rehearse the method of my
    pen.
No, prelate ; such is thy audacious wicked-
    ness,
Thy lewd, pestiferous, and dissentious
    pranks,   15
As very infants prattle of thy pride.
Thou art a most pernicious usurer ;
Froward by nature, enemy to peace ;
Lascivious, wanton, more than well
    beseems
A man of thy profession and degree ;   20

And for thy treachery, what's more
    manifest—
In that thou laid'st a trap to take my life,
As well at London Bridge as at the Tower ?
Beside, I fear me, if thy thoughts were
    sifted,
The King, thy sovereign, is not quite
    exempt   25
From envious malice of thy swelling heart.
   Win. Gloucester, I do defy thee. Lords,
    vouchsafe
To give me hearing what I shall reply.
If I were covetous, ambitious, or perverse,
As he will have me, how am I so poor ?   30
Or how haps it I seek not to advance
Or raise myself, but keep my wonted
    calling ?
And for dissension, who preferreth peace
More than I do, except I be provok'd ?
No, my good lords, it is not that offends ;   35
It is not that that hath incens'd the Duke :
It is because no one should sway but he ;
No one but he should be about the King ;
And that engenders thunder in his breast
And makes him roar these accusations
    forth.   40
But he shall know I am as good—
   Glo.   As good !
Thou bastard of my grandfather !
   Win. Ay, lordly sir ; for what are you,
    I pray,
But one imperious in another's throne ?
   Glo. Am I not Protector, saucy priest ? 45
   Win. And am not I a prelate of the
    church ?
   Glo. Yes, as an outlaw in a castle keeps,
And useth it to patronage his theft.
   Win. Unreverent Gloucester !
   Glo.   Thou art reverend
Touching thy spiritual function, not thy
    life.   50
   Win. Rome shall remedy this.
   War.   Roam thither then.
   Som. My lord, it were your duty to
    forbear.
   War. Ay, see the bishop be not overborne.
   Som. Methinks my lord should be
    religious,
And know the office that belongs to such. 55
   War. Methinks his lordship should be
    humbler ;
It fitteth not a prelate so to plead.
   Som. Yes, when his holy state is touch'd
    so near.
   War. State holy or unhallow'd, what of
    that ?
Is not his Grace Protector to the King ?   60
   Plan. [*Aside*] Plantagenet, I see, must
    hold his tongue,
Lest it be said ' Speak, sirrah, when you
    should ' ;
Must your bold verdict enter talk with
    lords ? '
Else would I have a fling at Winchester.

King. Uncles of Gloucester and of Winchester, 65
The special watchmen of our English weal,
I would prevail, if prayers might prevail,
To join your hearts in love and amity,
O, what a scandal is it to our crown 69
That two such noble peers as ye should jar!
Believe me, lords, my tender years can tell
Civil dissension is a viperous worm
That gnaws the bowels of the commonwealth.
[*A noise within:* Down
with the tawny coats.
What tumult's this?
War. An uproar, I dare warrant,
Begun through malice of the Bishop's men.
[*A noise again:* Stones! Stones!

Enter the MAYOR *of London, attended.*

May. O, my good lords, and virtuous Henry, 76
Pity the city of London, pity us!
The Bishop and the Duke of Gloucester's men,
Forbidden late to carry any weapon,
Have fill'd their pockets full of pebble stones 80
And, banding themselves in contrary parts,
Do pelt so fast at one another's pate
That many have their giddy brains knock'd out.
Our windows are broke down in every street,
And we for fear compell'd to shut our shops. 85

Enter in skirmish, the Retainers of Gloucester
and Winchester, *with bloody pates.*

King. We charge you, on allegiance to ourself,
To hold your slaught'ring hands and keep the peace.
Pray, uncle Gloucester, mitigate this strife.
1 Serv. Nay, if we be forbidden stones,
we'll fall to it with our teeth. 90
2 Serv. Do what ye dare, we are as resolute. [*Skirmish again.*
Glo. You of my household, leave this peevish broil,
And set this unaccustom'd fight aside.
3 Serv. My lord, we know your Grace to be a man 94
Just and upright, and for your royal birth
Inferior to none but to his Majesty;
And ere that we will suffer such a prince,
So kind a father of the commonweal,
To be disgraced by an inkhorn mate, 99
We and our wives and children all will fight
And have our bodies slaught'red by thy foes.
1 Serv. Ay, and the very parings of our nails
Shall pitch a field when we are dead.
[*Begin again.*
Glo. Stay, stay, I say!

And if you love me, as you say you do,
Let me persuade you to forbear awhile. 105
King. O, how this discord doth afflict my soul!
Can you, my Lord of Winchester, behold
My sighs and tears and will not once relent?
Who should be pitiful, if you be not?
Or who should study to prefer a peace, 110
If holy churchmen take delight in broils?
War. Yield, my Lord Protector; yield, Winchester;
Except you mean with obstinate repulse
To slay your sovereign and destroy the realm.
You see what mischief, and what murder too, 115
Hath been enacted through your enmity;
Then be at peace, except ye thirst for blood.
Win. He shall submit, or I will never yield.
Glo. Compassion on the King commands me stoop, 119
Or I would see his heart out ere the priest
Should ever get that privilege of me.
War. Behold, my Lord of Winchester, the Duke
Hath banish'd moody discontented fury,
As by his smoothed brows it doth appear;
Why look you still so stern and tragical? 125
Glo. Here, Winchester, I offer thee my hand.
King. Fie, uncle Beaufort! I have heard you preach
That malice was a great and grievous sin;
And will not you maintain the thing you teach, 129
But prove a chief offender in the same?
War. Sweet King! The Bishop hath a kindly gird.
For shame, my Lord of Winchester, relent;
What, shall a child instruct you what to do?
Win. Well, Duke of Gloucester, I will yield to thee; 134
Love for thy love and hand for hand I give.
Glo. [*Aside*] Ay, but, I fear me, with a hollow heart.—
See here, my friends and loving countrymen:
This token serveth for a flag of truce
Betwixt ourselves and all our followers.
So help me God, as I dissemble not! 140
Win. [*Aside*] So help me God, as I intend it not!
King. O loving uncle, kind Duke of Gloucester,
How joyful am I made by this contract!
Away, my masters! trouble us no more;
But join in friendship, as your lords have done. 145
1 Serv. Content: I'll to the surgeon's.
2 Serv. And so will I.
3 Serv. And I will see what physic the tavern affords.
[*Exeunt Servants, Mayor, &c.*

War. Accept this scroll, most gracious
    sovereign ;   149
Which in the right of Richard Plantagenet
We do exhibit to your Majesty.
    Glo. Well urg'd, my Lord of Warwick ;
    for, sweet prince,
An if your Grace mark every circumstance,
You have great reason to do Richard right ;
Especially for those occasions   155
At Eltham Place I told your Majesty.
    King. And those occasions, uncle, were of
    force ;
Therefore, my loving lords, our pleasure is
That Richard be restored to his blood.
    War. Let Richard be restored to his
    blood ;   160
So shall his father's wrongs be recompens'd.
    Win. As will the rest, so willeth Win-
    chester.
    King. If Richard will be true, not that
    alone
But all the whole inheritance I give   164
That doth belong unto the house of York,
From whence you spring by lineal descent.
    Plan. Thy humble servant vows obedi-
    ence
And humble service till the point of death.
    King. Stoop then and set your knee
    against my foot ;
And in reguerdon of that duty done   170
I girt thee with the valiant sword of York.
Rise, Richard, like a true Plantagenet,
And rise created princely Duke of York.
    Plan. And so thrive Richard as thy foes
    may fall !
And as my duty springs, so perish they 175
That grudge one thought against your
    Majesty !
    All. Welcome, high Prince, the mighty
    Duke of York !
    Som. [*Aside*] Perish, base Prince, ignoble
    Duke of York !
    Glo. Now will it best avail your Majesty
To cross the seas and to be crown'd in
    France :   180
The presence of a king engenders love
Amongst his subjects and his loyal friends,
As it disanimates his enemies.
    King. When Gloucester says the word,
    King Henry goes ;
For friendly counsel cuts off many foes. 185
    Glo. Your ships already are in readiness.
        [*Sennet. Flourish. Exeunt all but
        Exeter.*
    Exe. Ay, we may march in England or in
    France,
Not seeing what is likely to ensue.
This late dissension grown betwixt the peers
Burns under feigned ashes of forg'd love 190
And will at last break out into a flame ;
As fest'red members rot but by degree
Till bones and flesh and sinews fall away,
So will this base and envious discord breed.
And now I fear that fatal prophecy   195

Which in the time of Henry nam'd the
    Fifth
Was in the mouth of every sucking babe :
That Henry born at Monmouth should win
    all,   198
And Henry born at Windsor should lose all.
Which is so plain that Exeter doth wish
His days may finish ere that hapless time.
                  [*Exit.*

SCENE II. *France. Before Rouen.*

Enter LA PUCELLE *disguis'd, with four
Soldiers dressed like Countrymen, with
sacks upon their backs.*

    Puc. These are the city gates, the gates
    of Rouen,
Through which our policy must make a
    breach.
Take heed, be wary how you place your
    words ;
Talk like the vulgar sort of market-men
That come to gather money for their corn. 5
If we have entrance, as I hope we shall,
And that we find the slothful watch but
    weak,
I'll by a sign give notice to our friends,
That Charles the Dauphin may encounter
    them.
    1 Sold. Our sacks shall be a mean to sack
    the city,   10
And we be lords and rulers over Rouen ;
Therefore we'll knock.   [*Knocks.*
    Watch. [*Within*] Qui est là ?
    Puc. Paysans, pauvres gens de France—
Poor market-folks that come to sell their
    corn.   15
    Watch. Enter, go in ; the market-bell is
    rung.
    Puc. Now, Rouen, I'll shake thy bul-
    warks to the ground.
        [*La Pucelle, &c., enter the town.*

Enter CHARLES, BASTARD, ALENÇON,
    REIGNIER, *and* Forces.

    Char. Saint Denis bless this happy
    stratagem !
And once again we'll sleep secure in Rouen.
    Bast. Here ent'red Pucelle and her
    practisants ;   20
Now she is there, how will she specify
Here is the best and safest passage in ?
    Alen. By thrusting out a torch from
    yonder tower ;
Which once discern'd shows that her
    meaning is—
No way to that, for weakness, which she
    ent'red.   25

Enter LA PUCELLE, *on the top, thrusting out
a torch burning.*

    Puc. Behold, this is the happy wedding
    torch
That joineth Rouen unto her countrymen,

But burning fatal to the Talbotites. [*Exit.*
  Bast. See, noble Charles, the beacon of
    our friend ;   29
The burning torch in yonder turret stands.
  Char. Now shine it like a comet of
    revenge,
A prophet to the fall of all our foes !
  Alen. Defer no time, delays have
    dangerous ends ;
Enter, and cry ' The Dauphin ! ' presently,
And then do execution on the watch.   35
            [*Alarum. Exeunt.*

An alarum. Enter TALBOT *in an excursion.*

  Tal. France, thou shalt rue this treason
    with thy tears,
If Talbot but survive thy treachery.
Pucelle, that witch, that damned sorceress,
Hath wrought this hellish mischief un-
    awares,   39
That hardly we escap'd the pride of France.
                  [*Exit.*

An alarum ; excursions. BEDFORD *brought
in sick in a chair. Enter* TALBOT *and*
BURGUNDY *without ; within,* LA PUCELLE,
CHARLES, BASTARD, ALENÇON, *and*
REIGNIER, *on the walls.*

  Puc. Good morrow, gallants ! Want ye
    corn for bread ?
I think the Duke of Burgundy will fast
Before he'll buy again at such a rate.
'Twas full of darnel—do you like the taste ?
  Bur. Scoff on, vile fiend and shameless
    courtezan.   45
I trust ere long to choke thee with thine
    own,
And make thee curse the harvest of that
    corn.
  Char. Your Grace may starve, perhaps,
    before that time.
  Bed. O, let no words, but deeds, revenge
    this treason !
  Puc. What will you do, good grey-beard ?
    Break a lance,   50
And run a tilt at death within a chair ?
  Tal. Foul fiend of France and hag of all
    despite,
Encompass'd with thy lustful paramours,
Becomes it thee to taunt his valiant age 54
And twit with cowardice a man half dead ?
Damsel, I'll have a bout with you again,
Or else let Talbot perish with this shame.
  Puc. Are ye so hot, sir ? Yet, Pucelle,
    hold thy peace ;
If Talbot do but thunder, rain will follow.
    [*The English party whisper together
             in council.*
God speed the parliament ! Who shall be
    the Speaker ?   60
  Tal. Dare ye come forth and meet us in
    the field ?
  Puc. Belike your lordship takes us then
    for fools,

To try if that our own be ours or no.
  Tal. I speak not to that railing Hecate,
But unto thee, Alençon, and the rest.   65
Will ye, like soldiers, come and fight it out ?
  Alen. Signior, no.
  Tal. Signior, hang ! Base muleteers of
    France !
Like peasant foot-boys do they keep the
    walls,
And dare not take up arms like gentlemen.
  Puc. Away, captains ! Let's get us from
    the walls ;   71
For Talbot means no goodness by his looks.
God b'uy, my lord ; we came but to tell
    you
That we are here. [*Exeunt from the walls.*
  Tal. And there will we be too, ere it be
    long,   75
Or else reproach be Talbot's greatest fame !
Vow, Burgundy, by honour of thy house,
Prick'd on by public wrongs sustain'd in
    France,
Either to get the town again or die ;
And I, as sure as English Henry lives   80
And as his father here was conqueror,
As sure as in this late-betrayed town
Great Cœur-de-lion's heart was buried—
So sure I swear to get the town or die.
  Bur. My vows are equal partners with
    thy vows.   85
  Tal. But ere we go, regard this dying
    prince,
The valiant Duke of Bedford. Come, my
    lord,
We will bestow you in some better place,
Fitter for sickness and for crazy age.
  Bed. Lord Talbot, do not so dishonour
    me ;   90
Here will I sit before the walls of Rouen,
And will be partner of your weal or woe.
  Bur. Courageous Bedford, let us now
    persuade you.
  Bed. Not to be gone from hence ; for
    once I read
That stout Pendragon in his litter sick 95
Came to the field, and vanquished his foes.
Methinks I should revive the soldiers'
    hearts,
Because I ever found them as myself.
  Tal. Undaunted spirit in a dying breast !
Then be it so. Heavens keep old Bedford
    safe !   100
And now no more ado, brave Burgundy,
But gather we our forces out of hand
And set upon our boasting enemy.
    [*Exeunt against the town all but
         Bedford and attendants.*

An alarum ; excursions. Enter SIR JOHN
   FASTOLFE, *and a* Captain.

  Cap. Whither away, Sir John Fastolfe, in
    such haste ?
  Fast. Whither away ? To save myself by
    flight :   105

We are like to have the overthrow again.
Cap. What ! Will you fly, and leave Lord
    Talbot ?
Fast.   Ay,
All the Talbots in the world, to save my
    life.   [*Exit.*
Cap. Cowardly knight ! ill fortune follow
    thee !   [*Exit into the town.*

Retreat ; excursions. LA PUCELLE, ALEN-
    ÇON, *and* CHARLES *fly.*

Bed. Now, quiet soul, depart when
    heaven please,   110
For I have seen our enemies' overthrow.
What is the trust or strength of foolish
    man ?
They that of late were daring with their
    scoffs
Are glad and fain by flight to save them-
    selves.
        [*Bedford dies and is carried in by
            two in his chair.*

An alarum. Re-enter TALBOT, BURGUNDY,
    and the Rest.

Tal. Lost and recovered in a day again !
This is a double honour, Burgundy.   116
Yet heavens have glory for this victory !
Bur. Warlike and martial Talbot, Bur-
    gundy
Enshrines thee in his heart, and there erects
Thy noble deeds as valour's monuments. 120
Tal. Thanks, gentle Duke. But where is
    Pucelle now ?
I think her old familiar is asleep.
Now where's the Bastard's braves, and
    Charles his gleeks ?
What, all amort ?   Rouen hangs her head
    for grief
That such a valiant company are fled.   125
Now will we take some order in the town,
Placing therein some expert officers ;
And then depart to Paris to the King,
For there young Henry with his nobles lie.
Bur. What wills Lord Talbot pleaseth
    Burgundy.   130
Tal. But yet, before we go, let's not forget
The noble Duke of Bedford, late deceas'd,
But see his exequies fulfill'd in Rouen.
A braver soldier never couched lance,
A gentler heart did never sway in court ; 135
But kings and mightiest potentates must
    die,
For that's the end of human misery.
                            [*Exeunt.*

SCENE III. *The plains near Rouen.*

Enter CHARLES, *the* BASTARD, ALENÇON,
    LA PUCELLE, *and* Forces.

Puc. Dismay not, Princes, at this
    accident,
Nor grieve that Rouen is so recovered.
Care is no cure, but rather corrosive,
For things that are not to be remedied.
Let frantic Talbot triumph for a while   5
And like a peacock sweep along his tail ;
We'll pull his plumes and take away his
    train,
If Dauphin and the rest will be but rul'd.
Char. We have been guided by thee
    hitherto,
And of thy cunning had no diffidence ;   10
One sudden foil shall never breed distrust.
Bast. Search out thy wit for secret
    policies,
And we will make thee famous through the
    world.
Alen. We'll set thy statue in some holy
    place,
And have thee reverenc'd like a blessed
    saint.   15
Employ thee, then, sweet virgin, for our
    good.
Puc. Then thus it must be ; this doth
    Joan devise :
By fair persuasions, mix'd with sug'red
    words,
We will entice the Duke of Burgundy
To leave the Talbot and to follow us.   20
Char. Ay, marry, sweeting, if we could do
    that,
France were no place for Henry's warriors ;
Nor should that nation boast it so with
    us,
But be extirped from our provinces.
Alen. For ever should they be expuls'd
    from France,   25
And not have title of an earldom here.
Puc. Your honours shall perceive how I
    will work
To bring this matter to the wished end.
                        [*Drum sounds afar off.*
Hark ! by the sound of drum you may
    perceive
Their powers are marching unto Paris-
    ward.   30

*Here sound an English march. Enter, and
    pass over at a distance,* TALBOT *and his*
    Forces.

There goes the Talbot, with his colours
    spread,
And all the troops of English after him.

French march. Enter the DUKE OF
    BURGUNDY *and his* Forces.

Now in the rearward comes the Duke and
    his.
Fortune in favour makes him lag behind.
Summon a parley ; we will talk with him.
                    [*Trumpets sound a parley.*
Char. A parley with the Duke of Bur-
    gundy !   36
Bur. Who craves a parley with the
    Burgundy ?
Puc. The princely Charles of France, thy
    countryman.

Bur. What say'st thou, Charles ? for I am
    marching hence.
Char. Speak, Pucelle, and enchant him
    with thy words.   40
Puc. Brave Burgundy, undoubted hope
    of France !
Stay, let thy humble handmaid speak to
    thee.
Bur. Speak on ; but be not over-tedious.
Puc. Look on thy country, look on fertile
    France,
And see the cities and the towns defac'd 45
By wasting ruin of the cruel foe ;
As looks the mother on her lowly babe
When death doth close his tender dying
    eyes,
See, see the pining malady of France
Behold the wounds, the most unnatural
    wounds,   50
Which thou thyself hast given her woeful
    breast.
O, turn thy edged sword another way ;
Strike those that hurt, and hurt not those
    that help !
One drop of blood drawn from thy country's
    bosom
Should grieve thee more than streams of
    foreign gore.   55
Return therefore with a flood of tears,
And wash away thy country's stained
    spots.
Bur. Either she hath bewitch'd me with
    her words,
Or nature makes me suddenly relent.
Put. Besides, all French and France
    exclaims on thee,   60
Doubting thy birth and lawful progeny.
Who join'st thou with but with a lordly
    nation
That will not trust thee but for profit's
    sake ?
When Talbot hath set footing once in
    France,
And fashion'd thee that instrument of ill, 65
Who then but English Henry will be lord,
And thou be thrust out like a fugitive ?
Call we to mind—and mark but this for
    proof :
Was not the Duke of Orleans thy foe ?
And was he not in England prisoner ? 70
But when they heard he was thine enemy
They set him free without his ransom paid,
In spite of Burgundy and all his friends.
See then, thou fight'st against thy country-
    men,
And join'st with them will be thy slaughter-
    men.   75
Come, come, return ; return, thou wander-
    ing lord ;
Charles and the rest will take thee in their
    arms.
Bur. I am vanquished ; these haughty
    words of hers
Have batt'red me like roaring cannon-shot

608

And made me almost yield upon my knees.
Forgive me, country, and sweet country-
    men !   81
And, lords, accept this hearty kind embrace.
My forces and my power of men are yours ;
So, farewell, Talbot ; I'll no longer trust
    thee.
Puc. Done like a Frenchman—[*Aside*]
    turn and turn again.   85
Char. Welcome, brave Duke ! Thy friend-
    ship makes us fresh.
Bast. And doth beget new courage in our
    breasts.
Alen. Pucelle hath bravely play'd her
    part in this,
And doth deserve a coronet of gold.
Char. Now let us on, my lords, and join
    our powers,   90
And seek how we may prejudice the foe.
                                    [*Exeunt.*

SCENE IV. *Paris. The palace.*

Enter the KING, GLOUCESTER, WINCHESTER,
    YORK, SUFFOLK, SOMERSET, WARWICK,
    EXETER, VERNON, BASSET, *and* Others.
To them, with his Soldiers, TALBOT.

Tal. My gracious Prince, and honourable
    peers,
Hearing of your arrival in this realm,
I have awhile given truce unto my wars
To do my duty to my sovereign ;
In sign whereof, this arm that hath
    reclaim'd   5
To your obedience fifty fortresses,
Twelve cities, and seven walled towns of
    strength,
Beside five hundred prisoners of esteem,
Lets fall his sword before your Highness'
    feet,
And with submissive loyalty of heart   10
Ascribes the glory of his conquest got
First to my God and next unto your Grace.
                                    [*Kneels.*
King. Is this the Lord Talbot, uncle
    Gloucester,
That hath so long been resident in France ?
Glo. Yes, if it please your Majesty, my
    liege.   15
King. Welcome, brave captain and
    victorious lord !
When I was young, as yet I am not old,
I do remember how my father said
A stouter champion never handled sword.
Long since we were resolved of your truth,
Your faithful service, and your toil in
    war ;
Yet never have you tasted our reward,   22
Or been reguerdon'd with so much as
    thanks,
Because till now we never saw your face.
Therefore stand up ; and for these good
    deserts   25
We here create you Earl of Shrewsbury ;

And in our coronation take your place.
[*Sennet. Flourish. Exeunt all but
    Vernon and Basset.*
  Ver. Now, sir, to you, that were so hot
    at sea,
Disgracing of these colours that I wear
In honour of my noble Lord of York—   30
Dar'st thou maintain the former words
    thou spak'st ?
  Bas. Yes, sir ; as well as you dare
    patronage
The envious barking of your saucy tongue
Against my lord the Duke of Somerset.
  Ver. Sirrah, thy lord I honour as he is.   35
  Bas. Why, what is he ? As good a man
    as York !
  Ver. Hark ye : not so. In witness, take
    ye that.   [*Strikes him.*
  Bas. Villain, thou knowest the law of
    arms is such
That whoso draws a sword 'tis present
    death,
Or else this blow should broach thy dearest
    blood.   40
But I'll unto his Majesty and crave
I may have liberty to venge this wrong ;
When thou shalt see I'll meet thee to thy
    cost.
  Ver. Well, miscreant, I'll be there as soon
    as you ;   44
And, after, meet you sooner than you
    would.   [*Exeunt.*

ACT FOUR

SCENE I. *Paris. The palace.*

Enter the KING, GLOUCESTER, WINCHESTER,
    YORK, SUFFOLK, SOMERSET, WARWICK,
    TALBOT, EXETER, *the* GOVERNOR *of*
    Paris, *and* Others.

  Glo. Lord Bishop, set the crown upon his
    head.
  Win. God save King Henry, of that name
    the Sixth !
  Glo. Now, Governor of Paris, take your
    oath—   [*Governor kneels.*
That you elect no other king but him,
Esteem none friends but such as are his
    friends,   5
And none your foes but such as shall
    pretend
Malicious practices against his state.
This shall ye do, so help you righteous
    God !
        [*Exeunt Governor and his Train.*

Enter SIR JOHN FASTOLFE.

  Fast. My gracious sovereign, as I rode
    from Calais,
To haste unto your coronation,   10
A letter was deliver'd to my hands,
Writ to your Grace from th' Duke of
    Burgundy.

  Tal. Shame to the Duke of Burgundy and
    thee !
I vow'd, base knight, when I did meet thee
    next
To tear the Garter from thy craven's leg,   15
                    [*Plucking it off.*
Which I have done, because unworthily
Thou wast installed in that high degree.
Pardon me, princely Henry, and the rest :
This dastard, at the battle of Patay,   19
When but in all I was six thousand strong,
And that the French were almost ten to one,
Before we met or that a stroke was given,
Like to a trusty squire did run away ;
In which assault we lost twelve hundred
    men ;
Myself and divers gentlemen beside   25
Were there surpris'd and taken prisoners.
Then judge, great lords, if I have done amiss,
Or whether that such cowards ought to wear
This ornament of knighthood—yea or no.
  Glo. To say the truth, this fact was
    infamous   30
And ill beseeming any common man,
Much more a knight, a captain, and a
    leader.
  Tal. When first this order was ordain'd,
    my lords,
Knights of the Garter were of noble birth,
Valiant and virtuous, full of haughty
    courage,   35
Such as were grown to credit by the wars ;
Not fearing death nor shrinking for distress,
But always resolute in most extremes.
He then that is not furnish'd in this sort
Doth but usurp the sacred name of knight,
Profaning this most honourable order,   41
And should, if I were worthy to be judge,
Be quite degraded, like a hedge-born swain
That doth presume to boast of gentle blood.
  King. Stain to thy countrymen, thou
    hear'st thy doom.   45
Be packing, therefore, thou that wast a
    knight ;
Henceforth we banish thee on pain of death.
                    [*Exit Fastolfe.*
And now, my Lord Protector, view the
    letter
Sent from our uncle Duke of Burgundy.
  Glo. [*Viewing the superscription*] What
    means his Grace, that he hath
    chang'd his style ?   50
No more but plain and bluntly ' To the
    King ' !
Hath he forgot he is his sovereign ?
Or doth this churlish superscription
Pretend some alteration in good-will ?
What's here ? [*Reads*] ' I have, upon
    especial cause,   55
Mov'd with compassion of my country's
    wreck,
Together with the pitiful complaints
Of such as your oppression feeds upon,
Forsaken your pernicious faction,

And join'd with Charles, the rightful King
    of France.'   60
O monstrous treachery! Can this be so—
That in alliance, amity, and oaths,
There should be found such false dissemb-
    ling guile?
  King. What! Doth my uncle Burgundy
    revolt?
  Glo. He doth, my lord, and is become
    your foe.   65
  King. Is that the worst this letter doth
    contain?
  Glo. It is the worst, and all, my lord, he
    writes.
  King. Why then Lord Talbot there shall
    talk with him
And give him chastisement for this abuse.
How say you, my lord, are you not content?
  Tal. Content, my liege! Yes; but that I
    am prevented,   71
I should have begg'd I might have been
    employ'd.
  King. Then gather strength and march
    unto him straight;
Let him perceive how ill we brook his
    treason,
And what offence it is to flout his friends. 75
  Tal. I go, my lord, in heart desiring still
You may behold confusion of your foes.
                  [*Exit.*

    Enter VERNON *and* BASSET.

  Ver. Grant me the combat, gracious
    sovereign.
  Bas. And me, my lord, grant me the
    combat too.
  York. This is my servant: hear him,
    noble Prince.   80
  Som. And this is mine: sweet Henry,
    favour him.
  King. Be patient, lords, and give them
    leave to speak.
Say, gentlemen, what makes you thus
    exclaim,
And wherefore crave you combat, or with
    whom?
  Ver. With him, my lord; for he hath
    done me wrong.   85
  Bas. And I with him; for he hath done
    me wrong.
  King. What is that wrong whereof you
    both complain?
First let me know, and then I'll answer you.
  Bas. Crossing the sea from England into
    France,
This fellow here, with envious carping
    tongue,   90
Upbraided me about the rose I wear,
Saying the sanguine colour of the leaves
Did represent my master's blushing cheeks
When stubbornly he did repugn the truth
About a certain question in the law   95
Argu'd betwixt the Duke of York and him;
With other vile and ignominious terms—

In confutation of which rude reproach
And in defence of my lord's worthiness,
I crave the benefit of law of arms.   100
  Ver. And that is my petition, noble lord;
For though he seem with forged quaint
    conceit
To set a gloss upon his bold intent,
Yet know, my lord, I was provok'd by him,
And he first took exceptions at this badge,
Pronouncing that the paleness of this flower
Bewray'd the faintness of my master's
    heart.
  York. Will not this malice, Somerset, be
    left?
  Som. Your private grudge, my Lord of
    York, will out,   109
Though ne'er so cunningly you smother it.
  King. Good Lord, what madness rules in
    brainsick men,
When for so slight and frivolous a cause
Such factious emulations shall arise!
Good cousins both, of York and Somerset,
Quiet yourselves, I pray, and be at peace.
  York. Let this dissension first be tried by
    fight,   116
And then your Highness shall command a
    peace.
  Som. The quarrel toucheth none but us
    alone;
Betwixt ourselves let us decide it then.
  York. There is my pledge; accept it,
    Somerset.   120
  Ver. Nay, let it rest where it began at
    first.
  Bas. Confirm it so, mine honourable lord.
  Glo. Confirm it so? Confounded be your
    strife;
And perish ye, with your audacious prate!
Presumptuous vassals, are you not
    asham'd   125
With this immodest clamorous outrage
To trouble and disturb the King and us?
And you, my lords—methinks you do not
    well
To bear with their perverse objections,
Much less to take occasion from their
    mouths   130
To raise a mutiny betwixt yourselves.
Let me persuade you take a better course.
  Exe. It grieves his Highness. Good my
    lords, be friends.
  King. Come hither, you that would be
    combatants:
Henceforth I charge you, as you love our
    favour,   135
Quite to forget this quarrel and the cause.
And you, my lords, remember where we are:
In France, amongst a fickle wavering
    nation;
If they perceive dissension in our looks
And that within ourselves we disagree, 140
How will their grudging stomachs be pro-
    vok'd
To wilful disobedience, and rebel!

Beside, what infamy will there arise
When foreign princes shall be certified
That for a toy, a thing of no regard,   145
King Henry's peers and chief nobility
Destroy'd themselves and lost the realm of
    France !
O, think upon the conquest of my father,
My tender years ; and let us not forgo
That for a trifle that was bought with
    blood !   150
Let me be umpire in this doubtful strife.
I see no reason, if I wear this rose,
            [*Putting on a red rose.*
That any one should therefore be suspicious
I more incline to Somerset than York :
Both are my kinsmen, and I love them
    both.   155
As well they may upbraid me with my
    crown,
Because, forsooth, the King of Scots is
    crown'd.
But your discretions better can persuade
Than I am able to instruct or teach ;   159
And, therefore, as we hither came in peace,
So let us still continue peace and love.
Cousin of York, we institute your Grace
To be our Regent in these parts of France.
And, good my Lord of Somerset, unite
Your troops of horsemen with his bands of
    foot ;   165
And like true subjects, sons of your pro-
    genitors,
Go cheerfully together and digest
Your angry choler on your enemies.
Ourself, my Lord Protector, and the rest,
After some respite will return to Calais ;   170
From thence to England, where I hope ere
    long
To be presented by your victories
With Charles, Alençon, and that traitorous
    rout.
        [*Flourish.   Exeunt all but York,
        Warwick, Exeter, Vernon.*
    War. My Lord of York, I promise you,
    the King
Prettily, methought, did play the orator.
    York. And so he did ; but yet I like it
    not,   176
In that he wears the badge of Somerset.
    War. Tush, that was but his fancy ; blame
    him not ;
I dare presume, sweet prince, he thought
    no harm.
    York. An if I wist he did—but let it rest ;
Other affairs must now be managed.   181
            [*Exeunt all but Exeter.*
    Exe. Well didst thou, Richard, to
    suppress thy voice ;
For had the passions of thy heart burst out,
I fear we should have seen decipher'd there
More rancorous spite, more furious raging
    broils,   185
Than yet can be imagin'd or suppos'd.
But howsoe'er, no simple man that sees

This jarring discord of nobility,
This shouldering of each other in the court,
This factious bandying of their favourites,
But that it doth presage some ill event.
'Tis much when sceptres are in children's
    hands ;
But more when envy breeds unkind
    division :   193
There comes the ruin, there begins con-
    fusion.   [*Exit.*

    SCENE II.   *France.   Before Bordeaux.*

    Enter TALBOT, *with trump and drum.*

    Tal. Go to the gates of Bordeaux,
    trumpeter ;
Summon their general unto the wall.

Trumpet sounds a parley.   Enter, aloft, the
    General of the French, *and* Others.

English John Talbot, Captains, calls you
    forth,
Servant in arms to Harry King of England ;
And thus he would—Open your city gates,
Be humble to us, call my sovereign yours
And do him homage as obedient subjects,
And I'll withdraw me and my bloody
    power ;   8
But if you frown upon this proffer'd peace,
You tempt the fury of my three attendants,
Lean famine, quartering steel, and climbing
    fire ;
Who in a moment even with the earth
Shall lay your stately and air-braving
    towers,
If you forsake the offer of their love.
    Gen. Thou ominous and fearful owl of
    death,   15
Our nation's terror and their bloody scourge!
The period of thy tyranny approacheth.
On us thou canst not enter but by death ;
For, I protest, we are well fortified,
And strong enough to issue out and fight.   20
If thou retire, the Dauphin, well appointed,
Stands with the snares of war to tangle thee.
On either hand thee there are squadrons
    pitch'd
To wall thee from the liberty of flight,
And no way canst thou turn thee for redress
But death doth front thee with apparent
    spoil   26
And pale destruction meets thee in the face.
Ten thousand French have ta'en the sacra-
    ment
To rive their dangerous artillery
Upon no Christian soul but English Talbot.
Lo, there thou stand'st, a breathing valiant
    man,   31
Of an invincible unconquer'd spirit !
This is the latest glory of thy praise
That I, thy enemy, due thee withal ;
For ere the glass that now begins to run   35
Finish the process of his sandy hour,

These eyes that see thee now well coloured
Shall see thee withered, bloody, pale, and
    dead.   [Drum afar off.
Hark! hark!   The Dauphin's drum, a
    warning bell,
Sings heavy music to thy timorous soul; 40
And mine shall ring thy dire departure out.
                [Exit General.
  Tal. He fables not; I hear the enemy.
Out, some light horsemen, and peruse their
    wings.
O, negligent and heedless discipline!   44
How are we park'd and bounded in a pale—
A little herd of England's timorous deer,
Maz'd with a yelping kennel of French curs!
If we be English deer, be then in blood;
Not rascal-like to fall down with a pinch,
But rather, moody-mad and desperate
    stags,   50
Turn on the bloody hounds with heads of
    steel
And make the cowards stand aloof at bay.
Sell every man his life as dear as mine,
And they shall find dear deer of us, my
    friends.
God and Saint George, Talbot and Eng-
    land's right,   55
Prosper our colours in this dangerous fight!
                 [Exeunt.

SCENE III.   Plains in Gascony.

Enter YORK, with trumpet and many
    Soldiers. A Messenger meets him.

  York. Are not the speedy scouts return'd
    again
That dogg'd the mighty army of the
    Dauphin?
  Mess. They are return'd, my lord, and
    give it out
That he is march'd to Bordeaux with his
    power
To fight with Talbot; as he march'd along,
By your espials were discovered   6
Two mightier troops than that the Dauphin
    led,
Which join'd with him and made their
    march for Bordeaux.
  York. A plague upon that villain
    Somerset
That thus delays my promised supply   10
Of horsemen that were levied for this siege!
Renowned Talbot doth expect my aid,
And I am louted by a traitor villain
And cannot help the noble chevalier.
God comfort him in this necessity!   15
If he miscarry, farewell wars in France.

Enter SIR WILLIAM LUCY.

  Lucy. Thou princely leader of our
    English strength,
Never so needful on the earth of France,
Spur to the rescue of the noble Talbot,
Who now is girdled with a waist of iron 20
And hemm'd about with grim destruction.

To Bordeaux, warlike Duke! to Bordeaux,
    York!
Else, farewell Talbot, France, and Eng-
    land's honour.
  York. O God, that Somerset, who in
    proud heart
Doth stop my cornets, were in Talbot's
    place!   25
So should we save a valiant gentleman
By forfeiting a traitor and a coward.
Mad ire and wrathful fury makes me weep
That thus we die while remiss traitors sleep.
  Lucy. O, send some succour to the
    distress'd lord!   30
  York. He dies; we lose; I break my
    warlike word.
We mourn: France smiles. We lose: they
    daily get—
All long of this vile traitor Somerset.
  Lucy. Then God take mercy on brave
    Talbot's soul,
And on his son, young John, who two hours
    since   35
I met in travel toward his warlike father.
This seven years did not Talbot see his son;
And now they meet where both their lives
    are done.
  York. Alas, what joy shall noble Talbot
    have   39
To bid his young son welcome to his grave?
Away! vexation almost stops my breath,
That sund'red friends greet in the hour of
    death.
Lucy, farewell; no more my fortune can
But curse the cause I cannot aid the man.
Maine, Blois, Poictiers, and Tours, are won
    away   45
Long all of Somerset and his delay.
              [Exit with Forces.
  Lucy. Thus, while the vulture of sedition
Feeds in the bosom of such great com-
    manders,
Sleeping neglection doth betray to loss 49
The conquest of our scarce-cold conqueror,
That ever-living man of memory,
Henry the Fifth. Whiles they each other
    cross,
Lives, honours, lands, and all, hurry to loss.
                 [Exit.

SCENE IV.   Other plains of Gascony.

Enter SOMERSET, with his Forces; an
    Officer of Talbot's with him.

  Som. It is too late; I cannot send them
    now.
This expedition was by York and Talbot
Too rashly plotted; all our general force
Might with a sally of the very town
Be buckled with. The over-daring Talbot 5
Hath sullied all his gloss of former honour
By this unheedful, desperate, wild ad-
    venture.
York set him on to fight and die in shame

That, Talbot dead, great York might bear
    the name.
Off. Here is Sir William Lucy, who with
    me   10
Set from our o'er-match'd forces forth for aid.

Enter SIR WILLIAM LUCY.

Som. How now, Sir William! Whither
    were you sent?
Lucy. Whither, my lord! From bought
    and sold Lord Talbot,
Who, ring'd about with bold adversity,
Cries out for noble York and Somerset   15
To beat assailing death from his weak
    legions;
And whiles the honourable captain there
Drops bloody sweat from his war-wearied
    limbs
And, in advantage ling'ring, looks for rescue,
You, his false hopes, the trust of England's
    honour,   20
Keep off aloof with worthless emulation.
Let not your private discord keep away
The levied succours that should lend him aid,
While he, renowned noble gentleman,
Yield up his life unto a world of odds.   25
Orleans the Bastard, Charles, Burgundy,
Alençon, Reignier, compass him about,
And Talbot perisheth by your default.
Som. York set him on; York should
    have sent him aid.
Lucy. And York as fast upon your Grace
    exclaims,   30
Swearing that you withhold his levied host,
Collected for this expedition.
Som. York lies; he might have sent and
    had the horse.
I owe him little duty and less love,
And take foul scorn to fawn on him by
    sending.   35
Lucy. The fraud of England, not the force
    of France,
Hath now entrapp'd the noble-minded
    Talbot.
Never to England shall he bear his life,
But dies betray'd to fortune by your strife.
Som. Come, go; I will dispatch the
    horsemen straight;   40
Within six hours they will be at his aid.
Lucy. Too late comes rescue; he is ta'en
    or slain,
For fly he could not if he would have fled;
And fly would Talbot never, though he
    might.
Som. If he be dead, brave Talbot, then,
    adieu!   45
Lucy. His fame lives in the world, his
    shame in you.   [*Exeunt.*

SCENE V. *The English camp near Bordeaux.*

Enter TALBOT *and* JOHN *his son.*

Tal. O young John Talbot! I did send
    for thee

To tutor thee in stratagems of war,
That Talbot's name might be in thee
    reviv'd
When sapless age and weak unable limbs
Should bring thy father to his drooping
    chair.   5
But—O malignant and ill-boding stars!—
Now thou art come unto a feast of death,
A terrible and unavoided danger;
Therefore, dear boy, mount on my swiftest
    horse,   9
And I'll direct thee how thou shalt escape
By sudden flight. Come, dally not, be gone.
John. Is my name Talbot? and am I your
    son?
And shall I fly? O, if you love my mother,
Dishonour not her honourable name,
To make a bastard and a slave of me!   15
The world will say he is not Talbot's blood
That basely fled when noble Talbot stood.
Tal. Fly to revenge my death, if I be
    slain.
John. He that flies so will ne'er return
    again.
Tal. If we both stay, we both are sure
    to die.   20
John. Then let me stay; and, father, do
    you fly.
Your loss is great, so your regard should be;
My worth unknown, no loss is known in me;
Upon my death the French can little boast;
In yours they will, in you all hopes are lost.
Flight cannot stain the honour you have
    won;   26
But mine it will, that no exploit have done;
You fled for vantage, every one will swear;
But if I bow, they'll say it was for fear.
There is no hope that ever I will stay   30
If the first hour I shrink and run away.
Here, on my knee, I beg mortality,
Rather than life preserv'd with infamy.
Tal. Shall all thy mother's hopes lie in
    one tomb?
John. Ay, rather than I'll shame my
    mother's womb.   35
Tal. Upon my blessing I command thee
    go.
John. To fight I will, but not to fly the
    foe.
Tal. Part of thy father may be sav'd in
    thee.
John. No part of him but will be shame
    in me.
Tal. Thou never hadst renown, nor canst
    not lose it.   40
John. Yes, your renowned name; shall
    flight abuse it?
Tal. Thy father's charge shall clear thee
    from that stain.
John. You cannot witness for me, being
    slain.
If death be so apparent, then both fly.
Tal. And leave my followers here to fight
    and die?   45

My age was never tainted with such shame.
  John. And shall my youth be guilty of
    such blame ?
No more can I be severed from your side
Than can yourself yourself in twain divide.
Stay, go, do what you will, the like do I ; 50
For live I will not if my father die.
  Tal. Then here I take my leave of thee,
    fair son,
Born to eclipse thy life this afternoon.
Come, side by side together live and die ; 54
And soul with soul from France to heaven
    fly.   [*Exeunt.*

SCENE VI. *A field of battle.*

Alarum : excursions wherein JOHN TALBOT
is hemm'd about, and TALBOT *rescues him.*

  Tal. Saint George and victory ! Fight,
    soldiers, fight.
The Regent hath with Talbot broke his word
And left us to the rage of France his sword.
Where is John Talbot ? Pause and take thy
    breath ;
I gave thee life and rescu'd thee from
    death.   5
  John. O, twice my father, twice am I thy
    son !
The life thou gav'st me first was lost and
    done
Till with thy warlike sword, despite of fate,
To my determin'd time thou gav'st new
    date.
  Tal. When from the Dauphin's crest thy
    sword struck fire,   10
It warm'd thy father's heart with proud
    desire
Of bold-fac'd victory. Then leaden age,
Quicken'd with youthful spleen and warlike
    rage,
Beat down Alençon, Orleans, Burgundy, 14
And from the pride of Gallia rescued thee.
The ireful bastard Orleans, that drew blood
From thee, my boy, and had the maiden-
    hood
Of thy first fight, I soon encountered   18
And, interchanging blows, I quickly shed
Some of his bastard blood ; and in disgrace
Bespoke him thus : ' Contaminated, base,
And misbegotten blood I spill of thine,
Mean and right poor, for that pure blood
    of mine
Which thou didst force from Talbot, my
    brave boy '.
Here purposing the Bastard to destroy, 25
Came in strong rescue. Speak, thy father's
    care ;
Art thou not weary, John ? How dost thou
    fare ?
Wilt thou yet leave the battle, boy, and fly,
Now thou art seal'd the son of chivalry ?
Fly, to revenge my death when I am dead :
The help of one stands me in little stead.
O, too much folly is it, well I wot,   32

To hazard all our lives in one small boat !
If I to-day die not with Frenchmen's rage,
To-morrow I shall die with mickle age. 35
By me they nothing gain an if I stay :
'Tis but the short'ning of my life one day.
In thee thy mother dies, our household's
    name,
My death's revenge, thy youth, and Eng-
    land's fame.
All these and more we hazard by thy stay ; 40
All these are sav'd if thou wilt fly away.
  John. The sword of Orleans hath not
    made me smart ;
These words of yours draw life-blood from
    my heart.
On that advantage, bought with such a
    shame,   44
To save a paltry life and slay bright fame,
Before young Talbot from old Talbot fly,
The coward horse that bears me fall and
    die !
And like me to the peasant boys of France,
To be shame's scorn and subject of mis-
    chance !
Surely, by all the glory you have won,   50
An if I fly, I am not Talbot's son ;
Then talk no more of flight, it is no boot :
If son to Talbot, die at Talbot's foot.
  Tal. Then follow thou thy desp'rate sire
    of Crete,
Thou Icarus ; thy life to me is sweet.   55
If thou wilt fight, fight by thy father's side ;
And, commendable prov'd, let's die in
    pride.   [*Exeunt.*

SCENE VII. *Another part of the field.*

Alarum ; excursions. Enter old TALBOT *led
by a* Servant.

  Tal. Where is my other life ? Mine own
    is gone.
O, where's young Talbot ? Where is valiant
    John ?
Triumphant death, smear'd with captivity,
Young Talbot's valour makes me smile at
    thee.
When he perceiv'd me shrink and on my
    knee,   5
His bloody sword he brandish'd over me,
And like a hungry lion did commence
Rough deeds of rage and stern impatience ;
But when my angry guardant stood alone,
Tend'ring my ruin and assail'd of none, 10
Dizzy-ey'd fury and great rage of heart
Suddenly made him from my side to start
Into the clust'ring battle of the French ;
And in that sea of blood my boy did drench
His overmounting spirit ; and there died, 15
My Icarus, my blossom, in his pride.

Enter Soldiers, *bearing the body of John
Talbot.*

  Serv. O my dear lord, lo where your son
    is borne !

Tal. Thou antic Death, which laugh'st us
　　here to scorn,
Anon, from thy insulting tyranny,
Coupled in bonds of perpetuity,　　　　20
Two Talbots, winged through the lither
　　sky,
In thy despite shall scape mortality.
O thou whose wounds become hard-
　　favoured Death,
Speak to thy father ere thou yield thy
　　breath!
Brave Death by speaking, whether he will
　　or no;　　　　25
Imagine him a Frenchman and thy foe.
Poor boy! he smiles, methinks, as who
　　should say,
Had Death been French, then Death had
　　died to-day.
Come, come, and lay him in his father's
　　arms.
My spirit can no longer bear these harms. 30
Soldiers, adieu! I have what I would have,
Now my old arms are young John Talbot's
　　grave.　　　　[*Dies.*

Enter CHARLES, ALENÇON, BURGUNDY,
　　BASTARD, LA PUCELLE, *and* Forces.

　Char. Had York and Somerset brought
　　rescue in,
We should have found a bloody day of this.
　Bast. How the young whelp of Talbot's,
　　raging wood,　　　　35
Did flesh his puny sword in Frenchmen's
　　blood!
　Puc. Once I encount'red him, and thus
　　I said:
'Thou maiden youth, be vanquish'd by a
　　maid'.
But with a proud majestical high scorn
He answer'd thus: ' Young Talbot was not
　　born　　　　40
To be the pillage of a giglot wench'.
So, rushing in the bowels of the French,
He left me proudly, as unworthy fight.
　Bur. Doubtless he would have made a
　　noble knight.
See where he lies inhearsed in the arms　45
Of the most bloody nurser of his harms!
　Bast. Hew them to pieces, hack their
　　bones asunder,
Whose life was England's glory, Gallia's
　　wonder.
　Char. O, no; forbear! For that which
　　we have fled
During the life, let us not wrong it dead. 50

Enter SIR WILLIAM LUCY, *attended ; a*
　　French Herald *preceding.*

　Lucy. Herald, conduct me to the Dau-
　　phin's tent,
To know who hath obtain'd the glory of the
　　day.
　Char. On what submissive message art
　　thou sent?

　Lucy. Submission, Dauphin! 'Tis a mere
　　French word :　　　　54
We English warriors wot not what it means.
I come to know what prisoners thou hast
　　ta'en,
And to survey the bodies of the dead.
　Char. For prisoners ask'st thou? Hell
　　our prison is.
But tell me whom thou seek'st.
　Lucy. But where's the great Alcides of
　　the field,　　　　60
Valiant Lord Talbot, Earl of Shrewsbury,
Created for his rare success in arms
Great Earl of Washford, Waterford, and
　　Valence,
Lord Talbot of Goodrig and Urchinfield,
Lord Strange of Blackmere, Lord Verdun
　　of Alton,　　　　65
Lord Cromwell of Wingfield, Lord Furnival
　　of Sheffield,
The thrice victorious Lord of Falconbridge,
Knight of the noble order of Saint George,
Worthy Saint Michael, and the Golden
　　Fleece,
Great Marshal to Henry the Sixth　　70
Of all his wars within the realm of France?
　Puc. Here's a silly-stately style indeed!
The Turk, that two and fifty kingdoms hath,
Writes not so tedious a style as this.
Him that thou magnifi'st with all these
　　titles,　　　　75
Stinking and fly-blown lies here at our
　　feet.
　Lucy. Is Talbot slain—the Frenchmen's
　　only scourge,
Your kingdom's terror and black Nemesis?
O, were mine eye-balls into bullets turn'd,
That I in rage might shoot them at your
　　faces!　　　　80
O that I could but call these dead to life!
It were enough to fright the realm of
　　France.
Were but his picture left amongst you here,
It would amaze the proudest of you all.
Give me their bodies, that I may bear them
　　hence　　　　85
And give them burial as beseems their
　　worth.
　Puc. I think this upstart is old Talbot's
　　ghost,
He speaks with such a proud commanding
　　spirit.
For God's sake, let him have them; to keep
　　them here,　　　　89
They would but stink, and putrefy the air.
　Char. Go, take their bodies hence.
　Lucy. I'll bear them hence ; but from
　　their ashes shall be rear'd
A phœnix that shall make all France afeard.
　Char. So we be rid of them, do with them
　　what thou wilt.　　　　94
And now to Paris in this conquering vein!
All will be ours, now bloody Talbot's slain.
　　　　　　　　　　[*Exeunt.*

ACT FIVE

SCENE I. *London. The palace.*

Sennet. Enter the KING, GLOUCESTER, *and*
EXETER.

King. Have you perus'd the letters from
the Pope,
The Emperor, and the Earl of Armagnac ?
Glo. I have, my lord ; and their intent is
this :
They humbly sue unto your Excellence
To have a godly peace concluded of 5
Between the realms of England and of
France.
King. How doth your Grace affect their
motion ?
Glo. Well, my good lord, and as the only
means
To stop effusion of our Christian blood
And stablish quietness on every side. 10
King. Ay, marry, uncle ; for I always
thought
It was both impious and unnatural
That such immanity and bloody strife
Should reign among professors of one faith.
Glo. Beside, my lord, the sooner to effect
And surer bind this knot of amity, 16
The Earl of Armagnac, near knit to Charles,
A man of great authority in France,
Proffers his only daughter to your Grace
In marriage, with a large and sumptuous
dowry. 20
King. Marriage, uncle ! Alas, my years
are young !
And fitter is my study and my books
Than wanton dalliance with a paramour.
Yet call th' ambassadors, and, as you please,
So let them have their answers every one. 25
I shall be well content with any choice
Tends to God's glory and my country's
weal.

Enter WINCHESTER *in Cardinal's habit as*
CARDINAL BEAUFORT, *the* Papal Legate,
and two Ambassadors.

Exe. What ! Is my Lord of Winchester
install'd
And call'd unto a cardinal's degree ?
Then I perceive that will be verified 30
Henry the Fifth did sometime prophesy :
' If once he come to be a cardinal,
He'll make his cap co-equal with the
crown '.
King. My Lords Ambassadors, your
several suits
Have been consider'd and debated on. 35
Your purpose is both good and reasonable,
And therefore are we certainly resolv'd
To draw conditions of a friendly peace,
Which by my Lord of Winchester we mean
Shall be transported presently to France. 40
Glo. And for the proffer of my lord your
master,

I have inform'd his Highness so at large,
As, liking of the lady's virtuous gifts,
Her beauty, and the value of her dower,
He doth intend she shall be England's
Queen. 45
King. [*To Ambassador*] In argument and
proof of which contract,
Bear her this jewel, pledge of my affection.
And so, my Lord Protector, see them
guarded
And safely brought to Dover ; where,
inshipp'd,
Commit them to the fortune of the sea. 50
[*Exeunt all but Winchester and the
Legate.*
Win. Stay, my Lord Legate ; you shall
first receive
The sum of money which I promised
Should be delivered to his Holiness
For clothing me in these grave ornaments.
Leg. I will attend upon your lordship's
leisure. 55
Win. [*Aside*] Now Winchester will not
submit, I trow,
Or be inferior to the proudest peer.
Humphrey of Gloucester, thou shalt well
perceive
That neither in birth or for authority
The Bishop will be overborne by thee. 60
I'll either make thee stoop and bend thy
knee,
Or sack this country with a mutiny.
[*Exeunt.*

SCENE II. *France. Plains in Anjou.*

Enter CHARLES, BURGUNDY, ALENÇON,
BASTARD, REIGNIER, LA PUCELLE, *and*
Forces.

Char. These news, my lords, may cheer
our drooping spirits :
'Tis said the stout Parisians do revolt
And turn again unto the warlike French.
Alen. Then march to Paris, royal Charles
of France,
And keep not back your powers in dalliance.
Puc. Peace be amongst them, if they turn
to us ; 6
Else ruin combat with their palaces !

Enter a Scout.

Scout. Success unto our valiant general,
And happiness to his accomplices !
Char. What tidings send our scouts ? I
prithee speak. 10
Scout. The English army, that divided
was
Into two parties, is now conjoin'd in one,
And means to give you battle presently.
Char. Somewhat too sudden, sirs, the
warning is ;
But we will presently provide for them. 15
Bur. I trust the ghost of Talbot is not
there.

Now he is gone, my lord, you need not fear.
　　Puc. Of all base passions fear is most
　　　accurs'd.
Command the conquest, Charles, it shall be
　　thine,
Let Henry fret and all the world repine. 20
　　Char. Then on, my lords ; and France be
　　　fortunate !   [*Exeunt.*

SCENE III. *Before Angiers.*

Alarum ; excursions. Enter LA PUCELLE.

　　Puc. The Regent conquers and the
　　　Frenchmen fly.
Now help, ye charming spells and periapts ;
And ye choice spirits that admonish me
And give me signs of future accidents ;
　　　　　　　　　　　　　[*Thunder.*
You speedy helpers that are substitutes 5
Under the lordly monarch of the north,
Appear and aid me in this enterprise !

Enter Fiends.

This speedy and quick appearance argues
　　proof
Of your accustom'd diligence to me.
Now, ye familiar spirits that are cull'd 10
Out of the powerful regions under earth,
Help me this once, that France may get the
　　field.   [*They walk and speak not.*
O, hold me not with silence over-long !
Where I was wont to feed you with my
　　blood,
I'll lop a member off and give it you 15
In earnest of a further benefit,
So you do condescend to help me now.
　　　　　　　　　　[*They hang their heads.*
No hope to have redress ? My body shall
Pay recompense, if you will grant my suit.
　　　　　　　　　　[*They shake their heads.*
Cannot my body nor blood sacrifice 20
Entreat you to your wonted furtherance ?
Then take my soul—my body, soul, and all,
Before that England give the French the
　　foil.   [*They depart.*
See ! they forsake me. Now the time is
　　come
That France must vail her lofty-plumed
　　crest 25
And let her head fall into England's lap.
My ancient incantations are too weak,
And hell too strong for me to buckle with.
Now, France, thy glory droopeth to the
　　dust.   [*Exit.*

Excursions. Enter French *and* English,
　　fighting. LA PUCELLE *and* YORK *fight
　　hand to hand ; La Pucelle is taken. The
　　French fly.*

　　York. Damsel of France, I think I have
　　　you fast. 30
Unchain your spirits now with spelling
　　charms,
And try if they can gain your liberty.

A goodly prize, fit for the devil's grace !
See how the ugly witch doth bend her brows
As if, with Circe, she would change my
　　shape ! 35
　　Puc. Chang'd to a worser shape thou
　　　canst not be.
　　York. O, Charles the Dauphin is a proper
　　　man :
No shape but his can please your dainty
　　eye.
　　Puc. A plaguing mischief light on Charles
　　　and thee !
And may ye both be suddenly surpris'd 40
By bloody hands, in sleeping on your beds !
　　York. Fell banning hag ; enchantress,
　　　hold thy tongue.
　　Puc. I prithee give me leave to curse
　　　awhile.
　　York. Curse, miscreant, when thou
　　　comest to the stake.   [*Exeunt.*

Alarum. Enter SUFFOLK, *with* MARGARET
　　in his hand.

　　Suf. Be what thou wilt, thou art my
　　　prisoner.   [*Gazes on her.*
O fairest beauty, do not fear nor fly ! 46
For I will touch thee but with reverent
　　hands ;
I kiss these fingers for eternal peace,
And lay them gently on thy tender side.
Who art thou ? Say, that I may honour
　　thee. 50
　　Mar. Margaret my name, and daughter
　　　to a king,
The King of Naples—whosoe'er thou art.
　　Suf. An earl I am, and Suffolk am I
　　　call'd.
Be not offended, nature's miracle,
Thou art allotted to be ta'en by me. 55
So doth the swan her downy cygnets save,
Keeping them prisoner underneath her
　　wings.
Yet, if this servile usage once offend,
Go and be free again as Suffolk's friend.
　　　　　　　　　　[*She is going.*
O, stay ! [*Aside*] I have no power to let her
　　pass ; 60
My hand would free her, but my heart says
　　no.
As plays the sun upon the glassy streams,
Twinkling another counterfeited beam,
So seems this gorgeous beauty to mine eyes.
Fain would I woo her, yet I dare not speak.
I'll call for pen and ink, and write my mind.
Fie, de la Pole ! disable not thyself ;
Hast not a tongue ? Is she not here thy
　　prisoner ?
Wilt thou be daunted at a woman's sight ?
Ay, beauty's princely majesty is such 70
Confounds the tongue and makes the senses
　　rough.
　　Mar. Say, Earl of Suffolk, if thy name be
　　　so,
What ransom must I pay before I pass ?

For I perceive I am thy prisoner.
   Suf. [*Aside*] How canst thou tell she will
     deny thy suit,   75
Before thou make a trial of her love ?
   Mar. Why speak'st thou not ?   What
     ransom must I pay ?
   Suf. [*Aside*] She's beautiful, and there-
     fore to be woo'd ;
She is a woman, therefore to be won.
   Mar. Wilt thou accept of ransom—yea
     or no ?   80
   Suf. [*Aside*] Fond man, remember that
     thou hast a wife ;
Then how can Margaret be thy paramour ?
   Mar. I were best leave him, for he will
     not hear.
   Suf. [*Aside*] There all is marr'd ; there
     lies a cooling card.
   Mar. He talks at random ; sure, the man
     is mad.   85
   Suf. [*Aside*] And yet a dispensation may
     be had.
   Mar. And yet I would that you would
     answer me.
   Suf. [*Aside*] I'll win this Lady Margaret.
     For whom ?
Why, for my king ! Tush, that's a wooden
   thing !
   Mar. He talks of wood. It is some
     carpenter.   90
   Suf. [*Aside*] Yet so my fancy may be
     satisfied,
And peace established between these
   realms.
But there remains a scruple in that too ;
For though her father be the King of
   Naples,
Duke of Anjou and Maine, yet is he poor, 95
And our nobility will scorn the match.
   Mar. Hear ye, Captain—are you not at
     leisure ?
   Suf. [*Aside*] It shall be so, disdain they
     ne'er so much.
Henry is youthful, and will quickly yield.—
Madam, I have a secret to reveal.   100
   Mar. [*Aside*] What though I be en-
     thrall'd ? He seems a knight,
And will not any way dishonour me.
   Suf. Lady, vouchsafe to listen what I say.
   Mar. [*Aside*] Perhaps I shall be rescu'd
     by the French ;
And then I need not crave his courtesy. 105
   Suf. Sweet madam, give me hearing in a
     cause—
   Mar. [*Aside*] Tush ! women have been
     captivate ere now.
   Suf. Lady, wherefore talk you so ?
   Mar. I cry you mercy, 'tis but quid for
     quo.
   Suf. Say, gentle Princess, would you not
     suppose   110
Your bondage happy, to be made a queen ?
   Mar. To be a queen in bondage is more
     vile

Than is a slave in base servility ;
For princes should be free.
   Suf.   And so shall you,
If happy England's royal king be free. 115
   Mar. Why, what concerns his freedom
     unto me ?
   Suf. I'll undertake to make thee Henry's
     queen,
To put a golden sceptre in thy hand
And set a precious crown upon thy head,
If thou wilt condescend to be my—
   Mar.   What ?
   Suf. His love.   121
   Mar. I am unworthy to be Henry's wife.
   Suf. No, gentle madam ; I unworthy am
To woo so fair a dame to be his wife 124
And have no portion in the choice myself.
How say you, madam ? Are ye so content ?
   Mar. An if my father please, I am
     content.
   Suf. Then call our captains and our
     colours forth !
And, madam, at your father's castle walls
We'll crave a parley to confer with him. 130

Sound a parley. Enter REIGNIER *on the
     walls.*

See, Reignier, see, thy daughter prisoner !
   Reig. To whom ?
   Suf.   To me.
   Reig.   Suffolk, what remedy ?
I am a soldier and unapt to weep
Or to exclaim on fortune's fickleness.
   Suf. Yes, there is remedy enough, my
     lord.   135
Consent, and for thy honour give consent,
Thy daughter shall be wedded to my king,
Whom I with pain have woo'd and won
   thereto ;
And this her easy-held imprisonment 139
Hath gain'd thy daughter princely liberty.
   Reig. Speaks Suffolk as he thinks ?
   Suf.   Fair Margaret knows
That Suffolk doth not flatter, face, or feign.
   Reig. Upon thy princely warrant I
     descend   144
To give thee answer of thy just demand.
             [*Exit Reignier from the walls.*
   Suf. And here I will expect thy coming.

Trumpets sound. Enter REIGNIER *below.*

   Reig. Welcome, brave Earl, into our
     territories ;
Command in Anjou what your Honour
   pleases.
   Suf. Thanks, Reignier, happy for so sweet
     a child,
Fit to be made companion with a king.
What answer makes your Grace unto my
   suit ?   150
   Reig. Since thou dost deign to woo her
     little worth
To be the princely bride of such a lord,
Upon condition I may quietly

Enjoy mine own, the country Maine and
Anjou,   154
Free from oppression or the stroke of war,
My daughter shall be Henry's, if he please.

Suf. That is her ransom ; I deliver her.
And those two counties I will undertake
Your Grace shall well and quietly enjoy.

Reig. And I again, in Henry's royal name,
As deputy unto that gracious king,   161
Give thee her hand for sign of plighted
faith.

Suf. Reignier of France, I give thee
kingly thanks,
Because this is in traffic of a king.   164
[Aside] And yet, methinks, I could be well
content
To be mine own attorney in this case.—
I'll over then to England with this news,
And make this marriage to be solemniz'd.
So, farewell, Reignier.   Set this diamond
safe
In golden palaces, as it becomes.   170

Reig. I do embrace thee as I would
embrace
The Christian prince, King Henry, were he
here.

Mar. Farewell, my lord.   Good wishes,
praise, and prayers,
Shall Suffolk ever have of Margaret.
                                  [*She is going.*

Suf. Farewell, sweet madam.   But hark
you, Margaret—   175
No princely commendations to my king ?

Mar. Such commendations as becomes a
maid,
A virgin, and his servant, say to him.

Suf. Words sweetly plac'd and modestly
directed.
But, madam, I must trouble you again— 180
No loving token to his Majesty ?

Mar. Yes, my good lord : a pure unspotted heart,
Never yet taint with love, I send the King.

Suf. And this withal.   [*Kisses her.*

Mar. That for thyself—I will not so
presume   185
To send such peevish tokens to a king.
              [*Exeunt Reignier and Margaret.*

Suf. O, wert thou for myself !   But,
Suffolk, stay ;
Thou mayst not wander in that labyrinth :
There Minotaurs and ugly treasons lurk.
Solicit Henry with her wondrous praise. 190
Bethink thee on her virtues that surmount,
And natural graces that extinguish art ;
Repeat their semblance often on the seas,
That, when thou com'st to kneel at Henry's
feet,   194
Thou mayst bereave him of his wits with
wonder.   [*Exit.*

SCENE IV.   *Camp of the Duke of York in
Anjou.*

Enter YORK, WARWICK, *and* Others.

York. Bring forth that sorceress, condemn'd to burn.

Enter LA PUCELLE, *guarded, and a*
Shepherd.

Shep. Ah, Joan, this kills thy father's
heart outright !
Have I sought every country far and near,
And, now it is my chance to find thee out,
Must I behold thy timeless cruel death ? 5
Ah, Joan, sweet daughter Joan, I'll die
with thee !

Puc. Decrepit miser !   base ignoble
wretch !
I am descended of a gentler blood ;
Thou art no father nor no friend of mine.

Shep. Out, out !   My lords, an please you,
'tis not so ;   10
I did beget her, all the parish knows.
Her mother liveth yet, can testify
She was the first fruit of my bach'lorship.

War. Graceless, wilt thou deny thy
parentage ?

York. This argues what her kind of life
hath been—   15
Wicked and vile ; and so her death concludes.

Shep. Fie, Joan, that thou wilt be so
obstacle !
God knows thou art a collop of my flesh ;
And for thy sake have I shed many a tear.
Deny me not, I prithee, gentle Joan.   20

Puc. Peasant, avaunt !   You have
suborn'd this man
Of purpose to obscure my noble birth.

Shep. 'Tis true, I gave a noble to the
priest
The morn that I was wedded to her
mother.
Kneel down and take my blessing, good my
girl.   25
Wilt thou not stoop ?   Now cursed be the
time
Of thy nativity.   I would the milk
Thy mother gave thee when thou suck'dst
her breast
Had been a little ratsbane for thy sake.
Or else, when thou didst keep my lambs
a-field,   30
I wish some ravenous wolf had eaten thee.
Dost thou deny thy father, cursed drab ?
O, burn her, burn her !   Hanging is too
good.   [*Exit.*

York. Take her away ; for she hath liv'd
too long,
To fill the world with vicious qualities. 35

Puc. First let me tell you whom you have
condemn'd :
Not me begotten of a shepherd swain,
But issued from the progeny of kings ;
Virtuous and holy, chosen from above
By inspiration of celestial grace,   40
To work exceeding miracles on earth.
I never had to do with wicked spirits.

But you, that are polluted with your lusts,
Stain'd with the guiltless blood of inno-
cents,   44
Corrupt and tainted with a thousand vices,
Because you want the grace that others
have,
You judge it straight a thing impossible
To compass wonders but by help of
devils.
No, misconceived! Joan of Arc hath been
A virgin from her tender infancy,   50
Chaste and immaculate in very thought ;
Whose maiden blood, thus rigorously
effus'd,
Will cry for vengeance at the gates of
heaven.
    York. Ay, ay. Away with her to execu-
tion !
    War. And hark ye, sirs ; because she is
a maid,   55
Spare for no fagots, let there be enow.
Place barrels of pitch upon the fatal stake,
That so her torture may be shortened.
    Puc. Will nothing turn your unrelenting
hearts ?
Then, Joan, discover thine infirmity   60
That warranteth by law to be thy privilege:
I am with child, ye bloody homicides ;
Murder not then the fruit within my womb,
Although ye hale me to a violent death.
    York. Now heaven forfend ! The holy
maid with child !   65
    War. The greatest miracle that e'er ye
wrought :
Is all your strict preciseness come to this ?
    York. She and the Dauphin have been
juggling.
I did imagine what would be her refuge.
    War. Well, go to ; we'll have no bastards
live ;   70
Especially since Charles must father it.
    Puc. You are deceiv'd ; my child is none
of his :
It was Alençon that enjoy'd my love.
    York. Alençon, that notorious Machiavel!
It dies, an if it had a thousand lives.   75
    Puc. O, give me leave, I have deluded
you.
'Twas neither Charles nor yet the Duke I
nam'd,
But Reignier, King of Naples, that prevail'd.
    War. A married man ! That's most
intolerable.
    York. Why, here's a girl ! I think she
knows not well—   80
There were so many—whom she may
accuse.
    War. It's sign she hath been liberal and
free.
    York. And yet, forsooth, she is a virgin
pure.
Strumpet, thy words condemn thy brat and
thee
Use no entreaty, for it is in vain.   85

    Puc. Then lead me hence—with whom
I leave my curse :
May never glorious sun reflex his beams
Upon the country where you make abode ;
But darkness and the gloomy shade of
death
Environ you, till mischief and despair   90
Drive you to break your necks or hang
yourselves !   [Exit, guarded.
    York. Break thou in pieces and consume
to ashes,
Thou foul accursed minister of hell !

Enter CARDINAL BEAUFORT, attended.

    Car. Lord Regent, I do greet your
Excellence
With letters of commission from the King.
For know, my lords, the states of Christen-
dom,   96
Mov'd with remorse of these outrageous
broils,
Have earnestly implor'd a general peace
Betwixt our nation and the aspiring
French ;
And here at hand the Dauphin and his
train   100
Approacheth, to confer about some matter.
    York. Is all our travail turn'd to this
effect ?
After the slaughter of so many peers,
So many captains, gentlemen, and soldiers,
That in this quarrel have been overthrown
And sold their bodies for their country's
benefit,   106
Shall we at last conclude effeminate peace ?
Have we not lost most part of all the towns,
By treason, falsehood, and by treachery,
Our great progenitors had conquered ?   110
O Warwick, Warwick ! I foresee with grief
The utter loss of all the realm of France.
    War. Be patient, York. If we conclude a
peace,
It shall be with such strict and severe
covenants   114
As little shall the Frenchmen gain thereby.

Enter CHARLES, ALENÇON, BASTARD,
REIGNIER, and Others.

    Char. Since, lords of England, it is thus
agreed
That peaceful truce shall be proclaim'd in
France,
We come to be informed by yourselves
What the conditions of that league must be.
    York. Speak, Winchester ; for boiling
choler chokes   120
The hollow passage of my poison'd voice,
By sight of these our baleful enemies.
    Car. Charles, and the rest, it is enacted
thus :
That, in regard King Henry gives consent,
Of mere compassion and of lenity,   125
To ease your country of distressful war,
And suffer you to breathe in fruitful peace,

You shall become true liegemen to his
    crown ;
And, Charles, upon condition thou wilt
    swear
To pay him tribute and submit thyself, 130
Thou shalt be plac'd as viceroy under him,
And still enjoy thy regal dignity.
    Alen. Must he be then as shadow of
        himself ?
Adorn his temples with a coronet
And yet, in substance and authority,   135
Retain but privilege of a private man ?
This proffer is absurd and reasonless.
    Char. 'Tis known already that I am
        possess'd
With more than half the Gallian territories,
And therein reverenc'd for their lawful
    king.   140
Shall I, for lucre of the rest unvanquish'd,
Detract so much from that prerogative
As to be call'd but viceroy of the whole ?
No, Lord Ambassador ; I'll rather keep
That which I have than, coveting for more,
Be cast from possibility of all.   146
    York. Insulting Charles ! Hast thou by
        secret means
Us'd intercession to obtain a league,
And now the matter grows to compromise
Stand'st thou aloof upon comparison ? 150
Either accept the title thou usurp'st,
Of benefit proceeding from our king
And not of any challenge of desert,
Or we will plague thee with incessant wars.
    Reig. [*To Charles*] My lord, you do not
        well in obstinacy   155
To cavil in the course of this contract.
If once it be neglected, ten to one
We shall not find like opportunity.
    Alen. [*To Charles*] To say the truth, it is
        your policy   159
To save your subjects from such massacre
And ruthless slaughters as are daily seen
By our proceeding in hostility ;
And therefore take this compact of a
    truce,
Although you break it when your pleasure
    serves.
    War. How say'st thou, Charles ? Shall
        our condition stand ?   165
    Char. It shall ;
Only reserv'd, you claim no interest
In any of our towns of garrison.
    York. Then swear allegiance to his
        Majesty :
As thou art knight, never to disobey   170
Nor be rebellious to the crown of England—
Thou, nor thy nobles, to the crown of
    England.   [*Charles and the rest give
                tokens of fealty.*
So, now dismiss your army when ye please ;
Hang up your ensigns, let your drums be
    still,   174
For here we entertain a solemn peace.
                            [*Exeunt.*

SCENE V. *London. The palace.*

Enter SUFFOLK, *in conference with the*
    KING, GLOUCESTER *and* EXETER.

    King. Your wondrous rare description,
        noble Earl,
Of beauteous Margaret hath astonish'd me.
Her virtues, graced with external gifts,
Do breed love's settled passions in my
    heart ;
And like as rigour of tempestuous gusts 5
Provokes the mightiest hulk against the
    tide,
So am I driven by breath of her renown
Either to suffer shipwreck or arrive
Where I may have fruition of her love.
    Suf. Tush, my good lord! This super-
        ficial tale   10
Is but a preface of her worthy praise.
The chief perfections of that lovely dame,
Had I sufficient skill to utter them,
Would make a volume of enticing lines,
Able to ravish any dull conceit ;   15
And, which is more, she is not so divine,
So full-replete with choice of all delights,
But with as humble lowliness of mind
She is content to be at your command—
Command, I mean, of virtuous chaste
    intents,   20
To love and honour Henry as her lord.
    King. And otherwise will Henry ne'er
        presume.
Therefore, my Lord Protector, give consent
That Marg'ret may be England's royal
    Queen.
    Glo. So should I give consent to flatter
        sin.   25
You know, my lord, your Highness is
    betroth'd
Unto another lady of esteem.
How shall we then dispense with that
    contract,
And not deface your honour with reproach ?
    Suf. As doth a ruler with unlawful oaths ;
Or one that at a triumph, having vow'd 31
To try his strength, forsaketh yet the lists
By reason of his adversary's odds :
A poor earl's daughter is unequal odds,
And therefore may be broke without
    offence.   35
    Glo. Why, what, I pray, is Margaret
        more than that ?
Her father is no better than an earl,
Although in glorious titles he excel.
    Suf. Yes, my lord, her father is a king,
The King of Naples and Jerusalem ;   40
And of such great authority in France
As his alliance will confirm our peace,
And keep the Frenchmen in allegiance.
    Glo. And so the Earl of Armagnac may
        do,
Because he is near kinsman unto Charles. 45
    Exe. Beside, his wealth doth warrant a
        liberal dower ;

Where Reignier sooner will receive than
 give.
 Suf. A dow'r, my lords ! Disgrace not so
 your king,
That he should be so abject, base, and poor,
To choose for wealth and not for perfect
 love.   50
Henry is able to enrich his queen,
And not to seek a queen to make him
 rich.
So worthless peasants bargain for their
 wives,
As market-men for oxen, sheep, or horse.
Marriage is a matter of more worth   55
Than to be dealt in by attorneyship ;
Not whom we will, but whom his Grace
 affects,
Must be companion of his nuptial bed.
And therefore, lords, since he affects her
 most,
It most of all these reasons bindeth us   60
In our opinions she should be preferr'd ;
For what is wedlock forced but a hell,
An age of discord and continual strife ?
Whereas the contrary bringeth bliss,
And is a pattern of celestial peace.   65
Whom should we match with Henry, being
 a king,
But Margaret, that is daughter to a king ?
Her peerless feature, joined with her birth,
Approves her fit for none but for a
 king ;   69
Her valiant courage and undaunted spirit,
More than in women commonly is seen,
Will answer our hope in issue of a king ;
For Henry, son unto a conqueror,
Is likely to beget more conquerors,
If with a lady of so high resolve   75
As is fair Margaret he be link'd in love.
Then yield, my lords ; and here conclude
 with me

That Margaret shall be Queen, and none
 but she.
 King. Whether it be through force of
 your report,
My noble Lord of Suffolk, or for that   80
My tender youth was never yet attaint
With any passion of inflaming love,
I cannot tell ; but this I am assur'd,
I feel such sharp dissension in my breast,
Such fierce alarums both of hope and fear,
As I am sick with working of my thoughts.
Take therefore shipping ; post, my lord, to
 France ;
Agree to any covenants ; and procure
That Lady Margaret do vouchsafe to come
To cross the seas to England, and be
 crown'd   90
King Henry's faithful and anointed queen.
For your expenses and sufficient charge,
Among the people gather up a tenth.
Be gone, I say ; for till you do return
I rest perplexed with a thousand cares.   95
And you, good uncle, banish all offence :
If you do censure me by what you were,
Not what you are, I know it will excuse
This sudden execution of my will.   99
And so conduct me where, from company,
I may revolve and ruminate my grief.
                                   [*Exit.*
 Glo. Ay, grief, I fear me, both at first
 and last.
                 [*Exeunt Gloucester and Exeter.*
 Suf. Thus Suffolk hath prevail'd ; and
 thus he goes,
As did the youthful Paris once to Greece,
With hope to find the like event in love 105
But prosper better than the Troyan did.
Margaret shall now be Queen, and rule the
 King ;
But I will rule both her, the King, and
 realm.   [*Exit.*

THE SECOND PART OF
KING HENRY THE SIXTH

DRAMATIS PERSONÆ

KING HENRY THE SIXTH.
HUMPHREY, DUKE OF GLOUCESTER, *his uncle.*
CARDINAL BEAUFORT, BISHOP OF WINCHESTER, *great-uncle to the King.*
RICHARD PLANTAGENET, DUKE OF YORK.
EDWARD *and* RICHARD, *his sons.*
DUKE OF SOMERSET.
DUKE OF SUFFOLK.
DUKE OF BUCKINGHAM.
LORD CLIFFORD.
YOUNG CLIFFORD, *his son.*
EARL OF SALISBURY.
EARL OF WARWICK.
LORD SCALES.
LORD SAY.
SIR HUMPHREY STAFFORD.
WILLIAM STAFFORD, *his brother.*
SIR JOHN STANLEY.
VAUX.
MATTHEW GOFFE.
A Lieutenant, *a* Shipmaster, *a* Master's Mate, *and* WALTER WHITMORE.
Two Gentlemen, *prisoners with Suffolk.*
JOHN HUME *and* JOHN SOUTHWELL, *two priests.*

ROGER BOLINGBROKE, *a conjurer.*
A Spirit *raised by him.*
THOMAS HORNER, *an armourer.*
PETER, *his man.*
Clerk of Chatham.
Mayor of Saint Albans.
SAUNDER SIMPCOX, *an impostor.*
ALEXANDER IDEN, *a Kentish gentleman.*
JACK CADE, *a rebel.*
GEORGE BEVIS, JOHN HOLLAND, DICK the butcher, SMITH the weaver, MICHAEL, *&c., followers of Cade.*
Two Murderers.

MARGARET, *Queen to King Henry.*
ELEANOR, DUCHESS OF GLOUCESTER.
MARGERY JOURDAIN, *a witch.*
Wife *to Simpcox.*

Lords, Ladies, *and* Attendants ; Petitioners, Aldermen, *a* Herald, *a* Beadle, *a* Sheriff, Officers, Citizens, Prentices, Falconers, Guards, Soldiers, Messengers, &c.

THE SCENE : *England.*

ACT ONE

SCENE I. *London. The palace.*

Flourish of trumpets ; then hautboys. Enter the KING, DUKE HUMPHREY OF GLOUCESTER, SALISBURY, WARWICK, *and* CARDINAL BEAUFORT, *on the one side ; the* QUEEN, SUFFOLK, YORK, SOMERSET, *and* BUCKINGHAM, *on the other.*

Suf. As by your high imperial Majesty
I had in charge at my depart for France,
As procurator to your Excellence,
To marry Princess Margaret for your Grace ;
So, in the famous ancient city Tours,   5
In presence of the Kings of France and Sicil,
The Dukes of Orleans, Calaber, Bretagne, and Alençon,
Seven earls, twelve barons, and twenty reverend bishops,
I have perform'd my task, and was espous'd ;
And humbly now upon my bended knee,   10
In sight of England and her lordly peers,
Deliver up my title in the Queen
To your most gracious hands, that are the substance
Of that great shadow I did represent :
The happiest gift that ever marquis gave,   15
The fairest queen that ever king receiv'd.
King. Suffolk, arise. Welcome, Queen Margaret :
I can express no kinder sign of love
Than this kind kiss. O Lord, that lends me life,   19
Lend me a heart replete with thankfulness !
For thou hast given me in this beauteous face
A world of earthly blessings to my soul,
If sympathy of love unite our thoughts.
Queen. Great King of England, and my gracious lord,
The mutual conference that my mind hath had,   25
By day, by night, waking and in my dreams,
In courtly company or at my beads,
With you, mine alder-liefest sovereign,
Makes me the bolder to salute my king
With ruder terms, such as my wit affords   30
And over-joy of heart doth minister.

623

King. Her sight did ravish, but her grace in speech,
Her words y-clad with wisdom's majesty,
Makes me from wond'ring fall to weeping joys,
Such is the fulness of my heart's content. 35
Lords, with one cheerful voice welcome my love.

All. [*Kneeling*] Long live Queen Margaret, England's happiness!

Queen. We thank you all. [*Flourish.*

Suf. My Lord Protector, so it please your Grace,
Here are the articles of contracted peace 40
Between our sovereign and the French King Charles,
For eighteen months concluded by consent.

Glo. [*Reads*] ' Imprimis : It is agreed between the French King Charles and William de la Pole, Marquess of Suffolk, ambassador for Henry King of England, that the said Henry shall espouse the Lady Margaret, daughter unto Reignier King of Naples, Sicilia, and Jerusalem, and crown her Queen of England ere the thirtieth of May next ensuing.
Item : That the duchy of Anjou and the county of Maine shall be released and delivered to the King her father '—
[*Lets the paper fall.*

King. Uncle, how now !

Glo. Pardon me, gracious lord ; 50
Some sudden qualm hath struck me at the heart,
And dimm'd mine eyes, that I can read no further.

King. Uncle of Winchester, I pray read on.

Car. [*Reads*] ' Item : It is further agreed between them that the duchies of Anjou and Maine shall be released and delivered over to the King her father, and she sent over of the King of England's own proper cost and charges, without having any dowry.'

King. They please us well. Lord Marquess, kneel down :
We here create thee the first Duke of Suffolk,
And girt thee with the sword. Cousin of York, 60
We here discharge your Grace from being Regent
I' th' parts of France, till term of eighteen months
Be full expir'd. Thanks, uncle Winchester,
Gloucester, York, Buckingham, Somerset,
Salisbury, and Warwick ; 65
We thank you all for this great favour done
In entertainment to my princely queen.
Come, let us in, and with all speed provide
To see her coronation be perform'd.
[*Exeunt King, Queen, and Suffolk.*

Glo. Brave peers of England, pillars of the state, 70
To you Duke Humphrey must unload his grief—
Your grief, the common grief of all the land.
What ! did my brother Henry spend his youth,
His valour, coin, and people, in the wars ?
Did he so often lodge in open field, 75
In winter's cold and summer's parching heat,
To conquer France, his true inheritance ?
And did my brother Bedford toil his wits
To keep by policy what Henry got ?
Have you yourselves, Somerset, Buckingham, 80
Brave York, Salisbury, and victorious Warwick,
Receiv'd deep scars in France and Normandy ?
Or hath mine uncle Beaufort and myself,
With all the learned Council of the realm,
Studied so long, sat in the Council House 85
Early and late, debating to and fro
How France and Frenchmen might be kept in awe ?
And had his Highness in his infancy
Crowned in Paris, in despite of foes ?
And shall these labours and these honours die ? 90
Shall Henry's conquest, Bedford's vigilance,
Your deeds of war, and all our counsel die ?
O peers of England, shameful is this league !
Fatal this marriage, cancelling your fame,
Blotting your names from books of memory, 95
Razing the characters of your renown,
Defacing monuments of conquer'd France,
Undoing all, as all had never been !

Car. Nephew, what means this passionate discourse,
This peroration with such circumstance? 100
For France, 'tis ours ; and we will keep it still.

Glo. Ay, uncle, we will keep it if we can ;
But now it is impossible we should.
Suffolk, the new-made duke that rules the roast, 104
Hath given the duchy of Anjou and Maine
Unto the poor King Reignier, whose large style
Agrees not with the leanness of his purse.

Sal. Now, by the death of Him that died for all,
These counties were the keys of Normandy !
But wherefore weeps Warwick, my valiant son ? 110

War. For grief that they are past recovery ;
For were there hope to conquer them again
My sword should shed hot blood, mine eyes no tears.

Anjou and Maine! myself did win them
   both;
Those provinces these arms of mine did
   conquer;   115
And are the cities that I got with wounds
Deliver'd up again with peaceful words?
Mort Dieu!
   York. For Suffolk's duke, may he be
   suffocate,   119
That dims the honour of this warlike isle!
France should have torn and rent my very
   heart
Before I would have yielded to this league.
I never read but England's kings have had
Large sums of gold and dowries with their
   wives;
And our King Henry gives away his own 125
To match with her that brings no vantages.
   Glo. A proper jest, and never heard
   before,
That Suffolk should demand a whole
   fifteenth
For costs and charges in transporting her!
She should have stay'd in France, and
   starv'd in France,   130
Before—
   Car. My Lord of Gloucester, now ye grow
   too hot:
It was the pleasure of my lord the King.
   Glo. My Lord of Winchester, I know your
   mind;   134
'Tis not my speeches that you do mislike,
But 'tis my presence that doth trouble ye.
Rancour will out: proud prelate, in thy
   face
I see thy fury; if I longer stay
We shall begin our ancient bickerings.
Lordings, farewell; and say, when I am
   gone,   140
I prophesied France will be lost ere long.
                   [*Exit.*
   Car. So, there goes our Protector in a
   rage.
'Tis known to you he is mine enemy;
Nay, more, an enemy unto you all,   144
And no great friend, I fear me, to the King.
Consider, lords, he is the next of blood
And heir apparent to the English crown.
Had Henry got an empire by his marriage
And all the wealthy kingdoms of the west,
There's reason he should be displeas'd at it.
Look to it, lords; let not his smoothing
   words   151
Bewitch your hearts; be wise and circum-
   spect.
What though the common people favour
   him,
Calling him ' Humphrey, the good Duke of
   Gloucester',
Clapping their hands, and crying with loud
   voice   155
' Jesu maintain your royal excellence!'
With ' God preserve the good Duke
   Humphrey!'

I fear me, lords, for all this flattering gloss,
He will be found a dangerous Protector.
   Buck. Why should he then protect our
   sovereign,   160
He being of age to govern of himself?
Cousin of Somerset, join you with me,
And all together, with the Duke of Suffolk,
We'll quickly hoise Duke Humphrey from
   his seat.
   Car. This weighty business will not brook
   delay;   165
I'll to the Duke of Suffolk presently. [*Exit.*
   Som. Cousin of Buckingham, though
   Humphrey's pride
And greatness of his place be grief to us,
Yet let us watch the haughty cardinal;
His insolence is more intolerable   170
Than all the princes in the land beside:
If Gloucester be displac'd, he'll be Pro-
   tector.
   Buck. Or thou or I, Somerset, will be
   Protector,
Despite Duke Humphrey or the Cardinal.
        [*Exeunt Buckingham and Somerset.*
   Sal. Pride went before, ambition follows
   him.   175
While these do labour for their own prefer-
   ment,
Behoves it us to labour for the realm.
I never saw but Humphrey Duke of
   Gloucester
Did bear him like a noble gentleman.
Oft have I seen the haughty Cardinal— 180
More like a soldier than a man o' th' church,
As stout and proud as he were lord of
   all—
Swear like a ruffian and demean himself
Unlike the ruler of a commonweal.
Warwick my son, the comfort of my age, 185
Thy deeds, thy plainness, and thy house-
   keeping,
Hath won the greatest favour of the com-
   mons,
Excepting none but good Duke Humphrey.
And, brother York, thy acts in Ireland,
In bringing them to civil discipline,   190
Thy late exploits done in the heart of
   France
When thou wert Regent for our sovereign,
Have made thee fear'd and honour'd of the
   people:
Join we together for the public good,
In what we can, to bridle and suppress 195
The pride of Suffolk and the Cardinal,
With Somerset's and Buckingham's am-
   bition;
And, as we may, cherish Duke Humphrey's
   deeds
While they do tend the profit of the land.
   War. So God help Warwick, as he loves
   the land   200
And common profit of his country!
   York. And so says York—[*Aside*] for he
   hath greatest cause.

Sal. Then let's make haste away and look
    unto the main.
War. Unto the main ! O father, Maine is
    lost—
That Maine which by main force Warwick
    did win,   205
And would have kept so long as breath did
    last.
Main chance, father, you meant ; but I
    meant Maine,
Which I will win from France, or else be
    slain.
        [*Exeunt Warwick and Salisbury.*
  York. Anjou and Maine are given to the
    French ;
Paris is lost ; the state of Normandy   210
Stands on a tickle point now they are
    gone.
Suffolk concluded on the articles ;
The peers agreed ; and Henry was well
    pleas'd
To change two dukedoms for a duke's fair
    daughter.
I cannot blame them all : what is't to
    them ?   215
'Tis thine they give away, and not their
    own.
Pirates may make cheap pennyworths of
    their pillage,
And purchase friends, and give to cour-
    tezans,
Still revelling like lords till all be gone ;
While as the silly owner of the goods   220
Weeps over them and wrings his hapless
    hands
And shakes his head and trembling stands
    aloof,
While all is shar'd and all is borne away,
Ready to starve and dare not touch his
    own.
So York must sit and fret and bite his
    tongue,   225
While his own lands are bargain'd for and
    sold.
Methinks the realms of England, France,
    and Ireland,
Bear that proportion to my flesh and blood
As did the fatal brand Althæa burnt
Unto the prince's heart of Calydon.   230
Anjou and Maine both given unto the
    French !
Cold news for me, for I had hope of France,
Even as I have of fertile England's soil.
A day will come when York shall claim his
    own ;   234
And therefore I will take the Nevils' parts,
And make a show of love to proud Duke
    Humphrey,
And when I spy advantage, claim the
    crown,
For that's the golden mark I seek to hit.
Nor shall proud Lancaster usurp my right,
Nor hold the sceptre in his childish fist,   240
Nor wear the diadem upon his head,

Whose church-like humours fits not for a
    crown.
Then, York, be still awhile, till time do
    serve ;
Watch thou and wake, when others be
    asleep,
To pry into the secrets of the state ;   245
Till Henry, surfeiting in joys of love
With his new bride and England's dear-
    bought queen,
And Humphrey with the peers be fall'n at
    jars ;
Then will I raise aloft the milk-white rose,
With whose sweet smell the air shall be
    perfum'd,   250
And in my standard bear the arms of
    York,
To grapple with the house of Lancaster ;
And force perforce I'll make him yield the
    crown,
Whose bookish rule hath pull'd fair England
    down.   [*Exit.*

SCENE II. *The Duke of Gloucester's house.*

Enter DUKE HUMPHREY *and his wife*
ELEANOR.

  Duch. Why droops my lord, like over-
    ripen'd corn
Hanging the head at Ceres' plenteous load ?
Why doth the great Duke Humphrey knit
    his brows,
As frowning at the favours of the world ?
Why are thine eyes fix'd to the sullen earth,
Gazing on that which seems to dim thy
    sight ?   6
What see'st thou there ?   King Henry's
    diadem,
Enchas'd with all the honours of the world ?
If so, gaze on, and grovel on thy face
Until thy head be circled with the same.   10
Put forth thy hand, reach at the glorious
    gold.
What, is't too short ? I'll lengthen it with
    mine ;
And having both together heav'd it up,
We'll both together lift our heads to heaven,
And never more abase our sight so low   15
As to vouchsafe one glance unto the ground.
  Glo. O Nell, sweet Nell, if thou dost love
    thy lord,
Banish the canker of ambitious thoughts !
And may that thought, when I imagine ill
Against my king and nephew, virtuous
    Henry,   20
Be my last breathing in this mortal world !
My troublous dreams this night doth make
    me sad.
  Duch. What dream'd my lord ? Tell me,
    and I'll requite it
With sweet rehearsal of my morning's
    dream.
  Glo. Methought this staff, mine office-
    badge in court,   25

Was broke in twain; by whom I have
   forgot,
But, as I think, it was by th' Cardinal;
And on the pieces of the broken wand
Were plac'd the heads of Edmund Duke of
   Somerset
And William de la Pole, first Duke of
   Suffolk.   30
This was my dream; what it doth bode
   God knows.
   Duch. Tut, this was nothing but an
   argument
That he that breaks a stick of Gloucester's
   grove
Shall lose his head for his presumption.
But list to me, my Humphrey, my sweet
   Duke: 35
Methought I sat in seat of majesty
In the cathedral church of Westminster,
And in that chair where kings and queens
   were crown'd;
Where Henry and Dame Margaret kneel'd
   to me,
And on my head did set the diadem.   40
   Glo. Nay, Eleanor, then must I chide out-
   right.
Presumptuous dame, ill-nurtur'd Eleanor!
Art thou not second woman in the realm,
And the Protector's wife, belov'd of him?
Hast thou not worldly pleasure at com-
   mand   45
Above the reach or compass of thy thought?
And wilt thou still be hammering treachery
To tumble down thy husband and thyself
From top of honour to disgrace's feet?
Away from me, and let me hear no more! 50
   Duch. What, what, my lord! Are you so
   choleric
With Eleanor for telling but her dream?
Next time I'll keep my dreams unto myself
And not be check'd.
   Glo. Nay, be not angry; I am pleas'd
   again.   55

     Enter a Messenger.

   Mess. My Lord Protector, 'tis his High-
   ness' pleasure
You do prepare to ride unto Saint Albans,
Where as the King and Queen do mean to
   hawk.
   Glo. I go. Come, Nell, thou wilt ride with
   us?
   Duch. Yes, my good lord, I'll follow
   presently.   60
     [*Exeunt Gloucester and Messenger.*
Follow I must; I cannot go before,
While Gloucester bears this base and
   humble mind.
Were I a man, a duke, and next of blood,
I would remove these tedious stumbling-
   blocks
And smooth my way upon their headless
   necks;   65
And, being a woman, I will not be slack

To play my part in Fortune's pageant.
Where are you there, Sir John? Nay, fear
   not, man,
We are alone; here's none but thee and I.

     Enter HUME.

   Hume. Jesus preserve your royal Majesty!
   Duch. What say'st thou? Majesty! I am
   but Grace.   71
   Hume. But, by the grace of God and
   Hume's advice,
Your Grace's title shall be multiplied.
   Duch. What say'st thou, man? Hast
   thou as yet conferr'd
With Margery Jourdain, the cunning witch
   of Eie,   75
With Roger Bolingbroke, the conjurer?
And will they undertake to do me good?
   Hume. This they have promised, to show
   your Highness
A spirit rais'd from depth of underground
That shall make answer to such questions 80
As by your Grace shall be propounded
   him.
   Duch. It is enough; I'll think upon the
   questions;
When from Saint Albans we do make
   return
We'll see these things effected to the full.
Here, Hume, take this reward; make
   merry, man,   85
With thy confederates in this weighty cause.
     [*Exit.*
   Hume. Hume must make merry with the
   Duchess' gold;
Marry, and shall. But, how now, Sir John
   Hume!
Seal up your lips and give no words but
   mum:
The business asketh silent secrecy.   90
Dame Eleanor gives gold to bring the
   witch:
Gold cannot come amiss were she a devil.
Yet have I gold flies from another coast—
I dare not say from the rich Cardinal,
And from the great and new-made Duke of
   Suffolk;   95
Yet I do find it so; for, to be plain,
They, knowing Dame Eleanor's aspiring
   humour,
Have hired me to undermine the Duchess,
And buzz these conjurations in her brain.
They say 'A crafty knave does need no
   broker';   100
Yet am I Suffolk and the Cardinal's broker.
Hume, if you take not heed, you shall go
   near
To call them both a pair of crafty knaves.
Well, so it stands; and thus, I fear, at
   last
Hume's knavery will be the Duchess' wreck,
And her attainture will be Humphrey's fall.
Sort how it will, I shall have gold for all.
     [*Exit.*

Scene III. *London. The palace.*

Enter three or four Petitioners, PETER, *the
Armourer's man, being one.*

1 *Pet.* My masters, let's stand close ; my
Lord Protector will come this way by and
by, and then we may deliver our supplications in the quill.

2 *Pet.* Marry, the Lord protect him, for
he's a good man, Jesu bless him !   5

Enter SUFFOLK *and* QUEEN.

1 *Pet.* Here 'a comes, methinks, and the
Queen with him. I'll be the first, sure.

2 *Pet.* Come back, fool ; this is the Duke
of Suffolk and not my Lord Protector.   9

Suf. How now, fellow ! Wouldst anything with me ?

1 *Pet.* I pray, my lord, pardon me ; I
took ye for my Lord Protector.

Queen. [*Reads*] ' To my Lord Protector ! '
Are your supplications to his lordship ? Let
me see them. What is thine ?   15

1 *Pet.* Mine is, an't please your Grace,
against John Goodman, my Lord Cardinal's
man, for keeping my house and lands, and
wife and all, from me.

Suf. Thy wife too ! That's some wrong
indeed. What's yours ? What's here !
[*Reads*] ' Against the Duke of Suffolk, for
enclosing the commons of Melford.' How
now, sir knave !

2 *Pet.* Alas, sir, I am but a poor petitioner
of our whole township.   24

Peter. [*Presenting his petition*] Against my
master, Thomas Horner, for saying that
the Duke of York was rightful heir to
the crown.

Queen. What say'st thou ? Did the Duke
of York say he was rightful heir to the
crown ?   29

Peter. That my master was ? No, forsooth. My master said that he was, and
that the King was an usurper.

Suf. Who is there ?   [*Enter Servant.*
Take this fellow in, and send for his master
with a pursuivant presently. We'll hear
more of your matter before the King.
                [*Exit Servant with Peter.*

Queen. And as for you, that love to be
protected   35
Under the wings of our Protector's grace,
Begin your suits anew, and sue to him.
                [*Tears the supplications.*
Away, base cullions ! Suffolk, let them go.

All. Come, let's be gone.   [*Exeunt.*

Queen. My Lord of Suffolk, say, is this
the guise,   40
Is this the fashions in the court of England ?
Is this the government of Britain's isle,
And this the royalty of Albion's king ?
What, shall King Henry be a pupil still,
Under the surly Gloucester's governance ?

Am I a queen in title and in style,   46
And must be made a subject to a duke ?
I tell thee, Pole, when in the city Tours
Thou ran'st a tilt in honour of my love
And stol'st away the ladies' hearts of
France,   50
I thought King Henry had resembled thee
In courage, courtship, and proportion ;
But all his mind is bent to holiness,
To number Ave-Maries on his beads ;
His champions are the prophets and
apostles ;   55
His weapons, holy saws of sacred writ ;
His study is his tilt-yard, and his loves
Are brazen images of canonized saints.
I would the college of the Cardinals
Would choose him Pope, and carry him to
Rome,   60
And set the triple crown upon his head ;
That were a state fit for his holiness.

Suf. Madam, be patient. As I was cause
Your Highness came to England, so will I
In England work your Grace's full content.

Queen. Beside the haughty Protector,
have we Beaufort   66
The imperious churchman ; Somerset,
Buckingham,
And grumbling York ; and not the least of
these
But can do more in England than the King.

Suf. And he of these that can do most
of all   70
Cannot do more in England than the Nevils ;
Salisbury and Warwick are no simple peers.

Queen. Not all these lords do vex me half
so much
As that proud dame, the Lord Protector's
wife.
She sweeps it through the court with troops
of ladies,   75
More like an empress than Duke Humph-
rey's wife.
Strangers in court do take her for the
Queen.
She bears a duke's revenues on her back,
And in her heart she scorns our poverty ;
Shall I not live to be aveng'd on her ?   80
Contemptuous base-born callet as she is,
She vaunted 'mongst her minions t' other
day
The very train of her worst wearing gown
Was better worth than all my father's lands,
Till Suffolk gave two dukedoms for his
daughter.   85

Suf. Madam, myself have lim'd a bush
for her,
And plac'd a quire of such enticing birds
That she will light to listen to the lays,
And never mount to trouble you again.
So, let her rest. And, madam, list to me, 90
For I am bold to counsel you in this :
Although we fancy not the Cardinal,
Yet must we join with him and with the
lords,

Till we have brought Duke Humphrey in
    disgrace.
As for the Duke of York, this late com-
    plaint   95
Will make but little for his benefit.
So one by one we'll weed them all at last,
And you yourself shall steer the happy
    helm.

Sound a sennet. Enter the KING, DUKE
HUMPHREY, CARDINAL BEAUFORT,
BUCKINGHAM, YORK, SOMERSET SALIS-
BURY, WARWICK, *and the* DUCHESS OF
GLOUCESTER.

  King. For my part, noble lords, I care
    not which :
Or Somerset or York, all's one to me.   100
  York. If York have ill demean'd himself
    in France,
Then let him be denay'd the regentship.
  Som. If Somerset be unworthy of the
    place,
Let York be Regent ; I will yield to him.
  War. Whether your Grace be worthy, yea
    or no,   105
Dispute not that ; York is the worthier.
  Car. Ambitious Warwick, let thy betters
    speak.
  War. The Cardinal's not my better in the
    field.
  Buck. All in this presence are thy betters,
    Warwick.
  War. Warwick may live to be the best
    of all.   110
  Sal. Peace, son ! And show some reason,
    Buckingham,
Why Somerset should be preferr'd in this.
  Queen. Because the King, forsooth, will
    have it so.
  Glo. Madam, the King is old enough
    himself
To give his censure. These are no women's
    matters.   115
  Queen. If he be old enough, what needs
    your Grace
To be Protector of his Excellence ?
  Glo. Madam, I am Protector of the
    realm ;
And at his pleasure will resign my place.
  Suf. Resign it then, and leave thine
    insolence.   120
Since thou wert king—as who is king but
    thou ?—
The commonwealth hath daily run to
    wrack,
The Dauphin hath prevail'd beyond the
    'seas,
And all the peers and nobles of the realm
Have been as bondmen to thy sovereignty.
  Car. The commons hast thou rack'd ; the
    clergy's bags   126
Are lank and lean with thy extortions.
  Som. Thy sumptuous buildings and thy
    wife's attire

Have cost a mass of public treasury.
  Buck. Thy cruelty in execution   130
Upon offenders hath exceeded law,
And left thee to the mercy of the law.
  Queen. Thy sale of offices and towns in
    France,
If they were known, as the suspect is great,
Would make thee quickly hop without thy
    head. [*Exit Gloucester. The Queen
             drops her fan.*
Give me my fan. What, minion, can ye
    not ? [*She gives the Duchess a box
             on the ear.*
I cry your mercy, madam ; was it you ?
  Duch. Was't I ? Yea, I it was, proud
    Frenchwoman.
Could I come near your beauty with my
    nails,
I could set my ten commandments in your
    face.   140
  King. Sweet aunt, be quiet ; 'twas
    against her will.
  Duch. Against her will, good King ?
    Look to 't in time ;
She'll hamper thee and dandle thee like a
    baby.
Though in this place most master wear no
    breeches,
She shall not strike Dame Eleanor un-
    reveng'd.   [*Exit.*
  Buck. Lord Cardinal, I will follow
    Eleanor,   146
And listen after Humphrey, how he pro-
    ceeds.
She's tickled now ; her fume needs no
    spurs,
She'll gallop far enough to her destruction.
                        [*Exit.*

Re-enter GLOUCESTER.

  Glo. Now, lords, my choler being over-
    blown   150
With walking once about the quadrangle,
I come to talk of commonwealth affairs.
As for your spiteful false objections,
Prove them, and I lie open to the law ;
But God in mercy so deal with my soul   155
As I in duty love my king and country !
But to the matter that we have in hand :
I say, my sovereign, York is meetest man
To be your Regent in the realm of France.
  Suf. Before we make election, give me
    leave   160
To show some reason, of no little force,
That York is most unmeet of any man.
  York. I'll tell thee, Suffolk, why I am
    unmeet :
First, for I cannot flatter thee in pride ;
Next, if I be appointed for the place,   165
My Lord of Somerset will keep me here
Without discharge, money, or furniture,
Till France be won into the Dauphin's
    hands.
Last time I danc'd attendance on his will

Till Paris was besieg'd, famish'd, and lost.
  War. That can I witness ; and a fouler
    fact   171
Did never traitor in the land commit.
  Suf. Peace, headstrong Warwick !
  War. Image of pride, why should I hold
    my peace ?

Enter HORNER, *the Armourer, and his man*
PETER, *guarded.*

  Suf. Because here is a man accus'd of
    treason :   175
Pray God the Duke of York excuse himself !
  York. Doth any one accuse York for a
    traitor ?
  King. What mean'st thou, Suffolk ? Tell
    me, what are these ?
  Suf. Please it your Majesty, this is the
    man
That doth accuse his master of high
    treason ;   180
His words were these : that Richard Duke
    of York
Was rightful heir unto the English crown,
And that your Majesty was an usurper.
  King. Say, man, were these thy words ?
  Hor. An't shall please your Majesty, I
never said nor thought any such matter.
God is my witness, I am falsely accus'd by
the villain.
  Peter. [*Holding up his hands*] By these
ten bones, my lords, he did speak them to
me in the garret one night, as we were
scouring my Lord of York's armour. 190
  York. Base dunghill villain and mechan-
    ical,
I'll have thy head for this thy traitor's
    speech.
I do beseech your royal Majesty,
Let him have all the rigour of the law. 194
  Hor. Alas, my lord, hang me if ever I
spake the words. My accuser is my prentice;
and when I did correct him for his fault
the other day, he did vow upon his knees
he would be even with me. I have good
witness of this ; therefore I beseech your
Majesty, do not cast away an honest man
for a villain's accusation. 200
  King. Uncle, what shall we say to this
    in law ?
  Glo. This doom, my lord, if I may judge :
Let Somerset be Regent o'er the French,
Because in York this breeds suspicion ; 205
And let these have a day appointed them
For single combat in convenient place,
For he hath witness of his servant's malice.
This is the law, and this Duke Humphrey's
    doom.
  Som. I humbly thank your royal
    Majesty. 209
  Hor. And I accept the combat willingly.
  Peter. Alas, my lord, I cannot fight ; for
God's sake, pity my case ! The spite of
man prevaileth against me. O Lord, have

mercy upon me, I shall never be able to
fight a blow ! O Lord, my heart ! 214
  Glo. Sirrah, or you must fight or else be
    hang'd.
  King. Away with them to prison ; and
the day of combat shall be the last of the
next month.
Come, Somerset, we'll see thee sent away.
                [*Flourish. Exeunt.*

SCENE IV. *London. The Duke of*
Gloucester's garden.

Enter MARGERY JOURDAIN, *the witch ; the*
two priests, HUME *and* SOUTHWELL ; *and*
BOLINGBROKE.

  Hume. Come, my masters ; the Duchess,
I tell you, expects performance of your
promises.
  Boling. Master Hume, we are therefore
provided ; will her ladyship behold and
hear our exorcisms ?
  Hume. Ay, what else ? Fear you not her
courage.   5
  Boling. I have heard her reported to be
a woman of an invincible spirit ; but it
shall be convenient, Master Hume, that you
be by her aloft while we be busy below ;
and so I pray you go, in God's name, and
leave us. [*Exit Hume*] Mother Jourdain, be
you prostrate and grovel on the earth ;
John Southwell, read you ; and let us to
our work.   12

Enter DUCHESS *aloft, followed by* HUME.

  Duch. Well said, my masters ; and
welcome all. To this gear, the sooner the
better.
  Boling. Patience, good lady ; wizards
    know their times : 15
Deep night, dark night, the silent of the
    night,
The time of night when Troy was set on
    fire ;
The time when screech-owls cry and ban-
    dogs howl,
And spirits walk and ghosts break up their
    graves—
That time best fits the work we have in
    hand. 20
Madam, sit you, and fear not : whom we
    raise
We will make fast within a hallow'd
    verge.
  [*Here they do the ceremonies belonging, and*
    make the circle ; Bolingbroke or South-
    well reads : 'Conjuro te,' &c. It
    thunders and lightens terribly ; then the
    Spirit riseth.
  Spir. Adsum.
  M. Jourd. Asmath,   24
By the eternal God, whose name and power
Thou tremblest at, answer that I shall ask;

For till thou speak thou shalt not pass from
　　hence.
　Spir. Ask what thou wilt ; that I had
　　said and done.
　Boling. [*Reads*] ' First of the king : what
　　shall of him become ? '
　Spir. The Duke yet lives that Henry shall
　　depose ;　　　　　　　　　　　　　30
But him outlive, and die a violent death.
　　[*As the Spirit speaks, Southwell writes
　　　　　the answer.*
　Boling. ' What fates await the Duke of
　　Suffolk ? '
　Spir. By water shall he die and take his
　　end.
　Boling. ' What shall befall the Duke of
　　Somerset ? '
　Spir. Let him shun castles :　　　　35
Safer shall he be upon the sandy plains
Than where castles mounted stand.
Have done, for more I hardly can endure.
　Boling. Descend to darkness and the
　　burning lake ;
False fiend, avoid !　　　　　　　　40
　　[*Thunder and lightning. Exit Spirit.*

Enter the DUKE OF YORK *and the* DUKE OF
BUCKINGHAM *with their* Guard, *and break
in.*

　York. Lay hands upon these traitors and
　　their trash.
Beldam, I think we watch'd you at an inch.
What, madam, are you there ? The King
　　and commonweal
Are deeply indebted for this piece of pains ;
My Lord Protector will, I doubt it not,　45
See you well guerdon'd for these good
　　deserts.
　Duch. Not half so bad as thine to
　　England's king,
Injurious Duke, that threatest where's no
　　cause.
　Buck. True, madam, none at all. What
　　call you this ?
Away with them ! let them be clapp'd up
　　close,　　　　　　　　　　　　　50
And kept asunder. You, madam, shall
　　with us.
Stafford, take her to thee.
We'll see your trinkets here all forthcoming.
All, away ! [*Exeunt, above, Duchess and
　　　　　Hume, guarded ; below,
　　　　　Witch, Southwell and Bol-
　　　　　ingbroke, guarded.*
　York. Lord Buckingham, methinks you
　　watch'd her well.　　　　　　　　55
A pretty plot, well chosen to build upon !
Now, pray, my lord, let's see the devil's
　　writ.
What have we here ?　　　　　[*Reads.*
' The duke yet lives that Henry shall
　　depose ;
But him outlive, and die a violent death.' 60
Why, this is just

' Aio te, Æacida, Romanos vincere posse '.
Well, to the rest :
' Tell me what fate awaits the Duke of
　　Suffolk ? '
' By water shall he die and take his end.' 65
' What shall betide the Duke of Somerset?'
' Let him shun castles ;
Safer shall he be upon the sandy plains
Than where castles mounted stand.'
Come, come, my lords ;　　　　　　70
These oracles are hardly attain'd,
And hardly understood.
The King is now in progress towards Saint
　　Albans,
With him the husband of this lovely lady ;
Thither go these news as fast as horse can
　　carry them—　　　　　　　　　　75
A sorry breakfast for my Lord Protector.
　Buck. Your Grace shall give me leave,
　　my Lord of York,
To be the post, in hope of his reward.
　York. At your pleasure, my good lord.
　　Who's within there, ho ?　　　　　79

　　　　Enter a Servingman.

Invite my Lords of Salisbury and Warwick
To sup with me to-morrow night. Away !
　　　　　　　　　　　　　[*Exeunt.*

ACT TWO

SCENE I. *Saint Albans.*

Enter the KING, QUEEN, GLOUCESTER,
CARDINAL, *and* SUFFOLK, *with* Falconers
halloing.

　Queen. Believe me, lords, for flying at the
　　brook,
I saw not better sport these seven years'
　　day ;
Yet, by your leave, the wind was very high,
And ten to one old Joan had not gone out.
　King. But what a point, my lord, your
　　falcon made,　　　　　　　　　　5
And what a pitch she flew above the rest !
To see how God in all His creatures works !
Yea, man and birds are fain of climbing
　　high.
　Suf. No marvel, an it like your Majesty,
My Lord Protector's hawks do tow'r so
　　well ;　　　　　　　　　　　　　10
They know their master loves to be aloft,
And bears his thoughts above his falcon's
　　pitch.
　Glo. My lord, 'tis but a base ignoble mind
That mounts no higher than a bird can soar.
　Car. I thought as much ; he would be
　　above the clouds.　　　　　　　　15
　Glo. Ay, my lord Cardinal, how think you
　　by that ?
Were it not good your Grace could fly to
　　heaven ?
　King. The treasury of everlasting joy !
　Car. Thy heaven is on earth ; thine eyes
　　and thoughts

Beat on a crown, the treasure of thy heart ;
Pernicious Protector, dangerous peer,   21
That smooth'st it so with King and com-
    monweal.
  Glo. What, Cardinal, is your priesthood
    grown peremptory ?
Tantaene animis coelestibus irae ?
Churchmen so hot ? Good uncle, hide such
    malice ;   25
With such holiness can you do it ?
  Suf. No malice, sir ; no more than well
    becomes
So good a quarrel and so bad a peer.
  Glo. As who, my lord ?
  Suf.   Why, as you, my lord,
An't like your lordly Lord's Protectorship.
  Glo. Why, Suffolk, England knows thine
    insolence.   31
  Queen. And thy ambition, Gloucester.
  King.   I prithee, peace,
Good Queen, and whet not on these furious
    peers ;
For blessed are the peacemakers on earth.
  Car. Let me be blessed for the peace I
    make   36
Against this proud Protector with my
    sword !
  Glo. [*Aside to Cardinal*] Faith, holy uncle,
    would 'twere come to that !
  Car. [*Aside to Gloucester*] Marry, when
    thou dar'st.
  Glo. [*Aside to Cardinal*] Make up no
    factious numbers for the matter ;
In thine own person answer thy abuse.   41
  Car. [*Aside to Gloucester*] Ay, where thou
    dar'st not peep ; an if thou dar'st,
This evening on the east side of the grove.
  King. How now, my lords !
  Car.   Believe me, cousin Gloucester,
Had not your man put up the fowl so
    suddenly,   45
We had had more sport. [*Aside to Gloucester*]
    Come with thy two-hand sword.
  Glo. True, uncle.
  Car. [*Aside to Gloucester*] Are ye advis'd ?
    The east side of the grove ?
  Glo. [*Aside to Cardinal*] Cardinal, I am
    with you.
  King. Why, how now, uncle Gloucester !
  Glo. Talking of hawking ; nothing else,
    my lord.   50
[*Aside to Cardinal*] Now, by God's Mother,
    priest,
I'll shave your crown for this,
Or all my fence shall fail.
  Car. [*Aside to Gloucester*] Medice, teipsum ;
Protector, see to't well ; protect yourself.
  King. The winds grow high ; so do your
    stomachs, lords.   55
How irksome is this music to my heart !
When such strings jar, what hope of
    harmony ?
I pray, my lords, let me compound this
    strife.

Enter a Townsman of Saint Albans, *crying*
    ' A miracle ! '

  Glo. What means this noise ?
Fellow, what miracle dost thou proclaim? 60
  Towns. A miracle ! a miracle !
  Suf. Come to the King, and tell him what
    miracle.
  Towns. Forsooth, a blind man at Saint
    Albans shrine
Within this half hour hath receiv'd his sight;
A man that ne'er saw in his life before. 65
  King. Now God be prais'd that to
    believing souls
Gives light in darkness, comfort in despair !

Enter the Mayor of Saint Albans *and his*
Breth:en, *bearing* SIMPCOX *between two
in a chair ; his* Wife *and a* multitude
following.

  Car. Here comes the townsmen on pro-
    cession
To present your Highness with the man.
  King. Great is his comfort in this earthly
    vale,   70
Although by his sight his sin be multiplied.
  Glo. Stand by, my masters ; bring him
    near the King ;
His Highness' pleasure is to talk with him.
  King. Good fellow, tell us here the
    circumstance,
That we for thee may glorify the Lord. 75
What, hast thou been long blind and now
    restor'd ?
  Simp. Born blind, an't please your
Grace.
  Wife. Ay indeed was he.
  Suf. What woman is this ?
  Wife. His wife, an't like your worship. 80
  Glo. Hadst thou been his mother, thou
    couldst have better told.
  King. Where wert thou born ?
  Simp. At Berwick in the north, an't like
    your Grace.
  King. Poor soul, God's goodness hath
    been great to thee.
Let never day nor night unhallowed pass, 85
But still remember what the Lord hath
    done.
  Queen. Tell me, good fellow, cam'st thou
    here by chance,
Or of devotion, to this holy shrine ?
  Simp. God knows, of pure devotion ;
    being call'd   89
A hundred times and oft'ner, in my sleep,
By good Saint Alban, who said ' Simpcox,
    come,
Come, offer at my shrine, and I will help
    thee '.
  Wife. Most true, forsooth ; and many
    time and oft
Myself have heard a voice to call him so.
  Car. What, art thou lame ?
  Simp.   Ay, God Almighty help me !

Suf. How cam'st thou so ?
Simp.   A fall off of a tree. 96
Wife. A plum tree, master.
Glo. How long hast thou been blind ?
Simp. O, born so, master !
Glo. What, and wouldst climb a tree ?
Simp. But that in all my life, when I was
     a youth.
Wife. Too true ; and bought his climbing
     very dear. 100
Glo. Mass, thou lov'dst plums well, that
     wouldst venture so.
Simp. Alas, good master, my wife desir'd
     some damsons
And made me climb, with danger of my
life.
Glo. A subtle knave ! But yet it shall not
serve :
Let me see thine eyes ; wink now ; now
     open them ; 105
In my opinion yet thou seest not well.
Simp. Yes, master, clear as day, I thank
God and Saint Alban.
Glo. Say'st thou me so ? What colour is
     this cloak of ?
Simp. Red, master ; red as blood. 110
Glo. Why, that's well said. What colour
     is my gown of ?
Simp. Black, forsooth ; coal-black as jet.
King. Why, then, thou know'st what
     colour jet is of ?
Suf. And yet, I think, jet did he never see.
Glo. But cloaks and gowns before this
     day a many. 115
Wife. Never before this day in all his life.
Glo. Tell me, sirrah, what's my name ?
Simp. Alas, master, I know not.
Glo. What's his name ?
Simp. I know not. 120
Glo. Nor his ?
Simp. No, indeed, master.
Glo. What's thine own name ?
Simp. Saunder Simpcox, an if it please
     you, master.
Glo. Then, Saunder, sit there, the lying'st
knave in Christendom. If thou hadst been
born blind, thou mightst as well have
known all our names as thus to name the
several colours we do wear. Sight may
distinguish of colours ; but suddenly to
nominate them all, it is impossible. My
lords, Saint Alban here hath done a
miracle ; and would ye not think it cunning to be great that could restore this
cripple to his legs again ?
Simp. O master, that you could !
Glo. My masters of Saint Albans, have
you not beadles in your town, and things
call'd whips ? 135
Mayor. Yes, my lord, if it please your
Grace.
Glo. Then send for one presently.
Mayor. Sirrah, go fetch the beadle hither
     straight.   *[Exit an Attendant.*

Glo. Now fetch me a stool hither by and
by. [*A stool brought*] Now, sirrah, if you
mean to save yourself from whipping, leap
me over this stool and run away. 141
Simp. Alas, master, I am not able to
     stand alone !
You go about to torture me in vain.

Enter a Beadle *with whips.*

Glo. Well, sir, we must have you find
your legs. Sirrah beadle, whip him till he
leap over that same stool.
Bead. I will, my lord. Come on, sirrah ;
off with your doublet quickly. 147
Simp. Alas, master, what shall I do ? I
am not able to stand.
     [*After the Beadle hath hit him once, he
         leaps over the stool and runs away ;
         and they follow and cry ' A miracle ! '*
King. O God, seest Thou this, and bearest
     so long ? 150
Queen. It made me laugh to see the
     villain run.
Glo. Follow the knave, and take this
     drab away.
Wife. Alas, sir, we did it for pure
     need !
Glo. Let them be whipp'd through every
market town till they come to Berwick,
from whence they came.
     [*Exeunt Mayor, Beadle, Wife, &c.*
Car. Duke Humphrey has done a miracle
     to-day. 156
Suf. True ; made the lame to leap and fly
     away.
Glo. But you have done more miracles
     than I :
You made in a day, my lord, whole towns
     to fly.

Enter BUCKINGHAM.

King. What tidings with our cousin
     Buckingham ? 160
Buck. Such as my heart doth tremble to
     unfold :
A sort of naughty persons, lewdly bent,
Under the countenance and confederacy
Of Lady Eleanor, the Protector's wife,
The ringleader and head of all this rout, 165
Have practis'd dangerously against your
     state,
Dealing with witches and with conjurers,
Whom we have apprehended in the fact,
Raising up wicked spirits from under
     ground, 169
Demanding of King Henry's life and death
And other of your Highness' Privy Council,
As more at large your Grace shall under-
     stand.
Car. And so, my Lord Protector, by this
     means
Your lady is forthcoming yet at London.
This news, I think, hath turn'd your
     weapon's edge ; 175

'Tis like, my lord, you will not keep your
   hour.
   Glo. Ambitious churchman, leave to
      afflict my heart.
Sorrow and grief have vanquish'd all my
   powers;
And, vanquish'd as I am, I yield to thee
Or to the meanest groom.   180
   King. O God, what mischiefs work the
      wicked ones,
Heaping confusion on their own heads
   thereby!
   Queen. Gloucester, see here the tainture
      of thy nest;
And look thyself be faultless, thou wert
   best.
   Glo. Madam, for myself, to heaven I do
      appeal   185
How I have lov'd my King and common-
   weal;
And for my wife I know not how it
   stands.
Sorry I am to hear what I have heard.
Noble she is; but if she have forgot
Honour and virtue, and convers'd with
   such   190
As, like to pitch, defile nobility,
I banish her my bed and company
And give her as a prey to law and shame,
That hath dishonoured Gloucester's honest
   name.   194
   King. Well, for this night we will repose
      us here.
To-morrow toward London back again
To look into this business thoroughly
And call these foul offenders to their
   answers,   198
And poise the cause in justice' equal scales,
Whose beam stands sure, whose rightful
   cause prevails. [*Flourish. Exeunt.*

SCENE II. *London. The Duke of York's
         garden.*

Enter YORK, SALISBURY, *and* WARWICK.

   York. Now, my good Lords of Salisbury
      and Warwick,
Our simple supper ended, give me leave
In this close walk to satisfy myself
In craving your opinion of my title,
Which is infallible, to England's crown. 5
   Sal. My lord, I long to hear it at full.
   War. Sweet York, begin; and if thy
      claim be good,
The Nevils are thy subjects to command.
   York. Then thus:
Edward the Third, my lords, had seven
   sons;   10
The first, Edward the Black Prince, Prince
   of Wales;
The second, William of Hatfield; and the
   third,
Lionel Duke of Clarence; next to whom
Was John of Gaunt, the Duke of Lancaster;

The fifth was Edmund Langley, Duke of
   York;   15
The sixth was Thomas of Woodstock, Duke
   of Gloucester;
William of Windsor was the seventh and
   last.
Edward the Black Prince died before his
   father
And left behind him Richard, his only son,
Who, after Edward the Third's death,
   reign'd as king   20
Till Heny Bolingbroke, Duke of Lancaster,
The eldest son and heir of John of Gaunt,
Crown'd by the name of Henry the Fourth,
Seiz'd on the realm, depos'd the rightful
   king,
Sent his poor queen to France, from whence
   she came,   25
And him to Pomfret, where, as all you
   know,
Harmless Richard was murdered traitor-
   ously.
   War. Father, the Duke hath told the
      truth;
Thus got the house of Lancaster the crown.
   York. Which now they hold by force, and
      not by right;   30
For Richard, the first son's heir, being dead,
The issue of the next son should have
   reign'd.
   Sal. But William of Hatfield died without
      an heir.
   York. The third son, Duke of Clarence,
      from whose line
I claim the crown, had issue Philippe, a
   daughter,   35
Who married Edmund Mortimer, Earl of
   March;
Edmund had issue, Roger Earl of March;
Roger had issue, Edmund, Anne, and
   Eleanor.
   Sal. This Edmund, in the reign of Boling-
      broke,   39
As I have read, laid claim unto the crown;
And, but for Owen Glendower, had been
   king,
Who kept him in captivity till he died.
But, to the rest.
   York.   His eldest sister, Anne,
My mother, being heir unto the crown,
Married Richard Earl of Cambridge, who
   was   45
To Edmund Langley, Edward the Third's
   fifth son, son.
By her I claim the kingdom: she was
   heir
To Roger Earl of March, who was the son
Of Edmund Mortimer, who married
   Philippe,
Sole daughter unto Lionel Duke of Clarence;
So, if the issue of the elder son   51
Succeed before the younger, I am King.
   War. What plain proceedings is more
      plain than this?

Henry doth claim the crown from John of
    Gaunt,
The fourth son : York claims it from the
    third.   55
Till Lionel's issue fails, his should not reign.
It fails not yet, but flourishes in thee
And in thy sons, fair slips of such a stock.
Then, father Salisbury, kneel we together,
And in this private plot be we the first   60
That shall salute our rightful sovereign
With honour of his birthright to the crown.
    Both. Long live our sovereign Richard,
        England's King !
    York. We thank you, lords. But I am
        not your king
Till I be crown'd, and that my sword be
    stain'd   65
With heart-blood of the house of Lancaster;
And that's not suddenly to be perform'd,
But with advice and silent secrecy.
Do you as I do in these dangerous days :
Wink at the Duke of Suffolk's insolence,   70
At Beaufort's pride, at Somerset's ambi-
    tion,
At Buckingham, and all the crew of them,
Till they have snar'd the shepherd of the
    flock,
That virtuous prince, the good Duke
    Humphrey ;
'Tis that they seek ; and they, in seeking
    that,   75
Shall find their deaths, if York can
    prophesy.
    Sal. My lord, break we off ; we know
        your mind at full.
    War. My heart assures me that the Earl
        of Warwick
Shall one day make the Duke of York a
    king.   79
    York. And, Nevil, this I do assure myself,
Richard shall live to make the Earl of
    Warwick
The greatest man in England but the King.
                                                [Exeunt.

SCENE III. *London. A hall of justice.*

Sound trumpets. Enter the KING *and State :
the* QUEEN, GLOUCESTER, YORK, SUF-
FOLK, *and* SALISBURY, *with* Guard, *to
banish the Duchess. Enter, guarded, the*
DUCHESS OF GLOUCESTER, MARGERY
JOURDAIN, HUME, SOUTHWELL, *and*
BOLINGBROKE.

    King. Stand forth, Dame Eleanor Cob-
        ham, Gloucester's wife :
In sight of God and us, your guilt is great ;
Receive the sentence of the law for sins
Such as by God's book are adjudg'd to
    death.   4
You four, from hence to prison back again ;
From thence unto the place of execution :
The witch in Smithfield shall be burnt to
    ashes,

And you three shall be strangled on the
    gallows.
You, madam, for you are more nobly born,
Despoiled of your honour in your life,   10
Shall, after three days' open penance done,
Live in your country here in banishment
With Sir John Stanley in the Isle of Man.
    Duch. Welcome is banishment ; welcome
        were my death.
    Glo. Eleanor, the law, thou seest, hath
        judged thee.   15
I cannot justify whom the law condemns.
        *[Exeunt the Duchess and the other
                prisoners, guarded.*
Mine eyes are full of tears, my heart of
    grief.
Ah, Humphrey, this dishonour in thine age
Will bring thy head with sorrow to the
    ground !   19
I beseech your Majesty give me leave to go ;
Sorrow would solace, and mine age would
    ease.
    King. Stay, Humphrey Duke of Glouces-
        ter ; ere thou go,
Give up thy staff ; Henry will to himself
Protector be ; and God shall be my hope,
My stay, my guide, and lantern to my feet.
And go in peace, Humphrey, no less belov'd
Than when thou wert Protector to thy
    King.   27
    Queen. I see no reason why a king of years
Should be to be protected like a child.
God and King Henry govern England's
    realm !   30
Give up your staff, sir, and the King his
    realm.
    Glo. My staff ! Here, noble Henry, is my
        staff.
As willingly do I the same resign
As ere thy father Henry made it mine ;
And even as willingly at thy feet I leave it
As others would ambitiously receive it.   36
Farewell, good King ; when I am dead and
    gone,
May honourable peace attend thy throne !
                                                  [Exit.
    Queen. Why, now is Henry King, and
        Margaret Queen,
And Humphrey Duke of Gloucester scarce
    himself,   40
That bears so shrewd a maim : two pulls at
    once—
His lady banish'd and a limb lopp'd off.
This staff of honour raught, there let it
    stand
Where it best fits to be, in Henry's hand.
    Suf. Thus droops this lofty pine and
        hangs his sprays ;   45
Thus Eleanor's pride dies in her youngest
    days.
    York. Lords, let him go. Please it your
        Majesty,
This is the day appointed for the combat ;
And ready are the appellant and defendant,

The armourer and his man, to enter the
lists, 50
So please your Highness to behold the
fight.
Queen. Ay, good my lord ; for purposely
therefore
Left I the court, to see this quarrel
tried.
King. A God's name, see the lists and all
things fit ;
Here let them end it, and God defend the
right ! 55
York. I never saw a fellow worse bested,
Or more afraid to fight, than is the
appellant,
The servant of this armourer, my lords.

Enter at one door, HORNER, *the Armourer,
and his* Neighbours, *drinking to him so
much that he is drunk ; and he enters
with a drum before him and his staff with
a sand-bag fastened to it ; and at the
other door* PETER, *his man, with a drum
and sand-bag, and* Prentices *drinking to
him.*

1 *Neigh.* Here, neighbour Horner, I drink
to you in a cup of sack ; and fear not,
neighbour, you shall do well enough. 61
2 *Neigh.* And here, neighbour, here's a
cup of charneco.
3 *Neigh.* And here's a pot of good double
beer, neighbour ; drink, and fear not your
man. 65
Hor. Let it come, i' faith, and I'll pledge
you all ; and a fig for Peter !
1 *Pren.* Here, Peter, I drink to thee ; and
be not afraid.
2 *Pren.* Be merry, Peter, and fear not thy
master : fight for credit of the prentices. 71
Peter. I thank you all. Drink, and pray
for me, I pray you ; for I think I have
taken my last draught in this world. Here,
Robin, an if I die, I give thee my apron ;
and, Will, thou shalt have my hammer ;
and here, Tom, take all the money that I
have. O Lord bless me, I pray God ! for I
am never able to deal with my master, he
hath learnt so much fence already.
Sal. Come, leave your drinking and fall to
blows. Sirrah, what's thy name ? 80
Peter. Peter, forsooth.
Sal. Peter ? What more ?
Peter. Thump. 83
Sal. Thump ? Then see thou thump thy
master well.
Hor. Masters, I am come hither, as it
were, upon my man's instigation, to prove
him a knave and myself an honest man ;
and touching the Duke of York, I will take
my death I never meant him any ill, nor
the King, nor the Queen ; and therefore,
Peter, have at thee with a downright blow !
York. Dispatch—this knave's tongue
begins to double. 91

Sound, trumpets, alarum to the combatants ! [*Alarum. They fight, and
Peter strikes him down.*
Hor. Hold, Peter, hold ! I confess, I
confess treason. [*Dies.*
York. Take away his weapon. Fellow,
thank God, and the good wine in thy
master's way. 95
Peter. O God, have I overcome mine
enemies in this presence ? O Peter, thou
hast prevail'd in right !
King. Go, take hence that traitor from
our sight,
For by his death we do perceive his
guilt ;
And God in justice hath reveal'd to us 100
The truth and innocence of this poor fellow,
Which he had thought to have murder'd
wrongfully.
Come, fellow, follow us for thy reward.
[*Sound a flourish. Exeunt.*

Scene IV. *London. A street.*

Enter DUKE HUMPHREY *and his* Men, *in
mourning cloaks.*

Glo. Thus sometimes hath the brightest
day a cloud,
And after summer evermore succeeds
Barren winter, with his wrathful nipping
cold ;
So cares and joys abound, as seasons fleet.
Sirs, what's o'clock ?
Serv. Ten, my lord. 5
Glo. Ten is the hour that was appointed
me
To watch the coming of my punish'd
duchess.
Uneath may she endure the flinty streets
To tread them with her tender-feeling feet.
Sweet Nell, ill can thy noble mind abrook 10
The abject people gazing on thy face,
With envious looks, laughing at thy shame,
That erst did follow thy proud chariot
wheels
When thou didst ride in triumph through
the streets.
But, soft ! I think she comes, and I'll
prepare 15
My tear-stain'd eyes to see her miseries.

Enter the DUCHESS OF GLOUCESTER *in a
white sheet, and a taper burning in her
hand, with* SIR JOHN STANLEY, *the
Sheriff, and* Officers.

Serv. So please your Grace, we'll take her
from the sheriff.
Glo. No, stir not for your lives ; let her
pass by.
Duch. Come you, my lord, to see my open
shame ?
Now thou dost penance too. Look how
they gaze ! 20
See how the giddy multitude do point

And nod their heads and throw their eyes
  on thee !
Ah, Gloucester, hide thee from their hateful
  looks,
And, in thy closet pent up, rue my shame
And ban thine enemies, both mine and
  thine !   25
  Glo. Be patient, gentle Nell ; forget this
    grief.
  Duch. Ah, Gloucester, teach me to forget
    myself !
For whilst I think I am thy married wife
And thou a prince, Protector of this land,
Methinks I should not thus be led along, 30
Mail'd up in shame, with papers on my
  back,
And follow'd with a rabble that rejoice
To see my tears and hear my deep-fet
  groans.
The ruthless flint doth cut my tender feet,
And when I start, the envious people laugh
And bid me be advised how I tread.   36
Ah, Humphrey, can I bear this shameful
  yoke ?
Trowest thou that e'er I'll look upon the
  world
Or count them happy that enjoy the sun ?
No ; dark shall be my light and night my
  day ;   40
To think upon my pomp shall be my hell.
Sometime I'll say I am Duke Humphrey's
  wife,
And he a prince, and ruler of the land ;
Yet so he rul'd, and such a prince he was,
As he stood by whilst I, his forlorn duchess,
Was made a wonder and a pointing-stock
To every idle rascal follower.
But be thou mild, and blush not at my
  shame,
Nor stir at nothing till the axe of death
Hang over thee, as sure it shortly will. 50
For Suffolk—he that can do all in all
With her that hateth thee and hates us all—
And York, and impious Beaufort, that false
  priest,
Have all lim'd bushes to betray thy wings,
And, fly thou how thou canst, they'll tangle
  thee.   55
But fear not thou until thy foot be snar'd,
Nor never seek prevention of thy foes.
  Glo. Ah, Nell, forbear ! Thou aimest all
    awry.
I must offend before I be attainted ;
And had I twenty times so many foes, 60
And each of them had twenty times their
  power,
All these could not procure me any scathe
So long as I am loyal, true, and crimeless.
Wouldst have me rescue thee from this
  reproach ?
Why, yet thy scandal were not wip'd away,
But I in danger for the breach of law. 66
Thy greatest help is quiet, gentle Nell.
I pray thee sort thy heart to patience ;

These few days' wonder will be quickly
  worn.

        Enter a Herald.

  Her. I summon your Grace to his
    Majesty's Parliament,
Holden at Bury the first of this next month.
  Glo. And my consent ne'er ask'd herein
    before !   72
This is close dealing. Well, I will be there.
        [*Exit Herald.*
My Nell, I take my leave—and, master
  sheriff,
Let not her penance exceed the King's
  commission.   75
  Sher. An't please your Grace, here my
    commission stays ;
And Sir John Stanley is appointed now
To take her with him to the Isle of Man.
  Glo. Must you, Sir John, protect my lady
    here ?
  Stan. So am I given in charge, may't
    please your Grace.   80
  Glo. Entreat her not the worse in that I
    pray
You use her well ; the world may laugh
  again,
And I may live to do you kindness if
You do it her. And so, Sir John, farewell.
  Duch. What, gone, my lord, and bid me
    not farewell !   85
  Glo. Witness my tears, I cannot stay to
    speak.
        [*Exeunt Gloucester and Servants.*
  Duch. Art thou gone too ? All comfort go
    with thee !
For none abides with me. My joy is death—
Death, at whose name I oft have been
  afeard,
Because I wish'd this world's eternity. 90
Stanley, I prithee go, and take me hence ;
I care not whither, for I beg no favour,
Only convey me where thou art com-
  manded.
  Stan. Why, madam, that is to the Isle of
    Man,
There to be us'd according to your state. 95
  Duch. That's bad enough, for I am but
    reproach—
And shall I then be us'd reproachfully ?
  Stan. Like to a duchess and Duke
    Humphrey's lady,
According to that state you shall be us'd.
  Duch. Sheriff, farewell, and better than
    I fare,   100
Although thou hast been conduct of my
  shame.
  Sher. It is my office ; and, madam,
    pardon me.
  Duch. Ay, ay, farewell ; thy office is
    discharg'd.
Come, Stanley, shall we go ?
  Stan. Madam, your penance done, throw
    off this sheet,   105

637

And go we to attire you for our journey.
  Duch. My shame will not be shifted with
    my sheet.
No, it will hang upon my richest robes
And show itself, attire me how I can.   109
Go, lead the way ; I long to see my prison.
                                [*Exeunt.*

ACT THREE

SCENE I. *The Abbey at Bury St. Edmunds.*

Sound a sennet. Enter the KING, *the* QUEEN,
  CARDINAL, SUFFOLK, YORK, BUCKING-
  HAM, SALISBURY, *and* WARWICK, *to the*
  Parliament.

  King. I muse my Lord of Gloucester is
    not come.
'Tis not his wont to be the hindmost man,
Whate'er occasion keeps him from us now.
  Queen. Can you not see, or will ye not
    observe   4
The strangeness of his alter'd countenance ?
With what a majesty he bears himself ;
How insolent of late he is become,
How proud, how peremptory, and unlike
    himself ?
We know the time since he was mild and
    affable,
And if we did but glance a far-off look 10
Immediately he was upon his knee,
That all the court admir'd him for sub-
    mission.
But meet him now and be it in the morn,
When every one will give the time of day,
He knits his brow and shows an angry eye
And passeth by with stiff unbowed knee,
Disdaining duty that to us belongs.   17
Small curs are not regarded when they grin,
But great men tremble when the lion roars,
And Humphrey is no little man in England.
First note that he is near you in descent,
And should you fall he is the next will
    mount ;   22
Me seemeth, then, it is no policy—
Respecting what a rancorous mind he bears,
And his advantage following your decease—
That he should come about your royal
    person   26
Or be admitted to your Highness' Council.
By flattery hath he won the commons'
    hearts ;
And when he please to make commotion,
'Tis to be fear'd they all will follow him. 30
Now 'tis the spring, and weeds are shallow-
    rooted ;
Suffer them now, and they'll o'ergrow the
    garden
And choke the herbs for want of husbandry.
The reverent care I bear unto my lord
Made me collect these dangers in the Duke.
If it be fond, call it a woman's fear ; 36
Which fear if better reasons can supplant,
I will subscribe, and say I wrong'd the
    Duke.

My Lord of Suffolk, Buckingham, and
    York,
Reprove my allegation if you can,   40
Or else conclude my words effectual.
  Suf. Well hath your Highness seen into
    this duke ;
And had I first been put to speak my mind,
I think I should have told your Grace's tale.
The Duchess, by his subornation,   45
Upon my life, began her devilish practices ;
Or if he were not privy to those faults,
Yet by reputing of his high descent—
As next the King he was successive heir—
And such high vaunts of his nobility,   50
Did instigate the bedlam brainsick Duchess
By wicked means to frame our sovereign's
    fall.
Smooth runs the water where the brook is
    deep,
And in his simple show he harbours
    treason.
The fox barks not when he would steal the
    lamb.   55
No, no, my sovereign, Gloucester is a man
Unsounded yet, and full of deep deceit.
  Car. Did he not, contrary to form of law,
Devise strange deaths for small offences
    done ?
  York. And did he not, in his protector-
    ship,   60
Levy great sums of money through the
    realm
For soldiers' pay in France, and never sent
    it ?
By means whereof the towns each day
    revolted.
  Buck. Tut, these are petty faults to faults
    unknown
Which time will bring to light in smooth
    Duke Humphrey.   65
  King. My lords, at once : the care you
    have of us,
To mow down thorns that would annoy our
    foot,
Is worthy praise ; but shall I speak my
    conscience ?
Our kinsman Gloucester is as innocent 69
From meaning treason to our royal person
As is the sucking lamb or harmless dove :
The Duke is virtuous, mild, and too well
    given
To dream on evil or to work my downfall.
  Queen. Ah, what's more dangerous than
    this fond affiance ?
Seems he a dove ? His feathers are but
    borrow'd,   75
For he's disposed as the hateful raven.
Is he a lamb ? His skin is surely lent him,
For he's inclin'd as is the ravenous wolf.
Who cannot steal a shape that means
    deceit ?
Take heed, my lord ; the welfare of us all 80
Hangs on the cutting short that fraudful
    man.

Enter SOMERSET.

Som. All health unto my gracious
    sovereign !
King. Welcome, Lord Somerset. What
    news from France ?
Som. That all your interest in those
    territories
Is utterly bereft you ; all is lost.   85
    King. Cold news, Lord Somerset ; but
    God's will be done !
    York. [*Aside*] Cold news for me ; for I
    had hope of France
As firmly as I hope for fertile England.
Thus are my blossoms blasted in the bud,
And caterpillars eat my leaves away ;   90
But I will remedy this gear ere long,
Or sell my title for a glorious grave.

Enter GLOUCESTER.

Glo. All happiness unto my lord the
    King !
Pardon, my liege, that I have stay'd so
    long.
Suf. Nay, Gloucester, know that thou art
    come too soon,   95
Unless thou wert more loyal than thou art.
I do arrest thee of high treason here.
    Glo. Well, Suffolk, thou shalt not see me
    blush
Nor change my countenance for this arrest :
A heart unspotted is not easily daunted.   100
The purest spring is not so free from mud
As I am clear from treason to my sovereign.
Who can accuse me ? Wherein am I guilty ?
    York. 'Tis thought, my lord, that you
    took bribes of France
And, being Protector, stay'd the soldiers'
    pay ;   105
By means whereof his Highness hath lost
    France.
    Glo. Is it but thought so ? What are they
    that think it ?
I never robb'd the soldiers of their pay
Nor ever had one penny bribe from France.
So help me God, as I have watch'd the
    night—   110
Ay, night by night—in studying good for
    England !
That doit that e'er I wrested from the King,
Or any groat I hoarded to my use,
Be brought against me at my trial-day !
No ; many a pound of mine own proper
    store,   115
Because I would not tax the needy com-
    mons,
Have I dispursed to the garrisons,
And never ask'd for restitution.
    Car. It serves you well, my lord, to say
    so much.
    Glo. I say no more than truth, so help me
    God !   120
    York. In your protectorship you did
    devise

Strange tortures for offenders, never heard
    of,
That England was defam'd by tyranny.
    Glo. Why, 'tis well known that whiles I
    was Protector
Pity was all the fault that was in me ;   125
For I should melt at an offender's tears,
And lowly words were ransom for their
    fault.
Unless it were a bloody murderer,
Or foul felonious thief that fleec'd poor
    passengers,
I never gave them condign punishment.   130
Murder indeed, that bloody sin, I tortur'd
Above the felon or what trespass else.
    Suf. My lord, these faults are easy, quickly
    answer'd ;
But mightier crimes are laid unto your
    charge,   134
Whereof you cannot easily purge yourself.
I do arrest you in his Highness' name,
And here commit you to my Lord Cardinal
To keep until your further time of trial.
    King. My Lord of Gloucester, 'tis my
    special hope
That you will clear yourself from all
    suspence.   140
My conscience tells me you are innocent.
    Glo. Ah, gracious lord, these days are
    dangerous !
Virtue is chok'd with foul ambition,
And charity chas'd hence by rancour's
    hand ;
Foul subornation is predominant,   145
And equity exil'd your Highness' land.
I know their complot is to have my life ;
And if my death might make this island
    happy
And prove the period of their tyranny,
I would expend it with all willingness.   150
But mine is made the prologue to their
    play ;
For thousands more that yet suspect no
    peril
Will not conclude their plotted tragedy.
Beaufort's red sparkling eyes blab his
    heart's malice,   154
And Suffolk's cloudy brow his stormy hate ;
Sharp Buckingham unburdens with his
    tongue
The envious load that lies upon his heart ;
And dogged York, that reaches at the moon,
Whose overweening arm I have pluck'd
    back,
By false accuse doth level at my life.   160
And you, my sovereign lady, with the rest,
Causeless have laid disgraces on my head,
And with your best endeavour have stirr'd
    up
My liefest liege to be mine enemy ;
Ay, all of you have laid your heads to-
    gether—   165
Myself had notice of your conventicles—
And all to make away my guiltless life.

639

I shall not want false witness to condemn
    me
Nor store of treasons to augment my guilt.
The ancient proverb will be well effected:
'A staff is quickly found to beat a dog'. 171
   Car. My liege, his railing is intolerable.
If those that care to keep your royal person
From treason's secret knife and traitor's
    rage
Be thus upbraided, chid, and rated at, 175
And the offender granted scope of speech,
'Twill make them cool in zeal unto your
    Grace.
   Suf. Hath he not twit our sovereign lady
    here
With ignominious words, though clerkly
    couch'd,
As if she had suborned some to swear 180
False allegations to o'erthrow his state?
   Queen. But I can give the loser leave to
    chide.
   Glo. Far truer spoke than meant: I lose
    indeed.
Beshrew the winners, for they play'd me
    false!
And well such losers may have leave to
    speak. 185
   Buck. He'll wrest the sense, and hold us
    here all day.
Lord Cardinal, he is your prisoner.
   Car. Sirs, take away the Duke, and guard
    him sure.
   Glo. Ah, thus King Henry throws away
    his crutch
Before his legs be firm to bear his body! 190
Thus is the shepherd beaten from thy
    side,
And wolves are gnarling who shall gnaw
    thee first.
Ah, that my fear were false! ah, that it
    were!
For, good King Henry, thy decay I fear.
               [*Exit, guarded.*
   King. My lords, what to your wisdoms
    seemeth best 195
Do or undo, as if ourself were here.
   Queen. What, will your Highness leave
    the Parliament?
   King. Ay, Margaret; my heart is
    drown'd with grief,
Whose flood begins to flow within mine
    eyes;
My body round engirt with misery— 200
For what's more miserable than discontent?
Ah, uncle Humphrey, in thy face I see
The map of honour, truth, and loyalty!
And yet, good Humphrey, is the hour to
    come
That e'er I prov'd thee false or fear'd thy
    faith. 205
What louring star now envies thy estate
That these great lords, and Margaret our
    Queen,
Do seek subversion of thy harmless life?

Thou never didst them wrong, nor no man
    wrong;
And as the butcher takes away the calf, 210
And binds the wretch, and beats it when
    it strays,
Bearing it to the bloody slaughter-house,
Even so, remorseless, have they borne him
    hence;
And as the dam runs lowing up and down,
Looking the way her harmless young one
    went, 215
And can do nought but wail her darling's
    loss,
Even so myself bewails good Gloucester's
    case
With sad unhelpful tears, and with dimm'd
    eyes
Look after him, and cannot do him good,
So mighty are his vowed enemies. 220
His fortunes I will weep, and 'twixt each
    groan
Say 'Who's a traitor? Gloucester he is
    none'.   [*Exit.*
   Queen. Free lords, cold snow melts with
    the sun's hot beams:
Henry my lord is cold in great affairs,
Too full of foolish pity; and Gloucester's
    show 225
Beguiles him as the mournful crocodile
With sorrow snares relenting passengers;
Or as the snake, roll'd in a flow'ring bank,
With shining checker'd slough, doth sting a
    child
That for the beauty thinks it excellent. 230
Believe me, lords, were none more wise
    than I—
And yet herein I judge mine own wit good—
This Gloucester should be quickly rid the
    world
To rid us from the fear we have of him. 234
   Car. That he should die is worthy policy;
But yet we want a colour for his death.
'Tis meet he be condemn'd by course of law.
   Suf. But, in my mind, that were no
    policy:
The King will labour still to save his life;
The commons haply rise to save his life; 240
And yet we have but trivial argument,
More than mistrust, that shows him worthy
    death.
   York. So that, by this, you would not
    have him die.
   Suf. Ah, York, no man alive so fain as I!
   York. 'Tis York that hath more reason
    for his death. 245
But, my Lord Cardinal, and you, my Lord
    of Suffolk,
Say as you think, and speak it from your
    souls:
Were't not all one an empty eagle were
    set
To guard the chicken from a hungry kite
As place Duke Humphrey for the King's
    Protector? 250

Queen. So the poor chicken should be sure of death.

Suf. Madam, 'tis true; and were't not madness then
To make the fox surveyor of the fold?
Who being accus'd a crafty murderer,
His guilt should be but idly posted over, 255
Because his purpose is not executed.
No; let him die, in that he is a fox,
By nature prov'd an enemy to the flock,
Before his chaps be stain'd with crimson blood,
As Humphrey, prov'd by reasons, to my liege. 260
And do not stand on quillets how to slay him;
Be it by gins, by snares, by subtlety,
Sleeping or waking, 'tis no matter how,
So he be dead; for that is good deceit
Which mates him first that first intends deceit. 265

Queen. Thrice-noble Suffolk, 'tis resolutely spoke.

Suf. Not resolute, except so much were done,
For things are often spoke and seldom meant;
But that my heart accordeth with my tongue,
Seeing the deed is meritorious, 270
And to preserve my sovereign from his foe,
Say but the word, and I will be his priest.

Car. But I would have him dead, my Lord of Suffolk,
Ere you can take due orders for a priest;
Say you consent and censure well the deed,
And I'll provide his executioner— 276
I tender so the safety of my liege.

Suf. Here is my hand the deed is worthy doing.

Queen. And so say I.

York. And I. And now we three have spoke it, 280
It skills not greatly who impugns our doom.

Enter a Post.

Post. Great lords, from Ireland am I come amain
To signify that rebels there are up
And put the Englishmen unto the sword.
Send succours, lords, and stop the rage betime, 285
Before the wound do grow uncurable;
For, being green, there is great hope of help.

Car. A breach that craves a quick expedient stop!
What counsel give you in this weighty cause?

York. That Somerset be sent as Regent thither; 290
'Tis meet that lucky ruler be employ'd,
Witness the fortune he hath had in France.

Som. If York, with all his far-fet policy,
Had been the Regent there instead of me,
He never would have stay'd in France so long. 295

York. No, not to lose it all as thou hast done.
I rather would have lost my life betimes
Than bring a burden of dishonour home
By staying there so long till all were lost.
Show me one scar character'd on thy skin:
Men's flesh preserv'd so whole do seldom win. 301

Queen. Nay then, this spark will prove a raging fire,
If wind and fuel be brought to feed it with;
No more, good York; sweet Somerset, be still.
Thy fortune, York, hadst thou been Regent there, 305
Might happily have prov'd far worse than his.

York. What, worse than nought? Nay, then a shame take all!

Som. And in the number, thee that wishest shame!

Car. My Lord of York, try what your fortune is.
Th' uncivil kerns of Ireland are in arms 310
And temper clay with blood of Englishmen;
To Ireland will you lead a band of men,
Collected choicely, from each county some,
And try your hap against the Irishmen?

York. I will, my lord, so please his Majesty. 315

Suf. Why, our authority is his consent,
And what we do establish he confirms;
Then, noble York, take thou this task in hand.

York. I am content; provide me soldiers, lords,
Whiles I take order for mine own affairs. 320

Suf. A charge, Lord York, that I will see perform'd.
But now return we to the false Duke Humphrey.

Car. No more of him; for I will deal with him
That henceforth he shall trouble us no more.
And so break off; the day is almost spent.
Lord Suffolk, you and I must talk of that event. 326

York. My Lord of Suffolk, within fourteen days
At Bristol I expect my soldiers;
For there I'll ship them all for Ireland.

Suf. I'll see it truly done, my Lord of York. 　　　 [*Exeunt all but* York.

York. Now, York, or never, steel thy fearful thoughts 331
And change misdoubt to resolution;
Be that thou hop'st to be; or what thou art
Resign to death—it is not worth th' enjoying.
Let pale-fac'd fear keep with the meanborn man 335

And find no harbour in a royal heart.
Faster than spring-time show'rs comes
    thought on thought,
And not a thought but thinks on dignity.
My brain, more busy than the labouring
    spider,
Weaves tedious snares to trap mine ene-
    mies.   340
Well, nobles, well, 'tis politicly done
To send me packing with an host of men.
I fear me you but warm the starved snake,
Who, cherish'd in your breasts, will sting
    your hearts.
'Twas men I lack'd, and you will give them
    me ;   345
I take it kindly. Yet be well assur'd
You put sharp weapons in a madman's
    hands.
Whiles I in Ireland nourish a mighty band,
I will stir up in England some black storm
Shall blow ten thousand souls to heaven
    or hell ;   350
And this fell tempest shall not cease to rage
Until the golden circuit on my head,
Like to the glorious sun's transparent
    beams,
Do calm the fury of this mad-bred flaw.
And for a minister of my intent   355
I have seduc'd a headstrong Kentishman,
John Cade of Ashford,
To make commotion, as full well he can,
Under the title of John Mortimer.   359
In Ireland have I seen this stubborn Cade
Oppose himself against a troop of kerns,
And fought so long till that his thighs with
    darts
Were almost like a sharp-quill'd porpentine;
And in the end being rescu'd, I have
    seen
Him caper upright like a wild Morisco, 365
Shaking the bloody darts as he his bells.
Full often, like a shag-hair'd crafty kern,
Hath he conversed with the enemy,
And undiscover'd come to me again
And given me notice of their villainies. 370
This devil here shall be my substitute ;
For that John Mortimer, which now is dead,
In face, in gait, in speech, he doth resemble.
By this I shall perceive the commons'
    mind,
How they affect the house and claim of
    York.   375
Say he be taken, rack'd, and tortured ;
I know no pain they can inflict upon him
Will make him say I mov'd him to those
    arms.
Say that he thrive, as 'tis great like he will,
Why, then from Ireland come I with my
    strength,   380
And reap the harvest which that rascal
    sow'd ;
For Humphrey being dead, as he shall be,
And Henry put apart, the next for me.
        [*Exit.*

SCENE II.   *Bury St. Edmunds. A room of
    state.*

Enter two or three Murderers *running over
the stage, from the murder of Duke
Humphrey.*

1 *Mur.* Run to my Lord of Suffolk ; let
    him know
We have dispatch'd the Duke, as he com-
    manded.
2 *Mur.* O that it were to do ! What have
    we done ?
Didst ever hear a man so penitent ?

Enter SUFFOLK.

1 *Mur.* Here comes my lord.   5
Suf. Now, sirs, have you dispatch'd this
    thing ?
1 *Mur.* Ay, my good lord, he's dead.
Suf. Why, that's well said. Go, get you
    to my house ;
I will reward you for this venturous deed.
The King and all the peers are here at hand.
Have you laid fair the bed ? Is all things
    well,   11
According as I gave directions ?
1 *Mur.* 'Tis, my good lord.
Suf. Away ! be gone. [*Exeunt Murderers.*

Sound trumpets. Enter the KING, *the* QUEEN,
CARDINAL, SOMERSET, *with* Attendants.

  King. Go call our uncle to our presence
    straight ;   15
Say we intend to try his Grace to-day,
If he be guilty, as 'tis published.
  Suf. I'll call him presently, my noble
    lord.   [*Exit.*
  King. Lords, take your places ; and, I
    pray you all,
Proceed no straiter 'gainst our uncle
    Gloucester   20
Than from true evidence, of good esteem,
He be approv'd in practice culpable.
  Queen. God forbid any malice should
    prevail
That faultless may condemn a nobleman !
Pray God he may acquit him of suspicion !
  King. I thank thee, Meg ; these words
    content me much.   26

Re-enter SUFFOLK.

How now ! Why look'st thou pale ? Why
    tremblest thou ?
Where is our uncle ? What's the matter,
    Suffolk ?
  Suf. Dead in his bed, my lord ; Glouces-
    ter is dead.
  Queen. Marry, God forfend !   30
  Car. God's secret judgment ! I did dream
    to-night
The Duke was dumb and could not speak a
    word.   [*The King swoons.*
  Queen. How fares my lord ? Help, lords !
    The King is dead.

Som. Rear up his body ; wring him by
  the nose.
Queen. Run, go, help, help ! O Henry,
  ope thine eyes !   35
Suf. He doth revive again ; madam, be
  patient.
King. O heavenly God !
Queen.   How fares my gracious lord ?
Suf. Comfort, my sovereign ! Gracious
  Henry, comfort !
King. What, doth my Lord of Suffolk
  comfort me ?
Came he right now to sing a raven's note, 40
Whose dismal tune bereft my vital pow'rs ;
And thinks he that the chirping of a wren,
By crying comfort from a hollow breast,
Can chase away the first conceived sound ?
Hide not thy poison with such sug'red
  words ;   45
Lay not thy hands on me ; forbear, I say,
Their touch affrights me as a serpent's
  sting.
Thou baleful messenger, out of my sight !
Upon thy eye-balls murderous tyranny
Sits in grim majesty to fright the world. 50
Look not upon me, for thine eyes are
  wounding ;
Yet do not go away ; come, basilisk,
And kill the innocent gazer with thy sight ;
For in the shade of death I shall find joy—
In life but double death, now Gloucester's
  dead.   55
  Queen. Why do you rate my Lord of
  Suffolk thus ?
Although the Duke was enemy to him,
Yet he most Christian-like laments his
  death ;
And for myself—foe as he was to me—
Might liquid tears, or heart-offending
  groans,   60
Or blood-consuming sighs, recall his life,
I would be blind with weeping, sick with
  groans,
Look pale as primrose with blood-drinking
  sighs,
And all to have the noble Duke alive.
What know I how the world may deem of
  me ?   65
For it is known we were but hollow friends :
It may be judg'd I made the Duke away ;
So shall my name with slander's tongue be
  wounded,
And princes' courts be fill'd with my
  reproach.   69
This get I by his death. Ay me, unhappy !
To be a queen and crown'd with infamy !
  King. Ah, woe is me for Gloucester,
  wretched man !
  Queen. Be woe for me, more wretched
  than he is.
What, dost thou turn away, and hide thy
  face ?
I am no loathsome leper—look on me.   75
What, art thou like the adder waxen deaf ?

Be poisonous too, and kill thy forlorn
  Queen.
Is all thy comfort shut in Gloucester's
  tomb ?
Why, then Dame Margaret was ne'er thy
  joy.
Erect his statuē and worship it,   80
And make my image but an alehouse sign.
Was I for this nigh wreck'd upon the sea,
And twice by awkward wind from Eng-
  land's bank
Drove back again unto my native clime ?
What boded this but well-forewarning wind
Did seem to say ' Seek not a scorpion's
  nest,   86
Nor set no footing on this unkind shore ' ?
What did I then but curs'd the gentle
  gusts,
And he that loos'd them forth their brazen
  caves ;
And bid them blow towards England's
  blessed shore,   90
Or turn our stern upon a dreadful rock ?
Yet Æolus would not be a murderer,
But left that hateful office unto thee.
The pretty-vaulting sea refus'd to drown
  me,
Knowing that thou wouldst have me
  drown'd on shore
With tears as salt as sea through thy un-
  kindness ;   96
The splitting rocks cow'r'd in the sinking
  sands
And would not dash me with their ragged
  sides,
Because thy flinty heart, more hard than
  they,
Might in thy palace perish Margaret.   100
As far as I could ken thy chalky cliffs,
When from thy shore the tempest beat us
  back,
I stood upon the hatches in the storm ;
And when the dusky sky began to rob
My earnest-gaping sight of thy land's view,
I took a costly jewel from my neck—   106
A heart it was, bound in with diamonds—
And threw it towards thy land. The sea
  receiv'd it ;
And so I wish'd thy body might my heart.
And even with this I lost fair England's
  view,   110
And bid mine eyes be packing with my
  heart,
And call'd them blind and dusky spectacles
For losing ken of Albion's wished coast.
How often have I tempted Suffolk's
  tongue—
The agent of thy foul inconstancy—   115
To sit and witch me, as Ascanius did
When he to madding Dido would unfold
His father's acts commenc'd in burning
  Troy !
Am I not witch'd like her ? Or thou not
  false like him ?

Ay me, I can no more ! Die, Margaret, 120
For Henry weeps that thou dost live so long.

Noise within. Enter WARWICK, SALISBURY,
and many Commons.

War. It is reported, mighty sovereign,
That good Duke Humphrey traitorously is
 murd'red
By Suffolk and the Cardinal Beaufort's
 means.
The commons, like an angry hive of bees 125
That want their leader, scatter up and
 down
And care not who they sting in his revenge.
Myself have calm'd their spleenful mutiny
Until they hear the order of his death. 129
 King. That he is dead, good Warwick,
 'tis too true ;
But how he died God knows, not Henry.
Enter his chamber, view his breathless
 corpse,
And comment then upon his sudden death.
 War. That shall I do, my liege. Stay,
 Salisbury,   134
With the rude multitude till I return. [*Exit.*
  [*Exit Salisbury with the Commons.*
 King. O Thou that judgest all things,
 stay my thoughts—
My thoughts that labour to persuade my
 soul
Some violent hands were laid on Humph-
 rey's life !
If my suspect be false, forgive me, God ;
For judgment only doth belong to Thee. 140
Fain would I go to chafe his paly lips
With twenty thousand kisses and to drain
Upon his face an ocean of salt tears
To tell my love unto his dumb deaf trunk ;
And with my fingers feel his hand un-
 feeling ;   145
But all in vain are these mean obsequies ;
And to survey his dead and earthy image,
What were it but to make my sorrow
 greater ?

Bed put forth with the body. Enter WARWICK.

 War. Come hither, gracious sovereign,
 view this body.
 King. That is to see how deep my grave
 is made ;   150
For with his soul fled all my worldly solace,
For, seeing him, I see my life in death.
 War. As surely as my soul intends to live
With that dread King that took our state
 upon Him   154
To free us from his Father's wrathful curse,
I do believe that violent hands were laid
Upon the life of this thrice-famed Duke.
 Suf. A dreadful oath, sworn with a
 solemn tongue !
What instance gives Lord Warwick for his
 vow ?
 War. See how the blood is settled in his
 face.   160

Oft have I seen a timely-parted ghost,
Of ashy semblance, meagre, pale, and
 bloodless,
Being all descended to the labouring heart,
Who, in the conflict that it holds with death,
Attracts the same for aidance 'gainst the
 enemy,   165
Which with the heart there cools, and ne'er
 returneth
To blush and beautify the cheek again.
But see, his face is black and full of blood ;
His eye-balls further out than when he
 liv'd,   169
Staring full ghastly like a strangled man ;
His hair uprear'd, his nostrils stretch'd
 with struggling ;
His hands abroad display'd, as one that
 grasp'd
And tugg'd for life, and was by strength
 subdu'd.
Look, on the sheets his hair, you see, is
 sticking ;
His well-proportion'd beard made rough
 and rugged,   175
Like to the summer's corn by tempest
 lodged.
It cannot be but he was murd'red here :
The least of all these signs were probable.
 Suf. Why, Warwick, who should do the
 Duke to death ?
Myself and Beaufort had him in protection;
And we, I hope, sir, are no murderers. 181
 War. But both of you were vow'd Duke
 Humphrey's foes ;
And you, forsooth, had the good Duke to
 keep.
'Tis like you would not feast him like a
 friend ;
And 'tis well seen he found an enemy. 185
 Queen. Then you, belike, suspect these
 noblemen
As guilty of Duke Humphrey's timeless
 death.
 War. Who finds the heifer dead and
 bleeding fresh,
And sees fast by a butcher with an axe,
But will suspect 'twas he that made the
 slaughter ?   190
Who finds the partridge in the puttock's nest
But may imagine how the bird was dead,
Although the kite soar with unbloodied
 beak ?
Even so suspicious is this tragedy.
 Queen. Are you the butcher, Suffolk ?
 Where's your knife ?   195
Is Beaufort term'd a kite ? Where are his
 talons ?
 Suf. I wear no knife to slaughter sleeping
 men ;
But here's a vengeful sword, rusted with
 ease,
That shall be scoured in his rancorous heart
That slanders me with murder's crimson
 badge.   200

Say, if thou dar'st, proud Lord of Warwick-
    shire,
That I am faulty in Duke Humphrey's
    death. [*Exeunt Cardinal, Somerset,*
        and others.
  War. What dares not Warwick, if false
    Suffolk dare him ?
  Queen. He dares not calm his con-
    tumelious spirit,
Nor cease to be an arrogant controller, 205
Though Suffolk dare him twenty thousand
    times.
  War. Madam, be still—with reverence
    may I say ;
For every word you speak in his behalf
Is slander to your royal dignity.
  Suf. Blunt-witted lord, ignoble in
    demeanour,　　　　　　　210
If ever lady wrong'd her lord so much,
Thy mother took into her blameful bed
Some stern untutor'd churl, and noble stock
Was graft with crab-tree slip, whose fruit
    thou art,
And never of the Nevils' noble race.　215
  War. But that the guilt of murder
    bucklers thee,
And I should rob the deathsman of his fee,
Quitting thee thereby of ten thousand
    shames,
And that my sovereign's presence makes
    me mild,
I would, false murd'rous coward, on thy
    knee　　　　　　　　220
Make thee beg pardon for thy passed speech
And say it was thy mother that thou
    meant'st,
That thou thyself wast born in bastardy ;
And, after all this fearful homage done,　224
Give thee thy hire and send thy soul to hell,
Pernicious blood-sucker of sleeping men.
  Suf. Thou shalt be waking while I shed
    thy blood,
If from this presence thou dar'st go with
    me.
  War. Away even now, or I will drag thee
    hence.
Unworthy though thou art, I'll cope with
    thee,　　　　　　　　230
And do some service to Duke Humphrey's
    ghost. [*Exeunt Suffolk and Warwick.*
  King. What stronger breastplate than a
    heart untainted ?
Thrice is he arm'd that hath his quarrel
    just ;
And he but naked, though lock'd up in
    steel,
Whose conscience with injustice is cor-
    rupted.　　　　[*A noise within.*
  Queen. What noise is this ?　236

Re-enter SUFFOLK *and* WARWICK, *with their
    weapons drawn.*

  King. Why, how now, lords, your wrath-
    ful weapons drawn

Here in our presence !　Dare you be so
    bold ?
Why, what tumultuous clamour have we
    here ?
  Suf. The trait'rous Warwick, with the
    men of Bury,　　　　　240
Set all upon me, mighty sovereign.

      Re-enter SALISBURY.

  Sal. [*To the Commons within*] Sirs, stand
    apart, the King shall know your
    mind.
Dread lord, the commons send you word
    by me
Unless Lord Suffolk straight be done to
    death,
Or banished fair England's territories,　245
They will by violence tear him from your
    palace
And torture him with grievous ling'ring
    death.
They say by him the good Duke Humphrey
    died ;
They say in him they fear your Highness'
    death ;
And mere instinct of love and loyalty,　250
Free from a stubborn opposite intent,
As being thought to contradict your liking,
Makes them thus forward in his banish-
    ment.
They say, in care of your most royal person,
That if your Highness should intend to
    sleep　　　　　　　　255
And charge that no man should disturb
    your rest,
In pain of your dislike or pain of death,
Yet, notwithstanding such a strait edict,
Were there a serpent seen with forked
    tongue
That slily glided towards your Majesty,　260
It were but necessary you were wak'd,
Lest, being suffer'd in that harmful
    slumber,
The mortal worm might make the sleep
    eternal.
And therefore do they cry, though you
    forbid,
That they will guard you, whe'er you will
    or no,　　　　　　　　265
From such fell serpents as false Suffolk is ;
With whose envenomed and fatal sting
Your loving uncle, twenty times his worth,
They say, is shamefully bereft of life.
  Commons. [*Within*] An answer from the
    King, my Lord of Salisbury !　270
  Suf. 'Tis like the commons, rude un-
    polish'd hinds,
Could send such message to their sovereign;
But you, my lord, were glad to be employ'd,
To show how quaint an orator you are.
But all the honour Salisbury hath won　275
Is that he was the lord ambassador
Sent from a sort of tinkers to the King.

Commons. [*Within*] An answer from the King, or we will all break in!

King. Go, Salisbury, and tell them all from me   279
I thank them for their tender loving care;
And had I not been cited so by them,
Yet did I purpose as they do entreat;
For sure my thoughts do hourly prophesy
Mischance unto my state by Suffolk's means.
And therefore by His Majesty I swear, 285
Whose far unworthy deputy I am,
He shall not breathe infection in this air
But three days longer, on the pain of death.
                              [*Exit Salisbury.*

Queen. O Henry, let me plead for gentle Suffolk!

King. Ungentle Queen, to call him gentle Suffolk!   290
No more, I say; if thou dost plead for him,
Thou wilt but add increase unto my wrath.
Had I but said, I would have kept my word;
But when I swear, it is irrevocable.
If after three days' space thou here be'st found   295
On any ground that I am ruler of,
The world shall not be ransom for thy life.
Come, Warwick, come, good Warwick, go with me;
I have great matters to impart to thee.
                [*Exeunt all but Queen and Suffolk.*

Queen. Mischance and sorrow go along with you!   300
Heart's discontent and sour affliction
Be playfellows to keep you company!
There's two of you; the devil make a third,
And threefold vengeance tend upon your steps!

Suf. Cease, gentle Queen, these execra-tions,   305
And let thy Suffolk take his heavy leave.

Queen. Fie, coward woman and soft-hearted wretch,
Hast thou not spirit to curse thine enemy?

Suf. A plague upon them! Wherefore should I curse them?
Would curses kill as doth the mandrake's groan,   310
I would invent as bitter searching terms,
As curst, as harsh, and horrible to hear,
Deliver'd strongly through my fixed teeth,
With full as many signs of deadly hate,
As lean-fac'd Envy in her loathsome cave.
My tongue should stumble in mine earnest words,   316
Mine eyes should sparkle like the beaten flint,
Mine hair be fix'd an end, as one distract;
Ay, every joint should seem to curse and ban;
And even now my burden'd heart would break,   320

Should I not curse them. Poison be their drink!
Gall, worse than gall, the daintiest that they taste!
Their sweetest shade a grove of cypress trees!
Their chiefest prospect murd'ring basilisks!
Their softest touch as smart as lizards' stings!   325
Their music frightful as the serpent's hiss,
And boding screech-owls make the consort full!
All the foul terrors in dark-seated hell—

Queen. Enough, sweet Suffolk, thou torment'st thyself;
And these dread curses, like the sun 'gainst glass,   330
Or like an overcharged gun, recoil,
And turns the force of them upon thyself.

Suf. You bade me ban, and will you bid me leave?
Now, by the ground that I am banish'd from,
Well could I curse away a winter's night,   335
Though standing naked on a mountain top
Where biting cold would never let grass grow,
And think it but a minute spent in sport.

Queen. O, let me entreat thee cease! Give me thy hand,   339
That I may dew it with my mournful tears;
Nor let the rain of heaven wet this place
To wash away my woeful monuments.
O, could this kiss be printed in thy hand,
That thou might'st think upon these by the seal,
Through whom a thousand sighs are breath'd for thee!   345
So, get thee gone, that I may know my grief;
'Tis but surmis'd whiles thou art standing by,
As one that surfeits thinking on a want.
I will repeal thee or, be well assur'd,
Adventure to be banished myself;   350
And banished I am, if but from thee.
Go, speak not to me; even now be gone.
O, go not yet! Even thus two friends condemn'd
Embrace, and kiss, and take ten thousand leaves,
Loather a hundred times to part than die.
Yet now, farewell; and farewell life with thee!   356

Suf. Thus is poor Suffolk ten times banished,
Once by the King and three times thrice by thee.
'Tis not the land I care for, wert thou thence;
A wilderness is populous enough,   360
So Suffolk had thy heavenly company;
For where thou art, there is the world itself,
With every several pleasure in the world;

And where thou art not, desolation.   364
I can no more : Live thou to joy thy life ;
Myself no joy in nought but that thou liv'st.

          Enter VAUX.

    Queen. Whither goes Vaux so fast ? What
    news, I prithee ?
    Vaux. To signify unto his Majesty
That Cardinal Beaufort is at point of death;
For suddenly a grievous sickness took him
That makes him gasp, and stare, and catch
    the air,   371
Blaspheming God, and cursing men on
    earth.
Sometime he talks as if Duke Humphrey's
    ghost
Were by his side ; sometime he calls the
    King
And whispers to his pillow, as to him,   375
The secrets of his overcharged soul ;
And I am sent to tell his Majesty
That even now he cries aloud for him.
    Queen. Go tell this heavy message to the
    King.   [*Exit Vaux.*
Ay me ! What is this world ! What news
    are these ?   380
But wherefore grieve I at an hour's poor
    loss,
Omitting Suffolk's exile, my soul's treasure?
Why only, Suffolk, mourn I not for thee,
And with the southern clouds contend in
    tears—
Theirs for the earth's increase, mine for my
    sorrows ?   385
Now get thee hence : the King, thou
    know'st, is coming ;
If thou be found by me, thou art but dead.
    Suf. If I depart from thee I cannot live ;
And in thy sight to die, what were it else
But like a pleasant slumber in thy lap ?   390
Here could I breathe my soul into the air,
As mild and gentle as the cradle-babe
Dying with mother's dug between its lips ;
Where, from thy sight, I should be raging
    mad   394
And cry out for thee to close up mine eyes,
To have thee with thy lips to stop my
    mouth ;
So shouldst thou either turn my flying soul,
Or I should breathe it so into thy body,
And then it liv'd in sweet Elysium.
To die by thee were but to die in jest :   400
From thee to die were torture more than
    death.
O, let me stay, befall what may befall !
    Queen. Away ! Though parting be a
    fretful corrosive,
It is applied to a deathful wound.
To France, sweet Suffolk. Let me hear from
    thee ;   405
For whereso'er thou art in this world's
    globe
I'll have an Iris that shall find thee out.
    Suf. I go.

    Queen. And take my heart with thee.
                [*She kisses him.*
    Suf. A jewel, lock'd into the woefull'st
    cask
That ever did contain a thing of worth.   410
Even as a splitted bark, so sunder we :
This way fall I to death.
    Queen. This way for me. [*Exeunt severally.*

SCENE III.   *London.   Cardinal Beaufort's*
              bedchamber.

Enter the KING, SALISBURY, *and* WARWICK,
     to the CARDINAL *in bed.*

    King. How fares my lord ?   Speak,
    Beaufort, to thy sovereign.
    Car. If thou be'st Death I'll give thee
    England's treasure,
Enough to purchase such another island,
So thou wilt let me live and feel no pain.
    King. Ah, what a sign it is of evil life   5
Where death's approach is seen so terrible !
    War. Beaufort, it is thy sovereign speaks
    to thee.
    Car. Bring me unto my trial when you
    will.
Died he not in his bed ? Where should he
    die ?
Can I make men live, whe'er they will or
    no ?   10
O, torture me no more ! I will confess.
Alive again ? Then show me where he is ;
I'll give a thousand pound to look upon
    him.
He hath no eyes, the dust hath blinded
    them.
Comb down his hair ; look, look ! it stands
    upright,   15
Like lime-twigs set to catch my winged
    soul !
Give me some drink ; and bid the apothe-
    cary
Bring the strong poison that I bought of
    him.
    King. O Thou eternal Mover of the
    heavens,   19
Look with a gentle eye upon this wretch !
O, beat away the busy meddling fiend
That lays strong siege unto this wretch's
    soul,
And from his bosom purge this black
    despair !
    War. See how the pangs of death do
    make him grin.
    Sal. Disturb him not, let him pass
    peaceably.   25
    King. Peace to his soul, if God's good
    pleasure be !
Lord Card'nal, if thou think'st on heaven's
    bliss,
Hold up thy hand, make signal of thy
    hope.
He dies, and makes no sign : O God,
    forgive him !

War. So bad a death argues a monstrous
life. 30

King. Forbear to judge, for we are
sinners all.
Close up his eyes, and draw the curtain
close;
And let us all to meditation. [*Exeunt.*

ACT FOUR

Scene I. *The coast of Kent.*

*Alarum. Fight at sea. Ordnance goes off.
Enter a Lieutenant, a Shipmaster and
his Mate, and* WALTER WHITMORE, *with*
Sailors; SUFFOLK *and other* Gentlemen,
as prisoners.

Lieut. The gaudy, blabbing, and remorse-
ful day
Is crept into the bosom of the sea;
And now loud-howling wolves arouse the
jades
That drag the tragic melancholy night;
Who with their drowsy, slow, and flagging
wings 5
Clip dead men's graves, and from their
misty jaws
Breathe foul contagious darkness in the air.
Therefore bring forth the soldiers of our
prize;
For, whilst our pinnace anchors in the
Downs,
Here shall they make their ransom on the
sand, 10
Or with their blood stain this discoloured
shore.
Master, this prisoner freely give I thee;
And thou that art his mate make boot of
this;
The other, Walter Whitmore, is thy share.

1 Gent. What is my ransom, master, let
me know? 15

Mast. A thousand crowns, or else lay
down your head.

Mate. And so much shall you give, or off
goes yours.

Lieut. What, think you much to pay two
thousand crowns,
And bear the name and port of gentlemen?
Cut both the villains' throats—for die you
shall 20
The lives of those which we have lost in
fight
Be counterpois'd with such a petty sum!

1 Gent. I'll give it, sir; and therefore
spare my life.

2 Gent. And so will I, and write home for
it straight.

Whit. I lost mine eye in laying the prize
aboard, 25
[*To Suffolk*] And therefore, to revenge it,
shalt thou die;
And so should these, if I might have my
will.

Lieut. Be not so rash; take ransom, let
him live.

Suf. Look on my George, I am a gentleman:
Rate me at what thou wilt, thou shalt be
paid. 30

Whit. And so am I: my name is Walter
Whitmore.
How now! Why start'st thou? What,
doth death affright?

Suf. Thy name affrights me, in whose
sound is death.
A cunning man did calculate my birth
And told me that by water I should die; 35
Yet let not this make thee be bloody-
minded;
Thy name is Gualtier, being rightly
sounded.

Whit. Gualtier or Walter, which it is I
care not:
Never yet did base dishonour blur our
name
But with our sword we wip'd away the
blot; 40
Therefore, when merchant-like I sell
revenge,
Broke be my sword, my arms torn and
defac'd,
And I proclaim'd a coward through the
world.

Suf. Stay, Whitmore, for thy prisoner is
a prince,
The Duke of Suffolk, William de la Pole. 45

Whit. The Duke of Suffolk muffled up in
rags?

Suf. Ay, but these rags are no part of
the Duke:
Jove sometime went disguis'd, and why
not I?

Lieut. But Jove was never slain, as thou
shalt be.

Suf. Obscure and lowly swain, King
Henry's blood, 50
The honourable blood of Lancaster,
Must not be shed by such a jaded groom.
Hast thou not kiss'd thy hand and held
my stirrup,
Bareheaded plodded by my foot-cloth mule,
And thought thee happy when I shook my
head? 55
How often hast thou waited at my cup,
Fed from my trencher, kneel'd down at the
board,
When I have feasted with Queen Margaret?
Remember it, and let it make thee crest-
fall'n,
Ay, and allay thus thy abortive pride, 60
How in our voiding-lobby hast thou stood
And duly waited for my coming forth?
This hand of mine hath writ in thy behalf,
And therefore shall it charm thy riotous
tongue.

Whit. Speak, Captain, shall I stab the
forlorn swain? 65

Lieut. First let my words stab him, as he
    hath me.
Suf. Base slave, thy words are blunt, and
    so art thou.
Lieut. Convey him hence, and on our
    longboat's side
Strike off his head.
Suf.   Thou dar'st not, for thy own.
Lieut. Poole!
Suf. Poole?
Lieut. Ay, kennel, puddle, sink, whose
    filth and dirt
Troubles the silver spring where England
    drinks;
Now will I dam up this thy yawning mouth
For swallowing the treasure of the realm.
Thy lips, that kiss'd the Queen, shall sweep
    the ground;   75
And thou that smil'dst at good Duke
    Humphrey's death
Against the senseless winds shalt grin in
    vain,
Who in contempt shall hiss at thee again;
And wedded be thou to the hags of hell
For daring to affy a mighty lord   80
Unto the daughter of a worthless king,
Having neither subject, wealth, nor diadem.
By devilish policy art thou grown great,
And, like ambitious Sylla, overgorg'd
With gobbets of thy mother's bleeding
    heart.   85
By thee Anjou and Maine were sold to
    France;
The false revolting Normans thorough thee
Disdain to call us lord; and Picardy
Hath slain their governors, surpris'd our
    forts,
And sent the ragged soldiers wounded
    home.   90
The princely Warwick, and the Nevils all,
Whose dreadful swords were never drawn
    in vain,
As hating thee, are rising up in arms;
And now the house of York—thrust from
    the crown
By shameful murder of a guiltless king   95
And lofty proud encroaching tyranny—
Burns with revenging fire, whose hopeful
    colours
Advance our half-fac'd sun, striving to
    shine,
Under the which is writ 'Invitis nubibus'.
The commons here in Kent are up in
    arms;   100
And to conclude, reproach and beggary
Is crept into the palace of our King,
And all by thee. Away! convey him hence.
Suf. O that I were a god, to shoot forth
    thunder
Upon these paltry, servile, abject drudges!
Small things make base men proud: this
    villain here,   106
Being captain of a pinnace, threatens
    more

Than Bargulus, the strong Illyrian pirate.
Drones suck not eagles' blood but rob bee-
    hives.
It is impossible that I should die   110
By such a lowly vassal as thyself.
Thy words move rage and not remorse in
    me.
I go of message from the Queen to France:
I charge thee waft me safely cross the
    Channel.
Lieut. Walter—   115
Whit. Come, Suffolk, I must waft thee to
    thy death.
Suf. Gelidus timor occupat artus: it is
    thee I fear.
Whit. Thou shalt have cause to fear
    before I leave thee.
What, are ye daunted now? Now will ye
    stoop?
1 Gent. My gracious lord, entreat him,
    speak him fair.   120
Suf. Suffolk's imperial tongue is stern
    and rough,
Us'd to command, untaught to plead for
    favour.
Far be it we should honour such as
    these
With humble suit: no, rather let my
    head
Stoop to the block than these knees bow
    to any   125
Save to the God of heaven and to my king;
And sooner dance upon a bloody pole
Than stand uncover'd to the vulgar groom.
True nobility is exempt from fear:
More can I bear than you dare execute.   130
Lieut. Hale him away, and let him talk
    no more.
Suf. Come, soldiers, show what cruelty
    ye can,
That this my death may never be forgot—
Great men oft die by vile bezonians:
A Roman sworder and banditto slave   135
Murder'd sweet Tully; Brutus' bastard
    hand
Stabb'd Julius Cæsar; savage islanders
Pompey the Great; and Suffolk dies by
    pirates. [*Exit Walter with Suffolk.*
Lieut. And as for these, whose ransom we
    have set,
It is our pleasure one of them depart;   140
Therefore come you with us, and let him go.
    [*Exeunt all but the first Gentleman.*

Re-enter WHITMORE *with Suffolk's body.*

Whit. There let his head and lifeless
    body lie,
Until the Queen his mistress bury it. [*Exit.*
1 Gent. O barbarous and bloody spec-
    tacle!
His body will I bear unto the King.   145
If he revenge it not, yet will his friends;
So will the Queen, that living held him dear.
    [*Exit with the body.*

SCENE II. *Blackheath.*

Enter GEORGE BEVIS *and* JOHN HOLLAND.

Geo. Come and get thee a sword, though made of a lath; they have been up these two days.

John. They have the more need to sleep now, then.

Geo. I tell thee Jack Cade the clothier means to dress the commonwealth, and turn it, and set a new nap upon it.   6

John. So he had need, for 'tis threadbare. Well, I say it was never merry world in England since gentlemen came up.

Geo. O miserable age! Virtue is not regarded in handicraftsmen.   11

John. The nobility think scorn to go in leather aprons.

Geo. Nay, more, the King's Council are no good workmen.   14

John. True; and yet it is said ' Labour in thy vocation '; which is as much to say as ' Let the magistrates be labouring men'; and therefore should we be magistrates.

Geo. Thou hast hit it; for there's no better sign of a brave mind than a hard hand.

John. I see them! I see them! There's Best's son, the tanner of Wingham—   21

Geo. He shall have the skins of our enemies to make dog's leather of.

John. And Dick the butcher—

Geo. Then is sin struck down, like an ox, and iniquity's throat cut like a calf.   26

John. And Smith the weaver—

Geo. Argo, their thread of life is spun.

John. Come, come, let's fall in with them.

Drum.   Enter CADE, DICK *the Butcher,* SMITH *the Weaver, and a* Sawyer, *with infinite numbers.*

Cade. We John Cade, so term'd of our supposed father—   31

Dick. [*Aside*] Or rather, of stealing a cade of herrings.

Cade. For our enemies shall fall before us, inspired with the spirit of putting down kings and princes—command silence.   35

Dick. Silence!

Cade. My father was a Mortimer—

Dick. [*Aside*] He was an honest man and a good bricklayer.

Cade. My mother a Plantagenet—   40

Dick. [*Aside*] I knew her well; she was a midwife.

Cade. My wife descended of the Lacies—

Dick. [*Aside*] She was, indeed, a pedlar's daughter, and sold many laces.

Smith. [*Aside*] But now of late, not able to travel with her furr'd pack, she washes bucks here at home.   46

Cade. Therefore am I of an honourable house.

Dick. [*Aside*] Ay, by my faith, the field is honourable, and there was he born, under a hedge, for his father had never a house but the cage.   50

Cade. Valiant I am.

Smith. [*Aside*] 'A must needs; for beggary is valiant.

Cade. I am able to endure much.

Dick. [*Aside*] No question of that; for I have seen him whipt three market days together.   55

Cade. I fear neither sword nor fire.

Smith. [*Aside*] He need not fear the sword, for his coat is of proof.

Dick. [*Aside*] But methinks he should stand in fear of fire, being burnt i' th' hand for stealing of sheep.   60

Cade. Be brave, then, for your captain is brave, and vows reformation. There shall be in England seven halfpenny loaves sold for a penny; the three-hoop'd pot shall have ten hoops; and I will make it felony to drink small beer. All the realm shall be in common, and in Cheapside shall my palfrey go to grass. And when I am king— as king I will be—   67

All. God save your Majesty!

Cade. I thank you, good people—there shall be no money; all shall eat and drink on my score, and I will apparel them all in one livery, that they may agree like brothers and worship me their lord.   72

Dick. The first thing we do, let's kill all the lawyers.

Cade. Nay, that I mean to do. Is not this a lamentable thing, that of the skin of an innocent lamb should be made parchment? That parchment, being scribbl'd o'er, should undo a man? Some say the bee stings; but I say 'tis the bee's wax; for I did but seal once to a thing, and I was never mine own man since. How now! Who's there?   80

Enter some, bringing in the Clerk of Chatham.

Smith. The clerk of Chatham. He can write and read and cast accompt.

Cade. O monstrous!

Smith. We took him setting of boys' copies.

Cade. Here's a villain!   85

Smith. Has a book in his pocket with red letters in't.

Cade. Nay, then he is a conjurer.

Dick. Nay, he can make obligations and write court-hand.   89

Cade. I am sorry for't; the man is a proper man, of mine honour; unless I find him guilty, he shall not die. Come hither, sirrah, I must examine thee. What is thy name?

Clerk. Emmanuel.

Dick. They use to write it on the top of letters; 'twill go hard with you.   96

Cade. Let me alone. Dost thou use to write thy name, or hast thou a mark to thyself, like a honest plain-dealing man ?

Clerk. Sir, I thank God, I have been so well brought up that I can write my name.

All. He hath confess'd. Away with him ! He's a villain and a traitor. 103

Cade. Away with him, I say ! Hang him with his pen and inkhorn about his neck.

[*Exit one with the Clerk.*

Enter MICHAEL.

Mich. Where's our General ?

Cade. Here I am, thou particular fellow.

Mich. Fly, fly, fly ! Sir Humphrey Stafford and his brother are hard by, with the King's forces.

Cade. Stand, villain, stand, or I'll fell thee down. He shall be encount'red with a man as good as himself. He is but a knight, is 'a ? 112

Mich. No.

Cade. To equal him, I will make myself a knight presently. [*Kneels*] Rise up, Sir John Mortimer. [*Rises*] Now have at him ! 116

Enter SIR HUMPHREY STAFFORD *and* WILLIAM *his brother, with drum and* Soldiers.

Staf. Rebellious hinds, the filth and scum of Kent,
Mark'd for the gallows, lay your weapons down ;
Home to your cottages, forsake this groom ;
The King is merciful if you revolt. 120
W. Staf. But angry, wrathful, and inclin'd to blood,
If you go forward ; therefore yield or die.
Cade. As for these silken-coated slaves, I pass not ;
It is to you, good people, that I speak,
O'er whom, in time to come, I hope to reign ; 125
For I am rightful heir unto the crown.
Staf. Villain, thy father was a plasterer ;
And thou thyself a shearman, art thou not ?
Cade. And Adam was a gardener.
W. Staf. And what of that ? 130
Cade. Marry, this : Edmund Mortimer, Earl of March,
Married the Duke of Clarence' daughter, did he not ?
Staf. Ay, sir.
Cade. By her he had two children at one birth.
W. Staf. That's false. 135
Cade. Ay, there's the question ; but I say 'tis true.
The elder of them being put to nurse,
Was by a beggar-woman stol'n away,
And, ignorant of his birth and parentage,
Became a bricklayer when he came to age.
His son am I ; deny it if you can. 141

Dick. Nay, 'tis too true ; therefore he shall be king.
Smith. Sir, he made a chimney in my father's house, and the bricks are alive at this day to testify it ; therefore deny it not.
Staf. And will you credit this base drudge's words 146
That speaks he knows not what ?
All. Ay, marry, will we ; therefore get ye gone.
W. Staf. Jack Cade, the Duke of York hath taught you this. 149
Cade. [*Aside*] He lies, for I invented it myself—Go to, sirrah, tell the King from me that for his father's sake, Henry the Fifth, in whose time boys went to span-counter for French crowns, I am content he shall reign ; but I'll be Protector over him. 154
Dick. And furthermore, we'll have the Lord Say's head for selling the dukedom of Maine.
Cade. And good reason ; for thereby is England main'd and fain to go with a staff, but that my puissance holds it up. Fellow kings, I tell you that that Lord Say hath gelded the commonwealth and made it an eunuch ; and more than that, he can speak French, and therefore he is a traitor. 162
Staf. O gross and miserable ignorance !
Cade. Nay, answer if you can ; the Frenchmen are our enemies. Go to, then, I ask but this : can he that speaks with the tongue of an enemy be a good counsellor, or no ? 167
All. No, no ; and therefore we'll have his head.
W. Staf. Well, seeing gentle words will not prevail,
Assail them with the army of the King. 170
Staf. Herald, away ; and throughout every town
Proclaim them traitors that are up with Cade ;
That those which fly before the battle ends
May, even in their wives' and children's sight,
Be hang'd up for example at their doors. 175
And you that be the King's friends, follow me.
[*Exeunt the two Staffords and Soldiers.*
Cade. And you that love the commons follow me.
Now show yourselves men ; 'tis for liberty.
We will not leave one lord, one gentleman ;
Spare none but such as go in clouted shoon,
For they are thrifty honest men and such
As would—but that they dare not—take our parts. 182
Dick. They are all in order, and march toward us.
Cade. But then are we in order when we are most out of order. Come, march forward. [*Exeunt.*

SCENE III. *Another part of Blackheath.*

Alarums to the fight, wherein both the Staffords are slain. Enter CADE *and the rest.*

Cade. Where's Dick, the butcher of Ashford?

Dick. Here, sir.

Cade. They fell before thee like sheep and oxen, and thou behavedst thyself as if thou hadst been in thine own slaughter-house; therefore thus will I reward thee—the Lent shall be as long again as it is, and thou shalt have a licence to kill for a hundred lacking one.   7

Dick. I desire no more.

Cade. And, to speak truth, thou deserv'st no less. [*Putting on Sir Humphrey's brigandine*] This monument of the victory will I bear, and the bodies shall be dragged at my horse heels till I do come to London, where we will have the mayor's sword borne before us.   13

Dick. If we mean to thrive and do good, break open the gaols and let out the prisoners.   15

Cade. Fear not that, I warrant thee. Come, let's march towards London.
                                              [*Exeunt.*

SCENE IV. *London. The palace.*

Enter the KING *with a supplication, and the* QUEEN *with Suffolk's head; the* DUKE OF BUCKINGHAM, *and the* LORD SAY.

Queen. Oft have I heard that grief softens the mind
And makes it fearful and degenerate;
Think therefore on revenge and cease to weep.
But who can cease to weep, and look on this?
Here may his head lie on my throbbing breast;   5
But where's the body that I should embrace?

Buck. What answer makes your Grace to the rebels' supplication?

King. I'll send some holy bishop to entreat;   10
For God forbid so many simple souls
Should perish by the sword! And I myself,
Rather than bloody war shall cut them short,
Will parley with Jack Cade their general.
But stay, I'll read it over once again.

Queen. Ah, barbarous villains! Hath this lovely face
Rul'd like a wandering planet over me,   16
And could it not enforce them to relent
That were unworthy to behold the same?

King. Lord Say, Jack Cade hath sworn to have thy head.

Say. Ay, but I hope your Highness shall have his.

King. How now, madam!   21
Still lamenting and mourning for Suffolk's death?
I fear me, love, if that I had been dead,
Thou wouldst not have mourn'd so much for me.

Queen. No, my love, I should not mourn, but die for thee.   25

Enter a Messenger.

King. How now! What news? Why com'st thou in such haste?

Mess. The rebels are in Southwark; fly, my lord!
Jack Cade proclaims himself Lord Mortimer,
Descended from the Duke of Clarence' house,
And calls your Grace usurper, openly,   30
And vows to crown himself in Westminster.
His army is a ragged multitude
Of hinds and peasants, rude and merciless;
Sir Humphrey Stafford and his brother's death
Hath given them heart and courage to proceed.   35
All scholars, lawyers, courtiers, gentlemen,
They call false caterpillars and intend their death.

King. O graceless men! they know not what they do.

Buck. My gracious lord, retire to Killingworth   39
Until a power be rais'd to put them down.

Queen. Ah, were the Duke of Suffolk now alive,
These Kentish rebels would be soon appeas'd!

King. Lord Say, the traitors hate thee;
Therefore away with us to Killingworth.

Say. So might your Grace's person be in danger.   45
The sight of me is odious in their eyes;
And therefore in this city will I stay
And live alone as secret as I may.

Enter another Messenger.

2 Mess. Jack Cade hath gotten London Bridge.
The citizens fly and forsake their houses; 50
The rascal people, thirsting after prey,
Join with the traitor; and they jointly swear
To spoil the city and your royal court.

Buck. Then linger not, my lord; away, take horse.

King. Come, Margaret; God, our hope, will succour us.

Queen. My hope is gone, now Suffolk is deceas'd.   56

King. [*To Lord Say*] Farewell, my lord, trust not the Kentish rebels.

Buck. Trust nobody, for fear you be betray'd.

Say. The trust I have is in mine innocence,
And therefore am I bold and resolute.   60
[*Exeunt.*

SCENE V. *London. The Tower.*

Enter LORD SCALES *upon the Tower, walking. Then enter two or three Citizens, below.*

Scales. How now! Is Jack Cade slain?
1 *Cit.* No, my lord, nor likely to be slain;
for they have won the bridge, killing all
those that withstand them. The Lord
Mayor craves aid of your honour from the
Tower, to defend the city from the rebels. 5
Scales. Such aid as I can spare you shall
command,
But I am troubled here with them myself;
The rebels have assay'd to win the Tower.
But get you to Smithfield, and gather head,
And thither I will send you Matthew Goffe;
Fight for your King, your country, and
your lives;   11
And so, farewell, for I must hence again.
[*Exeunt.*

SCENE VI. *London. Cannon street.*

Enter JACK CADE *and the rest, and strikes his staff on London stone.*

Cade. Now is Mortimer lord of this city.
And here, sitting upon London Stone, I
charge and command that, of the city's
cost, the pissing-conduit run nothing but
claret wine this first year of our reign. And
now henceforward it shall be treason for
any that calls me other than Lord Mortimer.   6

Enter a Soldier, running.

Sold. Jack Cade! Jack Cade!
Cade. Knock him down there.
[*They kill him.*
Smith. If this fellow be wise, he'll never
call ye Jack Cade more; I think he hath
a very fair warning.   10
Dick. My lord, there's an army gathered
together in Smithfield.
Cade. Come then, let's go fight with them.
But first go and set London Bridge on fire;
and, if you can, burn down the Tower too.
Come, let's away.   [*Exeunt.*

SCENE VII. *London. Smithfield.*

Alarums. MATTHEW GOFFE *is slain, and all the rest. Then enter* JACK CADE, *with his company.*

Cade. So, sirs. Now go some and pull
down the Savoy; others to th' Inns of
Court; down with them all.
Dick. I have a suit unto your lordship.

Cade. Be it a lordship, thou shalt have it
for that word.   5
Dick. Only that the laws of England may
come out of your mouth.
John. [*Aside*] Mass, 'twill be sore law
then; for he was thrust in the mouth with
a spear, and 'tis not whole yet.
Smith. [*Aside*] Nay, John, it will be
stinking law; for his breath stinks with
eating toasted cheese.   11
Cade. I have thought upon it; it shall
be so. Away, burn all the records of the
realm. My mouth shall be the Parliament
of England.
John. [*Aside*] Then we are like to have
biting statutes, unless his teeth be pull'd
out.   16
Cade. And henceforward all things shall
be in common.

Enter a Messenger.

Mess. My lord, a prize, a prize! Here's
the Lord Say, which sold the towns in
France; he that made us pay one and
twenty fifteens, and one shilling to the
pound, the last subsidy.   21

Enter GEORGE BEVIS, *with the* LORD SAY.

Cade. Well, he shall be beheaded for it
ten times. Ah, thou say, thou serge, nay,
thou buckram lord! Now art thou within
point blank of our jurisdiction regal. What
canst thou answer to my Majesty for giving
up of Normandy unto Mounsieur Basimecu
the Dauphin of France? Be it known unto
thee by these presence, even the presence
of Lord Mortimer, that I am the besom
that must sweep the court clean of such
filth as thou art. Thou hast most traitorously corrupted the youth of the realm in
erecting a grammar school; and whereas,
before, our forefathers had no other books
but the score and the tally, thou hast
caused printing to be us'd, and, contrary
to the King, his crown, and dignity, thou
hast built a paper-mill. It will be proved
to thy face that thou hast men about thee
that usually talk of a noun and a verb, and
such abominable words as no Christian ear
can endure to hear. Thou hast appointed
justices of peace, to call poor men before
them about matters they were not able to
answer. Moreover, thou hast put them in
prison, and because they could not read,
thou hast hang'd them, when, indeed, only
for that cause they have been most worthy
to live. Thou dost ride in a foot-cloth, dost
thou not?   43
Say. What of that?
Cade. Marry, thou ought'st not to let thy
horse wear a cloak, when honester men
than thou go in their hose and doublets. 47
Dick. And work in their shirt too, as
myself, for example, that am a butcher.

Say. You men of Kent— 50
Dick. What say you of Kent?
Say. Nothing but this: 'tis ' bona terra, mala gens '.
Cade. Away with him, away with him! He speaks Latin.
Say. Hear me but speak, and bear me where you will. 55
Kent, in the Commentaries Cæsar writ,
Is term'd the civil'st place of all this isle.
Sweet is the country, because full of riches;
The people liberal, valiant, active, wealthy;
Which makes me hope you are not void of pity. 60
I sold not Maine, I lost not Normandy;
Yet, to recover them, would lose my life.
Justice with favour have I always done;
Pray'rs and tears have mov'd me, gifts could never. 64
When have I aught exacted at your hands,
But to maintain the King, the realm, and you?
Large gifts have I bestow'd on learned clerks,
Because my book preferr'd me to the King,
And seeing ignorance is the curse of God,
Knowledge the wing wherewith we fly to heaven, 70
Unless you be possess'd with devilish spirits
You cannot but forbear to murder me.
This tongue hath parley'd unto foreign kings
For your behoof. 74
Cade. Tut, when struck'st thou one blow in the field?
Say. Great men have reaching hands. Oft have I struck
Those that I never saw, and struck them dead.
Geo. O monstrous coward! What, to come behind folks?
Say. These cheeks are pale for watching for your good.
Cade. Give him a box o' th' ear, and that will make 'em red again. 81
Say. Long sitting to determine poor men's causes
Hath made me full of sickness and diseases.
Cade. Ye shall have a hempen caudle then, and the help of hatchet. 85
Dick. Why dost thou quiver, man?
Say. The palsy, and not fear, provokes me.
Cade. Nay, he nods at us, as who should say ' I'll be even with you '; I'll see if his head will stand steadier on a pole, or no. Take him away, and behead him. 90
Say. Tell me: wherein have I offended most?
Have I affected wealth or honour? Speak.
Are my chests fill'd up with extorted gold?
Is my apparel sumptuous to behold?
Whom have I injur'd, that ye seek my death? 95

These hands are free from guiltless blood-shedding,
This breast from harbouring foul deceitful thoughts.
O, let me live!
Cade. [*Aside*] I feel remorse in myself with his words; but I'll bridle it. He shall die, an it be but for pleading so well for his life. —Away with him! He has a familiar under his tongue; he speaks not o' God's name. Go, take him away, I say, and strike off his head presently, and then break into his son-in-law's house, Sir James Cromer, and strike off his head, and bring them both upon two poles hither. 106
All. It shall be done.
Say. Ah, countrymen! if when you make your pray'rs,
God should be so obdurate as yourselves,
How would it fare with your departed souls? 110
And therefore yet relent, and save my life.
Cade. Away with him, and do as I command ye. [*Exeunt some with Lord Say*] The proudest peer in the realm shall not wear a head on his shoulders, unless he pay me tribute; there shall not a maid be married, but she shall pay to me her maidenhead ere they have it. Men shall hold of me in capite; and we charge and command that their wives be as free as heart can wish or tongue can tell.
Dick. My lord, when shall we go to Cheapside, and take up commodities upon our bills? 120
Cade. Marry, presently.
All. O, brave!

Re-enter one *with the heads.*

Cade. But is not this braver? Let them kiss one another, for they lov'd well when they were alive. Now part them again, lest they consult about the giving up of some more towns in France. Soldiers, defer the spoil of the city until night; for with these borne before us instead of maces will we ride through the streets, and at every corner have them kiss. Away! [*Exeunt*

SCENE VIII. *Southwark.*

Alarum and retreat. Enter again CADE *and all his* Rabblement.

Cade. Up Fish Street! down Saint Magnus' Corner! Kill and knock down! Throw them into Thames! [*Sound a parley*] What noise is this I hear? Dare any be so bold to sound retreat or parley when I command them kill?

Enter BUCKINGHAM *and old* CLIFFORD, *attended.*

Buck. Ay, here they be that dare and will disturb thee.

Know, Cade, we come ambassadors from
   the King   6
Unto the commons whom thou hast misled;
And here pronounce free pardon to them
   all
That will forsake thee and go home in peace.
   Clif. What say ye, countrymen ? Will ye
   relent   10
And yield to mercy whilst 'tis offer'd you,
Or let a rebel lead you to your deaths ?
Who loves the King, and will embrace his
   pardon,
Fling up his cap and say ' God save his
   Majesty ! '   14
Who hateth him and honours not his father,
Henry the Fifth, that made all France to
   quake,
Shake he his weapon at us and pass by.
   All. God save the King ! God save the
   King !
   Cade. What, Buckingham and Clifford,
are ye so brave ? And you, base peasants,
do ye believe him ? Will you needs be
hang'd with your pardons about your
necks ? Hath my sword therefore broke
through London gates, that you should
leave me at the White Hart in Southwark ?
I thought ye would never have given out
these arms till you had recovered your
ancient freedom. But you are all recreants
and dastards, and delight to live in slavery
to the nobility. Let them break your backs
with burdens, take your houses over your
heads, ravish your wives and daughters
before your faces. For me, I will make
shift for one ; and so God's curse light
upon you all !   31
   All. We'll follow Cade, we'll follow Cade !
   Clif. Is Cade the son of Henry the Fifth,
That thus you do exclaim you'll go with
   him ?
Will he conduct you through the heart of
   France,   35
And make the meanest of you earls and
   dukes ?
Alas, he hath no home, no place to fly to ;
Nor knows he how to live but by the spoil,
Unless by robbing of your friends and us.
Were 't not a shame that whilst you live at
   jar   40
The fearful French, whom you late van-
   quished,
Should make a start o'er seas and vanquish
   you ?
Methinks already in this civil broil
I see them lording it in London streets,
Crying ' Villiago ! ' unto all they meet.   45
Better ten thousand base-born Cades mis-
   carry
Than you should stoop unto a Frenchman's
   mercy.
To France, to France, and get what you
   have lost ;
Spare England, for it is your native coast.

Henry hath money ; you are strong and
   manly.   50
God on our side, doubt not of victory.
   All. A Clifford ! a Clifford ! We'll follow
the King and Clifford.   53
   Cade. Was ever feather so lightly blown
to and fro as this multitude ? The name of
Henry the Fifth hales them to an hundred
mischiefs, and makes them leave me desolate. I see them lay their heads together to
surprise me. My sword make way for me
for here is no staying. In despite of the
devils and hell, have through the very
middest of you ! and heavens and honour
be witness that no want of resolution in
me, but only my followers' base and
ignominious treasons, makes me betake me
to my heels.   [*Exit.*
   Buck. What, is he fled ? Go some, and
follow him ;
And he that brings his head unto the King
Shall have a thousand crowns for his
   reward.   [*Exeunt some of them.*
Follow me, soldiers ; we'll devise a mean
To reconcile you all unto the King.   65
                              [*Exeunt.*

        Scene IX. *Killingworth Castle.*

Sound trumpets. Enter King, Queen, *and*
        Somerset, *on the terrace.*

   King. Was ever king that joy'd an
   earthly throne
And could command no more content
   than I ?
No sooner was I crept out of my cradle
But I was made a king, at nine months old.
Was never subject long'd to be a king   5
As I do long and wish to be a subject.

   Enter Buckingham *and old* Clifford.

   Buck. Health and glad tidings to your
   Majesty !
   King. Why, Buckingham, is the traitor
   Cade surpris'd ?
Or is he but retir'd to make him strong ?

Enter, below, Multitudes, *with halters about
      their necks.*

   Clif. He is fled, my lord, and all his
   powers do yield,   10
And humbly thus, with halters on their
   necks,
Expect your Highness' doom of life or
   death.
   King. Then, heaven, set ope thy ever-
   lasting gates,
To entertain my vows of thanks and praise !
Soldiers, this day have you redeem'd your
   lives,   15
And show'd how well you love your Prince
   and country.
Continue still in this so good a mind,
And Henry, though he be infortunate,

Assure yourselves, will never be unkind.
And so, with thanks and pardon to you all,
I do dismiss you to your several countries.
All. God save the King! God save the
King!   22

Enter a Messenger.

Mess. Please it your Grace to be adver-
tised
The Duke of York is newly come from
Ireland
And with a puissant and a mighty power 25
Of gallowglasses and stout kerns
Is marching hitherward in proud array,
And still proclaimeth, as he comes along,
His arms are only to remove from thee
The Duke of Somerset, whom he terms a
traitor.   30
King. Thus stands my state, 'twixt Cade
and York distress'd;
Like to a ship that, having scap'd a tempest,
Is straightway calm'd, and boarded with a
pirate;
But now is Cade driven back, his men
dispers'd,
And now is York in arms to second him. 35
I pray thee, Buckingham, go and meet him
And ask him what's the reason of these
arms.
Tell him I'll send Duke Edmund to the
Tower—
And, Somerset, we will commit thee thither
Until his army be dismiss'd from him. 40
Som. My lord,
I'll yield myself to prison willingly,
Or unto death, to do my country good.
King. In any case be not too rough in
terms,
For he is fierce and cannot brook hard
language.   45
Buck. I will, my lord, and doubt not so
to deal
As all things shall redound unto your good.
King. Come, wife, let's in, and learn to
govern better;
For yet may England curse my wretched
reign.   [*Flourish. Exeunt.*

SCENE X. *Kent. Iden's garden.*

Enter CADE.

Cade. Fie on ambitions! Fie on myself,
that have a sword and yet am ready to
famish! These five days have I hid me in
these woods and durst not peep out, for all
the country is laid for me; but now am I
so hungry that, if I might have a lease of
my life for a thousand years, I could stay
no longer. Wherefore, on a brick wall have
I climb'd into this garden, to see if I can
eat grass or pick a sallet another while,
which is not amiss to cool a man's stomach
this hot weather. And I think this word
'sallet' was born to do me good; for many

a time, but for a sallet, my brain-pan had
been cleft with a brown bill; and many a
time, when I have been dry, and bravely
marching, it hath serv'd me instead of a
quart-pot to drink in; and now the word
'sallet' must serve me to feed on.   15

Enter IDEN.

Iden. Lord, who would live turmoiled in
the court
And may enjoy such quiet walks as these?
This small inheritance my father left me
Contenteth me, and worth a monarchy.
I seek not to wax great by others' waning 20
Or gather wealth I care not with what envy;
Sufficeth that I have maintains my state,
And sends the poor well pleased from my
gate.
Cade. Here's the lord of the soil come to
seize me for a stray, for entering his fee-
simple without leave. Ah, villain, thou
wilt betray me, and get a thousand crowns
of the King by carrying my head to him;
but I'll make thee eat iron like an ostrich
and swallow my sword like a great pin ere
thou and I part.
Iden. Why, rude companion, whatsoe'er
thou be,   30
I know thee not; why then should I betray
thee?
Is't not enough to break into my garden
And like a thief to come to rob my grounds,
Climbing my walls in spite of me the owner,
But thou wilt brave me with these saucy
terms?   35
Cade. Brave thee? Ay, by the best blood
that ever was broach'd, and beard thee too.
Look on me well: I have eat no meat these
five days, yet come thou and thy five men
and if I do not leave you all as dead as a
door-nail, I pray God I may never eat
grass more.   40
Iden. Nay, it shall ne'er be said, while
England stands,
That Alexander Iden, an esquire of Kent,
Took odds to combat a poor famish'd man.
Oppose thy steadfast-gazing eyes to mine;
See if thou canst outface me with thy looks;
Set limb to limb, and thou art far the lesser;
Thy hand is but a finger to my fist,   47
Thy leg a stick compared with this
truncheon;
My foot shall fight with all the strength
thou hast,
And if mine arm be heaved in the air,   50
Thy grave is digg'd already in the earth.
As for words, whose greatness answers
words,
Let this my sword report what speech
forbears.   53
Cade. By my valour, the most complete
champion that ever I heard! Steel, if thou
turn the edge, or cut not out the burly-
bon'd clown in chines of beef ere thou sleep

in thy sheath, I beseech God on my knees
thou mayst be turn'd to hobnails. [*Here
they fight; Cade falls*] O, I am slain! famine
and no other hath slain me. Let ten
thousand devils come against me, and give
me but the ten meals I have lost, and I'd
defy them all. Wither, garden, and be
henceforth a burying place to all that do
dwell in this house, because the unconquered soul of Cade is fled.

Iden. Is't Cade that I have slain, that
 monstrous traitor ?   65
Sword, I will hallow thee for this thy deed
And hang thee o'er my tomb when I am
 dead.
Ne'er shall this blood be wiped from thy
 point,
But thou shalt wear it as a herald's coat 69
To emblaze the honour that thy master
 got.

Cade. Iden, farewell ; and be proud of
thy victory. Tell Kent from me she hath
lost her best man, and exhort all the world
to be cowards ; for I, that never feared
any, am vanquished by famine, not by
valour.   [*Dies.*

Iden. How much thou wrong'st me,
 heaven be my judge.   75
Die, damned wretch, the curse of her that
 bare thee !
And as I thrust thy body in with my
 sword,
So wish I I might thrust thy soul to hell.
Hence will I drag thee headlong by the
 heels   79
Unto a dunghill, which shall be thy grave,
And there cut off thy most ungracious head,
Which I will bear in triumph to the King,
Leaving thy trunk for crows to feed upon.
           [*Exit.*

ACT FIVE

Scene I. *Fields between Dartford and
   Blackheath.*

Enter York, *and his army of Irish, with
drum and colours.*

York. From Ireland thus comes York to
 claim his right
And pluck the crown from feeble Henry's
 head :
Ring bells aloud, burn bonfires clear and
 bright,
To entertain great England's lawful king.
Ah, sancta majestas ! who would not buy
 thee dear ?   5
Let them obey that knows not how to rule ;
This hand was made to handle nought but
 gold.
I cannot give due action to my words
Except a sword or sceptre balance it.
A sceptre shall it have, have I a soul, 10
On which I'll toss the flower-de-luce of
 France.

Enter Buckingham.

[*Aside*] Whom have we here ? Bucking-
ham, to disturb me ?
The King hath sent him, sure : I must
 dissemble.
Buck. York, if thou meanest well, I greet
 thee well.
York. Humphrey of Buckingham, I
 accept thy greeting.   15
Art thou a messenger, or come of pleasure ?
Buck. A messenger from Henry, our
 dread liege,
To know the reason of these arms in peace ;
Or why thou, being a subject as I am,
Against thy oath and true allegiance
 sworn,   20
Should raise so great a power without his
 leave,
Or dare to bring thy force so near the
 court.
York. [*Aside*] Scarce can I speak, my
 choler is so great.
O, I could hew up rocks and fight with
 flint,
I am so angry at these abject terms ; 25
And now, like Ajax Telamonius,
On sheep or oxen could I spend my fury.
I am far better born than is the King,
More like a king, more kingly in my
 thoughts ;
But I must make fair weather yet awhile, 30
Till Henry be more weak and I more
 strong.—
Buckingham, I prithee, pardon me
That I have given no answer all this while ;
My mind was troubled with deep melan-
 choly.
The cause why I have brought this army
 hither   35
Is to remove proud Somerset from the
 King,
Seditious to his Grace and to the state.
Buck. That is too much presumption on
 thy part ;
But if thy arms be to no other end,
The King hath yielded unto thy demand : 40
The Duke of Somerset is in the Tower.
York. Upon thine honour, is he prisoner ?
Buck. Upon mine honour, he is prisoner.
York. Then, Buckingham, I do dismiss
 my pow'rs.
Soldiers, I thank you all ; disperse your-
 selves ;   45
Meet me to-morrow in Saint George's field,
You shall have pay and everything you
 wish.
And let my sovereign, virtuous Henry,
Command my eldest son, nay, all my sons,
As pledges of my fealty and love. 50
I'll send them all as willing as I live :
Lands, goods, horse, armour, anything I
 have,
Is his to use, so Somerset may die.

Buck. York, I commend this kind sub-
        mission.
We twain will go into his Highness' tent. 55

Enter the KING, *and* Attendants.

King. Buckingham, doth York intend no
        harm to us,
That thus he marcheth with thee arm in
        arm ?
York. In all submission and humility
York doth present himself unto your
        Highness.
King. Then what intends these forces
        thou dost bring ?
York. To heave the traitor Somerset from
        hence,   61
And fight against that monstrous rebel
        Cade,
Who since I heard to be discomfited.

Enter IDEN, *with Cade's head.*

Iden. If one so rude and of so mean
        condition
May pass into the presence of a king,   65
Lo, I present your Grace a traitor's head,
The head of Cade, whom I in combat slew.
King. The head of Cade ! Great God,
        how just art Thou !
O, let me view his visage, being dead,
That living wrought me such exceeding
        trouble.   70
Tell me, my friend, art thou the man that
        slew him ?
Iden. I was, an't like your Majesty.
King. How art thou call'd ? And what
        is thy degree ?
Iden. Alexander Iden, that's my name ;
A poor esquire of Kent that loves his king.
Buck. So please it you, my lord, 'twere
        not amiss   76
He were created knight for his good service.
King. Iden, kneel down. [*He kneels*] Rise
        up a knight.
We give thee for reward a thousand marks,
And will that thou thenceforth attend on us.
Iden. May Iden live to merit such a
        bounty,   81
And never live but true unto his liege !

Enter the QUEEN *and* SOMERSET.

King. See, Buckingham ! Somerset
        comes with th' Queen :
Go, bid her hide him quickly from the
        Duke.
Queen. For thousand Yorks he shall not
        hide his head,   85
But boldly stand and front him to his face.
York. How now ! Is Somerset at liberty ?
Then, York, unloose thy long-imprisoned
        thoughts
And let thy tongue be equal with thy heart.
Shall I endure the sight of Somerset ? 90
False king, why hast thou broken faith
        with me,

Knowing how hardly I can brook abuse ?
King did I call thee ? No, thou art not
        king ;
Not fit to govern and rule multitudes,
Which dar'st not, no, nor canst not rule a
        traitor.   95
That head of thine doth not become a
        crown :
Thy hand is made to grasp a palmer's staff,
And not to grace an awful princely sceptre.
That gold must round engirt these brows
        of mine,
Whose smile and frown, like to Achilles'
        spear,   100
Is able with the change to kill and cure.
Here is a hand to hold a sceptre up,
And with the same to act controlling laws.
Give place. By heaven, thou shalt rule no
        more
O'er him whom heaven created for thy
        ruler.   105
Som. O monstrous traitor ! I arrest thee,
        York,
Of capital treason 'gainst the King and
        crown.
Obey, audacious traitor ; kneel for grace.
York. Wouldst have me kneel ? First let
        me ask of these,
If they can brook I bow a knee to man. 110
Sirrah, call in my sons to be my bail :
                            [*Exit Attendant.*
I know, ere they will have me go to ward,
They'll pawn their swords for my en-
        franchisement.
Queen. Call hither Clifford ; bid him
        come amain,
To say if that the bastard boys of York 115
Shall be the surety for their traitor father.
                            [*Exit Buckingham.*
York. O blood-bespotted Neapolitan,
Outcast of Naples, England's bloody
        scourge !
The sons of York, thy betters in their birth,
Shall be their father's bail ; and bane to
        those   120
That for my surety will refuse the boys !

Enter EDWARD *and* RICHARD
        PLANTAGENET.

See where they come : I'll warrant they'll
        make it good.

Enter CLIFFORD *and his* Son.

Queen. And here comes Clifford to deny
        their bail.
Clif. Health and all happiness to my lord
        the King !   [*Kneels.*
York. I thank thee, Clifford. Say, what
        news with thee ?   125
Nay, do not fright us with an angry look.
We are thy sovereign, Clifford, kneel again ;
For thy mistaking so, we pardon thee.
Clif. This is my King, York, I do not
        mistake ;

But thou mistakes me much to think I do.
To Bedlam with him! Is the man grown
    mad?   131
    King. Ay, Clifford; a bedlam and
        ambitious humour
Makes him oppose himself against his king.
    Clif. He is a traitor; let him to the
        Tower,
And chop away that factious pate of his. 135
    Queen. He is arrested, but will not obey;
His sons, he says, shall give their words for
    him.
    York. Will you not, sons?
    Edw. Ay, noble father, if our words will
        serve.
    Rich. And if words will not, then our
        weapons shall.   140
    Clif. Why, what a brood of traitors have
        we here!
    York. Look in a glass, and call thy image
        so:
I am thy king, and thou a false-heart
    traitor.
Call hither to the stake my two brave
    bears,   144
That with the very shaking of their chains
They may astonish these fell-lurking curs.
Bid Salisbury and Warwick come to me.

Enter the EARLS OF WARWICK *and*
    SALISBURY.

    Clif. Are these thy bears? We'll bait thy
        bears to death,
And manacle the berard in their chains,
If thou dar'st bring them to the baiting-
    place.   150
    Rich. Oft have I seen a hot o'erweening cur
Run back and bite, because he was with-
    held;
Who, being suffer'd, with the bear's fell
    paw,
Hath clapp'd his tail between his legs and
    cried;
And such a piece of service will you do, 155
If you oppose yourselves to match Lord
    Warwick.
    Clif. Hence, heap of wrath, foul indigested
        lump,
As crooked in thy manners as thy shape!
    York. Nay, we shall heat you thoroughly
        anon.
    Clif. Take heed, lest by your heat you
        burn yourselves.   160
    King. Why, Warwick, hath thy knee
        forgot to bow?
Old Salisbury, shame to thy silver hair,
Thou mad misleader of thy brainsick son!
What, wilt thou on thy death-bed play the
    ruffian   164
And seek for sorrow with thy spectacles?
O, where is faith? O, where is loyalty?
If it be banish'd from the frosty head,
Where shall it find a harbour in the earth?
Wilt thou go dig a grave to find out war

And shame thine honourable age with
    blood?   170
Why art thou old, and want'st experience?
Or wherefore dost abuse it, if thou hast it?
For shame! In duty bend thy knee to me,
That bows unto the grave with mickle age.
    Sal. My lord, I have considered with
        myself   175
The title of this most renowned duke,
And in my conscience do repute his Grace
The rightful heir to England's royal seat.
    King. Hast thou not sworn allegiance
        unto me?
    Sal. I have.   180
    King. Canst thou dispense with heaven
        for such an oath?
    Sal. It is great sin to swear unto a sin;
But greater sin to keep a sinful oath.
Who can be bound by any solemn vow
To do a murd'rous deed, to rob a man, 185
To force a spotless virgin's chastity,
To reave the orphan of his patrimony,
To wring the widow from her custom'd
    right,
And have no other reason for this wrong
But that he was bound by a solemn oath?
    Queen. A subtle traitor needs no sophister.
    King. Call Buckingham, and bid him arm
        himself.   192
    York. Call Buckingham, and all the
        friends thou hast,
I am resolv'd for death or dignity.
    Clif. The first I warrant thee, if dreams
        prove true.   195
    War. You were best to go to bed and
        dream again
To keep thee from the tempest of the field.
    Clif. I am resolv'd to bear a greater storm
Than any thou canst conjure up to-day;
And that I'll write upon thy burgonet, 200
Might I but know thee by thy household
    badge.
    War. Now, by my father's badge, old
        Nevil's crest,
The rampant bear chain'd to the ragged
    staff,
This day I'll wear aloft my burgonet,
As on a mountain-top the cedar shows, 205
That keeps his leaves in spite of any storm,
Even to affright thee with the view thereof.
    Clif. And from thy burgonet I'll rend thy
        bear
And tread it under foot with all contempt,
Despite the berard that protects the bear.
    Y. Clif. And so to arms, victorious
        father,   211
To quell the rebels and their complices.
    Rich. Fie! charity, for shame! Speak not
        in spite,
For you shall sup with Jesu Christ to-night.
    Y. Clif. Foul stigmatic, that's more than
        thou canst tell.   215
    Rich. If not in heaven, you'll surely sup
        in hell.   [*Exeunt severally.*

SCENE II. *Saint Albans.*

Alarums to the battle. Enter WARWICK.

War. Clifford of Cumberland, 'tis Warwick calls ;
And if thou dost not hide thee from the bear,
Now, when the angry trumpet sounds alarum
And dead men's cries do fill the empty air,
Clifford, I say, come forth and fight with me.   5
Proud northern lord, Clifford of Cumberland,
Warwick is hoarse with calling thee to arms.

Enter YORK.

How now, my noble lord ! what, all a-foot ?
York. The deadly-handed Clifford slew my steed ;
But match to match I have encount'red him,   10
And made a prey for carrion kites and crows
Even of the bonny beast he lov'd so well.

Enter old CLIFFORD.

War. Of one or both of us the time is come.
York. Hold, Warwick, seek thee out some other chase,   14
For I myself must hunt this deer to death.
War. Then, nobly, York ; 'tis for a crown thou fight'st.
As I intend, Clifford, to thrive to-day,
It grieves my soul to leave thee unassail'd.
                                                          [*Exit.*
Clif. What seest thou in me, York ? Why dost thou pause ?
York. With thy brave bearing should I be in love   20
But that thou art so fast mine enemy.
Clif. Nor should thy prowess want praise and esteem
But that 'tis shown ignobly and in treason.
York. So let it help me now against thy sword,
As I in justice and true right express it !   25
Clif. My soul and body on the action both !
York. A dreadful lay ! Address thee instantly.
                      [*They fight and Clifford falls.*
Clif. La fin couronne les œuvres. [*Dies.*
York. Thus war hath given thee peace, for thou art still.   29
Peace with his soul, heaven, if it be thy will !   [*Exit.*

Enter young CLIFFORD.

Y. Clif. Shame and confusion ! All is on the rout ;
Fear frames disorder, and disorder wounds
Where it should guard. O war, thou son of hell,
Whom angry heavens do make their minister,
Throw in the frozen bosoms of our part   35
Hot coals of vengeance ! Let no soldier fly.
He that is truly dedicate to war
Hath no self-love ; nor he that loves himself
Hath not essentially, but by circumstance,
The name of valour. [*Sees his father's body.*
                      O, let the vile world end
And the premised flames of the last day
Knit earth and heaven together !
Now let the general trumpet blow his blast,
Particularities and petty sounds   44
To cease ! Wast thou ordain'd, dear father,
To lose thy youth in peace and to achieve
The silver livery of advised age,
And in thy reverence and thy chair-days thus
To die in ruffian battle ? Even at this sight
My heart is turn'd to stone ; and while 'tis mine   50
It shall be stony. York not our old men spares ;
No more will I their babes. Tears virginal
Shall be to me even as the dew to fire ;
And beauty, that the tyrant oft reclaims,
Shall to my flaming wrath be oil and flax. 55
Henceforth I will not have to do with pity :
Meet I an infant of the house of York,
Into as many gobbets will I cut it
As wild Medea young Absyrtus did ;
In cruelty will I seek out my fame.   60
Come, thou new ruin of old Clifford's house ;
As did Æneas old Anchises bear,
So bear I thee upon my manly shoulders ;
But then Æneas bare a living load,
Nothing so heavy as these woes of mine.   65
                      [*Exit with the body.*

Enter RICHARD *and* SOMERSET *to fight. Somerset is killed.*

Rich. So, lie thou there ;
For underneath an alehouse' paltry sign,
The Castle in Saint Albans, Somerset
Hath made the wizard famous in his death.
Sword, hold thy temper ; heart, be wrathful still :   70
Priests pray for enemies, but princes kill.
                                                          [*Exit.*

Fight. Excursions. Enter KING, QUEEN, *and Others.*

Queen. Away, my lord ! You are slow ; for shame, away !
King. Can we outrun the heavens ? Good Margaret, stay.
Queen. What are you made of ? You'll nor fight nor fly.   74
Now is it manhood, wisdom, and defence,
To give the enemy way, and to secure us

By what we can, which can no more but fly.
                              [*Alarum afar off.*
If you be ta'en, we then should see the
      bottom
Of all our fortunes; but if we haply
      scape—
As well we may, if not through your
      neglect—   80
We shall to London get, where you are
      lov'd,
And where this breach now in our fortunes
      made
May readily be stopp'd.

    Re-enter young CLIFFORD.

  Y. Clif. But that my heart's on future
      mischief set,   84
I would speak blasphemy ere bid you fly;
But fly you must; uncurable discomfit
Reigns in the hearts of all our present
      parts.
Away, for your relief! and we will live
To see their day and them our fortune give.
Away, my lord, away!   [*Exeunt.*

  SCENE III. *Fields near Saint Albans.*

Alarum. Retreat. Enter YORK, RICHARD,
  WARWICK, *and* Soldiers, *with drum and
  colours.*

  York. Of Salisbury, who can report of
      him,
That winter lion, who in rage forgets
Aged contusions and all brush of time
And, like a gallant in the brow of youth,
Repairs him with occasion? This happy
      day   5
Is not itself, nor have we won one foot,
If Salisbury be lost.
  Rich.   My noble father,

Three times to-day I holp him to his horse,
Three times bestrid him, thrice I led him off,
Persuaded him from any further act;   10
But still where danger was, still there I
      met him;
And like rich hangings in a homely house,
So was his will in his old feeble body.
But, noble as he is, look where he comes.

    Enter SALISBURY.

  Sal. Now, by my sword, well hast thou
      fought to-day!
By th' mass, so did we all. I thank you,
      Richard: 16
God knows how long it is I have to live,
And it hath pleas'd Him that three times
      to-day
You have defended me from imminent
      death.
Well, lords, we have not got that which we
      have;   20
'Tis not enough our foes are this time fled,
Being opposites of such repairing nature.
  York. I know our safety is to follow
      them;
For, as I hear, the King is fled to London
To call a present court of Parliament. 25
Let us pursue him ere the writs go forth.
What says Lord Warwick? Shall we after
      them?
  War. After them? Nay, before them, if
      we can.
Now, by my faith, lords, 'twas a glorious
      day:
Saint Albans' battle, won by famous York,
Shall be eterniz'd in all age to come. 31
Sound drum and trumpets and to London
      all;
And more such days as these to us befall!
                              [*Exeunt.*

THE THIRD PART OF
KING HENRY THE SIXTH

DRAMATIS PERSONÆ

KING HENRY THE SIXTH.
EDWARD, PRINCE OF WALES, *his son.*
LOUIS XI, *King of France.*
DUKE OF SOMERSET.
DUKE OF EXETER.
EARL OF OXFORD.
EARL OF NORTHUMBERLAND.
EARL OF WESTMORELAND.
LORD CLIFFORD.
RICHARD PLANTAGENET, *Duke of York.*
EDWARD, *Earl of March, after-* ⎤
   wards King Edward IV, ⎟
EDMUND, *Earl of Rutland,* ⎟
GEORGE, *afterwards Duke of* ⎬ *his sons.*
   Clarence, ⎟
RICHARD, *afterwards Duke of* ⎟
   Gloucester, ⎦
DUKE OF NORFOLK.
MARQUIS OF MONTAGUE.
EARL OF WARWICK.
EARL OF PEMBROKE.
LORD HASTINGS.
LORD STAFFORD.

SIR JOHN MORTIMER, ⎤ *uncles to the*
SIR HUGH MORTIMER, ⎦ *Duke of York.*
HENRY, *Earl of Richmond, a youth.*
LORD RIVERS, *brother to Lady Grey.*
SIR WILLIAM STANLEY.
SIR JOHN MONTGOMERY.
SIR JOHN SOMERVILLE.
Tutor, *to Rutland.*
Mayor of York.
Lieutenant of the Tower.
A Nobleman.
Two Keepers.
A Huntsman.
A Son *that has killed his father.*
A Father *that has killed his son.*

QUEEN MARGARET.
LADY GREY, *afterwards Queen to Edward IV.*
BONA, *sister to the French Queen.*

Soldiers, Attendants, Messengers, Watchmen, &c.

THE SCENE: *England and France.*

ACT ONE

SCENE I. *London. The Parliament House.*

Alarum. Enter DUKE OF YORK, EDWARD, RICHARD, NORFOLK, MONTAGUE, WARWICK, *and* Soldiers, *with white roses in their hats.*

War. I wonder how the King escap'd our hands.
York. While we pursu'd the horsemen of the north,
He slily stole away and left his men;
Whereat the great Lord of Northumberland,
Whose warlike ears could never brook retreat,   5
Cheer'd up the drooping army, and himself,
Lord Clifford, and Lord Stafford, all abreast,
Charg'd our main battle's front, and, breaking in,
Were by the swords of common soldiers slain.
Edw. Lord Stafford's father, Duke of Buckingham,   10
Is either slain or wounded dangerous;
I cleft his beaver with a downright blow.

That this is true, father, behold his blood.
Mont. And, brother, here's the Earl of Wiltshire's blood,   14
Whom I encount'red as the battles join'd.
Rich. Speak thou for me, and tell them what I did.
   [*Throwing down Somerset's head.*
York. Richard hath best deserv'd of all my sons.
But is your Grace dead, my Lord of Somerset?
Norf. Such hope have all the line of John of Gaunt!
Rich. Thus do I hope to shake King Henry's head.   20
War. And so do I. Victorious Prince of York,
Before I see thee seated in that throne
Which now the house of Lancaster usurps,
I vow by heaven these eyes shall never close.
This is the palace of the fearful King,   25
And this the regal seat. Possess it, York;
For this is thine, and not King Henry's heirs'.
York. Assist me then, sweet Warwick, and I will;
For hither we have broken in by force.

Norf. We'll all assist you ; he that flies
   shall die.	30
York. Thanks, gentle Norfolk. Stay by
   me, my lords ;
And, soldiers, stay and lodge by me this
   night.	[*They go up.*
War. And when the King comes, offer
   him no violence,
Unless he seek to thrust you out perforce.
York. The Queen this day here holds her
   parliament,	35
But little thinks we shall be of her council.
By words or blows here let us win our right.
Rich. Arm'd as we are, let's stay within
   this house.
War. The bloody parliament shall this be
   call'd,	39
Unless Plantagenet, Duke of York, be King,
And bashful Henry depos'd, whose
   cowardice
Hath made us by-words to our enemies.
York. Then leave me not, my lords ; be
   resolute :
I mean to take possession of my right.
War. Neither the King, nor he that loves
   him best,	45
The proudest he that holds up Lancaster,
Dares stir a wing if Warwick shake his bells.
I'll plant Plantagenet, root him up who
   dares.
Resolve thee, Richard ; claim the English
   crown.	[*York occupies the throne*

Flourish. Enter KING HENRY, CLIFFORD,
NORTHUMBERLAND, WESTMORELAND, EX-
ETER, *and* Others, *with red roses in their
hats.*

K. Hen. My lords, look where the sturdy
   rebel sits,	50
Even in the chair of state ! Belike he
   means,
Back'd by the power of Warwick, that false
   peer,
To aspire unto the crown and reign as king.
Earl of Northumberland, he slew thy
   father ;
And thine, Lord Clifford ; and you both
   have vow'd revenge	55
On him, his sons, his favourites, and his
   friends.
North. If I be not, heavens be reveng'd
   on me !
Clif. The hope thereof makes Clifford
   mourn in steel.
West. What, shall we suffer this ? Let's
   pluck him down ;
My heart for anger burns ; I cannot brook
   it.	60
K. Hen. Be patient, gentle Earl of West-
   moreland.
Clif. Patience is for poltroons such as he ;
He durst not sit there had your father liv'd.
My gracious lord, here in the parliament
Let us assail the family of York.	65

North. Well hast thou spoken, cousin ;
   be it so.
K. Hen. Ah, know you not the city
   favours them,
And they have troops of soldiers at their
   beck ?
Exe. But when the Duke is slain they'll
   quickly fly.
K. Hen. Far be the thought of this from
   Henry's heart,	70
To make a shambles of the parliament
   house !
Cousin of Exeter, frowns, words, and
   threats,
Shall be the war that Henry means to use.
Thou factious Duke of York, descend my
   throne	74
And kneel for grace and mercy at my feet ;
I am thy sovereign.
York.	I am thine.
Exe. For shame, come down ; he made
   thee Duke of York.
York. 'Twas my inheritance, as the earl-
   dom was.
Exe. Thy father was a traitor to the
   crown.
War. Exeter, thou art a traitor to the
   crown	80
In following this usurping Henry.
Clif. Whom should he follow but his
   natural king ?
War. True, Clifford ; and that's Richard
   Duke of York.
K. Hen. And shall I stand, and thou sit in
   my throne ?
York. It must and shall be so ; content
   thyself.	85
War. Be Duke of Lancaster ; let him be
   King.
West. He is both King and Duke of
   Lancaster ;
And that the Lord of Westmoreland shall
   maintain.
War. And Warwick shall disprove it.
   You forget
That we are those which chas'd you from
   the field,	90
And slew your fathers, and with colours
   spread
March'd through the city to the palace
   gates.
North. Yes, Warwick, I remember it to
   my grief ;
And, by his soul, thou and thy house shall
   rue it.
West. Plantagenet, of thee, and these thy
   sons,	95
Thy kinsmen, and thy friends, I'll have
   more lives
Than drops of blood were in my father's
   veins.
Clif. Urge it no more ; lest that instead
   of words
I send thee, Warwick, such a messenger

As shall revenge his death before I stir. 100
  War. Poor Clifford, how I scorn his worthless threats !
  York. Will you we show our title to the crown ?
If not, our swords shall plead it in the field.
  K. Hen. What title hast thou, traitor, to the crown ?
Thy father was, as thou art, Duke of York ;
Thy grandfather, Roger Mortimer, Earl of March : 106
I am the son of Henry the Fifth,
Who made the Dauphin and the French to stoop,
And seiz'd upon their towns and provinces.
  War. Talk not of France, sith thou hast lost it all. 110
  K. Hen. The Lord Protector lost it, and not I :
When I was crown'd, I was but nine months old.
  Rich. You are old enough now, and yet methinks you lose.
Father, tear the crown from the usurper's head.
  Edw. Sweet father, do so ; set it on your head. 115
  Mont. Good brother, as thou lov'st and honourest arms,
Let's fight it out and not stand cavilling thus.
  Rich. Sound drums and trumpets, and the King will fly.
  York. Sons, peace !
  K. Hen. Peace thou ! and give King Henry leave to speak. 120
  War. Plantagenet shall speak first. Hear him, lords ;
And be you silent and attentive too,
For he that interrupts him shall not live.
  K. Hen. Think'st thou that I will leave my kingly throne, 124
Wherein my grandsire and my father sat ?
No ; first shall war unpeople this my realm;
Ay, and their colours, often borne in France,
And now in England to our heart's great sorrow,
Shall be my winding-sheet. Why faint you, lords ?
My title's good, and better far than his. 130
  War. Prove it, Henry, and thou shalt be King.
  K. Hen. Henry the Fourth by conquest got the crown.
  York. 'Twas by rebellion against his king.
  K. Hen. [*Aside*] I know not what to say ; my title's weak.—
Tell me, may not a king adopt an heir ? 135
  York. What then ?
  K. Hen. An if he may, then am I lawful King ;
For Richard, in the view of many lords,

Resign'd the crown to Henry the Fourth,
Whose heir my father was, and I am his. 140
  York. He rose against him, being his sovereign,
And made him to resign his crown perforce.
  War. Suppose, my lords, he did it unconstrain'd,
Think you 'twere prejudicial to his crown ?
  Exe. No ; for he could not so resign his crown 145
But that the next heir should succeed and reign.
  K. Hen. Art thou against us, Duke of Exeter ?
  Exe. His is the right, and therefore pardon me.
  York. Why whisper you, my lords, and answer not ?
  Exe. My conscience tells me he is lawful King. 150
  K. Hen. [*Aside*] All will revolt from me, and turn to him.
  North. Plantagenet, for all the claim thou lay'st,
Think not that Henry shall be so depos'd.
  War. Depos'd he shall be, in despite of all.
  North. Thou art deceiv'd. 'Tis not thy southern power 155
Of Essex, Norfolk, Suffolk, nor of Kent,
Which makes thee thus presumptuous and proud,
Can set the Duke up in despite of me.
  Clif. King Henry, be thy title right or wrong,
Lord Clifford vows to fight in thy defence.
May that ground gape, and swallow me alive, 161
Where I shall kneel to him that slew my father !
  K. Hen. O Clifford, how thy words revive my heart !
  York. Henry of Lancaster, resign thy crown.
What mutter you, or what conspire you, lords ? 165
  War. Do right unto this princely Duke of York ;
Or I will fill the house with armed men,
And over the chair of state, where now he sits,
Write up his title with usurping blood.
  [*He stamps with his foot and the Soldiers show themselves.*
  K. Hen. My Lord of Warwick, hear but one word : 170
Let me for this my life-time reign as king.
  York. Confirm the crown to me and to mine heirs,
And thou shalt reign in quiet while thou liv'st.
  K. Hen. I am content. Richard Plantagenet,
Enjoy the kingdom after my decease. 175

Clif. What wrong is this unto the Prince
   your son !
War. What good is this to England and
   himself !
West. Base, fearful, and despairing
   Henry !
Clif. How hast thou injur'd both thyself
   and us !
West. I cannot stay to hear these
   articles.   180
North. Nor I.
Clif. Come, cousin, let us tell the Queen
   these news.
West. Farewell, faint-hearted and degen-
   erate king,
In whose cold blood no spark of honour
   bides.
North. Be thou a prey unto the house of
   York   185
And die in bands for this unmanly deed !
Clif. In dreadful war mayst thou be
   overcome,
Or live in peace abandon'd and despis'd !
   [*Exeunt Northumberland, Clifford and*
      Westmoreland.
War. Turn this way, Henry, and regard
   them not.
Exe. They seek revenge, and therefore
   will not yield.   190
K. Hen. Ah, Exeter !
War. Why should you sigh, my lord ?
K. Hen. Not for myself, Lord Warwick,
   but my son,
Whom I unnaturally shall disinherit.
But be it as it may. [*To York*] I here entail
The crown to thee and to thine heirs for
   ever ;   195
Conditionally, that here thou take an
   oath
To cease this civil war, and, whilst I live,
To honour me as thy king and sovereign,
And neither by treason nor hostility   199
To seek to put me down and reign thyself.
York. This oath I willingly take, and will
   perform. [*Coming from the throne.*
War. Long live King Henry ! Planta-
   genet, embrace him.
K. Hen. And long live thou, and these
   thy forward sons !
York. Now York and Lancaster are
   reconcil'd.
Exe. Accurs'd be he that seeks to make
   them foes !   205
   [*Sennet. Here they come down.*
York. Farewell, my gracious lord ; I'll to
   my castle.
War. And I'll keep London with my
   soldiers.
Norf. And I to Norfolk with my
   followers.
Mont. And I unto the sea, from whence
   I came.   [*Exeunt the Yorkists.*
K. Hen. And I, with grief and sorrow, to
   the court.   210

Enter QUEEN MARGARET *and the* PRINCE
OF WALES.

Exe. Here comes the Queen, whose looks
   bewray her anger.
I'll steal away.
K. Hen.   Exeter, so will I.
Q. Mar. Nay, go not from me ; I will
   follow thee.
K. Hen. Be patient, gentle queen, and I
   will stay.
Q. Mar. Who can be patient in such
   extremes ?   215
Ah, wretched man ! Would I had died a
   maid,
And never seen thee, never borne thee son,
Seeing thou hast prov'd so unnatural a
   father !
Hath he deserv'd to lose his birthright
   thus ?   219
Hadst thou but lov'd him half so well as I,
Or felt that pain which I did for him once,
Or nourish'd him as I did with my blood,
Thou wouldst have left thy dearest heart-
   blood there
Rather than have made that savage duke
   thine heir,
And disinherited thine only son.   225
Prince. Father, you cannot disinherit
   me.
If you be King, why should not I succeed ?
K. Hen. Pardon me, Margaret ; pardon
   me, sweet son.
The Earl of Warwick and the Duke enforc'd
   me.
Q. Mar. Enforc'd thee ! Art thou King
   and wilt be forc'd ?   230
I shame to hear thee speak. Ah, timorous
   wretch !
Thou hast undone thyself, thy son, and me ;
And giv'n unto the house of York such
   head
As thou shalt reign but by their sufferance.
To entail him and his heirs unto the crown,
What is it but to make thy sepulchre   236
And creep into it far before thy time ?
Warwick is Chancellor and the lord of
   Calais ;
Stern Falconbridge commands the narrow
   seas ;
The Duke is made Protector of the realm ;
And yet shalt thou be safe ? Such safety
   finds   241
The trembling lamb environed with wolves.
Had I been there, which am a silly woman,
The soldiers should have toss'd me on their
   pikes
Before I would have granted to that act. 245
But thou prefer'st thy life before thine
   honour ;
And seeing thou dost, I here divorce myself
Both from thy table, Henry, and thy bed,
Until that act of parliament be repeal'd
Whereby my son is disinherited.   250

665

The northern lords that have forsworn thy
    colours
Will follow mine, if once they see them
    spread ;
And spread they shall be, to thy foul
    disgrace
And utter ruin of the house of York.
Thus do I leave thee. Come, son, let's
    away ;   255
Our army is ready ; come, we'll after them.
    K. Hen. Stay, gentle Margaret, and hear
    me speak.
    Q. Mar. Thou hast spoke too much
    already ; get thee gone.
    K. Hen. Gentle son Edward, thou wilt
    stay with me ?
    Q. Mar. Ay, to be murder'd by his
    enemies.   260
    Prince. When I return with victory from
    the field
I'll see your Grace ; till then I'll follow her.
    Q. Mar. Come, son, away ; we may not
    linger thus. [*Exeunt Queen Margaret
              and the Prince.*
    K. Hen. Poor queen ! How love to me
    and to her son
Hath made her break out into terms of
    rage !   265
Reveng'd may she be on that hateful Duke,
Whose haughty spirit, winged with desire,
Will cost my crown, and like an empty eagle
Tire on the flesh of me and of my son !
The loss of those three lords torments my
    heart.   270
I'll write unto them, and entreat them fair ;
Come, cousin, you shall be the messenger.
    Exe. And I, I hope, shall reconcile them
    all.   [*Exeunt.*

SCENE II. *Sandal Castle, near Wakefield, in
    Yorkshire.*

Flourish. Enter EDWARD, RICHARD, *and*
    MONTAGUE.

    Rich. Brother, though I be youngest, give
    me leave.
    Edw. No, I can better play the orator.
    Mont. But I have reasons strong and
    forcible.

Enter the DUKE OF YORK.

    York. Why, how now, sons and brother !
    at a strife ?   4
What is your quarrel ? How began it first ?
    Edw. No quarrel, but a slight contention.
    York. About what ?
    Rich. About that which concerns your
    Grace and us—
The crown of England, father, which is
    yours.
    York. Mine, boy ? Not till King Henry
    be dead.   10
    Rich. Your right depends not on his life
    or death.

    Edw. Now you are heir, therefore enjoy
    it now.
By giving the house of Lancaster leave to
    breathe,
It will outrun you, father, in the end.
    York. I took an oath that he should
    quietly reign.   15
    Edw. But for a kingdom any oath may be
    broken :
I would break a thousand oaths to reign
    one year. '
    Rich. No ; God forbid your Grace should
    be forsworn.
    York. I shall be, if I claim by open
    war.
    Rich. I'll prove the contrary, if you'll
    hear me speak.   20
    York. Thou canst not, son ; it is im-
    possible.
    Rich. An oath is of no moment, being not
    took
Before a true and lawful magistrate
That hath authority over him that swears.
Henry had none, but did usurp the place ;
Then, seeing 'twas he that made you to
    depose,   26
Your oath, my lord, is vain and frivolous.
Therefore, to arms. And, father, do but
    think
How sweet a thing it is to wear a crown,
Within whose circuit is Elysium   30
And all that poets feign of bliss and joy.
Why do we linger thus ? I cannot rest
Until the white rose that I wear be dy'd
Even in the lukewarm blood of Henry's
    heart.
    York. Richard, enough ; I will be King,
    or die.   35
Brother, thou shalt to London presently
And whet on Warwick to this enterprise.
Thou, Richard, shalt to the Duke of
    Norfolk
And tell him privily of our intent.   39
You, Edward, shall unto my Lord Cobham,
With whom the Kentishmen will willingly
    rise ;
In them I trust, for they are soldiers,
Witty, courteous, liberal, full of spirit.
While you are thus employ'd, what resteth
    more
But that I seek occasion how to rise,   45
And yet the King not privy to my drift,
Nor any of the house of Lancaster ?

Enter a Messenger.

But, stay. What news ? Why com'st thou
    in such post ?
    Mess. The Queen with all the northern
    earls and lords
Intend here to besiege you in your castle. 50
She is hard by with twenty thousand men ;
And therefore fortify your hold, my lord.
    York. Ay, with my sword. What !
    think'st thou that we fear them ?

Edward and Richard, you shall stay with
me ;   54
My brother Montague shall post to London.
Let noble Warwick, Cobham, and the rest,
Whom we have left protectors of the King,
With pow'rful policy strengthen themselves
And trust not simple Henry nor his oaths.
    Mont. Brother, I go ; I'll win them, fear
        it not.   60
And thus most humbly I do take my leave.
                                            [*Exit.*

Enter SIR JOHN *and* SIR HUGH
        MORTIMER.

    York. Sir John and Sir Hugh Mortimer,
        mine uncles !
You are come to Sandal in a happy hour ;
The army of the Queen mean to besiege us.
    Sir John. She shall not need ; we'll meet
        her in the field.   65
    York. What, with five thousand men ?
    Rich. Ay, with five hundred, father, for a
        need.
A woman's general ; what should we fear ?
                                    [*A march afar off.*
    Edw. I hear their drums. Let's set our
        men in order,
And issue forth and bid them battle
        straight.   70
    York. Five men to twenty ! Though the
        odds be great,
I doubt not, uncle, of our victory.
Many a battle have I won in France,
When as the enemy hath been ten to one ;
Why should I not now have the like
        success ?   [*Exeunt.*

SCENE III.   *Field of battle between Sandal
        Castle and Wakefield.*

Alarum.   Enter RUTLAND *and his* Tutor.

    Rut. Ah, whither shall I fly to scape their
        hands ?
Ah, tutor, look where bloody Clifford
        comes !

Enter CLIFFORD *and* Soldiers.

    Clif. Chaplain, away ! Thy priesthood
        saves thy life.
As for the brat of this accursed duke,
Whose father slew my father, he shall die. 5
    Tut. And I, my lord, will bear him com-
        pany.
    Clif. Soldiers, away with him !
    Tut. Ah, Clifford, murder not this
        innocent child,
Lest thou be hated both of God and man.
                        [*Exit, forced off by Soldiers.*
    Clif. How now, is he dead already ? Or
        is it fear   10
That makes him close his eyes ? I'll open
        them.
    Rut. So looks the pent-up lion o'er the
        wretch

That trembles under his devouring paws ;
And so he walks, insulting o'er his prey, 14
And so he comes, to rend his limbs asunder.
Ah, gentle Clifford, kill me with thy sword,
And not with such a cruel threat'ning look !
Sweet Clifford, hear me speak before I die.
I am too mean a subject for thy wrath ;
Be thou reveng'd on men, and let me live. 20
    Clif. In vain thou speak'st, poor boy ;
        my father's blood
Hath stopp'd the passage where thy words
        should enter.
    Rut. Then let my father's blood open it
        again :
He is a man, and, Clifford, cope with him.
    Clif. Had I thy brethren here, their lives
        and thine   25
Were not revenge sufficient for me ;
No, if I digg'd up thy forefathers' graves
And hung their rotten coffins up in chains,
It could not slake mine ire nor ease my
        heart.
The sight of any of the house of York   30
Is as a fury to torment my soul ;
And till I root out their accursed line
And leave not one alive, I live in hell.
Therefore—
    Rut. O, let me pray before I take my
        death !   35
To thee I pray : sweet Clifford, pity me.
    Clif. Such pity as my rapier's point
        affords.
    Rut. I never did thee harm ; why wilt
        thou slay me ?
    Clif. Thy father hath.
    Rut.   But 'twas ere I was born.
Thou hast one son ; for his sake pity me, 40
Lest in revenge thereof, sith God is just,
He be as miserably slain as I.
Ah, let me live in prison all my days ;
And when I give occasion of offence
Then let me die, for now thou hast no
        cause.   45
    Clif. No cause !
Thy father slew my father ; therefore, die.
                                        [*Stabs him.*
    Rut. Di faciant laudis summa sit ista
        tuae !   [*Dies.*
    Clif. Plantagenet, I come, Plantagenet !
And this thy son's blood cleaving to my
        blade   50
Shall rust upon my weapon, till thy blood,
Congeal'd with this, do make me wipe off
        both.   [*Exit.*

SCENE IV.   *Another part of the field.*

Alarum.   Enter the DUKE OF YORK.

    York. The army of the Queen hath got
        the field.
My uncles both are slain in rescuing me ;
And all my followers to the eager foe
Turn back and fly, like ships before the
        wind,

Or lambs pursu'd by hunger-starved
   wolves.   5
My sons—God knows what hath bechanced
   them ;
But this I know—they have demean'd
   themselves
Like men born to renown by life or death.
Three times did Richard make a lane to
   me,
And thrice cried ' Courage, father ! fight
   it out '.   10
And full as oft came Edward to my side
With purple falchion, painted to the hilt
In blood of those that had encount'red
   him.
And when the hardiest warriors did retire,
Richard cried ' Charge, and give no foot of
   ground '.   15
And cried ' A crown, or else a glorious
   tomb !
A sceptre, or an earthly sepulchre ! '
With this we charg'd again ; but out alas !
We bodg'd again ; as I have seen a swan
With bootless labour swim against the tide
And spend her strength with over-matching
   waves.   [A short alarum within.
Ah, hark ! The fatal followers do pursue,
And I am faint and cannot fly their fury ;
And were I strong, I would not shun their
   fury.
The sands are numb'red that make up my
   life ;   25
Here must I stay, and here my life must
   end.

Enter QUEEN MARGARET, CLIFFORD, NORTH-
UMBERLAND, *the* PRINCE OF WALES, *and*
Soldiers.

Come, bloody Clifford, rough Northumber-
   land,
I dare your quenchless fury to more rage ;
I am your butt, and I abide your shot.
   North. Yield to our mercy, proud
   Plantagenet.   30
   Clif. Ay, to such mercy as his ruthless
   arm
With downright payment show'd unto my
   father.
Now Phaethon hath tumbled from his car,
And made an evening at the noontide prick.
   York. My ashes, as the phœnix, may
   bring forth   35
A bird that will revenge upon you all ;
And in that hope I throw mine eyes to
   heaven,
Scorning whate'er you can afflict me with.
Why come you not ? What ! multitudes,
   and fear ?
   Clif. So cowards fight when they can fly
   no further ;   40
So doves do peck the falcon's piercing
   talons ;
So desperate thieves, all hopeless of their
   lives,

Breathe out invectives 'gainst the officers.
   York. O Clifford, but bethink thee once
   again,
And in thy thought o'errun my former
   time ;   45
And, if thou canst for blushing, view this
   face,
And bite thy tongue that slanders him with
   cowardice
Whose frown hath made thee faint and fly
   ere this !
   Clif. I will not bandy with thee word for
   word,
But buckler with thee blows, twice two for
   one.   50
   Q. Mar. Hold, valiant Clifford ; for a
   thousand causes
I would prolong awhile the traitor's life.
Wrath makes him deaf ; speak thou,
   Northumberland.
   North. Hold, Clifford ! do not honour him
   so much
To prick thy finger, though to wound his
   heart.   55
What valour were it, when a cur doth grin,
For one to thrust his hand between his
   teeth,
When he might spurn him with his foot
   away ?
It is war's prize to take all vantages ;
And ten to one is no impeach of valour.   60
   [*They lay hands on York, who struggles.*
   Clif. Ay, ay, so strives the woodcock
   with the gin.
   North. So doth the cony struggle in the
   net.
   York. So triumph thieves upon their con-
   quer'd booty ;
So true men yield, with robbers so o'er-
   match'd.
   North. What would your Grace have done
   unto him now ?   65
   Q. Mar. Brave warriors, Clifford and
   Northumberland,
Come, make him stand upon this molehill
   here
That raught at mountains with out-
   stretched arms,
Yet parted but the shadow with his hand.
What, was it you that would be England's
   king ?   70
Was't you that revell'd in our parliament
And made a preachment of your high
   descent ?
Where are your mess of sons to back you
   now ?
The wanton Edward and the lusty George ?
And where's that valiant crook-back
   prodigy,   75
Dicky your boy, that with his grumbling
   voice
Was wont to cheer his dad in mutinies ?
Or, with the rest, where is your darling
   Rutland ?

Look, York: I stain'd this napkin with the
blood 79
That valiant Clifford with his rapier's point
Made issue from the bosom of the boy;
And if thine eyes can water for his death,
I give thee this to dry thy cheeks withal.
Alas, poor York! but that I hate thee
deadly,
I should lament thy miserable state. 85
I prithee grieve to make me merry, York.
What, hath thy fiery heart so parch'd thine
entrails
That not a tear can fall for Rutland's death?
Why art thou patient, man? Thou shouldst
be mad;
And I to make thee mad do mock thee thus.
Stamp, rave, and fret, that I may sing and
dance. 91
Thou wouldst be fee'd, I see, to make me
sport;
York cannot speak unless he wear a crown.
A crown for York!—and, lords, bow low to
him.
Hold you his hands whilst I do set it on. 95
[*Putting a paper crown on his head.*
Ay, marry, sir, now looks he like a king!
Ay, this is he that took King Henry's chair,
And this is he was his adopted heir.
But how is it that great Plantagenet
Is crown'd so soon and broke his solemn
oath? 100
As I bethink me, you should not be King
Till our King Henry had shook hands with
death.
And will you pale your head in Henry's
glory,
And rob his temples of the diadem,
Now in his life, against your holy oath? 105
O, 'tis a fault too too unpardonable!
Off with the crown and with the crown his
head;
And, whilst we breathe, take time to do him
dead.

Clif. That is my office, for my father's
sake.

Q. Mar. Nay, stay; let's hear the orisons
he makes. 110

York. She-wolf of France, but worse than
wolves of France,
Whose tongue more poisons than the
adder's tooth!
How ill-beseeming is it in thy sex
To triumph like an Amazonian trull 114
Upon their woes whom fortune captivates!
But that thy face is visard-like, unchanging,
Made impudent with use of evil deeds,
I would assay, proud queen, to make thee
blush.
To tell thee whence thou cam'st, of whom
deriv'd,
Were shame enough to shame thee, wert
thou not shameless. 120
Thy father bears the type of King of
Naples,
Of both the Sicils and Jerusalem,
Yet not so wealthy as an English yeoman.
Hath that poor monarch taught thee to
insult?
It needs not, nor it boots thee not, proud
queen; 125
Unless the adage must be verified,
That beggars mounted run their horse to
death.
'Tis beauty that doth oft make women
proud;
But, God He knows, thy share thereof is
small.
'Tis virtue that doth make them most
admir'd; 130
The contrary doth make thee wond'red at.
'Tis government that makes them seem
divine;
The want thereof makes thee abominable.
Thou art as opposite to every good
As the Antipodes are unto us, 135
Or as the south to the septentrion.
O tiger's heart wrapp'd in a woman's hide!
How couldst thou drain the life-blood of
the child,
To bid the father wipe his eyes withal,
And yet be seen to bear a woman's face? 140
Women are soft, mild, pitiful, and flexible:
Thou stern, obdurate, flinty, rough, remorse-
less.
Bid'st thou me rage? Why, now thou
hast thy wish;
Wouldst have me weep? Why, now thou
hast thy will;
For raging wind blows up incessant
showers, 145
And when the rage allays, the rain begins.
These tears are my sweet Rutland's
obsequies;
And every drop cries vengeance for his
death
'Gainst thee, fell Clifford, and thee, false
Frenchwoman.

North. Beshrew me, but his passions
move me so 150
That hardly can I check my eyes from
tears.

York. That face of his the hungry
cannibals
Would not have touch'd, would not have
stain'd with blood;
But you are more inhuman, more inexor-
able— 154
O, ten times more—than tigers of Hyrcania.
See, ruthless queen, a hapless father's tears.
This cloth thou dipp'dst in blood of my
sweet boy,
And I with tears do wash the blood away.
Keep thou the napkin, and go boast of this;
And if thou tell'st the heavy story right, 160
Upon my soul, the hearers will shed tears;
Yea, even my foes will shed fast-falling
tears
And say 'Alas, it was a piteous deed!'

There, take the crown, and with the crown
   my curse;   164
And if thy need such comfort come to thee
As now I reap at thy too cruel hand!
Hard-hearted Clifford, take me from the
   world;
My soul to heaven, my blood upon your
   heads!
   North. Had he been slaughter-man to all
      my kin,   169
I should not for my life but weep with him,
To see how inly sorrow gripes his soul.
   Q. Mar. What, weeping-ripe, my Lord
      Northumberland?
Think but upon the wrong he did us all,
And that will quickly dry thy melting tears.
   Clif. Here's for my oath, here's for my
      father's death.   [*Stabbing him.*
   Q. Mar. And here's to right our gentle-
      hearted king.   [*Stabbing him.*
   York. Open Thy gate of mercy, gracious
      God!
My soul flies through these wounds to seek
   out Thee.   [*Dies.*
   Q. Mar. Off with his head, and set it on
   York gates;   179
So York may overlook the town of York.
           [*Flourish. Exeunt.*

ACT TWO

SCENE I. *A plain near Mortimer's Cross in
   Herefordshire.*

A march. Enter EDWARD, RICHARD, *and
   their* POWER.

   Edw. I wonder how our princely father
      scap'd,
Or whether he be scap'd away or no
From Clifford's and Northumberland's
   pursuit.
Had he been ta'en, we should have heard
   the news;
Had he been slain, we should have heard the
   news;   5
Or had he scap'd, methinks we should have
   heard
The happy tidings of his good escape.
How fares my brother? Why is he so sad?
   Rich. I cannot joy until I be resolv'd
Where our right valiant father is become. 10
I saw him in the battle range about,
And watch'd him how he singled Clifford
   forth.
Methought he bore him in the thickest
   troop
As doth a lion in a heard of neat;   14
Or as a bear, encompass'd round with dogs,
Who having pinch'd a few and made them
   cry,
The rest stand all aloof and bark at him.
So far'd our father with his enemies;
So fled his enemies my warlike father.
Methinks 'tis prize enough to be his son. 20

See how the morning opes her golden gates
And takes her farewell of the glorious sun.
How well resembles it the prime of youth,
Trimm'd like a younker prancing to his
   love!
   Edw. Dazzle mine eyes, or do I see three
      suns?   25
   Rich. Three glorious suns, each one a
      perfect sun;
Not separated with the racking clouds,
But sever'd in a pale clear-shining sky.
See, see! they join, embrace, and seem to
   kiss,
As if they vow'd some league inviolable. 30
Now are they but one lamp, one light, one
   sun.
In this the heaven figures some event.
   Edw. 'Tis wondrous strange, the like yet
      never heard of.
I think it cites us, brother, to the field,
That we, the sons of brave Plantagenet, 35
Each one already blazing by our meeds,
Should notwithstanding join our lights
   together
And overshine the earth, as this the world.
Whate'er it bodes, henceforward will I bear
Upon my target three fair shining suns. 40
   Rich. Nay, bear three daughters—by
      your leave I speak it,
You love the breeder better than the male.

Enter a MESSENGER, *blowing.*

But what art thou, whose heavy looks
   foretell
Some dreadful story hanging on thy
   tongue?
   Mess. Ah, one that was a woeful looker-
      on   45
When as the noble Duke of York was slain,
Your princely father and my loving lord!
   Edw. O, speak no more! for I have
      heard too much.
   Rich. Say how he died, for I will hear
      it all.   49
   Mess. Environed he was with many foes,
And stood against them as the hope of Troy
Against the Greeks that would have ent'red
   Troy.
But Hercules himself must yield to odds;
And many strokes, though with a little axe,
Hews down and fells the hardest-timber'd
   oak.   55
By many hands your father was subdu'd;
But only slaught'red by the ireful arm
Of unrelenting Clifford and the Queen,
Who crown'd the gracious Duke in high
   despite,
Laugh'd in his face; and when with grief
   he wept,   60
The ruthless Queen gave him to dry his
   cheeks
A napkin steeped in the harmless blood
Of sweet young Rutland, by rough Clifford
   slain;

And after many scorns, many foul taunts,
They took his head, and on the gates of
    York   65
They set the same ; and there it doth
    remain,
The saddest spectacle that e'er I view'd.
    Edw. Sweet Duke of York, our prop to
        lean upon,
Now thou art gone, we have no staff, no
    stay.
O Clifford, boist'rous Clifford, thou hast
    slain   70
The flow'r of Europe for his chivalry ;
And treacherously hast thou vanquish'd
    him,
For hand to hand he would have van-
    quish'd thee.
Now my soul's palace is become a prison.
Ah, would she break from hence, that this
    my body   75
Might in the ground be closed up in rest !
For never henceforth shall I joy again ;
Never, O never, shall I see more joy.
    Rich. I cannot weep, for all my body's
        moisture
Scarce serves to quench my furnace-
    burning heart ;   80
Nor can my tongue unload my heart's great
    burden,
For self-same wind that I should speak
    withal
Is kindling coals that fires all my breast,
And burns me up with flames that tears
    would quench.
To weep is to make less the depth of grief. 85
Tears then for babes ; blows and revenge
    for me !
Richard, I bear thy name ; I'll venge thy
    death,
Or die renowned by attempting it.
    Edw. His name that valiant duke hath
        left with thee ;   89
His dukedom and his chair with me is
    left.
    Rich. Nay, if thou be that princely eagle's
        bird,
Show thy descent by gazing 'gainst the sun;
For chair and dukedom, throne and king-
    dom, say :
Either that is thine, or else thou wert not
    his.

March. Enter WARWICK, MONTAGUE, *and
    their* Army.

    War. How now, fair lords ! What fare ?
        What news abroad ?   95
    Rich. Great Lord of Warwick, if we
        should recount
Our baleful news and at each word's
    deliverance
Stab poinards in our flesh till all were told,
The words would add more anguish than
    the wounds,
O valiant lord, the Duke of York is slain !

    Edw. O Warwick, Warwick ! that Plan-
        tagenet   101
Which held thee dearly as his soul's
    redemption
Is by the stern Lord Clifford done to death.
    War. Ten days ago I drown'd these news
        in tears ;
And now, to add more measure to your
    woes,   105
I come to tell you things sith then befall'n.
After the bloody fray at Wakefield fought,
Where your brave father breath'd his latest
    gasp,
Tidings, as swiftly as the posts could run,
Were brought me of your loss and his
    depart.   110
I, then in London, keeper of the King,
Muster'd my soldiers, gathered flocks of
    friends,
And very well appointed, as I thought,
March'd toward Saint Albans to intercept
    the Queen,
Bearing the King in my behalf along ;   115
For by my scouts I was advertised
That she was coming with a full intent
To dash our late decree in parliament
Touching King Henry's oath and your
    succession.   119
Short tale to make—we at St. Albans met,
Our battles join'd, and both sides fiercely
    fought ;
But whether 'twas the coldness of the King,
Who look'd full gently on his warlike queen,
That robb'd my soldiers of their heated
    spleen,
Or whether 'twas report of her success, 125
Or more than common fear of Clifford's
    rigour,
Who thunders to his captives blood and
    death,
I cannot judge ; but, to conclude with
    truth,
Their weapons like to lightning came and
    went :
Our soldiers', like the night-owl's lazy
    flight   130
Or like an idle thresher with a flail,
Fell gently down, as if they struck their
    friends.
I cheer'd them up with justice of our cause,
With promise of high pay and great
    rewards,   134
But all in vain ; they had no heart to
    fight,
And we in them no hope to win the day ;
So that we fled : the King unto the Queen ;
Lord George your brother, Norfolk, and
    myself,
In haste post-haste are come to join with
    you ;   139
For in the marches here we heard you were
Making another head to fight again.
    Edw. Where is the Duke of Norfolk,
        gentle Warwick ?

And when came George from Burgundy to
    England ?
    War. Some six miles off the Duke is with
    the soldiers ;
And for your brother, he was lately sent 145
From your kind aunt, Duchess of Burgundy,
With aid of soldiers to this needful war.
    Rich. 'Twas odds, belike, when valiant
    Warwick fled.
Oft have I heard his praises in pursuit,
But ne'er till now his scandal of retire. 150
    War. Nor now my scandal, Richard, dost
    thou hear ;
For thou shalt know this strong right hand
    of mine
Can pluck the diadem from faint Henry's
    head
And wring the awful sceptre from his fist,
Were he as famous and as bold in war 155
As he is fam'd for mildness, peace, and
    prayer.
    Rich. I know it well, Lord Warwick ;
    blame me not.
'Tis love I bear thy glories makes me speak.
But in this troublous time what's to be
    done ?   159
Shall we go throw away our coats of steel
And wrap our bodies in black mourning-
    gowns,
Numbering our Ave-Maries with our beads?
Or shall we on the helmets of our foes
Tell our devotion with revengeful arms ?
If for the last, say ' Ay ', and to it, lords. 165
    War. Why, therefore Warwick came to
    seek you out ;
And therefore comes my brother Montague.
Attend me, lords. The proud insulting
    Queen,
With Clifford and the haught Northumber-
    land,
And of their feather many moe proud birds,
Have wrought the easy-melting King like
    wax.   171
He swore consent to your succession,
His oath enrolled in the parliament ;
And now to London all the crew are gone
To frustrate both his oath and what beside
May make against the house of Lancaster.
Their power, I think, is thirty thousand
    strong.   177
Now if the help of Norfolk and myself,
With all the friends that thou, brave Earl
    of March,
Amongst the loving Welshmen canst pro-
    cure,   180
Will but amount to five and twenty
    thousand,
Why, Via ! to London will we march amain,
And once again bestride our foaming steeds,
And once again cry ' Charge upon our
    foes ! '
But never once again turn back and fly.
    Rich. Ay, now methinks I hear great
    Warwick speak.   186

Ne'er may he live to see a sunshine day
That cries ' Retire ! ' if Warwick bid him
    stay.
    Edw. Lord Warwick, on thy shoulder will
    I lean ;
And when thou fail'st—as God forbid the
    hour !—   190
Must Edward fall, which peril heaven
    forfend.
    War. No longer Earl of March, but Duke
    of York ;
The next degree is England's royal throne,
For King of England shalt thou be pro-
    claim'd
In every borough as we pass along ;   195
And he that throws not up his cap for joy
Shall for the fault make forfeit of his head.
King Edward, valiant Richard, Montague,
Stay we no longer, dreaming of renown,
But sound the trumpets and about our task.
    Rich. Then, Clifford, were thy heart as
    hard as steel,   201
As thou hast shown it flinty by thy deeds,
I come to pierce it or to give thee mine.
    Edw. Then strike up drums. God and
    Saint George for us !

Enter a Messenger.

    War. How now ! what news ?   205
    Mess. The Duke of Norfolk sends you
    word by me
The Queen is coming with a puissant host,
And craves your company for speedy
    counsel.
    War. Why, then it sorts ; brave warriors,
    let's away.   [*Exeunt.*

SCENE II. *Before York.*

Flourish.   Enter KING HENRY, QUEEN
    MARGARET, *the* PRINCE OF WALES,
    CLIFFORD, NORTHUMBERLAND, *with drum
    and trumpets.*

    Q. Mar. Welcome, my lord, to this brave
    town of York.
Yonder's the head of that arch-enemy
That sought to be encompass'd with your
    crown.
Doth not the object cheer your heart, my
    lord ?
    K. Hen. Ay, as the rocks cheer them that
    fear their wreck—   5
To see this sight, it irks my very soul.
Withhold revenge, dear God ; 'tis not my
    fault,
Nor wittingly have I infring'd my vow.
    Clif. My gracious liege, this too much
    lenity
And harmful pity must be laid aside.   10
To whom do lions cast their gentle looks?
Not to the beast that would usurp their
    den.
Whose hand is that the forest bear doth
    lick ?

Not his that spoils her young before her
 face.
Who scapes the lurking serpent's mortal
 sting ?   15
Not he that sets his foot upon her back.
The smallest worm will turn, being trodden
 on,
And doves will peck in safeguard of their
 brood.
Ambitious York did level at thy crown,
Thou smiling while he knit his angry brows.
He, but a Duke, would have his son a king,
And raise his issue like a loving sire : 22
Thou, being a king, bless'd with a goodly
 son,
Didst yield consent to disinherit him,
Which argued thee a most unloving father.
Unreasonable creatures feed their young ;
And though man's face be fearful to their
 eyes,   27
Yet, in protection of their tender ones,
Who hath not seen them—even with those
 wings
Which sometime they have us'd with fearful
 flight—   30
Make war with him that climb'd unto their
 nest,
Offering their own lives in their young's
 defence ?
For shame, my liege, make them your
 precedent !
Were it not pity that this goodly boy
Should lose his birthright by his father's
 fault,   35
And long hereafter say unto his child
' What my great-grandfather and grandsire
 got
My careless father fondly gave away ' ?
Ah, what a shame were this ! Look on the
 boy ;
And let his manly face, which promiseth 40
Successful fortune, steel thy melting heart
To hold thine own and leave thine own with
 him.
 K. Hen. Full well hath Clifford play'd the
 orator,
Inferring arguments of mighty force. 44
But, Clifford, tell me, didst thou never hear
That things ill got had ever bad success ?
And happy always was it for that son
Whose father for his hoarding went to hell ?
I'll leave my son my virtuous deeds behind;
And would my father had left me no more !
For all the rest is held at such a rate 51
As brings a thousand-fold more care to keep
Than in possession any jot of pleasure.
Ah, cousin York ! would thy best friends
 did know
How it doth grieve me that thy head is
 here !   55
 Q. Mar. My lord, cheer up your spirits ;
 our foes are nigh,
And this soft courage makes your followers
 faint.

You promis'd knighthood to our forward
 son :
Unsheathe your sword and dub him
 presently.
Edward, kneel down.   60
 K. Hen. Edward Plantagent, arise a
 knight ;
And learn this lesson : Draw thy sword in
 right.
 Prince. My gracious father, by your
 kingly leave,
I'll draw it as apparent to the crown,
And in that quarrel use it to the death. 65
 Clif. Why, that is spoken like a toward
 prince.

    Enter a Messenger.

 Mess. Royal commanders, be in readi-
 ness ;
For with a band of thirty thousand men
Comes Warwick, backing of the Duke of
 York,   69
And in the towns, as they do march along,
Proclaims him king, and many fly to him.
Darraign your battle, for they are at hand.
 Clif. I would your Highness would depart
 the field :
The Queen hath best success when you are
 absent.
 Q. Mar. Ay, good my lord, and leave us
 to our fortune.   75
 K. Hen. Why, that's my fortune too ;
 therefore I'll stay.
 North. Be it with resolution, then, to
 fight.
 Prince. My royal father, cheer these noble
 lords,
And hearten those that fight in your
 defence.
Unsheathe your sword, good father ; cry
 ' Saint George ! '   80

March. Enter EDWARD, GEORGE, RICHARD,
 WARWICK, NORFOLK, MONTAGUE, *and*
 Soldiers.

 Edw. Now, perjur'd Henry, wilt thou
 kneel for grace
And set thy diadem upon my head,
Or bide the mortal fortune of the field ?
 Q. Mar. Go rate thy minions, proud in-
 sulting boy.
Becomes it thee to be thus bold in terms 85
Before thy sovereign and thy lawful king ?
 Edw. I am his king, and he should bow
 his knee.
I was adopted heir by his consent :
Since when, his oath is broke ; for, as I
 hear,
You that are King, though he do wear the
 crown,   90
Have caus'd him by new act of parliament
To blot out me and put his own son in.
 Clif. And reason too :
Who should succeed the father but the son?

            673

Rich. Are you there, butcher ? O, I can-
 not speak !   95
Clif. Ay, crook-back, here I stand to
 answer thee,
Or any he, the proudest of thy sort.
 Rich. 'Twas you that kill'd young
  Rutland, was it not ?
Clif. Ay, and old York, and yet not
 satisfied.
Rich. For God's sake, lords, give signal
 to the fight.   100
War. What say'st thou, Henry ? Wilt
 thou yield the crown ?
Q. Mar. Why, how now, long-tongu'd
 Warwick ! Dare you speak ?
When you and I met at Saint Albans last
Your legs did better service than your
 hands.
War. Then 'twas my turn to fly, and now
 'tis thine.   105
Clif. You said so much before, and yet
 you fled.
War. 'Twas not your valour, Clifford,
 drove me thence.
North. No, nor your manhood that durst
 make you stay.
Rich. Northumberland, I hold thee rever-
 ently.
Break off the parley ; for scarce I can
 refrain   110
The execution of my big-swol'n heart
Upon that Clifford, that cruel child-killer.
 Clif. I slew thy father ; call'st thou him
 a child ?
Rich. Ay, like a dastard and a treacherous
 coward,
As thou didst kill our tender brother
 Rutland ;   115
But ere sunset I'll make thee curse the deed.
K. Hen. Have done with words, my lords,
 and hear me speak.
Q. Mar. Defy them then, or else hold
 close thy lips.
K. Hen. I prithee give no limits to my
 tongue :
I am a king, and privileg'd to speak. 120
 Clif. My liege, the wound that bred this
 meeting here
Cannot be cur'd by words ; therefore be
 still.
Rich. Then, executioner, unsheathe thy
 sword.
By Him that made us all, I am resolv'd
That Clifford's manhood lies upon his
 tongue.   125
 Edw. Say, Henry, shall I have my right,
 or no ?
A thousand men have broke their fasts
 to-day
That ne'er shall dine unless thou yield the
 crown.
 War. If thou deny, their blood upon thy
 head ;
For York in justice puts his armour on. 130

 Prince. If that be right which Warwick
 says is right,
There is no wrong, but every thing is right.
 Rich. Whoever got thee, there thy mother
 stands ;
For well I wot thou hast thy mother's
 tongue.
 Q. Mar. But thou art neither like thy sire
 nor dam ;   135
But like a foul misshapen stigmatic,
Mark'd by the destinies to be avoided,
As venom toads or lizards' dreadful stings.
 Rich. Iron of Naples hid with English
 gilt,
Whose father bears the title of a king— 140
As if a channel should be call'd the sea—
Sham'st thou not, knowing whence thou
 art extraught,
To let thy tongue detect thy base-born
 heart ?
 Edw. A wisp of straw were worth a
 thousand crowns   144
To make this shameless callet know herself.
Helen of Greece was fairer far than thou,
Although thy husband may be Menelaus ;
And ne'er was Agamemnon's brother
 wrong'd
By that false woman as this king by thee.
His father revell'd in the heart of France,
And tam'd the King, and made the Dauphin
 stoop ;   151
And had he match'd according to his
 state,
He might have kept that glory to this day ;
But when he took a beggar to his bed
And grac'd thy poor sire with his bridal
 day,   155
Even then that sunshine brew'd a show'r
 for him
That wash'd his father's fortunes forth of
 France
And heap'd sedition on his crown at home.
For what hath broach'd this tumult but thy
 pride ?
Hadst thou been meek, our title still had
 slept ;   160
And we, in pity of the gentle King,
Had slipp'd our claim until another age.
 Geo. But when we saw our sunshine made
 thy spring,
And that thy summer bred us no increase,
We set the axe to thy usurping root ; 165
And though the edge hath something hit
 ourselves,
Yet know thou, since we have begun to
 strike,
We'll never leave till we have hewn thee
 down,
Or bath'd thy growing with our heated
 bloods.   169
 Edw. And in this resolution I defy thee ;
Not willing any longer conference,
Since thou deniest the gentle King to
 speak.

Sound trumpets ; let our bloody colours
 wave,
And either victory or else a grave !
  Q. Mar. Stay, Edward.   175
  Edw. No, wrangling woman, we'll no
    longer stay ;
These words will cost ten thousand lives
    this day.   [*Exeunt.*

SCENE III. *A field of battle between Towton
    and Saxton, in Yorkshire.*

Alarum ; excursions. Enter WARWICK.

  War. Forspent with toil, as runners with
    a race,
I lay me down a little while to breathe ;
For strokes receiv'd and many blows repaid
Have robb'd my strong-knit sinews of their
    strength,   4
And spite of spite needs must I rest awhile.

Enter EDWARD, *running.*

  Edw. Smile, gentle heaven, or strike, un-
    gentle death ;
For this world frowns, and Edward's sun
    is clouded.
  War. How now, my lord ! What hap ?
    What hope of good ?

Enter GEORGE.

  Geo. Our hap is lost, our hope but sad
    despair ;
Our ranks are broke, and ruin follows us. 10
What counsel give you ? Whither shall we
    fly ?
  Edw. Bootless is flight : they follow us
    with wings ;
And weak we are, and cannot shun pursuit.

Enter RICHARD.

  Rich. Ah, Warwick, why hast thou with-
    drawn thyself ?
Thy brother's blood the thirsty earth hath
    drunk,   15
Broach'd with the steely point of Clifford's
    lance ;
And in the very pangs of death he cried,
Like to a dismal clangor heard from far,
' Warwick, revenge ! Brother, revenge my
    death '.
So, underneath the belly of their steeds, 20
That stain'd their fetlocks in his smoking
    blood,
The noble gentleman gave up the ghost.
  War. Then let the earth be drunken with
    our blood.
I'll kill my horse, because I will not fly.
Why stand we like soft-hearted women
    here,   25
Wailing our losses, whiles the foe doth rage,
And look upon, as if the tragedy
Were play'd in jest by counterfeiting actors?
Here on my knee I vow to God above
I'll never pause again, never stand still, 30

Till either death hath clos'd these eyes of
    mine
Or fortune given me measure of revenge.
  Edw. O Warwick, I do bend my knee
    with thine,
And in this vow do chain my soul to thine !
And ere my knee rise from the earth's cold
    face   35
I throw my hands, mine eyes, my heart to
    Thee,
Thou setter-up and plucker-down of kings,
Beseeching Thee, if with Thy will it stands
That to my foes this body must be prey,
Yet that Thy brazen gates of heaven may
    ope   40
And give sweet passage to my sinful soul.
Now, lords, take leave until we meet again,
Where'er it be, in heaven or in earth.
  Rich. Brother, give me thy hand ; and,
    gentle Warwick,
Let me embrace thee in my weary arms. 45
I that did never weep now melt with woe
That winter should cut off our spring-time
    so.
  War. Away, away ! Once more, sweet
    lords, farewell.
  Geo. Yet let us all together to our troops,
And give them leave to fly that will not
    stay,   50
And call them pillars that will stand to us ;
And if we thrive, promise them such re-
    wards
As victors wear at the Olympian games.
This may plant courage in their quailing
    breasts,
For yet is hope of life and victory.   55
Forslow no longer ; make we hence amain.
                                   [*Exeunt.*

SCENE IV. *Another part of the field.*

Excursions. Enter RICHARD *and* CLIFFORD.

  Rich. Now, Clifford, I have singled thee
    alone.
Suppose this arm is for the Duke of York,
And this for Rutland ; both bound to
    revenge,
Wert thou environ'd with a brazen wall.
  Clif. Now, Richard, I am with thee here
    alone.   5
This is the hand that stabb'd thy father
    York ;
And this the hand that slew thy brother
    Rutland ;
And here's the heart that triumphs in their
    death
And cheers these hands that slew thy sire
    and brother
To execute the like upon thyself ;   10
And so, have at thee !   [*They fight.*

Enter WARWICK ; *Clifford flies.*

  Rich. Nay, Warwick, single out some
    other chase ;

For I myself will hunt this wolf to death.
                                    [*Exeunt.*

SCENE V. *Another part of the field.*

Alarum. Enter KING HENRY *alone.*

K. Hen. This battle fares like to the
    morning's war,
When dying clouds contend with growing
    light,
What time the shepherd, blowing of his
    nails,
Can neither call it perfect day nor night.
Now sways it this way, like a mighty sea 5
Forc'd by the tide to combat with the
    wind;
Now sways it that way, like the selfsame
    sea
Forc'd to retire by fury of the wind.
Sometime the flood prevails, and then the
    wind;
Now one the better, then another best; 10
Both tugging to be victors, breast to breast,
Yet neither conqueror nor conquered.
So is the equal poise of this fell war.
Here on this molehill will I sit me down.
To whom God will, there be the victory! 15
For Margaret my queen, and Clifford too,
Have chid me from the battle, swearing
    both
They prosper best of all when I am thence.
Would I were dead, if God's good will were
    so!
For what is in this world but grief and woe?
O God! methinks it were a happy life 21
To be no better than a homely swain;
To sit upon a hill, as I do now,
To carve out dials quaintly, point by point,
Thereby to see the minutes how they run—
How many makes the hour full complete,
How many hours brings about the day,
How many days will finish up the year,
How many years a mortal man may live.
When this is known, then to divide the
    times— 30
So many hours must I tend my flock;
So many hours must I take my rest;
So many hours must I contemplate;
So many hours must I sport myself;
So many days my ewes have been with
    young; 35
So many weeks ere the poor fools will ean;
So many years ere I shall shear the fleece:
So minutes, hours, days, months, and years,
Pass'd over to the end they were created,
Would bring white hairs unto a quiet grave.
Ah, what a life were this! how sweet!
    how lovely! 41
Gives not the hawthorn bush a sweeter
    shade
To shepherds looking on their silly sheep,
Than doth a rich embroider'd canopy 44
To kings that fear their subjects' treachery?
O yes, it doth; a thousand-fold it doth.

And to conclude: the shepherd's homely
    curds,
His cold thin drink out of his leather bottle,
His wonted sleep under a fresh tree's shade,
All which secure and sweetly he enjoys, 50
Is far beyond a prince's delicates—
His viands sparkling in a golden cup,
His body couched in a curious bed,
When care, mistrust, and treason waits on
    him.

Alarum. Enter a Son *that hath kill'd his*
    Father, *at one door; and a* Father *that*
    hath kill'd his Son, *at another door.*

Son. Ill blows the wind that profits no-
    body. 55
This man whom hand to hand I slew in
    fight
May be possessed with some store of
    crowns;
And I, that haply take them from him now,
May yet ere night yield both my life and
    them
To some man else, as this dead man doth
    me. 60
Who's this? O God! It is my father's face,
Whom in this conflict I unwares have
    kill'd.
O heavy times, begetting such events!
From London by the King was I press'd
    forth;
My father, being the Earl of Warwick's
    man, 65
Came on the part of York, press'd by his
    master;
And I, who at his hands receiv'd my life,
Have by my hands of life bereaved him.
Pardon me, God, I knew not what I did.
And pardon, father, for I knew not thee. 70
My tears shall wipe away these bloody
    marks;
And no more words till they have flow'd
    their fill.
K. Hen. O piteous spectacle! O bloody
    times!
Whiles lions war and battle for their dens,
Poor harmless lambs abide their enmity. 75
Weep, wretched man; I'll aid thee tear for
    tear;
And let our hearts and eyes, like civil war,
Be blind with tears and break o'ercharg'd
    with grief.

Enter Father, *bearing of his* Son.

Fath. Thou that so stoutly hath resisted
    me,
Give me thy gold, if thou hast any gold; 80
For I have bought it with an hundred
    blows.
But let me see. Is this our foeman's face?
Ah, no, no, no, it is mine only son!
Ah, boy, if any life be left in thee,
Throw up thine eye! See, see what show'rs
    arise, 85

Blown with the windy tempest of my heart
Upon thy wounds, that kills mine eye and
    heart !
O, pity, God, this miserable age !
What stratagems, how fell, how butcherly,
Erroneous, mutinous, and unnatural,   90
This deadly quarrel daily doth beget !
O boy, thy father gave thee life too soon,
And hath bereft thee of thy life too late !
    K. Hen. Woe above woe ! grief more than
        common grief !
O that my death would stay these ruthful
    deeds !   95
O pity, pity, gentle heaven, pity !
The red rose and the white are on his face,
The fatal colours of our striving houses :
The one his purple blood right well re-
    sembles.
The other his pale cheeks, methinks, pre-
    senteth.   100
Wither one rose, and let the other flourish !
If you contend, a thousand lives must
    perish.
    Son. How will my mother for a father's
        death
Take on with me, and ne'er be satisfied !
    Fath. How will my wife for slaughter of
        my son   105
Shed seas of tears, and ne'er be satisfied !
    K. Hen. How will the country for these
        woeful chances
Misthink the King, and not be satisfied !
    Son. Was ever son so rued a father's
        death ?
    Fath. Was ever father so bemoan'd his
        son ?   110
    K. Hen. Was ever king so griev'd for
        subjects' woe ?
Much is your sorrow ; mine ten times so
    much.
    Son. I'll bear thee hence, where I may
        weep my fill.   [*Exit with the body.*
    Fath. These arms of mine shall be thy
        winding-sheet ;   114
My heart, sweet boy, shall be thy sepulchre,
For from my heart thine image ne'er shall
    go ;
My sighing breast shall be thy funeral bell ;
And so obsequious will thy father be,
Even for the loss of thee, having no more,
As Priam was for all his valiant sons.   120
I'll bear thee hence ; and let them fight
    that will,
For I have murdered where I should not
    kill.   [*Exit with the body.*
    K. Hen. Sad-hearted men, much over-
        gone with care,
Here sits a king more woeful than you are.

Alarums ; excursions. Enter QUEEN MAR-
GARET, PRINCE OF WALES, *and* EXETER.

    Prince. Fly, father, fly ; for all your
        friends are fled,   125
And Warwick rages like a chafed bull.

Away ! for death doth hold us in pursuit.
    Q. Mar. Mount you, my lord ; towards
        Berwick post amain.
Edward and Richard, like a brace of grey-
    hounds
Having the fearful flying hare in sight,   130
With fiery eyes sparkling for very wrath,
And bloody steel grasp'd in their ireful
    hands,
Are at our backs ; and therefore hence
    amain.
    Exe. Away ! for vengeance comes along
        with them.
Nay, stay not to expostulate ; make speed ;
Or else come after. I'll away before.   136
    K. Hen. Nay, take me with thee, good
        sweet Exeter.
Not that I fear to stay, but love to go
Whither the Queen intends.   Forward ;
    away !   [*Exeunt.*

SCENE VI.   *Another part of the field.*

A loud alarum. Enter CLIFFORD, *wounded.*

    Clif. Here burns my candle out ; ay, here
        it dies,
Which, whiles it lasted, gave King Henry
    light.
O Lancaster, I fear thy overthrow
More than my body's parting with my soul !
My love and fear glu'd many friends to thee ;
And, now I fall, thy tough commixture
    melts,   6
Impairing Henry, strength'ning misproud
    York.
The common people swarm like summer
    flies ;
And whither fly the gnats but to the sun ?
And who shines now but Henry's enemies ?
O Phœbus, hadst thou never given consent
That Phaethon should check thy fiery
    steeds,   12
Thy burning car never had scorch'd the
    earth !
And, Henry, hadst thou sway'd as kings
    should do,
Or as thy father and his father did,   15
Giving no ground unto the house of York,
They never then had sprung like summer
    flies ;
I and ten thousand in this luckless realm
Had left no mourning widows for our death ;
And thou this day hadst kept thy chair in
    peace.   20
For what doth cherish weeds but gentle air ?
And what makes robbers bold but too much
    lenity ?
Bootless are plaints, and cureless are my
    wounds.
No way to fly, nor strength to hold out
    flight.
The foe is merciless and will not pity ;   25
For at their hands I have deserv'd no pity.
The air hath got into my deadly wounds,

And much effuse of blood doth make me
    faint.
Come, York and Richard, Warwick and the
    rest ;   29
I stabb'd your fathers' bosoms : split my
    breast.   [*He faints.*

Alarum and retreat.   Enter EDWARD,
GEORGE, RICHARD, MONTAGUE, WAR-
WICK, *and* Soldiers.

  Edw. Now breathe we, lords.   Good
    fortune bids us pause
And smooth the frowns of war with peaceful
    looks.
Some troops pursue the bloody-minded
    Queen
That led calm Henry, though he were a
    king,
As doth a sail, fill'd with a fretting gust, 35
Command an argosy to stem the waves.
But think you, lords, that Clifford fled with
    them ?
  War. No, 'tis impossible he should
    escape ;
For, though before his face I speak the
    words,
Your brother Richard mark'd him for the
    grave ;   40
And, whereso'er he is, he's surely dead.
                        [*Clifford groans, and dies.*
  Rich. Whose soul is that which takes her
    heavy leave ?
A deadly groan, like life and death's
    departing.
See who it is.
  Edw.   And now the battle's ended,
If friend or foe, let him be gently used. 45
  Rich. Revoke that doom of mercy, for 'tis
    Clifford ;
Who not contented that he lopp'd the
    branch
In hewing Rutland when his leaves put
    forth,
But set his murd'ring knife unto the root
From whence that tender spray did sweetly
    spring—   50
I mean our princely father, Duke of York.
  War. From off the gates of York fetch
    down the head,
Your father's head, which Clifford placed
    there ;
Instead whereof let this supply the room.
Measure for measure must be answered. 55
  Edw. Bring forth that fatal screech-owl to
    our house,
That nothing sung but death to us and
    ours.
Now death shall stop his dismal threat'ning
    sound,
And his ill-boding tongue no more shall
    speak.   59
  War. I think his understanding is bereft.
Speak, Clifford, dost thou know who speaks
    to thee ?

Dark cloudy death o'ershades his beams of
    life,
And he nor sees nor hears us what we say.
  Rich. O, would he did ! and so, perhaps,
    he doth.
'Tis but his policy to counterfeit,   65
Because he would avoid such bitter taunts
Which in the time of death he gave our
    father.
  Geo. If so thou think'st, vex him with
    eager words.
  Rich. Clifford, ask mercy and obtain no
    grace.
  Edw. Clifford, repent in bootless peni-
    tence.   70
  War. Clifford, devise excuses for thy
    faults.
  Geo. While we devise fell tortures for thy
    faults.
  Rich. Thou didst love York, and I am son
    to York.
  Edw. Thou pitied'st Rutland, I will pity
    thee.
  Geo. Where's Captain Margaret, to fence
    you now ?   75
  War. They mock thee, Clifford ; swear as
    thou wast wont.
  Rich. What, not an oath ? Nay, then the
    world goes hard
When Clifford cannot spare his friends an
    oath.
I know by that he's dead ; and by my
    soul,   79
If this right hand would buy two hours' life,
That I in all despite might rail at him,
This hand should chop it off, and with the
    issuing blood
Stifle the villain whose unstanched thirst
York and young Rutland could not satisfy.
  War. Ay, but he's dead.   Off with the
    traitor's head,   85
And rear it in the place your father's stands.
And now to London with triumphant
    march,
There to be crowned England's royal King ;
From whence shall Warwick cut the sea to
    France,
And ask the Lady Bona for thy queen. 90
So shalt thou sinew both these lands to-
    gether ;
And, having France thy friend, thou shalt
    not dread
The scatt'red foe that hopes to rise again ;
For though they cannot greatly sting to
    hurt,
Yet look to have them buzz to offend thine
    ears.   95
First will I see the coronation ;
And then to Brittany I'll cross the sea
To effect this marriage, so it please my lord.
  Edw. Even as thou wilt, sweet Warwick,
    let it be ;
For in thy shoulder do I build my seat, 100
And never will I undertake the thing

Wherein thy counsel and consent is want-
  ing.
Richard, I will create thee Duke of
  Gloucester ;
And George, of Clarence ; Warwick, as
  ourself,
Shall do and undo as him pleaseth best. 105
  Rich. Let me be Duke of Clarence, George
  of Gloucester ;
For Gloucester's dukedom is too ominous.
  War. Tut, that's a foolish observation.
Richard, be Duke of Gloucester. Now to
  London
To see these honours in possession.   110
                                  [*Exeunt.*

ACT THREE

Scene I. *A chase in the north of England.*

Enter two Keepers, *with cross-bows in their
        hands.*

  1 *Keep.* Under this thick-grown brake
    we'll shroud ourselves,
For through this laund anon the deer will
  come ;
And in this covert will we make our stand,
Culling the principal of all the deer.
  2 *Keep.* I'll stay above the hill, so both
    may shoot.   5
  1 *Keep.* That cannot be ; the noise of thy
    cross-bow
Will scare the herd, and so my shoot is lost.
Here stand we both, and aim we at the best ;
And, for the time shall not seem tedious,
I'll tell thee what befell me on a day   10
In this self-place where now we mean to
  stand.
  2 *Keep.* Here comes a man ; let's stay
    till he be past.

Enter King Henry, *disguised, with a
        prayer-book.*

  K. Hen. From Scotland am I stol'n, even
    of pure love,
To greet mine own land with my wishful
  sight.
No, Harry, Harry, 'tis no land of thine ;   15
Thy place is fill'd, thy sceptre wrung from
  thee,
Thy balm wash'd off wherewith thou wast
  anointed.
No bending knee will call thee Cæsar now,
No humble suitors press to speak for right,
No, not a man comes for redress of thee ;   20
For how can I help them and not myself ?
  1 *Keep.* Ay, here's a deer whose skin's a
    keeper's fee.
This is the quondam king ; let's seize upon
  him.
  K. Hen. Let me embrace thee, sour
    adversity,
For wise men say it is the wisest course.   25
  2 *Keep.* Why linger we ? let us lay hands
    upon him.

  1 *Keep.* Forbear awhile ; we'll hear a
    little more.
  K. Hen. My Queen and son are gone to
    France for aid ;
And, as I hear, the great commanding
  Warwick
Is thither gone to crave the French King's
  sister   30
To wife for Edward. If this news be true,
Poor queen and son, your labour is but lost ;
For Warwick is a subtle orator,
And Lewis a prince soon won with moving
  words.
By this account, then, Margaret may win
  him ;   35
For she's a woman to be pitied much.
Her sighs will make a batt'ry in his breast ;
Her tears will pierce into a marble heart ;
The tiger will be mild whiles she doth
  mourn ;
And Nero will be tainted with remorse   40
To hear and see her plaints, her brinish
  tears.
Ay, but she's come to beg : Warwick, to
  give.
She, on his left side, craving aid for
  Henry :
He, on his right, asking a wife for Edward :
She weeps, and says her Henry is depos'd :
He smiles, and says his Edward is install'd ;
That she, poor wretch, for grief can speak
  no more ;
Whiles Warwick tells his title, smooths the
  wrong,
Inferreth arguments of mighty strength,
And in conclusion wins the King from her 50
With promise of his sister, and what else,
To strengthen and support King Edward's
  place.
O Margaret, thus 'twill be ; and thou, poor
  soul,
Art then forsaken, as thou went'st forlorn !
  2 *Keep.* Say, what art thou that talk'st of
    kings and queens ?   55
  K. Hen. More than I seem, and less than
    I was born to :
A man at least, for less I should not be ;
And men may talk of kings, and why not I ?
  2 *Keep.* Ay, but thou talk'st as if thou
    wert a king.
  K. Hen. Why, so I am—in mind ; and
    that's enough.   60
  2 *Keep.* But, if thou be a king, where is
    thy crown ?
  K. Hen. My crown is in my heart, not on
    my head ;
Not deck'd with diamonds and Indian
  stones,
Nor to be seen. My crown is call'd content ;
A crown it is that seldom kings enjoy.   65
  2 *Keep.* Well, if you be a king crown'd
    with content,
Your crown content and you must be con-
  tented

To go along with us ; for, as we think,
You are the king King Edward hath
    depos'd ;
And we his subjects, sworn in all allegiance,
Will apprehend you as his enemy.   71
  K. Hen. But did you never swear, and
    break an oath ?
  2 Keep. No, never such an oath ; nor will
    not now.
  K. Hen. Where did you dwell when I was
    King of England ?
  2 Keep. Here in this country, where we
    now remain.   75
  K. Hen. I was anointed king at nine
    months old ;
My father and my grandfather were kings ;
And you were sworn true subjects unto me ;
And tell me, then, have you not broke your
  oaths ?
  1 Keep. No ;   80
For we were subjects but while you were
  king.
  K. Hen. Why, am I dead ? Do I not
    breathe a man ?
Ah, simple men, you know not what you
  swear !
Look, as I blow this feather from my face,
And as the air blows it to me again,   85
Obeying with my wind when I do blow,
And yielding to another when it blows,
Commanded always by the greater gust,
Such is the lightness of you common men.
But do not break your oaths ; for of that
  sin   90
My mild entreaty shall not make you guilty.
Go where you will, the King shall be com-
  manded ;
And be you kings : command, and I'll obey.
  1 Keep. We are true subjects to the King,
    King Edward.
  K. Hen. So would you be again to
    Henry,   95
If he were seated as King Edward is.
  1 Keep. We charge you, in God's name
    and the King's,
To go with us unto the officers.
  K. Hen. In God's name, lead ; your
    King's name be obey'd ;
And what God will, that let your King
  perform ;   100
And what he will, I humbly yield unto.
                    [*Exeunt.*

    Scene II. *London. The palace.*

Enter King Edward, Gloucester, Clar-
    ence, *and* Lady Grey.

  K. Edw. Brother of Gloucester, at Saint
    Albans' field
This lady's husband, Sir Richard Grey, was
  slain,
His land then seiz'd on by the conqueror.
Her suit is now to repossess those lands ;
Which we in justice cannot well deny,   5

Because in quarrel of the house of York
The worthy gentleman did lose his life.
  Glo. Your Highness shall do well to grant
    her suit ;
It were dishonour to deny it her.
  K. Edw. It were no less ; but yet I'll
    make a pause.   10
  Glo. [*Aside to Clarence*] Yea, is it so ?
I see the lady hath a thing to grant,
Before the King will grant her humble suit.
  Clar. [*Aside to Gloucester*] He knows the
    game ; how true he keeps the wind !
  Glo. [*Aside to Clarence*] Silence !   15
  K. Edw. Widow, we will consider of your
    suit ;
And come some other time to know our
  mind.
  L. Grey. Right gracious lord, I cannot
    brook delay.
May it please your Highness to resolve me
  now ;   19
And what your pleasure is shall satisfy me.
  Glo. [*Aside*] Ay, widow ? Then I'll
    warrant you all your lands,
An if what pleases him shall pleasure
  you.
Fight closer or, good faith, you'll catch a
  blow.
  Clar. [*Aside to Gloucester*] I fear her not,
    unless she chance to fall.
  Glo. [*Aside to Clarence*] God forbid that,
    for he'll take vantages.   25
  K. Edw. How many children hast thou,
    widow, tell me.
  Clar. [*Aside to Gloucester*] I think he
    means to beg a child of her.
  Glo. [*Aside to Clarence*] Nay, then whip
    me ; he'll rather give her two.
  L. Grey. Three, my most gracious lord.
  Glo. [*Aside*] You shall have four if you'll
    be rul'd by him.   30
  K. Edw. 'Twere pity they should lose
    their father's lands.
  L. Grey. Be pitiful, dread lord, and grant
    it, then.
  K. Edw. Lords, give us leave ; I'll try
    this widow's wit.
  Glo. [*Aside*] Ay, good leave have you ; for
    you will have leave
Till youth take leave and leave you to the
  crutch.   35
        [*Gloucester and Clarence withdraw.*
  K. Edw. Now tell me, madam, do you
    love your children ?
  L. Grey. Ay, full as dearly as I love
    myself.
  K. Edw. And would you not do much to
    do them good ?
  L. Grey. To do them good I would
    sustain some harm.
  K. Edw. Then get your husband's lands,
    to do them good.   40
  L. Grey. Therefore I came unto your
    Majesty.

K. Edw. I'll tell you how these lands are
  to be got.

L. Grey. So shall you bind me to your
  Highness' service.

K. Edw. What service wilt thou do me
  if I give them ?

L. Grey. What you command that rests
  in me to do.   45

K. Edw. But you will take exceptions to
  my boon.

L. Grey. No, gracious lord, except I cannot do it.

K. Edw. Ay, but thou canst do what I
  mean to ask.

L. Grey. Why, then I will do what your
  Grace commands.

Glo. He plies her hard ; and much rain
  wears the marble.   50

Clar. As red as fire ! Nay, then her wax
  must melt.

L. Grey. Why stops my lord ? Shall I not
  hear my task ?

K. Edw. An easy task ; 'tis but to love
  a king.

L. Grey. That's soon perform'd, because
  I am a subject.

K. Edw. Why, then, thy husband's lands
  I freely give thee.   55

L. Grey. I take my leave with many
  thousand thanks.

Glo. The match is made ; she seals it
  with a curtsy.

K. Edw. But stay thee—'tis the fruits of
  love I mean.

L. Grey. The fruits of love I mean, my
  loving liege.

K. Edw. Ay, but, I fear me, in another
  sense.   60

What love, thinkst thou, I sue so much to
  get ?

L. Grey. My love till death, my humble
  thanks, my prayers ;

That love which virtue begs and virtue
  grants.

K. Edw. No, by my troth, I did not mean
  such love.

L. Grey. Why, then, you mean not as I
  thought you did.   65

K. Edw. But now you partly may perceive my mind.

L. Grey. My mind will never grant what
  I perceive

Your Highness aims at, if I aim aright.

K. Edw. To tell thee plain, I aim to lie
  with thee.

L. Grey. To tell you plain, I had rather
  lie in prison.   70

K. Edw. Why, then thou shalt not have
  thy husband's lands.

L. Grey. Why, then mine honesty shall be
  my dower ;

For by that loss I will not purchase them.

K. Edw. Therein thou wrong'st thy
  children mightily.

L. Grey. Herein your Highness wrongs
  both them and me.   75

But, mighty lord, this merry inclination
Accords not with the sadness of my suit.
Please you dismiss me, either with ay or no.

K. Edw. Ay, if thou wilt say ay to my
  request ;

No, if thou dost say no to my demand.   80

L. Grey. Then, no, my lord. My suit is at
  an end.

Glo. The widow likes him not ; she knits
  her brows.

Clar. He is the bluntest wooer in Christendom.

K. Edw. [*Aside*] Her looks doth argue her
  replete with modesty ;   84

Her words doth show her wit incomparable;
All her perfections challenge sovereignty.
One way or other, she is for a king ;
And she shall be my love, or else my queen.
Say that King Edward take thee for his
  queen ?

L. Grey. 'Tis better said than done, my
  gracious lord.   90

I am a subject fit to jest withal,
But far unfit to be a sovereign.

K. Edw. Sweet widow, by my state I
  swear to thee

I speak no more than what my soul intends;
And that is to enjoy thee for my love.   95

L. Grey. And that is more than I will
  yield unto.

I know I am too mean to be your queen,
And yet too good to be your concubine.

K. Edw. You cavil, widow ; I did mean
  my queen.

L. Grey. 'Twill grieve your Grace my sons
  should call you father.   100

K. Edw. No more than when my
  daughters call thee mother.

Thou art a widow, and thou hast some
  children ;

And, by God's Mother, I, being but a
  bachelor,

Have other some. Why, 'tis a happy thing
To be the father unto many sons.   105

Answer no more, for thou shalt be my
  queen.

Glo. The ghostly father now hath done
  his shrift.

Clar. When he was made a shriver, 'twas
  for shift.

K. Edw. Brothers, you muse what chat
  we two have had.

Glo. The widow likes it not, for she looks
  very sad.   110

K. Edw. You'd think it strange if I
  should marry her.

Clar. To who, my lord ?

K. Edw.   Why, Clarence, to myself.

Glo. That would be ten days' wonder at
  the least.

Clar. That's a day longer than a wonder
  lasts.

Glo. By so much is the wonder in
  extremes.   115
K. Edw. Well, jest on, brothers; I can
  tell you both
Her suit is granted for her husband's lands.

Enter a Nobleman.

Nob. My gracious lord, Henry your foe is
  taken
And brought your prisoner to your palace
  gate.
K. Edw. See that he be convey'd unto the
  Tower.   120
And go we, brothers, to the man that took
  him
To question of his apprehension.
Widow, go you along.   Lords, use her
  honourably.
         [*Exeunt all but Gloucester.*
Glo. Ay, Edward will use women honour-
  ably.
Would he were wasted, marrow, bones, and
  all,   125
That from his loins no hopeful branch may
  spring
To cross me from the golden time I look for!
And yet, between my soul's desire and me—
The lustful Edward's title buried:—
Is Clarence, Henry, and his son young
  Edward,   130
And all the unlook'd for issue of their
  bodies,
To take their rooms ere I can place myself.
A cold premeditation for my purpose!
Why, then I do but dream on sovereignty;
Like one that stands upon a promontory 135
And spies a far-off shore where he would
  tread,
Wishing his foot were equal with his eye;
And chides the sea that sunders him from
  thence,
Saying he'll lade it dry to have his way—
So do I wish the crown, being so far off; 140
And so I chide the means that keeps me
  from it;
And so I say I'll cut the causes off,
Flattering me with impossibilities.
My eye's too quick, my heart o'erweens too
  much,
Unless my hand and strength could equal
  them.   145
Well, say there is no kingdom then for
  Richard;
What other pleasure can the world afford?
I'll make my heaven in a lady's lap,
And deck my body in gay ornaments,
And witch sweet ladies with my words and
  looks.   150
O miserable thought! and more unlikely
Than to accomplish twenty golden crowns.
Why, love forswore me in my mother's
  womb;
And, for I should not deal in her soft laws,
She did corrupt frail nature with some bribe

To shrink mine arm up like a wither'd
  shrub;   156
To make an envious mountain on my back,
Where sits deformity to mock my body;
To shape my legs of an unequal size;
To disproportion me in every part,   160
Like to a chaos, or an unlick'd bear-whelp
That carries no impression like the dam.
And am I, then, a man to be belov'd?
O monstrous fault to harbour such a
  thought!   164
Then, since this earth affords no joy to me
But to command, to check, to o'erbear such
As are of better person than myself,
I'll make my heaven to dream upon the
  crown,
And whiles I live t' account this world but
  hell,
Until my misshap'd trunk that bears this
  head   170
Be round impaled with a glorious crown.
And yet I know not how to get the crown,
For many lives stand between me and
  home;
And I—like one lost in a thorny wood
That rents the thorns and is rent with the
  thorns,   175
Seeking a way and straying from the way;
Not knowing how to find the open air,
But toiling desperately to find it out—
Torment myself to catch the English crown;
And from that torment I will free myself
Or hew my way out with a bloody axe.
Why, I can smile, and murder whiles I
  smile,   182
And cry 'Content!' to that which grieves
  my heart,
And wet my cheeks with artificial tears,
And frame my face to all occasions.   185
I'll drown more sailors than the mermaid
  shall;
I'll slay more gazers than the basilisk;
I'll play the orator as well as Nestor,
Deceive more slily than Ulysses could,
And, like a Sinon, take another Troy.   190
I can add colours to the chameleon,
Change shapes with Proteus for advan-
  tages,
And set the murderous Machiavel to school.
Can I do this, and cannot get a crown?
Tut, were it farther off, I'll pluck it down.
                                   [*Exit.*

SCENE III. *France. The King's palace.*

Flourish.   Enter LEWIS *the French King,
  his sister* BONA, *his Admiral call'd*
  BOURBON;   PRINCE EDWARD, QUEEN
  MARGARET, *and the* EARL OF OXFORD.
  Lewis sits, and riseth up again.

Lewis. Fair Queen of England, worthy
  Margaret,
Sit down with us.   It ill befits thy state
And birth that thou shouldst stand while
  Lewis doth sit.

Q. Mar. No, mighty King of France.
    Now Margaret
Must strike her sail and learn a while to
    serve   5
Where kings command. I was, I must
    confess,
Great Albion's Queen in former golden
    days ;
But now mischance hath trod my title
    down
And with dishonour laid me on the ground,
Where I must take like seat unto my
    fortune,   10
And to my humble seat conform myself.
    Lewis. Why, say, fair Queen, whence
    springs this deep despair ?
    Q. Mar. From such a cause as fills mine
    eyes with tears
And stops my tongue, while heart is
    drown'd in cares.
    Lewis. Whate'er it be, be thou still like
    thyself,   15
And sit thee by our side. [*Seats her by him*]
    Yield not thy neck
To fortune's yoke, but let thy dauntless
    mind
Still ride in triumph over all mischance.
Be plain, Queen Margaret, and tell thy
    grief ;
It shall be eas'd, if France can yield relief. 20
    Q. Mar. Those gracious words revive my
    drooping thoughts
And give my tongue-tied sorrows leave to
    speak.
Now therefore be it known to noble Lewis
That Henry, sole possessor of my love,
Is, of a king, become a banish'd man, 25
And forc'd to live in Scotland a forlorn ;
While proud ambitious Edward Duke of
    York
Usurps the regal title and the seat
Of England's true-anointed lawful King.
This is the cause that I, poor Margaret, 30
With this my son, Prince Edward, Henry's
    heir,
Am come to crave thy just and lawful aid ;
And if thou fail us, all our hope is done.
Scotland hath will to help, but cannot
    help ;
Our people and our peers are both misled, 35
Our treasure seiz'd, our soldiers put to flight,
And, as thou seest, ourselves in heavy
    plight.
    Lewis. Renowned Queen, with patience
    calm the storm,
While we bethink a means to break it off.
    Q. Mar. The more we stay, the stronger
    grows our foe.   40
    Lewis. The more I stay, the more I'll
    succour thee.
    Q. Mar. O, but impatience waiteth on
    true sorrow.
And see where comes the breeder of my
    sorrow !

Enter WARWICK.

    Lewis. What's he approacheth boldly to
    our presence ?
    Q. Mar. Our Earl of Warwick, Edward's
    greatest friend.   45
    Lewis. Welcome, brave Warwick ! What
    brings thee to France ?
      [*He descends. She ariseth.*
    Q. Mar. Ay, now begins a second storm
    to rise ;
For this is he that moves both wind and
    tide.
    War. From worthy Edward, King of
    Albion,
My lord and sovereign, and thy vowed
    friend,   50
I come, in kindness and unfeigned love,
First to do greetings to thy royal person,
And then to crave a league of amity,
And lastly to confirm that amity
With nuptial knot, if thou vouchsafe to
    grant   55
That virtuous Lady Bona, thy fair sister,
To England's King in lawful marriage.
    Q. Mar. [*Aside*] If that go forward,
    Henry's hope is done.
    War. [*To Bona*] And, gracious madam, in
    our king's behalf,
I am commanded, with your leave and
    favour,   60
Humbly to kiss your hand, and with my
    tongue
To tell the passion of my sovereign's heart ;
Where fame, late ent'ring at his heedful
    ears,
Hath plac'd thy beauty's image and thy
    virtue.
    Q. Mar. King Lewis and Lady Bona, hear
    me speak   65
Before you answer Warwick. His demand
Springs not from Edward's well-meant
    honest love,
But from deceit bred by necessity ;
For how can tyrants safely govern home
Unless abroad they purchase great alliance?
To prove him tyrant this reason may
    suffice,   71
That Henry liveth still ; but were he
    dead,
Yet here Prince Edward stands, King
    Henry's son.
Look therefore, Lewis, that by this league
    and marriage
Thou draw not on thy danger and dishonour;
For though usurpers sway the rule a while
Yet heav'ns are just, and time suppresseth
    wrongs.   77
    War. Injurious Margaret !
    Prince.   And why not Queen ?
    War. Because thy father Henry did
    usurp ;
And thou no more art prince than she is
    queen.   80

Oxf. Then Warwick disannuls great John
 of Gaunt,
Which did subdue the greatest part of
 Spain ;
And, after John of Gaunt, Henry the
 Fourth,
Whose wisdom was a mirror to the wisest ;
And, after that wise prince, Henry the
 Fifth,   85
Who by his prowess conquered all France.
From these our Henry lineally descends.
 War. Oxford, how haps it in this smooth
  discourse
You told not how Henry the Sixth hath
 lost
All that which Henry the Fifth had gotten ?
Methinks these peers of France should smile
 at that.   91
But for the rest : you tell a pedigree
Of threescore and two years—a silly time
To make prescription for a kingdom's
 worth.
 Oxf. Why, Warwick, canst thou speak
  against thy liege, 95
Whom thou obeyed'st thirty and six years,
And not bewray thy treason with a blush ?
 War. Can Oxford that did ever fence the
  right
Now buckler falsehood with a pedigree ?
For shame ! Leave Henry, and call Edward
 king.   100
 Oxf. Call him my king by whose in-
  jurious doom
My elder brother, the Lord Aubrey Vere,
Was done to death ; and more than so, my
 father,
Even in the downfall of his mellow'd years,
When nature brought him to the door of
 death ?   105
No, Warwick, no ; while life upholds this
 arm,
This arm upholds the house of Lancaster.
 War. And I the house of York.
 Lewis. Queen Margaret, Prince Edward,
  and Oxford,
Vouchsafe at our request to stand aside 110
While I use further conference with War-
 wick.   [*They stand aloof.*
 Q. Mar. Heavens grant that Warwick's
  words bewitch him not !
 Lewis. Now, Warwick, tell me, even upon
  thy conscience,
Is Edward your true king ? for I were loath
To link with him that were not lawful
 chosen.   115
 War. Thereon I pawn my credit and
  mine honour.
 Lewis. But is he gracious in the people's
  eye ?
 War. The more that Henry was un-
  fortunate.
 Lewis. Then further : all dissembling set
  aside,
Tell me for truth the measure of his love 120

Unto our sister Bona.
 War.   Such it seems
As may beseem a monarch like himself.
Myself have often heard him say and swear
That this his love was an eternal plant
Whereof the root was fix'd in virtue's
 ground,   125
The leaves and fruit maintain'd with
 beauty's sun,
Exempt from envy, but not from disdain,
Unless the Lady Bona quit his pain.
 Lewis. Now, sister, let us hear your firm
  resolve.
 Bona. Your grant or your denial shall be
  mine.   130
[*To Warwick*] Yet I confess that often ere
 this day,
When I have heard your king's desert
 recounted,
Mine ear hath tempted judgment to desire.
 Lewis. Then, Warwick, thus : our sister
  shall be Edward's. 134
And now forthwith shall articles be drawn
Touching the jointure that your king must
 make,
Which with her dowry shall be counter-
 pois'd.
Draw near, Queen Margaret, and be a
 witness
That Bona shall be wife to the English
 king.
 Prince. To Edward, but not to the
  English king. 140
 Q. Mar. Deceitful Warwick, it was thy
  device
By this alliance to make void my suit.
Before thy coming, Lewis was Henry's
 friend.
 Lewis. And still is friend to him and
  Margaret.
But if your title to the crown be weak, 145
As may appear by Edward's good success,
Then 'tis but reason that I be releas'd
From giving aid which late I promised.
Yet shall you have all kindness at my
 hand
That your estate requires and mine can
 yield.   150
 War. Henry now lives in Scotland at his
  ease,
Where having nothing, nothing can he lose.
And as for you yourself, our quondam
 queen,
You have a father able to maintain you,
And better 'twere you troubled him than
 France.   155
 Q. Mar. Peace, impudent and shameless
  Warwick,
Proud setter up and puller down of kings !
I will not hence till with my talk and tears,
Both full of truth, I make King Lewis
 behold
Thy sly conveyance and thy lord's false
 love ;   160

For both of you are birds of self-same
    feather.
    [*Post blowing a horn within.*
Lewis. Warwick, this is some post to us
    or thee.

       Enter the Post.

Post. My lord ambassador, these letters
    are for you,
Sent from your brother, Marquis Montague.
These from our King unto your Majesty. 165
And, madam, these for you ; from whom I
    know not. [*They all read their letters.*
Oxf. I like it well that our fair Queen and
    mistress
Smiles at her news, while Warwick frowns
    at his.
Prince. Nay, mark how Lewis stamps as
    he were nettled.
I hope all's for the best. 170
    Lewis. Warwick, what are thy news ?
    And yours, fair Queen ?
Q. Mar. Mine such as fill my heart with
    unhop'd joys.
War. Mine full of sorrow and heart's
    discontent.
Lewis. What, has your king married the
    Lady Grey ? 174
And now, to soothe your forgery and his,
Sends me a paper to persuade me patience ?
Is this th' alliance that he seeks with
    France ?
Dare he presume to scorn us in this
    manner ?
Q. Mar. I told your Majesty as much
    before.
This proveth Edward's love and Warwick's
    honesty. 180
War. King Lewis, I here protest in sight
    of heaven,
And by the hope I have of heavenly bliss,
That I am clear from this misdeed of
    Edward's—
No more my king, for he dishonours me,
But most himself, if he could see his
    shame. 185
Did I forget that by the house of York
My father came untimely to his death ?
Did I let pass th' abuse done to my niece ?
Did I impale him with the regal crown ?
Did I put Henry from his native right ? 190
And am I guerdon'd at the last with shame?
Shame on himself ! for my desert is honour ;
And to repair my honour lost for him
I here renounce him and return to Henry.
My noble Queen, let former grudges pass,
And henceforth I am thy true servitor. 196
I will revenge his wrong to Lady Bona,
And replant Henry in his former state.
    Q. Mar. Warwick, these words have
    turn'd my hate to love ;
And I forgive and quite forget old faults, 200
And joy that thou becom'st King Henry's
    friend.

    War. So much his friend, ay, his un-
    feigned friend,
That if King Lewis vouchsafe to furnish us
With some few bands of chosen soldiers,
I'll undertake to land them on our coast 205
And force the tyrant from his seat by war.
'Tis not his new-made bride shall succour
    him ;
And as for Clarence, as my letters tell me,
He's very likely now to fall from him
For matching more for wanton lust than
    honour 210
Or than for strength and safety of our
    country.
    Bona. Dear brother, how shall Bona be
    reveng'd
But by thy help to this distressed queen ?
    Q. Mar. Renowned Prince, how shall
    poor Henry live 214
Unless thou rescue him from foul despair ?
    Bona. My quarrel and this English
    queen's are one.
    War. And mine, fair Lady Bona, joins
    with yours.
    Lewis. And mine with hers, and thine,
    and Margaret's.
Therefore, at last, I firmly am resolv'd
You shall have aid. 220
    Q. Mar. Let me give humble thanks for
    all at once.
    Lewis. Then, England's messenger, re-
    turn in post
And tell false Edward, thy supposed king,
That Lewis of France is sending over
    masquers
To revel it with him and his new bride. 225
Thou seest what's past ; go fear thy king
    withal.
    Bona. Tell him, in hope he'll prove a
    widower shortly,
I'll wear the willow-garland for his sake.
    Q. Mar. Tell him my mourning weeds are
    laid aside,
And I am ready to put armour on. 230
    War. Tell him from me that he hath done
    me wrong,
And therefore I'll uncrown him ere't be
    long.
There's thy reward ; be gone. [*Exit Post.*
    Lewis.   But, Warwick,
Thou and Oxford, with five thousand men,
Shall cross the seas and bid false Edward
    battle ; 235
And, as occasion serves, this noble Queen
And Prince shall follow with a fresh supply.
Yet, ere thou go, but answer me one doubt :
What pledge have we of thy firm loyalty ?
    War. This shall assure my constant
    loyalty : 240
That if our Queen and this young Prince
    agree,
I'll join mine eldest daughter and my
    joy
To him forthwith in holy wedlock bands.

Q. Mar. Yes, I agree, and thank you for
    your motion.
Son Edward, she is fair and virtuous,   245
Therefore delay not—give thy hand to
    Warwick ;
And with thy hand thy faith irrevocable
That only Warwick's daughter shall be
    thine.
    Prince. Yes, I accept her, for she well
    deserves it ;
And here, to pledge my vow, I give my
    hand.   250
            [*He gives his hand to Warwick.*
Lewis. Why stay we now ? These
    soldiers shall be levied ;
And thou, Lord Bourbon, our High
    Admiral,
Shall waft them over with our royal fleet.
I long till Edward fall by war's mischance
For mocking marriage with a dame of
    France. [*Exeunt all but Warwick.*
War. I came from Edward as ambas-
    sador,   256
But I return his sworn and mortal foe.
Matter of marriage was the charge he gave
    me,
But dreadful war shall answer his demand.
Had he none else to make a stale but me ?
Then none but I shall turn his jest to sorrow.
I was the chief that rais'd him to the crown,
And I'll be chief to bring him down again;
Not that I pity Henry's misery,
But seek revenge on Edward's mockery. 265
                      [*Exit.*

ACT FOUR

Scene I. *London. The palace.*

Enter Gloucester, Clarence, Somerset,
    and Montague.

  Glo. Now tell me, brother Clarence, what
    think you
Of this new marriage with the Lady Grey ?
Hath not our brother made a worthy
    choice ?
  Clar. Alas, you know 'tis far from hence
    to France !
How could he stay till Warwick made
    return ?   5
  Som. My lords, forbear this talk ; here
    comes the King.

Flourish. Enter King Edward, *attended ;*
  Lady Grey, *as Queen ;* Pembroke,
  Stafford, Hastings, *and* Others. *Four
  stand on one side, and four on the other.*

  Glo. And his well-chosen bride.
  Clar. I mind to tell him plainly what I
    think.
  K. Edw. Now, brother of Clarence, how
    like you our choice   9
That you stand pensive as half malcontent ?
  Clar. As well as Lewis of France or the
    Earl of Warwick,

Which are so weak of courage and in
    judgment
That they'll take no offence at our abuse.
  K. Edw. Suppose they take offence with-
    out a cause ;
They are but Lewis and Warwick : I am
    Edward,   15
Your King and Warwick's, and must have
    my will.
  Glo. And shall have your will, because our
    King.
Yet hasty marriage seldom proveth well.
  K. Edw. Yea, brother Richard, are you
    offended too ?
  Glo. Not I.   20
No, God forbid that I should wish them
    sever'd
Whom God hath join'd together ; ay, and
    'twere pity
To sunder them that yoke so well together.
  K. Edw. Setting your scorns and your
    mislike aside,
Tell me some reason why the Lady Grey 25
Should not become my wife and England's
    Queen.
And you too, Somerset and Montague,
Speak freely what you think.
  Clar. Then this is mine opinion : that
    King Lewis
Becomes your enemy for mocking him   30
About the marriage of the Lady Bona.
  Glo. And Warwick, doing what you gave
    in charge,
Is now dishonoured by this new marriage.
  K. Edw. What if both Lewis and War-
    wick be appeas'd
By such invention as I can devise ?   35
  Mont. Yet to have join'd with France in
    such alliance
Would more have strength'ned this our
    commonwealth
'Gainst foreign storms than any home-bred
    marriage.
  Hast. Why, knows not Montague that of
    itself
England is safe, if true within itself ?   40
  Mont. But the safer when 'tis back'd
    with France.
  Hast. 'Tis better using France than trust-
    ing France.
Let us be back'd with God, and with the
    seas   43
Which He hath giv'n for fence impregnable,
And with their helps only defend ourselves.
In them and in ourselves our safety lies.
  Clar. For this one speech Lord Hastings
    well deserves
To have the heir of the Lord Hungerford.
  K. Edw. Ay, what of that ? it was my
    will and grant ;
And for this once my will shall stand for
    law.   50
  Glo. And yet methinks your Grace hath
    not done well

To give the heir and daughter of Lord
    Scales
Unto the brother of your loving bride.
She better would have fitted me or Clarence;
But in your bride you bury brotherhood.
    Clar. Or else you would not have bestow'd
      the heir   56
Of the Lord Bonville on your new wife's
    son,
And leave your brothers to go speed else-
    where.
    K. Edw. Alas, poor Clarence! Is it for a
      wife
That thou art malcontent? I will provide
    thee.   60
    Clar. In choosing for yourself you show'd
      your judgment,
Which being shallow, you shall give me
    leave
To play the broker in mine own behalf;
And to that end I shortly mind to leave
    you.
    K. Edw. Leave me or tarry, Edward will
      be King,   65
And not be tied unto his brother's will.
    Q. Eliz. My lords, before it pleas'd his
      Majesty
To raise my state to title of a queen,
Do me but right, and you must all confess
That I was not ignoble of descent;   70
And meaner than myself have had like
    fortune.
But as this title honours me and mine,
So your dislikes, to whom I would be
    pleasing,
Doth cloud my joys with danger and with
    sorrow.
    K. Edw. My love, forbear to fawn upon
      their frowns.   75
What danger or what sorrow can befall
    thee,
So long as Edward is thy constant friend
And their true sovereign whom they must
    obey?
Nay, whom they shall obey, and love thee
    too,
Unless they seek for hatred at my hands; 80
Which if they do, yet will I keep thee
    safe,
And they shall feel the vengeance of my
    wrath.
    Glo. [*Aside*] I hear, yet say not much, but
    think the more.

        Enter a Post.

    K. Edw. Now, messenger, what letters or
      what news
From France?   85
    Mess. My sovereign liege, no letters, and
      few words,
But such as I, without your special pardon,
Dare not relate.
    K. Edw. Go to, we pardon thee; there-
    fore, in brief,

Tell me their words as near as thou canst
    guess them.   90
What answer makes King Lewis unto our
    letters?
    Mess. At my depart, these were his very
    words:
' Go tell false Edward, the supposed king,
That Lewis of France is sending over
    masquers
To revel it with him and his new bride '. 95
    K. Edw. Is Lewis so brave? Belike he
    thinks me Henry.
But what said Lady Bona to my marriage?
    Mess. These were her words, utt'red with
    mild disdain:
' Tell him, in hope he'll prove a widower
    shortly,
I'll wear the willow-garland for his sake '. 100
    K. Edw. I blame not her: she could say
    little less;
She had the wrong. But what said Henry's
    queen?
For I have heard that she was there in place.
    Mess. ' Tell him ' quoth she ' my mourn-
    ing weeds are done,
And I am ready to put armour on.'   105
    K. Edw. Belike she minds to play the
    Amazon.
But what said Warwick to these injuries?
    Mess. He, more incens'd against your
    Majesty
Than all the rest, discharg'd me with these
    words:
' Tell him from me that he hath done me
    wrong;   110
And therefore I'll uncrown him ere't be
    long '.
    K. Edw. Ha! durst the traitor breathe
    out so proud words?
Well, I will arm me, being thus forewarn'd.
They shall have wars and pay for their
    presumption.   114
But say, is Warwick friends with Margaret?
    Mess. Ay, gracious sovereign; they are
    so link'd in friendship
That young Prince Edward marries War-
    wick's daughter.
    Clar. Belike the elder; Clarence will have
    the younger.
Now, brother king, farewell, and sit you
    fast,
For I will hence to Warwick's other
    daughter;   120
That, though I want a kingdom, yet in
    marriage
I may not prove inferior to yourself.
You that love me and Warwick, follow me.
        [*Exit, and Somerset follows.*
    Glo. [*Aside*] Not I.   124
My thoughts aim at a further matter; I
Stay not for the love of Edward but the
    crown.
    K. Edw. Clarence and Somerset both
    gone to Warwick!

Yet am I arm'd against the worst can
    happen ;
And haste is needful in this desp'rate case.
Pembroke and Stafford, you in our behalf 130
Go levy men and make prepare for war ;
They are already, or quickly will be landed.
Myself in person will straight follow you.
        [Exeunt Pembroke and Stafford.
But ere I go, Hastings and Montague,
Resolve my doubt. You twain, of all the
    rest, 135
Are near to Warwick by blood and by
    alliance.
Tell me if you love Warwick more than me?
If it be so, then both depart to him :
I rather wish you foes than hollow friends.
But if you mind to hold your true obedience,
Give me assurance with some friendly vow,
That I may never have you in suspect.
  Mont. So God help Montague as he
    proves true !
  Hast. And Hastings as he favours
    Edward's cause !
  K. Edw. Now, brother Richard, will you
    stand by us ? 145
  Glo. Ay, in despite of all that shall
    withstand you.
  K. Edw. Why, so ! then am I sure of
    victory.
Now therefore let us hence, and lose no
    hour
Till we meet Warwick with his foreign
    pow'r.   [Exeunt.

SCENE II. A plain in Warwickshire.

Enter WARWICK and OXFORD, with French
    Soldiers.

  War. Trust me, my lord, all hitherto goes
    well ;
The common people by numbers swarm to
    us.

Enter CLARENCE and SOMERSET.

But see where Somerset and Clarence comes.
Speak suddenly, my lords—are we all
    friends ?
  Clar. Fear not that, my lord. 5
  War. Then, gentle Clarence, welcome
    unto Warwick ;
And welcome, Somerset. I hold it cowardice
To rest mistrustful where a noble heart
Hath pawn'd an open hand in sign of love ;
Else might I think that Clarence, Edward's
    brother, 10
Were but a feigned friend to our proceed-
    ings.
But welcome, sweet Clarence ; my daughter
    shall be thine.
And now what rests but, in night's cover-
    ture,
Thy brother being carelessly encamp'd,
His soldiers lurking in the towns about, 15
And but attended by a simple guard,

We may surprise and take him at our
    pleasure ?
Our scouts have found the adventure very
    easy ;
That as Ulysses and stout Diomede
With sleight and manhood stole to Rhesus'
    tents, 20
And brought from thence the Thracian
    fatal steeds,
So we, well cover'd with the night's black
    mantle,
At unawares may beat down Edward's
    guard
And seize himself—I say not 'slaughter him',
For I intend but only to surprise him. 25
You that will follow me to this attempt,
Applaud the name of Henry with your
    leader.   [They all cry ' Henry ! '
Why then, let's on our way in silent sort.
For Warwick and his friends, God and Saint
    George !   [Exeunt.

SCENE III. Edward's camp, near Warwick.

Enter three Watchmen, to guard the King's
    tent.

  1 Watch. Come on, my masters, each man
    take his stand ;
The King by this is set him down to sleep.
  2 Watch. What, will he not to bed ?
  1 Watch. Why, no ; for he hath made a
    solemn vow
Never to lie and take his natural rest 5
Till Warwick or himself be quite suppress'd.
  2 Watch. To-morrow then, belike, shall
    be the day,
If Warwick be so near as men report.
  3 Watch. But say, I pray, what nobleman
    is that 9
That with the King here resteth in his tent?
  1 Watch. 'Tis the Lord Hastings, the
    King's chiefest friend.
  3 Watch. O, is it so ? But why commands
    the King
That his chief followers lodge in towns
    about him,
While he himself keeps in the cold field ?
  2 Watch. 'Tis the more honour, because
    more dangerous. 15
  3 Watch. Ay, but give me worship and
    quietness ;
I like it better than a dangerous honour.
If Warwick knew in what estate he stands,
'Tis to be doubted he would waken him.
  1 Watch. Unless our halberds did shut up
    his passage. 20
  2 Watch. Ay, wherefore else guard we his
    royal tent
But to defend his person from night-foes ?

Enter WARWICK, CLARENCE, OXFORD,
SOMERSET, and French Soldiers, silent all.

  War. This is his tent ; and see where
    stand his guard.

Courage, my masters!   Honour now or
    never!
But follow me, and Edward shall be ours. 25
  1 *Watch*. Who goes there?
  2 *Watch*. Stay, or thou diest.
    [*Warwick and the rest cry all ' Warwick!
    Warwick!' and set upon the Guard,
    who fly, crying ' Arm! Arm!'
    Warwick and the rest following them.*

*The drum playing and trumpet sounding,
re-enter* WARWICK *and the* rest, *bringing
the* KING *out in his gown, sitting in a
chair.* GLOUCESTER *and* HASTINGS *fly
over the stage.*

  Som. What are they that fly there?
  War. Richard and Hastings. Let them
go; here is the Duke.
  K. Edw. The Duke! Why, Warwick,
    when we parted,   30
Thou call'dst me King?
  War.   Ay, but the case is alter'd.
When you disgrac'd me in my embassade,
Then I degraded you from being King,
And come now to create you Duke of York.
Alas, how should you govern any kingdom
That know not how to use ambassadors, 36
Nor how to be contented with one wife,
Nor how to use your brothers brotherly,
Nor how to study for the people's welfare,
Nor how to shroud yourself from enemies?
  K. Edw. Yea, brother of Clarence, art
    thou here too?   41
Nay, then I see that Edward needs must
    down.
Yet, Warwick, in despite of all mischance,
Of thee thyself and all thy complices,
Edward will always bear himself as King.
Though fortune's malice overthrow my
    state,   46
My mind exceeds the compass of her wheel.
  War. Then, for his mind, be Edward
    England's king;
             [*Takes off his crown.*
But Henry now shall wear the English
    crown
And be true King indeed; thou but the
    shadow.   50
My Lord of Somerset, at my request,
See that forthwith Duke Edward be con-
    vey'd
Unto my brother, Archbishop of York.
When I have fought with Pembroke and
    his fellows,
I'll follow you and tell what answer   55
Lewis and the Lady Bona send to him.
Now for a while farewell, good Duke of
    York.
  K. Edw. What fates impose, that men
    must needs abide;
It boots not to resist both wind and tide.
          [*They lead him out forcibly.*
  Oxf. What now remains, my lords, for us
    to do   60

But march to London with our soldiers?
  War. Ay, that's the first thing that we
    have to do;
To free King Henry from imprisonment,
And see him seated in the regal throne.
             [*Exeunt.*

SCENE IV.   *London.   The palace.*

Enter QUEEN ELIZABETH *and* RIVERS.

  Riv. Madam, what makes you in this
    sudden change?
  Q. Eliz. Why, brother Rivers, are you yet
    to learn
What late misfortune is befall'n King
    Edward?
  Riv. What, loss of some pitch'd battle
    against Warwick?
  Q. Eliz. No, but the loss of his own royal
    person.   5
  Riv. Then is my sovereign slain?
  Q. Eliz. Ay, almost slain, for he is taken
    prisoner;
Either betray'd by falsehood of his guard
Or by his foe surpris'd at unawares;
And, as I further have to understand, 10
Is new committed to the Bishop of York,
Fell Warwick's brother, and by that our
    foe.
  Riv. These news, I must confess, are full
    of grief;
Yet, gracious madam, bear it as you may:
Warwick may lose that now hath won the
    day.   15
  Q. Eliz. Till then, fair hope must hinder
    life's decay.
And I the rather wean me from despair
For love of Edward's offspring in my womb.
This is it that makes me bridle passion
And bear with mildness my misfortune's
    cross;   20
Ay, ay, for this I draw in many a tear
And stop the rising of blood-sucking sighs,
Lest with my sighs or tears I blast or drown
King Edward's fruit, true heir to th'
    English crown.
  Riv. But, madam, where is Warwick
    then become?   25
  Q. Eliz. I am inform'd that he comes
    towards London
To set the crown once more on Henry's
    head.
Guess thou the rest: King Edward's friends
    must down.
But to prevent the tyrant's violence—
For trust not him that hath once broken
    faith—   30
I'll hence forthwith unto the sanctuary
To save at least the heir of Edward's right.
There shall I rest secure from force and
    fraud.
Come, therefore, let us fly while we may fly:
If Warwick take us, we are sure to die. 35
             [*Exeunt.*

SCENE V. *A park near Middleham Castle in Yorkshire.*

Enter GLOUCESTER, LORD HASTINGS, SIR WILLIAM STANLEY, *and Others.*

Glo. Now, my Lord Hastings and Sir
　　William Stanley,
Leave off to wonder why I drew you hither
Into this chiefest thicket of the park.
Thus stands the case: you know our King,
　　my brother,
Is prisoner to the Bishop here, at whose
　　hands   5
He hath good usage and great liberty;
And often but attended with weak guard
Comes hunting this way to disport himself.
I have advertis'd him by secret means
That if about this hour he make this way,
Under the colour of his usual game,   11
He shall here find his friends, with horse
　　and men,
To set him free from his captivity.

Enter KING EDWARD *and a Huntsman with him.*

Hunt. This way, my lord; for this way
　　lies the game.
K. Edw. Nay, this way, man. See where
　　the huntsmen stand.   15
Now, brother of Gloucester, Lord Hastings,
　　and the rest,
Stand you thus close to steal the Bishop's
　　deer?
Glo. Brother, the time and case requireth
　　haste;
Your horse stands ready at the park corner.
K. Edw. But whither shall we then?
Hast. To Lynn, my lord; and shipt from
　　thence to Flanders.   21
Glo. Well guess'd, believe me; for that
　　was my meaning.
K. Edw. Stanley, I will requite thy
　　forwardness.
Glo. But wherefore stay we? 'Tis no
　　time to talk.
K. Edw. Huntsmen, what say'st thou?
　　Wilt thou go along?   25
Hunt. Better do so than tarry and be
　　hang'd.
Glo. Come then, away; let's ha' no more
　　ado.
K. Edw. Bishop, farewell. Shield thee
　　from Warwick's frown,
And pray that I may repossess the crown.
　　　　　　　　　　　　　　　[*Exeunt.*

SCENE VI. *London. The Tower.*

Flourish. Enter KING HENRY, CLARENCE, WARWICK, SOMERSET, *young* HENRY EARL OF RICHMOND, OXFORD, MONTAGUE, Lieutenant of the Tower, *and* Attendants.

K. Hen. Master Lieutenant, now that
　　God and friends
Have shaken Edward from the regal seat
And turn'd my captive state to liberty,
My fear to hope, my sorrows unto joys,   4
At our enlargement what are thy due fees?
Lieut. Subjects may challenge nothing of
　　their sov'reigns;
But if an humble prayer may prevail,
I then crave pardon of your Majesty.
K. Hen. For what, Lieutenant? For
　　well using me?
Nay, be thou sure I'll well requite thy
　　kindness,   10
For that it made my imprisonment a
　　pleasure;
Ay, such a pleasure as incaged birds
Conceive when, after many moody thoughts,
At last by notes of household harmony
They quite forget their loss of liberty.   15
But, Warwick, after God, thou set'st me
　　free,
And chiefly therefore I thank God and thee;
He was the author, thou the instrument.
Therefore, that I may conquer fortune's
　　spite
By living low where fortune cannot hurt
　　me,   20
And that the people of this blessed land
May not be punish'd with my thwarting
　　stars,
Warwick, although my head still wear the
　　crown,
I here resign my government to thee,
For thou art fortunate in all thy deeds.   25
War. Your Grace hath still been fam'd
　　for virtuous,
And now may seem as wise as virtuous
By spying and avoiding fortune's malice,
For few men rightly temper with the stars;
Yet in this one thing let me blame your
　　Grace,   30
For choosing me when Clarence is in place.
Clar. No, Warwick, thou art worthy of
　　the sway,
To whom the heav'ns in thy nativity
Adjudg'd an olive branch and laurel crown,
As likely to be blest in peace and war;   35
And therefore I yield thee my free consent.
War. And I choose Clarence only for
　　Protector.
K. Hen. Warwick and Clarence, give me
　　both your hands.
Now join your hands, and with your hands
　　your hearts,
That no dissension hinder government.   40
I make you both Protectors of this land,
While I myself will lead a private life
And in devotion spend my latter days,
To sin's rebuke and my Creator's praise.
War. What answers Clarence to his
　　sovereign's will?   45
Clar. That he consents, if Warwick yield
　　consent,

For on thy fortune I repose myself.
  War. Why, then, though loath, yet must
  I be content.
We'll yoke together, like a double shadow
To Henry's body, and supply his place ; 50
I mean, in bearing weight of government,
While he enjoys the honour and his ease.
And, Clarence, now then it is more than
  needful
Forthwith that Edward be pronounc'd a
  traitor,
And all his lands and goods confiscated. 55
  Clar. What else ? And that succession be
  determin'd.
  War. Ay, therein Clarence shall not want
  his part.
  K. Hen. But, with the first of all your
  chief affairs,
Let me entreat—for I command no more—
That Margaret your Queen and my son
  Edward 60
Be sent for to return from France with
  speed ;
For till I see them here, by doubtful fear
My joy of liberty is half eclips'd.
  Clar. It shall be done, my sovereign, with
  all speed.
  K. Hen. My Lord of Somerset, what
  youth is that, 65
Of whom you seem to have so tender care ?
  Som. My liege, it is young Henry, Earl
  of Richmond.
  K. Hen. Come hither, England's hope.
    [*Lays his hand on his head.*
        If secret powers
Suggest but truth to my divining thoughts,
This pretty lad will prove our country's
  bliss. 70
His looks are full of peaceful majesty ;
His head by nature fram'd to wear a crown,
His hand to wield a sceptre ; and himself
Likely in time to bless a regal throne.
Make much of him, my lords ; for this is
  he
Must help you more than you are hurt
  by me. 76

    Enter a Post.

  War. What news, my friend ?
  Post. That Edward is escaped from your
  brother
And fled, as he hears since, to Burgundy.
  War. Unsavoury news ! But how made
  he escape ? 80
  Post. He was convey'd by Richard Duke
  of Gloucester
And the Lord Hastings, who attended him
In secret ambush on the forest side
And from the Bishop's huntsmen rescu'd
  him ;
For hunting was his daily exercise. 85
  War. My brother was too careless of his
  charge.
But let us hence, my sovereign, to provide

A salve for any sore that may betide.
  [*Exeunt all but Somerset, Richmond, and
    Oxford.*
  Som. My lord, I like not of this flight of
  Edward's ;
For doubtless Burgundy will yield him
  help, 90
And we shall have more wars before't be
  long.
As Henry's late presaging prophecy
Did glad my heart with hope of this young
  Richmond,
So doth my heart misgive me, in these
  conflicts, 94
What may befall him to his harm and ours.
Therefore, Lord Oxford, to prevent the
  worst,
Forthwith we'll send him hence to Brittany,
Till storms be past of civil enmity.
  Oxf. Ay, for if Edward repossess the
  crown,
'Tis like that Richmond with the rest shall
  down. 100
  Som. It shall be so ; he shall to Brittany.
Come therefore, let's about it speedily.
                    [*Exeunt.*

    SCENE VII. *Before York.*

Flourish.   *Enter* KING EDWARD, GLOU-
CESTER, HASTINGS, *and* Soldiers.

  K. Edw. Now, brother Richard, Lord
  Hastings, and the rest,
Yet thus far fortune maketh us amends,
And says that once more I shall interchange
My waned state for Henry's regal crown.
Well have we pass'd and now repass'd the
  seas, 5
And brought desired help from Burgundy ;
What then remains, we being thus arriv'd
From Ravenspurgh haven before the gates
  of York,
But that we enter, as into our dukedom ?
  Glo. The gates made fast ! Brother, I like
  not this ; 10
For many men that stumble at the thresh-
  old
Are well foretold that danger lurks within.
  K. Edw. Tush, man, abodements must
  not now affright us.
By fair or foul means we must enter in,
For hither will our friends repair to us. 15
  Hast. My liege, I'll knock once more to
  summon them.

Enter, on the walls, the Mayor of York *and
his* Brethren.

  May. My lords, we were forewarned of
  your coming
And shut the gates for safety of ourselves,
For now we owe allegiance unto Henry.
  K. Edw. But, Master Mayor, if Henry be
  your King, 20
Yet Edward at the least is Duke of York.

May. True, my good lord; I know you
  for no less.
K. Edw. Why, and I challenge nothing
  but my dukedom,
As being well content with that alone.
Glo. [*Aside*] But when the fox hath once
  got in his nose,   25
He'll soon find means to make the body
  follow.
Hast. Why, Master Mayor, why stand
  you in a doubt ?
Open the gates; we are King Henry's
  friends.
May. Ay, say you so ? The gates shall
  then be open'd.   [*He descends.*
Glo. A wise stout captain, and soon
  persuaded !   30
Hast. The good old man would fain that
  all were well,
So 'twere not long of him; but being
  ent'red,
I doubt not, I, but we shall soon persuade
Both him and all his brothers unto reason.

Enter, below, the Mayor *and two* Aldermen.

K. Edw. So, Master Mayor. These gates
  must not be shut   35
But in the night or in the time of war.
What ! fear not, man, but yield me up the
  keys;   [*Takes his keys.*
For Edward will defend the town and
  thee,
And all those friends that deign to follow
  me.

March. Enter MONTGOMERY *with drum and*
  Soldiers.

Glo. Brother, this is Sir John Mont-
  gomery,   40
Our trusty friend, unless I be deceiv'd.
K. Edw. Welcome, Sir John ! But why
  come you in arms ?
Mont. To help King Edward in his time
  of storm,
As every loyal subject ought to do.
K. Edw. Thanks, good Montgomery; but
  we now forget   45
Our title to the crown, and only claim
Our dukedom till God please to send the
  rest.
Mont. Then fare you well, for I will hence
  again.
I came to serve a king and not a duke.   49
Drummer, strike up, and let us march
  away. [*The Drum begins to march.*
K. Edw. Nay, stay, Sir John, a while, and
  we'll debate
By what safe means the crown may be
  recover'd.
Mont. What talk you of debating ? In
  few words :
If you'll not here proclaim yourself our
  King,   54
I'll leave you to your fortune and be gone

To keep them back that come to succour
  you.
Why shall we fight, if you pretend no title ?
Glo. Why, brother, wherefore stand you
  on nice points ?
K. Edw. When we grow stronger, then
  we'll make our claim;
Till then 'tis wisdom to conceal our
  meaning.   60
Hast. Away with scrupulous wit ! Now
  arms must rule.
Glo. And fearless minds climb soonest
  unto crowns.
Brother, we will proclaim you out of hand ;
The bruit thereof will bring you many
  friends.
K. Edw. Then be it as you will ; for 'tis
  my right,   65
And Henry but usurps the diadem.
Mont. Ay, now my sovereign speaketh
  like himself ;
And now will I be Edward's champion.
Hast. Sound trumpet ; Edward shall be
  here proclaim'd.   69
Come, fellow soldier, make thou proclama-
  tion. [*Gives him a paper. Flourish.*
Sold. [*Reads*] ' Edward the Fourth, by
the grace of God, King of England and
France, and Lord of Ireland, &c.'
Mont. And whoso'er gainsays King
Edward's right,
By this I challenge him to single fight.
              [*Throws down his gauntlet.*
All. Long live Edward the Fourth !   75
K. Edw. Thanks, brave Montgomery, and
  thanks unto you all ;
If fortune serve me, I'll requite this
  kindness.
Now for this night let's harbour here in
  York ;
And when the morning sun shall raise his
  car
Above the border of this horizon,   80
We'll forward towards Warwick and his
  mates ;
For well I wot that Henry is no soldier.
Ah, froward Clarence, how evil it beseems
  thee
To flatter Henry and forsake thy brother !
Yet, as we may, we'll meet both thee and
  Warwick.   85
Come on, brave soldiers ; doubt not of the
  day,
And, that once gotten, doubt not of large
  pay.   [*Exeunt.*

SCENE VIII. *London. The palace.*

Flourish. Enter KING HENRY, WARWICK,
  MONTAGUE, CLARENCE, OXFORD, *and*
  EXETER.

War. What counsel, lords ? Edward from
  Belgia,
With hasty Germans and blunt Hollanders,

Hath pass'd in safety through the narrow
    seas
And with his troops doth march amain to
    London ;
And many giddy people flock to him.   5
  K. Hen. Let's levy men and beat him
    back again.
  Clar. A little fire is quickly trodden out,
Which, being suffer'd, rivers cannot quench.
  War. In Warwickshire I have true-
    hearted friends,
Not mutinous in peace, yet bold in war ; 10
Those will I muster up, and thou, son
    Clarence,
Shalt stir up in Suffolk, Norfolk, and in
    Kent,
The knights and gentlemen to come with
    thee.
Thou, brother Montague, in Buckingham,
Northampton, and in Leicestershire, shalt
    find   15
Men well inclin'd to hear what thou com-
    mand'st.
And thou, brave Oxford, wondrous well
    belov'd,
In Oxfordshire shalt muster up thy friends.
My sovereign, with the loving citizens,
Like to his island girt in with the ocean 20
Or modest Dian circled with her nymphs,
Shall rest in London till we come to him.
Fair lords, take leave and stand not to
    reply.
Farewell, my sovereign.
  K. Hen. Farewell, my Hector and my
    Troy's true hope.   25
  Clar. In sign of truth, I kiss your
    Highness' hand.
  K. Hen. Well-minded Clarence, be thou
    fortunate !
  Mont. Comfort, my lord ; and so I take
    my leave.
  Oxf. [*Kissing the King's hand*] And thus
    I seal my truth and bid adieu.
  K. Hen. Sweet Oxford, and my loving
    Montague,   30
And all at once, once more a happy fare-
    well.
  War. Farewell, sweet lords ; let's meet
    at Coventry.
    [*Exeunt all but the King and Exeter.*
  K. Hen. Here at the palace will I rest
    a while.
Cousin of Exeter, what thinks your lord-
    ship ?
Methinks the power that Edward hath in
    field   35
Should not be able to encounter mine.
  Exe. The doubt is that he will seduce the
    rest.
  K. Hen. That's not my fear ; my meed
    hath got me fame :
I have not stopp'd mine ears to their
    demands,   39
Nor posted off their suits with slow delays ;

My pity hath been balm to heal their
    wounds,
My mildness hath allay'd their swelling
    griefs,
My mercy dried their water-flowing tears ;
I have not been desirous of their wealth,
Nor much oppress'd them with great sub-
    sidies,   45
Nor forward of revenge, though they much
    err'd.
Then why should they love Edward more
    than me ?
No, Exeter, these graces challenge grace ;
And, when the lion fawns upon the lamb,
The lamb will never cease to follow him. 50
[*Shout within ' A Lancaster ! A Lancaster !'*
  Exe. Hark, hark, my lord ! What shouts
    are these ?

Enter KING EDWARD, GLOUCESTER, *and*
    Soldiers.

  K. Edw. Seize on the shame-fac'd Henry,
    bear him hence ;
And once again proclaim us King of
    England.
You are the fount that makes small brooks
    to flow.
Now stops thy spring ; my sea shall suck
    them dry,   55
And swell so much the higher by their ebb.
Hence with him to the Tower : let him
    not speak.
      [*Exeunt some with King Henry.*
And, lords, towards Coventry bend we our
    course,
Where peremptory Warwick now remains.
The sun shines hot ; and, if we use delay, 60
Cold biting winter mars our hop'd-for hay.
  Glo. Away betimes, before his forces join,
And take the great-grown traitor unawares.
Brave warriors, march amain towards
    Coventry.   [*Exeunt.*

ACT FIVE

SCENE I. *Coventry.*

Enter WARWICK, *the* Mayor of Coventry, *two*
Messengers, *and* Others *upon the walls.*

  War. Where is the post that came from
    valiant Oxford ?
How far hence is thy lord, mine honest
    fellow ?
  1 Mess. By this at Dunsmore, marching
    hitherward.
  War. How far off is our brother Mon-
    tague ?
Where is the post that came from Mon-
    tague ?   5
  2 Mess. By this at Daintry, with a
    puissant troop.

Enter SIR JOHN SOMERVILLE.

  War. Say, Somerville, what says my
    loving son ?

And by thy guess how nigh is Clarence
    now ?
Som. At Southam I did leave him with
    his forces,   9
And do expect him here some two hours
    hence.   [*Drum heard.*
War. Then Clarence is at hand ; I hear
    his drum.
Som. It is not his, my lord ; here
    Southam lies.
The drum your Honour hears marcheth
    from Warwick.
War. Who should that be ? Belike un-
    look'd for friends.
Som. They are at hand, and you shall
    quickly know.   15

March. Flourish. Enter KING EDWARD,
    GLOUCESTER, *and* Soldiers.

K. Edw. Go, trumpet, to the walls, and
    sound a parle.
Glo. See how the surly Warwick mans
    the wall.
War. O unbid spite ! Is sportful Edward
    come ?
Where slept our scouts or how are they
    seduc'd   19
That we could hear no news of his repair ?
K. Edw. Now, Warwick, wilt thou ope
    the city gates,
Speak gentle words, and humbly bend thy
    knee,
Call Edward King, and at his hands beg
    mercy ?
And he shall pardon thee these outrages.
War. Nay, rather, wilt thou draw thy
    forces hence,   25
Confess who set thee up and pluck'd thee
    down,
Call Warwick patron, and be penitent ?
And thou shalt still remain the Duke of
    York.
Glo. I thought, at least, he would have
    said the King ;
Or did he make the jest against his will ? 30
War. Is not a dukedom, sir, a goodly
    gift ?
Glo. Ay, by my faith, for a poor earl to
    give.
I'll do thee service for so good a gift.
War. 'Twas I that gave the kingdom to
    thy brother.
K. Edw. Why then 'tis mine, if but by
    Warwick's gift.   35
War. Thou art no Atlas for so great a
    weight ;
And, weakling, Warwick takes his gift
    again ;
And Henry is my King, Warwick his
    subject.
K. Edw. But Warwick's king is Edward's
    prisoner.
And, gallant Warwick, do but answer this :
What is the body when the head is off ? 41

Glo. Alas, that Warwick had no more
    forecast,
But, whiles he thought to steal the single
    ten,
The king was slily finger'd from the deck !
You left poor Henry at the Bishop's palace,
And ten to one you'll meet him in the
    Tower.   46
K. Edw. 'Tis even so ; yet you are
    Warwick still.
Glo. Come, Warwick, take the time ;
    kneel down, kneel down.
Nay, when ? Strike now, or else the iron
    cools.
War. I had rather chop this hand off at
    a blow,   50
And with the other fling it at thy face,
Than bear so low a sail to strike to thee.
K. Edw. Sail how thou canst, have wind
    and tide thy friend,
This hand, fast wound about thy coal-black
    hair,
Shall, whiles thy head is warm and new
    cut off,   55
Write in the dust this sentence with thy
    blood :
' Wind-changing Warwick now can change
    no more '.

Enter OXFORD, *with drum and colours.*

War. O cheerful colours ! See where
    Oxford comes.
Oxf. Oxford, Oxford, for Lancaster !   59
        [*He and his forces enter the city.*
Glo. The gates are open, let us enter too.
K. Edw. So other foes may set upon our
    backs.
Stand we in good array, for they no doubt
Will issue out again and bid us battle ;
If not, the city being but of small defence,
We'll quickly rouse the traitors in the same.
War. O, welcome, Oxford ! for we want
    thy help.   66

Enter MONTAGUE, *with drum and colours.*

Mont. Montague, Montague, for Lan-
    caster !
        [*He and his forces enter the city.*
Glo. Thou and thy brother both shall buy
    this treason
Even with the dearest blood your bodies
    bear.
K. Edw. The harder match'd, the greater
    victory.   70
My mind presageth happy gain and con-
    quest.

Enter SOMERSET, *with drum and colours.*

Som. Somerset, Somerset, for Lancaster !
        [*He and his forces enter the city.*
Glo. Two of thy name, both Dukes of
    Somerset,
Have sold their lives unto the house of
    York ;

And thou shalt be the third, if this sword
    hold.   75

Enter CLARENCE, *with drum and colours.*

  War. And lo where George of Clarence
    sweeps along,
Of force enough to bid his brother battle ;
With whom an upright zeal to right prevails
More than the nature of a brother's love.
  Clar. Clarence, Clarence, for Lancaster !
  K. Edw. Et tu Brute—wilt thou stab
    Cæsar too ?
A parley, sirrah, to George of Clarence.
    [*Sound a parley. Richard and Clarence*
        whisper.
  War. Come, Clarence, come. Thou wilt
    if Warwick call.   80
  Clar. [*Taking the red rose from his hat and*
throwing it at Warwick] Father of Warwick,
    know you what this means ?
Look here, I throw my infamy at thee.
I will not ruinate my father's house,
Who gave his blood to lime the stones
    together,
And set up Lancaster. Why, trowest thou,
    Warwick,   85
That Clarence is so harsh, so blunt, un-
    natural,
To bend the fatal instruments of war
Against his brother and his lawful King ?
Perhaps thou wilt object my holy oath.
To keep that oath were more impiety   90
Than Jephtha when he sacrific'd his
    daughter.
I am so sorry for my trespass made
That, to deserve well at my brother's hands,
I here proclaim myself thy mortal foe ;   94
With resolution whereso'er I meet thee—
As I will meet thee, if thou stir abroad—
To plague thee for thy foul misleading me.
And so, proud-hearted Warwick, I defy
    thee,   98
And to my brother turn my blushing cheeks.
Pardon me, Edward, I will make amends ;
And, Richard, do not frown upon my faults,
For I will henceforth be no more uncon-
    stant.
  K. Edw. Now welcome more, and ten
    times more belov'd,
Than if thou never hadst deserv'd our hate.
  Glo. Welcome, good Clarence ; this is
    brother-like.   105
  War. O passing traitor, perjur'd and
    unjust !
  K. Edw. What, Warwick, wilt thou leave
    the town and fight ?
Or shall we beat the stones about thine
    ears ?
  War. Alas, I am not coop'd here for
    defence !
I will away towards Barnet presently   110
And bid thee battle, Edward, if thou dar'st.
  K. Edw. Yes, Warwick, Edward dares
    and leads the way.

Lords, to the field ; Saint George and
    victory ! [*Exeunt Yorkists. March.*
    Warwick and his company follow.

SCENE II. *A field of battle near Barnet.*

Alarum and excursions.   *Enter* KING
EDWARD, *bringing forth* WARWICK
wounded.

  K. Edw. So, lie thou there. Die thou, and
    die our fear ;
For Warwick was a bug that fear'd us all.
Now, Montague, sit fast ; I seek for thee,
That Warwick's bones may keep thine
    company.   [*Exit.*
  War. Ah, who is nigh ? Come to me,
    friend or foe,   5
And tell me who is victor, York or War-
    wick ?
Why ask I that ? My mangled body shows,
My blood, my want of strength, my sick
    heart shows,
That I must yield my body to the earth
And, by my fall, the conquest to my foe. 10
Thus yields the cedar to the axe's edge,
Whose arms gave shelter to the princely
    eagle,
Under whose shade the ramping lion slept,
Whose top-branch overpeer'd Jove's spread-
    ing tree
And kept low shrubs from winter's pow'rful
    wind.   15
These eyes, that now are dimm'd with
    death's black veil,
Have been as piercing as the mid-day sun
To search the secret treasons of the world ;
The wrinkles in my brows, now fill'd with
    blood,
Were lik'ned oft to kingly sepulchres ;   20
For who liv'd King, but I could dig his
    grave ?
And who durst smile when Warwick bent
    his brow ?
Lo now my glory smear'd in dust and
    blood !
My parks, my walks, my manors, that I
    had,   25
Even now forsake me ; and of all my
    lands
Is nothing left me but my body's length.
Why, what is pomp, rule, reign, but earth
    and dust ?
And live we how we can, yet die we must.

Enter OXFORD *and* SOMERSET.

  Som. Ah, Warwick, Warwick ! wert thou
    as we are,
We might recover all our loss again.   30
The Queen from France hath brought a
    puissant power ;
Even now we heard the news. Ah, couldst
    thou fly !
  War. Why then, I would not fly. Ah,
    Montague,

If thou be there, sweet brother, take my
   hand,   34
And with thy lips keep in my soul a while!
Thou lov'st me not ; for, brother, if thou
   didst,
Thy tears would wash this cold congealed
   blood
That glues my lips and will not let me
   speak.
Come quickly, Montague, or I am dead.
   Som. Ah, Warwick ! Montague hath
   breath'd his last ;   40
And to the latest gasp cried out for
   Warwick,
And said ' Commend me to my valiant
   brother '.
And more he would have said ; and more
   he spoke,
Which sounded like a clamour in a vault,
That mought not be distinguish'd ; but at
   last,   45
I well might hear, delivered with a groan,
' O farewell, Warwick ! '
   War. Sweet rest his soul ! Fly, lords, and
   save yourselves ;
For Warwick bids you all farewell, to meet
   in heaven.   [*Dies.*
   Oxf. Away, away, to meet the Queen's
   great power !   50
      [*Here they bear away his body.*

SCENE III.   *Another part of the field.*

Flourish. Enter KING EDWARD *in triumph ;
with* GLOUCESTER, CLARENCE, *and the* rest.

   K. Edw. Thus far our fortune keeps an
   upward course,
And we are grac'd with wreaths of victory.
But in the midst of this bright-shining day
I spy a black, suspicious, threat'ning cloud
That will encounter with our glorious sun 5
Ere he attain his easeful western bed—
I mean, my lords, those powers that the
   Queen
Hath rais'd in Gallia have arriv'd our coast
And, as we hear, march on to fight with us.
   Clar. A little gale will soon disperse that
   cloud   10
And blow it to the source from whence it
   came ;
Thy very beams will dry those vapours up,
For every cloud engenders not a storm.
   Glo. The Queen is valued thirty thousand
   strong,
And Somerset, with Oxford, fled to her. 15
If she have time to breathe, be well assur'd
Her faction will be full as strong as ours.
   K. Edw. We are advertis'd by our loving
   friends
That they do hold their course toward
   Tewksbury ;
We, having now the best at Barnet field, 20
Will thither straight, for willingness rids
   way ;

And as we march our strength will be
   augmented
In every county as we go along.
Strike up the drum ; cry ' Courage ! ' and
   away.   [*Exeunt.*

SCENE IV.   *Plains near Tewksbury.*

Flourish. March. Enter QUEEN MARGARET,
PRINCE EDWARD, SOMERSET, OXFORD,
and Soldiers.

   Q. Mar. Great lords, wise men ne'er sit
   and wail their loss,
But cheerly seek how to redress their harms.
What though the mast be now blown over-
   board,   3
The cable broke, the holding-anchor lost,
And half our sailors swallow'd in the flood ;
Yet lives our pilot still. Is't meet that he
Should leave the helm and, like a fearful
   lad,
With tearful eyes add water to the sea
And give more strength to that which hath
   too much ;
Whiles, in his moan, the ship splits on the
   rock,   10
Which industry and courage might have
   sav'd ?
Ah, what a shame ! ah, what a fault were
   this !
Say Warwick was our anchor ; what of
   that ?
And Montague our top-mast ; what of
   him ?
Our slaught'red friends the tackles ; what
   of these ?   15
Why, is not Oxford here another anchor ?
And Somerset another goodly mast ?
The friends of France our shrouds and
   tacklings ?
And, though unskilful, why not Ned and I
For once allow'd the skilful pilot's charge ?
We will not from the helm to sit and weep,
But keep our course, though the rough wind
   say no,   22
From shelves and rocks that threaten us with
   wreck.
As good to chide the waves as speak them
   fair.
And what is Edward but a ruthless sea ? 25
What Clarence but a quicksand of deceit ?
And Richard but a ragged fatal rock ?
All these the enemies to our poor bark.
Say you can swim ; alas, 'tis but a while !
Tread on the sand ; why, there you quickly
   sink.   30
Bestride the rock ; the tide will wash you
   off,
Or else you famish—that's a threefold
   death.
This speak I, lords, to let you understand,
If case some one of you would fly from us,
That there's no hop'd-for mercy with the
   brothers   35

More than with ruthless waves, with sands,
    and rocks.
Why, courage then! What cannot be
    avoided
'Twere childish weakness to lament or fear.
   Prince. Methinks a woman of this valiant
    spirit
Should, if a coward heard her speak these
    words,   40
Infuse his breast with magnanimity
And make him naked foil a man-at-arms.
I speak not this as doubting any here;
For did I but suspect a fearful man,
He should have leave to go away betimes, 45
Lest in our need he might infect another
And make him of like spirit to himself.
If any such be here—as God forbid !—
Let him depart before we need his help.
   Oxf. Women and children of so high a
    courage,   50
And warriors faint ! Why, 'twere perpetual
    shame.
O brave young Prince! thy famous
    grandfather
Doth live again in thee. Long mayst thou
    live
To bear his image and renew his glories !
   Som. And he that will not fight for such a
    hope,   55
Go home to bed and, like the owl by day,
If he arise, be mock'd and wond'red at.
   Q. Mar. Thanks, gentle Somerset ; sweet
    Oxford, thanks.
   Prince. And take his thanks that yet
    hath nothing else.

        Enter a Messenger.

   Mess. Prepare you, lords, for Edward is
    at hand   60
Ready to fight ; therefore be resolute.
   Oxf. I thought no less. It is his policy
To haste thus fast, to find us unprovided.
   Som. But he's deceiv'd ; we are in
    readiness.
   Q. Mar. This cheers my heart, to see your
    forwardness.   65
   Oxf. Here pitch our battle ; hence we
    will not budge.

Flourish and march. Enter, at a distance,
KING EDWARD, GLOUCESTER, CLARENCE,
and Soldiers.

   K. Edw. Brave followers, yonder stands
    the thorny wood
Which, by the heavens' assistance and your
    strength,
Must by the roots be hewn up yet ere night.
I need not add more fuel to your fire,   70
For well I wot ye blaze to burn them out.
Give signal to the fight, and to it, lords.
   Q. Mar. Lords, knights, and gentlemen,
    what I should say
My tears gainsay ; for every word I speak,
Ye see, I drink the water of my eye.   75

Therefore, no more but this : Henry, your
    sovereign,
Is prisoner to the foe ; his state usurp'd,
His realm a slaughter-house, his subjects
    slain,
His statutes cancell'd, and his treasure
    spent ;
And yonder is the wolf that makes this
    spoil.   80
You fight in justice. Then, in God's name,
    lords,
Be valiant, and give signal to the fight.
       [*Alarum, retreat, excursions. Exeunt.*

   SCENE V. *Another part of the field.*

Flourish. Enter KING EDWARD, CLARENCE,
   GLOUCESTER, *and* Forces, *with* QUEEN
   MARGARET, OXFORD, *and* SOMERSET,
   prisoners.

   K. Edw. Now here a period of tumultuous
    broils.
Away with Oxford to Hames Castle
    straight ;
For Somerset, off with his guilty head.
Go, bear them hence ; I will not hear them
    speak.
   Oxf. For my part, I'll not trouble thee
    with words.   5
   Som. Nor I, but stoop with patience to
    my fortune.
       [*Exeunt Oxford and Somerset, guarded.*
   Q. Mar. So part we sadly in this troublous
    world,
To meet with joy in sweet Jerusalem.
   K. Edw. Is proclamation made that who
    finds Edward
Shall have a high reward, and he his life ? 10
   Glo. It is ; and lo where youthful Edward
    comes.

Enter Soldiers, *with* PRINCE EDWARD.

   K. Edw. Bring forth the gallant ; let us
    hear him speak.
What, can so young a man begin to prick ?
Edward, what satisfaction canst thou make
For bearing arms, for stirring up my
    subjects,   15
And all the trouble thou hast turn'd me to ?
   Prince. Speak like a subject, proud
    ambitious York.
Suppose that I am now my father's mouth ;
Resign thy chair, and where I stand kneel
    thou,
Whilst I propose the self-same words to
    thee   20
Which, traitor, thou wouldst have me
    answer to.
   Q. Mar. Ah, that thy father had been so
    resolv'd !
   Glo. That you might still have worn the
    petticoat
And ne'er have stol'n the breech from
    Lancaster.

Prince. Let Æsop fable in a winter's
   night ;   25
His currish riddles sorts not with this place.
Glo. By heaven, brat, I'll plague ye for
   that word.
Q. Mar. Ay, thou wast born to be a
   plague to men.
Glo. For God's sake, take away this
   captive scold.
Prince. Nay, take away this scolding
   crookback rather.   30
K. Edw. Peace, wilful boy, or I will charm
   your tongue.
Clar. Untutor'd lad, thou art too
   malapert.
Prince. I know my duty ; you are all
   undutiful.
Lascivious Edward, and thou perjur'd
   George,
And thou misshapen Dick, I tell ye all 35
I am your better, traitors as ye are ;
And thou usurp'st my father's right and
   mine.
K. Edw. Take that, the likeness of this
   railer here.   [*Stabs him.*
Glo. Sprawl'st thou ? Take that, to end
   thy agony.   [*Stabs him.*
Clar. And there's for twitting me with
   perjury.   [*Stabs him.*
Q. Mar. O, kill me too !   41
Glo. Marry, and shall. [*Offers to kill her.*
K. Edw. Hold, Richard, hold ; for we
   have done too much.
Glo. Why should she live to fill the world
   with words ?
K. Edw. What, doth she swoon ? Use
   means for her recovery.   45
Glo. Clarence, excuse me to the King my
   brother.
I'll hence to London on a serious matter ;
Ere ye come there, be sure to hear some
   news.
Clar. What ? what ?   49
Glo. The Tower ! the Tower !   [*Exit.*
Q. Mar. O Ned, sweet Ned, speak to thy
   mother, boy !
Canst thou not speak ? O traitors !
   murderers !
They that stabb'd Cæsar shed no blood at
   all,
Did not offend, nor were not worthy blame,
If this foul deed were by to equal it. 55
He was a man : this, in respect, a child ;
And men ne'er spend their fury on a child.
What's worse than murderer, that I may
   name it ?
No, no, my heart will burst, an if I speak—
And I will speak, that so my heart may
   burst.   60
Butchers and villains ! bloody cannibals !
How sweet a plant have you untimely
   cropp'd !
You have no children, butchers ; if you
   had,

The thought of them would have stirr'd up
   remorse.
But if you ever chance to have a child, 65
Look in his youth to have him so cut
   off
As, deathsmen, you have rid this sweet
   young prince !
K. Edw. Away with her ; go, bear her
   hence perforce.
Q. Mar. Nay, never bear me hence ;
   dispatch me here.
Here sheathe thy sword ; I'll pardon thee
   my death.   70
What, wilt thou not ? Then, Clarence, do
   it thou.
Clar. By heaven, I will not do thee so
   much ease.
Q. Mar. Good Clarence, do ; sweet
   Clarence, do thou do it.
Clar. Didst thou not hear me swear I
   would not do it ?
Q. Mar. Ay, but thou usest to forswear
   thyself.   75
'Twas sin before, but now 'tis charity.
What ! wilt thou not ? Where is that
   devil's butcher,
Hard-favour'd Richard ? Richard, where
   art thou ?
Thou art not here. Murder is thy alms-
   deed ;
Petitioners for blood thou ne'er put'st
   back.   80
K. Edw. Away, I say ; I charge ye bear
   her hence.
Q. Mar. So come to you and yours as to
   this prince ! [*Exit, led out forcibly.*
K. Edw. Where's Richard gone ?
Clar. To London, all in post ; and, as I
   guess,
To make a bloody supper in the Tower. 85
K. Edw. He's sudden, if a thing comes in
   his head.
Now march we hence. Discharge the
   common sort
With pay and thanks ; and let's away to
   London
And see our gentle queen how well she
   fares.
By this, I hope, she hath a son for me. 90
    [*Exeunt.*

SCENE VI. *London. The Tower.*

Enter KING HENRY *and* GLOUCESTER *with
the* Lieutenant, *on the walls.*

Glo. Good day, my lord. What, at your
   book so hard ?
K. Hen. Ay, my good lord—my lord, I
   should say rather.
'Tis sin to flatter ; ' good ' was little better.
' Good Gloucester ' and ' good devil ' were
   alike,
And both preposterous ; therefore, not
   ' good lord '.   5

Glo. Sirrah, leave us to ourselves; we
    must confer.   [*Exit Lieutenant.*
  K. Hen. So flies the reckless shepherd
    from the wolf;
So first the harmless sheep doth yield his
    fleece,
And next his throat unto the butcher's
    knife.
What scene of death hath Roscius now to
    act?   10
  Glo. Suspicion always haunts the guilty
    mind:
The thief doth fear each bush an officer.
  K. Hen. The bird that hath been limed
    in a bush
With trembling wings misdoubteth every
    bush;
And I, the hapless male to one sweet bird, 15
Have now the fatal object in my eye
Where my poor young was lim'd, was
    caught, and kill'd.
  Glo. Why, what a peevish fool was that
    of Crete
That taught his son the office of a fowl!
And yet, for all his wings, the fool was
    drown'd.   20
  K. Hen. I, Dædalus; my poor boy,
    Icarus;
Thy father, Minos, that denied our course;
The sun that sear'd the wings of my sweet
    boy,
Thy brother Edward; and thyself, the sea
Whose envious gulf did swallow up his life.
Ah, kill me with thy weapon, not with
    words!   26
My breast can better brook thy dagger's
    point
Than can my ears that tragic history.
But wherefore dost thou come? Is't for my
    life?   29
  Glo. Think'st thou I am an executioner?
  K. Hen. A persecutor I am sure thou art.
If murdering innocents be executing,
Why, then thou art an executioner.
  Glo. Thy son I kill'd for his presumption.
  K. Hen. Hadst thou been kill'd when first
    thou didst presume,   35
Thou hadst not liv'd to kill a son of mine.
And thus I prophesy, that many a thousand
Which now mistrust no parcel of my fear,
And many an old man's sigh, and many a
    widow's,   39
And many an orphan's water-standing
    eye—
Men for their sons, wives for their hus-
    bands,
Orphans for their parents' timeless death—
Shall rue the hour that ever thou wast born.
The owl shriek'd at thy birth—an evil sign;
The night-crow cried, aboding luckless
    time;   45
Dogs howl'd, and hideous tempest shook
    down trees;
The raven rook'd her on the chimney's top,

And chatt'ring pies in dismal discords sung;
Thy mother felt more than a mother's pain,
And yet brought forth less than a mother's
    hope,   50
To wit, an indigest deformed lump,
Not like the fruit of such a goodly tree.
Teeth hadst thou in thy head when thou
    wast born,
To signify thou cam'st to bite the world;
And if the rest be true which I have heard,
Thou cam'st—   56
  Glo. I'll hear no more. Die, prophet, in
    thy speech.   [*Stabs him.*
For this, amongst the rest, was I ordain'd.
  K. Hen. Ay, and for much more slaughter
    after this.
O, God forgive my sins and pardon thee!   60
                                 [*Dies.*
  Glo. What, will the aspiring blood of
    Lancaster
Sink in the ground? I thought it would
    have mounted.
See how my sword weeps for the poor
    King's death.
O, may such purple tears be alway shed
From those that wish the downfall of our
    house!   65
If any spark of life be yet remaining,
Down, down to hell; and say I sent thee
    thither—   [*Stabs him again.*
I, that have neither pity, love, nor fear.
Indeed, 'tis true that Henry told me of;
For I have often heard my mother say   70
I came into the world with my legs forward.
Had I not reason, think ye, to make haste
And seek their ruin that usurp'd our right?
The midwife wonder'd; and the women
    cried
'O, Jesus bless us, he is born with teeth!'
And so I was, which plainly signified   76
That I should snarl, and bite, and play the
    dog.
Then, since the heavens have shap'd my
    body so,
Let hell make crook'd my mind to answer it.
I have no brother, I am like no brother;   80
And this word 'love', which greybeards
    call divine,
Be resident in men like one another,
And not in me! I am myself alone.
Clarence, beware; thou keep'st me from
    the light,
But I will sort a pitchy day for thee;   85
For I will buzz abroad such prophecies
That Edward shall be fearful of his life;
And then to purge his fear, I'll be thy
    death.
King Henry and the Prince his son are gone.
Clarence, thy turn is next, and then the
    rest;   90
Counting myself but bad till I be best.
I'll throw thy body in another room,
And triumph, Henry, in thy day of doom.
                       [*Exit with the body.*

SCENE VII. *London. The palace.*

Flourish. Enter KING EDWARD, QUEEN
ELIZABETH, CLARENCE, GLOUCESTER,
HASTINGS, Nurse *with the young* PRINCE,
and Attendants.

K. Edw. Once more we sit in England's
    royal throne,
Repurchas'd with the blood of enemies.
What valiant foemen, like to autumn's
    corn,
Have we mow'd down in tops of all their
    pride !
Three Dukes of Somerset, threefold re-
    nown'd   5
For hardy and undoubted champions ;
Two Cliffords, as the father and the son ;
And two Northumberlands—two braver
    men
Ne'er spurr'd their coursers at the trumpet's
    sound ;
With them the two brave bears, Warwick
    and Montague,   10
That in their chains fetter'd the kingly
    lion
And made the forest tremble when they
    roar'd.
Thus have we swept suspicion from our seat
And made our footstool of security.
Come hither, Bess, and let me kiss my
    boy.   15
Young Ned, for thee thine uncles and
    myself
Have in our armours watch'd the winter's
    night,
Went all afoot in summer's scalding heat,
That thou might'st repossess the crown in
    peace ;
And of our labours thou shalt reap the gain.
    Glo. [*Aside*] I'll blast his harvest if your
    head were laid ;   21
For yet I am not look'd on in the world.

This shoulder was ordain'd so thick to
    heave ;
And heave it shall some weight or break my
    back.
Work thou the way—and that shall
    execute.   25
    K. Edw. Clarence and Gloucester, love
    my lovely queen ;
And kiss your princely nephew, brothers
    both.
    Clar. The duty that I owe unto your
    Majesty
I seal upon the lips of this sweet babe.
    K. Edw. Thanks, noble Clarence; worthy
    brother, thanks.   30
    Glo. And that I love the tree from whence
    thou sprang'st,
Witness the loving kiss I give the fruit.
[*Aside*] To say the truth, so Judas kiss'd
    his master
And cried ' All hail ! ' when as he meant
    all harm.
    K. Edw. Now am I seated as my soul
    delights,   35
Having my country's peace and brothers'
    loves.
    Clar. What will your Grace have done
    with Margaret ?
Reignier, her father, to the King of France
Hath pawn'd the Sicils and Jerusalem,
And hither have they sent it for her
    ransom.   40
    K. Edw. Away with her, and waft her
    hence to France.
And now what rests but that we spend the
    time
With stately triumphs, mirthful comic
    shows,
Such as befits the pleasure of the court ?
Sound drums and trumpets. Farewell, sour
    annoy !   45
For here, I hope, begins our lasting joy.
                [*Exeunt.*

KING RICHARD THE THIRD

DRAMATIS PERSONÆ

KING EDWARD THE FOURTH.
EDWARD, PRINCE OF WALES, *afterwards* KING EDWARD V,
RICHARD, DUKE OF YORK, } *sons to the King.*

GEORGE, DUKE OF CLARENCE,
RICHARD, DUKE OF GLOUCESTER, *afterwards* KING RICHARD III, } *brothers to the King*

A Young Son of Clarence (*Edward, Earl of Warwick*).
HENRY, EARL OF RICHMOND, *afterwards* KING HENRY VII.
CARDINAL BOURCHIER, ARCHBISHOP OF CANTERBURY.
THOMAS ROTHERHAM, ARCHBISHOP OF YORK.
JOHN MORTON, BISHOP OF ELY.
DUKE OF BUCKINGHAM.
DUKE OF NORFOLK.
EARL OF SURREY, *his son.*
EARL RIVERS, *brother to King Edward's Queen.*
MARQUIS OF DORSET *and* LORD GREY, *her sons.*
EARL OF OXFORD.
LORD HASTINGS.
LORD STANLEY, *called also* EARL OF DERBY.
LORD LOVEL.

SIR THOMAS VAUGHAN.
SIR RICHARD RATCLIFF.
SIR WILLIAM CATESBY.
SIR JAMES TYRREL.
SIR JAMES BLOUNT.
SIR WALTER HERBERT.
SIR ROBERT BRAKENBURY, *Lieutenant of the Tower.*
SIR WILLIAM BRANDON.
CHRISTOPHER URSWICK, *a priest.*
LORD MAYOR OF LONDON.
Sheriff of Wiltshire.
HASTINGS, *a pursuivant.*
TRESSEL *and* BERKELEY, *gentlemen attending on the Lady Anne.*

ELIZABETH, Queen to King Edward IV.
MARGARET, *widow of King Henry VI.*
DUCHESS OF YORK, *mother to King Edward IV, Clarence, and Gloucester.*
LADY ANNE, *widow of Edward Prince of Wales, son to King Henry VI; afterwards married to the Duke of Gloucester.*
A Young Daughter of Clarence (*Margaret Plantagenet, Countess of Salisbury*).

Ghosts, *of Richard's victims.*
Lords, Gentlemen, *and* Attendants; Priest, Scrivener, Page, Bishops, Aldermen, Citizens, Soldiers, Messengers, Murderers, Keeper.

THE SCENE: *England.*

ACT ONE

SCENE I. *London. A street.*

Enter RICHARD, DUKE OF GLOUCESTER, *solus.*

Glo. Now is the winter of our discontent
Made glorious summer by this sun of York;
And all the clouds that lour'd upon our house
In the deep bosom of the ocean buried.
Now are our brows bound with victorious wreaths;   5
Our bruised arms hung up for monuments;
Our stern alarums chang'd to merry meetings,
Our dreadful marches to delightful measures.
Grim-visag'd war hath smooth'd his wrinkled front,
And now, instead of mounting barbed steeds   10
To fright the souls of fearful adversaries,
He capers nimbly in a lady's chamber
To the lascivious pleasing of a lute.
But I—that am not shap'd for sportive tricks,
Nor made to court an amorous looking-glass—   15
I—that am rudely stamp'd, and want love's majesty
To strut before a wanton ambling nymph—
I—that am curtail'd of this fair proportion,
Cheated of feature by dissembling nature,
Deform'd, unfinish'd, sent before my time
Into this breathing world scarce half made up,   21
And that so lamely and unfashionable
That dogs bark at me as I halt by them—
Why, I, in this weak piping time of peace,
Have no delight to pass away the time,   25
Unless to spy my shadow in the sun
And descant on mine own deformity.
And therefore, since I cannot prove a lover
To entertain these fair well-spoken days,
I am determined to prove a villain   30
And hate the idle pleasures of these days.
Plots have I laid, inductions dangerous,

By drunken prophecies, libels, and dreams,
To set my brother Clarence and the King
In deadly hate the one against the other ;
And if King Edward be as true and just 36
As I am subtle, false, and treacherous,
This day should Clarence closely be mew'd
    up—
About a prophecy which says that G
Of Edward's heirs the murderer shall be. 40
Dive, thoughts, down to my soul. Here
    Clarence comes.

Enter CLARENCE, *guarded, and*
    BRAKENBURY.

Brother, good day. What means this armed
    guard
That waits upon your Grace ?
    Clar.   His Majesty,
Tend'ring my person's safety, hath ap-
    pointed
This conduct to convey me to th' Tower. 45
    Glo. Upon what cause ?
    Clar.   Because my name is George.
    Glo. Alack, my lord, that fault is none of
    yours :
He should, for that, commit your god-
    fathers.
O, belike his Majesty hath some intent
That you should be new-christ'ned in the
    Tower.   50
But what's the matter, Clarence ? May I
    know ?
    Clar. Yea, Richard, when I know ; for I
    protest
As yet I do not ; but, as I can learn,
He hearkens after prophecies and dreams,
And from the cross-row plucks the letter
    G,   55
And says a wizard told him that by G
His issue disinherited should be ;
And, for my name of George begins with G,
It follows in his thought that I am he.
These, as I learn, and such like toys as
    these   60
Hath mov'd his Highness to commit me
    now.
    Glo. Why, this it is when men are rul'd
    by women :
'Tis not the King that sends you to the
    Tower ;
My Lady Grey his wife, Clarence, 'tis she
That tempers him to this extremity.   65
Was it not she and that good man of
    worship,
Antony Woodville, her brother there,
That made him send Lord Hastings to the
    Tower,
From whence this present day he is
    delivered ?   69
We are not safe, Clarence ; we are not safe.
    Clar. By heaven, I think there is no man
    is secure
But the Queen's kindred, and night-walking
    heralds

That trudge betwixt the King and Mistress
    Shore.
Heard you not what an humble suppliant
Lord Hastings was, for her delivery ?   75
    Glo. Humbly complaining to her deity
Got my Lord Chamberlain his liberty.
I'll tell you what—I think it is our way,
If we will keep in favour with the King,
To be her men and wear her livery :   80
The jealous o'er-worn widow and herself,
Since that our brother dubb'd them gentle-
    women,
Are mighty gossips in our monarchy.
    Brak. I beseech your Graces both to
    pardon me :
His Majesty hath straitly given in charge 85
That no man shall have private conference,
Of what degree soever, with your brother.
    Glo. Even so ; an't please your worship,
    Brakenbury,
You may partake of any thing we say :
We speak no treason, man ; we say the
    King   90
Is wise and virtuous, and his noble queen
Well struck in years, fair, and not jealous ;
We say that Shore's wife hath a pretty foot,
A cherry lip, a bonny eye, a passing pleasing
    tongue ;
And that the Queen's kindred are made
    gentlefolks.   95
How say you, sir ? Can you deny all this ?
    Brak. With this, my lord, myself have
    nought to do.
    Glo. Nought to do with Mistress Shore !
    I tell thee, fellow,
He that doth naught with her, excepting one,
Were best to do it secretly alone.   100
    Brak. What one, my lord ?
    Glo. Her husband, knave ! Wouldst thou
    betray me ?
    Brak. I do beseech your Grace to pardon
    me, and withal
Forbear your conference with the noble
    Duke.
    Clar. We know thy charge, Brakenbury,
    and will obey.   105
    Glo. We are the Queen's abjects and must
    obey.
Brother, farewell ; I will unto the King ;
And whatsoe'er you will employ me in—
Were it to call King Edward's widow
    sister—
I will perform it to enfranchise you.   110
Meantime, this deep disgrace in brother-
    hood
Touches me deeper than you can imagine.
    Clar. I know it pleaseth neither of us well.
    Glo. Well, your imprisonment shall not be
    long ;
I will deliver you, or else lie for you.   115
Meantime, have patience.
    Clar.   I must perforce. Farewell.
        [*Exeunt Clarence, Brakenbury,
                and Guard.*

Glo. Go tread the path that thou shalt
　　ne'er return.
Simple, plain Clarence, I do love thee so
That I will shortly send thy soul to heaven,
If heaven will take the present at our hands.
But who comes here?　The new-delivered
　　Hastings?　　　　　　　　　　121

Enter LORD HASTINGS.

Hast. Good time of day unto my gracious
　　lord!
Glo. As much unto my good Lord
　　Chamberlain!
Well are you welcome to the open air.
How hath your lordship brook'd imprison-
　　ment?　　　　　　　　　　　　125
Hast. With patience, noble lord, as
　　prisoners must;
But I shall live, my lord, to give them
　　thanks
That were the cause of my imprisonment.
Glo. No doubt, no doubt; and so shall
　　Clarence too;
For they that were your enemies are his, 130
And have prevail'd as much on him as you.
Hast. More pity that the eagles should be
　　mew'd
Whiles kites and buzzards prey at liberty.
Glo. What news abroad?
Hast. No news so bad abroad as this at
　　home:　　　　　　　　　　　135
The King is sickly, weak, and melancholy,
And his physicians fear him mightily.
Glo. Now, by Saint John, that news is
　　bad indeed.
O, he hath kept an evil diet long
And overmuch consum'd his royal person!
'Tis very grievous to be thought upon. 141
Where is he?　In his bed?
Hast. He is.
Glo. Go you before, and I will follow you.
　　　　　　　　　　　　[Exit Hastings.
He cannot live, I hope, and must not die 145
Till George be pack'd with posthorse up to
　　heaven.
I'll in to urge his hatred more to Clarence
With lies well steel'd with weighty argu-
　　ments;
And, if I fail not in my deep intent,
Clarence hath not another day to live; 150
Which done, God take King Edward to his
　　mercy,
And leave the world for me to bustle in!
For then I'll marry Warwick's youngest
　　daughter.
What though I kill'd her husband and her
　　father?
The readiest way to make the wench
　　amends　　　　　　　　　　155
Is to become her husband and her father;
The which will I—not all so much for love
As for another secret close intent
By marrying her which I must reach unto.
But yet I run before my horse to market.

Clarence still breathes; Edward still lives
　　and reigns;　　　　　　　　　161
When they are gone, then must I count my
　　gains.　　　　　　　　　　[Exit.

SCENE II. *London. Another street.*

*Enter the corpse of King Henry the Sixth,
　　with* Halberds *to guard it;* LADY
　　ANNE *being the mourner, attended by*
　　TRESSEL *and* BERKELEY.

Anne. Set down, set down your honour-
　　able load—
If honour may be shrouded in a hearse,
Whilst I awhile obsequiously lament
Th' untimely fall of virtuous Lancaster.
Poor key-cold figure of a holy king!　5
Pale ashes of the house of Lancaster!
Thou bloodless remnant of that royal
　　blood!
Be it lawful that I invocate thy ghost
To hear the lamentations of poor Anne,
Wife to thy Edward, to thy slaughtered
　　son,　　　　　　　　　　　10
Stabb'd by the self-same hand that made
　　these wounds.
Lo, in these windows that let forth thy life
I pour the helpless balm of my poor eyes.
Curs'd be the hand that made these fatal
　　holes!
Cursed the heart that had the heart to
　　do it!　　　　　　　　　　15
Cursed the blood that let this blood from
　　hence!
More direful hap betide that hated wretch
That makes us wretched by the death of
　　thee
Than I can wish to adders, spiders, toads,
Or any creeping venom'd thing that lives!
If ever he have child, abortive be it,　21
Prodigious, and untimely brought to light,
Whose ugly and unnatural aspect
May fright the hopeful mother at the view,
And that be heir to his unhappiness!　25
If ever he have wife, let her be made
More miserable by the death of him
Than I am made by my young lord and
　　thee!
Come, now towards Chertsey with your
　　holy load,
Taken from Paul's to be interred there; 30
And still as you are weary of this weight
Rest you, whiles I lament King Henry's
　　corse.
　　　　　　　[The bearers take up the coffin.

Enter GLOUCESTER.

Glo. Stay, you that bear the corse, and
　　set it down.
Anne. What black magician conjures up
　　this fiend
To stop devoted charitable deeds?　35
Glo. Villains, set down the corse; or, by
　　Saint Paul,

703

I'll make a corse of him that disobeys!

1 Gent. My lord, stand back, and let the coffin pass.

Glo. Unmanner'd dog! Stand thou, when I command.
Advance thy halberd higher than my breast, 40
Or, by Saint Paul, I'll strike thee to my foot
And spurn upon thee, beggar, for thy boldness.

        [*The Bearers set down the coffin.*

Anne. What, do you tremble? Are you all afraid?
Alas, I blame you not, for you are mortal,
And mortal eyes cannot endure the devil. 45
Avaunt, thou dreadful minister of hell!
Thou hadst but power over his mortal body,
His soul thou canst not have; therefore, be gone.

Glo. Sweet saint, for charity, be not so curst.

Anne. Foul devil, for God's sake, hence and trouble us not; 50
For thou hast made the happy earth thy hell,
Fill'd it with cursing cries and deep exclaims.
If thou delight to view thy heinous deeds,
Behold this pattern of thy butcheries.
O, gentlemen, see, see! Dead Henry's wounds 55
Open their congeal'd mouths and bleed afresh.
Blush, blush, thou lump of foul deformity,
For 'tis thy presence that exhales this blood
From cold and empty veins where no blood dwells;
Thy deeds inhuman and unnatural 60
Provokes this deluge most unnatural.
O God, which this blood mad'st, revenge his death!
O earth, which this blood drink'st, revenge his death!
Either, heav'n, with lightning strike the murd'rer dead;
Or, earth, gape open wide and eat him quick, 65
As thou dost swallow up this good king's blood,
Which his hell-govern'd arm hath butchered.

Glo. Lady, you know no rules of charity,
Which renders good for bad, blessings for curses.

Anne. Villain, thou knowest nor law of God nor man: 70
No beast so fierce but knows some touch of pity.

Glo. But I know none, and therefore am no beast.

Anne. O wonderful, when devils tell the truth!

Glo. More wonderful when angels are so angry.
Vouchsafe, divine perfection of a woman, 75
Of these supposed crimes to give me leave
By circumstance but to acquit myself.

Anne. Vouchsafe, deffus'd infection of a man,
For these known evils but to give me leave
By circumstance to curse thy cursed self.

Glo. Fairer than tongue can name thee, let me have 81
Some patient leisure to excuse myself.

Anne. Fouler than heart can think thee, thou canst make
No excuse current but to hang thyself.

Glo. By such despair I should accuse myself. 85

Anne. And by despairing shalt thou stand excused
For doing worthy vengeance on thyself
That didst unworthy slaughter upon others.

Glo. Say that I slew them not?

Anne.   Then say they were not slain.
But dead they are, and, devilish slave, by thee. 90

Glo. I did not kill your husband.

Anne.   Why, then he is alive.

Glo. Nay, he is dead, and slain by Edward's hands.

Anne. In thy foul throat thou liest: Queen Margaret saw
Thy murd'rous falchion smoking in his blood;
The which thou once didst bend against her breast, 95
But that thy brothers beat aside the point.

Glo. I was provoked by her sland'rous tongue
That laid their guilt upon my guiltless shoulders.

Anne. Thou wast provoked by thy bloody mind,
That never dream'st on aught but butcheries. 100
Didst thou not kill this king?

Glo.   I grant ye.

Anne. Dost grant me, hedgehog? Then, God grant me too
Thou mayst be damned for that wicked deed!
O, he was gentle, mild, and virtuous!

Glo. The better for the King of Heaven, that hath him. 105

Anne. He is in heaven, where thou shalt never come.

Glo. Let him thank me that holp to send him thither,
For he was fitter for that place than earth.

Anne. And thou unfit for any place but hell.

Glo. Yes, one place else, if you will hear me name it. 110

Anne. Some dungeon.

Glo.   Your bed-chamber.
Anne. Ill rest betide the chamber where
thou liest !
Glo. So will it, madam, till I lie with you.
Anne. I hope so.
Glo.   I know so. But, gentle Lady Anne,
To leave this keen encounter of our wits, 115
And fall something into a slower method—
Is not the causer of the timeless deaths
Of these Plantagenets, Henry and Edward,
As blameful as the executioner ?
Anne. Thou wast the cause and most
accurs'd effect.   120
Glo. Your beauty was the cause of that
effect—
Your beauty that did haunt me in my sleep
To undertake the death of all the world
So I might live one hour in your sweet
bosom.
Anne. If I thought that, I tell thee,
homicide,   125
These nails should rend that beauty from
my cheeks.
Glo. These eyes could not endure that
beauty's wreck ;
You should not blemish it if I stood by.
As all the world is cheered by the sun,
So I by that ; it is my day, my life.   130
Anne. Black night o'ershade thy day, and
death thy life !
Glo. Curse not thyself, fair creature ;
thou art both.
Anne. I would I were, to be reveng'd on
thee.
Glo. It is a quarrel most unnatural,
To be reveng'd on him that loveth thee. 135
Anne. It is a quarrel just and reasonable,
To be reveng'd on him that kill'd my
husband.
Glo. He that bereft thee, lady, of thy
husband
Did it to help thee to a better husband.
Anne. His better doth not breathe upon
the earth.   140
Glo. He lives that loves thee better than
he could.
Anne. Name him.
Glo.   Plantagenet.
Anne.   Why, that was he.
Glo. The self-same name, but one of
better nature.
Anne. Where is he ?
Glo. Here. [*She spits at him*] Why dost
thou spit at me ?
Anne. Would it were mortal poison, for
thy sake !   145
Glo. Never came poison from so sweet a
place.
Anne. Never hung poison on a fouler
toad.
Out of my sight ! Thou dost infect mine
eyes.
Glo. Thine eyes, sweet lady, have in-
fected mine.

Anne. Would they were basilisks to
strike thee dead !   150
Glo. I would they were, that I might die
at once ;
For now they kill me with a living death.
Those eyes of thine from mine have drawn
salt tears,
Sham'd their aspects with store of childish
drops—
These eyes, which never shed remorseful
tear,   155
No, when my father York and Edward
wept
To hear the piteous moan that Rutland
made
When black-fac'd Clifford shook his sword
at him ;
Nor when thy warlike father, like a child,
Told the sad story of my father's death, 160
And twenty times made pause to sob and
weep
That all the standers-by had wet their
cheeks
Like trees bedash'd with rain—in that sad
time
My manly eyes did scorn an humble tear ;
And what these sorrows could not thence
exhale   165
Thy beauty hath, and made them blind
with weeping.
I never sued to friend nor enemy ;
My tongue could never learn sweet smooth-
ing word ;
But, now thy beauty is propos'd my fee,
My proud heart sues, and prompts my
tongue to speak.   170
                [*She looks scornfully at him.*
Teach not thy lip such scorn ; for it was
made
For kissing, lady, not for such contempt.
If thy revengeful heart cannot forgive,
Lo here I lend thee this sharp-pointed
sword ;
Which if thou please to hide in this true
breast   175
And let the soul forth that adoreth thee,
I lay it naked to the deadly stroke,
And humbly beg the death upon my knee.
                [*He lays his breast open ; she offers
at it with his sword.*
Nay, do not pause ; for I did kill King
Henry—
But 'twas thy beauty that provoked me. 180
Nay, now dispatch ; 'twas I that stabb'd
young Edward—
But 'twas thy heavenly face that set me on.
                [*She falls the sword.*
Take up the sword again, or take up me.
Anne. Arise, dissembler ; though I wish
thy death,
I will not be thy executioner.   185
Glo. Then bid me kill myself, and I will
do it.
Anne. I have already.

Glo.   That was in thy rage.
Speak it again, and even with the word
This hand, which for thy love did kill thy
    love,
Shall for thy love kill a far truer love ; 190
To both their deaths shalt thou be acces-
    sary.
  Anne. I would I knew thy heart.
  Glo. 'Tis figur'd in my tongue.
  Anne. I fear me both are false.
  Glo. Then never was man true.   195
  Anne. Well, well, put up your sword.
  Glo. Say, then, my peace is made.
  Anne. That shalt thou know hereafter.
  Glo. But shall I live in hope ?
  Anne. All men, I hope, live so.   200
  Glo. Vouchsafe to wear this ring.
  Anne. To take is not to give.
                  [*Puts on the ring.*
  Glo. Look how my ring encompasseth
    thy finger,
Even so thy breast encloseth my poor
    heart ;
Wear both of them, for both of them are
    thine.   205
And if thy poor devoted servant may
But beg one favour at thy gracious hand,
Thou dost confirm his happiness for ever.
  Anne. What is it ?
  Glo. That it may please you leave these
    sad designs   210
To him that hath most cause to be a
    mourner,
And presently repair to Crosby House ;
Where—after I have solemnly interr'd
At Chertsey monast'ry this noble king,
And wet his grave with my repentant
    tears—   215
I will with all expedient duty see you.
For divers unknown reasons, I beseech you,
Grant me this boon.
  Anne. With all my heart ; and much it
    joys me too
To see you are become so penitent.   220
Tressel and Berkeley, go along with me.
  Glo. Bid me farewell.
  Anne.   'Tis more than you deserve ;
But since you teach me how to flatter you,
Imagine I have said farewell already.
     [*Exeunt two gentlemen with Lady Anne.*
  Glo. Sirs, take up the corse.
  Gent.   Towards Chertsey, noble lord ?
  Glo. No, to White Friars ; there attend
    my coming.   226
             [*Exeunt all but Gloucester.*
Was ever woman in this humour woo'd ?
Was ever woman in this humour won ?
I'll have her ; but I will not keep her long.
What ! I that kill'd her husband and his
    father—   230
To take her in her heart's extremest hate,
With curses in her mouth, tears in her
    eyes,
The bleeding witness of my hatred by ;

Having God, her conscience, and these bars
    against me,
And I no friends to back my suit at all 235
But the plain devil and dissembling looks,
And yet to win her, all the world to nothing!
Ha !
Hath she forgot already that brave prince,
Edward, her lord, whom I, some three
    months since,   240
Stabb'd in my angry mood at Tewksbury ?
A sweeter and a lovelier gentleman—
Fram'd in the prodigality of nature,
Young, valiant, wise, and no doubt right
    royal—
The spacious world cannot again afford ; 245
And will she yet abase her eyes on me,
That cropp'd the golden prime of this sweet
    prince
And made her widow to a woeful bed ?
On me, whose all not equals Edward's
    moiety ?   249
On me, that halts and am misshapen thus ?
My dukedom to a beggarly denier,
I do mistake my person all this while.
Upon my life, she finds, although I cannot,
Myself to be a marv'llous proper man.
I'll be at charges for a looking-glass,   255
And entertain a score or two of tailors
To study fashions to adorn my body.
Since I am crept in favour with myself,
I will maintain it with some little cost.
But first I'll turn yon fellow in his grave,
And then return lamenting to my love. 261
Shine out, fair sun, till I have bought a
    glass,
That I may see my shadow as I pass. [*Exit.*

SCENE III. *London. The palace.*

Enter QUEEN ELIZABETH, LORD RIVERS,
and LORD GREY.

  Riv. Have patience, madam ; there's no
    doubt his Majesty
Will soon recover his accustom'd health.
  Grey. In that you brook it ill, it makes
    him worse ;
Therefore, for God's sake, entertain good
    comfort,
And cheer his Grace with quick and merry
    eyes.   5
  Q. Eliz. If he were dead, what would
    betide on me ?
  Grey. No other harm but loss of such a
    lord.
  Q. Eliz. The loss of such a lord includes
    all harms.
  Grey. The heavens have bless'd you with
    a goodly son
To be your comforter when he is gone.   10
  Q. Eliz. Ah, he is young ; and his
    minority
Is put unto the trust of Richard Gloucester,
A man that loves not me, nor none of
    you.

Riv. Is it concluded he shall be Protector ?

Q. Eliz. It is determin'd, not concluded yet ;   15
But so it must be, if the King miscarry.

Enter BUCKINGHAM *and* DERBY.

Grey. Here come the Lords of Buckingham and Derby.

Buck. Good time of day unto your royal Grace !

Der. God make your Majesty joyful as you have been.

Q. Eliz. The Countess Richmond, good my Lord of Derby,   20
To your good prayer will scarcely say amen.
Yet, Derby, notwithstanding she's your wife
And loves not me, be you, good lord, assur'd
I hate not you for her proud arrogance.

Derby. I do beseech you, either not believe   25
The envious slanders of her false accusers ;
Or, if she be accus'd on true report,
Bear with her weakness, which I think proceeds
From wayward sickness and no grounded malice.

Q. Eliz. Saw you the King to-day, my Lord of Derby ?

Der. But now he Duke of Buckingham and I
Are come from visiting his Majesty.

Q. Eliz. What likelihood of his amendment, lords ?

Buck. Madam, good hope ; his Grace speaks cheerfully.

Q. Eliz. God grant him health ! Did you confer with him ?   35

Buck. Ay, madam ; he desires to make atonement
Between the Duke of Gloucester and your brothers,
And between them and my Lord Chamberlain ;
And sent to warn them to his royal presence.

Q. Eliz. Would all were well ! But that will never be.   40
I fear our happiness is at the height.

Enter GLOUCESTER, HASTINGS, *and* DORSET.

Glo. They do me wrong, and I will not endure it.
Who is it that complains unto the King
That I, forsooth, am stern and love them not ?
By holy Paul, they love his Grace but lightly   45
That fill his ears with such dissentious rumours.
Because I cannot flatter and look fair,
Smile in men's faces, smooth, deceive, and cog,
Duck with French nods and apish courtesy,
I must be held a rancorous enemy.   50
Cannot a plain man live and think no harm
But thus his simple truth must be abus'd
With silken, sly, insinuating Jacks ?

Grey. To who in all this presence speaks your Grace ?

Glo. To thee, that hast nor honesty nor grace.   55
When have I injur'd thee ? when done thee wrong ?
Or thee, or thee, or any of your faction ?
A plague upon you all ! His royal Grace—
Whom God preserve better than you would wish !—
Cannot be quiet scarce a breathing while   60
But you must trouble him with lewd complaints.

Q. Eliz. Brother of Gloucester, you mistake the matter.
The King, on his own royal disposition
And not provok'd by any suitor else—
Aiming, belike, at your interior hatred   65
That in your outward action shows itself
Against my children, brothers, and myself—
Makes him to send that he may learn the ground.

Glo. I cannot tell ; the world is grown so bad   70
That wrens make prey where eagles dare not perch.
Since every Jack became a gentleman,
There's many a gentle person made a Jack.

Q. Eliz. Come, come, we know your meaning, brother Gloucester :
You envy my advancement and my friends' ;   75
God grant we never may have need of you !

Glo. Meantime, God grants that I have need of you.
Our brother is imprison'd by your means,
Myself disgrac'd, and the nobility
Held in contempt ; while great promotions
Are daily given to ennoble those   81
That scarce some two days since were worth a noble.

Q. Eliz. By Him that rais'd me to this careful height
From that contented hap which I enjoy'd,
I never did incense his Majesty   85
Against the Duke of Clarence, but have been
An earnest advocate to plead for him.
My lord, you do me shameful injury
Falsely to draw me in these vile suspects.

Glo. You may deny that you were not the mean   90
Of my Lord Hastings' late imprisonment.

Riv. She may, my lord ; for—

Glo. She may, Lord Rivers ? Why, who knows not so ?

She may do more, sir, than denying that:
She may help you to many fair prefer-
   ments   95
And then deny her aiding hand therein,
And lay those honours on your high desert.
What may she not? She may—ay, marry,
   may she—
  Riv. What, marry, may she?
  Glo. What, marry, may she? Marry
with a king,   100
A bachelor, and a handsome stripling too.
Iwis your grandam had a worser match.
  Q. Eliz. My Lord of Gloucester, I have
   too long borne
Your blunt upbraidings and your bitter
   scoffs.
By heaven, I will acquaint his Majesty 105
Of those gross taunts that oft I have
   endur'd.
I had rather be a country servant-maid
Than a great queen with this condition—
To be so baited, scorn'd, and stormed at.

Enter old QUEEN MARGARET, *behind.*

Small joy have I in being England's
   Queen.   110
  Q. Mar. And less'ned be that small, God,
   I beseech Him!
Thy honour, state, and seat, is due to me.
  Glo. What! Threat you me with telling
   of the King?
Tell him and spare not. Look what I have
   said
I will avouch't in presence of the King. 115
I dare adventure to be sent to th' Tow'r.
'Tis time to speak—my pains are quite
   forgot.
  Q. Mar. Out, devil! I do remember them
   too well:
Thou kill'dst my husband Henry in the
   Tower,
And Edward, my poor son, at Tewksbury.
  Glo. Ere you were queen, ay, or your
   husband king,   121
I was a pack-horse in his great affairs,
A weeder-out of his proud adversaries,
A liberal rewarder of his friends;
To royalize his blood I spent mine own. 125
  Q. Mar. Ay, and much better blood than
   his or thine.
  Glo. In all which time you and your
   husband Grey
Were factious for the house of Lancaster;
And, Rivers, so were you. Was not your
   husband   129
In Margaret's battle at Saint Albans slain?
Let me put in your minds, if you forget,
What you have been ere this, and what you
   are;
Withal, what I have been, and what I am.
  Q. Mar. A murd'rous villain, and so still
   thou art.
  Glo. Poor Clarence did forsake his father,
   Warwick,   135

Ay, and forswore himself—which Jesu
   pardon!—
  Q. Mar. Which God revenge!
  Glo. To fight on Edward's party for the
   crown;
And for his meed, poor lord, he is mewed up.
I would to God my heart were flint like
   Edward's,   140
Or Edward's soft and pitiful like mine.
I am too childish-foolish for this world.
  Q. Mar. Hie thee to hell for shame and
   leave this world,
Thou cacodemon; there thy kingdom is.
  Riv. My Lord of Gloucester, in those busy
   days   145
Which here you urge to prove us enemies,
We follow'd then our lord, our sovereign
   king.
So should we you, if you should be our king.
  Glo. If I should be! I had rather be a
   pedlar.
Far be it from my heart, the thought
   thereof!   150
  Q. Eliz. As little joy, my lord, as you
   suppose
You should enjoy were you this country's
   king,
As little joy you may suppose in me
That I enjoy, being the Queen thereof.
  Q. Mar. A little joy enjoys the Queen
   thereof;   155
For I am she, and altogether joyless.
I can no longer hold me patient.
                       [*Advancing.*
Hear me, you wrangling pirates, that fall
   out
In sharing that which you have pill'd from
   me.
Which of you trembles not that looks on
   me?   160
If not that, I am Queen, you bow like
   subjects,
Yet that, by you depos'd, you quake like
   rebels?
Ah, gentle villain, do not turn away!
  Glo. Foul wrinkled witch, what mak'st
   thou in my sight?
  Q. Mar. But repetition of what thou hast
   marr'd,   165
That will I make before I let thee go.
  Glo. Wert thou not banished on pain of
   death?
  Q. Mar. I was; but I do find more pain
   in banishment
Than death can yield me here by my
   abode.
A husband and a son thou ow'st to me; 170
And thou a kingdom; all of you allegiance.
This sorrow that I have by right is yours;
And all the pleasures you usurp are mine.
  Glo. The curse my noble father laid on
   thee,
When thou didst crown his warlike brows
   with paper   175

And with thy scorns drew'st rivers from his
   eyes,
And then to dry them gav'st the Duke a
   clout
Steep'd in the faultless blood of pretty
   Rutland—
His curses then from bitterness of soul
Denounc'd against thee are all fall'n upon
   thee;   180
And God, not we, hath plagu'd thy bloody
   deed.
  Q. Eliz. So just is God to right the
    innocent.
  Hast. O, 'twas the foulest deed to slay
    that babe,
And the most merciless that e'er was
   heard of!
  Riv. Tyrants themselves wept when it
    was reported.   185
  Dor. No man but prophesied revenge for
    it.
  Buck. Northumberland, then present,
    wept to see it.
  Q. Mar. What, were you snarling all
    before I came,
Ready to catch each other by the throat,
And turn you all your hatred now on me?
Did York's dread curse prevail so much
   with heaven   191
That Henry's death, my lovely Edward's
   death,
Their kingdom's loss, my woeful banish-
   ment,
Should all but answer for that peevish brat?
Can curses pierce the clouds and enter
   heaven?   195
Why then, give way, dull clouds, to my
   quick curses!
Though not by war, by surfeit die your
   king,
As ours by murder, to make him a king!
Edward thy son, that now is Prince of
   Wales,
For Edward our son, that was Prince of
   Wales,   200
Die in his youth by like untimely violence!
Thyself a queen, for me that was a queen,
Outlive thy glory, like my wretched self!
Long mayest thou live to wail thy children's
   death,
And see another, as I see thee now,   205
Deck'd in thy rights, as thou art stall'd in
   mine!
Long die thy happy days before thy death;
And, after many length'ned hours of grief,
Die neither mother, wife, nor England's
   Queen!
Rivers and Dorset, you were standers by,
And so wast thou, Lord Hastings, when my
   son   211
Was stabb'd with bloody daggers. God, I
   pray him,
That none of you may live his natural age,
But by some unlook'd accident cut off!

  Glo. Have done thy charm, thou hateful
    wither'd hag.   215
  Q. Mar. And leave out thee? Stay, dog,
    for thou shalt hear me.
If heaven have any grievous plague in store
Exceeding those that I can wish upon thee,
O, let them keep it till thy sins be ripe,
And then hurl down their indignation   220
On thee, the troubler of the poor world's
   peace!
The worm of conscience still be-gnaw thy
   soul!
Thy friends suspect for traitors while thou
   liv'st,
And take deep traitors for thy dearest
   friends!   224
No sleep close up that deadly eye of thine,
Unless it be while some tormenting dream
Affrights thee with a hell of ugly devils!
Thou elvish-mark'd, abortive, rooting hog,
Thou that wast seal'd in thy nativity
The slave of nature and the son of hell, 230
Thou slander of thy heavy mother's womb,
Thou loathed issue of thy father's loins,
Thou rag of honour, thou detested—
  Glo. Margaret!
  Q. Mar.   Richard!
  Glo.   Ha?
  Q. Mar.   I call thee not.
  Glo. I cry thee mercy then, for I did
    think   235
That thou hadst call'd me all these bitter
   names.
  Q. Mar. Why, so I did, but look'd for no
    reply.
O, let me make the period to my curse!
  Glo. 'Tis done by me, and ends in—
    Margaret.
  Q. Eliz. Thus have you breath'd your
    curse against yourself.   240
  Q. Mar. Poor painted queen, vain flourish
    of my fortune!
Why strew'st thou sugar on that bottled
   spider
Whose deadly web ensnareth thee about?
Fool, fool! thou whet'st a knife to kill
   thyself.
The day will come that thou shalt wish for
   me   245
To help thee curse this poisonous bunch-
   back'd toad.
  Hast. False-boding woman, end thy
    frantic curse,
Lest to thy harm thou move our patience.
  Q. Mar. Foul shame upon you! you have
    all mov'd mine.
  Riv. Were you well serv'd, you would be
    taught your duty.   250
  Q. Mar. To serve me well you all should
    do me duty,
Teach me to be your queen and you my
   subjects.
O, serve me well, and teach yourselves that
   duty!

Dor. Dispute not with her ; she is lunatic.

Q. Mar. Peace, Master Marquis, you are
 malapert ;   255
Your fire-new stamp of honour is scarce
 current.
O, that your young nobility could judge
What 'twere to lose it and be miserable !
They that stand high have many blasts to
 shake them,
And if they fall they dash themselves to
 pieces.   260

Glo. Good counsel, marry ; learn it, learn
 it, Marquis.

Dor. It touches you, my lord, as much
 as me.

Glo. Ay, and much more ; but I was born
 so high,
Our aery buildeth in the cedar's top,
And dallies with the wind, and scorns the
 sun.   265

Q. Mar. And turns the sun to shade—
 alas ! alas !
Witness my son, now in the shade of death,
Whose bright out-shining beams thy cloudy
 wrath
Hath in eternal darkness folded up.
Your aery buildeth in our aery's nest. 270
O God that seest it, do not suffer it ;
As it is won with blood, lost be it so !

Buck. Peace, peace, for shame, if not for
 charity !

Q. Mar. Urge neither charity nor shame
 to me.
Uncharitably with me have you dealt, 275
And shamefully my hopes by you are
 butcher'd.
My charity is outrage, life my shame ;
And in that shame still live my sorrow's
 rage !

Buck. Have done, have done.

Q. Mar. O princely Buckingham, I'll kiss
 thy hand   280
In sign of league and amity with thee.
Now fair befall thee and thy noble house !
Thy garments are not spotted with our
 blood,
Nor thou within the compass of my
 curse.

Buck. Nor no one here ; for curses never
 pass   285
The lips of those that breathe them in the
 air.

Q. Mar. I will not think but they ascend
 the sky
And there awake God's gentle-sleeping
 peace.
O Buckingham, take heed of yonder dog !
Look when he fawns, he bites ; and when
 he bites,   290
His venom tooth will rankle to the death :
Have not to do with him, beware of him ;
Sin, death, and hell, have set their marks
 on him,
And all their ministers attend on him.

Glo. What doth she say, my Lord of
 Buckingham ?   295

Buck. Nothing that I respect, my gracious
 lord.

Q. Mar. What, dost thou scorn me for my
 gentle counsel,
And soothe the devil that I warn thee
 from ?
O, but remember this another day,
When he shall split thy very heart with
 sorrow,   300
And say poor Margaret was a prophetess !
Live each of you the subjects to his hate,
And he to yours, and all of you to God's !
       [*Exit.*

Buck. My hair doth stand an end to hear
 her curses.

Riv. And so doth mine. I muse why she's
 at liberty.   305

Glo. I cannot blame her ; by God's holy
 Mother,
She hath had too much wrong ; and I
 repent
My part thereof that I have done to her.

Q. Eliz. I never did her any to my
 knowledge.

Glo. Yet you have all the vantage of her
 wrong.   310
I was too hot to do somebody good
That is too cold in thinking of it now.
Marry, as for Clarence, he is well repaid ;
He is frank'd up to fatting for his pains ;
God pardon them that are the cause thereof!

Riv. A virtuous and a Christian-like conclusion,   316
To pray for them that have done scathe
 to us !

Glo. So do I ever—[*Aside*] being well
 advis'd ;
For had I curs'd now, I had curs'd myself.

Enter CATESBY.

Cates. Madam, his Majesty doth call for
 you,   320
And for your Grace, and you, my gracious lords.

Q. Eliz. Catesby, I come. Lords, will you
 go with me ?

Riv. We wait upon your Grace.
    [*Exeunt all but Gloucester.*

Glo. I do the wrong, and first begin to
 brawl.
The secret mischiefs that I set abroach 325
I lay unto the grievous charge of others.
Clarence, who I indeed have cast in dark-
 ness,
I do beweep to many simple gulls ;
Namely, to Derby, Hastings, Buckingham ;
And tell them 'tis the Queen and her
 allies
That stir the King against the Duke my
 brother.   331
Now they believe it, and withal whet me
To be reveng'd on Rivers, Dorset, Grey ;

But then I sigh and, with a piece of
    Scripture,   334
Tell them that God bids us do good for evil.
And thus I clothe my naked villainy
With odd old ends stol'n forth of holy writ,
And seem a saint when most I play the
    devil.

Enter two Murderers.

But, soft, here come my executioners.   339
How now, my hardy stout resolved mates !
Are you now going to dispatch this thing ?
    1 *Murd.* We are, my lord, and come to
    have the warrant,
That we may be admitted where he is.
    Glo. Well thought upon ; I have it here
    about me.   [*Gives the warrant.*
When you have done, repair to Crosby
    Place.   345
But, sirs, be sudden in the execution,
Withal obdurate, do not hear him plead ;
For Clarence is well-spoken, and perhaps
May move your hearts to pity, if you mark
    him.
    1 *Murd.* Tut, tut, my lord, we will not
    stand to prate ;   350
Talkers are no good doers. Be assur'd
We go to use our hands and not our
    tongues.
    Glo. Your eyes drop millstones when
    fools' eyes fall tears.
I like you, lads ; about your business
    straight ;   355
Go, go, dispatch.
    1 *Murd.*   We will, my noble lord.
                          [*Exeunt.*

SCENE IV. *London. The Tower.*

Enter CLARENCE *and* Keeper.

    Keep. Why looks your Grace so heavily
    to-day ?
    Clar. O, I have pass'd a miserable night,
So full of fearful dreams, of ugly sights,
That, as I am a Christian faithful man,
I would not spend another such a night   5
Though 'twere to buy a world of happy
    days—
So full of dismal terror was the time !
    Keep. What was your dream, my lord ? I
    pray you tell me.
    Clar. Methoughts that I had broken from
    the Tower
And was embark'd to cross to Burgundy ; 10
And in my company my brother Gloucester,
Who from my cabin tempted me to walk
Upon the hatches.   Thence we look'd
    toward England,
And cited up a thousand heavy times,
During the wars of York and Lancaster,   15
That had befall'n us. As we pac'd along
Upon the giddy footing of the hatches,
Methought that Gloucester stumbled, and
    in falling

Struck me, that thought to stay him, over-
    board
Into the tumbling billows of the main.   20
O Lord, methought what pain it was to
    drown,
What dreadful noise of waters in my ears,
What sights of ugly death within my eyes !
Methoughts I saw a thousand fearful
    wrecks,
A thousand men that fishes gnaw'd upon,
Wedges of gold, great anchors, heaps of
    pearl,   26
Inestimable stones, unvalued jewels,
All scatt'red in the bottom of the sea ;
Some lay in dead men's skulls, and in the
    holes
Where eyes did once inhabit there were
    crept,   30
As 'twere in scorn of eyes, reflecting gems,
That woo'd the slimy bottom of the deep
And mock'd the dead bones that lay
    scatt'red by.
    Keep. Had you such leisure in the time
    of death
To gaze upon these secrets of the deep ? 35
    Clar. Methought I had ; and often did I
    strive
To yield the ghost, but still the envious
    flood
Stopp'd in my soul and would not let it
    forth
To find the empty, vast, and wand'ring
    air ;
But smother'd it within my panting bulk,
Who almost burst to belch it in the sea. 41
    Keep. Awak'd you not in this sore agony ?
    Clar. No, no, my dream was lengthen'd
    after life.
O, then began the tempest to my soul !
I pass'd, methought, the melancholy flood
With that sour ferryman which poets
    write of,   46
Unto the kingdom of perpetual night.
The first that there did greet my stranger
    soul
Was my great father-in-law, renowned
    Warwick,
Who spake aloud ' What scourge for per-
    jury   50
Can this dark monarchy afford false
    Clarence ? '
And so he vanish'd. Then came wand'ring
    by
A shadow like an angel, with bright hair
Dabbled in blood, and he shriek'd out
    aloud
' Clarence is come—false, fleeting, perjur'd
    Clarence,   55
That stabb'd me in the field by Tewksbury.
Seize on him, Furies, take him unto
    torment ! '
With that, methoughts, a legion of foul
    fiends
Environ'd me, and howled in mine ears

Such hideous cries that, with the very
   noise,   60
I trembling wak'd, and for a season after
Could not believe but that I was in hell,
Such terrible impression made my dream.
   Keep. No marvel, lord, though it
   affrighted you;
I am afraid, methinks, to hear you tell it. 65
   Clar. Ah, Keeper, Keeper, I have done
   these things
That now give evidence against my soul
For Edward's sake, and see how he requites
   me!
O God! If my deep prayers cannot appease
   Thee,
But Thou wilt be aveng'd on my misdeeds,
Yet execute Thy wrath in me alone;   71
O, spare my guiltless wife and my poor
   children!
Keeper, I prithee sit by me awhile;
My soul is heavy, and I fain would sleep.
   Keep. I will, my lord.   God give your
   Grace good rest.   [*Clarence sleeps.*

Enter BRAKENBURY *the Lieutenant.*

   Brak. Sorrow breaks seasons and repos-
   ing hours,   76
Makes the night morning and the noontide
   night.
Princes have but their titles for their
   glories,
An outward honour for an inward toil;
And for unfelt imaginations   80
They often feel a world of restless cares,
So that between their titles and low name
There's nothing differs but the outward
   fame.

Enter the two Murderers.

   1 *Murd.* Ho! who's here?
   Brak. What wouldst thou, fellow, and
   how cam'st thou hither?   85
   1 *Murd.* I would speak with Clarence, and
I came hither on my legs.
   Brak. What, so brief?
   2 *Murd.* 'Tis better, sir, than to be
tedious.   Let him see our commission and
talk no more.   [*Brakenbury reads it.*
   Brak. I am, in this, commanded to
deliver   91
The noble Duke of Clarence to your hands.
I will not reason what is meant hereby,
Because I will be guiltless from the meaning.
There lies the Duke asleep; and there the
   keys.   95
I'll to the King and signify to him
That thus I have resign'd to you my
   charge.
   1 *Murd.* You may, sir; 'tis a point of
wisdom.   Fare you well.
    [*Exeunt Brakenbury and Keeper.*
   2 *Murd.* What, shall I stab him as he
sleeps?   100

   1 *Murd.* No; he'll say 'twas done
cowardly, when he wakes.
   2 *Murd.* Why, he shall never wake until
the great judgment-day.
   1 *Murd.* Why, then he'll say we stabb'd
him sleeping.   106
   2 *Murd.* The urging of that word judgment hath bred a kind of remorse in me.
   1 *Murd.* What, art thou afraid?
   2 *Murd.* Not to kill him, having a
warrant; but to be damn'd for killing him,
from the which no warrant can defend me.
   1 *Murd.* I thought thou hadst been
resolute.   113
   2 *Murd.* So I am, to let him live.
   1 *Murd.* I'll back to the Duke of
Gloucester and tell him so.   116
   2 *Murd.* Nay, I prithee, stay a little. I
hope this passionate humour of mine will
change; it was wont to hold me but while
one tells twenty.   119
   1 *Murd.* How dost thou feel thyself now?
   2 *Murd.* Faith, some certain dregs of
conscience are yet within me.
   1 *Murd.* Remember our reward, when
the deed's done.
   2 *Murd.* Zounds, he dies; I had forgot
the reward.
   1 *Murd.* Where's thy conscience now?
   2 *Murd.* O, in the Duke of Gloucester's
purse!   127
   1 *Murd.* When he opens his purse to give
us our reward, thy conscience flies out.
   2 *Murd.* 'Tis no matter; let it go; there's
few or none will entertain it.   131
   1 *Murd.* What if it come to thee again?
   2 *Murd.* I'll not meddle with it—it makes
a man a coward: a man cannot steal, but
it accuseth him; a man cannot swear, but
it checks him; a man cannot lie with his
neighbour's wife, but it detects him. 'Tis
a blushing shamefac'd spirit that mutinies
in a man's bosom; it fills a man full of
obstacles: it made me once restore a purse
of gold that—by chance I found. It beggars
any man that keeps it. It is turn'd out of
towns and cities for a dangerous thing; and
every man that means to live well endeavours to trust to himself and live without it.
   1 *Murd.* Zounds, 'tis even now at my
elbow, persuading me not to kill the
Duke.   144
   2 *Murd.* Take the devil in thy mind and
believe him not; he would insinuate with
thee but to make thee sigh.
   1 *Murd.* I am strong-fram'd; he cannot
prevail with me.   148
   2 *Murd.* Spoke like a tall man that
respects thy reputation.   Come, shall we
fall to work?
   1 *Murd.* Take him on the costard with
the hilts of thy sword, and then chop him
in the malmsey-butt in the next room. 153

2 *Murd.* O excellent device ! and make a
sop of him.

1 *Murd.* Soft ! he wakes.

2 *Murd.* Strike !   155

1 *Murd.* No, we'll reason with him.

Clar. Where art thou, Keeper ? Give me
a cup of wine.

2 *Murd.* You shall have wine enough, my
lord, anon.

Clar. In God's name, what art thou ?

1 *Murd.* A man, as you are.   160

Clar. But not as I am, royal.

2 *Murd.* Nor you as we are, loyal.

Clar. Thy voice is thunder, but thy looks
are humble.

1 *Murd.* My voice is now the King's, my
looks mine own.

Clar. How darkly and how deadly dost
thou speak !   165
Your eyes do menace me. Why look you
pale ?
Who sent you hither ? Wherefore do you
come ?

2 *Murd.* To, to, to—

Clar. To murder me ?

Both Murd. Ay, ay.   170

Clar. You scarcely have the hearts to tell
me so,
And therefore cannot have the hearts to
do it.
Wherein, my friends, have I offended you ?

1 *Murd.* Offended us you have not, but
the King.   174

Clar. I shall be reconcil'd to him again.

2 *Murd.* Never, my lord ; therefore prepare to die.

Clar. Are you drawn forth among a world
of men
To slay the innocent ? What is my offence ?
Where is the evidence that doth accuse me?
What lawful quest have given their verdict
up   180
Unto the frowning judge, or who pro-
nounc'd
The bitter sentence of poor Clarence'
death ?
Before I be convict by course of law,
To threaten me with death is most un-
lawful.
I charge you, as you hope to have re-
demption   185
By Christ's dear blood shed for our
grievous sins,
That you depart and lay no hands on me.
The deed you undertake is damnable.

1 *Murd.* What we will do, we do upon
command.

2 *Murd.* And he that hath commanded
is our king.   190

Clar. Erroneous vassals ! the great King
of kings
Hath in the tables of his law commanded
That thou shalt do no murder. Will you
then

Spurn at his edict and fulfil a man's ?
Take heed ; for he holds vengeance in his
hand   195
To hurl upon their heads that break his
law.

2 *Murd.* And that same vengeance doth
he hurl on thee
For false forswearing, and for murder too :
Thou didst receive the sacrament to fight
In quarrel of the house of Lancaster.   200

1 *Murd.* And like a traitor to the name
of God
Didst break that vow ; and with thy
treacherous blade
Unripp'dst the bowels of thy sov'reign's
son.

2 *Murd.* Whom thou wast sworn to
cherish and defend.

1 *Murd.* How canst thou urge God's
dreadful law to us,   205
When thou hast broke it in such dear
degree ?

Clar. Alas ! for whose sake did I that ill
deed ?
For Edward, for my brother, for his sake.
He sends you not to murder me for this,   210
For in that sin he is as deep as I.
If God will be avenged for the deed,
O, know you yet He doth it publicly.
Take not the quarrel from His pow'rful
arm ;
He needs no indirect or lawless course   215
To cut off those that have offended Him.

1 *Murd.* Who made thee then a bloody
minister
When gallant-springing brave Plantagenet,
That princely novice, was struck dead by
thee ?

Clar. My brother's love, the devil, and
my rage.   220

1 *Murd.* Thy brother's love, our duty,
and thy faults,
Provoke us hither now to slaughter thee.

Clar. If you do love my brother, hate not
me ;
I am his brother, and I love him well.
If you are hir'd for meed, go back again,   225
And I will send you to my brother
Gloucester,
Who shall reward you better for my life
Than Edward will for tidings of my death.

2 *Murd.* You are deceiv'd : your brother
Gloucester hates you.

Clar. O, no, he loves me, and he holds
me dear.   230
Go you to him from me.

1 *Murd.*   Ay, so we will.

Clar. Tell him when that our princely
father York
Bless'd his three sons with his victorious
arm
And charg'd us from his soul to love each
other,   234
He little thought of this divided friendship.

713

Bid Gloucester think of this, and he will
    weep.
  1 *Murd.* Ay, millstones ; as he lesson'd
    us to weep.
  Clar. O, do not slander him, for he is
    kind.
  1 *Murd.* Right, as snow in harvest. Come,
    you deceive yourself :   240
'Tis he that sends us to destroy you here.
  Clar. It cannot be ; for he bewept my
    fortune
And hugg'd me in his arms, and swore
    with sobs
That he would labour my delivery.
  1 *Murd.* Why, so he doth, when he
    delivers you   245
From this earth's thraldom to the joys of
    heaven.
  2 *Murd.* Make peace with God, for you
    must die, my lord.
  Clar. Have you that holy feeling in your
    souls
To counsel me to make my peace with God,
And are you yet to your own souls so
    blind   250
That you will war with God by murd'ring
    me ?
O, sirs, consider : they that set you on
To do this deed will hate you for the deed.
  2 *Murd.* What shall we do ?
  Clar.   Relent, and save your souls.
  1 *Murd.* Relent ! No, 'tis cowardly and
    womanish.   255
  Clar. Not to relent is beastly, savage,
    devilish.
Which of you, if you were a prince's son,
Being pent from liberty as I am now,
If two such murderers as yourselves came
    to you,
Would not entreat for life ?   260
My friend, I spy some pity in thy looks ;
O, if thine eye be not a flatterer,
Come thou on my side and entreat for me—
As you would beg were you in my distress.
A begging prince what beggar pities not ?
  2 *Murd.* Look behind you, my lord. 266
  1 *Murd.* [*Stabbing him*] Take that, and
    that. If all this will not do,
I'll drown you in the malmsey-butt within.
                [*Exit with the body.*
  2 *Murd.* A bloody deed, and desperately
    dispatch'd !
How fain, like Pilate, would I wash my
    hands   270
Of this most grievous murder !

    Re-enter First Murderer.

  1 *Murd.* How now, what mean'st thou
    that thou help'st me not ?
By heavens, the Duke shall know how slack
    you have been !
  2 *Murd.* I would he knew that I had
    sav'd his brother !   274
Take thou the fee, and tell him what I say ;

For I repent me that the Duke is slain.
                    [*Exit.*
  1 *Murd.* So do not I. Go, coward as thou
    art.
Well, I'll go hide the body in some hole,
Till that the Duke give order for his burial ;
And when I have my meed, I will away ; 280
For this will out, and then I must not stay.
                    [*Exit.*

ACT TWO

  Scene I. *London. The palace.*

Flourish.   Enter King Edward *sick*,
  Queen Elizabeth, Dorset, Rivers,
  Hastings, Buckingham, Grey, *and*
  Others.

  K. Edw. Why, so. Now have I done a
    good day's work.
You peers, continue this united league.
I every day expect an embassage
From my Redeemer to redeem me hence ;
And more at peace my soul shall part to
    heaven,   5
Since I have made my friends at peace on
    earth.
Hastings and Rivers, take each other's
    hand ;
Dissemble not your hatred, swear your love.
  Riv. By heaven, my soul is purg'd from
    grudging hate ;
And with my hand I seal my true heart's
    love.   10
  Hast. So thrive I, as I truly swear the
    like !
  K. Edw. Take heed you dally not before
    your king ;
Lest He that is the supreme King of kings
Confound your hidden falsehood and award
Either of you to be the other's end.   15
  Hast. So prosper I, as I swear perfect
    love !
  Riv. And I, as I love Hastings with my
    heart !
  K. Edw. Madam, yourself is not exempt
    from this ;
Nor you, son Dorset ; Buckingham, nor
    you :
You have been factious one against the
    other.   20
Wife, love Lord Hastings, let him kiss your
    hand ;
And what you do, do it unfeignedly.
  Q. Eliz. There, Hastings ; I will never
    more remember
Our former hatred, so thrive I and mine !
  K. Edw. Dorset, embrace him ; Hastings,
    love Lord Marquis.   25
  Dor. This interchange of love, I here
    protest,
Upon my part shall be inviolable.
  Hast. And so swear I.   [*They embrace.*
  K. Edw. Now, princely Buckingham, seal
    thou this league

With thy embracements to my wife's allies,
And make me happy in your unity.   31
  Buck. [*To the Queen*] Whenever Bucking-
    ham doth turn his hate
Upon your Grace, but with all duteous love
Doth cherish you and yours, God punish me
With hate in those where I expect most
    love !   35
When I have most need to employ a friend
And most assured that he is a friend,
Deep, hollow, treacherous, and full of guile,
Be he unto me ! This do I beg of God
When I am cold in love to you or yours.   40
                    [*They embrace.*
  K. Edw. A pleasing cordial, princely
    Buckingham,
Is this thy vow unto my sickly heart.
There wanteth now our brother Gloucester
    here
To make the blessed period of this peace.
  Buck. And, in good time,
Here comes Sir Richard Ratcliff and the
    Duke.   45

     Enter GLOUCESTER, *and* RATCLIFF.

  Glo. Good morrow to my sovereign king
    and queen ;
And, princely peers, a happy time of day !
  K. Edw. Happy, indeed, as we have spent
    the day.
Gloucester, we have done deeds of charity,
Made peace of enmity, fair love of hate,   50
Between these swelling wrong-incensed
    peers.
  Glo. A blessed labour, my most sovereign
    lord.
Among this princely heap, if any here,
By false intelligence or wrong surmise,
Hold me a foe—   55
If I unwittingly, or in my rage,
Have aught committed that is hardly borne
To any in this presence, I desire
To reconcile me to his friendly peace :
'Tis death to me to be at enmity ;   60
I hate it, and desire all good men's love.
First, madam, I entreat true peace of you,
Which I will purchase with my duteous
    service ;
Of you, my noble cousin Buckingham,   64
If ever any grudge were lodg'd between us ;
Of you, and you, Lord Rivers, and of
    Dorset,
That all without desert have frown'd on
    me ;
Of you, Lord Woodville, and, Lord Scales,
    of you ;
Dukes, earls, lords, gentlemen—indeed, of
    all.
I do not know that Englishman alive
With whom my soul is any jot at odds   70
More than the infant that is born to-night.
I thank my God for my humility.
  Q. Eliz. A holy day shall this be kept
    hereafter.

I would to God all strifes were well com-
    pounded.
My sovereign lord, I do beseech your
    Highness   75
To take our brother Clarence to your grace.
  Glo. Why, madam, have I off'red love for
    this,
To be so flouted in this royal presence ?
Who knows not that the gentle Duke is
    dead ?   [*They all start.*
You do him injury to scorn his corse.   80
  K. Edw. Who knows not he is dead !
    Who knows he is ?
  Q. Eliz. All-seeing heaven, what a world
    is this !
  Buck. Look I so pale, Lord Dorset, as
    the rest ?
  Dor. Ay, my good lord ; and no man in
    the presence   84
But his red colour hath forsook his cheeks.
  K. Edw. Is Clarence dead ? The order
    was revers'd.
  Glo. But he, poor man, by your first
    order died,
And that a winged Mercury did bear ;
Some tardy cripple bare the countermand
That came too lag to see him buried.   90
God grant that some, less noble and less
    loyal,
Nearer in bloody thoughts, an not in blood,
Deserve not worse than wretched Clarence
    did,
And yet go current from suspicion !

          Enter DERBY.

  Der. A boon, my sovereign, for my
    service done !   95
  K. Edw. I prithee, peace ; my soul is full
    of sorrow.
  Der. I will not rise unless your Highness
    hear me.
  K. Edw. Then say at once what is it thou
    requests.
  Der. The forfeit, sovereign, of my
    servant's life ;
Who slew to-day a riotous gentleman   100
Lately attendant on the Duke of Norfolk.
  K. Edw. Have I a tongue to doom my
    brother's death,
And shall that tongue give pardon to a
    slave ?
My brother kill'd no man—his fault was
    thought,
And yet his punishment was bitter death.
Who sued to me for him ? Who, in my
    wrath,   106
Kneel'd at my feet, and bid me be advis'd ?
Who spoke of brotherhood ? Who spoke
    of love ?
Who told me how the poor soul did forsake
The mighty Warwick and did fight for
    me ?   110
Who told me, in the field at Tewksbury
When Oxford had me down, he rescued me

And said ' Dear Brother, live, and be a
   king ' ? 113
Who told me, when we both lay in the field
Frozen almost to death, how he did lap me
Even in his garments, and did give himself,
All thin and naked, to the numb cold
   night ?
All this from my remembrance brutish
   wrath
Sinfully pluck'd, and not a man of you 119
Had so much grace to put it in my mind.
But when your carters or your waiting-
   vassals
Have done a drunken slaughter and defac'd
The precious image of our dear Redeemer,
You straight are on your knees for pardon,
   pardon ;
And I, unjustly too, must grant it you. 125
                 [Derby rises.
But for my brother not a man would speak ;
Nor I, ungracious, speak unto myself
For him, poor soul. The proudest of you all
Have been beholding to him in his life ;
Yet none of you would once beg for his life.
O God, I fear thy justice will take hold 131
On me, and you, and mine, and yours, for
   this !
Come, Hastings, help me to my closet. Ah,
   poor Clarence !
      [Exeunt some with King and Queen.
   Glo. This is the fruits of rashness.
   Mark'd you not 134
How that the guilty kindred of the Queen
Look'd pale when they did hear of Clarence'
   death ?
O, they did urge it still unto the King !
God will revenge it. Come, lords, will you
   go
To comfort Edward with our company ?
   Buck. We wait upon your Grace. 140
                        [Exeunt.

SCENE II. London. The palace.

Enter the old DUCHESS OF YORK, with the
   Son and Daughter of Clarence.

   Son. Good grandam, tell us, is our father
   dead ?
   Duch. No, boy.
   Daugh. Why do you weep so oft, and beat
   your breast,
And cry ' O Clarence, my unhappy son ! ' ?
   Son. Why do you look on us, and shake
   your head, 5
And call us orphans, wretches, castaways,
If that our noble father were alive ?
   Duch. My pretty cousins, you mistake
   me both ;
I do lament the sickness of the King, 9
As loath to lose him, not your father's
   death ;
It were lost sorrow to wail one that's lost.
   Son. Then you conclude, my grandam,
   he is dead.

The King mine uncle is to blame for it.
God will revenge it ; whom I will im-
   portune
With earnest prayers all to that effect. 15
   Daugh. And so will I.
   Duch. Peace, children, peace ! The King
   doth love you well.
Incapable and shallow innocents,
You cannot guess who caus'd your father's
   death.
   Son. Grandam, we can ; for my good
   uncle Gloucester 20
Told me the King, provok'd to it by the
   Queen,
Devis'd impeachments to imprison him.
And when my uncle told me so, he wept,
And pitied me, and kindly kiss'd my cheek ;
Bade me rely on him as on my father, 25
And he would love me dearly as a child.
   Duch. Ah, that deceit should steal such
   gentle shape,
And with a virtuous vizor hide deep vice !
He is my son ; ay, and therein my shame ;
Yet from my dugs he drew not this deceit.
   Son. Think you my uncle did dissemble,
   grandam ? 31
   Duch. Ay, boy.
   Son. I cannot think it. Hark ! what noise
   is this ?

Enter QUEEN ELIZABETH, with her hair
   about her ears ; RIVERS and DORSET
   after her.

   Q. Eliz. Ah, who shall hinder me to wail
   and weep, 34
To chide my fortune, and torment myself ?
I'll join with black despair against my soul
And to myself become an enemy.
   Duch. What means this scene of rude
   impatience ?
   Q. Eliz. To make an act of tragic violence.
Edward, my lord, thy son, our king, is dead.
Why grow the branches when the root is
   gone ? 41
Why wither not the leaves that want their
   sap ?
If you will live, lament ; if die, be brief,
That our swift-winged souls may catch the
   King's,
Or like obedient subjects follow him 45
To his new kingdom of ne'er-changing
   night.
   Duch. Ah, so much interest have I in
   thy sorrow
As I had title in thy noble husband !
I have bewept a worthy husband's death,
And liv'd with looking on his images ; 50
But now two mirrors of his princely
   semblance
Are crack'd in pieces by malignant death,
And I for comfort have but one false glass,
That grieves me when I see my shame in
   him.
Thou art a widow, yet thou art a mother 55

And hast the comfort of thy children left;
But death hath snatch'd my husband from
    mine arms
And pluck'd two crutches from my feeble
    hands—
Clarence and Edward. O, what cause
    have I—
Thine being but a moiety of my moan— 60
To overgo thy woes and drown thy cries?
  Son. Ah, aunt, you wept not for our
    father's death!
How can we aid you with our kindred tears?
  Daugh. Our fatherless distress was left
    unmoan'd;
Your widow-dolour likewise be unwept! 65
  Q. Eliz. Give me no help in lamentation;
I am not barren to bring forth complaints.
All springs reduce their currents to mine
    eyes
That I, being govern'd by the watery moon,
May send forth plenteous tears to drown
    the world! 70
Ah for my husband, for my dear Lord
    Edward!
  Chil. Ah for our father, for our dear Lord
    Clarence!
  Duch. Alas for both, both mine, Edward
    and Clarence!
  Q. Eliz. What stay had I but Edward?
    and he's gone.
  Chil. What stay had we but Clarence?
    and he's gone. 75
  Duch. What stays had I but they? and
    they are gone.
  Q. Eliz. Was never widow had so dear a
    loss.
  Chil. Were never orphans had so dear a
    loss.
  Duch. Was never mother had so dear a
    loss.
Alas, I am the mother of these griefs! 80
Their woes are parcell'd, mine is general.
She for an Edward weeps, and so do I:
I for a Clarence weep, so doth not she.
These babes for Clarence weep, and so do I:
I for an Edward weep, so do not they. 85
Alas, you three on me, threefold distress'd,
Pour all your tears! I am your sorrow's
    nurse,
And I will pamper it with lamentation.
  Dor. Comfort, dear mother. God is much
    displeas'd
That you take with unthankfulness his
    doing. 90
In common worldly things 'tis call'd un-
    grateful
With dull unwillingness to repay a debt
Which with a bounteous hand was kindly
    lent;
Much more to be thus opposite with
    heaven,
For it requires the royal debt it lent you. 95
  Riv. Madam, bethink you, like a careful
    mother,

Of the young prince your son. Send straight
    for him;
Let him be crown'd; in him your comfort
    lives.
Drown desperate sorrow in dead Edward's
    grave,
And plant your joys in living Edward's
    throne. 100

Enter GLOUCESTER, BUCKINGHAM, DERBY,
    HASTINGS, *and* RATCLIFF.

  Glo. Sister, have comfort. All of us have
    cause
To wail the dimming of our shining star;
But none can help our harms by wailing
    them.
Madam, my mother, I do cry you mercy;
I did not see your Grace. Humbly on my
    knee 105
I crave your blessing.
  Duch. God bless thee; and put meekness
    in thy breast,
Love, charity, obedience, and true duty!
  Glo. Amen! [*Aside*] And make me die a
    good old man! 109
That is the butt end of a mother's blessing;
I marvel that her Grace did leave it out.
  Buck. You cloudy princes and heart-
    sorrowing peers,
That bear this heavy mutual load of moan,
Now cheer each other in each other's love.
Though we have spent our harvest of this
    king, 115
We are to reap the harvest of his son.
The broken rancour of your high-swol'n
    hearts,
But lately splinter'd, knit, and join'd to-
    gether,
Must gently be preserv'd, cherish'd, and
    kept.
Me seemeth good that, with some little
    train, 120
Forthwith from Ludlow the young prince
    be fet
Hither to London, to be crown'd our King.
  Riv. Why with some little train, my Lord
    of Buckingham?
  Buck. Marry, my lord, lest by a multitude
The new-heal'd wound of malice should
    break out, 125
Which would be so much the more
    dangerous
By how much the estate is green and yet
    ungovern'd;
Where every horse bears his commanding
    rein
And may direct his course as please
    himself, 129
As well the fear of harm as harm apparent,
In my opinion, ought to be prevented.
  Glo. I hope the King made peace with all
    of us;
And the compact is firm and true in me.
  Riv. And so in me; and so, I think, in all.

Yet, since it is but green, it should be put
To no apparent likelihood of breach,   136
Which haply by much company might be
    urg'd ;
Therefore I say with noble Buckingham
That it is meet so few should fetch the
    Prince.
  Hast. And so say I.   140
  Glo. Then be it so ; and go we to
    determine
Who they shall be that straight shall post
    to Ludlow.
Madam, and you, my sister, will you go
To give your censures in this business ?
  [*Exeunt all but Buckingham and Gloucester.*
  Buck. My lord, whoever journeys to the
    Prince,
For God sake, let not us two stay at home ;
For by the way I'll sort occasion,
As index to the story we late talk'd of,
To part the Queen's proud kindred from the
    Prince.   150
  Glo. My other self, my counsel's con-
    sistory,
My oracle, my prophet, my dear cousin,
I, as a child, will go by thy direction.
Toward Ludlow then, for we'll not stay
    behind.   [*Exeunt.*

    Scene III. *London. A street.*

Enter one Citizen *at one door, and* another
    at the other.

  1 *Cit.* Good morrow, neighbour. Whither
    away so fast ?
  2 *Cit.* I promise you, I scarcely know
    myself.
Hear you the news abroad ?
  1 *Cit.*   Yes, that the King is dead.
  2 *Cit.* Ill news, by'r lady ; seldom comes
    the better.
I fear, I fear 'twill prove a giddy world. 5

    Enter another Citizen.

  3 *Cit.* Neighbours, God speed !
  1 *Cit.*   Give you good morrow, sir.
  3 *Cit.* Doth the news hold of good King
    Edward's death ?
  2 *Cit.* Ay, sir, it is too true ; God help,
    the while !
  3 *Cit.* Then, masters, look to see a
    troublous world.
  1 *Cit.* No, no ; by God's good grace, his
    son shall reign.   10
  3 *Cit.* Woe to that land that's govern'd
    by a child.
  2 *Cit.* In him there is a hope of govern-
    ment,
Which, in his nonage, council under him,
And, in his full and ripened years, himself,
No doubt, shall then, and till then, govern
    well.   15
  1 *Cit.* So stood the state when Henry the
    Sixth

Was crown'd in Paris but at nine months
    old.
  3 *Cit.* Stood the state so ?   No, no, good
    friends, God wot ;
For then this land was famously enrich'd
With politic grave counsel ; then the King
Had virtuous uncles to protect his Grace. 21
  1 *Cit.* Why, so hath this, both by his
    father and mother.
  3 *Cit.* Better it were they all came by his
    father,
Or by his father there were none at all ;
For emulation who shall now be nearest 25
Will touch us all too near, if God prevent
    not.
O, full of danger is the Duke of Gloucester !
And the Queen's sons and brothers haught
    and proud ;
And were they to be rul'd, and not to
    rule,
This sickly land might solace as before. 30
  1 *Cit.* Come, come, we fear the worst ; all
    will be well.
  3 *Cit.* When clouds are seen, wise men
    put on their cloaks ;
When great leaves fall, then winter is at
    hand ;
When the sun sets, who doth not look for
    night ?
Untimely storms make men expect a
    dearth.   35
All may be well ; but, if God sort it so,
'Tis more than we deserve or I expect.
  2 *Cit.* Truly, the hearts of men are full
    of fear.
You cannot reason almost with a man
That looks not heavily and full of dread. 40
  3 *Cit.* Before the days of change, still is
    it so ;
By a divine instinct men's minds mistrust
Ensuing danger ; as by proof we see
The water swell before a boist'rous storm.
But leave it all to God. Whither away ? 45
  2 *Cit.* Marry, we were sent for to the
    justices.
  3 *Cit.* And so was I ; I'll bear you
    company.   [*Exeunt.*

    Scene IV. *London. The palace.*

Enter the Archbishop of York, *the young*
    Duke of York, Queen Elizabeth, *and*
    the Duchess of York.

  Arch. Last night, I hear, they lay at
    Stony Stratford,
And at Northampton they do rest to-night ;
To-morrow or next day they will be here.
  Duch. I long with all my heart to see the
    Prince.
I hope he is much grown since last I saw
    him.   5
  Q. Eliz. But I hear no ; they say my son
    of York
Has almost overta'en him in his growth.

York. Ay, mother ; but I would not have
　it so.
Duch. Why, my good cousin, it is good
　to grow.
York. Grandam, one night as we did sit
　at supper,   10
My uncle Rivers talk'd how I did grow
More than my brother. ' Ay,' quoth my
　uncle Gloucester
' Small herbs have grace : great weeds do
　grow apace.'
And since, methinks, I would not grow so
　fast,
Because sweet flow'rs are slow and weeds
　make haste.   15
Duch. Good faith, good faith, the saying
　did not hold
In him that did object the same to thee.
He was the wretched'st thing when he was
　young,
So long a-growing and so leisurely
That, if his rule were true, he should be
　gracious.   20
Arch. And so no doubt he is, my gracious
　madam.
Duch. I hope he is ; but yet let mothers
　doubt.
York. Now, by my troth, if I had been
　rememb'red,
I could have given my uncle's Grace a flout
To touch his growth nearer than he touch'd
　mine.   25
Duch. How, my young York ? I prithee
　let me hear it.
York. Marry, they say my uncle grew so
　fast
That he could gnaw a crust at two hours
　old.
'Twas full two years ere I could get a tooth.
Grandam, this would have been a biting
　jest.   30
Duch. I prithee, pretty York, who told
　thee this ?
York. Grandam, his nurse.
Duch. His nurse ! Why she was dead ere
　thou wast born.
York. If 'twere not she, I cannot tell who
　told me.
Q. Eliz. A parlous boy ! Go to, you are
　too shrewd.   35
Arch. Good madam, be not angry with
　the child.
Q. Eliz. Pitchers have ears.

　　　　　Enter a Messenger.

Arch. Here comes a messenger. What
　news ?
Mess. Such news, my lord, as grieves me
　to report.
Q. Eliz. How doth the Prince ?
Mess.　　　　Well, madam, and in health.
Duch. What is thy news ?   41
Mess.　　　　Lord Rivers and Lord Grey
Are sent to Pomfret, and with them

Sir Thomas Vaughan, prisoners.
Duch. Who hath committed them ?
Mess.　　　　　　The mighty Dukes,
Gloucester and Buckingham.
Arch.　　　　　　For what offence ?   45
Mess. The sum of all I can, I have
　disclos'd.
Why or for what the nobles were committed
Is all unknown to me, my gracious lord.
Q. Eliz. Ay me, I see the ruin of my
　house !   49
The tiger now hath seiz'd the gentle hind ;
Insulting tyranny begins to jet
Upon the innocent and aweless throne.
Welcome, destruction, blood, and massacre !
I see, as in a map, the end of all.
Duch. Accursed and unquiet wrangling
　days,   55
How many of you have mine eyes beheld !
My husband lost his life to get the crown ;
And often up and down my sons were
　toss'd
For me to joy and weep their gain and loss ;
And being seated, and domestic broils   60
Clean over-blown, themselves the con-
　querors
Make war upon themselves—brother to
　brother,
Blood to blood, self against self. O, pre-
　posterous
And frantic outrage, end thy damned
　spleen,
Or let me die, to look on death no more !   65
Q. Eliz. Come, come, my boy ; we will
　to sanctuary.
Madam, farewell.
Duch.　　　　Stay, I will go with you.
Q. Eliz. You have no cause.
Arch. [*To the Queen*] My gracious lady, go.
And thither bear your treasure and your
　goods.
For my part, I'll resign unto your Grace   70
The seal I keep ; and so betide to me
As well I tender you and all of yours !
Go, I'll conduct you to the sanctuary.
　　　　　　　　　　　　　　　[*Exeunt.*

ACT THREE

SCENE I. *London. A street.*

The trumpets sound. Enter the PRINCE OF
WALES, GLOUCESTER, BUCKINGHAM,
CATESBY, CARDINAL BOURCHIER, *and*
Others.

Buck. Welcome, sweet Prince, to London,
　to your chamber.
Glo. Welcome, dear cousin, my thoughts'
　sovereign.
The weary way hath made you melancholy.
Prince. No, uncle ; but our crosses on the
　way
Have made it tedious, wearisome, and
　heavy.   5

I want more uncles here to welcome me.
 Glo. Sweet Prince, the untainted virtue
  of your years
Hath not yet div'd into the world's deceit;
Nor more can you distinguish of a man
Than of his outward show; which, God He
  knows, 10
Seldom or never jumpeth with the heart.
Those uncles which you want were
  dangerous;
Your Grace attended to their sug'red
  words
But look'd not on the poison of their hearts.
God keep you from them and from such
  false friends! 15
 Prince. God keep me from false friends!
  but they were none.
 Glo. My lord, the Mayor of London comes
  to greet you.

 Enter the Lord Mayor *and his* Train.

 May. God bless your Grace with health
  and happy days!
 Prince. I thank you, good my lord, and
  thank you all.
I thought my mother and my brother
  York 20
Would long ere this have met us on the
  way.
Fie, what a slug is Hastings, that he comes
  not
To tell us whether they will come or no!

 Enter LORD HASTINGS.

 Buck. And, in good time, here comes the
  sweating lord.
 Prince. Welcome, my lord. What, will
  our mother come? 25
 Hast. On what occasion, God He knows,
  not I,
The Queen your mother and your brother
  York
Have taken sanctuary. The tender Prince
Would fain have come with me to meet
  your Grace, 29
But by his mother was perforce withheld.
 Buck. Fie, what an indirect and peevish
  course
Is this of hers? Lord Cardinal, will your
  Grace
Persuade the Queen to send the Duke of
  York
Unto his princely brother presently?
If she deny, Lord Hastings, go with him 35
And from her jealous arms pluck him
  perforce.
 Card. My Lord of Buckingham, if my
  weak oratory
Can from his mother win the Duke of York,
Anon expect him here; but if she be
  obdurate
To mild entreaties, God in heaven forbid 40
We should infringe the holy privilege
Of blessed sanctuary! Not for all this land

Would I be guilty of so deep a sin.
 Buck. You are too senseless-obstinate, my
  lord,
Too ceremonious and traditional. 45
Weigh it but with the grossness of this age,
You break not sanctuary in seizing him.
The benefit thereof is always granted
To those whose dealings have deserv'd the
  place
And those who have the wit to claim the
  place. 50
This Prince hath neither claim'd it nor
  deserv'd it,
And therefore, in mine opinion, cannot
  have it.
Then, taking him from thence that is not
  there,
You break no privilege nor charter there.
Oft have I heard of sanctuary men; 55
But sanctuary children never till now.
 Card. My lord, you shall overrule my
  mind for once.
Come on, Lord Hastings, will you go with
  me?
 Hast. I go, my lord.
 Prince. Good lords, make all the speedy
  haste you may. 60
  [*Exeunt Cardinal and Hastings.*
Say, uncle Gloucester, if our brother come,
Where shall we sojourn till our coronation?
 Glo. Where it seems best unto your royal
  self.
If I may counsel you, some day or two
Your Highness shall repose you at the
  Tower, 65
Then where you please and shall be thought
  most fit
For your best health and recreation.
 Prince. I do not like the Tower, of any
  place.
Did Julius Cæsar build that place, my lord?
 Glo. He did, my gracious lord, begin that
  place, 70
Which, since, succeeding ages have re-
  edified.
 Prince. Is it upon record, or else reported
Successively from age to age, he built it?
 Buck. Upon record, my gracious lord.
 Prince. But say, my lord, it were not
  regist'red, 75
Methinks the truth should live from age to
  age,
As 'twere retail'd to all posterity,
Even to the general all-ending day.
 Glo. [*Aside*] So wise so young, they say, do
  never live long.
 Prince. What say you, uncle? 80
 Glo. I say, without characters, fame lives
  long.
[*Aside*] Thus, like the formal vice, Iniquity,
I moralize two meanings in one word.
 Prince. That Julius Cæsar was a famous
  man;
With what his valour did enrich his wit, 85

His wit set down to make his valour live.
Death makes no conquest of this conqueror;
For now he lives in fame, though not in life.
I'll tell you what, my cousin Buckingham—
  Buck. What, my gracious lord ?   90
  Prince. An if I live until I be a man,
I'll win our ancient right in France again,
Or die a soldier as I liv'd a king.
  Glo. [*Aside*] Short summers lightly have a
    forward spring.

Enter young YORK, HASTINGS, *and the*
    CARDINAL.

  Buck. Now, in good time, here comes the
    Duke of York.   95
  Prince. Richard of York, how fares our
    loving brother ?
  York. Well my dread lord ; so must I
    call you now.
  Prince. Ay brother, to our grief, as it is
    yours.
Too late he died that might have kept that
    title,   99
Which by his death hath lost much majesty.
  Glo. How fares our cousin, noble Lord of
    York ?
  York. I thank you, gentle uncle. O, my
    lord,
You said that idle weeds are fast in growth.
The Prince my brother hath outgrown me
    far.
  Glo. He hath, my lord.
  York.   And therefore is he idle? 105
  Glo. O, my fair cousin, I must not say so.
  York. Then he is more beholding to you
    than I.
  Glo. He may command me as my
    sovereign ;
But you have power in me as in a kinsman.
  York. I pray you, uncle, give me this
    dagger.   110
  Glo. My dagger, little cousin ? With all
    my heart !
  Prince. A beggar, brother ?
  York. Of my kind uncle, that I know
    will give,
And being but a toy, which is no grief to
    give.
  Glo. A greater gift than that I'll give my
    cousin.   115
  York. A greater gift ! O, that's the
    sword to it !
  Glo. Ay, gentle cousin, were it light
    enough.
  York. O, then, I see you will part but
    with light gifts:
In weightier things you'll say a beggar nay.
  Glo. It is too heavy for your Grace to
    wear.   120
  York. I weigh it lightly, were it heavier.
  Glo. What, would you have my weapon,
    little lord ?
  York. I would, that I might thank you as
    you call me.

  Glo. How ?
  York. Little.   125
  Prince. My Lord of York will still be
    cross in talk.
Uncle, your Grace knows how to bear with
    him.
  York. You mean, to bear me, not to bear
    with me.
Uncle, my brother mocks both you and me ;
Because that I am little, like an ape, 130
He thinks that you should bear me on your
    shoulders.
  Buck. With what a sharp-provided wit he
    reasons !
To mitigate the scorn he gives his uncle
He prettily and aptly taunts himself.
So cunning and so young is wonderful. 135
  Glo. My lord, will't please you pass
    along ?
Myself and my good cousin Buckingham
Will to your mother, to entreat of her
To meet you at the Tower and welcome
    you.
  York. What, will you go unto the Tower,
    my lord ?   140
  Prince. My Lord Protector needs will
    have it so.
  York. I shall not sleep in quiet at the
    Tower.
  Glo. Why, what should you fear ?
  York. Marry, my uncle Clarence' angry
    ghost.
My grandam told me he was murder'd
    there.   145
  Prince. I fear no uncles dead.
  Glo. Nor none that live, I hope.
  Prince. An if they live, I hope I need not
    fear.
But come, my lord ; with a heavy heart,
Thinking on them, go I unto the Tower. 150
    [*A sennet.* *Exeunt all but Gloucester,*
    Buckingham, and Catesby.
  Buck. Think you, my lord, this little
    prating York
Was not incensed by his subtle mother
To taunt and scorn you thus opprobriously?
  Glo. No doubt, no doubt. O, 'tis a
    perilous boy ;   154
Bold, quick, ingenious, forward, capable.
He is all the mother's, from the top to
    toe.
  Buck. Well, let them rest. Come hither,
    Catesby.
Thou art sworn as deeply to effect what we
    intend
As closely to conceal what we impart.
Thou know'st our reasons urg'd upon the
    way.   160
What think'st thou ? Is it not an easy
    matter
To make William Lord Hastings of our
    mind,
For the instalment of this noble Duke
In the seat royal of this famous isle ?

Cate. He for his father's sake so loves the
    Prince   165
That he will not be won to aught against
    him.
Buck. What think'st thou then of
    Stanley ? Will not he ?
Cate. He will do all in all as Hastings
    doth.
Buck. Well then, no more but this : go,
    gentle Catesby,
And, as it were far off, sound thou Lord
    Hastings   170
How he doth stand affected to our purpose ;
And summon him to-morrow to the Tower,
To sit about the coronation.
If thou dost find him tractable to us,
Encourage him, and tell him all our
    reasons ;   175
If he be leaden, icy, cold, unwilling,
Be thou so too, and so break off the talk,
And give us notice of his inclination ;
For we to-morrow hold divided councils,
Wherein thyself shalt highly be employ'd.
    Glo. Commend me to Lord William. Tell
    him, Catesby,   181
His ancient knot of dangerous adversaries
To-morrow are let blood at Pomfret Castle ;
And bid my lord, for joy of this good news,
Give Mistress Shore one gentle kiss the
    more.   185
    Buck. Good Catesby, go effect this busi-
    ness soundly.
    Cate. My good lords both, with all the
    heed I can.
    Glo. Shall we hear from you, Catesby, ere
    we sleep ?
    Cate. You shall, my lord.   189
    Glo. At Crosby House, there shall you
    find us both.   [*Exit Catesby.*
    Buck. Now, my lord, what shall we do if
    we perceive
Lord Hastings will not yield to our com-
    plots ?
    Glo. Chop off his head—something we will
    determine.
And, look when I am King, claim thou of
    me
The earldom of Hereford and all the
    movables   195
Whereof the King my brother was possess'd.
    Buck. I'll claim that promise at your
    Grace's hand.
    Glo. And look to have it yielded with all
    kindness.   198
Come, let us sup betimes, that afterwards
We may digest our complots in some form.
                [*Exeunt.*

SCENE II. *Before Lord Hastings' house.*

Enter a Messenger *to the door of Hastings.*

Mess. My lord, my lord !   [*Knocking.*
Hast. [*Within*] Who knocks ?
Mess. One from the Lord Stanley.

Hast. [*Within*] What is't o'clock ?
Mess. Upon the stroke of four.   5

Enter LORD HASTINGS.

Hast. Cannot my Lord Stanley sleep
    these tedious nights ?
Mess. So it appears by that I have to say.
First, he commends him to your noble self.
Hast. What then ?
Mess. Then certifies your lordship that
    this night   10
He dreamt the boar had razed off his helm.
Besides, he says there are two councils
    kept,
And that may be determin'd at the one
Which may make you and him to rue at th'
    other.
Therefore he sends to know your lordship's
    pleasure—   15
If you will presently take horse with him
And with all speed post with him toward
    the north
To shun the danger that his soul divines.
    Hast. Go, fellow, go, return unto thy
    lord ;
Bid him not fear the separated council : 20
His honour and myself are at the one,
And at the other is my good friend Catesby;
Where nothing can proceed that toucheth
    us
Whereof I shall not have intelligence.
Tell him his fears are shallow, without
    instance ;   25
And for his dreams, I wonder he's so simple
To trust the mock'ry of unquiet slumbers.
To fly the boar before the boar pursues
Were to incense the boar to follow us
And make pursuit where he did mean no
    chase.   30
Go, bid thy master rise and come to me ;
And we will both together to the Tower,
Where, he shall see, the boar will use us
    kindly.
    Mess. I'll go, my lord, and tell him what
    you say.   [*Exit.*

Enter CATESBY.

    Cate. Many good morrows to my noble
    lord !   35
    Hast. Good morrow, Catesby; you are
    early stirring.
What news, what news, in this our tott'ring
    state ?
    Cate. It is a reeling world indeed, my
    lord ;
And I believe will never stand upright 39
Till Richard wear the garland of the realm.
    Hast. How, wear the garland ! Dost thou
    mean the crown ?
    Cate. Ay, my good lord.
    Hast. I'll have this crown of mine cut
    from my shoulders
Before I'll see the crown so foul misplac'd.
But canst thou guess that he doth aim at it ?

Cate. Ay, on my life; and hopes to find
    you forward   46
Upon his party for the gain thereof;
And thereupon he sends you this good
    news,
That this same very day your enemies,
The kindred of the Queen, must die at
    Pomfret.   50
    Hast. Indeed, I am no mourner for that
    news,
Because they have been still my adver-
    saries;
But that I'll give my voice on Richard's
    side
To bar my master's heirs in true descent,
God knows I will not do it to the death. 55
    Cate. God keep your lordship in that
    gracious mind!
    Hast. But I shall laugh at this a twelve
    month hence,
That they which brought me in my master's
    hate,
I live to look upon their tragedy.
Well, Catesby, ere a fortnight make me
    older,   60
I'll send some packing that yet think not
    on't.
    Cate. 'Tis a vile thing to die, my gracious
    lord,
When men are unprepar'd and look not
    for it.   65
    Hast. O monstrous, monstrous! And so
    falls it out
With Rivers, Vaughan, Grey; and so 'twill
    do
With some men else that think themselves
    as safe
As thou and I, who, as thou knowest, are
    dear   69
To princely Richard and to Buckingham.
    Cate. The Princes both make high account
    of you—
[*Aside*] For they account his head upon the
    bridge.
    Hast. I know they do, and I have well
    deserv'd it.

    Enter LORD STANLEY.

Come on, come on; where is your boar-
    spear, man?   74
Fear you the boar, and go so unprovided?
    Stan. My lord, good morrow; good
    morrow, Catesby.
You may jest on, but, by the holy rood,
I do not like these several councils, I.
    Hast. My lord, I hold my life as dear as
    yours,   80
And never in my days, I do protest,
Was it so precious to me as 'tis now.
Think you, but that I know our state
    secure,
I would be so triumphant as I am?
    Stan. The lords at Pomfret, when they
    rode from London,   85

Were jocund and suppos'd their states were
    sure,
And they indeed had no cause to mistrust;
But yet you see how soon the day o'ercast;
This sudden stab of rancour I misdoubt;
Pray God, I say, I prove a needless coward.
What, shall we toward the Tower? The
    day is spent.   91
    Hast. Come, come, have with you. Wot
    you what, my lord?
To-day the lords you talk'd of are beheaded.
    Stan. They, for their truth, might better
    wear their heads
Than some that have accus'd them wear
    their hats.   95
But come, my lord, let's away.

    Enter HASTINGS, *a pursuivant.*

    Hast. Go on before; I'll talk with this
    good fellow.
            [*Exeunt Stanley and Catesby.*
How now, Hastings! How goes the world
    with thee?
    Purs. The better that your lordship please
    to ask.
    Hast. I tell thee, man, 'tis better with me
    now   100
Than when thou met'st me last where now
    we meet:
Then was I going prisoner to the Tower
By the suggestion of the Queen's allies;
But now, I tell thee—keep it to thyself—
This day those enemies are put to death, 105
And I in better state than e'er I was.
    Purs. God hold it, to your honour's good
    content!
    Hast. Gramercy, Hastings; there, drink
    that for me. [*Throws him his purse.*
    Purs. I thank your honour.   [*Exit.*

    Enter a Priest.

    Pr. Well met, my lord; I am glad to see
    your honour.   110
    Hast. I thank thee, good Sir John, with
    all my heart.
I am in your debt for your last exercise;
Come the next Sabbath, and I will content
    you.   [*He whispers in his ear.*
    Pr. I'll wait upon your lordship.

    Enter BUCKINGHAM.

    Buck. What, talking with a priest, Lord
    Chamberlain!
Your friends at Pomfret, they do need the
    priest: 115
Your honour hath no shriving work in
    hand.
    Hast. Good faith, and when I met this
    holy man,
The men you talk of came into my mind.
What, go you toward the Tower?
    Buck. I do, my lord, but long I cannot
    stay there;   120
I shall return before your lordship thence.

Hast. Nay, like enough, for I stay dinner
there.

Buck. [*Aside*] And supper too, although
thou knowest it not.—
Come, will you go ?

Hast. I'll wait upon your lordship.
[*Exeunt.*

SCENE III. *Pomfret Castle.*

Enter SIR RICHARD RATCLIFF, *with* Halberds, *carrying the Nobles,* RIVERS, GREY,
and VAUGHAN, *to death.*

Riv. Sir Richard Ratcliff, let me tell thee
this :
To-day shalt thou behold a subject die
For truth, for duty, and for loyalty.

Grey. God bless the Prince from all the
pack of you !   5
A knot you are of damned blood-suckers.

Vaugh. You live that shall cry woe for
this hereafter.

Rat. Dispatch ; the limit of your lives
is out.

Riv. O Pomfret, Pomfret ! O thou bloody
prison,
Fatal and ominous to noble peers !   10
Within the guilty closure of thy walls
Richard the Second here was hack'd to
death ;
And, for more slander to thy dismal seat,
We give to thee our guiltless blood to drink.

Grey. Now Margaret's curse is fall'n upon
our heads,   15
When she exclaim'd on Hastings, you, and
I,
For standing by when Richard stabb'd her
son.

Riv. Then curs'd she Richard, then curs'd
she Buckingham,
Then curs'd she Hastings. O, remember,
God,
To hear her prayer for them, as now for us !
And for my sister, and her princely sons, 20
Be satisfied, dear God, with our true blood,
Which, as thou know'st, unjustly must be
spilt.

Rat. Make haste ; the hour of death is
expiate.

Riv. Come, Grey ; come, Vaughan ; let
us here embrace.
Farewell, until we meet again in heaven. 25
[*Exeunt.*

SCENE IV. *London. The Tower.*

Enter BUCKINGHAM, DERBY, HASTINGS,
the BISHOP OF ELY, RATCLIFF, LOVEL,
with Others *and seat themselves at a table.*

Hast. Now, noble peers, the cause why
we are met
Is to determine of the coronation.
In God's name speak—when is the royal
day ?

Buck. Is all things ready for the royal
time ?

Der. It is, and wants but nomination. 5

Ely. To-morrow then I judge a happy
day.

Buck. Who knows the Lord Protector's
mind herein ?
Who is most inward with the noble Duke ?

Ely. Your Grace, we think, should
soonest know his mind.   10

Buck. We know each other's faces ; for
our hearts,
He knows no more of mine than I of yours ;
Or I of his, my lord, than you of mine.
Lord Hastings, you and he are near in love.

Hast. I thank his Grace, I know he loves
me well ;   15
But for his purpose in the coronation
I have not sounded him, nor he deliver'd
His gracious pleasure any way therein.
But you, my honourable lords, may name
the time ;   19
And in the Duke's behalf I'll give my voice,
Which, I presume, he'll take in gentle part.

Enter GLOUCESTER.

Ely. In happy time, here comes the Duke
himself.

Glo. My noble lords and cousins all,
good morrow.
I have been long a sleeper, but I trust
My absence doth neglect no great design 25
Which by my presence might have been
concluded.

Buck. Had you not come upon your cue,
my lord,
William Lord Hastings had pronounc'd
your part—
I mean, your voice for crowning of the
King.

Glo. Than my Lord Hastings no man
might be bolder ;   30
His lordship knows me well and loves me
well.
My lord of Ely, when I was last in Holborn
I saw good strawberries in your garden
there.
I do beseech you send for some of them. 35

Ely. Marry and will, my lord, with all my
heart.   [*Exit.*

Glo. Cousin of Buckingham, a word with
you.   [*Takes him aside.*
Catesby hath sounded Hastings in our
business,
And finds the testy gentleman so hot   39
That he will lose his head ere give consent
His master's child, as worshipfully he
terms it,
Shall lose the royalty of England's throne.

Buck. Withdraw yourself awhile ; I'll go
with you.
[*Exeunt Gloucester and Buckingham.*

Der. We have not yet set down this day
of triumph.   44

To-morrow, in my judgment, is too sudden;
For I myself am not so well provided
As else I would be, were the day prolong'd.

Re-enter the BISHOP OF ELY.

Ely. Where is my lord the Duke of
Gloucester ?
I have sent for these strawberries.
  Hast. His Grace looks cheerfully and
smooth this morning ;   50
There's some conceit or other likes him well
When that he bids good morrow with such
spirit.
I think there's never a man in Christendom
Can lesser hide his love or hate than he ;
For by his face straight shall you know his
heart.   55
  Der. What of his heart perceive you in
his face
By any livelihood he show'd to-day ?
  Hast. Marry, that with no man here he
is offended ;
For, were he, he had shown it in his looks

Re-enter GLOUCESTER *and* BUCKINGHAM.

  Glo. I pray you all, tell me what they
deserve   61
That do conspire my death with devilish
plots
Of damned witchcraft, and that have
prevail'd
Upon my body with their hellish charms ?
  Hast. The tender love I bear your Grace,
my lord,   65
Makes me most forward in this princely
presence
To doom th' offenders, whosoe'er they be.
I say, my lord, they have deserved death.
  Glo. Then be your eyes the witness of
their evil.
Look how I am bewitch'd ; behold, mine
arm   70
Is like a blasted sapling wither'd up.
And this is Edward's wife, that monstrous
witch,
Consorted with that harlot strumpet Shore,
That by their witchcraft thus have marked
me.
  Hast. If they have done this deed, my
noble lord—   75
  Glo. If ?—thou protector of this damned
strumpet,
Talk'st thou to me of ifs ? Thou art a
traitor.
Off with his head ! Now by Saint Paul I
swear
I will not dine until I see the same.
Lovel and Ratcliff, look that it be done. 80
The rest that love me, rise and follow me.
      [*Exeunt all but Hastings, Lovell,
      and Ratcliff.*
  Hast. Woe, woe, for England ! not a whit
for me ;
For I, too fond, might have prevented this.

Stanley did dream the boar did raze our
helms,
And I did scorn it and disdain to fly. 85
Three times to-day my foot-cloth horse did
stumble,
And started when he look'd upon the
Tower,
As loath to bear me to the slaughter-house.
O, now I need the priest that spake to me !
I now repent I told the pursuivant, 90
As too triumphing, how mine enemies
To-day at Pomfret bloodily were butcher'd,
And I myself secure in grace and favour.
O Margaret, Margaret, now thy heavy curse
Is lighted on poor Hastings' wretched head !
  Rat. Come, come, dispatch ; the Duke
would be at dinner. 96
Make a short shrift ; he longs to see your
head.
  Hast. O momentary grace of mortal men,
Which we more hunt for than the grace of
God !
Who builds his hope in air of your good
looks   100
Lives like a drunken sailor on a mast,
Ready with every nod to tumble down
Into the fatal bowels of the deep.
  Lov. Come, come, dispatch ; 'tis bootless
to exclaim.
  Hast. O bloody Richard ! Miserable
England !   105
I prophesy the fearfull'st time to thee
That ever wretched age hath look'd upon.
Come, lead me to the block ; bear him my
head.
They smile at me who shortly shall be dead.
      [*Exeunt.*

SCENE V. *London. The Tower-walls.*

Enter GLOUCESTER *and* BUCKINGHAM *in
rotten armour, marvellous ill-favoured.*

  Glo. Come, cousin, canst thou quake and
change thy colour,
Murder thy breath in middle of a word,
And then again begin, and stop again,
As if thou were distraught and mad with
terror ?
  Buck. Tut, I can counterfeit the deep
tragedian ;   5
Speak and look back, and pry on every side,
Tremble and start at wagging of a straw,
Intending deep suspicion. Ghastly looks
Are at my service, like enforced smiles ;
And both are ready in their offices 10
At any time to grace my stratagems.
But what, is Catesby gone ?
  Glo. He is ; and, see, he brings the mayor
along.

Enter the Lord Mayor *and* CATESBY.

  Buck. Lord Mayor—
  Glo. Look to the drawbridge there ! 15
  Buck. Hark ! a drum.

Glo. Catesby, o'erlook the walls.

Buck. Lord Mayor, the reason we have sent—

Glo. Look back, defend thee ; here are enemies.

Buck. God and our innocence defend and guard us !   20

Enter LOVELL *and* RATCLIFF, *with Hastings' head.*

Glo. Be patient ; they are friends— Ratcliff and Lovel.

Lov. Here is the head of that ignoble traitor,
The dangerous and unsuspected Hastings.

Glo. So dear I lov'd the man that I must weep.
I took him for the plainest harmless creature   25
That breath'd upon the earth a Christian ;
Made him my book, wherein my soul recorded
The history of all her secret thoughts.
So smooth he daub'd his vice with show of virtue
That, his apparent open guilt omitted,   30
I mean his conversation with Shore's wife—
He liv'd from all attainder of suspects.

Buck. Well, well, he was the covert'st shelt'red traitor
That ever liv'd.
Would you imagine, or almost believe—   35
Were't not that by great preservation
We live to tell it—that the subtle traitor
This day had plotted, in the council-house,
To murder me and my good Lord of Gloucester.

May. Had he done so ?   40

Glo. What ! think you we are Turks or Infidels ?
Or that we would, against the form of law,
Proceed thus rashly in the villain's death
But that the extreme peril of the case,
The peace of England and our persons' safety,   45
Enforc'd us to this execution ?

May. Now, fair befall you ! He deserv'd his death ;
And your good Graces both have well proceeded
To warn false traitors from the like attempts.
I never look'd for better at his hands   50
After he once fell in with Mistress Shore.

Buck. Yet had we not determin'd he should die
Until your lordship came to see his end—
Which now the loving haste of these our friends,
Something against our meanings, have prevented—   55
Because, my lord, I would have had you heard

The traitor speak, and timorously confess
The manner and the purpose of his treasons;
That you might well have signified the same
Unto the citizens, who haply may   60
Misconster us in him and wail his death.

May. But, my good lord, your Grace's word shall serve
As well as I had seen and heard him speak ;
And do not doubt, right noble Princes both,
But I'll acquaint our duteous citizens   65
With all your just proceedings in this cause.

Glo. And to that end we wish'd your lordship here,
T' avoid the censures of the carping world.

Buck. Which since you come too late of our intent,   69
Yet witness what you hear we did intend.
And so, my good Lord Mayor, we bid farewell.   [*Exit Lord Mayor.*

Glo. Go, after, after, cousin Buckingham.
The Mayor towards Guildhall hies him in all post.
There, at your meet'st advantage of the time,
Infer the bastardy of Edward's children.   75
Tell them how Edward put to death a citizen
Only for saying he would make his son
Heir to the crown—meaning indeed his house,
Which by the sign thereof was termed so.
Moreover, urge his hateful luxury   80
And bestial appetite in change of lust,
Which stretch'd unto their servants, daughters, wives,
Even where his raging eye or savage heart
Without control lusted to make a prey.
Nay, for a need, thus far come near my person :   85
Tell them, when that my mother went with child
Of that insatiate Edward, noble York
My princely father then had wars in France
And, by true computation of the time,
Found that the issue was not his begot ;   90
Which well appeared in his lineaments,
Being nothing like the noble Duke my father.
Yet touch this sparingly, as 'twere far off ;
Because, my lord, you know my mother lives.

Buck. Doubt not, my lord, I'll play the orator   95
As if the golden plea for which I plead
Were for myself ; and so, my lord, adieu.

Glo. If you thrive well, bring them to Baynard's Castle ;
Where you shall find me well accompanied
With reverend fathers and well learned bishops.   100

Buck. I go ; and towards three or four o'clock

Look for the news that the Guildhall
affords.   [*Exit.*
  Glo. Go, Lovel, with all speed to Doctor
    Shaw.
[*To Catesby*] Go thou to Friar Penker. Bid
    them both
Meet me within this hour at Baynard's
    Castle. [*Exeunt all but Gloucester.*
Now will I go to take some privy order   106
To draw the brats of Clarence out of sight,
And to give order that no manner of person
Have any time recourse unto the Princes.
                                      [*Exit.*

SCENE VI. *London. A street.*

Enter a Scrivener.

  Scriv. Here is the indictment of the good
    Lord Hastings ;
Which in a set hand fairly is engross'd
That it may be to-day read o'er in Paul's.
And mark how well the sequel hangs to-
    gether :   4
Eleven hours I have spent to write it over,
For yesternight by Catesby was it sent me ;
The precedent was full as long a-doing ;
And yet within these five hours Hastings
    liv'd,
Untainted, unexamin'd, free, at liberty.
Here's a good world the while ! Who is so
    gross   10
That cannot see this palpable device ?
Yet who so bold but says he sees it not ?
Bad is the world ; and all will come to
    nought,
When such ill dealing must be seen in
    thought.   [*Exit.*

SCENE VII. *London. Baynard's Castle.*

Enter GLOUCESTER *and* BUCKINGHAM, *at
    several doors.*

  Glo. How now, how now ! What say the
    citizens ?
  Buck. Now, by the holy Mother of our
    Lord,
The citizens are mum, say not a word.
  Glo. Touch'd you the bastardy of
    Edward's children ?
  Buck. I did ; with his contract with
    Lady Lucy,   5
And his contract by deputy in France ;
Th' insatiate greediness of his desire,
And his enforcement of the city wives ;
His tyranny for trifles ; his own bastardy,
As being got, your father then in France,
And his resemblance, being not like the
    Duke.   11
Withal I did infer your lineaments,
Being the right idea of your father,
Both in your form and nobleness of mind ;
Laid open all your victories in Scotland, 15
Your discipline in war, wisdom in peace,
Your bounty, virtue, fair humility ;
Indeed, left nothing fitter for your purpose

Untouch'd or slightly handled in discourse.
And when mine oratory drew toward end
I bid them that did love their country's
    good   21
Cry ' God save Richard, England's royal
    King ! '
  Glo. And did they so ?
  Buck. No, so God help me, they spake not
    a word ;
But, like dumb statues or breathing stones,
Star'd each on other, and look'd deadly
    pale.   26
Which when I saw, I reprehended them,
And ask'd the Mayor what meant this
    wilful silence.
His answer was, the people were not used
To be spoke to but by the Recorder.   30
Then he was urg'd to tell my tale again.
' Thus saith the Duke, thus hath the Duke
    inferr'd '—
But nothing spoke in warrant from himself.
When he had done, some followers of mine
    own
At lower end of the hall hurl'd up their
    caps,   35
And some ten voices cried ' God save King
    Richard ! '
And thus I took the vantage of those few—
' Thanks,   gentle   citizens   and   friends,'
    quoth I
' This general applause and cheerful shout
Argues your wisdoms and your love to
    Richard '.   40
And even here brake off and came away.
  Glo. What, tongueless blocks were they ?
    Would they not speak ?
Will not the Mayor then and his brethren
    come ?
  Buck. The Mayor is here at hand. Intend
    some fear ;   45
Be not you spoke with but by mighty suit ;
And look you get a prayer-book in your
    hand,
And stand between two churchmen, good
    my lord ;
For on that ground I'll make a holy
    descant ;
And be not easily won to our requests.   50
Play the maid's part : still answer nay, and
    take it.
  Glo. I go ; and if you plead as well for
    them
As I can say nay to thee for myself,
No doubt we bring it to a happy issue.
  Buck. Go, go, up to the leads ; the Lord
    Mayor knocks.   [*Exit Gloucester.*

Enter the Lord Mayor, Aldermen, *and*
    Citizens.

Welcome, my lord.   I dance attendance
    here ;   56
I think the Duke will not be spoke withal.

Enter CATESBY.

Now, Catesby, what says your lord to my
   request ?
Cate. He doth entreat your Grace, my
   noble lord,
To visit him to-morrow or next day. 60
He is within, with two right reverend
   fathers,
Divinely bent to meditation ;
And in no worldly suits would he be mov'd,
To draw him from his holy exercise.
  Buck. Return, good Catesby, to the
   gracious Duke ; 65
Tell him, myself, the Mayor and Aldermen,
In deep designs, in matter of great moment,
No less importing than our general good,
Are come to have some conference with his
   Grace.
  Cate. I'll signify so much unto him
   straight. [*Exit.*
  Buck. Ah ha, my lord, this prince is not
   an Edward ! 71
He is not lolling on a lewd love-bed,
But on his knees at meditation ;
Not dallying with a brace of courtezans,
But meditating with two deep divines ; 75
Not sleeping, to engross his idle body,
But praying, to enrich his watchful soul.
Happy were England would this virtuous
   prince
Take on his Grace the sovereignty thereof ;
But, sure, I fear we shall not win him to it.
  May. Marry, God defend his Grace
   should say us nay ! 81
  Buck. I fear he will. Here Catesby comes
   again.

Re-enter CATESBY.

Now, Catesby, what says his Grace ?
  Cate. My lord,
He wonders to what end you have assembled
Such troops of citizens to come to him. 85
His Grace not being warn'd thereof before,
He fears, my lord, you mean no good to
   him.
  Buck. Sorry I am my noble cousin should
Suspect me that I mean no good to him. 89
By heaven, we come to him in perfect love ;
And so once more return and tell his Grace.
    [*Exit Catesby.*
When holy and devout religious men
Are at their beads, 'tis much to draw them
   thence,
So sweet is zealous contemplation.

Enter GLOUCESTER *aloft, between two*
  Bishops. CATESBY *returns.*

  May. See where his Grace stands 'tween
   two clergymen ! 95
  Buck. Two props of virtue for a Christian
   prince,
To stay him from the fall of vanity ;
And, see, a book of prayer in his hand,
True ornaments to know a holy man. 99
Famous Plantagenet, most gracious Prince,

Lend favourable ear to our requests,
And pardon us the interruption
Of thy devotion and right Christian zeal.
  Glo. My lord, there needs no such
   apology :
I do beseech your Grace to pardon me, 105
Who, earnest in the service of my God,
Deferr'd the visitation of my friends.
But, leaving this, what is your Grace's
   pleasure ?
  Buck. Even that, I hope, which pleaseth
   God above, 109
And all good men of this ungovern'd isle.
  Glo. I do suspect I have done some offence
That seems disgracious in the city's eye,
And that you come to reprehend my ignor-
   ance.
  Buck. You have, my lord. Would it
   might please your Grace,
On our entreaties, to amend your fault ! 115
  Glo. Else wherefore breathe I in a
   Christian land ?
  Buck. Know then, it is your fault that
   you resign
The supreme seat, the throne majestical,
The scept'red office of your ancestors,
Your state of fortune and your due of birth,
The lineal glory of your royal house, 121
To the corruption of a blemish'd stock ;
Whiles in the mildness of your sleepy
   thoughts,
Which here we waken to our country's
   good,
The noble isle doth want her proper limbs ;
Her face defac'd with scars of infamy, 126
Her royal stock graft with ignoble plants,
And almost should'red in the swallowing
   gulf
Of dark forgetfulness and deep oblivion.
Which to recure, we heartily solicit 130
Your gracious self to take on you the charge
And kingly government of this your land—
Not as protector, steward, substitute,
Or lowly factor for another's gain ; 134
But as successively, from blood to blood,
Your right of birth, your empery, your own.
For this, consorted with the citizens,
Your very worshipful and loving friends,
And by their vehement instigation,
In this just cause come I to move your
   Grace. 140
  Glo. I cannot tell if to depart in silence
Or bitterly to speak in your reproof
Best fitteth my degree or your condition.
If not to answer, you might haply think
Tongue-tied ambition, not replying,
   yielded 145
To bear the golden yoke of sovereignty,
Which fondly you would here impose on
   me ;
If to reprove you for this suit of yours,
So season'd with your faithful love to me,
Then, on the other side, I check'd my
   friends. 150

Therefore—to speak, and to avoid the first,
And then, in speaking, not to incur the last—
Definitively thus I answer you:
Your love deserves my thanks, but my desert
Unmeritable shuns your high request.   155
First, if all obstacles were cut away,
And that my path were even to the crown,
As the ripe revenue and due of birth,
Yet so much is my poverty of spirit,
So mighty and so many my defects,   160
That I would rather hide me from my greatness—
Being a bark to brook no mighty sea—
Than in my greatness covet to be hid,
And in the vapour of my glory smother'd.
But, God be thank'd, there is no need of me—   165
And much I need to help you, were there need.
The royal tree hath left us royal fruit
Which, mellow'd by the stealing hours of time,
Will well become the seat of majesty   169
And make, no doubt, us happy by his reign.
On him I lay that you would lay on me—
The right and fortune of his happy stars,
Which God defend that I should wring from him.
    Buck. My lord, this argues conscience in your Grace;
But the respects thereof are nice and trivial,   175
All circumstances well considered.
You say that Edward is your brother's son.
So say we too, but not by Edward's wife;
For first was he contract to Lady Lucy—
Your mother lives a witness to his vow—   180
And afterward by substitute betroth'd
To Bona, sister to the King of France.
These both put off, a poor petitioner,
A care-craz'd mother to a many sons,
A beauty-waning and distressed widow,   185
Even in the afternoon of her best days,
Made prize and purchase of his wanton eye,
Seduc'd the pitch and height of his degree
To base declension and loath'd bigamy.
By her, in his unlawful bed, he got   190
This Edward, whom our manners call the Prince.
More bitterly could I expostulate,
Save that, for reverence to some alive,
I give a sparing limit to my tongue.   194
Then, good my lord, take to your royal self
This proffer'd benefit of dignity;
If not to bless us and the land withal,
Yet to draw forth your noble ancestry
From the corruption of abusing times
Unto a lineal true-derived course.   200
    May. Do, good my lord; your citizens entreat you.
    Buck. Refuse not, mighty lord, this proffer'd love.

    Cate. O, make them joyful, grant their lawful suit!
    Glo. Alas, why would you heap this care on me?
I am unfit for state and majesty.   205
I do beseech you, take it not amiss:
I cannot nor I will not yield to you.
    Buck. If you refuse it—as, in love and zeal,
Loath to depose the child, your brother's son;   209
As well we know your tenderness of heart
And gentle, kind, effeminate remorse,
Which we have noted in you to your kindred
And egally indeed to all estates—
Yet know, whe'er you accept our suit or no,
Your brother's son shall never reign our king;   215
But we will plant some other in the throne
To the disgrace and downfall of your house;
And in this resolution here we leave you.
Come, citizens. Zounds, I'll entreat no more.
    Glo. O, do not swear, my lord of Buckingham.   [Exeunt Buckingham, Mayor, and Citizens.
    Cate. Call him again, sweet Prince, accept their suit.   221
If you deny them, all the land will rue it.
    Glo. Will you enforce me to a world of cares?
Call them again. I am not made of stones,
But penetrable to your kind entreaties,   225
Albeit against my conscience and my soul.

Re-enter BUCKINGHAM *and the* rest.

Cousin of Buckingham, and sage grave men,
Since you will buckle fortune on my back,
To bear my burden, whe'er I will or no,
I must have patience to endure the load;
But if black scandal or foul-fac'd reproach
Attend the sequel of your imposition,   232
Your mere enforcement shall acquittance me
From all the impure blots and stains thereof;
For God doth know, and you may partly see,   235
How far I am from the desire of this.
    May. God bless your Grace! We see it, and will say it.
    Glo. In saying so, you shall but say the truth.
    Buck. Then I salute you with this royal title—
Long live King Richard, England's worthy King!   240
    All. Amen.
    Buck. To-morrow may it please you to be crown'd?
    Glo. Even when you please, for you will have it so.

Buck. To-morrow, then, we will attend
    your Grace ;
And so, most joyfully, we take our leave.
Glo. [*To the Bishops*] Come, let us to our
    holy work again.   246
Farewell, my cousin ; farewell, gentle
    friends.   [*Exeunt.*

ACT FOUR

SCENE I. *London. Before the Tower.*

Enter QUEEN ELIZABETH, DUCHESS OF
YORK, *and* MARQUIS OF DORSET, *at one
door ;* ANNE DUCHESS OF GLOUCESTER,
leading LADY MARGARET PLANTAGENET,
*Clarence's young daughter, at another
door.*

Duch. Who meets us here ? My niece
    Plantagenet,
Led in the hand of her kind aunt of
    Gloucester ?
Now, for my life, she's wand'ring to the
    Tower,
On pure heart's love, to greet the tender
    Princes.
Daughter, well met.
Anne.   God give your Graces both 5
A happy and a joyful time of day !
Q. Eliz. As much to you, good sister !
    Whither away ?
Anne. No farther than the Tower ; and,
    as I guess,
Upon the like devotion as yourselves,
To gratulate the gentle Princes there.   10
Q. Eliz. Kind sister, thanks ; we'll enter
    all together.

Enter BRAKENBURY.

And in good time, here the lieutenant
    comes.
Master Lieutenant, pray you, by your leave,
How doth the Prince, and my young son
    of York ?
Brak. Right well, dear madam. By your
    patience,   15
I may not suffer you to visit them.
The King hath strictly charg'd the con-
    trary.
Q. Eliz. The King ! Who's that ?
Brak.   I mean the Lord Protector.
Q. Eliz. The Lord protect him from that
    kingly title !   20
Hath he set bounds between their love and
    me ?
I am their mother ; who shall bar me from
    them ?
Duch. I am their father's mother ; I will
    see them.
Anne. Their aunt I am in law, in love
    their mother.
Then bring me to their sights ; I'll bear thy
    blame,   25
And take thy office from thee on my peril.

Brak. No, madam, no. I may not leave
    it so ;
I am bound by oath, and therefore pardon
    me.   [*Exit.*

Enter STANLEY.

Stan. Let me but meet you, ladies, one
    hour hence,
And I'll salute your Grace of York as
    mother   30
And reverend looker-on of two fair queens.
[*To Anne*] Come, madam, you must straight
    to Westminster,
There to be crowned Richard's royal queen.
Q. Eliz. Ah, cut my lace asunder
That my pent heart may have some scope
    to beat,   35
Or else I swoon with this dead-killing news !
Anne. Despiteful tidings ! O unpleasing
    news !
Dor. Be of good cheer ; mother, how
    fares your Grace ?
Q. Eliz. O Dorset, speak not to me, get
    thee gone !
Death and destruction dogs thee at thy
    heels ;   40
Thy mother's name is ominous to children.
If thou wilt outstrip death, go cross the
    seas,
And live with Richmond, from the reach
    of hell.
Go, hie thee, hie thee from this slaughter-
    house,   44
Lest thou increase the number of the dead,
And make me die the thrall of Margaret's
    curse,
Nor mother, wife, nor England's counted
    queen.
Stan. Full of wise care is this your
    counsel, madam.
Take all the swift advantage of the hours ;
You shall have letters from me to my son 50
In your behalf, to meet you on the way.
Be not ta'en tardy by unwise delay.
Duch. O ill-dispersing wind of misery !
O my accursed womb, the bed of death !
A cockatrice hast thou hatch'd to the
    world,   55
Whose unavoided eye is murderous.
Stan. Come, madam, come ; I in all
    haste was sent.
Anne. And I with all unwillingness will
    go.   58
O, would to God that the inclusive verge
Of golden metal that must round my brow
Were red-hot stèel, to sear me to the brains !
Anointed let me be with deadly venom, 62
And die ere men can say ' God save the
    Queen ! '
Q. Eliz. Go, go, poor soul ; I envy not
    thy glory.
To feed my humour, wish thyself no harm.
Anne. No, why ? When he that is my
    husband now   66

Came to me, as I follow'd Henry's corse;
When scarce the blood was well wash'd
 from his hands
Which issued from my other angel husband,
And that dear saint which then I weeping
 follow'd—   70
O, when, I say, I look'd on Richard's face,
This was my wish: ' Be thou ' quoth I
 accurs'd
For making me, so young, so old a widow;
And when thou wed'st, let sorrow haunt
 thy bed;
And be thy wife, if any be so mad,   75
More miserable by the life of thee
Than thou hast made me by my dear lord's
 death '.
Lo, ere I can repeat this curse again,
Within so small a time, my woman's heart
Grossly grew captive to his honey words 80
And prov'd the subject of mine own soul's
 curse,
Which hitherto hath held my eyes from
 rest;
For never yet one hour in his bed
Did I enjoy the golden dew of sleep,
But with his timorous dreams was still
 awak'd.   85
Besides, he hates me for my father Warwick;
And will, no doubt, shortly be rid of me.
  Q. Eliz. Poor heart, adieu! I pity thy
   complaining.
  Anne. No more than with my soul I
   mourn for yours.
  Dor. Farewell, thou woeful welcomer
   of glory!   90
  Anne. Adieu, poor soul, that tak'st thy
   leave of it!
  Duch. [*To Dorset*] Go thou to Richmond,
   and good fortune guide thee!
[*To Anne*] Go thou to Richard, and good
 angels tend thee!
[*To Queen Elizabeth*] Go thou to sanctuary,
 and good thoughts possess thee!
I to my grave, where peace and rest lie
 with me!   95
Eighty odd years of sorrow have I seen,
And each hour's joy wreck'd with a week
 of teen.
  Q. Eliz. Stay, yet look back with me
   unto the Tower.
Pity, you ancient stones, those tender
 babes
Whom envy hath immur'd within your
 walls,   100
Rough cradle for such little pretty ones.
Rude ragged nurse, old sullen playfellow
For tender princes, use my babies well.
So foolish sorrows bids your stones farewell.
                                    [*Exeunt.*

SCENE II. *London. The palace.*

Sound a sennet. Enter RICHARD, *in pomp, as*
King; BUCKINGHAM, CATESBY, RATCLIFF,
LOVEL, *a Page, and Others.*

  K. Rich. Stand all apart. Cousin of
   Buckingham!
  Buck. My gracious sovereign?
  K. Rich. Give me thy hand.
   [*Here he ascendeth the throne. Souna.*
          Thus high, by thy advice
And thy assistance, is King Richard seated.
But shall we wear these glories for a day; 5
Or shall they last, and we rejoice in them?
  Buck. Still live they, and for ever let
   them last!
  K. Rich. Ah, Buckingham, now do I play
   the touch,
To try if thou be current gold indeed.
Young Edward lives—think now what I
 would speak.   10
  Buck. Say on, my loving lord.
  K. Rich. Why, Buckingham, I say I
   would be King.
  Buck. Why, so you are, my thrice-
   renowned lord.
  K. Rich. Ha! am I King? 'Tis so; but
   Edward lives.
  Buck. True, noble Prince.
  K. Rich.   O bitter consequence: 15
That Edward still should live—true noble
 Prince!
Cousin, thou wast not wont to be so dull.
Shall I be plain? I wish the bastards dead.
And I would have it suddenly perform'd.
What say'st thou now? Speak suddenly,
 be brief.   20
  Buck. Your Grace may do your pleasure.
  K. Rich. Tut, tut, thou art all ice; thy
   kindness freezes.
Say, have I thy consent that they shall
 die?
  Buck. Give me some little breath, some
   pause, dear lord,
Before I positively speak in this.   25
I will resolve you herein presently. [*Exit.*
  Cate. [*Aside to another*] The King is
   angry; see, he gnaws his lip.
  K. Rich. I will converse with iron-witted
   fools   [*Descends from the throne.*
And unrespective boys; none are for me
That look into me with considerate eyes. 30
High-reaching Buckingham grows circum-
 spect.
Boy!
  Page. My lord?
  K. Rich. Know'st thou not any whom
   corrupting gold
Will tempt unto a close exploit of death? 35
  Page. I know a discontented gentleman
Whose humble means match not his
 haughty spirit.
Gold were as good as twenty orators,
And will, no doubt, tempt him to anything.
  K. Rich. What is his name?
  Page.   His name, my lord, is Tyrrel. 40
  K. Rich. I partly know the man. Go, call
   him hither, boy.   [*Exit Page.*
The deep-revolving witty Buckingham

No more shall be the neighbour to my
    counsels.
Hath he so long held out with me, untir'd,
And stops he now for breath ? Well, be
    it so.   45

Enter STANLEY.

How now, Lord Stanley ! What's the
    news ?
  Stan. Know, my loving lord,
The Marquis Dorset, as I hear, is fled
To Richmond, in the parts where he abides.
                  [*Stands apart.*
  K. Rich. Come hither, Catesby. Rumour
    it abroad
That Anne, my wife, is very grievous sick ;
I will take order for her keeping close.   54
Inquire me out some mean poor gentleman,
Whom I will marry straight to Clarence'
    daughter—
The boy is foolish, and I fear not him.
Look how thou dream'st ! I say again,
    give out
That Anne, my queen, is sick and like to die.
About it ; for it stands me much upon   60
To stop all hopes whose growth may dam-
    age me.   [*Exit Catesby.*
I must be married to my brother's daughter,
Or else my kingdom stands on brittle glass.
Murder her brothers, and then marry her !
Uncertain way of gain ! But I am in   65
So far in blood that sin will pluck on sin.
Tear-falling pity dwells not in this eye.

Re-enter Page, *with* TYRREL.

Is thy name Tyrrel ?
  Tyr. James Tyrrel, and your most
    obedient subject.
  K. Rich. Art thou, indeed ?
  Tyr.   Prove me, my gracious lord.   70
  K. Rich. Dar'st thou resolve to kill a
    friend of mine ?
  Tyr. Please you ;
But I had rather kill two enemies.
  K. Rich. Why, then thou hast it.   Two
    deep enemies,
Foes to my rest, and my sweet sleep's
    disturbers,   75
Are they that I would have thee deal upon.
Tyrrel, I mean those bastards in the Tower.
  Tyr. Let me have open means to come to
    them,
And soon I'll rid you from the fear of them.
  K. Rich. Thou sing'st sweet music.
    Hark, come hither, Tyrrel.   80
Go, by this token. Rise, and lend thine ear.
                  [*Whispers.*
There is no more but so : say it is done,
And I will love thee and prefer thee for it.
  Tyr. I will dispatch it straight.   [*Exit.*

Re-enter BUCKINGHAM.

  Buck. My lord, I have consider'd in my
    mind

The late request that you did sound me in.
  K. Rich. Well, let that rest. Dorset is fled
    to Richmond.
  Buck. I hear the news, my lord.   90
  K. Rich. Stanley, he is your wife's son :
    well, look unto it.
  Buck. My lord, I claim the gift, my due
    by promise,
For which your honour and your faith is
    pawn'd :
Th' earldom of Hereford and the movables
Which you have promised I shall possess.
  K. Rich. Stanley, look to your wife ; if
    she convey   96
Letters to Richmond, you shall answer it.
  Buck. What says your Highness to my
    just request ?
  K. Rich. I do remember me : Henry the
    Sixth
Did prophesy that Richmond should be
    King,   100
When Richmond was a little peevish boy.
A king !—perhaps—
  Buck. My lord—
  K. Rich. How chance the prophet could
    not at that time
Have told me, I being by, that I should
    kill him ?   105
  Buck. My lord, your promise for the
    earldom—
  K. Rich. Richmond ! When last I was
    at Exeter,
The mayor in courtesy show'd me the
    castle
And call'd it Rugemount, at which name I
    started,
Because a bard of Ireland told me once 110
I should not live long after I saw Rich-
    mond.
  Buck. My lord—
  K. Rich. Ay, what's o'clock ?
  Buck. I am thus bold to put your Grace
    in mind   114
Of what you promis'd me.
  K. Rich.   Well, but what's o'clock?
  Buck. Upon the stroke of ten.
  K. Rich.   Well, let it strike.
  Buck. Why let it strike ?
  K. Rich. Because that like a Jack thou
    keep'st the stroke
Betwixt thy begging and my meditation.
I am not in the giving vein to-day.   120
  Buck. May it please you to resolve me in
    my suit.
  K. Rich. Thou troublest me ; I am not in
    the vein.
           [*Exeunt all but Buckingham.*
  Buck. And is it thus ? Repays he my
    deep service
With such contempt ? Made I him King
    for this ?   125
O, let me think on Hastings, and be gone
To Brecknock while my fearful head is on !
                    [*Exit.*

SCENE III. *London. The palace.*

Enter TYRREL.

Tyr. The tyrannous and bloody act is done,
The most arch deed of piteous massacre
That ever yet this land was guilty of.
Dighton and Forrest, who I did suborn
To do this piece of ruthful butchery, 5
Albeit they were flesh'd villains, bloody dogs,
Melted with tenderness and mild compassion,
Wept like two children in their deaths' sad story.
'O, thus' quoth Dighton 'lay the gentle babes'—
'Thus, thus,' quoth Forrest 'girdling one another 10
Within their alabaster innocent arms.
Their lips were four red roses on a stalk,
And in their summer beauty kiss'd each other.
A book of prayers on their pillow lay;
Which once,' quoth Forrest 'almost chang'd my mind; 15
But, O, the devil'—there the villain stopp'd;
When Dighton thus told on: 'We smothered
The most replenished sweet work of nature
That from the prime creation e'er she framed'.
Hence both are gone with conscience and remorse 20
They could not speak; and so I left them both,
To bear this tidings to the bloody King.

Enter KING RICHARD.

And here he comes. All health, my sovereign lord!
K. Rich. Kind Tyrrel, am I happy in thy news?
Tyr. If to have done the thing you gave in charge 25
Beget your happiness, be happy then,
For it is done.
K. Rich. But didst thou see them dead?
Tyr. I did, my lord.
K. Rich. And buried, gentle Tyrrel?
Tyr. The chaplain of the Tower ath buried them; 29
But where, to say the truth, I do not know.
K. Rich. Come to me, Tyrrel, soon at after supper,
When thou shalt tell the process of their death.
Meantime, but think how I may do thee good
And be inheritor of thy desire.
Farewell till then.
Tyr. I humbly take my leave. [*Exit.*

K. Rich. The son of Clarence have I pent up close; 36
His daughter meanly have I match'd in marriage;
The sons of Edward sleep in Abraham's bosom,
And Anne my wife hath bid this world good night.
Now, for I know the Britaine Richmond aims 40
At young Elizabeth, my brother's daughter,
And by that knot looks proudly on the crown,
To her go I, a jolly thriving wooer.

Enter RATCLIFF.

Rat. My lord!
K. Rich. Good or bad news, that thou com'st in so bluntly? 45
Rat. Bad news, my lord: Morton is fled to Richmond;
And Buckingham, back'd with the hardy Welshmen,
Is in the field, and still his power increaseth.
K. Rich. Ely with Richmond troubles me more near
Than Buckingham and his rash-levied strength. 50
Come, I have learn'd that fearful commenting
Is leaden servitor to dull delay;
Delay leads impotent and snail-pac'd beggary.
Then fiery expedition be my wing,
Jove's Mercury, and herald for a king! 55
Go, muster men. My counsel is my shield.
We must be brief when traitors brave the field. [*Exeunt.*

SCENE IV. *London. Before the palace.*

Enter old QUEEN MARGARET.

Q. Mar. So now prosperity begins to mellow
And drop into the rotten mouth of death.
Here in these confines slily have I lurk'd
To watch the waning of mine enemies.
A dire induction am I witness to, 5
And will to France, hoping the consequence
Will prove as bitter, black, and tragical.
Withdraw thee, wretched Margaret. Who comes here? [*Retires.*

Enter QUEEN ELIZABETH *and the* DUCHESS OF YORK.

Q. Eliz. Ah, my poor princes! ah, my tender babes! 9
My unblown flowers, new-appearing sweets!
If yet your gentle souls fly in the air
And be not fix'd in doom perpetual,
Hover about me with your airy wings
And hear your mother's lamentation.
Q. Mar. Hover about her; say that right for right 15

Hath dimm'd your infant morn to aged
    night.
  Duch. So many miseries have craz'd my
    voice
That my woe-wearied tongue is still and
    mute.
Edward Plantagenet, why art thou dead ?
  Q. Mar. Plantagenet doth quit Planta-
    genet, 20
Edward for Edward pays a dying debt.
  Q. Eliz. Wilt thou, O God, fly from such
    gentle lambs
And throw them in the entrails of the wolf ?
When didst thou sleep when such a deed
    was done ?
  Q. Mar. When holy Harry died, and my
    sweet son. 25
  Duch. Dead life, blind sight, poor mortal
    living ghost,
Woe's scene, world's shame, grave's due by
    life usurp'd,
Brief abstract and record of tedious days,
Rest thy unrest on England's lawful earth,
                 [*Sitting down.*
Unlawfully made drunk with innocent
    blood. 30
  Q. Eliz. Ah, that thou wouldst as soon
    afford a grave
As thou canst yield a melancholy seat !
Then would I hide my bones, not rest them
    here.
Ah, who hath any cause to mourn but we ?
            [*Sitting down by her.*
  Q. Mar. [*Coming forward*] If ancient
    sorrow be most reverend, 35
Give mine the benefit of seniory,
And let my griefs frown on the upper hand.
If sorrow can admit society,
           [*Sitting down with them.*
Tell o'er your woes again by viewing mine.
I had an Edward, till a Richard kill'd him ;
I had a husband, till a Richard kill'd him :
Thou hadst an Edward, till a Richard kill'd
    him ;
Thou hadst a Richard, till a Richard kill'd
    him. 42
  Duch. I had a Richard too, and thou
    didst kill him ;
I had a Rutland too, thou holp'st to kill
    him. 45
  Q. Mar. Thou hadst a Clarence too, and
    Richard kill'd him.
From forth the kennel of thy womb hath
    crept
A hell-hound that doth hunt us all to death.
That dog, that had his teeth before his eyes
To worry lambs and lap their gentle blood,
That foul defacer of God's handiwork, 51
That excellent grand tyrant of the earth
That reigns in galled eyes of weeping souls,
Thy womb let loose to chase us to our
    graves.
O upright, just, and true-disposing God,
How do I thank thee that this carnal cur

Preys on the issue of his mother's body 57
And makes her pew-fellow with others'
    moan !
  Duch. O Harry's wife, triumph not in my
    woes !
God witness with me, I have wept for
    thine. 60
  Q. Mar. Bear with me ; I am hungry for
    revenge,
And now I cloy me with beholding it.
Thy Edward he is dead, that kill'd my
    Edward ;
The other Edward dead, to quit my
    Edward ;
Young York he is but boot, because both
    they 65
Match'd not the high perfection of my loss.
Thy Clarence he is dead that stabb'd my
    Edward ;
And the beholders of this frantic play,
Th' adulterate Hastings, Rivers, Vaughan,
    Grey, 69
Untimely smother'd in their dusky graves.
Richard yet lives, hell's black intelligencer ;
Only reserv'd their factor to buy souls
And send them thither. But at hand, at
    hand,
Ensues his piteous and unpitied end.
Earth gapes, hell burns, fiends roar, saints
    pray, 75
To have him suddenly convey'd from hence.
Cancel his bond of life, dear God, I pray,
That I may live and say ' The dog is dead '.
  Q. Eliz. O, thou didst prophesy the time
    would come
That I should wish for thee to help me
    curse 80
That bottled spider, that foul bunch-back'd
    toad !
  Q. Mar. I call'd thee then vain flourish of
    my fortune ;
I call'd thee then poor shadow, painted
    queen,
The presentation of but what I was,
The flattering index of a direful pageant, 85
One heav'd a-high to be hurl'd down
    below,
A mother only mock'd with two fair babes,
A dream of what thou wast, a garish flag
To be the aim of every dangerous shot,
A sign of dignity, a breath, a bubble,
A queen in jest, only to fill the scene. 91
Where is thy husband now ? Where be thy
    brothers ?
Where be thy two sons ? Wherein dost
    thou joy ?
Who sues, and kneels, and says ' God save
    the Queen ' ?
Where be the bending peers that flattered
    thee ? 95
Where be the thronging troops that followed
    thee ?
Decline all this, and see what now thou art :
For happy wife, a most distressed widow ;

For joyful mother, one that wails the name;
For one being su'd to, one that humbly
    sues ;   100
For Queen, a very caitiff crown'd with care ;
For she that scorn'd at me, now scorn'd of
    me ;
For she being fear'd of all, now fearing one ;
For she commanding all, obey'd of none.
Thus hath the course of justice whirl'd
    about   105
And left thee but a very prey to time,
Having no more but thought of what thou
    wast
To torture thee the more, being what thou
    art.
Thou didst usurp my place, and dost thou
    not
Usurp the just proportion of my sorrow ?
Now thy proud neck bears half my
    burden'd yoke,   111
From which even here I slip my weary
    head
And leave the burden of it all on thee.
Farewell, York's wife, and queen of sad
    mischance ;
These English woes shall make me smile in
    France.   115
  Q. Eliz. O thou well skill'd in curses, stay
    awhile
And teach me how to curse mine enemies !
  Q. Mar. Forbear to sleep the nights, and
    fast the days ;
Compare dead happiness with living woe ;
Think that thy babes were sweeter than
    they were,   120
And he that slew them fouler than he is.
Bett'ring thy loss makes the bad-causer
    worse ;
Revolving this will teach thee how to curse.
  Q. Eliz. My words are dull ; O, quicken
    them with thine !
  Q. Mar. Thy woes will make them sharp
    and pierce like mine.   [Exit.
  Duch. Why should calamity be full of
    words ?   126
  Q. Eliz. Windy attorneys to their client
    woes,
Airy succeeders of intestate joys,
Poor breathing orators of miseries,
Let them have scope ; though what they
    will impart   130
Help nothing else, yet do they ease the
    heart.
  Duch. If so, then be not tongue-tied. Go
    with me,
And in the breath of bitter words let's
    smother
My damned son that thy two sweet sons
    smother'd.
The trumpet sounds ; be copious in
    exclaims.   135

Enter KING RICHARD *and his* Train,
    marching with drums and trumpets.

  K. Rich. Who intercepts me in my
    expedition ?
  Duch. O, she that might have intercepted
    thee,
By strangling thee in her accursed womb,
From all the slaughters, wretch, that thou
    hast done !
  Q. Eliz. Hidest thou that forehead with a
    golden crown   140
Where should be branded, if that right
    were right,
The slaughter of the Prince that ow'd that
    crown,
And the dire death of my poor sons and
    brothers ?
Tell me, thou villain slave, where are my
    children ?
  Duch. Thou toad, thou toad, where is thy
    brother Clarence ?   145
And little Ned Plantagenet, his son ?
  Q. Eliz. Where is the gentle Rivers,
    Vaughan, Grey ?
  Duch. Where is kind Hastings ?
  K. Rich. A flourish, trumpets ! Strike
    alarum, drums !
Let not the heavens hear these tell-tale
    women   149
Rail on the Lord's anointed. Strike, I say !
                        [Flourish. Alarums.
Either be patient and entreat me fair,
Or with the clamorous report of war
Thus will I drown your exclamations.
  Duch. Art thou my son ?
  K. Rich. Ay, I thank God, my father, and
    yourself.   155
  Duch. Then patiently hear my impatience.
  K. Rich. Madam, I have a touch of your
    condition
That cannot brook the accent of reproof.
  Duch. O, let me speak !
  K. Rich. Do, then ; but I'll not hear.
  Duch. I will be mild and gentle in my
    words.   160
  K. Rich. And brief, good mother ; for I
    am in haste.
  Duch. Art thou so hasty ? I have stay'd
    for thee,
God knows, in torment and in agony.
  K. Rich. And came I not at last to com-
    fort you ?
  Duch. No, by the holy rood, thou know'st
    it well   165
Thou cam'st on earth to make the earth my
    hell.
A grievous burden was thy birth to me ;
Tetchy and wayward was thy infancy ;
Thy school-days frightful, desp'rate, wild,
    and furious ;
Thy prime of manhood daring, bold, and
    venturous ;   170
Thy age confirm'd, proud, subtle, sly, and
    bloody,
More mild, but yet more harmful-kind in
    hatred.

What comfortable hour canst thou name
That ever grac'd me with thy company ?
  K. Rich. Faith, none but Humphrey
    Hour, that call'd your Grace   175
To breakfast once forth of my company.
If I be so disgracious in your eye,
Let me march on and not offend you,
    madam.
Strike up the drum.
  Duch.   I prithee hear me speak.
  K. Rich. You speak too bitterly.
  Duch.   Hear me a word ;   180
For I shall never speak to thee again.
  K. Rich. So.
  Duch. Either thou wilt die by God's just
    ordinance
Ere from this war thou turn a conqueror ;
Or I with grief and extreme age shall
    perish   185
And never more behold thy face again.
Therefore take with thee my most grievous
    curse,
Which in the day of battle tire thee more
Than all the complete armour that thou
    wear'st !
My prayers on the adverse party fight ;   190
And there the little souls of Edward's
    children
Whisper the spirits of thine enemies
And promise them success and victory.
Bloody thou art ; bloody will be thy end.
Shame serves thy life and doth thy death
    attend.   [*Exit.*
  Q. Eliz. Though far more cause, yet much
    less spirit to curse   196
Abides in me ; I say amen to her.
  K. Rich. Stay, madam, I must talk a
    word with you.
  Q. Eliz. I have no moe sons of the royal
    blood
For thee to slaughter. For my daughters,
    Richard,   200
They shall be praying nuns, not weeping
    queens ;
And therefore level not to hit their lives.
  K. Rich. You have a daughter call'd
    Elizabeth,
Virtuous and fair, royal and gracious.
  Q. Eliz. And must she die for this ? O, let
    her live,   205
And I'll corrupt her manners, stain her
    beauty,
Slander myself as false to Edward's bed,
Throw over her the veil of infamy ;
So she may live unscarr'd of bleeding
    slaughter,
I will confess she was not Edward's
    daughter.   210
  K. Rich. Wrong not her birth ; she is a
    royal Princess.
  Q. Eliz. To save her life I'll say she is
    not so.
  K. Rich. Her life is safest only in her
    birth.

  Q. Eliz. And only in that safety died her
    brothers.
  K. Rich. Lo, at their birth good stars were
    opposite.   215
  Q. Eliz. No, to their lives ill friends were
    contrary.
  K. Rich. All unavoided is the doom of
    destiny.
  Q. Eliz. True, when avoided grace makes
    destiny.
My babes were destin'd to a fairer death,
If grace had bless'd thee with a fairer life.
  K. Rich. You speak as if that I had slain
    my cousins.   221
  Q. Eliz. Cousins, indeed ; and by their
    uncle cozen'd
Of comfort, kingdom, kindred, freedom,
    life.
Whose hand soever lanc'd their tender
    hearts,
Thy head, all indirectly, gave direction.   225
No doubt the murd'rous knife was dull and
    blunt
Till it was whetted on thy stone-hard heart
To revel in the entrails of my lambs.
But that still use of grief makes wild grief
    tame,
My tongue should to thy ears not name my
    boys   230
Till that my nails were anchor'd in thine
    eyes ;
And I, in such a desp'rate bay of death,
Like a poor bark, of sails and tackling reft,
Rush all to pieces on thy rocky bosom.
  K. Rich. Madam, so thrive I in my enter-
    prise   235
And dangerous success of bloody wars,
As I intend more good to you or yours
Than ever you or yours by me were harm'd!
  Q. Eliz. What good is cover'd with the
    face of heaven,
To be discover'd, that can do me good ?   240
  K. Rich. Th' advancement of your
    children, gentle lady.
  Q. Eliz. Up to some scaffold, there to lose
    their heads ?
  K. Rich. Unto the dignity and height of
    Fortune,
The high imperial type of this earth's glory.
  Q. Eliz. Flatter my sorrow with report
    of it ;   245
Tell me what state, what dignity, what
    honour,
Canst thou demise to any child of mine ?
  K. Rich. Even all I have—ay, and myself
    and all
Will I withal endow a child of thine ;
So in the Lethe of thy angry soul   250
Thou drown the sad remembrance of those
    wrongs
Which thou supposest I have done to thee.
  Q. Eliz. Be brief, lest that the process of
    thy kindness
Last longer telling than thy kindness' date.

K. Rich. Then know, that from my soul I
    love thy daughter.   255

Q. Eliz. My daughter's mother thinks it
    with her soul.

K. Rich. What do you think ?

Q. Eliz. That thou dost love my daughter
    from thy soul.

So from thy soul's love didst thou love her
    brothers,

And from my heart's love I do thank thee
    for it.   260

K. Rich. Be not so hasty to confound my
    meaning.

I mean that with my soul I love thy
    daughter

And do intend to make her Queen of
    England.

Q. Eliz. Well, then, who dost thou mean
    shall be her king ?

K. Rich. Even he that makes her Queen.
    Who else should be ?   265

Q. Eliz. What, thou ?

K. Rich. Even so. How think you of it ?

Q. Eliz. How canst thou woo her ?

K. Rich.   That would I learn of you,

As one being best acquainted with her
    humour.

Q. Eliz. And wilt thou learn of me ?

K. Rich. Madam, with all my heart.

Q. Eliz. Send to her, by the man that
    slew her brothers,   271

A pair of bleeding hearts ; thereon engrave

'Edward' and 'York'. Then haply will she
    weep ;

Therefore present to her—as sometimes
    Margaret

Did to thy father, steep'd in Rutland's
    blood—   275

A handkerchief ; which, say to her, did
    drain

The purple sap from her sweet brother's
    body,

And bid her wipe her weeping eyes withal.

If this inducement move her not to love,

Send her a letter of thy noble deeds ;   280

Tell her thou mad'st away her uncle
    Clarence,

Her uncle Rivers ; ay, and for her sake

Mad'st quick conveyance with her good
    aunt Anne.

K. Rich. You mock me, madam ; this is
    not the way

To win your daughter.

Q. Eliz.   There is no other way ;   285

Unless thou couldst put on some other
    shape

And not be Richard that hath done all
    this.

K. Rich. Say that I did all this for love
    of her.

Q. Eliz. Nay, then indeed she cannot
    choose but hate thee,

Having bought love with such a bloody
    spoil.   290

K. Rich. Look what is done cannot be
    now amended.

Men shall deal unadvisedly sometimes,

Which after-hours gives leisure to repent.

If I did take the kingdom from your sons,

To make amends I'll give it to your
    daughter.   295

If I have kill'd the issue of your womb,

To quicken your increase I will beget

Mine issue of your blood upon your
    daughter.

A grandam's name is little less in love

Than is the doating title of a mother ;   300

They are as children but one step below,

Even of your metal, of your very blood ;

Of all one pain, save for a night of groans

Endur'd of her, for whom you bid like
    sorrow.   304

Your children were vexation to your youth;

But mine shall be a comfort to your age.

The loss you have is but a son being King,

And by that loss your daughter is made
    Queen.

I cannot make you what amends I would,

Therefore accept such kindness as I can.   310

Dorset your son, that with a fearful soul

Leads discontented steps in foreign soil,

This fair alliance quickly shall call home

To high promotions and great dignity.

The King, that calls your beauteous
    daughter wife,   315

Familiarly shall call thy Dorset brother ;

Again shall you be mother to a king,

And all the ruins of distressful times

Repair'd with double riches of content.

What ! we have many goodly days to
    see.

The liquid drops of tears that you have
    shed   321

Shall come again, transform'd to orient
    pearl,

Advantaging their loan with interest

Of ten times double gain of happiness.

Go, then, my mother, to thy daughter go ;

Make bold her bashful years with your
    experience ;   326

Prepare her ears to hear a wooer's tale ;

Put in her tender heart th' aspiring flame

Of golden sovereignty ; acquaint the
    Princess

With the sweet silent hours of marriage
    joys.   330

And when this arm of mine hath chastised

The petty rebel, dull-brain'd Buckingham,

Bound with triumphant garlands will I
    come,

And lead thy daughter to a conqueror's bed;

To whom I will retail my conquest won,   335

And she shall be sole victoress, Cæsar's
    Cæsar.

Q. Eliz. What were I best to say ? Her
    father's brother

Would be her lord ? Or shall I say her
    uncle ?

737

Or he that slew her brothers and her
    uncles ?
Under what title shall I woo for thee   340
That God, the law, my honour, and her love
Can make seem pleasing to her tender
    years ?

K. Rich. Infer fair England's peace by
    this alliance.
Q. Eliz. Which she shall purchase with
    still-lasting war.
K. Rich. Tell her the King, that may
    command, entreats.   345
Q. Eliz. That at her hands which the
    King's King forbids.
K. Rich. Say she shall be a high and
    mighty queen.
Q. Eliz. To wail the title, as her mother
    doth.
K. Rich. Say I will love her everlastingly.
Q. Eliz. But how long shall that title
    ' ever ' last ?   350
K. Rich. Sweetly in force unto her fair
    life's end.
Q. Eliz. But how long fairly shall her
    sweet life last ?
K. Rich. As long as heaven and nature
    lengthens it.
Q. Eliz. As long as hell and Richard likes
    of it.
K. Rich. Say I, her sovereign, am her
    subject low.   355
Q. Eliz. But she, your subject, loathes
    such sovereignty.
K. Rich. Be eloquent in my behalf to her.
Q. Eliz. An honest tale speeds best being
    plainly told.
K. Rich. Then plainly to her tell my
    loving tale.
Q. Eliz. Plain and not honest is too harsh
    a style.   360
K. Rich. Your reasons are too shallow and
    too quick.
Q. Eliz. O, no, my reasons are too deep
    and dead—
Too deep and dead, poor infants, in their
    graves.
K. Rich. Harp not on that string, madam;
    that is past.
Q. Eliz. Harp on it still shall I till heart-
    strings break.   365
K. Rich. Now, by my George, my garter,
    and my crown—
Q. Eliz. Profan'd, dishonour'd, and the
    third usurp'd.
K. Rich. I swear—
Q. Eliz.   By nothing; for this is no oath :
Thy George, profan'd, hath lost his lordly
    honour ;
Thy garter, blemish'd, pawn'd his knightly
    virtue ;   370
Thy crown, usurp'd, disgrac'd his kingly
    glory.
If something thou wouldst swear to be
    believ'd,

Swear then by something that thou hast
    not wrong'd.
K. Rich. Then, by my self—
Q. Eliz.   Thy self is self-misus'd.
K. Rich. Now, by the world—
Q. Eliz.   'Tis full of thy foul wrongs.
K. Rich. My father's death—
Q. Eliz.   Thy life hath it dishonour'd.
K. Rich. Why, then, by God—
Q. Eliz.   God's wrong is most of all.
If thou didst fear to break an oath with
    Him,
The unity the King my husband made
Thou hadst not broken, nor my brothers
    died.   380
If thou hadst fear'd to break an oath by
    Him,
Th' imperial metal, circling now thy head,
Had grac'd the tender temples of my child ;
And both the Princes had been breathing
    here,   384
Which now, two tender bedfellows for dust,
Thy broken faith hath made the prey for
    worms.
What canst thou swear by now ?
K. Rich.   The time to come.
Q. Eliz. That thou hast wronged in the
    time o'erpast ;
For I myself have many tears to wash
Hereafter time, for time past wrong'd by
    thee.   390
The children live whose fathers thou hast
    slaughter'd,
Ungovern'd youth, to wail it in their age ;
The parents live whose children thou hast
    butcher'd,
Old barren plants, to wail it with their age.
Swear not by time to come ; for that thou
    hast   395
Misus'd ere us'd, by times ill-us'd o'erpast.
K. Rich. As I intend to prosper and
    repent,
So thrive I in my dangerous affairs
Of hostile arms ! Myself myself confound !
Heaven and fortune bar me happy hours !
Day, yield me not thy light ; nor, night,
    thy rest !   401
Be opposite all planets of good luck
To my proceeding !—if, with dear heart's
    love,
Immaculate devotion, holy thoughts,
I tender not thy beauteous princely
    daughter.   405
In her consists my happiness and thine ;
Without her, follows to myself and thee,
Herself, the land, and many a Christian
    soul,
Death, desolation, ruin, and decay.
It cannot be avoided but by this ;   410
It will not be avoided but by this.
Therefore, dear mother—I must call you
    so—
Be the attorney of my love to her ;
Plead what I will be, not what I have been ;

Not my deserts, but what I will deserve. 415
Urge the necessity and state of times,
And be not peevish-fond in great designs.
  Q. Eliz. Shall I be tempted of the devil
    thus ?
  K. Rich. Ay, if the devil tempt you to do
    good.
  Q. Eliz. Shall I forget myself to be
    myself ?   420
  K. Rich. Ay, if your self's remembrance
    wrong yourself.
  Q. Eliz. Yet thou didst kill my children.
  K. Rich. But in your daughter's womb
    I bury them ;
Where, in that nest of spicery, they will
    breed   424
Selves of themselves, to your recomforture.
  Q. Eliz. Shall I go win my daughter to
    thy will ?
  K. Rich. And be a happy mother by the
    deed.
  Q. Eliz. I go. Write to me very shortly,
And you shall understand from me her
    mind.
  K. Rich. Bear her my true love's kiss ;
    and so, farewell.   430
      [*Kissing her. Exit Queen Elizabeth.*
Relenting fool, and shallow, changing
    woman !

    Enter RATCLIFF ; CATESBY *following.*

How now ! what news ?
  Rat. Most mighty sovereign, on the
    western coast
Rideth a puissant navy ; to our shores
Throng many doubtful hollow-hearted
    friends,   435
Unarm'd, and unresolv'd to beat them
    back.
'Tis thought that Richmond is their
    admiral ;
And there they hull, expecting but the aid
Of Buckingham to welcome them ashore.
  K. Rich. Some light-foot friend post to
    the Duke of Norfolk.   440
Ratcliff, thyself—or Catesby ; where is he ?
  Cate. Here, my good lord.
  K. Rich.   Catesby, fly to the Duke.
  Cate. I will, my lord, with all convenient
    haste.
  K. Rich. Ratcliff, come hither. Post to
    Salisbury ;
When thou com'st thither—[*To Catesby*]
    Dull, unmindful villain,
Why stay'st thou here, and go'st not to the
    Duke ?   445
  Cate. First, mighty liege, tell me your
    Highness' pleasure,
What from your Grace I shall deliver to
    him.
  K. Rich. O, true, good Catesby. Bid him
    levy straight
The greatest strength and power that he
    can make

And meet me suddenly at Salisbury.   450
  Cate. I go.   [*Exit.*
  Rat. What, may it please you, shall I do
    at Salisbury ?
  K. Rich. Why, what wouldst thou do
    there before I go ?
  Rat. Your Highness told me I should
    post before.   455
  K. Rich. My mind is chang'd.

    Enter LORD STANLEY.

      Stanley, what news with you.
  Stan. None good, my liege, to please you
    with the hearing ;
Nor none so bad but well may be reported.
  K. Rich. Hoyday, a riddle ! neither good
    nor bad !   460
What need'st thou run so many miles
    about,
When thou mayest tell thy tale the nearest
    way ?
Once more, what news ?
  Stan.   Richmond is on the seas.
  K. Rich. There let him sink, and be the
    seas on him !
White-liver'd runagate, what doth he
    there ?   465
  Stan. I know not, mighty sovereign, but
    by guess.
  K. Rich. Well, as you guess ?
  Stan. Stirr'd up by Dorset, Buckingham,
    and Morton,
He makes for England here to claim the
    crown.
  K. Rich. Is the chair empty ? Is the
    sword unsway'd ?   470
Is the King dead, the empire unpossess'd ?
What heir of York is there alive but we ?
And who is England's King but great
    York's heir ?
Then tell me what makes he upon the seas.
  Stan. Unless for that, my liege, I cannot
    guess.   475
  K. Rich. Unless for that he comes to be
    your liege,
You cannot guess wherefore the Welshman
    comes.
Thou wilt revolt and fly to him, I fear.
  Stan. No, my good lord ; therefore mis-
    trust me not.
  K. Rich. Where is thy power then, to
    beat him back ?   480
Where be thy tenants and thy followers ?
Are they not now upon the western shore,
Safe-conducting the rebels from their ships ?
  Stan. No, my good lord, my friends are in
    the north.
  K. Rich. Cold friends to me. What do
    they in the north,   485
When they should serve their sovereign in
    the west ?
  Stan. They have not been commanded,
    mighty King.
Pleaseth your Majesty to give me leave,

I'll muster up my friends and meet your
    Grace
Where and what time your Majesty shall
    please.   490
    K. Rich. Ay, ay, thou wouldst be gone to
    join with Richmond ;
But I'll not trust thee.
    Stan.   Most mighty sovereign,
You have no cause to hold my friendship
    doubtful.
I never was nor never will be false.   494
    K. Rich. Go, then, and muster men. But
    leave behind
Your son, George Stanley. Look your heart
    be firm,
Or else his head's assurance is but frail.
    Stan. So deal with him as I prove true
    to you.   [*Exit.*

Enter a Messenger.

    Mess. My gracious sovereign, now in
    Devonshire,   500
As I by friends am well advertised,
Sir Edward Courtney and the haughty
    prelate,
Bishop of Exeter, his elder brother,
With many moe confederates, are in arms.

Enter another Messenger.

    2 Mess. In Kent, my liege, the Guilfords
    are in arms ;   505
And every hour more competitors
Flock to the rebels, and their power grows
    strong.

Enter another Messenger.

    3 Mess. My lord, the army of great
    Buckingham—
    K. Rich. Out on you, owls ! Nothing but
    songs of death ?   [*He strikes him.*
There, take thou that till thou bring better
    news.   510
    3 Mess. The news I have to tell your
    Majesty
Is that by sudden floods and fall of waters
Buckingham's army is dispers'd and
    scatter'd ;
And he himself wand'red away alone,
No man knows whither.
    K. Rich.   I cry thee mercy.   515
There is my purse to cure that blow of
    thine.
Hath any well-advised friend proclaim'd
Reward to him that brings the traitor in ?
    3 Mess. Such proclamation hath been
    made, my lord.

Enter another Messenger.

    4 Mess. Sir Thomas Lovel and Lord
    Marquis Dorset,   520
'Tis said, my liege, in Yorkshire are in arms.
But this good comfort bring I to your
    Highness—
The Britaine navy is dispers'd by tempest.

Richmond in Dorsetshire sent out a boat
Unto the shore, to ask those on the banks
If they were his assistants, yea or no ;   526
Who answer'd him they came from
    Buckingham
Upon his party. He, mistrusting them,
Hois'd sail, and made his course again for
    Britaine.
    K. Rich. March on, march on, since we
    are up in arms ;   530
If not to fight with foreign enemies,
Yet to beat down these rebels here at home.

Re-enter CATESBY.

    Cate. My liege, the Duke of Buckingham
    is taken—
That is the best news. That the Earl of
    Richmond   534
Is with a mighty power landed at Milford
Is colder tidings, but yet they must be
    told.
    K. Rich. Away towards Salisbury ! While
    we reason here
A royal battle might be won and lost.
Some one take order Buckingham be
    brought   539
To Salisbury ; the rest march on with me.
             [*Flourish. Exeunt.*

SCENE V. *Lord Derby's house.*

Enter STANLEY and SIR CHRISTOPHER
URSWICK.

    Stan. Sir Christopher, tell Richmond this
    from me :
That in the sty of the most deadly boar
My son George Stanley is frank'd up in
    hold ;
If I revolt, off goes young George's head ;
The fear of that holds off my present aid.   5
So, get thee gone ; commend me to thy
    lord.
Withal say that the Queen hath heartily
    consented
He should espouse Elizabeth her daughter.
But tell me, where is princely Richmond
    now ?
    Chris. At Pembroke, or at Ha'rford west
    in Wales.
    Stan. What men of name resort to him ?
    Chris. Sir Walter Herbert, a renowned
    soldier ;
Sir Gilbert Talbot, Sir William Stanley,   10
Oxford, redoubted Pembroke, Sir James
    Blunt,
And Rice ap Thomas, with a valiant crew ;
And many other of great name and worth ;
And towards London do they bend their
    power,
If by the way they be not fought withal.   15
    Stan. Well, hie thee to thy lord ; I kiss
    his hand ;
My letter will resolve him of my mind.
Farewell.   [*Exeunt.*

ACT FIVE

SCENE I. *Salisbury. An open place.*

Enter the Sheriff *and* Guard, *with* BUCKING-
HAM, *led to execution.*

Buck. Will not King Richard let me speak
    with him ?
Sher. No, my good lord ; therefore be
    patient.
Buck. Hastings, and Edward's children,
    Grey, and Rivers,
Holy King Henry, and thy fair son Edward,
Vaughan, and all that have miscarried 5
By underhand corrupted foul injustice,
If that your moody discontented souls
Do through the clouds behold this present
    hour,
Even for revenge mock my destruction !
This is All-Souls' day, fellow, is it not ? 10
Sher. It is, my lord.
Buck. Why, then All-Souls' day is my
    body's doomsday.
This is the day which in King Edward's time
I wish'd might fall on me when I was found
False to his children and his wife's allies ;
This is the day wherein I wish'd to fall 16
By the false faith of him whom most I
    trusted ;
This, this All-Souls' day to my fearful soul
Is the determin'd respite of my wrongs ;
That high All-Seer which I dallied with 20
Hath turn'd my feigned prayer on my head
And given in earnest what I begg'd in jest.
Thus doth He force the swords of wicked
    men
To turn their own points in their masters'
    bosoms.
Thus Margaret's curse falls heavy on my
    neck. 25
' When he ' quoth she ' shall split thy heart
    with sorrow,
Remember Margaret was a prophetess.'
Come lead me, officers, to the block of
    shame ;
Wrong hath but wrong, and blame the due
    of blame.   [*Exeunt.*

SCENE II. *Camp near Tamworth.*

Enter RICHMOND, OXFORD, SIR JAMES
BLUNT, SIR WALTER HERBERT, *and*
Others, *with drum and colours.*

Richm. Fellows in arms, and my most
    loving friends,
Bruis'd underneath the yoke of tyranny,
Thus far into the bowels of the land
Have we march'd on without impediment ;
And here receive we from our father
    Stanley   — 5
Lines of fair comfort and encouragement.
The wretched, bloody, and usurping boar,
That spoil'd your summer fields and fruitful
    vines,
Swills your warm blood like wash, and
    makes his trough
In your embowell'd bosoms—this foul
    swine 10
Is now even in the centre of this isle,
Near to the town of Leicester, as we learn.
From Tamworth thither is but one day's
    march.
In God's name cheerly on, courageous
    friends,
To reap the harvest of perpetual peace 15
By this one bloody trial of sharp war.
Oxf. Every man's conscience is a thou-
    sand men,
To fight against this guilty homicide.
Herb. I doubt not but his friends will
    turn to us.
Blunt. He hath no friends but what are
    friends for fear, 20
Which in his dearest need will fly from him.
Richm. All for our vantage. Then in
    God's name march.
True hope is swift and flies with swallow's
    wings ;
Kings it makes gods, and meaner creatures
    kings.   [*Exeunt.*

SCENE III. *Bosworth Field.*

Enter KING RICHARD *in arms, with* NOR-
FOLK, RATCLIFF, *the* EARL OF SURREY,
and Others.

K. Rich. Here pitch our tent, even here
    in Bosworth field.
My Lord of Surrey, why look you so sad ?
Sur. My heart is ten times lighter than
    my looks.
K. Rich. My Lord of Norfolk !
Nor.   Here, most gracious liege.
K. Rich. Norfolk, we must have knocks ;
    ha ! must we not ? 5
Nor. We must both give and take, my
    loving lord.
K. Rich. Up with my tent ! Here will I
    lie to-night ;
    [*Soldiers begin to set up the King's tent.*
But where to-morrow ? Well, all's one for
    that.
Who hath descried the number of the
    traitors ?
Nor. Six or seven thousand is their
    utmost power. 10
K. Rich. Why, our battalia trebles that
    account ;
Besides, the King's name is a tower of
    strength,
Which they upon the adverse faction want.
Up with the tent ! Come, noble gentle-
    men,
Let us survey the vantage of the ground. 15
Call for some men of sound direction.
Let's lack no discipline, make no delay ;
For, lords, to-morrow is a busy day.
    [*Exeunt.*

Enter, on the other side of the Field, RICH-
MOND, SIR WILLIAM BRANDON, OXFORD,
DORSET, *and* Others. *Some pitch Rich-
mond's tent.*

Richm. The weary sun hath made a
    golden set,
And by the bright tract of his fiery car 20
Gives token of a goodly day to-morrow.
Sir William Brandon, you shall bear my
    standard.
Give me some ink and paper in my tent.
I'll draw the form and model of our battle,
Limit each leader to his several charge, 25
And part in just proportion our small
    power.
My Lord of Oxford—you, Sir William
    Brandon—
And you, Sir Walter Herbert—stay with
    me.
The Earl of Pembroke keeps his regiment ;
Good Captain Blunt, bear my good night to
    him, 30
And by the second hour in the morning
Desire the Earl to see me in my tent.
Yet one thing more, good Captain, do for
    me—
Where is Lord Stanley quarter'd, do you
    know ?
Blunt. Unless I have mista'en his colours
    much— 35
Which well I am assur'd I have not done—
His regiment lies half a mile at least
South from the mighty power of the
    King.
Richm. If without peril it be possible,
Sweet Blunt, make some good means to
    speak with him 40
And give him from me this most needful
    note.
Blunt. Upon my life, my lord, I'll under-
    take it ;
And so, God give you quiet rest to-night !
Richm. Good night, good Captain Blunt. 44
Come, gentlemen,
Let us consult upon to-morrow's business.
In to my tent ; the dew is raw and cold.
    [*They withdraw into the tent.*

Enter, to his tent, KING RICHARD, NORFOLK,
RATCLIFF, *and* CATESBY.

K. Rich. What is't o'clock ?
Cate.   It's supper-time, my lord ;
It's nine o'clock.
K. Rich.   I will not sup to-night.
Give me some ink and paper.
What, is my beaver easier than it was ? 50
And all my armour laid into my tent ?
Cate. It is, my liege ; and all things are
    in readiness.
K. Rich. Good Norfolk, hie thee to thy
    charge ;
Use careful watch, choose trusty sentinels.
Nor. I go, my lord. 55

K. Rich. Stir with the lark to-morrow,
    gentle Norfolk.
Nor. I warrant you, my lord.   [*Exit.*
K. Rich. Catesby !
Cate. My lord ?
K. Rich. Send out a pursuivant-at-arms
To Stanley's regiment ; bid him bring his
    power 60
Before sunrising, lest his son George fall
Into the blind cave of eternal night.
    [*Exit Catesby.*
Fill me a bowl of wine. Give me a watch.
Saddle white Surrey for the field to-morrow.
Look that my staves be sound, and not too
    heavy. 65
Ratcliff !
Rat. My lord ?
K. Rich. Saw'st thou the melancholy
    Lord Northumberland ?
Rat. Thomas the Earl of Surrey and
    himself,
Much about cock-shut time, from troop to
    troop 70
Went through the army, cheering up the
    soldiers.
K. Rich. So, I am satisfied. Give me a
    bowl of wine.
I have not that alacrity of spirit
Nor cheer of mind that I was wont to have.
Set it down. Is ink and paper ready ?
Rat. It is, my lord. 75
K. Rich. Bid my guard watch ; leave me.
Ratcliff, about the mid of night come to my
    tent
And help to arm me. Leave me, I say.
    [*Exit Ratcliff. Richard sleeps.*

Enter DERBY *to* RICHMOND *in his tent ;*
LORDS *attending.*

Der. Fortune and victory sit on thy
    helm !
Richm. All comfort that the dark night
    can afford 80
Be to thy person, noble father-in-law !
Tell me, how fares our loving mother ?
Der. I, by attorney, bless thee from
    thy mother,
Who prays continually for Richmond's
    good. 84
So much for that. The silent hours steal on,
And flaky darkness breaks within the east.
In brief, for so the season bids us be,
Prepare thy battle early in the morning,
And put thy fortune to the arbitrement 89
Of bloody strokes and mortal-staring war.
I, as I may—that which I would I cannot—
With best advantage will deceive the time
And aid thee in this doubtful shock of arms ;
But on thy side I may not be too forward,
Lest, being seen, thy brother, tender
    George, 95
Be executed in his father's sight.
Farewell ; the leisure and the fearful time
Cuts off the ceremonious vows of love

And ample interchange of sweet discourse
Which so-long-sund'red friends should dwell upon. 100
God give us leisure for these rites of love!
Once more, adieu; be valiant, and speed well!

Richm. Good lords, conduct him to his regiment.
I'll strive with troubled thoughts to take a nap,
Lest leaden slumber peise me down to-morrow 105
When I should mount with wings of victory.
Once more, good night, kind lords and gentlemen.
                                    [Exeunt all but Richmond.
O Thou, whose captain I account myself,
Look on my forces with a gracious eye;
Put in their hands Thy bruising irons of wrath, 110
That they may crush down with a heavy fall
The usurping helmets of our adversaries!
Make us Thy ministers of chastisement,
That we may praise Thee in the victory!
To Thee I do commend my watchful soul
Ere I let fall the windows of mine eyes.
Sleeping and waking, O, defend me still!
                                        [Sleeps.

Enter the Ghost *of young* PRINCE EDWARD, *son to Henry the Sixth.*

Ghost. [*To Richard*] Let me sit heavy on thy soul to-morrow!
Think how thou stabb'dst me in my prime of youth 119
At Tewksbury; despair, therefore, and die!
[*To Richmond*] Be cheerful, Richmond; for the wronged souls
Of butcher'd princes fight in thy behalf.
King Henry's issue, Richmond, comforts thee.

Enter the Ghost *of* HENRY THE SIXTH.

Ghost. [*To Richard*] When I was mortal, my anointed body
By thee was punched full of deadly holes.
Think on the Tower and me. Despair, and die! 126
Harry the Sixth bids thee despair and die.
[*To Richmond*] Virtuous and holy, be thou conqueror!
Harry, that prophesied thou shouldst be King,
Doth comfort thee in thy sleep. Live and flourish! 130

Enter the Ghost *of* CLARENCE.

Ghost. [*To Richard*] Let me sit heavy in thy soul to-morrow!
I that was wash'd to death with fulsome wine,
Poor Clarence, by thy guile betray'd to death!

To-morrow in the battle think on me,
And fall thy edgeless sword. Despair and die! 135
[*To Richmond*] Thou offspring of the house of Lancaster,
The wronged heirs of York do pray for thee.
Good angels guard thy battle! Live and flourish!

Enter the Ghosts *of* RIVERS, GREY, *and* VAUGHAN.

Riv. [*To Richard*] Let me sit heavy in thy soul to-morrow,
Rivers that died at Pomfret! Despair and die! 140
Grey. [*To Richard*] Think upon Grey, and let thy soul despair!
Vaugh. [*To Richard*] Think upon Vaughan, and with guilty fear
Let fall thy lance. Despair and die!
All. [*To Richmond*] Awake, and think our wrongs in Richard's bosom 144
Will conquer him. Awake and win the day.

Enter the Ghost *of* HASTINGS.

Ghost. [*To Richard*] Bloody and guilty, guiltily awake,
And in a bloody battle end thy days!
Think on Lord Hastings. Despair and die.
[*To Richmond*] Quiet untroubled soul, awake, awake!
Arm, fight, and conquer, for fair England's sake! 150

Enter the Ghosts *of the two young* Princes.

Ghosts. [*To Richard*] Dream on thy cousins smothered in the Tower.
Let us be lead within thy bosom, Richard,
And weigh thee down to ruin, shame, and death!
Thy nephews' souls bid thee despair and die.
[*To Richmond*] Sleep, Richmond, sleep in peace, and wake in joy; 155
Good angels guard thee from the boar's annoy!
Live, and beget a happy race of kings!
Edward's unhappy sons do bid thee flourish.

Enter the Ghost *of* LADY ANNE, *his wife.*

Ghost. [*To Richard*] Richard, thy wife, that wretched Anne thy wife
That never slept a quiet hour with thee 160
Now fills thy sleep with perturbations.
To-morrow in the battle think on me,
And fall thy edgeless sword. Despair and die.
[*To Richmond*] Thou quiet soul, sleep thou a quiet sleep;
Dream of success and happy victory! 165
Thy adversary's wife doth pray for thee.

Enter the Ghost *of* BUCKINGHAM.

Ghost. [*To Richard*] The first was I that help'd thee to the crown;

The last was I that felt thy tyranny.
O, in the battle think on Buckingham,
And die in terror of thy guiltiness!   170
Dream on, dream on of bloody deeds and
    death;
Fainting, despair; despairing, yield thy
    breath!
[*To Richmond*] I died for hope ere I could
    lend thee aid;
But cheer thy heart and be thou not
    dismay'd:
God and good angels fight on Richmond's
    side;   175
And Richard falls in height of all his pride.
    [*The Ghosts vanish. Richard starts
        out of his dream.*

    K. *Rich.* Give me another horse. Bind up
        my wounds.
Have mercy, Jesu! Soft! I did but dream.
O coward conscience, how dost thou afflict
    me!
The lights burn blue. It is now dead
    midnight.   180
Cold fearful drops stand on my trembling
    flesh.
What do I fear? Myself? There's none
    else by.
Richard loves Richard; that is, I am I.
Is there a murderer here? No—yes, I am.
Then fly. What, from myself? Great
    reason why—   185
Lest I revenge. What, myself upon myself!
Alack, I love myself. Wherefore? For any
    good
That I myself have done unto myself?
O, no! Alas, I rather hate myself   189
For hateful deeds committed by myself!
I am a villain; yet I lie, I am not.
Fool, of thyself speak well. Fool, do not
    flatter.
My conscience hath a thousand several
    tongues,   193
And every tongue brings in a several tale,
And every tale condemns me for a villain.
Perjury, perjury, in the high'st degree;
Murder, stern murder, in the dir'st degree;
All several sins, all us'd in each degree,
Throng to the bar, crying all 'Guilty!
    guilty!'
I shall despair. There is no creature loves
    me;   200
And if I die no soul will pity me:
And wherefore should they, since that I
    myself
Find in myself no pity to myself?
Methought the souls of all that I had
    murder'd
Came to my tent, and every one did threat
To-morrow's vengeance on the head of
    Richard.   206

    Enter RATCLIFF.

    Rat. My lord!
    K. *Rich.* Zounds, who is there?

    Rat. Ratcliff, my lord; 'tis I. The early
        village-cock
Hath twice done salutation to the morn;
Your friends are up and buckle on their
    armour.   211
    K. *Rich.* O Ratcliff, I have dream'd a
        fearful dream!
What think'st thou—will our friends prove
    all true?
    Rat. No doubt, my lord.
    K. *Rich.*   O Ratcliff, I fear, I fear.
    Rat. Nay, good my lord, be not afraid of
        shadows.   215
    K. *Rich.* By the apostle Paul, shadows
        to-night
Have struck more terror to the soul of
    Richard
Than can the substance of ten thousand
    soldiers
Armed in proof and led by shallow
    Richmond.   219
'Tis not yet near day. Come, go with
    me;
Under our tents I'll play the eaves-dropper,
To see if any mean to shrink from me.
                                        [*Exeunt.*

Enter the Lords *to* RICHMOND *sitting in his
        tent.*

    Lords. Good morrow, Richmond!
    Richm. Cry mercy, lords and watchful
        gentlemen,   224
That you have ta'en a tardy sluggard here.
    Lords. How have you slept, my lord?
    Richm. The sweetest sleep and fairest-
        boding dreams
That ever ent'red in a drowsy head
Have I since your departure had, my lords.
Methought their souls whose bodies Richard
    murder'd   230
Came to my tent and cried on victory.
I promise you my soul is very jocund
In the remembrance of so fair a dream.
How far into the morning is it, lords?
    Lords. Upon the stroke of four.   235
    Richm. Why, then 'tis time to arm and
        give direction.

        His Oration to his Soldiers.

More than I have said, loving countrymen,
The leisure and enforcement of the time
Forbids to dwell upon; yet remember this:
God and our good cause fight upon our side;
The prayers of holy saints and wronged
    souls,   241
Like high-rear'd bulwarks, stand before our
    faces;
Richard except, those whom we fight
    against
Had rather have us win than him they
    follow.
For what is he they follow? Truly, gentle-
    men,   245
A bloody tyrant and a homicide;

One rais'd in blood, and one in blood
   establish'd ;
One that made means to come by what he
   hath,
And slaughtered those that were the means
   to help him ;
A base foul stone, made precious by the
   foil   250
Of England's chair, where he is falsely set ;
One that hath ever been God's enemy.
Then if you fight against God's enemy,
God will in justice ward you as his soldiers ;
If you do sweat to put a tyrant down,   255
You sleep in peace, the tyrant being slain ;
If you do fight against your country's foes,
Your country's fat shall pay your pains the
   hire ;
If you do fight in safeguard of your wives,
Your wives shall welcome home the con-
   querors ;   260
If you do free your children from the sword,
Your children's children quits it in your
   age.
Then, in the name of God and all these
   rights,
Advance your standards, draw your willing
   swords.
For me, the ransom of my bold attempt   265
Shall be this cold corpse on the earth's cold
   face ;
But if I thrive, the gain of my attempt
The least of you shall share his part thereof.
Sound drums and trumpets boldly and
   cheerfully ;
God and Saint George ! Richmond and
   victory !   [*Exeunt.*

Re-enter KING RICHARD, RATCLIFF,
   Attendants, *and* Forces.

K. Rich. What said Northumberland as
   touching Richmond ?   271
Rat. That he was never trained up in
   arms.
K. Rich. He said the truth ; and what
   said Surrey then ?
Rat. He smil'd, and said ' The better for
   our purpose '.   274
K. Rich. He was in the right ; and so
   indeed it is.   [*Clock strikes.*
Tell the clock there. Give me a calendar.
Who saw the sun to-day ?
Rat.   Not I, my lord.
K. Rich. Then he disdains to shine ; for
   by the book
He should have brav'd the east an hour
   ago.
A black day will it be to somebody.   280
Ratcliff !
Rat. My lord ?
K. Rich. The sun will not be seen to-day;
The sky doth frown and lour upon our
   army.
I would these dewy tears were from the
   ground.   284

Not shine to-day ! Why, what is that to me
More than to Richmond ? For the selfsame
   heaven
That frowns on me looks sadly upon him.

          Enter NORFOLK.

Nor. Arm, arm, my lord ; the foe vaunts
   in the field.
K. Rich. Come, bustle, bustle ; caparison
   my horse ;
Call up Lord Stanley, bid him bring his
   power.   290
I will lead forth my soldiers to the plain,
And thus my battle shall be ordered :
My foreward shall be drawn out all in
   length,
Consisting equally of horse and foot ;
Our archers shall be placed in the midst. 295
John Duke of Norfolk, Thomas Earl of
   Surrey,
Shall have the leading of this foot and horse.
They thus directed, we will follow
In the main battle, whose puissance on
   either side   299
Shall be well winged with our chiefest horse.
This, and Saint George to boot ! What
   think'st thou, Norfolk ?
Nor. A good direction, warlike sovereign.
This found I on my tent this morning.
          [*He sheweth him a paper.*
K. Rich. [*Reads*]
   ' Jockey to Norfolk, be not so bold,
   For Dickon thy master is bought and
      sold.'   305
A thing devised by the enemy.
Go, gentlemen, every man unto his charge.
Let not our babbling dreams affright our
   souls ;
Conscience is but a word that cowards use,
Devis'd at first to keep the strong in awe.
Our strong arms be our conscience, swords
   our law.   311
March on, join bravely, let us to it pell-mell;
If not to heaven, then hand in hand to
   hell.

     His Oration to his Army.

What shall I say more than I have inferr'd?
Remember whom you are to cope withal—
A sort of vagabonds, rascals, and runaways,
A scum of Britaines, and base lackey
   peasants,   317
Whom their o'er-cloyed country vomits
   forth
To desperate adventures and assur'd
   destruction.
You sleeping safe, they bring to you unrest ;
You having lands, and bless'd with
   beauteous wives,
They would restrain the one, distain the
   other.   322
And who doth lead them but a paltry
   fellow,
Long kept in Britaine at our mother's cost ?

A milk-sop, one that never in his life   325
Felt so much cold as over shoes in snow ?
Let's whip these stragglers o'er the seas
   again ;
Lash hence these over-weening rags of
   France,
These famish'd beggars, weary of their
   lives ;
Who, but for dreaming on this fond exploit,
For want of means, poor rats, had hang'd
   themselves.   331
If we be conquered, let men conquer us,
And not these bastard Britaines, whom our
   fathers
Have in their own land beaten, bobb'd, and
   thump'd,
And, in record, left them the heirs of shame.
Shall these enjoy our lands ? lie with our
   wives,   336
Ravish our daughters ? [*Drum afar off*]
   Hark ! I hear their drum.
Fight, gentlemen of England ! Fight, bold
   yeomen !
Draw, archers, draw your arrows to the
   head !
Spur your proud horses hard, and ride in
   blood ;   340
Amaze the welkin with your broken staves !

    Enter a Messenger.

What says Lord Stanley ? Will he bring
   his power ?
  Mess. My lord, he doth deny to come.
  K. Rich. Off with his son George's head !
  Nor. My lord, the enemy is pass'd the
   marsh.   345
After the battle let George Stanley die.
  K. Rich. A thousand hearts are great
   within my bosom.
Advance our standards, set upon our foes ;
Our ancient word of courage, fair Saint
   George,   349
Inspire us with the spleen of fiery dragons !
Upon them ! Victory sits on our helms.
                  [*Exeunt.*

  SCENE IV. *Another part of the field.*

Alarum ; excursions. Enter NORFOLK *and*
  Forces ; *to him* CATESBY.

  Cate. Rescue, my Lord of Norfolk, rescue,
   rescue !
The King enacts more wonders than a man,
Daring an opposite to every danger.
His horse is slain, and all on foot he fights,
Seeking for Richmond in the throat of
   death.   5
Rescue, fair lord, or else the day is lost.

  Alarums. Enter KING RICHARD.

  K. Rich. A horse ! a horse ! my kingdom
   for a horse !
  Cate. Withdraw, my lord ; I'll help you
   to a horse

  K. Rich. Slave, I have set my life upon
   a cast
And I will stand the hazard of the die.   10
I think there be six Richmonds in the field ;
Five have I slain to-day instead of him.
A horse ! a horse ! my kingdom for a horse !
                  [*Exeunt.*

  SCENE V. *Another part of the field.*

Alarum. Enter RICHARD *and* RICHMOND ;
  *they fight ; Richard is slain. Retreat and
  Flourish.   Enter* RICHMOND, DERBY
  bearing the crown, with other* Lords.

  Richm. God and your arms be prais'd,
   victorious friends ;
The day is ours, the bloody dog is dead.
  Der. Courageous Richmond, well hast
   thou acquit thee !
Lo, here, this long-usurped royalty
From the dead temples of this bloody
   wretch   5
Have I pluck'd off, to grace thy brows
   withal.
Wear it, enjoy it, and make much of it.
  Richm. Great God of heaven, say Amen
   to all !
But, tell me is young George Stanley living.
  Der. He is, my lord, and safe in Leicester
   town,   10
Whither, if it please you, we may now with-
   draw us.
  Richm. What men of name are slain on
   either side ?
  Der. John Duke of Norfolk, Walter Lord
   Ferrers,
Sir Robert Brakenbury, and Sir William
   Brandon.
  Richm. Inter their bodies as becomes
   their births.   15
Proclaim a pardon to the soldiers fled
That in submission will return to us.
And then, as we have ta'en the sacrament,
We will unite the white rose and the red.
Smile heaven upon this fair conjunction,   20
That long have frown'd upon their enmity !
What traitor hears me, and says not amen ?
England hath long been mad, and scarr'd
   herself ;
The brother blindly shed the brother's
   blood,
The father rashly slaughter'd his own son, 25
The son, compell'd, been butcher to the
   sire ;
All this divided York and Lancaster,
Divided in their dire division,
O, now let Richmond and Elizabeth,
The true succeeders of each royal house,   30
By God's fair ordinance conjoin together !
And let their heirs, God, if thy will be so,
Enrich the time to come with smooth-fac'd
   peace,
With smiling plenty, and fair prosperous
   days !   34

Abate the edge of traitors, gracious Lord,
That would reduce these bloody days again
And make poor England weep in streams
    of blood !
Let them not live to taste this land's
    increase

That would with treason wound this fair
    land's peace !
Now civil wounds are stopp'd, peace lives
    again—   40
That she may long live here, God say amen!
              [*Exeunt.*

KING HENRY THE EIGHTH

DRAMATIS PERSONÆ

KING HENRY THE EIGHTH.
CARDINAL WOLSEY.
CARDINAL CAMPEIUS.
CAPUCIUS, *Ambassador from the Emperor Charles V.*
CRANMER, ARCHBISHOP OF CANTERBURY.
DUKE OF NORFOLK.
DUKE OF BUCKINGHAM.
DUKE OF SUFFOLK.
EARL OF SURREY.
Lord Chamberlain.
Lord Chancellor.
GARDINER, BISHOP OF WINCHESTER.
Bishop of Lincoln.
LORD ABERGAVENNY.
LORD SANDYS.
SIR HENRY GUILDFORD.
SIR THOMAS LOVELL.
SIR ANTHONY DENNY.
SIR NICHOLAS VAUX.
Secretaries *to Wolsey.*
CROMWELL, *servant to Wolsey.*

GRIFFITH, *gentleman-usher to Queen Katharine.*
Three Gentlemen.
DR. BUTTS, *physician to the King.*
Garter King-at-Arms.
Surveyor *to the Duke of Buckingham.*
BRANDON, *and a* Sergeant-at-Arms.
Doorkeeper of the Council Chamber.
Porter, *and his Man.*
Page *to Gardiner.*
A Crier.

QUEEN KATHARINE, *wife to King Henry, afterwards divorced.*
ANNE BULLEN, *her Maid of Honour, afterwards Queen.*
An old Lady, *friend to Anne Bullen.*
PATIENCE, *woman to Queen Katharine.*

Lord Mayor, Aldermen, Lords *and* Ladies *in the Dumb Shows ;* Women *attending upon the Queen ;* Scribes, Officers, Guards, *and other* Attendants ; Spirits.

THE SCENE: *London ; Westminster ; Kimbolton.*

THE PROLOGUE

I come no more to make you laugh ; things now
That bear a weighty and a serious brow,
Sad, high, and working, full of state and woe,
Such noble scenes as draw the eye to flow,
We now present. Those that can pity here 5
May, if they think it well, let fall a tear :
The subject will deserve it. Such as give
Their money out of hope they may believe
May here find truth too. Those that come to see
Only a show or two, and so agree 10
The play may pass, if they be still and willing,
I'll undertake may see away their shilling
Richly in two short hours. Only they
That come to hear a merry bawdy play,
A noise of targets, or to see a fellow 15
In a long motley coat guarded with yellow,
Will be deceiv'd ; for, gentle hearers, know,
To rank our chosen truth with such a show
As fool and fight is, beside forfeiting
Our own brains, and the opinion that we bring 20
To make that only true we now intend,
Will leave us never an understanding friend.
Therefore, for goodness sake, and as you are known
The first and happiest hearers of the town,
Be sad, as we would make ye. Think ye see
The very persons of our noble story 26
As they were living ; think you see them great,
And follow'd with the general throng and sweat
Of thousand friends ; then, in a moment, see
How soon this mightiness meets misery. 30
And if you can be merry then, I'll say
A man may weep upon his wedding-day.

ACT ONE

SCENE I. *London. The palace.*

Enter the DUKE OF NORFOLK *at one door ; at the other, the* DUKE OF BUCKINGHAM *and the* LORD ABERGAVENNY.

Buck. Good morrow, and well met. How have ye done
Since last we saw in France ?
Nor.   I thank your Grace,
Healthful ; and ever since a fresh admirer
Of what I saw there.
Buck.   An untimely ague 4
Stay'd me a prisoner in my chamber when
Those suns of glory, those two lights of men,
Met in the vale of Andren.
Nor.   'Twixt Guynes and Arde—
I was then present, saw them salute on horseback ;
Beheld them, when they lighted, how they clung

In their embracement, as they grew to-
    gether;   10
Which had they, what four thron'd ones
    could have weigh'd
Such a compounded one?

Buck.   All the whole time
I was my chamber's prisoner.

Nor.   Then you lost
The view of earthly glory; men might say,
Till this time pomp was single, but now
    married   15
To one above itself. Each following day
Became the next day's master, till the last
Made former wonders its. To-day the
    French,
All clinquant, all in gold, like heathen gods,
Shone down the English; and to-morrow
    they   20
Made Britain India: every man that stood
Show'd like a mine. Their dwarfish pages
    were
As cherubins, all gilt; the madams too,
Not us'd to toil, did almost sweat to bear
The pride upon them, that their very labour
Was to them as a painting. Now this
    masque   26
Was cried incomparable; and th' ensuing
    night
Made it a fool and beggar. The two kings,
Equal in lustre, were now best, now worst,
As presence did present them: him in eye
Still him in praise; and being present both,
'Twas said they saw but one, and no
    discerner   32
Durst wag his tongue in censure. When
    these suns—
For so they phrase 'em—by their heralds
    challeng'd
The noble spirits to arms, they did perform
Beyond thought's compass, that former
    fabulous story,   36
Being now seen possible enough, got credit,
That Bevis was believ'd.

Buck.   O, you go far!
Nor. As I belong to worship, and affect
In honour honesty, the tract of ev'rything
Would by a good discourser lose some life
Which action's self was tongue to. All was
    royal: 42
To the disposing of it nought rebell'd;
Order gave each thing view. The office did
Distinctly his full function.

Buck.   Who did guide—   45
I mean, who set the body and the limbs
Of this great sport together, as you guess?
Nor. One, certes, that promises no
    element
In such a business.

Buck.   I pray you, who, my lord?
Nor. All this was ord'red by the good
    discretion   50
Of the right reverend Cardinal of York.

Buck. The devil speed him! No man's pie
    is freed

From his ambitious finger. What had he
To do in these fierce vanities? I wonder
That such a keech can with his very bulk   55
Take up the rays o' th' beneficial sun,
And keep it from the earth.

Nor.   Surely, sir,
There's in him stuff that puts him to these
    ends;
For, being not propp'd by ancestry, whose
    grace   59
Chalks successors their way, nor call'd upon
For high feats done to th' crown, neither
    allied
To eminent assistants, but spider-like,
Out of his self-drawing web, 'a gives us
    note
The force of his own merit makes his way—
A gift that heaven gives for him, which
    buys   65
A place next to the King.

Aber.   I cannot tell
What heaven hath given him—let some
    graver eye
Pierce into that; but I can see his pride
Peep through each part of him. Whence
    has he that?
If not from hell, the devil is a niggard   70
Or has given all before, and he begins
A new hell in himself.

Buck.   Why the devil,
Upon this French going out, took he upon
    him—
Without the privity o' th' King—t'
    appoint
Who should attend on him? He makes up
    the file   75
Of all the gentry; for the most part such
To whom as great a charge as little honour
He meant to lay upon; and his own letter,
The honourable board of council out,
Must fetch him in he papers.

Aber.   I do know   80
Kinsmen of mine, three at the least, that
    have
By this so sicken'd their estates that never
They shall abound as formerly.

Buck.   O, many
Have broke their backs with laying manors
    on 'em
For this great journey. What did this
    vanity   85
But minister communication of
A most poor issue?

Nor.   Grievingly I think
The peace between the French and us not
    values
The cost that did conclude it.

Buck.   Every man,   89
After the hideous storm that follow'd, was
A thing inspir'd, and, not consulting, broke
Into a general prophecy—that this tempest,
Dashing the garment of this peace, aboded
The sudden breach on't.

Nor.   Which is budded out;

For France hath flaw'd the league, and
    hath attach'd 95
Our merchants' goods at Bordeaux.
    Aber. Is it therefore
Th' ambassador is silenc'd ?
    Nor. Marry, is't.
    Aber. A proper title of a peace, and
    purchas'd
At a superfluous rate !
    Buck. Why, all this business
Our reverend Cardinal carried.
    Nor. Like it your Grace, 100
The state takes notice of the private
    difference
Betwixt you and the Cardinal. I advise
    you—
And take it from a heart that wishes to-
    wards you
Honour and plenteous safety—that you
    read
The Cardinal's malice and his potency 105
Together ; to consider further, that
What his high hatred would effect wants
    not
A minister in his power. You know his
    nature,
That he's revengeful ; and I know his
    sword
Hath a sharp edge—it's long and't may be
    said 110
It reaches far, and where 'twill not extend,
Thither he darts it. Bosom up my counsel,
You'll find it wholesome. Lo, where comes
    that rock
That I advise your shunning.

Enter CARDINAL WOLSEY, *the purse borne
before him, certain of the* Guard, *and two
Secretaries with papers. The Cardinal in
his passage fixeth his eye on Buckingham,
and Buckingham on him, both full of
disdain.*

    Wol. The Duke of Buckingham's sur-
    veyor ? Ha ! 115
Where's his examination ?
    1 Secr. Here, so please you.
    Wol. Is he in person ready ?
    1 Secr. Ay, please your Grace.
    Wol. Well, we shall then know more, and
    Buckingham
Shall lessen this big look.
    [*Exeunt Wolsey and his Train.*
    Buck. This butcher's cur is venom-
    mouth'd, and I
Have not the power to muzzle him ; there-
    fore best 121
Not wake him in his slumber. A beggar's
    book
Outworths a noble's blood.
    Nor. What, are you chaf'd ?
Ask God for temp'rance ; that's th' appli-
    ance only
Which your disease requires.
    Buck. I read in's looks

Matter against me, and his eye revil'd 126
Me as his abject object. At this instant
He bores me with some trick. He's gone to
    th' King ;
I'll follow, and outstare him.
    Nor. Stay, my lord,
And let your reason with your choler
    question 130
What 'tis you go about. To climb steep
    hills
Requires slow pace at first. Anger is like
A full hot horse, who being allow'd his way,
Self-mettle tires him. Not a man in
    England
Can advise me like you ; be to yourself 135
As you would to your friend.
    Buck. I'll to the King,
And from a mouth of honour quite cry
    down
This Ipswich fellow's insolence ; or proclaim
There's difference in no persons.
    Nor. Be advis'd :
Heat not a furnace for your foe so hot 140
That it do singe yourself. We may outrun
By violent swiftness that which we run at,
And lose by over-running. Know you not
The fire that mounts the liquor till't run
    o'er
In seeming to augment it wastes it ? Be
    advis'd. 145
I say again there is no English soul
More stronger to direct you than yourself,
If with the sap of reason you would quench
Or but allay the fire of passion.
    Buck. Sir,
I am thankful to you, and I'll go along 150
By your prescription ; but this top-proud
    fellow—
Whom from the flow of gall I name not, but
From sincere motions, by intelligence,
And proofs as clear as founts in July when
We see each grain of gravel—I do know 155
To be corrupt and treasonous.
    Nor. Say not treasonous.
    Buck. To th' King I'll say't, and make
    my vouch as strong
As shore of rock. Attend : this holy fox,
Or wolf, or both—for he is equal rav'nous
As he is subtle, and as prone to mischief 160
As able to perform't, his mind and place
Infecting one another, yea, reciprocally—
Only to show his pomp as well in France
As here at home, suggests the King our
    master
To this last costly treaty, th' interview 165
That swallowed so much treasure and like a
    glass
Did break i' th' wrenching.
    Nor. Faith, and so it did.
    Buck. Pray, give me favour, sir : this
    cunning cardinal
The articles o' th' combination drew 169
As himself pleas'd ; and they were ratified
As he cried ' Thus let be ' to as much end

As give a crutch to th' dead.   But our
    Count-Cardinal
Has done this, and 'tis well; for worthy
    Wolsey,
Who cannot err, he did it.   Now this
    follows,
Which, as I take it, is a kind of puppy 175
To th' old dam treason: Charles the
    Emperor,
Under pretence to see the Queen his aunt—
For 'twas indeed his colour, but he came
To whisper Wolsey—here makes visita-
    tion—
His fears were that the interview betwixt
England and France might through their
    amity   181
Breed him some prejudice; for from this
    league
Peep'd harms that menac'd him—privily
Deals with our Cardinal; and, as I trow—
Which I do well, for I am sure the Emperor
Paid ere he promis'd; whereby his suit was
    granted   186
Ere it was ask'd—but when the way was
    made,
And pav'd with gold, the Emperor thus
    desir'd,
That he would please to alter the King's
    course,
And break the foresaid peace. Let the King
    know,   190
As soon he shall by me, that thus the
    Cardinal
Does buy and sell his honour as he pleases,
And for his own advantage.
    Nor.   I am sorry
To hear this of him, and could wish he were
Something mistaken in't.
    Buck.   No, not a syllable: 195
I do pronounce him in that very shape
He shall appear in proof.

Enter BRANDON, *a* Sergeant-at-Arms *before
    him, and two or three of the* Guard.

    Bran. Your office, sergeant: execute it.
    Serg.   Sir,
My lord the Duke of Buckingham, and Earl
Of Hereford, Stafford, and Northampton, I
Arrest thee of high treason, in the name
Of our most sovereign King.
    Buck.   Lo you, my lord,
The net has fall'n upon me! I shall perish
Under device and practice.
    Bran.   I am sorry
To see you ta'en from liberty, to look on 205
The business present; 'tis his Highness'
    pleasure
You shall to th' Tower.
    Buck.   It will help me nothing
To plead mine innocence; for that dye is
    on me
Which makes my whit'st part black. The
    will of heav'n
Be done in this and all things! I obey. 210

O my Lord Aberga'ny, fare you well!
    Bran. Nay, he must bear you company.
        [*To Abergavenny*] The King
Is pleas'd you shall to th' Tower, till you
    know
How he determines further.
    Aber.   As the Duke said,
The will of heaven be done, and the King's
    pleasure   215
By me obey'd.
    Bran.   Here is warrant from
The King t' attach Lord Montacute and
    the bodies
Of the Duke's confessor, John de la Car,
One Gilbert Peck, his chancellor—
    Buck.   So, so!
These are the limbs o' th' plot; no more, I
    hope.   220
    Bran. A monk o' th' Chartreux.
    Buck.   O, Nicholas Hopkins?
    Bran.   He.
    Buck. My surveyor is false. The o'er-
    great Cardinal
Hath show'd him gold; my life is spann'd
    already.
I am the shadow of poor Buckingham, 224
Whose figure even this instant cloud puts on
By dark'ning my clear sun.   My lord,
    farewell.   [*Exeunt.*

SCENE II. *London. The Council Chamber.*

Cornets. Enter KING HENRY, *leaning on
    the* CARDINAL'S *shoulder, the* Nobles, *and*
    SIR THOMAS LOVELL, *with Others.   The
    Cardinal places himself under the King's
    feet on his right side.*

    King. My life itself, and the best heart
    of it,
Thanks you for this great care; I stood i'
    th' level
Of a full-charg'd confederacy, and give
    thanks
To you that chok'd it. Let be call'd before
    us
That gentleman of Buckingham's.   In
    person   5
I'll hear him his confessions justify;
And point by point the treasons of his
    master
He shall again relate.

*A noise within, crying ' Room for the
    Queen!' Enter the* QUEEN, *usher'd by the*
    DUKES OF NORFOLK *and* SUFFOLK; *she
    kneels. The King riseth from his state,
    takes her up, kisses and placeth her by him.*

    Q. Kath. Nay, we must longer kneel: I
    am a suitor.
    King. Arise, and take place by us. Half
    your suit   10
Never name to us: you have half our
    power.
The other moiety ere you ask is given;

Repeat your will, and take it.
　Q. Kath.　　　　　　　　Thank your Majesty.
That you would love yourself, and in that
　　love
Not unconsidered leave your honour nor
The dignity of your office, is the point　16
Of my petition.
　King.　　　　　　　　Lady mine, proceed.
　Q. Kath. I am solicited, not by a few,
And those of true condition, that your
　　subjects
Are in great grievance : there have been
　　commissions　20
Sent down among 'em which hath flaw'd
　　the heart
Of all their loyalties ; wherein, although,
My good Lord Cardinal, they vent re-
　　proaches
Most bitterly on you as putter-on　24
Of these exactions, yet the King our
　　master—
Whose honour Heaven shield from soil !—
　　even he escapes not
Language unmannerly ; yea, such which
　　breaks
The sides of loyalty, and almost appears
In loud rebellion.
　Nor.　　　　　　Not almost appears—　29
It doth appear ; for, upon these taxations,
The clothiers all, not able to maintain
The many to them 'longing, have put off
The spinsters, carders, fullers, weavers,
　　who,
Unfit for other life, compell'd by hunger
And lack of other means, in desperate
　　manner　35
Daring th' event to th' teeth, are all in
　　uproar,
And danger serves among them.
　King.　　　　　　　　Taxation !
Wherein ? and what taxation ? My Lord
　　Cardinal,
You that are blam'd for it alike with us,
Know you of this taxation ?
　Wol.　　　　　　Please you, sir,　40
I know but of a single part in aught
Pertains to th' state, and front but in that
　　file
Where others tell steps with me.
　Q. Kath.　　　　　　　　No, my lord !
You know no more than others ! But you
　　frame
Things that are known alike, which are not
　　wholesome　45
To those which would not know them, and
　　yet must
Perforce be their acquaintance. These
　　exactions,
Whereof my sovereign would have note,
　　they are
Most pestilent to th' hearing ; and to bear
　　'em　49
The back is sacrifice to th' load. They say
They are devis'd by you, or else you suffer

Too hard an exclamation.
　King.　　　　　　　Still exaction !
The nature of it ? In what kind, let's know,
Is this exaction ?
　Q. Kath.　　　　I am much too venturous
In tempting of your patience, but am
　　bold'ned　55
Under your promis'd pardon. The subjects'
　　grief
Comes through commissions, which compels
　　from each
The sixth part of his substance, to be levied
Without delay ; and the pretence for this
Is nam'd your wars in France. This makes
　　bold mouths ;　60
Tongues spit their duties out, and cold
　　hearts freeze
Allegiance in them ; their curses now
Live where their prayers did ; and it's come
　　to pass
This tractable obedience is a slave
To each incensed will. I would your
　　Highness　65
Would give it quick consideration, for
There is no primer business.
　King.　　　　　　　By my life,
This is against our pleasure.
　Wol.　　　　　　And for me,
I have no further gone in this than by　69
A single voice ; and that not pass'd me but
By learned approbation of the judges. If I
　　am
Traduc'd by ignorant tongues, which
　　neither know
My faculties nor person, yet will be
The chronicles of my doing, let me say
'Tis but the fate of place, and the rough
　　brake　75
That virtue must go through. We must not
　　stint
Our necessary actions in the fear
To cope malicious censurers, which ever
As rav'nous fishes do a vessel follow　79
That is new-trimm'd, but benefit no further
Than vainly longing. What we oft do best,
By sick interpreters, once weak ones, is
Not ours, or not allow'd ; what worst, as oft
Hitting a grosser quality, is cried up
For our best act. If we shall stand still,　85
In fear our motion will be mock'd or carp'd
　　at,
We should take root here where we sit,
　　or sit
State-statues only.
　King.　　　　　　Things done well
And with a care exempt themselves from
　　fear :　89
Things done without example, in their issue
Are to be fear'd. Have you a precedent
Of this commission ? I believe, not any.
We must not rend our subjects from our
　　laws,
And stick them in our will. Sixth part of
　　each ?　94

A trembling contribution! Why, we take
From every tree lop, bark, and part o' th'
    timber;
And though we leave it with a root, thus
    hack'd,
The air will drink the sap. To every county
Where this is question'd send our letters
    with   99
Free pardon to each man that has denied
The force of this commission. Pray, look
    to't;
I put it to your care.
    Wol. [*Aside to the Secretary*] A word with
you.
Let there be letters writ to every shire
Of the King's grace and pardon. The
    grieved commons
Hardly conceive of me—let it be nois'd 105
That through our intercession this revoke-
    ment
And pardon comes. I shall anon advise you
Further in the proceeding. [*Exit Secretary.*

        Enter Surveyor.

    Q. Kath. I am sorry that the Duke of
    Buckingham   109
Is run in your displeasure.
    King.   It grieves many.
The gentleman is learn'd and a most rare
    speaker;
To nature none more bound; his training
    such
That he may furnish and instruct great
    teachers
And never seek for aid out of himself. Yet
    see,
When these so noble benefits shall prove 115
Not well dispos'd, the mind growing once
    corrupt,
They turn to vicious forms, ten times more
    ugly
Than ever they were fair. This man so
    complete,
Who was enroll'd 'mongst wonders, and
    when we,
Almost with ravish'd list'ning, could not
    find   120
His hour of speech a minute—he, my lady,
Hath into monstrous habits put the graces
That once were his, and is become as black
As if besmear'd in hell. Sit by us; you shall
    hear—
This was his gentleman in trust—of him 125
Things to strike honour sad. Bid him
    recount
The fore-recited practices, whereof
We cannot feel too little, hear too much.
    Wol. Stand forth, and with bold spirit
    relate what you,   129
Most like a careful subject, have collected
Out of the Duke of Buckingham.
    King.   Speak freely.
    Surv. First, it was usual with him—every
    day

It would infect his speech—that if the King
Should without issue die, he'll carry it so
To make the sceptre his. These very words
I've heard him utter to his son-in-law, 136
Lord Aberga'ny, to whom by oath he
    menac'd
Revenge upon the Cardinal.
    Wol.   Please your Highness, note
This dangerous conception in this point:
Not friended by his wish, to your high
    person   140
His will is most malignant, and it stretches
Beyond you to your friends.
    Q. Kath.   My learn'd Lord Cardinal,
Deliver all with charity.
    King.   Speak on.
How grounded he his title to the crown
Upon our fail? To this point hast thou
    heard him   145
At any time speak aught?
    Surv.   He was brought to this
By a vain prophecy of Nicholas Henton.
    King. What was that Henton?
    Surv.   Sir, a Chartreux friar,
His confessor, who fed him every minute
With words of sovereignty.
    King.   How know'st thou this?
    Surv. Not long before your Highness sped
    to France,   151
The Duke being at the Rose, within the
    parish
Saint Lawrence Poultney, did of me
    demand
What was the speech among the Londoners
Concerning the French journey. I replied
Men fear'd the French would prove per-
    fidious,   156
To the King's danger. Presently the Duke
Said 'twas the fear indeed and that he
    doubted
'Twould prove the verity of certain words
Spoke by a holy monk 'that oft' says he
'Hath sent to me, wishing me to permit 161
John de la Car, my chaplain, a choice
    hour
To hear from him a matter of some moment;
Whom after under the confession's seal
He solemnly had sworn that what he spoke
My chaplain to no creature living but 166
To me should utter, with demure confidence
This pausingly ensu'd: " Neither the King
    nor's heirs,
Tell you the Duke, shall prosper; bid him
    strive   169
To gain the love o' th' commonalty; the
    Duke
Shall govern England "'.
    Q. Kath.   If I know you well,
You were the Duke's surveyor, and lost
    your office
On the complaint o' th' tenants. Take good
    heed
You charge not in your spleen a noble
    person

And spoil your nobler soul. I say, take
heed;   175
Yes, heartily beseech you.
   King.   Let him on.
Go forward.
   Surv. On my soul, I'll speak but truth.
I told my lord the Duke, by th' devil's
   illusions
The monk might be deceiv'd, and that 'twas
   dangerous for him
To ruminate on this so far, until   180
It forg'd him some design, which, being
   believ'd,
It was much like to do. He answer'd
   ' Tush,
It can do me no damage '; adding further
That, had the King in his last sickness
   fail'd,
The Cardinal's and Sir Thomas Lovell's
   heads   185
Should have gone off.
   King. Ha! what, so rank? Ah ha!
There's mischief in this man. Canst thou
   say further?
   Surv. I can, my liege.
   King.   Proceed.
   Surv.   Being at Greenwich,
After your Highness had reprov'd the Duke
About Sir William Bulmer—
   King.   I remember   190
Of such a time: being my sworn servant,
The Duke retain'd him his. But on: what
   hence?
   Surv. ' If ' quoth he ' I for this had been
   committed—
As to the Tower I thought—I would have
   play'd
The part my father meant to act upon 195
Th' usurper Richard; who, being at
   Salisbury,
Made suit to come in's presence, which if
   granted,
As he made semblance of his duty, would
Have put his knife into him.'
   King.   A giant traitor!
   Wol. Now, madam, may his Highness live
   in freedom,   200
And this man out of prison?
   Q. Kath.   God mend all!
   King. There's something more would out
   of thee: what say'st?
   Surv. After 'the Duke his father' with
   the 'knife',
He stretch'd him, and, with one hand on his
   dagger,
Another spread on's breast, mounting his
   eyes,   205
He did discharge a horrible oath, whose
   tenour
Was, were he evil us'd, he would outgo
His father by as much as a performance
Does an irresolute purpose.
   King.   There's his period,
To sheath his knife in us. He is attach'd;

Call him to present trial. If he may   211
Find mercy in the law, 'tis his; if none,
Let him not seek't of us. By day and night!
He's traitor to th' height.   [*Exeunt.*

   SCENE III. *London. The palace.*

Enter the Lord Chamberlain *and* Lord
   Sandys.

   Cham. Is't possible the spells of France
   should juggle
Men into such strange mysteries?
   Sandys.   New customs,
Though they be never so ridiculous,
Nay, let 'em be unmanly, yet are follow'd.
   Cham. As far as I see, all the good our
   English   5
Have got by the late voyage is but merely
A fit or two o' th' face; but they are
   shrewd ones;
For when they hold 'em, you would swear
   directly
Their very noses had been counsellors   9
To Pepin or Clotharius, they keep state so.
   Sandys. They have all new legs, and lame
   ones. One would take it,
That never saw 'em pace before, the spavin
Or springhalt reign'd among 'em.
   Cham.   Death! my lord,
Their clothes are after such a pagan cut to't,
That sure th' have worn out Christendom.

   Enter Sir Thomas Lovell.

                           How now?   15
What news, Sir Thomas Lovell?
   Lov.   Faith, my lord,
I hear of none but the new proclamation
That's clapp'd upon the court gate.
   Cham.   What is't for?
   Lov. The reformation of our travell'd
   gallants,
That fill the court with quarrels, talk, and
   tailors.   20
   Cham. I am glad 'tis there. Now I would
   pray our monsieurs
To think an English courtier may be wise,
And never see the Louvre.
   Lov.   They must either,
For so run the conditions, leave those
   remnants   24
Of fool and feather that they got in France,
With all their honourable points of ignor-
   ance
Pertaining thereunto—as fights and fire-
   works;
Abusing better men than they can be,
Out of a foreign wisdom—renouncing clean
The faith they have in tennis, and tall
   stockings,   30
Short blist'red breeches, and those types of
   travel,
And understand again like honest men,
Or pack to their old playfellows. There, I
   take it,

They may, cum privilegio, wear away
The lag end of their lewdness and be
   laugh'd at.   35
  Sandys. 'Tis time to give 'em physic,
   their diseases
Are grown so catching.
  Cham.   What a loss our ladies
Will have of these trim vanities !
  Lov.   Ay, marry,
There will be woe indeed, lords : the sly
   whoresons
Have got a speeding trick to lay down
   ladies.   40
A French song and a fiddle has no fellow.
  Sandys. The devil fiddle 'em ! I am glad
   they are going,
For sure there's no converting of 'em. Now
An honest country lord, as I am, beaten
A long time out of play, may bring his
   plainsong   45
And have an hour of hearing ; and, by'r
   Lady,
Held current music too.
  Cham.   Well said, Lord Sandys ;
Your colt's tooth is not cast yet.
  Sandys.   No, my lord,
Nor shall not while I have a stump.
  Cham.   Sir Thomas,
Whither were you a-going ?
  Lov.   To the Cardinal's ;   50
Your lordship is a guest too.
  Cham.   O, 'tis true ;
This night he makes a supper, and a great
   one,
To many lords and ladies ; there will be
The beauty of this kingdom, I'll assure you.
  Lov. That churchman bears a bounteous
   mind indeed,   55
A hand as fruitful as the land that feeds us ;
His dews fall everywhere.
  Cham.   No doubt he's noble ;
He had a black mouth that said other of him.
  Sandys. He may, my lord ; has where-
   withal. In him
Sparing would show a worse sin than ill
   doctrine :   60
Men of his way should be most liberal,
They are set here for examples.
  Cham.   True, they are so ;
But few now give so great ones. My barge
   stays ;
Your lordship shall along. Come, good Sir
   Thomas,   64
We shall be late else ; which I would not be,
For I was spoke to, with Sir Henry
   Guildford,
This night to be comptrollers.
  Sandys.   I am your lordship's.
                      [*Exeunt.*

SCENE IV. *London. The Presence Chamber
    in York Place.*

*Hautboys. A small table under a state for
  the Cardinal, a longer table for the guests.*

Then enter ANNE BULLEN, *and divers
other* Ladies *and* Gentlemen, *as guests,
at one door ; at another door enter* SIR
HENRY GUILDFORD.

  Guild. Ladies, a general welcome from his
   Grace
Salutes ye all ; this night he dedicates
To fair content and you. None here, he
   hopes,
In all this noble bevy, has brought with her
One care abroad ; he would have all as
   merry   5
As, first, good company, good wine, good
   welcome,
Can make good people.

Enter Lord Chamberlain, LORD SANDYS,
   and SIR THOMAS LOVELL.

           O, my lord, y'are tardy,
The very thought of this fair company
Clapp'd wings to me.
  Cham. You are young, Sir Harry Guild-
   ford.
  Sandys. Sir Thomas Lovell, had the
   Cardinal   10
But half my lay thoughts in him, some of
   these
Should find a running banquet ere they
   rested
I think would better please 'em. By my life,
They are a sweet society of fair ones.
  Lov. O that your lordship were but now
   confessor   15
To one or two of these !
  Sandys.   I would I were ;
They should find easy penance.
  Lov.   Faith, how easy?
  Sandys. As easy as a down bed would
   afford it.
  Cham. Sweet ladies, will it please you
   sit ? Sir Harry,
Place you that side ; I'll take the charge of
   this.   20
His Grace is ent'ring. Nay, you must not
   freeze :
Two women plac'd together makes cold
   weather.
My Lord Sandys, you are one will keep 'em
   waking :
Pray sit between these ladies.
  Sandys.   By my faith,
And thank your lordship. By your leave,
   sweet ladies. [*Seats himself between
       Anne Bullen and another lady.*
If I chance to talk a little wild, forgive me ;
I had it from my father.
  Anne.   Was he mad, sir ?
  Sandys. O, very mad, exceeding mad, in
   love too.   28
But he would bite none ; just as I do now,
He would kiss you twenty with a breath.
                     [*Kisses her.*
  Cham.   Well said, my lord.

So, now y'are fairly seated. Gentlemen, 31
The penance lies on you if these fair
ladies
Pass away frowning.
Sandys. For my little cure,
Let me alone.

Hautboys. Enter CARDINAL WOLSEY,
attended ; and takes his state.

Wol. Y'are welcome, my fair guests.
That noble lady 35
Or gentleman that is not freely merry
Is not my friend. This, to confirm my
welcome—
And to you all, good health! [*Drinks.*
Sandys. Your Grace is noble.
Let me have such a bowl may hold my
thanks
And save me so much talking.
Wol. My Lord Sandys, 40
I am beholding to you. Cheer your
neighbours.
Ladies, you are not merry. Gentlemen,
Whose fault is this?
Sandys. The red wine first must rise
In their fair cheeks, my lord ; then we shall
have 'em 44
Talk us to silence.
Anne. You are a merry gamester,
My Lord Sandys.
Sandys. Yes, if I make my play.
Here's to your ladyship ; and pledge it,
madam,
For 'tis to such a thing—
Anne. You cannot show me.
Sandys. I told your Grace they would talk
anon. [*Drum and trumpet. Chambers
discharg'd.*
Wol. What's that?
Cham. Look out there, some of ye.
[*Exit a Servant.*
Wol. What warlike voice,
And to what end, is this? Nay, ladies, fear
not: 51
By all the laws of war y'are privileg'd.

Re-enter Servant.

Cham. How now! what is't?
Serv. A noble troop of strangers—
For so they seem. Th' have left their barge
and landed,
And hither make, as great ambassadors 55
From foreign princes.
Wol. Good Lord Chamberlain,
Go, give 'em welcome ; you can speak the
French tongue ;
And pray receive 'em nobly and conduct
'em
Into our presence, where this heaven of
beauty
Shall shine at full upon them. Some attend
him. 60
[*Exit Chamberlain attended. All rise,
and tables remov'd.*

You have now a broken banquet, but we'll
mend it.
A good digestion to you all ; and once more
I show'r a welcome on ye : welcome all.

Hautboys. Enter the KING, *and* Others, *as
maskers, habited like shepherds, usher'd
by the* Lord Chamberlain. *They pass
directly before the Cardinal, and gracefully
salute him.*

A noble company! What are their
pleasures?
Cham. Because they speak no English,
thus they pray'd 65
To tell your Grace, that, having heard by
fame
Of this so noble and so fair assembly
This night to meet here, they could do no
less,
Out of the great respect they bear to beauty,
But leave their flocks and, under your fair
conduct, 70
Crave leave to view these ladies and entreat
An hour of revels with 'em.
Wol. Say, Lord Chamberlain,
They have done my poor house grace ; for
which I pay 'em
A thousand thanks, and pray 'em take their
pleasures. [*They choose ladies. The
King chooses Anne Bullen.*
King. The fairest hand I ever touch'd!
O beauty, 75
Till now I never knew thee! [*Music. Dance.*
Wol. My lord!
Cham. Your Grace?
Wol. Pray tell 'em thus much from me :
There should be one amongst 'em, by his
person,
More worthy this place than myself ; to
whom, 79
If I but knew him, with my love and duty
I would surrender it.
Cham. I will, my lord.
[*He whispers to the Maskers.*
Wol. What say they?
Cham. Such a one, they all confess,
There is indeed ; which they would have
your Grace
Find out, and he will take it.
Wol. Let me see, then.
[*Comes from his state.*
By all your good leaves, gentlemen, here
I'll make 85
My royal choice.
King. [*Unmasking*] Ye have found him,
Cardinal.
You hold a fair assembly ; you do well,
lord.
You are a churchman, or, I'll tell you,
Cardinal,
I should judge now unhappily.
Wol. I am glad
Your Grace is grown so pleasant.
King. My Lord Chamberlain, 90

Prithee come hither: what fair lady's that?
  Cham. An't please your Grace, Sir
    Thomas Bullen's daughter—
The Viscount Rochford—one of her
    Highness' women.
  King. By heaven, she is a dainty one.
    Sweet heart,
I were unmannerly to take you out   95
And not to kiss you. A health, gentlemen!
Let it go round.
  Wol. Sir Thomas Lovell, is the banquet
    ready
I' th' privy chamber?
  Lov.   Yes, my lord.
  Wol.   Your Grace,
I fear, with dancing is a little heated. 100
  King. I fear, too much.
  Wol.   There's fresher air, my lord,
In the next chamber.
  King. Lead in your ladies, ev'ry one.
    Sweet partner,
I must not yet forsake you. Let's be merry:
Good my Lord Cardinal, I have half a
    dozen healths 105
To drink to these fair ladies, and a measure
To lead 'em once again; and then let's
    dream
Who's best in favour. Let the music
    knock it.   [*Exeunt, with trumpets.*

ACT TWO

SCENE I. *Westminster. A street.*

Enter two Gentlemen, at several doors.

  1 *Gent.* Whither away so fast?
  2 *Gent.*   O, God save ye!
Ev'n to the Hall, to hear what shall become
Of the great Duke of Buckingham.
  1 *Gent.*   I'll save you
That labour, sir. All's now done but the
    ceremony
Of bringing back the prisoner.
  2 *Gent.*   Were you there? 5
  1 *Gent.* Yes, indeed, was I.
  2 *Gent.*   Pray, speak what has happen'd.
  1 *Gent.* You may guess quickly what.
  2 *Gent.*   Is he found guilty?
  1 *Gent.* Yes, truly is he, and condemn'd
    upon't.
  2 *Gent.* I am sorry for't.
  1 *Gent.*   So are a number more.
  2 *Gent.* But, pray, how pass'd it? 10
  1 *Gent.* I'll tell you in a little. The great
    Duke
Came to the bar; where to his accusations
He pleaded still not guilty, and alleged
Many sharp reasons to defeat the law.
The King's attorney, on the contrary, 15
Urg'd on the examinations, proofs, con-
    fessions,
Of divers witnesses; which the Duke desir'd
To have brought, viva voce, to his face;
At which appear'd against him his surveyor,

Sir Gilbert Peck his chancellor, and John
    Car,   20
Confessor to him, with that devil-monk,
Hopkins, that made this mischief.
  2 *Gent.*   That was he
That fed him with his prophecies?
  1 *Gent.*   The same.
All these accus'd him strongly, which he
    fain
Would have flung from him; but indeed he
    could not;   25
And so his peers, upon this evidence,
Have found him guilty of high treason.
    Much
He spoke, and learnedly, for life; but all
Was either pitied in him or forgotten.
  2 *Gent.* After all this, how did he bear
    himself?   30
  1 *Gent.* When he was brought again to
    th' bar to hear
His knell rung out, his judgment, he was
    stirr'd
With such an agony he sweat extremely,
And something spoke in choler, ill and
    hasty;
But he fell to himself again, and sweetly 35
In all the rest show'd a most noble patience.
  2 *Gent.* I do not think he fears death.
  1 *Gent.*   Sure, he does not;
He never was so womanish; the cause
He may a little grieve at.
  2 *Gent.*   Certainly
The Cardinal is the end of this.
  1 *Gent.*   'Tis likely, 40
By all conjectures: first, Kildare's
    attainder,
Then deputy of Ireland, who remov'd,
Earl Surrey was sent thither, and in haste
    too,
Lest he should help his father.
  2 *Gent.*   That trick of state
Was a deep envious one.
  1 *Gent.*   At his return 45
No doubt he will requite it. This is noted,
And generally: whoever the King favours
The Cardinal instantly will find employ-
    ment,
And far enough from court too.
  2 *Gent.*   All the commons
Hate him perniciously, and, o' my con-
    science,   50
Wish him ten fathom deep: this Duke as
    much
They love and dote on; call him bounteous
    Buckingham,
The mirror of all courtesy—

Enter BUCKINGHAM *from his arraignment;*
  Tip-staves before him; the axe with the
  edge towards him; halberds on each side;
  accompanied with SIR THOMAS LOVELL,
  SIR NICHOLAS VAUX, SIR WILLIAM
  SANDYS, *and* common people, *etc.*

  1 *Gent.*   Stay there, sir,

And see the noble ruin'd man you speak of.

2 Gent. Let's stand close, and behold him.

Buck. All good people,
You that thus far have come to pity me, 56
Hear what I say, and then go home and
lose me.
I have this day receiv'd a traitor's judg-
ment,
And by that name must die; yet, heaven
bear witness,
And if I have a conscience, let it sink me 60
Even as the axe falls, if I be not faithful!
The law I bear no malice for my death:
'T has done, upon the premises, but justice.
But those that sought it I could wish more
Christians. 64
Be what they will, I heartily forgive 'em;
Yet let 'em look they glory not in mischief
Nor build their evils on the graves of great
men,
For then my guiltless blood must cry
against 'em.
For further life in this world I ne'er hope
Nor will I sue, although the King have
mercies 70
More than I dare make faults. You few
that lov'd me
And dare be bold to weep for Buckingham,
His noble friends and fellows, whom to
leave
Is only bitter to him, only dying,
Go with me like good angels to my end; 75
And as the long divorce of steel falls on me
Make of your prayers one sweet sacrifice,
And lift my soul to heaven. Lead on, a
God's name.

Lov. I do beseech your Grace, for charity,
If ever any malice in your heart 80
Were hid against me, now to forgive me
frankly.

Buck. Sir Thomas Lovell, I as free forgive
you
As I would be forgiven. I forgive all.
There cannot be those numberless offences
'Gainst me that I cannot take peace with.
No black envy 85
Shall mark my grave. Commend me to his
Grace;
And if he speak of Buckingham, pray tell
him
You met me half in heaven. My vows and
prayers
Yet are the King's, and, till my soul
forsake, 89
Shall cry for blessings on him. May he live
Longer than I have time to tell his years;
Ever belov'd and loving may his rule be;
And when old time shall lead him to his end,
Goodness and he fill up one monument!

Lov. To th' water side I must conduct
your Grace; 95
Then give my charge up to Sir Nicholas
Vaux,
Who undertakes you to your end.

Vaux.   Prepare there;
The Duke is coming; see the barge be
ready;
And fit it with such furniture as suits
The greatness of his person.

Buck.   Nay, Sir Nicholas, 100
Let it alone; my state now will but mock
me.
When I came hither I was Lord High
Constable
And Duke of Buckingham; now, poor
Edward Bohun.
Yet I am richer than my base accusers
That never knew what truth meant; I now
seal it; 105
And with that blood will make 'em one day
groan for't.
My noble father, Henry of Buckingham,
Who first rais'd head against usurping
Richard,
Flying for succour to his servant Banister,
Being distress'd, was by that wretch be-
tray'd 110
And without trial fell; God's peace be with
him!
Henry the Seventh succeeding, truly pity-
ing
My father's loss, like a most royal prince,
Restor'd me to my honours, and out of
ruins
Made my name once more noble. Now his
son, 115
Henry the Eighth, life, honour, name, and
all
That made me happy, at one stroke has
taken
For ever from the world. I had my trial,
And must needs say a noble one; which
makes me 119
A little happier than my wretched father;
Yet thus far we are one in fortunes: both
Fell by our servants, by those men we
lov'd most—
A most unnatural and faithless service.
Heaven has an end in all. Yet, you that
hear me, 124
This from a dying man receive as certain:
Where you are liberal of your loves and
counsels,
Be sure you be not loose; for those you
make friends
And give your hearts to, when they once
perceive
The least rub in your fortunes, fall away
Like water from ye, never found again 130
But where they mean to sink ye. All good
people,
Pray for me! I must now forsake ye; the
last hour
Of my long weary life is come upon me.
Farewell;
And when you would say something that
is sad, 135

Speak how I fell. I have done ; and God
　　forgive me !
　　　　[*Exeunt Buckingham and Train.*
1 *Gent.* O, this is full of pity ! Sir, it calls,
I fear, too many curses on their heads
That were the authors.
2 *Gent.*　　　　　If the Duke be guiltless,
'Tis full of woe ; yet I can give you inkling
Of an ensuing evil, if it fall,　　　　141
Greater than this.
1 *Gent.*　　Good angels keep it from us !
What may it be ? You do not doubt my
　　faith, sir ?
　　2 *Gent.* This secret is so weighty, 'twill
　　require
A strong faith to conceal it.
1 *Gent.*　　　　　Let me have it ;　145
I do not talk much.
2 *Gent.*　　　　I am confident.
You shall, sir. Did you not of late days hear
A buzzing of a separation
Between the King and Katharine ?
1 *Gent.*　　　　　Yes, but it held not ;
For when the King once heard it, out of
　　anger　　　150
He sent command to the Lord Mayor
　　straight
To stop the rumour and allay those tongues
That durst disperse it.
2 *Gent.*　　　　But that slander, sir,
Is found a truth now ; for it grows again
Fresher than e'er it was, and held for
　　certain　　　155
The King will venture at it. Either the
　　Cardinal
Or some about him near have, out of malice
To the good Queen, possess'd him with a
　　scruple
That will undo her. To confirm this too,
Cardinal Campeius is arriv'd and lately ;
As all think, for this business.
1 *Gent.*　　　　　'Tis the Cardinal ;
And merely to revenge him on the Emperor
For not bestowing on him at his asking
The archbishopric of Toledo, this is
　　purpos'd.
　　2 *Gent.* I think you have hit the mark ;
　　but is't not cruel　　　165
That she should feel the smart of this ? The
　　Cardinal
Will have his will, and she must fall.
1 *Gent.*　　　　　'Tis woeful.
We are too open here to argue this ;
Let's think in private more.　　　[*Exeunt.*

SCENE II. *London. The palace.*

Enter the Lord Chamberlain *reading this
letter.*

Cham. ' My lord,
　　　　The horses your lordship sent
for, with all the care I had, I saw well
chosen, ridden, and furnish'd. They were
young and handsome, and of the best breed
in the north. When they were ready to set
out for London, a man of my Lord Cardinal's, by commission, and main power,
took 'em from me, with this reason : his
master would be serv'd before a subject,
if not before the King ; which stopp'd our
mouths, sir.'
I fear he will indeed. Well, let him have
　　them.
He will have all, I think.

Enter to the Lord Chamberlain the DUKES OF
NORFOLK *and* SUFFOLK.

Nor. Well met, my Lord Chamberlain.　10
Cham. Good day to both your Graces.
Suf. How is the King employ'd ?
Cham.　　　　　I left him private,
Full of sad thoughts and troubles.
Nor.　　　　　What's the cause ?
Cham. It seems the marriage with his
　　brother's wife
Has crept too near his conscience.
Suf.　　　　No, his conscience　15
Has crept too near another lady.
Nor.　　　　　'Tis so ;
This is the Cardinal's doing ; the King-
　　Cardinal,
That blind priest, like the eldest son of
　　fortune,
Turns what he list. The King will know
　　him one day.
Suf. Pray God he do ! He'll never know
　　himself else.　　　20
Nor. How holily he works in all his
　　business !
And with what zeal ! For, now he has
　　crack'd the league
Between us and the Emperor, the Queen's
　　great nephew,
He dives into the King's soul and there
　　scatters
Dangers, doubts, wringing of the con-
　　science,　　　25
Fears, and despairs—and all these for his
　　marriage ;
And out of all these to restore the King,
He counsels a divorce, a loss of her
That like a jewel has hung twenty years
About his neck, yet never lost her lustre ;
Of her that loves him with that excellence
That angels love good men with ; even of
　　her
That, when the greatest stroke of fortune
　　falls,
Will bless the King—and is not this course
　　pious ?
Cham. Heaven keep me from such
　　counsel ! 'Tis most true　　　35
These news are everywhere ; every tongue
　　speaks 'em,
And every true heart weeps for't. All that
　　dare
Look into these affairs see this main end—

The French King's sister. Heaven will one
  day open
The King's eyes, that so long have slept
  upon   40
This bold bad man.
 Suf.   And free us from his slavery.
 Nor. We had need pray, and heartily, for
  our deliverance ;
Or this imperious man will work us all
From princes into pages. All men's
  honours   45
Lie like one lump before him, to be
  fashion'd
Into what pitch he please.
 Suf.   For me, my lords,
I love him not, nor fear him—there's my
  creed ;
As I am made without him, so I'll stand,
If the King please ; his curses and his
  blessings   50
Touch me alike ; th'are breath I not believe
  in.
I knew him, and I know him ; so I leave
  him
To him that made him proud—the Pope.
 Nor.   Let's in ;
And with some other business put the King
From these sad thoughts that work too
  much upon him.
My lord, you'll bear us company ?
 Cham.   Excuse me, 56
The King has sent me otherwhere ; besides,
You'll find a most unfit time to disturb him.
Health to your lordships !
 Nor. Thanks, my good Lord Chamberlain.
  [*Exit Lord Chamberlain ; and the
   King draws the curtain and sits
    reading pensively.*
 Suf. How sad he looks ; sure, he is much
  afflicted.   60
 King. Who's there, ha ?
 Nor.   Pray God he be not angry.
 K. Hen. Who's there, I say ? How dare
  you thrust yourselves
Into my private meditations ?
Who am I, ha ?
 Nor. A gracious king that pardons all
  offences   65
Malice ne'er meant. Our breach of duty
  this way
Is business of estate, in which we come
To know your royal pleasure.
 King.   Ye are too bold.
Go to ; I'll make ye know your times of
  business.
Is this an hour for temporal affairs, ha ? 70

Enter WOLSEY *and* CAMPEIUS *with a
  commission.*

Who's there ? My good Lord Cardinal ? O
  my Wolsey,
The quiet of my wounded conscience,
Thou art a cure fit for a King. [*To Campeius*]
  You're welcome,

Most learned reverend sir, into our kingdom.
Use us and it. [*To Wolsey*] My good lord,
  have great care
I be not found a talker.
 Wol.   Sir, you cannot. 76
I would your Grace would give us but an
  hour
Of private conference.
 King. [*To Norfolk and Suffolk*] We are
  busy ; go.
 Nor. [*Aside to Suffolk*] This priest has no
  pride in him !
 Suf. [*Aside to Norfolk*] Not to speak of !
I would not be so sick though for his place.
But this cannot continue.
 Nor. [*Aside to Suffolk*] If it do, 81
I'll venture one have-at-him.
 Suf. [*Aside to Norfolk*] I another.
     [*Exeunt Norfolk and Suffolk.*
 Wol. Your Grace has given a precedent
  of wisdom
Above all princes, in committing freely 84
Your scruple to the voice of Christendom.
Who can be angry now ? What envy reach
  you ?
The Spaniard, tied by blood and favour to
  her,
Must now confess, if they have any
  goodness,
The trial just and noble. All the clerks,
I mean the learned ones, in Christian
  kingdoms   90
Have their free voices. Rome the nurse of
  judgment,
Invited by your noble self, hath sent
One general tongue unto us, this good man,
This just and learned priest, Cardinal
  Campeius,
Whom once more I present unto your
  Highness.   95
 King. And once more in mine arms I bid
  him welcome,
And thank the holy conclave for their loves.
They have sent me such a man I would
  have wish'd for.
 Cam. Your Grace must needs deserve all
  strangers' loves,   99
You are so noble. To your Highness' hand
I tender my commission ; by whose
  virtue—
The court of Rome commanding—you, my
  Lord
Cardinal of York, are join'd with me their
  servant
In the unpartial judging of this business.
 King. Two equal men. The Queen shall
  be acquainted   105
Forthwith for what you come. Where's
  Gardiner ?
 Wol. I know your Majesty has always
  lov'd her
So dear in heart not to deny her that
A woman of less place might ask by law—
Scholars allow'd freely to argue for her. 110

King. Ay, and the best she shall have;
    and my favour
To him that does best. God forbid else.
    Cardinal,
Prithee call Gardiner to me, my new
    secretary;
I find him a fit fellow.   [*Exit Wolsey.*

    Re-enter WOLSEY *with* GARDINER.

    Wol. [*Aside to Gardiner*] Give me your
    hand: much joy and favour to you;
You are the King's now.
    Gard. [*Aside to Wolsey*] But to be com-
    manded   116
For ever by your Grace, whose hand has
    rais'd me.
    King. Come hither, Gardiner.
        [*Walks and whispers.*
    Cam. My Lord of York, was not one
    Doctor Pace
In this man's place before him?
    Wol.   Yes, he was. 120
    Cam. Was he not held a learned man?
    Wol.   Yes, surely.
    Cam. Believe me, there's an ill opinion
    spread then,
Even of yourself, Lord Cardinal.
    Wol.   How! Of me?
    Cam. They will not stick to say you envied
    him
And, fearing he would rise, he was so
    virtuous,   125
Kept him a foreign man still; which so
    griev'd him
That he ran mad and died.
    Wol.   Heav'n's peace be with him!
That's Christian care enough. For living
    murmurers
There's places of rebuke. He was a fool,
For he would needs be virtuous: that good
    fellow,   130
If I command him, follows my appoint-
    ment.
I will have none so near else. Learn this,
    brother,
We live not to be grip'd by meaner persons.
    King. Deliver this with modesty to th'
    Queen.   [*Exit Gardiner.*
The most convenient place that I can
    think of   135
For such receipt of learning is Blackfriars;
There ye shall meet about this weighty
    business—
My Wolsey, see it furnish'd. O, my lord,
Would it not grieve an able man to leave
So sweet a bedfellow? But, conscience,
    conscience!   140
O, 'tis a tender place! and I must leave her.
        [*Exeunt.*

    SCENE III. *London. The palace.*

    Enter ANNE BULLEN *and an old* Lady.

    Anne. Not for that neither. Here's the
    pang that pinches:

His Highness having liv'd so long with her,
    and she
So good a lady that no tongue could ever
Pronounce dishonour of her—by my life,
She never knew harm-doing—O, now, after
So many courses of the sun enthroned,   6
Still growing in a majesty and pomp, the
    which
To leave a thousand-fold more bitter than
'Tis sweet at first t' acquire—after this
    process,
To give her the avaunt, it is a pity   10
Would move a monster.
    Old L.   Hearts of most hard temper
Melt and lament for her.
    Anne.   O, God's will! much better
She ne'er had known pomp; though't be
    temporal,
Yet, if that quarrel, fortune, do divorce 14
It from the bearer, 'tis a sufferance panging
As soul and body's severing.
    Old L.   Alas, poor lady!
She's a stranger now again.
    Anne.   So much the more
Must pity drop upon her. Verily,
I swear 'tis better to be lowly born
And range with humble livers in content 20
Than to be perk'd up in a glist'ring grief
And wear a golden sorrow.
    Old L.   Our content
Is our best having.
    Anne.   By my troth and maidenhead,
I would not be a queen.
    Old L.   Beshrew me, I would,
And venture maidenhead for't; and so
    would you,   25
For all this spice of your hypocrisy.
You that have so fair parts of woman on
    you
Have too a woman's heart, which ever yet
Affected eminence, wealth, sovereignty;
Which, to say sooth, are blessings; and
    which gifts,   30
Saving your mincing, the capacity
Of your soft cheveril conscience would
    receive
If you might please to stretch it.
    Anne.   Nay, good troth.
    Old L. Yes, troth and troth. You would
    not be a queen!
    Anne. No, not for all the riches under
    heaven.   35
    Old L. 'Tis strange: a threepence bow'd
    would hire me,
Old as I am, to queen it. But, I pray you,
What think you of a duchess? Have you
    limbs
To bear that load of title?
    Anne.   No, in truth.
    Old L. Then you are weakly made. Pluck
    off a little;   40
I would not be a young count in your way
For more than blushing comes to. If your
    back

Cannot vouchsafe this burden, 'tis too weak
Ever to get a boy.
   Anne.   How you do talk!
I swear again I would not be a queen 45
For all the world.
   Old L.   In faith, for little England
You'd venture an emballing. I myself
Would for Carnarvonshire, although there
    long'd
No more to th' crown but that. Lo, who
    comes here?

     Enter the Lord Chamberlain.

   Cham. Good morrow, ladies. What were't
    worth to know 50
The secret of your conference?
   Anne.   My good lord,
Not your demand; it values not your
    asking.
Our mistress' sorrows we were pitying.
   Cham. It was a gentle business and
    becoming 54
The action of good women; there is hope
All will be well.
   Anne.   Now, I pray God, amen!
   Cham. You bear a gentle mind, and
    heav'nly blessings
Follow such creatures. That you may, fair
    lady,
Perceive I speak sincerely and high note's
Ta'en of your many virtues, the King's
    Majesty 60
Commends his good opinion of you to you,
    and
Does purpose honour to you no less flowing
Than Marchioness of Pembroke; to which
    title
A thousand pound a year, annual support,
Out of his grace he adds.
   Anne.   I do not know 65
What kind of my obedience I should
    tender;
More than my all is nothing, nor my prayers
Are not words duly hallowed, nor my wishes
More worth than empty vanities; yet
    prayers and wishes 69
Are all I can return. Beseech your lordship,
Vouchsafe to speak my thanks and my
    obedience,
As from a blushing handmaid, to his
    Highness;
Whose health and royalty I pray for.
   Cham.   Lady,
I shall not fail t'approve the fair conceit
The King hath of you. [*Aside*] I have
    perus'd her well:
Beauty and honour in her are so mingled 76
That they have caught the King; and who
    knows yet
But from this lady may proceed a gem
To lighten all this isle?—I'll to the King
And say I spoke with you.
   Anne.   My honour'd lord! 80
            [*Exit Lord Chamberlain.*

   Old L. Why, this it is: see, see!
I have been begging sixteen years in court—
Am yet a courtier beggarly—nor could
Come pat betwixt too early and too late
For any suit of pounds; and you, O fate!
A very fresh-fish here—fie, fie, fie upon 86
This compell'd fortune!—have your mouth
    fill'd up
Before you open it.
   Anne.   This is strange to me.
   Old L. How tastes it? Is it bitter?
    Forty pence, no. 89
There was a lady once—'tis an old story—
That would not be a queen, that would she
    not,
For all the mud in Egypt. Have you heard
    it?
   Anne. Come, you are pleasant.
   Old L.   With your theme I could
O'ermount the lark. The Marchioness of
    Pembroke! 94
A thousand pounds a year for pure respect!
No other obligation! By my life,
That promises moe thousands: honour's
    train
Is longer than his foreskirt. By this time
I know your back will bear a duchess. Say,
Are you not stronger than you were?
   Anne.   Good lady, 100
Make yourself mirth with your particular
    fancy,
And leave me out on't. Would I had no
    being,
If this salute my blood a jot; it faints me
To think what follows. 104
The Queen is comfortless, and we forgetful
In our long absence. Pray, do not deliver
What here y' have heard to her.
   Old L.   What do you think me?
                  [*Exeunt.*

SCENE IV. *London. A hall in Blackfriars.*

Trumpets, sennet, and cornets. Enter two
Vergers, *with short silver wands; next*
them, two Scribes, *in the habit of doctors;*
after them, the ARCHBISHOP OF CANTER-
BURY *alone; after him, the* BISHOPS OF
LINCOLN, ELY, ROCHESTER, *and* SAINT
ASAPH; *next them, with some small*
distance, follows a Gentleman *bearing the*
purse, with the great seal, and a Cardinal's
hat; then two Priests, *bearing each a*
silver cross; then a Gentleman Usher
bareheaded, accompanied with a Sergeant-
at-Arms *bearing a silver mace; then two*
Gentlemen *bearing two great silver pillars;*
after them, side by side, the two Cardinals,
WOLSEY *and* CAMPEIUS; *two* Noblemen
with the sword and mace. Then enter the
KING *and* QUEEN *and their* Trains. *The*
King *takes place under the cloth of state;*
the two Cardinals sit under him as judges.
The Queen takes place some distance from

the King. The Bishops place themselves on each side the court, in manner of a consistory; below them the Scribes. The Lords sit next the Bishops. The rest of the Attendants stand in convenient order about the stage.

Wol. Whilst our commission from Rome is read,
Let silence be commanded.
King.   What's the need?
It hath already publicly been read,
And on all sides th' authority allow'd;
You may then spare that time.
Wol.   Be't so; proceed. 5
Scribe. Say 'Henry King of England, come into the court'.
Crier. Henry King of England, &c.
King. Here.
Scribe. Say 'Katharine Queen of England, come into the court'.   11
Crier. Katharine Queen of England, &c.
[*The Queen makes no answer, rises out of her chair, goes about the court, comes to the King, and kneels at his feet; then speaks.*
Q. Kath. Sir, I desire you do me right and justice,
And to bestow your pity on me; for
I am a most poor woman and a stranger, 15
Born out of your dominions, having here
No judge indifferent, nor no more assurance
Of equal friendship and proceeding. Alas, sir,
In what have I offended you? What cause
Hath my behaviour given to your displeasure   20
That thus you should proceed to put me off
And take your good grace from me? Heaven witness,
I have been to you a true and humble wife,
At all times to your will conformable,
Ever in fear to kindle your dislike,   25
Yea, subject to your countenance—glad or sorry
As I saw it inclin'd. When was the hour
I ever contradicted your desire
Or made it not mine too? Or which of your friends   29
Have I not strove to love, although I knew
He were mine enemy? What friend of mine
That had to him deriv'd your anger did I
Continue in my liking? Nay, gave notice
He was from thence discharg'd? Sir, call to mind
That I have been your wife in this obedience   35
Upward of twenty years, and have been blest
With many children by you. If, in the course
And process of this time, you can report,

And prove it too against mine honour, aught,
My bond to wedlock or my love and duty,   40
Against your sacred person, in God's name,
Turn me away and let the foul'st contempt
Shut door upon me, and so give me up
To the sharp'st kind of justice. Please you, sir,
The King, your father, was reputed for 45
A prince most prudent, of an excellent
And unmatch'd wit and judgment; Ferdinand,
My father, King of Spain, was reckon'd one
The wisest prince that there had reign'd by many
A year before. It is not to be question'd 50
That they had gather'd a wise council to them
Of every realm, that did debate this business,
Who deem'd our marriage lawful. Wherefore I humbly
Beseech you, sir, to spare me till I may
Be by my friends in Spain advis'd, whose counsel   55
I will implore. If not, i' th' name of God,
Your pleasure be fulfill'd!
Wol.   You have here, lady,
And of your choice, these reverend fathers—men
Of singular integrity and learning,
Yea, the elect o' th' land, who are assembled   60
To plead your cause. It shall be therefore bootless
That longer you desire the court, as well
For your own quiet as to rectify
What is unsettled in the King.
Cam.   His Grace
Hath spoken well and justly; therefore, madam,   65
It's fit this royal session do proceed
And that, without delay, their arguments
Be now produc'd and heard.
Q. Kath.   Lord Cardinal,
To you I speak.
Wol.   Your pleasure, madam?
Q. Kath.   Sir,
I am about to weep; but, thinking that 70
We are a queen, or long have dream'd so, certain
The daughter of a king, my drops of tears
I'll turn to sparks of fire.
Wol.   Be patient yet.
Q. Kath. I will, when you are humble; nay, before,
Or God will punish me. I do believe, 75
Induc'd by potent circumstances, that
You are mine enemy, and make my challenge
You shall not be my judge; for it is you
Have blown this coal betwixt my lord and me—

Which God's dew quench! Therefore I say
    again,   80
I utterly abhor, yea, from my soul
Refuse you for my judge, whom yet once
    more
I hold my most malicious foe and think not
At all a friend to truth.
    Wol.   I do profess   84
You speak not like yourself, who ever yet
Have stood to charity and display'd th'
    effects
Of disposition gentle and of wisdom
O'ertopping woman's pow'r. Madam, you
    do me wrong :
I have no spleen against you, nor injustice
For you or any ; how far I have proceeded,
Or how far further shall, is warranted   91
By a commission from the Consistory,
Yea, the whole Consistory of Rome. You
    charge me
That I have blown this coal : I do deny it.
The King is present ; if it be known to him
That I gainsay my deed, how may he
    wound,   96
And worthily, my falsehood ! Yea, as much
As you have done my truth. If he know
That I am free of your report, he knows
I am not of your wrong. Therefore in him
It lies to cure me, and the cure is to   101
Remove these thoughts from you ; the
    which before
His Highness shall speak in, I do beseech
You, gracious madam, to unthink your
    speaking
And to say so no more.
    Q. Kath.   My lord, my lord,   105
I am a simple woman, much too weak
T' oppose your cunning. Y'are meek and
    humble-mouth'd ;
You sign your place and calling, in full
    seeming,
With meekness and humility ; but your
    heart
Is cramm'd with arrogancy, spleen, and
    pride.   110
You have, by fortune and his Highness'
    favours,
Gone slightly o'er low steps, and now are
    mounted
Where pow'rs are your retainers, and your
    words,
Domestics to you, serve your will as't please
Yourself pronounce their office. I must tell
    you   115
You tender more your person's honour
    than
Your high profession spiritual ; that again
I do refuse you for my judge and here,
Before you all, appeal unto the Pope,   119
To bring my whole cause 'fore his Holiness
And to be judg'd by him. [*She curtsies to the
    King, and offers to depart.*
    Cam.   The Queen is obstinate,
Stubborn to justice, apt to accuse it, and

Disdainful to be tried by't ; 'tis not well.
She's going away.
    King. Call her again.   125
    Crier. Katharine Queen of England, come
into the court.
    Gent. Usher. Madam, you are call'd back.
    Q. Kath. What need you note it ? Pray
        you keep your way ;
When you are call'd, return. Now the Lord
        help!
They vex me past my patience. Pray you
        pass on.   130
I will not tarry ; no, nor ever more
Upon this business my appearance make
In any of their courts. [*Exeunt Queen and
        her Attendants.*
    King.   Go thy ways, Kate.
That man i' th' world who shall report he
        has   134
A better wife, let him in nought be trusted
For speaking false in that. Thou art, alone—
If thy rare qualities, sweet gentleness,
Thy meekness saint-like, wife-like govern-
        ment,
Obeying in commanding, and thy parts
Sovereign and pious else, could speak thee
        out—   140
The queen of earthly queens. She's noble
        born ;
And like her true nobility she has
Carried herself towards me.
    Wol.   Most gracious sir,
In humblest manner I require your High-
        ness
That it shall please you to declare in
        hearing   145
Of all these ears—for where I am robb'd
        and bound,
There must I be unloos'd, although not
        there
At once and fully satisfied—whether ever I
Did broach this business to your Highness,
        or   149
Laid any scruple in your way which might
Induce you to the question on't, or ever
Have to you, but with thanks to God for
        such
A royal lady, spake one the least word that
        might   153
Be to the prejudice of her present state,
Or touch of her good person ?
    King.   My Lord Cardinal,
I do excuse you ; yea, upon mine honour,
I free you from't. You are not to be taught
That you have many enemies that know
        not
Why they are so, but, like to village curs,
Bark when their fellows do. By some of
        these   160
The Queen is put in anger. Y'are excus'd.
But will you be more justified ? You
        ever
Have wish'd the sleeping of this business ;
        never desir'd

It to be stirr'd; but oft have hind'red, oft,
The passages made toward it. On my
    honour,   165
I speak my good Lord Cardinal to this
    point,
And thus far clear him. Now, what mov'd
    me to't,
I will be bold with time and your attention.
Then mark th' inducement. Thus it came—
    give heed to't:
My conscience first receiv'd a tenderness,
Scruple, and prick, on certain speeches
    utter'd   171
By th' Bishop of Bayonne, then French
    ambassador,
Who had been hither sent on the debating
A marriage 'twixt the Duke of Orleans and
Our daughter Mary. I' th' progress of this
    business,   175
Ere a determinate resolution, he—
I mean the Bishop—did require a respite
Wherein he might the King his lord
    advertise
Whether our daughter were legitimate,
Respecting this our marriage with the
    dowager,   180
Sometimes our brother's wife. This respite
    shook
The bosom of my conscience, enter'd me,
Yea, with a splitting power, and made to
    tremble
The region of my breast, which forc'd such
    way   184
That many maz'd considerings did throng
And press'd in with this caution. First,
    methought
I stood not in the smile of heaven, who had
Commanded nature that my lady's womb,
If it conceiv'd a male child by me, should
Do no more offices of life to't than   190
The grave does to the dead; for her male
    issue
Or died where they were made, or shortly
    after
This world had air'd them. Hence I took
    a thought
This was a judgment on me, that my king-
    dom,
Well worthy the best heir o' th' world,
    should not   195
Be gladded in't by me. Then follows that
I weigh'd the danger which my realms
    stood in
By this my issue's fail, and that gave to me
Many a groaning throe. Thus hulling in
The wild sea of my conscience, I did steer
Toward this remedy, whereupon we are   201
Now present here together; that's to say
I meant to rectify my conscience, which
I then did feel full sick, and yet not well,
By all the reverend fathers of the land   205
And doctors learn'd. First, I began in
    private

With you, my Lord of Lincoln; you
    remember
How under my oppression I did reek,
When I first mov'd you.
    Lin.   Very well, my liege.
    King. I have spoke long; be pleas'd
    yourself to say   210
How far you satisfied me.
    Lin.   So please your Highness,
The question did at first so stagger me—
Bearing a state of mighty moment in't
And consequence of dread—that I com-
    mitted
The daring'st counsel which I had to doubt,
And did entreat your Highness to this
    course   216
Which you are running here.
    King.   I then mov'd you,
My Lord of Canterbury, and got your leave
To make this present summons. Un-
    solicited
I left no reverend person in this court,   220
But by particular consent proceeded
Under your hands and seals; therefore,
    go on,
For no dislike i' th' world against the
    person
Of the good Queen, but the sharp thorny
    points   224
Of my alleged reasons, drives this forward.
Prove but our marriage lawful, by my life
And kingly dignity, we are contented
To wear our mortal state to come with her,
Katharine our queen, before the primest
    creature
That's paragon'd o' th' world.
    Cam.   So please your Highness,
The Queen being absent, 'tis a needful
    fitness   231
That we adjourn this court till further day;
Meanwhile must be an earnest motion
Made to the Queen to call back her appeal
She intends unto his Holiness.
    King [*Aside*]   I may perceive   235
These cardinals trifle with me. I abhor
This dilatory sloth and tricks of Rome.
My learn'd and well-beloved servant,
    Cranmer,
Prithee return. With thy approach I know
My comfort comes along.—Break up the
    court;   240
I say, set on.
    [*Exeunt in manner as they enter'd.*

ACT THREE

Scene I. *London. The Queen's apartments.*

Enter the Queen *and her* Women, *as at
    work.*

    Q. Kath. Take thy lute, wench. My soul
    grows sad with troubles;
Sing and disperse 'em, if thou canst. Leave
    working.

SONG.

Orpheus with his lute made trees,
And the mountain tops that freeze,
   Bow themselves when he did sing ;   5
To his music plants and flowers
Ever sprung, as sun and showers
   There had made a lasting spring.

Every thing that heard him play,
Even the billows of the sea,   10
   Hung their heads and then lay by.
In sweet music is such art,
Killing care and grief of heart
   Fall asleep or hearing die.

Enter a Gentleman.

Q. Kath. How now ?   15
Gent. An't please your Grace, the two
   great Cardinals
Wait in the presence.
Q. Kath.   Would they speak with me ?
Gent. They will'd me say so, madam.
Q. Kath.   Pray their Graces
To come near. [*Exit Gentleman*] What can
   be their business
With me, a poor weak woman, fall'n from
   favour ?   20
I do not like their coming. Now I think on't,
They should be good men, their affairs as
   righteous ;
But all hoods make not monks.

Enter the two Cardinals, WOLSEY *and*
   CAMPEIUS.

Wol. Peace to your Highness !
Q. Kath. Your Graces find me here part
   of a housewife ;
I would be all, against the worst may
   happen.   25
What are your pleasures with me, reverend
   lords ?
Wol. May it please you, noble madam, to
   withdraw
Into your private chamber, we shall give
   you
The full cause of our coming.
Q. Kath.   Speak it here ;
There's nothing I have done yet, o' my
   conscience,   30
Deserves a corner. Would all other women
Could speak this with as free a soul as I do !
My lords, I care not—so much I am happy
Above a number—if my actions
Were tried by ev'ry tongue, ev'ry eye saw
   'em,   35
Envy and base opinion set against 'em,
I know my life so even. If your business
Seek me out, and that way I am wife in,
Out with it boldly ; truth loves open
   dealing.   39
Wol. Tanta est erga te mentis integritas,
regina serenissima—
Q. Kath. O, good my lord, no Latin !
I am not such a truant since my coming,

As not to know the language I have liv'd in;
A strange tongue makes my cause more
   strange, suspicious ;   45
Pray speak in English. Here are some will
   thank you,
If you speak truth, for their poor mistress'
   sake ;
Believe me, she has had much wrong. Lord
   Cardinal,
The willing'st sin I ever yet committed
May be absolv'd in English.
Wol.   Noble lady,   50
I am sorry my integrity should breed,
And service to his Majesty and you,
So deep suspicion, where all faith was
   meant.
We come not by the way of accusation
To taint that honour every good tongue
   blesses,   55
Nor to betray you any way to sorrow—
You have too much, good lady ; but to
   know
How you stand minded in the weighty
   difference
Between the King and you, and to deliver,
Like free and honest men, our just opinions
And comforts to your cause.
Cam.   Most honour'd madam,
My Lord of York, out of his noble nature,
Zeal and obedience he still bore your Grace,
Forgetting, like a good man, your late
   censure
Both of his truth and him—which was too
   far—   65
Offers, as I do, in a sign of peace,
His service and his counsel.
Q. Kath. [*Aside*]   To betray me.—
My lords, I thank you both for your good
   wills ;
Ye speak like honest men—pray God ye
   prove so !
But how to make ye suddenly an answer,   70
In such a point of weight, so near mine
   honour,
More near my life, I fear, with my weak wit,
And to such men of gravity and learning,
In truth I know not. I was set at work
Among my maids, full little, God knows,
   looking   75
Either for such men or such business.
For her sake that I have been—for I feel
The last fit of my greatness—good your
   Graces,
Let me have time and counsel for my cause.
Alas, I am a woman, friendless, hopeless !
Wol. Madam, you wrong the King's love
   with these fears ;   81
Your hopes and friends are infinite.
Q. Kath.   In England
But little for my profit ; can you think,
   lords,
That any Englishman dare give me counsel?
Or be a known friend, 'gainst his Highness'
   pleasure—

Though he be grown so desperate to be
　　honest—　　　　　　　　　　　　　86
And live a subject ? Nay, forsooth, my
　　friends,
They that must weigh out my afflictions,
They that my trust must grow to, live not
　　here ;
They are, as all my other comforts, far
　　hence,　　　　　　　　　　　　　90
In mine own country, lords.
　　Cam.　　　　　　　I would your Grace
Would leave your griefs, and take my
　　counsel.
　　Q. Kath.　　　　　　　How, sir ?
　　Cam. Put your main cause into the King's
　　protection ;
He's loving and most gracious. 'Twill be
　　much
Both for your honour better and your
　　cause ;　　　　　　　　　　　　　95
For if the trial of the law o'ertake ye
You'll part away disgrac'd.
　　Wol.　　　　　　He tells you rightly.
　　Q. Kath. Ye tell me what ye wish for
　　both—my ruin.
Is this your Christian counsel ? Out upon
　　ye !　　　　　　　　　　　　　　　99
Heaven is above all yet : there sits a Judge
That no king can corrupt.
　　Cam.　　　　Your rage mistakes us.
　　Q. Kath. The more shame for ye ; holy
　　men I thought ye,
Upon my soul, two reverend cardinal
　　virtues ;
But cardinal sins and hollow hearts I fear
　　ye,
Mend 'em, for shame, my lords. Is this
　　your comfort ?　　　　　　　　　105
The cordial that ye bring a wretched lady—
A woman lost among ye, laugh'd at,
　　scorn'd ?
I will not wish ye half my miseries :
I have more charity ; but say I warn'd ye.
Take heed, for heaven's sake take heed, lest
　　at once　　　　　　　　　　　　110
The burden of my sorrows fall upon ye.
　　Wol. Madam, this is a mere distraction ;
You turn the good we offer into envy.
　　Q. Kath. Ye turn me into nothing. Woe
　　upon ye,
And all such false professors ! Would you
　　have me—　　　　　　　　　　115
If you have any justice, any pity,
If ye be any thing but churchmen's habits—
Put my sick cause into his hands that hates
　　me ?
Alas ! has banish'd me his bed already,
His love too long ago ! I am old, my lords,
And all the fellowship I hold now with him
Is only my obedience. What can happen
To me above this wretchedness ? All your
　　studies
Make me a curse like this.
　　Cam.　　　　Your fears are worse.

　　Q. Kath. Have I liv'd thus long—let me
　　speak myself,　　　　　　　　　125
Since virtue finds no friends—a wife, a true
　　one ?
A woman, I dare say without vain-glory,
Never yet branded with suspicion ?
Have I with all my full affections
Still met the King, lov'd him next heav'n,
　　obey'd him,　　　　　　　　　130
Been, out of fondness, superstitious to him,
Almost forgot my prayers to content him,
And am I thus rewarded ? 'Tis not well,
　　lords.
Bring me a constant woman to her husband,
One that ne'er dream'd a joy beyond his
　　pleasure,　　　　　　　　　　135
And to that woman, when she has done
　　most,
Yet will I add an honour—a great patience.
　　Wol. Madam, you wander from the good
　　we aim at.
　　Q. Kath. My lord, I dare not make myself
　　so guilty,
To give up willingly that noble title　140
Your master wed me to : nothing but death
Shall e'er divorce my dignities.
　　Wol.　　　　　　　Pray hear me.
　　Q. Kath. Would I had never trod this
　　English earth,
Or felt the flatteries that grow upon it !
Ye have angels' faces, but heaven knows
　　your hearts.　　　　　　　　　145
What will become of me now, wretched
　　lady ?
I am the most unhappy woman living.
[*To her Women*] Alas, poor wenches, where
　　are now your fortunes ?
Shipwreck'd upon a kingdom, where no
　　pity,
No friends, no hope ; no kindred weep for
　　me ;　　　　　　　　　　　　150
Almost no grave allow'd me. Like the lily,
That once was mistress of the field, and
　　flourish'd,
I'll hang my head and perish.
　　Wol.　　　　　　　If your Grace
Could but be brought to know our ends are
　　honest,
You'd feel more comfort. Why should we,
　　good lady,　　　　　　　　　155
Upon what cause, wrong you ? Alas, our
　　places,
The way of our profession is against it ;
We are to cure such sorrows, not to sow 'em.
For goodness' sake, consider what you do ;
How you may hurt yourself, ay, utterly　160
Grow from the King's acquaintance, by this
　　carriage.
The hearts of princes kiss obedience,
So much they love it ; but to stubborn
　　spirits
They swell and grow as terrible as storms.
I know you have a gentle, noble temper,　165
A soul as even as a calm. Pray think us

Those we profess, peace-makers, friends,
   and servants.
  Cam. Madam, you'll find it so. You
   wrong your virtues
With these weak women's fears. A noble
   spirit,
As yours was put into you, ever casts 170
Such doubts as false coin from it. The King
   loves you ;
Beware you lose it not. For us, if you please
To trust us in your business, we are ready
To use our utmost studies in your service.
  Q. Kath. Do what ye will, my lords ; and
   pray forgive me 175
If I have us'd myself unmannerly ;
You know I am a woman, lacking wit
To make a seemly answer to such persons.
Pray do my service to his Majesty ;
He has my heart yet, and shall have my
   prayers 180
While I shall have my life. Come, reverend
   fathers,
Bestow your counsels on me ; she now begs
That little thought, when she set footing
   here,
She should have bought her dignities so
   dear.   [*Exeunt.*

SCENE II. *London. The palace.*

Enter the DUKE OF NORFOLK, *the* DUKE OF
SUFFOLK, *the* EARL OF SURREY, *and the*
Lord Chamberlain.

  Nor. If you will now unite in your
   complaints
And force them with a constancy, the
   Cardinal
Cannot stand under them : if you omit
The offer of this time, I cannot promise
But that you shall sustain moe new
   disgraces 5
With these you bear already.
  Sur.   I am joyful
To meet the least occasion that may give
   me
Remembrance of my father-in-law, the
   Duke, 8
To be reveng'd on him.
  Suf.   Which of the peers
Have uncontemn'd gone by him, or at least
Strangely neglected ? When did he regard
The stamp of nobleness in any person
Out of himself ?
  Cham.   My lords, you speak your plea-
   sures.
What he deserves of you and me I know ;
What we can do to him—though now the
   time 15
Gives way to us—I much fear. If you
   cannot
Bar his access to th' King, never attempt
Anything on him ; for he hath a witchcraft
Over the King in's tongue.
  Nor.   O, fear him not !

His spell in that is out ; the King hath
   found 20
Matter against him that for ever mars
The honey of his language. No, he's
   settled,
Not to come off, in his displeasure.
  Sur.   Sir,
I should be glad to hear such news as this
Once every hour.
  Nor.   Believe it, this is true : 25
In the divorce his contrary proceedings
Are all unfolded ; wherein he appears
As I would wish mine enemy.
  Sur.   How came
His practices to light ?
  Suf.   Most strangely
  Sur.   O, how, how ?
  Suf. The Cardinal's letters to the Pope
   miscarried, 30
And came to th' eye o' th' King ; wherein
   was read
How that the Cardinal did entreat his
   Holiness
To stay the judgment o' th' divorce ; for if
It did take place, ' I do ' quoth he ' perceive
My king is tangled in affection to 35
A creature of the Queen's, Lady Anne
   Bullen '.
  Sur. Has the King this ?
  Suf.   Believe it.
  Sur.   Will this work ?
  Cham. The King in this perceives him
   how he coasts
And hedges his own way. But in this point
All his tricks founder, and he brings his
   physic 40
After his patient's death : the King already
Hath married the fair lady.
  Sur.   Would he had !
  Suf. May you be happy in your wish, my
   lord !
For. I profess, you have it.
  Sur.   Now, all my joy
Trace the conjunction !
  Suf.   My amen to't !
  Nor.   All men's ! 45
  Suf. There's order given for her corona-
   tion ;
Marry, this is yet but young, and may be
   left
To some ears unrecounted. But, my lords,
She is a gallant creature, and complete
In mind and feature. I persuade me from
   her 50
Will fall some blessing to this land, which
   shall
In it be memoriz'd.
  Sur.   But will the King
Digest this letter of the Cardinal's ?
The Lord forbid !
  Nor.   Marry, amen !
  Suf.   No, no ;
There be moe wasps that buzz about his
   nose 55

Will make this sting the sooner. Cardinal
    Campeius
Is stol'n away to Rome; hath ta'en no
    leave;
Has left the cause o' th' King unhandled, and
Is posted, as the agent of our Cardinal,
To second all his plot. I do assure you   60
The King cried 'Ha!' at this.
    Cham.   Now, God incense him,
And let him cry 'Ha!' louder!
    Nor.   But, my lord,
When returns Cranmer?
    Suf. He is return'd, in his opinions;
    which
Have satisfied the King for his divorce,   65
Together with all famous colleges
Almost in Christendom. Shortly, I believe,
His second marriage shall be publish'd, and
Her coronation. Katharine no more   69
Shall be call'd queen, but princess dowager
And widow to Prince Arthur.
    Nor.   This same Cranmer's
A worthy fellow, and hath ta'en much pain
In the King's business.
    Suf.   He has; and we shall see him
For it an archbishop.
    Nor.   So I hear.
    Suf.   'Tis so.

     Enter WOLSEY *and* CROMWELL.

The Cardinal!
    Nor. Observe, observe, he's moody.
    Wol. The packet, Cromwell,   76
Gave't you the King?
    Crom. To his own hand, in's bedchamber.
    Wol. Look'd he o' th' inside of the paper?
    Crom.   Presently
He did unseal them; and the first he
    view'd,
He did it with a serious mind; a heed   80
Was in his contenance. You he bade
Attend him here this morning.
    Wol.   Is he ready
To come abroad?
    Crom.   I think by this he is.
    Wol. Leave me awhile. [*Exit Cromwell.*
[*Aside*] It shall be to the Duchess of
    Alençon,   85
The French King's sister; he shall marry her.
Anne Bullen! No, I'll no Anne Bullens for
    him;
There's more in't than fair visage. Bullen!
No, we'll no Bullens. Speedily I wish
To hear from Rome. The Marchioness of
    Pembroke!   90
    Nor. He's discontented.
    Suf.   May be he hears the King
Does whet his anger to him.
    Sur.   Sharp enough,
Lord, for thy justice!
    Wol. [*Aside*] The late Queen's gentle-
    woman, a knight's daughter,
To be her mistress' mistress! The Queen's
    queen!   95

This candle burns not clear. 'Tis I must
    snuff it;
Then out it goes. What though I know her
    virtuous
And well deserving? Yet I know her for
A spleeny Lutheran; and not wholesome
    to
Our cause that she should lie i' th' bosom of
Our hard-rul'd King. Again, there is
    sprung up   101
An heretic, an arch one, Cranmer; one
Hath crawl'd into the favour of the King,
And is his oracle.
    Nor.   He is vex'd at something.

  Enter the KING, *reading of a schedule, and*
          LOVELL.

    Sur. I would 'twere something that would
    fret the string,   105
The master-cord on's heart!
    Suf.   The King, the King!
    King. What piles of wealth hath he
    accumulated
To his own portion! And what expense by
    th' hour
Seems to flow from him! How, i' th' name
    of thrift,
Does he rake this together?—Now, my
    lords,   110
Saw you the Cardinal?
    Nor.   My lord, we have
Stood here observing him. Some strange
    commotion
Is in his brain: he bites his lip and starts,
Stops on a sudden, looks upon the ground,
Then lays his finger on his temple; straight
Springs out into fast gait; then stops again,
Strikes his breast hard; and anon he casts
His eye against the moon. In most strange
    postures   118
We have seen him set himself.
    King.   It may well be
There is a mutiny in's mind. This morning
Papers of state he sent me to peruse,
As I requir'd; and wot you what I found
There—on my conscience, put unwittingly?
Forsooth, an inventory, thus importing 124
The several parcels of his plate, his treasure,
Rich stuffs, and ornaments of household;
    which
I find at such proud rate that it outspeaks
Possession of a subject.
    Nor.   It's heaven's will;
Some spirit put this paper in the packet
To bless your eye withal.
    King.   If we did think 130
His contemplation were above the earth
And fix'd on spiritual object, he should still
Dwell in his musings; but I am afraid
His thinkings are below the moon, not
    worth
His serious considering.
    [*The King takes his seat and whispers
    Lovell, who goes to the Cardinal.*

Wol. Heaven forgive me !   135
Ever God bless your Highness !
King.   Good, my lord,
You are full of heavenly stuff, and bear the
          inventory
Of your best graces in your mind ; the
          which
You were now running o'er. You have
          scarce time   139
To steal from spiritual leisure a brief span
To keep your earthly audit ; sure, in that
I deem you an ill husband, and am glad
To have you therein my companion.
Wol.   Sir,
For holy offices I have a time ; a time   144
To think upon the part of business which
I bear i' th' state ; and nature does require
Her times of preservation, which perforce
I, her frail son, amongst my brethren
          mortal,
Must give my tendance to.
King.   You have said well.
Wol. And ever may your Highness yoke
          together,   150
As I will lend you cause, my doing well
With my well saying !
King.   'Tis well said again ;
And 'tis a kind of good deed to say well ;
And yet words are no deeds. My father
          lov'd you :
He said he did ; and with his deed did
          crown   155
His word upon you. Since I had my office
I have kept you next my heart ; have not
          alone
Employ'd you where high profits might
          come home,
But par'd my present havings to bestow
My bounties upon you.
Wol. [*Aside*] What should this mean ? 160
Sur. [*Aside*] The Lord increase this
          business !
King.   Have I not made you
The prime man of the state ? I pray you
          tell me
If what I now pronounce you have found
          true ;
And, if you may confess it, say withal
If you are bound to us or no. What say
          you ?   165
Wol. My sovereign, I confess your royal
          graces,
Show'r'd on me daily, have been more than
          could
My studied purposes requite ; which went
Beyond all man's endeavours.   My en-
          deavours,
Have ever come too short of my desires, 170
Yet fil'd with my abilities ; mine own ends
Have been mine so that evermore they
          pointed
To th' good of your most sacred person and
The profit of the state. For your great
          graces

Heap'd upon me, poor undeserver, I   175
Can nothing render but allegiant thanks ;
My pray'rs to heaven for you ; my loyalty,
Which ever has and ever shall be growing,
Till death, that winter, kill it.
King.   Fairly answer'd !
A loyal and obedient subject is   180
Therein illustrated ; the honour of it
Does pay the act of it, as, i' th' contrary,
The foulness is the punishment. I presume
That, as my hand has open'd bounty to you,
My heart dropp'd love, my pow'r rain'd
          honour, more   185
On you than any, so your hand and heart,
Your brain, and every function of your
          power,
Should, notwithstanding that your bond of
          duty,
As 'twere in love's particular, be more
To me, your friend, than any.
Wol.   I do profess   190
That for your Highness' good I ever
          labour'd
More than mine own ; that am, have, and
          will be—
Though all the world should crack their
          duty to you,
And throw it from their soul ; though
          perils did
Abound as thick as thought could make
          'em, and   195
Appear in forms more horrid—yet my duty,
As doth a rock against the chiding flood,
Should the approach of this wild river
          break,
And stand unshaken yours.
King.   'Tis nobly spoken.
Take notice, lords, he has a loyal breast, 200
For you have seen him open 't. Read o'er
          this ;   [*Giving him papers.*
And after, this ; and then to breakfast
          with
What appetite you have. [*Exit the King,
          frowning upon the Cardinal ; the
          Nobles throng after him, smiling
          and whispering.*
Wol.   What should this mean ?
What sudden anger's this ? How have I
          reap'd it ?
He parted frowning from me, as if ruin   205
Leap'd from his eyes ; so looks the chafed
          lion
Upon the daring huntsman that has gall'd
          him—
Then makes him nothing. I must read this
          paper ;
I fear, the story of his anger. 'Tis so ;
This paper has undone me. 'Tis th'
          account   210
Of all that world of wealth I have drawn
          together
For mine own ends ; indeed, to gain the
          popedom,
And fee my friends in Rome. O negligence,

Fit for a fool to fall by ! What cross devil
Made me put this main secret in the packet
I sent the King ? Is there no way to cure
    this ?   216
No new device to beat this from his brains ?
I know 'twill stir him strongly ; yet I know
A way, if it take right, in spite of fortune,
Will bring me off again. What's this ? ' To
    th' Pope.'   220
The letter, as I live, with all the business
I writ to's Holiness. Nay then, farewell !
I have touch'd the highest point of all my
    greatness,
And from that full meridian of my glory
I haste now to my setting. I shall fall   225
Like a bright exhalation in the evening,
And no man see me more.

Re-enter to Wolsey the DUKES OF NORFOLK
and SUFFOLK, *the* EARL OF SURREY, *and
the* Lord Chamberlain.

Nor. Hear the King's pleasure, Cardinal,
    who commands you
To render up the great seal presently
Into our hands, and to confine yourself 230
To Asher House, my Lord of Winchester's,
Till you hear further from his Highness.
Wol.   Stay :
Where's your commission, lords ? Words
    cannot carry
Authority so weighty.
Suf.   Who dare cross 'em,
Bearing the King's will from his mouth
    expressly ?   235
Wol. Till I find more than will or words
    to do it—
I mean your malice—know, officious lords,
I dare and must deny it. Now I feel
Of what coarse metal ye are moulded—
    envy ;
How eagerly ye follow my disgraces, 240
As if it fed ye ; and how sleek and wanton
Ye appear in every thing may bring my
    ruin !
Follow your envious courses, men of malice;
You have Christian warrant for 'em, and
    no doubt   244
In time will find their fit rewards. That seal
You ask with such a violence, the King—
Mine and your master—with his own hand
    gave me ;
Bade me enjoy it, with the place and
    honours,
During my life ; and, to confirm his good-
    ness,
Tied it by letters-patents. Now, who'll take
    it ?   250
Sur. The King, that gave it.
Wol.   It must be himself then.
Sur. Thou art a proud traitor, priest.
Wol.   Proud lord, thou liest.
Within these forty hours Surrey durst
    better
Have burnt that tongue than said so.

Sur.   Thy ambition,
Thou scarlet sin, robb'd this bewailing land
Of noble Buckingham, my father-in-law.
The heads of all thy brother cardinals, 257
With thee and all thy best parts bound
    together,
Weigh'd not a hair of his. Plague of your
    policy !
You sent me deputy for Ireland ; 260
Far from his succour, from the King, from
    all
That might have mercy on the fault thou
    gav'st him ;
Whilst your great goodness, out of holy
    pity,
Absolv'd him with an axe.
Wol.   This, and all else 264
This talking lord can lay upon my credit,
I answer is most false. The Duke by law
Found his deserts ; how innocent I was
From any private malice in his end,
His noble jury and foul cause can witness.
If I lov'd many words, lord, I should tell
    you   270
You have as little honesty as honour,
That in the way of loyalty and truth
Toward the King, my ever royal master,
Dare mate a sounder man than Surrey can
    be
And all that love his follies.
Sur.   By my soul, 275
Your long coat, priest, protects you ; thou
    shouldst feel
My sword i' th' life-blood of thee else. My
    lords,
Can ye endure to hear this arrogance ?
And from this fellow ? If we live thus
    tamely,
To be thus jaded by a piece of scarlet, 280
Farewell nobility ! Let his Grace go
    forward
And dare us with his cap like larks.
Wol.   All goodness
Is poison to thy stomach.
Sur.   Yes, that goodness
Of gleaning all the land's wealth into one,
Into your own hands, Cardinal, by extor-
    tion ;   285
The goodness of your intercepted packets
You writ to th' Pope against the King ;
    your goodness,
Since you provoke me, shall be most
    notorious.
My Lord of Norfolk, as you are truly noble,
As you respect the common good, the
    state
Of our despis'd nobility, our issues, 291
Whom, if he live, will scarce be gentlemen—
Produce the grand sum of his sins, the
    articles
Collected from his life. I'll startle you
Worse than the sacring bell, when the
    brown wench   295
Lay kissing in your arms, Lord Cardinal.

Wol. How much, methinks, I could despise this man,
But that I am bound in charity against it!
  Nor. Those articles, my lord, are in the King's hand;
But, thus much, they are foul ones.
  Wol.   So much fairer 300
And spotless shall mine innocence arise,
When the King knows my truth.
  Sur.   This cannot save you.
I thank my memory I yet remember
Some of these articles; and out they shall.
Now, if you can blush and cry guilty, Cardinal, 305
You'll show a little honesty.
  Wol.   Speak on, sir;
I dare your worst objections. If I blush,
It is to see a nobleman want manners.
  Sur. I had rather want those than my head. Have at you!
First, that without the King's assent or knowledge 310
You wrought to be a legate; by which power
You maim'd the jurisdiction of all bishops.
  Nor. Then, that in all you writ to Rome, or else
To foreign princes, ' Ego et Rex meus'
Was still inscrib'd; in which you brought the King 315
To be your servant.
  Suf. Then, that without the knowledge
Either of King or Council, when you went
Ambassador to the Emperor, you made bold
To carry into Flanders the great seal. 319
  Sur. Item, you sent a large commission
To Gregory de Cassado, to conclude,
Without the King's will or the state's allowance,
A league between his Highness and Ferrara.
  Suf. That out of mere ambition you have caus'd
Your holy hat to be stamp'd on the King's coin. 325
  Sur. Then, that you have sent innumerable substance,
By what means got I leave to your own conscience,
To furnish Rome and to prepare the ways 328
You have for dignities, to the mere undoing
Of all the kingdom. Many more there are,
Which, since they are of you, and odious,
I will not taint my mouth with.
  Cham.   O my lord,
Press not a falling man too far! 'Tis virtue.
His faults lie open to the laws; let them,
Not you, correct him. My heart weeps to see him 335
So little of his great self.
  Sur.   I forgive him.
  Suf. Lord Cardinal, the King's further pleasure is—

Because all those things you have done of late,
By your power legatine within this kingdom,
Fall into th' compass of a præmunire— 340
That therefore such a writ be sued against you:
To forfeit all your goods, lands, tenements,
Chattels, and whatsoever, and to be
Out of the King's protection. This is my charge.
  Nor. And so we'll leave you to your meditations 345
How to live better. For your stubborn answer
About the giving back the great seal to us,
The King shall know it, and, no doubt, shall thank you.
So fare you well, my little good Lord Cardinal. [*Exeunt all but Wolsey.*
  Wol. So farewell to the little good you bear me. 350
Farewell, a long farewell, to all my greatness!
This is the state of man: to-day he puts forth
The tender leaves of hopes; to-morrow blossoms
And bears his blushing honours thick upon him; 354
The third day comes a frost, a killing frost,
And when he thinks, good easy man, full surely
His greatness is a-ripening, nips his root,
And then he falls, as I do. I have ventur'd,
Like little wanton boys that swim on bladders,
This many summers in a sea of glory; 360
But far beyond my depth. My high-blown pride
At length broke under me, and now has left me,
Weary and old with service, to the mercy
Of a rude stream, that must for ever hide me.
Vain pomp and glory of this world, I hate ye; 365
I feel my heart new open'd. O, how wretched
Is that poor man that hangs on princes' favours!
There is betwixt that smile we would aspire to,
That sweet aspect of princes, and their ruin
More pangs and fears than wars or women have; 370
And when he falls, he falls like Lucifer,
Never to hope again.

Enter CROMWELL, *standing amazed.*

                    Why, how now, Cromwell!
  Crom. I have no power to speak, sir.
  Wol.   What, amaz'd
At my misfortunes? Can thy spirit wonder

A great man should decline ? Nay, an you
   weep,   375
I am fall'n indeed.
   Crom.   How does your Grace ?
   Wol.   Why, well ;
Never so truly happy, my good Cromwell.
I know myself now, and I feel within me
A peace above all earthly dignities,
A still and quiet conscience. The King has
   cur'd me,   380
I humbly thank his Grace ; and from these
   shoulders,
These ruin'd pillars, out of pity, taken
A load would sink a navy—too much
   honour.
O, 'tis a burden, Cromwell, 'tis a burden
Too heavy for a man that hopes for heaven !
   Crom. I am glad your Grace has made
      that right use of it.   386
   Wol. I hope I have. I am able now,
   methinks,
Out of a fortitude of soul I feel,
To endure more miseries and greater far
Than my weak-hearted enemies dare offer.
What news abroad ?
   Crom.   The heaviest and the worst
Is your displeasure with the King.
   Wol.   God bless him !
   Crom. The next is that Sir Thomas More
      is chosen   393
Lord Chancellor in your place.
   Wol.   That's somewhat sudden.
But he's a learned man. May he continue
Long in his Highness' favour, and do justice
For truth's sake and his conscience ; that
   his bones,
When he has run his course and sleeps in
   blessings,
May have a tomb of orphans' tears wept on
   him !
What more ?
   Crom. That Cranmer is return'd with
      welcome,   400
Install'd Lord Archbishop of Canterbury.
   Wol. That's news indeed.
   Crom.   Last, that the Lady Anne,
Whom the King hath in secrecy long
   married,
This day was view'd in open as his queen,
Going to chapel ; and the voice is now 405
Only about her coronation.
   Wol. There was the weight that pull'd me
      down. O Cromwell,
The King has gone beyond me. All my
   glories
In that one woman I have lost for ever.
No sun shall ever usher forth mine honours,
Or gild again the noble troops that waited
Upon my smiles. Go get thee from me,
   Cromwell ;
I am a poor fall'n man, unworthy now
To be thy lord and master. Seek the King ;
That sun, I pray, may never set ! I have
   told him   415

What and how true thou art. He will
   advance thee ;
Some little memory of me will stir him—
I know his noble nature—not to let
Thy hopeful service perish too. Good
   Cromwell,
Neglect him not ; make use now, and
   provide   420
For thine own future safety.
   Crom.   O my lord,
Must I then leave you ? Must I needs forgo
So good, so noble, and so true a master ?
Bear witness, all that have not hearts of
   iron,
With what a sorrow Cromwell leaves his
   lord.   425
The King shall have my service ; but my
   prayers
For ever and for ever shall be yours.
   Wol. Cromwell, I did not think to shed a
   tear
In all my miseries ; but thou hast forc'd me,
Out of thy honest truth, to play the woman.
Let's dry our eyes ; and thus far hear me,
   Cromwell,   431
And when I am forgotten, as I shall be,
And sleep in dull cold marble, where no
   mention
Of me more must be heard of, say I taught
   thee—
Say Wolsey, that once trod the ways of
   glory,   435
And sounded all the depths and shoals of
   honour,
Found thee a way, out of his wreck, to
   rise in—
A sure and safe one, though thy master
   miss'd it.
Mark but my fall and that that ruin'd me.
Cromwell, I charge thee, fling away
   ambition :   440
By that sin fell the angels. How can man
   then,
The image of his Maker, hope to win by it ?
Love thyself last ; cherish those hearts that
   hate thee ;
Corruption wins not more than honesty.
Still in thy right hand carry gentle peace
To silence envious tongues. Be just, and
   fear not ;   446
Let all the ends thou aim'st at be thy
   country's,
Thy God's, and truth's ; then, if thou fall'st,
   O Cromwell,
Thou fall'st a blessed martyr !
Serve the King, and—prithee lead me
   in.   450
There take an inventory of all I have
To the last penny ; 'tis the King's. My
   robe,
And my integrity to heaven, is all
I dare now call mine own. O Cromwell,
   Cromwell !   454
Had I but serv'd my God with half the zeal

I serv'd my King, he would not in mine age
Have left me naked to mine enemies.
   Crom. Good sir, have patience.
   Wol.   So I have. Farewell
The hopes of court! My hopes in heaven
   do dwell.   [*Exeunt.*

ACT FOUR

Scene I. *A street in Westminster.*

Enter two Gentlemen, *meeting one another.*

   1 *Gent.* Y'are well met once again.
   2 *Gent.*   So are you.
   1 *Gent.* You come to take your stand
   here, and behold
The Lady Anne pass from her coronation?
   2 *Gent.* 'Tis all my business. At our last
   encounter
The Duke of Buckingham came from his
   trial.   5
   1 *Gent.* 'Tis very true. But that time
   offer'd sorrow;
This, general joy.
   2 *Gent.*   'Tis well. The citizens,
I am sure, have shown at full their royal
   minds—
As, let 'em have their rights, they are ever
   forward—
In celebration of this day with shows,   10
Pageants, and sights of honour.
   1 *Gent.*   Never greater,
Nor, I'll assure you, better taken, sir.
   2 *Gent.* May I be bold to ask what that
   contains,
That paper in your hand?
   1 *Gent.*   Yes; 'tis the list   15
Of those that claim their offices this day,
By custom of the coronation.
The Duke of Suffolk is the first, and claims
To be High Steward; next, the Duke of
   Norfolk,
He to be Earl Marshal. You may read the
   rest.
   2 *Gent.* I thank you, sir; had I not
   known those customs,   20
I should have been beholding to your paper.
But, I beseech you, what's become of
   Katharine,
The Princess Dowager? How goes her
   business?
   1 *Gent.* That I can tell you too. The
   Archbishop
Of Canterbury, accompanied with other   25
Learned and reverend fathers of his order,
Held a late court at Dunstable, six miles off
From Ampthill, where the Princess lay;
   to which
She was often cited by them, but appear'd
   not.
And, to be short, for not appearance and   30
The King's late scruple, by the main assent
Of all these learned men, she was divorc'd,
And the late marriage made of none effect;

Since which she was removed to Kimbolton,
Where she remains now sick.
   2 *Gent.*   Alas, good lady! 35
                            [*Trumpets.*
The trumpets sound. Stand close, the
   Queen is coming.   [*Hautboys.*

   The Order of the Coronation.

1. *A lively flourish of trumpets.*
2. *Then two* Judges.
3. Lord Chancellor, *with purse and mace
   before him.*
4. Choristers *singing.*   [*Music.*
5. Mayor of London, *bearing the mace.
   Then Garter, in his coat of arms,
   and on his head he wore a gilt
   copper crown.*
6. Marquis Dorset, *bearing a sceptre of
   gold, on his head a demi-coronal of
   gold. With him, the* Earl of
   Surrey, *bearing the rod of silver
   with the dove, crowned with an earl's
   coronet. Collars of Esses.*
7. Duke of Suffolk, *in his robe of estate,
   his coronet on his head, bearing a
   long white wand, as High Steward.
   With him, the* Duke of Norfolk,
   with the rod of marshalship, a
   coronet on his head. Collars of
   Esses.*
8. *A canopy borne by four of the* Cinque-
   ports; *under it the* Queen *in her
   robe; in her hair richly adorned
   with pearl, crowned. On each side
   her, the* Bishops of London *and*
   Winchester.
9. *The old* Duchess of Norfolk, *in a
   coronal of gold, wrought with flowers,
   bearing the Queen's train.*
10. *Certain* Ladies *or* Countesses, *with plain
   circlets of gold without flowers.*

   [*Exeunt, first passing over the stage in
   order and state, and then a great
   flourish of trumpets.*

   2 *Gent.* A royal train, believe me. These
   I know.
Who's that that bears the sceptre?
   1 *Gent.*   Marquis Dorset;
And that the Earl of Surrey, with the rod.
   2 *Gent.* A bold brave gentleman. That
   should be
The Duke of Suffolk?
   1 *Gent.* 'Tis the same—High Steward.   41
   2 *Gent.* And that my Lord of Norfolk?
   1 *Gent.*   Yes.
   2 *Gent.* [*Looking on the Queen*] Heaven
   bless thee!
Thou hast the sweetest face I ever look'd
   on.
Sir, as I have a soul, she is an angel;
Our king has all the Indies in his arms,   45
And more and richer, when he strains that
   lady;

I cannot blame his conscience.

1 Gent.   They that bear
The cloth of honour over her are four barons
Of the Cinque-ports.

2 Gent. Those men are happy; and so are
all are near her.   50
I take it she that carries up the train
Is that old noble lady, Duchess of Norfolk.

1 Gent. It is; and all the rest are countesses.

2 Gent. Their coronets say so. These are
stars indeed,
And sometimes falling ones.

1 Gent.   No more of that.   55

[*Exit Procession, with a great flourish
of trumpets.*

Enter a third Gentleman.

God save you, sir! Where have you been
broiling?

3 Gent. Among the crowd i' th' Abbey,
where a finger
Could not be wedg'd in more; I am stifled
With the mere rankness of their joy.

2 Gent.   You saw
The ceremony?

3 Gent.   That I did.

1 Gent.   How was it?   60

3 Gent. Well worth the seeing.

2 Gent.   Good sir, speak it to us.

3 Gent. As well as I am able. The rich stream
Of lords and ladies, having brought the Queen
To a prepar'd place in the choir, fell off
A distance from her, while her Grace sat down   65
To rest awhile, some half an hour or so,
In a rich chair of state, opposing freely
The beauty of her person to the people.
Believe me, sir, she is the goodliest woman
That ever lay by man; which when the people   70
Had the full view of, such a noise arose
As the shrouds make at sea in a stiff tempest,
As loud, and to as many tunes; hats, cloaks—
Doublets, I think—flew up, and had their faces
Been loose, this day they had been lost. Such joy   75
I never saw before. Great-bellied women,
That had not half a week to go, like rams
In the old time of war, would shake the press,
And make 'em reel before 'em. No man living
Could say 'This is my wife' there, all were woven   80
So strangely in one piece.

2 Gent.   But what follow'd?

3 Gent. At length her Grace rose, and
with modest paces
Came to the altar, where she kneel'd, and saintlike
Cast her fair eyes to heaven, and pray'd devoutly,
Then rose again, and bow'd her to the people;   85
When by the Archbishop of Canterbury
She had all the royal makings of a queen:
As holy oil, Edward Confessor's crown,
The rod, and bird of peace, and all such emblems
Laid nobly on her; which perform'd, the choir,   90
With all the choicest music of the kingdom,
Together sung 'Te Deum'. So she parted,
And with the same full state pac'd back again
To York Place, where the feast is held.

1 Gent.   Sir,
You must no more call it York Place: that's past;   95
For since the Cardinal fell that title's lost.
'Tis now the King's, and call'd Whitehall.

3 Gent.   I know it;
But 'tis so lately alter'd that the old name
Is fresh about me.

2 Gent.   What two reverend bishops
Were those that went on each side of the Queen?   100

3 Gent. Stokesly and Gardiner: the one
of Winchester,
Newly preferr'd from the King's secretary;
The other, London.

2 Gent.   He of Winchester
Is held no great good lover of the Archbishop's,
The virtuous Cranmer.

3 Gent.   All the land knows that;   105
However, yet there is no great breach. When it comes,
Cranmer will find a friend will not shrink from him.

2 Gent. Who may that be, I pray you?

3 Gent.   Thomas Cromwell,
A man in much esteem with th' King, and truly
A worthy friend. The King has made him Master   110
O' th' Jewel House,
And one, already, of the Privy Council.

2 Gent. He will deserve more.

3 Gent.   Yes, without all doubt.
Come, gentlemen, ye shall go my way, which
Is to th' court, and there ye shall be my guests:
Something I can command. As I walk thither,   116
I'll tell ye more.

Both.   You may command us, sir.

[*Exeunt.*

SCENE II. *Kimbolton.*

Enter KATHARINE, *Dowager, sick ; led
between* GRIFFITH, *her Gentleman Usher,
and* PATIENCE, *her woman.*

Grif. How does your Grace ?
Kath.   O Griffith, sick to death !
My legs like loaden branches bow to th'
    earth,
Willing to leave their burden.   Reach a
    chair.
So—now, methinks, I feel a little ease.
Didst thou not tell me, Griffith, as thou
    led'st me,
That the great child of honour, Cardinal   5
    Wolsey,
Was dead ?
Grif.   Yes, madam ; but I think your
    Grace,
Out of the pain you suffer'd, gave no ear
    to't.
Kath. Prithee, good Griffith, tell me how
    he died.
If well, he stepp'd before me, happily,   10
For my example.
Grif.   Well, the voice goes, madam ;
For after the stout Earl Northumberland
Arrested him at York and brought him
    forward,
As a man sorely tainted, to his answer,
He fell sick suddenly, and grew so ill   15
He could not sit his mule.
Kath.   Alas, poor man !
Grif. At last, with easy roads, he came to
    Leicester,
Lodg'd in the abbey ; where the reverend
    abbot,
With all his covent, honourably receiv'd
    him ;
To whom he gave these words : ' O father
    Abbot,
An old man, broken with the storms of   20
    state,
Is come to lay his weary bones among ye ;
Give him a little earth for charity ! '
So went to bed ; where eagerly his sickness
Pursu'd him still.   And three nights after
    this,
About the hour of eight—which he himself   25
Foretold should be his last—full of repent-
    ance,
Continual meditations, tears, and sorrows,
He gave his honours to the world again,
His blessed part to heaven, and slept in
    peace.
Kath. So may he rest ; his faults lie   30
    gently on him !
Yet thus far, Griffith, give me leave to
    speak him,
And yet with charity.   He was a man
Of an unbounded stomach, ever ranking
Himself with princes ;   one that, by
    suggestion,   35

Tied all the kingdom.   Simony was fair
    play ;
His own opinion was his law.   I' th' presence
He would say untruths, and be ever double
Both in his words and meaning.   He was
    never,
But where he meant to ruin, pitiful.   40
His promises were, as he then was, mighty ;
But his performance, as he is now, nothing.
Of his own body he was ill, and gave
The clergy ill example.
Grif.   Noble madam,
Men's evil manners live in brass : their
    virtues
We write in water.   May it please your   45
    Highness
To hear me speak his good now ?
Kath.   Yes, good Griffith ;
I were malicious else.
Grif.   This Cardinal,
Though from an humble stock, undoubtedly
Was fashion'd to much honour from his
    cradle.
He was a scholar, and a ripe and good one ;   50
Exceeding wise, fair-spoken, and persuad-
    ing ;
Lofty and sour to them that lov'd him not,
But to those men that sought him sweet
    as summer.
And though he were unsatisfied in getting—   54
Which was a sin—yet in bestowing, madam—
He was most princely : ever witness for him
Those twins of learning that he rais'd in
    you,
Ipswich and Oxford !   One of which fell
    with him,
Unwilling to outlive the good that did it ;   59
The other, though unfinish'd, yet so
    famous,
So excellent in art, and still so rising,
That Christendom shall ever speak his
    virtue.
His overthrow heap'd happiness upon him ;
For then, and not till then, he felt himself,
And found the blessedness of being little.   66
And, to add greater honours to his age
Than man could give him, he died fearing
    God.
Kath. After my death I wish no other
    herald,
No other speaker of my living actions,   70
To keep mine honour from corruption,
But such an honest chronicler as Griffith.
Whom I most hated living, thou hast made
    me,
With thy religious truth and modesty,
Now in his ashes honour.   Peace be with
    him !   75
Patience, be near me still, and set me
    lower :
I have not long to trouble thee.   Good
    Griffith,
Cause the musicians play me that sad note
I nam'd my knell, whilst I sit meditating

On that celestial harmony I go to.　　80
　　　　　　[*Sad and solemn music.*
Grif. She is asleep. Good wench, let's sit
　　down quiet,
For fear we wake her.　Softly, gentle
　　Patience.

The Vision.

*Enter, solemnly tripping one after another,
six Personages clad in white robes, wearing
on their heads garlands of bays, and golden
vizards on their faces ; branches of bays or
palm in their hands. They first congee unto
her, then dance ; and, at certain changes, the
first two hold a spare garland over her head,
at which the other four make reverent curls es.
Then the two that held the garland deliver the
same to the other next two, who observe the
same order in their changes, and holding the
garland over her head ; which done, they
deliver the same garland to the last two, who
likewise observe the same order ; at which, as
it were by inspiration, she makes in her sleep
signs of rejoicing, and holdeth up her hands
to heaven. And so in their dancing vanish,
carrying the garland with them. The music
continues.*

Kath. Spirits of peace, where are ye ?
　　Are ye all gone ?
And leave me here in wretchedness behind
　　ye ?
Grif. Madam, we are here.
Kath.　　　　　　It is not you I call for.
Saw ye none enter since I slept ?
Grif.　　　　　　None, madam.　86
Kath. No ?　Saw you not, even now, a
　　blessed troop
Invite me to a banquet ; whose bright
　　faces
Cast thousand beams upon me, like the
　　sun ?
They promis'd me eternal happiness,　90
And brought me garlands, Griffith, which
　　I feel
I am not worthy yet to wear.　I shall,
　　assuredly.
Grif. I am most joyful, madam, such
　　good dreams
Possess your fancy.
Kath.　　　　　　Bid the music leave,
They are harsh and heavy to me.
　　　　　　　　　　[*Music ceases.*
Pat.　　　　　　Do you note　95
How much her Grace is alter'd on the
　　sudden ?
How long her face is drawn !　How pale she
　　looks,
And of an earthy cold !　Mark her eyes.
Grif. She is going, wench.　Pray, pray.
Pat.　　　　　　Heaven comfort her !

Enter a Messenger.

Mess. An't like your Grace—

Kath.　　　　　　You are a saucy fellow.
Deserve we no more reverence ?
Grif.　　　　　　You are to blame,　101
Knowing she will not lose her wonted
　　greatness,
To use so rude behaviour.　Go to, kneel.
Mess. I humbly do entreat your High-
　　ness' pardon ;
My haste made me unmannerly.　There is
　　staying　　　　　　105
A gentleman, sent from the King, to see
　　you.
Kath. Admit him entrance, Griffith ; but
　　this fellow
Let me ne'er see again.　[*Exit Messenger.*

Enter Lord Capucius.

　　　　　　　　If my sight fail not,
You should be Lord Ambassador from the
　　Emperor,　　　　　　109
My royal nephew, and your name Capucius.
Cap. Madam, the same—your servant.
Kath.　　　　　　O, my Lord,
The times and titles now are alter'd
　　strangely
With me since first you knew me.　But, I
　　pray you,
What is your pleasure with me ?
Cap.　　　　　　Noble lady,
First, mine own service to your Grace ; the
　　next,　　　　　　115
The King's request that I would visit
　　you,
Who grieves much for your weakness, and
　　by me
Sends you his princely commendations
And heartily entreats you take good
　　comfort.
Kath. O my good lord, that comfort
　　comes too late,
'Tis like a pardon after execution :　121
That gentle physic, given in time, had cur'd
　　me ;
But now I am past all comforts here, but
　　prayers.
How does his Highness ?
Cap.　　　　　Madam, in good health.
Kath. So may he ever do !　and ever
　　flourish　　　　　　125
When I shall dwell with worms, and my
　　poor name
Banish'd the kingdom !　Patience, is that
　　letter
I caus'd you write yet sent away ?
Pat.　　　　　　No, madam.
　　　　　　[*Giving it to Katharine.*
Kath. Sir, I most humbly pray you to
　　deliver
This to my lord the King.
Cap.　　　　　Most willing, madam.　130
Kath. In which I have commended to his
　　goodness
The model of our chaste loves, his young
　　daughter—

The dews of heaven fall thick in blessings on her !—
Beseeching him to give her virtuous breeding—   134
She is young, and of a noble modest nature;
I hope she will deserve well—and a little
To love her for her mother's sake, that lov'd him,
Heaven knows how dearly. My next poor petition
Is that his noble Grace would have some pity
Upon my wretched women that so long 140
Have follow'd both my fortunes faithfully ;
Of which there is not one, I dare avow—
And now I should not lie—but will deserve,
For virtue and true beauty of the soul,
For honesty and decent carriage,   145
A right good husband, let him be a noble ;
And sure those men are happy that shall have 'em.
The last is for my men—they are the poorest,
But poverty could never draw 'em from me—
That they may have their wages duly paid 'em,   150
And something over to remember me by.
If heaven had pleas'd to have given me longer life
And able means, we had not parted thus.
These are the whole contents ; and, good my lord,   154
By that you love the dearest in this world,
As you wish Christian peace to souls departed,
Stand these poor people's friend, and urge the King
To do me this last right.
    Cap.   By heaven, I will,
Or let me lose the fashion of a man !
    Kath. I thank you, honest lord. Remember me   160
In all humility unto his Highness ;
Say his long trouble now is passing
Out of this world. Tell him in death I bless'd him,
For so I will. Mine eyes grow dim. Farewell,   164
My lord. Griffith, farewell. Nay, Patience,
You must not leave me yet. I must to bed ;
Call in more women. When I am dead, good wench,
Let me be us'd with honour ; strew me over
With maiden flowers, that all the world may know
I was a chaste wife to my grave. Embalm me,   170
Then lay me forth ; although unqueen'd, yet like
A queen, and daughter to a king, inter me.
I can no more. [*Exeunt, leading Katharine.*

ACT FIVE

SCENE I. *London. A gallery in the palace.*

Enter GARDINER, BISHOP OF WINCHESTER, *a Page with a torch before him, met by* SIR THOMAS LOVELL.

    Gar. It's one o'clock, boy, is't not ?
    Boy.   It hath struck.
    Gar. These should be hours for necessities,
Not for delights ; times to repair our nature
With comforting repose, and not for us
To waste these times. Good hour of night, Sir Thomas !
Whither so late ?
    Lov. Came you from the King, my lord ? 6
    Gar. I did, Sir Thomas, and left him at primero
With the Duke of Suffolk.
    Lov.   I must to him too,
Before he go to bed. I'll take my leave.
    Gar. Not yet, Sir Thomas Lovell. What's the matter ?   10
It seems you are in haste. An if there be
No great offence belongs to't, give your friend
Some touch of your late business. Affairs that walk—
As they say spirits do—at midnight, have
In them a wilder nature than the business
That seeks despatch by day.
    Lov.   My lord, I love you ;
And durst commend a secret to your ear 17
Much weightier than this work. The Queen's in labour,
They say in great extremity, and fear'd
She'll with the labour end.
    Gar.   The fruit she goes with 20
I pray for heartily, that it may find
Good time, and live ; but for the stock, Sir Thomas,
I wish it grubb'd up now.
    Lov.   Methinks I could
Cry thee amen ; and yet my conscience says   24
She's a good creature, and, sweet lady, does
Deserve our better wishes.
    Gar.   But, sir, sir—
Hear me, Sir Thomas. Y'are a gentleman
Of mine own way ; I know you wise, religious ;
And, let me tell you, it will ne'er be well—
'Twill not, Sir Thomas Lovell, take't of me—   30
Till Cranmer, Cromwell, her two hands, and she,
Sleep in their graves.
    Lov.   Now, sir, you speak of two
The most remark'd i' th' kingdom. As for Cromwell,
Beside that of the Jewel House, is made Master
O' th' Rolls, and the King's secretary ; further, sir,   35

Stands in the gap and trade of moe prefer-
    ments,
With which the time will load him. Th'
    Archbishop
Is the King's hand and tongue, and who
    dare speak
One syllable against him?
   Gar.   Yes, yes, Sir Thomas,
There are that dare; and I myself have
    ventur'd   40
To speak my mind of him; and indeed this
    day,
Sir—I may tell it you—I think I have
Incens'd the lords o' th' Council, that
    he is—
For so I know he is, they know he is—
A most arch heretic, a pestilence   45
That does infect the land; with which they
    moved
Have broken with the King, who hath so
    far
Given ear to our complaint—of his great
    grace
And princely care, foreseeing those fell
    mischiefs
Our reasons laid before him—hath com-
    manded   50
To-morrow morning to the Council board
He be convented. He's a rank weed, Sir
    Thomas,
And we must root him out. From your
    affairs
I hinder you too long—good night, Sir
    Thomas.   54
   Lov. Many good nights, my lord; I rest
    your servant.
             [Exeunt Gardiner and Page.

Enter the KING *and the* DUKE OF SUFFOLK.

   King. Charles, I will play no more to-
    night;
My mind's not on't; you are too hard for
    me.
   Suf. Sir, I did never win of you before.
   King. But little, Charles;
Nor shall not, when my fancy's on my play.
Now, Lovell, from the Queen what is the
    news?   61
   Lov. I could not personally deliver to her
What you commanded me, but by her
    woman
I sent your message; who return'd her
    thanks
In the great'st humbleness, and desir'd
    your Highness
Most heartily to pray for her.
   King.   What say'st thou, ha? 66
To pray for her? What, is she crying out?
   Lov. So said her woman; and that her
    suff'rance made
Almost each pang a death.
   King.   Alas, good lady!
   Suf. God safely quit her of her burden,
    and   70

With gentle travail, to the gladding of
Your Highness with an heir!
   King.   'Tis midnight, Charles;
Prithee to bed; and in thy pray'rs re-
    member
Th' estate of my poor queen. Leave me
    alone,
For I must think of that which company 75
Will not be friendly to.
   Suf.   I wish your Highness
A quiet night, and my good mistress will
Remember in my prayers.
   King.   Charles, good night.
                      [Exit Suffolk.

   Enter SIR ANTHONY DENNY.

Well, sir, what follows?
   Den. Sir, I have brought my lord the
    Archbishop,   80
As you commanded me.
   King.   Ha! Canterbury?
   Den. Ay, my good lord.
   King. 'Tis true. Where is he, Denny?
   Den. He attends your Highness' pleasure.
   King.   Bring him to us.
                      [Exit Denny.
   Lov. [*Aside*] This is about that which the
    bishop spake.
I am happily come hither.   85

   Re-enter DENNY, *with* CRANMER.

   King. Avoid the gallery.
                 [Lovell seems to stay.
        Ha! I have said. Be gone.
What!   *[Exeunt Lovell and Denny.*
   Cran. [*Aside*] I am fearful—wherefore
    frowns he thus?
'Tis his aspect of terror. All's not well.
   King. How now, my lord? You do
    desire to know
Wherefore I sent for you.
   Cran. [*Kneeling*] It is my duty 90
T' attend your Highness' pleasure.
   King.   Pray you, arise,
My good and gracious Lord of Canterbury.
Come, you and I must walk a turn together;
I have news to tell you; come, come, give
    me your hand.   94
Ah, my good lord, I grieve at what I speak,
And am right sorry to repeat what follows.
I have, and most unwillingly, of late
Heard many grievous—I do say, my lord,
Grievous—complaints of you; which, being
    consider'd,
Have mov'd us and our Council that you
    shall   100
This morning come before us; where I
    know
You cannot with such freedom purge
    yourself
But that, till further trial in those charges
Which will require your answer, you must
    take   104
Your patience to you and be well contented

To make your house our Tow'r. You a
brother of us,
It fits we thus proceed, or else no witness
Would come against you.
　　Cran.　　I humbly thank your Highness,
And am right glad to catch this good
occasion
Most throughly to be winnowed where my
chaff　　110
And corn shall fly asunder; for I know
There's none stands under more calumnious
tongues
Than I myself, poor man.
　　King.　　Stand up, good Canterbury;
Thy truth and thy integrity is rooted
In us, thy friend. Give me thy hand, stand
up;　　115
Prithee let's walk. Now, by my holidame,
What manner of man are you? My lord,
I look'd
You would have given me your petition
that
I should have ta'en some pains to bring
together
Yourself and your accusers, and to have
heard you　　120
Without indurance further.
　　Cran.　　Most dread liege,
The good I stand on is my truth and
honesty;
If they shall fail, I with mine enemies
Will triumph o'er my person; which I
weigh not,
Being of those virtues vacant. I fear
nothing　　125
What can be said against me.
　　King.　　Know you not
How your state stands i' th' world, with
the whole world?
Your enemies are many, and not small; their
practices
Must bear the same proportion; and not
ever
The justice and the truth o' th' question
carries　　130
The due o' th' verdict with it; at what ease
Might corrupt minds procure knaves as
corrupt
To swear against you? Such things have
been done.
You are potently oppos'd, and with a
malice　　134
Of as great size. Ween you of better luck,
I mean in perjur'd witness, than your
Master,
Whose minister you are, whiles here He
liv'd
Upon this naughty earth? Go to, go to;
You take a precipice for no leap of danger,
And woo your own destruction.
　　Cran.　　God and your Majesty
Protect mine innocence, or I fall into　　141
The trap is laid for me!
　　King.　　Be of good cheer;

They shall no more prevail than we give
way to.
Keep comfort to you, and this morning see
You do appear before them; if they shall
chance,　　145
In charging you with matters, to commit
you,
The best persuasions to the contrary
Fail not to use, and with what vehemency
Th' occasion shall instruct you. If en-
treaties
Will render you no remedy, this ring　　150
Deliver them, and your appeal to us
There make before them. Look, the good
man weeps!
He's honest, on mine honour. God's blest
Mother!
I swear he is true-hearted, and a soul　　154
None better in my kingdom. Get you gone,
And do as I have bid you. 　[*Exit Cranmer.*
He has strangled his language in his tears.

Enter Old Lady.

　　Gent. [*Within*] Come back; what mean
you?
　　Old L. I'll not come back; the tidings
that I bring
Will make my boldness manners. Now,
good angels
Fly o'er thy royal head, and shade thy
person　　160
Under their blessed wings!
　　King.　　Now, by thy looks
I guess thy message. Is the Queen de-
liver'd?
Say ay, and of a boy.
　　Old L.　　Ay, ay, my liege;
And of a lovely boy. The God of Heaven
Both now and ever bless her! 'Tis a girl,
Promises boys hereafter. Sir, your queen
Desires your visitation, and to be　　167
Acquainted with this stranger; 'tis as like you
As cherry is to cherry.
　　King.　　Lovell!

Enter Lovell.

　　Lov.　　Sir?
　　King. Give her an hundred marks. I'll
to the Queen. 　[*Exit.*
　　Old L. An hundred marks? By this light,
I'll ha' more!　　171
An ordinary groom is for such payment.
I will have more, or scold it out of him.
Said I for this the girl was like to him? I'll
Have more, or else unsay't; and now, while
'tis hot,
I'll put it to the issue. 　[*Exeunt.*

Scene II. *Lobby before the Council Chamber.*

Enter Cranmer, Archbishop of Canterbury.

　　Cran. I hope I am not too late; and yet
the gentleman

That was sent to me from the Council pray'd me
To make great haste. All fast? What means this? Ho!
Who waits there? Sure you know me?

Enter Keeper.

Keep.   Yes, my lord;
But yet I cannot help you.   5
Cran. Why?
Keep. Your Grace must wait till you be call'd for.

Enter DOCTOR BUTTS.

Cran.   So.
Butts. [*Aside*] This is a piece of malice. I am glad
I came this way so happily; the King
Shall understand it presently.   [*Exit.*
Cran [*Aside*]   'Tis Butts,   10
The King's physician; as he pass'd along,
How earnestly he cast his eyes upon me!
Pray heaven he sound not my disgrace!
    For certain,
This is of purpose laid by some that hate me—   14
God turn their hearts! I never sought their malice—
To quench mine honour; they would shame to make me
Wait else at door, a fellow councillor,
'Mong boys, grooms, and lackeys. But their pleasures   18
Must be fulfill'd, and I attend with patience.

Enter the KING *and* BUTTS *at a window above.*

Butts. I'll show your Grace the strangest sight—
King.   What's that, Butts?
Butts. I think your Highness saw this many a day.
King. Body a me, where is it?
Butts.   There my lord:
The high promotion of his Grace of Canterbury;
Who holds his state at door, 'mongst pursuivants,
Pages, and footboys.
King.   Ha, 'tis he indeed.   25
Is this the honour they do one another?
'Tis well there's one above 'em yet. I had thought
They had parted so much honesty among 'em—
At least good manners—as not thus to suffer   29
A man of his place, and so near our favour,
To dance attendance on their lordships' pleasures,
And at the door too, like a post with packets.
By holy Mary, Butts, there's knavery!

Let 'em alone, and draw the curtain close;
We shall hear more anon.   [*Exeunt.*

SCENE III. *The Council Chamber.*

A Council table brought in, with chairs and stools, and placed under the state. Enter Lord Chancellor, places himself at the upper end of the table on the left hand, a seat being left void above him, as for Canterbury's seat. DUKE OF SUFFOLK, DUKE OF NORFOLK, SURREY, LORD CHAMBERLAIN, GARDINER, *seat themselves in order on each side;* CROMWELL *at lower end, as secretary.* Keeper *at the door.*

Chan. Speak to the business, master secretary;
Why are we met in council?
Crom.   Please your honours,
The chief cause concerns his Grace of Canterbury.
Gar. Has he had knowledge of it?
Crom.   Yes.
Nor.   Who waits there?
Keep. Without, my noble lords?
Gar.   Yes.
Keep.   My Lord Archbishop;
And has done half an hour, to know your pleasures.   6
Chan. Let him come in.
Keep.   Your Grace may enter now.

CRANMER *approaches the Council table.*

Chan. My good Lord Archbishop, I am very sorry
To sit here at this present, and behold
That chair stand empty; but we all are men,   10
In our own natures frail and capable
Of our flesh; few are angels; out of which frailty
And want of wisdom, you, that best should teach us,
Have misdemean'd yourself, and not a little,
Toward the King first, then his laws, in filling   15
The whole realm by your teaching and your chaplains—
For so we are inform'd—with new opinions,
Divers and dangerous; which are heresies,
And, not reform'd, may prove pernicious.
Gar. Which reformation must be sudden too,   20
My noble lords; for those that tame wild horses
Pace 'em not in their hands to make 'em gentle,
But stop their mouths with stubborn bits and spur 'em
Till they obey the manage. If we suffer,
Out of our easiness and childish pity   25
To one man's honour, this contagious sickness,

Farewell all physic; and what follows then?
Commotions, uproars, with a general taint
Of the whole state; as of late days our neighbours,
The upper Germany, can dearly witness, 30
Yet freshly pitied in our memories.

  Cran. My good lords, hitherto in all the progress
Both of my life and office, I have labour'd,
And with no little study, that my teaching
And the strong course of my authority 35
Might go one way, and safely; and the end
Was ever to do well. Nor is there living—
I speak it with a single heart, my lords—
A man that more detests, more stirs against,
Both in his private conscience and his place, 40
Defacers of a public peace than I do.
Pray heaven the King may never find a heart
With less allegiance in it! Men that make
Envy and crooked malice nourishment
Dare bite the best. I do beseech your lordships 45
That, in this case of justice, my accusers,
Be what they will, may stand forth face to face
And freely urge against me.

  Suf.   Nay, my lord,
That cannot be; you are a councillor, 49
And by that virtue no man dare accuse you.

  Gar. My lord, because we have business of more moment,
We will be short with you. 'Tis his Highness' pleasure
And our consent, for better trial of you,
From hence you be committed to the Tower;
Where, being but a private man again, 55
You shall know many dare accuse you boldly,
More than, I fear, you are provided for.

  Cran. Ah, my good Lord of Winchester, I thank you;
You are always my good friend; if your will pass,
I shall both find your lordship judge and juror, 60
You are so merciful. I see your end—
'Tis my undoing. Love and meekness, lord,
Become a churchman better than ambition;
Win straying souls with modesty again,
Cast none away. That I shall clear myself,
Lay all the weight ye can upon my patience,
I make as little doubt as you do conscience
In doing daily wrongs. I could say more,
But reverence to your calling makes me modest. 69

  Gar. My lord, my lord, you are a sectary;
That's the plain truth. Your painted gloss discovers,
To men that understand you, words and weakness.

  Crom. My Lord of Winchester, y'are a little,
By your good favour, too sharp; men so noble,
However faulty, yet should find respect 75
For what they have been; 'tis a cruelty
To load a falling man.

  Gar.   Good Master Secretary,
I cry your honour mercy; you may, worst
Of all this table, say so.

  Crom.   Why, my lord?

  Gar. Do not I know you for a favourer 80
Of this new sect? Ye are not sound.

  Crom.   Not sound?

  Gar. Not sound, I say.

  Crom. Would you were half so honest!
Men's prayers then would seek you, not their fears.

  Gar. I shall remember this bold language.

  Crom.   Do.
Remember your bold life too.

  Chan.   This is too much; 85
Forbear, for shame, my lords.

  Gar.   I have done.

  Crom.   And I.

  Chan. Then thus for you, my lord: it stands agreed,
I take it, by all voices, that forthwith
You be convey'd to th' Tower a prisoner;
There to remain till the King's further pleasure 90
Be known unto us. Are you all agreed, lords?

  All. We are.

  Cran. Is there no other way of mercy,
But I must needs to th' Tower, my lords?

  Gar.   What other
Would you expect? You are strangely troublesome.
Let some o' th' guard be ready there.

Enter the Guard.

  Cran.   For me? 95
Must I go like a traitor thither?

  Gar.   Receive him,
And see him safe i' th' Tower.

  Cran.   Stay, good my lords,
I have a little yet to say. Look there, my lords;
By virtue of that ring I take my cause 99
Out of the gripes of cruel men and give it
To a most noble judge, the King my master.

  Cham. This is the King's ring.

  Sur.   'Tis no counterfeit.

  Suf. 'Tis the right ring, by heav'n. I told ye all,
When we first put this dangerous stone a-rolling,
'Twould fall upon ourselves.

  Nor.   Do you think, my lords, 105
The King will suffer but the little finger
Of this man to be vex'd?

  Cham.   'Tis now too certain;

How much more is his life in value with
   him !
Would I were fairly out on't !
  Crom.   My mind gave me,
In seeking tales and informations   110
Against this man—whose honesty the devil
And his disciples only envy at—
Ye blew the fire that burns ye. Now have
   at ye !

Enter the KING *frowning on them ; he takes
   his seat.*

  Gar. Dread sovereign, how much are we
   bound to heaven   114
In daily thanks, that gave us such a prince ;
Not only good and wise but most religious ;
One that in all obedience makes the church
The chief aim of his honour and, to
   strengthen
That holy duty, out of dear respect,
His royal self in judgment comes to hear   120
The cause betwixt her and this great
   offender.
  King. You were ever good at sudden
   commendations,
Bishop of Winchester. But know I come
   not
To hear such flattery now, and in my
   presence   124
They are too thin and bare to hide offences.
To me you cannot reach you play the
   spaniel,
And think with wagging of your tongue to
   win me ;
But whatsoe'er thou tak'st me for, I'm sure
Thou hast a cruel nature and a bloody.
[*To* Cranmer] Good man, sit down. Now let
   me see the proudest   130
He that dares most but wag his finger at
   thee.
By all that's holy, he had better starve
Than but once think this place becomes thee
   not.
  Sur. May it please your Grace—
  King.   No, sir, it does not please me.
I had thought I had had men of some
   understanding
And wisdom of my Council ; but I find
   none.   136
Was it discretion, lords, to let this man,
This good man—few of you deserve that
   title—
This honest man, wait like a lousy footboy
At chamber door ? and one as great as you
   are ?   140
Why, what a shame was this ! Did my
   commission
Bid ye so far forget yourselves ? I gave ye
Power as he was a councillor to try him,
Not as a groom. There's some of ye, I see,
More out of malice than integrity,   145
Would try him to the utmost, had ye mean ;
Which ye shall never have while I live.
  Chan.   Thus far,

My most dread sovereign, may it like your
   Grace
To let my tongue excuse all. What was
   purpos'd   149
Concerning his imprisonment was rather—
If there be faith in men—meant for his
   trial
And fair purgation to the world, than
   malice,
I'm sure, in me.
  King. Well, well, my lords, respect him ;
Take him, and use him well, he's worthy
   of it.
I will say thus much for him : if a prince   155
May be beholding to a subject, I
Am for his love and service so to him.
Make me no more ado, but all embrace him ;
Be friends, for shame, my lords ! My Lord
   of Canterbury,   159
I have a suit which you must not deny me :
That is, a fair young maid that yet wants
   baptism ;
You must be godfather, and answer for her.
  Cran. The greatest monarch now alive
   may glory   163
In such an honour ; how may I deserve it,
That am a poor and humble subject to you?
  King. Come, come, my lord, you'd spare
   your spoons. You shall have
Two noble partners with you : the old
   Duchess of Norfolk
And Lady Marquis Dorset. Will these
   please you ?
Once more, my Lord of Winchester, I
   charge you,   170
Embrace and love this man.
  Gar.   With a true heart
And brother-love I do it.
  Cran.   And let heaven
Witness how dear I hold this confirmation.
  King. Good man, those joyful tears show
   thy true heart.
The common voice, I see, is verified   175
Of thee, which says thus : ' Do my Lord of
   Canterbury
A shrewd turn and he's your friend for
   ever '.
Come, lords, we trifle time away ; I long
To have this young one made a Christian.
As I have made ye one, lords, one remain ;
So I grow stronger, you more honour gain.
                     [*Exeunt.*

SCENE IV. *The palace yard.*

Noise and tumult within. Enter PORTER *and
   his Man.*

  Port. You'll leave your noise anon, ye
rascals. Do you take the court for Paris
garden ? Ye rude slaves, leave your gaping.
  [*Within*: Good master porter, I belong to
th' larder.
  Port. Belong to th' gallows, and be
hang'd, ye rogue ! Is this a place to roar

in ? Fetch me a dozen crab-tree staves,
and strong ones : these are but switches to
'em. I'll scratch your heads. You must be
seeing christenings ? Do you look for ale
and cakes here, you rude rascals?

Man. Pray, sir, be patient ; 'tis as much
impossible,
Unless we sweep 'em from the door with
cannons,   11
To scatter 'em as 'tis to make 'em sleep
On May-day morning ; which will never be.
We may as well push against Paul's as stir
'em.

Port. How got they in, and be hang'd ? 15

Man. Alas, I know not : how gets the
tide in ?
As much as one sound cudgel of four foot—
You see the poor remainder—could
distribute,
I made no spare, sir.

Port.   You did nothing, sir.

Man. I am not Samson, nor Sir Guy, nor
Colbrand,
To mow 'em down before me ; but if I
spar'd any   21
That had a head to hit, either young or old,
He or she, cuckold or cuckold-maker,
Let me ne'er hope to see a chine again ;
And that I would not for a cow, God save
her !   25

[*Within* : Do you hear, master porter ?

Port. I shall be with you presently, good
master puppy. Keep the door close, sirrah.

Man. What would you have me do ? 29

Port. What should you do, but knock 'em
down by th' dozens ? Is this Moorfields to
muster in ? Or have we some strange
Indian with the great tool come to court,
the women so besiege us ? Bless me, what
a fry of fornication is at door ! On my
Christian conscience, this one christening
will beget a thousand : here will be father,
godfather, and all together.   36

Man. The spoons will be the bigger, sir.
There is a fellow somewhat near the door,
he should be a brazier by his face, for, o'
my conscience, twenty of the dog-days now
reign in's nose ; all that stand about him
are under the line, they need no other
penance. That fire-drake did I hit three
times on the head, and three times was his
nose discharged against me ; he stands
there like a mortar-piece, to blow us. There
was a haberdasher's wife of small wit near
him, that rail'd upon me till her pink'd
porringer fell off her head, for kindling such
a combustion in the state. I miss'd the
meteor once, and hit that woman, who cried
out ' Clubs ! ' when I might see from far
some forty truncheoners draw to her
succour, which were the hope o' th' Strand,
where she was quartered. They fell on ; I
made good my place. At length they came
to th' broomstaff to me ; I defied 'em still ;

when suddenly a file of boys behind 'em,
loose shot, deliver'd such a show'r of
pebbles that I was fain to draw mine
honour in and let 'em win the work : the
devil was amongst 'em, I think surely.   56

Port. These are the youths that thunder
at a playhouse and fight for bitten apples ;
that no audience but the tribulation of
Tower-hill or the limbs of Limehouse, their
dear brothers, are able to endure. I have
some of 'em in Limbo Patrum, and there
they are like to dance these three days ;
besides the running banquet of two beadles
that is to come.

Enter the Lord Chamberlain.

Cham. Mercy o' me, what a multitude are
here !
They grow still too ; from all parts they
are coming,   65
As if we kept a fair here ! Where are these
porters,
These lazy knaves ? Y'have made a fine
hand, fellows.
There's a trim rabble let in : are all these
Your faithful friends o' th' suburbs ? We
shall have
Great store of room, no doubt, left for the
ladies,   70
When they pass back from the christening.

Port.   An't please your honour,
We are but men ; and what so many may
do,
Not being torn a pieces, we have done.
An army cannot rule 'em.

Cham.   As I live,
If the King blame me for't, I'll lay ye all 75
By th' heels, and suddenly ; and on your
heads
Clap round fines for neglect. Y'are lazy
knaves ;
And here ye lie baiting of bombards, when
Ye should do service. Hark ! the trumpets
sound ;   79
Th'are come already from the christening.
Go break among the press and find a way
out
To let the troop pass fairly, or I'll find
A Marshalsea shall hold ye play these two
months.

Port. Make way there for the Princess.

Man.   You great fellow,
Stand close up, or I'll make your head ache.

Port. You i' th' camlet, get up o' th' rail ;
I'll peck you o'er the pales else. [*Exeunt.*

SCENE V. *The palace.*

Enter Trumpets, *sounding* ; *then two* Aldermen, Lord Mayor, Garter, CRANMER,
DUKE OF NORFOLK, *with his marshal's
staff*, DUKE OF SUFFOLK, *two* Noblemen
*bearing great standing-bowls for the
christening gifts* ; *then four* Noblemen

bearing a canopy, under which the
DUCHESS OF NORFOLK, *godmother, bearing
the child richly habited in a mantle, &c.,
train borne by a* Lady ; *then follows the*
MARCHIONESS DORSET, *the other godmother, and* Ladies. *The troop pass once
about the stage, and Garter speaks.*

Gart. Heaven, from thy endless goodness,
send prosperous life, long and ever-happy,
to the high and mighty Princess of England,
Elizabeth !

Flourish. Enter KING *and* Guard.

Cran. [*Kneeling*] And to your royal
　　Grace and the good Queen !
My noble partners and myself thus pray : 5
All comfort, joy, in this most gracious lady,
Heaven ever laid up to make parents happy,
May hourly fall upon ye !
　　King. Thank you, good Lord Archbishop.
What is her name ?
　　Cran.　　　　　Elizabeth.
　　King.　　　　　　　Stand up, lord.
　　　　[*The King kisses the child.*
With this kiss take my blessing : God pro-
　　tect thee !　　　　　　　　　　　10
Into whose hand I give thy life.
　　Cran.　　　　　　Amen.
　　King. My noble gossips, y'have been too
　　prodigal ;
I thank ye heartily. So shall this lady,
When she has so much English.
　　Cran.　　　　Let me speak, sir,
For heaven now bids me ; and the words
　　I utter　　　　　　　　　　　　15
Let none think flattery, for they'll find 'em
　　truth.
This royal infant—heaven still move about
　　her !—
Though in her cradle, yet now promises
Upon this land a thousand thousand
　　blessings,
Which time shall bring to ripeness. She
　　shall be—　　　　　　　　　　　20
But few now living can behold that good-
　　ness—
A pattern to all princes living with her,
And all that shall succeed. Saba was never
More covetous of wisdom and fair virtue
Than this pure soul shall be. All princely
　　graces　　　　　　　　　　　　25
That mould up such a mighty piece as
　　this is,
With all the virtues that attend the good,
Shall still be doubled on her. Truth shall
　　nurse her,
Holy and heavenly thoughts still counsel
　　her ;
She shall be lov'd and fear'd. Her own
　　shall bless her :
Her foes shake like a field of beaten corn, 31
And hang their heads with sorrow. Good
　　grows with her ;

In her days every man shall eat in safety
Under his own vine what he plants, and
　　sing
The merry songs of peace to all his neigh-
　　bours.　　　　　　　　　　　　35
God shall be truly known ; and those
　　about her
From her shall read the perfect ways of
　　honour,
And by those claim their greatness, not by
　　blood.
Nor shall this peace sleep with her ; but as
　　when
The bird of wonder dies, the maiden
　　phœnix,　　　　　　　　　　　　40
Her ashes new create another heir
As great in admiration as herself,
So shall she leave her blessedness to one—
When heaven shall call her from this cloud
　　of darkness—
Who from the sacred ashes of her honour 45
Shall star-like rise, as great in fame as she
　　was,
And so stand fix'd. Peace, plenty, love,
　　truth, terror,
That were the servants to this chosen
　　infant,
Shall then be his, and like a vine grow to
　　him ;
Wherever the bright sun of heaven shall
　　shine,　　　　　　　　　　　　50
His honour and the greatness of his name
Shall be, and make new nations ; he shall
　　flourish,
And like a mountain cedar reach his
　　branches
To all the plains about him ; our children's
　　children
Shall see this and bless heaven.
　　King.　　　　　Thou speakest wonders.
　　Cran. She shall be, to the happiness of
　　England,　　　　　　　　　　　56
An aged princess ; many days shall see
　　her,
And yet no day without a deed to crown it.
Would I had known no more ! But she
　　must die—
She must, the saints must have her—yet a
　　virgin ;　　　　　　　　　　　60
A most unspotted lily shall she pass
To th' ground, and all the world shall
　　mourn her.
　　King. O Lord Archbishop,
Thou hast made me now a man ; never
　　before
This happy child did I get anything.　65
This oracle of comfort has so pleas'd me
That when I am in heaven I shall desire
To see what this child does, and praise my
　　Maker.
I thank ye all. To you, my good Lord
　　Mayor,
And you, good brethren, I am much be-
　　holding ;　　　　　　　　　　70

I have receiv'd much honour by your
    presence,
And ye shall find me thankful. Lead the
    way, lords;
Ye must all see the Queen, and she must
    thank ye,
She will be sick else. This day, no man
    think
Has business at his house; for all shall
    stay.   75
This little one shall make it holiday.
                               [*Exeunt.*

THE EPILOGUE

'Tis ten to one this play can never please
All that are here. Some come to take their
    ease

And sleep an act or two; but those, we fear,
W'have frighted with our trumpets; so,
    'tis clear,
They'll say 'tis nought; others to hear the
    city   5
Abus'd extremely, and to cry 'That's
    witty!'
Which we have not done neither; that,
    I fear,
All the expected good w'are like to hear
For this play at this time is only in   9
The merciful construction of good women;
For such a one we show'd 'em. If they
    smile
And say 'twill do, I know within a while
All the best men are ours; for 'tis ill hap
If they hold when their ladies bid 'em clap.

TROILUS AND CRESSIDA

DRAMATIS PERSONÆ

PRIAM, *King of Troy.*

HECTOR,
TROILUS,
PARIS, } *his sons.*
DEIPHOBUS,
HELENUS,

MARGARELON, *a bastard son of Priam.*

ÆNEAS,
ANTENOR, } *Trojan commanders.*

CALCHAS, *a Trojan priest, taking part with the Greeks.*

PANDARUS, *uncle to Cressida.*

AGAMEMNON, *the Greek general.*

MENELAUS, *his brother.*

ACHILLES,
AJAX, } *Greek commanders.*

ULYSSES,
NESTOR,
DIOMEDES, } *Greek commanders.*
PATROCLUS,

THERSITES, *a deformed and scurrilous Greek.*

ALEXANDER, *servant to Cressida.*
Servant *to Troilus.*
Servant *to Paris.*
Servant *to Diomedes.*

HELEN, *wife to Menelaus.*
ANDROMACHE, *wife to Hector.*
CASSANDRA, *daughter to Priam, a prophetess.*
CRESSIDA, *daughter to Calchas.*

Trojan *and* Greek Soldiers, *and* Attendants.

THE SCENE : *Troy and the Greek camp before it.*

PROLOGUE

In Troy, there lies the scene. From isles of
    Greece
The princes orgillous, their high blood
    chaf'd,
Have to the port of Athens sent their ships
Fraught with the ministers and instruments
Of cruel war. Sixty and nine that wore   5
Their crownets regal from th' Athenian bay
Put forth toward Phrygia ; and their vow
    is made
To ransack Troy, within whose strong
    immures
The ravish'd Helen, Menelaus' queen,
With wanton Paris sleeps—and that's the
    quarrel.   10
To Tenedos they come,
And the deep-drawing barks do there
    disgorge
Their war-like fraughtage. Now on Dardan
    plains
The fresh and yet unbruised Greeks do
    pitch
Their brave pavilions : Priam's six-gated
    city,   15
Dardan, and Tymbria, Helias, Chetas,
    Troien,
And Antenorides, with massy staples
And corresponsive and fulfilling bolts,
Sperr up the sons of Troy.
Now expectation, tickling skittish spirits 20
On one and other side, Troyan and Greek,
Sets all on hazard—and hither am I come
A Prologue arm'd, but not in confidence
Of author's pen or actor's voice, but suited
In like conditions as our argument,   25
To tell you, fair beholders, that our play
Leaps o'er the vaunt and firstlings of those
    broils,
Beginning in the middle ; starting thence
    away
To what may be digested in a play.
Like or find fault ; do as your pleasures
    are ;   30
Now good or bad, 'tis but the chance of war.

ACT ONE

SCENE I. *Troy. Before Priam's palace.*

Enter TROILUS *armed, and* PANDARUS.

  Tro. Call here my varlet ; I'll unarm
    again.
Why should I war without the walls of
    Troy
That find such cruel battle here within ?
Each Troyan that is master of his heart,
Let him to field ; Troilus, alas, hath
    none!
  Pan. Will this gear ne'er be mended ? 6
  Tro. The Greeks are strong, and skilful to
    their strength,
Fierce to their skill, and to their fierceness
    valiant ;
But I am weaker than a woman's tear,   9
Tamer than sleep, fonder than ignorance,
Less valiant than the virgin in the night,
And skilless as unpractis'd infancy.
  Pan. Well, I have told you enough of
this ; for my part, I'll not meddle nor make
no farther. He that will have a cake out of
the wheat must needs tarry the grinding. 16
  Tro. Have I not tarried ?

Pan. Ay, the grinding; but you must tarry the bolting.

Tro. Have I not tarried?

Pan. Ay, the bolting; but you must tarry the leavening.   21

Tro. Still have I tarried.

Pan. Ay, to the leavening; but here's yet in the word 'hereafter' the kneading, the making of the cake, the heating of the oven, and the baking; nay, you must stay the cooling too, or you may chance to burn your lips.   26

Tro. Patience herself, what goddess e'er she be,
Doth lesser blench at suff'rance than I do.
At Priam's royal table do I sit;
And when fair Cressid comes into my
      thoughts—   30
So, traitor, then she comes when she is
      thence.

Pan. Well, she look'd yesternight fairer than ever I saw her look, or any woman else.

Tro. I was about to tell thee: when my
      heart,
As wedged with a sigh, would rive in twain,
Lest Hector or my father should perceive
      me,   36
I have, as when the sun doth light a storm,
Buried this sigh in wrinkle of a smile.
But sorrow that is couch'd in seeming
      gladness
Is like that mirth fate turns to sudden
      sadness.   40

Pan. An her hair were not somewhat darker than Helen's—well, go to—there were no more comparison between the women. But, for my part, she is my kins-woman; I would not, as they term it, praise her, but I would somebody had heard her talk yesterday, as I did. I will not dispraise your sister Cassandra's wit; but—   46

Tro. O Pandarus! I tell thee, Pan-darus—
When I do tell thee there my hopes lie
      drown'd,
Reply not in how many fathoms deep
They lie indrench'd. I tell thee I am mad
In Cressid's love. Thou answer'st 'She is
      fair '—   51
Pourest in the open ulcer of my heart—
Her eyes, her hair, her cheek, her gait, her
      voice,
Handlest in thy discourse. O, that her hand,
In whose comparison all whites are ink 55
Writing their own reproach; to whose soft
      seizure
The cygnet's down is harsh, and spirit of
      sense
Hard as the palm of ploughman! This thou
      tell'st me,
As true thou tell'st me, when I say I love
      her;

But, saying thus, instead of oil and balm, 60
Thou lay'st in every gash that love hath
      given me
The knife that made it.

Pan. I speak no more than truth.

Tro. Thou dost not speak so much.   64

Pan. Faith, I'll not meddle in it. Let her be as she is: if she be fair, 'tis the better for her; an she be not, she has the mends in her own hands.   67

Tro. Good Pandarus!   How now, Pandarus!

Pan. I have had my labour for my travail, ill thought on of her and ill thought on of you; gone between and between, but small thanks for my labour.   71

Tro. What, art thou angry, Pandarus? What, with me?

Pan. Because she's kin to me, therefore she's not so fair as Helen. An she were not kin to me, she would be as fair a Friday as Helen is on Sunday. But what care I? I care not an she were a blackamoor; 'tis all one to me.   77

Tro. Say I she is not fair?

Pan. I do not care whether you do or no. She's a fool to stay behind her father. Let her to the Greeks; and so I'll tell her the next time I see her. For my part, I'll meddle nor make no more i' th' matter. 82

Tro. Pandarus!

Pan. Not I.

Tro. Sweet Pandarus!   85

Pan. Pray you, speak no more to me: I will leave all as I found it, and there an end.
                        [*Exit. Sound alarum.*

Tro. Peace, you ungracious clamours!
      Peace, rude sounds!
Fools on both sides! Helen must needs be
      fair,
When with your blood you daily paint her
      thus.   90
I cannot fight upon this argument;
It is too starv'd a subject for my sword.
But Pandarus—O gods, how do you plague
      me!
I cannot come to Cressid but by Pandar;
And he's as tetchy to be woo'd to woo 95
As she is stubborn-chaste against all suit.
Tell me, Apollo, for thy Daphne's love,
What Cressid is, what Pandar, and what
      we?
Her bed is India; there she lies, a pearl;
Between our Ilium and where she resides
Let it be call'd the wild and wand'ring
      flood;   101
Ourself the merchant, and this sailing
      Pandar
Our doubtful hope, our convoy, and our
      bark.

Alarum. Enter ÆNEAS.

Æne. How now, Prince Troilus! Where-fore not afield?

Tro. Because not there. This woman's
    answer sorts,
For womanish it is to be from thence. 106
What news, Æneas, from the field to-day ?
  Æne. That Paris is returned home, and
    hurt.
Tro. By whom, Æneas ?
  Æne.   Troilus, by Menelaus.
Tro. Let Paris bleed : 'tis but a scar to
    scorn ; 110
Paris is gor'd with Menelaus' horn.
                  [*Alarum.*
  Æne. Hark what good sport is out of
    town to-day !
Tro. Better at home, if ' would I might '
    were ' may '.
But to the sport abroad. Are you bound
    thither ? 114
  Æne. In all swift haste.
Tro.   Come, go we then together.
                  [*Exeunt.*

SCENE II. *Troy. A street.*

Enter CRESSIDA *and her man* ALEXANDER.

  Cres. Who were those went by ?
  Alex.   Queen Hecuba and Helen.
  Cres. And whither go they ?
  Alex.   Up to the eastern tower,
Whose height commands as subject all the
    vale,
To see the battle. Hector, whose patience
Is as a virtue fix'd, to-day was mov'd. 5
He chid Andromache, and struck his
    armourer ;
And, like as there were husbandry in war,
Before the sun rose he was harness'd light,
And to the field goes he ; where every
    flower
Did as a prophet weep what it foresaw 10
In Hector's wrath.
  Cres.   What was his cause of anger ?
  Alex. The noise goes, this : there is
    among the Greeks
A lord of Troyan blood, nephew to Hector ;
They call him Ajax.
  Cres.   Good ; and what of him ?
  Alex. They say he is a very man per se 15
And stands alone.
  Cres. So do all men, unless they are
drunk, sick, or have no legs.
  Alex. This man, lady, hath robb'd many
beasts of their particular additions : he is
as valiant as the lion, churlish as the bear,
slow as the elephant—a man into whom
nature hath so crowded humours that his
valour is crush'd into folly, his folly sauced
with discretion. There is no man hath a
virtue that he hath not a glimpse of, nor
any man an attaint but he carries some
stain of it ; he is melancholy without cause
and merry against the hair ; he hath the
joints of every thing ; but everything so
out of joint that he is a gouty Briareus,

many hands and no use, or purblind Argus,
all eyes and no sight. 29
  Cres. But how should this man, that
makes me smile, make Hector angry ?
  Alex. They say he yesterday cop'd
Hector in the battle and struck him down,
the disdain and shame whereof hath ever
since kept Hector fasting and waking.

Enter PANDARUS.

  Cres. Who comes here ? 35
  Alex. Madam, your uncle Pandarus.
  Cres. Hector's a gallant man.
  Alex. As may be in the world, lady.
  Pan. What's that ? What's that ?
  Cres. Good morrow, uncle Pandarus. 40
  Pan. Good morrow, cousin Cressid. What
do you talk of ?—Good morrow, Alex-
ander.—How do you, cousin ? When were
you at Ilium ?
  Cres. This morning, uncle. 44
  Pan. What were you talking of when I
came ? Was Hector arm'd and gone ere you
came to Ilium ? Helen was not up, was she ?
  Cres. Hector was gone ; but Helen was
not up.
  Pan. E'en so. Hector was stirring early.
  Cres. That were we talking of, and of his
anger. 50
  Pan. Was he angry ?
  Cres. So he says here.
  Pan. True, he was so ; I know the cause
too ; he'll lay about him to-day, I can tell
them that. And there's Troilus will not
come far behind him ; let them take heed
of Troilus, I can tell them that too. 56
  Cres. What, is he angry too ?
  Pan. Who, Troilus ? Troilus is the better
man of the two.
  Cres. O Jupiter ! there's no comparison.
  Pan. What, not between Troilus and
Hector ? Do you know a man if you see
him ? 63
  Cres. Ay, if I ever saw him before and
knew him.
  Pan. Well, I say Troilus is Troilus.
  Cres. Then you say as I say, for I am
sure he is not Hector. 66
  Pan. No, nor Hector is not Troilus in
some degrees.
  Cres. 'Tis just to each of them : he is
himself.
  Pan. Himself ! Alas, poor Troilus ! I
would he were !
  Cres. So he is. 70
  Pan. Condition I had gone barefoot to
India.
  Cres. He is not Hector.
  Pan. Himself ! no, he's not himself.
Would 'a were himself ! Well, the gods are
above ; time must friend or end. Well,
Troilus, well ! I would my heart were in
her body ! No, Hector is not a better man
than Troilus. 76

Cres. Excuse me.

Pan. He is elder.

Cres. Pardon me, pardon me.

Pan. Th' other's not come to't; you shall tell me another tale when th' other's come to't. Hector shall not have his wit this year. 82

Cres. He shall not need it if he have his own.

Pan. Nor his qualities.

Cres. No matter. 85

Pan. Nor his beauty.

Cres. 'Twould not become him: his own's better.

Pan. You have no judgment, niece. Helen herself swore th' other day that Troilus, for a brown favour, for so 'tis, I must confess—not brown neither— 90

Cres. No, but brown.

Pan. Faith, to say truth, brown and not brown.

Cres. To say the truth, true and not true.

Pan. She prais'd his complexion above Paris.

Cres. Why, Paris hath colour enough. 95

Pan. So he has.

Cres. Then Troilus should have too much. If she prais'd him above, his complexion is higher than his; he having colour enough, and the other higher, is too flaming a praise for a good complexion. I had as lief Helen's golden tongue had commended Troilus for a copper nose. 101

Pan. I swear to you I think Helen loves him better than Paris.

Cres. Then she's a merry Greek indeed.

Pan. Nay, I am sure she does. She came to him th' other day into the compass'd window—and you know he has not past three or four hairs on his chin— 107

Cres. Indeed a tapster's arithmetic may soon bring his particulars therein to a total.

Pan. Why, he is very young, and yet will he within three pound lift as much as his brother Hector.

Cres. Is he so young a man and so old a lifter?

Pan. But to prove to you that Helen loves him: she came and puts me her white hand to his cloven chin—

Cres. Juno have mercy! How came it cloven? 115

Pan. Why, you know, 'tis dimpled. I think his smiling becomes him better than any man in all Phrygia.

Cres. O, he smiles valiantly!

Pan. Does he not? 119

Cres. O yes, an 'twere a cloud in autumn!

Pan. Why, go to, then! But to prove to you that Helen loves Troilus—

Cres. Troilus will stand to the proof, if you'll prove it so.

Pan. Troilus! Why, he esteems her no more than I esteem an addle egg. 126

Cres. If you love an addle egg as well as you love an idle head, you would eat chickens i' th' shell.

Pan. I cannot choose but laugh to think how she tickled his chin. Indeed, she has a marvell's white hand, I must needs confess.

Cres. Without the rack. 132

Pan. And she takes upon her to spy a white hair on his chin.

Cres. Alas, poor chin! Many a wart is richer. 135

Pan. But there was such laughing! Queen Hecuba laugh'd that her eyes ran o'er.

Cres. With millstones.

Pan. And Cassandra laugh'd.

Cres. But there was a more temperate fire under the pot of her eyes. Did her eyes run o'er too? 141

Pan. And Hector laugh'd.

Cres. At what was all this laughing?

Pan. Marry, at the white hair that Helen spied on Troilus' chin. 145

Cres. An't had been a green hair I should have laugh'd too.

Pan. They laugh'd not so much at the hair as at his pretty answer.

Cres. What was his answer? 150

Pan. Quoth she 'Here's but two and fifty hairs on your chin, and one of them is white'.

Cres. This is her question.

Pan. That's true; make no question of that. 'Two and fifty hairs,' quoth he 'and one white. That white hair is my father, and all the rest are his sons.' 'Jupiter!' quoth she 'which of these hairs is Paris my husband?' 'The forked one;' quoth he 'pluck't out and give it him.' But there was such laughing! and Helen so blush'd, and Paris so chaf'd; and all the rest so laugh'd that it pass'd. 161

Cres. So let it now; for it has been a great while going by.

Pan. Well, cousin, I told you a thing yesterday; think on't. 165

Cres. So I do.

Pan. I'll be sworn 'tis true; he will weep you, an 'twere a man born in April.

Cres. And I'll spring up in his tears, an 'twere a nettle against May. 170

[*Sound a retreat.*

Pan. Hark! they are coming from the field. Shall we stand up here and see them as they pass toward Ilium? Good niece, do, sweet niece Cressida.

Cres. At your pleasure. 174

Pan. Here, here, here's an excellent place; here we may see most bravely. I'll tell you them all by their names as they pass by; but mark Troilus above the rest.

ÆNEAS passes.

Cres. Speak not so loud. 178

Pan. That's Æneas. Is not that a brave man? He's one of the flowers of Troy, I can tell you. But mark Troilus; you shall see anon.   181

ANTENOR *passes.*

Cres. Who's that?
Pan. That's Antenor. He has a shrewd wit, I can tell you; and he's a man good enough; he's one o' th' soundest judgments in Troy, whosoever, and a proper man of person. When comes Troilus? I'll show you Troilus anon. If he see me, you shall see him nod at me.   187
Cres. Will he give you the nod?
Pan. You shall see.
Cres. If he do, the rich shall have more.

HECTOR *passes.*

Pan. That's Hector, that, that, look you, that; there's a fellow! Go thy way, Hector! There's a brave man, niece. O brave Hector! Look how he looks. There's a countenance! Is't not a brave man?
Cres. O, a brave man!   195
Pan. Is 'a not? It does a man's heart good. Look you what hacks are on his helmet! Look you yonder, do you see? Look you there. There's no jesting; there's laying on; take't off who will, as they say. There be hacks.   200
Cres. Be those with swords?
Pan. Swords! anything, he cares not; an the devil come to him, it's all one. By God's lid, it does one's heart good. Yonder comes Paris, yonder comes Paris.   204

PARIS *passes.*

Look ye yonder, niece; is't not a gallant man too, is't not? Why, this is brave now. Who said he came hurt home to-day? He's not hurt. Why, this will do Helen's heart good now, ha! Would I could see Troilus now! You shall see Troilus anon.

HELENUS *passes.*

Cres. Who's that?   210
Pan. That's Helenus. I marvel where Troilus is. That's Helenus. I think he went not forth to-day. That's Helenus.
Cres. Can Helenus fight, uncle?   214
Pan. Helenus! no. Yes, he'll fight indifferent well. I marvel where Troilus is. Hark! do you not hear the people cry 'Troilus'? Helenus is a priest.
Cres. What sneaking fellow comes yonder?   218

TROILUS *passes.*

Pan. Where? yonder? That's Deiphobus. 'Tis Troilus. There's a man, niece. Hem! Brave Troilus, the prince of chivalry!   221
Cres. Peace, for shame, peace!
Pan. Mark him; note him. O brave

Troilus! Look well upon him, niece; look you how his sword is bloodied, and his helm more hack'd than Hector's; and how he looks, and how he goes! O admirable youth! he never saw three and twenty. Go thy way, Troilus, go thy way. Had I a sister were a grace or a daughter a goddess, he should take his choice. O admirable man! Paris? Paris is dirt to him; and, I warrant, Helen, to change, would give an eye to boot.   231
Cres. Here comes more.

Common Soldiers *pass.*

Pan. Asses, fools, dolts! chaff and bran, chaff and bran! porridge after meat! I could live and die in the eyes of Troilus. Ne'er look, ne'er look; the eagles are gone. Crows and daws, crows and daws! I had rather be such a man as Troilus than Agamemnon and all Greece.
Cres. There is amongst the Greeks Achilles, a better man than Troilus.   240
Pan. Achilles? A drayman, a porter, a very camel!
Cres. Well, well.
Pan. Well, well! Why, have you any discretion? Have you any eyes? Do you know what a man is? Is not birth, beauty, good shape, discourse, manhood, learning, gentleness, virtue, youth, liberality, and such like, the spice and salt that season a man?   247
Cres. Ay, a minc'd man; and then to be bak'd with no date in the pie, for then the man's date is out.
Pan. You are such a woman! A man knows not at what ward you lie.   251
Cres. Upon my back, to defend my belly; upon my wit, to defend my wiles; upon my secrecy, to defend mine honesty; my mask, to defend my beauty; and you, to defend all these; and at all these wards I lie at, at a thousand watches.   256
Pan. Say one of your watches.
Cres. Nay, I'll watch you for that; and that's one of the chiefest of them too. If I cannot ward what I would not have hit, I can watch you for telling how I took the blow; unless it swell past hiding, and then it's past watching.   262
Pan. You are such another!

Enter Troilus' Boy.

Boy. Sir, my lord would instantly speak with you.
Pan. Where?   265
Boy. At your own house; there he unarms him.
Pan. Good boy, tell him I come.
[*Exit Boy.*
I doubt he be hurt. Fare ye well, good niece.
Cres. Adieu, uncle.

791

Pan. I will be with you, niece, by and by.
Cres. To bring, uncle.   271
Pan. Ay, a token from Troilus.
Cres. By the same token, you are a
  bawd.   [*Exit Pandarus.*
Words, vows, gifts, tears, and love's full
  sacrifice,
He offers in another's enterprise ;   275
But more in Troilus thousand-fold I see
Than in the glass of Pandar's praise may be,
Yet hold I off. Women are angels, wooing :
Things won are done ; joy's soul lies in the
  doing.
That she belov'd knows nought that knows
  not this :   280
Men prize the thing ungain'd more than
  it is.
That she was never yet that ever knew
Love got so sweet as when desire did sue ;
Therefore this maxim out of love I teach :
Achievement is command ; ungain'd,
  beseech.   285
Then though my heart's content firm love
  doth bear,
Nothing of that shall from mine eyes
  appear.   [*Exit.*

SCENE III. *The Grecian camp.   Before
         Agamemnon's tent.*

Sennet. Enter AGAMEMNON, NESTOR, ULYS-
  SES, DIOMEDES, MENELAUS, *and* Others.

 Agam. Princes,
What grief hath set these jaundies o'er your
  cheeks ?
The ample proposition that hope makes
In all designs begun on earth below
Fails in the promis'd largeness ; checks and
  disasters   5
Grow in the veins of actions highest rear'd,
As knots, by the conflux of meeting sap,
Infects the sound pine, and diverts his
  grain
Tortive and errant from his course of
  growth.
Nor, princes, is it matter new to us   10
That we come short of our suppose so far
That after seven years' siege yet Troy walls
  stand ;
Sith every action that hath gone before,
Whereof we have record, trial did draw
Bias and thwart, not answering the aim,   15
And that unbodied figure of the thought
That gave't surmised shape. Why then,
  you princes,
Do you with cheeks abash'd behold our
  works
And call them shames, which are, indeed,
  nought else
But the protractive trials of great Jove 20
To find persistive constancy in men ;
The fineness of which metal is not found
In fortune's love ? For then the bold and
  coward,

The wise and fool, the artist and unread,   24
The hard and soft, seem all affin'd and kin.
But in the wind and tempest of her frown
Distinction, with a broad and powerful fan,
Puffing at all, winnows the light away ;
And what hath mass or matter by itself
Lies rich in virtue and unmingled.   30
  Nest. With due observance of thy godlike
    seat,
Great Agamemnon, Nestor shall apply
Thy latest words. In the reproof of chance
Lies the true proof of men. The sea being
  smooth,   34
How many shallow bauble boats dare sail
Upon her patient breast, making their way
With those of nobler bulk !
But let the ruffian Boreas once enrage
The gentle Thetis, and anon behold
The strong-ribb'd bark through liquid
  mountains cut,   40
Bounding between the two moist elements
Like Perseus' horse.   Where's then the
  saucy boat,
Whose weak untimber'd sides but even now
Co-rivall'd greatness ? Either to harbour
  fled
Or made a toast for Neptune. Even so 45
Doth valour's show and valour's worth
  divide
In storms of fortune ; for in her ray and
  brightness
The herd hath more annoyance by the
  breese
Than by the tiger ; but when the splitting
  wind
Makes flexible the knees of knotted oaks, 50
And flies fled under shade—why, then the
  thing of courage,
As rous'd with rage, with rage doth
  sympathise,
And with an accent tun'd in self-same key
Retorts to chiding fortune.
  Ulyss.   Agamemnon,
Thou great commander, nerve and bone of
  Greece,   55
Heart of our numbers, soul and only spirit
In whom the tempers and the minds of all
Should be shut up—hear what Ulysses
  speaks.
Besides the applause and approbation
The which, [*To Agamemnon*] most mighty,
  for thy place and sway,   60
[*To Nestor*] And, thou most reverend, for
  thy stretch'd-out life,
I give to both your speeches—which were
  such
As Agamemnon and the hand of Greece
Should hold up high in brass ; and such
  again
As venerable Nestor, hatch'd in silver, 65
Should with a bond of air, strong as the
  axle-tree
On which heaven rides, knit all the Greekish
  ears

To his experienc'd tongue—yet let it please
  both,
Thou great, and wise, to hear Ulysses
  speak.
   Agam. Speak, Prince of Ithaca ; and be't
  of less expect   70
That matter needless, of importless burden,
Divide thy lips than we are confident,
When rank Thersites opes his mastic jaws,
We shall hear music, wit, and oracle.
   Ulyss. Troy, yet upon his basis, had been
  down,   75
And the great Hector's sword had lack'd a
  master,
But for these instances :
The specialty of rule hath been neglected ;
And look how many Grecian tents do stand
Hollow upon this plain, so many hollow
  factions.   80
When that the general is not like the hive,
To whom the foragers shall all repair,
What honey is expected ? Degree being
  vizarded,
Th' unworthiest shows as fairly in the mask.
The heavens themselves, the planets, and
  this centre,   85
Observe degree, priority, and place,
Insisture, course, proportion, season, form,
Office, and custom, in all line of order ;
And therefore is the glorious planet Sol
In noble eminence enthron'd and spher'd 90
Amidst the other, whose med'cinable eye
Corrects the ill aspects of planets evil,
And posts, like the commandment of a
  king,
Sans check, to good and bad. But when the
  planets
In evil mixture to disorder wander,   95
What plagues and what portents, what
  mutiny,
What raging of the sea, shaking of earth,
Commotion in the winds ! Frights, changes,
  horrors,
Divert and crack, rend and deracinate,
The unity and married calm of states   100
Quite from their fixture ! O, when degree
  is shak'd,
Which is the ladder of all high designs,
The enterprise is sick ! How could com-
  munities,
Degrees in schools, and brotherhoods in
  cities,   104
Peaceful commerce from dividable shores,
The primogenity and due of birth,
Prerogative of age, crowns, sceptres,
  laurels,
But by degree, stand in authentic place ?
Take but degree away, untune that string,
And hark what discord follows ! Each
  thing melts   110
In mere oppugnancy : the bounded waters
Should lift their bosoms higher than the
  shores,
And make a sop of all this solid globe ;

Strength should be lord of imbecility,
And the rude son should strike his father
  dead ;   115
Force should be right ; or, rather, right and
  wrong—
Between whose endless jar justice resides—
Should lose their names, and so should
  justice too.
Then everything includes itself in power,
Power into will, will into appetite ;   120
And appetite, an universal wolf,
So doubly seconded with will and power,
Must make perforce an universal prey,
And last eat up himself. Great Agamem-
  non,
This chaos, when degree is suffocate,   125
Follows the choking.
And this neglection of degree it is
That by a pace goes backward, with a
  purpose
It hath to climb. The general 's disdain'd
By him one step below, he by the next,   130
That next by him beneath ; so every step,
Exampl'd by the first pace that is sick
Of his superior, grows to an envious fever
Of pale and bloodless emulation.
And 'tis this fever that keeps Troy on foot,
Not her own sinews. To end a tale of
  length,   136
Troy in our weakness stands, not in her
  strength.
   Nest. Most wisely hath Ulysses here dis-
  cover'd
The fever whereof all our power is sick.
   Agam. The nature of the sickness found,
  Ulysses,   140
What is the remedy ?
   Ulyss. The great Achilles, whom opinion
  crowns
The sinew and the forehand of our host,
Having his ear full of his airy fame,
Grows dainty of his worth, and in his tent
Lies mocking our designs ; with him
  Patroclus   146
Upon a lazy bed the livelong day
Breaks scurril jests ;
And with ridiculous and awkward action—
Which, slanderer, he imitation calls—   150
He pageants us. Sometime, great Aga-
  memnon,
Thy topless deputation he puts on ;
And like a strutting player whose conceit
Lies in his hamstring, and doth think it rich
To hear the wooden dialogue and sound 155
'Twixt his stretch'd footing and the
  scaffoldage—
Such to-be-pitied and o'er-wrested seeming
He acts thy greatness in ; and when he
  speaks
'Tis like a chime a-mending ; with terms
  unsquar'd,
Which, from the tongue of roaring Typhon
  dropp'd,   160
Would seem hyperboles. At this fusty stuff

The large Achilles, on his press'd bed
   lolling,
From his deep chest laughs out a loud
   applause ;
Cries ' Excellent ! 'tis Agamemnon just.
Now play me Nestor ; hem, and stroke thy
   beard,   165
As he being drest to some oration '.
That's done—as near as the extremest ends
Of parallels, as like as Vulcan and his wife ;
Yet god Achilles still cries ' Excellent !
'Tis Nestor right.   Now play him me,
   Patroclus,   170
Arming to answer in a night alarm '.
And then, forsooth, the faint defects of age
Must be the scene of mirth : to cough and
   spit
And, with a palsy-fumbling on his gorget,
Shake in and out the rivet.   And at this
   sport   175
Sir Valour dies ;   cries   ' O, enough,
   Patroclus ;
Or give me ribs of steel !   I shall split all
In pleasure of my spleen '.   And in this
   fashion
All our abilities, gifts, natures, shapes,
Severals and generals of grace exact,   180
Achievements, plots, orders, preventions,
Excitements to the field or speech for truce,
Success or loss, what is or is not, serves
As stuff for these two to make paradoxes.
   Nest. And in the imitation of these
   twain—   185
Who, as Ulysses says, opinion crowns
With an imperial voice—many are infect.
Ajax is grown self-will'd and bears his head
In such a rein, in full as proud a place   189
As broad Achilles : keeps his tent like him ;
Makes factious feasts ; rails on our state of
   war
Bold as an oracle, and sets Thersites,
A slave whose gall coins slanders like a
   mint,
To match us in comparisons with dirt,
To weaken and discredit our exposure,   195
How rank soever rounded in with danger.
   Ulyss. They tax our policy and call it
   cowardice,
Count wisdom as no member of the war,
Forestall prescience, and esteem no act
But that of hand.   The still and mental
   parts   200
That do contrive how many hands shall
   strike
When fitness calls them on, and know, by
   measure
Of their observant toil, the enemies'
   weight—
Why, this hath not a finger's dignity :
They call this bed-work, mapp'ry, closet-
   war ;   205
So that the ram that batters down the wall,
For the great swinge and rudeness of his
   poise,

They place before his hand that made the
   engine,
Or those that with the fineness of their souls
By reason guide his execution.   210
   Nest. Let this be granted, and Achilles'
   horse
Makes many Thetis' sons.   [*Tucket.*
   Agam. What trumpet ? Look, Menelaus.
   Men. From Troy.

Enter ÆNEAS.

   Agam. What would you fore our tent ?
   Æne. Is this great Agamemnon's tent, I
   pray you ?   216
   Agam. Even this.
   Æne. May one that is a herald and a
   prince
Do a fair message to his kingly eyes ?
   Agam. With surety stronger than Achilles'
   arm   220
Fore all the Greekish heads, which with one
   voice
Call Agamemnon head and general.
   Æne. Fair leave and large security. How
   may
A stranger to those most imperial looks
Know them from eyes of other mortals ?
   Agam.   How ?
   Æne. Ay ;   226
I ask, that I might waken reverence,
And bid the cheek be ready with a blush
Modest as Morning when she coldly eyes
The youthful Phœbus.   230
Which is that god in office, guiding men ?
Which is the high and mighty Agamemnon?
   Agam. This Troyan scorns us, or the men
   of Troy
Are ceremonious courtiers.
   Æne. Courtiers as free, as debonair, un-
   arm'd,   235
As bending angels ; that's their fame in
   peace.
But when they would seem soldiers, they
   have galls,
Good arms, strong joints, true swords ;
   and, Jove's accord,   238
Nothing so full of heart. But peace, Æneas,
Peace, Troyan ; lay thy finger on thy lips.
The worthiness of praise distains his worth,
If that the prais'd himself bring the praise
   forth ;
But what the repining enemy commends,
That breath fame blows ; that praise, sole
   pure, transcends.
   Agam. Sir, you of Troy, call you yourself
   Æneas ?   245
   Æne. Ay, Greek, that is my name.
   Agam. What's your affair, I pray you ?
   Æne. Sir, pardon ; 'tis for Agamemnon's
   ears.
   Agam. He hears nought privately that
   comes from Troy.
   Æne. Nor I from Troy come not to
   whisper with him ;   250

I bring a trumpet to awake his ear,
To set his sense on the attentive bent,
And then to speak.
　Agam.　　　　Speak frankly as the wind ;
It is not Agamemnon's sleeping hour.　254
That thou shalt know, Troyan, he is awake,
He tells thee so himself.
　Æne.　　　　　　　Trumpet, blow loud,
Send thy brass voice through all these lazy
　　　tents ;
And every Greek of mettle, let him know
What Troy means fairly shall be spoke
　　　aloud.　　　　　[*Sound trumpet.*
We have, great Agamemnon, here in Troy
A prince called Hector—Priam is his
　　　father—　261
Who in this dull and long-continued truce
Is resty grown ; he bade me take a trumpet
And to this purpose speak : Kings, princes,
　　　lords !　264
If there be one among the fair'st of Greece
That holds his honour higher than his ease,
That seeks his praise more than he fears his
　　　peril,
That knows his valour and knows not his
　　　fear,
That loves his mistress more than in con-
　　　fession　269
With truant vows to her own lips he loves,
And dare avow her beauty and her worth
In other arms than hers—to him this
　　　challenge.
Hector, in view of Troyans and of Greeks,
Shall make it good or do his best to do it :
He hath a lady wiser, fairer, truer,　275
Than ever Greek did couple in his arms ;
And will to-morrow with his trumpet call
Mid-way between your tents and walls of
　　　Troy
To rouse a Grecian that is true in love.
If any come, Hector shall honour him ;　280
If none, he'll say in Troy, when he retires,
The Grecian dames are sunburnt and not
　　　worth
The splinter of a lance.　Even so much.
　Agam. This shall be told our lovers, Lord
　　　Æneas.　284
If none of them have soul in such a kind,
We left them all at home.　But we are
　　　soldiers ;
And may that soldier a mere recreant prove
That means not, hath not, or is not in
　　　love.
If then one is, or hath, or means to be,
That one meets Hector ; if none else, I am
　　　he.　290
　Nest. Tell him of Nestor, one that was a
　　　man
When Hector's grandsire suck'd.　He is old
　　　now ;
But if there be not in our Grecian mould
One noble man that hath one spark of fire
To answer for his love, tell him from me　295
I'll hide my silver beard in a gold beaver,

And in my vantbrace put this wither'd
　　　brawn,
And, meeting him, will tell him that my
　　　lady
Was fairer than his grandame, and as chaste
As may be in the world.　His youth in flood,
I'll prove this truth with my three drops of
　　　blood.　301
　Æne. Now heavens forfend such scarcity
　　　of youth !
　Ulyss. Amen.
　Agam. Fair Lord Æneas, let me touch
　　　your hand ;
To our pavilion shall I lead you, first.　305
Achilles shall have word of this intent ;
So shall each lord of Greece, from tent to
　　　tent.
Yourself shall feast with us before you go,
And find the welcome of a noble foe.
　　　　[*Exeunt all but Ulysses and Nestor.*
　Ulyss. Nestor !　310
　Nest. What says Ulysses ?
　Ulyss. I have a young conception in my
　　　brain ;
Be you my time to bring it to some shape.
　Nest. What is't ?
　Ulyss. This 'tis :　315
Blunt wedges rive hard knots.　The seeded
　　　pride
That hath to this maturity blown up
In rank Achilles must or now be cropp'd
Or, shedding, breed a nursery of like evil
To overbulk us all.
　Nest.　　　　　Well, and how ?　320
　Ulyss This challenge that the gallant
　　　Hector sends,
However it is spread in general name,
Relates in purpose only to Achilles.
　Nest. True.　The purpose is perspicuous
　　　even as substance　324
Whose grossness little characters sum up ;
And, in the publication, make no strain
But that Achilles, were his brain as barren
As banks of Libya—though, Apollo knows,
'Tis dry enough—will with great speed of
　　　judgment,
Ay, with celerity, find Hector's purpose　330
Pointing on him.
　Ulyss. And wake him to the answer,
　　　think you ?
　Nest. Why, 'tis most meet.　Who may
　　　you else oppose
That can from Hector bring those honours
　　　off,
If not Achilles ?　Though't be a sportful
　　　combat,　335
Yet in this trial much opinion dwells ;
For here the Troyans taste our dear'st
　　　repute
With their fin'st palate ; and trust to me,
　　　Ulysses,
Our imputation shall be oddly pois'd
In this vile action ; for the success,　340
Although particular, shall give a scantling

795

Of good or bad unto the general ;
And in such indexes, although small pricks
To their subsequent volumes, there is seen
The baby figure of the giant mass   345
Of things to come at large. It is suppos'd
He that meets Hector issues from our
      choice ;
And choice, being mutual act of all our
      souls,
Makes merit her election, and doth boil,
As 'twere from forth us all, a man distill'd
Out of our virtues ; who miscarrying,   351
What heart receives from hence a conquer-
      ing part,
To steel a strong opinion to themselves ?
Which entertain'd, limbs are his instru-
      ments,
In no less working than are swords and
      bows   355
Directive by the limbs.
  Ulyss.   Give pardon to my speech.
Therefore 'tis meet Achilles meet not
      Hector.
Let us, like merchants, show our foulest
      wares
And think perchance they'll sell ; if not,
      the lustre   360
Of the better yet to show shall show the
      better,
By showing the worst first. Do not consent
That ever Hector and Achilles meet ;
For both our honour and our shame in this
Are dogg'd with two strange followers.   365
  Nest. I see them not with my old eyes.
      What are they ?
  Ulyss. What glory our Achilles shares
      from Hector,
Were he not proud, we all should wear with
      him ;
But he already is too insolent ;
And it were better parch in Afric sun   370
Than in the pride and salt scorn of his
      eyes,
Should he scape Hector fair. If he were
      foil'd,
Why, then we do our main opinion crush
In taint of our best man. No, make a
      lott'ry ;
And, by device, let blockish Ajax draw   375
The sort to fight with Hector. Among our-
      selves
Give him allowance for the better man ;
For that will physic the, great Myrmidon,
Who broils in loud applause, and make him
      fall
His crest, that prouder than blue Iris bends.
If the dull brainless Ajax come safe off, 381
We'll dress him up in voices ; if he fail,
Yet go we under our opinion still
That we have better men. But, hit or miss,
Our project's life this shape of sense
      assumes—   385
Ajax employ'd plucks down Achilles'
      plumes.

  Nest. Now, Ulysses, I begin to relish thy
      advice ;
And I will give a taste thereof forthwith
To Agamemnon. Go we to him straight.   390
Two curs shall tame each other : pride
      alone
Must tarre the mastiffs on, as 'twere their
      bone.   [*Exeunt.*

ACT TWO

SCENE I. *The Grecian camp.*

Enter AJAX *and* THERSITES.

  Ajax. Thersites !
  Ther. Agamemnon—how if he had boils
full, all over, generally ?
  Ajax. Thersites !
  Ther. And those boils did run—say so.
Did not the general run then ? Were not
that a botchy core ?   6
  Ajax. Dog !
  Ther. Then there would come some
matter from him ; I see none now.
  Ajax. Thou bitch-wolf's son, canst thou
not hear ? Feel, then.   [*Strikes him.*
  Ther. The plague of Greece upon thee,
thou mongrel beef-witted lord !   13
  Ajax. Speak, then, thou whinid'st leaven,
speak. I will beat thee into handsomeness.
  Ther. I shall sooner rail thee into wit and
holiness ; but I think thy horse will sooner
con an oration than thou learn a prayer
without book. Thou canst strike, canst
thou ? A red murrain o' thy jade's tricks !
  Ajax. Toadstool, learn me the proclamation.   20
  Ther. Dost thou think I have no sense,
thou strikest me thus ?
  Ajax. The proclamation !
  Ther. Thou art proclaim'd a fool, I think.
  Ajax. Do not, porpentine, do not ; my
fingers itch.   25
  Ther. I would thou didst itch from head
to foot and I had the scratching of thee ; I
would make thee the loathsomest scab in
Greece. When thou art forth in the
incursions, thou strikest as slow as another.
  Ajax. I say, the proclamation.   30
  Ther. Thou grumblest and railest every
hour on Achilles ; and thou art as full of
envy at his greatness as Cerberus is at
Proserpina's beauty—ay, that thou bark'st
at him.
  Ajax. Mistress Thersites !
  Ther. Thou shouldst strike him.   35
  Ajax. Cobloaf !
  Ther. He would pun thee into shivers
with his fist, as a sailor breaks a biscuit.
  Ajax. You whoreson cur !   [*Strikes him.*
  Ther. Do, do.   40
  Ajax. Thou stool for a witch !
  Ther. Ay, do, do ; thou sodden-witted
lord ! Thou hast no more brain than I have
in mine elbows ; an assinico may tutor

thee. You scurvy valiant ass! Thou art here but to thrash Troyans, and thou art bought and sold among those of any wit like a barbarian slave. If thou use to beat me, I will begin at thy heel and tell what thou art by inches, thou thing of no bowels, thou!

Ajax. You dog!

Ther. You scurvy lord!   50

Ajax. You cur!   [*Strikes him.*

Ther. Mars his idiot! Do, rudeness; do, camel; do, do.

Enter ACHILLES *and* PATROCLUS.

Achil. Why, how now, Ajax! Wherefore do you thus?

How now, Thersites! What's the matter, man?

Ther. You see him there, do you?   55

Achil. Ay; what's the matter?

Ther. Nay, look upon him.

Achil. So I do. What's the matter?

Ther. Nay, but regard him well.

Achil. Well! why, so I do.   60

Ther. But yet you look not well upon him; for who some ever you take him to be, he is Ajax.

Achil. I know that, fool.

Ther. Ay, but that fool knows not himself.

Ajax. Therefore I beat thee.   65

Ther. Lo, lo, lo, lo, what modicums of wit he utters! His evasions have ears thus long. I have bobb'd his brain more than he has beat my bones. I will buy nine sparrows for a penny, and his pia mater is not worth the ninth part of a sparrow. This lord, Achilles, Ajax—who wears his wit in his belly and his guts in his head—I'll tell you what I say of him.   72

Achil. What?

Ther. I say this Ajax—

       [*Ajax offers to strike him.*

Achil. Nay, good Ajax.   75

Ther. Has not so much wit—

Achil. Nay, I must hold you.

Ther. As will stop the eye of Helen's needle, for whom he comes to fight.

Achil. Peace, fool!   80

Ther. I would have peace and quietness, but the fool will not—he there; that he; look you there.

Ajax. O thou damned cur! I shall—

Achil. Will you set your wit to a fool's?

Ther. No, I warrant you; the fool's will shame it.   85

Patr. Good words, Thersites.

Achil. What's the quarrel?

Ajax. I bade the vile owl go learn me the tenour of the proclamation, and he rails upon me.

Ther. I serve thee not.   90

Ajax. Well, go to, go to.

Ther. I serve here voluntary.

Achil. Your last service was suff'rance; 'twas not voluntary. No man is beaten voluntary. Ajax was here the voluntary, and you as under an impress.   95

Ther. E'en so; a great deal of your wit too lies in your sinews, or else there be liars. Hector shall have a great catch an he knock out either of your brains: 'a were as good crack a fusty nut with no kernel.

Achil. What, with me too, Thersites? 100

Ther. There's Ulysses and old Nestor—whose wit was mouldy ere your grandsires had nails on their toes—yoke you like draught oxen, and make you plough up the wars.

Achil. What, what?

Ther. Yes, good sooth. To Achilles, to Ajax, to—   105

Ajax. I shall cut out your tongue.

Ther. 'Tis no matter; I shall speak as much as thou afterwards.

Patr. No more words, Thersites; peace!

Ther. I will hold my peace when Achilles' brach bids me, shall I?   111

Achil. There's for you, Patroclus.

Ther. I will see you hang'd like clotpoles ere I come any more to your tents. I will keep where there is wit stirring, and leave the faction of fools.   [*Exit.*

Patr. A good riddance.   116

Achil. Marry, this, sir, is proclaim'd through all our host,

That Hector, by the fifth hour of the sun,

Will with a trumpet 'twixt our tents and Troy,

To-morrow morning, call some knight to arms   120

That hath a stomach; and such a one that dare

Maintain I know not what; 'tis trash. Farewell.

Ajax. Farewell. Who shall answer him?

Achil. I know not; 'tis put to lott'ry. Otherwise

He knew his man.   125

Ajax. O, meaning you! I will go learn more of it.   [*Exeunt.*

SCENE II. *Troy. Priam's palace.*

Enter PRIAM, HECTOR, TROILUS, PARIS, *and* HELENUS.

Pri. After so many hours, lives, speeches, spent,

Thus once again says Nestor from the Greeks:

' Deliver Helen, and all damage else—

As honour, loss of time, travail, expense,

Wounds, friends, and what else dear that is consum'd   5

In hot digestion of this cormorant war—

Shall be struck off'. Hector, what say you to't?

Hect. Though no man lesser fears the
 Greeks than I,
As far as toucheth my particular,
Yet, dread Priam, 10
There is no lady of more softer bowels,
More spongy to suck in the sense of fear,
More ready to cry out ' Who knows what
 follows ? '
Than Hector is. The wound of peace is
 surety,
Surety secure ; but modest doubt is call'd
The beacon of the wise, the tent that
 searches 16
To th' bottom of the worst. Let Helen go.
Since the first sword was drawn about this
 question,
Every tithe soul 'mongst many thousand
 dismes
Hath been as dear as Helen—I mean, of
 ours. 20
If we have lost so many tenths of ours
To guard a thing not ours, nor worth to us,
Had it our name, the value of one ten,
What merit's in that reason which denies
The yielding of her up ?
 Tro.   Fie, fie, my brother ! 25
Weigh you the worth and honour of a king,
So great as our dread father's, in a scale
Of common ounces ? Will you with
 counters sum
The past-proportion of his infinite,
And buckle in a waist most fathomless 30
With spans and inches so diminutive
As fears and reasons ? Fie, for godly shame !
 Hel. No marvel though you bite so sharp
 at reasons,
You are so empty of them. Should not our
 father
Bear the great sway of his affairs with
 reasons, 35
Because your speech hath none that tells
 him so ?
 Tro. You are for dreams and slumbers,
 brother priest ;
You fur your gloves with reason. Here are
 your reasons :
You know an enemy intends you harm ;
You know a sword employ'd is perilous, 40
And reason flies the object of all harm.
Who marvels, then, when Helenus beholds
A Grecian and his sword, if he do set
The very wings of reason to his heels
And fly like chidden Mercury from Jove, 45
Or like a star disorb'd ? Nay, if we talk of
 reason,
Let's shut our gates and sleep. Manhood
 and honour
Should have hare hearts, would they but fat
 their thoughts
With this cramm'd reason. Reason and
 respect
Make livers pale and lustihood deject. 50
 Hect. Brother, she is not worth what she
 doth cost

The keeping.
 Tro. What's aught but as 'tis valued ?
 Hect. But value dwells not in particular
 will :
It holds his estimate and dignity
As well wherein 'tis precious of itself 55
As in the prizer. 'Tis mad idolatry
To make the service greater than the god ;
And the will dotes that is attributive
To what infectiously itself affects,
Without some image of th' affected merit. 60
 Tro. I take to-day a wife, and my election
Is led on in the conduct of my will ;
My will enkindled by mine eyes and ears,
Two traded pilots 'twixt the dangerous
 shores
Of will and judgment : how may I avoid, 65
Although my will distaste what it elected,
The wife I chose ? There can be no evasion
To blench from this and to stand firm by
 honour.
We turn not back the silks upon the
 merchant
When we have soil'd them ; nor the re-
 mainder viands 70
We do not throw in unrespective sieve,
Because we now are full. It was thought
 meet
Paris should do some vengeance on the
 Greeks ;
Your breath with full consent bellied his
 sails ;
The seas and winds, old wranglers, took a
 truce, 75
And did him service. He touch'd the ports
 desir'd ;
And for an old aunt whom the Greeks held
 captive
He brought a Grecian queen, whose youth
 and freshness
Wrinkles Apollo's, and makes stale the
 morning.
Why keep we her ? The Grecians keep our
 aunt. 80
Is she worth keeping ? Why, she is a pearl
Whose price hath launch'd above a
 thousand ships,
And turn'd crown'd kings to merchants.
If you'll avouch 'twas wisdom Paris went—
As you must needs, for you all cried ' Go,
 go '— 85
If you'll confess he brought home worthy
 prize—
As you must needs, for you all clapp'd your
 hands,
And cried ' Inestimable ! '—why do you
 now
The issue of your proper wisdoms rate,
And do a deed that never fortune did— 90
Beggar the estimation which you priz'd
Richer than sea and land ? O theft most
 base,
That we have stol'n what we do fear to
 keep !

But thieves unworthy of a thing so stol'n
That in their country did them that
disgrace   95
We fear to warrant in our native place!
  Cas. [*Within*] Cry, Troyans, cry.
  Pri.   What noise, what shriek is this?
  Pro. 'Tis our mad sister; I do know her
voice.
  Cas. [*Within*] Cry, Troyans.
  Hect. It is Cassandra.   100

        Enter CASSANDRA, *raving.*

  Cas. Cry, Troyans, cry. Lend me ten
thousand eyes,
And I will fill them with prophetic tears.
  Hect. Peace, sister, peace.
  Cas. Virgins and boys, mid-age and
wrinkled eld,   104
Soft infancy, that nothing canst but cry,
Add to my clamours. Let us pay betimes
A moiety of that mass of moan to come.
Cry, Troyans, cry. Practise your eyes with
tears.
Troy must not be, nor goodly Ilion stand;
Our firebrand brother, Paris, burns us all.
Cry, Troyans, cry, A Helen and a woe!   111
Cry, cry. Troy burns, or else let Helen go.
                                            [*Exit.*
  Hect. Now, youthful Troilus, do not these
high strains
Of divination in our sister work
Some touches of remorse, or is your blood
So madly hot that no discourse of reason,
Nor fear of bad success in a bad cause,   117
Can qualify the same?
  Tro.   Why, brother Hector,
We may not think the justness of each act
Such and no other than event doth form it;
Nor once deject the courage of our minds
Because Cassandra's mad. Her brain-sick
raptures   122
Cannot distaste the goodness of a quarrel
Which hath our several honours all engag'd
To make it gracious. For my private part,
I am no more touch'd than all Priam's sons;
And Jove forbid there should be done
amongst us   127
Such things as might offend the weakest
spleen
To fight for and maintain.
  Par. Else might the world convince of
levity   130
As well my undertakings as your counsels;
[   ] I attest the gods, your full consent
Gave wings to my propension, and cut off
All fears attending on so dire a project.
For what, alas, can these my single arms?
What propugnation is in one man's valour
To stand the push and enmity of those
This quarrel would excite? Yet, I protest,
Were I alone to pass the difficulties,
And had as ample power as I have will,   140
Paris should ne'er retract what he hath
done

Nor faint in the pursuit.
  Pri.   Paris, you speak
Like one besotted on your sweet delights.
You have the honey still, but these the gall;
So to be valiant is no praise at all.   145
  Par. Sir, I propose not merely to myself
The pleasures such a beauty brings with it;
But I would have the soil of her fair rape
Wip'd off in honourable keeping her.
What treason were it to the ransack'd
queen,   150
Disgrace to your great worths, and shame
to me,
Now to deliver her possession up
On terms of base compulsion! Can it be
That so degenerate a strain as this
Should once set footing in your generous
bosoms?   155
There's not the meanest spirit on our party
Without a heart to dare or sword to draw
When Helen is defended; nor none so
noble
Whose life were ill bestow'd or death un-
fam'd
Where Helen is the subject. Then, I say, 160
Well may we fight for her whom we know
well
The world's large spaces cannot parallel.
  Hect. Paris and Troilus, you have both
said well;
And on the cause and question now in hand
Have gloz'd, but superficially; not much
Unlike young men, whom Aristotle thought
Unfit to hear moral philosophy.
The reasons you allege do more conduce
To the hot passion of distemp'red blood
Than to make up a free determination   170
'Twixt right and wrong; for pleasure and
revenge
Have ears more deaf than adders to the
voice
Of any true decision. Nature craves
All dues be rend'red to their owners. Now,
What nearer debt in all humanity   175
Than wife is to the husband? If this law
Of nature be corrupted through affection;
And that great minds, of partial indulgence
To their benumbed wills, resist the same;
There is a law in each well-order'd nation
To curb those raging appetites that are   181
Most disobedient and refractory.
If Helen, then, be wife to Sparta's king—
As it is known she is—these moral laws
Of nature and of nations speak aloud   185
To have her back return'd. Thus to persist
In doing wrong extenuates not wrong,
But makes it much more heavy. Hector's
opinion
Is this, in way of truth. Yet, ne'er the less,
My spritely brethren, I propend to you   190
In resolution to keep Helen still;
For 'tis a cause that hath no mean depend-
ence
Upon our joint and several dignities.

Tro. Why, there you touch'd the life of
  our design.
Were it not glory that we more affected 195
Than the performance of our heaving
  spleens,
I would not wish a drop of Troyan blood
Spent more in her defence. But, worthy
  Hector,
She is a theme of honour and renown,
A spur to valiant and magnanimous deeds,
Whose present courage may beat down our
  foes,   201
And fame in time to come canonize us ;
For I presume brave Hector would not
  lose
So rich advantage of a promis'd glory   204
As smiles upon the forehead of this action
For the wide world's revenue.

  Hect.   I am yours,
You valiant offspring of great Priamus.
I have a roisting challenge sent amongst
The dull and factious nobles of the Greeks
Will strike amazement to their drowsy
  spirits.   210
I was advertis'd their great general slept,
Whilst emulation in the army crept.
This, I presume, will wake him.   [*Exeunt.*

SCENE III. *The Grecian camp. Before the
  tent of Achilles.*

Enter THERSITES, *solus.*

  Ther. How now, Thersites ! What, lost
in the labyrinth of thy fury ? Shall the
elephant Ajax carry it thus ? He beats me,
and I rail at him. O worthy satisfaction !
Would it were otherwise : that I could beat
him, whilst he rail'd at me ! 'Sfoot, I'll
learn to conjure and raise devils, but I'll
see some issue of my spiteful execrations.
Then there's Achilles, a rare engineer ! If
Troy be not taken till these two undermine
it, the walls will stand till they fall of themselves.   O thou great thunder-darter of
Olympus, forget that thou art Jove, the
king of gods, and, Mercury, lose all the
serpentine craft of thy caduceus, if
ye take not that little little less-than-
little wit from them that they have !
which short-arm'd ignorance itself knows
is so abundant scarce, it will not in
circumvention deliver a fly from a
spider without drawing their massy irons
and cutting the web.   After this, the
vengeance on the whole camp ! or, rather,
the Neapolitan bone-ache ! for that, methinks, is the curse depending on those that
war for a placket. I have said my prayers ;
and devil Envy say 'Amen'. What ho ! my
Lord Achilles !   20

Enter PATROCLUS.

  Patr. Who's there ?   Thersites ! Good
Thersites, come in and rail.

  Ther. If I could 'a rememb'red a gilt
counterfeit, thou wouldst not have slipp'd
out of my contemplation ; but it is no
matter ; thyself upon thyself ! The common curse of mankind, folly and ignorance,
be thine in great revenue ! Heaven bless
thee from a tutor, and discipline come not
near thee ! Let thy blood be thy direction
till thy death. Then if she that lays thee
out says thou art a fair corse, I'll be sworn
and sworn upon't she never shrouded any
but lazars. Amen. Where's Achilles ? 31
  Patr. What, art thou devout ? Wast thou
in prayer ?
  Ther. Ay, the heavens hear me !
  Patr. Amen.

Enter ACHILLES.

  Achil. Who's there ?   35
  Patr. Thersites, my lord.
  Achil. Where, where ? O, where ? Art
thou come ? Why, my cheese, my diges-
tion, why hast thou not served thyself in
to my table so many meals ? Come, what's
Agamemnon ?   40
  Ther. Thy commander, Achilles. Then
tell me, Patroclus, what's Achilles ?
  Patr. Thy lord, Thersites. Then tell me,
I pray thee, what's Thersites ?
  Ther. Thy knower, Patroclus. Then tell
me, Patroclus, what art thou ?   46
  Patr. Thou must tell that knowest.
  Achil. O, tell, tell !
  Ther. I'll decline the whole question.
Agememnon commands Achilles ; Achilles
is my lord ; I am Patroclus' knower ; and
Patroclus is a fool.   51
  Patr. You rascal !
  Ther. Peace, fool ! I have not done.
  Achil. He is a privileg'd man. Proceed,
Thersites.
  Ther. Agamemnon is a fool ; Achilles is
a fool ; Thersites is a fool ; and, as afore-
said, Patroclus is a fool.   56
  Achil. Derive this ; come.
  Ther. Agamemnon is a fool to offer to
command Achilles ; Achilles is a fool to be
commanded of Agamemnon ; Thersites is
a fool to serve such a fool ; and this
Patroclus is a fool positive.   61
  Patr. Why am I a fool ?
  Ther. Make that demand of the Creator.
It suffices me thou art. Look you, who
comes here ?
  Achil. Come, Patroclus, I'll speak with
nobody. Come in with me, Thersites.   66
                                           [*Exit.*
  Ther. Here is such patchery, such
juggling, and such knavery. All the argument is a whore and a cuckold—a good
quarrel to draw emulous factions and bleed
to death upon. Now the dry serpigo on the
subject, and war and lechery confound all !
                                           [*Exit.*

Enter Agamemnon, Ulysses, Nestor,
Diomedes, Ajax, *and* Calcas.

Agam. Where is Achilles ?   72
Patr. Within his tent ; but ill-dispos'd,
my lord.
Agam. Let it be known to him that we
are here.
He shent our messengers ; and we lay by 75
Our appertainings, visiting of him.
Let him be told so ; lest, perchance, he
think
We dare not move the question of our
place
Or know not what we are.
Patr.   I shall say so to him. [*Exit.*
Ulyss. We saw him at the opening of his
tent.   80
He is not sick.
Ajax. Yes, lion-sick, sick of proud heart.
You may call it melancholy, if you will
favour the man ; but, by my head, 'tis
pride. But why, why ? Let him show us a
cause. A word, my lord.   85
                    [*Takes Agamemnon aside.*
Nest. What moves Ajax thus to bay at
him ?
Ulyss. Achilles hath inveigled his fool
from him.
Nest. Who, Thersites ?
Ulyss. He.   89
Nest. Then will Ajax lack matter, if he
have lost his argument.
Ulyss. No ; you see he is his argument
that has his argument—Achilles.
Nest. All the better ; their fraction is
more our wish than their faction. But it
was a strong composure a fool could
disunite !   96
Ulyss. The amity that wisdom knits not,
folly may easily untie.

Re-enter Patroclus.

Here comes Patroclus.
Nest. No Achilles with him.   100
Ulyss. The elephant hath joints, but none
for courtesy ; his legs are legs for necessity,
not for flexure.
Patr. Achilles bids me say he is much
sorry
If any thing more than your sport and
pleasure
Did move your greatness and this noble
state   105
To call upon him ; he hopes it is no other
But for your health and your digestion
sake,
An after-dinner's breath.
Agam.   Hear you, Patroclus.
We are too well acquainted with these
answers ;
But his evasion, wing'd thus swift with
scorn,   110
Cannot outfly our apprehensions.

Much attribute he hath, and much the
reason
Why we ascribe it to him. Yet all his
virtues,
Not virtuously on his own part beheld, 114
Do in our eyes begin to lose their gloss ;
Yea, like fair fruit in an unwholesome dish,
Are like to rot untasted. Go and tell him
We come to speak with him ; and you shall
not sin
If you do say we think him over-proud
And under-honest, in self-assumption
greater   120
Than in the note of judgment ; and
worthier than himself
Here tend the savage strangeness he puts
on,
Disguise the holy strength of their com-
mand,
And underwrite in an observing kind   124
His humorous predominance ; yea, watch
His pettish lunes, his ebbs, his flows, as if
The passage and whole carriage of this
action
Rode on his tide. Go tell him this, and add
That if he overhold his price so much
We'll none of him, but let him, like an
engine   130
Not portable, lie under this report :
Bring action hither ; this cannot go to war.
A stirring dwarf we do allowance give
Before a sleeping giant. Tell him so.
Patr. I shall, and bring his answer
presently.   [*Exit.*
Agam. In second voice we'll not be
satisfied ;
We come to speak with him. Ulysses,
enter you.   [*Exit Ulysses.*
Ajax. What is he more than another ?
Agam. No more than what he thinks he is.
Ajax. Is he so much ? Do you not think
he thinks himself a better man than I am ?
Agam. No question.   142
Ajax. Will you subscribe his thought and
say he is ?
Agam. No, noble Ajax ; you are as
strong, as valiant, as wise, no less noble,
much more gentle, and altogether more
tractable.   146
Ajax. Why should a man be proud ?
How doth pride grow ? I know not what
pride is.
Agam. Your mind is the clearer, Ajax,
and your virtues the fairer. He that is
proud eats up himself. Pride is his own
glass, his own trumpet, his own chronicle ;
and whatever praises itself but in the deed
devours the deed in the praise.   153

Re-enter Ulysses.

Ajax. I do hate a proud man as I do hate
the engend'ring of toads.
Nest. [*Aside*] And yet he loves himself :
is't not strange ?

Ulyss. Achilles will not to the field to-
    morrow.
Agam. What's his excuse?
Ulyss.   He doth rely on none;
But carries on the stream of his dispose,
Without observance or respect of any,   160
In will peculiar and in self-admission.
Agam. Why will he not, upon our fair
    request,
Untent his person and share the air with us?
Ulyss. Things small as nothing, for
    request's sake only,
He makes important; possess'd he is with
    greatness,   165
And speaks not to himself but with a pride
That quarrels at self-breath.   Imagin'd
    worth
Holds in his blood such swol'n and hot
    discourse
That 'twixt his mental and his active parts
Kingdom'd Achilles in commotion rages,   170
And batters down himself.   What should I
    say?
He is so plaguy proud that the death tokens
    of it
Cry 'No recovery'.
Agam.   Let Ajax go to him.
Dear lord, go you and greet him in his tent.
'Tis said he holds you well; and will be led
At your request a little from himself.   176
Ulyss. O Agamemnon, let it not be so!
We'll consecrate the steps that Ajax makes
When they go from Achilles.   Shall the
    proud lord
That bastes his arrogance with his own
    seam   180
And never suffers matter of the world
Enter his thoughts, save such as doth
    revolve
And ruminate himself—shall he be wor-
    shipp'd
Of that we hold an idol more than he?
No, this thrice-worthy and right valiant
    lord   185
Shall not so stale his palm, nobly acquir'd,
Nor, by my will, assubjugate his merit,
As amply titled as Achilles is,
By going to Achilles.   189
That were to enlard his fat-already pride,
And add more coals to Cancer when he
    burns
With entertaining great Hyperion.
This lord go to him! Jupiter forbid,
And say in thunder 'Achilles go to him'.
Nest. [*Aside*] O, this is well! He rubs the
    vein of him.
Dio. [*Aside*] And how his silence drinks
    up this applause!   196
Ajax. If I go to him, with my armed fist
I'll pash him o'er the face.
Agam. O, no, you shall not go.
Ajax. An 'a be proud with me I'll pheeze
    his pride.   200
Let me go to him.

Ulyss. Not for the worth that hangs upon
    our quarrel.
Ajax. A paltry, insolent fellow!
Nest. [*Aside*] How he describes himself!
Ajax. Can he not be sociable?   205
Ulyss. [*Aside*] The raven chides black-
ness.
Ajax. I'll let his humours blood.
Agam. [*Aside*] He will be the physician
that should be the patient.
Ajax. An all men were a my mind—   210
Ulyss. [*Aside*] Wit would be out of
fashion.
Ajax. 'A should not bear it so, 'a should
eat's words first.   Shall pride carry it?
Nest. [*Aside*] An 'twould, you'd carry
half.
Ulyss. [*Aside*] 'A would have ten shares.
Ajax. I will knead him, I'll make him
supple.   216
Nest. [*Aside*] He's not yet through warm.
Force him with praises; pour in, pour in;
his ambition is dry.
Ulyss. [*To Agamemnon*] My lord, you feed
too much on this dislike.
Nest. Our noble general, do not do so.
Dio. You must prepare to fight without
    Achilles.   221
Ulyss. Why 'tis this naming of him does
    him harm.
Here is a man—but 'tis before his face;
I will be silent.
Nest.   Wherefore should you so?
He is not emulous, as Achilles is.   225
Ulyss. Know the whole world, he is as
    valiant.
Ajax. A whoreson dog, that shall palter
with us thus!   Would he were a Troyan!
Nest. What a vice were it in Ajax now—
Ulyss. If he were proud.   230
Dio. Or covetous of praise.
Ulyss. Ay, or surly borne.
Dio. Or strange, or self-affected.
Ulyss. Thank the heavens, lord, thou art
    of sweet composure;
Praise him that gat thee, she that gave thee
    suck;   235
Fam'd be thy tutor, and thy parts of
    nature
Thrice-fam'd beyond, beyond all erudition;
But he that disciplin'd thine arms to fight—
Let Mars divide eternity in twain
And give him half; and, for thy vigour, 240
Bull-bearing Milo his addition yield
To sinewy Ajax.   I will not praise thy
    wisdom,
Which, like a bourn, a pale, a shore, con-
    fines
Thy spacious and dilated parts.   Here's
    Nestor,
Instructed by the antiquary times—   245
He must, he is, he cannot but be wise;
But pardon, father Nestor, were your
    days

As green as Ajax' and your brain so
    temper'd,
You should not have the eminence of him,
But be as Ajax.
    Ajax.   Shall I call you father?
    Nest. Ay, my good son.
    Dio.   Be rul'd by him, Lord Ajax.
    Ulyss. There is no tarrying here ; the
    hart Achilles   252
Keeps thicket. Please it our great general
To call together all his state of war ;
Fresh kings are come to Troy. To-morrow
We must with all our main of power stand
    fast ;   256
And here's a lord—come knights from east
    to west
And cull their flower, Ajax shall cope the
    best.
    Agam. Go we to council. Let Achilles
    sleep.   259
Light boats sail swift, though greater hulks
    draw deep.   [*Exeunt.*

ACT THREE

SCENE I. *Troy. Priam's palace.*

Music sounds within. Enter PANDARUS
and a Servant.

    Pan. Friend, you—pray you, a word. Do
you not follow the young Lord Paris ?
    Serv. Ay, sir, when he goes before me.
    Pan. You depend upon him, I mean ?
    Serv. Sir, I do depend upon the lord. 5
    Pan. You depend upon a notable gentle-
man ; I must needs praise him.
    Serv. The lord be praised !
    Pan. You know me, do you not ?
    Serv. Faith, sir, superficially.   10
    Pan. Friend, know me better : I am the
Lord Pandarus.
    Serv. I hope I shall know your honour
better.
    Pan. I do desire it.
    Serv. You are in the state of grace. 14
    Pan. Grace ! Not so, friend ; honour and
lordship are my titles. What music is this ?
    Serv. I do but partly know, sir ; it is
music in parts.
    Pan. Know you the musicians ?
    Serv. Wholly, sir.
    Pan. Who play they to ?   20
    Serv. To the hearers, sir.
    Pan. At whose pleasure, friend ?
    Serv. At mine, sir, and theirs that love
music.
    Pan. Command, I mean, friend.
    Serv. Who shall I command, sir ?   25
    Pan. Friend, we understand not one
another : I am too courtly, and thou art
too cunning. At whose request do these
men play ?
    Serv. That's to't, indeed, sir. Marry, sir,
at the request of Paris my lord, who is

there in person ; with him the mortal
Venus, the heart-blood of beauty, love's
invisible soul—   32
    Pan. Who, my cousin, Cressida ?
    Serv. No, sir, Helen. Could not you find
out that by her attributes ?   35
    Pan. It should seem, fellow, that thou
hast not seen the Lady Cressida. I come
to speak with Paris from the Prince Troilus ;
I will make a complimental assault upon
him, for my business seethes.   39
    Serv. Sodden business ! There's a stew'd
phrase indeed !

Enter PARIS *and* HELEN, *attended.*

    Pan. Fair be to you, my lord, and to all
this fair company ! Fair desires, in all fair
measure, fairly guide them—especially to
you, fair queen ! Fair thoughts be your fair
pillow.   44
    Helen. Dear lord, you are full of fair
words.
    Pan. You speak your fair pleasure, sweet
queen. Fair prince, here is good broken
music.   47
    Par. You have broke it, cousin ; and by
my life, you shall make it whole again ; you
shall piece it out with a piece of your
performance.
    Helen. He is full of harmony.   50
    Pan. Truly, lady, no.
    Helen. O, sir—
    Pan. Rude, in sooth ; in good sooth, very
rude.
    Par. Well said, my lord. Well, you say so
in fits.
    Pan. I have business to my lord, dear
queen. My lord, will you vouchsafe me a
word ?   56
    Helen. Nay, this shall not hedge us out.
We'll hear you sing, certainly.
    Pan. Well, sweet queen, you are pleasant
with me. But, marry, thus, my lord : my
dear lord and most esteemed friend, your
brother Troilus—   61
    Helen. My Lord Pandarus, honey-sweet
lord—
    Pan. Go to, sweet queen, go to—com-
mends himself most affectionately to you—
    Helen. You shall not bob us out of our
melody. If you do, our melancholy upon
your head !   66
    Pan. Sweet queen, sweet queen ; that's
a sweet queen, i' faith.
    Helen. And to make a sweet lady sad is a
sour offence.
    Pan. Nay, that shall not serve your turn ;
that shall it not, in truth, la. Nay, I care
not for such words ; no, no.—And, my lord,
he desires you that, if the King call for him
at supper, you will make his excuse.
    Helen. My Lord Pandarus !   74
    Pan. What says my sweet queen, my very
very sweet queen ?

Par. What exploit's in hand ?   Where sups he to-night ?

Helen. Nay, but, my lord—

Pan. What says my sweet queen ?—My cousin will fall out with you.

Helen. You must not know where he sups.   80

Par. I'll lay my life, with my disposer Cressida.

Pan. No, no, no such matter ; you are wide.   Come, your disposer is sick.

Par. Well, I'll make's excuse.

Pan. Ay, good my lord.   Why should you say Cressida ?   No, your poor disposer's sick.   86

Par. I spy

Pan. You spy !   What do you spy ?— Come, give me an instrument.   Now, sweet queen.

Helen. Why, this is kindly done.   90

Pan. My niece is horribly in love with a thing you have, sweet queen.

Helen. She shall have it, my lord, if it be not my Lord Paris.   94

Pan. He !   No, she'll none of him ; they two are twain.

Helen. Falling in, after falling out, may make them three.

Pan. Come, come.   I'll hear no more of this ; I'll sing you a song now.   99

Helen. Ay, ay, prithee now.   By my troth, sweet lord, thou hast a fine forehead.

Pan. Ay, you may, you may.

Helen. Let thy song be love.   This love will undo us all.   O Cupid, Cupid, Cupid !

Pan. Love !   Ay, that it shall, i' faith.   105

Par. Ay, good now, love, love, nothing but love.

Pan. In good troth, it begins so. [*Sings*]

Love, love, nothing but love, still love, still
    more !
    For, oh, love's bow
    Shoots buck and doe ;   110
    The shaft confounds
    Not that it wounds,
But tickles still the sore.
These lovers cry, O ho, they die !
    Yet that which seems the wound to kill
Doth turn O ho ! to ha ! ha ! he !   116
    So dying love lives still.
O ho ! a while, but ha ! ha ! ha !
O ho ! groans out for ha ! ha ! ha !—hey ho !

Helen. In love, i' faith, to the very tip of the nose.   121

Par. He eats nothing but doves, love ; and that breeds hot blood, and hot blood begets hot thoughts, and hot thoughts beget hot deeds, and hot deeds is love.   124

Pan. Is this the generation of love : hot blood, hot thoughts, and hot deeds ?   Why, they are vipers.   Is love a generation of vipers ?   Sweet lord, who's a-field today ?

Par. Hector, Deiphobus, Helenus, An-

tenor, and all the gallantry of Troy.   I would fain have arm'd to-day, but my Nell would not have it so.   How chance my brother Troilus went not ?   131

Helen. He hangs the lip at something. You know all, Lord Pandarus.

Pan. Not I, honey-sweet queen.   I long to hear how they sped to-day.   You'll remember your brother's excuse ?   136

Par. To a hair.

Pan. Farewell, sweet queen.

Helen. Commend me to your niece.   139

Pan. I will, sweet queen.   [*Exit.*
                                   [*Sound a retreat.*

Par. They're come from the field.   Let us
    to Priam's hall
To greet the warriors.   Sweet Helen, I must
    woo you
To help unarm our Hector.   His stubborn
    buckles,
With these your white enchanting fingers
    touch'd,
Shall more obey than to the edge of steel 145
Or force of Greekish sinews ; you shall do
    more
Than all the island kings—disarm great
    Hector.

Helen. 'Twill make us proud to be his
    servant, Paris ;
Yea, what he shall receive of us in duty
Gives us more palm in beauty than we
    have,   150
Yea, overshines ourself.

Par. Sweet, above thought I love thee.
                                          [*Exeunt.*

Scene II.   *Troy.   Pandarus' orchard.*

Enter PANDARUS *and* Troilus' *Boy, meeting.*

Pan. How now !   Where's thy master ? At my cousin Cressida's ?

Boy. No, sir ; he stays for you to conduct him thither.

Enter TROILUS.

Pan. O, here he comes.   How now, how now !   5

Tro. Sirrah, walk off.   [*Exit Boy.*

Pan. Have you seen my cousin ?

Tro. No, Pandarus.   I stalk about her
    door
Like a strange soul upon the Stygian banks
Staying for waftage.   O, be thou my
    Charon,   10
And give me swift transportation to these
    fields
Where I may wallow in the lily beds
Propos'd for the deserver !   O gentle
    Pandar,
From Cupid's shoulder pluck his painted
    wings,
And fly with me to Cressid !   15

Pan. Walk here i' th' orchard, I'll bring her straight.   [*Exit.*

Tro. I am giddy ; expectation whirls me
    round.
Th' imaginary relish is so sweet
That it enchants my sense ; what will
    it be
When that the wat'ry palate tastes indeed
Love's thrice-repured nectar ?   Death, I
    fear me ;   21
Swooning destruction ; or some joy too
    fine,
Too subtle-potent, tun'd too sharp in
    sweetness,
For the capacity of my ruder powers.
I fear it much ; and I do fear besides   25
That I shall lose distinction in my joys ;
As doth a battle, when they charge on
    heaps
The enemy flying.

Re-enter PANDARUS.

Pan. She's making her ready, she'll come
straight ; you must be witty now.   She
does so blush, and fetches her wind so
short, as if she were fray'd with a sprite.
I'll fetch her.   It is the prettiest villain;
she fetches her breath as short as a new-
ta'en sparrow.   [*Exit.*
Tro. Even such a passion doth embrace
    my bosom.
My heart beats thicker than a feverous
    pulse,   35
And all my powers do their bestowing lose,
Like vassalage at unawares encount'ring
The eye of majesty.

Re-enter PANDARUS *with* CRESSIDA.

Pan. Come, come, what need you blush ?
Shame's a baby.—Here she is now ; swear
the oaths now to her that you have sworn
to me.—What, are you gone again ?   You
must be watch'd ere you be made tame,
must you ?   Come your ways, come your
ways ; an you draw backward, we'll put
you i' th' fills.—Why do you not speak to
her ?—Come, draw this curtain and let's
see your picture.   Alas the day, how loath
you are to offend daylight !   An 'twere
dark, you'd close sooner.   So, so ; rub on,
and kiss the mistress.   How now, a kiss in
fee-farm !   Build there, carpenter ; the air
is sweet.   Nay, you shall fight your hearts
out ere I part you.   The falcon as the tercel,
for all the ducks i' th' river.   Go to, go to. 52
Tro. You have bereft me of all words,
lady.
Pan. Words pay no debts, give her deeds;
but she'll bereave you o' th' deeds too, if
she call your activity in question.   What,
billing again ?   Here's ' In witness whereof
the parties interchangeably'.   Come in, come
in ;   I'll go get a fire.   [*Exit.*
Cres. Will you walk in, my lord ?   59
Tro. O Cressid, how often have I wish'd
me thus !

Cres. Wish'd, my lord !   The gods grant—
O my lord !
Tro. What should they grant ?   What
makes this pretty abruption ?   What too
curious dreg espies my sweet lady in the
fountain of our love ?   64
Cres. More dregs than water, if my fears
have eyes.
Tro. Fears make devils of cherubins ;
they never see truly.
Cres. Blind fear, that seeing reason leads,
finds safer footing than blind reason
stumbling without fear.   To fear the worst
oft cures the worse.   70
Tro. O, let my lady apprehend no fear !
In all Cupid's pageant there is presented no
monster.
Cres. Nor nothing monstrous neither ?
Tro. Nothing, but our undertakings when
we vow to weep seas, live in fire, eat rocks,
tame tigers ;   thinking it harder for our
mistress to devise imposition enough than
for us to undergo any difficulty imposed.
This is the monstruosity in love, lady, that
the will is infinite, and the execution confin'd ; that the desire is boundless, and the
act a slave to limit.   80
Cres. They say all lovers swear more performance than they are able, and yet
reserve an ability that they never perform ;
vowing more than the perfection of ten,
and discharging less than the tenth part of
one.   They that have the voice of lions
and the act of hares, are they not monsters ?   86
Tro. Are there such ?   Such are not we.
Praise us as we are tasted, allow us as we
prove ;   our head shall go bare till merit
crown it.   No perfection in reversion shall
have a praise in present.   We will not name
desert before his birth ; and, being born,
his addition shall be humble.   Few words
to fair faith : Troilus shall be such to
Cressid as what envy can say worst shall
be a mock for his truth ; and what truth
can speak truest not truer than Troilus.   95
Cres. Will you walk in, my lord ?

Re-enter PANDARUS.

Pan. What, blushing still ?   Have you
not done talking yet ?
Cres. Well, uncle, what folly I commit, I
dedicate to you.   100
Pan. I thank you for that ; if my lord
get a boy of you, you'll give him me.   Be
true to my lord ; if he flinch, chide me
for it.
Tro. You know now your hostages : your
uncle's word and my firm faith.   105
Pan. Nay, I'll give my word for her too :
our kindred, though they be long ere they
are wooed, they are constant being won ;
they are burs, I can tell you ; they'll stick
where they are thrown.

805

Cres. Boldness comes to me now and
  brings me heart.   110
Prince Troilus, I have lov'd you night and
  day
For many weary months.
  Tro. Why was my Cressid then so hard
  to win?
  Cres. Hard to seem won; but I was won,
  my lord,
With the first glance that ever—pardon
  me.   115
If I confess much, you will play the tyrant.
I love you now; but till now not so much
But I might master it. In faith, I lie;
My thoughts were like unbridled children,
  grown
Too headstrong for their mother. See, we
  fools!   120
Why have I blabb'd? Who shall be true
  to us,
When we are so unsecret to ourselves?
But, though I lov'd you well, I woo'd you
  not;
And yet, good faith, I wish'd myself a
  man,
Or that we women had men's privilege 125
Of speaking first. Sweet, bid me hold my
  tongue,
For in this rapture I shall surely speak
The thing I shall repent. See, see, your
  silence,
Cunning in dumbness, from my weakness
  draws   129
My very soul of counsel. Stop my mouth.
  Tro. And shall, albeit sweet music issues
  thence.
  Pan. Pretty, i' faith.
  Cres. My lord, I do beseech you, pardon
  me;
'Twas not my purpose thus to beg a kiss.
I am asham'd. O heavens! what have I
  done?   135
For this time will I take my leave, my lord.
  Tro. Your leave, sweet Cressid!
  Pan. Leave! An you take leave till to-
morrow morning—
  Cres. Pray you, content you.
  Tro. What offends you, lady?   140
  Cres. Sir, mine own company.
  Tro. You cannot shun yourself.
  Cres. Let me go and try.
I have a kind of self resides with you;
But an unkind self, that it self will leave 145
To be another's fool. I would be gone.
Where is my wit? I know not what I speak.
  Tro. Well know they what they speak
  that speak so wisely.
  Cres. Perchance, my lord, I show more
  craft than love;
And fell so roundly to a large confession 150
To angle for your thoughts; but you are
  wise—
Or else you love not; for to be wise and
  love

Exceeds man's might; that dwells with
  gods above.
  Tro. O that I thought it could be in a
  woman—
As, if it can, I will presume in you—   155
To feed for aye her lamp and flames of love;
To keep her constancy in plight and youth,
Outliving beauty's outward, with a mind
That doth renew swifter than blood decays!
Or that persuasion could but thus convince
  me   160
That my integrity and truth to you
Might be affronted with the match and
  weight
Of such a winnowed purity in love.
How were I then uplifted! but, alas,
I am as true as truth's simplicity,   165
And simpler than the infancy of truth.
  Cres. In that I'll war with you.
  Tro.   O virtuous fight,
When right with right wars who shall be
  most right!
True swains in love shall in the world to
  come
Approve their truth by Troilus, when their
  rhymes,   170
Full of protest, of oath, and big compare,
Want similes, truth tir'd with iteration—
As true as steel, as plantage to the moon,
As sun to day, as turtle to her mate,
As iron to adamant, as earth to th' centre—
Yet, after all comparisons of truth,   176
As truth's authentic author to be cited,
'As true as Troilus' shall crown up the
  verse
And sanctify the numbers.
  Cres.   Prophet may you be!
If I be false, or swerve a hair from truth, 180
When time is old and hath forgot itself,
When waterdrops have worn the stones of
  Troy,
And blind oblivion swallow'd cities up,
And mighty states characterless are grated
To dusty nothing—yet let memory   185
From false to false, among false maids in
  love,
Upbraid my falsehood when th' have said
  'As false
As air, as water, wind, or sandy earth,
As fox to lamb, or wolf to heifer's calf,
Pard to the hind, or stepdame to her son'—
Yea, let them say, to stick the heart of
  falsehood,   191
'As false as Cressid'.
  Pan. Go to, a bargain made; seal it, seal
it; I'll be the witness. Here I hold your
hand; here my cousin's. If ever you prove
false one to another, since I have taken
such pains to bring you together, let all
pitiful goers-between be call'd to the
world's end after my name—call them all
Pandars; let all constant men be Troiluses,
all false women Cressids, and all brokers
between Pandars. Say 'Amen'.   200

Tro. Amen.

Cres. Amen.

Pan. Amen. Whereupon I will show you
a chamber and a bed ; which bed, because
it shall not speak of your pretty encounters,
press it to death. Away ! 205
And Cupid grant all tongue-tied maidens
here,
Bed, chamber, pander, to provide this gear !
[*Exeunt.*

SCENE III. *The Greek camp.*

Flourish. Enter AGAMEMNON, ULYSSES,
DIOMEDES, NESTOR, AJAX, MENELAUS,
and CALCHAS.

Cal. Now, Princes, for the service I have
done,
Th' advantage of the time prompts me
aloud
To call for recompense. Appear it to your
mind
That, through the sight I bear in things to
come,
I have abandon'd Troy, left my possession, 5
Incurr'd a traitor's name, expos'd myself
From certain and possess'd conveniences
To doubtful fortunes, sequest'ring from
me all
That time, acquaintance, custom, and con-
dition, 9
Made tame and most familiar to my nature;
And here, to do you service, am become
As new into the world, strange, un-
acquainted—
I do beseech you, as in way of taste,
To give me now a little benefit
Out of those many regist'red in promise, 15
Which you say live to come in my behalf.

Agam. What wouldst thou of us, Troyan?
Make demand.

Cal. You have a Troyan prisoner call'd
Antenor,
Yesterday took ; Troy holds him very dear.
Oft have you—often have you thanks
therefore— 20
Desir'd my Cressid in right great exchange,
Whom Troy hath still denied ; but this
Antenor,
I know, is such a wrest in their affairs
That their negotiations all must slack 24
Wanting his manage ; and they will almost
Give us a prince of blood, a son of Priam,
In change of him. Let him be sent, great
Princes,
And he shall buy my daughter ; and her
presence
Shall quite strike off all service I have done
In most accepted pain.

Agam.   Let Diomedes bear him, 30
And bring us Cressid hither. Calchas shall
have
What he requests of us. Good Diomed,
Furnish you fairly for this interchange ;

Withal, bring word if Hector will to-
morrow
Be answer'd in his challenge. Ajax is ready.

Dio. This shall I undertake ; and 'tis a
burden 36
Which I am proud to bear.
[*Exeunt Diomedes and Calchas.*

ACHILLES *and* PATROCLUS *stand in their
tent.*

Ulyss. Achilles stands i' th' entrance of
his tent.
Please it our general pass strangely by him,
As if he were forgot ; and, Princes all, 40
Lay negligent and loose regard upon him.
I will come last. 'Tis like he'll question me
Why such unplausive eyes are bent, why
turn'd on him ?
If so, I have derision med'cinable
To use between your strangeness and his
pride, 45
Which his own will shall have desire to
drink.
It may do good. Pride hath no other glass
To show itself but pride ; for supple knees
Feed arrogance and are the proud man's
fees.

Agam. We'll execute your purpose, and
put on 50
A form of strangeness as we pass along.
So do each lord ; and either greet him not,
Or else disdainfully, which shall shake him
more
Than if not look'd on. I will lead the way.

Achil. What comes the general to speak
with me ? 55
You know my mind, I'll fight no more
'gainst Troy.

Agam. What says Achilles ? Would he
aught with us ?

Nest. Would you, my lord, aught with
the general ?

Achil. No.

Nest. Nothing, my lord. 60

Agam. The better.
[*Exeunt Agamemnon and Nestor.*

Achil. Good day, good day.

Men. How do you ? How do you ? [*Exit.*

Achil. What, does the cuckold scorn me ?

Ajax. How now, Patroclus ? 65

Achil. Good morrow, Ajax.

Ajax. Ha ?

Achil. Good morrow.

Ajax. Ay, and good next day too. [*Exit.*

Achil. What mean these fellows ? Know
they not Achilles ? 70

Patr. They pass by strangely. They were
us'd to bend,
To send their smiles before them to Achilles,
To come as humbly as they us'd to creep
To holy altars.

Achil.   What, am I poor of late ?
'Tis certain, greatness, once fall'n out with
fortune, 75

Must fall out with men too. What the
    declin'd is,
He shall as soon read in the eyes of others
As feel in his own fall; for men, like
    butterflies,
Show not their mealy wings but to the
    summer;
And not a man for being simply man   80
Hath any honour, but honour for those
    honours
That are without him, as place, riches, and
    favour,
Prizes of accident, as oft as merit;
Which when they fall, as being slippery
    standers,
The love that lean'd on them as slippery
    too,   85
Doth one pluck down another, and together
Die in the fall. But 'tis not so with me:
Fortune and I are friends; I do enjoy
At ample point all that I did possess
Save these men's looks; who do, methinks,
    find out   90
Something not worth in me such rich
    beholding
As they have often given. Here is Ulysses.
I'll interrupt his reading.
How now, Ulysses!
    Ulyss.   Now, great Thetis' son!
    Achil. What are you reading?
    Ulyss.   A strange fellow here
Writes me that man—how dearly ever
    parted,   96
How much in having, or without or in—
Cannot make boast to have that which he
    hath,
Nor feels not what he owes, but by
    reflection;
As when his virtues shining upon others   100
Heat them, and they retort that heat again
To the first giver.
    Achil.   This is not strange, Ulysses.
The beauty that is borne here in the face
The bearer knows not, but commends itself
To others' eyes; nor doth the eye itself—
That most pure spirit of sense—behold
    itself,   106
Not going from itself; but eye to eye
    opposed
Salutes each other with each other's form;
For speculation turns not to itself
Till it hath travell'd, and is mirror'd there
Where it may see itself. This is not strange
    at all.   111
    Ulyss. I do not strain at the position—
It is familiar—but at the author's drift;
Who, in his circumstance, expressly proves
That no man is the lord of anything,   115
Though in and of him there be much
    consisting,
Till he communicate his parts to others;
Nor doth he of himself know them for
    aught
Till he behold them formed in th' applause

Where th' are extended; who, like an arch,
    reverb'rate   120
The voice again; or, like a gate of steel
Fronting the sun, receives and renders back
His figure and his heat. I was much rapt in
    this;
And apprehended here immediately
Th' unknown Ajax. Heavens, what a man
    is there!   125
A very horse that has he knows not what!
Nature, what things there are
Most abject in regard and dear in use!
What things again most dear in the esteem
And poor in worth! Now shall we see to-
    morrow—   130
An act that very chance doth throw upon
    him—
Ajax renown'd. O heavens, what some men
    do,
While some men leave to do!
How some men creep in skittish Fortune's
    hall,
Whiles others play the idiots in her eyes!   135
How one man eats into another's pride,
While pride is fasting in his wantonness!
To see these Grecian lords!—why, even
    already
They clap the lubber Ajax on the shoulder,
As if his foot were on brave Hector's breast,
And great Troy shrinking.   141
    Achil. I do believe it; for they pass'd by
    me
As misers do by beggars—neither gave to
    me
Good word nor look. What, are my deeds
    forgot?
    Ulyss. Time hath, my lord, a wallet at his
    back,   145
Wherein he puts alms for oblivion,
A great-siz'd monster of ingratitudes.
Those scraps are good deeds past, which are
    devour'd
As fast as they are made, forgot as soon
As done. Perseverance, dear my lord,   150
Keeps honour bright. To have done is to
    hang
Quite out of fashion, like a rusty mail
In monumental mock'ry. Take the instant
    way;
For honour travels in a strait so narrow
Where one but goes abreast. Keep then the
    path,   155
For emulation hath a thousand sons
That one by one pursue; if you give way,
Or hedge aside from the direct forthright,
Like to an ent'red tide they all rush by
And leave you hindmost;   160
Or, like a gallant horse fall'n in first rank,
Lie there for pavement to the abject rear,
O'er-run and trampled on. Then what they
    do in present,
Though less than yours in past, must
    o'ertop yours;
For Time is like a fashionable host,   165

That slightly shakes his parting guest by
    th' hand ;
And with his arms out-stretch'd, as he
    would fly,
Grasps in the comer.   The welcome ever
    smiles,
And farewell goes out sighing. O, let not
    virtue seek
Remuneration for the thing it was ;   170
For beauty, wit,
High birth, vigour of bone, desert in service,
Love, friendship, charity, are subjects all
To envious and calumniating Time.
One touch of nature makes the whole world
    kin—   175
That all with one consent praise new-born
    gawds,
Though they are made and moulded of
    things past,
And give to dust that is a little gilt
More laud than gilt o'er-dusted.   179
The present eye praises the present object.
Then marvel not, thou great and complete
    man,
That all the Greeks begin to worship Ajax,
Since things in motion sooner catch the eye
Than what stirs not. The cry went once on
    thee,
And still it might, and yet it may again, 185
If thou wouldst not entomb thyself alive
And case thy reputation in thy tent,
Whose glorious deeds but in these fields of
    late
Made emulous missions 'mongst the gods
    themselves,
And drave great Mars to faction.
    Achil.   Of this my privacy 190
I have strong reasons.
    Ulyss.   But 'gainst your privacy
The reasons are more potent and heroical.
'Tis known, Achilles, that you are in love
With one of Priam's daughters.
    Achil.   Ha ! known !
    Ulyss. Is that a wonder ?   195
The providence that's in a watchful state
Knows almost every grain of Plutus' gold ;
Finds bottom in th' uncomprehensive
    deeps ;
Keeps pace with thought, and almost, like
    the gods,   199
Do thoughts unveil in their dumb cradles.
There is a mystery—with whom relation
Durst never meddle—in the soul of state,
Which hath an operation more divine
Than breath or pen can give expressure to.
All the commerce that you have had with
    Troy   205
As perfectly is ours as yours, my lord ;
And better would it fit Achilles much
To throw down Hector than Polyxena.
But it must grieve young Pyrrhus now at
    home,
When fame shall in our island, sound her
    trump,   210

And all the Greekish girls shall tripping
    sing
' Great Hector's sister did Achilles win ;
But our great Ajax bravely beat down
    him '.
Farewell, my lord. I as your lover speak.
The fool slides o'er the ice that you should
    break.   [*Exit.*
    Patr. To this effect, Achilles, have I
    mov'd you.   216
A woman impudent and mannish grown
Is not more loath'd than an effeminate
    man
In time of action. I stand condemn'd for
    this ;
They think my little stomach to the war 220
And your great love to me restrains you
    thus.
Sweet, rouse yourself ; and the weak
    wanton Cupid
Shall from your neck unloose his amorous
    fold,
And, like a dew-drop from the lion's mane,
Be shook to airy air.
    Achil. Shall Ajax fight with Hector ?
    Patr. Ay, and perhaps receive much
    honour by him.   226
    Achil. I see my reputation is at stake ;
My fame is shrewdly gor'd.
    Patr.   O, then, beware :
Those wounds heal ill that men do give
    themselves ;
Omission to do what is necessary   230
Seals a commission to a blank of danger ;
And danger, like an ague, subtly taints
Even then when they sit idly in the sun.
    Achil. Go call Thersites hither, sweet
    Patroclus.
I'll send the fool to Ajax, and desire him 235
T' invite the Troyan lords, after the
    combat,
To see us here unarm'd. I have a woman's
    longing,
An appetite that I am sick withal,   238
To see great Hector in his weeds of peace ;
To talk with him, and to behold his visage,
Even to my full of view.

        Enter THERSITES.

             A labour sav'd !
    Ther. A wonder !
    Achil. What ?
    Ther. Ajax goes up and down the field
asking for himself.   245
    Achil. How so ?
    Ther. He must fight singly to-morrow
with Hector, and is so prophetically proud
of an heroical cudgelling that he raves in
saying nothing.
    Achil. How can that be ?   250
    Ther. Why, 'a stalks up and down like a
peacock—a stride and a stand ; ruminates
like an hostess that hath no arithmetic but
her brain to set down her reckoning, bites

his lip with a politic regard, as who should
say 'There were wit in this head, an 'twould
out '; and so there is ; but it lies as coldly
in him as fire in a flint, which will not show
without knocking. The man's undone for
ever ; for if Hector break not his neck i'
th' combat, he'll break't himself in vain-
glory. He knows not me. I said ' Good
morrow, Ajax '; and he replies ' Thanks,
Agamemnon'. What think you of this man
that takes me for the general ? He's grown
a very land fish, languageless, a monster.
A plague of opinion ! A man may wear it
on both sides, like a leather jerkin.   264

Achil. Thou must be my ambassador to
him, Thersites.

Ther. Who, I ? Why, he'll answer nobody ; he professes not answering. Speaking is for beggars : he wears his tongue in's
arms. I will put on his presence. Let
Patroclus make his demands to me, you
shall see the pageant of Ajax.   269

Achil. To him, Patroclus. Tell him I
humbly desire the valiant Ajax to invite
the most valorous Hector to come unarm'd
to my tent ; and to procure safe conduct
for his person of the magnanimous and
most illustrious six-or-seven-times-honour'd
Captain General of the Grecian army,
et cetera, Agamemnon. Do this.   275

Patr. Jove bless great Ajax !

Ther. Hum !

Patr. I come from the worthy Achilles—

Ther. Ha !   279

Patr. Who most humbly desires you to
invite Hector to his tent—

Ther. Hum !

Patr. And to procure safe conduct from
Agamemnon.

Ther. Agamemnon !

Patr. Ay, my lord.   285

Ther. Ha !

Patr. What say you to't ?

Ther. God buy you, with all my heart.

Patr. Your answer, sir.   289

Ther. If to-morrow be a fair day, by
eleven of the clock it will go one way or
other. Howsoever, he shall pay for me ere
he has me.

Patr. Your answer, sir.

Ther. Fare ye well, with all my heart.

Achil. Why, but he is not in this tune,
is he ?   295

Ther. No, but he's out a tune thus.
What music will be in him when Hector has
knock'd out his brains I know not ; but, I
am sure, none ; unless the fiddler Apollo
get his sinews to make catlings on.   299

Achil. Come, thou shalt bear a letter to
him straight.

Ther. Let me carry another to his horse ;
for that's the more capable creature.

Achil. My mind is troubled, like a
    fountain stirr'd ;

And I myself see not the bottom of it.   304
        [*Exeunt Achilles and Patroclus.*

Ther. Would the fountain of your mind
were clear again, that I might water an ass
at it. I had rather be a tick in a sheep
than such a valiant ignorance.   [*Exit.*

ACT FOUR

Scene I. *Troy. A street.*

Enter, at one side, ÆNEAS, *and Servant with
a torch ; at another,* PARIS, DEIPHOBUS,
ANTENOR, DIOMEDES *the Grecian, and
Others, with torches.*

Par. See, ho ! Who is that there ?

Dei.   It is the Lord Æneas.

Æne. Is the Prince there in person ?
Had I so good occasion to lie long
As you, Prince Paris, nothing but heavenly
        business   5
Should rob my bed-mate of my company.

Dio. That's my mind too. Good morrow,
        Lord Æneas.

Par. A valiant Greek, Æneas—take his
        hand :
Witness the process of your speech, wherein
You told how Diomed, a whole week by
        days,   10
Did haunt you in the field.

Æne.   Health to you, valiant sir,
During all question of the gentle truce ;
But when I meet you arm'd, as black
        defiance
As heart can think or courage execute.   15

Dio. The one and other Diomed em-
        braces.
Our bloods are now in calm ; and so long
        health !
But when contention and occasion meet,
By Jove, I'll play the hunter for thy life
With all my force, pursuit, and policy.   20

Æne. And thou shalt hunt a lion, that
        will fly
With his face backward. In humane
        gentleness,
Welcome to Troy ! now, by Anchises' life,
Welcome indeed ! By Venus' hand I swear
No man alive can love in such a sort   25
The thing he means to kill, more excellently.

Dio. We sympathise. Jove let Æneas
        live,
If to my sword his fate be not the glory,
A thousand complete courses of the sun !
But in mine emulous honour let him die   30
With every joint a wound, and that to-
        morrow !

Æne. We know each other well.

Dio. We do ; and long to know each
        other worse.

Par. This is the most despiteful'st gentle
        greeting,
The noblest hateful love, that e'er I heard
        of.   35

What business, lord, so early?

Æne. I was sent for to the King; but
why, I know not.

Par. His purpose meets you: 'twas to
bring this Greek   38
To Calchas' house, and there to render him,
For the enfreed Antenor, the fair Cressid.
Let's have your company; or, if you please,
Haste there before us.   I constantly
believe—
Or rather call my thought a certain know-
ledge—
My brother Troilus lodges there to-night.
Rouse him and give him note of our
approach,   45
With the whole quality wherefore; I fear
We shall be much unwelcome.

Æne.   That I assure you:
Troilus had rather Troy were borne to
Greece
Than Cressid borne from Troy.

Par.   There is no help;
The bitter disposition of the time   50
Will have it so. On, lord; we'll follow you.

Æne. Good morrow, all.

[*Exit with servant.*

Par. And tell me, noble Diomed—faith,
tell me true,
Even in the soul of sound good-fellowship—
Who in your thoughts deserves fair Helen
best,   55
Myself or Menelaus?

Dio.   Both alike:
He merits well to have her that doth seek
her,
Not making any scruple of her soilure,
With such a hell of pain and world of
charge;
And you as well to keep her that defend
her,   60
Not palating the taste of her dishonour,
With such a costly loss of wealth and
friends.
He like a puling cuckold would drink up
The lees and dregs of a flat tamed piece;
You, like a lecher, out of whorish loins   65
Are pleas'd to breed out your inheritors.
Both merits pois'd, each weighs nor less
nor more;
But he as he, the heavier for a whore.

Par. You are too bitter to your country-
woman.

Dio. She's bitter to her country. Hear
me, Paris: 70
For every false drop in her bawdy veins
A Grecian's life hath sunk; for every
scruple
Of her contaminated carrion weight
A Troyan hath been slain; since she could
speak,
She hath not given so many good words
breath   75
As for her Greeks and Troyans suff'red
death.

Par. Fair Diomed, you do as chapmen do,
Dispraise the thing that you desire to buy;
But we in silence hold this virtue well: 79
We'll not commend what we intend to sell.
Here lies our way.   [*Exeunt.*

SCENE II. *Troy. The court of Pandarus'
house.*

Enter TROILUS *and* CRESSIDA.

Tro. Dear, trouble not yourself; the
morn is cold.

Cres. Then, sweet my lord, I'll call mine
uncle down;
He shall unbolt the gates.

Tro.   Trouble him not;
To bed, to bed! Sleep kill those pretty
eyes,
And give as soft attachment to thy senses 5
As infants' empty of all thought!

Cres.   Good morrow, then.

Tro. I prithee now, to bed.

Cres.   Are you aweary of me?

Tro. O Cressida! but that the busy day,
Wak'd by the lark, hath rous'd the ribald
crows,
And dreaming night will hide our joys no
longer,   10
I would not from thee.

Cres.   Night hath been too brief.

Tro. Beshrew the witch! with venomous
wights she stays
As tediously as hell, but flies the grasps of
love
With wings more momentary-swift than
thought.
You will catch cold, and curse me.

Cres.   Prithee tarry. 15
You men will never tarry.
O foolish Cressid! I might have still held
off,
And then you would have tarried. Hark!
there's one up.

Pan. [*Within*] What's all the doors open
here?

Tro. It is your uncle.   20

Enter PANDARUS.

Cres. A pestilence on him! Now will he
be mocking.
I shall have such a life!

Pan. How now, how now! How go
maidenheads? Here, you maid! Where's
my cousin Cressid?

Cres. Go hang yourself, you naughty
mocking uncle.   25
You bring me to do, and then you flout me
too.

Pan. To do what? to do what? Let her
say what. What have I brought you to do?

Cres. Come, come, beshrew your heart!
You'll ne'er be good,
Nor suffer others.   30

Pan. Ha, ha! Alas, poor wretch! a poor

capocchia! hast not slept to-night? Would
he not, a naughty man, let it sleep? A
bugbear take him!

Cres. Did not I tell you? Would he were
　　knock'd i' th' head! [*One knocks.*
Who's that at door? Good uncle, go and
　　see.　　　　　　　　　　　　　　　35
My lord, come you again into my chamber.
You smile and mock me, as if I meant
　　naughtily.

Tro. Ha! ha!

Cres. Come, you are deceiv'd, I think of
　　no such thing.　　　　　　[*Knock.*
How earnestly they knock! Pray you
　　come in:　　　　　　　　　　　40
I would not for half Troy have you seen
　　here. [*Exeunt Troilus and Cressida.*

Pan. Who's there? What's the matter?
Will you beat down the door? How now?
What's the matter?

Enter ÆNEAS.

Æne. Good morrow, lord, good morrow.

Pan. Who's there? My lord Æneas? By
　　my troth,　　　　　　　　　　45
I knew you not. What news with you so
　　early?

Æne. Is not Prince Troilus here?

Pan. Here! What should he do here?

Æne. Come, he is here, my lord; do not
　　deny him.　　　　　　　　　　49
It doth import him much to speak with me.

Pan. Is he here, say you? It's more than
I know, I'll be sworn. For my own part,
I came in late. What should he do here?　53

Æne. Who!—nay, then. Come, come,
you'll do him wrong ere you are ware;
you'll be so true to him to be false to him.
Do not you know of him, but yet go fetch
him hither; go.　　　　　　　　　57

Re-enter TROILUS.

Tro. How now! What's the matter?

Æne. My lord, I scarce have leisure to
　　salute you,
My matter is so rash. There is at hand　60
Paris your brother, and Deiphobus,
The Grecian Diomed, and our Antenor
Deliver'd to us; and for him forthwith,
Ere the first sacrifice, within this hour,
We must give up to Diomedes' hand　　65
The Lady Cressida.

Tro.　　　　　　Is it so concluded?

Æne. By Priam, and the general state of
　　Troy.
They are at hand and ready to effect it.

Tro. How my achievements mock me!
I will go meet them; and, my lord Æneas,
We met by chance; you did not find me
　　here.　　　　　　　　　　　　71

Æne. Good, good, my lord, the secrets of
　　neighbour Pandar
Have not more gift in taciturnity.
　　　　　[*Exeunt Troilus and Æneas.*

Pan. Is't possible? No sooner got but
lost? The devil take Antenor! The young
prince will go mad. A plague upon Antenor!
I would they had broke's neck.　　　76

Re-enter CRESSIDA.

Cres. How now! What's the matter?
Who was here?

Pan. Ah, ah!

Cres. Why sigh you so profoundly?
Where's my lord? Gone? Tell me, sweet
uncle, what's the matter?　　　　　80

Pan. Would I were as deep under the
earth as I am above!

Cres. O the gods! What's the matter?

Pan. Pray thee, get thee in. Would thou
hadst ne'er been born! I knew thou
wouldst be his death! O, poor gentleman!
A plague upon Antenor!　　　　　86

Cres. Good uncle, I beseech you, on my
knees I beseech you, what's the matter?

Pan. Thou must be gone, wench, thou
must be gone; thou art chang'd for
Antenor; thou must to thy father, and be
gone from Troilus. 'Twill be his death;
'twill be his bane; he cannot bear it.　92

Cres. O you immortal gods! I will not
go.

Pan. Thou must.

Cres. I will not, uncle. I have forgot my
father;　　　　　　　　　　　　95
I know no touch of consanguinity,
No kin, no love, no blood, no soul so near
　　me
As the sweet Troilus. O you gods divine,
Make Cressid's name the very crown of
　　falsehood,
If ever she leave Troilus! Time, force, and
　　death,　　　　　　　　　　　100
Do to this body what extremes you can,
But the strong base and building of my love
Is as the very centre of the earth,
Drawing all things to it. I'll go in and
　　weep—

Pan. Do, do.　　　　　　　　　105

Cres. Tear my bright hair, and scratch
　　my praised cheeks,
Crack my clear voice with sobs and break
　　my heart,
With sounding 'Troilus'. I will not go from
Troy.　　　　　　　　　　　[*Exeunt.*

SCENE III.　*Troy. A street before Pandarus'
　　　　house.*

Enter PARIS, TROILUS, ÆNEAS, DEIPHOBUS,
　　ANTENOR, *and* DIOMEDES.

Par. It is great morning; and the hour
　　prefix'd
For her delivery to this valiant Greek
Comes fast upon. Good my brother
　　Troilus,
Tell you the lady what she is to do,　　4
And haste her to the purpose.

Tro.   Walk into her house.
I'll bring her to the Grecian presently ;
And to his hand when I deliver her,
Think it an altar, and thy brother Troilus
A priest, there off'ring to it his own heart.
                                        [*Exit.*

Par. I know what 'tis to love,   10
And would, as I shall pity, I could help !
Please you walk in, my lords.   [*Exeunt.*

SCENE IV. *Troy. Pandarus' house.*

Enter PANDARUS *and* CRESSIDA.

Pan. Be moderate, be moderate.
Cres. Why tell you me of moderation ?
The grief is fine, full, perfect, that I taste,
And violenteth in a sense as strong
As that which causeth it.   How can I
      moderate it ?   5
If I could temporize with my affections
Or brew it to a weak and colder palate,
The like allayment could I give my grief.
My love admits no qualifying dross ;   9
No more my grief, in such a precious loss.

Enter TROILUS.

Pan. Here, here, here he comes.   Ah,
sweet ducks !
Cres. O Troilus ! Troilus !
                          [*Embracing him.*
Pan. What a pair of spectacles is here !
Let me embrace too.   ' O heart,' as the
goodly saying is,

      O heart, heavy heart,   15
   Why sigh'st thou without breaking ?

where he answers again

   Because thou canst not ease thy smart
      By friendship nor by speaking.   19

There was never a truer rhyme.   Let us cast
away nothing, for we may live to have need
of such a verse.   We see it, we see it.   How
now, lambs !
Tro. Cressid, I love thee in so strain'd a
      purity
That the bless'd gods, as angry with my
      fancy,
More bright in zeal than the devotion
      which   25
Cold lips blow to their deities, take thee
      from me.
Cres. Have the gods envy ?
Pan. Ay, ay, ay, ay ; 'tis too plain a case.
Cres. And is it true that I must go from
      Troy ?
Tro. A hateful truth.
Cres.   What, and from Troilus too ?   30
Tro. From Troy and Troilus.
Cres.   Is't possible ?
Tro. And suddenly ; where injury of
      chance
Puts back leave-taking, justles roughly by
All time of pause, rudely beguiles our lips
Of all rejoindure, forcibly prevents   35

Our lock'd embrasures, strangles our dear
      vows
Even in the birth of our own labouring
      breath.
We two, that with so many thousand sighs
Did buy each other, must poorly sell
      ourselves   39
With the rude brevity and discharge of one.
Injurious time now with a robber's haste
Crams his rich thievery up, he knows not
      how.
As many farewells as be stars in heaven,
With distinct breath and consign'd kisses
      to them,
He fumbles up into a loose adieu,   45
And scants us with a single famish'd kiss,
Distasted with the salt of broken tears.
Æne. [*Within*] My lord, is the lady ready ?
Tro. Hark ! you are call'd.   Some say the
      Genius so
Cries ' Come ' to him that instantly must
      die.   50
Bid them have patience ; she shall come
      anon.
Pan. Where are my tears ?   Rain, to lay
this wind, or my heart will be blown up by
th' root ?   [*Exit.*
Cres. I must then to the Grecians ?
Tro.   No remedy.
Cres. A woeful Cressid 'mongst the merry
      Greeks !   55
When shall we see again ?
Tro. Hear me, my love.   Be thou but true
      of heart—
Cres. I true ! how now !   What wicked
      deem is this ?
Tro. Nay, we must use expostulation
      kindly,
For it is parting from us.   60
I speak not ' Be thou true ' as fearing thee,
For I will throw my glove to Death himself
That there's no maculation in thy heart ;
But ' Be thou true ' say I to fashion in
My sequent protestation : be thou true,   65
And I will see thee.
Cres. O, you shall be expos'd, my lord, to
      dangers
As infinite as imminent ! But I'll be true.
Tro. And I'll grow friend with danger.
      Wear this sleeve.
Cres. And you this glove.   When shall I
      see you ?   70
Tro. I will corrupt the Grecian sentinels
To give thee nightly visitation.
But yet be true.
Cres.   O heavens ! ' Be true ' again !
Tro. Hear why I speak it, love.
The Grecian youths are full of quality ;   75
They're loving, well compos'd with gifts of
      nature,
And flowing o'er with arts and exercise.
How novelties may move, and parts with
      person,
Alas, a kind of godly jealousy,

Which I beseech you call a virtuous sin, 80
Makes me afeard.
   Cres.   O heavens ! you love me not.
   Tro. Die I a villain, then !
In this I do not call your faith in question
So mainly as my merit. I cannot sing, 84
Nor heel the high lavolt, nor sweeten talk,
Nor play at subtle games—fair virtues all,
To which the Grecians are most prompt and
    pregnant ;
But I can tell that in each grace of these
There lurks a still and dumb-discoursive
    devil
That tempts most cunningly. But be not
    tempted. 90
   Cres. Do you think I will ?
   Tro. No.
But something may be done that we will
    not ;
And sometimes we are devils to ourselves,
When we will tempt the frailty of our
    powers, 95
Presuming on their changeful potency.
   Æne. [*Within*] Nay, good my lord !
   Tro. Come, kiss ; and let us part.
   Par. [*Within*] Brother Troilus !
   Tro.   Good brother, come you hither ;
And bring Æneas and the Grecian with you.
   Cres. My lord, will you be true ? 100
   Tro. Who, I ? Alas, it is my vice, my
    fault !
Whiles others fish with craft for great
    opinion,
I with great truth catch mere simplicity ;
Whilst some with cunning gild their copper
    crowns,
With truth and plainness I do wear mine
    bare. 105

Enter ÆNEAS, PARIS, ANTENOR, DEI-
   PHOBUS, *and* DIOMEDES.

Fear not my truth : the moral of my wit
Is ' plain and true ' ; there's all the reach
    of it.
Welcome, Sir Diomed ! Here is the lady
Which for Antenor we deliver you ; 109
At the port, lord, I'll give her to thy hand,
And by the way possess thee what she is.
Entreat her fair ; and, by my soul, fair
    Greek,
If e'er thou stand at mercy of my sword,
Name Cressid, and thy life shall be as safe
As Priam is in Ilion.
   Dio.   Fair Lady Cressid, 115
So please you, save the thanks this prince
    expects.
The lustre in your eye, heaven in your
    cheek,
Pleads your fair usage ; and to Diomed
You shall be mistress, and command him
    wholly.
   Tro. Grecian, thou dost not use me
    courteously 120
To shame the zeal of my petition to thee

In praising her. I tell thee, lord of Greece,
She is as far high-soaring o'er thy praises
As thou unworthy to be call'd her servant.
I charge thee use her well, even for my
    charge ; 125
For, by the dreadful Pluto, if thou dost not,
Though the great bulk Achilles be thy
    guard,
I'll cut thy throat.
   Dio.   O, be not mov'd, Prince Troilus.
Let me be privileg'd by my place and
    message
To be a speaker free : when I am hence 130
I'll answer to my lust. And know you, lord,
I'll nothing do on charge : to her own
    worth
She shall be priz'd. But that you say
    ' Be't so ',
I speak it in my spirit and honour, ' No '.
   Tro. Come, to the port. I'll tell thee,
    Diomed, 135
This brave shall oft make thee to hide thy
    head.
Lady, give me your hand ; and, as we walk,
To our own selves bend we our needful talk.
   [*Exeunt Troilus, Cressida, and Diomedes.*
                   [*Sound trumpet.*
   Par. Hark ! Hector's trumpet.
   Æne. How have we spent this morning !
The Prince must think me tardy and remiss,
That swore to ride before him to the field.
   Par. 'Tis Troilus' fault. Come, come to
    field with him.
   Dei. Let us make ready straight.
   Æne. Yea, with a bridegroom's fresh
    alacrity
Let us address to tend on Hector's heels. 145
The glory of our Troy doth this day lie
On his fair worth and single chivalry.
                       [*Exeunt.*

SCENE V. *The Grecian Camp. Lists set out.*

Enter AJAX, *armed ;* AGAMEMNON, ACHIL-
   LES, PATROCLUS, MENELAUS, ULYSSES,
   NESTOR, *and* Others.

   Agam. Here art thou in appointment
    fresh and fair,
Anticipating time with starting courage.
Give with thy trumpet a loud note to Troy,
Thou dreadful Ajax, that the appalled air
May pierce the head of the great com-
    batant, 5
And hale him hither.
   Ajax. Thou, trumpet, there's my purse.
Now crack thy lungs and split thy brazen
    pipe ;
Blow, villain, till thy sphered bias cheek
Out-swell the colic of puff'd Aquilon.
Come, stretch thy chest, and let thy eyes
    spout blood : 10
Thou blowest for Hector. [*Trumpet sounds.*
   Ulyss. No trumpet answers.
   Achil.   'Tis but early days.

Enter DIOMEDES, *with* CRESSIDA.

Agam. Is not yond Diomed, with Calchas'
    daughter ?
Ulyss. 'Tis he, I ken the manner of his
    gait :
He rises on the toe. That spirit of his   15
In aspiration lifts him from the earth.
Agam. Is this the lady Cressid ?
Dio.   Even she.
Agam. Most dearly welcome to the
    Greeks, sweet lady.
Nest. Our general doth salute you with a
    kiss.
Ulyss. Yet is the kindness but particular ;
'Twere better she were kiss'd in general. 21
Nest. And very courtly counsel : I'll
    begin.
So much for Nestor.
Achil. I'll take that winter from your
    lips, fair lady.
Achilles bids you welcome.   25
Men. I had good argument for kissing
    once.
Patr. But that's no argument for kissing
    now ;
For thus popp'd Paris in his hardiment,
And parted thus you and your argument.
Ulyss. O deadly gall, and theme of all
    our scorns !   30
For which we lose our heads to gild his
    horns.
Patr. The first was Menelaus' kiss ; this,
    mine—   [*Kisses her again.*
Patroclus kisses you.
Men.   O, this is trim !
Patr. Paris and I kiss evermore for him.
Men. I'll have my kiss, sir. Lady, by
    your leave.   35
Cres. In kissing, do you render or receive?
Patr. Both take and give.
Cres.   I'll make my match to live,
The kiss you take is better than you give ;
Therefore no kiss.
Men. I'll give you boot ; I'll give you
    three for one.   40
Cres. You are an odd man ; give even or
    give none.
Men. An odd man, lady ? Every man is
    odd.
Cres. No, Paris is not ; for you know 'tis
    true
That you are odd, and he is even with you.
Men. You fillip me o' th' head.
Cres.   No, I'll be sworn. 45
Ulyss. It were no match, your nail against
    his horn.
May I, sweet lady, beg a kiss of you ?
Cres. You may.
Ulyss.   I do desire it.
Cres.   Why, beg then.
Ulyss. Why then, for Venus' sake give
    me a kiss
When Helen is a maid again, and his. 50

Cres. I am your debtor ; claim it when
    'tis due.
Ulyss. Never's my day, and then a kiss
    of you.
Dio. Lady, a word. I'll bring you to your
    father.   [*Exit with Cressida.*
Nest. A woman of quick sense.
Ulyss.   Fie, fie upon her !
There's language in her eye, her cheek, her
    lip,   55
Nay, her foot speaks ; her wanton spirits
    look out
At every joint and motive of her body.
O these encounterers so glib of tongue
That give a coasting welcome ere it comes,
And wide unclasp the tables of their
    thoughts   60
To every ticklish reader ! Set them down
For sluttish spoils of opportunity,
And daughters of the game.
                    [*Trumpet within.*
All. The Troyans' trumpet.

Enter HECTOR, *armed* ; ÆNEAS, TROILUS,
    PARIS, HELENUS, *and other* Trojans,
    with Attendants.

Agam.   Yonder comes the troop.
Æne. Hail, all the state of Greece ! What
    shall be done   65
To him that victory commands ? Or do you
    purpose
A victor shall be known ? Will you the
    knights
Shall to the edge of all extremity
Pursue each other, or shall they be divided
By any voice or order of the field ?   70
Hector bade ask.
Agam. Which way would Hector have it?
Æne. He cares not ; he'll obey conditions.
Achil. 'Tis done like Hector ; but
    securely done,
A little proudly, and great deal misprizing
The knight oppos'd.
Æne.   If not Achilles, sir, 75
What is your name ?
Achil.   If not Achilles, nothing.
Æne. Therefore Achilles. But whate'er,
    know this :
In the extremity of great and little
Valour and pride excel themselves in
    Hector ;
The one almost as infinite as all,   80
The other blank as nothing. Weigh him
    well,
And that which looks like pride is courtesy.
This Ajax is half made of Hector's blood ;
In love whereof half Hector stays at
    home ;
Half heart, half hand, half Hector comes to
    seek   85
This blended knight, half Troyan and half
    Greek.
Achil. A maiden battle then ? O, I
    perceive you !

Re-enter DIOMEDES.

Agam. Here is Sir Diomed. Go, gentle
        knight,
Stand by our Ajax. As you and Lord Æneas
Consent upon the order of their fight,   90
So be it ; either to the uttermost,
Or else a breath. The combatants being kin
Half stints their strife before their strokes
        begin.
        [*Ajax and Hector enter the lists.*
Ulyss. They are oppos'd already.
Agam. What Troyan is that same that
        looks so heavy ?   95
Ulyss. The youngest son of Priam, a true
        knight ;
Not yet mature, yet matchless ; firm of
        word ;
Speaking in deeds and deedless in his
        tongue ;
Not soon provok'd, nor being provok'd
        soon calm'd ;
His heart and hand both open and both
        free ;   100
For what he has he gives, what thinks he
        shows,
Yet gives he not till judgment guide his
        bounty,
Nor dignifies an impair thought with
        breath ;
Manly as Hector, but more dangerous ;
For Hector in his blaze of wrath subscribes
To tender objects, but he in heat of action
Is more vindicative than jealous love.   107
They call him Troilus, and on him erect
A second hope as fairly built as Hector.
Thus says Æneas, one that knows the
        youth   110
Even to his inches, and, with private soul,
Did in great Ilion thus translate him to me.
        [*Alarum. Hector and Ajax fight.*
Agam. They are in action.
Nest. Now, Ajax, hold thine own !
Tro.   Hector, thou sleep'st ;
Awake thee.   115
Agam. His blows are well dispos'd. There,
        Ajax !   [*Trumpets cease.*
Dio. You must no more.
Æne.   Princes, enough, so please you.
Ajax. I am not warm yet ; let us fight
        again.
Dio. As Hector pleases.
Hect.   Why, then will I no more.
Thou art, great lord, my father's sister's
        son,   120
A cousin-german to great Priam's seed ;
The obligation of our blood forbids
A gory emulation 'twixt us twain :
Were thy commixtion Greek and Troyan so
That thou could'st say ' This hand is
        Grecian all,   125
And this is Troyan ; the sinews of this leg
All Greek, and this all Troy ; my mother's
        blood

Runs on the dexter cheek, and this sinister
Bounds in my father's ' ; by Jove multi-
        potent,
Thou shouldst not bear from me a Greekish
        member   130
Wherein my sword had not impressure
        made
Of our rank feud ; but the just gods gainsay
That any drop thou borrow'dst from thy
        mother,
My sacred aunt, should by my mortal
        sword
Be drained ! Let me embrace thee, Ajax.   135
By him that thunders, thou hast lusty
        arms ;
Hector would have them fall upon him
        thus.
Cousin, all honour to thee !
Ajax.   I thank thee, Hector.
Thou art too gentle and too free a man.
I came to kill thee, cousin, and bear hence
A great addition earned in thy death.   141
Hect. Not Neoptolemus so mirable,
On whose bright crest Fame with her loud'st
        Oyes
Cries ' This is he ' could promise to himself
A thought of added honour torn from
        Hector.   145
Æne. There is expectance here from both
        the sides
What further you will do.
Hect.   We'll answer it :
The issue is embracement. Ajax, farewell.
Ajax. If I might in entreaties find success,
As seld I have the chance, I would desire
My famous cousin to our Grecian tents.
Dio. 'Tis Agamemnon's wish ; and great
        Achilles
Doth long to see unarm'd the valiant
        Hector.
Hect. Æneas, call my brother Troilus to
        me,
And signify this loving interview   155
To the expecters of our Troyan part ;
Desire them home. Give me thy hand, my
        cousin ;
I will go eat with thee, and see your knights.

*Agamemnon and the rest of the Greeks come
        forward.*

Ajax. Great Agamemnon comes to meet
        us here.
Hect. The worthiest of them tell me name
        by name ;   160
But for Achilles, my own searching eyes
Shall find him by his large and portly size.
Agam. Worthy all arms ! as welcome as
        to one
That would be rid of such an enemy.
But that's no welcome. Understand more
        clear,   165
What's past and what's to come is strew'd
        with husks
And formless ruin of oblivion ;

But in this extant moment, faith and troth,
Strain'd purely from all hollow bias-
    drawing,
Bids thee with most divine integrity,   170
From heart of very heart, great Hector,
    welcome.
  Hect. I thank thee, most imperious
    Agamemnon.
  Agam. [*To Troilus*] My well-fam'd lord of
    Troy, no less to you.
  Men. Let me confirm my princely
    brother's greeting.
You brace of warlike brothers, welcome
    hither.   175
  Hect. Who must we answer?
  Æne.   The noble Menelaus.
  Hect. O you, my lord? By Mars his
    gauntlet, thanks!
Mock not that I affect the untraded oath;
Your quondam wife swears still by Venus'
    glove.
She's well, but bade me not commend her
    to you.   180
  Men. Name her not now, sir; she's a
    deadly theme.
  Hect. O, pardon; I offend.
  Nest. I have, thou gallant Troyan, seen
    thee oft,
Labouring for destiny, make cruel way
Through ranks of Greekish youth; and I
    have seen thee,   185
As hot as Perseus, spur thy Phrygian steed,
Despising many forfeits and subduements,
When thou hast hung thy advanced sword
    i' th' air,
Not letting it decline on the declined;
That I have said to some my standers-by
' Lo, Jupiter is yonder, dealing life!'   191
And I have seen thee pause and take thy
    breath,
When that a ring of Greeks have hemm'd
    thee in,
Like an Olympian wrestling. This have I
    seen;
But this thy countenance, still lock'd in
    steel,   195
I never saw till now. I knew thy grandsire,
And once fought with him. He was a
    soldier good,
But, by great Mars, the captain of us all,
Never like thee. O, let an old man embrace
    thee;
And, worthy warrior, welcome to our tents.
  Æne. 'Tis the old Nestor.   201
  Hect. Let me embrace thee, good old
    chronicle,
That hast so long walk'd hand in hand with
    time.
Most reverend Nestor, I am glad to clasp
    thee.
  Nest. I would my arms could match thee
    in contention   205
As they contend with thee in courtesy.
  Hect. I would they could.

  Nest. Ha!
By this white beard, I'd fight with thee
    to-morrow.
Well, welcome, welcome! I have seen the
    time.   210
  Ulyss. I wonder now how yonder city
    stands,
When we have here her base and pillar
    by us.
  Hect. I know your favour, Lord Ulysses,
    well.
Ah, sir, there's many a Greek and Troyan
    dead,
Since first I saw yourself and Diomed   215
In Ilion on your Greekish embassy.
  Ulyss. Sir, I foretold you then what
    would ensue.
My prophecy is but half his journey yet;
For yonder walls, that pertly front your
    town,
Yond towers, whose wanton tops do buss
    the clouds,   220
Must kiss their own feet.
  Hect.   I must not believe you.
There they stand yet; and modestly I
    think
The fall of every Phrygian stone will cost
A drop of Grecian blood. The end crowns
    all;
And that old common arbitrator, Time,   225
Will one day end it.
  Ulyss.   So to him we leave it.
Most gentle and most valiant Hector,
    welcome.
After the General, I beseech you next
To feast with me and see me at my tent.
  Achil. I shall forestall thee, Lord Ulysses,
    thou!   230
Now, Hector, I have fed mine eyes on thee;
I have with exact view perus'd thee,
    Hector,
And quoted joint by joint.
  Hect.   Is this Achilles?
  Achil. I am Achilles.
  Hect. Stand fair, I pray thee; let me look
    on thee.   235
  Achil. Behold thy fill.
  Hect.   Nay, I have done already.
  Achil. Thou art too brief. I will the
    second time,
As I would buy thee, view thee limb by
    limb.
  Hect. O, like a book of sport thou'lt read
    me o'er;
But there's more in me than thou under-
    stand'st.   240
Why dost thou so oppress me with thine
    eye?
  Achil. Tell me, you heavens, in which
    part of his body
Shall I destroy him? Whether there, or
    there, or there?
That I may give the local wound a
    name,

And make distinct the very breach where-
out   245
Hector's great spirit flew.   Answer me,
heavens.
Hect. It would discredit the blest gods,
proud man,
To answer such a question.   Stand again.
Think'st thou to catch my life so pleasantly
As to prenominate in nice conjecture   250
Where thou wilt hit me dead ?
Achil.   I tell thee yea.
Hect. Wert thou an oracle to tell me so,
I'd not believe thee.   Henceforth guard
thee well ;
For I'll not kill thee there, nor there, nor
there ;
But, by the forge that stithied Mars his
helm,   255
I'll kill thee everywhere, yea, o'er and o'er.
You wisest Grecians, pardon me this brag.
His insolence draws folly from my lips ;
But I'll endeavour deeds to match these
words,
Or may I never—
Ajax.   Do not chafe thee, cousin ;   260
And you, Achilles, let these threats alone
Till accident or purpose bring you to't.
You may have every day enough of Hector,
If you have stomach.   The general state,
I fear,   264
Can scarce entreat you to be odd with him.
Hect. I pray you let us see you in the
field ;
We have had pelting wars since you refus'd
The Grecians' cause.
Achil.   Dost thou entreat me, Hector ?
To-morrow do I meet thee, fell as death ;
To-night all friends.
Hect.   Thy hand upon that match. 270
Agam. First, all you peers of Greece, go
to my tent ;
There in the full convive we ; afterwards,
As Hector's leisure and your bounties shall
Concur together, severally entreat him.
Beat loud the tabourines, let the trumpets
blow,   275
That this great soldier may his welcome
know.
[*Exeunt all but Troilus and Ulysses.*
Tro. My Lord Ulysses, tell me, I beseech
you,
In what place of the field doth Calchas
keep ?
Ulyss. At Menelaus' tent, most princely
Troilus.   279
There Diomed doth feast with him to-night,
Who neither looks upon the heaven nor
earth,
But gives all gaze and bent of amorous view
On the fair Cressid.
Tro. Shall I, sweet lord, be bound to you
so much,
After we part from Agamemnon's tent, 285
To bring me thither ?

Ulyss.   You shall command me, sir.
As gentle tell me of what honour was
This Cressida in Troy ? Had she no lover
there
That wails her absence ?
Tro. O, sir, to such as boasting show
their scars   290
A mock is due.   Will you walk on, my lord ?
She was belov'd, she lov'd ; she is, and
doth ;
But still sweet love is food for fortune's
tooth.   [*Exeunt.*

ACT FIVE

SCENE I.   *The Grecian camp.   Before the*
tent of Achilles.

Enter ACHILLES *and* PATROCLUS.

Achil. I'll heat his blood with Greekish
wine to-night,
Which with my scimitar I'll cool to-morrow.
Patroclus, let us feast him to the height.
Patr. Here comes Thersites.

Enter THERSITES.

Achil.   How now, thou core of envy !
Thou crusty batch of nature, what's the
news ?   5
Ther. Why, thou picture of what thou
seemest, and idol of idiot worshippers,
here's a letter for thee.
Achil. From whence, fragment ?
Ther. Why, thou full dish of fool, from
Troy.
Patr. Who keeps the tent now ?   10
Ther. The surgeon's box or the patient's
wound.
Patr. Well said Adversity ! and what
needs these tricks ?
Ther. Prithee, be silent, boy ; I profit
not by thy talk ; thou art said to be
Achilles' male varlet.
Patr. Male varlet, you rogue ! What's
that ?   15
Ther. Why, his masculine whore. Now,
the rotten diseases of the south, the guts-
griping ruptures, catarrhs, loads o' gravel
in the back, lethargies, cold palsies, raw
eyes, dirt-rotten livers, wheezing lungs,
bladders full of imposthume, sciaticas,
limekilns i' th' palm, incurable bone-ache,
and the rivelled fee-simple of the tetter,
take and take again such preposterous
discoveries !   22
Patr. Why, thou damnable box of envy,
thou, what meanest thou to curse thus ?
Ther. Do I curse thee ?   25
Patr. Why, no, you ruinous butt ; you
whoreson indistinguishable cur, no.
Ther. No !   Why art thou, then, exasperate, thou idle immaterial skein of
sleid silk, thou green sarcenet flap for a
sore eye, thou tassel of a prodigal's purse,

thou? Ah, how the poor world is pest'red
with such water-flies—diminutives of
nature!   32
  Patr. Out, gall!
  Ther. Finch egg!
  Achil. My sweet Patroclus, I am thwarted
      quite   35
From my great purpose in to-morrow's
      battle.
Here is a letter from Queen Hecuba,
A token from her daughter, my fair love,
Both taxing me and gaging me to keep
An oath that I have sworn. I will not break
      it.   40
Fall Greeks; fail fame; honour or go or
      stay;
My major vow lies here, this I'll obey.
Come, come, Thersites, help to trim my
      tent;
This night in banqueting must all be spent.
Away, Patroclus!   [*Exit with Patroclus.*
  Ther. With too much blood and too little
brain these two may run mad; but, if with
too much brain and too little blood they do,
I'll be a curer of madmen. Here's Agamemnon, an honest fellow enough, and one that
loves quails, but he has not so much brain
as ear-wax; and the goodly transformation
of Jupiter there, his brother, the bull, the
primitive statue and oblique memorial of
cuckolds, a thrifty shoeing-horn in a chain,
hanging at his brother's leg—to what form
but that he is, should wit larded with
malice, and malice forced with wit, turn
him to? To an ass, were nothing: he is
both ass and ox. To an ox, were nothing:
he is both ox and ass. To be a dog, a mule,
a cat, a fitchew, a toad, a lizard, an owl, a
puttock, or a herring without a roe, I would
not care; but to be Menelaus, I would
conspire against destiny. Ask me not what
I would be, if I were not Thersites; for I
care not to be the louse of a lazar, so I were
not Menelaus. Hey-day! sprites and fires!

Enter HECTOR, TROILUS, AJAX, AGAMEM-
    NON, ULYSSES, NESTOR, MENELAUS, *and*
    DIOMEDES, *with lights.*

  Agam. We go wrong, we go wrong.
  Ajax.   No, yonder 'tis;
There, where we see the lights.
  Hect.   I trouble you.   65
  Ajax. No, not a whit.

            Re-enter ACHILLES.

  Ulyss. Here comes himself to guide you.
  Achil. Welcome, brave Hector; welcome
      Princes all.
  Agam. So now, fair Prince of Troy, I bid
      good night;
Ajax commands the guard to tend on you.
  Hect. Thanks, and good night to the
      Greeks' general.   70
  Men. Good night, my lord.

  Hect. Good night, sweet Lord Menelaus.
  Ther. Sweet draught! ' Sweet ' quoth 'a?
Sweet sink, sweet sewer!
  Achil. Good night and welcome, both at
      once, to those
That go or tarry.   75
  Agam. Good night.
            [*Exeunt Agamemnon and Menelaus.*
  Achil. Old Nestor tarries; and you too,
      Diomed,
Keep Hector company an hour or two.
  Dio. I cannot, lord; I have important
      business,
The tide whereof is now. Good night, great
      Hector.   80
  Hect. Give me your hand.
  Ulyss. [*Aside to Troilus*] Follow his torch;
      he goes to Calchas' tent;
I'll keep you company.
  Tro.   Sweet sir, you honour me.
  Hect. And so, good night. [*Exit Diomedes;
            Ulysses and Troilus following.*
  Achil.   Come, come, enter my tent. 85
            [*Exeunt all but Thersites.*
  Ther. That same Diomed's a false-
hearted rogue, a most unjust knave; I will
no more trust him when he leers than I will
a serpent when he hisses. He will spend his
mouth and promise, like Brabbler the
hound; but when he performs, astronomers
foretell it: it is prodigious, there will come
some change; the sun borrows of the moon
when Diomed keeps his word. I will rather
leave to see Hector than not to dog him.
They say he keeps a Troyan drab, and uses
the traitor Calchas' tent. I'll after. Nothing
but lechery! All incontinent varlets!   95
                                               [*Exit.*

     SCENE II. *The Grecian camp. Before
                Calchas' tent.*

            Enter DIOMEDES.

  Dio. What, are you up here, ho? Speak.
  Cal. [*Within*] Who calls?
  Dio. Diomed. Calchas, I think. Where's
your daughter?
  Cal. [*Within*] She comes to you.

Enter TROILUS *and* ULYSSES, *at a distance;
            after them* THERSITES.

  Ulyss. Stand where the torch may not
      discover us.

            Enter CRESSIDA.

  Tro. Cressid comes forth to him.
  Dio. How now, my charge!
  Cres. Now, my sweet guardian! Hark, a
      word with you.   [*Whispers.*
  Tro. Yea, so familiar!
  Ulyss. She will sing any man at first sight.
  Ther. And any man may sing her, if he
can take her cliff; she's noted.   11
  Dio. Will you remember?

Cres. Remember ? Yes.

Dio. Nay, but do, then ;
And let your mind be coupled with your
   words. 15

Tro. What shall she remember ?

Ulyss. List !

Cres. Sweet honey Greek, tempt me no
   more to folly.

Ther. Roguery !

Dio. Nay, then— 20

Cres. I'll tell you what—

Dio. Fo, fo ! come, tell a pin ; you are
   a forsworn—

Cres. In faith, I cannot. What would you
   have me do ?

Ther. A juggling trick, to be secretly
open.

Dio. What did you swear you would
   bestow on me ? 25

Cres. I prithee, do not hold me to mine
   oath ;
Bid me do anything but that, sweet
   Greek.

Dio. Good night.

Tro. Hold, patience !

Ulyss. How now, Troyan ! 30

Cres. Diomed !

Dio. No. no, good night ; I'll be your
   fool no more.

Tro. Thy better must.

Cres. Hark ! a word in your ear.

Tro. O plague and madness ! 35

Ulyss. You are moved, Prince ; let us
   depart, I pray,
Lest your displeasure should enlarge itself
To wrathful terms. This place is danger-
   ous ;
The time right deadly ; I beseech you, go.

Tro. Behold, I pray you.

Ulyss. Nay, good my lord, go off ;
You flow to great distraction ; come, my
   lord. 41

Tro. I prithee stay.

Ulyss. You have not patience ; come.

Tro. I pray you, stay ; by hell and all
   hell's torments,
I will not speak a word.

Dio. And so, good night.

Cres. Nay, but you part in anger.

Tro. Doth that grieve thee ? O withered
   truth !

Ulyss. How now, my lord ?

Tro. By Jove, I will be patient. 46

Cres. Guardian ! Why, Greek !

Dio. Fo, fo ! adieu ! you palter.

Cres. In faith, I do not. Come hither
   once again.

Ulyss. You shake, my lord, at something ;
   will you go ? 50
You will break out.

Tro. She strokes his cheek.

Ulyss. Come, come.

Tro. Nay, stay ; by Jove, I will not speak
   a word :

There is between my will and all offences
A guard of patience. Stay a little while. 54

Ther. How the devil luxury, with his fat
rump and potato finger, tickles these together ! Fry, lechery, fry !

Dio. But will you, then ?

Cres. In faith, I will, lo ; never trust me
   else.

Dio. Give me some token for the surety
   of it. 59

Cres. I'll fetch you one. [*Exit.*

Ulyss. You have sworn patience.

Tro. Fear me not, my lord ;
I will not be myself, nor have cognition
Of what I feel. I am all patience.

Re-enter CRESSIDA.

Ther. Now the pledge ; now, now, now !

Cres. Here, Diomed, keep this sleeve. 65

Tro. O beauty ! where is thy faith ?

Ulyss. My lord !

Tro. I will be patient ; outwardly I will.

Cres. You look upon that sleeve ; behold
   it well.
He lov'd me—O false wench !—Give't me
   again.

Dio. Whose was't ? 70

Cres. It is no matter, now I ha't again.
I will not meet with you to-morrow night.
I prithee, Diomed, visit me no more.

Ther. Now she sharpens. Well said,
whetstone.

Dio. I shall have it.

Cres. What, this ?

Dio. Ay, that.

Cres. O all you gods ! O pretty, pretty
   pledge ! 76
Thy master now lies thinking on his bed
Of thee and me, and sighs, and takes my
   glove,
And gives memorial dainty kisses to it,
As I kiss thee. Nay, do not snatch it from
   me ; 80
He that takes that doth take my heart
   withal.

Dio. I had your heart before ; this follows
   it.

Tro. I did swear patience.

Cres. You shall not have it, Diomed ;
   faith, you shall not ;
I'll give you something else. 85

Dio. I will have this. Whose was it ?

Cres. It is no matter.

Dio. Come, tell me whose it was.

Cres. 'Twas one's that lov'd me better
   than you will. 88
But, now you have it, take it.

Dio. Whose was it ?

Cres. By all Diana's waiting women yond,
And by herself, I will not tell you whose.

Dio. To-morrow will I wear it on my
   helm,
And grieve his spirit that dares not
   challenge it.

Tro. Wert thou the devil and wor'st it on thy horn,
It should be challeng'd.   95
    Cres. Well, well, 'tis done, 'tis past; and yet it is not;
I will not keep my word.
    Dio.   Why, then farewell;
Thou never shalt mock Diomed again.
    Cres. You shall not go. One cannot speak a word
But it straight starts you.
    Dio.   I do not like this fooling. 100
    Ther. Nor I, by Pluto; but that that likes not you
Pleases me best.
    Dio. What, shall I come? The hour—
    Cres. Ay, come—O Jove! Do come. I shall be plagu'd.
    Dio. Farewell till then.
    Cres.   Good night. I prithee come.
                            [*Exit Diomedes.*
Troilus, farewell! One eye yet looks on thee;   105
But with my heart the other eye doth see.
Ah, poor our sex! this fault in us I find,
The error of our eye directs our mind.
What error leads must err; O, then conclude,
Minds sway'd by eyes are full of turpitude.
                                    [*Exit.*
    Ther. A proof of strength she could not publish more,   111
Unless she said 'My mind is now turn'd whore'.
    Ulyss. All's done, my lord.
    Tro.   It is.
    Ulyss.   Why stay we, then?
    Tro. To make a recordation to my soul
Of every syllable that here was spoke. 115
But if I tell how these two did coact,
Shall I not lie in publishing a truth?
Sith yet there is a credence in my heart,
An esperance so obstinately strong,   119
That doth invert th' attest of eyes and ears;
As if those organs had deceptious functions
Created only to calumniate.
Was Cressid here?
    Ulyss.   I cannot conjure, Troyan.
    Tro. She was not, sure.
    Ulyss.   Most sure she was.
    Tro. Why, my negation hath no taste of madness.   125
    Ulyss. Nor mine, my lord. Cressid was here but now.
    Tro. Let it not be believ'd for womanhood.
Think, we had mothers; do not give advantage
To stubborn critics, apt, without a theme,
For depravation, to square the general sex
By Cressid's rule. Rather think this not Cressid.   131
    Ulyss. What hath she done, Prince, that can soil our mothers?

Tro. Nothing at all, unless that this were she.
    Ther. Will 'a swagger himself out on's own eyes?
    Tro. This she? No; this is Diomed's Cressida.   135
If beauty have a soul, this is not she;
If souls guide vows, if vows be sanctimonies,
If sanctimony be the gods' delight,
If there be rule in unity itself,   139
This was not she. O madness of discourse,
That cause sets up with and against itself!
Bifold authority! where reason can revolt
Without perdition, and loss assume all reason   143
Without revolt: this is, and is not, Cressid.
Within my soul there doth conduce a fight
Of this strange nature, that a thing inseparate
Divides more wider than the sky and earth;
And yet the spacious breadth of this division
Admits no orifex for a point as subtle
As Ariachne's broken woof to enter.   150
Instance, O instance! strong as Pluto's gates;
Cressid is mine, tied with the bonds of heaven.
Instance, O instance! strong as heaven itself:
The bonds of heaven are slipp'd, dissolv'd, and loos'd;
And with another knot, five-finger-tied, 155
The fractions of her faith, orts of her love,
The fragments, scraps, the bits, and greasy relics
Of her o'er-eaten faith, are bound to Diomed.
    Ulyss. May worthy Troilus be halfattach'd
With that which here his passion doth express?   160
    Tro. Ay, Greek; and that shall be divulged well
In characters as red as Mars his heart
Inflam'd with Venus. Never did young man fancy
With so eternal and so fix'd a soul.   164
Hark, Greek: as much as I do Cressid love,
So much by weight hate I her Diomed.
That sleeve is mine that he'll bear on his helm;
Were it a casque compos'd by Vulcan's skill
My sword should bite it. Not the dreadful spout
Which shipmen do the hurricano call,   170
Constring'd in mass by the almighty sun,
Shall dizzy with more clamour Neptune's ear
In his descent than shall my prompted sword
Falling on Diomed.
    Ther. He'll tickle it for his concupy. 175

821

Tro. O Cressid! O false Cressid! false,
false, false!
Let all untruths stand by thy stained name,
And they'll seem glorious.
    Ulyss.   O, contain yourself;
Your passion draws ears hither.

Enter ÆNEAS.

Æne. I have been seeking you this hour,
    my lord.   180
Hector, by this, is arming him in Troy;
Ajax, your guard, stays to conduct you
    home.
    Tro. Have with you, Prince.   My
    courteous lord, adieu.
Farewell, revolted fair!—and, Diomed,
Stand fast and wear a castle on thy head.
    Ulyss. I'll bring you to the gates.
    Tro. Accept distracted thanks.   187
            [*Exeunt Troilus, Æneas, and Ulysses.*
    Ther. Would I could meet that rogue
Diomed! I would croak like a raven; I
would bode, I would bode. Patroclus will
give me anything for the intelligence of this
whore; the parrot will not do more for an
almond than he for a commodious drab.
Lechery, lechery! Still wars and lechery!
Nothing else holds fashion. A burning devil
take them!   [*Exit.*

SCENE III. *Troy. Before Priam's palace.*

Enter HECTOR *and* ANDROMACHE.

And. When was my lord so much un-
    gently temper'd
To stop his ears against admonishment?
Unarm, unarm, and do not fight to-day.
    Hect. You train me to offend you; get
    you in.
By all the everlasting gods, I'll go.   5
    And. My dreams will, sure, prove
    ominous to the day.
    Hect. No more, I say.

Enter CASSANDRA.

Cas.   Where is my brother Hector?
And. Here, sister, arm'd, and bloody in
    intent.
Consort with me in loud and dear petition,
Pursue we him on knees; for I have
    dreamt
Of bloody turbulence, and this whole night
Hath nothing been but shapes and forms
    of slaughter.
    Cas. O, 'tis true!
    Hect.   Ho! bid my trumpet sound.
    Cas. No notes of sally, for the heavens,
    sweet brother!
    Hect. Be gone, I say. The gods have
    heard me swear.   15
    Cas. The gods are deaf to hot and peevish
    vows;
They are polluted off'rings, more abhorr'd
Than spotted livers in the sacrifice.

And. O, be persuaded! Do not count it
    holy
To hurt by being just. It is as lawful, 20
For we would give much, to use violent
    thefts
And rob in the behalf of charity.
    Cas. It is the purpose that makes strong
    the vow;
But vows to every purpose must not hold.
Unarm, sweet Hector.
    Hect.   Hold you still, I say. 25
Mine honour keeps the weather of my
    fate.
Life every man holds dear; but the dear
    man
Holds honour far more precious dear than
    life.

Enter TROILUS.

How now, young man! Mean'st thou to
    fight to-day?   29
    And. Cassandra, call my father to
    persuade.   [*Exit Cassandra.*
    Hect. No, faith, young Troilus; doff thy
    harness, youth;
I am to-day i' th' vein of chivalry.
Let grow thy sinews till their knots be
    strong,
And tempt not yet the brushes of the war.
Unarm thee, go; and doubt thou not,
    brave boy,   35
I'll stand to-day for thee and me and Troy.
    Tro. Brother, you have a vice of mercy
    in you
Which better fits a lion than a man.
    Hect. What vice is that, good Troilus?
    Chide me for it.
    Tro. When many times the captive
    Grecian falls,   40
Even in the fan and wind of your fair
    sword,
You bid them rise and live.
    Hect. O, 'tis fair play!
    Tro.   Fool's play, by heaven, Hector.
    Hect. How now! how now!
    Tro.   For th' love of all the gods,
Let's leave the hermit Pity with our
    mother!   45
And when we have our armours buckled on,
The venom'd vengeance ride upon our
    swords,
Spur them to ruthful work, rein them from
    ruth!
    Hect. Fie, savage, fie!
    Tro.   Hector, then 'tis wars.
    Hect. Troilus, I would not have you fight
    to-day.   50
    Tro. Who should withhold me?
Not fate, obedience, nor the hand of Mars
Beck'ning with fiery truncheon my retire;
Not Priamus and Hecuba on knees,
Their eyes o'ergalled with recourse of tears;
Nor you, my brother, with your true sword
    drawn,   56

Oppos'd to hinder me, should stop my way,
But by my ruin.

Re-enter CASSANDRA, *with* PRIAM.

   Cas. Lay hold upon him, Priam, hold him
    fast ;
He is thy crutch ; now if thou lose thy
    stay,   60
Thou on him leaning, and all Troy on
    thee,
Fall all together.
   Pri.   Come, Hector, come, go back.
Thy wife hath dreamt ; thy mother hath
    had visions ;
Cassandra doth foresee ; and I myself
Am like a prophet suddenly enrapt   65
To tell thee that this day is ominous.
Therefore, come back.
   Hect.   Æneas is a-field ;
And I do stand engag'd to many Greeks,
Even in the faith of valour, to appear
This morning to them.
   Pri.   Ay, but thou shalt not go. 70
   Hect. I must not break my faith.
You know me dutiful ; therefore, dear sir,
Let me not shame respect ; but give me
    leave
To take that course by your consent and
    voice   74
Which you do here forbid me, royal Priam,
   Cas. O Priam, yield not to him !
   And.   Do not, dear father.
   Hect. Andromache, I am offended with
    you.
Upon the love you bear me, get you in.
               [*Exit Andromache.*
   Tro. This foolish, dreaming, superstitious
    girl
Makes all these bodements.
   Cas.   O, farewell, dear Hector ! 80
Look how thou diest. Look how thy eye
    turns pale.
Look how thy wounds do bleed at many
    vents.
Hark how Troy roars ; how Hecuba cries
    out ;
How poor Andromache shrills her dolours
    forth ;
Behold distraction, frenzy, and amaze-
    ment,   85
Like witless antics, one another meet,
And all cry, Hector ! Hector's dead ! O
    Hector !
   Tro. Away, away !
   Cas. Farewell !—yet, soft ! Hector I
    take my leave.
Thou dost thyself and all our Troy deceive.
                     [*Exit.*
   Hect. You are amaz'd, my liege, at her
    exclaim.   91
Go in, and cheer the town ; we'll forth, and
    fight,
Do deeds worth praise and tell you them at
    night.

   Pri. Farewell. The gods with safety
    stand about thee ! [*Exeunt severally*
               Priam and Hector. Alarums.
   Tro. They are at it, hark ! Proud
    Diomed, believe,   95
I come to lose my arm or win my sleeve.

Enter PANDARUS.

   Pan. Do you hear, my lord ? Do you
hear ?
   Tro. What now ?
   Pan. Here's a letter come from yond
poor girl.
   Tro. Let me read.   100
   Pan. A whoreson tisick, a whoreson
rascally tisick so troubles me, and the
foolish fortune of this girl, and what one
thing, what another, that I shall leave you
one o' th's days ; and I have a rheum in
mine eyes too, and such an ache in my
bones that unless a man were curs'd I
cannot tell what to think on't. What says
she there ?   107
   Tro. Words, words, mere words, no
    matter from the heart ;
Th' effect doth operate another way.
               [*Tearing the letter.*
Go, wind, to wind, there turn and change
    together.   110
My love with words and errors still she
    feeds,
But edifies another with her deeds.
[*Pan.* Why but heare you.
   Tro. Hence broker-lackey. Ignominy and
    shame
Pursue thy life and live aye with thy name!]
               [*Exeunt severally.*

SCENE IV. *The plain between Troy and the
Grecian camp.*

Enter THERSITES. *Excursions.*

   Ther. Now they are clapper-clawing one
another ; I'll go look on. That dissembling
abominable varlet, Diomed, has got that
same scurvy doting foolish young knave's
sleeve of Troy there in his helm. I would
fain see them meet, that that same young
Troyan ass that loves the whore there
might send that Greekish whoremasterly
villain with the sleeve back to the dissembling luxurious drab of a sleeve-less
errand. A th' t'other side, the policy of
those crafty swearing rascals—that stale
old mouse-eaten dry cheese, Nestor, and
that same dog-fox, Ulysses—is not prov'd
worth a blackberry. They set me up, in
policy, that mongrel cur, Ajax, against
that dog of as bad a kind, Achilles ; and
now is the cur Ajax prouder than the cur
Achilles, and will not arm to-day ; whereupon the Grecians begin to proclaim
barbarism, and policy grows into an ill
opinion.   16

Enter DIOMEDES, TROILUS *following.*

Soft ! here comes sleeve, and t'other.

Tro. Fly not ; for shouldst thou take the
    river Styx
I would swim after.

Dio.   Thou dost miscall retire.
I do not fly ; but advantageous care   20
Withdrew me from the odds of multitude.
Have at thee.

Ther. Hold thy whore, Grecian ; now for
thy whore, Troyan—now the sleeve, now
the sleeve !
            [*Exeunt Troilus and Diomedes fighting.*

Enter HECTOR.

Hect. What art thou, Greek ? Art thou
    for Hector's match ?   25
Art thou of blood and honour ?

Ther. No, no—I am a rascal ; a scurvy
railing knave ; a very filthy rogue.

Hect. I do believe thee. Live.   [*Exit.*

Ther. God-a-mercy, that thou wilt
believe me ; but a plague break thy neck
for frighting me ! What's become of the
wenching rogues ? I think they have
swallowed one another. I would laugh at
that miracle. Yet, in a sort, lechery eats
itself. I'll seek them.   [*Exit.*

SCENE V. *Another part of the plain.*

Enter DIOMEDES *and a* Servant.

Dio. Go, go, my servant, take thou
    Troilus' horse ;
Present the fair steed to my lady Cressid.
Fellow, commend my service to her beauty;
Tell her I have chastis'd the amorous
    Troyan,
And am her knight by proof.

Serv.   I go, my lord.   5
                                   [*Exit.*

Enter AGAMEMNON.

Agam. Renew, renew ! The fierce Poly-
    damus
Hath beat down Menon ; bastard Mar-
    garelon
Hath Doreus prisoner,
And stands colossus-wise, waving his beam,
Upon the pashed corses of the kings   10
Epistrophus and Cedius. Polixenes is slain;
Amphimacus and Thoas deadly hurt ;
Patroclus ta'en, or slain ; and Palamedes
Sore hurt and bruis'd. The dreadful
    Sagittary
Appals our numbers. Haste we, Diomed, 15
To reinforcement, or we perish all.

Enter NESTOR.

Nest. Go, bear Patroclus' body to
    Achilles,
And bid the snail-pac'd Ajax arm for
    shame.

There is a thousand Hectors in the field ;
Now here he fights on Galathe his horse, 20
And there lacks work ; anon he's there
    afoot,
And there they fly or die, like scaled sculls
Before the belching whale ; then is he
    yonder,
And there the strawy Greeks, ripe for his
    edge,
Fall down before him like the mower's
    swath.   25
Here, there, and everywhere, he leaves and
    takes ;
Dexterity so obeying appetite
That what he will he does, and does so
    much
That proof is call'd impossibility.

Enter ULYSSES.

Ulyss. O, courage, courage, Princes !
    Great Achilles   30
Is arming, weeping, cursing, vowing
    vengeance.
Patroclus' wounds have rous'd his drowsy
    blood,
Together with his mangled Myrmidons,
That noseless, handless, hack'd and chipp'd,
    come to him,
Crying on Hector. Ajax hath lost a friend
And foams at mouth, and he is arm'd and
    at it,   36
Roaring for Troilus ; who hath done to-day
Mad and fantastic execution,
Engaging and redeeming of himself
With such a careless force and forceless care
As if that luck, in very spite of cunning,
Bade him win all.   42

Enter AJAX.

Ajax. Troilus ! thou coward Troilus !
                                   [*Exit.*
Dio. Ay, there, there.

Nest. So, so, we draw together.   [*Exit.*

Enter ACHILLES.

Achil. Where is this Hector ?
Come, come, thou boy-queller, show thy
    face ;   45
Know what it is to meet Achilles angry.
Hector ! where's Hector ? I will none but
    Hector.   [*Exeunt.*

SCENE VI. *Another part of the plain.*

Enter AJAX.

Ajax. Troilus, thou coward Troilus, show
    thy head.

Enter DIOMEDES.

Dio. Troilus, I say ! Where's Troilus ?
Ajax.   What wouldst thou ?
Dio. I would correct him.
Ajax. Were I the general, thou shouldst
    have my office

Ere that correction. Troilus, I say ! What,
   Troilus !   5

Enter TROILUS.

Tro. O traitor Diomed ! Turn thy false
   face, thou traitor,
And pay thy life thou owest me for my
   horse.
Dio. Ha ! art thou there ?
Ajax. I'll fight with him alone. Stand,
   Diomed.   9
Dio. He is my prize. I will not look upon.
Tro. Come, both, you cogging Greeks ;
   have at you both. [*Exeunt fighting.*

Enter HECTOR.

Hect. Yea, Troilus ? O, well fought, my
   youngest brother !

Enter ACHILLES.

Achil. Now do I see thee, ha ! Have at
   thee, Hector !
Hect. Pause, if thou wilt.
Achil. I do disdain thy courtesy, proud
   Troyan.   15
Be happy that my arms are out of use ;
My rest and negligence befriends thee now,
But thou anon shalt hear of me again ;
Till when, go seek thy fortune.   [*Exit.*
Hect.   Fare thee well.
I would have been much more a fresher
   man,   20
Had I expected thee.

Re-enter TROILUS.

          How now, my brother !
Tro. Ajax hath ta'en Æneas. Shall it be ?
No, by the flame of yonder glorious heaven,
He shall not carry him ; I'll be ta'en too,
Or bring him off. Fate, hear me what I say :
I reck not though thou end my life to-day.
                       [*Exit.*

Enter One *in armour.*

Hect. Stand, stand, thou Greek ; thou
   art a goodly mark.
No ? wilt thou not ? I like thy armour
   well ;
I'll frush it and unlock the rivets all
But I'll be master of it. Wilt thou not,
   beast, abide ?   30
Why then, fly on ; I'll hunt thee for thy
   hide.   [*Exeunt.*

SCENE VII. *Another part of the plain.*

Enter ACHILLES, *with* Myrmidons.

Achil. Come here about me, you my
   Myrmidons ;
Mark what I say. Attend me where I wheel ;
Strike not a stroke, but keep yourselves in
   breath ;
And when I have the bloody Hector found,

Empale him with your weapons round
   about ;   5
In fellest manner execute your arms.
Follow me, sirs, and my proceedings eye.
It is decreed Hector the great must die.
                     [*Exeunt.*

Enter MENELAUS *and* PARIS, *fighting ; then*
          THERSITES.

Ther. The cuckold and the cuckold-
maker are at it. Now, bull ! now, dog !
'Loo, Paris, 'loo ! now my double-horn'd
Spartan ! 'loo, Paris, 'loo ! The bull has
the game. Ware horns, ho !   12
          [*Exeunt Paris and Menelaus.*

Enter MARGARELON.

Mar. Turn, slave, and fight.
Ther. What art thou ?
Mar. A bastard son of Priam's.   15
Ther. I am a bastard too ; I love
bastards. I am a bastard begot, bastard
instructed, bastard in mind, bastard in
valour, in everything illegitimate. One
bear will not bite another, and wherefore
should one bastard ? Take heed, the
quarrel's most ominous to us : if the son
of a whore fight for a whore, he tempts
judgment. Farewell, bastard.   [*Exit.*
Mar. The devil take thee, coward !
                       [*Exit.*

SCENE VIII. *Another part of the plain.*

Enter HECTOR.

Hect. Most putrified core so fair without,
Thy goodly armour thus hath cost thy life.
Now is my day's work done ; I'll take good
   breath :
Rest, sword ; thou hast thy fill of blood
   and death !   [*Disarms.*

Enter ACHILLES *and his* Myrmidons.

Achil. Look, Hector, how the sun begins
   to set ;   5
How ugly night comes breathing at his
   heels ;
Even with the vail and dark'ning of the
   sun,
To close the day up, Hector's life is done.
Hect. I am unarm'd ; forego this vantage,
   Greek.   9
Achil. Strike, fellows, strike ; this is the
   man I seek.   [*Hector falls.*
So, Ilion, fall thou next ! Come, Troy, sink
   down ;
Here lies thy heart, thy sinews, and thy
   bone.
On, Myrmidons, and cry you all amain
' Achilles hath the mighty Hector slain '.
             [*A retreat sounded.*
Hark ! a retire upon our Grecian part.   15
Myr. The Troyan trumpets sound the
   like, my lord.

Achil. The dragon wing of night o'er-
        spreads the earth
And, stickler-like, the armies separates.
My half-supp'd sword, that frankly would
        have fed,
Pleas'd with this dainty bait, thus goes to
        bed.   [*Sheathes his sword.*
Come, tie his body to my horse's tail;   21
Along the field I will the Troyan trail.
                                        [*Exeunt.*

SCENE IX. *Another part of the plain.*

Sound retreat. Shout. Enter AGAMEMNON,
    AJAX, MENELAUS, NESTOR, DIOMEDES,
    and the rest, marching.

  Agam. Hark! hark! what shout is this?
  Nest. Peace, drums!
  Soldiers. [*Within*] Achilles! Achilles!
Hector's slain. Achilles!
  Dio. The bruit is Hector's slain, and by
    Achilles.
  Ajax. If it be so, yet bragless let it be; 5
Great Hector was as good a man as he.
  Agam. March patiently along. Let one be
        sent
To pray Achilles see us at our tent.
If in his death the gods have us befriended;
Great Troy is ours, and our sharp wars are
        ended.   [*Exeunt.*

SCENE X. *Another part of the plain.*

Enter ÆNEAS, PARIS, ANTENOR, *and*
    DEIPHOBUS.

  Æne. Stand, ho! yet are we masters of
        the field.
Never go home; here starve we out the
        night.

Enter TROILUS.

  Tro. Hector is slain.
  All.   Hector! The gods forbid!
  Tro. He's dead, and at the murderer's
        horse's tail,
In beastly sort, dragg'd through the shame-
        ful field.   5
Frown on, you heavens, effect your rage
        with speed.
Sit, gods, upon your thrones, and smile at
        Troy.
I say at once let your brief plagues be
        mercy,
And linger not our sure destructions on.
  Æne. My lord, you do discomfort all the
        host.   10
  Tro. You understand me not that tell me
        so.
I do not speak of flight, of fear of death,
But dare all imminence that gods and men
Address their dangers in. Hector is gone.
Who shall tell Priam so, or Hecuba?   15

Let him that will a screech-owl aye be
        call'd
Go in to Troy, and say there 'Hector's
        dead'.
There is a word will Priam turn to stone;
Make wells and Niobes of the maids and
        wives,   19
Cold statues of the youth; and, in a word,
Scare Troy out of itself. But, march away;
Hector is dead; there is no more to say.
Stay yet. You vile abominable tents,
Thus proudly pight upon our Phrygian
        plains,
Let Titan rise as early as he dare,   25
I'll through and through you. And, thou
        great-siz'd coward,
No space of earth shall sunder our two
        hates;
I'll haunt thee like a wicked conscience
        still,
That mouldeth goblins swift as frenzy's
        thoughts.
Strike a free march to Troy. With comfort
        go;   30
Hope of revenge shall hide our inward woe.

Enter PANDARUS.

  Pan. But hear you, hear you!
  Tro. Hence, broker-lackey. Ignominy
        and shame
Pursue thy life and live aye with thy name!
                            [*Exeunt all but Pandarus.*
  Pan. A goodly medicine for my aching
bones! O world! world! world! thus is the
poor agent despis'd! O traitors and bawds,
how earnestly are you set a work, and how
ill requited! Why should our endeavour
be so lov'd, and the performance so loathed?
What verse for it? What instance for it?
Let me see—   40

Full merrily the humble-bee doth sing
Till he hath lost his honey and his sting;
And being once subdu'd in armed tail,
Sweet honey and sweet notes together fail.

Good traders in the flesh, set this in your
painted cloths.
As many as be here of pander's hall,   46
Your eyes, half out, weep out at Pandar's
        fall;
Or, if you cannot weep, yet give some
        groans,
Though not for me, yet for your aching
        bones.
Brethren and sisters of the hold-door trade,
Some two months hence my will shall here
        be made.   51
It should be now, but that my fear is this,
Some galled goose of Winchester would hiss.
Till then I'll sweat and seek about for eases,
And at that time bequeath you my diseases.
                                        [*Exit.*

CORIOLANUS

DRAMATIS PERSONÆ

CAIUS MARCIUS, *afterwards* CAIUS MARCIUS CORIOLANUS.
TITUS LARTIUS, ⎱ *Generals against the*
COMINIUS, ⎰ *Volscians.*
MENENIUS AGRIPPA, *friend to Coriolanus.*
SICINIUS VELUTUS, ⎱ *Tribunes of the*
JUNIUS BRUTUS, ⎰ *People.*
YOUNG MARCIUS, *son to Coriolanus.*
A Roman Herald.
NICANOR, *a Roman.*
TULLUS AUFIDIUS, *General of the Volscians.*
Lieutenant *to Aufidius.*
Conspirators *with Aufidius.*

ADRIAN, *a Volscian.*
A Citizen of Antium.
Two Volscian Guards.

VOLUMNIA, *mother to Coriolanus.*
VIRGILIA, *wife to Coriolanus.*
VALERIA, *friend to Virgilia.*
Gentlewoman *attending on Virgilia.*

Roman *and* Volscian Senators, Patricians, Ædiles, Lictors, Soldiers, Citizens, Messengers, Servants to Aufidius, *and other* Attendants.

THE SCENE: *Rome and the neighbourhood; Corioli and the neighbourhood; Antium.*

ACT ONE

SCENE I. *Rome. A street.*

Enter a company of mutinous Citizens, *with staves, clubs, and other weapons.*

1 *Cit.* Before we proceed any further, hear me speak.

All. Speak, speak.

1 *Cit.* You are all resolv'd rather to die than to famish?

All. Resolv'd, resolv'd. 5

1 *Cit.* First, you know Caius Marcius is chief enemy to the people.

All. We know't, we know't.

1 *Cit.* Let us kill him, and we'll have corn at our own price. Is't a verdict? 10

All. No more talking on't; let it be done. Away, away!

2 *Cit.* One word, good citizens. 13

1 *Cit.* We are accounted poor citizens, the patricians good. What authority surfeits on would relieve us; if they would yield us but the superfluity while it were wholesome, we might guess they relieved us humanely; but they think we are too dear. The leanness that afflicts us, the object of our misery, is as an inventory to particularize their abundance; our sufferance is a gain to them. Let us revenge this with our pikes ere we become rakes; for the gods know I speak this in hunger for bread, not in thirst for revenge.

2 *Cit.* Would you proceed especially against Caius Marcius? 25

1 *Cit.* Against him first; he's a very dog to the commonalty.

2 *Cit.* Consider you what services he has done for his country?

1 *Cit.* Very well, and could be content to give him good report for't but that he pays himself with being proud. 32

2 *Cit.* Nay, but speak not maliciously.

1 *Cit.* I say unto you, what he hath done famously he did it to that end; though soft-conscienc'd men can be content to say it was for his country, he did it to please his mother and to be partly proud, which he is, even to the altitude of his virtue.

2 *Cit.* What he cannot help in his nature you account a vice in him. You must in no way say he is covetous. 41

1 *Cit.* If I must not, I need not be barren of accusations; he hath faults, with surplus, to tire in repetition. [*Shouts within*] What shouts are these? The other side o' th' city is risen. Why stay we prating here? To th' Capitol! 46

All. Come, come.

1 *Cit.* Soft! who comes here?

Enter MENENIUS AGRIPPA.

2 *Cit.* Worthy Menenius Agrippa; one that hath always lov'd the people. 50

1 *Cit.* He's one honest enough; would all the rest were so!

Men. What work's, my countrymen, in hand? Where go you
With bats and clubs? The matter? Speak, I pray you.

1 *Cit.* Our business is not unknown to th' Senate; they have had inkling this fortnight what we intend to do, which now we'll show 'em in deeds. They say poor suitors have strong breaths; they shall know we have strong arms too.

Men. Why, masters, my good friends, mine honest neighbours, 60
Will you undo yourselves?

1 *Cit.* We cannot, sir ; we are undone
  already.
  Men. I tell you, friends, most charitable
  care
Have the patricians of you. For your
  wants,
Your suffering in this dearth, you may as
  well   65
Strike at the heaven with your staves as
  lift them
Against the Roman state ; whose course
  will on
The way it takes, cracking ten thousand
  curbs
Of more strong link asunder than can ever
Appear in your impediment. For the
  dearth,   70
The gods, not the patricians, make it, and
Your knees to them, not arms, must help.
  Alack,
You are transported by calamity
Thither where more attends you ; and you
  slander
The helms o' th' state, who care for you
  like fathers,   75
When you curse them as enemies.
  1 *Cit.* Care for us ! True, indeed ! They
ne'er car'd for us yet. Suffer us to famish,
and their storehouses cramm'd with grain ;
make edicts for usury, to support usurers ;
repeal daily any wholesome act established
against the rich, and provide more piercing
statutes daily to chain up and restrain the
poor. If the wars eat us not up, they will ;
and there's all the love they bear us.
  Men. Either you must   85
Confess yourselves wondrous malicious,
Or be accus'd of folly. I shall tell you
A pretty tale. It may be you have heard it ;
But, since it serves my purpose, I will
  venture
To stale't a little more.   90
  1 *Cit.* Well, I'll hear it, sir ; yet you
must not think to fob off our disgrace with
a tale. But, an't please you, deliver.
  Men. There was a time when all the
  body's members
Rebell'd against the belly ; thus accus'd it :
That only like a gulf it did remain   96
I' th' midst o' th' body, idle and unactive,
Still cupboarding the viand, never bearing
Like labour with the rest ; where th' other
  instruments
Did see and hear, devise, instruct, walk,
  feel,   100
And, mutually participate, did minister
Unto the appetite and affection common
Of the whole body. The belly answer'd—
  1 *Cit.* Well, sir, what answer made the
belly ?
  Men. Sir, I shall tell you. With a kind of
  smile,   105
Which ne'er came from the lungs, but even
  thus—

For look you, I may make the belly smile
As well as speak—it tauntingly replied
To th' discontented members, the mutinous
  parts
That envied his receipt ; even so most fitly
As you malign our senators for that   111
They are not such as you.
  1 *Cit.*   Your belly's answer—What ?
The kingly crowned head, the vigilant eye,
The counsellor heart, the arm our soldier,
Our steed the leg, the tongue our trumpeter,
With other muniments and petty helps   116
Is this our fabric, if that they—
  Men.   What then ?
Fore me, this fellow speaks ! What then ?
  What then ?
  1 *Cit.* Should by the cormorant belly be
  restrain'd,
Who is the sink o' th' body—
  Men.   Well, what then ? 120
  1 *Cit.* The former agents, if they did
  complain,
What could the belly answer ?
  Men.   I will tell you ;
If you'll bestow a small—of what you have
  little—
Patience awhile, you'st hear the belly's
  answer.
  1 *Cit.* Y'are long about it.
  Men.   Note me this, good friend :
Your most grave belly was deliberate,   126
Not rash like his accusers, and thus
  answered.
' True is it, my incorporate friends,' quoth
  he
' That I receive the general food at first
Which you do live upon ; and fit it is,   130
Because I am the storehouse and the shop
Of the whole body. But, if you do remem-
  ber,
I send it through the rivers of your blood,
Even to the court, the heart, to th' seat
  o' th' brain ;   134
And, through the cranks and offices of man,
The strongest nerves and small inferior
  veins
From me receive that natural competency
Whereby they live. And though that all
  at once
You, my good friends '—this says the
  belly ; mark me.
  1 *Cit.* Ay, sir ; well, well.
  Men.   ' Though all at once cannot
See what I do deliver out to each,   141
Yet I can make my audit up, that all
From me do back receive the flour of all,
And leave me but the bran.' What say
  you to't ?
  1 *Cit.* It was an answer. How apply you
this ?
  Men. The senators of Rome are this good
  belly,   146
And you the mutinous members ; for,
  examine

Their counsels and their cares, digest things
    rightly
Touching the weal o' th' common, you shall
    find
No public benefit which you receive   150
But it proceeds or comes from them to you,
And no way from yourselves. What do you
    think,
You, the great toe of this assembly ?
  1 *Cit.* I the great toe ? Why the great
    toe ?
  Men. For that, being one o' th' lowest,
    basest, poorest,
Of this most wise rebellion, thou goest
    foremost.   156
Thou rascal, that art worst in blood to run,
Lead'st first to win some vantage.
But make you ready your stiff bats and
    clubs.
Rome and her rats are at the point of
    battle ;   160
The one side must have bale.

      Enter CAIUS MARCIUS.

            Hail, noble Marcius !
  Mar. Thanks. What's the matter, you
    dissentious rogues
That, rubbing the poor itch of your opinion,
Make yourselves scabs ?
  1 *Cit.* We have ever your good word.
  Mar. He that will give good words to
    thee will flatter
Beneath abhorring. What would you have,
    you curs,   166
That like nor peace nor war ? The one
    affrights you,
The other makes you proud. He that trusts
    to you,
Where he should find you lions, finds you
    hares ;
Where foxes, geese ; you are no surer, no,
Than is the coal of fire upon the ice   171
Or hailstone in the sun. Your virtue is
To make him worthy whose offence subdues
    him,
And curse that justice did it. Who deserves
    greatness
Deserves your hate ; and your affections
    are   175
A sick man's appetite, who desires most
    that
Which would increase his evil. He that
    depends
Upon your favours swims with fins of lead,
And hews down oaks with rushes. Hang ye!
    Trust ye ?   179
With every minute you do change a mind
And call him noble that was now your hate,
Him vile that was your garland. What's
    the matter
That in these several places of the city
You cry against the noble Senate, who,
Under the gods, keep you in awe, which
    else   185

Would feed on one another ? What's their
    seeking ?
  Men. For corn at their own rates, whereof
    they say
The city is well stor'd.
  Mar.   Hang 'em ! They say !
They'll sit by th' fire and presume to know
What's done i' th' Capitol, who's like to
    rise,   190
Who thrives and who declines ; side
    factions, and give out
Conjectural marriages, making parties
    strong,
And feebling such as stand not in their
    liking
Below their cobbled shoes. They say there's
    grain enough !
Would the nobility lay aside their ruth   195
And let me use my sword, I'd make a quarry
With thousands of these quarter'd slaves,
    as high
As I could pick my lance.
  Men. Nay, these are almost thoroughly
    persuaded ;
For though abundantly they lack discre-
    tion,   200
Yet are they passing cowardly. But, I
    beseech you,
What says the other troop ?
  Mar.   They are dissolv'd. Hang 'em !
They said they were an-hungry ; sigh'd
    forth proverbs—
That hunger broke stone walls, that dogs
    must eat,
That meat was made for mouths, that the
    gods sent not
Corn for the rich men only. With these
    shreds   206
They vented their complainings ; which
    being answer'd,
And a petition granted them—a strange
    one,
To break the heart of generosity   209
And make bold power look pale—they
    threw their caps
As they would hang them on the horns o'
    th' moon,
Shouting their emulation.
  Men.   What is granted them ?
  Mar. Five tribunes, to defend their
    vulgar wisdoms,
Of their own choice. One's Junius Brutus—
Sicinius Velutus, and I know not. 'Sdeath !
The rabble should have first unroof'd the
    city   216
Ere so prevail'd with me ; it will in time
Win upon power and throw forth greater
    themes
For insurrection's arguing.
  Men.   This is strange.
  Mar. Go get you home, you fragments.

      Enter a Messenger, *hastily.*

  Mess. Where's Caius Marcius ?

Mar.   Here. What's the matter?

Mess. The news is, sir, the Volsces are in
        arms.

Mar. I am glad on't; then we shall ha'
        means to vent
Our musty superfluity. See, our best elders.

Enter COMINIUS, TITUS LARTIUS, *with other*
Senators; JUNIUS BRUTUS *and* SICINIUS
VELUTUS.

1 Sen. Marcius, 'tis true that you have
        lately told us :   225
The Volsces are in arms.

Mar.   They have a leader,
Tullus Aufidius, that will put you to't.
I sin in envying his nobility;
And were I anything but what I am,
I would wish me only he.

Com.   You have fought together? 230

Mar. Were half to half the world by th'
        ears, and he
Upon my party, I'd revolt, to make
Only my wars with him. He is a lion
That I am proud to hunt.

1 Sen.   Then, worthy Marcius,
Attend upon Cominius to these wars.   235

Com. It is your former promise.

Mar.   Sir, it is;
And I am constant. Titus Lartius, thou
Shalt see me once more strike at Tullus'
        face.
What, art thou stiff? Stand'st out?

Lart.   No, Caius Marcius;
I'll lean upon one crutch and fight with
        t'other   240
Ere stay behind this business.

Men.   O, true bred!

1 Sen. Your company to th' Capitol;
        where, I know,
Our greatest friends attend us.

Lart. [*To Cominius*]   Lead you on.
[*To Marcius*] Follow Cominius; we must
        follow you;
Right worthy you priority.

Com.   Noble Marcius! 245

1 Sen. [*To the Citizens*] Hence to your
        homes; be gone.

Mar.   Nay, let them follow.
The Volsces have much corn: take these
        rats thither
To gnaw their garners.   Worshipful
        mutineers,
Your valour puts well forth: pray follow.
        [*Citizens steal away. Exeunt all but
                Sicinius and Brutus.*

Sic. Was ever man so proud as is this
        Marcius?   250

Bru. He has no equal.

Sic. When we were chosen tribunes for
        the people—

Bru. Mark'd you his lip and eyes?

Sic.   Nay, but his taunts!

Bru. Being mov'd, he will not spare to
        gird the gods.

Sic. Bemock the modest moon.   255

Bru. The present wars devour him! He
        is grown
Too proud to be so valiant.

Sic.   Such a nature,
Tickled with good success, disdains the
        shadow
Which he treads on at noon. But I do
        wonder
His insolence can brook to be commanded
Under Cominius.   261

Bru.   Fame, at the which he aims—
In whom already he is well grac'd—cannot
Better be held nor more attain'd than by
A place below the first; for what miscarries
Shall be the general's fault, though he
        perform   265
To th' utmost of a man, and giddy censure
Will then cry out of Marcius ' O, if he
Had borne the business!'

Sic.   Besides, if things go well,
Opinion, that so sticks on Marcius, shal!
Of his demerits rob Cominius.

Bru.   Come.   270
Half all Cominius' honours are to Marcius,
Though Marcius earn'd them not; and all
        his faults
To Marcius shall be honours, though indeed
In aught he merit not.

Sic.   Let's hence and hear
How the dispatch is made, and in what
        fashion,   275
More than his singularity, he goes
Upon this present action.

Bru.   Let's along.
                              [*Exeunt.*

SCENE II. *Corioli. The Senate House.*

Enter TULLUS AUFIDIUS *with* Senators *of*
                Corioli.

1 Sen. So, your opinion is, Aufidius,
That they of Rome are ent'red in our
        counsels
And know how we proceed.

Auf.   Is it not yours?
What ever have been thought on in this
        state
That could be brought to bodily act ere
        Rome   5
Had circumvention? 'Tis not four days
        gone
Since I heard thence; these are the words
        —I think
I have the letter here; yes, here it is:
[*Reads*] ' They have press'd a power, but it
        is not known
Whether for east or west. The dearth is
        great;   10
The people mutinous; and it is rumour'd,
Cominius, Marcius your old enemy,
Who is of Rome worse hated than of you,
And Titius Lartius, a most valiant Roman,
These three lead on this preparation   15

Whither 'tis bent. Most likely 'tis for you ;
Consider of it '.
  1 Sen.   Our army's in the field ;
We never yet made doubt but Rome was
    ready
To answer us.
  Auf.   Nor did you think it folly
To keep your great pretences veil'd till
    when   20
They needs must show themselves ; which
    in the hatching,
It seem'd, appear'd to Rome. By the
    discovery
We shall be short'ned in our aim, which
    was
To take in many towns ere almost Rome
Should know we were afoot.
  2 Sen.   Noble Aufidius, 25
Take your commission ; hie you to your
    bands ;
Let us alone to guard Corioli.
If they set down before's, for the remove
Bring up your army ; but I think you'll
    find
Th'have not prepar'd for us.
  Auf.   O, doubt not that ! 30
I speak from certainties. Nay more,
Some parcels of their power are forth
    already,
And only hitherward. I leave your honours.
If we and Caius Marcius chance to meet,
'Tis sworn between us we shall ever strike
Till one can do no more.
  All.   The gods assist you !
  Auf. And keep your honours safe !
  1 Sen.   Farewell.
  2 Sen.   Farewell.
  All. Farewell.   [*Exeunt.*

    SCENE III. *Rome. Marcius' house.*

Enter VOLUMNIA *and* VIRGILIA, *mother and
wife to Marcius ; they set them down on
two low stools and sew.*

  Vol. I pray you, daughter, sing, or express yourself in a more comfortable sort.
If my son were my husband, I should
freelier rejoice in that absence wherein he
won honour than in the embracements of
his bed where he would show most love.
When yet he was but tender-bodied, and
the only son of my womb ; when youth
with comeliness pluck'd all gaze his way ;
when, for a day of kings' entreaties, a
mother should not sell him an hour from
her beholding ; I, considering how honour
would become such a person—that it was
no better than picture-like to hang by th'
wall, if renown made it not stir—was
pleas'd to let him seek danger where he
was like to find fame. To a cruel war I sent
him, from whence he return'd his brows
bound with oak. I tell thee, daughter, I
sprang not more in joy at first hearing he

was a man-child than now in first seeing
he had prov'd himself a man.
  Vir. But had he died in the business,
madam, how then ?   19
  Vol. Then his good report should have
been my son ; I therein would have found
issue. Hear me profess sincerely : had I a
dozen sons, each in my love alike, and none
less dear than thine and my good Marcius,
I had rather had eleven die nobly for their
country than one voluptuously surfeit out
of action.   25

    Enter a Gentlewoman.

  Gent. Madam, the Lady Valeria is come
to visit you.
  Vir. Beseech you give me leave to retire
myself.
  Vol. Indeed you shall not.
Methinks I hear hither your husband's
    drum ;   29
See him pluck Aufidius down by th'
    hair ;
As children from a bear, the Volsces shun-
    ning him.
Methinks I see him stamp thus, and call
    thus :
' Come on, you cowards ! You were got in
    fear,
Though you were born in Rome '. His
    bloody brow
With his mail'd hand then wiping, forth
    he goes,   35
Like to a harvest-man that's task'd to mow
Or all or lose his hire.
  Vir. His bloody brow ? O Jupiter, no
    blood !
  Vol. Away, you fool ! It more becomes
    a man
Than gilt his trophy. The breasts of
    Hecuba,   40
When she did suckle Hector, look'd not
    lovelier
Than Hector's forehead when it spit forth
    blood
At Grecian sword, contemning. Tell
    Valeria
We are fit to bid her welcome.
                [*Exit Gentlewoman.*
  Vir. Heavens bless my lord from fell
    Aufidius !   45
  Vol. He'll beat Aufidius' head below his
    knee
And tread upon his neck.

Re-enter Gentlewoman, *with* VALERIA *and
an* Usher.

  Val. My ladies both, good day to you.
  Vol. Sweet madam !
  Vir. I am glad to see your ladyship. 50
  Val. How do you both ? You are
manifest housekeepers. What are you sewing here ? A fine spot, in good faith. How
does your little son ?

Vir. I thank your ladyship ; well, good madam.

Vol. He had rather see the swords and hear a drum than look upon his schoolmaster. 56

Val. O' my word, the father's son ! I'll swear 'tis a very pretty boy. O' my troth, I look'd upon him a Wednesday half an hour together ; has such a confirm'd countenance ! I saw him run after a gilded butterfly ; and when he caught it he let it go again, and after it again, and over and over he comes, and up again, catch'd it again ; or whether his fall enrag'd him, or how 'twas, he did so set his teeth and tear it. O, I warrant, how he mammock'd it ! 65

Vol. One on's father's moods.

Val. Indeed, la, 'tis a noble child.

Vir. A crack, madam.

Val. Come, lay aside your stitchery ; I must have you play the idle huswife with me this afternoon. 70

Vir. No, good madam ; I will not out of doors.

Val. Not out of doors !

Vol. She shall, she shall.

Vir. Indeed, no, by your patience ; I'll not over the threshold till my lord return from the wars. 75

Val. Fie, you confine yourself most unreasonably ; come, you must go visit the good lady that lies in.

Vir. I will wish her speedy strength, and visit her with my prayers ; but I cannot go thither.

Vol. Why, I pray you ? 80

Vir. 'Tis not to save labour, nor that I want love.

Val. You would be another Penelope ; yet they say all the yarn she spun in Ulysses' absence did but fill Ithaca full of moths. Come, I would your cambric were sensible as your finger, that you might leave pricking it for pity. Come, you shall go with us. 86

Vir. No, good madam, pardon me ; indeed I will not forth.

Val. In truth, la, go with me ; and I'll tell you excellent news of your husband. 90

Vir. O, good madam, there can be none yet.

Val. Verily, I do not jest with you ; there came news from him last night.

Vir. Indeed, madam ?

Val. In earnest, it's true ; I heard a senator speak it. Thus it is : the Volsces have an army forth ; against whom Cominius the general is gone, with one part of our Roman power. Your lord and Titus Lartius are set down before their city Corioli ; they nothing doubt prevailing, and to make it brief wars. This is true, on mine honour ; and so, I pray, go with us.

Vir. Give me excuse, good madam ; I will obey you in everything hereafter.

Vol. Let her alone, lady ; as she is now, she will but disease our better mirth. 105

Val. In troth, I think she would. Fare you well, then. Come, good sweet lady. Prithee, Virgilia, turn thy solemness out o' door and go along with us.

Vir. No, at a word, madam ; indeed I must not. I wish you much mirth. 110

Val. Well then, farewell. [*Exeunt.*

SCENE IV. *Before Corioli.*

Enter MARCIUS, TITUS LARTIUS, *with drum and colours, with* Captains *and* Soldiers. *To them a* Messenger.

Mar. Yonder comes news ; a wager— they have met.

Lart. My horse to yours—no.

Mar. 'Tis done.

Lart. Agreed.

Mar. Say, has our general met the enemy ?

Mess. They lie in view, but have not spoke as yet.

Lart. So, the good horse is mine.

Mar. I'll buy him of you.

Lart. No, I'll nor sell nor give him ; lend you him I will 6
For half a hundred years. Summon the town.

Mar. How far off lie these armies ?

Mess. Within this mile and half.

Mar. Then shall we hear their 'larum, and they ours.
Now, Mars, I prithee, make us quick in work, 10
That we with smoking swords may march from hence
To help our fielded friends ! Come, blow thy blast.

They sound a parley. Enter two Senators *with* Others, *on the walls of Corioli.*

Tullus Aufidius, is he within your walls ?

1 *Sen.* No, nor a man that fears you less than he :
That's lesser than a little. [*Drum afar off*]
Hark, our drums 15
Are bringing forth our youth. We'll break our walls
Rather than they shall pound us up ; our gates,
Which yet seem shut, we have but pinn'd with rushes ;
They'll open of themselves. [*Alarum far off*]
Hark you far off !
There is Aufidius. List what work he makes 20
Amongst your cloven army.

Mar. O, they are at it !

Lart. Their noise be our instruction. Ladders, ho !

Enter the army of the Volsces.

Mar. They fear us not, but issue forth
    their city.
Now put your shields before your hearts,
    and fight
With hearts more proof than shields. Ad-
    vance, brave Titus.   25
They do disdain us much beyond our
    thoughts,
Which makes me sweat with wrath. Come
    on, my fellows.
He that retires, I'll take him for a Volsce,
And he shall feel mine edge.

*Alarum. The Romans are beat back to their
    trenches. Re-enter* MARCIUS, *cursing.*

Mar. All the contagion of the south light
    on you,   30
You shames of Rome ! you herd of—Boils
    and plagues
Plaster you o'er, that you may be abhorr'd
Farther than seen, and one infect another
Against the wind a mile ! You souls of
    geese
That bear the shapes of men, how have you
    run   35
From slaves that apes would beat ! Pluto
    and hell !
All hurt behind ! Backs red, and faces
    pale
With flight and agued fear ! Mend and
    charge home,
Or, by the fires of heaven, I'll leave the foe
And make my wars on you. Look to't.
    Come on ;   40
If you'll stand fast we'll beat them to their
    wives,
As they us to our trenches. Follow me.

*Another alarum. The Volsces fly, and
    Marcius follows them to the gates.*

So, now the gates are ope ; now prove
    good seconds ;   43
'Tis for the followers fortune widens them,
Not for the fliers. Mark me, and do the like.
    [*Marcius enters the gates.*
1 Sol. Fool-hardiness ; not I.
2 Sol. Not I.   [*Marcius is shut in.*
1 Sol. See, they have shut him in.
All.   To th' pot, I warrant him.
    [*Alarum continues.*

Re-enter TITUS LARTIUS.

Lart. What is become of Marcius ?
All.   Slain, sir, doubtless.
1 Sol. Following the fliers at the very
    heels,   50
With them he enters ; who, upon the
    sudden,
Clapp'd to their gates. He is himself alone,
To answer all the city.
Lart.   O noble fellow !
Who sensibly outdares his senseless sword,

And when it bows stand'st up. Thou art
    left, Marcius ;
A carbuncle entire, as big as thou art, 56
Were not so rich a jewel. Thou wast a
    soldier
Even to Cato's wish, not fierce and terrible
Only in strokes ; but with thy grim looks
    and   59
The thunder-like percussion of thy sounds
Thou mad'st thine enemies shake, as if the
    world
Were feverous and did tremble.

Re-enter MARCIUS, *bleeding, assaulted by the
    Enemy.*

1 Sol.   Look, sir.
Lart.   O, 'tis Marcius !
Let's fetch him off, or make remain alike.
    [*They fight, and all enter the city.*

SCENE V. *Within Corioli. A street.*

Enter certain Romans, *with spoils.*

1 Rom. This will I carry to Rome.
2 Rom. And I this.
3 Rom. A murrain on't ! I took this for
silver.   [*Alarum continues still afar off.*

Enter MARCIUS *and* TITUS LARTIUS *with a
    trumpetor.*

Mar. See here these movers that do prize
    their hours
At a crack'd drachma ! Cushions, leaden
    spoons,   5
Irons of a doit, doublets that hangmen
    would
Bury with those that wore them, these base
    slaves,
Ere yet the fight be done, pack up. Down
    with them !   [*Exeunt pillagers.*
And hark, what noise the general makes !
    To him !
There is the man of my soul's hate,
    Aufidius,   10
Piercing our Romans ; then, valiant Titus,
    take
Convenient numbers to make good the city;
Whilst I, with those that have the spirit,
    will haste
To help Cominius.
Lart.   Worthy sir, thou bleed'st ;
Thy exercise hath been too violent   15
For a second course of fight.
Mar.   Sir, praise me not ;
My work hath yet not warm'd me. Fare
    you well ;
The blood I drop is rather physical
Than dangerous to me. To Aufidius thus
I will appear, and fight.
Lart.   Now the fair goddess, Fortune,
Fall deep in love with thee, and her great
    charms   21
Misguide thy opposers' swords ! Bold
    gentleman,

Prosperity be thy page !
 Mar.   Thy friend no less
Than those she placeth highest ! So farewell.
 Lart. Thou worthiest Marcius ! 25
       [*Exit Marcius.*
Go sound thy trumpet in the market-place ;
Call thither all the officers o' th' town,
Where they shall know our mind. Away !
       [*Exeunt.*

SCENE VI. *Near the camp of Cominius.*

Enter COMINIUS, *as it were in retire, with*
 Soldiers.

 Com. Breathe you, my friends. Well
  fought ; we are come off
Like Romans, neither foolish in our stands
Nor cowardly in retire. Believe me, sirs,
We shall be charg'd again. Whiles we have
  struck,
By interims and conveying gusts we have
  heard   5
The charges of our friends. The Roman
  gods,
Lead their successes as we wish our own,
That both our powers, with smiling fronts
  encount'ring,
May give you thankful sacrifice !

   Enter a Messenger.

       Thy news ?
 Mess. The citizens of Corioli have issued
And given to Lartius and to Marcius battle ;
I saw our party to their trenches driven,
And then I came away.
 Com.   Though thou speak'st truth,
Methinks thou speak'st not well. How long
  is't since ?
 Mess. Above an hour, my lord. 15
 Com. 'Tis not a mile ; briefly we heard
  their drums.
How couldst thou in a mile confound an
  hour,
And bring thy news so late ?
 Mess.   Spies of the Volsces
Held me in chase, that I was forc'd to wheel
Three or four miles about ; else had I, sir,
Half an hour since brought my report. 21

   Enter MARCIUS.

 Com.   Who's yonder
That does appear as he were flay'd ? O
  gods !
He has the stamp of Marcius, and I have
Before-time seen him thus.
 Mar.   Come I too late ?
 Com. The shepherd knows not thunder
  from a tabor
More than I know the sound of Marcius'
  tongue   26
From every meaner man.
 Mar.   Come I too late ?
 Com. Ay, if you come not in the blood
  of others,

But mantled in your own.
 Mar.   O ! let me clip ye
In arms as sound as when I woo'd, in heart
As merry as when our nuptial day was
  done,   31
And tapers burn'd to bedward.
 Com.   Flower of warriors,
How is't with Titus Lartius ?
 Mar. As with a man busied about
  decrees :
Condemning some to death and some to
  exile ;   35
Ransoming him or pitying, threat'ning th'
  other ;
Holding Corioli in the name of Rome
Even like a fawning greyhound in the leash,
To let him slip at will.
 Com.   Where is that slave
Which told me they had beat you to your
  trenches ?   40
Where is he ? Call him hither.
 Mar.   Let him alone ;
He did inform the truth. But for our
  gentlemen,
The common file—a plague ! tribunes for
  them !
The mouse ne'er shunn'd the cat as they
  did budge
From rascals worse than they.
 Com. But how prevail'd you ? 45
 Mar. Will the time serve to tell ? I do
  not think.
Where is the enemy ? Are you lords o' th'
  field ?
If not, why cease you till you are so ?
 Com.   Marcius,
We have at disadvantage fought, and did
Retire to win our purpose.   50
 Mar. How lies their battle ? Know you
  on which side
They have plac'd their men of trust ?
 Com.   As I guess, Marcius,
Their bands i' th' vaward are the Antiates,
Of their best trust ; o'er them Aufidius,
Their very heart of hope.
 Mar.   I do beseech you, 55
By all the battles wherein we have fought,
By th' blood we have shed together, by th'
  vows
We have made to endure friends, that you
  directly
Set me against Aufidius and his Antiates ;
And that you not delay the present, but, 60
Filling the air with swords advanc'd and
  darts,
We prove this very hour.
 Com.   Though I could wish
You were conducted to a gentle bath
And balms applied to you, yet dare I never
Deny your asking : take your choice of
  those   65
That best can aid your action.
 Mar.   Those are they
That most are willing. If any such be here—

As it were sin to doubt—that love this
  painting
Wherein you see me smear'd ; if any fear
Lesser his person than an ill report ;   70
If any think brave death outweighs bad
  life
And that his country's dearer than himself ;
Let him alone, or so many so minded,
Wave thus to express his disposition,
And follow Marcius.   75
  [*They all shout and wave their swords, take
  him up in their arms and cast up their caps.*
O, me alone ! Make you a sword of me ?
If these shows be not outward, which of you
But is four Volsces ? None of you but is
Able to bear against the great Aufidius
A shield as hard as his. A certain number,
Though thanks to all, must I select from
  all ; the rest   81
Shall bear the business in some other fight,
As cause will be obey'd. Please you to
  march ;
And four shall quickly draw out my com-
  mand,
Which men are best inclin'd.
  Com.   March on, my fellows ;   85
Make good this ostentation, and you shall
Divide in all with us.   [*Exeunt.*

Scene VII. *The gates of Corioli.*

Titus Lartius, *having set a guard upon
  Corioli, going with drum and trumpet
  toward Cominius and Caius Marcius,
  enters with a* Lieutenant, *other* Soldiers,
  and a Scout.

Lart. So, let the ports be guarded ; keep
  your duties
As I have set them down. If I do send,
  dispatch
Those centuries to our aid ; the rest will
  serve
For a short holding. If we lose the field
We cannot keep the town.
  Lieut.   Fear not our care, sir.   5
Lart. Hence, and shut your gates upon's.
Our guider, come ; to th' Roman camp
  conduct us.   [*Exeunt.*

Scene VIII. *A field of battle between the
  Roman and the Volscian camps.*

Alarum, as in battle. Enter Marcius *and*
  Aufidius *at several doors.*

  Mar. I'll fight with none but thee, for I
  do hate thee
Worse than a promise-breaker.
  Auf.   We hate alike :
Not Afric owns a serpent I abhor
More than thy fame and envy. Fix thy
  foot.
  Mar. Let the first budger die the other's
  slave,   5
And the gods doom him after !

  Auf.   If I fly, Marcius,
Halloa me like a hare.
  Mar. Within these three hours, Tullus,
Alone I fought in your Corioli walls,
And made what work I pleas'd. 'Tis not my
  blood
Wherein thou seest me mask'd. For thy
  revenge   10
Wrench up thy power to th' highest.
  Auf.   Wert thou the Hector
That was the whip of your bragg'd progeny,
Thou shouldst not scape me here.
  [*Here they fight, and certain* Volsces
  come in the aid of Aufidius. Marcius
  fights till they be driven in breathless.
Officious, and not valiant, you have sham'd
  me   14
In your condemned seconds.   [*Exeunt.*

Scene IX. *The Roman camp.*

*Flourish. Alarum. A retreat is sounded.
  Enter, at one door,* Cominius *with the
  Romans ; at another door,* Marcius, *with
  his arm in a scarf.*

  Com. If I should tell thee o'er this thy
  day's work,
Thou't not believe thy deeds ; but I'll
  report it
Where senators shall mingle tears with
  smiles ;
Where great patricians shall attend, and
  shrug,
I' th' end admire ; where ladies shall be
  frighted   5
And, gladly quak'd, hear more ; where the
  dull tribunes,
That with the fusty plebeians hate thine
  honours,
Shall say against their hearts ' We thank
  the gods
Our Rome hath such a soldier '.
Yet cam'st thou to a morsel of this feast,   10
Having fully din'd before.

Enter Titus Lartius, *with his* Power, *from
  the pursuit.*

  Lart. O General,
Here is the steed, we the caparison.
Hadst thou beheld—
  Mar.   Pray now, no more ; my mother,
Who has a charter to extol her blood,
When she does praise me grieves me. I
  have done   15
As you have done—that's what I can ;
  induc'd
As you have been—that's for my country :
He that has but effected his good will
Hath overta'en mine act.
  Com.   You shall not be
The grave of your deserving ; Rome must
  know   20
The value of her own. 'Twere a conceal-
  ment

Worse than a theft, no less than a traducement,
To hide your doings and to silence that
Which, to the spire and top of praises vouch'd,
Would seem but modest. Therefore, I beseech you, 25
In sign of what you are, not to reward
What you have done, before our army hear me.
  Mar. I have some wounds upon me, and they smart
To hear themselves rememb'red.
  Com.   Should they not, 29
Well might they fester 'gainst ingratitude
And tent themselves with death. Of all the horses—
Whereof we have ta'en good, and good store—of all
The treasure in this field achiev'd and city,
We render you the tenth ; to be ta'en forth
Before the common distribution at 35
Your only choice.
  Mar.   I thank you, General,
But cannot make my heart consent to take
A bribe to pay my sword. I do refuse it,
And stand upon my common part with those
That have beheld the doing. 40
  [*A long flourish. They all cry* ' Marcius, Marcius! ' *cast up their caps and lances. Cominius and Lartius stand bare.*
May these same instruments which you profane
Never sound more ! When drums and trumpets shall
I' th' field prove flatterers, let courts and cities be
Made all of false-fac'd soothing. When steel grows 44
Soft as the parasite's silk, let him be made
An overture for th' wars. No more, I say.
For that I have not wash'd my nose that bled,
Or foil'd some debile wretch, which without note
Here's many else have done, you shout me forth
In acclamations hyperbolical, 51
As if I lov'd my little should be dieted
In praises sauc'd with lies.
  Com.   Too modest are you ;
More cruel to your good report than grateful 54
To us that give you truly. By your patience,
If 'gainst yourself you be incens'd, we'll put you—
Like one that means his proper harm—in manacles,
Then reason safely with you. Therefore be it known,
As to us, to all the world, that Caius Marcius

Wears this war's garland ; in token of the which, 60
My noble steed, known to the camp, I give him,
With all his trim belonging ; and from this time,
For what he did before Corioli, call him
With all th' applause and clamour of the host,
Caius Marcius Coriolanus. 65
Bear th' addition nobly ever !
  [*Flourish. Trumpets sound, and drums.*
  All. Caius Marcius Coriolanus !
  Cor. I will go wash ;
And when my face is fair you shall perceive
Whether I blush or no. Howbeit, I thank you ; 70
I mean to stride your steed, and at all times
To undercrest your good addition
To th' fairness of my power.
  Com.   So, to our tent ;
Where, ere we do repose us, we will write
To Rome of our success. You, Titus Lartius, 75
Must to Corioli back. Send us to Rome
The best, with whom we may articulate
For their own good and ours.
  Lart.   I shall, my lord.
  Cor. The gods begin to mock me. I, that now
Refus'd most princely gifts, am bound to beg 80
Of my Lord General.
  Com.   Take't—'tis yours ; what is't ?
  Cor. I sometime lay here in Corioli
At a poor man's house ; he us'd me kindly.
He cried to me ; I saw him prisoner ;
But then Aufidius was within my view, 85
And wrath o'erwhelm'd my pity. I request you
To give my poor host freedom.
  Com.   O, well begg'd !
Were he the butcher of my son, he should
Be free as is the wind. Deliver him, Titus.
  Lart. Marcius, his name ?
  Cor.   By Jupiter, forgot ! 90
I am weary ; yea, my memory is tir'd.
Have we no wine here ?
  Com.   Go we to our tent.
The blood upon your visage dries ; 'tis time
It should be look'd to. Come.   [*Exeunt.*

SCENE X. *The camp of the Volsces.*

A flourish. Cornets. Enter TULLUS AUFIDIUS *bloody, with two or three* Soldiers.

  Auf. The town is ta'en.
  1 Sol. 'Twill be deliver'd back on good condition.
  Auf. Condition !
I would I were a Roman ; for I cannot,
Being a Volsce, be that I am. Condition ? 5
What good condition can a treaty find

I' th' part that is at mercy? Five times, Marcius,
I have fought with thee; so often hast
    thou beat me;
And wouldst do so, I think, should we
    encounter
As often as we eat. By th' elements,   10
If e'er again I meet him beard to beard,
He's mine or I am his. Mine emulation
Hath not that honour in't it had; for
    where
I thought to crush him in an equal force,
True sword to sword, I'll potch at him some
    way,   15
Or wrath or craft may get him.

1 Sol.   He's the devil.

Auf. Bolder, though not so subtle. My
    valour's poison'd
With only suff'ring stain by him; for him
Shall fly out of itself. Nor sleep nor
    sanctuary,
Being naked, sick, nor fane nor Capitol, 20
The prayers of priests nor times of sacrifice,
Embarquements all of fury, shall lift up
Their rotten privilege and custom 'gainst
My hate to Marcius. Where I find him,
    were it
At home, upon my brother's guard, even
    there,   25
Against the hospitable canon, would I
Wash my fierce hand in's heart. Go you to
    th' city;
Learn how 'tis held, and what they are
    that must
Be hostages for Rome.

1 Sol.   Will not you go?

Auf. I am attended at the cypress grove;
    I pray you—   30
'Tis south the city mills—bring me word
    thither
How the world goes, that to the pace of it
I may spur on my journey.

1 Sol.   I shall, sir. [*Exeunt.*

ACT TWO

SCENE I. *Rome. A public place.*

Enter MENENIUS, *with the two Tribunes of
    the people,* SICINIUS *and* BRUTUS.

Men. The augurer tells me we shall have
news to-night.

Bru. Good or bad?

Men. Not according to the prayer of the
people, for they love not Marcius.

Sic. Nature teaches beasts to know their
friends.   5

Men. Pray you, who does the wolf love?

Sic. The lamb.

Men. Ay, to devour him, as the hungry
plebeians would the noble Marcius.

Bru. He's a lamb indeed, that baes like
a bear.   10

Men. He's a bear indeed, that lives like
a lamb. You two are old men; tell me one
thing that I shall ask you.

Both Trib. Well, sir.

Men. In what enormity is Marcius poor
in that you two have not in abundance? 15

Bru. He's poor in no one fault, but stor'd
with all.

Sic. Especially in pride.

Bru. And topping all others in boasting.

Men. This is strange now. Do you two
know how you are censured here in the city
—I mean of us o' th' right-hand file? Do
you?   21

Both Trib. Why, how are we censur'd?

Men. Because you talk of pride now—
will you not be angry?

Both Trib. Well, well, sir, well.   25

Men. Why, 'tis no great matter; for a
very little thief of occasion will rob you of
a great deal of patience. Give your dispositions the reins, and be angry at your
pleasures—at the least, if you take it as
a pleasure to you in being so. You blame
Marcius for being proud?   30

Bru. We do it not alone, sir.

Men. I know you can do very little alone;
for your helps are many, or else your actions
would grow wondrous single: your abilities
are too infant-like for doing much alone.
You talk of pride. O that you could turn
your eyes toward the napes of your necks,
and make but an interior survey of your
good selves! O that you could!   37

Both. What then, sir?

Men. Why, then you should discover a
brace of unmeriting, proud, violent, testy
magistrates—alias fools—as any in Rome.

Sic. Menenius, you are known well
enough too.   42

Men. I am known to be a humorous
patrician, and one that loves a cup of hot
wine with not a drop of allaying Tiber in't;
said to be something imperfect in favouring
the first complaint, hasty and tinder-like
upon too trivial motion; one that converses
more with the buttock of the night than
with the forehead of the morning. What I
think I utter, and spend my malice in my
breath. Meeting two such wealsmen as you
are—I cannot call you Lycurguses—if the
drink you give me touch my palate adversely, I make a crooked face at it. I
cannot say your worships have deliver'd
the matter well, when I find the ass in compound with the major part of your syllables;
and though I must be content to bear with
those that say you are reverend grave men,
yet they lie deadly that tell you have
good faces. If you see this in the map of
my microcosm, follows it that I am known
well enough too? What harm can your
bisson conspectuities glean out of this
character, if I be known well enough too? 60

Bru. Come, sir, come, we know you well enough.

Men. You know neither me, yourselves, nor any thing. You are ambitious for poor knaves' caps and legs ; you wear out a good wholesome forenoon in hearing a cause between an orange-wife and a fosset-seller, and then rejourn the controversy of threepence to a second day of audience. When you are hearing a matter between party and party, if you chance to be pinch'd with the colic, you make faces like mummers, set up the bloody flag against all patience, and, in roaring for a chamber-pot, dismiss the controversy bleeding, the more entangled by your hearing. All the peace you make in their cause is calling both the parties knaves. You are a pair of strange ones. 74

Bru. Come, come, you are well understood to be a perfecter giber for the table than a necessary bencher in the Capitol. 77

Men. Our very priests must become mockers, if they shall encounter such ridiculous subjects as you are. When you speak best unto the purpose, it is not worth the wagging of your beards ; and your beards deserve not so honourable a grave as to stuff a botcher's cushion or to be entomb'd in an ass's pack-saddle. Yet you must be saying Marcius is proud ; who, in a cheap estimation, is worth all your predecessors since Deucalion ; though peradventure some of the best of 'em were hereditary hangmen. God-den to your worships. More of your conversation would infect my brain, being the herdsmen of the beastly plebeians. I will be bold to take my leave of you. 89

[*Brutus and Sicinius go aside.*

Enter VOLUMNIA, VIRGILIA, *and* VALERIA.

How now, my as fair as noble ladies—and the moon, were she earthly, no nobler—whither do you follow your eyes so fast ?

Vol. Honourable Menenius, my boy Marcius approaches ; for the love of Juno let's go.

Men. Ha ! Marcius coming home ? 95

Vol. Ay, worthy Menenius, and with most prosperous approbation.

Men. Take my cap, Jupiter, and I thank thee. Hoo ! Marcius coming home !

Vol., Vir. Nay, 'tis true. 100

Vol. Look, here's a letter from him ; the state hath another, his wife another ; and I think there's one at home for you.

Men. I will make my very house reel to-night. A letter for me ? 105

Vir. Yes, certain, there's a letter for you ; I saw't.

Men. A letter for me ! It gives me an estate of seven years' health ; in which time I will make a lip at the physician. The most sovereign prescription in Galen is but empiricutic and, to this preservative, of no better report than a horse-drench. Is he not wounded ? He was wont to come home wounded. 112

Vir. O, no, no, no.

Vol. O, he is wounded, I thank the gods for't.

Men. So do I too, if it be not too much. Brings 'a victory in his pocket ? The wounds become him. 116

Vol. On's brows, Menenius, he comes the third time home with the oaken garland.

Men. Has he disciplin'd Aufidius soundly ?

Vol. Titus Lartius writes they fought together, but Aufidius got off. 121

Men. And 'twas time for him too, I'll warrant him that ; an he had stay'd by him, I would not have been so fidius'd for all the chests in Corioli and the gold that's in them. Is the Senate possess'd of this ? 125

Vol. Good ladies, let's go. Yes, yes, yes : the Senate has letters from the General, wherein he gives my son the whole name of the war ; he hath in this action outdone his former deeds doubly. 129

Val. In troth, there's wondrous things spoke of him.

Men. Wondrous ! Ay, I warrant you, and not without his true purchasing.

Vir. The gods grant them true !

Vol. True ! pow, waw. 134

Men. True ! I'll be sworn they are true. Where is he wounded ? [*To the Tribunes*] God save your good worships ! Marcius is coming home ; he has more cause to be proud. Where is he wounded ?

Vol. I' th' shoulder and i' th' left arm ; there will be large cicatrices to show the people when he shall stand for his place. He received in the repulse of Tarquin seven hurts i' th' body. 142

Men. One i' th' neck and two i' th' thigh—there's nine that I know.

Vol. He had before this last expedition twenty-five wounds upon him. 146

Men. Now it's twenty-seven ; every gash was an enemy's grave. [*A shout and flourish*] Hark ! the trumpets.

Vol. These are the ushers of Marcius. Before him he carries noise, and behind him he leaves tears : 150
Death, that dark spirit, in's nervy arm doth lie,
Which, being advanc'd, declines, and then men die.

A sennet. Trumpets sound. Enter COMINIUS *the General, and* TITUS LARTIUS ; *between them,* CORIOLANUS, *crown'd with an oaken garland ; with* Captains *and* Soldiers *and a* Herald.

Her. Know, Rome, that all alone Marcius did fight

Within Corioli gates, where he hath won,
With fame, a name to Caius Marcius ; these
In honour follows Coriolanus.   156
Welcome to Rome, renowned Coriolanus !
                              [*Flourish.*
  All.   Welcome to Rome, renowned
    Coriolanus !
  Cor. No more of this, it does offend my
    heart.
Pray now, no more.
  Com.   Look, sir, your mother !
  Cor.   O, 160
You have, I know, petition'd all the gods
For my prosperity !   [*Kneels.*
  Vol.   Nay, my good soldier, up ;
My gentle Marcius, worthy Caius, and
By deed-achieving honour newly nam'd—
What is it ? Coriolanus must I call thee ?
But, O, thy wife !
  Cor.   My gracious silence, hail !
Wouldst thou have laugh'd had I come
    coffin'd home,   167
That weep'st to see me triumph ? Ah, my
    dear,
Such eyes the widows in Corioli wear,
And mothers that lack sons.
  Men.   Now the gods crown thee!
  Cor. And live you yet ? [*To Valeria*] O my
    sweet lady, pardon.   171
  Vol. I know not where to turn.
O, welcome home ! And welcome, General.
And y'are welcome all.
  Men. A hundred thousand welcomes. I
    could weep
And I could laugh ; I am light and heavy.
    Welcome !
A curse begin at very root on's heart   176
That is not glad to see thee ! You are
    three
That Rome should dote on ; yet, by the
    faith of men,
We have some old crab trees here at home
    that will not
Be grafted to your relish. Yet welcome,
    warriors.   180
We call a nettle but a nettle, and
The faults of fools but folly.
  Com.   Ever right.
  Cor. Menenius ever, ever.
  Her. Give way there, and go on.
  Cor. [*To his wife and mother*] Your hand,
    and yours.
Ere in our own house I do shade my head,
The good patricians must be visited ;   186
From whom I have receiv'd not only
    greetings,
But with them change of honours.
  Vol.   I have lived
To see inherited my very wishes,
And the buildings of my fancy ; only 190
There's one thing wanting, which I doubt
    not but
Our Rome will cast upon thee.
  Cor.   Know, good mother,

I had rather be their servant in my way
Than sway with them in theirs.
  Com.   On, to the Capitol.
    [*Flourish. Cornets. Exeunt in state, as
    before. Brutus and Sicinius come
    forward.*
  Bru. All tongues speak of him and the
    bleared sights   195
Are spectacled to see him. Your prattling
    nurse
Into a rapture lets her baby cry
While she chats him ; the kitchen malkin
    pins
Her richest lockram 'bout her reechy neck,
Clamb'ring the walls to eye him ; stalls,
    bulks, windows,   200
Are smother'd up, leads fill'd and ridges
    hors'd
With variable complexions, all agreeing
In earnestness to see him.   Seld-shown
    flamens
Do press among the popular throngs and
    puff   204
To win a vulgar station ; our veil'd dames
Commit the war of white and damask in
Their nicely gawded cheeks to th' wanton
    spoil
Of Phœbus' burning kisses. Such a pother,
As if that whatsoever god who leads him
Were slily crept into his human powers, 210
And gave him graceful posture.
  Sic.   On the sudden
I warrant him consul.
  Bru.   Then our office may
During his power go sleep.
  Sic. He cannot temp'rately transport his
    honours
From where he should begin and end, but
    will   215
Lose those he hath won.
  Bru.   In that there's comfort.
  Sic.   Doubt not
The commoners, for whom we stand, but they
Upon their ancient malice will forget
With the least cause these his new honours ;
    which
That he will give them make I as little
    question   220
As he is proud to do't.
  Bru.   I heard him swear,
Were he to stand for consul, never would he
Appear i' th' market-place, nor on him put
The napless vesture of humility ;   224
Nor, showing, as the manner is, his wounds
To th' people, beg their stinking breaths.
  Sic.   'Tis right.
  Bru. It was his word. O, he would miss
    it rather
Than carry it but by the suit of the gentry
    to him
And the desire of the nobles.
  Sic.   I wish no better
Than have him hold that purpose, and to
    put it   230

In execution.
    Bru.   'Tis most like he will.
    Sic. It shall be to him then as our good
        wills :
A sure destruction.
    Bru.   So it must fall out
To him or our authorities. For an end,
We must suggest the people in what hatred
He still hath held them ; that to's power
        he would   236
Have made them mules, silenc'd their
        pleaders, and
Dispropertied their freedoms ; holding
        them
In human action and capacity
Of no more soul nor fitness for the world 240
Than camels in their war, who have their
        provand
Only for bearing burdens, and sore blows
For sinking under them.
    Sic.   This, as you say, suggested
At some time when his soaring insolence
Shall touch the people—which time shall not
        want,   245
If he be put upon't, and that's as easy
As to set dogs on sheep—will be his fire
To kindle their dry stubble; and their
        blaze
Shall darken him for ever.

        Enter a Messenger.

    Bru.   What's the matter ?
    Mess. You are sent for to the Capitol.
    'Tis thought
That Marcius shall be consul.   251
I have seen the dumb men throng to see
        him and
The blind to hear him speak ; matrons
        flung gloves,
Ladies and maids their scarfs and hand-
        kerchers,   254
Upon him as he pass'd ; the nobles bended
As to Jove's statue, and the commons
        made
A shower and thunder with their caps and
        shouts.
I never saw the like.
    Bru.   Let's to the Capitol,
And carry with us ears and eyes for th'
        time,   259
But hearts for the event.
    Sic.   Have with you. [*Exeunt.*

    SCENE II. *Rome. The Capitol.*

Enter two Officers, *to lay cushions, as it
    were in the Capitol.*

    1 *Off.* Come, come, they are almost here.
How many stand for consulships ?
    2 *Off.* Three, they say ; but 'tis thought
of every one Coriolanus will carry it.
    1 *Off.* That's a brave fellow ; but he's
vengeance proud and loves not the common
people.   6

    2 *Off.* Faith, there have been many great
men that have flatter'd the people, who
ne'er loved them ; and there be many that
they have loved, they know not wherefore ;
so that, if they love they know not why,
they hate upon no better a ground. Therefore, for Coriolanus neither to care whether
they love or hate him manifests the true
knowledge he has in their disposition, and
out of his noble carelessness lets them
plainly see't.   14
    1 *Off.* If he did not care whether he had
their love or no, he waved indifferently
'twixt doing them neither good nor harm ;
but he seeks their hate with greater devotion than they can render it him, and leaves
nothing undone that may fully discover him
their opposite. Now to seem to affect the
malice and displeasure of the people is as
bad as that which he dislikes—to flatter
them for their love.   22
    2 *Off.* He hath deserved worthily of his
country ; and his ascent is not by such
easy degrees as those who, having been
supple and courteous to the people,
bonneted, without any further deed to have
them at all, into their estimation and report;
but he hath so planted his honours in their
eyes and his actions in their hearts that for
their tongues to be silent and not confess
so much were a kind of ingrateful injury ;
to report otherwise were a malice that,
giving itself the lie, would pluck reproof
and rebuke from every ear that heard it. 32
    1 *Off.* No more of him ; he's a worthy
man. Make way, they are coming.

A Sennet. Enter the Patricians *and the*
    Tribunes *of the People,* Lictors *before
    them ;* CORIOLANUS, MENENIUS, COM-
    INIUS *the* Consul. *Sicinius and Brutus
    take their places by themselves. Corio-
    lanus stands.*

    Men. Having determin'd of the Volsces,
        and   35
To send for Titus Lartius, it remains,
As the main point of this our after-meeting,
To gratify his noble service that
Hath thus stood for his country. Therefore
        please you,
Most reverend and grave elders, to desire 40
The present consul and last general
In our well-found successes to report
A little of that worthy work perform'd
By Caius Marcius Coriolanus ; whom
We met here both to thank and to re-
        member   45
With honours like himself. [*Coriolanus sits.*
    1 *Sen.*   Speak, good Cominius.
Leave nothing out for length, and make us
        think
Rather our state's defective for requital
Than we to stretch it out. Masters o' th'
        people,

We do request your kindest ears   and,
    after,   50
Your loving motion toward the common
    body,
To yield what passes here.
Sic.   We are convented
Upon a pleasing treaty, and have hearts
Inclinable to honour and advance
The theme of our assembly.
Bru.   Which the rather 55
We shall be bless'd to do, if he remember
A kinder value of the people than
He hath hereto priz'd them at.
Men.   That's off, that's off ;
I would you rather had been silent. Please
    you
To hear Cominius speak ?
Bru.   Most willingly. 60
But yet my caution was more pertinent
Than the rebuke you give it.
Men.   He loves your people ;
But tie him not to be their bedfellow.
Worthy Cominius, speak.
    [*Coriolanus rises, and offers to go away.*
            Nay, keep your place.
    1 *Sen.* Sit, Coriolanus, never shame to
        hear   65
What you have nobly done.
Cor.   Your Honours' pardon.
I had rather have my wounds to heal again
Than hear say how I got them.
Bru.   Sir, I hope
My words disbench'd you not.
Cor.   No, sir ; yet oft,
When blows have made me stay, I fled from
    words.   70
You sooth'd not, therefore hurt not. But
    your people,
I love them as they weigh—
Men.   Pray now, sit down.
Cor. I had rather have one scratch my
    head i' th' sun
When the alarum were struck than idly sit
To hear my nothings monster'd.   [*Exit.*
Men.   Masters of the people, 75
Your multiplying spawn how can he
    flatter—
That's thousand to one good one—when
    you now see
He had rather venture all his limbs for
    honour
Than one on's ears to hear it ? Proceed,
    Cominius.
Com. I shall lack voice ; the deeds of
    Coriolanus   80
Should not be utter'd feebly. It is held
That valour is the chiefest virtue and
Most dignifies the haver. If it be,
The man I speak of cannot in the world 84
Be singly counterpois'd. At sixteen years,
When Tarquin made a head for Rome, he
    fought
Beyond the mark of others ; our then
    Dictator,

Whom with all praise I point at, saw him
    fight
When with his Amazonian chin he drove
The bristled lips before him ; he bestrid 90
An o'erpress'd Roman and i' th' consul's
    view
Slew three opposers ; Tarquin's self he met,
And struck him on his knee. In that day's
    feats,
When he might act the woman in the scene,
He prov'd best man i' th' field, and for his
    meed   95
Was brow-bound with the oak. His pupil age
Man-ent'red thus, he waxed like a sea,
And in the brunt of seventeen battles since
He lurch'd all swords of the garland. For
    this last,
Before and in Corioli, let me say   100
I cannot speak him home. He stopp'd the
    fliers,
And by his rare example made the coward
Turn terror into sport ; as weeds before
A vessel under sail, so men obey'd
And fell below his stem. His sword, death's
    stamp,   105
Where it did mark, it took ; from face to foot
He was a thing of blood, whose every
    motion
Was tim'd with dying cries. Alone he
    ent'red
The mortal gate of th' city, which he
    painted   109
With shunless destiny ; aidless came off,
And with a sudden re-enforcement struck
Corioli like a planet. Now all's his.
When by and by the din of war 'gan pierce
His ready sense, then straight his doubled
    spirit
Re-quick'ned what in flesh was fatigate, 115
And to the battle came he ; where he did
Run reeking o'er the lives of men, as if
'Twere a perpetual spoil ; and till we call'd
Both field and city ours he never stood
To ease his breast with panting.
Men.   Worthy man ! 120
1 *Sen.* He cannot but with measure fit the
    honours
Which we devise him.
Com.   Our spoils he kick'd at,
And look'd upon things precious as they
    were
The common muck of the world. He covets
    less
Than misery itself would give, rewards 125
His deeds with doing them, and is content
To spend the time to end it.
Men.   He's right noble ;
Let him be call'd for.
1 *Sen.*   Call Coriolanus.
Off. He doth appear.

Re-enter CORIOLANUS.

Men. The Senate, Coriolanus, are well
    pleas'd   130

To make thee consul.
Cor.   I do owe them still
My life and services.
Men.   It then remains
That you do speak to the people.
Cor.   I do beseech you
Let me o'erleap that custom; for I cannot
Put on the gown, stand naked, and entreat
    them   135
For my wounds' sake to give their suffrage.
    Please you
That I may pass this doing.
Sic.   Sir, the people
Must have their voices; neither will they
    bate
One jot of ceremony.
Men.   Put them not to't.
Pray you go fit you to the custom, and   140
Take to you, as your predecessors have,
Your honour with your form.
Cor.   It is a part
That I shall blush in acting, and might well
Be taken from the people.
Bru.   Mark you that?
Cor. To brag unto them 'Thus I did,
    and thus!'   145
Show them th' unaching scars which I
    should hide,
As if I had receiv'd them for the hire
Of their breath only!
Men.   Do not stand upon't.
We recommend to you, Tribunes of the
    People,
Our purpose to them; and to our noble
    consul   150
Wish we all joy and honour.
Sen. To Coriolanus come all joy and
    honour!
    [Flourish. Cornets. Then exeunt all
        but Sicinius and Brutus.
Bru. You see how he intends to use the
    people.
Sic. May they perceive's intent! He will
    require them
As if he did contemn what he requested   155
Should be in them to give.
Bru.   Come, we'll inform them
Of our proceedings here. On th' market-
    place
I know they do attend us.   [Exeunt.

SCENE III. Rome. The Forum.

Enter seven or eight Citizens.

1 Cit. Once, if he do require our voices,
we ought not to deny him.
2 Cit. We may, sir, if we will.   3
3 Cit. We have power in ourselves to do
it, but it is a power that we have no power
to do; for if he show us his wounds and
tell us his deeds, we are to put our tongues
into those wounds and speak for them; so,
if he tell us his noble deeds, we must also
tell him our noble acceptance of them.

Ingratitude is monstrous, and for the
multitude to be ingrateful were to make a
monster of the multitude; of the which we
being members should bring ourselves to
be monstrous members.
1 Cit. And to make us no better thought
of, a little help will serve; for once we stood
up about the corn, he himself stuck not to
call us the many-headed multitude.   16
3 Cit. We have been call'd so of many;
not that our heads are some brown, some
black, some abram, some bald, but that
our wits are so diversely colour'd; and
truly I think if all our wits were to issue
out of one skull, they would fly east, west,
north, south, and their consent of one
direct way should be at once to all the
points o' th' compass.
2 Cit. Think you so? Which way do you
judge my wit would fly?   25
3 Cit. Nay, your wit will not so soon out
as another man's will—'tis strongly wedg'd
up in a block-head; but if it were at
liberty 'twould sure southward.
2 Cit. Why that way?   29
3 Cit. To lose itself in a fog; where being
three parts melted away with rotten dews,
the fourth would return for conscience' sake,
to help to get thee a wife.
2 Cit. You are never without your tricks;
you may, you may.   34
3 Cit. Are you all resolv'd to give your
voices? But that's no matter, the greater
part carries it. I say, if he would incline to
the people, there was never a worthier man.

Enter CORIOLANUS, in a gown of humility,
with MENENIUS.

Here he comes, and in the gown of humility.
Mark his behaviour. We are not to stay
all together, but to come by him where he
stands, by ones, by twos, and by threes.
He's to make his requests by particulars,
wherein every one of us has a single honour,
in giving him our own voices with our own
tongues; therefore follow me, and I'll
direct you how you shall go by him.   45
All. Content, content. [Exeunt Citizens.
Men. O sir, you are not right; have you
    not known
The worthiest men have done't?
Cor.   What must I say?
'I pray, sir'—Plague upon't! I cannot
    bring
My tongue to such a pace. 'Look, sir, my
    wounds!   50
I got them in my country's service, when
Some certain of your brethren roar'd, and
    ran
From th' noise of our own drums.'
Men.   O me, the gods!
You must not speak of that. You must
    desire them
To think upon you.

Cor.   Think upon me ? Hang 'em !
I would they would forget me, like the
virtues   56
Which our divines lose by 'em.

Men.   You'll mar all.
I'll leave you. Pray you speak to 'em, I
     pray you,
In wholesome manner.   [*Exit.*

Re-enter three of the Citizens.

Cor.   Bid them wash their faces
And keep their teeth clean. So, here comes
     a brace.   60
You know the cause, sir, of my standing
     here.

3 Cit. We do, sir ; tell us what hath
     brought you to't.

Cor. Mine own desert.

2 Cit. Your own desert ?   65

Cor. Ay, not mine own desire.

3 Cit. How, not your own desire ?

Cor. No, sir, 'twas never my desire yet to
trouble the poor with begging.

3 Cit. You must think, if we give you
anything, we hope to gain by you.   71

Cor. Well then, I pray, your price o' th'
consulship ?

1 Cit. The price is to ask it kindly.

Cor. Kindly, sir, I pray let me ha't. I
have wounds to show you, which shall be
yours in private. Your good voice, sir ;
what say you ?   76

2 Cit. You shall ha' it, worthy sir.

Cor. A match, sir. There's in all two
worthy voices begg'd. I have your alms.
Adieu.

3 Cit. But this is something odd.   80

2 Cit. An 'twere to give again—but 'tis
no matter.   [*Exeunt the three Citizens.*

Re-enter two other Citizens.

Cor. Pray you now, if it may stand with
the tune of your voices that I may be
consul, I have here the customary gown.

4 Cit. You have deserved nobly of your
country, and you have not deserved nobly.

Cor. Your enigma ?   87

4 Cit. You have been a scourge to her
enemies ; you have been a rod to her
friends. You have not indeed loved the
common people.   90

Cor. You should account me the more
virtuous, that I have not been common in
my love. I will, sir, flatter my sworn
brother, the people, to earn a dearer
estimation of them ; 'tis a condition they
account gentle ; and since the wisdom of
their choice is rather to have my hat than
my heart, I will practise the insinuating
nod and be off to them most counterfeitly.
That is, sir, I will counterfeit the bewitch-
ment of some popular man and give it
bountiful to the desirers. Therefore,
beseech you I may be consul.   100

5 Cit. We hope to find you our friend ;
and therefore give you our voices heartily.

4 Cit. You have received many wounds
for your country.   104

Cor. I will not seal your knowledge with
showing them. I will make much of your
voices, and so trouble you no farther.

Both Cit. The gods give you joy, sir,
heartily !   [*Exeunt Citizens.*

Cor. Most sweet voices !
Better it is to die, better to starve,   110
Than crave the hire which first we do
     deserve.
Why in this wolvish toge should I stand
     here
To beg of Hob and Dick that do appear
Their needless vouches ? Custom calls me
     to't.
What custom wills, in all things should we
     do't,   115
The dust on antique time would lie un-
     swept,
And mountainous error be too highly
     heap'd
For truth to o'erpeer. Rather than fool
     it so,
Let the high office and the honour go
To one that would do thus. I am half
     through :   120
The one part suffered, the other will I do.

Re-enter three Citizens *more.*

Here come moe voices.
Your voices. For your voices I have
     fought ;
Watch'd for your voices ; for your voices
     bear
Of wounds two dozen odd ; battles thrice
     six   125
I have seen and heard of ; for your voices
     have
Done many things, some less, some more.
     Your voices ?
Indeed, I would be consul.

6 Cit. He has done nobly, and cannot go
without any honest man's voice.   130

7 Cit. Therefore let him be consul. The
gods give him joy, and make him good
friend to the people !

All. Amen, amen. God save thee, noble
consul !   [*Exeunt Citizens.*

Cor. Worthy voices !

Re-enter MENENIUS *with* BRUTUS *and*
SICINIUS.

Men. You have stood your limitation,
     and the tribunes
Endue you with the people's voice.
     Remains   136
That, in th' official marks invested, you
Anon do meet the Senate.

Cor.   Is this done ?

Sic. The custom of request you have
     discharg'd.

The people do admit you, and are sum-
 mon'd   140
To meet anon, upon your approbation.
Cor. Where ? At the Senate House ?
Sic.   There, Coriolanus.
Cor. May I change these garments ?
Sic.   You may, sir.
Cor. That I'll straight do, and, knowing
 myself again,
Repair to th' Senate House.   145
 Men. I'll keep you company. Will you
  along ?
 Bru. We stay here for the people.
 Sic.   Fare you well.
  [*Exeunt Coriolanus and Menenius.*
He has it now ; and by his looks methinks
'Tis warm at's heart.
 Bru.   With a proud heart he wore
His humble weeds. Will you dismiss the
 people ?   150

   Re-enter Citizens.

 Sic. How now, my masters ! Have you
  chose this man ?
 1 Cit. He has our voices, sir.
 Bru. We pray the gods he may deserve
  your loves.
 2 Cit. Amen, sir. To my poor unworthy
  notice,
He mock'd us when he begg'd our voices.
 3 Cit.   Certainly ; 155
He flouted us downright.
 1 Cit. No, 'tis his kind of speech—he did
  not mock us.
 2 Cit. Not one amongst us, save yourself,
  but says
He us'd us scornfully. He should have
 show'd us
His marks of merit, wounds receiv'd for's
 country.   160
 Sic. Why, so he did, I am sure.
 All. No, no ; no man saw 'em.
 3 Cit. He said he had wounds which he
  could show in private,
And with his hat, thus waving it in scorn,
' I would be consul ;' says he ' aged
 custom   165
But by your voices will not so permit me ;
Your voices therefore '. When we granted
 that,
Here was ' I thank you for your voices.
 Thank you,
Your most sweet voices. Now you have left
 your voices,
I have no further with you '. Was not this
 mockery ?   170
 Sic. Why either were you ignorant to
  see't,
Or, seeing it, of such childish friendliness
To yield your voices ?
 Bru.   Could you not have told him—
As you were lesson'd—when he had no
 power
But was a petty servant to the state, 175

He was your enemy ; ever spake against
Your liberties and the charters that you
 bear
I' th' body of the weal ; and now, arriving
A place of potency and sway o' th' state,
If he should still malignantly remain 180
Fast foe to th' plebeii, your voices might
Be curses to yourselves ? You should have
 said
That as his worthy deeds did claim no less
Than what he stood for so his gracious
 nature   184
Would think upon you for your voices, and
Translate his malice towards you into love,
Standing your friendly lord.
 Sic.   Thus to have said,
As you were fore-advis'd, had touch'd his
 spirit
And tried his inclination ; from him pluck'd
Either his gracious promise, which you
 might,   190
As cause had call'd you up, have held him
 to ;
Or else it would have gall'd his surly nature,
Which easily endures not article
Tying him to aught. So, putting him to
 rage,
You should have ta'en th' advantage of his
 choler   195
And pass'd him unelected.
 Bru.   Did you perceive
He did solicit you in free contempt
When he did need your loves ; and do you
 think
That his contempt shall not be bruising to
 you
When he hath power to crush ? Why, had
 your bodies   200
No heart among you ? Or had you tongues
 to cry
Against the rectorship of judgment ?
 Sic.   Have you
Ere now denied the asker, and now again,
Of him that did not ask but mock, bestow
Your su'd-for tongues ?   205
 3 Cit. He's not confirm'd : we may deny
  him yet.
 2 Cit. And will deny him ;
I'll have five hundred voices of that sound.
 1 Cit. I twice five hundred, and their
  friends to piece 'em.
 Bru. Get you hence instantly, and tell
  those friends   210
They have chose a consul that will from
 them take
Their liberties, make them of no more voice
Than dogs, that are as often beat for
 barking
As therefore kept to do so.
 Sic.   Let them assemble ;
And, on a safer judgment, all revoke 215
Your ignorant election. Enforce his pride
And his old hate unto you ; besides, forget
 not

With what contempt he wore the humble
   weed;
How in his suit he scorn'd you; but your
   loves,   219
Thinking upon his services, took from
   you
Th' apprehension of his present portance,
Which, most gibingly, ungravely, he did
   fashion
After the inveterate hate he bears you.
  Bru.   Lay
A fault on us, your tribunes, that we
   labour'd,
No impediment between, but that you
   must   225
Cast your election on him.
  Sic.   Say you chose him
More after our commandment than as
   guided
By your own true affections; and that
   your minds,
Pre-occupied with what you rather must do
Than what you should, made you against
   the grain   230
To voice him consul. Lay the fault on us.
  Bru. Ay, spare us not. Say we read
   lectures to you,
How youngly he began to serve his country,
How long continued; and what stock he
   springs of—
The noble house o' th' Marcians; from
   whence came   235
That Ancus Marcius, Numa's daughter's
   son,
Who, after great Hostilius, here was king;
Of the same house Publius and Quintus
   were,
That our best water brought by conduits
   hither;
And Censorinus, nobly named so,   240
Twice being by the people chosen censor,
Was his great ancestor.
  Sic.   One thus descended,
That hath beside well in his person wrought
To be set high in place, we did commend
To your remembrances; but you have
   found,   245
Scaling his present bearing with his past,
That he's your fixed enemy, and revoke
Your sudden approbation.
  Bru.   Say you ne'er had done't—
Harp on that still—but by our putting on;
And presently, when you have drawn your
   number   250
Repair to th' Capitol.
  Citizens.   We will so; almost all
Repent in their election. [*Exeunt Plebeians.*
  Bru.   Let them go on;
This mutiny were better put in hazard
Than stay, past doubt, for greater.
If, as his nature is, he fall in rage   255
With their refusal, both observe and answer
The vantage of his anger.
  Sic.   To th' Capitol, come.

We will be there before the stream o' th'
   people;
And this shall seem, as partly 'tis, their
   own,   259
Which we have goaded onward.   [*Exeunt.*

ACT THREE

Scene I. *Rome. A street.*

Cornets.   Enter Coriolanus, Menenius,
all the Gentry, Cominius, Titus Lartius,
and other Senators.

  Cor. Tullus Aufidius, then, had made new
   head?
  Lart. He had, my lord; and that it was
   which caus'd
Our swifter composition.
  Cor. So then the Volsces stand but as
   at first,
Ready, when time shall prompt them, to
   make road   5
Upon's again.
  Com.   They are worn, Lord Consul, so
That we shall hardly in our ages see
Their banners wave again.
  Cor.   Saw you Aufidius?
  Lart. On safeguard he came to me, and
   did curse   9
Against the Volsces, for they had so vilely
Yielded the town. He is retir'd to Antium.
  Cor. Spoke he of me?
  Lart.   He did, my lord.
  Cor.   How? What?
  Lart. How often he had met you, sword
   to sword;
That of all things upon the earth he
   hated
Your person most; that he would pawn
   his fortunes   15
To hopeless restitution, so he might
Be call'd your vanquisher.
  Cor.   At Antium lives he?
  Lart. At Antium.
  Cor. I wish I had a cause to seek him
   there,   19
To oppose his hatred fully. Welcome home.

Enter Sicinius *and* Brutus.

Behold, these are the tribunes of the people,
The tongues o' th' common mouth. I do
   despise them,
For they do prank them in authority,
Against all noble sufferance.
  Sic. Pass no further.
  Cor.   Ha! What is that?   25
  Bru. It will be dangerous to go on—no
   further.
  Cor. What makes this change?
  Men. The matter?
  Com. Hath he not pass'd the noble and
   the common?
  Bru. Cominius, no.
  Cor.   Have I had children's voices? 30

1 Sen. Tribunes, give way : he shall to th'
    market-place.
Bru. The people are incens'd against him.
Sic.   Stop,
Or all will fall in broil.
Cor.   Are these your herd ?
Must these have voices, that can yield them
    now
And straight disclaim their tongues ? What
    are your offices ?   35
You being their mouths, why rule you not
    their teeth ?
Have you not set them on ?
Men.   Be calm, be calm.
Cor. It is a purpos'd thing, and grows by
    plot,
To curb the will of the nobility ;   39
Suffer't, and live with such as cannot rule
Nor ever will be rul'd.
Bru.   Call't not a plot.
The people cry you mock'd them ; and of
    late,
When corn was given them gratis, you
    repin'd ;
Scandal'd the suppliants for the people,
    call'd them   44
Time-pleasers, flatterers, foes to nobleness.
Cor. Why, this was known before.
Bru.   Not to them all.
Cor. Have you inform'd them sithence ?
Bru.   How ? I inform them !
Com. You are like to do such business.
Bru.   Not unlike
Each way to better yours.
Cor. Why then should I be consul ? By
    yond clouds,   50
Let me deserve so ill as you, and make me
Your fellow tribune.
Sic.   You show too much of that
For which the people stir ; if you will pass
To where you are bound, you must enquire
    your way,   54
Which you are out of, with a gentler spirit,
Or never be so noble as a consul,
Nor yoke with him for tribune.
Men.   Let's be calm.
Com. The people are abus'd ; set on. This
    palt-ring
Becomes not Rome ; nor has Coriolanus
Deserv'd this so dishonour'd rub, laid
    falsely   60
I' th' plain way of his merit.
Cor.   Tell me of corn !
This was my speech, and I will speak't
    again—
Men. Not now, not now.
1 Sen.   Not in this heat, sir, now.
Cor. Now, as I live, I will.
My nobler friends, I crave their par-
    dons.   65
For the mutable, rank-scented meiny, let
    them
Regard me as I do not flatter, and
Therein behold themselves. I say again,

In soothing them we nourish 'gainst our
    Senate   69
The cockle of rebellion, insolence, sedition,
Which we ourselves have plough'd for,
    sow'd, and scatter'd,
By mingling them with us, the honour'd
    number,
Who lack not virtue, no, nor power, but that
Which they have given to beggars.
Men.   Well, no more.
1 Sen. No more words, we beseech you.
Cor.   How ? no more !
As for my country I have shed my blood, 76
Not fearing outward force, so shall my
    lungs
Coin words till their decay against those
    measles
Which we disdain should tetter us, yet
    sought
The very way to catch them.
Bru.   You speak o' th' people 80
As if you were a god, to punish ; not
A man of their infirmity.
Sic.   'Twere well
We let the people know't.
Men.   What, what ? his choler ?
Cor. Choler !
Were I as patient as the midnight sleep, 85
By Jove, 'twould be my mind !
Sic.   It is a mind
That shall remain a poison where it is,
Not poison any further.
Cor.   Shall remain !
Hear you this Triton of the minnows ?
    Mark you
His absolute ' shall ' ?
Com.   'Twas from the canon.
Cor.   ' Shall ' ! 90
O good but most unwise patricians ! Why,
You grave but reckless senators, have you
    thus
Given Hydra here to chose an officer
That with his peremptory 'shall ', being but
The horn and noise o' th' monster's, wants
    not spirit   95
To say he'll turn your current in a ditch,
And make your channel his ? If he have
    power,
Then vail your ignorance ; if none, awake
Your dangerous lenity. If you are learn'd,
Be not as common fools ; if you are not, 100
Let them have cushions by you. You are
    plebeians,
If they be senators ; and they are no less,
When, both your voices blended, the
    great'st taste
Most palates theirs. They choose their
    magistrate ;   104
And such a one as he, who puts his ' shall ',
His popular ' shall ', against a graver bench
Than ever frown'd in Greece. By Jove
    himself,
It makes the consuls base ; and my soul
    aches

To know, when two authorities are up,
Neither supreme, how soon confusion   110
May enter 'twixt the gap of both and take
The one by th' other.
    Com.   Well, on to th' market-place.
    Cor. Whoever gave that counsel to give
       forth
The corn o' th' storehouse gratis, as 'twas
       us'd
Sometime in Greece—
    Men.   Well, well, no more of that.   115
    Cor. Though there the people had more
      absolute pow'r—
I say they nourish'd disobedience, fed
The ruin of the state.
    Bru.   Why shall the people give
One that speaks thus their voice ?
    Cor.   I'll give my reasons,
More worthier than their voices. They
    know the corn   120
Was not our recompense, resting well
    assur'd
They ne'er did service for't ; being press'd
    to th' war,
Even when the navel of the state was
    touch'd,
They would not thread the gates. This kind
    of service
Did not deserve corn gratis. Being i' th'
    war,   125
Their mutinies and revolts, wherein they
    show'd
Most valour, spoke not for them. Th'
    accusation
Which they have often made against the
    Senate,
All cause unborn, could never be the
    native   129
Of our so frank donation. Well, what then ?
How shall this bosom multiplied digest
The Senate's courtesy ? Let deeds express
What's like to be their words : ' We did
    request it ;
We are the greater poll, and in true fear
They gave us our demands'. Thus we
    debase   135
The nature of our seats, and make the
    rabble
Call our cares fears ; which will in time
Break ope the locks o' th' Senate and bring
    in
The crows to peck the eagles.
    Men.   Come, enough.
    Bru. Enough, with over measure.
    Cor.   No, take more.   140
What may be sworn by, both divine and
    human,
Seal what I end withal ! This double
    worship,
Where one part does disdain with cause,
    the other
Insult without all reason ; where gentry,
    title, wisdom,
Cannot conclude but by the yea and no   145

Of general ignorance—it must omit
Real necessities, and give way the while
To unstable slightness. Purpose so barr'd,
    it follows
Nothing is done to purpose. Therefore,
    beseech you—   149
You that will be less fearful than discreet ;
That love the fundamental part of state
More than you doubt the change on't ; that
    prefer
A noble life before a long, and wish
To jump a body with a dangerous physic
That's sure of death without it—at once
    pluck out   155
The multitudinous tongue ; let them not
    lick
The sweet which is their poison. Your
    dishonour
Mangles true judgment, and bereaves the
    state
Of that integrity which should become't,
Not having the power to do the good it
    would,   160
For th' ill which doth control't.
    Bru.   Has said enough.
    Sic. Has spoken like a traitor and shall
    answer
As traitors do.
    Cor.   Thou wretch, despite o'erwhelm
    thee !
What should the people do with these bald
    tribunes,   164
On whom depending, their obedience fails
To the greater bench ? In a rebellion,
When what's not meet, but what must be,
    was law,
Then were they chosen ; in a better hour
Let what is meet be said it must be meet,
And throw their power i' th' dust.   170
    Bru. Manifest treason !
    Sic.   This a consul ? No.
    Bru. The ædiles, ho !

            Enter an Ædile.

           Let him be apprehended.
    Sic. Go call the people, [*Exit Ædile*] in
    whose name myself
Attach thee as a traitorous innovator,
A foe to th' public weal. Obey, I charge
    thee,   175
And follow to thine answer.
    Cor.   Hence, old goat !
    Patricians. We'll surety him.
    Com.   Ag'd sir, hands off.
    Cor. Hence, rotten thing ! or I shall shake
    thy bones
Out of thy garments.
    Sic.   Help, ye citizens !

Enter a rabble of Plebeians, *with the* Ædiles.

    Men. On both sides more respect.   180
    Sic. Here's he that would take from you
    all your power.
    Bru. Seize him, ædiles.

Plebeians. Down with him ! down with him !

2 Sen. Weapons, weapons, weapons !

[*They all bustle about Coriolanus.*

All. Tribunes ! patricians ! citizens ! What, ho ! Sicinius ! Brutus ! Coriolanus ! Citizens !

Patricians. Peace, peace, peace ; stay, hold, peace !   187

Men. What is about to be ? I am out of breath ;

Confusion's near ; I cannot speak. You Tribunes

To th' people—Coriolanus, patience !   190 Speak, good Sicinius.

Sic.   Hear me, people ; peace !

Plebeians. Let's hear our tribune. Peace ! Speak, speak, speak.

Sic. You are at point to lose your liberties.   194

Marcius would have all from you ; Marcius, Whom late you have nam'd for consul.

Men.   Fie, fie, fie ! This is the way to kindle, not to quench.

1 Sen. To unbuild the city, and to lay all flat.

Sic. What is the city but the people ?

Plebeians.   True,

The people are the city.   200

Bru. By the consent of all we were establish'd

The people's magistrates.

Plebeians.   You so remain.

Men. And so are like to do.

Com. That is the way to lay the city flat, To bring the roof to the foundation,   205 And bury all which yet distinctly ranges In heaps and piles of ruin.

Sic.   This deserves death.

Bru. Or let us stand to our authority Or let us lose it. We do here pronounce, Upon the part o' th' people, in whose power We were elected theirs : Marcius is worthy Of present death.

Sic.   Therefore lay hold of him ; Bear him to th' rock Tarpeian, and from thence

Into destruction cast him.

Bru.   Ædiles, seize him.

Plebeians. Yield, Marcius, yield.

Men. Hear me one word ; beseech you, Tribunes,   215

Hear me but a word.

Æd. Peace, peace !

Men. Be that you seem, truly your country's friend,

And temp'rately proceed to what you would Thus violently redress.

Bru.   Sir, those cold ways,   220 That seem like prudent helps, are very poisonous

Where the disease is violent. Lay hands upon him

And bear him to the rock.

[*Coriolanus draws his sword.*

Cor.   No : I'll die here. There's some among you have beheld me fighting ;

Come, try upon yourselves what you have seen me.   225

Men. Down with that sword ! Tribunes, withdraw awhile.

Bru. Lay hands upon him.

Men.   Help Marcius, help, You that be noble ; help him, young and old.

Plebeians. Down with him, down with him ! [*In this mutiny the Tribunes, the Ædiles, and the People are beat in.*

Men. Go, get you to your house ; be gone, away.   230

All will be nought else.

2 Sen. Get you gone.

Cor.   Stand fast ; We have as many friends as enemies.

Men. Shall it be put to that ?

1 Sen.   The gods forbid ! I prithee, noble friend, home to thy house ; Leave us to cure this cause.

Men.   For 'tis a sore upon us 235 You cannot tent yourself : be gone, beseech you.

Com. Come, sir, along with us.

Cor. I would they were barbarians, as they are,

Though in Rome litter'd   not Romans, as they are not,   239

Though calved i' th' porch o' th' Capitol.

Men.   Be gone. Put not your worthy rage into your tongue ; One time will owe another.

Cor.   On fair ground I could beat forty of them.

Men.   I could myself Take up a brace o' th' best of them ; yea, the two tribunes.

Com. But now 'tis odds beyond arithmetic,   245

And manhood is call'd foolery when it stands

Against a falling fabric. Will you hence, Before the tag return ? whose rage doth rend Like interrupted waters, and o'erbear What they are us'd to bear.

Men.   Pray you be gone. 250 I'll try whether my old wit be in request With those that have but little ; this must be patch'd

With cloth of any colour.

Com.   Nay, come away.

[*Exeunt Coriolanus and Cominius, with others.*

Pat. This man has marr'd his fortune.

Men. His nature is too noble for the world :   255

He would not flatter Neptune for his trident,

Or Jove for's power to thunder. His heart's his mouth ;

What his breast forges, that his tongue
    must vent ;
And, being angry, does forget that ever
He heard the name of death.   260
                    [*A noise within.*
Here's goodly work !
  Pat. I would they were a-bed.
  Men. I would they were in Tiber.
What the vengeance, could he not speak
    'em fair ?

Re-enter BRUTUS *and* SICINIUS, *with the*
    Rabble *again.*

  Sic. Where is this viper
That would depopulate the city and   264
Be every man himself ?
  Men.   You worthy Tribunes—
  Sic. He shall be thrown down the
    Tarpeian rock
With rigorous hands ; he hath resisted law,
And therefore law shall scorn him further
    trial
Than the severity of the public power,
Which he so sets at nought.
  1 Cit.   He shall well know   270
The noble tribunes are the people's mouths,
And we their hands.
  Plebeians. He shall, sure on't.
  Men.   Sir, sir—
  Sic. Peace !
  Men. Do not cry havoc, where you
    should but hunt   275
With modest warrant.
  Sic.   Sir, how comes't that you
Have holp to make this rescue ?
  Men.   Hear me speak.
As I do know the consul's worthiness,
So can I name his faults.
  Sic.   Consul ! What consul ?
  Men. The consul Coriolanus.
  Bru.   He consul ! 280
  Plebeians. No, no, no, no, no.
  Men. If, by the tribune's leave, and
    yours, good people,
I may be heard, I would crave a word or
    two ;
The which shall turn you to no further
    harm
Than so much loss of time.
  Sic.   Speak briefly, then, 285
For we are peremptory to dispatch
This viperous traitor ; to eject him hence
Were but one danger, and to keep him here
Our certain death ; therefore it is decreed
He dies to-night.
  Men.   Now the good gods forbid 290
That our renowned Rome, whose gratitude
Towards her deserved children is enroll'd
In Jove's own book, like an unnatural dam
Should now eat up her own !
  Sic. He's a disease that must be cut
    away. 295
  Men. O, he's a limb that has but a
    disease—

Mortal, to cut it off : to cure it, easy.
What has he done to Rome that's worthy
    death ?
Killing our enemies, the blood he hath
    lost—
Which I dare vouch is more than that he
    hath 300
By many an ounce—he dropt it for his
    country ;
And what is left, to lose it by his country
Were to us all that do't and suffer it
A brand to th' end o' th' world.
  Sic.   This is clean kam.
  Bru. Merely awry. When he did love his
    country, 305
It honour'd him.
  Sic.   The service of the foot,
Being once gangren'd, is not then respected
For what before it was.
  Bru.   We'll hear no more.
Pursue him to his house and pluck him
    thence,
Lest his infection, being of catching
    nature, 310
Spread further.
  Men.   One word more, one word !
This tiger-footed rage, when it shall find
The harm of unscann'd swiftness, will, too
    late,
Tie leaden pounds to's heels.   Proceed by
    process,
Lest parties—as he is belov'd—break out,
And sack great Rome with Romans. 316
  Bru.   If it were so—
  Sic. What do ye talk ?
Have we not had a taste of his obedience—
Our ædiles smote, ourselves resisted ?
    Come !
  Men. Consider this : he has been bred
    i' th' wars
Since 'a could draw a sword, and is ill
    school'd 321
In bolted language ; meal and bran
    together
He throws without distinction.   Give me
    leave,
I'll go to him and undertake to bring
    him
Where he shall answer by a lawful form, 325
In peace, to his utmost peril.
  1 Sen.   Noble Tribunes,
It is the humane way ; the other course
Will prove too bloody, and the end of it
Unknown to the beginning.
  Sic.   Noble Menenius,
Be you then as the people's officer. 330
Masters, lay down your weapons.
  Bru.   Go not home.
  Sic. Meet on the market-place. We'll
    attend you there ;
Where, if you bring not Marcius, we'll
    proceed
In our first way.
  Men.   I'll bring him to you.

[*To the Senators*] Let me desire your com-
            pany ; he must come,   335
Or what is worst will follow.
1 *Sen.*   Pray you let's to him.
                                    [*Exeunt.*

SCENE II. *Rome. The house of Coriolanus.*

    Enter CORIOLANUS *with* Nobles.

    Cor. Let them pull all about mine ears,
            present me
Death on the wheel or at wild horses' heels ;
Or pile ten hills on the Tarpeian rock,
That the precipitation might down stretch
Below the beam of sight ; yet will I still 5
Be thus to them.
    1 *Pat.*   You do the nobler.
    Cor. I muse my mother
Does not approve me further, who was
            wont
To call them woollen vassals, things created
To buy and sell with groats ; to show bare
            heads   10
In congregations, to yawn, be still, and
            wonder,
When one but of my ordinance stood up
To speak of peace or war.

            Enter VOLUMNIA.

                          I talk of you :
Why did you wish me milder ? Would you
            have me
False to my nature ? Rather say I play 15
The man I am.
    Vol.   O, sir, sir, sir,
I would have had you put your power well
            on
Before you had worn it out.
    Cor.   Let go.
    Vol. You might have been enough the
            man you are   19
With striving less to be so ; lesser had been
The thwartings of your dispositions, if
You had not show'd them how ye were
            dispos'd,
Ere they lack'd power to cross you.
    Cor.   Let them hang.
    Vol. Ay, and burn too.

    Enter MENENIUS *with the* Senators.

    Men. Come, come, you have been too
            rough, something too rough ;   25
You must return and mend it.
    1 *Sen.*   There's no remedy,
Unless, by not so doing, our good city
Cleave in the midst and perish.
    Vol.   Pray be counsell'd ;
I have a heart as little apt as yours,   29
But yet a brain that leads my use of anger
To better vantage.
    Men.   Well said, noble woman !
Before he should thus stoop to th' herd,
            but that
The violent fit o' th' time craves it as physic

For the whole state, I would put mine
            armour on,
Which I can scarcely bear.
    Cor.   What must I do ?   35
    Men. Return to th' tribunes.
    Cor.   Well, what then, what then ?
    Men. Repent what you have spoke.
    Cor. For them ! I cannot do it to the
            gods ;
Must I then do't to them ?
    Vol.   You are too absolute ;
Though therein you can never be too noble
But when extremities speak. I have heard
            you say   41
Honour and policy, like unsever'd friends,
I' th' war do grow together ; grant that,
            and tell me
In peace what each of them by th' other
            lose
That they combine not there.
    Cor.   Tush, tush !
    Men.   A good demand.
    Vol. If it be honour in your wars to seem
The same you are not, which for your best
            ends   47
You adopt your policy, how is it less or
            worse
That it shall hold companionship in peace
With honour as in war ; since that to both
It stands in like request ?
    Cor.   Why force you this ?
    Vol. Because that now it lies you on to
            speak   52
To th' people, not by your own instruction,
Nor by th' matter which your heart
            prompts you,
But with such words that are but roted in
Your tongue, though but bastards and
            syllables   56
Of no allowance to your bosom's truth.
Now, this no more dishonours you at all
Than to take in a town with gentle words,
Which else would put you to your fortune
            and   60
The hazard of much blood.
I would dissemble with my nature where
My fortunes and my friends at stake
            requir'd
I should do so in honour. I am in this
Your wife, your son, these senators, the
            nobles ;   65
And you will rather show our general louts
How you can frown, than spend a fawn
            upon 'em
For the inheritance of their loves and safe-
            guard
Of what that want might ruin.
    Men.   Noble lady !
Come, go with us, speak fair ; you may
            salve so,   70
Not what is dangerous present, but the loss
Of what is past.
    Vol.   I prithee now, my son,
Go to them with this bonnet in thy hand ;

And thus far having stretch'd it—here be
    with them—
Thy knee bussing the stones—for in such
    business   75
Action is eloquence, and the eyes of th'
    ignorant
More learned than the ears—waving thy
    head,
Which often thus correcting thy stout heart,
Now humble as the ripest mulberry
That will not hold the handling. Or say to
    them   80
Thou art their soldier and, being bred in
    broils,
Hast not the soft way which, thou dost
    confess,
Were fit for thee to use, as they to claim,
In asking their good loves; but thou wilt
    frame
Thyself, forsooth, hereafter theirs, so far 85
As thou hast power and person.
Men.   This but done
Even as she speaks, why, their hearts were
    yours;
For they have pardons, being ask'd, as free
As words to little purpose.
Vol.   Prithee now,
Go, and be rul'd; although I know thou
    hadst rather   90
Follow thine enemy in a fiery gulf
Than flatter him in a bower.

Enter COMINIUS.

                  Here is Cominius.
  Com. I have been i' th' market-place;
    and, sir, 'tis fit
You make strong party, or defend yourself
By calmness or by absence; all's in anger.
  Men. Only fair speech.
  Com.   I think 'twill serve, if he
Can thereto frame his spirit.
  Vol.   He must and will.
Prithee now, say you will, and go about it.
  Cor. Must I go show them my unbarb'd
    sconce? Must I
With my base tongue give to my noble
    heart   100
A lie that it must bear? Well, I will do't;
Yet, were there but this single plot to lose,
This mould of Marcius, they to dust should
    grind it,
And throw't against the wind. To th'
    market-place!
You have put me now to such a part which
    never   105
I shall discharge to th' life.
  Com.   Come, come, we'll prompt you.
  Vol. I prithee now, sweet son, as thou
    hast said
My praises made thee first a soldier, so,
To have my praise for this, perform a part
Thou hast not done before.
  Cor.   Well, I must do't. 110
Away, my disposition, and possess me

Some harlot's spirit! My throat of war be
    turn'd,
Which quier'd with my drum, into a pipe
Small as an eunuch or the virgin voice
That babies lulls asleep! The smiles of
    knaves   115
Tent in my cheeks, and schoolboys' tears
    take up
The glasses of my sight! A beggar's tongue
Make motion through my lips, and my
    arm'd knees,   118
Who bow'd but in my stirrup, bend like his
That hath receiv'd an alms! I will not do't,
Lest I surcease to honour mine own truth,
And by my body's action teach my mind
A most inherent baseness.
  Vol.   At thy choice, then.
To beg of thee, it is my more dishonour
Than thou of them. Come all to ruin. Let
Thy mother rather feel thy pride than fear
Thy dangerous stoutness; for I mock at
    death
With as big heart as thou. Do as thou list.
Thy valiantness was mine, thou suck'dst it
    from me;
But owe thy pride thyself.
  Cor.   Pray be content. 130
Mother, I am going to the market-place;
Chide me no more. I'll mountebank their
    loves,
Cog their hearts from them, and come home
    belov'd
Of all the trades in Rome. Look, I am
    going.
Commend me to my wife. I'll return
    consul,   135
Or never trust to what my tongue can do
I' th' way of flattery further.
  Vol.   Do your will. [*Exit.*
  Com. Away! The tribunes do attend
    you. Arm yourself
To answer mildly; for they are prepar'd
With accusations, as I hear, more strong
Than are upon you yet.   141
  Cor. The word is 'mildly'. Pray you let
    us go.
Let them accuse me by invention; I
Will answer in mine honour.
  Men.   Ay, but mildly. 144
  Cor. Well, mildly be it then—mildly.
                         [*Exeunt.*

Scene III. *Rome. The Forum.*

Enter SICINIUS *and* BRUTUS.

  Bru. In this point charge him home, that
    he affects
Tyrannical power. If he evade us there,
Enforce him with his envy to the people,
And that the spoil got on the Antiates
Was ne'er distributed.   5

Enter an ÆDILE.

                  What, will he come?

Æd. He's coming

Bru. How accompanied ?

Æd. With old Menenius, and those senators
That always favour'd him.

Sic. Have you a catalogue
Of all the voices that we have procur'd,
Set down by th' poll ?

Æd. I have ; 'tis ready. 10

Sic. Have you collected them by tribes ?

Æd. I have.

Sic. Assemble presently the people hither;
And when they hear me say ' It shall be so
I' th' right and strength o' th' commons'
be it either
For death, for fine, or banishment, then let them, 15
If I say fine, cry ' Fine !'—if death, cry
' Death ! '
Insisting on the old prerogative
And power i' th' truth o' th' cause.

Æd. I shall inform them.

Bru. And when such time they have
begun to cry, 19
Let them not cease, but with a din confus'd
Enforce the present execution
Of what we chance to sentence.

Æd. Very well.

Sic. Make them be strong, and ready for
this hint,
When we shall hap to give't them.

Bru. Go about it.
[*Exit Ædile.*
Put him to choler straight. He hath been
us'd 25
Ever to conquer, and to have his worth
Of contradiction ; being once chaf'd, he
cannot
Be rein'd again to temperance ; then he
speaks
What's in his heart, and that is there which
looks
With us to break his neck.

Enter CORIOLANUS, MENENIUS, *and* COM-
INIUS, *with* Others.

Sic. Well, here he comes. 30

Men. Calmly, I do beseech you.

Cor. Ay, as an ostler, that for th' poorest
piece
Will bear the knave by th' volume. Th'
honour'd gods
Keep Rome in safety, and the chairs of
justice
Supplied with worthy men ! plant love
among's ! 35
Throng our large temples with the shows of
peace,
And not our streets with war !

1 Sen. Amen, amen !

Men. A noble wish.

Re-enter the Ædile, *with the* Plebeians.

Sic. Draw near, ye people.

Æd. List to your tribunes. Audience !
peace, I say !

Cor. First, hear me speak.

Both Tri. Well, say. Peace, ho !

Cor. Shall I be charg'd no further than
this present ? 42
Must all determine here ?

Sic. I do demand,
If you submit you to the people's voices,
Allow their officers, and are content 45
To suffer lawful censure for such faults
As shall be prov'd upon you.

Cor. I am content.

Men. Lo, citizens, he says he is content.
The warlike service he has done, consider ;
think
Upon the wounds his body bears, which
show 50
Like graves i' th' holy churchyard.

Cor. Scratches with briers,
Scars to move laughter only.

Men. Consider further,
That when he speaks not like a citizen, 53
You find him like a soldier ; do not take
His rougher accents for malicious sounds,
But, as I say, such as become a soldier
Rather than envy you.

Com. Well, well ! No more.

Cor. What is the matter,
That being pass'd for consul with full voice,
I am so dishonour'd that the very hour 60
You take it off again ?

Sic. Answer to us.

Cor. Say then ; 'tis true, I ought so.

Sic. We charge you that you have con-
triv'd to take
From Rome all season'd office, and to wind
Yourself into a power tyrannical ; 65
For which you are a traitor to the people.

Cor. How—traitor ?

Men. Nay, temperately ! Your promise.

Cor. The fires i' th' lowest hell fold in the
people !
Call me their traitor ! Thou injurious
tribune !
Within thine eyes sat twenty thousand
deaths 70
In thy hands clutch'd as many millions, in
Thy lying tongue both numbers, I would
say
' Thou liest ' unto thee with a voice as free
As I do pray the gods.

Sic. Mark you this, people ?

Plebeians. To th' rock, to th' rock, with
him ! 75

Sic. Peace !
We need not put new matter to his charge.
What you have seen him do and heard him
speak,
Beating your officers, cursing yourselves,
Opposing laws with strokes, and here
defying 80
Those whose great power must try him—
even this,

So criminal and in such capital kind,
Deserves th' extremest death.

Bru.   But since he hath
Serv'd well for Rome—
   Cor.   What do you prate of service ?
   Bru. I talk of that that know it.   85
   Cor. You !
   Men. Is this the promise that you made
      your mother ?
   Com. Know, I pray you—
   Cor.   I'll know no further.
Let them pronounce the steep Tarpeian
     death,
Vagabond exile, flaying, pent to linger   90
But with a grain a day, I would not buy
Their mercy at the price of one fair word,
Nor check my courage for what they can
     give,
To have't with saying ' Good morrow '.
   Sic.   For that he has—
As much as in him lies—from time to time
Envied against the people, seeking means
To pluck away their power ; as now at last
Given hostile strokes, and that not in the
     presence
Of dreaded justice, but on the ministers
That do distribute it—in the name o' th'
     people,   100
And in the power of us the tribunes, we,
Ev'n from this instant, banish him our city,
In peril of precipitation
From off the rock Tarpeian, never more
To enter our Rome gates.   I' th' people's
     name,   105
I say it shall be so.
   Plebeians. It shall be so, it shall be so !
Let him away !
He's banish'd, and it shall be so.
   Com. Hear me, my masters and my
     common friends—
   Sic. He's sentenc'd ; no more hearing.
   Com.   Let me speak.
I have been consul, and can show for Rome
Her enemies' marks upon me. I do love
My country's good with a respect more
     tender,
More holy and profound, than mine own
     life,
My dear wife's estimate, her womb's
     increase   115
And treasure of my loins. Then if I would
Speak that—
   Sic.   We know your drift. Speak what ?
   Bru. There's no more to be said, but he is
     banish'd,
As enemy to the people and his country.
It shall be so.   120
   Plebeians. It shall be so, it shall be so.
   Cor. You common cry of curs, whose
breath I hate
As reek o' th' rotten fens, whose loves I
     prize
As the dead carcasses of unburied men
That do corrupt my air—I banish you.   125

And here remain with your uncertainty !
Let every feeble rumour shake your hearts ;
Your enemies, with nodding of their plumes,
Fan you into despair ! Have the power still
To banish your defenders, till at length   130
Your ignorance—which finds not till it
     feels,
Making but reservation of yourselves
Still your own foes—deliver you
As most abated captives to some nation   134
That won you without blows ! Despising
For you the city, thus I turn my back ;
There is a world elsewhere.
    [*Exeunt Coriolanus, Cominius, Men-*
    enius, with the other Patricians.
   Æd. The people's enemy is gone, is gone !
    [*They all shout and throw up their caps.*
   Plebeians. Our enemy is banish'd, he is
gone ! Hoo-oo !
   Sic. Go see him out at gates, and follow
him,   140
As he hath follow'd you, with all despite ;
Give him deserv'd vexation. Let a guard
Attend us through the city.
   Plebeians. Come, come, let's see him out
at gates ; come !
The gods preserve our noble tribunes !
   Come.   [*Exeunt.*

ACT FOUR

SCENE I. *Rome. Before a gate of the city.*

Enter CORIOLANUS, VOLUMNIA, VIRGILIA,
MENENIUS, COMINIUS, *with the young*
Nobility *of Rome.*

   Cor. Come, leave your tears ; a brief
     farewell. The beast
With many heads butts me away. Nay,
     mother,
Where is your ancient courage ? You were
     us'd
To say extremities was the trier of spirits ;
That common chances common men could
     bear ;   5
That when the sea was calm all boats alike
Show'd mastership in floating ; fortune's
     blows,
When most struck home, being gentle
     wounded craves
A noble cunning. You were us'd to load me
With precepts that would make invincible
The heart that conn'd them.   11
   Vir. O heavens ! O heavens !
   Cor.   Nay, I prithee, woman—
   Vol. Now the red pestilence strike all
     trades in Rome,
And occupations perish !
   Cor.   What, what, what !
I shall be lov'd when I am lack'd. Nay,
     mother,   15
Resume that spirit when you were wont
     to say,
If you had been the wife of Hercules,

Six of his labours you'd have done, and
    sav'd
Your husband so much sweat. Cominius,
Droop not ; adieu. Farewell, my wife, my
    mother.   20
I'll do well yet.   Thou old and true
    Menenius,
Thy tears are salter than a younger man's
And venomous to thine eyes. My sometime
    General,
I have seen thee stern, and thou hast oft
    beheld
Heart-hard'ning spectacles ; tell these sad
    women   25
'Tis fond to wail inevitable strokes,
As 'tis to laugh at 'em. My mother, you wot
    well
My hazards still have been your solace ;
    and
Believe't not lightly—though I go alone,
Like to a lonely dragon, that his fen   30
Makes fear'd and talk'd of more than
    seen—your son
Will or exceed the common or be caught
With cautelous baits and practice.
  Vol.   My first son,
Whither wilt thou go ?   Take good
    Cominius
With thee awhile ; determine on some
    course   35
More than a wild exposture to each chance
That starts i' th' way before thee.
  Vir.   O the gods !
  Com. I'll follow thee a month, devise
    with thee
Where thou shalt rest, that thou mayst
    hear of us,   39
And we of thee ; so, if the time thrust
    forth
A cause for thy repeal, we shall not send
O'er the vast world to seek a single man,
And lose advantage, which doth ever cool
I' th' absence of the needer.
  Cor.   Fare ye well ;
Thou hast years upon thee, and thou art
    too full   45
Of the wars' surfeits to go rove with one
That's yet unbruis'd ; bring me but out
    at gate.
Come, my sweet wife, my dearest mother,
    and
My friends of noble touch ; when I am
    forth,
Bid me farewell, and smile.   I pray you
    come.   50
While I remain above the ground you shall
Hear from me still, and never of me aught
But what is like me formerly.
  Men.   That's worthily
As any ear can hear. Come, let's not
    weep.
If I could shake off but one seven years   55
From these old arms and legs, by the good
    gods,

I'd with thee every foot.
  Cor.   Give me thy hand.
Come.   [*Exeunt.*

SCENE II. *Rome. A street near the gate.*

Enter the two Tribunes, SICINIUS *and*
    BRUTUS, *with the Ædile.*

  Sic. Bid them all home ; he's gone, and
    we'll no further.
The nobility are vex'd, whom we see have
    sided
In his behalf.
  Bru.   Now we have shown our power,
Let us seem humbler after it is done
Than when it was a-doing.
  Sic.   Bid them home.   5
Say their great enemy is gone, and they
Stand in their ancient strength.
  Bru.   Dismiss them home.
                       [*Exit Ædile.*
Here comes his mother.

Enter VOLUMNIA, VIRGILIA, *and* MENENIUS.

  Sic.   Let's not meet her.
  Bru.   Why ?
  Sic. They say she's mad.
  Bru. They have ta'en note of us ; keep
    on your way.   10
  Vol. O, y'are well met ; th' hoarded
    plague o' th' gods
Requite your love !
  Men.   Peace, peace, be not so loud.
  Vol If that I could for weeping, you
    should hear—
Nay, and you shall hear some. [*To Brutus*]
    Will you be gone ?
  Vir. [*To Sicinius*] You shall stay too. I
    would I had the power   15
To say so to my husband.
  Sic.   Are you mankind ?
  Vol. Ay, fool ; is that a shame ? Note
    but this, fool :
Was not a man my father   Hadst thou
    foxship
To banish him that struck more blows for
    Rome
Than thou hast spoken words ?
  Sic.   O blessed heavens !   20
  Vol. Moe noble blows than ever thou wise
    words ;
And for Rome's good. I'll tell thee what—
    yet go !
Nay, but thou shalt stay too. I would my
    son
Were in Arabia, and thy tribe before him,
His good sword in his hand.
  Sic.   What then ?
  Vir.   What then !   25
He'd make an end of thy posterity.
  Vol. Bastards and all.
Good man, the wounds that he does bear
    for Rome !
  Men. Come, come, peace.

Sic. I would he had continued to his
  country   30
As he began, and not unknit himself
The noble knot he made.
 Bru.   I would he had.
 Vol. 'I would he had'! 'Twas you
incens'd the rabble—
Cats that can judge as fitly of his worth
As I can of those mysteries which heaven 35
Will not have earth to know.
 Bru.   Pray, let's go.
 Vol. Now, pray, sir, get you gone ;
You have done a brave deed. Ere you go,
 hear this :
As far as doth the Capitol exceed
The meanest house in Rome, so far my
 son—   40
This lady's husband here, this, do you
 see ?—
Whom you have banish'd does exceed you
 all.
 Bru. Well, well, we'll leave you.
 Sic.   Why stay we to be baited
With one that wants her wits ?
         [*Exeunt Tribunes.*
 Vol.   Take my prayers with you.
I would the gods had nothing else to do 45
But to confirm my curses. Could I meet 'em
But once a day, it would unclog my heart
Of what lies heavy to't.
 Men.   You have told them home,
And, by my troth, you have cause. You'll
 sup with me ?
 Vol. Anger's my meat ; I sup upon
 myself,   50
And so shall starve with feeding. Come,
 let's go.
Leave this faint puling and lament as I do,
In anger, Juno-like. Come, come, come.
     [*Exeunt Volumnia and Virgilia.*
 Men. Fie, fie, fie !   [*Exit.*

Scene III. *A highway between Rome and
Antium.*

Enter a Roman *and a* Volsce, *meeting.*

 Rom. I know you well, sir, and you know
me : your name, I think, is Adrian.
 Vols. It is so, sir. Truly, I have forgot
you.
 Rom. I am a Roman ; and my services
are, as you are, against 'em. Know you me
yet ?   5
 Vols. Nicanor ? No !
 Rom. The same, sir.
 Vols. You had more beard when I last
saw you, but your favour is well appear'd
by your tongue. What's the news in Rome?
I have a note from the Volscian state, to
find you out there. You have well saved me
a day's journey.   12
 Rom. There hath been in Rome strange
insurrections : the people against the
senators, patricians, and nobles.

 Vols. Hath been ! Is it ended, then ?
Our state thinks not so ; they are in a
most warlike preparation, and hope to
come upon them in the heat of their
division.   17
 Rom. The main blaze of it is past, but a
small thing would make it flame again ; for
the nobles receive so to heart the banishment of that worthy Coriolanus that they
are in a ripe aptness to take all power from
the people, and to pluck from them their
tribunes for ever. This lies glowing, I can
tell you, and is almost mature for the violent
breaking out.   24
 Vols. Coriolanus banish'd !
 Rom. Banish'd, sir.
 Vols. You will be welcome with this
intelligence, Nicanor.   28
 Rom. The day serves well for them now.
I have heard it said the fittest time to
corrupt a man's wife is when she's fall'n
out with her husband. Your noble Tullus
Aufidius will appear well in these wars, his
great opposer, Coriolanus, being now in
no request of his country.
 Vols. He cannot choose. I am most
fortunate thus accidentally to encounter
you ; you have ended my business, and I
will merrily accompany you home.   36
 Rom. I shal' between this and supper tell
you most strange things 'rom Rome, all
tending to the good of their adversaries.
Have you an army ready, say you ?
 Vols. A most royal one : the centurions
a_d their charges, distinctly billeted,
already in th' entertainment, and to be on
foot at an hour's warning.   42
 Rom. I am joyful to hear of their readiness, and am the man, I think, that shall
set them in present action. So, sir, heartily
well met, and most glad of your company.
 Vols. You take my part from me, sir. I
have the most cause to be glad of yours. 47
 Rom. Well, let us go together. [*Exeunt.*

Scene IV. ~~Antium. Before Aufidius's
house.~~

Enter Coriolanus, *in mean apparel,
disguis'd and muffled.*

 Cor. A goodly city is this Antium. City,
'Tis I that made thy widows ; many an
 heir
Of these fair edifices fore my wars
Have I heard groan and drop. Then know
 me not,
Lest that thy wives with spits and boys
 with stones,
In puny battle slay me.

      Enter a Citizen.

        Save you, sir.
 Cit. And you.
 Cor.   Direct me, if it be your will,

855

Where great Aufidius lies. Is he in Antium?

  Cit. He is, and feasts the nobles of the
state   9

At his house this night.

  Cor.   Which is his house, beseech you ?

  Cit. This here before you.

  Cor.   Thank you, sir ; farewell.

                        [Exit Citizen.

O world, thy slippery turns ! Friends now
    fast sworn,

Whose double bosoms seems to wear one
    heart,

Whose hours, whose bed, whose meal and
    exercise

Are still together, who twin, as 'twere, in
    love   15

Unseparable, shall within this hour,

On a dissension of a doit, break out

To bitterest enmity ; so fellest foes,

Whose passions and whose plots have
    broke their sleep   19

To take the one the other, by some chance,

Some trick not worth an egg, shall grow
    dear friends

And interjoin their issues. So with me :

My birthplace hate I, and my love's upon

This enemy town. I'll enter. If he slay me,

He does fair justice ; if he give me way, 25

I'll do his country service.   *[Exit.*

SCENE V. *Antium. Aufidius's house*

  Music plays. Enter a Servingman.

  1 *Serv.* Wine, wine, wine ! What service
is here ! I think our fellows are asleep.

                        [Exit.

    Enter another Servingman.

  2 *Serv.* Where's Cotus ? My master calls
for him. Cotus !   *[Exit.*

    Enter CORIOLANUS.

  Cor. A goodly house. The feast smells
well, but I   5
Appear not like a guest.

  Re-enter the first Servingman.

  1 *Serv.* What would you have, friend ?
Whence are you ? Here's no place for you :
pray go to the door.   *[Exit.*

  Cor. I have deserv'd no better entertainment
In being Coriolanus.   10

  Re-enter second Servant.

  2 *Serv.* Whence are you, sir ? Has the
porter his eyes in his head that he gives
entrance to such companions ? Pray get
you out.

  Cor. Away !

  2 *Serv.* Away ? Get you away.   15

  Cor. Now th' art troublesome.

  2 *Serv.* Are you so brave ? I'll have you
talk'd with anon.

Enter a third Servingman. *The first meets
him.*

  3 *Serv.* What fellow's this ?   19

  1 *Serv.* A strange one as ever I look'd on.
I cannot get him out o' th' house. Prithee
call my master to him.

  3 *Serv.* What have you to do here, fellow?
Pray you avoid the house.

  Cor. Let me but stand—I will not hurt
your hearth.   25

  3 *Serv.* What are you ?

  Cor. A gentleman.

  3 *Serv.* A marv'llous poor one.

  Cor. True, so I am.   29

  3 *Serv.* Pray you, poor gentleman, take
up some other station ; here's no place for
you. Pray you avoid. Come.

  Cor. Follow your function, go and batten
on cold bits. *[Pushes him away from him.*

  3 *Serv.* What, you will not ? Prithee tell
my master what a strange guest he has
here.   35

  2 *Serv.* And I shall.   *[Exit.*

  3 *Serv.* Where dwell'st thou ?

  Cor. Under the canopy.

  3 *Serv.* Under the canopy ?

  Cor. Ay.   40

  3 *Serv.* Where's that ?

  Cor. I' th' city of kites and crows.

  3 *Serv.* I' th' city of kites and crows !
What an ass it is ! Then thou dwell'st with
daws too ?

  Cor. No, I serve not thy master.   45

  3 *Serv.* How, sir ! Do you meddle with
my master ?

  Cor. Ay ; 'tis an honester service than to
meddle with thy mistress. Thou prat'st and
prat'st ; serve with thy trencher ; hence !

                    [Beats him away.

Enter AUFIDIUS *with the second* Servingman.

  Auf. Where is this fellow ?   50

  2 *Serv.* Here, sir ; I'd have beaten him
like a dog, but for disturbing the lords
within.

  Auf. Whence com'st thou ? What
    wouldst thou ? Thy name ?

Why speak'st not ? Speak, man. What's
    thy name ?

  Cor. [*Unmuffling*]   If, Tullus,

Not yet thou know'st me, and, seeing me,
    dost not   55

Think me for the man I am, necessity

Commands me name myself.

  Auf.   What is thy name ?

  Cor. A name unmusical to the Volscians'
    ears,

And harsh in sound to thine.

  Auf.   Say, what's thy name ?

Thou hast a grim appearance, and thy
    face

Bears a command in't ; though thy tackle's
    torn,   61

Thou show'st a noble vessel. What's thy
  name?
  Cor. Prepare thy brow to frown—know'st
    thou me yet?
  Auf. I know thee not. Thy name?
  Cor. My name is Caius Marcius, who hath
    done   65
To thee particularly, and to all the Volsces,
Great hurt and mischief; thereto witness
  may
My surname, Coriolanus. The painful
  service,
The extreme dangers, and the drops of
  blood
Shed for my thankless country, are re-
    quited   70
But with that surname—a good memory
And witness of the malice and displeasure
Which thou shouldst bear me. Only that
    name remains;
The cruelty and envy of the people,
Permitted by our dastard nobles, who   75
Have all forsook me, hath devour'd the rest,
And suffer'd me by th' voice of slaves to be
Whoop'd out of Rome. Now this extremity
Hath brought me to thy hearth; not out
    of hope,
Mistake me not, to save my life; for if 80
I had fear'd death, of all the men i' th'
    world
I would have 'voided thee; but in mere
    spite,
To be full quit of those my banishers,
Stand I before thee here. Then if thou hast
A heart of wreak in thee, that wilt revenge
Thine own particular wrongs and stop those
    maims   86
Of shame seen through thy country, speed
    thee straight
And make my misery serve thy turn. So
    use it
That my revengeful services may prove
As benefits to thee; for I will fight   90
Against my cank'red country with the
    spleen
Of all the under fiends. But if so be
Thou dar'st not this, and that to prove
    more fortunes
Th'art tir'd, then, in a word, I also am
Longer to live most weary, and present 95
My throat to thee and to thy ancient malice;
Which not to cut would show thee but a
    fool,
Since I have ever followed thee with hate,
Drawn tuns of blood out of thy country's
    breast,
And cannot live but to thy shame, unless 100
It be to do thee service.
  Auf.   O Marcius, Marcius!
Each word thou hast spoke hath weeded
    from my heart
A root of ancient envy. If Jupiter
Should from yond cloud speak divine
    things,

And say ''Tis true', I'd not believe them
    more   105
Than thee, all noble Marcius. Let me twine
Mine arms about that body, where against
My grainèd ash an hundred times hath
    broke
And scarr'd the moon with splinters; here
    I clip
The anvil of my sword, and do contest 110
As hotly and as nobly with thy love
As ever in ambitious strength I did
Contend against thy valour. Know thou
    first,
I lov'd the maid I married; never man
Sigh'd truer breath; but that I see thee
    here,   115
Thou noble thing, more dances my rapt
    heart
Than when I first my wedded mistress saw
Bestride my threshold. Why, thou Mars, I
    tell thee
We have a power on foot, and I had purpose
Once more to hew thy target from thy
    brawn,   120
Or lose mine arm for't. Thou hast beat me out
Twelve several times, and I have nightly
    since
Dreamt of encounters 'twixt thyself and
    me—
We have been down together in my sleep,
Unbuckling helms, fisting each other's
    throat—   125
And wak'd half dead with nothing. Worthy
    Marcius,
Had we no other quarrel else to Rome but
    that
Thou art thence banish'd, we would muster
    all
From twelve to seventy, and, pouring war
Into the bowels of ungrateful Rome,   130
Like a bold flood o'erbea . O, come, go in,
And take our friendly senators by th' hands,
Who now are here, taking their leaves of me
Who am prepar'd against your territories,
Though not for Rome itself.
  Cor.   You bless me, gods! 135
  Auf. Therefore, most absolute sir, if thou
    wilt have
The leading of thine own revenges, take
Th' one half of my commission, and set
    down—
As best thou art experienc'd, since thou
    know'st
Thy country's strength and weakness—
    thine own ways,
Whether to knock against the gates of
    Rome,   141
Or rudely visit them in parts remote
To fright them ere destroy. But come in;
Let me commend thee first to those that
    shall
Say yea to thy desires. A thousand
    welcomes!   145
And more a friend than e'er an enemy;

Yet, Marcius, that was much. Your hand ;
  most welcome !
        [*Exeunt Coriolanus and Aufidius.*

        The two Servingmen *come forward.*

1 *Serv.* Here's a strange alteration !
2 *Serv.* By my hand, I had thought to
have strucken him with a cudgel ; and yet
my mind gave me his clothes made a false
report of him.   151
1 *Serv.* What an arm he has ! He turn'd
me about with his finger and his thumb, as
one would set up a top.
2 *Serv.* Nay, I knew by his face that there
was something in him ; he had, sir, a kind
of face, methought—I cannot tell how to
term it.   156
1 *Serv.* He had so, looking as it were—
Would I were hang'd, but I thought there
was more in him than I could think.
2 *Serv.* So did I, I'll be sworn. He is
simply the rarest man i' th' world.   161
1 *Serv.* I think he is ; but a greater
soldier than he you wot one.
2 *Serv.* Who, my master ?
1 *Serv.* Nay, it's no matter for that.   165
2 *Serv.* Worth six on him.
1 *Serv.* Nay, not so neither ; but I take
him to be the greater soldier.
2 *Serv.* Faith, look you, one cannot tell
how to say that ; for the defence of a town
our general is excellent.
1 *Serv.* Ay, and for an assault too.   171

        Re-enter the third Servingman.

3 *Serv.* O slaves, I can tell you news—
news, you rascals !
Both. What, what, what ? Let's partake.
3 *Serv.* I would not be a Roman, of all
nations ; I had as lief be a condemn'd
man.
Both. Wherefore ? wherefore ?   177
3 *Serv.* Why, here's he that was wont to
thwack our general—Caius Marcius.
1 *Serv.* Why do you say ' thwack our
general ' ?   180
3 *Serv.* I do not say ' thwack our general',
but he was always good enough for him.
2 *Serv.* Come, we are fellows and friends.
He was ever too hard for him, I have heard
him say so himself.
1 *Serv.* He was too hard for him directly,
to say the troth on't ; before Corioli he
scotch'd him and notch'd him like a
carbonado.   187
2 *Serv.* An he had been cannibally given,
he might have broil'd and eaten him too.
1 *Serv.* But more of thy news !   190
3 *Serv.* Why, he is so made on here
within as if he were son and heir to Mars ;
set at upper end o' th' table ; no question
asked him by any of the senators but they
stand bald before him. Our general himself
makes a mistress of him, sanctifies himself

with's hand, and turns up the white o' th'
eye to his discourse. But the bottom of the
news is, our general is cut i' th' middle and
but one half of what he was yesterday, for
the other has half by the entreaty and grant
of the whole table. He'll go, he says, and
sowl the porter of Rome gates by th' ears ;
he will mow all down before him, and leave
his passage poll'd.
2 *Serv.* And he's as like to do't as any
man I can imagine.   204
3 *Serv.* Do't ! He will do't ; for look you,
sir, he has as many friends as enemies ;
which friends, sir, as it were, durst not—
look you, sir—show themselves, as we term
it, his friends, whilest he's in directitude.
1 *Serv.* Directitude ? What's that ?   209
3 *Serv.* But when they shall see, sir, his
crest up again and the man in blood, they
will out of their burrows, like conies after
rain, and revel all with him.
1 *Serv.* But when goes this forward ?   213
3 *Serv.* To-morrow, to-day, presently.
You shall have the drum struck up this
afternoon ; 'tis as it were a parcel of their
feast, and to be executed ere they wipe
their lips.
2 *Serv.* Why, then we shall have a stirring
world again. This peace is nothing but to
rust iron, increase tailors, and breed ballad-
makers.   220
1 *Serv.* Let me have war, say I ; it exceeds peace as far as day does night ; it's
spritely, waking, audible, and full of vent.
Peace is a very apoplexy, lethargy ;
mull'd, deaf, sleepy, insensible ; a getter
of more bastard children than war's a
destroyer of men.   225
2 *Serv.* 'Tis so ; and as war in some sort
may be said to be a ravisher, so it cannot
be denied but peace is a great maker of
cuckolds.
1 *Serv.* Ay, and it makes men hate one
another.
3 *Serv.* Reason : because they then less
need one another. The wars for my money.
I hope to see Romans as cheap as Volscians.
They are rising, they are rising.   232
Both. In, in, in, in !   [*Exeunt.*

SCENE VI. *Rome. A public place.*

    Enter the two Tribunes, SICINIUS *and*
                  BRUTUS.

Sic. We hear not of him, neither need
      we fear him.
His remedies are tame. The present peace
And quietness of the people, which before
Were in wild hurry, here do make his
      friends
Blush that the world goes well ; who rather
      had,   5
Though they themselves did suffer by't,
      behold

Dissentious numbers pest'ring streets than
    see
Our tradesmen singing in their shops, and
    going
About their functions friendly.

Enter MENENIUS.

Bru. We stood to't in good time. Is this
    Menenius ?
Sic. 'Tis he, 'tis he. O, he is grown most
    kind   11
Of late. Hail, sir !
Men.   Hail to you both !
Sic. Your Coriolanus is not much miss'd
But with his friends. The commonwealth
    doth stand,
And so would do, were he more angry at it.
Men. All's well, and might have been
    much better if   16
He could have temporiz'd.
Sic.   Where is he, hear you ?
Men. Nay, I hear nothing ; his mother
    and his wife
Hear nothing from him.

Enter three or four Citizens.

Citizens. The gods preserve you both !
Sic.   God-den, our neighbours.
Bru. God-den to you all, god-den to you
    all.   21
1 *Cit.* Ourselves, our wives, and children,
    on our knees
Are bound to pray for you both.
Sic.   Live and thrive !
Bru. Farewell, kind neighbours ; we
    wish'd Coriolanus
Had lov'd you as we did.
Citizens.   Now the gods keep you ! 25
Both Tri. Farewell, farewell.
                     [*Exeunt Citizens.*
Sic. This is a happier and more comely
    time
Than when these fellows ran about the
    streets
Crying confusion.
Bru.   Caius Marcius was
A worthy officer i' th' war, but insolent, 30
O'ercome with pride, ambitious past all
    thinking,
Self-loving—
Sic.   And affecting one sole throne,
Without assistance.
Men.   I think not so.
Sic. We should by this, to all our
    lamentation,
If he had gone forth consul, found it so. 35
Bru. The gods have well prevented it,
    and Rome
Sits safe and still without him.

Enter an ÆDILE.

Æd.   Worthy tribunes,
There is a slave, whom we have put in
    prison,

Reports the Volsces with two several
    powers
Are ent'red in the Roman territories,   40
And with the deepest malice of the war
Destroy what lies before 'em.
Men.   'Tis Aufidius,
Who, hearing of our Marcius' banishment,
Thrusts forth his horns again into the world,
Which were inshell'd when Marcius stood
    for Rome,   45
And durst not once peep out.
Sic. Come, what talk you of Marcius ?
Bru. Go see this rumourer whipp'd. It
    cannot be
The Volsces dare break with us.
Men.   Cannot be !
We have record that very well it can ; 50
And three examples of the like hath been
Within my age. But reason with the fellow
Before you punish him, where he heard
    this,
Lest you shall chance to whip your
    information
And beat the messenger who bids beware 55
Of what is to be dreaded.
Sic.   Tell not me.
I know this cannot be.
Bru.   Not possible.

Enter a Messenger.

Mess. The nobles in great earnestness are
    going
All to the Senate House   some news is
    come   59
That turns their countenances.
Sic.   'Tis this slave—
Go whip him fore the people's eyes—his
    raising,
Nothing but his report.
Mess.   Yes, worthy sir,
The slave's report is seconded, and more,
More fearful, is deliver'd.
Sic.   What more fearful ?
Mess. It is spoke freely out of many
    mouths—   65
How probable I do not know—that Marcius,
Join'd with Aufidius, leads a power 'gainst
    Rome,
And vows revenge as spacious as between
The young'st and oldest thing.
Sic.   This is most likely !
Bru. Rais'd only that the weaker sort
    may wish   70
Good Marcius home again.
Sic.   The very trick on't.
Men. This is unlikely.
He and Aufidius can no more atone
Than violent'st contrariety.

Enter a second Messenger.

2 *Mess.* You are sent for to the Senate. 75
A fearful army, led by Caius Marcius
Associated with Aufidius, rages
Upon our territories, and have already

O'erborne their way, consum'd with fire
   and took
What lay before them.   80

Enter COMINIUS.

Com. O, you have made good work!
Men.   What news? what news?
Com. You have holp to ravish your own
   daughters and
To melt the city leads upon your pates,
To see your wives dishonour'd to your
   noses—
   Men. What's the news? What's the
   news?   85
Com. Your temples burned in their
   cement, and
Your franchises, whereon you stood,
   confin'd
Into an auger's bore.
   Men.   Pray now, your news?
You have made fair work, I fear me. Pray,
   your news.
If Marcius should be join'd wi' th' Volscians—
   Com.   If! 90
He is their god; he leads them like a thing
Made by some other deity than Nature,
That shapes man better; and they follow
   him
Against us brats with no less confidence
Than boys pursuing summer butterflies, 95
Or butchers killing flies.
   Men.   You have made good work,
You and your apron men; you that stood
   so much
Upon the voice of occupation and   98
The breath of garlic-eaters!
   Com.   He'll shake
Your Rome about your ears.
   Men.   As Hercules
Did shake down mellow fruit. You have
   made fair work!
Bru. But is this true, sir?
   Com.   Ay; and you'll look pale
Before you find it other. All the regions
Do smilingly revolt, and who resists
Are mock'd for valiant ignorance,   105
And perish constant fools. Who is't can
   blame him?
Your enemies and his find something in
   him.
Men. We are all undone unless
The noble man have mercy.
   Com.   Who shall ask it?
The tribunes cannot do't for shame; the
   people   110
Deserve such pity of him as the wolf
Does of the shepherds; for his best friends,
   if they
Should say 'Be good to Rome'—they
   charg'd him even
As those should do that had deserv'd his
   hate,
And therein show'd like enemies.
   Men.   'Tis true; 115

If he were putting to my house the brand
That should consume it, I have not the face
To say 'Beseech you, cease'. You have
   made fair hands,
You and your crafts! You have crafted
   fair!
   Com.   You have brought
A trembling upon Rome, such as was never
S' incapable of help.
   Both Tri.   Say not we brought it.
   Men. How! Was't we? We lov'd him,
   but, like beasts   122
And cowardly nobles, gave way unto your
   clusters,
Who did hoot him out o' th' city.
   Com.   But I fear
They'll roar him in again. Tullus Aufidius,
The second name of men, obeys his points
As if he were his officer. Desperation 127
Is all the policy, strength, and defence,
That Rome can make against them.

Enter a *troop of* Citizens.

   Men.   Here comes the clusters.
And is Aufidius with him? You are they
That made the air unwholesome when you
   cast   131
Your stinking greasy caps in hooting at
Coriolanus' exile. Now he's coming,
And not a hair upon a soldier's head
Which will not prove a whip; as many
   coxcombs   135
As you threw caps up will he tumble down,
And pay you for your voices. 'Tis no
   matter;
If he could burn us all into one coal,
We have deserv'd it.
   Plebeians. Faith, we hear fearful news.
   1 Cit.   For mine own part,
When I said banish him, I said 'twas pity.
   2 Cit. And so did I.   142
   3 Cit. And so did I; and, to say the
truth, so did very many of us. That we did,
we did for the best; and though we will-
ingly consented to his banishment, yet it
was against our will.   146
   Com. Y'are goodly things, you voices!
   Men.   You have made
Good work, you and your cry! Shall's to
   the Capitol?
   Com. O, ay, what else?
           [*Exeunt Cominius and Menenius.*
   Sic. Go masters, get you home; be not
   dismay'd;   150
These are a side that would be glad to have
This true which they so seem to fear. Go
   home,
And show no sign of fear.
   1 Cit. The gods be good to us! Come,
masters, let's home. I ever said we were i'
th' wrong when we banish'd him.   156
   2 Cit. So did we all. But come, let's
home.   [*Exeunt Citizens.*
   Bru. I do not like this news.

Sic. Nor I.

Bru. Let's to the Capitol. Would half my
    wealth   160
Would buy this for a lie !

Sic.   Pray let's go. [*Exeunt.*

SCENE VII. *A camp at a short distance from
Rome.*

Enter AUFIDIUS *with his* Lieutenant.

Auf. Do they still fly to th' Roman ?

Lieu. I do not know what witchcraft's
    in him, but
Your soldiers use him as the grace fore
    meat,
Their talk at table, and their thanks at end ;
And you are dark'ned in this action, sir,   5
Even by your own.

Auf.   I cannot help it now,
Unless by using means I lame the foot
Of our design. He bears himself more
    proudlier,
Even to my person, than I thought he
    would
When first I did embrace him ; yet his
    nature   10
In that's no changeling, and I must excuse
What cannot be amended.

Lieu.   Yet I wish, sir—
I mean, for your particular—you had not
Join'd in commission with him, but either
Had borne the action of yourself, or else   15
To him had left it solely.

Auf. I understand thee well ; and be
    thou sure,
When he shall come to his account, he
    knows not
What I can urge against him. Although it
    seems,
And so he thinks, and is no less apparent   20
To th' vulgar eye, that he bears all things
    fairly
And shows good husbandry for the Volscian
    state,
Fights dragon-like, and does achieve as
    soon
As draw his sword ; yet he hath left undone
That which shall break his neck or hazard
    mine   25
Whene'er we come to our account.

Lieu. Sir, I beseech you, think you he'll
    carry Rome ?

Auf. All places yield to him ere he sits
    down,
And the nobility of Rome are his ;
The senators and patricians love him too. 30
The tribunes are no soldiers, and their
    people
Will be as rash in the repeal as hasty
To expel him thence. I think he'll be to
    Rome
As is the osprey to the fish, who takes it
By sovereignty of nature. First he was   35
A noble servant to them, but he could not

Carry his honours even. Whether 'twas
    pride,
Which out of daily fortune ever taints
The happy man ; whether defect of judg-
    ment,
To fail in the disposing of those chances 40
Which he was lord of ; or whether nature,
Not to be other than one thing, not moving
From th' casque to th' cushion, but com-
    manding peace
Even with the same austerity and garb
As he controll'd the war ; but one of
    these—   45
As he hath spices of them all—not all,
For I dare so far free him—made him
    fear'd,
So hated, and so banish'd. But he has a
    merit
To choke it in the utt'rance. So our virtues
Lie in th' interpretation of the time ;   50
And power, unto itself most commendable,
Hath not a tomb so evident as a chair
T' extol what it hath done.
One fire drives out one fire ; one nail, one
    nail ;
Rights by rights falter, strengths by
    strengths do fail.
Come, let's away. When, Caius, Rome is
    thine,   56
Thou art poor'st of all ; then shortly art
    thou mine.   [*Exeunt.*

ACT FIVE

SCENE I. *Rome. A public place.*

Enter MENENIUS, COMINIUS, SICINIUS *and*
BRUTUS *the two Tribunes, with* Others.

Men. No, I'll not go. You hear what he
    hath said
Which was sometime his general, who lov'd
    him
In a most dear particular. He call'd me
    father ;
But what o' that ? Go, you that banish'd
    him :   4
A mile before his tent fall down, and knee
The way into his mercy. Nay, if he coy'd
To hear Cominius speak, I'll keep at home.

Com. He would not seem to know me.

Men.   Do you hear ?

Com. Yet one time he did call me by my
    name.
I urg'd our old acquaintance, and the drops
That we have bled together. ' Coriolanus '
He would not answer to ; forbad all names;
He was a kind of nothing, titleless,
Till he had forg'd himself a name i' th' fire
Of burning Rome.

Men.   Why, so ! You have made good
    work.   15
A pair of tribunes that have wrack'd for
    Rome
To make coals cheap—a noble memory !

Com. I minded him how royal 'twas to
    pardon
When it was less expected ; he replied,
It was a bare petition of a state   20
To one whom they had punish'd.
    Men.   Very well.
Could he say less ?
    Com. I offer'd to awaken his regard
For's private friends ; his answer to me
    was,
He could not stay to pick them in a pile 25
Of noisome musty chaff. He said 'twas
    folly,
For one poor grain or two, to leave unburnt
And still to nose th' offence.
    Men.   For one poor grain or two !
I am one of those. His mother, wife, his
    child,
And this brave fellow too—we are the
    grains :   30
You are the musty chaff, and you are smelt
Above the moon. We must be burnt for
    you.
    Sic. Nay, pray be patient ; if you refuse
    your aid
In this so never-needed help, yet do not
Upbraid's with our distress. But sure, if
    you   35
Would be your country's pleader, your
    good tongue,
More than the instant army we can make,
Might stop our countryman.
    Men.   No ; I'll not meddle.
    Sic. Pray you go to him.
    Men.   What should I do ?
    Bru. Only make trial what your love
    can do   40
For Rome, towards Marcius.
    Men.   Well, and say that Marcius
Return me, as Cominius is return'd,
Unheard—what then ?
But as a discontented friend, grief-shot
With his unkindness ? Say't be so ?
    Sic.   Yet your good will 45
Must have that thanks from Rome after the
    measure
As you intended well.
    Men.   I'll undertake't ;
I think he'll hear me. Yet to bite his lip
And hum at good Cominius much unhearts
    me.   49
He was not taken well : he had not din'd ;
The veins unfill'd, our blood is cold, and
    then
We pout upon the morning, are unapt
To give or to forgive ; but when we have
    stuff'd
These pipes and these conveyances of our
    blood
With wine and feeding, we have suppler
    souls   55
Than in our priest-like fasts. Therefore I'll
    watch him
Till he be dieted to my request,

And then I'll set upon him.
    Bru. You know the very road into his
    kindness
And cannot lose your way.
    Men.   Good faith, I'll prove him, 60
Speed how it will. I shall ere long have
    knowledge
Of my success.   [*Exit.*
    Com.   He'll never hear him.
    Sic.   Not ?
    Com. I tell you he does sit in gold, his eye
Red as 'twould burn Rome, and his injury
The gaoler to his pity. I kneel'd before him;
'Twas very faintly he said ' Rise ' ; dis-
    miss'd me   66
Thus with his speechless hand. What he
    would do,
He sent in writing after me ; what he
    would not,
Bound with an oath to yield to his con-
    ditions ;
So that all hope is vain,   70
Unless his noble mother and his wife,
Who, as I hear, mean to solicit him
For mercy to his country. Therefore let's
    hence,
And with our fair entreaties haste them on.
                                       [*Exeunt.*

SCENE II. *The Volscian camp before
    Rome.*

Enter MENENIUS *to the* Watch *on guard.*

1 *Watch.* Stay. Whence are you ?
2 *Watch.*   Stand, and go back.
    Men. You guard like men, 'tis well ; but,
    by your leave,
I am an officer of state and come
To speak with Coriolanus.
1 *Watch.*   From whence ?
    Men.   From Rome.
1 *Watch.* You may not pass ; you must
    return. Our general   5
Will no more hear from thence.
2 *Watch.* You'll see your Rome embrac'd
    with fire before
You'll speak with Coriolanus.
    Men.   Good my friends,
If you have heard your general talk of
    Rome   9
And of his friends there, it is lots to blanks
My name hath touch'd your ears : it is
    Menenius.
1 *Watch.* Be it so ; go back. The virtue
    of your name
Is not here passable.
    Men.   I tell thee, fellow,
Thy general is my lover. I have been
The book of his good acts whence men have
    read   15
His fame unparallel'd haply amplified ;
For I have ever verified my friends—
Of whom he's chief—with all the size that
    verity

Would without lapsing suffer. Nay, some-
    times,
Like to a bowl upon a subtle ground,   20
I have tumbled past the throw, and in his
    praise
Have almost stamp'd the leasing ; there-
    fore, fellow,
I must have leave to pass.
    1 *Watch.* Faith, sir, if you had told as
many lies in his behalf as you have uttered
words in your own, you should not pass
here ; no, though it were as virtuous to lie
as to live chastely. Therefore go back.
    Men. Prithee, fellow, remember my name
is Menenius, always factionary on the party
of your general.   29
    2 *Watch.* Howsoever you have been his
liar, as you say you have, I am one that,
telling true under him, must say you cannot
pass. Therefore go back.
    Men. Has he din'd, canst thou tell ? For
I would not speak with him till after dinner.
    1 *Watch.* You are a Roman, are you ?   35
    Men. I am as thy general is.
    1 *Watch.* Then you should hate Rome, as
he does. Can you, when you have push'd
out your gates the very defender of them,
and in a violent popular ignorance given
your enemy your shield, think to front his
revenges with the easy groans of old
women, the virginal palms of your daughters, or with the palsied intercession of such
a decay'd dotant as you seem to be ? Can
you think to blow out the intended fire
your city is ready to flame in with such
weak breath as this ? No, you are deceiv'd ;
therefore back to Rome and prepare for
your execution. You are condemn'd ; our
general has sworn you out of reprieve and
pardon.
    Men. Sirrah, if thy captain knew I were
here, he would use me with estimation.   50
    1 *Watch.* Come, my captain knows you
not.
    Men. I mean thy general.
    1 *Watch.* My general cares not for you.
Back, I say ; go, lest I let forth your half
pint of blood. Back—that's the utmost of
your having. Back.   55
    Men. Nay, but fellow, fellow—

Enter CORIOLANUS *with* AUFIDIUS.

    Cor. What's the matter ?
    Men. Now, you companion, I'll say an
errand for you ; you shall know now that
I am in estimation ; you shall perceive that
a Jack guardant cannot office me from my
son Coriolanus. Guess but by my entertainment with him if thou stand'st not i' th'
state of hanging, or of some death more
long in spectatorship and crueller in suffering ; behold now presently, and swoon for
what's to come upon thee. The glorious gods
sit in hourly synod about thy particular

prosperity, and love thee no worse than thy
old father Menenius does ! O my son ! my
son ! thou art preparing fire for us ; look
thee, here's water to quench it. I was
hardly moved to come to thee ; but being
assured none but myself could move thee,
I have been blown out of your gates with
sighs, and conjure thee to pardon Rome and
thy petitionary countrymen. The good gods
assuage thy wrath, and turn the dregs of
it upon this varlet here ; this, who, like a
block, hath denied my access to thee.   75
    Cor. Away !
    Men. How ! away !
    Cor. Wife, mother, child, I know not.
        My affairs
Are servanted to others. Though I owe
My revenge properly, my remission lies   80
In Volscian breasts. That we have been
    familiar,
Ingrate forgetfulness shall poison rather
Than pity note how much. Therefore be
    gone.
Mine ears against your suits are stronger
    than
Your gates against my force. Yet, for I
    lov'd thee,   85
Take this along ; I writ it for thy sake
                         [*Gives a letter.*
And would have sent it. Another word,
    Menenius,
I will not hear thee speak. This man,
    Aufidius,
Was my belov'd in Rome ; yet thou
    behold'st.
    Auf. You keep a constant temper.   90
        [*Exeunt Coriolanus and Aufidius.*
    1 *Watch.* Now, sir, is your name Men-
enius ?
    2 *Watch.* 'Tis a spell, you see, of much
power ! You know the way home again.
    1 *Watch.* Do you hear how we are shent
for keeping your greatness back ?   95
    2 *Watch.* What cause, do you think, I
have to swoon ?
    Men. I neither care for th' world nor your
general ; for such things as you, I can
scarce think there's any, y'are so slight.
He that hath a will to die by himself fears
it not from another. Let your general do
his worst. For you, be that you are, long ;
and your misery increase with your age !
I say to you, as I was said to : Away ! [*Exit.*
    1 *Watch.* A noble fellow, I warrant
him.   103
    2 *Watch.* The worthy fellow is our general;
he's the rock, the oak not to be wind-
shaken.   [*Exeunt.*

SCENE III. *The tent of Coriolanus.*

Enter CORIOLANUS, AUFIDIUS, *and* Others.

    Cor. We will before the walls of Rome
        to-morrow

Set down our host. My partner in this action,
You must report to th' Volscian lords how plainly
I have borne this business.
Auf. Only their ends
You have respected; stopp'd your ears against 5
The general suit of Rome; never admitted
A private whisper—no, not with such friends
That thought them sure of you.
Cor. This last old man,
Whom with a crack'd heart I have sent to Rome,
Lov'd me above the measure of a father; 10
Nay, godded me indeed. Their latest refuge
Was to send him; for whose old love I have—
Though I show'd sourly to him—once more offer'd
The first conditions, which they did refuse
And cannot now accept. To grace him only, 15
That thought he could do more, a very little
I have yielded to; fresh embassies and suits,
Nor from the state nor private friends, hereafter
Will I lend ear to. [*Shout within*] Ha! what shout is this? 20
Shall I be tempted to infringe my vow
In the same time 'tis made? I will not.

Enter, in mourning habits, VIRGILIA, VOLUMNIA, VALERIA, *young* MARCIUS, *with* Attendants.

My wife comes foremost, then the honour'd mould
Wherein this trunk was fram'd, and in her hand
The grandchild to her blood. But out, affection!
All bond and privilege of nature, break! 25
Let it be virtuous to be obstinate.
What is that curtsy worth? or those doves' eyes,
Which can make gods forsworn? I melt, and am not
Of stronger earth than others. My mother bows,
As if Olympus to a molehill should 30
In supplication nod; and my young boy
Hath an aspect of intercession which
Great nature cries 'Deny not'. Let the Volsces
Plough Rome and harrow Italy; I'll never
Be such a gosling to obey instinct, but stand 35
As if a man were author of himself
And knew no other kin.
Vir. My lord and husband!

Cor. These eyes are not the same I wore in Rome.
Vir. The sorrow that delivers us thus chang'd
Makes you think so.
Cor. Like a dull actor now 40
I have forgot my part and I am out,
Even to a full disgrace. Best of my flesh,
Forgive my tyranny; but do not say,
For that, 'Forgive our Romans'. O, a kiss
Long as my exile, sweet as my revenge! 45
Now, by the jealous queen of heaven, that kiss
I carried from thee, dear, and my true lip
Hath virgin'd it e'er since. You gods! I prate,
And the most noble mother of the world
Leave unsaluted. Sink, my knee, i' th' earth; [*Kneels.*
Of thy deep duty more impression show 51
Than that of common sons.
Vol. O, stand up blest!
Whilst with no softer cushion than the flint
I kneel before thee, and unproperly
Show duty, as mistaken all this while 55
Between the child and parent. [*Kneels.*
Cor. What's this?
Your knees to me, to your corrected son?
Then let the pebbles on the hungry beach
Fillip the stars; then let the mutinous winds
Strike the proud cedars 'gainst the fiery sun, 60
Murd'ring impossibility, to make
What cannot be slight work.
Vol. Thou art my warrior;
I holp to frame thee. Do you know this lady?
Cor. The noble sister of Publicola,
The moon of Rome, chaste as the icicle 65
That's curdied by the frost from purest snow,
And hangs on Dian's temple—dear Valeria!
Vol. This is a poor epitome of yours,
Which by th' interpretation of full time
May show like all yourself.
Cor. The god of soldiers, 70
With the consent of supreme Jove, inform
Thy thoughts with nobleness, that thou mayst prove
To shame unvulnerable, and stick i' th' wars
Like a great sea-mark, standing every flaw,
And saving those that eye thee!
Vol. Your knee, sirrah. 75
Cor. That's my brave boy.
Vol. Even he, your wife, this lady, and myself,
Are suitors to you.
Cor. I beseech you, peace!
Or, if you'd ask, remember this before:
The thing I have forsworn to grant may never 80
Be held by you denials. Do not bid me

Dismiss my soldiers, or capitulate
Again with Rome's mechanics. Tell me not
Wherein I seem unnatural; desire not
T'allay my rages and revenges with   85
Your colder reasons.
     Vol.   O, no more, no more!
You have said you will not grant us
     any thing—
For we have nothing else to ask but that
Which you deny already; yet we will ask,
That, if you fail in our request, the blame
May hang upon your hardness; therefore
     hear us.   91
     Cor. Aufidius, and you Volsces, mark;
     for we'll
Hear nought from Rome in private. Your
     request?
     Vol. Should we be silent and not speak,
     our raiment   94
And state of bodies would bewray what life
We have led since thy exile. Think with
     thyself
How more unfortunate than all living
     women
Are we come hither; since that thy sight,
     which should
Make our eyes flow with joy, hearts dance
     with comforts,
Constrains them weep and shake with fear
     and sorrow,   100
Making the mother, wife, and child, to see
The son, the husband, and the father, tear-
     ing
His country's bowels out. And to poor we
Thine enmity's most capital: thou bar'st
     us   104
Our prayers to the gods, which is a comfort
That all but we enjoy. For how can we,
Alas, how can we for our country pray,
Whereto we are bound, together with thy
     victory,
Whereto we are bound? Alack, or we must
     lose
The country, our dear nurse, or else thy
     person,   110
Our comfort in the country. We must find
An evident calamity, though we had
Our wish, which side should win; for either
     thou
Must as a foreign recreant be led   114
With manacles through our streets, or
     else
Triumphantly tread on thy country's ruin,
And bear the palm for having bravely shed
Thy wife and children's blood. For myself,
     son,
I purpose not to wait on fortune till
These wars determine; if I can not per-
     suade thee   120
Rather to show a noble grace to both parts
Than seek the end of one, thou shalt no
     sooner
March to assault thy country than to
     tread—

Trust to't, thou shalt not—on thy mother's
     womb
That brought thee to this world.
     Vir.   Ay, and mine,   125
That brought you forth this boy to keep
     your name
Living to time.
     Boy.   'A shall not tread on me!
I'll run away till I am bigger, but then I'll
     fight.
     Cor. Not of a woman's tenderness to be
Requires nor child nor woman's face to see.
I have sat too long.   [*Rising.*
     Vol.   Nay, go not from us thus.
If it were so that our request did tend
To save the Romans, thereby to destroy
The Volsces whom you serve, you might
     condemn us   134
As poisonous of your honour. No, our suit
Is that you reconcile them: while the
     Volsces
May say ' This mercy we have show'd ', the
     Romans
' This we receiv'd ', and each in either side
Give the all-hail to thee, and cry ' Be
     blest
For making up this peace! ' Thou know'st,
     great son,   140
The end of war's uncertain; but this
     certain,
That, if thou conquer Rome, the benefit
Which thou shalt thereby reap is such a
     name
Whose repetition will be dogg'd with
     curses;
Whose chronicle thus writ: ' The man was
     noble,   145
But with his last attempt he wip'd it out,
Destroy'd his country, and his name
     remains
To th' ensuing age abhorr'd '. Speak to me,
     son.
Thou hast affected the fine strains of
     honour,
To imitate the graces of the gods,   150
To tear with thunder the wide cheeks o'
     th' air,
And yet to charge thy sulphur with a bolt
That should but rive an oak. Why dost not
     speak?
Think'st thou it honourable for a noble man
Still to remember wrongs?   Daughter,
     speak you: 155
He cares not for your weeping. Speak thou,
     boy;
Perhaps thy childishness will move him
     more
Than can our reasons. There's no man in
     the world
More bound to's mother, yet here he lets
     me prate
Like one i' th' stocks. Thou hast never in
     thy life   160
Show'd thy dear mother any courtesy,

When she, poor hen, fond of no second
    brood,
Has cluck'd thee to the wars, and safely
    home
Loaden with honour. Say my request's
    unjust,
And spurn me back ; but if it be not so, 165
Thou art not honest, and the gods will
    plague thee,
That thou restrain'st from me the duty
    which
To a mother's part belongs. He turns away.
Down, ladies ; let us shame him with our
    knees.
To his surname Coriolanus 'longs more
    pride   170
Than pity to our prayers. Down. An end ;
This is the last. So we will home to Rome,
And die among our neighbours. Nay,
    behold's !
This boy, that cannot tell what he would
    have
But kneels and holds up hands for fellow-
    ship,   175
Does reason our petition with more strength
Than thou hast to deny't. Come, let us go.
This fellow had a Volscian to his mother ;
His wife is in Corioli, and his child
Like him by chance. Yet give us our
    dispatch.   180
I am hush'd until our city be afire,
And then I'll speak a little.
        [He holds her by the hand, silent.
    Cor.   O mother, mother !
What have you done ? Behold, the heavens
    do ope,
The gods look down, and this unnatural
    scene   184
They laugh at. O my mother, mother ! O !
You have won a happy victory to Rome ;
But for your son—believe it, O, believe it !—
Most dangerously you have with him
    prevail'd,
If not most mortal to him. But let it come.
Aufidius, though I cannot make true wars,
I'll frame convenient peace. Now, good
    Aufidius,   191
Were you in my stead, would you have
    heard
A mother less, or granted less, Aufidius ?
    Auf.   I was mov'd withal.
    Cor.   I dare be sworn you were !
And, sir, it is no little thing to make   195
Mine eyes to sweat compassion. But, good
    sir,
What peace you'll make, advise me. For
    my part,
I'll not to Rome, I'll back with you ; and
    pray you
Stand to me in this cause. O mother ! wife !
    Auf. [Aside] I am glad thou hast set thy
    mercy and thy honour   200
At difference in thee. Out of that I'll work
Myself a former fortune.

    Cor. [To the ladies] Ay, by and by ;
But we will drink together ; and you shall
    bear
A better witness back than words, which
    we,   204
On like conditions, will have counter-seal'd.
Come, enter with us. Ladies, you deserve
To have a temple built you. All the
    swords
In Italy, and her confederate arms,
Could not have made this peace. [Exeunt.

SCENE IV. Rome. A public place.

Enter MENENIUS and SICINIUS.

    Men. See you yond coign o' th' Capitol,
yond corner-stone ?
    Sic. Why, what of that ?
    Men. If it be possible for you to displace
it with your little finger, there is some hope
the ladies of Rome, especially his mother,
may prevail with him. But I say there is
no hope in't ; our throats are sentenc'd,
and stay upon execution.
    Sic. Is't possible that so short a time can
alter the condition of a man ?   10
    Men. There is difference between a grub
and a butterfly ; yet your butterfly was a
grub. This Marcius is grown from man to
dragon ; he has wings, he's more than a
creeping thing.
    Sic. He lov'd his mother dearly.   15
    Men. So did he me ; and he no more
remembers his mother now than an eight-
year-old horse. The tartness of his face
sours ripe grapes ; when he walks, he
moves like an engine and the ground
shrinks before his treading. He is able to
pierce a corslet with his eye, talks like a
knell, and his hum is a battery. He sits in
his state as a thing made for Alexander.
What he bids be done is finish'd with his
bidding. He wants nothing of a god but
eternity, and a heaven to throne in.
    Sic. Yes—mercy, if you report him
truly.   25
    Men. I paint him in the character. Mark
what mercy his mother shall bring from
him. There is no more mercy in him than
there is milk in a male tiger ; that shall our
poor city find. And all this is 'long of you.
    Sic. The gods be good unto us !   30
    Men. No, in such a case the gods will not
be good unto us. When we banish'd him we
respected not them ; and, he returning to
break our necks, they respect not us.

Enter a Messenger.

    Mess. Sir, if you'd save your life, fly to
your house.   34
The plebeians have got your fellow tribune
And hale him up and down ; all swearing if
The Roman ladies bring not comfort home
They'll give him death by inches.

Enter another Messenger.

Sic.   What's the news ?
2 Mess. Good news, good news ! The
    ladies have prevail'd,
The Volscians are dislodg'd, and Marcius
    gone.   40
A merrier day did never yet greet Rome,
No, not th' expulsion of the Tarquins.
Sic.   Friend,
Art thou certain this is true ? Is't most
    certain ?
2 Mess. As certain as I know the sun is
    fire.
Where have you lurk'd, that you make
    doubt of it ?   45
Ne'er through an arch so hurried the blown
    tide
As the recomforted through th' gates.
    Why, hark you ! [*Trumpets, haut-
        boys, drums beat, all together.*
The trumpets, sackbuts, psalteries, and
    fifes,
Tabors and cymbals, and the shouting
    Romans,
Make the sun dance. Hark you !
                            [*A shout within.*
Men.   This is good news. 50
I will go meet the ladies. This Volumnia
Is worth of consuls, senators, patricians,
A city full ; of tribunes such as you,
A sea and land full. You have pray'd well
    to-day :
This morning for ten thousand of your
    throats   55
I'd not have given a doit. Hark, how they
    joy ! [*Sound still with the shouts.*
Sic. First, the gods bless you for your
    tidings ; next,
Accept my thankfulness.
2 Mess.   Sir, we have all
Great cause to give great thanks.
Sic.   They are near the city ?
Mess. Almost at point to enter.
Sic.   We'll meet them, 60
And help the joy.   [*Exeunt.*

SCENE V. *Rome. A street near the gate.*

Enter two Senators *with* VOLUMNIA, VIR-
    GILIA, VALERIA, *passing over the stage,
    with other Lords.*

1 Sen. Behold our patroness, the life of
    Rome !
Call all your tribes together, praise the
    gods,
And make triumphant fires ; strew flowers
    before them.   3
Unshout the noise that banish'd Marcius,
Repeal him with the welcome of his mother ;
Cry ' Welcome, ladies, welcome ! '
All.   Welcome, ladies,
Welcome ! [*A flourish with drums and
            trumpets. Exeunt.*

SCENE VI. *Corioli. A public place.*

Enter TULLUS AUFIDIUS, *with* Attendants.

Auf. Go tell the lords o' th' city I am
    here ;
Deliver them this paper ; having read it,
Bid them repair to th' market-place,
    where I,
Even in theirs and in the commons' ears,
Will vouch the truth of it. Him I accuse 5
The city ports by this hath enter'd and
Intends t' appear before the people, hoping
To purge himself with words. Dispatch.
                            [*Exeunt Attendants.*

Enter three or four Conspirators *of
        Aufidius' faction.*

                                Most welcome !
1 Con. How is it with our general ?
Auf.   Even so 10
As with a man by his own alms empoison'd,
And with his charity slain.
2 Con.   Most noble sir,
If you do hold the same intent wherein
You wish'd us parties, we'll deliver you
Of your great danger.
Auf.   Sir, I cannot tell ; 15
We must proceed as we do find the people.
3 Con. The people will remain uncertain
    whilst
'Twixt you there's difference ; but the fall
    of either
Makes the survivor heir of all.
Auf.   I know it ;
And my pretext to strike at him admits 20
A good construction. I rais'd him, and I
    pawn'd
Mine honour for his truth ; who being so
    heighten'd,
He watered his new plants with dews of
    flattery,
Seducing so my friends ; and to this end
He bow'd his nature, never known before
But to be rough, unswayable, and free. 26
3 Con. Sir, his stoutness
When he did stand for consul, which he lost
By lack of stooping—
Auf.   That I would have spoke of.
Being banish'd for't, he came unto my
    hearth,   30
Presented to my knife his throat. I took
    him ;
Made him joint-servant with me ; gave
    him way
In all his own desires ; nay, let him choose
Out of my files, his projects to accomplish,
My best and freshest men ; serv'd his
    designments   35
In mine own person ; holp to reap the fame
Which he did end all his, and took some
    pride
To do myself this wrong. Till, at the last,
I seem'd his follower, not partner ; and

He wag'd me with his countenance as if 40
I had been mercenary.

1 *Con.* So he did, my lord.
The army marvell'd at it ; and, in the last,
When he had carried Rome and that we
 look'd
For no less spoil than glory—

Auf. There was it ;
For which my sinews shall be stretch'd upon
 him. 45
At a few drops of women's rheum, which
 are
As cheap as lies, he sold the blood and
 labour
Of our great action ; therefore shall he die,
And I'll renew me in his fall. But, hark ! 49
 [*Drums and trumpets sound, with great
  shouts of the people.*

1 *Con.* Your native town you enter'd like
 a post,
And had no welcomes home ; but he
 returns
Splitting the air with noise.

2 *Con.* And patient fools,
Whose children he hath slain, their base
 throats tear
With giving him glory.

3 *Con.* Therefore, at your vantage,
Ere he express himself or move the people
With what he would say, let him feel your
 sword, 56
Which we will second. When he lies along,
After your way his tale pronounc'd shall
 bury
His reasons with his body.

Auf. Say no more :
Here come the lords. 60

 Enter the Lords *of the city.*

Lords. You are most welcome home.
Auf. I have not deserv'd it.
But, worthy lords, have you with heed
 perused
What I have written to you ?
Lords. We have.
1 *Lord.* And grieve to hear't.
What faults he made before the last, I think
Might have found easy fines ; but there 'to
 end 65
Where he was to begin, and give away
The benefit of our levies, answering us
With our own charge, making a treaty
 where
There was a yielding—this admits no
 excuse.
Auf. He approaches ; you shall hear
 him. 70

Enter CORIOLANUS, *marching with drum
and colours : the* Commoners *being with
him.*

Cor. Hail, lords ! I am return'd your
 soldier ;
No more infected with my country's love

Than when I parted hence, but still sub-
 sisting
Under your great command. You are to
 know 74
That prosperously I have attempted, and
With bloody passage led your wars even to
The gates of Rome. Our spoils we have
 brought home
Doth more than counterpoise a full third
 part
The charges of the action. We have made
 peace
With no less honour to the Antiates 80
Than shame to th' Romans ; and we here
 deliver,
Subscrib'd by th' consuls and patricians,
Together with the seal o' th' Senate, what
We have compounded on.
Auf. Read it not, noble lords ;
But tell the traitor in the highest degree 85
He hath abus'd your powers.
Cor. Traitor ! How now ?
Auf. Ay, traitor, Marcius.
Cor. Marcius !
Auf. Ay, Marcius, Caius Marcius ! Dost
 thou think
I'll grace thee with that robbery, thy stol'n
 name
Coriolanus, in Corioli ? 90
You lords and heads o' th' state, perfidi-
 ously
He has betray'd your business and given up,
For certain drops of salt, your city Rome—
I say your city—to his wife and mother ;
Breaking his oath and resolution like 95
A twist of rotten silk ; never admitting
Counsel o' th' war ; but at his nurse's
 tears
He whin'd and roar'd away your victory,
That pages blush'd at him, and men of
 heart
Look'd wond'ring each at others.
Cor. Hear'st thou, Mars ? 100
Auf. Name not the god, thou boy of tears—
Cor. Ha !
Auf. —no more.
Cor. Measureless liar, thou hast made my
 heart
Too great for what contains it. 'Boy'! O
 slave !
Pardon me, lords, 'tis the first time that
 ever 105
I was forc'd to scold. Your judgments, my
 grave lords,
Must give this cur the lie ; and his own
 notion—
Who wears my stripes impress'd upon him,
 that
Must bear my beating to his grave—shall
 join
To thrust the lie unto him. 110
1 *Lord.* Peace, both, and hear me speak.
Cor. Cut me to pieces, Volsces ; men and
 lads,

Stain all your edges on me. ' Boy '! False
    hound !
It you have writ your annals true, 'tis there
That, like an eagle in a dove-cote, I   115
Flutter'd your Volscians in Corioli.
Alone I did it. ' Boy '!
  Auf.   Why, noble lords,
Will you be put in mind of his blind
    fortune,
Which was your shame, by this unholy
    braggart,
Fore your own eyes and ears ?
  Conspirators.   Let him die for't. 120
  All the people. Tear him to pieces. Do it
presently. He kill'd my son. My daughter.
He kill'd my cousin Marcus. He kill'd my
father.
  2 *Lord.* Peace, ho ! No outrage—peace !
The man is noble, and his fame folds in 125
This orb o' th' earth. His last offences to us
Shall have judicious hearing.   Stand,
    Aufidius,
And trouble not the peace.
  Cor.   O that I had him,
With six Aufidiuses, or more—his tribe,
To use my lawful sword !
  Auf.   Insolent villain ! 130
  Conspirators. Kill, kill, kill, kill, kill him !
    [*The Conspirators draw and kill
    Coriolanus, who falls. Aufidius
    stands on him.*
  Lords. Hold, hold, hold, hold !
  Auf. My noble masters, hear me speak.
1 *Lord.*   O Tullus !
2 *Lord.* Thou hast done a deed whereat
    valour will weep.

3 *Lord.* Tread not upon him. Masters all,
    be quiet ;
Put up your swords.   135
  Auf. My lords, when you shall know—as
    in this rage,
Provok'd by him, you cannot—the great
    danger
Which this man's life did owe you, you'll
    rejoice
That he is thus cut off. Please it your
    honours
To call me to your Senate, I'll deliver 140
Myself your loyal servant, or endure
Your heaviest censure.
1 *Lord.*   Bear from hence his body,
And mourn you for him. Let him be
    regarded
As the most noble corse that ever herald
Did follow to his urn.
2 *Lord.*   His own impatience 145
Takes from Aufidius a great part of
    blame.
Let's make the best of it.
  Auf.   My rage is gone,
And I am struck with sorrow. Take him up.
Help, three o' th' chiefest soldiers ; I'll be
    one.
Beat thou the drum, that it speak mourn-
    fully ;   150
Trail your steel pikes. Though in this city
    he
Hath widowed and unchilded many a one,
Which to this hour bewail the injury,
Yet he shall have a noble memory.   154
Assist. [*Exeunt, bearing the body of Corio-
    lanus. A dead march sounded.*

TITUS ANDRONICUS

DRAMATIS PERSONÆ

SATURNINUS, *son to the late Emperor of Rome, afterwards Emperor.*
BASSIANUS, *brother to Saturninus.*
TITUS ANDRONICUS, *a noble Roman.*
MARCUS ANDRONICUS, *Tribune of the People, and brother to Titus.*
LUCIUS,
QUINTUS,
MARTIUS, } *sons to Titus Andronicus.*
MUTIUS,
YOUNG LUCIUS, *a boy, son to Lucius.*
PUBLIUS, *son to Marcus Andronicus.*
SEMPRONIUS,
CAIUS, } *kinsmen to Titus.*
VALENTINE,

ÆMILIUS, *a noble Roman.*
ALARBUS,
DEMETRIUS, } *sons to Tamora.*
CHIRON,
AARON, *a Moor, beloved by Tamora.*
A Captain.
A Messenger.
A Clown.

TAMORA, *Queen of the Goths.*
LAVINIA, *daughter to Titus Andronicus.*
A Nurse, *and a black Child.*

Romans *and* Goths, Senators, Tribunes, Officers, Soldiers, *and* Attendants.

THE SCENE: *Rome and the neighbourhood.*

ACT ONE

SCENE I. *Rome. Before the Capitol.*

Flourish. Enter the Tribunes *and* Senators *aloft; and then enter below* SATURNINUS *and his* Followers *at one door, and* BASSIANUS *and his* Followers *at the other, with drums and trumpets.*

Sat. Noble patricians, patrons of my right,
Defend the justice of my cause with arms;
And, countrymen, my loving followers,
Plead my successive title with your swords.
I am his first-born son that was the last 5
That ware the imperial diadem of Rome;
Then let my father's honours live in me,
Nor wrong mine age with this indignity.

Bas. Romans, friends, followers, favourers of my right,
If ever Bassianus, Cæsar's son, 10
Were gracious in the eyes of royal Rome,
Keep then this passage to the Capitol;
And suffer not dishonour to approach
The imperial seat, to virtue consecrate,
To justice, continence, and nobility; 15
But let desert in pure election shine;
And, Romans, fight for freedom in your choice.

Enter MARCUS ANDRONICUS *aloft, with the crown.*

Marc. Princes, that strive by factions and by friends
Ambitiously for rule and empery,
Know that the people of Rome, for whom we stand 20
A special party, have by common voice
In election for the Roman empery
Chosen Andronicus, surnamed Pius
For many good and great deserts to Rome.
A nobler man, a braver warrior, 25
Lives not this day within the city walls.
He by the Senate is accited home,
From weary wars against the barbarous Goths,
That with his sons, a terror to our foes,
Hath yok'd a nation strong, train'd up in arms. 30
Ten years are spent since first he undertook
This cause of Rome, and chastised with arms
Our enemies' pride; five times he hath return'd
Bleeding to Rome, bearing his valiant sons
In coffins from the field; *and at this day
To the monument of that Andronici
Done sacrifice of expiation,
And slain the noblest prisoner of the Goths.*
And now at last, laden with honour's spoils,
Returns the good Andronicus to Rome,
Renowned Titus, flourishing in arms.
Let us entreat, by honour of his name
Whom worthily you would have now succeed, 40
And in the Capitol and Senate's right,
Whom you pretend to honour and adore,
That you withdraw you and abate your strength,
Dismiss your followers, and, as suitors should,
Plead your deserts in peace and humbleness. 45

Sat. How fair the Tribune speaks to calm my thoughts!

Bas. Marcus Andronicus, so I do affy
In thy uprightness and integrity,
And so I love and honour thee and thine,

Thy noble brother Titus and his sons,   50
And her to whom my thoughts are humbled
      all,
Gracious Lavinia, Rome's rich ornament,
That I will here dismiss my loving friends,
And to my fortunes and the people's favour
Commit my cause in balance to be weigh'd.
                  [*Exeunt the soldiers of Bassianus.*
  Sat. Friends, that have been thus forward
      in my right,   56
I thank you all and here dismiss you all,
And to the love and favour of my country
Commit myself, my person, and the cause.
                  [*Exeunt the soldiers of Saturninus.*
Rome, be as just and gracious unto me   60
As I am confident and kind to thee.
Open the gates and let me in.
  Bas. Tribunes, and me, a poor competitor.
                  [*Flourish. They go up into the
                          Senate House.*

              Enter a Captain.

  Cap. Romans, make way.   The good
      Andronicus,
Patron of virtue, Rome's best champion,   65
Successful in the battles that he fights,
With honour and with fortune is return'd
From where he circumscribed with his
      sword
And brought to yoke the enemies of Rome.

*Sound drums and trumpets, and then enter
  MARTIUS and MUTIUS, two of Titus' sons;
  and then two Men bearing a coffin covered
  with black; then LUCIUS and QUINTUS,
  two other sons; then TITUS ANDRONICUS;
  and then TAMORA the Queen of Goths, with
  her three sons, ALARBUS, DEMETRIUS and
  CHIRON, with AARON the Moor, and
  Others, as many as can be.   Then set down
  the coffin and Titus speaks.*

  Tit. Hail, Rome, victorious in thy mourn-
      ing weeds!   70
Lo, as the bark that hath discharg'd her
      fraught
Returns with precious lading to the bay
From whence at first she weigh'd her
      anchorage,
Cometh Andronicus, bound with laurel
      boughs,
To re-salute his country with his tears,   75
Tears of true joy for his return to Rome.
Thou great defender of this Capitol,
Stand gracious to the rites that we intend!
Romans, of five and twenty valiant sons,
Half of the number that King Priam had,
Behold the poor remains, alive and dead!
These that survive let Rome reward with
      love;   82
These that I bring unto their latest home,
With burial amongst their ancestors.
Here Goths have given me leave to sheathe
      my sword.   85

Titus, unkind, and careless of thine own,
Why suffer'st thou thy sons, unburied yet,
To hover on the dreadful shore of Styx?
Make way to lay them by their brethren.
                  [*They open the tomb.*
There greet in silence, as the dead are wont,
And sleep in peace, slain in your country's
      wars.   91
O sacred receptacle of my joys,
Sweet cell of virtue and nobility,
How many sons hast thou of mine in
      store
That thou wilt never render to me more!   95
  Luc. Give us the proudest prisoner of the
      Goths,
That we may hew his limbs, and on a pile
Ad manes fratrum sacrifice his flesh
Before this earthy prison of their bones,
That so the shadows be not unappeas'd,   100
Nor we disturb'd with prodigies on earth.
  Tit. I give him you—the noblest that
      survives,
The eldest son of this distressed queen.
  Tam. Stay, Roman brethren!   Gracious
      conqueror,
Victorious Titus, rue the tears I shed,   105
A mother's tears in passion for her son;
And if thy sons were ever dear to thee,
O, think my son to be as dear to me!
Sufficeth not that we are brought to Rome
To beautify thy triumphs, and return   110
Captive to thee and to thy Roman yoke;
But must my sons be slaughtered in the
      streets
For valiant doings in their country's cause?
O, if to fight for king and commonweal
Were piety in thine, it is in these.   115
Andronicus, stain not thy tomb with blood.
Wilt thou draw near the nature of the gods?
Draw near them then in being merciful.
Sweet mercy is nobility's true badge.   119
Thrice-noble Titus, spare my first-born son.
  Tit. Patient yourself, madam, and pardon
      me.
These are their brethren, whom your Goths
      beheld
Alive and dead; and for their brethren
      slain
Religiously they ask a sacrifice.   124
To this your son is mark'd, and die he must
T' appease their groaning shadows that are
      gone.
  Luc. Away with him, and make a fire
      straight;
And with our swords, upon a pile of wood,
Let's hew his limbs till they be clean con-
      sum'd.
                  [*Exeunt Titus' sons, with Alarbus.*
  Tam. O cruel, irreligious piety!   130
  Chi. Was never Scythia half so barbarous!
  Dem. Oppose not Scythia to ambitious
      Rome.
Alarbus goes to rest, and we survive
To tremble under Titus' threat'ning look.

Then, madam, stand resolv'd, but hope
    withal   135
The self-same gods that arm'd the Queen
    of Troy
With opportunity of sharp revenge
Upon the Thracian tyrant in his tent
May favour Tamora. the queen of Goths—
When Goths were Goths and Tamora was
    queen—   140
To quit the bloody wrongs upon her foes.

Re-enter LUCIUS, QUINTUS, MARTIUS, *and*
MUTIUS, *the sons of Andronicus, with their
swords bloody.*

Luc. See, lord and father, how we have
    perform'd
Our Roman rites : Alarbus' limbs are
    lopp'd,
And entrails feed the sacrificing fire,
Whose smoke like incense doth perfume the
    sky.   145
Remaineth nought but to inter our brethren,
And with loud 'larums welcome them to
    Rome.
Tit. Let it be so, and let Andronicus
Make this his latest farewell to their souls.

*Sound trumpets and lay the coffin in the
    tomb.*

In peace and honour rest you here, my
    sons ;   150
Rome's readiest champions, repose you
    here in rest,
Secure from worldly chances and mishaps !
Here lurks no treason, here no envy swells,
Here grow no damned drugs, here are no
    storms,
No noise, but silence and eternal sleep. 155
In peace and honour rest you here, my sons !

Enter LAVINIA.

Lav. In peace and honour live Lord Titus
    long ;
My noble lord and father, live in fame !
Lo, at this tomb my tributary tears
I render for my brethren's obsequies ; 160
And at thy feet I kneel, with tears of joy
Shed on this earth for thy return to
    Rome.
O, bless me here with thy victorious hand,
Whose fortunes Rome's best citizens
    applaud !
Tit. Kind Rome, that hast thus lovingly
    reserv'd   165
The cordial of mine age to glad my heart !
Lavinia, live ; outlive thy father's days,
And fame's eternal date, for virtue's praise !

Enter, above, MARCUS ANDRONICUS *and*
Tribunes ; *re-enter* SATURNINUS, BASSI-
ANUS, *and* Attendants.

Marc. Long live Lord Titus, my beloved
    brother,
Gracious triumpher in the eyes of Rome !

Tit. Thanks, gentle Tribune, noble
    brother Marcus.   171
Marc. And welcome, nephews, from
    successful wars,
You that survive and you that sleep in
    fame.
Fair lords, your fortunes are alike in all
That in your country's service drew your
    swords ;   175
But safer triumph is this funeral pomp
That hath aspir'd to Solon's happiness
And triumphs over chance in honour's bed.
Titus Andronicus, the people of Rome,
Whose friend in justice thou hast ever
    been,   180
Send thee by me, their Tribune and their
    trust,
This palliament of white and spotless hue ;
And name thee in election for the empire
With these our late-deceased Emperor's
    sons :
Be candidatus then, and put it on,   185
And help to set a head on headless Rome.
Tit. A better head her glorious body fits
Than his that shakes for age and feebleness.
What should I don this robe and trouble
    you ?
Be chosen with proclamations to-day,   190
To-morrow yield up rule, resign my life,
And set abroad new business for you all ?
Rome, I have been thy soldier forty years,
And led my country's strength successfully,
And buried one and twenty valiant sons,
Knighted in field, slain manfully in arms,
In right and service of their noble country.
Give me a staff of honour for mine age,
But not a sceptre to control the world.
Upright he held it, lords, that held it last.
Marc. Titus, thou shalt obtain and ask
    the empery.   201
Sat. Proud and ambitious Tribune, canst
    thou tell ?
Tit. Patience, Prince Saturninus.
Sat.   Romans, do me right.
Patricians, draw your swords, and sheathe
    them not
Till Saturninus be Rome's Emperor.   205
Andronicus, would thou were shipp'd to
    hell
Rather than rob me of the people's hearts !
Luc. Proud Saturnine, interrupter of the
    good
That noble-minded Titus means to thee !
Tit. Content thee, Prince ; I will restore
    to thee   210
The people's hearts, and wean them from
    themselves.
Bas. Andronicus, I do not flatter thee,
But honour thee, and will do till I die.
My faction if thou strengthen with thy
    friends,
I will most thankful be ; and thanks to
    men   215
Of noble minds is honourable meed.

Tit. People of Rome, and people's
      Tribunes here,
I ask your voices and your suffrages :
Will ye bestow them friendly on Androni-
      cus ?
  Trib. To gratify the good Andronicus, 220
And gratulate his safe return to Rome,
The people will accept whom he admits.
  Tit. Tribunes, I thank you ; and this suit
      I make,
That you create our Emperor's eldest son,
Lord Saturnine ; whose virtues will, I hope,
Reflect on Rome as Titan's rays on earth,
And ripen justice in this commonweal.
Then, if you will elect by my advice,
Crown him, and say ' Long live our
      Emperor ! '
  Marc. With voices and applause of every
      sort,   230
Patricians and plebeians, we create
Lord Saturninus Rome's great Emperor ;
And say 'Long live our Emperor Saturnine!'
      [*A long flourish till they come down.*
  Sat. Titus Andronicus, for thy favours
      done
To us in our election this day   235
I give thee thanks in part of thy deserts,
And will with deeds requite thy gentleness ;
And for an onset, Titus, to advance
Thy name and honourable family,
Lavinia will I make my emperess,   240
Rome's royal mistress, mistress of my heart,
And in the sacred Pantheon her espouse.
Tell me, Andronicus, doth this motion
      please thee ?
  Tit. It doth, my worthy lord, and in this
      match   244
I hold me highly honoured of your Grace,
And here in sight of Rome, to Saturnine,
King and commander of our commonweal,
The wide world's Emperor, do I consecrate
My sword, my chariot, and my prisoners,
Presents well worthy Rome's imperious
      lord ;   250
Receive them then, the tribute that I owe,
Mine honour's ensigns humbled at thy feet.
  Sat. Thanks, noble Titus, father of my
      life.
How proud I am of thee and of thy gifts
Rome shall record ; and when I do forget
The least of these unspeakable deserts, 256
Romans, forget your fealty to me.
  Tit. [*To Tamora*] Now, madam, are you
      prisoner to an emperor ;
To him that for your honour and your state
Will use you nobly and your followers. 260
  Sat. [*Aside*] A goodly lady, trust me ; of
      the hue
That I would choose, were I to choose
      anew.—
Clear up, fair Queen, that cloudy counten-
      ance ;
Though chance of war hath wrought this
      change of cheer,

Thou com'st not to be made a scorn in
      Rome—   265
Princely shall be thy usage every way.
Rest on my word, and let not discontent
Daunt all your hopes. Madam, he comforts
      you
Can make you greater than the Queen of
      Goths.   269
Lavinia, you are not displeas'd with this ?
  Lav. Not I, my lord, sith true nobility
Warrants these words in princely courtesy.
  Sat. Thanks, sweet Lavinia. Romans, let
      us go.
Ransomless here we set our prisoners free.
Proclaim our honours, lords, with trump
      and drum.   [*Flourish.*
  Bas. Lord Titus, by your leave, this maid
      is mine.   [*Seizing Lavinia.*
  Tit. How, sir ! Are you in earnest then,
      my lord ?   277
  Bas. Ay, noble Titus, and resolv'd withal
To do myself this reason and this right.
  Marc. Suum cuique is our Roman justice:
This prince in justice seizeth but his own.
  Luc. And that he will and shall, if Lucius
      live.
  Tit. Traitors, avaunt ! Where is the
      Emperor's guard ?
Treason, my lord—Lavinia is surpris'd !
  Sat. Surpris'd ! By whom ?
  Bas.   By him that justly may 285
Bear his betroth'd from all the world away.
      [*Exeunt Bassianus and Marcus
                      with Lavinia.*
  Mut. Brothers, help to convey her hence
      away,
And with my sword I'll keep this door safe.
      [*Exeunt Lucius, Quintus, and Martius.*
  Tit. Follow, my lord, and I'll soon bring
      her back.
  Mut. My lord, you pass not here.
  Tit.   What, villain boy ! 290
Bar'st me my way in Rome ?
  Mut.   Help, Lucius, help !
      [*Titus kills him. During the fray, exeunt
      Saturninus, Tamora, Demetrius,
      Chiron, and Aaron.*

                Re-enter Lucius.

  Luc. My lord, you are unjust, and more
      than so :
In wrongful quarrel you have slain your
      son.
  Tit. Nor thou nor he are any sons of
      mine ;
My sons would never so dishonour me. 295

Re-enter aloft the Emperor *with* Tamora
and her two Sons, *and* Aaron *the Moor.*

Traitor, restore Lavinia to the Emperor.
  Luc. Dead, if you will ; but not to be his
      wife,
That is another's lawful promis'd love.
                              [*Exit.*

Sat. No, Titus, no; the Emperor needs
  her not,
Nor her, nor thee, nor any of thy stock. 300
I'll trust by leisure him that mocks me
  once;
Thee never, nor thy traitorous haughty
  sons,
Confederates all thus to dishonour me.
Was there none else in Rome to make a
  stale
But Saturnine? Full well, Andronicus, 305
Agree these deeds with that proud brag of
  thine
That saidst I begg'd the empire at thy
  hands.
  Tit. O monstrous! What reproachful
    words are these?
  Sat. But go thy ways; go, give that
    changing piece
To him that flourish'd for her with his
  sword. 310
A valiant son-in-law thou shalt enjoy;
One fit to bandy with thy lawless sons,
To ruffle in the commonwealth of Rome.
  Tit. These words are razors to my
    wounded heart.
  Sat. And therefore, lovely Tamora, Queen
    of Goths,
That, like the stately Phœbe 'mongst her
  nymphs, 316
Dost overshine the gallant'st dames of
  Rome,
If thou be pleas'd with this my sudden
  choice,
Behold, I choose thee, Tamora, for my
  bride
And will create thee Emperess of Rome. 320
Speak, Queen of Goths, dost thou applaud
  my choice?
And here I swear by all the Roman gods—
Sith priest and holy water are so near,
And tapers burn so bright, and every-
  thing
In readiness for Hymenæus stand— 325
I will not re-salute the streets of Rome,
Or climb my palace, till from forth this
  place
I lead espous'd my bride along with me.
  Tam. And here in sight of heaven to
    Rome I swear, 329
If Saturnine advance the Queen of Goths,
She will a handmaid be to his desires,
A loving nurse, a mother to his youth.
  Sat. Ascend, fair queen, Pantheon.
    Lords, accompany
Your noble Emperor and his lovely bride,
Sent by the heavens for Prince Saturnine,
Whose wisdom hath her fortune conquered;
There shall we consummate our spousal
  rites. [*Exeunt all but Titus.*
  Tit. I am not bid to wait upon this bride.
Titus, when wert thou wont to walk alone,
Dishonoured thus, and challenged of
  wrongs? 340

Re-enter MARCUS, *and Titus' sons,* LUCIUS,
  QUINTUS, *and* MARTIUS.

  Marc. O Titus, see, O, see what thou hast
    done!
In a bad quarrel slain a virtuous son.
  Tit. No, foolish Tribune, no; no son of
    mine—
Nor thou, nor these, confederates in the
  deed
That hath dishonoured all our family; 345
Unworthy brother and unworthy sons!
  Luc. But let us give him burial, as
    becomes;
Give Mutius burial with our bretheren.
  Tit. Traitors, away! He rests not in this
    tomb.
This monument five hundred years hath
  stood, 350
Which I have sumptuously re-edified;
Here none but soldiers and Rome's
  servitors
Repose in fame; none basely slain in
  brawls.
Bury him where you can, he comes not
  here.
  Marc. My lord, this is impiety in you. 355
My nephew Mutius' deeds do plead for him;
He must be buried with his bretheren.
  Quin. ⎱ And shall, or him we will accom-
  Mart. ⎰   pany.
  Tit. 'And shall'! What villain was it
    spake that word?
  Quin. He that would vouch it in any
    place but here. 360
  Tit. What, would you bury him in my
    despite?
  Marc. No, noble Titus, but entreat of
    thee
To pardon Mutius and to bury him.
  Tit. Marcus, even thou hast struck upon
    my crest,
And with these boys mine honour thou hast
  wounded. 365
My foes I do repute you every one;
So trouble me no more, but get you gone.
  Mart. He is not with himself; let us
    withdraw.
  Quin. Not I, till Mutius' bones be buried.
    [*The brother and the sons kneel.*
  Marc. Brother, for in that name doth
    nature plead— 370
  Quin. Father, and in that name doth
    nature speak—
  Tit. Speak thou no more, if all the rest
    will speed.
  Marc. Renowned Titus, more than half
    my soul—
  Luc. Dear father, soul and substance of
    us all— 37
  Marc. Suffer thy brother Marcus to inter
His noble nephew here in virtue's nest,
That died in honour and Lavinia's cause.
Thou art a Roman—be not barbarous.

The Greeks upon advice did bury Ajax,
That slew himself ; and wise Laertes' son
Did graciously plead for his funerals.   381
Let not young Mutius, then, that was thy joy,
Be barr'd his entrance here.
 Tit.   Rise, Marcus, rise ;
The dismal'st day is this that e'er I saw,
To be dishonoured by my sons in Rome !
Well, bury him, and bury me the next. 386
    [*They put Mutius in the tomb.*
 Luc. There lie thy bones, sweet Mutius, with thy friends,
Till we with trophies do adorn thy tomb.
 All. [*Kneeling*] No man shed tears for noble Mutius ;
He lives in fame that died in virtue's cause.
 Marc. My lord—to step out of these dreary dumps—   391
How comes it that the subtle Queen of Goths
Is of a sudden thus advanc'd in Rome ?
 Tit. I know not, Marcus, but I know it is—
Whether by device or no, the heavens can tell.   395
Is she not, then, beholding to the man
That brought her for this high good turn so far ?
 Marc. Yes, and will nobly him remunerate.

 Flourish. Re-enter the EMPEROR, TAMORA *and her two* Sons, *with the* MOOR, *at one door ; at the other door,* BASSIANUS *and* LAVINIA, *with* Others.

 Sat. So, Bassianus, you have play'd your prize :
God give you joy, sir, of your gallant bride !
 Bas. And you of yours, my lord ! I say no more,   401
Nor wish no less ; and so I take my leave.
 Sat. Traitor, if Rome have law or we have power,
Thou and thy faction shall repent this rape.
 Bas. Rape, call you it, my lord, to seize my own,   405
My true betrothed love, and now my wife ?
But let the laws of Rome determine all ;
Meanwhile am I possess'd of that is mine.
 Sat. 'Tis good, sir. You are very short with us ;
But if we live we'll be as sharp with you. 410
 Bas. My lord, what I have done, as best I may,
Answer I must, and shall do with my life.
Only thus much I give your Grace to know :
By all the duties that I owe to Rome,
This noble gentleman, Lord Titus here, 415
Is in opinion and in honour wrong'd,
That, in the rescue of Lavinia,
With his own hand did slay his youngest son,
In zeal to you, and highly mov'd to wrath

To be controll'd in that he frankly gave. 420
Receive him then to favour, Saturnine,
That hath express'd himself in all his deeds
A father and a friend to thee and Rome.
 Tit. Prince Bassianus, leave to plead my deeds.
'Tis thou and those that have dishonoured me.   425
Rome and the righteous heavens be my judge
How I have lov'd and honoured Saturnine !
 Tam. My worthy lord, if ever Tamora
Were gracious in those princely eyes of thine,   429
Then hear me speak indifferently for all ;
And at my suit, sweet, pardon what is past.
 Sat. What, madam ! be dishonoured openly,
And basely put it up without revenge ?
 Tam. Not so, my lord ; the gods of Rome forfend
I should be author to dishonour you ! 435
But on mine honour dare I undertake
For good Lord Titus' innocence in all,
Whose fury not dissembled speaks his griefs.
Then at my suit look graciously on him ;
Lose not so noble a friend on vain suppose,
Nor with sour looks afflict his gentle heart.
[*Aside to Sat.*] My lord, be rul'd by me, be won at last ;   442
Dissemble all your griefs and discontents.
You are but newly planted in your throne ;
Lest, then, the people, and patricians too,
Upon a just survey take Titus' part, 446
And so supplant you for ingratitude,
Which Rome reputes to be a heinous sin,
Yield at entreats, and then let me alone ;
I'll find a day to massacre them all, 450
And raze their faction and their family,
The cruel father and his traitorous sons,
To whom I sued for my dear son's life ;
And make them know what 'tis to let a queen
Kneel in the streets and beg for grace in vain.—   455
Come, come, sweet Emperor ; come, Andronicus.
Take up this good old man, and cheer the heart
That dies in tempest of thy angry frown.
 Sat. Rise, Titus, rise ; my Empress hath prevail'd.
 Tit. I thank your Majesty and her, my lord ;   460
These words, these looks, infuse new life in me.
 Tam. Titus, I am incorporate in Rome,
A Roman now adopted happily,
And must advise the Emperor for his good.
This day all quarrels die, Andronicus ; 465
And let it be mine honour, good my lord,
That I have reconcil'd your friends and you.
For you, Prince Bassianus, I have pass'd
My word and promise to the Emperor 469

That you will be more mild and tractable.
And fear not, lords—and you, Lavinia.
By my advice, all humbled on your knees,
You shall ask pardon of his Majesty.
  Luc. We do, and vow to heaven and to
    his Highness   474
That what we did was mildly as we might,
Tend'ring our sister's honour and our own.
  Marc. That on mine honour here do I
    protest.
  Sat. Away, and talk not ; trouble us no
    more.
  Tam. Nay, nay, sweet Emperor, we must
    all be friends.
The Tribune and his nephews kneel for
    grace.   480
I will not be denied. Sweet heart, look
    back.
  Sat. Marcus, for thy sake, and thy
    brother's here,
And at my lovely Tamora's entreats,
I do remit these young men's heinous
    faults.
Stand up.   485
Lavinia, though you left me like a churl,
I found a friend ; and sure as death I swore
I would not part a bachelor from the priest.
Come, if the Emperor's court can feast two
    brides,
You are my guest, Lavinia, and your
    friends.   490
This day shall be a love-day, Tamora.
  Tit. To-morrow, an it please your
    Majesty
To hunt the panther and the hart with me,
With horn and hound we'll give your Grace
    bonjour.
  Sat. Be it so, Titus, and gramercy too.
         [*Exeunt. Sound trumpets.*

ACT TWO

SCENE I. *Rome. Before the palace.*

Enter AARON.

  Aar. Now climbeth Tamora Olympus'
    top,
Safe out of Fortune's shot, and sits aloft,
Secure of thunder's crack or lightning flash,
Advanc'd above pale envy's threat'ning
    reach.
As when the golden sun salutes the morn, 5
And, having gilt the ocean with his beams,
Gallops the zodiac in his glistering coach
And overlooks the highest-peering hills,
So Tamora.
Upon her wit doth earthly honour wait, 10
And virtue stoops and trembles at her
    frown.
Then, Aaron, arm thy heart and fit thy
    thoughts
To mount aloft with thy imperial mistress,
And mount her pitch whom thou in triumph
    long

Hast prisoner held, fett'red in amorous
    chains,   15
And faster bound to Aaron's charming eyes
Than is Prometheus tied to Caucasus.
Away with slavish weeds and servile
    thoughts !
I will be bright and shine in pearl and gold,
To wait upon this new-made emperess. 20
To wait, said I ?   To wanton with this
    queen,
This goddess, this Semiramis, this nymph,
This siren that will charm Rome's
    Saturnine,
And see his shipwreck and his common-
    weal's.
Hullo ! what storm is this ?   25

Enter CHIRON *and* DEMETRIUS, *braving.*

  Dem. Chiron, thy years wants wit, thy
    wits wants edge
And manners, to intrude where I am
    grac'd,
And may, for aught thou knowest, affected
    be.
  Chi. Demetrius, thou dost over-ween
    in all ;
And so in this, to bear me down with
    braves.   30
'Tis not the difference of a year or two
Makes me less gracious or thee more
    fortunate :
I am as able and as fit as thou
To serve and to deserve my mistress' grace ;
And that my sword upon thee shall approve,
And plead my passions for Lavinia's love.
  Aar. [*Aside*] Clubs, clubs ! These lovers
    will not keep the peace.   37
  Dem. Why, boy, although our mother,
    unadvis'd,
Gave you a dancing-rapier by your side,
Are you so desperate grown to threat your
    friends ?   40
Go to ; have your lath glued within your
    sheath
Till you know better how to handle it.
  Chi. Meanwhile, sir, with the little skill
    I have,
Full well shalt thou perceive how much I
    dare.
  Dem. Ay, boy, grow ye so brave ?
                    [*They draw.*
  Aar. [*Coming forward*] Why, how now,
    lords !   45
So near the Emperor's palace dare ye draw
And maintain such a quarrel openly ?
Full well I wot the ground of all this grudge :
I would not for a million of gold
The cause were known to them it most
    concerns ;   50
Nor would your noble mother for much
    more
Be so dishonoured in the court of Rome.
For shame, put up.
  Dem.   Not I, till I have sheath'd

My rapier in his bosom, and withal
Thrust those reproachful speeches down
    his throat   55
That he hath breath'd in my dishonour
    here.
  Chi. For that I am prepar'd and full
    resolv'd,
Foul-spoken coward, that thund'rest with
    thy tongue,
And with thy weapon nothing dar'st
    perform.
  Aar. Away, I say!   60
Now, by the gods that warlike Goths adore,
This petty brabble will undo us all.
Why, lords, and think you not how
    dangerous
It is to jet upon a prince's right?
What, is Lavinia then become so loose,   65
Or Bassianus so degenerate,
That for her love such quarrels may be
    broach'd
Without controlment, justice, or revenge?
Young lords, beware; an should the
    Empress know
This discord's ground, the music would not
    please.   70
  Chi. I care not, I, knew she and all the
    world:
I love Lavinia more than all the world.
  Dem. Youngling, learn thou to make
    some meaner choice:
Lavinia is thine elder brother's hope.
  Aar. Why, are ye mad, or know ye not
    in Rome
How furious and impatient they be,   76
And cannot brook competitors in love?
I tell you, lords, you do but plot your deaths
By this device.
  Chi.   Aaron, a thousand deaths
Would I propose to achieve her whom I
    love.   80
  Aar. To achieve her—How?
  Dem. Why mak'st thou it so strange?
She is a woman, therefore may be woo'd;
She is a woman, therefore may be won;
She is Lavinia, therefore must be lov'd.
What, man! more water glideth by the mill
Than wots the miller of; and easy it is   86
Of a cut loaf to steal a shive, we know.
Though Bassianus be the Emperor's
    brother,
Better than he have worn Vulcan's badge.
  Aar. [*Aside*] Ay, and as good as Saturni-
    nus may.   90
  Dem. Then why should he despair that
    knows to court it
With words, fair looks, and liberality?
What, hast not thou full often struck a doe,
And borne her cleanly by the keeper's nose?
  Aar. Why, then, it seems some certain
    snatch or so
Would serve your turns.
  Chi.   Ay, so the turn were served. 96
  Dem. Aaron, thou hast hit it.

  Aar.   Would you had hit it too!
Then should not we be tir'd with this ado.
Why, hark ye, hark ye! and are you such
    fools
To square for this? Would it offend you,
    then,   100
That both should speed?
  Chi. Faith, not me.
  Dem.   Nor me, so I were one.
  Aar. For shame, be friends, and join for
    that you jar.
'Tis policy and stratagem must do   104
That you affect; and so must you resolve
That what you cannot as you would
    achieve,
You must perforce accomplish as you may.
Take this of me: Lucrece was not more
    chaste
Than this Lavinia, Bassianus' love.
A speedier course than ling'ring languish-
    ment   110
Must we pursue, and I have found the path.
My lords, a solemn hunting is in hand;
There will the lovely Roman ladies troop;
The forest walks are wide and spacious,
And many unfrequented plots there are 115
Fitted by kind for rape and villainy.
Single you thither then this dainty doe,
And strike her home by force if not by
    words.
This way, or not at all, stand you in hope.
Come, come, our Empress, with her sacred
    wit   120
To villainy and vengeance consecrate,
Will we acquaint with all what we intend;
And she shall file our engines with advice
That will not suffer you to square your-
    selves,
But to your wishes' height advance you
    both.   125
The Emperor's court is like the house of
    Fame,
The palace full of tongues, of eyes, and ears;
The woods are ruthless, dreadful, deaf, and
    dull.
There speak and strike, brave boys, and
    take your turns;
There serve your lust, shadowed from
    heaven's eye,   130
And revel in Lavinia's treasury.
  Chi. Thy counsel, lad, smells of no
    cowardice.
  Dem. Sit fas aut nefas, till I find the
    stream
To cool this heat, a charm to calm these
    fits,   134
Per Styga, per manes vehor.   [*Exeunt.*

SCENE II. *A forest near Rome.*

Enter TITUS ANDRONICUS, *and his three
sons,* LUCIUS, QUINTUS, MARTIUS, *making
a noise with hounds and horns; and*
MARCUS.

Tit. The hunt is up, the morn is bright
    and grey,
The fields are fragrant, and the woods are
    green.
Uncouple here, and let us make a bay,
And wake the Emperor and his lovely
    bride,
And rouse the Prince, and ring a hunter's
    peal,   5
That all the court may echo with the noise.
Sons, let it be your charge, as it is ours,
To attend the Emperor's person carefully.
I have been troubled in my sleep this night,
But dawning day new comfort hath
    inspir'd.   10

*Here a cry of hounds, and wind horns in a
peal. Then enter* SATURNINUS, TAMORA,
BASSIANUS, LAVINIA, CHIRON, DE-
METRIUS, *and their* Attendants.

Many good morrows to your Majesty !
Madam, to you as many and as good !
I promised your Grace a hunter's peal.
    Sat. And you have rung it lustily, my
    lords—   14
Somewhat too early for new-married ladies.
    Bas. Lavinia, how say you ?
    Lav.   I say no ;
I have been broad awake two hours and
    more.
    Sat. Come on then, horse and chariots
    let us have,
And to our sport. [*To Tamora*] Madam,
    now shall ye see
Our Roman hunting.
    Marc.   I have dogs, my lord,   20
Will rouse the proudest panther in the
    chase,
And climb the highest promontory top.
    Tit. And I have horse will follow where
    the game
Makes way, and run like swallows o'er the
    plain.
    Dem. Chiron, we hunt not, we, with horse
    nor hound,   25
But hope to pluck a dainty doe to ground.
                                          [*Exeunt.*

SCENE III. *A lonely part of the forest.*

Enter AARON *alone, with a bag of gold.*

    Aar. He that had wit would think that
    I had none,
To bury so much gold under a tree
And never after to inherit it.
Let him that thinks of me so abjectly
Know that this gold must coin a stratagem,
Which, cunningly effected, will beget   6
A very excellent piece of villainy.
And so repose, sweet gold, for their unrest
                                 [*Hides the gold.*
That have their alms out of the Empress'
    chest.

Enter TAMORA *alone, to the Moor.*

Tam. My lovely Aaron, wherefore look'st
    thou sad   10
When everything doth make a gleeful
    boast ?
The birds chant melody on every bush ;
The snakes lie rolled in the cheerful sun ;
The green leaves quiver with the cooling
    wind
And make a chequer'd shadow on the
    ground ;   15
Under their sweet shade, Aaron, let us sit,
And whilst the babbling echo mocks the
    hounds,
Replying shrilly to the well-tun'd horns,
As if a double hunt were heard at once,
Let us sit down and mark their yellowing
    noise ;   20
And—after conflict such as was suppos'd
The wand'ring prince and Dido once en-
    joyed,
When with a happy storm they were
    surpris'd,
And curtain'd with a counsel-keeping
    cave—
We may, each wreathed in the other's
    arms,   25
Our pastimes done, possess a golden
    slumber,
Whiles hounds and horns and sweet
    melodious birds
Be unto us as is a nurse's song
Of lullaby to bring her babe asleep.
    Aar. Madam, though Venus govern your
    desires,   30
Saturn is dominator over mine.
What signifies my deadly-standing eye,
My silence and my cloudy melancholy,
My fleece of woolly hair that now uncurls
Even as an adder when she doth unroll   35
To do some fatal execution ?
No, madam, these are no venereal signs.
Vengeance is in my heart, death in my
    hand,
Blood and revenge are hammering in my
    head.
Hark, Tamora, the empress of my soul,   40
Which never hopes more heaven than rests
    in thee—
This is the day of doom for Bassianus ;
His Philomel must lose her tongue to-day,
Thy sons make pillage of her chastity,
And wash their hands in Bassianus' blood.
Seest thou this letter ? Take it up, I pray
    thee,   46
And give the King this fatal-plotted scroll.
Now question me no more ; we are
    espied.
Here comes a parcel of our hopeful booty,
Which dreads not yet their lives' destruc-
    tion.   50

Enter BASSIANUS *and* LAVINIA.

    Tam. Ah, my sweet Moor, sweeter to me
    than life !

Aar. No more, great Empress: Bassianus
 comes.
Be cross with him ; and I'll go fetch thy
 sons
To back thy quarrels, whatsoe'er they be.
         [*Exit.*
 Bas. Who have we here ? Rome's royal
  Emperess,   55
Unfurnish'd of her well-beseeming troop ?
Or is it Dian, habited like her,
Who hath abandoned her holy groves
To see the general hunting in this forest ?
 Tam. Saucy controller of my private
  steps !   60
Had I the pow'r that some say Dian had,
Thy temples should be planted presently
With horns, as was Actæon's ; and the
 hounds
Should drive upon thy new-transformed
 limbs,
Unmannerly intruder as thou art ! 65
 Lav. Under your patience, gentle
  Emperess,
'Tis thought you have a goodly gift in
 horning,
And to be doubted that your Moor and you
Are singled forth to try thy experiments.
Jove shield your husband from his hounds
 to-day !   70
'Tis pity they should take him for a stag.
 Bas. Believe me, Queen, your swarth
  Cimmerian
Doth make your honour of his body's hue,
Spotted, detested, and abominable.
Why are you sequest'red from all your
 train,   75
Dismounted from your snow-white goodly
 steed,
And wand'red hither to an obscure plot,
Accompanied but with a barbarous Moor,
If foul desire had not conducted you ?
 Lav. And, being intercepted in your
  sport,   80
Great reason that my noble lord be rated
For sauciness. I pray you let us hence,
And let her joy her raven-coloured love ;
This valley fits the purpose passing well.
 Bas. The King my brother shall have
  notice of this.   85
 Lav. Ay, for these slips have made him
  noted long.
Good king, to be so mightily abused !
 Tam. Why, I have patience to endure all
  this.

   Enter Chiron *and* Demetrius.

 Dem. How now, dear sovereign, and our
  gracious mother !
Why doth your Highness look so pale and
 wan ?   90
 Tam. Have I not reason, think you, to
  look pale ?
These two have 'ticed me hither to this
 place.

A barren detested vale you see it is :
The trees, though summer, yet forlorn and
 lean,   94
Overcome with moss and baleful mistletoe :
Here never shines the sun ; here nothing
 breeds,
Unless the nightly owl or fatal raven.
And when they show'd me this abhorred pit,
They told me, here, at dead time of the
 night,
A thousand fiends, a thousand hissing
 snakes,   100
Ten thousand swelling toads, as many
 urchins,
Would make such fearful and confused cries
As any mortal body hearing it
Should straight fall mad or else die
 suddenly.
No sooner had they told this hellish tale 105
But straight they told me they would bind
 me here
Unto the body of a dismal yew,
And leave me to this miserable death.
And then they call'd me foul adulteress,
Lascivious Goth, and all the bitterest terms
That ever ear did hear to such effect ; 111
And had you not by wondrous fortune
 come,
This vengeance on me had they executed.
Revenge it, as you love your mother's
 life,   114
Or be ye not henceforth call'd my children.
 Dem. This is a witness that I am thy son.
        [*Stabs Bassianus.*
 Chi. And this for me, struck home to
  show my strength. [*Also stabs.*
 Lav. Ay, come, Semiramis—nay, bar-
  barous Tamora,
For no name fits thy nature but thy own !
 Tam. Give me the poniard ; you shall
  know, my boys,   120
Your mother's hand shall right your
 mother's wrong.
 Dem. Stay, madam, here is more belongs
  to her ;
First thrash the corn, then after burn the
 straw.
This minion stood upon her chastity,
Upon her nuptial vow, her loyalty, 125
And with that painted hope braves your
 mightiness ;
And shall she carry this unto her grave ?
 Chi. An if she do, I would I were an
  eunuch.
Drag hence her husband to some secret
 hole,   129
And make his dead trunk pillow to our lust.
 Tam. But when ye have the honey we
  desire,
Let not this wasp outlive, us both to sting.
 Chi. I warrant you, madam, we will
  make that sure.
Come, mistress, now perforce we will enjoy
That nice-preserved honesty of yours. 135

879

Lav. O Tamora ! thou bearest a woman's
    face—

Tam. I will not hear her speak ; away
    with her !

Lav. Sweet lords, entreat her hear me but
    a word.

Dem. Listen, fair madam : let it be your
    glory   139
To see her tears ; but be your heart to them
As unrelenting flint to drops of rain.

Lav. When did the tiger's young ones
    teach the dam ?
O, do not learn her wrath—she taught it
    thee ;
The milk thou suck'dst from her did turn
    to marble,   144
Even at thy teat thou hadst thy tyranny.
Yet every mother breeds not sons alike :
[*To Chiron*] Do thou entreat her show a
    woman's pity.

Chi. What, wouldst thou have me prove
    myself a bastard ?

Lav. 'Tis true, the raven doth not hatch
    a lark.   149
Yet have I heard—O, could I find it now !—
The lion, mov'd with pity, did endure
To have his princely paws par'd all away.
Some say that ravens foster forlorn children,
The whilst their own birds famish in their
    nests ;   154
O, be to me, though thy hard heart say no,
Nothing so kind, but something pitiful !

Tam. I know not what it means ; away
    with her !

Lav. O, let me teach thee ! For my
    father's sake,
That gave thee life when well he might
    have slain thee,
Be not obdurate, open thy deaf ears.   160

Tam. Hadst thou in person ne'er offended
    me,
Even for his sake am I pitiless.
Remember, boys, I pour'd forth tears in
    vain
To save your brother from the sacrifice ;
But fierce Andronicus would not relent.   165
Therefore away with her, and use her as
    you will ;
The worse to her the better lov'd of me.

Lav. O Tamora, be call'd a gentle queen,
And with thine own hands kill me in this
    place !   169
For 'tis not life that I have begg'd so long ;
Poor I was slain when Bassianus died.

Tam. What beg'st thou, then ? Fond
    woman, let me go.

Lav. 'Tis present death I beg ; and one
    thing more,
That womanhood denies my tongue to tell :
O, keep me from their worse than killing
    lust,   175
And tumble me into some loathsome pit,
Where never man's eye may behold my
    body ;

Do this, and be a charitable murderer.

Tam. So should I rob my sweet sons of
    their fee ;
No, let them satisfy their lust on thee.   180

Dem. Away ! for thou hast stay'd us here
    too long.

Lav. No grace ? no womanhood ? Ah,
    beastly creature,
The blot and enemy to our general name !
Confusion fall—

Chi. Nay, then I'll stop your mouth.
    Bring thou her husband.   185
This is the hole where Aaron bid us hide
    him.

[*Demetrius throws the body of Bassianus
into the pit ; then exeunt Demetrius and
Chiron, dragging off Lavinia.*

Tam. Farewell, my sons ; see that you
    make her sure.
Ne'er let my heart know merry cheer indeed
Till all the Andronici be made away.   189
Now will I hence to seek my lovely Moor,
And let my spleenful sons this trull
    deflower.   [*Exit.*

Re-enter AARON, *with two of Titus' sons,*
    QUINTUS *and* MARTIUS.

Aar. Come on, my lords, the better foot
    before ;
Straight will I bring you to the loathsome
    pit
Where I espied the panther fast asleep.

Quin. My sight is very dull, whate'er it
    bodes.   195

Mart. And mine, I promise you ; were it
    not for shame,
Well could I leave our sport to sleep awhile.
                      [*Falls into the pit.*

Quin. What, art thou fallen ? What
    subtle hole is this,
Whose mouth is covered with rude-growing
    briers,
Upon whose leaves are drops of new-shed
    blood   200
As fresh as morning dew distill'd on
    flowers ?
A very fatal place it seems to me.
Speak, brother, hast thou hurt thee with
    the fall ?

Mart. O brother, with the dismal'st
    object hurt
That ever eye with sight made heart
    lament !   205

Aar. [*Aside*] Now will I fetch the King
    to find them here,
That he thereby may have a likely guess
How these were they that made away his
    brother.   [*Exit.*

Mart. Why dost not comfort me, and
    help me out
From this unhallow'd and blood-stained
    hole ?   210

Quin. I am surprised with an uncouth
    fear ;

A chilling sweat o'er-runs my trembling
  joints ;
My heart suspects more than mine eye can
  see.
  Mart. To prove thou hast a true divining
    heart,   214
Aaron and thou look down into this den,
And see a fearful sight of blood and death.
  Quin. Aaron is gone, and my compassion-
    ate heart
Will not permit mine eyes once to behold
The thing whereat it trembles by surmise ;
O, tell me who it is, for ne'er till now   220
Was I a child to fear I know not what.
  Mart. Lord Bassianus lies beray'd in
    blood,
All on a heap, like to a slaughtered lamb,
In this detested, dark, blood-drinking pit.
  Quin. If it be dark, how dost thou know
    'tis he ?   225
  Mart. Upon his bloody finger he doth wear
A precious ring that lightens all this hole,
Which, like a taper in some monument,
Doth shine upon the dead man's earthy
  cheeks,   229
And shows the ragged entrails of this pit ;
So pale did shine the moon on Pyramus
When he by night lay bath'd in maiden
  blood.
O brother, help me with thy fainting
  hand—
If fear hath made thee faint, as me it
  hath—
Out of this fell devouring receptacle,   235
As hateful as Cocytus' misty mouth.
  Quin. Reach me thy hand, that I may
    help thee out,
Or, wanting strength to do thee so much
  good,
I may be pluck'd into the swallowing womb
Of this deep pit, poor Bassianus' grave.   240
I have no strength to pluck thee to the
  brink.
  Mart. Nor I no strength to climb without
    thy help.
  Quin. Thy hand once more ; I will not
    loose again,
Till thou art here aloft, or I below.
Thou canst not come to me—I come to
  thee.   [*Falls in.*

Enter the EMPEROR *and* ¸AARON *the Moor.*

  Sat. Along with me ! I'll see what hole
    is here,   246
And what he is that now is leapt into it.
Say, who art thou that lately didst descend
Into this gaping hollow of the earth ?
  Mart. The unhappy sons of old An-
    dronicus,   250
Brought hither in a most unlucky hour,
To find thy brother Bassianus dead.
  Sat. My brother dead ! I know thou dost
    but jest :
He and his lady both are at the lodge   254

Upon the north side of this pleasant chase ;
'Tis not an hour since I left them there.
  Mart. We know not where you left them
    all alive ;
But, out alas ! here have we found him
  dead.

Re-enter TAMORA, *with* Attendants ; TITUS
  ANDRONICUS *and* LUCIUS.

  Tam. Where is my lord the King ?
  Sat. Here, Tamora ; though griev'd with
    killing grief.   260
  Tam. Where is thy brother Bassianus ?
  Sat. Now to the bottom dost thou search
    my wound ;
Poor Bassianus here lies murdered.
  Tam. Then all too late I bring this fatal
    writ,
The complot of this timeless tragedy ;   265
And wonder greatly that man's face can
  fold
In pleasing smiles such murderous tyranny.
                  [*She giveth Saturnine a letter.*
  Sat. [*Reads*] ' An if we miss to meet him
    handsomely,
Sweet huntsman—Bassianus 'tis we mean—
Do thou so much as dig the grave for him.
Thou know'st our meaning. Look for thy
  reward   271
Among the nettles at the elder-tree
Which overshades the mouth of that same
  pit
Where we decreed to bury Bassianus.
Do this, and purchase us thy lasting
  friends.'   275
O Tamora ! was ever heard the like ?
This is the pit and this the elder-tree.
Look, sirs, if you can find the huntsman
  out
That should have murdered Bassianus here.
  Aar. My gracious lord, here is the bag of
    gold.   280
  Sat. [*To Titus*] Two of thy whelps, fell
    curs of bloody kind,
Have here bereft my brother of his life.
Sirs, drag them from the pit unto the prison;
There let them bide until we have devis'd
Some never-heard-of torturing pain for
  them.   285
  Tam. What, are they in this pit ? O
    wondrous thing !
How easily murder is discovered !
  Tit. High Emperor, upon my feeble knee
I beg this boon, with tears not lightly shed,
That this fell fault of my accursed sons—
Accursed if the fault be prov'd in them—
  Sat. If it be prov'd ! You see it is
    apparent.
Who found this letter ? Tamora, was it
  you ?
  Tam. Andronicus himself did take it up.
  Tit. I did, my lord, yet let me be their
    bail ;   295
For, by my fathers' reverend tomb, I vow

They shall be ready at your Highness'
 will
To answer their suspicion with their lives.
 Sat. Thou shalt not bail them ; see thou
  follow me.
Some bring the murdered body, some the
 murderers ;   300
Let them not speak a word—the guilt is
 plain ;
For, by my soul, were there worse end than
 death,
That end upon them should be executed.
 Tam. Andronicus, I will entreat the King.
Fear not thy sons ; they shall do well
 enough.   305
 Tit. Come, Lucius, come ; stay not to
  talk with them.   [*Exeunt.*

SCENE IV. *Another part of the forest.*

Enter the Empress' *sons,* DEMETRIUS *and*
CHIRON, *with* LAVINIA, *her hands cut off,
and her tongue cut out, and ravish'd.*

 Dem. So, now go tell, an if thy tongue can
  speak,
Who 'twas that cut thy tongue and ravish'd
 thee.
 Chi. Write down thy mind, bewray thy
  meaning so,
An if thy stumps will let thee play the
 scribe.
 Dem. See how with signs and tokens she
  can scrowl.   5
 Chi. Go home, call for sweet water, wash
  thy hands.
 Dem. She hath no tongue to call, nor
  hands to wash ;
And so let's leave her to her silent walks.
 Chi. An 'twere my cause, I should go hang
  myself.
 Dem. If thou hadst hands to help thee
  knit the cord.   10
    [*Exeunt Demetrius and Chiron.*

Wind horns. Enter MARCUS, *from hunting.*

 Marc. Who is this ?—my niece, that flies
  away so fast ?
Cousin, a word : where is your husband ?
If I do dream, would all my wealth would
 wake me !
If I do wake, some planet strike me down,
That I may slumber an eternal sleep ! 15
Speak, gentle niece. What stern ungentle
 hands
Hath lopp'd, and hew'd, and made thy
 body bare
Of her two branches—those sweet orna-
 ments
Whose circling shadows kings have sought
 to sleep in,
And might not gain so great a happiness 20
As half thy love ? Why dost not speak to
 me ?
Alas, a crimson river of warm blood,

Like to a bubbling fountain stirr'd with
 wind,
Doth rise and fall between thy rosed lips,
Coming and going with thy honey breath.
But sure some Tereus hath deflowered thee,
And, lest thou shouldst detect him, cut thy
 tongue.   27
Ah, now thou turn'st away thy face for
 shame !
And notwithstanding all this loss of blood—
As from a conduit with three issuing
 spouts—   30
Yet do thy cheeks look red as Titan's face
Blushing to be encount'red with a cloud.
Shall I speak for thee ? Shall I say 'tis so ?
O, that I knew thy heart, and knew the
 beast,   34
That I might rail at him to ease my mind !
Sorrow concealed, like an oven stopp'd,
Doth burn the heart to cinders where it is.
Fair Philomel, why she but lost her
 tongue,
And in a tedious sampler sew'd her mind ;
But, lovely niece, that mean is cut from
 thee.   40
A craftier Tereus, cousin, hast thou met,
And he hath cut those pretty fingers off
That could have better sew'd than Philo-
 mel.
O, had the monster seen those lily hands
Tremble like aspen leaves upon a lute 45
And make the silken strings delight to kiss
 them,
He would not then have touch'd them for
 his life !
Or had he heard the heavenly harmony
Which that sweet tongue hath made,
He would have dropp'd his knife, and fell
 asleep,   50
As Cerberus at the Thracian poet's feet.
Come, let us go, and make thy father
 blind,
For such a sight will blind a father's eye ;
One hour's storm will drown the fragrant
 meads,
What will whole months of tears thy
 father's eyes ?   55
Do not draw back, for we will mourn with
 thee ;
O, could our mourning ease thy misery !
        [*Exeunt.*

ACT THREE

SCENE I. *Rome. A street.*

Enter the Judges, Tribunes, *and* Senators,
with Titus' *two sons* MARTIUS *and*
QUINTUS *bound, passing on the stage to
the place of execution, and* TITUS *going
before, pleading.*

 Tit. Hear me, grave fathers ; noble
  Tribunes, stay !
For pity of mine age, whose youth was
 spent

In dangerous wars whilst you securely
    slept ;
For all my blood in Rome's great quarrel
    shed,
For all the frosty nights that I have
    watch'd,   5
And for these bitter tears, which now you
    see
Filling the aged wrinkles in my cheeks,
Be pitiful to my condemned sons,
Whose souls are not corrupted as 'tis
    thought.
For two and twenty sons I never wept, 10
Because they died in honour's lofty bed.
    [*Andronicus lieth down, and the Judges
    pass by him with the prisoners, and
    exeunt.*
For these, Tribunes, in the dust I write
My heart's deep languor and my soul's sad
    tears.
Let my tears stanch the earth's dry
    appetite ;
My sons' sweet blood will make it shame
    and blush.   15
O earth, I will befriend thee more with rain
That shall distil from these two ancient
    urns,
Than youthful April shall with all his
    show'rs.
In summer's drought I'll drop upon thee
    still ;
In winter with warm tears I'll melt the
    snow   20
And keep eternal spring-time on thy face,
So thou refuse to drink my dear sons'
    blood.

Enter LUCIUS *with his weapon drawn.*

O reverend Tribunes ! O gentle aged men !
Unbind my sons, reverse the doom of
    death,
And let me say, that never wept before, 25
My tears are now prevailing orators.
    Luc. O noble father, you lament in vain ;
The Tribunes hear you not, no man is by,
And you recount your sorrows to a stone.
    Tit. Ah, Lucius, for thy brothers let me
    plead !   30
Grave Tribunes, once more I entreat of you.
    Luc. My gracious lord, no tribune hears
    you speak.
    Tit. Why, 'tis no matter, man : if they
    did hear,
They would not mark me ; if they did
    mark,
They would not pity me ; yet plead I must,
And bootless unto them.   36
Therefore I tell my sorrows to the stones ;
Who though they cannot answer my
    distress,
Yet in some sort they are better than the
    Tribunes,
For that they will not intercept my tale. 40
When I do weep, they humbly at my feet

Receive my tears, and seem to weep with
    me ;
And were they but attired in grave weeds,
Rome could afford no tribunes like to these.
A stone is soft as wax : tribunes more hard
    than stones.   45
A stone is silent and offendeth not,
And tribunes with their tongues doom men
    to death.   [*Rises.*
But wherefore stand'st thou with thy
    weapon drawn ?
    Luc. To rescue my two brothers from
    their death ;
For which attempt the judges have pro-
    nounc'd   50
My everlasting doom of banishment.
    Tit. O happy man ! they have befriended
    thee.
Why, foolish Lucius, dost thou not perceive
That Rome is but a wilderness of tigers ?
Tigers must prey, and Rome affords no
    prey   55
But me and mine ; how happy art thou
    then
From these devourers to be banished !
But who comes with our brother Marcus
    here ?

Enter MARCUS *with* LAVINIA.

    Marc. Titus, prepare thy aged eyes to
    weep,
Or if not so, thy noble heart to break. 60
I bring consuming sorrow to thine age.
    Tit. Will it consume me ? Let me see it
    then.
    Marc. This was thy daughter.
    Tit. Why, Marcus, so she is.
    Luc. Ay me ! this object kills me.
    Tit. Faint-hearted boy, arise, and look
    upon her.   65
Speak, Lavinia, what accursed hand
Hath made thee handless in thy father's
    sight ?
What fool hath added water to the sea,
Or brought a fagot to bright-burning Troy ?
My grief was at the height before thou
    cam'st,   70
And now like Nilus it disdaineth bounds.
Give me a sword, I'll chop off my hands
    too,
For they have fought for Rome, and all in
    vain ;
And they have nurs'd this woe in feeding
    life ;   74
In bootless prayer have they been held up,
And they have serv'd me to effectless use.
Now all the service I require of them
Is that the one will help to cut the other.
'Tis well, Lavinia, that thou hast no hands ;
For hands to do Rome service is but vain.
    Luc. Speak, gentle sister, who hath
    martyr'd thee ?   81
    Marc. O, that delightful engine of her
    thoughts

883

That blabb'd them with such pleasing
    eloquence
Is torn from forth that pretty hollow cage,
Where like a sweet melodious bird it sung
Sweet varied notes, enchanting every ear !
    Luc. O, say thou for her, who hath done
      this deed ?
    Marc. O, thus I found her straying in the
      park,
Seeking to hide herself as doth the deer 89
That hath receiv'd some unrecuring wound.
    Tit. It was my dear, and he that wounded
      her
Hath hurt me more than had he kill'd me
    dead ;
For now I stand as one upon a rock,
Environ'd with a wilderness of sea,
Who marks the waxing tide grow wave by
    wave,   95
Expecting ever when some envious surge
Will in his brinish bowels swallow him.
This way to death my wretched sons are
    gone ;
Here stands my other son, a banish'd man,
And here my brother, weeping at my woes.
But that which gives my soul the greatest
    spurn   101
Is dear Lavinia, dearer than my soul.
Had I but seen thy picture in this plight,
It would have madded me ; what shall I do
Now I behold thy lively body so ?   105
Thou hast no hands to wipe away thy tears,
Nor tongue to tell me who hath martyr'd
    thee ;
Thy husband he is dead, and for his death
Thy brothers are condemn'd, and dead by
    this.
Look, Marcus ! Ah, son Lucius, look on
    her !   110
When I did name her brothers, then fresh
    tears
Stood on her cheeks, as doth the honey dew
Upon a gath'red lily almost withered.
    Marc. Perchance she weeps because they
      kill'd her husband ;
Perchance because she knows them inno-
    cent.   115
    Tit. If they did kill thy husband, then
      be joyful,
Because the law hath ta'en revenge on
    them.
No, no, they would not do so foul a deed ;
Witness the sorrow that their sister makes.
Gentle Lavinia, let me kiss thy lips,   120
Or make some sign how I may do thee ease.
Shall thy good uncle and thy brother
    Lucius
And thou and I sit round about some
    fountain,
Looking all downwards to behold our
    cheeks
How they are stain'd, like meadows yet not
    dry   125
With miry slime left on them by a flood ?

And in the fountain shall we gaze so long,
Till the fresh taste be taken from that
    clearness,
And made a brine-pit with our bitter tears ?
Or shall we cut away our hands like thine ?
Or shall we bite our tongues, and in dumb
    shows   131
Pass the remainder of our hateful days ?
What shall we do ? Let us that have our
    tongues
Plot some device of further misery
To make us wonder'd at in time to come.
    Luc. Sweet father, cease your tears ; for
      at your grief   136
See how my wretched sister sobs and weeps.
    Marc. Patience, dear niece. Good Titus,
      dry thine eyes.
    Tit. Ah, Marcus, Marcus ! Brother, well
      I wot
Thy napkin cannot drink a tear of mine, 140
For thou, poor man, hast drown'd it with
    thine own.
    Luc. Ah, my Lavinia, I will wipe thy
      cheeks.
    Tit. Mark, Marcus, mark ! I understand
      her signs.
Had she a tongue to speak, now would she
    say   144
That to her brother which I said to thee :
His napkin, with his true tears all bewet,
Can do no service on her sorrowful cheeks.
O, what a sympathy of woe is this—
As far from help as Limbo is from bliss !

    Enter AARON *the Moor.*

    Aar. Titus Andronicus, my lord the
      Emperor   150
Sends thee this word, that, if thou love thy
    sons,
Let Marcus, Lucius, or thyself, old Titus,
Or any one of you, chop off your hand
And send it to the King : he for the same
Will send thee hither both thy sons alive,
And that shall be the ransom for their fault.
    Tit. O gracious Emperor ! O gentle
      Aaron !
Did ever raven sing so like a lark   158
That gives sweet tidings of the sun's uprise?
With all my heart I'll send the Emperor
    my hand.
Good Aaron, wilt thou help to chop it off ?
    Luc. Stay, father ! for that noble hand of
      thine,
That hath thrown down so many enemies,
Shall not be sent. My hand will serve the
    turn,   165
My youth can better spare my blood than
    you,
And therefore mine shall save my brothers'
    lives.
    Marc. Which of your hands hath not
      defended Rome
And rear'd aloft the bloody battle-axe,
Writing destruction on the enemy's castle ?

O, none of both but are of high desert! 171
My hand hath been but idle; let it serve
To ransom my two nephews from their
    death;
Then have I kept it to a worthy end.
    Aar. Nay, come, agree whose hand shall
        go along,   175
For fear they die before their pardon come.
    Marc. My hand shall go.
    Luc.   By heaven, it shall not go!
    Tit. Sirs, strive no more; such with'red
        herbs as these
Are meet for plucking up, and therefore
    mine.
    Luc. Sweet father, if I shall be thought
        thy son,   180
Let me redeem my brothers both from
    death.
    Marc. And for our father's sake and
        mother's care,
Now let me show a brother's love to thee.
    Tit. Agree between you; I will spare my
        hand.
    Luc. Then I'll go fetch an axe.   185
    Marc. But I will use the axe.
            [*Exeunt Lucius and Marcus.*
    Tit. Come hither, Aaron, I'll deceive
        them both;
Lend me thy hand, and I will give thee
    mine.
    Aar. [*Aside*] If that be call'd deceit, I will
        be honest,
And never whilst I live deceive men so; 190
But I'll deceive you in another sort,
And that you'll say ere half an hour pass.
            [*He cuts off Titus' hand.*

    Re-enter LUCIUS *and* MARCUS.

    Tit. Now stay your strife. What shall be
        is dispatch'd.
Good Aaron, give his Majesty my hand;
Tell him it was a hand that warded him 195
From thousand dangers; bid him bury it.
More hath it merited—that let it have.
As for my sons, say I account of them
As jewels purchas'd at an easy price;
And yet dear too, because I bought mine
    own.   200
    Aar. I go, Andronicus; and for thy hand
Look by and by to have thy sons with thee.
    [*Aside*] Their heads I mean. O, how this
        villainy
Doth fat me with the very thoughts of
    it!
Let fools do good, and fair men call for
    grace: 205
Aaron will have his soul black like his face.
            [*Exit.*
    Tit. O, here I lift this one hand up to
        heaven,
And bow this feeble ruin to the earth;
If any power pities wretched tears,
To that I call! [*To Lavinia*] What, would'st
    thou kneel with me?   210

Do, then, dear heart; for heaven shall hear
    our prayers,
Or with our sighs we'll breathe the welkin
    dim
And stain the sun with fog, as sometime
    clouds
When they do hug him in their melting
    bosoms.   214
    Marc. O brother, speak with possibility,
And do not break into these deep extremes.
    Tit. Is not my sorrow deep, having no
        bottom?
Then be my passions bottomless with them.
    Marc. But yet let reason govern thy
        lament.
    Tit. If there were reason for these
        miseries,   220
Then into limits could I bind my woes.
When heaven doth weep, doth not the
    earth o'erflow?
If the winds rage, doth not the sea wax
    mad,
Threat'ning the welkin with his big-swol'n
    face?   224
And wilt thou have a reason for this coil?
I am the sea; hark how her sighs do
    blow.
She is the weeping welkin, I the earth;
Then must my sea be moved with her sighs;
Then must my earth with her continual
    tears   229
Become a deluge, overflow'd and drown'd;
For why my bowels cannot hide her woes,
But like a drunkard must I vomit them.
Then give me leave; for losers will have
    leave
To ease their stomachs with their bitter
    tongues.

Enter a MESSENGER, *with two heads and a
    hand.*

    Mess. Worthy Andronicus, ill art thou
        repaid   235
For that good hand thou sent'st the
    Emperor.
Here are the heads of thy two noble sons;
And here's thy hand, in scorn to thee sent
    back—
Thy grief their sports, thy resolution
    mock'd,
That woe is me to think upon thy woes, 240
More than remembrance of my father's
    death.   [*Exit.*
    Marc. Now let hot Ætna cool in Sicily,
And be my heart an ever-burning hell!
These miseries are more than may be borne.
To weep with them that weep doth ease
    some deal,   245
But sorrow flouted at is double death.
    Luc. Ah, that this sight should make so
        deep a wound,
And yet detested life not shrink thereat!
That ever death should let life bear his
    name,

885

Where life hath no more interest but to
 breathe ! [*Lavinia kisses Titus.*
 Marc. Alas, poor heart, that kiss is
 comfortless   251
As frozen water to a starved snake.
 Tit. When will this fearful slumber have
 an end ?
 Marc. Now farewell, flatt'ry; die,
 Andronicus.
Thou dost not slumber : see thy two sons'
 heads,   255
Thy warlike hand, thy mangled daughter
 here ;
Thy other banish'd son with this dear sight
Struck pale and bloodless; and thy
 brother, I,
Even like a stony image, cold and numb.
Ah ! now no more will I control thy griefs.
Rent off thy silver hair, thy other hand
Gnawing with thy teeth ; and be this
 dismal sight
The closing up of our most wretched eyes.
Now is a time to storm ; why art thou still ?
 Tit. Ha, ha, ha !   265
 Marc. Why dost thou laugh ? It fits not
 with this hour.
 Tit. Why, I have not another tear to
 shed ;
Besides, this sorrow is an enemy,
And would usurp upon my wat'ry eyes
And make them blind with tributary tears.
Then which way shall I find Revenge's
 cave ?   271
For these two heads do seem to speak to me,
And threat me I shall never come to bliss
Till all these mischiefs be return'd again
Even in their throats that have committed
 them.   275
Come, let me see what task I have to do.
You heavy people, circle me about,
That I may turn me to each one of you
And swear unto my soul to right your
 wrongs.
The vow is made. Come, brother, take a
 head,   280
And in this hand the other will I bear.
And, Lavinia, thou shalt be employ'd in
 this ;
Bear thou my hand, sweet wench, between
 thy teeth.
As for thee, boy, go, get thee from my
 sight ;   284
Thou art an exile, and thou must not stay.
Hie to the Goths and raise an army there ;
And if ye love me, as I think you do,
Let's kiss and part, for we have much to do.
      [*Exeunt all but Lucius.*
 Luc. Farewell, Andronicus, my noble
 father,
The woefull'st man that ever liv'd in
 Rome.   290
Farewell, proud Rome ; till Lucius come
 again,
He leaves his pledges dearer than his life.

Farewell, Lavinia, my noble sister ;
O, would thou wert as thou tofore hast
 been !
But now nor Lucius nor Lavinia lives 295
But in oblivion and hateful griefs.
If Lucius live, he will requite your wrongs
And make proud Saturnine and his emperess
Beg at the gates like Tarquin and his queen.
Now will I to the Goths, and raise a pow'r
To be reveng'd on Rome and Saturnine.
         [*Exit.*

  Scene II. *Rome. Titus' house.*

A banquet. Enter Titus, Marcus,
Lavinia, *and the boy* Young Lucius.

 Tit. So so, now sit ; and look you eat
 no more
Than will preserve just so much strength
 in us
As will revenge these bitter woes of ours.
Marcus, unknit that sorrow-wreathen knot ;
Thy niece and I, poor creatures, want our
 hands,   5
And cannot passionate our tenfold grief
With folded arms. This poor right hand of
 mine
Is left to tyrannize upon my breast ;
Who, when my heart, all mad with misery,
Beats in this hollow prison of my flesh, 10
Then thus I thump it down.
[*To Lavinia*] Thou map of woe, that thus
 dost talk in signs !
When thy poor heart beats with out-
 rageous beating,
Thou canst not strike it thus to make it
 still.
Wound it with sighing, girl, kill it with
 groans ;   15
Or get some little knife between thy teeth
And just against thy heart make thou a
 hole,
That all the tears that thy poor eyes let fall
May run into that sink and, soaking in,
Drown the lamenting fool in sea-salt tears.
 Marc. Fie, brother, fie ! Teach her not
 thus to lay   21
Such violent hands upon her tender life.
 Tit. How now ! Has sorrow made thee
 dote already ?
Why, Marcus, no man should be mad but I.
What violent hands can she lay on her life ?
Ah, wherefore dost thou urge the name of
 hands ?   26
To bid Æneas tell the tale twice o'er
How Troy was burnt and he made miser-
 able ?
O, handle not the theme, to talk of hands,
Lest we remember still that we have none.
Fie, fie, how franticly I square my talk,
As if we should forget we had no hands,
If Marcus did not name the word of hands !
Come, let's fall to ; and, gentle girl, eat
 this :

Here is no drink. Hark, Marcus, what she
   says—   35
I can interpret all her martyr'd signs ;
She says she drinks no other drink but
   tears,
Brew'd with her sorrow, mesh'd upon her
   cheeks.
Speechless complainer, I will learn thy
   thought ;
In thy dumb action will I be as perfect 40
As begging hermits in their holy prayers.
Thou shalt not sigh, nor hold thy stumps
   to heaven,
Nor wink, nor nod, nor kneel, nor make a
   sign,
But I of these will wrest an alphabet,
And by still practice learn to know thy
   meaning.   45
  Boy. Good grandsire, leave these bitter
   deep laments ;
Make my aunt merry with some pleasing
   tale.
  Marc. Alas, the tender boy, in passion
   mov'd,
Doth weep to see his grandsire's heaviness.
  Tit. Peace, tender sapling ; thou art
   made of tears,   50
And tears will quickly melt thy life away.
   [*Marcus strikes the dish with a knife.*
What dost thou strike at, Marcus, with thy
   knife ?
  Marc. At that that I have kill'd, my
   lord—a fly.
  Tit. Out on thee, murderer, thou kill'st
   my heart !   54
Mine eyes are cloy'd with view of tyranny ;
A deed of death done on the innocent
Becomes not Titus' brother. Get thee
   gone;
I see thou art not for my company.
  Marc. Alas, my lord, I have but kill'd a
   fly.
  Tit. ' But ' ! How if that fly had a father
   and mother ?   60
How would he hang his slender gilded wings
And buzz lamenting doings in the air !
Poor harmless fly,
That with his pretty buzzing melody
Came here to make us merry ! And thou
   hast kill'd him.   65
  Marc. Pardon me, sir ; it was a black
   ill-favour'd fly,
Like to the Empress' Moor ; therefore I
   kill'd him.
  Tit. O, O, O !
Then pardon me for reprehending thee,
For thou hast done a charitable deed.   70
Give me thy knife, I will insult on him,
Flattering myself as if it were the Moor
Come hither purposely to poison me.
There's for thyself, and that's for Tamora.
Ah, sirrah !   75
Yet, I think, we are not brought so low
But that between us we can kill a fly

That comes in likeness of a coal-black Moor.
  Marc. Alas, poor man ! grief has so
   wrought on him,   79
He takes false shadows for true substances.
  Tit. Come, take away. Lavinia, go with
   me ;
I'll to thy closet, and go read with thee
Sad stories chanced in the times of old.
Come, boy, and go with me ; thy sight is
   young,   84
And thou shalt read when mine begin to
   dazzle.   [*Exeunt.*

ACT FOUR

    Scene I. *Rome. Titus' garden.*

Enter Young Lucius *and* Lavinia *running after him, and the boy flies from
her with his books under his arm. Enter*
Titus *and* Marcus.

  Boy. Help, grandsire, help ! my aunt
   Lavinia
Follows me everywhere, I know not why.
Good uncle Marcus, see how swift she
   comes !
Alas, sweet aunt, I know not what you
   mean.
  Marc. Stand by me, Lucius ; do not fear
   thine aunt.
  Tit. She loves thee, boy, too well to do
   thee harm.   6
  Boy. Ay, when my father was in Rome
   she did.
  Marc. What means my niece Lavinia by
   these signs ?
  Tit. Fear her not, Lucius ; somewhat
   doth she mean.
See, Lucius, see how much she makes of
   thee.   10
Somewhither would she have thee go with
   her.
Ah, boy, Cornelia never with more care
Read to her sons than she hath read to thee
Sweet poetry and Tully's Orator.
  Marc. Canst thou not guess wherefore she
   plies thee thus ?   15
  Boy. My lord, I know not, I, nor can I
   guess,
Unless some fit or frenzy do possess her ;
For I have heard my grandsire say full oft
Extremity of griefs would make men mad ;
And I have read that Hecuba of Troy   20
Ran mad for sorrow. That made me to
   fear;
Although, my lord, I know my noble aunt
Loves me as dear as e'er my mother did,
And would not, but in fury, fright my
   youth ;
Which made me down to throw my books,
   and fly—   25
Causeless, perhaps. But pardon me, sweet
   aunt ;
And, madam, if my uncle Marcus go,

I will most willingly attend your ladyship.
  Marc. Lucius, I will. [*Lavinia turns
      over with her stumps the books
      which Lucius has let fall.*
  Tit. How now, Lavinia! Marcus, what
    means this ?   30
Some book there is that she desires to see.
Which is it, girl, of these ?—Open them,
boy.—
But thou art deeper read and better skill'd ;
Come and take choice of all my library,   34
And so beguile thy sorrow, till the heavens
Reveal the damn'd contriver of this deed.
Why lifts she up her arms in sequence thus ?
  Marc. I think she means that there were
    more than one
Confederate in the fact ; ay, more there
    was,
Or else to heaven she heaves them for
    revenge.   40
  Tit. Lucius, what book is that she tosseth
    so ?
  Boy. Grandsire, 'tis Ovid's Metamorpho-
    ses ;
My mother gave it me.
  Marc.   For love of her that's gone,
Perhaps she cull'd it from among the rest.
  Tit. Soft ! So busily she turns the leaves !
    Help her.   46
What would she find ? Lavinia, shall I
    read ?
This is the tragic tale of Philomel
And treats of Tereus' treason and his rape ;
And rape, I fear, was root of thy annoy.   50
  Marc. See, brother, see! Note how she
    quotes the leaves.
  Tit. Lavinia, wert thou thus surpris'd,
    sweet girl,
Ravish'd and wrong'd as Philomela was,
Forc'd in the ruthless, vast, and gloomy
    woods ?
See, see !   55
Ay, such a place there is where we did
    hunt—
O, had we never, never hunted there !—
Pattern'd by that the poet here describes,
By nature made for murders and for rapes.
  Marc. O, why should nature build so foul
    a den,   60
Unless the gods delight in tragedies ?
  Tit. Give signs, sweet girl, for here are
    none but friends,
What Roman lord it was durst do the deed.
Or slunk not Saturnine, as Tarquin erst,
That left the camp to sin in Lucrece' bed ?
  Marc. Sit down, sweet niece ; brother, sit
    down by me.   66
Apollo, Pallas, Jove, or Mercury,
Inspire me, that I may this treason find !
My lord, look here ! Look here, Lavinia !
    [*He writes his name with his staff, and
      guides it with feet and mouth.*
This sandy plot is plain ; guide, if thou
    canst,   70

This after me. I have writ my name
Without the help of any hand at all.
Curs'd be that heart that forc'd us to this
    shift !
Write thou, good niece, and here display at
    last
What God will have discovered for revenge.
Heaven guide thy pen to print thy sorrows
    plain,   76
That we may know the traitors and the
    truth ! [*She takes the staff in her
    mouth and guides it with her stumps,
    and writes.*
O, do ye read, my lord, what she hath
    writ ?
' Stuprum—Chiron—Demetrius.'
  Marc. What, what! the lustful sons of
    Tamora   80
Performers of this heinous bloody deed ?
  Tit. Magni Dominator poli,
Tam lentus audis scelera ? tam lentus
    vides ?
  Marc. O, calm thee, gentle lord ! although
    I know
There is enough written upon this earth 85
To stir a mutiny in the mildest thoughts,
And arm the minds of infants to exclaims.
My lord, kneel down with me ; Lavinia,
    kneel ;
And kneel, sweet boy, the Roman Hector's
    hope ;
And swear with me—as, with the woeful
    fere   90
And father of that chaste dishonoured
    dame,
Lord Junius Brutus sware for Lucrece
    rape—
That we will prosecute, by good advice,
Mortal revenge upon these traitorous
    Goths,
And see their blood or die with this
    reproach.   95
  Tit. 'Tis sure enough, an you knew how ;
But if you hunt these bear-whelps, then
    beware:
The dam will wake ; and if she wind ye
    once,
She's with the lion deeply still in league,
And lulls him whilst she playeth on her
    back,   100
And when he sleeps will she do what she
    list.
You are a young huntsman, Marcus ; let
    alone ;
And come, I will go get a leaf of brass,
And with a gad of steel will write these
    words,
And lay it by. The angry northern wind 105
Will blow these sands like Sibyl's leaves
    abroad,
And where's our lesson, then ? Boy, what
    say you ?
  Boy. I say, my lord, that if I were a
    man

Their mother's bedchamber should not be
  safe
For these base bondmen to the yoke of
  Rome.   110
  Marc. Ay, that's my boy! Thy father
  hath full oft
For his ungrateful country done the like.
  Boy. And, uncle, so will I, an if I live.
  Tit. Come, go with me into mine
  armoury.
Lucius, I'll fit thee; and withal my boy 115
Shall carry from me to the Empress' sons
Presents that I intend to send them both.
Come, come; thou'lt do my message, wilt
  thou not?
  Boy. Ay, with my dagger in their bosoms,
  grandsire.
  Tit. No, boy, not so; I'll teach thee
  another course.   120
Lavinia, come. Marcus, look to my house.
Lucius and I'll go brave it at the court;
Ay, marry, will we, sir! and we'll be waited
  on. [Exeunt Titus, Lavinia, and
                      Young Lucius.
  Marc. O heavens, can you hear a good
  man groan
And not relent, or not compassion him? 125
Marcus, attend him in his ecstasy,
That hath more scars of sorrow in his heart
Than foemen's marks upon his batt'red
  shield,
But yet so just that he will not revenge.
Revenge the heavens for old Andronicus!
                                    [Exit.

SCENE II. Rome. The palace.

Enter AARON, DEMETRIUS and CHIRON, at
one door; and at the other door, YOUNG
LUCIUS and another with a bundle of
weapons, and verses writ upon them.

  Chi. Demetrius, here's the son of Lucius;
He hath some message to deliver us.
  Aar. Ay, some mad message from his mad
  grandfather.
  Boy. My lords, with all the humbleness
  I may,
I greet your honours from Andronicus— 5
[Aside] And pray the Roman gods confound
  you both!
  Dem. Gramercy, lovely Lucius. What's
  the news?
  Boy. [Aside] That you are both de-
  cipher'd, that's the news,
For villains mark'd with rape.—May it
  please you,
My grandsire, well-advis'd, hath sent by me
The goodliest weapons of his armoury 11
To gratify your honourable youth,
The hope of Rome; for so he bid me say;
And so I do, and with his gifts present
Your lordships, that, whenever you have
  need,   15
You may be armed and appointed well.

And so I leave you both—[Aside] like
  bloody villains.
          [Exeunt Young Lucius and Attendant.
  Dem. What's here? A scroll, and written
  round about.
Let's see:
  [Reads] 'Integer vitae, scelerisque purus, 20
          Non eget Mauri iaculis, nec arcu.'
  Chi. O, 'tis a verse in Horace, I know it
  well;
I read it in the grammar long ago.
  Aar. Ay, just—a verse in Horace. Right,
  you have it.   24
[Aside] Now, what a thing it is to be an ass!
Here's no sound jest! The old man hath
  found their guilt,
And sends them weapons wrapp'd about
  with lines
That wound, beyond their feeling, to the
  quick.
But were our witty Empress well afoot,
She would applaud Andronicus' conceit. 30
But let her rest in her unrest awhile—
And now, young lords, was't not a happy
  star
Led us to Rome, strangers, and more than
  so,
Captives, to be advanced to this height?
It did me good before the palace gate   35
To brave the Tribune in his brother's
  hearing.
  Dem. But me more good to see so great a
  lord
Basely insinuate and send us gifts.
  Aar. Had he not reason, Lord De-
  metrius?
Did you not use his daughter very friendly?
  Dem. I would we had a thousand Roman
  dames   41
At such a bay, by turn to serve our lust.
  Chi. A charitable wish and full of love.
  Aar. Here lacks but your mother for to
  say amen.
  Chi. And that would she for twenty
  thousand more.   45
  Dem. Come, let us go and pray to all the
  gods
For our beloved mother in her pains.
  Aar. [Aside] Pray to the devils; the gods
  have given us over.
                          [Trumpets sound.
  Dem. Why do the Emperor's trumpets
  flourish thus?
  Chi. Belike, for joy the Emperor hath a
  son.   50
  Dem. Soft! who comes here?

Enter Nurse, with a blackamoor Child.

  Nur. Good morrow, lords.
O, tell me, did you see Aaron the Moor?
  Aar. Well, more or less, or ne'er a whit
  at all,
Here Aaron is; and what with Aaron now?
  Nur. O gentle Aaron, we are all undone!

Now help, or woe betide thee evermore ! 56
  Aar. Why, what a caterwauling dost thou
    keep !
What dost thou wrap and fumble in thy
    arms ?
  Nur. O, that which I would hide from
    heaven's eye :
Our Empress' shame and stately Rome's
    disgrace ! 60
She is delivered, lords ; she is delivered.
  Aar. To whom ?
  Nur.   I mean she is brought a-bed.
  Aar. Well, God give her good rest ! What
    hath he sent her ?
  Nur. A devil.
  Aar.   Why, then she is the devil's
    dam ;
A joyful issue. 65
  Nur. A joyless, dismal, black, and
    sorrowful issue !
Here is the babe, as loathsome as a toad
Amongst the fair-fac'd breeders of our
    clime ;
The Empress sends it thee, thy stamp, thy
    seal,
And bids thee christen it with thy dagger's
    point. 70
  Aar. Zounds, ye whore ! Is black so base
    a hue ?
Sweet blowse, you are a beauteous blossom
    sure.
  Dem. Villain, what hast thou done ?
  Aar. That which thou canst not undo.
  Chi. Thou hast undone our mother. 75
  Aar. Villain, I have done thy mother.
  Dem. And therein, hellish dog, thou hast
    undone her.
Woe to her chance, and damn'd her loathed
    choice !
Accurs'd the offspring of so foul a fiend !
  Chi. It shall not live. 80
  Aar. It shall not die.
  Nur. Aaron, it must ; the mother wills
    it so.
  Aar. What, must it, nurse ? Then let no
    man but I
Do execution on my flesh and blood.
  Dem. I'll broach the tadpole on my
    rapier's point. 85
Nurse, give it me ; my sword shall soon
    dispatch it.
  Aar. Sooner this sword shall plough thy
    bowels up. [*Takes the Child from
    the Nurse, and draws.*
Stay, murderous villains, will you kill your
    brother !
Now, by the burning tapers of the sky
That shone so brightly when this boy was
    got, 90
He dies upon my scimitar's sharp point
That touches this my first-born son and heir.
I tell you, younglings, not Enceladus,
With all his threat'ning band of Typhon's
    brood,

Nor great Alcides, nor the god of war, 95
Shall seize this prey out of his father's
    hands.
What, what, ye sanguine, shallow-hearted
    boys !
Ye white-lim'd walls ! ye alehouse painted
    signs !
Coal-black is better than another hue
In that it scorns to bear another hue ; 100
For all the water in the ocean
Can never turn the swan's black legs to
    white,
Although she lave them hourly in the flood.
Tell the Empress from me I am of age
To keep mine own—excuse it how she can.
  Dem. Wilt thou betray thy noble mistress
    thus ? 106
  Aar. My mistress is my mistress : this
    my self,
The vigour and the picture of my youth.
This before all the world do I prefer ;
This maugre all the world will I keep safe,
Or some of you shall smoke for it in Rome.
  Dem. By this our mother is for ever
    sham'd. 112
  Chi. Rome will despise her for this foul
    escape.
  Nur. The Emperor in his rage will doom
    her death.
  Chi. I blush to think upon this ignomy.
  Aar. Why, there's the privilege your
    beauty bears : 116
Fie, treacherous hue, that will betray with
    blushing
The close enacts and counsels of thy heart!
Here's a young lad fram'd of another leer.
Look how the black slave smiles upon the
    father, 120
As who should say ' Old lad, I am thine
    own'.
He is your brother, lords, sensibly fed
Of that self-blood that first gave life to you ;
And from your womb where you imprisoned
    were
He is enfranchised and come to light. 125
Nay, he is your brother by the surer side,
Although my seal be stamped in his face.
  Nur. Aaron, what shall I say unto the
    Empress ?
  Dem. Advise thee, Aaron, what is to be
    done,
And we will all subscribe to thy advice. 130
Save thou the child, so we may all be safe.
  Aar. Then sit we down and let us all
    consult.
My son and I will have the wind of you :
Keep there ; now talk at pleasure of your
    safety. [*They sit.*
  Dem. How many women saw this child
    of his ? 135
  Aar. Why, so, brave lords ! When we
    join in league
I am a lamb ; but if you brave the Moor,
The chafed boar, the mountain lioness,

890

The ocean swells not so as Aaron storms.
But say, again, how many saw the child? 140
  Nur. Cornelia the midwife and myself ;
And no one else but the delivered Empress.
  Aar. The Emperess, the midwife, and
    yourself.
Two may keep counsel when the third's
    away :
Go to the Empress, tell her this I said. 145
                    [*He kills her.*
Weeke weeke !
So cries a pig prepared to the spit.
  Dem. What mean'st thou, Aaron ?
    Wherefore didst thou this ?
  Aar. O Lord, sir, 'tis a deed of policy.
Shall she live to betray this guilt of ours—
A long-tongu'd babbling gossip ? No, lords,
    no.   151
And now be it known to you my full intent:
Not far, one Muliteus, my countryman—
His wife but yesternight was brought to
    bed ;
His child is like to her, fair as you are. 155
Go pack with him, and give the mother
    gold,
And tell them both the circumstance of all,
And how by this their child shall be
    advanc'd,
And be received for the Emperor's heir
And substituted in the place of mine, 160
To calm this tempest whirling in the court ;
And let the Emperor dandle him for his
    own.
Hark ye, lords. You see I have given her
    physic,   [*Pointing to the Nurse.*
And you must needs bestow her funeral ;
The fields are near, and you are gallant
    grooms.   165
This done, see that you take no longer days,
But send the midwife presently to me.
The midwife and the nurse well made
    away,
Then let the ladies tattle what they please.
  Chi. Aaron, I see thou wilt not trust the
    air   170
With secrets.
  Dem.   For this care of Tamora,
Herself and hers are highly bound to thee.
        [*Exeunt Demetrius and Chiron,
           bearing off the dead Nurse.*
  Aar. Now to the Goths, as swift as
    swallow flies,
There to dispose this treasure in mine
    arms,
And secretly to greet the Empress' friends.
Come on, you thick-lipp'd slave, I'll bear
    you hence ;   176
For it is you that puts us to our shifts.
I'll make you feed on berries and on roots,
And feed on curds and whey, and suck the
    goat,
And cabin in a cave, and bring you up 180
To be a warrior and command a camp.
                    [*Exit with the child.*

SCENE III. *Rome. A public place.*

Enter TITUS, *bearing arrows with letters on
   the ends of them ; with him* MARCUS,
   YOUNG LUCIUS, *and other gentlemen,*
   PUBLIUS, SEMPRONIUS, *and* CAIUS, *with
   bows.*

  Tit. Come, Marcus, come ; kinsmen, this
    is the way.
Sir boy, let me see your archery ;
Look ye draw home enough, and 'tis there
    straight.
Terras Astraea reliquit,
Be you rememb'red, Marcus ; she's gone,
    she's fled.   5
Sirs, take you to your tools. You, cousins,
    shall
Go sound the ocean and cast your nets ;
Happily you may catch her in the sea ;
Yet there's as little justice as at land.
No ; Publius and Sempronius, you must
    do it ;   10
'Tis you must dig with mattock and with
    spade,
And pierce the inmost centre of the earth ;
Then, when you come to Pluto's region,
I pray you deliver him this petition.
Tell him it is for justice and for aid,   15
And that it comes from old Andronicus,
Shaken with sorrows in ungrateful Rome.
Ah, Rome !   Well, well, I made thee
    miserable
What time I threw the people's suffrages
On him that thus doth tyrannize o'er me. 20
Go get you gone ; and pray be careful all,
And leave you not a man-of-war un-
    search'd.
This wicked Emperor may have shipp'd her
    hence ;
And, kinsmen, then we may go pipe for
    justice.   24
  Marc. O Publius, is not this a heavy case,
To see thy noble uncle thus distract ?
  Pub. Therefore, my lords, it highly us
    concerns
By day and night t'attend him carefully,
And feed his humour kindly as we may
Till time beget some careful remedy.   30
  Marc. Kinsmen, his sorrows are past
    remedy.
Join with the Goths, and with revengeful
    war
Take wreak on Rome for this ingratitude,
And vengeance on the traitor Saturnine.
  Tit. Publius, how now ? How now, my
    masters ?   35
What, have you met with her ?
  Pub. No, my good lord ; but Pluto sends
    you word,
If you will have Revenge from hell, you
    shall.
Marry, for Justice, she is so employ'd,
He thinks, with Jove in heaven, or some-
    where else,   40

891

So that perforce you must needs stay a time.
  Tit. He doth me wrong to feed me with delays.
I'll dive into the burning lake below
And pull her out of Acheron by the heels.
Marcus, we are but shrubs, no cedars we, 45
No big-bon'd men fram'd of the Cyclops' size ;
But metal, Marcus, steel to the very back,
Yet wrung with wrongs more than our backs can bear ;
And, sith there's no justice in earth nor hell,
We will solicit heaven, and move the gods
To send down Justice for to wreak our wrongs. 51
Come, to this gear. You are a good archer, Marcus. [*He gives them the arrows.*
' Ad Jovem ' that's for you ; here ' Ad Apollinem '.
' Ad Martem ' that's for myself.
Here, boy, ' To Pallas ' ; here ' To Mercury '. 55
' To Saturn ' Caius—not to Saturnine :
You were as good to shoot against the wind.
To it, boy. Marcus, loose when I bid.
Of my word, I have written to effect ;
There's not a god left unsolicited. 60
  Marc. Kinsmen, shoot all your shafts into the court ;
We will afflict the Emperor in his pride.
  Tit. Now, masters, draw. [*They shoot*] O, well said, Lucius !
Good boy, in Virgo's lap ! Give it Pallas.
  Marc. My lord, I aim a mile beyond the moon ; 65
Your letter is with Jupiter by this.
  Tit. Ha ! ha !
Publius, Publius, what hast thou done ?
See, see, thou hast shot off one of Taurus' horns.
  Marc. This was the sport, my lord : when Publius shot, 70
The Bull, being gall'd, gave Aries such a knock
That down fell both the Ram's horns in the court ;
And who should find them but the Empress' villain ?
She laugh'd, and told the Moor he should not choose 74
But give them to his master for a present.
  Tit. Why, there it goes ! God give his lordship joy !

Enter the Clown, *with a basket and two pigeons in it.*

News, news from heaven ! Marcus, the post is come.
Sirrah, what tidings ? Have you any letters ? 78
Shall I have justice ? What says Jupiter ?
  Clo. Ho, the gibbet-maker ? He says that he hath taken them down again, for the man must not be hang'd till the next week.
  Tit. But what says Jupiter, I ask thee ?
  Clo. Alas, sir, I know not Jupiter ; I never drank with him in all my life. 85
  Tit. Why, villain, art not thou the carrier ?
  Clo. Ay, of my pigeons, sir ; nothing else.
  Tit. Why, didst thou not come from heaven ?
  Clo. From heaven ! Alas, sir, I never came there. God forbid I should be so bold to press to heaven in my young days. Why, I am going with my pigeons to the Tribunal Plebs, to take up a matter of brawl betwixt my uncle and one of the Emperal's men. 93
  Marc. Why, sir, that is as fit as can be to serve for your oration ; and let him deliver the pigeons to the Emperor from you.
  Tit. Tell me, can you deliver an oration to the Emperor with a grace ?
  Clo. Nay, truly, sir, I could never say grace in all my life.
  Tit. Sirrah, come hither. Make no more ado, 100
But give your pigeons to the Emperor ;
By me thou shalt have justice at his hands.
Hold, hold ! Meanwhile here's money for thy charges.
Give me pen and ink. Sirrah, can you with a grace deliver up a supplication ? 105
  Clo. Ay, sir.
  Tit. Then here is a supplication for you. And when you come to him, at the first approach you must kneel ; then kiss his foot ; then deliver up your pigeons ; and then look for your reward. I'll be at hand, sir ; see you do it bravely. 111
  Clo. I warrant you, sir ; let me alone.
  Tit. Sirrah, hast thou a knife ? Come, let me see it.
Here, Marcus, fold it in the oration ;
For thou hast made it like an humble suppliant. 115
And when thou hast given it to the Emperor,
Knock at my door, and tell me what he says.
  Clo. God be with you, sir ; I will.
  Tit. Come, Marcus, let us go. Publius, follow me. [*Exeunt.*

SCENE IV. *Rome. Before the palace.*

Enter the EMPEROR, *and the* EMPRESS *and her two sons,* DEMETRIUS *and* CHIRON ; *Lords and Others. The Emperor brings the arrows in his hand that Titus shot at him.*

  Sat. Why, lords, what wrongs are these ! Was ever seen
An emperor in Rome thus overborne,
Troubled, confronted thus ; and, for the extent

Of egal justice, us'd in such contempt ?
My lords, you know, as know the mightful
  gods,   5
However these disturbers of our peace
Buzz in the people's ears, there nought hath
  pass'd
But even with law against the wilful sons
Of old Andronicus. And what an if
His sorrows have so overwhelm'd his wits,
Shall we be thus afflicted in his wreaks, 11
His fits, his frenzy, and his bitterness ?
And now he writes to heaven for his redress.
See, here's ' To Jove ' and this ' To
  Mercury ';
This ' To Apollo '; this ' To the God of
  War '—   15
Sweet scrolls to fly about the streets of
  Rome !
What's this but libelling against the Senate,
And blazoning our unjustice every where ?
A goodly humour, is it not, my lords ?
As who would say in Rome no justice were.
But if I live, his feigned ecstasies   21
Shall be no shelter to these outrages ;
But he and his shall know that justice lives
In Saturninus' health ; whom, if she sleep,
He'll so awake as he in fury shall   25
Cut off the proud'st conspirator that lives.
  Tam. My gracious lord, my lovely
  Saturnine,
Lord of my life, commander of my thoughts,
Calm thee, and bear the faults of Titus' age,
Th' effects of sorrow for his valiant sons, 30
Whose loss hath pierc'd him deep and
  scarr'd his heart ;
And rather comfort his distressed plight
Than prosecute the meanest or the best
For these contempts. [*Aside*] Why, thus it
  shall become
High-witted Tamora to gloze with all.   35
But, Titus, I have touch'd thee to the quick,
Thy life-blood out ; if Aaron now be wise,
Then is all safe, the anchor in the port.

            Enter Clown.

How now, good fellow !   Wouldst thou
  speak with us ?
  Clo. Yes, forsooth, an your mistriship be
Emperial.   40
  Tam. Empress I am, but yonder sits the
  Emperor.
  Clo. 'Tis he.—God and Saint Stephen
give you godden. I have brought you a
letter and a couple of pigeons here.
              [*Saturninus reads the letter.*
  Sat. Go take him away, and hang him
presently.   45
  Clo. How much money must I have ?
  Tam. Come, sirrah, you must be hang'd.
  Clo. Hang'd ! by'r lady, then I have
brought up a neck to a fair end.
                            [*Exit guarded.*
  Sat. Despiteful and intolerable wrongs !
Shall I endure this monstrous villainy ? 51

I know from whence this same device
  proceeds.
May this be borne—as if his traitorous sons
That died by law for murder of our brother
Have by my means been butchered wrong-
  fully ?   55
Go drag the villain hither by the hair ;
Nor age nor honour shall shape privilege.
For this proud mock I'll be thy slaughter-
  man,
Sly frantic wretch, that holp'st to make me
  great,
In hope thyself should govern Rome and
  me.   60

        Enter Nuntius ÆMILIUS.

What news with thee, Æmilius ?
  Æmil. Arm, my lords ! Rome never had
    more cause.
The Goths have gathered head ; and with
    a power
Of high resolved men, bent to the spoil,
They hither march amain, under conduct
Of Lucius, son to old Andronicus ;   66
Who threats in course of this revenge to do
As much as ever Coriolanus did.
  Sat. Is warlike Lucius general of the
    Goths ?
These tidings nip me, and I hang the head
As flowers with frost, or grass beat down
    with storms.   71
Ay, now begins our sorrows to approach.
'Tis he the common people love so much ;
Myself hath often heard them say—
When I have walked like a private man—
That Lucius' banishment was wrongfully,
And they have wish'd that Lucius were
    their emperor.
  Tam. Why should you fear ? Is not your
    city strong ?
  Sat. Ay, but the citizens favour Lucius,
And will revolt from me to succour him. 80
  Tam. King, be thy thoughts imperious
    like thy name !
Is the sun dimm'd, that gnats do fly in it ?
The eagle suffers little birds to sing,
And is not careful what they mean thereby,
Knowing that with the shadow of his wings
He can at pleasure stint their melody ;   86
Even so mayest thou the giddy men of
    Rome.
Then cheer thy spirit ; for know thou,
    Emperor,
I will enchant the old Andronicus
With words more sweet, and yet more
    dangerous,   90
Than baits to fish or honey-stalks to sheep,
When as the one is wounded with the bait,
The other rotted with delicious feed.
  Sat. But he will not entreat his son for us.
  Tam. If Tamora entreat him, then he will ;
For I can smooth and fill his aged ears 96
With golden promises, that, were his heart
Almost impregnable, his old ears deaf,

Yet should both ear and heart obey my
    tongue.
[*To Æmilius*] Go thou before to be our
    ambassador ;   100
Say that the Emperor requests a parley
Of warlike Lucius, and appoint the meeting
Even at his father's house, the old An-
    dronicus.
    Sat. Æmilius, do this message honour-
    ably ;   104
And if I stand on hostage for his safety,
Bid him demand what pledge will please
    him best.
    Æmil. Your bidding shall I do effectually.
                                            [*Exit.*
    Tam. Now will I to that old Andronicus,
And temper him with all the art I have,
To pluck proud Lucius from the warlike
    Goths.   110
And now, sweet Emperor, be blithe again,
And bury all thy fear in my devices.
    Sat. Then go successantly, and plead to
    him.   [*Exeunt.*

ACT FIVE

SCENE I. *Plains near Rome.*

Enter LUCIUS *with an army of* Goths *with
    drums and colours.*

    Luc. Approved warriors and my faithful
    friends,
I have received letters from great Rome
Which signifies what hate they bear their
    Emperor
And how desirous of our sight they are.
Therefore, great lords, be, as your titles
    witness,   5
Imperious and impatient of your wrongs ;
And wherein Rome hath done you any
    scath,
Let him make treble satisfaction.
    1 Goth. Brave slip, sprung from the great
    Andronicus,
Whose name was once our terror, now our
    comfort,   10
Whose high exploits and honourable deeds
Ingrateful Rome requites with foul con-
    tempt,
Be bold in us : we'll follow where thou
    lead'st,
Like stinging bees in hottest summer's day,
Led by their master to the flow'red fields,
And be aveng'd on cursed Tamora.   16
    All the Goths. And as he saith, so say we
    all with him.
    Luc. I humbly thank him, and I thank
    you all.
But who comes here, led by a lusty Goth ?

Enter a Goth, *leading* AARON *with his* Child
    in his arms.

    2 Goth. Renowned Lucius, from our
    troops I stray'd   20

To gaze upon a ruinous monastery ;
And as I earnestly did fix mine eye
Upon the wasted building, suddenly
I heard a child cry underneath a wall.
I made unto the noise, when soon I heard
The crying babe controll'd with this
    discourse :   26
' Peace, tawny slave, half me and half thy
    dam !
Did not thy hue bewray whose brat thou
    art,
Had nature lent thee but thy mother's look,
Villain, thou mightst have been an
    emperor ;   30
But where the bull and cow are both milk-
    white,
They never do beget a coal-black calf.
Peace, villain, peace ! '—even thus he rates
    the babe—
' For I must bear thee to a trusty Goth,
Who, when he knows thou art the Empress'
    babe,   35
Will hold thee dearly for thy mother's sake'.
With this, my weapon drawn, I rush'd upon
    him,
Surpris'd him suddenly, and brought him
    hither
To use as you think needful of the man.
    Luc. O worthy Goth, this is the incarnate
    devil   40
That robb'd Andronicus of his good hand ;
This is the pearl that pleas'd your Empress'
    eye ;
And here's the base fruit of her burning
    lust.
Say, wall-ey'd slave, whither wouldst thou
    convey
This growing image of thy fiend-like face ?
Why dost not speak ? What, deaf ? Not a
    word ?   46
A halter, soldiers ! Hang him on this tree,
And by his side his fruit of bastardy.
    Aar. Touch not the boy, he is of royal
    blood.
    Luc. Too like the sire for ever being good.
First hang the child, that he may see it
    sprawl—   51
A sight to vex the father's soul withal.
Get me a ladder. [*A ladder brought, which
                    Aaron is made to climb.*
    Aar.   Lucius, save the child,
And bear it from me to the Emperess.
If thou do this, I'll show thee wondrous
    things   55
That highly may advantage thee to hear ;
If thou wilt not, befall what may befall,
I'll speak no more but ' Vengeance rot you
    all ! '
    Luc. Say on ; an if it please me which
    thou speak'st,
Thy child shall live, and I will see it
    nourish'd.   60
    Aar. An if it please thee ! Why, assure
    thee, Lucius,

894

'Twill vex thy soul to hear what I shall
    speak ;
For I must talk of murders, rapes, and
    massacres,
Acts of black night, abominable deeds,
Complots of mischief, treason, villainies, 65
Ruthful to hear, yet piteously perform'd ;
And this shall all be buried in my death,
Unless thou swear to me my child shall
    live.
  Luc. Tell on thy mind ; I say thy child
    shall live.
  Aar. Swear that he shall, and then I will
    begin.   70
  Luc. Who should I swear by ? Thou
    believest no god ;
That granted, how canst thou believe an
    oath ?
  Aar. What if I do not ?—as indeed I do
    not ;
Yet, for I know thou art religious
And hast a thing within thee called con-
    science,   75
With twenty popish tricks and ceremonies
Which I have seen thee careful to observe,
Therefore I urge thy oath. For that I know
An idiot holds his bauble for a god,
And keeps the oath which by that god he
    swears,   80
To that I'll urge him. Therefore thou shalt
    vow
By that same god—what god soe'er it be
That thou adorest and hast in reverence—
To save my boy, to nourish and bring him
    up ;
Or else I will discover nought to thee.   85
  Luc. Even by my god I swear to thee I
    will.
  Aar. First know thou, I begot him on the
    Empress.
  Luc. O most insatiate and luxurious
    woman !
  Aar. Tut, Lucius, this was but a deed of
    charity
To that which thou shalt hear of me anon.
'Twas her two sons that murdered Bas-
    sianus ;   91
They cut thy sister's tongue, and ravish'd
    her,
And cut her hands, and trimm'd her as
    thou sawest.
  Luc. O detestable villain ! Call'st thou
    that trimming ?
  Aar. Why, she was wash'd, and cut, and
    trimm'd, and 'twas   95
Trim sport for them which had the doing
    of it.
  Luc. O barbarous beastly villains like
    thyself !
  Aar. Indeed, I was their tutor to instruct
    them.
That codding spirit had they from their
    mother,
As sure a card as ever won the set ;   100

That bloody mind, I think, they learn'd
    of me,
As true a dog as ever fought at head.
Well, let my deeds be witness of my worth.
I train'd thy brethren to that guileful hole
Where the dead corpse of Bassianus lay ;
I wrote the letter that thy father found,
And hid the gold within that letter men-
    tion'd,
Confederate with the queen and her two
    sons ;
And what not done, that thou hast cause
    to rue,   109
Wherein I had no stroke of mischief in it ?
I play'd the cheater for thy father's hand,
And, when I had it, drew myself apart
And almost broke my heart with extreme
    laughter.
I pried me through the crevice of a wall,
When, for his hand, he had his two sons'
    heads ;   115
Beheld his tears, and laugh'd so heartily
That both mine eyes were rainy like to his ;
And when I told the Empress of this sport,
She swooned almost at my pleasing tale,
And for my tidings gave me twenty kisses.
  Goth. What, canst thou say all this and
    never blush ?   121
  Aar. Ay, like a black dog, as the saying is.
  Luc. Art thou not sorry for these heinous
    deeds ?
  Aar. Ay, that I had not done a thousand
    more.
Even now I curse the day—and yet, I
    think,   125
Few come within the compass of my curse—
Wherein I did not some notorious ill :
As kill a man, or else devise his death ;
Ravish a maid, or plot the way to do it ;
Accuse some innocent, and forswear myself;
Set deadly enmity between two friends ;
Make poor men's cattle break their necks ;
Set fire on barns and hay-stacks in the
    night,
And bid the owners quench them with their
    tears.
Oft have I digg'd up dead men from their
    graves,   135
And set them upright at their dear friends'
    door
Even when their sorrows almost was forgot,
And on their skins, as on the bark of trees,
Have with my knife carved in Roman
    letters
' Let not your sorrow die, though I am
    dead '.   140
Tut, I have done a thousand dreadful
    things
As willingly as one would kill a fly ;
And nothing grieves me heartily indeed
But that I cannot do ten thousand more.
  Luc. Bring down the devil, for he must
    not die   145
So sweet a death as hanging presently.

895

Aar. If there be devils, would I were a devil,
To live and burn in everlasting fire,
So I might have your company in hell
But to torment you with my bitter tongue!
   Luc. Sirs, stop his mouth, and let him speak no more. 151

Enter ÆMILIUS.

   Goth. My lord, there is a messenger from Rome
Desires to be admitted to your presence.
   Luc. Let him come near.
Welcome, Æmilius. What's the news from Rome? 155
   Æmil. Lord Lucius, and you Princes of the Goths,
The Roman Emperor greets you all by me;
And, for he understands you are in arms,
He craves a parley at your father's house,
Willing you to demand your hostages, 160
And they shall be immediately deliver'd.
   1 *Goth.* What says our general?
   Luc. Æmilius, let the Emperor give his pledges
Unto my father and my uncle Marcus. 164
And we will come. March away. [*Exeunt.*

Scene II. *Rome. Before Titus' house.*

Enter TAMORA, *and her two sons,* DE-
METRIUS *and* CHIRON, *disguised.*

   Tam. Thus, in this strange and sad habiliment,
I will encounter with Andronicus,
And say I am Revenge, sent from below
To join with him and right his heinous wrongs.
Knock at his study, where they say he keeps 5
To ruminate strange plots of dire revenge;
Tell him Revenge is come to join with him,
And work confusion on his enemies.

They knock, and TITUS *opens his study door, above.*

   Tit. Who doth molest my contemplation?
Is it your trick to make me ope the door, 10
That so my sad decrees may fly away
And all my study be to no effect?
You are deceiv'd; for what I mean to do
See here in bloody lines I have set down;
And what is written shall be executed. 15
   Tam. Titus, I am come to talk with thee.
   Tit. No, not a word. How can I grace my talk,
Wanting a hand to give it that accord?
Thou hast the odds of me; therefore no more.
   Tam. If thou didst know me, thou wouldst talk with me. 20
   Tit. I am not mad, I know thee well enough:

Witness this wretched stump, witness these crimson lines;
Witness these trenches made by grief and care;
Witness the tiring day and heavy night;
Witness all sorrow that I know thee well 25
For our proud Empress, mighty Tamora.
Is not thy coming for my other hand?
   Tam. Know thou, sad man, I am not Tamora:
She is thy enemy and I thy friend.
I am Revenge, sent from th' infernal kingdom 30
To ease the gnawing vulture of thy mind
By working wreakful vengeance on thy foes.
Come down and welcome me to this world's light;
Confer with me of murder and of death;
There's not a hollow cave or lurking-place,
No vast obscurity or misty vale, 36
Where bloody murder or detested rape
Can couch for fear but I will find them out;
And in their ears tell them my dreadful name—
Revenge, which makes the foul offender quake. 40
   Tit. Art thou Revenge? and art thou sent to me
To be a torment to mine enemies?
   Tam. I am; therefore come down and welcome me.
   Tit. Do me some service ere I come to thee.
Lo, by thy side where Rape and Murder stands; 45
Now give some surance that thou art Revenge—
Stab them, or tear them on thy chariot wheels;
And then I'll come and be thy waggoner
And whirl along with thee about the globes.
Provide thee two proper palfreys, black as jet, 50
To hale thy vengeful waggon swift away,
And find out murderers in their guilty caves;
And when thy car is loaden with their heads,
I will dismount, and by thy waggon wheel
Trot, like a servile footman, all day long, 55
Even from Hyperion's rising in the east
Until his very downfall in the sea.
And day by day I'll do this heavy task,
So thou destroy Rapine and Murder there.
   Tam. These are my ministers, and come with me. 60
   Tit. Are they thy ministers? What are they call'd?
   Tam. Rape and Murder; therefore called so
'Cause they take vengeance of such kind of men.
   Tit. Good Lord, how like the Empress' sons they are!

And you the Empress! But we worldly
　　men　65
Have miserable, mad, mistaking eyes.
O sweet Revenge, now do I come to thee;
And, if one arm's embracement will content
　　thee,
I will embrace thee in it by and by.
　　　　　　　　　　　　　　[*Exit above.*

Tam. This closing with him fits his
　　lunacy.　70
Whate'er I forge to feed his brain-sick
　　humours,
Do you uphold and maintain in your
　　speeches,
For now he firmly takes me for Revenge;
And, being credulous in this mad thought,
I'll make him send for Lucius his son,　75
And whilst I at a banquet hold him sure,
I'll find some cunning practice out of hand
To scatter and disperse the giddy Goths,
Or, at the least, make them his enemies.
See, here he comes, and I must ply my
　　theme.　80

Enter TITUS, *below.*

Tit. Long have I been forlorn, and all for
　　thee.
Welcome, dread Fury, to my woeful house.
Rapine and Murder, you are welcome too.
How like the Empress and her sons you are!
Well are you fitted, had you but a Moor.　85
Could not all hell afford you such a devil?
For well I wot the Empress never wags
But in her company there is a Moor;
And, would you represent our queen
　　aright,
It were convenient you had such a devil.　90
But welcome as you are. What shall we do?

Tam. What wouldst thou have us do,
　　Andronicus?
Dem. Show me a murderer, I'll deal with
　　him.
Chi. Show me a villain that hath done a
　　rape,
And I am sent to be reveng'd on him.　95
Tam. Show me a thousand that hath
　　done thee wrong,
And I will be revenged on them all.
Tit. Look round about the wicked streets
　　of Rome,
And when thou find'st a man that's like
　　thyself,　99
Good Murder, stab him; he's a murderer.
Go thou with him, and when it is thy hap
To find another that is like to thee,
Good Rapine, stab him; he is a ravisher.
Go thou with them; and in the Emperor's
　　court
There is a queen, attended by a Moor;　105
Well shalt thou know her by thine own
　　proportion,
For up and down she doth resemble thee.
I pray thee, do on them some violent death;
They have been violent to me and mine.

Tam. Well hast thou lesson'd us; this
　　shall we do.　110
But would it please thee, good Andronicus,
To send for Lucius, thy thrice-valiant son,
Who leads towards Rome a band of warlike
　　Goths,
And bid him come and banquet at thy
　　house;　114
When he is here, even at thy solemn feast,
I will bring in the Empress and her sons,
The Emperor himself, and all thy foes;
And at thy mercy shall they stoop and
　　kneel,
And on them shalt thou ease thy angry
　　heart.
What says Andronicus to this device?　120
Tit. Marcus, my brother! 'Tis sad Titus
　　calls.

Enter MARCUS.

Go, gentle Marcus, to thy nephew Lucius;
Thou shalt inquire him out among the
　　Goths.　123
Bid him repair to me, and bring with him
Some of the chiefest princes of the Goths;
Bid him encamp his soldiers where they are.
Tell him the Emperor and the Empress too
Feast at my house, and he shall feast with
　　them.
This do thou for my love; and so let him,
As he regards his aged father's life.　130
Marc. This will I do, and soon return
　　again.　[*Exit.*
Tam. Now will I hence about thy
　　business,
And take my ministers along with me.
Tit. Nay, nay, let Rape and Murder stay
　　with me,
Or else I'll call my brother back again,　135
And cleave to no revenge but Lucius.
Tam. [*Aside to her sons*] What say you,
　　boys? Will you abide with him,
Whiles I go tell my lord the Emperor
How I have govern'd our determin'd jest?
Yield to his humour, smooth and speak him
　　fair,　140
And tarry with him till I turn again.
Tit. [*Aside*] I knew them all, though they
　　suppos'd me mad,
And will o'er-reach them in their own
　　devices,
A pair of cursed hell-hounds and their dam.
Dem. Madam, depart at pleasure; leave
　　us here.　145
Tam. Farewell, Andronicus, Revenge
　　now goes
To lay a complot to betray thy foes.
Tit. I know thou dost; and, sweet
　　Revenge, farewell. [*Exit Tamora.*
Chi. Tell us, old man, how shall we be
　　employ'd?
Tit. Tut, I have work enough for you to
　　do.　150
Publius, come hither, Caius, and Valentine.

897

Enter PUBLIUS, CAIUS, *and* VALENTINE.

Pub. What is your will ?
Tit. Know you these two ?
Pub. The Empress' sons, I take them :
Chiron, Demetrius.   155
Tit. Fie, Publius, fie ! thou art too much
      deceiv'd.
The one is Murder, and Rape is the other's
      name ;
And therefore bind them, gentle Publius—
Caius and Valentine, lay hands on them.
Oft have you heard me wish for such an
      hour,   160
And now I find it ; therefore bind them
      sure,
And stop their mouths if they begin to cry.
      [*Exit. They lay hold on Chiron and
                              Demetrius.*
Chi. Villains, forbear ! we are the
      Empress' sons.
Pub. And therefore do we what we are
      commanded.
Stop close their mouths, let them not speak
      a word.   165
Is he sure bound ? Look that you bind
      them fast.

Re-enter TITUS ANDRONICUS *with a knife,
      and* LAVINIA *with a basin.*

Tit. Come, come, Lavinia ; look, thy foes
      are bound.
Sirs, stop their mouths, let them not speak
      to me ;
But let them hear what fearful words I
      utter.
O villains, Chiron and Demetrius !   170
Here stands the spring whom you have
      stain'd with mud ;
This goodly summer with your winter
      mix'd.
You kill'd her husband ; and for that vile
      fault
Two of her brothers were condemn'd to
      death,
My hand cut off and made a merry jest ;   175
Both her sweet hands, her tongue, and that
      more dear
Than hands or tongue, her spotless chastity,
Inhuman traitors, you constrain'd and
      forc'd.
What would you say, if I should let you
      speak ?
Villains, for shame you could not beg for
      grace.   180
Hark, wretches ! how I mean to martyr you.
This one hand yet is left to cut your throats,
Whiles that Lavinia 'tween her stumps doth
      hold
The basin that receives your guilty blood.
You know your mother means to feast with
      me,   185
And calls herself Revenge, and thinks me
      mad.

Hark, villains ! I will grind your bones to
      dust,
And with your blood and it I'll make a
      paste ;
And of the paste a coffin I will rear,
And make two pasties of your shameful
      heads ;   190
And bid that strumpet, your unhallowed
      dam,
Like to the earth, swallow her own increase.
This is the feast that I have bid her to,
And this the banquet she shall surfeit on ;
For worse than Philomel you us'd my
      daughter,   195
And worse than Progne I will be reveng'd.
And now prepare your throats. Lavinia,
      come,
Receive the blood ; and when that they are
      dead,
Let me go grind their bones to powder
      small,
And with this hateful liquor temper it ;   200
And in that paste let their vile heads be
      bak'd.
Come, come, be every one officious
To make this banquet, which I wish may
      prove
More stern and bloody than the Centaurs'
      feast.   [*He cuts their throats.*
So.
Now bring them in, for I will play the cook,
And see them ready against their mother
      comes.   206
      [*Exeunt, bearing the dead bodies.*

SCENE III. *The court of Titus' house.*

Enter LUCIUS, MARCUS, *and the* Goths, *with*
AARON *prisoner, and his* Child *in the arms
of an* Attendant.

Luc. Uncle Marcus, since 'tis my father's
      mind
That I repair to Rome, I am content.
1 Goth. And ours with thine, befall what
      fortune will.
Luc. Good uncle, take you in this
      barbarous Moor,
This ravenous tiger, this accursed devil ;   5
Let him receive no sust'nance, fetter him,
Till he be brought unto the Empress' face
For testimony of her foul proceedings.
And see the ambush of our friends be
      strong ;
I fear the Emperor means no good to us.   10
Aar. Some devil whisper curses in my ear,
And prompt me that my tongue may utter
      forth
The venomous malice of my swelling heart !
Luc. Away, inhuman dog, unhallowed
      slave !
Sirs, help our uncle to convey him in.   15
      [*Exeunt Goths with Aaron. Flourish
                                          within.*
The trumpets show the Emperor is at hand.

Sound trumpets. Enter SATURNINUS *and*
TAMORA, *with* ÆMILIUS, *Tribunes, Sen-*
ators, and Others.

Sat. What, hath the firmament moe suns
 than one ?

Luc. What boots it thee to call thyself a
 sun ?

Marc. Rome's Emperor, and nephew,
 break the parle ;
These quarrels must be quietly debated. 20
The feast is ready which the careful Titus
Hath ordain'd to an honourable end,
For peace, for love, for league, and good to
 Rome.
Please you, therefore, draw nigh and take
 your places.

Sat. Marcus, we will. [*A table brought in.*
     The company sit down.

Trumpets sounding, enter TITUS *like a cook,*
placing the dishes, and LAVINIA *with a*
veil over her face ; also YOUNG LUCIUS,
and Others.

Tit. Welcome, my lord ; welcome, dread
 Queen ;   26
Welcome, ye warlike Goths ; welcome,
 Lucius ;
And welcome all. Although the cheer be
 poor,
'Twill fill your stomachs ; please you eat
 of it.

Sat. Why art thou thus attir'd, Andronicus ?   30

Tit. Because I would be sure to have all
 well
To entertain your Highness and your
 Empress.

Tam. We are beholding to you, good
 Andronicus.

Tit. An if your Highness knew my heart,
 you were.
My lord the Emperor, resolve me this : 35
Was it well done of rash Virginius
To slay his daughter with his own right
 hand,
Because she was enforc'd, stain'd, and
 deflower'd ?

Sat. It was, Andronicus.

Tit. Your reason, mighty lord.   40

Sat. Because the girl should not survive
 her shame,
And by her presence still renew his sorrows.

Tit. A reason mighty, strong, and
 effectual ;
A pattern, precedent, and lively warrant
For me, most wretched, to perform the like.
Die, die, Lavinia, and thy shame with thee ;
      [*He kills her.*
And with thy shame thy father's sorrow die!

Sat. What hast thou done, unnatural and
 unkind ?

Tit. Kill'd her for whom my tears have
 made me blind.

I am as woeful as Virginius was,   50
And have a thousand times more cause than
 he
To do this outrage ; and it now is done.

Sat. What, was she ravish'd ? Tell who
 did the deed.

Tit. Will't please you eat ? Will't please
 your Highness feed ?

Tam. Why hast thou slain thine only
 daughter thus ?   55

Tit. Not I ; 'twas Chiron and Demetrius.
They ravish'd her, and cut away her
 tongue ;
And they, 'twas they, that did her all this
 wrong.

Sat. Go, fetch them hither to us presently.

Tit. Why, there they are, both baked in
 this pie,   60
Whereof their mother daintily hath fed,
Eating the flesh that she herself hath bred.
'Tis true, 'tis true : witness my knife's
 sharp point. [*He stabs the Empress.*

Sat. Die, frantic wretch, for this accursed
 deed !   [*He stabs Titus.*

Luc. Can the son's eye behold his father
 bleed ?   65
There's meed for meed, death for a deadly
 deed. [*He stabs Saturninus. A great*
 tumult. Lucius, Marcus, and their
 friends go up into the balcony.

Marc. You sad-fac'd men, people and
 sons of Rome,
By uproars sever'd, as a flight of fowl
Scatter'd by winds and high tempestuous
 gusts,
O, let me teach you how to knit again   70
This scatter'd corn into one mutual sheaf,
These broken limbs again into one body ;
Lest Rome herself be bane unto herself,
And she whom mighty kingdoms curtsy to,
Like a forlorn and desperate castaway,   75
Do shameful execution on herself.
But if my frosty signs and chaps of age,
Grave witnesses of true experience,
Cannot induce you to attend my words,
[*To Lucius*] Speak, Rome's dear friend, as
 erst our ancestor,   80
When with his solemn tongue he did
 discourse
To love-sick Dido's sad attending ear
The story of that baleful burning night,
When subtle Greeks surpris'd King Priam's
 Troy.   84
Tell us what Sinon hath bewitch'd our ears,
Or who hath brought the fatal engine in
That gives our Troy, our Rome, the civil
 wound.
My heart is not compact of flint nor steel ;
Nor can I utter all our bitter grief,
But floods of tears will drown my oratory 90
And break my utt'rance, even in the
 time
When it should move ye to attend me most,
And force you to commiseration.

Here's Rome's young Captain, let him tell
    the tale;
While I stand by and weep to hear him
    speak. 95
  Luc. Then, gracious auditory, be it known
    to you
That Chiron and the damn'd Demetrius
Were they that murd'red our Emperor's
    brother;
And they it were that ravished our sister.
For their fell faults our brothers were
    beheaded, 100
Our father's tears despis'd, and basely
    cozen'd
Of that true hand that fought Rome's
    quarrel out
And sent her enemies unto the grave.
Lastly, myself unkindly banished,
The gates shut on me, and turn'd weeping
    out, 105
To beg relief among Rome's enemies;
Who drown'd their enmity in my true tears,
And op'd their arms to embrace me as a
    friend.
I am the turned forth, be it known to
    you,
That have preserv'd her welfare in my
    blood 110
And from her bosom took the enemy's
    point,
Sheathing the steel in my advent'rous body.
Alas! you know I am no vaunter, I;
My scars can witness, dumb although they
    are,
That my report is just and full of truth. 115
But, soft! methinks I do digress too much,
Citing my worthless praise. O, pardon me!
For when no friends are by, men praise
    themselves.
  Marc. Now is my turn to speak. Behold
    the child. [*Pointing to the child in
        an Attendant's arms.*
Of this was Tamora delivered, 120
The issue of an irreligious Moor,
Chief architect and plotter of these woes.
The villain is alive in Titus' house,
Damn'd as he is, to witness this is true.
Now judge what cause had Titus to revenge
These wrongs unspeakable, past patience,
Or more than any living man could bear.
Now have you heard the truth: what say
    you, Romans?
Have we done aught amiss, show us where-
    in,
And, from the place where you behold us
    pleading, 130
The poor remainder of Andronici
Will hand in hand all headlong hurl our-
    selves,
And on the ragged stones beat forth our
    souls,
And make a mutual closure of our house.
Speak, Romans, speak; and if you say we
    shall, 135

Lo, hand in hand, Lucius and I will fall.
  Æmil. Come, come, thou reverend man
    of Rome,
And bring our Emperor gently in thy hand,
Lucius our Emperor; for well I know
The common voice do cry it shall be so. 140
  All. Lucius, all hail, Rome's royal
    Emperor!
  Marc. Go, go into old Titus' sorrowful
    house,
And hither hale that misbelieving Moor
To be adjudg'd some direful slaught'ring
    death,
As punishment for his most wicked life. 145
    [*Exeunt some Attendants. Lucius,
      Marcus, and the others descend.*
  All. Lucius, all hail, Rome's gracious
    governor!
  Luc. Thanks, gentle Romans! May I
    govern so
To heal Rome's harms and wipe away her
    woe!
But, gentle people, give me aim awhile,
For nature puts me to a heavy task. 150
Stand all aloof; but, uncle, draw you near
To shed obsequious tears upon this trunk.
O, take this warm kiss on thy pale cold lips,
    [*Kisses Titus.*
These sorrowful drops upon thy blood-
    stain'd face,
The last true duties of thy noble son! 155
  Marc. Tear for tear and loving kiss for
    kiss
Thy brother Marcus tenders on thy lips.
O, were the sum of these that I should
    pay
Countless and infinite, yet would I pay
    them!
  Luc. Come hither, boy; come, come, and
    learn of us 160
To melt in showers. Thy grandsire lov'd
    thee well;
Many a time he danc'd thee on his knee,
Sung thee asleep, his loving breast thy
    pillow;
Many a story hath he told to thee,
And bid thee bear his pretty tales in mind
And talk of them when he was dead and
    gone. 166
  Marcus. How many thousand times hath
    these poor lips,
When they were living, warm'd themselves
    on thine!
O, now, sweet boy, give them their latest
    kiss!
Bid him farewell; commit him to the
    grave; 170
Do them that kindness, and take leave of
    them.
  Boy. O grandsire, grandsire! ev'n with
    all my heart
Would I were dead, so you did live again!
O Lord, I cannot speak to him for weeping;
My tears will choke me, if I ope my mouth.

Re-enter Attendants *with* AARON.

A Roman. You sad Andronici, have done
    with woes ;   176
Give sentence on this execrable wretch
That hath been breeder of these dire events.
    Luc. Set him breast-deep in earth, and
    famish him ;
There let him stand and rave and cry for
    food.   180
If any one relieves or pities him,
For the offence he dies. This is our doom.
Some stay to see him fast'ned in the earth.
    Aar. Ah, why should wrath be mute and
    fury dumb ?
I am no baby, I, that with base prayers   185
I should repent the evils I have done ;

Ten thousand worse than ever yet I did
Would I perform, if I might have my will.
If one good deed in all my life I did,
I do repent it from my very soul.   190
    Luc. Some loving friends convey the
    Emperor hence,
And give him burial in his father's grave.
My father and Lavinia shall forthwith
Be closed in our household's monument.
As for that ravenous tiger, Tamora,   195
No funeral rite, nor man in mourning weed,
No mournful bell shall ring her burial ;
But throw her forth to beasts and birds
    to prey.
Her life was beastly and devoid of pity,
And being dead, let birds on her take pity.
                [Exeunt.

ROMEO AND JULIET

DRAMATIS PERSONÆ

CHORUS.

ESCALUS, *Prince of Verona.*

PARIS, *a young nobleman, kinsman to the Prince.*

MONTAGUE, } *heads of two houses at vari-*
CAPULET, } *ance with each other.*

An Old Man, *of the Capulet family.*

ROMEO, *son to Montague.*

MERCUTIO, *kinsman to the Prince, and friend to Romeo.*

BENVOLIO, *nephew to Montague, and friend to Romeo.*

TYBALT, *nephew to Lady Capulet.*

FRIAR LAWRENCE, } *Franciscans.*
FRIAR JOHN, }

BALTHASAR, *servant to Romeo.*

SAMPSON, } *servants to Capulet.*
GREGORY, }

PETER, *servant to Juliet's nurse.*

ABRAHAM, *servant to Montague.*

An Apothecary.

Three Musicians.

An Officer.

LADY MONTAGUE, *wife to Montague.*

LADY CAPULET, *wife to Capulet.*

JULIET, *daughter to Capulet.*

Nurse *to Juliet.*

Citizens of Verona ; Gentlemen and Gentle-women of both houses ; Maskers, Torchbearers, Pages, Guards, Watch-men, Servants, and Attendants.

THE SCENE : *Verona and Mantua.*

THE PROLOGUE

Enter CHORUS.

Two households, both alike in dignity,
In fair Verona, where we lay our scene,
From ancient grudge break to new mutiny,
Where civil blood makes civil hands un-
    clean.   4
From forth the fatal loins of these two foes
A pair of star-cross'd lovers take their
    life ;
Whose misadventur'd piteous overthrows
Doth with their death bury their parents'
    strife.
The fearful passage of their death-mark'd
    love,   9
And the continuance of their parents' rage,
Which, but their children's end, nought
    could remove,
Is now the two hours' traffic of our stage ;
The which if you with patient ears attend,
What here shall miss, our toil shall strive to
    mend.   [*Exit.*

ACT ONE

SCENE I. *Verona. A public place.*

Enter SAMPSON *and* GREGORY, *of the house of Capulet, with swords and bucklers on.*

Sam. Gregory, on my word, we'll not carry coals.

Gre. No, for then we should be colliers.

Sam. I mean, an we be in choler, we'll draw.

Gre. Ay, while you live, draw your neck out of collar.   5

Sam. I strike quickly, being moved.

Gre. But thou art not quickly moved to strike.

Sam. A dog of the house of Montague moves me.

Gre. To move is to stir, and to be valiant is to stand ; therefore, if thou art moved, thou run'st away.   10

Sam. A dog of that house shall move me to stand. I will take the wall of any man or maid of Montague's.

Gre. That shows thee a weak slave ; for the weakest goes to the wall.   14

Sam. 'Tis true ; and therefore women, being the weaker vessels, are ever thrust to the wall ; therefore I will push Montague's men from the wall and thrust his maids to the wall.

Gre. The quarrel is between our masters and us their men.   20

Sam. 'Tis all one ; I will show myself a tyrant. When I have fought with the men, I will be civil with the maids—I will cut off their heads.

Gre. The heads of the maids ?   24

Sam. Ay, the heads of the maids, or their maidenheads ; take it in what sense thou wilt.   26

Gre. They must take it in sense that feel it.

Sam. Me they shall feel while I am able to stand ; and 'tis known I am a pretty piece of flesh.

Gre. 'Tis well thou art not fish ; if thou hadst, thou hadst been poor-John. Draw thy tool ; here comes two of the house of Montagues.   32

Enter two other Servingmen,
ABRAHAM *and* BALTHASAR.

Sam. My naked weapon is out ; quarrel,
I will back thee.

Gre. How ? turn thy back and run ?   35

Sam. Fear me not.

Gre. No, marry ; I fear thee !

Sam. Let us take the law of our sides ;
let them begin.

Gre. I will frown as I pass by, and let
them take it as they list.   40

Sam. Nay, as they dare. I will bite my
thumb at them, which is disgrace to them
if they bear it.

Abr. Do you bite your thumb at us, sir ?

Sam. I do bite my thumb, sir.   44

Abr. Do you bite your thumb at us, sir ?

Sam. [*Aside to Gregory*] Is the law of our
side, if I say ay ?

Gre. [*Aside to Sampson*] No.

Sam. No, sir, I do not bite my thumb at
you, sir ; but I bite my thumb, sir.

Gre. Do you quarrel, sir ?   50

Abr. Quarrel, sir ! No, sir.

Sam. But if you do, sir, I am for you. I
serve as good a man as you.

Abr. No better ?

Sam. Well, sir.   55

Enter BENVOLIO.

Gre. [*Aside to Sampson*] Say 'better' ;
here comes one of my master's kinsmen.

Sam. Yes, better, sir.

Abr. You lie.   59

Sam. Draw, if you be men. Gregory,
remember thy swashing blow. [*They fight.*

Ben. Part, fools ! [*Beats down their swords.*
Put up your swords ; you know not what
you do.   63

Enter TYBALT.

Tyb. What, art thou drawn among these
heartless hinds ?
Turn thee, Benvolio ; look upon thy death.

Ben. I do but keep the peace ; put up
thy sword,   66
Or manage it to part these men with me.

Tyb. What, drawn, and talk of peace ! I
hate the word,   68
As I hate hell, all Montagues, and thee.
Have at thee, coward !   [*They fight.*

Enter an Officer, *and three or four* Citizens
with clubs or partisans.

Officer. Clubs, bills, and partisans ! Strike !
beat them down.

Citizens. Down with the Capulets !
Down with the Montagues !

Enter Old CAPULET *in his gown, and his*
Wife.

Cap. What noise is this ? Give me my
long sword, ho !

Lady C. A crutch, a crutch ! Why call
you for a sword ?

Cap. My sword, I say ! Old Montague is
come,   75
And flourishes his blade in spite of me.

Enter Old MONTAGUE *and his Wife.*

Mon. Thou villain Capulet !—Hold me
not, let me go.

Lady M. Thou shalt not stir one foot to
seek a foe.

Enter PRINCE ESCALUS, *with his* Train.

Prin. Rebellious subjects, enemies to
peace,   79
Profaners of this neighbour-stained steel—
Will they not hear ? What, ho ! you men,
you beasts,
That quench the fire of your pernicious rage
With purple fountains issuing from your
veins !
On pain of torture, from those bloody hands
Throw your mistempered weapons to the
ground,   85
And hear the sentence of your moved
prince.
Three civil brawls, bred of an airy word,
By thee, old Capulet, and Montague,
Have thrice disturb'd the quiet of our
streets
And made Verona's ancient citizens   90
Cast by their grave beseeming ornaments
To wield old partisans, in hands as old,
Cank'red with peace, to part your cank'red
hate.
If ever you disturb our streets again,   94
Your lives shall pay the forfeit of the peace.
For this time all the rest depart away.
You, Capulet, shall go along with me ;
And, Montague, come you this afternoon,
To know our farther pleasure in this case,
To old Free-town, our common judgment-
place.   100
Once more, on pain of death, all men
depart. [*Exeunt all but Montague,
his Wife, and Benvolio.*

Mon. Who set this ancient quarrel new
abroach ?
Speak, nephew ; were you by when it
began ?

Ben. Here were the servants of your
adversary   104
And yours, close fighting ere I did approach.
I drew to part them ; in the instant came
The fiery Tybalt, with his sword prepar'd ;
Which, as he breath'd defiance to my
ears,
He swung about his head and cut the winds,
Who, nothing hurt withal, hiss'd him in
scorn.   110
While we were interchanging thrusts and
blows,
Came more and more, and fought on part
and part,

Till the Prince came, who parted either part.

   Lady M. O, where is Romeo ? Saw you him to-day ?

Right glad I am he was not at this fray. 115

   Ben. Madam, an hour before the worshipp'd sun

Peer'd forth the golden window of the east,
A troubled mind drew me to walk abroad ;
Where, underneath the grove of sycamore
That westward rooteth from this city side,
So early walking did I see your son. 121
Towards him I made ; but he was ware of me
And stole into the covert of the wood.
I, measuring his affections by my own,
Which then most sought where most might not be found, 125
Being one too many by my weary self,
Pursu'd my humour, not pursuing his,
And gladly shunn'd who gladly fled from me.

   Mon. Many a morning hath he there been seen,

With tears augmenting the fresh morning's dew, 130
Adding to clouds more clouds with his deep sighs ;
But all so soon as the all-cheering sun
Should in the farthest east begin to draw
The shady curtains from Aurora's bed, 134
Away from light steals home my heavy son,
And private in his chamber pens himself,
Shuts up his windows, locks fair daylight out,
And makes himself an artificial night.
Black and portentous must this humour prove, 139
Unless good counsel may the cause remove.

   Ben. My noble uncle, do you know the cause ?

   Mon. I neither know it nor can learn of him.

   Ben. Have you importun'd him by any means ?

   Mon. Both by myself and many other friends.

But he, his own affections' counsellor, 145
Is to himself—I will not say how true ;
But to himself so secret and so close,
So far from sounding and discovery,
As is the bud bit with an envious worm,
Ere he can spread his sweet leaves to the air, 150
Or dedicate his beauty to the sun.
Could we but learn from whence his sorrows grow,
We would as willingly give cure as know.

Enter ROMEO.

   Ben. See where he comes. So please you step aside ; 154
I'll know his grievance or be much denied.

   Mon. I would thou wert so happy by thy stay
To hear true shrift. Come, madam, let's away.

            [Exeunt Montague and his Wife.

   Ben. Good morrow, cousin.

   Rom.   Is the day so young ?

   Ben. But new struck nine.

   Rom.   Ay me ! sad hours seem long.
Was that my father that went hence so fast ? 160

   Ben. It was. What sadness lengthens Romeo's hours ?

   Rom. Not having that which having makes them short.

   Ben. In love ?

   Rom. Out—

   Ben. Of love ? 165

   Rom. Out of her favour where I am in love.

   Ben. Alas that love, so gentle in his view,
Should be so tyrannous and rough in proof!

   Rom. Alas that love, whose view is muffled still,
Should without eyes see pathways to his will ! 170
Where shall we dine ? O me ! What fray was here ?
Yet tell me not, for I have heard it all.
Here's much to do with hate, but more with love.
Why then, O brawling love ! O loving hate!
O anything, of nothing first create ! 175
O heavy lightness ! serious vanity !
Mis-shapen chaos of well-seeming forms !
Feather of lead, bright smoke, cold fire, sick health !
Still-waking sleep, that is not what it is !
This love feel I, that feel no love in this. 180
Dost thou not laugh ?

   Ben.   No, coz, I rather weep.

   Rom. Good heart, at what ?

   Ben.   At thy good heart's oppression.

   Rom. Why, such is love's transgression.
Griefs of mine own lie heavy in my breast,
Which thou wilt propagate, to have it prest
With more of thine. This love that thou hast shown 186
Doth add more grief to too much of mine own.
Love is a smoke rais'd with the fume of sighs ;
Being purg'd, a fire sparkling in lovers' eyes ;
Being vex'd, a sea nourish'd with loving tears. 190
What is it else ? A madness most discreet,
A choking gall, and a preserving sweet.
Farewell, my coz.

   Ben.   Soft ! I will go along ;
An if you leave me so, you do me wrong.

   Rom. Tut, I have lost myself ; I am not here : 195
This is not Romeo, he's some other where.

Ben. Tell me in sadness who is that you
love.
Rom. What, shall I groan and tell thee?
Ben.   Groan! Why, no;
But sadly tell me who.
Rom. Bid a sick man in sadness make his
will.   200
Ah, word ill urg'd to one that is so ill!
In sadness, cousin, I do love a woman.
Ben. I aim'd so near when I suppos'd you
lov'd.
Rom. A right good markman! And she's
fair I love.
Ben. A right fair mark, fair coz, is soonest
hit.   205
Rom. Well, in that hit you miss: she'll
not be hit
With Cupid's arrow. She hath Dian's wit,
And in strong proof of chastity well arm'd,
From Love's weak childish bow she lives
unharm'd.   209
She will not stay the siege of loving terms,
Nor bide th' encounter of assailing eyes,
Nor ope her lap to saint-seducing gold.
O, she is rich in beauty; only poor
That, when she dies, with beauty dies her
store.
Ben. Then she hath sworn that she will
still live chaste?   215
Rom. She hath, and in that sparing
makes huge waste;
For beauty, starv'd with her severity,
Cuts beauty off from all posterity.
She is too fair, too wise, wisely too fair,
To merit bliss by making me despair.   220
She hath forsworn to love, and in that vow
Do I live dead that live to tell it now.
Ben. Be rul'd by me: forget to think of her.
Rom. O, teach me how I should forget to
think!
Ben. By giving liberty unto thine eyes.
Examine other beauties.
Rom.   'Tis the way   226
To call hers, exquisite, in question more.
These happy masks that kiss fair ladies'
brows,
Being black, puts us in mind they hide the
fair.
He that is strucken blind cannot forget 230
The precious treasure of his eyesight lost.
Show me a mistress that is passing fair,
What doth her beauty serve but as a note
Where I may read who pass'd that passing
fair?   234
Farewell; thou canst not teach me to forget.
Ben. I'll pay that doctrine or else die in
debt.   [*Exeunt.*

SCENE II. *A street.*

Enter CAPULET, COUNTY PARIS, *and the*
Clown, *his servant.*

Cap. But Montague is bound as well as I,
In penalty alike; and 'tis not hard, I think,

For men so old as we to keep the peace.
Par. Of honourable reckoning are you
both,
And pity 'tis you liv'd at odds so long.   5
But now, my lord, what say you to my suit?
Cap. But saying o'er what I have said
before:
My child is yet a stranger in the world,
She hath not seen the change of fourteen
years;
Let two more summers wither in their
pride   10
Ere we may think her ripe to be a bride.
Par. Younger than she are happy
mothers made.
Cap. And too soon marr'd are those so
early made.
Earth hath swallowed all my hopes but she;
She is the hopeful lady of my earth.   15
But woo her, gentle Paris, get her heart;
My will to her consent is but a part.
And, she agreed, within her scope of choice
Lies my consent and fair according voice.
This night I hold an old accustom'd feast,
Whereto I have invited many a guest,   21
Such as I love; and you among the store,
One more, most welcome, makes my num-
ber more.
At my poor house look to behold this night
Earth-treading stars that make dark
heaven light.   25
Such comfort as do lusty young men feel
When well-apparell'd April on the heel
Of limping winter treads, even such delight
Among fresh female buds shall you this
night
Inherit at my house. Hear all, all see,   30
And like her most whose merit most shall
be;
Which on more view of many, mine, being
one,
May stand in number, though in reck'ning
none.
Come, go with me. [*To Servant, giving him
a paper*] Go, sirrah, trudge about
Through fair Verona; find those persons
out   35
Whose names are written there, and to
them say
My house and welcome on their pleasure
stay.   [*Exeunt Capulet and Paris.*
Serv. Find them out whose names are
written here! It is written that the shoe-
maker should meddle with his yard and the
tailor with his last, the fisher with his pencil
and the painter with his nets; but I am
sent to find those persons whose names are
here writ, and can never find what names
the writing person hath here writ. I must
to the learned. In good time!   44

Enter BENVOLIO *and* ROMEO.

Ben. Tut, man, one fire burns out another's burning,

One pain is less'ned by another's anguish;
Turn giddy, and be holp by backward
  turning;
One desperate grief cures with another's
  languish.
Take thou some new infection to thy
  eye,
And the rank poison of the old will die. 50
  Rom. Your plantain leaf is excellent for
    that.
  Ben. For what, I pray thee?
  Rom.   For your broken shin.
  Ben. Why, Romeo, art thou mad?
  Rom. Not mad, but bound more than a
    madman is;   54
Shut up in prison, kept without my food,
Whipt and tormented, and—God-den,
  good fellow.
  Serv. God gi' go'den. I pray, sir, can you
    read?
  Rom. Ay, mine own fortune in my misery.
  Serv. Perhaps you have learned it with-
out book. But I pray, can you read any-
thing you see?   60
  Rom. Ay, if I know the letters and the
language.
  Serv. Ye say honestly; rest you merry!
  Rom. Stay, fellow; I can read.   63
  [*He reads the list*] 'Signior Martino and
his wife and daughters; County Anselme
and his beauteous sisters; the lady widow
of Vitruvio; Signior Placentio and his
lovely nieces; Mercutio and his brother
Valentine; mine uncle Capulet, his wife,
and daughters; my fair niece Rosaline
and Livia; Signior Valentio and his cousin
Tybalt; Lucio and the lively Helena.' 70
A fair assembly. [*Gives back the paper*]
  Whither should they come?
  Serv. Up.
  Rom. Whither?
  Serv. To supper. To our house.
  Rom. Whose house?   75
  Serv. My master's.
  Rom. Indeed, I should have ask'd you
    that before.
  Serv. Now I'll tell you without asking:
my master is the great rich Capulet; and
if you be not of the house of Montagues, I
pray come and crush a cup of wine. Rest
you merry!   [*Exit.*
  Ben. At this same ancient feast of
    Capulet's   82
Sups the fair Rosaline whom thou so loves,
With all the admired beauties of Verona.
Go thither, and with unattainted eye   85
Compare her face with some that I shall
  show,
And I will make thee think thy swan a
  crow.
  Rom. When the devout religion of mine
    eye
Maintains such falsehood, then turn tears
    to fires;

And these, who, often drown'd, could never
  die,   90
Transparent heretics, be burnt for liars!
One fairer than my love! The all-seeing
  sun
Ne'er saw her match since first the world
  begun.
  Ben. Tut, you saw her fair, none else
    being by,
Herself pois'd with herself in either eye; 95
But in that crystal scales let there be
  weigh'd
Your lady's love against some other maid
That I will show you shining at this feast,
And she shall scant show well that now
    seems best.
  Rom. I'll go along, no such sight to be
    shown,   100
But to rejoice in splendour of mine own.
                            [*Exeunt.*

SCENE III. *Capulet's house.*

Enter LADY CAPULET *and* Nurse.

  Lady C. Nurse, where's my daughter?
    Call her forth to me.
  Nurse. Now, by my maidenhead at
    twelve year old,
I bade her come. What, lamb! what, lady-
  bird!
God forbid! Where's this girl? What,
  Juliet!

Enter JULIET.

  Jul. How now, who calls?   5
  Nurse. Your mother.
  Jul. Madam, I am here. What is your will?
  Lady C. This is the matter. Nurse, give
    leave awhile,
We must talk in secret. Nurse, come back
    again;
I have rememb'red me, thou's hear our
    counsel.   10
Thou knowest my daughter's of a pretty
    age.
  Nurse. Faith, I can tell her age unto an
    hour.
  Lady C. She's not fourteen.
  Nurse.   I'll lay fourteen of my teeth—
And yet, to my teen be it spoken, I have but
    four—
She's not fourteen. How long is it now 15
To Lammas-tide?
  Lady C.   A fortnight and odd days.
  Nurse. Even or odd, of all days in the
    year,
Come Lammas Eve at night shall she be
    fourteen.
Susan and she—God rest all Christian
    souls!—   19
Were of an age. Well, Susan is with God;
She was too good for me. But, as I said,
On Lammas Eve at night shall she be
    fourteen;

That shall she, marry ; I remember it well.
'Tis since the earthquake now eleven years ;
And she was wean'd—I never shall forget
   it—   25
Of all the days of the year, upon that day ;
For I had then laid wormwood to my dug,
Sitting in the sun under the dove-house
   wall ;
My lord and you were then at Mantua.
Nay, I do bear a brain. But, as I said,   30
When it did taste the wormwood on the
   nipple
Of my dug, and felt it bitter, pretty fool,
To see it tetchy, and fall out with the
   dug !
Shake, quoth the dove-house. 'Twas no
   need, I trow,
To bid me trudge.   35
And since that time it is eleven years ;
For then she could stand high-lone ; nay,
   by th' rood,
She could have run and waddled all about ;
For even the day before, she broke her
   brow ;
And then my husband—God be with his
   soul !   40
'A was a merry man—took up the child.
' Yea,' quoth he ' dost thou fall upon thy
   face ?
Thou wilt fall backward when thou hast
   more wit,
Wilt thou not, Jule ? ' And, by my
   holidam,
The pretty wretch left crying, and said
   ' Ay '.   45
To see, now, how a jest shall come about !
I warrant, an I should live a thousand
   years,
I never should forget it : ' Wilt thou not,
   Jule ? ' quoth he ;
And, pretty fool, it stinted, and said ' Ay '.
   Lady C. Enough of this ; I pray thee
     hold thy peace.   50
   Nurse. Yes, madam. Yet I cannot choose
   but laugh
To think it should leave crying and say
   ' Ay '.
And yet, I warrant, it had upon it brow
A bump as big as a young cock'rel's stone—
A perilous knock ; and it cried bitterly. 55
' Yea,' quoth my husband ' fall'st upon thy
   face ?
Thou wilt fall backward when thou comest
   to age ;
Wilt thou not, Jule ? ' It stinted, and said
   ' Ay '.
   Jul. And stint thou too, I pray thee,
     nurse, say I.
   Nurse. Peace, I have done. God mark
     thee to his grace !   60
Thou wast the prettiest babe that e'er I
   nurs'd ;
An I might live to see thee married once,
I have my wish.

   Lady C. Marry, that ' marry ' is the very
     theme   64
I came to talk of. Tell me, daughter Juliet,
How stands your dispositions to be married ?
   Jul. It is an honour that I dream not of.
   Nurse. An honour ! Were not I thine
   only nurse,
I would say thou hadst suck'd wisdom
   from thy teat.
   Lady C. Well, think of marriage now.
     Younger than you,   70
Here in Verona, ladies of esteem,
Are made already mothers. By my count,
I was your mother much upon these years
That you are now a maid. Thus, then, in
   brief :
The valiant Paris seeks you for his love. 75
   Nurse. A man, young lady ! lady, such a
   man
As all the world—why, he's a man of
   wax.
   Lady C. Verona's summer hath not such
   a flower.
   Nurse. Nay, he's a flower ; in faith, a
   very flower.
   Lady C. What say you ? Can you love
     the gentleman ?   80
This night you shall behold him at our
   feast ;
Read o'er the volume of young Paris' face,
And find delight writ there with beauty's
   pen ;
Examine every married lineament,
And see how one another lends content ; 85
And what obscur'd in this fair volume lies
Find written in the margent of his eyes.
This precious book of love, this unbound
   lover,
To beautify him, only lacks a cover.
The fish lives in the sea, and 'tis much
   pride   90
For fair without the fair within to hide.
That book in many's eyes doth share the
   glory
That in gold clasps locks in the golden
   story ;
So shall you share all that he doth possess,
By having him making yourself no less. 95
   Nurse. No less ! Nay, bigger ; women
   grow by men.
   Lady C. Speak briefly, can you like of
   Paris' love ?
   Jul. I'll look to like, if looking liking
   move ;
But no more deep will I endart mine eye
Than your consent gives strength to make
   it fly.   100

          Enter a Servant.

   Serv. Madam, the guests are come, supper
serv'd up, you call'd, my young lady ask'd
for, the nurse curs'd in the pantry, and
everything in extremity. I must hence to
wait ; I beseech you, follow straight.

Lady C. We follow thee. [*Exit Servant*]
  Juliet, the County stays.   105
Nurse. Go, girl, seek happy nights to
  happy days.   [*Exeunt.*

SCENE IV. *A street.*

Enter ROMEO, MERCUTIO, BENVOLIO, *with
five or six other* Maskers; Torch-bearers.

Rom. What, shall this speech be spoke
    for our excuse ?
Or shall we on without apology ?
  Ben. The date is out of such prolixity.
We'll have no Cupid hoodwink'd with a
    scarf,
Bearing a Tartar's painted bow of lath,   5
Scaring the ladies like a crow-keeper ;
Nor no without-book prologue, faintly
    spoke
After the prompter, for our entrance ;
But, let them measure us by what they will,
We'll measure them a measure, and be
    gone.   10
  Rom. Give me a torch ; I am not for this
    ambling ;
Being but heavy, I will bear the light.
  Mer. Nay, gentle Romeo, we must have
    you dance.
  Rom. Not I, believe me. You have danc-
    ing shoes
With nimble soles : I have a soul of lead   15
So stakes me to the ground I cannot move.
  Mer. You are a lover ; borrow Cupid's
    wings
And soar with them above a common
    bound.
  Rom. I am too sore enpierced with his
    shaft
To soar with his light feathers ; and so
    bound   20
I cannot bound a pitch above dull woe.
Under love's heavy burden do I sink.
  Mer. And to sink in it should you burden
    love ;
Too great oppression for a tender thing.
  Rom. Is love a tender thing ? It is too
    rough,   25
Too rude, too boist'rous, and it pricks like
    thorn.
  Mer. If love be rough with you, be rough
    with love ;
Prick love for pricking, and you beat love
    down.
Give me a case to put my visage in.
                      [*Putting on a mask.*
A visor for a visor ! What care I   30
What curious eye doth quote deformities ?
Here are the beetle brows shall blush for me.
  Ben. Come, knock and enter ; and no
    sooner in
But every man betake him to his legs.
  Rom. A torch for me. Let wantons, light
    of heart,   35
Tickle the senseless rushes with their heels ;

For I am proverb'd with a grandsire phrase ;
I'll be a candle-holder and look on ;
The game was ne'er so fair, and I am done.
  Mer. Tut, dun's the mouse, the con-
    stable's own word ;   40
If thou art Dun, we'll draw thee from the
    mire
Of this sir-reverence love, wherein thou
    stickest
Up to the ears. Come, we burn daylight, ho !
  Rom. Nay, that's not so.
  Mer.   I mean, sir, in delay
We waste our lights in vain—like lights by
    day.   45
Take our good meaning, for our judgment
    sits
Five times in that ere once in our five wits.
  Rom. And we mean well in going to this
    mask ;
But 'tis no wit to go.
  Mer.   Why, may one ask ?   49
  Rom. I dreamt a dream to-night.
  Mer.   And so did I.
  Rom. Well, what was yours ?
  Mer.   That dreamers often lie.
  Rom. In bed asleep, while they do dream
    things true.
  Mer. O, then I see Queen Mab hath been
    with you.
She is the fairies' midwife, and she comes
In shape no bigger than an agate stone   55
On the fore-finger of an alderman,
Drawn with a team of little atomies
Athwart men's noses as they lie asleep ;
Her waggon-spokes made of long spinners'
    legs ;
The cover, of the wings of grasshoppers ;   60
Her traces, of the smallest spider's web ;
Her collars, of the moonshine's wat'ry
    beams ;
Her whip, of cricket's bone ; the lash, of
    film ;
Her waggoner, a small grey-coated gnat,
Not half so big as a round little worm   65
Prick'd from the lazy finger of a maid.
Her chariot is an empty hazel-nut,
Made by the joiner squirrel or old grub,
Time out o' mind the fairies' coachmakers.
And in this state she gallops night by
    night
Through lovers' brains, and then they
    dream of love ;   71
O'er courtiers' knees, that dream on curtsies
    straight ;
O'er lawyers' fingers, who straight dream
    on fees ;
O'er ladies' lips, who straight on kisses
    dream,
Which oft the angry Mab with blisters
    plagues,   75
Because their breaths with sweetmeats
    tainted are.
Sometime she gallops o'er a courtier's nose,
And then dreams he of smelling out a suit ;

And sometime comes she with a tithe-pig's
    tail,
Tickling a parson's nose as 'a lies asleep, 80
Then dreams he of another benefice.
Sometime she driveth o'er a soldier's neck,
And then dreams he of cutting foreign
    throats,
Of breaches, ambuscadoes, Spanish blades,
Of healths five fathom deep; and then
    anon   85
Drums in his ear, at which he starts and
    wakes,
And, being thus frighted, swears a prayer
    or two,
And sleeps again. This is that very Mab
That plats the manes of horses in the night;
And bakes the elf-locks in foul sluttish hairs,
Which once untangled much misfortune
    bodes.   91
This is the hag, when maids lie on their
    backs,
That presses them and learns them first to
    bear,
Making them women of good carriage.   94
This is she—
    Rom.   Peace, peace, Mercutio, peace!
Thou talk'st of nothing.
    Mer.   True, I talk of dreams,
Which are the children of an idle brain,
Begot of nothing but vain fantasy;
Which is as thin of substance as the air,
And more inconstant than the wind, who
    woos   100
Even now the frozen bosom of the north,
And, being anger'd, puffs away from thence,
Turning his side to the dew-dropping south.
    Ben. This wind you talk of blows us from
    ourselves:
Supper is done, and we shall come too
    late.
    Rom. I fear, too early; for my mind
    misgives   106
Some consequence, yet hanging in the stars,
Shall bitterly begin his fearful date
With this night's revels and expire the term
Of a despised life clos'd in my breast,   110
By some vile forfeit of untimely death.
But He that hath the steerage of my course
Direct my sail! On, lusty gentlemen.
    Ben. Strike, drum.
    [*They march about the stage. Exeunt.*

    Scene V. *Capulet's house.*

Enter the Maskers. Servingmen *come forth
    with napkins.*

    1 *Serv.* Where's Potpan, that he helps
not to take away? He shift a trencher! He
scrape a trencher!
    2 *Serv.* When good manners shall lie all
in one or two men's hands, and they unwash'd too, 'tis a foul thing.   4
    1 *Serv.* Away with the join-stools, remove
the court-cubbert, look to the plate. Good

thou, save me a piece of marchpane; and
as thou loves me let the porter let in Susan
Grindstone and Nell. Antony, and Potpan!
    2 *Serv.* Ay, boy, ready.   9
    1 *Serv.* You are look'd for and call'd for,
ask'd for and sought for, in the great
chamber.
    3 *Serv.* We cannot be here and there too.
Cheerly, boys! Be brisk a while, and the
longer liver take all!   [*Servants retire.*

Enter CAPULET, *with all the* Guests *and*
    Gentlewomen *to the Maskers.*

    Cap. Welcome, gentlemen! Ladies that
    have their toes
Unplagu'd with corns will have a bout with
    you.   15
Ah ha, my mistresses! which of you all
Will now deny to dance? She that makes
    dainty,
She I'll swear hath corns; am I come near
    ye now?
Welcome, gentlemen! I have seen the day
That I have worn a visor and could tell 20
A whispering tale in a fair lady's ear,
Such as would please. 'Tis gone, 'tis gone,
    'tis gone!
You are welcome, gentlemen. Come,
    musicians, play.
A hall, a hall! give room; and foot it, girls.
          [*Music plays, and they dance.*
More light, you knaves; and turn the
    tables up,   25
And quench the fire, the room is grown too
    hot.
Ah, sirrah, this unlook'd-for sport comes
    well.
Nay, sit, nay, sit, good cousin Capulet,
For you and I are past our dancing days.
How long is't now since last yourself and I
Were in a mask?
    2 *Cap.*   By'r Lady, thirty years.   31
    Cap. What, man? 'tis not so much, 'tis
    not so much.
'Tis since the nuptial of Lucentio,
Come Pentecost as quickly as it will,
Some five and twenty years; and then we
    mask'd.   35
    2 *Cap.* 'Tis more, 'tis more: his son is
    elder, sir;
His son is thirty.
    Cap.   Will you tell me that?
His son was but a ward two years ago.
    Rom. [*To a servant*] What lady's that
    which doth enrich the hand
Of yonder knight?   40
    Serv. I know not, sir.
    Rom. O, she doth teach the torches to
    burn bright!
It seems she hangs upon the cheek of night
As a rich jewel in an Ethiop's ear—
Beauty too rich for use, for earth too dear!
So shows a snowy dove trooping with
    crows   46

As yonder lady o'er her fellows shows.
The measure done, I'll watch her place of
    stand,
And, touching hers, make blessed my rude
    hand.
Did my heart love till now? Forswear it,
    sight;   50
For I ne'er saw true beauty till this night.
   Tyb. This, by his voice, should be a
    Montague.
Fetch me my rapier, boy. What, dares
    the slave
Come hither, cover'd with an antic face,
To fleer and scorn at our solemnity? 55
Now, by the stock and honour of my kin,
To strike him dead I hold it not a sin.
   Cap. Why, how now, kinsman! Where-
    fore storm you so?
   Tyb. Uncle, this is a Montague, our foe;
A villain, that is hither come in spite 60
To scorn at our solemnity this night.
   Cap. Young Romeo, is it?
   Tyb.   'Tis he, that villain Romeo.
   Cap. Content thee, gentle coz, let him
    alone.
'A bears him like a portly gentleman;
And, to say truth, Verona brags of him 65
To be a virtuous and well-govern'd youth.
I would not for the wealth of all this town
Here in my house do him disparagement.
Therefore be patient, take no note of him;
It is my will; the which if thou respect, 70
Show a fair presence and put off these
    frowns,
An ill-beseeming semblance for a feast.
   Tyb. It fits, when such a villain is a guest.
I'll not endure him.
   Cap.   He shall be endur'd. 74
What, goodman boy! I say he shall. Go to;
Am I the master here or you? Go to.
You'll not endure him! God shall mend my
    soul!
You'll make a mutiny among my guests!
You will set cock-a-hoop! You'll be the
    man!
   Tyb. Why, uncle, 'tis a shame.
   Cap.   Go to, go to; 80
You are a saucy boy. Is't so, indeed?
This trick may chance to scathe you. I
    know what:
You must contrary me. Marry, 'tis time.—
Well said, my hearts!—You are a princox;
    go.
Be quiet, or—More light, more light!—For
    shame! 85
I'll make you quiet. What!—Cheerly, my
    hearts!
   Tyb. Patience perforce with wilful choler
    meeting
Makes my flesh tremble in their different
    greeting. 88
I will withdraw; but this intrusion shall,
Now seeming sweet, convert to bitt'rest
    gall.   *[Exit.*

   Rom. [*To Juliet*] If I profane with my un-
    worthiest hand 91
This holy shrine, the gentle fine is this:
My lips, two blushing pilgrims, ready stand
To smooth that rough touch with a tender
    kiss.
   Jul. Good pilgrim, you do wrong your
    hand too much, 95
Which mannerly devotion shows in this;
For saints have hands that pilgrims' hands
    do touch,
And palm to palm is holy palmers' kiss.
   Rom. Have not saints lips, and holy
    palmers too?
   Jul. Ay, pilgrim, lips that they must use
    in pray'r. 100
   Rom. O, then, dear saint, let lips do what
    hands do!
They pray; grant thou, lest faith turn to
    despair.
   Jul. Saints do not move, though grant
    for prayers' sake.
   Rom. Then move not while my prayer's
    effect I take. 104
Thus from my lips by thine my sin is
    purg'd.   *[Kissing her.*
   Jul. Then have my lips the sin that they
    have took.
   Rom. Sin from my lips? O trespass
    sweetly urg'd!
Give me my sin again.   *[Kissing her.*
   Jul.   You kiss by th' book.
   Nurse. Madam, your mother craves a
    word with you. 109
   Rom. What is her mother?
   Nurse.   Marry, bachelor,
Her mother is the lady of the house,
And a good lady, and a wise and virtuous.
I nurs'd her daughter that you talk'd
    withal.
I tell you, he that can lay hold of her 114
Shall have the chinks.
   Rom.   Is she a Capulet?
O dear account! my life is my foe's debt.
   Ben. Away, be gone; the sport is at the
    best.
   Rom. Ay, so I fear; the more is my
    unrest.
   Cap. Nay, gentlemen, prepare not to be
    gone; 119
We have a trifling foolish banquet towards.
Is it e'en so? Why, then I thank you all;
I thank you, honest gentlemen; good
    night.
More torches here! [*Exeunt Maskers*] Come
    on then, let's to bed.
Ah, sirrah, by my fay, it waxes late;
I'll to my rest. 125
       [Exeunt all but Juliet and Nurse.
   Jul. Come hither, nurse. What is yond
    gentleman?
   Nurse. The son and heir of old Tiberio.
   Jul. What's he that now is going out of
    door?

Nurse. Marry, that I think be young
    Petruchio.
Jul. What's he that follows there, that
    would not dance ?   130
Nurse. I know not.
Jul. Go ask his name.—If he be married,
My grave is like to be my wedding bed.
Nurse. His name is Romeo, and a
    Montague ;
The only son of your great enemy.   135
   Jul. My only love sprung from my only
    hate !
Too early seen unknown, and known too
    late !
Prodigious birth of love it is to me,
That I must love a loathed enemy.
   Nurse. What's this ? What's this ?
   Jul.   A rhyme I learnt even now
Of one I danc'd withal.
            [*One calls within ' Juliet '.*
Nurse.   Anon, anon !   141
Come, let's away ; the strangers all are
    gone.   [*Exeunt.*

ACT TWO

PROLOGUE

Enter CHORUS.

Now old desire doth in his death-bed lie,
And young affection gapes to be his heir ;
That fair for which love groan'd for and
    would die,
With tender Juliet match'd, is now not fair.
Now Romeo is belov'd, and loves again,   5
Alike bewitched by the charm of looks ;
But to his foe suppos'd he must complain,
And she steal love's sweet bait from fearful
    hooks.
Being held a foe, he may not have access
To breathe such vows as lovers use to
    swear;   10
And she as much in love, her means much
    less
To meet her new beloved any where.
But passion lends them power, time means,
    to meet,
Temp'ring extremities with extreme sweet.
                     [*Exit.*

SCENE I. *A lane by the wall of Capulet's*
         orchard.

Enter ROMEO.

   Rom. Can I go forward when my heart is
    here ?
Turn back, dull earth, and find thy centre
    out.
      [*He climbs the wall and leaps down*
                    within it.

Enter BENVOLIO *with* MERCUTIO.

   Ben. Romeo ! my cousin, Romeo !
    Romeo !
   Mer.   He is wise,

And, on my life, hath stol'n him home to
    bed.
   Ben. He ran this way, and leapt this
    orchard wall.   5
Call, good Mercutio.
   Mer.   Nay, I'll conjure too.
Romeo ! humours ! madman ! passion !
    lover !
Appear thou in the likeness of a sigh ;
Speak but one rhyme and I am satisfied ;
Cry but ' Ay me ! ' pronounce but ' love '
    and ' dove ' ;   10
Speak to my gossip Venus one fair word,
One nickname for her purblind son and
    heir,
Young Adam Cupid, he that shot so trim
When King Cophetua lov'd the beggar-
    maid !
He heareth not, he stirreth not, he moveth
    not ;   15
The ape is dead, and I must conjure him.
I conjure thee by Rosaline's bright eyes,
By her high forehead and her scarlet lip,
By her fine foot, straight leg, and quivering
    thigh,   19
And the demesnes that there adjacent lie,
That in thy likeness thou appear to us.
   Ben. An if he hear thee, thou wilt anger
    him.
   Mer. This cannot anger him : 'twould
    anger him
To raise a spirit in his mistress' circle
Of some strange nature, letting it there
    stand   25
Till she had laid it and conjur'd it down ;
That were some spite. My invocation
Is fair and honest : in his mistress' name,
I conjure only but to raise up him.
   Ben. Come, he hath hid himself among
    these trees   30
To be consorted with the humorous night :
Blind is his love, and best befits the
    dark.
   Mer. If love be blind, love cannot hit the
    mark.
Now will he sit under a medlar tree,
And wish his mistress were that kind of
    fruit   35
As maids call medlars when they laugh
    alone.
O Romeo, that she were, O that she were
An open et cetera, thou a pop'rin pear !
Romeo, good night. I'll to my truckle bed ;
This field-bed is too cold for me to sleep.   40
Come, shall we go ?
   Ben.   Go, then ; for 'tis in vain
To seek him here that means not to be
    found.   [*Exeunt.*

SCENE II. *Capulet's orchard.*

Enter ROMEO.

   Rom. He jests at scars that never felt a
    wound.

Enter JULIET *above at a window.*

But, soft! What light through yonder
  window breaks?
It is the east, and Juliet is the sun.
Arise, fair sun, and kill the envious moon,
Who is already sick and pale with grief   5
That thou her maid art far more fair than
  she.
Be not her maid, since she is envious;
Her vestal livery is but sick and green,
And none but fools do wear it; cast it off.
It is my lady; O, it is my love!   10
O that she knew she were!
She speaks, yet she says nothing. What of
  that?
Her eye discourses; I will answer it.
I am too bold, 'tis not to me she speaks;
Two of the fairest stars in all the heaven,
Having some business, do entreat her eyes
To twinkle in their spheres till they return.
What if her eyes were there, they in her
  head?
The brightness of her cheek would shame
  those stars,
As daylight doth a lamp; her eyes in
  heaven   20
Would through the airy region stream so
  bright
That birds would sing, and think it were
  not night.
See how she leans her cheek upon her hand!
O that I were a glove upon that hand,   24
That I might touch that cheek!
  Jul.   Ay me!
  Rom.   She speaks.
O, speak again, bright angel, for thou art
As glorious to this night, being o'er my
  head,
As is a winged messenger of heaven
Unto the white-upturned wond'ring eyes
Of mortals that fall back to gaze on him, 30
When he bestrides the lazy-pacing clouds
And sails upon the bosom of the air.
  Jul. O Romeo, Romeo! wherefore art
  thou Romeo?
Deny thy father and refuse thy name;   34
Or, if thou wilt not, be but sworn my love,
And I'll no longer be a Capulet.
  Rom. [*Aside*] Shall I hear more, or shall
  I speak at this?
  Jul. 'Tis but thy name that is my enemy;
Thou art thyself, though not a Montague.
What's Montague? It is nor hand, nor
  foot,   40
Nor arm, nor face, nor any other part
Belonging to a man. O, be some other
  name!
What's in a name? That which we call a
  rose
By any other name would smell as sweet;
So Romeo would, were he not Romeo
  call'd,   45
Retain that dear perfection which he owes

Without that title. Romeo, doff thy name;
And for thy name, which is no part of thee,
Take all myself.
  Rom.   I take thee at thy word:
Call me but love, and I'll be new baptiz'd;
Henceforth I never will be Romeo.   51
  Jul. What man art thou, that, thus be-
  screen'd in night,
So stumblest on my counsel?
  Rom.   By a name
I know not how to tell thee who I am:
My name, dear saint, is hateful to myself,
Because it is an enemy to thee;   56
Had I it written, I would tear the word.
  Jul. My ears have yet not drunk a
  hundred words
Of thy tongue's uttering, yet I know the
  sound:
Art thou not Romeo, and a Montague? 60
  Rom. Neither, fair maid, if either thee
  dislike.
  Jul. How cam'st thou hither, tell me, and
  wherefore?
The orchard walls are high and hard to
  climb;
And the place death, considering who thou
  art,
If any of my kinsmen find thee here.   65
  Rom. With love's light wings did I o'er-
  perch these walls,
For stony limits cannot hold love out;
And what love can do, that dares love
  attempt.
Therefore thy kinsmen are no stop to me.
  Jul. If they do see thee, they will murder
  thee.   70
  Rom. Alack, there lies more peril in thine
  eye
Than twenty of their swords; look thou
  but sweet,
And I am proof against their enmity.
  Jul. I would not for the world they saw
  thee here.
  Rom. I have night's cloak to hide me
  from their eyes;   75
And but thou love me, let them find me
  here.
My life were better ended by their hate
Than death prorogued wanting of thy love.
  Jul. By whose direction found'st thou
  out this place?
  Rom. By love, that first did prompt me
  to enquire;   80
He lent me counsel, and I lent him eyes.
I am no pilot; yet, wert thou as far
As that vast shore wash'd with the farthest
  sea,
I should adventure for such merchandise.
  Jul. Thou knowest the mask of night is
  on my face,   85
Else would a maiden blush bepaint my
  cheek
For that which thou hast heard me speak
  to-night.

Fain would I dwell on form, fain, fain deny
What I have spoke; but farewell compli-
    ment!
Dost thou love me? I know thou wilt say
    ay,   90
And I will take thy word; yet, if thou
    swear'st,
Thou mayst prove false; at lovers' per-
    juries
They say Jove laughs. O gentle Romeo,
If thou dost love, pronounce it faithfully.
Or, if thou think'st I am too quickly won,
I'll frown, and be perverse, and say thee
    nay,   96
So thou wilt woo; but else, not for the
    world.
In truth, fair Montague, I am too fond;
And therefore thou mayst think my
    haviour light;
But trust me, gentleman, I'll prove more
    true   100
Than those that have more cunning to be
    strange.
I should have been more strange, I must
    confess,
But that thou overheard'st, ere I was
    ware,
My true love's passion. Therefore pardon
    me,   104
And not impute this yielding to light love,
Which the dark night hath so discovered.
    Rom. Lady, by yonder blessed moon I
    vow,
That tips with silver all these fruit-tree
    tops—
    Jul. O, swear not by the moon, th' incon-
    stant moon,   109
That monthly changes in her circled orb,
Lest that thy love prove likewise variable.
    Rom. What shall I swear by?
    Jul.   Do not swear at all;
Or, if thou wilt, swear by thy gracious self,
Which is the god of my idolatry,
And I'll believe thee.
    Rom.   If my heart's dear love— 115
    Jul. Well, do not swear. Although I joy
    in thee,
I have no joy of this contract to-night:
It is too rash, too unadvis'd, too sudden;
Too like the lightning, which doth cease to
    be
Ere one can say ' It lightens'. Sweet, good
    night!   120
This bud of love, by summer's ripening
    breath,
May prove a beauteous flow'r when next
    we meet.
Good night, good night! As sweet repose
    and rest
Come to thy heart as that within my breast!
    Rom. O, wilt thou leave me so un-
    satisfied?   125
    Jul. What satisfaction canst thou have
    to-night?

    Rom. Th' exchange of thy love's faithful
    vow for mine.
    Jul. I gave thee mine before thou didst
    request it;
And yet I would it were to give again.
    Rom. Wouldst thou withdraw it? For
    what purpose, love?   130
    Jul. But to be frank, and give it thee
    again.
And yet I wish but for the thing I have.
My bounty is as boundless as the sea,
My love as deep: the more I give to thee,
The more I have, for both are infinite. 135
        [*Nurse calls within.*
I hear some noise within. Dear love,
    adieu!—
Anon, good nurse!—Sweet Montague, be
    true.
Stay but a little, I will come again. [*Exit.*
    Rom. O blessed, blessed night! I am
    afeard,
Being in night, all this is but a dream, 140
Too flattering-sweet to be substantial.

    Re-enter JULIET *above.*

    Jul. Three words, dear Romeo, and good
    night indeed.
If that thy bent of love be honourable,
Thy purpose marriage, send me word to-
    morrow,
By one that I'll procure to come to thee,
Where and what time thou wilt perform
    the rite;   146
And all my fortunes at thy foot I'll lay,
And follow thee, my lord, throughout the
    world.
    Nurse. [*Within*] Madam!
    Jul. I come anon.—But if thou meanest
    not well,   150
I do beseech thee—
    Nurse. [*Within*] Madam!
    Jul.   By and by, I come—
To cease thy suit, and leave me to my grief.
To-morrow will I send.
    Rom.   So thrive my soul—
    Jul. A thousand times good night! [*Exit.*
    Rom. A thousand times the worse, to
    want thy light.   155
Love goes toward love as school-boys from
    their books;
But love from love, toward school with
    heavy looks.

    Re-enter JULIET *above.*

    Jul. Hist! Romeo, hist!—O for a
    falc'ner's voice,
To lure this tassel-gentle back again!
Bondage is hoarse, and may not speak
    aloud;   160
Else would I tear the cave where Echo lies,
And make her airy tongue more hoarse
    than mine
With repetition of my Romeo's name.
Romeo!

Rom. It is my soul that calls upon my
    name.   165
How silver-sweet sound lovers' tongues by
    night,
Like softest music to attending ears !
    Jul. Romeo !
    Rom.   My dear ?
    Jul.   At what o'clock to-morrow
Shall I send to thee ?
    Rom.   By the hour of nine.
    Jul. I will not fail. 'Tis twenty years till
    then.   170
I have forgot why I did call thee back.
    Rom. Let me stand here till thou remem-
    ber it.
    Jul. I shall forget, to have thee still stand
    there,
Rememb'ring how I love thy company.
    Rom. And I'll still stay, to have thee still
    forget,   175
Forgetting any other home but this.
    Jul. 'Tis almost morning. I would have
    thee gone ;
And yet no farther than a wanton's bird,
That lets it hop a little from her hand,
Like a poor prisoner in his twisted gyves,
And with a silk thread plucks it back again,
So loving-jealous of his liberty.   182
    Rom. I would I were thy bird.
    Jul.   Sweet, so would I.
Yet I should kill thee with much cherishing.
Good night, good night ! Parting is such
    sweet sorrow   185
That I shall say good night till it be
    morrow.   [*Exit.*
    Rom. Sleep dwell upon thine eyes, peace
    in thy breast !
Would I were sleep and peace, so sweet to
    rest !   188
Hence will I to my ghostly father's cell,
His help to crave and my dear hap to tell.
                          [*Exit.*

    SCENE III.   *Friar Lawrence's cell.*

    Enter FRIAR LAWRENCE *with a basket.*

    Fri. L. The gray-ey'd morn smiles on the
    frowning night,
Check'ring the eastern clouds with streaks
    of light ;
And fleckel'd darkness like a drunkard reels
From forth day's path and Titan's fiery
    wheels.   4
Now, ere the sun advance his burning eye
The day to cheer and night's dank dew to
    dry,
I must up-fill this osier cage of ours
With baleful weeds and precious-juiced
    flowers.
The earth that's nature's mother is her
    tomb ;
What is her burying grave, that is her
    womb.   10
And from her womb children of divers kind

We sucking on her natural bosom find ;
Many for many virtues excellent,
None but for some, and yet all different.
O, mickle is the powerful grace that lies   15
In plants, herbs, stones, and their true
    qualities ;
For nought so vile that on the earth doth
    live
But to the earth some special good doth
    give ;
Nor aught so good but, strain'd from that
    fair use,
Revolts from true birth, stumbling on
    abuse :   20
Virtue itself turns vice, being misapplied,
And vice sometime's by action dignified.
Within the infant rind of this weak flower
Poison hath residence, and medicine power;
For this, being smelt, with that part cheers
    each part ;   25
Being tasted, slays all senses with the heart.
Two such opposed kings encamp them still
In man as well as herbs—grace and rude
    will ;
And where the worser is predominant,
Full soon the canker death eats up that
    plant.   30

             Enter ROMEO.

    Rom. Good morrow, father !
    Fri. L.   Benedicite !
What early tongue so sweet saluteth me ?
Young son, it argues a distempered head
So soon to bid good morrow to thy bed.
Care keeps his watch in every old man's
    eye,   35
And where care lodges sleep will never lie ;
But where unbruised youth with unstuff'd
    brain
Doth couch his limbs, there golden sleep
    doth reign.
Therefore thy earliness doth me assure   39
Thou art uprous'd with some distemp'r-
    ature ;
Or if not so, then here I hit it right—
Our Romeo hath not been in bed to-night.
    Rom. That last is true ; the sweeter rest
    was mine.
    Fri. L. God pardon sin ! Wast thou with
    Rosaline ?
    Rom. With Rosaline, my ghostly father ?
    No ;   45
I have forgot that name, and that name's
    woe.
    Fri. L. That's my good son ; but where
    hast thou been then ?
    Rom. I'll tell thee ere thou ask it me
    again.
I have been feasting with mine enemy ;
Where, on a sudden, one hath wounded me 50
That's by me wounded ; both our remedies
Within thy help and holy physic lies.
I bear no hatred, blessed man, for, lo,
My intercession likewise steads my foe.

Fri. L. Be plain, good son, and homely
　　in thy drift ;　　　　　　　　　　　55
Riddling confession finds but riddling
　　shrift.
　　Rom. Then plainly know my heart's dear
　　　　love is set
On the fair daughter of rich Capulet.
As mine on hers, so hers is set on mine ;
And all combin'd, save what thou must
　　combine　　　　　　　　　　　　60
By holy marriage. When, and where, and
　　how,
We met, we woo'd, and made exchange of
　　vow,
I'll tell thee as we pass ; but this I pray,
That thou consent to marry us to-day.
　　Fri. L. Holy Saint Francis ! What a
　　　　change is here !　　　　　　　　65
Is Rosaline, that thou didst love so dear,
So soon forsaken ? Young men's love, then,
　　lies
Not truly in their hearts, but in their eyes.
Jesu Maria, what a deal of brine
Hath wash'd thy sallow cheeks for Rosa-
　　line !　　　　　　　　　　　　　70
How much salt water thrown away in
　　waste,
To season love, that of it doth not taste !
The sun not yet thy sighs from heaven
　　clears,
Thy old groans yet ring in mine ancient
　　ears ;　　　　　　　　　　　　74
Lo, here upon thy cheek the stain doth sit
Of an old tear that is not wash'd off yet.
If e'er thou wast thyself, and these woes
　　thine,
Thou and these woes were all for Rosaline.
And art thou chang'd ? Pronounce this
　　sentence, then :
Women may fall, when there's no strength
　　in men.　　　　　　　　　　　　80
　　Rom. Thou chid'st me oft for loving
　　　　Rosaline.
　　Fri. L. For doting, not for loving, pupil
　　　　mine.
　　Rom. And bad'st me bury love.
　　Fri. L.　　　　　　　　Not in a grave
To lay one in, another out to have.
　　Rom. I pray thee chide me not ; her I
　　　　love now　　　　　　　　　　85
Doth grace for grace and love for love
　　allow ;
The other did not so.
　　Fri. L.　　　　　　O, she knew well
Thy love did read by rote that could not
　　spell.
But come, young waverer, come, go with
　　me,
In one respect I'll thy assistant be ;　　90
For this alliance may so happy prove
To turn your households' rancour to pure
　　love.
　　Rom. O, let us hence ; I stand on sudden
　　　　haste.

　　Fri. L. Wisely and slow ; they stumble
　　　　that run fast.　　　　　　[*Exeunt.*

　　　　　SCENE IV. *A street.*

　　　Enter BENVOLIO *and* MERCUTIO.

　　Mer. Where the devil should this Romeo
　　　　be ?
Came he not home to-night ?
　　Ben. Not to his father's ; I spoke with
　　　　his man.
　　Mer. Why, that same pale hard-hearted
　　　　wench, that Rosaline,　　　　　4
Torments him so that he will sure run mad.
　　Ben. Tybalt, the kinsman to old Capulet,
Hath sent a letter to his father's house.
　　Mer. A challenge, on my life.
　　Ben. Romeo will answer it.
　　Mer. Any man that can write may
answer a letter.　　　　　　　　　　10
　　Ben. Nay, he will answer the letter's
master, how he dares, being dared.
　　Mer. Alas, poor Romeo, he is already
dead : stabb'd with a white wench's black
eye ; run through the ear with a love-
song ; the very pin of his heart cleft with
the blind bow-boy's butt-shaft. And is he a
man to encounter Tybalt ?　　　　　17
　　Ben. Why, what is Tybalt ?
　　Mer. More than Prince of Cats. O,
he's the courageous captain of compliments. He fights as you sing prick-
song : keeps time, distance, and proportion ; he rests his minim rests, one, two,
and the third in your bosom ; the very
butcher of a silk button, a duellist, a
duellist ; a gentleman of the very first
house, of the first and second cause. Ah,
the immortal passado ! the punto reverso !
the hay !—　　　　　　　　　　　　26
　　Ben. The what ?
　　Mer. The pox of such antic, lisping,
affecting fantasticoes ; these new tuners
of accent !—' By Jesu, a very good blade !
a very tall man ! a very good whore ! '
Why, is not this a lamentable thing, grandsire, that we should be thus afflicted with
these strange flies, these fashion-mongers,
these pardon me's, who stand so much on
the new form that they cannot sit at ease
on the old bench ? O, their bones, their
bones !　　　　　　　　　　　　　35

　　　　　Enter ROMEO.

　　Ben. Here comes Romeo, here comes
Romeo.
　　Mer. Without his roe, like a dried herring.
O flesh, flesh, how art thou fishified ! Now is
he for the numbers that Petrarch flow'd in ;
Laura, to his lady, was a kitchen-wench—
marry, she had a better love to berhyme
her ; Dido, a dowdy ; Cleopatra, a gipsy ;
Helen and Hero, hildings and harlots ;
Thisbe, a gray eye or so, but not to

the purpose—Signior Romeo, bon jour!
There's a French salutation to your French
slop. You gave us the counterfeit fairly last
night.

Rom. Good morrow to you both. What
counterfeit did I give you?

Mer. The slip, sir, the slip; can you not
conceive?

Rom. Pardon, good Mercutio; my business was great, and in such a case as mine
a man may strain courtesy. 50

Mer. That's as much as to say, such a
case as yours constrains a man to bow in
the hams.

Rom. Meaning, to curtsy.

Mer. Thou hast most kindly hit it.

Rom. A most courteous exposition. 55

Mer. Nay, I am the very pink of courtesy.

Rom. Pink for flower.

Mer. Right.

Rom. Why, then is my pump well
flower'd. 59

Mer. Sure wit! Follow me this jest now
till thou hast worn out thy pump, that,
when the single sole of it is worn, the jest
may remain, after the wearing, solely
singular.

Rom. O single-sol'd jest, solely singular
for the singleness! 65

Mer. Come between us, good Benvolio;
my wits faints.

Rom. Swits and spurs, swits and spurs;
or I'll cry a match. 68

Mer. Nay, if our wits run the wild-goose
chase, I am done; for thou hast more of
the wild goose in one of thy wits than, I
am sure, I have in my whole five. Was I
with you there for the goose? 72

Rom. Thou wast never with me for anything when thou wast not there for the
goose.

Mer. I will bite thee by the ear for that
jest. 75

Rom. Nay, good goose, bite not.

Mer. Thy wit is a very bitter sweeting;
it is a most sharp sauce.

Rom. And is it not then well serv'd in to
a sweet goose?

Mer. O, here's a wit of cheveril, that
stretches from an inch narrow to an ell
broad! 81

Rom. I stretch it out for that word
'broad', which, added to the goose, proves
thee far and wide a broad goose. 84

Mer. Why, is not this better now than
groaning for love? Now art thou sociable,
now art thou Romeo; now art thou what
thou art by art as well as by nature; for
this drivelling love is like a great natural
that runs lolling up and down to hide his
bauble in a hole.

Ben. Stop there, stop there. 90

Mer. Thou desirest me to stop in my tale
against the hair.

Ben. Thou wouldst else have made thy
tale large.

Mer. O, thou art deceiv'd: I would have
made it short; for I was come to the whole
depth of my tale, and meant, indeed, to
occupy the argument no longer. 96

Rom. Here's goodly gear!

Enter Nurse *and her man,* PETER.

Mer. A sail, a sail!

Ben. Two, two; a shirt and a smock.

Nurse. Peter! 100

Peter. Anon.

Nurse. My fan, Peter.

Mer. Good Peter, to hide her face; for
her fan's the fairer face. 104

Nurse. God ye good morrow, gentlemen.

Mer. God ye good den, fair gentlewoman.

Nurse. Is it good den?

Mer. 'Tis no less, I tell ye; for the
bawdy hand of the dial is now upon the
prick of noon.

Nurse. Out upon you! What a man are
you? 110

Rom. One, gentlewoman, that God hath
made himself to mar.

Nurse. By my troth, it is well said. 'For
himself to mar' quoth 'a! Gentlemen, can
any of you tell me where I may find the
young Romeo? 115

Rom. I can tell you; but young Romeo
will be older when you have found him than
he was when you sought him. I am the
youngest of that name, for fault of a worse.

Nurse. You say well. 120

Mer. Yea, is the worst well? Very well
took, i' faith; wisely, wisely.

Nurse. If you be he, sir, I desire some
confidence with you. 124

Ben. She will indite him to some supper.

Mer. A bawd, a bawd, a bawd! So ho!

Rom. What hast thou found?

Mer. No hare, sir; unless a hare, sir, in a
lenten pie, that is something stale and hoar
ere it be spent.

[*He walks by them and sings.*

> An old hare hoar, 130
> And an old hare hoar,
> Is very good meat in Lent;
> But a hare that is hoar
> Is too much for a score,
> When it hoars ere it be spent. 135

Romeo, will you come to your father's?
We'll to dinner thither.

Rom. I will follow you.

Mer. Farewell, ancient lady; farewell,
[*Sings*] lady, lady, lady. 140

[*Exeunt Mercutio and Benvolio.*

Nurse. I pray you, sir, what saucy
merchant was this that was so full of his
ropery? 142

Rom. A gentleman, nurse, that loves to

hear himself talk, and will speak more in
a minute than he will stand to in a month.

Nurse. An 'a speak anything against me,
I'll take him down, an 'a were lustier than
he is, and twenty such Jacks; and if I
cannot, I'll find those that shall. Scurvy
knave! I am none of his flirt-gills; I am
none of his skains-mates. And thou must
stand by too, and suffer every knave to use
me at his pleasure?   151

Pet. I saw no man use you at his pleasure;
if I had, my weapon should quickly have
been out, I warrant you. I dare draw as
soon as another man, if I see occasion in a
good quarrel, and the law on my side. 155

Nurse. Now, afore God, I am so vex'd
that every part about me quivers. Scurvy
knave!—Pray you, sir, a word; and as I
told you, my young lady bid me enquire
you out; what she bid me say I will keep
to myself. But first let me tell ye, if ye
should lead her in a fool's paradise, as they
say, it were a very gross kind of behaviour,
as they say; for the gentlewoman is young;
and, therefore, if you should deal double
with her, truly it were an ill thing to be
off'red to any gentlewoman, and very weak
dealing.   165

Rom. Nurse, commend me to thy lady
and mistress. I protest unto thee—

Nurse. Good heart, and, i' faith, I will
tell her as much. Lord, Lord! she will be a
joyful woman.

Rom. What wilt thou tell her, nurse?
Thou dost not mark me.   171

Nurse. I will tell her, sir, that you do
protest; which, as I take it, is a gentleman-
like offer.

Rom. Bid her devise
Some means to come to shrift this after-
noon;   175
And there she shall at Friar Lawrence' cell
Be shriv'd and married. Here is for thy
pains.

Nurse. No, truly, sir; not a penny.

Rom. Go to; I say you shall.

Nurse. This afternoon, sir? Well, she
shall be there.   180

Rom. And stay, good nurse—behind the
abbey wall
Within this hour my man shall be with
thee,
And bring thee cords made like a tackled
stair;
Which to the high top-gallant of my joy
Must be my convoy in the secret night. 185
Farewell; be trusty, and I'll quit thy pains.
Farewell; commend me to thy mistress.

Nurse. Now God in heaven bless thee!—
Hark you, sir.

Rom. What say'st thou, my dear nurse?

Nurse. Is your man secret? Did you
ne'er hear say   190
Two may keep counsel, putting one away?

Rom. I warrant thee my man's as true as
steel.

Nurse. Well, sir. My mistress is the
sweetest lady—Lord, Lord! when 'twas a
little prating thing! O, there is a nobleman
in town, one Paris, that would fain lay
knife aboard; but she, good soul, had as
lief see a toad, a very toad, as see him. I
anger her sometimes, and tell her that Paris
is the properer man; but, I'll warrant you,
when I say so she looks as pale as any clout
in the versal world. Doth not rosemary and
Romeo begin both with a letter?   201

Rom. Ay, nurse; what of that? Both
with an R.

Nurse. Ah, mocker! that's the dog's
name. R is for the—no, I know it begins
with some other letter. And she hath the
prettiest sententious of it, of you and rosemary, that it would do you good to hear it.

Rom. Commend me to thy lady. 207

Nurse. Ay, a thousand times.—Peter!

Pet. Anon.

Nurse. [*Handing him her fan*] Before and
apace.   [*Exeunt.*

Scene V. *Capulet's orchard.*

Enter Juliet.

Jul. The clock struck nine when I did
    send the nurse;
In half an hour she promis'd to return.
Perchance she cannot meet him—that's not
    so.
O, she is lame! Love's heralds should be
    thoughts,
Which ten times faster glide than the sun's
    beams   5
Driving back shadows over louring hills;
Therefore do nimble-pinion'd doves draw
    Love,
And therefore hath the wind-swift Cupid
    wings.
Now is the sun upon the highmost hill
Of this day's journey; and from nine till
    twelve   10
Is three long hours, yet she is not come.
Had she affections and warm youthful
    blood,
She would be as swift in motion as a ball;
My words would bandy her to my sweet
    love,
And his to me.   15
But old folks—many feign as they were
    dead;
Unwieldy, slow, heavy, and pale as lead.

Enter Nurse *and* Peter.

O God, she comes! O honey nurse, what
    news?
Hast thou met with him? Send thy man
    away.

Nurse. Peter, stay at the gate.   20
                                  [*Exit Peter.*

Jul. Now, good sweet nurse—O Lord,
    why look'st thou sad ?
Though news be sad, yet tell them merrily ;
If good, thou shamest the music of sweet
    news
By playing it to me with so sour a face.
    Nurse. I am aweary, give me leave a
        while ;   25
Fie, how my bones ache ! What a jaunce
    have I had !
    Jul. I would thou hadst my bones and I
        thy news.
Nay, come, I pray thee speak ; good, good
    nurse, speak.
    Nurse. Jesu, what haste ? Can you not
        stay a while ?
Do you not see that I am out of breath ? 30
    Jul. How art thou out of breath, when
        thou hast breath
To say to me that thou art out of breath ?
The excuse that thou dost make in this
    delay   33
Is longer than the tale thou dost excuse.
Is thy news good or bad ? Answer to that ;
Say either, and I'll stay the circumstance.
Let me be satisfied, is't good or bad ?   37
    Nurse. Well, you have made a simple
choice ; you know not how to choose a
man. Romeo ! no, not he ; though his face
be better than any man's, yet his leg excels
all men's ; and for a hand, and a foot, and
a body, though they be not to be talk'd on,
yet they are past compare. He is not the
flower of courtesy, but I'll warrant him as
gentle as a lamb. Go thy ways, wench ;
serve God. What, have you din'd at home ?
    Jul. No, no. But all this did I know
        before.   46
What says he of our marriage ? What of
    that ?
    Nurse. Lord, how my head aches ! What
        a head have I !
It beats as it would fall in twenty pieces.
My back a t' other side—ah, my back, my
    back !   50
Beshrew your heart for sending me about
To catch my death with jauncing up and
    down !
    Jul. I' faith, I am sorry that thou art not
        well.
Sweet, sweet, sweet nurse, tell me, what
    says my love ?   54
    Nurse. Your love says like an honest
gentleman, and a courteous, and a kind,
and a handsome, and, I warrant, a virtuous
—Where is your mother ?
    Jul. Where is my mother ! Why, she is
        within ;
Where should she be ? How oddly thou
    repliest !
' Your love says like an honest gentle-
    man,   60
Where is your mother ? '
    Nurse.   O God's lady dear !

Are you so hot ? Marry, come up, I trow ;
Is this the poultice for my aching bones ?
Henceforward, do your messages yourself.
    Jul. Here's such a coil ! Come, what says
        Romeo ?   65
    Nurse. Have you got leave to go to shrift
        to-day ?
    Jul. I have.
    Nurse. Then hie you hence to Friar
        Lawrence' cell ;
There stays a husband to make you a wife.
Now comes the wanton blood up in your
    cheeks ;   70
They'll be in scarlet straight at any news.
Hie you to church ; I must another way,
To fetch a ladder, by the which your love
Must climb a bird's nest soon when it is
    dark.   74
I am the drudge, and toil in your delight ;
But you shall bear the burden soon at
    night.
Go ; I'll to dinner ; hie you to the cell.
    Jul. Hie to high fortune ! Honest nurse,
        farewell.   [*Exeunt.*

SCENE VI. *Friar Lawrence's cell.*

Enter FRIAR LAWRENCE *and* ROMEO.

    Fri. L. So smile the heavens upon this
        holy act
That after-hours with sorrow chide us not !
    Rom. Amen, amen ! But come what
        sorrow can,
It cannot countervail the exchange of joy
That one short minute gives me in her
    sight.   5
Do thou but close our hands with holy
    words,
Then love-devouring death do what he
    dare ;
It is enough I may but call her mine.
    Fri. L. These violent delights have violent
        ends,
And in their triumph die ; like fire and
    powder,   10
Which, as thy kiss, consume. The sweetest
    honey
Is loathsome in his own deliciousness,
And in the taste confounds the appetite.
Therefore love moderately : long love doth
    so ;
Too swift arrives as tardy as too slow.   15

Enter JULIET.

Here comes the lady. O, so light a foot
Will ne'er wear out the everlasting flint.
A lover may bestride the gossamer
That idles in the wanton summer air
And yet not fall, so light is vanity.   20
    Jul. Good even to my ghostly confessor.
    Fri. L. Romeo shall thank thee, daughter,
        for us both.
    Jul. As much to him, else is his thanks
        too much.

Rom. Ah, Juliet, if the measure of thy joy
Be heap'd like mine, and that thy skill be
          more   25
To blazon it, then sweeten with thy breath
This neighbour air, and let rich music's
          tongue
Unfold the imagin'd happiness that both
Receive in either by this dear encounter.

Jul. Conceit, more rich in matter than in
          words,   30
Brags of his substance, not of ornament.
They are but beggars that can count their
          worth;
But my true love is grown to such excess
I cannot sum up sum of half my wealth.

Fri. L. Come, come with me, and we will
          make short work;   35
For, by your leaves, you shall not stay
          alone
Till holy church incorporate two in one.
                                    [*Exeunt.*

ACT THREE

SCENE I. *A public place.*

Enter MERCUTIO, BENVOLIO, Page, *and*
          Servants.

Ben. I pray thee, good Mercutio, let's
          retire.
The day is hot, the Capulets abroad,
And if we meet we shall not scape a brawl;
For now, these hot days, is the mad blood
          stirring.   4
Mer. Thou art like one of these fellows
that, when he enters the confines of a
tavern, claps me his sword upon the table,
and says ' God send me no need of thee ! '
and by the operation of the second cup
draws him on the drawer, when, indeed,
there is no need.
Ben. Am I like such a fellow ?   10
Mer. Come, come, thou art as hot a Jack
in thy mood as any in Italy; and as soon
moved to be moody, and as soon moody to
be moved.
Ben. And what to ?   14
Mer. Nay, an there were two such, we
should have none shortly, for one would
kill the other. Thou ! why, thou wilt
quarrel with a man that hath a hair more
or a hair less in his beard than thou hast.
Thou wilt quarrel with a man for cracking
nuts, having no other reason but because
thou hast hazel eyes. What eye but such
an eye would spy out such a quarrel ? Thy
head is as full of quarrels as an egg is full
of meat; and yet thy head hath been
beaten as addle as an egg for quarrelling.
Thou hast quarrell'd with a man for coughing in the street, because he hath wakened
thy dog that hath lain asleep in the sun.
Didst thou not fall out with a tailor for
wearing his new doublet before Easter ?
With another for tying his new shoes with

old riband ? And yet thou wilt tutor me
from quarrelling !   29
Ben. An I were so apt to quarrel as thou
art, any man should buy the fee simple of
my life for an hour and a quarter.
Mer. The fee simple ! O simple !

Enter TYBALT *and* Others.

Ben. By my head, here comes the
Capulets.
Mer. By my heel, I care not.   35
Tyb. Follow me close, for I will speak to
          them.
Gentlemen, good den; a word with one of
          you.
Mer. And but one word with one of us ?
Couple it with something; make it a word
and a blow.
Tyb. You shall find me apt enough to
that, sir, an you will give me occasion.   41
Mer. Could you not take some occasion
without giving ?
Tyb. Mercutio, thou consortest with
Romeo.
Mer. Consort ! What, dost thou make us
minstrels ? An thou make minstrels of us,
look to hear nothing but discords. Here's
my fiddlestick; here's that shall make you
dance. Zounds, consort !   47
Ben. We talk here in the public haunt of
          men;
Either withdraw unto some private place,
Or reason coldly of your grievances,   50
Or else depart; here all eyes gaze on us.
Mer. Men's eyes were made to look, and
          let them gaze;
I will not budge for no man's pleasure, I.

Enter ROMEO.

Tyb. Well, peace be with you, sir. Here
          comes my man.
Mer. But I'll be hang'd, sir, if he wear
          your livery.   55
Marry, go before to field, he'll be your
          follower;
Your worship in that sense may call him
          man.
Tyb. Romeo, the love I bear thee can
          afford
No better term than this : thou art a
          villain.
Rom. Tybalt, the reason that I have to
          love thee   60
Doth much excuse the appertaining rage
To such a greeting. Villain am I none;
Therefore, farewell; I see thou knowest
          me not.
Tyb. Boy, this shall not excuse the
          injuries
That thou hast done me; therefore turn
          and draw.   65
Rom. I do protest I never injur'd thee,
But love thee better than thou canst devise
Till thou shalt know the reason of my love;

And so, good Capulet—which name I
    tender
As dearly as mine own—be satisfied.   70
    Mer. O calm, dishonourable, vile sub-
        mission !
Alla stoccata carries it away.   [*Draws.*
Tybalt, you rat-catcher, will you walk ?
    Tyb. What wouldst thou have with me ?
    Mer. Good King of Cats, nothing but one
of your nine lives ; that I mean to make
bold withal, and, as you shall use me here-
after, dry-beat the rest of the eight. Will
you pluck your sword out of his pilcher by
the ears ? Make haste, lest mine be about
your ears ere it be out.   79
    Tyb. I am for you.   [*Draws.*
    Rom. Gentle Mercutio, put thy rapier up.
    Mer. Come, sir, your passado. [*They fight.*
    Rom. Draw, Benvolio ; beat down their
        weapons.
Gentlemen, for shame, forbear this outrage!
Tybalt ! Mercutio ! the Prince expressly
    hath   85
Forbid this bandying in Verona streets.
Hold, Tybalt ! Good Mercutio !
    [*Tybalt under Romeo's arm thrusts Mer-
        cutio in, and flies with his friends.*
    Mer.   I am hurt.
A plague a both your houses ! I am sped.
Is he gone and hath nothing ?
    Ben.   What, art thou hurt ?
    Mer. Ay, ay, a scratch, a scratch ; marry,
        'tis enough.   90
Where is my page ? Go, villain, fetch a
    surgeon.   [*Exit Page.*
    Rom. Courage, man ; the hurt cannot be
        much.   92
    Mer. No, 'tis not so deep as a well, nor so
wide as a church door, but 'tis enough,
'twill serve. Ask for me to-morrow, and
you shall find me a grave man. I am
peppered, I warrant, for this world. A
plague a both your houses ! Zounds, a dog,
a rat, a mouse, a cat, to scratch a man to
death ! A braggart, a rogue, a villain, that
fights by the book of arithmetic ! Why
the devil came you between us ? I was hurt
under your arm.   100
    Rom. I thought all for the best.
    Mer. Help me into some house, Benvolio,
    or I shall faint.
A plague a both your houses !
They have made worms' meat of me.   104
I have it, and soundly too—Your houses !
    [*Exeunt Mercutio and Benvolio.*
    Rom. This gentleman, the Prince's near
    ally,
My very friend, hath got this mortal hurt
In my behalf ; my reputation stain'd
With Tybalt's slander—Tybalt, that an
    hour
Hath been my cousin. O sweet Juliet,   110
Thy beauty hath made me effeminate,
And in my temper soft'ned valour's steel !

Re-enter BENVOLIO.

    Ben. O Romeo, Romeo, brave Mercutio
        is dead !
That gallant spirit hath aspir'd the clouds,
Which too untimely here did scorn the
    earth.   115
    Rom. This day's black fate on moe days
        doth depend ;
This but begins the woe others must end.

Re-enter TYBALT.

    Ben. Here comes the furious Tybalt back
        again.
    Rom. Alive in triumph and Mercutio
        slain !
Away to heaven respective lenity,   120
And fire-ey'd fury be my conduct now !
Now, Tybalt, take the ' villain ' back again
That late thou gav'st me ; for Mercutio's
    soul
Is but a little way above our heads,
Staying for thine to keep him company. 125
Either thou or I, or both, must go with him.
    Tyb. Thou, wretched boy, that didst con-
        sort him here,
Shalt with him hence.
    Rom.   This shall determine that.
        [*They fight ; Tybalt falls.*
    Ben. Romeo, away, be gone.
The citizens are up, and Tybalt slain.   130
Stand not amaz'd. The Prince will doom
    thee death
If thou art taken. Hence, be gone, away !
    Rom. O, I am fortune's fool !
    Ben.   Why dost thou stay ?
        [*Exit Romeo.*

Enter Citizens.

    1 *Cit.* Which way ran he that kill'd
        Mercutio ?   134
Tybalt, that murderer, which way ran he ?
    Ben. There lies that Tybalt.
    1 *Cit.*   Up, sir, go with me ;
I charge thee in the Prince's name, obey.

Enter PRINCE, *attended* ; MONTAGUE, CAPU-
    LET, *their* Wives, *and All.*

    Prin. Where are the vile beginners of this
        fray ?   138
    Ben. O noble Prince, I can discover all
The unlucky manage of this fatal brawl :
There lies the man, slain by young Romeo,
That slew thy kinsman, brave Mercutio.
    Lady C. Tybalt, my cousin ! O my
        brother's child !
O Prince ! O husband ! O, the blood is
    spill'd
Of my dear kinsman ! Prince, as thou art
    true,   145
For blood of ours shed blood of Montague.
O cousin, cousin !
    Prin. Benvolio, who began this bloody
        fray ?

Ben. Tybalt, here slain, whom Romeo's
    hand did slay;
Romeo that spoke him fair, bid him
    bethink   150
How nice the quarrel was, and urg'd withal
Your high displeasure. All this, uttered
With gentle breath, calm look, knees
    humbly bow'd,
Could not take truce with the unruly spleen
Of Tybalt, deaf to peace, but that he tilts
With piercing steel at bold Mercutio's
    breast;   156
Who, all as hot, turns deadly point to
    point,
And, with a martial scorn, with one hand
    beats
Cold death aside, and with the other sends
It back to Tybalt, whose dexterity   160
Retorts it. Romeo he cries aloud
'Hold, friends! friends, part!' and,
    swifter than his tongue,
His agile arm beats down their fatal points,
And 'twixt them rushes; underneath
    whose arm   164
An envious thrust from Tybalt hit the life
Of stout Mercutio; and then Tybalt fled;
But by and by comes back to Romeo,
Who had but newly entertain'd revenge,
And to't they go like lightning; for ere I
Could draw to part them was stout Tybalt
    slain;   170
And as he fell did Romeo turn and fly.
This is the truth, or let Benvolio die.

    Lady C. He is a kinsman to the Mon-
    tague,
Affection makes him false, he speaks not
    true;
Some twenty of them fought in this black
    strife,   175
And all those twenty could but kill one life.
I beg for justice, which thou, Prince, must
    give:
Romeo slew Tybalt, Romeo must not live.

    Prin. Romeo slew him; he slew Mercutio.
Who now the price of his dear blood doth
    owe?   180

    Mon. Not Romeo, Prince; he was Mer-
    cutio's friend;
His fault concludes but what the law should
    end,
The life of Tybalt.

    Prin.   And for that offence,
Immediately we do exile him hence.   184
I have an interest in your hate's proceeding,
My blood for your rude brawls doth lie
    a-bleeding;
But I'll amerce you with so strong a fine
That you shall all repent the loss of mine.
I will be deaf to pleading and excuses,
Nor tears nor prayers shall purchase out
    abuses;   190
Therefore use none. Let Romeo hence in
    haste,
Else when he is found that hour is his last.

Bear hence this body, and attend our will:
Mercy but murders, pardoning those that
    kill.   [*Exeunt.*

    SCENE II.   *Capulet's orchard.*

    Enter JULIET.

    Jul. Gallop apace, you fiery-footed steeds
Towards Phœbus' lodging; such a wag-
    goner
As Phaethon would whip you to the west,
And bring in cloudy night immediately.
Spread thy close curtain, love-performing
    night,   5
That runaways' eyes may wink, and
    Romeo
Leap to these arms, untalk'd of and unseen.
Lovers can see to do their amorous rites
By their own beauties; or if love be blind,
It best agrees with night. Come, civil night,
Thou sober-suited matron, all in black,   11
And learn me how to lose a winning match,
Play'd for a pair of stainless maidenhoods;
Hood my unmann'd blood, bating in my
    cheeks,
With thy black mantle, till strange love,
    grown bold,   15
Think true love acted simple modesty.
Come, night; come, Romeo; come, thou
    day in night;
For thou wilt lie upon the wings of night
Whiter than new snow on a raven's back.
Come, gentle night, come, loving black-
    brow'd night,   20
Give me my Romeo; and, when he shall
    die,
Take him and cut him out in little stars,
And he will make the face of heaven so fine
That all the world will be in love with night,
And pay no worship to the garish sun.   25
O, I have bought the mansion of a love,
But not possess'd it; and though I am
    sold,
Not yet enjoy'd. So tedious is this day
As is the night before some festival   29
To an impatient child that hath new robes,
And may not wear them. O, here comes my
    nurse,

    Enter Nurse *with cords.*

And she brings news; and every tongue
    that speaks
But Romeo's name speaks heavenly
    eloquence.
Now, nurse, what news? What hast thou
    there? The cords
That Romeo bid thee fetch?

    Nurse.   Ay, ay, the cords.   35
            [*Throws them down.*

    Jul. Ay, me! what news? Why dost
    thou wring thy hands?

    Nurse. Ah, well-a-day! he's dead, he's
    dead, he's dead.
We are undone, lady, we are undone.

Alack the day! he's gone, he's kill'd, he's
 dead.
 Jul. Can heaven be so envious?
 Nurse.   Romeo can, 40
Though heaven cannot. O Romeo,
 Romeo!
Who ever would have thought it? Romeo!
 Jul. What devil art thou that dost
  torment me thus?
This torture should be roar'd in dismal hell.
Hath Romeo slain himself? Say thou
 but 'I',   45
And that bare vowel I shall poison more
Than the death-darting eye of cockatrice.
I am not I if there be such an 'I';
Or those eyes shut that makes thee answer
 'I'.   49
If he be slain, say 'I'; or if not, 'No';
 Nurse. I saw the wound, I saw it with
  mine eyes—
God save the mark!—here on his manly
 breast.
A piteous corse, a bloody piteous corse;
Pale, pale as ashes, all bedaub'd in blood, 55
All in gore-blood. I swounded at the sight.
 Jul. O, break, my heart! poor bankrupt,
  break at once!
To prison, eyes; ne'er look on liberty.
Vile earth, to earth resign; end motion
 here;   59
And thou and Romeo press one heavy bier!
 Nurse. O Tybalt, Tybalt, the best friend
  I had!
O courteous Tybalt! honest gentleman!
That ever I should live to see thee dead!
 Jul. What storm is this that blows so
  contrary?   64
Is Romeo slaught'red, and is Tybalt dead?
My dearest cousin and my dearer lord?
Then, dreadful trumpet, sound the general
 doom;
For who is living if those two are gone?
 Nurse. Tybalt is gone, and Romeo ban-
  ished;
Romeo that kill'd him, he is banished. 70
 Jul. O God! Did Romeo's hand shed
  Tybalt's blood?
 Nurse. It did, it did; alas the day, it
  did!
 Jul. O serpent heart, hid with a flow'ring
  face!
Did ever dragon keep so fair a cave?
Beautiful tyrant! fiend angelical! 75
Dove-feather'd raven! wolfish-ravening
 lamb!
Despised substance of divinest show!
Just opposite to what thou justly seem'st,
A damned saint, an honourable villain!
O nature, what hadst thou to do in hell, 80
When thou didst bower the spirit of a
 fiend
In mortal paradise of such sweet flesh?
Was ever book containing such vile matter

So fairly bound? O, that deceit should
 dwell
In such a gorgeous palace!
 Nurse.   There's no trust, 85
No faith, no honesty in men; all perjur'd,
All forsworn, all naught, all dissemblers.
Ah, where's my man? Give me some aqua
 vitæ.
These griefs, these woes, these sorrows,
 make me old.
Shame come to Romeo!
 Jul.   Blister'd be thy tongue 90
For such a wish! He was not born to
 shame:
Upon his brow shame is asham'd to sit;
For 'tis a throne where honour may be
 crown'd
Sole monarch of the universal earth.
O, what a beast was I to chide at him! 95
 Nurse. Will you speak well of him that
  kill'd your cousin?
 Jul. Shall I speak ill of him that is my
  husband?
Ah, poor my lord, what tongue shall smooth
 thy name,
When I, thy three-hours wife, have
 mangled it?
But wherefore, villain, didst thou kill my
 cousin?   100
That villain cousin would have kill'd my
 husband.
Back, foolish tears, back to your native
 spring;
Your tributary drops belong to woe,
Which you, mistaking, offer up to joy.
My husband lives that Tybalt would have
 slain,   105
And Tybalt's dead that would have slain
 my husband.
All this is comfort; wherefore weep I
 then?
Some word there was, worser than Tybalt's
 death,
That murd'red me; I would forget it fain,
But, O, it presses to my memory 110
Like damned guilty deeds to sinners'
 minds:
'Tybalt is dead, and Romeo banished'.
That 'banished', that one word 'banished',
Hath slain ten thousand Tybalts. Tybalt's
 death
Was woe enough, if it had ended there; 115
Or if sour woe delights in fellowship
And needly will be rank'd with other griefs
Why followed not, when she said 'Tybalt's
 dead',
Thy father or thy mother, nay, or both,
Which modern lamentation might have
 mov'd?   120
But, with a rear-ward following Tybalt's
 death,
'Romeo is banished'—to speak that word
Is father, mother, Tybalt, Romeo, Juliet,
All slain, all dead. 'Romeo is banished'—

There is no end, no limit, measure, bound,
In that word's death; no words can that
    woe sound.   126
Where is my father and my mother, nurse?
   Nurse. Weeping and wailing over Ty-
    balt's corse.
Will you go to them? I will bring you
    thither.
   Jul. Wash they his wounds with tears!
    Mine shall be spent,   130
When theirs are dry, for Romeo's banish-
    ment.
Take up those cords. Poor ropes, you are
    beguil'd,
Both you and I, for Romeo is exil'd;
He made you for a highway to my bed,
But I, a maid, die maiden-widowed.   135
Come, cords; come, nurse; I'll to my
    wedding-bed;
And death, not Romeo, take my maiden-
    head!
   Nurse. Hie to your chamber; I'll find
    Romeo
To comfort you. I wot well where he is.
Hark ye, your Romeo will be here at night.
I'll to him; he is hid at Lawrence' cell.
   Jul. O, find him! give this ring to my
    true knight,   142
And bid him come to take his last farewell.
                    [*Exeunt.*

Scene III.   *Friar Lawrence's cell.*

   Enter FRIAR LAWRENCE.

   Fri. L. Romeo, come forth; come forth,
    thou fearful man;
Affliction is enamour'd of thy parts,
And thou art wedded to calamity.

   Enter ROMEO.

   Rom. Father, what news? What is the
    Prince's doom?
What sorrow craves acquaintance at my
    hand   5
That I yet know not?
   Fri. L.   Too familiar
Is my dear son with such sour company;
I bring thee tidings of the Prince's doom.
   Rom. What less than doomsday is the
    Prince's doom?
   Fri. L. A gentler judgment vanish'd from
    his lips—   10
Not body's death, but body's banishment.
   Rom. Ha, banishment! Be merciful, say
    'death';
For exile hath more terror in his look,
Much more than death. Do not say 'banish-
    ment'.
   Fri. L. Here from Verona art thou
    banished.   15
Be patient, for the world is broad and wide.
   Rom. There is no world without Verona
    walls,
But purgatory, torture, hell itself.

Hence banished is banish'd from the world,
And world's exile is death. Then 'banished'
Is death mis-term'd; calling death 'ban-
    ished',   21
Thou cut'st my head off with a golden axe,
And smilest upon the stroke that murders
    me.
   Fri. L. O deadly sin! O rude unthank-
    fulness!
Thy fault our law calls death; but the kind
    Prince,   25
Taking thy part, hath rush'd aside the law,
And turn'd that black word death to
    banishment.
This is dear mercy, and thou seest it not.
   Rom. 'Tis torture, and not mercy;
    heaven is here   29
Where Juliet lives, and every cat, and dog,
And little mouse, every unworthy thing,
Live here in heaven and may look on her;
But Romeo may not. More validity,
More honourable state, more courtship
    lives
In carrion flies than Romeo. They may
    seize   35
On the white wonder of dear Juliet's hand,
And steal immortal blessing from her lips;
Who, even in pure and vestal modesty,
Still blush, as thinking their own kisses
    sin;
But Romeo may not—he is banished.   40
This may flies do, when I from this must fly;
They are free men, but I am banished.
And sayest thou yet that exile is not death?
Hadst thou no poison mix'd, no sharp-
    ground knife,
No sudden mean of death, though ne'er so
    mean,   45
But 'banished' to kill me—'banished'?
O friar, the damned use that word in hell;
Howling attends it; how hast thou the
    heart,
Being a divine, a ghostly confessor,
A sin-absolver, and my friend profess'd, 50
To mangle me with that word 'banished'?
   Fri. L. Thou fond mad man, hear me
    a little speak.
   Rom. O, thou wilt speak again of banish-
    ment.
   Fri. L. I'll give thee armour to keep off
    that word;
Adversity's sweet milk, philosophy,   55
To comfort thee, though thou art banished.
   Rom. Yet 'banished'? Hang up philo-
    sophy;
Unless philosophy can make a Juliet,
Displant a town, reverse a prince's doom,
It helps not, it prevails not. Talk no more.
   Fri. L. O, then I see that madmen have
    no ears.   61
   Rom. How should they, when that wise
    men have no eyes?
   Fri. L. Let me dispute with thee of thy
    estate.

Rom. Thou canst not speak of that thou
    dost not feel.
Wert thou as young as I, Juliet thy love, 65
An hour but married, Tybalt murdered,
Doting like me, and like me banished,
Then mightst thou speak, then mightst
    thou tear thy hair,
And fall upon the ground, as I do now, 69
Taking the measure of an unmade grave.
                [*Knocking within.*
    Fri. L. Arise ; one knocks. Good
      Romeo, hide thyself.
    Rom. Not I ; unless the breath of heart-
      sick groans,
Mist-like, enfold me from the search of eyes.
                    [*Knocking.*
Fri. L. Hark how they knock ! Who's
    there ? Romeo, arise ;
Thou wilt be taken.—Stay awhile.—Stand
    up ;   [*Knocking.*
Run to my study.—By and by.—God's
    will,   76
What simpleness is this !—I come, I come.
                    [*Knocking.*
Who knocks so hard ? Whence come you ?
    What's your will ?
    Nurse. [*Within*] Let me come in and you
      shall know my errand ;
I come from Lady Juliet.
    Fri. L.   Welcome, then. 80

        Enter Nurse.

Nurse. O holy friar, O, tell me, holy friar,
Where's my lady's lord, where's Romeo ?
Fri. L. There on the ground, with his own
    tears made drunk.
Nurse. O, he is even in my mistress' case,
Just in her case !
    Fri. L.   O woeful sympathy !
Piteous predicament !
    Nurse.   Even so lies she, 85
Blubb'ring and weeping, weeping and
    blubb'ring.
Stand up, stand up ; stand, an you be a
    man ;
For Juliet's sake, for her sake, rise and
    stand ;
Why should you fall into so deep an O ? 90
Rom. Nurse !
Nurse. Ah, sir ! ah, sir ! Well, death's
    the end of all.
    Rom. Spakest thou of Juliet ? How is it
    with her ?
Doth not she think me an old murderer, 94
Now I have stain'd the childhood of our joy
With blood remov'd but little from her
    own ?
Where is she ? and how doth she ? and
    what says
My conceal'd lady to our cancell'd love ?
    Nurse. O, she says nothing, sir, but weeps
    and weeps ;
And now falls on her bed, and then starts
    up,   100

And Tybalt calls ; and then on Romeo
    cries,
And then down falls again.
    Rom.   As if that name,
Shot from the deadly level of a gun,
Did murder her ; as that name's cursed
    hand
Murder'd her kinsman. O, tell me, friar,
    tell me, 105
In what vile part of this anatomy
Doth my name lodge ? Tell me that I may
    sack
The hateful mansion. [*Drawing his sword.*
    Fri. L.   Hold thy desperate hand.
Art thou a man ? Thy form cries out thou
    art :
Thy tears are womanish ; thy wild acts
    denote 110
The unreasonable fury of a beast.
Unseemly woman in a seeming man !
And ill-beseeming beast in seeming both !
Thou hast amaz'd me. By my holy
    order,
I thought thy disposition better temper'd.
Hast thou slain Tybalt ? Wilt thou slay
    thyself ? 116
And slay thy lady that in thy life lives,
By doing damned hate upon thyself ?
Why railest thou on thy birth, the heaven,
    and earth ?
Since birth, and heaven, and earth, all three
    do meet 120
In thee at once ; which thou at once
    wouldst lose.
Fie, fie ! thou shamest thy shape, thy love,
    thy wit ;
Which, like a usurer, abound'st in all,
And usest none in that true use indeed
Which should bedeck thy shape, thy love,
    thy wit. 125
Thy noble shape is but a form of wax,
Digressing from the valour of a man ;
Thy dear love sworn but hollow perjury,
Killing that love which thou hast vow'd to
    cherish ; 129
Thy wit, that ornament to shape and love,
Misshapen in the conduct of them both,
Like powder in a skilless soldier's flask,
Is set afire by thine own ignorance,
And thou dismemb'red with thine own
    defence. 134
What, rouse thee, man ! Thy Juliet is alive,
For whose dear sake thou wast but lately
    dead ;
There art thou happy. Tybalt would kill
    thee,
But thou slewest Tybalt ; there art thou
    happy too.
The law, that threat'ned death, becomes
    thy friend,
And turns it to exile ; there art thou
    happy. 140
A pack of blessings lights upon thy back ;
Happiness courts thee in her best array ;

But, like a misbehav'd and sullen wench,
Thou pout'st upon thy fortune and thy love.
Take heed, take heed, for such die miser-
    able.   145
Go, get thee to thy love, as was decreed,
Ascend her chamber, hence and comfort
    her.
But look thou stay not till the watch be set,
For then thou canst not pass to Mantua,
Where thou shalt live till we can find a
    time   150
To blaze your marriage, reconcile your
    friends,
Beg pardon of the Prince, and call thee
    back
With twenty hundred thousand times more
    joy
Than thou went'st forth in lamentation.
Go before, nurse; commend me to thy
    lady;   155
And bid her hasten all the house to bed,
Which heavy sorrow makes them apt unto;
Romeo is coming.
    Nurse. O Lord, I could have stay'd here
        all the night   159
To hear good counsel; O, what learning is!
My lord, I'll tell my lady you will come.
    Rom. Do so, and bid my sweet prepare
        to chide.
    Nurse. Here, sir, a ring she bid me give
        you, sir.
Hie you, make haste, for it grows very late.
                                    [*Exit.*
    Rom. How well my comfort is reviv'd by
        this!   165
    Fri. L. Go hence; good night; and here
        stands all your state:
Either be gone before the watch be set,
Or by the break of day disguis'd from
    hence.
Sojourn in Mantua; I'll find out your man,
And he shall signify from time to time 170
Every good hap to you that chances here.
Give me thy hand. 'Tis late; farewell;
    good night.
    Rom. But that a joy past joy calls out
        on me,
It were a grief so brief to part with thee.
Farewell.   [*Exeunt.*

SCENE IV. *Capulet's house.*

Enter CAPULET, LADY CAPULET, *and* PARIS.

    Cap. Things have fall'n out, sir, so un-
        luckily
That we have had no time to move our
    daughter.
Look you, she lov'd her kinsman Tybalt
    dearly,
And so did I. Well, we were born to die.
'Tis very late; she'll not come down to-
    night.   5
I promise you, but for your company,
I would have been abed an hour ago.

    Par. These times of woe afford no time
        to woo.
Madam, good night; commend me to your
    daughter.
    Lady C. I will, and know her mind early
        to-morrow;   10
To-night she's mew'd up to her heaviness.
    Cap. Sir Paris, I will make a desperate
        tender
Of my child's love. I think she will be
    rul'd
In all respects by me; nay, more, I doubt
    it not.
Wife, go you to her ere you go to bed; 15
Acquaint her here of my son Paris' love
And bid her, mark you me, on Wednesday
    next—
But, soft! what day is this?
    Par.   Monday, my lord.
    Cap. Monday! ha, ha! Well, Wednesday
        is too soon.
A Thursday let it be; a Thursday, tell
    her,   20
She shall be married to this noble earl.
Will you be ready? Do you like this haste?
We'll keep no great ado—a friend or two;
For, hark you, Tybalt being slain so late,
It may be thought we held him carelessly,
Being our kinsman, if we revel much;   26
Therefore we'll have some half a dozen
    friends,
And there an end. But what say you to
    Thursday?
    Par. My lord, I would that Thursday
        were to-morrow.
    Cap. Well, get you gone; a Thursday be
        it then.   30
Go you to Juliet ere you go to bed;
Prepare her, wife, against this wedding-day.
Farewell, my lord. Light to my chamber,
    ho!
Afore me, it is so very very late
That we may call it early by and by.   35
Good night.   [*Exeunt.*

SCENE V. *Capulet's orchard.*

Enter ROMEO *and* JULIET, *aloft.*

    Jul. Wilt thou be gone? It is not yet
        near day;
It was the nightingale, and not the lark,
That pierc'd the fearful hollow of thine ear;
Nightly she sings on yond pomegranate
    tree.
Believe me, love, it was the nightingale. 5
    Rom. It was the lark, the herald of the
        morn,
No nightingale. Look, love, what envious
    streaks
Do lace the severing clouds in yonder east;
Night's candles are burnt out, and jocund
    day   9
Stands tiptoe on the misty mountain tops.
I must be gone and live, or stay and die.

925

Jul. Yond light is not daylight ; I know
    it, I :
It is some meteor that the sun exhales
To be to thee this night a torch-bearer,
And light thee on thy way to Mantua ; 15
Therefore stay yet ; thou need'st not to be
    gone.
    Rom. Let me be ta'en, let me be put to
    death ;
I am content, so thou wilt have it so.
I'll say yon grey is not the morning's eye,
'Tis but the pale reflex of Cynthia's brow ;
Nor that is not the lark whose notes do beat
The vaulty heaven so high above our heads.
I have more care to stay than will to go.
Come death, and welcome ! Juliet wills
    it so.
How is't, my soul ? Let's talk—it is not
    day. 25
    Jul. It is, it is ; hie hence, be gone, away!
It is the lark that sings so out of tune,
Straining harsh discords and unpleasing
    sharps.
Some say the lark makes sweet division ;
This doth not so, for she divideth us. 30
Some say the lark and loathed toad change
    eyes ;
O, now I would they had chang'd voices
    too !
Since arm from arm that voice doth us
    affray,
Hunting thee hence with hunts-up to the
    day.
O, now be gone ! More light and light it
    grows. 35
    Rom. More light and light—more dark
    and dark our woes !

Enter Nurse.

Nurse. Madam !
Jul. Nurse ?
Nurse. Your lady mother is coming to
    your chamber.
The day is broke ; be wary, look about. 40
    [*Exit.*
    Jul. Then, window, let day in and let life
    out.
    Rom. Farewell, farewell ! One kiss, and
    I'll descend. [*He goeth down.*
    Jul. Art thou gone so, love—lord, ay,
    husband, friend !
I must hear from thee every day in the
    hour,
For in a minute there are many days ; 45
O, by this count I shall be much in years
Ere I again behold my Romeo !
    Rom. Farewell !
I will omit no opportunity
That may convey my greetings, love, to
    thee. 50
    Jul. O, think'st thou we shall ever meet
    again ?
    Rom. I doubt it not ; and all these woes
    shall serve

For sweet discourses in our times to
    come.
    Jul. O God, I have an ill-divining soul !
Methinks I see thee, now thou art below, 55
As one dead in the bottom of a tomb ;
Either my eyesight fails or thou look'st
    pale.
    Rom. And trust me, love, in my eye so do
    you ;
Dry sorrow drinks our blood. Adieu, adieu!
    [*Exit below.*
    Jul. O Fortune, Fortune ! all men call
    thee fickle. 60
If thou art fickle, what dost thou with him
That is renown'd for faith ? Be fickle,
    Fortune ;
For then, I hope, thou wilt not keep him
    long,
But send him back.
    Lady C. [*Within*] Ho, daughter ! are you
    up ?
    Jul. Who is't that calls ? It is my lady
    mother. 65
Is she not down so late, or up so early ?
What unaccustom'd cause procures her
    hither ?

Enter LADY CAPULET.

    Lady C. Why, how now, Juliet !
    Jul.   Madam, I am not well.
    Lady C. Evermore weeping for your
    cousin's death ?
What, wilt thou wash him from his grave
    with tears ? 70
An if thou couldst, thou couldst not make
    him live ;
Therefore have done. Some grief shows
    much of love ;
But much of grief shows still some want of
    wit.
    Jul. Yet let me weep for such a feeling
    loss.
    Lady C. So shall you feel the loss, but not
    the friend 75
Which you weep for.
    Jul.   Feeling so the loss,
I cannot choose but ever weep the friend.
    Lady C. Well, girl, thou weep'st not so
    much for his death
As that the villain lives which slaughter'd
    him.
    Jul. What villain, madam ?
    Lady C.   That same villain, Romeo.
    Jul. [*Aside*] Villain and he be many miles
    asunder !— 81
God pardon him ! I do, with all my heart ;
And yet no man like he doth grieve my
    heart.
    Lady C. That is because the traitor
    murderer lives.
    Jul. Ay, madam, from the reach of these
    my hands. 85
Would none but I might venge my cousin's
    death !

Lady C. We will have vengeance for it,
　　fear thou not;
Then weep no more. I'll send to one in
　　Mantua—
Where that same banish'd runagate doth
　　live— 　　　　　　　　　　　　　　89
Shall give him such an unaccustom'd dram
That he shall soon keep Tybalt company;
And then I hope thou wilt be satisfied.
　　Jul. Indeed I never shall be satisfied
With Romeo till I behold him—dead—
Is my poor heart so for a kinsman vex'd. 95
Madam, if you could find out but a man
To bear a poison, I would temper it,
That Romeo should, upon receipt thereof,
Soon sleep in quiet. O, how my heart
　　abhors
To hear him nam'd, and cannot come to
　　him, 　　　　　　　　　　　　　　100
To wreak the love I bore my cousin Tybalt
Upon his body that hath slaughter'd him!
　　Lady C. Find thou the means, and I'll
　　find such a man.
But now I'll tell thee joyful tidings, girl.
　　Jul. And joy comes well in such a needy
　　time. 　　　　　　　　　　　　　　105
What are they, beseech your ladyship?
　　Lady C. Well, well, thou hast a careful
　　father, child;
One who, to put thee from thy heaviness,
Hath sorted out a sudden day of joy
That thou expects not, nor I look'd not
　　for. 　　　　　　　　　　　　　　110
　　Jul. Madam, in happy time, what day is
　　that?
　　Lady C. Marry, my child, early next
　　Thursday morn
The gallant, young, and noble gentleman,
The County Paris, at Saint Peter's Church,
Shall happily make thee there a joyful
　　bride. 　　　　　　　　　　　　　115
　　Jul. Now, by Saint Peter's Church, and
　　Peter too,
He shall not make me there a joyful bride.
I wonder at this haste, that I must wed
Ere he that should be husband comes to
　　woo. 　　　　　　　　　　　　　　119
I pray you tell my lord and father, madam,
I will not marry yet; and when I do, I
　　swear
It shall be Romeo, whom you know I hate,
Rather than Paris. These are news indeed!
　　Lady C. Here comes your father; tell
　　him so yourself, 　　　　　　　　124
And see how he will take it at your hands.

Enter CAPULET *and* Nurse.

　　Cap. When the sun sets, the air doth
　　drizzle dew;
But for the sunset of my brother's son
It rains downright.
How now! a conduit, girl? What, still in
　　tears? 　　　　　　　　　　　　　129
Evermore show'ring? In one little body

Thou counterfeit'st a bark, a sea, a wind;
For still thy eyes, which I may call the
　　sea,
Do ebb and flow with tears. The bark thy
　　body is,
Sailing in this salt flood; the winds thy
　　sighs,
Who, raging with thy tears, and they with
　　them, 　　　　　　　　　　　　　135
Without a sudden calm will overset
Thy tempest-tossed body. How now, wife!
Have you delivered to her our decree?
　　Lady C. Ay, sir; but she will none, she
　　gives you thanks. 　　　　　　　139
I would the fool were married to her grave!
　　Cap. Soft! take me with you, take me
　　with you, wife.
How will she none? Doth she not give us
　　thanks?
Is she not proud? Doth she not count her
　　blest,
Unworthy as she is, that we have wrought
So worthy a gentleman to be her bride-
　　groom? 　　　　　　　　　　　　145
　　Jul. Not proud you have, but thankful
　　that you have.
Proud can I never be of what I hate,
But thankful even for hate that is meant
　　love.
　　Cap. How how, how how, chopt logic!
　　What is this?
'Proud'—and 'I thank you'—and 'I
　　thank you not'— 　　　　　　　150
And yet 'not proud'? Mistress minion,
　　you,
Thank me no thankings, nor proud me no
　　prouds,
But fettle your fine joints 'gainst Thursday
　　next,
To go with Paris to Saint Peter's Church,
Or I will drag thee on a hurdle thither. 155
Out, you green-sickness carrion! Out, you
　　baggage!
You tallow-face!
　　Lady C. Fie, fie! what, are you mad?
　　Jul. Good father, I beseech you on my
　　knees,
Hear me with patience but to speak a word.
　　Cap. Hang thee, young baggage! dis-
　　obedient wretch! 　　　　　　　160
I tell thee what—get thee to church a
　　Thursday,
Or never after look me in the face.
Speak not, reply not, do not answer me;
My fingers itch. Wife, we scarce thought
　　us blest 　　　　　　　　　　　164
That God had lent us but this only child;
But now I see this one is one too much,
And that we have a curse in having her.
Out on her, hilding!
　　Nurse. 　　　　　　God in heaven bless her!
You are to blame, my lord, to rate her so.
　　Cap. And why, my Lady Wisdom? Hold
　　your tongue, 　　　　　　　　170

Good Prudence; smatter with your gossips,
   go.
  Nurse. I speak no treason.
  Cap.   O, God-i-goden!
  Nurse. May not one speak?
  Cap.   Peace, you mumbling fool!
Utter your gravity o'er a gossip's bowl,
For here we need it not.
  Lady C.   You are too hot. 175
  Cap. God's bread! it makes me mad:
Day, night, hour, tide, time, work, play,
Alone, in company, still my care hath been
To have her match'd; and having now
   provided
A gentleman of noble parentage,   180
Of fair demesnes, youthful, and nobly
   train'd,
Stuff'd, as they say, with honourable parts,
Proportion'd as one's thought would wish a
   man—
And then to have a wretched puling fool,
A whining mammet, in her fortune's
   tender,   185
To answer 'I'll not wed, I cannot love,
I am too young, I pray you pardon me'!
But, an you will not wed, I'll pardon you.
Graze where you will, you shall not house
   with me.   189
Look to 't, think on't; I do not use to jest.
Thursday is near; lay hand on heart,
   advise:
An you be mine, I'll give you to my friend;
An you be not, hang, beg, starve, die in the
   streets,
For, by my soul, I'll ne'er acknowledge
   thee,   194
Nor what is mine shall never do thee good.
Trust to't, bethink you, I'll not be forsworn.
                     [*Exit.*
  Jul. Is there no pity sitting in the clouds
That sees into the bottom of my grief?
O, sweet my mother, cast me not away!
Delay this marriage for a month, a week; 201
Or, if you do not, make the bridal bed
In that dim monument where Tybalt lies.
  Lady C. Talk not to me, for I'll not
   speak a word;
Do as thou wilt, for I have done with thee.
                     [*Exit.*
  Jul. O God!—O nurse! how shall this be
   prevented?   205
My husband is on earth, my faith in
   heaven;
How shall that faith return again to earth,
Unless that husband send it me from
   heaven
By leaving earth? Comfort me, counsel
   me.
Alack, alack, that heaven should practise
   stratagems   210
Upon so soft a subject as myself!
What say'st thou! Hast thou not a word
   of joy?
Some comfort, nurse.

  Nurse.   Faith, here it is:
Romeo is banished; and all the world to
   nothing
That he dares ne'er come back to challenge
   you;   215
Or, if he do, it needs must be by stealth.
Then, since the case so stands as now it
   doth,
I think it best you married with the
   County.
O, he's a lovely gentleman!
Romeo 's a dishclout to him; an eagle,
   madam,   220
Hath not so green, so quick, so fair an eye
As Paris hath. Beshrew my very heart,
I think you are happy in this second match,
For it excels your first; or, if it did not,
Your first is dead, or 'twere as good he
   were   225
As living here and you no use of him.
  Jul. Speak'st thou from thy heart?
  Nurse. And from my soul too, else
   beshrew them both.
  Jul. Amen!
  Nurse. What?   230
  Jul. Well, thou hast comforted me
   marvellous much.
Go in; and tell my lady I am gone,
Having displeas'd my father, to Lawrence'
   cell
To make confession, and to be absolv'd.
  Nurse. Marry, I will; and this is wisely
   done.   [*Exit.*
  Jul. Ancient damnation! O most wicked
   fiend!   236
Is it more sin to wish me thus forsworn,
Or to dispraise my lord with that same
   tongue
Which she hath prais'd him with above
   compare   239
So many thousand times? Go, counsellor;
Thou and my bosom henceforth shall be
   twain.
I'll to the friar to know his remedy;
If all else fail, myself have power to die.
                     [*Exit.*

ACT FOUR

SCENE I. *Friar Lawrence's cell.*

Enter FRIAR LAWRENCE *and* COUNTY PARIS.

  Fri. L. On Thursday, sir? The time is
   very short.
  Par. My father Capulet will have it so,
And I am nothing slow to slack his haste.
  Fri. L. You say you do not know the
   lady's mind:
Uneven is the course; I like it not.   5
  Par. Immoderately she weeps for Tybalt's
   death,
And therefore have I little talk'd of love;
For Venus smiles not in a house of tears.
Now, sir, her father counts it dangerous
That she do give her sorrow so much sway,

And in his wisdom hastes our marriage, 11
To stop the inundation of her tears ;
Which, too much minded by herself alone,
May be put from her by society.
Now do you know the reason of this haste.
 Fri. L. [*Aside*] I would I knew not why
  it should be slow'd.— 16
Look, sir, here comes the lady toward my
 cell.

    Enter JULIET.

 Par. Happily met, my lady and my wife !
 Jul. That may be, sir, when I may be a
  wife.
 Par. That may be must be, love, on
  Thursday next. 20
 Jul. What must be shall be.
 Fri. L.   That's a certain text.
 Par. Come you to make confession to this
  father ?
 Jul. To answer that, I should confess to
  you.
 Par. Do not deny to him that you love
  me. 24
 Jul. I will confess to you that I love him.
 Par. So will ye, I am sure, that you love
  me.
 Jul. If I do so, it will be of more price
Being spoke behind your back than to your
 face.
 Par. Poor soul, thy face is much abus'd
  with tears.
 Jul. The tears have got small victory by
  that, 30
For it was bad enough before their spite.
 Par. Thou wrong'st it more than tears
  with that report.
 Jul. That is no slander, sir, which is a
  truth ;
And what I spake, I spake it to my face.
 Par. Thy face is mine, and thou hast
  sland'red it. 35
 Jul. It may be so, for it is not mine own.
Are you at leisure, holy father, now,
Or shall I come to you at evening mass ?
 Fri. L. My leisure serves me, pensive
  daughter, now.
My lord, we must entreat the time alone. 40
 Par. God shield I should disturb devo-
  tion !
Juliet, on Thursday early will I rouse ye ;
Till then, adieu, and keep this holy kiss.
         [*Exit.*
 Jul. O, shut the door, and when thou
  hast done so,
Come weep with me—past hope, past cure,
 past help. 45
 Fri. L. O, Juliet, I already know thy
  grief ;
It strains me past the compass of my wits.
I hear thou must, and nothing may pro-
 rogue it,
On Thursday next be married to this
 County.

 Jul. Tell me not, friar, that thou hear'st
  of this, 50
Unless thou tell me how I may prevent it ;
If, in thy wisdom, thou canst give no help,
Do thou but call my resolution wise,
And with this knife I'll help it presently.
God join'd my heart and Romeo's, thou our
 hands ; 55
And ere this hand, by thee to Romeo's seal'd,
Shall be the label to another deed,
Or my true heart with treacherous revolt
Turn to another, this shall slay them both.
Therefore, out of thy long-experienc'd time,
Give me some present counsel ; or, behold,
'Twixt my extremes and me this bloody
 knife
Shall play the umpire, arbitrating that
Which the commission of thy years and art
Could to no issue of true honour bring. 65
Be not so long to speak ; I long to die,
If what thou speak'st speak not of remedy.
 Fri. L. Hold, daughter ; I do spy a kind
  of hope,
Which craves as desperate an execution
As that is desperate which we would pre-
 vent. 70
If, rather than to marry County Paris,
Thou hast the strength of will to slay
 thyself,
Then is it likely thou wilt undertake
A thing like death to chide away this shame,
That cop'st with death himself to scape
 from it ; 75
And, if thou dar'st, I'll give thee remedy.
 Jul. O, bid me leap, rather than marry
  Paris,
From off the battlements of any tower,
Or walk in thievish ways, or bid me lurk
Where serpents are ; chain me with roaring
 bears, 80
Or hide me nightly in a charnel house,
O'er-cover'd quite with dead men's rattling
 bones,
With reeky shanks and yellow chapless
 skulls ;
Or bid me go into a new-made grave,
And hide me with a dead man in his
 shroud— 85
Things that, to hear them told, have made
 me tremble—
And I will do it without fear or doubt,
To live an unstain'd wife to my sweet love.
 Fri. L. Hold, then ; go home, be merry,
  give consent 89
To marry Paris. Wednesday is to-morrow ;
To-morrow night look that thou lie alone,
Let not the nurse lie with thee in thy
 chamber.
Take thou this vial, being then in bed,
And this distilled liquor drink thou off ;
When presently through all thy veins shall
 run 95
A cold and drowsy humour ; for no pulse
Shall keep his native progress, but surcease;

            929

No warmth, no breath, shall testify thou
 livest ;
The roses in thy lips and cheeks shall fade
To paly ashes, thy eyes' windows fall, 100
Like death when he shuts up the day of life;
Each part, depriv'd of supple government,
Shall, stiff and stark and cold, appear like
 death ;
And in this borrow'd likeness of shrunk
 death 104
Thou shalt continue two and forty hours,
And then awake as from a pleasant sleep.
Now, when the bridegroom in the morning
 comes
To rouse thee from thy bed, there art thou
 dead.
Then, as the manner of our country is,
In thy best robes, uncovered on the bier,
Thou shalt be borne to that same ancient
 vault 111
Where all the kindred of the Capulets lie.
In the meantime, against thou shalt awake,
Shall Romeo by my letters know our drift,
And hither shall he come ; and he and I
Will watch thy waking, and that very night
Shall Romeo bear thee hence to Mantua.
And this shall free thee from this present
 shame,
If no inconstant toy nor womanish fear
Abate thy valour in the acting it. 120
 Jul. Give me, give me ! O, tell not me of
  fear !
 Fri. L. Hold ; get you gone, be strong
  and prosperous
In this resolve. I'll send a friar with speed
To Mantua, with my letters to thy lord.
 Jul. Love give me strength ! and strength
  shall help afford. 125
Farewell, dear father ! [*Exeunt.*

SCENE II. *Capulet's house.*

Enter CAPULET, LADY CAPULET, Nurse, *and
 two or three* Servingmen.

 Cap. So many guests invite as here are
  writ. [*Exit a Servingman.*
Sirrah, go hire me twenty cunning cooks.
 Serv. You shall have none ill, sir ; for
I'll try if they can lick their fingers.
 Cap. How canst thou try them so ? 5
 Serv. Marry, sir, 'tis an ill cook that
cannot lick his own fingers ; therefore he
that cannot lick his fingers goes not with
me.
 Cap. Go, be gone.
      [*Exit second Servingman.*
We shall be much unfurnish'd for this
 time. 10
What, is my daughter gone to Friar
 Lawrence ?
 Nurse. Ay, forsooth.
 Cap. Well, he may chance to do some
good on her :
A peevish self-will'd harlotry it is.

Enter JULIET.

 Nurse. See where she comes from shrift
  with merry look. 15
 Cap. How now, my headstrong ! Where
  have you been gadding ?
 Jul. Where I have learnt me to repent the
  sin
Of disobedient opposition
To you and your behests ; and am enjoin'd
By holy Lawrence to fall prostrate here, 20
To beg your pardon. Pardon, I beseech
 you.
Henceforward I am ever rul'd by you.
 Cap. Send for the County ; go tell him
  of this.
I'll have this knot knit up to-morrow
 morning.
 Jul. I met the youthful lord at Lawrence'
  cell, 25
And gave him what becomed love I might,
Not stepping o'er the bounds of modesty.
 Cap. Why, I am glad on't ; this is well—
  stand up—
This is as't should be. Let me see the
 County ; 29
Ay, marry, go, I say, and fetch him hither.
Now, afore God, this reverend holy friar,
All our whole city is much bound to him.
 Jul. Nurse, will you go with me into my
  closet
To help me sort such needful ornaments
As you think fit to furnish me to-morrow ?
 Lady C. No, not till Thursday ; there is
  time enough. 36
 Cap. Go, nurse, go with her. We'll to
  church to-morrow.
     [*Exeunt Juliet and Nurse.*
 Lady C. We shall be short in our pro-
  vision ;
'Tis now near night.
 Cap.   Tush, I will stir about,
And all things shall be well, I warrant thee,
 wife. 40
Go thou to Juliet, help to deck up her ;
I'll not to bed to-night ; let me alone.
I'll play the huswife for this once. What,
 ho !
They are all forth ; well, I will walk myself
To County Paris, to prepare up him 45
Against to-morrow. My heart is wondrous
 light
Since this same wayward girl is so reclaim'd.
          [*Exeunt.*

SCENE III. *Juliet's chamber.*

Enter JULIET *and* Nurse.

 Jul. Ay, those attires are best ; but,
  gentle nurse,
I pray thee, leave me to myself to-night,
For I have need of many orisons
To move the heavens to smile upon my
 state,

Which well thou knowest is cross and full
   of sin.   5

Enter LADY CAPULET.

Lady C. What, are you busy, ho? Need
   you my help?
Jul. No, madam; we have cull'd such
   necessaries
As are behoveful for our state to-morrow.
So please you, let me now be left alone,   9
And let the nurse this night sit up with
   you;
For I am sure you have your hands full all
In this so sudden business.
Lady C.   Good night.
Get thee to bed, and rest; for thou hast
   need.
     [*Exeunt Lady Capulet and Nurse.*
Jul. Farewell! God knows when we shall
   meet again.
I have a faint cold fear thrills through my
   veins,   15
That almost freezes up the heat of life;
I'll call them back again to comfort me.
Nurse!—What should she do here?
My dismal scene I needs must act alone.
Come, vial.   20
What if this mixture do not work at all?
Shall I be married, then, to-morrow morn-
   ing?
No, no; this shall forbid it. Lie thou there.
     [*Laying down her dagger.*
What if it be a poison which the friar
Subtly hath minist'red to have me dead,   25
Lest in this marriage he should be dis-
   honour'd,
Because he married me before to Romeo?
I fear it is; and yet methinks it should
   not,
For he hath still been tried a holy man.
How if, when I am laid into the tomb,   30
I wake before the time that Romeo
Come to redeem me? There's a fearful
   point.
Shall I not then be stifled in the vault,
To whose foul mouth no healthsome air
   breathes in,
And there die strangled ere my Romeo
   comes?   35
Or, if I live, is it not very like
The horrible conceit of death and night,
Together with the terror of the place—
As in a vault, an ancient receptacle
Where for this many hundred years the
   bones   40
Of all my buried ancestors are pack'd;
Where bloody Tybalt, yet but green in
   earth,
Lies fest'ring in his shroud; where, as they
   say,
At some hours in the night spirits resort—
Alack, alack, is it not like that I,   45
So early waking—what with loathsome
   smells,

And shrieks like mandrakes' torn out of the
   earth,
That living mortals, hearing them, run
   mad—
O, if I wake, shall I not be distraught,
Environed with all these hideous fears,   50
And madly play with my forefathers'
   joints,
And pluck the mangled Tybalt from his
   shroud,
And, in this rage, with some great kins-
   man's bone,
As with a club, dash out my desp'rate
   brains?   54
O, look! methinks I see my cousin's ghost
Seeking out Romeo, that did spit his body
Upon a rapier's point. Stay, Tybalt, stay.
Romeo, I come. This do I drink to thee.
     [*She drinks and falls upon her bed*
             within the curtains.

SCENE IV.   *Capulet's house.*

Enter LADY CAPULET *and* Nurse.

Lady C. Hold, take these keys, and fetch
   more spices, nurse.
Nurse. They call for dates and quinces in
   the pastry.

Enter CAPULET.

Cap. Come, stir, stir, stir! The second
   cock hath crow'd,
The curfew bell hath rung, 'tis three o'clock.
Look to the bak'd meats, good Angelica;   5
Spare not for cost.
Nurse.   Go, you cot-quean, go,
Get you to bed; faith, you'll be sick to-
   morrow
For this night's watching.
Cap. No, not a whit; what! I have
   watch'd ere now
All night for lesser cause, and ne'er been
   sick.   10
Lady C. Ay, you have been a mouse-hunt
   in your time;
But I will watch you from such watching
   now.
     [*Exeunt Lady Capulet and Nurse.*
Cap. A jealous-hood, a jealous-hood!

Enter three or four Servingmen *with spits
and logs and baskets.*

                    Now, fellow,
What is there?
1 *Fellow.* Things for the cook, sir; but I
   know not what.   15
Cap. Make haste, make haste. [*Exit*
   1 *Fellow*] Sirrah, fetch drier logs;
Call Peter; he will show thee where they are.
2 *Fellow.* I have a head, sir, that will find
   out logs,
And never trouble Peter for the matter.
Cap. Mass, and well said; a merry
   whoreson, ha!   20

Thou shalt be logger-head. [*Exit 2 Fellow*]
   Good faith, 'tis day ;
The County will be here with music straight,
For so he said he would. [*Play music*] I
   hear him near.
Nurse ! Wife ! What, ho ! What, nurse,
   I say !

      Re-enter Nurse.

Go waken Juliet, go and trim her up ; 25
I'll go and chat with Paris. Hie, make
   haste,
Make haste. The bridegroom he is come
   already.
Make haste, I say.   [*Exeunt.*

   SCENE V. *Juliet's chamber.*

      Enter Nurse.

Nurse. Mistress ! What, mistress ! Juliet!
   Fast, I warrant her, she.
Why, lamb ! Why, lady ! Fie, you slug-a-
   bed !
Why, love, I say ! madam ! sweetheart !
   Why, bride !
What, not a word ? You take your penny-
   worths now.
Sleep for a week ; for the next night, I
   warrant,   5
The County Paris hath set up his rest
That you shall rest but little. God forgive
   me !
Marry, and amen. How sound is she asleep !
I needs must wake her. Madam, madam,
   madam !   9
Ay, let the County take you in your bed ;
He'll fright you up, i' faith. Will it not be ?
                 [*Draws the curtains.*
What, dress'd, and in your clothes, and
   down again !
I must needs wake you. Lady ! lady ! lady !
Alas, alas ! Help, help ! my lady 's dead !
O well-a-day that ever I was born !   15
Some aqua-vitæ, ho ! My lord ! My lady !

     Enter LADY CAPULET.

Lady C. What noise is here ?
Nurse.   O lamentable day !
Lady C. What is the matter ?
Nurse.   Look, look ! O heavy day !
Lady C. O me, O me ! My child, my only
   life,
Revive, look up, or I will die with thee ! 20
Help, help ! Call help.

     Enter CAPULET.

Cap. For shame, bring Juliet forth ; her
   lord is come.
Nurse. She's dead, deceas'd, she's dead ;
   alack the day !
Lady C. Alack the day, she's dead, she's
   dead, she's dead !
Cap. Ha ! let me see her. Out, alas ! she's
   cold ;   25

Her blood is settled, and her joints are stiff.
Life and these lips have long been separ-
   ated.
Death lies on her like an untimely frost
Upon the sweetest flower of all the field.
   Nurse. O lamentable day !
   Lady C.   O woeful time ! 30
   Cap. Death, that hath ta'en her hence to
   make me wail,
Ties up my tongue and will not let me
   speak.

   Enter FRIAR LAWRENCE *and* COUNTY
      PARIS, *with* Musicians.

   Fri. L. Come, is the bride ready to go to
   church ?
   Cap. Ready to go, but never to return.
O son, the night before thy wedding day 35
Hath Death lain with thy wife. There
   she lies,
Flower as she was, deflowered by him.
Death is my son-in-law, Death is my heir ;
My daughter he hath wedded ; I will die,
And leave him all ; life, living, all is
   Death's.   40
   Par. Have I thought long to see this
   morning's face,
And doth it give me such a sight as this ?
   Lady C. Accurs'd, unhappy, wretched,
   hateful day !
Most miserable hour that e'er time saw
In lasting labour of his pilgrimage !   45
But one, poor one, one poor and loving
   child,
But one thing to rejoice and solace in,
And cruel Death hath catch'd it from my
   sight !
   Nurse. O woe ! O woeful, woeful, woeful
   day !
Most lamentable day, most woeful day 50
That ever, ever, I did yet behold !
O day ! O day ! O day ! O hateful day !
Never was seen so black a day as this.
O woeful day, O woeful day !
   Par. Beguil'd, divorced, wronged, spited,
   slain !   55
Most detestable Death, by thee beguil'd,
By cruel cruel thee quite overthrown !
O love ! O life !—not life, but love in
   death !
   Cap. Despis'd, distressed, hated, mar-
   tyr'd, kill'd !—   59
Uncomfortable time, why cam'st thou now
To murder, murder our solemnity ?
O child ! O child ! my soul, and not my
   child !
Dead art thou ; alack, my child is dead,
And with my child my joys are buried.
   Fri. L. Peace, ho, for shame ! Confusion's
   cure lives not   65
In these confusions. Heaven and yourself
Had part in this fair maid ; now heaven
   hath all,
And all the better is it for the maid.

Your part in her you could not keep from
    death,
But heaven keeps his part in eternal life. 70
The most you sought was her promotion,
For 'twas your heaven she should be
    advanc'd ;
And weep ye now, seeing she is advanc'd
Above the clouds, as high as heaven itself ?
O, in this love, you love your child so ill 75
That you run mad, seeing that she is
    well.
She's not well married that lives married
    long,
But she's best married that dies married
    young.
Dry up your tears, and stick your rosemary
On this fair corse, and, as the custom is, 80
In all her best array bear her to church ;
For though fond nature bids us all lament,
Yet nature's tears are reason's merriment.
  Cap. All things that we ordained festival
Turn from their office to black funeral : 85
Our instruments to melancholy bells,
Our wedding cheer to a sad burial feast,
Our solemn hymns to sullen dirges change ;
Our bridal flowers serve for a buried corse ;
And all things change them to the contrary.
  Fri. L. Sir, go you in ; and, madam, go
    with him ;   91
And go, Sir Paris. Every one prepare
To follow this fair corse unto her grave.
The heavens do lour upon you for some ill ;
Move them no more by crossing their high
    will.   95
    [*Exeunt all but Nurse and Musicians.*
  1 Mus. Faith, we may put up our pipes
and be gone.
  Nurse. Honest good fellows, ah, put up,
    put up ;
For well you know this is a pitiful case.
                    [*Exit.*
  1 Mus. Ay, by my troth, the case may be
amended.   99

         Enter PETER.

  Pet. Musicians, O, musicians, 'Heart's
ease ', ' Heart's ease ' ! O, an you will have
me live, play ' Heart's ease '.
  1 Mus. Why ' Heart's ease ' ?
  Pet. O, musicians, because my heart itself
plays ' My heart is full of woe '. O, play me
some merry dump to comfort me.   105
  1 Mus. Not a dump we ! 'Tis no time to
play now.
  Pet. You will not, then ?
  1 Mus. No.
  Pet. I will then give it you soundly.
  1 Mus. What will you give us ?   110
  Pet. No money, on my faith, but the
gleek. I will give you the minstrel.
  1 Mus. Then will I give you the serving-
creature.
  Pet. Then will I lay the serving-creature's
dagger on your pate. I will carry no

crotchets : I'll re you, I'll fa you ; do you
note me ?   116
  1 Mus. An you re us and fa us, you note
us.
  2 Mus. Pray you put up your dagger, and
put out your wit.
  Pet. Then have at you with my wit ! I
will dry-beat you with an iron wit, and put
up my iron dagger. Answer me like men.

' When griping grief the heart doth wound
    And doleful dumps the mind oppress,
  Then music with her silver sound '— 125

Why ' silver sound ' ? Why ' music with
her silver sound ' ? What say you, Simon
Catling ?
  1 Mus. Marry, sir, because silver hath a
sweet sound.
  Pet. Pretty ! What say you, Hugh
Rebeck ?   130
  2 Mus. I say ' silver sound ' because
musicians sound for silver.
  Pet. Pretty too ! What say you, James
Soundpost ?
  3 Mus. Faith, I know not what to say.
  Pet. O, I cry you mercy, you are the
singer ; I will say for you. It is ' music
with her silver sound ' because musicians
have no gold for sounding.   137

' Then music with her silver sound
    With speedy help doth lend redress.'

                    [*Exit.*
  1 Mus. What a pestilent knave is this
same !
  2 Mus. Hang him, Jack ! Come, we'll in
here ; tarry for the mourners, and stay
dinner.   [*Exeunt.*

          ACT FIVE

    SCENE I. *Mantua. A street.*

      Enter ROMEO.

  Rom. If I may trust the flattering truth
    of sleep,
My dreams presage some joyful news at
    hand.
My bosom's lord sits lightly in his throne,
And all this day an unaccustom'd spirit
Lifts me above the ground with cheerful
    thoughts.   5
I dreamt my lady came and found me
    dead—
Strange dream, that gives a dead man leave
    to think !—
And breath'd such life with kisses in my
    lips
That I reviv'd, and was an emperor.   9
Ah me ! how sweet is love itself possess'd,
When but love's shadows are so rich in joy !

   Enter BALTHASAR, *Romeo's man.*

News from Verona ! How now, Balthasar !

Dost thou not bring me letters from the friar?
How doth my lady? Is my father well?
How fares my Juliet? That I ask again, 15
For nothing can be ill if she be well.
    Bal. Then she is well, and nothing can be ill.
Her body sleeps in Capels' monument,
And her immortal part with angels lives.
I saw her laid low in her kindred's vault, 20
And presently took post to tell it you.
O, pardon me for bringing these ill news,
Since you did leave it for my office, sir.
    Rom. Is it e'en so? Then I defy you, stars.
Thou knowest my lodging: get me ink and paper, 25
And hire post-horses; I will hence to-night.
    Bal. I do beseech you, sir, have patience;
Your looks are pale and wild, and do import 28
Some misadventure.
    Rom.   Tush, thou art deceiv'd;
Leave me, and do the thing I bid thee do.
Hast thou no letters to me from the friar?
    Bal. No, my good lord.
    Rom.   No matter; get thee gone,
And hire those horses; I'll be with thee straight.   [*Exit Balthasar.*
Well, Juliet, I will lie with thee to-night.
Let's see for means. O mischief, thou art swift 35
To enter in the thoughts of desperate men!
I do remember an apothecary,
And hereabouts 'a dwells, which late I noted
In tatt'red weeds, with overwhelming brows, 39
Culling of simples. Meagre were his looks;
Sharp misery had worn him to the bones;
And in his needy shop a tortoise hung,
An alligator stuff'd, and other skins
Of ill-shap'd fishes; and about his shelves
A beggarly account of empty boxes, 45
Green earthen pots, bladders, and musty seeds,
Remnants of packthread, and old cakes of roses,
Were thinly scattered, to make up a show.
Noting this penury, to myself I said
' An if a man did need a poison now, 50
Whose sale is present death in Mantua,
Here lives a caitiff wretch would sell it him '.
O, this same thought did but forerun my need;
And this same needy man must sell it me.
As I remember, this should be the house. 55
Being holiday, the beggar's shop is shut.
What, ho! Apothecary!

    Enter Apothecary.

    Ap.   Who calls so loud?

    Rom. Come hither, man. I see that thou art poor. 58
Hold, there is forty ducats; let me have
A dram of poison, such soon-speeding gear
As will disperse itself through all the veins
That the life-weary taker may fall dead,
And that the trunk may be discharg'd of breath
As violently as hasty powder fir'd 64
Doth hurry from the fatal cannon's womb.
    Ap. Such mortal drugs I have; but Mantua's law
Is death to any he that utters them.
    Rom. Art thou so bare and full of wretchedness
And fearest to die? Famine is in thy cheeks, 69
Need and oppression starveth in thy eyes,
Contempt and beggary hangs upon thy back,
The world is not thy friend, nor the world's law;
The world affords no law to make thee rich;
Then be not poor, but break it and take this.
    Ap. My poverty but not my will consents. 75
    Rom. I pay thy poverty and not thy will.
    Ap. Put this in any liquid thing you will
And drink it off; and if you had the strength
Of twenty men, it would dispatch you straight.
    Rom. There is thy gold—worse poison to men's souls, 80
Doing more murder in this loathsome world
Than these poor compounds that thou mayst not sell.
I sell thee poison: thou hast sold me none.
Farewell; buy food, and get thyself in flesh. 84
Come, cordial and not poison, go with me
To Juliet's grave; for there must I use thee.   [*Exeunt.*

    SCENE II. *Friar Lawrence's cell.*

    Enter FRIAR JOHN.

    Fri. J. Holy Franciscan friar! Brother, ho!

    Enter FRIAR LAWRENCE.

    Fri. L. This same should be the voice of Friar John.
Welcome from Mantua! What says Romeo?
Or, if his mind be writ, give me his letter.
    Fri. J. Going to find a barefoot brother out, 5
One of our order, to associate me,
Here in this city visiting the sick,
And finding him, the searchers of the town,
Suspecting that we both were in a house
Where the infectious pestilence did reign,

Seal'd up the doors, and would not let us
    forth,   11
So that my speed to Mantua there was
    stay'd.
  Fri. L. Who bare my letter, then, to
    Romeo ?
  Fri. J. I could not send it—here it is
    again—
Nor get a messenger to bring it thee,   15
So fearful were they of infection.
  Fri. L. Unhappy fortune!   By my
    brotherhood,
The letter was not nice, but full of charge
Of dear import ; and the neglecting it
May do much danger.   Friar John, go
    hence ;   20
Get me an iron crow, and bring it straight
Unto my cell.
  Fri. J. Brother, I'll go and bring it thee.
                    [*Exit.*
  Fri. L. Now must I to the monument
    alone.
Within this three hours will fair Juliet
    wake ;   25
She will beshrew me much that Romeo
Hath had no notice of these accidents.
But I will write again to Mantua,
And keep her at my cell till Romeo come—
Poor living corse, clos'd in a dead man's
    tomb !   [*Exit.*

SCENE III. *Verona. A churchyard ; in it
    the tomb of the Capulets.*

Enter PARIS, *and his* Page *bearing flowers
    and a torch.*

  Par. Give me thy torch, boy ; hence, and
    stand aloof ;
Yet put it out, for I would not be seen.
Under yond yew trees lay thee all along,
Holding thy ear close to the hollow ground ;
So shall no foot upon the churchyard
    tread—   5
Being loose, unfirm, with digging up of
    graves—
But thou shalt hear it. Whistle then to me,
As signal that thou hearest something
    approach.
Give me those flowers. Do as I bid thee, go.
  Page. [*Aside*] I am almost afraid to stand
    alone   10
Here in the churchyard ; yet I will
    adventure.   [*Retires.*
  Par. Sweet flower, with flowers thy bridal
    bed I strew—
O woe, thy canopy is dust and stones !—
Which with sweet water nightly I will dew ;
Or, wanting that, with tears distill'd by
    moans.   15
The obsequies that I for thee will keep,
Nightly shall be to strew thy grave and
    weep.   [*The Page whistles.*
The boy gives warning something doth
    approach.

What cursed foot wanders this way to-
    night   19
To cross my obsequies and true love's rite ?
What, with a torch ! Muffle me, night,
    awhile.   [*Retires.*

Enter ROMEO *and* BALTHASAR, *with a torch,
    a mattock, and a crow of iron.*

  Rom. Give me that mattock and the
    wrenching iron.
Hold, take this letter ; early in the morning
See thou deliver it to my lord and father.
Give me the light ; upon thy life I charge
    thee,   25
Whate'er thou hearest or seest, stand all
    aloof
And do not interrupt me in my course.
Why I descend into this bed of death
Is partly to behold my lady's face,
But chiefly to take thence from her dead
    finger   30
A precious ring—a ring that I must use
In dear employment ; therefore hence, be
    gone.
But if thou, jealous, dost return to pry
In what I farther shall intend to do,
By heaven, I will tear thee joint by joint, 35
And strew this hungry churchyard with thy
    limbs.
The time and my intents are savage-wild,
More fierce and more inexorable far
Than empty tigers or the roaring sea.
  Bal. I will be gone, sir, and not trouble
    ye.   40
  Rom. So shalt thou show me friendship.
    Take thou that ;
Live and be prosperous ; and farewell, good
    fellow.
  Bal. [*Aside*] For all this same, I'll hide
    me hereabout ;
His looks I fear, and his intents I doubt.
                    [*Retires.*
  Rom. Thou detestable maw, thou womb
    of death,   45
Gorg'd with the dearest morsel of the earth,
Thus I enforce thy rotten jaws to open,
        [*Breaking open the tomb.*
And, in despite, I'll cram thee with more
    food.
  Par. This is that banish'd haughty
    Montague
That murd'red my love's cousin—with
    which grief   50
It is supposed the fair creature died—
And here is come to do some villainous
    shame
To the dead bodies. I will apprehend him.
Stop thy unhallowed toil, vile Montague.
Can vengeance be pursued further than
    death ?   55
Condemned villain, I do apprehend thee.
Obey, and go with me ; for thou must die.
  Rom. I must indeed ; and therefore came
    I hither.

Good gentle youth, tempt not a desp'rate
man ;
Fly hence, and leave me. Think upon these
gone ; 60
Let them affright thee. I beseech thee,
youth,
Put not another sin upon my head
By urging me to fury ; O, be gone !
By heaven, I love thee better than myself,
For I come hither arm'd against myself. 65
Stay not, be gone ; live, and hereafter say
A madman's mercy bid thee run away.
    Par. I do defy thy conjuration,
And apprehend thee for a felon here. 69
    Rom. Wilt thou provoke me ? Then have
at thee, boy ! [*They fight.*
    Page. O lord, they fight ! I will go call
the watch. [*Exit. Paris falls.*
    Par. O, I am slain ! If thou be merciful,
Open the tomb, lay me with Juliet. [*Dies.*
    Rom. In faith, I will. Let me peruse this
face. 74
Mercutio's kinsman, noble County Paris !
What said my man, when my betossed soul
Did not attend him as we rode ? I think
He told me Paris should have married
Juliet.
Said he not so, or did I dream it so ?
Or am I mad, hearing him talk of Juliet, 80
To think it was so ? O, give me thy hand,
One writ with me in sour misfortune's book!
I'll bury thee in a triumphant grave.
A grave ? O no ! A lantern, slaught'red
youth ; 84
For here lies Juliet, and her beauty makes
This vault a feasting presence full of light.
Death, lie thou there, by a dead man
interr'd.
            [*Laying Paris in the tomb.*
How oft when men are at the point of
death
Have they been merry ! Which their keep-
ers call
A lightning before death. O, how may I 90
Call this a lightning ? O my love ! my wife !
Death, that hath suck'd the honey of thy
breath,
Hath had no power yet upon thy beauty.
Thou art not conquer'd ; beauty's ensign
yet
Is crimson in thy lips and in thy cheeks, 95
And death's pale flag is not advanced there.
Tybalt, liest thou there in thy bloody
sheet ?
O, what more favour can I do to thee
Than with that hand that cut thy youth in
twain
To sunder his that was thine enemy ? 100
Forgive me, cousin. Ah, dear Juliet,
Why art thou yet so fair ? Shall I believe
That unsubstantial Death is amorous,
And that the lean abhorred monster keeps
Thee here in dark to be his paramour ? 105
For fear of that I still will stay with thee,

And never from this palace of dim night
Depart again. Here, here will I remain
With worms that are thy chambermaids. O,
here
Will I set up my everlasting rest, 110
And shake the yoke of inauspicious stars
From this world-wearied flesh. Eyes, look
your last.
Arms, take your last embrace. And, lips,
O you
The doors of breath, seal with a righteous
kiss
A dateless bargain to engrossing death ! 115
Come, bitter conduct, come, unsavoury
guide.
Thou desperate pilot, now at once run on
The dashing rocks thy sea-sick weary bark.
Here's to my love ! [*Drinks*] O true apothe-
cary ! 119
Thy drugs are quick. Thus with a kiss I die.
                                [*Falls.*

Enter FRIAR LAWRENCE, *with lantern, crow,
and spade.*

    Fri. L. Saint Francis be my speed ! How
oft to-night
Have my old feet stumbled at graves !
Who's there ?
    Bal. Here's one, a friend, and one that
knows you well.
    Fri. L. Bliss be upon you ! Tell me, good
my friend,
What torch is yond that vainly lends his
light 125
To grubs and eyeless skulls ? As I discern,
It burneth in the Capels' monument.
    Bal. It doth so, holy sir ; and there's my
master,
One that you love.
    Fri. L.   Who is it ?
    Bal.   Romeo.
    Fri. L. How long hath he been there ?
    Bal.   Full half an hour.
    Fri. L. Go with me to the vault.
    Bal.   I dare not, sir. 131
My master knows not but I am gone
hence,
And fearfully did menace me with death,
If I did stay to look on his intents.
    Fri. L. Stay, then, I'll go alone ; fear
comes upon me ; 135
O, much I fear some ill unthrifty thing.
    Bal. As I did sleep under this yew tree
here,
I dreamt my master and another fought,
And that my master slew him.
    Fri. L.   Romeo !
Alack, alack, what blood is this which
stains 140
The stony entrance of this sepulchre ?
What mean these masterless and gory
swords
To lie discolour'd by this place of peace ?
                        [*Enters the tomb.*

Romeo! O, pale! Who else? What, Paris
  too?
And steep'd in blood? Ah, what an unkind
  hour   145
Is guilty of this lamentable chance!
The lady stirs.   [*Juliet wakes.*
   Jul. O comfortable friar! Where is my
    lord?
I do remember well where I should be,
And there I am. Where is my Romeo? 150
                      [*Noise within.*
   Fri. L. I hear some noise. Lady, come
    from that nest
Of death, contagion, and unnatural sleep;
A greater power than we can contradict
Hath thwarted our intents. Come, come
  away;   154
Thy husband in thy bosom there lies dead;
And Paris too. Come, I'll dispose of thee
Among a sisterhood of holy nuns.
Stay not to question, for the watch is
  coming;
Come, go, good Juliet. I dare no longer
  stay.   159
   Jul. Go, get thee hence, for I will not
    away.   [*Exit Friar Lawrence.*
What's here? A cup, clos'd in my true
  love's hand?
Poison, I see, hath been his timeless end.
O churl! drunk all, and left no friendly
  drop
To help me after? I will kiss thy lips;
Haply some poison yet doth hang on them,
To make me die with a restorative. 166
                      [*Kisses him.*
Thy lips are warm.
   1 Watch. [*Within*] Lead, boy. Which
way?
   Jul. Yea, noise? Then I'll be brief. O
    happy dagger!
        [*Snatching Romeo's dagger.*
This is thy sheath; there rust, and let me
  die.
   [*She stabs herself and falls on Romeo's
    body.*

   Enter Watch, *with* Paris's Page.

   Page. This is the place; there, where the
    torch doth burn.   170
   1 Watch. The ground is bloody; search
    about the churchyard.
Go, some of you, whoe'er you find attach.
         [*Exeunt some of the Watch.*
Pitiful sight! here lies the County slain;
And Juliet bleeding, warm, and newly dead,
Who here hath lain this two days buried.
Go, tell the Prince; run to the Capulets;
Raise up the Montagues; some others
  search. [*Exeunt others of the Watch.*
We see the ground whereon these woes do
  lie;
But the true ground of all these piteous
  woes   179
We cannot without circumstance descry.

   Re-enter some of the Watch *with* BALTHASAR.

   2 Watch. Here's Romeo's man; we found
    him in the churchyard.
   1 Watch. Hold him in safety till the
    Prince come hither.

   Re-enter FRIAR LAWRENCE *and another*
    Watchman.

   3 Watch. Here is a friar that trembles,
    sighs, and weeps;
We took this mattock and this spade from
  him,
As he was coming from this churchyard's
  side.   185
   1 Watch. A great suspicion; stay the
    friar too.

   Enter the PRINCE *and* Attendants.

   Prince. What misadventure is so early up,
That calls our person from our morning
  rest?

   Enter CAPULET, LADY CAPULET, *and* Others.

   Cap. What should it be that is so shriek'd
    abroad?
   Lady C. The people in the street cry
    ' Romeo ',   190
Some ' Juliet ' and some ' Paris '; and all
  run,
With open outcry, toward our monument.
   Prince. What fear is this which startles
    in our ears?
   1 Watch. Sovereign, here lies the County
    Paris slain;   194
And Romeo dead; and Juliet, dead before,
Warm and new kill'd.
   Prince. Search, seek, and know how this
    foul murder comes.
   1 Watch. Here is a friar, and slaughter'd
    Romeo's man,
With instruments upon them fit to open
These dead men's tombs.   200
   Cap. O heavens! O wife, look how our
    daughter bleeds!
This dagger hath mista'en, for, lo, his house
Is empty on the back of Montague,
And it mis-sheathed in my daughter's
  bosom.
   Lady C. O me! this sight of death is as a
    bell   205
That warns my old age to a sepulchre.

   Enter MONTAGUE *and* Others.

   Prince. Come, Montague, for thou art
    early up
To see thy son and heir more early down.
   Mon. Alas, my liege, my wife is dead
    to-night;
Grief of my son's exile hath stopp'd her
  breath.   210
What further woe conspires against mine
  age?
   Prince. Look, and thou shalt see.

Mon. O thou untaught! what manners is in this,
To press before thy father to a grave?

Prince. Seal up the mouth of outrage for a while,   215
Till we can clear these ambiguities,
And know their spring, their head, their true descent:
And then will I be general of your woes,
And lead you even to death. Meantime forbear,
And let mischance be slave to patience.   220
Bring forth the parties of suspicion.

Fri. L. I am the greatest, able to do least,
Yet most suspected, as the time and place
Doth make against me, of this direful murder;
And here I stand, both to impeach and purge   225
Myself condemned and myself excus'd.

Prince. Then say at once what thou dost know in this.

Fri. L. I will be brief, for my short date of breath
Is not so long as is a tedious tale.
Romeo, there dead, was husband to that Juliet;   230
And she, there dead, that Romeo's faithful wife.
I married them; and their stol'n marriage-day
Was Tybalt's doomsday, whose untimely death
Banish'd the new-made bridegroom from this city;   234
For whom, and not for Tybalt, Juliet pin'd.
You, to remove that siege of grief from her,
Betroth'd, and would have married her perforce,
To County Paris. Then comes she to me,
And with wild looks bid me devise some mean
To rid her from this second marriage,   240
Or in my cell there would she kill herself.
Then gave I her, so tutor'd by my art,
A sleeping potion; which so took effect
As I intended, for it wrought on her
The form of death. Meantime I writ to Romeo   245
That he should hither come as this dire night
To help to take her from her borrowed grave,
Being the time the potion's force should cease.   248
But he which bore my letter, Friar John,
Was stay'd by accident, and yesternight
Return'd my letter back. Then all alone
At the prefixed hour of her waking   252
Came I to take her from her kindred's vault;
Meaning to keep her closely at my cell
Till I conveniently could send to Romeo.
But when I came, some minute ere the time

Of her awakening, here untimely lay   257
The noble Paris and true Romeo dead.
She wakes; and I entreated her come forth,
And bear this work of heaven with patience.
But then a noise did scare me from the tomb,   261
And she, too desperate, would not go with me,
But, as it seems, did violence on herself.
All this I know, and to the marriage
Her nurse is privy; and if ought in this   265
Miscarried by my fault, let my old life
Be sacrific'd, some hour before his time,
Unto the rigour of severest law.

Prince. We still have known thee for a holy man.
Where's Romeo's man? What can he say to this?   270

Bal. I brought my master news of Juliet's death;
And then in post he came from Mantua
To this same place, to this same monument.
This letter he early bid me give his father;
And threat'ned me with death, going in the vault,   275
If I departed not and left him there.

Prince. Give me the letter, I will look on it.
Where is the County's page that rais'd the watch?
Sirrah, what made your master in this place?

Page. He came with flowers to strew his lady's grave;   280
And bid me stand aloof, and so I did.
Anon comes one with light to ope the tomb;
And by and by my master drew on him;
And then I ran away to call the watch.

Prince. This letter doth make good the friar's words,   285
Their course of love, the tidings of her death;
And here he writes that he did buy a poison
Of a poor pothecary, and therewithal
Came to this vault to die, and lie with Juliet.
Where be these enemies?   Capulet, Montague,   290
See what a scourge is laid upon your hate,
That heaven finds means to kill your joys with love!
And I, for winking at your discords too,
Have lost a brace of kinsmen. All are punish'd.

Cap. O brother Montague, give me thy hand.   295
This is my daughter's jointure, for no more
Can I demand.

Mon.   But I can give thee more;
For I will raise her statue in pure gold,
That whiles Verona by that name is known,
There shall no figure at such rate be set   300
As that of true and faithful Juliet.

Cap. As rich shall Romeo's by his lady's
  lie—
Poor sacrifices of our enmity !
 Prince. A glooming peace this morning
  with it brings ;   304
The sun for sorrow will not show his head.

Go hence, to have more talk of these sad
  things ;
Some shall be pardon'd and some punished ;
For never was a story of more woe
Than this of Juliet and her Romeo. 309
        [Exeunt.

TIMON OF ATHENS

DRAMATIS PERSONÆ

TIMON of Athens.
LUCIUS, ⎫
LUCULLUS, ⎬ flattering lords.
SEMPRONIUS, ⎭
VENTIDIUS, one of Timon's false friends.
ALCIBIADES, an Athenian captain.
APEMANTUS, a churlish philosopher.
FLAVIUS, steward to Timon.
FLAMINIUS, ⎫
LUCILIUS, ⎬ Timon's servants.
SERVILIUS, ⎭
CAPHIS, ⎫
PHILOTUS, ⎪
TITUS, ⎬ servants to Timon's creditors.
HORTENSIUS, ⎪
Poet. ⎭

Painter.
Jeweller.
Merchant.
Mercer.
An Old Athenian.
Three Strangers.
A Page.
A Fool.

PHRYNIA, ⎫
TIMANDRA, ⎬ mistresses to Alcibiades.

CUPID, ⎫
AMAZONS, ⎬ in the Mask.

Lords, Senators, Officers, Soldiers, Servants, Thieves, and Attendants.

THE SCENE: Athens and the neighbouring woods.

ACT ONE

SCENE I. Athens. Timon's house.

Enter Poet, Painter, Jeweller, Merchant, *and* Mercer, *at several doors.*

Poet. Good day, sir.
Pain. I am glad y'are well.
Poet. I have not seen you long; how goes the world?
Pain. It wears, sir, as it grows.
Poet. Ay, that's well known.
But what particular rarity? What strange,
Which manifold record not matches? See,
Magic of bounty, all these spirits thy power
Hath conjur'd to attend! I know the merchant.
Pain. I know them both; th' other's a jeweller.
Mer. O, 'tis a worthy lord!
Jew. Nay, that's most fix'd.
Mer. A most incomparable man; breath'd, as it were,
To an untirable and continuate goodness. 11
He passes.
Jew. I have a jewel here—
Mer. O, pray let's see't. For the Lord Timon, sir?
Jew. If he will touch the estimate. But for that—
Poet. When we for recompense have prais'd the vile,
It stains the glory in that happy verse 17
Which aptly sings the good.
Mer. [*Looking at the jewel*] 'Tis a good form.
Jew. And rich. Here is a water, look ye.

Pain. You are rapt, sir, in some work, some dedication 21
To the great lord.
Poet. A thing slipp'd idly from me.
Our poesy is as a gum, which oozes
From whence 'tis nourish'd. The fire i' th' flint
Shows not till it be struck: our gentle flame 25
Provokes itself, and like the current flies
Each bound it chafes. What have you there?
Pain. A picture, sir. When comes your book forth?
Poet. Upon the heels of my presentment, sir.
Let's see your piece.
Pain. 'Tis a good piece. 30
Poet. So 'tis; this comes off well and excellent.
Pain. Indifferent.
Poet. Admirable. How this grace
Speaks his own standing! What a mental power
This eye shoots forth! How big imagination 35
Moves in this lip! To th' dumbness of the gesture
One might interpret.
Pain. It is a pretty mocking of the life.
Here is a touch; is't good?
Poet. I will say of it
It tutors nature. Artificial strife 40
Lives in these touches, livelier than life.

Enter certain Senators, *and pass over.*

Pain. How this lord is followed!

Poet. The senators of Athens—happy man !

Pain. Look, moe !

Poet. You see this confluence, this great flood of visitors. 45
I have in this rough work shap'd out a man
Whom this beneath world doth embrace and hug
With amplest entertainment. My free drift
Halts not particularly, but moves itself
In a wide sea of tax. No levell'd malice 50
Infects one comma in the course I hold,
But flies an eagle flight, bold and forth on,
Leaving no tract behind.

Pain. How shall I understand you ?

Poet.   I will unbolt to you.
You see how all conditions, how all minds— 55
As well of glib and slipp'ry creatures as
Of grave and austere quality, tender down
Their services to Lord Timon. His large fortune,
Upon his good and gracious nature hanging,
Subdues and properties to his love and tendance 60
All sorts of hearts ; yea, from the glass-fac'd flatterer
To Apemantus, that few things loves better
Than to abhor himself ; even he drops down
The knee before him, and returns in peace
Most rich in Timon's nod.

Pain. I saw them speak together. 65

Poet. Sir, I have upon a high and pleasant hill
Feign'd Fortune to be thron'd. The base o' th' mount
Is rank'd with all deserts, all kind of natures
That labour on the bosom of this sphere
To propagate their states. Amongst them all 70
Whose eyes are on this sovereign lady fix'd
One do I personate of Lord Timon's frame,
Whom Fortune with her ivory hand wafts to her ;
Whose present grace to present slaves and servants
Translates his rivals.

Pain. 'Tis conceiv'd to scope. 75
This throne, this Fortune, and this hill, methinks,
With one man beckon'd from the rest below,
Bowing his head against the steepy mount
To climb his happiness, would be well express'd
In our condition.

Poet.   Nay, sir, but hear me on. 80
All those which were his fellows but of late—
Some better than his value—on the moment
Follow his strides, his lobbies fill with tendance,
Rain sacrificial whisperings in his ear,
Make sacred even his stirrup, and through him 85
Drink the free air.

Pain.   Ay, marry, what of these ?

Poet. When Fortune in her shift and change of mood
Spurns down her late beloved, all his dependants,
Which labour'd after him to the mountain's top
Even on their knees and hands, let him slip down, 90
Not one accompanying his declining foot.

Pain. 'Tis common.
A thousand moral paintings I can show
That shall demonstrate these quick blows of Fortune's
More pregnantly than words. Yet you do well 95
To show Lord Timon that mean eyes have seen
The foot above the head.

Trumpets sound. Enter TIMON, *addressing himself courteously to every suitor, a* Messenger *from Ventidius talking with him ;* LUCILIUS *and other* Servants *following.*

Tim. Imprison'd is he, say you ?

Mess. Ay, my good lord. Five talents is his debt ;
His means most short, his creditors most strait.
Your honourable letter he desires 100
To those have shut him up ; which failing,
Periods his comfort.

Tim.   Noble Ventidius ! Well.
I am not of that feather to shake off
My friend when he must need me. I do know him
A gentlemen that well deserves a help, 105
Which he shall have. I'll pay the debt, and free him.

Mess. Your lordship ever binds him.

Tim. Commend me to him ; I will send his ransom ;
And being enfranchis'd, bid him come to me.
'Tis not enough to help the feeble up, 110
But to support him after. Fare you well.

Mess. All happiness to your honour !
                                    [*Exit.*

Enter an Old Athenian.

Old Ath. Lord Timon, hear me speak.

Tim.   Freely, good father.

Old Ath. Thou hast a servant nam'd Lucilius.

Tim. I have so ; what of him ? 115

Old Ath. Most noble Timon, call the man before thee.

Tim. Attends he here, or no ? Lucilius !
Luc. Here, at your lordship's service.
Old Ath. This fellow here, Lord Timon,
    this thy creature,   119
By night frequents my house. I am a man
That from my first have been inclin'd to
    thrift,
And my estate deserves an heir more rais'd
Than one which holds a trencher.
Tim.   Well ; what further ?
Old Ath. One only daughter have I, no
    kin else,
On whom I may confer what I have got. 125
The maid is fair, o' th' youngest for a
    bride,
And I have bred her at my dearest cost
In qualities of the best. This man of thine
Attempts her love ; I prithee, noble lord,
Join with me to forbid him her resort ; 130
Myself have spoke in vain.
Tim.   The man is honest.
Old Ath. Therefore he will be, Timon.
His honesty rewards him in itself ;
It must not bear my daughter.
Tim.   Does she love him ?
Old Ath. She is young and apt :   135
Our own precedent passions do instruct us
What levity's in youth.
Tim.   Love you the maid ?
Luc. Ay, my good lord, and she accepts
    of it.
Old Ath. If in her marriage my consent be
    missing,
I call the gods to witness I will choose 140
Mine heir from forth the beggars of the
    world,
And dispossess her all.
Tim.   How shall she be endow'd,
If she be mated with an equal husband ?
Old Ath. Three talents on the present ; in
    future, all.
Tim. This gentleman of mine hath serv'd
    me long ;
To build his fortune I will strain a little, 146
For 'tis a bond in men. Give him thy
    daughter :
What you bestow, in him I'll counterpoise,
And make him weigh with her.
Old Ath.   Most noble lord,
Pawn me to this your honour, she is his. 150
Tim. My hand to thee ; mine honour on
    my promise.
Luc. Humbly I thank your lordship.
    Never may
That state or fortune fall into my keeping
Which is not owed to you !
    [*Exeunt Lucilius and Old Athenian.*
Poet. [*Presenting his poem*] Vouchsafe
    my labour, and long live your
    lordship !   155
Tim. I thank you ; you shall hear from
    me anon ;
Go not away. What have you there, my
    friend ?

Pain. A piece of painting, which I do
    beseech
Your lordship to accept.
Tim.   Painting is welcome.
The painting is almost the natural man ; 160
For since dishonour traffics with man's
    nature,
He is but outside ; these pencill'd figures
    are
Even such as they give out. I like your
    work,
And you shall find I like it ; wait attend-
    ance
Till you hear further from me.
Pain.   The gods preserve ye ! 165
Tim. Well fare you, gentleman. Give me
    your hand ;
We must needs dine together. Sir, your
    jewel
Hath suffered under praise.
Jew.   What, my lord ! Dispraise ?
Tim. A mere satiety of commendations.
If I should pay you for't as 'tis extoll'd, 170
It would unclew me quite.
Jew.   My lord, 'tis rated
As those which sell would give ; but you
    well know
Things of like value, differing in the owners,
Are prized by their masters. Believe't, dear
    lord,
You mend the jewel by the wearing it. 175
Tim. Well mock'd.

Enter APEMANTUS.

Mer. No, my good lord ; he speaks the
    common tongue,
Which all men speak with him.
Tim. Look who comes here ; will you be
    chid ?
Jew. We'll bear, with your lordship.
Mer.   He'll spare none.
Tim. Good morrow to thee, gentle Ape-
    mantus !   181
Apem. Till I be gentle, stay thou for thy
    good morrow ;
When thou art Timon's dog, and these
    knaves honest.
Tim. Why dost thou call them knaves ?
    Thou know'st them not.
Apem. Are they not Athenians ?   185
Tim. Yes.
Apem. Then I repent not.
Jew. You know me, Apemantus ?
Apem. Thou know'st I do ; I call'd thee
by thy name.
Tim. Thou art proud, Apemantus.   190
Apem. Of nothing so much as that I am
not like Timon.
Tim. Whither art going ?
Apem. To knock out an honest Athen-
ian's brains.
Tim. That's a deed thou't die for.   195
Apem. Right, if doing nothing be death
by th' law.

Tim. How lik'st thou this picture, Apemantus ?

Apem. The best, for the innocence.

Tim. Wrought he not well that painted it?

Apem. He wrought better that made the painter ; and yet he's but a filthy piece of work.   201

Pain. Y'are a dog.

Apem. Thy mother's of my generation ; what's she, if I be a dog ?

Tim. Wilt dine with me, Apemantus ?

Apem. No ; I eat not lords.   206

Tim. An thou shouldst, thou'dst anger ladies.

Apem. O, they eat lords ; so they come by great bellies.

Tim. That's a lascivious apprehension.

Apem. So thou apprehend'st it take it for thy labour.   211

Tim. How dost thou like this jewel, Apemantus ?

Apem. Not so well as plain dealing, which will not cost a man a doit.   214

Tim. What dost thou think 'tis worth ?

Apem. Not worth my thinking. How now, poet !

Poet. How now, philosopher !

Apem. Thou liest.

Poet. Art not one ?

Apem. Yes.   220

Poet. Then I lie not.

Apem. Art not a poet ?

Poet. Yes.

Apem. Then thou liest. Look in thy last work, where thou hast feign'd him a worthy fellow.   225

Poet. That's not feign'd—he is so.

Apem. Yes, he is worthy of thee, and to pay thee for thy labour. He that loves to be flattered is worthy o' th' flatterer. Heavens, that I were a lord !   229

Tim. What wouldst do then, Apemantus ?

Apem. E'en as Apemantus does now : hate a lord with my heart.

Tim. What, thyself ?

Apem. Ay.

Tim. Wherefore ?   235

Apem. That I had no angry wit to be a lord.—Art not thou a merchant ?

Mer. Ay, Apemantus.

Apem. Traffic confound thee, if the gods will not !

Mer. If traffic do it, the gods do it.   240

Apem. Traffic's thy god, and thy god confound thee !

Trumpet sounds. Enter a Messenger.

Tim. What trumpet's that ?

Mess. 'Tis Alcibiades, and some twenty horse,

All of companionship.

Tim. Pray entertain them ; give them guide to us.
          [*Exeunt some Attendants.*

You must needs dine with me. Go not you hence   246
Till I have thank'd you. When dinner's done
Show me this piece. I am joyful of your sights.

Enter ALCIBIADES, *with the* rest.

Most welcome, sir !   [*They salute.*

Apem. So, so, there !

Aches contract and starve your supple joints !   250
That there should be small love amongst these sweet knaves,
And all this courtesy ! The strain of man's bred out
Into baboon and monkey.

Alcib. Sir, you have sav'd my longing, and I feed
Most hungerly on your sight.

Tim.   Right welcome, sir ! 255
Ere we depart we'll share a bounteous time
In different pleasures. Pray you, let us in.
          [*Exeunt all but Apemantus.*

Enter two Lords.

1 Lord. What time o' day is't, Apemantus ?

Apem. Time to be honest.

1 Lord. That time serves still.   260

Apem. The more accursed thou that still omit'st it.

2 Lord. Thou art going to Lord Timon's feast.

Apem. Ay ; to see meat fill knaves and wine heat fools.

2 Lord. Fare thee well, fare thee well.

Apem. Thou art a fool to bid me farewell twice.   265

2 Lord. Why, Apemantus ?

Apem. Shouldst have kept one to thyself, for I mean to give thee none.

1 Lord. Hang thyself.   269

Apem. No, I will do nothing at thy bidding ; make thy requests to thy friend.

2 Lord. Away, unpeaceable dog, or I'll spurn thee hence.

Apem. I will fly, like a dog, the heels o' th' ass.   [*Exit.*

1 Lord. He's opposite to humanity. Come, shall we in   275
And taste Lord Timon's bounty ? He outgoes
The very heart of kindness.

2 Lord. He pours it out : Plutus, the god of gold,
Is but his steward ; no meed but he repays
Sevenfold above itself ; no gift to him   280
But breeds the giver a return exceeding
All use of quittance.

1 Lord.   The noblest mind he carries
That ever govern'd man.

2 Lord. Long may he live in fortunes ! Shall we in ?   284

1 Lord. I'll keep you company. [*Exeunt.*

SCENE II. *A room of state in Timon's house.*

Hautboys playing loud music. A great banquet serv'd in; FLAVIUS and Others attending; and then enter LORD TIMON, the States, the Athenian Lords, VENTIDIUS, which Timon redeem'd from prison. Then comes, dropping after all, APEMANTUS, discontentedly, like himself.

Ven. Most honoured Timon,
It hath pleas'd the gods to remember my
father's age,
And call him to long peace.
He is gone happy, and has left me rich.
Then, as in grateful virtue I am bound   5
To your free heart, I do return those talents,
Doubled with thanks and service, from
whose help
I deriv'd liberty.
   Tim. O, by no means,
Honest Ventidius! You mistake my love;
I gave it freely ever; and there's none   10
Can truly say he gives, if he receives.
If our betters play at that game, we must
not dare
To imitate them: faults that are rich are fair.
   Ven. A noble spirit!
   Tim. Nay, my lords, ceremony was but
devis'd at first   15
To set a gloss on faint deeds, hollow
welcomes,
Recanting goodness, sorry ere 'tis shown;
But where there is true friendship there
needs none.
Pray, sit; more welcome are ye to my
fortunes
Than my fortunes to me.   [*They sit.* 20
   1 Lord. My lord, we always have confess'd it.
   Apem. Ho, ho, confess'd it! Hang'd it,
have you not?
   Tim. O, Apemantus, you are welcome.
   Apem.   No; 24
You shall not make me welcome.
I come to have thee thrust me out of doors.
   Tim. Fie, th'art a churl; ye have got a
humour there
Does not become a man; 'tis much to
blame.
They say, my lords, Ira furor brevis est;
but yond man is ever angry. Go, let him
have a table by himself; for he does
neither affect company nor is he fit for't
indeed.   31
   Apem. Let me stay at thine apperil,
Timon.
I come to observe; I give thee warning
on't.
   Tim. I take no heed of thee. Th'art an
Athenian, therefore welcome. I myself
would have no power; prithee let my meat
make thee silent.   36

   Apem. I scorn thy meat; 'twould choke
me, for I should ne'er flatter thee. O you
gods, what a number of men eats Timon,
and he sees 'em not! It grieves me to see
so many dip their meat in one man's blood;
and all the madness is, he cheers them up
too.   41
I wonder men dare trust themselves with
men.
Methinks they should invite them without
knives:
Good for their meat and safer for their lives.
There's much example for't; the fellow
that sits next him now, parts bread with
him,
pledges the breath of him in a divided
draught, is the readiest man to kill him.
'T has been proved. If I were a huge man
I should fear to drink at meals,
Lest they should spy my windpipe's
dangerous notes.   50
Great men should drink with harness on
their throats.
   Tim. My lord, in heart! and let the
health go round.
   2 Lord. Let it flow this way, my good
lord.
   Apem. Flow this way! A brave fellow!
He keeps his tides well. Those healths will
make thee and thy state look ill, Timon.
Here's that which is too weak to be a
sinner, honest water, which ne'er left man
i' th' mire.
This and my food are equals; there's no
odds.
Feasts are too proud to give thanks to the
gods.

Apemantus' Grace.

Immortal gods, I crave no pelf;   60
I pray for no man but myself.
Grant I may never prove so fond
To trust man on his oath or bond,
Or a harlot for her weeping,
Or a dog that seems a-sleeping,   65
Or a keeper with my freedom,
Or my friends, if I should need 'em.
Amen. So fall to't.
Rich men sin, and I eat root.
              [*Eats and drinks.*
Much good dich thy good heart, Apemantus!   70
   Tim. Captain Alcibiades, your heart's in
the field now.
   Alcib. My heart is ever at your service,
my lord.
   Tim. You had rather be at a breakfast
of enemies than a dinner of friends.
   Alcib. So they were bleeding new, my
lord, there's no meat like 'em; I could wish
my best friend at such a feast.   77
   Apem. Would all those flatterers were
thine enemies then, that then thou mightst
kill 'em, and bid me to 'em.
   1 Lord. Might we but have that happi-

ness, my lord, that you would once use our hearts, whereby we might express some part of our zeals, we should think ourselves for ever perfect.   83

Tim. O, no doubt, my good friends, but the gods themselves have provided that I shall have much help from you. How had you been my friends else ? Why have you that charitable title from thousands, did not you chiefly belong to my heart ? I have told more of you to myself than you can with modesty speak in your own behalf ; and thus far I confirm you. O you gods, think I, what need we have any friends if we should ne'er have need of 'em ? They were the most needless creatures living, should we ne'er have use for 'em ; and would most resemble sweet instruments hung up in cases, that keep their sounds to themselves. Why, I have often wish'd myself poorer, that I might come nearer to you. We are born to do benefits ; and what better or properer can we call our own than the riches of our friends ? O, what a precious comfort 'tis to have so many like brothers commanding one another's fortunes ! O, joy's e'en made away ere't can be born ! Mine eyes cannot hold out water, methinks. To forget their faults, I drink to you.   103

Apem. Thou weep'st to make them drink, Timon.

2 Lord. Joy had the like conception in our eyes,
And at that instant like a babe sprung up.

Apem. Ho, ho ! I laugh to think that babe a bastard.   107

3 Lord. I promise you, my lord, you mov'd me much.

Apem. Much !   [*Sound tucket.*

Tim. What means that trump ?

Enter a Servant.

How now ?   110

Serv. Please you, my lord, there are certain ladies most desirous of admittance.

Tim. Ladies ! What are their wills ?

Serv. There comes with them a fore-runner, my lord, which bears that office to signify their pleasures.   115

Tim. I pray let them be admitted.

Enter CUPID.

Cup. Hail to thee, worthy Timon, and to all
That of his bounties taste ! The five best Senses
Acknowledge thee their patron, and come freely   119
To gratulate thy plenteous bosom. Th' Ear, Taste, Touch, Smell, pleas'd from thy table rise ;
They only now come but to feast thine eyes.

Tim. They're welcome all ; let 'em have kind admittance.

Music, make their welcome. [*Exit Cupid.*

1 Lord. You see, my lord, how ample y'are belov'd.   125

Music. Re-enter CUPID, *with a* Masque of Ladies as Amazons, *with lutes in their hands, dancing and playing.*

Apem. Hoy-day, what a sweep of vanity comes this way !
They dance ? They are mad women.
Like madness is the glory of this life,
As this pomp shows to a little oil and root.
We make ourselves fools to disport ourselves,   130
And spend our flatteries to drink those men
Upon whose age we void it up again
With poisonous spite and envy.
Who lives that's not depraved or depraves ?
Who dies that bears not one spurn to their graves   135
Of their friends' gift ?
I should fear those that dance before me now
Would one day stamp upon me. 'T has been done :
Men shut their doors against a setting sun.

The Lords rise from table, with much adoring of Timon ; and to show their loves, each single out an Amazon, and all dance, men with women, a lofty strain or two to the hautboys, and cease.

Tim. You have done our pleasures much grace, fair ladies,   140
Set a fair fashion on our entertainment,
Which was not half so beautiful and kind ;
You have added worth unto't and lustre,
And entertain'd me with mine own device ;
I am to thank you for't.   145

1 Lady. My lord, you take us even at the best.

Apem. Faith, for the worst is filthy, and would not hold taking, I doubt me.

Tim. Ladies, there is an idle banquet attends you ;
Please you to dispose yourselves.   150

All Ladies. Most thankfully, my lord.
                 [*Exeunt Cupid and Ladies.*

Tim. Flavius !

Flav. My lord ?

Tim.   The little casket bring me hither.

Flav. Yes, my lord. [*Aside*] More jewels yet !
There is no crossing him in's humour,   155
Else I should tell him—well i' faith, I should—
When all's spent, he'd be cross'd then, an he could.
'Tis pity bounty had not eyes behind,
That man might ne'er be wretched for his mind.   [*Exit.*

1 Lord. Where be our men ?   160

Serv. Here, my lord, in readiness.
2 Lord. Our horses!

Re-enter FLAVIUS, *with the caske..*

Tim. O my friends,
I have one word to say to you. Look you,
my good lord,
I must entreat you honour me so much 165
As to advance this jewel; accept it and
wear it,
Kind my lord.
1 Lord. I am so far already in your gifts—
All. So are we all.

Enter a Servant.

Serv. My lord, there are certain nobles of
the Senate newly alighted and come to
visit you. 171
Tim. They are fairly welcome.
⸰ [*Exit Servant.*
Flav. I beseech your honour, vouchsafe
me a word; it does concern you near.
Tim. Near! Why then, another time
I'll hear thee. I prithee let's be provided
to show them entertainment.
Flav. [*Aside*] I scarce know how. 177

Enter another Servant.

2 Serv. May it please your honour, Lord
Lucius, out of his free love, hath presented
to you four milk-white horses, trapp'd in
silver.
Tim. I shall accept them fairly. Let the
presents 181
Be worthily entertain'd. [*Exit Servant.*

Enter a third Servant.

How now! What news?
3 Serv. Please you, my lord, that honour-
able gentleman, Lord Lucullus, entreats
your company to-morrow to hunt with him
and has sent your honour two brace of
greyhounds. 186
Tim. I'll hunt with him; and let them
be receiv'd,
Not without fair reward. [*Exit Servant.*
Flav. [*Aside*] What will this come to?
He commands us to provide and give great
gifts,
And all out of an empty coffer; 190
Nor will he know his purse, or yield me this,
To show him what a beggar his heart is,
Being of no power to make his wishes good.
His promises fly so beyond his state 194
That what he speaks is all in debt; he owes
For ev'ry word. He is so kind that he now
Pays interest for't; his land's put to their
books.
Well, would I were gently put out of office
Before I were forc'd out! 200
Happier is he that has no friend to feed
Than such that do e'en enemies exceed.
I bleed inwardly for my lord. [*Exit.*
Tim. You do yourselves much wrong;

You bate too much of your own merits.
Here, my lord, a trifle of our love.
2 Lord. With more than common thanks
I will receive it. 206
3 Lord. O, he's the very soul of bounty!
Tim. And now I remember, my lord, you
gave good words the other day of a bay
courser I rode on. 'Tis yours because you
lik'd it. 210
3 Lord. O, I beseech you pardon me, my
lord, in that.
Tim. You may take my word, my lord:
I know no man
Can justly praise but what he does affect.
I weigh my friend's affection with mine
own.
I'll tell you true; I'll call to you. 216
All Lords. O, none so welcome!
Tim. I take all and your several visita-
tions
So kind to heart 'tis not enough to give;
Methinks I could deal kingdoms to my
friends 220
And ne'er be weary. Alcibiades,
Thou art a soldier, therefore seldom rich.
It comes in charity to thee; for all thy
living
Is 'mongst the dead, and all the lands thou
hast
Lie in a pitch'd field. 225
Alcib. Ay, defil'd land my lord.
1 Lord. We are so virtuously bound—
Tim. And so am I to you.
2 Lord. So infinitely endear'd—
Tim. All to you. Lights, more lights! 230
1 Lord. The best of happiness, honour,
and fortunes, keep with you, Lord Timon!
Tim. Ready for his friends.
[*Exeunt all but Apemantus and Timon.*
Apem. What a coil's here!
Serving of becks and jutting-out of
bums!
I doubt whether their legs be worth the
sums 235
That are given for 'em. Friendship's full of
dregs:
Methinks false hearts should never have
sound legs.
Thus honest fools lay out their wealth on
curtsies.
Tim. Now, Apemantus, if thou wert not
sullen
I would be good to thee. 240
Apem. No, I'll nothing; for if I should
be brib'd too, there would be none left to
rail upon thee, and then thou wouldst sin
the faster. Thou giv'st so long, Timon, I
fear me thou wilt give away thyself in
paper shortly. What needs these feasts,
pomps, and vainglories? 245
Tim. Nay, an you begin to rail on society
once, I am sworn not to give regard to you.
Farewell; and come with better music.
[*Exit.*

Apem. So. Thou wilt not hear me now:
thou shalt not then. I'll lock thy heaven
from thee. 250
O that men's ears should be
To counsel deaf, but not to flattery! [*Exit.*

ACT TWO

Scene I. *A Senator's house.*

Enter a Senator, *with papers in his hand.*

Sen. And late, five thousand. To Varro
　　　and to Isidore
He owes nine thousand; besides my former
　　　sum,
Which makes it five and twenty. Still in
　　　motion
Of raging waste? It cannot hold; it will not.
If I want gold, steal but a beggar's dog 5
And give it Timon, why, the dog coins gold.
If I would sell my horse and buy twenty moe
Better than he, why, give my horse to
　　　Timon,
Ask nothing, give it him, it foals me
　　　straight,
And able horses. No porter at his gate, 10
But rather one that smiles and still invites
All that pass by. It cannot hold; no reason
Can sound his state in safety. Caphis, ho!
Caphis, I say!

Enter Caphis.

Cap. Here, sir; what is your pleasure?
Sen. Get on your cloak and haste you to
　　　Lord Timon; 15
Importune him for my moneys; be not
　　　ceas'd
With slight denial, nor then silenc'd when
' Commend me to your master ' and the cap
Plays in the right hand, thus; but tell him
My uses cry to me, I must serve my turn 20
Out of mine own; his days and times are
　　　past,
And my reliances on his fracted dates
Have smit my credit. I love and honour
　　　him,
But must not break my back to heal his
　　　finger.
Immediate are my needs, and my relief 25
Must not be toss'd and turn'd to me in
　　　words,
But find supply immediate. Get you gone;
Put on a most importunate aspect,
A visage of demand; for I do fear, 29
When every feather sticks in his own wing,
Lord Timon will be left a naked gull,
Which flashes now a phœnix. Get you gone.
Caph. I go, sir.
Sen. 　　　　　　Take the bonds along
　　　with you,
And have the dates in compt.
Caph. 　　　　　　　　I will, sir.
Sen. 　　　　　　　　　　　Go. 35
　　　　　　　　　　　　　　[*Exeunt.*

Scene II. *Before Timon's house.*

Enter Flavius, *Timon's steward, with many
　　　bills in his hand.*

Flav. No care, no stop! So senseless of
　　　expense
That he will neither know how to main-
　　　tain it
Nor cease his flow of riot; takes no account
How things go from him, nor resumes no
　　　care
Of what is to continue. Never mind 5
Was to be so unwise to be so kind.
What shall be done? He will not hear
　　　till feel.
I must be round with him. Now he comes
　　　from hunting.
Fie, fie, fie, fie!

Enter Caphis, *and the* Servants *of* Isidore
　　　and Varro.

Caph. Good even, Varro. What, you come
for money? 10
Var. Serv. Is't not your business too?
Caph. It is. And yours too, Isidore?
Isid. Serv. It is so.
Caph. Would we were all discharg'd! 14
Var. Serv. I fear it.
Caph. Here comes the lord.

Enter Timon *and his* Train, *with*
　　　Alcibiades.

Tim. So soon as dinner's done we'll forth
　　　again,
My Alcibiades.—With me? What is your
　　　will?
Caph. My lord, here is a note of certain
dues.
Tim. Dues! Whence are you?
Caph. Of Athens here, my lord.
Tim. Go to my steward. 21
Caph. Please it your lordship, he hath put
me off
To the succession of new days this month.
My master is awak'd by great occasion
To call upon his own, and humbly prays
you 25
That with your other noble parts you'll
suit
In giving him his right.
Tim. 　　　　　　Mine honest friend,
I prithee but repair to me next morning.
Caph. Nay, good my lord—
Tim. 　　　　　　Contain thyself, good friend.
Var. Serv. One Varro's servant, my good
lord— 30
Isid. Serv. From Isidore: he humbly
prays your speedy payment—
Caph. If you did know, my lord, my
master's wants—
Var. Serv. 'Twas due on forfeiture, my
lord, six weeks and past. 35
Isid. Serv. Your steward puts me off, my

947

lord; and I am sent expressly to your lordship.

Tim. Give me breath.

I do beseech you, good my lords, keep on; I'll wait upon you instantly.

[*Exeunt Alcibiades and Lords.*

[*To Flavius*] Come hither. Pray you, 40
How goes the world that I am thus encount'red
With clamorous demands of date-broke bonds
And the detention of long-since-due debts, Against my honour?

Flav.   Please you, gentlemen,
The time is unagreeable to this business. 45
Your importunacy cease till after dinner,
That I may make his lordship understand
Wherefore you are not paid.

Tim.   Do so, my friends.
See them well entertain'd.   [*Exit.*

Flav.   Pray draw near. [*Exit.*

Enter APEMANTUS and Fool.

Caph. Stay, stay, here comes the fool with Apemantus. Let's ha' some sport with 'em.

Var. Serv. Hang him, he'll abuse us!

Isid. Serv. A plague upon him, dog!

Var. Serv. How dost, fool?   55

Apem. Dost dialogue with thy shadow?

Var. Serv. I speak not to thee.

Apem. No, 'tis to thyself. [*To the Fool*] Come away.

Isid Serv. [*To Var. Serv.*] There's the fool hangs on your back already.

Apem. No, thou stand'st single; th'art not on him yet.

Caph. Where's the fool now?   61

Apem. He last ask'd the question. Poor rogues and usurers' men! Bawds between gold and want!

All Serv. What are we, Apemantus?

Apem. Asses.   65

All Serv. Why?

Apem. That you ask me what you are, and do not know yourselves. Speak to 'em, fool.

Fool. How do you, gentlemen?

All Serv. Gramercies, good fool. How does your mistress?   71

Fool. She's e'en setting on water to scald such chickens as you are. Would we could see you at Corinth!

Apem. Good! gramercy.

Enter Page.

Fool. Look you, here comes my mistress' page.   75

Page [*To the Fool*] Why, how now, Captain? What do you in this wise company? How dost thou, Apemantus?

Apem. Would I had a rod in my mouth, that I might answer thee profitably!

Page. Prithee, Apemantus, read me the superscription of these letters; I know not which is which.   81

Apem. Canst not read?

Page. No.

Apem. There will little learning die, then, that day thou art hang'd. This is to Lord Timon; this to Alcibiades. Go; thou wast born a bastard, and thou't die a bawd. 87

Page. Thou wast whelp'd a dog, and thou shalt famish a dog's death. Answer not: I am gone.   [*Exit Page.*

Apem. E'en so thou outrun'st grace. Fool, I will go with you to Lord Timon's. 91

Fool. Will you leave me there?

Apem. If Timon stay at home. You three serve three usurers?

All Serv. Ay; would they serv'd us! 95

Apem. So would I—as good a trick as ever hangman serv'd thief.

Fool. Are you three usurers' men?

All Serv. Ay, fool.   99

Fool. I think no usurer but has a fool to his servant. My mistress is one, and I am her fool. When men come to borrow of your masters, they approach sadly and go away merry; but they enter my mistress' house merrily and go away sadly. The reason of this?

Var. Serv. I could render one.   105

Apem. Do it then, that we may account thee a whoremaster and a knave; which notwithstanding, thou shalt be no less esteemed.   108

Var. Serv. What is a whoremaster, fool?

Fool. A fool in good clothes, and something like thee. 'Tis a spirit. Sometime 't appears like a lord; sometime like a lawyer; sometime like a philosopher, with two stones moe than's artificial one. He is very often like a knight; and, generally, in all shapes that man goes up and down in from fourscore to thirteen, this spirit walks in.   115

Var. Serv. Thou art not altogether a fool.

Fool. Nor thou altogether a wise man. As much foolery as I have, so much wit thou lack'st.

Apem. That answer might have become Apemantus.

Var. Serv. Aside, aside; here comes Lord Timon.   120

Re-enter TIMON and FLAVIUS.

Apem. Come with me, fool, come.

Fool. I do not always follow lover, elder brother, and woman; sometime the philosopher. [*Exeunt Apemantus and Fool.*

Flav Pray you walk near; I'll speak with you anon.   [*Exeunt Servants.*

Tim. You make me marvel wherefore ere this time   125
Had you not fully laid my state before me,
That I might so have rated my expense
As I had leave of means.

Flav.   You would not hear me
At many leisures I propos'd.
Tim.   Go to;   129
Perchance some single vantages you took
When my indisposition put you back,
And that unaptness made your minister
Thus to excuse yourself.
Flav.   O my good lord,
At many times I brought in my accounts,
Laid them before you; you would throw
    them off   135
And say you found them in mine honesty.
When, for some trifling present, you have
    bid me
Return so much, I have shook my head and
    wept;
Yea, 'gainst th' authority of manners,
    pray'd you   139
To hold your hand more close. I did endure
Not seldom, nor no slight checks, when I
    have
Prompted you in the ebb of your estate
And your great flow of debts. My lov'd
    lord,
Though you hear now—too late!—yet
    now's a time:
The greatest of your having lacks a half 145
To pay your present debts.
Tim.   Let all my land be sold.
Flav. 'Tis all engag'd, some forfeited and
    gone;
And what remains will hardly stop the
    mouth
Of present dues. The future comes apace;
What shall defend the interim? And at
    length   150
How goes our reck'ning?
Tim. To Lacedæmon did my land extend.
Flav. O my good lord, the world is but
    a word;
Were it all yours to give it in a breath,
How quickly were it gone!
Tim.   You tell me true. 155
Flav. If you suspect my husbandry or
    falsehood,
Call me before th' exactest auditors
And set me on the proof. So the gods bless
    me,
When all our offices have been oppress'd
With riotous feeders, when our vaults have
    wept   160
With drunken spilth of wine, when every
    room
Hath blaz'd with lights and bray'd with
    minstrelsy,
I have retir'd me to a wasteful cock
And set mine eyes at flow.
Tim.   Prithee no more.
Flav. 'Heavens,' have I said 'the bounty
    of this lord!
How many prodigal bits have slaves and
    peasants   166
This night englutted! Who is not Lord
    Timon's?

What heart, head, sword, force, means, but
    is Lord Timon's?
Great Timon, noble, worthy, royal Timon!'
Ah! when the means are gone that buy
    this praise,   170
The breath is gone whereof this praise is
    made.
Feast-won, fast-lost; one cloud of winter
    show'rs,
These flies are couch'd.
Tim.   Come, sermon me no further.
No villainous bounty yet hath pass'd my
    heart;
Unwisely, not ignobly, have I given.   175
Why dost thou weep? Canst thou the con-
    science lack
To think I shall lack friends? Secure thy
    heart:
If I would broach the vessels of my love,
And try the argument of hearts by borrow-
    ing,   179
Men and men's fortunes could I frankly use
As I can bid thee speak.
Flav.   Assurance bless your thoughts!
Tim. And, in some sort, these wants of
    mine are crown'd
That I account them blessings; for by these
Shall I try friends. You shall perceive how
    you
Mistake my fortunes; I am wealthy in my
    friends.   185
Within there! Flaminius! Servilius!

Enter FLAMINIUS, SERVILIUS, *and another*
    Servant.

Servants. My lord! my lord!
Tim. I will dispatch you severally—you
to Lord Lucius; to Lord Lucullus you; I
hunted with his honour to-day. You to
Sempronius. Commend me to their loves;
and I am proud, say, that my occasions
have found time to use 'em toward a supply
of money. Let the request be fifty talents.
Flam. As you have said, my lord.
                            [*Exeunt Servants.*
Flav. [*Aside*] Lord Lucius and Lucullus?
Humh!   195
Tim. Go you, sir, to the senators,
Of whom, even to the state's best health,
    I have
Deserv'd this hearing. Bid 'em send o' th'
    instant
A thousand talents to me.
Flav.   I have been bold,
For that I knew it the most general way, 200
To them to use your signet and your name;
But they do shake their heads, and I am
    here
No richer in return.
Tim.   Is't true? Can't be?
Flav. They answer, in a joint and
    corporate voice,
That now they are at fall, want treasure,
    cannot   205

Do what they would, are sorry—you are
    honourable—
But yet they could have wish'd—they know
    not—
Something hath been amiss—a noble
    nature
May catch a wrench—would all were well !—
    'tis pity—
And so, intending other serious matters, 210
After distasteful looks, and these hard
    fractions,
With certain half-caps and cold-moving
    nods,
They froze me into silence.
  Tim.   You gods, reward them !
Prithee, man, look cheerly. These old
    fellows   214
Have their ingratitude in them hereditary.
Their blood is cak'd, 'tis cold, it seldom
    flows ;
'Tis lack of kindly warmth they are not
    kind ;
And nature, as it grows again toward earth,
Is fashion'd for the journey dull and heavy.
Go to Ventidius. Prithee be not sad, 220
Thou art true and honest ; ingeniously I
    speak,
No blame belongs to thee. Ventidius lately
Buried his father, by whose death he's
    stepp'd
Into a great estate. When he was poor,
Imprison'd, and in scarcity of friends, 225
I clear'd him with five talents. Greet him
    from me,
Bid him suppose some good necessity
Touches his friend, which craves to be
    rememb'red
With those five talents. That had, give't
    these fellows
To whom 'tis instant due. Nev'r speak or
    think   230
That Timon's fortunes 'mong his friends
    can sink.
  Flav. I would I could not think it.
That thought is bounty's foe ;
Being free itself, it thinks all others so.
                            [*Exeunt.*

ACT THREE

Scene I. *Lucullus' house.*

Flaminius *waiting to speak with Lucullus.*
    Enter a Servant *to him.*

  Serv. I have told my lord of you ; he is
coming down to you.
  Flam. I thank you, sir.

Enter Lucullus.

  Serv. Here's my lord.   4
  Lucul. [*Aside*] One of Lord Timon's men ?
A gift, I warrant. Why, this hits right ; I
dreamt of a silver basin and ewer to-night—
Flaminius, honest Flaminius, you are very
respectively welcome, sir. Fill me some

wine. [*Exit Servant*] And how does that
honourable, complete, free-hearted gentleman of Athens, thy very bountiful good
lord and master ?   11
  Flam. His health is well, sir.
  Lucul. I am right glad that his health
is well, sir. And what hast thou there under
thy cloak, pretty Flaminius ?   15
  Flam. Faith, nothing but an empty box,
sir, which in my lord's behalf I come to
entreat your honour to supply ; who,
having great and instant occasion to use
fifty talents, hath sent to your lordship to
furnish him, nothing doubting your present
assistance therein.   20
  Lucul. La, la, la, la ! ' Nothing doubting '
says he ? Alas, good lord ! a noble gentleman 'tis, if he would not keep so good a
house. Many a time and often I ha' din'd
with him and told him on't ; and come
again to supper to him of purpose to have
him spend less ; and yet he would embrace
no counsel, take no warning by my coming.
Every man has his fault, and honesty is
his. I ha' told him on't, but I could ne'er
get him from't.

Re-enter Servant, *with wine.*

  Serv. Please your lordship, here is the
wine.   30
  Lucul. Flaminius, I have noted thee
always wise. Here's to thee.
  Flam. Your lordship speaks your pleasure.
  Lucul. I have observed thee always for
a towardly prompt spirit, give thee thy
due, and one that knows what belongs to
reason, and canst use the time well, if the
time use thee well. Good parts in thee. [*To
Servant*] Get you gone, sirrah. [*Exit
Servant*] Draw nearer, honest Flaminius.
Thy lord's a bountiful gentleman ; but
thou art wise, and thou know'st well
enough, although thou com'st to me, that
this is no time to lend money, especially
upon bare friendship without security.
Here's three solidares for thee. Good boy,
wink at me, and say thou saw'st me not.
Fare thee well.   44
  Flam. Is't possible the world should so
    much differ,
And we alive that liv'd ? Fly, damned
    baseness,
To him that worships thee.
              [*Throwing the money back.*
  Lucul. Ha ! Now I see thou art a fool,
and fit for thy master.   [*Exit.*
  Flam. May these add to the number that
    may scald thee !   50
Let molten coin be thy damnation,
Thou disease of a friend and not himself !
Has friendship such a faint and milky heart
It turns in less than two nights ? O you
    gods,

I feel my master's passion ! This slave   55
Unto his honour has my lord's meat in
    him ;
Why should it thrive and turn to nutriment
When he is turn'd to poison ?
O, may diseases only work upon't !
And when he's sick to death, let not that
    part of nature   60
Which my lord paid for be of any power
To expel sickness, but prolong his hour !
                                    [Exit.

SCENE II. A public place.

Enter LUCIUS, with three Strangers.

Luc. Who, the Lord Timon ? He is my
very good friend, and an honourable
gentleman.

1 Stran. We know him for no less, though
we are but strangers to him. But I can tell
you one thing, my lord, and which I hear
from common rumours : now Lord Timon's
happy hours are done and past, and his
estate shrinks from him.

Luc. Fie, no : do not believe it ; he
cannot want for money.   9

2 Stran. But believe you this, my lord,
that not long ago one of his men was with
the Lord Lucullus to borrow so many
talents ; nay, urg'd extremely for't, and
showed what necessity belong'd to't, and
yet was denied.

Luc. How ?

2 Stran. I tell you, denied, my lord.   15

Luc. What a strange case was that !
Now, before the gods, I am asham'd on't.
Denied that honourable man ! There was
very little honour show'd in't. For my own
part, I must needs confess I have received
some small kindnesses from him, as money,
plate, jewels, and such-like trifles, nothing
comparing to his ; yet, had he mistook
him and sent to me, I should ne'er have
denied his occasion so many talents.   23

Enter SERVILIUS.

Ser. See, by good hap, yonder's my lord ;
I have sweat to see his honour.—My
honour'd lord !   25

Luc. Servilius ? You are kindly met, sir.
Fare thee well ; commend me to thy
honourable virtuous lord, my very exquisite friend.   28

Ser. May it please your honour, my lord
hath sent—

Luc. Ha ! What has he sent ? I am so
much endeared to that lord ; he's ever
sending. How shall I thank him, think'st
thou ? And what has he sent now ?

Ser. Has only sent his present occasion
now, my lord, requesting your lordship to
supply his instant use with so many talents.

Luc. I know his lordship is but merry
    with me ;   36
He cannot want fifty-five hundred talents.

Ser. But in the mean time he wants
    less, my lord.
If his occasion were not virtuous
I should not urge it half so faithfully.   40

Luc. Dost thou speak seriously, Servilius ?

Ser. Upon my soul, 'tis true, sir.

Luc. What a wicked beast was I to disfurnish myself against such a good time,
when I might ha' shown myself honourable !
How unluckily it happ'ned that I should
purchase the day before for a little part
and undo a great deal of honour ! Servilius,
now before the gods, I am not able to do—
the more beast, I say ! I was sending to
use Lord Timon myself, these gentlemen
can witness ; but I would not for the
wealth of Athens I had done't now. Commend me bountifully to his good lordship,
and I hope his honour will conceive the
fairest of me, because I have no power to
be kind. And tell him this from me : I count
it one of my greatest afflictions, say, that I
cannot pleasure such an honourable
gentleman. Good Servilius, will you befriend me so far as to use mine own words
to him ?   57

Ser. Yes, sir, I shall.

Luc. I'll look you out a good turn,
Servilius.   [Exit Servilius.
True, as you said, Timon is shrunk indeed ;
And he that's once denied will hardly speed.
                                    [Exit.

1 Stran. Do you observe this, Hostilius ?

2 Stran. Ay, too well.

1 Stran. Why, this is the world's soul ;
    and just of the same piece
Is every flatterer's spirit. Who can call him
    his friend
That dips in the same dish ? For, in my
    knowing,   65
Timon has been this lord's father,
And kept his credit with his purse ;
Supported his estate ; nay, Timon's money
Has paid his men their wages. He ne'er
    drinks
But Timon's silver treads upon his lip ;   70
And yet—O, see the monstrousness of man
When he looks out in an ungrateful shape !—
He does deny him, in respect of his,
What charitable men afford to beggars.

3 Stran. Religion groans at it.

1 Stran.   For mine own part,
I never tasted Timon in my life,   76
Nor came any of his bounties over me
To mark me for his friend ; yet I protest,
For his right noble mind, illustrious virtue,
And honourable carriage,   80
Had his necessity made use of me,
I would have put my wealth into donation,
And the best half should have return'd to
    him,   83
So much I love his heart. But I perceive
Men must learn now with pity to dispense ;
For policy sits above conscience. [Exeunt.

SCENE III. *Sempronius' house.*

Enter SEMPRONIUS *and a* Servant of Timon's.

Sem. Must he needs trouble me in't ?
Hum ! 'Bove all others ?
He might have tried Lord Lucius or
Lucullus ;
And now Ventidius is wealthy too,
Whom he redeem'd from prison. All these
Owe their estates unto him.
Serv. My lord, 5
They have all been touch'd and found base
metal, for
They have all denied him.
Sem. How ! Have they denied him ?
Has Ventidius and Lucullus denied him ?
And does he send to me ? Three ? Humh !
It shows but little love or judgment in him.
Must I be his last refuge ? His friends, like
physicians, 11
Thrice give him over. Must I take th' cure
upon me ?
Has much disgrac'd me in't ; I'm angry
at him,
That might have known my place. I see no
sense for't,
But his occasions might have woo'd me
first ; 15
For, in my conscience, I was the first man
That e'er received gift from him.
And does he think so backwardly of me now
That I'll requite it last ? No ;
So it may prove an argument of laughter 20
To th' rest, and I 'mongst lords be thought
a fool.
I'd rather than the worth of thrice the sum
Had sent to me first, but for my mind's
sake ;
I'd such a courage to do him good. But
now return, 24
And with their faint reply this answer join :
Who bates mine honour shall not know my
coin. [*Exit.*
Serv. Excellent ! Your lordship's a goodly
villain. The devil knew not what he did
when he made man politic—he cross'd him-
self by't ; and I cannot think but, in the
end, the villainies of man will set him clear.
How fairly this lord strives to appear foul !
Takes virtuous copies to be wicked, like
those that under hot ardent zeal would set
whole realms on fire.
Of such a nature is his politic love.
This was my lord's best hope ; now all are
fled, 35
Save only the gods. Now his friends are
dead,
Doors that were ne'er acquainted with their
wards
Many a bounteous year must be employ'd
Now to guard sure their master.
And this is all a liberal course allows : 40

Who cannot keep his wealth must keep his
house. [*Exit.*

SCENE IV. *A hall in Timon's house.*

Enter two of Varro's Men, *meeting* Lucius'
Servant, *and Others, all being servants of
Timon's creditors, to wait for his coming
out. Then enter* TITUS *and* HORTENSIUS.

1 Var. Serv. Well met ; good morrow,
Titus and Hortensius.
Tit. The like to you, kind Varro.
Hor. Lucius ! What, do we meet together ?
Luc. Serv. Ay, and I think one business
does command us all ; for mine is money.
Tit. So is theirs and ours. 6

Enter PHILOTUS.

Luc. Serv. And Sir Philotus too !
Phi. Good day at once.
Luc. Serv. Welcome, good brother, what
do you think the hour ?
Phi. Labouring for nine.
Luc. Serv. So much ?
Phi. Is not my lord seen yet ?
Luc. Serv. Not yet.
Phi. I wonder on't ; he was wont to shine
at seven.
Luc. Serv. Ay, but the days are wax'd
shorter with him ; 11
You must consider that a prodigal course
Is like the sun's, but not like his recover-
able.
I fear
'Tis deepest winter in Lord Timon's purse ;
That is, one may reach deep enough and yet
Find little.
Phi. I am of your fear for that. 17
Tit. I'll show you how t' observe a strange
event.
Your lord sends now for money.
Hor. Most true, he does.
Tit. And he wears jewels now of Timon's
gift, 20
For which I wait for money.
Hor. It is against my heart.
Luc. Serv. Mark how strange it shows
Timon in this should pay more than he
owes :
And e'en as if your lord should wear rich
jewels
And send for money for 'em. 25
Hor. I'm weary of this charge, the gods
can witness ;
I know my lord hath spent of Timon's
wealth,
And now ingratitude makes it worse than
stealth.
1 Var. Serv. Yes, mine's three thousand
crowns ; what's yours ?
Luc. Serv. Five thousand mine. 30
1 Var. Serv. 'Tis much deep ; and it
should seem by th' sum
Your master's confidence was above mine,

Else surely his had equall'd.

Enter FLAMINIUS.

Tit. One of Lord Timon's men.
Luc. Serv. Flaminius! Sir, a word. Pray,
is my lord ready to come forth?   36
Flam. No, indeed, he is not.
Tit. We attend his lordship; pray signify
so much.
Flam. I need not tell him that; he knows
you are too diligent.   [*Exit.* 40

Enter FLAVIUS, *in a cloak, muffled.*

Luc. Serv. Ha! Is not that his steward
muffled so? He goes away in a cloud.
Call him, call him.
Tit. Do you hear, sir?
2 Var. Serv. By your leave, sir.   44
Flav. What do ye ask of me, my friend?
Tit. We wait for certain money here, sir.
Flav.   Ay,
If money were as certain as your waiting,
'Twere sure enough.
Why then preferr'd you not your sums and
bills
When your false masters eat of my lord's
meat?   50
Then they could smile, and fawn upon his
debts,
And take down th' int'rest into their
glutt'nous maws.
You do yourselves but wrong to stir me up;
Let me pass quietly.
Believe't, my lord and I have made an end:
I have no more to reckon, he to spend.   56
Luc. Serv. Ay, but this answer will not
serve.
Flav. If 'twill not serve, 'tis not so base
as you,
For you serve knaves.   [*Exit.*
1 Var. Serv. How! What does his cashier'd
worship mutter?   61
2 Var. Serv. No matter what; he's poor,
and that's revenge enough. Who can speak
broader than he that has no house to put
his head in? Such may rail against great
buildings.   65

Enter SERVILIUS.

Tit. O, here's Servilius; now we shall
know some answer.
Ser. If I might beseech you, gentlemen,
to repair some other hour, I should derive
much from't; for take't of my soul, my
lord leans wondrously to discontent. His
comfortable temper has forsook him; he's
much out of health and keeps his chamber.
Luc. Serv. Many do keep their chambers
are not sick;
And if it be so far beyond his health,
Methinks he should the sooner pay his
debts,   75
And make a clear way to the gods.
Ser.   Good gods!
Tit. We cannot take this for answer, sir.

Flam. [*Within*] Servilius, help! My lord!
my lord!

Enter TIMON, *in a rage,* FLAMINIUS
following.

Tim. What, are my doors oppos'd against
my passage?
Have I been ever free, and must my house 80
Be my retentive enemy, my gaol?
The place which I have feasted, does it now,
Like all mankind, show me an iron heart?
Luc. Serv. Put in now, Titus.
Tit. My lord, here is my bill.   85
Luc. Serv. Here's mine.
Hor. And mine, my lord.
Both Var. Serv. And ours, my lord
Phi. All our bills.
Tim. Knock me down with 'em; cleave
me to the girdle.
Luc. Serv. Alas, my lord—   91
Tim. Cut my heart in sums.
Tit. Mine, fifty talents.
Tim. Tell out my blood.
Luc. Serv. Five thousand crowns, my lord.
Tim. Five thousand drops pays that.
What yours? and yours?   96
1 Var. Serv. My lord—
2 Var. Serv. My lord—
Tim. Tear me, take me, and the gods fall
upon you!   [*Exit.*
Hor. Faith, I perceive our masters may
throw their caps at their money. These
debts may well be call'd desperate ones,
for a madman owes 'em.   [*Exeunt.*

Re-enter TIMON *and* FLAVIUS.

Tim. They have e'en put my breath from
me, the slaves.
Creditors? Devils!   106
Flav. My dear lord—
Tim. What if it should be so?
Flam. My lord—
Tim. I'll have it so. My steward!   110
Flav. Here, my lord.
Tim. So fitly? Go, bid all my friends
again:
Lucius, Lucullus, and Sempronius—all.
I'll once more feast the rascals.   113
Flav.   O my lord,
You only speak from your distracted soul;
There is not so much left to furnish out
A moderate table.
Tim.   Be it not in thy care.
Go, I charge thee, invite them all; let in
the tide   119
Of knaves once more; my cook and I'll
provide.   [*Exeunt.*

SCENE V. *The Senate House.*

Enter three Senators *at one door,* ALCIBIADES
meeting them, with Attendants.

1 Sen. My lord, you have my voice to't:
the fault's bloody.

'Tis necessary he should die :
Nothing emboldens sin so much as mercy.
  2 *Sen.* Most true ; the law shall bruise
    him.
  Alcib. Honour, health, and compassion,
    to the Senate !
  1 *Sen.* Now, Captain ?   6
  Alcib. I am an humble suitor to your
    virtues ;
For pity is the virtue of the law,
And none but tyrants use it cruelly.
It pleases time and fortune to lie heavy 10
Upon a friend of mine, who in hot blood
Hath stepp'd into the law, which is past
    depth
To those that without heed do plunge
    into't.
He is a man, setting his fate aside,
Of comely virtues ;   15
Nor did he soil the fact with cowardice—
An honour in him which buys out his
    fault—
But with a noble fury and fair spirit,
Seeing his reputation touch'd to death,
He did oppose his foe ;   20
And with such sober and unnoted passion
He did behove his anger ere 'twas spent,
As if he had but prov'd an argument.
  1 *Sen.* You undergo too strict a paradox,
Striving to make an ugly deed look fair ; 25
Your words have took such pains as if they
    labour'd
To bring manslaughter into form and set
Quarrelling upon the head of valour ; which,
    indeed,
Is valour misbegot, and came into the
    world   29
When sects and factions were newly born.
He's truly valiant that can wisely suffer
The worst that man can breathe,
And make his wrongs his outsides,
To wear them like his raiment, carelessly,
And ne'er prefer his injuries to his heart,
To bring it into danger.   35
If wrongs be evils, and enforce us kill,
What folly 'tis to hazard life for ill !
  Alcib. My lord—
  1 *Sen.*   You cannot make gross sins look
    clear :
To revenge is no valour, but to bear.
  Alcib. My lords, then, under favour,
    pardon me   40
If I speak like a captain :
Why do fond men expose themselves to
    battle,
And not endure all threats ? Sleep upon't,
And let the foes quietly cut their throats,
Without repugnancy ? If there be   45
Such valour in the bearing, what make we
Abroad ? Why, then, women are more
    valiant,
That stay at home, if bearing carry it ;
And the ass more captain than the lion ;
    the fellow

Loaden with irons wiser than the judge, 50
If wisdom be in suffering. O my lords,
As you are great, be pitifully good.
Who cannot condemn rashness in cold
    blood ?
To kill, I grant, is sin's extremest gust ;
But, in defence, by mercy, 'tis most just. 55
To be in anger is impiety ;
But who is man that is not angry ?
Weigh but the crime with this.
  2 *Sen.* You breathe in vain.
  Alcib.   In vain ! His service done
At Lacedaemon and Byzantium   60
Were a sufficient briber for his life.
  1 *Sen.* What's that ?
  Alcib. Why, I say, my lords, has done
    fair service,
And slain in fight many of your enemies ;
How full of valour did he bear himself
In the last conflict, and made plenteous
    wounds !   65
  2 *Sen.* He has made too much plenty
    with 'em.
He's a sworn rioter ; he has a sin that often
Drowns him and takes his valour prisoner.
If there were no foes, that were enough
To overcome him. In that beastly fury 70
He has been known to commit outrages
And cherish factions. 'Tis inferr'd to us
His days are foul and his drink dangerous.
  1 *Sen.* He dies.
  Alcib.   Hard fate ! He might have died
    in war.
My lords, if not for any parts in him— 75
Though his right arm might purchase his
    own time,
And be in debt to none—yet, more to move
    you,
Take my deserts to his, and join 'em both ;
And, for I know your reverend ages love
Security, I'll pawn my victories, all   80
My honours to you, upon his good returns.
If by this crime he owes the law his life,
Why, let the war receive't in valiant gore ;
For law is strict, and war is nothing more.
  1 *Sen.* We are for law : he dies. Urge it
    no more   85
On height of our displeasure. Friend or
    brother,
He forfeits his own blood that spills an-
    other.
  Alcib. Must it be so ? It must not be. My
    lords,
I do beseech you, know me.
  2 *Sen.* How !   90
  Alcib. Call me to your remembrances.
  3 *Sen.* What !
  Alcib. I cannot think but your age has
    forgot me ;
It could not else be I should prove so base
To sue, and be denied such common grace.
My wounds ache at you.
  1 *Sen.*   Do you dare our anger ?
'Tis in few words, but spacious in effect : 97

We banish thee for ever.
  Alcib.   Banish me!
Banish your dotage! Banish usury
That makes the Senate ugly.   100
  1 *Sen.* If after two days' shine Athens
      contain thee,
Attend our weightier judgment. And, not
      to swell our spirit,
He shall be executed presently.
                              [*Exeunt Senators.*
  Alcib. Now the gods keep you old enough
      that you may live   104
Only in bone, that none may look on you!
I'm worse than mad; I have kept back
      their foes,
While they have told their money and let
      out
Their coin upon large interest, I myself   108
Rich only in large hurts. All those for
      this?
Is this the balsam that the usuring Senate
Pours into captains' wounds? Banishment!
It comes not ill; I hate not to be banish'd;
It is a cause worthy my spleen and fury,
That I may strike at Athens. I'll cheer up
My discontented troops, and lay for hearts.
'Tis honour with most lands to be at odds;
Soldiers should brook as little wrongs as
      gods.   [*Exit.*

SCENE VI. *A banqueting hall in Timon's
      house.*

Music. Tables set out; Servants *attending.
  Enter divers* Lords, *friends of Timon, at
  several doors.*

  1 *Lord.* The good time of day to you, sir.
  2 *Lord.* I also wish it to you. I think this
honourable lord did but try us this other
day.
  1 *Lord.* Upon that were my thoughts
tiring when we encount'red. I hope it is
not so low with him as he made it seem in
the trial of his several friends.   6
  2 *Lord.* It should not be, by the persuasion of his new feasting.
  1 *Lord.* I should think so. He hath sent
me an earnest inviting, which many my
near occasions did urge me to put off; but
he hath conjur'd me beyond them, and I
must needs appear.   12
  2 *Lord.* In like manner was I in debt to
my importunate business, but he would not
hear my excuse. I am sorry, when he sent
to borrow of me, that my provision was out.
  1 *Lord.* I am sick of that grief too, as I
understand how all things go.
  2 *Lord.* Every man here's so. What
would he have borrowed of you?   20
  1 *Lord.* A thousand pieces.
  2 *Lord.* A thousand pieces!
  1 *Lord.* What of you?
  2 *Lord.* He sent to me, sir—here he
comes.

Enter TIMON *and* Attendants.

  Tim. With all my heart, gentlemen both!
And how fare you?   26
  1 *Lord.* Ever at the best, hearing well of
your lordship.
  2 *Lord.* The swallow follows not summer
more willing than we your lordship.   30
  Tim. [*Aside*] Nor more willingly leaves
winter; such summer-birds are men—
Gentlemen, our dinner will not recompense
this long stay; feast your ears with the
music awhile, if they will fare so harshly 'o
th' trumpet's sound; we shall to't presently.   35
  1 *Lord.* I hope it remains not unkindly
with your lordship that I return'd you an
empty messenger.
  Tim. O sir, let it not trouble you.
  2 *Lord.* My noble lord—   39
  Tim. Ah, my good friend, what cheer?
  2 *Lord.* My most honourable lord, I am
e'en sick of shame that, when your lordship
this other day sent to me, I was so unfortunate a beggar.
  Tim. Think not on't, sir.
  2 *Lord.* If you had sent but two hours
before—   45
  Tim. Let it not cumber your better
remembrance. [*The banquet brought in.*
Come, bring in all together.
  2 *Lord.* All cover'd dishes!
  1 *Lord.* Royal cheer, I warrant you.
  3 *Lord.* Doubt not that, if money and the
season can yield it.   51
  1 *Lord.* How do you? What's the news?
  3 *Lord.* Alcibiades is banish'd. Hear you
of it?
  1 *& 2 Lord.* Alcibiades banish'd!
  3 *Lord.* 'Tis so, be sure of it.   55
  1 *Lord.* How? how?
  2 *Lord.* I pray you, upon what?
  Tim. My worthy friends, will you draw
near?
  3 *Lord.* I'll tell you more anon Here's a
noble feast toward.   60
  2 *Lord.* This is the old man still.
  3 *Lord.* Will't hold? Will't hold?
  2 *Lord.* It does; but time will—and so—
  3 *Lord.* I do conceive.   64
  Tim. Each man to his stool with that
spur as he would to the lip of his mistress;
your diet shall be in all places alike. Make
not a city feast of it, to let the meat cool
ere we can agree upon the first place. Sit,
sit. The gods require our thanks: 69

You great benefactors, sprinkle our
society with thankfulness. For your own
gifts make yourselves prais'd; but reserve
still to give, lest your deities be despised.
Lend to each man enough, that one need
not lend to another; for were your god-
heads to borrow of men, men would forsake

the gods. Make the meat be beloved more than the man that gives it. Let no assembly of twenty be without a score of villains. If there sit twelve women at the table, let a dozen of them be—as they are. The rest of your foes, O gods, the Senators of Athens, together with the common lag of people, what is amiss in them, you gods, make suitable for destruction. For these my present friends, as they are to me nothing, so in nothing bless them, and to nothing are they welcome.

Uncover, dogs, and lap. 85
[*The dishes are uncovered and seen to be full of warm water.*
Some speak. What does his lordship mean ?
Some other. I know not.
Tim. May you a better feast never behold,
You knot of mouth-friends ! Smoke and lukewarm water
Is your perfection. This is Timon's last ; 90
Who, stuck and spangled with your flatteries,
Washes it off, and sprinkles in your faces
[*Throwing the water in their faces.*
Your reeking villainy. Live loath'd and long,
Most smiling, smooth, detested parasites,
Courteous destroyers, affable wolves, meek bears, 95
You fools of fortune, trencher friends, time's flies,
Cap and knee slaves, vapours, and minute-jacks !
Of man and beast the infinite malady
Crust you quite o'er ! What, dost thou go ?
Soft, take thy physic first ; thou too, and thou. 100
Stay, I will lend thee money, borrow none.
[*Throws the dishes at them, and drives them out.*
What, all in motion ? Henceforth be no feast
Whereat a villain's not a welcome guest.
Burn house ! Sink Athens ! Henceforth hated be
Of Timon man and all humanity ! [*Exit.*

Re-enter the Lords.

1 Lord. How now, my lords !
2 Lord. Know you the quality of Lord Timon's fury ?
3 Lord. Push ! Did you see my cap ?
4 Lord. I have lost my gown. 109
1 Lord. He's but a mad lord, and nought but humours sways him. He gave me a jewel th' other day, and now he has beat it out of my hat. Did you see my jewel ?
3 Lord. Did you see my cap ?
2 Lord. Here 'tis. 115
4 Lord. Here lies my gown.

1 Lord. Let's make no stay.
2 Lord. Lord Timon's mad.
3 Lord. I feel't upon my bones.
4 Lord. One day he gives us diamonds, next day stones. [*Exeunt.*

ACT FOUR

SCENE I. *Without the walls of Athens.*

Enter TIMON.

Tim. Let me look back upon thee. O thou wall
That girdles in those wolves, dive in the earth
And fence not Athens ! Matrons, turn incontinent.
Obedience, fail in children ! Slaves and fools,
Pluck the grave wrinkled Senate from the bench
And minister in their steads. To general filths 5
Convert, o' th' instant, green virginity.
Do't in your parents' eyes. Bankrupts, hold fast ;
Rather than render back, out with your knives
And cut your trusters' throats. Bound servants, steal : 10
Large-handed robbers your grave masters are,
And pill by law. Maid, to thy master's bed :
Thy mistress is o' th' brothel. Son of sixteen,
Pluck the lin'd crutch from thy old limping sire,
With it beat out his brains. Piety and fear, 14
Religion to the gods, peace, justice, truth,
Domestic awe, night-rest, and neighbourhood,
Instruction, manners, mysteries, and trades,
Degrees, observances, customs and laws,
Decline to your confounding contraries 20
And let confusion live. Plagues incident to men,
Your potent and infectious fevers heap
On Athens, ripe for stroke. Thou cold sciatica,
Cripple our senators, that their limbs may halt
As lamely as their manners. Lust and liberty, 25
Creep in the minds and marrows of our youth;
That 'gainst the stream of virtue they may strive
And drown themselves in riot. Itches, blains, 28
Sow all th' Athenian bosoms, and their crop
Be general leprosy ! Breath infect breath,
That their society, as their friendship, may
Be merely poison ! Nothing I'll bear from thee

But nakedness, thou detestable town !
Take thou that too, with multiplying bans.
Timon will to the woods, where he shall
    find
Th' unkindest beast more kinder than man-
    kind.   36
The gods confound—hear me, you good gods
    all—
The Athenians both within and out that
    wall !
And grant, as Timon grows, his hate may
    grow
To the whole race of mankind, high and
    low !   40
Amen.   [*Exit.*

SCENE II. *Athens. Timon's house.*

Enter FLAVIUS, *with two or three* Servants.

 1 *Serv.* Hear you, Master Steward,
    where's our master ?
Are we undone, cast off, nothing remaining?
 Flav. Alack, my fellows, what should I
    say to you ?
Let me be recorded by the righteous gods,
I am as poor as you.
 1 *Serv.*   Such a house broke ! 5
So noble a master fall'n ! All gone, and not
One friend to take his fortune by the arm
And go along with him ?
 2 *Serv.*   As we do turn our backs
From our companion, thrown into his
    grave,
So his familiars to his buried fortunes   10
Slink all away ; leave their false vows with
    him,
Like empty purses pick'd ; and his poor
    self,
A dedicated beggar to the air,
With his disease of all-shunn'd poverty,
Walks, like contempt, alone. More of our
    fellows.   15

Enter other Servants.

 Flav. All broken implements of a ruin'd
    house.
 3 *Serv.* Yet do our hearts wear Timon's
    livery ;
That see I by our faces. We are fellows still,
Serving alike in sorrow. Leak'd is our bark ;
And we, poor mates, stand on the dying
    deck,   20
Hearing the surges threat. We must all
    part
Into this sea of air.
 Flav.   Good fellows all,
The latest of my wealth I'll share amongst
    you.
Wherever we shall meet, for Timon's sake,
Let's yet be fellows ; let's shake our heads
    and say,   25
As 'twere a knell unto out master's fortune,
' We have seen better days'. Let each take
    some.   [*Giving them money.*

Nay, put out all your hands. Not one word
    more !
Thus part we rich in sorrow, parting poor.
            [*Embrace, and part several ways.*
O the fierce wretchedness that glory brings
    us !   30
Who would not wish to be from wealth
    exempt,
Since riches point to misery and contempt ?
Who would be so mock'd with glory, or to
    live
But in a dream of friendship,
To have his pomp, and all what state
    compounds,   35
But only painted, like his varnish'd friends?
Poor honest lord, brought low by his own
    heart,
Undone by goodness ! Strange, unusual
    blood,
When man's worst sin is he does too much
    good !   39
Who then dares to be half so kind again ?
For bounty, that makes gods, does still mar
    men.
My dearest lord—blest to be most
    accurst,
Rich only to be wretched—thy great
    fortunes
Are made thy chief afflictions. Alas, kind
    lord !   44
He's flung in rage from this ingrateful seat
Of monstrous friends ; nor has he with
    him to
Supply his life, or that which can com-
    mand it.
I'll follow and enquire him out.   48
I'll ever serve his mind with my best
    will ;
Whilst I have gold, I'll be his steward still.
                                        [*Exit.*

SCENE III. *The woods near the sea-shore.
            Before Timon's cave.*

Enter TIMON *in the woods.*

 Tim. O blessed breeding sun, draw from
    the earth
Rotten humidity ; below thy sister's orb
Infect the air ! Twinn'd brothers of one
    womb—
Whose procreation, residence, and birth,
Scarce is dividant—touch them with
    several fortunes ;   5
The greater scorns the lesser. Not nature,
To whom all sores lay siege, can bear great
    fortune
But by contempt of nature.
Raise me this beggar and deny't that lord :
The senator shall bear contempt hereditary,
The beggar native honour.   11
It is the pasture lards the rother's sides,
The want that makes him lean. Who dares,
    who dares,
In purity of manhood stand upright,

957

And say ' This man's a flatterer ' ? If one
    be,   15
So are they all ; for every grise of fortune
Is smooth'd by that below. The learned
    pate
Ducks to the golden fool. All's oblique ;
There's nothing level in our cursed natures
But direct villainy. Therefore be abhorr'd
All feasts, societies, and throngs of men ! 21
His semblable, yea, himself, Timon disdains.
Destruction fang mankind ! Earth, yield
    me roots.   [*Digging.*
Who seeks for better of thee, sauce his
    palate
With thy most operant poison. What is
    here ?   25
Gold ? Yellow, glittering, precious gold ?
No, gods,
I am no idle votarist. Roots, you clear
    heavens !
Thus much of this will make black white,
    foul fair,
Wrong right, base noble, old young, coward
    valiant.
Ha, you gods ! why this ? What, this, you
    gods ? Why, this   30
Will lug your priests and servants from
    your sides,
Pluck stout men's pillows from below their
    heads—
This yellow slave
Will knit and break religions, bless th'
    accurs'd,   34
Make the hoar leprosy ador'd, place thieves
And give them title, knee, and approbation,
With senators on the bench. This is it
That makes the wappen'd widow wed
    again—
She whom the spital-house and ulcerous
    sores
Would cast the gorge at this embalms and
    spices   40
To th' April day again. Come, damn'd
    earth,
Thou common whore of mankind, that puts
    odds
Among the rout of nations, I will make thee
Do thy right nature.   [*March afar off.*
                    Ha ! a drum ? Th'art quick,
But yet I'll bury thee. Thou't go, strong
    thief,   45
When gouty keepers of thee cannot stand.
Nay, stay thou out for earnest.
                        [*Keeping some gold.*

Enter ALCIBIADES, *with drum and fife, in
    warlike manner ; and* PHRYNIA *and*
TIMANDRA.

Alcib. What art thou there ? Speak.
Tim. A beast, as thou art. The canker
    gnaw thy heart
For showing me again the eyes of man !
    Alcib. What is thy name ? Is man so
        hateful to thee

That art thyself a man ?   51
    Tim. I am Misanthropos, and hate man-
        kind.
For thy part, I do wish thou wert a dog,
That I might love thee something.
    Alcib.   I know thee well ;
But in thy fortunes am unlearn'd and
    strange.   55
    Tim. I know thee too ; and more than
        that I know thee
I not desire to know. Follow thy drum ;
With man's blood paint the ground, gules,
    gules.
Religious canons, civil laws, are cruel ;
Then what should war be ? This fell whore
    of thine   60
Hath in her more destruction than thy
    sword
For all her cherubin look.
    Phry.   Thy lips rot off !
    Tim. I will not kiss thee ; then the rot
        returns
To thine own lips again.
    Alcib. How came the noble Timon to this
        change ?   65
    Tim. As the moon does, by wanting light
        to give.
But then renew I could not, like the moon ;
There were no suns to borrow of.
    Alcib.   Noble Timon,
What friendship may I do thee ?
    Tim.   None, but to
Maintain my opinion.
    Alcib.   What is it, Timon ? 71
    Tim. Promise me friendship, but perform
none. If thou wilt not promise, the gods
plague thee, for thou art a man ! If thou
dost perform, confound thee, for thou art
a man !   75
    Alcib. I have heard in some sort of thy
        miseries.
    Tim. Thou saw'st them when I had
        prosperity.
    Alcib. I see them now ; then was a
        blessed time.
    Tim. As thine is now, held with a brace
        of harlots.
    Timan. Is this th' Athenian minion whom
        the world
Voic'd so regardfully ?
    Tim.   Art thou Timandra ? 81
    Timan. Yes.
    Tim. Be a whore still ; they love thee not
        that use thee.
Give them diseases, leaving with thee their
    lust.
Make use of thy salt hours. Season the
    slaves   85
For tubs and baths ; bring down rose-
    cheek'd youth
To the tub-fast and the diet.
    Timan.   Hang thee, monster !
    Alcib. Pardon him, sweet Timandra, for
        his wits

Are drown'd and lost in his calamities.   89
I have but little gold of late, brave Timon,
The want whereof doth daily make revolt
In my penurious band.   I have heard, and
     griev'd,
How cursed Athens, mindless of thy worth,
Forgetting thy great deeds, when neighbour
     states,
But for thy sword and fortune, trod upon
     them—   95
   Tim. I prithee beat thy drum and get
     thee gone.
   Alcib. I am thy friend, and pity thee, dear
     Timon.
   Tim. How dost thou pity him whom thou
     dost trouble ?
I had rather be alone.
   Alcib.   Why, fare thee well ;
Here is some gold for thee.
   Tim.   Keep it : I cannot eat it.   100
   Alcib. When I have laid proud Athens on
     a heap—
   Tim. War'st thou 'gainst Athens ?
   Alcib.   Ay, Timon, and have cause.
   Tim. The gods confound them all in thy
     conquest ;
And thee after, when thou hast conquer'd !
   Alcib. Why me, Timon ?
   Tim.   That by killing of villains   105
Thou wast born to conquer my country.
Put up thy gold. Go on. Here's gold. Go
     on.
Be as a planetary plague, when Jove
Will o'er some high-vic'd city hang his
     poison   109
In the sick air ; let not thy sword skip one.
Pity not honour'd age for his white beard ;
He is an usurer. Strike me the counterfeit
     matron :
It is her habit only that is honest,
Herself's a bawd. Let not the virgin's cheek
Make soft thy trenchant sword ; for those
     milk paps   115
That through the window bars bore at men's
     eyes
Are not within the leaf of pity writ,
But set them down horrible traitors. Spare
     not the babe
Whose dimpled smiles from fools exhaust
     their mercy ;
Think it a bastard whom the oracle   120
Hath doubtfully pronounc'd thy throat
     shall cut,
And mince it sans remorse. Swear against
     abjects ;
Put armour on thine ears and on thine eyes,
Whose proof nor yells of mothers, maids,
     nor babes,
Nor sight of priests in holy vestments
     bleeding,   125
Shall pierce a jot. There's gold to pay thy
     soldiers.
Make large confusion ; and, thy fury spent,
Confounded be thyself ! Speak not, be gone.

   Alcib. Hast thou gold yet ? I'll take the
     gold thou givest me,
Not all thy counsel.   130
   Tim. Dost thou, or dost thou not,
     heaven's curse upon thee !
   Phr. & Timan. Give us some gold, good
     Timon. Hast thou more ?
   Tim. Enough to make a whore forswear
     her trade,
And to make whores a bawd. Hold up, you
     sluts,
Your aprons mountant ; you are not
     oathable,   135
Although I know you'll swear, terribly
     swear,
Into strong shudders and to heavenly agues,
Th' immortal gods that hear you. Spare
     your oaths ;
I'll trust to your conditions. Be whores
     still ;
And he whose pious breath seeks to convert
     you—   140
Be strong in whore, allure him, burn him
     up ;
Let your close fire predominate his smoke,
And be no turncoats. Yet may your pains
     six months
Be quite contrary ! And thatch your poor
     thin roofs
With burdens of the dead—some that were
     hang'd,   145
No matter. Wear them, betray with them.
     Whore still ;
Paint till a horse may mire upon your face.
A pox of wrinkles !
   Phr. & Timan. Well, more gold. What
     then ?
Believe't that we'll do anything for gold.
   Tim. Consumptions sow   150
In hollow bones of man ; strike their sharp
     shins,
And mar men's spurring. Crack the lawyer's
     voice,
That he may never more false title plead,
Nor sound his quillets shrilly. Hoar the
     flamen,
That scolds against the quality of flesh   155
And not believes himself. Down with the
     nose,
Down with it flat, take the bridge quite
     away
Of him that, his particular to foresee,
Smells from the general weal. Make curl'd-
     pate ruffians bald,   159
And let the unscarr'd braggarts of the war
Derive some pain from you. Plague all,
That your activity may defeat and quell
The source of all erection. There's more
     gold.
Do you damn others, and let this damn
     you,
And ditches grave you all !   165
   Phr. & Timan. More counsel with more
     money, bounteous Timon.

Tim. More whore, more mischief first; I have given you earnest.

Alcib. Strike up the drum towards Athens. Farewell, Timon;
If I thrive well, I'll visit thee again.

Tim. If I hope well, I'll never see thee more.   170

Alcib. I never did thee harm.

Tim. Yes, thou spok'st well of me.

Alcib.   Call'st thou that harm?

Tim. Men daily find it. Get thee away, and take
Thy beagles with thee.

Alcib.   We but offend him. Strike.
                [*Drum beats. Exeunt all but Timon.*

Tim. That nature, being sick of man's unkindness,   175
Should yet be hungry! Common mother, thou,   [*Digging.*
Whose womb unmeasurable and infinite breast
Teems and feeds all; whose self-same mettle,
Whereof thy proud child, arrogant man, is puff'd,   179
Engenders the black toad and adder blue,
The gilded newt and eyeless venom'd worm,
With all th' abhorred births below crisp heaven
Whereon Hyperion's quick'ning fire doth shine—
Yield him, who all thy human sons doth hate,
From forth thy plenteous bosom, one poor root!   185
Ensear thy fertile and conceptious womb,
Let it no more bring out ingrateful man!
Go great with tigers, dragons, wolves, and bears;
Teem with new monsters whom thy upward face
Hath to the marbled mansion all above 190
Never presented!—O, a root! Dear thanks!—
Dry up thy marrows, vines, and plough-torn leas,
Whereof ingrateful man, with liquorish draughts
And morsels unctuous, greases his pure mind,
That from it all consideration slips—   195

Enter APEMANTUS.

More man? Plague, plague!

Apem. I was directed hither. Men report
Thou dost affect my manners and dost use them.

Tim. 'Tis, then, because thou dost not keep a dog,
Whom I would imitate. Consumption catch thee!   200

Apem. This is in thee a nature but infected,
A poor unmanly melancholy sprung

From change of fortune. Why this spade, this place?
This slave-like habit and these looks of care?
Thy flatterers yet wear silk, drink wine, lie soft,   205
Hug their diseas'd perfumes, and have forgot
That ever Timon was. Shame not these woods
By putting on the cunning of a carper.
Be thou a flatterer now, and seek to thrive
By that which has undone thee: hinge thy knee,   210
And let his very breath whom thou'lt observe
Blow off thy cap; praise his most vicious strain,
And call it excellent. Thou wast told thus;
Thou gav'st thine ears, like tapsters that bade welcome,
To knaves and all approachers. 'Tis most just   215
That thou turn rascal; hadst thou wealth again
Rascals should have't. Do not assume my likeness.

Tim. Were I like thee, I'd throw away myself.

Apem. Thou hast cast away thyself, being like thyself;
A madman so long, now a fool. What, think'st   220
That the bleak air, thy boisterous chamberlain,
Will put thy shirt on warm? Will these moist trees,
That have outliv'd the eagle, page thy heels
And skip when thou point'st out? Will the cold brook,   224
Candied with ice, caudle thy morning taste
To cure thy o'ernight's surfeit? Call the creatures
Whose naked natures live in all the spite
Of wreakful heaven, whose bare unhoused trunks,
To the conflicting elements expos'd,   229
Answer mere nature—bid them flatter thee.
O, thou shalt find—

Tim.   A fool of thee. Depart.

Apem. I love thee better now than e'er I did.

Tim. I hate thee worse.

Apem.   Why?

Tim.   Thou flatter'st misery.

Apem. I flatter not, but say thou art a caitiff.

Tim. Why dost thou seek me out?

Apem.   To vex thee.   235

Tim. Always a villain's office or a fool's.
Dost please thyself in't?

Apem.   Ay.

Tim.   What, a knave too?

Apem. If thou didst put this sour-cold habit on

You should have fear'd false times when
    you did feast :
Suspect still comes where an estate is least.
That which I show, heaven knows, is merely
    love, 515
Duty, and zeal, to your unmatched mind,
Care of your food and living ; and believe
    it,
My most honour'd lord,
For any benefit that points to me,
Either in hope or present, I'd exchange 520
For this one wish, that you had power and
    wealth
To requite me by making rich yourself.

    Tim. Look thee, 'tis so ! Thou singly
    honest man,
Here, take. The gods, out of my misery,
Have sent thee treasure. Go, live rich and
    happy, 525
But thus condition'd : thou shalt build
    from men ;
Hate all, curse all, show charity to none,
But let the famish'd flesh slide from the
    bone
Ere thou relieve the beggar. Give to dogs
What thou deniest to men ; let prisons
    swallow 'em, 530
Debts wither 'em to nothing. Be men like
    blasted woods,
And may diseases lick up their false bloods !
And so, farewell and thrive.

    Flav.   O, let me stay
And comfort you, my master.

    Tim.   If thou hat'st curses,
Stay not ; fly whilst thou art blest and
    free. 535
Ne'er see thou man, and let me ne'er see
    thee.   *[Exeunt severally.*

ACT FIVE

SCENE I. *The woods. Before Timon's cave.*

Enter Poet *and* Painter.

    Pain. As I took note of the place, it
cannot be far where he abides.

    Poet. What's to be thought of him ?

    Poet. What have you now to present
unto him ?

    Pain. Nothing at this time but my
visitation ; only I will promise him an
excellent piece.

    Poet. I must serve him so too, tell him
of an intent that's coming toward him. 21

    Pain. Good as the best. Promising is the
very air o' th' time ; it opens the eyes of
expectation. Performance is ever the duller
for his act, and but in the plainer and
simpler kind of people the deed of saying
is quite out of use. To promise is most
courtly and fashionable ; performance is a
kind of will or testament which argues a
great sickness in his judgment that makes
it.

Enter TIMON *from his cave.*

    Tim. [*Aside*] Excellent workman ! Thou
canst not paint a man so bad as is thyself.30

    Poet. I am thinking what I shall say I
have provided for him. It must be a
personating of himself ; a satire against the
softness of prosperity, with a discovery of
the infinite flatteries that follow youth and
opulency. 34

    Tim. [*Aside*] Must thou needs stand for a
villain in thine own work ? Wilt thou whip
thine own faults in other men ? Do so, I
have gold for thee.

    Poet. Nay, let's seek him ;
Then do we sin against our own estate
When we may profit meet and come too
    late. 40

    Pain. True ;
When the day serves, before black-
    corner'd night,
Find what thou want'st by free and offer'd
    light.
Come.

    Tim. [*Aside*] I'll meet you at the turn.
What a god's gold, 45
That he is worshipp'd in a baser temple
Than where swine feed !
'Tis thou that rig'st the bark and plough'st
    the foam,

Settlest admired reverence in a slave.   49
To thee be worship ! and thy saints for aye
Be crown'd with plagues, that thee alone
  obey !
Fit I meet them. [*Advancing from his cave.*
  Poet. Hail, worthy Timon !
  Pain.   Our late noble master !
  Tim. Have I once liv'd to see two honest
    men ?
  Poet. Sir,   55
Having often of your open bounty tasted,
Hearing you were retir'd, your friends
  fall'n off,
Whose thankless natures—O abhorred
  spirits !—
Not all the whips of heaven are large
  enough—
What ! to you,   60
Whose star-like nobleness gave life and
  influence
To their whole being !   I am rapt, and
  cannot cover
The monstrous bulk of this ingratitude
With any size of words.
  Tim. Let it go naked : men may see't the
    better.   65
You that are honest, by being what you are,
Make them best seen and known.
  Pain.   He and myself
Have travail'd in the great show'r of your
  gifts,
And sweetly felt it.
  Tim.   Ay, you are honest men.
  Pain. We are hither come to offer you our
    service.   70
  Tim. Most honest men ! Why, how shall
    I requite you ?
Can you eat roots, and drink cold water—
    No ?
  Both. What we can do, we'll do, to do you
    service.
  Tim. Y'are honest men. Y'have heard
    that I have gold ;
I am sure you have. Speak truth ; y'are
  honest men.   75
  Pain. So it is said, my noble lord ; but
    therefore
Came not my friend nor I.
  Tim. Good honest men ! Thou draw'st a
    counterfeit
Best in all Athens. Th'art indeed the best ;
Thou counterfeit'st most lively.
  Pain.   So, so, my lord.   80
  Tim. E'en so, sir, as I say. [*To the Poet*]
    And for thy fiction,
Why, thy verse swells with stuff so fine and
  smooth
That thou art even natural in thine art.
But for all this, my honest-natur'd friends,
I must needs say you have a little fault.   85
Marry, 'tis not monstrous in you ; neither
  wish I
You take much pains to mend.
  Both.   Beseech your honour

To make it known to us.
  Tim.   You'll take it ill.
  Both. Most thankfully, my lord.
  Tim.   Will you indeed ?
  Both. Doubt it not, worthy lord.   90
  Tim. There's never a one of you but
    trusts a knave
That mightily deceives you.
  Both.   Do we, my lord ?
  Tim. Ay, and you hear him cog, see him
    dissemble,
Know his gross patchery, love him, feed
  him,
Keep in your bosom ; yet remain assur'd 95
That he's a made-up villain.
  Pain. I know not such, my lord.
  Poet.   Nor I.
  Tim. Look you, I love you well ; I'll give
    you gold,
Rid me these villains from your companies.
Hang them or stab them, drown them in a
  draught,   100
Confound them by some course, and come
  to me,
I'll give you gold enough.
  Both. Name them, my lord ; let's know
    them.
  Tim. You that way, and you this—but
    two in company ;
Each man apart, all single and alone,   105
Yet an arch-villain keeps him company.
[*To the Painter*] If, where thou art, two
    villains shall not be,
Come not near him. [*To the Poet*] If thou
    wouldst not reside
But where one villain is, then him aban-
    don.—
Hence, pack ! there's gold ; you came for
    gold, ye slaves.   110
[*To the Painter*] You have work for me ;
    there's payment ; hence !
[*To the Poet*] You are an alchemist ; make
    gold of that.—
Out, rascal dogs !
                   [*Beats and drives them out.*

Enter FLAVIUS *and two* Senators.

  Flav. It is vain that you would speak
    with Timon ;
For he is set so only to himself   115
That nothing but himself which looks like
    man
Is friendly with him.
  1 Sen.   Bring us to his cave.
It is our part and promise to th' Athenians
To speak with Timon.
  2 Sen.   At all times alike
Men are not still the same ; 'twas time and
    griefs   120
That fram'd him thus. Time, with his fairer
    hand,
Offering the fortunes of his former days,
The former man may make him. Bring us
    to him,

And chance it as it may.
Flav.   Here is his cave.
Peace and content be here! Lord Timon!
Timon!   125
Look out, and speak to friends. Th'
Athenians
By two of their most reverend Senate greet
thee.
Speak to them, noble Timon.

Enter TIMON *out of his cave.*

Tim. Thou sun that comforts, burn.
Speak and be hang'd!   129
For each true word a blister, and each false
Be as a cauterizing to the root o' th' tongue,
Consuming it with speaking!
1 *Sen.*   Worthy Timon—
Tim. Of none but such as you, and you
of Timon.
1 *Sen.* The senators of Athens greet thee,
Timon.
Tim. I thank them; and would send
them back the plague,   135
Could I but catch it for them.
1 *Sen.*   O, forget
What we are sorry for ourselves in thee.
The senators with one consent of love
Entreat thee back to Athens, who have
thought
On special dignities, which vacant lie   140
For thy best use and wearing.
2 *Sen.*   They confess
Toward thee forgetfulness too general,
gross;
Which now the public body, which doth
seldom
Play the recanter, feeling in itself
A lack of Timon's aid, hath sense withal 145
Of it own fail, restraining aid to Timon,
And send forth us to make their sorrowed
render,
Together with a recompense more fruitful
Than their offence can weigh down by the
dram;
Ay, even such heaps and sums of love and
wealth   150
As shall to thee blot out what wrongs were
theirs
And write in thee the figures of their love,
Ever to read them thine.
Tim.   You witch me in it;
Surprise me to the very brink of tears.   154
Lend me a fool's heart and a woman's eyes,
And I'll beweep these comforts, worthy
senators.
1 *Sen.* Therefore so please thee to return
with us,
And of our Athens, thine and ours, to take
The captainship, thou shalt be met with
thanks,
Allow'd with absolute power, and thy good
name   160
Live with authority. So soon we shall drive
back

Of Alcibiades th' approaches wild,
Who, like a boar too savage, doth root up
His country's peace.
2 *Sen.*   And shakes his threat'ning sword
Against the walls of Athens.
1 *Sen.*   Therefore, Timon—
Tim. Well, sir, I will. Therefore I will,
sir, thus: 166
If Alcibiades kill my countrymen,
Let Alcibiades know this of Timon,
That Timon cares not. But if he sack fair
Athens,
And take our goodly aged men by th'
beards,   170
Giving our holy virgins to the stain
Of contumelious, beastly, mad-brain'd war,
Then let him know—and tell him Timon
speaks it
In pity of our aged and our youth—   174
I cannot choose but tell him that I care
not,
And let him take't at worst; for their knives
care not,
While you have throats to answer. For
myself,
There's not a whittle in th' unruly camp
But I do prize it at my love before
The reverend'st throat in Athens. So I
leave you   180
To the protection of the prosperous gods,
As thieves to keepers.
Flav.   Stay not, all's in vain.
Tim. Why, I was writing of my epitaph;
It will be seen to-morrow. My long sickness
Of health and living now begins to mend,
And nothing brings me all things. Go, live
still;   186
Be Alcibiades your plague, you his,
And last so long enough!
1 *Sen.*   We speak in vain.
Tim. But yet I love my country, and am
not
One that rejoices in the common wreck,   190
As common bruit doth put it.
1 *Sen.*   That's well spoke.
Tim. Commend me to my loving country-
men—
1 *Sen.* These words become your lips as
they pass thorough them.
2 *Sen.* And enter in our ears like great
triumphers
In their applauding gates.
Tim.   Commend me to them,   195
And tell them that, to ease them of their
griefs,
Their fears of hostile strokes, their aches,
losses,
Their pangs of love, with other incident
throes
That nature's fragile vessel doth sustain
In life's uncertain voyage, I will some kindness do them—   200
I'll teach them to prevent wild Alcibiades'
wrath.

To castigate thy pride, 'twere well; but
    thou
Dost it enforcedly. Thou'dst courtier be
    again   240
Wert thou not beggar. Willing misery
Outlives incertain pomp, is crown'd before.
The one is filling still, never complete;
The other, at high wish. Best state, con-
    tentless,   244
Hath a distracted and most wretched being,
Worse than the worst, content.
Thou should'st desire to die, being miser-
    able.
    Tim. Not by his breath that is more
    miserable.
Thou art a slave whom Fortune's tender
    arm   249
With favour never clasp'd, but bred a dog.
Hadst thou, like us from our first swath,
    proceeded
The sweet degrees that this brief world
    affords
To such as may the passive drugs of it
Freely command, thou wouldst have
    plung'd thyself
In general riot, melted down thy youth 255
In different beds of lust, and never learn'd
The icy precepts of respect, but followed
The sug'red game before thee. But myself,
Who had the world as my confectionary;
The mouths, the tongues, the eyes, and
    hearts of men
At duty, more than I could frame employ-
    ment;   261
That numberless upon me stuck, as leaves
Do on the oak, have with one winter's
    brush
Fell from their boughs, and left me open,
    bare   264
For every storm that blows—I to bear this,
That never knew but better, is some burden.
Thy nature did commence in sufferance;
    time
Hath made thee hard in't. Why shouldst
    thou hate men?
They never flatter'd thee. What hast thou
    given?   269
If thou wilt curse, thy father, that poor rag,
Must be thy subject; who, in spite, put
    stuff
To some she-beggar and compounded thee
Poor rogue hereditary. Hence, be gone.
If thou hadst not been born the worst of
    men,
Thou hadst been a knave and flatterer.
    Apem.   Art thou proud yet?
    Tim. Ay, that I am not thee.
    Apem.   I, that I was 276
No prodigal.
    Tim.   I, that I am one now.
Were all the wealth I have shut up in thee,
I'd give thee leave to hang it. Get thee
    gone.   279
That the whole life of Athens were in this!

Thus would I eat it.   [*Eating a root.*
    Apem.   Here! I will mend thy feast.
        [*Offering him food.*
    Tim. First mend my company: take
    away thyself.
    Apem. So I shall mend mine own by th'
    lack of thine.
    Tim. 'Tis not well mended so; it is but
    botch'd.
If not, I would it were.   285
    Apem. What wouldst thou have to
    Athens?
    Tim. Thee thither in a whirlwind. If thou
    wilt,
Tell them there I have gold; look, so I
    have.   288
    Apem. Here is no use for gold.
    Tim.   The best and truest;
For here it sleeps and does no hired harm.
    Apem. Where liest a nights, Timon?
    Tim.   Under that's above me.
Where feed'st thou a days, Apemantus?
    Apem. Where my stomach finds meat;
or rather, where I eat it.   295
    Tim. Would poison were obedient, and
knew my mind!
    Apem. Where wouldst thou send it?
    Tim. To sauce thy dishes.
    Apem. The middle of humanity thou
never knewest, but the extremity of both
ends. When thou wast in thy gilt and thy
perfume, they mock'd thee for too much
curiosity; in thy rags thou know'st none,
but art despis'd for the contrary. There's
a medlar for thee; eat it.
    Tim. On what I hate I feed not.
    Apem. Dost hate a medlar?   305
    Tim. Ay, though it look like thee.
    Apem. An th'hadst hated medlars sooner,
thou shouldst have loved thyself better
now. What man didst thou ever know
unthrift that was beloved after his means?
    Tim. Who, without those means thou
ta.k'st of, didst thou ever know belov'd?
    Apem. Myself.   312
    Tim. I understand thee: thou hadst some
means to keep a dog.
    Apem. What things in the world canst
thou nearest compare to thy flatterers? 316
    Tim. Women nearest; but men, men are
the things themselves. What wouldst thou
do with the world, Apemantus, if it lay in
thy power?
    Apem. Give it the beasts, to be rid of the
men.   320
    Tim. Wouldst thou have thyself fall in
the confusion of men, and remain a beast
with the beasts?
    Apem. Ay, Timon.
    Tim. A beastly ambition, which the gods
grant thee t' attain to! If thou wert the
lion, the fox would beguile thee; if thou
wert the lamb, the fox would eat thee; if
thou wert the fox, the lion would suspect

thee, when, peradventure, thou wert accus'd by the ass. If thou wert the ass, thy dulness would torment thee; and still thou liv'dst but as a breakfast to the wolf. If thou wert the wolf, thy greediness would afflict thee, and oft thou shouldst hazard thy life for thy dinner. Wert thou the unicorn, pride and wrath would confound thee, and make thine own self the conquest of thy fury. Wert thou a bear, thou wouldst be kill'd by the horse; wert thou a horse, thou wouldst be seiz'd by the leopard; wert thou a leopard, thou wert german to the lion, and the spots of thy kindred were jurors on thy life. All thy safety were remotion, and thy defence absence. What beast couldst thou be that were not subject to a beast? And what a beast art thou already, that seest not thy loss in transformation!

Apem. If thou couldst please me with speaking to me, thou mightst have hit upon it here. The commonwealth of Athens is become a forest of beasts. 345

Tim. How has the ass broke the wall, that thou art out of the city?

Apem. Yonder comes a poet and a painter. The plague of company light upon thee! I will fear to catch it, and give way. When I know not what else to do, I'll see thee again. 351

Tim. When there is nothing living but thee, thou shalt be welcome. I had rather be a beggar's dog than Apemantus.

Apem. Thou art the cap of all the fools alive. 355

Tim. Would thou wert clean enough to spit upon!

Apem. A plague on thee! thou art too bad to curse.

Tim. All villains that do stand by thee are pure.

Apem. There is no leprosy but what thou speak'st.

Tim. If I name thee. 360
I'll beat thee—but I should infect my hands

Apem. I would my tongue could rot them off!

Tim. Away, thou issue of a mangy dog! Choler does kill me that thou art alive; I swoon to see thee.

Apem. Would thou wouldst burst!

Tim. Away,
Thou tedious rogue! I am sorry I shall lose

A stone by thee. [*Throws a stone at him.*

Apem. Beast!

Tim. Slave! 370

Apem. Toad!

Tim. Rogue, rogue, rogue!
I am sick of this false world, and will love nought
But even the mere necessities upon't. 374
Then, Timon, presently prepare thy grave;

Lie where the light foam of the sea may beat
Thy gravestone daily; make thine epitaph,
That death in me at others' lives may laugh.
[*Looks at the gold*] O thou sweet king-killer, and dear divorce
'Twixt natural son and sire! thou bright defiler 380
Of Hymen's purest bed! thou valiant Mars!
Thou ever young, fresh, lov'd, and delicate wooer,
Whose blush doth thaw the consecrated snow
That lies on Dian's lap! thou visible god,
That sold'rest close impossibilities, 385
And mak'st them kiss! that speak'st with every tongue
To every purpose! O thou touch of hearts!
Think thy slave man rebels, and by thy virtue
Set them into confounding odds, that beasts
May have the world in empire!

Apem. Would 'twere so! 390
But not till I am dead. I'll say th' hast gold.
Thou wilt be throng'd to shortly.

Tim. Throng'd to?

Apem. Ay.

Tim. Thy back, I prithee.

Apem. Live, and love thy misery!

Tim. Long live so, and so die! [*Exit Apemantus*] I am quit.
Moe things like men? Eat, Timon, and abhor them. 395

Enter the Banditti.

1 *Ban.* Where should he have this gold? It is some poor fragment, some slender ort of his remainder. The mere want of gold and the falling-from of his friends drove him into this melancholy. 399

2 *Ban.* It is nois'd he hath a mass of treasure.

3 *Ban.* Let us make the assay upon him; if he care not for't, he will supply us easily; if he covetously reserve it, how shall's get it?

2 *Ban.* True; for he bears it not about him. 'Tis hid.

1 *Ban.* Is not this he? 405

Banditti. Where?

2 *Ban.* 'Tis his description.

3 *Ban.* He; I know him.

Banditti. Save thee, Timon!

Tim. Now, thieves? 410

Banditti. Soldiers, not thieves.

Tim. Both too, and women's sons.

Banditti. We are not thieves, but men that much do want.

Tim. Your greatest want is, you want much of meat.
Why should you want? Behold, the earth hath roots;

1 Sen. I like this well; he will return
 again.
 Tim. I have a tree, which grows here in
 my close,
That mine own use invites me to cut down,
And shortly must I fell it. Tell my friends,
Tell Athens, in the sequence of degree 206
From high to low throughout, that whoso
 please
To stop affliction, let him take his haste,
Come hither, ere my tree hath felt the axe,
And hang himself. I pray you do my
 greeting.   210
 Flav. Trouble him no further; thus you
 still shall find him.
 Tim. Come not to me again; but say to
 Athens
Timon hath made his everlasting mansion
Upon the beached verge of the salt flood,
Who once a day with his embossed froth 215
The turbulent surge shall cover. Thither
 come,
And let my gravestone be your oracle.
Lips, let sour words go by and language
 end:
What is amiss, plague and infection mend!
Graves only be men's works and death their
 gain!   220
Sun, hide thy beams. Timon hath done his
 reign. *[Exit Timon into his cave.*
 1 Sen. His discontents are unremovably
Coupled to nature.
 2 Sen. Our hope in him is dead. Let us
 return   224
And strain what other means is left unto us
In our dear peril.
 1 Sen.   It requires swift foot.
            [Exeunt.

 Scene II. *Before the walls of Athens.*

Enter two other Senators *with a* Messenger.

 1 Sen. Thou hast painfully discover'd;
 are his files
As full as thy report?
 Mess.   I have spoke the least.
Besides, his expedition promises
Present approach.
 2 Sen. We stand much hazard if they
 bring not Timon.   5
 Mess. I met a courier, one mine ancient
 friend,
Whom, though in general part we were
 oppos'd,
Yet our old love had a particular force,
And made us speak like friends. This man
 was riding
From Alcibiades to Timon's cave   10
With letters of entreaty, which imported
His fellowship i' th' cause against your city,
In part for his sake mov'd.

Enter the other Senators, *from Timon.*

 1 Sen.   Here come our brothers.

 3 Sen. No talk of Timon, nothing of him
 expect.
The enemies' drum is heard, and fearful
 scouring   15
Doth choke the air with dust. In, and
 prepare.
Ours is the fall, I fear; our foes the snare.
             [Exeunt.

 Scene III. *The woods. Timon's cave,*
   and a rude tomb seen.

Enter a Soldier *in the woods, seeking Timon.*

 Sold. By all description this should be
 the place.
Who's here? Speak, ho! No answer?
 What is this?
Timon is dead, who hath outstretch'd his
 span.
Some beast rear'd this; here does not live
 a man.
Dead, sure; and this his grave. What's on
 this tomb
I cannot read; the character I'll take with
 wax.   6
Our captain hath in every figure skill,
An ag'd interpreter, though young in days;
Before proud Athens he's set down by this,
Whose fall the mark of his ambition is. 10
              [Exit.

 Scene IV. *Before the walls of Athens.*

Trumpets sound. Enter Alcibiades *with
 his* Powers *before Athens.*

 Alcib. Sound to this coward and lascivious
 town
Our terrible approach.

Sound a parley. The Senators *appear upon
 the walls.*

Till now you have gone on and fill'd the
 time
With all licentious measure, making your
 wills
The scope of justice; till now, myself, and
 such   5
As slept within the shadow of your power,
Have wander'd with our travers'd arms,
 and breath'd
Our sufferance vainly. Now the time is
 flush,
When crouching marrow, in the bearer
 strong,
Cries of itself ' No more!' Now breathless
 wrong   10
Shall sit and pant in your great chairs of
 ease,
And pursy insolence shall break his wind
With fear and horrid flight.
 1 Sen.   Noble and young,
When thy first griefs were but a mere
 conceit,
Ere thou hadst power or we had cause of
 fear,   15

We sent to thee, to give thy rages balm,
To wipe out our ingratitude with loves
Above their quantity.
   2 *Sen.*   So did we woo
Transformed Timon to our city's love
By humble message and by promis'd
   means.   20
We were not all unkind, nor all deserve
The common stroke of war.
   1 *Sen.*   These walls of ours
Were not erected by their hands from whom
You have receiv'd your griefs; nor are
   they such
That these great tow'rs, trophies, and
   schools, should fall
For private faults in them.
   2 *Sen.*   Nor are they living 26
Who were the motives that you first went
   out;
Shame, that they wanted cunning, in excess
Hath broke their hearts. March, noble lord,
Into our city with thy banners spread. 30
By decimation and a tithed death—
If thy revenges hunger for that food
Which nature loathes—take thou the
   destin'd tenth,
And by the hazard of the spotted die
Let die the spotted.
   1 *Sen.*   All have not offended; 35
For those that were, it is not square to
   take,
On those that are, revenge: crimes, like
   lands,
Are not inherited. Then, dear countryman,
Bring in thy ranks, but leave without thy
   rage;
Spare thy Athenian cradle, and those kin 40
Which, in the bluster of thy wrath, must
   fall
With those that have offended. Like a
   shepherd
Approach the fold and cull th' infected
   forth,
But kill not all together.
   2 *Sen.*   What thou wilt,
Thou rather shalt enforce it with thy smile
Than hew to't with thy sword.
   1 *Sen.*   Set but thy foot
Against our rampir'd gates and they shall
   ope, 47
So thou wilt send thy gentle heart before
To say thou't enter friendly.
   2 *Sen.*   Throw thy glove,
Or any token of thine honour else, 50

That thou wilt use the wars as thy redress
And not as our confusion, all thy powers
Shall make their harbour in our town till we
Have seal'd thy full desire.
   Alcib.   Then there's my glove;
Descend, and open your uncharged ports. 55
Those enemies of Timon's and mine own,
Whom you yourselves shall set out for
   reproof,
Fall, and no more. And, to atone your fears
With my more noble meaning, not a man
Shall pass his quarter or offend the stream
Of regular justice in your city's bounds, 61
But shall be render'd to your public laws
At heaviest answer.
   Both.   'Tis most nobly spoken.
   Alcib. Descend, and keep your words.
       [*The Senators descend and open the gates.*

       Enter a Soldier *as a Messenger.*

   Sol. My noble General, Timon is dead;
Entomb'd upon the very hem o' th' sea; 66
And on his grave-stone this insculpture,
   which
With wax I brought away, whose soft im-
   pression
Interprets for my poor ignorance.

       Alcibiades reads the Epitaph.

' Here lies a wretched corse, of wretched
   soul bereft; 70
Seek not my name. A plague consume you
   wicked caitiffs left!
Here lie I, Timon, who alive all living men
   did hate.
Pass by, and curse thy fill; but pass, and
   stay not here thy gait.'

These well express in thee thy latter spirits.
Though thou abhorr'dst in us our human
   griefs, 75
Scorn'dst our brain's flow, and those our
   droplets which
From niggard nature fall, yet rich conceit
Taught thee to make vast Neptune weep
   for aye
On thy low grave, on faults forgiven. Dead
Is noble Timon, of whose memory 80
Hereafter more. Bring me into your city,
And I will use the olive, with my sword;
Make war breed peace, make peace stint
   war, make each
Prescribe to other, as each other's leech.
Let our drums strike.   [*Exeunt.*

JULIUS CÆSAR

DRAMATIS PERSONÆ

JULIUS CÆSAR.
OCTAVIUS CÆSAR, ⎱ Triumvirs after the
MARCUS ANTONIUS, ⎰ death of Julius
M. ÆMIL. LEPIDUS, ⎰ Cæsar.
CICERO,
PUBLIUS, ⎱ senators.
POPILIUS LENA, ⎰
MARCUS BRUTUS,
CASSIUS,
CASCA,
TREBONIUS, conspirators against
LIGARIUS, Julius Cæsar.
DECIUS BRUTUS,
METELLUS CIMBER,
CINNA,
FLAVIUS and MARULLUS, tribunes.
ARTEMIDORUS, a sophist of Cnidos.
A Soothsayer.

CINNA, a poet.
Another Poet.
LUCILIUS,
TITINIUS, ⎱ friends to Brutus and
MESSALA, ⎰ Cassius.
YOUNG CATO,
VOLUMNIUS,
VARRO,
CLITUS,
CLAUDIUS, ⎱ servants to Brutus.
STRATO, ⎰
LUCIUS,
DARDANIUS,
PINDARUS, servant to Cassius.

CALPHURNIA, wife to Cæsar.
PORTIA, wife to Brutus.

Senators, Citizens, Guards, Attendants, &c.

THE SCENE: Rome; near Sardis; near Philippi.

ACT ONE

SCENE I. Rome. A street.

Enter FLAVIUS, MARULLUS, and certain
Commoners over the stage.

Flav. Hence! home, you idle creatures,
get you home.
Is this a holiday? What! know you not,
Being mechanical, you ought not walk
Upon a labouring day without the sign
Of your profession? Speak, what trade art
thou?   5
1 Cit. Why, sir, a carpenter.
Mar. Where is thy leather apron and thy
rule?
What dost thou with thy best apparel on?
You, sir, what trade are you?
2 Cit. Truly, sir, in respect of a fine
workman, I am but, as you would say, a
cobbler.   11
Mar. But what trade art thou? Answer
me directly.
2 Cit. A trade, sir, that I hope I may use
with a safe conscience, which is indeed, sir,
a mender of bad soles.
Mar. What trade, thou knave? Thou
naughty knave, what trade?   15
2 Cit. Nay, I beseech you, sir, be not out
with me; yet, if you be out, sir, I can
mend you.
Mar. What mean'st thou by that? Mend
me, thou saucy fellow!
2 Cit. Why, sir, cobble you.   20
Flav. Thou art a cobbler, art thou?

2 Cit. Truly, sir, all that I live by is with
the awl. I meddle with no tradesman's
matters nor women's matters, but with awl.
I am indeed, sir, a surgeon to old shoes.
When they are in great danger, I re-cover
them. As proper men as ever trod upon
neat's leather have gone upon my handiwork.
Flav. But wherefore art not in thy shop
to-day?
Why dost thou lead these men about the
streets?   29
2 Cit. Truly, sir, to wear out their shoes,
to get myself into more work. But indeed,
sir, we make holiday to see Cæsar, and to
rejoice in his triumph.
Mar. Wherefore rejoice? What conquest
brings he home?
What tributaries follow him to Rome,
To grace in captive bonds his chariot
wheels?   35
You blocks, you stones, you worse than
senseless things!
O you hard hearts, you cruel men of Rome,
Knew you not Pompey? Many a time and
oft
Have you climb'd up to walls and battle-
ments,
To tow'rs and windows, yea, to chimney-
tops,   40
Your infants in your arms, and there have
sat
The livelong day, with patient expectation,
To see great Pompey pass the streets of
Rome.

And when you saw his chariot but appear,
Have you not made an universal shout, 45
That Tiber trembled underneath her banks,
To hear the replication of your sounds
Made in her concave shores ?
And do you now put on your best attire ?
And do you now cull out a holiday ? 50
And do you now strew flowers in his way
That comes in triumph over Pompey's
blood ?
Be gone !
Run to your houses, fall upon your knees,
Pray to the gods to intermit the plague 55
That needs must light on this ingratitude.
  Flav. Go, go, good countrymen, and for
this fault
Assemble all the poor men of your sort ;
Draw them to Tiber banks, and weep your
tears
Into the channel, till the lowest stream 60
Do kiss the most exalted shores of all.
             [*Exeunt all the Commoners.*
See whe'r their basest metal be not mov'd ;
They vanish tongue-tied in their guiltiness.
Go you down that way towards the Capitol ;
This way will I. Disrobe the images 65
If you do find them deck'd with ceremonies.
  Mar. May we do so ?
You know it is the feast of Lupercal.
  Flav. It is no matter ; let no images 69
Be hung with Cæsar's trophies. I'll about,
And drive away the vulgar from the streets ;
So do you too, where you perceive them
thick.
These growing feathers pluck'd from
Cæsar's wing
Will make him fly an ordinary pitch,
Who else would soar above the view of
men, 75
And keep us all in servile fearfulness.
                     [*Exeunt.*

SCENE II. *Rome. A public place.*

Music. Enter CÆSAR ; ANTONY, *for the
course ;* CALPHURNIA, PORTIA, DECIUS,
CICERO, BRUTUS, CASSIUS, *and* CASCA ;
a great crowd following, among them a
Soothsayer ; *after them,* MARULLUS *and*
FLAVIUS.

  Cæs. Calphurnia.
  Casca.   Peace, ho ! Cæsar speaks.
                    [*Music ceases.*
  Cæs. Calphurnia.
  Cal. Here, my lord.
  Cæs. Stand you directly in Antonius'
way
When he doth run his course. Antonius !
  Ant. Cæsar, my lord. 5
  Cæs. Forget not in your speed, Antonius,
To touch Calphurnia ; for our elders say,
The barren, touched in this holy chase, 8
Shake off their sterile curse.
  Ant.   I shall remember.

When Cæsar says ' Do this ', it is perform'd.
  Cæs. Set on, and leave no ceremony out.
                      [*Music.*
  Sooth. Cæsar !
  Cæs. Ha ! Who calls ?
  Casca. Bid every noise be still. Peace yet
again.   [*Music ceases.*
  Cæs. Who is it in the press that calls on
me ? 15
I hear a tongue, shriller than all the music,
Cry ' Cæsar ! ' Speak. Cæsar is turn'd to
hear.
  Sooth. Beware the ides of March.
  Cæs.   What man is that ?
  Bru. A soothsayer bids you beware the
ides of March.
  Cæs. Set him before me ; let me see his
face. 20
  Cas. Fellow, come from the throng ; look
upon Cæsar.
  Cæs. What say'st thou to me now? Speak
once again.
  Sooth. Beware the ides of March.
  Cæs. He is a dreamer ; let us leave him.
    Pass. [*Sennet. Exeunt all but Brutus
                     and Cassius.*
  Cas. Will you go see the order of the
course ? 25
  Bru. Not I.
  Cas. I pray you do.
  Bru. I am not gamesome : I do lack
some part
Of that quick spirit that is in Antony. 29
Let me not hinder, Cassius, your desires ;
I'll leave you.
  Cas. Brutus, I do observe you now of
late ;
I have not from your eyes that gentleness
And show of love as I was wont to have.
You bear too stubborn and too strange a
hand 35
Over your friend that loves you.
  Bru.   Cassius,
Be not deceiv'd. If I have veil'd my look,
I turn the trouble of my countenance
Merely upon myself. Vexed I am
Of late with passions of some difference, 40
Conceptions only proper to myself,
Which give some soil, perhaps, to my
behaviours ;
But let not therefore my good friends be
griev'd—
Among which number, Cassius, be you
one—
Nor construe any further my neglect 45
Than that poor Brutus, with himself at
war,
Forgets the shows of love to other men.
  Cas. Then, Brutus, I have much mistook
your passion,
By means whereof this breast of mine hath
buried
Thoughts of great value, worthy cogita-
tions. 50

Tell me, good Brutus, can you see your
    face ?
   Bru. No, Cassius ; for the eye sees not
    itself
But by reflection, by some other things.
   Cas. 'Tis just ;
And it is very much lamented, Brutus,   55
That you have no such mirrors as will turn
Your hidden worthiness into your eye,
That you might see your shadow. I have
    heard,
Where many of the best respect in Rome—
Except immortal Cæsar—speaking of
    Brutus,
And groaning underneath this age's yoke,
Have wish'd that noble Brutus had his eyes.
   Bru. Into what dangers would you lead
    me, Cassius,
That you would have me seek into myself
For that which is not in me ?   65
   Cas. Therefore, good Brutus, be prepar'd
    to hear ;
And since you know you cannot see yourself
So well as by reflection, I, your glass,
Will modestly discover to yourself
That of yourself which you yet know
    not of.   70
And be not jealous on me, gentle Brutus :
Were I a common laughter, or did use
To stale with ordinary oaths my love
To every new protester ; if you know   74
That I do fawn on men and hug them hard,
And after scandal them ; or if you know
That I profess myself in banqueting
To all the rout, then hold me dangerous.
         [*Flourish and shout.*
   Bru. What means this shouting ? I do
    fear the people
Choose Cæsar for their king.
   Cas.   Ay, do you fear it ?   80
Then must I think you would not have
    it so.
   Bru. I would not, Cassius ; yet I love
    him well.
But wherefore do you hold me here so long?
What is it that you would impart to me ?
If it be aught toward the general good,   85
Set honour in one eye and death i' th'
    other,
And I will look on both indifferently ;
For let the gods so speed me as I love
The name of honour more than I fear death.
   Cas. I know that virtue to be in you,
    Brutus,   90
As well as I do know your outward favour.
Well, honour is the subject of my story.
I cannot tell what you and other men
Think of this life ; but, for my single self,
I had as lief not be as live to be   95
In awe of such a thing as I myself.
I was born free as Cæsar ; so were you.
We both have fed as well, and we can both
Endure the winter's cold as well as he.
For once, upon a raw and gusty day,   100

The troubled Tiber chafing with her shores,
Cæsar said to me ' Dar'st thou, Cassius, now
Leap in with me into this angry flood,
And swim to yonder point ? ' Upon the
    word,
Accoutred as I was, I plunged in   105
And bade him follow. So indeed he did.
The torrent roar'd, and we did buffet it
With lusty sinews, throwing it aside
And stemming it with hearts of controversy;
But ere we could arrive the point propos'd,
Cæsar cried ' Help me, Cassius, or I sink ! '
I, as Æneas, our great ancestor,   112
Did from the flames of Troy upon his
    shoulder
The old Anchises bear, so from the waves
    of Tiber
Did I the tired Cæsar. And this man   115
Is now become a god ; and Cassius is
A wretched creature, and must bend his
    body
If Cæsar carelessly but nod on him.
He had a fever when he was in Spain,
And when the fit was on him I did mark   120
How he did shake. 'Tis true, this god did
    shake.
His coward lips did from their colour fly,
And that same eye, whose bend doth awe
    the world,
Did lose his lustre. I did hear him groan.
Ay, and that tongue of his, that bade the
    Romans   125
Mark him, and write his speeches in their
    books,
Alas ! it cried ' Give me some drink,
    Titinius '
As a sick girl. Ye gods ! it doth amaze me
A man of such a feeble temper should
So get the start of the majestic world,   130
And bear the palm alone. [*Shout. Flourish.*
   Bru. Another general shout !
I do believe that these applauses are
For some new honours that are heap'd on
    Cæsar.
   Cas. Why, man, he doth bestride the
    narrow world   135
Like a Colossus, and we petty men
Walk under his huge legs, and peep about
To find ourselves dishonourable graves.
Men at some time are masters of their fates:
The fault, dear Brutus, is not in our stars,
But in ourselves, that we are underlings.
' Brutus ' and ' Cæsar '. What should be in
    that ' Cæsar ' ?   142
Why should that name be sounded more
    than yours ?
Write them together : yours is as fair a
    name.
Sound them : it doth become the mouth as
    well.   145
Weigh them : it as heavy. Conjure with
    'em :
' Brutus ' will start a spirit as soon as
    ' Cæsar '.

Now, in the names of all the gods at once,
Upon what meat doth this our Cæsar feed,
That he is grown so great ? Age, thou art
   sham'd !   150
Rome, thou has lost the breed of noble
   bloods !
When went there by an age, since the great
   flood,
But it was fam'd with more than with one
   man ?
When could they say, till now, that talk'd
   of Rome,
That her wide walls encompass'd but one
   man ?   155
Now is it Rome indeed, and room enough,
When there is in it but one only man.
O ! you and I have heard our fathers say
There was a Brutus once that would have
   brook'd
Th' eternal devil to keep his state in Rome
As easily as a king.   161
   Bru. That you do love me, I am nothing
   jealous ;
What you would work me to, I have some
   aim ;
How I have thought of this, and of these
   times,   164
I shall recount hereafter. For this present,
I would not, so with love I might entreat
   you,
Be any further mov'd. What you have said
I will consider ; what you have to say
I will with patience hear ; and find a time
Both meet to hear and answer such high
   things.   170
Till then, my noble friend, chew upon this :
Brutus had rather be a villager
Than to repute himself a son of Rome
Under these hard conditions as this time
Is like to lay upon us.   175
   Cas. I am glad that my weak words
Have struck but thus much show of fire
   from Brutus.

     Re-enter CÆSAR *and his* Train.

   Bru. The games are done, and Cæsar is
   returning.
   Cas. As they pass by, pluck Casca by the
   sleeve,   179
And he will, after his sour fashion, tell you
What hath proceeded worthy note to-day.
   Bru. I will do so. But, look you, Cassius,
The angry spot doth glow on Cæsar's brow,
And all the rest look like a chidden train ;
Calphurnia's cheek is pale, and Cicero   185
Looks with such ferret and such fiery eyes
As we have seen him in the Capitol,
Being cross'd in conference by some
   senators.
   Cas. Casca will tell us what the matter is.
   Cæs. Antonius !   190
   Ant. Cæsar ?
   Cæs. Let me have men about me that
   are fat ;

Sleek-headed men, and such as sleep o'
   nights.
Yond Cassius has a lean and hungry look ;
He thinks too much. Such men are
   dangerous.   195
   Ant. Fear him not, Cæsar, he's not
   dangerous ;
He is a noble Roman, and well given.
   Cæs. Would he were fatter ! But I fear
   him not.
Yet if my name were liable to fear,
I do not know the man I should avoid 200
So soon as that spare Cassius. He reads
   much,
He is a great observer, and he looks
Quite through the deeds of men. He loves
   no plays,
As thou dost, Antony ; he hears no music.
Seldom he smiles, and smiles in such a sort
As if he mock'd himself, and scorn'd his
   spirit   206
That could be mov'd to smile at anything.
Such men as he be never at heart's ease
Whiles they behold a greater than them-
   selves,
And therefore are they very dangerous. 210
I rather tell thee what is to be fear'd
Than what I fear ; for always I am Cæsar.
Come on my right hand, for this ear is deaf,
And tell me truly what thou think'st of him.
     [*Sennet. Exeunt Cæsar and his Train.*
   Casca. You pull'd me by the cloak.
   Would you speak with me ?   215
   Bru. Ay, Casca ; tell us what hath
   chanc'd to-day,
That Cæsar looks so sad ?
   Casca. Why, you were with him, were
   you not ?
   Bru. I should not then ask Casca what
   had chanc'd.   219
   Casca. Why, there was a crown offer'd
him ; and being offer'd him, he put it by
with the back of his hand, thus ; and then
the people fell a-shouting.
   Bru. What was the second noise for ?
   Casca. Why, for that too.   224
   Cas. They shouted thrice ; what was the
   last cry for ?
   Casca. Why, for that too.
   Bru. Was the crown offer'd him thrice ?
   Casca. Ay, marry, was't, and he put it by
thrice, every time gentler than other ; and
at every putting by mine honest neighbours
shouted.   230
   Cas. Who offer'd him the crown ?
   Casca. Why, Antony.
   Bru. Tell us the manner of it, gentle
   Casca.   233
   Casca. I can as well be hang'd as tell the
manner of it : it was mere foolery ; I did
not mark it. I saw Mark Antony offer him
a crown—yet 'twas not a crown neither,
'twas one of these coronets—and, as I told
you, he put it by once ; but for all that,

to my thinking, he would fain have had it.
Then he offered it to him again ; then he
put it by again ; but to my thinking, he
was very loath to lay his fingers off it. And
then he offered it the third time ; he put
it the third time by ; and still as he refus'd
it, the rabblement hooted, and clapp'd
their chopt hands, and threw up their
sweaty night-caps, and uttered such a deal
of stinking breath because Cæsar refus'd
the crown, that it had almost choked
Cæsar ; for he swooned and fell down at it.
And for mine own part I durst not laugh,
for fear of opening my lips and receiving
the bad air.   249

Cas. But soft, I pray you.   What, did
    Cæsar swoon ?

Casca. He fell down in the market-place,
and foam'd at mouth, and was speechless.

Bru. 'Tis very like. He hath the falling
    sickness.

Cas. No, Cæsar hath it not ; but you,
    and I,
And honest Casca, we have the falling
    sickness.   255

Casca. I know not what you mean by
that, but I am sure Cæsar fell down. If the
tag-rag people did not clap him and hiss
him, according as he pleas'd and displeas'd
them, as they use to do the players in the
theatre, I am no true man.   260

Bru. What said he when he came unto
    himself ?

Casca. Marry, before he fell down, when
he perceiv'd the common herd was glad he
refus'd the crown, he pluckt me ope his
doublet, and offer'd them his throat to cut.
An I had been a man of any occupation,
if I would not have taken him at a word,
I would I might go to hell among the
rogues. And so he fell. When he came to
himself again, he said, if he had done or
said anything amiss, he desir'd their
worships to think it was his infirmity. Three
or four wenches, where I stood, cried ' Alas,
good soul ! ' and forgave him with all their
hearts. But there's no heed to be taken of
them ; if Cæsar had stabb'd their mothers,
they would have done no less.

Bru. And after that, he came thus sad
    away ?   275

Casca. Ay.

Cas. Did Cicero say anything ?

Casca. Ay, he spoke Greek.

Cas. To what effect ?   279

Casca. Nay, an I tell you that, I'll ne'er
look you i' th' face again. But those that
understood him smil'd at one another, and
shook their heads ; but for mine own part,
it was Greek to me. I could tell you more
news too : Marullus and Flavius, for
pulling scarfs off Cæsar's images, are put
to silence. Fare you well. There was more
foolery yet, if I could remember it.   286

Cas. Will you sup with me to-night,
Casca ?

Casca. No, I am promis'd forth.

Cas. Will you dine with me to-morrow ?

Casca. Ay, if I be alive, and your mind
hold, and your dinner worth the eating. 291

Cas. Good ; I will expect you.

Casca. Do so. Farewell, both.   [*Exit.*

Bru. What a blunt fellow is this grown
    to be !
He was quick mettle when he went to
    school.   295

Cas. So is he now, in execution
Of any bold or noble enterprise,
However he puts on this tardy form.
This rudeness is a sauce to his good wit,
Which gives men stomach to digest his
    words   300
With better appetite.

Bru. And so it is. For this time I will
    leave you.
To-morrow, if you please to speak with me,
I will come home to you ; or, if you will,
Come home to me, and I will wait for you.

Cas. I will do so. Till then, think of the
    world.   [*Exit Brutus.*
Well, Brutus, thou art noble ; yet, I see,
Thy honourable metal may be wrought
From that it is dispos'd. Therefore it is
    meet
That noble minds keep ever with their
    likes ;   310
For who so firm that cannot be seduc'd ?
Cæsar doth bear me hard ; but he loves
    Brutus.
If I were Brutus now and he were Cassius,
He should not humour me. I will this night,
In several hands, in at his windows throw,
As if they came from several citizens, 316
Writings, all tending to the great opinion
That Rome holds of his name ; wherein
    obscurely
Cæsar's ambition shall be glanced at.
And, after this, let Cæsar seat him sure ; 320
For we will shake him, or worse days
    endure.   [*Exit.*

SCENE III.   *Rome.   A street.*

*Thunder and lightning. Enter, from opposite
    sides,* CASCA, *with his sword drawn,
    and* CICERO.

Cic. Good even, Casca.   Brought you
    Cæsar home ?
Why are you breathless ? and why stare
    you so ?

Casca. Are not you mov'd, when all the
    sway of earth
Shakes like a thing unfirm ? O Cicero,
I have seen tempests when the scolding
    winds   5
Have riv'd the knotty oaks, and I have seen
Th' ambitious ocean swell, and rage, and
    foam,

To be exalted with the threat'ning clouds;
But never till to-night, never till now,
Did I go through a tempest dropping fire. 10
Either there is a civil strife in heaven,
Or else the world, too saucy with the gods,
Incenses them to send destruction.
   Cic. Why, saw you any thing more
     wonderful?
   Casca. A common slave—you know him
     well by sight—   15
Held up his left hand, which did flame and
   burn
Like twenty torches join'd; and yet his
   hand,
Not sensible of fire, remain'd unscorch'd.
Besides—I ha' not since put up my sword—
Against the Capitol I met a lion,   20
Who glaz'd upon me, and went surly by
Without annoying me; and there were
   drawn
Upon a heap a hundred ghastly women,
Transformed with their fear, who swore
   they saw
Men, all in fire, walk up and down the
   streets.   25
And yesterday the bird of night did sit,
Even at noon-day, upon the market-place,
Hooting and shrieking. When these
   prodigies
Do so conjointly meet, let not men say
' These are their reasons—they are natural ',
For I believe they are portentous things 31
Unto the climate that they point upon.
   Cic. Indeed, it is a strange-disposed time;
But men may construe things after their
   fashion,
Clean from the purpose of the things them-
   selves.   35
Comes Cæsar to the Capitol to-morrow?
   Casca. He doth; for he did bid Antonius
Send word to you he would be there to-
   morrow.
   Cic. Good night, then, Casca; this
   disturbed sky   39
Is not to walk in.
   Casca.   Farewell, Cicero. [*Exit Cicero.*

     Enter CASSIUS.

   Cas. Who's there?
   Casca.   A Roman.
   Cas.   Casca, by your voice.
   Casca. Your ear is good. Cassius, what
   night is this!
   Cas. A very pleasing night to honest men.
   Casca. Who ever knew the heavens
   menace so?
   Cas. Those that have known the earth so
   full of faults.   45
For my part, I have walk'd about the
   streets,
Submitting me unto the perilous night,
And, thus unbraced, Casca, as you see,
Have bar'd my bosom to the thunder-
   stone;

And when the cross blue lightning seem'd
   to open   50
The breast of heaven, I did present myself
Even in the aim and very flash of it.
   Casca. But wherefore did you so much
   tempt the heavens?
It is the part of men to fear and tremble
When the most mighty gods by tokens send
Such dreadful heralds to astonish us.   56
   Cas. You are dull, Casca, and those
   sparks of life
That should be in a Roman you do want,
Or else you use not. You look pale, and
   gaze,
And put on fear, and cast yourself in
   wonder,   60
To see the strange impatience of the
   heavens;
But if you would consider the true cause—
Why all these fires, why all these gliding
   ghosts,
Why birds and beasts, from quality and
   kind;   64
Why old men, fools, and children calculate;
Why all these things change from their
   ordinance,
Their natures and preformed faculties,
To monstrous quality—why, you shall find
That heaven hath infus'd them with these
   spirits,
To make them instruments of fear and
   warning   70
Unto some monstrous state.
Now could I, Casca, name to thee a man
Most like this dreadful night
That thunders, lightens, opens graves, and
   roars
As doth the lion in the Capitol;   75
A man no mightier than thyself or me
In personal action, yet prodigious grown,
And fearful, as these strange eruptions are.
   Casca. 'Tis Cæsar that you mean, is it
   not, Cassius?
   Cas. Let it be who it is; for Romans
   now   80
Have thews and limbs like to their an-
   cestors.
But woe the while! our fathers' minds are
   dead,
And we are govern'd with our mothers'
   spirits;
Our yoke and sufferance show us womanish.
   Casca. Indeed they say the senators to-
   morrow   85
Mean to establish Cæsar as a king;
And he shall wear his crown by sea and
   land,
In every place save here in Italy.
   Cas. I know where I will wear this dagger
   then;   89
Cassius from bondage will deliver Cassius.
Therein, ye gods, you make the weak most
   strong;
Therein, ye gods, you tyrants do defeat.

Nor stony tower, nor walls of beaten brass,
Nor airless dungeon, nor strong links of
   iron,   94
Can be retentive to the strength of spirit ;
But life, being weary of these worldly bars,
Never lacks power to dismiss itself.
If I know this, know all the world besides,
That part of tyranny that I do bear,
I can shake off at pleasure. [*Thunder still.*
   Casca.   So can I ;   100
So every bondman in his own hand bears
The power to cancel his captivity.
   Cas. And why should Cæsar be a tyrant,
   then ?   103
Poor man ! I know he would not be a wolf
But that he sees the Romans are but sheep ;
He were no lion, were not Romans hinds.
Those that with haste will make a mighty
   fire
Begin it with weak straws. What trash is
   Rome,
What rubbish, and what offal, when it
   serves
For the base matter to illuminate   110
So vile a thing as Cæsar ! But, O grief,
Where hast thou led me ? I perhaps speak
   this
Before a willing bondman ; then I know
My answer must be made. But I am arm'd,
And dangers are to me indifferent.   115
   Casca. You speak to Casca, and to such
   a man
That is no fleering tell-tale. Hold, my hand.
Be factious for redress of all these griefs,
And I will set this foot of mine as far
As who goes farthest.
   Cas.   There's a bargain made. 120
Now know you, Casca, I have mov'd
   already
Some certain of the noblest-minded
   Romans
To undergo with me an enterprise
Of honourable-dangerous consequence ;
And I do know by this they stay for me 125
In Pompey's porch ; for now, this fearful
   night,
There is no stir or walking in the streets,
And the complexion of the element
In favour's like the work we have in hand,
Most bloody, fiery, and most terrible.   130

      Enter CINNA.

   Casca. Stand close awhile, for here comes
   one in haste.
   Cas. 'Tis Cinna, I do know him by his
   gait ;
He is a friend. Cinna, where haste you so ?
   Cin. To find out you. Who's that ?
   Metellus Cimber ?
   Cas. No, it is Casca, one incorporate 135
To our attempts. Am I not stay'd for,
   Cinna ?
   Cin. I am glad on't. What a fearful
   night is this !

There's two or three of us have seen strange
   sights.
   Cas. Am I not stay'd for ? Tell me. 139
   Cin. Yes, you are. O Cassius, if you could
But win the noble Brutus to our party—
   Cas. Be you content. Good Cinna, take
   this paper,
And look you lay it in the prætor's chair,
Where Brutus may but find it ; and throw
   this
In at his window ; set this up with wax 145
Upon old Brutus' statue. All this done,
Repair to Pompey's porch, where you shall
   find us.
Is Decius Brutus and Trebonius there ?
   Cin. All but Metellus Cimber, and he's
   gone   149
To seek you at your house. Well, I will hie,
And so bestow these papers as you bade me.
   Cas. That done, repair to Pompey's
   theatre.   [*Exit Cinna.*
Come, Casca, you and I will yet ere day
See Brutus at his house. Three parts of him
Is ours already, and the man entire   155
Upon the next encounter yields him ours.
   Casca. O, he sits high in all the people's
   hearts ;
And that which would appear offence in us
His countenance, like richest alchemy,
Will change to virtue and to worthiness. 160
   Cas. Him and his worth and our great
   need of him
You have right well conceited. Let us go,
For it is after midnight ; and ere day
We will awake him and be sure of him.
                  [*Exeunt.*

           ACT TWO

      SCENE I. *Rome.*

   Enter BRUTUS *in his orchard.*

   Bru. What, Lucius, ho !
I cannot by the progress of the stars
Give guess how near to day. Lucius, I say !
I would it were my fault to sleep so soundly.
When, Lucius, when ? Awake, I say !
   What, Lucius !   5

      Enter LUCIUS.

   Luc. Call'd you, my lord ?
   Bru. Get me a taper in my study, Lucius;
When it is lighted, come and call me here.
   Luc. I will, my lord.   [*Exit.*
   Bru. It must be by his death ; and for
   my part,   10
I know no personal cause to spurn at him,
But for the general : he would be crown'd.
How that might change his nature, there's
   the question.
It is the bright day that brings forth the
   adder,
And that craves wary walking. Crown him
   —that !   15
And then, I grant, we put a sting in him

That at his will he may do danger with.
Th' abuse of greatness is, when it disjoins
Remorse from power ; and to speak truth
    of Cæsar,
I have not known when his affections
    sway'd   20
More than his reason. But 'tis a common
    proof
That lowliness is young ambition's ladder,
Whereto the climber-upward turns his face;
But when he once attains the upmost
    round,
He then unto the ladder turns his back, 25
Looks in the clouds, scorning the base
    degrees
By which he did ascend. So Cæsar may.
Then, lest he may, prevent. And since the
    quarrel
Will bear no colour for the thing he is,
Fashion it thus—that what he is, aug-
    mented,   30
Would run to these and these extremities ;
And therefore think him as a serpent's egg,
Which, hatch'd, would as his kind grow
    mischievous,
And kill him in the shell.

Re-enter LUCIUS.

Luc. The taper burneth in your closet,
    sir.   35
Searching the window for a flint, I found
This paper, thus seal'd up ; and I am sure
It did not lie there when I went to bed.
                      [Giving him a letter.
Bru. Get you to bed again, it is not day.
Is not to-morrow, boy, the ides of March ?
Luc. I know not, sir.   41
Bru. Look in the calendar, and bring me
    word.
Luc. I will, sir.   *[Exit.*
Bru. The exhalations, whizzing in the air,
Give so much light that I may read by
    them.   *[Opens the letter and reads.*
' Brutus, thou sleep'st. Awake, and see
    thyself.
Shall Rome, &c. Speak, strike, redress !
Brutus, thou sleep'st ; awake.'
Such instigations have been often dropp'd
Where I have took them up.   50
' Shall Rome, &c.' Thus must I piece it out :
Shall Rome stand under one man's awe ?
    What, Rome ?
My ancestors did from the streets of Rome
The Tarquin drive, when he was call'd a
    king.   54
' Speak, strike, redress ! ' Am I entreated
To speak and strike ? O Rome, I make
    thee promise,
If the redress will follow, thou receivest
Thy full petition at the hand of Brutus !

Re-enter LUCIUS.

Luc. Sir, March is wasted fifteen days.
                      [Knocking within.

Bru. 'Tis good. Go to the gate ; some-
    body knocks.   *[Exit Lucius.*
Since Cassius first did whet me against
    Cæsar,   61
I have not slept.
Between the acting of a dreadful thing
And the first motion, all the interim is
Like a phantasma or a hideous dream. 65
The Genius and the mortal instruments
Are then in council ; and the state of man,
Like to a little kingdom, suffers then
The nature of an insurrection.

Re-enter LUCIUS.

Luc. Sir, 'tis your brother Cassius at
    the door   70
Who doth desire to see you.
Bru.   Is he alone ?
Luc. No, sir, there are moe with him.
Bru.   Do you know them ?
Luc. No, sir ; their hats are pluck'd
    about their ears
And half their faces buried in their cloaks,
That by no means I may discover them 75
By any mark of favour
Bru.   Let 'em enter.
                        [Exit Lucius.
They are the faction. O conspiracy,
Sham'st thou to show thy dang'rous brow
    by night,   78
When evils are most free ? O, then by day
Where wilt thou find a cavern dark enough
To mask thy monstrous visage ? Seek none,
    conspiracy ;
Hide it in smiles and affability !
For if thou path, thy native semblance on,
Not Erebus itself were dim enough
To hide thee from prevention.   85

Enter the conspirators, CASSIUS, CASCA,
    DECIUS, CINNA, METELLUS CIMBER,
    and TREBONIUS.

Cas. I think we are too bold upon your
    rest.
Good morrow, Brutus. Do we trouble you?
Bru. I have been up this hour, awake all
    night.
Know I these men that come along with
    you ?
Cas. Yes, every man of them ; and no
    man here   90
But honours you ; and every one doth wish
You had but that opinion of yourself
Which every noble Roman bears of you.
This is Trebonius.
Bru.   He is welcome hither.
Cas. This, Decius Brutus.
Bru.   He is welcome too. 95
Cas. This, Casca ; this, Cinna ;
And this, Metellus Cimber.
Bru.   They are all welcome.
What watchful cares do interpose them-
    selves
Betwixt your eyes and night ?

Cas. Shall I entreat a word ?   100
　　　　　　　　　　[*They whisper.*
Dec. Here lies the east. Doth not the day
　　break here ?
Casca. No.
Cin. O, pardon, sir, it doth ; and yon
　　grey lines
That fret the clouds are messengers of day.
Casca. You shall confess that you are
　　both deceiv'd.   105
Here, as I point my·sword, the sun arises ;
Which is a great way growing on the south,
Weighing the youthful season of the year.
Some two months hence up higher toward
　　the north
He first presents his fire ; and the high east
Stands as the Capitol, directly here.   111
Bru. Give me your hands all over, one
　　by one.
Cas. And let us swear our resolution.
Bru. No, not an oath. If not the face
　　of men,
The sufferance of our souls, the time's
　　abuse,   115
If these be motives weak, break off be-
　　times,
And every man hence to his idle bed.
So let high-sighted tyranny range on,
Till each man drop by lottery. But if these,
As I am sure they do, bear fire enough   120
To kindle cowards, and to steel with valour
The melting spirits of women, then,
　　countrymen,
What need we any spur but our own cause
To prick us to redress ? What other bond
Than secret Romans that have spoke the
　　word   125
And will not palter ? And what other oath
Than honesty to honesty engæg'd
That this shall be or we will fall for it ?
Swear priests and cowards and men
　　cautelous,   129
Old feeble carrions and such suffering souls
That welcome wrongs ; unto bad causes
　　swear
Such creatures as men doubt ; but do not
　　stain
The even virtue of our enterprise,
Nor th' insuppressive mettle of our spirits,
To think that or our·cause or our perform-
　　ance   135
Did need an oath ; when every drop of
　　blood
That every Roman bears, and nobly bears,
Is guilty of a several bastardy,
If he do break the smallest particle   139
Of any promise that hath pass'd from him.
Cas. But what of Cicero ? Shall we
　　sound him ?
I think he will stand very strong with us.
Casca. Let us not leave him out.
Cin.　　　　　　No, by no means.
Met. O, let us have him ; for his silver
　　hairs

Will purchase us a good opinion,   145
And buy men's voices to commend our
　　deeds.
It shall be said his judgment rul'd our
　　hands ;
Our youths and wildness shall no whit
　　appear,
But all be buried in his gravity.
Bru. O, name him not ! Let us not break
　　with him ;   150
For he will never follow any thing
That other men begin.
Cas.　　　　　Then leave him out.
Casca. Indeed he is not fit.
Dec. Shall no man else be touch'd but
　　only Cæsar ?
Cas. Decius, well urg'd. I think it is not
　　meet   155
Mark Antony, so well belov'd of Cæsar,
Should outlive Cæsar We shall find of
　　him
A shrewd contriver ; and you know his
　　means,
If he improve them, may well stretch so far
As to annoy us all ; which to prevent,   160
Let Antony and Cæsar fall together.
Bru. Our course will seem too bloody,
　　Caius Cassius, ·
To cut the head off and then hack the
　　limbs—
Like wrath in death and envy afterwards ;
For Antony is but a limb of Cæsar.   165
Let's be sacrificers, but not butchers, Caius.
We all stand up against the spirit of Cæsar,
And in the spirit of men there is no blood.
O that we then could come by Cæsar's
　　spirit,
And not dismember Cæsar ! But, alas,   170
Cæsar must bleed for it ! And, gentle
　　friends,
Let's kill him boldly, but not wrathfully ;
Let's carve him as a dish fit for the gods,
Not hew him as a carcase fit for hounds ;
And let our hearts, as subtle masters do, 175
Stir up their servants to an act of rage,
And after seem to chide 'em. This shall
　　make
Our purpose necessary, and not envious ;
Which so appearing to the common eyes,
We shall be call'd purgers, not murderers.
And for Mark Antony, think not of him ;
For he can do no more than Cæsar's arm
When Cæsar's head is off.
Cas.　　　　　Yet I fear him ;
For in the engrafted love he bears to
　　Cæsar—
Bru. Alas, good Cassius, do not think of
　　him !   185
If he love Cæsar, all that he can do
Is ·to himself take thought and die for
　　Cæsar ;
And that were much he should, for he is
　　given
To sports, to wildness, and much company.

Treb. There is no fear in him. Let him
 not die ;   190
For he will live, and laugh at this hereafter.
         [Clock strikes.
 Bru. Peace ! Count the clock.
 Cas.   The clock hath stricken three.
 Treb. 'Tis time to part.
 Cas.   But it is doubtful yet
Whether Cæsar will come forth to-day or
 no ;
For he is superstitious grown of late,   195
Quite from the main opinion he held once
Of fantasy, of dreams, and ceremonies.
It may be these apparent prodigies,
The unaccustom'd terror of this night,
And the persuasion of his augurers,   200
May hold him from the Capitol to-day.
 Dec. Never fear that. If he be so resolv'd,
I can o'ersway him ; for he loves to hear
That unicorns may be betray'd with trees,
And bears with glasses, elephants with
 holes,   205
Lions with toils, and men with flatterers ;
But when I tell him he hates flatterers,
He says he does, being then most flattered.
Let me work ;
For I can give his humour the true bent,   210
And I will bring him to the Capitol.
 Cas. Nay, we will all of us be there to
 fetch him.
 Bru. By the eighth hour. Is that the
 uttermost ?
 Cin. Be that the uttermost, and fail not
 then.
 Met. Caius Ligarius doth bear Cæsar
 hard,   215
Who rated him for speaking well of Pom-
 pey.
I wonder none of you have thought of him.
 Bru. Now, good Metellus, go along by
 him.
He loves me well, and I have given him
 reasons ;   219
Send him but hither, and I'll fashion him.
 Cas. The morning comes upon's. We'll
 leave you, Brutus.
And, friends, disperse yourselves ; but all
 remember
What you have said, and show yourselves
 true Romans.
 Bru. Good gentlemen, look fresh and
 merrily ;
Let not our looks put on our purposes,   225
But bear it as our Roman actors do,
With untir'd spirits and formal constancy.
And so good morrow to you every one.
       [Exeunt all but Brutus.
Boy ! Lucius ! Fast asleep ? It is no
 matter ;
Enjoy the honey-heavy dew of slumber.   230
Thou hast no figures nor no fantasies
Which busy care draws in the brains of
 men ;
Therefore thou sleep'st so sound.

        Enter PORTIA.

 Por. Brutus, my lord !
 Bru. Portia, what mean you ? Wherefore
 rise you now ?
It is not for your health thus to commit   235
Your weak condition to the raw cold
 morning.
 Por. Nor for yours neither. Y'have un-
 gently, Brutus,
Stole from my bed ; and yesternight at
 supper
You suddenly arose and walk'd about,   239
Musing and sighing, with your arms across;
And when I ask'd you what the matter was,
You star'd upon me with ungentle looks.
I urg'd you further ; then you scratch'd
 your head
And too impatiently stamp'd with your
 foot.
Yet I insisted ; yet you answer'd not,   245
But with an angry wafture of your hand
Gave sign for me to leave you. So I did,
Fearing to strengthen that impatience
Which seem'd too much enkindled ; and
 withal
Hoping it was but an effect of humour,   250
Which sometime hath his hour with every
 man.
It will not let you eat, nor talk, nor sleep ;
And, could it work so much upon your
 shape
As it hath much prevail'd on your con-
 dition,
I should not know you Brutus. Dear my
 lord,   255
Make me acquainted with your cause of
 grief.
 Bru. I am not well in health, and that
 is all.
 Por. Brutus is wise, and, were he not in
 health,
He would embrace the means to come by it.
 Bru. Why, so I do. Good Portia, go to
 bed.   260
 Por. Is Brutus sick, and is it physical
To walk unbraced and suck up the humours
Of the dank morning ? What, is Brutus
 sick,
And will he steal out of his wholesome bed,
To dare the vile contagion of the night,   265
And tempt the rheumy and unpurged air
To add unto his sickness ? No, my Brutus ;
You have some sick offence within your
 mind,
Which by the right and virtue of my
 place
I ought to know of ; and upon my knees   270
I charm you, by my once-commended
 beauty,
By all your vows of love, and that great
 vow
Which did incorporate and make us one,
That you unfold to me, your self, your half,

And reason to my love is liable.
  Cæs. How foolish do your fears seem
    now, Calphurnia !
I am ashamed I did yield to them.   106
Give me my robe, for I will go.

Enter BRUTUS, LIGARIUS, METELLUS, CASCA,
  TREBONIUS, CINNA, *and* PUBLIUS.

And look where Publius is come to fetch me.
  Pub. Good morrow, Cæsar.
  Cæs.   Welcome, Publius.
What, Brutus, are you stirr'd so early too ?
Good morrow, Casca. Caius Ligarius,   111
Cæsar was ne'er so much your enemy
As that same ague which hath made you
    lean.
What is't o'clock ?
  Bru.   Cæsar, 'tis strucken eight.
  Cæs. I thank you for your pains and
    courtesy.   115

Enter ANTONY.

See ! Antony, that revels long o' nights,
Is notwithstanding up. Good morrow,
  Antony.
  Ant. So to most noble Cæsar.
  Cæs.   Bid them prepare within.
I am to blame to be thus waited for.
Now, Cinna.   Now, Metellus.   What,
  Trebonius !   120
I have an hour's talk in store for you.
Remember that you call on me to-day ;
Be near me, that I may remember you.
  Treb. Cæsar, I will. [*Aside*] And so near
    will I be,
That your best friends shall wish I had
    been further.   125
  Cæs. Good friends, go in and taste some
    wine with me ;
And we, like friends, will straightway go
    together.
  Bru. [*Aside*] That every like is not the
    same, O Cæsar,
The heart of Brutus earns to think upon !
                    [*Exeunt.*

SCENE III. *Rome. A street near the Capitol.*

Enter ARTEMIDORUS *reading a paper.*

  Art. ' Cæsar, beware of Brutus ; take
heed of Cassius ; come not near Casca ;
have an eye to Cinna ; trust not Trebonius ; mark well Metellus Cimber ;
Decius Brutus loves thee not ; thou hast
wrong'd Caius Ligarius. There is but one
mind in all these men, and it is bent against
Cæsar. If thou beest not immortal, look
about you. Security gives way to conspiracy. The mighty gods defend thee !   6
            Thy lover,
            ARTEMIDORUS.'

Here will I stand till Cæsar pass along,
And as a suitor will I give him this.
My heart laments that virtue cannot live   10

Out of the teeth of emulation.
If thou read this, O Cæsar, thou mayest
  live ;
If not, the fates with traitors do contrive.
                    [*Exit.*

SCENE IV. *Rome. Before the house of*
              Brutus.

Enter PORTIA *and* LUCIUS.

  Por. I prithee, boy, run to the Senate
    House.
Stay not to answer me, but get thee gone.
Why dost thou stay ?
  Luc.   To know my errand, madam.
  Por. I would have had thee there and
    here again,
Ere I can tell thee what thou shouldst do
    there.   5
[*Aside*] O constancy, be strong upon my
    side !
Set a huge mountain 'tween my heart and
    tongue !
I have a man's mind, but a woman's might.
How hard it is for women to keep counsel !—
Art thou here yet ?
  Luc.   Madam, what should I do ?   10
Run to the Capitol, and nothing else ?
And so return to you, and nothing else ?
  Por. Yes, bring me word, boy, if thy lord
    look well,
For he went sickly forth ; and take good
    note
What Cæsar doth, what suitors press to
    him.   15
Hark, boy ! What noise is that ?
  Luc. I hear none, madam.
  Por.   Prithee listen well.
I heard a bustling rumour, like a fray,
And the wind brings it from the Capitol.
  Luc. Sooth, madam, I hear nothing.

Enter the SOOTHSAYER.

  Por.   Come hither, fellow. 20
Which way hast thou been ?
  Sooth.   At mine own house, good lady.
  Por. What is't o'clock ?
  Sooth.   About the ninth hour, lady.
  Por. Is Cæsar yet gone to the Capitol ?
  Sooth. Madam, not yet. I go to take my
    stand,
To see him pass on to the Capitol.   25
  Por. Thou hast some suit to Cæsar, hast
    thou not ?
  Sooth. That I have, lady. If it will please
    Cæsar
To be so good to Cæsar as to hear me,
I shall beseech him to befriend himself.
  Por. Why, know'st thou any harm's
    intended towards him ?   30
  Sooth. None that I know will be, much
    that I fear may chance.
Good morrow to you. Here the street is
    narrow ;

The throng that follows Cæsar at the heels,
Of senators, of prætors, common suitors,
Will crowd a feeble man almost to death. 35
I'll get me to a place more void, and there
Speak to great Cæsar as he comes along.
[*Exit.*

Por. I must go in. [*Aside*] Ay me, how
weak a thing
The heart of woman is! O Brutus, 39
The heavens speed thee in thine enterprise!
Sure the boy heard me.—Brutus hath a suit
That Cæsar will not grant.—O, I grow
faint.—
Run, Lucius, and commend me to my lord;
Say I am merry. Come to me again, 44
And bring me word what he doth say to
thee. [*Exeunt severally.*

ACT THREE.

SCENE I. *Rome. A street before the Capitol.*

Flourish. Enter CÆSAR, BRUTUS, CASSIUS,
CASCA, DECIUS, METELLUS, TREBONIUS,
CINNA, ANTONY, LEPIDUS, ARTEMI-
DORUS, POPILIUS, PUBLIUS, *and the*
Soothsayer.

Cæs. The ides of March are come.
Sooth. Ay, Cæsar, but not gone.
Art. Hail, Cæsar! Read this schedule.
Dec. Trebonius doth desire you to o'er-
read,
At your best leisure, this his humble suit. 5
Art. O Cæsar, read mine first; for mine's
a suit
That touches Cæsar nearer. Read it, great
Cæsar.
Cæs. What touches us ourself shall be
last serv'd.
Art. Delay not, Cæsar; read it instantly.
Cæs. What, is the fellow mad?
Pub. Sirrah, give place. 10
Cas. What, urge you your petitions in the
street?
Come to the Capitol.

Cæsar enters the Capitol, the rest following.

Pop. I wish your enterprise to-day may
thrive.
Cas. What enterprise, Popilius?
Pop. Fare you well.
[*Advances to Cæsar.*
Bru. What said Popilius Lena? 15
Cas. He wish'd to-day our enterprise
might thrive.
I fear our purpose is discovered.
Bru. Look how he makes to Cæsar.
Mark him.
Cas. Casca, be sudden, for we fear pre-
vention.
Brutus, what shall be done? If this be
known, 20
Cassius or Cæsar never shall turn back,
For I will slay myself.

Bru. Cassius, be constant.
Popilius Lena speaks not of our purposes;
For look, he smiles, and Cæsar doth not
change.
Cas. Trebonius knows his time; for look
you, Brutus, 25
He draws Mark Antony out of the way.
[*Exeunt Antony and Trebonius.*
Dec. Where is Metellus Cimber? Let him
go
And presently prefer his suit to Cæsar.
Bru. He is address'd; press near and
second him.
Cin. Casca, you are the first that rears
your hand. 30
Cæs. Are we all ready? What is now
amiss
That Cæsar and his Senate must redress?
Met. Most high, most mighty, and most
puissant Cæsar, 33
Metellus Cimber throws before thy seat
An humble heart. [*Kneeling.*
Cæs. I must prevent thee, Cimber.
These couchings and these lowly courtesies
Might fire the blood of ordinary men,
And turn pre-ordinance and first decree
Into the law of children. Be not fond 39
To think that Cæsar bears such rebel blood
That will be thaw'd from the true quality
With that which melteth fools—I mean,
sweet words,
Low-crooked curtsies, and base spaniel
fawning.
Thy brother by decree is banished;
If thou dost bend, and pray, and fawn for
him, 45
I spurn thee like a cur out of my way.
Know, Cæsar doth not wrong; nor without
cause
Will he be satisfied.
Met. Is there no voice more worthy than
my own 49
To sound more sweetly in great Cæsar's ear
For the repealing of my banish'd brother?
Bru. I kiss thy hand, but not in flattery,
Cæsar,
Desiring thee that Publius Cimber may
Have an immediate freedom of repeal. 54
Cæs. What, Brutus!
Cas. Pardon, Cæsar! Cæsar, pardon!
As low as to thy foot doth Cassius fall,
To beg enfranchisement for Publius Cimber.
Cæs. I could be well mov'd, if I were as
you;
If I could pray to move, prayers would
move me;
But I am constant as the northern star, 60
Of whose true-fix'd and resting quality
There is no fellow in the firmament.
The skies are painted with unnumb'red
sparks,
They are all fire, and every one doth shine;
But there's but one in all doth hold his
place. 65

So in the world : 'tis furnish'd well with men,
And men are flesh and blood, and apprehensive ;
Yet in the number I do know but one
That unassailable holds on his rank,
Unshak'd of motion ; and that I am he, 70
Let me a little show it, even in this—
That I was constant Cimber should be banish'd,
And constant do remain to keep him so.
  Cin. O Cæsar !
  Cæs.   Hence ! Wilt thou lift up Olympus ?
  Dec. Great Cæsar !
  Cæs.   Doth not Brutus bootless kneel ?   75
  Casca. Speak, hands, for me !
        [*They stab Cæsar. Casca strikes the first, Brutus the last blow.*
  Cæs. Et tu, Brute ?—Then fall, Cæsar !
                                    [*Dies.*
  Cin. Liberty ! Freedom ! Tyranny is dead !
Run hence, proclaim, cry it about the streets.
  Cas. Some to the common pulpits, and cry out   80
' Liberty, freedom, and enfranchisement ! '
  Bru. People and Senators, be not affrighted ;
Fly not ; stand still. Ambition's debt is paid.
  Casca. Go to the pulpit, Brutus.
  Dec. And Cassius too.   85
  Bru. Where's Publius ?
  Cin. Here, quite confounded with this mutiny.
  Met. Stand fast together, lest some friend of Cæsar's
Should chance—
  Bru. Talk not of standing. Publius, good cheer !   90
There is no harm intended to your person,
Nor to no Roman else. So tell them, Publius.
  Cas. And leave us, Publius, lest that the people,
Rushing on us, should do your age some mischief.
  Bru. Do so ; and let no man abide this deed   95
But we the doers.

                Re-enter TREBONIUS.

  Cas. Where is Antony ?
  Tre.   Fled to his house amaz'd.
Men, wives, and children, stare, cry out, and run,
As it were doomsday.
  Bru.   Fates, we will know your pleasures.
That we shall die, we know ; 'tis but the time,   100

And drawing days out, that men stand upon.
  Cas. Why, he that cuts off twenty years of life
Cuts off so many years of fearing death.
  Bru. Grant that, and then is death a benefit.
So are we Cæsar's friends, that have abrid'g   105
His time of fearing death. Stoop, Romans, stoop,
And let us bathe our hands in Cæsar's blood
Up to the elbows, and besmear our swords.
Then walk we forth, even to the market-place,   109
And waving our red weapons o'er our heads,
Let's all cry ' Peace, freedom, and liberty ! '
  Cas. Stoop then, and wash. How many ages hence
Shall this our lofty scene be acted over
In states unborn and accents yet unknown !
  Bru. How many times shall Cæsar bleed in sport,   115
That now on Pompey's basis lies along
No worthier than the dust !
  Cas.   So oft as that shall be,
So often shall the knot of us be call'd
The men that gave their country liberty.
  Dec. What, shall we forth ?
  Cas.   Ay, every man away. 120
Brutus shall lead, and we will grace his heels
With the most boldest and best hearts of Rome.

                Enter a Servant.

  Bru. Soft, who comes here ? A friend of Antony's.
  Serv. Thus, Brutus, did my master bid me kneel ;   124
Thus did Mark Antony bid me fall down ;
And, being prostrate, thus he bade me say :
Brutus is noble, wise, valiant, and honest ;
Cæsar was mighty, bold, royal, and loving.
Say I love Brutus, and I honour him ;
Say I fear'd Cæsar, honour'd him, and lov'd him.   130
If Brutus will vouchsafe that Antony
May safely come to him, and be resolv'd
How Cæsar hath deserv'd to lie in death,
Mark Antony shall not love Cæsar dead
So well as Brutus living ; but will follow 135
The fortunes and affairs of noble Brutus
Thorough the hazards of this untrod state
With all true faith. So says my master Antony.
  Bru. Thy master is a wise and valiant Roman ;
I never thought him worse.   140
Tell him, so please him come unto this place,
He shall be satisfied and, by my honour,
Depart untouch'd.

                                    983

Serv. I'll fetch him presently. [*Exit.*
Bru. I know that we shall have him well
  to friend.
Cas. I wish we may. But yet have I a
  mind   145
That fears him much; and my misgiving
  still
Falls shrewdly to the purpose.

Re-enter ANTONY.

Bru. But here comes Antony. Welcome,
  Mark Antony.
Ant. O mighty Cæsar! dost thou lie so
  low?
Are all thy conquests, glories, triumphs,
  spoils,   150
Shrunk to this little measure? Fare thee
  well.
I know not, gentlemen, what you intend,
Who else must be let blood, who else is rank.
If I myself, there is no hour so fit
As Cæsar's death's hour; nor no instru-
  ment   155
Of half that worth as those your swords,
  made rich
With the most noble blood of all this world.
I do beseech ye, if you bear me hard,
Now, whilst your purpled hands do reek
  and smoke,   159
Fulfil your pleasure. Live a thousand years,
I shall not find myself so apt to die.
No place will please me so, no mean of
  death,
As here by Cæsar, and by you cut off,   163
The choice and master spirits of this age.
Bru. O Antony! beg not your death of us.
Though now we must appear bloody and
  cruel,
As by our hands and this our present act
You see we do; yet see you but our hands,
And this the bleeding business they have
  done.   169
Our hearts you see not; they are pitiful;
And pity to the general wrong of Rome,
As fire drives out fire, so pity pity,
Hath done this deed on Cæsar. For your
  part,
To you our swords have leaden points,
  Mark Antony;
Our arms in strength of malice, and our
  hearts   175
Of brothers' temper, do receive you in
With all kind love, good thoughts, and
  reverence.
Cas. Your voice shall be as strong as any
  man's
In the disposing of new dignities.
Bru. Only be patient till we have
  appeas'd   180
The multitude, beside themselves with fear,
And then we will deliver you the cause
Why I, that did love Cæsar when I struck
  him,
Have thus proceeded.   183

Ant. I doubt not of your wisdom.
Let each man render me his bloody hand.
First, Marcus Brutus, will I shake with you;
Next, Caius Cassius, do I take your hand;
Now, Decius Brutus, yours; now yours,
  Metellus;
Yours, Cinna; and, my valiant Casca,
  yours.
Though last, not least in love, yours, good
  Trebonius.   190
Gentlemen all—alas, what shall I say?
My credit now stands on such slippery
  ground
That one of two bad ways you must conceit
  me,
Either a coward or a flatterer.
That I did love thee, Cæsar, O, 'tis true! 195
If then thy spirit look upon us now,
Shall it not grieve thee dearer than thy
  death
To see thy Antony making his peace,
Shaking the bloody fingers of thy foes,
Most noble! in the presence of thy corse?
Had I as many eyes as thou hast wounds,
Weeping as fast as they stream forth thy
  blood,   202
It would become me better than to close
In terms of friendship with thine enemies.
Pardon me, Julius! Here wast thou bay'd,
  brave hart;
Here didst thou fall; and here thy hunters
  stand,   206
Sign'd in thy spoil, and crimson'd in thy
  lethe.
O world, thou wast the forest to this hart;
And this indeed, O world, the heart of thee!
How like a deer strucken by many princes
Dost thou here lie!   211
Cas. Mark Antony—
Ant.   Pardon me, Caius Cassius.
The enemies of Cæsar shall say this;
Then, in a friend, it is cold modesty.
Cas. I blame you not for praising Cæsar
  so;   215
But what compact mean you to have with
  us?
Will you be prick'd in number of our
  friends,
Or shall we on, and not depend on you?
Ant. Therefore I took your hands; but
  was indeed
Sway'd from the point by looking down on
  Cæsar.   220
Friends am I with you all, and love you all,
Upon this hope, that you shall give me
  reasons
Why and wherein Cæsar was dangerous.
Bru. Or else were this a savage spectacle.
Our reasons are so full of good regard   225
That were you, Antony, the son of Cæsar,
You should be satisfied.
Ant.   That's all I seek;
And am moreover suitor that I may
Produce his body to the market-place

And, in the pulpit, as becomes a friend, 230
Speak in the order of his funeral.
  Bru. You shall, Mark Antony.
  Cas.   Brutus, a word with you.
[*Aside to Brutus*] You know not what you
  do. Do not consent
That Antony speak in his funeral.
Know you how much the people may be
  mov'd   235
By that which he will utter ?
  Bru. [*Aside to Cassius*] By your pardon—
I will myself into the pulpit first,
And show the reason of our Cæsar's
  death.
What Antony shall speak, I will protest
He speaks by leave and by permission ; 240
And that we are contented Cæsar shall
Have all true rites and lawful ceremonies.
It shall advantage more than do us wrong.
  Cas. I know not what may fall I like it
  not.
  Bru. Mark Antony, here, take you
  Cæsar's body.   245
You shall not in your funeral speech blame
  us,
But speak all good you can devise of
  Cæsar ;
And say you do't by our permission ;
Else shall you not have any hand at all
About his funeral. And you shall speak 250
In the same pulpit whereto I am going,
After my speech is ended.
  Ant.   Be it so ;
I do desire no more.
  Bru. Prepare the body then, and follow
  us.   [*Exeunt all but Antony.*
  Ant. O, pardon me, thou bleeding piece
  of earth,   255
That I am meek and gentle with these
  butchers !
Thou art the ruins of the noblest man
That ever lived in the tide of times.
Woe to the hand that shed this costly
  blood !
Over thy wounds now do I prophesy— 260
Which like dumb mouths do ope their
  ruby lips
To beg the voice and utterance of my
  tongue—
A curse shall light upon the limbs of men ;
Domestic fury and fierce civil strife
Shall cumber all the parts of Italy ;   265
Blood and destruction shall be so in use,
And dreadful objects so familiar,
That mothers shall but smile when they
  behold
Their infants quartered with the hands of
  war,   269
All pity chok'd with custom of fell deeds ;
And Cæsar's spirit, ranging for revenge,
With Até by his side come hot from hell,
Shall in these confines with a monarch's
  voice
Cry ' Havoc ! ' and let slip the dogs of war,

That this foul deed shall smell above the
  earth   275
With carrion men, groaning for burial.

        Enter Octavius' Servant.

You serve Octavius Cæsar, do you not ?
  Serv. I do, Mark Antony.
  Ant. Cæsar did write for him to come to
  Rome.
  Serv. He did receive his letters, and is
  coming,   280
And bid me say to you by word of mouth—
O Cæsar !   [*Seeing the body.*
  Ant. Thy heart is big, get thee apart and
  weep.
Passion, I see, is catching ; for mine eyes,
Seeing those beads of sorrow stand in thine,
Began to water. Is thy master coming ?
  Serv. He lies to-night within seven leagues
  of Rome.
  Ant. Post back with speed, and tell him
  what hath chanc'd.
Here is a mourning Rome, a dangerous
  Rome,
No Rome of safety for Octavius yet ;   290
Hie hence and tell him so. Yet stay awhile ;
Thou shalt not back till I have borne this
  corse
Into the market-place. There shall I try,
In my oration, how the people take
The cruel issue of these bloody men ;   295
According to the which thou shalt discourse
To young Octavius of the state of things.
Lend me your hand.
         [*Exeunt with Cæsar's body.*

    Scene II. *Rome. The Forum.*

  Enter Brutus *and* Cassius, *with the*
    Plebeians.

  Citizens. We will be satisfied ! Let us be
  satisfied !
  Bru. Then follow me, and give me
  audience, friends.
Cassius, go you into the other street,
And part the numbers.
Those that will hear me speak, let 'em stay
  here ;   5
Those that will follow Cassius, go with him ;
And public reasons shall be rendered
Of Cæsar's death.
  1 *Pleb.*   I will hear Brutus speak.
  2 *Pleb.* I will hear Cassius, and compare
  their reasons,
When severally we hear them rendered. 10
   [*Exit Cassius, with some of the Plebeians.*
        Brutus goes into the pulpit.
  3 *Pleb.* The noble Brutus is ascended.
  Silence !
  Bru. Be patient till the last.
Romans, countrymen, and lovers ! hear me
for my cause, and be silent, that you may
hear. Believe me for mine honour, and
have respect to mine honour, that you may

believe. Censure me in your wisdom, and
awake your senses, that you may the better
judge. If there be any in this assembly, any
dear friend of Cæsar's, to him I say that
Brutus' love to Cæsar was no less than his.
If then that friend demand why Brutus
rose against Cæsar, this is my answer:
Not that I lov'd Cæsar less, but that I
lov'd Rome more. Had you rather Cæsar
were living, and die all slaves, than that
Cæsar were dead, to live all free men? As
Cæsar lov'd me, I weep for him; as he was
fortunate, I rejoice at it; as he was valiant,
I honour him; but—as he was ambitious,
I slew him. There is tears for his love; joy
for his fortune; honour for his valour;
and death for his ambition. Who is here
so base that would be a bondman? If any,
speak; for him have I offended. Who is
here so rude that would not be a Roman?
If any, speak; for him have I offended.
Who is here so vile that will not love his
country? If any, speak; for him have I
offended. I pause for a reply.

All. None, Brutus, none. 34

Bru. Then none have I offended. I have
done no more to Cæsar than you shall do
to Brutus. The question of his death is
enroll'd in the Capitol; his glory not
extenuated, wherein he was worthy; nor
his offences enforc'd, for which he suffered
death. 39

Enter MARK ANTONY *and* Others *with
Cæsar's body.*

Here comes his body, mourn'd by Mark
Antony, who, though he had no hand in
his death, shall receive the benefit of his
dying, a place in the commonwealth, as
which of you shall not? With this I depart,
that, as I slew my best lover for the good
of Rome, I have the same dagger for myself, when it shall please my country to
need my death. 46

All. Live, Brutus! live, live!

1 *Pleb.* Bring him with triumph home
unto his house.

2 *Pleb.* Give him a statue with his
ancestors.

3 *Pleb.* Let him be Cæsar.

4 *Pleb.* Cæsar's better parts 50
Shall be crown'd in Brutus.

1 *Pleb.* We'll bring him to his house with
shouts and clamours.

Bru. My countrymen—

2 *Pleb.* Peace, silence! Brutus speaks.

1 *Pleb.* Peace, ho!

Bru. Good countrymen, let me depart
alone, 55
And for my sake stay here with Antony.
Do grace to Cæsar's corpse, and grace his
speech
Tending to Cæsar's glories, which Mark
Antony,

By our permission, is allow'd to make.
I do entreat you, not a man depart 60
Save I alone, till Antony have spoke. [*Exit.*

1 *Pleb.* Stay, ho! and let us hear Mark
Antony.

3 *Pleb.* Let him go up into the public chair.
We'll hear him. Noble Antony, go up.

Ant. For Brutus' sake I am beholding
to you. [*Goes up.* 65

4 *Pleb.* What does he say of Brutus?

3 *Pleb.* He says, for Brutus' sake
He finds himself beholding to us all.

4 *Pleb.* 'Twere best he speak no harm of
Brutus here.

1 *Pleb.* This Cæsar was a tyrant.

3 *Pleb.* Nay, that's certain.
We are blest that Rome is rid of him. 70

2 *Pleb.* Peace! let us hear what Antony
can say.

Ant. You gentle Romans—

All. Peace, ho! let us hear him.

Ant. Friends, Romans, countrymen, lend
me your ears;
I come to bury Cæsar, not to praise him.
The evil that men do lives after them; 75
The good is oft interred with their bones;
So let it be with Cæsar. The noble Brutus
Hath told you Cæsar was ambitious.
If it were so, it was a grievous fault;
And grievously hath Cæsar answer'd it. 80
Here, under leave of Brutus and the rest—
For Brutus is an honourable man;
So are they all, all honourable men—
Come I to speak in Cæsar's funeral.
He was my friend, faithful and just to
me;
But Brutus says he was ambitious, 86
And Brutus is an honourable man.
He hath brought many captives home to
Rome,
Whose ransoms did the general coffers fill;
Did this in Cæsar seem ambitious? 90
When that the poor have cried, Cæsar hath
wept;
Ambition should be made of sterner stuff.
Yet Brutus says he was ambitious;
And Brutus is an honourable man.
You all did see that on the Lupercal 95
I thrice presented him a kingly crown,
Which he did thrice refuse. Was this
ambition?
Yet Brutus says he was ambitious;
And sure he is an honourable man. 99
I speak not to disprove what Brutus spoke,
But here I am to speak what I do know.
You all did love him once, not without
cause;
What cause withholds you, then, to mourn
for him?
O judgment, thou art fled to brutish beasts,
And men have lost their reason! Bear with
me; 105
My heart is in the coffin there with Cæsar,
And I must pause till it come back to me.

1 Pleb. Methinks there is much reason in his sayings.

2 Pleb. If thou consider rightly of the matter,

Cæsar has had great wrong.

3 Pleb.   Has he, masters! 110

I fear there will a worse come in his place.

4 Pleb. Mark'd ye his words? He would not take the crown;

Therefore 'tis certain he was not ambitious.

1 Pleb. If it be found so, some will dear abide it.

2 Pleb. Poor soul! his eyes are red as fire with weeping.   115

3 Pleb. There's not a nobler man in Rome than Antony.

4 Pleb. Now mark him, he begins again to speak.

Ant. But yesterday the word of Cæsar might

Have stood against the world: now lies he there,

And none so poor to do him reverence. 120

O masters, if I were dispos'd to stir

Your hearts and minds to mutiny and rage,

I should do Brutus wrong, and Cassius wrong,

Who, you all know, are honourable men.

I will not do them wrong; I rather choose

To wrong the dead, to wrong myself and you,   126

Than I will wrong such honourable men.

But here's a parchment with the seal of Cæsar;

I found it in his closet—'tis his will.   129

Let but the commons hear this testament,

Which, pardon me, I do not mean to read,

And they would go and kiss dead Cæsar's wounds

And dip their napkins in his sacred blood;

Yea, beg a hair of him for memory

And, dying, mention it within their wills, 135

Bequeathing it as a rich legacy

Unto their issue.

4 Pleb. We'll hear the will. Read it, Mark Antony.

All. The will, the will! We will hear Cæsar's will.

Ant. Have patience, gentle friends, I must not read it;   140

It is not meet you know how Cæsar lov'd you.

You are not wood, you are not stones, but men;

And being men, hearing the will of Cæsar,

It will inflame you, it will make you mad.

'Tis good you know not that you are his heirs;   145

For if you should, O, what would come of it?

4 Pleb. Read the will; we'll hear it, Antony!

You shall read us the will—Cæsar's will.

Ant. Will you be patient? Will you stay awhile?

I have o'ershot myself to tell you of it. 150

I fear I wrong the honourable men

Whose daggers have stabb'd Cæsar; I do fear it.

4 Pleb. They were traitors. Honourable men!

All. The will! the testament!

2 Pleb. They were villains, murderers. The will! Read the will.   156

Ant. You will compel me, then, to read the will?

Then make a ring about the corpse of Cæsar,

And let me show you him that made the will.

Shall I descend? and will you give me leave?   160

All. Come down.

2 Pleb. Descend.   [*Antony comes down.*

3 Pleb. You shall have leave.

4 Pleb. A ring! Stand round.

1 Pleb. Stand from the hearse, stand from the body.

2 Pleb. Room for Antony, most noble Antony!   166

Ant. Nay, press not so upon me; stand far off.

All. Stand back. Room! Bear back.

Ant. If you have tears, prepare to shed them now.   169

You all do know this mantle. I remember

The first time ever Cæsar put it on;

'Twas on a summer's evening, in his tent,

That day he overcame the Nervii.

Look! in this place ran Cassius' dagger through;   174

See what a rent the envious Casca made;

Through this the well-beloved Brutus stabb'd,

And as he pluck'd his cursed steel away,

Mark how the blood of Cæsar follow'd it,

As rushing out of doors, to be resolv'd

If Brutus so unkindly knock'd or no; 180

For Brutus, as you know, was Cæsar's angel.

Judge, O you gods, how dearly Cæsar lov'd him!

This was the most unkindest cut of all;

For when the noble Cæsar saw him stab,

Ingratitude, more strong than traitors' arms,   185

Quite vanquish'd him. Then burst his mighty heart;

And in his mantle muffling up his face,

Even at the base of Pompey's statua,

Which all the while ran blood, great Cæsar fell.   189

O, what a fall was there, my countrymen!

Then I, and you, and all of us fell down,

Whilst bloody treason flourish'd over us.

O, now you weep, and I perceive you feel

The dint of pity. These are gracious drops.

Kind souls, what weep you when you but
   behold   195
Our Cæsar's vesture wounded ? Look you
   here,
Here is himself, marr'd as you see with
   traitors.
  1 Pleb. O piteous spectacle !
  2 Pleb. O noble Cæsar !
  3 Pleb. O woeful day !   200
  4 Pleb. O traitors, villains !
  1 Pleb. O most bloody sight !
  2 Pleb. We will be reveng'd.
  All. Revenge ! About ! Seek ! Burn !
Fire ! Kill ! Slay ! Let not a traitor
live !   205
  Ant. Stay, countrymen.
  1 Pleb. Peace there ! Hear the noble
Antony.
  2 Pleb. We'll hear him, we'll follow him,
we'll die with him.
  Ant. Good friends, sweet friends, let me
not stir you up   210
To such a sudden flood of mutiny.
They that have done this deed are honour-
   able.
What private griefs they have, alas, I know
   not,
That made them do it ; they are wise and
   honourable,
And will, no doubt, with reasons answer
   you.   215
I come not, friends, to steal away your
   hearts ;
I am no orator, as Brutus is,
But, as you know me all, a plain blunt man,
That love my friend ; and that they know
   full well   219
That gave me public leave to speak of him.
For I have neither wit, nor words, nor
   worth,
Action, nor utterance, nor the power of
   speech,
To stir men's blood ; I only speak right on.
I tell you that which you yourselves do
   know ;
Show you sweet Cæsar's wounds, poor poor
   dumb mouths,
And bid them speak for me. But were I
   Brutus,   226
And Brutus Antony, there were an Antony
Would ruffle up your spirits, and put a
   tongue
In every wound of Cæsar, that should move
The stones of Rome to rise and mutiny. 230
  All. We'll mutiny.
  1 Pleb. We'll burn the house of Brutus.
  3 Pleb. Away, then ! Come seek the
conspirators.
  Ant. Yet hear me, countrymen ; yet hear
me speak.
  All. Peace, ho ! Hear Antony, most
noble Antony.
  Ant. Why, friends, you go to do you
know not what.

Wherein hath Cæsar thus deserv'd your
   loves ?   237
Alas, you know not ! I must tell you, then :
You have forgot the will I told you of.
  All. Most true. The will ! Let's stay and
hear the will.   240
  Ant. Here is the will, and under Cæsar's
seal :
To every Roman citizen he gives,
To every several man, seventy-five drach-
   mas.
  2 Pleb. Most noble Cæsar ! We'll revenge
his death.
  3 Pleb. O royal Cæsar !   245
  Ant. Hear me with patience.
  All. Peace, ho !
  Ant. Moreover, he hath left you all his
   walks,
His private arbours, and new-planted
   orchards,   249
On this side Tiber ; he hath left them you,
And to your heirs for ever—common
   pleasures,
To walk abroad and recreate yourselves.
Here was a Cæsar ! When comes such
   another ?
  1 Pleb. Never, never ! Come away, away !
We'll burn his body in the holy place, 255
And with the brands fire the traitors'
   houses.
Take up the body.
  2 Pleb. Go, fetch fire.
  3 Pleb. Pluck down benches.
  4 Pleb. Pluck down forms, windows, any
thing.   [*Exeunt Plebeians with the body.*
  Ant. Now let it work. Mischief, thou art
afoot,   261
Take thou what course thou wilt.

Enter a Servant.

                How now, fellow !
  Serv. Sir, Octavius is already come to
Rome.
  Ant. Where is he ?
  Serv. He and Lepidus are at Cæsar's
house.   265
  Ant. And thither will I straight to visit
him.
He comes upon a wish. Fortune is merry,
And in this mood will give us any thing.
  Serv. I heard him say Brutus and Cassius
Are rid like madmen through the gates of
Rome.   270
  Ant. Belike they had some notice of the
people,
How I had mov'd them. Bring me to
Octavius.   [*Exeunt.*

SCENE III. *Rome. A street.*

Enter CINNA *the Poet, and after him the*
Plebeians.

  Cin. I dreamt to-night that I did feast
with Cæsar,

And things unluckily charge my fantasy.
I have no will to wander forth of doors,
Yet something leads me forth.

1 Pleb. What is your name ?   5
2 Pleb. Whither are you going ?
3 Pleb. Where do you dwell ?
4 Pleb. Are you a married man or a bachelor ?
2 Pleb. Answer every man directly.
1 Pleb. Ay, and briefly.   10
4 Pleb. Ay, and wisely.
3 Pleb. Ay, and truly, you were best.
Cin. What is my name ? Whither am I going ? Where do I dwell ? Am I a married man or a bachelor ? Then to answer every man directly and briefly, wisely and truly : wisely, I say I am a bachelor.   16
2 Pleb. That's as much as to say they are fools that marry. You'll bear me a bang for that, I fear. Proceed directly.
Cin. Directly, I am going to Cæsar's funeral.   20
1 Pleb. As a friend or an enemy ?
Cin. As a friend.
2 Pleb. That matter is answered directly.
4 Pleb. For your dwelling—briefly.
Cin. Briefly, I dwell by the Capitol.   25
3 Pleb. Your name, sir, truly.
Cin. Truly, my name is Cinna.
1 Pleb. Tear him to pieces ; he's a conspirator !
Cin. I am Cinna the poet, I am Cinna the poet.
4 Pleb. Tear him for his bad verses, tear him for his bad verses !   31
Cin. I am not Cinna the conspirator.
4 Pleb. It is no matter, his name's Cinna ; pluck but his name out of his heart, and turn him going.
3 Pleb. Tear him, tear him ! Come, brands, ho ! fire-brands ! To Brutus', to Cassius' ! Burn all ! Some to Decius' house, and some to Casca's ; some to Ligarius'. Away, go !   38
[Exeunt all the Plebeians with Cinna.

ACT FOUR

Scene I. *Rome. Antony's house.*

Enter Antony, Octavius, *and* Lepidus.

Ant. These many, then, shall die ; their names are prick'd.
Oct. Your brother too must die. Consent you, Lepidus ?
Lep. I do consent.
Oct.   Prick him down, Antony.
Lep. Upon condition Publius shall not live,
Who is your sister's son, Mark Antony.   5
Ant. He shall not live ; look, with a spot I damn him.
But, Lepidus, go you to Cæsar's house ;
Fetch the will hither, and we shall determine
How to cut off some charge in legacies.

Lep. What, shall I find you here ?   10
Oct. Or here or at the Capitol.
[Exit Lepidus.
Ant. This is a slight unmeritable man,
Meet to be sent on errands. Is it fit,
The threefold world divided, he should stand
One of the three to share it ?
Oct.   So you thought him,   15
And took his voice who should be prick'd to die
In our black sentence and proscription.
Ant. Octavius, I have seen more days than you ;
And though we lay these honours on this man,   19
To ease ourselves of divers sland'rous loads,
He shall but bear them as the ass bears gold,
To groan and sweat under the business,
Either led or driven as we point the way ;
And having brought our treasure where we will,
Then take we down his load, and turn him off,   25
Like to the empty ass, to shake his ears
And graze in commons.
Oct.   You may do your will ;
But he's a tried and valiant soldier.
Ant. So is my horse, Octavius, and for that
I do appoint him store of provender.   30
It is a creature that I teach to fight,
To wind, to stop, to run directly on,
His corporal motion govern'd by my spirit.
And, in some taste, is Lepidus but so :
He must be taught, and train'd, and bid go forth ;   35
A barren-spirited fellow ; one that feeds
On abjects, orts, and imitations,
Which, out of use and stal'd by other men,
Begin his fashion. Do not talk of him
But as a property. And now, Octavius,   40
Listen great things : Brutus and Cassius
Are levying powers ; we must straight make head ;
Therefore let our alliance be combin'd,
Our best friends made, our means stretch'd ;
And let us presently go sit in council   45
How covert matters may be best disclos'd,
And open perils surest answered.
Oct. Let us do so ; for we are at the stake,
And bay'd about with many enemies ;
And some that smile have in their hearts, I fear,   50
Millions of mischiefs.   *[Exeunt.*

Scene II. *The Camp near Sardis. Before the tent of Brutus.*

Drum. Enter Brutus, Lucilius, Lucius, *and the* Army. Titinius *and* Pindarus *meet them.*

Bru. Stand, ho !
Lucil. Give the word, ho ! and stand.

Bru. What now, Lucilius ? Is Cassius
  near ?
Lucil. He is at hand, and Pindarus is
  come
To do you salutation from his master.   5
Bru. He greets me well. Your master,
  Pindarus,
In his own change, or by ill officers,
Hath given me some worthy cause to wish
Things done undone ; but if he be at hand
I shall be satisfied.
Pin.   I do not doubt   10
But that my noble master will appear
Such as he is, full of regard and honour.
Bru. He is not doubted. A word,
  Lucilius,
How he receiv'd you ; let me be resolv'd.
Lucil. With courtesy and with respect
  enough,   15
But not with such familiar instances
Nor with such free and friendly conference
As he hath us'd of old.
Bru.   Thou hast describ'd
A hot friend cooling. Ever note, Lucilius,
When love begins to sicken and decay,   20
It useth an enforced ceremony.
There are no tricks in plain and simple
  faith ;
But hollow men, like horses hot at hand,
Make gallant show and promise of their
  mettle ;
But when they should endure the bloody
  spur,   25
They fall their crests, and like deceitful
  jades
Sink in the trial. Comes his army on ?
Lucil. They mean this night in Sardis to
  be quarter'd.
The greater part, the horse in general,
Are come with Cassius.   [*Low march within.*
Bru.   Hark ! he is arriv'd :   30
March gently on to meet him.

Enter CASSIUS *and his* Powers.

Cas. Stand, ho !
Bru. Stand, ho ! Speak the word along.
1 *Sold.* Stand !
2 *Sold.* Stand !   35
3 *Sold.* Stand !
Cas. Most noble brother, you have done
  me wrong.
Bru. Judge me, you gods ! wrong I mine
  enemies ?
And, if not so, how should I wrong a
  brother ?
Cas. Brutus, this sober form of yours
  hides wrongs ;   40
And when you do them—
Bru.   Cassius, be content ;
Speak your griefs softly ; I do know you
  well.
Before the eyes of both our armies here,
Which should perceive nothing but love
  from us,

Let us not wrangle. Bid them move away ;
Then in my tent, Cassius, enlarge your
  griefs,   46
And I will give you audience.
Cas.   Pindarus,
Bid our commanders lead their charges off
A little from this ground.
Bru. Lucilius, do you the like ; and let
  no man   50
Come to our tent till we have done our con-
  ference.
Let Lucius and Titinius guard our door.
                       [*Exeunt.*

SCENE III. *The Camp near Sardis. Within
the tent of Brutus.*

Enter BRUTUS *and* CASSIUS.

Cas. That you have wrong'd me doth
  appear in this :
You have condemn'd and noted Lucius
  Pella
For taking bribes here of the Sardians ;
Wherein my letters, praying on his side,   4
Because I knew the man, were slighted off.
Bru. You wrong'd yourself to write in
  such a case.
Cas. In such a time as this it is not meet
That every nice offence should bear his
  comment.
Bru. Let me tell you, Cassius, you your-
  self
Are much condemn'd to have an itching
  palm,   10
To sell and mart your offices for gold
To undeservers.
Cas.   I an itching palm !
You know that you are Brutus that speaks
  this,
Or, by the gods, this speech were else your
  last.
Bru. The name of Cassius honours this
  corruption,   15
And chastisement doth therefore hide his
  head.
Cas. Chastisement !
Bru. Remember March, the ides of
  March remember :
Did not great Julius bleed for justice sake ?
What villain touch'd his body, that did
  stab,   20
And not for justice ? What, shall one of us,
That struck the foremost man of all this
  world
But for supporting robbers, shall we now
Contaminate our fingers with base bribes,
And sell the mighty space of our large
  honours   25
For so much trash as may be grasped thus ?
I had rather be a dog and bay the moon
Than such a Roman.
Cas.   Brutus, bait not me !
I'll not endure it. You forget yourself,
To hedge me in. I am a soldier, I,   30

Mes. Then like a Roman bear the truth
    I tell:
For certain she is dead, and by strange
    manner.
    Bru. Why, farewell, Portia. We must
    die, Messala.
With meditating that she must die once,
I have the patience to endure it now.   190
    Mes. Even so great men great losses
    should endure.
    Cas. I have as much of this in art as you,
But yet my nature could not bear it so.
    Bru. Well, to our work alive. What do
    you think
Of marching to Philippi presently?   195
    Cas. I do not think it good.
    Bru.   Your reason?
    Cas.   This it is:
'Tis better that the enemy seek us;
So shall he waste his means, weary his
    soldiers,
Doing himself offence, whilst we, lying
    still,
Are full of rest, defence, and nimbleness.   200
    Bru. Good reasons must, of force, give
    place to better.
The people 'twixt Philippi and this ground
Do stand but in a forc'd affection;
For they have grudg'd us contribution.
The enemy, marching along by them,   205
By them shall make a fuller number up,
Come on refresh'd, new-added, and en-
    courag'd;
From which advantage shall we cut him
    off,
If at Philippi we do face him there,
These people at our back.
    Cas.   Hear me, good brother.   210
    Bru. Under your pardon. You must note
    beside
That we have tried the utmost of our
    friends,
Our legions are brim full, our cause is ripe.
The enemy increaseth every day:
We, at the height, are ready to decline.   215
There is a tide in the affairs of men
Which, taken at the flood, leads on to
    fortune;
Omitted, all the voyage of their life
Is bound in shallows and in miseries.
On such a full sea are we now afloat,   220
And we must take the current when it
    serves,
Or lose our ventures.
    Cas.   Then, with your will, go on;
We'll along ourselves and meet them at
    Philippi.
    Bru. The deep of night is crept upon our
    talk,
And nature must obey necessity,   225
Which we will niggard with a little rest.
There is no more to say?
    Cas.   No more. Good night:
Early to-morrow will we rise, and hence.

    Bru. Lucius! [*Enter* LUCIUS] My gown.
    [*Exit Lucius*] Farewell, good Messala.
Good night, Titinius. Noble, noble Cassius,
Good night, and good repose!
    Cas.   O my dear brother,
This was an ill beginning of the night!
Never come such division 'tween our souls!
Let it not, Brutus.
    Bru.   Everything is well.   234
    Cas. Good night, my lord.
    Bru.   Good night, good brother.
    Tit. and Mes. Good night, Lord Brutus.
    Bru.   Farewell, every one.
    [*Exeunt Cassius, Titinius, and Messala.*

    Re-enter LUCIUS *with the gown.*

Give me the gown. Where is thy instru-
    ment?
    Luc. Here in the tent.
    Bru.   What, thou speak'st drowsily?
Poor knave, I blame thee not; thou art
    o'erwatch'd.
Call Claudius and some other of my men;   240
I'll have them sleep on cushions in my tent.
    Luc. Varro and Claudius!

    Enter VARRO *and* CLAUDIUS.

    Var. Calls my lord?
    Bru. I pray you, sirs, lie in my tent and
    sleep;
It may be I shall raise you by and by   245
On business to my brother Cassius.
    Var. So please you we will stand and
    watch your pleasure.
    Bru. I will not have it so. Lie down, good
    sirs;
It may be I shall otherwise bethink me.
Look, Lucius, here's the book I sought
    for so;   250
I put it in the pocket of my gown.
    [*Varro and Claudius lie down.*
    Luc. I was sure your lordship did not
    give it me.
    Bru. Bear with me, good boy, I am much
    forgetful.
Canst thou hold up thy heavy eyes awhile,
And touch thy instrument a strain or two?
    Luc. Ay, my lord, an't please you.
    Bru.   It does, my boy.
I trouble thee too much, but thou art
    willing.   257
    Luc. It is my duty, sir.
    Bru. I should not urge thy duty past thy
    might;
I know young bloods look for a time of
    rest.
    Luc. I have slept, my lord, already.   261
    Bru. It was well done; and thou shalt
    sleep again;
I will not hold thee long. If I do live,
I will be good to thee.
    [*Music and a song. Lucius falls asleep.*
This is a sleepy tune. O murd'rous slumber!
Layest thou thy leaden mace upon my boy,

That plays thee music ? Gentle knave, good
    night.   267
I will not do thee so much wrong to wake
    thee.
If thou dost nod, thou break'st thy instru-
    ment ;
I'll take it from thee ; and, good boy,
    good night.   270
Let me see, let me see ; is not the leaf
    turn'd down
Where I left reading ? Here it is, I think.
                     [*Sits down.*

Enter the Ghost of CÆSAR.

How ill this taper burns ! Ha ! who comes
    here ?
I think it is the weakness of mine eyes
That shapes this monstrous apparition. 275
It comes upon me.   Art thou any thing ?
Art thou some god, some angel, or some
    devil,
That mak'st my blood cold and my hair to
    stare ?
Speak to me what thou art.
  Ghost. Thy evil spirit, Brutus.
  Bru.   Why com'st thou ? 280
  Ghost. To tell thee thou shalt see me at
    Philippi.
  Bru. Well ; then I shall see thee again ?
  Ghost. Ay, at Philippi.
  Bru. Why, I will see thee at Philippi,
    then.   [*Exit Ghost.*
Now I have taken heart thou vanishest. 285
Ill spirit, I would hold more talk with
    thee.
Boy ! Lucius ! Varro ! Claudius ! Sirs,
    awake !
Claudius !
  Luc. The strings, my lord, are false.
  Bru. He thinks he still is at his instru-
    ment.   290
Lucius, awake !
  Luc. My lord !
  Bru. Didst thou dream, Lucius, that
    thou so criedst out ?
  Luc. My lord, I do not know that I did
    cry.
  Bru. Yes, that thou didst. Didst thou see
    any thing ?
  Luc. Nothing, my lord.   296
  Bru. Sleep again, Lucius. Sirrah Claud-
    ius !
[*To Varro*] Fellow thou, awake !
  Var. My lord ?
  Clau. My lord ?   300
  Bru. Why did you so cry out, sirs, in
    your sleep ?
  Both. Did we, my lord ?
  Bru.   Ay. Saw you any thing ?
  Var. No, my lord, I saw nothing.
  Clau.   Nor I, my lord.
  Bru. Go and commend me to my brother
    Cassius ;   304
Bid him set on his pow'rs betimes before,

And we will follow.
  Var. and Clau. It shall be done, my lord.
                       [*Exeunt.*

ACT FIVE

SCENE I. *Near Philippi.*

Enter OCTAVIUS, ANTONY, *and their* Army.

  Oct. Now, Antony, our hopes are
    answered.
You said the enemy would not come down,
But keep the hills and upper regions ;
It proves not so. Their battles are at hand ;
They mean to warn us at Philippi here, 5
Answering before we do demand of them.
  Ant. Tut, I am in their bosoms, and I
    know
Wherefore they do it.   They could be
    content
To visit other places, and come down   9
With fearful bravery, thinking by this face
To fasten in our thoughts that they have
    courage ;
But 'tis not so.

Enter a Messenger.

  Mess.   Prepare you, generals :
The enemy comes on in gallant show ;
Their bloody sign of battle is hung out,
And something to be done immediately. 15
  Ant. Octavius, lead your battle softly on,
Upon the left hand of the even field.
  Oct. Upon the right hand I : keep thou
    the left.
  Ant. Why do you cross me in this
    exigent ?   19
  Oct. I do not cross you ; but I will do so.
                       [*March.*

Drum. Enter BRUTUS, CASSIUS, *and their*
    Army ; LUCILIUS, TITINIUS, MESSALA,
        and Others.

  Bru. They stand, and would have parley.
  Cas. Stand fast, Titinius ; we must out
    and talk.
  Oct. Mark Antony, shall we give sign of
    battle ?
  Ant. No, Cæsar, we will answer on their
    charge.
Make forth ; the generals would have some
    words.   25
  Oct. Stir not until the signal.
  Bru. Words before blows.   Is it so,
    countrymen ?
  Oct. Not that we love words better, as
    you do.
  Bru. Good words are better than bad
    strokes, Octavius.
  Ant. In your bad strokes, Brutus, you
    give good words ;   30
Witness the hole you made in Cæsar's heart,
Crying ' Long live ! Hail, Cæsar ! '
  Cas.   Antony,
The posture of your blows are yet unknown ;

But for your words, they rob the Hybla
    bees,
And leave them honeyless.
    Ant.   Not stingless too ? 35
    Bru. O yes, and soundless too ;
For you have stol'n their buzzing, Antony,
And very wisely threat before you sting.
    Ant. Villains, you did not so when your
    vile daggers
Hack'd one another in the sides of Cæsar. 40
You show'd your teeth like apes, and
    fawn'd like hounds,
And bow'd like bondmen, kissing Cæsar's
    feet ;
Whilst damned Casca, like a cur, behind
Struck Cæsar on the neck. O you flatterers !
    Cas. Flatterers ! Now, Brutus, thank
    yourself : 45
This tongue had not offended so to-day
If Cassius might have rul'd.
    Oct. Come, come, the cause. If arguing
    make us sweat,
The proof of it will turn to redder drops.
Look, 50
I draw a sword against conspirators ;
When think you that the sword goes up
    again ?
Never till Cæsar's three and thirty wounds
Be well aveng'd, or till another Cæsar
Have added slaughter to the sword of
    traitors. 55
    Bru. Cæsar, thou canst not die by
    traitors' hands,
Unless thou bring'st them with thee.
    Oct.   So I hope.
I was not born to die on Brutus' sword.
    Bru. O, if thou wert the noblest of thy
    strain,
Young man, thou couldst not die more
    honourable. 60
    Cas. A peevish schoolboy, worthless of
    such honour,
Join'd with a masker and a reveller !
    Ant. Old Cassius still !
    Oct.   Come, Antony ; away !
Defiance, traitors, hurl we in your teeth.
If you dare fight to-day, come to the field ;
If not, when you have stomachs. [*Exeunt
    Octavius, Antony, and their Army.*
    Cas. Why, now, blow wind, swell billow,
    and swim bark ! 67
The storm is up, and all is on the hazard.
    Bru. Ho, Lucilius ! hark, a word with
    you.
    Lucil. My lord.
    [*Brutus and Lucilius converse apart.*
    Cas. Messala.
    Mes.   What says my general ?
    Cas.   Messala, 70
This is my birth-day ; as this very day
Was Cassius born. Give me thy hand
    Messala.
Be thou my witness that against my will,
As Pompey was, am I compell'd to set

Upon one battle all our liberties. 75
You know that I held Epicurus strong,
And his opinion ; now I change my mind,
And partly credit things that do presage.
Coming from Sardis, on our former ensign
Two mighty eagles fell ; and there they
    perch'd, 80
Gorging and feeding from our soldiers'
    hands,
Who to Philippi here consorted us.
This morning are they fled away and gone,
And in their steads do ravens, crows, and
    kites,
Fly o'er our heads and downward look
    on us 85
As we were sickly prey. Their shadows
    seem
A canopy most fatal, under which
Our army lies, ready to give up the ghost.
    Mes. Believe not so.
    Cas.   I but believe it partly ;
For I am fresh of spirit and resolv'd 90
To meet all perils very constantly.
    Bru. Even so, Lucilius.
    Cas.   Now, most noble Brutus,
The gods to-day stand friendly, that we
    may,
Lovers in peace, lead on our days to age !
But, since the affairs of men rest still in-
    certain, 95
Let's reason with the worst that may befall.
If we do lose this battle, then is this
The very last time we shall speak together.
What are you then determined to do ? 99
    Bru. Even by the rule of that philosophy
By which I did blame Cato for the death
Which he did give himself—I know not
    how,
But I do find it cowardly and vile,
For fear of what might fall, so to prevent
The time of life—arming myself with
    patience 105
To stay the providence of some high powers
That govern us below.
    Cas.   Then, if we lose this battle,
You are contented to be led in triumph
Thorough the streets of Rome ?
    Bru. No, Cassius, no. Think not, thou
    noble Roman, 110
That ever Brutus will go **bound** to Rome ;
He bears too great a mind. **But this** same
    day
Must end that work the **ides of** March
    begun,
And whether we shall meet again **I know**
    not.
Therefore our everlasting farewell take : 115
For ever and for ever farewell, Cassius !
If we do meet again, why, we shall smile ;
If not, why then this parting was well made.
    Cas. For ever and for ever farewell,
    Brutus !
If we do meet again, we'll smile indeed ; 120
If not, 'tis true this parting was well made.

Bru. Why then, lead on. O that a man
    might know
The end of this day's business ere it come !
But it sufficeth that the day will end, 124
And then the end is known. Come, ho !
    away !   [*Exeunt.*

SCENE II. *Near Philippi. The field of
    battle.*

Alarum. Enter BRUTUS *and* MESSALA.

Bru. Ride, ride, Messala, ride, and give
    these bills
Unto the legions on the other side .
                            [*Loud alarum.*
Let them set on at once ; for I perceive
But cold demeanour in Octavius' wing, 4
And sudden push gives them the overthrow.
Ride, ride, Messala ; let them all come
    down.   [*Exeunt.*

SCENE III. *Another part of the field.*

Alarums. Enter CASSIUS *and* TITINIUS.

Cas. O, look, Titinius, look, the villains
    fly !
Myself have to mine own turn'd enemy.
This ensign here of mine was turning back ;
I slew the coward, and did take it from him.
    Tit. O Cassius, Brutus gave the word too
        early,   5
Who, having some advantage on Octavius,
Took it too eagerly. His soldiers fell to
    spoil,
Whilst we by Antony are all enclos'd.

Enter PINDARUS.

Pin. Fly further off, my lord, fly further
    off ;
Mark Antony is in your tents, my lord ; 10
Fly, therefore, noble Cassius, fly far off.
    Cas. This hill is far enough. Look, look,
        Titinius.
Are those my tents where I perceive the fire?
    Tit. They are, my lord.
    Cas.   Titinius, if thou lovest me,
Mount thou my horse and hide thy spurs
    in him,   15
Till he have brought thee up to yonder
    troops
And here again, 'that I may rest assur'd
Whether yond troops are friend or enemy.
    Tit. I will be here again even with a
        thought.   [*Exit.*
    Cas. Go, Pindarus, get higher on that
        hill ;   20
My sight was ever thick ; regard Titinius,
And tell me what thou not'st about the
    field.   [*Pindarus goes up.*
This day I breathed first. Time is come
    round,
And where I did begin there shall I end ;
My life is run his compass. Sirrah, what
    news ?   25

Pin. [*Above*] O my lord !
Cas. What news ?
Pin. Titinius is enclosed round about
With horsemen that make to him on the
    spur ;
Yet he spurs on. Now they are almost on
    him.   30
Now Titinius ! Now some light. O, he
    lights too !
He's ta'en.   [*Shout.*
And hark ! They shout for joy.
    Cas. Come down ; behold no more.
O, coward that I am to live so long   34
To see my best friend ta'en before my face !

Enter PINDARUS.

Come hither, sirrah.
In Parthia did I take thee prisoner ;
And then I swore thee, saving of thy life,
That whatsoever I did bid thee do
Thou shouldst attempt it. Come now, keep
    thine oath ;
Now be a freeman, and with this good
    sword,   41
That ran through Cæsar's bowels, search
    this bosom.
Stand not to answer ; here, take thou the
    hilts ;
And when my face is cover'd, as 'tis now,
Guide thou the sword. [*Pindarus stabs him.*
                    Cæsar, thou art reveng'd, 45
Even with the sword that kill'd thee. [*Dies.*
    Pin. So, I am free ; yet would not so
        have been,
Durst I have done my will. O Cassius ! 48
Far from this country Pindarus shall run,
Where never Roman shall take note of him.
                                    [*Exit.*

Re-enter TITINIUS, *with* MESSALA.

Mes. It is but change, Titinius ; for
    Octavius
Is overthrown by noble Brutus' power,
As Cassius' legions are by Antony.
    Tit. These tidings will well comfort
        Cassius.
Mes. Where did you leave him ?
Tit.   All disconsolate, 55
With Pindarus, his bondman, on this hill.
Mes. Is not that he that lies upon the
    ground ?
Tit. He lies not like the living. O my
    heart !
Mes. Is not that he ?
Tit.   No, this was he, Messala ;
But Cassius is no more. O setting sun, 60
As in thy red rays thou dost sink to night,
So in his red blood Cassius' day is set !
The sun of Rome is set. Our day is gone ;
Clouds, dews, and dangers come ; our deeds
    are done.   64
Mistrust of my success hath done this deed.
    Mes. Mistrust of good success hath done
        this deed.

O hateful error, melancholy's child,
Why dost thou show to the apt thoughts of
    men
The things that are not ?   O error, soon
    conceiv'd,
Thou never com'st unto a happy birth,   70
But kill'st the mother that engend'red
    thee !
  Tit. What, Pindarus !   Where art thou,
    Pindarus ?
  Mes. Seek him, Titinius, whilst I go to
    meet
The noble Brutus, thrusting this report
Into his ears.   I may say ' thrusting ' it ; 75
For piercing steel and darts envenomed
Shall be as welcome to the ears of Brutus
As tidings of this sight.
  Tit.   Hie you, Messala,
And I will seek for Pindarus the while.
                              [*Exit Messala.*
Why didst thou send me forth, brave
    Cassius ?   80
Did I not meet thy friends, and did not they
Put on my brows this wreath of victory,
And bid me give it thee ?   Didst thou not
    hear thy shouts ?
Alas, thou hast misconstrued every thing !
But hold thee, take this garland on thy
    brow ;   85
Thy Brutus bid me give it thee, and I
Will do his bidding.   Brutus, come apace,
And see how I regarded Caius Cassius.
By your leave, gods.   This is a Roman's part.
Come, Cassius' sword, and find Titinius'
    heart.   [*Dies.*

Alarum. Re-enter MESSALA, *with* BRUTUS,
    YOUNG CATO, STRATO, VOLUMNIUS,
    and LUCILIUS.

  Bru. Where, where, Messala, doth his
    body lie ?   91
  Mes. Lo yonder, and Titinius mourning it.
  Bru. Titinius' face is upward.
  Cato.   He is slain.
  Bru. O Julius Cæsar, thou art mighty yet !
Thy spirit walks abroad and turns our
    swords   95
In our own proper entrails.   [*Low alarums.*
  Cato.   Brave Titinius !
Look whe'r he have not crown'd dead
    Cassius !
  Bru. Are yet two Romans living such as
    these ?
The last of all the Romans, fare thee well !
It is impossible that ever Rome   100
Should breed thy fellow.   Friends, I owe
    moe tears
To this dead man than you shall see me pay.
I shall find time, Cassius, I shall find time.
Come, therefore, and to Thasos send his
    body.
His funerals shall not be in our camp,   105
Lest it discomfort us.   Lucilius, come ;
And come, young Cato ; let us to the field.

Labeo and Flavius set our battles on.
'Tis three o'clock ; and, Romans, yet ere
    night
We shall try fortune in a second fight.   110
                              [*Exeunt.*

SCENE IV.   *Another part of the field.*

Alarum. Enter BRUTUS, MESSALA, YOUNG
    CATO, LUCILIUS, *and* FLAVIUS.

  Bru. Yet, countrymen, O, yet hold up
    your heads !
  Cato. What bastard doth not ?   Who will
    go with me ?
I will proclaim my name about the field :
I am the son of Marcus Cato, ho !
A foe to tyrants, and my country's friend. 5
I am the son of Marcus Cato, ho !

        Enter Soldiers and fight.

  Bru. And I am Brutus, Marcus Brutus, I
Brutus, my country's friend !   Know me for
    Brutus !   [*Exit.   Young Cato falls.*
  Lucil. O young and noble Cato, art thou
    down ?   9
Why, now thou diest as bravely as Titinius,
And mayst be honour'd, being Cato's son.
  1 Sold. Yield, or thou diest.
  Lucil.   Only I yield to die.
[*Offering money*] There is so much that thou
    wilt kill me straight.   13
Kill Brutus, and be honour'd in his death.
  1 Sold. We must not.   A noble prisoner !

          Enter ANTONY.

  2 Sold. Room, ho !   Tell Antony Brutus
    is ta'en.
  1 Sold. I'll tell the news.   Here comes the
    general.
Brutus is ta'en !   Brutus is ta'en, my lord !
  Ant. Where is he ?
  Lucil. Safe, Antony ; Brutus is safe
    enough.   20
I dare assure thee that no enemy
Shall ever take alive the noble Brutus.
The gods defend him from so great a shame !
When you do find him, or alive or dead,
He will be found like Brutus, like himself.
  Ant. This is not Brutus, friend ; but, I
    assure you,   26
A prize no less in worth.   Keep this man safe ;
Give him all kindness.   I had rather have
Such men my friends than enemies.   Go on,
And see whe'r Brutus be alive or dead ;   30
And bring us word unto Octavius' tent
How everything is chanc'd.   [*Exeunt.*

SCENE V.   *Another part of the field.*

Enter BRUTUS, DARDANIUS, CLITUS,
    STRATO, *and* VOLUMNIUS.

  Bru. Come, poor remains of friends, rest
    on this rock.
  Cli. Statilius show'd the torch-light ; but,
    my lord,

                                           997

He came not back. He is or ta'en or slain.
   Bru. Sit thee down, Clitus. Slaying is the
     word ;
It is a deed in fashion. Hark thee, Clitus. 5
                   [*Whispering.*
   Cli. What, I, my lord ? No, not for all
     the world.
   Bru. Peace, then, no words.
   Cli.   I'll rather kill myself.
   Bru. Hark thee, Dardanius !
   Dar.   Shall I do such a deed ?
   Cli. O Dardanius !
   Dar. O Clitus !   10
   Cli. What ill request did Brutus make
     to thee ?
   Dar. To kill him, Clitus. Look, he
     meditates.
   Cli. Now is that noble vessel full of grief,
That it runs over even at his eyes.
   Bru. Come hither, good Volumnius ; list
     a word.   15
   Vol. What says my lord ?
   Bru.   Why, this, Volumnius :
The ghost of Cæsar hath appear'd to me
Two several times by night—at Sardis once,
And this last night here in Philippi fields.
I know my hour is come.
   Vol.   Not so, my lord. 20
   Bru. Nay, I am sure it is, Volumnius.
Thou seest the world, Volumnius, how it
     goes :
Our enemies have beat us to the pit ;
                   [*Low alarums.*
It is more worthy to leap in ourselves
Than tarry till they push us. Good
     Volumnius,   25
Thou know'st that we two went to school
     together ;
Even for that our love of old, I prithee,
Hold thou my sword-hilts whilst I run on it.
   Vol. That's not an office for a friend, my
     lord.   [*Alarum still.*
   Cli. Fly, fly, my lord ; there is no tarry-
     ing here.   30
   Bru. Farewell to you ; and you ; and
     you, Volumnius.
Strato, thou hast been all this while asleep ;
Farewell to thee too, Strato. Countrymen,
My heart doth joy that yet in all my life
I found no man but he was true to me. 35
I shall have glory by this losing day,
More than Octavius and Mark Antony
By this vile conquest shall attain unto.
So fare you well at once ; for Brutus'
     tongue
Hath almost ended his life's history.   40
Night hangs upon mine eyes ; my bones
     would rest,
That have but labour'd to attain this hour.
     [*Alarum. Cry within ' Fly, fly, fly ! '*

   Cli. Fly, my lord, fly.
   Bru.   Hence ! I will follow.
     [*Exeunt Clitus, Dardanius, and
               Volumnius.*
I prithee, Strato, stay thou by thy lord ;
Thou art a fellow of a good respect ;   45
Thy life hath had some smatch of honour
     in it.
Hold then my sword, and turn away thy
     face,
While I do run upon it. Wilt thou, Strato ?
   Stra. Give me your hand first. Fare you
     well, my lord.
   Bru. Farewell, good Strato. Cæsar, now
     be still.   50
I kill'd not thee with half so good a will.
     [*He runs on his sword, and dies.*

Alarum. Retreat. Enter OCTAVIUS, AN-
TONY, MESSALA, LUCILIUS, *and the* Army.

   Oct. What man is that ?
   Mes. My master's man. Strato, where is
     thy master ?
   Stra. Free from the bondage you are in,
     Messala.
The conquerors can but make a fire of him ;
For Brutus only overcame himself,   56
And no man else hath honour by his death.
   Lucil. So Brutus should be found. I
     thank thee, Brutus,
That thou hast prov'd Lucilius' saying true.
   Oct. All that serv'd Brutus, I will enter-
     tain them.   60
Fellow, wilt thou bestow thy time with me ?
   Stra. Ay, if Messala will prefer me to you.
   Oct. Do so, good Messala.
   Mes. How died my master, Strato ?
   Stra. I held the sword, and he did run
     on it.   65
   Mes. Octavius, then take him to follow
     thee,
That did the latest service to my master.
   Ant. This was the noblest Roman of them
     all.
All the conspirators save only he
Did that they did in envy of great Cæsar ;
He only in a general honest thought   71
And common good to all made one of them.
His life was gentle ; and the elements
So mix'd in him that Nature might stand up
And say to all the world ' This was a man!'
   Oct. According to his virtue let us use
     him,   76
With all respect and rites of burial.
Within my tent his bones to-night shall
     lie,
Most like a soldier, ordered honourably.
So call the field to rest, and let's away 80
To part the glories of this happy day.
                    [*Exeunt.*

MACBETH

DRAMATIS PERSONÆ

DUNCAN, *King of Scotland.*
MALCOLM, }
DONALBAIN, } *his sons.*
MACBETH, }
BANQUO, } *Generals of the King's army.*
MACDUFF, }
LENNOX, }
ROSS, }
MENTEITH, } *Noblemen of Scotland.*
ANGUS, }
CAITHNESS, }
FLEANCE, *son to Banquo.*
SIWARD, *Earl of Northumberland, General of the English forces.*
YOUNG SIWARD, *his son.*
SEYTON, *an officer attending on Macbeth.*
BOY, *son to Macduff.*

A Sergeant.
A Porter.
An Old Man.
An English Doctor.
A Scots Doctor.

LADY MACBETH.
LADY MACDUFF.
Gentlewoman *attending on Lady Macbeth.*

THE WEIRD SISTERS.
HECATE.
The Ghost *of Banquo.*
Apparitions.

Lords, Gentlemen, Officers, Soldiers, Murderers, Attendants, *and* Messengers.

THE SCENE : *Scotland and England.*

ACT ONE

SCENE I. *An open place.*

Thunder and lightning. Enter three Witches.

1 Witch. When shall we three meet again ?
In thunder, lightning, or in rain ?
2 Witch. When the hurlyburly's done,
When the battle's lost and won.
3 Witch. That will be ere the set of sun. 5
1 Witch. Where the place ?
2 Witch. Upon the heath.
3 Witch. There to meet with Macbeth.
1 Witch. I come, Graymalkin.
2 Witch. Paddock calls.
3 Witch. Anon !
All. Fair is foul, and foul is fair : 10
Hover through the fog and filthy air.
[*Witches vanish.*

SCENE II. *A camp near Forres.*

Alarum within. Enter KING DUNCAN,
MALCOLM, DONALBAIN, LENNOX, *with*
Attendants, *meeting a bleeding* Sergeant.

Dun. What bloody man is that ? He can report,
As seemeth by his plight, of the revolt
The newest state.
Mal. This is the sergeant
Who like a good and hardy soldier fought
'Gainst my captivity. Hail, brave friend !
Say to the King the knowledge of the broil
As thou didst leave it.
Serg. Doubtful it stood,
As two spent swimmers that do cling together
And choke their art. The merciless Macdonwald—
Worthy to be a rebel, for to that   10
The multiplying villainies of nature
Do swarm upon him—from the Western Isles
Of kerns and gallowglasses is supplied ;
And Fortune, on his damned quarrel smiling,
Show'd like a rebel's whore. But all's too weak ;   15
For brave Macbeth—well he deserves that name—
Disdaining Fortune, with his brandish'd steel
Which smok'd with bloody execution,
Like valour's minion, carv'd out his passage
Till he fac'd the slave ;   20
Which ne'er shook hands, nor bade farewell to him,
Till he unseam'd him from the nave to th' chaps,
And fix'd his head upon our battlements.
Dun. O valiant cousin ! worthy gentleman !
Serg. As whence the sun gins his reflection   25
Shipwrecking storms and direful thunders break,
So from that spring whence comfort seem'd to come
Discomfort swells. Mark, King of Scotland, mark :

No sooner justice had, with valour arm'd,
Compell'd these skipping kerns to trust
their heels,   30
But the Norweyan lord, surveying vantage,
With furbish'd arms and new supplies of
men,
Began a fresh assault.
Dun.   Dismay'd not this
Our captains, Macbeth and Banquo?
Serg.   Yes;
As sparrows eagles, or the hare the lion. 35
If I say sooth, I must report they were
As cannons overcharg'd with double
cracks;
So they doubly redoubled strokes upon the
foe.
Except they meant to bathe in reeking
wounds,   40
Or memorize another Golgotha,
I cannot tell—
But I am faint; my gashes cry for help.
Dun. So well thy words become thee as
thy wounds;   44
They smack of honour both.—Go get him
surgeons. [*Exit Sergeant, attended.*

Enter Ross.

Who comes here?
Mal.   The worthy Thane of Ross.
Len. What a haste looks through his
eyes!
So should he look that seems to speak
things strange.
Ross. God save the King!
Dun. Whence cam'st thou, worthy
thane?
Ross.   From Fife, great King,
Where the Norweyan banners flout the
sky   50
And fan our people cold.
Norway himself, with terrible numbers,
Assisted by that most disloyal traitor
The Thane of Cawdor, began a dismal
conflict,
Till that Bellona's bridegroom, lapp'd in
proof,   55
Confronted him with self-comparisons,
Point against point rebellious, arm 'gainst
arm,
Curbing his lavish spirit; and to conclude,
The victory fell on us.
Dun. Great happiness!
Ross. That now   60
Sweno, the Norways' king, craves com-
position;
Nor would we deign him burial of his men
Till he disbursed, at Saint Colme's Inch,
Ten thousand dollars to our general use.
Dun. No more that Thane of Cawdor
shall deceive   65
Our bosom interest.   Go pronounce his
present death,
And with his former title greet Macbeth.
Ross. I'll see it done.

Dun. What he hath lost, noble Macbeth
hath won.   [*Exeunt.*

SCENE III.   *A blasted heath.*

Thunder.   Enter the three Witches.

1 Witch. Where hast thou been, sister?
2 Witch. Killing swine.
3 Witch. Sister, where thou?
1 Witch. A sailor's wife had chestnuts in
her lap,
And mounch'd, and mounch'd, and
mounch'd.
' Give me ' quoth I.   5
' Aroint thee, witch!' the rump-fed
ronyon cries.
Her husband's to Aleppo gone, master o'
th' Tiger;
But in a sieve I'll thither sail
And, like a rat without a tail,
I'll do, I'll do, and I'll do.   10
2 Witch. I'll give thee a wind.
1 Witch. Th'art kind.
3 Witch. And I another.
1 Witch. I myself have all the other;
And the very ports they blow,   15
All the quarters that they know
I' th' shipman's card.
I'll drain him dry as hay:
Sleep shall neither night nor day
Hang upon his pent-house lid;   20
He shall live a man forbid;
Weary sev'nights, nine times nine,
Shall he dwindle, peak, and pine.
Though his bark cannot be lost,
Yet it shall be tempest-tost.   25
Look what I have.
2 Witch. Show me, show me.
1 Witch. Here I have a pilot's thumb,
Wreck'd as homeward he did come.
                              [*Drum within.*
3 Witch. A drum, a drum!   30
Macbeth doth come.
All. The Weird Sisters, hand in hand,
Posters of the sea and land,
Thus do go about, about;
Thrice to thine, and thrice to mine,   35
And thrice again, to make up nine.
Peace! The charm's wound up.

Enter MACBETH *and* BANQUO.

Macb. So foul and fair a day I have not
seen.
Ban. How far is't call'd to Forres? What
are these,
So wither'd, and so wild in their attire,   40
That look not like th' inhabitants o' th'
earth,
And yet are on't? Live you, or are you
aught
That man may question? You seem to
understand me,
By each at once her choppy finger laying

Upon her skinny lips.   You should be
women,   45
And yet your beards forbid me to interpret
That you are so.

  Macb. Speak, if you can.   What are you ?

  1 *Witch.* All hail, Macbeth ! Hail to thee,
    Thane of Glamis !

  2 *Witch.* All hail, Macbeth ! Hail to thee,
    Thane of Cawdor !

  3 *Witch.* All hail, Macbeth, that shalt
    be King hereafter !   50

  Ban. Good sir, why do you start, and
    seem to fear
Things that do sound so fair ? I' th' name
of truth,
Are ye fantastical, or that indeed
Which outwardly ye show ?   My noble
partner
You greet with present grace and great
prediction   55
Of noble having and of royal hope,
That he seems rapt withal.   To me you
speak not.
If you can look into the seeds of time
And say which grain will grow and which
will not,
Speak then to me, who neither beg nor fear
Your favours nor your hate.   61

  1 *Witch.* Hail !

  2 *Witch.* Hail !

  3 *Witch.* Hail !

  1 *Witch.*   Lesser than Macbeth, and
    greater.   65

  2 *Witch.* Not so happy, yet much happier.

  3 *Witch.* Thou shalt get kings, though
    thou be none.
So, all hail, Macbeth and Banquo !

  1 *Witch.* Banquo and Macbeth, all hail !

  Macb. Stay, you imperfect speakers, tell
    me more.   70
By Sinel's death I know I am Thane of
Glamis ;
But how of Cawdor ? The Thane of Cawdor
lives,
A prosperous gentleman ; and to be King
Stands not within the prospect of belief,
No more than to be Cawdor.   Say from
whence   75
You owe this strange intelligence, or why
Upon this blasted heath you stop our way
With such prophetic greeting ?   Speak, I
charge you.   [*Witches vanish.*

  Ban. The earth hath bubbles, as the
    water has,
And these are of them.   Whither are they
vanish'd ?   80

  Macb. Into the air ; and what seem'd
    corporal melted
As breath into the wind.   Would they had
stay'd !

  Ban. Were such things here as we do
    speak about ?
Or have we eaten on the insane root
That takes the reason prisoner ?   85

  Macb. Your children shall be kings.

  Ban.   You shall be King.

  Macb. And Thane of Cawdor too ; went
    it not so ?

  Ban. To th' self-same tune and words.
    Who's here ?

       Enter ROSS *and* ANGUS.

  Ross. The King hath happily receiv'd,
    Macbeth,
The news of thy success ; and when he
reads   90
Thy personal venture in the rebels' fight,
His wonders and his praises do contend
Which should be thine or his.   Silenc'd with
that,
In viewing o'er the rest o' th' self-same day,
He finds thee in the stout Norweyan ranks,
Nothing afeard of what thyself didst make,
Strange images of death.   As thick as
tale
Came post with post, and every one did
bear
Thy praises in his kingdom's great defence,
And pour'd them down before him.

  Ang.   We are sent 100
To give thee, from our royal master,
thanks ;
Only to herald thee into his sight,
Not pay thee.

  Ross. And, for an earnest of a greater
    honour,
He bade me, from him, call thee Thane of
Cawdor ;   105
In which addition, hail, most worthy
Thane !
For it is thine.

  Ban.   What, can the devil speak true ?

  Macb. The Thane of Cawdor lives ; why
    do you dress me
In borrowed robes ?

  Ang.   Who was the Thane lives yet ;
But under heavy judgment bears that life
Which he deserves to lose.   Whether he was
combin'd   111
With those of Norway, or did line the rebel
With hidden help and vantage, or that
with both
He labour'd in his country's wreck, I know
not ;
But treasons capital, confess'd and prov'd,
Have overthrown him.

  Macb. [*Aside*] Glamis, and Thane of
    Cawdor !   116
The greatest is behind.—Thanks for your
pains.
[*Aside to Banquo*] Do you not hope your
children shall be kings,
When those that gave the Thane of Cawdor
to me
Promis'd no less to them ?

  Ban. [*Aside to Macbeth*] That, trusted
    home,   120
Might yet enkindle you unto the crown,

Besides the Thane of Cawdor. But 'tis strange ;
And oftentimes to win us to our harm,
The instruments of darkness tell us truths,
Win us with honest trifles, to betray's 125
In deepest consequence.—
Cousins, a word, I pray you.
   Macb. [*Aside*]   Two truths are told,
As happy prologues to the swelling act
Of the imperial theme.—I thank you, gentlemen.
[*Aside*] This supernatural soliciting 130
Cannot be ill ; cannnot be good. If ill,
Why hath it given me earnest of success,
Commencing in a truth ? I am Thane of Cawdor.
If good, why do I yield to that suggestion
Whose horrid image doth unfix my hair 135
And make my seated heart knock at my ribs
Against the use of nature ? Present fears
Are less than horrible imaginings.
My thought, whose murder yet is but fantastical,
Shakes so my single state of man
That function is smother'd in surmise, 140
And nothing is but what is not.
   Ban. Look how our partner's rapt.
   Macb. [*Aside*] If chance will have me King, why, chance may crown me,
Without my stir.
   Ban.   New honours come upon him,
Like our strange garments, cleave not to their mould 145
But with the aid of use.
   Macb. [*Aside*] Come what come may,
Time and the hour runs through the roughest day.
   Ban. Worthy Macbeth, we stay upon your leisure.
   Macb. Give me your favour. My dull brain was wrought
With things forgotten. Kind gentlemen, your pains 150
Are regist'red where every day I turn
The leaf to read them. Let us toward the King.
[*Aside to Banquo*] Think upon what hath chanc'd ; and, at more time,
The interim having weigh'd it, let us speak 154
Our free hearts each to other.
   Ban. [*Aside to Macbeth*]   Very gladly.
   Macb. [*Aside to Banquo*] Till then, enough.—Come, friends. [*Exeunt.*

SCENE IV. *Forres. The palace.*

Flourish. Enter DUNCAN, MALCOLM, DONALBAIN, LENNOX *and* Attendants.

   Dun. Is execution done on Cawdor ? Are not
Those in commission yet return'd ?
   Mal.   My liege,

They are not yet come back. But I have spoke
With one that saw him die ; who did report
That very frankly he confess'd his treasons,
Implor'd your Highness' pardon, and set forth 6
A deep repentance. Nothing in his life
Became him like the leaving it : he died
As one that had been studied in his death
To throw away the dearest thing he ow'd 10
As 'twere a careless trifle.
   Dun.   There's no art
To find the mind's construction in the face.
He was a gentleman on whom I built
An absolute trust.

Enter MACBETH, BANQUO, ROSS, *and* ANGUS.

                    O worthiest cousin !
The sin of my ingratitude even now 15
Was heavy on me. Thou art so far before
That swiftest wing of recompense is slow
To overtake thee. Would thou hadst less deserv'd,
That the proportion both of thanks and payment
Might have been mine ! Only I have left to say, 20
More is thy due than more than all can pay.
   Macb. The service and the loyalty I owe,
In doing it, pays itself. Your Highness' part
Is to receive our duties ; and our duties
Are to your throne and state children and servants, 25
Which do but what they should by doing everything
Safe toward your love and honour.
   Dun.   Welcome hither.
I have begun to plant thee, and will labour
To make thee full of growing. Noble Banquo,
That hast no less deserv'd, nor must be known 30
No less to have done so, let me infold thee
And hold thee to my heart.
   Ban.   There if I grow,
The harvest is your own.
   Dun.   My plenteous joys,
Wanton in fulness, seek to hide themselves
In drops of sorrow. Sons, kinsmen, thanes,
And you whose places are the nearest, know 36
We will establish our estate upon
Our eldest, Malcolm, whom we name hereafter
The Prince of Cumberland ; which honour must
Not unaccompanied invest him only, 40
But signs of nobleness, like stars, shall shine
On all deservers. From hence to Inverness,
And bind us further to you.
   Macb. The rest is labour, which is not us'd for you.

I'll be myself the harbinger, and make joyful   45
The hearing of my wife with your approach;
So, humbly take my leave.
  Dun.   My worthy Cawdor !
  Macb. [*Aside*] The Prince of Cumberland !
That is a step,
On which I must fall down, or else o'er-leap,
For in my way it lies. Stars, hide your fires ;   50
Let not light see my black and deep desires.
The eye wink at the hand ; yet let that be
Which the eye fears, when it is done, to see.
                      [*Exit.*
  Dun. True, worthy Banquo : he is full so valiant ;
And in his commendations I am fed ;   55
It is a banquet to me. Let's after him,
Whose care is gone before to bid us welcome.
It is a peerless kinsman. [*Flourish. Exeunt.*

Scene V. *Inverness. Macbeth's castle.*

Enter Lady Macbeth, *reading a letter.*

  Lady M. ' They met me in the day of success ; and I have learn'd by the perfect'st report they have more in them than mortal knowledge. When I burn'd in desire to question them further, they made themselves air, into which they vanish'd. Whiles I stood rapt in the wonder of it, came missives from the King, who all-hail'd me " Thane of Cawdor " ; by which title, before, these weird sisters saluted me, and referr'd me to the coming on of time, with " Hail, king that shalt be ! " This have I thought good to deliver thee, my dearest partner of greatness, that thou mightst not lose the dues of rejoicing by being ignorant of what greatness is promis'd thee. Lay it to thy heart, and farewell.'
Glamis thou art, and Cawdor ; and shalt be
What thou art promis'd. Yet do I fear thy nature ;
It is too full o' th' milk of human kindness
To catch the nearest way. Thou wouldst be great ;   15
Art not without ambition, but without
The illness should attend it. What thou wouldst highly,
That wouldst thou holily ; wouldst not play false,
And yet wouldst wrongly win.
Thou'dst have, great Glamis, that which cries
' Thus thou must do ' if thou have it ;   20
And that which rather thou dost fear to do
Than wishest should be undone. Hie thee hither,
That I may pour my spirits in thine ear,
And chastise with the valour of my tongue
All that impedes thee from the golden round   25

Which fate and metaphysical aid doth seem
To have thee crown'd withal.

        Enter a Messenger.

                  What is your tidings ?
  Mess. The King comes here to-night.
  Lady M.   Thou'rt mad to say it.
Is not thy master with him ? who, were't so,
Would have inform'd for preparation.   30
  Mess. So please you, it is true. Our Thane is coming.
One of my fellows had the speed of him,
Who, almost dead for breath, had scarcely more
Than would make up his message.
  Lady M.   Give him tending :
He brings great news.   [*Exit Messenger.*
          The raven himself is hoarse 35
That croaks the fatal entrance of Duncan
Under my battlements. Come, you spirits
That tend on mortal thoughts, unsex me here ;
And fill me, from the crown to the toe, top-full
Of direst cruelty. Make thick my blood,   40
Stop up th' access and passage to remorse,
That no compunctious visitings of nature
Shake my fell purpose nor keep peace between
Th' effect and it. Come to my woman's breasts,
And take my milk for gall, you murd'ring ministers,   45
Wherever in your sightless substances
You wait on nature's mischief. Come, thick night,
And pall thee in the dunnest smoke of hell,
That my keen knife see not the wound it makes,
Nor heaven peep through the blanket of the dark   50
To cry ' Hold, hold '.

        Enter Macbeth.

     Great Glamis ! Worthy Cawdor !
Greater than both, by the all-hail hereafter !
Thy letters have transported me beyond
This ignorant present, and I feel now
The future in the instant.
  Macb.   My dearest love, 55
Duncan comes here to-night.
  Lady M.   And when goes hence ?
  Macb. To-morrow—as he purposes.
  Lady M.   O, never
Shall sun that morrow see !
Your face, my thane, is as a book where men
May read strange matters. To beguile the time,   60
Look like the time ; bear welcome in your eye,
Your hand, your tongue ; look like th' innocent flower,

But be the serpent under't. He that's
    coming
Must be provided for ; and you shall put
This night's great business into my dis-
    patch ;   65
Which shall to all our nights and days to
    come
Give solely sovereign sway and masterdom.
Macb. We will speak further.
    Lady M.   Only look up clear.
To alter favour ever is to fear.   69
Leave all the rest to me.   [*Exeunt.*

SCENE VI. *Inverness.   Before Macbeth's
                    castle.*

Hautboys and torches.   Enter DUNCAN,
    MALCOLM, DONALBAIN, BANQUO, LEN-
    NOX, MACDUFF, ROSS, ANGUS, *and*
    Attendants.

    Dun. This castle hath a pleasant seat ;
        the air
Nimbly and sweetly recommends itself
Unto our gentle senses.
    Ban.   This guest of summer,
The temple-haunting martlet, does approve
By his lov'd mansionry that the heaven's
    breath   5
Smells wooingly here ; no jutty, frieze,
Buttress, nor coign of vantage, but this bird
Hath made her pendent bed and procreant
    cradle.
Where they most breed and haunt, I have
    observ'd
The air is delicate.

            Enter LADY MACBETH.

    Dun. See, see, our honour'd hostess ! 10
The love that follows us sometime is our
    trouble,
Which still we thank as love. Herein I teach
    you
How you shall bid God 'ield us for your
    pains,
And thank us for your trouble.
    Lady M.   All our service
In every point twice done, and then done
    double,   15
Were poor and single business to contend
Against those honours deep and broad
    wherewith
Your Majesty loads our house ; for those
    of old,
And the late dignities heap'd up to them,
We rest your hermits.
    Dun.   Where's the Thane of Cawdor ?
We cours'd him at the heels and had a
    purpose   21
To be his purveyor ; but he rides well,
And his great love, sharp as his spur, hath
    holp him
To his home before us. Fair and noble
    hostess,   24
We are your guest to-night.

Lady M.   Your servants ever
Have theirs, themselves, and what is theirs,
    in compt,
To make their audit at your Highness'
    pleasure,
Still to return your own.
    Dun.   Give me your hand ;
Conduct me to mine host. We love him
    highly,   29
And shall continue our graces towards him.
By your leave, hostess.   [*Exeunt.*

SCENE VII. *Inverness.   Macbeth's castle.*

*Hautboys, torches.   Enter a Sewer, and divers
    Servants with dishes and service over the
    stage.   Then enter* MACBETH.

    Macb. If it were done when 'tis done,
        then 'twere well
It were done quickly. If th' assassination
Could trammel up the consequence, and
    catch,
With his surcease, success ; that but this
    blow
Might be the be-all and the end-all here— 5
But here upon this bank and shoal of time—
We'd jump the life to come. But in these
    cases
We still have judgment here, that we but
    teach
Bloody instructions, which being taught
    return
To plague th' inventor. This even-handed
    justice   10
Commends th' ingredience of our poison'd
    chalice
To our own lips. He's here in double trust :
First, as I am his kinsman and his subject—
Strong both against the deed ; then, as his
    host,
Who should against his murderer shut the
    door,   15
Not bear the knife myself. Besides, this
    Duncan
Hath borne his faculties so meek, hath been
So clear in his great office, that his virtues
Will plead like angels, trumpet-tongu'd,
    against
The deep damnation of his taking-off ;   20
And pity, like a naked new-born babe,
Striding the blast, or heaven's cherubin
    hors'd
Upon the sightless couriers of the air,
Shall blow the horrid deed in every eye,
That tears shall drown the wind. I have
    no spur   25
To prick the sides of my intent, but only
Vaulting ambition, which o'er-leaps itself,
And falls on th' other.

            Enter LADY MACBETH.

            How now ! What news ?
    Lady M. He has almost supp'd. Why
        have you left the chamber ?   29

Macb. Hath he ask'd for me?
Lady M.   Know you not he has?
Macb. We will proceed no further in this
        business.
He hath honour'd me of late; and I have
        bought
Golden opinions from all sorts of people,
Which would be worn now in their newest
        gloss,
Not cast aside so soon.
    Lady M.   Was the hope drunk 35
Wherein you dress'd yourself? Hath it
        slept since,
And wakes it now to look so green and pale
At what it did so freely? From this time
Such I account thy love. Art thou afeard
To be the same in thine own act and valour
As thou art in desire? Wouldst thou have
        that   41
Which thou esteem'st the ornament of life,
And live a coward in thine own esteem,
Letting ' I dare not ' wait upon ' I would ',
Like the poor cat i' th' adage?
    Macb.   Prithee, peace; 45
I dare do all that may become a man;
Who dares do more is none.
    Lady M.   What beast was't then
That made you break this enterprise to me?
When you durst do it, then you were a
        man;
And to be more than what you were, you
        wouid   50
Be so much more the man. Nor time nor
        place
Did then adhere, and yet you would make
        both;
They have made themselves, and that their
        fitness now
Does unmake you. I have given suck, and
        know
How tender 'tis to love the babe that milks
        me—   55
I would, while it was smiling in my face,
Have pluck'd my nipple from his boneless
        gums,
And dash'd the brains out, had I so sworn
As you have done to this.
    Macb. If we should fail?
    Lady M.   We fail!
But screw your courage to the sticking
        place,   60
And we'll not fail. When Duncan is
        asleep—
Whereto the rather shall his day's hard
        journey
Soundly invite him—his two chamberlains
Will I with wine and wassail so convince
That memory, the warder of the brain, 65
Shall be a fume, and the receipt of reason
A limbec only. When in swinish sleep
Their drenched natures lie as in a death,
What cannot you and I perform upon
Th' unguarded Duncan? what not put
        upon   70

His spongy officers, who shall bear the
        guilt
Of our great quell?
    Macb.   Bring forth men-children only;
For thy undaunted mettle should compose
Nothing but males. Will it not be receiv'd,
When we have mark'd with blood those
        sleepy two   75
Of his own chamber, and us'd their very
        daggers,
That they have done 't?
    Lady M.   Who dares receive it other,
As we shall make our griefs and clamour
        roar
Upon his death?
    Macb.   I am settled, and bend up
Each corporal agent to this terrible feat. 80
Away, and mock the time with fairest show;
False face must hide what the false heart
        doth know.   [*Exeunt.*

ACT TWO

Scene I. *Inverness. Court of Macbeth's
        castle.*

Enter Banquo, *and* Fleance *with a torch
        before him.*

Ban. How goes the night, boy?
Fle. The moon is down; I have not
        heard the clock.
Ban. And she goes down at twelve.
Fle.   I take 't, 'tis later, sir.
Ban. Hold, take my sword. There's
        husbandry in heaven;
Their candles are all out. Take thee that
        too.   5
A heavy summons lies like lead upon me,
And yet I would not sleep. Merciful powers
Restrain in me the cursed thoughts that
        nature
Gives way to in repose!

Enter Macbeth *and a* Servant *with a torch.*
                          Give me my sword.
Who's there?   10
    Macb. A friend.
    Ban. What, sir, not yet at rest? The
        king's a-bed.
He hath been in unusual pleasure, and
Sent forth great largess to your offices.
This diamond he greets your wife withal, 15
By the name of most kind hostess; and
        shut up
In measureless content.
    Macb.   Being unprepar'd,
Our will became the servant to defect;
Which else should free have wrought.
    Ban.   All's well.
I dreamt last night of the three Weird
        Sisters.   20
To you they have show'd some truth.
    Macb.   I think not of them;
Yet, when we can entreat an hour to serve,

We would spend it in some words upon that business,
If you would grant the time.
   Ban.   At your kind'st leisure.
   Macb. If you shall cleave to my consent, when 'tis,   25
It shall make honour for you.
   Ban.   So I lose none
In seeking to augment it, but still keep
My bosom franchis'd and allegiance clear,
I shall be counsell'd.
   Macb.   Good repose the while !
   Ban. Thanks, sir ; the like to you !   30
        [Exeunt Banquo and Fleance.
   Macb. Go bid thy mistress, when my drink is ready,
She strike upon the bell. Get thee to bed.
        [Exit Servant.
Is this a dagger which I see before me,
The handle toward my hand ? Come, let me clutch thee.
I have thee not, and yet I see thee still.   35
Art thou not, fatal vision, sensible
To feeling as to sight ? or art thou but
A dagger of the mind, a false creation,
Proceeding from the heat-oppressed brain ?
I see thee yet, in form as palpable   40
As this which now I draw.
Thou marshall'st me the way that I was going ;
And such an instrument I was to use.
Mine eyes are made the fools o' th' other senses,
Or else worth all the rest. I see thee still ;
And on thy blade and dudgeon gouts of blood,   46
Which was not so before. There's no such thing :
It is the bloody business which informs
Thus to mine eyes. Now o'er the one half-world
Nature seems dead, and wicked dreams abuse   50
The curtain'd sleep ; now witchcraft celebrates
Pale Hecate's offerings ; and wither'd murder,
Alarum'd by his sentinel, the wolf,
Whose howl's his watch, thus with his stealthy pace,
With Tarquin's ravishing strides, towards his design   55
Moves like a ghost. Thou sure and firm-set earth,
Hear not my steps which way they walk, for fear
Thy very stones prate of my whereabout
And take the present horror from the time,
Which now suits with it. Whiles I threat, he lives ;   60
Words to the heat of deeds too cold breath gives.   *[A bell rings.*
I go, and it is done ; the bell invites me.
Hear it not, Duncan, for it is a knell

That summons thee to heaven or to hell.
        [Exit.

SCENE II. *Inverness. Macbeth's castle.*

Enter LADY MACBETH.

   Lady M. That which hath made them drunk hath made me bold ;
What hath quench'd them hath given me fire. Hark ! Peace !
It was the owl that shriek'd, the fatal bell-man,
Which gives the stern'st good-night. He is about it.
The doors are open ; and the surfeited grooms   5
Do mock their charge with snores. I have drugg'd their possets,
That death and nature do contend about them,
Whether they live or die.
   Macb. [*Within*] Who's there ! What, ho !
   Lady M. Alack ! I am afraid they have awak'd,
And 'tis not done. Th' attempt, and not the deed,   10
Confounds us. Hark ! I laid their daggers ready ;
He could not miss 'em. Had he not resembled
My father as he slept, I had done't.

Enter MACBETH.

                 My husband !
   Macb. I have done the deed. Didst thou not hear a noise ?
   Lady M. I heard the owl scream and the crickets cry.   15
Did not you speak ?
   Macb.   When ?
   Lady M.   Now.
   Macb.   As I descended ?
   Lady M. Ay.
   Macb. Hark !
Who lies i' th' second chamber ?
   Lady M.   Donalbain.
   Macb. This is a sorry sight.   20
        [Looking on his hands.
   Lady M. A foolish thought to say a sorry sight.
   Macb. There's one did laugh in's sleep, and one cried ' Murder ! '
That they did wake each other. I stood and heard them ;
But they did say their prayers, and address'd them   24
Again to sleep.
   Lady M. There are two lodg'd together.
   Macb. One cried ' God bless us ', and ' Amen ' the other,
As they had seen me with these hangman's hands.
List'ning their fear, I could not say ' Amen '

When they did say ' God bless us! '
  Lady M. Consider it not so deeply.   30
  Macb. But wherefore could not I pro-
    nounce ' Amen ' ?
I had most need of blessing, and ' Amen '
Stuck in my throat.
  Lady M.   These deeds must not be
    thought
After these ways : so, it will make us
    mad.
  Macb. Methought I heard a voice cry
    ' Sleep no more ;   35
Macbeth does murder sleep '—the innocent
    sleep,
Sleep that knits up the ravell'd sleave of
    care,
The death of each day's life, sore labour's
    bath,
Balm of hurt minds, great nature's second
    course,   39
Chief nourisher in life's feast.
  Lady M.   What do you mean ?
  Macb. Still it cried ' Sleep no more ' to
    all the house ;
' Glamis hath murder'd sleep ; and there-
    fore Cawdor
Shall sleep no more—Macbeth shall sleep
    no more '.
  Lady M. Who was it that thus cried ?
    Why, worthy Thane,
You do unbend your noble strength to
    think   45
So brainsickly of things. Go get some
    water
And wash this filthy witness from your
    hand.
Why did you bring these daggers from the
    place ?
They must lie there. Go carry them, and
    smear
The sleepy grooms with blood.
  Macb.   I'll go no more : 50
I am afraid to think what I have done ;
Look on't again I dare not.
  Lady M.   Infirm of purpose !
Give me the daggers. The sleeping and the
    dead
Are but as pictures ; 'tis the eye of
    childhood   54
That fears a painted devil. If he do bleed,
I'll gild the faces of the grooms withal,
For it must seem their guilt.
          [*Exit. Knocking within.*
  Macb.   Whence is that knocking ?
How is't with me, when every noise appals
    me ?
What hands are here ? Ha ! they pluck
    out mine eyes.
Will all great Neptune's ocean wash this
    blood   60
Clean from my hand ? No ; this my hand
    will rather
The multitudinous seas incarnadine,
Making the green one red.

       Re-enter LADY MACBETH.

  Lady M. My hands are of your colour ;
    but I shame
To wear a heart so white. [*Knock*] I hear
    a knocking   65
At the south entry ; retire we to our
    chamber.
A little water clears us of this deed.
How easy is it then ! Your constancy
Hath left you unattended. [*Knock*] Hark !
    more knocking.
Get on your nightgown, lest occasion call
    us   70
And show us to be watchers. Be not lost
So poorly in your thoughts.
  Macb. To know my deed, 'twere best not
    know myself.   [*Knock.*
Wake Duncan with thy knocking ! I would
    thou couldst !   [*Exeunt.*

  SCENE III. *Inverness. Macbeth's castle.*

    Knocking within. Enter a PORTER.

  Porter. Here's a knocking indeed ! If a
man were porter of hell-gate, he should
have old turning the key. [*Knock*] Knock,
knock, knock ! Who's there, i' th' name
of Beelzebub ? Here's a farmer that hang'd
himself on th' expectation of plenty. Come
in time ; have napkins enow about you ;
here you'll sweat for't. [*Knock*] Knock,
knock ! Who's there, i' th' other devil's
name ? Faith, here's an equivocator, that
could swear in both the scales against either
scale ; who committed treason enough for
God's sake, yet could not equivocate to
heaven. O, come in, equivocator. [*Knock*]
Knock, knock, knock ! Who's there ?
Faith, here's an English tailor come hither
for stealing out of a French hose. Come in,
tailor, here you may roast your goose.
[*Knock*] Knock, knock ; never at quiet !
What are you ? But this place is too cold
for hell. I'll devil-porter it no further. I
had thought to have let in some of all
professions that go the primrose way to
th' everlasting bonfire. [*Knock*] Anon,
anon ! [*Opens the gate*] I pray you remember
the porter.

    Enter MACDUFF *and* LENNOX.

  Macd. Was it so late, friend, ere you
went to bed, that you do lie so late ?   22
  Port. Faith, sir, we were carousing till
the second cock ; and drink, sir, is a great
provoker of three things.
  Macd. What three things does drink
especially provoke ?   26
  Port. Marry, sir, nose-painting, sleep, and
urine. Lechery, sir, it provokes and un-
provokes : it provokes the desire, but it
takes away the performance. Therefore
much drink may be said to be an equivo-

cator with lechery: it makes him, and it mars him; it sets him on, and it takes him off; it persuades him, and disheartens him; makes him stand to, and not stand to; in conclusion, equivocates him in a sleep, and, giving him the lie, leaves him.

Macd. I believe drink gave thee the lie last night.   35

Port. That it did, sir, i' the very throat on me; but I requited him for his lie; and, I think, being too strong for him, though he took up my legs sometime, yet I made a shift to cast him.

Macd. Is thy master stirring?   40

Enter MACBETH.

Our knocking has awak'd him; here he comes.

Len. Good morrow, noble sir!

Macb.   Good morrow, both!

Macd. Is the King stirring, worthy Thane?

Macb.   Not yet.

Macd. He did command me to call timely on him;
I have almost slipp'd the hour.

Macb.   I'll bring you to him.   45

Macd. I know this is a joyful trouble to you;
But yet 'tis one.

Macb. The labour we delight in physics pain.
This is the door.

Macd.   I'll make so bold to call, 49
For 'tis my limited service. [*Exit Macduff.*

Len. Goes the King hence to-day?

Macb. He does: he did appoint so.

Len. The night has been unruly. Where we lay,
Our chimneys were blown down; and, as they say,
Lamentings heard i' th' air, strange screams of death,
And prophesying, with accents terrible,   55
Of dire combustion and confus'd events
New hatch'd to th' woeful time; the obscure bird
Clamour'd the livelong night. Some say the earth
Was feverous and did shake.

Macb.   'Twas a rough night.

Len. My young remembrance cannot parallel   60
A fellow to it.

Re-enter MACDUFF.

Macd. O horror, horror, horror! Tongue nor heart
Cannot conceive nor name thee.

Macb. ⎫
Len. ⎬   What's the matter?

Macd. Confusion now hath made his masterpiece.
Most sacrilegious murder hath broke ope

The Lord's anointed temple, and stole thence   66
The life o' th' building.

Macb.   What is't you say—the life?

Len. Mean you his Majesty?

Macd. Approach the chamber, and destroy your sight   69
With a new Gorgon. Do not bid me speak;
See, and then speak yourselves.

[*Exeunt Macbeth and Lennox.*
Awake, awake!
Ring the alarum bell. Murder and treason!
Banquo and Donalbain! Malcolm! awake!
Shake off this downy sleep, death's counterfeit,   74
And look on death itself. Up, up, and see
The great doom's image! Malcolm! Banquo!
As from your graves rise up and walk like sprites
To countenance this horror! Ring the bell.

[*Bell rings.*

Enter LADY MACBETH.

Lady M. What's the business,   79
That such a hideous trumpet calls to parley
The sleepers of the house? Speak, speak!

Macd. O gentle lady,
'Tis not for you to hear what I can speak!
The repetition in a woman's ear
Would murder as it fell.

Enter BANQUO.

                    O Banquo, Banquo,
Our royal master's murder'd!

Lady M.   Woe, alas! 85
What, in our house?

Ban.   Too cruel any where.
Dear Duff, I prithee contradict thyself,
And say it is not so.

Re-enter MACBETH, LENNOX, *with* ROSS.

Macb. Had I but died an hour before this chance,
I had liv'd a blessed time; for, from this instant,   90
There's nothing serious in mortality—
All is but toys; renown and grace is dead;
The wine of life is drawn, and the mere lees
Is left this vault to brag of.

Enter MALCOLM *and* DONALBAIN.

Don. What is amiss?

Macb. You are, and do not know't. 95
The spring, the head, the fountain of your blood,
Is stopp'd; the very source of it is stopp'd.

Macd. Your royal father's murder'd.

Mal.   O, by whom?

Len. Those of his chamber, as it seem'd, had done't.
Their hands and faces were all badg'd with blood;   100

So were their daggers, which unwip'd we
    found
Upon their pillows.   They star'd and were
    distracted ;
No man's life was to be trusted with them.
  Macb. O, yet I do repent me of my fury
That I did kill them.
  Macd.   Wherefore did you so ?
  Macb. Who can be wise, amaz'd,
    temp'rate, and furious,   107
Loyal and neutral, in a moment ? No man.
The expedition of my violent love
Outrun the pauser reason.   Here lay
    Duncan,   110
His silver skin lac'd with his golden blood ;
And his gash'd stabs look'd like a breach
    in nature
For ruin's wasteful entrance : there, the
    murderers,
Steep'd in the colours of their trade, their
    daggers
Unmannerly breech'd with gore.   Who
    could refrain,   115
That had a heart to love, and in that heart
Courage to make's love known ?
  Lady M.   Help me hence, ho !
  Macd. Look to the lady.
  Mal. [*Aside to Donalbain*] Why do we hold
    our tongues that most may claim
This argument for ours ?
  Don. [*Aside to Malcolm*] What should be
    spoken
Here, where our fate, hid in an auger-hole,
May rush and seize us ? Let's away.
Our tears are not yet brew'd.
  Mal. [*Aside to Donalbain*] Nor our strong
    sorrow
Upon the foot of motion.
  Ban. Look to the lady.
           [*Lady Macbeth is carried out.*
And when we have our naked frailties hid,
That suffer in exposure, let us meet,   126
And question this most bloody piece of
    work,
To know it further. Fears and scruples
    shake us.
In the great hand of God I stand, and
    thence
Against the undivulg'd pretence I fight 130
Of treasonous malice.
  Macd.   And so do I.
  All.   So all.
  Macb. Let's briefly put on manly readi-
    ness
And meet i' th' hall together.
  All.   Well contented.
    [*Exeunt all but Malcolm and Donalbain.*
  Mal. What will you do ? Let's not con-
    sort with them.
To show an unfelt sorrow is an office   135
Which the false man does easy. I'll to
    England.
  Don. To Ireland I ; our separated
    fortune

Shall keep us both the safer. Where we are,
There's daggers in men's smiles ; the near
    in blood,   139
The nearer bloody.
  Mal.   This murderous shaft that's shot
Hath not yet lighted ; and our safest way
Is to avoid the aim. Therefore to horse ;
And let us not be dainty of leave-taking,
But shift away. There's warrant in that
    theft   144
Which steals itself, when there's no mercy
    left.   [*Exeunt.*

SCENE IV. *Inverness. Without Macbeth's
castle.*

Enter Ross *with an* Old Man.

  Old M. Threescore and ten I can remem-
    ber well ;
Within the volume of which time I have
    seen
Hours dreadful and things strange ; but
    this sore night
Hath trifled former knowings.
  Ross.   Ah, good father,
Thou seest, the heavens, as troubled with
    man's act,   5
Threatens his bloody stage. By th' clock
    'tis day,
And yet dark night strangles the travelling
    lamp.
Is't night's predominance, or the day's
    shame,
That darkness does the face of earth en-
    tomb,
When living light should kiss it ?
  Old M.   'Tis unnatural, 10
Even like the deed that's done. On Tuesday
    last,
A falcon, tow'ring in her pride of place,
Was by a mousing owl hawk'd at and kill'd.
  Ross. And Duncan's horses—a thing
    most strange and certain—
Beautous and swift, the minions of their
    race,   15
Turn'd wild in nature, broke their stalls,
    flung out,
Contending 'gainst obedience, as they
    would make
War with mankind.
  Old M.   'Tis said they eat each other.
  Ross. They did so ; to the amazement of
    mine eyes,   19
That look'd upon't.

Enter MACDUFF.

           Here comes the good Macduff.
How goes the world, sir, now ?
  Macd.   Why, see you not ?
  Ross. Is't known who did this more than
    bloody deed ?
  Macd. Those that Macbeth hath slain.
  Ross.   Alas, the day !
What good could they pretend ?

Macd. They were suborn'd.
Malcolm and Donalbain, the King's two
     sons,   25
Are stol'n away and fled ; which puts upon
     them
Suspicion of the deed.
Ross.   'Gainst nature still.
Thriftless ambition, that wilt ravin up
Thine own life's means ! Then 'tis most like
The sovereignty will fall upon Macbeth. 30
     Macd. He is already nam'd, and gone to
          Scone
To be invested.
Ross.   Where is Duncan's body ?
Macd. Carried to Colmekill,
The sacred storehouse of his predecessors
And guardian of their bones.
Ross.   Will you to Scone ? 35
Macd. No, cousin, I'll to Fife.
Ross.   Well, I will thither.
Macd. Well, may you see things well
     done there ! Adieu,
Lest our old robes sit easier than our new.
Ross. Farewell, father.
     Old M. God's benison go with you, and
          with those   40
That would make good of bad, and friends
     of foes.   [*Exeunt.*

ACT THREE

SCENE I. *Forres. The palace.*

Enter BANQUO.

Ban. Thou hast it now—King, Cawdor,
     Glamis, all
As the weird women promis'd ; and I fear
Thou play'dst most foully for't ; yet it was
     said
It should not stand in thy posterity ;
But that myself should be the root and
     father   5
Of many kings. If there come truth from
     them—
As upon thee, Macbeth, their speeches
     shine—
Why, by the verities on thee made good,
May they not be my oracles as well
And set me up in hope ? But, hush, no
     more.   10

Sennet sounded. Enter MACBETH *as King,*
LADY MACBETH *as Queen ;* LENNOX,
ROSS, *Lords, Ladies, and Attendants.*

Macb. Here's our chief guest.
Lady M.   If he had been forgotten,
It had been as a gap in our great feast,
And all-thing unbecoming.
     Macb. To-night we hold a solemn supper,
          sir,
And I'll request your presence.
Ban.   Let your Highness 15
Command upon me ; to the which my
     duties

Are with a most indissoluble tie
For ever knit.
     Macb. Ride you this afternoon ?
Ban.   Ay, my good lord.
     Macb. We should have else desir'd your
          good advice—   20
Which still hath been both grave and
     prosperous—
In this day's council ; but we'll take to-
     morrow.
Is't far you ride ?
     Ban. As far, my lord, as will fill up the
          time
'Twixt this and supper. Go not my horse
     the better,   25
I must become a borrower of the night
For a dark hour or twain.
     Macb.   Fail not our feast.
Ban. My lord, I will not.
     Macb. We hear our bloody cousins are
          bestow'd   29
In England and in Ireland, not confessing
Their cruel parricide, filling their hearers
With strange invention ; but of that to-
     morrow,
When therewithal we shall have cause of
     state
Craving us jointly. Hie you to horse ;
     adieu,
Till you return at night. Goes Fleance with
     you ?   35
     Ban. Ay, my good lord ; our time does
          call upon's.
Macb. I wish your horses swift and sure
     of foot,
And so I do commend you to their backs.
Farewell.   [*Exit Banquo.*
Let every man be master of his time 40
Till seven at night ; to make society
The sweeter welcome, we will keep ourself
Till supper-time alone. While then, God be
     with you !
     [*Exeunt all but Macbeth and a Servant.*
Sirrah, a word with you. Attend those men
     our pleasure ?   45
     Serv. They are, my lord, without the
          palace gate.
Macb. Bring them before us.
                              [*Exit Servant.*
                    To be thus is nothing,
But to be safely thus. Our fears in Banquo
Stick deep ; and in his royalty of nature
Reigns that which would be fear'd. 'Tis
     much he dares,   50
And to that dauntless temper of his mind
He hath a wisdom that doth guide his
     valour
To act in safety. There is none but he
Whose being I do fear ; and under him
My Genius is rebuk'd, as it is said 55
Mark Antony's was by Cæsar. He chid the
     Sisters
When first they put the name of King upon
     me,

And bade them speak to him; then, prophet-like,
They hail'd him father to a line of kings.
Upon my head they plac'd a fruitless crown
And put a barren sceptre in my gripe,   61
Thence to be wrench'd with an unlineal hand,
No son of mine succeeding. If't be so,
For Banquo's issue have I fil'd my mind;
For them the gracious Duncan have I murder'd;   65
Put rancours in the vessel of my peace
Only for them, and mine eternal jewel
Given to the common enemy of man
To make them kings—the seeds of Banquo kings!
Rather than so, come, Fate, into the list,   70
And champion me to th' utterance! Who's there?

Re-enter Servant *and two* Murderers.

Now go to the door and stay there till we call.   [*Exit Servant.*
Was it not yesterday we spoke together?
1 *Mur.* It was, so please your Highness.
Macb.   Well then, now
Have you consider'd of my speeches? Know   75
That it was he, in the times past, which held you
So under fortune; which you thought had been
Our innocent self. This I made good to you
In our last conference, pass'd in probation with you,
How you were borne in hand, how cross'd, the instruments,   80
Who wrought with them, and all things else that might
To half a soul and to a notion craz'd
Say 'Thus did Banquo'.
1 *Mur.*   You made it known to us.
Macb. I did so; and went further, which is now   84
Our point of second meeting. Do you find
Your patience so predominant in your nature
That you can let this go? Are you so gospell'd,
To pray for this good man and for his issue,
Whose heavy hand hath bow'd you to the grave
And beggar'd yours for ever?
1 *Mur.*   We are men, my liege.   90
Macb. Ay, in the catalogue ye go for men;
As hounds, and greyhounds, mongrels, spaniels, curs,
Shoughs, water-rugs, and demi-wolves, are clept
All by the name of dogs. The valued file
Distinguishes the swift, the slow, the subtle,   95
The house-keeper, the hunter, every one

According to the gift which bounteous nature
Hath in him clos'd; whereby he does receive
Particular addition, from the bill   99
That writes them all alike; and so of men.
Now, if you have a station in the file,
Not i' th' worst rank of manhood, say't;
And I will put that business in your bosoms
Whose execution takes your enemy off,
Grapples you to the heart and love of us,
Who wear our health but sickly in his life,
Which in his death were perfect.
2 *Mur.*   I am one, my liege,
Whom the vile blows and buffets of the world
Hath so incens'd that I am reckless what
I do to spite the world.
1 *Mur.*   And I another,   110
So weary with disasters, tugg'd with fortune,
That I would set my life on any chance,
To mend it or be rid on't.
Macb.   Both of you
Know Banquo was your enemy.
Both Mur.   True, my lord.
Macb. So is he mine; and in such bloody distance   115
That every minute of his being thrusts
Against my near'st of life; and though I could
With bare-fac'd power sweep him from my sight,
And bid my will avouch it, yet I must not,
For certain friends that are both his and mine,   120
Whose loves I may not drop, but wail his fall
Who I myself struck down. And thence it is
That I to your assistance do make love,
Masking the business from the common eye
For sundry weighty reasons.
2 *Mur.*   We shall, my lord,   125
Perform what you command us.
1 *Mur.*   Though our lives—
Macb. Your spirits shine through you. Within this hour at most,
I will advise you where to plant yourselves,
Acquaint you with the perfect spy o' th' time,
The moment on't; for 't must be done to-night,   130
And something from the palace; always thought
That I require a clearness; and with him,
To leave no rubs nor botches in the work,
Fleance his son, that keeps him company,
Whose absence is no less material to me   135
Than is his father's, must embrace the fate
Of that dark hour. Resolve yourselves apart;
I'll come to you anon.
Both Mur.   We are resolv'd, my lord.

Macb. I'll call upon you straight ; abide
within. [*Exeunt Murderers.*
It is concluded : Banquo, thy soul's flight
If it find heaven must find it out to-night.
[*Exit.*

SCENE II. *Forres. The palace.*

Enter LADY MACBETH *and a* Servant.

Lady M. Is Banquo gone from court ?
Serv. Ay, madam, but returns again to-
night.
Lady M. Say to the King I would attend
his leisure
For a few words.
Serv. Madam, I will. [*Exit.*
Lady M. Nought's had, all's spent,
Where our desire is got without content. 5
'Tis safer to be that which we destroy,
Than by destruction dwell in doubtful joy.

Enter MACBETH.

How now, my lord ! Why do you keep
alone,
Of sorriest fancies your companions making,
Using those thoughts which should indeed
have died 10
With them they think on ? Things without
all remedy
Should be without regard. What's done is
done.
Macb. We have scotch'd the snake, not
kill'd it ;
She'll close, and be herself, whilst our poor
malice
Remains in danger of her former tooth. 15
But let the frame of things disjoint, both
the worlds suffer,
Ere we will eat our meal in fear and sleep
In the affliction of these terrible dreams
That shake us nightly. Better be with the
dead,
Whom we, to gain our peace, have sent to
peace, 20
Than on the torture of the mind to lie
In restless ecstasy. Duncan is in his grave ;
After life's fitful fever he sleeps well ;
Treason has done his worst ; nor steel, nor
poison,
Malice domestic, foreign levy, nothing, 25
Can touch him further.
Lady M. Come on.
Gentle my lord, sleek o'er your rugged
looks ;
Be bright and jovial among your guests
to-night.
Macb. So shall I, love ; and so, I pray,
be you. 29
Let your remembrance apply to Banquo ;
Present him eminence, both with eye and
tongue—
Unsafe the while, that we
Must lave our honours in these flattering
streams,
And make our faces vizards to our hearts,

Disguising what they are.
Lady M. You must leave this.
Macb. O, full of scorpions is my mind,
dear wife ! 36
Thou know'st that Banquo, and his
Fleance, lives.
Lady M. But in them nature's copy's not
eterne.
Macb. There's comfort yet ; they are
assailable.
Then be thou jocund. Ere the bat hath
flown 40
His cloister'd flight ; ere to black Hecate's
summons
The shard-borne beetle with his drowsy
hums
Hath rung night's yawning peal, there shall
be done
A deed of dreadful note.
Lady M. What's to be done ?
Macb. Be innocent of the knowledge,
dearest chuck, 45
Till thou applaud the deed. Come, seeling
night,
Scarf up the tender eye of pitiful day,
And with thy bloody and invisible hand
Cancel and tear to pieces that great bond
Which keeps me pale. Light thickens, and
the crow 50
Makes wing to th' rooky wood ;
Good things of day begin to droop and
drowse,
Whiles night's black agents to their preys
do rouse.
Thou marvell'st at my words ; but hold
thee still :
Things bad begun make strong themselves
by ill. 55
So, prithee go with me. [*Exeunt.*

SCENE III. *Forres. The approaches to the
palace.*

Enter three Murderers.

1 *Mur.* But who did bid thee join with us?
3 *Mur.* Macbeth.
2 *Mur.* He needs not our mistrust, since
he delivers
Our offices, and what we have to do,
To the direction just.
1 *Mur.* Then stand with us.
The west yet glimmers with some streaks
of day ; 5
Now spurs the lated traveller apace
To gain the timely inn, and near approaches
The subject of our watch.
3 *Mur.* Hark ! I hear horses.
Ban. [*Within*] Give us a light there, ho !
2 *Mur.* Then 'tis he ; the rest
That are within the note of expectation 10
Already are i' th' court.
1 *Mur.* His horses go about.
3 *Mur.* Almost a mile ; but he does
usually,

So all men do, from hence to th' palace gate
Make it their walk.

Enter BANQUO, *and* FLEANCE *with a torch.*

   2 *Mur.*   A light, a light !
   3 *Mur.*   'Tis he.
   1 *Mur.* Stand to 't.   15
   Ban. It will be rain to-night.
   1 *Mur.*   Let it come down.
                    [*Stabs Banquo.*
   Ban. O, treachery ! Fly, good Fleance,
fly, fly, fly.
Thou mayst revenge. O slave !   18
         [*Dies. Fleance escapes.*
   3 *Mur.* Who did strike out the light ?
   1 *Mur.*   Was't not the way ?
   3 *Mur.* There's but one down ; the son
is fled.
   2 *Mur.*   We have lost
Best half of our affair.
   1 *Mur.*   Well, let's away,
And say how much is done.   [*Exeunt.*

      SCENE IV. *Forres. The palace.*

Banquet prepar'd. Enter MACBETH, LADY
   MACBETH, ROSS, LENNOX, Lords, *and*
   Attendants.

   Macb. You know your own degrees, sit
down.
At first and last the hearty welcome.
   Lords. Thanks to your Majesty.
   Macb. Our self will mingle with society
And play the humble host.
Our hostess keeps her state ; but in best
time   5
We will require her welcome.
   Lady M. Pronounce it for me, sir, to all
   our friends ;
For my heart speaks they are welcome.

   Enter First Murderer to the door.

   Macb. See, they encounter thee with
   their hearts' thanks.
Both sides are even ; here I'll sit i' th'
   midst.   10
Be large in mirth ; anon we'll drink a
   measure
The table round.   [*Going to the door.*
There's blood upon thy face.
   Mur.   'Tis Banquo's then.
   Macb. 'Tis better thee without than he
   within.   14
Is he despatch'd ?
   Mur.   My lord, his throat is cut ;
That I did for him.
   Macb.   Thou art the best o' th' cut-
   throats ;
Yet he's good that did the like for Fleance.
If thou didst it, thou art the nonpareil.
   Mur. Most royal sir—Fleance is 'scap'd.
   Macb. Then comes my fit again. I had
   else been perfect,   21

Whole as the marble, founded as the rock,
As broad and general as the casing air,
But now I am cabin'd, cribb'd, confin'd,
   bound in
To saucy doubts and fears. But Banquo's
   safe ?   25
   Mur. Ay, my good lord. Safe in a ditch
   he bides,
With twenty trenched gashes on his head,
The least a death to nature.
   Macb.   Thanks for that.
There the grown serpent lies ; the worm
   that's fled   29
Hath nature that in time will venom breed,
No teeth for th' present. Get thee gone ;
   to-morrow
We'll hear, ourselves, again.
                  [*Exit Murderer.*
   Lady M. My royal lord,
You do not give the cheer ; the feast is sold
That is not often vouch'd, while 'tis
   a-making,
'Tis given with welcome. To feed were best
   at home :   35
From thence the sauce to meat is ceremony;
Meeting were bare without it.

   Enter the Ghost of BANQUO *and sits in
   Macbeth's place.*

   Macb.   Sweet remembrancer !
Now good digestion wait on appetite,
And health on both !
   Len.   May't please your Highness sit ?
   Macb. Here had we now our country's
   honour roof'd,   40
Were the grac'd person of our Banquo
   present ;
Who may I rather challenge for unkindness
Than pity for mischance.
   Ross.   His absence, sir,
Lays blame upon his promise. Please 't
   your Highness
To grace us with your royal company. 45
   Macb. The table 's full.
   Len.   Here is a place reserv'd, sir.
   Macb. Where ?
   Len.   Here, my good lord.
What is't that moves your Highness ?
   Macb. Which of you have done this ?
   Lords.   What, my good lord ?
   Macb. Thou canst not say I did it ; never
   shake   50
Thy gory locks at me.
   Ross. Gentlemen, rise ; his Highness is
   not well.
   Lady M. Sit, worthy friends. My lord is
   often thus,
And hath been from his youth. Pray you,
   keep seat.
The fit is momentary ; upon a thought 55
He will again be well. If much you note
   him,
You shall offend him and extend his
   passion.

Feed, and regard him not.—Are you a man?
  Macb. Ay, and a bold one that dare look
    on that
Which might appal the devil.
  Lady M.   O proper stuff! 60
This is the very painting of your fear;
This is the air-drawn dagger which you said
Led you to Duncan. O, these flaws and
    starts—
Impostors to true fear—would well become
A woman's story at a winter's fire,   65
Authoriz'd by her grandam. Shame itself!
Why do you make such faces? When all's
    done,
You look but on a stool.
  Macb.   Prithee see there.
Behold! look! lo! how say you?
Why, what care I? If thou canst nod,
    speak too.   70
If charnel-houses and our graves must send
Those that we bury back, our monuments
Shall be the maws of kites.   [*Exit Ghost.*
  Lady M. What, quite unmann'd in folly?
  Macb. If I stand here, I saw him.
  Lady M.   Fie, for shame!
  Macb. Blood hath been shed ere now, i'
    th' olden time,   75
Ere humane statute purg'd the gentle weal;
Ay, and since too, murders have been
    perform'd
Too terrible for the ear. The time has been
That when the brains were out the man
    would die,
And there an end; but now they rise again,
With twenty mortal murders on their
    crowns,   81
And push us from our stools. This is more
    strange
Than such a murder is.
  Lady M.   My worthy lord,
Your noble friends do lack you.
  Macb.   I do forget.
Do not muse at me, my most worthy
    friends;   85
I have a strange infirmity, which is nothing
To those that know me. Come, love and
    health to all;
Then I'll sit down. Give me some wine, fill
    full.

          Enter Ghost.

I drink to the general joy o' th' whole table,
And to our dear friend Banquo, whom we
    miss.   90
Would he were here! To all, and him, we
    thirst,
And all to all.
  Lords.   Our duties, and the pledge.
  Macb. Avaunt, and quit my sight. Let
    the earth hide thee.
Thy bones are marrowless, thy blood is cold;
Thou hast no speculation in those eyes   95
Which thou dost glare with!
  Lady M.   Think of this, good peers,

But as a thing of custom. 'Tis no other;
Only it spoils the pleasure of the time.
  Macb. What man dare, I dare.
Approach thou like the rugged Russian
    bear,   100
The arm'd rhinoceros, or th' Hyrcan tiger;
Take any shape but that, and my firm
    nerves
Shall never tremble. Or be alive again,
And dare me to the desert with thy sword;
If trembling I inhabit, then protest me   105
The baby of a girl. Hence, horrible shadow!
Unreal mock'ry, hence!   [*Exit Ghost.*
          Why, so; being gone,
I am a man again. Pray you, sit still.
  Lady M. You have displac'd the mirth,
    broke the good meeting,
With most admir'd disorder.
  Macb.   Can such things be,   110
And overcome us like a summer's cloud,
Without our special wonder? You make
    me strange
Even to the disposition that I owe,
When now I think you can behold such
    sights   114
And keep the natural ruby of your cheeks,
When mine is blanch'd with fear.
  Ross.   What sights, my lord?
  Lady M. I pray you speak not; he
    grows worse and worse;
Question enrages him. At once, good night.
Stand not upon the order of your going,
But go at once.
  Len. Good night; and better health 120
Attend his Majesty!
  Lady M.   A kind good night to all!
        [*Exeunt Lords and Attendants.*
  Macb. It will have blood; they say blood
    will have blood.
Stones have been known to move, and trees
    to speak;
Augurs and understood relations have
By maggot-pies and choughs and rooks
    brought forth   125
The secret'st man of blood. What is the
    night?
  Lady M. Almost at odds with morning,
    which is which.
  Macb. How say'st thou that Macduff
    denies his person
At our great bidding?
  Lady M.   Did you send to him, sir?
  Macb. I hear it by the way; but I will
    send—   130
There's not a one of them but in this house
I keep a servant fee'd—I will to-morrow.
And betimes I will to the Weird Sisters:
More shall they speak; for now I am bent
    to know
By the worst means the worst. For mine
    own good   135
All causes shall give way. I am in blood
Stepp'd in so far that, should I wade no
    more,

Returning were as tedious as go o'er.
Strange things I have in head that will to
    hand,
Which must be acted ere they may be
    scann'd.   140
  Lady M. You lack the season of all
    natures, sleep.
  Macb. Come, we'll to sleep. My strange
    and self-abuse
Is the initiate fear that wants hard use.
We are yet but young in deed. [*Exeunt.*

SCENE V. A heath.

Thunder. Enter the three Witches, *meeting*
HECATE.

  1 *Witch.* Why, how now, Hecat! You
    look angerly.
  Hec. Have I not reason, beldams as you
    are,
Saucy and overbold? How did you dare
To trade and traffic with Macbeth
In riddles and affairs of death;   5
And I, the mistress of your charms,
The close contriver of all harms,
Was never call'd to bear my part,
Or show the glory of our art?
And, which is worse, all you have done   10
Hath been but for a wayward son,
Spiteful and wrathful; who, as others do,
Loves for his own ends, not for you.
But make amends now. Get you gone,
And at the pit of Acheron   15
Meet me i' th' morning; thither he
Will come to know his destiny.
Your vessels and your spells provide,
Your charms, and everything beside.
I am for th' air; this night I'll spend   20
Unto a dismal and a fatal end.
Great business must be wrought ere noon.
Upon the corner of the moon
There hangs a vap'rous drop profound;
I'll catch it ere it come to ground;   25
And that, distill'd by magic sleights,
Shall raise such artificial sprites
As, by the strength of their illusion,
Shall draw him on to his confusion.   29
He shall spurn fate, scorn death, and bear
His hopes 'bove wisdom, grace, and fear;
And you all know security
Is mortals' chiefest enemy.
        [*Music and a song within:*
        ' Come away, come away, etc.'
Hark! I am call'd; my little spirit, see,
Sits in a foggy cloud, and stays for me. 35
                [*Exit.*
  1 *Witch.* Come, let's make haste; she'll
    soon be back again. [*Exeunt.*

SCENE VI. Forres. The palace.

Enter LENNOX *and another* Lord.

  Len. My former speeches have but hit
    your thoughts,
Which can interpret farther. Only I say

Things have been strangely borne. The
    gracious Duncan
Was pitied of Macbeth. Marry, he was
    dead.
And the right-valiant Banquo walk'd too
    late;   5
Whom, you may say, if't please you,
    Fleance kill'd,
For Fleance fled. Men must not walk too
    late.
Who cannot want the thought how
    monstrous
It was for Malcolm and for Donalbain
To kill their gracious father? Damned
    fact!   10
How it did grieve Macbeth! Did he not
    straight,
In pious rage, the two delinquents tear,
That were the slaves of drink and thralls of
    sleep?
Was not that nobly done? Ay, and wisely
    too;
For 'twould have anger'd any heart alive 15
To hear the men deny't. So that, I say,
He has borne all things well; and I do
    think
That had he Duncan's sons under his key—
As, an't please heaven, he shall not—they
    should find
What 'twere to kill a father; so should
    Fleance.   20
But peace! For from broad words, and
    'cause he fail'd
His presence at the tyrant's feast, I hear,
Macduff lives in disgrace. Sir, can you tell
Where he bestows himself?
  Lord.   The son of Duncan,
From whom this tyrant holds the due of
    birth,   25
Lives in the English court, and is receiv'd
Of the most pious Edward with such grace
That the malevolence of fortune nothing
Takes from his high respect; thither
    Macduff   29
Is gone to pray the holy King upon his aid
To wake Northumberland and warlike
    Siward,
That by the help of these—with Him above
To ratify the work—we may again
Give to our tables meat, sleep to our
    nights,
Free from our feasts and banquets bloody
    knives,   35
Do faithful homage and receive free
    honours—
All which we pine for now. And this report
Hath so exasperate the King that he
Prepares for some attempt of war.
  Len.   Sent he to Macduff?
  Lord. He did; and with an absolute
    ' Sir, not I!'   40
The cloudy messenger turns me his back
And hums, as who should say ' You'll rue
    the time

That clogs me with this answer'.

Len.   And that well might
Advise him to a caution t' hold what
    distance
His wisdom can provide. Some holy angel
Fly to the court of England and unfold 46
His message ere he come, that a swift
    blessing
May soon return to this our suffering
    country
Under a hand accurs'd!

Lord.   I'll send my prayers with him.
                                    [*Exeunt.*

ACT FOUR

SCENE I. *A dark cave. In the middle, a
    cauldron boiling.*

Thunder. Enter the three Witches.

1 *Witch.* Thrice the brinded cat hath
    mew'd.
2 *Witch.* Thrice and once the hedge-pig
    whin'd.
3 *Witch.* Harpier cries; 'tis time, 'tis
    time.
1 *Witch.* Round about the cauldron go;
    In the poison'd entrails throw.   5
    Toad that under cold stone
    Days and nights has thirty-one
    Swelt'red venom sleeping got
    Boil thou first i' th' charmed pot.
All. Double, double toil and trouble; 10
    Fire burn, and cauldron bubble.
2 *Witch.* Fillet of a fenny snake,
    In the cauldron boil and bake;
    Eye of newt, and toe of frog,
    Wool of bat, and tongue of dog,   15
    Adder's fork, and blind-worm's sting,
    Lizard's leg, and howlet's wing—
    For a charm of pow'rful trouble,
    Like a hell-broth boil and bubble.
All. Double, double toil and trouble; 20
    Fire burn, and cauldron bubble.
3 *Witch.* Scale of dragon, tooth of wolf,
    Witch's mummy, maw and gulf
    Of the ravin'd salt-sea shark,
    Root of hemlock digg'd i' th' dark, 25
    Liver of blaspheming Jew,
    Gall of goat, and slips of yew
    Sliver'd in the moon's eclipse,
    Nose of Turk, and Tartar's lips,
    Finger of birth-strangled babe   30
    Ditch-deliver'd by a drab—
    Make the gruel thick and slab;
    Add thereto a tiger's chaudron,
    For th' ingredience of our cauldron.
All. Double, double toil and trouble; 35
    Fire burn, and cauldron bubble.
2 *Witch.* Cool it with a baboon's blood,
    Then the charm is firm and good.

Enter HECATE.

Hec. O, well done! I commend your
    pains;

And every one shall share i' th' gains.   40
And now about the cauldron sing,
Like elves and fairies in a ring,
Enchanting all that you put in.
        [*Music and a song:* 'Black spirits,
                    etc.' *Exit Hecate.*
2 *Witch.* By the pricking of my thumbs,
Something wicked this way comes.   45
Open, locks, whoever knocks.

Enter MACBETH.

Macb. How now, you secret, black, and
    midnight hags!
What is't you do?
All.   A deed without a name.
Macb. I conjure you by that which you
    profess—   50
Howe'er you come to know it—answer
    me.
Though you untie the winds and let them
    fight
Against the churches; though the yesty
    waves
Confound and swallow navigation up;
Though bladed corn be lodg'd and trees
    blown down;   55
Though castles topple on their warders'
    heads;
Though palaces and pyramids do slope
Their heads to their foundations; though
    the treasure
Of nature's germens tumble all together,
Even till destruction sicken—answer me 60
To what I ask you.
    1 *Witch.*   Speak.
    2 *Witch.*   Demand.
    3 *Witch.*   We'll answer.
1 *Witch.* Say, if thou'dst rather hear it
    from our mouths,
Or from our masters?
Macb.   Call 'em; let me see 'em.
1 *Witch.* Pour in sow's blood that hath
    eaten
Her nine farrow; grease that's sweaten 65
From the murderer's gibbet throw
Into the flame.
All.   Come, high or low;
Thyself and office deftly show.

Thunder. First Apparition, an Armed Head.

Macb. Tell me, thou unknown power—
1 *Witch.*   He knows thy thought.
Hear his speech, but say thou nought. 70
App. Macbeth! Macbeth! Macbeth!
    Beware Macduff;
Beware the Thane of Fife. Dismiss me.
    Enough.   [*He descends.*
Macb. Whate'er thou art, for thy good
    caution, thanks;
Thou hast harp'd my fear aright. But one
    word more—
1 *Witch.* He will not be commanded.
    Here's another,   75
More potent than the first.

Thunder. Second Apparition, *a Bloody Child.*

App. Macbeth ! Macbeth ! Macbeth !
Macb. Had I three ears, I'd hear thee.
App. Be bloody, bold, and resolute ;
laugh to scorn   79
The pow'r of man, for none of woman born
Shall harm Macbeth.   [*Descends.*
Macb. Then live, Macduff ; what need I
fear of thee ?
But yet I'll make assurance double sure
And take a bond of fate. Thou shalt not
live ;
That I may tell pale-hearted fear it lies, 85
And sleep in spite of thunder.

Thunder.   Third Apparition, *a Child Crowned, with a tree in his hand.*

                              What is this
That rises like the issue of a king,
And wears upon his baby brow the round
And top of sovereignty ?
All.   Listen, but speak not to't.
App. Be lion-mettled, proud, and take no
care
Who chafes, who frets, or where conspirers
are ;   91
Macbeth shall never vanquish'd be until
Great Birnam wood to high Dunsinane Hill
Shall come against him.   [*Descends.*
Macb.   That will never be.
Who can impress the forest, bid the tree 95
Unfix his earth-bound root ? Sweet bode-
ments, good !
Rebellion's head rise never till the wood
Of Birnam rise, and our high-plac'd
Macbeth
Shall live the lease of nature, pay his breath
To time and mortal custom. Yet my heart
Throbs to know one thing ; tell me, if
your art   101
Can tell so much—shall Banquo's issue ever
Reign in this kingdom ?
All.   Seek to know no more.
Macb. I will be satisfied. Deny me this,
And an eternal curse fall on you ! Let me
know.   105
Why sinks that cauldron, and what noise
is this ?   [*Hautboys.*
1 *Witch.* Show !
2 *Witch.* Show !
3 *Witch.* Show !
All. Show his eyes, and grieve his heart ;
Come like shadows, so depart !   111

A Show of eight Kings, and BANQUO *last ; the last king with a glass in his hand.*

Macb. Thou art too like the spirit of
Banquo ; down !
Thy crown does sear mine eye-balls. And
thy hair,
Thou other gold-bound brow, is like the
first.

A third is like the former. Filthy hags ! 115
Why do you show me this ? A fourth ?
Start, eyes.
What, will the line stretch out to th' crack
of doom ?
Another yet ? A seventh ? I'll see no more.
And yet the eighth appears, who bears a
glass
Which shows me many more ; and some I
see   120
That twofold balls and treble sceptres carry.
Horrible sight ! Now I see 'tis true ;
For the blood-bolter'd Banquo smiles upon
me,
And points at them for his. [*The show
vanishes*] What ! is this so ?
1 *Witch.* Ay, sir, all this is so. But why
Stands Macbeth thus amazedly ?   126
Come, sisters, cheer we up his sprites,
And show the best of our delights ;
I'll charm the air to give a sound,
While you perform your antic round ;   130
That this great king may kindly say,
Our duties did his welcome pay.

Music. The Witches dance, and vanish.

Macb. Where are they ? Gone ? Let this
pernicious hour
Stand aye accursed in the calendar.
Come in, without there.

                    Enter LENNOX.

Len.   What's your Grace's will ? 135
Macb. Saw you the Weird Sisters ?
Len.   No, my lord.
Macb. Came they not by you ?
Len.   No, indeed, my lord.
Macb. Infected be the air whereon they
ride ;
And damn'd all those that trust them ! I
did hear   139
The galloping of horse. Who was't came by ?
Len. 'Tis two or three, my lord, that
bring you word
Macduff is fled to England.
Macb.   Fled to England !
Len. Ay, my good lord.
Macb. [*Aside*] Time, thou anticipat'st
my dread exploits.
The flighty purpose never is o'ertook   145
Unless the deed go with it. From this
moment
The very firstlings of my heart shall be
The firstlings of my hand. And even now,
To crown my thoughts with acts, be it
thought and done :
The castle of Macduff I will surprise,   150
Seize upon Fife, give to the edge o' th'
sword
His wife, his babes, and all unfortunate
souls
That trace him in his line. No boasting like
a fool :
This deed I'll do before this purpose cool.

But no more sights !—Where are these
  gentlemen ?   155
Come, bring me where they are.   [*Exeunt.*

SCENE II. *Fife. Macduff's castle.*

Enter LADY MACDUFF, *her* Son, *and* ROSS.

Lady Macd. What had he done to make
  him fly the land ?
Ross. You must have patience, madam.
L. Macd.   He had none ;
His flight was madness. When our actions
  do not,
Our fears do make us traitors.
  Ross.   You know not
Whether it was his wisdom or his fear. 5
  L. Macd. Wisdom ! To leave his wife, to
  leave his babes,
His mansion, and his titles, in a place
From whence himself does fly ? He loves
  us not ;
He wants the natural touch ; for the poor
  wren,
The most diminutive of birds, will fight, 10
Her young ones in her nest, against the
  owl.
All is the fear, and nothing is the love ;
As little is the wisdom, where the flight
So runs against all reason.
  Ross.   My dearest coz,
I pray you, school yourself. But, for your
  husband,   15
He is noble, wise, judicious, and best knows
The fits o' th' season. I dare not speak
  much further ;
But cruel are the times, when we are
  traitors
And do not know ourselves ; when we hold
  rumour
From what we fear, yet know not what we
  fear,   20
But float upon a wild and violent sea
Each way and none.   I take my leave of
  you ;
Shall not be long but I'll be here again.
Things at the worst will cease, or else climb
  upward
To what they were before.—My pretty
  cousin,   25
Blessing upon you !
  L. Macd. Father'd he is, and yet he's
  fatherless.
Ross. I am so much a fool, should I stay
  longer,
It would be my disgrace and your dis-
  comfort.
I take my leave at once.   [*Exit.*
  L. Macd. Sirrah, your father's dead ;
And what will you do now ? How will you
  live ?   31
  Son. As birds do, mother.
  L. Macd. What, with worms and flies ?
  Son. With what I get, I mean ; and so do
  they.

L. Macd. Poor bird ! thou'dst never fear
  the net nor lime,
The pitfall nor the gin.   35
  Son. Why should I, mother ? Poor birds
  they are not set for.
My father is not dead, for all your saying.
  L. Macd. Yes, he is dead. How wilt thou
  do for a father ?
  Son. Nay, how will you do for a husband?
  L. Macd. Why, I can buy me twenty at
  any market.
  Son. Then you'll buy 'em to sell again. 41
  L. Macd. Thou speak'st with all thy wit ;
  and yet, i' faith,
With wit enough for thee.
  Son. Was my father a traitor, mother ?
  L. Macd. Ay, that he was.   45
  Son. What is a traitor ?
  L. Macd. Why, one that swears and lies.
  Son. And be all traitors that do so ?
  L. Macd. Every one that does so is a
  traitor, and must be hang'd.   50
  Son. And must they all be hang'd that
  swear and lie ?
  L. Macd. Every one.
  Son. Who must hang them ?
  L. Macd. Why, the honest men.   54
  Son. Then the liars and swearers are
  fools ; for there are liars and swearers enow
  to beat the honest men and hang up them.
  L. Macd. Now, God help thee, poor
  monkey ! But how wilt thou do for a
  father ?   59
  Son. If he were dead, you'd weep for him;
  if you would not, it were a good sign that I
  should quickly have a new father.
  L. Macd. Poor prattler, how thou talk'st !

Enter a Messenger.

  Mess. Bless you, fair dame ! I am not to
  you known,
Though in your state of honour I am perfect.
I doubt some danger does approach you
  nearly.   66
If you will take a homely man's advice,
Be not found here ; hence, with your little
  ones.
To fright you thus, methinks, I am too
  savage ;
To do worse to you were fell cruelty,   70
Which is too nigh your person. Heaven
  preserve you !
I dare abide no longer.   [*Exit.*
  L. Macd.   Whither should I fly ?
I have done no harm. But I remember now
I am in this earthly world, where to do
  harm
Is often laudable, to do good sometime 75
Accounted dangerous folly. Why then, alas,
Do I put up that womanly defence
To say I have done no harm ?

Enter Murderers.

What are these faces ?

1 *Mur.* Where is your husband ?
L. Macd. I hope, in no place so un-
   sanctified   80
Where such as thou mayst find him.
  1 *Mur.*   He's a traitor.
  Son. Thou liest, thou shag-ear'd villain.
  1 *Mur.* What, you egg ? [*Stabbing him.*
Young fry of treachery !
  Son.   He has kill'd me, mother.
Run away, I pray you.   [*Dies.*
  [*Exit Lady Macduff, crying ' Murder ! '*

SCENE III. *England. Before King Edward's
palace.*

Enter MALCOLM *and* MACDUFF.

  Mal. Let us seek out some desolate
   shade, and there
Weep our sad bosoms empty.
  Macd.   Let us rather
Hold fast the mortal sword, and like good
  men
Bestride our down-fall'n birthdom. Each
  new morn
New widows howl, new orphans cry ; new
  sorrows   5
Strike heaven on the face, that it resounds
As if it felt with Scotland and yell'd out
Like syllable of dolour.
  Mal.   What I believe, I'll wail ;
What know, believe ; and what I can
  redress,
As I shall find the time to friend, I will. 10
What you have spoke, it may be so per-
  chance.
This tyrant, whose sole name blisters our
  tongues,
Was once thought honest ; you have lov'd
  him well ;
He hath not touch'd you yet. I am young ;
  but something
You may deserve of him through me ; and
  wisdom   15
To offer up a weak, poor, innocent lamb
T' appease an angry god.
  Macd. I am not treacherous.
  Mal.   But Macbeth is.
A good and virtuous nature may recoil
In an imperial charge. But I shall crave
  your pardon ;   20
That which you are, my thoughts cannot
  transpose ;
Angels are bright still, though the brightest
  fell.
Though all things foul would wear the brows
  of grace,
Yet grace must still look so.
  Macd.   I have lost my hopes.
  Mal. Perchance even there where I did
  find my doubts.   25
Why in that rawness left you wife and
  child,
Those precious motives, those strong knots
  of love,

Without leave-taking ? I pray you,
Let not my jealousies be your dishonours,
But mine own safeties. You may be rightly
  just,   30
Whatever I shall think.
  Macd.   Bleed, bleed, poor country.
Great tyranny, lay thou thy basis sure,
For goodness dare not check thee. Wear
  thou thy wrongs,
The title is affeer'd. Fare thee well, lord.
I would not be the villain that thou think'st
For the whole space that's in the tyrant's
  grasp   36
And the rich East to boot.
  Mal.   Be not offended.
I speak not as in absolute fear of you.
I think our country sinks beneath the yoke ;
It weeps, it bleeds ; and each new day a
  gash   40
Is added to her wounds. I think withal
There would be hands uplifted in my right ;
And here, from gracious England, have I
  offer
Of goodly thousands. But, for all this,
When I shall tread upon the tyrant's head,
Or wear it on my sword, yet my poor
  country   46
Shall have more vices than it had before ;
More suffer, and more sundry ways than
  ever,
By him that shall succeed.
  Macd.   What should he be ?
  Mal. It is myself I mean ; in whom I
  know   50
All the particulars of vice so grafted
That, when they shall be open'd, black
  Macbeth
Will seem as pure as snow ; and the poor
  state
Esteem him as a lamb, being compar'd
With my confineless harms.
  Macd.   Not in the legions 55
Of horrid hell can come a devil more
  damn'd
In evils to top Macbeth.
  Mal.   I grant him bloody,
Luxurious, avaricious, false, deceitful,
Sudden, malicious, smacking of every sin
That has a name ; but there's no bottom,
  none,   60
In my voluptuousness. Your wives, your
  daughters,
Your matrons, and your maids, could not
  fill up
The cistern of my lust ; and my desire
All continent impediments would o'erbear
That did oppose my will. Better Macbeth
Than such an one to reign.
  Macd.   Boundless intemperance
In nature is a tyranny ; it hath been 67
Th' untimely emptying of the happy throne
And fall of many kings. But fear not yet
To take upon you what is yours. You may
Convey your pleasures in a spacious plenty,

And yet seem cold, the time you may so
    hoodwink.
We have willing dames enough ; there
    cannot be
That vulture in you to devour so many
As will to greatness dedicate themselves, 75
Finding it so inclin'd.
    Mal.   With this there grows
In my most ill-compos'd affection such
A stanchless avarice that, were I King,
I should cut off the nobles for their
    lands,
Desire his jewels, and this other's house ; 80
And my more-having would be as a sauce
To make me hunger more, that I should
    forge
Quarrels unjust against the good and loyal,
Destroying them for wealth.
    Macd.   This avarice
Sticks deeper, grows with more pernicious
    root   85
Than summer-seeming lust ; and it hath
    been
The sword of our slain kings. Yet do not
    fear ;
Scotland hath foisons to fill up your will
Of your mere own. All these are portable,
With other graces weigh'd.   90
    Mal. But I have none. The king-
    becoming graces,
As justice, verity, temp'rance, stableness,
Bounty, perseverance, mercy, lowliness,
Devotion, patience, courage, fortitude,
I have no relish of them ; but abound   95
In the division of each several crime,
Acting it many ways. Nay, had I pow'r, I
    should
Pour the sweet milk of concord into hell,
Uproar the universal peace, confound
All unity on earth.
    Macd.   O Scotland, Scotland !   100
    Mal. If such a one be fit to govern, speak.
I am as I have spoken.
    Macd.   Fit to govern !
No, not to live ! O nation miserable,
With an untitled tyrant bloody-scept'red,
When shalt thou see thy wholesome days
    again,   105
Since that the truest issue of thy throne
By his own interdiction stands accurs'd
And does blaspheme his breed ? Thy royal
    father
Was a most sainted king ; the queen that
    bore thee,
Oft'ner upon her knees than on her feet, 110
Died every day she liv'd. Fare thee well !
These evils thou repeat'st upon thyself
Hath banish'd me from Scotland. O my
    breast,
Thy hope ends here !
    Mal.   Macduff, this noble passion,
Child of integrity, hath from my soul   115
Wip'd the black scruples, reconcil'd my
    thoughts

To thy good truth and honour. Devilish
    Macbeth
By many of these trains hath sought to win
    me
Into his power ; and modest wisdom plucks
    me   119
From over-credulous haste. But God above
Deal between thee and me ; for even now
I put myself to thy direction, and
Unspeak mine own detraction, here abjure
The taints and blames I laid upon myself
For strangers to my nature. I am yet   125
Unknown to woman, never was forsworn,
Scarcely have coveted what was mine own,
At no time broke my faith, would not be-
    tray
The devil to his fellow, and delight
No less in truth than life. My first false
    speaking   130
Was this upon myself. What I am truly
Is thine and my poor country's to com-
    mand :
Whither indeed, before thy here-approach,
Old Siward with ten thousand warlike men
Already at a point was setting forth.   135
Now we'll together ; and the chance of
    goodness
Be like our warranted quarrel ! Why are
    you silent ?
    Macd. Such welcome and unwelcome
    things at once
'Tis hard to reconcile.

Enter a Doctor.

    Mal. Well ; more anon. Comes the King
    forth, I pray you ?   140
    Doct. Ay, sir. There are a crew of
    wretched souls
That stay his cure. Their malady convinces
The great assay of art ; but at his touch,
Such sanctity hath heaven given his hand,
They presently amend.
    Mal.   I thank you, doctor. [*Exit Doctor.*
    Macd. What's the disease he means ?
    Mal.   'Tis called the evil :
A most miraculous work in this good king ;
Which often since my here-remain in
    England
I have seen him do. How he solicits heaven,
Himself best knows ; but strangely-visited
    people,   150
All swoln and ulcerous, pitiful to the eye,
The mere despair of surgery, he cures,
Hanging a golden stamp about their necks,
Put on with holy prayers ; and 'tis spoken,
To the succeeding royalty he leaves   155
The healing benediction. With this strange
    virtue,
He hath a heavenly gift of prophecy ;
And sundry blessings hang about his throne
That speak him full of grace.

Enter ROSS.

    Macd.   See, who comes here ?

Mal. My countryman; but yet I know
    him not.   160
Macd. My ever gentle cousin, welcome
    hither.
Mal. I know him now.   Good God
    betimes remove
The means that makes us strangers!
Ross.   Sir, amen.
Macd. Stands Scotland where it did?
Ross.   Alas, poor country,
Almost afraid to know itself! It cannot 165
Be call'd our mother, but our grave; where
    nothing,
But who knows nothing, is once seen to
    smile;
Where sighs, and groans, and shrieks, that
    rent the air,
Are made, not mark'd; where violent
    sorrow seems   169
A modern ecstasy; the dead man's knell
Is there scarce ask'd for who; and good
    men's lives
Expire before the flowers in their caps,
Dying or ere they sicken.
Macd.   O, relation
Too nice, and yet too true!
Mal. What's the newest grief?
Ross. That of an hour's age doth hiss the
    speaker: 175
Each minute teems a new one.
Macd.   How does my wife?
Ross. Why, well.
Macd.   And all my children?
Ross.   Well too.
Macd. The tyrant has not batter'd at
    their peace?
Ross. No; they were well at peace when
    I did leave 'em.
Macd. Be not a niggard of your speech.
    How goes't?   180
Ross. When I came hither to transport
    the tidings,
Which I have heavily borne, there ran a
    rumour
Of many worthy fellows that were out;
Which was to my belief witness'd the
    rather
For that I saw the tyrant's power afoot. 185
Now is the time of help; your eye in
    Scotland
Would create soldiers, make our women
    fight,
To doff their dire distresses.
Mal.   Be't their comfort
We are coming thither. Gracious England
    hath
Lent us good Siward and ten thousand
    men—   190
An older and a better soldier none
That Christendom gives out.
Ross.   Would I could answer
This comfort with the like! But I have
    words
That would be howl'd out in the desert air,

Where hearing should not latch them.
Macd.   What concern they?
The general cause, or is it a fee-grief 196
Due to some single breast?
Ross.   No mind that's honest
But in it shares some woe, though the main
    part
Pertains to you alone.
Macd.   If it be mine,
Keep it not from me; quickly let me
    have it.   200
Ross. Let not your ears despise my
    tongue for ever,
Which shall possess them with the heaviest
    sound
That ever yet they heard.
Macd.   Humh! I guess at it.
Ross. Your castle is surpris'd; your wife
    and babes
Savagely slaughter'd.   To relate the
    manner,   205
Were, on the quarry of these murder'd deer,
To add the death of you.
Mal.   Merciful heaven!
What, man! Ne'er pull your hat upon your
    brows;
Give sorrow words. The grief that does not
    speak
Whispers the o'erfraught heart and bids it
    break.   210
Macd. My children too?
Ross.   Wife, children, servants, all
That could be found.
Macd.   And I must be from thence!
My wife kill'd too?
Ross.   I have said.
Mal.   Be comforted.
Let's make us med'cines of our great
    revenge
To cure this deadly grief.   215
Macd. He has no children. All my pretty
    ones?
Did you say all? O hell-kite! All?
What, all my pretty chickens and their dam
At one fell swoop?
Mal. Dispute it like a man.
Macd.   I shall do so; 220
But I must also feel it as a man.
I cannot but remember such things were
That were most precious to me. Did heaven
    look on,
And would not take their part? Sinful
    Macduff,
They were all struck for thee—nought that
    I am;   225
Not for their own demerits, but for mine,
Fell slaughter on their souls. Heaven rest
    them now!
Mal. Be this the whetstone of your
    sword. Let grief
Convert to anger; blunt not the heart,
    enrage it.
Macd. O, I could play the woman with
    mine eyes   230

And braggart with my tongue! But, gentle heavens,
Cut short all intermission; front to front
Bring thou this fiend of Scotland and myself;
Within my sword's length set him; if he scape,
Heaven forgive him too!
Mal. This tune goes manly. 235
Come, go we to the King. Our power is ready;
Our lack is nothing but our leave. Macbeth
Is ripe for shaking, and the pow'rs above
Put on their instruments. Receive what cheer you may; 239
The night is long that never finds the day.
[*Exeunt.*

ACT FIVE

SCENE I. *Dunsinane. Macbeth's castle.*

Enter a Doctor of Physic *and a* Waiting-Gentlewoman.

Doct. I have two nights watch'd with you, but can perceive no truth in your report. When was it she last walk'd?
Gent. Since his Majesty went into the field, I have seen her rise from her bed, throw her nightgown upon her, unlock her closet, take forth paper, fold it, write upon't, read it, afterwards seal it, and again return to bed; yet all this while in a most fast sleep. 8
Doct. A great perturbation in nature, to receive at once the benefit of sleep and do the effects of watching! In this slumb'ry agitation, besides her walking and other actual performances, what, at any time, have you heard her say? 13
Gent. That, sir, which I will not report after her.
Doct. You may to me; and 'tis most meet you should.
Gent. Neither to you nor any one, having no witness to confirm my speech.

Enter LADY MACBETH, *with a taper.*

Lo you, here she comes! This is her very guise; and, upon my life, fast asleep. Observe her; stand close.
Doct. How came she by that light? 20
Gent. Why, it stood by her. She has light by her continually; 'tis her command.
Doct. You see her eyes are open.
Gent. Ay, but their sense is shut.
Doct. What is it she does now? Look how she rubs her hands. 26
Gent. It is an accustomed action with her, to seem thus washing her hands; I have known her continue in this a quarter of an hour.
Lady M. Yet here's a spot. 30
Doct. Hark, she speaks. I will set down what comes from her, to satisfy my remembrance the more strongly.
Lady M. Out, damned spot! out, I say! One, two; why then 'tis time to do't. Hell is murky. Fie, my lord, fie! a soldier, and afeard? What need we fear who knows it, when none can call our pow'r to account? Yet who would have thought the old man to have had so much blood in him?
Doct. Do you mark that? 39
Lady M. The Thane of Fife had a wife; where is she now? What, will these hands ne'er be clean? No more o' that, my lord, no more o' that; you mar all with this starting.
Doct. Go to, go to; you have known what you should not. 45
Gent. She has spoke what she should not, I am sure of that. Heaven knows what she has known.
Lady M. Here's the smell of the blood still. All the perfumes of Arabia will not sweeten this little hand. Oh, oh, oh! 50
Doct. What a sigh is there! The heart is sorely charg'd.
Gent. I would not have such a heart in my bosom for the dignity of the whole body.
Doct. Well, well, well. 55
Gent. Pray God it be, sir.
Doct. This disease is beyond my practice. Yet I have known those which have walk'd in their sleep who have died holily in their beds. 59
Lady M. Wash your hands, put on your nightgown, look not so pale. I tell you yet again, Banquo's buried; he cannot come out on's grave.
Doct. Even so? 63
Lady M. To bed, to bed; there's knocking at the gate. Come, come, come, come, give me your hand. What's done cannot be undone. To bed, to bed, to bed. [*Exit.*
Doct. Will she go now to bed?
Gent. Directly.
Doct. Foul whisp'rings are abroad. Unnatural deeds
Do breed unnatural troubles; infected minds 70
To their deaf pillows will discharge their secrets.
More needs she the divine than the physician.
God, God forgive us all. Look after her;
Remove from her the means of all annoyance,
And still keep eyes upon her. So, good night. 75
My mind she has mated, and amaz'd my sight.
I think, but dare not speak.
Gent. Good night, good doctor.
[*Exeunt.*

SCENE II. *The country near Dunsinane.*

Drum and colours.   Enter MENTEITH,
CAITHNESS, ANGUS, LENNOX, *and* Soldiers.

  Ment. The English pow'r is near, led on
    by Malcolm,
His uncle Siward, and the good Macduff.
Revenges burn in them; for their dear
    causes
Would to the bleeding and the grim alarm
Excite the mortified man.
  Ang.   Near Birnam wood
Shall we well meet them; that way are
    they coming.   6
  Caith. Who knows if Donalbain be with
    his brother?
  Len. For certain, sir, he is not; I have
    a file
Of all the gentry. There is Siward's son,
And many unrough youths that even now
Protest their first of manhood.
  Ment.   What does the tyrant?
  Caith. Great Dunsinane he strongly
    fortifies.   12
Some say he's mad; others, that lesser
    hate him,
Do call it valiant fury; but for certain
He cannot buckle his distemper'd cause 15
Within the belt of rule.
  Ang.   Now does he feel
His secret murders sticking on his hands;
Now minutely revolts upbraid his faith-
    breach;
Those he commands move only in com-
    mand,   19
Nothing in love. Now does he feel his title
Hang loose about him, like a giant's robe
Upon a dwarfish thief.
  Ment.   Who then shall blame
His pester'd senses to recoil and start,
When all that is within him does condemn
Itself for being there?
  Caith.   Well, march we on 25
To give obedience where 'tis truly ow'd.
Meet we the med'cine of the sickly weal;
And with him pour we in our country's
    purge
Each drop of us.
  Len.   Or so much as it needs
To dew the sovereign flower and drown the
    weeds.   30
Make we our march towards Birnam.
                [*Exeunt, marching.*

SCENE III. *Dunsinane.   Macbeth's castle.*

Enter MACBETH, Doctor, *and* Attendants.

  Macb. Bring me no more reports; let
    them fly all.
Till Birnam wood remove to Dunsinane
I cannot taint with fear. What's the boy
    Malcolm?
Was he not born of woman? The spirits
    that know

All mortal consequences have pronounc'd
    me thus: 5
'Fear not, Macbeth; no man that's born
    of woman
Shall e'er have power upon thee'. Then fly,
    false thanes,
And mingle with the English epicures.
The mind I sway by and the heart I bear
Shall never sag with doubt nor shake with
    fear.   10

Enter Servant.

The devil damn thee black, thou cream-
    fac'd loon!
Where got'st thou that goose look?
  Serv. There is ten thousand—
  Macb.   Geese, villain?
  Serv.   Soldiers, sir.
  Macb. Go, prick thy face, and over-red
    thy fear,
Thou lily-liver'd boy.   What soldiers,
    patch?   15
Death of thy soul! Those linen cheeks of
    thine
Are counsellors to fear.   What soldiers,
    whey-face?
  Serv. The English force, so please you.
  Macb. Take thy face hence. [*Exit Servant.*
    Seyton!—I am sick at heart,
When I behold—Seyton, I say!—This push
Will cheer me ever, or disseat me now. 21
I have liv'd long enough. My way of life
Is fall'n into the sear, the yellow leaf;
And that which should accompany old age,
As honour, love, obedience, troops of
    friends,   25
I must not look to have; but, in their stead,
Curses not loud but deep, mouth-honour,
    breath,
Which the poor heart would fain deny, and
    dare not.
Seyton!

Enter SEYTON.

  Sey. What's your gracious pleasure?
  Macb.   What news more?
  Sey. All is confirm'd, my lord, which was
    reported.   31
  Macb. I'll fight till from my bones my
    flesh be hack'd.
Give me my armour.
  Sey.   'Tis not needed yet.
  Macb. I'll put it on.
Send out moe horses, skirr the country
    round;   35
Hang those that talk of fear. Give me mine
    armour.
How does your patient, doctor?
  Doct.   Not so sick, my lord,
As she is troubled with thick-coming
    fancies   38
That keep her from her rest.
  Macb.   Cure her of that.
Canst thou not minister to a mind diseas'd,

Pluck from the memory a rooted sorrow,
Raze out the written troubles of the brain,
And with some ,sweet oblivious antidote
Cleanse the stuff'd bosom of that perilous stuff
Which weighs upon the heart ?
Doct. Therein the patient 45
Must minister to himself.
Macb. Throw physic to the dogs—I'll none of it.
Come, put mine armour on ; give me my staff.
Seyton, send out. Doctor, the thanes fly from me.
Come, sir, dispatch. If thou couldst, doctor, cast 50
The water of my land, find her disease,
And purge it to a sound and pristine health,
I would applaud thee to the very echo,
That should applaud again.—Pull't off, I say.—
What rhubarb, senna, or what purgative drug, 55
Would scour these English hence ? Hear'st thou of them ?
Doct. Ay, my good lord. Your royal preparation
Makes us hear something.
Macb. Bring it after me.
I will not be afraid of death and bane
Till Birnam Forest come to Dunsinane. 60
[*Exeunt all but the Doctor.*
Doct. Were I from Duninsane away and clear,
Profit again should hardly draw me here.
[*Exit.*

SCENE IV. *Before Birnam Wood.*

Drum and colours. Enter MALCOLM, SIWARD, MACDUFF, Siward's Son, MENTEITH, CAITHNESS, ANGUS, LENNOX, ROSS, *and* Soldiers, *marching.*

Mal. Cousins, I hope the days are near at hand
That chambers will be safe.
Ment. We doubt it nothing.
Siw. What wood is this before us ?
Ment. The wood of Birnam.
Mal. Let every soldier hew him down a bough
And bear't before him ; thereby shall we shadow 5
The numbers of our host, and make discovery
Err in report of us.
Sold. It shall be done.
Siw. We learn no other but the confident tyrant
Keeps still in Dunsinane, and will endure
Our setting down before't.
Mal. 'Tis his main hope ; 10
For where there is advantage to be given,

Both more and less have given him the revolt ;
And none serve with him but constrained things,
Whose hearts are absent too.
Macd. Let our just censures
Attend the true event, and put we on 15
Industrious soldiership.
Siw. The time approaches
That will with due decision make us know
What we shall say we have, and what we owe.
Thoughts speculative their unsure hopes relate,
But certain issue strokes must arbitrate ; 20
Towards which advance the war.
[*Exeunt, marching.*

SCENE V. *Dunsinane. Macbeth's castle.*

Enter MACBETH, SEYTON, *and* Soldiers, *with drum and colours.*

Macb. Hang out our banners on the outward walls ;
The cry is still ' They come '. Our castle's strength
Will laugh a siege to scorn. Here let them lie
Till famine and the ague eat them up.
Were they not forc'd with those that should be ours, 5
We might have met them dareful, beard to beard,
And beat them backward home.
[*A cry within of women.*
What is that noise ?
Sey. It is the cry of women, my good lord.
[*Exit.*
Macb. I have almost forgot the taste of fears.
The time has been my senses would have cool'd 10
To hear a night-shriek, and my fell of hair
Would at a dismal treatise rouse and stir
As life were in't. I have supp'd full with horrors ;
Direness, familiar to my slaughterous thoughts,
Cannot once start me.

Re-enter SEYTON.

Wherefore was that cry ? 15
Sey. The Queen, my lord, is dead.
Macb. She should have died hereafter ;
There would have been a time for such a word.
To-morrow, and to-morrow, and to-morrow,
Creeps in this petty pace from day to day
To the last syllable of recorded time, 21
And all our yesterdays have lighted fools
The way to dusty death. Out, out, brief candle !
Life's but a walking shadow, a poor player,

That struts and frets his hour upon the
stage,   25
And then is heard no more ; it is a tale
Told by an idiot, full of sound and fury,
Signifying nothing.

Enter a Messenger.

Thou com'st to use thy tongue ; thy story
quickly.
  Mess. Gracious my lord,   30
I should report that which I say I saw,
But know not how to do't.
  Macb.   Well, say, sir.
  Mess. As I did stand my watch upon the
hill,
I look'd toward Birnam, and anon me-
thought
The wood began to move.
  Macb.   Liar and slave ! 35
  Mess. Let me endure your wrath, if't be
not so.
Within this three mile may you see it
coming ;
I say, a moving grove.
  Macb.   If thou speak'st false,
Upon the next tree shalt thou hang alive,
Till famine cling thee. If thy speech be
sooth,   40
I care not if thou dost for me as much.
I pull in resolution, and begin
To doubt th' equivocation of the fiend
That lies like truth. ' Fear not, till Birnam
wood   44
Do come to Dunsinane.' And now a wood
Comes toward Dunsinane. Arm, arm, and
out.
If this which he avouches does appear,
There is nor flying hence nor tarrying here.
I gin to be aweary of the sun,
And wish th' estate o' th' world were now
undone.   50
Ring the alarum bell. Blow wind, come
wrack ;
At least we'll die with harness on our back.
[*Exeunt.*

SCENE VI. *Dunsinane. Before the castle.*

Drum and colours.   Enter MALCOLM,
SIWARD, MACDUFF, *and their Army with
boughs.*

  Mal. Now near enough ; your leavy
screens throw down,
And show like those you are. You, worthy
uncle,
Shall with my cousin, your right noble
son,
Lead our first battle ; worthy Macduff and
we
Shall take upon's what else remains to do,
According to our order.
  Siw.   Fare you well.   6
Do we but find the tyrant's power to-night,
Let us be beaten, if we cannot fight.

  Macd. Make all our trumpets speak ;
give them all breath,   9
Those clamorous harbingers of blood and
death.   [*Exeunt.*

SCENE VII. *Another part of the field.*

Enter MACBETH.

  Macb. They have tied me to a stake ; I
cannot fly,
But bear-like I must fight the course.
What's he
That was not born of woman ? Such a one
Am I to fear, or none.   4

Enter young SIWARD.

  Yo. Siw. What is thy name ?
  Macb.   Thou'lt be afraid to hear it.
  Yo. Siw. No ; though thou call'st thyself
a hotter name
Than any is in hell.
  Macb.   My name's Macbeth.
  Yo. Siw. The devil himself could not
pronounce a title
More hateful to mine ear.
  Macb.   No, nor more fearful.
  Yo. Siw. Thou liest, abhorred tyrant ;
with my sword   10
I'll prove the lie thou speak'st.
      [*Fight, and young Siward slain.*
  Macb. Thou wast born of woman.
But swords I smile at, weapons laugh to
scorn,
Brandish'd by man that's of a woman born.
[*Exit.*

Alarums.   Enter MACDUFF.

  Macd. That way the noise is.   Tyrant,
show thy face.
If thou beest slain and with no stroke of
mine,   15
My wife and children's ghosts will haunt me
still.
I cannot strike at wretched kerns whose
arms
Are hir'd to bear their staves ; either thou,
Macbeth,
Or else my sword with an unbattered
edge
I sheathe again undeeded.   There thou
shouldst be ;   20
By this great clatter, one of greatest note
Seems bruited. Let me find him, Fortune,
And more I beg not.   [*Exit. Alarums.*

Enter MALCOLM *and old* SIWARD.

  Siw. This way, my lord.   The castle's
gently rend'red ;   24
The tyrant's people on both sides do
fight ;
The noble thanes do bravely in the war ;
The day almost itself professes yours,
And little is to do.
  Mal.   We have met with foes

That strike beside us.

Siw.   Enter, sir, the castle.
                    [*Exeunt. Alarum.*

SCENE VIII. *Another part of the field.*

Enter MACBETH.

Macb. Why should I play the Roman
        fool, and die
On mine own sword ? Whiles I see lives,
        the gashes
Do better upon them.

Enter MACDUFF.

Macd.   Turn, hell-hound, turn.
Macb. Of all men else I have avoided
        thee.
But get thee back ; my soul is too much
        charg'd   5
With blood of thine already.
Macd.   I have no words—
My voice is in my sword : thou bloodier
        villain
Than terms can give thee out.
                    [*Fight. Alarum.*
Macb.   Thou losest labour.
As easy mayst thou the intrenchant air
With thy keen sword impress as make me
        bleed.   10
Let fall thy blade on vulnerable crests ;
I bear a charmed life, which must not yield
To one of woman born.
Macd.   Despair thy charm ;
And let the angel whom thou still hast
        serv'd
Tell thee Macduff was from his mother's
        womb   15
Untimely ripp'd.
Macb. Accursed be that tongue that tells
        me so,
For it hath cow'd my better part of man ;
And be these juggling fiends no more
        believ'd
That palter with us in a double sense,   20
That keep the word of promise to our ear,
And break it to our hope ! I'll not fight
        with thee.
Macd. Then yield thee, coward,
And live to be the show and gaze o' th'
        time.
We'll have thee, as our rarer monsters are,
Painted upon a pole, and underwrit   26
' Here may you see the tyrant '.
Macb.   I will not yield,
To kiss the ground before young Malcolm's
        feet
And to be baited with the rabble's curse.
Though Birnam wood be come to Dunsi-
        nane,   30
And thou oppos'd, being of no woman born,
Yet I will try the last. Before my body
I throw my warlike shield. Lay on,
        Macduff ;
And damn'd be him that first cries ' Hold,
        enough!' [*Exeunt, fighting. Alarums.*

*Retreat and flourish. Enter, with drum and
colours,* MALCOLM, SIWARD, ROSS, LEN-
NOX, ANGUS, CAITHNESS, MENTEITH, *and*
Soldiers.

Mal. I would the friends we miss were
        safe arriv'd.   35
Siw. Some must go off ; and yet, by these
        I see,
So great a day as this is cheaply bought.
Mal. Macduff is missing, and your noble
        son.
Ross. Your son, my lord, has paid a
        soldier's debt :
He only liv'd but till he was a man ;   40
The which no sooner had his prowess con-
        firm'd
In the unshrinking station where he fought,
But like a man he died.
Siw.   Then he is dead ?
Ross. Ay, and brought off the field.
        Your cause of sorrow
Must not be measur'd by his worth, for
        then   45
It hath no end.
Siw.   Had he his hurts before ?
Ross. Ay, on the front.
Siw.   Why, then, God's soldier be he !
Had I as many sons as I have hairs,
I would not wish them to a fairer death.
And so his knell is knoll'd.
Mal.   He's worth more sorrow,   50
And that I'll spend for him.
Siw.   He's worth no more.
They say he parted well and paid his
        score ;
And so, God be with him ! Here comes
        newer comfort.

Re-enter MACDUFF, *with* MACBETH'S *head.*

Macd. Hail, King ! for so thou art.
        Behold where stands
Th' usurper's cursed head. The time is
        free.   55
I see thee compass'd with thy kingdom's
        pearl
That speak my salutation in their minds ;
Whose voices I desire aloud with mine—
Hail, King of Scotland !
All. Hail, King of Scotland ! [*Flourish.*
Mal. We shall not spend a large expense
        of time   60
Before we reckon with your several loves,
And make us even with you. My Thanes
        and kinsmen,
Henceforth be Earls, the first that ever
        Scotland
In such an honour nam'd. What's more to
        do,
Which would be planted newly with the
        time—   65
As calling home our exil'd friends abroad
That fled the snares of watchful tyranny ;
Producing forth the cruel ministers

Of this dead butcher, and his fiend-like
    queen,
Who, as 'tis thought, by self and violent
    hands   70
Took off her life—this, and what needful
    else

That calls upon us, by the grace of Grace,
We will perform in measure, time, and
    place.
So thanks to all at once and to each one, 74
Whom we invite to see us crown'd at Scone.
                 [*Flourish. Exeunt.*

HAMLET, PRINCE OF DENMARK

DRAMATIS PERSONÆ

CLAUDIUS, *King of Denmark.*
HAMLET, *son to the former and nephew to the present King.*
POLONIUS, *Lord Chamberlain.*
HORATIO, *friend to Hamlet.*
LAERTES, *son to Polonius.*
VOLTEMAND,
CORNELIUS,
ROSENCRANTZ,
GUILDENSTERN, } *courtiers.*
OSRIC,
A Gentleman,
A Priest.
MARCELLUS, } *officers.*
BERNARDO,

FRANCISCO, *a soldier.*
REYNALDO, *servant to Polonius.*
Players.
Two Clowns, *grave-diggers.*
FORTINBRAS, *Prince of Norway.*
A Norwegian Captain.
English Ambassadors.

GERTRUDE, *Queen of Denmark, and mother of Hamlet.*
OPHELIA, *daughter to Polonius.*

Ghost of Hamlet's Father.

Lords, Ladies, Officers, Soldiers, Sailors, Messengers, *and* Attendants.

THE SCENE : *Denmark.*

ACT ONE

SCENE I. *Elsinore. The guard-platform of the Castle.*

FRANCISCO *at his post. Enter to him* BERNARDO.

Ber. Who's there ?
Fran. Nay, answer me.   Stand and unfold yourself.
Ber. Long live the King !
Fran. Bernardo ?
Ber. He.   5
Fran. You come most carefully upon your hour.
Ber. 'Tis now struck twelve ; get thee to bed, Francisco.
Fran. For this relief much thanks. 'Tis bitter cold,
And I am sick at heart.
Ber. Have you had quiet guard ?
Fran.   Not a mouse stirring.
Ber. Well, good night.   11
If you do meet Horatio and Marcellus,
The rivals of my watch, bid them make haste.

Enter HORATIO *and* MARCELLUS.

Fran. I think I hear them. Stand, ho ! Who is there ?
Hor. Friends to this ground.
Mar.   And liegemen to the Dane.   15
Fran. Give you good night.
Mar.   O, farewell, honest soldier !
Who hath reliev'd you ?
Fran.   Bernardo hath my place.
Give you good night.   [*Exit.*
Mar.   Holla, Bernado !
Ber.   Say—

What, is Horatio there?
Hor.   A piece of him.
Ber. Welcome, Horatio; welcome, good Marcellus.   20
Hor. What, has this thing appear'd again to-night ?
Ber. I have seen nothing.
Mar. Horatio says 'tis but our fantasy,
And will not let belief take hold of him
Touching this dreaded sight, twice seen of us ;   25
Therefore I have entreated him along
With us to watch the minutes of this night,
That, if again this apparition come,
He may approve our eyes and speak to it.
Hor. Tush, tush, 'twill not appear.
Ber.   Sit down awhile,
And let us once again assail your ears,   31
That are so fortified against our story,
What we have two nights seen.
Hor.   Well, sit we down,
And let us hear Bernardo speak of this.
Ber. Last night of all,   35
When yond same star that's westward from the pole
Had made his course t' illume that part of heaven
Where now it burns, Marcellus and myself,
The bell then beating one—

Enter Ghost.

Mar. Peace, break thee off ; look where it comes again.   40
Ber. In the same figure, like the King that's dead.
Mar. Thou art a scholar ; speak to it, Horatio.
Ber. Looks 'a not like the King ? Mark it, Horatio.

Hor. Most like. It harrows me with fear
and wonder.
Ber. It would be spoke to.
Mar.   Question it, Horatio. 45
Hor. What art thou that usurp'st this
time of night
Together with that fair and warlike form
In which the majesty of buried Denmark
Did sometimes march ? By heaven I charge
thee, speak !
Mar. It is offended.
Ber.   See, it stalks away. 50
Hor. Stay! speak, speak ! I charge thee,
speak !   [*Exit Ghost.*
Mar. 'Tis gone, and will not answer.
Ber. How now, Horatio ! You tremble
and look pale.
Is not this something more than fantasy ?
What think you on't ?   55
Hor. Before my God, I might not this
believe
Without the sensible and true avouch
Of mine own eyes.
Mar.   Is it not like the King ?
Hor. As thou art to thyself :
Such was the very armour he had on 60
When he the ambitious Norway combated ;
So frown'd he once when, in an angry parle,
He smote the sledded Polacks on the ice.
'Tis strange.
Mar. Thus twice before, and jump at this
dead hour,   65
With martial stalk hath he gone by our
watch.
Hor. In what particular thought to work
I know not ;
But, in the gross and scope of mine opinion,
This bodes some strange eruption to our
state.
Mar. Good now, sit down, and tell me,
he that knows,   70
Why this same strict and most observant
watch
So nightly toils the subject of the land ;
And why such daily cast of brazen cannon,
And foreign mart for implements of war ;
Why such impress of shipwrights, whose
sore task   75
Does not divide the Sunday from the week ;
What might be toward, that this sweaty
haste
Doth make the night joint-labourer with
the day :
Who is't that can inform me ?
Hor.   That can I ;
At least, the whisper goes so. Our last
king,   80
Whose image even but now appear'd to us,
Was, as you know, by Fortinbras of Nor-
way,
Thereto prick'd on by a most emulate
pride,
Dar'd to the combat ; in which our valiant
Hamlet—

For so this side of our known world esteem'd
him—   85
Did slay this Fortinbras ; who, by a seal'd
compact,
Well ratified by law and heraldry,
Did forfeit, with his life, all those his lands
Which he stood seiz'd of, to the conqueror ;
Against the which a moiety competent 90
Was gaged by our king ; which had
return'd
To the inheritance of Fortinbras,
Had he been vanquisher ; as, by the same
comart
And carriage of the article design'd,
His fell to Hamlet. Now, sir, young
Fortinbras,   95
Of unimproved mettle hot and full,
Hath in the skirts of Norway, here and
there,
Shark'd up a list of lawless resolutes,
For food and diet, to some enterprise
That hath a stomach in't ; which is no
other,   100
As it doth well appear unto our state,
But to recover of us, by strong hand
And terms compulsatory, those foresaid
lands
So by his father lost ; and this, I take it,
Is the main motive of our preparations, 105
The source of this our watch, and the chief
head
Of this post-haste and romage in the land.
Ber. I think it be no other but e'en so.
Well may it sort, that this portentous figure
Comes armed through our watch ; so like
the King   110
That was and is the question of these wars.
Hor. A mote it is to trouble the mind's
eye.
In the most high and palmy state of Rome,
A little ere the mightiest Julius fell,
The graves stood tenantless, and the
sheeted dead   115
Did squeak and gibber in the Roman
streets ;
As, stars with trains of fire, and dews of
blood,
Disasters in the sun ; and the moist star
Upon whose influence Neptune's empire
stands   119
Was sick almost to doomsday with eclipse ;
And even the like precurse of fear'd events,
As harbingers preceding still the fates
And prologue to the omen coming on,
Have heaven and earth together demon-
strated
Unto our climatures and countrymen. 125

Re-enter Ghost.

But, soft, behold ! Lo, where it comes
again !
I'll cross it, though it blast me. Stay,
illusion.   [*Ghost spreads its arms.*
If thou hast any sound or use of voice,

Speak to me.
If there be any good thing to be done, 130
That may to thee do ease and grace to me,
Speak to me.
If thou art privy to thy country's fate,
Which happily foreknowing may avoid,
O, speak! 135
Or if thou hast uphoarded in thy life
Extorted treasure in the womb of earth,
For which, they say, you spirits oft walk
    in death, [*The cock crows.*
Speak of it. Stay, and speak. Stop it,
    Marcellus.
  Mar. Shall I strike at it with my
    partisan? 140
Hor. Do, if it will not stand.
Ber. 'Tis here!
Hor. 'Tis here!
Mar. 'Tis gone! [*Exit Ghost.*
We do it wrong, being so majestical,
To offer it the show of violence;
For it is, as the air, invulnerable, 145
And our vain blows malicious mockery.
  Ber. It was about to speak, when the
    cock crew.
  Hor. And then it started like a guilty
    thing
Upon a fearful summons. I have heard
The cock, that is the trumpet to the morn,
Doth with his lofty and shrill-sounding
    throat 151
Awake the god of day; and at his warning,
Whether in sea or fire, in earth or air,
Th' extravagant and erring spirit hies
To his confine; and of the truth herein 155
This present object made probation.
  Mar. It faded on the crowing of the cock.
Some say that ever 'gainst that season
    comes
Wherein our Saviour's birth is celebrated,
This bird of dawning singeth all night long;
And then, they say, no spirit dare stir
    abroad, 161
The nights are wholesome, then no planets
    strike,
No fairy takes, nor witch hath power to
    charm,
So hallowed and so gracious is that time.
  Hor. So have I heard, and do in part
    believe it. 165
But look, the morn, in russet mantle clad,
Walks o'er the dew of yon high eastward hill.
Break we our watch up; and, by my
    advice,
Let us impart what we have seen to-night
Unto young Hamlet; for, upon my life, 170
This spirit, dumb to us, will speak to him.
Do you consent we shall acquaint him
    with it,
As needful in our loves, fitting our duty?
  Mar. Let's do't, I pray; and I this
    morning know
Where we shall find him most convenient.
           [*Exeunt.*

SCENE II. *Elsinore. The Castle.*

Flourish. Enter CLAUDIUS KING OF DEN-
MARK, GERTRUDE THE QUEEN, *and* Coun-
cillors, *including* POLONIUS, *his son*
LAERTES, VOLTEMAND, CORNELIUS, *and*
HAMLET.

  King. Though yet of Hamlet our dear
    brother's death
The memory be green; and that it us
    befitted
To bear our hearts in grief, and our whole
    kingdom
To be contracted in one brow of woe;
Yet so far hath discretion fought with
    nature 5
That we with wisest sorrow think on him,
Together with remembrance of ourselves.
Therefore our sometime sister, now our
    queen,
Th' imperial jointress to this warlike state,
Have we, as 'twere with a defeated joy, 10
With an auspicious and a dropping eye,
With mirth in funeral, and with dirge in
    marriage,
In equal scale weighing delight and dole,
Taken to wife; nor have we herein barr'd
Your better wisdoms, which have freely
    gone 15
With this affair along. For all, our thanks.
Now follows that you know: young
    Fortinbras,
Holding a weak supposal of our worth,
Or thinking by our late dear brother's
    death
Our state to be disjoint and out of frame, 20
Co-leagued with this dream of his advan-
    tage—
He hath not fail'd to pester us with message
Importing the surrender of those lands
Lost by his father, with all bands of law,
To our most valiant brother. So much for
    him. 25
Now for ourself, and for this time of
    meeting,
Thus much the business is: we have here
    writ
To Norway, uncle of young Fortinbras—
Who, impotent and bed-rid, scarcely hears
Of this his nephew's purpose—to suppress
His further gait herein, in that the levies,
The lists, and full proportions, are all made
Out of his subject; and we here dispatch
You, good Cornelius, and you, Voltemand,
For bearers of this greeting to old Norway;
Giving to you no further personal power
To business with the King more than the
    scope
Of these delated articles allow.
Farewell; and let your haste commend
    your duty.
  Cor. ⎱ In that and all things will we
  Vol. ⎰ show our duty. 40

King. We doubt it nothing, heartily
   farewell.
   [*Exeunt Voltemand and Cornelius.*
And now, Laertes, what's the news with
   you ?
You told us of some suit ; what is't,
   Laertes ?
You cannot speak of reason to the Dane
And lose your voice. What wouldst thou
   beg, Laertes,   45
That shall not be my offer, not thy asking ?
The head is not more native to the heart,
The hand more instrumental to the mouth,
Than is the throne of Denmark to thy
   father.
What wouldst thou have, Laertes ?
   Laer.   My dread lord, 50
Your leave and favour to return to France ;
From whence though willingly I came to
   Denmark
To show my duty in your coronation,
Yet now, I must confess, that duty done,
My thoughts and wishes bend again toward
   France,   55
And bow them to your gracious leave and
   pardon.
   King. Have you your father's leave ?
   What says Polonius ?
   Pol. 'A hath, my lord, wrung from me
   my slow leave
By laboursome petition ; and at last
Upon his will I seal'd my hard consent. 60
I do beseech you, give him leave to go.
   King. Take thy fair hour, Laertes ; time
   be thine,
And thy best graces spend it at thy will !
But now, my cousin Hamlet, and my son—
   Ham. [*Aside*] A little more than kin, and
   less than kind.   65
   King. How is it that the clouds still hang
   on you ?
   Ham. Not so, my lord ; I am too much
   in the sun.
   Queen. Good Hamlet, cast thy nighted
   colour off,
And let thine eye look like a friend on
   Denmark.
Do not for ever with thy vailed lids   70
Seek for thy noble father in the dust.
Thou know'st 'tis common—all that lives
   must die,
Passing through nature to eternity.
   Ham. Ay, madam, it is common.
   Queen.   If it be,
Why seems it so particular with thee ? 75
   Ham. Seems, madam ! Nay, it is ; I
   know not seems.
'Tis not alone my inky cloak, good mother,
Nor customary suits of solemn black,
Nor windy suspiration of forc'd breath,
No, nor the fruitful river in the eye,   80
Nor the dejected haviour of the visage,
Together with all forms, moods, shapes of
   grief,

That can denote me truly. These, indeed,
   seem ;
For they are actions that a man might play;
But I have that within which passes
   show—   85
These but the trappings and the suits of
   woe.
   King. 'Tis sweet and commendable in
   your nature, Hamlet,
To give these mourning duties to your
   father ;
But you must know your father lost a
   father ;
That father lost lost his ; and the survivor
   bound,   90
In filial obligation, for some term
To do obsequious sorrow. But to persever
In obstinate condolement is a course
Of impious stubbornness ; 'tis unmanly
   grief ;
It shows a will most incorrect to heaven, 95
A heart unfortified, a mind impatient,
An understanding simple and unschool'd ;
For what we know must be, and is as
   common
As any the most vulgar thing to sense, 99
Why should we in our peevish opposition
Take it to heart ? Fie ! 'tis a fault to heaven,
A fault against the dead, a fault to nature,
To reason most absurd ; whose common
   theme
Is death of fathers, and who still hath cried,
From the first corse till he that died to-day,
' This must be so '. We pray you throw to
   earth   106
This unprevailing woe, and think of us
As of a father ; for let the world take
   note
You are the most immediate to our throne ;
And with no less nobility of love   110
Than that which dearest father bears his
   son
Do I impart toward you. For your intent
In going back to school in Wittenberg,
It is most retrograde to our desire ;
And we beseech you bend you to remain 115
Here, in the cheer and comfort of our eye,
Our chiefest courtier, cousin, and our son.
   Queen. Let not thy mother lose her
   prayers, Hamlet :
I pray thee stay with us ; go not to
   Wittenberg.
   Ham. I shall in all my best obey you,
   madam.   120
   King. Why, 'tis a loving and a fair reply.
Be as ourself in Denmark. Madam, come ;
This gentle and unforc'd accord of Hamlet
Sits smiling to my heart ; in grace whereof,
No jocund health that Denmark drinks
   to-day   125
But the great cannon to the clouds shall
   tell,
And the King's rouse the heaven shall bruit
   again,

Re-speaking earthly thunder. Come away.
[*Flourish. Exeunt all but Hamlet.*
Ham. O, that this too too solid flesh
would melt,
Thaw, and resolve itself into a dew !   130
Or that the Everlasting had not fix'd
His canon 'gainst self-slaughter ! O God !
God !
How weary, stale, flat, and unprofitable,
Seem to me all the uses of this world !
Fie on't ! Ah, fie ! 'tis an unweeded garden,
That grows to seed ; things rank and gross
in nature   136
Possess it merely. That it should come to
this !
But two months dead ! Nay, not so much,
not two.
So excellent a king that was to this
Hyperion to a satyr ; so loving to my
mother,   140
That he might not beteem the winds of
heaven
Visit her face too roughly. Heaven and
earth !
Must I remember ? Why, she would hang
on him
As if increase of appetite had grown
By what it fed on ; and yet, within a
month—   145
Let me not think on't. Frailty, thy name
is woman !—
A little month, or ere those shoes were old
With which she followed my poor father's
body,
Like Niobe, all tears—why she, even she—
O God ! a beast that wants discourse of
reason   150
Would have mourn'd longer—married with
my uncle,
My father's brother ; but no more like my
father
Than I to Hercules. Within a month,
Ere yet the salt of most unrighteous tears
Had left the flushing in her galled eyes,   155
She married. O, most wicked speed, to
post
With such dexterity to incestuous sheets !
It is not, nor it cannot come to good.
But break, my heart, for I must hold my
tongue.

Enter HORATIO, MARCELLUS, *and*
BERNARDO.

Hor. Hail to your lordship !
Ham.   I am glad to see you well. 160
Horatio—or I do forget myself.
Hor. The same, my lord, and your poor
servant ever.
Ham. Sir, my good friend. I'll change
that name with you.
And what make you from Wittenberg,
Horatio ?
Marcellus ?   165
Mar. My good lord !

Ham. I am very glad to see you. [*To
Bernardo*] Good even, sir.—
But what, in faith, make you from Witten-
berg ?
Hor. A truant disposition, good my lord.
Ham. I would not hear your enemy say
so ;   170
Nor shall you do my ear that violence,
To make it truster of your own report
Against yourself. I know you are no truant.
But what is your affair in Elsinore ?
We'll teach you to drink deep ere you
depart.   175
Hor. My lord, I came to see your father's
funeral.
Ham. I prithee do not mock me, fellow-
student ;
I think it was to see my mother's wedding.
Hor. Indeed, my lord, it followed hard
upon.
Ham. Thrift, thrift, Horatio ! The
funeral bak'd-meats   180
Did coldly furnish forth the marriage
tables.
Would I had met my dearest foe in heaven
Or ever I had seen that day, Horatio !
My father—methinks I see my father.
Hor. Where, my lord ?
Ham.   In my mind's eye, Horatio. 185
Hor. I saw him once ; 'a was a goodly
king.
Ham. 'A was a man, take him for all
in all,
I shall not look upon his like again.
Hor. My lord, I think I saw him yester-
night.
Ham. Saw who ?   190
Hor. My lord, the King your father.
Ham.   The King my father !
Hor. Season your admiration for a while
With an attent ear, till I may deliver,
Upon the witness of these gentlemen,
This marvel to you.
Ham.   For God's love, let me hear.
Hor. Two nights together had these
gentlemen,   196
Marcellus and Bernardo, on their watch,
In the dead waste and middle of the night,
Been thus encount'red. A figure like your
father,
Armed at point exactly, cap-a-pe,   200
Appears before them, and with solemn
march
Goes slow and stately by them ; thrice he
walk'd
By their oppress'd and fear-surprised eyes,
Within his truncheon's length ; whilst
they, distill'd
Almost to jelly with the act of fear,   205
Stand dumb and speak not to him. This
to me
In dreadful secrecy impart they did ;
And I with them the third night kept the
watch ;

Where, as they had delivered, both in time,
Form of the thing, each word made true
   and good,   210
The apparition comes. I knew your father ;
These hands are not more like.
Ham.   But where was this ?
Mar. My lord, upon the platform where
   we watch.
Ham. Did you not speak to it ?
Hor.   My lord, I did ;
But answer made it none ; yet once me-
   thought   215
It lifted up it head and did address
Itself to motion, like as it would speak ;
But even then the morning cock crew
   loud,
And at the sound it shrunk in haste away
And vanish'd from our sight.
Ham.   'Tis very strange. 220
Hor. As I do live, my honour'd lord, 'tis
   true ;
And we did think it writ down in our duty
To let you know of it.
Ham. Indeed, indeed, sirs, but this
   troubles me.
Hold you the watch to-night ?
All.   We do, my lord. 225
Ham. Arm'd, say you ?
All.   Arm'd, my lord.
Ham. From top to toe ?
All.   My lord, from head to foot.
Ham. Then saw you not his face ?
Hor. O yes, my lord ; he wore his beaver
   up.
Ham. What, look'd he frowningly ?   230
Hor. A countenance more in sorrow than
   in anger.
Ham. Pale or red ?
Hor. Nay, very pale.
Ham.   And fix'd his eyes upon you ?
Hor. Most constantly.
Ham.   I would I had been there.
Hor. It would have much amaz'd you. 235
Ham. Very like, very like. Stay'd it long?
Hor. While one with moderate haste
   might tell a hundred.
Both. Longer, longer.
Hor. Not when I saw't.
Ham. His beard was grizzl'd—no ?   239
Hor. It was, as I have seen it in his life,
A sable silver'd.
Ham.   I will watch to-night ;
Perchance 'twill walk again.
Hor.   I warr'nt it will.
Ham. If it assume my noble father's
   person,
I'll speak to it, though hell itself should
   gape   244
And bid me hold my peace. I pray you all,
If you have hitherto conceal'd this sight,
Let it be tenable in your silence still ;
And whatsomever else shall hap to-night,
Give it an understanding, but no tongue ;
I will requite your loves. So, fare you well—

Upon the platform, 'twixt eleven and
   twelve,   251
I'll visit you.
All.   Our duty to your honour.
Ham. Your loves, as mine to you ; fare-
   well.   [*Exeunt all but Hamlet.*
My father's spirit in arms ! All is not well.
I doubt some foul play. Would the night
   were come !   255
Till then sit still, my soul. Foul deeds will
   rise,
Though all the earth o'erwhelm them, to
   men's eyes.   [*Exit.*

SCENE III. *Elsinore. The house of Polonius.*

Enter LAERTES *and* OPHELIA *his sister.*

Laer. My necessaries are embark'd.
   Farewell.
And, sister, as the winds give benefit
And convoy is assistant, do not sleep,
But let me hear from you.
Oph.   Do you doubt that ?
Laer. For Hamlet, and the trifling of his
   favour,   5
Hold it a fashion and a toy in blood,
A violet in the youth of primy nature,
Forward not permanent, sweet not lasting,
The perfume and suppliance of a minute ;
No more.
Oph.   No more but so ?
Laer.   Think it no more ; 10
For nature crescent does not grow alone
In thews and bulk, but as this temple
   waxes,
The inward service of the mind and soul
Grows wide withal. Perhaps he loves you
   now,   14
And now no soil nor cautel doth besmirch
The virtue of his will ; but you must fear,
His greatness weigh'd, his will is not his
   own ;
For he himself is subject to his birth :
He may not, as unvalued persons do,
Carve for himself ; for on his choice
   depends   20
The sanity and health of this whole state ;
And therefore must his choice be circum-
   scrib'd
Unto the voice and yielding of that body
Whereof he is the head. Then if he says he
   loves you,
It fits your wisdom so far to believe it 25
As he in his particular act and place
May give his saying deed ; which is no
   further
Than the main voice of Denmark goes
   withal.
Then weigh what loss your honour may
   sustain,
If with too credent ear you list his songs, 30
Or lose your heart, or your chaste treasure
   open
To his unmast'red importunity.

Fear it, Ophelia, fear it, my dear sister;
And keep you in the rear of your affection,
Out of the shot and danger of desire.   35
The chariest maid is prodigal enough
If she unmask her beauty to the moon.
Virtue itself scapes not calumnious strokes;
The canker galls the infants of the spring
Too oft before their buttons be disclos'd; 40
And in the morn and liquid dew of youth
Contagious blastments are most imminent.
Be wary, then; best safety lies in fear:
Youth to itself rebels, though none else
    near.
  Oph. I shall the effect of this good lesson
    keep   45
As watchman to my heart. But, good my
    brother,
Do not, as some ungracious pastors do,
Show me the steep and thorny way to
    heaven,
Whiles, like a puff'd and reckless libertine,
Himself the primrose path of dalliance
    treads   50
And recks not his own rede.
    Laer.   O, fear me not!

         Enter POLONIUS.

I stay too long. But here my father comes.
A double blessing is a double grace;
Occasion smiles upon a second leave.
  Pol. Yet here, Laertes! Aboard, aboard,
    for shame!   55
The wind sits in the shoulder of your sail,
And you are stay'd for. There—my bless-
    ing with thee!
And these few precepts in thy memory
Look thou character. Give thy thoughts no
    tongue,
Nor any unproportion'd thought his act. 60
Be thou familiar, but by no means vulgar.
Those friends thou hast, and their adoption
    tried,
Grapple them to thy soul with hoops of
    steel;
But do not dull thy palm with entertain-
    ment
Of each new-hatch'd, unfledg'd courage.
    Beware   65
Of entrance to a quarrel; but, being in,
Bear't that th' opposed may beware of thee.
Give every man thy ear, but few thy
    voice;
Take each man's censure, but reserve thy
    judgment.
Costly thy habit as thy purse can buy, 70
But not express'd in fancy; rich, not
    gaudy;
For the apparel oft proclaims the man;
And they in France of the best rank and
    station
Are of a most select and generous choice in
    that.
Neither a borrower nor a lender be;   75
For loan oft loses both itself and friend,

And borrowing dulls the edge of husbandry.
This above all—to thine own self be true,
And it must follow, as the night the day,
Thou canst not then be false to any man. 80
Farewell; my blessing season this in thee!
  Laer. Most humbly do I take my leave,
    my lord.
  Pol. The time invites you; go, your
    servants tend.
  Laer. Farewell, Ophelia; and remember
    well
What I have said to you.
  Oph.   'Tis in my memory lock'd, 85
And you yourself shall keep the key of it.
  Laer. Farewell.   [*Exit.*
  Pol. What is't, Ophelia, he hath said to
    you?
  Oph. So please you, something touching
    the Lord Hamlet.
  Pol. Marry, well bethought!   90
'Tis told me he hath very oft of late
Given private time to you; and you
    yourself
Have of your audience been most free and
    bounteous.
If it be so—as so 'tis put on me,
And that in way of caution—I must tell
    you   95
You do not understand yourself so clearly
As it behoves my daughter and your
    honour.
What is between you? Give me up the
    truth.
  Oph. He hath, my lord, of late made
    many tenders
Of his affection to me.   100
  Pol. Affection! Pooh! You speak like a
    green girl,
Unsifted in such perilous circumstance.
Do you believe his tenders, as you call
    them?
  Oph. I do not know, my lord, what I
    should think.
  Pol. Marry, I will teach you: think
    yourself a baby   105
That you have ta'en these tenders for true
    pay
Which are not sterling. Tender yourself
    more dearly;
Or—not to crack the wind of the poor
    phrase,
Running it thus—you'll tender me a fool.
  Oph. My lord, he hath importun'd me
    with love   110
In honourable fashion.
  Pol. Ay, fashion you may call it; go to,
    go to.
  Oph. And hath given countenance to his
    speech, my lord,
With almost all the holy vows of heaven.
  Pol. Ay, springes to catch woodcocks! I
    do know,   115
When the blood burns, how prodigal the
    soul

Lends the tongue vows. These blazes, daughter,
Giving more light than heat—extinct in both,   118
Even in their promise, as it is a-making—
You must not take for fire. From this time
Be something scanter of your maiden presence ;
Set your entreatments at a higher rate
Than a command to parle. For Lord Hamlet,
Believe so much in him, that he is young,
And with a larger tether may he walk   125
Than may be given you. In few, Ophelia,
Do not believe his vows ; for they are brokers,
Not of that dye which their investments show,
But mere implorators of unholy suits,   129
Breathing like sanctified and pious bonds,
The better to beguile. This is for all—
I would not, in plain terms, from this time forth
Have you so slander any moment leisure
As to give words or talk with the Lord Hamlet.   134
Look to't, I charge you. Come your ways.
   Oph. I shall obey, my lord.   [*Exeunt.*

SCENE IV. *Elsinore. The guard-platform of the Castle.*

Enter HAMLET, HORATIO, *and* MARCELLUS.

   Ham. The air bites shrewdly ; it is very cold.
   Hor. It is a nipping and an eager air.
   Ham. What hour now ?
   Hor.   I think it lacks of twelve.
   Mar. No, it is struck.
   Hor. Indeed ? I heard it not. It then draws near the season   5
Wherein the spirit held his wont to walk.
      [*A flourish of trumpets, and two pieces
                   go off.*
What does this mean, my lord ?
   Ham. The King doth wake to-night and takes his rouse,
Keeps wassail, and the swagg'ring up-spring reels,
And, as he drains his draughts of Rhenish down,   10
The kettle-drum and trumpet thus bray out
The triumph of his pledge.
   Hor.   Is it a custom ?
   Ham. Ay, marry, is't ;
But to my mind, though I am native here
And to the manner born, it is a custom   15
More honour'd in the breach than the observance.
This heavy-headed revel east and west
Makes us traduc'd and tax'd of other nations ;
They clepe us drunkards, and with swinish phrase

Soil our addition ; and, indeed, it takes   20
From our achievements, though perform'd at height,
The pith and marrow of our attribute.
So, oft it chances in particular men
That, for some vicious mole of nature in them,
As in their birth, wherein they are not guilty,   25
Since nature cannot choose his origin ;
By the o'ergrowth of some complexion,
Oft breaking down the pales and forts of reason ;
Or by some habit that too much o'er-leavens
The form of plausive manners—that these men,   30
Carrying, I say, the stamp of one defect,
Being nature's livery or fortune's star,
His virtues else, be they as pure as grace,
As infinite as man may undergo,   34
Shall in the general censure take corruption
From that particular fault. The dram of eale
Doth all the noble substance of a doubt
To his own scandal.

           Enter Ghost.

   Hor.   Look, my lord, it comes.
   Ham. Angels and ministers of grace defend us !   39
Be thou a spirit of health or goblin damn'd,
Bring with thee airs from heaven or blasts from hell,
Be thy intents wicked or charitable,
Thou com'st in such a questionable shape
That I will speak to thee. I'll call thee Hamlet,   44
King, father, royal Dane. O, answer me !
Let me not burst in ignorance, but tell
Why thy canoniz'd bones, hearsed in death,
Have burst their cerements ; why the sepulchre
Wherein we saw thee quietly enurn'd   49
Hath op'd his ponderous and marble jaws
To cast thee up again. What may this mean
That thou, dead corse, again in complete steel
Revisits thus the glimpses of the moon,
Making night hideous, and we fools of nature
So horridly to shake our disposition   55
With thoughts beyond the reaches of our souls ?
Say, why is this ? wherefore? What should we do ?   [*Ghost beckons Hamlet.*
   Hor. It beckons you to go away with it,
As if it some impartment did desire
To you alone.
   Mar.   Look with what courteous action
It waves you to a more removed ground. 61
But do not go with it.
   Hor.   No, by no means.

Ham. It will not speak ; then I will
follow it.
Hor. Do not, my lord.
Ham. Why, what should be the fear ?
I do not set my life at a pin's fee ;   65
And for my soul, what can it do to that,
Being a thing immortal as itself ?
It waves me forth again ; I'll follow it.
Hor. What if it tempt you toward the
flood, my lord,
Or to the dreadful summit of the cliff   70
That beetles o'er his base into the sea,
And there assume some other horrible
form,
Which might deprive your sovereignty of
reason
And draw you into madness ? Think of it :
The very place puts toys of desperation,   75
Without more motive, into every brain
That looks so many fathoms to the sea
And hears it roar beneath.
Ham.   It waves me still.
Go on ; I'll follow thee.   79
Mar. You shall not go, my lord.
Ham.   Hold off your hands.
Hor. Be rul'd ; you shall not go.
Ham.   My fate cries out,
And makes each petty arture in this body
As hardy as the Nemean lion's nerve.
                        [*Ghost beckons.*
Still am I call'd. Unhand me, gentlemen.
By heaven, I'll make a ghost of him that
lets me.   85
I say, away ! Go on ; I'll follow thee.
                        [*Exeunt Ghost and Hamlet.*
Hor. He waxes desperate with imagina-
tion.
Mar. Let's follow ; 'tis not fit thus to
obey him.
Hor. Have after. To what issue will this
come ?
Mar. Something is rotten in the state of
Denmark.   90
Hor. Heaven will direct it.
Mar.   Nay, let's follow him.
                        [*Exeunt.*

SCENE V. *Elsinore. The battlements of
the Castle.*

Enter Ghost *and* HAMLET.

Ham. Whither ,wilt thou lead me ?
Speak. I'll go no further.
Ghost. Mark me.
Ham.   I will.
Ghost.   My hour is almost come,
When I to sulph'rous and tormenting
flames
Must render up myself.
Ham.   Alas, poor ghost !
Ghost. Pity me not, but lend thy serious
hearing   5
To what I shall unfold.
Ham.   Speak ; I am bound to hear.

Ghost. So art thou to revenge, when thou
shalt hear.
Ham. What ?
Ghost. I am thy father's spirit,
Doom'd for a certain term to walk the
night,   10
And for the day confin'd to fast in fires,
Till the foul crimes done in my days of
nature
Are burnt and purg'd away. But that I am
forbid
To tell the secrets of my prison-house,
I could a tale unfold whose lightest word   15
Would harrow up thy soul, freeze thy young
blood,
Make thy two eyes, like stars, start from
their spheres,
Thy knotted and combined locks to part,
And each particular hair to stand an end,
Like quills upon the fretful porpentine.   20
But this eternal blazon must not be
To ears of flesh and blood. List, list, O, list !
If thou didst ever thy dear father love—
Ham. O God !
Ghost. Revenge his foul and most un-
natural murder.
Ham. Murder !   26
Ghost. Murder most foul, as in the best
it is ;
But this most foul, strange, and unnatural.
Ham. Haste me to know't, that I, with
wings as swift
As meditation or the thoughts of love,   30
May sweep to my revenge.
Ghost.   I find thee apt ;
And duller shouldst thou be than the fat
weed
That roots itself in ease on Lethe wharf,
Wouldst thou not stir in this. Now, Ham-
let, hear :
'Tis given out that, sleeping in my
orchard,   35
A serpent stung me ; so the whole ear of
Denmark
Is by a forged process of my death
Rankly abus'd ; but know, thou noble
youth,
The serpent that did sting thy father's life
Now wears his crown.
Ham.   O my prophetic soul !   40
My uncle !
Ghost. Ay, that incestuous, that adulter-
ate beast,
With witchcraft of his wits, with traitorous
gifts—
O wicked wit and gifts that have the power
So to seduce !—won to his shameful lust   45
The will of my most seeming virtuous
queen.
O Hamlet, what a falling off was there,
From me, whose love was of that dignity
That it went hand in hand even with the
vow   49
I made to her in marriage ; and to decline

Upon a wretch whose natural gifts were
   poor
To those of mine !
But virtue, as it never will be moved,
Though lewdness court it in a shape of
   heaven,
So lust, though to a radiant angel link'd, 55
Will sate itself in a celestial bed
And prey on garbage.
But soft ! methinks I scent the morning air.
Brief let me be. Sleeping within my orchard,
My custom always of the afternoon,   60
Upon my secure hour thy uncle stole,
With juice of cursed hebona in a vial,
And in the porches of my ears did pour
The leperous distilment ; whose effect
Holds such an enmity with blood of man 65
That swift as quicksilver it courses through
The natural gates and alleys of the body ;
And with a sudden vigour it doth posset
And curd, like eager droppings into milk,
The thin and wholesome blood. So did it
   mine ;   70
And a most instant tetter bark'd about,
Most lazar-like, with vile and loathsome
   crust,
All my smooth body.
Thus was I, sleeping, by a brother's hand
Of life, of crown, of queen, at once dis-
   patch'd ;   75
Cut off even in the blossoms of my sin,
Unhous'led, disappointed, unanel'd ;
No reck'ning made, but sent to my account
With all my imperfections on my head.
O, horrible ! O, horrible ! most horrible !
If thou hast nature in thee, bear it not ;
Let not the royal bed of Denmark be
A couch for luxury and damned incest.
But, howsomever thou pursuest this act,
Taint not thy mind, nor let thy soul
   contrive   85
Against thy mother aught ; leave her to
   heaven,
And to those thorns that in her bosom
   lodge
To prick and sting her. Fare thee well at
   once.
The glowworm shows the matin to be near,
And gins to pale his uneffectual fire.   90
Adieu, adieu, adieu ! Remember me. [*Exit.*
  Ham. O all you host of heaven ! O earth !
   What else ?
And shall I couple hell ? O, fie ! Hold,
   hold, my heart ;
And you, my sinews, grow not instant old,
But bear me stiffly up. Remember thee ! 95
Ay, thou poor ghost, whiles memory holds
   a seat
In this distracted globe. Remember thee !
Yea, from the table of my memory
I'll wipe away all trivial fond records,
All saws of books, all forms, all pressures
   past,   100
That youth and observation copied there,

And thy commandment all alone shall live
Within the book and volume of my brain,
Unmix'd with baser matter.   Yes, by
   heaven !
O most pernicious woman !   105
O villain, villain, smiling, damned villain !
My tables—meet it is I set it down
That one may smile, and smile, and be a
   villain ;
At least I am sure it may be so in Denmark.
                       [*Writing.*
So, uncle, there you are. Now to my word :
It is ' Adieu, adieu ! Remember me '.   111
I have sworn't.
  Hor. [*Within*] My lord, my lord !

    Enter HORATIO *and* MARCELLUS.

  Mar. Lord Hamlet !
  Hor. Heavens secure him !
  Ham. So be it !
  Mar. Illo, ho, ho, my lord !   115
  Ham. Hillo, ho, ho, boy ! Come, bird,
   come.
  Mar. How is't, my noble lord ?
  Hor.   What news, my lord ?
  Ham. O, wonderful !
  Hor. Good my lord, tell it.
  Ham.   No ; you will reveal it.
  Hor. Not I, my lord, by heaven !
  Mar.   Nor I, my lord.   120
  Ham. How say you, then ; would heart
   of man once think it ?
But you'll be secret ?
  Both.   Ay, by heaven, my lord !
  Ham. There's never a villain dwelling in
   all Denmark
But he's an arrant knave.
  Hor. There needs no ghost, my lord, come
   from the grave   125
To tell us this.
  Ham. Why, right ; you are in the right ;
And so, without more circumstance at all,
I hold it fit that we shake hands and part ;
You, as your business and desire shall point
  you—
For every man hath business and desire, 130
Such as it is ; and for my own poor part,
Look you, I will go pray.
  Hor. These are but wild and whirling
   words, my lord.
  Ham. I am sorry they offend you, heartily;
Yes, faith, heartily.
  Hor.   There's no offence, my lord. 135
  Ham. Yes, by Saint Patrick, but there is,
   Horatio,
And much offence too. Touching this vision
  here—
It is an honest ghost, that let me tell you.
For your desire to know what is between us,
O'ermaster't as you may. And now, good
  friends,   140
As you are friends, scholars, and soldiers,
Give me one poor request.
  Hor. What is't, my lord ? We will.

Ham. Never make known what you have
    seen to-night.
Both. My lord, we will not.
Ham.   Nay, but swear't.
Hor.   In faith,
My lord, not I.
  Mar.   Nor I, my lord, in faith. 146
Ham. Upon my sword.
Mar. We have sworn, my lord, already.
Ham. Indeed, upon my sword, indeed.
Ghost. [*Cries under the stage*] Swear.
Ham. Ha, ha, boy ! say'st thou so ? Art
    thou there, truepenny ?   150
Come on. You hear this fellow in the
    cellarage :
Consent to swear.
  Hor.   Propose the oath, my lord.
Ham. Never to speak of this that you
    have seen,
Swear by my sword.
  Ghost. [*Beneath*] Swear.   155
Ham. Hic et ubique ? Then we'll shift
    our ground.
Come hither, gentlemen,
And lay your hands again upon my sword.
Swear by my sword
Never to speak of this that you have heard.
  Ghost [*Beneath*] Swear, by his sword. 161
  Ham. Well said, old mole ! Canst work
    i' th' earth so fast ?
A worthy pioneer ! Once more remove,
    good friends.
  Hor. O day and night, but this is
    wondrous strange !
  Ham. And therefore as a stranger give it
    welcome.   165
There are more things in heaven and earth,
    Horatio,
Than are dreamt of in your philosophy.
But come.
Here, as before, never, so help you mercy,
How strange or odd some'er I bear myself—
As I perchance hereafter shall think meet
To put an antic disposition on—   172
That you, at such times, seeing me, never
    shall,
With arms encumb'red thus, or this head-
    shake,
Or by pronouncing of some doubtful phrase,
As 'Well, well, we know ' or ' We could, an
    if we would '   176
Or ' If we list to speak ' or ' There be, an if
    they might '
Or such ambiguous giving out, to note
That you know aught of me—this do swear,
So grace and mercy at your most need help
    you.   180
  Ghost. [*Beneath*] Swear.
  Ham. Rest, rest, perturbed spirit ! So,
    gentlemen,
With all my love I do commend me to you ;
And what so poor a man as Hamlet is   185
May do t'express his love and friending to
    you,

God willing, shall not lack. Let us go in
    together ;
And still your fingers on your lips, I pray.
The time is out of joint. O cursed spite,
That ever I was born to set it right !   190
Nay, come, let's go together.   [*Exeunt.*

ACT TWO

SCENE I. *Elsinore. The house of Polonius.*

Enter POLONIUS *and* REYNALDO.

  Pol. Give him this money and these
    notes, Reynaldo.
  Rey. I will, my lord.
  Pol. You shall do marvellous wisely, good
    Reynaldo,
Before you visit him, to make inquire
Of his behaviour.
  Rey.   My lord, I did intend it. 5
  Pol. Marry, well said ; very well said.
    Look you, sir,
Enquire me first what Danskers are in
    Paris ;
And how, and who, what means, and where
    they keep,
What company, at what expense ; and
    finding
By this encompassment and drift of
    question   10
That they do know my son, come you more
    nearer
Than your particular demands will touch it.
Take you, as 'twere, some distant know-
    ledge of him ;
As thus : ' I know his father and his friends,
And in part him '. Do you mark this,
    Reynaldo ?   15
  Rey. Ay, very well, my lord.
  Pol. ' And in part him—but ' you may
    say ' not well ;
But if't be he I mean, he's very wild ;
Addicted so and so ' ; and there put on him
What forgeries you please ; marry, none so
    rank   20
As may dishonour him ; take heed of that ;
But, sir, such wanton, wild, and usual slips
As are companions noted and most known
To youth and liberty.
  Rey.   As gaming, my lord.
  Pol. Ay, or drinking, fencing, swearing,
    quarrelling,   25
Drabbing—you may go so far.
  Rey. My lord, that would dishonour him.
  Pol. Faith, no ; as you may season it in
    the charge.
You must not put another scandal on him,
That he is open to incontinency ;   30
That's not my meaning. But breathe his
    faults so quaintly
That they may seem the taints of liberty ;
The flash and outbreak of a fiery mind,
A savageness in unreclaimed blood,
Of general assault.

Rey.   But, my good lord— 35
Pol. Wherefore should you do this ?
Rey.   Ay, my lord,
I would know that.
Pol.   Marry, sir, here's my drift,
And I believe it is a fetch of warrant :
You laying these slight sullies on my son,
As 'twere a thing a little soil'd wi' th' work-
            ing,   40
Mark you,
Your party in converse, him you would
            sound,
Having ever seen in the prenominate crimes
The youth you breathe of guilty, be assur'd
He closes with you in this consequence :
' Good sir ' or so, or ' friend ' or ' gentle-
            man '   46
According to the phrase or the addition
Of man and country.
Rey.   Very good, my lord.
Pol. And then, sir, does 'a this—'a does—
What was I about to say ? By the mass,
I was about to say something ; where did I
leave ?   51
Rey. At ' closes in the consequence ', at
' friend or so ' and ' gentleman'.
Pol. At ' closes in the consequence '—
            ay, marry,
He closes thus : ' I know the gentleman ;
I saw him yesterday, or t'other day,   56
Or then, or then ; with such, or such ; and,
            as you say,
There was 'a gaming ; there o'ertook in's
            rouse ;
There falling out at tennis ' ; or perchance
' I saw him enter such a house of sale ' 60
Videlicet, a brothel, or so forth. See you now
Your bait of falsehood take this carp of
            truth ;
And thus do we of wisdom and of reach,
With windlasses and with assays of bias, 65
By indirections find directions out :
So, by my former lecture and advice,
Shall you my son. You have me, have you
            not ?
Rey. My lord, I have.
Pol.   God buy ye ; fare ye well.
Rey. Good my lord !   70
Pol. Observe his inclination in yourself.
Rey. I shall, my lord.
Pol. And let him ply his music.
Rey.   Well, my lord.
Pol. Farewell !   [*Exit Reynaldo.*

Enter OPHELIA.

How now, Ophelia ! What's the matter?
Oph. O my lord, my lord, I have been so
            affrighted !   75
Pol. With what, i' th' name of God ?
Oph. My lord, as I was sewing in my
            closet,
Lord Hamlet, with his doublet all unbrac'd,
No hat upon his head, his stockings fouled,
Ungart'red and down-gyved to his ankle ;

Pale as his shirt, his knees knocking each
            other,   81
And with a look so piteous in purport
As if he had been loosed out of hell
To speak of horrors—he comes before me.
Pol. Mad for thy love ?
Oph.   My lord, I do not know,
But truly I do fear it.
Pol.   What said he ? 86
Oph. He took me by the wrist, and held
            me hard ;
Then goes he to the length of all his arm,
And, with his other hand thus o'er his
            brow,
He falls to such perusal of my face   90
As 'a would draw it. Long stay'd he so.
At last, a little shaking of mine arm,
And thrice his head thus waving up and
            down,
He rais'd a sigh so piteous and profound
As it did seem to shatter all his bulk 95
And end his being. That done, he lets me
            go,
And, with his head over his shoulder turn'd,
He seem'd to find his way without his eyes ;
For out adoors he went without their helps
And to the last bended their light on me.
Pol. Come, go with me. I will go seek
            the King.   101
This is the very ecstasy of love,
Whose violent property fordoes itself,
And leads the will to desperate under-
            takings
As oft as any passion under heaven   105
That does afflict our natures. I am sorry—
What, have you given him any hard words
            of late ?
Oph. No, my good lord ; but, as you did
            command,
I did repel his letters, and denied
His access to me.
Pol.   That hath made him mad. 110
I am sorry that with better heed and judg-
            ment
I had not quoted him. I fear'd he did but
            trifle,
And meant to wreck thee ; but beshrew my
            jealousy !
By heaven, it is as proper to our age   114
To cast beyond ourselves in our opinions
As it is common for the younger sort
To lack discretion. Come, go we to the
            King.
This must be known ; which, being kept
            close, might move
More grief to hide than hate to utter love.
Come.   [*Exeunt.* 120

SCENE II. *Elsinore. The Castle.*

Flourish.   Enter KING, QUEEN, ROSEN-
CRANTZ, GUILDENSTERN, *and* Attendants.

King. Welcome, dear Rosencrantz and
            Guildenstern !

Moreover that we much did long to see you,
The need we have to use you did provoke
Our hasty sending. Something have you
    heard
Of Hamlet's transformation ; so I call it, 5
Sith nor th' exterior nor the inward man
Resembles that it was. What it should be,
More than his father's death, that thus hath
    put him
So much from th' understanding of himself,
I cannot deem of. I entreat you both   10
That, being of so young days brought up
    with him,
And sith so neighboured to his youth and
    haviour,
That you vouchsafe your rest here in our
    court   13
Some little time ; so by your companies
To draw him on to pleasures, and to gather,
So much as from occasion you may glean,
Whether aught to us unknown afflicts him
    thus
That, open'd, lies within our remedy.
    Queen. Good gentlemen, he hath much
    talk'd of you ;   19
And sure I am two men there is not living
To whom he more adheres. If it will please
    you
To show us so much gentry and good will
As to expend your time with us awhile
For the supply and profit of our hope,
Your visitation shall receive such thanks 25
As fits a king's remembrance.
    Ros.   Both your Majesties
Might, by the sovereign power you have of
    us,
Put your dread pleasures more into com-
    mand
Than to entreaty.
    Guil.   But we both obey, 29
And here give up ourselves, in the full bent,
To lay our service freely at your feet,
To be commanded.
    King. Thanks, Rosencrantz and gentle
    Guildenstern.
    Queen. Thanks, Guildenstern and gentle
    Rosencrantz.
And I beseech you instantly to visit   35
My too much changed son. Go, some of you,
And bring these gentlemen where Hamlet
    is.
    Guil. Heavens make our presence and
    our practices
Pleasant and helpful to him !
    Queen.   Aye amen !
    [*Exeunt Rosencrantz, Guildenstern,*
    and some Attendants.

    Enter POLONIUS.

    Pol. Th' ambassadors from Norway, my
    good lord,   40
Are joyfully return'd.
    King. Thou still hast been the father of
    good news.

    Pol. Have I, my lord ? I assure you, my
    good liege,
I hold my duty, as I hold my soul,   44
Both to my God and to my gracious King ;
And I do think—or else this brain of mine
Hunts not the trail of policy so sure
As it hath us'd to do—that I have found
The very cause of Hamlet's lunacy.
    King. O, speak of that ; that do I long
    to hear.   50
    Pol. Give first admittance to th' am-
    bassadors ;
My news shall be the fruit to that great
    feast.
    King. Thyself do grace to them, and
    bring them in.   [*Exit Polonius.*
He tells me, my dear Gertrude, he hath
    found
The head and source of all your son's
    distemper.   55
    Queen. I doubt it is no other but the main,
His father's death and our o'erhasty
    marriage.
    King. Well, we shall sift him.

    Re-enter POLONIUS, *with* VOLTEMAND *and*
              CORNELIUS.

          Welcome, my good friends !
Say, Voltemand, what from our brother
    Norway ?
    Volt. Most fair return of greetings and
    desires.   60
Upon our first, he sent out to suppress
His nephew's levies; which to him appear'd
To be a preparation 'gainst the Polack ;
But, better look'd into, he truly found
It was against your Highness. Whereat
    griev'd,   65
That so his sickness, age, and impotence,
Was falsely borne in hand, sends out
    arrests
On Fortinbras ; which he, in brief, obeys ;
Receives rebuke from Norway ; and, in
    fine,
Makes vow before his uncle never more 70
To give th' assay of arms against your
    Majesty.
Whereon old Norway, overcome with joy,
Gives him threescore thousand crowns in
    annual fee,
And his commission to employ those
    soldiers,
So levied as before, against the Polack ; 75
With an entreaty, herein further shown,
    [*Gives a paper.*
That it might please you to give quiet pass
Through your dominions for this enterprise,
On such regards of safety and allowance
As therein are set down.
    King.   It likes us well ; 80
And at our more considered time we'll read,
Answer, and think upon this business.
Meantime we thank you for your well-took
    labour.

Go to your rest; at night we'll feast
    together.
Most welcome home!
    [*Exeunt Ambassadors and Attendants.*
Pol.   This business is well ended. 85
My liege, and madam, to expostulate
What majesty should be, what duty is,
Why day is day, night night, and time is
    time,
Were nothing, but to waste night, day, and
    time.
Therefore, since brevity is the soul of wit, 90
And tediousness the limbs and outward
    flourishes,
I will be brief. Your noble son is mad.
Mad call I it; for, to define true madness,
What is't but to be nothing else but mad?
But let that go.
    Queen.   More matter with less art. 95
Pol. Madam, I swear I use no art at all.
That he's mad, 'tis true: 'tis true 'tis pity;
And pity 'tis 'tis true. A foolish figure!
But farewell it, for I will use no art.
Mad let us grant him, then; and now
    remains   100
That we find out the cause of this effect;
Or rather say the cause of this defect,
For this effect defective comes by cause.
Thus it remains, and the remainder thus.
Perpend.   105
I have a daughter—have while she is
    mine—
Who in her duty and obedience, mark,
Hath given me this. Now gather, and
    surmise.   [*Reads.*
    'To the celestial, and my soul's idol, the
most beautified Ophelia.' That's an ill
phrase, a vile phrase; 'beautified' is a vile
phrase. But you shall hear. Thus: [*Reads.*
' In her excellent white bosom, these, &c.'
    Queen. Came this from Hamlet to her?
    Pol. Good madam, stay awhile; I will be
faithful.   [*Reads.*
    ' Doubt thou the stars are fire;   115
        Doubt that the sun doth move;
        Doubt truth to be a liar;
        But never doubt I love.
O dear Ophelia, I am ill at these numbers.
I have not art to reckon my groans; but
that I love thee best, O most best, believe
it. Adieu.   121
        Thine evermore, most dear lady, whilst
            this machine is to him, HAMLET.'
This, in obedience, hath my daughter
    shown me;
And more above, hath his solicitings,   125
As they fell out by time, by means, and
    place,
All given to mine ear.
    King.   But how hath she
Receiv'd his love?
    Pol.   What do you think of me?
    King. As of a man faithful and honour-
    able.

Pol. I would fain prove so. But what
    might you think,   130
When I had seen this hot love on the wing,
As I perceiv'd it, I must tell you that,
Before my daughter told me—what might
    you,
Or my dear Majesty your queen here,
    think,
If I had play'd the desk or table-book; 135
Or given my heart a winking, mute and
    dumb;
Or look'd upon this love with idle sight—
What might you think? No, I went round
    to work,
And my young mistress thus I did bespeak:
' Lord Hamlet is a prince out of thy
    star;
This must not be'. And then I prescripts
    gave her,   141
That she should lock herself from his resort,
Admit no messengers, receive no tokens.
Which done, she took the fruits of my
    advice;
And he repelled, a short tale to make, 145
Fell into a sadness, then into a fast,
Thence to a watch, thence into a weakness,
Thence to a lightness, and, by this declen-
    sion,   148
Into the madness wherein now he raves
And all we mourn for.
    King.   Do you think 'tis this?
    Queen. It may be, very like.
    Pol. Hath there been such a time—I
        would fain know that—
That I have positively said ' 'Tis so ',
When it prov'd otherwise?
    King.   Not that I know.
    Pol. Take this from this, if this be other-
        wise.   155
If circumstances lead me, I will find
Where truth is hid, though it were hid
    indeed
Within the centre.
    King.   How may we try it further?
    Pol. You know sometimes he walks four
        hours together,
Here in the lobby.
    Queen.   So he does, indeed.   160
    Pol. At such a time I'll loose my daughter
        to him.
Be you and I behind an arras then;
Mark the encounter: if he love her not,
And be not from his reason fall'n thereon,
Let me be no assistant for a state,   165
But keep a farm and carters.
    King.   We will try it.

    Enter HAMLET, *reading on a book.*

    Queen. But look where sadly the poor
        wretch comes reading.
    Pol. Away, I do beseech you, both away!
I'll board him presently. O, give me leave.
                        [*Exeunt King and Queen.*
How does my good Lord Hamlet?   170

Ham. Well, God-a-mercy.

Pol. Do you know me, my lord ?

Ham. Excellent well ; you are a fish-monger.

Pol. Not I, my lord.

Ham. Then I would you were so honest a man.   175

Pol. Honest, my lord !

Ham. Ay, sir ; to be honest, as this world goes, is to be one man pick'd out of ten thousand.

Pol. That's very true, my lord.   179

Ham. For if the sun breed maggots in a dead dog, being a good kissing carrion— Have you a daughter ?

Pol. I have, my lord.

Ham. Let her not walk i' th' sun. Conception is a blessing. But as your daughter may conceive—friend, look to't.

Pol. How say you by that ? [*Aside*] Still harping on my daughter. Yet he knew me not at first ; 'a said I was a fishmonger. 'A is far gone, far gone. And truly in my youth I suff'red much extremity for love. Very near this. I'll speak to him again.— What do you read, my lord ?   190

Ham. Words, words, words.

Pol. What is the matter, my lord ?

Ham. Between who ?

Pol. I mean, the matter that you read, my lord.   194

Ham. Slanders, sir ; for the satirical rogue says here that old men have grey beards ; that their faces are wrinkled ; their eyes purging thick amber and plum-tree gum ; and that they have a plentiful lack of wit, together with most weak hams —all which, sir, though I most powerfully and potently believe, yet I hold it not honesty to have it thus set down ; for you yourself, sir, shall grow old as I am, if, like a crab, you could go backward.

Pol. [*Aside*] Though this be madness, yet there is method in't.—Will you walk out of the air, my lord ?   205

Ham. Into my grave ?

Pol. Indeed, that's out of the air. [*Aside*] How pregnant sometimes his replies are ! a happiness that often madness hits on, which reason and sanity could not so prosperously be delivered of. I will leave him, and suddenly contrive the means of meeting between him and my daughter. —My lord, I will take my leave of you.   213

Ham. You cannot, sir, take from me anything that I will more willingly part withal —except my life, except my life, except my life.   216

Enter ROSENCRANTZ *and* GUILDENSTERN.

Pol. Fare you well, my lord.

Ham. These tedious old fools !

Pol. You go to seek the Lord Hamlet ; there he is.

Ros. [*To Polonius*] God save you, sir !
[*Exit Polonius.*

Guil. My honour'd lord !   221

Ros. My most dear lord !

Ham. My excellent good friends ! How dost thou, Guildenstern ? Ah, Rosencrantz ! Good lads, how do you both ?   225

Ros. As the indifferent children of the earth.

Guil. Happy in that we are not over-happy ;
On fortune's cap we are not the very button.

Ham. Nor the soles of her shoe ?

Ros. Neither, my lord.   230

Ham. Then you live about her waist, or in the middle of her favours ?

Guil. Faith, her privates we.

Ham. In the secret parts of Fortune ? O, most true ; she is a strumpet. What news ?

Ros. None, my lord, but that the world's grown honest.   236

Ham. Then is doomsday near. But your news is not true. Let me question more in particular. What have you, my good friends, deserved at the hands of Fortune, that she sends you to prison hither ?   240

Guil. Prison, my lord !

Ham. Denmark's a prison.

Ros. Then is the world one.

Ham. A goodly one ; in which there are many confines, wards, and dungeons, Denmark being one o' th' worst.   246

Ros. We think not so, my lord.

Ham. Why, then, 'tis none to you ; for there is nothing either good or bad, but thinking makes it so. To me it is a prison.

Ros. Why, then your ambition makes it one ; 'tis too narrow for your mind.   252

Ham. O God, I could be bounded in a nutshell and count myself a king of infinite space, were it not that I have bad dreams.

Guil. Which dreams indeed are ambition; for the very substance of the ambitious is merely the shadow of a dream.   258

Ham. A dream itself is but a shadow.

Ros. Truly, and I hold ambition of so airy and light a quality that it is but a shadow's shadow.   261

Ham. Then are our beggars bodies, and our monarchs and outstretch'd heroes the beggars' shadows. Shall we to th' court ? for, by my fay, I cannot reason.

Both. We'll wait upon you.   265

Ham. No such matter. I will not sort you with the rest of my servants ; for, to speak to you like an honest man, I am most dreadfully attended. But, in the beaten way of friendship, what make you at Elsinore ?

Ros. To visit you, my lord ; no other occasion.   270

Ham. Beggar that I am, I am even poor in thanks ; but I thank you ; and sure, dear friends, my thanks are too dear a half-penny. Were you not sent for ? Is it your own inclining ? Is it a free visitation ? Come, come, deal justly with me. Come, come ; nay, speak.   275

Guil. What should we say, my lord ?

Ham. Why any thing. But to th' purpose : you were sent for ; and there is a kind of confession in your looks, which your modesties have not craft enough to colour ; I know the good King and Queen have sent for you.   280

Ros. To what end, my lord ?

Ham. That you must teach me. But let me conjure you by the rights of our fellow-ship, by the consonancy of our youth, by the obligation of our ever-preserved love, and by what more dear a better proposer can charge you withal, be even and direct with me, whether you were sent for or no ?

Ros. [*Aside to Guildenstern*] What say you ?

Ham. [*Aside*] Nay, then, I have an eye of you.—If you love me, hold not off.   290

Guil. My lord, we were sent for.

Ham. I will tell you why ; so shall my anticipation prevent your discovery, and your secrecy to the King and Queen moult no feather. I have of late—but wherefore I know not—lost all my mirth, forgone all custom of exercises ; and indeed it goes so heavily with my disposition that this goodly frame, the earth, seems to me a sterile promontory ; this most excellent canopy the air, look you, this brave o'er-hanging firmament, this majestical roof fretted with golden fire—why, it appeareth no other thing to me than a foul and pestilent congregation of vapours. What a piece of work is a man ! How noble in reason ! how infinite in faculties ! in form and moving, how express and admirable ! in action, how like an angel ! in apprehen-sion, how like a god ! the beauty of the world ! the paragon of animals ! And yet, to me, what is this quintessence of dust ? Man delights not me—no, nor woman neither, though by your smiling you seem to say so.   309

Ros. My lord, there was no such stuff in my thoughts.

Ham. Why did ye laugh, then, when I said ' Man delights not me ' ?

Ros. To think, my lord, if you delight not in man, what lenten entertainment the players shall receive from you. We coted them on the way ; and hither are they coming to offer you service.   316

Ham. He that plays the king shall be welcome—his Majesty shall have tribute on me ; the adventurous knight shall use his foil and target ; the lover shall not sigh gratis ; the humorous man shall end his part in peace ; the clown shall make those laugh whose lungs are tickle a' th' sere ; and the lady shall say her mind freely, or the blank verse shall halt for't. What players are they ?   323

Ros. Even those you were wont to take such delight in—the tragedians of the city.

Ham. How chances it they travel ? Their residence, both in reputation and profit, was better both ways.

Ros. I think their inhibition comes by the means of the late innovation.   329

Ham. Do they hold the same estimation they did when I was in the city ? Are they so followed ?

Ros. No, indeed, are they not.

Ham. How comes it ? Do they grow rusty ?   333

Ros. Nay, their endeavour keeps in the wonted pace ; but there is, sir, an eyrie of children, little eyases, that cry out on the top of question, and are most tyrannically clapp'd for't. These are now the fashion, and so berattle the common stages—so they call them—that many wearing rapiers are afraid of goose quills and dare scarce come thither.   340

Ham. What, are they children ? Who maintains 'em ? How are they escoted ? Will they pursue the quality no longer than they can sing ? Will they not say after-wards, if they should grow themselves to common players—as it is most like, if their means are no better—their writers do them wrong to make them exclaim against their own succession ?   347

Ros. Faith, there has been much to-do on both sides ; and the nation holds it no sin to tarre them to controversy. There was for a while no money bid for argument, unless the poet and the player went to cuffs in the question.   352

Ham. Is't possible ?

Guil. O, there has been much throwing about of brains.   355

Ham. Do the boys carry it away ?

Ros. Ay, that they do, my lord—Hercules and his load too.

Ham. It is not very strange ; for my uncle is King of Denmark, and those that would make mows at him while my father lived give twenty, forty, fifty, a hundred ducats apiece for his picture in little. 'Sblood, there is something in this more than natural, if philosophy could find it out.   [*A flourish.*]

Guil. There are the players.   365

Ham. Gentlemen, you are welcome to Elsinore. Your hands, come then ; th' appur-tenance of welcome is fashion and ceremony. Let me comply with you in this garb ; lest my extent to the players, which, I tell you, must show fairly outwards, should more appear like entertainment than yours. You

are welcome. But my uncle-father and
aunt-mother are deceived.   372

Guil. In what, my dear lord ?

Ham. I am but mad north-north-west ;
when the wind is southerly I know a hawk
from a handsaw.   375

Re-enter POLONIUS.

Pol. Well be with you, gentlemen !

Ham. Hark you, Guildenstern, and you
too—at each ear a hearer : that great baby
you see there is not yet out of his swaddling
clouts.

Ros. Happily he is the second time come
to them ; for they say an old man is twice
a child.   381

Ham. I will prophesy he comes to tell me
of the players ; mark it. You say right,
sir : a Monday morning ; 'twas then indeed.

Pol. My lord, I have news to tell you. 385

Ham. My lord, I have news to tell you.
When Roscius was an actor in Rome—

Pol. The actors are come hither, my lord.

Ham. Buzz, buzz !

Pol. Upon my honour—   390

Ham. Then came each actor on his ass—

Pol. The best actors in the world, either
for tragedy, comedy, history, pastoral,
pastoral-comical, historical-pastoral, tragi-
cal-historical, tragical-comical-historical-
pastoral, scene individable, or poem unlimited. Seneca cannot be too heavy nor
Plautus too light. For the law of writ and
the liberty, these are the only men.   397

Ham. O Jephthah, judge of Israel, what
a treasure hadst thou !

Pol. What a treasure had he, my lord ?

Ham. Why—   401

' One fair daughter, and no more,
   The which he loved passing well '.

Pol. [*Aside*] Still on my daughter.

Ham. Am I not i' th' right, old Jephthah?

Pol. If you call me Jephthah, my lord, I
have a daughter that I love passing well.

Ham. Nay, that follows not.

Pol. What follows then, my lord ?

Ham. Why—   410

' As by lot, God wot '

and then, you know,

' It came to pass, as most like it was '.

The first row of the pious chanson will show
you more ; for look where my abridgment
comes.   415

Enter the Players.

You are welcome, masters ; welcome, all.—
I am glad to see thee well.—Welcome, good
friends.—O, my old friend ! Why thy face is
valanc'd since I saw thee last ; com'st thou
to beard me in Denmark ?—What, my
young lady and mistress ! By'r lady, your
ladyship is nearer to heaven than when I
saw you last by the altitude of a chopine.

Pray God, your voice, like a piece of uncurrent gold, be not crack'd within the
ring.—Masters, you are all welcome. We'll
e'en to't like French falconers, fly at anything we see. We'll have a speech straight.
Come, give us a taste of your quality ;
come, a passionate speech.

1 Play. What speech, my good lord ? 427

Ham. I heard thee speak me a speech
once, but it was never acted ; or, if it was,
not above once ; for the play, I remember,
pleas'd not the million ; 'twas caviary to
the general. But it was—as I received it,
and others whose judgments in such
matters cried in the top of mine—an
excellent play, well digested in the scenes,
set down with as much modesty as cunning.
I remember one said there were no sallets
in the lines to make the matter savoury,
nor no matter in the phrase that might
indict the author of affectation ; but call'd it
an honest method, as wholesome as sweet,
and by very much more handsome than
fine. One speech in it I chiefly lov'd : 'twas
Æneas' tale to Dido ; and thereabout of it
especially where he speaks of Priam's
slaughter. If it live in your memory, begin
at this line—let me see, let me see :   443

' The rugged Pyrrhus, like th' Hyrcanian
      beast,'

'Tis not so ; it begins with Pyrrhus.   445

' The rugged Pyrrhus, he whose sable arms,
Black as his purpose, did the night re-
      semble
When he lay couched in the ominous
      horse,
Hath now this dread and black com-
      plexion smear'd
With heraldry more dismal ;   head to
      foot   450
Now is he total gules, horridly trick'd
With blood of fathers, mothers, daughters,
      sons,
Bak'd and impasted with the parching
      streets,
That lend a tyrannous and damned light
To their lord's murder. Roasted in wrath
      and fire,   455
And thus o'er-sized with coagulate gore,
With eyes like carbuncles, the hellish
      Pyrrhus
Old grandsire Priam seeks.'

So proceed you.

Pol. Fore God, my lord, well spoken,
with good accent and good discretion. 461

1 Play.   'Anon he finds him
Striking too short at Greeks ; his antique
      sword,
Rebellious to his arm, lies where it falls,
Repugnant to command. Unequal match'd,
Pyrrhus at Priam drives, in rage strikes
      wide ;   466

But with the whiff and wind of his fell
    sword
Th' unnerved father falls. Then senseless
    Ilium,   468
Seeming to feel this blow, with flaming top
Stoops to his base, and with a hideous crash
Takes prisoner Pyrrhus' ear. For, lo ! his
    sword,   471
Which was declining on the milky head
Of reverend Priam, seem'd i' th' air to stick.
So, as a painted tyrant, Pyrrhus stood
And, like a neutral to his will and matter,
Did nothing.   476
But as we often see, against some storm,
A silence in the heavens, the rack stand
    still,
The bold winds speechless, and the orb
    below
As hush as death, anon the dreadful
    thunder   480
Doth rend the region ; so, after Pyrrhus'
    pause,
A roused vengeance sets him new a-work ;
And never did the Cyclops' hammers fall
On Mars's armour, forg'd for proof eterne,
With less remorse than Pyrrhus' bleeding
    sword   485
Now falls on Priam.
Out, out, thou strumpet, Fortune ! All you
    gods,
In general synod, take away her power ;
Break all the spokes and fellies from her
    wheel,
And bowl the round nave down the hill
    of heaven,   490
As low as to the fiends.'
    Pol. This is too long.
    Ham. It shall to the barber's, with your
beard. Prithee say on. He's for a jig, or a
tale of bawdry, or he sleeps. Say on ; come
to Hecuba.   495
    1 Play. ' But who, ah, who had seen the
    mobled queen—'
    Ham. ' The mobled queen ' ?
    Pol. That's good ; ' mobled queen ' is
good.
    1 Play. ' Run barefoot up and down,
    threat'ning the flames   499
With bisson rheum ; a clout upon that head
Where late the diadem stood, and for a robe,
About her lank and all o'er-teemed loins,
A blanket, in the alarm of fear caught up—
Who this had seen, with tongue in venom
    steep'd,
'Gainst Fortune's state would treason have
    pronounc'd.   505
But if tne gods themselves did see her then,
When she saw Pyrrhus make malicious
    sport
In mincing with his sword her husband's
    limbs,
The instant burst of clamour that she
    made—   509
Unless things mortal move them not at all—

Would have made milch the burning eyes of
    heaven,
And passion in the gods.'
    Pol. Look whe'er he has not turn'd his
colour, and has tears in 's eyes. Prithee no
more.   514
    Ham. 'Tis well ; I'll have thee speak out
the rest of this soon.—Good my lord, will
you see the players well bestowed ? Do
you hear : let them be well used ; for
they are the abstract and brief chronicles
of the time ; after your death you were
better have a bad epitaph than their ill
report while you live.   520
    Pol. My lord, I will use them according
to their desert.
    Ham. God's bodykins, man, much better.
Use every man after his desert, and who
shall scape whipping ? Use them after
your own honour and dignity : the less
they deserve, the more merit is in your
bounty. Take them in.   527
    Pol. Come, sirs.
    Ham. Follow him, friends. We'll hear a
play to-morrow. Dost thou hear me, old
friend ; can you play ' The Murder of
Gonzago ' ?
    1 Play. Ay, my lord.   533
    Ham. We'll ha't to-morrow night. You
could, for a need, study a speech of some
dozen or sixteen lines which I would set
down and insert in't, could you not ?
    1 Play. Ay, my lord.   537
    Ham. Very well. Follow that lord ; and
look you mock him not. [*Exeunt Polonius
and Players*] My good friends, I'll leave you
till night. You are welcome to Elsinore. 540
    Ros. Good my lord !
    [*Exeunt Rosencrantz and Guildenstern.*
    Ham. Ay, so God buy to you ! Now I am
    alone.
O, what a rogue and peasant slave am I !
Is it not monstrous that this player here,
But in a fiction, in a dream of passion, 545
Could force his soul so to his own conceit
That from her working all his visage
    wann'd ;
Tears in his eyes, distraction in's aspect,
A broken voice, and his whole function
    suiting
With forms to his conceit ? And all for
    nothing !   550
For Hecuba !
What's Hecuba to him or he to Hecuba,
That he should weep for her ? What would
    he do,
Had he the motive and the cue for passion
That I have ? He would drown the stage
    with tears,   555
And cleave the general ear with horrid
    speech ;
Make mad the guilty, and appal the free,
Confound the ignorant, and amaze indeed
The very faculties of eyes and ears.

Yet I,   560
A dull and muddy-mettl'd rascal, peak,
Like John-a-dreams, unpregnant of my
      cause,
And can say nothing ; no, not for a king
Upon whose property and most dear life
A damn'd defeat was made. Am I a
      coward ?   565
Who calls me villain, breaks my pate across,
Plucks off my beard and blows it in my face,
Tweaks me by the nose, gives me the lie i'
      th' throat
As deep as to the lungs ? Who does me
      this ?
Ha !   570
'Swounds, I should take it ; for it cannot be
But I am pigeon-liver'd and lack gall
To make oppression bitter, or ere this
I should 'a fatted all the region kites
With this slave's offal. Bloody, bawdy
      villain !   575
Remorseless, treacherous, lecherous, kind-
      less villain !
O, vengeance !
Why, what an ass am I ! This is most
      brave,
That I, the son of a dear father murder'd,
Prompted to my revenge by heaven and
      hell,   580
Must, like a whore, unpack my heart with
      words,
And fall a-cursing like a very drab,
A scullion ! Fie upon't ! foh !
About, my brains. Hum—I have heard
That guilty creatures, sitting at a play, 585
Have by the very cunning of the scene
Been struck so to the soul that presently
They have proclaim'd their malefactions ;
For murder, though it have no tongue, will
      speak
With most miraculous organ. I'll have
      these players   590
Play something like the murder of my
      father
Before mine uncle. I'll observe his looks ;
I'll tent him to the quick. If 'a do blench,
I know my course. The spirit that I have
      seen   594
May be a devil ; and the devil hath power
T' assume a pleasing shape ; yea, and
      perhaps
Out of my weakness and my melancholy,
As he is very potent with such spirits,
Abuses me to damn me. I'll have grounds
More relative than this. The play's the
      thing   600
Wherein I'll catch the conscience of the
      King.   [Exit.

ACT THREE

SCENE I. *Elsinore. The Castle.*

Enter KING, QUEEN, POLONIUS, OPHELIA,
  ROSENCRANTZ, *and* GUILDENSTERN.

King. And can you by no drift of con-
      ference
Get from him why he puts on this confusion,
Grating so harshly all his days of quiet
With turbulent and dangerous lunacy ?
      Ros. He does confess he feels himself
      distracted,   5
But from what cause 'a will by no means
      speak.
      Guil. Nor do we find him forward to be
      sounded ;
But, with a crafty madness, keeps aloof
When we would bring him on to some con-
      fession
Of his true state.
      Queen.   Did he receive you well ? 10
      Ros. Most like a gentleman.
      Guil. But with much forcing of his
      disposition.
      Ros. Niggard of question ; but of our
      demands
Most free in his reply.
      Queen.   Did you assay him
To any pastime ?   15
      Ros. Madam, it so fell out that certain
      players
We o'er-raught on the way. Of these we
      told him ;
And there did seem in him a kind of joy
To hear of it. They are here about the
      court,
And, as I think, they have already order 20
This night to play before him.
      Pol.   'Tis most true ;
And he beseech'd me to entreat your
      Majesties
To hear and see the matter.
      King. With all my heart ; and it doth
      much content me
To hear him so inclin'd.   25
Good gentlemen, give him a further edge,
And drive his purpose into these delights.
      Ros. We shall, my lord.
            [*Exeunt Rosencrantz and Guildenstern.*
      King.   Sweet Gertrude, leave us too ;
For we have closely sent for Hamlet hither,
That he, as 'twere by accident, may here 30
Affront Ophelia.
Her father and myself—lawful espials—
Will so bestow ourselves that, seeing un-
      seen,
We may of their encounter frankly judge,
And gather by him, as he is behav'd,   35
If 't be th' affliction of his love or no
That thus he suffers for.
      Queen.   I shall obey you ;
And for your part, Ophelia, I do wish
That your good beauties be the happy cause
Of Hamlet's wildness ; so shall I hope your
      virtues   40
Will bring him to his wonted way again,
To both your honours.
      Oph.   Madam, I wish it may.
                                   [*Exit Queen.*

Pol. Ophelia, walk you here.—Gracious, so please you,
We will bestow ourselves.—Read on this book ;   44
That show of such an exercise may colour
Your loneliness.—We are oft to blame in this :
'Tis too much prov'd, that with devotion's visage
And pious action we do sugar o'er
The devil himself.
   King. [*Aside*] O, 'tis too true !
How smart a lash that speech doth give my conscience !   50
The harlot's cheek, beautied with plast'ring art,
Is not more ugly to the thing that helps it
Than is my deed to my most painted word.
O heavy burden !   54
   Pol. I hear him coming ; let's withdraw, my lord. [*Exeunt King and Polonius.*

Enter HAMLET.

Ham. To be, or not to be—that is the question ;
Whether 'tis nobler in the mind to suffer
The slings and arrows of outrageous fortune,
Or to take arms against a sea of troubles,
And by opposing end them ? To die, to sleep—   60
No more ; and by a sleep to say we end
The heart-ache and the thousand natural shocks
That flesh is heir to. 'Tis a consummation
Devoutly to be wish'd. To die, to sleep ;
To sleep, perchance to dream. Ay, there's the rub ;   65
For in that sleep of death what dreams may come,
When we have shuffled off this mortal coil,
Must give us pause. There's the respect
That makes calamity of so long life ;
For who would bear the whips and scorns of time,   70
Th' oppressor's wrong, the proud man's contumely,
The pangs of despis'd love, the law's delay,
The insolence of office, and the spurns
That patient merit of th' unworthy takes,
When he himself might his quietus make 75
With a bare bodkin ? Who would these fardels bear,
To grunt and sweat under a weary life,
But that the dread of something after death—
The undiscover'd country, from whose bourn
No traveller returns—puzzles the will,   80
And makes us rather bear those ills we have
Than fly to others that we know not of ?
Thus conscience does make cowards of us all ;
And thus the native hue of resolution

Is sicklied o'er with the pale cast of thought,   85
And enterprises of great pitch and moment,
With this regard, their currents turn awry
And lose the name of action.—Soft you now !
The fair Ophelia.—Nymph, in thy orisons
Be all my sins rememb'red.
   Oph.   Good my lord, 90
How does your honour for this many a day?
   Ham. I humbly thank you ; well, well, well.
   Oph. My lord, I have remembrances of yours
That I have longed long to re-deliver.
I pray you now receive them.
   Ham.   No, not I ; 95
I never gave you aught.
   Oph. My honour'd lord, you know right well you did,
And with them words of so sweet breath compos'd
As made the things more rich ; their perfume lost,   99
Take these again ; for to the noble mind
Rich gifts wax poor when givers prove unkind.
There, my lord.
   Ham. Ha, ha ! Are you honest ?
   Oph. My lord ?
   Ham. Are you fair ?   105
   Oph. What means your lordship ?
   Ham. That if you be honest and fair, your honesty should admit no discourse to your beauty.
   Oph. Could beauty, my lord, have better commerce than with honesty ?   110
   Ham. Ay, truly ; for the power of beauty will sooner transform honesty from what it is to a bawd than the force of honesty can translate beauty into his likeness. This was sometime a paradox, but now the time gives it proof. I did love you once.   115
   Oph. Indeed, my lord, you made me believe so.
   Ham. You should not have believ'd me ; for virtue cannot so inoculate our old stock but we shall relish of it. I loved you not.
   Oph. I was the more deceived.   120
   Ham. Get thee to a nunnery. Why wouldst thou be a breeder of sinners ? I am myself indifferent honest, but yet I could accuse me of such things that it were better my mother had not borne me : I am very proud, revengeful, ambitious ; with more offences at my beck than I have thoughts to put them in, imagination to give them shape, or time to act them in. What should such fellows as I do crawling between earth and heaven ? We are arrant knaves, all ; believe none of us. Go thy ways to a nunnery. Where's your father ?   130
   Oph. At home, my lord.
   Ham. Let the doors be shut upon him,

that he may play the fool nowhere but in's own house. Farewell.

Oph. O, help him, you sweet heavens ! 134

Ham. If thou dost marry, I'll give thee this plague for thy dowry : be thou as chaste as ice, as pure as snow, thou shalt not escape calumny. Get thee to a nunnery, go, farewell. Or, if thou wilt needs marry, marry a fool ; for wise men know well enough what monsters you make of them. To a nunnery, go ; and quickly too. Farewell. 140

Oph. O heavenly powers, restore him !

Ham. I have heard of your paintings too, well enough ; God hath given you one face, and you make yourselves another. You jig and amble, and you lisp, and nickname God's creatures, and make your wantonness your ignorance. Go to, I'll no more on't ; it hath made me mad. I say we will have no moe marriage : those that are married already, all but one, shall live ; the rest shall keep as they are. To a nunnery, go. [*Exit.*

Oph. O, what a noble mind is here o'er-thrown ! 150
The courtier's, soldier's, scholar's, eye, tongue, sword ;
Th' expectancy and rose of the fair state,
The glass of fashion and the mould of form,
Th' observ'd of all observers—quite, quite down ! 154
And I, of ladies most deject and wretched,
That suck'd the honey of his music vows,
Now see that noble and most sovereign reason,
Like sweet bells jangled, out of time and harsh ;
That unmatch'd form and feature of blown youth
Blasted with ecstasy. O, woe is me 160
T' have seen what I have seen, see what I see !

Re-enter KING *and* POLONIUS.

King. Love ! His affections do not that way tend ;
Nor what he spake, though it lack'd form a little,
Was not like madness. There's something in his soul 164
O'er which his melancholy sits on brood ;
And I do doubt the hatch and the disclose
Will be some danger ; which to prevent
I have in quick determination
Thus set it down : he shall with speed to England 169
For the demand of our neglected tribute.
Haply the seas and countries different,
With variable objects, shall expel
This something-settled matter in his heart
Whereon his brains still beating puts him thus

From fashion of himself. What think you on't ? 175

Pol. It shall do well. But yet do I believe
The origin and commencement of his grief
Sprung from neglected love. How now, Ophelia !
You need not tell us what Lord Hamlet said ;
We heard it all. My lord, do as you please ;
But if you hold it fit, after the play 181
Let his queen mother all alone entreat him
To show his grief. Let her be round with him ;
And I'll be plac'd, so please you, in the ear
Of all their conference. If she find him not,
To England send him ; or confine him where 186
Your wisdom best shall think.

King. It shall be so :
Madness in great ones must not unwatch'd go. [*Exeunt.*

SCENE II. *Elsinore. The Castle.*

Enter HAMLET *and three of the* Players.

Ham. Speak the speech, I pray you, as I pronounc'd it to you, trippingly on the tongue ; but if you mouth it, as many of our players do, I had as lief the town-crier spoke my lines. Nor do not saw the air too much with your hand, thus, but use all gently ; for in the very torrent, tempest, and, as I may say, whirlwind of your passion, you must acquire and beget a temperance that may give it smoothness. O, it offends me to the soul to hear a robustious periwig-pated fellow tear a passion to tatters, to very rags, to split the ears of the groundlings, who, for the most part, are capable of nothing but inexplicable dumb shows and noise. I would have such a fellow whipp'd for o'erdoing Termagant ; it out-herods Herod. Pray you avoid it. 14

1 Play. I warrant your honour.

Ham. Be not too tame neither, but let your own discretion be your tutor. Suit the action to the word, the word to the action ; with this special observance, that you o'er-step not the modesty of nature ; for anything so o'erdone is from the purpose of playing, whose end, both at the first and now, was and is to hold, as 'twere, the mirror up to nature ; to show virtue her own feature, scorn her own image, and the very age and body of the time his form and pressure. Now, this overdone or come tardy off, though it makes the unskilful laugh, cannot but make the judicious grieve ; the censure of the which one must, in your allowance, o'erweigh a whole theatre of others. O, there be players that I have seen play—and heard others praise, and that highly—not to speak it profanely, that, neither having th' accent of Christians, nor the gait of Christian, pagan, nor man, have so strutted and bellowed that I have thought some of Nature's journeymen had made men, and not made them well, they imitated humanity so abominably.   34

1 *Play.* I hope we have reform'd that indifferently with us, sir.

Ham. O, reform it altogether. And let those that play your clowns speak no more than is set down for them; for there be of them that will themselves laugh, to set on some quantity of barren spectators to laugh too, though in the meantime some necessary question of the play be then to be considered. That's villainous, and shows a most pitiful ambition in the fool that uses it. Go, make you ready.   [*Exeunt Players.*

Enter POLONIUS, ROSENCRANTZ, *and* GUILDENSTERN.

How now, my lord! Will the King hear this piece of work?   45

Pol. And the Queen too, and that presently.

Ham. Bid the players make haste.
          [*Exit Polonius.*
Will you two help to hasten them?

Ros. Ay, my lord.   [*Exeunt they two.*

Ham. What, ho, Horatio!   50

Enter HORATIO.

Hor. Here, sweet lord, at your service.

Ham. Horatio, thou art e'en as just a man
As e'er my conversation cop'd withal.

Hor. O my dear lord!

Ham.   Nay, do not think I flatter;
For what advancement may I hope from thee,   55
That no revenue hast but thy good spirits
To feed and clothe thee? Why should the poor be flatter'd?
No, let the candied tongue lick absurd pomp,
And crook the pregnant hinges of the knee
Where thrift may follow fawning. Dost thou hear?   60
Since my dear soul was mistress of her choice
And could of men distinguish her election,
Sh'hath seal'd thee for herself; for thou hast been
As one, in suff'ring all, that suffers nothing;
A man that Fortune's buffets and rewards 65
Hast ta'en with equal thanks; and blest are those
Whose blood and judgment are so well comeddled
That they are not a pipe for Fortune's finger
To sound what stop she please. Give me that man
That is not passion's slave, and I will wear him   70
In my heart's core, ay, in my heart of heart,

As I do thee. Something too much of this.
There is a play to-night before the King;
One scene of it comes near the circumstance
Which I have told thee of my father's death.
I prithee, when thou seest that act afoot,
Even with the very comment of thy soul
Observe my uncle. If his occulted guilt
Do not itself unkennel in one speech,
It is a damned ghost that we have seen, 80
And my imaginations are as foul
As Vulcan's stithy. Give him heedful note;
For I mine eyes will rivet to his face;
And, after, we will both our judgments join
In censure of his seeming.

Hor.   Well, my lord. 85
If 'a steal aught the whilst this play is playing,
And scape detecting, I will pay the theft.

Enter trumpets and kettledrums. Danish march. Sound a flourish. Enter KING, QUEEN, POLONIUS, OPHELIA, ROSENCRANTZ, GUILDENSTERN, *and other* Lords *attendant, with the* Guard *carrying torches.*

Ham. They are coming to the play; I must be idle.
Get you a place.

King. How fares our cousin Hamlet? 90

Ham. Excellent, i' faith; of the chameleon's dish. I eat the air, promise-cramm'd; you cannot feed capons so.

King. I have nothing with this answer, Hamlet; these words are not mine.   94

Ham. No, nor mine now. [*To Polonius*] My lord, you play'd once i' th' university, you say?

Pol. That did I, my lord, and was accounted a good actor.

Ham. What did you enact?   99

Pol. I did enact Julius Cæsar; I was kill'd i' th' Capitol; Brutus kill'd me.

Ham. It was a brute part of him to kill so capital a calf there. Be the players ready?

Ros. Ay, my lord; they stay upon your patience.

Queen. Come hither, my dear Hamlet, sit by me.   105

Ham. No, good mother; here's metal more attractive.

Pol. [*To the King*] O, ho! do you mark that?

Ham. Lady, shall I lie in your lap?
          [*Lying down at Ophelia's feet.*

Oph. No, my lord.   109

Ham. I mean, my head upon your lap?

Oph. Ay, my lord.

Ham. Do you think I meant country matters?

Oph. I think nothing, my lord.

Ham. That's a fair thought to lie between maids' legs.

Oph. What is, my lord?   115

Ham. Nothing.

Oph. You are merry, my lord.

Ham. Who, I ?

Oph. Ay, my lord.   119

Ham. O God, your only jig-maker ! What should a man do but be merry ? For look you how cheerfully my mother looks, and my father died within's two hours.

Oph. Nay, 'tis twice two months, my lord.   123

Ham. So long ? Nay then, let the devil wear black, for I'll have a suit of sables. O heavens ! die two months ago, and not forgotten yet ? Then there's hope a great man's memory may outlive his life half a year ; but, by'r lady, 'a must build churches, then ; or else shall 'a suffer not thinking on, with the hobby-horse, whose epitaph is ' For O, for O, the hobby-horse is forgot ! '   130

The trumpet sounds. Hautboys play. The Dumb Show enters.

Enter a King and a Queen, very lovingly ; the Queen embracing him and he her. She kneels, and makes show of protestation unto him. He takes her up, and declines his head upon her neck. He lies him down upon a bank of flowers ; she, seeing him asleep, leaves him. Anon comes in a Fellow, takes off his crown, kisses it, pours poison in the sleeper's ears, and leaves him. The Queen returns ; finds the King dead, and makes passionate action. The Poisoner, with some two or three Mutes, comes in again, seeming to condole with her. The dead body is carried away. The Poisoner woos the Queen with gifts : she seems harsh awhile, but in the end accepts his love.   [Exeunt.

Oph. What means this, my lord ?

Ham. Marry, this is miching mallecho ; it means mischief.

Oph. Belike this show imports the argument of the play.   135

Enter Prologue.

Ham. We shall know by this fellow : the players cannot keep counsel ; they'll tell all.

Oph. Will 'a tell us what this show meant ?   138

Ham. Ay, or any show that you will show him. Be not you asham'd to show, he'll not shame to tell you what it means.   141

Oph. You are naught, you are naught. I'll mark the play.

Pro. For us, and for our tragedy,
   Here stooping to your clemency,   145
   We beg your hearing patiently. [*Exit.*

Ham. Is this a prologue, or the posy of a ring ?

Oph. 'Tis brief, my lord.

Ham. As woman's love.

Enter the Player King *and* Queen.

P. King. Full thirty times hath Phœbus'
   cart gone round   150
Neptune's salt wash and Tellus' orbed
   ground,
And thirty dozen moons with borrowed sheen
About the world have times twelve thirties
   been,
Since love our hearts and Hymen did our
   hands
Unite comutual in most sacred bands.   155

P. Queen. So many journeys may the sun
   and moon
Make us again count o'er ere love be done !
But, woe is me, you are so sick of late,   158
So far from cheer and from your former state,
That I distrust you. Yet, though I distrust,
Discomfort you, my lord, it nothing must ;
For women fear too much even as they love,
And women's fear and love hold quantity,
In neither aught, or in extremity.
Now, what my love is, proof hath made you
   know ;
And as my love is siz'd, my fear is so.   165
Where love is great, the littlest doubts are fear ;
Where little fears grow great, great love grows
   there.

P. King. Faith, I must leave thee, love, and
   shortly too :   168
My operant powers their functions leave to do ;
And thou shalt live in this fair world behind,
Honour'd, belov'd ; and haply one as kind
For husband shalt thou—

P. Queen.   O, confound the rest !
Such love must needs be treason in my breast.
In second husband let me be accurst !   174
None wed the second but who kill'd the first.

Ham. That's wormwood, wormwood.

P. Queen. The instances that second
   marriage move
Are base respects of thrift, but none of love.
A second time I kill my husband dead,
When second husband kisses me in bed.   180

P. King. I do believe you think what now
   you speak ;
But what we do determine oft we break.
Purpose is but the slave to memory,
Of violent birth, but poor validity ;
Which now, the fruit unripe, sticks on the
   tree ;   185
But fall unshaken when they mellow be.
Most necessary 'tis that we forget
To pay ourselves what to ourselves is debt.
What to ourselves in passion we propose,
The passion ending, doth the purpose lose. 190
The violence of either grief or joy
Their own enactures with themselves destroy.
Where joy most revels grief doth most lament ;
Grief joys, joy grieves, on slender accident.
This world is not for aye ; nor 'tis not strange
That even our loves should with our fortunes
   change ;   196
For 'tis a question left us yet to prove,

Whether love lead fortune or else fortune love.
The great man down, you mark his favourite
    flies ;   199
The poor advanc'd makes friends of enemies.
And hitherto doth love on fortune tend ;
For who not needs shall never lack a friend,
And who in want a hollow friend doth try,
Directly seasons him his enemy.
But, orderly to end where I begun,   205
Our wills and fates do so contrary run
That our devices still are overthrown ;
Our thoughts are ours, their ends none of our
    own.
So think thou wilt no second husband wed ;
But die thy thoughts when thy first lord is
    dead.   210
  P. Queen. Nor earth to me give food, nor
    heaven light,
Sport and repose lock from me day and
    night,
To desperation turn my trust and hope,
An anchor's cheer in prison be my scope,
Each opposite that blanks the face of joy 215
Meet what I would have well, and it destroy,
Both here and hence pursue me lasting strife,
If, once a widow, ever I be wife !
  Ham. If she should break it now !
  P. King. 'Tis deeply sworn. Sweet, leave
    me here awhile ;   220
My spirits grow dull, and fain I would
    beguile
The tedious day with sleep.   [*Sleeps.*
  P. Queen.   *Sleep rock thy brain,*
And never come mischance between us twain !
                        [*Exit.*
  Ham. Madam, how like you this play ?
  Queen. The lady doth protest too much,
methinks.   225
  Ham. O, but she'll keep her word.
  King. Have you heard the argument ? Is
there no offence in't ?
  Ham. No, no ; they do but jest, poison
in jest ; no offence i' th' world.   230
  King. What do you call the play ?
  Ham. ' The Mouse-trap.' Marry, how ?
Tropically. This play is the image of a
murder done in Vienna : Gonzago is the
duke's name ; his wife, Baptista. You shall
see anon. 'Tis a knavish piece of work ;
but what of that ? Your Majesty, and we
that have free souls, it touches us not. Let
the galled jade wince, our withers are
unwrung.

        Enter LUCIANUS.

This is one Lucianus, nephew to the King.
  Oph. You are as good as a chorus, my
lord.   239
  Ham. I could interpret between you and
your love, if I could see the puppets
dallying.
  Oph. You are keen, my lord, you are keen.
  Ham. It would cost you a groaning to
take off mine edge.

  Oph. Still better, and worse.   245
  Ham. So you mis-take your husbands.—
Begin, murderer ; pox, leave thy damnable
faces and begin. Come ; the croaking raven
doth bellow for revenge.
  Luc. Thoughts black, hands apt, drugs fit,
    and time agreeing ;   249
Confederate season, else no creature seeing ;
Thou mixture rank, of midnight weeds
    collected,
With Hecat's ban thrice blasted, thrice
    infected,
Thy natural magic and dire property
On wholesome life usurps immediately. 254
          [*Pours the poison in his ears.*
  Ham. 'A poisons him i' th' garden for his
estate. His name's Gonzago. The story is
extant, and written in very choice Italian.
You shall see anon how the murderer gets
the love of Gonzago's wife.
  Oph. The King rises.
  Ham. What, frighted with false fire ! 260
  Queen. How fares my lord ?
  Pol. Give o'er the play.
  King. Give me some light. Away !
  Pol. Lights, lights, lights !
      [*Exeunt all but Hamlet and Horatio.*
  Ham. Why, let the strucken deer go
    weep,   265
    The hart ungalled play ;
  For some must watch, while some
    must sleep ;
    Thus runs the world away. 268
Would not this, sir, and a forest of feathers
—if the rest of my fortunes turn Turk with
me—with two Provincial roses on my raz'd
shoes, get me a fellowship in a cry of players,
sir ?
  Hor. Half a share.
  Ham. A whole one, I.   274
    For thou dost know, O Damon dear,
    This realm dismantled was
    Of Jove himself ; and now reigns
    here
    A very, very—paiock.
  Hor. You might have rhym'd.
  Ham. O good Horatio, I'll take the
ghost's word for a thousand pound. Didst
perceive ?   281
  Hor. Very well, my lord.
  Ham. Upon the talk of the poisoning.
  Hor. I did very well note him.
  Ham. Ah, ha ! Come, some music. Come,
the recorders.   286
  For if the King like not the comedy,
  Why, then, belike he likes it not, perdy.
Come, some music.

Re-enter ROSENCRANTZ *and* GUILDENSTERN.

  Guil. Good my lord, vouchsafe me a
word with you.   290
  Ham. Sir, a whole history.
  Guil. The King, sir—
  Ham. Ay, sir, what of him ?

Guil. Is, in his retirement, marvellous distemp'red.

Ham. With drink, sir? 295

Guil. No, my lord, rather with choler.

Ham. Your wisdom should show itself more richer to signify this to his doctor; for for me to put him to his purgation would perhaps plunge him into far more choler.

Guil. Good my lord, put your discourse into some frame, and start not so wildly from my affair. 301

Ham. I am tame, sir. Pronounce.

Guil. The Queen, your mother, in most great affliction of spirit, hath sent me to you.

Ham. You are welcome. 305

Guil. Nay, good my lord, this courtesy is not of the right breed. If it shall please you to make me a wholesome answer, I will do your mother's commandment; if not, your pardon and my return shall be the end of my business. 310

Ham. Sir, I cannot.

Ros. What, my lord?

Ham. Make you a wholesome answer; my wit's diseas'd. But, sir, such answer as I can make, you shall command; or rather, as you say, my mother. Therefore no more, but to the matter: my mother, you say— 316

Ros. Then thus she says: your behaviour hath struck her into amazement and admiration.

Ham. O wonderful son, that can so stonish a mother! But is there no sequel at the heels of this mother's admiration? Impart. 321

Ros. She desires to speak with you in her closet ere you go to bed.

Ham. We shall obey, were she ten times our mother. Have you any further trade with us? 325

Ros. My lord, you once did love me.

Ham. And do still, by these pickers and stealers.

Ros. Good my lord, what is your cause of distemper? You do surely bar the door upon your own liberty, if you deny your griefs to your friend. 330

Ham. Sir, I lack advancement.

Ros. How can that be, when you have the voice of the King himself for your succession in Denmark? 333

Ham. Ay, sir, but 'While the grass grows'—the proverb is something musty.

Re-enter the Players, *with recorders.*

O, the recorders! Let me see one. To withdraw with you—why do you go about to recover the wind of me, as if you would drive me into a toil?

Guil. O my lord, if my duty be too bold, my love is too unmannerly. 340

Ham. I do not well understand that. Will you play upon this pipe?

Guil. My lord, I cannot.

Ham. I pray you.

Guil. Believe me, I cannot. 345

Ham. I do beseech you.

Guil. I know no touch of it, my lord.

Ham. It is as easy as lying: govern these ventages with your fingers and thumb, give it breath with your mouth, and it will discourse most eloquent music. Look you, these are the stops. 351

Guil. But these cannot I command to any utterance of harmony; I have not the skill. 353

Ham. Why, look you now, how unworthy a thing you make of me! You would play upon me; you would seem to know my stops; you would pluck out the heart of my mystery; you would sound me from my lowest note to the top of my compass; and there is much music, excellent voice, in this little organ, yet cannot you make it speak. 'Sblood, do you think I am easier to be play'd on than a pipe? Call me what instrument you will, though you can fret me, yet you cannot play upon me.

Re-enter POLONIUS.

God bless you, sir!

Pol. My lord, the Queen would speak with you, and presently. 365

Ham. Do you see yonder cloud that's almost in shape of a camel?

Pol. By th' mass, and 'tis like a camel indeed.

Ham. Methinks it is like a weasel.

Pol. It is back'd like a weasel. 370

Ham. Or like a whale?

Pol. Very like a whale.

Ham. Then I will come to my mother by and by. [*Aside*] They fool me to the top of my bent.—I will come by and by. 375

Pol. I will say so. [*Exit Polonius.*

Ham. 'By and by' is easily said. [*Exeunt all but Hamlet.*
'Tis now the very witching time of night,
When churchyards yawn, and hell itself breathes out
Contagion to this world. Now could I drink hot blood, 380
And do such bitter business as the day
Would quake to look on. Soft! now to my mother.
O heart, lose not thy nature; let not ever
The soul of Nero enter this firm bosom.
Let me be cruel, not unnatural: 385
I will speak daggers to her, but use none.
My tongue and soul in this be hypocrites—
How in my words somever she be shent,
To give them seals never, my soul, consent!
[*Exit.*

SCENE III. *Elsinore. The Castle.*

Enter KING, ROSENCRANTZ, *and* GUILDEN-
STERN.

King. I like him not ; nor stands it safe
        with us
To let his madness range. Therefore pre-
        pare you ;
I your commission will forthwith dispatch,
And he to England shall along with you.
The terms of our estate may not endure 5
Hazard so near's as doth hourly grow
Out of his brows.
    Guil.   We will ourselves provide.
Most holy and religious fear it is
To keep those many many bodies safe
That live and feed upon your Majesty. 10
    Ros. The single and peculiar life is bound
With all the strength and armour of the
        mind
To keep itself from noyance ; but much
        more
That spirit upon whose weal depends and
        rests   14
The lives of many. The cease of majesty
Dies not alone, but like a gulf doth draw
What's near it with it. It is a massy wheel,
Fix'd on the summit of the highest mount,
To whose huge spokes ten thousand lesser
        things
Are mortis'd and adjoin'd ; which when it
        falls,   20
Each small annexment, petty consequence,
Attends the boist'rous ruin. Never alone
Did the king sigh, but with a general groan.
    King. Arm you, I pray you, to this
        speedy voyage ;
For we will fetters put about this fear, 25
Which now goes too free-footed.
    Ros.   We will haste us.
        [*Exeunt Rosencrantz and Guildenstern.*

Enter POLONIUS.

    Pol. My lord, he's going to his mother's
        closet.
Behind the arras I'll convey myself
To hear the process. I'll warrant she'll tax
        him home ;
And, as you said, and wisely was it said, 30
'Tis meet that some more audience than a
        mother,
Since nature makes them partial, should
        o'erhear
The speech, of vantage. Fare you well, my
        liege.
I'll call upon you ere you go to bed, 34
And tell you what I know.
    King.   Thanks, dear my lord.
                                [*Exit Polonius.*
O, my offence is rank, it smells to heaven ;
It hath the primal eldest curse upon't—
A brother's murder ! Pray can I not,
Though inclination be as sharp as will. 39

My stronger guilt defeats my strong intent,
And, like a man to double business bound,
I stand in pause where I shall first begin,
And both neglect. What if this cursed hand
Were thicker than itself with brother's
        blood,
Is there not rain enough in the sweet
        heavens   45
To wash it white as snow ? Whereto serves
        mercy
But to confront the visage of offence ?
And what's in prayer but this twofold
        force,
To be forestalled ere we come to fall,
Or pardon'd being down ? Then I'll look
        up ;   50
My fault is past. But, O, what form of
        prayer
Can serve my turn ? ' Forgive me my foul
        murder ' !
That cannot be ; since I am still possess'd
Of those effects for which I did the mur-
        der—
My crown, mine own ambition, and my
        queen.   55
May one be pardon'd and retain th' offence?
In the corrupted currents of this world
Offence's gilded hand may shove by justice;
And oft 'tis seen the wicked prize itself
Buys out the law. But 'tis not so above : 60
There is no shuffling ; there the action lies
In his true nature ; and we ourselves com-
        pell'd,
Even to the teeth and forehead of our
        faults,
To give in evidence. What then ? What
        rests ?   64
Try what repentance can. What can it not ?
Yet what can it when one can not repent ?
O wretched state ! O bosom black as
        death !
O limed soul, that, struggling to be free,
Art more engag'd! Help, angels. Make assay!
Bow, stubborn knees ; and, heart, with
        strings of steel,   70
Be soft as sinews of the new-born babe.
All may be well.   [*Retires and kneels.*

Enter HAMLET.

    Ham. Now might I do it pat, now 'a is
        a-praying ;
And now I'll do't—and so 'a goes to
        heaven,
And so am I reveng'd. That would be
        scann'd :   75
A villain kills my father ; and for that,
I, his sole son, do this same villain send
To heaven.
Why, this is hire and salary, not revenge.
'A took my father grossly, full of bread, 80
With all his crimes broad blown, as flush as
        May ;
And how his audit stands who knows save
        heaven ?

But in our circumstance and course of thought
'Tis heavy with him; and am I then reveng'd
To take him in the purging of his soul, 85
When he is fit and season'd for his passage ? No.
Up, sword, and know thou a more horrid hent.
When he is drunk asleep, or in his rage ;
Or in th' incestuous pleasure of his bed ; 90
At game, a-swearing, or about some act
That has no relish of salvation in't—
Then trip him, that his heels may kick at heaven,
And that his soul may be as damn'd and black 94
As hell, whereto it goes. My mother stays.
This physic but prolongs thy sickly days.
[*Exit.*

King. [*Rising*] My words fly up, my thoughts remain below.
Words without thoughts never to heaven go. [*Exit.*

SCENE IV. *The Queen's closet.*

Enter QUEEN *and* POLONIUS.

Pol. 'A will come straight. Look you lay home to him ;
Tell him his pranks have been too broad to bear with,
And that your Grace hath screen'd and stood between
Much heat and him. I'll silence me even here. 4
Pray you be round with him.
Ham. [*Within*] Mother, mother, mother !
Queen. I'll warrant you. Fear me not.
Withdraw, I hear him coming.
[*Polonius goes behind the arras.*

Enter HAMLET.

Ham. Now, mother, what's the matter ?
Queen. Hamlet, thou hast thy father much offended.
Ham. Mother, you have my father much offended. 10
Queen. Come, come, you answer with an idle tongue.
Ham. Go, go, you question with a wicked tongue.
Queen. Why, how now, Hamlet !
Ham. What's the matter now ?
Queen. Have you forgot me ?
Ham. No, by the rood, not so :
You are the Queen, your husband's brother's wife ; 15
And—would it were not so !—you are my mother.
Queen. Nay then, I'll set those to you that can speak.
Ham. Come, come, and sit you down ; you shall not budge.

You go not till I set you up a glass 19
Where you may see the inmost part of you.
Queen. What wilt thou do ? Thou wilt not murder me ?
Help, help, ho !
Pol. [*Behind*] What, ho! help, help, help!
Ham. [*Draws*] How now ! a rat ?
Dead, for a ducat, dead ! [*Kills Polonius with a pass through the arras.*
Pol. [*Behind*] O, I am slain !
Queen. O me, what hast thou done ?
Ham. Nay, I know not :
Is it the King ? 26
Queen. O, what a rash and bloody deed is this !
Ham. A bloody deed !—almost as bad, good mother,
As kill a king and marry with his brother.
Queen. As kill a king !
Ham. Ay, lady, it was my word. 30
[*Parting the arras.*
Thou wretched, rash, intruding fool, farewell !
I took thee for thy better. Take thy fortune.
Thou find'st to be too busy is some danger.
Leave wringing of your hands. Peace ; sit you down, 34
And let me wring your heart ; for so I shall,
If it be made of penetrable stuff ;
If damned custom have not braz'd it so
That it be proof and bulwark against sense.
Queen. What have I done that thou dar'st wag thy tongue
In noise so rude against me ?
Ham. Such an act 40
That blurs the grace and blush of modesty ;
Calls virtue hypocrite ; takes off the rose
From the fair forehead of an innocent love,
And sets a blister there ; makes marriage-vows
As false as dicers' oaths. O, such a deed 45
As from the body of contraction plucks
The very soul, and sweet religion makes
A rhapsody of words. Heaven's face does glow
O'er this solidity and compound mass 49
With heated visage, as against the doom—
Is thought-sick at the act.
Queen. Ay me, what act,
That roars so loud and thunders in the index ?
Ham. Look here upon this picture and on this,
The counterfeit presentment of two brothers. 54
See what a grace was seated on this brow ;
Hyperion's curls ; the front of Jove himself ;
An eye like Mars, to threaten and command;
A station like the herald Mercury
New lighted on a heaven-kissing hill—
A combination and a form indeed 60
Where every god did seem to set his seal,

To give the world assurance of a man.
This was your husband. Look you now
   what follows :
Here is your husband, like a mildew'd ear
Blasting his wholesome brother. Have you
   eyes ?   65
Could you on this fair mountain leave to
   feed,
And batten on this moor ? Ha ! have you
   eyes ?
You cannot call it love ; for at your age
The heyday in the blood is tame, it's
   humble,
And waits upon the judgment ; and what
   judgment   70
Would step from this to this ? Sense, sure,
   you have,
Else could you not have motion ; but sure
   that sense
Is apoplex'd ; for madness would not err,
Nor sense to ecstasy was ne'er so thrall'd
But it reserv'd some quantity of choice 75
To serve in such a difference. What devil
   was't
That thus hath cozen'd you at hoodman-
   blind ?
Eyes without feeling, feeling without sight,
Ears without hands or eyes, smelling sans
   all,
Or but a sickly part of one true sense   80
Could not so mope. O shame ! where is thy
   blush ?
Rebellious hell,
If thou canst mutine in a matron's bones,
To flaming youth let virtue be as wax
And melt in her own fire ; proclaim no
   shame   85
When the compulsive ardour gives the
   charge,
Since frost itself as actively doth burn,
And reason panders will.
   Queen.   O Hamlet, speak no more !
Thou turn'st my eyes into my very soul ;
And there I see such black and grained
   spots   90
As will not leave their tinct.
   Ham.   Nay, but to live
In the rank sweat of an enseamed bed,
Stew'd in corruption, honeying and making
   love
Over the nasty sty !
   Queen.   O, speak to me no more !
These words like daggers enter in my ears ;
No more, sweet Hamlet.
   Ham.   A murderer and a villain !
A slave that is not twentieth part the tithe
Of your precedent lord ; a vice of kings ;
A cutpurse of the empire and the rule,   99
That from a shelf the precious diadem stole
And put it in his pocket !
   Queen. No more !

          Enter Ghost.

   Ham. A king of shreds and patches—

Save me, and hover o'er me with your
   wings,
You heavenly guards ! What would your
   gracious figure ?
   Queen. Alas, he's mad !   105
   Ham. Do you not come your tardy son to
   chide,
That, laps'd in time and passion, lets go by
Th' important acting of your dread com-
   mand ?
O, say !
   Ghost. Do not forget ; this visitation 110
Is but to whet thy almost blunted purpose.
But look, amazement on thy mother sits.
O, step between her and her fighting soul !
Conceit in weakest bodies strongest works.
Speak to her, Hamlet.   115
   Ham. How is it with you, lady ?
   Queen.   Alas, how is't with you,
That you do bend your eye on vacancy,
And with th' incorporal air do hold
   discourse ?
Forth at your eyes your spirits wildly peep ;
And, as the sleeping soldiers in th' alarm,
Your bedded hairs like life in excrements
Start up and stand an end. O gentle son,
Upon the heat and flame of thy distemper
Sprinkle cool patience ! Whereon do you
   look ?
   Ham. On him, on him ! Look you how
   pale he glares.   125
His form and cause conjoin'd, preaching to
   stones,
Would make them capable.—Do not look
   upon me,
Lest with this piteous action you convert
My stern effects ; then what I have to do
Will want true colour—tears perchance for
   blood.   130
   Queen. To whom do you speak this ?
   Ham. Do you see nothing there ?
   Queen. Nothing at all ; yet all that is
   I see.
   Ham. Nor did you nothing hear ?
   Queen. No, nothing but ourselves.
   Ham. Why, look you there. Look how it
   steals away.
My father, in his habit as he liv'd !   135
Look where he goes even now out at the
   portal.   [*Exit Ghost.*
   Queen. This is the very coinage of your
   brain.
This bodiless creation ecstasy
Is very cunning in.
   Ham.   Ecstasy !
My pulse as yours doth temperately keep
   time,   140
And makes as healthful music. It is not
   madness
That I have utt'red. Bring me to the test,
And I the matter will re-word which
   madness
Would gambol from. Mother, for love of
   grace,

Lay not that flattering unction to your
    soul,   145
That not your trespass but my madness
    speaks:
It will but skin and film the ulcerous place,
Whiles rank corruption, mining all within,
Infects unseen. Confess yourself to heaven;
Repent what's past; avoid what is to come;
And do not spread the compost on the
    weeds,   151
To make them ranker. Forgive me this my
    virtue;
For in the fatness of these pursy times
Virtue itself of vice must pardon beg,
Yea, curb and woo for leave to do him good.
    Queen. O Hamlet, thou hast cleft my
    heart in twain.   156
    Ham. O, throw away the worser part
    of it,
And live the purer with the other half.
Good night—but go not to my uncle's bed;
Assume a virtue, if you have it not.   160
That monster custom, who all sense doth
    eat,
Of habits devil, is angel yet in this,
That to the use of actions fair and good
He likewise gives a frock or livery
That aptly is put on. Refrain to-night; 165
And that shall lend a kind of easiness
To the next abstinence; the next more
    easy;
For use almost can change the stamp of
    nature,
And either curb the devil, or throw him
    out,
With wondrous potency. Once more, good
    night;   170
And when you are desirous to be blest,
I'll blessing beg of you. For this same lord
I do repent; but Heaven hath pleas'd
    it so,
To punish me with this, and this with me,
That I must be their scourge and minister.
I will bestow him, and will answer well
The death I gave him. So, again, good
    night.
I must be cruel only to be kind;
Thus bad begins and worse remains behind.
One word more, good lady.
    Queen.   What shall I do? 180
    Ham. Not this, by no means, that I bid
    you do:
Let the bloat King tempt you again to bed;
Pinch wanton on your cheek; call you his
    mouse;
And let him, for a pair of reechy kisses,
Or paddling in your neck with his damn'd
    fingers,   185
Make you to ravel all this matter out,
That I essentially am not in madness,
But mad in craft. 'Twere good you let him
    know;
For who that's but a queen, fair, sober,
    wise,

Would from a paddock, from a bat, a gib,
Such dear concernings hide? Who would
    do so?   191
No, in despite of sense and secrecy,
Unpeg the basket on the house's top,
Let the birds fly, and, like the famous ape,
To try conclusions, in the basket creep 195
And break your own neck down.
    Queen. Be thou assur'd, if words be made
    of breath
And breath of life, I have no life to breathe
What thou hast said to me.
    Ham. I must to England; you know
    that?
    Queen.   Alack, 200
I had forgot. 'Tis so concluded on.
    Ham. There's letters seal'd; and my two
    school-fellows,
Whom I will trust as I will adders fang'd—
They bear the mandate; they must sweep
    my way   204
And marshal me to knavery. Let it work;
For 'tis the sport to have the engineer
Hoist with his own petar; and't shall go
    hard
But I will delve one yard below their mines
And blow them at the moon. O, 'tis most
    sweet   209
When in one line two crafts directly meet.
This man shall set me packing.
I'll lug the guts into the neighbour room.
Mother, good night. Indeed, this coun-
    sellor
Is now most still, most secret, and most
    grave,
Who was in life a foolish prating knave. 215
Come, sir, to draw toward an end with you.
Good night, mother.   [*Exeunt severally;
                         Hamlet tugging in Polonius.*

ACT FOUR

SCENE I. *Elsinore. The Castle.*

Enter KING, QUEEN, ROSENCRANTZ, *and*
    GUILDENSTERN.

    King. There's matter in these sighs, these
    profound heaves,
You must translate; 'tis fit we understand
    them.
Where is your son?
    Queen. Bestow this place on us a little
    while.
        [*Exeunt Rosencrantz and Guildenstern.*
Ah, mine own lord, what have I seen to-
    night!   5
    King. What, Gertrude? How does
    Hamlet?
    Queen. Mad as the sea and wind, when
    both contend
Which is the mightier. In his lawless fit,
Behind the arras hearing something stir,
Whips out his rapier, cries 'A rat, a rat!'
And in this brainish apprehension kills 11

The unseen good old man.

King.   O heavy deed !
It had been so with us had we been there.
His liberty is full of threats to all—
To you yourself, to us, to every one.   15
Alas, how shall this bloody deed be
    answer'd ?
It will be laid to us, whose providence
Should have kept short, restrain'd, and out
    of haunt,
This mad young man. But so much was our
    love,
We would not understand what was most
    fit ;   20
But, like the owner of a foul disease,
To keep it from divulging, let it feed
Even on the pith of life. Where is he gone ?
Queen. To draw apart the body he hath
    kill'd ;   24
O'er whom his very madness, like some ore
Among a mineral of metals base,
Shows itself pure : 'a weeps for what is
    done.
King. O Gertrude, come away !
The sun no sooner shall the mountains
    touch
But we will ship him hence ; and this vile
    deed   30
We must with all our majesty and skill
Both countenance and excuse. Ho,
    Guildenstern !

Re-enter ROSENCRANTZ *and* GUILDENSTERN.

Friends, both go join you with some further
    aid :
Hamlet in madness hath Polonius slain,
And from his mother's closet hath he
    dragg'd him ;   35
Go seek him out ; speak fair, and bring the
    body
Into the chapel. I pray you haste in this.
    [*Exeunt Rosencrantz and Guildenstern.*
Come, Gertrude, we'll call up our wisest
    friends
And let them know both what we mean to
    do
And what's untimely done ; so haply
    slander—   40
Whose whisper o'er the world's diameter,
As level as the cannon to his blank,
Transports his pois'ned shot—may miss our
    name,
And hit the woundless air. O, come away !
My soul is full of discord and dismay.   45
    [*Exeunt.*

SCENE II. *Elsinore. The Castle.*

Enter HAMLET.

Ham. Safely stow'd.
Gentlemen. [*Within*] Hamlet ! Lord Hamlet !
Ham. But soft ! What noise ? Who calls
on Hamlet ? O, here they come !

Enter ROSENCRANTZ *and* GUILDENSTERN.

Ros. What have you done, my lord, with
    the dead body ?   5
Ham. Compounded it with dust, whereto
    'tis kin.
Ros. Tell us where 'tis, that we may take
    it thence
And bear it to the chapel.
Ham. Do not believe it.
Ros. Believe what ?   10
Ham. That I can keep your counsel, and
not mine own. Besides, to be demanded
of a sponge—what replication should be
made by the son of a king ?   13
Ros. Take you me for a sponge, my lord ?
Ham. Ay, sir ; that soaks up the King's
countenance, his rewards, his authorities.
But such officers do the King best service
in the end : he keeps them, like an ape an
apple in the corner of his jaw; first mouth'd,
to be last swallowed ; when he needs what
you have glean'd, it is but squeezing you
and, sponge, you shall be dry again.   20
Ros. I understand you not, my lord.
Ham. I am glad of it ; a knavish speech
sleeps in a foolish ear.
Ros. My lord, you must tell us where the
body is, and go with us to the King.   25
Ham. The body is with the King, but the
King is not with the body. The King is a
thing—
Guil. A thing, my lord !
Ham. Of nothing. Bring me to him.
Hide fox, and all after.   [*Exeunt.* 30

SCENE III. *Elsinore. The Castle.*

Enter KING, *attended.*

King. I have sent to seek him, and to find
    the body.
How dangerous is it that this man goes
    loose !
Yet must not we put the strong law on
    him :
He's lov'd of the distracted multitude,
Who like not in their judgment but their
    eyes;   5
And where 'tis so, th' offender's scourge is
    weigh'd,
But never the offence. To bear all smooth
    and even,
This sudden sending him away must seem
Deliberate pause. Diseases desperate
    grown
By desperate appliance are reliev'd,   10
Or not at all.

Enter ROSENCRANTZ.

          How now ! what hath befall'n ?
Ros. Where the dead body is bestow'd,
    my lord,
We cannot get from him.
King.   But where is he ?

Ros. Without, my lord ; guarded, to know your pleasure.

King. Bring him before us.   15

Ros. Ho, Guildenstern ! bring in the lord.

Enter HAMLET *and* GUILDENSTERN.

King. Now, Hamlet, where's Polonius ?

Ham. At supper.

King. At supper ! Where ?   19

Ham. Not where he eats, but where 'a is eaten ; a certain convocation of politic worms are e'en at him. Your worm is your only emperor for diet : we fat all creatures else to fat us, and we fat ourselves for maggots ; your fat king and your lean beggar is but variable service—two dishes, but to one table. That's the end.   25

King. Alas, alas !

Ham. A man may fish with the worm that hath eat of a king, and eat of the fish that hath fed of that worm.

King. What dost thou mean by this ?

Ham. Nothing but to show you how a king may go a progress through the guts of a beggar.   31

King. Where is Polonius ?

Ham. In heaven ; send thither to see ; if your messenger find him not there, seek him i' th' other place yourself. But if, indeed, you find him not within this month, you shall nose him as you go up the stairs into the lobby.   37

King [*To Attendants*] Go seek him there.

Ham. 'A will stay till you come.

[*Exeunt Attendants.*

King. Hamlet, this deed, for thine especial safety—   40
Which we do tender, as we dearly grieve
For that which thou hast done—must send thee hence
With fiery quickness. Therefore prepare thyself ;
The bark is ready, and the wind at help, 44
Th' associates tend, and everything is bent
For England.

Ham.   For England !

King.   Ay, Hamlet.

Ham.   Good !

King. So is it, if thou knew'st our purposes.

Ham. I see a cherub that sees them.
But, come ; for England ! Farewell, dear mother.

King. Thy loving father, Hamlet.   50

Ham. My mother : father and mother is man and wife; man and wife is one flesh; and so, my mother. Come, for England. [*Exit.*

King. Follow him at foot ; tempt him with speed aboard ;   54
Delay it not ; I'll have him hence to-night.
Away ! for everything is seal'd and done
That else leans on th' affair. Pray you make haste.

[*Exeunt all but the King.*

And, England, if my love thou hold'st at aught—
As my great power thereof may give thee sense,
Since yet thy cicatrice looks raw and red 60
After the Danish sword, and thy free awe
Pays homage to us—thou mayst not coldly set
Our sovereign process ; which imports at full,
By letters congruing to that effect,
The present death of Hamlet. Do it, England :   65
For like the hectic in my blood he rages,
And thou must cure me. Till I know 'tis done,
Howe'er my haps, my joys were ne'er begun.   [*Exit.*

SCENE IV. *A plain in Denmark.*

Enter FORTINBRAS *with his* Army *over the stage.*

Fort. Go, Captain, from me greet the Danish king.
Tell him that by his licence Fortinbras
Craves the conveyance of a promis'd march
Over his kingdom. You know the rendezvous.
If that his Majesty would aught with us, 5
We shall express our duty in his eye ;
And let him know so.

Cap.   I will do't, my lord.

Fort. Go softly on.

[*Exeunt all but the Captain.*

Enter HAMLET, ROSENCRANTZ, GUILDENSTERN, *and* Others.

Ham. Good sir, whose powers are these ?

Cap. They are of Norway, sir.   10

Ham. How purpos'd, sir, I pray you ?

Cap. Against some part of Poland.

Ham. Who commands them, sir ?

Cap. The nephew to old Norway, Fortinbras.

Ham. Goes it against the main of Poland, sir,   15
Or for some frontier ?

Cap. Truly to speak, and with no addition,
We go to gain a little patch of ground
That hath in it no profit but the name.
To pay five ducats, five, I would not farm it ;   20
Nor will it yield to Norway or the Pole
A ranker rate should it be sold in fee.

Ham. Why, then the Polack never will defend it.

Cap. Yes, it is already garrison'd.

Ham. Two thousand souls and twenty thousand ducats   25
Will not debate the question of this straw.
This is th' imposthume of much wealth and peace,

That inward breaks, and shows no cause
　　without
Why the man dies. I humbly thank you,
　　sir.　　　　　　　　　　　　　　　28
　　Cap. God buy you, sir.　　　　[*Exit.*
　　Ros. Will't please you go, my lord?
　　Ham. I'll be with you straight. Go a little
　　before.　　　[*Exeunt all but Hamlet.*
How all occasions do inform against me,
And spur my dull revenge! What is a man,
If his chief good and market of his time
Be but to sleep and feed? A beast, no
　　more!　　　　　　　　　　　　　35
Sure he that made us with such large
　　discourse,
Looking before and after, gave us not
That capability and godlike reason
To fust in us unus'd. Now, whether it be
Bestial oblivion, or some craven scruple 40
Of thinking too precisely on th' event—
A thought which, quarter'd, hath but one
　　part wisdom
And ever three parts coward—I do not
　　know
Why yet I live to say ' This thing's to do',
Sith I have cause, and will, and strength,
　　and means,　　　　　　　　　　45
To do't. Examples gross as earth exhort
　　me :
Witness this army, of such mass and charge,
Led by a delicate and tender prince,
Whose spirit, with divine ambition puff'd,
Makes mouths at the invisible event,　50
Exposing what is mortal and unsure
To all that fortune, death, and danger, dare,
Even for an egg-shell. Rightly to be great
Is not to stir without great argument,
But greatly to find quarrel in a straw,　55
When honour's at the stake. How stand
　　I, then,
That have a father kill'd, a mother stain'd,
Excitements of my reason and my blood,
And let all sleep, while to my shame I see
The imminent death of twenty thousand
　　men　　　　　　　　　　　　　60
That, for a fantasy and trick of fame,
Go to their graves like beds, fight for a plot
Whereon the numbers cannot try the cause,
Which is not tomb enough and continent
To hide the slain? O, from this time forth,
My thoughts be bloody, or be nothing
　　worth !　　　　　　　　　　[*Exit.*

SCENE V. *Elsinore. The Castle.*

Enter QUEEN, HORATIO, *and a* Gentleman.

　　Queen. I will not speak with her.
　　Gent. She is importunate, indeed distract.
Her mood will needs be pitied.
　　Queen.　　　　What would she have?
　　Gent. She speaks much of her father;
　　says she hears
There's tricks i' th' world, and hems, and
　　beats her heart ;　　　　　　　5

Spurns enviously at straws ; speaks things
　　in doubt,
That carry but half sense. Her speech is
　　nothing,
Yet the unshaped use of it doth move
The hearers to collection ; they yawn
　　at it,
And botch the words up fit to their own
　　thoughts ;　　　　　　　　　10
Which, as her winks and nods and gestures
　　yield them,
Indeed would make one think there might
　　be thought,
Though nothing sure, yet much unhappily.
　　Hor. 'Twere good she were spoken with ;
　　for she may strew
Dangerous conjectures in ill-breeding
　　minds.　　　　　　　　　　15
　　Queen. Let her come in. [*Exit Gentleman.*
[*Aside*] To my sick soul, as sin's true nature
　　is,
Each toy seems prologue to some great
　　amiss.
So full of artless jealousy is guilt,
It spills itself in fearing to be spilt.　20

Enter OPHELIA *distracted.*

　　Oph. Where is the beautous Majesty of
　　Denmark ?
　　Queen. How now, Ophelia !
　　Oph. [*Sings*]
　　　　How should I your true love know
　　　　　From another one ?
　　　　By his cockle hat and staff,　　25
　　　　　And his sandal shoon.
　　Queen. Alas, sweet lady, what imports
　　this song ?
　　Oph. Say you ? Nay, pray you mark.
[*Sings*] He is dead and gone, lady,
　　　　　He is dead and gone ;　　30
　　　　At his head a grass-green turf,
　　　　　At his heels a stone.
O, ho !
　　Queen. Nay, but, Ophelia—
　　Oph.　　　　　　　Pray you mark.
[*Sings*] White his shroud as the mountain
　　snow—

Enter KING.

　　Queen. Alas, look here, my lord.　35
　　Oph. Larded with sweet flowers ;
　　　Which bewept to the grave did
　　　　not go
　　　With true-love showers.
　　King. How do you, pretty lady ?　39
　　Oph. Well, God dild you ! They say the
owl was a baker's daughter. Lord, we know
what we are, but know not what we may
be. God be at your table !
　　King. Conceit upon her father.
　　Oph. Pray let's have no words of this ;
but when they ask you what it means, say
you this :　　　　　　　　　　45

[*Sings*] To-morrow is Saint Valentine's day,
    All in the morning betime,
And I a maid at your window,
    To be your Valentine.

    Then up he rose, and donn'd his
        clothes, 50
    And dupp'd the chamber-door;
Let in the maid, that out a maid
    Never departed more.

King. Pretty Ophelia!

Oph. Indeed, la, without an oath, I'll
make an end on't. 55

[*Sings*] By Gis and by Saint Charity,
    Alack, and fie for shame!
Young men will do't, if they come
    to't;
By Cock, they are to blame.

Quoth she ' Before you tumbled
    me, 60
You promis'd me to wed '.

He answers:

' So would I 'a done, by yonder
    sun,
An thou hadst not come to my
    bed '.

King. How long hath she been thus? 65

Oph. I hope all will be well. We must be
patient; but I cannot choose but weep to
think they would lay him i' th' cold ground.
My brother shall know of it; and so I
thank you for your good counsel. Come,
my coach! Good night, ladies; good night,
sweet ladies, good night, good night. [*Exit.*

King. Follow her close; give her good
watch, I pray you.
      [*Exeunt Horatio and Gentleman.*
O, this is the poison of deep grief; it springs
All from her father's death. And now
    behold—
O Gertrude, Gertrude!
When sorrows come, they come not single
    spies, 75
But in battalions! First, her father slain;
Next, your son gone, and he most violent
    author
Of his own just remove; the people
    muddied,
Thick and unwholesome in their thoughts
    and whispers
For good Polonius' death; and we have
    done but greenly 80
In hugger-mugger to inter him; poor
    Ophelia
Divided from herself and her fair judg-
    ment,
Without the which we are pictures, or mere
    beasts;
Last, and as much containing as all these,
Her brother is in secret come from France;
Feeds on his wonder, keeps himself in
    clouds, 86
And wants not buzzers to infect his ear

With pestilent speeches of his father's
    death;
Wherein necessity, of matter beggar'd,
Will nothing stick our person to arraign 90
In ear and ear. O my dear Gertrude, this,
Like to a murd'ring piece, in many places
Gives me superfluous death. [*A noise within.*

Queen. Alack, what noise is this?

King. Attend!

Enter a Gentleman.

Where are my Switzers? Let them guard
    the door.
What is the matter?

Gent.   Save yourself, my lord: 95
The ocean, overpeering of his list,
Eats not the flats with more impitious
    haste
Than young Laertes, in a riotous head,
O'erbears your officers. The rabble call him
    lord; 99
And, as the world were now but to begin,
Antiquity forgot, custom not known,
The ratifiers and props of every word,
They cry ' Choose we; Laertes shall be
    king '.
Caps, hands, and tongues, applaud it to the
    clouds,
' Laertes shall be king, Laertes king '. 105

Queen. How cheerfully on the false trail
    they cry!   [*Noise within.*
O, this is counter, you false Danish dogs!

King. The doors are broke.

Enter LAERTES, *with* Others, *in arms.*

Laer. Where is this king?—Sirs, stand
    you all without.

All. No, let's come in.

Laer.   I pray you give me leave.

All. We will, we will.   [*Exeunt.* 111

Laer. I thank you. Keep the door.—O
    thou vile king,
Give me my father!

Queen.   Calmly, good Laertes.

Laer. That drop of blood that's calm
    proclaims me bastard;
Cries cuckold to my father; brands the
    harlot 115
Even here, between the chaste unsmirched
    brow
Of my true mother.

King.   What is the cause, Laertes,
That thy rebellion looks so giant-like?
Let him go, Gertrude; do not fear our
    person:
There's such divinity doth hedge a king 120
That treason can but peep to what it
    would,
Acts little of his will. Tell me, Laertes,
Why thou art thus incens'd. Let him go,
    Gertrude.
Speak, man.

Laer. Where is my father?

King.   Dead.

Or is it some abuse, and no such thing?
   Laer. Know you the hand?   50
   King. 'Tis Hamlet's character. 'Naked'!
And in a postcript here, he says ' alone '.
Can you devise me?
   Laer. I am lost in it, my lord. But let
him come;   55
It warms the very sickness in my heart
That I shall live and tell him to his teeth
' Thus didest thou '.
   King.   If it be so, Laertes—
As how should it be so, how otherwise?—
Will you be rul'd by me?
   Laer.   Ay, my lord;
So you will not o'errule me to a peace.   60
   King. To thine own peace. If he be now
return'd,
As checking at his voyage, and that he
means
No more to undertake it, I will work him
To an exploit now ripe in my device,
Under the which he shall not choose but
fall;   65
And for his death, no wind of blame shall
breathe;
But even his mother shall uncharge the
practice
And call it accident.
   Laer.   My lord, I will be rul'd
The rather, if you could devise it so
That I might be the organ.
   King.   It falls right.   70
You have been talk'd of since your travel
much,
And that in Hamlet's hearing, for a quality
Wherein they say you shine. Your sum of
parts
Did not together pluck such envy from him
As did that one; and that, in my regard,   75
Of the unworthiest siege.
   Laer.   What is that, my lord?
   King. A very riband in the cap of youth,
Yet needful too; for youth no less becomes
The light and careless livery that it wears
Than settled age his sables and his weeds,
Importing health and graveness. Two
months since   81
Here was a gentleman of Normandy—
I have seen myself, and serv'd against, the
French,
And they can well on horseback; but this
gallant
Had witchcraft in't; he grew unto his seat,
And to such wondrous doing brought his
horse,   86
As had he been incorps'd and demi-natur'd
With the brave beast. So far he topp'd my
thought,
That I, in forgery of shapes and tricks,
Come short of what he did.
   Laer.   A Norman was't?   90
   King. A Norman.
   Laer. Upon my life, Lamord.
   King.   The very same.

   Laer. I know him well. He is the brooch
indeed
And gem of all the nation.
   King. He made confession of you;   95
And gave you such a masterly report
For art and exercise in your defence,
And for your rapier most especial,
That he cried out 'twould be a sight indeed
If one could match you. The scrimers of
their nation   100
He swore had neither motion, guard, nor
eye,
If you oppos'd them. Sir, this report of his
Did Hamlet so envenom with his envy
That he could nothing do but wish and beg
Your sudden coming o'er, to play with you.
Now, out of this—
   Laer.   What out of this, my lord?
   King. Laertes, was your father dear to
you?
Or are you like the painting of a sorrow,
A face without a heart?
   Laer.   Why ask you this?   109
   King. Not that I think you did not love
your father?
But that I know love is begun by time,
And that I see, in passages of proof,
Time qualifies the spark and fire of it.
There lives within the very flame of love
A kind of wick or snuff that will abate it;
And nothing is at a like goodness still;
For goodness, growing to a pleurisy,   117
Dies in his own too much. That we would
do,
We should do when we would; for this
' would ' changes,
And hath abatements and delays as many
As there are tongues, are hands, are
accidents;   121
And then this ' should ' is like a spend-
thrift's sigh
That hurts by easing. But to the quick of
th' ulcer:
Hamlet comes back; what would you
undertake   124
To show yourself in deed your father's son
More than in words?
   Laer.   To cut his throat i' th' church.
   King. No place, indeed, should murder
sanctuarize;
Revenge should have no bounds. But, good
Laertes,
Will you do this? Keep close within your
chamber.
Hamlet return'd shall know you are come
home.   130
We'll put on those shall praise your
excellence,
And set a double varnish on the fame
The Frenchman gave you; bring you, in
fine, together,
And wager on your heads. He, being
remiss,   134
Most generous, and free from all contriving,

Will not peruse the foils ; so that with ease
Or with a little shuffling, you may choose
A sword unbated, and, in a pass of practice,
Requite him for your father.
　Laer.　　　　　　　I will do't ;
And for that purpose I'll anoint my sword.
I bought an unction of a mountebank, 141
So mortal that but dip a knife in it,
Where it draws blood no cataplasm so rare,
Collected from all simples that have virtue
Under the moon, can save the thing from
　death　　　　　　　　　　　　145
That is but scratch'd withal. I'll touch my
　point
With this contagion, that, if I gall him
　slightly,
It may be death.
　King.　　　Let's further think of this ;
Weigh what convenience both of time and
　means
May fit us to our shape. If this should
　fail,　　　　　　　　　　　　150
And that our drift look through our bad
　performance,
'Twere better not assay'd, therefore this
　project
Should have a back or second, that might
　hold
If this did blast in proof. Soft ! let me
　see.
We'll make a solemn wager on your cun-
　nings—　　　　　　　　　　155
I ha't.
When in your motion you are hot and dry—
As make your bouts more violent to that
　end—
And that he calls for drink, I'll have pre-
　ferr'd him　　　　　　　　　159
A chalice for the nonce; whereon but sipping,
If he by chance escape your venom'd stuck,
Our purpose may hold there. But stay ;
　what noise ?

Enter QUEEN.

　Queen. One woe doth tread upon an-
　other's heel,
So fast they follow. Your sister's drown'd,
　Laertes.　　　　　　　　　165
　Laer. Drown'd ! O, where ?
　Queen. There is a willow grows aslant the
　brook
That shows his hoar leaves in the glassy
　stream ;
Therewith fantastic garlands did she make
Of crowflowers, nettles, daisies, and long
　purples　　　　　　　　　170
That liberal shepherds give a grosser name,
But our cold maids do dead men's fingers
　call them.
There, on the pendent boughs her coronet
　weeds
Clamb'ring to hang, an envious sliver
　broke ;　　　　　　　　　174
When down her weedy trophies and herself

Fell in the weeping brook. Her clothes
　spread wide　　　　　　　　176
And, mermaid-like, awhile they bore her up;
Which time she chanted snatches of old
　lauds,
As one incapable of her own distress,
Or like a creature native and indued　180
Unto that element ; but long it could not
　be
Till that her garments, heavy with their
　drink,
Pull'd the poor wretch from her melodious
　lay
To muddy death.
　Laer.　　　　Alas, then she is drown'd !
　Queen. Drown'd, drown'd.　　　185
　Laer. Too much of water hast thou, poor
　Ophelia,
And therefore I forbid my tears ; but yet
It is our trick ; nature her custom holds,
Let shame say what it will. When these
　are gone,
The woman will be out. Adieu, my lord. 190
I have a speech o' fire that fain would blaze
But that this folly douts it.　　[*Exit.*
　King.　　　　Let's follow, Gertrude.
How much I had to do to calm his rage !
Now fear I this will give it start again ; 194
Therefore let's follow.　　　[*Exeunt.*

ACT FIVE

SCENE I. *Elsinore. A churchyard.*

Enter two Clowns *with spades and picks.*

1 *Clo.* Is she to be buried in Christian
burial when she wilfully seeks her own
salvation ?

2 *Clo.* I tell thee she is ; therefore make
her grave straight. The crowner hath sat
on her, and finds it Christian burial.　　5

1 *Clo.* How can that be, unless she
drown'd herself in her own defence ?

2 *Clo.* Why, 'tis found so.

1 *Clo.* It must be ' se offendendo ' ; it
cannot be else. For here lies the point : if
I drown myself wittingly, it argues an act ;
and an act hath three branches—it is to
act, to do, to perform ; argal, she drown'd
herself wittingly.　　　　　　13

2 *Clo.* Nay, but hear you, Goodman
Delver.

1 *Clo.* Give me leave. Here lies the
water ; good. Here stands the man ;
good. If the man go to this water and
drown himself, it is, will he, nill he, he
goes—mark you that ; but if the water
come to him and drown him, he drowns
not himself. Argal, he that is not guilty
of his own death shortens not his own life.

2 *Clo.* But is this law ?　　　21

1 *Clo.* Ay, marry, is't ; crowner's quest
law.

2 *Clo.* Will you ha the truth an't ? If

this had not been a gentlewoman, she should have been buried out a Christian burial. 25

1 Clo. Why, there thou say'st; and the more pity that great folk should have count'nance in this world to drown or hang themselves more than their even Christen. Come, my spade. There is no ancient gentlemen but gard'ners, ditchers, and grave-makers; they hold up Adam's profession. 31

2 Clo. Was he a gentleman?

1 Clo. 'A was the first that ever bore arms.

2 Clo. Why, he had none. 34

1 Clo. What, art a heathen? How dost thou understand the Scripture? The Scripture says Adam digg'd. Could he dig without arms? I'll put another question to thee. If thou answerest me not to the purpose, confess thyself—

2 Clo. Go to. 40

1 Clo. What is he that builds stronger than either the mason, the shipwright, or the carpenter?

2 Clo. The gallows-maker; for that frame outlives a thousand tenants. 44

1 Clo. I like thy wit well; in good faith the gallows does well; but how does it well? It does well to those that do ill. Now thou dost ill to say the gallows is built stronger than the church; argal, the gallows may do well to thee. To 't again, come. 49

2 Clo. Who builds stronger than a mason, a shipwright, or a carpenter?

1 Clo. Ay, tell me that, and unyoke.

2 Clo. Marry, now I can tell.

1 Clo. To 't.

2 Clo. Mass, I cannot tell. 55

Enter HAMLET *and* HORATIO, *afar off.*

1 Clo. Cudgel thy brains no more about it, for your dull ass will not mend his pace with beating; and when you are ask'd this question next, say 'a grave-maker': the houses he makes lasts till doomsday. Go, get thee to Yaughan; fetch me a stoup of liquor. [*Exit Second Clown.*
[*Digs and sings*] In youth, when I did love, did love, 61
  Methought it was very sweet,
To contract-o-the time for-a my behove,
  O, methought there-a-was nothing-a meet.

Ham. Has this fellow no feeling of his business, that 'a sings in grave-making? 66

Hor. Custom hath made it in him a property of easiness.

Ham. 'Tis e'en so; the hand of little employment hath the daintier sense. 70

1 Clo. [*Sings*] But age, with his stealing steps,

Hath clawed me in his clutch,
And hath shipped me intil the land,
  As if I had never been such. 74
[*Throws up a skull.*
Ham. That skull had a tongue in it, and could sing once. How the knave jowls it to the ground, as if 'twere Cain's jawbone, that did the first murder! This might be the pate of a politician, which this ass now o'erreaches; one that would circumvent God, might it not? 80

Hor. It might, my lord.

Ham. Or of a courtier; which could say 'Good morrow, sweet lord! How dost thou, sweet lord?' This might be my Lord Such-a-one, that praised my Lord Such-a-one's horse, when 'a meant to beg it—might it not?

Hor. Ay, my lord. 85

Ham. Why, e'en so; and now my Lady Worm's, chapless, and knock'd about the mazard with a sexton's spade. Here's fine revolution, an we had the trick to see't. Did these bones cost no more the breeding but to play at loggats with them? Mine ache to think on't. 90

1 Clo. [*Sings*] A pick-axe and a spade, a spade,
  For and a shrouding sheet:
O, a pit of clay for to be made
  For such a guest is meet.
[*Throws up another skull.*
Ham. There's another. Why may not that be the skull of a lawyer? Where be his quiddities now, his quillets, his cases, his tenures, and his tricks? Why does he suffer this rude knave now to knock him about the sconce with a dirty shovel, and will not tell him of his action of battery? Hum! This fellow might be in's time a great buyer of land, with his statutes, his recognizances, his fines, his double vouchers, his recoveries. Is this the fine of his fines, and the recovery of his recoveries, to have his fine pate full of fine dirt? Will his vouchers vouch him no more of his purchases, and double ones too, than the length and breadth of a pair of indentures? The very conveyances of his lands will scarcely lie in this box; and must th' inheritor himself have no more, ha?

Hor. Not a jot more, my lord.

Ham. Is not parchment made of sheepskins? 110

Hor. Ay, my lord, and of calves' skins too.

Ham. They are sheep and calves which seek out assurance in that. I will speak to this fellow. Whose grave's this, sirrah?

1 Clo. Mine, sir. 115
[*Sings*] O, a pit of clay for to be made
  For such a guest is meet.

Ham. I think it be thine indeed, for thou liest in't.

1 Clo. You lie out on't, sir, and therefore 'tis not yours. For my part, I do not lie in't, yet it is mine. 120

Ham. Thou dost lie in't, to be in't and say it is thine ; 'tis for the dead, not for the quick ; therefore thou liest.

1 Clo. 'Tis a quick lie, sir ; 'twill away again from me to you. 125

Ham. What man dost thou dig it for ?

1 Clo. For no man, sir.

Ham. What woman, then ?

1 Clo. For none neither.

Ham. Who is to be buried in't ? 130

1 Clo. One that was a woman, sir ; but, rest her soul, she's dead.

Ham. How absolute the knave is ! We must speak by the card, or equivocation will undo us. By the Lord, Horatio, this three years I have took note of it : the age is grown so picked that the toe of the peasant comes so near the heel of the courtier, he galls his kibe. How long hast thou been a grave-maker ?

1 Clo. Of all the days i' th' year, I came to't that day that our last King Hamlet overcame Fortinbras. 140

Ham. How long is that since ?

1 Clo. Cannot you tell that ? Every fool can tell that : it was that very day that young Hamlet was born—he that is mad, and sent into England.

Ham. Ay, marry, why was he sent into England ? 145

1 Clo. Why, because 'a was mad : 'a shall recover his wits there ; or, if 'a do not, 'tis no great matter there.

Ham. Why ?

1 Clo. 'Twill not be seen in him there : there the men are as mad as he. 150

Ham. How came he mad ?

1 Clo. Very strangely, they say.

Ham. How strangely ?

1 Clo. Faith, e'en with losing his wits.

Ham. Upon what ground ? 155

1 Clo. Why, here in Denmark. I have been sexton here, man and boy, thirty years.

Ham. How long will a man lie i' th' earth ere he rot ?

1 Clo. Faith, if 'a be not rotten before 'a die—as we have many pocky corses now-a-days that will scarce hold the laying in—'a will last you some eight year or nine year. A tanner will last you nine year. 163

Ham. Why he more than another ?

1 Clo. Why, sir, his hide is so tann'd with his trade that 'a will keep out water a great while ; and your water is a sore decayer of your whoreson dead body. Here's a skull now ; this skull has lien you i' th' earth three and twenty years.

Ham. Whose was it ? 170

1 Clo. A whoreson mad fellow's it was. Whose do you think it was ?

Ham. Nay, I know not.

1 Clo. A pestilence on him for a mad rogue ! 'A poured a flagon of Rhenish on my head once. This same skull, sir, was, sir, Yorick's skull, the King's jester. 176

Ham. This ?

1 Clo. E'en that.

Ham. Let me see. [Takes the skull] Alas, poor Yorick ! I knew him, Horatio : a fellow of infinite jest, of most excellent fancy ; he hath borne me on his back a thousand times. And now how abhorred in my imagination it is ! My gorge rises at it. Here hung those lips that I have kiss'd I know not how oft. Where be your gibes now, your gambols, your songs, your flashes of merriment that were wont to set the table on a roar ? Not one now to mock your own grinning—quite chap-fall'n ? Now get you to my lady's chamber, and tell her, let her paint an inch thick, to this favour she must come ; make her laugh at that. Prithee, Horatio, tell me one thing.

Hor. What's that, my lord ? 191

Ham. Dost thou think Alexander look'd a this fashion i' th' earth ?

Hor. E'en so.

Ham. And smelt so ? Pah ! 195
[Throws down the skull.

Hor. E'en so, my lord.

Ham. To what base uses we may return, Horatio ! Why may not imagination trace the noble dust of Alexander till 'a find it stopping a bung-hole ? 199

Hor. 'Twere to consider too curiously to consider so.

Ham. No, faith, not a jot ; but to follow him thither with modesty enough, and likelihood to lead it, as thus : Alexander died, Alexander was buried, Alexander returneth to dust ; the dust is earth ; of earth we make loam ; and why of that loam whereto he was converted might they not stop a beer-barrel ? 206

Imperious Cæsar, dead and turn'd to clay,
Might stop a hole to keep the wind away.
O, that that earth which kept the world in awe
Should patch a wall t' expel the winter's flaw ! 210
But soft ! but soft ! awhile. Here comes the King.

Enter the KING, QUEEN, LAERTES, in funeral procession after the coffin, with Priest and Lords attendant.

The Queen, the courtiers. Who is this they follow ?
And with such maimed rites ? This doth betoken
The corse they follow did with desperate hand
Fordo it own life. 'Twas of some estate. 215

Couch we awhile and mark.
                    [*Retiring with Horatio.*
Laer. What ceremony else ?
Ham. That is Laertes, a very noble youth.
Mark.
    Laer. What ceremony else ?
    Priest. Her obsequies have been as far
        enlarg'd   220
As we have warrantise. Her death was
        doubtful ;
And, but that great command o'ersways
        the order,
She should in ground unsanctified have
        lodg'd
Till the last trumpet ; for charitable
        prayers,
Shards, flints, and pebbles, should be
        thrown on her ;   225
Yet here she is allow'd her virgin crants,
Her maiden strewments, and the bringing
        home
Of bell and burial.
    Laer. Must there no more be done ?
    Priest.   No more be done.
We should profane the service of the dead
To sing sage requiem and such rest to her
As to peace-parted souls.
    Laer.   Lay her i' th' earth ;
And from her fair and unpolluted flesh
May violets spring ! I tell thee, churlish
        priest,
A minist'ring angel shall my sister be   235
When thou liest howling.
    Ham.   What, the fair Ophelia !
    Queen. Sweets to the sweet ; farewell !
                    [*Scattering flowers.*
I hop'd thou shouldst have been my
        Hamlet's wife ;
I thought thy bride-bed to have deck'd,
        sweet maid,
And not have strew'd thy grave.
    Laer.   O, treble woe   240
Fall ten times treble on that cursed head
Whose wicked deed thy most ingenious sense
Depriv'd thee of! Hold off the earth awhile,
Till I have caught her once more in mine
        arms.   [*Leaps into the grave.*
Now pile your dust upon the quick and
        dead,   245
Till of this flat a mountain you have made
T' o'er-top old Pelion or the skyish head
Of blue Olympus.
    Ham. [*Advancing*] What is he whose grief
Bears such an emphasis, whose phrase of
        sorrow
Conjures the wand'ring stars, and makes
        them stand   250
Like wonder-wounded hearers ? This is I,
Hamlet the Dane.   [*Leaps into the grave.*
    Laer. The devil take thy soul !
                    [*Grappling with him.*
    Ham.   Thou pray'st not well.
I prithee take thy fingers from my throat ;
For, though I am not splenitive and rash,

Yet have I in me something dangerous,   256
Which let thy wiseness fear. Hold off thy
        hand.
    King. Pluck them asunder.
    Queen. Hamlet ! Hamlet !
    All. Gentlemen !
    Hor. Good my lord, be quiet.
            [*The Attendants part them, and
                they come out of the grave.*
    Ham. Why, I will fight with him upon
        this theme   260
Until my eyelids will no longer wag.
    Queen. O my son, what theme ?
    Ham. I lov'd Ophelia : forty thousand
        brothers
Could not, with all their quantity of love,
Make up my sum. What wilt thou do for
        her ?   265
    King. O, he is mad, Laertes.
    Queen. For love of God, forbear him.
    Ham. 'Swounds, show me what th'owt
        do :
Woo't weep, woo't fight, woo't fast, woo't
        tear thyself,
Woo't drink up eisel, eat a crocodile ?   270
I'll do't. Dost come here to whine ?
To outface me with leaping in her grave ?
Be buried quick with her, and so will I ;
And, if thou prate of mountains, let them
        throw
Millions of acres on us, till our ground,   275
Singeing his pate against the burning zone,
Make Ossa like a wart ! Nay, an thou'lt
        mouth,
I'll rant as well as thou.
    Queen.   This is mere madness ;
And thus awhile the fit will work on him ;
Anon, as patient as the female dove   280
When that her golden couplets are dis-
        clos'd,
His silence will sit drooping.
    Ham.   Hear you, sir :
What is the reason that you use me thus ?
I lov'd you ever. But it is no matter.
Let Hercules himself do what he may,   285
The cat will mew, and dog will have his day.
                                        [*Exit.*
    King. I pray thee, good Horatio, wait
        upon him.   [*Exit Horatio.*
[*To Laertes*] Strengthen your patience in our
        last night's speech ;
We'll put the matter to the present push.—
Good Gertrude, set some watch over your
        son.—   290
This grave shall have a living monument.
An hour of quiet shortly shall we see ;
Till then in patience our proceeding be.
                                        [*Exeunt.*

SCENE II. *Elsinore. The Castle.*

Enter HAMLET *and* HORATIO.

Ham. So much for this, sir ; now shall
        you see the other.

You do remember all the circumstance ?

Hor. Remember it, my lord !

Ham. Sir, in my heart there was a kind
of fighting
That would not let me sleep. Methought I
lay 5
Worse than the mutines in the bilboes.
Rashly,
And prais'd be rashness for it—let us know,
Our indiscretion sometime serves us well,
When our deep plots do pall ; and that
should learn us
There's a divinity that shapes our ends, 10
Rough-hew them how we will.

Hor. That is most certain.

Ham. Up from my cabin,
My sea-gown scarf'd about me, in the dark
Grop'd I to find out them ; had my desire ;
Finger'd their packet, and in fine withdrew
To mine own room again, making so bold,
My fears forgetting manners, to unseal 17
Their grand commission ; where I found,
Horatio,
Ah, royal knavery ! an exact command,
Larded with many several sorts of reasons,
Importing Denmark's health and England's
too, 21
With, ho ! such bugs and goblins in my
life—
That, on the supervise, no leisure bated,
No, not to stay the grinding of the axe,
My head should be struck off.

Hor. Is't possible ? 25

Ham. Here's the commission ; read it at
more leisure.
But wilt thou hear now how I did proceed ?

Hor. I beseech you.

Ham. Being thus benetted round with
villainies—
Ere I could make a prologue to my brains, 30
They had begun the play—I sat me down ;
Devis'd a new commission ; wrote it fair.
I once did hold it, as our statists do,
A baseness to write fair, and labour'd much
How to forget that learning ; but, sir, now
It did me yeoman's service. Wilt thou
know 36
Th' effect of what I wrote ?

Hor. Ay, good my lord.

Ham. An earnest conjuration from the
King,
As England was his faithful tributary,
As love between them like the palm might
flourish, 40
As peace should still her wheaten garland
wear
And stand a comma 'tween their amities,
And many such like as-es of great charge,
That, on the view and knowing of these
contents, 44
Without debatement further more or less,
He should those bearers put to sudden death,
Not shriving-time allow'd.

Hor. How was this seal'd ?

Ham. Why, even in that was heaven
ordinant.
I had my father's signet in my purse, 49
Which was the model of that Danish seal ;
Folded the writ up in the form of th' other ;
Subscrib'd it, gave't th' impression, plac'd
it safely,
The changeling never known. Now, the
next day
Was our sea-fight ; and what to this was
sequent
Thou knowest already. 55

Hor. So Guildenstern and Rosencrantz go
to't.

Ham. Why, man, they did make love to
this employment ;
They are not near my conscience ; their
defeat
Does by their own insinuation grow : 59
'Tis dangerous when the baser nature comes
Between the pass and fell incensed points
Of mighty opposites.

Hor. Why, what a king is this !

Ham. Does it not, think thee, stand me
now upon—
He that hath kill'd my king and whor'd my
mother ;
Popp'd in between th' election and my
hopes ; 65
Thrown out his angle for my proper life,
And with such coz'nage—is't not perfect
conscience
To quit him with this arm ? And is't not to
be damn'd
To let this canker of our nature come
In further evil ? 70

Hor. It must be shortly known to him
from England
What is the issue of the business there.

Ham. It will be short ; the interim is
mine,
And a man's life's no more than to say
' one '.
But I am very sorry, good Horatio, 75
That to Laertes I forgot myself ;
For by the image of my cause I see
The portraiture of his. I'll court his
favours.
But sure the bravery of his grief did put me
Into a tow'ring passion.

Hor. Peace ; who comes here ? 80

Enter young OSRIC.

Osr. Your lordship is right welcome back
to Denmark.

Ham. I humbly thank you, sir. [*Aside to
Horatio*] Dost know this water-fly ? 83

Hor. [*Aside to Hamlet*] No, my good lord.

Ham. [*Aside to Horatio*] Thy state is the
more gracious ; for 'tis a vice to know him.
He hath much land, and fertile. Let a beast
be lord of beasts, and his crib shall stand
at the king's mess. 'Tis a chough ; but,
as I say, spacious in the possession of dirt.

Osr. Sweet lord, if your lordship were at leisure, I should impart a thing to you from his Majesty. 91

Ham. I will receive it, sir, with all diligence of spirit. Put your bonnet to his right use; 'tis for the head.

Osr. I thank your lordship; it is very hot. 94

Ham. No, believe me, 'tis very cold; the wind is northerly.

Osr. It is indifferent cold, my lord, indeed.

Ham. But yet methinks it is very sultry and hot for my complexion. 99

Osr. Exceedingly, my lord; it is very sultry, as 'twere—I cannot tell how. But, my lord, his Majesty bade me signify to you that 'a has laid a great wager on your head. Sir, this is the matter—

Ham. I beseech you, remember. 104

[*Hamlet moves him to put on his hat.*

Osr. Nay, good my lord; for my ease, in good faith. Sir, here is newly come to court Laertes; believe me, an absolute gentleman, full of most excellent differences, of very soft society and great showing. Indeed, to speak feelingly of him, he is the card or calendar of gentry, for you shall find in him the continent of what part a gentleman would see. 111

Ham. Sir, his definement suffers no perdition in you; though, I know, to divide him inventorially would dozy th' arithmetic of memory, and yet but yaw neither in respect of his quick sail. But, in the verity of extolment, I take him to be a soul of great article, and his infusion of such dearth and rareness as, to make true diction of him, his semblable is his mirror, and who else would trace him, his umbrage, nothing more.

Osr. Your lordship speaks most infallibly of him. 120

Ham. The concernancy, sir? Why do we wrap the gentleman in our more rawer breath?

Osr. Sir?

Hor. [*Aside to Hamlet*] Is't not possible to understand in another tongue? You will to't, sir, really. 125

Ham. What imports the nomination of this gentleman?

Osr. Of Laertes?

Hor. [*Aside*] His purse is empty already; all's golden words are spent. 130

Ham. Of him, sir.

Osr. I know you are not ignorant—

Ham. I would you did, sir; yet, in faith, if you did, it would not much approve me. Well, sir.

Osr. You are not ignorant of what excellence Laertes is— 136

Ham. I dare not confess that, lest I should compare with him in excellence; but to know a man well were to know himself. 139

Osr. I mean, sir, for his weapon; but in the imputation laid on him by them, in his meed he's unfellowed.

Ham. What's his weapon?

Osr. Rapier and dagger.

Ham. That's two of his weapons—but well. 144

Osr. The King, sir, hath wager'd with him six Barbary horses; against the which he has impon'd, as I take it, six French rapiers and poniards, with their assigns, as girdle, hangers, and so—three of the carriages, in faith, are very dear to fancy, very responsive to the hilts, most delicate carriages, and of very liberal conceit. 150

Ham. What call you the carriages?

Hor. [*Aside to Hamlet*] I knew you must be edified by the margent ere you had done.

Osr. The carriages, sir, are the hangers.

Ham. The phrase would be more germane to the matter if we could carry a cannon by our sides. I would it might be hangers till then. But on: six Barbary horses against six French swords, their assigns, and three liberal conceited carriages; that's the French bet against the Danish. Why is this all impon'd, as you call it? 160

Osr. The King, sir, hath laid, sir, that in a dozen passes between yourself and him he shall not exceed you three hits; he hath laid on twelve for nine, and it would come to immediate trial if your lordship would vouchsafe the answer. 165

Ham. How if I answer no?

Osr. I mean, my lord, the opposition of your person in trial.

Ham. Sir, I will walk here in the hall. If it please his Majesty, it is the breathing time of day with me; let the foils be brought, the gentleman willing, and the King hold his purpose, I will win for him an I can; if not, I will gain nothing but my shame and the odd hits.

Osr. Shall I redeliver you e'en so?

Ham. To this effect, sir, after what flourish your nature will. 176

Osr. I commend my duty to your lordship.

Ham. Yours, yours. [*Exit Osric*] He does well to commend it himself; there are no tongues else for's turn.

Hor. This lapwing runs away with the shell on his head. 181

Ham. 'A did comply, sir, with his dug before 'a suck'd it. Thus has he, and many more of the same bevy, that I know the drossy age dotes on, only got the tune of the time and outward habit of encounter—a kind of yesty collection, which carries them through and through the most fann'd and winnowed opinions; and do but blow them to their trial, the bubbles are out. 188

Enter a Lord.

Lord. My lord, his Majesty commended

him to you by young Osric, who brings back
to him that you attend him in the hall. He
sends to know if your pleasure hold to play
with Laertes, or that you will take longer
time.

Ham. I am constant to my purposes ;
they follow the king's pleasure : if his fitness speaks, mine is ready now—or whensoever, provided I be so able as now. 195

Lord. The King and Queen and all are
coming down.

Ham. In happy time.

Lord. The Queen desires you to use some
gentle entertainment to Laertes before you
fall to play. 199

Ham. She well instructs me. [*Exit Lord.*

Hor. You will lose this wager, my lord.

Ham. I do not think so ; since he went
into France I have been in continual
practice. I shall win at the odds. But thou
wouldst not think how ill all's here about
my heart ; but it is no matter. 205

Hor. Nay, good my lord—

Ham. It is but foolery ; but it is such a
kind of gain-giving as would perhaps trouble
a woman.

Hor. If your mind dislike anything, obey
it. I will forestall their repair hither, and
say you are not fit. 210

Ham. Not a whit, we defy augury :
there is a special providence in the fall of
a sparrow. If it be now, 'tis not to come ;
if it be not to come, it will be now ; if it
be not now, yet it will come—the readiness
is all. Since no man owes of aught he
leaves, what is't to leave betimes ? Let be.

A table prepared. Trumpets, Drums, *and*
Officers *with cushions, foils and daggers.*
Enter KING, QUEEN, LAERTES, *and all*
the State.

King. Come, Hamlet, come, and take
this hand from me. [*The King puts
Laertes's hand into Hamlet's.*

Ham. Give me your pardon, sir. I have
done you wrong ;
But pardon 't, as you are a gentleman.
This presence knows, 220
And you must needs have heard how I am
punish'd
With a sore distraction. What I have done
That might your nature, honour, and
exception,
Roughly awake, I here proclaim was mad-
ness.
Was 't Hamlet wrong'd Laertes ? Never
Hamlet. 225
If Hamlet from himself be ta'en away,
And when he's not himself does wrong
Laertes,
Then Hamlet does it not, Hamlet denies it.
Who does it, then? His madness. If't be so,
Hamlet is of the faction that is wrong'd ;
His madness is poor Hamlet's enemy. 231

Sir, in this audience,
Let my disclaiming from a purpos'd evil
Free me so far in your most generous
thoughts 234
That I have shot my arrow o'er the house
And hurt my brother.
Laer.   I am satisfied in nature,
Whose motive in this case should stir me
most
To my revenge ; but in my terms of honour
I stand aloof, and will no reconcilement
Till by some elder masters of known
honour 240
I have a voice and precedent of peace
To keep my name ungor'd—but till that
time
I do receive your offer'd love like love,
And will not wrong it.
Ham.   I embrace it freely ;
And will this brother's wager frankly play.
Give us the foils. Come on.
Laer.   Come, one for me.
Ham. I'll be your foil, Laertes ; in mine
ignorance 247
Your skill shall, like a star i' th' darkest
night,
Stick fiery off indeed.
Laer.   You mock me, sir.
Ham. No, by this hand. 250
King. Give them the foils, young Osric.
Cousin Hamlet,
You know the wager ?
Ham.   Very well, my lord ;
Your Grace has laid the odds a' th' weaker
side.
King. I do not fear it : I have seen you
both ;
But since he's better'd, we have therefore
odds. 255
Laer. This is too heavy ; let me see
another.
Ham. This likes me well. These foils
have all a length ?
[*They prepare to play.*
Osr. Ay, my good lord.
King. Set me the stoups of wine upon
that table.
If Hamlet give the first or second hit, 260
Or quit in answer of the third exchange,
Let all the battlements their ordnance fire ;
The King shall drink to Hamlet's better
breath,
And in the cup an union shall he throw,
Richer than that which four successive
kings 265
In Denmark's crown have worn. Give me
the cups ;
And let the kettle to the trumpet speak,
The trumpet to the cannoneer without,
The cannons to the heavens, the heaven to
earth,
' Now the King drinks to Hamlet '. Come,
begin— 270
And you, the judges, bear a wary eye.

Ham. Come on, sir.

Laer. Come, my lord.   [*They play.*

Ham. One.

Laer. No.

Ham. Judgment ?

Osr. A hit, a very palpable hit.

Laer. Well, again.

King. Stay, give me drink. Hamlet, this
     pearl is thine ;

Here's to thy health.

         [*Drum, trumpets, and shot.*

         Give him the cup. 275

   Ham. I'll play this bout first ; set it by
     awhile.

Come.   [*They play.*

Another hit ; what say you ?

   Laer. A touch, a touch, I do confess't.

King. Our son shall win.

Queen. He's fat, and scant of breath.

Here, Hamlet, take my napkin, rub thy
     brows.   280

The Queen carouses to thy fortune, Hamlet.

   Ham. Good madam !

   King. Gertrude, do not drink.

   Queen. I will, my lord ; I pray you
     pardon me.

   King. [*Aside*] It is the poison'd cup ; it is
     too late.

   Ham. I dare not drink yet, madam ; by
     and by.   285

   Queen. Come, let me wipe thy face.

   Laer. My lord, I'll hit him now.

   King.   I do not think't.

   Laer. [*Aside*] And yet it is almost against
     my conscience.

   Ham. Come, for the third. Laertes, you
     do but dally ;   289

I pray you pass with your best violence ;

I am afeard you make a wanton of me.

   Laer. Say you so ? Come on. [*They play.*

   Osr. Nothing, neither way.

   Laer. Have at you now ! [*Laertes wounds
     Hamlet : then, in scuffling, they change
     rapiers, and Hamlet wounds Laertes.*

   King. Part them ; they are incens'd.

   Ham. Nay, come again. [*The Queen falls.*

   Osr. Look to the Queen there, ho !

   Hor. They bleed on both sides. How is it,
     my lord ?

   Osr. How is't, Laertes ?   297

   Laer. Why, as a woodcock, to mine own
     springe, Osric ;

I am justly kill'd with mine own treachery.

   Ham. How does the Queen ?

   King.   She swoons to see them bleed.

   Queen. No, no, the drink, the drink ! O
     my dear Hamlet !   301

The drink, the drink ! I am poison'd. [*Dies.*

   Ham. O, villainy ! Ho ! let the door be
     lock'd.

Treachery ! seek it out.   [*Laertes falls.*

   Laer. It is here, Hamlet. Hamlet, thou
     art slain ;   305

No med'cine in the world can do thee good ;

In thee there is not half an hour's life ;

The treacherous instrument is in thy hand,

Unbated and envenom'd. The foul practice

Hath turn'd itself on me ; lo, here I lie, 310

Never to rise again. Thy mother's poison'd.

I can no more. The King, the King's to
     blame.

   Ham. The point envenom'd too !

Then, venom, to thy work. [*Stabs the King.*

   All. Treason ! treason !   315

   King. O, yet defend me, friends ; I am
     but hurt.

   Ham. Here, thou incestuous, murd'rous,
     damned Dane,

Drink off this potion. Is thy union here ?

Follow my mother.   [*King dies.*

   Laer.   He is justly serv'd :

It is a poison temper'd by himself.   320

Exchange forgiveness with me, noble
     Hamlet.

Mine and my father's death come not upon
     thee,

Nor thine on me !   [*Dies.*

   Ham. Heaven make thee free of it ! I
     follow thee.

I am dead, Horatio. Wretched queen,
     adieu !   325

You that look pale and tremble at this
     chance,

That are but mutes or audience to this
     act,

Had I but time, as this fell sergeant Death

Is strict in his arrest, O, I could tell you—

But let it be. Horatio, I am dead :   330

Thou livest ; report me and my cause
     aright

To the unsatisfied.

   Hor.   Never believe it.

I am more an antique Roman than a Dane ;

Here's yet some liquor left.

   Ham.   As th'art a man,

Give me the cup. Let go. By heaven, I'll
     ha't.   335

O God ! Horatio, what a wounded name,

Things standing thus unknown, shall live
     behind me !

If thou didst ever hold me in thy heart,

Absent thee from felicity awhile,

And in this harsh world draw thy breath in
     pain,   340

To tell my story.

       [*March afar off, and shot within.*

          What warlike noise is this ?

   Osr. Young Fortinbras, with conquest
     come from Poland,

To th' ambassadors of England gives

This warlike volley.

   Ham.   O, I die, Horatio !

The potent poison quite o'er-crows my
     spirit.   345

I cannot live to hear the news from
     England,

But I do prophesy th' election lights

On Fortinbras ; he has my dying voice.

So tell him, with th' occurrents, more and less,   349
Which have solicited—the rest is silence.
                                        [Dies.
  Hor. Now cracks a noble heart. Good night, sweet prince,
And flights of angels sing thee to thy rest !
                                        [March within.
Why does the drum come hither ?

Enter FORTINBRAS *and* English Ambassadors, *with drum, colours, and* Attendants.

  Fort. Where is this sight ?
  Hor.   What is it you would see ?
If aught of woe or wonder, cease your search.   355
  Fort. This quarry cries on havoc. O proud death,
What feast is toward in thine eternal cell
That thou so many princes at a shot
So bloodily hast struck ?
  1 Amb.   The sight is dismal ;
And our affairs from England come too late :   360
The ears are senseless that should give us hearing
To tell him his commandment is fulfill'd,
That Rosencrantz and Guildenstern are dead.
Where should we have our thanks ?
  Hor.   Not from his mouth,
Had it th' ability of life to thank you : 365
He never gave commandment for their death.
But since, so jump upon this bloody question,
You from the Polack wars, and you from England,
Are here arrived, give order that these bodies

High on a stage be placed to the view ; 370
And let me speak to th' yet unknowing world
How these things came about. So shall you hear
Of carnal, bloody, and unnatural acts ;
Of accidental judgments, casual slaughters ;
Of deaths put on by cunning and forc'd cause ;   375
And, in this upshot, purposes mistook
Fall'n on th' inventors' heads—all this can I
Truly deliver.
  Fort.   Let us haste to hear it,
And call the noblest to the audience.
For me, with sorrow I embrace my fortune ;   380
I have some rights of memory in this kingdom,
Which now to claim my vantage doth invite me.
  Hor. Of that I shall have also cause to speak,
And from his mouth whose voice will draw on more.   384
But let this same be presently perform'd,
Even while men's minds are wild, lest more mischance
On plots and errors happen.
  Fort.   Let four captains
Bear Hamlet like a soldier to the stage ;
For he was likely, had he been put on,
To have prov'd most royal ; and for his passage   390
The soldier's music and the rite of war
Speak loudly for him.
Take up the bodies. Such a sight as this
Becomes the field, but here shows much amiss.   394
Go, bid the soldiers shoot. [*Exeunt marching.*
                    A peal of ordnance shot off.

KING LEAR

DRAMATIS PERSONÆ

LEAR, *King of Britain.*
KING OF FRANCE.
DUKE OF BURGUNDY.
DUKE OF CORNWALL.
DUKE OF ALBANY.
EARL OF KENT.
EARL OF GLOUCESTER.
EDGAR, *son to Gloucester.*
EDMUND, *bastard son to Gloucester.*
CURAN, *a courtier.*
Old Man, *tenant to Gloucester.*
Doctor.

Fool.
OSWALD, *steward to Goneril.*
A Captain, *employed by Edmund.*
Gentleman *attendant on Cordelia.*
A Herald.
Servants *to Cornwall.*

GONERIL,
REGAN,   } *daughters to Lear.*
CORDELIA,

Knights *attending on Lear*, Officers, Messengers, Soldiers, *and* Attendants.

THE SCENE : *Britain.*

ACT ONE

SCENE I. *King Lear's palace.*

Enter KENT, GLOUCESTER, *and* EDMUND.

Kent. I thought the King had more affected the Duke of Albany than Cornwall.

Glo. It did always seem so to us ; but now, in the division of the kingdom, it appears not which of the Dukes he values most ; for equalities are so weigh'd that curiosity in neither can make choice of either's moiety.   6

Kent. Is not this your son, my lord ?

Glo. His breeding, sir, hath been at my charge. I have so often blush'd to acknowledge him that now I am braz'd to't.   10

Kent. I cannot conceive you.

Glo. Sir, this young fellow's mother could ; whereupon she grew round-womb'd, and had indeed, sir, a son for her cradle ere she had a husband for her bed. Do you smell a fault ?   15

Kent. I cannot wish the fault undone, the issue of it being so proper.

Glo. But I have a son, sir, by order of law, some year elder than this, who yet is no dearer in my account. Though this knave came something saucily to the world before he was sent for, yet was his mother fair ; there was good sport at his making, and the whoreson must be acknowledged.—Do you know this noble gentleman, Edmund ?

Edm. No, my lord.   25

Glo. My Lord of Kent. Remember him hereafter as my honourable friend.

Edm. My services to your lordship.

Kent. I must love you, and sue to know you better.

Edm. Sir, I shall study deserving.   30

Glo. He hath been out nine years, and away he shall again. [*Sennet*] The King is coming.

Enter One bearing a coronet ; then LEAR, *then the* DUKES OF ALBANY *and* CORNWALL, *next* GONERIL, REGAN, CORDELIA, *with* Followers.

Lear. Attend the Lords of France and Burgundy, Gloucester.

Glo. I shall, my liege.
        [*Exeunt Gloucester and Edmund.*

Lear. Meantime we shall express our darker purpose.   35
Give me the map there. Know that we have divided
In three our kingdom ; and 'tis our fast intent
To shake all cares and business from our age,
Conferring them on younger strengths, while we
Unburden'd crawl toward death. Our son of Cornwall,   40
And you, our no less loving son of Albany,
We have this hour a constant will to publish
Our daughters' several dowers, that future strife
May be prevented now. The Princes, France and Burgundy,
Great rivals in our youngest daughter's love,   45
Long in our court have made their amorous sojourn,
And here are to be answer'd. Tell me, my daughters—
Since now we will divest us both of rule,
Interest of territory, cares of state—
Which of you shall we say doth love us most ?   50

1073

That we our largest bounty may extend
Where nature doth with merit challenge. Goneril,
Our eldest-born, speak first.

   Gon. Sir, I love you more than word can
     wield the matter;
Dearer than eyesight, space, and liberty; 55
Beyond what can be valued, rich or rare;
No less than life, with grace, health, beauty,
   honour;
As much as child e'er lov'd, or father
   found;
A love that makes breath poor and speech
   unable; 59
Beyond all manner of so much I love you.

   Cor. [*Aside*] What shall Cordelia speak?
   Love, and be silent.

   Lear. Of all these bounds, even from this
   line to this,
With shadowy forests and with champains
   rich'd,
With plenteous rivers and wide-skirted
   meads,
We make thee lady: to thine and Albany's
   issues 65
Be this perpetual.—What says our second
   daughter,
Our dearest Regan, wife of Cornwall?
   Speak.

   Reg. I am made of that self metal as my
   sister,
And prize me at her worth. In my true
   heart
I find she names my very deed of love; 70
Only she comes too short, that I profess
Myself an enemy to all other joys
Which the most precious square of sense
   possesses,
And find I am alone felicitate 74
In your dear Highness' love.

   Cor. [*Aside*]   Then poor Cordelia!
And yet not so; since I am sure my love's
More ponderous than my tongue.

   Lear. To thee and thine hereditary ever
Remain this ample third of our fair
   kingdom;
No less in space, validity, and pleasure, 80
Than that conferr'd on Goneril.—Now, our
   joy,
Although our last and least; to whose
   young love
The vines of France and milk of Burgundy
Strive to be interess'd; what can you say
   to draw
A third more opulent than your sisters?
   Speak. 85

   Cor. Nothing, my lord.

   Lear. Nothing!

   Cor. Nothing.

   Lear. Nothing will come of nothing.
   Speak again.

   Cor. Unhappy that I am, I cannot heave
My heart into my mouth. I love your
   Majesty 91

According to my bond; no more nor less.

   Lear. How, how, Cordelia! Mend your
     speech a little, 93
Lest you may mar your fortunes.

   Cor.   Good my lord,
You have begot me, bred me, lov'd me; I
Return those duties back as are right fit,
Obey you, love you, and most honour you.
Why have my sisters husbands, if they say
They love you all? Haply, when I shall
   wed,
That lord whose hand must take my plight
   shall carry 100
Half my love with him, half my care and
   duty.
Sure I shall never marry like my sisters,
To love my father all.

   Lear. But goes thy heart with this?

   Cor.   Ay, my good lord.

   Lear. So young and so untender? 105

   Cor. So young, my lord, and true.

   Lear. Let it be so! Thy truth, then, be
   thy dower!
For, by the scared radiance of the sun,
The mysteries of Hecat and the night;
By all the operation of the orbs 110
From whom we do exist and cease to be;
Here I disclaim all my paternal care,
Propinquity and property of blood,
And as a stranger to my heart and me
Hold thee from this for ever. The barbarous
   Scythian, 115
Or he that makes his generation messes
To gorge his appetite, shall to my bosom
Be as well neighbour'd, pitied, and reliev'd,
As thou my sometime daughter.

   Kent.   Good my liege—

   Lear. Peace, Kent! 120
Come not between the dragon and his
   wrath.
I lov'd her most, and thought to set my
   rest
On her kind nursery. [*To Cordelia*] Hence,
   and avoid my sight!—
So be my grave my peace as here I give
Her father's heart from her! Call France—
   Who stirs? 125
Call Burgundy. Cornwall and Albany,
With my two daughters' dowers digest this
   third.
Let pride, which she calls plainness, marry
   her.
I do invest you jointly with my power,
Pre-eminence, and all the large effects 130
That troop with majesty. Ourself, by
   monthly course,
With reservation of an hundred knights,
By you to be sustain'd, shall our abode
Make with you by due turn. Only we shall
   retain 134
The name, and all th' addition to a king:
The sway, revenue, execution of the rest,
Beloved sons, be yours; which to confirm,
This coronet part between you.

Kent.   Royal Lear,
Whom I have ever honour'd as my king,
Lov'd as my father, as my master follow'd,
As my great patron thought on in my
      prayers—   141
  Lear. The bow is bent and drawn ; make
      from the shaft.
  Kent. Let it fall rather, though the fork
      invade
The region of my heart.   Be Kent un-
      mannerly
When Lear is mad.   What wouldst thou do,
      old man ?   145
Think'st thou that duty shall have dread
      to speak
When power to flattery bows ?   To plain-
      ness honour's bound
When majesty falls to folly.   Reserve thy
      state ;
And in thy best consideration check
This hideous rashness.   Answer my life my
      judgment :   150
Thy youngest daughter does not love thee
      least ;
Nor are those empty-hearted whose low
      sounds
Reverb no hollowness.
  Lear.   Kent, on thy life, no more !
  Kent. My life I never held but as a pawn
To wage against thine enemies ; nor fear
      to lose it,   155
Thy safety being motive.
  Lear.   Out of my sight !
  Kent. See better, Lear ; and let me still
      remain
The true blank of thine eye.
  Lear. Now by Apollo—
  Kent.   Now, by Apollo, King,
Thou swear'st thy gods in vain.
  Lear.   O, vassal ! miscreant !
      [*Laying his hand on his sword.*
  Alb. and Corn. Dear sir, forbear.   161
  Kent. Do ;
Kill thy physician, and the fee bestow
Upon the foul disease.   Revoke thy gift,
Or, whilst I can vent clamour from my
      throat,   165
I'll tell thee thou dost evil.
  Lear.   Hear me, recreant ;
On thine allegiance, hear me.
That thou hast sought to make us break
      our vows—
Which we durst never yet—and with
      strain'd pride
To come betwixt our sentence and our
      power—   170
Which nor our nature nor our place can
      bear ;
Our potency made good, take thy reward.
Five days we do allot thee for provision
To shield thee from disasters of the world,
And on the sixth to turn thy hated back 175
Upon our kingdom ; if, on the tenth day
      following,

Thy banish'd trunk be found in our
      dominions,
The moment is thy death.   Away ! by
      Jupiter,
This shall not be revok'd.
  Kent. Fare thee well, King.   Sith thus
      thou wilt appear,   180
Freedom lives hence, and banishment is
      here.
[*To Cordelia*] The gods to their dear shelter
      take thee, maid,
That justly think'st, and hast most rightly
      said !
[*To Regan and Goneril*] And your large
      speeches may your deeds approve,
That good effects may spring from words of
      love !   185
Thus Kent, O princes, bids you all adieu ;
He'll shape his old course in a country new.
                                      [*Exit.*

Flourish.   Re-enter GLOUCESTER, *with*
  FRANCE, BURGUNDY, *and* Attendants.

  Glo. Here's France and Burgundy, my
      noble lord.
  Lear. My Lord of Burgundy,
We first address toward you, who with this
      king   190
Hath rivall'd for our daughter.   What in
      the least
Will you require in present dower with her,
Or cease your quest of love ?
  Bur.   Most royal Majesty,
I crave no more than hath your Highness
      offer'd,
Nor will you tender less.
  Lear.   Right noble Burgundy, 195
When she was dear to us, we did hold her
      so ;
But now her price is fallen.   Sir, there she
      stands :
If aught within that little seeming sub-
      stance,
Or all of it, with our displeasure piec'd,
And nothing more, may fitly like your
      Grace,   200
She's there, and she is yours.
  Bur.   I know no answer.
  Lear. Will you, with those infirmities she
      owes,
Unfriended, new-adopted to our hate,
Dower'd with our curse, and stranger'd
      with our oath,   204
Take her or leave her ?
  Bur.   Pardon me, royal sir ;
Election makes not up in such conditions.
  Lear. Then leave her, sir ; for, by the
      pow'r that made me,   207
I tell you all her wealth. [*To France*] For
      you, great King,
I would not from your love make such a
      stray
To match you where I hate ; therefore
      beseech you   210

T' avert your liking a more worthier way,
Than on a wretch whom nature is asham'd
Almost t' acknowledge hers.
    France.   This is most strange,
That she, whom even but now was your
        best object,
The argument of your praise, balm of your
        age,   215
The best, the dearest, should in this trice
        of time
Commit a thing so monstrous to dismantle
So many folds of favour. Sure her offence
Must be of such unnatural degree
That monsters it, or your fore-vouch'd
        affection   220
Fall into taint—which to believe of her
Must be a faith that reason without miracle
Should never plant in me.
    Cor.   I yet beseech your Majesty—
If for I want that glib and oily art
To speak and purpose not, since what I well
        intend   225
I'll do't before I speak—that you make
        known
It is no vicious blot, murder, or foulness,
No unchaste action or dishonoured step,
That hath depriv'd me of your grace and
        favour;
But even for want of that for which I am
        richer—   230
A still-soliciting eye, and such a tongue
That I am glad I have not, though not to
        have it
Hath lost me in your liking.
    Lear.   Better thou
Hadst not been born than not t' have
        pleas'd me better.
    France. Is it but this? A tardiness in
        nature,   235
Which often leaves the history unspoke
That it intends to do! My Lord of Bur-
        gundy,
What say you to the lady? Love's not
        love
When it is mingled with regards that
        stands
Aloof from th' entire point. Will you have
        her?   240
She is herself a dowry.
    Bur.   Royal king,
Give but that portion which yourself
        propos'd,
And here I take Cordelia by the hand,
Duchess of Burgundy.
    Lear. Nothing! I have sworn; I am
        firm.   245
    Bur. I am sorry, then, you have so lost
        a father
That you must lose a husband.
    Cor.   Peace be with Burgundy!
Since that respects of fortune are his love
I shall not be his wife.
    France. Fairest Cordelia, that art most
        rich, being poor;   250

Most choice, forsaken; and most lov'd,
        despis'd!
Thee and thy virtues here I seize upon,
Be it lawful I take up what's cast away.
Gods, gods! 'tis strange that from their
        cold'st neglect   254
My love should kindle to inflam'd respect.
Thy dow'rless daughter, King, thrown to
        my chance,
Is queen of us, of ours, and our fair France.
Not all the dukes of wat'rish Burgundy
Can buy this unpriz'd precious maid of me.
Bid them farewell, Cordelia, though un-
        kind;   260
Thou losest here, a better where to find.
    Lear. Thou hast her, France; let her be
        thine; for we
Have no such daughter, nor shall ever see
That face of hers again. [*To Cordelia*] There-
        fore be gone
Without our grace, our love, our benison.
Come, noble Burgundy.   266
    [*Flourish. Exeunt Lear, Burgundy, Corn-
    wall, Albany, Gloucester, and Attendants.*
    France. Bid farewell to your sisters.
    Cor. The jewels of our father, with wash'd
        eyes
Cordelia leaves you. I know you what you
        are;
And, like a sister, am most loath to call   270
Your faults as they are named. Love well
        our father.
To your professed bosoms I commit him;
But yet, alas, stood I within his grace,
I would prefer him to a better place.
So, farewell to you both.   275
    Reg. Prescribe not us our duty.
    Gon.   Let your study
Be to content your lord, who hath receiv'd
        you
At fortune's alms. You have obedience
        scanted,
And well are worth the want that you have
        wanted.
    Cor. Time shall unfold what plighted
        cunning hides,   280
Who covers faults, at last with shame
        derides.
Well may you prosper!
    France.   Come, my fair Cordelia.
        [*Exeunt France and Cordelia.*
    Gon. Sister, it is not little I have to say
of what most nearly appertains to us both.
I think our father will hence to-night.   285
    Reg. That's most certain, and with you;
next month with us.
    Gon. You see how full of changes his age
is; the observation we have made of it
hath not been little. He always lov'd our
sister most; and with what poor judgment
he hath now cast her off appears too grossly.
    Reg. 'Tis the infirmity of his age; yet he
hath ever but slenderly known himself.   293
    Gon. The best and soundest of his time

hath been but rash; then must we look from his age to receive not alone the imperfections of long-engraffed condition, but therewithal the unruly waywardness that infirm and choleric years bring with them.

Reg. Such unconstant starts are we like to have from him as this of Kent's banishment.   300

Gon. There is further compliment of leave-taking between France and him. Pray you, let us hit together; if our father carry authority with such disposition as he bears, this last surrender of his will but offend us.

Reg. We shall further think of it.   305

Gon. We must do something, and i' th' heat.   *[Exeunt.*

Scene II. *Gloucester's castle.*

Enter EDMUND *with a letter.*

Edm. Thou, Nature, art my goddess; to
    thy law
My services are bound. Wherefore should I
Stand in the plague of custom, and permit
The curiosity of nations to deprive me,
For that I am some twelve or fourteen
    moonshines   5
Lag of a brother? Why bastard? Where-
    fore base?
When my dimensions are as well compact,
My mind as generous, and my shape as
    true,
As honest madam's issue? Why brand
    they us
With base? with baseness? bastardy?
    base, base?   10
Who, in the lusty stealth of nature, take
More composition and fierce quality
Than doth, within a dull, stale, tired bed,
Go to th' creating a whole tribe of fops
Got 'tween asleep and wake? Well then, 15
Legitimate Edgar, I must have your land.
Our father's love is to the bastard Edmund
As to th' legitimate. Fine word 'legiti-
    mate'!
Well, my legitimate, if this letter speed, 19
And my invention thrive, Edmund the base
Shall top th' legitimate. I grow; I prosper.
Now, gods, stand up for bastards.

Enter GLOUCESTER.

Glo. Kent banish'd thus! and France in
    choler parted!
And the King gone to-night! Prescrib'd his
    pow'r!
Confin'd to exhibition! All this done   25
Upon the gad! Edmund, how now! What
    news?
Edm. So please your lordship, none.
                [Putting up the letter.
Glo. Why so earnestly seek you to put up
that letter?

Edm. I know no news, my lord.
Glo. What paper were you reading?   30
Edm. Nothing, my lord.
Glo. No? What needed then that terrible dispatch of it into your pocket? The quality of nothing hath not such need to hide itself. Let's see. Come, if it be nothing, I shall not need spectacles.   35
Edm. I beseech you, sir, pardon me. It is a letter from my brother that I have not all o'er-read; and for so much as I have perus'd, I find it not fit for your o'er-looking.
Glo. Give me the letter, sir.   39
Edm. I shall offend either to detain or give it. The contents, as in part I understand them, are to blame.
Glo. Let's see, let's see.
Edm. I hope, for my brother's justification, he wrote this but as an essay or taste of my virtue.   44
Glo. [*Reads*] 'This policy and reverence of age makes the world bitter to the best of our times; keeps our fortunes from us till our oldness cannot relish them. I begin to find an idle and fond bondage in the oppression of aged tyranny, who sways, not as it hath power, but as it is suffer'd. Come to me, that of this I may speak more. If our father would sleep till I wak'd him, you should enjoy half his revenue for ever, and live the beloved of your brother.
                  EDGAR.'   51
Hum—Conspiracy! 'Sleep till I wak'd him, you should enjoy half his revenue.' My son Edgar! Had he a hand to write this? a heart and a brain to breed it in? When came this to you? Who brought it?
Edm. It was not brought me, my lord; there's the cunning of it. I found it thrown in at the casement of my closet.   58
Glo. You know the character to be your brother's?
Edm. If the matter were good, my lord, I durst swear it were his; but in respect of that, I would fain think it were not.   62
Glo. It is his.
Edm. It is his hand, my lord; but I hope his heart is not in the contents.   65
Glo. Has he never before sounded you in this business?
Edm. Never, my lord; but I have heard him oft maintain it to be fit that, sons at perfect age and fathers declin'd, the father should be as ward to the son, and the son manage his revenue.   71
Glo. O villain, villain! His very opinion in the letter! Abhorred villain! Unnatural, detested, brutish villain! Worse than brutish! Go, sirrah, seek him; I'll apprehend him. Abominable villain! Where is he?   75
Edm. I do not well know, my lord. If it shall please you to suspend your indigna-

tion against my brother till you can derive from him better testimony of his intent, you should run a certain course ; where, if you violently proceed against him, mistaking his purpose, it would make a great gap in your own honour, and shake in pieces the heart of his obedience. I dare pawn down my life for him that he hath writ this to feel my affection to your honour, and to no other pretence of danger.

Glo. Think you so ? 85

Edm. If your honour judge it meet, I will place you where you shall hear us confer of this, and by an auricular assurance have your satisfaction ; and that without any further delay than this very evening.

Glo. He cannot be such a monster. 90

Edm. Nor is not, sure.

Glo. To his father, that so tenderly and entirely loves him. Heaven and earth ! Edmund, seek him out ; wind me into him, I pray you. Frame the business after your own wisdom. I would unstate myself to be in a due resolution. 96

Edm. I will seek him, sir, presently ; convey the business as I shall find means, and acquaint you withal.

Glo. These late eclipses in the sun and moon portend no good to us. Though the wisdom of nature can reason it thus and thus, yet nature finds itself scourg'd by the sequent effects : love cools, friendship falls off, brothers divide ; in cities, mutinies ; in countries, discord ; in palaces, treason ; and the bond crack'd 'twixt son and father. This villain of mine comes under the prediction : there's son against father. The King falls from bias of nature : there's father against child. We have seen the best of our time : machinations, hollowness, treachery, and all ruinous disorders, follow us disquietly to our graves. Find out this villain, Edmund ; it shall lose thee nothing ; do it carefully. And the noble and true-hearted Kent banish'd ! His offence, honesty ! 'Tis strange. [*Exit.*

Edm. This is the excellent foppery of the world, that, when we are sick in fortune, often the surfeits of our own behaviour, we make guilty of our disasters the sun, the moon, and stars ; as if we were villains on necessity ; fools by heavenly compulsion ; knaves, thieves, and treachers, by spherical predominance ; drunkards, liars, and adulterers, by an enforc'd obedience of planetary influence ; and all that we are evil in, by a divine thrusting on—an admirable evasion of whoremaster man, to lay his goatish disposition on the charge of a star ! My father compounded with my mother under the Dragon's tail, and my nativity was under Ursa Major, so that it

follows I am rough and lecherous. Fut, I should have been that I am, had the maidenliest star in the firmament twinkled on my bastardizing. Edgar ! 127

Enter EDGAR.

Pat ! He comes like the catastrophe of the old comedy. My cue is villainous melancholy, with a sigh like Tom o' Bedlam.—O, these eclipses do portend these divisions ! fa, sol, la, mi. 131

Edg. How now, brother Edmund ! What serious contemplation are you in ?

Edm. I am thinking, brother, of a prediction I read this other day what should follow these eclipses. 135

Edg. Do you busy yourself with that ?

Edm. I promise you, the effects he writes of succeed unhappily ; as of unnaturalness between the child and the parent ; death, dearth, dissolutions of ancient amities ; divisions in state, menaces and maledictions against king and nobles ; needless diffidences, banishment of friends, dissipation of cohorts, nuptial breaches, and I know not what. 142

Edg. How long have you been a sectary astronomical ?

Edm. Come, come ! When saw you my father last ?

Edg. The night gone by. 145

Edm. Spake you with him ?

Edg. Ay, two hours together.

Edm. Parted you in good terms ? Found you no displeasure in him by word nor countenance ?

Edg. None at all. 150

Edm. Bethink yourself wherein you may have offended him ; and at my entreaty forbear his presence, until some little time hath qualified the heat of his displeasure, which at this instant so rageth in him that with the mischief of your person it would scarcely allay. 155

Edg. Some villain hath done me wrong.

Edm. That's my fear. I pray you have a continent forbearance till the speed of his rage goes slower ; and, as I say, retire with me to my lodging, from whence I will fitly bring you to hear my lord speak. Pray ye go ; there's my key. If you do stir abroad, go arm'd. 161

Edg. Arm'd, brother !

Edm. Brother, I advise you to the best. I am no honest man if there be any good meaning toward you. I have told you what I have seen and heard—but faintly ; nothing like the image and horror of it. Pray you, away. 167

Edg. Shall I hear from you anon ?

Edm. I do serve you in this business.

[*Exit Edgar.*

A credulous father ! and a brother noble, Whose nature is so far from doing harms

That he suspects none; on whose foolish
    honesty
My practices ride easy! I see the business.
Let me, if not by birth, have lands by wit:
All with me's meet that I can fashion fit. 175
                                        [Exit.

SCENE III. *The Duke of Albany's palace.*

Enter GONERIL *and* OSWALD, *her steward.*

  Gon. Did my father strike my gentleman
for chiding of his fool?
  Osw. Ay, madam.
  Gon. By day and night, he wrongs me;
    every hour
He flashes into one gross crime or other 5
That sets us all at odds. I'll not endure it.
His knights grow riotous, and himself up-
    braids us
On every trifle. When he returns from
    hunting,
I will not speak with him; say I am sick.
If you come slack of former services, 10
You shall do well; the fault of it I'll
    answer.   [*Horns within.*
  Osw. He's coming, madam; I hear him.
  Gon. Put on what weary negligence you
    please,
You and your fellows; I'd have it come to
    question.
If he distaste it, let him to my sister, 15
Whose mind and mine, I know, in that are
    one,
Not to be overrul'd. Idle old man,
That still would manage those authorities
That he hath given away! Now, by my
    life,
Old fools are babes again, and must be us'd
With checks as flatteries, when they are
    seen abus'd. 21
Remember what I have said.
  Osw.   Well, madam.
  Gon. And let his knights have colder
    looks among you;
What grows of it, no matter. Advise your
    fellows so.
I would breed from hence occasions, and I
    shall, 25
That I may speak. I'll write straight to my
    sister
To hold my very course. Prepare for
    dinner.   [*Exeunt.*

SCENE IV. *A hall in Albany's palace.*

Enter KENT, *disguised.*

  Kent. If but as well I other accents
    borrow
That can my speech defuse, my good intent
May carry through itself to that full issue
For which I raz'd my likeness. Now,
    banish'd Kent,
If thou canst serve where thou dost stand
    condemn'd, 5

So may it come thy master whom thou
    lov'st
Shall find thee full of labours.

Horns within.   Enter LEAR, *Knights, and*
    Attendants.

  Lear. Let me not stay a jot for dinner;
go get it ready. [*Exit an Attendant*] How
now! What art thou?
  Kent. A man, sir.   10
  Lear. What dost thou profess? What
wouldst thou with us?
  Kent. I do profess to be no less than I
seem, to serve him truly that will put me
in trust, to love him that is honest, to
converse with him that is wise and says
little, to fear judgment, to fight when I
cannot choose, and to eat no fish.   17
  Lear. What art thou?
  Kent. A very honest-hearted fellow, and
as poor as the King.   20
  Lear. If thou be'st as poor for a subject
as he's for a king, thou art poor enough.
What wouldst thou?
  Kent. Service.
  Lear. Who wouldst thou serve?
  Kent. You.   25
  Lear. Dost thou know me, fellow?
  Kent. No, sir; but you have that in
your countenance which I would fain call
master.
  Lear. What's that?
  Kent. Authority.   30
  Lear. What services canst thou do?
  Kent. I can keep honest counsel, ride,
run, mar a curious tale in telling it, and
deliver a plain message bluntly. That
which ordinary men are fit for, I am
qualified in; and the best of me is
diligence.   35
  Lear. How old art thou?
  Kent. Not so young, sir, to love a woman
for singing, nor so old to dote on her for
anything: I have years on my back forty-
eight.   39
  Lear. Follow me; thou shalt serve me.
If I like thee no worse after dinner, I will
not part from thee yet. Dinner, ho, dinner!
Where's my knave? my fool?—Go you and
call my fool hither.   [*Exit an Attendant.*

Enter OSWALD.

You, you, sirrah, where's my daughter? 44
  Osw. So please you—   [*Exit.*
  Lear. What says the fellow there? Call
the clotpoll back. [*Exit a Knight*] Where's
my fool, ho? I think the world's asleep.

Re-enter Knight.

  How now! Where's that mongrel?
  Knight. He says, my lord, your daughter
is not well.   50
  Lear. Why came not the slave back to me
when I call'd him?

Knight. Sir, he answered me in the roundest manner he would not.

Lear. He would not! 55

Knight. My lord, I know not what the matter is; but, to my judgment, your Highness is not entertain'd with that ceremonious affection as you were wont; there's a great abatement of kindness appears as well in the general dependants as in the Duke himself also and your daughter. 61

Lear. Ha! say'st thou so?

Knight. I beseech you pardon me, my lord, if I be mistaken; for my duty cannot be silent when I think your Highness wrong'd. 65

Lear. Thou but rememb'rest me of mine own conception. I have perceived a most faint neglect of late, which I have rather blamed as mine own jealous curiosity than as a very pretence and purpose of unkindness. I will look further into't. But where's my fool? I have not seen him this two days. 71

Knight. Since my young lady's going into France, sir, the fool hath much pined away.

Lear. No more of that; I have noted it well. Go you and tell my daughter I would speak with her. [*Exit an Attendant*] Go you, call hither my fool. [*Exit another Attendant.*

Re-enter OSWALD.

O, you sir, you! Come you hither, sir. Who am I, sir? 77

Osw. My lady's father.

Lear. 'My lady's father'! my lord's knave! you whoreson dog! you slave! you cur! 80

Osw. I am none of these, my lord; I beseech your pardon.

Lear. Do you bandy looks with me, you rascal! [*Striking him.*

Osw. I'll not be strucken, my lord. 84

Kent. Nor tripp'd neither, you base football player. [*Tripping up his heels.*

Lear. I thank thee, fellow; thou serv'st me, and I'll love thee. 87

Kent. Come, sir, arise, away! I'll teach you differences. Away, away! If you will measure your lubber's length again, tarry; but away! Go to! Have you wisdom? So. [*Pushes Oswald out.*

Lear. Now, my friendly knave, I thank thee; there's earnest of thy service. 93 [*Giving Kent money.*

Enter FOOL.

Fool. Let me hire him too; here's my coxcomb. [*Offering Kent his cap.*

Lear. How now, my pretty knave! How dost thou? 95

Fool. Sirrah, you were best take my coxcomb.

Kent. Why, fool?

Fool. Why? For taking one's part that's out of favour. Nay, an thou canst not smile as the wind sits, thou'lt catch cold shortly. There, take my coxcomb. Why, this fellow has banish'd two on's daughters, and did the third a blessing against his will; if thou follow him, thou must needs wear my coxcomb.—How now, nuncle! Would I had two coxcombs and two daughters!

Lear. Why, my boy? 105

Fool. If I gave them all my living, I'd keep my coxcombs myself. There's mine; beg another of thy daughters.

Lear. Take heed, sirrah—the whip. 109

Fool. Truth's a dog must to kennel; he must be whipp'd out, when Lady the brach may stand by th' fire and stink.

Lear. A pestilent gall to me!

Fool. Sirrah, I'll teach thee a speech.

Lear. Do. 115

Fool. Mark it, nuncle:
Have more than thou showest,
Speak less than thou knowest,
Lend less than thou owest,
Ride more than thou goest, 120
Learn more than thou trowest,
Set less than thou throwest;
Leave thy drink and thy whore,
And keep in-a-door,
And thou shalt have more 125
Than two tens to a score.

Kent. This is nothing, fool.

Fool. Then 'tis like the breath of an unfee'd lawyer—you gave me nothing for't. Can you make no use of nothing, nuncle?

Lear. Why, no, boy; nothing can be made out of nothing. 132

Fool. [*To Kent*] Prithee tell him, so much the rent of his land comes to; he will not believe a fool.

Lear. A bitter fool! 135

Fool. Dost thou know the difference, my boy, between a bitter fool and a sweet one?

Lear. No, lad; teach me.

Fool. That lord that counsell'd thee
To give away thy land, 140
Come place him here by me—
Do thou for him stand.
The sweet and bitter fool
Will presently appear;
The one in motley here, 145
The other found out there.

Lear. Dost thou call me fool, boy?

Fool. All thy other titles thou hast given away; that thou wast born with. 149

Kent. This is not altogether fool, my lord.

Fool. No, faith, lords and great men will not let me; if I had a monopoly out, they would have part on't. And ladies too—they will not let me have all the fool to myself; they'll be snatching. Nuncle, give me an egg, and I'll give thee two crowns. 155

Lear. What two crowns shall they be?

Fool. Why, after I have cut the egg i' th' middle and eat up the meat, the two crowns of the egg. When thou clovest thy crown i' th' middle, and gav'st away both parts, thou bor'st thine ass on thy back o'er the dirt. Thou hadst little wit in thy bald crown when thou gav'st thy golden one away. If I speak like myself in this, let him be whipp'd that first finds it so. 163
[*Sings*] Fools had ne'er less grace in a year ;
          For wise men are grown foppish,
          And know not how their wits to wear,
                    Their manners are so apish.

Lear. When were you wont to be so full of songs, sirrah ?   169
Fool. I have us'd it, nuncle, e'er since thou mad'st thy daughters thy mothers ; for when thou gav'st them the rod, and put'st down thine own breeches
[*Sings*] Then they for sudden joy did weep,
          And I for sorrow sung,
          That such a king should play bo-peep   175
          And go the fools among.
Prithee, nuncle, keep a schoolmaster that can teach thy fool to lie. I would fain learn to lie.
Lear. An you lie, sirrah, we'll have you whipp'd.   179
Fool. I marvel what kin thou and thy daughters are. They'll have me whipp'd for speaking true : thou'lt have me whipp'd for lying ; and sometimes I am whipp'd for holding my peace. I had rather be any kind o' thing than a fool ; and yet I would not be thee, nuncle ; thou hast pared thy wit o' both sides, and left nothing i' th' middle. Here comes one o' th' parings.   186

Enter GONERIL.

Lear. How now, daughter ! What makes that frontlet on ? You are too much of late i' th' frown.   189
Fool. Thou wast a pretty fellow when thou hadst no need to care for her frowning; now thou art an O without a figure. I am better than thou art now: I am a fool, thou art nothing. [*To Goneril*] Yes, forsooth, I will hold my tongue ; so your face bids me, though you say nothing. Mum, mum !
    He that keeps nor crust nor crumb,
    Weary of all, shall want some.   197
[*Pointing to Lear*] That's a sheal'd peascod.
Gon. Not only, sir, this your all-licens'd fool,
But other of your insolent retinue   200
Do hourly carp and quarrel, breaking forth
In rank and not-to-be-endured riots. Sir,
I had thought, by making this well known unto you,
To have found a safe redress ; but now grow fearful,

By what yourself too late have spoke and done,   205
That you protect this course, and put it on
By your allowance ; which if you should, the fault
Would not scape censure, nor the redresses sleep,   208
Which, in the tender of a wholesome weal,
Might in their working do you that offence
Which else were shame, that then necessity
Will call discreet proceeding.
Fool. For, you know, nuncle,
The hedge-sparrow fed the cuckoo so long
That it's had it head bit off by it young.   215
So, out went the candle, and we were left darkling.
Lear. Are you our daughter ?
Gon. I would you would make use of your good wisdom,
Whereof I know you are fraught, and put away   220
These dispositions which of late transport you
From what you rightly are.
Fool. May not an ass know when the cart draws the horse ? Whoop, Jug ! I love thee.
Lear. Does any here know me ? This is not Lear.   225
Does Lear walk thus ? speak thus ? Where are his eyes ?
Either his notion weakens, or his discernings
Are lethargied.—Ha ! waking ? 'Tis not so.—
Who is it that can tell me who I am ?
Fool. Lear's shadow.   230
Lear. I would learn that ; for, by the marks of sovereignty, knowledge, and reason, I should be false persuaded I had daughters.
Fool. Which they will make an obedient father.
Lear. Your name, fair gentlewoman ?   235
Gon. This admiration, sir, is much o' th' savour
Of other your new pranks. I do beseech you
To understand my purposes aright.
As you are old and reverend, should be wise.
Here do you keep a hundred knights and squires ;   240
Men so disorder'd, so debosh'd and bold,
That this our court, infected with their manners,
Shows like a riotous inn. Epicurism and lust
Makes it more like a tavern or a brothel
Than a grac'd palace. The shame itself doth speak   245
For instant remedy. Be then desir'd
By her that else will take the thing she begs
A little to disquantity your train ;
And the remainders that shall still depend
To be such men as may besort your age,   250
Which know themselves and you.

Lear.   Darkness and devils !
Saddle my horses ; call my train together.
Degenerate bastard ! I'll not trouble thee ;
Yet have I left a daughter.
  Gon. You strike my people ; and your
      disorder'd rabble   255
Make servants of their betters.

Enter ALBANY.

  Lear. Woe that too late repents !—O, sir,
      are you come ?
Is it your will ? Speak, sir.—Prepare my
      horses.
Ingratitude, thou marble-hearted fiend,
More hideous when thou show'st thee in a
      child   260
Than the sea-monster !
  Alb.   Pray, sir, be patient.
  Lear. [*To Goneril*] Detested kite ! thou
      liest :
My train are men of choice and rarest parts,
That all particulars of duty know ;
And in the most exact regard support   265
The worships of their name.—O most small
      fault,
How ugly didst thou in Cordelia show !
Which, like an engine, wrench'd my frame
      of nature
From the fix'd place ; drew from my heart
      all love   269
And added to the gall. O Lear, Lear, Lear !
Beat at this gate that let thy folly in
              [*Striking his head.*
And thy dear judgment out ! Go, go, my
      people. [*Exeunt Kent and Knights.*
  Alb. My lord, I am guiltless, as I am
      ignorant
Of what hath moved you.
  Lear.   It may be so, my lord.
Hear, Nature, hear ; dear goddess, hear. 275
Suspend thy purpose, if thou didst intend
To make this creature fruitful.
Into her womb convey sterility ;
Dry up in her the organs of increase ;   279
And from her derogate body never spring
A babe to honour her ! If she must
      teem,
Create her child of spleen, that it may live
And be a thwart disnatur'd torment to her.
Let it stamp wrinkles in her brow of youth,
With cadent tears fret channels in her
      cheeks,   285
Turn all her mother's pains and benefits
To laughter and contempt, that she may
      feel
How sharper than a serpent's tooth it is
To have a thankless child. Away, away !
                        [*Exit.*
  Alb. Now, gods that we adore, whereof
      comes this ?   290
  Gon. Never afflict yourself to know more
      of it ;
But let his disposition have that scope
As dotage gives it.

1082

Re-enter LEAR.

  Lear. What, fifty of my followers at a
      clap !
Within a fortnight !
  Alb.   What's the matter, sir ?
  Lear. I'll tell thee. [*To Goneril*] Life and
      death ! I am asham'd   296
That thou hast power to shake my man-
      hood thus ;
That these hot tears, which break from me
      perforce,
Should make thee worth them. Blasts and
      fogs upon thee !
Th' untented woundings of a father's curse
Pierce every sense about thee !—Old fond
      eyes,   301
Beweep this cause again, I'll pluck ye
      out,
And cast you, with the waters that you
      loose,
To temper clay. Ha ! Is't come to this ?
Let it be so. I have another daughter, 305
Who, I am sure, is kind and comfortable.
When she shall hear this of thee, with her
      nails
She'll flay thy wolfish visage. Thou shalt
      find
That I'll resume the shape which thou dost
      think
I have cast off for ever.   310
                        [*Exit Lear.*
  Gon.   Do you mark that ?
  Alb. I cannot be so partial, Goneril,
To the great love I bear you—
  Gon. Pray you, content.—What, Oswald,
      ho !
[*To the Fool*] You, sir, more knave than
      fool, after your master.   315
  Fool. Nuncle Lear, nuncle Lear, tarry—
take the fool with thee.
      A fox, when one has caught her,
      And such a daughter,
      Should sure to the slaughter, 320
      If my cap would buy a halter.
      So the fool follows after. [*Exit.*
  Gon. This man hath had good counsel. A
      hundred knights !
'Tis politic and safe to let him keep
At point a hundred knights—yes, that on
      every dream,   325
Each buzz, each fancy, each complaint,
      dislike,
He may enguard his dotage with their
      pow'rs,
And hold our lives in mercy. Oswald, I say!
  Alb. Well, you may fear too far.
  Gon.   Safer than trust too far.
Let me still take away the harms I fear, 330
Not fear still to be taken. I know his heart.
What he hath utter'd I have writ my
      sister.
If she sustain him and his hundred knights,
When I have show'd th' unfitness—

That tend upon my father ?   95
  Glo. I know not, madam. 'Tis too bad,
too bad.
  Edm. Yes, madam, he was of that
consort.
  Reg. No marvel, then, though he were ill
affected.
'Tis they have put him on the old man's
death,
To have th' expense and waste of his
revenues.   100
I have this present evening from my sister
Been well inform'd of them ; and with such
cautions
That, if they come to sojourn at my house,
I'll not be there.
  Corn.   Nor I, assure thee, Regan.
Edmund, I hear that you have shown your
father   105
A child-like office.
  Edm.   It was my duty, sir.
  Glo. He did bewray his practice, and
receiv'd
This hurt you see, striving to apprehend him.
  Corn. Is he pursued ?
  Glo.   Ay, my good lord.
  Corn. If he be taken, he shall never more
Be fear'd of doing harm. Make your own
purpose,   111
How in my strength you please. For you,
Edmund,
Whose virtue and obedience doth this
instant
So much commend itself, you shall be ours.
Natures of such deep trust we shall much
need ;   115
You we first seize on.
  Edm.   I shall serve you, sir,
Truly, however else.
  Glo.   For him I thank your Grace.
  Corn. You know not why we came to
visit you—
  Reg. Thus out of season, threading dark-
ey'd night :   119
Occasions, noble Gloucester, of some poise,
Wherein we must have use of your advice.
Our father he hath writ, so hath our sister,
Of differences, which I best thought it fit
To answer from our home ; the several
messengers
From hence attend dispatch. Our good old
friend,   125
Lay comforts to your bosom, and bestow
Your needful counsel to our businesses,
Which craves the instant use.
  Glo.   I serve you, madam.
Your Graces are right welcome. [*Exeunt.*

  SCENE II. *Before Gloucester's castle.*

  Enter KENT *and* OSWALD *severally.*

  Osw. Good dawning to thee, friend. Art
of this house ?
  Kent. Ay.

  Osw. Where may we set our horses ?
  Kent. I' th' mire.
  Osw. Prithee, if thou lov'st me, tell me. 5
  Kent. I love thee not.
  Osw. Why then, I care not for thee.
  Kent. If I had thee in Lipsbury pinfold, I
would make thee care for me.
  Osw. Why dost thou use me thus ? I
know thee not.   10
  Kent. Fellow, I know thee.
  Osw. What dost thou know me for ?
  Kent. A knave, a rascal, an eater of
broken meats ; a base, proud, shallow,
beggarly, three-suited, hundred-pound,
filthy, worsted-stocking knave ; a lily-
liver'd, action-taking, whoreson, glass-
gazing, superserviceable, finical rogue ;
one-trunk-inheriting slave ; one that
wouldst be a bawd in way of good service,
and art nothing but the composition of a
knave, beggar, coward, pander, and the
son and heir of a mongrel bitch ; one whom
I will beat into clamorous whining, if thou
deny'st the least syllable of thy addition.
  Osw. Why, what a monstrous fellow art
thou, thus to rail on one that is neither
known of thee nor knows thee ?   24
  Kent. What a brazen-fac'd varlet art
thou, to deny thou knowest me ! Is it two
days since I tripp'd up thy heels and beat
thee before the King ? Draw, you rogue ;
for, though it be night, yet the moon
shines ; I'll make a sop o' th' moonshine
of you ; you whoreson cullionly barber-
monger, draw.   [*Drawing his sword.*
  Osw. Away ! I have nothing to do with
thee.   31
  Kent. Draw, you rascal. You come with
letters against the King, and take Vanity
the puppet's part against the royalty of her
father. Draw, you rogue, or I'll so carbonado your shanks. Draw, you rascal ; come
your ways.
  Osw. Help, ho ! murder ! help.   36
  Kent. Strike, you slave ; stand, rogue,
stand ; you neat slave, strike.

                  [*Beating him.*
  Osw. Help, ho ! murder ! murder !

Enter EDMUND *with his rapier drawn,*
GLOUCESTER, CORNWALL, REGAN, *and*
Servants.

  Edm. How now ! What's the matter ?
Part !   40
  Kent. With you, goodman boy, an you
please. Come, I'll flesh ye ; come on, young
master.
  Glo. Weapons ! arms ! What's the matter
here ?
  Corn. Keep peace, upon your lives ;
He dies that strikes again. What is the
matter ?   45
  Reg. The messengers from our sister and
the King.

Corn. What is your difference ? Speak.

Osw. I am scarce in breath, my lord.

Kent. No marvel, you have so bestirr'd
your valour. You cowardly rascal, nature
disclaims in thee : a tailor made thee.   51

Corn. Thou art a strange fellow. A tailor
make a man ?

Kent. Ay, a tailor, sir. A stone-cutter or
a painter could not have made him so ill,
though they had been but two years o' th'
trade.   55

Corn. Speak yet, how grew your quarrel ?

Osw. This ancient ruffian, sir, whose life I
have spar'd at suit of his grey beard—

Kent. Thou whoreson zed ! thou unnecessary letter ! My lord, if you will give
me leave, I will tread this unbolted villain
into mortar, and daub the wall of a jakes
with him.—Spare my grey beard, you
wagtail ?   62

Corn. Peace, sirrah !

You beastly knave, know you no reverence?

Kent. Yes, sir ; but anger hath a
privilege.   65

Corn. Why art thou angry ?

Kent. That such a slave as this should
        wear a sword,

Who wears no honesty. Such smiling
        rogues as these,

Like rats, oft bite the holy cords a-twain

Which are too intrinse t' unloose ; smooth
        every passion   70

That in the natures of their lords rebel ;

Bring oil to fire, snow to their colder moods;

Renege, affirm, and turn their halcyon
        beaks

With every gale and vary of their masters,

Knowing nought, like dogs, but following.

A plague upon your epileptic visage !   76

Smile you my speeches, as I were a fool ?

Goose, if I had you upon Sarum plain,

I'd drive ye cackling home to Camelot.

Corn. What, are thou mad, old fellow ?

Glo. How fell you out ? Say that.   81

Kent. No contraries hold more antipathy

Than I and such a knave.

Corn. Why dost thou call him knave ?
What is his fault ?

Kent. His countenance likes me not.   85

Corn. No more, perchance, does mine,
        nor his, nor hers.

Kent. Sir, 'tis my occupation to be plain :
I have seen better faces in my time
Than stands on any shoulder that I see
Before me at this instant.

Corn.   This is some fellow 90
Who, having been prais'd for bluntness,
        doth affect

A saucy roughness, and constrains the garb
Quite from his nature. He cannot flatter,
        he,

An honest mind and plain—he must speak
        truth.

An they will take it, so ; if not, he's plain.

These kind of knaves I know, which in this
        plainness   96

Harbour more craft and more corrupter
        ends

Than twenty silly ducking observants

That stretch their duties nicely.   99

Kent. Sir, in good faith, in sincere verity,
Under th' allowance of your great aspect,
Whose influence, like the wreath of radiant
        fire

On flickering Phœbus' front—

Corn.   What mean'st by this ?

Kent. To go out of my dialect, which you
discommend so much. I know, sir, I am no
flatterer. He that beguil'd you in a plain
accent was a plain knave ; which, for my
part, I will not be, though I should win
your displeasure to entreat me to't.

Corn. What was th' offence you gave
        him ?

Osw.   I never gave him any.   110
It pleas'd the King his master very late
To strike at me, upon his misconstruction ;
When he, compact, and flattering his dis-
        pleasure,

Tripp'd me behind ; being down, insulted,
        rail'd,

And put upon him such a deal of man   115
That worthied him, got praises of the
        King

For him attempting who was self-subdu'd ;
And in the fleshment of this dread exploit,
Drew on me here again.

Kent. None of these rogues and cowards
But Ajax is their fool.

Corn.   Fetch forth the stocks. 120
You stubborn ancient knave, you reverend
        braggart,

We'll teach you.

Kent.   Sir, I am too old to learn.
Call not your stocks for me ; I serve the
        King,

On whose employment I was sent to you.
You shall do small respect, show too bold
        malice   125

Against the grace and person of my master,
Stocking his messenger.

Corn. Fetch forth the stocks. As I have
        life and honour,

There shall he sit till noon.

Reg. Till noon ! Till night, my lord ; and
        all night too.   130

Kent. Why, madam, if I were your
        father's dog,

You should not use me so.

Reg.   Sir, being his knave, I will.

Corn. This is a fellow of the self-same
        colour

Our sister speaks of. Come, bring away the
        stocks.   [*Stocks brought out.*

Glo. Let me beseech your Grace not to do
        so.   135

His fault is much, and the good King his
        master

Will check him for't ; your purpos'd low
    correction
Is such as basest and contemned'st wretches
For pilf'rings and most common trespasses
Are punish'd with. The King must take
    it ill   140
That he, so slightly valued in his messenger,
Should have him thus restrained.
    Corn.   I'll answer that.
    Reg. My sister may receive it much more
    worse
To have her gentleman abus'd, assaulted,
For following her affairs. Put in his legs. 145
        [*Kent is put in the stocks.*
Come, my good lord, away.
      [*Exeunt all but Gloucester and Kent.*
    Glo. I am sorry for thee, friend ; 'tis the
    Duke's pleasure
Whose disposition, all the world well knows,
Will not be rubb'd nor stopp'd. I'll entreat
    for thee.
    Kent. Pray, do not, sir. I have watch'd
    and travell'd hard ;   150
Some time I shall sleep out, the rest I'll
    whistle.
A good man's fortune may grow out at
    heels.
Give you good morrow !
    Glo.   The Duke's to blame in this ;
'Twill be ill taken.   [*Exit.*
    Kent. Good King, that must approve the
    common saw,   155
Thou out of heaven's benediction com'st
To the warm sun !
Approach, thou beacon to this under globe,
That by thy comfortable beams I may
Peruse this letter.   Nothing almost sees
    miracles   160
But misery. I know 'tis from Cordelia,
Who hath most fortunately been inform'd
Of my obscured course. [*Reads*] ' —and
    shall find time
From this enormous state—seeking to give
Losses their remedies.' All weary and o'er-
    watch'd,   165
Take vantage, heavy eyes, not to behold
This shameful lodging.
Fortune, good night ; smile once more ;
    turn thy wheel.   [*He sleeps.*

SCENE III.   *The open country.*

Enter EDGAR.

    Edg. I heard myself proclaim'd,
And by the happy hollow of a tree
Escap'd the hunt. No port is free ; no place
That guard and most unusual vigilance
Does not attend my taking. Whiles I may
    scape   5
I will preserve myself ; and am bethought
To take the basest and most poorest shape
That ever penury in contempt of man
Brought near to beast. My face I'll grime
    with filth,

Blanket my loins, elf all my hairs in knots,
And with presented nakedness outface   11
The winds and persecutions of the sky.
The country gives me proof and precedent
Of Bedlam beggars, who, with roaring
    voices,
Strike in their numb'd and mortified bare
    arms   15
Pins, wooden pricks, nails, sprigs of rose-
    mary ;
And with this horrible object, from low
    farms,
Poor pelting villages, sheep-cotes, and mills,
Sometimes with lunatic bans, sometime
    with prayers,
Enforce their charity.   Poor Turlygod !
    poor Tom !   20
That's something yet. Edgar I nothing am.
      [*Exit.*

SCENE IV.   *Before Gloucester's castle.*

Enter LEAR, Fool, *and* Gentleman, *to* KENT
    in the stocks.

    Lear. 'Tis strange that they should so
    depart from home,
And not send back my messenger.
    Gent.   As I learn'd,
The night before there was no purpose in
    them
Of this remove.
    Kent.   Hail to thee, noble master !
    Lear. Ha !   5
Mak'st thou this shame thy pastime ?
    Kent.   No, my lord.
    Fool. Ha, ha ! he wears cruel garters.
Horses are tied by the heads, dogs and
bears by th' neck, monkeys by th' loins,
and men by th' legs. When a man's over-
lusty at legs, then he wears wooden nether-
stocks.   10
    Lear. What's he that hath so much thy
    place mistook
To set thee here ?
    Kent.   It is both he and she,
Your son and daughter.
    Lear. No.
    Kent. Yes.   15
    Lear. No, I say.
    Kent. I say, yea.
    Lear. No, no ; they would not.
    Kent. Yes, they have.
    Lear. By Jupiter, I swear, no.   20
    Kent. By Juno, I swear, ay.
    Lear.   They durst not do't ;
They could not, would not do't ; 'tis worse
    than murder
To do upon respect such violent outrage.
Resolve me with all modest haste which
    way
Thou might'st deserve or they impose this
    usage,   25
Coming from us.
    Kent.   My lord, when at their home

I did commend your Highness' letters to
    them,
Ere I was risen from the place that show'd
My duty kneeling, came there a reeking
    post,
Stew'd in his haste, half breathless, panting
    forth   30
From Goneril his mistress salutations ;
Deliver'd letters, spite of intermission,
Which presently they read ; on whose con-
    tents
They summon'd up their meiny, straight
    took horse,
Commanded me to follow and attend   35
The leisure of their answer, gave me cold
    looks ;
And meeting here the other messenger,
Whose welcome I perceiv'd had poison'd
    mine,
Being the very fellow which of late   39
Display'd so saucily against your Highness,
Having more man than wit about me, drew.
He rais'd the house with loud and coward
    cries.
Your son and daughter found this trespass
    worth
The shame which here it suffers.
    Fool. Winter's not gone yet, if the wild
geese fly that way.   46
          Fathers that wear rags
             Do make their children blind ;
          But fathers that bear bags
             Shall see their children kind.   50
          Fortune, that arrant whore,
          Ne'er turns the key to th' poor.
But, for all this, thou shalt have as many
dolours for thy daughters as thou canst
tell in a year.
    Lear. O, how this mother swells up to-
    ward my heart !   55
Hysterica passio—down, thou climbing
    sorrow,
Thy element's below.   Where is this
    daughter ?
    Kent. With the earl, sir, here within.
    Lear.   Follow me not ;
Stay here.   [*Exit.*
    Gent. Made you no more offence but what
    you speak of ?   60
    Kent. None.
How chance the King comes with so small
    a number ?
    Fool. An thou hadst been set i' th' stocks
for that question, thou'dst well deserv'd it.
    Kent. Why, fool ?   65
    Fool. We'll set thee to school to an ant,
to teach thee there's no labouring i' th'
winter. All that follow their noses are led
by their eyes but blind men ; and there's
not a nose among twenty but can smell him
that's stinking. Let go thy hold when a
great wheel runs down a hill, lest it break
thy neck with following; but the great
one that goes upward, let him draw thee

after. When a wise man gives thee better
counsel, give me mine again. I would have
none but knaves follow it, since a fool
gives it.   75
    That sir which serves and seeks for gain,
        And follows but for form,
    Will pack when it begins to rain,
        And leave thee in the storm.
    But I will tarry ; the fool will stay 80
        And let the wise man fly.
    The knave turns fool that runs away ;
        The fool no knave, perdy.
    Kent. Where learn'd you this, fool ?
    Fool. Not i' th' stocks, fool.   85

    Re-enter LEAR *and* GLOUCESTER.

    Lear. Deny to speak with me ! They are
    sick ! They are weary !
They have travell'd all the night ! Mere
    fetches ;
The images of revolt and flying off.
Fetch me a better answer.
    Glo.   My dear lord,
You know the fiery quality of the Duke ; 90
How unremovable and fix'd he is
In his own course.
    Lear. Vengeance ! plague ! death ! con-
    fusion !
Fiery ? What quality ? Why Gloucester,
    Gloucester,
I'd speak with the Duke of Cornwall and
    his wife.   95
    Glo. Well, my good lord, I have inform'd
    them so.
    Lear. Inform'd them ! Dost thou under-
    stand me, man ?
    Glo. Ay, my good lord.
    Lear. The King would speak with Corn-
    wall ; the dear father
Would with his daughter speak ; commands
    their service.   100
Are they inform'd of this ? My breath and
    blood !
Fiery ? the fiery Duke ? Tell the hot Duke
    that—
No, but not yet. May be he is not well.
Infirmity doth still neglect all office
Whereto our health is bound ; we are not
    ourselves   105
When nature, being oppress'd, commands
    the mind
To suffer with the body. I'll forbear ;
And am fallen out with my more headier
    will
To take the indispos'd and sickly fit
For the sound man. Death on my state !
    Wherefore   110
Should he sit here ? This act persuades me
That this remotion of the Duke and her
Is practice only. Give me my servant forth.
Go tell the Duke and's wife I'd speak with
    them—
Now, presently. Bid them come forth and
    hear me,   115

Or at their chamber door I'll beat the drum
Till it cry sleep to death.

  Glo. I would have all well betwixt you.
                            [*Exit.*

  Lear. O me, my heart, my rising heart!
But, down.   119

  Fool. Cry to it, nuncle, as the cockney did
to the eels when she put 'em i' th' paste
alive; she knapp'd 'em o' th' coxcombs
with a stick, and cried ' Down, wantons,
down'. 'Twas her brother that, in pure
kindness to his horse, butter'd his hay. 124

Enter CORNWALL, REGAN, GLOUCESTER,
     and Servants.

  Lear. Good morrow to you both.
  Corn.   Hail to your Grace!
                 [*Kent here set at liberty.*
  Reg. I am glad to see your Highness.
  Lear. Regan, I think you are; I know
     what reason
I have to think so. If thou shouldst not be
     glad,
I would divorce me from thy mother's
     tomb,
Sepulchring an adultress. [*To Kent*] O, are
     you free?   130
Some other time for that.—Beloved Regan,
Thy sister's naught. O Regan, she hath
     tied
Sharp-tooth'd unkindness, like a vulture,
     here.   [*Points to his heart.*
I can scarce speak to thee; thou'lt not
     believe   134
With how deprav'd a quality—O Regan!
  Reg. I pray you, sir, take patience. I have
     hope
You less know how to value her desert
Than she to scant her duty.
  Lear.   Say, how is that?
  Reg. I cannot think my sister in the least
Would fail her obligation. If, sir, perchance
She have restrain'd the riots of your
     followers,   141
'Tis on such ground, and to such wholesome
     end,
As clears her from all blame.
  Lear. My curses on her!
  Reg.   O, sir, you are old;
Nature in you stands on the very verge 145
Of her confine. You should be rul'd and led
By some discretion that discerns your state
Better than you yourself. Therefore I pray
     you
That to our sister you do make return;
Say you have wrong'd her, sir.
  Lear.   Ask her forgiveness?
Do you but mark how this becomes the
     house: 151
' Dear daughter, I confess that I am old;
                     [*Kneeling.*
Age is unnecessary; on my knees I beg
That you'll vouchsafe me raiment, bed, and
     food'.

  Reg. Good sir, no more; these are un-
     sightly tricks.   155
Return you to my sister.
  Lear. [*Rising*] Never, Regan.
She hath abated me of half my train;
Look'd black upon me; struck me with her
     tongue,
Most serpent-like, upon the very heart.
All the stor'd vengeances of heaven fall 160
On her ingrateful top! Strike her young
     bones,
You taking airs, with lameness.
  Corn.   Fie, sir, fie!
  Lear. You nimble lightnings, dart your
     blinding flames
Into her scornful eyes. Infect her beauty,
You fen-suck'd fogs, drawn by the pow'rful
     sun   165
To fall and blast her pride.
  Reg.   O the blest gods!
So will you wish on me when the rash mood
     is on.
  Lear. No, Regan, thou shalt never have
     my curse:
Thy tender-hefted nature shall not give 170
Thee o'er to harshness. Her eyes are fierce,
     but thine
Do comfort and not burn. 'Tis not in thee
To grudge my pleasures, to cut off my train,
To bandy hasty words, to scant my sizes,
And, in conclusion, to oppose the bolt 175
Against my coming in; thou better know'st
The offices of nature, bond of childhood,
Effects of courtesy, dues of gratitude;
Thy half o' th' kingdom hast thou not forgot,
Wherein I thee endow'd.
  Reg.   Good sir, to th' purpose. 180
  Lear. Who put my man i' th' stocks?
                 [*Tucket within.*
  Corn.   What trumpet's that?
  Reg. I know't—my sister's. This
     approves her letter,
That she would soon be here.

Enter OSWALD.

               Is your lady come?
  Lear. This is a slave whose easy-borrow'd
     pride   184
Dwells in the fickle grace of her he follows.
Out, varlet, from my sight!
  Corn.   What means your Grace?

Enter GONERIL.

  Lear. Who stock'd my servant? Regan,
     I have good hope
Thou didst not know on't.—Who comes
     here? O heavens,
If you do love old men, if your sweet sway
Allow obedience, if you yourselves are old,
Make it your cause; send down, and take
     my part.   191
[*To Goneril*] Art not asham'd to look upon
     this beard?—
O Regan, will you take her by the hand?

Gon. Why not by th' hand, sir ?   How
  have I offended ?
All's not offence that indiscretion finds,   195
And dotage terms so.
  Lear.   O sides, you are too tough !
Will you yet hold ?—How came my man
  i' th' stocks ?
  Corn. I set him there, sir ; but his own
    disorders
Deserv'd much less advancement.
  Lear.   You ! did you ?
  Reg. I pray you, father, being weak,
    seem so.   200
If, till the expiration of your month,
You will return and sojourn with my sister,
Dismissing half your train, come then to
  me.
I am now from home, and out of that
  provision
Which shall be needful for your entertain-
  ment.   205
  Lear. Return to her, and fifty men
    dismiss'd ?
No, rather I abjure all roofs, and choose
To wage against the enmity o' th' air,
To be a comrade with the wolf and owl—
Necessity's sharp pinch ! Return with her ?
Why, the hot-blooded France, that dower-
  less took   211
Our youngest born—I could as well be
  brought
To knee this throne, and, squire-like,
  pension beg
To keep base life afoot.   Return with her ?
Persuade me rather to be slave and sumpter
To this detested groom. [*Pointing to Oswald.*
  Gon.   At your choice, sir.
  Lear. I prithee, daughter, do not make
    me mad.   217
I will not trouble thee, my child ; farewell.
We'll no more meet, no more see one
  another.
But yet thou art my flesh, my blood, my
  daughter ;   220
Or rather a disease that's in my flesh,
Which I must needs call mine ; thou art a
  boil,
A plague-sore, or embossed carbuncle
In my corrupted blood.   But I'll not chide
  thee ;
Let shame come when it will, I do not
  call it ;   225
I do not bid the Thunder-bearer shoot,
Nor tell tales of thee to high-judging Jove.
Mend when thou canst ; be better at thy
  leisure ;
I can be patient ; I can stay with Regan,
I and my hundred knights.
  Reg.   Not altogether so. 230
I look'd not for you yet, nor am provided
For your fit welcome.   Give ear, sir, to my
  sister ;
For those that mingle reason with your
  passion

Must be content to think you old, and so—
But she knows what she does.
  Lear.   Is this well spoken ? 235
  Reg. I dare avouch it, sir.   What, fifty
    followers ?
Is it not well ? What should you need of
  more ?
Yea, or so many, sith that both charge and
  danger
Speak 'gainst so great a number ? How in
  one house   239
Should many people under two commands
Hold amity ? 'Tis hard ; almost impossible.
  Gon. Why might not you, my lord,
    receive attendance
From those that she calls servants, or from
  mine ?
  Reg. Why not, my lord ? If then they
    chanc'd to slack ye,
We could control them.   If you will come
  to me—   245
For now I spy a danger—I entreat you
To bring but five and twenty.   To no
  more
Will I give place or notice.
  Lear. I gave you all.
  Reg.   And in good time you gave it.
  Lear. Made you my guardians, my de-
    positaries ;   250
But kept a reservation to be followed
With such a number.   What, must I come
  to you
With five and twenty, Regan ? Said you so?
  Reg. And speak't again, my lord.   No
    more with me.
  Lear. Those wicked creatures yet do look
    well-favour'd   255
When others are more wicked ; not being
  the worst
Stands in some rank of praise. [*To Goneril*]
  I'll go with thee.
Thy fifty yet doth double five and twenty,
And thou art twice her love.
  Gon.   Hear me, my lord :
What need you five and twenty, ten, or
  five,   260
To follow in a house where twice so many
Have a command to tend you ?
  Reg.   What need one ?
  Lear. O, reason not the need !   Our
    basest beggars
Are in the poorest thing superfluous.
Allow not nature more than nature needs,
Man's life is cheap as beast's.   Thou art a
  lady ;   266
If only to go warm were gorgeous,
Why, nature needs not what thou gorgeous
  wear'st,
Which scarcely keeps thee warm.   But, for
  true need—
You heavens, give me that patience,
  patience I need.   270
You see me here, you gods, a poor old
  man,

Their scanted courtesy.
Lear.   My wits begin to turn.
Come on, my boy. How dost, my boy ? Art
        cold ?
I am cold myself. Where is this straw, my
        fellow ?
The art of our necessities is strange   70
That can make vile things precious. Come,
        your hovel.
Poor fool and knave, I have one part in my
        heart
That's sorry yet for thee.
Fool. [*Sings*] He that has and a little tiny
        wit
With heigh-ho, the wind and the rain—   75
Must make content with his fortunes fit,
Though the rain it raineth every day.
Lear. True, my good boy. Come, bring us
        to this hovel.
                [*Exeunt Lear and Kent.*
Fool. This is a brave night to cool a
courtezan. I'll speak a prophecy ere I go.
        When priests are more in word than
                matter ;   81
        When brewers mar their malt with
                water ;
        When nobles are their tailors' tutors ;
        No heretics burn'd, but wenches' suitors;
        When every case in law is right ;   85
        No squire in debt, nor no poor knight ;
        When slanders do not live in tongues ;
        Nor cutpurses come not to throngs ;
        When usurers tell their gold i' th' field ;
        And bawds and whores do churches
                build—   90
        Then shall the realm of Albion
        Come to great confusion.
        Then comes the time, who lives to see't,
        That going shall be us'd with feet.   94
This prophecy Merlin shall make, for I live
before his time.   [*Exit.*

SCENE III.   *Gloucester's castle.*

Enter GLOUCESTER *and* EDMUND.

Glo. Alack, alack, Edmund, I like not
this unnatural dealing. When I desired
their leave that I might pity him, they took
from me the use of mine own house, charg'd
me, on pain of perpetual displeasure, neither
to speak of him, entreat for him, or any
way sustain him.   6
Edm. Most savage and unnatural !
Glo. Go to ; say you nothing. There is
division between the Dukes ; and a worse
matter than that. I have received a letter
this night—'tis dangerous to be spoken ; I
have lock'd the letter in my closet. These
injuries the King now bears will be revenged
home ; there is part of a power already
footed. We must incline to the King. I will
look him, and privily relieve him. Go you
and maintain talk with the Duke, that my
charity be not of him perceived ; if he ask

for me, I am ill, and gone to bed. If I die
for it, as no less is threatened me, the King
my old master must be relieved. There is
strange things toward, Edmund ; pray
you be careful.   [*Exit.*
Edm. This courtesy forbid thee shall the
        Duke   21
Instantly know, and of that letter too.
This seems a fair deserving, and must draw
        me
That which my father loses—no less than
        all.
The younger rises, when the old doth fall.
                                        [*Exit.*

SCENE IV.   *Before a hovel on the heath.*

Storm still.   Enter LEAR, KENT, *and* Fool.

Kent. Here is the place, my lord ; good
        my lord, enter.
The tyranny of the open night's too rough
For nature to endure.
Lear.   Let me alone.
Kent. Good my lord, enter here.
Lear.   Wilt break my heart ?
Kent. I had rather break mine own.
        Good my lord, enter.   5
Lear. Thou think'st 'tis much that this
        contentious storm
Invades us to the skin ; so 'tis to thee,
But where the greater malady is fix'd,
The lesser is scarce felt. Thou'dst shun a
        bear ;
But if thy flight lay toward the roaring sea,
Thou'dst meet the bear i' th' mouth. When
        the mind's free   11
The body's delicate ; this tempest in my
        mind
Doth from my senses take all feeling else,
Save what beats there. Filial ingratitude !
Is it not as this mouth should tear this hand
For lifting food to't ? But I will punish
        home.   16
No, I will weep no more. In such a night,
To shut me out ! Pour on ; I will endure.
In such a night as this ! O Regan, Goneril !
Your old kind father, whose frank heart
        gave all !   20
O, that way madness lies ; let me shun
        that ;
No more of that.
Kent.   Good my lord, enter here.
Lear. Prithee go in thyself ; seek thine
        own ease.
This tempest will not give me leave to
        ponder
On things would hurt me more. But I'll go
        in.   25
[*To the Fool*] In, boy ; go first.—You house-
        less poverty—
Nay, get thee in. I'll pray, and then I'll
        sleep.   [*Exit Fool.*
Poor naked wretches, wheresoe'er you are,
That bide the pelting of this pitiless storm,

How shall your houseless heads and unfed
    sides,   30
Your loop'd and window'd raggedness,
    defend you
From seasons such as these ? O, I have
    ta'en
Too little care of this ! Take physic,
    pomp ;
Expose thyself to feel what wretches feel,
That thou mayst shake the superflux to
    them,   35
And show the heavens more just.
    Edg. [*Within*] Fathom and half, fathom
and half ! Poor Tom !

    Enter Fool *from the hovel.*

    Fool. Come not in here, nuncle, here's a
spirit. Help me, help me !   40
    Kent. Give me thy hand. Who's there ?
    Fool. A spirit, a spirit. He says his
name's poor Tom.
    Kent. What art thou that dost grumble
there i' th' straw ?
Come forth.

    Enter EDGAR, *disguised as a madman.*

    Edg. Away ! the foul fiend follows me. 45
Through the sharp hawthorn blows the cold
    wind.
Humh ! go to thy cold bed and warm thee.
    Lear. Didst thou give all to thy daugh-
ters ? And art thou come to this ?   49
    Edg. Who gives anything to poor Tom ?
whom the foul fiend hath led through fire
and through flame, through ford and whirl-
pool, o'er bog and quagmire ; that hath laid
knives under his pillow and halters in his
pew, set ratsbane by his porridge; made
him proud of heart, to ride on a bay
trotting-horse over four-inched bridges, to
course his own shadow for a traitor. Bless
thy five wits ! Tom's a-cold. O, do de, do
de, do de. Bless thee from whirlwinds, star-
blasting, and taking ! Do poor Tom some
charity, whom the foul fiend vexes. There
could I have him now—and there—and
there again—and there.   [*Storm still.*
    Lear. What, has his daughters brought
him to this pass ?
Could'st thou save nothing ? Would'st thou
    give 'em all ?
    Fool. Nay, he reserv'd a blanket, else we
had been all sham'd.   65
    Lear. Now all the plagues that in the
    pendulous air
Hang fated o'er men's faults light on thy
    daughters !
    Kent. He hath no daughters, sir.
    Lear. Death, traitor ! Nothing could
    have subdu'd nature
To such a lowness but his unkind daugh-
    ters.
Is it the fashion that discarded fathers 71
Should have thus little mercy on their flesh?

Judicious punishment ! 'twas this flesh
    begot
Those pelican daughters.
    Edg. Pillicock sat on Pillicock-hill. 75
        Alow, alow, loo, loo !
    Fool. This cold night will turn us all to
fools and madmen.
    Edg. Take heed o' th' foul fiend ; obey
thy parents ; keep thy words justly ; swear
not ; commit not with man's sworn spouse ;
set not thy sweet heart on proud array.
Tom's a-cold.   82
    Lear. What hast thou been ?
    Edg. A serving-man, proud in heart and
mind ; that curl'd my hair ; wore gloves
in my cap ; serv'd the lust of my mistress'
heart, and did the act of darkness with her ;
swore as many oaths as I spake words, and
broke them in the sweet face of heaven ;
one that slept in the contriving of lust, and
wak'd to do it. Wine lov'd I deeply, dice
dearly ; and in woman out-paramour'd the
Turk. False of heart, light of ear, bloody of
hand ; hog in sloth, fox in stealth, wolf in
greediness, dog in madness, lion in prey.
Let not the creaking of shoes nor the
rustling of silks betray thy poor heart to
woman. Keep thy foot out of brothels, thy
hand out of plackets, thy pen from lenders'
books, and defy the foul fiend.   96
Still through the hawthorn blows the cold
    wind.
Says suum, mun, nonny.
Dolphin my boy, boy, sessa ! let him trot
by.   [*Storm still.*
    Lear. Why, thou wert better in a grave
than to answer with thy uncover'd body
this extremity of the skies. Is man no
more than this ? Consider him well. Thou
ow'st the worm no silk, the beast no hide,
the sheep no wool, the cat no perfume. Ha !
here's three on's are sophisticated ! Thou
art the thing itself : unaccommodated man
is no more but such a poor, bare, forked
animal as thou art. Off, off, you lendings !
Come, unbutton here.   108

    [*Tearing off his clothes.*

    Enter GLOUCESTER *with a torch.*

    Fool. Prithee, nuncle, be contented ; 'tis
a naughty night to swim in. Now a little
fire in a wild field were like an old lecher's
heart—a small spark, all the rest on's body
cold. Look, here comes a walking fire. 112
    Edg. This is the foul fiend Flibbertigibbet;
he begins at curfew, and walks till the first
cock ; he gives the web and the pin, squenes
the eye, and makes the hare-lip ; mildews
the white wheat, and hurts the poor
creature of earth. 117
        Swithold footed thrice the 'old ;
        He met the nightmare and her nine-
          fold ;
        Bid her alight   120

And her troth plight,
And aroint thee, witch, aroint thee !
Kent. How fares your Grace ?
Lear. What's he ?   124
Kent. Who's there ? What is't you seek ?
Glo. What are you there ? Your names ?
Edg. Poor Tom ; that eats the swimming
frog, the toad, the tadpole, the wall-newt,
and the water ; that in the fury of his
heart, when the foul fiend rages, eats cow-
dung for sallets, swallows the old rat and
the ditch-dog, drinks the green mantle of
the standing pool ; who is whipp'd from
tithing to tithing, and stock-punish'd,
and imprison'd ; who hath had three suits
to his back, six shirts to his body—
Horse to ride, and weapon to wear ;
But mice and rats, and such small deer,
Have been Tom's food for seven long
year.   136
Beware my follower. Peace, Smulkin ;
peace, thou fiend !
Glo. What, hath your Grace no better
company ?
Edg. The prince of darkness is a gentle-
man ; Modo he's call'd, and Mahu. 140
Glo. Our flesh and blood, my lord, is
grown so vile
That it doth hate what gets it.
Edg. Poor Tom's a-cold.
Glo. Go in with me : my duty cannot
suffer
T' obey in all your daughters' hard com-
mands.   145
Though their injunction be to bar my
doors,
And let this tyrannous night take hold upon
you,
Yet have I ventur'd to come seek you
out,
And bring you where both fire and food is
ready.
Lear. First let me talk with this philoso-
pher.   150
What is the cause of thunder ?
Kent. Good my lord, take his offer ; go
into th' house.
Lear. I'll talk a word with this same
learned Theban.
What is your study ?
Edg. How to prevent the fiend and to kill
vermin.   155
Lear. Let me ask you one word in private.
Kent. Importune him once more to go,
my lord ;
His wits begin t' unsettle.   [*Storm still.*
Glo.   Canst thou blame him ?
His daughters seek his death. Ah, that good
Kent !—
He said it would be thus—poor, banish'd
man !   160
Thou sayest the King grows mad ; I'll tell
thee, friend,
I am almost mad myself. I had a son,

Now outlaw'd from my blood ; he sought
my life
But lately, very late. I lov'd him, friend—
No father his son dearer. True to tell
thee,
The grief hath craz'd my wits. What a
night's this !   166
I do beseech your Grace—
Lear.   O, cry you mercy, sir.
Noble philosopher, your company.
Edg. Tom's a-cold.
Glo. In, fellow, there, into th' hovel ;
keep thee warm.   170
Lear. Come, let's in all.
Kent.   This way, my lord.
Lear.   With him ;
I will keep still with my philosopher.
Kent. Good my lord, soothe him ; let him
take the fellow.
Glo. Take him you on.   174
Kent. Sirrah, come on ; go along with us.
Lear. Come, good Athenian.
Glo. No words, no words ! Hush.
Edg. Child Rowland to the dark tower
came,
His word was still ' Fie, foh, and
fum,   179
I smell the blood of a British man '.
                              [*Exeunt.*

SCENE V. *Gloucester's castle.*

Enter CORNWALL *and* EDMUND.

Corn. I will have my revenge ere I depart
his house.
Edm. How, my lord, I may be censured,
that nature thus gives way to loyalty,
something fears me to think of.
Corn. I now perceive it was not altogether your brother's evil disposition made
him seek his death ; but a provoking merit,
set a-work by a reprovable badness in
himself.   7
Edm. How malicious is my fortune, that
I must repent to be just ! This is the
letter he spoke of, which approves him an
intelligent party to the advantages of
France. O heavens ! that this treason
were not, or not I the detector !   12
Corn. Go with me to the Duchess.
Edm. If the matter of this paper be
certain, you have mighty business in hand.
Corn. True or false, it hath made thee
Earl of Gloucester. Seek out where thy
father is, that he may be ready for our
apprehension.   18
Edm. [*Aside*] If I find him comforting the
King, it will stuff his suspicion more fully.
—I will persever in my course of loyalty,
though the conflict be sore between that
and my blood.   22
Corn. I will lay trust upon thee ; and
thou shalt find a dearer father in my love.
                              [*Exeunt.*

Scene VI. *An outhouse of Gloucester's castle.*

Enter Kent *and* Gloucester.

Glo. Here is better than the open air; take it thankfully. I will piece out the comfort with what addition I can. I will not be long from you. 3

Kent. All the pow'r of his wits have given way to his impatience. The gods reward your kindness! [*Exit Gloucester.*

Enter Lear, Edgar, *and* Fool.

Edg. Fraterretto calls me, and tells me Nero is an angler in the lake of darkness. Pray, innocent, and beware the foul fiend.

Fool. Prithee, nuncle, tell me whether a madman be a gentleman or a yeoman? 10

Lear. A king, a king!

Fool. No; he's a yeoman that has a gentleman to his son; for he's a mad yeoman that sees his son a gentleman before him.

Lear. To have a thousand with red burning spits 15
Come hizzing in upon 'em—

Edg. The foul fiend bites my back.

Fool. He's mad that trusts in the tameness of a wolf, a horse's health, a boy's love, or a whore's oath.

Lear. It shall be done; I will arraign them straight. 20
[*To Edgar*] Come, sit thou here, most learned justicer.
[*To the Fool*] Thou, sapient sir, sit here.—Now, you she-foxes!

Edg. Look where he stands and glares! Want'st thou eyes at trial, madam?
Come o'er the bourn, Bessy, to me. 25

Fool. Her boat hath a leak,
And she must not speak,
Why she dares not come over to thee.

Edg. The foul fiend haunts poor Tom in the voice of a nightingale. Hoppedance cries in Tom's belly for two white herring. Croak not, black angel; I have no food for thee. 32

Kent. How do you, sir? Stand you not so amaz'd.
Will you lie down and rest upon the cushions?

Lear. I'll see their trial first. Bring in their evidence. 35
[*To Edgar*] Thou robed man of justice, take thy place.
[*To the Fool*] And thou, his yoke-fellow of equity,
Bench by his side. [*To Kent*] You are o' th' commission,
Sit you too.

Edg. Let us deal justly. 40
Sleepest or wakest thou, jolly shepherd?
Thy sheep be in the corn;

And for one blast of thy minikin mouth,
Thy sheep shall take no harm.
Pur! the cat is grey. 45

Lear. Arraign her first; 'tis Goneril. I here take my oath before this honourable assembly she kick'd the poor King her father.

Fool. Come hither, mistress. Is your name Goneril?

Lear. She cannot deny it. 50

Fool. Cry you mercy, I took you for a joint-stool.

Lear. And here's another, whose warp'd looks proclaim
What store her heart is made on. Stop her there!
Arms, arms, sword, fire! Corruption in the place!
False justicer, why hast thou let her scape?

Edg. Bless thy five wits! 56

Kent. O pity! Sir, where is the patience now
That you so oft have boasted to retain?

Edg. [*Aside*] My tears begin to take his part so much
They mar my counterfeiting. 60

Lear. The little dogs and all,
Tray, Blanch, and Sweetheart, see, they bark at me.

Edg. Tom will throw his head at them. Avaunt, you curs!
Be thy mouth or black or white, 65
Tooth that poisons if it bite;
Mastiff, greyhound, mongrel grim,
Hound or spaniel, brach or lym,
Or bobtail tike or trundle-tail—
Tom will make him weep and wail; 70
For, with throwing thus my head,
Dogs leapt the hatch, and all are fled.
Do de, de, de. Sessa! Come, march to wakes and fairs and market-towns. Poor Tom, thy horn is dry. 74

Lear. Then let them anatomize Regan; see what breeds about her heart. Is there any cause in nature that make these hard hearts? [*To Edgar*] You, sir, I entertain for one of my hundred; only I do not like the fashion of your garments. You will say they are Persian, but let them be chang'd. 80

Kent. Now, good my lord, lie here and rest awhile.

Lear. Make no noise, make no noise; draw the curtains. So, so. We'll go to supper i' th' morning.

Fool. And I'll go to bed at noon. 85

Re-enter Gloucester.

Glo. Come hither, friend. Where is the King my master?

Kent. Here, sir; but trouble him not—his wits are gone.

Glo. Good friend, I prithee, take him in thy arms;

I have o'erheard a plot of death upon him.
There is a litter ready; lay him in't   90
And drive toward Dover, friend, where thou
    shalt meet
Both welcome and protection. Take up thy
    master;
If thou shouldst dally half an hour, his life,
With thine, and all that offer to defend
    him,
Stand in assured loss. Take up, take up; 95
And follow me, that will to some provision
Give thee quick conduct.
    Kent.   Oppressed nature sleeps.
This rest might yet have balm'd thy broken
    sinews,
Which, if convenience will not allow,
Stand in hard cure. [*To the Fool*] Come,
    help to bear thy master;   100
Thou must not stay behind.
    Glo.   Come, come, away.
                    [*Exeunt all but Edgar.*
    Edg. When we our betters see bearing
    our woes,
We scarcely think our miseries our foes.
Who alone suffers suffers most i' th' mind,
Leaving free things and happy shows
    behind;   105
But then the mind much sufferance doth
    o'erskip
When grief hath mates, and bearing fellow-
    ship.
How light and portable my pain seems now,
When that which makes me bend makes the
    King bow;
He childed as I father'd! Tom, away! 110
Mark the high noises; and thyself bewray,
When false opinion, whose wrong thoughts
    defile thee,
In thy just proof repeals and reconciles
    thee.
What will hap more to-night, safe scape the
    King!   114
Lurk, lurk.   [*Exit.*

SCENE VII. *Gloucester's castle.*

Enter CORNWALL, REGAN, GONERIL,
    EDMUND, *and* Servants.

    Corn. [*To Goneril*] Post speedily to my
lord your husband; show him this letter.
The army of France is landed.—Seek out
the traitor Gloucester.
                    [*Exeunt some of the Servants.*
    Reg. Hang him instantly.
    Gon. Pluck out his eyes.   5
    Corn. Leave him to my displeasure.
Edmund, keep you our sister company.
The revenges we are bound to take upon
your traitorous father are not fit for your
beholding. Advise the Duke, where you
are going, to a most festinate preparation;
we are bound to the like. Our posts shall be
swift and intelligent betwixt us. Farewell,
dear sister; farewell, my Lord of Gloucester.

Enter OSWALD.

How now! where's the King?
    Osw. My Lord of Gloucester hath con-
    vey'd him hence.
Some five or six and thirty of his knights, 15
Hot questrists after him, met him at
    gate;
Who, with some other of the lord's de-
    pendants,
Are gone with him toward Dover, where
    they boast
To have well-armed friends.
    Corn.   Get horses for your mistress.
    Gon. Farewell, sweet lord, and sister. 20
    Corn. Edmund, farewell. [*Exeunt Goneril,
                    Edmund, and Oswald.*
            Go seek the traitor Gloucester,
Pinion him like a thief, bring him before us.
                    [*Exeunt other Servants.*
Though well we may not pass upon his life
Without the form of justice, yet our power
Shall do a court'sy to our wrath, which men
May blame, but not control.

Enter GLOUCESTER, *brought in by two or
                    three.*

            Who's there? the traitor?
    Reg. Ingrateful fox! 'tis he.   27
    Corn. Bind fast his corky arms.
    Glo. What means your Graces? Good my
    friends, consider
You are my guests; do me no foul play,
    friends.   30
    Corn. Bind him, I say. [*Servants bind him.*
    Reg.   Hard, hard. O filthy traitor!
    Glo. Unmerciful lady as you are, I'm
    none.
    Corn. To this chair bind him. Villain,
    thou shalt find—
                    [*Regan plucks his beard.*
    Glo. By the kind gods, 'tis most ignobly
    done
To pluck me by the beard.   35
    Reg. So white, and such a traitor!
    Glo.   Naughty lady,
These hairs which thou dost ravish from my
    chin
Will quicken and accuse thee. I am your
    host.
With robbers' hands my hospitable favours
You should not ruffle thus. What will you
    do?   40
    Corn. Come, sir, what letters had you late
    from France?
    Reg. Be simple-answer'd, for we know
    the truth.
    Corn. And what confederacy have you
    with the traitors
Late footed in the kingdom?
    Reg. To whose hands you have sent the
    lunatic King:
Speak.   46
    Glo. I have a letter guessingly set down,

Which came from one that's of a neutral
heart,
And not from one oppos'd.
Corn.   Cunning.
Reg.   And false.
Corn. Where hast thou sent the King?
Glo.   To Dover. 50
Reg. Wherefore to Dover? Wast thou
not charg'd at peril—
Corn. Wherefore to Dover? Let him
first answer that.
Glo. I am tied to the stake, and I must
stand the course.
Reg. Wherefore to Dover?
Glo. Because I would not see thy cruel
nails   55
Pluck out his poor old eyes; nor thy fierce
sister
In his anointed flesh rash boarish fangs.
The sea, with such a storm as his bare
head
In hell-black night endur'd, would have
buoy'd up
And quench'd the stelled fires.   60
Yet, poor old heart, he holp the heavens
to rain.
If wolves had at thy gate howl'd that dern
time,
Thou shouldst have said 'Good porter,
turn the key'.
All cruels else subscribe; but I shall see
The winged vengeance overtake such
children.   65
Corn. See't shalt thou never. Fellows,
hold the chair.
Upon these eyes of thine I'll set my foot.
Glo. He that will think to live till he be
old,
Give me some help!—O cruel! O you gods!
Reg. One side will mock another; th'
other too.   70
Corn. If you see vengeance—
1 Serv.   Hold your hand, my lord.
I have serv'd you ever since I was a child;
But better service have I never done you,
Than now to bid you hold.
Reg.   How now, you dog!
1 Serv. If you did wear a beard upon
your chin   75
I'd shake it on this quarrel. What do you
mean?
Corn. My villain! [*They draw and fight.*
1 Serv. Nay, then come on, and take the
chance of anger.
                    [*Cornwall is wounded.*
Reg. Give me thy sword. A peasant stand
up thus! [*She takes a sword and stabs
                    him from behind.*
1 Serv. O, I am slain! My lord, you have
one eye left   80
To see some mischief on him. O! [*Dies.*
Corn. Lest it see more, prevent it. Out
vile jelly!
Where is thy lustre now?

Glo. All dark and comfortless! Where's
my son Edmund?   84
Edmund, enkindle all the sparks of nature
To quit this horrid act.
Reg.   Out, treacherous villain!
Thou call'st on him that hates thee. It
was he
That made the overture of thy treasons
to us;
Who is too good to pity thee.
Glo. O my follies! Then Edgar was
abus'd.   90
Kind gods, forgive me that, and prosper
him.
Reg. Go thrust him out at gates and let
him smell
His way to Dover.   [*Gloucester led out.*
How is't my lord? How look you?
Corn. I have receiv'd a hurt. Follow me,
lady.
Turn out that eyeless villain; throw this
slave   95
Upon the dunghill. Regan, I bleed apace.
Untimely comes this hurt. Give me your
arm. [*Exit Cornwall, led by Regan.*
2 Serv. I'll never care what wickedness I
do,
If this man come to good.
3 Serv.   If she live long,
And in the end meet the old course of death,
Women will all turn monsters.   101
2 Serv. Let's follow the old Earl and get
the Bedlam
To lead him where he would. His roguish
madness
Allows itself to anything.
3 Serv. Go thou. I'll fetch some flax and
whites of eggs   105
To apply to his bleeding face. Now heaven
help him!   [*Exeunt.*

ACT FOUR

SCENE I. *The Heath.*

Enter EDGAR.

Edg. Yet better thus and known to be
contemn'd,
Than still contemn'd and flatter'd. To be
worst,
The lowest and most dejected thing of
fortune,
Stands still in esperance, lives not in fear.
The lamentable change is from the best; 5
The worst returns to laughter. Welcome,
then,
Thou unsubstantial air that I embrace!
The wretch that thou hast blown unto the
worst
Owes nothing to thy blasts.

Enter GLOUCESTER, *led by an* Old Man.

                    But who comes here?
My father, poorly led? World, world, O
world!   10

But that thy strange mutations make us
 hate thee,
Life would not yield to age.
 Old Man. O my good lord, I have been
your tenant, and your father's tenant, these
fourscore years.
 Glo. Away, get thee away; good friend,
 be gone.   15
Thy comforts can do me no good at all;
Thee they may hurt.
 Old Man. You cannot see your way.
 Glo. I have no way, and therefore want
 no eyes;
I stumbled when I saw: full oft 'tis seen 20
Our means secure us, and our mere defects
Prove our commodities. O dear son Edgar,
The food of thy abused father's wrath!
Might I but live to see thee in my touch,
I'd say I had eyes again!
 Old Man. How now! Who's there? 25
 Edg. [*Aside*] O gods! Who is't can say
 ' I am at the worst ' ?
I am worse than e'er I was.
 Old Man. 'Tis poor mad Tom.
 Edg. [*Aside*] And worse I may be yet.
 The worst is not
So long as we can say ' This is the worst '.
 Old Man. Fellow, where goest?
 Glo.   Is it a beggar-man? 30
 Old Man. Madman and beggar too.
 Glo. He has some reason, else he could
 not beg.
I' th' last night's storm I such a fellow saw;
Which made me think a man a worm. My
 son
Came then into my mind; and yet my
 mind   35
Was then scarce friends with him. I have
 heard more since.
As flies to wanton boys are we to th' gods—
They kill us for their sport.
 Edg. [*Aside*]   How should this be?
Bad is the trade that must play fool to
 sorrow,
Ang'ring itself and others.—Bless thee,
 master!   40
 Glo. Is that the naked fellow?
 Old Man.   Ay, my lord.
 Glo. Then, prithee, get thee away. If for
 my sake
Thou wilt o'ertake us hence a mile or twain
I' th' way toward Dover, do it for ancient
 love;
And bring some covering for this naked
 soul,   45
Which I'll entreat to lead me.
 Old Man.   Alack, sir, he is mad.
 Glo. 'Tis the times' plague when madmen
 lead the blind.
Do as I bid thee, or rather do thy pleasure;
Above the rest, be gone.
 Old Man. I'll bring him the best 'parel
 that I have,   50
Come on't what will.   [*Exit.*

 Glo. Sirrah, naked fellow!
 Edg. Poor Tom's a-cold. [*Aside*] I cannot
 daub it further.
 Glo. Come hither, fellow.
 Edg. [*Aside*] And yet I must.—Bless thy
 sweet eyes, they bleed.   55
 Glo. Know'st thou the way to Dover?
 Edg. Both stile and gate, horse-way and
footpath. Poor Tom hath been scar'd out
of his good wits. Bless thee, good man's son,
from the foul fiend! Five fiends have been
in poor Tom at once: of lust, as Obidicut;
Hobbididence, prince of dumbness; Mahu,
of stealing; Modo, of murder; Flibberti-
gibbet, of mopping and mowing, who since
possesses chambermaids and waiting-
women. So, bless thee, master!
 Glo. Here, take this purse, thou whom the
 heavens' plagues   65
Have humbled to all strokes. That I am
 wretched
Makes thee the happier. Heavens, deal so
 still!
Let the superfluous and lust-dieted man
That slaves your ordinance, that will not
 see
Because he does not feel, feel your power
 quickly;   70
So distribution should undo excess,
And each man have enough. Dost thou
 know Dover?
 Edg. Ay, master.
 Glo. There is a cliff whose high and
 bending head
Looks fearfully in the confined deep: 75
Bring me but to the very brim of it
And I'll repair the misery thou dost bear
With something rich about me. From that
 place
I shall no leading need.
 Edg.   Give me thy arm; 79
Poor Tom shall lead thee.   [*Exeunt.*

SCENE II. *Before the Duke of Albany's
palace.*

Enter GONERIL *and* EDMUND.

 Gon. Welcome, my lord. I marvel our
 mild husband
Not met us on the way.

Enter OSWALD.

     Now, where's your master?
 Osw. Madam, within, but never man so
 chang'd.
I told him of the army that was landed;
He smil'd at it. I told him you were
 coming;   5
His answer was ' The worse '. Of Glou-
 cester's treachery,
And of the loyal service of his son,
When I inform'd him, then he call'd me sot,
And told me I had turn'd the wrong side
 out.

What most he should dislike seems pleasant
to him ; 10
What like, offensive.
   Gon. [*To Edmund*] Then shall you go no
further.
It is the cowish terror of his spirit
That dares not undertake ; he'll not feel
wrongs
Which tie him to an answer. Our wishes on
the way
May prove effects. Back, Edmund, to my
brother ; 15
Hasten his musters and conduct his pow'rs.
I must change arms at home, and give the
distaff
Into my husband's hands. This trusty
servant
Shall pass between us. Ere long you are
like to hear,
If you dare venture in your own behalf, 20
A mistress's command. Wear this ; spare
speech. [*Giving a favour.*
Decline your head ; this kiss, if it durst
speak,
Would stretch thy spirits up into the air.
Conceive, and fare thee well.
   Edm. Yours in the ranks of death.
   Gon.   My most dear Gloucester.
              [*Exit Edmund.*
O, the difference of man and man ! 26
To thee a woman's services are due.
My fool usurps my body.
   Osw.   Madam, here comes my lord.
                 [*Exit.*

Enter ALBANY.

   Gon. I have been worth the whistle.
   Alb.   O Goneril !
You are not worth the dust which the rude
wind 30
Blows in your face. I fear your disposition :
That nature which contemns it origin
Cannot be border'd certain in itself ;
She that herself will sliver and disbranch
From her material sap perforce must wither
And come to deadly use. 36
   Gon. No more ; the text is foolish.
   Alb. Wisdom and goodness to the vile
seem vile ;
Filths savour but themselves. What have
you done ?
Tigers, not daughters, what have you
perform'd ? 40
A father, and a gracious aged man,
Whose reverence even the head-lugg'd bear
would lick,
Most barbarous, most degenerate, have
you madded.
Could my good brother suffer you to do it ?
A man, a Prince, by him so benefited ! 45
If that the heavens do not their visible
spirits
Send quickly down to tame these vile
offences,

It will come
Humanity must perforce prey on itself,
Like monsters of the deep.
   Gon.   Milk-liver'd man ! 50
That bear'st a cheek for blows, a head for
wrongs ;
Who hast not in thy brows an eye discern-
ing
Thine honour from thy suffering ; that not
know'st
Fools do those villains pity who are
punish'd
Ere they have done their mischief. Where's
thy drum ? 55
France spreads his banners in our noiseless
land,
With plumed helm thy state begins to
threat,
Whil'st thou, a moral fool, sits still, and
cries
' Alack, why does he so ? '
   Alb.   See thyself, devil !
Proper deformity shows not in the fiend
So horrid as in woman.
   Gon.   O vain fool ! 61
   Alb. Thou changed and self-cover'd
thing, for shame !
Be-monster not thy feature. Were't my
fitness
To let these hands obey my blood,
They are apt enough to dislocate and tear
Thy flesh and bones. Howe'er thou art a
fiend, 66
A woman's shape doth shield thee.
   Gon. Marry, your manhood—mew !

Enter a Messenger.

   Alb. What news ?
   Mess. O, my good lord, the Duke of
Cornwall's dead, 70
Slain by his servant, going to put out
The other eye of Gloucester.
   Alb.   Gloucester's eyes !
   Mess. A servant that he bred, thrill'd
with remorse,
Oppos'd against the act, bending his sword
To his great master ; who, thereat enrag'd,
Flew on him, and amongst them fell'd him
dead ; 76
But not without that harmful stroke which
since
Hath pluck'd him after.
   Alb.   This shows you are above,
You justicers, that these our nether crimes
So speedily can venge ! But, O poor
Gloucester ! 80
Lost he his other eye ?
   Mess.   Both, both, my lord.
This letter, madam, craves a speedy
answer ;
'Tis from your sister.
   Gon. [*Aside*] One way I like this well ;
But being widow, and my Gloucester with
her,

May all the building in my fancy pluck 85
Upon my hateful life. Another way
The news is not so tart.—I'll read, and
    answer.   [*Exit.*
  Alb. Where was his son, when they did
    take his eyes?
  Mess. Come with my lady hither.
  Alb.   He is not here.
  Mess. No, my good lord; I met him back
    again.   90
  Alb. Knows he the wickedness?
  Mess. Ay, my good lord; 'twas he in-
    form'd against him
And quit the house on purpose that their
    punishment
Might have the freer course.
  Alb.   Gloucester, I live
To thank thee for the love thou show'dst
    the King,   95
And to revenge thine eyes. Come hither,
    friend:
Tell me what more thou know'st. [*Exeunt.*

SCENE III. *The French camp near Dover.*

    Enter KENT *and a* Gentleman.

  Kent. Why the King of France is so
suddenly gone back know you no reason?
  Gent. Something he left imperfect in the
state, which since his coming forth is
thought of, which imports to the kingdom
so much fear and danger that his personal
return was most required and necessary. 6
  Kent. Who hath he left behind him
general?
  Gent. The Marshal of France, Monsieur
La Far.
  Kent. Did your letters pierce the Queen
to any demonstration of grief?   10
  Gent. Ay, sir; she took them, read them
in my presence,
And now and then an ample tear trill'd
    down
Her delicate cheek. It seem'd she was a
    queen
Over her passion, who, most rebel-like,
Sought to be king o'er her.
  Kent.   O, then it mov'd her. 15
  Gent. Not to a rage; patience and
    sorrow strove
Who should express her goodliest. You
    have seen
Sunshine and rain at once: her smiles and
    tears
Were like a better way. Those happy smilets
That play'd on her ripe lip seem'd not to
    know   20
What guests were in her eyes, which parted
    thence
As pearls from diamonds dropp'd. In
    brief,
Sorrow would be a rarity most beloved
If all could so become it.
  Kent.   Made she no verbal question?

  Gent. Faith, once or twice she heav'd the
    name of father   25
Pantingly forth, as if it press'd her heart;
Cried 'Sisters! sisters! Shame of ladies!
    Sisters!
Kent! father! sisters! What i' th' storm?
    i' th' night?
Let pity not be believ'd!' There she shook
The holy water from her heavenly eyes, 30
And clamour moisten'd; then away she
    started
To deal with grief alone.
  Kent.   It is the stars,
The stars above us, govern our conditions;
Else one self mate and make could not beget
Such different issues. You spoke not with
    her since?   35
  Gent. No.
  Kent. Was this before the King return'd?
  Gent.   No, since.
  Kent. Well, sir, the poor distressed Lear's
    i' th' town;
Who sometime in his better tune re-
    members   39
What we are come about, and by no means
Will yield to see his daughter.
  Gent.   Why, good sir?
  Kent. A sovereign shame so elbows him;
    his own unkindness,
That stripp'd her from his benediction,
    turn'd her
To foreign casualties, gave her dear rights
To his dog-hearted daughters—these things
    sting   45
His mind so venomously that burning
    shame
Detains him from Cordelia.
  Gent.   Alack, poor gentleman!
  Kent. Of Albany's and Cornwall's powers
    you heard not?
  Gent. 'Tis so; they are afoot.
  Kent. Well, sir, I'll bring you to our
    master Lear,   50
And leave you to attend him. Some dear
    cause
Will in concealment wrap me up awhile;
When I am known aright, you shall not
    grieve
Lending me this acquaintance. I pray you
    go   54
Along with me.   [*Exeunt.*

SCENE IV. *The French camp. A tent.*

Enter with drum and colours, CORDELIA,
    Doctor, *and* Soldiers.

  Cor. Alack, 'tis he! Why, he was met
    even now
As mad as the vex'd sea, singing aloud,
Crown'd with rank fumiter and furrow
    weeds,
With hardocks, hemlock, nettles, cuckoo-
    flow'rs,
Darnel, and all the idle weeds that grow 5

In our sustaining corn. A century send
   forth ;
Search every acre in the high-grown field,
And bring him to our eye. [*Exit an Officer.*
           What can man's wisdom,
In the restoring his bereaved sense ?
He that helps him, take all my outward
   worth.   10
  Doct. There is means, madam.
Our foster-nurse of nature is repose,
The which he lacks ; that to provoke in
   him
Are many simples operative, whose power
Will close the eye of anguish.
  Cor.   All blest secrets, 15
All you unpublish'd virtues of the earth,
Spring with my tears ; be aidant and
   remediate,
In the good man's distress. Seek, seek for
   him ;
Lest his ungovern'd rage dissolve the life
That wants the means to lead it.

        Enter a Messenger.

  Mess. News, madam :   20
The British pow'rs are marching hither-
   ward.
  Cor. 'Tis known before ; our preparation
   stands
In expectation of them. O dear father !
It is thy business that I go about ;
Therefore great France   25
My mourning and importun'd tears hath
   pitied.
No blown ambition doth our arms incite,
But love, dear love, and our ag'd father's
   right.
Soon may I hear and see him ! [*Exeunt.*

    SCENE V. *Gloucester's castle.*

    Enter REGAN *and* OSWALD.

  Reg. But are my brother's pow'rs set
   forth ?
  Osw.   Ay madam.
  Reg. Himself in person there ?
  Osw.   Madam, with much ado.
Your sister is the better soldier.
  Reg. Lord Edmund spake not with your
   lord at home ?
  Osw. No, madam.   5
  Reg. What might import my sister's letter
   to him ?
  Osw. I know not, lady.
  Reg. Faith, he is posted hence on serious
   matter.
It was great ignorance, Gloucester's eyes
   being out,
To let him live ; where he arrives he moves
All hearts against us. Edmund, I think, is
   gone   11
In pity of his misery, to dispatch
His nighted life ; moreover, to descry
The strength o' th' enemy.

  Osw. I must needs after him, madam,
   with my letter.   15
  Reg. Our troops set forth to-morrow :
   stay with us ;
The ways are dangerous.
  Osw.   I may not, madam :
My lady charg'd my duty in this business.
  Reg. Why should she write to Edmund ?
   Might not you
Transport her purposes by word ? Belike
Some things—I know not what. I'll love
   thee much—   21
Let me unseal the letter.
  Osw.   Madam, I had rather—
  Reg. I know your lady does not love her
   husband ;
I am sure of that ; and at her late being
   here
She gave strange œillades and most speak-
   ing looks   25
To noble Edmund. I know you are of her
   bosom.
  Osw. I, madam ?
  Reg. I speak in understanding ; y'are,
   I know't.
Therefore I do advise you take this note.
My lord is dead ; Edmund and I have
   talk'd ;   30
And more convenient is he for my hand
Than for your lady's. You may gather
   more.
If you do find him, pray you give him
   this ;
And when your mistress hears thus much
   from you,
I pray desire her call her wisdom to her. 35
So fare you well.
If you do chance to hear of that blind
   traitor,
Preferment falls on him that cuts him off.
  Osw. Would I could meet him, madam !
   I should show
What party I do follow.
  Reg.   Fare thee well. 40
             [*Exeunt.*

    SCENE VI. *The country near Dover.*

  Enter GLOUCESTER, *and* EDGAR *dressed like
    a peasant.*

  Glo. When shall I come to th' top of that
   same hill ?
  Edg. You do climb up it now ; look how
   we labour.
  Glo. Methinks the ground is even.
  Edg.   Horrible steep.
Hark, do you hear the sea ?
  Glo.   No, truly.
  Edg. Why then, your other senses grow
   imperfect   5
By your eyes' anguish.
  Glo.   So may it be indeed.
Methinks thy voice is alter'd, and thou
   speak'st

In better phrase and matter than thou
    didst.
   Edg. Y'are much deceiv'd : in nothing
    am I chang'd
But in my garments.
   Glo.   Methinks y'are better spoken.
   Edg. Come on, sir ; here's the place.
    Stand still. How fearful   11
And dizzy 'tis to cast one's eyes so low !
The crows and choughs that wing the mid-
    way air
Show scarce so gross as beetles. Half-way
    down
Hangs one that gathers samphire—dreadful
    trade !   15
Methinks he seems no bigger than his head.
The fishermen that walk upon the beach
Appear like mice ; and yond tall anchoring
    bark
Diminish'd to her cock ; her cock, a buoy
Almost too small for sight. The murmuring
    surge   20
That on th' unnumb'red idle pebble chafes
Cannot be heard so high. I'll look no more ;
Lest my brain turn, and the deficient sight
Topple down headlong.
   Glo.   Set me where you stand.
   Edg. Give me your hand. You are now
    within a foot   25
Of th' extreme verge. For all beneath the
    moon
Would I not leap upright.
   Glo.   Let go my hand.
Here, friend, 's another purse ; in it a
    jewel
Well worth a poor man's taking. Fairies
    and gods   29
Prosper it with thee ! Go thou further off ;
Bid me farewell, and let me hear thee going.
   Edg. Now fare ye well, good sir.
   Glo.   With all my heart.
   Edg. Why I do trifle thus with his despair
Is done to cure it.
   Glo. [*Kneeling*] O you mighty gods !
This world I do renounce, and in your
    sights   35
Shake patiently my great affliction off.
If I could bear it longer, and not fall
To quarrel with your great opposeless wills,
My snuff and loathed part of nature should
Burn itself out. If Edgar live, O, bless him !
[*Rising*] Now, fellow, fare thee well.
   Edg.   Gone, sir ; farewell,
      [*Gloucester casts himself down.*
And yet I know not how conceit may rob
The treasury of life, when life itself
Yields to the theft. Had he been where he
    thought,
By this had thought been past.—Alive or
    dead ?   45
Ho, you sir ! friend ! Hear you, sir !
    Speak !—
Thus might he pass indeed. Yet he revives—
What are you, sir ?

   Glo.   Away, and let me die.
   Edg. Hadst thou been aught but gos-
    samer, feathers, air,
So many fathom down precipitating,   50
Thou'dst shiver'd like an egg ; but thou
    dost breathe,
Hast heavy substance, bleed'st not,
    speak'st, art sound.
Ten masts at each make not the altitude
Which thou hast perpendicularly fell.
Thy life's a miracle. Speak yet again.   55
   Glo. But have I fall'n, or no ?
   Edg. From the dread summit of this
    chalky bourn.
Look up a-height ; the shrill-gorg'd lark so
    far
Cannot be seen or heard. Do but look up.
   Glo. Alack, I have no eyes.   60
Is wretchedness depriv'd that benefit,
To end itself by death ? 'Twas yet some
    comfort,
When misery could beguile the tyrant's rage
And frustrate his proud will.
   Edg.   Give me your arm.
Up—so. How is't ? Feel you your legs ?
    You stand.   65
   Glo. Too well, too well.
   Edg.   This is above all strangeness.
Upon the crown o' th' cliff what thing was
    that
Which parted from you ?
   Glo.   A poor unfortunate beggar.
   Edg. As I stood here below, methought
    his eyes
Were two full moons ; he had a thousand
    noses,   70
Horns whelk'd and waved like the enridged
    sea.
It was some fiend ; therefore, thou happy
    father,
Think that the clearest gods, who make
    them honours
Of men's impossibilities, have preserved
    thee.
   Glo. I do remember now. Henceforth I'll
    bear   75
Affliction till it do cry out itself
' Enough, enough ' and die. That thing
    you speak of
I took it for a man ; often 'twould say,
' The fiend, the fiend '. He led me to that
    place.   79
   Edg. Bear free and patient thoughts.

Enter LEAR, *fantastically dressed with weeds.*

      But who comes here ?
The safer sense will ne'er accommodate
His master thus.
   Lear. No, they cannot touch me for
coining ; I am the King himself.
   Edg. O thou side-piercing sight !   85
   Lear. Nature's above art in that respect.
There's your press-money. That fellow
handles his bow like a crow-keeper ; draw

me a clothier's yard.　Look, look, a mouse !
Peace, peace ; this piece of toasted cheese
will do't.　There's my gauntlet ;　I'll prove
it on a giant.　Bring up the brown bills.
O, well flown, bird ! i' the clout, i' the clout
—hewgh !　Give the word.　　　　　　　92
　　Edg.　Sweet marjoram.
　　Lear.　Pass.
　　Glo.　I know that voice.　　　　　　95
　　Lear.　Ha ! Goneril, with a white beard !
They flatter'd me like a dog, and told me
I had white hairs in my beard ere the
black ones were there.　To say ' ay ' and ' no '
to everything that I said !　' Ay ' and ' no '
too was no good divinity.　When the rain
came to wet me once, and the wind to make
me chatter ; when the thunder would not
peace at my bidding ; there I found 'em,
there I smelt 'em out.　Go to, they are not
men o' their words.　They told me I was
everything ; 'tis a lie—I am not ague-
proof.　　　　　　　　　　　　　　　105
　　Glo.　The trick of that voice I do well
　　　　remember.
Is't not the King ?
　　Lear.　　　　　　Ay, every inch a king.
When I do stare, see how the subject
　　　quakes.
I pardon that man's life.　What was thy
　　cause ?
Adultery ?　　　　　　　　　　　　　110
Thou shalt not die.　Die for adultery ?　No.
The wren goes to't, and the small gilded fly
Does lecher in my sight.
Let copulation thrive ; for Gloucester's
　　　bastard son　　　　　　　　　　114
Was kinder to his father than my daughters
Got 'tween the lawful sheets.
To't, luxury, pell-mell, for I lack soldiers.
Behold yond simp'ring dame
Whose face between her forks presages
　　snow,
That minces virtue and does shake the
　　head　　　　　　　　　　　　　120
To hear of pleasure's name—
The fitchew nor the soiled horse goes to't
With a more riotous appetite.
Down from the waist they are centaurs,
Though women all above ;　　　　　125
But to the girdle do the gods inherit,
Beneath is all the fiends' ;
There's hell, there's darkness, there is the
　　sulphurous pit—
Burning, scalding, stench, consumption.
Fie, fie, fie ! pah, pah ! Give me an ounce of
civit, good apothecary, to sweeten my
imagination.　There's money for thee.　131
　　Glo.　O, let me kiss that hand !
　　Lear.　Let me wipe it first ; it smells of
　　　mortality.
　　Glo.　O ruin'd piece of nature !　This great
　　　world
Shall so wear out to nought.　Dost thou
　　know me ?　　　　　　　　　　135

　　Lear.　I remember thine eyes well enough.
Dost thou squiny at me ?　No, do thy
worst, blind Cupid ;　I'll not love.　Read
thou this challenge ; mark but the penning
of it.
　　Glo.　Were all thy letters suns, I could not
　　　see one.　　　　　　　　　　140
　　Edg.　[*Aside*]　I would not take this from
　　　report.　It is,
And my heart breaks at it.
　　Lear.　Read.
　　Glo.　What, with the case of eyes ?　　144
　　Lear.　O, ho, are you there with me ?
No eyes in your head nor no money in your
purse ?　Your eyes are in a heavy case, your
purse in a light ; yet you see how this
world goes.
　　Glo.　I see it feelingly.　　　　　149
　　Lear.　What, art mad ?　A man may see
how this world goes with no eyes.　Look
with thine ears.　See how yond justice rails
upon yond simple thief.　Hark, in thine ear :
change places and, handy-dandy, which is
the justice, which is the thief ?　Thou hast
seen a farmer's dog bark at a beggar ?　155
　　Glo.　Ay, sir.
　　Lear.　And the creature run from the cur ?
There thou mightst behold the great image
of authority : a dog's obey'd in office.
Thou rascal beadle, hold thy bloody
　　hand.
Why dost thou lash that whore ?　Strip thy
　　own back ;　　　　　　　　　　161
Thou hotly lusts to use her in that kind
For which thou whip'st her.　The usurer
　　hangs the cozener.
Through tatter'd clothes small vices do
　　appear ;
Robes and furr'd gowns hide all.　Plate sin
　　with gold,　　　　　　　　　　165
And the strong lance of justice hurtless
　　breaks ;
Arm it in rags, a pigmy's straw does pierce
　　it.
None does offend, none—I say none ; I'll
　　able 'em.
Take that of me, my friend, who have the
　　power
To seal th' accuser's lips.　Get thee glass
　　eyes,　　　　　　　　　　　　170
And, like a scurvy politician, seem
To see the things thou dost not.　Now, now,
　　now, now !
Pull off my boots.　Harder, harder—so.
　　Edg.　O, matter and impertinency mix'd !
Reason in madness !　　　　　　　176
　　Lear.　If thou wilt weep my fortunes, take
　　my eyes.
I know thee well enough ; thy name is
　　Gloucester.
Thou must be patient ; we came crying
　　hither.
Thou know'st the first time that we smell
　　the air　　　　　　　　　　　180

We wawl and cry. I will preach to thee.
Mark.
Glo. Alack, alack the day!
Lear. When we are born, we cry that we
are come
To this great stage of fools. This a good
block!
It were a delicate stratagem to shoe   185
A troop of horse with felt; I'll put't in
proof;
And when I have stol'n upon these son-in-
laws,
Then kill, kill, kill, kill, kill, kill!

Enter a Gentleman, *with* Attendants.

Gent. O, here he is: lay hand upon
him.—Sir,
Your most dear daughter—   190
Lear. No rescue? What, a prisoner? I
am even
The natural fool of fortune. Use me well;
You shall have ransom. Let me have
surgeons;
I am cut to th' brains.
Gent.   You shall have any thing.
Lear. No seconds? All myself?   195
Why, this would make a man a man of
salt,
To use his eyes for garden water-pots,
Ay, and laying Autumn's dust.
Gent.   Good sir—
Lear. I will die bravely, like a smug
bridegroom. What!   200
I will be jovial. Come, come; I am a king,
My masters, know you that.
Gent. You are a royal one, and we obey
you.
Lear. Then there's life in't. Nay, an you
get it, you shall get it by running. Sa, sa,
sa, sa. [*Exit running; Attendants follow.*
Gent. A sight most pitiful in the meanest
wretch,   206
Past speaking of in a king! Thou hast one
daughter
Who redeems nature from the general curse
Which twain have brought her to.
Edg. Hail, gentle sir.
Gent. Sir, speed you; what's your will?
Edg. Do you hear aught, sir, of a battle
toward?   211
Gent. Most sure and vulgar; every one
hears that
Which can distinguish sound.
Edg.   But, by your favour,
How near's the other army?
Gent. Near and on speedy foot; the main
descry   215
Stands on the hourly thought.
Edg.   I thank you, sir; that's all.
Gent. Though that the Queen on special
cause is here,
Her army is mov'd on.
Edg.   I thank you, sir. [*Exit Gentleman.*

Glo. You ever-gentle gods, take my
breath from me;
Let not my worser spirit tempt me again   220
To die before you please.
Edg.   Well pray you, father.
Glo. Now, good sir, what are you?
Edg. A most poor man, made tame to
fortune's blows,
Who, by the art of known and feeling
sorrows,
Am pregnant to good pity. Give me your
hand;   225
I'll lead you to some biding.
Glo.   Hearty thanks;
The bounty and the benison of heaven
To boot, and boot!

Enter OSWALD.

Osw. A proclaim'd prize! Most happy!
That eyeless head of thine was first fram'd
flesh
To raise my fortunes. Thou old unhappy
traitor,   230
Briefly thyself remember. The sword is out
That must destroy thee.
Glo.   Now let thy friendly hand
Put strength enough to't. [*Edgar interposes.*
Osw.   Wherefore, bold peasant,
Dar'st thou support a publish'd traitor?
Hence;
Lest that th' infection of his fortune take
Like hold on thee. Let go his arm.   236
Edg. Chill not let go, zir, without vurther
'casion.
Osw. Let go, slave, or thou diest.
Edg. Good gentleman, go your gait, and
let poor volk pass. An chud ha' bin
zwagger'd out of my life, 'twould not ha'
bin zo long as 'tis by a vortnight. Nay,
come not near th' old man; keep out, che
vor ye, or Ice try whether your costard or
my ballow be the harder. Chill be plain
with you.
Osw. Out, dunghill!   245
Edg. Chill pick your teeth, zir. Come;
no matter vor your foins. [*They fight.*
Osw. Slave, thou hast slain me. Villain,
take my purse;
If ever thou wilt thrive, bury my body,
And give the letters which thou find'st
about me   250
To Edmund Earl of Gloucester. Seek him
out
Upon the English party. O, untimely
death!
Death!   [*He dies.*
Edg. I know thee well; a serviceable
villain,
As duteous to the vices of thy mistress   255
As badness would desire.
Glo.   What, is he dead?
Edg. Sit you down, father; rest you.
Let's see these pockets; the letters that he
speaks of

May be my friends. He's dead ; I am only
sorry 259
He had no other death's-man. Let us see.
Leave, gentle wax ; and, manners, blame
us not :
To know our enemies' minds we'd rip their
hearts ;
Their papers is more lawful.
[Reads] ' Let our reciprocal vows be
rememb'red. You have many opportunities
to cut him off ; if your will want not, time
and place will be fruitfully offer'd. There
is nothing done if he return the conqueror :
then am I the prisoner, and his bed my
gaol ; from the loathed warmth whereof
deliver me, and supply the place for your
labour. 268
Your (wife, so I would say) affectionate
servant, GONERIL.'
O indistinguish'd space of woman's will !
A plot upon her virtuous husband's life ;
And the exchange my brother ! Here, in
the sands
Thee I'll rake up, the post unsanctified
Of murderous lechers ; and in the mature
time 275
With this ungracious paper strike the sight
Of the death-practis'd duke. For him 'tis
well
That of thy death and business I can tell.
Glo. The King is mad ; how stiff is my
vile sense,
That I stand up, and have ingenious
feeling 280
Of my huge sorrows ! Better I were
distract ;
So should my thoughts be sever'd from my
griefs,
And woes by wrong imaginations lose
The knowledge of themselves.
[Drum afar off.
Edg. Give me your hand.
Far off methinks I hear the beaten drum.
Come, father, I'll bestow you with a friend.
[Exeunt.

SCENE VII. A tent in the French camp.

Music. Enter CORDELIA, KENT, Doctor,
and Gentleman.

Cor. O thou good Kent, how shall I live
and work
To match thy goodness ? My life will be
too short,
And every measure fail me.
Kent. To be acknowledg'd, madam, is
o'erpaid.
All my reports go with the modest truth ;
Nor more nor clipp'd, but so. 6
Cor. Be better suited.
These weeds are memories of those worser
hours ;
I prithee put them off.
Kent. Pardon, dear madam ;

Yet to be known shortens my made intent :
My boon I make it that you know me not
Till time and I think meet. 11
Cor. Then be't so, my good lord. [To the
Doctor] How does the King ?
Doct. Madam, sleeps still.'
Cor. O you kind gods,
Cure this great breach in his abused nature !
Th' untun'd and jarring senses, O, wind
up 16
Of this child-changed father !
Doct. So please your Majesty
That we may wake the King ; he hath slept
long.
Cor. Be govern'd by your knowledge, and
proceed
I' th' sway of your own will. [To the
gentleman] Is he array'd ? 20
Gent. Ay, madam ; in the heaviness of
sleep
We put fresh garments on him.
Doct. Be by, good madam, when we do
awake him ;
I doubt not of his temperance.
Cor. Very well.
Doct. Please you, draw near. Louder the
music there ! 25

He draws the curtains and discovers LEAR
asleep in bed.

Cor. O my dear father ! Restoration hang
Thy medicine on my lips, and let this kiss
Repair those violent harms that my two
sisters
Have in thy reverence made.
Kent. Kind and dear princess !
Cor. Had you not been their father, these
white flakes 30
Did challenge pity of them. Was this a
face
To be oppos'd against the warring winds ?
To stand against the deep dread bolted
thunder ?
In the most terrible and nimble stroke
Of quick cross lightning ? to watch—poor
perdu !— 35
With this thin helm ? Mine enemy's dog,
Though he had bit me, should have stood
that night
Against my fire ; and wast thou fain, poor
father,
To hovel thee with swine and rogues forlorn,
In short and musty straw ? Alack, alack !
'Tis wonder that thy life and wits at once
Had not concluded all.—He wakes ; speak
to him. 42
Doct. Madam, do you ; 'tis fittest.
Cor. How does my royal lord ? How fares
your Majesty ?
Lear. You do me wrong to take me out
o' th' grave.
Thou art a soul in bliss ; but I am bound 46
Upon a wheel of fire, that mine own tears
Do scald like molten lead.

Cor. Sir, do you know me?

Lear. You are a spirit, I know. Where did you die?

Cor. Still, still far wide! 50

Doct. He's scarce awake; let him alone awhile.

Lear. Where have I been? Where am I? Fair daylight?
I am mightily abus'd. I should e'en die with pity
To see another thus. I know not what to say.
I will not swear these are my hands. Let's see. 55
I feel this pin prick. Would I were assur'd
Of my condition!

Cor. O, look upon me, sir,
And hold your hands in benediction o'er me.
No, sir, you must not kneel.

Lear. Pray, do not mock me:
I am a very foolish fond old man, 60
Fourscore and upward, not an hour more nor less;
And, to deal plainly,
I fear I am not in my perfect mind.
Methinks I should know you, and know this man;
Yet I am doubtful; for I am mainly ignorant 65
What place this is; and all the skill I have
Remembers not these garments; nor I know not
Where I did lodge last night. Do not laugh at me;
For, as I am a man, I think this lady
To be my child Cordelia.

Cor. And so I am, I am. 70

Lear. Be your tears wet? Yes, faith. I pray weep not;
If you have poison for me I will drink it.
I know you do not love me; for your sisters
Have, as I do remember, done me wrong:
You have some cause, they have not.

Cor. No cause, no cause. 75

Lear. Am I in France?

Kent. In your own kingdom, sir.

Lear. Do not abuse me.

Doct. Be comforted, good madam. The great rage,
You see, is kill'd in him; and yet it is danger 79
To make him even o'er the time he has lost.
Desire him to go in; trouble him no more
Till further settling.

Cor. Will't please your Highness walk?

Lear. You must bear with me.
Pray you now, forget and forgive; I am old and foolish. 85

[*Exeunt all but Kent and Gentleman.*

Gent. Holds it true, sir, that the Duke of Cornwall was so slain?

Kent. Most certain, sir.

Gent. Who is conductor of his people?

Kent. As 'tis said, the bastard son of Gloucester. 90

Gent. They say Edgar, his banish'd son, is with the Earl of Kent in Germany.

Kent. Report is changeable. 'Tis time to look about; the powers of the kingdom approach apace.

Gent. The arbitrement is like to be bloody. Fare you well, sir. [*Exit.*

Kent. My point and period will be throughly wrought, 97
Or well or ill, as this day's battle's fought. [*Exit.*

ACT FIVE

SCENE I. *The British camp near Dover.*

Enter, with drum and colours, EDMUND, REGAN, *Gentlemen, and* Soldiers.

Edm. Know of the Duke if his last purpose hold,
Or whether since he is advis'd by aught
To change the course. He's full of alteration
And self-reproving—bring his constant pleasure. [*Exit an Officer.*

Reg. Our sister's man is certainly miscarried. 5

Edm. 'Tis to be doubted, madam.

Reg. Now, sweet lord,
You know the goodness I intend upon you.
Tell me—but truly—but then speak the truth—
Do you not love my sister?

Edm. In honour'd love.

Reg. But have you never found my brother's way 10
To the forfended place?

Edm. That thought abuses you.

Reg. I am doubtful that you have been conjunct
And bosom'd with her, as far as we call hers.

Edm. No, by mine honour, madam.

Reg. I never shall endure her. Dear my lord, 15
Be not familiar with her.

Edm. Fear me not.
She and the Duke her husband!

Enter, with drum and colours, ALBANY, GONERIL, *and* Soldiers.

Gon. [*Aside*] I had rather lose the battle than that sister
Should loosen him and me.

Alb. Our very loving sister, well be-met.
Sir, this I heard: the King is come to his daughter 21
With others whom the rigour of our state
Forc'd to cry out. Where I could not be honest
I never yet was valiant. For this business,
It touches us as France invades our land, 25

Not bolds the King, with others whom, I
  fear,
Most just and heavy causes make oppose.
  Edm. Sir, you speak nobly.
  Reg.   Why is this reason'd ?
  Gon. Combine together 'gainst the enemy;
For these domestic-door particulars   30
Are not the question here.
  Alb.   Let's then determine
With th' ancient of war on our proceeding.
  Edm. I shall attend you presently at
    your tent.
  Reg. Sister, you'll go with us ?
  Gon. No.   35
  Reg. 'Tis most convenient ; pray you go
    with us.
  Gon. [*Aside*] O, ho, I know the riddle.—
    I will go.

As they are going out, enter EDGAR, *disguised.*

  Edg. If e'er your Grace had speech with
    man so poor,
Hear me one word.
  Alb.   I'll overtake you.—Speak.
    [*Exeunt all but Albany and Edgar.*
  Edg. Before you fight the battle, ope this
    letter.   40
If you have victory, let the trumpet sound
For him that brought it ; wretched though
    I seem
I can produce a champion that will prove
What is avouched there. If you miscarry,
Your business of the world hath so an end,
And machination ceases. Fortune love you!
  Alb. Stay till I have read the letter.
  Edg.   I was forbid it.
When time shall serve, let but the herald
    cry,   48
And I'll appear again.
  Alb. Why, fare thee well. I will o'erlook
    thy paper.   [*Exit Edgar.*

       Re-enter EDMUND.

  Edm. The enemy's in view ; draw up
    your powers.   51
Here is the guess of their true strength and
    forces
By diligent discovery ; but your haste
Is now urg'd on you.
  Alb.   We will greet the time. [*Exit.*
  Edm. To both these sisters have I sworn
    my love ;   55
Each jealous of the other, as the stung
Are of the adder. Which of them shall I
    take ?
Both ? one ? or neither ? Neither can be
    enjoy'd,
If both remain alive : to take the widow,
Exasperates, makes mad her sister Goneril ;
And hardly shall I carry out my side,   61
Her husband being alive. Now then, we'll
    use
His countenance for the battle ; which
    being done,

Let her who would be rid of him devise
His speedy taking off. As for the mercy 65
Which he intends to Lear and to Cordelia—
The battle done, and they within our power,
Shall never see his pardon ; for my state
Stands on me to defend, not to debate.
                  [*Exit.*

SCENE II. *A field between the two camps.*

*Alarum within. Enter, with drum and
colours, the* Powers of France *over the
stage,* CORDELIA *with her* Father *in her
hand, and exeunt.*

    Enter EDGAR *and* GLOUCESTER.

  Edg. Here, father, take the shadow of
    this tree
For your good host ; pray that the right
    may thrive.
If ever I return to you again
I'll bring you comfort.
  Glo.   Grace go with you, sir !
                [*Exit Edgar.*

Alarum and retreat within. Re-enter EDGAR.

  Edg. Away, old man ; give me thy hand ;
    away !   5
King Lear hath lost, he and his daughter
    ta'en.
Give me thy hand ; come on.
  Glo. No further, sir ; a man may rot even
    here.
  Edg. What, in ill thoughts again ? Men
    must endure
Their going hence, even as their coming
    hither :   10
Ripeness is all. Come on.
  Glo.   And that's true too.
                  [*Exeunt.*

SCENE III. *The British camp near Dover.*

Enter, in conquest, with drum and colours,
EDMUND ; LEAR *and* CORDELIA *prisoners ;*
Soldiers, Captain.

  Edm. Some officers take them away.
    Good guard,
Until their greater pleasures first be known
That are to censure them.
  Cor.   We are not the first
Who with best meaning have incurr'd the
    worst.
For thee, oppressed King, am I cast down ;
Myself could else out-frown false Fortune's
    frown.   6
Shall we not see these daughters and these
    sisters ?
  Lear. No, no, no, no ! Come, let's away
    to prison.
We two alone will sing like birds i' th' cage ;
When thou dost ask me blessing, I'll kneel
    down   10
And ask of thee forgiveness ; so we'll live,
And pray, and sing, and tell old tales, and
    laugh

At gilded butterflies, and hear poor rogues
Talk of court news ; and we'll talk with
    them too—
Who loses and who wins ; who's in, who's
    out—   15
And take upon's the mystery of things
As if we were God's spies ; and we'll wear
    out
In a wall'd prison packs and sects of great
    ones
That ebb and flow by th' moon.
    Edm.   Take them away.
    Lear. Upon such sacrifices, my Cordelia,
The gods themselves throw incense. Have I
    caught thee ?   21
He that parts us shall bring a brand from
    heaven
And fire us hence like foxes. Wipe thine
    eyes ;
The good years shall devour them, flesh and
    fell,
Ere they shall make us weep. We'll see 'em
    starv'd first.   25
Come. [*Exeunt Lear and Cordelia, guarded.*
    Edm. Come hither, Captain ; hark.
[*Giving a paper*] Take thou this note ; go
    follow them to prison.
One step I have advanc'd thee ; if thou dost
As this instructs thee, thou dost make thy
    way   30
To noble fortunes. Know thou this, that
    men
Are as the time is ; to be tender-minded
Does not become a sword. Thy great em-
    ployment
Will not bear question ; either say thou'lt
    do't,
Or thrive by other means.
    Capt.   I'll do't, my lord. 35
    Edm. About it ; and write happy when
    th' hast done.
Mark—I say, instantly ; and carry it so
As I have set it down.
    Capt. I cannot draw a cart nor eat
    dried oats ;   39
If it be man's work, I'll do't.   [*Exit.*

Flourish. Enter ALBANY, GONERIL, REGAN,
    and Soldiers.

    Alb. Sir, you have show'd to-day your
    valiant strain,
And fortune led you well. You have the
    captives   42
Who were the opposites of this day's strife ;
I do require them of you, so to use them
As we shall find their merits and our safety
May equally determine.
    Edm.   Sir, I thought it fit
To send the old and miserable king
To some retention and appointed guard ;
Whose age has charms in it, whose title
    more,
To pluck the common bosom on his side, 50
And turn our impress'd lances in our eyes

Which do command them. With him I sent
    the Queen,
My reason all the same ; and they are ready
To-morrow, or at further space, t' appear
Where you shall hold your session. At this
    time   55
We sweat and bleed ; the friend hath lost
    his friend ;
And the best quarrels, in the heat, are
    curs'd
By those that feel their sharpness.
The question of Cordelia and her father
Requires a fitter place.
    Alb.   Sir, by your patience, 60
I hold you but a subject of this war,
Not as a brother.
    Reg.   That's as we list to grace him.
Methinks our pleasure might have been
    demanded
Ere you had spoke so far.   He led our
    powers,
Bore the commission of my place and
    person,   65
The which immediacy may well stand up
And call itself your brother.
    Gon.   Not so hot.
In his own grace he doth exalt himself,
More than in your addition.
    Reg.   In my rights,
By me invested, he compeers the best. 70
    Alb. That were the most, if he should
    husband you.
    Reg. Jesters do oft prove prophets.
    Gon.   Holla, holla !
That eye that told you so look'd but
    asquint.
    Reg. Lady, I am not well ; else I should
    answer
From a full-flowing stomach. General, 75
Take thou my soldiers, prisoners, patri-
    mony ;
Dispose of them, of me ; the walls is
    thine.
Witness the world that I create thee here
My lord and master.
    Gon.   Mean you to enjoy him ?
    Alb. The let-alone lies not in your good
    will.   80
    Edm. Nor in thine, lord.
    Alb.   Half-blooded fellow, yes.
    Reg. [*To Edmund*] Let the drum strike,
    and prove my title thine.
    Alb. Stay yet ; hear reason. Edmund, I
    arrest thee
On capital treason ; and, in thy attaint,
                 [*Pointing to Goneril.*
This gilded serpent. For your claim, fair
    sister,   85
I bar it in the interest of my wife ;
'Tis she is sub-contracted to this lord,
And I, her husband, contradict your banns.
If you will marry, make your loves to me—
My lady is bespoke.
    Gon.   An interlude !   90

Alb. Thou art arm'd, Gloster. Let the
     trumpet sound.
If none appear to prove upon thy person
Thy heinous, manifest, and many treasons,
There is my pledge ; [*Throwing down a glove.*
                    I'll make it on thy heart,
Ere I taste bread, thou art in nothing less
Than I have here proclaim'd thee.
Reg. Sick, O, sick !
Gon. [*Aside*] If not, I'll ne'er trust
     medicine.   97
Edm. There's my exchange. [*Throwing
down a glove*]. What in the world he is
That names me traitor, villain-like he lies.
Call by thy trumpet : he that dares
     approach,   100
On him, on you, who not, I will maintain
My truth and honour firmly.
Alb. A herald, ho !
Edm.   A herald, ho, a herald !
Alb. Trust to thy single virtue ; for thy
     soldiers,
All levied in my name, have in my name 105
Took their discharge.
Reg.   My sickness grows upon me.
Alb. She is not well ; convey her to my
     tent.   [*Exit Regan, led.*

          Enter a Herald.

Come hither, herald. Let the trumpet
     sound,
And read out this.   109
Herald. [*Reads*] ' If any man of quality
or degree within the lists of the army will
maintain upon Edmund, supposed Earl of
Gloucester, that he is a manifold traitor,
let him appear by the third sound of the
trumpet. He is bold in his defence.'   114
Sound, trumpet.   [1 *Trumpet.*
Herald. Again !   [2 *Trumpet.*
Herald. Again !   [3 *Trumpet.*
          [*Trumpet answers within.*

Enter EDGAR, *armed, at the third sound, a
     trumpet before him.*

Alb. Ask him his purposes, why he
     appears
Upon this call o' th' trumpet.
Herald.   What are you ?
Your name, your quality, and why you
     answer   120
This present summons ?
Edg.   Know, my name is lost,
By treason's tooth bare-gnawn and canker-
     bit ;
Yet am I noble as the adversary
I come to cope.
Alb.   Which is that adversary ?
Edg. What's he that speaks for Edmund
     Earl of Gloucester ?   125
Edm. Himself. What say'st thou to him ?
Edg.   Draw thy sword,
That, if my speech offend a noble heart,
Thy arm may do thee justice ; here is mine.

Behold, it is the privilege of mine honours,
My oath, and my profession. I protest—
Maugre thy strength, youth, place, and
     eminence,   131
Despite thy victor sword and fire-new
     fortune,
Thy valour and thy heart—thou art a
     traitor ;
False to thy gods, thy brother, and thy
     father ;
Conspirant 'gainst this high illustrious
     prince ;   135
And, from th' extremest upward of thy
     head
To the descent and dust below thy foot,
A most toad-spotted traitor. Say thou
     ' No ',
This sword, this arm, and my best spirits,
     are bent   139
To prove upon thy heart, whereto I speak,
Thou liest.
Edm. In wisdom I should ask thy name ;
But, since thy outside looks so fair and
     warlike,
And that thy tongue some say of breeding
     breathes,   143
What safe and nicely I might well delay
By rule of knighthood, I disdain and spurn.
Back do I toss these treasons to thy head ;
With the hell-hated lie o'erwhelm thy
     heart ;
Which—for they yet glance by and scarcely
     bruise—
This sword of mine shall give them instant
     way
Where they shall rest for ever. Trumpets,
     speak.   150
          [*Alarums. They fight. Edmund falls.*
Alb. Save him, save him !
Gon.   This is practice, Gloucester.
By th' law of war thou wast not bound
     to answer
An unknown opposite ; thou art not
     vanquish'd,
But cozen'd and beguil'd,
Alb.   Shut your mouth, dame,
Or with this paper shall I stopple it. Hold,
     sir.   155
Thou worse than any name, read thine own
     evil.
No tearing, lady ; I perceive you know it.
Gon. Say, if I do—the laws are mine, not
     thine.   158
Who can arraign me for't ?
Alb.   Most monstrous ! O !
Know'st thou this paper ?
Gon. Ask me not what I know. [*Exit.*
Alb. Go after her. She's desperate ;
     govern her.   [*Exit an Officer.*
Edm. What you have charg'd me with,
     that have I done,
And more, much more ; the time will bring
     it out.
'Tis past, and so am I. But what art thou

That hast this fortune on me ? If thou'rt
    noble,   165
I do forgive thee.
    Edg.   Let's exchange charity.
I am no less in blood than thou art,
    Edmund ;
If more, the more th' hast wrong'd me.
My name is Edgar, and thy father's son.
The gods are just, and of our pleasant vices
Make instruments to plague us :   171
The dark and vicious place where thee he
    got
Cost him his eyes.
    Edm.   Th' hast spoken right, 'tis true ;
The wheel is come full circle ; I am here.
    Alb. Methought thy very gait did
    prophesy   175
A royal nobleness. I must embrace thee.
Let sorrow split my heart if ever I
Did hate thee or thy father !
    Edg.   Worthy prince,
I know't.
    Alb.   Where have you hid yourself ?
How have you known the miseries of your
    father ?   180
    Edg. By nursing them, my lord. List a
    brief tale ;
And when 'tis told, O that my heart would
    burst !
The bloody proclamation to escape
That follow'd me so near—O our lives'
    sweetness,   184
That we the pain of death would hourly die
Rather than die at once !—taught me to
    shift
Into a madman's rags, t' assume a
    semblance
That very dogs disdain'd ; and in this habit
Met I my father with his bleeding rings,
Their precious stones new lost ; became his
    guide,   190
Led him, begg'd for him, sav'd him from
    despair ;
Never—O fault !—reveal'd myself unto him
Until some half-hour past, when I was
    arm'd ;
Not sure, though hoping, of this good
    success,
I ask'd his blessing, and from first to last
Told him my pilgrimage. But his flaw'd
    heart—   196
Alack, too weak the conflict to support !—
'Twixt two extremes of passion, joy and
    grief,
Burst smilingly.
    Edm. This speech of yours hath mov'd
    me,
And shall perchance do good ; but speak
    you on ;   200
You look as you had something more to say.
    Alb. If there be more, more woeful, hold
    it in ;
For I am almost ready to dissolve,
Hearing of this.

    Edg.   This would have seem'd a period
To such as love not sorrow ; but another,
To amplify too much, would make much
    more,   206
And top extremity.
Whilst I was big in clamour, came there in
    a man
Who, having seen me in my worst estate,
Shunn'd my abhorr'd society ; but then,
    finding   210
Who 'twas that so endur'd, with his strong
    arms
He fastened on my neck and bellowed out
As he'd burst heaven ; threw him on my
    father ;
Told the most piteous tale of Lear and him
That ever ear receiv'd ; which in recounting
His grief grew puissant, and the strings of
    life   216
Began to crack. Twice then the trumpets
    sounded
And there I left him tranc'd.
    Alb.   But who was this ?
    Edg. Kent, sir, the banish'd Kent, who
    in disguise
Follow'd his enemy king, and did him
    service   220
Improper for a slave.

Enter a Gentleman *with a bloody knife.*

    Gent. Help, help, O, help !
    Edg.   What kind of help ?
    Alb.   Speak, man.
    Edg. What means this bloody knife ?
    Gent.   'Tis hot, it smokes ;
It came even from the heart of—O, she's
    dead !
    Alb. Who dead ? Speak, man.   225
    Gent. Your lady, sir, your lady ! and her
    sister
By her is poison'd ; she confesses it.
    Edm. I was contracted to them both. All
    three
Now marry in an instant.
    Edg.   Here comes Kent.

Enter KENT.

    Alb. Produce the bodies, be they alive or
    dead.   [*Exit Gentleman.* 230
This judgment of the heavens, that makes
    us tremble,
Touches us not with pity.   O, is this he ?
The time will not allow the compliment
Which very manners urges.
    Kent.   I am come
To bid my king and master aye good night.
Is he not here ?
    Alb.   Great thing of us forgot !
Speak, Edmund, where's the King ? and
    where's Cordelia ? [*The bodies of
    Goneril and Regan are brought in.*
See'st thou this object, Kent ?
    Kent. Alack, why thus ?
    Edm.   Yet Edmund was belov'd.

The one the other poison'd for my sake, 240
And after slew herself.

Alb. Even so. Cover their faces.

Edm. I pant for life. Some good I mean
    to do,
Despite of mine own nature. Quickly
    send—
Be brief in it—to th' castle ; for my writ
Is on the life of Lear and on Cordelia. 246
Nay, send in time.

Alb.   Run, run, O, run !

Edg. To who, my lord ? Who has the
    office ? Send
Thy token of reprieve. 249

Edm. Well thought on. Take my sword ;
Give it the Captain.

Alb.   Haste thee, for thy life.
                [*Exit Edgar.*

Edm. He hath commission from thy wife
    and me
To hang Cordelia in the prison, and
To lay the blame upon her own despair,
That she fordid herself. 255

Alb. The gods defend her ! Bear him
    hence awhile. [*Edmund is borne off.*

Enter LEAR, *with* CORDELIA *dead in his
arms* ; EDGAR, Captain, *and* Others
following.

Lear. Howl, howl, howl, howl ! O, you
    are men of stones !
Had I your tongues and eyes, I'd use them
    so
That heaven's vault should crack. She's
    gone for ever.
I know when one is dead and when one
    lives ; 260
She's dead as earth. Lend me a looking-
    glass ;
If that her breath will mist or stain the
    stone,
Why, then she lives.

Kent.   Is this the promis'd end ?

Edg. Or image of that horror ?

Alb.   Fall and cease !

Lear. This feather stirs ; she lives. If it
    be so, 265
It is a chance which does redeem all sorrows
That ever I have felt.

Kent. O my good master ! [*Kneeling.*

Lear. Prithee away.

Edg.   'Tis noble Kent, your friend.

Lear. A plague upon you, murderers,
    traitors all !
I might have sav'd her ; now she's gone for
    ever.
Cordelia, Cordelia ! stay a little. Ha ! 270
What is't thou say'st ? Her voice was ever
    soft,
Gentle, and low—an excellent thing in
    woman.
I kill'd the slave that was a-hanging thee.

Capt. 'Tis true, my lords, he did.

Lear.   Did I not, fellow ?

I have seen the day, with my good biting
    falchion, 276
I would have made them skip : I am old
    now,
And these same crosses spoil me. Who are
    you ?
Mine eyes are not o' th' best. I'll tell you
    straight.

Kent. If fortune brag of two she lov'd and
    hated, 280
One of them we behold.

Lear. This is a dull sight. Are you not
    Kent ?

Kent.   The same—
Your servant Kent. Where is your servant
    Caius ?

Lear. He's a good fellow, I can tell you
    that ;
He'll strike, and quickly too. He's dead and
    rotten. 285

Kent. No, my good lord ; I am the very
    man—

Lear. I'll see that straight.

Kent. That from your first of difference
    and decay
Have follow'd your sad steps.

Lear.   You are welcome hither.

Kent. Nor no man else ! All's cheerless,
    dark, and deadly. 290
Your eldest daughters have fordone them-
    selves
And desperately are dead.

Lear.   Ay, so I think.

Alb. He knows not what he says ; and
    vain is it
That we present us to him.

Edg.   Very bootless. 294

Enter a Messenger.

Mess. Edmund is dead, my lord.

Alb.   That's but a trifle here.
You lords and noble friends, know our
    intent.
What comfort to this great decay may come
Shall be applied. For us, we will resign
During the life of this old Majesty,
To him our absolute power. [*To Edgar and
    Kent*] You to your rights ; 300
With boot, and such addition as your
    honours
Have more than merited. All friends shall
    taste
The wages of their virtue, and all foes
The cup of their deservings. O, see, see !

Lear. And my poor fool is hang'd ! No,
    no, no life ! 305
Why should a dog, a horse, a rat have life,
And thou no breath at all ? Thou'lt come
    no more,
Never, never, never, never, never.
Pray you undo this button. Thank you, sir.
Do you see this ? Look on her. Look, her
    lips. 310
Look there, look there !   [*He dies.*

Edg.   He faints. My lord, my lord !
Kent. Break, heart ; I prithee break.
Edg.   Look up, my lord,
Kent. Vex not his ghost. O, let him pass !
    He hates him
That would upon the rack of this tough
    world
Stretch him out longer.
Edg.   He is gone indeed. 315
Kent. The wonder is he hath endur'd so
    long :
He but usurp'd his life.
Alb. Bear them from hence. Our present
    business

Is general woe. [*To Kent and Edgar*] Friends
    of my soul, you twain
Rule in this realm and the gor'd state
    sustain.   320
    Kent. I have a journey, sir, shortly to go.
My master calls me ; I must not say no.
    Edg. The weight of this sad time we must
        obey ;
Speak what we feel, not what we ought to
    say.
The oldest hath borne most ; we that are
    young   325
Shall never see so much nor live so long.
                            [*Exeunt with a dead march.*

OTHELLO, THE MOOR OF VENICE

DRAMATIS PERSONÆ

DUKE OF VENICE.
BRABANTIO, *a Senator, father to Desdemona.*
Other Senators.
GRATIANO, *brother to Brabantio,* } *two noble Venetians.*
LODOVICO, *kinsman to Brabantio,*
OTHELLO, *the Moor, in the service of Venice.*
CASSIO, *his honourable Lieutenant.*
IAGO, *his Ancient, a villain.*
RODERIGO, *a gull'd Venetian gentleman.*

MONTANO, *Governor of Cyprus, before Othello.*
Clown, *servant to Othello.*
DESDEMONA, *daughter to Brabantio, and wife to Othello.*
EMILIA, *wife to Iago.*
BIANCA, *a courtezan, in love with Cassio.*
Gentlemen of Cyprus, Sailors, Officers, Messenger, Musicians, Herald, Attendants, &c.

THE SCENE: *Venice ; Cyprus.*

ACT ONE

SCENE I. *Venice. A street.*

Enter RODERIGO *and* IAGO.

Rod. Tush, never tell me ; I take it much
    unkindly
That you, Iago, who has had my purse
As if the strings were thine, shouldst know
    of this.
Iago. 'Sblood, but you will not hear me.
If ever I did dream of such a matter,   5
Abhor me.
    Rod. Thou told'st me thou didst hold him
    in thy hate.
    Iago. Despise me if I do not. Three great
    ones of the city,
In personal suit to make me his lieutenant,
Off-capp'd to him ; and, by the faith of
    man,   10
I know my price, I am worth no worse a
    place.
But he, as loving his own pride and
    purposes,
Evades them with a bombast circumstance
Horribly stuff'd with epithets of war ;
And, in conclusion,   15
Nonsuits my mediators ; 'For, certes,' says
    he
' I have already chose my officer'.
And what was he ?
Forsooth, a great arithmetician,
One Michael Cassio, a Florentine,   20
A fellow almost damn'd in a fair wife,
That never set a squadron in the field,
Nor the division of a battle knows
More than a spinster ; unless the bookish
    theoric,
Wherein the toged consuls can propose 25
As masterly as he—mere prattle, without
    practice,
Is all his soldiership. But he, sir, had the
    election ;

And I, of whom his eyes had seen the proof
At Rhodes, at Cyprus, and on other
    grounds,
Christian and heathen, must be be-lee'd
    and calm'd   30
By debitor and creditor—this counter-
    caster,
He, in good time, must his lieutenant be,
And I, God bless the mark! his Moorship's
    ancient.
    Rod. By heaven, I rather would have
    been his hangman !
    Iago. Why, there's no remedy ; 'tis the
    curse of service: 35
Preferment goes by letter and affection,
Not by the old gradation, where each
    second
Stood heir to the first. Now, sir, be judge
    yourself
Whether I in any just term am affin'd
To love the Moor.
    Rod.   I would not follow him, then.
    Iago. O, sir, content you.   41
I follow him to serve my turn upon him :
We cannot all be masters, nor all masters
Cannot be truly follow'd. You shall mark
Many a duteous and knee-crooking knave
That, doting on his own obsequious
    bondage,   46
Wears out his time, much like his master's
    ass,
For nought but provender ; and when he's
    old, cashier'd.
Whip me such honest knaves. Others there
    are
Who, trimm'd in forms and visages of
    duty,
Keep yet their hearts attending on them-
    selves ;   51
And, throwing but shows of service on
    their lords,
Do well thrive by 'em and, when they have
    lin'd their coats,

Do themselves homage—these fellows have
    some soul ;
And such a one do I profess myself.   55
For, sir,
It is as sure as you are Roderigo,
Were I the Moor, I would not be Iago.
In following him I follow but myself—
Heaven is my judge, not I for love and
    duty,   60
But seeming so for my peculiar end.
For when my outward action doth demon-
    strate
The native act and figure of my heart
In compliment extern, 'tis not long after
But I will wear my heart upon my sleeve 65
For daws to peck at : I am not what I am.
    Rod. What a full fortune does the thick-
    lips owe,
If he can carry't thus !
    Iago.   Call up her father.
Rouse him, make after him, poison his
    delight,
Proclaim him in the streets ; incense her
    kinsmen,   70
And, though he in a fertile climate dwell,
Plague him with flies ; though that his joy
    be joy,
Yet throw such changes of vexation on't
As it may lose some colour.
    Rod. Here is her father's house. I'll call
    aloud.   75
    Iago. Do, with like timorous accent and
    dire yell
As when, by night and negligence, the fire
Is spied in populous cities.
    Rod. What, ho, Brabantio ! Signior
    Brabantio, ho !
    Iago. Awake ! What, ho, Brabantio !
    Thieves, thieves, thieves !   80
Look to your house, your daughter, and
    your bags.
Thieves ! thieves !

    BRABANTIO *appears above at a window.*

    Bra. What is the reason of this terrible
    summons ?
What is the matter there ?   84
    Rod. Signior, is all your family within ?
    Iago. Are your doors lock'd ?
    Bra.   Why, wherefore ask you this ?
    Iago. Zounds, sir, you're robb'd ; for
    shame, put on your gown ;
Your heart is burst ; you have lost half
    your soul.
Even now, very now, an old black ram
Is tupping your white ewe. Arise, arise ; 90
Awake the snorting citizens with the bell,
Or else the devil will make a grandsire of
    you.
Arise, I say.
    Bra.   What, have you lost your wits ?
    Rod. Most reverend signior, do you know
    my voice ?
    Bra. Not I ; what are you ?   95

    Rod. My name is Roderigo.
    Bra.   The worser welcome !
I have charg'd thee not to haunt about my
    doors ;
In honest plainness thou hast heard me say
My daughter is not for thee ; and now, in
    madness,
Being full of supper and distempering
    draughts,   100
Upon malicious bravery dost thou come
To start my quiet.
    Rod. Sir, sir, sir—
    Bra.   But thou must needs be sure
My spirit and my place have in their power
To make this bitter to thee.
    Rod.   Patience, good sir.
    Bra. What tell'st thou me of robbing ?
    This is Venice ;   106
My house is not a grange.
    Rod.   Most grave Brabantio,
In simple and pure soul I come to you. 108
    Iago. Zounds, sir, you are one of those
that will not serve God if the devil bid you.
Because we come to do you service, and
you think we are ruffians, you'll have your
daughter cover'd with a Barbary horse ;
you'll have your nephews neigh to you ;
you'll have coursers for cousins and gennets
for germans.
    Bra. What profane wretch art thou ? 115
    Iago. I am one, sir, that comes to tell you
your daughter and the Moor are now
making the beast with two backs.
    Bra. Thou art a villain.
    Iago.   You are—a Senator.
    Bra. This thou shalt answer ; I know
    thee, Roderigo.   120
    Rod. Sir, I will answer anything. But I
    beseech you,
If't be your pleasure and most wise con-
    sent—
As partly I find it is—that your fair
    daughter,
At this odd-even and dull watch o' th'
    night,
Transported with no worse nor better
    guard   125
But with a knave of common hire, a
    gondolier,
To the gross clasps of a lascivious Moor—
If this be known to you, and your allowance,
We then have done you bold and saucy
    wrongs ;
But if you know not this, my manners tell
    me   130
We have your wrong rebuke. Do not
    believe
That, from the sense of all civility,
I thus would play and trifle with your
    reverence.
Your daughter, if you have not given her
    leave,
I say again, hath made a gross revolt ; 135
Tying her duty, beauty, wit, and fortunes,

In an extravagant and wheeling stranger
Of here and everywhere. Straight satisfy
    yourself.
If she be in her chamber or your house,
Let loose on me the justice of the state 140
For thus deluding you.
  Bra. Strike on the tinder, ho !
Give me a taper ; call up all my people.
This accident is not unlike my dream.
Belief of it oppresses me already.
Light, I say ; light !   [*Exit from above.*
  Iago.   Farewell ; for I must leave you.
It seems not meet nor wholesome to my
    place 146
To be producted—as if I stay I shall—
Against the Moor ; for I do know the state,
However this may gall him with some
    check,
Cannot with safety cast him ; for he's
    embark'd 150
With such loud reason to the Cyprus wars,
Which even now stands in act, that, for
    their souls,
Another of his fathom they have none
To lead their business ; in which regard,
Though I do hate him as I do hell pains, 155
Yet, for necessity of present life,
I must show out a flag and sign of love,
Which is indeed but sign. That you shall
    surely find him,
Lead to the Sagittary the raised search ; 159
And there will I be with him. So, farewell.
    [*Exit.*

Enter below, BRABANTIO, *in his night gown,
and* Servants *with torches.*

  Bra. It is too true an evil. Gone she is ;
And what's to come of my despised time
Is nought but bitterness. Now, Roderigo,
Where didst thou see her ?—O unhappy
    girl !—
With the Moor, say'st thou ?—Who would
    be a father ?— 165
How didst thou know 'twas she ?—O, thou
    deceivest me
Past thought !—What said she to you ?—
    Get moe tapers ;
Raise all my kindred.—Are they married
    think you ?
  Rod. Truly, I think they are.
  Bra. O heaven ! How got she out ? O
    treason of the blood ! 170
Fathers, from hence trust not your
    daughters' minds
By what you see them act. Is there not
    charms
By which the property of youth and maid-
    hood
May be abus'd ? Have you not read,
    Roderigo,
Of some such thing ?
  Rod.   Yes, sir, I have indeed. 175
  Bra. Call up my brother.—O that you
    had had her !—

Some one way, some another.—Do you
    know
Where we may apprehend her and the
    Moor ?
  Rod. I think I can discover him, if you
    please 179
To get good guard, and go along with me.
  Bra. Pray lead me on. At every house
    I'll call ;
I may command at most.—Get weapons,
    ho !
And raise some special officers of night.—
On, good Roderigo ; I'll deserve your pains.
    [*Exeunt.*

SCENE II. *Venice. Another street.*

Enter OTHELLO, IAGO, *and* Attendants *with
torches.*

  Iago. Though in the trade of war I have
    slain men,
Yet do I hold it very stuff o' th' conscience
To do no contriv'd murder. I lack iniquity
Sometime to do me service. Nine or ten
    times
I had thought to have yerk'd him here
    under the ribs. 5
  Oth. 'Tis better as it is.
  Iago.   Nay, but he prated,
And spoke such scurvy and provoking terms
Against your honour
That, with the little godliness I have,
I did full hard forbear him. But I pray,
    sir, 10
Are you fast married ? For be assur'd of
    this,
That the magnifico is much beloved,
And hath in his effect a voice potential
As double as the Duke's. He will divorce
    you,
Or put upon you what restraint and
    grievance 15
That law, with all his might to enforce it on,
Will give him cable.
  Oth.   Let him do his spite.
My services which I have done the signiory
Shall out-tongue his complaints. 'Tis yet
    to know—
Which, when I know that boasting is an
    honour, 20
I shall promulgate—I fetch my life and
    being
From men of royal siege ; and my demerits
May speak unbonneted to as proud a
    fortune
As this that I have reach'd. For know,
    Iago,
But that I love the gentle Desdemona, 25
I would not my unhoused free condition
Put into circumscription and confine
For the seas' worth.

Enter CASSIO *and* Officers *with torches.*

    But look what lights come yonder.

Iago. Those are the raised father and his friends.

You were best go in.

Oth.   Not I; I must be found.
My parts, my title, and my perfect soul 31
Shall manifest me rightly. Is it they?

Iago. By Janus, I think no.

Oth. The servants of the Duke and my lieutenant—

The goodness of the night upon you, friends!   35
What is the news?

Cas. The Duke does greet you, General;
And he requires your haste-post-haste appearance
Even on the instant.

Oth.   What is the matter, think you?

Cas. Something from Cyprus, as I may divine.
It is a business of some heat: the galleys 40
Have sent a dozen sequent messengers
This very night at one another's heels;
And many of the consuls, rais'd and met,
Are at the Duke's already. You have been hotly call'd for;
When, being not at your lodging to be found,   45
The Senate hath sent about three several quests
To search you out.

Oth.   'Tis well I am found by you.
I will but spend a word here in the house,
And go with you.   [*Exit.*

Cas. Ancient, what makes he here?

Iago. Faith, he to-night hath boarded a land carrack.   50
If it prove lawful prize, he's made for ever.

Cas. I do not understand.

Iago.   He's married.

Cas.   To who?

Re-enter OTHELLO.

Iago. Marry, to—Come, Captain, will you go?

Oth. Have with you.

Enter BRABANTIO, RODERIGO, *and* Officers *with torches and weapons.*

Cas. Here comes another troop to seek for you.

Iago. It is Brabantio. General, be advis'd;   55
He comes to bad intent.

Oth.   Holla! stand there.

Rod. Signior, it is the Moor.

Bra.   Down with him, thief.
              [*They draw on both sides.*

Iago. You, Roderigo; come, sir, I am for you.

Oth. Keep up your bright swords, for the dew will rust them.

Good signior, you shall more command with years   60
Than with your weapons.

Bra. O thou foul thief, where hast thou stow'd my daughter?
Damn'd as thou art, thou hast enchanted her;
For I'll refer me to all things of sense,
If she in chains of magic were not bound, 65
Whether a maid so tender, fair, and happy,
So opposite to marriage that she shunn'd
The wealthy curled darlings of our nation,
Would ever have, to incur a general mock,
Run from her guardage to the sooty bosom
Of such a thing as thou—to fear, not to delight.   71
Judge me the world, if 'tis not gross in sense
That thou hast practis'd on her with foul charms,
Abus'd her delicate youth with drugs or minerals
That weakens motion. I'll have't disputed on;   75
'Tis probable, and palpable to thinking.
I therefore apprehend and do attach thee
For an abuser of the world, a practiser
Of arts inhibited and out of warrant.
Lay hold upon him. If he do resist, 80
Subdue him at his peril.

Oth.   Hold your hands,
Both you of my inclining and the rest.
Were it my cue to fight, I should have known it
Without a prompter. Where will you that I go
To answer this your charge?

Bra.   To prison; till fit time
Of law and course of direct session 86
Call thee to answer.

Oth.   What if I do obey?
How may the Duke be therewith satisfied,
Whose messengers are here about my side,
Upon some present business of the state, 90
To bring me to him.

1 Off. 'Tis true, most worthy signior;
The Duke's in council, and your noble self,
I am sure, is sent for.

Bra.   How! The Duke in council!
In this time of the night! Bring him away.
Mine's not an idle cause. The Duke himself,
Or any of my brothers of the state, 96
Cannot but feel this wrong as 'twere their own;
For if such actions may have passage free,
Bond-slaves and pagans shall our statesmen be.   [*Exeunt.*

SCENE III. *Venice. A council-chamber.*

Enter DUKE *and* Senators, *set at a table with lights; and* Attendants.

Duke. There is no composition in these news
That gives them credit.

1 Sen. Indeed, they are disproportion'd;
My letters say a hundred and seven galleys.

Duke. And mine a hundred and forty.
2 *Sen.* And mine two hundred.
But though they jump not on a just
account— 5
As in these cases, where the aim reports,
'Tis oft with difference—yet do they all
confirm
A Turkish fleet, and bearing up to Cyprus.
Duke. Nay, it is possible enough to
judgment.
I do not so secure me in the error 10
But the main article I do approve
In fearful sense.
Sailor. [*Within*] What, ho! what, ho!
what, ho!

Enter Sailor.

Officer. A messenger from the galleys.
Duke. Now, what's the business?
Sail. The Turkish preparation makes for
Rhodes;
So was I bid report here to the state 15
By Signior Angelo.
Duke. How say you by this change?
1 *Sen.* This cannot be,
By no assay of reason. 'Tis a pageant
To keep us in false gaze. When we consider
The importancy of Cyprus to the Turk, 20
And let ourselves again but understand
That as it more concerns the Turk than
Rhodes,
So may he with more facile question bear
it,
For that it stands not in such warlike brace,
But altogether lacks th' abilities 25
That Rhodes is dress'd in—if we make
thought of this,
We must not think the Turk is so unskilful
To leave that latest which concerns him
first,
Neglecting an attempt of ease and gain
To wake and wage a danger profitless. 30
Duke. Nay, in all confidence, he's not for
Rhodes.
Officer. Here is more news.

Enter a Messenger.

Mess. The Ottomites, reverend and
gracious,
Steering with due course toward the isle of
Rhodes,
Have there injointed them with an after
fleet. 35
1 *Sen.* Ay, so I thought. How many, as
you guess?
Mess. Of thirty sail; and now they do
restem
Their backward course, bearing with frank
appearance
Their purposes toward Cyprus. Signior
Montano,
Your trusty and most valiant servitor, 40
With his free duty recommends you thus,
And prays you to believe him.

Duke. 'Tis certain, then, for Cyprus.
Marcus Lucchese, is not he in town?
1 *Sen.* He's now in Florence. 45
Duke. Write from us: wish him post-
post-haste dispatch.

Enter BRABANTIO, OTHELLO, IAGO,
RODERIGO, *and* Officers.

1 *Sen.* Here comes Brabantio and the
valiant Moor.
Duke. Valiant Othello, we must straight
employ you
Against the general enemy Ottoman.
[*To Brabantio*] I did not see you; welcome,
gentle signior; 50
We lack'd your counsel and your help to-
night.
Bra. So did I yours. Good your Grace,
pardon me:
Neither my place, nor aught I heard of
business,
Hath rais'd me from my bed; nor doth the
general care 54
Take hold on me; for my particular grief
Is of so flood-gate and o'erbearing nature
That it engluts and swallows other sorrows,
And it is still itself.
Duke. Why, what's the matter?
Bra. My daughter! O, my daughter!
All. Dead?
Bra. Ay, to me.
She is abus'd, stol'n from me, and cor-
rupted, 60
By spells and medicines bought of mounte-
banks;
For nature so preposterously to err,
Being not deficient, blind, or lame of sense,
Sans witchcraft could not.
Duke. Whoe'er he be that in this foul
proceeding 65
Hath thus beguil'd your daughter of herself,
And you of her, the bloody book of law
You shall yourself read in the bitter letter
After your own sense; yea, though our
proper son
Stood in your action.
Bra. Humbly I thank your Grace.
Here is the man—this Moor whom now, it
seems, 71
Your special mandate for the state affairs
Hath hither brought.
All. We are very sorry for't.
Duke. [*To Othello*] What, in your own
part, can you say to this?
Bra. Nothing, but this is so. 75
Oth. Most potent, grave, and reverend
signiors,
My very noble and approv'd good masters:
That I have ta'en away this old man's
daughter,
It is most true; true, I have married her—
The very head and front of my offending 80
Hath this extent, no more. Rude am I in
my speech,

And little blest with the soft phrase of
    peace ;
For since these arms of mine had seven
    years' pith,
Till now some nine moons wasted, they
    have us'd
Their dearest action in the tented field ; 85
And little of this great world can I speak
More than pertains to feats of broil and
    battle ;
And therefore little shall I grace my cause
In speaking for myself.   Yet, by your
    gracious patience,
I will a round unvarnish'd tale deliver 90
Of my whole course of love—what drugs,
    what charms,
What conjuration, and what mighty magic,
For such proceedings am I charg'd withal,
I won his daughter.
    Bra.   A maiden never bold,
Of spirit so still and quiet that her motion
Blush'd at herself ; and she—in spite of
    nature,   96
Of years, of country, credit, every thing—
To fall in love with what she fear'd to look
    on !
It is a judgment maim'd and most im-
    perfect
That will confess perfection so could err 100
Against all rules of nature, and must be
    driven
To find out practices of cunning hell,
Why this should be.   I therefore vouch
    again
That with some mixtures powerful o'er the
    blood,   104
Or with some dram conjur'd to this effect,
He wrought upon her.
    Duke.   To vouch this is no proof—
Without more wider and more overt test
Than these thin habits and poor likelihoods
Of modern seeming do prefer against him.
    1 Sen. But, Othello, speak.   110
Did you by indirect and forced courses
Subdue and poison this young maid's
    affections ?
Or came it by request, and such fair
    question
As soul to soul affordeth ?
    Oth.   I do beseech you,
Send for the lady to the Sagittary,   115
And let her speak of me before her father.
If you do find me foul in her report,
The trust, the office, I do hold of you
Not only take away, but let your sentence
Even fall upon my life.
    Duke.   Fetch Desdemona hither. 120
    Oth. Ancient, conduct them ; you best
    know the place.
        [Exeunt Iago and Attendants.
And, till she come, as faithful as to heaven
I do confess the vices of my blood,
So justly to your grave ears I'll present
How I did thrive in this fair lady's love, 125

And she in mine.
    Duke. Say it, Othello.
    Oth. Her father lov'd me, oft invited me ;
Still question'd me the story of my life
From year to year—the battles, sieges,
    fortunes,   130
That I have pass'd.
I ran it through, even from my boyish days
To th' very moment that he bade me tell it ;
Wherein I spake of most disastrous chances,
Of moving accidents by flood and field ; 135
Of hairbreadth scapes · i' th' imminent
    deadly breach ;
Of being taken by the insolent foe
And sold to slavery ; of my redemption
    thence,
And portance in my travel's history ;
Wherein of antres vast and deserts idle, 140
Rough quarries, rocks, and hills whose
    heads touch heaven,
It was my hint to speak—such was the
    process ;
And of the Cannibals that each other eat,
The Anthropophagi, and men whose heads
Do grow beneath their shoulders.   This to
    hear   145
Would Desdemona seriously incline ;
But still the house affairs would draw her
    thence ;
Which ever as she could with haste
    dispatch,
She'd come again, and with a greedy ear
Devour up my discourse.   Which I observ-
    ing,   150
Took once a pliant hour, and found good
    means
To draw from her a prayer of earnest heart
That I would all my pilgrimage dilate,
Whereof by parcels she had something
    heard,
But not intentively.   I did consent,   155
And often did beguile her of her tears,
When I did speak of some distressful stroke
That my youth suffer'd.   My story being
    done,
She gave me for my pains a world of
    sighs ;
She swore, in faith, 'twas strange, 'twas
    passing strange ;   160
'Twas pitiful, 'twas wondrous pitiful.
She wish'd she had not heard it ; yet she
    wish'd
That heaven had made her such a man. She
    thank'd me ;
And bade me, if I had a friend that lov'd
    her,
I should but teach him how to tell my
    story,   165
And that would woo her.   Upon this hint
    I spake ;
She lov'd me for the dangers I had pass'd ;
And I lov'd her that she did pity them.
This only is the witchcraft I have us'd.
Here comes the lady ; let her witness it. 170

Enter DESDEMONA, IAGO, *and* Attendants.

Duke. I think this tale would win my
   daughter too.
Good Brabantio,
Take up this mangled matter at the best.
Men do their broken weapons rather use
Than their bare hands.
Bra.   I pray you hear her speak.
If she confess that she was half the wooer,
Destruction on my head if my bad blame
Light on the man! Come hither, gentle
   mistress.   178
Do you perceive in all this noble company
Where most you owe obedience?
Des.   My noble father,
I do perceive here a divided duty: 181
To you I am bound for life and education;
My life and education both do learn me
How to respect you; you are the lord of
   duty—
I am hitherto your daughter; but here's
   my husband,   185
And so much duty as my mother show'd
To you, preferring you before her father,
So much I challenge that I may profess
Due to the Moor, my lord.
Bra.   God bu'y, I ha done.
Please it your Grace, on to the state
   affairs—   190
I had rather to adopt a child than get it.
Come hither, Moor:
I here do give thee that with all my
   heart
Which, but thou hast already, with all my
   heart
I would keep from thee. For your sake,
   jewel,   195
I am glad at soul I have no other child;
For thy escape would teach me tyranny,
To hang clogs on them. I have done, my
   lord.
Duke. Let me speak like yourself, and lay
   a sentence
Which, as a grise or step, may help these
   lovers   200
Into your favour.
When remedies are past, the griefs are
   ended
By seeing the worst, which late on hopes
   depended.
To mourn a mischief that is past and gone
Is the next way to draw new mischief on.
What cannot be preserv'd when fortune
   takes,   206
Patience her injury a mockery makes.
The robb'd that smiles steals something
   from the thief;
He robs himself that spends a bootless
   grief.
Bra. So let the Turk of Cyprus us beguile:
We lose it not so long as we can smile.   211
He bears the sentence well that nothing
   bears

But the free comfort which from thence he
   hears;
But he bears both the sentence and the
   sorrow
That to pay grief must of poor patience
   borrow.   215
These sentences, to sugar or to gall,
Being strong on both sides, are equivocal.
But words are words: I never yet did hear
That the bruis'd heart was pierced through
   the ear.
I humbly beseech you proceed to th' affairs
of state.   220
Duke. The Turk with a most mighty
preparation makes for Cyprus. Othello, the
fortitude of the place is best known to you;
and though we have there a substitute of
most allowed sufficiency, yet opinion, a
sovereign mistress of effects, throws a more
safer voice on you. You must therefore be
content to slubber the gloss of your new
fortunes with this more stubborn and
boisterous expedition.
Oth. The tyrant custom, most grave
   senators,
Hath made the flinty and steel couch of
   war   230
My thrice-driven bed of down. I do agnize
A natural and prompt alacrity
I find in hardness; and would undertake
This present wars against the Ottomites.
Most humbly, therefore, bending to your
   state,   235
I crave fit disposition for my wife;
Due reference of place and exhibition;
With such accommodation and besort
As levels with her breeding.
Duke.   If you please,
Be't at her father's.
Bra.   I'll not have it so.   240
Oth. Nor I.
Des.   Nor I. I would not there reside,
To put my father in impatient thoughts
By being in his eye. Most gracious Duke,
To my unfolding lend your prosperous ear,
And let me find a charter in your voice 245
T' assist my simpleness.
Duke. What would you, Desdemona?
Des. That I did love the Moor to live
   with him,
My downright violence and storm of
   fortunes
May trumpet to the world. My heart's
   subdu'd   250
Even to the very quality of my lord:
I saw Othello's visage in his mind;
And to his honours and his valiant parts
Did I my soul and fortunes consecrate.
So that, dear lords, if I be left behind,   255
A moth of peace, and he go to the war,
The rites for why I love him are bereft me,
And I a heavy interim shall support
By his dear absence. Let me go with him.
Oth. Let her have your voice.

Vouch with me, heaven, I therefore beg
    it not
To please the palate of my appetite ;
Nor to comply with heat—the young affects
In me defunct—and proper satisfaction ;
But to be free and bounteous to her
    mind.
And heaven defend your good souls that
    you think   266
I will your serious and great business
    scant
For she is with me. No, when light-wing'd
    toys
Of feather'd Cupid seel with wanton dull-
    ness
My speculative and offic'd instruments, 270
That my disports corrupt and taint my
    business,
Let huswives make a skillet of my helm,
And all indign and base adversities
Make head against my estimation !
    Duke. Be it as you shall privately
        determine,   275
Either for her stay or going. Th' affair cries
    haste,
And speed must answer it. You must away
    to-night.
    Des. To-night, my lord !
    Duke.   This night.
    Oth.   With all my heart.
    Duke. At nine i' th' morning here we'll
        meet again.
Othello, leave some officer behind,   280
And he shall our commission bring to
    you ;
With such things else of quality and respect
As doth import you.
    Oth. So please your Grace, my ancient ;
A man he is of honesty and trust.
To his conveyance I assign my wife, 285
With what else needful your good Grace
    shall think
To be sent after me.
    Duke.   Let it be so.
Good night to every one. [*To Brabantio*]
    And, noble signior,
If virtue no delighted beauty lack,   289
Your son-in-law is far more fair than black.
    1 *Sen.* Adieu, brave Moor ; use Desde-
        mona well.
    Bra. Look to her, Moor, if thou hast eyes
        to see :
She has deceiv'd her father, and may thee.
        [*Exeunt Duke, Senators, Officers, &c.*
    Oth. My life upon her faith !—Honest
    Iago,
My Desdemona must I leave to thee.   295
I prithee let thy wife attend on her ;
And bring them after in the best advantage.
Come, Desdemona, I have but an hour
Of love, of worldly matter and direction,
To spend with thee. We must obey the
    time.   300
        [*Exeunt Othello and Desdemona.*

    Rod. Iago !
    Iago. What say'st thou, noble heart ?
    Rod. What will I do, thinkest thou ?
    Iago. Why, go to bed and sleep.   304
    Rod. I will incontinently drown myself.
    Iago. Well, if thou dost, I shall never love
thee after it. Why, thou silly gentleman !
    Rod. It is silliness to live when to live is
torment ; and then have we a prescription
to die when death is our physician.   310
    Iago. O villainous ! I ha look'd upon the
world for four times seven years ; and since
I could distinguish betwixt a benefit and
an injury, I never found a man that knew
how to love himself. Ere I would say I
would drown myself for the love of a
guinea-hen, I would change my humanity
with a baboon.   316
    Rod. What should I do ? I confess it is
my shame to be so fond, but it is not in my
virtue to amend it.
    Iago. Virtue ? A fig ! 'Tis in ourselves
that we are thus or thus. Our bodies are our
gardens to the which our wills are gardeners ; so that if we will plant nettles or
sow lettuce, set hyssop and weed up thyme,
supply it with one gender of herbs or
distract it with many, either to have it
sterile with idleness or manur'd with industry—why, the power and corrigible
authority of this lies in our wills. If the
balance of our lives had not one scale of
reason to poise another of sensuality, the
blood and baseness of our natures would
conduct us to most preposterous conclusions. But we have reason to cool our
raging motions, our carnal stings, our un-
bitted lusts ; whereof I take this that you
call love to be a sect or scion.
    Rod. It cannot be.   332
    Iago. It is merely a lust of the blood and
a permission of the will. Come, be a man.
Drown thyself ? Drown cats and blind
puppies ! I have profess'd me thy friend,
and I confess me knit to thy deserving with
cables of perdurable toughness. I could
never better stead thee than now. Put
money in thy purse ; follow thou the wars ;
defeat thy favour with an usurp'd beard.
I say, put money in thy purse. It cannot
be long that Desdemona should continue
her love to the Moor—put money in thy
purse—nor he his to her : it was a violent
commencement in her, and thou shalt see an
answerable sequestration—put but money
in thy purse. These Moors are changeable
in their wills—fill thy purse with money.
The food that to him now is as luscious as
locusts shall be to him shortly as acerbe as
the coloquintida. She must change for
youth ; when she is sated with his body, she
will find the error of her choice. Therefore
put money in thy purse. If thou wilt needs
damn thyself, do it a more delicate way

than drowning. Make all the money thou
canst. If sanctimony and a frail vow
betwixt an erring barbarian and a super-
subtle Venetian be not too hard for my
wits and all the tribe of hell, thou shalt
enjoy her ; therefore make money. A pox
a drowning thyself ! 'Tis clean out of the
way. Seek thou rather to be hang'd in
compassing thy joy than to be drown'd
and go without her.

   Rod. Wilt thou be fast to my hopes, if I
depend on the issue ? 360

   Iago. Thou art sure of me—go make
money. I have told thee often, and I retell
thee again and again I hate the Moor.
My cause is hearted : thine hath no less
reason. Let us be conjunctive in our
revenge against him. If thou canst cuckold
him, thou dost thyself a pleasure, me a
sport. There are many events in the womb
of time which will be delivered. Traverse ;
go ; provide thy money. We will have more
of this to-morrow. Adieu. 369

   Rod. Where shall we meet i' th' morning ?

   Iago. At my lodging.

   Rod. I'll be with thee betimes.

   Iago. Go to ; farewell. Do you hear,
Roderigo ?

   Rod. What say you ? 374

   Iago. No more of drowning, do you hear ?

   Rod. I am chang'd.

   Iago. Go to ; farewell. Put money
enough in your purse.

   Rod. I'll sell all my land. [*Exit Roderigo.*

   Iago. Thus do I ever make my fool my
    purse ;
For I mine own gain'd knowledge should
    profane
If I would time expend with such a snipe
But for my sport and profit. I hate the
    Moor ; 380
And it is thought abroad that 'twixt my
    sheets
'Has done my office. I know not if't be
    true ;
Yet I, for mere suspicion in that kind, 383
Will do as if for surety. He holds me well ;
The better shall my purpose work on him.
Cassio's a proper man. Let me see now :
To get his place, and to plume up my will
In double knavery. How, how ? Let's see :
After some time to abuse Othello's ear
That he is too familiar with his wife. 390
He hath a person and a smooth dispose
To be suspected—fram'd to make women
    false.
The Moor is of a free and open nature
That thinks men honest that but seem to
    be so ;
And will as tenderly be led by th' nose 395
As asses are.
I ha't—it is engender'd. Hell and night
Must bring this monstrous birth to the
    world's light. [*Exit.*

ACT TWO

SCENE I. *Cyprus. A sea-port.*

Enter MONTANO, *Governor of Cyprus, with
two other* Gentlemen.

   Mon. What from the cape can you
    discern at sea ?

   1 *Gent.* Nothing at all ; it is a high-
    wrought flood.
I cannot 'twixt the heaven and the main
Descry a sail.

   Mon. Methinks the wind hath spoke
    aloud at land ; 5
A fuller blast ne'er shook our battlements.
If it ha ruffian'd so upon the sea,
What ribs of oak, when mountains melt on
    them,
Can hold the mortise ? What shall we hear
    of this ? 9

   2 *Gent.* A segregation of the Turkish fleet.
For do but stand upon the banning shore,
The chidden billow seems to pelt the
    clouds ;
The wind-shak'd surge, with high and
    monstrous mane,
Seems to cast water on the burning Bear,
And quench the guards of th' ever-fired
    pole. 15
I never did like molestation view
On the enchafed flood.

   Mon. If that the Turkish fleet
Be not enshelter'd and embay'd, they are
    drown'd :
It is impossible they bear it out.

Enter a third Gentleman.

   3 *Gent.* News, lads ! Your wars are done.
The desperate tempest hath so bang'd the
    Turk 21
That their designment halts. A noble ship
    of Venice
Hath seen a grievous wreck and sufferance
On most part of their fleet.

   Mon. How ! Is this true ?

   3 *Gent.* The ship is here put in,
A Veronesa ; Michael Cassio, 26
Lieutenant to the warlike Moor Othello,
Is come ashore : the Moor himself at sea,
And is in full commission here for Cyprus.

   Mon. I am glad on't ; 'tis a worthy
    governor. 30

   3 *Gent.* But this same Cassio, though he
    speak of comfort
Touching the Turkish loss, yet he looks
    sadly
And prays the Moor be safe ; for they were
    parted
With foul and violent tempest.

   Mon. Pray heaven he be ;
For I have serv'd him, and the man
    commands 35
Like a full soldier. Let's to the sea-side, ho !
As well to see the vessel that's come in

As to throw out our eyes for brave Othello,
Even till we make the main and th' aerial
      blue
An indistinct regard.
  3 *Gent.*   Come, let's do so ;   40
For every minute is expectancy
Of more arrivance.

             Enter CASSIO.

  Cas. Thanks you, the valiant of this war-
      like isle,
That so approve the Moor.   O, let the
      heavens
Give him defence against their elements,   45
For I have lost him on a dangerous sea !
  Mon. Is he well shipp'd ?
  Cas. His bark is stoutly timber'd, and his
      pilot
Of very expert and approv'd allowance ;
Therefore my hopes, not surfeited to death,
Stand in bold cure.   51
         [*Within :* A sail, a sail, a sail !

        Enter a Messenger.

  Cas. What noise ?
  Mess. The town is empty ; on the brow
      o' th' sea
Stand ranks of people, and they cry ' A
      sail ! '
  Cas. My hopes do shape him for the
      Governor.   [*A shot.*
  2 *Gent.* They do discharge the shot of
      courtesy :   56
Our friend at least.
  Cas.   I pray you, sir, go forth,
And give us truth who 'tis that is arriv'd.
  2 *Gent.* I shall.   [*Exit.*
  Mon. But, good Lieutenant, is your
      general wiv'd ?   60
  Cas. Most fortunately : he hath achiev'd
      a maid
That paragons description and wild fame ;
One that excels the quirks of blazoning
      pens,
And in th' essential vesture of creation
Does tire the ingener.

      Re-enter second Gentleman.

                     Now, who has put in ?
  2 *Gent.* 'Tis one Iago, ancient to the
      General.   66
  Cas. 'Has had most favourable and
      happy speed.
Tempests themselves, high seas, and howl-
      ing winds,
The gutter'd rocks, and congregated sands,
Traitors ensteep'd to enclog the guiltless
      keel,
As having sense of beauty, do omit   71
Their mortal natures, letting go safely by
The divine Desdemona.
  Mon.   What is she ?
  Cas. She that I spake of—our great
      Captain's Captain,

Left in the conduct of the bold Iago ;   75
Whose footing here anticipates our thoughts
A se'nnight's speed.   Great Jove, Othello
      guard,
And swell his sail with thine own powerful
      breath,
That he may bless this bay with his tall
      ship,
Make love's quick pants in Desdemona's
      arms,   80
Give renew'd fire to our extincted spirits,
And bring all Cyprus comfort !

Enter DESDEMONA, IAGO, EMILIA, RODE-
      RIGO, *and* Attendants.

                           O, behold,
The riches of the ship is come ashore !
Ye men of Cyprus, let her have your knees.
Hail to thee, lady ! and the grace of
      heaven,   85
Before, behind thee, and on every hand,
Enwheel thee round !
  Des.   I thank you, valiant Cassio.
What tidings can you tell me of my lord ?
  Cas. He is not yet arriv'd ; nor know I
      aught   89
But that he's well, and will be shortly here.
  Des. O, but I fear !   How lost you
      company ?
  Cas. The great contention of the sea and
      skies
Parted our fellowship.
           [*Within :* A sail, a sail !
           But hark—' A sail ! '   [*A shot.*
  2 *Gent.* They give their greeting to the
      citadel :
This likewise is a friend.
  Cas.   So speaks this voice.
See for the news.   [*Exit Gentleman.*
Good ancient, you are welcome.   [*To
      Emilia*] Welcome, mistress.   96
Let it not gall your patience, good Iago,
That I extend my manners ; 'tis my
      breeding
That gives me this bold show of courtesy.
                            [*Kissing her.*
  Iago. Sir, would she give you so much of
      her lips   100
As of her tongue she oft bestows on me,
You'd have enough.
  Des. Alas, she has no speech !
  Iago.   I know too much
I find it aye when I ha list to sleep.
Marry, before your ladyship, I grant,   105
She puts her tongue a little in her heart
And chides with thinking.
  Emil.   You ha little cause to say so.
  Iago. Come on, come on ; you are
pictures out a-doors, bells in your parlours,
wildcats in your kitchens, saints in your
injuries, devils being offended, players in
your huswifery, and huswives in your beds.
  Des. O, fie upon thee, slanderer !
  Iago. Nay, it is true, or else I am a Turk :

You rise to play, and go to bed to work. 115
Emil. You shall not write my praise.
Iago. No, let me not.
Des. What wouldst write of me if thou
    shouldst praise me ?
Iago. O gentle lady, do not put me to't ;
For I am nothing if not critical.
Des. Come on, assay.—There's one gone
    to the harbour ? 120
Iago. Ay, madam.
Des. I am not merry ; but I do beguile
The thing I am by seeming otherwise.
Come, how wouldst thou praise me ? 124
Iago. I am about it ; but, indeed, my
invention comes from my pate as birdlime
does from frieze—it plucks out brains and
all. But my Muse labours, and thus she is
deliver'd :
If she be fair and wise—fairness and wit,
The one's for use, the other useth it. 130
    Des. Well prais'd. How if she be black
    and witty ?
    Iago. If she be black, and thereto have
    a wit,
She'll find a white that shall her blackness
    hit.
    Des. Worse and worse !
    Emil. How if fair and foolish ? 135
Iago. She never yet was foolish that was
    fair ;
For even her folly help'd her to an heir.
Des. These are old fond paradoxes to
make fools laugh i' th' alehouse. What
miserable praise hast thou for her that's
foul and foolish ? 140
Iago. There's none so foul, and foolish
    thereunto,
But does foul pranks which fair and wise
    ones do.
Des. O heavy ignorance ! that praises
the worst best. But what praise couldst
thou bestow on a deserving woman indeed
—one that, in the authority of her merits,
did justly put on the vouch of very malice
itself ? 146
Iago. She that was ever fair, and never
    proud ;
Had tongue at will, and yet was never loud ;
Never lack'd gold, and yet went never
    gay ;
Fled from her wish, and yet said ' Now I
    may ' ; 150
She that, being ang'red, her revenge being
    nigh,
Bade her wrong stay and her displeasure
    fly ;
She that in wisdom never was so frail
To change the cod's head for the salmon's
    tail ;
She that could think, and ne'er disclose her
    mind ; 155
See suitors following, and not look behind :
She was a wight, if ever such wight were—
    Des. To do what ?

Iago. To suckle fools and chronicle small
    beer. 159
Des. O most lame and impotent conclusion ! Do not learn of him, Emilia,
though he be thy husband. How say you,
Cassio ? Is he not a most profane and
liberal counsellor ?
Cas. He speaks home, madam. You may
relish him more in the soldier than in the
scholar. 165
Iago. [*Aside*] He takes her by the palm.
Ay, well said, whisper. With as little a
web as this will I ensnare as great a fly as
Cassio. Ay, smile upon her, do ; I will
gyve thee in thine own courtship. You say
true ; 'tis so, indeed. If such tricks as
these strip you out of your lieutenantry, it
had been better you had not kiss'd your
three fingers so oft, which now again you
are most apt to play the sir in. Very good ;
well kissed ! and excellent courtesy ! 'Tis
so, indeed. Yet again your fingers to your
lips ? Would they were clyster-pipes for
your sake ! [*Trumpet within.*
The Moor ! I know his trumpet.
Cas. 'Tis truly so.
Des. Let's meet him, and receive him.
Cas. Lo, where he comes !

Enter OTHELLO *and* Attendants.

Oth. O my fair warrior !
Des. My dear Othello ! 180
Oth. It gives me wonder great as my
    content
To see you here before me. O my soul's joy !
If after every tempest come such calms,
May the winds blow till they have waken'd
    death,
And let the labouring bark climb hills of
    seas 185
Olympus-high and duck again as low
As hell's from heaven. If it were now to die,
'Twere now to be most happy ; for I fear
My soul hath her content so absolute
That not another comfort like to this 190
Succeeds in unknown fate.
Des. The heavens forbid
But that our loves and comforts should
    increase
Even as our days do grow !
Oth. Amen to that, sweet powers !
I cannot speak enough of this content ;
It stops me here ; it is too much of joy. 195
And this, and this, the greatest discords be
    [*They kiss.*
That e'er our hearts shall make !
Iago. [*Aside*] O, you are well tun'd now !
But I'll set down the pegs that make this
    music,
As honest as I am.
Oth. Come, let us to the castle.
News, friends : our wars are done ; the
    Turks are drown'd. 200
How do our old acquaintance of the isle ?

Honey, you shall be well desir'd in Cyprus;
I have found great love amongst them. O
    my sweet,
I prattle out of fashion, and I dote
In mine own comforts. I prithee, good
    Iago,   205
Go to the bay, and disembark my coffers;
Bring thou the Master to the Citadel;
He is a good one, and his worthiness
Does challenge much respect.   Come,
    Desdemona,
Once more well met at Cyprus.   210
            [*Exeunt all but Iago and Roderigo.*
Iago. [*To one leaving*] Do thou
meet me presently at the harbour. [*To
Roderigo*] Come hither.   If thou be'st
valiant—as they say base men being in
love have then a nobility in their natures
more than is native to them—list me. The
Lieutenant to-night watches on the court
of guard.   First, I must tell thee this:
Desdemona is directly in love with him. 216
Rod. With him! Why, 'tis not possible.
Iago. Lay thy finger thus, and let thy
soul be instructed.   Mark me with what
violence she first lov'd the Moor, but for
bragging and telling her fantastical lies.
To love him still for prating?—let
not thy discreet heart think it.   Her eye
must be fed; and what delight shall she
have to look on the devil?   When the
blood is made dull with the act of sport,
there should be—again to inflame it, and
to give satiety a fresh appetite—loveliness
in favour, sympathy in years, manners,
and beauties—all which the Moor is
defective in.   Now for want of these
requir'd conveniences, her delicate tenderness will find itself abus'd, begin to heave
the gorge, disrelish and abhor the Moor;
very nature will instruct her in it, and
compel her to some second choice.   Now,
sir, this granted—as it is a most pregnant
and unforc'd position—who stands so
eminent in the degree of this fortune as
Cassio does?   A knave very voluble; no
further conscionable than in putting on the
mere form of civil and humane seeming,
for the better compassing of his salt and
most hidden loose affection?   Why, none;
why, none.   A slipper and subtle knave;
a finder-out of occasion; that has an eye
can stamp and counterfeit advantages,
though true advantage never present itself;
a devilish knave!   Besides, the knave is
handsome, young, and hath all those
requisites in him that folly and green minds
look after; a pestilent complete knave, and
the woman hath found him already.   244
Rod. I cannot believe that in her; she's
full of most blest condition.
Iago. Blest fig's end!   The wine she
drinks is made of grapes.   If she had been
blest, she would never have lov'd the

Moor.   Blest pudding!   Didst thou not see
her paddle with the palm of his hand?
Didst not mark that?
Rod. Yes, that I did; but that was but
courtesy.   251
Iago. Lechery, by this hand; an index
and obscure prologue to the history of lust
and foul thoughts.   They met so near with
their lips that their breaths embrac'd together.   Villainous thoughts, Roderigo!
When these mutualities so marshal the
way, hard at hand comes the master and
main exercise, th' incorporate conclusion.
Pish!   But, sir, be you rul'd by me; I
have brought you from Venice.   Watch
you to-night; for your command, I'll lay't
upon you.   Cassio knows you not; I'll not
be far from you.   Do you find some occasion
to anger Cassio, either by speaking too
loud, or tainting his discipline, or from
what other course you please, which the
time shall more favourably minister.
Rod. Well.   265
Iago. Sir, he's rash, and very sudden in
choler, and haply with his truncheon may
strike at you; provoke him that he may;
for even out of that will I cause these of
Cyprus to mutiny, whose qualification shall
come into no true taste again but by the
displanting of Cassio. So shall you have a
shorter journey to your desires by the
means I shall then have to prefer them;
and the impediment most profitably
remov'd, without the which there were no
expectation of our prosperity.   274
Rod. I will do this, if you can bring it to
any opportunity.
Iago. I warrant thee.   Meet me by and
by at the citadel.   I must fetch his
necessaries ashore.   Farewell.
Rod. Adieu.   [*Exit.*
Iago. That Cassio loves her, I do well
        believe it;   280
That she loves him, 'tis apt and of great
        credit.
The Moor, howbeit that I endure him not,
Is of a constant, loving, noble nature;
And I dare think he'll prove to Desdemona
A most dear husband.   Now I do love her
        too;   285
Not out of absolute lust, though per-
        adventure
I stand accountant for as great a sin,
But partly led to diet my revenge,
For that I do suspect the lustful Moor
Hath leap'd into my seat; the thought
        whereof   290
Doth like a poisonous mineral gnaw my
        inwards;
And nothing can nor shall content my
        soul
Till I am even'd with him, wife for wife;
Or failing so, yet that I put the Moor
At least into a jealousy so strong   295

That judgment cannot cure. Which thing
    to do,
If this poor trash of Venice, whom I trash
For his quick hunting, stand the putting on,
I'll have our Michael Cassio on the hip,   299
Abuse him to the Moor in the rank garb—
For I fear Cassio with my night-cap too ;
Make the Moor thank me, love me, and
    reward me,
For making him egregiously an ass,
And practising upon his peace and quiet
Even to madness.   'Tis here, but yet
    confus'd :   305
Knavery's plain face is never seen till us'd.
                       [*Exit.*

SCENE II. *Cyprus. A street.*

*Enter Othello's Herald with a proclamation ;
People following.*

Her. It is Othello's pleasure, our noble
and valiant general, that, upon certain
tidings now arriv'd, importing the mere
perdition of the Turkish fleet, every man
put himself into triumph ; some to dance,
some to make bonfires, each man to what
sport and revels his addiction leads him ;
for, besides these beneficial news, it is the
celebration of his nuptial. So much was his
pleasure should be proclaimed. All offices
are open ; and there is full liberty of
feasting from this present hour of five till
the bell have told eleven. Heaven bless the
isle of Cyprus and our noble general
Othello !   [*Exeunt.*

SCENE III   *Cyprus. The citadel.*

Enter OTHELLO, DESDEMONA, CASSIO, *and*
Attendants.

Oth. Good Michael, look you to the guard
    to-night.
Let's teach ourselves that honourable stop,
Not to outsport discretion.
  Cas. Iago hath direction what to do ;
But, notwithstanding, with my personal
    eye   5
Will I look to't.
  Oth.   Iago is most honest.
Michael, good night. To-morrow with your
    earliest
Let me have speech with you. [*To Desde-
mona*] Come, my dear love,
The purchase made, the fruits are to ensue ;
That profit's yet to come twixt me and
    you.—   10
Good night. [*Exeunt Othello, Desdemona,
            and Attendants.*

Enter IAGO.

  Cas. Welcome, Iago ; we must to the
    watch.
  Iago. Not this hour, Lieutenant ; 'tis not
yet ten a clock. Our general cast us

thus early for the love of his Desdemona ;
who let us not therefore blame. He hath
not yet made wanton the night with her ;
and she is sport for Jove.   17
  Cas. She is a most exquisite lady.
  Iago. And, I'll warrant her, full of game.
  Cas. Indeed, she is a most fresh and
delicate creature.
  Iago. What an eye she has ! Methinks it
sounds a parley to provocation.
  Cas. An inviting eye ; and yet methinks
right modest.
  Iago. And when she speaks, is it not an
alarm to love ?
  Cas. She is indeed perfection.   25
  Iago. Well, happiness to their sheets !
Come, Lieutenant, I have a stoup of wine ;
and here without are a brace of Cyprus
gallants that would fain have a measure
to the health of the black Othello.
  Cas. Not to-night, good Iago . I have
very poor and unhappy brains for drinking ;
I could well wish courtesy would invent
some other custom of entertainment.   32
  Iago. O, they are our friends—but one
cup ; I'll drink for you.
  Cas. I have drunk but one cup to-night,
and that was craftily qualified too, and
behold what innovation it makes here. I
am unfortunate in the infirmity, and dare
not task my weakness with any more.
  Iago. What, man ! 'Tis a night of revels.
The gallants desire it.   40
  Cas. Where are they ?
  Iago. Here at the door ; I pray you call
    them in.
  Cas. I'll do't ; but it dislikes me. [*Exit.*
  Iago. If I can fasten but one cup upon
    him,
With that which he hath drunk to-night
    already,   45
He'll be as full of quarrel and offence
As my young mistress' dog. Now my sick
    fool Roderigo,
Whom love hath turn'd almost the wrong
    side outward,
To Desdemona hath to-night carous'd   49
Potations pottle deep ; and he's to watch.
Three else of Cyprus—noble swelling
    spirits,
That hold their honours in a wary distance,
The very elements of this warlike isle—
Have I to-night fluster'd with flowing cups,
And they watch too. Now, 'mongst this
    flock of drunkards   55
Am I to put our Cassio in some action
That may offend the isle—but here they
    come.

Re-enter CASSIO *with* MONTANO, *and* Gentlemen, *followed by* Servant *with wine.*

If consequence do but approve my dream,
My boat sails freely, both with wind and
    stream.

Yet surely Cassio, I believe, receiv'd
From him that fled some strange indignity
Which patience could not pass.
Oth.   I know, Iago,
Thy honesty and love doth mince this
    matter,
Making it light to Cassio. Cassio, I love
    thee ;   240
But never more be officer of mine.

    Re-enter DESDEMONA, *attended.*

Look if my gentle love be not rais'd up.
I'll make thee an example.
  Des. What is the matter, dear ?
  Oth.   All's well now, sweeting ;
Come away to bed. [*To Montano*] Sir, for
    your hurts,   245
Myself will be your surgeon. Lead him off.
                  [*Montano is led off*].
Iago, look with care about the town,
And silence those whom this vile brawl
    distracted.
Come, Desdemona ; 'tis the soldiers' life
To have their balmy slumbers wak'd with
    strife.   250
      [*Exeunt all but Iago and Cassio.*
  Iago. What, are you hurt, Lieutenant ?
  Cas. Ay, past all surgery.
  Iago. Marry, God forbid !
  Cas. Reputation, reputation, reputation !
O, I have lost my reputation ! I have lost
the immortal part of myself, and what
remains is bestial. My reputation, Iago, my
reputation !   257
  Iago. As I am an honest man, I had thought
you had receiv'd some bodily wound ; there
is more sense in that than in reputation.
Reputation is an idle and most false imposition ; oft got without merit, and lost
without deserving. You have lost no
reputation at all, unless you repute yourself
such a loser. What, man ! there are more
ways to recover the General again ; you are
but now cast in his mood, a punishment
more in policy than in malice ; even so
as one would beat his offenceless dog to
affright an imperious lion. Sue to him
again, and he's yours.   267
  Cas. I will rather sue to be despis'd than
to deceive so good a commander with so
slight, so drunken, and so indiscreet an
officer. Drunk ! And speak parrot ! And
squabble, swagger, swear ! And discourse
fustian with one's own shadow ! O thou
invisible spirit of wine, if thou hast no
name to be known by, let us call thee devil !
  Iago. What was he that you follow'd
with your sword ? What had he done to
you ?   276
  Cas. I know not.
  Iago. Is't possible ?
  Cas. I remember a mass of things, but
nothing distinctly ; a quarrel, but nothing
wherefore. O God, that men should put an

enemy in their mouths to steal away their
brains ! That we should with joy, pleasance, revel and applause, transform ourselves into beasts !
  Iago. Why, but you are now well enough.
How come you thus recovered ?   285
  Cas. It hath pleas'd the devil drunkenness to give place to the devil wrath. One
unperfectness shows me another, to make
me frankly despise myself.
  Iago. Come, you are too severe a moraller.
As the time, the place, and the condition
of this country stands, I could heartily
wish this had not so befall'n ; but since it
is as it is, mend it for your own good.   292
  Cas. I will ask him for my place again :
he shall tell me I am a drunkard. Had I as
many mouths as Hydra, such an answer
would stop them all. To be now a sensible
man, by and by a fool, and presently a
beast ! O strange ! Every inordinate cup
is unblest, and the ingredience is a devil.
  Iago. Come, come, good wine is a good
familiar creature if it be well us'd ; exclaim
no more against it. And, good Lieutenant,
I think you think I love you.   301
  Cas. I have well approv'd it, sir. I
drunk !
  Iago. You or any man living may be
drunk at a time, man. I'll tell you what
you shall do. Our General's wife is now
the General—I may say so in this respect,
for that he hath devoted and given up
himself to the contemplation, mark, and
denotement, of her parts and graces—
confess yourself freely to her ; importune
her help to put you in your place again :
she is of so free, so kind, so apt, so blessed
a disposition, she holds it a vice in her
goodness not to do more than she is
requested. This broken joint between you
and her husband entreat her to splinter ;
and, my fortunes against any lay worth
naming, this crack of your love shall grow
stronger than it was before.   315
  Cas. You advise me well.
  Iago. I protest, in the sincerity of love
and honest kindness.
  Cas. I think it freely ; and betimes in the
morning I will beseech the virtuous
Desdemona to undertake for me. I am
desperate of my fortunes if they check me
here.
  Iago. You are in the right. Good night,
Lieutenant ; I must to the watch.
  Cas. Good night, honest Iago.   [*Exit.*
  Iago. And what's he, then, that says I
    play the villain ?   325
When this advice is free I give and honest,
Probal to thinking, and indeed the course
To win the Moor again ? For 'tis most easy
The inclining Desdemona to subdue   329
In any honest suit : she's fram'd as fruitful
As the free elements. And then for her

To win the Moor—were't to renounce his
  baptism,
All seals and symbols of redeemed sin—
His soul is so enfetter'd to her love
That she may make, unmake, do what she
  list,   335
Even as her appetite shall play the god
With his weak function. How am I, then,
  a villain
To counsel Cassio to this parallel course,
Directly to his good ? Divinity of hell !
When devils will their blackest sins put on,
They do suggest at first with heavenly
  shows,   341
As I do now ; for whiles this honest fool
Plies Desdemona to repair his fortunes,
And she for him pleads strongly to the
  Moor,
I'll pour this pestilence into his ear— 345
That she repeals him for her body's lust ;
And by how much she strives to do him
  good
She shall undo her credit with the Moor.
So will I turn her virtue into pitch ;   349
And out of her own goodness make the net
That shall enmesh them all.

Enter RODERIGO.

                    How now, Roderigo !
Rod. I do follow here in the chase, not
like a hound that hunts, but one that fills
up the cry. My money is almost spent ;
I have been to-night exceedingly well
cudgell'd ; and I think the issue will be—
I shall have so much experience for my
pains as that comes to ; and so, with no
money at all, and a little more wit, return
again to Venice.   357
  Iago. How poor are they that have not
patience !
What wound did ever heal but by degrees ?
Thou know'st we work by wit, and not by
  witchcraft ;   360
And wit depends on dilatory time.
Does't not go well ? Cassio hath beaten
  thee,
And thou, by that small hurt, hast cashier'd
Cassio.
Though other things grow fair against the
  sun,
Yet fruits that blossom first will first be
  ripe.   365
Content thyself awhile. By th' mass, 'tis
  morning !
Pleasure and action make the hours seem
  short.
Retire thee ; go where thou art billeted.
Away, I say ; thou shalt know more here-
after.
Nay, get thee gone.   [*Exit Roderigo.*
            Two things are to be done :
My wife must move for Cassio to her
  mistress ;   371
I'll set her on ;

Myself awhile to draw the Moor apart
And bring him jump when he may Cassio
  find
Soliciting his wife. Ay, that's the way ; 375
Dull not device by coldness and delay.
                              [*Exit.*

ACT THREE

SCENE I. *Cyprus. Before the citadel.*

Enter CASSIO, *with* Musicians.

Cas. Masters, play here ; I will content
  your pains.
Something that's brief ; and bid ' Good
  morrow, General '.   [*Music.*

Enter Clown.

  Clo. Why masters, ha your instruments
been in Naples, that they speak i' th'
nose thus ?
  1 *Mus.* How, sir, how ?   5
  Clo. Are these, I pray, call'd wind
instruments ?
  1 *Mus.* Ay, marry, are they, sir.
  Clo. O, thereby hangs a tail.
  1 *Mus.* Whereby hangs a tale, sir ? 9
  Clo. Marry, sir, by many a wind instrument that I know. But, masters, here's
money for you ; and the General so likes
your music that he desires you, of all loves,
to make no more noise with it.
  1 *Mus.* Well, sir, we will not.   14
  Clo. If you have any music that may not
be heard, to't again ; but, as they say, to
hear music the General does not greatly
care.
  1 *Mus.* We have none such, sir.   18
  Clo. Then put up your pipes in your bag,
for I'll away. Go ; vanish into air ; away.
                      [*Exeunt Musicians.*
  Cas. Dost thou hear, my honest friend ?
  Clo. No, I hear not your honest friend ;
I hear you.   22
  Cas. Prithee keep up thy quillets.
There's a poor piece of gold for thee. If
the gentlewoman that attends the General's
wife be stirring, tell her there's one Cassio
entreats her a little favour of speech. Wilt
thou do this ?   26
  Clo. She is stirring, sir ; if she will stir
hither, I shall seem to notify unto her.
  Cas. Do, good my friend.   [*Exit Clown.*

Enter IAGO.

                    In happy time, Iago.
  Iago. You have not been abed, then ? 30
  Cas. Why, no ; the day had broke before
  we parted.
I have made bold, Iago,
To send in to your wife : my suit to her
Is that she will to virtuous Desdemona
Procure me some access.
  Iago.   I'll send her to you presently ;
And I'll devise a mean to draw the Moor 36

Out of the way, that your converse and
    business
May be more free.
    Cas. I humbly thank you for't. [*Exit
    Iago*] I never knew
A Florentine more kind and honest.   40

       Enter EMILIA.

    Emil. Good morrow, good Lieutenant. I
    am sorry
For your displeasure; but all will sure
    be well.
The General and his wife are talking of it;
And she speaks for you stoutly: the Moor
    replies   44
That he you hurt is of great fame in Cyprus
And great affinity, and that in wholesome
    wisdom
He might not but refuse you; but he
    protests he loves you,
And needs no other suitor but his likings
To take the safest occasion by the front
To bring you in again.
    Cas.   Yet, I beseech you,
If you think fit, or that it may be done, 51
Give me advantage of some brief discourse
With Desdemona alone.
    Emil.   Pray you come in.
I will bestow you where you shall have
    time
To speak your bosom freely.
    Cas.   I am much bound to you.
                                    [*Exeunt.*

    SCENE II. *Cyprus. The citadel.*

Enter OTHELLO, IAGO, *and* Gentlemen.

    Oth. These letters give, Iago, to the pilot;
And by him do my duties to the Senate.
That done, I will be walking on the works;
Repair there to me.
    Iago.   Well, my good lord, I'll do't.
    Oth. This fortification, gentlemen—shall
    we see't?   5
    Gent. We'll wait upon your lordship.
                                      [*Exeunt.*

SCENE III. *Cyprus. The garden of the
                citadel.*

Enter DESDEMONA, CASSIO, *and* EMILIA.

    Des. Be thou assur'd, good Cassio, I will
    do
All my abilities in thy behalf.
    Emil. Good madam, do. I warrant it
    grieves my husband
As if the case were his.
    Des. O, that's an honest fellow. Do not
    doubt, Cassio,   5
But I will have my lord and you again
As friendly as you were.
    Cas.   Bounteous madam,
Whatever shall become of Michael Cassio,
He's never any thing but your true servant.

    Des. I know't—I thank you. You do love
    my lord;   10
You have known him long; and be you
    well assur'd
He shall in strangeness stand no farther off
Than in a politic distance.
    Cas.   Ay, but, lady,
That policy may either last so long,
Or feed upon such nice and waterish diet,
Or breed itself so out of circumstances, 16
That, I being absent, and my place
    supplied,
My general will forget my love and service.
    Des. Do not doubt that; before Emilia
    here
I give thee warrant of thy place. Assure
    thee,   20
If I do vow a friendship, I'll perform it
To the last article. My lord shall never
    rest;
I'll watch him tame, and talk him out of
    patience;
His bed shall seem a school, his board a
    shrift;
I'll intermingle everything he does   25
With Cassio's suit. Therefore be merry,
    Cassio;
For thy solicitor shall rather die
Than give thy cause away.

      Enter OTHELLO *and* IAGO.

    Emil. Madam, here comes my lord.
    Cas. Madam, I'll take my leave.   30
    Des. Why, stay, and hear me speak.
    Cas. Madam, not now. I am very ill at
    ease,
Unfit for mine own purposes.
    Des. Well, do your discretion.   34
                               [*Exit Cassio.*
    Iago. Ha! I like not that.
    Oth.   What dost thou say?
    Iago. Nothing, my lord; or if—I know
    not what.
    Oth. Was not that Cassio parted from my
    wife?
    Iago. Cassio, my lord! No, sure, I cannot
    think it,
That he would sneak away so guilty-like, 40
Seeing your coming.
    Oth.   I do believe 'twas he.
    Des. How now, my lord!
I have been talking with a suitor here,
A man that languishes in your displeasure.
    Oth. Who is't you mean?   45
    Des. Why, your lieutenant, Cassio. Good
    my lord,
If I have any grace or power to move you,
His present reconciliation take;
For if he be not one that truly loves you,
That errs in ignorance, and not in cunning,
I have no judgment in an honest face. 51
I prithee call him back.
    Oth.   Went he hence now?
    Des. Yes, faith; so humbled

That he hath left part of his grief with me
To suffer with him. Good love, call him
   back. 55
  Oth. Not now, sweet Desdemona; some
   other time.
  Des. But shall't be shortly?
  Oth.   The sooner, sweet, for you.
  Des. Shall't be to-night at supper?
  Oth.   No, not to-night.
  Des. To-morrow dinner, then?
  Oth.   I shall not dine at home;
I meet the captains at the citadel. 60
  Des. Why, then, to-morrow night, or
   Tuesday morn,
On Tuesday noon or night, on Wednesday
   morn,
I prithee name the time; but let it not
Exceed three days. I'faith, he's penitent;
And yet his trespass, in our common
   reason— 65
Save that, they say, the wars must make
   example
Out of her best—is not almost a fault
T' incur a private check. When shall he
   come?
Tell me, Othello—I wonder in my soul 69
What you would ask me that I should
   deny,
Or stand so mamm'ring on. What!
   Michael Cassio,
That came a-wooing with you, and so many
   a time,
When I have spoke of you dispraisingly,
Hath ta'en your part—to have so much
   to do
To bring him in! By'r Lady, I could do
   much— 75
  Oth. Prithee, no more; let him come
   when he will;
I will deny thee nothing.
  Des.   Why, this is not a boon;
'Tis as I should entreat you wear your
   gloves,
Or feed on nourishing dishes, or keep you
   warm,
Or sue to you to do a peculiar profit 80
To your own person. Nay, when I have
   a suit
Wherein I mean to touch your love indeed,
It shall be full of poise and difficult weight,
And fearful to be granted.
  Oth.   I will deny thee nothing.
Whereon I do beseech thee grant me this,
To leave me but a little to myself. 86
  Des. Shall I deny you? No; farewell,
   my lord.
  Oth. Farewell, my Desdemona. I'll come
   to thee straight.
  Des. Emilia, come.—Be as your fancies
   teach you;
Whate'er you be, I am obedient. 90
       [*Exeunt Desdemona and Emilia.*
  Oth. Excellent wretch! Perdition catch
   my soul

But I do love thee; and when I love thee
   not
Chaos is come again.
  Iago. My noble lord!
  Oth.   What dost thou say, Iago?
  Iago. Did Michael Cassio, when you
   woo'd my lady, 95
Know of your love?
  Oth. He did, from first to last. Why dost
   thou ask?
  Iago. But for a satisfaction of my
   thought—
No further harm.
  Oth.   Why of thy thought, Iago?
  Iago. I did not think he had been
   acquainted with her. 100
  Oth. O, yes; and went between us very
   often.
  Iago. Indeed!
  Oth. Indeed? Ay, indeed. Discern'st
   thou aught in that?
Is he not honest?
  Iago.   Honest, my lord? 105
  Oth. Honest? Ay, honest.
  Iago.   My lord, for aught I know.
  Oth. What dost thou think?
  Iago.   Think, my lord?
  Oth. Think, my lord! By heaven, he
   echoes me, 110
As if there were some monster in his
   thought
Too hideous to be shown. Thou dost mean
   something:
I heard thee say but now thou lik'st not
   that,
When Cassio left my wife. What didst
   not like? 114
And when I told thee he was of my counsel
In my whole course of wooing, thou criedst
   ' Indeed! '
And didst contract and purse thy brow
   together,
As if thou then hadst shut up in thy brain
Some horrible conceit. If thou dost love
   me,
Show me thy thought. 120
  Iago. My lord, you know I love you.
  Oth.   I think thou dost;
And for I know thou art full of love and
   honesty,
And weigh'st thy words before thou giv'st
   them breath,
Therefore these stops of thine affright me
   the more;
For such things in a false disloyal knave 125
Are tricks of custom; but in a man that's
   just
They are close delations, working from the
   heart
That passion cannot rule.
  Iago.   For Michael Cassio,
I dare presume I think that he is honest.
  Oth. I think so too.
  Iago.   Men should be that they seem;

Or those that be not, would they might
    seem none!   131
  Oth. Certain, men should be what they
    seem.
  Iago. Why then, I think Cassio's an
    honest man.
  Oth. Nay, yet there's more in this.   134
I prithee speak to me as to thy thinkings,
As thou dost ruminate; and give thy worst
    of thoughts
The worst of words.
  Iago.   Good my lord, pardon me.
Though I am bound to every act of duty,
I am not bound to that all slaves are free
    to—
Utter my thoughts. Why, say they are vile
    and false,   140
As where's that palace whereinto foul things
Sometimes intrude not? Who has that
    breast so pure
But some uncleanly apprehensions
Keep leets and law-days, and in sessions sit
With meditations lawful?   145
  Oth. Thou dost conspire against thy
    friend, Iago,
If thou but think'st him wrong'd, and
    mak'st his ear
A stranger to thy thoughts.
  Iago.   I do beseech you,
Though I perchance am vicious in my guess,
As, I confess, it is my nature's plague   150
To spy into abuses, and oft my jealousy
Shapes faults that are not—that your
    wisdom
From one that so imperfectly conjects,
Would take no notice; nor build yourself
    a trouble
Out of his scattering and unsure obser-
    vance.   155
It were not for your quiet nor your good,
Nor for my manhood, honesty, or wisdom,
To let you know my thoughts.
  Oth. Zounds! What dost thou mean?
  Iago. Good name in man and woman,
    dear my lord,
Is the immediate jewel of their souls: 160
Who steals my purse steals trash; 'tis
    something, nothing;
'Twas mine, 'tis his, and has been slave to
    thousands;
But he that filches from me my good
    name
Robs me of that which not enriches him
And makes me poor indeed.   165
  Oth. By heaven, I'll know thy thoughts.
  Iago. You cannot, if my heart were in
    your hand;
Nor shall not, whilst 'tis in my custody.
  Oth. Ha!
  Iago. O, beware, my lord, of jealousy;
It is the green-ey'd monster which doth
    mock   170
The meat it feeds on. That cuckold lives
    in bliss

Who, certain of his fate, loves not his
    wronger;
But, O, what damned minutes tells he o'er
Who dotes, yet doubts, suspects, yet
    strongly loves!
  Oth. O misery!   175
  Iago. Poor and content is rich, and rich
    enough;
But riches fineless is as poor as winter
To him that ever fears he shall be poor.
Good God, the souls of all my tribe defend
From jealousy!
  Oth.   Why, why is this?   180
Think'st thou I'd make a life of jealousy,
To follow still the changes of the moon
With fresh suspicions? No; to be once in
    doubt
Is once to be resolv'd. Exchange me for a
    goat   184
When I shall turn the business of my soul
To such exsufflicate and blown surmises
Matching thy inference. 'Tis not to make
    me jealous
To say my wife is fair, feeds well, loves
    company,
Is free of speech, sings, plays, and dances
    well;   189
Where virtue is, these are more virtuous.
Nor from mine own weak merits will I
    draw
The smallest fear or doubt of her revolt;
For she had eyes, and chose me. No, Iago;
I'll see before I doubt; when I doubt,
    prove;
And, on the proof, there is no more but
    this—   195
Away at once with love or jealousy!
  Iago. I am glad of this; for now I shall
    have reason
To show the love and duty that I bear you
With franker spirit. Therefore, as I am
    bound,
Receive it from me. I speak not yet of
    proof.   200
Look to your wife; observe her well with
    Cassio;
Wear your eyes thus, not jealous nor secure.
I would not have your free and noble
    nature
Out of self-bounty be abus'd; look to't.
I know our country disposition well: 205
In Venice they do let God see the pranks
They dare not show their husbands; their
    best conscience
Is not to leave't undone, but keep't un-
    known.
  Oth. Dost thou say so?
  Iago. She did deceive her father, marry-
    ing you;   210
And when she seem'd to shake and fear
    your looks,
She lov'd them most.
  Oth.   And so she did.
  Iago.   Why, go to then!

She that, so young, could give out such a
  seeming,
To seel her father's eyes up close as oak—
He thought 'twas witchcraft. But I am
  much to blame;   215
I humbly do beseech you of your pardon
For too much loving you.
  Oth.   I am bound to thee for ever.
  Iago. I see this hath a little dash'd your
    spirits.
  Oth. Not a jot, not a jot.
  Iago.   I'faith, I fear it has.
I hope you will consider what is spoke   220
Comes from my love; but I do see you are
  mov'd.
I am to pray you not to strain my speech
To grosser issues nor to larger reach
Than to suspicion.
  Oth. I will not.
  Iago.   Should you do so, my lord, 225
My speech should fall into such vile success
Which my thoughts aim'd not. Cassio's
  my worthy friend—
My lord, I see you are mov'd.
  Oth.   No, not much mov'd.
I do not think but Desdemona's honest.
  Iago. Long live she so! and long live you
    to think so!   230
  Oth. And yet, how nature erring from
    itself—
  Iago. Ay, there's the point: as—to be
    bold with you—
Not to affect many proposed matches
Of her own clime, complexion, and degree,
Whereto we see in all things nature tends—
Foh! one may smell in such a will most
  rank,   236
Foul disproportion, thoughts unnatural.
But pardon me—I do not in position
Distinctly speak of her; though I may fear
Her will, recoiling to her better judgment,
May fall to match you with her country
  forms,   241
And happily repent.
  Oth.   Farewell, farewell.
If more thou dost perceive, let me know
  more;
Set on thy wife to observe. Leave me,
  Iago.   244
  Iago. My lord, I take my leave. [*Going.*
  Oth. Why did I marry? This honest
    creature doubtless
Sees and knows more—much more than he
  unfolds.
  Iago. [*Returning*] My lord, I would I
    might entreat your honour
To scan this thing no further; leave it to
  time.   249
Although 'tis fit that Cassio have his place,
For, sure, he fills it up with great ability,
Yet if you please to hold him off awhile,
You shall by that perceive him and his
  means.   253
Note if your lady strain his entertainment

With any strong or vehement importunity;
Much will be seen in that. In the mean
  time
Let me be thought too busy in my fears—
As worthy cause I have to fear I am—
And hold her free, I do beseech your honour.
  Oth. Fear not my government.   260
  Iago. I once more take my leave. [*Exit.*
  Oth. This fellow's of exceeding honesty,
And knows all qualities, with a learned
  spirit,
Of human dealing. If I do prove her
  haggard,
Though that her jesses were my dear heart-
  strings,   265
I'd whistle her off and let her down the
  wind
To prey at fortune. Haply, for I am black
And have not those soft parts of conversa-
  tion
That chamberers have, or for I am declin'd
Into the vale of years—yet that's not
  much—   270
She's gone; I am abus'd; and my relief
Must be to loathe her. O curse of marriage,
That we can call these delicate creatures
  ours,
And not their appetites! I had rather be a
  toad,
And live upon the vapour of a dungeon,   275
Than keep a corner in the thing I love
For others' uses. Yet 'tis the plague of
  great ones;
Prerogativ'd are they less than the base;
'Tis destiny unshunnable, like death;   279
Even then this forked plague is fated to us
When we do quicken. Look where she
  comes.

Re-enter DESDEMONA *and* EMILIA.

If she be false, O, then heaven mocks itself!
I'll not believe it.
  Des.   How now, my dear Othello?
Your dinner, and the generous islanders
By you invited, do attend your presence.
  Oth. I am to blame.
  Des.   Why do you speak so faintly?
Are you not well?
  Oth. I have a pain upon my forehead
    here.
  Des. Faith, that's with watching; 'twill
    away again.   289
Let me but bind it hard, within this hour
It will be well.
    [*He puts the handkerchief from him,
        and she drops it.*
  Oth.   Your napkin is too little.
Let it alone. Come, I'll go in with you.
  Des. I am very sorry that you are not
    well.
      [*Exeunt Othello and Desdemona.*
  Emil. I am glad I have found this napkin.
This was her first remembrance from the
  Moor.   295

My wayward husband hath a hundred times
Woo'd me to steal it ; but she so loves the token—
For he conjur'd her she should ever keep it—
That she reserves it evermore about her
To kiss and talk to. I'll ha the work ta'en out,   300
And give't Iago. What he'll do with it Heaven knows, not I ;
I nothing but to please his fantasy.

Re-enter IAGO.

Iago. How now ! What do you here alone ?
Emil. Do not you chide ; I have a thing for you.   305
Iago. You have a thing for me ?
It is a common thing !
Emil. Ha !
Iago. To have a foolish wife.
Emil. O, is that all ? What will you give me now
For that same handkerchief ?
Iago.   What handkerchief ?
Emil. What handkerchief !   311
Why that the Moor first gave to Desdemona ;
That which so often you did bid me steal.
Iago. Hast stole it from her ?
Emil. No, faith ; she let it drop by negligence,   315
And to the advantage, I, being here, took't up.
Look, here it is.
Iago.   A good wench ! Give it me.
Emil. What will you do with't, that you have been so earnest
To have me filch it ?
Iago.   Why, what's that to you ?
                    [*Snatching it.*
Emil. If it be not for some purpose of import,   320
Give me't again. Poor lady, she'll run mad
When she shall lack it.
Iago. Be not acknown on't ; I have use for it.
Go, leave me.   [*Exit Emilia.*
I will in Cassio's lodging lose this napkin,
And let him find it. Trifles light as air   326
Are to the jealous confirmations strong
As proofs of holy writ ; this may do something.
The Moor already changes with my poison.
Dangerous conceits are in their natures poisons   330
Which at the first are scarce found to distaste
But, with a little act upon the blood,
Burn like the mines of sulphur.

Re-enter OTHELLO.

                  I did say so.

Look where he comes ! Not poppy, nor mandragora,
Nor all the drowsy syrups of the world,   335
Shall ever medicine thee to that sweet sleep
Which thou owed'st yesterday.
  Oth. Ha ! ha ! false to me, to me ?
  Iago. Why, how now, General ? No more of that.
  Oth. Avaunt ! be gone ! Thou hast set me on the rack.
I swear 'tis better to be much abus'd   340
Than but to know 't a little.
  Iago.   How now, my lord !
  Oth. What sense had I in her stol'n hours of lust ?
I saw 't not, thought it not, it harm'd not me.
I slept the next night well, fed well, was free and merry ;
I found not Cassio's kisses on her lips.   345
He that is robb'd, not wanting what is stol'n,
Let him not know't, and he's not robb'd at all.
  Iago. I am sorry to hear this.
  Oth. I had been happy if the general camp,   349
Pioneers and all, had tasted her sweet body,
So I had nothing known. O, now for ever
Farewell the tranquil mind ! farewell content !
Farewell the plumed troops, and the big wars
That makes ambition virtue ! O, farewell !
Farewell the neighing steed and the shrill trump,   355
The spirit-stirring drum, th' ear-piercing fife,
The royal banner, and all quality,
Pride, pomp, and circumstance, of glorious war !
And O ye mortal engines whose rude throats
Th' immortal Jove's dread clamours counterfeit,   360
Farewell ! Othello's occupation's gone.
  Iago. Is't possible, my lord ?
  Oth. Villain, be sure thou prove my love a whore—
           [*Taking him by the throat.*
Be sure of it ; give me the ocular proof ;
Or, by the worth of man's eternal soul,   365
Thou hadst been better have been born a dog
Than answer my wak'd wrath.
  Iago.   Is't come to this ?
  Oth. Make me to see't ; or, at the least, so prove it
That the probation bear no hinge nor loop
To hang a doubt on ; or woe upon thy life !
  Iago. My noble lord—   371
  Oth. If thou dost slander her and torture me,
Never pray more ; abandon all remorse ;

On horror's head horrors accumulate ;
Do deeds to make heaven weep, all earth
    amaz'd ;   375
For nothing canst thou to damnation add
Greater than that.
   Iago.   O grace ! O heaven forgive me !
Are you a man ? Have you a soul or
    sense ?—
God buy you ; take mine office. O wretched
    fool,   379
That liv'st to make thine honesty a vice !
O monstrous world ! Take note, take note,
    O world,
To be direct and honest is not safe.
I thank you for this profit ; and from hence
I'll love no friend, sith love breeds such
    offence.   384
   Oth. Nay, stay. Thou shouldst be honest.
   Iago. I should be wise ; for honesty's a
    fool,
And loses that it works for.
   Oth.   By the world,
I think my wife be honest, and think she
    is not ;
I think that thou art just, and think thou
    art not.
I'll have some proof. Her name, that was
    as fresh   390
As Dian's visage, is now begrim'd and black
As mine own face. If there be cords or
    knives,
Poison, or fire, or suffocating streams,
I'll not endure it. Would I were satisfied !
   Iago. I see, sir, you are eaten up with
    passion ;   395
I do repent me that I put it to you.
You would be satisfied ?
   Oth.   Would ! Nay, and I will.
   Iago. And may ; but how—how satisfied,
    my lord ?
Would you, the supervisor, grossly gape
    on—   399
Behold her topp'd ?
   Oth.   Death and damnation ! O !
   Iago. It were a tedious difficulty, I think,
To bring them to that prospect. Damn
    them, then,
If ever mortal eyes do see them bolster
More than their own ! What then ? How
    then ?   404
What shall I say ? Where's satisfaction ?
It is impossible you should see this,
Were they as prime as goats, as hot as
    monkeys,
As salt as wolves in pride, and fools as gross
As ignorance made drunk. But yet, I say,
If imputation and strong circumstances   410
Which lead directly to the door of truth
Will give you satisfaction, you might
    have't.
   Oth. Give me a living reason she's dis-
    loyal.
   Iago. I do not like the office ;   414
But, sith I am enter'd in this cause so far,

Prick'd to't by foolish honesty and love,
I will go on. I lay with Cassio lately,
And, being troubled with a raging tooth,
I could not sleep.
There are a kind of men so loose of soul   420
That in their sleeps will mutter their affairs:
One of this kind is Cassio.
In sleep I heard him say ' Sweet Desde-
    mona,
Let us be wary, let us hide our loves ',
And then, sir, would he gripe and wring my
    hand,   425
Cry ' O sweet creature ! ' then kiss me
    hard,
As if he pluck'd up kisses by the roots,
That grew upon my lips—then laid his leg
Over my thigh—and sigh'd, and kiss'd, and
    then
Cried ' Cursed fate that gave thee to the
    Moor ! '   430
   Oth. O monstrous ! monstrous !
   Iago.   Nay, this was but his dream.
   Oth. But this denoted a foregone con-
    clusion.
   Iago. 'Tis a shrewd doubt, though it be
    but a dream.
And this may help to thicken other proofs
That do demonstrate thinly.
   Oth. I'll tear her all to pieces.
   Iago. Nay, but be wise ; yet we see
    nothing done ;   436
She may be honest yet. Tell me but this :
Have you not sometimes seen a handker-
    chief
Spotted with strawberries in your wife's
    hand ?
   Oth. I gave her such a one ; 'twas my
    first gift.   440
   Iago. I know not that ; but such a
    handkerchief—
I am sure it was your wife's—did I to-day
See Cassio wipe his beard with.
   Oth.   If it be that—
   Iago. If it be that, or any that was hers,
It speaks against her with the other proofs.
   Oth. O that the slave had forty thousand
    lives !   446
One is too poor, too weak for my revenge.
Now do I see 'tis true. Look here, Iago—
All my fond love thus do I blow to heaven.
'Tis gone.   450
Arise, black vengeance, from the hollow
    hell.
Yield up, O love, thy crown and hearted
    throne
To tyrannous hate ! Swell, bosom, with
    thy fraught,
For 'tis of aspics' tongues.
   Iago.   Yet be content.
   Oth. O, blood, blood, blood !   455
   Iago. Patience, I say ; your mind per-
    haps may change.
   Oth. Never, Iago. Like to the Pontic sea,
Whose icy current and compulsive course

Ne'er feels retiring ebb, but keeps due on
To the Propontic and the Hellespont ;　460
Even so my bloody thoughts, with violent
　　pace,
Shall ne'er look back, ne'er ebb to humble
　　love,
Till that a capable and wide revenge
Swallow them up. [*He kneels*] Now, by yond
　　marble heaven,
In the due reverence of a sacred vow　465
I here engage my words.
　　Iago. [*Kneeling*] Do not rise yet.
Witness, you ever-burning lights above,
You elements that clip us round about,
Witness that here Iago doth give up
The execution of his wit, hands, heart,　470
To wrong'd Othello's service !　Let him
　　command,
And· to obey shall be in me remorse,
What bloody business ever.　[*They rise.*
　　Oth.　　　　　　I greet thy love,
Not with vain thanks, but with acceptance
　　bounteous,
And will upon the instant put thee to't.　475
Within these three days let me hear thee
　　say
That Cassio's not alive.
　　Iago.　　　　My friend is dead ;
'Tis done at your request.　But let her live.
　　Oth. Damn her, lewd minx ! O, damn her,
　　damn her !　　　　　　　　479
Come, go with me apart ; I will withdraw
To furnish me with some swift means of
　　death
For the fair devil.　Now art thou my
　　lieutenant.
　　Iago. I am your own for ever.　[*Exeunt.*

Scene IV. *Cyprus. Before the citadel.*

Enter Desdemona, Emilia, *and* Clown.

　　Des. Do you know, sirrah, where the
Lieutenant Cassio lies ?
　　Clo. I dare not say he lies anywhere.
　　Des. Why, man ?
　　Clo. He's a soldier ; and for one to say
a soldier lies, 'tis stabbing.　　　　5
　　Des. Go to.　Where lodges he ?
　　Clo. To tell you where he lodges is to tell
you where I lie.
　　Des. Can anything be made of this ?　9
　　Clo. I know not where he lodges ; and
for me to devise a lodging, and say he lies
here or he lies there, were to lie in mine
own throat.
　　Des. Can you inquire him out, and be
edified by report ?
　　Clo. I will catechize the world for him ;
that is, make questions, and by them
answer.　　　　　　　　15
　　Des. Seek him ; bid him come hither :
tell him I have mov'd my lord on his
behalf, and hope all will be well.
　　Clo. To do this is within the compass of

man's wit ; and therefore I will attempt
the doing it.　　　　　　　　　　[*Exit.*
　　Des. Where should I lose the hand-
　　kerchief, Emilia ?
　　Emil. I know not, madam.　　　　21
　　Des. Believe me, I had rather lose my
　　purse
Full of crusadoes ; and but my noble Moor
Is true of mind, and made of no such
　　baseness
As jealous creatures are, it were enough　25
To put him to ill thinking.
　　Emil.　　　　　Is he not jealous ?
　　Des. Who, he ? I think the sun where he
　　was born
Drew all such humours from him.

　　　　　　Enter Othello.

　　Emil.　　　　　Look where he comes.
　　Des. I will not leave him now till Cassio
Be call'd to him. How is't with you, my
　　lord ?　　　　　　　　　　　　30
　　Oth. Well, my good lady. [*Aside*] O,
　　hardness to dissemble !—
How do you, Desdemona ?
　　Des.　　　　Well, my good lord.
　　Oth. Give me your hand.　This hand is
　　moist, my lady.
　　Des. It yet hath felt no age nor known
　　no sorrow.
　　Oth. This argues fruitfulness and liberal
　　heart :　　　　　　　　　　　35
Hot, hot, and moist. This hand of yours
　　requires
A sequester from liberty, fasting and
　　prayer,
Much castigation, exercise devout ;
For here's a young and sweating devil here
That commonly rebels.　'Tis a good hand,
A frank one.
　　Des.　　　You may indeed say so ;　41
For 'twas that hand that gave away my
　　heart.
　　Oth. A liberal hand. The hearts of old
　　gave hands ;
But our new heraldry is hands, not hearts.
　　Des. I cannot speak of this. Come now,
　　your promise.　　　　　　　　45
　　Oth. What promise, chuck ?
　　Des. I have sent to bid Cassio come
　　speak with you.
　　Oth. I have a salt and sorry rheum
　　offends me ;
Lend me thy handkerchief.
　　Des.　　　　　Here, my lord.　50
　　Oth. That which I gave you.
　　Des.　　　　I have it not about me.
　　Oth. Not ?
　　Des.　　　No, faith, my lord.
　　Oth. That's a fault. That handkerchief　55
Did an Egyptian to my mother give.
She was a charmer, and could almost read
The thoughts of people ; she told her, while
　　she kept it,

'Twould make her amiable, and subdue my
        father
Entirely to her love ; but if she lost it, 60
Or made a gift of it, my father's eye
Should hold her loathely, and his spirits
        should hunt
After new fancies. She, dying, gave it me,
And bid me, when my fate would have me
        wive, 64
To give it her. I did so ; and take heed on't;
Make it a darling like your precious eye ;
To lose't or give't away were such perdition
As nothing else could match.

Des.   Is't possible ?

Oth. 'Tis true. There's magic in the web
        of it.
A sibyl that had numb'red in the world 70
The sun to course two hundred compasses
In her prophetic fury sew'd the work ;
The worms were hallowed that did breed
        the silk ;
And it was dy'd in mummy which the
        skilful
Conserv'd of maidens' hearts.

Des.   I'faith ! Is't true ? 75

Oth. Most veritable ; therefore look to't
        well.

Des. Then would to God that I had never
        seen't !

Oth. Ha ! Wherefore ?

Des. Why do you speak so startingly and
        rash ?

Oth. Is't lost ? Is't gone ? Speak. Is 't
        out o' th' way ? 80

Des. Heaven bless us !

Oth. Say you ?

Des. It is not lost ; but what an if it
        were ?

Oth. How ! 84

Des. I say it is not lost.

Oth.   Fetch't, let me see't.

Des. Why, so I can, sir, but I will not
        now.
This is a trick to put me from my suit :
Pray you let Cassio be receiv'd again.

Oth. Fetch me the handkerchief : my
        mind misgives. 90

Des. Come, come ;
You'll never meet a more sufficient man.

Oth. The handkerchief !

Des.   I pray talk me of Cassio.

Oth. The handkerchief !

Des.   A man that all his time
Hath founded his good fortunes on your
        love, 95
Shar'd dangers with you—

Oth.   The handkerchief !

Des. I'faith, you are to blame.

Oth. Zounds !   [*Exit Othello.*

Emil. Is not this man jealous ? 100

Des. I ne'er saw this before.
Sure there's some wonder in this hand-
        kerchief ;
I am most unhappy in the loss of it.

Emil. 'Tis not a year or two shows us a
        man.
They are all but stomachs, and we all but
        food ; 105
They eat us hungerly, and when they are
        full,
They belch us.

        Enter CASSIO *and* IAGO.

        Look you, Cassio and my husband.

Iago. There is no other way ; 'tis she
        must do 't.
And, lo, the happiness ! Go and importune
        her.

Des. How now, good Cassio, what's the
        news with you ? 110

Cas. Madam, my former suit. I do
        beseech you
That by your virtuous means I may again
Exist, and be a member of his love
Whom I, with all the office of my heart,
Entirely honour. I would not be delay'd.
If my offence be of such mortal kind 116
That nor my service past, nor present
        sorrows,
Nor purpos'd merit in futurity,
Can ransom me into his love again,
But to know so must be my benefit ; 120
So shall I clothe me in a forc'd content,
And shut myself up in some other course,
To fortune's alms.

Des.   Alas, thrice-gentle Cassio !
My advocation is not now in tune ;
My lord is not my lord ; nor should I know
        him, 125
Were he in favour as in humour alter'd.
So help me every spirit sanctified,
As I have spoken for you all my best,
And stood within the blank of his dis-
        pleasure
For my free speech ! You must awhile be
        patient. 130
What I can do I will ; and more I will
Than for myself I dare ; let that suffice you.

Iago. Is my lord angry ?

Emil.   He went hence but now,
And certainly in strange unquietness.

Iago. Can he be angry ? I have seen the
        cannon 135
When it hath blown his ranks into the
        air,
And, like the devil, from his very arm
Puff'd his own brother—and is he angry ?
Something of moment, then. I will go meet
        him. 139
There's matter in't indeed, if he be angry.

Des. I prithee do so.   [*Exit Iago.*
                Something sure of state
Either from Venice, or some unhatch'd
        practice
Made demonstrable here in Cyprus to him,
Hath puddled his clear spirit ; and in such
        cases
Men's natures wrangle with inferior things, 144

Though great ones are their object. 'Tis
    even so ;
For let our finger ache, and it endues
Our other healthful members even to a
    sense
Of pain. Nay, we must think, men are not
    gods,
Nor of them look for such observancy   150
As fits the bridal. Beshrew me much,
    Emilia,
I was—unhandsome warrior as I am—
Arraigning his unkindness with my soul ;
But now I find I had suborn'd the witness,
And he's indicted falsely.   155
    Emil. Pray heaven it be state matters,
        as you think,
And no conception nor no jealous toy
Concerning you.
    Des. Alas the day, I never gave him
        cause !
    Emil. But jealous souls will not be
        answer'd so ;   160
They are not ever jealous for the cause,
But jealous for they are jealous. 'Tis a
    monster
Begot upon it self, born on it self.
    Des. Heaven keep that monster from
        Othello's mind !
    Emil. Lady, amen.   165
    Des. I will go seek him. Cassio, walk
        hereabout.
If I do find him fit, I'll move your suit,
And seek to effect it to my uttermost.
    Cas. I humbly thank your ladyship.   169
        [*Exeunt Desdemona and Emilia.*

        Enter BIANCA.

    Bian. Save you, friend Cassio !
    Cas.   What make you from home ?
How is it with you, my most fair Bianca ?
I' faith, sweet love, I was coming to your
    house.
    Bian. And I was going to your lodging,
        Cassio.
What, keep a week away ? seven days and
    nights ?
Eightscore eight hours ? and lovers' absent
    hours,   175
More tedious than the dial eight score
    times ?
O weary reckoning !
    Cas.   Pardon me, Bianca.
I have this while with leaden thoughts
    been press'd ;
But I shall in a more continuate time
Strike off this score of absence. Sweet
    Bianca,   180
        [*Giving her Desdemona's handkerchief.*
Take me this work out.
    Bian.   O Cassio, whence came this ?
This is some token from a newer friend :
To the felt absence now I feel a cause.
Is't come to this ? Well, well.
    Cas.   Go to, woman !

Throw your vile guesses in the devil's
    teeth,   185
From whence you have them. You are
    jealous now
That this is from some mistress, some
    remembrance.
No, by my faith, Bianca.
    Bian.   Why, whose is it ?
    Cas. I know not neither ; I found it in
        my chamber.   189
I like the work well ; ere it be demanded—
As like enough it will—I would have it
    copied.
Take it, and do't ; and leave me for this
    time.
    Bian. Leave you ! Wherefore ?
    Cas. I do attend here on the General ;
And think it no addition, nor my wish,   195
To have him see me woman'd.
    Bian.   Why, I pray you ?
    Cas. Not that I love you not.
    Bian.   But that you do not love me.
I pray you bring me on the way a little ;
And say if I shall see you soon at night.
    Cas. 'Tis but a little way that I can bring
        you,   200
For I attend here ; but I'll see you soon.
    Bian. 'Tis very good ; I must be circum-
        stanc'd.   [*Exeunt.*

        ACT FOUR

    SCENE I. *Cyprus. Before the citadel.*

        Enter OTHELLO *and* IAGO.

    Iago. Will you think so ?
    Oth.   Think so, Iago ?
    Iago.   What,
To kiss in private ?
    Oth.   An unauthoriz'd kiss.
    Iago. Or to be naked with her friend abed
An hour or more, not meaning any harm ?
    Oth. Naked abed, Iago, and not mean
        harm !   5
It is hypocrisy against the devil.
They that mean virtuously and yet do so,
The devil their virtue tempts, and they
    tempt heaven.
    Iago. So they do nothing, 'tis a venial
        slip ;
But if I give my wife a handkerchief—   10
    Oth. What then ?
    Iago. Why, then 'tis hers, my lord ; and,
        being hers,
She may, I think, bestow't on any man.
    Oth. She is protectress of her honour too :
May she give that ?   15
    Iago. Her honour is an essence that's not
        seen ;
They have it very oft that have it not.
But, for the handkerchief—
    Oth. By heaven, I would most gladly
        have forgot it.   19
Thou said'st—O, it comes o'er my memory

As doth the raven o'er the infected house,
Boding to all—he had my handkerchief.

Iago. Ay, what of that ?

Oth. That's not so good now.

Iago. What
If I had said I had seen him do you wrong ?
Or heard him say—as knaves be such
abroad,   25
Who having, by their own importunate
suit,
Or voluntary dotage of some mistress,
Convinced or supplied them, cannot choose
But they must blab—

Oth. Hath he said anything ?

Iago. He hath, my lord ; but be you well
assur'd,   30
No more than he'll unswear.

Oth. What hath he said ?

Iago. Faith, that he did—I know not
what he did.

Oth. What ? what ?

Iago. Lie—

Oth. With her ?

Iago. With her, on her ; what you will.

Oth. Lie with her—lie on her ? We say
lie on her when they belie her. Lie with
her. Zounds, that's fulsome. Handkerchief
—confessions—handkerchief ! To confess,
and be hang'd for his labour—first, to be
hang'd, and then to confess. I tremble at
it. Nature would not invest herself in such
shadowing passion without some instruction. It is not words that shakes me thus—
pish !—noses, ears, and lips. Is't possible ?
Confess ! Handkerchief ! O devil !

[*Falls in a trance.*

Iago. Work on,   44
My medicine, work. Thus credulous fools
are caught ;
And many worthy and chaste dames even
thus,
All guiltless, meet reproach. What, ho !
my lord !
My lord, I say ! Othello !

Enter CASSIO.

How now, Cassio !

Cas. What's the matter ?

Iago. My lord is fall'n into an epilepsy. 50
This is his second fit ; he had one yesterday.

Cas. Rub him about the temples.

Iago. No, forbear.
The lethargy must have his quiet course ;
If not, he foams at mouth, and by and by
Breaks out to savage madness. Look, he
stirs.   55
Do you withdraw yourself a little while ;
He will recover straight ; when he is
gone,
I would on great occasion speak with you.

[*Exit Cassio.*

How is it, General ? Have you not hurt
your head ?

Oth. Dost thou mock me ?

Iago. I mock you ? No, by heaven !
Would you would bear your fortune like a
man !   61

Oth. A horned man's a monster and a
beast.

Iago. There's many a beast then in a
populous city,
And many a civil monster.

Oth. Did he confess it ?

Iago. Good sir, be a man ; 65
Think every bearded fellow that's but
yok'd
May draw with you ; there's millions now
alive
That nightly lie in those unproper beds
Which they dare swear peculiar : your case
is better.
O, 'tis the spite of hell, the fiend's arch-
mock,   70
To lip a wanton in a secure couch,
And to suppose her chaste ! No, let me
know ;
And knowing what I am, I know what she
shall be.

Oth. O, thou art wise ; 'tis certain.

Iago. Stand you awhile apart.
Confine yourself but in a patient list. 75
Whilst you were here o'erwhelmed with
your grief—
A passion most unsuiting such a man—
Cassio came hither ; I shifted him away,
And laid good 'scuse upon your ecstasy ;
Bade him anon return, and here speak with
me ;   80
The which he promis'd. Do but encave
yourself,
And mark the fleers, the gibes, and notable
scorns,
That dwell in every region of his face ;
For I will make him tell the tale anew—
Where, how, how oft, how long ago, and
when,   85
He hath, and is again to cope your wife.
I say, but mark his gesture. Marry,
patience ;
Or I shall say you are all in all in spleen,
And nothing of a man.

Oth. Dost thou hear, Iago ?
I will be found most cunning in my
patience ;   90
But—dost thou hear ?—most bloody.

Iago. That's not amiss ;
But yet keep time in all. Will you with-
draw ? [*Othello withdraws.*
Now will I question Cassio of Bianca,
A huswife that by selling her desires
Buys herself bread and clothes ; it is a
creature   95
That dotes on Cassio, as 'tis the strumpet's
plague
To beguile many and be beguil'd by one.
He, when he hears of her, cannot restrain
From the excess of laughter.

Re-enter CASSIO.

                                    Here he comes.
As he shall smile Othello shall go mad ;   100
And his unbookish jealousy must construe
Poor Cassio's smiles, gestures, and light
    behaviours,
Quite in the wrong.   How do you now,
    Lieutenant ?
    Cas. The worser that you give me the
        addition
Whose want even kills me.   105
    Iago. Ply Desdemona well, and you are
        sure on't.
Now, if this suit lay in Bianca's dower,
How quickly should you speed !
    Cas.   Alas, poor caitiff !
    Oth. Look how he laughs already !   109
    Iago. I never knew a woman love man so.
    Cas. Alas, poor rogue ! I think, i' faith,
        she loves me.
    Oth. Now he denies it faintly, and laughs
        it out.
    Iago. Do you hear, Cassio ?
    Oth.   Now he importunes him
To tell it o'er.   Go to ; well said, well said.
    Iago. She gives it out that you shall
        marry her.   115
Do you intend it ?
    Cas. Ha, ha, ha !
    Oth. Do you triumph, Roman ? Do you
triumph ?
    Cas. I marry her ! What, a customer ! I
prithee bear some charity to my wit ; do
not think it so unwholesome. Ha, ha, ha !
    Oth. So, so, so, so—they laugh that
wins.   122
    Iago. Faith, the cry goes that you marry
her.
    Cas. Prithee say true.
    Iago. I am a very villain else.   125
    Oth. Ha you scor'd me ? Well.
    Cas. This is the monkey's own giving
out : she is persuaded I will marry her,
out of her own love and flattery, not out
of my promise.
    Oth. Iago beckons me ; now he begins
the story.   130
    Cas. She was here even now ; she haunts
me in every place. I was t'other day talking
on the sea-bank with certain Venetians,
and thither comes the bauble—by this
hand, she falls me thus about my neck.
    Oth. Crying ' O dear Cassio ! ' as it were :
his gesture imports it.
    Cas. So hangs, and lolls, and weeps upon
me ; so hales, and pulls me. Ha, ha, ha !
    Oth. Now he tells how she pluck'd him
to my chamber. O, I see that nose of yours,
but not that dog I shall throw't to.   141
    Cas. Well, I must leave her company.

Enter BIANCA.

    Iago. Before me ! Look where she comes.

    Cas. 'Tis such another fitchew ! marry, a
perfum'd one. What do you mean by this
haunting of me ?   145
    Bian. Let the devil and his dam haunt
you. What did you mean by that same
handkerchief you gave me even now ? I
was a fine fool to take it. I must take out
the whole work—a likely piece of work
that you should find it in your chamber
and know not who left it there ! This is
some minx's token, and I must take out
the work ? There—give it your hobby-
horse. Wheresoever you had it, I'll take
out no work on't.   153
    Cas. How now, my sweet Bianca ! how
now ! how now !
    Oth. By heaven, that should be my
handkerchief !   155
    Bian. An you'll come to supper to-night,
you may ; an you will not, come when you
are next prepar'd for.   [*Exit.*
    Iago. After her, after her.
    Cas. Faith, I must ; she'll rail i' th'
street else.
    Iago. Will you sup there ?   160
    Cas. Faith, I intend so.
    Iago. Well, I may chance to see you ; for
I would very fain speak with you.
    Cas. Prithee come ; will you ?
    Iago. Go to ; say no more. [*Exit Cassio.*
    Oth. [*Coming forward*] How shall I
murder him, Iago ?   166
    Iago. Did you perceive how he laugh'd at
his vice ?
    Oth. O Iago !
    Iago. And did you see the handker-
chief ?
    Oth. Was that mine ?   170
    Iago. Yours, by this hand. And to see
how he prizes the foolish woman your wife !
She gave it him, and he hath giv'n it his
whore.
    Oth. I would have him nine years a-
killing. A fine woman ! a fair woman ! a
sweet woman !   175
    Iago. Nay, you must forget that.
    Oth. Ay, let her rot, and perish, and be
damn'd to-night ; for she shall not live.
No, my heart is turn'd to stone ; I strike
it, and it hurts my hand. O, the world
hath not a sweeter creature ; she might lie
by an emperor's side and command him
tasks.   181
    Iago. Nay, that's not your way.
    Oth. Hang her ! I do but say what she
is : so delicate with her needle, an admirable musician—O, she will sing the
savageness out of a bear !—of so high and
plenteous wit and invention.   186
    Iago. She's the worse for all this.
    Oth. O, a thousand, a thousand times—
and then of so gentle a condition.
    Iago. Ay, too gentle.   190
    Oth. Nay, that's certain. But yet the

pity of it, Iago! O, Iago, the pity of it, Iago!

Iago. If you be so fond over her iniquity, give her patent to offend; for, if it touch not you, it comes near nobody.   195

Oth. I will chop her into messes. Cuckold me!

Iago. O, 'tis foul in her.

Oth. With mine officer!

Iago. That's fouler.   199

Oth. Get me some poison, Iago—this night. I'll not expostulate with her, lest her body and beauty unprovide my mind again—this night, Iago.

Iago. Do it not with poison; strangle her in her bed, even the bed she hath contaminated.   204

Oth. Good, good; the justice of it pleases; very good.

Iago. And for Cassio—let me be his undertaker. You shall hear more by midnight.   207

Oth. Excellent good.   [*A trumpet.*
              What trumpet is that same?

Iago. I warrant, something from Venice.

Enter LODOVICO, DESDEMONA, *and*
                    Attendants.

'Tis Lodovico—this comes from the Duke. See, your wife 's with him.

Lod. God save thee, worthy General!

Oth.   With all my heart, sir.

Lod. The Duke and Senators of Venice greet you.   [*Gives him a packet.*

Oth. I kiss the instrument of their pleasures.   [*Opens the packet and reads.*

Des. And what's the news, good cousin Lodovico?   214

Iago. I am very glad to see you, signior; Welcome to Cyprus.

Lod. I thank you. How does Lieutenant Cassio?

Iago.   Lives, sir.

Des. Cousin, there's fall'n between him and my lord
An unkind breach; but you shall make all well.   220

Oth. Are you sure of that?

Des. My lord?

Oth. [*Reads*] ' This fail you not to do as you will '—

Lod. He did not call; he's busy in the paper.
Is there division 'twixt thy lord and Cassio?   225

Des. A most unhappy one. I would do much
T' atone them, for the love I bear to Cassio.

Oth. Fire and brimstone!

Des. My lord?

Oth. Are you wise?   230

Des. What, is he angry?

Lod.   May be the letter mov'd him;

For, as I think, they do command him home,
Deputing Cassio in his government.

Des. By my troth, I am glad on't.

Oth. Indeed!

Des. My lord?

Oth. I am glad to see you mad.

Des.   Why, sweet Othello?

Oth. Devil!   [*Striking her.*

Des. I have not deserv'd this.   237

Lod. My lord, this would not be believ'd in Venice,
Though I should swear I saw't. 'Tis very much.
Make her amends; she weeps.

Oth.   O devil, devil!   240
If that the earth could teem with woman's tears,
Each drop she falls would prove a crocodile.
Out of my sight!

Des.   I will not stay to offend you.
                                        [*Going.*

Lod. Truly, an obedient lady.   244
I do beseech your lordship, call her back.

Oth. Mistress!

Des. My lord?

Oth. What would you with her, sir?

Lod.   Who, I, my lord?

Oth. Ay; you did wish that I would make her turn.   249
Sir, she can turn, and turn, and yet go on,
And turn again; and she can weep, sir, weep;
And she's obedient, as you say, obedient,
Very obedient.—Proceed you in your tears.—
Concerning this, sir,—O, well-painted passion!—   254
I am commanded home.—Get you away;
I'll send for you anon.—Sir, I obey the mandate,
And will return to Venice.—Hence, avaunt!
                              [*Exit Desdemona.*
Cassio shall have my place. And, sir, to-night,
I do entreat that we may sup together.
You are welcome, sir, to Cyprus.—Goats and monkeys!   [*Exit.*

Lod. Is this the noble Moor whom our full Senate   261
Call all in all sufficient? Is this the nature
Whom passion could not shake, whose solid virtue
The shot of accident nor dart of chance
Could neither graze nor pierce?

Iago.   He is much chang'd.

Lod. Are his wits safe? Is he not light of brain?   266

Iago. He's that he is. I may not breathe my censure.
What he might be, if what he might he is not,
I would to heaven he were!

Lod.   What, strike his wife!

Iago. Faith, that was not so well; yet
    would I knew   270
That stroke would prove the worst!
    Lod.   Is it his use?
Or did the letters work upon his blood,
And new-create this fault?
    Iago.   Alas, alas!
It is not honesty in me to speak
What I have seen and known. You shall
    observe him;   275
And his own courses will denote him so
That I may save my speech. Do but go
    after,
And mark how he continues.
    Lod. I am sorry that I am deceiv'd in
    him.   [*Exeunt.*

SCENE II. *Cyprus. The citadel.*

Enter OTHELLO *and* EMILIA.

Oth. You have seen nothing, then?
Emil. Nor ever heard, nor ever did
    suspect.
Oth. Yes, you have seen Cassio and she
    together.
Emil. But then I saw no harm, and then
    I heard
Each syllable that breath made up between
    them.   5
Oth. What, did they never whisper?
Emil.   Never, my lord.
Oth. Nor send you out o' th' way?
Emil. Never.
Oth. To fetch her fan, her gloves, her
    mask, nor nothing?
Emil. Never, my lord.   10
Oth. That's strange.
Emil. I durst, my lord, to wager she is
    honest,
Lay down my soul at stake. If you think
    other,
Remove your thought—it doth abuse your
    bosom.
If any wretch have put this in your head, 15
Let heaven requite it with the serpent's
    curse;
For if she be not honest, chaste, and
    true,
There's no man happy; the purest of their
    wives
Is foul as slander.
    Oth.   Bid her come hither. Go.
                    [*Exit Emilia.*
She says enough; yet she's a simple bawd
That cannot say as much. This is a subtle
    whore,   21
A closet-lock-and-key of villainous secrets;
And yet she'll kneel and pray; I have seen
    her do't.

Re-enter EMILIA *with* DESDEMONA.

Des. My lord, what is your will?
Oth. Pray you chuck, come hither. 24
Des. What is your pleasure?

Oth. Let me see your eyes; look in my
    face.
Des. What horrible fancy's this?
Oth. [*To Emilia*] Some of your function,
    mistress:
Leave procreants alone, and shut the
    door;
Cough, or cry hem, if any body come. 29
Your mystery, your mystery; nay,
    dispatch.   [*Exit Emilia.*
Des. Upon my knees, what doth your
    speech import?
I understand a fury in your words,
But not the words.
    Oth. Why, what art thou?
Des. You wife, my lord; your true and
    loyal wife.   35
Oth. Come, swear it, damn thyself; lest,
being like one of heaven, the devils them-
selves should fear to seize thee; therefore
be double-damn'd—swear thou art honest.
Des. Heaven doth truly know it.
Oth. Heaven truly knows that thou art
    false as hell.
Des. To whom, my lord? With whom?
    How am I false?   41
Oth. Ah, Desdemona! away! away!
    away!
Des. Alas the heavy day! Why do you
    weep?
Am I the motive of these tears, my lord?
If haply you my father do suspect   45
An instrument of this your calling back,
Lay not your blame on me; if you have
    lost him,
Why, I have lost him too.
    Oth.   Had it pleas'd heaven
To try me with affliction; had they rain'd
All kind of sores and shames on my bare
    head,   50
Steep'd me in poverty to the very lips,
Given to captivity me and my utmost
    hopes,
I should have found in some place of my
    soul
A drop of patience; but, alas, to make me
The fixed figure for the time of scorn 55
To point his slow unmoving finger at!—
    O, O!
Yet could I bear that too; well, very well;
But there, where I have garner'd up my
    heart,
Where either I must live or bear no life,
The fountain from the which my current
    runs,   60
Or else dries up—to be discarded thence!
Or keep it as a cistern for foul toads
To knot and gender in! Turn thy com-
    plexion there,
Patience, thou young and rose-lipp'd
    cherubin—
Ay, here, look grim as hell.   65
Des. I hope my noble lord esteems me
    honest.

Oth. O, ay ; as summer flies are in the shambles,
That quicken even with blowing. O thou weed
Who art so lovely fair and smell'st so sweet
That the sense aches at thee !
Would thou had'st never been born !   70
Des. Alas, what ignorant sin have I committed ?
Oth. Was this fair paper, this most goodly book,
Made to write ' whore ' upon ? What committed !
Committed ! O thou public commoner !
I should make very forges of my cheeks   75
That would to cinders burn up modesty,
Did I but speak thy deeds. What committed !
Heaven stops the nose at it, and the moon winks ;
The bawdy wind, that kisses all it meets,
Is hush'd within the hollow mine of earth
And will not hear it. What committed ! 81
Impudent strumpet !
Des.   By heaven, you do me wrong.
Oth. Are not you a strumpet ?
Des.   No, as I am a Christian.
If to preserve this vessel for my lord
From any other foul unlawful touch   85
Be not to be a strumpet, I am none.
Oth. What, not a whore ?
Des.   No, as I shall be sav'd.
Oth. Is't possible ?
Des. O, heaven forgive us !
Oth.   I cry you mercy, then.
I took you for that cunning whore of Venice   90
That married with Othello.—You, mistress,
That have the office opposite to Saint Peter
And keeps the gate of hell !

Re-enter EMILIA.

                You, you, ay you !
We ha done our course ; there's money for your pains.
I pray you turn the key, and keep our counsel.   [*Exit.*
Emil. Alas, what does this gentleman conceive ?   96
How do you, madam ? How do you, my good lady ?
Des. Faith, half asleep.
Emil. Good madam, what's the matter with my lord ?
Des. With who ?   100
Emil. Why, with my lord, madam.
Des. Who is thy lord ?
Emil.   He that is yours, sweet lady.
Des. I have none. Do not talk to me, Emilia ;
I cannot weep, nor answers have I none
But what should go by water. Prithee, to-night   105

Lay on my bed my wedding sheets—remember ;
And call thy husband hither.
Emil. Here's a change indeed !   [*Exit.*
Des. 'Tis meet I should be us'd so, very meet.
How have I been behav'd, that he might stick   109
The small'st opin.on on my great'st abuse ?

Re-enter EMILIA *with* IAGO.

Iago. What is your pleasure, madam ? How is't with you ?
Des. I cannot tell. Those that do teach young babes
Do it with gentle means and easy tasks.
He might have chid me so ; for, in good faith,
I am a child to chiding.
Iago. What is the matter, lady ?   115
Emil. Alas, Iago, my lord hath so bewhor'd her,
Thrown such despite and heavy terms upon her
That true hearts cannot bear it.
Des. Am I that name, Iago ?
Iago.   What name, fair lady ?
Des. Such as she says my lord did say I was.   120
Emil. He call'd her whore. A beggar in his drink
Could not have laid such terms upon his callat.
Iago. Why did he so ?
Des. I do not know ; I am sure I am none such.
Iago. Do not weep, do not weep. Alas, the day !   125
Emil. Hath she forsook so many noble matches,
Her father, and her country, and her friends,
To be call'd whore ? Would it not make one weep ?
Des. It is my wretched fortune.
Iago.   Beshrew him for't !
How comes this trick upon him ?
Des.   Nay, heaven doth know.
Emil. I will be hang'd if some eternal villain,   131
Some busy and insinuating rogue,
Some cogging, cozening slave, to get some office,
Have not devis'd this slander ; I'll be hang'd else.
Iago. Fie, there is no such man ; it is impossible.   135
Des. If any such there be, heaven pardon him !
Emil. A halter pardon him ! and hell gnaw his bones !
Why should he call her whore ? Who keeps her company ?
What place, what time, what form, what likelihood ?

The Moor's abus'd by some outrageous
    knave, 140
Some base notorious knave, some scurvy
    fellow.
O heaven, that such companions thou'dst
    unfold,
And put in every honest hand a whip
To lash the rascals naked through the world
Even from the east to the west!
    Iago.   Speak within door. 145
    Emil. O, fie upon them! Some such squire
    he was
That turn'd your wit the seamy side
    without
And made you to suspect me with the Moor.
    Iago. You are a fool; go to.
    Des.   O God! Iago,
What shall I do to win my lord again? 150
Good friend, go to him; for, by this light
    of heaven,
I know not how I lost him. Here I kneel.
If e'er my will did trespass 'gainst his
    love,
Either in discourse of thought or actual
    deed, 154
Or that mine eyes, mine ears, or any sense,
Delighted them in any other form,
Or that I do not yet, and ever did,
And ever will—though he do shake me off
To beggarly divorcement—love him dearly,
Comfort forswear me! Unkindness may do
    much; 160
And his unkindness may defeat my life,
But never taint my love. I cannot say
    ' whore ';
It does abhor me now I speak the word;
To do the act that might the addition earn,
Not the world's mass of vanity could make
    me. 165
    Iago. I pray you be content; 'tis but his
    humour.
The business of the state does him offence,
And he does chide with you.
    Des. If 'twere no other!
    Iago.   It is but so, I warrant.
        [*Trumpets within.*
Hark how these instruments summon you
    to supper. 170
The messengers of Venice stay the meat.
Go in, and weep not; all things shall be
    well.
        [*Exeunt Desdemona and Emilia.*

    Enter RODERIGO.

How now, Roderigo!
    Rod. I do not find that thou deal'st justly
with me.
    Iago. What in the contrary? 175
    Rod. Every day thou daff'st me with
some device, Iago; and rather, as it seems
to me now, keep'st from me all conveniency than suppliest me with the least
advantage of hope. I will indeed, no longer
endure it; nor am I yet persuaded to put

up in peace what already I have foolishly
suffer'd. 181
    Iago. Will you hear me, Roderigo?
    Rod. Faith, I have heard too much; for
your words and performances are no kin
together.
    Iago. You charge me most unjustly. 185
    Rod. With nought but truth. I have
wasted myself out of my means. The jewels
you have had from me to deliver to
Desdemona would half have corrupted a
votarist. You have told me she hath
receiv'd them, and return'd me expectations
and comforts of sudden respect and
acquaintance; but I find none. 191
    Iago. Well; go to; very well.
    Rod. Very well! go to! I cannot go to,
man, nor 'tis not very well; by this hand,
I say 'tis very scurvy, and begin to find
myself fopt in it. 195
    Iago. Very well.
    Rod. I tell you 'tis not very well. I will
make myself known to Desdemona. If she
will return me my jewels, I will give over
my suit and repent my unlawful solicita-
tion; if not, assure yourself I will seek
satisfaction of you.
    Iago. You have said now. 201
    Rod. Ay, and said nothing but what I
protest intendment of doing.
    Iago. Why, now I see there's mettle in
thee; and even from this instant do build
on thee a better opinion than ever before.
Give me thy hand, Roderigo. Thou hast
taken against me a most just exception;
but yet, I protest, I have dealt most
directly in thy affair.
    Rod. It hath not appear'd. 209
    Iago. I grant, indeed, it hath not
appear'd; and your suspicion is not without wit and judgment. But, Roderigo, if
thou hast that in thee indeed, which I
have greater reason to believe now than
ever—I mean purpose, courage, and
valour—this night show it; if thou the
next night following enjoy not Desdemona, take me from this world with
treachery, and devise engines for my life.
    Rod. Well, what is it? Is it within
reason and compass? 218
    Iago. Sir, there is especial commission
come from Venice to depute Cassio in
Othello's place. 220
    Rod. Is that true? Why, then Othello
and Desdemona return again to Venice.
    Iago. O, no; he goes into Mauritania,
and taketh away with him the fair Desdemona, unless his abode be linger'd here by
some accident; wherein none can be so
determinate as the removing of Cassio. 226
    Rod. How do you mean removing of him?
    Iago. Why, by making him uncapable of
Othello's place—knocking out his brains.
    Rod. And that you would have me to do?

Iago. Ay, an if you dare do yourself a profit and right. He sups to-night with a harlotry, and thither will I go to him—he knows not yet of his honourable fortune. If you will watch his going thence, which I will fashion to fall out between twelve and one, you may take him at your pleasure. I will be near to second your attempt, and he shall fall between us. Come, stand not amaz'd at it, but go along with me; I will show you such a necessity in his death that you shall think yourself bound to put it on him. It is now high supper-time, and the night grows to waste. About it.   241

Rod. I will hear further reason for this.

Iago. And you shall be satisfied. [*Exeunt.*

SCENE III. *Cyprus. The citadel.*

Enter OTHELLO, DESDEMONA, LODOVICO, EMILIA, *and* Attendants.

Lod. I do beseech you, sir, trouble yourself no further.

Oth. O, pardon me; 'twill do me good to walk.

Lod. Madam, good night; I humbly thank your ladyship.

Des. Your honour is most welcome.

Oth. Will you walk, sir? O, Desdemona!

Des. My lord?   6

Oth. Get you to bed on th' instant; I will be return'd forthwith. Dispatch your attendant there. Look 't be done.

Des. I will, my lord. [*Exeunt Othello, Lodovico, and Attendants.*

Emil. How goes it now? He looks gentler than he did.   10

Des. He says he will return incontinent. He hath commanded me to go to bed, And bade me to dismiss you.

Emil.   Dismiss me!

Des. It was his bidding; therefore, good Emilia, Give me my nightly wearing, and adieu. 15 We must not now displease him.

Emil. I would you had never seen him.

Des. So would not I: my love doth so approve him That even his stubbornness, his checks, his frowns— Prithee unpin me—have grace and favour in them.   20

Emil. I have laid those sheets you bade me on the bed.

Des. All's one. Good faith, how foolish are our minds! If I do die before thee, prithee shroud me In one of these same sheets.

Emil.   Come, come, you talk.

Des. My mother had a maid call'd Barbary: 25 She was in love; and he she lov'd prov'd mad,

And did forsake her. She had a song of ' willow '; An old thing 'twas, but it express'd her fortune, And she died singing it. That song to-night Will not go from my mind; I have much to do   30 But to go hang my head all at one side And sing it like poor Barbary. Prithee dispatch.

Emil. Shall I go fetch your night-gown?

Des. No, unpin me here. This Lodovico is a proper man.

Emil. A very handsome man.   35

Des. He speaks well.

Emil. I know a lady in Venice would have walk'd barefoot to Palestine for a touch of his nether lip.

Des. [*Sings*] The poor soul sat sighing by a sycamore tree, Sing all a green willow;   40 Her hand on her bosom, her head on her knee. Sing willow, willow, willow. The fresh streams ran by her, and murmur'd her moans; Sing willow, willow, willow; Her salt tears fell from her and soft'ned the stones;   45 Sing willow— Lay by these— willow, willow.— Prithee, hie thee; he'll come anon.— Sing all a green willow must be my garland. Let nobody blame him; his scorn I approve—   50 Nay, that's not next. Hark! who is 't that knocks?

Emil. It is the wind.

Des. [*Sings*] I call'd my love false love; but what said he then? Sing willow, willow, willow: If I court moe women, you'll couch with moe men—   55 So, get thee gone; good night. Mine eyes do itch; Doth that bode weeping?

Emil.   'Tis neither here nor there.

Des. I have heard it said so. O, these men, these men! Dost thou in conscience think—tell me, Emilia— That there be women do abuse their husbands   60 In such gross kind?

Emil. There be some such, no question.

Des. Wouldst thou do such a deed for all the world?

Emil. Why, would not you?

Des.   No, by this heavenly light!

Emil. Nor I neither by this heavenly light; I might do 't as well i' th' dark.   65

Des. Wouldst thou do such a deed for all
    the world ?

Emil. The world's a huge thing.
It is a great price for a small vice.

Des. Good troth, I think thou wouldst
not.

Emil. By my troth, I think I should ;
and undo't when I had done it. Marry, I
would not do such a thing for a joint-ring,
nor for measures of lawn, nor for gowns,
petticoats, nor caps, nor any petty exhibition ; but for all the whole world—ud's
pity, who would not make her husband a
cuckold to make him a monarch ? I should
venture purgatory for't.   75

Des. Beshrew me, if I would do such a
wrong for the whole world.

Emil. Why, the wrong is but a wrong i'
th' world ; and having the world for your
labour, 'tis a wrong in your own world, and
you might quickly make it right.   80

Des. I do not think there is any such
woman.

Emil. Yes, a dozen ; and as many to th'
vantage as would store the world they
play'd for.
But I do think it is their husbands' faults
If wives do fall. Say that they slack their
    duties,   85
And pour our treasures into foreign laps ;
Or else break out in peevish jealousies,
Throwing restraint upon us ; or say they
    strike us,
Or scant our former having in despite ;
Why, we have galls ; and though we have
    some grace,   90
Yet have we some revenge. Let husbands
    know
Their wives have sense like them ; they see
    and smell,
And have their palates both for sweet and
    sour
As husbands have. What is it that they do
When they change us for others ? Is it
    sport ?   95
I think it is. And doth affection breed it ?
I think it doth. Is't frailty that thus errs ?
It is so too. And have not we affections,
Desires for sport, and frailty, as men have ?
Then let them use us well ; else let them
    know   100
The ills we do their ills instruct us so.

Des. Good night, good night. God me
    such uses send,
Not to pick bad from bad, but by bad
    mend !   [*Exeunt.*

ACT FIVE

SCENE I. *Cyprus. A street.*

Enter IAGO *and* RODERIGO.

Iago. Here, stand behind this bulk ;
straight will he come.

Wear thy good rapier bare, and put it
    home.
Quick, quick ; fear nothing ; I'll be at thy
    elbow.
It makes us or it mars us ; think on that,
And fix most firm thy resolution.   5

Rod. Be near at hand ; I may miscarry
    in't.

Iago. Here, at thy hand. Be bold, and
    take thy stand.   [*Withdraws.*

Rod. I have no great devotion to the
    deed ;
And yet he hath given me satisfying
    reasons—
'Tis but a man gone. Forth, my sword ;
    he dies.   10

Iago. I have rubb'd this young quat
    almost to the sense,
And he grows angry. Now, whether he kill
    Cassio
Or Cassio him, or each do kill the other,
Every way makes my gain. Live Roderigo,
He calls me to a restitution large   15
Of gold and jewels that I bobb'd from him
As gifts to Desdemona ;
It must not be. If Cassio do remain,
He hath a daily beauty in his life
That makes me ugly ; and besides, the
    Moor   20
May unfold me to him ; there stand I in
    much peril.
No, he must die. Be 't so. I hear him
    coming.

Enter CASSIO.

Rod. I know his gait, 'tis he. Villain,
    thou diest !   [*Thrusts at Cassio.*

Cas. That thrust had been mine enemy
    indeed
But that my coat is better than thou
    know'st.   25
I will make proof of thine. [*Draws, and
            wounds Roderigo.*

Rod. O, I am slain ! [*Iago stabs Cassio
    from behind in the leg, and exit.*

Cas. I am maim'd for ever. Help, ho !
    murder ! murder !   [*Falls.*

Enter OTHELLO *at a distance.*

Oth. The voice of Cassio. Iago keeps his
    word.

Rod. O, villain that I am !

Oth. It is even so.

Cas. O, help, ho ! light ! a surgeon ! 30

Oth. 'Tis he. O brave Iago, honest and
    just,
That hast such noble sense of thy friend's
    wrong !
Thou teachest me—minion, your dear lies
    dead,
And your unblest fate hies. Strumpet, I
    come.
Forth of my heart those charms, thine eyes,
    are blotted ;   35

Thy bed, lust-stain'd, shall with lust's blood
be spotted. [*Exit.*

Enter LODOVICO *and* GRATIANO *at a distance.*

Cas. What, ho! No watch? No passage?
Murder! murder!
Gra. 'Tis some mischance; the voice is
very direful.
Cas. O, help!
Lod. Hark!
Rod. O wretched villain!   40
Lod. Two or three groan. 'Tis heavy
night;
These may be counterfeits; let's think't
unsafe
To come in to the cry without more help.
Rod. Nobody come? Then shall I bleed
to death.   45

Re-enter IAGO *with a light.*

Lod. Hark!
Gra. Here's one comes in his shirt, with
light and weapons.
Iago. Who's there? Whose noise is this
that cries on murder?
Lod. We do not know.
Iago.   Did not you hear a cry?
Cas. Here, here! For heaven's sake,
help me!
Iago.   What's the matter?
Gra. This is Othello's ancient, as I take it.
Lod. The same indeed; a very valiant
fellow.   52
Iago. What are you here that cry so
grievously?
Cas. Iago? O, I am spoil'd, undone by
villains!
Give me some help.   55
Iago. O me, Lieutenant! What villains
have done this?
Cas. I think that one of them is here-
about,
And cannot make away.
Iago.   O treacherous villains!—
[*To Lodovico and Gratiano*] What are you
there? Come in, and give some
help.
Rod. O, help me there!   60
Cas. That's one of them.
Iago. O murd'rous slave! O villain!
[*Stabs Roderigo.*
Rod. O damn'd Iago! O inhuman dog!
Iago. Kill men i' th' dark! Where 'be
these bloody thieves?
How silent is this town! Ho! murder!
murder!
What may you be? Are you of good or
evil?   65
Lod. As you shall prove us, praise us.
Iago. Signior Lodovico?
Lod. He, sir.
Iago. I cry you mercy. Here's Cassio
hurt by villains.
Gra. Cassio!   70

Iago. How is't, brother?
Cas. My leg is cut in two.
Iago. Marry, heaven forbid!
Light, gentlemen. I'll bind it with my
shirt.

Enter BIANCA.

Bian. What is the matter, ho? Who is't
that cried?
Iago. Who is't that cried!   75
Bian. O my dear Cassio!
My sweet Cassio! O Cassio, Cassio, Cassio!
Iago. O notable strumpet! Cassio, may
you suspect
Who they should be that have thus
mangled you?
Cas. No.   80
Gra. I am sorry to find you thus; I have
been to seek you.
Iago. Lend me a garter. So.
O, for a chair, to bear him easily hence!
Bian. Alas, he faints! O Cassio, Cassio,
Cassio!
Iago. Gentlemen all, I do suspect this
trash   85
To be a party in this injury.
Patience awhile, good Cassio. Come,
come;
Lend me a light. Know we this face or no?
Alas, my friend and my dear countryman
Roderigo? No—yes, sure; O heaven!
Roderigo.   90
Gra. What, of Venice?
Iago. Even he, sir; did you know him?
Gra.   Know him! Ay.
Iago. Signior Gratiano? I cry your gentle
pardon;
These bloody accidents must excuse my
manners,
That so neglected you.
Gra.   I am glad to see you.   95
Iago. How do you, Cassio?—O, a chair,
a chair!
Gra. Roderigo!
Iago. He, he, 'tis he. [*A chair brought in.*
O, that's well said; the chair.
Some good man bear him carefully from
hence;
I'll fetch the General's surgeon. [*To Bianca*]
For you, mistress,   100
Save you your labour.—He that lies slain
here, Cassio,
Was my dear friend. What malice was
between you?
Cas. None in the world; nor do I know
the man.
Iago. [*To Bianca*] What, look you
pale?—O, bear him out o' th' air.
[*Cassio and Roderigo are borne off.*
Stay you, good gentlemen.—Look you pale,
mistress?—   105
Do you perceive the gastness of her eye?—
Nay, an you stare, we shall hear more
anon.—

Behold her well; I pray you look upon her.
Do you see, gentlemen? Nay, guiltiness
will speak
Though tongues were out of use.   110

Enter EMILIA.

  Emil. 'Las, what's the matter? What's
    the matter, husband?
  Iago. Cassio hath here been set on in the
    dark
By Roderigo and fellows that are 'scap'd.
He's almost slain, and Roderigo quite dead.
  Emil. Alas, good gentleman! Alas, good
    Cassio!   115
  Iago. This is the fruits of whoring.
    Prithee, Emilia,
Go know of Cassio where he supp'd to-
    night.—
What, do you shake at that?
  Bian. He supp'd at my house; but I
    therefore shake not.
  Iago. O, did he so? I charge you go
    with me.   120
  Emil. Fie, fie upon thee, strumpet!
  Bian. I am no strumpet, but of life as
    honest
As you that thus abuse me.
  Emil.   As I! Foh! Fie upon thee!
  Iago. Kind gentlemen, let's go see poor
    Cassio dress'd.—
Come, mistress, you must tell's another
    tale.   125
Emilia, run you to the citadel,
And tell my lord and lady what hath
    happ'd.
Will you go on afore? [*Aside*] This is the
    night
That either makes me or fordoes me quite.
                 [*Exeunt.*

SCENE II. *Cyprus. The citadel.*

DESDEMONA *in her bed. Enter* OTHELLO
with a light.

  Oth. It is the cause, it is the cause, my
    soul—
Let me not name it to you, you chaste
    stars—
It is the cause. Yet I'll not shed her blood,
Nor scar that whiter skin of hers than snow,
And smooth as monumental alabaster.   5
Yet she must die, else she'll betray more
    men.
Put out the light, and then put out the
    light.
If I quench thee, thou flaming minister,
I can again thy former light restore,
Should I repent me; but once put out
    thy light,   10
Thou cunning'st pattern of excelling
    nature,
I know not where is that Promethean heat
That can thy light relume. When I have
    pluck'd thy rose,

I cannot give it vital growth again;
It needs must wither. I'll smell thee on
    the tree.   [*Kissing her.* 15
O balmy breath, that dost almost persuade
Justice to break her sword! One more, one
    more.
Be thus when thou art dead, and I will
    kill thee,
And love thee after. One more, and that's
    the last: 19
So sweet was ne'er so fatal. I must weep,
But they are cruel tears. This sorrow's
    heavenly;
It strikes where it doth love. She wakes.
  Des. Who's there? Othello?
  Oth. Ay, Desdemona.
  Des. Will you come to bed, my lord?
  Oth. Have you pray'd to-night, Desde-
    mona?   25
  Des. Ay, my lord.
  Oth. If you bethink yourself of any crime
Unreconcil'd as yet to heaven and grace,
Solicit for it straight.
  Des.   Alack, my lord,
What may you mean by that?   30
  Oth. Well, do it, and be brief; I will
    walk by.
I would not kill thy unprepared spirit;
No, heaven forfend!—I would not kill
    thy soul.   33
  Des. Talk you of killing?
  Oth.   Ay, I do.
  Des.   Then heaven
Have mercy on me!
  Oth.   Amen, with all my heart!
  Des. If you say so, I hope you will not
    kill me.
  Oth. Humh!
  Des. And yet I fear you; for you're
    fatal then   40
When your eyes roll so. Why I should fear
I know not,
Since guiltiness I know not; but yet I feel
    I fear.
  Oth. Think on thy sins.
  Des.   They are loves I bear to you.
  Oth. Ay, and for that thou diest.
  Des. That death's unnatural that kills for
    loving.   45
Alas, why gnaw you so your nether lip?
Some bloody passion shakes your very
    frame.
These are portents; but yet I hope, I hope,
They do not point on me.
  Oth. Peace, and be still.
  Des.   I will so. What's the matter? 50
  Oth. That handkerchief which I so lov'd
    and gave thee
Thou gav'st to Cassio.
  Des.   No, by my life and soul!
Send for the man and ask him.
  Oth.   Sweet soul, take heed,
Take heed of perjury; thou art on thy
    death-bed.

Des. Ay, but not yet to die.
Oth.   Yes, presently. 55
Therefore confess thee freely of thy sin ;
For to deny each article with oath
Cannot remove nor choke the strong conception
That I do groan withal. Thou art to die. 59
   Des. Then, Lord have mercy on me !
   Oth.   I say, amen.
   Des. And have you mercy too ! I never did
Offend you in my life ; never lov'd Cassio
But with such general warranty of heaven
As I might love. I never gave him token.
   Oth. By heaven, I saw my handkerchief
in's hand. 65
O perjur'd woman ! thou dost stone my heart,
And mak'st me call what I intend to do
A murder, which I thought a sacrifice.
I saw the handkerchief.
   Des.   He found it, then ;
I never gave it him. Send for him hither ;
Let him confess a truth.
   Oth.   He hath confess'd. 71
   Des. What, my lord ?
   Oth.   That he hath—ud's death !—
us'd thee.
   Des. How ? unlawfully ?
   Oth.   Ay.
   Des. He will not say so.
   Oth.   No, his mouth is stopp'd ;
Honest Iago hath ta'en order for't. 76
   Des. O, my fear interprets ! What, is he dead ?
   Oth. Had all his hairs been lives, my great revenge
Had stomach for them all. 79
   Des. Alas, he is betray'd, and I undone !
   Oth. Out, strumpet ! Weep'st thou for him to my face ?
   Des. O, banish me, my lord, but kill me not !
   Oth. Down, strumpet.
   Des. Kill me to-morrow ; let me live to-night.
   Oth. Nay, an you strive— 85
   Des. But half an hour !
   Oth. Being done, there is no pause.
   Des. But while I say one prayer !
   Oth. It is too late. [*Smothers her.*
   Des. O Lord, Lord, Lord !
   Emil. [*Within*] My lord, my lord !
what, ho ! my lord, my lord !
   Oth. What voice is this ? Not dead ? not yet quite dead ?
I that am cruel am yet merciful ; 90
I would not have thee linger in thy pain.
So, so.
   Emil. [*Within*] What, ho ! my lord, my lord !
   Oth. Who's there ?
   Emil. [*Within*] O, good my lord, I'd speak a word with you !

   Oth. Yes—'tis Emilia—by and by. She's dead.
'Tis like she comes to speak of Cassio's death ; 95
The noise was high. Ha ! no more moving ?
Still as the grave. Shall she come in ? Were't good ?
I think she stirs again. No. What's the best ?
If she come in she'll sure speak to my wife.
My wife ! my wife ! what wife ? I have no wife. 100
O insupportable ! O heavy hour !
Methinks it should be now a huge eclipse
Of sun and moon, and that th' affrighted globe
Did yawn at alteration.
   Emil. [*Within*] I do beseech you that
I may speak with you. O good my lord ! 105
   Oth. I had forgot thee : O, come in, Emilia.
Soft, by and by. Let me the curtains draw.
Where art thou ? [*Unlocks the door.*

Enter EMILIA.

   What's the matter with thee now ?
   Emil. O, my good lord, yonder's foul murders done !
   Oth. What, now ? 110
   Emil. But now, my lord.
   Oth. It is the very error of the moon ;
She comes more nearer earth than she was wont,
And makes men mad.
   Emil. Cassio, my lord, hath kill'd a young Venetian 115
Call'd Roderigo.
   Oth.   Roderigo kill'd !
And Cassio kill'd !
   Emil.   No, Cassio, is not kill'd.
   Oth. Not Cassio kill'd ! Then murder's out of tune,
And sweet revenge grows harsh.
   Des. O, falsely, falsely murder'd !
   Emil.   O Lord, what cry is that ?
   Oth. That ! what ? 121
   Emil. Out and alas ! that was my lady's voice.
Help ! help, ho ! help ! O lady, speak again !
Sweet Desdemona ! O sweet mistress, speak !
   Des. A guiltless death I die. 125
   Emil. O, who hath done this deed ?
   Des. Nobody. I myself. Farewell.
Commend me to my kind lord. O, farewell !
[*She dies.*
   Oth. Why, how should she be murd'red ?
   Emil.   Alas, who knows ?
   Oth. You heard her say herself it was not I. 130
   Emil. She said so. I must needs report a truth.

Oth. She's like a liar gone to burning hell :

'Twas I that kill'd her.

Emil.   O, the more angel she,
And you the blacker devil !

Oth. She turn'd to folly, and she was a whore.   135

Emil. Thou dost belie her, and thou art a devil.

Oth. She was false as water.

Emil.   Thou art rash as fire to say
That she was false. O, she was heavenly true !

Oth. Cassio did top her ; ask thy husband else.   139
O, I were damn'd beneath all depth in hell
But that I did proceed upon just grounds
To this extremity. Thy husband knew it all.

Emil. My husband !

Oth. Thy husband.

Emil. That she was false to wedlock ?   145

Oth. Ay, with Cassio. Nay, had she been true,
If heaven would make me such another world
Of one entire and perfect chrysolite,
I'd not have sold her for it.

Emil. My husband !

Oth. Ay, 'twas he that told me on her first.   150
An honest man he is, and hates the slime
That sticks on filthy deeds.

Emil. My husband !

Oth. What needs this iterance, woman ?
I say thy husband.

Emil. O mistress, villainy hath made mocks with love !
My husband say that she was false !

Oth.   He, woman ;   155
I say thy husband ; dost understand the word ?
My friend, thy husband—honest, honest Iago.

Emil. If he say so, may his pernicious soul
Rot half a grain a day ! He lies to th' heart.
She was too fond of her most filthy bargain.

Oth. Ha !   161

Emil. Do thy worst :
This deed of thine is no more worthy heaven
Than thou wast worthy her.

Oth.   Peace, you were best.

Emil. Thou hast not half that power to do me harm   165
As I have to be hurt. O gull ! O dolt !
As ignorant as dirt ! Thou hast done a deed—
I care not for thy sword ; I'll make thee known,
Though I lost twenty lives. Help ! help, ho ! help !

The Moor hath kill'd my mistress ! Murder ! murder !   170

Enter MONTANO, GRATIANO, IAGO, *and Others.*

Mon. What is the matter ? How now, General !

Emil. O, are you come, Iago ? You have done well,
That men must lay their murders on your neck.

Gra. What is the matter ?

Emil. Disprove this villain, if thou be'st a man :   175
He says thou told'st him that his wife was false.
I know thou didst not ; thou'rt not such a villain.
Speak, for my heart is full.

Iago. I told him what I thought, and told no more
Than what he found himself was apt and true.   180

Emil. But did you ever tell him she was false ?

Iago. I did.

Emil. You told a lie—an odious, damned lie.
Upon my soul, a lie—a wicked lie.
She false with Cassio ! Did you say with Cassio ?   185

Iago. With Cassio, mistress. Go to, charm your tongue.

Emil. I will not charm my tongue ; I am bound to speak :
My mistress here lies murdered in her bed.

All. O heavens forfend !

Emil. And your reports have set the murder on.   190

Oth. Nay, stare not, masters : it is true, indeed.

Gra. 'Tis a strange truth.

Mon. O monstrous act !

Emil. Villainy, villainy, villainy !
I think upon't. I think—I smell't. villainy !
I thought so then. I'll kill myself for grief.   195
O villainy, villainy !

Iago. What, are you mad ? I charge you get you home.

Emil. Good gentlemen, let me have leave to speak.
'Tis proper I obey him, but not now.
Perchance, Iago, I will ne'er go home.   200

Oth. O ! O ! O !   [*Falls on the bed.*

Emil.   Nay, lay thee down and roar ;
For thou hast kill'd the sweetest innocent
That e'er did lift up eye.

Oth. [*Rising*]   O, she was foul !
I scarce did know you, uncle. There lies your niece,
Whose breath indeed these hands have newly stopp'd.   205

I know this act shows horrible and grim.
  Gra. Poor Desdemona! I am glad thy
    father's dead.
Thy match was mortal to him, and pure
    grief
Shore his old thread atwain. Did he live
    now,
This sight would make him do a desperate
    turn, 210
Yea, curse his better angel from his side,
And fall to reprobance.
  Oth. 'Tis pitiful; but yet Iago knows
That she with Cassio hath the act of shame
A thousand times committed; Cassio
    confess'd it; 215
And she did gratify his amorous works
With that recognizance and pledge of love
Which I first gave her; I saw it in his
    hand.
It was a handkerchief, an antique token
My father gave my mother. 220
  Emil. O God! O heavenly God!
  Iago. Zounds, hold your peace.
  Emil. 'Twill out, 'twill out. I, peace!
No, I will speak as liberal as the north.
Let heaven and men and devils, let them all,
All, all, cry shame against me, yet I'll
    speak. 225
  Iago. Be wise, and get you home.
  Emil.   I will not.
    [*Iago offers to stab his wife.*
  Gra. Fie! Your sword upon a woman?
  Emil. O thou dull Moor! That hand-
    kerchief thou speak'st of
I found by fortune, and did give my
    husband;
For often with a solemn earnestness— 230
More than indeed belong'd to such a trifle—
He begg'd of me to steal it.
  Iago.   Villainous whore!
  Emil. She give it Cassio! No, alas, I
    found it,
And I did give't my husband.
  Iago.   Filth, thou liest.
  Emil. By heaven, I do not, I do not,
    gentlemen. 235
O murderous coxcomb! What should such
    a fool
Do with so good a wife? [*The Moor runs
    at Iago; Montano and others disarm
    the Moor. Iago kills his wife and escapes.*
  Oth. Are there no stones in heaven but
what serves for the thunder? Precious
villain!
  Gra. The woman falls; sure he hath
    kill'd his wife.
  Emil. Ay, ay. O, lay me by my mistress'
    side. 240
  Gra. He's gone, but his wife's kill'd.
  Mon. 'Tis a notorious villain. Take you
    this weapon,
Which I have here recover'd from the Moor.
Come, guard the door without; let him
    not pass,

But kill him rather. I'll after that same
    villain, 245
For 'tis a damned slave.
    [*Exeunt Montano, Gratiano, and others.*
  Oth. I am not valiant neither—
But every puny whipster gets my sword.
But why should honour outlive honesty?
Let it go all.
  Emil. What did thy song bode, lady?
Hark, canst thou hear me? I will play the
    swan, 250
And die in music. [*Sings*] Willow, willow,
    willow.—
Moor, she was chaste; she lov'd thee, cruel
    Moor;
So come my soul to bliss, as I speak true;
So speaking as I think, alas, I die.
    [*She dies.*
  Oth. I have another weapon in this
    chamber; 255
It was a sword of Spain, the ice-brook's
    temper.
O, here it is. Uncle, I must come forth.
  Gra. [*Within*] If thou attempt it, it will
    cost thee dear;
Thou hast no weapon, and perforce must
    suffer.
  Oth. Look in upon me, then, and speak
    with me, 260
Or, naked as I am, I will assault thee.

        Re-enter GRATIANO.

  Gra. What is the matter?
  Oth.   Behold, I have a weapon;
A better never did itself sustain
Upon a soldier's thigh. I have seen the day
That with this little arm and this good
    sword 265
I have made my way through more
    impediments
Than twenty times your stop. But, O vain
    boast!
Who can control his fate? 'Tis not so now.
Be not afraid though you do see me
    weapon'd; 269
Here is my journey's end, here is my butt,
And very sea-mark of my utmost sail.
Do you go back dismay'd? 'Tis a lost fear;
Man but a rush against Othello's breast,
And he retires. Where should Othello go?
Now, how dost thou look now? O ill-
    starr'd wench! 275
Pale as thy smock! When we shall meet at
    compt,
This look of thine will hurl my soul from
    heaven,
And fiends will snatch at it. Cold, cold, my
    girl!
Even like thy chastity. O cursed, cursed
    slave!
Whip me, ye devils, 280
From the possession of this heavenly sight.
Blow me about in winds, roast me in
    sulphur,

Wash me in steep-down gulfs of liquid fire.
O Desdemona! Dead! Desdemona! Dead!
O! O!   285

Enter LODOVICO, MONTANO, CASSIO *carried
in a chair, and* Officers, *with* IAGO *prisoner.*

Lod. Where is this rash and most un-
fortunate man?
Oth. That's he that was Othello—here
I am.
Lod. Where is that viper? Bring the
villain forth.
Oth. I look down towards his feet—but
that's a fable.   289
If that thou be'st a devil, I cannot kill thee.
                              [*Wounds* Iago.
Lod. Wrench his sword from him.
Iago. I bleed, sir; but not kill'd.
Oth. I am not sorry neither: I'd have
thee live;
For, in my sense, 'tis happiness to die.
Lod. O thou Othello, that was once so
good,
Fall'n in the practice of a damned slave, 295
What shall be said to thee?
Oth.   Why, any thing:
An honourable murderer, if you will;
For nought I did in hate, but all in honour.
Lod. This wretch hath part confess'd his
villainy.   299
Did you and he consent in Cassio's death?
Oth. Ay.
Cas. Dear General, I never gave you
cause.
Oth. I do believe it, and I ask your
pardon.
Will you, I pray, demand that demi-devil
Why he hath thus ensnar'd my soul and
body?   305
Iago. Demand me nothing. What you
know, you know.
From this time forth I never will speak
word.
Lod. What, not to pray?
Gra.   Torments will ope your lips.
Oth. Well, thou dost best.
Lod. Sir, you shall understand what hath
befall'n,   310
Which, as I think, you know not. Here is
a letter
Found in the pocket of the slain Roderigo;
And here another: the one of them
imports
The death of Cassio to be undertook
By Roderigo.   315
Oth. O villain!
Cas.   Most heathenish and most gross!
Lod. Now here's another discontented
paper,
Found in his pocket too; and this, it seems,
Roderigo meant t' have sent this damned
villain;
But that, belike, Iago in the nick   320
Came in and satisfied him.

Oth.   O thou pernicious caitiff!
How came you, Cassio, by that hand-
kerchief
That was my wife's?
Cas.   I found it in my chamber;
And he himself confess'd it even now
That there he dropp'd it for a special
purpose   325
Which wrought to his desire.
Oth.   O fool! fool! fool!
Cas. There is besides in Roderigo's letter,
How he upbraids Iago that he made him
Brave me upon the watch; whereon it
came
That I was cast; and even but now he
spake,   330
After long seeming dead, Iago hurt him,
Iago set him on.
Lod. You must forsake this room and go
with us.
Your power and your command is taken off,
And Cassio rules in Cyprus. For this slave,
If there be any cunning cruelty   336
That can torment him much and hold him
long,
It shall be his. You shall close prisoner rest
Till that the nature of your fault be known
To the Venetian state. Come, bring away.
Oth. Soft you; a word or two before
you go.   341
I have done the state some service, and
they know't—
No more of that. I pray you, in your
letters,
When you shall these unlucky deeds relate,
Speak of me as I am; nothing extenuate,
Nor set down aught in malice. Then must
you speak   346
Of one that lov'd not wisely, but too well;
Of one not easily jealous, but, being
wrought,
Perplexed in the extreme; of one whose
hand,   349
Like the base Indian, threw a pearl away
Richer than all his tribe; of one whose
subdu'd eyes,
Albeit unused to the melting mood,
Drops tears as fast as the Arabian trees
Their med'cinable gum. Set you down this:
And say besides that in Aleppo once,   355
Where a malignant and a turban'd Turk
Beat a Venetian and traduc'd the state,
I took by th' throat the circumcised dog,
And smote him—thus. [*He stabs himself.*
Lod. O bloody period!
Gra.   All that is spoke is marr'd. 360
Oth. I kiss'd thee ere I kill'd thee. No
way but this—
Killing my self, to die upon a kiss.
                    [*Falls on the bed and dies.*
Cas. This did I fear, but thought he had
no weapon;
For he was great of heart.
Lod. [*To* Iago]   O Spartan dog,

More fell than anguish, hunger, or the sea !
Look on the tragic loading of this bed. 366
This is thy work.—The object poisons
    sight ;
Let it be hid. Gratiano, keep the house,
And seize upon the fortunes of the Moor,
For they succeed on you. To you, Lord
    Governor, 370

Remains the censure of this hellish
    villain ;
The time, the place, the torture—O, enforce
    it !
Myself will straight aboard ; and to the
    state
This heavy act with heavy heart relate.
                      [*Exeunt.*

ANTONY AND CLEOPATRA

DRAMATIS PERSONÆ

MARK ANTONY,
OCTAVIUS CÆSAR, } Triumvirs.
M. ÆMILIUS LEPIDUS,
SEXTUS POMPEIUS.

DOMITIUS ENOBARBUS,
VENTIDIUS,
EROS,
SCARUS, } friends to Antony.
DERCETAS,
DEMETRIUS,
PHILO,

MÆCENAS,
AGRIPPA,
DOLABELLA,
PROCULEIUS, } friends to Cæsar.
THYREUS,
GALLUS,

MENAS,
MENECRATES, } friends to Pompey.
VARRIUS,

TAURUS, Lieutenant-General to Cæsar.
CANIDIUS, Lieutenant-General to Antony.
SILIUS, an Officer in Ventidius's army.
EUPHRONIUS, an ambassador from Antony
to Cæsar.

ALEXAS,
MARDIAN,
SELEUCUS, } attendants on Cleopatra.
DIOMEDES,
A Soothsayer.
A Clown.

CLEOPATRA, Queen of Egypt.
OCTAVIA, sister to Cæsar and wife to
Antony.
CHARMIAN, } ladies attending on
IRAS, } Cleopatra.

Officers, Soldiers, Messengers, and
Attendants.

THE SCENE : The Roman Empire.

ACT ONE

SCENE I. Alexandria. Cleopatra's palace.

Enter DEMETRIUS *and* PHILO.

Phi. Nay, but this dotage of our general's
O'erflows the measure. Those his goodly
eyes,
That o'er the files and musters of the war
Have glow'd like plated Mars, now bend,
now turn,
The office and devotion of their view   5
Upon a tawny front. His captain's heart,
Which in the scuffles of great fights hath
burst
The buckles on his breast, reneges all
temper,
And is become the bellows and the fan
To cool a gipsy's lust.

Flourish. Enter ANTONY, CLEOPATRA, *her
Ladies, the Train, with* Eunuchs *fanning
her.*

Look where they come !
Take but good note, and you shall see in
him   11
The triple pillar of the world transform'd
Into a strumpet's fool. Behold and see.
Cleo. If it be love indeed, tell me how
much.
Ant. There's beggary in the love that can
be reckon'd.   15
Cleo. I'll set a bourn how far to be
belov'd.

Ant. Then must thou needs find out new
heaven, new earth.

Enter a Messenger.

Mess. News, my good lord, from Rome.
Ant.   Grates me the sum.
Cleo. Nay, hear them, Antony.   19
Fulvia perchance is angry ; or who knows
If the scarce-bearded Cæsar have not sent
His pow'rful mandate to you : ' Do this
or this ;
Take in that kingdom and enfranchise that ;
Perform't, or else we damn thee '.
Ant.   How, my love ?
Cleo. Perchance ? Nay, and most like,   25
You must not stay here longer ; your
dismission
Is come from Cæsar ; therefore hear it,
Antony.
Where's Fulvia's process ? Cæsar's I would
say ? Both ?
Call in the messengers. As I am Egypt's
Queen,
Thou blushest, Antony, and that blood of
thine   30
Is Cæsar's homager. Else so thy cheek
pays shame
When shrill-tongu'd Fulvia scolds. The
messengers !
Ant. Let Rome in Tiber melt, and the
wide arch
Of the rang'd empire fall ! Here is my
space.   34
Kingdoms are clay ; our dungy earth alike

Feeds beast as man. The nobleness of life
Is to do thus [*embracing*], when such a
    mutual pair
And such a twain can do't, in which I
    bind,
On pain of punishment, the world to weet
We stand up peerless.
  Cleo.   Excellent falsehood! 40
Why did he marry Fulvia, and not love her?
I'll seem the fool I am not. Antony
Will be himself.
  Ant.   But stirr'd by Cleopatra.
Now for the love of Love and her soft
    hours,
Let's not confound the time with con-
    ference harsh;   45
There's not a minute of our lives should
    stretch
Without some pleasure now. What sport
    to-night?
  Cleo. Hear the ambassadors.
  Ant.   Fie, wrangling queen!
Whom everything becomes—to chide, to
    laugh,   49
To weep; whose every passion fully strives
To make itself in thee fair and admir'd.
No messenger but thine, and all alone
To-night we'll wander through the streets
    and note
The qualities of people. Come, my queen;
Last night you did desire it. Speak not
    to us.   55
    [*Exeunt Antony and Cleopatra, with
          the Train.*
  Dem. Is Cæsar with Antonius priz'd so
    slight?
  Phi. Sir, sometimes when he is not
    Antony,
He comes too short of that great property
Which still should go with Antony.
  Dem.   I am full sorry
That he approves the common liar, who 60
Thus speaks of him at Rome; but I will
    hope
Of better deeds to-morrow. Rest you
    happy!   [*Exeunt.*

SCENE II. *Alexandria. Cleopatra's palace.*

Enter CHARMIAN, IRAS, ALEXAS, *and a
    Soothsayer.*

  Char. Lord Alexas, sweet Alexas, most
anything Alexas, almost most absolute
Alexas, where's the soothsayer that you
prais'd so to th' Queen? O that I knew
this husband, which you say must charge
his horns with garlands!   5
  Alex. Soothsayer!
  Sooth. Your will?
  Char. Is this the man? Is't you, sir, that
    know things?
  Sooth. In nature's infinite book of secrecy
A little I can read.
  Alex.   Show him your hand. 10

Enter ENOBARBUS.

  Eno. Bring in the banquet quickly;
    wine enough
Cleopatra's health to drink.
  Char. Good sir, give me good fortune.
  Sooth. I make not, but foresee.
  Char. Pray, then, forsee me one. 15
  Sooth. You shall be yet far fairer than
    you are.
  Char. He means in flesh.
  Iras. No, you shall paint when you are
    old.
  Char. Wrinkles forbid!
  Alex. Vex not his prescience; be
attentive.   20
  Char. Hush!
  Sooth. You shall be more beloving than
    beloved.
  Char. I had rather heat my liver with
drinking.
  Alex. Nay, hear him. 24
  Char. Good now, some excellent fortune!
Let me be married to three kings in a fore-
noon, and widow them all. Let me have a
child at fifty, to whom Herod of Jewry may
do homage. Find me to marry me with
Octavius Cæsar, and companion me with
my mistress.
  Sooth. You shall outlive the lady whom
    you serve.
  Char. O, excellent! I love long life better 30
than figs.
  Sooth. You have seen and prov'd a fairer
    former fortune
Than that which is to approach.
  Char. Then belike my children shall have
no names. Prithee, how many boys and
wenches must I have? 35
  Sooth. If every of your wishes had a
womb,
And fertile every wish, a million.
  Char. Out, fool! I forgive thee for a
witch.
  Alex. You think none but your sheets are
privy to your wishes. 40
  Char. Nay, come, tell Iras hers.
  Alex. We'll know all our fortunes.
  Eno. Mine, and most of our fortunes,
to-night, shall be—drunk to bed.
  Iras. There's a palm presages chastity,
if nothing else. 45
  Char. E'en as the o'erflowing Nilus
presageth famine.
  Iras. Go, you wild bedfellow, you cannot
soothsay.
  Char. Nay, if an oily palm be not a
fruitful prognostication, I cannot scratch
mine ear. Prithee, tell her but a worky-day
fortune. 50
  Sooth. Your fortunes are alike.
  Iras. But how, but how? Give me
particulars.
  Sooth. I have said.

Iras. Am I not an inch of fortune better than she ?

Char. Well, if you were but an inch of fortune better than I, where would you choose it ?   56

Iras. Not in my husband's nose.

Char. Our worser thoughts heavens mend ! Alexas—come, his fortune, his fortune ! O, let him marry a woman that cannot go, sweet Isis, I beseech thee ! And let her die too, and give him a worse ! And let worse follow worse, till the worst of all follow him laughing to his grave, fiftyfold a cuckold ! Good Isis, hear me this prayer, though thou deny me a matter of more weight ; good Isis, I beseech thee !   64

Iras. Amen. Dear goddess, hear that prayer of the people ! For, as it is a heart-breaking to see a handsome man loose-wiv'd, so it is a deadly sorrow to behold a foul knave uncuckolded. Therefore, dear Isis, keep decorum, and fortune him accordingly !

Char. Amen.   70

Alex. Lo now, if it lay in their hands to make me a cuckold, they would make themselves whores but they'ld do't !

Enter CLEOPATRA.

Eno. Hush ! Here comes Antony.

Char.   Not he ; the Queen.

Cleo. Saw you my lord ?

Eno.   No, lady.

Cleo. Was he not here ?

Char.   No, madam.

Cleo. He was dispos'd to mirth ; but on the sudden

A Roman thought hath struck him. Enobarbus !   80

Eno. Madam ?

Cleo. Seek him, and bring him hither. Where's Alexas ?

Alex. Here, at your service. My lord approaches.

Enter ANTONY, *with* a Messenger *and* Attendants.

Cleo. We will not look upon him. Go with us. [*Exeunt Cleopatra, Enobarbus, and the rest.*

Mess. Fulvia thy wife first came into the field.   85

Ant. Against my brother Lucius ?

Mess. Ay.

But soon that war had end, and the time's state

Made friends of them, jointing their force 'gainst Cæsar,

Whose better issue in the war from Italy 90

Upon the first encounter drave them.

Ant.   Well, what worst ?

Mess. The nature of bad news infects the teller.

Ant. When it concerns the fool or coward. On !

Things that are past are done with me. 'Tis thus :

Who tells me true, though in his tale lie death,   95

I hear him as he flatter'd.

Mess.   Labienus—

This is stiff news—hath with his Parthian force

Extended Asia from Euphrates,

His conquering banner shook from Syria

To Lydia and to Ionia,   100

Whilst—

Ant.   Antony, thou wouldst say.

Mess.   O, my lord !

Ant. Speak to me home ; mince not the general tongue ;

Name Cleopatra as she is call'd in Rome.

Rail thou in Fulvia's phrase, and taunt my faults

With such full licence as both truth and malice   105

Have power to utter. O, then we bring forth weeds

When our quick minds lie still, and our ills told us

Is as our earing. Fare thee well awhile.

Mess. At your noble pleasure.   [*Exit.*

Ant. From Sicyon, ho, the news ! Speak there !   110

1 *Att.* The man from Sicyon—is there such an one ?

2 *Att.* He stays upon your will.

Ant.   Let him appear.

These strong Egyptian fetters I must break,

Or lose myself in dotage.

Enter another Messenger *with a letter.*

What are you ?

2 *Mess.* Fulvia thy wife is dead.

Ant.   Where died she ?

2 *Mess.* In Sicyon.   116

Her length of sickness, with what else more serious

Importeth thee to know, this bears.

[*Gives the letter.*

Ant.   Forbear me.

[*Exit Messenger.*

There's a great spirit gone ! Thus did I desire it.

What our contempts doth often hurl from us   120

We wish it ours again ; the present pleasure,

By revolution low'ring, does become

The opposite of itself. She's good, being gone ;

The hand could pluck her back that shov'd her on.

I must from this enchanting queen break off.   125

Ten thousand harms, more than the ills I know,

My idleness doth hatch.   How now,
    Enobarbus!

Re-enter ENOBARBUS.

Eno. What's your pleasure, sir?
Ant. I must with haste from hence.
Eno. Why, then we kill all our women.
We see how mortal an unkindness is to
them; if they suffer our departure, death's
the word.   132
Ant. I must be gone.
Eno. Under a compelling occasion, let
women die. It were pity to cast them away
for nothing, though between them and a
great cause they should be esteemed nothing. Cleopatra, catching but the least noise
of this, dies instantly; I have seen her die
twenty times upon far poorer moment. I
do think there is mettle in death, which
commits some loving act upon her, she hath
such a celerity in dying.   140
Ant. She is cunning past man's thought.
Eno. Alack, sir, no! Her passions are
made of nothing but the finest part of pure
love. We cannot call her winds and waters
sighs and tears; they are greater storms
and tempests than almanacs can report.
This cannot be cunning in her; if it be, she
makes a show'r of rain as well as Jove.
Ant. Would I had never seen her!   147
Eno. O sir, you had then left unseen a
wonderful piece of work, which not to have
been blest withal would have discredited
your travel.   150
Ant. Fulvia is dead.
Eno. Sir?
Ant. Fulvia is dead.
Eno. Fulvia?
Ant. Dead.   155
Eno. Why, sir, give the gods a thankful
sacrifice. When it pleaseth their deities to
take the wife of a man from him, it shows
to man the tailors of the earth; comforting
therein that when old robes are worn out
there are members to make new. If there
were no more women but Fulvia, then had
you indeed a cut, and the case to be
lamented. This grief is crown'd with consolation: your old smock brings forth a
new petticoat; and indeed the tears live
in an onion that should water this sorrow.
Ant. The business she hath broached in
    the state   165
Cannot endure my absence.
Eno. And the business you have broach'd
here cannot be without you; especially
that of Cleopatra's, which wholly depends
on your abode.
Ant. No more light answers. Let our
    officers   170
Have notice what we purpose. I shall
    break
The cause of our expedience to the Queen,
And get her leave to part. For not alone

The death of Fulvia, with more urgent
    touches,
Do strongly speak to us; but the letters
    too   175
Of many our contriving friends in Rome
Petition us at home. Sextus Pompeius
Hath given the dare to Cæsar, and com-
    mands
The empire of the sea; our slippery people,
Whose love is never link'd to the deserver
Till his deserts are past, begin to throw
Pompey the Great and all his dignities   182
Upon his son; who, high in name and
    power,
Higher than both in blood and life, stands
    up
For the main soldier; whose quality, going
    on,   185
The sides o' th' world may danger. Much
    is breeding
Which, like the courser's hair, hath yet but
    life
And not a serpent's poison. Say our
    pleasure,
To such whose place is under us, requires
Our quick remove from hence.   190
Eno. I shall do't.   [*Exeunt.*

SCENE III. *Alexandria. Cleopatra's palace.*

Enter CLEOPATRA, CHARMIAN, IRAS, *and*
    ALEXAS.

Cleo. Where is he?
Char.   I did not see him since.
Cleo. See where he is, who's with him,
    what he does.
I did not send you. If you find him sad,
Say I am dancing; if in mirth, report
That I am sudden sick. Quick, and return.
                     [*Exit Alexas.*
Char. Madam, methinks, if you did love
    him dearly,   6
You do not hold the method to enforce
The like from him.
Cleo.   What should I do I do not?
Char. In each thing give him way; cross
    him in nothing.
Cleo. Thou teachest like a fool—the way
    to lose him.   10
Char. Tempt him not so too far; I wish,
    forbear;
In time we hate that which we often fear.

Enter ANTONY.

But here comes Antony.
Cleo.   I am sick and sullen.
Ant. I am sorry to give breathing to my
    purpose—
Cleo. Help me away, dear Charmian; I
    shall fall.   15
It cannot be thus long; the sides of nature
Will not sustain it.
Ant.   Now, my dearest queen—
Cleo. Pray you, stand farther from me.

Ant.   What's the matter ?
Cleo. I know by that same eye there's
      some good news.
What says the married woman ? You may
      go.   20
Would she had never given you leave to
      come !
Let her not say 'tis I that keep you here—
I have no power upon you ; hers you
      are.
  Ant. The gods best know—
  Cleo.   O, never was there queen
So mightily betray'd ! Yet at the first   25
I saw the treasons planted.
  Ant.   Cleopatra—
  Cleo. Why should I think you can be
      mine and true,
Though you in swearing shake the thronèd
      gods,
Who have been false to Fulvia ? Riotous
      madness,
To be entangled with those mouth-made
      vows,   30
Which break themselves in swearing !
  Ant.   Most sweet queen—
  Cleo. Nay, pray you seek no colour for
      your going,
But bid farewell, and go. When you sued
      staying,
Then was the time for words. No going
      then !
Eternity was in our lips and eyes,   35
Bliss in our brows' bent, none our parts
      so poor
But was a race of heaven. They are so still,
Or thou, the greatest soldier of the world,
Art turn'd the greatest liar.
  Ant.   How now, lady !
  Cleo. I would I had thy inches. Thou
      shouldst know   40
There were a heart in Egypt.
  Ant.   Hear me, Queen :
The strong necessity of time commands
Our services awhile ; but my full heart
Remains in use with you. Our Italy
Shines o'er with civil swords : Sextus
      Pompeius   45
Makes his approaches to the port of Rome ;
Equality of two domestic powers
Breed scrupulous faction ; the hated,
      grown to strength,
Are newly grown to love. The condemn'd
      Pompey,
Rich in his father's honour, creeps apace   50
Into the hearts of such as have not thrived
Upon the present state, whose numbers
      threaten ;
And quietness, grown sick of rest, would
      purge
By any desperate change. My more
      particular,
And that which most with you should safe
      my going,   55
Is Fulvia's death.

  Cleo. Though age from folly could not
      give me freedom,
It does from childishness. Can Fulvia die ?
  Ant. She's dead, my queen.   59
Look here, and at thy sovereign leisure read
The garboils she awak'd. At the last, best.
See when and where she died.
  Cleo.   O most false love !
Where be the sacred vials thou shouldst fill
With sorrowful water ? Now I see, I see,
In Fulvia's death how mine receiv'd shall
      be.   65
  Ant. Quarrel no more, but be prepar'd to
      know
The purposes I bear ; which are, or cease,
As you shall give th' advice. By the fire
That quickens Nilus' slime, I go from hence
Thy soldier, servant, making peace or war
As thou affects.
  Cleo.   Cut my lace, Charmian, come !
But let it be ; I am quickly ill and well—
So Antony loves.
  Ant.   My precious queen, forbear,
And give true evidence to his love, which
      stands
An honourable trial.
  Cleo.   So Fulvia told me.   75
I prithee turn aside and weep for her ;
Then bid adieu to me, and say the tears
Belong to Egypt. Good now, play one scene
Of excellent dissembling, and let it look
Like perfect honour.
  Ant.   You'll heat my blood ; no more.
  Cleo. You can do better yet ; but this is
      meetly.   81
  Ant. Now, by my sword—
  Cleo.   And target. Still he mends ;
But this is not the best. Look, prithee,
      Charmian,
How this Herculean Roman does become
The carriage of his chafe.   85
  Ant. I'll leave you, lady.
  Cleo.   Courteous lord, one word.
Sir, you and I must part—but that's not it.
Sir, you and I have lov'd—but there's
      not it.
That you know well. Something it is I
      would—
O, my oblivion is a very Antony,   90
And I am all forgotten !
  Ant.   But that your royalty
Holds idleness your subject, I should take
      you
For idleness itself.
  Cleo.   'Tis sweating labour
To bear such idleness so near the heart
As Cleopatra this. But, sir, forgive me ; 95
Since my becomings kill me when they do
      not
Eye well to you. Your honour calls you
      hence ;
Therefore be deaf to my unpitied folly,
And all the gods go with you ! Upon your
      sword

Sit laurel victory, and smooth success 100
Be strew'd before your feet!

Ant.   Let us go. Come.
Our separation so abides and flies
That thou, residing here, goes yet with me,
And I, hence fleeting, here remain with thee.
Away!   [*Exeunt.*

SCENE IV. *Rome. Cæsar's house.*

Enter OCTAVIUS CÆSAR, *reading a letter*; LEPIDUS, *and their* Train.

Cæs. You may see, Lepidus, and henceforth know,
It is not Cæsar's natural vice to hate
Our great competitor. From Alexandria
This is the news: he fishes, drinks, and wastes
The lamps of night in revel; is not more manlike 5
Than Cleopatra, nor the queen of Ptolemy
More womanly than he; hardly gave audience, or
Vouchsaf'd to think he had partners. You shall find there
A man who is the abstract of all faults 9
That all men follow.

Lep.   I must not think there are
Evils enow to darken all his goodness.
His faults, in him, seem as the spots of heaven,
More fiery by night's blackness; hereditary
Rather than purchas'd; what he cannot change
Than what he chooses. 15

Cæs. You are too indulgent. Let's grant it is not
Amiss to tumble on the bed of Ptolemy,
To give a kingdom for a mirth, to sit
And keep the turn of tippling with a slave,
To reel the streets at noon, and stand the buffet 20
With knaves that smell of sweat. Say this becomes him—
As his composure must be rare indeed
Whom these things cannot blemish—yet must Antony
No way excuse his foils when we do bear
So great weight in his lightness. If he fill'd 25
His vacancy with his voluptuousness,
Full surfeits and the dryness of his bones
Call on him for't! But to confound such time
That drums him from his sport and speaks as loud
As his own state and ours—'tis to be chid
As we rate boys who, being mature in knowledge, 31
Pawn their experience to their present pleasure,
And so rebel to judgment.

Enter a Messenger.

Lep.   Here's more news.
Mess. Thy biddings have been done; and every hour, 34
Most noble Cæsar, shalt thou have report
How 'tis abroad. Pompey is strong at sea,
And it appears he is belov'd of those
That only have fear'd Cæsar. To the ports
The discontents repair, and men's reports
Give him much wrong'd.

Cæs.   I should have known no less. 40
It hath been taught us from the primal state
That he which is was wish'd until he were;
And the ebb'd man, ne'er lov'd till ne'er worth love,
Comes dear'd by being lack'd. This common body,
Like to a vagabond flag upon the stream,
Goes to and back, lackeying the varying tide, 46
To rot itself with motion.

Mess.   Cæsar, I bring thee word
Menecrates and Menas, famous pirates,
Make the sea serve them, which they ear and wound 49
With keels of every kind. Many hot inroads
They make in Italy; the borders maritime
Lack blood to think on't, and flush youth revolt.
No vessel can peep forth but 'tis as soon
Taken as seen; for Pompey's name strikes more
Than could his war resisted.

Cæs.   Antony, 55
Leave thy lascivious wassails. When thou once
Was beaten from Modena, where thou slew'st
Hirtius and Pansa, consuls, at thy heel
Did famine follow; whom thou fought'st against,
Though daintily brought up, with patience more 60
Than savages could suffer. Thou didst drink
The stale of horses and the gilded puddle
Which beasts would cough at. Thy palate then did deign
The roughest berry on the rudest hedge;
Yea, like the stag when snow the pasture sheets, 65
The barks of trees thou brows'd. On the Alps
It is reported thou didst eat strange flesh,
Which some did die to look on. And all this—
It wounds thine honour that I speak it now— 69
Was borne so like a soldier that thy cheek
So much as lank'd not.

Lep. 'Tis pity of him.

Cæs.   Let his shames quickly

Drive him to Rome. 'Tis time we twain
Did show ourselves i' th' field ; and to that
　　　end　　　　　　　　　　　　　　　74
Assemble we immediate council. Pompey
Thrives in our idleness.
　　Lep.　　　　　　　To-morrow, Cæsar,
I shall be furnish'd to inform you rightly
Both what by sea and land I can be able
To front this present time.
　　Cæs.　　　　　　Till which encounter
It is my business too. Farewell.　　　80
　　Lep. Farewell, my lord. What you shall
　　　know meantime
Of stirs abroad, I shall beseech you, sir,
To let me be partaker.
　　Cæs.　　　　　　Doubt not, sir ;
I knew it for my bond.　　　　[*Exeunt.*

　　Scene V. *Alexandria. Cleopatra's
　　　　　　palace.*

Enter CLEOPATRA, CHARMIAN, IRAS, *and*
　　　　　MARDIAN.

　　Cleo. Charmian !
　　Char. Madam ?
　　Cleo. Ha, ha !
Give me to drink mandragora.
　　Char.　　　　　　Why, madam ?
　　Cleo. That I might sleep out this great
　　　gap of time　　　　　　　　5
My Antony is away.
　　Char.　　　　You think of him too much.
　　Cleo. O, 'tis treason !
　　Char.　　　　Madam, I trust, not so.
　　Cleo. Thou, eunuch Mardian !
　　Mar. What's your Highness' pleasure ?
　　Cleo. Not now to hear thee sing ; I take
　　　no pleasure
In aught an eunuch has. 'Tis well for
　　　thee　　　　　　　　　　　10
That, being unseminar'd, thy freer thoughts
May not fly forth of Egypt. Hast thou
　　　affections ?
　　Mar. Yes, gracious madam.
　　Cleo. Indeed ?
　　Mar. Not in deed, madam ; for I can do
　　　nothing　　　　　　　　　　15
But what indeed is honest to be done.
Yet have I fierce affections, and think
What Venus did with Mars.
　　Cleo.　　　　　　O Charmian,
Where think'st thou he is now ? Stands he
　　　or sits he ?
Or does he walk ? or is he on his horse ? 20
O happy horse, to bear the weight of An-
　　　tony !
Do bravely, horse ; for wot'st thou whom
　　　thou mov'st ?
The demi-Atlas of this earth, the arm
And burgonet of men. He's speaking now,
Or murmuring ' Where's my serpent of old
　　　Nile ? '　　　　　　　　　　25
For so he calls me. Now I feed myself
With most delicious poison. Think on me,

That am with Phœbus' amorous pinches
　　　black,
And wrinkled deep in time ? Broad-
　　　fronted Cæsar,
When thou wast here above the ground,
　　　I was　　　　　　　　　　30
A morsel for a monarch ; and great
　　　Pompey
Would stand and make his eyes grow in my
　　　brow ;
There would he anchor his aspect and die
With looking on his life.

　　　　Enter ALEXAS.

　　Alex. Sovereign of Egypt, hail !
　　Cleo. How much unlike art thou Mark
　　　Antony !　　　　　　　　　35
Yet, coming from him, that great med'cine
　　　hath
With his tinct gilded thee.
How goes it with my brave Mark Antony ?
　　Alex. Last thing he did, dear Queen,
He kiss'd—the last of many doubled
　　　kisses—　　　　　　　　　40
This orient pearl. His speech sticks in my
　　　heart.
　　Cleo. Mine ear must pluck it thence.
　　Alex.　　　　　' Good friend,' quoth he
' Say the firm Roman to great Egypt sends
This treasure of an oyster ; at whose
　　　foot,
To mend the petty present, I will piece 45
Her opulent throne with kingdoms. All the
　　　East,
Say thou, shall call her mistress.' So he
　　　nodded,
And soberly did mount an arm-gaunt steed,
Who neigh'd so high that what I would
　　　have spoke
Was beastly dumb'd by him.
　　Cleo.　　　　What, was he sad or merry ?
　　Alex. Like to the time o' th' year between
　　　the extremes　　　　　　　51
Of hot and cold ; he was nor sad nor merry.
　　Cleo. O well-divided disposition ! Note
　　　him,
Note him, good Charmian ; 'tis the man ;
　　　but note him !　　　　　　54
He was not sad, for he would shine on those
That make their looks by his ; he was not
　　　merry,
Which seem'd to tell them his remembrance
　　　lay
In Egypt with his joy ; but between both.
O heavenly mingle ! Be'st thou sad or
　　　merry,
The violence of either thee becomes,　　60
So does it no man else. Met'st thou my
　　　posts ?
　　Alex. Ay, madam, twenty several
　　　messengers.
Why do you send so thick ?
　　Cleo.　　　　　Who's born that day
When I forget to send to Antony

Shall die a beggar. Ink and paper, Char-
     mian.   65
Welcome, my good Alexas. Did I, Char-
     mian,
Ever love Cæsar so ?
     Char.   O that brave Cæsar !
     Cleo. Be chok'd with such another
          emphasis !
Say ' the brave Antony '.
     Char.   The valiant Cæsar !
     Cleo. By Isis, I will give thee bloody
          teeth   70
If thou with Cæsar paragon again
My man of men.
     Char.   By your most gracious pardon,
I sing but after you.
     Cleo.   My salad days,
When I was green in judgment, cold in
     blood,
To say as I said then. But come, away ! 75
Get me ink and paper.
He shall have every day a several greeting,
Or I'll unpeople Egypt.
                                      [*Exeunt.*

ACT TWO

Scene I. *Messina. Pompey's house.*

Enter Pompey, Menecrates, *and* Menas,
     in warlike manner.

     Pom. If the great gods be just, they shall
          assist
The deeds of justest men.
     Mene.   Know, worthy Pompey,
That what they do delay they not deny.
     Pom. Whiles we are suitors to their
          throne, decays
The thing we sue for.
     Mene.   We, ignorant of ourselves, 5
Beg often our own harms, which the wise
     pow'rs
Deny us for our good ; so find we profit
By losing of our prayers.
     Pom.   I shall do well.
The people love me, and the sea is mine ;
My powers are crescent, and my auguring
     hope   10
Says it will come to th' full. Mark Antony
In Egypt sits at dinner, and will make
No wars without doors. Cæsar gets money
     where
He loses hearts. Lepidus flatters both, 14
Of both is flatter'd ; but he neither loves,
Nor either cares for him.
     Men.   Cæsar and Lepidus
Are in the field. A mighty strength they
     carry.
     Pom. Where have you this ? 'Tis false.
     Men.   From Silvius, sir.
     Pom. He dreams. I know they are in
          Rome together,
Looking for Antony. But all the charms
     of love,   20
Salt Cleopatra, soften thy wan'd lip !

Let witchcraft join with beauty, lust with
     both ;
Tie up the libertine in a field of feasts,
Keep his brain fuming. Epicurean cooks
Sharpen with cloyless sauce his appetite, 25
That sleep and feeding may prorogue his
     honour
Even till a Lethe'd dullness—

Enter Varrius.

                            How now, Varrius !
     Var. This is most certain that I shall
          deliver :
Mark Antony is every hour in Rome   29
Expected. Since he went from Egypt 'tis
A space for farther travel.
     Pom.   I could have given less matter
A better ear. Menas, I did not think
This amorous surfeiter would have donn'd
     his helm
For such a petty war ; his soldiership
Is twice the other twain. But let us rear 35
The higher our opinion, that our stirring
Can from the lap of Egypt's widow pluck
The ne'er-lust-wearied Antony.
     Men.   I cannot hope
Cæsar and Antony shall well greet together.
His wife that's dead did trespasses to
     Cæsar ;   40
His brother warr'd upon him ; although, I
     think,
Not mov'd by Antony.
     Pom.   I know not, Menas,
How lesser enmities may give way to
     greater.
Were't not that we stand up against them
     all,
'Twere pregnant they should square be-
     tween themselves ;   45
For they have entertained cause enough
To draw their swords. But how the fear
     of us
May cement their divisions, and bind up
The petty difference we yet not know.
Be't as our gods will have't ! It only stands
Our lives upon to use our strongest hands.
Come, Menas.   [*Exeunt.*

Scene II. *Rome. The house of Lepidus.*

Enter Enobarbus *and* Lepidus.

     Lep. Good Enobarbus, 'tis a worthy
          deed,
And shall become you well, to entreat your
     captain
To soft and gentle speech.
     Eno.   I shall entreat him
To answer like himself. If Cæsar move him,
Let Antony look over Cæsar's head   5
And speak as loud as Mars. By Jupiter,
Were I the wearer of Antonius' beard,
I would not shave't to-day.
     Lep.   'Tis not a time
For private stomaching.

Eno.   Every time
Serves for the matter that is then born
   in't.   10
  Lep. But small to greater matters must
   give way.
  Eno. Not if the small come first.
  Lep.   Your speech is passion !
But pray you stir no embers up. Here
  comes
The noble Antony.

    Enter ANTONY *and* VENTIDIUS.

  Eno.   And yonder, Cæsar.

    Enter CÆSAR, MÆCENAS, *and* AGRIPPA.

  Ant. If we compose well here, to Parthia.
Hark, Ventidius.   16
    Cæs. I do not know, Mæcenas. Ask
   Agrippa.
  Lep. Noble friends,
That which combin'd us was most great,
  and let not
A leaner action rend us. What's amiss,
May it be gently heard. When we debate 20
Our trivial difference loud, we do commit
Murder in healing wounds. Then, noble
  partners,
The rather for I earnestly beseech,
Touch you the sourest points with sweetest
  terms,
Nor curstness grow to th' matter.
  Ant.   'Tis spoken well. 25
Were we before our armies, and to fight,
I should do thus.   [*Flourish.*
    Cæs. Welcome to Rome.
  Ant. Thank you.
  Cæs. Sit.   30
  Ant. Sit, sir.
  Cæs. Nay, then.   [*They sit.*
  Ant. I learn you take things ill which are
  not so,
Or being, concern you not.
  Cæs.   I must be laugh'd at
If, or for nothing or a little, I   35
Should say myself offended, and with you
Chiefly i' th' world ; more laugh'd at that
  I should
Once name you derogately when to sound
  your name
It not concern'd me.
  Ant.   My being in Egypt, Cæsar,
What was't to you ?   40
  Cæs. No more than my residing here at
  Rome
Might be to you in Egypt. Yet, if you
  there
Did practise on my state, your being in
  Egypt
Might be my question.
  Ant.   How intend you—practis'd ?
  Cæs. You may be pleas'd to catch at mine
  intent   45
By what did here befall me. Your wife and
  brother

Made wars upon me, and their contestation
Was theme for you ; you were the word of
  war.
  Ant. You do mistake your business ; my
  brother never
Did urge me in his act. I did inquire it, 50
And have my learning from some true
  reports
That drew their swords with you. Did he
  not rather
Discredit my authority with yours,
And make the wars alike against my
  stomach,
Having alike your cause ? Of this my
  letters   55
Before did satisfy you. If you'll patch a
  quarrel,
As matter whole you have not to make it
  with,
It must not be with this.
  Cæs.   You praise yourself
By laying defects of judgment to me ; but
You patch'd up your excuses.
  Ant.   Not so, not so ;
I know you could not lack, I am certain
  on't,   61
Very necessity of this thought, that I,
Your partner in the cause 'gainst which he
  fought,
Could not with graceful eyes attend those
  wars
Which fronted mine own peace. As for my
  wife,   65
I would you had her spirit in such another !
The third o' th' world is yours, which with
  a snaffle
You may pace easy, but not such a wife.
  Eno. Would we had all such wives, that
  the men might go to wars with the women !
  Ant. So much uncurbable, her garboils,
  Cæsar,   71
Made out of her impatience—which not
  wanted
Shrewdness of policy too—I grieving grant
Did you too much disquiet. For that you
  must
But say I could not help it.
  Cæs.   I wrote to you 75
When rioting in Alexandria ; you
Did pocket up my letters, and with taunts
Did gibe my missive out of audience.
  Ant.   Sir,
He fell upon me ere admitted. Then
Three kings I had newly feasted, and did
  want   80
Of what I was i' th' morning ; but next day
I told him of myself, which was as much
As to have ask'd him pardon. Let this
  fellow
Be nothing of our strife ; if we contend,
Out of our question wipe him.
  Cæs.   You have broken 85
The article of your oath, which you shall
  never

Have tongue to charge me with.
   Lep.   Soft, Cæsar!
   Ant.   No;
Lepidus, let him speak.
The honour is sacred which he talks on
   now,
Supposing that I lack'd it. But on, Cæsar:
The article of my oath—   91
   Cæs. To lend me arms and aid when I
   requir'd them,
The which you both denied.
   Ant.   Neglected, rather;
And then when poisoned hours had bound
   me up
From mine own knowledge. As nearly as I
   may,   95
I'll play the penitent to you; but mine
   honesty
Shall not make poor my greatness, nor my
   power
Work without it. Truth is, that Fulvia,
To have me out of Egypt, made wars here;
For which myself, the ignorant motive, do
So far ask pardon as befits mine honour
To stoop in such a case.
   Lep.   'Tis noble spoken.
   Mæc. If it might please you to enforce no
   further
The griefs between ye—to forget them
   quite
Were to remember that the present need 105
Speaks to atone you.
   Lep.   Worthily spoken, Mæcenas.
   Eno. Or, if you borrow one another's love
for the instant, you may, when you hear
no more words of Pompey, return it again.
You shall have time to wrangle in when you
have nothing else to do.   110
   Ant. Thou art a soldier only. Speak no
   more.
   Eno. That truth should be silent I had
almost forgot.
   Ant. You wrong this presence; therefore
   speak no more.
   Eno. Go to, then—your considerate
stone!
   Cæs. I do not much dislike the matter,
   but   115
The manner of his speech; for't cannot be
We shall remain in friendship, our con-
   ditions
So diff'ring in their acts. Yet if I knew
What hoop should hold us stanch, from
   edge to edge
O' th' world, I would pursue it.
   Agr. Give me leave, Cæsar.
   Cæs.   Speak, Agrippa. 121
   Agr. Thou hast a sister by the mother's
   side,
Admir'd Octavia. Great Mark Antony
Is now a widower.
   Cæs.   Say not so, Agrippa.
If Cleopatra heard you, your reproof   125
Were well deserv'd of rashness.

   Ant. I am not married, Cæsar. Let me
   hear
Agrippa further speak.
   Agr. To hold you in perpetual amity,
To make you brothers, and to knit your
   hearts   130
With an unslipping knot, take Antony
Octavia to his wife; whose beauty claims
No worse a husband than the best of men;
Whose virtue and whose general graces
   speak
That which none else can utter. By this
   marriage,   135
All little jealousies, which now seem great,
And all great fears, which now import their
   dangers,
Would then be nothing. Truths would be
   tales,
Where now half tales be truths. Her love
   to both   140
Would each to other, and all loves to both,
Draw after her. Pardon what I have spoke;
For 'tis a studied, not a present thought,
By duty ruminated.
   Ant.   Will Cæsar speak?
   Cæs. Not till he hears how Antony is
   touch'd
With what is spoke already.
   Ant.   What power is in Agrippa,
If I would say ' Agrippa, be it so',   146
To make this good?
   Cæs.   The power of Cæsar, and
His power unto Octavia.
   Ant.   May I never
To this good purpose, that so fairly shows,
Dream of impediment! Let me have thy
   hand.   150
Further this act of grace; and from this
   hour
The heart of brothers govern in our loves
And sway our great designs!
   Cæs.   There is my hand.
A sister I bequeath you, whom no brother
Did ever love so dearly. Let her live   155
To join our kingdoms and our hearts; and
   never
Fly off our loves again!
   Lep.   Happily, amen!
   Ant. I did not think to draw my sword
   'gainst Pompey;
For he hath laid strange courtesies and
   great   159
Of late upon me. I must thank him only,
Lest my remembrance suffer ill report;
At heel of that, defy him.
   Lep.   Time calls upon's.
Of us must Pompey presently be sought,
Or else he seeks out us.
   Ant.   Where lies he?   164
   Cæs. About the Mount Misenum.
   Ant. What is his strength by land?
   Cæs. Great and increasing; but by sea
He is an absolute master.
   Ant.   So is the fame.

Would we had spoke together! Haste we
for it.
Yet, ere we put ourselves in arms, dispatch
we
The business we have talk'd of.
 Cæs.   With most gladness;
And do invite you to my sister's view, 171
Whither straight I'll lead you.
 Ant.   Let us, Lepidus,
Not lack your company.
 Lep.   Noble Antony,
Not sickness should detain me.
   [*Flourish. Exeunt all but Enobarbus,*
      Agrippa, Mæcenas.
 Mæc. Welcome from Egypt, sir. 175
 Eno. Half the heart of Cæsar, worthy
Mæcenas! My honourable friend, Agrippa!
 Agr. Good Enobarbus!
 Mæc. We have cause to be glad that
matters are so well digested. You stay'd
well by't in Egypt. 180
 Eno. Ay, sir; we did sleep day out of
countenance and made the night light with
drinking.
 Mæc. Eight wild boars roasted whole at
a breakfast, and but twelve persons there.
Is this true? 184
 Eno. This was but as a fly by an eagle.
We had much more monstrous matter of
feast, which worthily deserved noting.
 Mæc. She's a most triumphant lady, if
report be square to her.
 Eno. When she first met Mark Antony
she purs'd up his heart, upon the river of
Cydnus. 191
 Agr. There she appear'd indeed! Or my
reporter devis'd well for her.
 Eno. I will tell you.
The barge she sat in, like a burnish'd
throne, 195
Burn'd on the water. The poop was beaten
gold;
Purple the sails, and so perfumed that
The winds were love-sick with them; the
oars were silver,
Which to the tune of flutes kept stroke, and
made 199
The water which they beat to follow faster,
As amorous of their strokes. For her own
person,
It beggar'd all description. She did lie
In her pavilion, cloth-of-gold, of tissue,
O'erpicturing that Venus where we see
The fancy out-work nature. On each side
her 205
Stood pretty dimpled boys, like smiling
Cupids,
With divers-colour'd fans, whose wind did
seem
To glow the delicate cheeks which they did
cool, 208
And what they undid did.
 Agr.   O, rare for Antony!
 Eno. Her gentlewomen, like the Nereides,

So many mermaids, tended her i' th' eyes,
And made their bends adornings. At the
helm
A seeming mermaid steers. The silken tackle
Swell with the touches of those flower-soft
hands
That yarely frame the office. From the
barge 215
A strange invisible perfume hits the sense
Of the adjacent wharfs. The city cast
Her people out upon her; and Antony,
Enthron'd i' th' market-place, did sit alone,
Whistling to th' air; which, but for
vacancy, 220
Had gone to gaze on Cleopatra too,
And made a gap in nature.
 Agr.   Rare Egyptian!
 Eno. Upon her landing, Antony sent to
her,
Invited her to supper. She replied 224
It should be better he became her guest;
Which she entreated. Our courteous
Antony,
Whom ne'er the word of 'No' woman heard
speak,
Being barber'd ten times o'er, goes to the
feast,
And for his ordinary pays his heart
For what his eyes eat only.
 Agr.   Royal wench! 230
She made great Cæsar lay his sword to bed.
He ploughed her, and she cropp'd.
 Eno.   I saw her once
Hop forty paces through the public street;
And, having lost her breath, she spoke, and
panted,
That she did make defect perfection, 235
And, breathless, pow'r breathe forth.
 Mæc. Now Antony must leave her
utterly.
 Eno. Never! He will not.
Age cannot wither her, nor custom stale
Her infinite variety. Other women cloy 240
The appetites they feed, but she makes
hungry
Where most she satisfies; for vilest things
Become themselves in her, that the holy
priests
Bless her when she is riggish.
 Mæc. If beauty, wisdom, modesty, can
settle 245
The heart of Antony, Octavia is
A blessed lottery to him.
 Agr.   Let us go.
Good Enobarbus, make yourself my guest
Whilst you abide here.
 Eno. Humbly, sir, I thank you. [*Exeunt.*

  SCENE III. *Rome. Cæsar's house.*

Enter ANTONY, CÆSAR, OCTAVIA *between*
     them.

 Ant. The world and my great office will
sometimes

Divide me from your bosom.

Octa. All which time
Before the gods my knee shall bow my
 prayers
To them for you.

Ant. Good night, sir. My Octavia,
Read not my blemishes in the world's
 report. 5
I have not kept my square; but that to
 come
Shall all be done by th' rule. Good night,
 dear lady.

Octa. Good night, sir.

Cæs. Good night.
 [*Exeunt Cæsar and Octavia.*

Enter Soothsayer.

Ant. Now, sirrah, you do wish yourself
 in Egypt? 10

Sooth. Would I had never come from
thence, nor you thither!

Ant. If you can—your reason.

Sooth. I see it in my motion, have it not
in my tongue; but yet hie you to Egypt
again. 15

Ant. Say to me,
Whose fortunes shall rise higher, Cæsar's or
 mine?

Sooth. Cæsar's.
Therefore, O Antony, stay not by his side.
Thy dæmon, that thy spirit which keeps
 thee, is 20
Noble, courageous, high, unmatchable,
Where Cæsar's is not; but near him thy
 angel
Becomes a fear, as being o'erpow'r'd.
 Therefore
Make space enough between you.

Ant. Speak this no more.

Sooth. To none but thee; no more but
 when to thee. 25
If thou dost play with him at any game,
Thou art sure to lose; and of that natural
 luck
He beats thee 'gainst the odds. Thy lustre
 thickens
When he shines by. I say again, thy spirit
Is all afraid to govern thee near him; 30
But, he away, 'tis noble.

Ant. Get thee gone.
Say to Ventidius I would speak with him.
 [*Exit Soothsayer.*
He shall to Parthia.—Be it art or hap,
He hath spoken true. The very dice obey
 him; 34
And in our sports my better cunning faints
Under his chance. If we draw lots, he
 speeds;
His cocks do win the battle still of mine,
When it is all to nought, and his quails ever
Beat mine, inhoop'd, at odds. I will to
 Egypt;
And though I make this marriage for my
 peace, 40

I' th' East my pleasure lies.

Enter VENTIDIUS.

O, come, Ventidius,
You must to Parthia. Your commission's
 ready;
Follow me and receive't. [*Exeunt.*

SCENE IV. *Rome. A street.*

Enter LEPIDUS, MÆCENAS, *and* AGRIPPA.

Lep. Trouble yourselves no further. Pray
 you hasten
Your generals after.

Agr. Sir, Mark Antony
Will e'en but kiss Octavia, and we'll follow.

Lep. Till I shall see you in your soldier's
 dress,
Which will become you both, farewell.

Mæc. We shall, 5
As I conceive the journey, be at th' Mount
Before you, Lepidus.

Lep. Your way is shorter;
My purposes do draw me much about.
You'll win two days upon me.

Both. Sir, good success!

Lep. Farewell. [*Exeunt.*

SCENE V. *Alexandria. Cleopatra's palace.*

Enter CLEOPATRA, CHARMIAN, IRAS, *and*
 ALEXAS.

Cleo. Give me some music—music, moody
 food
Of us that trade in love.

All. The music, ho!

Enter MARDIAN the Eunuch.

Cleo. Let it alone! Let's to billiards.
 Come, Charmian.

Char. My arm is sore; best play with
 Mardian.

Cleo. As well a woman with an eunuch
 play'd 5
As with a woman. Come, you'll play with
 me, sir?

Mar. As well as I can, madam.

Cleo. And when good will is show'd,
 though't come too short,
The actor may plead pardon. I'll none now.
Give me mine angle—we'll to th' river.
 There, 10
My music playing far off, I will betray
Tawny-finn'd fishes; my bended hook
 shall pierce
Their slimy jaws; and as I draw them up
I'll think them every one an Antony,
And say 'Ah ha! Y'are caught'.

Char. 'Twas merry when 15
You wager'd on your angling; when your
 diver
Did hang a salt fish on his hook, which he
With fervency drew up.

Cleo. That time? O times!

I laugh'd him out of patience; and that
   night
I laugh'd him into patience; and next
   morn,   20
Ere the ninth hour, I drunk him to his bed,
Then put my tires and mantles on him,
   whilst
I wore his sword Philippan.

      Enter a Messenger.

                 O! from Italy?
Ram thou thy fruitful tidings in mine ears,
That long time have been barren.
   Mess.   Madam, madam— 25
   Cleo. Antony's dead! If thou say so,
      villain,
Thou kill'st thy mistress; but well and
   free,
If thou so yield him, there is gold, and here
My bluest veins to kiss—a hand that kings
Have lipp'd, and trembled kissing.   30
   Mess. First, madam, he is well.
   Cleo.   Why, there's more gold.
But, sirrah, mark, we use
To say the dead are well. Bring it to
   that,
The gold I give thee will I melt and pour
Down thy ill-uttering throat.   35
   Mess. Good madam, hear me.
   Cleo.   Well, go to, I will.
But there's no goodness in thy face. If
   Antony
Be free and healthful—why so tart a favour
To trumpet such good tidings? If not well,
Thou shouldst come like a Fury crown'd
   with snakes,   40
Not like a formal man.
   Mess.   Will't please you hear me?
   Cleo. I have a mind to strike thee ere
      thou speak'st.
Yet, if thou say Antony lives, is well,
Or friends with Cæsar, or not captive to
   him,
I'll set thee in a shower of gold, and hail 45
Rich pearls upon thee.
   Mess.   Madam, he's well.
   Cleo.   Well said.
   Mess. And friends with Cæsar.
   Cleo.   Th'art an honest man.
   Mess. Cæsar and he are greater friends
      than ever.
   Cleo. Make thee a fortune from me.
   Mess.   But yet, madam—
   Cleo. I do not like ' but yet '. It does
      allay   50
The good precedence; fie upon ' but yet '!
' But yet ' is as a gaoler to bring forth
Some monstrous malefactor. Prithee,
   friend,
Pour out the pack of matter to mine ear,
The good and bad together. He's friends
   with Cæsar;   55
In state of health, thou say'st; and, thou
   say'st, free.

   Mess. Free, madam! No; I made no
      such report.
He's bound unto Octavia.
   Cleo.   For what good turn?
   Mess. For the best turn i' th' bed.
   Cleo.   I am pale, Charmian.
   Mess. Madam, he's married to Octavia.
   Cleo. The most infectious pestilence upon
      thee!   [*Strikes him down.*
   Mess. Good madam, patience.
   Cleo.   What say you? Hence,
               [*Strikes him.*
Horrible villain! or I'll spurn thine eyes
Like balls before me; I'll unhair thy head;
       [*She hales him up and down.*
Thou shalt be whipp'd with wire and stew'd
   in brine,   65
Smarting in ling'ring pickle.
   Mess.   Gracious madam,
I that do bring the news made not the
   match.
   Cleo. Say 'tis not so, a province I will
      give thee,
And make thy fortunes proud. The blow
   thou hadst
Shall make thy peace for moving me to
   rage;   70
And I will boot thee with what gift beside
Thy modesty can beg.
   Mess.   He's married, madam.
   Cleo. Rogue, thou hast liv'd too long.
             [*Draws a knife.*
   Mess.   Nay, then I'll run.
What mean you, madam? I have made
   no fault.   [*Exit.*
   Char. Good madam, keep yourself within
      yourself: 75
The man is innocent.
   Cleo. Some innocents scape not the
      thunderbolt.
Melt Egypt into Nile! and kindly creatures
Turn all to serpents! Call the slave again.
Though I am mad, I will not bite him. Call!
   Char. He is afear'd to come.
   Cleo.   I will not hurt him.
These hands do lack nobility, that they
   strike   82
A meaner than myself; since I myself
Have given myself the cause.

      Enter the Messenger *again.*

                 Come hither, sir.
Though it be honest, it is never good   85
To bring bad news. Give to a gracious
   message
An host of tongues; but let ill tidings tell
Themselves when they be felt.
   Mess.   I have done my duty.
   Cleo. Is he married?
I cannot hate thee worser than I do   90
If thou again say ' Yes '.
   Mess.   He's married, madam.
   Cleo. The gods confound thee! Dost thou
      hold there still?

Mess. Should I lie, madam?

Cleo. O, I would thou didst,
So half my Egypt were submerg'd and made
A cistern for scal'd snakes! Go, get thee hence. 95
Hadst thou Narcissus in thy face, to me
Thou wouldst appear most ugly. He is married?

Mess. I crave your Highness' pardon.

Cleo. He is married?

Mess. Take no offence that I would not offend you;
To punish me for what you make me do 100
Seems much unequal. He's married to Octavia.

Cleo. O, that his fault should make a knave of thee
That art not what th'art sure of! Get thee hence.
The merchandise which thou hast brought from Rome
Are all too dear for me. Lie they upon thy hand, 105
And be undone by 'em! [*Exit Messenger.*

Char. Good your Highness, patience.

Cleo. In praising Antony I have disprais'd Cæsar.

Char. Many times, madam.

Cleo. I am paid for't now. Lead me from hence, 109
I faint. O Iras, Charmian! 'Tis no matter.
Go to the fellow, good Alexas; bid him
Report the feature of Octavia, her years,
Her inclination; let him not leave out
The colour of her hair. Bring me word quickly. [*Exit Alexas.*
Let him for ever go—let him not, Charmian— 115
Though he be painted one way like a Gorgon,
The other way's a Mars. [*To Mardian*]
Bid you Alexas
Bring me word how tall she is.—Pity me, Charmian,
But do not speak to me. Lead me to my chamber. [*Exeunt.*

SCENE VI. *Near Misenum.*

Flourish. Enter POMPEY *and* MENAS *at one door, with drum and trumpet; at another,* CÆSAR, ANTONY, LEPIDUS, ENOBARBUS, MÆCENAS, AGRIPPA, *with* Soldiers *marching.*

Pom. Your hostages I have, so have you mine;
And we shall talk before we fight.

Cæs. Most meet
That first we come to words; and therefore have we
Our written purposes before us sent; 4
Which if thou hast considered, let us know
If 'twill tie up thy discontented sword

And carry back to Sicily much tall youth
That else must perish here.

Pom. To you all three,
The senators alone of this great world, 9
Chief factors for the gods: I do not know
Wherefore my father should revengers want,
Having a son and friends, since Julius Cæsar,
Who at Philippi the good Brutus ghosted,
There saw you labouring for him. What was't
That mov'd pale Cassius to conspire? and what 15
Made the all-honour'd honest Roman, Brutus,
With the arm'd rest, courtiers of beauteous freedom,
To drench the Capitol, but that they would
Have one man but a man? And that is it
Hath made me rig my navy, at whose burden 20
The anger'd ocean foams; with which I meant
To scourge th' ingratitude that despiteful Rome
Cast on my noble father.

Cæs. Take your time.

Ant. Thou canst not fear us, Pompey, with thy sails;
We'll speak with thee at sea; at land thou know'st 25
How much we do o'er-count thee.

Pom. At land, indeed,
Thou dost o'er-count me of my father's house.
But since the cuckoo builds not for himself,
Remain in't as thou mayst.

Lep. Be pleas'd to tell us—
For this is from the present—how you take
The offers we have sent you.

Cæs. There's the point.

Ant. Which do not be entreated to, but weigh
What it is worth embrac'd.

Cæs. And what may follow,
To try a larger fortune.

Pom. You have made me offer
Of Sicily, Sardinia; and I must 35
Rid all the sea of pirates; then to send
Measures of wheat to Rome; this 'greed upon,
To part with unhack'd edges and bear back
Our targes undinted.

All. That's our offer.

Pom. Know, then,
I came before you here a man prepar'd 40
To take this offer; but Mark Antony
Put me to some impatience. Though I lose
The praise of it by telling, you must know,
When Cæsar and your brother were at blows, 44
Your mother came to Sicily and did find
Her welcome friendly.

Ant.   I have heard it, Pompey,
And am well studied for a liberal thanks
Which I do owe you.
Pom.   Let me have your hand.
I did not think, sir, to have met you here.
   Ant. The beds i' th' East are soft ; and
        thanks to you,   50
That call'd me timelier than my purpose
        hither ;
For I gave gained by't.
   Cæs.   Since I saw you last
There is a change upon you.
   Pom.   Well, I know not
What counts harsh fortune casts upon my
        face ;
But in my bosom shall she never come   55
To make my heart her vassal.
   Lep.   Well met here.
   Pom. I hope so, Lepidus. Thus we are
        agreed.
I crave our composition may be written,
And seal'd between us.
   Cæs.   That's the next to do.
   Pom. We'll feast each other ere we part,
        and let's   60
Draw lots who shall begin.
   Ant.   That will I, Pompey.
   Pom. No, Antony, take the lot ;
But, first or last, your fine Egyptian
        cookery
Shall have the fame. I have heard that
        Julius Cæsar
Grew fat with feasting there.
   Ant.   You have heard much.   65
   Pom. I have fair meanings, sir.
   Ant.   And fair words to them.
   Pom. Then so much have I heard ;
And I have heard Apollodorus carried—
   Eno. No more of that ! He did so.
   Pom.   What, I pray you ?
   Eno. A certain queen to Cæsar in a
        mattress.   70
   Pom. I know thee now. How far'st thou,
        soldier ?
   Eno.   Well ;
And well am like to do, for I perceive
Four feasts are toward.
   Pom.   Let me shake thy hand.
I never hated thee ; I have seen thee
        fight,
When I have envied thy behaviour.
   Eno.   Sir,
I never lov'd you much ; but I ha' prais'd
        ye   76
When you have well deserv'd ten times as
        much
As I have said you did.
   Pom.   Enjoy thy plainness ;
It nothing ill becomes thee.
Aboard my galley I invite you all.   80
Will you lead, lords ?
   All. Show's the way sir.
   Pom.   Come.
   [*Exeunt all but Enobarbus and Menas.*

   Men. [*Aside*] Thy father, Pompey, would
        ne'er have made this treaty.—
You and I have known, sir.
   Eno. At sea, I think.
   Men. We have, sir.   85
   Eno. You have done well by water.
   Men. And you by land.
   Eno. I will praise any man that will praise
me ; though it cannot be denied what I
have done by land.   89
   Men. Nor what I have done by water.
   Eno. Yes, something you can deny for
your own safety : you have been a great
thief by sea.
   Men. And you by land.
   Eno. There I deny my land service. But
give me your hand, Menas ; if our eyes had
authority, here they might take two thieves
kissing.   96
   Men. All men's faces are true, whatsome-
'er their hands are.
   Eno. But there is never a fair woman has
a true face.
   Men. No slander : they steal hearts. 99
   Eno. We came hither to fight with you.
   Men. For my part, I am sorry it is turn'd
to a drinking. Pompey doth this day laugh
away his fortune.
   Eno. If he do, sure he cannot weep't
back again.
   Men. Y'have said, sir. We look'd not
for Mark Antony here. Pray you, is he
married to Cleopatra ?   105
   Eno. Cæsar's sister is call'd Octavia.
   Men. True, sir ; she was the wife of
Caius Marcellus.
   Eno. But she is now the wife of Marcus
Antonius.
   Men. Pray ye, sir ?
   Eno. 'Tis true.   110
   Men. Then is Cæsar and he for ever knit
together.
   Eno. If I were bound to divine of this
unity, I would not prophesy so.
   Men. I think the policy of that purpose
made more in the marriage than the love of
the parties.   115
   Eno. I think so too. But you shall find
the band that seems to tie their friendship
together will be the very strangler of their
amity : Octavia is of a holy, cold, and still
conversation.   119
   Men. Who would not have his wife so ?
   Eno. Not he that himself is not so ; which
is Mark Antony. He will to his Egyptian
dish again ; then shall the sighs of Octavia
blow the fire up in Cæsar, and, as I said
before, that which is the strength of their
amity shall prove the immediate author of
their variance. Antony will use his affection
where it is ; he married but his occasion
here.   127
   Men. And thus it may be. Come, sir, will
you aboard ? I have a health for you.

Eno. I shall take it, sir. We have us'd
our throats in Egypt.   131
Men. Come, let's away.   [*Exeunt.*

SCENE VII. *On board Pompey's galley, off
Misenum.*

Music plays. Enter two or three Servants
with a banquet.

1 *Serv.* Here they'll be, man. Some o'
their plants are ill-rooted already; the
least wind i' th' world will blow them down.
2 *Serv.* Lepidus is high-colour'd.
1 *Serv.* They have made him drink alms-
drink.   5
2 *Serv.* As they pinch one another by the
disposition, he cries out ' No more ! ';
reconciles them to his entreaty and himself
to th' drink.
1 *Serv.* But it raises the greater war
between him and his discretion.   10
2 *Serv.* Why, this it is to have a name in
great men's fellowship. I had as lief have
a reed that will do me no service as a
partizan I could not heave.
1 *Serv.* To be call'd into a huge sphere,
and not to be seen to move in't, are the
holes where eyes should be, which pitifully
disaster the cheeks.   16

A sennet sounded. Enter CÆSAR, ANTONY,
LEPIDUS, POMPEY, AGRIPPA, MÆCENAS,
ENOBARBUS, MENAS, *with other* Cap-
tains.

Ant. [*To Cæsar*] Thus do they, sir: they
take the flow o' th' Nile
By certain scales i' th' pyramid; they
know
By th' height, the lowness, or the mean, if
dearth
Or foison follow. The higher Nilus swells 20
The more it promises; as it ebbs, the
seedsman
Upon the slime and ooze scatters his grain,
And shortly comes to harvest.
Lep. Y'have strange serpents there.
Ant. Ay, Lepidus.   25
Lep. Your serpent of Egypt is bred now
of your mud by the operation of your sun ;
so is your crocodile.
Ant. They are so.
Pom. Sit—and some wine ! A health to
Lepidus !
Lep. I am not so well as I should be, but
I'll ne'er out.   30
Eno. Not till you have slept. I fear me
you'll be in till then.
Lep. Nay, certainly, I have heard the
Ptolemies' pyramises are very goodly
things. Without contradiction I have
heard that.   35
Men. [*Aside to Pompey*] Pompey, a word.
Pom. [*Aside to Menas*] Say in mine ear;
what is't ?

Men. [*Aside to Pompey*] Forsake thy seat,
I do beseech thee, Captain,
And hear me speak a word.
Pom. [*Whispers in's ear*] Forbear me till
anon—
This wine for Lepidus !
Lep. What manner o' thing is your
crocodile ?   40
Ant. It is shap'd, sir, like itself, and it is
as broad as it hath breadth; it is just so
high as it is, and moves with it own
organs. It lives by that which nourisheth
it, and the elements once out of it, it
transmigrates.
Lep. What colour is it of ?   45
Ant. Of it own colour too.
Lep. 'Tis a strange serpent.
Ant. 'Tis so. And the tears of it are wet.
Cæs. Will this description satisfy him ?
Ant. With the health that Pompey gives
him, else he is a very epicure.   51
Pom. [*Aside to Menas*] Go, hang, sir,
hang ! Tell me of that ! Away !
Do as I bid you.—Where's this cup I call'd
for ?
Men. [*Aside to Pompey*] If for the sake of
merit thou wilt hear me,   54
Rise from thy stool.
Pom. [*Aside to Menas*] I think th'art
mad. [*Rises and walks aside*] The
matter ?
Men. I have ever held my cap off to thy
fortunes.
Pom. Thou hast serv'd me with much
faith. What's else to say ?—
Be jolly, lords.
Ant.   These quicksands, Lepidus,
Keep off them, for you sink.   59
Men. Wilt thou be lord of all the world ?
Pom.   What say'st thou ?
Men. Wilt thou be lord of the whole
world ? That's twice.   61
Pom. How should that be ?
Men.   But entertain it,
And though thou think me poor, I am the
man
Will give thee all the world.
Pom.   Hast thou drunk well ?
Men. No, Pompey, I have kept me from
the cup.   65
Thou art, if thou dar'st be, the earthly
Jove ;
Whate'er the ocean pales or sky inclips
Is thine, if thou wilt ha't.
Pom.   Show me which way.
Men. These three world-sharers, these
competitors,   69
Are in thy vessel. Let me cut the cable ;
And when we are put off, fall to their
throats.
All there is thine.
Pom. Ah, this thou shouldst have done,
And not have spoke on't. In me 'tis
villainy:

In thee't had been good service. Thou
    must know
'Tis not my profit that does lead mine
    honour : 75
Mine honour, it. Repent that e'er thy
    tongue
Hath so betray'd thine act. Being done
    unknown,
I should have found it afterwards well done,
But must condemn it now. Desist, and
    drink.

Men. [*Aside*] For this, 80
I'll never follow thy pall'd fortunes more.
Who seeks, and will not take when once 'tis
    offer'd,
Shall never find it more.

Pom. This health to Lepidus !

Ant. Bear him ashore, I'll pledge it for
    him, Pompey.

Eno. Here's to thee, Menas !

Men.   Enobarbus, welcome ! 85

Pom. Fill till the cup be hid.

Eno. There's a strong fellow, Menas.
    [*Pointing to the Servant who carries off*
                    Lepidus.

Men. Why ?

Eno. 'A bears the third part of the
    world, man ; see'st not ?

Men. The third part, then, is drunk.
    Would it were all,
That it might go on wheels ! 91

Eno. Drink thou ; increase the reels.

Men. Come.

Pom. This is not yet an Alexandrian
    feast.

Ant. It ripens towards it. Strike the
    vessels, ho ! 95
Here's to Cæsar !

Cæs.   I could well forbear 't.
It's monstrous labour when I wash my
    brain
And it grows fouler.

Ant.   Be a child o' th' time.

Cæs. Possess it, I'll make answer.
But I had rather fast from all four days 100
Than drink so much in one.

Eno. [*To Antony*] Ha, my brave emperor !
Shall we dance now the Egyptian Bac-
    chanals
And celebrate our drink ?

Pom.   Let's ha't, good soldier.

Ant. Come, let's all take hands,
Till that the conquering wine hath steep'd
    our sense 105
In soft and delicate Lethe.

Eno.   All take hands.
Make battery to our ears with the loud
    music,
The while I'll place you ; then the boy
    shall sing ;
The holding every man shall bear as loud
As his strong sides can volley. 110
    [*Music plays. Enobarbus places them
               hand in hand.*

The Song.

Come, thou monarch of the vine,
Plumpy Bacchus with pink eyne !
In thy fats our cares be drown'd,
With thy grapes our hairs be crown'd.
Cup us till the world go round, 115
Cup us till the world go round !

Cæs. What would you more ? Pompey,
    good night. Good brother,
Let me request you off ; our graver busi-
    ness
Frowns at this levity. Gentle lords, let's
    part ;
You see we have burnt our cheeks. Strong
    Enobarb 120
Is weaker than the wine, and mine own
    tongue
Splits what it speaks. The wild disguise
    hath almost
Antick'd us all. What needs more words ?
    Good night.
Good Antony, your hand.

Pom.   I'll try you on the shore.

Ant. And shall, sir. Give's your hand.

Pom.   O Antony,
You have my father's house—but what ?
    We are friends. 126
Come, down into the boat.

Eno.   Take heed you fall not.
    [*Exeunt all but Enobarbus and Menas.*
Menas, I'll not on shore.

Men.   No, to my cabin.
These drums ! these trumpets, flutes ! what !
Let Neptune hear we bid a loud farewell
To these great fellows. Sound and be
    hang'd, sound out ! 131
    [*Sound a flourish, with drums.*

Eno. Hoo ! says 'a. There's my cap.

Men. Hoo ! Noble Captain, come.
                          [*Exeunt.*

ACT THREE

SCENE I. *A plain in Syria.*

Enter VENTIDIUS, *as it were in triumph,
with* SILIUS *and other* Romans, Officers
and Soldiers ; *the dead body of* PACORUS
borne before him.

Ven. Now, darting Parthia, art thou
    struck, and now
Pleas'd fortune does of Marcus Crassus'
    death
Make me revenger. Bear the King's son's
    body
Before our army. Thy Pacorus, Orodes,
Pays this for Marcus Crassus.

Sil.   Noble Ventidius,
Whilst yet with Parthian blood thy sword
    is warm 6
The fugitive Parthians follow ; spur
    through Media,
Mesopotamia, and the shelters whither

The routed fly. So thy grand captain,
    Antony,   9
Shall set thee on triumphant chariots and
Put garlands on thy head.
  Ven.   O Silius, Silius,
I have done enough. A lower place, note
    well,
May make too great an act ; for learn this,
    Silius :
Better to leave undone than by our deed
Acquire too high a fame when him we
    serve's away.   15
Cæsar and Antony have ever won
More in their officer, than person. Sossius,
One of my place in Syria, his lieutenant,
For quick accumulation of renown,
Which he achiev'd by th' minute, lost his
    favour.   20
Who does i' th' wars more than his captain
    can
Becomes his captain's captain ; and
    ambition,
The soldier's virtue, rather makes choice
    of loss
Than gain which darkens him.
I could do more to do Antonius good,   25
But 'twould offend him ; and in his offence
Should my performance perish.
  Sil.   Thou hast, Ventidius, that
Without the which a soldier and his
    sword
Grants scarce distinction. Thou wilt write
    to Antony ?
  Ven. I'll humbly signify what in his
    name,   30
That magical word of war, we have effected;
How, with his banners, and his well-paid
    ranks,
The ne'er-yet-beaten horse of Parthia
We have jaded out o' th' field.
  Sil.   Where is he now ?
  Ven. He purposeth to Athens ; whither,
    with what haste   35
The weight we must convey with's will
    permit,
We shall appear before him.—On, there ;
    pass along.   *[Exeunt.*

SCENE II. *Rome. Cæsar's house.*

Enter AGRIPPA *at one door,* ENOBARBUS *at
    another.*

  Agr. What, are the brothers parted ?
  Eno. They have dispatch'd with Pom-
    pey ; he is gone ;
The other three are sealing. Octavia weeps
To part from Rome ; Cæsar is sad ; and
    Lepidus,
Since Pompey's feast, as Menas says, is
    troubled   5
With the green sickness.
  Agr.   'Tis a noble Lepidus.
  Eno. A very fine one. O, how he loves
    Cæsar !

  Agr. Nay, but how dearly he adores
    Mark Antony !
  Eno. Cæsar ? Why he's the Jupiter of
    men.
  Agr. What's Antony ? The god of
    Jupiter.   10
  Eno. Spake you of Cæsar ? How ! the
    nonpareil !
  Agr. O, Antony ! O thou Arabian bird !
  Eno. Would you praise Cæsar, say
    ' Cæsar '—go no further.
  Agr. Indeed, he plied them both with
    excellent praises.
  Eno. But he loves Cæsar best. Yet he
    loves Antony.   15
Hoo ! hearts, tongues, figures, scribes,
    bards, poets, cannot
Think, speak, cast, write, sing, number—
    hoo !—
His love to Antony. But as for Cæsar,
Kneel down, kneel down, and wonder.
  Agr.   Both he loves.
  Eno. They are his shards, and he their
    beetle. [*Trumpets within*] So— 20
This is to horse. Adieu, noble Agrippa.
  Agr. Good fortune, worthy soldier, and
    farewell.

Enter CÆSAR, ANTONY, LEPIDUS, *and*
    OCTAVIA.

  Ant. No further, sir.
  Cæs. You take from me a great part of
    myself ;
Use me well in't. Sister, prove such a
    wife   25
As my thoughts make thee, and as my
    farthest band
Shall pass on thy approof. Most noble
    Antony,
Let not the piece of virtue which is set
Betwixt us as the cement of our love
To keep it builded be the ram to batter 30
The fortress of it ; for better might we
Have lov'd without this mean, if on both
    parts
This be not cherish'd.
  Ant.   Make me not offended
In your distrust.
  Cæs.   I have said.
  Ant.   You shall not find,
Though you be therein curious, the least
    cause   35
For what you seem to fear. So the gods
    keep you,
And make the hearts of Romans serve your
    ends !
We will here part.
  Cæs. Farewell, my dearest sister, fare
    thee well.
The elements be kind to thee and make 40
Thy spirits all of comfort ! Fare thee well.
  Octa. My noble brother !
  Ant. The April's in her eyes. It is love's
    spring,

And these the showers to bring it on. Be
  cheerful.
  Octa. Sir, look well to my husband's
house ; and—
  Cæs. What, 45
Octavia ?
  Octa. I'll tell you in your ear.
  Ant. Her tongue will not obey her heart,
  nor can
Her heart inform her tongue—the swan's
  down feather,
That stands upon the swell at the full of
  tide,
And neither way inclines. 50
  Eno. [*Aside to Agrippa*] Will Cæsar weep ?
  Agr. [*Aside to Enobarbus*] He has a cloud
  in's face.
  Eno. [*Aside to Agrippa*] He were the
  worse for that, were he a horse ;
So is he, being a man.
  Agr. [*Aside to Enobarbus*] Why, Eno-
  barbus,
When Antony found Julius Cæsar dead,
He cried almost to roaring ; and he wept 55
When at Philippi he found Brutus slain.
  Eno. [*Aside to Agrippa*] That year, in-
  deed, he was troubled with a rheum ;
What willingly he did confound he wail'd,
Believe't—till I weep too.
  Cæs. No, sweet Octavia,
You shall hear from me still ; the time
  shall not 60
Out-go my thinking on you.
  Ant. Come, sir, come ;
I'll wrestle with you in my strength of love.
Look here I have you ; thus I let you go,
And give you to the gods.
  Cæs. Adieu ; be happy !
  Lep. Let all the number of the stars give
  light 65
To thy fair way !
  Cæs. Farewell, farewell ! [*Kisses Octavia.*
  Ant. Farewell !

    [*Trumpets sound. Exeunt.*

Scene III. *Alexandria. Cleopatra's palace.*

Enter Cleopatra, Charmian, Iras, *and*
    Alexas.

  Cleo. Where is the fellow ?
  Alex. Half afeard to come.
  Cleo. Go to, go to.

    Enter the Messenger *as before.*

    Come hither, sir.
  Alex. Good Majesty,
Herod of Jewry dare not look upon you
But when you are well pleas'd.
  Cleo. That Herod's head
I'll have. But how, when Antony is gone, 5
Through whom I might command it ?
    Come thou near.
  Mess. Most gracious Majesty !
  Cleo. Didst thou behold Octavia ?

  Mess. Ay, dread Queen.
  Cleo. Where ?
  Mess. Madam, in Rome
I look'd her in the face, and saw her led
Between her brother and Mark Antony. 10
  Cleo. Is she as tall as me ?
  Mess. She is not, madam.
  Cleo. Didst hear her speak ? Is she shrill-
  tongu'd or low ?
  Mess. Madam, I heard her speak : she is
  low voic'd.
  Cleo. That's not so good. He cannot like
  her long. 14
  Char. Like her ? O Isis ! 'tis impossible.
  Cleo. I think so, Charmian. Dull of
tongue and dwarfish !
What majesty is in her gait ? Remember,
If e'er thou look'dst on majesty.
  Mess. She creeps.
Her motion and her station are as one ;
She shows a body rather than a life, 20
A statue than a breather.
  Cleo. Is this certain ?
  Mess. Or I have no observance.
  Char. Three in Egypt
Cannot make better note.
  Cleo. He's very knowing ;
I do perceive't. There's nothing in her yet.
The fellow has good judgment.
  Char. Excellent. 25
  Cleo. Guess at her years, I prithee.
  Mess. Madam,
She was a widow.
  Cleo. Widow ? Charmian, hark !
  Mess. And I do think she's thirty.
  Cleo. Bear'st thou her face in mind ? Is't
long or round ?
  Mess. Round even to faultiness. 30
  Cleo. For the most part, too, they are
  foolish that are so.
Her hair, what colour ?
  Mess. Brown, madam ; and her forehead
As low as she would wish it.
  Cleo. There's gold for thee.
Thou must not take my former sharpness
  ill. 34
I will employ thee back again ; I find thee
Most fit for business. Go make thee ready ;
Our letters are prepar'd. [*Exit Messenger.*
  Char. A proper man.
  Cleo. Indeed, he is so. I repent me much
That so I harried him. Why, methinks, by
  him,
This creature's no such thing.
  Char. Nothing, madam. 40
  Cleo. The man hath seen some majesty,
  and should know.
  Char. Hath he seen majesty ? Isis else
  defend,
And serving you so long !
  Cleo. I have one thing more to ask him
  yet, good Charmian.
But 'tis no matter ; thou shalt bring him
  to me 45

Where I will write. All may be well
enough.

Char. I warrant you, madam. [*Exeunt.*

SCENE IV. *Athens. Antony's house.*

Enter ANTONY *and* OCTAVIA.

Ant. Nay, nay, Octavia, not only that—
That were excusable, that and thousands
more
Of semblable import—but he hath wag'd
New wars 'gainst Pompey; made his will,
and read it
To public ear; 5
Spoke scantly of me; when perforce he
could not
But pay me terms of honour, cold and
sickly
He vented them, most narrow measure
lent me;
When the best hint was given him, he not
took't,
Or did it from his teeth.
Octa. O my good lord, 10
Believe not all; or if you must believe,
Stomach not all. A more unhappy lady,
If this division chance, ne'er stood between,
Praying for both parts.
The good gods will mock me presently 15
When I shall pray 'O, bless my lord and
husband!'
Undo that prayer by crying out as loud
'O, bless my brother!' Husband win, win
brother,
Prays, and destroys the prayer; no mid-
way
'Twixt these extremes at all.
Ant. Gentle Octavia, 20
Let your best love draw to that point
which seeks
Best to preserve it. If I lose mine
honour,
I lose myself; better I were not yours
Than yours so branchless. But, as you
requested,
Yourself shall go between's. The mean-
time, lady, 25
I'll raise the preparation of a war
Shall stain your brother. Make your soonest
haste;
So your desires are yours.
Octa. Thanks to my lord.
The Jove of power make me, most weak,
most weak,
Your reconciler! Wars 'twixt you twain
would be 30
As if the world should cleave, and that
slain men
Should solder up the rift.
Ant. When it appears to you where this
begins,
Turn your displeasure that way, for our
faults
Can never be so equal that your love 35

Can equally move with them. Provide your
going;
Choose your own company, and command
what cost
Your heart has mind to. [*Exeunt.*

SCENE V. *Athens. Antony's house.*

Enter ENOBARBUS *and* EROS, *meeting.*

Eno. How now, friend Eros!
Eros. There's strange news come, sir.
Eno. What, man?
Eros. Cæsar and Lepidus have made wars
upon Pompey. 5
Eno. This is old. What is the success?
Eros. Cæsar, having made use of him in
the wars 'gainst Pompey, presently denied
him rivality, would not let him partake in
the glory of the action; and not resting
here, accuses him of letters he had formerly
wrote to Pompey; upon his own appeal,
seizes him. So the poor third is up, till
death enlarge his confine. 12
Eno. Then, world, thou hast a pair of
chaps—no more;
And throw between them all the food thou
hast,
They'll grind the one the other. Where's
Antony? 15
Eros. He's walking in the garden—thus,
and spurns
The rush that lies before him; cries 'Fool
Lepidus!'
And threats the throat of that his officer
That murd'red Pompey.
Eno. Our great navy's rigg'd.
Eros. For Italy and Cæsar. More,
Domitius: 20
My lord desires you presently; my news
I might have told hereafter.
Eno. 'Twill be naught;
But let it be. Bring me to Antony.
Eros. Come, sir. [*Exeunt.*

SCENE VI. *Rome. Cæsar's house.*

Enter CÆSAR, AGRIPPA, *and* MÆCENAS.

Cæs. Contemning Rome, he has done all
this and more
In Alexandria. Here's the manner of't:
I' th' market-place, on a tribunal silver'd,
Cleopatra and himself in chairs of gold
Were publicly enthron'd; at the feet sat 5
Cæsarion, whom they call my father's son,
And all the unlawful issue that their lust
Since then hath made between them. Unto
her
He gave the stablishment of Egypt; made
her
Of lower Syria, Cyprus, Lydia, 10
Absolute queen.
Mæc. This in the public eye?
Cæs. I' th' common show-place, where
they exercise.

His sons he there proclaim'd the kings of
    kings :
Great Media, Parthia, and Armenia,
He gave to Alexander; to Ptolemy he
    assign'd   15
Syria, Cilicia, and Phœnicia. She
In th' habiliments of the goddess Isis
That day appear'd; and oft before gave
    audience,
As 'tis reported, so.

Mæc.   Let Rome be thus
Inform'd.

Agr.   Who, queasy with his insolence   20
Already, will their good thoughts call from
    him.

Cæs.   The people knows it, and have now
    receiv'd
His accusations.

Agr.   Who does he accuse ?

Cæs. Cæsar; and that, having in Sicily
Sextus Pompeius spoil'd, we had not rated
    him   25
His part o' th' isle. Then does he say he
    lent me
Some shipping, unrestor'd. Lastly, he frets
That Lepidus of the triumvirate
Should be depos'd; and, being, that we
    detain
All his revenue.

Agr.   Sir, this should be answer'd.   30

Cæs. 'Tis done already, and the messenger
    gone.
I have told him Lepidus was grown too
    cruel,
That he his high authority abus'd,
And did deserve his change. For what I
    have conquer'd
I grant him part; but then, in his Armenia
And other of his conquer'd kingdoms, I   36
Demand the like.

Mæc.   He'll never yield to that.

Cæs. Nor must not then be yielded to
    in this.

    Enter OCTAVIA, *with her* Train.

Octa. Hail, Cæsar, and my lord ! hail,
    most dear Cæsar !

Cæs. That ever I should call thee cast-
    away !   40

Octa. You have not call'd me so, nor have
    you cause.

Cæs. Why have you stol'n upon us thus ?
    You come not
Like Cæsar's sister. The wife of Antony
Should have an army for an usher, and
The neighs of horse to tell of her approach
Long ere she did appear. The trees by th'
    way   46
Should have borne men, and expectation
    fainted,
Longing for what it had not. Nay, the dust
Should have ascended to the roof of heaven,
Rais'd by your populous troops. But you
    are come   50

A market-maid to Rome, and have pre-
    vented
The ostentation of our love, which left
    unshown
Is often left unlov'd. We should have met
    you
By sea and land, supplying every stage
With an augmented greeting.

Octa.   Good my lord,   55
To come thus was I not constrain'd, but
    did it
On my free will. My lord, Mark Antony,
Hearing that you prepar'd for war,
    acquainted
My grieved ear withal; whereon I begg'd
His pardon for return.

Cæs.   Which soon he granted,   60
Being an obstruct 'tween his lust and him.

Octa. Do not say so, my lord.

Cæs.   I have eyes upon him,
And his affairs come to me on the wind.
Where is he now ?

Octa.   My lord, in Athens.

Cæs. No, my most wronged sister :
    Cleopatra   65
Hath nodded him to her. He hath given
    his empire
Up to a whore, who now are levying
The kings o' th' earth for war. He hath
    assembled
Bocchus, the king of Libya ; Archelaus
Of Cappadocia ; Philadelphos, king   70
Of Paphlagonia ; the Thracian king,
    Adallas ;
King Manchus of Arabia ; King of Pont ;
Herod of Jewry ; Mithridates, king
Of Comagene ; Polemon and Amyntas,
The kings of Mede and Lycaonia, with a   75
More larger list of sceptres.

Octa.   Ay me most wretched,
That have my heart parted betwixt two
    friends,
That does afflict each other !

Cæs.   Welcome hither.
Your letters did withhold our breaking
    forth,
Till we perceiv'd both how you were wrong
    led   80
And we in negligent danger. Cheer your
    heart ;
Be you not troubled with the time, which
    drives
O'er your content these strong necessities,
But let determin'd things to destiny
Hold unbewail'd their way. Welcome to
    Rome ;   85
Nothing more dear to me. You are abus'd
Beyond the mark of thought, and the high
    gods,
To do you justice, make their ministers
Of us and those that love you. Best of
    comfort,
And ever welcome to us.

Agr.   Welcome, lady.   90

Mæc. Welcome, dear madam.
Each heart in Rome does love and pity you;
Only th' adulterous Antony, most large
In his abominations, turns you off,
And gives his potent regiment to a trull 95
That noises it against us.
  Octa.   Is it so, sir ?
  Cæs. Most certain.   Sister, welcome.
     Pray you
Be ever known to patience. My dear'st
     sister !   [*Exeunt.*

SCENE VII. *Antony's camp near Actium.*

  Enter CLEOPATRA *and* ENOBARBUS.

  Cleo. I will be even with thee, doubt it
    not.
  Eno. But why, why, why ?
  Cleo. Thou hast forspoke my being in
    these wars,
And say'st it is not fit.
  Eno.   Well, is it, is it ?
  Cleo. Is't not denounc'd against us ?
    Why should not we   5
Be there in person ?
  Eno. [*Aside*] Well, I could reply :
If we should serve with horse and mares
    together
The horse were merely lost ; the mares
    would bear
A soldier and his horse.
  Cleo.   What is't you say ?
  Eno. Your presence needs must puzzle
    Antony ;   10
Take from his heart, take from his brain,
    from 's time,
What should not then be spar'd. He is
    already
Traduc'd for levity ; and 'tis said in Rome
That Photinus an eunuch and your maids
Manage this war.
  Cleo.   Sink Rome, and their tongues rot
That speak against us ! A charge we bear i'
    th' war,   16
And, as the president of my kingdom, will
Appear there for a man. Speak not against
    it ;
I will not stay behind.

  Enter ANTONY *and* CANIDIUS.

  Eno.   Nay, I have done.
Here comes the Emperor.
  Ant.   Is it not strange, Canidius,
That from Tarentum and Brundusium 21
He could so quickly cut the Ionian sea,
And take in Toryne ?—You have heard
    on't, sweet ?
  Cleo. Celerity is never more admir'd
Than by the negligent.
  Ant.   A good rebuke, 25
Which might have well becom'd the best of
    men
To taunt at slackness. Canidius, we
Will fight with him by sea.

  Cleo.   By sea ! What else ?
  Can. Why will my lord do so ?
  Ant.   For that he dares us to 't.
  Eno. So hath my lord dar'd him to single
    fight.   30
  Can. Ay, and to wage this battle at
    Pharsalia,
Where Cæsar fought with Pompey. But
    these offers,
Which serve not for his vantage, he shakes
    off ;
And so should you.
  Eno.   Your ships are not well mann'd ;
Your mariners are muleteers, reapers,
    people   35
Ingross'd by swift impress. In Cæsar's fleet
Are those that often have 'gainst Pompey
    fought ;
Their ships are yare ; yours heavy. No
    disgrace
Shall fall you for refusing him at sea,
Being prepar'd for land.
  Ant.   By sea, by sea. 40
  Eno. Most worthy sir, you therein throw
    away
The absolute soldiership you have by land ;
Distract your army, which doth most
    consist
Of war-mark'd footmen ; leave unex-
    ecuted
Your own renowned knowledge ; quite
    forgo   45
The way which promises assurance ; and
Give up yourself merely to chance and
    hazard
From firm security.
  Ant.   I'll fight at sea.
  Cleo. I have sixty sails, Cæsar none
    better.
  Ant. Our overplus of shipping will we
    burn,   50
And, with the rest full-mann'd, from th'
    head of Actium
Beat th' approaching Cæsar. But if we fail,
We then can do't at land.

     Enter a Messenger.

            Thy business ?
  Mess. The news is true, my lord : he is
    descried ;
Cæsar has taken Toryne.   55
  Ant. Can he be there in person ? 'Tis
    impossible—
Strange that his power should be. Canidius,
Our nineteen legions thou shalt hold by
    land,
And our twelve thousand horse. We'll to
    our ship.
Away, my Thetis !

     Enter a Soldier.

     How now, worthy soldier ? 60
  Sold. O noble Emperor, do not fight by
    sea ;

Trust not to rotten planks. Do you mis-
    doubt
This sword and these my wounds ? Let th'
    Egyptians
And the Phœnicians go a-ducking ; we 64
Have us'd to conquer standing on the earth
And fighting foot to foot.
Ant.   Well, well—away.
        [*Exeunt Antony, Cleopatra, and*
                      Enobarbus.
Sold. By Hercules, I think I am i' th'
    right.
Can. Soldier, thou art ; but his whole
    action grows
Not in the power on't. So our leader's led,
And we are women's men.
Sold.   You keep by land
The legions and the horse whole, do you
    not ?   71
Can. Marcus Octavius, Marcus Justeius,
Publicola, and Cælius are for sea ;
But we keep whole by land. This speed of
    Cæsar's
Carries beyond belief.
Sold.   While he was yet in Rome,
His power went out in such distractions as
Beguil'd all spies.
Can.   Who's his lieutenant, hear you ?
Sold. They say one Taurus.
Can.   Well I know the man.

       Enter a Messenger.

Mess. The Emperor calls Canidius.
Can. With news the time's with labour
    and throes forth   80
Each minute some.   [*Exeunt.*

    SCENE VIII. *A plain near Actium.*

Enter CÆSAR, *with his Army, marching.*

Cæs. Taurus !
Taur. My lord ?
Cæs. Strike not by land ; keep whole ;
    provoke not battle
Till we have done at sea. Do not exceed 4
The prescript of this scroll. Our fortune lies
Upon this jump.   [*Exeunt.*

    SCENE IX. *Another part of the plain.*

    Enter ANTONY *and* ENOBARBUS.

Ant. Set we our squadrons on yond side
    o' th' hill,
In eye of Cæsar's battle ; from which place
We may the number of the ships behold,
And so proceed accordingly.   [*Exeunt.*

    SCENE X. *Another part of the plain.*

CANIDIUS *marcheth with his land Army one
    way over the stage, and* TAURUS, *the
    Lieutenant of Cæsar, the other way.
    After their going in is heard the noise
    of a sea-fight.*

    Alarum. Enter ENOBARBUS.

Eno. Naught, naught, all naught ! I can
    behold no longer.
Th' Antoniad, the Egyptian admiral,
With all their sixty, fly and turn the rudder.
To see't mine eyes are blasted.

       Enter SCARUS.

Scar.   Gods and goddesses,
All the whole synod of them !
Eno.   What's thy passion ? 5
Scar. The greater cantle of the world is
    lost
With very ignorance ; we have kiss'd away
Kingdoms and provinces.
Eno.   How appears the fight ?
Scar. On our side like the token'd
    pestilence,
Where death is sure. Yon ribaudred nag of
    Egypt—   10
Whom leprosy o'ertake !—i' th' midst o'
    th' fight,
When vantage like a pair of twins appear'd,
Both as the same, or rather ours the elder—
The breese upon her, like a cow in June—
Hoists sails and flies.   15
Eno.   That I beheld ;
Mine eyes did sicken at the sight and could
    not
Endure a further view.
Scar.   She once being loof'd,
The noble ruin of her magic, Antony,
Claps on his sea-wing, and, like a doting
    mallard,   20
Leaving the fight in height, flies after her.
I never saw an action of such shame ;
Experience, manhood, honour, ne'er before
Did violate so itself.
Eno.   Alack, alack !

       Enter CANIDIUS.

Can. Our fortune on the sea is out of
    breath,   25
And sinks most lamentably. Had our
    general
Been what he knew himself, it had gone
    well.
O, he has given example for our flight
Most grossly by his own !
Eno.   Ay, are you thereabouts ?
Why then, good night indeed.   30
Can. Toward Peloponnesus are they
    fled.
Scar. 'Tis easy to't ; and there I will
    attend
What further comes.
Can.   To Cæsar will I render
My legions and my horse ; six kings already
Show me the way of yielding.
Eno.   I'll yet follow 35
The wounded chance of Antony, though my
    reason
Sits in the wind against me.   [*Exeunt.*

SCENE XI. *Alexandria. Cleopatra's palace.*

Enter ANTONY *with* Attendants.

Ant. Hark! the land bids me tread no
    more upon't;
It is asham'd to bear me. Friends, come
    hither.
I am so lated in the world that I
Have lost my way for ever. I have a ship
Laden with gold; take that; divide it.
    Fly, 5
And make your peace with Cæsar.
All.   Fly? Not we!
    Ant. I have fled myself, and have in-
        structed cowards
To run and show their shoulders. Friends,
    be gone;
I have myself resolv'd upon a course
Which has no need of you; be gone. 10
My treasure's in the harbour, take it. O,
I follow'd that I blush to look upon.
My very hairs do mutiny; for the white
Reprove the brown for rashness, and they
    them
For fear and doting. Friends, be gone;
    you shall 15
Have letters from me to some friends that
    will
Sweep your way for you. Pray you look
    not sad,
Nor make replies of loathness; take the
    hint
Which my despair proclaims. Let that be
    left
Which leaves itself. To the sea-side
    straight way. 20
I will possess you of that ship and treasure.
Leave me, I pray, a little; pray you now;
Nay, do so, for indeed I have lost command;
Therefore I pray you. I'll see you by and
    by.   [*Sits down.*

Enter CLEOPATRA, *led by* CHARMIAN *and*
    IRAS, EROS *following.*

    Eros. Nay, gentle madam, to him! Com-
        fort him. 25
    Iras. Do, most dear Queen.
    Char. Do? Why, what else?
    Cleo. Let me sit down. O Juno!
    Ant. No, no, no, no, no.
    Eros. See you here, sir? 30
    Ant. O, fie, fie, fie!
    Char. Madam!
    Iras. Madam, O good Empress!
    Eros. Sir, sir!
    Ant. Yes, my lord, yes. He at Philippi
        kept 35
His sword e'en like a dancer, while I struck
The lean and wrinkled Cassius; and 'twas I
That the mad Brutus ended; he alone
Dealt on lieutenantry, and no practice had
In the brave squares of war. Yet now—no
    matter. 40
    Cleo. Ah, stand by!

    Eros. The Queen, my lord, the Queen!
    Iras. Go to him, madam, speak to him.
He is unqualitied with very shame.
    Cleo. Well then, sustain me. O! 45
    Eros. Most noble sir, arise; the Queen
        approaches.
Her head's declin'd, and death will seize her
    but
Your comfort makes the rescue.
    Ant. I have offended reputation—
A most unnoble swerving.
    Eros.   Sir, the Queen. 50
    Ant. O, whither hast thou led me, Egypt?
        See
How I convey my shame out of thine
    eyes
By looking back what I have left behind
'Stroy'd in dishonour.
    Cleo.   O my lord, my lord, 54
Forgive my fearful sails! I little thought
You would have followed.
    Ant.   Egypt, thou knew'st too well
My heart was to thy rudder tied by th'
    strings,
And thou shouldst tow me after. O'er my
    spirit
Thy full supremacy thou knew'st, and that
Thy beck might from the bidding of the
    gods 60
Command me.
    Cleo.   O, my pardon!
    Ant.   Now I must
To the young man send humble treaties,
    dodge
And palter in the shifts of lowness, who
With half the bulk o' th' world play'd as I
    pleas'd,
Making and marring fortunes. You did
    know 65
How much you were my conqueror, and
    that
My sword, made weak by my affection,
    would
Obey it on all cause.
    Cleo.   Pardon, pardon!
    Ant. Fall not a tear, I say; one of them
        rates
All that is won and lost. Give me a kiss; 70
Even this repays me.
We sent our schoolmaster; is 'a come back?
Love, I am full of lead. Some wine,
Within there, and our viands! Fortune
    knows
We scorn her most when most she offers
    blows.   [*Exeunt.*

SCENE XII. *Cæsar's camp in Egypt.*

Enter CÆSAR, AGRIPPA, DOLABELLA,
    THYREUS, *with* Others.

    Cæs. Let him appear that's come from
        Antony.
Know you him?
    Dol.   Cæsar, 'tis his schoolmaster:

An argument that he is pluck'd, when
    hither
He sends so poor a pinion of his wing,   4
Which had superfluous kings for messengers
Not many moons gone by.

Enter EUPHRONIUS, *Ambassador from*
Antony.

Cæs.   Approach, and speak.
Eup. Such as I am, I come from Antony.
I was of late as petty to his ends
As is the morn-dew on the myrtle leaf
To his grand sea.
Cæs.   Be't so. Declare thine office. 10
Eup. Lord of his fortunes he salutes thee,
    and
Requires to live in Egypt; which not
    granted,
He lessens his requests and to thee sues
To let him breathe between the heavens
    and earth,
A private man in Athens. This for him. 15
Next, Cleopatra does confess thy greatness,
Submits her to thy might, and of thee craves
The circle of the Ptolemies for her heirs,
Now hazarded to thy grace.
Cæs.   For Antony,
I have no ears to his request. The Queen 20
Of audience nor desire shall fail, so she
From Egypt drive her all-disgraced friend,
Or take his life there. This if she perform,
She shall not sue unheard. So to them both.
Eup. Fortune pursue thee!
Cæs.   Bring him through the bands.
                    [*Exit Euphronius.*
[*To Thyreus*] To try thy eloquence, now 'tis
    time. Dispatch; 26
From Antony win Cleopatra. Promise,
And in our name, what she requires; add
    more,
From thine invention, offers. Women are
    not
In their best fortunes strong; but want
    will perjure 30
The ne'er-touch'd vestal. Try thy cunning,
    Thyreus;
Make thine own edict for thy pains, which
    we
Will answer as a law.
Thyr.   Cæsar, I go.
Cæs. Observe how Antony becomes his
    flaw,
And what thou think'st his very action
    speaks 35
In every power that moves.
Thyr.   Cæsar, I shall. [*Exeunt.*

SCENE XIII. *Alexandria. Cleopatra's*
palace.

Enter CLEOPATRA, ENOBARBUS, CHARMIAN,
and IRAS.

Cleo. What shall we do, Enobarbus?
Eno.   Think, and die.

Cleo. Is Antony or we in fault for this?
Eno. Antony only, that would make his
    will
Lord of his reason. What though you
    fled
From that great face of war, whose several
    ranges 5
Frighted each other? Why should he
    follow?
The itch of his affection should not then
Have nick'd his captainship, at such a
    point,
When half to half the world oppos'd, he
    being
The mered question. 'Twas a shame no
    less 10
Than was his loss, to course your flying
    flags
And leave his navy gazing.
Cleo.   Prithee, peace.

Enter EUPHRONIUS, *the Ambassador; with*
ANTONY.

Ant. Is that his answer?
Eup. Ay, my lord.
Ant. The Queen shall then have courtesy,
    so she 15
Will yield us up.
Eup.   He says so.
Ant.   Let her know't.
To the boy Cæsar send this grizzled head,
And he will fill thy wishes to the brim
With principalities.
Cleo.   That head, my lord?
Ant. To him again. Tell him he wears
    the rose 20
Of youth upon him; from which the world
    should note
Something particular. His coin, ships,
    legions,
May be a coward's, whose ministers would
    prevail
Under the service of a child as soon
As i' th' command of Cæsar. I dare him
    therefore 25
To lay his gay comparisons apart,
And answer me declin'd, sword against
    sword,
Ourselves alone. I'll write it. Follow me.
           [*Exeunt Antony and Euphronius.*
Eno. [*Aside*] Yes, like enough high-
    battled Cæsar will
Unstate his happiness, and be stag'd to th'
    show 30
Against a sworder! I see men's judgments
    are
A parcel of their fortunes, and things out-
    ward
Do draw the inward quality after them,
To suffer all alike. That he should dream,
Knowing all measures, the full Cæsar will 35
Answer his emptiness! Cæsar, thou hast
    subdu'd
His judgment too.

Enter a Servant.

Serv. A messenger from Cæsar.

Cleo. What, no more ceremony? See, my women!

Against the blown rose may they stop their nose

That kneel'd unto the buds. Admit him, sir. [*Exit Servant.*

Eno. [*Aside*] Mine honesty and I begin to square. 41

The loyalty well held to fools does make

Our faith mere folly. Yet he that can endure

To follow with allegiance a fall'n lord

Does conquer him that did his master conquer, 45

And earns a place i' th' story.

Enter THYREUS.

Cleo. Cæsar's will?

Thyr. Hear it apart.

Cleo. None but friends : say boldly.

Thyr. So, haply, are they friends to Antony.

Eno. He needs as many, sir, as Cæsar has,

Or needs not us. If Cæsar please, our master 50

Will leap to be his friend. For us, you know

Whose he is we are, and that is Cæsar's.

Thyr. So.

Thus then, thou most renown'd : Cæsar entreats

Not to consider in what case thou stand'st

Further than he is Cæsar.

Cleo. Go on. Right royal! 55

Thyr. He knows that you embrace not Antony

As you did love, but as you fear'd him.

Cleo. O!

Thyr. The scars upon your honour, therefore, he

Does pity, as constrained blemishes,

Not as deserv'd.

Cleo. He is a god, and knows 60

What is most right. Mine honour was not yielded,

But conquer'd merely.

Eno. [*Aside*] To be sure of that,

I will ask Antony. Sir, sir, thou art so leaky

That we must leave thee to thy sinking, for

Thy dearest quit thee. [*Exit.*

Thyr. Shall I say to Cæsar 65

What you require of him? For he partly begs

To be desir'd to give. It much would please him

That of his fortunes you should make a staff

To lean upon. But it would warm his spirits

To hear from me you had left Antony, 70

And put yourself under his shroud,

The universal landlord.

Cleo. What's your name?

Thyr. My name is Thyreus.

Cleo. Most kind messenger,

Say to great Cæsar this : in deputation

I kiss his conqu'ring hand. Tell him I am prompt 75

To lay my crown at 's feet, and there to kneel.

Tell him from his all-obeying breath I hear

The doom of Egypt.

Thyr. 'Tis your noblest course.

Wisdom and fortune combating together,

If that the former dare but what it can, 80

No chance may shake it. Give me grace to lay

My duty on your hand.

Cleo. Your Cæsar's father oft,

When he hath mus'd of taking kingdoms in,

Bestow'd his lips on that unworthy place,

As it rain'd kisses.

Re-enter ANTONY *and* ENOBARBUS.

Ant. Favours, by Jove that thunders!

What art thou, fellow?

Thyr. One that but performs

The bidding of the fullest man, and worthiest 87

To have command obey'd.

Eno. [*Aside*] You will be whipt.

Ant. Approach there.—Ah, you kite!—

Now, gods and devils!

Authority melts from me. Of late, when I cried ' Ho!' 90

Like boys unto a muss, kings would start forth

And cry ' Your will? ' Have you no ears? I am

Antony yet.

Enter Servants.

Take hence this Jack and whip him.

Eno. 'Tis better playing with a lion's whelp

Than with an old one dying.

Ant. Moon and stars! 95

Whip him. Were't twenty of the greatest tributaries

That do acknowledge Cæsar, should I find them

So saucy with the hand of she here—what's her name

Since she was Cleopatra? Whip him, fellows, 99

Till like a boy you see him cringe his face,

And whine aloud for mercy. Take him hence.

Thyr. Mark Antony—

Ant. Tug him away. Being whipt,

Bring him again : the Jack of Cæsar's shall

Bear us an errand to him. 104

[*Exeunt Servants with Thyreus.*

You were half blasted ere I knew you. Ha!

Have I my pillow left unpress'd in Rome,

Forborne the getting of a lawful race,

And by a gem of women, to be abus'd

By one that looks on feeders?
   Cleo.   Good my lord—
   Ant. You have been a boggler ever. 110
But when we in our viciousness grow
   hard—
O misery on't !—the wise gods seel our eyes,
In our own filth drop our clear judgments,
   make us
Adore our errors, laugh at's while we strut
To our confusion.
   Cleo.   O, is't come to this ? 115
   Ant. I found you as a morsel cold upon
Dead Cæsar's trencher. Nay, you were a
   fragment
Of Cneius Pompey's, besides what hotter
   hours,
Unregist'red in vulgar fame, you have
Luxuriously pick'd out ; for I am sure, 120
Though you can guess what temperance
   should be,
You know not what it is.
   Cleo.   Wherefore is this ?
   Ant. To let a fellow that will take
   rewards, 123
And say ' God quit you ! ' be familiar with
My playfellow, your hand, this kingly seal
And plighter of high hearts ! O that I were
Upon the hill of Basan to outroar
The horned herd ! For I have savage cause,
And to proclaim it civilly were like
A halter'd neck which does the hangman
   thank 130
For being yare about him.

   Re-enter a Servant *with* THYREUS.

           Is he whipt ?
   Serv. Soundly, my lord.
   Ant.   Cried he ? and begg'd 'a pardon ?
   Serv. He did ask favour.
   Ant. If that thy father live, let him
   repent
Thou wast not made his daughter ; and be
   thou sorry
To follow Cæsar in his triumph, since 136
Thou hast been whipt for following him.
   Henceforth
The white hand of a lady fever thee !
Shake thou to look on't. Get thee back to
   Cæsar ;
Tell him thy entertainment ; look thou say
He makes me angry with him ; for he
   seems 141
Proud and disdainful, harping on what I
   am,
Not what he knew I was. He makes me
   angry ;
And at this time most easy 'tis to do't,
When my good stars, that were my former
   guides, 145
Have empty left their orbs and shot their
   fires
Into th' abysm of hell. If he mislike
My speech and what is done, tell him he
   has

Hipparchus, my enfranched bondman,
   whom
He may at pleasure whip or hang or
   torture, 150
As he shall like, to quit me. Urge it thou.
Hence with thy stripes, be gone.
               [*Exit Thyreus.*
   Cleo. Have you done yet ?
   Ant.   Alack, our terrene moon
Is now eclips'd, and it portends alone
The fall of Antony.
   Cleo.   I must stay his time. 155
   Ant. To flatter Cæsar, would you mingle
   eyes
With one that ties his points ?
   Cleo.   Not know me yet ?
   Ant. Cold-hearted toward me ?
   Cleo.   Ah, dear, if I be so,
From my cold heart let heaven engender
   hail,
And poison it in the source, and the first
   stone 160
Drop in my neck ; as it determines, so
Dissolve my life ! The next Cæsarion smite!
Till by degrees the memory of my womb,
Together with my brave Egyptians all, 164
By the discandying of this pelleted storm,
Lie graveless, till the flies and gnats of Nile
Have buried them for prey.
   Ant.   I am satisfied.
Cæsar sits down in Alexandria, where
I will oppose his fate. Our force by land
Hath nobly held ; our sever'd navy too 170
Have knit again, and fleet, threat'ning
   most sea-like.
Where hast thou been, my heart ? Dost
   thou hear, lady ?
If from the field I shall return once more
To kiss these lips, I will appear in blood.
I and my sword will earn our chronicle. 175
There's hope in't yet.
   Cleo. That's my brave lord !
   Ant. I will be treble-sinew'd, hearted,
   breath'd,
And fight maliciously. For when mine
   hours 179
Were nice and lucky, men did ransom lives
Of me for jests ; but now I'll set my teeth,
And send to darkness all that stop me.
   Come,
Let's have one other gaudy night. Call to
   me
All my sad captains ; fill our bowls once
   more ;
Let's mock the midnight bell.
   Cleo.   It is my birthday. 185
I had thought t'have held it poor ; but
   since my lord
Is Antony again, I will be Cleopatra.
   Ant. We'll yet do well.
   Cleo. Call all his noble captains to my
   lord.
   Ant. Do so, we'll speak to them ; and
   to-night I'll force 190

The wine peep through their scars. Come
    on, my queen,
There's sap in't yet. The next time I do
    fight
I'll make death love me ; for I will contend
Even with his pestilent scythe.
                    [*Exeunt all but Enobarbus.*
    Eno. Now he'll outstare the lightning.
    To be furious   195
Is to be frighted out of fear, and in that
    mood
The dove will peck the estridge ; and I see
    still
A diminution in our captain's brain
Restores his heart. When valour preys on
    reason,   199
It eats the sword it fights with. I will seek
Some way to leave him.   [*Exit.*

ACT FOUR

SCENE I. *Cæsar's camp before Alexandria.*

Enter CÆSAR, AGRIPPA, *and* MÆCENAS,
with his Army ; *Cæsar reading a letter.*

    Cæs. He calls me boy, and chides as he
        had power
To beat me out of Egypt. My messenger
He hath whipt with rods ; dares me to
    personal combat,
Cæsar to Antony. Let the old ruffian know
I have many other ways to die, meantime
Laugh at his challenge.
    Mæc.   Cæsar must think, 6
When one so great begins to rage, he's
    hunted
Even to falling. Give him no breath, but
    now
Make boot of his distraction. Never anger
Made good guard for itself.
    Cæs.   Let our best heads
Know that to-morrow the last of many
    battles   11
We mean to fight. Within our files there
    are
Of those that serv'd Mark Antony but late
Enough to fetch him in. See it done ;   14
And feast the army ; we have store to do't,
And they have earn'd the waste. Poor
    Antony !   [*Exeunt.*

SCENE II. *Alexandria. Cleopatra's palace.*

Enter ANTONY, CLEOPATRA, ENOBARBUS,
CHARMIAN, IRAS, ALEXAS, *with* Others.

    Ant. He will not fight with me, Domitius?
    Eno.   No.
    Ant. Why should he not ?
    Eno. He thinks, being twenty times of
        better fortune,
He is twenty men to one.
    Ant.   To-morrow, soldier,
By sea and land I'll fight. Or I will live, 5
Or bathe my dying honour in the blood

Shall make it live again. Woo't thou fight
    well ?
    Eno. I'll strike, and cry ' Take all '.
    Ant.   Well said ; come on.
Call forth my household servants ; let's
    to-night
Be bounteous at our meal.

        Enter three or four Servitors.

                    Give me thy hand, 10
Thou hast been rightly honest. So hast
    thou ;
Thou, and thou, and thou. You have
    serv'd me well,
And kings have been your fellows.
    Cleo. [*Aside to Enobarbus*] What means
        this ?
    Eno. [*Aside to Cleopatra*] 'Tis one of those
        odd tricks which sorrow shoots
Out of the mind.
    Ant. And thou art honest too.   15
I wish I could be made so many men,
And all of you clapp'd up together in
An Antony, that I might do you service
So good as you have done.
    Serv.   The gods forbid !
    Ant. Well, my good fellows, wait on me
        to-night.   20
Scant not my cups, and make as much
    of me
As when mine empire was your fellow too,
And suffer'd my command.
    Cleo. [*Aside to Enobarbus*] What does he
        mean ?
    Eno. [*Aside to Cleopatra*] To make his
        followers weep.
    Ant.   Tend me to-night ;
May be it is the period of your duty.   25
Haply you shall not see me more ; or if,
A mangled shadow. Perchance to-morrow
You'll serve another master. I look on
    you
As one that takes his leave. Mine honest
    friends,
I turn you not away ; but, like a master 30
Married to your good service, stay till death.
Tend me to-night two hours, I ask no more,
And the gods yield you for't !
    Eno.   What mean you, sir,
To give them this discomfort ? Look, they
    weep ;   34
And I, an ass, am onion-ey'd. For shame !
Transform us not to women.
    Ant.   Ho, ho, ho !
Now the witch take me if I meant it thus !
Grace grow where those drops fall ! My
    hearty friends,
You take me in too dolorous a sense ;
For I spake to you for your comfort, did
    desire you   40
To burn this night with torches. Know, my
    hearts,
I hope well of to-morrow, and will lead you
Where rather I'll expect victorious life

Than death and honour. Let's to supper, come,
And drown consideration.   [*Exeunt.*

SCENE III. *Alexandria. Before Cleopatra's palace.*

Enter a Company of Soldiers.

1 *Sold.* Brother, good night. To-morrow is the day.
2 *Sold.* It will determine one way. Fare you well.
Heard you of nothing strange about the streets ?
1 *Sold.* Nothing. What news ?
2 *Sold.* Belike 'tis but a rumour. Good night to you.   5
1 *Sold.* Well, sir, good night.

They meet other Soldiers.

2 *Sold.* Soldiers, have careful watch.
1 *Sold.* And you. Good night, good night.
        [*The two companies separate and place themselves in every corner of the stage.*
2 *Sold.* Here we. And if to-morrow   9
Our navy thrive, I have an absolute hope
Our landmen will stand up.
3 *Sold.*   'Tis a brave army,
And full of purpose.
        [*Music of the hautboys is under the stage.*
2 *Sold.*   Peace, what noise ?
3 *Sold.*   List, list !
2 *Sold.* Hark !
3 *Sold.*   Music i' th' air.
4 *Sold.*   Under the earth.
5 *Sold.* It signs well, does it not ?
4 *Sold.*   No.
3 *Sold.*   Peace, I say !
What should this mean ?   15
2 *Sold.* 'Tis the god Hercules, whom Antony lov'd,
Now leaves him.
3 *Sold.* Walk ; let's see if other watchmen
Do hear what we do.
2 *Sold.*   How now, masters !   19
Soldiers. [*Speaking together*] How now !
How now ! Do you hear this ?
1 *Sold.*   Ay ; is't not strange ?
3 *Sold.* Do you hear, masters ? Do you hear ?
1 *Sold.* Follow the noise so far as we have quarter ;
Let's see how it will give off.   25
Soldiers. Content. 'Tis strange. [*Exeunt.*

SCENE IV. *Alexandria. Cleopatra's palace.*

Enter ANTONY *and* CLEOPATRA, CHARMIAN, IRAS, *with* Others.

Ant. Eros ! mine armour, Eros !
Cleo.   Sleep a little.
Ant. No, my chuck. Eros ! Come, mine armour, Eros !

Enter EROS *with armour.*

Come, good fellow, put mine iron on.
If fortune be not ours to-day, it is
Because we brave her. Come.
Cleo.   Nay, I'll help too.   5
What's this for ?
Ant.   Ah, let be, let be ! Thou art
The armourer of my heart. False, false ; this, this.
Cleo. Sooth, la, I'll help. Thus it must be.
Ant.   Well, well ;
We shall thrive now. Seest thou, my good fellow ?
Go put on thy defences.
Eros.   Briefly, sir.   10
Cleo. Is not this buckled well ?
Ant.   Rarely, rarely !
He that unbuckles this, till we do please
To daff't for our repose, shall hear a storm.
Thou fumblest, Eros, and my queen's a squire
More tight at this than thou. Dispatch. O love,   15
That thou couldst see my wars to-day, and knew'st
The royal occupation ! Thou shouldst see
A workman in't.

Enter an armed Soldier.

          Good-morrow to thee. Welcome.
Thou look'st like him that knows a warlike charge.
To business that we love we rise betime,   20
And go to't with delight.
Sold.   A thousand, sir,
Early though't be, have on their riveted trim,
And at the port expect you.
        [*Shout. Flourish of trumpets within.*

Enter Captains *and* Soldiers.

Capt. The morn is fair. Good morrow, General.
All. Good morrow, General.
Ant.   'Tis well blown, lads.   25
This morning, like the spirit of a youth
That means to be of note, begins betimes.
So, so. Come, give me that. This way.
Well said.
Fare thee well, dame, whate'er becomes of me.
This is a soldier's kiss. Rebukeable,   30
And worthy shameful check it were, to stand
On more mechanic compliment ; I'll leave thee
Now like a man of steel. You that will fight,
Follow me close ; I'll bring you to't. Adieu.
        [*Exeunt Antony, Eros, Captains and Soldiers.*
Char. Please you retire to your chamber ?
Cleo.   Lead me.

He goes forth gallantly. That he and
    Cæsar might   36
Determine this great war in single fight !
Then, Antony—but now. Well, on.
                              [*Exeunt.*

SCENE V. *Alexandria. Antony's camp.*

Trumpets sound. Enter ANTONY *and* EROS,
    a Soldier meeting them.

  Sold. The gods make this a happy day
    to Antony !
  Ant. Would thou and those thy scars had
    once prevail'd
To make me fight at land !
  Sold.   Hadst thou done so
The kings that have revolted, and the
    soldier
That has this morning left thee, would have
    still   5
Followed thy heels.
  Ant.   Who's gone this morning ?
  Sold.   Who ?
One ever near thee. Call for Enobarbus,
He shall not hear thee ; or from Cæsar's
    camp
Say ' I am none of thine'.
  Ant.   What say'st thou ?
  Sold.   Sir,
He is with Cæsar.
  Eros.   Sir, his chests and treasure
He has not with him.
  Ant.   Is he gone ?
  Sold.   Most certain.
  Ant. Go, Eros, send his treasure after ;
    do it ;   12
Detain no jot, I charge thee. Write to
    him—
I will subscribe—gentle adieus and greet-
    ings ;
Say that I wish he never find more cause 15
To change a master. O, my fortunes have
Corrupted honest men ! Dispatch. Eno-
    barbus !   [*Exeunt.*

SCENE VI. *Alexandria. Cæsar's camp.*

Flourish.   Enter AGRIPPA, CÆSAR, *with*
    DOLABELLA *and* ENOBARBUS.

  Cæs. Go forth, Agrippa, and begin the
    fight.
Our will is Antony be took alive ;
Make it so known.
  Agr.   Cæsar, I shall.   [*Exit.*
  Cæs. The time of universal peace is near.
Prove this a prosp'rous day, the three-
    nook'd world   6
Shall bear the olive freely.

Enter a Messenger.

  Mess.   Antony
Is come into the field.
  Cæs.   Go charge Agrippa
Plant those that have revolted in the vant,

That Antony may seem to spend his fury 10
Upon himself. [*Exeunt all but Enobarbus.*
  Eno. Alexas did revolt and went to
    Jewry on
Affairs of Antony ; there did dissuade
Great Herod to incline himself to Cæsar
And leave his master Antony.   For this
    pains   15
Cæsar hath hang'd him. Canidius and the
    rest
That fell away have entertainment, but
No honourable trust. I have done ill,
Of which I do accuse myself so sorely
That I will joy no more.

Enter a Soldier of Cæsar's.

  Sold. Enobarbus, Antony   20
Hath after thee sent all thy treasure, with
His bounty overplus. The messenger
Came on my guard, and at thy tent is now
Unloading of his mules.
  Eno.   I give it you.
  Sold. Mock not, Enobarbus.   25
I tell you true. Best you saf'd the bringer
Out of the host. I must attend mine office,
Or would have done't myself. Your emperor
Continues still a Jove.   [*Exit.*
  Eno. I am alone the villain of the earth,
And feel I am so most. O Antony,   31
Thou mine of bounty, how wouldst thou
    have paid
My better service, when my turpitude
Thou dost so crown with gold ! This blows
    my heart.
If swift thought break it not, a swifter mean
Shall outstrike thought ; but thought will
    do't, I feel.   36
I fight against thee ? No ! I will go seek
Some ditch wherein to die ; the foul'st best
    fits
My latter part of life.   [*Exit.*

SCENE VII. *Field of battle between the
    camps.*

Alarum. Drums and trumpets. Enter
    AGRIPPA *and* Others.

  Agr. Retire. We have engag'd ourselves
    too far.
Cæsar himself has work, and our oppression
Exceeds what we expected.   [*Exeunt.*

Alarums. Enter ANTONY, *and* SCARUS
    wounded.

  Scar. O my brave Emperor, this is fought
    indeed !
Had we done so at first, we had driven
    them home   5
With clouts about their heads.
  Ant.   Thou bleed'st apace.
  Scar. I had a wound here that was like
    a T,
But now 'tis made an H.
  Ant.   They do retire.

Ant. Too late, good Diomed. Call my
　　guard, I prithee.
Dio. What, ho! the Emperor's guard!
　　The guard, what ho!
Come, your lord calls!　　　　　　　130

Enter four or five of the Guard *of Antony.*

Ant. Bear me, good friends, where
　　Cleopatra bides;
'Tis the last service that I shall command
　　you.
1 Guard. Woe, woe are we, sir, you may
　　not live to wear
All your true followers out.
All.　　　　　　　　　　Most heavy day!
Ant. Nay, good my fellows, do not please
　　sharp fate　　　　　　　　　　135
To grace it with your sorrows. Bid that
　　welcome
Which comes to punish us, and we punish
　　it,
Seeming to bear it lightly. Take me up.
I have led you oft; carry me now, good
　　friends,
And have my thanks for all.　　　　140
　　　　　　[*Exeunt, bearing Antony.*

SCENE XV. *Alexandria. A monument.*

Enter CLEOPATRA *and her* Maids *aloft, with*
CHARMIAN *and* IRAS.

Cleo. O Charmian, I will never go from
　　hence!
Char. Be comforted, dear madam.
Cleo.　　　　　　　　No, I will not.
All strange and terrible events are welcome,
But comforts we despise; our size of
　　sorrow,　　　　　　　　　　　4
Proportion'd to our cause, must be as great
As that which makes it.

Enter DIOMEDES, *below.*

　　　　　　　　How now! Is he dead?
Dio. His death's upon him, but not dead.
Look out o' th' other side your monument;
His guard have brought him thither.

Enter, below, ANTONY, *borne by the* Guard.

Cleo. O sun,
Burn the great sphere thou mov'st in!
　　Darkling stand　　　　　　　10
The varying shore o' th' world. O Antony,
Antony, Antony! Help, Charmian; help,
　　Iras, help;
Help, friends below! Let's draw him
　　hither.
Ant.　　　　　　　　Peace!
Not Cæsar's valour hath o'erthrown Antony,
But Antony's hath triumph'd on itself.　15
Cleo. So it should be, that none but
　　Antony
Should conquer Antony; but woe 'tis so!
Ant. I am dying, Egypt, dying; only
I here importune death awhile, until

Of many thousand kisses the poor last　20
I lay upon thy lips.
Cleo.　　　　　　　I dare not, dear.
Dear my lord, pardon! I dare not,
Lest I be taken. Not th' imperious show
Of the full-fortun'd Cæsar ever shall
Be brooch'd with me. If knife, drugs,
　　serpents, have　　　　　　　25
Edge, sting, or operation, I am safe.
Your wife Octavia, with her modest eyes
And still conclusion, shall acquire no
　　honour
Demuring upon me. But come, come,
　　Antony—
Help me, my women—we must draw thee
　　up;　　　　　　　　　　　30
Assist, good friends.
Ant.　　　　　O, quick, or I am gone.
Cleo. Here's sport indeed! How heavy
　　weighs my lord!
Our strength is all gone into heaviness;
That makes the weight. Had I great Juno's
　　power,
The strong-wing'd Mercury should fetch
　　thee up,　　　　　　　　　35
And set thee by Jove's side. Yet come a
　　little.
Wishers were ever fools. O come, come,
　　come,
　　　[*They heave Antony aloft to Cleopatra.*
And welcome, welcome! Die where thou
　　hast liv'd.
Quicken with kissing. Had my lips that
　　power,
Thus would I wear them out.
All.　　　　　　　　A heavy sight!　40
Ant. I am dying, Egypt, dying.
Give me some wine, and let me speak a
　　little.
Cleo. No, let me speak; and let me rail
　　so high
That the false huswife Fortune break her
　　wheel,　　　　　　　　　　44
Provok'd by my offence.
Ant.　　　　　One word, sweet queen:
Of Cæsar seek your honour, with your
　　safety. O!
Cleo. They do not go together.
Ant.　　　　　　　Gentle, hear me:
None about Cæsar trust but Proculeius.
Cleo. My resolution and my hands I'll
　　trust;
None about Cæsar.　　　　　　　50
Ant. The miserable change now at my
　　end
Lament nor sorrow at; but please your
　　thoughts
In feeding them with those my former
　　fortunes
Wherein I liv'd the greatest prince o' th'
　　world,
The noblest; and do now not basely die, 55
Not cowardly put off my helmet to
My countryman—a Roman by a Roman

Valiantly vanquish'd. Now my spirit is
    going ;
I can no more.
    Cleo.   Noblest of men, woo't die ?
Hast thou no care of me ? Shall I abide 60
In this dull world, which in thy absence is
No better than a sty ? O, see, my women,
                              [*Antony dies.*
The crown o' th' earth doth melt. My lord !
O, wither'd is the garland of the war,
The soldier's pole is fall'n ! Young boys and
    girls   65
Are level now with men. The odds is gone,
And there is nothing left remarkable
Beneath the visiting moon.   [*Swoons.*
    Char. O, quietness, lady !
    Iras. She's dead too, our sovereign.
    Char. Lady !
    Iras. Madam !
    Char. O madam, madam, madam !   70
    Iras. Royal Egypt, Empress !
    Char. Peace, peace, Iras !
    Cleo. No more but e'en a woman, and
    commanded
By such poor passion as the maid that milks
And does the meanest chares. It were for
    me   75
To throw my sceptre at the injurious gods ;
To tell them that this world did equal theirs
Till they had stol'n our jewel. All's but
    nought ;
Patience is sottish, and impatience does
Become a dog that's mad. Then is it sin 80
To rush into the secret house of death
Ere death dare come to us ? How do you,
    women ?
What, what ! good cheer ! Why, how now,
    Charmian !
My noble girls ! Ah, women, women, look,
Our lamp is spent, it's out ! Good sirs, take
    heart.   85
We'll bury him ; and then, what's brave,
    what's noble,
Let's do it after the high Roman fashion,
And make death proud to take us. Come,
    away ;
This case of that huge spirit now is cold.
Ah, women, women ! Come ; we have no
    friend   90
But resolution and the briefest end.
    [*Exeunt; those above bearing off Antony's
                    body.*

ACT FIVE

SCENE I. *Alexandria. Cæsar's camp.*

Enter CÆSAR, AGRIPPA, DOLABELLA, MÆ-
CENAS, GALLUS, PROCULEIUS, *and* Others,
his Council of War.

    Cæs. Go to him, Dolabella, bid him yield ;
Being so frustrate, tell him he mocks
The pauses that he makes.
    Dol.   Cæsar, I shall. [*Exit.*

Enter DERCETAS *with the sword of Antony.*

    Cæs. Wherefore is that ? And what art
    thou that dar'st
Appear thus to us ?
    Der.   I am call'd Dercetas ; 5
Mark Antony I serv'd, who best was
    worthy
Best to be serv'd. Whilst he stood up and
    spoke,
He was my master, and I wore my life
To spend upon his haters. If thou please
To take me to thee, as I was to him   10
I'll be to Cæsar ; if thou pleasest not,
I yield thee up my life.
    Cæs.   What is't thou say'st ?
    Der. I say, O Cæsar, Antony is dead.
    Cæs. The breaking of so great a thing
    should make
A greater crack. The round world   15
Should have shook lions into civil streets,
And citizens to their dens. The death of
    Antony
Is not a single doom : in the name lay
A moiety of the world.
    Der.   He is dead, Cæsar,
Not by a public minister of justice,   20
Nor by a hired knife ; but that self hand
Which writ his honour in the acts it did
Hath, with the courage which the heart did
    lend it,
Splitted the heart. This is his sword ;   24
I robb'd his wound of it ; behold it stain'd
With his most noble blood.
    Cæs.   Look you sad, friends ?
The gods rebuke me, but it is tidings
To wash the eyes of kings.
    Agr.   And strange it is
That nature must compel us to lament 29
Our most persisted deeds.
    Mæc.   His taints and honours
Wag'd equal with him.
    Agr.   A rarer spirit never
Did steer humanity. But you gods will
    give us
Some faults to make us men. Cæsar is
    touch'd.
    Mæc. When such a spacious mirror's set
    before him,
He needs must see himself.
    Cæs.   O Antony,   35
I have follow'd thee to this ! But we do
    lance
Diseases in our bodies. I must perforce
Have shown to thee such a declining day
Or look on thine ; we could not stall
    together
In the whole world. But yet let me lament,
With tears as sovereign as the blood of
    hearts,   41
That thou, my brother, my competitor
In top of all design, my mate in empire,
Friend and companion in the front of war,
The arm of mine own body, and the heart

Where mine his thoughts did kindle—that
    our stars,   46
Unreconciliable, should divide
Our equalness to this. Hear me, good
    friends—

        Enter an Egyptian.

But I will tell you at some meeter season.
The business of this man looks out of him ;
We'll hear him what he says. Whence are
    you ?   51
    Egyp. A poor Egyptian, yet the Queen,
    my mistress,
Confin'd in all she has, her monument,
Of thy intents desires instruction,
That she preparedly may frame herself   55
To th' way she's forc'd to.
    Cæs.   Bid her have good heart.
She soon shall know of us, by some of ours,
How honourable and how kindly we   58
Determine for her ; for Cæsar cannot learn
To be ungentle.
    Egyp. So the gods preserve thee ! [*Exit.*
    Cæs. Come hither, Proculeius. Go and
    say   61
We purpose her no shame. Give her what
    comforts
The quality of her passion shall require,
Lest, in her greatness, by some mortal
    stroke
She do defeat us ; for her life in Rome   65
Would be eternal in our triumph. Go,
And with your speediest bring us what she
    says,
And how you find of her.
    Pro.   Cæsar, I shall. [*Exit.*
    Cæs. Gallus, go you along. [*Exit Gallus.*
              Where's Dolabella,
To second Proculeius ?
    All.   Dolabella !   70
    Cæs. Let him alone, for I remember now
How he's employ'd ; he shall in time be
    ready.
Go with me to my tent, where you shall see
How hardly I was drawn into this war,
How calm and gentle I proceeded still   75
In all my writings. Go with me, and see
What I can show in this.   [*Exeunt.*

Scene II. *Alexandria.   The monument.*

Enter CLEOPATRA, CHARMIAN, IRAS, *and*
        MARDIAN.

    Cleo. My desolation does begin to make
A better life. 'Tis paltry to be Cæsar :
Not being Fortune, he's but Fortune's
    knave,
A minister of her will ; and it is great
To do that thing that ends all other deeds,
Which shackles accidents and bolts up
    change,   6
Which sleeps, and never palates more the
    dug,
The beggar's nurse and Cæsar's.

Enter, to the gates of the monument, PRO-
    CULEIUS, GALLUS, *and* Soldiers.

    Pro. Cæsar sends greeting to the Queen
    of Egypt ;   9
And bids thee study on what fair demands
Thou mean'st to have him grant thee.
    Cleo.   What's thy name ?
    Pro. My name is Proculeius.
    Cleo.   Antony
Did tell me of you, bade me trust you ; but
I do not greatly care to be deceiv'd,
That have no use for trusting. If your
    master   15
Would have a queen his beggar, you must
    tell him
That majesty, to keep decorum, must
No less beg than a kingdom. If he please
To give me conquer'd Egypt for my son,
He gives me so much of mine own as I   20
Will kneel to him with thanks.
    Pro.   Be of good cheer ;
Y'are fall'n into a princely hand ; fear
    nothing.
Make your full reference freely to my lord,
Who is so full of grace that it flows over
On all that need. Let me report to him   25
Your sweet dependency, and you shall find
A conqueror that will pray in aid for
    kindness
Where he for grace is kneel'd to.
    Cleo.   Pray you tell him
I am his fortune's vassal and I send him
The greatness he has got. I hourly learn   30
A doctrine of obedience, and would gladly
Look him i' th' face.
    Pro.   This I'll report, dear lady.
Have comfort, for I know your plight is
    pitied
Of him that caus'd it.
    Gal. You see how easily she may be
    surpris'd.   35
[*Here Proculeius and two of the Guard ascend
the monument by a ladder placed against a
window, and come behind Cleopatra. Some
of the Guard unbar and open the gates.*
Guard her till Cæsar come.   [*Exit.*
    Iras. Royal Queen !
    Char. O Cleopatra ! thou art taken,
    Queen !
    Cleo. Quick, quick, good hands.
                [*Drawing a dagger.*
    Pro.   Hold, worthy lady, hold,
                [*Disarms her.*
Do not yourself such wrong, who are in this
Reliev'd, but not betray'd.
    Cleo.   What, of death too,
That rids our dogs of languish ?
    Pro.   Cleopatra,
Do not abuse my master's bounty by   43
Th' undoing of yourself. Let the world see
His nobleness well acted, which your death
Will never let come forth.
    Cleo.   Where art thou, death ?

Come hither, come! Come, come, and take
a queen
Worth many babes and beggars!
Pro.   O, temperance, lady!
Cleo. Sir, I will eat no meat; I'll not
drink, sir;
If idle talk will once be necessary,   50
I'll not sleep neither. This mortal house
I'll ruin,
Do Cæsar what he can. Know, sir, that I
Will not wait pinion'd at your master's
court,
Nor once be chastis'd with the sober eye
Of dull Octavia. Shall they hoist me up, 55
And show me to the shouting varletry
Of censuring Rome? Rather a ditch in
Egypt
Be gentle grave unto me! Rather on
Nilus' mud
Lay me stark-nak'd, and let the water-flies
Blow me into abhorring! Rather make   60
My country's high pyramides my gibbet,
And hang me up in chains!
Pro.   You do extend
These thoughts of horror further than you
shall
Find cause in Cæsar.

Enter DOLABELLA.

Dol. Proculeius,
What thou hast done thy master Cæsar
knows,   65
And he hath sent for thee. For the Queen,
I'll take her to my guard.
Pro.   So, Dolabella,
It shall content me best. Be gentle to her.
[*To Cleopatra*] To Cæsar I will speak what
you shall please,
If you'll employ me to him.
Cleo.   Say I would die. 70
        [*Exeunt Proculeius and Soldiers.*
Dol. Most noble Empress, you have
heard of me?
Cleo. I cannot tell.
Dol.   Assuredly you know me.
Cleo. No matter, sir, what I have heard
or known.
You laugh when boys or women tell their
dreams;
Is't not your trick?
Dol.   I understand not, madam. 75
Cleo. I dreamt there was an Emperor
Antony—
O, such another sleep, that I might see
But such another man!
Dol.   If it might please ye—
Cleo. His face was as the heav'ns, and
therein stuck
A sun and moon, which kept their course
and lighted   80
The little O, the earth.
Dol.   Most sovereign creature—
Cleo. His legs bestrid the ocean; his
rear'd arm

Crested the world. His voice was propertied
As all the tuned spheres, and that to
friends;
But when he meant to quail and shake the
orb,   85
He was as rattling thunder. For his bounty,
There was no winter in't; an autumn
'twas
That grew the more by reaping. His
delights
Were dolphin-like: they show'd his back
above
The element they liv'd in. In his livery 90
Walk'd crowns and crownets; realms and
islands were
As plates dropp'd from his pocket.
Dol.   Cleopatra—
Cleo. Think you there was or might be
such a man
As this I dreamt of?
Dol.   Gentle madam, no.
Cleo. You lie, up to the hearing of the
gods.   95
But if there be nor ever were one such,
It's past the size of dreaming. Nature wants
stuff
To vie strange forms with fancy; yet t'
imagine
An Antony were nature's piece 'gainst
fancy,
Condemning shadows quite.
Dol.   Hear me, good madam. 100
Your loss is, as yourself, great; and you
bear it
As answering to the weight. Would I might
never
O'ertake pursu'd success, but I do feel,
By the rebound of yours, a grief that smites
My very heart at root.
Cleo.   I thank you, sir. 105
Know you what Cæsar means to do with
me?
Dol. I am loath to tell you what I would
you knew.
Cleo. Nay, pray you, sir.
Dol.   Though he be honourable—
Cleo. He'll lead me, then, in triumph?
Dol. Madam, he will. I know't.   110
                            [*Flourish.*
Within. Make way there—Cæsar!

Enter CÆSAR; GALLUS, PROCULEIUS,
MÆCENAS, SELEUCUS, *and others of his*
Train.

Cæs. Which is the Queen of Egypt?
Dol. It is the Emperor, madam.
                        [*Cleopatra kneels*
Cæs. Arise, you shall not kneel.
I pray you, rise; rise, Egypt.
Cleo.   Sir, the gods
Will have it thus; my master and my lord
I must obey.
Cæs.   Take to you no hard thoughts.
The record of what injuries you did us, 117

Though written in our flesh, we shall remember
As things but done by chance.
   Cleo.   Sole sir o' th' world,
I cannot project mine own cause so well 120
To make it clear, but do confess I have
Been laden with like frailties which before
Have often sham'd our sex.
   Cæs.   Cleopatra, know
We will extenuate rather than enforce.
If you apply yourself to our intents— 125
Which towards you are most gentle—you shall find
A benefit in this change; but if you seek
To lay on me a cruelty by taking
Antony's course, you shall bereave yourself
Of my good purposes, and put your children 130
To that destruction which I'll guard them from,
If thereon you rely. I'll take my leave.
   Cleo. And may, through all the world. 'Tis yours, and we,
Your scutcheons and your signs of conquest, shall
Hang in what place you please. Here, my good lord. 135
   Cæs. You shall advise me in all for Cleopatra.
   Cleo. This is the brief of money, plate, and jewels,
I am possess'd of. 'Tis exactly valued,
Not petty things admitted. Where's Seleucus?
   Sel. Here, madam. 140
   Cleo. This is my treasurer; let him speak, my lord,
Upon his peril, that I have reserv'd
To myself nothing. Speak the truth, Seleucus.
   Sel. Madam, 144
I had rather seal my lips than to my peril
Speak that which is not.
   Cleo.   What have I kept back?
   Sel. Enough to purchase what you have made known.
   Cæs. Nay, blush not, Cleopatra; I approve
Your wisdom in the deed.
   Cleo.   See, Cæsar! O, behold,
How pomp is followed! Mine will now be yours; 150
And, should we shift estates, yours would be mine.
The ingratitude of this Seleucus does
Even make me wild. O slave, of no more trust
Than love that's hir'd! What, goest thou back? Thou shalt
Go back, I warrant thee; but I'll catch thine eyes 155
Though they had wings. Slave, soulless villain, dog!
O rarely base!

   Cæs. Good Queen, let us entreat you.
   Cleo. O Cæsar, what a wounding shame is this,
That thou vouchsafing here to visit me,
Doing the honour of thy lordliness 160
To one so meek, that mine own servant should
Parcel the sum of my disgraces by
Addition of his envy! Say, good Cæsar,
That I some lady trifles have reserv'd,
Immoment toys, things of such dignity 165
As we greet modern friends withal; and say
Some nobler token I have kept apart
For Livia and Octavia, to induce
Their mediation—must I be unfolded
With one that I have bred? The gods! It smites me 170
Beneath the fall I have. [*To Seleucus*]
     Prithee go hence;
Or I shall show the cinders of my spirits
Through th' ashes of my chance. Wert thou a man,
Thou wouldst have mercy on me.
   Cæs.   Forbear, Seleucus.
     [*Exit Seleucus.*
   Cleo. Be it known that we, the greatest, are misthought 175
For things that others do; and when we fall
We answer others' merits in our name,
Are therefore to be pitied.
   Cæs.   Cleopatra,
Not what you have reserv'd, nor what acknowledg'd,
Put we i' th' roll of conquest. Still be't yours, 180
Bestow it at your pleasure; and believe
Cæsar's no merchant, to make prize with you
Of things that merchants sold. Therefore be cheer'd;
Make not your thoughts your prisons. No, dear Queen;
For we intend so to dispose you as 185
Yourself shall give us counsel. Feed and sleep.
Our care and pity is so much upon you
That we remain your friend; and so, adieu.
   Cleo. My master and my lord!
   Cæs.   Not so. Adieu.
   [*Flourish. Exeunt Cæsar and his Train.*
   Cleo. He words me, girls, he words me, that I should not 190
Be noble to myself. But hark thee, Charmian! [*Whispers Charmian.*
   Iras. Finish, good lady; the bright day is done,
And we are for the dark.
   Cleo.   Hie thee again.
I have spoke already, and it is provided;
Go put it to the haste.
   Char.   Madam, I will. 195

Re-enter DOLABELLA.

Dol. Where's the Queen ?
Char.   Behold, sir. [*Exit.*
Cleo.   Dolabella !
Dol. Madam, as thereto sworn by your
    command,
Which my love makes religion to obey,
I tell you this : Cæsar through Syria
Intends his journey, and within three
    days   200
You with your children will he send
    before.
Make your best use of this ; I have
    perform'd
Your pleasure and my promise.
Cleo.   Dolabella,
I shall remain your debtor.
Dol.   I your servant.
Adieu, good Queen ; I must attend on
    Cæsar.   205
Cleo. Farewell, and thanks.
                              [*Exit Dolabella.*
    Now, Iras, what think'st thou ?
Thou an Egyptian puppet shall be shown
In Rome as well as I. Mechanic slaves,
With greasy aprons, rules, and hammers,
    shall
Uplift us to the view ; in their thick
    breaths,   210
Rank of gross diet, shall we be enclouded,
And forc'd to drink their vapour.
Iras.   The gods forbid !
Cleo. Nay, 'tis most certain, Iras. Saucy
    lictors
Will catch at us like strumpets, and scald
    rhymers   214
Ballad us out o' tune ; the quick comedians
Extemporally will stage us, and present
Our Alexandrian revels ; Antony
Shall be brought drunken forth, and I shall
    see
Some squeaking Cleopatra boy my great-
    ness
I' th' posture of a whore.
Iras.   O the good gods !   220
Cleo. Nay, that's certain.
Iras. I'll never see't, for I am sure mine
    nails
Are stronger than mine eyes.
Cleo.   Why, that's the way
To fool their preparation and to conquer
Their most absurd intents.

Enter CHARMIAN.

                    Now, Charmian !   225
Show me, my women, like a queen. Go
    fetch
My best attires. I am again for Cydnus,
To meet Mark Antony. Sirrah, Iras, go.
Now, noble Charmian, we'll dispatch
    indeed ;
And when thou hast done this chare, I'll
    give thee leave

To play till doomsday. Bring our crown
    and all.   231
                    [*Exit Iras. A noise within.*
Wherefore's this noise ?

Enter a Guardsman.

Guard.   Here is a rural fellow
That will not be denied your Highness'
    presence.
He brings you figs.   234
Cleo. Let him come in. [*Exit Guardsman.*
                    What poor an instrument
May do a noble deed ! He brings me liberty.
My resolution's plac'd, and I have nothing
Of woman in me. Now from head to foot
I am marble-constant ; now the fleeting
    moon
No planet is of mine.   239

Re-enter Guardsman *and* Clown, *with a
    basket.*

Guard. This is the man.
Cleo.   Avoid, and leave him.
                              [*Exit Guardsman.*
Hast thou the pretty worm of Nilus there
That kills and pains not ?
Clown. Truly, I have him. But I would
not be the party that should desire you to
touch him, for his biting is immortal ; those
that do die of it do seldom or never recover.
Cleo. Remember'st thou any that have
died on't ?   248
Clown. Very many, men and women too.
I heard of one of them no longer than
yesterday : a very honest woman, but
something given to lie, as a woman should
not do but in the way of honesty ; how she
died of the biting of it, what pain she felt—
truly she makes a very good report o' th'
worm. But he that will believe all that
they say shall never be saved by half that
they do. But this is most falliable, the
worm's an odd worm.
Cleo. Get thee hence ; farewell.   257
Clown. I wish you all joy of the worm.
                         [*Sets down the basket.*
Cleo. Farewell.
Clown. You must think this, look you,
that the worm will do his kind.   261
Cleo. Ay, ay ; farewell.
Clown. Look you, the worm is not to be
trusted but in the keeping of wise people ;
for indeed there is no goodness in the worm.
Cleo. Take thou no care ; it shall be
heeded.   266
Clown. Very good. Give it nothing, I
pray you, for it is not worth the feeding.
Cleo. Will it eat me ?   269
Clown. You must not think I am so
simple but I know the devil himself will
not eat a woman. I know that a woman
is a dish for the gods, if the devil dress her
not. But truly, these same whoreson devils
do the gods great harm in their women, for

in every ten that they make the devils mar
five.   275
 Cleo. Well, get thee gone ; farewell.
 Clown. Yes, forsooth. I wish you joy o'
th' worm.   [*Exit.*

 Re-enter IRAS, *with a robe, crown, &c.*

 Cleo. Give me my robe, put on my crown ;
  I have
Immortal longings in me. Now no more
The juice of Egypt's grape shall moist this
 lip.   280
Yare, yare, good Iras ; quick. Methinks I
 hear
Antony call. I see him rouse himself
To praise my noble act. I hear him mock
The luck of Cæsar, which the gods give men
To excuse their after wrath. Husband, I
 come.   285
Now to that name my courage prove my
 title !
I am fire and air ; my other elements
I give to baser life. So, have you done ?
Come then, and take the last warmth of
 my lips.
Farewell, kind Charmian. Iras, long fare-
 well.   290
   [*Kisses them. Iras falls and dies.*
Have I the aspic in my lips ? Dost fall ?
If thou and nature can so gently part,
The stroke of death is as a lover's pinch,
Which hurts and is desir'd. Dost thou lie
 still ?
If thus thou vanishest, thou tell'st the
 world   295
It is not worth leave-taking.
 Char. Dissolve, thick cloud, and rain,
  that I may say
The gods themselves do weep.
 Cleo.   This proves me base.
If she first meet the curled Antony,
He'll make demand of her, and spend that
 kiss   300
Which is my heaven to have. Come, thou
 mortal wretch,
  [*To an asp, which she applies to her breast.*
With thy sharp teeth this knot intrinsicate
Of life at once untie. Poor venomous fool,
Be angry, and dispatch. O couldst thou
 speak,   304
That I might hear thee call great Cæsar ass
Unpolicied !
 Char. O Eastern star !
 Cleo.   Peace, peace !
Dost thou not see my baby at my breast
That sucks the nurse asleep ?
 Char.   O, break ! O, break !
 Cleo. As sweet as balm, as soft as air, as
  gentle—
O Antony ! Nay, I will take thee too : 310
  [*Applying another asp to her arm.*
What should I stay—   [*Dies.*
 Char. In this vile world ? So, fare thee
  well.

Now boast thee, death, in thy possession
 lies
A lass unparallel'd. Downy windows, close;
And golden Phœbus never be beheld 315
Of eyes again so royal ! Your crown's
 awry ;
I'll mend it and then play—

 Enter the Guard, *rushing in.*

 1 *Guard.* Where's the Queen ?
 Char. Speak softly, wake her not.
 1 *Guard.* Cæsar hath sent—
 Char.   Too slow a messenger.
      [*Applies an asp.*
O, come apace, dispatch. I partly feel thee.
 1 *Guard.* Approach, ho ! All's not well :
  Cæsar's beguil'd.   321
 2 *Guard.* There's Dolabella sent from
  Cæsar ; call him.
 1 *Guard.* What work is here ! Charmian,
  is this well done ?
 Char. It is well done, and fitting for a
  princess
Descended of so many royal kings. 325
Ah, soldier !   [*Charmian dies.*

 Re-enter DOLABELLA.

 Dol. How goes it here ?
 2 *Guard.*   All dead.
 Dol.   Cæsar, thy thoughts
Touch their effects in this. Thyself art
 coming
To see perform'd the dreaded act which
 thou
So sought'st to hinder.   330
 Within. A way there, a way for Cæsar!

 Re-enter CÆSAR *and all his* Train.

 Dol. O sir, you are too sure an augurer :
That you did fear is done.
 Cæs. Bravest at the last,
She levell'd at our purposes, and being
 royal,
Took her own way. The manner of their
 deaths ?   334
I do not see them bleed.
 Dol. Who was last with them ?
 1 *Guard.* A simple countryman that
  brought her figs.
This was his basket.
 Cæs. Poison'd then.
 1 *Guard.*   O Cæsar,
This Charmian liv'd but now ; she stood
 and spake.
I found her trimming up the diadem
On her dead mistress. Tremblingly she
 stood,   340
And on the sudden dropp'd.
 Cæs. O noble weakness !
If they had swallow'd poison 'twould
 appear
By external swelling ; but she looks like
 sleep,
As she would catch another Antony

In her strong toil of grace.

Dol.   Here on her breast 345
There is a vent of blood, and something blown ;
The like is on her arm.

   1 Guard. This is an aspic's trail ; and these fig-leaves
Have slime upon them, such as th' aspic leaves
Upon the caves of Nile.

   Cæs.   Most probable 350
That so she died ; for her physician tells me
She hath pursu'd conclusions infinite
Of easy ways to die. Take up her bed,
And bear her women from the monument.
She shall be buried by her Antony ;   355
No grave upon the earth shall clip in it
A pair so famous. High events as these
Strike those that make them ; and their story is
No less in pity than his glory which
Brought them to be lamented. Our army shall   360
In solemn show attend this funeral,
And then to Rome. Come, Dolabella, see
High order in this great solemnity.

                            [*Exeunt.*

CYMBELINE

DRAMATIS PERSONÆ

CYMBELINE, King of Britain.
CLOTEN, son to the Queen by a former husband.
POSTHUMUS LEONATUS, a gentleman, husband to Imogen.
BELARIUS, a banished lord, disguised under the name of MORGAN.
GUIDERIUS, }
ARVIRAGUS, } sons to Cymbeline, disguised under the names of POLYDORE and CADWAL, supposed sons to Belarius.
PHILARIO, friend to Posthumus, }
IACHIMO, friend to Philario, } Italians.
A French Gentleman, friend to Philario.
CAIUS LUCIUS, General of the Roman Forces.
A Roman Captain.
Two British Captains.

PISANIO, servant to Posthumus.
CORNELIUS, a physician.
Two Lords of Cymbeline's court.
Two Gentlemen of the same.
Two Gaolers.

QUEEN, wife to Cymbeline.
IMOGEN, daughter to Cymbeline by a former queen.
HELEN, a lady attending on Imogen.

Apparitions.

Lords, Ladies, Roman Senators, Tribunes, a Soothsayer, a Dutch Gentleman, a Spanish Gentleman, Musicians, Officers, Captains, Soldiers, Messengers and Attendants.

THE SCENE: Britain; Italy.

ACT ONE

SCENE I. Britain. The garden of Cymbeline's palace.

1 *Gent.* You do not meet a man but frowns; our bloods
No more obey the heavens than our courtiers
Still seem as does the King's.
2 *Gent.*   But what's the matter?
1 *Gent.* His daughter, and the heir of's kingdom, whom
He purpos'd to his wife's sole son—a widow   5
That late he married—hath referr'd herself
Unto a poor but worthy gentleman. She's wedded;
Her husband banish'd; she imprison'd. All
Is outward sorrow, though I think the King
Be touch'd at very heart.
2 *Gent.*   None but the King?   10
1 *Gent.* He that hath lost her too. So is the Queen,
That most desir'd the match. But not a courtier,
Although they wear their faces to the bent
Of the King's looks, hath a heart that is not
Glad at the thing they scowl at.
2 *Gent.*   And why so?   15
1 *Gent.* He that hath miss'd the Princess is a thing
Too bad for bad report; and he that hath her—
I mean that married her, alack, good man!
And therefore banish'd—is a creature such
As, to seek through the regions of the earth
For one his like, there would be something failing   21
In him that should compare. I do not think
So fair an outward and such stuff within
Endows a man but he.
2 *Gent.*   You speak him far.
1 *Gent.* I do extend him, sir, within himself;   25
Crush him together rather than unfold
His measure duly.
2 *Gent.*   What's his name and birth?
1 *Gent.* I cannot delve him to the root; his father
Was call'd Sicilius, who did join his honour
Against the Romans with Cassibelan,   30
But had his titles by Tenantius, whom
He serv'd with glory and admir'd success,
So gain'd the sur-addition Leonatus;
And had, besides this gentleman in question,
Two other sons, who, in the wars o' th' time,   35
Died with their swords in hand; for which their father,
Then old and fond of issue, took such sorrow
That he quit being; and his gentle lady,
Big of this gentleman, our theme, deceas'd
As he was born. The King he takes the babe   40
To his protection, calls him Posthumus Leonatus,
Breeds him and makes him of his bed-chamber,
Puts to him all the learnings that his time

Could make him the receiver of ; which he
took,
As we do air, fast as 'twas minist'red,   45
And in's spring became a harvest, liv'd in
court—
Which rare it is to do—most prais'd, most
lov'd,
A sample to the youngest ; to th' more
mature
A glass that feated them ; and to the
graver
A child that guided dotards.   To his
mistress,   50
For whom he now is banish'd—her own
price
Proclaims how she esteem'd him and his
virtue ;
By her election may be truly read
What kind of man he is.
    2 Gent.   I honour him
Even out of your report. But pray you tell
me,   55
Is she sole child to th' King ?
    1 Gent.   His only child.
He had two sons—if this be worth your
hearing,
Mark it—the eldest of them at three years
old,
I' th' swathing clothes the other, from
their nursery
Were stol'n ; and to this hour no guess in
knowledge   60
Which way they went.
    2 Gent. How long is this ago ?
    1 Gent.   Some twenty years.
    2 Gent. That a king's children should be
so convey'd,
So slackly guarded, and the search so slow
That could not trace them !
    1 Gent.   Howsoe'er 'tis strange, 65
Or that the negligence may well be laugh'd
at,
Yet is it true, sir.
    2 Gent.   I do well believe you.
    1 Gent. We must forbear ; here comes
the gentleman,
The Queen, and Princess.   [*Exeunt.*

Enter the QUEEN, POSTHUMUS, *and*
IMOGEN.

    Queen. No, be assur'd you shall not find
me, daughter,
After the slander of most stepmothers, 71
Evil-ey'd unto you. You're my prisoner, but
Your gaoler shall deliver you the keys
That lock up your restraint. For you,
Posthumus,
So soon as I can win th' offended King, 75
I will be known your advocate. Marry, yet
The fire of rage is in him, and 'twere good
You lean'd unto his sentence with what
patience
Your wisdom may inform you.

    Post.   Please your Highness,
I will from hence to-day.
    Queen.   You know the peril. 80
I'll fetch a turn about the garden, pitying
The pangs of barr'd affections, though the
King
Hath charg'd you should not speak
together.   [*Exit.*
    Imo.   O
Dissembling courtesy ! How fine this
tyrant
Can tickle where she wounds ! My dearest
husband,   85
I something fear my father's wrath, but
nothing—
Always reserv'd my holy duty—what
His rage can do on me. You must be gone ;
And I shall here abide the hourly shot
Of angry eyes, not comforted to live   90
But that there is this jewel in the world
That I may see again.
    Post.   My queen ! my mistress !
O lady, weep no more, lest I give cause
To be suspected of more tenderness
Than doth become a man. I will remain 95
The loyal'st husband that did e'er plight
troth ;
My residence in Rome at one Philario's,
Who to my father was a friend, to me
Known but by letter ; thither write, my
queen,
And with mine eyes I'll drink the words
you send,   100
Though ink be made of gall.

Re-enter QUEEN.

    Queen.   Be brief, I pray you.
If the King come, I shall incur I know not
How much of his displeasure. [*Aside*] Yet
I'll move him   103
To walk this way. I never do him wrong
But he does buy my injuries, to be friends ;
Pays dear for my offences.   [*Exit.*
    Post. Should we be taking leave
As long a term as yet we have to live,
The loathness to depart would grow.
Adieu !
    Imo. Nay, stay a little.   109
Were you but riding forth to air yourself,
Such parting were too petty. Look here,
love :
This diamond was my mother's ; take it,
heart ;
But keep it till you woo another wife,
When Imogen is dead.
    Post.   How, how ? Another ? 114
You gentle gods, give me but this I have,
And cere up my embracements from a next
With bonds of death ! Remain, remain
thou here   [*Puts on the ring.*
While sense can keep it on. And, sweetest,
fairest,
As I my poor self did exchange for you,
To your so infinite loss, so in our trifles 120

I still win of you. For my sake wear
this ;
It is a manacle of love ; I'll place it
Upon this fairest prisoner.
                    [*Puts a bracelet on her arm.*
Imo.   O the gods !
When shall we see again ?

Enter CYMBELINE *and* Lords.

Post.   Alack, the King !
Cym. Thou basest thing, avoid ; hence
    from my sight !
If after this command thou fraught the
court   126
With thy unworthiness, thou diest. Away !
Thou'rt poison to my blood.
Post.   The gods protect you,
And bless the good remainders of the
    court !
I am gone.   [*Exit.*
Imo. There cannot be a pinch in death
More sharp than this is.
Cym.   O disloyal thing,
That shouldst repair my youth, thou
    heap'st   132
A years' age on me !
Imo.   I beseech you, sir,
Harm not yourself with your vexation.
I am senseless of your wrath ; a touch
    more rare   135
Subdues all pangs, all fears.
Cym.   Past grace ? obedience ?
Imo. Past hope, and in despair ; that
    way past grace.
Cym. That mightst have had the sole son
    of my queen !
Imo. O blessed that I might not ! I chose
    an eagle,
And did avoid a puttock.   140
Cym. Thou took'st a beggar, wouldst
    have made my throne
A seat for baseness.
Imo.   No ; I rather added
A lustre to it.
Cym.   O thou vile one !
Imo.   Sir,
It is your fault that I have lov'd Post-
    humus.   144
You bred him as my playfellow, and he is
A man worth any woman ; overbuys me
Almost the sum he pays.
Cym.   What, art thou mad ?
Imo. Almost, sir. Heaven restore me !
    Would I were
A neat-herd's daughter, and my Leonatus
Our neighbour shepherd's son !

Re-enter QUEEN.

Cym.   Thou foolish thing !
[*To the Queen*] They were again together.
    You have done   151
Not after our command. Away with her,
And pen her up.
Queen. Beseech your patience.—Peace,

Dear lady daughter, peace !—Sweet sov-
    ereign,
Leave us to ourselves, and make yourself
    some comfort
Out of your best advice.
Cym.   Nay, let her languish 156
A drop of blood a day and, being aged,
Die of this folly.   [*Exit, with Lords.*

Enter PISANIO.

Queen.   Fie ! you must give way.
Here is your servant. How now, sir ! What
    news ?
Pis. My lord your son drew on my
    master.
Queen.   Ha ! 160
No harm, I trust, is done ?
Pis.   There might have been,
But that my master rather play'd than
    fought,
And had no help of anger ; they were
    parted
By gentlemen at hand.
Queen.   I am very glad on't.
Imo. Your son's my father's friend ; he
    takes his part   165
To draw upon an exile ! O brave sir !
I would they were in Afric both together ;
Myself by with a needle, that I might
    prick
The goer-back. Why came you from your
    master ?
Pis. On his command. He would not
    suffer me   170
To bring him to the haven ; left these notes
Of what commands I should be subject to,
When't pleas'd you to employ me.
Queen.   This hath been
Your faithful servant. I dare lay mine
    honour   174
He will remain so.
Pis.   I humbly thank your Highness.
Queen. Pray walk awhile.
Imo.   About some half-hour hence,
Pray you speak with me. You shall at
    least
Go see my lord aboard. For this time leave
    me.   [*Exeunt.*

SCENE II. *Britain. A public place.*

Enter CLOTEN *and two* Lords.

1 *Lord.* Sir, I would advise you to shift a
shirt ; the violence of action hath made
you reek as a sacrifice. Where air comes
out, air comes in ; there's none abroad so
wholesome as that you vent.
    Clo. If my shirt were bloody, then to
shift it. Have I hurt him ?   6
    2 *Lord.* [*Aside*] No, faith ; not so much
as his patience.
    1 *Lord.* Hurt him ! His body's a passable
carcass if he be not hurt. It is a through-
fare for steel if it be not hurt.   10

2 Lord. [*Aside*] His steel was in debt ; it went o' th' back side the town.

Clo. The villain would not stand me.

2 Lord. [*Aside*] No ; but he fled forward still, toward your face. 15

1 Lord. Stand you ? You have land enough of your own ; but he added to your having, gave you some ground.

2 Lord. [*Aside*] As many inches as you have oceans. Puppies ! 20

Clo. I would they had not come between us.

2 Lord. [*Aside*] So would I, till you had measur'd how long a fool you were upon the ground.

Clo. And that she should love this fellow, and refuse me ! 25

2 Lord. [*Aside*] If it be a sin to make a true election, she is damn'd.

1 Lord. Sir, as I told you always, her beauty and her brain go not together ; she's a good sign, but I have seen small reflection of her wit. 30

2 Lord. [*Aside*] She shines not upon fools, lest the reflection should hurt her.

Clo. Come, I'll to my chamber. Would there had been some hurt done !

2 Lord. [*Aside*] I wish not so ; unless it had been the fall of an ass, which is no great hurt. 36

Clo. You'll go with us ?

1 Lord. I'll attend your lordship.

Clo. Nay, come, let's go together.

2 Lord. Well, my lord. [*Exeunt.*

SCENE III. *Britain. Cymbeline's palace.*

Enter IMOGEN *and* PISANIO.

Imo. I would thou grew'st unto the shores o' th' haven,
And questioned'st every sail ; if he should write,
And I not have it, 'twere a paper lost,
As offer'd mercy is. What was the last
That he spake to thee ?

Pis. It was : his queen, his queen ! 5

Imo. Then wav'd his handkerchief ?

Pis. And kiss'd it, madam.

Imo. Senseless linen, happier therein than I !
And that was all ?

Pis. No, madam ; for so long
As he could make me with his eye, or care
Distinguish him from others, he did keep
The deck, with glove, or hat, or handkerchief,
Still waving, as the fits and stirs of's mind
Could best express how slow his soul sail'd on,
How swift his ship.

Imo. Thou shouldst have made him
As little as a crow, or less, ere left 15
To after-eye him.

Pis. Madam, so I did.

Imo. I would have broke mine eye-strings, crack'd them but
To look upon him, till the diminution
Of space had pointed him sharp as my needle ; 19
Nay, followed him till he had melted from
The smallness of a gnat to air, and then
Have turn'd mine eye and wept. But, good Pisanio,
When shall we hear from him ?

Pis. Be assur'd, madam,
With his next vantage.

Imo. I did not take my leave of him, but had 25
Most pretty things to say. Ere I could tell him
How I would think on him at certain hours
Such thoughts and such ; or I could make him swear
The shes of Italy should not betray
Mine interest and his honour ; or have charg'd him, 30
At the sixth hour of morn, at noon, at midnight,
T' encounter me with orisons, for then
I am in heaven for him ; or ere I could
Give him that parting kiss which I had set
Betwixt two charming words, comes in my father, 35
And like the tyrannous breathing of the north
Shakes all our buds from growing.

Enter a Lady.

Lady. The Queen, madam,
Desires your Highness' company.

Imo. Those things I bid you do, get them dispatch'd. 39
I will attend the Queen.

Pis. Madam, I shall. [*Exeunt.*

SCENE IV. *Rome. Philario's house.*

Enter PHILARIO, IACHIMO, *a* Frenchman, *a* Dutchman, *and a* Spaniard.

Iach. Believe it, sir, I have seen him in Britain. He was then of a crescent note, expected to prove so worthy as since he hath been allowed the name of. But I could then have look'd on him without the help of admiration, though the catalogue of his endowments had been tabled by his side, and I to peruse him by items. 6

Phi. You speak of him when he was less furnish'd than now he is with that which makes him both without and within. 9

French. I have seen him in France ; we had very many there could behold the sun with as firm eyes as he.

Iach. This matter of marrying his king's daughter, wherein he must be weighed rather by her value than his own, words him, I doubt not, a great deal from the matter. 15

French. And then his banishment.

Iach. Ay, and the approbation of those that weep this lamentable divorce under her colours are wonderfully to extend him, be it but to fortify her judgment, which else an easy battery might lay flat, for taking a beggar, without less quality. But how comes it he is to sojourn with you ? How creeps acquaintance ?   22

Phi. His father and I were soldiers together, to whom I have been often bound for no less than my life.

Enter POSTHUMUS.

Here comes the Briton. Let him be so entertained amongst you as suits with gentlemen of your knowing to a stranger of his quality. I beseech you all be better known to this gentleman, whom I commend to you as a noble friend of mine. How worthy he is I will leave to appear hereafter, rather than story him in his own hearing.   31

French. Sir, we have known together in Orleans.

Post. Since when I have been debtor to you for courtesies, which I will be ever to pay and yet pay still.   34

French. Sir, you o'errate my poor kindness. I was glad I did atone my countryman and you ; it had been pity you should have been put together with so mortal a purpose as then each bore, upon importance of so slight and trivial a nature.   39

Post. By your pardon, sir, I was then a young traveller ; rather shunn'd to go even with what I heard than in my every action to be guided by others' experiences ; but upon my mended judgment—if I offend not to say it is mended—my quarrel was not altogether slight.   44

French. Faith, yes, to be put to the arbitrement of swords, and by such two that would by all likelihood have confounded one the other or have fall'n both.

Iach. Can we, with manners, ask what was the difference ?   49

French. Safely, I think. 'Twas a contention in public, which may, without contradiction, suffer the report. It was much like an argument that fell out last night, where each of us fell in praise of our country mistresses ; this gentleman at that time vouching—and upon warrant of bloody affirmation—his to be more fair, virtuous, wise, chaste, constant, qualified, and less attemptable, than any the rarest of our ladies in France.   57

Iach. That lady is not now living, or this gentleman's opinion, by this, worn out.

Post. She holds her virtue still, and I my mind.   60

Iach. You must not so far prefer her fore ours of Italy.

Post. Being so far provok'd as I was in France, I would abate her nothing, though I profess myself her adorer, not her friend.

Iach. As fair and as good—a kind of hand-in-hand comparison—had been something too fair and too good for any lady in Britain. If she went before others I have seen as that diamond of yours outlustres many I have beheld, I could not but believe she excelled many ; but I have not seen the most precious diamond that is, nor you the lady.   72

Post. I prais'd her as I rated her. So do I my stone.

Iach. What do you esteem it at ?

Post. More than the world enjoys.   75

Iach. Either your unparagon'd mistress is dead, or she's outpriz'd by a trifle.

Post. You are mistaken : the one may be sold or given, if there were wealth enough for the purchase or merit for the gift ; the other is not a thing for sale, and only the gift of the gods.   81

Iach. Which the gods have given you ?

Post. Which by their graces I will keep.

Iach. You may wear her in title yours ; but you know strange fowl light upon neighbouring ponds. Your ring may be stol'n too. So your brace of unprizable estimations, the one is but frail and the other casual ; a cunning thief, or a that-way-accomplish'd courtier, would hazard the winning both of first and last.   89

Post. Your Italy contains none so accomplish'd a courtier to convince the honour of my mistress, if in the holding or loss of that you term her frail. I do nothing doubt you have store of thieves ; notwithstanding, I fear not my ring.

Phi. Let us leave here, gentlemen.   95

Post. Sir, with all my heart. This worthy signior, I thank him, makes no stranger of me ; we are familiar at first.

Iach. With five times so much conversation I should get ground of your fair mistress ; make her go back even to the yielding, had I admittance and opportunity to friend.   102

Post. No, no.

Iach. I dare thereupon pawn the moiety of my estate to your ring, which, in my opinion, o'ervalues it something. But I make my wager rather against your confidence than her reputation ; and, to bar your offence herein too, I durst attempt it against any lady in the world.

Post. You are a great deal abus'd in too bold a persuasion, and I doubt not you sustain what y'are worthy of by your attempt.   111

Iach. What's that ?

Post. A repulse ; though your attempt, as you call it, deserve more—a punishment too.

Phi. Gentlemen, enough of this. It came in too suddenly ; let it die as it was born, and I pray you be better acquainted. 117

Iach. Would I had put my estate and my neighbour's on th' approbation of what I have spoke !

Post. What lady would you choose to assail ? 120

Iach. Yours, whom in constancy you think stands so safe. I will lay you ten thousand ducats to your ring that, commend me to the court where your lady is, with no more advantage than the opportunity of a second conference, and I will bring from thence that honour of hers which you imagine so reserv'd. 126

Post. I will wage against your gold gold to it. My ring I hold dear as my finger ; 'tis part of it.

Iach. You are a friend, and therein the wiser. If you buy ladies' flesh at a million a dram, you cannot preserve it from tainting. But I see you have some religion in you, that you fear. 132

Post. This is but a custom in your tongue; you bear a graver purpose, I hope.

Iach. I am the master of my speeches, and would undergo what's spoken, I swear.

Post. Will you ? I shall but lend my diamond till your return. Let there be covenants drawn between's. My mistress exceeds in goodness the hugeness of your unworthy thinking. I dare you to this match : here's my ring. 141

Phi. I will have it no lay.

Iach. By the gods, it is one. If I bring you no sufficient testimony that I have enjoy'd the dearest bodily part of your mistress, my ten thousand ducats are yours ; so is your diamond too. If I come off, and leave her in such honour as you have trust in, she your jewel, this your jewel, and my gold are yours—provided I have your commendation for my more free entertainment. 149

Post. I embrace these conditions ; let us have articles betwixt us. Only, thus far you shall answer : if you make your voyage upon her, and give me directly to understand you have prevail'd, I am no further your enemy—she is not worth our debate; if she remain unseduc'd, you not making it appear otherwise, for your ill opinion and th' assault you have made to her chastity you shall answer me with your sword. 157

Iach. Your hand—a covenant ! We will have these things set down by lawful counsel, and straight away for Britain, lest the bargain should catch cold and starve. I will fetch my gold and have our two wagers recorded. 161

Post. Agreed.

[*Exeunt Posthumus and Iachimo.*

French. Will this hold, think you ? 164

Phi. Signior Iachimo will not from it. Pray let us follow 'em. [*Exeunt.*

SCENE V. *Britain. Cymbeline's palace.*

Enter QUEEN, Ladies, *and* CORNELIUS.

Queen. Whiles yet the dew's on ground gather those flowers ;
Make haste ; who has the note of them ?
Lady. I, madam.
Queen. Dispatch. [*Exeunt Ladies.*
Now, Master Doctor, have you brought those drugs ?
Cor. Pleaseth your Highness, ay. Here they are, madam. 5
[*Presenting a box.*
But I beseech your Grace, without offence—
My conscience bids me ask—wherefore you have
Commanded of me these most poisonous compounds,
Which are the movers of a languishing death,
But, though slow, deadly ?
Queen. I wonder, Doctor, 10
Thou ask'st me such a question. Have I not been
Thy pupil long ? Hast thou not learn'd me how
To make perfumes ? distil ? preserve ? yea, so
That our great king himself doth woo me oft
For my confections ? Having thus far proceeded— 15
Unless thou think'st me devilish—is't not meet
That I did amplify my judgment in
Other conclusions ? I will try the forces
Of these thy compounds on such creatures as
We count not worth the hanging—but none human— 20
To try the vigour of them, and apply
Allayments to their act, and by them gather
Their several virtues and effects.
Cor. Your Highness
Shall from this practice but make hard your heart ;
Besides, the seeing these effects will be 25
Both noisome and infectious.
Queen. O, content thee.

Enter PISANIO.

[*Aside*] Here comes a flattering rascal ; upon him
Will I first work. He's for his master,
And enemy to my son.—How now, Pisanio !
Doctor, your service for this time is ended ;
Take your own way.
Cor. [*Aside*] I do suspect you, madam ;
But you shall do no harm.
Queen. [*To Pisanio*] Hark thee, a word.

Cor. [*Aside*] I do not like her. She doth
    think she has
Strange ling'ring poisons. I do know her
    spirit,
And will not trust one of her malice with 35
A drug of such damn'd nature. Those she
    has
Will stupefy and dull the sense awhile,
Which first perchance she'll prove on cats
    and dogs,
Then afterward up higher; but there is
No danger in what show of death it makes,
More than the locking up the spirits a time,
To be more fresh, reviving. She is fool'd
With a most false effect; and I the truer
So to be false with her.
    Queen. No further service, Doctor,
Until I send for thee.
    Cor. I humbly take my leave. 45
                    [*Exit.*
    Queen. Weeps she still, say'st thou?
    Dost thou think in time
She will not quench, and let instructions
    enter
Where folly now possesses? Do thou work.
When thou shalt bring me word she loves
    my son,
I'll tell thee on the instant thou art then 50
As great as is thy master; greater, for
His fortunes all lie speechless, and his name
Is at last gasp. Return he cannot, nor
Continue where he is. To shift his being
Is to exchange one misery with another, 55
And every day that comes comes to decay
A day's work in him. What shalt thou
    expect
To be depender on a thing that leans,
Who cannot be new built, nor has no
    friends
So much as but to prop him?
          [*The Queen drops the box.*
          Pisanio takes it up.
          Thou tak'st up 60
Thou know'st not what; but take it for
    thy labour.
It is a thing I made, which hath the King
Five times redeem'd from death. I do not
    know
What is more cordial. Nay, I prithee
    take it;
It is an earnest of a further good 65
That I mean to thee. Tell thy mistress how
The case stands with her; do't as from
    thyself.
Think what a chance thou changest on;
    but think
Thou hast thy mistress still; to boot, my
    son,
Who shall take notice of thee. I'll move the
    King 70
To any shape of thy preferment, such
As thou'lt desire; and then myself, I
    chiefly,
That set thee on to this desert, am bound

To load thy merit richly. Call my women.
Think on my words. [*Exit Pisanio.*
        A sly and constant knave, 75
Not to be shak'd; the agent for his master,
And the remembrancer of her to hold
The hand-fast to her lord. I have given him
    that
Which, if he take, shall quite unpeople her
Of leigers for her sweet; and which she
    after, 80
Except she bend her humour, shall be
    assur'd
To taste of too.

    Re-enter PISANIO *and* Ladies.

        So, so. Well done, well done.
The violets, cowslips, and the primroses,
Bear to my closet. Fare thee well, Pisanio;
Think on my words. [*Exeunt Queen and Ladies.*
    Pis. And shall do. 85
But when to my good lord I prove untrue
I'll choke myself—there's all I'll do for you.
                   [*Exit.*

  SCENE VI. *Britain. The palace.*

    Enter IMOGEN *alone.*

    Imo. A father cruel and a step-dame
    false;
A foolish suitor to a wedded lady
That hath her husband banish'd. O, that
    husband!
My supreme crown of grief! and those
    repeated
Vexations of it! Had I been thief-stol'n, 5
As my two brothers, happy! but most
    miserable
Is the desire that's glorious. Blessed be
    those,
How mean soe'er, that have their honest
    wills,
Which seasons comfort. Who may this be?
    Fie! 9

    Enter PISANIO *and* IACHIMO.

    Pis. Madam, a noble gentleman of Rome
Comes from my lord with letters.
    Iach. Change you, madam?
The worthy Leonatus is in safety,
And greets your Highness dearly.
               [*Presents a letter.*
    Imo. Thanks, good sir.
You're kindly welcome.
    Iach. [*Aside*] All of her that is out of
    door most rich! 15
If she be furnish'd with a mind so rare,
She is alone th' Arabian bird, and I
Have lost the wager. Boldness be my
    friend!
Arm me, audacity, from head to foot! 19
Or, like the Parthian, I shall flying fight;
Rather, directly fly.
    Imo. [*Reads*] ' He is one of the noblest

note, to whose kindnesses I am most infinitely tied. Reflect upon him accordingly,
as you value your trust.   LEONATUS.'

So far I read aloud;   25
But even the very middle of my heart
Is warm'd by th' rest and takes it thankfully.
You are as welcome, worthy sir, as I
Have words to bid you; and shall find it so
In all that I can do.
      Iach.   Thanks, fairest lady.   30
What, are men mad? Hath nature given
            them eyes
To see this vaulted arch and the rich crop
Of sea and land, which can distinguish
            'twixt
The fiery orbs above and the twinn'd stones
Upon the number'd beach, and can we
            not   35
Partition make with spectacles so precious
'Twixt fair and foul?
      Imo.   What makes your admiration?
      Iach. It cannot be i' th' eye, for apes and
            monkeys,
'Twixt two such shes, would chatter this
            way and
Contemn with mows the other; nor i' th'
            judgment,   40
For idiots in this case of favour would
Be wisely definite; nor i' th' appetite;
Sluttery, to such neat excellence oppos'd,
Should make desire vomit emptiness,
Not so allur'd to feed.   45
      Imo. What is the matter, trow?
      Iach.   The cloyed will—
That satiate yet unsatisfied desire, that tub
Both fill'd and running—ravening first the
            lamb,
Longs after for the garbage.
      Imo.   What, dear sir,
Thus raps you? Are you well?
      Iach. Thanks, madam; well.—Beseech
            you, sir,   51
Desire my man's abode where I did leave
            him.
He's strange and peevish.
      Pis.   I was going, sir,
To give him welcome.   [*Exit.*
      Imo. Continues well my lord? His
            health beseech you?   55
      Iach. Well, madam.
      Imo. Is he dispos'd to mirth? I hope
            he is.
      Iach. Exceeding pleasant; none a
            stranger there
So merry and so gamesome. He is call'd
The Britain reveller.
      Imo.   When he was here   60
He did incline to sadness, and oft-times
Not knowing why.
      Iach.   I never saw him sad.
There is a Frenchman his companion, one
An eminent monsieur that, it seems, much
            loves

A Gallian girl at home. He furnaces   65
The thick sighs from him; whiles the jolly
            Briton—
Your lord, I mean—laughs from's free
            lungs, cries ' O,
Can my sides hold, to think that man—
            who knows
By history, report, or his own proof,
What woman is, yea, what she cannot
            choose   70
But must be—will's free hours languish for
Assured bondage?'
      Imo.   Will my lord say so?
      Iach. Ay, madam, with his eyes in flood
            with laughter.
It is a recreation to be by
And hear him mock the Frenchman. But
            heavens know   75
Some men are much to blame.
      Imo.   Not he, I hope.
      Iach. Not he; but yet heaven's bounty
            towards him might
Be us'd more thankfully. In himself, 'tis
            much;
In you, which I account his, beyond all
            talents.
Whilst I am bound to wonder, I am bound
To pity too.
      Imo.   What do you pity, sir?   81
      Iach. Two creatures heartily.
      Imo.   Am I one, sir?
You look on me: what wreck discern you
            in me
Deserves your pity?
      Iach.   Lamentable! What,
To hide me from the radiant sun and
            solace   85
I' th' dungeon by a snuff?
      Imo.   I pray you, sir,
Deliver with more openness your answers
To my demands. Why do you pity me?
      Iach. That others do,
I was about to say, enjoy your——But   90
It is an office of the gods to venge it,
Not mine to speak on't.
      Imo.   You do seem to know
Something of me, or what concerns me;
            pray you—
Since doubting things go ill often hurts
            more
Than to be sure they do; for certainties   95
Either are past remedies, or, timely
            knowing,
The remedy then born—discover to me
What both you spur and stop.
      Iach.   Had I this cheek
To bathe my lips upon; this hand, whose
            touch,
Whose every touch, would force the feeler's
            soul   100
To th' oath of loyalty; this object, which
Takes prisoner the wild motion of mine eye,
Fixing it only here; should I, damn'd then,
Slaver with lips as common as the stairs

That mount the Capitol ; join gripes with
　　hands　　　　　　　　　　　　　　　105
Made hard with hourly falsehood—false-
　　hood as
With labour ; then by-peeping in an eye
Base and illustrious as the smoky light
That's fed with stinking tallow—it were fit
That all the plagues of hell should at one
　　time　　　　　　　　　　　　　　　110
Encounter such revolt.
　　Imo.　　　　　　　My lord, I fear,
Has forgot Britain.
　　Iach.　　　　　　And himself. Not I
Inclin'd to this intelligence pronounce
The beggary of his change ; but 'tis your
　　graces
That from my mutest conscience to my
　　tongue　　　　　　　　　　　　　115
Charms this report out.
　　Imo.　　　　　　Let me hear no more.
　　Iach. O dearest soul, your cause doth
　　strike my heart
With pity that doth make me sick ! A lady
So fair, and fasten'd to an empery,
Would make the great'st king double, to be
　　partner'd　　　　　　　　　　　　120
With tomboys hir'd with that self exhibi-
　　tion
Which your own coffers yield ! with
　　diseas'd ventures
That play with all infirmities for gold
Which rottenness can lend nature ! such
　　boil'd stuff　　　　　　　　　　　124
As well might poison poison ! Be reveng'd ;
Or she that bore you was no queen, and you
Recoil from your great stock.
　　Imo.　　　　　　　　Reveng'd ?
How should I be reveng'd ? If this be
　　true—
As I have such a heart that both mine ears
Must not in haste abuse—if it be true,　130
How should I be reveng'd ?
　　Iach.　　　　　　Should he make me
Live like Diana's priest betwixt cold sheets,
Whiles he is vaulting variable ramps,
In your despite, upon your purse ? Re-
　　venge it.　　　　　　　　　　　134
I dedicate myself to your sweet pleasure,
More noble than that runagate to your bed,
And will continue fast to your affection,
Still close as sure.
　　Imo.　　　　　　What ho, Pisanio !
　　Iach. Let me my service tender on your
　　lips.
　　Imo. Away ! I do condemn mine ears
　　that have　　　　　　　　　　　140
So long attended thee. If thou wert
　　honourable,
Thou wouldst have told this tale for virtue,
　　not
For such an end thou seek'st, as base as
　　strange.
Thou wrong'st a gentleman who is as far
From thy report as thou from honour ; and

Solicits here a lady that disdains　　　146
Thee and the devil alike.—What ho,
　　Pisanio !—
The King my father shall be made ac-
　　quainted
Of thy assault. If he shall think it fit
A saucy stranger in his court to mart　150
As in a Romish stew, and to expound
His beastly mind to us, he hath a court
He little cares for, and a daughter who
He not respects at all.—What ho, Pisanio !
　　Iach. O happy Leonatus ! I may say　155
The credit that thy lady hath of thee
Deserves thy trust, and thy most perfect
　　goodness
Her assur'd credit. Blessed live you long,
A lady to the worthiest sir that ever
Country call'd his ! and you his mistress,
　　only　　　　　　　　　　　　　160
For the most worthiest fit ! Give me your
　　pardon.
I have spoke this to know if your affiance
Were deeply rooted, and shall make your
　　lord
That which he is new o'er ; and he is one
The truest manner'd, such a holy witch　165
That he enchants societies into him,
Half all men's hearts are his.
　　Imo.　　　　　　You make amends.
　　Iach. He sits 'mongst men like a de-
　　scended god :
He hath a kind of honour sets him off　169
More than a mortal seeming. Be not angry,
Most mighty Princess, that I have ad-
　　ventur'd
To try your taking of a false report, which
　　hath
Honour'd with confirmation your great
　　judgment
In the election of a sir so rare,
Which you know cannot err. The love I
　　bear him　　　　　　　　　　　175
Made me to fan you thus ; but the gods
　　made you,
Unlike all others, chaffless. Pray your
　　pardon.
　　Imo. All's well, sir ; take my pow'r i' th'
　　court for yours.
　　Iach. My humble thanks. I had almost
　　forgot
T' entreat your Grace but in a small
　　request,　　　　　　　　　　　180
And yet of moment too, for it concerns
Your lord ; myself and other noble friends
Are partners in the business.
　　Imo.　　　　　　Pray what is't ?
　　Iach. Some dozen Romans of us, and
　　your lord—
The best feather of our wing—have mingled
　　sums　　　　　　　　　　　　　185
To buy a present for the Emperor ;
Which I, the factor for the rest, have done
In France. 'Tis plate of rare device, and
　　jewels

Of rich and exquisite form, their values
    great;
And I am something curious, being
    strange, 190
To have them in safe stowage. May it
    please you
To take them in protection?
  Imo. Willingly;
And pawn mine honour for their safety.
    Since
My lord hath interest in them, I will keep
    them
In my bedchamber.
  Iach. They are in a trunk, 195
Attended by my men. I will make bold
To send them to you only for this night;
I must aboard to-morrow.
  Imo. O, no, no.
  Iach. Yes, I beseech; or I shall short my
    word
By length'ning my return. From Gallia 200
I cross'd the seas on purpose and on
    promise
To see your Grace.
  Imo. I thank you for your pains.
But not away to-morrow!
  Iach. O, I must, madam.
Therefore I shall beseech you, if you please
To greet your ʌord with writing, do't to-
    night. 205
I have outstood my time, which is material
To th' tender of our present.
  Imo. I will write
Send your trunk to me; it shall safe be
    kept
And truly yielded you. You're very
    welcome. [*Exeunt.*

ACT TWO

SCENE I. *Britain. Before Cymbeline's
palace.*

Enter CLOTEN *and the two* Lords.

  Clo. Was there ever man had such luck!
When I kiss'd the jack, upon an up-cast to
be hit away! I had a hundred pound on't;
and then a whoreson jackanapes must take
me up for swearing, as if I borrowed mine
oaths of him, and might not spend them at
my pleasure. 5
  1 Lord. What got he by that? You have
broke his pate with your bowl. 7
  2 Lord. [*Aside*] If his wit had been like
him that broke it, it would have run all out.
  Clo. When a gentleman is dispos'd to
swear, it is not for any standers-by to
curtail his oaths. Ha? 11
  2 Lord. No, my lord; [*Aside*] nor crop the
ears of them.
  Clo. Whoreson dog! I give him satisfaction? Would he had been one of my rank!
  2 Lord. [*Aside*] To have smell'd like a
fool. 16

  Clo. I am not vex'd more at anything in
th' earth. A pox on't! I had rather not
be so noble as I am; they dare not fight
with me, because of the Queen my mother.
Every jackslave hath his bellyfull of
fighting, and I must go up and down like a
cock that nobody can match. 21
  2 Lord. [*Aside*] You are cock and capon
too; and you crow, cock, with your comb
on.
  Clo. Sayest thou?
  2 Lord. It is not fit your lordship should
undertake every companion that you give
offence to. 26
  Clo. No, I know that; but it is fit I
should commit offence to my inferiors.
  2 Lord. Ay, it is fit for your lordship
only.
  Clo. Why, so I say. 30
  1 Lord. Did you hear of a stranger that's
come to court to-night?
  Clo. A stranger, and I not know on't?
  2 Lord. [*Aside*] He's a strange fellow
himself, and knows it not. 35
  1 Lord. There's an Italian come, and, 'tis
thought, one of Leonatus' friends.
  Clo. Leonatus? A banish'd rascal; and
he's another, whatsoever he be. Who told
you of this stranger?
  1 Lord. One of your lordship's pages. 40
  Clo. Is it fit I went to look upon him? Is
there no derogation in't?
  2 Lord. You cannot derogate, my lord.
  Clo. Not easily, I think.
  2 Lord. [*Aside*] You are a fool granted;
therefore your issues, being foolish, do not
derogate. 46
  Clo. Come, I'll go see this Italian. What
I have lost to-day at bowls I'll win to-night
of him. Come, go.
  2 Lord. I'll attend your lordship.
        [*Exeunt Cloten and First Lord.*
That such a crafty devil as is his mother 50
Should yield the world this ass! A woman
    that
Bears all down with her brain; and this
    her son
Cannot take two from twenty, for his
    heart,
And leave eighteen. Alas, poor princess,
Thou divine Imogen, what thou endur'st,
Betwixt a father by thy step-dame
    govern'd, 56
A mother hourly coining plots, a wooer
More hateful than the foul expulsion is
Of thy dear husband, than that horrid act
Of the divorce he'd make! The heavens
    ho.d firm 60
The walls of thy dear honour, keep un-
    shak'd
That temple, thy fair mind, that thou mayst
    stand
T' enjoy thy banish'd lord and this great
    land! [*Exit.*

SCENE II. *Britain. Imogen's bedchamber in Cymbeline's palace; a trunk in one corner.*

Enter IMOGEN *in her bed, and a* Lady *attending.*

Imo. Who's there? My woman? Helen?
Lady.   Please you, madam.
Imo. What hour is it?
Lady.   Almost midnight, madam.
Imo. I have read three hours then. Mine eyes are weak;
Fold down the leaf where I have left. To bed.   4
Take not away the taper, leave it burning;
And if thou canst awake by four o' th' clock,
I prithee call me. Sleep hath seiz'd me wholly.   [*Exit Lady.*
To your protection I commend me, gods.
From fairies and the tempters of the night
Guard me, beseech ye!   10
          [*Sleeps. Iachimo comes from the trunk.*
Iach. The crickets sing, and man's o'er-labour'd sense
Repairs itself by rest. Our Tarquin thus
Did softly press the rushes ere he waken'd
The chastity he wounded. Cytherea,
How bravely thou becom'st thy bed! fresh lily,   15
And whiter than the sheets! That I might touch!
But kiss; one kiss! Rubies unparagon'd,
How dearly they do't! 'Tis her breathing that
Perfumes the chamber thus. The flame o' th' taper
Bows toward her and would under-peep her lids   20
To see th' enclosed lights, now canopied
Under these windows white and azure, lac'd
With blue of heaven's own tinct. But my design
To note the chamber. I will write all down:
Such and such pictures; there the window; such   25
Th' adornment of her bed; the arras, figures—
Why, such and such; and the contents o' th' story.
Ah, but some natural notes about her body
Above ten thousand meaner movables
Would testify, t' enrich mine inventory.   30
O sleep, thou ape of death, lie dull upon her!
And be her sense but as a monument,
Thus in a chapel lying! Come off, come off;
          [*Taking off her bracelet.*
As slippery as the Gordian knot was hard!
'Tis mine; and this will witness outwardly,
As strongly as the conscience does within,

To th' madding of her lord. On her left breast   37
A mole cinque-spotted, like the crimson drops
I' th' bottom of a cowslip. Here's a voucher
Stronger than ever law could make; this secret   40
Will force him think I have pick'd the lock and ta'en
The treasure of her honour. No more. To what end?
Why should I write this down that's riveted,
Screw'd to my memory? She hath been reading late
The tale of Tereus; here the leaf's turn'd down   45
Where Philomel gave up. I have enough.
To th' trunk again, and shut the spring of it.
Swift, swift, you dragons of the night, that dawning
May bare the raven's eye! I lodge in fear;
Though this a heavenly angel, hell is here.
          [*Clock strikes.*
One, two, three. Time, time!   51
          [*Exit into the trunk.*

SCENE III. *Cymbeline's palace. An antechamber adjoining Imogen's apartments.*

Enter CLOTEN *and* Lords.

1 Lord. Your lordship is the most patient man in loss, the most coldest that ever turn'd up ace.

Clo. It would make any man cold to lose.

1 Lord. But not every man patient after the noble temper of your lordship. You are most hot and furious when you win.   6

Clo. Winning will put any man into courage. If I could get this foolish Imogen, I should have gold enough. It's almost morning, is't not?

1 Lord. Day, my lord.   10

Clo. I would this music would come. I am advised to give her music a mornings; they say it will penetrate.

Enter Musicians.

Come on, tune. If you can penetrate her with your fingering, so. We'll try with tongue too. If none will do, let her remain; but I'll never give o'er. First, a very excellent good-conceited thing; after, a wonderful sweet air, with admirable rich words to it—and then let her consider.   18

Song.

Hark, hark! the lark at heaven's gate sings,
    And Phœbus 'gins arise,   20
His steeds to water at those springs
    On chalic'd flow'rs that lies;
And winking Mary-buds begin

To ope their golden eyes.
With everything that pretty bin,   25
   My lady sweet, arise ;
     Arise, arise !

So, get you gone. If this penetrate, I will
consider your music the better ; if it do
not, it is a vice in her ears which horsehairs
and calves' guts, nor the voice of unpaved
eunuch to boot, can never amend.   31
               [Exeunt Musicians.

Enter CYMBELINE *and* QUEEN.

  2 *Lord.* Here comes the King.
  Clo. I am glad I was up so late, for that's
the reason I was up so early. He cannot
choose but take this service I have done
fatherly.—Good morrow to your Majesty
and to my gracious mother.   36
  Cym. Attend you here the door of our
    stern daughter ?
Will she not forth ?
  Clo. I have assail'd her with musics, but
she vouchsafes no notice.   40
  Cym. The exile of her minion is too new ;
She hath not yet forgot him ; some more
    time
Must wear the print of his remembrance
    out,
And then she's yours.
  Queen. You are most bound to th' King,
Who lets go by no vantages that may   45
Prefer you to his daughter. Frame yourself
To orderly solicity, and be friended
With aptness of the season ; make denials
Increase your services ; so seem as if
You were inspir'd to do those duties which
You tender to her ; that you in all obey her,
Save when command to your dismission
    tends,   52
And therein you are senseless.
  Clo.   Senseless ? Not so.

Enter a Messenger.

  Mess. So like you, sir, ambassadors from
    Rome ;
The one is Caius Lucius.
  Cym.   A worthy fellow,   55
Albeit he comes on angry purpose now ;
But that's no fault of his. We must receive
    him
According to the honour of his sender ;
And towards himself, his goodness fore-
    spent on us,   59
We must extend our notice. Our dear son,
When you have given good morning to
    your mistress,
Attend the Queen and us ; we shall have
    need
T' employ you towards this Roman. Come,
    our queen.   [*Exeunt all but Cloten.*
  Clo. If she be up, I'll speak with her ;
    if not,

Let her lie still and dream. By your leave,
    ho !   [*Knocks.*
I know her women are about her ; what   66
If I do line one of their hands ? 'Tis gold
Which buys admittance ; oft it doth—yea,
    and makes
Diana's rangers false themselves, yield up
Their deer to th' stand o' th' stealer ; and
    'tis gold   70
Which makes the true man kill'd and saves
    the thief ;
Nay, sometime hangs both thief and true
    man. What
Can it not do and undo ? I will make
One of her women lawyer to me, for
I yet not understand the case myself.   75
By your leave.   [*Knocks.*

Enter a Lady.

  Lady. Who's there that knocks ?
  Clo.   A gentleman.
  Lady.   No more ?
  Clo. Yes, and a gentlewoman's son.
  Lady.   That's more
Than some whose tailors are as dear as
    yours
Can justly boast of. What's your lordship's
    pleasure ?   80
  Clo. Your lady's person ; is she ready ?
  Lady.   Ay,
To keep her chamber.
  Clo. There is gold for you ; sell me your
    good report.
  Lady. How ? My good name ? or to
    report of you
What I shall think is good ? The Princess !

Enter IMOGEN.

  Clo. Good morrow, fairest sister. Your
    sweet hand.   [*Exit Lady.*
  Imo. Good morrow, sir. You lay out too
    much pains   87
For purchasing but trouble. The thanks I
    give
Is telling you that I am poor of thanks,
And scarce can spare them.
  Clo.   Still I swear I love you.   90
  Imo. If you but said so, 'twere as deep
    with me.
If you swear still, your recompense is still
That I regard it not.
  Clo.   This is no answer.
  Imo. But that you shall not say I yield,
    being silent,
I would not speak. I pray you spare me.
    Faith,   95
I shall unfold equal discourtesy
To your best kindness ; one of your great
    knowing
Should learn, being taught, forbearance.
  Clo. To leave you in your madness 'twere
    my sin ;
I will not.   100
  Imo. Fools are not mad folks.

Clo. Do you call me fool ?
Imo.   As I am mad, I do ;
If you'll be patient, I'll no more be mad ;
That cures us both. I am much sorry, sir, 105
You put me to forget a lady's manners
By being verbal ; and learn now, for all,
That I, which know my heart, do here pronounce,
By th' very truth of it, I care not for you,
And am so near the lack of charity
To accuse myself I hate you ; which I had
     rather 110
You felt than make 't my boast.
Clo.   You sin against
Obedience, which you owe your father. For
The contract you pretend with that base
     wretch,
One bred of alms and foster'd with cold
     dishes,
With scraps o' th' court—it is no contract,
     none. 115
And though it be allowed in meaner
     parties—
Yet who than he more mean ?—to knit
     their souls—
On whom there is no more dependency
But brats and beggary—in self-figur'd knot,
Yet you are curb'd from that enlargement
     by 120
The consequence o' th' crown, and must
     not foil
The precious note of it with a base slave,
A hilding for a livery, a squire's cloth,
A pantler—not so eminent !
Imo.   Profane fellow !
Wert thou the son of Jupiter, and no more
But what thou art besides, thou wert too
     base 126
To be his groom. Thou wert dignified
     enough,
Even to the point of envy, if 'twere made
Comparative for your virtues to be styl'd
The under-hangman of his kingdom, and
     hated 130
For being preferr'd so well.
Clo.   The south fog rot him !
Imo. He never can meet more mischance
     than come
To be but nam'd of thee. His mean'st
     garment
That ever hath but clipp'd his body is
     dearer 134
In my respect than all the hairs above thee,
Were they all made such men. How now,
Pisanio !

Enter PISANIO.

Clo. ' His garments ' ! Now the devil—
Imo. To Dorothy my woman hie thee
     presently.
Clo. ' His garment ' !
Imo.   I am sprited with a fool ;
Frighted, and ang'red worse. Go bid my
     woman 140

Search for a jewel that too casually
Hath left mine arm. It was thy master's ;
     shrew me,
If I would lose it for a revenue
Of any king's in Europe ! I do think
I saw't this morning ; confident I am 145
Last night 'twas on mine arm ; I kiss'd it.
I hope it be not gone to tell my lord
That I kiss aught but he.
Pis.   'Twill not be lost.
Imo. I hope so. Go and search.
                      [*Exit Pisanio.*
Clo.   You have abus'd me.
' His meanest garment ' !
Imo.   Ay, I said so, sir. 150
If you will make 't an action, call witness
     to 't.
Clo. I will inform your father.
Imo.   Your mother too.
She's my good lady and will conceive, I
     hope,
But the worst of me. So I leave you, sir,
To th' worst of discontent.   [*Exit.*
Clo.   I'll be reveng'd. 155
' His mean'st garment ' ! Well.   [*Exit.*

Scene IV. *Rome. Philario's house.*

Enter POSTHUMUS *and* PHILARIO.

Post. Fear it not, sir ; I would I were so
     sure
To win the King as I am bold her honour
Will remain hers.
Phi. What means do you make to him ?
Post. Not any ; but abide the change of
     time,
Quake in the present winter's state, and
     wish 5
That warmer days would come. In these
     fear'd hopes
I barely gratify your love ; they failing,
I must die much your debtor.
Phi. Your very goodness and your
     company
O'erpays all I can do. By this your king 10
Hath heard of great Augustus. Caius
     Lucius
Will do's commission throughly ; and I
     think
He'll grant the tribute, send th' arrearages,
Or look upon our Romans, whose remembrance
Is yet fresh in their grief.
Post.   I do believe, 15
Statist though I am none, nor like to be,
That this will prove a war ; and you shall
     hear
The legions now in Gallia sooner landed
In our not-fearing Britain than have
     tidings
Of any penny tribute paid. Our countrymen 20
Are men more order'd than when Julius
     Cæsar

Smil'd at their lack of skill, but found their
　courage
Worthy his frowning at. Their discipline,
Now mingled with their courages, will
　make known
To their approvers they are people such 25
That mend upon the world.

　　　　　Enter IACHIMO.

Phi.　　　　　　　　See! Iachimo!
Post. The swiftest harts have posted you
　by land,
And winds of all the corners kiss'd your
　sails,
To make your vessel nimble.
Phi.　　　　　　　　Welcome, sir.
Post. I hope the briefness of your answer
　made　　　　　　　　　　　　　30
The speediness of your return.
Iach.　　　　　　　　Your lady
Is one of the fairest that I have look'd
　upon.
Post. And therewithal the best; or let
　her beauty
Look through a casement to allure false
　hearts,　　　　　　　　　　　34
And be false with them.
Iach.　　　　Here are letters for you.
Post. Their tenour good, I trust.
Iach.　　　　　　　'Tis very like.
Phi. Was Caius Lucius in the Britain
　court
When you were there?
Iach.　　　　　He was expected then,
But not approach'd.
Post.　　　　　All is well yet.
Sparkles this stone as it was wont, or is't
　not　　　　　　　　　　　　　40
Too dull for your good wearing?
Iach.　　　　　　If I have lost it,
I should have lost the worth of it in gold.
I'll make a journey twice as far t' enjoy
A second night of such sweet shortness
　which　　　　　　　　　　　　44
Was mine in Britain; for the ring is won.
Post. The stone's too hard to come by.
Iach.　　　　　　　Not a whit,
Your lady being so easy.
Post.　　　　　　Make not, sir,
Your loss your sport. I hope you know
　that we　　　　　　　　　　　48
Must not continue friends.
Iach.　　　　　Good sir, we must,
If you keep covenant. Had I not brought
The knowledge of your mistress home, I
　grant
We were to question farther; but I now
Profess myself the winner of her honour,
Together with your ring; and not the
　wronger
Of her or you, having proceeded but 55
By both your wills.
Post.　　　If you can make't apparent
That you have tasted her in bed, my hand

And ring is yours. If not, the foul opinion
You had of her pure honour gains or loses
Your sword or mine, or masterless leaves
　both　　　　　　　　　　　　60
To who shall find them.
Iach.　　　　　Sir, my circumstances,
Being so near the truth as I will make
　them,
Must first induce you to believe—whose
　strength
I will confirm with oath; which I doubt
　not
You'll give me leave to spare when you
　shall find　　　　　　　　　　65
You need it not.
Post.　　　　　　Proceed.
Iach.　　　　　First, her bedchamber,
Where I confess I slept not, but profess
Had that was well worth watching—it was
　hang'd　　　　　　　　　　　68
With tapestry of silk and silver; the story,
Proud Cleopatra when she met her Roman
And Cydnus swell'd above the banks, or for
The press of boats or pride. A piece of
　work
So bravely done, so rich, that it did strive
In workmanship and value; which I
　wonder'd
Could be so rarely and exactly wrought, 75
Since the true life on't was—
Post.　　　　　　This is true;
And this you might have heard of here, by
　me
Or by some other.
Iach.　　　　　More particulars
Must justify my knowledge.
Post.　　　　　　So they must,
Or do your honour injury.
Iach.　　　　　　The chimney 80
Is south the chamber, and the chimney-
　piece
Chaste Dian bathing. Never saw I figures
So likely to report themselves. The cutter
Was as another nature, dumb; outwent
　her,
Motion and breath left out.
Post.　　　　　This is a thing 85
Which you might from relation likewise
　reap,
Being, as it is, much spoke of.
Iach.　　　　The roof o' th' chamber
With golden cherubins is fretted; her
　andirons—
I had forgot them—were two winking
　Cupids　　　　　　　　　　　89
Of silver, each on one foot standing, nicely
Depending on their brands.
Post.　　　　　This is her honour!
Let it be granted you have seen all this, and
　praise
Be given to your remembrance; the
　description
Of what is in her chamber nothing saves
The wager you have laid.

Iach.   Then, if you can, 95
[*Shows the bracelet.*
Be pale. I beg but leave to air this jewel.
See !
And now 'tis up again. It must be married
To that your diamond ; I'll keep them.
Post.   Jove !
Once more let me behold it. Is it that
Which I left with her ?
Iach.   Sir—I thank her—that. 100
She stripp'd it from her arm ; I see her yet ;
Her pretty action did outsell her gift,
And yet enrich'd it too. She gave it me,
and said
She priz'd it once.
Post.   May be she pluck'd it off
To send it me.
Iach.   She writes so to you, doth she ?
Post. O, no, no, no ! 'tis true. Here, take
this too ;   [*Gives the ring.*
It is a basilisk unto mine eye,   107
Kills me to look on't. Let there be no
honour
Where there is beauty ;   truth where
semblance ; love
Where there's another man. The vows of
women   110
Of no more bondage be to where they are
made
Than they are to their virtues, which is
nothing.
O, above measure false !
Phi.   Have patience, sir,
And take your ring again ; 'tis not yet
won.
It may be probable she lost it, or   115
Who knows if one her women, being cor-
rupted,
Hath stol'n it from her ?
Post.   Very true ;
And so I hope he came by't. Back my
ring.   118
Render to me some corporal sign about her,
More evident than this ; for this was stol'n.
Iach. By Jupiter, I had it from her arm !
Post. Hark you, he swears ; by Jupiter
he swears.
'Tis true—nay, keep the ring, 'tis true. I
am sure
She would not lose it. Her attendants are
All sworn and honourable—they induc'd to
steal it !   125
And by a stranger ! No, he hath enjoy'd
her.
The cognizance of her incontinency
Is this : she hath bought the name of
whore thus dearly.
There, take thy hire ; and all the fiends of
hell
Divide themselves between you !
Phi.   Sir, be patient ; 130
This is not strong enough to be believ'd
Of one persuaded well of.
Post.   Never talk on't ;

She hath been colted by him.
Iach.   If you seek
For further satisfying, under her breast—
Worthy the pressing—lies a mole, right
proud   135
Of that most delicate lodging. By my life,
I kiss'd it ; and it gave me present hunger
To feed again, though full.   You do
remember
This stain upon her ?
Post.   Ay, and it doth confirm
Another stain, as big as hell can hold, 140
Were there no more but it.
Iach.   Will you hear more ?
Post. Spare your arithmetic ; never count
the turns.
Once, and a million !
Iach.   I'll be sworn—
Post.   No swearing.
If you will swear you have not done't,
you lie ;
And I will kill thee if thou dost deny 145
Thou'st made me cuckold.
Iach.   I'll deny nothing.
Post. O that I had her here to tear her
limb-meal !
I will go there and do't, i' th' court, before
Her father. I'll do something—   [*Exit.*
Phi.   Quite besides
The government of patience ! You have
won.   150
Let's follow him and pervert the present
wrath
He hath against himself.
Iach.   With all my heart.
[*Exeunt.*

SCENE V. *Rome. Another room in Philario's
house.*

Enter POSTHUMUS.

Post. Is there no way for men to be, but
women
Must be half-workers ? We are all bastards,
And that most venerable man which I
Did call my father was I know not where
When I was stamp'd. Some coiner with his
tools   5
Made me a counterfeit ; yet my mother
seem'd
The Dian of that time. So doth my wife
The nonpareil of this.   O, vengeance,
vengeance !
Me of my lawful pleasure she restrain'd,
And pray'd me oft forbearance ; did it
with   10
A pudency so rosy, the sweet view on't
Might well have warm'd old Saturn ; that
I thought her
As chaste as unsunn'd snow. O, all the
devils !
This yellow Iachimo in an hour—was't not?
Or less !—at first ? Perchance he spoke not,
but,   15

Like a full-acorn'd boar, a German one,
Cried ' O ! ' and mounted ; found no
   opposition
But what he look'd for should oppose and
   she
Should from encounter guard. Could I find
   out
The woman's part in me ! For there's no
   motion   20
That tends to vice in man but I affirm
It is the woman's part. Be it lying, note it,
The woman's ; flattering, hers ; deceiving,
   hers ;
Lust and rank thoughts, hers, hers ;
   revenges, hers ;
Ambitions, covetings, change of prides,
   disdain,   25
Nice longing, slanders, mutability,
All faults that man may name, nay, that
   hell knows,
Why, hers, in part or all : but rather all ;
For even to vice
They are not constant, but are changing
   still   30
One vice but of a minute old for one
Not half so old as that. I'll write against
   them,
Detest them, curse them. Yet 'tis greater
   skill   33
In a true hate to pray they have their will :
The very devils cannot plague them better.
             [*Exit.*

ACT THREE

SCENE I. *Britain. A hall in Cymbeline's
palace.*

Enter in state, CYMBELINE, QUEEN,
CLOTEN, *and Lords a one door, and at
another* CAIUS LUCIUS *and Attendants.*

Cym. Now say, what would Augustus
   Cæsar with us ?
Luc. When Julius Cæsar—whose remem-
   brance yet
Lives in men's eyes, and will to ears and
   tongues
Be theme and hearing ever—was in this
   Britain,
And conquer'd it, Cassibelan, thine uncle, 5
Famous in Cæsar's praises no whit less
Than in his feats deserving it, for him
And his succession granted Rome a tribute,
Yearly three thousand pounds, which by
   thee lately
Is left untender'd.
   Queen.   And, to kill the marvel, 10
Shall be so ever.
   Clo.   There be many Cæsars
Ere such another Julius. Britain is
A world by itself, and we will nothing pay
For wearing our own noses.
   Queen.   That opportunity,
Which then they had to take from 's, to
   resume   15

We have again. Remember, sir, my liege,
The kings your ancestors, together with
The natural bravery of your isle, which
   stands
As Neptune's park, ribb'd and pal'd in
With rocks unscalable and roaring waters,
With sands that will not bear your enemies'
   boats
But suck them up to th' top-mast. A kind 21
   of conquest
Cæsar made here ; but made not here his
   brag
Of ' came, and saw, and overcame '. With
   shame—
The first that ever touch'd him—he was
   carried   25
From off our coast, twice beaten ; and his
   shipping—
Poor ignorant baubles !—on our terrible seas,
Like egg-shells mov'd upon their surges,
   crack'd
As easily 'gainst our rocks ; for joy whereof
The fam'd Cassibelan, who was once at
   point—   30
O, giglot fortune !—to master Cæsar's
   sword,
Made Lud's Town with rejoicing fires bright
And Britons strut with courage.
   Clo. Come, there's no more tribute to be
paid. Our kingdom is stronger than it was
at that time ; and, as I said, there is no
moe such Cæsars. Other of them may have
crook'd noses ; but to owe such straight
arms, none.
   Cym. Son, let your mother end.   38
   Clo. We have yet many among us can
gripe as hard as Cassibelan. I do not say
I am one ; but I have a hand. Why tribute ?
Why should we pay tribute ? If Cæsar can
hide the sun from us with a blanket, or put
the moon in his pocket, we will pay him
tribute for light ; else, sir, no more tribute,
pray you now.
   Cym. You must know,   45
Till the injurious Romans did extort
This tribute from us, we were free. Cæsar's
   ambition—
Which swell'd so much that it did almost
   stretch
The sides o' th' world—against all colour
   here
Did put the yoke upon's ; which to shake
   off
Becomes a warlike people, whom we reckon 50
Ourselves to be.
   Clo.   We do.
   Cym.   Say then to Cæsar
Our ancestor was that Mulmutius which
Ordain'd our laws—whose use the sword
   of Cæsar
Hath too much mangled ; whose repair and
   franchise   55
Shall, by the power we hold, be our good
   deed,

Though Rome be therefore angry. Mul-
    mutius made our laws,
Who was the first of Britain which did put
His brows within a golden crown, and
    call'd
Himself a king.
    Luc.   I am sorry, Cymbeline, 60
That I am to pronounce Augustus Cæsar—
Cæsar, that hath moe kings his servants
    than
Thyself domestic officers—thine enemy.
Receive it from me, then : war and con-
    fusion
In Cæsar's name pronounce I 'gainst thee ;
    look 65
For fury not to be resisted. Thus defied,
I thank thee for myself.
    Cym.   Thou art welcome, Caius.
Thy Cæsar knighted me ; my youth I spent
Much under him ; of him I gather'd honour,
Which he to seek of me again, perforce, 70
Behoves me keep at utterance. I am perfect
That the Pannonians and Dalmatians for
Their liberties are now in arms, a precedent
Which not to read would show the Britons
    cold ;
So Cæsar shall not find them.
    Luc.   Let proof speak. 75
    Clo. His Majesty bids you welcome.
Make pastime with us a day or two, or
longer. If you seek us afterwards in other
terms, you shall find us in our salt-water
girdle. If you beat us out of it, it is yours ;
if you fall in the adventure, our crows shall
fare the better for you ; and there's an end.
    Luc. So, sir.   82
    Cym. I know your master's pleasure, and
    he mine ;
All the remain is, welcome.   [*Exeunt.*

SCENE II. *Britain. Another room in
    Cymbeline's palace.*

Enter PISANIO *reading of a letter.*

    Pis. How ? of adultery ?   Wherefore
    write you not
What monsters her accuse ?   Leonatus !
O master, what a strange infection
Is fall'n into thy ear ! What false Italian—
As poisonous-tongu'd as handed—hath
    prevail'd 5
On thy too ready hearing ? Disloyal ? No.
She's punish'd for her truth, and undergoes,
More goddess-like than wife-like, such
    assaults
As would take in some virtue. O my
    master !
Thy mind to her is now as low as were 10
Thy fortunes. How ? that I should murder
    her ?
Upon the love, and truth, and vows, which I
Have made to thy command ? I, her ? Her
    blood ?
If it be so to do good service, never

Let me be counted serviceable. How look I
That I should seem to lack humanity 16
So much as this fact comes to ? [*Reads*]
    ' Do't. The letter
That I have sent her, by her own command
Shall give thee opportunity.' O damn'd
    paper,
Black as the ink that's on thee ! Senseless
    bauble, 20
Art thou a fedary for this act, and look'st
So virgin-like without ? Lo here she comes.

        Enter IMOGEN.

I am ignorant in what I am commanded.
    Imo. How now, Pisanio !
    Pis. Madam, here is a letter from my
    lord. 25
    Imo. Who ? thy lord ? That is my lord—
    Leonatus ?
O, learn'd indeed were that astronomer
That knew the stars as I his characters ;
He'd lay the future open. You good gods,
Let what is here contain'd relish of love, 30
Of my lord's health, of his content ; yet
    not
That we two are asunder—let that grieve
    him !
Some griefs are med'cinable ; that is one of
    them,
For it doth physic love—of his content,
All but in that. Good wax, thy leave.
    Blest be 35
You bees that make these locks of counsel !
    Lovers
And men in dangerous bonds pray not
    alike ;
Though forfeiters you cast in prison, yet 38
You clasp young Cupid's tables. Good
    news, gods !   [*Reads.*

    ' Justice, and your father's wrath, should
he take me in his dominion, could not be so
cruel to me as you, O the dearest of creatures, would even renew me with your eyes.
Take notice that I am in Cambria, at
Milford Haven. What your own love will
out of this advise you, follow. So he wishes
you all happiness that remains loyal to his
vow, and your increasing in love 45
                 LEONATUS POSTHUMUS.'

O for a horse with wings ! Hear'st thou,
    Pisanio ?
He is at Milford Haven. Read, and tell me
How far 'tis thither. If one of mean affairs
May plod it in a week, why may not I 50
Glide thither in a day ? Then, true
    Pisanio—
Who long'st like me to see thy lord, who
    long'st—
O, let me 'bate !—but not like me, yet
    long'st,
But in a fainter kind—O, not like me,
For mine's beyond beyond !—say, and
    speak thick— 55

Love's counsellor should fill the bores of
 hearing
To th' smothering of the sense—how far
 it is
To this same blessed Milford. And by th'
 way
Tell me how Wales was made so happy as
T' inherit such a haven. But first of all, 60
How we may steal from hence; and for the
 gap
That we shall make in time from our hence-
 going
And our return, to excuse. But first, how
 get hence.
Why should excuse be born or ere begot?
We'll talk of that hereafter. Prithee speak,
How many score of miles may we well ride
'Twixt hour and hour?
 Pis.   One score 'twixt sun and sun,
Madam, 's enough for you, and too much
 too.   68
 Imo. Why, one that rode to's execution,
 man,
Could never go so slow. I have heard of
 riding wagers
Where horses have been nimbler than the
 sands   71
That run i' th' clock's behalf. But this is
 fool'ry.
Go bid my woman feign a sickness; say
She'll home to her father; and provide me
 presently
A riding suit, no costlier than would fit 75
A franklin's huswife.
 Pis. Madam, you're best consider.
 Imo. I see before me, man. Nor here, nor
 here,
Nor what ensues, but have a fog in them
That I cannot look through. Away, I
 prithee;
Do as I bid thee. There's no more to say;
Accessible is none but Milford way. 81
        [*Exeunt.*

SCENE III. *Wales. A mountainous country
 with a cave.*

Enter from the cave BELARIUS, GUIDERIUS,
 and ARVIRAGUS.

 Bel. A goodly day not to keep house
 with such
Whose roof's as low as ours! Stoop, boys;
 this gate
Instructs you how t' adore the heavens,
 and bows you
To a morning's holy office. The gates of
 monarchs
Are arch'd so high that giants may jet
 through   5
And keep their impious turbans on without
Good morrow to the sun. Hail, thou fair
 heaven!
We house i' th' rock, yet use thee not so
 hardly

As prouder livers do.
 Gui.   Hail, heaven!
 Arv.   Hail, heaven!
 Bel. Now for our mountain sport. Up to
 yond hill,   10
Your legs are young; I'll tread these flats.
 Consider,
When you above perceive me like a crow,
That it is place which lessens and sets off;
And you may then revolve what tales I
 have told you
Of courts, of princes, of the tricks in war. 15
This service is not service so being done,
But being so allow'd. To apprehend thus
Draws us a profit from all things we see,
And often to our comfort shall we find
The sharded beetle in a safer hold 20
Than is the full-wing'd eagle. O, this life
Is nobler than attending for a check,
Richer than doing nothing for a bribe,
Prouder than rustling in unpaid-for silk:
Such gain the cap of him that makes him
 fine,   25
Yet keeps his book uncross'd. No life to
 ours!
 Gui. Out of your proof you speak. We,
 poor unfledg'd,
Have never wing'd from view o' th' nest,
 nor know not
What air's from home. Haply this life is
 best,
If quiet life be best; sweeter to you 30
That have a sharper known; well corres-
 ponding
With your stiff age. But unto us it is
A cell of ignorance, travelling abed,
A prison for a debtor that not dares
To stride a limit.
 Arv.   What should we speak of 35
When we are old as you? When we shall
 hear
The rain and wind beat dark December,
 how,
In this our pinching cave, shall we dis-
 course
The freezing hours away? We have seen
 nothing;   39
We are beastly: subtle as the fox for prey,
Like warlike as the wolf for what we eat.
Our valour is to chase what flies; our cage
We make a choir, as doth the prison'd bird,
And sing our bondage freely.
 Bel.   How you speak!
Did you but know the city's usuries, 45
And felt them knowingly—the art o' th'
 court,
As hard to leave as keep, whose top to
 climb
Is certain falling, or so slipp'ry that
The fear's as bad as falling; the toil o' th'
 war,   49
A pain that only seems to seek out danger
I' th' name of fame and honour, which dies
 i' th' search,

And hath as oft a sland'rous epitaph
As record of fair act; nay, many times,
Doth ill deserve by doing well; what's
   worse—
Must curtsy at the censure. O, boys, this
   story   55
The world may read in me; my body's
   mark'd
With Roman swords, and my report was
   once
First with the best of note. Cymbeline
   lov'd me;
And when a soldier was the theme, my
   name
Was not far off. Then was I as a tree   60
Whose boughs did bend with fruit; but in
   one night
A storm, or robbery, call it what you will,
Shook down my mellow hangings, nay, my
   leaves,
And left me bare to weather.
   Gui.   Uncertain favour!
   Bel. My fault being nothing—as I have
     told you oft—   65
But that two villains, whose false oaths
   prevail'd
Before my perfect honour, swore to
   Cymbeline
I was confederate with the Romans. So
Follow'd my banishment, and this twenty
   years
This rock and these demesnes have been my
   world,   70
Where I have liv'd at honest freedom, paid
More pious debts to heaven than in all
The fore-end of my time. But up to th'
   mountains!
This is not hunters' language. He that
   strikes
The venison first shall be the lord o' th'
   feast;   75
To him the other two shall minister;
And we will fear no poison, which attends
In place of greater state. I'll meet you in
   the valleys.
       [*Exeunt Guiderius and Arviragus.*
How hard it is to hide the sparks of nature!
These boys know little they are sons to th'
   King,   80
Nor Cymbeline dreams that they are alive.
They think they are mine; and though
   train'd up thus meanly
I' th' cave wherein they bow, their thoughts
   do hit
The roofs of palaces, and nature prompts
   them   84
In simple and low things to prince it much
Beyond the trick of others. This Polydore,
The heir of Cymbeline and Britain, who
The King his father call'd Guiderius—Jove!
When on my three-foot stool I sit and tell
The warlike feats I have done, his spirits
   fly out   90
Into my story; say ' Thus mine enemy fell,

And thus I set my foot on's neck '; even
   then
The princely blood flows in his cheek, he
   sweats,
Strains his young nerves, and puts himself
   in posture
That acts my words. The younger brother,
   Cadwal,   95
Once Arviragus, in as like a figure
Strikes life into my speech, and shows
   much more
His own conceiving. Hark, the game is
   rous'd!
O Cymbeline, heaven and my conscience
   knows   99
Thou didst unjustly banish me! Whereon,
At three and two years old, I stole these
   babes,
Thinking to bar thee of succession as
Thou refts me of my lands. Euriphile,
Thou wast their nurse; they took thee for
   their mother,
And every day do honour to her grave. 105
Myself, Belarius, that am Morgan call'd,
They take for natural father. The game
   is up.   [*Exit.*

SCENE IV. *Wales, near Milford Haven.*

     Enter PISANIO *and* IMOGEN.

   Imo. Thou told'st me, when we came
     from horse, the place
Was near at hand. Ne'er long'd my mother
   so
To see me first as I have now. Pisanio!
   Man!
Where is Posthumus? What is in thy mind
That makes thee stare thus? Wherefore
   breaks that sigh   5
From th' inward of thee? One but painted
   thus
Would be interpreted a thing perplex'd
Beyond self-explication. Put thyself
Into a haviour of less fear, ere wildness
Vanquish my staider senses. What's the
   matter?   10
Why tender'st thou that paper to me with
A look untender? If't be summer news,
Smile to't before; if winterly, thou need'st
But keep that count'nance still. My
   husband's hand?
That drug-damn'd Italy hath out-craftied
   him,   15
And he's at some hard point. Speak, man;
   thy tongue
May take off some extremity, which to read
Would be even mortal to me.
   Pis.   Please you read,
And you shall find me, wretched man, a
   thing
The most disdain'd of fortune.   20
   Imo. [*Reads*] ' Thy mistress, Pisanio,
hath play'd the strumpet in my bed, the
testimonies whereof lie bleeding in me. I

speak not out of weak surmises, but from
proof as strong as my grief and as certain
as I expect my revenge. That part thou,
Pisanio, must act for me, if thy faith be not
tainted with the breach of hers. Let thine
own hands take away her life; I shall give
thee opportunity at Milford Haven; she
hath my letter for the purpose; where, if
thou fear to strike, and to make me certain
it is done, thou art the pander to her
dishonour, and equally to me disloyal.' 29
  Pis. What shall I need to draw my
    sword? The paper
Hath cut her throat already. No, 'tis
  slander, 31
Whose edge is sharper than the sword,
  whose tongue
Outvenoms all the worms of Nile, whose
  breath
Rides on the posting winds and doth belie
All corners of the world. Kings, queens,
  and states, 35
Maids, matrons, nay, the secrets of the
  grave,
This viperous slander enters. What cheer,
  madam?
  Imo. False to his bed? What is it to be
    false?
To lie in watch there, and to think on him?
To weep twixt clock and clock? If sleep
  charge nature,
To break it with a fearful dream of him, 41
And cry myself awake? That's false to's
  bed,
Is it?
  Pis. Alas, good lady!
  Imo. I false! Thy conscience witness!
Iachimo,
Thou didst accuse him of incontinency; 45
Thou then look'dst like a villain; now,
  methinks,
Thy favour's good enough. Some jay of
  Italy,
Whose mother was her painting, hath be-
  tray'd him.
Poor I am stale, a garment out of fashion,
And for I am richer than to hang by th'
  walls 50
I must be ripp'd. To pieces with me! O,
Men's vows are women's traitors! All good
  seeming,
By thy revolt, O husband, shall be thought
Put on for villainy; not born where't
  grows,
But worn a bait for ladies.
  Pis. Good madam, hear me. 55
  Imo. True honest men being heard, like
    false Æneas,
Were, in his time, thought false; and
  Sinon's weeping
Did scandal many a holy tear, took pity
From most true wretchedness. So thou,
  Posthumus,
Wilt lay the leaven on all proper men: 60

Goodly and gallant shall be false and
  perjur'd
From thy great fail. Come, fellow, be thou
  honest;
Do thou thy master's bidding; when thou
  seest him,
A little witness my obedience. Look! 64
I draw the sword myself; take it, and hit
The innocent mansion of my love, my
  heart.
Fear not; 'tis empty of all things but
  grief;
Thy master is not there, who was indeed
The riches of it. Do his bidding; strike.
Thou mayst be valiant in a better cause, 70
But now thou seem'st a coward.
  Pis. Hence, vile instrument!
Thou shalt not damn my hand.
  Imo. Why, I must die;
And if I do not by thy hand, thou art
No servant of thy master's. Against self-
  slaughter
There is a prohibition so divine 75
That cravens my weak hand. Come, here's
  my heart—
Something's afore't. Soft, soft! we'll no
  defence!—
Obedient as the scabbard. What is here?
The scriptures of the loyal Leonatus
All turn'd to heresy? Away, away, 80
Corrupters of my faith! you shall no more
Be stomachers to my heart. Thus may
  poor fools
Believe false teachers; though those that
  are betray'd
Do feel the treason sharply, yet the traitor
Stands in worse case of woe. And thou,
  Posthumus,
That didst set up my disobedience 'gainst
  the King
My father, and make me put into contempt
  the suits
Of princely fellows, shalt hereafter find
It is no act of common passage but 90
A strain of rareness; and I grieve myself
To think, when thou shalt be disedg'd by her
That now thou tirest on, how thy memory
Will then be pang'd by me. Prithee
  dispatch.
The lamb entreats the butcher. Where's
  thy knife? 95
Thou art too slow to do thy master's
  bidding,
When I desire it too.
  Pis. O gracious lady,
Since I receiv'd command to do this
  business
I have not slept one wink.
  Imo. Do't, and to bed then.
  Pis. I'll wake mine eyeballs first.
  Imo. Wherefore then
Didst undertake it? Why hast thou
  abus'd 101
So many miles with a pretence? This place?

Mine action and thine own? our horses'
    labour?
The time inviting thee? the perturb'd
    court,   104
For my being absent?—whereunto I never
Purpose return. Why hast thou gone so far
To be unbent when thou hast ta'en thy
    stand,
Th' elected deer before thee?
    Pis.   But to win time
To lose so bad employment, in the which
I have consider'd of a course. Good lady,
Hear me with patience.
    Imo.   Talk thy tongue weary—speak.
I have heard I am a strumpet, and mine
    ear,   112
Therein false struck, can take no greater
    wound,
Nor tent to bottom that. But speak.
    Pis.   Then, madam,
I thought you would not back again.
    Imo.   Most like— 115
Bringing me here to kill me.
    Pis.   Not so, neither;
But if I were as wise as honest, then
My purpose would prove well. It cannot be
But that my master is abus'd. Some
    villain,
Ay, and singular in his art, hath done you
    both   120
This cursed injury.
    Imo. Some Roman courtezan!
    Pis.   No, on my life!
I'll give but notice you are dead, and send
    him
Some bloody sign of it, for 'tis commanded
I should do so. You shall be miss'd at
    court,   125
And that will well confirm it.
    Imo.   Why, good fellow,
What shall I do the while? where bide?
    how live?
Or in my life what comfort, when I am
Dead to my husband?
    Pis.   If you'll back to th' court—
    Imo. No court, no father, nor no more
    ado   130
With that harsh, noble, simple nothing—
That Cloten, whose love-suit hath been to
    me
As fearful as a siege.
    Pis.   If not at court,
Then not in Britain must you bide.
    Imo.   Where then?
Hath Britain all the sun that shines? Day,
    night,   135
Are they not but in Britain? I' th' world's
    volume
Our Britain seems as of it, but not n't;
In a great pool a swan's nest. Prithee
    think
There's livers out of Britain.
    Pis.   I am most glad
You think of other place. Th' ambassador,

Lucius the Roman, comes to Milford
    Haven   141
To-morrow. Now, if you could wear a
    mind
Dark as your fortune is, and but disguise
That which t' appear itself must not yet be
But by self-danger, you should tread a
    course   145
Pretty and full of view; yea, happily, near
The residence of Posthumus; so nigh, at
    least,
That though his actions were not visible, yet
Report should render him hourly to your
    ear
As truly as he moves.
    Imo.   O! for such means, 150
Though peril to my modesty, not death
    on't,
I would adventure.
    Pis.   Well then, here's the point:
You must forget to be a woman; change
Command into obedience; fear and nice-
    ness—
The handmaids of all women, or, more
    truly,   155
Woman it pretty self—into a waggish
    courage;
Ready in gibes, quick-answer'd, saucy, and
As quarrelous as the weasel. Nay, you
    must
Forget that rarest treasure of your cheek,
Exposing it—but, O, the harder heart! 160
Alack, no remedy!—to the greedy touch
Of common-kissing Titan, and forget
Your laboursome and dainty trims wherein
You made great Juno angry.
    Imo.   Nay, be brief;
I see into thy end, and am almost 165
A man already.
    Pis.   First, make yourself but like one.
Fore-thinking this, I have already fit—
'Tis in my cloak-bag—doublet, hat, hose, all
That answer to them. Would you, in their
    serving,
And with what imitation you can borrow
From youth of such a season, fore noble
    Lucius   171
Present yourself, desire his service, tell him
Wherein you're happy—which will make
    him know
If that his head have ear in music; doubt-
    less
With joy he will embrace you; for he's
    honourable,   175
And, doubling that, most holy. Your means
    abroad—
You have me, rich; and I will never fail
Beginning nor supplyment.
    Imo.   Thou art all the comfort
The gods will diet me with. Prithee away!
There's more to be consider'd; but we'll
    even   180
All that good time will give us. This
    attempt

I am soldier to, and will abide it with
A prince's courage. Away, I prithee.
   Pis. Well, madam, we must take a short
     farewell,
Lest, being miss'd, I be suspected of   185
Your carriage from the court. My noble
    mistress,
Here is a box ; I had it from the Queen.
What's in't is precious. If you are sick
    at sea
Or stomach-qualm'd at land, a dram of this
Will drive away distemper. To some shade,
And fit you to your manhood. May the gods
Direct you to the best !
   Imo.   Amen. I thank thee.
                 [Exeunt severally.

   Scene V. *Britain. Cymbeline's palace.*

   Enter Cymbeline, Queen, Cloten,
       Lucius, *and* Lords.

   Cym. Thus far ; and so farewell.
   Luc.   Thanks, royal sir.
My emperor hath wrote ; I must from
    hence,
And am right sorry that I must report ye
My master's enemy.
   Cym.   Our subjects, sir,   4
Will not endure his yoke ; and for ourself
To show less sovereignty than they, must
    needs
Appear unkinglike.
   Luc.   So, sir. I desire of you
A conduct overland to Milford Haven.
Madam, all joy befall your Grace, and you !
   Cym. My lords, you are appointed for
    that office ;   10
The due of honour in no point omit.
So farewell, noble Lucius.
   Luc.   Your hand, my lord.
   Clo. Receive it friendly ; but from this
    time forth
I wear it as your enemy.
   Luc.   Sir, the event   14
Is yet to name the winner. Fare you well.
   Cym. Leave not the worthy Lucius, good
    my lords,
Till he have cross'd the Severn. Happiness !
            [Exeunt Lucius and Lords.
   Queen. He goes hence frowning ; but it
    honours us
That we have given him cause.
   Clo.   'Tis all the better ;
Your valiant Britons have their wishes in it.
   Cym. Lucius hath wrote already to the
    Emperor   21
How it goes here. It fits us therefore ripely
Our chariots and our horsemen be in
    readiness.
The pow'rs that he already hath in Gallia
Will soon be drawn to head, from whence
    he moves   25
His war for Britain.
   Queen.   'Tis not sleepy business,

But must be look'd to speedily and strongly.
   Cym. Our expectation that it would be
    thus
Hath made us forward. But, my gentle
    queen,
Where is our daughter ? She hath not
    appear'd   30
Before the Roman, nor to us hath tender'd
The duty of the day. She looks us like
A thing more made of malice than of duty ;
We have noted it. Call her before us, for
We have been too slight in sufferance.
                [Exit a Messenger.
   Queen.   Royal sir.
Since the exile of Posthumus, most retir'd
Hath her life been ; the cure whereof, my
    lord,   37
'Tis time must do. Beseech your Majesty,
Forbear sharp speeches to her ; she's a lady
So tender of rebukes that words are strokes,
And strokes death to her.

      Re-enter Messenger.

   Cym.   Where is she, sir ? How
Can her contempt be answer'd ?
   Mess.   Please you, sir,
Her chambers are all lock'd, and there's no
    answer
That will be given to th' loud noise we
    make.
   Queen. My lord, when last I went to visit
    her,   45
She pray'd me to excuse her keeping close ;
Whereto constrain'd by her infirmity
She should that duty leave unpaid to you
Which daily she was bound to proffer. This
She wish'd me to make known ; but our
    great court   50
Made me to blame in memory.
   Cym.   Her doors lock'd ?
Not seen of late ? Grant, heavens, that
    which I fear
Prove false !   *[Exit.*
   Queen. Son, I say, follow the King.
   Clo. That man of hers, Pisanio, her old
    servant,   55
I have not seen these two days.
   Queen.   Go, look after.
                   [Exit Cloten.
Pisanio, thou that stand'st so for Posthu-
    mus !
He hath a drug of mine. I pray his absence
Proceed by swallowing that ; for he
    believes
It is a thing most precious. But for her, 60
Where is she gone ? Haply despair hath
    seiz'd her ;
Or, wing'd with fervour of her love, she's
    flown
To her desir'd Posthumus. Gone she is
To death or to dishonour, and my end
Can make good use of either. She being
    down,   65
I have the placing of the British crown.

Re-enter CLOTEN.

How now, my son ?

Clo.   'Tis certain she is fled.
Go in and cheer the King. He rages ; none
Dare come about him.

Queen.   All the better. May
This night forestall him of the coming day !
                                    [*Exit.*

Clo. I love and hate her ; for she's fair
  and royal,   71
And that she hath all courtly parts more
  exquisite
Than lady, ladies, woman. From every one
The best she hath, and she, of all com-
  pounded,   74
Outsells them all. I love her therefore ; but
Disdaining me and throwing favours on
The low Posthumus slanders so her judg-
  ment
That what's else rare is chok'd ; and in that
  point
I will conclude to hate her, nay, indeed,
To be reveng'd upon her. For when fools
Shall—   81

Enter PISANIO.

Who is here ? What, are you packing,
  sirrah ?
Come hither. Ah, you precious pander !
  Villain,
Where is thy lady ? In a word, or else
Thou art straightway with the fiends.

Pis.   O good my lord !

Clo. Where is thy lady ? or, by Jupiter—
I will not ask again. Close villain,   86
I'll have this secret from thy heart, or rip
Thy heart to find it. Is she with Posthu-
  mus ?
From whose so many weights of baseness
  cannot
A dram of worth be drawn.

Pis.   Alas, my lord,   90
How can she be with him ? When was she
  miss'd ?
He is in Rome.

Clo.   Where is she, sir ? Come nearer.
No farther halting ! Satisfy me home
What is become of her.

Pis. O my all-worthy lord !

Clo.   All-worthy villain !   95
Discover where thy mistress is at once,
At the next word. No more of ' worthy
  lord ' !
Speak, or thy silence on the instant is   98
Thy condemnation and thy death.

Pis.   Then, sir,
This paper is the history of my knowledge
Touching her flight. [*Presenting a letter.*

Clo.   Let's see't. I will pursue her
Even to Augustus' throne.

Pis. [*Aside*]   Or this or perish.
She's far enough ; and what he learns by
  this

May prove his travel, not her danger.

Clo.   Humh !

Pis. [*Aside*] I'll write to my lord she's
  dead. O Imogen,   105
Safe mayst thou wander, safe return again !

Clo. Sirrah, is this letter true ?

Pis. Sir, as I think.   108

Clo. It is Posthumus' hand ; I know't.
Sirrah, if thou wouldst not be a villain, but
do me true service, undergo those employ-
ments wherein I should have cause to use
thee with a serious industry—that is, what
villainy soe'er I bid thee do, to perform it
directly and truly—I would think thee an
honest man ; thou shouldst neither want
my means for thy relief nor my voice for
thy preferment.   116

Pis. Well, my good lord.

Clo. Wilt thou serve me ? For since
patiently and constantly thou hast stuck
to the bare fortune of that beggar Posthumus, thou canst not, in the course of
gratitude, but be a diligent follower of
mine. Wilt thou serve me ?   122

Pis. Sir, I will.

Clo. Give me thy hand ; here's my purse.
Hast any of thy late master's garments in
thy possession ?   125

Pis. I have, my lord, at my lodging, the
same suit he wore when he took leave of
my lady and mistress.

Clo. The first service thou dost me, fetch
that suit hither. Let it be thy first service ;
go.   129

Pis. I shall, my lord.   [*Exit.*

Clo. Meet thee at Milford Haven ! I
forgot to ask him one thing ; I'll remember't anon. Even there, thou villain
Posthumus, will I kill thee. I would these
garments were come. She said upon a time
—the bitterness of it I now belch from my
heart—that she held the very garment of
Posthumus in more respect than my noble
and natural person, together with the
adornment of my qualities. With that suit
upon my back will I ravish her ; first kill
him, and in her eyes. There shall she see
my valour, which will then be a torment
to her contempt. He on the ground, my
speech of insultment ended on his dead
body, and when my lust hath dined—
which, as I say, to vex her I will execute
in the clothes that she so prais'd—to the
court I'll knock her back, foot her home
again. She hath despis'd me rejoicingly,
and I'll be merry in my revenge.   146

Re-enter PISANIO, *with the clothes.*

Be those the garments ?

Pis. Ay, my noble lord.

Clo. How long is't since she went to
Milford Haven ?

Pis. She can scarce be there yet.   150

Clo. Bring this apparel to my chamber ;

that is the second thing that I have commanded thee. The third is that thou wilt
be a voluntary mute to my design. Be but
duteous and true, preferment shall tender
itself to thee. My revenge is now at
Milford; would I had wings to follow it!
Come, and be true.   [Exit.

Pis. Thou bid'st me to my loss; for
    true to thee
Were to prove false, which I will never be,
To him that is most true. To Milford go,
And find not her whom thou pursuest.
    Flow, flow,   160
You heavenly blessings, on her! This fool's
    speed
Be cross'd with slowness! Labour be his
    meed!   [Exit.

SCENE VI. *Wales. Before the cave of*
Belarius.

Enter IMOGEN *alone, in boy's clothes.*

Imo. I see a man's life is a tedious one.
I have tir'd myself, and for two nights
    together
Have made the ground my bed. I should
    be sick
But that my resolution helps me. Milford,
When from the mountain-top Pisanio
    show'd thee,   5
Thou wast within a ken. O Jove! I think
Foundations fly the wretched; such, I
    mean,
Where they should be reliev'd.   Two
    beggars told me
I could not miss my way. Will poor folks
    lie,   9
That have afflictions on them, knowing 'tis
A punishment or trial? Yes; no wonder,
When rich ones scarce tell true. To lapse in
    fulness
Is sorer than to lie for need; and falsehood
Is worse in kings than beggars. My dear
    lord!
Thou art one o' th' false ones. Now I think
    on thee   15
My hunger's gone; but even before, I was
At point to sink for food. But what is this?
Here is a path to't; 'tis some savage hold.
I were best not call; I dare not call. Yet
    famine,
Ere clean it o'erthrow nature, makes it
    valiant.   20
Plenty and peace breeds cowards; hard-
    ness ever
Of hardiness is mother. Ho! who's here?
If anything that's civil, speak; if savage,
Take or lend. Ho! No answer? Then I'll
    enter.   24
Best draw my sword; and if mine enemy
But fear the sword, like me, he'll scarcely
    look on't.
Such a foe, good heavens!
             [Exit into the cave.

Enter BELARIUS, GUIDERIUS, *and*
ARVIRAGUS.

Bel. You, Polydore, have prov'd best
    woodman and
Are master of the feast. Cadwal and I
Will play the cook and servant; 'tis our
    match.   30
The sweat of industry would dry and die
But for the end it works to. Come, our
    stomachs
Will make what's homely savoury; weari-
    ness
Can snore upon the flint, when resty sloth
Finds the down pillow hard. Now, peace
    be here,   35
Poor house, that keep'st thyself!
Gui.   I am throughly weary.
Arv. I am weak with toil, yet strong in
    appetite.
Gui. There is cold meat i' th' cave; we'll
    browse on that
Whilst what we have kill'd be cook'd.
Bel. [*Looking into the cave*] Stay, come
    not in.   39
But that it eats our victuals, I should think
Here were a fairy.
Gui.   What's the matter, sir?
Bel. By Jupiter, an angel! or, if not,
An earthly paragon! Behold diviness
No elder than a boy!

Re-enter IMOGEN.

Imo. Good masters, harm me not.   45
Before I enter'd here I call'd, and thought
To have begg'd or bought what I have
    took. Good troth,
I have stol'n nought; nor would not
    though I had found
Gold strew'd i' th' floor. Here's money for
    my meat.
I would have left it on the board, so soon   50
As I had made my meal, and parted
With pray'rs for the provider.
Gui.   Money, youth?
Arv. All gold and silver rather turn to
    dirt,
As 'tis no better reckon'd but of those   54
Who worship dirty gods.
Imo.   I see you're angry.
Know, if you kill me for my fault, I should
Have died had I not made it.
Bel.   Whither bound?
Imo. To Milford Haven.
Bel.   What's your name?
Imo. Fidele, sir. I have a kinsman who
Is bound for Italy; he embark'd at Mil-
    ford;   60
To whom being going, almost spent with
    hunger,
I am fall'n in this offence.
Bel.   Prithee, fair youth,
Think us no churls, nor measure our good
    minds

By this rude place we live in. Well en-
counter'd !   65
'Tis almost night ; you shall have better
cheer
Ere you depart, and thanks to stay and
eat it.
Boys, bid him welcome.
    Gui.   Were you a woman, youth,
I should woo hard but be your groom. In
honesty
I bid for you as I'd buy.
    Arv.   I'll make't my comfort   70
He is a man. I'll love him as my brother ;
And such a welcome as I'd give to him
After long absence, such is yours. Most
welcome !
Be sprightly, for you fall 'mongst friends.
    Imo.   'Mongst friends,
If brothers. [*Aside*] Would it had been so
that they   75
Had been my father's sons ! Then had my
prize
Been less, and so more equal ballasting
To thee, Posthumus.
    Bel. He wrings at some distress.
    Gui. Would I could free't !
    Arv.   Or I, whate'er it be,
What pain it cost, what danger ! Gods !
    Bel.   [*Whispering*] Hark, boys. 80
    Imo. [*Aside*] Great men,
That had a court no bigger than this cave,
That did attend themselves, and had the
virtue
Which their own conscience seal'd them,
laying by   84
That nothing-gift of differing multitudes,
Could not out-peer these twain. Pardon
me, gods !
I'd change my sex to be companion with
them,
Since Leonatus' false.
    Bel. It shall be so.
Boys, we'll go dress our hunt. Fair youth,
come in.
Discourse is heavy, fasting ; when we have
supp'd,   90
We'll mannerly demand thee of thy story,
So far as thou wilt speak it.
    Gui.   Pray draw near.
    Arv. The night to th' owl and morn to th'
lark less welcome.
    Imo. Thanks, sir.   94
    Arv.   I pray draw near.   [*Exeunt.*

SCENE VII. *Rome. A public place.*

Enter two Roman Senators *and* Tribunes.

    1 *Sen.* This is the tenour of the Emperor's
writ :
That since the common men are now in
action
'Gainst the Pannonians and Dalmatians,
And that the legions now in Gallia are
Full weak to undertake our wars against   5

The fall'n-off Britons, that we do incite
The gentry to this business. He creates
Lucius proconsul ; and to you, the
tribunes,
For this immediate levy, he commands   9
His absolute commission. Long live Cæsar !
    Tri. Is Lucius general of the forces ?
    2 *Sen.*   Ay.
    Tri. Remaining now in Gallia ?
    1 *Sen.*   With those legions
Which I have spoke of, whereunto your
levy
Must be supplyant. The words of your
commission
Will tie you to the numbers and the time   15
Of their dispatch.
    Tri.   We will discharge our duty.
                     [*Exeunt.*

ACT FOUR

SCENE I. *Wales. Near the cave of Belarius.*

Enter CLOTEN *alone.*

    Clo. I am near to th' place where they
should meet, if Pisanio have mapp'd it
truly. How fit his garments serve me ! Why
should his mistress, who was made by him
that made the tailor, not be fit too ? The
rather—saving reverence of the word—for
'tis said a woman's fitness comes by fits.
Therein I must play the workman. I dare
speak it to myself, for it is not vain-glory
for a man and his glass to confer in his own
chamber—I mean, the lines of my body
are as well drawn as his ; no less young,
more strong, not beneath him in fortunes,
beyond him in the advantage of the time,
above him in birth, alike conversant in
general services, and more remarkable in
single oppositions. Yet this imperceiverant
thing loves him in my despite. What
mortality is ! Posthumus, thy head, which
now is growing upon thy shoulders, shall
within this hour be off ; thy mistress enforced ; thy garments cut to pieces before
her face ; and all this done, spurn her
home to her father, who may, haply, be a
little angry for my so rough usage ; but
my mother, having power of his testiness,
shall turn all into my commendations. My
horse is tied up safe. Out, sword, and to a
sore purpose ! Fortune, put them into my
hand. This is the very description of their
meeting-place ; and the fellow dares not
deceive me.   [*Exit.*

SCENE II. *Wales. Before the cave of*
Belarius.

Enter, from the cave, BELARIUS, GUIDERIUS,
ARVIRAGUS, *and* IMOGEN.

    Bel. [*To Imogen*] You are not well.
Remain here in the cave ;
We'll come to you after hunting.

Arv. [*To Imogen*]   Brother, stay here.
Are we not brothers ?
Imo.   So man and man should be ;
But clay and clay differs in dignity,
Whose dust is both alike. I am very sick. 5
Gui. Go you to hunting ; I'll abide with
        him.
Imo. So sick I am not, yet I am not well ;
But not so citizen a wanton as
To seem to die ere sick. So please you, leave
        me ;
Stick to your journal course. The breach
        of custom   10
Is breach of all. I am ill, but your being
        by me
Cannot amend me ; society is no comfort
To one not sociable. I am not very sick,
Since I can reason of it. Pray you trust me
        here.
I'll rob none but myself ; and let me die, 15
Stealing so poorly.
Gui.   I love thee ; I have spoke it.
How much the quantity, the weight as
        much
As I do love my father.
Bel.   What ? how ? how ?
Arv. If it be sin to say so, sir, I yoke me
In my good brother's fault. I know not
        why   20
I love this youth, and I have heard you say
Love's reason's without reason. The bier
        at door,
And a demand who is't shall die, I'd say
' My father, not this youth '.
Bel. [*Aside*]   O noble strain !
O worthiness of nature ! breed of great-
        ness !   25
Cowards father cowards and base things
        sire base.
Nature hath meal and bran, contempt and
        grace.
I'm not their father ; yet who this should
        be
Doth miracle itself, lov'd before me.—
'Tis the ninth hour o' th' morn.
Arv. Brother, farewell.   30
Imo. I wish ye sport.
Arv. You health. [*To Belarius*] So please
        you, sir.
Imo. [*Aside*] These are kind creatures.
Gods, what lies I have heard !
Our courtiers say all's savage but at
        court.
Experience, O, thou disprov'st report !
Th' imperious seas breed monsters ; for the
        dish,   35
Poor tributary rivers as sweet fish.
I am sick still ; heart-sick. Pisanio,
I'll now taste of thy drug. [*Swallows some.*
Gui. I could not stir him.
He said he was gentle, but unfortunate ;
Dishonestly afflicted, but yet honest.   40
Arv. Thus did he answer me ; yet said
        hereafter

I might know more.
Bel.   To th' field, to th' field !
We'll leave you for this time. Go in and
        rest.
Arv. We'll not be long away.
Bel.   Pray be not sick,
For you must be our huswife.
Imo.   Well, or ill,   45
I am bound to you.
Bel.   And shalt be ever.
        [*Exit Imogen into the cave.*
This youth, howe'er distress'd, appears he
        hath had
Good ancestors.
Arv.   How angel-like he sings !
Gui. But his neat cookery ! He cut our
        roots in characters,   50
And sauc'd our broths as Juno had been
        sick,
And he her dieter.
Arv.   Nobly he yokes
A smiling with a sigh, as if the sigh
Was that it was for not being such a smile ;
The smile mocking the sigh that it would
        fly   55
From so divine a temple to commix
With winds that sailors rail at.
Gui.   I do note
That grief and patience, rooted in him both,
Mingle their spurs together.
Arv.   Grow patience !
And let the stinking elder, grief, untwine 60
His perishing root with the increasing vine !
Bel. It is great morning. Come, away !
        Who's there ?

        Enter CLOTEN.

Clo. I cannot find those runagates ; that
        villain
Hath mock'd me. I am faint.
Bel.   Those runagates ?
Means he not us ? I partly know him ; 'tis
Cloten, the son o' th' Queen. I fear some
        ambush.   66
I saw him not these many years, and yet
I know 'tis he. We are held as outlaws.
        Hence !
Gui. He is but one ; you and my brother
        search
What companies are near. Pray you away ;
Let me alone with him.
        [*Exeunt Belarius and Arviragus.*
Clo.   Soft ! What are you
That fly me thus ? Some villain moun-
        taineers ?
I have heard of such. What slave art thou ?
Gui.   A thing
More slavish did I ne'er than answering
' A slave ' without a knock.
Clo.   Thou art a robber,   75
A law-breaker, a villain. Yield thee, thief.
Gui. To who ? To thee ? What art
        thou ? Have not I
An arm as big as thine, a heart as big ?

Thy words, I grant, are bigger, for I wear
not
My dagger in my mouth. Say what thou
art;   80
Why I should yield to thee.
  Clo.   Thou villain base,
Know'st me not by my clothes?
  Gui.   No, nor thy tailor, rascal,
Who is thy grandfather; he made those
clothes,
Which, as it seems, make thee.
  Clo.   Thou precious varlet,
My tailor made them not.
  Gui.   Hence, then, and thank   85
The man that gave them thee. Thou art
some fool;
I am loath to beat thee.
  Clo.   Thou injurious thief,
Hear but my name, and tremble.
  Gui.   What's thy name?
  Clo. Cloten, thou villain.
  Gui. Cloten, thou double villain, be thy
name,   90
I cannot tremble at it. Were it toad, or
adder, spider,
'Twould move me sooner.
  Clo.   To thy further fear,
Nay, to thy mere confusion, thou shalt
know
I am son to th' Queen.
  Gui.   I'm sorry for't; not seeming
So worthy as thy birth.
  Clo.   Art not afeard?   95
  Gui. Those that I reverence, those I fear—
the wise:
At fools I laugh, not fear them.
  Clo.   Die the death.
When I have slain thee with my proper
hand,
I'll follow those that even now fled hence,
And on the gates of Lud's Town set your
heads.   100
Yield, rustic mountaineer.
                                   [Exeunt, fighting.

Re-enter BELARIUS and ARVIRAGUS.

  Bel. No company's abroad.
  Arv. None in the world; you did mistake
him, sure.
  Bel. I cannot tell; long is it since I saw
him,
But time hath nothing blurr'd those lines
of favour   105
Which then he wore; the snatches in his
voice,
And burst of speaking, were as his. I am
absolute
'Twas very Cloten.
  Arv.   In this place we left them.
I wish my brother make good time with
him,
You say he is so fell.
  Bel.   Being scarce made up,   110
I mean to man, he had not apprehension

Of roaring terrors; for defect of judgment
Is oft the cease of fear.

Re-enter GUIDERIUS with Cloten's head.

                         But, see, thy brother.
  Gui. This Cloten was a fool, an empty
purse;
There was no money in't. Not Hercules
Could have knock'd out his brains, for he
had none;   116
Yet I not doing this, the fool had borne
My head as I do his.
  Bel.   What hast thou done?
  Gui. I am perfect what: cut off one
Cloten's head,
Son to the Queen, after his own report;   120
Who call'd me traitor, mountaineer, and
swore
With his own single hand he'd take us in,
Displace our heads where—thank the
gods!—they grow,
And set them on Lud's Town.
  Bel.   We are all undone.
  Gui. Why, worthy father, what have we
to lose   125
But that he swore to take, our lives? The
law
Protects not us; then why should we be
tender
To let an arrogant piece of flesh threat us,
Play judge and executioner all himself,
For we do fear the law? What company
Discover you abroad?
  Bel.   No single soul   131
Can we set eye on, but in all safe reason
He must have some attendants. Though
his humour
Was nothing but mutation—ay, and that
From one bad thing to worse—not frenzy,
not   135
Absolute madness could so far have rav'd,
To bring him here alone. Although perhaps
It may be heard at court that such as we
Cave here, hunt here, are outlaws, and in
time
May make some stronger head—the which
he hearing,   140
As it is like him, might break out and
swear
He'd fetch us in; yet is't not probable
To come alone, either he so undertaking
Or they so suffering. Then on good ground
we fear,
If we do fear this body hath a tail   145
More perilous than the head.
  Arv.   Let ordinance
Come as the gods foresay it. Howsoe'er,
My brother hath done well.
  Bel.   I had no mind
To hunt this day; the boy Fidele's sickness
Did make my way long forth.
  Gui.   With his own sword,
Which he did wave against my throat, I
have ta'en   151

                                                              1223

His head from him. I'll throw't into the creek
Behind our rock, and let it to the sea
And tell the fishes he's the Queen's son, Cloten.
That's all I reck. [*Exit.*
Bel. I fear 'twill be reveng'd. 155
Would, Polydore, thou hadst not done't! though valour
Becomes thee well enough.
Arv. Would I had done't,
So the revenge alone pursu'd me! Polydore,
I love thee brotherly, but envy much
Thou hast robb'd me of this deed. I would revenges, 160
That possible strength might meet, would seek us through,
And put us to our answer.
Bel. Well, 'tis done.
We'll hunt no more to-day, nor seek for danger
Where there's no profit. I prithee to our rock. 164
You and Fidele play the cooks; I'll stay
Till hasty Polydore return, and bring him
To dinner presently.
Arv. Poor sick Fidele!
I'll willingly to him; to gain his colour
I'd let a parish of such Clotens' blood,
And praise myself for charity. [*Exit.*
Bel. O thou goddess, 170
Thou divine Nature, thou thyself thou blazon'st
In these two princely boys! They are as gentle
As zephyrs blowing below the violet,
Not wagging his sweet head; and yet as rough,
Their royal blood enchaf'd, as the rud'st wind 175
That by the top doth take the mountain pine
And make him stoop to th' vale. 'Tis wonder
That an invisible instinct should frame them
To royalty unlearn'd, honour untaught,
Civility not seen from other, valour 180
That wildly grows in them, but yields a crop
As if it had been sow'd. Yet still it's strange
What Cloten's being here to us portends,
Or what his death will bring us.

Re-enter GUIDERIUS.

Gui. Where's my brother?
I have sent Cloten's clotpoll down the stream, 185
In embassy to his mother; his body's hostage
For his return. [*Solemn music.*
Bel. My ingenious instrument!

Hark, Polydore, it sounds. But what occasion
Hath Cadwal now to give it motion? Hark!
Gui. Is he at home?
Bel. He went hence even now. 190
Gui. What does he mean? Since death of my dear'st mother
It did not speak before. All solemn things
Should answer solemn accidents. The matter?
Triumphs for nothing and lamenting toys
Is jollity for apes and grief for boys. 195
Is Cadwal mad?

Re-enter ARVIRAGUS, *with* IMOGEN *as dead, bearing her in his arms.*

Bel. Look, here he comes,
And brings the dire occasion in his arms
Of what we blame him for!
Arv. The bird is dead
That we have made so much on. I had rather
Have skipp'd from sixteen years of age to sixty, 200
To have turn'd my leaping time into a crutch,
Than have seen this.
Gui. O sweetest, fairest lily!
My brother wears thee not the one half so well
As when thou grew'st thyself.
Bel. O melancholy!
Who ever yet could sound thy bottom? find 205
The ooze to show what coast thy sluggish crare
Might'st easiliest harbour in? Thou blessed thing!
Jove knows what man thou mightst have made; but I,
Thou diedst, a most rare boy, of melancholy.
How found you him?
Arv. Stark, as you see; 210
Thus smiling, as some fly had tickled slumber,
Not as death's dart, being laugh'd at; his right cheek
Reposing on a cushion.
Gui. Where?
Arv. O' th' floor;
His arms thus leagu'd. I thought he slept, and put
My clouted brogues from off my feet, whose rudeness 215
Answer'd my steps too loud.
Gui. Why, he but sleeps.
If he be gone he'll make his grave a bed;
With female fairies will his tomb be haunted,
And worms will not come to thee.
Arv. With fairest flowers,
Whilst summer lasts and I live here, Fidele,

I'll sweeten thy sad grave. Thou shalt not
    lack   221
The flower that's like thy face, pale
    primrose ; nor
The azur'd hare-bell, like thy veins ; no, nor
The leaf of eglantine, whom not to slander,
Out-sweet'ned not thy breath. The rud-
    dock would,   225
With charitable bill—O bill, sore shaming
Those rich-left heirs that let their fathers
    lie
Without a monument !—bring thee all this ;
Yea, and furr'd moss besides, when flow'rs
    are none,
To winter-ground thy corse—
    Gui.   Prithee have done, 230
And do not play in wench-like words with
    that
Which is so serious. Let us bury him,
And not protract with admiration what
Is now due debt. To th' grave.
    Arv.   Say, where shall's lay him ?
    Gui. By good Euriphile, our mother.
    Arv.   Be't so ;
And let us, Polydore, though now our
    voices   236
Have got the mannish crack, sing him to
    th' ground,
As once to our mother ; use like note and
    words,
Save that Euriphile must be Fidele.
    Gui. Cadwal,   240
I cannot sing. I'll weep, and word it with
    thee ;
For notes of sorrow out of tune are worse
Than priests and fanes that lie.
    Arv.   We'll speak it, then.
    Bel. Great griefs, I see, med'cine the less,
    for Cloten
Is quite forgot. He was a queen's son,
    boys ;   245
And though he came our enemy, remember
He was paid for that. Though mean and
    mighty rotting
Together have one dust, yet reverence—
That angel of the world—doth make
    distinction
Of place 'tween high and low. Our foe was
    princely ;   250
And though you took his life, as being our
    foe,
Yet bury him as a prince.
    Gui.   Pray you fetch him hither.
Thersites' body is as good as Ajax',
When neither are alive.
    Arv.   If you'll go fetch him,
We'll say our song the whilst. Brother,
    begin.   [*Exit Belarius.*
    Gui. Nay, Cadwal, we must lay his head
    to th' East ;   256
My father hath a reason for't.
    Arv.   'Tis true.
    Gui. Come on, then, and remove him.
    Arv.   So. Begin.

                  Song.
  Gui. Fear no more the heat o' th' sun
    Nor the furious winter's rages ; 260
  Thou thy worldly task hast done,
    Home art gone, and ta'en thy
    wages.
  Golden lads and girls all must,
    As chimney-sweepers, come to dust.

  Arv. Fear no more the frown o' th' great ;
    Thou art past the tyrant's stroke.
  Care no more to clothe and eat ;
    To thee the reed is as the oak.
  The sceptre, learning, physic, must
  All follow this and come to dust. 270

  Gui. Fear no more the lightning flash,
  Arv.   Nor th' all-dreaded thunder-stone ;
  Gui. Fear not slander, censure rash ;
  Arv. Thou hast finish'd joy and moan.
  Both. All lovers young, all lovers must 275
  Consign to thee and come to dust.

  Gui. No exorciser harm thee !
  Arv. Nor no witchcraft charm thee !
  Gui. Ghost unlaid forbear thee !
  Arv. Nothing ill come near thee ! 280
  Both. Quiet consummation have,
  And renowned be thy grave !

Re-enter BELARIUS *with the body of Cloten.*

  Gui. We have done our obsequies. Come,
    lay him down.
  Bel. Here's a few flowers ; but 'bout
    midnight, more.
The herbs that have on them cold dew o'
    th' night   285
Are strewings fit'st for graves. Upon their
    faces.
You were as flow'rs, now wither'd. Even so
These herblets shall which we upon you
    strew.
Come on, away. Apart upon our knees.
The ground that gave them first has them
    again.   290
Their pleasures here are past, so is their
    pain.   [*Exeunt all but Imogen.*
  Imo. [*Awaking*] Yes, sir, to Milford
    Haven. Which is the way ?
I thank you. By yond bush ? Pray, how
    far thither ?
'Ods pittikins ! can it be six mile yet ?
I have gone all night. Faith, I'll lie down
    and sleep.   295
But, soft ! no bedfellow. O gods and god-
    desses !   [*Seeing the body.*
These flow'rs are like the pleasures of the
    world ;
This bloody man, the care on't. I hope I
    dream ;
For so I thought I was a cave-keeper,
And cook to honest creatures. But 'tis not
    so ;   300
'Twas but a bolt of nothing, shot at
    nothing,

Which the brain makes of fumes. Our very
    eyes
Are sometimes, like our judgments, blind.
    Good faith,
I tremble still with fear ; but if there be
Yet left in heaven as small a drop of
    pity
As a wren's eye, fear'd gods, a part of it !
The dream's here still. Even when I wake
    it is
Without me, as within me ; not imagin'd,
    felt.
A headless man ? The garments of
    Posthumus ? 309
I know the shape of's leg ; this is his hand,
His foot Mercurial, his Martial thigh,
The brawns of Hercules ; but his Jovial
    face—
Murder in heaven ! How ! 'Tis gone.
    Pisanio,
All curses madded Hecuba gave the Greeks,
And mine to boot, be darted on thee !
    Thou, 315
Conspir'd with that irregulous devil,
    Cloten,
Hath here cut off my lord. To write and
    read
Be henceforth treacherous ! Damn'd
    Pisanio
Hath with his forged letters—damn'd
    Pisanio— 319
From this most bravest vessel of the world
Struck the main-top. O Posthumus ! alas,
Where is thy head ? Where's that ? Ay me !
    where's that ?
Pisanio might have kill'd thee at the heart,
And left this head on. How should this be ?
    Pisanio ?
'Tis he and Cloten ; malice and lucre in
    them 325
Have laid this woe here. O, 'tis pregnant,
    pregnant !
The drug he gave me, which he said was
    precious
And cordial to me, have I not found it
Murd'rous to th' senses ? That confirms it
    home. 329
This is Pisanio's deed, and Cloten. O !
Give colour to my pale cheek with thy
    blood,
That we the horrider may seem to those
Which chance to find us. O, my lord, my
    lord ! [*Falls fainting on the body.*

Enter LUCIUS, *Captains, and a* Soothsayer.

  Cap. To them the legions garrison'd in
    Gallia,
After your will, have cross'd the sea,
    attending 335
You here at Milford Haven ; with your ships,
They are in readiness.
  Luc. But what from Rome ?
  Cap. The Senate hath stirr'd up the
    confiners

And gentlemen of Italy, most willing
    spirits, 339
That promise noble service ; and they
    come
Under the conduct of bold Iachimo,
Sienna's brother.
  Luc. When expect you them ?
  Cap. With the next benefit o' th' wind.
  Luc. This forwardness
Makes our hopes fair. Command our pres-
    ent numbers
Be muster'd ; bid the captains look to't.
    Now, sir, 345
What have you dream'd of late of this war's
    purpose ?
  Sooth. Last night the very gods show'd
    me a vision—
I fast and pray'd for their intelligence—
    thus :
I saw Jove's bird, the Roman eagle, wing'd
From the spongy south to this part of the
    west, 350
There vanish'd in the sunbeams ; which
    portends,
Unless my sins abuse my divination,
Success to th' Roman host.
  Luc. Dream often so,
And never false. Soft, ho ! what trunk is
    here
Without his top ? The ruin speaks that
    sometime 355
It was a worthy building. How ? a page ?
Or dead or sleeping on him ? But dead,
    rather ;
For nature doth abhor to make his bed
With the defunct, or sleep upon the dead.
Let's see the boy's face.
  Cap. He's alive, my lord. 360
  Luc. He'll then instruct us of this body.
    Young one,
Inform us of thy fortunes ; for it seems
They crave to be demanded. Who is this
Thou mak'st thy bloody pillow ? Or who
    was he
That, otherwise than noble nature did, 365
Hath alter'd that good picture ? What's
    thy interest
In this sad wreck ? How came't ? Who
    is't ? What art thou ?
  Imo. I am nothing ; or if not,
Nothing to be were better. This was my
    master,
A very valiant Briton and a good, 370
That here by mountaineers lies slain. Alas !
There is no more such masters. I may
    wander
From east to occident ; cry out for service ;
Try many, all good ; serve truly ; never
Find such another master.
  Luc. 'Lack, good youth ! 375
Thou mov'st no less with thy complaining
    than
Thy master in bleeding. Say his name,
    good friend.

Imo. Richard du Champ. [*Aside*] If I do lie, and do   378
No harm by it, though the gods hear, I hope
They'll pardon it.—Say you, sir ?
    Luc.   Thy name ?
    Imo.   Fidele, sir.
    Luc. Thou dost approve thyself the very same ;
Thy name well fits thy faith, thy faith thy name.
Wilt take thy chance with me ?   I will not say   385
Thou shalt be so well master'd ; but, be sure,
No less belov'd.   The Roman Emperor's letters,
Sent by a consul to me, should not sooner
Than thine own worth prefer thee.   Go with me.
    Imo. I'll follow, sir. But first, an't please the gods,   390
I'll hide my master from the flies, as deep
As these poor pickaxes can dig ; and when
With wild wood-leaves and weeds I ha' strew'd his grave,
And on it said a century of prayers,
Such as I can, twice o'er, I'll weep and sigh ;
And leaving so his service, follow you,   396
So please you entertain me.
    Luc.   Ay, good youth ;
And rather father thee than master thee.
My friends,
The boy hath taught us manly duties ; let us   400
Find out the prettiest daisied plot we can,
And make him with our pikes and partisans
A grave. Come, arm him. Boy, he is preferr'd
By thee to us ; and he shall be interr'd
As soldiers can. Be cheerful ; wipe thine eyes.   405
Some falls are means the happier to arise.
                                    [*Exeunt.*

SCENE III.   *Britain. Cymbeline's palace.*

Enter CYMBELINE, *Lords,* PISANIO, *and* Attendants.

    Cym. Again ! and bring me word how 'tis with her.   [*Exit an Attendant.*
A fever with the absence of her son ;
A madness, of which her life's in danger. Heavens,
How deeply you at once do touch me ! Imogen,
The great part of my comfort, gone ; my queen   5
Upon a desperate bed, and in a time
When fearful wars point at me ; her son gone,
So needful for this present. It strikes me past
The hope of comfort. But for thee, fellow,
Who needs must know of her departure and   10
Dost seem so ignorant, we'll enforce it from thee
By a sharp torture.
    Pis.   Sir, my life is yours ;
I humbly set it at your will ; but for my mistress,
I nothing know where she remains, why gone,
Nor when she purposes return.   Beseech your Highness,   15
Hold me your loyal servant.
    Lord.   Good my liege,
The day that she was missing he was here.
I dare be bound he's true and shall perform
All parts of his subjection loyally.   For Cloten,   19
There wants no diligence in seeking him,
And will no doubt be found.
    Cym.   The time is troublesome.
[*To Pisanio*] We'll slip you for a season ; but our jealousy
Does yet depend.
    Lord.   So please your Majesty,
The Roman legions, all from Gallia drawn,
Are landed on your coast, with a supply   25
Of Roman gentlemen by the Senate sent.
    Cym. Now for the counsel of my son and queen !
I am amaz'd with matter.
    Lord.   Good my liege,
Your preparation can affront no less
Than what you hear of.   Come more, for more you're ready.   30
The want is but to put those pow'rs in motion
That long to move.
    Cym.   I thank you. Let's withdraw,
And meet the time as it seeks us. We fear not
What can from Italy annoy us ; but
We grieve at chances here.   Away !   35
                        [*Exeunt all but Pisanio.*
    Pis. I heard no letter from my master since
I wrote him Imogen was slain. 'Tis strange.
Nor hear I from my mistress, who did promise
To yield me often tidings. Neither know I
What is betid to Cloten, but remain   40
Perplex'd in all.   The heavens still must work.
Wherein I am false I am honest ; not true, to be true.
These present wars shall find I love my country,
Even to the note o' th' King, or I'll fall in them.
All other doubts, by time let them be clear'd :   45
Fortune brings in some boats that are not steer'd.   [*Exit.*

SCENE IV. *Wales. Before the cave of Belarius.*

Enter BELARIUS, GUIDERIUS, *and* ARVIRAGUS.

Gui. The noise is round about us.
Bel.   Let us from it.
Arv. What pleasure, sir, find we in life,
    to lock it
From action and adventure?
Gui.   Nay, what hope
Have we in hiding us? This way the Romans
Must or for Britons slay us, or receive us 5
For barbarous and unnatural revolts
During their use, and slay us after.
Bel.   Sons,
We'll higher to the mountains; there secure us.
To the King's party there's no going. Newness
Of Cloten's death—we being not known, not muster'd 10
Among the bands—may drive us to a render
Where we have liv'd, and so extort from's that
Which we have done, whose answer would be death,
Drawn on with torture.
Gui.   This is, sir, a doubt
In such a time nothing becoming you 15
Nor satisfying us.
Arv.   It is not likely
That when they hear the Roman horses neigh,
Behold their quarter'd fires, have both their eyes
And ears so cloy'd importantly as now,
That they will waste their time upon our note, 20
To know from whence we are.
Bel.   O, I am known
Of many in the army. Many years,
Though Cloten then but young, you see, not wore him
From my remembrance. And, besides, the King
Hath not deserv'd my service nor your loves, 25
Who find in my exile the want of breeding,
The certainty of this hard life; aye hopeless
To have the courtesy your cradle promis'd,
But to be still hot summer's tanlings and
The shrinking slaves of winter.
Gui.   Than be so, 30
Better to cease to be. Pray, sir, to th' army.
I and my brother are not known; yourself
So out of thought, and thereto so o'ergrown,
Cannot be question'd.
Arv.   By this sun that shines,

I'll thither. What thing is't that I never 35
Did see man die! scarce ever look'd on blood
But that of coward hares, hot goats, and venison!
Never bestrid a horse, save one that had
A rider like myself, who ne'er wore rowel
Nor iron on his heel! I am asham'd 40
To look upon the holy sun, to have
The benefit of his blest beams, remaining
So long a poor unknown.
Gui.   By heavens, I'll go!
If you will bless me, sir, and give me leave,
I'll take the better care; but if you will not, 45
The hazard therefore due fall on me by
The hands of Romans!
Arv.   So say I. Amen.
Bel. No reason I, since of your lives you set
So slight a valuation, should reserve
My crack'd one to more care. Have with you, boys! 50
If in your country wars you chance to die,
That is my bed too, lads, and there I'll lie.
Lead, lead. [*Aside*] The time seems long; their blood thinks scorn
Till it fly out and show them princes born.
                                  [*Exeunt.*

ACT FIVE

SCENE I. *Britain. The Roman camp.*

Enter POSTHUMUS *alone, with a bloody handkerchief.*

Post. Yea, bloody cloth, I'll keep thee; for I wish'd
Thou shouldst be colour'd thus. You married ones,
If each of you should take this course, how many
Must murder wives much better than themselves
For wrying but a little! O Pisanio! 5
Every good servant does not all commands;
No bond but to do just ones. Gods! if you
Should have ta'en vengeance on my faults, I never
Had liv'd to put on this; so had you saved
The noble Imogen to repent, and struck 10
Me, wretch more worth your vengeance. But alack,
You snatch some hence for little faults; that's love,
To have them fall no more. You some permit
To second ills with ills, each elder worse,
And make them dread it, to the doers' thrift. 15
But Imogen is your own. Do your best wills,
And make me blest to obey. I am brought hither
Among th' Italian gentry, and to fight

Against my lady's kingdom. 'Tis enough
That, Britain, I have kill'd thy mistress;
    peace!   20
I'll give no wound to thee. Therefore, good
    heavens,
Hear patiently my purpose. I'll disrobe me
Of these Italian weeds, and suit myself
As does a Britain peasant. So I'll fight
Against the part I come with; so I'll die   25
For thee, O Imogen, even for whom my life
Is every breath a death. And thus un-
    known,
Pitied nor hated, to the face of peril
Myself I'll dedicate. Let me make men
    know
More valour in me than my habits show.   30
Gods, put the strength o' th' Leonati in me!
To shame the guise o' th' world, I will begin
The fashion—less without and more
    within.   [Exit.

SCENE II. *Britain. A field of battle between
    the British and Roman camps.*

Enter LUCIUS, IACHIMO, *and the* Roman
    Army *at one door, and the* Britain Army
    at another, LEONATUS POSTHUMUS *follow-
    ing like a poor soldier. They march over
    and go out. Alarums. Then enter again,
    in skirmish,* IACHIMO *and* POSTHUMUS.
    *He vanquisheth and disarmeth Iachimo,
    and then leaves him.*

Iach. The heaviness and guilt within my
    bosom
Takes off my manhood. I have belied a
    lady,
The Princess of this country, and the air
    on't
Revengingly enfeebles me; or could this
    carl,   4
A very drudge of nature's, have subdu'd me
In my profession? Knighthoods and
    honours borne
As I wear mine are titles but of scorn.
If that thy gentry, Britain, go before
This lout as he exceeds our lords, the odds
Is that we scarce are men, and you are
    gods.   [Exit.

The battle continues; the Britons *fly;* CYM-
BELINE *is taken. Then enter to his rescue*
BELARIUS, GUIDERIUS, *and* ARVIRAGUS.

Bel. Stand, stand! We have th' ad-
    vantage of the ground;   11
The lane is guarded; nothing routs us but
The villainy of our fears.
    Gui. and Arv. Stand, stand, and fight!

Re-enter POSTHUMUS, *and seconds the*
    Britons; *they rescue Cymbeline, and
    exeunt. Then re-enter* LUCIUS *and*
    IACHIMO, *with* IMOGEN.

Luc. Away, boy, from the troops, and
    save thyself;

For friends kill friends, and the disorder's
    such   15
As war were hoodwink'd.
    Iach.   'Tis their fresh supplies.
    Luc. It is a day turn'd strangely. Or
    betimes
Let's reinforce or fly.   [Exeunt.

SCENE III. *Another part of the field.*

Enter POSTHUMUS *and a* Britain Lord.

Lord. Cam'st thou from where they made
    the stand?
    Post.   I did:
Though you, it seems, come from the fliers.
    Lord.   I did.
    Post. No blame be to you, sir, for all was
    lost,
But that the heavens fought. The King
    himself
Of his wings destitute, the army broken, 5
And but the backs of Britons seen, all
    flying,
Through a straight lane—the enemy, full-
    hearted,
Lolling the tongue with slaught'ring, hav-
    ing work
More plentiful than tools to do't, struck
    down
Some mortally, some slightly touch'd, some
    falling   10
Merely through fear, that the strait path
    was damm'd
With dead men hurt behind, and cowards
    living
To die with length'ned shame.
    Lord.   Where was this lane?
    Post. Close by the battle, ditch'd, and
    wall'd with turf,
Which gave advantage to an ancient
    soldier—   15
An honest one, I warrant, who deserv'd
So long a breeding as his white beard came
    to,
In doing this for's country. Athwart the
    lane
He, with two striplings—lads more like to
    run
The country base than to commit such
    slaughter;   20
With faces fit for masks, or rather fairer
Than those for preservation cas'd or
    shame—
Made good the passage, cried to those that
    fled
' Our Britain's harts die flying, not our
    men.
To darkness fleet souls that fly backwards!
    Stand;   25
Or we are Romans and will give you that,
Like beasts, which you shun beastly, and
    may save
But to look back in frown. Stand, stand!'
    These three,

Three thousand confident, in act as many—
For three performers are the file when all 30
The rest do nothing—with this word
   ' Stand, stand ! '
Accommodated by the place, more charm-
   ing
With their own nobleness, which could
   have turn'd
A distaff to a lance, gilded pale looks,
Part shame, part spirit renew'd ; that some
   turn'd coward 35
But by example—O, a sin in war
Damn'd in the first beginners !—gan to
   look
The way that they did and to grin like
   lions
Upon the pikes o' th' hunters. Then began
A stop i' th' chaser, a retire ; anon 40
A rout, confusion thick. Forthwith they
   fly,
Chickens, the way which they stoop'd
   eagles ; slaves,
The strides they victors made ; and now
   our cowards,
Like fragments in hard voyages, became
The life o' th' need. Having found the
   back-door open 45
Of the unguarded hearts, heavens, how
   they wound !
Some slain before, some dying, some their
   friends
O'erborne i' th' former wave. Ten chas'd
   by one
Are now each one the slaughterman of
   twenty.
Those that would die or ere resist are
   grown 50
The mortal bugs o' th' field.
   Lord. This was strange chance :
A narrow lane, an old man, and two boys.
   Post. Nay, do not wonder at it ; you are
   made 53
Rather to wonder at the things you hear
Than to work any. Will you rhyme upon't,
And vent it for a mock'ry ? Here is one :
' Two boys, an old man (twice a boy), a
   lane,
Preserv'd the Britons, was the Romans'
   bane'.
   Lord. Nay, be not angry, sir.
   Post. 'Lack, to what end ?
Who dares not stand his foe I'll be his
   friend ; 60
For if he'll do as he is made to do,
I know he'll quickly fly my friendship too.
You have put me into rhyme.
   Lord. Farewell ; you're angry.
                      [*Exit.*
   Post. Still going ? This is a lord ! O
   noble misery,
To be i' th' field and ask ' What news ? ' of
   me ! 65
To-day how many would have given their
   honours

To have sav'd their carcasses ! took heel
   to do't,
And yet died too ! I, in mine own woe
   charm'd,
Could not find death where I did hear him
   groan,
Nor feel him where he struck. Being an
   ugly monster, 70
'Tis strange he hides him in fresh cups, soft
   beds,
Sweet words ; or hath moe ministers than
   we
That draw his knives i' th' war. Well, I
   will find him ;
For being now a favourer to the Briton,
No more a Briton, I have resum'd again 75
The part I came in. Fight I will no more,
But yield me to the veriest hind that shall
Once touch my shoulder. Great the
   slaughter is
Here made by th' Roman ; great the
   answer be
Britons must take. For me, my ransom's
   death ; 80
On either side I come to spend my breath,
Which neither here I'll keep nor bear
   again,
But end it by some means for Imogen.

Enter two British Captains *and* Soldiers.

   1 *Cap.* Great Jupiter be prais'd ! Lucius
   is taken.
'Tis thought the old man and his sons were
   angels. 85
   2 *Cap.* There was a fourth man, in a silly
   habit,
That gave th' affront with them.
   1 *Cap.* So 'tis reported ;
But none of 'em can be found. Stand !
   who's there ?
   Post. A Roman,
Who had not now been drooping here if
   seconds 90
Had answer'd him.
   2 *Cap.* Lay hands on him ; a dog !
A leg of Rome shall not return to tell
What crows have peck'd them here. He
   brags his service,
As if he were of note. Bring him to th'
   King.

Enter CYMBELINE, BELARIUS, GUIDERIUS,
ARVIRAGUS, PISANIO, *and* Roman Captives. *The Captains present Posthumus
to Cymbeline, who delivers him over to a
Gaoler. Exeunt omnes.*

       SCENE IV. *Britain. A prison.*

    Enter POSTHUMUS *and two* Gaolers.

   1 *Gaol.* You shall not now be stol'n, you
   have locks upon you ;
So graze as you find pasture.

2 *Gaol.*   Ay, or a stomach.
Post. Most welcome, bondage ! for thou
        art a way,
I think, to liberty. Yet am I better
Than one that's sick o' th' gout, since he
        had rather   5
Groan so in perpetuity than be cur'd
By th' sure physician death, who is the key
T' unbar these locks. My conscience, thou
        art fetter'd
More than my shanks and wrists ; you good
        gods, give me   9
The penitent instrument to pick that bolt,
Then, free for ever ! Is't enough I am
        sorry ?
So children temporal fathers do appease ;
Gods are more full of mercy. Must I
        repent,
I cannot do it better than in gyves,   14
Desir'd more than constrain'd. To satisfy,
If of my freedom 'tis the main part, take
No stricter render of me than my all.
I know you are more clement than vile
        men,   18
Who of their broken debtors take a third,
A sixth, a tenth, letting them thrive again
On their abatement ; that's not my desire.
For Imogen's dear life take mine ; and
        though
'Tis not so dear, yet 'tis a life ; you coin'd
        it.
'Tween man and man they weigh not every
        stamp ;
Though light, take pieces for the figure's
        sake ;   25
You rather mine, being yours. And so,
        great pow'rs,
If you will take this audit, take this life,
And cancel these cold bonds. O Imogen !
I'll speak to thee in silence.   [*Sleeps.*

Solemn Music. Enter, as in an apparition,
SICILIUS LEONATUS, *father to Posthumus,
an old man attired like a warrior ; leading
in his hand an ancient matron, his Wife,
and mother to Posthumus, with music
before them. Then, after other music,
follows the two young* LEONATI, *brothers
to Posthumus, with wounds, as they died
in the wars. They circle Posthumus round
as he lies sleeping.*

Sici. No more, thou thunder-master,
        show   30
        Thy spite on mortal flies.
With Mars fall out, with Juno chide,
        That thy adulteries
        Rates and revenges.
Hath my poor boy done aught but well, 35
        Whose face I never saw ?
I died whilst in the womb he stay'd
        Attending nature's law ;
Whose father then, as men report
        Thou orphans' father art,   40

Thou shouldst have been, and shielded him
        From this earth-vexing smart.
Mother. Lucina lent not me her aid,
        But took me in my throes,
That from me was Posthumus ripp'd,   43
        Came crying 'mongst his foes,
        A thing of pity.
Sici. Great Nature like his ancestry
        Moulded the stuff so fair
That he deserv'd the praise o' th' world 50
        As great Sicilius' heir.
1 *Bro.* When once he was mature for man,
        In Britain where was he
That could stand up his parallel,
        Or fruitful object be   55
In eye of Imogen, that best
        Could deem his dignity ?
Mother. With marriage wherefore was he
        mock'd,
        To be exil'd and thrown
From Leonati seat and cast   60
        From her his dearest one,
        Sweet Imogen ?
Sici. Why did you suffer Iachimo,
        Slight thing of Italy,
To taint his nobler heart and brain   65
        With needless jealousy,
And to become the geeck and scorn
        O' th' other's villainy ?
2 *Bro.* For this from stiller seats we came,
        Our parents and us twain,   70
That, striking in our country's cause,
        Fell bravely and were slain,
Our fealty and Tenantius' right
        With honour to maintain.
1 *Bro.* Like hardiment Posthumus hath
        To Cymbeline perform'd.   76
Then, Jupiter, thou king of gods,
        Why hast thou thus adjourn'd
The graces for his merits due,
        Being all to dolours turn'd ?   80
Sici. Thy crystal window ope ; look out ;
        No longer exercise
Upon a valiant race thy harsh
        And potent injuries.
Mother. Since, Jupiter, our son is good,
        Take off his miseries.   86
Sici. Peep through thy marble mansion.
        Help !
        Or we poor ghosts will cry
To th' shining synod of the rest
        Against thy deity.   90
Brothers. Help, Jupiter ! or we appeal,
        And from thy justice fly.

JUPITER *descends in thunder and lightning,
sitting upon an eagle. He throws a
thunderbolt. The Ghosts fall on their
knees.*

Jup. No more, you petty spirits of region low,
Offend our hearing ; hush ! How dare you ghosts   94
Accuse the Thunderer whose bolt, you know,
Sky-planted, batters all rebelling coasts ?
Poor shadows of Elysium, hence, and rest
Upon your never-withering banks of flow'rs.
Be not with mortal accidents opprest :   99
No care of yours it is ; you know 'tis ours.
Whom best I love I cross ; to make my gift,
The more delay'd, delighted. Be content ;
Your low-laid son our godhead will uplift ;
His comforts thrive, his trials well are spent.   104
Our Jovial star reign'd at his birth, and in
Our temple was he married. Rise, and fade !
He shall be lord of Lady Imogen,
And happier much by his affliction made.
This tablet lay upon his breast, wherein
Our pleasure his full fortune doth confine ;
And so, away ; no farther with your din
Express impatience, lest you stir up mine.
Mount, eagle, to my palace crystalline.
                                        [*Ascends.*
Sici. He came in thunder ; his celestial breath   114
Was sulphurous to smell ; the holy eagle
Stoop'd, as to foot us. His ascension is
More sweet than our blest fields. His royal bird
Prunes the immortal wing, and cloys his beak,
As when his god is pleas'd.
All.   Thanks, Jupiter !
Sici. The marble pavement closes, he is enter'd   120
His radiant roof. Away ! and, to be blest,
Let us with care perform his great behest.
                                        [*Ghosts vanish.*
Post. [*Waking*] Sleep, thou hast been a grandsire and begot
A father to me ; and thou hast created
A mother and two brothers. But, O scorn,
Gone ! They went hence so soon as they were born.   126
And so I am awake. Poor wretches, that depend
On greatness' favour, dream as I have done ;
Wake and find nothing. But, alas, I swerve ;
Many dream not to find, neither deserve,
And yet are steep'd in favours ; so am I,
That have this golden chance, and know not why.   132
What fairies haunt this ground ? A book ? O rare one !
Be not, as is our fangled world, a garment
Nobler than that it covers. Let thy effects
So follow to be most unlike our courtiers,
As good as promise.   137

[*Reads*] ' When as a lion's whelp shall, to himself unknown, without seeking find, and be embrac'd by a piece of tender air ; and when from a stately cedar shall be lopp'd branches which, being dead many years, shall after revive, be jointed to the old stock, and freshly grow ; then shall Posthumus end his miseries, Britain be fortunate and flourish in peace and plenty.'

'Tis still a dream, or else such stuff as madmen
Tongue, and brain not ; either both or nothing,   145
Or senseless speaking, or a speaking such
As sense cannot untie. Be what it is,
The action of my life is like it, which
I'll keep, if but for sympathy.

Re-enter Gaoler.

Gaol. Come, sir, are you ready for death ?
Post. Over-roasted rather ; ready long ago.   151
Gaol. Hanging is the word, sir ; if you be ready for that, you are well cook'd.
Post. So, if I prove a good repast to the spectators, the dish pays the shot.   155
Gaol. A heavy reckoning for you, sir. But the comfort is, you shall be called to no more payments, fear no more tavern bills, which are often the sadness of parting, as the procuring of mirth. You come in faint for want of meat, depart reeling with too much drink ; sorry that you have paid too much, and sorry that you are paid too much ; purse and brain both empty ; the brain the heavier for being too light, the purse too light, being drawn of heaviness. O, of this contradiction you shall now be quit. O, the charity of a penny cord ! It sums up thousands in a trice. You have no true debitor and creditor but it ; of what's past, is, and to come, the discharge. Your neck, sir, is pen, book, and counters ; so the acquittance follows.
Post. I am merrier to die than thou art to live.   170
Gaol. Indeed, sir, he that sleeps feels not the toothache. But a man that were to sleep your sleep, and a hangman to help him to bed, I think he would change places with his officer ; for look you, sir, you know not which way you shall go.   175
Post. Yes indeed do I, fellow.
Gaol. Your death has eyes in's head, then ; I have not seen him so pictur'd. You must either be directed by some that take upon them to know, or to take upon yourself that which I am sure you do not know, or jump the after-inquiry on your own peril. And how you shall speed in your journey's end, I think you'll never return to tell one.
Post. I tell thee, fellow, there are none want eyes to direct them the way I am

going, but such as wink and will not use
them.　　　　　　　　　　　　　　186

Gaol. What an infinite mock is this, that
a man should have the best use of eyes to
see the way of blindness ! I am sure
hanging's the way of winking.

Enter a Messenger.

Mess. Knock off his manacles ; bring
your prisoner to the King.　　　　　191

Post. Thou bring'st good news : I am
call'd to be made free.

Gaol. I'll be hang'd, then.

Post. Thou shalt be then freer than a
gaoler ; no bolts for the dead.　　　196
　　　　　　　[Exeunt Posthumus and Messenger.

Gaol. Unless a man would marry a
gallows and beget young gibbets, I never
saw one so prone. Yet, on my conscience,
there are verier knaves desire to live, for all
he be a Roman ; and there be some of
them too that die against their wills ; so
should I, if I were one. I would we were
all of one mind, and one mind good. O,
there were desolation of gaolers and gal-
lowses ! I speak against my present profit,
but my wish hath a preferment in't. *[Exit.*

SCENE V. *Britain. Cymbeline's tent.*

Enter CYMBELINE, BELARIUS, GUIDERIUS,
ARVIRAGUS, PISANIO, Lords, Officers, *and*
Attendants.

Cym. Stand by my side, you whom the
gods have made
Preservers of my throne. Woe is my
heart
That the poor soldier that so richly fought,
Whose rags sham'd gilded arms, whose
naked breast
Stepp'd before targes of proof, cannot be
found.　　　　　　　　　　　5
He shall be happy that can find him, if
Our grace can make him so.

Bel.　　　　　　I never saw
Such noble fury in so poor a thing ;
Such precious deeds in one that promis'd
nought
But beggary and poor looks.

Cym.　　　　No tidings of him ? 10

Pis. He hath been search'd among the
dead and living,
But no trace of him.

Cym.　　　To my grief, I am
The heir of his reward ; *[To Belarius,
Guiderius and Arviragus]* which I will add
To you, the liver, heart, and brain, of
Britain,
By whom I grant she lives. 'Tis now the
time　　　　　　　　　　　15
To ask of whence you are. Report it.

Bel.　　　　　　　　　Sir,
In Cambria are we born, and gentlemen ;

Further to boast were neither true nor
modest,　　　　　　　　　　18
Unless I add we are honest.

Cym.　　　　　　Bow your knees.
Arise my knights o' th' battle ; I create you
Companions to our person, and will fit you
With dignities becoming your estates.

Enter CORNELIUS *and* Ladies.

There's business in these faces. Why so
sadly
Greet you our victory ? You look like
Romans,
And not o' th' court of Britain.

Cor.　　　　　Hail, great King ! 25
To sour your happiness I must report
The Queen is dead.

Cym.　　　Who worse than a physician
Would this report become ? But I consider
By med'cine life may be prolong'd, yet
death
Will seize the doctor too. How ended she ?

Cor. With horror, madly dying, like her
life ;　　　　　　　　　　31
Which, being cruel to the world, concluded
Most cruel to herself. What she confess'd
I will report, so please you ; these her
women
Can trip me if I err, who with wet cheeks 35
Were present when she finish'd.

Cym.　　　　　　Prithee say.

Cor. First, she confess'd she never lov'd
you ; only
Affected greatness got by you, not you ;
Married your royalty, was wife to your
place ;
Abhorr'd your person.

Cym.　　　　She alone knew this ; 40
And but she spoke it dying, I would not
Believe her lips in opening it. Proceed.

Cor. Your daughter, whom she bore in
hand to love
With such integrity, she did confess　44
Was as a scorpion to her sight ; whose life,
But that her flight prevented it, she had
Ta'en off by poison.

Cym.　　　O most delicate fiend !
Who is't can read a woman ? Is there
more ?

Cor. More, sir, and worse. She did con-
fess she had
For you a mortal mineral, which, being
took,　　　　　　　　　　50
Should by the minute feed on life, and,
ling'ring,
By inches waste you. In which time she
purpos'd,
By watching, weeping, tendance, kissing, to
O'ercome you with her show ; and in time,
When she had fitted you with her craft, to
work　　　　　　　　　　55
Her son into th' adoption of the crown ;
But failing of her end by his strange
absence,

Grew shameless-desperate, open'd, in de-
    spite
Of heaven and men, her purposes, re-
    pented   59
The evils she hatch'd were not effected ; so,
Despairing, died.
    Cym.   Heard you all this, her women ?
    Lady. We did, so please your Highness.
    Cym.   Mine eyes
Were not in fault, for she was beautiful ;
Mine ears, that heard her flattery ; nor my
    heart,
That thought her like her seeming. It had
    been vicious   65
To have mistrusted her ; yet, O my
    daughter !
That it was folly in me thou mayst say,
And prove it in thy feeling. Heaven mend
    all !

Enter LUCIUS, IACHIMO, *the* Soothsayer, *and
other* Roman Prisoners, *guarded ;* POS-
THUMUS *behind, and* IMOGEN.

Thou com'st not, Caius, now for tribute ;
    that
The Britons have raz'd out, though with
    the loss   70
Of many a bold one, whose kinsmen have
    made suit
That their good souls may be appeas'd
    with slaughter
Of you their captives, which ourself have
    granted ;
So think of your estate.
    Luc. Consider, sir, the chance of war. The
    day   75
Was yours by accident ; had it gone with
    us,
We should not, when the blood was cool,
    have threaten'd
Our prisoners with the sword. But since the
    gods
Will have it thus, that nothing but our lives
May be call'd ransom, let it come. Sufficeth
A Roman with a Roman's heart can suffer.
Augustus lives to think on't ; and so much
For my peculiar care. This one thing only
I will entreat : my boy, a Briton born,
Let him be ransom'd. Never master had   85
A page so kind, so duteous, diligent,
So tender over his occasions, true,
So feat, so nurse-like ; let his virtue join
With my request, which I'll make bold
    your Highness
Cannot deny ; he hath done no Briton
    harm   90
Though he have serv'd a Roman. Save
    him, sir,
And spare no blood beside.
    Cym.   I have surely seen him ;
His favour is familiar to me. Boy,
Thou hast look'd thyself into my grace,
And art mine own. I know not why,
    wherefore   95

To say ' Live, boy '. Ne'er thank thy
    master. Live ;
And ask of Cymbeline what boon thou wilt,
Fitting my bounty and thy state, I'll give
    it ;
Yea, though thou do demand a prisoner,
The noblest ta'en.
    Imo.   I humbly thank your Highness.
    Luc. I do not bid thee beg my life, good
    lad,   101
And yet I know thou wilt.
    Imo.   No, no ! Alack,
There's other work in hand. I see a
    thing
Bitter to me as death ; your life, good
    master,
Must shuffle for itself.
    Luc.   The boy disdains me, 105
He leaves me, scorns me. Briefly die their
    joys
That place them on the truth of girls and
    boys.
Why stands he so perplex'd ?
    Cym.   What wouldst thou, boy ?
I love thee more and more ; think more
    and more
What's best to ask. Know'st him thou
    look'st on ? Speak,   110
Wilt have him live ? Is he thy kin ? thy
    friend ?
    Imo. He is a Roman, no more kin to me
Than I to your Highness ; who, being born
    your vassal,
Am something nearer.
    Cym.   Wherefore ey'st him so ?
    Imo. I'll tell you, sir, in private, if you
    please   115
To give me hearing.
    Cym.   Ay, with all my heart,
And lend my best attention. What's thy
    name ?
    Imo. Fidele, sir.
    Cym.   Thou'rt my good youth, my page ;
I'll be thy master. Walk with me ; speak
    freely.   119
    [*Cymbeline and Imogen converse apart.*
    Bel. Is not this boy reviv'd from death ?
    Arv.   One sand another
Not more resembles—that sweet rosy lad
Who died, and was Fidele. What think
    you ?
    Gui. The same dead thing alive.
    Bel. Peace, peace ! see further. He eyes
    us not ; forbear.
Creatures may be alike ; were't he, I am
    sure   125
He would have spoke to us.
    Gui.   But we saw him dead.
    Bel. Be silent ; let's see further.
    Pis. [*Aside*]   It is my mistress.
Since she is living, let the time run on
To good or bad.
    [*Cymbeline and Imogen advance.*
    Cym. Come, stand thou by our side ; 129

Make thy demand aloud. [*To Iachimo*] Sir,
  step you forth ;
Give answer to this boy, and do it freely,
Or, by our greatness and the grace of it,
Which is our honour, bitter torture shall
Winnow the truth from falsehood. On,
  speak to him.
  Imo. My boon is that this gentleman may
render   135
Of whom he had this ring.
  Post. [*Aside*]   What's that to him ?
  Cym. That diamond upon your finger,
  say
How came it yours ?
  Iach. Thou'lt torture me to leave un-
  spoken that
Which to be spoke would torture thee.
  Cym.   How ? me ?   140
  Iach. I am glad to be constrain'd to utter
  that
Which torments me to conceal. By villainy
I got this ring ; 'twas Leonatus' jewel,
Whom thou didst banish ; and—which
  more may grieve thee,
As it doth me—a nobler sir ne'er liv'd   145
'Twixt sky and ground. Wilt thou hear
  more, my lord ?
  Cym. All that belongs to this.
  Iach.   That paragon, thy daughter,
For whom my heart drops blood and my
  false spirits
Quail to remember—Give me leave, I faint.
  Cym. My daughter ? What of her ? Re-
  new thy strength ;   150
I had rather thou shouldst live while nature
  will
Than die ere I hear more. Strive, man, and
  speak.
  Iach. Upon a time—unhappy was the
  clock
That struck the hour !—it was in Rome—
  accurs'd
The mansion where !—'twas at a feast—
  O, would   155
Our viands had been poison'd, or at least
Those which I heav'd to head !—the good
  Posthumus—
What should I say ? he was too good to be
Where ill men were, and was the best of all
Amongst the rar'st of good ones—sitting
  sadly,   160
Hearing us praise our loves of Italy
For beauty that made barren the swell'd
  boast
Of him that best could speak ; for feature,
  laming
The shrine of Venus or straight-pight
  Minerva,
Postures beyond brief nature ; for con-
  dition,   165
A shop of all the qualities that man
Loves woman for ; besides that hook of
  wiving,
Fairness which strikes the eye—

  Cym.   I stand on fire.
Come to the matter.
  Iach.   All too soon I shall,
Unless thou wouldst grieve quickly. This
  Posthumus,   170
Most like a noble lord in love and one
That had a royal lover, took his hint ;
And not dispraising whom we prais'd—
  therein
He was as calm as virtue—he began
His mistress' picture ; which by his tongue
  being made,   175
And then a mind put in't, either our brags
Were crack'd of kitchen trulls, or his
  description
Prov'd us unspeaking sots.
  Cym.   Nay, nay, to th' purpose.
  Iach. Your daughter's chastity—there it
  begins.
He spake of her as Dian had hot dreams 180
And she alone were cold ; whereat I,
  wretch,
Made scruple of his praise, and wager'd
  with him
Pieces of gold 'gainst this which then he
  wore
Upon his honour'd finger, to attain   184
In suit the place of's bed, and win this ring
By hers and mine adultery. He, true
  knight,
No lesser of her honour confident
Than I did truly find her, stakes this ring ;
And would so, had it been a carbuncle
Of Phœbus' wheel ; and might so safely,
  had it   190
Been all the worth of's car. Away to
  Britain
Post I in this design. Well may you, sir,
Remember me at court, where I was taught
Of your chaste daughter the wide difference
'Twixt amorous and villainous. Being thus
  quench'd   195
Of hope, not longing, mine Italian brain
Gan in your duller Britain operate
Most vilely ; for my vantage, excellent ;
And, to be brief, my practice so prevail'd
That I return'd with simular proof enough
To make the noble Leonatus mad,   201
By wounding his belief in her renown
With tokens thus and thus ; averring notes
Of chamber-hanging, pictures, this her
  bracelet—   204
O cunning, how I got it !—nay, some marks
Of secret on her person, that he could not
But think her bond of chastity quite
  crack'd,
I having ta'en the forfeit. Whereupon—
Methinks I see him now—
  Post. [*Coming forward*] Ay, so thou dost,
Italian fiend ! Ay me, most credulous fool,
Egregious murderer, thief, anything   211
That's due to all the villains past, in being,
To come ! O, give me cord, or knife, or
  poison,

Some upright justicer! Thou, King, send
    out
For torturers ingenious. It is I   215
That all th' abhorred things o' th' earth
    amend
By being worse than they. I am Posthu-
    mus,
That kill'd thy daughter; villain-like, I
    lie—   218
That caus'd a lesser villain than myself,
A sacrilegious thief, to do't. The temple
Of virtue was she; yea, and she herself.
Spit, and throw stones, cast mire upon me,
    set
The dogs o' th' street to bay me. Every
    villain
Be call'd Posthumus Leonatus, and
Be villainy less than 'twas! O Imogen!   225
My queen, my life, my wife! O Imogen,
Imogen, Imogen!
    Imo.   Peace, my lord. Hear, hear!
    Post. Shall's have a play of this? Thou
    scornful page,
There lie thy part. [*Strikes her. She falls.*
    Pis.   O gentlemen, help!
Mine and your mistress! O, my lord
    Posthumus!   230
You ne'er kill'd Imogen till now. Help,
    help!
Mine honour'd lady!
    Cym.   Does the world go round?
    Post. How comes these staggers on me?
    Pis.   Wake, my mistress!
    Cym. If this be so, the gods do mean to
    strike me
To death with mortal joy.
    Pis. How fares my mistress?
    Imo.   O, get thee from my sight; 236
Thou gav'st me poison. Dangerous fellow,
    hence!
Breathe not where princes are.
    Cym.   The tune of Imogen!
    Pis. Lady,   239
The gods throw stones of sulphur on me, if
That box I gave you was not thought by me
A precious thing! I had it from the Queen.
    Cym. New matter still?
    Imo.   It poison'd me.
    Cor.   O gods!
I left out one thing which the Queen
    confess'd,
Which must approve thee honest. 'If
    Pisanio   245
Have' said she 'given his mistress that
    confection
Which I gave him for cordial, she is serv'd
As I would serve a rat.'
    Cym.   What's this, Cornelius?
    Cor. The Queen, sir, very oft importun'd
    me   249
To temper poisons for her; still pretending
The satisfaction of her knowledge only
In killing creatures vile, as cats and dogs,
Of no esteem. I, dreading that her purpose

Was of more danger, did compound for her
A certain stuff, which, being ta'en, would
    cease   255
The present pow'r of life, but in short time
All offices of nature should again
Do their due functions. Have you ta'en
    of it?
    Imo. Most like I did, for I was dead.
    Bel.   My boys,
There was our error.
    Gui.   This is sure Fidele. 260
    Imo. Why did you throw your wedded
    lady from you?
Think that you are upon a rock, and now
Throw me again.   [*Embracing him.*
    Post. Hang there like fruit, my soul,
Till the tree die!
    Cym. How now, my flesh? my child?
What, mak'st thou me a dullard in this
    act?   265
Wilt thou not speak to me?
    Imo. [*Kneeling*]   Your blessing, sir.
    Bel. [*To Guiderius and Arviragus*]
Though you did love this youth, I blame
    ye not;
You had a motive for't.
    Cym.   My tears that fall
Prove holy water on thee! Imogen,   269
Thy mother's dead.
    Imo.   I am sorry for't, my lord.
    Cym. O, she was naught, and long of her
    it was
That we meet here so strangely; but her
    son
Is gone, we know not how nor where.
    Pis.   My lord,
Now fear is from me, I'll speak troth.
    Lord Cloten,
Upon my lady's missing, came to me   275
With his sword drawn, foam'd at the
    mouth, and swore,
If I discover'd not which way she was gone,
It was my instant death. By accident
I had a feigned letter of my master's
Then in my pocket, which directed him 280
To seek her on the mountains near to
    Milford;
Where, in a frenzy, in my master's gar-
    ments,
Which he enforc'd from me, away he posts
With unchaste purpose, and with oath to
    violate
My lady's honour. What became of him 285
I further know not.
    Gui.   Let me end the story:
I slew him there.
    Cym.   Marry, the gods forfend!
I would not thy good deeds should from
    my lips
Pluck a hard sentence. Prithee, valiant
    youth,
Deny't again.
    Gui. I have spoke it, and I did it. 290
    Cym. He was a prince.

Gui. A most incivil one. The wrongs he
    did me
Were nothing prince-like; for he did pro-
    voke me
With language that would make me spurn
    the sea,   294
If it could so roar to me. I cut off's head,
And am right glad he is not standing here
To tell this tale of mine.
    Cym.   I am sorry for thee.
By thine own tongue thou art condemn'd,
    and must
Endure our law. Thou'rt dead.
    Imo.   That headless man
I thought had been my lord.
    Cym.   Bind the offender, 300
And take him from our presence.
    Bel.   Stay, sir King.
This man is better than the man he slew,
As well descended as thyself, and hath
More of thee merited than a band of
    Clotens
Had ever scar for. [*To the Guard*] Let his
    arms alone;   305
They were not born for bondage.
    Cym.   Why, old soldier,
Wilt thou undo the worth thou art unpaid
    for
By tasting of our wrath? How of descent
As good as we?
    Arv.   In that he spake too far. 309
    Cym. And thou shalt die for't.
    Bel.   We will die all three;
But I will prove that two on's are as good
As I have given out him. My sons, I must
For mine own part unfold a dangerous
    speech,
Though haply well for you.
    Arv.   Your danger's ours.
    Gui. And our good his.
    Bel.   Have at it then by leave! 315
Thou hadst, great King, a subject who
Was call'd Belarius.
    Cym.   What of him? He is
A banish'd traitor.
    Bel.   He it is that hath
Assum'd this age; indeed a banish'd man;
I know not how a traitor.
    Cym.   Take him hence, 320
The whole world shall not save him.
    Bel.   Not too hot.
First pay me for the nursing of thy sons,
And let it be confiscate all, so soon
As I have receiv'd it.
    Cym.   Nursing of my sons?
    Bel. I am too blunt and saucy: here's
    my knee.   325
Ere I arise I will prefer my sons;
Then spare not the old father. Mighty sir,
These two young gentlemen that call me
    father,
And think they are my sons, are none of
    mine;   329
They are the issue of your loins, my liege,

And blood of your begetting.
    Cym.   How? my issue?
    Bel. So sure as you your father's. I, old
    Morgan,
Am that Belarius whom you sometime
    banish'd.
Your pleasure was my mere offence, my
    punishment   334
Itself, and all my treason; that I suffer'd
Was all the harm I did. These gentle
    princes—
For such and so they are—these twenty
    years
Have I train'd up; those arts they have
    as I
Could put into them. My breeding was,
    sir, as
Your Highness knows. Their nurse,
    Euriphile,   340
Whom for the theft I wedded, stole these
    children
Upon my banishment; I mov'd her to't,
Having receiv'd the punishment before
For that which I did then. Beaten for
    loyalty
Excited me to treason. Their dear loss, 345
The more of you 'twas felt, the more it
    shap'd
Unto my end of stealing them. But,
    gracious sir,
Here are your sons again, and I must lose
Two of the sweet'st companions in the
    world.   349
The benediction of these covering heavens
Fall on their heads like dew! for they are
    worthy
To inlay heaven with stars.
    Cym.   Thou weep'st and speak'st.
The service that you three have done is
    more
Unlike than this thou tell'st. I lost my
    children.   354
If these be they, I know not how to wish
A pair of worthier sons.
    Bel.   Be pleas'd awhile.
This gentleman, whom I call Polydore,
Most worthy prince, as yours, is true
    Guiderius;
This gentleman, my Cadwal, Arviragus,
Your younger princely son; he, sir, was
    lapp'd   360
In a most curious mantle, wrought by th'
    hand
Of his queen mother, which for more
    probation
I can with ease produce.
    Cym.   Guiderius had
Upon his neck a mole, a sanguine star;
It was a mark of wonder.
    Bel.   This is he, 365
Who hath upon him still that natural
    stamp.
It was wise nature's end in the donation,
To be his evidence now.

Cym.   O, what am I ?
A mother to the birth of three ? Ne'er
        mother
Rejoic'd deliverance more. Blest pray you
        be,   370
That, after this strange starting from your
        orbs,
You may reign in them now ! O Imogen,
Thou hast lost by this a kingdom.
        Imo.   No, my lord ;
I have got two worlds by't. O my gentle
        brothers,   374
Have we thus met ? O, never say here-
        after
But I am truest speaker ! You call'd me
        brother,
When I was but your sister : I you brothers,
When we were so indeed.
        Cym.   Did you e'er meet ?
Arv. Ay, my good lord.
Gui.   And at first meeting lov'd,
Continu'd so until we thought he died. 380
Cor. By the Queen's dram she swallow'd.
Cym.   O rare instinct !
When shall I hear all through ? This fierce
        abridgment
Hath to it circumstantial branches, which
Distinction should be rich in. Where ? how
        liv'd you ?
And when came you to serve our Roman
        captive ?   385
How parted with your brothers ? how first
        met them ?
Why fled you from the court ? and whither ?
        These,
And your three motives to the battle, with
I know not how much more, should be
        demanded,
And all the other by-dependances,   390
From chance to chance ; but nor the time
        nor place
Will serve our long interrogatories. See,
Posthumus anchors upon Imogen ;
And she, like harmless lightning, throws
        her eye
On him, her brothers, me, her master,
        hitting   395
Each object with a joy ; the counterchange
Is severally in all. Let's quit this ground,
And smoke the temple with our sacrifices.
[*To Belarius*] Thou art my brother ; so we'll
        hold thee ever.
    Imo. You are my father too, and did
        relieve me   400
To see this gracious season.
    Cym.   All o'erjoy'd
Save these in bonds. Let them be joyful
        too,
For they shall taste our comfort.
    Imo.   My good master,
I will yet do you service.
    Luc.   Happy be you !
Cym. The forlorn soldier, that so nobly
        fought,   405

He would have well becom'd this place and
        grac'd
The thankings of a king.
    Post.   I am, sir,
The soldier that did company these three
In poor beseeming ; 'twas a fitment for
The purpose I then follow'd. That I was he,
Speak, Iachimo. I had you down, and
        might   411
Have made you finish.
    Iach. [*Kneeling*]   I am down again ;
But now my heavy conscience sinks my
        knee,
As then your force did. Take that life,
        beseech you,   414
Which I so often owe ; but your ring first,
And here the bracelet of the truest princess
That ever swore her faith.
    Post.   Kneel not to me.
The pow'r that I have on you is to spare
        you ;
The malice towards you to forgive you.
        Live,
And deal with others better.
    Cym.   Nobly doom'd ! 420
We'll learn our freeness of a son-in-law ;
Pardon's the word to all.
    Arv.   You holp us, sir,
As you did mean indeed to be our brother ;
Joy'd are we that you are.   424
    Post. Your servant, Princes. Good my
        lord of Rome,
Call forth your soothsayer. As I slept, me-
        thought
Great Jupiter, upon his eagle back'd,
Appear'd to me, with other spritely shows
Of mine own kindred. When I wak'd, I
        found   429
This label on my bosom ; whose containing
Is so from sense in hardness that I can
Make no collection of it. Let him show
His skill in the construction.
    Luc.   Philarmonus !
Sooth. Here, my good lord.
Luc.   Read, and declare the meaning.

Sooth. [*Reads*] ' When as a lion's whelp
shall, to himself unknown, without seeking
find, and be embrac'd by a piece of tender
air ; and when from a stately cedar shall be
lopp'd branches which, being dead many
years, shall after revive, be jointed to the
old stock, and freshly grow ; then shall
Posthumus end his miseries, Britain be
fortunate and flourish in peace and plenty.'

Thou, Leonatus, art the lion's whelp ; 441
The fit and apt construction of thy name,
Being Leo-natus, doth import so much.
[*To Cymbeline*] The piece of tender air, thy
        virtuous daughter,
Which we call ' mollis aer', and ' mollis aer'
We term it ' mulier ' ; which ' mulier ' I
        divine   446
Is this most constant wife, who even now

Answering the letter of the oracle,
Unknown to you, unsought, were clipp'd about
With this most tender air.
   Cym.   This hath some seeming. 450
   Sooth. The lofty cedar, royal Cymbeline,
Personates thee ; and thy lopp'd branches point
Thy two sons forth, who, by Belarius stol'n,
For many years thought dead, are now reviv'd, 454
To the majestic cedar join'd, whose issue
Promises Britain peace and plenty.
   Cym.   Well,
My peace we will begin. And, Caius Lucius,
Although the victor, we submit to Cæsar
And to the Roman empire, promising 459
To pay our wonted tribute, from the which
We were dissuaded by our wicked queen,
Whom heavens in justice, both on her and hers,
Have laid most heavy hand.
   Sooth. The fingers of the pow'rs above do tune
The harmony of this peace. The vision 465

Which I made known to Lucius ere the stroke
Of yet this scarce-cold battle, at this instant
Is full accomplish'd ; for the Roman eagle,
From south to west on wing soaring aloft,
Lessen'd herself and in the beams o' th' sun 470
So vanish'd ; which foreshow'd our princely eagle,
Th' imperial Cæsar, should again unite
His favour with the radiant Cymbeline,
Which shines here in the west.
   Cym.   Laud we the gods ;
And let our crooked smokes climb to their nostrils 475
From our bless'd altars. Publish we this peace
To all our subjects. Set we forward ; let
A Roman and a British ensign wave
Friendly together. So through Lud's Town march ;
And in the temple of great Jupiter 480
Our peace we'll ratify ; seal it with feasts.
Set on there ! Never was a war did cease,
Ere bloody hands were wash'd, with such a peace.   *[Exeunt.*

PERICLES, PRINCE OF TYRE

DRAMATIS PERSONÆ

GOWER, *as Chorus.*

ANTIOCHUS, *King of Antioch.*
PERICLES, *Prince of Tyre.*
HELICANUS,⎫
ESCANES, ⎬ *two lords of Tyre.*
SIMONIDES, *King of Pentapolis.*
CLEON, *Governor of Tharsus.*
LYSIMACHUS, *Governor of Mytilene.*
CERIMON, *a ˉord of Ephesus.*
THALIARD, *a lord of Antioch.*
PHILEMON, *servant to Cerimon.*
LEONINE, *servant to Dionyza.*
MARSHAL.

A Pander.
BOULT, *his servant.*

The Daughter of Antiochus.
DIONYZA, *wife to Cleon.*
THAISA, *daughter to Simonides.*
MARINA, *daughter to Pericles and Thaisa.*
LYCHORIDA, *nurse to Marina.*
A Bawd.

DIANA.

Lords, Ladies, Knights, Gentlemen, Sailors,
    Pirates, Fishermen, *and* Messengers.

THE SCENE : *Dispersedly in various countries.*

ACT ONE

Antioch. Before the palace.

Enter GOWER.

To sing a song that old was sung,
From ashes ancient Gower is come,
Assuming man's infirmities,
To glad your ear and please your eyes.
It hath been sung at festivals,   5
On ember-eves and holy-ales ;
And lords and ladies in their lives
Have read it for restoratives.
The purchase is to make men glorious ;
Et bonum quo antiquius, eo melius.   10
If you, born in those latter times,
When wit's more ripe, accept my rhymes,
And that to hear an old man sing
May to your wishes pleasure bring,
I life would wish, and that I might   15
Waste it for you, like taper-ˉight.
This Antioch, then, Antiochus the Great
Built up, this city, for his chiefest seat ;
The fairest in all Syria—
I tell you what mine authors say.   20
This king unto him took a fere,
Who died and left a female heir,
So buxom, blithe, and full of face,
As heaven had lent her all his grace ;
With whom the father liking took,   25
And her to incest did provoke.
Bad child! Worse father! To entice his own
To evil should be done by none.
But custom what they did begin
Was with long use account no sin.   30
The beauty of this sinful dame
Made many princes thither frame
To seek her as a bed-fellow,
In marriage-pleasures play-fellow ;
Which to prevent he made a law—   35

To keep her still, and men in awe—
That whoso ask'd her for his wife,
His riddle told not, lost his life.
So for her many a wight did die,
As yon grim looks do testify.   40
What now ensues to the judgment of your
    eye
I give, my cause who best can justify.
                                              [*Exit.*

SCENE I. *Antioch. The palace.*

Enter ANTIOCHUS, PRINCE PERICLES, *and*
    Followers.

Ant. Young Prince of Tyre, you have at
    large received
The danger of the task you undertake.
Per. I have, Antiochus, and, with a soul
Embold'ned with the glory of her praise,
Think death no hazard in this enterprise. 5
Ant. Bring in our daughter, clothed like
    a bride   [*Music.*
For the embracements even of Jove him-
    self ;
At whose conception, till Lucina reigned,
Nature this dowry gave to glad her
    presence :
The senate-house of planets all did sit, 10
To knit in her their best perfections.

Enter the Daughter of Antiochus.

Per. See where she comes, apparell'd like
    the spring,
Graces her subjects, and her thoughts the
    king
Of every virtue gives renown to men.   14
Her face the book of praises, where is read
Nothing but curious pleasures, as from
    thence
Sorrow were ever raz'd, and testy wrath
Could never be her mild companion.

You gods that made me man, and sway
in love,
That have inflam'd desire in my breast   20
To taste the fruit of yon celestial tree,
Or die in the adventure, be my helps,
As I am son and servant to your will,
To compass such a boundless happiness !
    Ant. Prince Pericles—   25
    Per. That would be son to great Antio-
chus.
    Ant. Before thee stands this fair
Hesperides,
With golden fruit, but dangerous to be
touch'd ;
For death-like dragons here affright thee
hard.   29
Her face, like heaven, enticeth thee to view
Her countless glory, which desert must
gain ;
And which, without desert, because thine eye
Presumes to reach, all the whole heap must
die.
Yon sometimes famous princes, like thyself,
Drawn by report, advent'rous by desire,   35
Tell thee, with speechless tongues and
semblance pale,
That, without covering, save yon field of
stars,
Here they stand martyrs, slain in Cupid's
wars ;   38
And with dead cheeks advise thee to desist
For going on death's net, whom none resist.
    Per. Antiochus, I thank thee, who hath
taught
My frail mortality to know itself,
And by those fearful objects to prepare
This body, like to them, to what I must ;
For death remembered should be like a
mirror,   45
Who tells us life's but breath, to trust it
error.
I'll make my will then, and, as sick men do,
Who know the world, see heaven, but,
feeling woe,
Gripe not at earthly joys as erst they did ;
So I bequeath a happy peace to you   50
And all good men, as every prince should
do ;
My riches to the earth from whence they
came ;
[*To the Princess*] But my unspotted fire of
love to you.
Thus ready for the way of life or death,
I wait the sharpest blow, Antiochus.   55
    Ant. Scorning advice, read the con-
clusion then ;
Which read and not expounded, 'tis decreed,
As these before thee, thou thyself shalt
bleed.
    Daugh. Of all 'say'd yet, mayst thou
prove prosperous !
Of all 'say'd yet, I wish thee happiness ! 60
    Per. Like a bold champion I assume the
lists,

Nor ask advice of any other thought
But faithfulness and courage.   [*Reads.*
The Riddle.
I am no viper, yet I feed   64
On mother's flesh which did me breed.
I sought a husband, in which labour
I found that kindness in a father.
He's father, son, and husband mild ;
I mother, wife, and yet his child.
How they may be, and yet in two,   70
As you will live, resolve it you.

[*Aside*] Sharp physic is the last. But, O you
powers
That give heaven countless eyes to view
men's acts,
Why cloud they not their sights perpetually,
If this be true, which makes me pale to
read it ?   75
Fair glass of light, I lov'd you, and could
still,
Were not this glorious casket stor'd with ill.
But I must tell you now my thoughts
revolt ;
For he's no man on whom perfections wait
That, knowing sin within, will touch the
gate.   80
You are a fair viol, and your sense the
strings ;
Who, finger'd to make man his lawful
music,
Would draw heaven down, and all the gods,
to hearken ;
But, being play'd upon before your time,
Hell only danceth at so harsh a chime.   85
Good sooth, I care not for you.
    Ant. Prince Pericles, touch not, upon thy
life,
For that's an article within our law
As dangerous as the rest.   Your time's
expir'd :
Either expound now, or receive your
sentence.   90
    Per. Great King,
Few love to hear the sins they love to act ;
'Twould braid yourself too near for me to
tell it.
Who has a book of all that monarchs do,
He's more secure to keep it shut than
shown ;   95
For vice repeated is like the wand'ring
wind,
Blows dust in others' eyes, to spread itself ;
And yet the end of all is bought thus dear,
The breath is gone, and the sore eyes see
clear
To stop the air would hurt them. The blind
mole casts   100
Copp'd hills towards heaven, to tell the
earth is throng'd
By man's oppression, and the poor worm
doth die for't.
Kings are earth's gods ; in vice their law's
their will ;

And if Jove stray, who dares say Jove doth
    ill ?
It is enough you know ; and it is fit,   105
What being more known grows worse, to
    smother it.
All love the womb that their first being
    bred ;
Then give my tongue like leave to love my
    head.
    Ant. [*Aside*] Heaven, that I had thy
    head ! He has found the meaning.
But I will gloze with him.—Young Prince
    of Tyre,   110
Though by the tenour of our strict edict,
Your exposition misinterpreting,
We might proceed to cancel of your days ;
Yet hope, succeeding from so fair a tree
As your fair self, doth tune us otherwise. 115
Forty days longer we do respite you ;
If by which time our secret be undone,
This mercy shows we'll joy in such a son ;
And until then your entertain shall be 119
As doth befit our honour and your worth.
            [*Exeunt all but Pericles.*
    Per. How courtesy would seem to cover
    sin,
When what is done is like an hypocrite,
The which is good in nothing but in sight !
If it be true that I interpret false,
Then were it certain you were not so bad 125
As with foul incest to abuse your soul ;
Where now you're both a father and a son
By your untimely claspings with your
    child—
Which pleasure fits a husband, not a
    father—
And she an eater of her mother's flesh 130
By the defiling of her parent's bed ;
And both like serpents are, who, though
    they feed
On sweetest flowers, yet they poison breed.
Antioch, farewell ! for wisdom sees those
    men   134
Blush not in actions blacker than the night
Will shun no course to keep them from the
    light.
One sin I know another doth provoke :
Murder's as near to lust as flame to smoke.
Poison and treason are the hands of sin,
Ay, and the targets to put off the shame. 140
Then, lest my life be cropp'd to keep you
    clear,
By flight I'll shun the danger which I fear.
                    [*Exit.*

      Re-enter ANTIOCHUS.

    Ant. He hath found the meaning,
For which we mean to have his head.
He must not live to trumpet forth my
    infamy,   145
Nor tell the world Antiochus doth sin
In such a loathed manner ;
And therefore instantly this prince must
    die ;

For by his fall my honour must keep high.
Who attends us there ?   150

      Enter THALIARD.

    Thal. Doth your Highness call ?
    Ant. Thaliard, you are of our chamber,
    and our mind partakes
Her private actions to your secrecy ;
And for your faithfulness we will advance
    you.   155
Thaliard, behold here's poison and here's
    gold ;
We hate the Prince of Tyre, and thou must
    kill him.
It fits thee not to ask the reason why,
Because we bid it. Say, is it done ?
    Thal.   My lord,
'Tis done.   160
    Ant. Enough.

      Enter a Messenger.

Let your breath cool yourself, telling your
    haste.
    Mess. My lord, Prince Pericles is fled.
                      [*Exit.*
    Ant. As thou wilt live, fly after ; and like
an arrow shot from a well-experienc'd
archer hits the mark his eye doth level at,
so thou never return unless thou say Prince
Pericles is dead.
    Thal. My lord, if I can get him within my
pistol's length I'll make him sure enough.
So, farewell to your Highness. 170
    Ant. Thaliard, adieu ! [*Exit Thaliard*] Till
    Pericles be dead
My heart can lend no succour to my head.
                      [*Exit.*

    SCENE II. *Tyre. The palace.*

    Enter PERICLES *with his Lords.*

    Per. Let none disturb us. [*Exeunt Lords.*
Why should this change of thoughts,
The sad companion, dull-ey'd melancholy,
Be my so us'd a guest as not an hour
In the day's glorious walk, or peaceful
    night,
The tomb where grief should sleep, can
    breed me quiet ? 5
Here pleasures court mine eyes, and mine
    eyes shun them,
And danger, which I fear'd, is at Antioch,
Whose arm seems far too short to hit me
    here.
Yet neither pleasure's art can joy my
    spirits,
Nor yet the other's distance comfort me. 10
Then it is thus : the passions of the mind,
That have their first conception by mis-
    dread,
Have after-nourishment and life by care ;
And what was first but fear what might be
    done 14
Grows elder now, and cares it be not done.
And so with me. The great Antiochus—

'Gainst whom I am too little to contend,
Since he's so great can make his will his act—
Will think me speaking, though I swear to
    silence;
Nor boots it me to say I honour him,   20
If he suspect I may dishonour him;
And what may make him blush in being
    known,
He'll stop the course by which it might be
    known.
With hostile forces he'll o'erspread the land,
And with th' ostent of war will look so huge
Amazement shall drive courage from the
    state;
Our men be vanquish'd ere they do resist,
And subjects punish'd that ne'er thought
    offence;
Which care of them, not pity of myself—
Who am no more but as the tops of trees 30
Which fence the roots they grow by and
    defend them—
Makes both my body pine and soul to
    languish,
And punish that before that he would
    punish.

Enter HELICANUS *and all the* Lords.

1 *Lord.* Joy and all comfort in your
    sacred breast!
2 *Lord.* And keep your mind till you
    return to us,   35
Peaceful and comfortable!
    Hel. Peace, peace, and give experience
    tongue.
They do abuse the king that flatter him,
For flattery is the bellows blows up sin;
The thing the which is flattered but a spark,
To which that blast gives heat and stronger
    glowing;   41
Whereas reproof, obedient, and in order,
Fits kings as they are men, for they may err.
When Signior Sooth here does proclaim a
    peace,
He flatters you, makes war upon your life.
Prince, pardon me, or strike me if you
    please;   46
I cannot be much lower than my knees.
                                    [*Kneels.*
    Per. All leave us else; but let your cares
    o'erlook
What shipping and what lading's in our
    haven,
And then return to us. [*Exeunt Lords*]
    Helicanus, thou   50
Hast moved us. What seest thou in our
    looks?
    Hel. An angry brow, dread lord.
    Per. If there be such a dart in princes'
    frowns,
How durst thy tongue move anger to our
    face?
    Hel. How dare the plants look up to
    heaven, from whence   55
They have their nourishment?

    Per.   Thou know'st I have power
To take thy life from thee.
    Hel. I have ground the axe myself;
Do but you strike the blow.
    Per.   Rise, prithee, rise. 60
Sit down. Thou art no flatterer.
I thank thee for't; and heaven forbid
That kings should let their ears hear their
    faults hid!
Fit counsellor and servant for a prince,
Who by thy wisdom mak'st a prince thy
    servant,   64
What wouldst thou have me do?
    Hel.   To bear with patience
Such griefs as you yourself do lay upon
    yourself.
    Per. Thou speak'st like a physician,
    Helicanus,
That ministers a potion unto me
That thou wouldst tremble to receive
    thyself.
Attend me, then: I went to Antioch,   70
Where, as thou know'st, against the face of
    death,
I sought the purchase of a glorious beauty,
From whence an issue I might propagate
Are arms to princes and bring joys to
    subjects.
Her face was to mine eye beyond all
    wonder;   75
The rest—hark in thine ear—as black as
    incest;
Which by my knowledge found, the sinful
    father
Seem'd not to strike, but smooth. But thou
    know'st this,
'Tis time to fear when tyrants seem to kiss.
Which fear so grew in me I hither fled   80
Under the covering of a careful night,
Who seem'd my good protector; and, be-
    ing here,
Bethought me what was past, what might
    succeed.
I knew him tyrannous; and tyrants' fears
Decrease not, but grow faster than the
    years;   85
And should he doubt it, as no doubt he
    doth,
That I should open to the list'ning air
How many worthy princes' bloods were
    shed
To keep his bed of blackness unlaid ope,
To lop that doubt, he'll fill this land with
    arms,   90
And make pretence of wrong that I have
    done him;
When all, for mine, if I may call offence,
Must feel war's blow, who spares not
    innocence;
Which love to all, of which thyself art one,
Who now reprov'dst me for't—
    Hel.   Alas, sir!   95
    Per. Drew sleep out of mine eyes, blood
    from my cheeks,

1243

Musings into my mind, with thousand
 doubts
How I might stop this tempest ere it came ;
And, finding little comfort to relieve them,
I thought it princely charity to grieve them.
 Hel. Well, my lord, since you have given
  me leave to speak, 101
Freely will I speak. Antiochus you fear,
And justly too, I think, you fear the tyrant,
Who either by public war or private treason
Will take away your life. 105
Therefore, my lord, go travel for a while
Till that his rage and anger be forgot,
Or till the Destinies do cut his thread of life.
Your rule direct to any ; if to me,
Day serves not light more faithful than I'll
 be. 110
 Per. I do not doubt thy faith ;
But should he wrong my liberties in my
 absence ?
 Hel. We'll mingle our bloods together in
 the earth,
From whence we had our being and our birth.
 Per. Tyre, I now look from thee then,
  and to Tharsus 115
Intend my travel, where I'll hear from thee ;
And by whose letters I'll dispose myself.
The care I had and have of subjects' good
On thee I lay, whose wisdom's strength can
 bear it.
I'll take thy word for faith, not ask thine
 oath : 120
Who shuns not to break one will sure crack
 both.
But in our orbs we'll live so round and safe
That time of both this truth shall ne'er
 convince,
Thou show'dst a subject's shine, I a true
 prince. [*Exeunt.*

SCENE III. *Tyre. The palace.*

Enter THALIARD.

 Thal. So, this is Tyre, and this the court.
Here must I kill King Pericles ; and if I do
it not, I am sure to be hang'd at home. 'Tis
dangerous. Well, I perceive he was a wise
fellow and had good discretion that, being
bid to ask what he would of the king,
desired he might know none of his secrets.
Now do I see he had some reason for't ; for
if a king bid a man be a villain, he's bound
by the indenture of his oath to be one.
Husht ! here comes the lords of Tyre.

Enter HELICANUS, ESCANES, *with other*
 Lords.

 Hel. You shall not need, my fellow peers
of Tyre, 10
Further to question me of your king's
 departure :
His seal'd commission, left in trust with me,
Does speak sufficiently he's gone to travel.
 Thal. [*Aside*] How ! the king gone !

 Hel. If further yet you will be satisfied 15
Why, as it were unlicens'd of your loves,
He would depart, I'll give some light unto
 you.
Being at Antioch—
 Thal. [*Aside*] What from Antioch ?
 Hel. Royal Antiochus, on what cause I
 know not,
Took some displeasure at him ; at least he
 judg'd so ; 20
And doubting lest that he had err'd or
 sinn'd,
To show his sorrow, he'd correct himself ;
So puts himself unto the shipman's toil,
With whom each minute threatens life or
 death. 24
 Thal. [*Aside*] Well, I perceive
I shall not be hang'd now although I would ;
But since he's gone, the King's seas must
 please
He scap'd the land to perish at the seas.
I'll present myself.—Peace to the Lords of
 Tyre !
 Hel. Lord Thaliard from Antiochus is
 welcome.
 Thal. From him I come 30
With message unto princely Pericles ;
But since my landing I have understood
Your lord has betook himself to unknown
 travels,
Now message must return from whence it
 came.
 Hel. We have no reason to desire it, 35
Commended to our master, not to us ;
Yet, ere you shall depart, this we desire—
As friends to Antioch, we may feast in Tyre.
     [*Exeunt.*

SCENE IV. *Tharsus. The Governor's house.*

Enter CLEON *the Governor of Tharsus, with*
 DIONYZA *his wife, and* Others.

 Cle. My Dionyza, shall we rest us here,
And by relating tales of others' griefs
See if 'twill teach us to forget our own ?
 Dio. That were to blow at fire in hope to
 quench it ;
For who digs hills because they do aspire 5
Throws down one mountain to cast up a
 higher.
O my distressed lord, even such our griefs
 are !
Here they are but felt and seen with
 mischief's eyes,
But like to groves, being topp'd, they higher
 rise.
 Cle. O Dionyza, 10
Who wanteth food, and will not say he
 wants it,
Or can conceal his hunger till he famish ?
Our tongues and sorrows to sound deep
Our woes into the air ; our eyes to weep ?
Till tongues fetch breath that may pro-
 claim them louder ; 15

That, if heaven slumber while their
      creatures want,
They may awake their helps to comfort them.
I'll then discourse our woes, felt several
      years,
And, wanting breath to speak, help me
      with tears.
      Dio. I'll do my best, sir.   20
      Cle. This Tharsus, o'er which I have the
      government,
A city on whom plenty held full hand,
For Riches strew'd herself even in her
      streets;
Whose towers bore heads so high they
      kiss'd the clouds,
And strangers ne'er beheld but wond'red at;   24
Whose men and dames so jetted and
      adorn'd,
Like one another's glass to trim them by;
Their tables were stor'd full, to glad the
      sight,
And not so much to feed on as delight;   29
All poverty was scorn'd, and pride so great
The name of help grew odious to repeat.
      Dio. O, 'tis too true!
      Cle. But see what heaven can do! By
      this our change
These mouths who but of late earth, sea,
      and air,
Were all too little to content and please,   35
Although they gave their creatures in
      abundance,
As houses are defil'd for want of use,
They are now starv'd for want of exercise.
Those palates who, not yet two summers
      younger,   39
Must have inventions to delight the taste,
Would now be glad of bread, and beg for it.
Those mothers who to nouzle up their babes
Thought nought too curious are ready now
To eat those little darlings whom they lov'd.
So sharp are hunger's teeth that man and
      wife   45
Draw lots who first shall die to lengthen life.
Here stands a lord, and there a lady
      weeping;
Here many sink, yet those which see them
      fall
Have scarce strength left to give them
      burial.
Is not this true?   50
      Dio. Our cheeks and hollow eyes do
      witness it.
      Cle. O, let those cities that of Plenty's cup
And her prosperities so largely taste,
With their superfluous riots, hear these
      tears!
The misery of Tharsus may be theirs.   55

      Enter a Lord.

      Lord. Where's the Lord Governor?
      Cle. Here.
Speak out thy sorrows which thou bring'st
      in haste,
For comfort is too far for us to expect.
      Lord. We have descried, upon our neigh-
      bouring shore,   60
A portly sail of ships make hitherward.
      Cle. I thought as much.
One sorrow never comes but brings an heir
That may succeed as his inheritor;
And so in ours: some neighbouring nation,
Taking advantage of our misery,   66
Hath stuff'd the hollow vessels with their
      power,
To beat us down, the which are down
      already;
And make a conquest of unhappy me,
Whereas no glory's got to overcome.   70
      Lord. That's the least fear; for by the
      semblance
Of their white flags display'd, they bring
      us peace,
And come to us as favourers, not as foes.
      Cle. Thou speak'st like him's untutor'd
      to repeat:
Who makes the fairest show means most
      deceit.   75
But bring they what they will and what
      they can,
What need we fear?
Our ground's the lowest, and we are half-
      way there.
Go tell their general we attend him here,
To know for what he comes, and whence
      he comes,   80
And what he craves.
      Lord. I go, my lord.   [*Exit.*
      Cle. Welcome is peace, if he on peace
      consist;
If wars, we are unable to resist.

      Enter PERICLES, *with* Attendants.

      Per. Lord Governor, for so we hear you
      are,   85
Let not our ships and number of our men
Be like a beacon fir'd t' amaze your eyes.
We have heard your miseries as far as Tyre,
And seen the desolation of your streets;   89
Nor come we to add sorrow to your tears,
But to relieve them of their heavy load;
And these our ships you happily may think
Are like the Troyan horse was stuff'd
      within
With bloody veins, expecting overthrow,
Are stor'd with corn to make your needy
      bread,   95
And give them life whom hunger starv'd
      half dead.
      All. The gods of Greece protect you!
And we'll pray for you.   [*They kneel.*
      Per.   Arise, I pray you, rise.
We do not look for reverence, but for love,
And harbourage for ourself, our ships, and
      men.   100
      Cle. The which when any shall not gratify,
Or pay you with unthankfulness in thought,
Be it our wives, our children, or ourselves,

The curse of heaven and men succeed their
    evils !
Till when—the which I hope shall ne'er be
    seen—   105
Your Grace is welcome to our town and us.
  Per. Which welcome we'll accept ; feast
  here awhile,
Until our stars that frown lend us a smile.
                  [*Exeunt.*

ACT TWO

Enter GOWER.

  Gow. Here have you seen a mighty king
His child iwis to incest bring ;
A better prince and benign lord,
That will prove awful both in deed and
  word.
Be quiet then, as men should be,   5
Till he hath pass'd necessity.
I'll show you those in troubles reign,
Losing a mite, a mountain gain.
The good in conversation,
To whom I give my benison,   10
Is still at Tharsus, where each man
Thinks all is writ he speken can ;
And, to remember what he does,
Build his statue to make him glorious.
But tidings to the contrary   15
Are brought your eyes. What need speak I ?

Dumb show.

Enter, at one door, PERICLES, *talking with*
CLEON ; *all the* Train *with them. Enter, at
another door, a* Gentleman *with a letter to
Pericles ; Pericles shows the letter to Cleon.
Pericles gives the Messenger a reward, and
knights him. Exit Pericles at one door and
Cleon at another.*

Good Helicane, that stay'd at home,
Not to eat honey like a drone
From others' labours ; for though he strive
To killen bad, keep good alive ;   20
And, to fulfil his prince' desire,
Sends word of all that haps in Tyre :
How Thaliard came full bent with sin
And had intent to murder him ;
And that in Tharsus was not best   25
Longer for him to make his rest.
He, doing so, put forth to seas,
Where when men been, there's seldom ease ;
For now the wind begins to blow ;
Thunder above and deeps below   30
Makes such unquiet that the ship
Should house him safe is wreck'd and split ;
And he, good prince, having all lost,
By waves from coast to coast is toss'd.
All perishen of man, of pelf,   35
Ne aught escapen but himself ;
Till fortune, tir'd with doing bad,
Threw him ashore, to give him glad.
And here he comes. What shall be next,
Pardon old Gower—this longs the text. 40
                  [*Exit.*

SCENE I. *Pentapolis. An open place by the
           seaside.*

Enter PERICLES, *wet.*

  Per. Yet cease your ire, you angry stars
  of heaven !
Wind, rain, and thunder, remember earthly
  man
Is but a substance that must yield to you ;
And I, as fits my nature, do obey you.
Alas, the sea hath cast me on the rocks, 5
Wash'd me from shore to shore, and left me
  breath
Nothing to think on but ensuing death.
Let it suffice the greatness of your powers
To have bereft a prince of all his fortunes ;
And having thrown him from your wat'ry
  grave,   10
Here to have death in peace is all he'll crave.

Enter three Fishermen.

  1 Fish. What, ho, Pilch !
  2 Fish. Ha, come and bring away the
nets.
  1 Fish. What, Patchbreech, I say !
  3 Fish. What say you, master ?   15
  1 Fish. Look how thou stirr'st now.
Come away, or I'll fetch thee with a
wanion.
  3 Fish. Faith, master, I am thinking of
the poor men that were cast away before us
even now.   19
  1 Fish. Alas, poor souls ! It grieved my
heart to hear what pitiful cries they made
to us to help them, when, well-a-day, we
could scarce help ourselves.
  3 Fish. Nay, master, said not I as much
when I saw the porpas how he bounc'd and
tumbled ? They say they're half fish, half
flesh. A plague on them ! They ne'er come
but I look to be wash'd. Master, I marvel
how the fishes live in the sea.   27
  1 Fish. Why, as men do a-land—the
great ones eat up the little ones. I can
compare our rich misers to nothing so fitly
as to a whale : 'a plays and tumbles, driving the poor fry before him, and at last
devours them all at a mouthful. Such
whales have I heard on a'th' land, who never
leave gaping till they've swallow'd the
whole parish, church, steeple, bells, and all.
  Per. [*Aside*] A pretty moral.   35
  3 Fish. But, master, if I had been the
sexton, I would have been that day in the
belfry.
  2 Fish. Why, man ?
  3 Fish. Because he should have swallowed
me too ; and when I had been in his belly
I would have kept such a jangling of the
bells that he should never have left till he
cast bells, steeple, church, and parish up
again. But if the good King Simonides were
of my mind—
  Per. [*Aside*] Simonides !

3 *Fish.* We would purge the land of these drones that rob the bee of her honey.

Per. [*Aside*] How from the finny subject of the sea
These fishers tell the infirmities of men,
And from their wat'ry empire recollect   50
All that may men approve or men detect!—
Peace be at your labour, honest fishermen!

2 *Fish.* Honest—good fellow! What's that? If it be a day fits you, scratch't out of the calendar, and nobody look after it.   55

Per. May see the sea hath cast upon your coast—

2 *Fish.* What a drunken knave was the sea to cast thee in our way!

Per. A man whom both the waters and the wind
In that vast tennis-court hath made the ball   60
For them to play upon entreats you pity him;
He asks of you that never us'd to beg.

1 *Fish.* No, friend, cannot you beg? Here's them in our country of Greece gets more with begging than we can do with working.   65

2 *Fish.* Canst thou catch any fishes, then?

Per. I never practis'd it.

2 *Fish.* Nay, then thou wilt starve, sure; for here's nothing to be got now-a-days unless thou canst fish for't.   70

Per. What I have been I have forgot to know;
But what I am want teaches me to think on:
A man throng'd up with cold; my veins are chill,
And have no more of life than may suffice
To give my tongue that heat to ask your help;   75
Which if you shall refuse, when I am dead,
For that I am a man, pray see me buried.

1 *Fish.* Die quoth-a? Now gods forbid't! And I have a gown here! Come, put it on; keep thee warm. Now, afore me, a handsome fellow! Come, thou shalt go home, and we'll have flesh for holidays, fish for fasting days, and moreo'er puddings and flapjacks; and thou shalt be welcome.

Per. I thank you, sir.

2 *Fish.* Hark you, my friend; you said you could not beg.   86

Per. I did but crave.

2 *Fish.* But crave! Then I'll turn craver too, and so I shall scape whipping.

Per. Why, are all your beggars whipp'd, then?   90

2 *Fish.* O, not all, my friend, not all! For if all your beggars were whipp'd, I would wish no better office than to be beadle. But, master, I'll go draw up the net.

[*Exit with Third Fisherman.*

Per. [*Aside*] How well this honest mirth becomes their labour!

1 *Fish.* Hark you, sir; do you know where ye are?   95

Per. Not well.

1 *Fish.* Why, I'll tell you: this is call'd Pentapolis, and our king the good Simonides.

Per. The good Simonides, do you call him?

1 *Fish.* Ay, sir; and he deserves so to be call'd for his peaceable reign and good government.   101

Per. He is a happy king, since he gains from his subjects the name of good by his government. How far is his court distant from this shore?

1 *Fish.* Marry, sir, half a day's journey; and I'll tell you, he hath a fair daughter, and to-morrow is her birthday, and there are princes and knights come from all parts of the world to joust and tourney for her love.

Per. Were my fortunes equal to my desires, I could wish to make one there.   110

1 *Fish.* O sir, things must be as they may; and what a man cannot get he may lawfully deal for—his wife's soul.   113

Re-enter Second *and* Third Fishermen, *drawing up a net.*

2 *Fish.* Help, master, help! Here's a fish hangs in the net like a poor man's right in the law; 'twill hardly come out. Ha! Bots on't! 'Tis come at last, and 'tis turn'd to a rusty armour.

Per. An armour, friends! I pray you let me see it.
Thanks, Fortune, yet, that after all my crosses
Thou givest me somewhat to repair myself;   120
And though it was mine own, part of my heritage
Which my dead father did bequeath to me,
With this strict charge, even as he left his life:
' Keep it, my Pericles. It hath been a shield
'Twixt me and death;' and pointed to this brace   125
' For that it sav'd me, keep it. In like necessity—
The which the gods protect thee from!—may't defend thee!'
It kept where I kept, I so dearly lov'd it;
Till the rough seas, that spare not any man,
Took it in rage, though calm'd have given't again—   130
I thank thee for't. My shipwreck now's no ill,
Since I have here my father's gift in his will.

1 *Fish.* What mean you, sir?

Per. To beg of you, kind friends, this coat of worth,
For it was sometime target to a king;   135

I know it by this mark. He lov'd me
dearly,
And for his sake I wish the having of it ;
And that you'd guide me to your sovereign's
court,
Where with it I may appear a gentleman ;
And if that ever my low fortune's better, 140
I'll pay your bounties ; till then rest your
debtor.

1 *Fish.* Why, wilt thou tourney for the
lady ?

Per. I'll show the virtue I have borne in
arms.

1 *Fish.* Why, do'e take it, and the gods
give thee good on't ! 145

2 *Fish.* Ay, but hark you, my friend ;
'twas we that made up this garment
through the rough seams of the waters ;
there are certain condolements, certain
vails. I hope, sir, if you thrive, you'll
remember from whence you had them. 150

Per. Believe't, I will.
By your furtherance I am cloth'd in steel ;
And spite of all the rapture of the sea
This jewel holds his building on my arm.
Unto thy value I will mount myself 155
Upon a courser whose delightful steps
Shall make the gazer joy to see him tread.
Only, my friend, I yet am unprovided
Of a pair of bases. 159

2 *Fish.* We'll sure provide. Thou shalt
have my best gown to make thee a pair ;
and I'll bring thee to the court myself.

Per. Then honour be but a goal to my
will ; 163
This day I'll rise, or else add ill to ill.
[*Exeunt.*

SCENE II. *Pentapolis. A public way or
platform leading to the lists. A pavilion
by the side of it for the reception of the
King, Princess, Lords, &c.*

Enter SIMONIDES, THAISA, *Lords, and*
Attendants.

Sim. Are the knights ready to begin the
triumph ?

1 *Lord.* They are, my liege ;
And stay your coming to present themselves.

Sim. Return them we are ready ; and
our daughter here,
In honour of whose birth these triumphs
are, 5
Sits here like beauty's child, whom nature
gat
For men to see, and seeing wonder at.
[*Exit a Lord.*

Thai. It pleaseth you, my royal father,
to express
My commendations great, whose merit's
less.

Sim. It's fit it should be so ; for princes
are 10

A model which heaven makes like to itself :
As jewels lose their glory if neglected,
So princes their renowns if not respected.
'Tis now your honour, daughter, to enter-
tain
The labour of each knight in his device. 15

Thai. Which, to preserve mine honour,
I'll perform.

Enter a Knight ; *he passes over, and his*
Squire *presents his shield to the Princess.*

Sim. Who is the first that doth prefer
himself ?

Thai. A knight of Sparta, my renowned
father ;
And the device he bears upon his shield
Is a black Ethiope reaching at the sun ; 20
The word, ' Lux tua vita mihi'.

Sim. He loves you well that holds his life
of you.

The Second Knight *passes by.*

Who is the second that presents himself ?
Thai. A prince of Macedon, my royal
father ;
And the device he bears upon his shield 25
Is an arm'd knight that's conquer'd by a
lady ;
The motto thus, in Spanish, ' Piu por
dulzura que por fuerza'.

The Third Knight *passes by.*

Sim. And what's the third ?
Thai. The third of Antioch ;
And his device a wreath of chivalry ;
The word, ' Me pompæ provexit apex'. 30

The Fourth Knight *passes by.*

Sim. What is the fourth ?
Thai. A burning torch that's turned up-
side down ;
The word, ' Quod me alit, me extinguit'.
Sim. Which shows that beauty hath his
power and will,
Wh.ch can as well inflame as it can kill. 35

The Fifth Knight *passes by.*

Thai. The fifth, an hand environed with
clouds,
Holding out gold that's by the touchstone
tried ;
The motto thus, ' Sic spectanda fides'.

PERICLES *as* Sixth Knight *passes by.*

Sim. And what's the sixth and last, the
which the knight himself 40
With such a graceful courtesy deliver'd ?
Thai. He seems to be a stranger ; but his
present is
A withered branch, that's only green at
top ;
The motto, ' In hac spe vivo '.
Sim. A pretty moral ; 45
From the dejected state wherein he is,

He hopes by you his fortunes yet may
    flourish.
  1 *Lord.* He had need mean better than
    his outward show
Can any way speak in his just commend ;
For by his rusty outside he appears   50
To have practis'd more the whipstock than
    the lance.
  2 *Lord.* He well may be a stranger, for he
    comes
To an honour'd triumph strangely furnished.
  3 *Lord.* And on set purpose let his
    armour rust
Until this day, to scour it in the dust. 55
  Sim. Opinion's but a fool, that makes us
    scan
The outward habit by the inward man.
But stay, the knights are coming. We will
    withdraw
Into the gallery.   [*Exeunt.*
    [*Great shouts within, and all cry*
           ' The mean knight ! '

SCENE III. *Pentapolis. A hall of state. A*
    banquet prepared.

Enter KING SIMONIDES, THAISA, Ladies,
  Lords, Knights, *from tilting, and*
    Attendants.

  Sim. Knights !
To say you're welcome were superfluous.
To place upon the volume of your deeds,
As in a title-page, your worth in arms
Were more than you expect, or more than's
    fit,   5
Since every worth in show commends itself.
Prepare for mirth, for mirth becomes a feast ;
You are princes and my guests.
  Thai. But you my knight and guest ;
To whom this wreath of victory I give, 10
And crown you king of this day's happiness.
  Per. 'Tis more by fortune, lady, than my
    merit.
  Sim. Call it by what you will, the day is
    yours ;
And here I hope is none that envies it. 14
In framing an artist, art hath thus decreed,
To make some good, but others to exceed ;
And you are her labour'd scholar. Come,
    queen o' th' feast—
For, daughter, so you are—here take your
    place.
Marshal the rest as they deserve their
    grace.
  Knights. We are honour'd much by good
    Simonides.   20
  Sim. Your presence glads our days.
    Honour we love ;
For who hates honour hates the gods above.
  Marshal. Sir, yonder is your place.
  Per.   Some other is more fit.
  1 *Knight.* Contend not, sir ; for we are
    gentlemen   24
That neither in our hearts nor outward eyes

Envy the great nor shall the low despise.
  Per. You are right courteous knights.
  Sim.   Sit, sir, sit.
[*Aside*] By Jove, I wonder, that is king of
    thoughts,   28
These cates resist me, he not thought upon.
  Thai. [*Aside*] By Juno, that is queen of
    marriage,
All viands that I eat do seem unsavoury,
Wishing him my meat.—Sure he's a gallant
    gentleman.
  Sim. He's but a country gentleman ;
Has done no more than other knights have
    done ;
Has broken a staff or so ; so let it pass. 35
  Thai. [*Aside*] To me he seems like dia-
    mond to glass.
  Per. [*Aside*] Yon king's to me like to my
    father's picture,
Which tells me in that glory once he was ;
Had princes sit like stars about his throne,
And he the sun, for them to reverence ; 40
None that beheld him but, like lesser lights,
Did vail their crowns to his supremacy :
Where now his son's like a glowworm in the
    night,
The which hath fire in darkness, none in
    light.   44
Whereby I see that Time's the king of men ;
He's both their parent, and he is their
    grave,
And gives them what he will, not what they
    crave.
  Sim. What, are you merry, knights ?
  1 *Knight.* Who can be other in this royal
    presence ?
  Sim. Here, with a cup that's stor'd unto
    the brim—   50
As you do love, fill to your mistress' lips—
We drink this health to you.
  Knights.   We thank your Grace.
  Sim. Yet pause awhile.
Yon knight doth sit too melancholy,
As if the entertainment in our court 55
Had not a show might countervail his
    worth.
Note it not you, Thaisa ?
  Thai.   What is't
To me, my father ?
  Sim.   O, attend, my daughter :
Princes, in this, should live like gods above,
Who freely give to every one that comes 61
To honour them ;
And princes not doing so are like to gnats,
Which make a sound, but kill'd are
    wond'red at.   64
Therefore to make his entertain more sweet,
Here, say we drink this standing-bowl of
    wine to him.
  Thai. Alas, my father, it befits not me
Unto a stranger knight to be so bold :
He may my proffer take for an offence,
Since men take women's gifts for impud-
    ence.   70

Sim. How !
Do as I bid you, or you'll move me else.

Thai. [*Aside*] Now, by the gods, he could
not please me better.

Sim. And furthermore tell him we desire
to know of him

Of whence he is, his name and parentage. 75

Thai. The King my father, sir, has drunk
to you.

Per. I thank him.

Thai. Wishing it so much blood unto
your life.

Per. I thank both him and you, and
pledge him freely.

Thai. And further he desires to know of
you 80

Of whence you are, your name and parentage.

Per. A gentleman of Tyre—my name,
Pericles ;

My education been in arts and arms ; 83
Who, looking for adventures in the world,
Was by the rough seas reft of ships and men,
And after shipwreck driven upon this shore.

Thai. He thanks your Grace ; names
himself Pericles,
A gentleman of Tyre,
Who only by misfortune of the seas, 89
Bereft of ships and men, cast on this shore.

Sim. Now, by the gods, I pity his
misfortune,
And will awake him from his melancholy.
Come, gentlemen, we sit too long on trifles
And waste the time which looks for other
revels. 94
Even in your armours, as you are address'd,
Will very well become a soldier's dance.
I will not have excuse, with saying this
Loud music is too harsh for ladies' heads,
Since they love men in arms as well as beds.
[*They dance.*

So, this was well ask'd, 'twas so well
perform'd. 100
Come, sir ;
Here is a lady that wants breathing too ;
And I have heard you knights of Tyre
Are excellent in making ladies trip ;
And that their measures are as excellent.

Per. In those that practise them they are,
my lord. 105

Sim. O, that's as much as you would be
denied
Of your fair courtesy. [*The Knights and
Ladies dance*] Unclasp, unclasp.

Thanks, gentlemen, to all ; all have done
well,
[*To Pericles*] But you the best.—Pages and
lights, to conduct
These knights unto their several lodgings !—
Yours, sir, 110
We have given order to be next our own.

Per. I am at your Grace's pleasure.

Sim. Princes, it is too late to talk of love,
And that's the mark I know you level at.

Therefore each one betake him to his rest ;
To-morrow all for speeding do their best.
[*Exeunt.*

SCENE IV. *Tyre. The Governor's house.*

Enter HELICANUS *and* ESCANES.

Hel. No, Escanes ; know this of me—
Antiochus from incest liv'd not free ;
For which, the most high gods not minding
longer
To withhold the vengeance that they had
in store,
Due to this heinous capital offence, 5
Even in the height and pride of all his
glory,
When he was seated in a chariot
Of an inestimable value, and his daughter
with him,
A fire from heaven came and shrivell'd up
Their bodies, even to loathing ; for they so
stunk 10
That all those eyes ador'd them ere their
fall
Scorn now their hand should give them
burial.

Esca. 'Twas very strange.

Hel. And yet but justice ; for though
This king were great, his greatness was no
guard
To bar heaven's shaft, but sin had his
reward. 15

Esca. 'Tis very true.

Enter two or three Lords.

1 Lord. See, not a man in private conference
Or council has respect with him but he.

2 Lord. It shall no longer grieve without
reproof.

3 Lord. And curs'd be he that will not
second it ! 20

1 Lord. Follow me, then. Lord Helicane,
a word.

Hel. With me ? and welcome. Happy
day, my lords.

1 Lord. Know that our griefs are risen to
the top,
And now at length they overflow their
banks.

Hel. Your griefs ! for what ? Wrong not
your prince you love. 25

1 Lord. Wrong not yourself, then, noble
Helicane ;
But if the prince do live, let us salute him,
Or know what ground's made happy by his
breath.
If in the world he live, we'll seek him out ;
If in his grave he rest, we'll find him there ;
And be resolv'd he lives to govern us, 31
Or, dead, give's cause to mourn his funeral,
And leave us to our free election.

2 Lord. Whose death's indeed the
strongest in our censure ;

And knowing this kingdom, if without a
    head,   35
Like goodly buildings left without a roof,
Soon fall to ruin, your noble self,
That best know how to rule and how to reign,
We thus submit unto—our sovereign.
    All. Live, noble Helicane !   40
    Hel. By honour's cause, forbear your
      suffrages.
If that you love Prince Pericles, forbear.
Take I your wish, I leap into the seas,
Where's hourly trouble for a minute's ease.
A twelvemonth longer let me entreat you 45
To forbear the absence of your king ;
If in which time expir'd he not return,
I shall with aged patience bear your yoke.
But if I cannot win you to this love,
Go search like nobles, like noble subjects, 50
And in your search spend your adventurous
    worth ;
Whom if you find, and win unto return,
You shall like diamonds sit about his crown.
    1 Lord. To wisdom he's a fool that will
      not yield ;
And since Lord Helicane enjoineth us,   55
We with our travels will endeavour it.
    Hel. Then you love us, we you, and we'll
      clasp hands :
When peers thus knit, a kingdom ever
    stands.   [*Exeunt.*

    SCENE V. *Pentapolis. The palace.*

Enter SIMONIDES, *reading of a letter, at one
    door. The Knights meet him.*

    1 Knight. Good morrow to the good
      Simonides.
    Sim. Knights, from my daughter this I
      let you know,
That for this twelvemonth she'll not under-
    take
A married life.
Her reason to herself is only known,   5
Which from her by no means can I get.
    2 Knight. May we not get access to her,
      my lord ?
    Sim. Faith, by no means ; she hath so
      strictly tied her
To her chamber that it is impossible.
One twelve moons more she'll wear Diana's
    livery.   10
This by the eye of Cynthia hath she vow'd,
And on her virgin honour will not break it.
    3 Knight. Loath to bid farewell, we take
      our leaves.   [*Exeunt Knights.*
    Sim. So,
They are well despatch'd. Now to my
    daughter's letter.   15
She tells me here she'll wed the stranger
    knight,
Or never more to view nor day nor light.
'Tis well, mistress ; your choice agrees
    with mine ;
I like that well. Nay, how absolute she's in't,

Not minding whether I dislike or no !   20
Well, I do commend her choice ;
And will no longer have it be delay'd.
Soft ! here he comes : I must dissemble it.

    Enter PERICLES.

    Per. All fortune to the good Simonides !
    Sim. To you as much, sir ! I am behold-
      ing to you   25
For your sweet music this last night. I do
Protest my ears were never better fed
With such delightful pleasing harmony.
    Per. It is your Grace's pleasure to com-
      mend ;
Not my desert.
    Sim.   Sir, you are music's master. 30
    Per. The worst of all her scholars, my
      good lord.
    Sim. Let me ask you one thing :
What do you think of my daughter, sir ?
    Per. A most virtuous princess.
    Sim. And she is fair too, is she not ?   35
    Per. As a fair day in summer—wondrous
      fair.
    Sim. Sir, my daughter thinks very well
      of you ;
Ay, so well that you must be her master,
And she will be your scholar ; therefore
    look to it.   39
    Per. I am unworthy for her schoolmaster.
    Sim. She thinks not so ; peruse this
      writing else.
    Per. [*Aside*] What's here ?
A letter, that she loves the knight of Tyre.
'Tis the king's subtlety to have my life.—
O, seek not to entrap me, gracious lord, 45
A stranger and distressed gentleman,
That never aim'd so high to love your
    daughter,
But bent all offices to honour her !
    Sim. Thou hast bewitch'd my daughter,
      and thou art
A villain.
    Per.   By the gods, I have not.   50
Never did thought of mine levy offence ;
Nor never did my actions yet commence
A deed might gain her love or your dis-
    pleasure.
    Sim. Traitor, thou liest.
    Per.   Traitor !
    Sim.   Ay, traitor.
    Per. Even in his throat—unless it be the
      King—   55
That calls me traitor I return the lie.
    Sim. [*Aside*] Now, by the gods, I do
      applaud his courage.
    Per. My actions are as noble as my
      thoughts,
That never relish'd of a base descent.   59
I came unto your court for honour's cause,
And not to be a rebel to her state ;
And he that otherwise accounts of me,
This sword shall prove he's honour's
    enemy.

Sim. No?
Here comes my daughter, she can witness
it.   65
     Enter THAISA.

Per. Then, as you are as virtuous as fair,
Resolve your angry father if my tongue
Did e'er solicit, or my hand subscribe
To any syllable that made love to you.
 Thai. Why, sir, say if you had, 70
Who takes offence at that would make me
  glad?
 Sim. Yea, mistress, are you so peremp-
  tory?
[*Aside*] I am glad on't with all my heart.—
I'll tame you; I'll bring you in subjection.
Will you, not having my consent, 75
Bestow your love and your affections
Upon a stranger?—[*Aside*] who, for aught
  I know,
May be, nor can I think the contrary,
As great in blood as I myself.— 79
Therefore, hear you, mistress: either frame
Your will to mine—and you, sir, hear you,
Either be rul'd by me—or I will make
  you—
Man and wife.
Nay, come, your hands and lips must seal
  it too;
And being join'd, I'll thus your hopes
  destroy,
          85
And for further grief—God give you joy!
What, are you both pleas'd?
 Thai.   Yes, if you love me, sir.
 Per. Even as my life my blood that
  fosters it.
 Sim. What, are you both agreed?
 Both. Yes, if't please your Majesty. 90
 Sim. It pleaseth me so well that I will
  see you wed;
And then, with what haste you can, get
  you to bed.   [*Exeunt.*

ACT THREE

Enter GOWER.

Gow. Now sleep yslaked hath the rout;
No din but snores the house about,
Made louder by the o'er-fed breast
Of this most pompous marriage feast.
The cat, with eyne of burning coal, 5
Now couches fore the mouse's hole;
And crickets sing at the oven's mouth,
Aye the blither for their drouth.
Hymen hath brought the bride to bed,
Where, by the loss of maidenhead, 10
A babe is moulded. Be attent,
And time that is so briefly spent
With your fine fancies quaintly eche.
What's dumb in show I'll plain with speech.

Dumb Show.

Enter PERICLES *and* SIMONIDES *at one door,
with* Attendants; *a Messenger meets*

them, *kneels, and gives Pericles a letter.
Pericles shows it Simonides; the Lords
kneel to Pericles. Then enter* THAISA,
with child, with LYCHORIDA, *a nurse. The
King shows her the letter; she rejoices.
She and Pericles take leave of her father,
and depart with Lychorida and their
Attendants. Then exeunt Simonides and
the rest.*

By many a dern and painful perch 15
Of Pericles the careful search,
By the four opposing coigns
Which the world together joins,
Is made with all due diligence
That horse and sail and high expense 20
Can stead the quest. At last from Tyre—
Fame answering the most strange inquire—
To the court of King Simonides
Are letters brought, the tenour these:
Antiochus and his daughter dead, 25
The men of Tyrus on the head
Of Helicanus would set on
The crown of Tyre, but he will none.
The mutiny he there hastes t' oppress;
Says to 'em, if King Pericles 30
Come not home in twice six moons,
He, obedient to their dooms,
Will take the crown. The sum of this,
Brought hither to Pentapolis,
Y-ravished the regions round, 35
And every one with claps can sound
' Our heir-apparent is a king!
Who dream'd, who thought of such a
  thing?'
Brief, he must hence depart to Tyre.
His queen with child makes her desire— 40
Which who shall cross?—along to go.
Omit we all their dole and woe.
Lychorida, her nurse, she takes,
And so to sea. Their vessel shakes
On Neptune's billow; half the flood 45
Hath their keel cut: but fortune's mood
Varies again; the grizzled north
Disgorges such a tempest forth
That, as a duck for life that dives,
So up and down the poor ship drives. 50
The lady shrieks, and, well-a-near,
Does fall in travail with her fear;
And what ensues in this fell storm
Shall for itself itself perform.
I nill relate, action may 55
Conveniently the rest convey;
Which might not what by me is told.
In your imagination hold
This stage the ship, upon whose deck
The sea-toss'd Pericles appears to speak. 60
            [*Exit.*

SCENE I. *Enter* PERICLES, *a-shipboard.*

Per. Thou god of this great vast, rebuke
  these surges,
Which wash both heaven and hell; and
  thou that hast

Upon the winds command, bind them in
    brass,
Having call'd them from the deep ! O, still
Thy deaf'ning dreadful thunders ; gently
    quench   5
Thy nimble sulphurous flashes !—O, how,
    Lychorida,
How does my queen ?—Thou stormest
    venomously ;
Wilt thou spit all thyself ?   The seaman's
    whistle
Is as a whisper in the ears of death,
Unheard.—Lychorida !—Lucina, O   10
Divinest patroness, and midwife gentle
To those that cry by night, convey thy
    deity
Aboard our dancing boat ; make swift the
    pangs
Of my queen's travails !

    Enter LYCHORIDA, *with an* Infant.

                Now, Lychorida !
  Lyc. Here is a thing too young for such
    a place,   15
Who, if it had conceit, would die, as I
Am like to do. Take in your arms this piece
Of your dead queen.
  Per.   How, how, Lychorida ?
  Lyc. Patience, good sir ; do not assist
    the storm.   19
Here's all that is left living of your queen—
A little daughter. For the sake of it,
Be manly, and take comfort.
  Per.   O you gods !
Why do you make us love your goodly gifts,
And snatch them straight away ? We here
    below   24
Recall not what we give, and therein may
Use honour with you.
  Lyc. Patience, good sir, even for this
    charge.
  Per. Now, mild may be thy life !
For a more blusterous birth had never babe ;
Quiet and gentle thy conditions ! for
Thou art the rudeliest welcome to this
    world   30
That ever was prince's child. Happy what
    follows !
Thou hast as chiding a nativity
As fire, air, water, earth, and heaven, can
    make,
To herald thee from the womb.   34
Even at the first thy loss is more than can
Thy portage quit with all thou canst find
    here.
Now the good gods throw their best eyes
    upon't !

    Enter two Sailors.

  1 Sail. What courage, sir ? God save you !
  Per. Courage enough : I do not fear the
    flaw ;
It hath done to me the worst. Yet, for the
    love   40

Of this poor infant, this fresh-new seafarer,
I would it would be quiet.
  1 Sail. Slack the bolins there.—Thou
wilt not, wilt thou ? Blow, and split thyself.
  2 Sail. But sea-room, an the brine and
cloudy billow kiss the moon, I care not. 46
  1 Sail. Sir, your queen must overboard :
the sea works high, the wind is loud, and
will not lie till the ship be clear'd of the
dead.
  Per. That's your superstition.   50
  1 Sail. Pardon us, sir ; with us at sea it
hath been still observed, and we are strong
in custom. Therefore briefly yield 'er ; for
she must overboard straight.
  Per. As you think meet. Most wretched
    queen !
  Lyc. Here she lies, sir.   55
  Per. A terrible childbed hast thou had,
    my dear ;
No light, no fire. Th' unfriendly elements
Forgot thee utterly ; nor have I time
To give thee hallow'd to thy grave, but
    straight
Must cast thee, scarcely coffin'd, in the
    ooze ;   60
Where, for a monument upon thy bones,
And aye-remaining lamps, the belching
    whale
And humming water must o'erwhelm thy
    corpse,
Lying with simple shells. O Lychorida, 64
Bid Nestor bring me spices, ink and paper,
My casket and my jewels ; and bid
    Nicander
Bring me the satin coffer. Lay the babe
Upon the pillow. Hie thee, whiles I say
A priestly farewell to her. Suddenly,
    woman.   [*Exit Lychorida.*
  2 Sail. Sir, we have a chest beneath the
hatches, caulk'd and bitumed ready.   71
  Per. I thank thee. Mariner, say what
    coast is this ?
  2 Sail. We are near Tharsus.
  Per. Thither, gentle mariner,
Alter thy course for Tyre. When canst thou
    reach it ?
  2 Sail. By break of day, if the wind
cease.   76
  Per. O, make for Tharsus !
There will I visit Cleon, for the babe
Cannot hold out to Tyrus ; there I'll leave it
At careful nursing. Go thy ways, good
    mariner :   80
I'll bring the body presently.   [*Exeunt.*

  SCENE II. *Ephesus. Cerimon's house.*

  Enter CERIMON, *with a* Servant, *and some*
    Persons *who have been shipwrecked.*

  Cer. Philemon, ho !

    Enter PHILEMON.

  Phil. Doth my lord call ?

Cer. Get fire and meat for these poor men.
'T'as been a turbulent and stormy night.

    Serv. I have been in many; but such a
night as this,
Till now, I ne'er endured.   6

    Cer. Your master will be dead ere you
       return;
There's nothing can be minist'red to nature
That can recover him. [*To Philemon*] Give
       this to the pothecary,
And tell me how it works.
               [*Exeunt all but Cerimon.*

       Enter two Gentlemen.

    1 Gent. Good morrow.   10
    2 Gent. Good morrow to your lordship.
    Cer. Gentlemen, why do you stir so early?
    1 Gent. Sir,
Our lodgings, standing bleak upon the sea,
Shook as the earth did quake;   15
The very principals did seem to rend,
And all to topple. Pure surprise and fear
Made me to quit the house.

    2 Gent. That is the cause we trouble you
       so early;
'Tis not our husbandry.
    Cer.   O, you say well. 20
    1 Gent. But I much marvel that your
       lordship, having
Rich tire about you, should at these early
       hours
Shake off the golden slumber of repose.
'Tis most strange   24
Nature should be so conversant with pain,
Being thereto not compell'd.
    Cer.   I hold it ever
Virtue and cunning were endowments
       greater
Than nobleness and riches: careless heirs
May the two latter darken and expend;
But immortality attends the former,   30
Making a man a god. 'Tis known I ever
Have studied physic, through which secret
       art,
By turning o'er authorities, I have,
Together with my practice, made familiar
To me and to my aid the blest infusions 35
That dwell in vegetives, in metals, stones;
And I can speak of the disturbances
That nature works, and of her cures; which
       doth give me
A more content in course of true delight
Than to be thirsty after tottering honour,
Or tie my treasure up in silken bags,   41
To please the fool and death.
    2 Gent. Your honour has through
       Ephesus pour'd forth
Your charity, and hundreds call themselves
Your creatures, who by you have been
       restor'd: 45
And not your knowledge, your personal
       pain, but even
Your purse, still open, hath built Lord
       Cerimon

Such strong renown as time shall never raze.

    Enter two or three Servants *with a chest.*

    1 Ser. So, lift there.
    Cer. What's that?   50
    1 Serv. Sir, even now did the sea toss
up upon our shore this chest. 'Tis of some
wreck.
    Cer. Set't down, let's look upon't.
    2 Gent. 'Tis like a coffin, sir.
    Cer.   Whate'er it be, 55
'Tis wondrous heavy. Wrench it open
       straight.
If the sea's stomach be o'ercharg'd with
       gold,
'Tis a good constraint of fortune it belches
       upon us.
    2 Gent. 'Tis so, my lord.
    Cer. How close 'tis caulk'd and bitumed!
Did the sea cast it up?   61
    1 Serv. I never saw so huge a billow, sir,
as toss'd it upon shore.
    Cer. Wrench it open. Soft! It smells
most sweetly in my sense.
    2 Gent. A delicate odour.   66
    Cer. As ever hit my nostril. So, up with it.
O you most potent gods! What's here?
       A corse!
    1 Gent. Most strange!   69
    Cer. Shrouded in cloth of state; balm'd
and entreasur'd with full bags of spices.
A passport too. Apollo, perfect me in the
characters!   [*Reads from a scroll.*

    Here I give to understand—
    If e'er this coffin drives a-land—
    I, King Pericles, have lost   75
    This queen, worth all our mundane cost.
    Who finds her, give her burying;
    She was the daughter of a king.
    Besides this treasure for a fee,
    The gods requite his charity!   80
If thou livest, Pericles, thou hast a heart
That ever cracks for woe! This chanc'd
       to-night.
    2 Gent. Most likely, sir.
    Cer.   Nay, certainly to-night;
For look how fresh she looks! They were
       too rough
That threw her in the sea. Make a fire
       within.   85
Fetch hither all my boxes in my closet.
               [*Exit a servant.*
Death may usurp on nature many hours,
And yet the fire of life kindle again
The o'erpress'd spirits. I heard of an
       Egyptian
That had nine hours lien dead,   90
Who was by good appliance recovered.

    Re-enter a Servant, *with boxes, napkins, and
       fire.*

Well said, well said! The fire and cloths.
The rough and woeful music that we have,

Cause it to sound, beseech you.
The vial once more. How thou stirr'st, thou
    block ! 95
The music there ! I pray you give her air.
    Gentlemen,
This queen will live ; nature awakes ; a
    warmth
Breathes out of her. She hath not been
    entranc'd 99
Above five hours. See how she gins to blow
Into life's flower again !
    1 Gent.   The heavens,
Through you, increase our wonder, and set up
Your fame for ever.
    Cer.   She is alive. Behold,
Her eyelids, cases to those heavenly jewels
Which Pericles hath lost, begin to part 105
Their fringes of bright gold ; the diamonds
Of a most praised water do appear,
To make the world twice rich. Live, and
    make
Us weep to hear your fate, fair creature,
Rare as you seem to be.   [She moves.
    Thai. O dear Diana, where am I ?
Where's my lord ? What world is this ? 111
    2 Gent. Is not this strange ?
    1 Gent. Most rare.
    Cer. Hush, my gentle neighbours !
Lend me your hands : to the next chamber
    bear her ; 115
Get linen. Now this matter must be look'd
    to,
For her relapse is mortal.
Come, come ; and Æsculapius guide us !
        [Exeunt, carrying her away.

SCENE III. *Tharsus. Cleon's house.*

Enter PERICLES, CLEON, DIONYZA, *and*
    LYCHORIDA *with* MARINA *in her arms.*

    Per. Most honour'd Cleon, I must needs
        be gone ;
My twelve months are expir'd, and Tyrus
    stands
In a litigious peace. You and your lady
Take from my heart all thankfulness ! The
    gods
Make up the rest upon you !   5
    Cle. Your shafts of fortune, though they
        hurt you mortally,
Yet glance full wand'ringly on us.
    Dio.   O your sweet queen !
That the strict Fates had pleas'd you had
    brought her hither,
To have bless'd mine eyes with her !
    Per.   We cannot but obey
The powers above us. Could I rage and
    roar 10
As doth the sea she lies in, yet the end
Must be as 'tis. My gentle babe Marina,
    whom,
For she was born at sea, I have nam'd so,
    here
I charge your charity withal, leaving her

The infant of your care ; beseeching you 15
To give her princely training, that she may
Be manner'd as she is born.
    Cle. Fear not, my lord, but think
Your grace, that fed my country with your
    corn,
For which the people's prayers still fall
    upon you,
Must in your child be thought on. If
    neglection 20
Should therein make me vile, the common
    body,
By you reliev'd, would force me to my duty.
But if to that my nature need a spur,
The gods revenge it upon me and mine
To the end of generation !
    Per.   I believe you ; 25
Your honour and your goodness teach me
    to't
Without your vows. Till she be married,
    madam,
By bright Diana, whom we honour all, 28
Unscissor'd shall this hair of mine remain,
Though I show ill in't. So I take my
    leave.
Good madam, make me blessed in your care
In bringing up my child.
    Dio.   I have one myself,
Who shall not be more dear to my respect
Than yours, my lord.
    Per. Madam, my thanks and prayers.
    Cle. We'll bring your Grace e'en to the
        edge o' th' shore, 35
Then give you up to the mask'd Neptune and
The gentlest winds of heaven.
    Per.   I will embrace
Your offer. Come, dearest madam. O, no
    tears,
Lychorida, no tears.
Look to your little mistress, on whose
    grace 40
You may depend hereafter. Come, my lord.
        [Exeunt.

SCENE IV. *Ephesus. Cerimon's house.*

Enter CERIMON *and* THAISA.

    Cer. Madam, this letter, and some certain
        jewels,
Lay with you in your coffer ; which are
At your command. Know you the char-
    acter ?
    Thai. It is my lord's.   4
That I was shipp'd at sea I well remember,
Even on my eaning time ; but whether
    there
Delivered, by the holy gods,
I cannot rightly say. But since King
    Pericles,
My wedded lord, I ne'er shall see again,
A vestal livery will I take me to,   10
And never more have joy.
    Cer. Madam, if this you purpose as ye
        speak,

Diana's temple is not distant far,
Where you may abide till your date
    expire.
Moreover, if you please, a niece of mine 15
Shall there attend you.
   Thai. My recompense is thanks, that's all;
Yet my good will is great, though the gift
    small.   [*Exeunt.*

ACT FOUR

Enter GOWER.

   Gow. Imagine Pericles arriv'd at Tyre,
Welcom'd and settled to his own desire.
His woeful queen we leave at Ephesus,
Unto Diana there a votaress.
Now to Marina bend your mind,   5
Whom our fast-growing scene must find
At Tharsus, and by Cleon train'd
In music, letters; who hath gain'd
Of education all the grace,   9
Which makes her both the heart and place
Of general wonder. But, alack,
That monster Envy, oft the wrack
Of earned praise, Marina's life
Seeks to take off by treason's knife.
And in this kind hath our Cleon   15
One daughter, and a wench full grown,
Even ripe for marriage-rite; this maid
Hight Philoten; and it is said
For certain in our story, she
Would ever with Marina be.   20
Be't when she weav'd the sleided silk
With fingers long, small, white as milk;
Or when she would with sharp needle wound
The cambric, which she made more sound
By hurting it; or when to th' lute   25
She sung, and made the night-bird mute,
That still records with moan; or when
She would with rich and constant pen
Vail to her mistress Dian; still
This Philoten contends in skill   30
With absolute Marina. So
The dove of Paphos might with the crow
Vie feathers white. Marina gets
All praises, which are paid as debts,
And not as given. This so darks   35
In Philoten all graceful marks
That Cleon's wife, with envy rare,
A present murderer does prepare
For good Marina, that her daughter
Might stand peerless by this slaughter. 40
The sooner her vile thoughts to stead,
Lychorida, our nurse, is dead;
And cursed Dionyza hath
The pregnant instrument of wrath
Prest for this blow. The unborn event 45
I do commend to your content;
Only I carry winged time
Post on the lame feet of my rhyme;
Which never could I so convey
Unless your thoughts went on my way. 50
Dionyza does appear,
With Leonine, a murderer.   [*Exit.*

SCENE I.   *Tharsus.*   *An open place near
    the seashore.*

Enter DIONYZA and LEONINE.

   Dio. Thy oath remember; thou hast
    sworn to do't.
'Tis but a blow, which never shall be known.
Thou canst not do a thing in the world so
    soon
To yield thee so much profit. Let not con-
    science,
Which is but cold, inflaming love in thy
    bosom,   5
Inflame too nicely; nor let pity, which
Even women have cast off, melt thee, but be
A soldier to thy purpose.
   Leon. I will do't; but yet she is a goodly
    creature.
   Dio. The fitter, then, the gods should
    have her.
Here she comes weeping for her only
    mistress' death.
Thou art resolv'd?   12
   Leon. I am resolv'd.

Enter MARINA *with a basket of flowers.*

   Mar. No, I will rob Tellus of her weed,
To strew thy green with flowers. The
    yellows, blues,   15
The purple violets, and marigolds,
Shall as a carpet hang upon thy grave
While summer days do last. Ay me! poor
    maid,
Born in a tempest, when my mother died,
This world to me is like a lasting storm, 20
Whirring me from my friends.
   Dio. How now, Marina! Why do you
    keep alone?
How chance my daughter is not with you?
    Do not
Consume your blood with sorrowing; you
    have
A nurse of me. Lord, how your favour's
    chang'd   25
With this unprofitable woe! Come,
Give me your flowers. On the sea margent
Walk with Leonine; the air is quick there,
And it pierces and sharpens the stomach.
    Come,
Leonine, take her by the arm, walk with
    her.   30
   Mar. No, I pray you;
I'll not bereave you of your servant.
   Dio.   Come, come;
I love the king your father, and yourself,
With more than foreign heart. We every
    day   35
Expect him here. When he shall come, and
    find
Our paragon to all reports thus blasted,
He will repent the breadth of his great
    voyage;
Blame both my lord and me that we have
    taken

No care to your best courses. Go, I pray
    you,   40
Walk, and be cheerful once again ; reserve
That excellent complexion which did steal
The eyes of young and old. Care not for me ;
I can go home alone.
    Mar.   Well, I will go ;
But yet I have no desire to it.   45
    Dio. Come, come, I know 'tis good for
    you.
Walk half an hour, Leonine, at the least.
Remember what I have said.
    Leon.   I warrant you, madam.
    Dio. I'll leave you, my sweet lady, for
    a while.   49
Pray walk softly ; do not heat your blood.
What ! I must have care of you.
    Mar.   My thanks, sweet madam.
                       [Exit Dionyza.
Is this wind westerly that blows ?
    Leon.   South-west.
    Mar. When I was born the wind was
    north.
    Leon.   Was't so ?
    Mar. My father, as nurse says, did never
    fear,
But cried ' Good seamen ! ' to the sailors,
    galling   55
His kingly hands hauling ropes ;
And, clasping to the mast, endur'd a sea
That almost burst the deck.
    Leon. When was this ?
    Mar. When I was born.   60
Never was waves nor wind more violent ;
And from the ladder-tackle washes off
A canvas-climber. ' Ha ! ' says one ' wolt
    out ? '
And with a dropping industry they skip
From stern to stern ; the boatswain
    whistles, and   65
The master calls, and trebles their confusion.
    Leon. Come, say your prayers.
    Mar.   What mean you ?
    Leon. If you require a little space for
    prayer,
I grant it. Pray ; but be not tedious, for 70
The gods are quick of ear, and I am sworn
To do my work with haste.
    Mar.   Why will you kill me ?
    Leon. To satify my lady.
    Mar. Why would she have me kill'd ?
Now, as I can remember, by my troth,   75
I never did her hurt in all my life.
I never spake bad word, nor did ill turn
To any living creature. Believe me, la,
I never kill'd a mouse, nor hurt a fly ;
I trod upon a worm against my will,   80
But I wept for it. How have I offended,
Wherein my death might yield her any profit,
Or my life imply her any danger ?
    Leon.   My commission
Is not to reason of the deed, but do't.   85
    Mar. You will not do't for all the world,
    I hope.

You are well-favour'd, and your looks fore-
    show
You have a gentle heart. I saw you lately
When you caught hurt in parting two that
    fought.
Good sooth, it show'd well in you. Do so
    now :   90
Your lady seeks my life ; come you be-
    tween,
And save poor me, the weaker.
    Leon.   I am sworn,
And will dispatch.   *[Seizes her.*

          Enter Pirates.

    1 Pirate. Hold, villain !
                   [Leonine runs away.
    2 Pirate. A prize ! a prize !   95
    3 Pirate. Half part, mates, half part !
Come, let's have her aboard suddenly.
      [Exeunt Pirates with Marina.

      Re-enter LEONINE.

    Leon. These roguing thieves serve the
    great pirate Valdes,
And they have seiz'd Marina. Let her go ;
There's no hope she will return. I'll swear
    she's dead   100
And thrown into the sea. But I'll see
    further.
Perhaps they will but please themselves
    upon her,
Not carry her aboard. If she remain,
Whom they have ravish'd must by me be
    slain.   *[Exit.*

    SCENE II. *Mytilene. A brothel.*

    Enter Pander, Bawd, *and* BOULT.

    Pand. Boult !
    Boult. Sir ?
    Pand. Search the market narrowly.
Mytilene is full of gallants. We lost too
much money this mart by being too
wenchless.   5
    Bawd. We were never so much out of
creatures. We have but poor three, and
they can do no more than they can do ;
and they with continual action are even as
good as rotten.   9
    Pand. Therefore let's have fresh ones,
whate'er we pay for them. If there be not
a conscience to be us'd in every trade, we
shall never prosper.
    Bawd. Thou say'st true ; 'tis not our
bringing up of poor bastards—as, I think,
I have brought up some eleven—   15
    Boult. Ay, to eleven ; and brought them
down again. But shall I search the market ?
    Bawd. What else, man ? The stuff we
have, a strong wind will blow it to pieces,
they are so pitifully sodden.
    Pand. Thou sayest true ; they are too
unwholesome, o' conscience. The poor
Transylvanian is dead that lay with the
little baggage.   22

Boult. Ay, she quickly poop'd him ; she made her roast meat for worms. But I'll go search the market.   [*Exit.*

Pand. Three or four thousand chequins were as pretty a proportion to live quietly, and so give over.

Bawd. Why to give over, I pray you ? Is it a shame to get when we are old ?   28

Pand. O, our credit comes not in like the commodity, nor the commodity wages not with the danger ; therefore, if in our youths we could pick up some pretty estate, 'twere not amiss to keep our door hatch'd. Besides, the sore terms we stand upon with the gods will be strong with us for giving o'er.

Bawd. Come, other sorts offend as well as we.   35

Pand. As well as we ! Ay, and better too ; we offend worse. Neither is our profession any trade ; it's no calling. But here comes Boult.

Re-enter BOULT, *with the* Pirates *and* MARINA.

Boult. [*To Marina*] Come your ways.— My masters, you say she's a virgin ?   40

1 *Pirate.* O, sir, we doubt it not.

Boult. Master, I have gone through for this piece you see. If you like her, so ; if not, I have lost my earnest.

Bawd. Boult, has she any qualities ?   45

Boult. She has a good face, speaks well, and has excellent good clothes ; there's no farther necessity of qualities can make her be refus'd.

Bawd. What's her price, Boult ?

Boult. I cannot be bated one doit of a thousand pieces.   51

Pand. Well, follow me, my masters ; you shall have your money presently. Wife, take her in ; instruct her what she has to do, that she may not be raw in her entertainment.   [*Exeunt Pander and Pirates.*

Bawd. Boult, take you the marks of her— the colour of her hair, complexion, height, her age, with warrant of her virginity ; and cry ' He that will give most shall have her first '. Such a maidenhead were no cheap thing, if men were as they have been. Get this done as I command you.   61

Boult. Performance shall follow.   [*Exit.*

Mar. Alack that Leonine was so slack, so slow !

He should have struck, not spoke ; or that these pirates,

Not enough barbarous, had not o'erboard thrown me

For to seek my mother !   66

Bawd. Why lament you, pretty one ?

Mar. That I am pretty.

Bawd. Come, the gods have done their part in you.

Mar. I accuse them not.   70

Bawd. You are light into my hands, where you are like to live.

Mar. The more my fault
To scape his hands where I was like to die.

Bawd. Ay, and you shall live in pleasure.

Mar. No.   76

Bawd. Yes, indeed shall you, and taste gentlemen of all fashions. You shall fare well ; you shall have the difference of all complexions. What ! do you stop your ears ?   80

Mar. Are you a woman ?

Bawd. What would you have me be, an I be not a woman ?   83

Mar. An honest woman, or not a woman.

Bawd. Marry, whip thee, gosling ! I think I shall have something to do with you. Come, you're a young foolish sapling, and must be bow'd as I would have you.

Mar. The gods defend me !   89

Bawd. If it please the gods to defend you by men, then men must comfort you, men must feed you, men must stir you up. Boult's return'd.

Re-enter BOULT.

Now, sir, hast thou cried her through the market ?

Boult. I have cried her almost to the number of her hairs ; I have drawn her picture with my voice.   95

Bawd. And I prithee tell me how dost thou find the inclination of the people, especially of the younger sort ?

Boult. Faith, they listened to me as they would have hearkened to their father's testament. There was a Spaniard's mouth so wat'red that he went to bed to her very description.   102

Bawd. We shall have him here to-morrow with his best ruff on.

Boult. To-night, to-night. But, mistress, do you know the French knight that cowers i' th' hams ?   106

Bawd. Who ? Monsieur Veroles ?

Boult. Ay, he ; he offered to cut a caper at the proclamation ; but he made a groan at it, and swore he would see her to-morrow.   110

Bawd. Well, well ; as for him, he brought his disease hither : here he does but repair it. I know he will come in our shadow to scatter his crowns in the sun.

Boult. Well, if we had of every nation a traveller, we should lodge them with this sign.   115

Bawd. [*To Marina*] Pray you, come hither awhile. You have fortunes coming upon you. Mark me : you must seem to do that fearfully which you commit willingly ; to despise profit where you have most gain. To weep that you live as ye do makes pity in your lovers ; seldom but that pity begets you a good opinion, and that opinion a mere profit.   122

Mar. I understand you not.

Boult. O, take her home, mistress, take her home. These blushes of hers must be quench'd with some present practice.   126

Bawd. Thou sayest true, i' faith, so they must; for your bride goes to that with shame which is her way to go with warrant.

Boult. Faith, some do, and some do not. But, mistress, if I have bargain'd for the joint—   131

Bawd. Thou mayst cut a morsel off the spit.

Boult. I may so.

Bawd. Who should deny it? Come, young one, I like the manner of your garments well.   135

Boult. Ay, by my faith, they shall not be chang'd yet.

Bawd. Boult, spend thou that in the town; report what a sojourner we have; you'll lose nothing by custom. When nature fram'd this piece she meant thee a good turn; therefore say what a paragon she is, and thou hast the harvest out of thine own report.   142

Boult. I warrant you, mistress, thunder shall not so awake the beds of eels as my giving out her beauty stir up the lewdly inclined. I'll bring home some to-night.

Bawd. Come your ways; follow me.

Mar. If fires be hot, knives sharp, or waters deep,
Untied I still my virgin knot will keep.
Diana aid my purpose!   149

Bawd. What have we to do with Diana? Pray you will you go with us?   [*Exeunt.*

SCENE III. *Tharsus. Cleon's house.*

Enter CLEON *and* DIONYZA.

Dio. Why are you foolish? Can it be undone?

Cle. O Dionyza, such a piece of slaughter
The sun and moon ne'er look'd upon!

Dio.   I think
You'll turn a child again.

Cle. Were I chief lord of all this spacious world,   5
I'd give it to undo the deed. O lady,
Much less in blood than virtue, yet a princess
To equal any single crown o' th' earth
I' th' justice of compare! O villain Leonine!
Whom thou hast pois'ned too.   10
If thou hadst drunk to him, 't had been a kindness
Becoming well thy fact. What canst thou say
When noble Pericles shall demand his child?

Dio. That she is dead. Nurses are not the Fates,
To foster it, nor ever to preserve.   15
She died at night; I'll say so. Who can cross it?
Unless you play the pious innocent,
And for an honest attribute cry out
'She died by foul play'.

Cle.   O, go to. Well, well.
Of all the faults beneath the heavens the gods   20
Do like this worst.

Dio.   Be one of those that thinks
The petty wrens of Tharsus will fly hence,
And open this to Pericles. I do shame
To think of what a noble strain you are,
And of how coward a spirit.

Cle.   To such proceeding
Who ever but his approbation added,   26
Though not his prime consent, he did not flow
From honourable sources.

Dio.   Be it so, then.
Yet none does know, but you, how she came dead,
Nor none can know, Leonine being gone.
She did distain my child, and stood between   31
Her and her fortunes. None would look on her,
But cast their gazes on Marina's face;
Whilst ours was blurted at, and held a mawkin,
Not worth the time of day. It pierc'd me thorough;   35
And though you call my course unnatural,
You not your child well loving, yet I find
It greets me as an enterprise of kindness
Perform'd to your sole daughter.

Cle.   Heavens forgive it!

Dio. And as for Pericles,   40
What should he say? We wept after her hearse,
And yet we mourn; her monument
Is almost finish'd, and her epitaphs
In glittering golden characters express
A general praise to her, and care in us   45
At whose expense 'tis done.

Cle.   Thou art like the harpy,
Which, to betray, dost, with thine angel's face,
Seize with thine eagle's talons.

Dio. You are like one that superstitiously
Doth swear to the gods that winter kills the flies;   50
But yet I know you'll do as I advise.
[*Exeunt.*

SCENE IV. *Before Marina's monument at Tharsus.*

Enter GOWER.

Gow. Thus time we waste, and longest leagues make short;

Sail seas in cockles, have an wish but for't ;
Making, to take our imagination,
From bourn to bourn, region to region.
By you being pardon'd, we commit no
    crime   5
To use one langauge in each several clime
Where our scenes seem to live. I do beseech
    you
To learn of me, who stand i' th' gaps to
    teach you
The stages of our story. Pericles   9
Is now again thwarting the wayward seas,
Attended on by many a lord and knight,
To see his daughter, all his life's delight.
Old Helicanus goes along. Behind
Is left to govern it, you bear in mind,
Old Escanes, whom Helicanus late   15
Advanc'd in time to great and high estate.
Well-sailing ships and bounteous winds
    have brought
This king to Tharsus—think this pilot
    thought ;
So with his steerage shall your thoughts
    grow on—
To fetch his daughter home, who first is
    gone.   20
Like motes and shadows see them move
    awhile ;
Your ears unto your eyes I'll reconcile.

Dumb show.

Enter PERICLES, *at one door, with all his*
    Train : CLEON *and* DIONYZA *at the other.*
    Cleon shows Pericles the tomb of Marina,
    whereat Pericles makes lamentation, puts on
    sackcloth, and in a mighty passion departs.
    Then exeunt Cleon and Dionyza.

See how belief may suffer by foul show !
This borrowed passion stands for true old
    woe ;
And Pericles, in sorrow all devour'd,   25
With sighs shot through and biggest tears
    o'ershower'd,
Leaves Tharsus, and again embarks. He
    swears
Never to wash his face nor cut his hairs ;
He puts on sackcloth, and to sea. He bears
A tempest which his mortal vessel tears,   30
And yet he rides it out. Now please you wit
The epitaph is for Marina writ
By wicked Dionyza. [*Reads the inscription*
                  on Marina's monument.
' The fairest, sweetest, and best lies here,
Who withered in her spring of year.   35
She was of Tyrus the King's daughter,
On whom foul death hath made this
    slaughter ;
Marina was she call'd ; and at her birth,
Thetis, being proud, swallowed some part o'
    th' earth ;
Therefore the earth, fearing to be o'er-
    flowed,   40
Hath Thetis' birth-child on the heavens
    bestowed ;

Wherefore she does—and swears she'll
    never stint—
Make raging battery upon shores of flint.'
No visor does become black villainy
So well as soft and tender flattery.   45
Let Pericles believe his daughter's dead,
And bear his courses to be ordered
By Lady Fortune ; while our scene must
    play
His daughter's woe and heavy well-a-day
In her unholy service. Patience, then,   50
And think you now are all in Mytilen.
                        [*Exit.*

SCENE V. *Mytilene. A street before the*
        brothel.

Enter, from the brothel, two Gentlemen.

1 *Gent.* Did you ever hear the like ?
2 *Gent.* No, nor never shall do in such a
place as this, she being once gone.   3
1 *Gent.* But to have divinity preach'd
there ! Did you ever dream of such a thing ?
2 *Gent.* No, no. Come, I am for no more
bawdy-houses. Shall's go hear the vestals
sing ?
1 *Gent.* I'll do anything now that is
virtuous ; but I am out of the road of
rutting for ever.   [*Exeunt.*

SCENE VI. *Mytilene. A room in the brothel.*

Enter Pander, Bawd, and BOULT.

Pand. Well, I had rather than twice the
worth of her she had ne'er come here.
Bawd. Fie, fie, upon her ! She's able to
freeze the god Priapus, and undo a whole
generation. We must either get her
ravished or be rid of her. When she should
do for clients her fitment, and do me the
kindness of our profession, she has me her
quirks, her reasons, her master-reasons, her
prayers, her knees ; that she would make
a puritan of the devil, if he should cheapen
a kiss of her.
Boult. Faith, I must ravish her, or she'll   10
disfurnish us of all our cavalleria and make
our swearers priests.
Pand. Now the pox upon her green-
sickness for me !
Bawd. Faith there's no way to be rid on't
but by the way to the pox. Here comes the
Lord Lysimachus disguised.   16
Boult. We should have both lord and
lown, if the peevish baggage would but give
way to customers.

Enter LYSIMACHUS

Lys. How now ! How a dozen of
virginities ?
Bawd. Now, the gods to bless your
Honour !
Boult. I am glad to see your Honour in   20
good health.

Lys. You may so ; 'tis the better for you that your resorters stand upon sound legs. How now! Wholesome iniquity have you, that a man may deal withal and defy the surgeon ?   25

Bawd. We have here one, sir, if she would —but there never came her like in Mytilene.

Lys. If she'd do the deed of darkness, thou wouldst say.

Bawd. Your Honour knows what 'tis to say well enough.   31

Lys. Well, call forth, call forth.

Boult. For flesh and blood, sir, white and red, you shall see a rose ; and she were a rose indeed, if she had but—   35

Lys. What, prithee ?

Boult. O, sir, I can be modest.

Lys. That dignifies the renown of a bawd no less than it gives a good report to a number to be chaste.   *[Exit Boult.*

Bawd. Here comes that which grows to the stalk—never plucked yet, I can assure you.   41

Re-enter BOULT *with* MARINA.

Is she not a fair creature ?

Lys. Faith, she would serve after a long voyage at sea. Well, there's for you. Leave us.

Bawd. I beseech your Honour, give me leave : a word, and I'll have done presently.   46

Lys. I beseech you, do.

Bawd. [*Aside to Marina*] First, I would have you note this is an honourable man.

Mar. I desire to find him so, that I may worthily note him.   51

Bawd. Next, he's the governor of this country, and a man whom I am bound to.

Mar. If he govern the country, you are bound to him indeed ; but how honourable he is in that I know not.

Bawd. Pray you, without any more virginal fencing, will you use him kindly ? He will line your apron with gold.

Mar. What he will do graciously I will thankfully receive.   60

Lys. Ha' you done ?

Bawd. My lord, she's not pac'd yet ; you must take some pains to work her to your manage. Come, we will leave his Honour and her together. Go thy ways.

    [*Exeunt Bawd, Pander, and Boult.*

Lys. Now, pretty one, how long have you been at this trade ?   66

Mar. What trade, sir ?

Lys. Why, I cannot name't but I shall offend.

Mar. I cannot be offended with my trade. Please you to name it.   70

Lys. How long have you been of this profession ?

Mar. E'er since I can remember.

Lys. Did you go to't so young ? Were you a gamester at five or at seven ?   75

Mar. Earlier too, sir, if now I be one.

Lys. Why, the house you dwell in proclaims you to be a creature of sale.

Mar. Do you know this house to be a place of such resort, and will come into't ? I hear say you're of honourable parts, and are the governor of this place.   80

Lys. Why, hath your principal made known unto you who I am ?

Mar. Who is my principal ?   83

Lys. Why, your herb-woman ; she that sets seeds and roots of shame and iniquity. O, you have heard something of my power, and so stand aloof for more serious wooing. But I protest to thee, pretty one, my authority shall not see thee, or else look friendly upon thee. Come, bring me to some private place. Come, come.   90

Mar. If you were born to honour, show it now ;

If put upon you, make the judgment good That thought you worthy of it.

Lys. How's this ? how's this ? Some more ; be sage.

Mar.   For me,

That am a maid, though most ungentle fortune   95

Have plac'd me in this sty, where, since I came,

Diseases have been sold dearer than physic—

That the gods

Would set me free from this unhallowed place,

Though they did change me to the meanest bird   100

That flies i' th' purer air !

Lys.   I did not think

Thou couldst have spoke so well ; ne'er dreamt thou couldst.

Had I brought hither a corrupted mind,

Thy speech had altered it. Hold, here's gold for thee :

Persever in that clear way thou goest,   105

And the gods strengthen thee !

Mar. The good gods preserve you !

Lys. For me, be you thoughten

That I came with no ill intent ; for to me

The very doors and windows savour vilely.

Fare thee well. Thou art a piece of virtue, and   110

I doubt not but thy training hath been noble.

Hold, here's more gold for thee.

A curse upon him, die he like a thief,

That robs thee of thy goodness ! If thou dost

Hear from me, it shall be for thy good.   115

Re-enter BOULT.

Boult. I beseech your Honour, one piece for me.

Lys. Avaunt, thou damned door keeper!
Your house, but for this virgin that doth
    prop it, 118
Would sink and overwhelm you. Away!
                       [*Exit.*

Boult. How's this? We must take another course with you. If your peevish
chastity, which is not worth a breakfast in
the cheapest country under the cope, shall
undo a whole household, let me be gelded
like a spaniel. Come your ways.

Mar. Whither would you have me? 125

Boult. I must have your maidenhead
taken off, or the common hangman shall
execute it. Come your ways. We'll have
no more gentlemen driven away. Come
your ways, I say. 129

Re-enter BAWD.

Bawd. How now! What's the matter?

Boult. Worse and worse, mistress; she
has here spoken holy words to the Lord
Lysimachus.

Bawd. O abominable!

Boult. She makes our profession as it
were to stink afore the face of the gods. 135

Bawd. Marry, hang her up for ever!

Boult. The nobleman would have dealt
with her like a nobleman, and she sent him
away as cold as a snowball; saying his
prayers too. 139

Bawd. Boult, take her away; use her at
thy pleasure. Crack the glass of her
virginity, and make the rest malleable.

Boult. An if she were a thornier piece of
ground than she is, she shall be ploughed.

Mar. Hark, hark, you gods! 145

Bawd. She conjures. Away with her.
Would she had never come within my
doors! Marry, hang you! She's born to
undo us. Will you not go the way of
womenkind? Marry, come up, my dish of
chastity with rosemary and bays! [*Exit.*

Boult. Come, mistress; come your ways
with me. 151

Mar. Whither wilt thou have me?

Boult. To take from you the jewel you
hold so dear.

Mar. Prithee tell me one thing first.

Boult. Come now, your one thing. 155

Mar. What canst thou wish thine enemy
to be?

Boult. Why, I could wish him to be my
master, or, rather, my mistress.

Mar. Neither of these are so bad as thou
    art, 159
Since they do better thee in their command.
Thou hold'st a place for which the pained'st
    fiend
Of hell would not in reputation change;
Thou art the damned doorkeeper to every
Coistrel that comes inquiring for his Tib;
To the choleric fisting of every rogue 165
Thy ear is liable; thy food is such

As hath been belch'd on by infected lungs.

Boult. What would you have me do? Go
to the wars, would you, where a man may
serve seven years for the loss of a leg, and
have not money enough in the end to buy
him a wooden one? 171

Mar. Do anything but this thou doest.
    Empty
Old receptacles, or common shores, of filth;
Serve by indenture to the common hang-
    man. 174
Any of these ways are yet better than this;
For what thou professest, a baboon, could
    he speak,
Would own a name too dear. That the gods
Would safely deliver me from this place!
Here, here's gold for thee.
If that thy master would gain by me, 180
Proclaim that I can sing, weave, sew, and
    dance,
With other virtues which I'll keep from
    boast;
And I will undertake all these to teach.
I doubt not but this populous city will
Yield many scholars. 185

Boult. But can you teach all this you
speak of?

Mar. Prove that I cannot, take me home
    again
And prostitute me to the basest groom
That doth frequent your house.

Boult. Well, I will see what I can do for
thee. If I can place thee, I will. 191

Mar. But amongst honest women?

Boult. Faith, my acquaintance lies little
amongst them. But since my master and
mistress have bought you, there's no going
but by their consent. Therefore I will make
them acquainted with your purpose, and I
doubt not but I shall find them tractable
enough. Come, I'll do for thee what I can;
come your ways. [*Exeunt.*

ACT FIVE

Enter GOWER.

Gow. Marina thus the brothel scapes and
    chances
Into an honest house, our story says.
She sings like one immortal, and she dances
As goddess-like to her admired lays;
Deep clerks she dumbs; and with her
    needle composes 5
Nature's own shape of bud, bird, branch,
    or berry,
That even her art sisters the natural roses;
Her inkle, silk, twin with the rubied cherry;
That pupils lacks she none of noble race,
Who pour their bounty on her; and her
    gain 10
She gives the cursed bawd. Here we her
    place;
And to her father turn our thoughts again,

Where we left him on the sea. We there him
    lost ;
Whence, driven before the winds, he is
    arriv'd
Here where his daughter dwells ; and on
    this coast   15
Suppose him now at anchor.   The city
    striv'd
God Neptune's annual feast to keep ; from
    whence
Lysimachus our Tyrian ship espies,
His banners sable, trimm'd with rich
    expense ;   19
And to him in his barge with fervour hies.
In your supposing once more put your
    sight.
Of heavy Pericles, think this his bark ;
Where what is done in action, more, if
    might,
Shall be discover'd ; please you sit and
    hark.   [*Exit.*

SCENE I. *On board Pericles' ship, off*
Mytilene. A pavilion on deck with a
curtain before it ; Pericles within it,
reclining on a couch. A barge lying beside
the Tyrian vessel.

Enter two Sailors, one belonging to the
Tyrian vessel, the other to the barge ; to
them HELICANUS.

  Tyr. Sail. [*To the Sailor of Mytilene*]
Where is Lord Helicanus ? He can resolve
you.
O, here he is.
Sir, there is a barge put off from Mytilene,
And in it is Lysimachus the Governor,
Who craves to come aboard. What is your
    will ?   5
  Hel. That he have his. Call up some
    gentlemen.
  Tyr. Sail. Ho, gentlemen ! my lord calls.

  Enter two or three Gentlemen.

  1 *Gent.* Doth your lordship call ?
  Hel. Gentlemen, there is some of worth
    would come aboard ;
I pray greet him fairly.   10
    [*The Gentlemen and the two Sailors*
    descend, and go on board the barge.

Enter, from thence, LYSIMACHUS *and Lords,*
with the Gentlemen and the two Sailors.

  Tyr. Sail. Sir,
This is the man that can, in aught you
    would,
Resolve you.
  Lys. Hail, reverend sir ! The gods pre-
    serve you !   14
  Hel. And you, sir, to outlive the age I am,
And die as I would do.
  Lys.   You wish me well.
Being on shore, honouring of Neptune's
    triumphs,
Seeing this goodly vessel ride before us,

I made to it, to know of whence you are. 19
  Hel. First, what is your place ?
  Lys.   I am the Governor
Of this place you lie before.
  Hel. Sir,
Our vessel is of Tyre, in it the King ;
A man who for this three months hath not
    spoken
To any one, nor taken sustenance   25
But to prorogue his grief.
  Lys. Upon what ground is his dis-
    temperature ?
  Hel. 'Twould be too tedious to repeat ;
But the main grief springs from the loss
Of a beloved daughter and a wife.   30
  Lys. May we not see him ?
  Hel. You may ;
But bootless is your sight—he will not speak
To any.
  Lys. Yet let me obtain my wish.
  Hel. Behold him. [*Pericles discovered*] This
    was a goodly person   35
Till the disaster that, one mortal night,
Drove him to this.
  Lys. Sir King, all hail !   The gods
    preserve you !
Hail, royal sir !
  Hel. It is in vain ; he will not speak to
    you.   40
  1 *Lord.* Sir, we have a maid in Mytilene,
    I durst wager,
Would win some words of him.
  Lys.   'Tis well bethought.
She, questionless, with her sweet harmony
And other chosen attractions, would allure,
And make a batt'ry through his deafen'd
    parts,   46
Which now are midway stopp'd.
She is all happy as the fairest of all,
And, with her fellow maids, is now upon
The leafy shelter that abuts against 50
The island's side. [*He whispers First Lord,*
    who goes off in the barge of Lysimachus.
  Hel. Sure, all's effectless ; yet nothing
    we'll omit
That bears recovery's name. But, since
    your kindness
We have stretch'd thus far, let us beseech
    you   54
That for our gold we may provision have,
Wherein we are not destitute for want,
But weary for the staleness.
  Lys.   O sir, a courtesy
Which if we should deny, the most just gods
For every graff would send a caterpillar,
And so inflict our province. Yet once more
Let me entreat to know at large the cause
Of your king's sorrow.
  Hel. Sit, sir, I will recount it to you. 62
But, see, I am prevented.

  Re-enter, from the barge, First Lord, with
    MARINA *and another Girl.*

  Lys.   O, here is

The lady that I sent for. Welcome, fair one!
Is't not a goodly presence ?
    Hel.   She's a gallant lady. 65
    Lys. She's such a one that, were I well
        assur'd
Came of gentle kind and noble stock,
I'd wish no better choice, and think me
        rarely wed.
Fair one, all goodness that consists in
        bounty   69
Expect even here, where is a kingly patient.
If that thy prosperous and artificial feat
Can draw him but to answer thee in aught,
Thy sacred physic shall receive such pay
As thy desires can wish.
    Mar.   Sir, I will use
My utmost skill in his recovery,
Provided   75
That none but I and my companion maid
Be suffered to come near him.
    Lys.   Come, let us leave her ;
And the gods make her prosperous !
                              [*Marina sings.*
    Lys. Mark'd he your music ?
    Mar.   No, nor look'd on us.
    Lys. See, she will speak to him.   80
    Mar. Hail sir ! my lord, lend ear.
    Per. Hum, ha !
    Mar. I am a maid,
My lord, that ne'er before invited eyes,
But have been gaz'd on like a comet. She
        speaks,   85
My lord, that, may be, hath endur'd a grief
Might equal yours, if both were justly
        weigh'd.
Though wayward fortune did malign my
        state,
My derivation was from ancestors   89
Who stood equivalent with mighty kings ;
But time hath rooted out my parentage,
And to the world and awkward casualties
Bound me in servitude. [*Aside*] I will desist;
But there is something glows upon my cheek,
And whispers in mine ear ' Go not till he
        speak '.   95
    Per. My fortunes—parentage—good par-
        entage—
To equal mine !—was it not thus ? What
        say you ?
    Mar. I said, my lord, if you did know my
        parentage
You would not do me violence.   99
    Per. I do think so. Pray you turn your
        eyes upon me.
You are like something that—What
        countrywoman ?
Here of these shores ?
    Mar.   No, nor of any shores.
Yet I was mortally brought forth, and am
No other than I appear.
    Per. I am great with woe, and shall
        deliver weeping.   105
My dearest wife was like this maid, and
        such a one

My daughter might have been : my queen's
        square brows ;
Her stature to an inch ; as wand-like
        straight ;
As silver voic'd ; her eyes as jewel-like,
And cas'd as richly ; in pace another Juno ;
Who starves the ears she feeds, and makes
        them hungry   111
The more she gives them speech. Where do
        you live ?
    Mar. Where I am but a stranger. From
        the deck
You may discern the place.
    Per.   Where were you bred ?
And how achiev'd you these endowments,
        which   115
You make more rich to owe ?
    Mar. If I should tell my history, it would
        seem
Like lies, disdain'd in the reporting.
    Per.   Prithee speak.
Falseness cannot come from thee ; for thou
        lookest
Modest as Justice, and thou seem'st a
        palace   120
For the crown'd Truth to dwell in. I will
        believe thee,
And make my senses credit thy relation
To points that seem impossib.e ; for thou
        lookest
Like one I lov'd indeed. What were thy
        friends ?
D dst thou not say, when I did push thee
        back—   125
Which was when I perceiv'd thee—that
        thou cam'st
From good descending ?
    Mar.   So indeed I did.
    Per. Report thy parentage. I think thou
        said'st
Thou hadst been toss'd from wrong to
        injury,
And that thou thought'st thy griefs might
        equal mine,   130
If both were opened.
    Mar.   Some such thing
I said, and said no more but what my
        thoughts
Did warrant me was likely.
    Per.   Tell thy story.
If thine consider'd prove the thousand part
Of my endurance, thou art a man, and I 135
Have suffered like a girl. Yet thou dost look
Like Patience gazing on kings' graves, and
        smiling
Extremity out of act. What were thy
        friends ?
How lost thou them ? Thy name, my most
        kind virgin ?
Recount, I do beseech thee. Come, sit by
        me.   140
    Mar. My name is Marina.
    Per.   O, I am mock'd,
And thou by some incensed god sent hither

To make the world to laugh at me.
Mar.   Patience, good sir,
Or here I'll cease.
Per.   Nay, I'll be patient.
Thou little know'st how thou dost startle
me   145
To call thyself Marina.
Mar. The name
Was given me by one that had some power,
My father, and a king.
Per.   How! a king's daughter?
And call'd Marina?
Mar.   You said you would believe me;
But, not to be a troubler of your peace,   150
I will end here.
Per.   But are you flesh and blood?
Have you a working pulse, and are no fairy?
Motion! Well; speak on. Where were
you born?
And wherefore call'd Marina?
Mar.   Call'd Marina
For I was born at sea.
Per.   At sea! what mother?   155
Mar. My mother was the daughter of a
king;
Who died the minute I was born,
As my good nurse Lychorida hath oft
Delivered weeping.
Per.   O, stop there a little!
[*Aside*] This is the rarest dream that e'er
dull sleep   160
Did mock sad fools withal. This cannot be:
My daughter's buried.—Well, where were
you bred?
I'll hear you more, to th' bottom of your
story,
And never interrupt you.
Mar. You scorn; believe me, 'twere
best I did give o'er.   165
Per. I will believe you by the syllable
Of what you shall deliver. Yet give me
leave—
How came you in these parts? where were
you bred?
Mar. The King my father did in Tharsus
leave me;
Till cruel Cleon, with his wicked wife,   170
Did seek to murder me; and having woo'd
A villain to attempt it, who having drawn
to do't,
A crew of pirates came and rescued me;
Brought me to Mytilene. But, good sir,
Whither will you have me? Why do you
weep? It may be   175
You think me an impostor. No, good
faith;
I am the daughter to King Pericles,
If good King Pericles be.
Per. Ho, Helicanus!
Hel.   Calls my lord?   180
Per. Thou art a grave and noble coun-
sellor,
Most wise in general. Tell me, if thou canst,
What this maid is, or what is like to be,

That thus hath made me weep?
Hel.   I know not; but
Here is the regent, sir, of Mytilene   185
Speaks nobly of her.
Lys.   She never would tell
Her parentage; being demanded that,
She would sit still and weep.
Per. O Helicanus, strike me, honour'd
sir;
Give me a gash, put me to present pain,   190
Lest this great sea of joys rushing upon me
O'erbear the shores of my mortality,
And drown me with their sweetness. O,
come hither,
Thou that beget'st him that did thee beget;
Thou that wast born at sea, buried at
Tharsus,   195
And found at sea again! O Helicanus,
Down on thy knees, thank the holy gods as
loud
As thunder threatens us. This is Marina.
What was thy mother's name? Tell me but
that,   199
For truth can never be confirm'd enough,
Though doubts did ever sleep.
Mar.   First, sir, I pray,
What is your title?
Per. I am Pericles of Tyre; but tell me
now
My drown'd queen's name, as in the rest
you said
Thou hast been godlike perfect,   205
The heir of kingdoms and another life
To Pericles thy father.
Mar. Is it no more to be your daughter
than
To say my mother's name was Thaisa?
Thaisa was my mother, who did end
The minute I began.   210
Per. Now blessing on thee! Rise; thou
art my child.
Give me fresh garments. Mine own,
Helicanus;
She is not dead at Tharsus, as she should
have been
By savage Cleon. She shall tell thee all;
When thou shalt kneel, and justify in
knowledge   215
She is thy very princess. Who is this?
Hel. Sir, 'tis the Governor of Mytilene,
Who, hearing of your melancholy state,
Did come to see you.
Per.   I embrace you.   220
Give me my robes. I am wild in my be-
holding.
O heavens bless my girl! But hark, what
music?
Tell Helicanus, my Marina, tell him
O'er, point by point, for yet he seems to
doubt,
How sure you are my daughter. But, what
music?   225
Hel. My lord, I hear none.
Per. None?

The music of the spheres !   List, my
  Marina.
   Lys. It is not good to cross him ; give
    him way.
  Per. Rarest sounds ! Do ye not hear ?
  Lys. My lord, I hear.   [*Music.*
  Per. Most heavenly music !   231
It nips me unto list'ning, and thick slumber
Hangs upon mine eyes : let me rest. [*Sleeps.*
  Lys. A pillow for his head.
So, leave him all. Well, my companion-
  friends,   235
If this but answer to my just belief,
I'll well remember you.
          [*Exeunt all but Pericles.*

DIANA *appears to Pericles as in a vision.*

  Dia. My temple stands in Ephesus. Hie
   thee thither,
And do upon mine altar sacrifice.
There, when my maiden priests are met
  together,   240
Before the people all,
Reveal how thou at sea didst lose thy
  wife.
To mourn thy crosses, with thy daughter's,
  call,
And give them repetition to the life.   244
Or perform my bidding or thou liv'st in woe;
Do it, and happy—by my silver bow !
Awake and tell thy dream.   [*Disappears.*
  Per. Celestial Dian, goddess argentine,
I will obey thee. Helicanus!

  Re-enter HELICANUS, LYSIMACHUS,
       MARINA, &c.

  Hel   Sir ?
  Per. My purpose was for Tharsus, there
   to strike   250
The inhospitable Cleon ; but I am
For other service first : toward Ephesus
Turn our blown sails ; eftsoons I'll tell thee
  why.
[*To Lysimachus*] Shall we refresh us, sir,
  upon your shore,
And give you gold for such provision   255
As our intents will need ?
  Lys. Sir,
With all my heart ; and when you come
  ashore
I have another suit.
  Per.   You shall prevail,   259
Were it to woo my daughter ; for it seems
You have been noble towards her.
  Lys. Sir, lend me your arm.
  Per. Come, my Marina.   [*Exeunt.*

SCENE II. *Ephesus. Before the Temple of
    Diana.*

    Enter GOWER.

  Gow. Now our sands are almost run ;
More a little, and then dumb.
This, my last boon, give me,

For such kindness must relieve me—
That you aptly will suppose   5
What pageantry, what feats, what shows,
What minstrelsy, and pretty din,
The regent made in Mytilen
To greet the King. So he thrived,
That he is promis'd to be wived   10
To fair Marina ; but in no wise
Till he had done his sacrifice,
As Dian bade ; whereto being bound,
The interim, pray you, all confound.
In feather'd briefness sails are fill'd, 15
And wishes fall out as they're will'd.
At Ephesus the temple see,
Our king, and all his company.
That he can hither come so soon,   19
Is by your fancies' thankful doom. [*Exit.*

SCENE III. *Ephesus. The Temple of Diana ;*
  THAISA *standing near the altar as High
  Priestess ; a number of* Virgins *on each
  side ;* CERIMON *and other* Inhabitants *of
  Ephesus attending.*

Enter PERICLES, *with his* Train ; LYSIMA-
  CHUS, HELICANUS, MARINA, *and a* Lady.

  Per. Hail, Dian ! to perform thy just
   command,
I here confess myself the King of Tyre ;
Who, frighted from my country, did wed
At Pentapolis the fair Thaisa.
At sea in childbed died she, but brought
  forth   5
A maid-child, call'd Marina ; who, O
  goddess,
Wears yet thy silver livery. She at Tharsus
Was nurs'd with Cleon ; who at fourteen
  years
He sought to murder ; but her better stars
Brought her to Mytilene ; 'gainst whose
  shore   10
Riding, her fortunes brought the maid
  aboard us,
Where, by her own most clear remem-
  brance, she
Made known herself my daughter.
  Thai.   Voice and favour !
You are, you are—O royal Pericles !
                [*Swoons.*
  Per. What means the nun ? She dies !
   Help, gentlemen !
  Cer. Noble sir,
If you have told Diana's altar true,
This is your wife.
  Per. Reverend appearer, no ;
I threw her o'erboard with these very arms.
  Cer. Upon this coast, I warrant you.
  Per.   'Tis most certain.
  Cer. Look to the lady. O, she's but over-
   joy'd.   21
Early in blustering morn this lady was
Thrown upon this shore. I op'd the coffin,
Found there rich jewels : recover'd her, and
  plac'd her

Here in Diana's temple.

Per.   May we see them?

Cer. Great sir, they shall be brought you
  to my house,   26
Whither I invite you. Look, Thaisa is
Recovered.

Thai. O, let me look!
If he be none of mine, my sanctity   30
Will to my sense bend no licentious ear,
But curb it, spite of seeing. O, my lord,
Are you not Pericles? Like him you
  spake,
Like him you are. Did you not name a
  tempest,   34
A birth and death?

Per.   The voice of dead Thaisa!

Thai. That Thaisa am I, supposed dead
And drown'd.

Per. Immortal Dian!

Thai.   Now I know you better.
When we with tears parted Pentapolis,
The King my father gave you such a ring.
         [*Shows a ring.*

Per. This, this! No more, you gods!
  your present kindness   41
Makes my past miseries sports. You shall
  do well
That on the touching of her lips I may
Melt and no more be seen. O, come, be
  buried
A second time within these arms!

Mar.   My heart
Leaps to be gone into my mother's bosom.
         [*Kneels to Thaisa.*

Per. Look who kneels here! Flesh of thy
  flesh, Thaisa;   47
Thy burden at the sea, and call'd Marina,
For she was yielded there.

Thai.   Blest and mine own!

Hel. Hail, madam, and my queen!

Thai.   I know you not.

Per. You have heard me say, when I did
  fly from Tyre,   51
I left behind an ancient substitute.
Can you remember what I call'd the man?
I have nam'd him oft.

Thai.   'Twas Helicanus then.

Per. Still confirmation.   55
Embrace him, dear Thaisa; this is he.
Now do I long to hear how you were found;
How possibly preserv'd; and who to
  thank,
Besides the gods, for this great miracle. 59

Thai. Lord Cerimon, my lord—this man
Through whom the gods have shown their
  power—that can
From first to last resolve you.

Per.   Reverend sir,
The gods can have no mortal officer

More like a god than you. Will you deliver
How this dead queen re-lives?

Cer.   I will, my lord.
Beseech you, first, go with me to my
  house,   66
Where shall be shown you all was found
  with her;
How she came plac'd here in the temple;
No needful thing omitted.

Per. Pure Dian, bless thee for thy vision!
  I   70
Will offer night-oblations to thee. Thaisa,
This Prince, the fair-betrothed of your
  daughter,
Shall marry her at Pentapolis. And now,
This ornament   74
Makes me look dismal will I clip to form;
And what this fourteen years no razor
  touch'd,
To grace thy marriage-day I'll beautify.

Thai. Lord Cerimon hath letters of good
  credit, sir,
My father's dead.

Per. Heavens make a star of him! Yet
  there, my queen,   80
We'll celebrate their nuptials, and ourselves
Will in that kingdom spend our following
  days.
Our son and daughter shall in Tyrus
  reign.
Lord Cerimon, we do our longing stay   84
To hear the rest untold. Sir, lead's the way.
           [*Exeunt.*

Enter GOWER.

Gow. In Antiochus and his daughter you
  have heard
Of monstrous lust the due and just reward:
In Pericles, his queen, and daughter, seen,
Although assail'd with fortune fierce and
  keen,
Virtue preserv'd from fell destruction's
  blast,   90
Led on by heaven, and crown'd with joy
  at last.
In Helicanus may you well descry
A figure of truth, of faith, of loyalty;
In reverend Cerimon there well appears 94
The worth that learned charity aye wears.
For wicked Cleon and his wife, when fame
Had spread their cursed deed, and honour'd
  name
Of Pericles, to rage the city turn,
That him and his they in his palace burn;
The gods for murder seemed so content 100
To punish—although not done, but meant.
So, on your patience evermore attending,
New joy wait on you! Here our play has
  ending.   [*Exit.*

VENUS AND ADONIS

Vilia miretur vulgus : mihi flavus Apollo
Pocula Castalia plena ministret aqua.

TO THE

RIGHT HONORABLE HENRIE WRIOTHESLEY,

EARLE OF SOUTHAMPTON, AND BARON OF TITCHFIELD.

RIGHT HONOURABLE,

I KNOW not how I shall offend in dedicating my unpolisht lines to your Lordship, nor how the worlde will censure mee for choosing so strong a proppe to support so weake a burthen, onelye if your Honour seeme but pleased, I account my selfe highly praised, and vowe to take advantage of all idle houres, till I have honoured you with some graver labour. But if the first heire of my invention prove deformed, I shall be sorie it had so noble a god-father : and never after eare so barren a land, for feare it yeeld me still so bad a harvest, I leave it to your Honourable survey, and your Honor to your hearts content which I wish may alwaies answere your owne wish, and the worlds hopefull expectation.

Your Honors in all dutie,

WILLIAM SHAKESPEARE.

EVEN as the sun with purple-colour'd face
Had ta'en his last leave of the weeping
 morn,
Rose-cheek'd Adonis hied him to the chase ;
Hunting he lov'd, but love he laugh'd to
 scorn,
 Sick-thoughted Venus makes amain unto
  him,   5
 And like a bold-fac'd suitor gins to woo
  him.

' Thrice fairer than myself,' thus she began,
' The field's chief flower, sweet above com-
 pare,
Stain to all nymphs, more lovely than a
 man,   9
More white and red than doves or roses are ;
 Nature that made thee, with herself at
  strife,
 Saith that the world hath ending with
  thy life.

' Vouchsafe, thou wonder, to alight thy
 steed,   13
And rein his proud head to the saddle-bow ;
If thou wilt deign this favour, for thy meed
A thousand honey secrets shalt thou know.
 Here come and sit, where never serpent
  hisses,
 And being set, I'll smother thee with
  kisses ;

' And yet not cloy thy lips with loath'd
 satiety,   19
But rather famish them amid their plenty,
Making them red and pale with fresh
 variety—

Ten kisses short as one, one long as twenty.
 A summer's day will seem an hour but
  short,
 Being wasted in such time-beguiling
  sport.'

With this she seizeth on his sweating palm,
The precedent of pith and livelihood, 26
And, trembling in her passion, calls it balm,
Earth's sovereign salve to do a goddess
 good.
 Being so enrag'd, desire doth lend her
  force
 Courageously to pluck him from his
  horse.   30

Over one arm the lusty courser's rein,
Under her other was the tender boy,
Who blush'd and pouted in a dull disdain,
With leaden appetite, unapt to toy ; 34
 She red and hot as coals of glowing fire,
 He red for shame, but frosty in desire.

The studded bridle on a ragged bough
Nimbly she fastens—O, how quick is
 love !
The steed is stalled up, and even now
To tie the rider she begins to prove : 40
 Backward she push'd him, as she would
  be thrust,
 And govern'd him in strength, though
  not in lust.

So soon was she along as he was down,
Each leaning on their elbows and their
 hips ;
Now doth she stroke his cheek, now doth
 he frown,   45

1268

And gins to chide, but soon she stops his
lips,
And kissing speaks, with lustful language broken :
' If thou wilt chide, thy lips shall never
open '.

He burns with bashful shame ; she with
her tears
Doth quench the maiden burning of his
cheeks ; 50
Then with her windy sighs and golden
hairs
To fan and blow them dry again she seeks.
He saith she is immodest, blames her
miss ;
What follows more she murders with a
kiss.

Even as an empty eagle, sharp by fast, 55
Tires with her beak on feathers, flesh, and
bone,
Shaking her wings, devouring all in haste,
Till either gorge be stuff'd, or prey be gone ;
Even so she kiss'd his brow, his cheek,
his chin, 59
And where she ends she doth anew begin.

Forc'd to content, but never to obey,
Panting he lies and breatheth in her face ;
She feedeth on the steam as on a prey,
And calls it heavenly moisture, air of grace,
Wishing her cheeks were gardens full of
flowers, 65
So they were dew'd with such distilling
showers.

Look how a bird lies tangled in a net,
So fast'ned in her arms Adonis lies ;
Pure shame and aw'd resistance made him
fret, 69
Which bred more beauty in his angry eyes.
Rain added to a river that is rank
Perforce will force it overflow the bank.

Still she entreats, and prettily entreats,
For to a pretty ear she tunes her tale ;
Still is he sullen, still he lours and frets, 75
'Twixt crimson shame and anger ashy-pale ;
Being red, she loves him best ; and being
white,
Her best is better'd with a more delight.

Look how he can, she cannot choose but
love ; 79
And by her fair immortal hand she swears
From his soft bosom never to remove
Till he take truce with her contending tears,
Which long have rain'd, making her
cheeks all wet ;
And one sweet kiss shall pay this count-
less debt.

Upon this promise did he raise his chin, 85
Like a dive-dapper peering through a wave,
Who, being look'd on, ducks as quickly in ;
So offers he to give what she did crave ;

But when her lips were ready for his pay,
He winks, and turns his lips another way.

Never did passenger in summer's heat 91
More thirst for drink than she for this good
turn :
Her help she sees, but help she cannot get ;
She bathes in water, yet her fire must burn.
' O, pity,' gan she cry ' flint-hearted
boy ! 95
'Tis but a kiss I beg ; why art thou coy ?

' I have been wooed, as I entreat thee now,
Even by the stern and direful god of war,
Whose sinewy neck in battle ne'er did bow,
Who conquers where he comes in every jar ;
Yet hath he been my captive and my
slave, 101
And begg'd for that which thou unask'd
shalt have.

' Over my altars hath he hung his lance,
His batt'red shield, his uncontrolled crest,
And for my sake hath learn'd to sport and
dance, 105
To toy, to wanton, dally, smile, and jest,
Scorning his churlish drum and ensign
red,
Making my arms his field, his tent my bed.

' Thus he that overrul'd I overswayed,
Leading him prisoner in a red-rose chain ;
Strong-temper'd steel his stronger strength
obeyed, 111
Yet was he servile to my coy disdain.
O, be not proud, nor brag not of thy
might,
For mast'ring her that foil'd the god of
fight !

' Touch but my lips with those fair lips of
thine ; 115
Though mine be not so fair, yet are they
red—
The kiss shall be thine own as well as mine.
What seest thou in the ground ? Hold up
thy head ;
Look in mine eyeballs ; there thy beauty
lies.
Then why not lips on lips, since eyes in
eyes ? 120

' Art thou asham'd to kiss ? Then wink
again,
And I will wink ; so shall the day seem
night.
Love keeps his revels where there are but
twain ;
Be bold to play ; our sport is not in sight.
These blue-vein'd violets whereon we
lean 125
Never can blab, nor know not what we
mean.

' The tender spring upon thy tempting lip
Shows thee unripe ; yet mayst thou well
be tasted ; 128

Make use of time, let not advantage slip;
Beauty within itself should not be wasted.
 Fair flowers that are not gath'red in
  their prime
 Rot and consume themselves in little
  time.

'Were I hard-favour'd, foul, or wrinkled-
  old,
Ill-nurtur'd, crooked, churlish, harsh in
 voice,
O'er-worn, despised, rheumatic, and cold,
Thick-sighted, barren, lean, and lacking
 juice,   136
 Then mightst thou pause, for then I
  were not for thee;
 But having no defects, why dost abhor
  me?

'Thou canst not see one wrinkle in my
  brow;
Mine eyes are grey, and bright, and quick
 in turning;   140
My beauty as the spring doth yearly grow,
My flesh is soft and plump, my marrow
 burning;
 My smooth moist hand, were it with thy
  hand felt,
 Would in thy palm dissolve or seem to
  melt.

'Bid me discourse, I will enchant thine ear,
Or, like a fairy, trip upon the green, 146
Or, like a nymph, with long dishevelled
 hair,
Dance on the sands, and yet no footing
 seen.
 Love is a spirit all compact of fire,
 Not gross to sink, but light, and will
  aspire.   150

'Witness this primrose bank whereon I lie:
These forceless flowers like sturdy trees
 support me;
Two strengthless doves will draw me
 through the sky
From morn till night, even where I list to
 sport me.
 Is love so light, sweet boy, and may it be
 That thou should think it heavy unto
  thee?   156

'Is thine own heart to thine own face
 affected?
Can thy right hand seize love upon thy
 left?
Then woo thyself, be of thyself rejected;
Steal thine own freedom, and complain on
 theft.   160
 Narcissus so himself himself forsook,
 And died to kiss his shadow in the brook.

'Torches are made to light, jewels to wear,
Dainties to taste, fresh beauty for the use,
Herbs for their smell, and sappy plants to
 bear: 165

Things growing to themselves are growth's
 abuse.
 Seeds spring from seeds, and beauty
  breedeth beauty;
 Thou wast begot—to get it is thy duty.

'Upon the earth's increase why shouldst
  thou feed,   169
Unless the earth with thy increase be fed?
By law of nature thou art bound to breed,
That thine may live when thou thyself art
 dead;
 And so in spite of death thou dost
  survive,
 In that thy likeness still is left alive.'

By this the love-sick queen began to sweat,
For where they lay the shadow had forsook
 them,   176
And Titan, tired in the mid-day heat,
With burning eye did hotly overlook them;
 Wishing Adonis had his team to guide,
 So he were like him, and by Venus' side.

And now Adonis, with a lazy sprite, 181
And with a heavy, dark, disliking eye,
His louring brows o'erwhelming his fair
 sight,
Like misty vapours when they blot the sky,
 Souring his cheeks, cries 'Fie, no more
  of love!   185
 The sun doth burn my face; I must
  remove'.

'Ay me,' quoth Venus 'young, and so un-
  kind!
What bare excuses mak'st thou to be gone!
I'll sigh celestial breath, whose gentle wind
Shall cool the heat of this descending
 sun;   190
 I'll make a shadow for thee of my hairs;
 If they burn too, I'll quench them with
  my tears.

'The sun that shines from heaven shines
 but warm,
And lo, I lie between that sun and thee;
The heat I have from thence doth little
 harm;   195
Thine eye darts forth the fire that burneth
 me;
 And were I not immortal, life were done
 Between this heavenly and earthly sun.

'Art thou obdurate, flinty, hard as steel?
Nay, more than flint, for stone at rain
 relenteth.   200
Art thou a woman's son, and canst not feel
What 'tis to love? how want of love
 tormenteth?
 O, had thy mother borne so hard a mind,
 She had not brought forth thee, but died
  unkind!

'What am I, that thou shouldst contemn
 me this?   205
Or what great danger dwells upon my suit?

What were thy lips the worse for one poor
    kiss ?
Speak, fair ; but speak fair words, or else
    be mute.
  Give me one kiss ; I'll give it thee again,
  And one for int'rest, if thou wilt have
    twain.   210

' Fie, lifeless picture, cold and senseless
    stone,
Well-painted idol, image dull and dead,
Statue contenting but the eye alone,
  Thing like a man, but of no woman bred !
    Thou art no man, though of a man's
      complexion,   215
    For men will kiss even by their own
      direction.'

This said, impatience chokes her pleading
    tongue,
And swelling passion doth provoke a pause ;
Red cheeks and fiery eyes blaze forth her
    wrong ;
Being judge in love, she cannot right her
    cause ;   220
  And now she weeps, and now she fain
    would speak,
  And now her sobs do her intendments
    break.

Sometime she shakes her head, and then
    his hand ;   223
Now gazeth she on him, now on the ground ;
Sometime her arms infold him like a band ;
She would, he will not in her arms be
    bound ;
  And when from thence he struggles to be
    gone,
  She locks her lily fingers one in one.

' Fondling,' she saith ' since I have hemm'd
    thee here
Within the circuit of this ivory pale,   230
I'll be a park, and thou shalt be my deer ;
Feed where thou wilt, on mountain or in
    dale ;
  Graze on my lips ; and if those hills be
    dry,
  Stray lower, where the pleasant foun-
    tains lie.

' Within this limit is relief enough,   235
Sweet bottom-grass, and high delightful
    plain,
Round rising hillocks, brakes obscure and
    rough,
To shelter thee from tempest and from
    rain ;
  Then be my deer, since I am such a park ;
  No dog shall rouse thee, though a
    thousand bark.'   240

At this Adonis smiles as in disdain,
That in each cheek appears a pretty dimple.
Love made those hollows, if himself were
    slain,
He might be buried in a tomb so simple ;

Foreknowing well, if there he came to lie,
Why, there Love liv'd and there he could
    not die.   246

These lovely caves, these round enchanting
    pits,
Open'd their mouths to swallow Venus'
    liking.
Being mad before, how doth she now for
    wits ?
Struck dead at first, what needs a second
    striking ?   250
  Poor queen of love, in thine own law
    forlorn,
  To love a cheek that smiles at thee in
    scorn !

Now which way shall she turn ? What shall
    she say ?
Her words are done, her woes the more
    increasing ;
The time is spent, her object will away,   255
And from her twining arms doth urge
    releasing.
  ' Pity ! ' she cries ' Some favour, some
    remorse ! '
  Away she springs, and hasteth to his
    horse.

But, lo, from forth a copse that neighbours
    by,
A breeding jennet, lusty, young, and
    proud,   260
Adonis' trampling courser doth espy,
And forth she rushes, snorts, and neighs
    aloud ;
  The strong-neck'd steed, being tied unto
    a tree,
  Breaketh his rein, and to her straight
    goes he.   264

Imperiously he leaps, he neighs, he bounds,
And now his woven girths he breaks
    asunder ;
The bearing earth with his hard hoof he
    wounds,
Whose hollow womb resounds like heaven's
    thunder ;
  The iron bit he crusheth 'tween his teeth,
  Controlling what he was controlled with.

His ears up-prick'd ; his braided hanging
    mane   271
Upon his compass'd crest now stand on end;
His nostrils drink the air, and forth again,
As from a furnace, vapours doth he send ;
  His eye, which scornfully glisters like fire,
  Shows his hot courage and his high
    desire.   276

Sometime he trots, as if he told the steps,
With gentle majesty and modest pride ;
Anon he rears upright, curvets, and leaps,
As who should say ' Lo, thus my strength
    is tried,   280
  And this I do to captivate the eye
  Of the fair breeder that is standing by'.

What recketh he his rider's angry stir,
His flattering ' Holla ' or his ' Stand, I
say ' ?
What cares he now for curb, or pricking
spur ?   285
For rich caparisons, or trappings gay ?
　He sees his love, and nothing else he sees,
　Nor nothing else with his proud sight
　agrees.

Look when a painter would surpass the
life   289
In limning out a well-proportioned steed,
His art with nature's workmanship at
strife,
As if the dead the living should exceed ;
　So did this horse excel a common one
　In shape, in courage, colour, pace, and
　bone.

Round-hoof'd, short-jointed, fetlocks shag
and long,   295
Broad breast, full eye, small head, and
nostril wide,
High crest, short ears, straight legs and
passing strong,
Thin mane, thick tail, broad buttock,
tender hide ;
　Look what a horse should have he did
　not lack,   299
　Save a proud rider on so proud a back.

Sometime he scuds far off, and there he
stares ;
Anon he starts at stirring of a feather ;
To bid the wind a base he now prepares,
And whe'r he run or fly they know not
whether ;
　For through his mane and tail the high
　wind sings,   305
　Fanning the hairs, who wave like
　feath'red wings.

He looks upon his love and neighs unto her ;
She answers him as if she knew his mind ;
Being proud, as females are, to see him woo
her,
She puts on outward strangeness, seems
unkind,   310
　Spurns at his love, and scorns the heat
　he feels,
　Beating his kind embracements with her
　heels.

Then, like a melancholy malcontent,
He vails his tail, that, like a falling plume,
Cool shadow to his melting buttock lent
He stamps, and bites the poor flies in his
fume.   316
　His love, perceiving how he was enrag'd,
　Grew kinder, and his fury was assuag'd.

His testy master goeth about to take him,
When, lo, the unback'd breeder, full of fear,
Jealous of catching, swiftly doth forsake
him,   321
With her the horse, and left Adonis there.

As they were mad, unto the wood they
hie them,
Out-stripping crows that strive to over-
fly them.   324

All swol'n with chafing, down Adonis sits,
Banning his boist'rous and unruly beast ;
And now the happy season once more
fits
That love-sick Love by pleading may be
blest ;
　For lovers say the heart hath treble
　wrong,
　When it is barr'd the aidance of the
　tongue.   330

An oven that is stopp'd, or river stay'd,
Burneth more hotly, swelleth with more
rage ;
So of concealed sorrow may be said :
Free vent of words love's fire doth assuage ;
　But when the heart's attorney once is
　mute,   335
　The client breaks, as desperate in his
　suit.

He sees her coming, and begins to glow
Even as a dying coal revives with wind,
And with his bonnet hides his angry brow,
Looks on the dull earth with disturbed
mind,   340
　Taking no notice that she is so nigh,
　For all askance he holds her in his eye.

O what a sight it was, wistly to view
How she came stealing to the wayward boy !
To note the fighting conflict of her hue ! 345
How white and red each other did destroy !
　But now her cheek was pale, and by and
　by
　It flash'd forth fire, as lightning from the
　sky.

Now was she just before him as he sat,
And like a lowly lover down she kneels ; 350
With one fair hand she heaveth up his hat,
Her other tender hand his fair cheek feels :
　His tend'rer cheek receives her soft hand's
　print
　As apt as new-fall'n snow takes any dint.

O, what a war of looks was then between
them,   355
Her eyes, petitioners, to his eyes suing !
His eyes saw her eyes as they had not seen
them ;
Her eyes wooed still, his eyes disdain'd the
wooing ;
　And all this dumb play had his acts made
　plain
　With tears which chorus-like her eyes did
　rain.   360

Full gently now she takes him by the hand,
A lily prison'd in a gaol of snow,
Or ivory in an alabaster band ;
So white a friend engirts so white a foe.

This beauteous combat, wilful and un-
    willing,   365
Showed like two silver doves that sit a-
    billing.

Once more the engine of her thoughts
    began :
' O fairest mover on this mortal round,
Would thou wert as I am, and I a man,
My heart all whole as thine, thy heart my
    wound !   370
    For one sweet look thy help I would
        assure thee,
    Though nothing but my body's bane
        would cure thee '.

' Give me my hand ' saith he. ' Why dost
    thou feel it ? '
' Give me my heart,' saith she ' and thou
    shalt have it.   374
O, give it me, lest thy hard heart do steel it,
And being steel'd, soft sighs can never
    grave it ;
    Then love's deep groans I never shall
        regard,
    Because Adonis' heart hath made mine
        hard.'

' For shame,' he cries ' let go, and let me
    go ;   379
My day's delight is past, my horse is gone,
And 'tis your fault I am bereft him so.
I pray you hence, and leave me here alone ;
    For all my mind, my thought, my busy
        care,
    Is how to get my palfrey from the mare.'

Thus she replies : ' Thy palfrey, as he
    should,   385
Welcomes the warm approach of sweet
    desire.
Affection is a coal that must be cool'd ;
Else, suffer'd, it will set the heart on fire.
    The sea hath bounds, but deep desire
        hath none,
    Therefore no marvel though thy horse be
        gone.   390

' How like a jade he stood, tied to the
    tree,
Servilely master'd with a leathern rein !
But when he saw his love, his youth's fair
    fee,
He held such petty bondage in disdain,
    Throwing the base thong from his bend-
        ing crest,   395
    Enfranchising his mouth, his back, his
        breast.

' Who sees his true-love in her naked bed,
Teaching the sheets a whiter hue than
    white,
But, when his glutton eye so full hath
    fed,
His other agents aim at like delight ?   400
    Who is so faint that dares not be so bold
    To touch the fire, the weather being cold ?

' Let me excuse thy courser, gentle boy ;
And learn of him, I heartily beseech thee,
To take advantage on presented joy ;   405
Though I were dumb, yet his proceedings
    teach thee.
    O, learn to love ! The lesson is but plain,
    And once made perfect never lost again'.

' I know not love,' quoth he ' nor will not
    know it,
Unless it be a boar, and then I chase it.   410
'Tis much to borrow, and I will not owe it.
My love to love is love but to disgrace it ;
    For I have heard it is a life in death,
    That laughs, and weeps, and all but with
        a breath.

' Who wears a garment shapeless and un-
    finish'd ?   415
Who plucks the bud before one leaf put
    forth ?
If springing things be any jot diminish'd,
They wither in their prime, prove nothing
    worth.
    The colt that's back'd and burden'd
        being young
    Loseth his pride and never waxeth
        strong.   420

' You hurt my hand with wringing ; let us
    part,
And leave this idle theme, this bootless chat;
Remove your siege from my unyielding
    heart ;
To love's alarms it will not ope the gate.
    Dismiss your vows, your feigned tears,
        your flatt'ry ;   425
    For where a heart is hard they make no
        batt'ry.'

' What ! canst thou talk ? ' quoth she
      ' Hast thou a tongue ?
O, would thou hadst not, or I had no
    hearing !
Thy mermaid's voice hath done me double
    wrong ;
I had my load before, now press'd with
    bearing :   430
    Melodious discord, heavenly tune harsh
        sounding,
    Ear's deep-sweet music, and heart's
        deep-sore wounding.

' Had I no eyes but ears, my ears would
    love
That inward beauty and invisible ;
Or were I deaf, thy outward parts would
    move   435
Each part in me that were but sensible.
    Though neither eyes nor ears, to hear
        nor see,
    Yet should I be in love by touching thee.

' Say that the sense of feeling were bereft
    me,
And that I could not see, nor hear, nor
    touch,   440

And nothing but the very smell were left
   me,
Yet would my love to thee be still as much ;
  For from the stillitory of thy face
    excelling
   Comes breath perfum'd, that breedeth
    love by smelling.

' But, O, what banquet wert thou to the
   taste,   445
Being nurse and feeder of the other four !
Would they not wish the feast might ever
   last,
And bid Suspicion double-lock the door,
  Lest Jealousy, that sour unwelcome
    guest,
   Should by his stealing in disturb the
    feast ? '   450

Once more the ruby-colour'd portal open'd
Which to his speech did honey passage
   yield ;
Like a red morn, that ever yet betoken'd
Wreck to the seaman, tempest to the field,
  Sorrow to shepherds, woe unto the birds,
  Gusts and foul flaws to herdmen and to
    herds.   456

This ill presage advisedly she marketh.
Even as the wind is hush'd before it raineth,
Or as the wolf doth grin before he barketh,
Or as the berry breaks before it staineth,
  Or like the deadly bullet of a gun,   461
  His meaning struck her ere his words
    begun.

And at his look she flatly falleth down,
For looks kill love, and love by looks
   reviveth ;
A smile recures the wounding of a frown.
But blessed bankrupt that by love so
   thriveth !   466
  The silly boy, believing she is dead,
  Claps her pale cheek till clapping makes
    it red ;

And all-amaz'd brake off his late intent,
For sharply he did think to reprehend her,
Which cunning love did wittily prevent.
Fair fall the wit that can so well defend her !
  For on the grass she lies as she were slain,
  Till his breath breatheth life in her again.

He wrings her nose, he strikes her on the
   cheeks,   475
He bends her fingers, holds her pulses hard,
He chafes her lips, a thousand ways he
   seeks
To mend the hurt that his unkindness
   marr'd ;
  He kisses her ; and she, by her good will,
  Will never rise, so he will kiss her still. 480

The night of sorrow now is turn'd to day :
Her two blue windows faintly she up-
   heaveth,
Like the fair sun when in his fresh array

He cheers the morn and all the earth
   relieveth ;   484
And as the bright sun glorifies the sky,
So is her face illumin'd with her eye ;

Whose beams upon his hairless face are
   fix'd,
As if from thence they borrowed all their
   shine.   488
Were never four such lamps together mix'd,
Had not his clouded with his brows' repine ;
  But hers, which through the crystal tears
    gave light,
  Shone like the moon in water seen by
    night.

' O, where am I ? ' quoth she ' in earth or
   heaven,
Or in the ocean drench'd, or in the fire ?
What hour is this ? or morn, or weary
   even ?   495
Do I delight to die, or life desire ?
  But now I liv'd, and life was death's
    annoy ;
  But now I died, and death was lively joy.

' O, thou didst kill me ! Kill me once again.
Thy eyes' shrewd tutor, that hard heart of
   thine,   500
Hath taught them scornful tricks, and such
   disdain
That they have murd'red this poor heart of
   mine ;
  And these mine eyes, true leaders to their
    queen,
  But for thy piteous lips no more had seen.

' Long may they kiss each other, for this
   cure !   505
O, never let their crimson liveries wear !
And as they last, their verdure still endure,
To drive infection from the dangerous year !
  That the star-gazers, having writ on
    death,
  May say the plague is banish'd by thy
    breath.   510

' Pure lips, sweet seals in my soft lips
   imprinted,
What bargains may I make, still to be
   sealing ?
To sell myself I can be well contented,
So thou wilt buy, and pay, and use good
   dealing ;
  Which purchase if thou make, for fear of
    slips   515
  Set thy seal manual on my wax-red lips.

' A thousand kisses buys my heart from
   me ;
And pay them at thy leisure, one by one.
What is ten hundred touches unto thee ?
Are they not quickly told, and quickly
   gone ?   520
  Say for non-payment that the debt
    should double,
  Is twenty hundred kisses such a trouble ? '

'Fair queen,' quoth he ' if any love you
owe me,
Measure my strangeness with my unripe
years ;   524
Before I know myself, seek not to know me;
No fisher but the ungrown fry forbears.
  The mellow plum doth fall, the green
    sticks fast,
  Or being early pluck'd is sour to taste.

' Look, the world's comforter, with weary
    gait,   529
His day's hot task hath ended in the west ;
The owl, night's herald, shrieks ; 'tis very
    late ;
The sheep are gone to fold, birds to their
    nest ;
  And coal-black clouds that shadow
    heaven's light
  Do summon us to part and bid good
    night.

' Now let me say " good night ", and so say
    you ;   535
If you will say so, you shall have a kiss.'
' Good night ' quoth she ; and, ere he says
    ' adieu ',
The honey fee of parting tend'red is :
  Her arms do lend his neck a sweet
    embrace ;
  Incorporate then they seem ; face grows
    to face.   540

Till, breathless, he disjoin'd, and backward
    drew
The heavenly moisture, that sweet coral
    mouth,
Whose precious taste her thirsty lips well
    knew,
Whereon they surfeit, yet complain on
    drouth.
  He with her plenty press'd, she faint with
    dearth,   545
  Their lips together glued, fall to the
    earth.

Now quick desire hath caught the yielding
    prey,
And glutton-like she feeds, yet never
    filleth ;
Her lips are conquerors, his lips obey, 549
Paying what ransom the insulter willeth ;
  Whose vulture thought doth pitch the
    price so high
  That she will draw his lips' rich treasure
    dry.

And having felt the sweetness of the spoil,
With blindfold fury she begins to forage ;
Her face doth reek and smoke, her blood
    doth boil,   555
And careless lust stirs up a desperate
    courage ;
  Planting oblivion, beating reason back,
  Forgetting shame's pure blush, and
    honour's wrack.

Hot, faint, and weary, with her hard
    embracing,
Like a wild bird being tam'd with too much
    handling,   560
Or as the fleet-foot roe that's tir'd with
    chasing,
Or like the froward infant still'd with
    dandling,
  He now obeys and now no more resisteth,
  While she takes all she can, not all she
    listeth.

What wax so frozen but dissolves with
    temp'ring,   565
And yields at last to every light impression?
Things out of hope are compass'd oft with
    vent'ring,
Chiefly in love, whose leave exceeds com-
    mission.
  Affection faints not like a pale-fac'd
    coward,
  But then wooes best when most his
    choice is froward.   570

When he did frown, O, had she then gave
    over,
Such nectar from his lips she had not
    suck'd.
Foul words and frowns must not repel a
    lover ;
What though the rose have prickles, yet 'tis
    pluck'd.
  Were beauty under twenty locks kept
    fast,   575
  Yet love breaks through and picks them
    all at last.

For pity now she can no more detain him ;
The poor fool prays her that he may depart.
She is resolv'd no longer to restrain him ;
Bids him farewell, and look well to her
    heart,   580
  The which, by Cupid's bow she doth
    protest,
  He carries thence incaged in his breast.

' Sweet boy,' she says ' this night I'll waste
    in sorrow,
For my sick heart commands mine eyes to
    watch.
Tell me, love's master, shall we meet to-
    morrow ?   585
Say, shall we ? shall we ? wilt thou make
    the match ? '
  He tells her no ; to-morrow he intends
  To hunt the boar with certain of his
    friends.

' The boar ! ' quoth she, whereat a sudden
    pale,
Like lawn being spread upon the blushing
    rose,   590
Usurps her cheek ; she trembles at his
    tale,
And on his neck her yoking arms she
    throws ;

She sinketh down, still hanging by his neck,
He on her belly falls, she on her back.

Now is she in the very lists of love,   595
Her champion mounted for the hot encounter.
All is imaginary she doth prove ;
He will not manage her, although he mount her.
　That worse than Tantalus' is her annoy,
　To clip Elysium and to lack her joy.   600

Even so poor birds, deceiv'd with painted grapes,
Do surfeit by the eye and pine the maw ;
Even so she languisheth in her mishaps,
As those poor birds that helpless berries saw.
　The warm effects which she in him finds missing   605
　She seeks to kindle with continual kissing.

But all in vain ; good queen, it will not be.
She hath assay'd as much as may be prov'd ;
Her pleading hath deserv'd a greater fee ;
She's Love, she loves, and yet she is not lov'd.   610
　'Fie, fie,' he says 'you crush me ; let me go ;
　You have no reason to withhold me so.'

'Thou hadst been gone,' quoth she 'sweet boy, ere this,
But that thou told'st me thou wouldst hunt the boar.   614
O, be advis'd ! Thou know'st not what it is
With javelin's point a churlish swine to gore,
Whose tushes never sheath'd he whetteth still,
　Like to a mortal butcher bent to kill.

'On his bow-back he hath a battle set
Of bristly pikes that ever threat his foes ;
His eyes like glow-worms shine when he doth fret ;   621
His snout digs sepulchres where'er he goes ;
　Being mov'd, he strikes whate'er is in his way,
　And whom he strikes his cruel tushes slay.

'His brawny sides, with hairy bristles armed,   625
Are better proof than thy spear's point can enter ;
His short thick neck cannot be easily harmed ;
Being ireful, on the lion he will venter.
　The thorny brambles and embracing bushes,
　As fearful of him, part ; through whom he rushes.   630

'Alas, he nought esteems that face of thine,
To which Love's eyes pays tributary gazes ;
Nor thy soft hands, sweet lips, and crystal eyne,
Whose full perfection all the world amazes ;
　But having thee at vantage—wondrous dread !—   635
　Would root these beauties as he roots the mead.

'O, let him keep his loathsome cabin still !
Beauty hath nought to do with such foul fiends.
Come not within his danger by thy will.
They that thrive well take counsel of their friends.   640
　When thou didst name the boar, not to dissemble,
　I fear'd thy fortune, and my joints did tremble.

'Didst thou not mark my face ? Was it not white ?
Sawest thou not signs of fear lurk in mine eye ?
Grew I not faint ? And fell I not downright ?   645
Within my bosom, whereon thou dost lie,
　My boding heart pants, beats, and takes no rest,
　But, like an earthquake, shakes thee on my breast.

'For where Love reigns, disturbing Jealousy
Doth call himself Affection's sentinel ;   650
Gives false alarms, suggesteth mutiny,
And in a peaceful hour doth cry " Kill, kill ! "
　Distemp'ring gentle Love in his desire,
　As air and water do abate the fire.

'This sour informer, this bate-breeding spy,   655
This canker that eats up Love's tender spring,
This carry-tale, dissentious Jealousy,
That sometime true news, sometime false doth bring,
　Knocks at my heart, and whispers in mine ear,
　That if I love thee I thy death should fear ;   660

'And, more than so, presenteth to mine eye
The picture of an angry chafing boar,
Under whose sharp fangs on his back doth lie
An image like thyself, all stain'd with gore ;
　Whose blood upon the fresh flowers being shed   665
　Doth make them droop with grief and hang the head.

'What should I do, seeing thee so indeed,
That tremble at th' imagination ?

The thought of it doth make my faint heart
bleed,
And fear doth teach it divination : 670
I prophesy thy death, my living sorrow,
If thou encounter with the boar to-
morrow.

'But if thou needs wilt hunt, be rul'd by
me ;
Uncouple at the timorous flying hare,
Or at the fox which lives by subtlety, 675
Or at the roe which no encounter dare.
Pursue these fearful creatures o'er the
downs,
And on thy well-breath'd horse keep
with thy hounds.

'And when thou hast on foot the purblind
hare,
Mark the poor wretch, to overshoot his
troubles, 680
How he outruns the wind, and with what
care
He cranks and crosses with a thousand
doubles.
The many musits through the which he
goes
Are like a labyrinth to amaze his foes.

'Sometime he runs among a flock of sheep,
To make the cunning hounds mistake their
smell, 686
And sometime where earth-delving conies
keep,
To stop the loud pursuers in their yell ;
And sometime sorteth with a herd of
deer.
Danger deviseth shifts ; wit waits on
fear. 690

'For there his smell with others being
mingled,
The hot scent-snuffing hounds are driven
to doubt,
Ceasing their clamorous cry till they have
singled
With much ado the cold fault cleanly out.
Then do they spend their mouths ; echo
replies, 695
As if another chase were in the skies.

'By this, poor Wat, far off upon a hill,
Stands on his hinder legs with list'ning
ear,
To hearken if his foes pursue him still ;
Anon their loud alarums he doth hear ; 700
And now his grief may be compared well
To one sore sick that hears the passing-
bell.

'Then shalt thou see the dew-bedabbled
wretch
Turn and return, indenting with the way ;
Each envious briar his weary legs do
scratch, 705
Each shadow makes him stop, each murmur stay ;

For misery is trodden on by many,
And being low never reliev'd by any.

'Lie quietly and hear a little more ;
Nay, do not struggle, for thou shalt not
rise. 710
To make thee hate the hunting of the
boar,
Unlike myself thou hear'st me moralize,
Applying this to that, and so to so ;
For love can comment upon every woe.

'Where did I leave ? ' 'No matter where ; '
quoth he 715
'Leave me, and then the story aptly ends.
The night is spent.' 'Why, what of that ? '
quoth she.
'I am,' quoth he 'expected of my friends ;
And now 'tis dark, and going I shall fall.'
'In night,' quoth she 'desire sees best
of all. 720

'But if thou fall, O, then imagine this,
The earth in love with thee thy footing
trips,
And all is but to rob thee of a kiss.
Rich preys make true-men thieves ; so do
thy lips 724
Make modest Dian cloudy and forlorn,
Lest she should steal a kiss, and die
forsworn.

'Now of this dark night I perceive the
reason :
Cynthia for shame obscures her silver shine,
Till forging Nature be condemn'd of
treason
For stealing moulds from heaven that were
divine, 730
Wherein she fram'd thee in high heaven's
despite,
To shame the sun by day and her by
night.

'And therefore hath she brib'd the
Destinies
To cross the curious workmanship of
Nature,
To mingle beauty with infirmities, 735
And pure perfection with impure defeature,
Making it subject to the tyranny
Of mad mischances and much misery :

'As burning fevers, agues pale and faint,
Life-poisoning pestilence, and frenzies
wood, 740
The marrow-eating sickness whose attaint
Disorder breeds by heating of the blood,
Surfeits, imposthumes, grief, and damn'd
despair,
Swear Nature's death for framing thee
so fair.

'And not the least of all these maladies 745
But in one minute's fight brings beauty
under.
Both favour, savour, hue, and qualities,

Whereat th' impartial gazer late did
　　wonder,
　　Are on the sudden wasted, thaw'd, and
　　　done,
　　As mountain snow melts with the midday
　　　sun.　　750

' Therefore, despite of fruitless chastity,
Love-lacking vestals, and self-loving nuns,
That on the earth would breed a scarcity
And barren dearth of daughters and of
　　sons,
　　Be prodigal : the lamp that burns by
　　　night　　755
　　Dries up his oil to lend the world his
　　　light.

' What is thy body but a swallowing grave,
Seeming to bury that posterity
Which by the rights of time thou needs
　　must have,　　759
If thou destroy them not in dark obscurity ?
If so, the world will hold thee in disdain,
Sith in thy pride so fair a hope is slain.

' So in thyself thyself art made away—
A mischief worse than civil home-bred
　　strife,
Or theirs whose desperate hands themselves
　　do slay,　　765
Or butcher-sire that reaves his son of life.
　　Foul cank'ring rust the hidden treasure
　　　frets,
　　But gold that's put to use more gold
　　　begets.'

' Nay, then,' quoth Adon ' you will fall
　　again
Into your idle over-handled theme ;　　770
The kiss I gave you is bestow'd in vain,
And all in vain you strive against the
　　stream ;
　　For, by this black-fac'd night, desire's
　　　foul nurse,
　　Your treatise makes me like you worse
　　　and worse.

' If love have lent you twenty thousand
　　tongues,　　775
And every tongue more moving than your
　　own,
Bewitching like the wanton mermaid's
　　songs,
Yet from mine ear the tempting tune is
　　blown ;
　　For know, my heart stands armed in
　　　mine ear,　　779
　　And will not let a false sound enter there,

' Lest the deceiving harmony should run
Into the quiet closure of my breast ;
And then my little heart were quite undone,
In his bedchamber to be barr'd of rest.
　　No, lady, no ; my heart longs not to
　　　groan,　　785
　　But soundly sleeps, while now it sleeps
　　　alone.

' What have you urg'd that I cannot
　　reprove ?
The path is smooth that leadeth on to
　　danger ;
I hate not love, but your device in love,
That lends embracements unto every
　　stranger.　　790
　　You do it for increase ! O strange excuse,
　　When reason is the bawd to lust's abuse !

' Call it not love, for Love to heaven is fled,
Since sweating lust on earth usurp'd his
　　name ;
Under whose simple semblance he hath fed
Upon fresh beauty, blotting it with blame ;
　　Which the hot tyrant stains and soon
　　　bereaves,　　797
　　As caterpillars do the tender leaves.

' Love comforteth like sunshine after rain,
But Lust's effect is tempest after sun ;　　800
Love's gentle spring doth always fresh
　　remain :
Lust's winter comes ere summer half be
　　done.
　　Love surfeits not : Lust like a glutton
　　　dies.
　　Love is all truth : Lust full of forged lies.

' More I could tell, but more I dare not
　　say ;　　805
The text is old, the orator too green.
Therefore, in sadness, now I will away ;
My face is full of shame, my heart of teen ;
　　Mine ears that to your wanton talk
　　　attended
　　Do burn themselves for having so
　　　offended.'　　810

With this he breaketh from the sweet
　　embrace
Of those fair arms which bound him to her
　　breast,
And homeward through the dark laund
　　runs apace ;
Leaves Love upon her back, deeply dis-
　　tress'd.
　　Look how a bright star shooteth from the
　　　sky,　　815
　　So glides he in the night from Venus' eye ;

Which after him she darts, as one on shore
Gazing upon a late-embarked friend,
Till the wild waves will have him seen no
　　more,
Whose ridges with the meeting clouds
　　contend ;　　820
　　So did the merciless and pitchy night
　　Fold in the object that did feed her sight.

Whereat amaz'd, as one that unaware
Hath dropp'd a precious jewel in the flood,
Or stonish'd as night-wand'rers often are,
Their light blown out in some mistrustful
　　wood ;　　826
　　Even so confounded in the dark she lay,
　　Having lost the fair discovery of her way.

And now she beats her heart, whereat it
    groans,
That all the neighbour caves, as seeming
    troubled, 830
Make verbal repetition of her moans ;
Passion on passion deeply is redoubled :
' Ay me ! ' she cries, and twenty times,
    ' Woe, woe ! '
    And twenty echoes twenty times cry so.

She, marking them, begins a wailing note,
And sings extemporally a woeful ditty—
How love makes young men thrall, and old
    men dote ; 837
How love is wise in folly, foolish-witty.
    Her heavy anthem still concludes in woe,
    And still the choir of echoes answer so.

Her song was tedious, and outwore the
    night, 841
For lovers' hours are long, though seeming
    short ;
If pleas'd themselves, others, they think,
    delight
In such-like circumstance, with such-like
    sport.
    Their copious stories, oftentimes begun,
    End without audience and are never
    done. 846

For who hath she to spend the night withal
But idle sounds resembling parasits,
Like shrill-tongu'd tapsters answering
    every call,
Soothing the humour of fantastic wits ? 850
    She says ' 'Tis so '; they answer all
    ' 'Tis so ';
    And would say after her, if she said ' No '.

Lo, here the gentle lark, weary of rest,
From his moist cabinet mounts up on high,
And wakes the morning, from whose silver
    breast 855
The sun ariseth in his majesty ;
    Who doth the world so gloriously behold
    That cedar-tops and hills seem burnish'd
    gold.

Venus salutes him with this fair good-
    morrow : 859
' O thou clear god, and patron of all light,
From whom each lamp and shining star
    doth borrow
The beauteous influence that makes him
    bright,
    There lives a son that suck'd an earthly
    mother
    May lend thee light, as thou dost lend
    to other '.

This said, she hasteth to a myrtle grove, 865
Musing the morning is so much o'erworn,
And yet she hears no tidings of her love ;
She hearkens for his hounds and for his
    horn.
    Anon she hears them chant it lustily,
    And all in haste she coasteth to the cry.

And as she runs, the bushes in the way
Some catch her by the neck, some kiss her
    face, 872
Some twine about her thigh to make her
    stay ;
She wildly breaketh their strict
    embrace,
    Like a milch doe whose swelling dugs
    do ache 875
    Hasting to feed her fawn hid in some
    brake.

By this, she hears the hounds are at a bay ;
Whereat she starts, like one that spies an
    adder
Wreath'd up in fatal folds just in his way,
The fear whereof doth make him shake and
    shudder ; 880
    Even so the timorous yelping of the
    hounds
    Appals her senses and her spirit con-
    founds.

For now she knows it is no gentle chase,
But the blunt boar, rough bear, or lion
    proud,
Because the cry remaineth in one place, 885
Where fearfully the dogs exclaim aloud.
    Finding their enemy to be so curst,
    They all strain court'sy who shall cope
    him first.

This dismal cry rings sadly in her ear,
Through which it enters to surprise her
    heart, 890
Who, overcome by doubt and bloodless
    fear,
With cold-pale weakness numbs each feel-
    ing part ;
    Like soldiers, when their captain once
    doth yield,
    They basely fly and dare not stay the
    field.

Thus stands she in a trembling ecstasy ; 895
Till, cheering up her senses all dismay'd,
She tells them 'tis a causeless fantasy,
And childish error that they are afraid ;
    Bids them leave quaking, bids them fear
    no more—
    And with that word she spied the hunted
    boar, 900

Whose frothy mouth, bepainted all with
    red,
Like milk and blood being mingled both
    together,
A second fear through all her sinews spread,
Which madly hurries her she knows not
    whither :
    This way she runs, and now she will no
    further, 905
    But back retires to rate the boar for
    murther.

A thousand spleens bear her a thousand
    ways ;

She treads the path that she untreads
again ;
Her more than haste is mated with delays,
Like the proceedings of a drunken brain,
Full of respects, yet nought at all respect-
ing,   911
In hand with all things, nought at all
effecting.

Here kennell'd in a brake she finds a
hound,
And asks the weary caitiff for his master ;
And there another licking of his wound, 915
'Gainst venom'd sores the only sovereign
plaster ;
And here she meets another sadly
scowling,
To whom she speaks, and he replies with
howling.

When he hath ceas'd his ill-resounding
noise,
Another flap-mouth'd mourner, black and
grim,
Against the welkin volleys out his voice ;   920
Another and another answer him,
Clapping their proud tails to the ground
below,
Shaking their scratch'd ears, bleeding as
they go.

Look how the world's poor people are
amazed   925
At apparitions, signs, and prodigies,
Whereon with fearful eyes they long have
gazed,
Infusing them with dreadful prophecies ;
So she at these sad signs draws up her
breath,   929
And, sighing it again, exclaims on Death.

' Hard-favour'd tyrant, ugly, meagre, lean,
Hateful divorce of love,'—thus chides she
Death—
' Grim-grinning ghost, earth's worm, what
dost thou mean
To stifle beauty, and to steal his breath,
Who when he liv'd, his breath and beauty
set   935
Gloss on the rose, smell to the violet ?

' If he be dead—O no, it cannot be,
Seeing his beauty, thou shouldst strike
at it.
O yes, it may ; thou hast no eyes to see,
But hatefully at random dost thou hit. 940
Thy mark is feeble age ; but thy false
dart
Mistakes that aim and cleaves an infant's
heart.

' Hadst thou but bid beware, then he had
spoke,
And hearing him thy power had lost his
power.
The Destinies will curse thee for this   944
stroke :

They bid thee crop a weed ; thou pluck'st a
flower.
Love's golden arrow at him should have
fled,
And not Death's ebon dart, to strike him
dead.

' Dost thou drink tears, that thou provok'st
such weeping ?   949
What may a heavy groan advantage thee ?
Why hast thou cast into eternal sleeping
Those eyes that taught all other eyes to see ?
Now Nature cares not for thy mortal
vigour,
Since her best work is ruin'd with thy
rigour.'

Here overcome, as one full of despair,   955
She vail'd her eyelids, who, like sluices,
stopp'd
The crystal tide that from her two cheeks
fair
In the sweet channel of her bosom dropp'd ;
But through the floodgates breaks the
silver rain,
And with his strong course opens them
again.   960

O, how her eyes and tears did lend and
borrow !
Her eye seen in the tears, tears in her eye ;
Both crystals, where they view'd each
other's sorrow—
Sorrow that friendly sighs sought still to
dry ;
But like a stormy day, now wind, now
rain,   965
Sighs dry her cheeks, tears make them
wet again.

Variable passions throng her constant woe,
As striving who should best become her
grief ;
All entertain'd, each passion labours so
That every present sorrow seemeth chief,
But none is best.   Then join they all
together,   971
Like many clouds consulting for foul
weather.

By this, far off she hears some huntsman
hollow ;
A nurse's song ne'er pleas'd her babe so
well.
The dire imagination she did follow   975
This sound of hope doth labour to expel ;
For now reviving joy bids her rejoice,
And flatters her it is Adonis' voice.

Whereat her tears began to turn their tide,
Being prison'd in her eye like pearls in
glass ;   980
Yet sometimes falls an orient drop beside,
Which her cheek melts, as scorning it
should pass
To wash the foul face of the sluttish
ground,

Who is but drunken when she seemeth
   drown'd.

O hard-believing love, how strange it
   seems   985
Not to believe, and yet too credulous !
Thy weal and woe are both of them ex-
   tremes ;
Despair and hope makes thee ridiculous :
   The one doth flatter thee in thoughts
     unlikely,
   In likely thoughts the other kills thee
     quickly.   990

Now she unweaves the web that she hath
   wrought :
Adonis lives, and Death is not to blame ;
It was not she that call'd him all to nought.
Now she adds honours to his hateful name :
   She clepes him king of graves, and grave
     for kings,   995
   Imperious supreme of all mortal things.

' No, no,' quoth she ' sweet Death, I did
   but jest ;
Yet pardon me I felt a kind of fear
When as I met the boar, that bloody beast
Which knows no pity but is still severe.   1000
   Then, gentle shadow—truth I must
     confess—
   I rail'd on thee, fearing my love's
     decesse.

' 'Tis not my fault ; the boar provok'd my
   tongue ;
Be wreak'd on him, invisible commander ;
'Tis he, foul creature, that hath done thee
   wrong ;   1005
I did but act ; he's author of thy slander.
   Grief hath two tongues, and never woman
     yet
   Could rule them both without ten
     women's wit.'

Thus, hoping that Adonis is alive,
Her rash suspect she doth extenuate ;   1010
And that his beauty may the better thrive,
With Death she humbly doth insinuate ;
   Tells him of trophies, statues, tombs,
     and stories
   His victories, his triumphs, and his
     glories.

' O Jove,' quoth she ' how much a fool
   was I   1015
To be of such a weak and silly mind
To wail his death who lives, and must not
   die
Till mutual overthrow of mortal kind !
   For he being dead, with him is beauty
     slain,
   And, beauty dead, black chaos comes
     again.   1020

' Fie, fie, fond love, thou art so full of fear
As one with treasure laden, hemm'd with
   thieves ;

Trifles, unwitnessed with eye or ear,
Thy coward heart with false bethinking
   grieves.'
   Even at this word she hears a merry
     horn,   1025
   Whereat she leaps that was but late
     forlorn.

As falcons to the lure away she flies ;
The grass stoops not, she treads on it so
   light ;
And in her haste unfortunately spies
The foul boar's conquest on her fair
   delight ;   1030
   Which seen, her eyes, as murd'red with
     the view,
   Like stars asham'd of day, themselves
     withdrew ;

Or as the snail, whose tender horns being
   hit,
Shrinks backward in his shelly cave with
   pain,
And there, all smoth'red up, in shade doth
   sit,   1035
Long after fearing to creep forth again ;
   So at his bloody view her eyes are fled
   Into the deep-dark cabins of her head ;

Where they resign their office and their
   light
To the disposing of her troubled brain ;   1040
Who bids them still consort with ugly
   night,
And never wound the heart with looks
   again ;
   Who, like a king perplexed in his throne,
   By their suggestion gives a deadly groan.

Whereat each tributary subject quakes ;
As when the wind, imprison'd in the
   ground,   1046
Struggling for passage, earth's foundation
   shakes,
Which with cold terror doth men's minds
   confound.
   This mutiny each part doth so surprise
   That from their dark beds once more leap
     her eyes ;   1050

And, being open'd, threw unwilling light
Upon the wide wound that the boar had
   trench'd
In his soft flank ; whose wonted lily white
With purple tears that his wound wept was
   drench'd.
   No flow'r was nigh, no grass, herb, leaf,
     or weed,   1055
   But stole his blood and seem'd with him
     to bleed.

This solemn sympathy poor Venus noteth.
Over one shoulder doth she hang her head ;
Dumbly she passions, franticly she doteth ;
She thinks he could not die, he is not dead.
   Her voice is stopp'd, her joints forget to
     bow ;   1061

Her eyes are mad that they have wept
 till now.

Upon his hurt she looks so steadfastly
That her sight dazzling makes the wound
  seem three ;   1064
And then she reprehends her mangling eye
That makes more gashes where no breach
  should be.
 His face seems twain, each several limb
  is doubled ;
 For oft the eye mistakes, the brain being
  troubled.

' My tongue cannot express my grief for
 one,
And yet ' quoth she ' behold two Adons
 dead.   1070
My sighs are blown away, my salt tears
 gone,
Mine eyes are turn'd to fire, my heart to
 lead ;
 Heavy heart's lead melt at mine eyes'
  red fire !
 So shall I die by drops of hot desire.

' Alas, poor world, what treasure hast thou
 lost !   1075
What face remains alive that's worth the
 viewing ?
Whose tongue is music now ? What canst
 thou boast
Of things long since, or any thing ensuing ?
 The flowers are sweet, their colours fresh
  and trim ;
 But true-sweet beauty liv'd and died
  with him.   1080

' Bonnet nor veil henceforth no creature
 wear ;
Nor sun nor wind will ever strive to kiss
 you :
Having no fair to lose, you need not
 fear ;
The sun doth scorn you, and the wind doth
 hiss you.
 But when Adonis liv'd, sun and sharp air
 Lurk'd like two thieves to rob him of his
  fair ;   1086

' And therefore would he put his bonnet on,
Under whose brim the gaudy sun would
 peep ;
The wind would blow it off, and, being
 gone,
Play with his locks. Then would Adonis
 weep ;   1090
 And straight, in pity of his tender years,
 They both would strive who first should
  dry his tears.

' To see his face the lion walk'd along
Behind some hedge, because he would not
 fear him.   1094
To recreate himself when he hath song,
The tiger would be tame and gently hear
 him.

If he had spoke, the wolf would leave his
 prey,
And never fright the silly lamb that day.

' When he beheld his shadow in the brook,
The fishes spread on it their golden gills ;
When he was by, the birds such pleasure
 took   1101
That some would sing, some other in their
 bills
 Would bring him mulberries and ripe-
  red cherries ;
 He fed them with his sight, they him
  with berries.

' But this foul, grim, and urchin-snouted
 boar,   1105
Whose downward eye still looketh for a
 grave,
Ne'er saw the beauteous livery that he
 wore :
Witness the entertainment that he gave.
 If he did see his face, why then I know
 He thought to kiss him, and hath kill'd
  him so.   1110

' 'Tis true, 'tis true ; thus was Adonis slain :
He ran upon the boar with his sharp spear,
Who did not whet his teeth at him again,
But by a kiss thought to persuade him
 there ;
 And nuzzling in his flank, the loving
  swine   1115
 Sheath'd unaware the tusk in his soft
  groin.

' Had I been tooth'd like him, I must
 confess,
With kissing him I should have kill'd him
 first ;
But he is dead, and never did he bless
My youth with his ; the more am I accurst.'
 With this, she falleth in the place she
  stood,   1121
 And stains her face with his congealed
  blood.

She looks upon his lips, and they are pale ;
She takes him by the hand, and that is cold ;
She whispers in his ears a heavy tale, 1125
As if they heard the woeful words she told ;
 She lifts the coffer-lids that close his eyes,
 Where, lo, two lamps burnt out in dark-
  ness lies ;   1128

Two glasses where herself herself beheld
A thousand times, and now no more reflect,
Their virtue lost wherein they late excell'd,
And every beauty robb'd of his effect.
 ' Wonder of time,' quoth she ' this is my
  spite,   1133
 That, thou being dead, the day should
  yet be light.

' Since thou art dead, lo, here I prophesy
Sorrow on love hereafter shall attend :
It shall be waited on with jealousy,

Find sweet beginning but unsavoury end,
Ne'er settled equally, but high or low,
That all love's pleasure shall not match
    his woe.   1140

' It shall be fickle, false, and full of fraud,
Bud and be blasted in a breathing while,
The bottom poison, and the top o'erstraw'd
With sweets that shall the truest sight
    beguile ;
    The strongest body shall it make most
      weak,   1145
    Strike the wise dumb, and teach the fool
      to speak.

' It shall be sparing, and too full of riot,
Teaching decrepit age to tread the
    measures ;
The staring ruffian shall it keep in quiet,
Pluck down the rich, enrich the poor with
    treasures ;   1150
    It shall be raging mad, and silly mild,
    Make the young old, the old become a
      child.

' It shall suspect where is no cause of
    fear ;
It shall not fear where it should most
    mistrust ;
It shall be merciful, and too severe,   1155
And most deceiving when it seems most
    just ;
    Perverse it shall be where it shows most
      toward,
    Put fear to valour, courage to the
      coward.

' It shall be cause of war and dire events,
And set dissension 'twixt the son and sire,
Subject and servile to all discontents,   1161
As dry combustious matter is to fire.
    Sith in his prime death doth my love
      destroy,
    They that love best their loves shall not
      enjoy.'   1164

By this, the boy that by her side lay kill'd
Was melted like a vapour from her sight,

And in his blood that on the ground lay
    spill'd
A purple flow'r sprung up, check'red with
    white,
    Resembling well his pale cheeks, and the
      blood
    Which in round drops upon their white-
      ness stood.   1170

She bows her head the new-sprung flow'r
    to smell,
Comparing it to her Adonis' breath ;
And says within her bosom it shall dwell,
Since he himself is reft from her by death ;
    She crops the stalk, and in the breach
      appears   1175
    Green dropping sap, which she compares
      to tears.

' Poor flow'r,' quoth she ' this was thy
    father's guise—
Sweet issue of a more sweet-smelling sire—
For every little grief to wet his eyes.
To grow unto himself was his desire,   1180
    And so 'tis thine ; but know, it is as good
    To wither in my breast as in his blood.

' Here was thy father's bed, here in my
    breast ;
Thou art the next of blood, and 'tis thy
    right.
Lo, in this hollow cradle take thy rest ;   1185
My throbbing heart shall rock thee day and
    night ;
    There shall not be one minute in an hour
    Wherein I will not kiss my sweet love's
      flow'r.'

Thus weary of the world, away she hies,
And yokes her silver doves ; by whose
    swift aid   1190
Their mistress, mounted, through the
    empty skies
In her light chariot quickly is convey'd,
    Holding their course to Paphos, where
      their queen
    Means to immure herself, and not be seen.

THE RAPE OF LUCRECE

TO THE

RIGHT HONOURABLE HENRY WRIOTHESLEY,

EARLE OF SOUTHAMPTON, AND BARON OF TITCHFIELD.

THE love I dedicate to your Lordship is without end : wherof this Pamphlet without beginning is but a superfluous Moity. The warrant I have of your Honourable disposition, not the worth of my untutord Lines makes it assured of acceptance. What I have done is yours, what I have to doe is yours, being part in all I have, devoted yours. Were my worth greater my duety would shew greater, meane time, as it is, it is bound to your Lordship ; To whom I wish long life still lengthned with all happinesse.

Your Lordships in all duety.

WILLIAM SHAKESPEARE.

THE ARGUMENT.

LUCIUS TARQUINIUS (for his excessive pride surnamed Superbus), after he had caused his own father-in-law, Servius Tullius, to be cruelly murd'red, and, contrary to the Roman laws and customs, not requiring or staying for the people's suffrages, had possessed himself of the kingdom, went, accompanied with his sons and other noblemen of Rome, to besiege Ardea ; during which siege, the principal men of the army meeting one evening at the tent of Sextus Tarquinius, the King's son, in their discourses after supper every one commended the virtues of his own wife ; among whom Collatinus extolled the incomparable chastity of his wife Lucretia. In that pleasant humour they all posted to Rome ; and intending by their secret and sudden arrival to make trial of that which every one had before avouched, only Collatinus finds his wife (though it were late in the night) spinning amongst her maids ; the other ladies were all found dancing and revelling, or in several disports. Whereupon the noblemen yielded Collatinus the victory, and his wife the fame. At that time Sextus Tarquinius, being inflamed with Lucrece' beauty, yet smothering his passions for the present, departed with the rest back to the camp ; from whence he shortly after privily withdrew himself, and was (according to his estate) royally entertained and lodged by Lucrece at Collatium. The same night he treacherously stealeth into her chamber, violently ravish'd her, and early in the morning speedeth away. Lucrece, in this lamentable plight, hastily dispatcheth messengers, one to Rome for her father, another to the camp for Collatine. They came, the one accompanied with Junius Brutus, the other with Publius Valerius ; and, finding Lucrece attired in mourning habit, demanded the cause of her sorrow. She, first taking an oath of them for her revenge, revealed the actor and whole manner of his dealing, and withal suddenly stabbed herself. Which done, with one consent they all vowed to root out the whole hated family of the Tarquins ; and, bearing the dead body to Rome, Brutus acquainted the people with the doer and manner of the vile deed, with a bitter invective against the tyranny of the King ; wherewith the people were so moved, that with one consent and a general acclamation the Tarquins were all exiled, and the state government changed from kings to consuls.

FROM the besieged Ardea all in post,
Borne by the trustless wings of false desire,
Lust-breathed Tarquin leaves the Roman host,
And to Collatium bears the lightless fire
Which, in pale embers hid, lurks to aspire 5
   And girdle with embracing flames the waist
     Of Collatine's fair love, Lucrece the chaste.

Haply that name of ' chaste ' unhap'ly set
This bateless edge on his keen appetite ;

When Collatine unwisely did not let   10
To praise the clear unmatched red and white
Which triumph'd in that sky of his delight,
   Where mortal stars, as bright as heaven's beauties,
     With pure aspects did him peculiar duties.   14

For he the night before, in Tarquin's tent,
Unlock'd the treasure of his happy state—
What priceless wealth the heavens had him lent

In the possession of his beauteous mate ;
Reck'ning his fortune at such high-proud
 rate,
 That kings might be espoused to more
  fame, 20
 But king nor peer to such a peerless
  dame.

O happiness enjoy'd but of a few !
And, if possess'd, as soon decay'd and done
As is the morning's silver-melting dew 24
Against the golden splendour of the sun !
An expir'd date, cancell'd ere well begun :
 Honour and beauty, in the owner's arms,
 Are weakly fortress'd from a world of
  harms.

Beauty itself doth of itself persuade
The eyes of men without an orator ; 30
What needeth then apologies be made
To set forth that which is so singular ?
Or why is Collatine the publisher
 Of that rich jewel he should keep un-
  known 34
 From thievish ears, because it is his own ?

Perchance his boast of Lucrece' sov'reignty
Suggested this proud issue of a king ;
For by our ears our hearts oft tainted be.
Perchance that envy of so rich a thing,
Braving compare, disdainfully did sting 40
 His high-pitch'd thoughts that meaner
  men should vaunt
 That golden hap which their superiors
  want.

But some untimely thought did instigate
His all-too-timeless speed, if none of those.
His honour, his affairs, his friends, his state,
Neglected all, with swift intent he goes 46
To quench the coal which in his liver glows.
 O rash false heat, wrapp'd in repentant
  cold,
 Thy hasty spring still blasts and ne'er
  grows old ! 49

When at Collatium this false lord arrived,
Well was he welcom'd by the Roman dame,
Within whose face beauty and virtue
 strived
Which of them both should underprop her
 fame :
When virtue bragg'd, beauty would blush
 for shame ;
 When beauty boasted blushes, in despite
 Virtue would stain that o'er with silver
  white. 56

But beauty, in that white intituled,
From Venus' doves doth challenge that fair
 field ;
Then virtue claims from beauty beauty's
 red,
Which virtue gave the golden age to gild 60
Their silver cheeks, and call'd it then their
 shield ;
 Teaching them thus to use it in the fight,

When shame assail'd, the red should
 fence the white.

This heraldry in Lucrece' face was seen,
Argued by beauty's red and virtue's
 white ; 65
Of either's colour was the other queen,
Proving from world's minority their right ;
Yet their ambition makes them still to fight,
 The sovereignty of either being so great
 That oft they interchange each other's
  seat. 70

This silent war of lilies and of roses
Which Tarquin view'd in her fair face's
 field,
In their pure ranks his traitor eye encloses ;
Where, lest between them both it should be
 kill'd, 74
The coward captive vanquished doth yield
 To those two armies that would let him
  go
 Rather than triumph in so false a foe.

Now thinks he that her husband's shallow
 tongue—
The niggard prodigal that prais'd her so—
In that high task hath done her beauty
 wrong, 80
Which far exceeds his barren skill to show ;
Therefore that praise which Collatine doth
 owe
 Enchanted Tarquin answers with sur-
  mise,
 In silent wonder of still-gazing eyes.

This earthly saint, adored by this devil, 85
Little suspecteth the false worshipper ;
For unstain'd thoughts do seldom dream
 on evil ;
Birds never lim'd no secret bushes fear.
So guiltless she securely gives good cheer
 And reverend welcome to her princely
  guest, 90
 Whose inward ill no outward harm
  express'd ;

For that he colour'd with his high estate,
Hiding base sin in pleats of majesty ;
That nothing in him seem'd inordinate, 94
Save sometime too much wonder of his eye,
Which, having all, all could not satisfy ;
 But, poorly rich, so wanteth in his store
 That cloy'd with much he pineth still for
  more.

But she that never cop'd with stranger eyes
Could pick no meaning from their parling
 looks, 100
Nor read the subtle-shining secrecies
Writ in the glassy margents of such books.
She touch'd no unknown baits, nor fear'd
 no hooks ;
 Nor could she moralize his wanton sight,
 More than his eyes were open'd to the
  light. 105

He stories to her ears her husband's fame,
Won in the fields of fruitful Italy ;
And decks with praises Collatine's high name,
Made glorious by his manly chivalry,
With bruised arms and wreaths of victory.
  Her joy with heav'd-up hand she doth express, 111
  And, wordless, so greets heaven for his success.

Far from the purpose of his coming thither
He makes excuses for his being there.
No cloudy show of stormy blust'ring weather 115
Doth yet in his fair welkin once appear ;
Till sable Night, mother of Dread and Fear,
  Upon the world dim darkness doth display,
  And in her vaulty prison stows the Day.

For then is Tarquin brought unto his bed,
Intending weariness with heavy sprite ;
For, after supper, long he questioned 122
With modest Lucrece, and wore out the night.
Now leaden slumber with life's strength doth fight ;
  And every one to rest themselves betake,
  Save thieves, and cares, and troubled minds that wake. 126

As one of which doth Tarquin lie revolving
The sundry dangers of his will's obtaining ;
Yet ever to obtain his will resolving,
Though weak-built hopes persuade him to abstaining ; 130
Despair to gain doth traffic oft for gaining ;
  And when great treasure is the meed proposed,
  Though death be adjunct, there's no death supposed.

Those that much covet are with gain so fond
That what they have not, that which they possess 135
They scatter and unloose it from their bond,
And so, by hoping more, they have but less ;
Or, gaining more, the profit of excess
  Is but to surfeit, and such griefs sustain
  That they prove bankrupt in this poor-rich gain. 140

The aim of all is but to nurse the life
With honour, wealth, and ease in waning age ;
And in this aim there is such thwarting strife
That one for all or all for one we gage :
As life for honour in fell battle's rage ; 145
  Honour for wealth ; and oft that wealth doth cost
  The death of all, and all together lost.

So that in vent'ring ill we leave to be
The things we are for that which we expect ;

And this ambitious foul infirmity, 150
In having much, torments us with defect
Of that we have ; so then we do neglect
  The thing we have and, all for want of wit,
  Make something nothing by augmenting it.

Such hazard now must doting Tarquin make, 155
Pawning his honour to obtain his lust ;
And for himself himself he must forsake—
Then where is truth if there be no self-trust ?
When shall he think to find a stranger just,
  When he himself himself confounds, betrays 160
  To sland'rous tongues and wretched hateful days ?

Now stole upon the time the dead of night,
When heavy sleep had clos'd up mortal eyes ;
No comfortable star did lend his light,
No noise but owls' and wolves' death-boding cries ; 165
Now serves the season that they may surprise
  The silly lambs. Pure thoughts are dead and still,
  While lust and murder wake to stain and kill.

And now this lustful lord leap'd from his bed, 169
Throwing his mantle rudely o'er his arm ;
Is madly toss'd between desire and dread ;
Th' one sweetly flatters, th' other feareth harm ;
But honest Fear, bewitch'd with lust's foul charm, 173
  Doth too too oft betake him to retire,
  Beaten away by brain-sick rude desire.

His falchion on a flint he softly smiteth,
That from the cold stone sparks of fire do fly,
Whereat a waxen torch forthwith he lighteth,
Which must be lode-star to his lustful eye ;
And to the flame thus speaks advisedly : 180
  ' As from this cold flint I enforc'd this fire,
  So Lucrece must I force to my desire '.

Here pale with fear he doth premeditate
The dangers of his loathsome enterprise,
And in his inward mind he doth debate 185
What following sorrow may on this arise ;
Then, looking scornfully, he doth despise
  His naked armour of still-slaughtered lust,
  And justly thus controls his thoughts unjust :

' Fair torch, burn out thy light, and lend it not 190

To darken her whose light excelleth thine ;
And die, unhallowed thoughts, before you
    blot
With your uncleanness that which is divine ;
Offer pure incense to so pure a shrine :
    Let fair humanity abhor the deed   195
    That spots and stains love's modest
        snow-white weed.

' O shame to knighthood and to shining
        arms !
O foul dishonour to my household's grave !
O impious act including all foul harms !
A martial man to be soft fancy's slave ! 200
True valour still a true respect should have;
    Then my digression is so vile, so base,
    That it will live engraven in my face.

' Yea, though I die, the scandal will survive
And be an eyesore in my golden coat ; 205
Some loathsome dash the herald will
        contrive
To cipher me how fondly I did dote ;
That my posterity, sham'd with the note,
    Shall curse my bones, and hold it for no
        sin   209
    To wish that I their father had not been.

' What win I if I gain the thing I seek ?
A dream, a breath, a froth of fleeting joy.
Who buys a minute's mirth to wail a week ?
Or sells eternity to get a toy ?
For one sweet grape who will the vine
        destroy ?   215
    Or what fond beggar, but to touch the
        crown,
    Would with the sceptre straight be
        strucken down ?

' If Collatinus dream of my intent,   218
Will he not wake, and in a desp'rate rage
Post hither, this vile purpose to prevent—
This siege that hath engirt his marriage,
This blur to youth, this sorrow to the sage,
    This dying virtue, this surviving shame,
    Whose crime will bear an ever-during
        blame ?

' O, what excuse can my invention make
When thou shalt charge me with so black a
        deed ?   226
Will not my tongue be mute, my frail joints
        shake,
Mine eyes forgo their light, my false heart
        bleed ?
The guilt being great, the fear doth still
        exceed ;
    And extreme fear can neither fight nor
        fly,   230
    But coward-like with trembling terror
        die.

' Had Collatinus kill'd my son or sire,
Or lain in ambush to betray my life,
Or were he not my dear friend, this desire
Might have excuse to work upon his wife,
As in revenge or quittal of such strife ;

But as he is my kinsman, my dear friend,
The shame and fault finds no excuse nor
        end.   238

' Shameful it is—ay, if the fact be known ;
Hateful it is—there is no hate in loving ;
I'll beg her love—but she is not her own—
The worst is but denial and reproving.
My will is strong, past reason's weak
        removing ;
    Who fears a sentence or an old man's saw
    Shall by a painted cloth be kept in awe.'

Thus, graceless, holds he disputation   246
'Tween frozen conscience and hot-burning
        will,
And with good thoughts makes dispensa-
        tion,
Urging the worser sense for vantage still ;
    Which in a moment doth confound and kill
    All pure effects, and doth so far proceed
    That what is vile shows like a virtuous
        deed.

Quoth he ' She took me kindly by the hand
And gaz'd for tidings in my eager eyes,
Fearing some hard news from the warlike
        band   255
Where her beloved Collatinus lies.
O how her fear did make her colour rise !
    First red as roses that on lawn we lay,
    Then white as lawn, the roses took away.

' And how her hand in my hand being
        lock'd   260
Forc'd it to tremble with her loyal fear !
Which struck her sad, and then it faster
        rock'd
Until her husband's welfare she did hear ;
Whereat she smiled with so sweet a cheer
    That had Narcissus seen her as she stood
    Self-love had never drown'd him in the
        flood.   266

' Why hunt I then for colour or excuses ?
All orators are dumb when beauty plead-
        eth ;
Poor wretches have remorse in poor abuses;
Love thrives not in the heart that shadows
        dreadeth ;   270
Affection is my captain, and he leadeth ;
    And when his gaudy banner is display'd,
    The coward fights and will not be dis-
        may'd.

' Then, childish fear avaunt ! debating die !
Respect and reason wait on wrinkled age !
My heart shall never countermand mine
        eye ;   276
Sad pause and deep regard beseems the
        sage ;
My part is youth, and beats these from the
        stage :
    Desire my pilot is, beauty my prize ;
    Then who fears sinking where such
        treasure lies ? '   280

As corn o'ergrown by weeds, so heedful fear
Is almost chok'd by unresisted lust.
Away he steals with open list'ning ear,
Full of foul hope, and full of fond mistrust;
Both which, as servitors to the unjust, 285
 So cross him with their opposite per-
  suasion
 That now he vows a league, and now
  invasion.

Within his thought her heavenly image sits,
And in the selfsame seat sits Collatine.
That eye which looks on her confounds his
  wits; 290
That eye which him beholds, as more
  divine,
Unto a view so false will not incline;
 But with a pure appeal seeks to the heart,
 Which once corrupted takes the worser
  part; 294

And therein heartens up his servile powers,
Who, flatt'red by their leader's jocund
  show,
Stuff up his lust, as minutes fill up hours;
And as their captain, so their pride doth
  grow,
Paying more slavish tribute than they owe.
 By reprobate desire thus madly led, 300
 The Roman lord marcheth to Lucrece'
  bed.

The locks between her chamber and his
  will,
Each one by him enforc'd, retires his ward;
But, as they open, they all rate his ill,
Which drives the creeping thief to some
  regard. 305
The threshold grates the door to have him
  heard;
 Night-wand'ring weasels shriek to see
  him there;
 They fright him, yet he still pursues his
  fear.

As each unwilling portal yields him way,
Through little vents and crannies of the
  place 310
The wind wars with his torch, to make him
  stay,
And blows the smoke of it into his face,
Extinguishing his conduct in this case;
 But his hot heart, which fond desire doth
  scorch,
 Puffs forth another wind that fires the
  torch; 315

And, being lighted, by the light he spies
Lucretia's glove, wherein her needle sticks;
He takes it from the rushes where it lies,
And griping it, the needle his finger pricks,
As who should say 'This glove to wanton
  tricks 320
 Is not inur'd. Return again in haste;
 Thou seest our mistress' ornaments are
  chaste'.

But all these poor forbiddings could not
  stay him;
He in the worst sense consters their denial:
The doors, the wind, the glove that did
  delay him, 325
He takes for accidental things of trial;
Or as those bars which stop the hourly dial,
 Who with a ling'ring stay his course doth
  let,
 Till every minute pays the hour his debt.

'So, so,' quoth he 'these lets attend the
  time, 330
Like little frosts that sometime threat the
  spring,
To add a more rejoicing to the prime,
And give the sneaped birds more cause to
  sing.
Pain pays the income of each precious
  thing:
 Huge rocks, high winds, strong pirates,
  shelves and sands, 335
 The merchant fears, ere rich at home he
  lands.'

Now is he come unto the chamber door
That shuts him from the heaven of his
  thought,
Which with a yielding latch, and with no
  more,
Hath barr'd him from the blessed thing he
  sought. 340
So from himself impiety hath wrought
 That for his prey to pray he doth begin,
 As if the heavens should countenance his
  sin.

But in the midst of his unfruitful prayer,
Having solicited th' eternal power, 345
That his foul thoughts might compass his
  fair fair,
And they would stand auspicious to the
  hour,
Even there he starts—quoth he 'I must
  deflow'r.
 The powers to whom I pray abhor this
  fact; 349
 How can they then assist me in the act?

'Then Love and Fortune be my gods, my
  guide!
My will is back'd with resolution.
Thoughts are but dreams till their effects
  be tried;
The blackest sin is clear'd with absolution;
Against love's fire fear's frost hath dissolu-
  tion. 355
 The eye of heaven is out, and misty night
 Covers the shame that follows sweet
  delight'.

This said, his guilty hand pluck'd up the
  latch,
And with his knee the door he opens wide.
The dove sleeps fast that this night-owl
  will catch. 360

Thus treason works ere traitors be espied.
Who sees the lurking serpent steps aside;
But she, sound sleeping, fearing no such
thing,
Lies at the mercy of his mortal sting.

Into the chamber wickedly he stalks, 365
And gazeth on her yet unstained bed.
The curtains being close, about he walks,
Rolling his greedy eyeballs in his head.
By their high treason is his heart misled,
Which gives the watchword to his hand
full soon 370
To draw the cloud that hides the silver
moon.

Look as the fair and fiery-pointed sun,
Rushing from forth a cloud, bereaves our
sight;
Even so, the curtain drawn, his eyes begun
To wink, being blinded with a greater light;
Whether it is that she reflects so bright
That dazzleth them, or else some shame
supposed; 377
But blind they are, and keep themselves
enclosed.

O, had they in that darksome prison died,
Then had they seen the period of their
ill! 380
Then Collatine again by Lucrece' side
In his clear bed might have reposed still;
But they must ope, this blessed league to
kill;
And holy-thoughted Lucrece to their
sight
Must sell her joy, her life, her world's
delight. 385

Her lily hand her rosy cheek lies under,
Coz'ning the pillow of a lawful kiss;
Who, therefore angry, seems to part in
sunder,
Swelling on either side to want his bliss;
Between whose hills her head entombed is;
Where, like a virtuous monument, she
lies, 391
To be admir'd of lewd unhallowed eyes.

Without the bed her other fair hand was,
On the green coverlet; whose perfect white
Show'd like an April daisy on the grass, 395
With pearly sweat, resembling dew of night.
Her eyes, like marigolds, had sheath'd their
light,
And canopied in darkness sweetly lay,
Till they might open to adorn the day.

Her hair, like golden threads, play'd with
her breath— 400
O modest wantons! wanton modesty!—
Showing life's triumph in the map of death,
And death's dim look in life's mortality.
Each in her sleep themselves so beautify,
As if between them twain there were no
strife, 405

But that life liv'd in death, and death
in life.

Her breasts, like ivory globes circled with
blue,
A pair of maiden worlds unconquered,
Save of their lord no bearing yoke they
knew,
And him by oath they truly honoured. 410
These worlds in Tarquin new ambition
bred,
Who like a foul usurper went about
From this fair throne to heave the owner
out.

What could he see but mightily he noted?
What did he note but strongly he desired?
What he beheld, on that he firmly doted,
And in his will his wilful eye he tired. 417
With more than admiration he admired
Her azure veins, her alabaster skin,
Her coral lips, her snow-white dimpled
chin. 420

As the grim lion fawneth o'er his prey,
Sharp hunger by the conquest satisfied,
So o'er this sleeping soul doth Tarquin stay,
His rage of lust by gazing qualified;
Slack'd, not suppress'd; for standing by
her side, 425
His eye, which late this mutiny restrains,
Unto a greater uproar tempts his veins;

And they, like straggling slaves for pillage
fighting,
Obdurate vassals, fell exploits effecting,
In bloody death and ravishment delighting,
Nor children's tears nor mothers' groans
respecting, 431
Swell in their pride, the onset still expect-
ing.
Anon his beating heart, alarum striking,
Gives the hot charge and bids them do
their liking.

His drumming heart cheers up his burning
eye, 435
His eye commends the leading to his hand;
His hand, as proud of such a dignity,
Smoking with pride, march'd on to make
his stand
On her bare breast, the heart of all her land;
Whose ranks of blue veins, as his hand
did scale, 440
Left their round turrets destitute and
pale.

They, must'ring to the quiet cabinet
Where their dear governess and lady lies,
Do tell her she is dreadfully beset, 444
And fright her with confusion of their cries:
She, much amaz'd, breaks ope her lock'd-
up eyes,
Who, peeping forth this tumult to be-
hold,
Are by his flaming torch dimm'd and
controll'd.

Imagine her as one in dead of night
From forth dull sleep by dreadful fancy
　waking,　　　　　　　　　　　　450
That thinks she hath beheld some ghastly
　sprite
Whose grim aspect sets every joint a-
　shaking—
What terror 'tis! but she, in worser taking,
　From sleep disturbed, heedfully doth
　　view
　The sight which makes supposed terror
　　true.　　　　　　　　　　　　455

Wrapp'd and confounded in a thousand
　fears,
Like to a new-kill'd bird she trembling lies;
She dares not look; yet, winking, there
　appears
Quick-shifting antics, ugly in her eyes.
Such shadows are the weak brain's for-
　geries,　　　　　　　　　　　　460
　Who, angry that the eyes fly from their
　　lights,
　In darkness daunts them with more
　　dreadful sights.

His hand, that yet remains upon her
　breast—
Rude ram, to batter such an ivory wall!—
May feel her heart, poor citizen, distress'd,
Wounding itself to death, rise up and fall,
Beating her bulk, that his hand shakes
　withal.　　　　　　　　　　　　467
　This moves in him more rage and lesser
　　pity,
　To make the breach and enter this sweet
　　city.

First like a trumpet doth his tongue begin
To sound a parley to his heartless foe,　471
Who o'er the white sheet peers her whiter
　chin,
The reason of this rash alarm to know,
Which he by dumb demeanour seeks to
　show;
　But she with vehement prayers urgeth
　　still　　　　　　　　　　　　475
　Under what colour he commits this ill.

Thus he replies: ' The colour in thy face,
That even for anger makes the lily pale
And the red rose blush at her own disgrace,
Shall plead for me and tell my loving tale.
Under that colour am I come to scale　481
　Thy never-conquered fort. The fault is
　　thine,
　For those thine eyes betray thee unto
　　mine.

' Thus I forestall thee, if thou mean to
　chide:　　　　　　　　　　　　484
Thy beauty hath ensnar'd thee to this night,
Where thou with patience must my will
　abide,
My will that marks thee for my earth's
　delight,

Which I to conquer sought with all my
　might;　　　　　　　　　　　　488
　But as reproof and reason beat it dead,
　By thy bright beauty was it newly bred.

' I see what crosses my attempt will bring;
I know what thorns the growing rose
　defends;
I think the honey guarded with a sting:
All this beforehand counsel comprehends.
But Will is deaf and hears no heedful
　friends;　　　　　　　　　　　495
　Only he hath an eye to gaze on beauty,
　And dotes on what he looks, 'gainst law
　　or duty.

' I have debated, even in my soul,
What wrong, what shame, what sorrow I
　shall breed;　　　　　　　　　499
But nothing can Affection's course control,
Or stop the headlong fury of his speed.
I know repentant tears ensue the deed,
　Reproach, disdain, and deadly enmity;
　Yet strive I to embrace mine infamy'.

This said, he shakes aloft his Roman blade,
Which, like a falcon tow'ring in the skies,
Coucheth the fowl below with his wings'
　shade,
Whose crooked beak threats if he mount he
　dies.
So under his insulting falchion lies　　509
　Harmless Lucretia, marking what he tells
　With trembling fear, as fowl hear falcon's
　　bells.

' Lucrece,' quoth he ' this night I must
　enjoy thee.
If thou deny, then force must work my way,
For in thy bed I purpose to destroy thee;
That done, some worthless slave of thine
　I'll slay,　　　　　　　　　　515
To kill thine honour with thy life's decay;
　And in thy dead arms do I mean to place
　　him,
　Swearing I slew him, seeing thee embrace
　　him.

' So thy surviving husband shall remain
The scornful mark of every open eye;　520
Thy kinsmen hang their heads at this
　disdain,
Thy issue blurr'd with nameless bastardy;
And thou, the author of their obloquy,
　Shalt have thy trespass cited up in
　　rhymes,
　And sung by children in succeeding
　　times.　　　　　　　　　　　525

' But if thou yield, I rest thy secret friend:
The fault unknown is as a thought unacted;
A little harm done to a great good end
For lawful policy remains enacted.
The poisonous simple sometime is com-
　pacted　　　　　　　　　　　530
　In a pure compound; being so applied,
　His venom in effect is purified.

' Then, for thy husband and thy children's
      sake,
Tender my suit ; bequeath not to their lot
The shame that from them no device can
      take,   535
The blemish that will never be forgot ;
Worse than a slavish wipe or birth-hour's
      blot ;
   For marks descried in men's nativity
   Are nature's faults, not their own in-
      famy.'

Here with a cockatrice' dead-killing eye 540
He rouseth up himself, and makes a pause ;
While she, the picture of pure piety,
Like a white hind under the grype's sharp
      claws,
Pleads, in a wilderness where are no
      laws,
   To the rough beast that knows no gentle
      right,   545
   Nor aught obeys but his foul appetite.

But when a black-fac'd cloud the world
      doth threat,
In his dim mist th' aspiring mountains
      hiding,
From earth's dark womb some gentle gust
      doth get,
Which blows these pitchy vapours from
      their biding,   550
Hind'ring their present fall by this divid-
      ing ;
   So his unhallowed haste her words de-
      lays,
   And moody Pluto winks while Orpheus
      plays.

Yet, foul night-waking cat, he doth but
      dally,
While in his holdfast foot the weak mouse
      panteth ;   555
Her sad behaviour feeds his vulture folly,
A swallowing gulf that even in plenty
      wanteth ;
His ear her prayers admits, but his heart
      granteth
   No penetrable entrance to her plaining.
   Tears harden lust, though marble wear
      with raining.   560

Her pity-pleading eyes are sadly fixed
In the remorseless wrinkles of his face ;
Her modest eloquence with sighs is mixed,
Which to her oratory adds more grace.
She puts the period often from his place,
   And midst the sentence so her accent
      breaks   566
   That twice she doth begin ere once she
      speaks.

She conjures him by high almighty Jove,
By knighthood, gentry, and sweet friend-
      ship's oath,   569
By her untimely tears, her husband's love,
By holy human law, and common troth,

By heaven and earth, and all the power of
      both,
   That to his borrowed bed he make retire,
   And stoop to honour, not to foul desire.

Quoth she ' Reward not hospitality   575
With such black payment as thou hast
      pretended ;
Mud not the fountain that gave drink to
      thee ;
Mar not the thing that cannot be amended ;
End thy ill aim before thy shoot be ended.
   He is no woodman that doth bend his
      bow   580
   To strike a poor unseasonable doe.

' My husband is thy friend—for his sake
      spare me ;
Thyself art mighty—for thine own sake
      leave me ;
Myself a weakling—do not then ensnare me;
Thou look'st not like deceit—do not deceive
      me.   585
   My sighs like whirlwinds labour hence to
      heave me.
   If ever man were mov'd with woman's
      moans,
   Be moved with my tears, my sighs, my
      groans ;

' All which together, like a troubled ocean,
Beat at thy rocky and wrack-threat'ning
      heart ;   590
To soften it with their continual motion ;
For stones dissolv'd to water do convert.
O, if no harder than a stone thou art,
   Melt at my tears, and be compassionate !
   Soft pity enters at an iron gate.   595

' In Tarquin's likeness I did entertain thee ;
Hast thou put on his shape to do him
      shame ?
To all the host of heaven I complain me
Thou wrong'st his honour, wound'st his
      princely name.
Thou art not what thou seem'st ; and if the
      same,   600
   Thou seem'st not what thou art, a god,
      a king ;
   For kings like gods should govern every-
      thing.

' How will thy shame be seeded in thine
      age,
When thus thy vices bud before thy spring !
If in thy hope thou dar'st do such outrage,
What dar'st thou not when once thou art a
      king ?   606
O, be remem'bred, no outrageous thing
   From vassal actors can be wip'd away ;
   Then kings' misdeeds cannot be hid in
      clay.

' This deed will make thee only lov'd for
      fear,   610
But happy monarchs still are fear'd for
      love ;

With foul offenders thou perforce must
    bear,
When they in thee the like offences prove.
If but for fear of this, thy will remove ;
    For princes are the glass, the school, the
      book,
      Where subjects' eyes do learn, do read,
        do look.   616

' And wilt thou be the school where Lust
    shall learn ?
Must he in thee read lectures of such
    shame ?
Wilt thou be glass wherein it shall discern
Authority for sin, warrant for blame,   620
To privilege dishonour in thy name ?
    Thou back'st reproach against long-
      living laud,
      And mak'st fair reputation but a bawd.

' Hast thou command ? By him that gave
    it thee,   624
From a pure heart command thy rebel will ;
Draw not thy sword to guard iniquity,
For it was lent thee all that brood to
    kill.
Thy princely office how canst thou fulfil,
    When, pattern'd by thy fault, foul Sin
      may say
      He learn'd to sin and thou didst teach
        the way ?   630

' Think but how vile a spectacle it were
To view thy present trespass in another.
Men's faults do seldom to themselves
    appear ;
Their own transgressions partially they
    smother :
This guilt would seem death-worthy in thy
    brother.   635
    O, how are they wrapp'd in with infamies
    That from their own misdeeds askance
      their eyes !

' To thee, to thee, my heav'd-up hands
    appeal,
Not to seducing lust, thy rash relier ;
I sue for exil'd majesty's repeal ;   640
Let him return and flatt'ring thoughts
    retire :
His true respect will prison false desire,
    And wipe the dim mist from thy doting
      eyne,
      That thou shalt see thy state, and pity
        mine '.

' Have done ; ' quoth he ' my uncontrolled
    tide   645
Turns not, but swells the higher by this let.
Small lights are soon blown out ; huge fires
    abide,
And with the wind in greater fury fret.
The petty streams that pay a daily debt
    To their salt sovereign, with their fresh
      falls' haste,   650
      Add to his flow, but alter not his taste.'

' Thou art ' quoth she ' a sea, a sovereign
    king ;
And, lo, there falls into thy boundless flood
Black lust, dishonour, shame, misgovern-
    ing,   654
Who seek to stain the ocean of thy blood.
If all these petty ills shall change thy good,
    Thy sea within a puddle's womb is
      hearsed,
      And not the puddle in thy sea dispersed.

' So shall these slaves be king, and thou
    their slave ;
Thou nobly base, they basely dignified ; 660
Thou their fair life, and they thy fouler
    grave ;
Thou loathed in their shame, they in thy
    pride.
The lesser thing should not the greater hide ;
    The cedar stoops not to the base shrub's
      foot,   664
      But low shrubs wither at the cedar's root.

' So let thy thoughts, low vassals to thy
    state '—
' No more ; ' quoth he ' by heaven, I will
    not hear thee !
Yield to my love ; if not, enforced hate,
Instead of love's coy touch, shall rudely
    tear thee ;   669
That done, despitefully I mean to bear thee
    Unto the base bed of some rascal groom,
    To be thy partner in this shameful doom.'

This said, he sets his foot upon the light,
For light and lust are deadly enemies ; 674
Shame folded up in blind concealing night,
    When most unseen, then most doth
      tyrannize.
The wolf hath seiz'd his prey ; the poor
    lamb cries
    Till with her own white fleece her voice
      controll'd
      Entombs her outcry in her lips' sweet
        fold ;   679

For with the nightly linen that she wears
He pens her piteous clamours in her head,
Cooling his hot face in the chastest tears
That ever modest eyes with sorrow shed.
O, that prone lust should stain so pure a
    bed !   684
    The spots whereof could weeping purify,
    Her tears should drop on them perpetu-
      ally.

But she hath lost a dearer thing than
    life,
And he hath won what he would lose again.
This forced league doth force a further
    strife,   689
This momentary joy breeds months of pain,
This hot desire converts to cold disdain ;
    Pure Chastity is rifled of her store,
    And Lust, the thief, far poorer than
      before.

Look as the full-fed hound or gorged hawk,
Unapt for tender smell or speedy flight, 695
Make slow pursuit, or altogether bauk
The prey wherein by nature they delight ;
So surfeit-taking Tarquin fares this night :
His taste delicious, in digestion souring,
Devours his will, that liv'd by foul
devouring. 700

O, deeper sin than bottomless conceit
Can comprehend in still imagination !
Drunken Desire must vomit his receipt,
Ere he can see his own abomination. 704
While Lust is in his pride, no exclamation
Can curb his heat or rein his rash desire,
Till, like a jade, Self-will himself doth
tire.

And then with lank and lean discolour'd
cheek,
With heavy eye, knit brow, and strength-
less pace, 709
Feeble Desire, all recreant, poor, and meek,
Like to a bankrupt beggar wails his case.
The flesh being proud, Desire doth fight
with Grace,
For there it revels ; and when that
decays,
The guilty rebel for remission prays. 714

So fares it with this faultful lord of Rome,
Who this accomplishment so hotly chased ;
For now against himself he sounds this
doom,
That through the length of times he stands
disgraced :
Besides, his soul's fair temple is defaced.
To whose weak ruins muster troops of
cares, 720
To ask the spotted princess how she fares.

She says her subjects with foul insurrection
Have batter'd down her consecrated wall,
And by their mortal fault brought in sub-
jection
Her immortality, and made her thrall 725
To living death and pain perpetual ;
Which in her prescience she controlled
still,
But her foresight could not forestall their
will.

Ev'n in this thought through the dark
night he stealeth,
A captive victor that hath lost in gain ; 730
Bearing away the wound that nothing
healeth,
The scar that will despite of cure remain,
Leaving his spoil perplex'd in greater pain.
She bears the load of lust he left behind,
And he the burthen of a guilty mind. 735

He like a thievish dog creeps sadly thence,
She like a wearied lamb lies panting there ;
He scowls and hates himself for his offence,
She, desperate, with her nails her flesh doth
tear. 739

He faintly flies, sweating with guilty fear ;
She stays, exclaiming on the direful
night ;
He runs, and chides his vanish'd loath'd
delight.

He thence departs a heavy convertite,
She there remains a hopeless castaway ;
He in his speed looks for the morning
light ; 745
She prays she never may behold the day.
' For day ' quoth she ' night's scapes doth
open lay ;
And my true eyes have never practis'd
how 748
To cloak offences with a cunning brow.

' They think not but that every eye can see
The same disgrace which they themselves
behold ;
And therefore would they still in darkness
be,
To have their unseen sin remain untold ;
For they their guilt with weeping will un-
fold,
And grave, like water that doth eat in
steel, 755
Upon my cheeks what helpless shame
I feel.'

Here she exclaims against repose and rest,
And bids her eyes hereafter still be blind.
She wakes her heart by beating on her
breast,
And bids it leap from thence, where it may
find 760
Some purer chest to close so pure a mind.
Frantic with grief thus breathes she forth
her spite
Against the unseen secrecy of night :

' O comfort-killing Night, image of hell !
Dim register and notary of shame ! 765
Black stage for tragedies and murders fell !
Vast sin-concealing chaos ! nurse of blame !
Blind muffled bawd ! dark harbour for
defame !
Grim cave of death ! whisp'ring con-
spirator,
With close-tongu'd treason and the
ravisher ! 770

' O hateful, vaporous, and foggy night !
Since thou art guilty of my cureless crime,
Muster thy mists to meet the eastern light,
Make war against proportion'd course of
time ;
Or if thou wilt permit the sun to climb 775
His wonted height, yet ere he go to bed,
Knit poisonous clouds about his golden
head.

' With rotten damps ravish the morning
air ;
Let their exhal'd unwholesome breaths
make sick
The life of purity, the supreme fair, 780

Ere he arrive his weary noontide prick ;
And let thy musty vapours march so thick
That in their smoky ranks his smoth'red
light
May set at noon and make perpetual
night.

'Were Tarquin Night, as he is but Night's
child, 785
The silver-shining queen he would distain ;
Her twinkling handmaids too, by him
defil'd,
Through Night's black bosom should not
peep again ;
So should I have co-partners in my pain ;
And fellowship in woe doth woe assuage,
As palmers' chat makes short their
pilgrimage. 791

'Where now I have no one to blush with
me,
To cross their arms and hang their heads
with mine,
To mask their brows and hide their infamy;
But I alone alone must sit and pine, 795
Seasoning the earth with show'rs of silver
brine,
Mingling my talk with tears, my grief
with groans,
Poor wasting monuments of lasting
moans.

'O Night, thou furnace of foul reeking
smoke, 799
Let not the jealous Day behold that face
Which underneath thy black all-hiding
cloak
Immodestly lies martyr'd with disgrace !
Keep still possession of thy gloomy place,
That all the faults which in thy reign are
made 804
May likewise be sepulcher'd in thy shade.

'Make me not object to the tell-tale Day.
The light will show, character'd in my brow,
The story of sweet chastity's decay,
The impious breach of holy wedlock vow ;
Yea, the illiterate, that know not how 810
To cipher what is writ in learned books,
Will quote my loathsome trespass in my
looks.

'The nurse, to still her child, will tell my
story,
And fright her crying babe with Tarquin's
name ;
The orator, to deck his oratory, 815
Will couple my reproach to Tarquin's
shame ;
Feast-finding minstrels, tuning my defame,
Will tie the hearers to attend each line,
How Tarquin wronged me, I Collatine.

'Let my good name, that senseless reputa-
tion, 820
For Collatine's dear love be kept unspotted;
If that be made a theme for disputation,

The branches of another root are rotted,
And undeserv'd reproach to him allotted
That is as clear from this attaint of mine
As I ere this was pure to Collatine. 826

'O unseen shame ! invisible disgrace !
O unfelt sore ! crest-wounding, private scar !
Reproach is stamp'd in Collatinus' face,
And Tarquin's eye may read the mot
afar,
How he in peace is wounded, not in war.
Alas, how many bear such shameful
blows, 832
Which not themselves but he that gives
them knows !

'If, Collatine, thine honour lay in me,
From me by strong assault it is bereft. 835
My honey lost, and I, a drone-like bee,
Have no perfection of my summer left,
But robb'd and ransack'd by injurious
theft.
In thy weak hive a wand'ring wasp hath
crept,
And suck'd the honey which thy chaste
bee kept. 840

'Yet am I guilty of thy honour's wrack—
Yet for thy honour did I entertain him ;
Coming from thee, I could not put him
back,
For it had been dishonour to disdain him ;
Besides of weariness he did complain him,
And talk'd of virtue—O unlook'd-for
evil, 846
When virtue is profan'd in such a devil !

'Why should the worm intrude the maiden
bud ?
Or hateful cuckoos hatch in sparrows' nests?
Or toads infect fair founts with venom
mud ? 850
Or tyrant folly lurk in gentle breasts ?
Or kings be breakers of their own behests ?
But no perfection is so absolute
That some impurity doth not pollute.

'The aged man that coffers up his gold 855
Is plagu'd with cramps and gouts and pain-
ful fits,
And scarce hath eyes his treasure to behold,
But like still-pining Tantalus he sits,
And useless barns the harvest of his wits,
Having no other pleasure of his gain 860
But torment that it cannot cure his pain.

'So then he hath it, when he cannot use
it,
And leaves it to be mast'red by his young ;
Who in their pride do presently abuse it.
Their father was too weak, and they too
strong, 865
To hold their cursed-blessed fortune long.
The sweets we wish for turn to loathed
sours
Even in the moment that we call them
ours.

'Unruly blasts wait on the tender spring;
Unwholesome weeds take root with
    precious flow'rs;   870
The adder hisses where the sweet birds sing;
What virtue breeds iniquity devours.
We have no good that we can say is ours,
    But ill-annexed Opportunity
    Or kills his life or else his quality.   875

'O Opportunity, thy guilt is great!
'Tis thou that execut'st the traitor's
    treason;
Thou sets the wolf where he the lamb may
    get;
Whoever plots the sin, thou 'point'st the
    season;
'Tis thou that spurn'st at right, at law, at
    reason;   880
    And in thy shady cell, where none may
      spy him,
    Sits Sin, to seize the souls that wander
      by him.

'Thou makest the vestal violate her oath;
Thou blowest the fire when temperance is
    thaw'd;
Thou smotherest honesty, thou murth'rest
    troth;   885
Thou foul abettor! thou notorious bawd!
Thou plantest scandal and displacest laud.
    Thou ravisher, thou traitor, thou false
      thief,
    Thy honey turns to gall, thy joy to grief!

'Thy secret pleasure turns to open shame,
Thy private feasting to a public fast,   891
Thy smoothing titles to a ragged name,
Thy sug'red tongue to bitter wormwood
    taste;
Thy violent vanities can never last.
    How comes it then, vile Opportunity,   895
    Being so bad, such numbers seek for thee?

'When wilt thou be the humble suppliant's
    friend,
And bring him where his suit may be
    obtained?
When wilt thou sort an hour great strifes
    to end?
Or free that soul which wretchedness hath
    chained?   900
Give physic to the sick, ease to the pained?
    The poor, lame, blind, halt, creep, cry
      out for thee;
    But they ne'er meet with Opportunity.

'The patient dies while the physician
    sleeps;   904
The orphan pines while the oppressor feeds;
Justice is feasting while the widow weeps;
Advice is sporting while infection breeds;
Thou grant'st no time for charitable deeds;
    Wrath, envy, treason, rape, and murder's
      rages,
    Thy heinous hours wait on them as their
      pages.   910

'When Truth and Virtue have to do with
    thee,
A thousand crosses keep them from thy aid;
They buy thy help, but Sin ne'er gives a
    fee;   913
He gratis comes, and thou art well apaid
As well to hear as grant what he hath said.
    My Collatine would else have come to me
    When Tarquin did, but he was stay'd by
      thee.

'Guilty thou art of murder and of theft,
Guilty of perjury and subornation,
Guilty of treason, forgery, and shift,   920
Guilty of incest, that abomination:
An accessary by thine inclination
    To all sins past, and all that are to come,
    From the creation to the general doom.

'Mis-shapen Time, copesmate of ugly
    Night,   925
Swift subtle post, carrier of grisly care,
Eater of youth, false slave to false delight,
Base watch of woes, sin's packhorse,
    virtue's snare;
Thou nursest all, and murd'rest all that are.
    O hear me then, injurious, shifting Time!
    Be guilty of my death, since of my crime.

'Why hath thy servant Opportunity   932
Betray'd the hours thou gav'st me to
    repose?
Cancell'd my fortunes and enchained me
To endless date of never-ending woes?
Time's office is to fine the hate of foes,   934
    To eat up errors by opinion bred,
    Not spend the dowry of a lawful bed.

'Time's glory is to calm contending kings,
To unmask falsehood, and bring truth to
    light,   940
To stamp the seal of time in aged things,
To wake the morn, and sentinel the night,
To wrong the wronger till he render right;
    To ruinate proud buildings with thy
      hours,
    And smear with dust their glitt'ring
      golden tow'rs;   945

'To fill with worm-holes stately monu-
    ments,
To feed oblivion with decay of things,
To blot old books and alter their contents,
To pluck the quills from ancient ravens'
    wings,
To dry the old oak's sap, and cherish
    springs;   950
    To spoil antiquities of hammer'd steel,
    And turn the giddy round of Fortune's
      wheel;

'To show the beldam daughters of her
    daughter,
To make the child a man, the man a child,
To slay the tiger that doth live by slaughter,
To tame the unicorn and lion wild,   956
To mock the subtle in themselves beguil'd,

To cheer the ploughman with increaseful crops,
And waste huge stones with little water-drops.

'Why work'st thou mischief in thy pilgrim-age,   960
Unless thou couldst return to make amends?
One poor retiring minute in an age
Would purchase thee a thousand thousand friends,
Lending him wit that to bad debtors lends.
    O, this dread night, wouldst thou one hour come back,
    I could prevent this storm, and shun thy wrack!   966

'Thou ceaseless lackey to Eternity,
With some mischance cross Tarquin in his flight;
Devise extremes beyond extremity
To make him curse this cursed crimeful night;   970
Let ghastly shadows his lewd eyes affright.
    And the dire thought of his committed evil
    Shape every bush a hideous shapeless devil.

'Disturb his hours of rest with restless trances,   974
Afflict him in his bed with bedrid groans;
Let there bechance him pitiful mischances
To make him moan, but pity not his moans.
Stone him with hard'ned hearts harder than stones;
    And let mild women to him lose their mildness,
    Wilder to him than tigers in their wildness.   980

'Let him have time to tear his curled hair,
Let him have time against himself to rave,
Let him have time of Time's help to despair,
Let him have time to live a loathed slave,
Let him have time a beggar's orts to crave;
    And time to see one that by alms doth live   986
    Disdain to him disdained scraps to give.

'Let him have time to see his friends his foes,
And merry fools to mock at him resort;
Let him have time to mark how slow time goes
In time of sorrow, and how swift and short   990
His time of folly and his time of sport;
    And ever let his unrecalling crime
    Have time to wail th' abusing of his time.

'O Time, thou tutor both to good and bad,
Teach me to curse him that thou taught'st this ill!   996
At his own shadow let the thief run mad,
Himself himself seek every hour to kill!

Such wretched hands such wretched blood should spill;
For who so base would such an office have   1000
As sland'rous death's-man to so base a slave?

'The baser is he, coming from a king,
To shame his hope with deeds degenerate.
The mightier man, the mightier is the thing
That makes him honour'd or begets him hate;   1005
For greatest scandal waits on greatest state.
    The moon being clouded presently is miss'd,
    But little stars may hide them when they list.

'The crow may bathe his coal-black wings in mire   1009
And unperceiv'd fly with the filth away;
But if the like the snow-white swan desire,
The stain upon his silver down will stay.
Poor grooms are sightless night, kings glorious day.   1013
    Gnats are unnoted wheresoe'er they fly,
    But eagles gaz'd upon with every eye.

'Out, idle words, servants to shallow fools!
Unprofitable sounds, weak arbitrators!
Busy yourselves in skill-contending schools,
Debate where leisure serves with dull debaters;
To trembling clients be you mediators.   1020
    For me, I force not argument a straw,
    Since that my case is past the help of law.

'In vain I rail at Opportunity,
At Time, at Tarquin, and uncheerful Night;
In vain I cavil with mine infamy,   1025
In vain I spurn at my confirm'd despite:
This helpless smoke of words doth me no right.
    The remedy indeed to do me good
    Is to let forth my foul defiled blood.

'Poor hand, why quiver'st thou at this decree?   1030
Honour thyself to rid me of this shame;
For if I die my honour lives in thee,
But if I live thou liv'st in my defame.
Since thou couldst not defend thy loyal dame,
    And wast afeard to scratch her wicked foe,   1035
    Kill both thyself and her for yielding so'.

This said, from her betumbled couch she starteth
To find some desp'rate instrument of death,
But this no slaughterhouse no tool imparteth
To make more vent for passage of her breath,   1040

Which thronging through her lips so vanisheth
  As smoke from Ætna, that in air consumes,
  Or that which from discharged cannon fumes.

' In vain,' quoth she ' I live, and seek in vain
Some happy mean to end a hapless life. 1045
I fear'd by Tarquin's falchion to be slain,
Yet for the self-same purpose seek a knife;
But when I fear'd I was a loyal wife;
  So am I now—O no, that cannot be;
  Of that true type hath Tarquin rifled me.

' O, that is gone for which I sought to live,
And therefore now I need not fear to die.
To clear this spot by death, at least I give
A badge of fame to slander's livery;
A dying life to living infamy. 1055
  Poor helpless help, the treasure stol'n away,
  To burn the guiltless casket where it lay!

' Well, well, dear Collatine, thou shalt not know
The stained taste of violated troth;
I will not wrong thy true affection so 1060
To flatter thee with an infringed oath;
This bastard graff shall never come to growth;
  He shall not boast who did thy stock pollute
  That thou art doting father of his fruit.

' Nor shall he smile at thee in secret thought, 1065
Nor laugh with his companions at thy state;
But thou shalt know thy interest was not bought
Basely with gold, but stol'n from forth thy gate.
For me, I am the mistress of my fate, 1069
  And with my trespass never will dispense,
  Till life to death acquit my forc'd offence.

' I will not poison thee with my attaint,
Nor fold my fault in cleanly coin'd excuses;
My sable ground of sin I will not paint
To hide the truth of this false night's abuses. 1075
My tongue shall utter all; mine eyes like sluices,
  As from a mountain-spring that feeds a dale,
  Shall gush pure streams to purge my impure tale.'

By this, lamenting Philomel had ended
The well-tun'd warble of her nightly sorrow, 1080
And solemn night with slow-sad gait descended
To ugly hell; when lo, the blushing morrow

Lends light to all fair eyes that light will borrow;
  But cloudy Lucrece shames herself to see,
  And therefore still in night would cloist'red be. 1085

Revealing day through every cranny spies,
And seems to point her out where she sits weeping;
To whom she sobbing speaks: ' O eye of eyes,
Why pry'st thou through my window? Leave thy peeping;
Mock with thy tickling beams eyes that are sleeping; 1090
  Brand not my forehead with thy piercing light,
  For day hath nought to do what's done by night'.

Thus cavils she with every thing she sees.
True grief is fond and testy as a child,
Who wayward once, his mood with nought agrees. 1095
Old woes, not infant sorrows, bear them mild:
Continuance tames the one; the other wild,
  Like an unpractis'd swimmer plunging still
  With too much labour drowns for want of skill.

So she, deep drenched in a sea of care, 1100
Holds disputation with each thing she views,
And to herself all sorrow doth compare;
No object but her passion's strength renews,
And as one shifts, another straight ensues.
  Sometime her grief is dumb and hath no words; 1105
  Sometime 'tis mad and too much talk affords.

The little birds that tune their morning's joy
Make her moans mad with their sweet melody;
For mirth doth search the bottom of annoy;
Sad souls are slain in merry company; 1110
Grief best is pleas'd with grief's society.
  True sorrow then is feelingly suffic'd
  When with like semblance it is sympathiz'd.

'Tis double death to drown in ken of shore;
He ten times pines that pines beholding food; 1115
To see the salve doth make the wound ache more;
Great grief grieves most at that would do it good;
Deep woes roll forward like a gentle flood,
  Who, being stopp'd, the bounding banks o'erflows;

Grief dallied with nor law nor limit
knows.   1120

'You mocking birds,' quoth she 'your
tunes entomb
Within your hollow-swelling feathered
breasts,
And in my hearing be you mute and dumb.
My restless discord loves no stops nor rests ;
A woeful hostess brooks not merry guests.
Relish your nimble notes to pleasing ears;
Distress likes dumps when time is kept
with tears.   1127

'Come, Philomel, that sing'st of ravish-
ment,
Make thy sad grove in my dishevell'd hair.
As the dank earth weeps at thy languish-
ment,   1130
So I at each sad strain will strain a tear,
And with deep groans the diapason bear ;
For burthen-wise I'll hum on Tarquin
still,
While thou on Tereus descants better
skill.

'And whiles against a thorn thou bear'st
thy part   1135
To keep thy sharp woes waking, wretched I,
To imitate thee well, against my heart
Will fix a sharp knife to affright mine
eye ;
Who, if it wink, shall thereon fall and die.
These means, as frets upon an instru-
ment,   1140
Shall tune our heartstrings to true
languishment.

'And for, poor bird, thou sing'st not in the
day,
As shaming any eye should thee behold,
Some dark deep desert, seated from the
way,
That knows not parching heat nor freezing
cold,   1145
Will we find out ; and there we will unfold
To creatures stern sad tunes, to change
their kinds.
Since men prove beasts, let beasts bear
gentle minds.'

As the poor frighted deer, that stands at
gaze,
Wildly determining which way to fly, 1150
Or one encompass'd with a winding maze
That cannot tread the way out readily ;
So with herself is she in mutiny,
To live or die which of the twain were
better,
When life is sham'd, and death reproach's
debtor.   1155

'To kill myself,' quoth she 'alack, what
were it,
But with my body my poor soul's pollution ?
They that lose half with greater patience
bear it

Than they whose whole is swallowed in
confusion.   1159
That mother tries a merciless conclusion
Who, having two sweet babes, when
death takes one,
Will slay the other and be nurse to none.

'My body or my soul, which was the
dearer,
When the one pure, the other made divine ?
Whose love of either to myself was nearer,
When both were kept for heaven and
Collatine ?   1166
Ay me ! the bark pill'd from the lofty pine,
His leaves will wither and his sap decay ;
So must my soul, her bark being pill'd
away.

'Her house is sack'd, her quiet interrupted,
Her mansion batter'd by the enemy ; 1171
Her sacred temple spotted, spoil'd, cor-
rupted,
Grossly engirt with daring infamy ;
Then let it not be call'd impiety
If in this blemish'd fort I make some
hole   1175
Through which I may convey this
troubled soul.

'Yet die I will not till my Collatine
Have heard the cause of my untimely
death ;
That he may vow, in that sad hour of mine,
Revenge on him that made me stop my
breath.   1180
My stained blood to Tarquin I'll bequeath,
Which by him tainted shall for him be
spent,
And as his due writ in my testament.

'My honour I'll bequeath unto the knife
That wounds my body so dishonoured. 1185
'Tis honour to deprive dishonour'd life :
The one will live, the other being dead.
So of shame's ashes shall my fame be bred ;
For in my death I murther shameful
scorn.
My shame so dead, mine honour is new
born.   1190

'Dear lord of that dear jewel I have lost,
What legacy shall I bequeath to thee ?
My resolution, love, shall be thy boast,
By whose example thou reveng'd mayst be.
How Tarquin must be us'd, read it in me :
Myself, thy friend, will kill myself, thy
foe ;   1196
And for my sake serve thou false Tarquin
so.

'This brief abridgment of my will I make :
My soul and body to the skies and ground ;
My resolution, husband, do thou take ; 1200
Mine honour be the knife's that makes my
wound ;
My shame be his that did my fame con-
found ;

And all my fame that lives disbursed be
To those that live and think no shame
 of me.   1204

' Thou, Collatine, shalt oversee this will.
How was I overseen that thou shalt see it !
My blood shall wash the slander of mine ill ;
My life's foul deed, my life's fair end shall
 free it.
Faint not, faint heart, but stoutly say
 " So be it ".
 Yield to my hand ; my hand shall con-
  quer thee ;   1210
 Thou dead, both die, and both shall
  victors be.'

This plot of death when sadly she had
 laid,
And wip'd the brinish pearl from her bright
 eyes,
With untun'd tongue she hoarsely calls
 her maid,   1214
Whose swift obedience to her mistress hies ;
For fleet-wing'd duty with thought's
 feathers flies.
 Poor Lucrece' cheeks unto her maid
  seem so
 As winter meads when sun doth melt
  their snow.

Her mistress she doth give demure good-
 morrow
With soft-slow tongue, true mark of
 modesty,   1220
And sorts a sad look to her lady's sorrow,
For why her face wore sorrow's livery ;
But durst not ask of her audaciously
 Why her two suns were cloud-eclipsed so,
 Nor why her fair cheeks over-wash'd
  with woe.   1225

But as the earth doth weep, the sun being
 set,
Each flower moist'ned like a melting eye ;
Even so the maid with swelling drops gan
 wet
Her circled eyne, enforc'd by sympathy
Of those fair suns set in her mistress' sky,
 Who in a salt-wav'd ocean quench their
  light,   1231
 Which makes the maid weep like the
  dewy night.

A pretty while these pretty creatures stand,
Like ivory conduits coral cisterns filling :
One justly weeps ; the other takes in hand
No cause but company of her drops
 spilling.   1236
Their gentle sex to weep are often willing ;
 Grieving themselves to guess at others'
  smarts,
 And then they drown their eyes, or
  break their hearts.

For men have marble, women waxen minds,
And therefore are they form'd as marble
 will ;   1241

The weak oppress'd, th' impression of
 strange kinds
Is form'd in them by force, by fraud, or
 skill.
Then call them not the authors of their
 ill,
 No more than wax shall be accounted
  evil   1245
 Wherein is stamp'd the semblance of a
  devil.

Their smoothness, like a goodly champaign
 plain,
Lays open all the little worms that creep ;
In men, as in a rough-grown grove, remain
Cave-keeping evils that obscurely sleep.
Through crystal walls each little mote will
 peep.   1251
 Though men can cover crimes with bold
  stern looks,
 Poor women's faces are their own faults'
  books.

No man inveigh against the withered
 flow'r,
But chide rough winter that the flow'r hath
 kill'd.   1255
Not that devour'd, but that which doth
 devour,
Is worthy blame. O, let it not be hild
Poor women's faults that they are so
 fulfill'd
 With men's abuses ! those proud lords to
  blame
 Make weak-made women tenants to their
  shame.   1260

The precedent whereof in Lucrece view,
Assail'd by night with circumstances strong
Of present death and shame that might
 ensue
By that her death, to do her husband
 wrong.
Such danger to resistance did belong   1265
 That dying fear through all her body
  spread ;
 And who cannot abuse a body dead ?

By this, mild patience bid fair Lucrece
 speak
To the poor counterfeit of her complaining.
' My girl,' quoth she ' on what occasion
 break   1270
Those tears from thee that down thy cheeks
 are raining ?
If thou dost weep for grief of my sustaining,
 Know, gentle wench, it small avails my
  mood ;
 If tears could help, mine own would do
  me good.

' But tell me, girl, when went '—and there
 she stay'd   1275
Till after a deep groan—' Tarquin from
 hence ? '
' Madam, ere I was up,' replied the maid

'The more to blame my sluggard negligence.
Yet with the fault I thus far can dispense:
Myself was stirring ere the break of day,
And ere I rose was Tarquin gone away.

'But, lady, if your maid may be so bold,
She would request to know your heaviness.'
'O, peace!' quoth Lucrece 'If it should be told,
The repetition cannot make it less,   1285
For more it is than I can well express;
And that deep torture may be call'd a hell,
When more is felt than one hath power to tell.

'Go, get me hither paper, ink, and pen—
Yet save that labour, for I have them here.
What should I say?—One of my husband's men   1291
Bid thou be ready, by and by, to bear
A letter to my lord, my love, my dear.
Bid him with speed prepare to carry it;
The cause craves haste, and it will soon be writ.'   1295

Her maid is gone, and she prepares to write,
First hovering o'er the paper with her quill.
Conceit and grief an eager combat fight;
What wit sets down is blotted straight with will;   1299
This is too curious-good, this blunt and ill:
Much like a press of people at a door,
Throng her inventions, which shall go before.

At last she thus begins: 'Thou worthy lord
Of that unworthy wife that greeteth thee,
Health to thy person! Next vouchsafe t' afford—   1305
If ever, love, thy Lucrece thou wilt see—
Some present speed to come and visit me.
So I commend me from our house in grief;
My woes are tedious, though my words are brief'.

Here folds she up the tenour of her woe,
Her certain sorrow writ uncertainly.   1311
By this short schedule Collatine may know
Her grief, but not her grief's true quality;
She dares not thereof make discovery,
Lest he should hold it her own gross abuse,   1315
Ere she with blood had stain'd her stain'd excuse.

Besides, the life and feeling of her passion
She hoards, to spend when he is by to hear her;
When sighs and groans and tears may grace the fashion
Of her disgrace, the better so to clear her
From that suspicion which the world might bear her.   1321

To shun this blot, she would not blot the letter
With words, till action might become them better.

To see sad sights moves more than hear them told;
For then the eye interprets to the ear   1325
The heavy motion that it doth behold,
When every part a part of woe doth bear.
'Tis but a part of sorrow that we hear:
Deep sounds make lesser noise than shallow fords,
And sorrow ebbs, being blown with wind of words.   1330

Her letter now is seal'd, and on it writ
'At Ardea to my lord with more than haste'.
The post attends, and she delivers it,
Charging the sour-fac'd groom to hie as fast
As lagging fowls before the northern blast.
Speed more than speed but dull and slow she deems: 1336
Extremity still urgeth such extremes.

The homely villain curtsies to her low;
And blushing on her, with a steadfast eye
Receives the scroll without or yea or no,
And forth with bashful innocence doth hie.
But they whose guilt within their bosoms lie   1342
Imagine every eye beholds their blame;
For Lucrece thought he blush'd to see her shame.

When, silly groom . God wot, it was defect
Of spirit, life, and bold audacity.   1346
Such harmless creatures have a true respect
To talk in deeds, while others saucily
Promise more speed but do it leisurely.
Even so, this pattern of the worn-out age
Pawn'd honest looks, but laid no words to gage.   1351

His kindled duty kindled her mistrust,
That two red fires in both their faces blazed;
She thought he blush'd as knowing Tarquin's lust,
And, blushing with him, wistly on him gazed;   1355
Her earnest eye did make him more amazed;
The more she saw the blood his cheeks replenish,
The more she thought he spied in her some blemish.

But long she thinks till he return again,
And yet the duteous vassal scarce is gone.
The weary time she cannot entertain,   1361
For now 'tis stale to sigh, to weep, and groan;
So woe hath wearied woe, moan tired moan,
That she her plaints a little while doth stay,
Pausing for means to mourn some newer way.   1365

At last she calls to mind where hangs a
   piece
Of skilful painting, made for Priam's Troy ;
Before the which is drawn the power of
   Greece
For Helen's rape the city to destroy,
Threat'ning cloud-kissing Ilion with annoy;
   Which the conceited painter drew so
     proud,   1371
     As heaven, it seem'd, to kiss the turrets
     bow'd.

A thousand lamentable objects there,
In scorn of nature, art gave lifeless life :
Many a dry drop seem'd a weeping tear
Shed for the slaught'red husband by the
   wife ;   1376
The red blood reek'd to show the painter's
   strife ;
     And dying eyes gleam'd forth their ashy
     lights,
     Like dying coals burnt out in tedious
     nights.

There might you see the labouring pioneer
Begrim d with sweat and smeared all with
   dust ;   1381
And from the towers of Troy there would
   appear
The very eyes of men through loopholes
   thrust,
Gazing upon the Greeks with little lust.
     Such sweet observance in this work was
     had   1385
     That one might see those far-off eyes
     look sad.

In great commanders grace and majesty
You might behold, triumphing in their
   faces ;
In youth, quick bearing and dexterity ;
And here and there the painter inter-
   laces
Pale cowards marching on with trembling
   paces,   1391
     Which heartless peasants did so well
     resemble
     That one would swear he saw them quake
     and tremble.

In Ajax and Ulysses, O what art
Of physiognomy might one behold !   1395
The face of either cipher'd either's heart ;
Their face their manners most expressly
   told :
In Ajax' eyes blunt rage and rigour roll'd ;
     But the mild glance that sly Ulysses lent
     Show'd deep regard and smiling govern-
     ment.   1400

There pleading might you see grave Nestor
   stand,
As 'twere encouraging the Greeks to fight,
Making such sober action with his hand
That it beguil'd attention, charm'd the
   sight.

In speech, it seem'd, his beard all silver
   white   1405
Wagg'd up and down, and from his lips
   did fly
Thin winding breath, which purl'd up to
   the sky.

About him were a press of gaping faces,
Wh.ch seem'd to swallow up his sound
   advice,
All jointly list'ning, but with several graces,
As if some mermaid did their ears entice ;
Some high, some low—the painter was so
   nice—   1412
     The scalps of many, almost hid behind,
     To jump up higher seem'd to mock the
     mind.

Here one man's hand lean'd on another's
   head,   1415
His nose being shadowed by his neighbour's
   ear ;
Here one being throng'd bears back, all
   boll'n and red ;
Another smother'd seems to pelt and swear;
And in their rage such signs of rage they
   bear,   1419
     As, but for loss of Nestor's golden words,
     It seem'd they would debate with angry
     swords.

For much imaginary work was there ;
Conceit deceitful, so compact, so kind,
That for Achilles' image stood his spear,
Grip'd in an armed hand ; himself, behind
Was left unseen, save to the eye of mind :
     A hand, a toot, a face a leg, a head,   1427
     Stood for the whole to be imagined.

And from the walls of strong-besieged Troy
When their brave hope, bold Hector,
   march'd to field,   1430
Stood many Troyan mothers, sharing joy
To see their youthful sons bright weapons
   wield ;
And to their hope they such odd action
   yield
     That through their light joy seemed to
     appear,
     Like bright things stain'd, a kind of
     heavy fear.   1435

And from the strond of Dardan where they
   fought,
To Simois' reedy banks, the red blood ran,
Whose waves to imitate the battle sought
With swelling ridges ; and their ranks
   began   1439
To break upon the galled shore, and than
     Retire again, till meeting greater ranks
     They join, and shoot their foam at
     Simois' banks.

To this well-painted piece is Lucrece come,
To find a face where all distress is stell'd.
Many she sees where cares have carved
   some,   1445

But none where all distress and dolour
dwell'd,
Till she despairing Hecuba beheld,
  Staring on Priam's wounds with her old
eyes,
    Which bleeding under Pyrrhus' proud
foot lies.

In her the painter had anatomiz'd   1450
Time's ruin, beauty's wrack, and grim care's
reign;
Her cheeks with chaps and wrinkles were
disguis'd;
Of what she was no semblance did remain:
Her blue blood chang'd to black in every
vein,
  Wanting the spring that those shrunk
pipes had fed,   1455
    Show'd life imprison'd in a body dead.

On this sad shadow Lucrece spends her eyes,
And shapes her sorrow to the beldam's
woes,
Who nothing wants to answer her but cries,
And bitter words to ban her cruel foes: 1460
The painter was no god to lend her those;
  And therefore Lucrece swears he did her
wrong
    To give her so much grief and not a
tongue.

'Poor instrument,' quoth she 'without a
sound,
I'll tune thy woes with my lamenting
tongue,   1465
And drop sweet balm in Priam's painted
wound,
And rail on Pyrrhus that hath done him
wrong,
And with my tears quench Troy that burns
so long;
  And with my knife scratch out the angry
eyes   1469
    Of all the Greeks that are thine enemies.

'Show me the strumpet that began this
stir,
That with my nails her beauty I may tear.
Thy heat of lust, fond Paris, did incur
This load of wrath that burning Troy doth
bear.   1474
  Thy eye kindled the fire that burneth here;
  And here in Troy, for trespass of thine
eye,
    The sire, the son, the dame, and daughter
die.

'Why should the private pleasure of some
one
Become the public plague of many moe?
Let sin, alone committed, light alone   1480
Upon his head that hath transgressed so;
Let guiltless souls be freed from guilty woe.
  For one's offence why should so many
fall,
    To plague a private sin in general?

'Lo, here weeps Hecuba, here Priam dies,
Here manly Hector faints, here Troilus
sounds;   1486
Here friend by friend in bloody channel lies,
And friend to friend gives unadvised
wounds,
And one man's lust these many lives confounds.
  Had doting Priam check'd his son's
desire,   1490
    Troy had been bright with fame, and not
with fire.'

Here feelingly she weeps Troy's painted
woes;
For sorrow, like a heavy-hanging bell,
Once set on ringing, with his own weight
goes;
Then little strength rings out the doleful
knell;   1495
  So Lucrece set a-work sad tales doth tell
    To pencill'd pensiveness and colour'd
sorrow;
    She lends them words, and she their looks
doth borrow.

She throws her eyes about the painting
round,   1499
And who she finds forlorn she doth lament.
At last she sees a wretched image bound
That piteous looks to Phrygian shepherds
lent;
His face, though full of cares, yet show'd
content:
  Onward to Troy with the blunt swains
he goes,
    So mild that Patience seem'd to scorn
his woes.   1505

In him the painter labour'd with his skill
To hide deceit, and give the harmless show
An humble gait, calm looks, eyes wailing
still,
A brow unbent, that seem'd to welcome
woe;   1509
  Cheeks neither red nor pale, but mingled so
    That blushing red no guilty instance
gave,
    Nor ashy pale the fear that false hearts
have;

But, like a constant and confirmed devil,
He entertain'd a show so seeming just,
And therein so ensconc'd his secret evil,
That jealousy itself could not mistrust   1516
False-creeping craft and perjury should
thrust
  Into so bright a day such black-fac'd
storms,
    Or blot with hell-born sin such saint-like
forms.

The well-skill'd workman this mild image
drew   1520
For perjur'd Sinon, whose enchanting story
The credulous old Priam after slew;

Whose words, like wildfire, burnt the shin-
ing glory
Of rich-built Ilion, that the skies were sorry,
   And little stars shot from their fixed
     places,   1525
   When their glass fell wherein they view'd
     their faces.

This picture she advisedly perus'd,
And chid the painter for his wondrous
   skill ;
Saying, some shape in Sinon's was abus'd,
So fair a form lodg'd not a mind so ill ; 1530
And still on him she gaz'd, and gazing
   still
   Such signs of truth in his plain face she
     spied
   That she concludes the picture was
     belied.

' It cannot be ' quoth she ' that so much
   guile '
She would have said ' can lurk in such a
   look '   1535
But Tarquin's shape came in her mind the
   while,
And from her tongue ' can lurk ' from
   ' cannot ' took ;
   It cannot be ' she in that sense forsook,
     And turn'd it thus : ' It cannot be, I find,
     But such a face should bear a wicked
     mind ;   1540

' For even as subtle Sinon here is painted,
So sober-sad, so weary, and so mild,
As if with grief or travail he had fainted,
To me came Tarquin armed ; so beguil'd 1545
With outward honesty, but yet defil'd
   With inward vice. As Priam him did
     cherish,
   So did I Tarquin ; so my Troy did perish.

' Look, look, how list'ning Priam wets his
   eyes,
To see those borrowed tears that Sinon
   sheds.
Priam, why art thou old, and yet not wise ?
For every tear he falls a Troyan bleeds ;
His eye drops fire, no water thence pro-
   ceeds ;   1552
   Those round clear pearls of his that move
     thy pity
   Are balls of quenchless fire to burn thy
     city.

' Such devils steal effects from lightless
   hell ;   1555
For Sinon in his fire doth quake with cold,
And in that cold hot burning fire doth
   dwell ;
These contraries such unity do hold
Only to flatter fools, and make them bold ;
   So Priam's trust false Sinon's tears doth
     flatter   1560
   That he finds means to burn his Troy
     with water '.

Here, all enrag'd, such passion her assails
That patience is quite beaten from her
   breast.
She tears the senseless Sinon with her nails,
Comparing him to that unhappy guest 1565
Whose deed hath made herself herself
   detest.
   At last she smilingly with this gives o'er :
   ' Fool ! fool ! ' quoth she ' his wounds
     will not be sore.'

Thus ebbs and flows the current of her
   sorrow,
And time doth weary time with her com-
   plaining.   1570
She looks for night, and then she longs for
   morrow,
And both she thinks too long with her
   remaining.
Short time seems long in sorrow's sharp
   sustaining ;
   Though woe be heavy, yet it seldom
     sleeps ;
   And they that watch see time how slow
     it creeps.   1575

Which all this time hath overslipp'd her
   thought
That she with painted images hath spent,
Being from the feeling of her own grief
   brought
By deep surmise of others' detriment, 1579
Losing her woes in shows of discontent.
   It easeth some, though none it ever
     cured,
   To think their dolour others have
     endured.

But now the mindful messenger, come back,
Brings home his lord and other company ;
Who finds his Lucrece clad in mourning
   black,   1585
And round about her tear-distained eye
Blue circles stream'd, like rainbows in the
   sky.
These water-galls in her dim element
Foretell new storms to those already
   spent.

Which when her sad-beholding husband
   saw,   1590
Amazedly in her sad face he stares :
Her eyes, though sod in tears, look'd red
   and raw,
Her lively colour kill'd with deadly cares.
He hath no power to ask her how she fares ;
   Both stood like old acquaintance in a
     trance,   1595
   Met far from home, wond'ring each
     other's chance.

At last he takes her by the bloodless
   hand,
And thus begins : ' What uncouth ill event
Hath thee befall'n, that thou dost trembling stand ?

Sweet love, what spite hath thy fair colour
    spent ? 1600
Why art thou thus attir'd in discontent ?
  Unmask, dear dear, this moody heavi-
    ness,
  And tell thy grief, that we may give
    redress '.

Three times with sighs she gives her sorrow
    fire
Ere once she can discharge one word of
    woe ; 1605
At length address'd to answer his desire,
She modestly prepares to let them know
Her honour is ta'en prisoner by the foe ;
  While Collatine and his consorted lords
  With sad attention long to hear her
    words. 1610

And now this pale swan in her wat'ry nest
Begins the sad dirge of her certain ending.
' Few words ' quoth she ' shall fit the
    trespass best,
Where no excuse can give the fault amend-
    ing :
In me moe woes than words are now
    depending ; 1615
  And my laments would be drawn out too
    long
  To tell them all with one poor tired
    tongue.

' Then be this all the task it hath to say :
Dear husband, in the interest of thy bed
A stranger came and on that pillow lay 1620
Where thou wast wont to rest thy weary
    head ;
And what wrong else may be imagined
  By foul enforcement might be done to me
  From that, alas, thy Lucrece is not free.

' For in the dreadful dead of dark mid-
    night, 1625
With shining falchion in my chamber came
A creeping creature, with a flaming light,
And softly cried " Awake, thou Roman
    dame, 1628
And entertain my love ; else lasting shame
  On thee and thine this night I will inflict,
  If thou my love's desire do contradict.

' " For some hard-favour'd groom of thine "
    quoth he
" Unless thou yoke thy liking to my will,
I'll murder straight, and then I'll slaughter
    thee, 1634
And swear I found you where you did
    fulfil
The loathsome act of lust, and so did kill
  The lechers in their deed : this act will be
  My fame, and thy perpetual infamy ".

' With this I did begin to start and cry,
And then against my heart he set his sword,
Swearing, unless I took all patiently, 1641
I should not live to speak another word,
So should my shame still rest upon record,

And never be forgot in mighty Rome
Th' adulterate death of Lucrece and her
    groom. 1645

' Mine enemy was strong, my poor self
    weak,
And far the weaker with so strong a fear.
My bloody judge forbade my tongue to
    speak ;
No rightful plea might plead for justice
    there.
His scarlet lust came evidence to swear 1650
  That my poor beauty had purloin'd his
    eyes,
  And when the judge is robb'd, the
    prisoner dies.

' O, teach me how to make mine own excuse !
Or, at the least, this refuge let me find :
Though my gross blood be stain'd with this
    abuse, 1655
Immaculate and spotless is my mind ;
That was not forc'd ; that never was
    inclin'd
  To accessary yieldings, but still pure
  Doth in her poison'd closet yet endure.'

Lo, here, the hopeless merchant of this loss,
With head declin'd and voice damm'd up
    with woe, 1661
With sad-set eyes and wretched arms
    across,
From lips new-waxen pale begins to blow
The grief away that stops his answer so ;
  But wretched as he is he strives in vain ;
  What he breathes out his breath drinks
    up again. 1666

As through an arch the violent roaring tide
Outruns the eye that doth behold his haste,
Yet in the eddy boundeth in his pride
Back to the strait that forc'd him on so
    fast, 1670
In rage sent out, recall'd in rage, being
    past ;
  Even so his sighs, his sorrows, make a
    saw,
  To push grief on, and back the same
    grief draw.

Which speechless woe of his poor she
    attendeth, 1674
And his untimely frenzy thus awaketh :
' Dear lord, thy sorrow to my sorrow
    lendeth
Another power ; no flood by raining
    slaketh.
My woe too sensible thy passion maketh
  More feeling-painful. Let it then suffice
  To drown one woe, one pair of weeping
    eyes. 1680

And for my sake, when I might charm
    thee so,
For she that was thy Lucrece, now attend
    me :
Be suddenly revenged on my foe,

Thine, mine, his own; suppose thou dost
    defend me
From what is past. The help that thou
    shalt lend me   1685
  Comes all too late, yet let the traitor die;
  For sparing justice feeds iniquity.

' But ere I name him, you, fair lords,'
    quoth she,
Speaking to those that came with Collatine,
' Shall plight your honourable faiths to me
With swift pursuit to venge this wrong of
    mine;   1691
For 'tis a meritorious fair design
  To chase injustice with revengeful arms:
  Knights, by their oaths, should right
    poor ladies' harms'.

At this request, with noble disposition 1695
Each present lord began to promise aid,
As bound in knighthood to her imposition,
Longing to hear the hateful foe bewray'd.
But she, that yet her sad task hath not
    said,
  The protestation stops. ' O speak,' quoth
    she   1700
  ' How may this forced stain be wip'd
    from me ?

' What is the quality of my offence,
Being constrain'd with dreadful circum-
    stance ?
May my pure mind with the foul act
    dispense,
My low-declined honour to advance ? 1705
May any terms acquit me from this chance?
  The poisoned fountain clears itself again;
  And why not I from this compelled
    stain ? '

With this, they all at once began to say
Her body's stain her mind untainted
    clears;
While with a joyless smile she turns away
The face, that map which deep impression
    bears   1712
Of hard misfortune, carv'd in it with tears.
  ' No, no,' quoth she ' no dame hereafter
    living
  By my excuse shall claim excuse's
    giving.'   1715

Here with a sigh, as if her heart would
    break,
She throws forth Tarquin's name: ' He,
    he ' she says,
But more than ' he ' her poor tongue could
    not speak;
Till after many accents and delays,
Untimely breathings, sick, and short assays,
  She utters this: ' He, he, fair lords, 'tis
    he,   1721
  That guides this hand to give this wound
    to me '.

Even here she sheathed in her harmless
    breast

A harmful knife, that thence her soul un-
    sheathed.   1724
That blow did bail it from the deep unrest
Of that polluted prison where it breathed.
Her contrite sighs unto the clouds be-
    queathed
  Her winged sprite, and through her
    wounds doth fly
  Life's lasting date from cancell'd destiny.

Stone-still, astonish'd with this deadly
    deed,   1730
Stood Collatine and all his lordly crew;
Till Lucrece' father, that beholds her bleed,
Himself on her self-slaught'red body threw,
And from the purple fountain Brutus drew
  The murd'rous knife, and, as it left the
    place,   1735
  Her blood, in poor revenge, held it in
    chase;

And bubbling from her breast, it doth
    divide
In two slow rivers, that the crimson blood
Circles her body in on every side,   1739
Who like a late-sack'd island vastly stood
Bare and unpeopled in this fearful flood.
  Some of her blood still pure and red
    remain'd,
  And some look'd black, and that false
    Tarquin stain'd.

About the mourning and congealed face
Of that black blood a wat'ry rigol goes, 1745
Which seems to weep upon the tainted
    place;
And ever since, as pitying Lucrece' woes,
Corrupted blood some watery token shows;
  And blood untainted still doth red abide,
  Blushing at that which is so putrified.

' Daughter, dear daughter,' old Lucretius
    cries,   1751
' That life was mine which thou hast here
    deprived.
If in the child the father's image lies,
Where shall I live now Lucrece is unlived ?
Thou wast not to this end from me derived.
  If children predecease progenitors, 1756
  We are their offspring, and they none of
    ours.

' Poor broken glass, I often did behold
In thy sweet semblance my old age new
    born;
But now that fair fresh mirror, dim and
    old,   1760
Shows me a bare-bon'd death by time out-
    worn;
O, from thy cheeks my image thou hast
    torn,
  And shiver'd all the beauty of my glass
  That I no more can see what once I was

' O time, cease thou thy course and last no
    longer,   176
If they surcease to be that shou'd survive.

Shall rotten death make conquest of the
    stronger,
And leave the falt'ring feeble souls alive?
The old bees die, the young possess their
    hive.
    Then live, sweet Lucrece, live again, and
      see   1770
    Thy father die, and not thy father thee.'

By this starts Collatine as from a dream,
And bids Lucretius give his sorrow place;
And then in key-cold Lucrece' bleeding
    stream
He falls, and bathes the pale fear in his
    face,   .   1775
And counterfeits to die with her a space;
    Till manly shame bids him possess his
      breath,
    And live, to be revenged on her death.

The deep vexation of his inward soul
Hath serv'd a dumb arrest upon his
    tongue;   1780
Who, mad that sorrow should his use
    control,
Or keep him from heart-easing words so
    long,
Begins to talk; but through his lips do
    throng
    Weak words, so thick come, in his poor
      heart's aid,
    That no man could distinguish what he
      said.   1785

Yet sometime 'Tarquin' was pronounced
    plain,
But through his teeth, as if the name he
    tore.
This windy tempest, till it blow up rain,
Held back his sorrow's tide, to make it
    more;
At last it rains, and busy winds give o'er;
    Then son and father weep with equal
      strife,   1791
    Who should weep most for daughter or
      for wife.

The one doth call her his, the other his,
Yet neither may possess the claim they lay.
The father says 'She's mine'. 'O, mine
    she is!'   1795
Replies her husband. 'Do not take away
My sorrow's interest; let no mourner
    say
    He weeps for her, for she was only mine,
    And only must be wail'd by Collatine.'

'O,' quoth Lucretius 'I did give that life
Which she too early and too late hath
    spill'd.'   1801
'Woe, woe,' quoth Collatine 'she was my
    wife,
I owed her, and 'tis mine that she hath
    kill'd.'
'My daughter!' and 'My wife!' with
    clamours fill'd

The dispers'd air, who, holding Lucrece'
    life,   1805
    Answer'd their cries, 'My daughter!'
    and 'My wife!'

Brutus, who pluck'd the knife from
    Lucrece' side,
Seeing such emulation in their woe,
Began to clothe his wit in state and pride,
Burying in Lucrece' wound his folly's show.
He with the Romans was esteemed so 1811
    As silly jeering idiots are with kings,
    For sportive words and utt'ring foolish
      things.

But now he throws that shallow habit by
Wherein deep policy did him disguise, 1815
And arm'd his long-hid wits advisedly
To check the tears in Collatinus' eyes.
'Thou wronged lord of Rome,' quoth he
    'arise;
    Let my unsounded self, suppos'd a fool,
    Now set thy long-experienc'd wit to
      school.   1820

'Why, Collatine, is woe the cure for woe?
Do wounds help wounds, or grief help
    grievous deeds?
Is it revenge to give thyself a blow,
For his foul act by whom thy fair wife
    bleeds?
Such childish humour from weak minds
    proceeds.   1825
    Thy wretched wife mistook the matter so,
    To slay herself that should have slain her
      foe.

'Courageous Roman, do not steep thy
    heart
In such relenting dew of amentations,
But kneel with me, and help to bear thy
    part   1830
To rouse our Roman gods with invocations
That they will suffer these abominations—
    Since Rome herself in them doth stand
      disgraced—
    By our strong arms from forth her fair
      streets chased.

'Now by the Capitol that we adore, 1835
And by this chaste blood so unjustly
    stained,
By heaven's fair sun that breeds the fat
    earth's store,
By all our country rights in Rome main-
    tained,
And by chaste Lucrece' soul that late com-
    plained
    Her wrongs to us, and by this bloody
      knife,   1840
    We will revenge the death of this true
      wife.'

This said, he struck his hand upon his
    breast,
And kiss'd the fatal knife to end his vow;
And to his protestation urg'd the rest,

Who, wond'ring at him, did his words
    allow ; 1845
Then jointly to the ground their knees they
    bow
  And that deep vow which Brutus made
    before
  He doth again repeat, and that they
    swore.

When they had sworn to this advised doom,
They did conclude to bear dead Lucrece
    thence, 1850
To show her bleeding body thorough Rome,
And so to publish Tarquin's foul offence ;
Which being done with speedy diligence,
  The Romans plausibly did give consent
  To Tarquin's everlasting banishment.

SONNETS

TO. THE. ONLIE. BEGETTER. OF.
THESE. INSUING. SONNETS.
MR. W. H. ALL. HAPPINESSE.
AND. THAT. ETERNITIE.
PROMISED.
BY.
OUR. EVER-LIVING. POET.
WISHETH.
THE. WELL-WISHING.
ADVENTURER. IN.
SETTING.
FORTH.

T. T.

1

From fairest creatures we desire increase,
That thereby beauty's rose might never die,
But as the riper should by time decease,
His tender heir might bear his memory;
But thou, contracted to thine own bright eyes, 5
Feed'st thy light's flame with self-substantial fuel,
Making a famine where abundance lies,
Thyself thy foe, to thy sweet self too cruel.
Thou that art now the world's fresh ornament
And only herald to the gaudy spring, 10
Within thine own bud buriest thy content,
And, tender churl, mak'st waste in niggarding.
　　Pity the world, or else this glutton be,
　　To eat the world's due, by the grave and thee.

2

When forty winters shall besiege thy brow,
And dig deep trenches in thy beauty's field,
Thy youth's proud livery, so gaz'd on now,
Will be a tatter'd weed of small worth held.
Then being ask'd where all thy beauty lies,
Where all the treasure of thy lusty days, 6
To say within thine own deep-sunken eyes
Were an all-eating shame and thriftless praise.
How much more praise deserv'd thy beauty's use,
If thou couldst answer ' This fair child of mine 10
Shall sum my count, and make my old excuse '
Proving his beauty by succession thine !
　　This were to be new made when thou art old,
　　And see thy blood warm when thou feel'st it cold.

3

Look in thy glass, and tell the face thou viewest
Now is the time that face should form another;
Whose fresh repair if now thou not renewest,
Thou dost beguile the world, unbless some mother.
For where is she so fair whose unear'd womb 5
Disdains the tillage of thy husbandry ?
Or who is he so fond will be the tomb
Of his self-love, to stop posterity ?
Thou art thy mother's glass, and she in thee
Calls back the lovely April of her prime ; 10
So thou through windows of thine age shalt see,
Despite of wrinkles, this thy golden time.
　　But if thou live rememb'red not to be,
　　Die single, and thine image dies with thee.

4

Unthrifty loveliness, why dost thou spend
Upon thyself thy beauty's legacy ?
Nature's bequest gives nothing, but doth lend,
And, being frank, she lends to those are free.
Then, beauteous niggard, why dost thou abuse 5
The bounteous largess given thee to give ?
Profitless usurer, why dost thou use
So great a sum of sums, yet canst not live ?
For having traffic with thyself alone,
Thou of thyself thy sweet self dost deceive.
Then how when nature calls thee to be gone, 11
What acceptable audit canst thou leave ?
　　Thy unus'd beauty must be tomb'd with thee,
　　Which, used, lives th' executor to be.

5

Those hours that with gentle work did frame
The lovely gaze where every eye doth dwell
Will play the tyrants to the very same,
And that unfair which fairly doth excel ;
For never-resting time leads summer on 5
To hideous winter, and confounds him there ;
Sap check'd with frost and lusty leaves quite gone,
Beauty o'ersnow'd, and bareness every where.
Then, were not summer's distillation left
A liquid prisoner pent in walls of glass, 10
Beauty's effect with beauty were bereft,

Nor it, nor no remembrance what it was;
   But flowers distill'd, though they with
      winter meet,
     Leese but their show: their substance
      still lives sweet.

6

Then let not winter's ragged hand deface
In thee thy summer ere thou be distill'd;
Make sweet some vial; treasure thou some
    place
With beauty's treasure ere it be self-kill'd.
That use is not forbidden usury   5
Which happies those that pay the willing
    loan—
That's for thyself to breed an other thee,
Or ten times happier, be it ten for one;
Ten times thy self were happier than thou
    art,
If ten of thine ten times refigur'd thee.   10
Then what could Death do if thou shouldst
    depart,
Leaving thee living in posterity?
   Be not self-will'd, for thou art much too
    fair
   To be death's conquest and make worms
    thine heir.

7

Lo, in the orient when the gracious light
Lifts up his burning head, each under eye
Doth homage to his new-appearing sight,
Serving with looks his sacred majesty;
And having climb'd the steep-up heavenly
    hill,   5
Resembling strong youth in his middle age,
Yet mortal looks adore his beauty still,
Attending on his golden pilgrimage;
But when from highmost pitch, with weary
    car,
Like feeble age he reeleth from the day, 10
The eyes, 'fore duteous, now converted are
From his low tract and look another way;
   So thou, thyself outgoing in thy noon,
   Unlook'd on diest, unless thou get a son.

8

Music to hear, why hear'st thou music
    sadly?
Sweets with sweets war not, joy delights in
    joy.
Why lov'st thou that which thou receiv'st
    not gladly,
Or else receiv'st with pleasure thine annoy?
If the true concord of well-tuned sounds, 5
By unions married, do offend thine ear,
They do but sweetly chide thee, who con-
    founds
In singleness the parts that thou shouldst
    bear.
Mark how one string, sweet husband to
    another,
Strikes each in each by mutual ordering; 10

Resembling sire, and child, and happy
    mother,
Who, all in one, one pleasing note do sing;
   Whose speechless song, being many,
    seeming one,
   Sings this to thee: 'Thou single wilt
    prove none'.

9

Is it for fear to wet a widow's eye
That thou consum'st thyself in single life?
Ah! if thou issueless shalt hap to die,
The world will wail thee like a makeless
    wife: 4
The world will be thy widow, and still weep
That thou no form of thee hast left behind,
When every private widow well may keep,
By children's eyes, her husband's shape in
    mind.
Look what an unthrift in the world doth
    spend
Shifts but his place, for still the world
    enjoys it;   10
But beauty's waste hath in the world an
    end,
And kept unus'd, the user so destroys it.
   No love toward others in that bosom sits
   That on himself such murd'rous shame
    commits.

10

For shame! deny that thou bear'st love to
    any,
Who for thy self art so unprovident.
Grant, if thou wilt, thou art belov'd of
    many,
But that thou none lov'st is most evident;
For thou art so possess'd with murd'rous
    hate   5
That 'gainst thyself thou stick'st not to
    conspire,
Seeking that beauteous roof to ruinate
Which to repair should be thy chief desire.
O, change thy thought, that I may change
    my mind!   9
Shall hate be fairer lodg'd than gentle love?
Be, as thy presence is, gracious and kind,
Or to thy self at least kind-hearted prove;
   Make thee an other self for love of me,
   That beauty still may live in thine or
    thee.

11

As fast as thou shalt wane, so fast thou
    grow'st
In one of thine, from that which thou
    departest;
And that fresh blood which youngly thou
    bestow'st
Thou mayst call thine when thou from
    youth convertest.
Herein lives wisdom, beauty, and increase;

Without this folly, age, and cold decay. 6
If all were minded so, the times should
cease,
And threescore year would make the world
away.
Let those whom Nature hath not made for
store,
Harsh, featureless, and rude, barrenly
perish.   10
Look whom she best endow'd she gave the
more ;
Which bounteous gift thou shouldst in
bounty cherish ;
  She carv'd thee for her seal, and meant
  thereby
  Thou shouldst print more, not let that
  copy die.

12

When I do count the clock that tells the
time,
And see the brave day sunk in hideous
night ;
When I behold the violet past prime,
And sable curls all silver'd o'er with white ;
When lofty trees I see barren of leaves,   5
Which erst from heat did canopy the herd,
And summer's green all girded up in sheaves
Borne on the bier with white and bristly
beard ;
Then of thy beauty do I question make
That thou among the wastes of time must
go,   10
Since sweets and beauties do themselves
forsake,
And die as fast as they see others grow ;
  And nothing 'gainst Time's scythe can
  make defence
  Save breed, to brave him when he takes
  thee hence.

13

O that you were yourself ! But, love, you
are
No longer yours than you your self here
live.
Against this coming end you should pre-
pare,
And your sweet semblance to some other
give.
So should that beauty which you hold in
lease   5
Find no determination ; then you were
Your self again, after your self's decease,
When your sweet issue your sweet form
should bear.
Who lets so fair a house fall to decay,   9
Which husbandry in honour might uphold
Against the stormy gusts of winter's day
And barren rage of death's eternal cold ?
  O, none but unthrifts ! Dear my love,
  you know
  You had a father : let your son say so.

14

Not from the stars do I my judgment pluck,
And yet methinks I have astronomy ;
But not to tell of good or evil luck,
Of plagues, of dearths, or seasons' quality ;
Nor can I fortune to brief minutes tell,   5
Pointing to each his thunder, rain, and
wind,
Or say with princes if it shall go well
By oft predict that I in heaven find ;
But from thine eyes my knowledge I derive,
And, constant stars, in them I read such
art   10
As truth and beauty shall together thrive,
If from thy self to store thou wouldst con-
vert.
  Or else of thee this I prognosticate :
  Thy end is truth's and beauty's doom
  and date.

15

When I consider every thing that grows
Holds in perfection but a little moment,
That this huge stage presenteth nought but
shows
Whereon the stars in secret influence com-
ment ;
When I perceive that men as plants in-
crease,   5
Cheered and check'd even by the self-same
sky,
Vaunt in their youthful sap, at height
decrease,
And wear their brave state out of memory ;
Then the conceit of this inconstant stay
Sets you most rich in youth before my
sight,   10
Where wasteful Time debateth with
Decay
To change your day of youth to sullied
night ;
  And all in war with Time for love of you,
  As he takes from you, I engraft you new.

16

But wherefore do not you a mightier way
Make war upon this bloody tyrant Time ?
And fortify your self in your decay
With means more blessed than my barren
rhyme ?
Now stand you on the top of happy hours,
And many maiden gardens, yet unset,   6
With virtuous wish would bear your living
flowers,
Much liker than your painted counterfeit ;
So should the lines of life that life repair, 9
Which this, Time's pencil or my pupil pen,
Neither in inward worth, nor outward fair,
Can make you live your self in eyes of men.
  To give away your self keeps your self
  still ;
  And you must live, drawn by your own
  sweet skill.

17

Who will believe my verse in time to come,
If it were fill'd with your most high deserts?
Though yet, heaven knows, it is but as a tomb
Which hides your life and shows not half your parts.
If I could write the beauty of your eyes 5
And in fresh numbers number all your graces,
The age to come would say ' This poet lies ;
Such heavenly touches ne'er touch'd earthly faces '.
So should my papers, yellowed with their age,
Be scorn'd, like old men of less truth than tongue ; 10
And your true rights be term'd a poet's rage,
And stretched metre of an antique song.
   But were some child of yours alive that time,
   You should live twice—in it, and in my rhyme.

18

Shall I compare thee to a summer's day ?
Thou art more lovely and more temperate.
Rough winds do shake the darling buds of May,
And summer's lease hath all too short a date : 4
Sometime too hot the eye of heaven shines,
And often is his gold complexion dimm'd ;
And every fair from fair some time declines,
By chance, or nature's changing course, untrimm'd ;
But thy eternal summer shall not fade 9
Nor lose possession of that fair thou ow'st ;
Nor shall Death brag thou wand'rest in his shade,
When in eternal lines to time thou grow'st.
   So long as men can breathe or eyes can see,
   So long lives this, and this gives life to thee.

19

Devouring Time, blunt thou the lion's paws,
And make the earth devour her own sweet brood ;
Pluck the keen teeth from the fierce tiger's jaws,
And burn the long-liv'd phœnix in her blood ; 4
Make glad and sorry seasons as thou fleet'st,
And do whate'er thou wilt, swift-footed Time,
To the wide world and all her fading sweets;
But I forbid thee one most heinous crime :
O, carve not with thy hours my love's fair brow,
Nor draw no lines there with thine antique pen ; 10
Him in thy course untainted do allow
For beauty's pattern to succeeding men.
   Yet, do thy worst, old Time. Despite thy wrong,
   My love shall in my verse ever live young.

20

A woman's face, with Nature's own hand painted,
Hast thou, the Master Mistress of my passion ;
A woman's gentle heart, but not acquainted
With shifting change, as is false woman's fashion ;
An eye more bright than theirs, less false in rolling, 5
Gilding the object whereupon it gazeth ;
A man in hue all hues in his controlling,
Which steals men's eyes and women's souls amazeth.
And for a woman wert thou first created ;
Till Nature, as she wrought thee, fell a-doting, 10
And by addition me of thee defeated
By adding one thing to my purpose nothing.
   But since she prick'd thee out for women's pleasure,
   Mine be thy love, and thy love's use their treasure.

21

So is it not with me as with that Muse,
Stirr'd by a painted beauty to his verse ;
Who heaven itself for ornament doth use,
And every fair with his fair doth rehearse,
Making a couplement of proud compare 5
With sun and moon, with earth and sea's rich gems,
With April's first-born flowers, and all things rare
That heaven's air in this huge rondure hems.
O, let me, true in love, but truly write,
And then believe me, my love is as fair 10
As any mother's child, though not so bright
As those gold candles fix'd in heaven's air.
   Let them say more that like of hearsay well :
   I will not praise that purpose not to sell.

22

My glass shall not persuade me I am old
So long as youth and thou are of one date ;
But when in thee time's furrows I behold,
Then look I death my days should expiate.
For all that beauty that doth cover thee 5
Is but the seemly raiment of my heart,
Which in thy breast doth live, as thine in me ;
How can I then be elder than thou art ?

O, therefore, love, be of thyself so wary,
As I not for myself but for thee will;   10
Bearing thy heart, which I will keep so chary
As tender nurse her babe from faring ill.
   Presume not on thy heart when mine is slain;
   Thou gav'st me thine, not to give back again.

23

As an unperfect actor on the stage
Who with his fear is put besides his part,
Or some fierce thing replete with too much rage,
Whose strength's abundance weakens his own heart;
So I, for fear of trust, forget to say   5
The perfect ceremony of love's rite,
And in mine own love's strength seem to decay,
O'ercharg'd with burthen of mine own love's might.
O, let my looks be then the eloquence
And dumb presagers of my speaking breast;
Who plead for love, and look for recompense,   11
More than that tongue that more hath more express'd.
   O, learn to read what silent love hath writ!
   To hear with eyes belongs to love's fine wit.

24

Mine eye hath play'd the painter and hath stell'd
Thy beauty's form in table of my heart;
My body is the frame wherein 'tis held,
And perspective it is best painter's art.
For through the painter must you see his skill   5
To find where your true image pictur'd lies,
Which in my bosom's shop is hanging still,
That hath his windows glazed with thine eyes.
Now see what good turns eyes for eyes have done:
Mine eyes have drawn thy shape, and thine for me   10
Are windows to my breast, where through the sun
Delights to peep, to gaze therein on thee;
   Yet eyes this cunning want to grace their art:
   They draw but what they see, know not the heart.

25

Let those who are in favour with their stars
Of public honour and proud titles boast,
Whilst I, whom fortune of such triumph bars,
Unlook'd for joy in that I honour most.
Great princes' favourites their fair leaves spread   5
But as the marigold at the sun's eye;
And in themselves their pride lies buried,
For at a frown they in their glory die.
The painful warrior famoused for fight,
After a thousand victories once foil'd,   10
Is from the book of honour razed quite,
And all the rest forgot for which he toil'd.
   Then happy I, that love and am beloved
   Where I may not remove nor be removed.

26

Lord of my love, to whom in vassalage
Thy merit hath my duty strongly knit,
To thee I send this written embassage,
To witness duty, not to show my wit;
Duty so great, which wit so poor as mine   5
May make seem bare, in wanting words to show it,
But that I hope some good conceit of thine
In thy soul's thought, all naked, will bestow it;
Till whatsoever star that guides my moving
Points on me graciously with fair aspect,   10
And puts apparel on my tattered loving
To show me worthy of thy sweet respect.
   Then may I dare to boast how I do love thee;
   Till then not show my head where thou mayst prove me.

27

Weary with toil, I haste me to my bed,
The dear repose for limbs with travel tired;
But then begins a journey in my head
To work my mind when body's work's expired;
For then my thoughts, from far where I abide,   5
Intend a zealous pilgrimage to thee,
And keep my drooping eyelids open wide,
Looking on darkness which the blind do see;
Save that my soul's imaginary sight   9
Presents thy shadow to my sightless view,
Which, like a jewel hung in ghastly night,
Makes black night beauteous and her old face new.
   Lo, thus, by day my limbs, by night my mind,
   For thee, and for myself, no quiet find.

28

How can I then return in happy plight
That am debarr'd the benefit of rest?
When day's oppression is not eas'd by night,
But day by night and night by day oppress'd?   4
And each, though enemies to either's reign,
Do in consent shake hands to torture me,
The one by toil, the other to complain

How far I toil, still farther off from thee.
I tell the day, to please him, thou art bright
And dost him grace when clouds do blot
   the heaven ;   10
So flatter I the swart-complexion'd night,
When sparkling stars twire not, thou gild'st
   the even.
  But day doth daily draw my sorrows
    longer,
  And night doth nightly make grief's
    strength seem stronger.

29

When in disgrace with Fortune and men's
   eyes,
I all alone beweep my outcast state,
And trouble deaf heaven with my bootless
   cries,
And look upon myself, and curse my fate,
Wishing me like to one more rich in hope, 5
Featur'd like him, like him with friends
   possess'd,
Desiring this man's art, and that man's
   scope,
With what I most enjoy contented least ;
Yet in these thoughts myself almost despis-
   ing,   9
Haply I think on thee, and then my state,
Like to the lark at break of day arising
From sullen earth, sings hymns at heaven's
   gate ;
  For thy sweet love rememb'red such
    wealth brings
  That then I scorn to change my state
    with kings.

30

When to the sessions of sweet silent
   thought
I summon up remembrance of things past,
I sigh the lack of many a thing I sought,
And with old woes new wail my dear time's
   waste.
Then can I drown an eye, unus'd to flow, 5
For precious friends hid in death's dateless
   night,
And weep afresh love's long since cancell'd
   woe,
And moan th' expense of many a vanish'd
   sight.
Then can I grieve at grievances foregone,
And heavily from woe to woe tell o'er   10
The sad account of fore-bemoaned moan,
Which I new pay as if not paid before.
  But if the while I think on thee, dear
    friend,
  All losses are restor'd, and sorrows end.

31

Thy bosom is endeared with all hearts
Which I by lacking have supposed dead ;
And there reigns love and all love's loving
   parts,

And all those friends which I thought
   buried.
How many a holy and obsequious tear 5
Hath dear religious love stol'n from mine
   eye,
As interest of the dead, which now appear
But things remov'd that hidden in thee
   lie !
Thou art the grave where buried love doth
   live,   9
Hung with the trophies of my lovers gone,
Who all their parts of me to thee did give ;
That due of many now is thine alone.
  Their images I lov'd I view in thee,
  And thou, all they, hast all the all of me.

32

If thou survive my well-contented day
When that churl Death my bones with dust
   shall cover,
And shalt by fortune once more re-survey
These poor rude lines of thy deceased
   lover,
Compare them with the bett'ring of the
   time,   5
And though they be outstripp'd by every
   pen,
Reserve them for my love, not for their
   rhyme,
Exceeded by the height of happier men.
O, then vouchsafe me but this loving
   thought :
' Had my friend's Muse grown with this
   growing age,   10
A dearer birth than this his love had
   brought,
To march in ranks of better equipage ;
  But since he died, and poets better prove,
  Theirs for their style I'll read, his for his
    love '.

33

Full many a glorious morning have I seen
Flatter the mountain-tops with sovereign
   eye,
Kissing with golden face the meadows
   green,
Gilding pale streams with heavenly
   alchemy ;
Anon permit the basest clouds to ride 5
With ugly rack on his celestial face,
And from the forlorn world his visage hide,
Stealing unseen to west with this disgrace.
Even so my sun one early morn did shine
With all triumphant splendour on my
   brow ;   10
But out, alack ! he was but one hour
   mine,
The region cloud hath mask'd him from me
   now.
  Yet him for this my love no whit dis-
    daineth ;
  Suns of the world may stain when
    heaven's sun staineth.

34

Why didst thou promise such a beauteous
    day,
And make me travel forth without my
    cloak,
To let base clouds o'ertake me in my way,
Hiding thy brav'ry in their rotten smoke ?
'Tis not enough that through the cloud thou
    break   5
To dry the rain on my storm-beaten face,
For no man well of such a salve can speak
That heals the wound, and cures not the
    disgrace.
Nor can thy shame give physic to my grief ;
Though thou repent, yet I have still the
    loss.   10
Th' offender's sorrow lends but weak relief
To him that bears the strong offence's cross.
    Ah ! but those tears are pearl which thy
        love sheds,
    And they are rich, and ransom all ill
        deeds.

35

No more be griev'd at that which thou hast
    done :
Roses have thorns, and silver fountains
    mud ;
Clouds and eclipses stain both moon and
    sun,
And loathsome canker lives in sweetest bud.
All men make faults, and even I in this,   5
Authorizing thy trespass with compare,
Myself corrupting, salving thy amiss,
Excusing thy sins more than thy sins are ;
For to thy sensual fault I bring in sense—
Thy adverse party is thy advocate—   10
And 'gainst myself a lawful plea commence ;
Such civil war is in my love and hate
    That I an accessary needs must be
    To that sweet thief which sourly robs
        from me.

36

Let me confess that we two must be twain,
Although our undivided loves are one ;
So shall those blots that do with me remain,
Without thy help, by me be borne alone.
In our two loves there is but one respect,   5
Though in our lives a separable spite,
Which though it alter not love's sole effect,
Yet doth it steal sweet hours from love's
    delight.
I may not evermore acknowledge thee,
Lest my bewailed guilt should do thee
    shame ;   10
Nor thou with public kindness honour me,
Unless thou take that honour from thy
    name.
    But do not so ; I love thee in such sort
    As, thou being mine, mine is thy good
        report.

37

As a decrepit father takes delight
To see his active child do deeds of youth,
So I, made lame by Fortune's dearest spite,
Take all my comfort of thy worth and
    truth ;
For whether beauty, birth, or wealth, or
    wit,   5
Or any of these all, or all, or more,
Entitled in thy parts do crowned sit,
I make my love engrafted to this store.
So then I am not lame, poor, nor despis'd,
Whilst that this shadow doth such sub-
    stance give   10
That I in thy abundance am suffic'd,
And by a part of all thy glory live.
    Look what is best, that best I wish in
        thee ;
    This wish I have ; then ten times happy
        me !

38

How can my Muse want subject to invent,
While thou dost breathe that pour'st into
    my verse
Thine own sweet argument, too excellent
For every vulgar paper to rehearse ?
O, give thyself the thanks if aught in me   5
Worthy perusal stand against thy sight ;
For who's so dumb that cannot write to
    thee,
When thou thy self dost give invention
    light ?
Be thou the tenth Muse, ten times more in
    worth
Than those old nine which rhymers in-
    vocate ;   10
And he that calls on thee, let him bring
    forth
Eternal numbers to outlive long date.
    If my slight Muse do please these curious
        days,
    The pain be mine, but thine shall be the
        praise.

39

O, how thy worth with manners may I sing,
When thou art all the better part of me ?
What can mine own praise to mine own self
    bring ?
And what is't but mine own, when I praise
    thee ?
Even for this let us divided live,   5
And our dear love lose name of single one,
That by this separation I may give
That due to thee which thou deserv'st
    alone.
O absence, what a torment wouldst thou
    prove,
Were it not thy sour leisure gave sweet
    leave   10
To entertain the time with thoughts of love ;

Which time and thoughts so sweetly doth
deceive,
And that thou teachest how to make one
twain,
By praising him here who doth hence
remain !

40

Take all my loves, my love, yea, take them
all ;
What hast thou then more than thou hadst
before ?
No love, my love, that thou mayst true love
call ;
All mine was thine before thou hadst this
more.   4
Then if for my love thou my love receivest,
I cannot blame thee, for my love thou usest ;
But yet be blam'd, if thou thyself deceivest
By wilful taste of what thyself refusest.
I do forgive thy robb'ry, gentle thief,   9
Although thou steal thee all my poverty ;
And yet love knows it is a greater grief
To bear love's wrong than hate's known
injury.
   Lascivious grace, in whom all ill well
   shows,
   Kill me with spites ; yet we must not be
   foes.

41

Those pretty wrongs that liberty commits
When I am sometime absent from thy
heart,
Thy beauty and thy years full well befits,
For still temptation follows where thou art.
Gentle thou art, and therefore to be won,
Beauteous thou art, therefore to be assailed;
And when a woman woos, what woman's
son   7
Will sourly leave her till she have prevailed ?
Ay me ! but yet thou mightst my seat
forbear,
And chide thy beauty and thy straying
youth,   10
Who lead thee in their riot even there
Where thou art forc'd to break a twofold
truth :
   Hers, by thy beauty tempting her to thee,
   Thine, by thy beauty being false to me.

42

That thou hast her, it is not all my grief,
And yet it may be said I lov'd her dearly ;
That she hath thee is of my wailing chief,
A loss in love that touches me more nearly.
Loving offenders, thus I will excuse ye :   5
Thou dost love her because thou know'st I
love her,
And for my sake even so doth she abuse me,
Suff'ring my friend for my sake to approve
her.

If I lose thee, my loss is my love's gain,
And, losing her, my friend hath found that
loss ;   10
Both find each other, and I lose both twain,
And both for my sake lay on me this
cross.
   But here's the joy : my friend and I are
   one ;
   Sweet flattery ! then she loves but me
   alone.

43

When most I wink, then do mine eyes best
see,
For all the day they view things un-
respected ;
But when I sleep, in dreams they look on
thee,
And, darkly bright, are bright in dark
directed ;
Then thou whose shadow shadows doth
make bright,   5
How would thy shadow's form form happy
show
To the clear day with thy much clearer
light,
When to unseeing eyes thy shade shines so !
How would, I say, mine eyes be blessed
made
By looking on thee in the living day,   10
When in dead night thy fair imperfect
shade
Through heavy sleep on sightless eyes doth
stay !
   All days are nights to see till I see
   thee,
   And nights bright days when dreams do
   show thee me.

44

If the dull substance of my flesh were
thought,
Injurious distance should not stop my way ;
For then, despite of space, I would be
brought
From limits far remote, where thou dost
stay.
No matter then, although my foot did
stand   5
Upon the farthest earth remov'd from thee,
For nimble thought can jump both sea and
land
As soon as think the place where he would
be.
But ah ! thought kills me that I am not
thought,
To leap large lengths of miles when thou
art gone,   10
But that, so much of earth and water
wrought,
I must attend time's leisure with my moan,
   Receiving nought by elements so slow
   But heavy tears, badges of either's woe.

45

The other two, slight air and purging fire,
Are both with thee, wherever I abide ;
The first my thought, the other my desire,
These present-absent with swift motion
slide.   4
For when these quicker elements are gone
In tender embassy of love to thee,
My life, being made of four, with two alone
Sinks down to death, oppress'd with
melancholy ;
Until life's composition be recured
By those swift messengers return'd from
thee,   10
Who even but now come back again,
assured
Of thy fair health, recounting it to me.
    This told, I joy ; but then no longer glad,
    I send them back again, and straight
    grow sad.

46

Mine eye and heart are at a mortal war
How to divide the conquest of thy sight ;
Mine eye my heart thy picture's sight
would bar,
My heart mine eye the freedom of that
right.
My heart doth plead that thou in him dost
lie,   5
A closet never pierc'd with crystal eyes ;
But the defendant doth that plea deny,
And says in him thy fair appearance lies.
To 'cide this title is impanelled
A quest of thoughts, all tenants to the
heart ;   10
And by their verdict is determined
The clear eye's moiety and the dear heart's
part—
    As thus : mine eye's due is thine out-
    ward part,
    And my heart's right thine inward love
    of heart.

47

Betwixt mine eye and heart a league is took,
And each doth good turns now unto the
other.
When that mine eye is famish'd for a look,
Or heart in love with sighs himself doth
smother ;
With my love's picture then my eye doth
feast,   5
And to the painted banquet bids my heart ;
Another time mine eye is my heart's guest,
And in his thoughts of love doth share a
part ;
So, either by thy picture or my love,
Thyself away art present still with me ;   10
For thou not farther than my thoughts
canst move,
And I am still with them, and they with
thee ;

Or if they sleep, thy picture in my sight
Awakes my heart to heart's and eye's
delight.

48

How careful was I when I took my way,
Each trifle under truest bars to thrust,
That to my use it might unused stay
From hands of falsehood, in sure wards of
trust !
But thou, to whom my jewels trifles are,   5
Most worthy comfort, now my greatest
grief,
Thou, best of dearest, and mine only care,
Art left the prey of every vulgar thief.
Thee have I not lock'd up in any chest,
Save where thou art not, though I feel thou
art,   10
Within the gentle closure of my breast,
From whence at pleasure thou mayst come
and part ;
    And even thence thou wilt be stol'n, I
    fear,
    For truth proves thievish for a prize so
    dear.

49

Against that time, if ever that time come,
When I shall see thee frown on my defects,
When as thy love hath cast his utmost sum,
Call'd to that audit by advis'd respects ;
Against that time when thou shalt strangely
pass   5
And scarcely greet me with that sun, thine
eye,
When love, converted from the thing it was,
Shall reasons find of settled gravity—
Against that time do I ensconce me here
Within the knowledge of mine own desert,
And this my hand against myself uprear,   11
To guard the lawful reasons on thy part :
    To leave poor me thou hast the strength
    of laws,
    Since why to love I can allege no cause.

50

How heavy do I journey on the way,
When what I seek—my weary travel's
end—
Doth teach that ease and that repose to say
' Thus far the miles are measur'd from thy
friend ! '   4
The beast that bears me, tired with my woe,
Plods dully on, to bear that weight in me,
As if by some instinct the wretch did know
His rider lov'd not speed being made from
thee.
The bloody spur cannot provoke him on   9
That sometimes anger thrusts into his hide,
Which heavily he answers with a groan,
More sharp to me than spurring to his side ;
    For that same groan doth put this in my
    mind :
    My grief lies onward, and my joy behind.

51

Thus can my love excuse the slow offence
Of my dull bearer, when from thee I speed:
From where thou art why should I haste me
  thence?
Till I return, of posting is no need.
O, what excuse will my poor beast then
  find,   5
When swift extremity can seem but slow?
Then should I spur, though mounted on the
  wind;
In winged speed no motion shall I know.
Then can no horse with my desire keep
  pace;
Therefore desire, of perfect'st love being
  made,   10
Shall weigh no dull flesh in his fiery race;
But love, for love, thus shall excuse my
  jade:
  Since from thee going he went wilful
    slow,
  Towards thee I'll run, and give him leave
    to go.

52

So am I as the rich whose blessed key
Can bring him to his sweet up-locked
  treasure,
The which he will not ev'ry hour survey,
For blunting the fine point of seldom
  pleasure.   4
Therefore are feasts so solemn and so rare,
Since seldom coming, in the long year set,
Like stones of worth they thinly placed are,
Or captain jewels in the carcanet.
So is the time that keeps you as my chest,
Or as the wardrobe which the robe doth
  hide,   10
To make some special instant special blest
By new unfolding his imprison'd pride.
  Blessed are you, whose worthiness gives
    scope,
  Being had, to triumph, being lack'd, to
    hope.

53

What is your substance, whereof are you
  made,
That millions of strange shadows on you
  tend?
Since every one hath, every one, one
  shade,
And you, but one, can every shadow lend.
Describe Adonis, and the counterfeit   5
Is poorly imitated after you;
On Helen's cheek all art of beauty set,
And you in Grecian tires are painted new.
Speak of the spring and foison of the year:
The one doth shadow of your beauty show,
The other as your bounty doth appear,   11
And you in every blessed shape we know.
  In all external grace you have some part,
  But you like none, none you, for constant
    heart.

54

O, how much more doth beauty beauteous
  seem
By that sweet ornament which truth doth
  give!
The rose looks fair, but fairer we it deem
For that sweet odour which doth in it
  live.
The canker-blooms have full as deep a dye
As the perfumed tincture of the roses,   6
Hang on such thorns, and play as wantonly
When summer's breath their masked buds
  discloses;
But for their virtue only is their show,   9
They lived unwoo'd, and unrespected fade;
Die to themselves. Sweet roses do not so:
Of their sweet deaths are sweetest odours
  made.
  And so of you, beauteous and lovely
    youth,
  When that shall vade, by verse distills
    your truth.

55

Not marble nor the gilded monuments
Of princes shall outlive this pow'rful
  rhyme;
But you shall shine more bright in these
  contents
Than unswept stone, besmear'd with
  sluttish time.   4
When wasteful war shall statues overturn,
And broils root out the work of masonry,
Nor Mars his sword nor war's quick fire
  shall burn
The living record of your memory.
'Gainst death and all-oblivious enmity
Shall you pace forth; your praise shall still
  find room,   10
Even in the eyes of all posterity
That wear this world out to the ending
  doom.
  So, till the judgment that yourself arise,
  You live in this, and dwell in lovers' eyes.

56

Sweet love, renew thy force; be it not
  said
Thy edge should blunter be than appetite,
Which but to-day by feeding is allay'd,
To-morrow sharp'ned in his former might.
So, love, be thou; although to-day thou
  fill   5
Thy hungry eyes, even till they wink with
  fulness,
To-morrow see again, and do not kill
The spirit of love with a perpetual dulness.
Let this sad int'rim like the ocean be
Which parts the shore where two con-
  tracted new   10
Come daily to the banks, that, when they
  see

Return of love, more blest may be the view;
  Or call it winter, which, being full of care,
  Makes summer's welcome thrice more
    wish'd, more rare.

57

Being your slave, what should I do but
    tend
Upon the hours and times of your desire?
I have no precious time at all to spend,
Nor services to do, till you require.
Nor dare I chide the world-without-end
    hour,   5
Whilst I, my sovereign, watch the clock for
    you,
Nor think the bitterness of absence sour,
When you have bid your servant once
    adieu;
Nor dare I question with my jealous
    thought   9
Where you may be, or your affairs suppose,
But, like a sad slave, stay and think of
    nought
Save where you are how happy you make
    those.
  So true a fool is love that in your will,
  Though you do anything, he thinks no ill.

58

That god forbid that made me first your
    slave
I should in thought control your times of
    pleasure,
Or at your hand th' account of hours to
    crave,
Being your vassal bound to stay your
    leisure!
O, let me suffer, being at your beck,   5
Th' imprison'd absence of your liberty,
And patience, tame to sufferance, bide each
    check
Without accusing you of injury.
Be where you list; your charter is so
    strong   9
That you yourself may privilege your time
To what you will; to you it doth belong
Your self to pardon of self-doing crime.
  I am to wait, though waiting so be hell;
  Not blame your pleasure, be it ill or well.

59

If there be nothing new, but that which is
Hath been before, how are our brains
    beguil'd,
Which labouring for invention bear amiss
The second burthen of a former child!   4
O, that record could with a backward look,
Even of five hundred courses of the sun,
Show me your image in some antique book,
Since mind at first in character was done!
That I might see what the old world could
    say   9

To this composed wonder of your frame;
Whether we are mended, or whe'er better
    they,
Or whether revolution be the same.
  O, sure I am, the wits of former days
    To subjects worse have given admiring
    praise.

60

Like as the waves make towards the
    pebbled shore,
So do our minutes hasten to their end;
Each changing place with that which goes
    before,
In sequent toil all forwards do contend.
Nativity, once in the main of light,   5
Crawls to maturity, wherewith being
    crown'd,
Crooked eclipses 'gainst his glory fight,
And Time that gave doth now his gift con-
    found.
Time doth transfix the flourish set on
    youth,   9
And delves the parallels in beauty's brow,
Feeds on the rarities of nature's truth,
And nothing stands but for his scythe to
    mow.
  And yet to times in hope my verse shall
    stand,
  Praising thy worth, despite his cruel
    hand.

61

Is it thy will thy image should keep open
My heavy eyelids to the weary night?
Dost thou desire my slumbers should be
    broken,
While shadows like to thee do mock my
    sight?   4
Is it thy spirit that thou send'st from thee
So far from home into my deeds to pry,
To find out shames and idle hours in me,
The scope and tenour of thy jealousy?
O no! thy love, though much, is not so
    great: 9
It is my love that keeps mine eye awake;
Mine own true love that doth my rest defeat
To play the watchman ever for thy sake.
  For thee watch I, whilst thou dost wake
    elsewhere,
  From me far off, with others all too near.

62

Sin of self-love possesseth all mine eye,
And all my soul, and all my every part;
And for this sin there is no remedy,
It is so grounded inward in my heart.
Methinks no face so gracious is as mine,   5
No shape so true, no truth of such account,
And for myself mine own worth do define
As I all other in all worths surmount.
But when my glass shows me myself indeed,

Beated and chopt with tann'd antiquity, 10
Mine own self-love quite contrary I read ;
Self so self-loving were iniquity.
   'Tis thee, my self, that for myself I praise,
   Painting my age with beauty of thy days.

63

Against my love shall be as I am now,
With Time's injurious hand crush'd and
   o'erworn ;
When hours have drain'd his blood, and
   fill'd his brow
With lines and wrinkles ; when his youthful
   morn
Hath travell'd on to age's steepy night ; 5
And all those beauties whereof now he's
   king
Are vanishing or vanish'd out of sight,
Stealing away the treasure of his spring—
For such a time do I now fortify
Against confounding age's cruel knife, 10
That he shall never cut from memory
My sweet love's beauty, though my lover's
   life.
   His beauty shall in these black lines be
     seen,
   And they shall live, and he in them still
     green.

64

When I have seen by Time's fell hand
   defaced
The rich proud cost of outworn buried age ;
When sometime lofty towers I see down-
   rased,
And brass eternal slave to mortal rage ;
When I have seen the hungry ocean gain 5
Advantage on the kingdom of the shore,
And the firm soil win of the wat'ry main,
Increasing store with loss, and loss with
   store ;
When I have seen such interchange of state,
Or state itself confounded to decay ; 10
Ruin hath taught me thus to ruminate—
That Time will come and take my love
   away.
   This thought is as a death, which cannot
     choose
   But weep to have that which it fears to
     lose.

65

Since brass, nor stone, nor earth, nor
   boundless sea,
But sad mortality o'ersways their power,
How with this rage shall beauty hold a plea,
Whose action is no stronger than a flower ?
O, how shall summer's honey breath hold
   out 5
Against the wrackful siege of batt'ring days,
When rocks impregnable are not so stout,
Nor gates of steel so strong, but Time
   decays ?

O fearful meditation ! Where, alack,
Shall Time's best jewel from Time's chest
   lie hid ? 10
Or what strong hand can hold his swift foot
   back ?
Or who his spoil of beauty can forbid ?
   O, none, unless this miracle have might,
   That in black ink my love may still shine
     bright.

66

Tir'd with all these, for restful death I cry :
As, to behold desert a beggar born,
And needy nothing trimm'd in jollity,
And purest faith unhappily forsworn,
And gilded honour shamefully misplac'd, 5
And maiden virtue rudely strumpeted,
And right perfection wrongfully disgrac'd,
And strength by limping sway disabled,
And art made tongue-tied by authority,
And folly, doctor-like, controlling skill, 10
And simple truth miscall'd simplicity,
And captive good attending captain ill—
   Tir'd with all these, from these would I
     be gone,
   Save that, to die, I leave my love alone.

67

Ah ! wherefore with infection should he live
And with his presence grace impiety,
That sin by him advantage should achieve,
And lace itself with his society ?
Why should false painting imitate his
   cheek, 5
And steal dead seeming of his living hue ?
Why should poor beauty indirectly seek
Roses of shadow, since his rose is true ?
Why should he live now Nature bankrupt is,
Beggar'd of blood to blush through lively
   veins ? 10
For she hath no exchequer now but his,
And, proud of many, lives upon his gains.
   O, him she stores, to show what wealth
     she had
   In days long since, before these last so
     bad.

68

Thus is his cheek the map of days outworn,
When beauty liv'd and died as flowers do
   now,
Before these bastard signs of fair were born,
Or durst inhabit on a living brow ;
Before the golden tresses of the dead, 5
The right of sepulchres, were shorn away
To live a second life on second head,
Ere beauty's dead fleece made another gay.
In him those holy antique hours are seen,
Without all ornament, itself and true, 10
Making no summer of another's green,
Robbing no old to dress his beauty new ;
   And him as for a map doth Nature store,
   To show false Art what beauty was of
     yore.

69

Those parts of thee that the world's eye
    doth view
Want nothing that the thought of hearts
    can mend.
All tongues, the voice of souls, give thee
    that due,
Utt'ring bare truth, even so as foes com-
    mend.
Thine outward thus with outward praise is
    crown'd ;   5
But those same tongues that give thee so
    thine own
In other accents do this praise confound
By seeing farther than the eye hath shown.
They look into the beauty of thy mind,
And that, in guess, they measure by thy
    deeds ;   10
Then, churls, their thoughts, although their
    eyes were kind,
To thy fair flower add the rank smell of
    weeds.
    But why thy odour matcheth not thy
      show,
    The soil is this—that thou dost common
      grow.

70

That thou art blam'd shall not be thy
    defect,
For slander's mark was ever yet the fair ;
The ornament of beauty is suspect,   3
A crow that flies in heaven's sweetest air.
So thou be good, slander doth but approve
Thy worth the greater, being woo'd of time;
For canker vice the sweetest buds doth love,
And thou present'st a pure unstained prime.
Thou hast pass'd by the ambush of young
    days,   9
Either not assail'd, or victor being charg'd ;
Yet this thy praise cannot be so thy praise
To tie up envy, evermore enlarg'd.
    If some suspect of ill mask'd not thy
      show,
    Then thou alone kingdoms of hearts
      shouldst owe.

71

No longer mourn for me when I am dead
Than you shall hear the surly sullen bell
Give warning to the world that I am fled
From this vile world, with vilest worms to
    dwell.
Nay, if you read this line, remember not 5
The hand that writ it ; for I love you so,
That I in your sweet thoughts would be
    forgot,
If thinking on me then should make you
    woe.
O, if, I say, you look upon this verse, 9
When I perhaps compounded am with clay,
Do not so much as my poor name rehearse,
But let your love even with my life decay ;
    Lest the wise world should look into your
      moan,
    And mock you with me after I am gone.

72

O, lest the world should task you to recite
What merit liv'd in me, that you should
    love
After my death, dear love, forget me quite,
For you in me can nothing worthy prove ;
Unless you would devise some virtuous lie,
To do more for me than mine own desert,
And hang more praise upon deceased I 7
Than niggard truth would willingly impart.
O, lest your true love may seem false in
    this,
That you for love speak well of me untrue,
My name be buried where my body is,   11
And live no more to shame nor me nor you !
    For I am sham'd by that which I bring
      forth,
    And so should you, to love things nothing
      worth.

73

That time of year thou mayst in me behold
When yellow leaves, or none, or few, do
    hang
Upon those boughs which shake against the
    cold,
Bare ruin'd choirs where late the sweet
    birds sang.
In me thou seest the twilight of such day 5
As after sunset fadeth in the west,
Which by and by black night doth take
    away,
Death's second self, that seals up all in rest.
In me thou seest the glowing of such fire
That on the ashes of his youth doth lie, 10
As the death-bed whereon it must expire,
Consum'd with that which it was nourish'd
    by.
    This thou perceiv'st which makes thy
      love more strong,
    To love that well which thou must leave
      ere long.

74

But be contented. When that fell arrest
Without all bail shall carry me away,
My life hath in this line some interest,
Which for memorial still with thee shall
    stay.
When thou reviewest this, thou dost review
The very part was consecrate to thee. 6
The earth can have but earth, which is his
    due ;
My spirit is thine, the better part of me.
So then thou hast but lost the dregs of life,
The prey of worms, my body being dead ;
The coward conquest of a wretch's knife,

Too base of thee to be remembered.   12
  The worth of that is that which it contains,
  And that is this, and this with thee remains.

75

So are you to my thoughts as food to life,
Or as sweet-season'd showers are to the ground ;
And for the peace of you I hold such strife
As 'twixt a miser and his wealth is found :
Now proud as an enjoyer, and anon   5
Doubting the filching age will steal his treasure ;
Now counting best to be with you alone,
Then better'd that the world may see my pleasure ;
Sometime all full with feasting on your sight,
And by and by clean starved for a look ;   10
Possessing or pursuing no delight
Save what is had or must from you be took.
  Thus do I pine and surfeit day by day,
  Or gluttoning on all, or all away.

76

Why is my verse so barren of new pride ?
So far from variation or quick change ?
Why, with the time, do I not glance aside
To new-found methods and to compounds strange ?
Why write I still all one, ever the same,   5
And keep invention in a noted weed,
That every word doth almost tell my name,
Showing their birth, and where they did proceed ?
O, know, sweet love, I always write of you,
And you and love are still my argument ;   10
So all my best is dressing old words new,
Spending again what is already spent ;
  For as the sun is daily new and old,
  So is my love still telling what is told.

77

Thy glass will show thee how thy beauties wear,
Thy dial how thy precious minutes waste ;
The vacant leaves thy mind's imprint will bear,
And of this book this learning mayst thou taste.
The wrinkles which thy glass will truly show   5
Of mouthed graves will give thee memory ;
Thou by thy dial's shady stealth mayst know
Time's thievish progress to eternity.
Look what thy memory cannot contain
Commit to these waste blanks, and thou shalt find   10

Those children nurs'd, deliver'd from thy brain,
To take a new acquaintance of thy mind.
  These offices, so oft as thou wilt look,
  Shall profit thee, and much enrich thy book.

78

So oft have I invok'd thee for my Muse,
And found such fair assistance in my verse,
As every alien pen hath got my use,
And under thee their poesy disperse.
Thine eyes, that taught the dumb on high to sing   5
And heavy ignorance aloft to fly,
Have added feathers to the learned's wing
And given grace a double majesty.
Yet be most proud of that which I compile,
Whose influence is thine, and born of thee :
In others' works thou dost but mend the style,   11
And arts with thy sweet graces graced be ;
  But thou art all my art, and dost advance
  As high as learning my rude ignorance.

79

Whilst I alone did call upon thy aid,
My verse alone had all thy gentle grace ;
But now my gracious numbers are decay'd,
And my sick Muse doth give another place.
I grant, sweet love, thy lovely argument   5
Deserves the travail of a worthier pen ;
Yet what of thee thy poet doth invent
He robs thee of, and pays it thee again.   8
He lends thee virtue, and he stole that word
From thy behaviour ; beauty doth he give,
And found it in thy cheek ; he can afford
No praise to thee but what in thee doth live.
  Then thank him not for that which he doth say,
  Since what he owes thee thou thyself dost pay.

80

O, how I faint when I of you do write,
Knowing a better spirit doth use your name
And in the praise thereof spends all his might
To make me tongue-tied, speaking of your fame !   4
But since your worth, wide as the ocean is,
The humble as the proudest sail doth bear,
My saucy bark, inferior far to his,
On your broad main doth wilfully appear.
Your shallowest help will hold me up afloat,
Whilst he upon your soundless deep doth ride ;   10
Or, being wreck'd, I am a worthless boat,
He of tall building and of goodly pride.
  Then if he thrive, and I be cast away,
  The worst was this : my love was my decay.

81

Or I shall live your epitaph to make,
Or you survive when I in earth am rotten ;
From hence your memory death cannot take,
Although in me each part will be forgotten.
Your name from hence immortal life shall have,   5
Though I, once gone, to all the world must die ;
The earth can yield me but a common grave,
When you entombed in men's eyes shall lie.
Your monument shall be my gentle verse,
Which eyes not yet created shall o'er-read ;
And tongues to be your being shall rehearse,
When all the breathers of this world are dead.   12
    You still shall live, such virtue hath my pen,
    Where breath most breathes, even in the mouths of men.

82

I grant thou wert not married to my Muse,
And therefore mayst without attaint o'er-look
The dedicated words which writers use
Of their fair subject, blessing every book.
Thou art as fair in knowledge as in hue,   5
Finding thy worth a limit past my praise,
And therefore art enforc'd to seek anew
Some fresher stamp of the time-bettering days.
And do so, love ; yet when they have devis'd
What strained touches rhetoric can lend,   10
Thou truly fair wert truly sympathiz'd
In true plain words by thy true-telling friend :
    And their gross painting might be better us'd
    Where cheeks need blood ; in thee it is abus'd.

83

I never saw that you did painting need,
And therefore to your fair no painting set ;
I found, or thought I found, you did exceed
The barren tender of a poet's debt ;
And therefore have I slept in your report,   5
That you your self, being extant, well might show
How far a modern quill doth come too short,
Speaking of worth, what worth in you doth grow.
This silence for my sin you did impute,
Which shall be most my glory, being dumb ;
For I impair not beauty, being mute,   11
When others would give life, and bring a tomb.

There lives more life in one of your fair eyes
Than both your poets can in praise devise.

84

Who is it that says most which can say more
Than this rich praise—that you alone are you ?
In whose confine immured is the store
Which should example where your equal grew ?
Lean penury within that pen doth dwell   5
That to his subject lends not some small glory ;
But he that writes of you, if he can tell
That you are you, so dignifies his story.
Let him but copy what in you is writ,
Not making worse what nature made so clear,   10
And such a counterpart shall fame his wit,
Making his style admired every where.
    You to your beauteous blessings add a curse,
    Being fond on praise, which makes your praises worse.

85

My tongue-tied Muse in manners holds her still,
While comments of your praise, richly compil'd,
Reserve their character with golden quill
And precious phrase by all the Muses fil'd.
I think good thoughts, whilst other write good words,   5
And, like unlettered clerk, still cry ' Amen '
To every hymn that able spirit affords
In polish'd form of well-refined pen.
Hearing you prais'd, I say ' 'Tis so, 'tis true ',
And to the most of praise add something more ;   10
But that is in my thought, whose love to you,
Though words come hindmost, holds his rank before.
    Then others for the breath of words respect,
    Me for my dumb thoughts, speaking in effect.

86

Was it the proud full sail of his great verse,
Bound for the prize of all-too-precious you,
That did my ripe thoughts in my brain inhearse,
Making their tomb the womb wherein they grew ?
Was it his spirit, by spirits taught to write   5
Above a mortal pitch, that struck me dead ?
No, neither he, nor his compeers by night

Giving him aid, my verse astonished.
He nor that affable familiar ghost
Which nightly gulls him with intelligence,
As victors, of my silence cannot boast :   11
I was not sick of any fear from thence.
   But when your countenance fill'd up his
      line,
   Then lack'd I matter ; that enfeebled
      mine.

87

Farewell ! thou art too dear for my
    possessing,
And like enough thou know'st thy estimate.
The charter of thy worth gives thee re-
    leasing ;
My bonds in thee are all determinate.   4
For how do I hold thee but by thy granting?
And for that riches where is my deserving ?
The cause of this fair gift in me is wanting,
And so my patent back again is swerving.
Thy self thou gav'st, thy own worth then
    not knowing,
Or me, to whom thou gav'st it, else mis-
    taking ;   10
So thy great gift, upon misprision growing,
Comes home again, on better judgment
    making.
   Thus have I had thee, as a dream doth
      flatter :
   In sleep a king, but waking no such
      matter.

88

When thou shalt be dispos'd to set me light,
And place my merit in the eye of scorn,
Upon thy side against myself I'll fight,
And prove thee virtuous, though thou art
    forsworn.
With mine own weakness being best
    acquainted,   5
Upon thy part I can set down a story
Of faults conceal'd, wherein I am attainted ;
That thou, in losing me, shall win much
    glory.
And I by this will be a gainer too ;
For bending all my loving thoughts on
    thee,   10
The injuries that to myself I do,
Doing thee vantage, double vantage me.
   Such is my love, to thee I so belong,
   That for thy right myself will bear all
      wrong.

89

Say that thou didst forsake me for some
    fault,
And I will comment upon that offence ;
Speak of my lameness, and I straight will
    halt ;
Against thy reasons making no defence.
Thou canst not, love, disgrace me half so
    ill,   5

To set a form upon desired change,
As I'll myself disgrace, knowing thy will.
I will acquaintance strangle and look
    strange,
Be absent from thy walks, and in my
    tongue
Thy sweet beloved name no more shall
    dwell,   10
Lest I, too much profane, should do it
    wrong,
And haply of our old acquaintance tell.
   For thee, against myself I'll vow debate,
   For I must ne'er love him whom thou
      dost hate.

90

Then hate me when thou wilt ; if ever,
    now ;
Now while the world is bent my deeds to
    cross,
Join with the spite of fortune, make me
    bow,
And do not drop in for an after-loss.
Ah, do not, when my heart hath scap'd this
    sorrow,   5
Come in the rearward of a conquer'd woe ;
Give not a windy night a rainy morrow,
To linger out a purpos'd overthrow.
If thou wilt leave me, do not leave me
    last,
When other petty griefs have done their
    spite,   10
But in the onset come ; so shall I taste
At first the very worst of fortune's might ;
   And other strains of woe, which now seem
      woe,
   Compar'd with loss of thee will not
      seem so.

91

Some glory in their birth, some in their
    skill,
Some in their wealth, some in their body's
    force ;
Some in their garments, though new-
    fangled ill ;
Some in their hawks and hounds, some in
    their horse ;
And every humour hath his adjunct
    pleasure,   5
Wherein it finds a joy above the rest ;
But these particulars are not my measure :
All these I better in one general best.
Thy love is better than high birth to me,
Richer than wealth, prouder than garments'
    cost,   10
Of more delight than hawks and horses be ;
And, having thee, of all men's pride I
    boast—
   Wretched in this alone, that thou mayst
      take
   All this away, and me most wretched
      make.

92

But do thy worst to steal thy self away,
For term of life thou art assured mine ;
And life no longer than thy love will stay,
For it depends upon that love of thine. 4
Then need I not to fear the worst of wrongs,
When in the least of them my life hath end.
I see a better state to me belongs
Than that which on thy humour doth
    depend.
Thou canst not vex me with inconstant
    mind,
Since that my life on thy revolt doth lie. 10
O what a happy title do I find,
Happy to have thy love, happy to die !
    But what's so blessed-fair that fears no
    blot ?
    Thou mayst be false, and yet I know it
    not.

93

So shall I live, supposing thou art true,
Like a deceived husband ; so love's face
May still seem love to me, though alter'd
    new—
Thy looks with me, thy heart in other
    place. 4
For there can live no hatred in thine eye ;
Therefore in that I cannot know thy
    change.
In many's looks the false heart's history
Is writ in moods and frowns and wrinkles
    strange ;
But heaven in thy creation did decree
That in thy face sweet love should ever
    dwell ; 10
Whate'er thy thoughts or thy heart's work-
    ings be,
Thy looks should nothing thence but
    sweetness tell.
    How like Eve's apple doth thy beauty
    grow,
    If thy sweet virtue answer not thy show !

94

They that have power to hurt and will do
    none,
That do not do the thing they most do show,
Who, moving others, are themselves as
    stone,
Unmoved, cold, and to temptation slow—
They rightly do inherit Heaven's graces, 5
And husband nature's riches from expense ;
They are the lords and owners of their faces,
Others but stewards of their excellence.
The summer's flow'r is to the summer sweet
Though to itself it only live and die ; 10
But if that flow'r with base infection meet,
The basest weed outbraves his dignity.
    For sweetest things turn sourest by their
    deeds :
    Lilies that fester smell far worse than
    weeds.

95

How sweet and lovely dost thou make the
    shame
Which, like a canker in the fragrant rose,
Doth spot the beauty of thy budding name !
O, in what sweets dost thou thy sins
    enclose ! 4
That tongue that tells the story of thy days,
Making lascivious comments on thy sport,
Cannot dispraise but in a kind of praise :
Naming thy name blesses an ill report.
O, what a mansion have those vices got 9
Which for their habitation chose out thee,
Where beauty's veil doth cover every blot,
And all things turns to fair that eyes can see !
    Take heed, dear heart, of this large
    privilege ;
    The hardest knife ill-us'd doth lose his
    edge.

96

Some say thy fault is youth, some wanton-
    ness ;
Some say thy grace is youth and gentle
    sport ;
Both grace and faults are lov'd of more and
    less :
Thou mak'st faults graces that to thee
    resort.
As on the finger of a throned queen 5
The basest jewel will be well esteem'd ;
So are those errors that in thee are seen
To truths translated and for true things
    deem'd.
How many lambs might the stern wolf
    betray, 9
If like a lamb he could his looks translate !
How many gazers mightst thou lead away,
If thou wouldst use the strength of all thy
    state !
    But do not so ; I love thee in such sort,
    As, thou being mine, mine is thy good
    report.

97

How like a winter hath my absence been
From thee, the pleasure of the fleeting year !
What freezings have I felt, what dark days
    seen !
What old December's bareness everywhere !
And yet this time remov'd was summer's
    time, 5
The teeming autumn, big with rich increase,
Bearing the wanton burden of the prime,
Like widowed wombs after their lord's
    decease ;
Yet this abundant issue seem'd to me 9
But hope of orphans, and unfathered fruit ;
For summer and his pleasures wait on thee,
And, thou away, the very birds are mute ;
    Or, if they sing, 'tis with so dull a cheer
    That leaves look pale, dreading the
    winter's near.

98

From you have I been absent in the spring,
When proud-pied April, dress'd in all his trim,
Hath put a spirit of youth in every thing,
That heavy Saturn laugh'd and leap'd with him.
Yet nor the lays of birds, nor the sweet smell   5
Of different flowers in odour and in hue,
Could make me any summer's story tell,
Or from their proud lap pluck them where they grew ;
Nor did I wonder at the lily's white,   9
Nor praise the deep vermilion in the rose :
They were but sweet, but figures of delight,
Drawn after you, you pattern of all those.
    Yet seem'd it winter still, and, you away,
    As with your shadow I with these did play.

99

The forward violet thus did I chide :
Sweet thief, whence didst thou steal thy sweet that smells,
If not from my love's breath ? The purple pride
Which on thy soft cheek for complexion dwells
In my love's veins thou hast too grossly dy'd.   5
The lily I condemned for thy hand,
And buds of marjoram had stol'n thy hair ;
The roses fearfully on thorns did stand,
One blushing shame, another white despair;
A third, nor red nor white, had stol'n of both,   10
And to his robb'ry had annex'd thy breath;
But, for his theft, in pride of all his growth
A vengeful canker eat him up to death.
    More flowers I noted, yet I none could see
    But sweet or colour it had stol'n from thee.

100

Where art thou, Muse, that thou forget'st so long
To speak of that which gives thee all thy might ?
Spend'st thou thy fury on some worthless song,
Dark'ning thy power to lend base subjects light ?
Return, forgetful Muse, and straight redeem   5
In gentle numbers time so idly spent ;
Sing to the ear that doth thy lays esteem
And gives thy pen both skill and argument.
Rise, resty Muse, my love's sweet face survey,
If Time have any wrinkle graven there ;   10
If any, be a satire to decay,
And make Time's spoils despised everywhere.
    Give my love fame faster than Time wastes life ;
    So thou prevent'st his scythe and crooked knife.

101

O truant Muse, what shall be thy amends
For thy neglect of truth in beauty dy'd ?
Both truth and beauty on my love depends;
So dost thou too, and therein dignified.
Make answer, Muse. Wilt thou not haply say   5
' Truth needs no colour with his colour fix'd ;
Beauty no pencil, beauty's truth to lay ;
But best is best, if never intermix'd ' ?
Because he needs no praise, wilt thou be dumb ?
Excuse not silence so ; for't lies in thee   10
To make him much outlive a gilded tomb,
And to be prais'd of ages yet to be.
    Then do thy office, Muse. I teach thee how
    To make him seem long hence as he shows now.

102

My love is strength'ned, though more weak in seeming ;
I love not less, though less the show appear ;
That love is merchandiz'd whose rich esteeming
The owner's tongue doth publish every where.
Our love was new, and then but in the spring,   5
When I was wont to greet it with my lays ;
As Philomel in summer's front doth sing,
And stops her pipe in growth of riper days.
Not that the summer is less pleasant now
Than when her mournful hymns did hush the night,   10
But that wild music burthens every bough,
And sweets grown common lose their dear delight.
    Therefore, like her, I sometime hold my tongue,
    Because I would not dull you with my song.

103

Alack, what poverty my Muse brings forth,
That, having such a scope to show her pride,
The argument all bare is of more worth
Than when it hath my added praise beside !
O, blame me not, if I no more can write !   5
Look in your glass, and there appears a face
That over-goes my blunt invention quite,
Dulling my lines, and doing me disgrace.

Were it not sinful then, striving to mend,
To mar the subject that before was well ?
For to no other pass my verses tend   11
Than of your graces and your gifts to tell ;
  And more, much more, than in my verse
    can sit
    Your own glass shows you, when you
    look in it.

104

To me, fair friend, you never can be old,
For as you were when first your eye I ey'd,
Such seems your beauty still.   Three
    winters cold
Have from the forests shook three summers'
    pride,
Three beauteous springs to yellow autumn
    turn'd   5
In process of the seasons have I seen,
Three April perfumes in three hot Junes
    burn'd,
Since first I saw you fresh, which yet are
    green.
Ah, yet doth beauty, like a dial-hand,
Steal from his figure, and no pace per-
    ceiv'd ;   10
So your sweet hue, which methinks still
    doth stand,
Hath motion, and mine eye may be
    deceiv'd.
  For fear of which, hear this, thou age
    unbred :
  Ere you were born was beauty's summer
    dead.

105

Let not my love be call'd idolatry,
Nor my beloved as an idol show,
Since all alike my songs and praises be
To one, of one, still such, and ever so.
Kind is my love to-day, to-morrow kind, 5
Still constant in a wondrous excellence ;
Therefore my verse, to constancy confin'd,
One thing expressing, leaves out difference.
' Fair, kind, and true ' is all my argument,
' Fair, kind, and true ' varying to other
    words ;   10
And in this change is my invention spent,
Three themes in one, which wondrous scope
    affords.
  Fair, kind, and true, have often liv'd
    alone,
  Which three, till now, never kept seat
    in one.

106

When in the chronicle of wasted time
I see descriptions of the fairest wights,
And beauty making beautiful old rhyme
In praise of ladies dead and lovely knights,
Then, in the blazon of sweet beauty's best,
Of hand, of foot, of lip, of eye, of brow,   6
I see their antique pen would have ex-
    press'd
Even such a beauty as you master now.

So all their praises are but prophecies
Of this our time, all you prefiguring ;   10
And, for they look'd but with divining
    eyes,
They had not skill enough your worth to
    sing ;
  For we, which now behold these present
    days,
  Have eyes to wonder, but lack tongues
    to praise.

107

Not mine own fears, nor the prophetic soul
Of the wide world dreaming on things to
    come,
Can yet the lease of my true love control,
Suppos'd as forfeit to a confin'd doom.   4
The mortal moon hath her eclipse endur'd,
And the sad augurs mock their own pres-
    age ;
Incertainties now crown themselves assur'd,
And peace proclaims olives of endless age.
Now with the drops of this most balmy
    time
My love looks fresh, and Death to me
    subscribes,   10
Since spite of him I'll live in this poor
    rhyme,
While he insults o'er dull and speechless
    tribes.
  And thou in this shalt find thy monu-
    ment,
  When tyrants' crests and tombs of brass
    are spent.

108

What's in the brain that ink may character
Which hath not figur'd to thee my true
    spirit ?
What's new to speak, what new to register,
That may express my love or thy dear
    merit ?
Nothing, sweet boy ; but yet, like prayers
    divine,   5
I must each day say o'er the very same ;
Counting no old thing old, thou mine, I
    thine,
Even as when first I hallowed thy fair
    name.
So that eternal love in love's fresh case
Weighs not the dust and injury of age,   10
Nor gives to necessary wrinkles place,
But makes antiquity for aye his page ;
  Finding the first conceit of love there
    bred,
  Where time and outward form would
    show it dead.

109

O, never say that I was false of heart,
Though absence seem'd my flame to qualify!
As easy might I from my self depart
As from my soul, which in thy breast doth
    lie :   4

That is my home of love. If I have rang'd,
Like him that travels, I return again,
Just to the time, not with the time ex-
      chang'd,
So that my self bring water for my stain.
Never believe, though in my nature reign'd
All frailties that besiege all kinds of blood,
That it could so preposterously be stain'd
To leave for nothing all thy sum of good ;
   For nothing this wide universe I call   13
   Save thou, my rose ; in it thou art my all.

110

Alas, 'tis true I have gone here and there
And made myself a motley to the view,
Gor'd mine own thoughts, sold cheap what
      is most dear,
Made old offences of affections new.   4
Most true it is that I have look'd on truth
Askance and strangely ; but, by all above,
These blenches gave my heart another
      youth,
And worse essays prov'd thee my best of
      love.
Now all is done, have what shall have no
      end ;
Mine appetite I never more will grind   10
On newer proof, to try an older friend,
A god in love, to whom I am confin'd.
   Then give me welcome, next my heaven
      the best,
   Even to thy pure and most most loving
      breast.

111

O, for my sake do you with Fortune chide,
The guilty goddess of my harmful deeds,
That did not better for my life provide
Than public means which public manners
      breeds.
Thence comes it that my name receives a
      brand,   5
And almost thence my nature is subdu'd
To what it works in, like the dyer's hand.
Pity me then, and wish I were renew'd ;
Whilst, like a willing patient, I will drink
Potions of eisel, 'gainst my strong in-
      fection ;   10
No bitterness that I will bitter think,
Nor double penance, to correct correction.
   Pity me then, dear friend, and I assure
      ye,
   Even that your pity is enough to cure me.

112

Your love and pity doth th' impression fill
Which vulgar scandal stamp'd upon my
      brow ;
For what care I who calls me well or ill,
So you o'ergreen my bad, my good allow ?
You are my all the world, and I must strive
To know my shames and praises from your
      tongue ;   6

None else to me, nor I to none alive,
That my steel'd sense or changes right or
      wrong.
In so profound abysm I throw all care
Of others' voices that my adder's sense   10
To critic and to flatterer stopped are.
Mark how with my neglect I do dispense :
   You are so strongly in my purpose bred
   That all the world besides methinks are
      dead.

113

Since I left you, mine eye is in my mind ;
And that which governs me to go about
Doth part his function, and is partly blind,
Seems seeing, but effectually is out ;
For it no form delivers to the heart   5
Of bird, of flow'r, or shape, which it doth
      latch ;
Of his quick objects hath the mind no part,
Nor his own vision holds what it doth
      catch;
For if it see the rud'st or gentlest sight,
The most sweet favour or deformed'st
      creature,   10
The mountain or the sea, the day or night,
The crow or dove, it shapes them to your
      feature.
   Incapable of more, replete with you,
   My most true mind thus mak'th mine
      eye untrue.

114

Or whether doth my mind, being crown'd
      with you,
Drink up the monarch's plague, this
      flattery ?
Or whether shall I say mine eye saith true,
And that your love taught it this alchemy
To make of monsters and things indigest   5
Such cherubins as your sweet self resemble,
Creating every bad a perfect best
As fast as objects to his beams assemble ?
O, 'tis the first ; 'tis flatt'ry in my seeing,
And my great mind most kingly drinks
      it up.   10
Mine eye well knows what with his gust is
      'greeing,
And to his palate doth prepare the cup.
   If it be poison'd, 'tis the lesser sin
   That mine eye loves it, and doth first
      begin.

115

Those lines that I before have writ do lie ;
Even those that said I could not love you
      dearer ;
Yet then my judgment knew no reason
      why
My most full flame should afterwards burn
      clearer.
But reckoning Time, whose million'd
      accidents   5

Creep in 'twixt vows and change decrees of
    kings,
Tan sacred beauty, blunt the sharp'st
    intents,
Divert strong minds to th' course of alt'ring
    things—
Alas, why, fearing of Time's tyranny,
Might I not then say ' Now I love you
    best '   10
When I was certain o'er incertainty,
Crowning the present, doubting of the rest?
    Love is a babe ; then might I not say so,
    To give full growth to that which still
        doth grow ?

116

Let me not to the marriage of true minds
Admit impediments. Love is not love
Which alters when it alteration finds,
Or bends with the remover to remove.
O, no ! it is an ever-fixed mark,   5
That looks on tempests and is never shaken;
It is the star to every wand'ring bark,
Whose worth's unknown, although his
    height be taken.
Love's not Time's fool, though rosy lips and
    cheeks   9
Within his bending sickle's compass come ;
Love alters not with his brief hours and
    weeks,
But bears it out even to the edge of doom.
    If this be error, and upon me prov'd,
    I never writ, nor no man ever lov'd.

117

Accuse me thus : that I have scanted all
Wherein I should your great deserts repay ;
Forgot upon your dearest love to call,
Whereto all bonds do tie me day by day ;
That I have frequent been with unknown
    minds,   5
And given to time your own dear-purchas'd
    right ;
That I have hoisted sail to all the winds
Which should transport me farthest from
    your sight.
Book both my wilfulness and errors down,
And on just proof surmise accumulate ;   10
Bring me within the level of your frown,
But shoot not at me in your wakened hate ;
    Since my appeal says I did strive to
        prove
    The constancy and virtue of your love.

118

Like as to make our appetites more keen
With eager compounds we our palate urge,
As to prevent our maladies unseen
We sicken to shun sickness when we purge ;
Even so, being full of your ne'er-cloying
    sweetness,   5
To bitter sauces did I frame my feeding,

And, sick of welfare, found a kind of
    meetness
To be diseas'd ere that there was true
    needing.
Thus policy in love, t' anticipate
The ills that were not, grew to faults
    assured,   10
And brought to medicine a healthful state,
Which, rank of goodness, would by ill be
    cured.
    But thence I learn, and find the lesson
        true,
    Drugs poison him that so fell sick of you.

119

What potions have I drunk of Siren tears,
Distill'd from limbecks foul as hell within,
Applying fears to hopes, and hopes to fears,
Still losing when I saw my self to win !
What wretched errors hath my heart com-
    mitted,   5
Whilst it hath thought it self so blessed
    never !
How have mine eyes out of their spheres
    been fitted
In the distraction of this madding fever !
O benefit of ill ! Now I find true
That better is by evil still made better ;   10
And ruin'd love, when it is built anew,
Grows fairer than at first, more strong, far
    greater.
    So I return rebuk'd to my content,
    And gain by ill thrice more than I have
        spent.

120

That you were once unkind befriends me
    now,
And for that sorrow which I then did feel
Needs must I under my transgression bow,
Unless my nerves were brass or hammered
    steel.   4
For if you were by my unkindness shaken,
As I by yours, y'have pass'd a hell of time ;
And I, a tyrant, have no leisure taken
To weigh how once I suffered in your crime.
O that our night of woe might have remem-
    b'red   9
My deepest sense how hard true sorrow hits,
And soon to you, as you to me, then
    tend'red
The humble salve which wounded bosoms
    fits !
    But that your trespass now becomes a
        fee ;
    Mine ransoms yours, and yours must
        ransom me.

121

'Tis better to be vile than vile esteemed,
When not to be receives reproach of being,
And the just pleasure lost, which is so
    deemed

Not by our feeling, but by others' seeing.
For why should others' false adulterate eyes
Give salutation to my sportive blood ?　6
Or on my frailties why are frailer spies,
Which in their wills count bad what I think
　　good ?
No ; I am that I am ; and they that level
At my abuses reckon up their own.　10
I may be straight though they themselves
　　be bevel :
By their rank thoughts my deeds must not
　　be shown,
　Unless this general evil they maintain :
　All men are bad, and in their badness
　　reign.

122

Thy gift, thy tables, are within my brain
Full character'd with lasting memory,
Which shall above that idle rank remain
Beyond all date, even to eternity ;
Or at the least so long as brain and heart　5
Have faculty by nature to subsist ;
Till each to raz'd oblivion yield his part
Of thee, thy record never can be miss'd.
That poor retention could not so much
　　hold,
Nor need I tallies thy dear love to score ;　10
Therefore to give them from me was I bold,
To trust those tables that receive thee more.
　To keep an adjunct to remember thee
　Were to import forgetfulness in me.

123

No, Time, thou shalt not boast that I do
　　change.
Thy pyramids built up with newer might
To me are nothing novel, nothing strange ;
They are but dressings of a former sight.　4
Our dates are brief, and therefore we admire
What thou dost foist upon us that is old,
And rather make them born to our desire
Than think that we before have heard them
　　told.
Thy registers and thee I both defy,　9
Not wond'ring at the present nor the past,
For thy records and what we see doth lie,
Made more or less by thy continual haste.
　This I do vow, and this shall ever be :
　I will be true, despite thy scythe and
　　thee.

124

If my dear love were but the child of state,
It might for Fortune's bastard be un-
　　father'd,
As subject to Time's love or to Time's hate,
Weeds among weeds, or flowers with flowers
　　gather'd.
No, it was builded far from accident ;　5
It suffers not in smiling pomp, nor falls
Under the blow of thralled discontent,
Whereto th' inviting time our fashion calls.

It fears not Policy, that heretic,
Which works on leases of short-numb'red
　　hours,　10
But all alone stands hugely politic,
That it nor grows with heat nor drowns
　　with show'rs.
　To this I witness call the fools of time,
　Which die for goodness, who have liv'd
　　for crime.

125

Were't aught to me I bore the canopy,
With my extern the outward honouring,
Or laid great bases for eternity,
Which proves more short than waste or
　　ruining ?
Have I not seen dwellers on form and
　　favour　5
Lose all, and more, by paying too much
　　rent,
For compound sweet forgoing simple
　　savour—
Pitiful thrivers, in their gazing spent ?
No, let me be obsequious in thy heart,
And take thou my oblation, poor but free,
Which is not mix'd with seconds, knows no
　　art　11
But mutual render, only me for thee.
　Hence, thou suborn'd informer ! A true
　　soul,
　When most impeach'd, stands least in
　　thy control.

126

O thou, my lovely boy, who in thy power
Dost hold Time's fickle glass, his sickle
　　hour ;
Who hast by waning grown, and therein
　　show'st
Thy lovers withering as thy sweet self
　　grow'st ;
If Nature, sovereign mistress over wrack,　5
As thou goest onwards, still will pluck thee
　　back,
She keeps thee to this purpose, that her
　　skill
May time disgrace, and wretched minutes
　　kill.
Yet fear her, O thou minion of her pleasure !
She may detain, but not still keep, her
　　treasure ;　10
　Her audit, though delay'd, answer'd
　　must be,
　And her quietus is to render thee.

127

In the old age black was not counted fair,
Or if it were, it bore not beauty's name ;
But now is black beauty's successive heir,
And beauty slander'd with a bastard
　　shame ;
For since each hand hath put on nature's
　　power,　5

Fairing the foul with art's false borrow'd
    face,
Sweet beauty hath no name, no holy
    bower,
But is profan'd, if not lives in disgrace.
Therefore my mistress' brows are raven
    black,   9
Her eyes so suited, and they mourners seem
At such who, not born fair, no beauty lack,
Sland'ring creation with a false esteem.
  Yet so they mourn, becoming of their
    woe,
  That every tongue says beauty should
    look so.

128

How oft, when thou, my music, music
    play'st
Upon that blessed wood whose motion
    sounds
With thy sweet fingers, when thou gently
    sway'st
The wiry concord that mine ear confounds,
Do I envy those jacks that nimble leap 5
To kiss the tender inward of thy hand,
Whilst my poor lips, which should that
    harvest reap,
At the wood's boldness by thee blushing
    stand !
To be so tickled, they would change their
    state
And situation with those dancing chips 10
O'er whom thy fingers walk with gentle
    gait,
Making dead wood more blest than living
    lips.
  Since saucy jacks so happy are in this,
  Give them thy fingers, me thy lips to kiss.

129

Th' expense of spirit in a waste of shame
Is lust in action ; and till action, lust
Is perjur'd, murd'rous, bloody, full of
    blame,
Savage, extreme, rude, cruel, not to trust ;
Enjoy'd no sooner but despised straight ; 5
Past reason hunted, and, no sooner had,
Past reason hated, as a swallowed bait,
On purpose laid to make the taker mad—
Mad in pursuit, and in possession so ;   9
Had, having, and in quest to have, extreme;
A bliss in proof, and prov'd, a very woe ;
Before, a joy propos'd ; behind, a dream.
  All this the world well knows ; yet none
    knows well
  To shun the heaven that leads men to this
    hell.

130

My mistress' eyes are nothing like the sun ;
Coral is far more red than her lips' red ;
If snow be white, why then her breasts are
    dun ;
If hairs be wires, black wires grow on her
    head.

I have seen roses damask'd, red and white,
But no such roses see I in her cheeks ;   6
And in some perfumes is there more delight
Than in the breath that from my mistress
    reeks.
I love to hear her speak, yet well I know
That music hath a far more pleasing sound ;
I grant I never saw a goddess go—   11
My mistress when she walks treads on the
    ground.
  And yet, by heaven, I think my love as
    rare
  As any she belied with false compare.

131

Thou art as tyrannous, so as thou art,
As those whose beauties proudly make them
    cruel ;
For well thou know'st to my dear doting
    heart
Thou art the fairest and most precious
    jewel.
Yet, in good faith, some say that thee
    behold   5
Thy face hath not the power to make love
    groan.
To say they err I dare not be so bold,
Although I swear it to myself alone.
And, to be sure that is not false I swear,
A thousand groans, but thinking on thy
    face,   10
One on another's neck, do witness bear
Thy black is fairest in my judgment's place.
  In nothing art thou black save in thy
    deeds,
  And thence this slander, as I think,
    proceeds.

132

Thine eyes I love, and they, as pitying me,
Knowing thy heart torments me with
    disdain,
Have put on black, and loving mourners be,
Looking with pretty ruth upon my pain.
And truly not the morning sun of heaven 5
Better becomes the grey cheeks of the east,
Nor that full star that ushers in the even
Doth half that glory to the sober west,
As those two mourning eyes become thy
    face.
O, let it then as well beseem thy heart   10
To mourn for me, since mourning doth thee
    grace,
And suit thy pity like in every part.
  Then will I swear beauty herself is black,
  And all they foul that thy complexion
    lack.

133

Beshrew that heart that makes my heart
    to groan
For that deep wound it gives my friend and
    me !

Is't not enough to torture me alone,
But slave to slavery my sweet'st friend
    must be ?
Me from my self thy cruel eye hath taken, 5
And my next self thou harder hast en-
    grossed ;
Of him, my self, and thee, I am forsaken ;
A torment thrice three-fold thus to be
    crossed.
Prison my heart in thy steel bosom's ward,
But then my friend's heart let my poor
    heart bail ;   10
Whoe'er keeps me, let my heart be his
    guard ;
Thou canst not then use rigour in my gaol.
    And yet thou wilt ; for I, being pent in
      thee,
    Perforce am thine, and all that is in me.

134

So now I have confess'd that he is thine,
And I myself am mortgag'd to thy will ;
My self I'll forfeit, so that other mine
Thou wilt restore to be my comfort still.
But thou wilt not, nor he will not be free, 5
For thou art covetous, and he is kind ;
He learn'd but surety-like to write for me
Under that bond that him as fast doth bind.
The statute of thy beauty thou wilt take,
Thou usurer that put'st forth all to use, 10
And sue a friend came debtor for my sake ;
So him I lose through my unkind abuse.
    Him have I lost ; thou hast both him
      and me ;
    He pays the whole, and yet am I not free.

135

Whoever hath her wish, thou hast thy
    Will,
And Will to boot, and Will in over-plus ;
More than enough am I that vex thee still,
To thy sweet will making addition thus. 4
Wilt thou, whose will is large and spacious,
Not once vouchsafe to hide my will in
    thine ?
Shall will in others seem right gracious,
And in my will no fair acceptance shine ?
The sea, all water, yet receives rain still,
And in abundance addeth to his store ; 10
So thou, being rich in Will, add to thy Will
One will of mine, to make thy large Will
    more.
    Let no unkind, no fair beseechers kill ;
    Think all but one, and me in that one
      Will.

136

If thy soul check thee that I come so near,
Swear to thy blind soul that I was thy Will,
And will, thy soul knows, is admitted there;
Thus far for love my love-suit, sweet, fulfil.
Will will fulfil the treasure of thy love, 5
Ay, fill it full with wills, and my will one.

In things of great receipt with ease we
    prove
Among a number one is reckon'd none.
Then in the number let me pass untold,
Though in thy store's account I one must
    be ;   10
For nothing hold me, so it please thee hold
That nothing me, a something sweet to
    thee ;
    Make but my name thy love, and love
      that still,
    And then thou lov'st me, for my name
      is Will.

137

Thou blind fool, Love, what dost thou to
    mine eyes
That they behold, and see not what they
    see ?
They know what beauty is, see where it lies,
Yet what the best is take the worst to be.
If eyes, corrupt by over-partial looks, 5
Be anchor'd in the bay where all men ride,
Why of eyes' falsehood hast thou forged
    hooks,
Whereto the judgment of my heart is tied ?
Why should my heart think that a several
    plot,
Which my heart knows the wide world's
    common place ?   10
Or mine eyes, seeing this, say this is not,
To put fair truth upon so foul a face ?
    In things right true my heart and eyes
      have erred,
    And to this false plague are they now
      transferred.

138

When my love swears that she is made of
    truth,
I do believe her, though I know she lies,
That she might think me some untutor'd
    youth,
Unlearned in the world's false subtleties.
Thus vainly thinking that she thinks me
    young,   5
Although she knows my days are past the
    best,
Simply I credit her false-speaking tongue ;
On both sides thus is simple truth sup-
    press'd.
But wherefore says she not she is unjust ?
And wherefore say not I that I am old ? 10
O, love's best habit is in seeming trust,
And age in love loves not to have years told.
    Therefore I lie with her, and she with me,
    And in our faults by lies we flattered be.

139

O, call not me to justify the wrong
That thy unkindness lays upon my heart ;
Wound me not with thine eye, but with thy
    tongue ;

Use power with power, and slay me not by
    art.
Tell me thou lov'st elsewhere ; but in my
    sight,   5
Dear heart, forbear to glance thine eye
    aside.
What need'st thou wound with cunning,
    when thy might
Is more than my o'erpress'd defence can
    bide ?
Let me excuse thee : ah ! my love well
    knows
Her pretty looks have been mine enemies ;
And therefore from my face she turns my
    foes,   11
That they elsewhere might dart their
    injuries.
    Yet do not so ; but since I am near slain,
    Kill me outright with looks and rid my
      pain.

140

Be wise as thou art cruel ; do not press
My tongue-tied patience with too much
    disdain ;
Lest sorrow lend me words, and words
    express
The manner of my pity-wanting pain.
If I might teach thee wit, better it were,   5
Though not to love, yet, love, to tell me so ;
As testy sick men, when their deaths be
    near,
No news but health from their physicians
    know.
For, if I should despair, I should grow mad,
And in my madness might speak ill of
    thee.
Now this ill-wresting world is grown so bad
Mad slanderers by mad ears believed be.   12
    That I may not be so, nor thou belied,
    Bear thine eyes straight, though thy
      proud heart go wide.

141

In faith, I do not love thee with mine eyes,
For they in thee a thousand errors note ;
But 'tis my heart that loves what they
    despise,
Who in despite of view is pleas'd to dote.
Nor are mine ears with thy tongue's tune
    delighted ;   5
Nor tender feeling to base touches prone,
Nor taste nor smell desire to be invited
To any sensual feast with thee alone ;
But my five wits nor my five senses can
Dissuade one foolish heart from serving
    thee,   10
Who leaves unsway'd the likeness of a man,
Thy proud heart's slave and vassal wretch
    to be.
    Only my plague thus far I count my gain,
    That she that makes me sin awards me
      pain.

142

Love is my sin, and thy dear virtue hate,
Hate of my sin, grounded on sinful loving.
O, but with mine compare thou thine own
    state,
And thou shalt find it merits not reproving ;
Or, if it do, not from those lips of thine,   5
That have profan'd their scarlet ornaments,
And seal'd false bonds of love as oft as
    mine ;
Robb'd others' beds' revenues of their
    rents.
Be it lawful I love thee as thou lov'st those
Whom thine eyes woo as mine importune
    thee.   10
Root pity in thy heart, that, when it grows,
Thy pity may deserve to pitied be.
    If thou dost seek to have what thou dost
    hide,
    By self-example mayst thou be denied !

143

Lo as a careful huswife runs to catch
One of her feathered creatures broke away,
Sets down her babe, and makes all swift
    dispatch
In pursuit of the thing she would have stay;
Whilst her neglected child holds her in
    chase,   5
Cries to catch her whose busy care is
    bent
To follow that which flies before her face,
Not prizing her poor infant's discontent ;
So run'st thou after that which flies from
    thee,
Whilst I thy babe chase thee afar behind ;
But if thou catch thy hope, turn back to
    me,   11
And play the mother's part, kiss me, be
    kind.
    So will I pray that thou mayst have thy
      Will,
    If thou turn back and my loud crying
      still.

144

Two loves I have, of comfort and despair,
Which like two spirits do suggest me still ;
The better angel is a man right fair,
The worser spirit a woman colour'd ill.
To win me soon to hell, my female evil   5
Tempteth my better angel from my side,
And would corrupt my saint to be a devil,
Wooing his purity with her foul pride.
And whether that my angel be turn'd fiend,
Suspect I may, yet not directly tell ;   10
But being both from me, both to each
    friend,
I guess one angel in another's hell.
    Yet this shall I ne'er know, but live in
      doubt,
    Till my bad angel fire my good one out.

145

Those lips that Love's own hand did make
Breath'd forth the sound that said ' I hate '
To me that languish'd for her sake ;
But when she saw my woeful state,
Straight in her heart did mercy come,   5
Chiding that tongue that ever sweet
Was us'd in giving gentle doom ;
And taught it thus anew to greet :
' I hate ' she alter'd with an end
That follow'd it as gentle day   10
Doth follow night, who like a fiend
From heaven to hell is flown away :
      ' I hate ' from hate away she threw,
      And sav'd my life, saying ' not you '.

146

Poor soul, the centre of my sinful earth,
[My sinful earth] these rebel pow'rs that
            thee array,
Why dost thou pine within and suffer
            dearth,
Painting thy outward walls so costly gay ?
Why so large cost, having so short a lease,   5
Dost thou upon thy fading mansion spend ?
Shall worms, inheritors of this excess,
Eat up thy charge ? Is this thy body's end ?
Then, soul, live thou upon thy servant's
            loss,
And let that pine to aggravate thy store ;   10
Buy terms divine in selling hours of dross ;
Within be fed, without be rich no more.
      So shalt thou feed on Death, that feeds
            on men,
      And, Death once dead, there's no more
            dying then.

147

My love is as a fever, longing still
For that which longer nurseth the disease ;
Feeding on that which doth preserve the ill,
Th' uncertain sickly appetite to please.
My Reason, the physician to my Love,   5
Angry that his prescriptions are not kept,
Hath left me, and I desperate now approve
Desire is death, which physic did except.
Past cure I am, now reason is past care,
And frantic mad with evermore unrest ;   10
My thoughts and my discourse as mad men's
            are,
At random from the truth vainly express'd ;
      For I have sworn thee fair, and thought
            thee bright,
      Who art as black as hell, as dark as night.

148

O me, what eyes hath Love put in my head,
Which have no correspondence with true
            sight !
Or, if they have, where is my judgment fled,
That censures falsely what they see aright ?

If that be fair whereon my false eyes dote,   5
What means the world to say it is not so ?
If it be not, then love doth well denote
Love's eye is not so true as all men's—no,
How can it ? O, how can Love's eye be
            true,
That is so vex'd with watching and with
            tears ?   10
No marvel then though I mistake my view :
The sun itself sees not till heaven clears.
      O cunning Love ! with tears thou keep'st
            me blind,
      Lest eyes well seeing thy foul faults
            should find.

149

Canst thou, O cruel ! say I love thee not,
When I against myself with thee partake ?
Do I not think on thee when I forgot
Am of myself, all tyrant, for thy sake ?
Who hateth thee that I do call my friend ?   5
On whom frown'st thou that I do fawn
            upon ?
Nay, if thou lour'st on me, do I not spend
Revenge upon myself with present moan ?
What merit do I in myself respect
That is so proud thy service to despise,   10
When all my best doth worship thy defect,
Commanded by the motion of thine eyes ?
      But, love, hate on, for now I know thy
            mind :
      Those that can see thou lov'st, and I am
            blind.

150

O, from what pow'r hast thou this pow'rful
            might
With insufficiency my heart to sway ?
To make me give the lie to my true sight,
And swear that brightness doth not grace
            the day ?
Whence hast thou this becoming of things
            ill,   5
That in the very refuse of thy deeds
There is such strength and warrantise of
            skill
That in my mind thy worst all best exceeds?
Who taught thee how to make me love thee
            more,   9
The more I hear and see just cause of hate ?
O, though I love what others do abhor,
With others thou shouldst not abhor my
            state ;
      If thy unworthiness rais'd love in me,
      More worthy I to be belov'd of thee.

151

Love is too young to know what con-
            science is ;
Yet who knows not conscience is born of
            love ?
Then, gentle cheater, urge not my amiss,
Lest guilty of my faults thy sweet self prove.

For thou betraying me, I do betray   5
My nobler part to my gross body's treason;
My soul doth tell my body that he may
Triumph in love; flesh stays no farther
   reason,
But, rising at thy name, doth point out thee
As his triumphant prize. Proud of this
   pride,   10
He is contented thy poor drudge to be,
To stand in thy affairs, fall by thy side.
   No want of conscience hold it that I call
   Her 'love' for whose dear love I rise
   and fall.

152

In loving thee thou know'st I am forsworn,
But thou art twice forsworn, to me love
   swearing;
In act thy bed-vow broke, and new faith
   torn
In vowing new hate after new love bearing.
But why of two oaths' breach do I accuse
   thee,
When I break twenty? I am perjur'd most;   5
For all my vows are oaths but to misuse
   thee,
And all my honest faith in thee is lost;
For I have sworn deep oaths of thy deep
   kindness,
Oaths of thy love, thy truth, thy constancy;
And, to enlighten thee, gave eyes to blind-
   ness,   11
Or made them swear against the thing they
   see;
   For I have sworn thee fair—more per-
   jur'd I,
   To swear against the truth so foul a lie!

153

Cupid laid by his brand, and fell asleep.
A maid of Dian's this advantage found,
And his love-kindling fire did quickly steep
In a cold valley-fountain of that ground;
Which borrow'd from this holy fire of
   Love
A dateless lively heat, still to endure,   6
And grew a seething bath, which yet men
   prove
Against strange maladies a sovereign cure.
But at my mistress' eye Love's brand new-
   fired,
The boy for trial needs would touch my
   breast;   10
I, sick withal, the help of bath desired,
And thither hied, a sad distemper'd guest,
   But found no cure. The bath for my
   help lies
   Where Cupid got new fire—my mistress'
   eyes.

154

The little love-god, lying once asleep,
Laid by his side his heart-inflaming brand,
Whilst many nymphs that vow'd chaste life
   to keep
Came tripping by; but in her maiden
   hand
The fairest votary took up that fire   5
Which many legions of true hearts had
   warm'd;
And so the general of hot desire
Was sleeping by a virgin hand disarm'd.
This brand she quenched in a cool well
   by,
Which from Love's fire took heat perpetual,
Growing a bath and healthful remedy   11
For men diseas'd; but I, my mistress'
   thrall,
   Came there for cure, and this by that
   I prove:
   Love's fire heats water, water cools not
   love.

A LOVER'S COMPLAINT

From off a hill whose concave womb re-
        worded
A plaintful story from a sist'ring vale,
My spirits t' attend this double voice
        accorded,
And down I laid to list the sad-tun'd tale;
Ere long espied a fickle maid full pale,   5
Tearing of papers, breaking rings a-twain,
Storming her world with sorrow's wind and
        rain.

Upon her head a platted hive of straw,
Which fortified her visage from the sun,
Whereon the thought might think some-
        time it saw   10
The carcase of a beauty spent and done.
Time had not scythed all that youth begun,
Nor youth all quit; but, spite of heaven's
        fell rage,
Some beauty peep'd through lattice of
        sear'd age.   14

Oft did she heave her napkin to her eyne,
Which on it had conceited characters,
Laund'ring the silken figures in the brine
That seasoned woe had pelleted in tears,
And often reading what contents it bears;
As often shrieking undistinguish'd woe,   20
In clamours of all size, both high and low.

Sometimes her levell'd eyes their carriage
        ride,
As they did batt'ry to the spheres intend;
Sometime diverted their poor balls are tied
To th' orbed earth; sometimes they do
        extend   25
Their view right on; anon their gazes lend
To every place at once, and nowhere fix'd,
The mind and sight distractedly commix'd.

Her hair, nor loose nor tied in formal plat,
Proclaim'd in her a careless hand of pride;
For some, untuck'd, descended her sheav'd
        hat,   31
Hanging her pale and pined cheek beside;
Some in her threaden fillet still did bide,
And, true to bondage, would not break
        from thence,   34
Though slackly braided in loose negligence.

A thousand favours from a maund she drew
Of amber, crystal, and of beaded jet,
Which one by one she in a river threw,
Upon whose weeping margent she was set;
Like usury, applying wet to wet,   40
Or monarch's hands that lets not bounty fall
Where want cries some but where excess
        begs all.

Of folded schedules had she many a one,
Which she perus'd, sigh'd, tore, and gave
        the flood;

Crack'd many a ring of posied gold and
        bone,   45
Bidding them find their sepulchres in mud;
Found yet moe letters sadly penn'd in
        blood,
With sleided silk feat and affectedly
Enswath'd and seal'd to curious secrecy.   49

These often bath'd she in her fluxive eyes,
And often kiss'd, and often gan to tear;
Cried 'O false blood, thou register of
        lies,
What unapproved witness dost thou bear!
Ink would have seem'd more black and
        damned here!'   54
This said, in top of rage the lines she rents,
Big discontent so breaking their contents.

A reverend man that graz'd his cattle nigh,
Sometime a blusterer that the ruffle knew
Of court, of city, and had let go by   59
The swiftest hours observed as they flew,
Towards this afflicted fancy fastly drew;
And, privileg'd by age, desires to know
In brief the grounds and motives of her woe.

So slides he down upon his grained bat,
And comely distant sits he by her side;   65
When he again desires her, being sat,
Her grievance with his hearing to divide.
If that from him there may be aught
        applied
Which may her suffering ecstasy assuage,
'Tis promis'd in the charity of age.   70

'Father,' she says 'though in me you
        behold
The injury of many a blasting hour,
Let it not tell your judgment I am old;
Not age, but sorrow, over me hath power.
I might as yet have been a spreading
        flower,   75
Fresh to myself, if I had self-applied
Love to myself, and to no love beside.

'But woe is me! too early I attended   78
A youthful suit—it was to gain my grace—
O! one by nature's outwards so commended
That maidens' eyes stuck over all his face.
Love lack'd a dwelling and made him her
        place;
And when in his fair parts she did abide,
She was new lodg'd and newly deified.

'His browny locks did hang in crooked
        curls;   85
And every light occasion of the wind
Upon his lips their silken parcels hurls.
What's sweet to do, to do will aptly find:
Each eye that saw him did enchant the
        mind;
For on his visage was in little drawn   90

What largeness thinks in Paradise was sawn.

'Small show of man was yet upon his chin;
His phœnix down began but to appear,
Like unshorn velvet, on that termless skin,
Whose bare out-bragg'd the web it seem'd to wear;   95
Yet show'd his visage by that cost more dear;
And nice affections wavering stood in doubt
If best were as it was, or best without.

'His qualities were beauteous as his form,
For maiden-tongu'd he was, and thereof free;   100
Yet, if men mov'd him, was he such a storm
As oft 'twixt May and April is to see,
When winds breathe sweet, unruly though they be.
His rudeness so with his authoriz'd youth
Did livery falseness in a pride of truth.   105

'Well could he ride, and often men would say
"That horse his mettle from his rider takes:
Proud of subjection, noble by the sway,
What rounds, what bounds, what course, what stop he makes!"   109
And controversy hence a question takes,
Whether the horse by him became his deed,
Or he his manage by th' well-doing steed.

'But quickly on this side the verdict went:
His real habitude gave life and grace
To appertainings and to ornament,   115
Accomplish'd in himself, not in his case.
All aids, themselves made fairer by their place,
Came for additions; yet their purpos'd trim
Piec'd not his grace, but were all grac'd by him.

'So on the tip of his subduing tongue   120
All kind of arguments and question deep,
All replication prompt, and reason strong,
For his advantage still did wake and sleep.
To make the weeper laugh, the laugher weep,
He had the dialect and different skill,   125
Catching all passions in his craft of will;

'That he did in the general bosom reign
Of young, of old, and sexes both enchanted,
To dwell with him in thoughts, or to remain
In personal duty, following where he haunted.   130
Consents bewitch'd, ere he desire, have granted,
And dialogu'd for him what he would say,
Ask'd their own wills, and made their wills obey.

'Many there were that did his picture get,
To serve their eyes, and in it put their mind;   135
Like fools that in th' imagination set
The goodly objects which abroad they find
Of lands and mansions, theirs in thought assign'd;
And labouring in moe pleasures to bestow them
Than the true gouty landlord which doth owe them.   140

'So many have, that never touch'd his hand,
Sweetly suppos'd them mistress of his heart.
My woeful self, that did in freedom stand,
And was my own fee-simple, not in part,
What with his art in youth, and youth in art,   145
Threw my affections in his charmed power,
Reserv'd the stalk and gave him all my flower.

'Yet did I not, as some my equals did,
Demand of him, nor being desired yielded;
Finding myself in honour so forbid,   150
With safest distance I mine honour shielded.
Experience for me many bulwarks builded
Of proofs new-bleeding, which remain'd the foil   153
Of this false jewel, and his amorous spoil.

'But ah! who ever shunn'd by precedent
The destin'd ill she must herself assay?
Or forc'd examples, 'gainst her own content,
To put the by-past perils in her way?
Counsel may stop awhile what will not stay;
For when we rage, advice is often seen   160
By blunting us to make our wits more keen.

'Nor gives it satisfaction to our blood
That we must curb it upon others' proof,
To be forbod the sweets that seem so good   164
For fear of harms that preach in our behoof.
O appetite, from judgment stand aloof!
The one a palate hath that needs will taste,
Though Reason weep, and cry "It is thy last".

'For further I could say "This man's untrue",
And knew the patterns of his foul beguiling;   170
Heard where his plants in others' orchards grew;
Saw how deceits were gilded in his smiling;
Knew vows were ever brokers to defiling;
Thought characters and words merely but art,   174
And bastards of his foul adulterate heart.

'And long upon these terms I held my city,
Till thus he gan besiege me: "Gentle maid,
Have of my suffering youth some feeling pity,
And be not of my holy vows afraid.   179
That's to ye sworn to none was ever said;

For feasts of love I have been call'd unto,
Till now did ne'er invite nor never woo.

' " All my offences that abroad you see
Are errors of the blood, none of the mind ;
Love made them not ; with acture they
     may be,   185
Where neither party is nor true nor kind.
They sought their shame that so their
     shame did find ;
And so much less of shame in me remains
By how much of me their reproach contains.

' " Among the many that mine eyes have
     seen,   190
Not one whose flame my heart so much as
     warmed,
Or my affection put to th' smallest teen,
Or any of my leisures ever charmed.
Harm have I done to them, but ne'er was
     harmed ;
Kept hearts in liveries, but mine own was
     free,   195
And reign'd commanding in his monarchy.

' " Look here what tributes wounded fancies
     sent me,
Of pallid pearls and rubies red as blood ;
Figuring that they their passions likewise
     lent me
Of grief and blushes, aptly understood 200
In bloodless white and the encrimson'd
     mood—
Effects of terror and dear modesty,
Encamp'd in hearts, but fighting outwardly.

' " And, lo, behold these talents of their
     hair,   204
With twisted metal amorously empleach'd,
I have receiv'd from many a several fair,
Their kind acceptance weepingly beseech'd,
With the annexions of fair gems enrich'd,
And deep-brain'd sonnets that did amplify
Each stone's dear nature, worth, and
     quality.   210

' " The diamond—why, 'twas beautiful and
     hard,
Whereto his invis'd properties did tend ;
The deep-green em'rald, in whose fresh
     regard
Weak sights their sickly radiance do amend ;
The heaven-hu'd sapphire and the opal
     blend   215
With objects manifold ; each several stone,
With wit well blazon'd, smil'd, or made
     some moan.

' " Lo, all these trophies of affections hot,
Of pensiv'd and subdu'd desires the tender,
Nature hath charg'd me that I hoard them
     not,   220
But yield them up where I myself must
     render—
That is, to you, my origin and ender ;
For these, of force, must your oblations be,
Since I their altar, you enpatron me.

' " O, then, advance of yours that phraseless
     hand   225
Whose white weighs down the airy scale of
     praise ;
Take all these similes to your own com-
     mand,
Hallowed with sighs that burning lungs did
     raise ;   228
What me, your minister, for you obeys,
Works under you ; and to your audit comes
Their distract parcels in combined sums.

' " Lo, this device was sent me from a nun,
Or sister sanctified, of holiest note,
Which late her noble suit in court did shun,
Whose rarest havings made the blossoms
     dote ;   235
For she was sought by spirits of richest coat,
But kept cold distance, and did thence
     remove
To spend her living in eternal love.

" But, O my sweet, what labour is't to
     leave
The thing we have not, mast'ring what not
     strives,   240
Paling the place which did no form receive,
Playing patient sports in unconstrained
     gyves !
She that her fame so to herself contrives,
The scars of battle scapeth by the flight,
And makes her absence valiant, not her
     might.   245

' " O, pardon me, in that my boast is true !
The accident which brought me to her eye
Upon the moment did her force subdue,
And now she would the caged cloister fly.
Religious love put out religion's eye.   250
Not to be tempted, would she be immur'd,
And now, to tempt all, liberty procur'd.

' " How mighty then you are, O, hear me
     tell !   253
The broken bosoms that to me belong
Have emptied all their fountains in my well,
And mine I pour your ocean all among.
I strong o'er them, and you o'er me being
     strong,
Must for your victory us all congest,
As compound love to physic your cold
     breast.

' " My parts had pow'r to charm a sacred
     nun,   260
Who, disciplin'd, ay, dieted in grace,
Believ'd her eyes when they t' assail begun,
All vows and consecrations giving place.
O most potential love ! vow, bond, nor
     space,
In thee hath neither sting, knot, nor
     confine,   265
For thou art all, and all things else are
     thine.

' " When thou impressest, what are pre-
     cepts worth

Of stale example ? When thou wilt inflame,
How coldly those impediments stand forth,
Of wealth, of filial fear, law, kindred, fame !
Love's arms are peace, 'gainst rule, 'gainst
    sense, 'gainst shame,   271
And sweetens, in the suff'ring pangs it bears,
The aloes of all forces, shocks, and fears.

' " Now all these hearts that do on mine
    depend,
Feeling it break, with bleeding groans they
    pine,   275
And supplicant their sighs to you extend,
To leave the batt'ry that you make 'gainst
    mine,
Lending soft audience to my sweet design,
And credent soul to that strong-bonded
    oath,   279
That shall prefer and undertake my troth ".

' This said, his wat'ry eyes he did dismount,
Whose sights till then were levell'd on my
    face ;
Each cheek a river running from a fount
With brinish current downward flow'd
    apace.
O, how the channel to the stream gave
    grace !   285
Who glaz'd with crystal gate the glowing
    roses
That flame through water which their hue
    encloses.

' O father, what a hell of witchcraft lies
In the small orb of one particular tear !
But with the inundation of the eyes   290
What rocky heart to water will not wear ?
What breast so cold that is not warmed
    here ?
O cleft effect ! cold modesty, hot wrath,
Both fire from hence and chill extincture
    hath.   294

' For lo, his passion, but an art of craft,
Even there resolv'd my reason into tears ;
There my white stole of chastity I daff'd,
Shook off my sober guards and civil fears ;
Appear to him as he to me appears,

All melting ; though our drops this diff'r-
    ence bore :   300
His poison'd me, and mine did him restore.

' In him a plenitude of subtle matter,
Applied to cautels, all strange forms re-
    ceives,
Of burning blushes or of weeping water,
Or swooning paleness ; and he takes and
    leaves,   305
In either's aptness, as it best deceives,
To blush at speeches rank, to weep at woes,
Or to turn white and swoon at tragic
    shows ;

' That not a heart which in his level came
Could scape the hail of his all-hurting
    aim,   310
Showing fair nature is both kind and tame ;
And, veil'd in them, did win whom he would
    maim.
Against the thing he sought he would
    exclaim ;
When he most burn'd in heart-wish'd
    luxury,
He preach'd pure maid and prais'd cold
    chastity.   315

' Thus merely with the garment of a Grace
The naked and concealed fiend he cover'd,
That th' unexperient gave the tempter
    place,
Which, like a cherubin, above them hover'd.
Who, young and simple, would not be so
    lover'd ?   320
Ay me ! I fell ; and yet do question make
What I should do again for such a sake.

' O, that infected moisture of his eye,
O, that false fire which in his cheek so
    glowed,
O, that forc'd thunder from his heart did
    fly,   325
O, that sad breath his spongy lungs
    bestowed,
O, all that borrowed motion, seeming owed,
Would yet again betray the fore-betray'd,
And new pervert a reconciled maid ! '

1

When my love swears that she is made of truth,
I do believe her, though I know she lies,
That she might think me some untutor'd youth,
Unskilful in the world's false forgeries.   4
Thus vainly thinking that she thinks me young,
Although I know my years be past the best,
I smiling credit her false-speaking tongue,
Outfacing faults in love with love's ill rest.
But wherefore says my love that she is young?
And wherefore say not I that I am old?   10
O, love's best habit is a soothing tongue,
And age in loves not to have years told.
  Therefore I'll lie with love, and love with me,
    Since that our faults in love thus smother'd be.

2

Two loves I have, of comfort and despair,
That like two spirits do suggest me still;
My better angel is a man right fair,
My worser spirit a woman colour'd ill.
To win me soon to hell, my female evil   5
Tempteth my better angel from my side,
And would corrupt my saint to be a devil,
Wooing his purity with her fair pride.
And whether that my angel be turn'd fiend,
Suspect I may, yet not directly tell;   10
For being both to me, both to each friend,
I guess one angel in another's hell.
  The truth I shall not know, but live in doubt,
    Till my bad angel fire my good one out.

3

Did not the heavenly rhetoric of thine eye,
'Gainst whom the world could not hold argument,
Persuade my heart to this false perjury?
Vows for thee broke deserve not punishment.
A woman I forswore; but I will prove,   5
Thou being a goddess, I forswore not thee:
My vow was earthly, thou a heavenly love;
Thy grace being gain'd cures all disgrace in me.
My vow was breath, and breath a vapour is;
Then, thou fair sun, that on this earth doth shine,   10
Exhale this vapour vow; in thee it is:
If broken, then it is no fault of mine.
  If by me broke, what fool is not so wise
    To break an oath, to win a paradise?

4

Sweet Cytherea, sitting by a brook
With young Adonis, lovely, fresh, and green,
Did court the lad with many a lovely look,
Such looks as none could look but beauty's queen.
She told him stories to delight his ear;   5
She show'd him favours to allure his eye;
To win his heart she touch'd him here and there:
Touches so soft still conquer chastity.
But whether unripe years did want conceit,
Or he refus'd to take her figured proffer,   10
The tender nibbler would not touch the bait,
But smile and jest at every gentle offer.
  Then fell she on her back, fair queen, and toward:
    He rose and ran away; ah, fool too froward!

5

If love make me forsworn, how shall I swear to love?
O never faith could hold, if not to beauty vowed;
Though to myself forsworn, to thee I'll constant prove;
Those thoughts, to me like oaks, to thee like osiers bowed.
Study his bias leaves and makes his book thine eyes,   5
Where all those pleasures live that art can comprehend.
If knowledge be the mark, to know thee shall suffice;
Well learned is that tongue that well can thee commend;
All ignorant that soul that sees thee without wonder;
Which is to me some praise, that I thy parts admire.   10
Thine eye Jove's lightning seems, thy voice his dreadful thunder,
Which, not to anger bent, is music and sweet fire.
  Celestial as thou art, O, do not love that wrong,
    To sing heaven's praise with such an earthly tongue.

6

Scarce had the sun dried up the dewy morn,
And scarce the herd gone to the hedge for shade,
When Cytherea, all in love forlorn,
A longing tarriance for Adonis made
Under an osier growing by a brook,   5

A brook where Adon us'd to cool his spleen.
Hot was the day ; she hotter that did look
For his approach that often there had been.
Anon he comes, and throws his mantle by,
And stood stark naked on the brook's green
   brim.   10
The sun look'd on the world with glorious
   eye,
Yet not so wistly as this queen on him.
  He, spying her, bounc'd in whereas he
    stood ;
  ' O Jove,' quoth she ' why was not I a
    flood ? '

7

Fair is my love, but not so fair as fickle ;
Mild as a dove, but neither true nor trusty ;
Brighter than glass, and yet, as glass is,
   brittle ;
Softer than wax, and yet, as iron, rusty ; 4
A lily pale, with damask dye to grace her ;
None fairer, nor none falser to deface her.

Her lips to mine how often hath she joined,
Between each kiss her oaths of true love
   swearing !
How many tales to please me hath she
   coined,
Dreading my love, the loss whereof still
   fearing !   10
  Yet, in the midst of all her pure pro-
    testings,
  Her faith, her oaths, her tears, and all,
    were jestings.

She burn'd with love, as straw with fire
   flameth,
She burn'd out love, as soon as straw out-
   burneth ;
She fram'd the love, and yet she foil'd the
   framing,   15
She bade love last, and yet she fell
   a-turning.
  Was this a lover, or a lecher whether ?
  Bad in the best, though excellent in
    neither.

8

If music and sweet poetry agree,
As they must needs, the sister and the
   brother,
Then must the love be great 'twixt thee
   and me,
Because thou lov'st the one, and I the
   other.
Dowland to thee is dear, whose heavenly
   touch   5
Upon the lute doth ravish human sense ;
Spenser to me, whose deep conceit is such
As, passing all conceit, needs no defence.
Thou lov'st to hear the sweet melodious
   sound
That Phœbus' lute, the queen of music,
   makes ;   10
And I in deep delight am chiefly drown'd

Whenas himself to singing he betakes.
  One god is god of both, as poets feign ;
  One knight loves both, and both in thee
    remain.

9

Fair was the morn, when the fair queen of
   love,

*   *   *   *   *   *   *

Paler for sorrow than her milk-white dove,
For Adon's sake, a youngster proud and
   wild,
Her stand she takes upon a steep-up hill. 5
Anon Adonis comes with horn and hounds ;
She, silly queen, with more than love's good
   will,
Forbade the boy he should not pass those
   grounds.
' Once ' quoth she ' did I see a fair sweet
   youth
Here in these brakes deep-wounded with a
   boar,   10
Deep in the thigh, a spectacle of ruth !
See in my thigh,' quoth she ' here was the
   sore.'
  She showed hers ; he saw more wounds
    than one,
  And blushing fled, and left her all alone.

10

Sweet rose, fair flower, untimely pluck'd,
   soon vaded,
Pluck'd in the bud, and vaded in the spring !
Bright orient pearl, alack, too timely
   shaded !
Fair creature, kill'd too soon by death's
   sharp sting !
Like a green plum that hangs upon a tree, 5
And falls, through wind, before the fall
   should be.

I weep for thee, and yet no cause I have ;
For why thou lefts me nothing in thy will.
And yet thou lefts me more than I did
   crave ;
For why I craved nothing of thee still.   10
  O yes, dear friend, I pardon crave of
    thee !
  Thy discontent thou didst bequeath to
    me.

11

Venus, with Adonis sitting by her
Under a myrtle shade, began to woo him.
She told the youngling how god Mars did
   try her,
And as he fell to her, she fell to him.
' Even thus ' quoth she ' the warlike god
   embrac'd me.'   5
And then she clipp'd Adonis in her arms.
' Even thus ' quoth she ' the warlike god
   unlac'd me '
As if the boy should use like loving charms.
' Even thus ' quoth she ' he seized on my
   lips '   9

And with her lips on his did act the seizure ;
And as she fetched breath, away he skips,
And would not take her meaning nor her
   pleasure.
  Ah ! that I had my lady at this bay,
  To kiss and clip me till I run away !

12

Crabbed age and youth cannot live to-
   gether :
Youth is full of pleasance, age is full of care;
Youth like summer morn, age like winter
   weather ;
Youth like summer brave, age like winter
   bare.
Youth is full of sport, age's breath is short ;
Youth is nimble, age is lame ;   6
Youth is hot and bold, age is weak and
   cold ;
Youth is wild, and age is tame.
Age, I do abhor thee ; youth, I do adore
   thee.
O, my love, my love is young !   10
Age, I do defy thee.
O sweet shepherd, hie thee,
For methinks thou stays too long.

13

Beauty is but a vain and doubtful good,
A shining gloss that vadeth suddenly ;
A flower that dies when first it gins to bud ;
A brittle glass that's broken presently ; 4
  A doubtful good, a gloss, a glass, a flower,
  Lost, vaded, broken, dead within an
    hour.

And as goods lost are seld or never found,
As vaded gloss no rubbing will refresh,
As flowers dead lie withered on the ground,
As broken glass no cement can redress ; 10
  So beauty, blemish'd once, for ever lost,
  In spite of physic, painting, pain, and
    cost.

14

Good night, good rest. Ah, neither be my
   share !
She bade good night that kept my rest
   away,
And daff'd me to a cabin hang'd with care,
To descant on the doubts of my decay.
  ' Farewell,' quoth she ' and 'come again
    to-morrow.'   5
  Fare well I could not, for I supp'd with
    sorrow.

Yet at my parting sweetly did she smile,
In scorn or friendship, nill I construe
   whether :
'T may be she joy'd to jest at my exile ;
'T may be again to make me wander
   thither—   10
  ' Wander ', a word for shadows like
    myself
  As take the pain but cannot pluck the pelf.

Lord, how mine eyes throw gazes to the
   east !
My heart doth charge the watch ; the
   morning rise   14
Doth cite each moving sense from idle rest,
Not daring trust the office of mine eyes.
  While Philomela sits and sings, I sit and
    mark,
  And wish her lays were tuned like the
    lark ;

For she doth welcome daylight with her
   ditty,   19
And drives away dark dreaming night.
The night so pack'd, I post unto my pretty;
Heart hath his hope, and eyes their wished
   sight ;
  Sorrow chang'd to solace, and solace
    mix'd with sorrow ;
  For why she sigh'd, and bade me come
    to-morrow.

Were I with her, the night would post too
   soon ;   25
But now are minutes added to the hours ;
To spite me now, each minute seems a
   moon ;
Yet not for me, shine sun to succour flowers !
  Pack night, peep day ; good day, of
    night now borrow ;
  Short, night, to-night, and length thyself
    to-morrow.   30

15

It was a lording's daughter, the fairest one
   of three,
That liked of her master as well as well
   might be,
Till looking on an Englishman, the fairest
   that eye could see,
Her fancy fell a-turning.
Long was the combat doubtful that love
   with love did fight,   5
To leave the master loveless, or kill the
   gallant knight ;
To put in practice either, alas, it was a spite
   Unto the silly damsel !
But one must be refused ; more mickle was
   the pain
That nothing could be used to turn them
   both to gain,   10
For of the two the trusty knight was
   wounded with disdain.
  Alas, she could not help it !
Thus art with arms contending was victor
   of the day,
Which by a gift of learning did bear the
   maid away.
Then, lullaby, the learned man hath got the
   lady gay ;   15
  For now my song is ended.

16

On a day, alack the day !
Love, whose month was ever May,

Spied a blossom passing fair,
Playing in the wanton air.
Through the velvet leaves the wind,　5
All unseen, gan passage find ;
That the lover, sick to death,
Wish'd himself the heaven's breath.
' Air,' quoth he ' thy cheeks may blow ;
Air, would I might triumph so !　10
But, alas, my hand hath sworn
Ne'er to pluck thee from thy thorn ;
Vow, alack, for youth unmeet,
Youth, so apt to pluck a sweet.
Thou for whom Jove would swear　15
Juno but an Ethiope were ;
And deny himself for Jove,
Turning mortal for thy love.'

17

My flocks feed not,
My ewes breed not,
My rams speed not,
　All is amiss ;
Love is dying,　5
Faith's defying,
Heart's denying,
　Causer of this.
All my merry jigs are quite forgot,
All my lady's love is lost, God wot.　10
Where her faith was firmly fix'd in love,
There a nay is plac'd without remove.
One silly cross
Wrought all my loss.　14
　O frowning Fortune, cursed fickle dame !
For now I see
Inconstancy
　More in women than in men remain.

In black mourn I,
All fears scorn I,　20
Love hath forlorn me,
　Living in thrall ;
Heart is bleeding,
All help needing,
O cruel speeding,　25
　Fraughted with gall !
My shepherd's pipe can sound no deal ;
My wether's bell rings doleful knell ;
My curtail dog, that wont to have play'd,
Plays not at all, but seems afraid.　30
With sighs so deep,
Procures to weep,
　In howling wise, to see my doleful
　　plight.
How sighs resound
Through heartless ground,　35
　Like a thousand vanquish'd men in
　　bloody fight !

Clear wells spring not,
Sweet birds sing not,
Green plants bring not
　Forth their dye.　40
Herds stand weeping,
Flocks all sleeping,

Nymphs back peeping
　Fearfully.　44
All our pleasure known to us poor swains,
All our merry meetings on the plains,
All our evening sport from us is fled,
All our love is lost, for Love is dead.
Farewell, sweet lass ;
Thy like ne'er was　50
　For a sweet content, the cause of all my
　　moan.
Poor Corydon
Must live alone ;
　Other help for him I see that there is
　　none.

18

When as thine eye hath chose the dame,
And stall'd the deer that thou shouldst
　strike,
Let reason rule things worthy blame,
As well as fancy, partial wight ;
　Take counsel of some wiser head,　5
　Neither too young nor yet unwed.

And when thou com'st thy tale to tell,
Smooth not thy tongue with filed talk,
Lest she some subtle practice smell—
　A cripple soon can find a halt,　10
　But plainly say thou lov'st her well,
　And set her person forth to sell.

And to her will frame all thy ways ;
Spare not to spend, and chiefly there
Where thy desert may merit praise　15
By ringing in thy lady's ear.
　The strongest castle, tower, and town,
　The golden bullet beats it down.

Serve always with assured trust,
And in thy suit be humble-true ;　20
Unless thy lady prove unjust,
Press never thou to choose a new.
　When time shall serve, be thou not slack
　To proffer, though she put thee back.

What though her frowning brows be bent,
Her cloudy looks will calm ere night ;　26
And then too late she will repent
That thus dissembled her delight ;
　And twice desire, ere it be day,
　That which with scorn she put away.　30

What though she strive to try her strength,
And ban and brawl and say thee nay ?
Her feeble force will yield at length,
When craft hath taught her thus to say :
　' Had women been so strong as men,　35
　In faith, you had not had it then '.

The wiles and guiles that women work,
Dissembled with an outward show,
The tricks and toys that in them lurk,　39
The cock that treads them shall not know.
　Have you not heard it said full oft,
　A woman's nay doth stand for nought ?

Think women still to strive with men
To sin, and never for to saint ;
There is no heaven—be holy then—   45
When time with age shall them attaint.
    Were kisses all the joys in bed,
    One woman would another wed.

But soft ; enough—too much I fear ;
Lest that my mistress hear my song ;   50
She will not stick to round me on th' ear,
To teach my tongue to be so long.
    Yet will she blush, here be it said,
    To hear her secrets so bewray'd.

19

Live with me, and be my love,
And we will all the pleasures prove
That hills and valleys, dales and fields,
And all the craggy mountains yields.

There will we sit upon the rocks,   5
And see the shepherds feed their flocks,
By shallow rivers, by whose falls
Melodious birds sing madrigals.

There will I make thee a bed of roses,
With a thousand fragrant posies,   10
A cap of flowers, and a kirtle
Embroidered all with leaves of myrtle ;

A belt of straw and ivy buds,
With coral clasps and amber studs.
And if these pleasures may thee move,   15
Then live with me and be my love.

LOVE'S ANSWER

If that the world and love were young,
And truth in every shepherd's tongue,
These pretty pleasures might me move,
To live with thee and be thy love.   20

20

As it fell upon a day,
In the merry month of May,
Sitting in a pleasant shade
Which a grove of myrtles made,
Beasts did leap and birds did sing,   5
Trees did grow and plants did spring ;
Every thing did banish moan,
Save the nightingale alone.

She, poor bird, as all forlorn,
Lean'd her breast up-till a thorn,   10
And there sung the dolefull'st ditty,
That to hear it was great pity.
' Fie, fie, fie ! ' now would she cry ;
' Teru, Teru ! ' by and by ;
That to hear her so complain   15
Scarce I could from tears refrain ;
For her griefs, so lively shown,
Made me think upon mine own.
Ah, thought I, thou mourn'st in vain ;
None takes pity on thy pain :   20
Senseless trees, they cannot hear thee ;
Ruthless bears, they will not cheer thee.
King Pandion, he is dead ;
All thy friends are lapp'd in lead :
All thy fellow birds do sing,   25
Careless of thy sorrowing.
Even so, poor bird, like thee,
None alive will pity me.
Whilst as fickle Fortune smil'd,
Thou and I were both beguil'd.   30
Every one that flatters thee
Is no friend in misery.
Words are easy, like the wind ;
Faithful friends are hard to find.
Every man will be thy friend   35
Whilst thou hast wherewith to spend ;
But if store of crowns be scant,
No man will supply thy want.
If that one be prodigal,
Bountiful they will him call,   40
And with such-like flattering,
' Pity but he were a king '.
If he be addict to vice,
Quickly him they will entice ;
If to women he be bent,   45
They have at commandement ;
But if Fortune once do frown,
Then farewell his great renown.
They that fawn'd on him before
Use his company no more.   50
He that is thy friend indeed,
He will help thee in thy need ;
If thou sorrow, he will weep ;
If thou wake, he cannot sleep.
Thus of every grief in heart   55
He with thee doth bear a part.
These are certain signs to know
Faithful friend from flatt'ring foe.

THE PHŒNIX AND TURTLE

LET the bird of loudest lay,
On the sole Arabian tree,
Herald sad and trumpet be,
To whose sound chaste wings obey.

But thou shrieking harbinger, 5
Foul precurrer of the fiend,
Augur of the fever's end,
To this troop come thou not near.

From this session interdict
Every fowl of tyrant wing, 10
Save the eagle, feath'red king:
Keep the obsequy so strict.

Let the priest in surplice white,
That defunctive music can,
Be the death-divining swan, 15
Lest the requiem lack his right.

And thou treble-dated crow,
That thy sable gender mak'st
With the breath thou giv'st and tak'st
'Mongst our mourners shalt thou go. 20

Here the anthem doth commence:
Love and constancy is dead;
Phœnix and the turtle fled
In a mutual flame from hence.

So they lov'd as love in twain 25
Had the essence but in one;
Two distincts, division none:
Number there in love was slain.

Hearts remote, yet not asunder;
Distance, and no space was seen 30
'Twixt this turtle and his queen;
But in them it were a wonder.

So between them love did shine
That the turtle saw his right
Flaming in the phœnix' sight: 35
Either was the other's mine.

Property was thus appalled,
That the self was not the same;
Single nature's double name
Neither two nor one was called. 40

Reason, in itself confounded,
Saw division grow together,
To themselves yet either neither,
Simple were so well compounded,

That it cried 'How true a twain 45
Seemeth this concordant one!
Love hath reason, reason none,
If what parts can so remain'.

Whereupon it made this threne
To the phœnix and the dove, 50
Co-supremes and stars of love,
As chorus to their tragic scene.

THRENOS

Beauty, truth, and rarity,
Grace in all simplicity,
Here enclos'd in cinders lie. 55

Death is now the phœnix' nest;
And the turtle's loyal breast
To eternity doth rest,

Leaving no posterity—
'Twas not their infirmity, 60
It was married chastity.

Truth may seem, but cannot be;
Beauty brag, but 'tis not she:
Truth and beauty buried be.

To this urn let those repair 65
That are either true or fair;
For these dead birds sigh a prayer.

APPENDIX

THIS transcript, reproduced in type-facsimile, of 147 lines from the manuscript of the play of *Sir Thomas More*, is included by the generous permission of Sir Walter Greg, who made it, and the syndics of the Cambridge University Press. It can be studied with complete advantage only in the context for which Dr. Greg designed it—namely, *Shakespeare's Hand in Sir Thomas More*,* a study from all angles of the authorship of these lines by a group of scholars who proved, beyond reasonable question, that Shakespeare wrote them, and that chance has preserved for us, in addition to the six, possibly seven, genuine signatures, this

*By Alfred W. Pollard, W. W. Greg, E. Maunde Thompson, J. Dover Wilson and R. W. Chambers. Cambridge University Press, 1923.

Lincolne	Peace heare me, he that will not fee [a red] hearing at a harry Fol. 8ª grote, butter at a levenpence a pou[nde, meale at] nyne ſhillingę a Buſhell and Beeff at fower nob[les a ſtone, lyſ]t to me	
~~other~~ Geo bett	yt will Come to that paſſę yf ſtrain[gers be ſu]fferd mark him	
Linco	our Countrie is a great eating Country, argo they eate more in our Countrey then they do in their owne	5
~~other~~ betts clow	by a half penny loff a day troy waight	
Linc	they bring in ſtraing rootes, which is meerly to the vndoing of poor prentizes, for whatę ~~a watrie~~ a ſorry pſnyp to a good hart	
~~oth~~ william	traſh traſh, : they breed ſore eyes and tis enough to infect the Cytty wᵗ the palſey	10
Lin	nay yt has infected yt wᵗ the palſey, for theiſe baſterdę of dung as you knowe they growe in Dvng haue infected vs, and yt is our infeccion will make the Cytty ſhake which ptly Coms through the eating of pſnyps	15
~~o~~ Clown · betts Enter	trewe and pumpions togeather	
ſeriant	what ſay yoᵘ to the mercy of the king do yoᵘ refuſe yt	
Lin	yoᵘ woold haue [vs] vppon thipp woold yoᵘ no marry do we not, we accept of the kingę mercy but wee will ſhowe no mercy vppŏ the ſtraingers	20
ſeriaunt	yoᵘ ar the ſimpleſt thingę that eū ſtood in ſuch a queſtion	
Lin	now prenty how ſay yoᵘ prentiſſes ſymple downe wᵗʰ him	

3 *Beeff*] the first *e* has been altered from some other letter.   5 *Linco*] *in* has two minims only but the first is dotted.   8 *of*] the final curl of the *f* has been carried round in such a way as to resemble *o*   10 *william*] *m* has two minims only.   *traſh,:*] so T, but the lower dot may be accidental: M prints a semi-colon.   12 *dung*] *un* has five minims.   17 ʻThe initial letter of the speaker's name, whether it be regarded as minuscule (T) or majuscule (M), is certainly of an Italian type.   18 *haue*] T *have* perhaps by an accidental slip; the word occurs elsewhere eight times always spelt *haue*, Dyce read *haue* here, and the very obscure original seems to me to have *u* rather than *v*   19 *ſhowe*] *w* blotted, possibly altered.   22 The marginal and interlined words were added later.   *prenty*] *n* is represented by one minim only, and *y* is doubtful.

extensive specimen of the dramatist's handwriting. Though only a comparison of the transcript with a facsimile of the original will make clear the full implications of this discovery, the reader has here before him a fragment of the master's composition, transcribed with a care that will permit him to understand more adequately than any description the difficulties confronting Heminge and Condell in their editorial labours. The 147 lines occupy both sides of a leaf of paper and one side of a second leaf, and form part of a scene Shakespeare contributed to a piece by some fellow playwrights. The original author or authors had difficulty with the licenser of plays. That official was not troubled by the play's protagonist being More, a martyr to the cause of Catholicism : a Protestant audience under the Protestant Elizabeth had

all	prentiſſes ſymple prentiſſes ſymple	
	Enter the L maier Surrey	
	Shrewſbury	25
~~Sher~~ Maior	hold in the kinge name hold	
Surrey	frende maſters Countrymen	
mayer	peace how peace J ~~fh~~ Charg yoᵘ keep the peace	
Shro·	my maſters Countrymen	
~~Sher~~ Williamson	The noble Earle of Shrewſbury lette hear him	30
Ge bette	weele heare the Earle of Surrey	
Linc	the earle of Shrewſbury	
bette	weele heare both	
all	both both both both	
Linc	Peace J ſay peace ar yoᵘ men of Wiſdome ~~ar or~~ what ar yoᵘ	35
Surr	~~But~~ what yoᵘ will haue them but not men of wiſdome	
all	weele not heare my L of Surrey, ~~all~~ no no no no no no ——————————————————————————————Shrewſbury ſhr	
moor	whiles they ar ore the banck of their obedyenc thus will they bere downe all thinge	40
Linc	Shreiff moor ſpeakes ſhall we heare ſhreef moor ſpeake	
Doll	Lette heare him a keepes a plentyfull ſhrevaltry, and a made my	

26 *Sher*] this must be a slip for *Shre*   27 The rule has been accidentally omitted after this line.
29 *Shro·*] the last letter certainly seems to be *o* but D always writes *Shrewſbury* elsewhere.   30 C wrote his alteration on the top of D's original.   30, 32 *Shrewſbury*] M, T *Shrowſbury*   38 *all no... ſhr*] added later; the deletion is probably by C.   *Shrewſbury*] so M: T *Shrowſbury* (the letter is indistinguishable).   40 *thinge*] I am unable to read the end of this word.
42 *ſhrevaltry,*] so M: T *shrevaltry.* but it is clearly a comma I think

a sufficiently catholic attitude to understand and appreciate his character. But a series of episodes in which he is represented as intervening in person to quell the ' ill May-day ' riot of 1517 so disturbed the licenser that after marking several passages for omission he turned back and wrote at the beginning of the manuscript :

' Leave out the insurrection wholly and the cause thereof and begin with Sir Thomas More at the Mayor's sessions with a report afterwards of his good service done being Sheriff of London upon a mutiny against the Lombards. Only by a short report and not otherwise at your own perils.—TYLLNEY '.

The constant danger of attack on the foreign colonies in London from riotous native elements was too present to the licenser's mind to

	Brother Arther watchin[s] Seriant Safes yeoman letę heare ſhreeve moore	
all	Shreiue moor moor more Shreue moore	45
moor	[ev]en by the rule yoᵘ haue among yoʳ ſealues Comand ſtill audience	FOL. 8ᵇ
all	[S]urrey Sury	
all	moor moor	
Lincolne bettę	peace pęace ſcilens peace	50
moor	Yoᵘ that haue voyce and Credyt wᵗ the ~mv~ nvmber Comaund them to a ſtilnes	
Lincolne	a plaigue on them they will not hold their peace the deule Cannot rule them	
moor	Then what a rough and ryotous charge haue yoᵘ to Leade thoſe that the deule Cannot rule good maſters heare me ſpeake	55
Doll	J byth mas will we moor thart a good howſkeeper and J thanck thy good worſhip for my Brother Arthur watchins	
all	peace peace	60
moor	look what yoᵘ do offend yoᵘ Cry vppŏ that is the peace; not [on] of yoᵘ heare preſent had there ſuch fellowes lyvd when yoᵘ wer babes that coold haue topt the peace, as nowe yoᵘ woold the peace wherin yoᵘ haue till nowe growne vp had bin tane from yoᵘ, and the bloody tymes coold not haue brought yoᵘ to ~theiſe~ the ſtate of men alas poor thingę what is yt yoᵘ haue gott although we graunt yoᵘ geat the thing yoᵘ ſeeke	65

43 *Safes*] *af* seems to me to have disappeared entirely except perhaps for the extreme tail of the *f*. *yeoman*] *o* altered, probably by C, from some other small letter. 45 This line with the rule above it was added later. 59 *watchins*] *c* altered, apparently from the beginning of *h*

allow him to pass episodes which showed historical precedent for such attempts. At some stage in the struggle to fit the play for official favour the author or authors sought the help of Shakespeare, not as some unknown or prentice playwright, but as one whose dexterity and experience would supply the resource required.

Shakespeare's scene opens with the rioters led by Lincoln crying out against the foreigners. To them enters a Sergeant-at-Arms, followed by the Lord Mayor with the Earls of Surrey and Shrewsbury and Sir Thomas More. The crowd cry down the Mayor and Earls but are willing to give More a hearing. The interpretation of the typographical detail of the transcript will be clear from Dr. Greg's own analysis :

' The author wrote the text, at any rate of the first two pages, continuously, dividing the speeches by rules but without indicating the

D̶Bett	marry the removing of the ſtraingers wch cannot choofe but much h̶e̶l̶p̶e advauntage the poor handycraftes of the Cytty	70
moor	graunt them remoued and graunt that this yor y̶ noyce hath Chidd downe all the matie of Jngland ymagin that yo^u ſee the wretched ſtraingers	
	their babyes at their back℮, a̶n̶d their poor lug̃age^w^t plodding tooth port℮ and coſt℮ for tranfportacion and that yo^u ſytt as king℮ in your deſyres aucthoryty quyte ſylenct by yor braule and yo^u in ruff of yor y̶o opynions cloth̃d	75
	what had yo^u gott; Jle tell yo^u, yo^u had taught how inſolenc and ſtrong hand ſhoold prevayle how orderd ſhoold be quelld, and by this patterne not on of yo^u ſhoold lyve an aged man for other ruffians as their fancies wrought	80
	wth ſealf ſame hand ſealf reaſons and ſealf right woold ſhark on yo^u and men lyke ravenous fiſhes woold feed on on another	85
Doll	before god that℮ as trewe as the goſpell.	
Bett℮ lincoln	nay this a ſound fellowe J tell yo^u lets mark him	
moor	Let me ſett vp before yor thoughts good freind℮ on ſuppoſytion, which if yo^u will marke yo^u ſhall pceaue howe horrible a ſhape your ynnovation beres, firſt tis a ſinn which oft thappoſtle did forwarne vs of vrging obedienc to aucthory[ty] and twere i̶n̶ no error yf J told yo^u all yo^u wer in armes gainſt g[od]	90
		95

70 The D appears to have been crossed out by both D and C.   71 *handycraftes*] the *e* is represented only by a small blot between *t* and *s*   72 *noyce*] *y* altered from *w*   73 *matie*] sic, by a slip from *matie* i.e. *maieſtie* (cf. l. 121).   75 *and* was crossed out, and *w^t* interlined to replace it, by D. Neither M nor T notices the alteration.   80 *gott;*] so T: M prints a comma, but the original seems to have ·;·   82 *orderd*] so T: M *ordcre*: doubtful, but in either case an error for *order* 85 *hand*] there is a very small dot after this word, some stop may possibly be intended.   89 *lincoln*] so M: T *Lincoln* (perhaps a slip).   93 *your*] M, T *yor* but the reading though indistinct is hardly open to question.   94 *vrging*] so M: T *urging* (an accidental slip).

speakers. He then read it through, inserting the prefixes and at the same time making certain additions to the text, some words at the beginning of l. 22, at the end of l. 38, and the whole of l. 45. . . . The addition of the speakers' names was certainly perfunctory, especially on the first page, but, apart from the unsatisfactory condition of the deleted passage on the third, I do not find any evidence of haste or carelessness in composition '.

The scene, however, does not stand in its final state exactly as Shakespeare left it. The heavier type indicates additions and alterations by a second hand, that of a playhouse reviser who tried to clarify and pull together certain details of the original. One instance only of his efforts can be commented on here : he has deleted ll. 112-14 and substituted a phrase of his own. Shakespeare's omission of punctuation

all

marry god forbid that

moo

nay certainly yo^u ar
for to the king god hath his offyc lent
of dread of Juftyce, power and Comaund
hath bid him rule, and willd yo^u to obay   100
and to add ampler mafie to this
he god hath not le only lent the king his figure
          &
his throne his fword, but gyven him his owne name
calls him a god on earth, what do yo^u then
ryfing gainft him that god himfealf enftalls   105
but ryfe gainft god, what do yo^u to yor fowles
in doing this o defperat ar as you are·
wafh your foule mynds w^t teares and thofe fame hand{
that yo^u lyke rebells lyft againft the peace
lift vp for peace, and your vnreuerent knees   110
that make them your feet   to kneele to be forgyven.
is fafer warrs, then euer yo^u can make·
               in in to yor obediene·
whofe difcipline is ryot; why euen yor warrs hurly
    tell me but this
cannot peed but by obediene what rebell captaine
       n
as mutyes ar incident, by his name   115
can ftill the rout who will obay th a traytor
or howe can well that pclamation founde
when ther is no adicion but a rebell
to quallyfy a rebell, youle put downe ftraingers

FOL. 9ª

101 and] n has three minims.   102 vnly] so M: T souly (withdrawn; see above, p. 76, note). 103 his (deleted)] so M: T hys (withdrawn; see above, p. 76, note). The & is really written on the top of his not between the lines.   110 and] for an attempted alteration see final note.   111 There is a slightly wider space after feet and a break may have been intended as in l. 95. to kneele] so M: T fo kneele (an accidental misprint due to a broken letter).   112-4 With the exception of the single word warrs (which he crossed out, adding hurly in its place) these lines were left standing by D. All the other deletions are in darker ink, presumably by C, who added the interlined words in the third line.   113 warrs] so M: T warre altered to warri (see final note).   obedienc·] T omits the stop, but I do not think that the mark can be accidental.   117 founde] un has three minims only.   118 ther] r altered from ir.

marks and capital letters, his insertion of the phrase ' in in to your obedience ' and the extra-metrical nature of the conclusion of l. 114 puzzled the reviser. He took the phrase ' to kneel to be forgiven ' with what goes before instead of with what follows, and in his determination to have it all tidy scored out the troublesome passage and inserted a join of his own contriving.

Had this manuscript gone as it stands to the printer it needs no imagination to picture the difficulties that would have confronted the compositor. It is true that these three pages were composed by Shakespeare in circumstances very different from those in which he wrote his own plays. But the handwriting, with all the difficulties and irregularities recorded in Dr. Greg's notes, would be the same ; there would be the same minimum of punctuation and capitalization, and possibly, in places, the same insertions, extra-metrical lines, and loose ends. These by themselves would be sufficient to explain many of the

kill them cutt their throts poffeffe their howfes   120
and leade the matie of lawe in liom

~~alas alas~~
to flipp him lyke a hound; ~~fayeng~~ fay nowe the king
as he is clement,. yf thoffendor moorne
fhoold fo much com to fhort of your great trefpas
   as but to banyfh yo^u, whether woold yo^u go·   125
what Country by the nature of yor error
fhoold gyve you harber go yo^u to ffraunc or flanders
to any Jarman pvince, ~~to~~ fpane or portigall
nay any where ~~why yo^u~~ that not adheres to Jngland
why yo^u muft neede be ftraingers, woold yo^u be pleafd   130
to find a nation of fuch barbarous temper
that breaking out in hiddious violence
woold not afoord yo^u, an abode on earth
whett their detefted knyves againft yor throtes
fpurne yo^u lyke dogge, and lyke as yf that god   135
owed not nor made not yo^u, nor that the elamente

                     yor
wer not all appropriat to ~~their~~ Comforte·
but Charterd vnto them, what woold yo^u thinck
to be thus vfd, this is the ftraingers cafe
all   and this your momtanifh inhumanyty   140

<hr>

fayth a faies trewe letts ~~vs~~ do as we may be boon by

121 *matie*] contraction mark omitted as in l. 73.   122 *fayeng*] M, T *saying* but there is no doubt of the reading. The substituted words, interlined by D, were deleted by C.   123 *clement,*.] M, T print a comma only, but there seems clearly to be a point after it.   125 The writing avoids a small hole in the paper.   127 *flanders*] the *r* is malformed.   130 *ftraingers*,] T's comma is better than M's point, but the mark may be accidental.   131 *barbarous*] second *r* altered from *b* (not from *k* as T suggests).   136 *elamente*] T adds a comma but the mark is in the paper only. 137 *their*] M, T *ther* but there is little doubt of the reading.   140 *all*] belongs properly to the next line where T prints it.   *momtanifh*] T *mountanish* noting '*un* only three minims': the writer's intention is quite obscure.   *inhumanyty*] so M; T adds a point but it appears to be no more than a flick of the tail of *y*   141 *vs*] M and T both describe the deletion as being in modern ink, but on re-examination I am unable to distinguish it from that of other deletions and therefore ascribe it to C. The writer probably intended *lett vs* but forgot to cross out the *s*

blunders that mar the Good Quartos and that must have stood in the transcripts prepared by scriveners working from Shakespeare's papers. The three pages of *Sir Thomas More* here transcribed must, when they were new and fresh, have presented an appearance that might reasonably be described as scarcely blotted; but careful study can discover beneath the discolourings and blurrings that now overlay them the many pitfalls that would await a printer. We need not therefore be surprised, though we may regret, that even with Shakespeare's papers in their possession Heminge and Condell did not succeed in giving us the perfect text. Only the most unrelaxing vigilance and supervision can arrest the brood of error that haunt the printing-house and the copyist's desk alike. The three pages from Shakespeare's own hand may show the reader some of the loopholes through which those intruders have found their way into Shakespeare's text.

~~all~~ Linco   weele be ruld by you mafter moor yf youle ftand our
                         freind to pcure our pdon

moor,   Submyt you to theife noble gentlemen
                         entreate their mediation to the kinge   145
                         gyve vp yor fealf to forme obay the maieftrate
                         and thers no doubt, but mercy may be found   yf you fo feek [yt]

147 *found*] *un* has three minims only.   *you*] *ou* malformed.   *yt*] M *is*: T omits. D certainly wrote something after *seek* and the addition seems to me to improve the sense. The visible traces can be read *yt* (hardly *it*), but at the same time they are rather widely separated from the preceding word, and it is possible that they represent an *&* or some other sign indicating that the original text was to resume at this point.

FINAL NOTE ON CERTAIN READINGS IN Ll. 103–14.

103 *bis* (deleted)] The curious symbol superimposed on this word has certainly not the form of the *&* usual in English hands. It may, however, I think, be a loose attempt at rendering the print form of ampersand, which though rare is not unknown in manuscripts of the period. Since the ink in which the symbol is written is identical with that of the original writing, it seems unlikely that a second hand is involved in the alteration. This also applies to the contraction mark of *maiie* in l. 101.

110 *and your*] T notes: 'a word was underlined for insertion between these two words, but it appears to have been wiped out while the ink was still wet. The traces of the letters seem to suggest *bend*.' It appears that *and* was crossed out and the word, whatever it was, interlined to replace it. But the whole alteration, which was probably never completed, has been erased. The traces are very illegible, but to me they suggest the letters *hye* rather than *bend*.

113 *warrs*] T *warre* noting that the writer 'altered *warre* to *warrs* by interlining a long *s*.' I am not myself able to detect any indication of a final *e*, and believe the supposed *f* to be the upward curl of the regular English final *s*.

112–4 In these difficult lines, if the original writer intended the interlined words *in in to yor obedienc·* as a substitute for the two half-lines *why euen...by obedienc* (as has been suggested) one would have expected him to delete the latter. But, with the substitution of *hurly* for *warrs* he left the passage as it was, and must, I think, have meant it to stand. I conjecture that a stop was intended after *feet* in l. 111, and that *in in to yor obedienc·* should be inserted between *ryot;* and *why*. The whole passage is clumsy but I no longer think, as I was once inclined to do, that the author was conscious of having left it in confusion.

GLOSSARY

abate, to shorten, *Mid. N. Dr.*, 3.ii.432; to except, *L. Lab. Lost*, 5.ii.540; to lessen, *Tam. Shrew*, Ind. i.135.

abhor, to disgust, *Oth.*, 4.ii.163; shudder from, *Mer. Wives Win.*, 3.v.14; to reject, *Hen. 8*, 2.iv.81.

abject, *adj.*, despised, *Hen. 8*, 1.i.127; servile, *Mer. Ven.*, 4.i.92; *noun*, contemptible thing, *Jul. Caes.*, 4.i.37.

abode, to foretell, *Hen. 8*, 1.i.93.

abortives, untimely births, *John*, 3.iv.158.

abram, auburn, *Cor.*, 2.iii.18.

abridgement, what cuts short or passes the time, *Ham.*, 2.ii.415; *Mid. N. Dr.*, 5.i.39.

abrook, to tolerate, *2 Hen. 6*, 2.iv.10.

abruption, abrupt breaking off, *Troil. and Cres.*, 3.ii.63.

Absey-book, a book to teach the ABC of a subject, *John*, 1.i.196.

absolute, perfect, *Hen. 5*, 3.vii.25; positive, *Ham.*, 5.i.133; decided, *M. Meas.*, 3.i.5.

aby, to pay penalty for, *Mid. N. Dr.*, 3.ii.175.

accite, to summon, *Titus*, 1.i.27; to excite, *2 Hen. 4*, 2.ii.56.

accommodate, to furnish or equip, *2 Hen. 4*, 3.ii.65.

accomplice, comrade (but not in crime), *1 Hen. 6*, 5.ii.9.

accomplish, to arm completely, *Hen. 5*, 4. Prol. 12; to furnish, *Rich. 2*, 2.i.177.

ache, pronounced ' aitch ' at *Much Ado*, 3.iv.48, where it is represented by H.

Acheron, one of the five rivers of the lower world, but called a lake at *Titus*, 4.iii.44; stands for hell itself at *Mac.*, 3.v.15.

ackown, be not acknown, admit no knowledge of, *Oth.*, 3.iii.323.

aconitum, poison from wolf's-bane, *2 Hen. 4*, 4.iv.48.

action-taking, sheltering behind the law, *Lear*, 2.ii.16.

acture, action, *Lov. Comp.*, 185.

Adam (i) *the picture of old Adam*, because the officer had a coat of strong leather, and Adam, after the Fall, wore skins, *Com. Err.*, 4.iii.13. (ii) Adam Bell, famous as an archer, *Much Ado*, 1.i.224; *Rom. and Jul.*, 2.i.13.

adamant, very hard substance, *1 Hen. 6*, 1.iv.52; lode-stone, *Mid. N. Dr.*, 2.i.195.

addiction, natural inclination, *Oth.*, 2.ii.5.

addition, description or title acquired by habits or service, *Troil. and Cres.*, 2.iii.241.

address, to prepare, *As You Like*, 5.iv.150; to equip, *Troil. and Cres.*, 5.x.14.

admiral, flagship, *Ant. and Cleo.*, 3.x.2.

advertisement, information, warning, *1 Hen. 4*, 3.ii.172; *All's Well*, 4.iii.197.

advice, thought, *Two Gent. Ver.*, 2.iv.203, 204.

aedile, Roman official responsible for public order and public works, *Cor.*, 3.i.172.

aery, nest and young of eagle, *Rich. 3*, 1.iii.264; applied to the young actors of the boys' companies, *Ham.*, 2.ii.335.

affect, aim at, *Cor.*, 3.iii.1; love, *Tw. Night*, 2.v.22.

affection, affectation, *L. Lab. Lost*, 5.i.4.

affeer, confirm, *Mac.*, 4.iii.34.

affiance, trust, *Cym.*, 1.vi.162.

affront, to meet, confront, *Ham.*, 3.i.31.

affy, to trust, betroth, *Titus*, 1.i.47; *Tam. Shrew*, 4.iv.49.

agate, small figure like that cut on stone of seal-ring, *2 Hen. 4*, 1.ii.16.

Agenor, King of Tyre and father of Europa, *Tam. Shrew*, 1.i.163.

aglet-baby, small figure on lace-tag, *Tam. Shrew*, 1.ii.77.

agnize, acknowledge, *Oth.*, 1.iii.231.

a-hold, directly into the wind, *Tem.*, 1.i.46.

aim, conjecture, *Oth.*, 1.iii.6; term of encouragement, *John*, 2.i.196.

Ajax, Greek hero before Troy with more brawn than brains, *Troil. and Cres.*, 2.i.70; with pun (see jakes), *L. Lab. Lost*, 5.ii.572.

alderliefest, dearest of all, *2 Hen. 6*, 1.i.28.

Alecto, one of the Furies, *2 Hen. 4*, 5.v.37.

a-life, dearly, *Win. Tale*, 4.iv.255.

All-hallond eve, eve of All Saints' day, *M. Meas.*, 2.i.120.

All-hallowmas, 1st Nov., *Mer. Wives Win.*, 1.i.185.

All-hallown summer, summer lasting into winter and so vigour of manhood in age, *1 Hen. 4*, 1.ii.153.

all hid, hide and seek, *L. Lab. Lost*, 4.iii.74.

allicholy, melancholy, *Mer. Wives Win.*, 1.iv.138.

Almain, German, *Oth.*, 2.iii.77.

alms drink, taken on another's behalf, *Ant. and Cleo.*, 2.vii.5.

ames-ace, both aces, lowest throw with two dice, *All's Well*, 2.iii.77.

amort, *all amort*, almost dead, *Tam. Shrew*, 4.iii.36.

anchor, hermit, *Ham.*, 3.ii.214.

ancient, from ensign or standard-bearer, *Oth.*, 1.i.33.

angel, gold coin stamped with image of angel, worth about ten shillings, *Mer. Ven.*, 2.vii.55-7.

Anthropophagi, cannibals, *Oth.*, 1.iii.144; *Anthropophaginian*, *Mer. Wives Win.*, 4.v.8.

antic, odd, unusual, *Ham.*, 1.v.172.

antre, cave, *Oth.*, 1.iii.140.

appellant, challenger, *Rich. 2*, 1.iii.4.

apple-john, a sound but wither'd-looking apple, *1 Hen. 4*, 3.iii.4.

aqua-vitæ, whisky, *Mer. Wives Win.*, 2.ii.271.

Aquilon, north wind, *Troil. and Cres.*, 4.v.9.

Arabian bird, phoenix, *Ant. and Cleo.*, 3.ii.12.

arch, patron, *Lear*, 2.i.59.

argal, argo, ergo, therefore, *Ham.*, 5.i.12.

Ariachne, Arachne, changed to a spider for pride in her weaving by Athene, *Troil. and Cres.*, 5.ii.150.

arm-gaunt (doubtful), *Ant. and Cleo.*, 1.v.48.

armipotent, strong in arms, *L. Lab. Lost*, 5.ii.636.

aroint, away ! *Mac.*, 1.iii.6.

Arthur (i) *Arthur's show*, display of archery by London company called Prince Arthur's Knights, *2 Hen. 4*, 3.ii.272. (ii) *Arthur's bosom*, malapropism for Abraham's bosom, *Hen. 5*, 2.iii.9.

artist, learned practitioner, *Troil. and Cres.*, 1.iii.24.

assinego, ass, *Troil. and Cres.*, 2.i.43.

Astraea, goddess of Justice, *Titus*, 4.iii.4.

atone, unite, *Cor.*, 4.vi.73.

Atropos, one of the Fates, *2 Hen. 4*, 2.iv.189.

auricular, through the ear, *Lear*, 1.ii.88.

bacare, go back, *Tam. Shrew*, 2.i.73.

back-friend, the officer who arrests you from behind, *Com. Err.*, 4.ii.37.

backsword-man, a single-stick performer, *2 Hen. 4*, 3.ii.63.

back-trick, a movement in some dance, *Tw. Night*, 1.iii.115.

baffle, to proclaim one a perjured knight, *1 Hen. 4*, 1.ii.98; shame, *Tw. Night*, 2.v.142.

bait, to set on dogs to worry an animal, as in a baiting-place, *2 Hen. 6*, 5.i.150; to catch as with a bait, *Com. Err.*, 2.i.94.

baldrick, cross belt from shoulder to carry sword or bugle, *Much Ado*, 1.i.209.

balk, to miss an opportunity or prey, *Tw. Night*, 3.ii.23; chop logic, *Tam. Shrew*, 1.i.34.

ballow, cudgel, *Lear*, 4.vi.243.

ban, prohibit, *Oth.*, 2.i.11; curse, *2 Hen. 6*, 3.ii.333.

bandy, to exchange blows or words or looks (as strokes in a rally at tennis), *Lear*, 1.iv.83.

bank, sea-shore, *Troil. and Cres.* 1.iii.328; sand-bank, *Mac.*, 1.vii.6; to take in (as banker at card game), *John*, 5.ii.104.

Barbason, a devil, *Mer. Wives Win.*, 2.ii.265.

barbed, protected on breast and flanks, of horse, *Rich. 3*, 1.i.10.

barful, difficult, *Tw. Night*, 1.iv.40.

barm, yeast, *Mid. N. Dr.*, 2.i.38.

barne, child, *Much Ado*, 3.iv.42.

barnacle, a goose, *Tem.*, 4.1.247.

Bartholomew, *-tide,* 24th August, *Hen. 5*, 5.ii.303; *boar-pig*, kind sold at Bartholomew fair, *2 Hen. 4*, 2.iv.221.

base, course, as at game of prisoners' base, *Cym.*, 5.iii.20.

base-court, lower court of castle (as *basse-cour* in French), *Rich. 2*, 3.iii.176.

bases, cloth extensions to knee, worn by mounted knights, *Per.*, 2.i.159.

Basilisco, character in play of 'Soliman and Perseda', *John*, 1.i.244.

basilisk, the fabled cockatrice that kills with its look, *Win. Tale*, 1.ii.388; cannon, *Hen. 5*, 5.ii.17.

basimecu, corruption of 'baisez ma queue', *2 Hen. 6*, 4.vii.26.

basta, enough ! *Tam. Shrew*, 1.i.193.

bastard, sweet wine from Spain, *1 Hen. 4*, 2.iv.25.

bate, beat or flutter like a bird's wings, *Rom. and Jul.*, 3.ii.14; to blunt or weaken, *Timon*, 3.iii.26.

bat-fowling, catching birds at night by dazzling them with a light, *Tem.*, 2.i.176.

batler, wooden instrument for use in washing clothes, *As You Like*, 2.iv.46.

batten, eat voraciously, *Ham.*, 3.iv.67.

bavin, brushwood, easily kindled, *1 Hen. 4*, 3.ii.61.

bawbling, of little account, *Tw. Night*, 5.i.48.

bawcock, stout fellow (French, *beau coq*), *Hen. 5*, 3.ii.24.

bay, to pursue with barking, to bring the quarry to a stand, *Mid. N. Dr.*, 4.i.110.

beagle, a small type of hound, *Tw. Night*, 2.iii.168.

beam, in contrast to the 'mote', as in Matthew's gospel, *L. Lab. Lost*, 4.iii.158.

bear, to obtain, *Oth.*, 1.iii.23; to regard with hate, *Jul. Caes.*, 2.i.215.

bear-herd *or* **bear-ward** (berrord), one who keeps a bear for exhibition, *Much Ado*, 2.i.34.

bearing-cloth, christening robe, *1 Hen. 6*, 1.iii.42.

beated, (*perhaps*) lined or wrinkled, *Son.*, 62, 10.

beaver, face-piece of helmet, *Ham.*, 1.ii.229; the helmet as a whole, *1 Hen. 4*, 4.i.104.

bedlam (i) an asylum, the word being derived from Bethlehem, the name of the London hospital, *2 Hen. 6*, 5.i.131; (ii) a crazed person, *John*, 2.i.183.

beetle (i) a heavy rammer for flattening earth, *2 Hen. 4*, 1.ii.215. (ii) overhanging, *Rom. and Jul.*, 1.iv.32.

beldam, a grandmother, old woman, *Lucrece*, 953.

be-lee'd, cut off from the wind and so stationary, *Oth.*, 1.i.30.

bell (book and candle), expression used in excommunication, *John*, 3.iii.12.

bell-wether, sheep carrying bell round neck to guide the flock, *As You Like*, 3.ii.71.

be-mete, to thrash, *Tam. Shrew*, 4.iii.112.

bench, the seat of authority, or those who sit in it, *Cor.*, 3.i.106.

bend, glance, *Jul. Caes.*, 1.ii.123.

benevolence, a loan exacted by the king on the pretext that the payment is a gesture of good will, *Rich. 2*, 2.i.250.

beray, to befoul, *Titus*, 2.iii.222.

bergomask, a rustic dance, *Mid. N. Dr.*, 5.i.350.

berrord, *see* bear-herd.

beshrew (a good-natured imprecation), plague on or curse whatever follows, *Rom. and Jul.*, 5.ii.26.

beteem, to allow, *Ham.*, 1.ii.141.

Bevis, of Southampton, whose prodigies were told by the early romancers, *Hen. 8*, 1.i.38.

bezonian, a needy rascal, *2 Hen. 6*, 4.i.134.

bias, oblique course, like the curve made by the bowl, *Ham.*, 2.i.65.

bifold, twofold, *Troil. and Cres.*, 5.ii.142.

bigamy, marriage with a widow as in *Rich. 3*, 3.vii.189.

biggen, night-cap, *2 Hen. 4*, 4.v.27.

bilbo, a sword, good swords were made in Bilbao, *Mer. Wives Win.*, 3.v.98.

bilboes, irons for mutinous sailors, *Ham.*, 5.ii.6.

bill, a weapon like a pole-axe; *bills*, the troops so armed, *Lear*, 4.vi.91.

bird-bolt, blunted arrow for shooting birds, *L. Lab. Lost*, 4.iii.20.

bisson, blind, blinding, *Ham.*, 2.ii.500.

Black Monday, Easter Monday, *Mer. Ven.*, 2.v.24 (from storm of 1360 when English troops outside Paris suffered greatly).

blank (i) white spot in centre of target, aiming point, *Ham.*, 4.i.42; (ii) a document to be filled in as the holder decides, *Rich. 2*, 2.i.250.

blazon, (i) coat of arms, *Mer. Wives Win.*, 5.v.62. (ii) from the meaning of describing a coat of arms it comes to mean merely a description or announcement, *Ham.*, 1.v.21.

blear, to hoodwink, *Tam. Shrew*, 5.i.104.

blister'd, puffed out, *Hen. 8*, 1.iii.31.

block, wooden shape on which hats are moulded, *Much Ado*, 1.i.63.

blood-bolter'd, the hair matted with blood, *Mac.*, 4.i.123.

blow, to puff up, *Tw. Night*, 2.v.40; to burst, *Ant. and Cleo.*, 4.vi.34; to defile with their (flies') eggs, *Ant. and Cleo.*, 5.ii.60.

blue-bottle, the beadle, because of his blue coat, *2 Hen. 4*, 5.iv.20.

blue-caps, the Scots with their blue-bonnets, *1 Hen. 4*, 2.iv.347.

bob, a hit or quip, *As You Like*, 2.vii.55.

bob, to steal or cheat, *Troil. and Cres.*, 3.i.65.

bodement, omen, *Mac.*, 4.i.96.

bodkin, dagger, *Ham.*, 3.i.76.

boggler, selfishly unstable, *Ant. and Cleo.*, 3.xiii.110.

bollen, swollen, *Lucrece*, 1417.

bolt, short blunt-headed arrow, *Hen. 5*, 3.vii.119.

bolt, to sift, *Win. Tale*, 4.iv.356.

bolter, for sifting flour, *1 Hen. 4*, 3.iii.69.

bombard, leather bottle for drink, *1 Hen. 4*, 2.iv.436.

bombast, cotton-wool stuffing, *L. Lab. Lost*, 5.ii.769.

bona-roba, showy wanton, *2 Hen. 4*, 3.ii.22.

bones, rural musical instrument, *Mid. N. Dr.*, 4.i.27; bobbins, *Tw. Night*, 2.iv.44.

boot, something extra thrown in, *Troil. and Cres.*, 4.v.40; plunder, *2 Hen. 6*, 4.i.13.

boot-hose, a stocking covering the leg like a jack-boot, *Tam. Shrew*, 3.ii.63.

Boreas, north wind, *Troil. and Cres.*, 1.iii.38.

bosky, with trees and undergrowth, *Tem.*, 4.i.81.

botch (i) *noun*, careless bit in work, *Mac.*, 3.i.133; (ii) *verb*, to patch, *Ham.*, 4.v.10.

bottom (i) valley, *Ven. and Ad.*, 236; (ii) ship, *Mer. Ven.*, 1.i.42; (iii) ball of thread, with *verb* meaning to wind on a core like a ball of thread, *Two Gent. Ver.*, 3.ii.53.

bourn, boundary, but brook in *Lear*, 3.vi.25.

bow hand, the left hand that holds the bow, *L. Lab. Lost*, 4.i.126.

GLOSSARY

brace, armour for the arms, hence armour as a whole, and state of defence, *Oth.*, 1.iii.24.

brach, a kind of hound, *Lear*, 3.vi.68.

bravery, show of courage, *Oth.*, 1.i.101; display as of clothes or feelings, *Tam. Shrew*, 4.iii.57.

brawl, a dance, *L. Lab. Lost*, 3.i.8.

breese, gadfly, *Ant. and Cleo.*, 3.x.14.

Briareus, a hundred-handed giant, *Troil. and Cres.*, 1.ii.28.

brib'd, stolen, *Mer. Wives Win.*, 5.v.22.

brinded, striped, *Mac.*, 4.i.1.

broach, to pierce (broach a cask), *Timon*, 2.ii.178; open a discussion, or enter on some business, *Ant. and Cleo.*, 1.ii.165.

brock, badger, *Tw. Night*, 2.v.95.

brooch, an ornament, so applied to one who is an ornament to his circle, *Ham.*, 4.vii.93.

Brownist, an adherent of the Puritan sect which adopted the principles propagated by Robert Browne about 1580, *Tw. Night*, 3.ii.29.

bruit, *noun,* report, hearsay, *Troil. and Cres.*, 5.ix.4; *verb,* publish broadcast, *Ham.* 1.ii.127.

bubukle, a portmanteau word from ' bubo', an abscess, and carbuncle, *Hen.* 5, 3.vi.99.

buck, the pile of soiled clothes for washing, 2 *Hen.* 6, 4.ii.46; *-ing,* washing, *Mer. Wives Win.*, 3.iii.115; *-basket,* dirty clothes basket, *Mer. Wives Win.*, 3.v.126.

buck, a stag, *Troil. and Cres.*, 3.i.110; named by sportsmen according to the year of its age; 1st fawn, 2nd pricket, 3rd sorell, 4th sore, 5th buck of the first head, 6th a buck, *L. Lab. Lost*, 4.ii.54 sqq. plays upon these terms.

Bucklersbury, the street where the apothecaries sold herbs, *Mer. Wives Win.*, 3.iii.62.

buckram, coarse linen specially treated, 1 *Hen.* 4, 2.iv.186.

buff, strong leather from ox-hide, used for jacket of soldiers, bailiffs, *Com. Err.*, 4.ii.36.

bug, a thing causing fear, 3 *Hen.* 6, 5.ii.2.

bugle, black bead of glass, *As You Like*, 3.v.47.

bulk, framework before shop, *Oth.*, 5.i.1.

bully, often prefixed to express admiration or affection, *Mid. N. Dr.*, 4.ii.18.

bum-baily, bailiff, *Tw. Night*, 3.iv.168.

burden, bass accompaniment to tune, *As You Like*, 3.ii.232; refrain, *Tem.*, 1.ii.380.

burgonet, light helmet, 2 *Hen.* 6, 5.i.200.

buss, *noun and verb,* kiss, 2 *Hen.* 4, 2.iv.258.

buzzard, a hawk of a type useless for falconry, *Tam. Shrew*, 2.i.206.

cacodemon, evil spirit, *Rich.* 3, 1.iii.144.

caddis, garter-tape, *Win. Tale*, 4.iv.205.

cade, herring-barrel, 2 *Hen.* 6, 4.ii.32.

cadent, falling, *Lear*, 1.iv.285.

Cadmus, founder and king of Thebes, *Mid. N. Dr.*, 4.i.109.

caduceus, Mercury's wand, *Troil. and Cres.*, 2.iii.11.

Cain-coloured, reddish, the traditional colour of his hair, *Mer. Wives Win.*, 1.iv.21.

Calipolis, wife of Muly Mahamet in Peele's ' Alcazar', 2 *Hen.* 4, 2.iv.169.

caliver, musket, 1 *Hen.* 4, 4.ii.19.

call, decoy, *John*, 3.iv.174.

callat, contemptuous term for a woman, *Win. Tale*, 2.iii.90.

Cambyses vein, in the style of the old play ' Cambises, King of Percia', 1 *Hen.* 4, 2.iv.376.

canary (i) sweet wine from the Canaries, *Tw. Night*, 1.iii.79; (ii) Spanish dance, *All's Well*, 2.i.73.

canker, ulcer-like evil or sore, 2 *Hen.* 6, 1.ii.18; evil that like caterpillar destroys promise of our nature, *Ham.*, 5.ii.69.

canon, church law, then any rule, *e.g.*, grammatical, as in *Cor.*, 3.i.90.

cantle, a part cut out, *Ant. and Cleo.*, 3.x.6.

canton, song, *Tw. Night*, 1.v.254.

canzonet, short song, *L. Lab. Lost*, 4.ii.115.

cap-a-pe, from head to foot, *Ham.*, 1.ii.200.

Capitol, temple of Jupiter at Rome, *Jul. Caes.*, 1.iii.20.

capocchia, simpleton, *Troil. and Cres.*, 4.ii.31.

carack, galleon, *Oth.*, 1.ii.50.

carbonado, meat prepared for cooking by scoring with knife, *Cor.*, 4.v.187.

carcanet, a necklace, *Com. Err.*, 3.i.4.

cardecue, ' quart d'ecu ', French silver coin, *All's Well*, 4.iii.259.

Carduus Benedictus, the blessed thistle, regarded as a kind of cure-all, *Much Ado*, 3.iv.65.

carpet, *consideration,* for services not on the field of battle, *Tw. Night*, 3.iv.224.

Cataian, a Chinaman, *Tw. Night*, 2.iii.73.

cataplasm, poultice, *Ham.*, 4.vii.143.

catch, musical composition for several voices, *Tw. Night*, 2.iii.86.

cater-cousins, intimates, *Mer. Ven.*, 2.ii.119.

cat-o'-mountain, a spotted creature as in Bishop's version of *Jer.*, xiii.23, ' May a man of Inde chaunge his skinne, and the catte of the mountaine her spots', *Tem.*, 4.i.260.

cautel, deceit, *Ham.*, 1.iii.15.

cautelous, crafty, *Jul. Caes.*, 2.i.129.

caviary, salted roe of sturgeon, *Ham.*, 2.ii.430.

cerecloth, winding-sheet, *Mer. Ven.*, 2.vii.51.

chace, term from tennis, *Hen.* 5, 1.ii.266.

champaign, flat country where view is extensive, *Tw. Night*, 2.v.142.

champion, to challenge, *Mac.*, 3.i.71.

changeling, child left by the fairies for one they have stolen, *Mid. N. Dr.*, 2.i.120 (here, a child adopted by the fairies).

chanson, song, *Ham.*, 2.ii.414.

chape, the scabbard, or its metal point, *All's Well*, 4.iii.136.

chapless, with lower jaw gone, *Ham.*, 5.i.87.

chapman, merchant, *L. Lab. Lost*, 2.i.16.

character, *noun,* writing; *verb,* to write, *Ham.*, 1.iii.59.

chare, chore, *Ant. and Cleo.*, 4.xv.75.

charge-house (doubtful) perhaps a school, *L. Lab. Lost*, 5.i.70.

Chartreux, the Charterhouse in London, *Hen.* 8, 1.ii.148.

chaudron, entrails, *Mac.*, 4.i.33.

chequin, gold coin, *Per.*, 4.ii.25.

cheveril, flexible leather, easily manipulated, *Tw. Night*, 3.i.11.

chewet, a jackdaw, and so applied to the talkative, 1 *Hen.* 4, 5.i.29.

chopine, shoe with high sole, *Ham.*, 2.ii.422.

chough, crow or jackdaw, *Tem.*, 2.i.257.

chrisom, a child still in its christening-robe, *Hen.* 5, 2.iii.11.

chrysolite, a precious green stone, *Oth.*, 5.ii.148.

cicatrice, a mark of, or like, a scar, *Cor.*, 2.i.140.

cinquepace, brisk dance, *Tw. Night*, 1.iii.122.

Cinque-ports, five English channel ports, *Hen.* 8, 4.i.49.

Circe, the enchantress, a draught from whose cup turned men to swine, *Com. Err.*, 5.i.270.

citizen, city-bred, *Cym.*, 4.ii.8.

cittern, a guitar-like instrument, often with a curiously carved head, *L. Lab. Lost*, 5.ii.603.

civet, perfume, *Lear*, 4.vi.130.

clack-dish, beggar's wooden disk with lid for clacking, *M. Meas.*, 3 ii.118.

clearstories, upper range of windows in cathedral, *Tw. Night*, 4.ii.37.

clepe, to call, *Ham.*, 1.iv.19.

clerk, scholar, *Mid. N. Dr.*, 5.i.93.

clew, ball of thread, *All's Well*, 1.iii.173.

climatures, regions, *Ham.*, 1.i.125.

cling, shrivel up, *Mac.*, 5.v.40.

clinquant, glittering, *Hen.* 8, 1.i.19.

clip, embrace, *John*, 5.ii.34.

clipper, one who pares off the edges of coin of the realm, *Hen.* 5, 4.i.225.

clisterpipe, syringe, *Oth.*, 2.i.175.

clout, mark at archery, 2 *Hen.* 4, 3.ii.45.

cobloaf, a little loaf with a round head, *Troil. and Cres.*, 2.i.36.

cock, perversion of 'God', in oaths, 2 *Hen. 4*, v.i.1.

cockatrice, *see* basilisk.

cockle, the tares that grow with the corn, so of evil disposition, *Cor.*, 3.i.70.

cockle shell, scallop shell worn by pilgrims returning from shrine of St. James of Compostella in Spain, *Ham.*, 4.v.25.

cockney, useless fellow, *Tw. Night*, 4.i.13.

Cocytus, one of the five rivers of the underworld, *Titus*, 2.iii.236.

coffin, pie-crust, *Titus*, 5.ii.190.

cog, cheat, wheedle, *Timon*, 5.i.93.

cognizance, a device worn by a gentleman's retainers, so a token, 1 *Hen. 6*, 2.iv.108.

coign, projecting corner, *Mac.*, 1.vi.7.

coil, troublesome affair, *Ham.*, 3.i.67.

coistrel, knave, *Tw. Night*, 1.iii.37.

Colbrand, Danish giant, conquered by Sir Guy of Warwick, *Hen. 8*, 5.iv.20.

collection, inference, *Ham.*, 4.v.9.

collied, overcast and troubled, *Oth.*, 2.iii.198.

Colme-kill, Iona (Columba's cell), *Mac.*, 2.iv.33.

coloquintida, drug from bitter-apple, *Oth.*, 1.iii.347.

Colossus, huge bronze statue of Apollo at harbour of Rhodes, *Jul. Caes.*, 1.ii.136.

colour, (often) deceitful appearance, *Two Gent. Ver.*, 4.ii.3.

comart, bargain, agreement, *Ham.*, 1.i.93.

combination, alliance, treaty, *Hen. 8*, 1.ii.169.

comedle, mingle, *Ham.*, 3.ii.67.

commodity, profit, *John*, 2.i.574; merchandise.

competitor, partner, *Ant. and Cleo.*, 5.i.42.

complexion, appearance as governed by the predominant 'humour', *L. Lab. Lost*, 1.ii.81.

compt, reckoning and so Day of Judgment, *Oth.*, 5.ii.276.

con, learn, *Jul Caes.*, 4.iii.97.

conceit, thought, *Mer. Ven.*, 1.i.92.

congied, taken ceremonious farewell, *All's Well*, 4.iii.83.

conscience, knowledge (shading off when of right and wrong into modern meaning), *Ham.*, 3.i.83.

constringe, drawn together, *Troil. and Cres.*, 5.ii.171.

contraction, pledged faith, *Ham.*, 3.iv.46.

conversion, promotion, *John*, 1.i.189.

convince, overpower, *Mac.*, 1.vii.64.

cony-catch, to cheat, *Mer. Wives Win.*, 1.iii.31.

copatain, high-crowned hat, *Tam. Shrew*, 5.i.57.

copp'd, pointed, *Per.*, 1.i.101.

copy, example to follow, as at head of a copy-book, *All's Well*, 1.ii.46; notion of pattern combined with that of tenure, by copyhold, *Mac.*, 3.ii.38.

coranto, a dance, *Hen. 5*, 3.v.33.

Corinth, Corinthian, life in Corinth was supposed to be very gay, 1 *Hen. 4*, 2.iv.11.

corky, pithless, *Lear*, 3.vii.28.

cornet, body of mounted troops, 1 *Hen. 6*, 4.iii.25.

corollary, some extra, *Tem.*, 4.i.57.

corporal, a senior rank in Shakespeare's day, *L. Lab. Lost*, 3.i.177.

costard, head, from name for large apple, *Rich. 3*, 1.iv.151.

cote, pass (from coursing, when one dog outruns the other), *Ham.*, 2.ii.315.

Cotswold, Cotsall, this district in Gloucestershire was famous for its coursing contests, *Mer. Wives Win.*, 1.i.80.

counter, used with *hunting* when dogs follow the scent in the wrong direction; play on this meaning and counter = debtors' prison in *Com. Err.*, 4.ii.39.

counterfeit, portrait, *Mer. Ven.*, 3.ii.115.

counter-gate, debtors' prison, *Mer. Wives Win.*, 3.iii.67.

courage, disposition, desire, comrade (as Folio reads for 'courage' at *Ham.*, 1.iii.65).

court-hand, style of script used in legal documents, 2 *Hen. 6*, 4.ii.89.

cousin, coz, a relative of some kind, or courtesy title, *John*, 3.iii.17.

cozen, to cheat, *Lucrece*, 387.

cozier, cobbler, *Tw. Night*, 2.iii.86.

crack, bright lad ('young rascal'), *Cor.*, 1.iii.68.

crank (i) *noun*, twisting passages, *Cor.*, 1.i.135; (ii) *verb*, to twist and turn, *Ven. and Ad.*, 682.

crants, a garland, *Ham.*, 5.i.226.

crare, small coasting vessel, *Cym.*, 4.ii.206.

cross-row, the alphabet, the row in the primer containing it being marked with a cross, *Rich. 3*, 1.i.55.

crow-flower, buttercup, or (perhaps) Ragged Robin, *Ham.*, 4.vii.170.

crow-keeper, scare-crow, *Lear*, 4.vi.88.

crown-imperial, a kind of lily, *Win. Tale*, 4.iv.126.

crusado, Portuguese gold coin stamped with a cross, *Oth.*, 3.iv.23.

cry, pack of hounds or rascals, *Cor.*, 3.iii.121.

cry aim, 'good shot!' *John*, 2.i.196.

cullion, low fellow, *Hen. 5*, 3.ii.20.

culverin, cannon, long in proportion to its calibre, 1 *Hen. 4*, 2.iii.50.

cunning (i) *noun*, knowledge, skill; (ii) *adj.*, learned, clever (not always in bad sense as to-day), *Rom. and Jul.*, 4.ii.2.

Cupid's flower, love-in-idleness, the pansy, *Mid. N. Dr.*, 2.i.168 and 4.i.70.

curiosity, critical examination, *Lear*, 1.i.6.

curious, careful, *All's Well*, 1.ii.20; finely made, *Ven. and Ad.*, 734.

curst, sharp in tone or temper, *Tw. Night*, 3.ii.39.

cushes, thigh-armour, 1 *Hen. 4*, 4.i.105.

custalorum, nonsense for 'Custos Rotulorum' Keeper of the Rolls, *Mer. Wives Win.*, 1.i.6.

cut, working-horse or gelding, so as term of contempt, and the point of *Tw. Night*, 2.v.81.

cynic, blunt fellow like Diogenes, *Jul. Caes.*, 4.iii.131.

cypress, garment of crape, *Tw. Night*, 3.i.118.

daff, put off, thrust aside, 1 *Hen. 4*, 4.i.96.

Dagonet, Arthur's fool, 2 *Hen. 4*, 3.ii.272.

Damascus, regarded as the place where Cain killed Abel, 1 *Hen. 6*, 1.iii.39.

dancing horse, a performing horse called Morocco exhibited by its owner Banks about 1590, *L. Lab. Lost*, 1.ii.53.

dancing-rapier, for show only, *Titus*, 2.i.39.

Daphne, a nymph loved by Apollo and turned to a laurel tree, *Mid. N. Dr.*, 2.i.231.

dare (fowling term) to render the bird immobile by dazzling it by some device, *Hen. 5*, 4.ii.36.

darraign, set in order, 3 *Hen. 6*, 2.ii.72.

daub, keep up the pretence, *Lear*, 4.i.53.

daubery, pretence, *Mer. Wives Win.*, 4.ii.155.

day-bed, couch, *Tw. Night*, 2.v.45.

dearth, value, *Ham.*, 5.ii.117.

death-practis'd, marked for death by his enemies, *Lear*, 4.vi.277.

death-token, the mark of the plague and so of death, *Troil. and Cres.*, 2.iii.172.

debile, feeble, *Cor.*, 1.ix.48.

deboshed, debauched, *Lear*, 1.iv.241.

decimation, execution of every tenth man, *Timon*, 5.iv.31.

deck, pack of cards, 3 *Hen. 6*, 5.i.44.

decoct, heat up, *Hen. 5*, 3.v.20.

defunctive, funereal, *Phoenix*, 13.

degree, the principle of order by which persons (or objects) stand in proper relation to one another, *Troil. and Cres.*, 1.iii.109.

delate, dilate, express at length, *Ham.*, 1.ii.38.

delation, expression of accusation, *Oth.*, 3.iii.127.

demerit, (i) merit, *Oth.*, 1.ii.22; (ii) fault, *Mac.*, 4.iii.226.

demi-cannon, gun of large calibre, *Tam. Shrew*, 4.iii.88.

denier, French copper coin of small value, *Rich. 3*, 1.ii.251.

dependency, objects depending, *Cym.*, 2.iii.118.

depose (i) set aside, *Rich.* 2, 3.ii.56; (ii) assert on oath, *M. Meas.*, 5.i.196; (iii) examine on oath, *Rich.* 2, 1.iii.30.

deputation, office of deputy, *Troil. and Cres.*, 1.iii.152; 1 *Hen.* 4, 4.iii.87.

dern, dark, *Lear*, 3.vii.62.

derogate, unworthy, to prove unworthy of position or descent, *Lear*, i.iv.280.

descant, comment (from the term that refers to the upper and more elaborate part of a musical composition), *Rich.* 3, 3.vii.49.

determinate, purposed, conclusive, *Tw. Night* 2.i.9; *Oth.*, 4.ii.226.

determination, decision, *Troil. and Cres.*, 2.ii.173.

determine, end, *Cor.*, 3.iii.43.

deuce-ace, throw of two and one at dice, *L. Lab. Lost*, 1.ii.46.

dexter, right, *Troil. and Cres.*, 4.v.128.

dial, watch, *As You Like*, 2.vii.20.

diapason, bass part, *Lucrece*, 1132.

difference, distinction of rank or descent or character, *All's Well*, 2.iii.119.

diffidence, distrust, 1 *Hen.* 6, 3.iii.10.

digression, transgression, *L. Lab. Lost*, 1.ii.112.

dilate, *see* delate.

dilemmas, alternatives, *All's Well*, 3.vi.67.

disaster, unfavourable aspect, *Ham.* 1.i.118.

discandy, melt, *Ant. and Cleo.*, 4.xii.22.

discernings, faculties requisite for judgment, *Lear*, 1.iv.227.

discomfortable, discouraging, *Rich.* 2, 3.ii.36.

discontent, one not satisfied with his conditions, *Ant. and Cleo.*, 1.iv.39.

discourse, power or process of reasoning, *Ham.*, 4.iv.36; *Troil. and Cres.*, 5.ii.140.

discover, to reveal what is known to the speaker, *Rom. and Jul.*, 3.i.39; to find out, *Rich.* 2, 2.iii.33.

discovery, revelation, *Ham.*, 2.ii.293.

discreet, indiscreet, 2 *Hen.* 4, 2.iv.240.

disguise, state of drunkenness, *Ant. and Cleo.*, 2.vii.122.

disme, tenth man, *Troil. and Cres.*, 2.ii.19.

dismount, draw sword from its scabbard, *Tw. Night*, 3.iv.213.

dispark, open land to public use, *Rich.* 2, 3.i.23.

dispose, *noun*, disposal, *Two Gent. Ver.* 2.vii.86; disposition, *Troil. and Cres.*, 2.iii.159; *verb*, arrange, *John*, 3.iv.11.

disposer, one who has the matter in her control, *Troil. and Cres.*, 3.i.81.

disposition, arrangement, *Oth.*, 1.iii.236; behaviour, mood, *Ham.*, 1.v.172.

disproperty, to take away from their possession, *Cor.*, 2.i.238.

distance, dissension, *Mac.*, 3.i.115; space between fencers, *Rom. and Jul.*, 2.iv.21.

distemperature, lack of order and so inclemency in weather or illness in man, *Mid. N. Dr.*, 2.i.106; *Per.*, 5.i.27.

distinction, judgment, *Troil. and Cres.*, 3.ii.26; the clear and true apprehension of the matter, *Cym.*, 5.v.384.

distinctly, in several separate parts, *Tem.*, 1.ii.200.

distinguishment, distinction, *Win. Tale*, 2.i.86.

distract, *adj.*, divided, and so divided in mind, crazed, *Lov. Comp.*, 231; *Jul. Caes.*, 4.iii.153; *verb*, to divide out, *Oth.*, 1.iii.323.

distrain, to take legal possession of goods, etc., to cover debt, to take over, *Rich.* 2, 2.iii.131.

distressful, earned by toil and sweat, *Hen.* 5, 4.i.266.

divers, diverse, unorthodox in *Hen.* 8, 5.iii.18.

division, proper disposition of forces, *Oth.*, 1.i.23; decorative elaboration of a musical theme, 1 *Hen.* 4, 3.i.210.

doctrine, precept, principle, learning, *L. Lab. Lost*, 4.iii.346.

document, a piece of instruction, *Ham.*, 4.v.175.

doit, a Dutch coin of small value, *Cor.*, 4.iv.17.

dollar, English name for German thaler, a large silver coin, *Mac.*, 1.ii.64.

dominical, letter which was printed in red in the almanacs, so a reference to the lady's hair and complexion, *L. Lab. Lost*, 5.ii.44.

doom, judgment, 2 *Hen.* 6, 3.i.281; *day of doom, doomsday*, day of one's death, 3 *Hen.* 6, 5.vi.93; *Rom. and Jul.*, 5.iii.233.

double-fatal, the yew yielding the wood for bow and poisonous berries, *Rich.* 2, 3.ii.117.

doublet and hose, the dress of a man, hence his characteristics, *As You Like*, 3.ii.204; 2 *Hen.* 6, 4.vii.47, implies that plain men have to go simply dressed without a cloak.

dout, extinguish, *Hen.* 5, 4.ii.11.

dowlas, coarse linen, 1 *Hen.* 4, 3.iii.68.

dowle, feather, *Tem.*, 3.iii.65.

doxy, beggar's trull, *Win. Tale*, 4.iii.2.

drachma, silver coin of antiquity, *Jul. Caes.*, 3.ii.243.

draught, cesspool, *Timon*, 5.i.100.

draw dry-foot, to track by the scent of the footmarks, *Com. Err.*, 4.ii.39.

drawer, tapster, 1 *Hen.* 4, 2.iv.7.

dribbling, falling wide of the mark, *M. Meas.*, 1.iii.2.

drift, design, intention, *Rom. and Jul.*, 4.i.114; *Troil. and Cres.*, 3.iii.113.

drollery, puppet-show, *Tem.*, 3.iii.21.

drumble, to move slowly, *Mer. Wives Win.*, 3.iii.130.

ducat, gold coin of about ten shillings value, Italian silver coin, *Ham.*, 2.ii.362.

dudgeon, kind of wood used in dagger-hilts, so the hilt itself, *Mac.*, 2.i.46.

duello, the rules and etiquette of duelling, *L. Lab. Lost*, 1.ii.169.

dump, melancholy tune, *Two Gent. Ver.*, 3.ii.85.

dup, open, *Ham.*, 4.v.51.

durance, lasting nature, *Com. Err.*, 4.iii.24.

eager, sharp, cutting, physically or mentally, *Rich.* 2, 1.i.49; acid, *Ham.*, 1.v.69.

eagerly, relentlessly, *Hen.* 8, 4.ii.24.

eale (perhaps) for evil at *Ham.*, 1.iv.36.

ean, to give birth, *Mer. Ven.*, 1.iii.82.

ear, plough, cultivate, *Rich.* 2, 3.ii.212.

earn, yearn, *Hen.* 5, 2.iii.3.

earnest, token payment as pledge of some service or obligation, *Hen.* 5, 5.i.58.

eche, eke out, *Per.*, 3.Prol.13.

ecstasy, out of one's normal state, madness, stupor, *Tem.*, 3.iii.108; *Ham.*, 2.i.102.

effigies, image, *As You Like*, 2.vii.193.

eftsoons, soon, *Per.*, 5.i.253.

egregious, notable, *Cym.*, 5.v.211.

eisel, vinegar, *Ham.*, 5.i.270.

eld, old age, *M. Meas.*, 3.i.36.

elder-gun, child's toy gun, *Hen.* 5, 4.i.196.

elf, tangle, *Lear*, 2.iii.10.

elf-locks, tangled strands, *Rom. and Jul.*, 1.iv.90.

elm, used as a prop for vines, *Com. Err.*, 2.ii.173.

embarquements, restraints, *Cor.*, 1.x.22.

embossed (i) swollen, *As You Like*, 2.vii.67; (ii) with mouth covered with foam from exertion, *Tam. Shrew*, Ind.i.15.

empiric, empiricutic, unprofessional or quack practitioner and his type of prescription, *All's Well*, 2.i.121; *Cor.*, 2.i.110.

emulous (in both good and bad sense) seeking praise or glory, *Troil. and Cres.*, 2.iii.225.

enew, to drive, as the falcon, the prey into the water, *M. Meas.*, 3.i.92.

enfeoff'd, became the vassal of, gave himself up to, 1 *Hen.* 4, 3.ii.69.

engine, contrivance, weapon of war, *Troil. and Cres.*, 1.iii.208; *Oth.*, 4.ii.216.

engineer, ingener, an inventive mind in words or of devices of war, *Oth.*, 2.i.65.

ensconce, take shelter, *Mer. Wives Win.*, 3.iii.77.

enseamed, greasy, *Ham.*, 3.iv.92.

entertain, receive, as a follower, *Lear*, 3.vi.78.

Ephesian, companion, *Mer. Wives Win.*, 4.v.16.

epithet, epitheton, expression, *Oth.*, 1.i.14.

GLOSSARY

equinox, equal poise, as day and night are equal at the equinox, *Oth.*, 2.iii.116.

ergo, therefore, *Com. Err.*, 4.iii.51.

eringo, candied sweetmeat, *Mer. Wives Win.*, 5.v.19.

escoted, maintained, *Ham.*, 2.ii.342.

esperance, hope, *Lear*, 4.i.4; Percy's battle-cry, 1 *Hen.* 4, 5.ii.97.

estridge, ostrich, 1 *Hen.* 4, 4.i.98.

even Christian, fellow Christian, *Ham.*, 5.i.28.

evitate, avoid, *Mer. Wives Win.*, 5.v.215.

exactly, completely, *Ham.*, 1.ii.200.

except, object, play on legal phrase ' except as before excepted ' at *Tw. Night*, 1.iii.6.

exception, objection, *Ham.*, 5.ii.223.

excitement, encouragement, *Ham.*, 4.iv.58.

excrement, what grows from the body as nails or hair, *Ham.*, 3.iv.121.

exempt, separated from, free from, *As You Like*, 2.i.15; *Timon*, 4.ii.31.

exhalation, meteor, *Jul. Caes.*, 2.1.44.

exhale, draw (your sword), *Hen.* 5, 2.i.60.

exhibition, a maintenance allowance, *Two Gent. Ver.*, 1.iii.69.

exigent, crisis, *Jul. Caes.*, 5.i.19.

exorciser, exorcist, one who calls up spirits, *Cym.*, 4.ii.277.

expectancy, one in whom hopes are placed, *Ham.*, 3.i.152.

expedience, haste, purpose requiring haste, *Ant. and Cleo.*, 1.ii.172.

expiate (literally) ended—the hour of execution has come, *Rich.* 3, 3.iii.23.

expostulate, to discuss, *Ham.*, 2.ii.86.

exposture, exposure, *Cor.*, 4.i.36.

express (as in ' express likeness ') true to divine pattern, *Ham.*, 2.ii.304.

expressure, description, *Tw. Night*, 2.iii.147.

exsufflicate, puffed out, *Oth.*, 3.iii.186.

extemporal, extempore, *L. Lab. Lost*, 4.ii.47.

extirp, to weed out, *M. Meas.*, 3.ii.95.

extraught, descended, 3 *Hen.* 6, 2.ii.142.

extravagancy, extravagant, wandering, *Ham.*, 1.i.154.

eyas, young hawk in training, *Ham.*, 2.ii.335; so *eyas-musket* of a boy at *Mer. Wives Win.*, 3.iii.18.

eye-glass, lens of eye, *Win. Tale*, 1.ii.268.

face, to trim a garment, *Tam. Shrew*, 4.iii.122.

face royal, refers to effigy on gold coin called ' a royal ', 2 *Hen.* 4, 1.ii.22.

facinerous, wicked, *All's Well*, 2.iii.28.

fact, what has been done, action, *Mac.*, 3.vi.10; way of acting, *Win. Tale*, 3.ii.83.

faction, a party group, *Jul. Caes.*, 2.i.77.

fadge, come off, *Tw. Night*, 2.ii.31.

fading, refrain of popular song, *Win. Tale*, 4.iv.193.

fairing, present, *L. Lab. Lost*, 5.ii.2.

faitor, cheat (but Pistol's meaning, if any, is doubtful), 2 *Hen.* 4, 2.iv.150.

falling sickness, epilepsy, *Jul. Caes.*, 1.ii.253.

fame, rumour, *Ant. and Cleo.*, 2.ii.167; reputation, *Ant. and Cleo.*, 3.i.15.

fan, winnowing-fan, *Troil. and Cres.*, 1.iii.27.

fanatical phantasime, individual with crazy but fixed notions, *L. Lab. Lost*, 5.i.16.

fang, seize, *Timon*, 4.iii.23.

fantastic, merely in the fancy, *Rich.* 2, 1.iii.299; unusual, almost incredible, *Troil. and Cres.*, 5.v.38.

fantastico, foolish conceited individual, *Rom. and Jul.*, 2.iv.28.

fantasy, mere fancy, *Ham.*, 1.i.54; musings prompted by responsibility or care, *Jul. Caes.*, 2.i.231.

fap, drunk, *Mer. Wives Win.*, 1.i.160.

farborough, third borough, constable, *L. Lab. Lost*, 1.i.182.

farced, stuffed out with the appearance of dignity, *Hen.* 5, 4.i.259.

fardel, pack or burden, *Ham.*, 3.i.76.

farrow, litter of pigs, *Mac.*, 4.i.65.

farthingale, hooped petticoat, *Mer. Wives Win.*, 3.iii.55.

fashions, a disease in horses, *Tam. Shrew*, 3.ii.49.

fat, hot, 1 *Hen.* 4, 2.iv.1. (*cp. Ham.*, 5.ii.279).

fat, vat, *Ant. and Cleo.*, 2.vii.113.

fatigate, exhausted, *Cor.*, 2.ii.115.

fault, break in the scent in hunting, *Tw. Night*, 2.v.117.

favour, mercy, *Ant. and Cleo.*, 3.xiii.133; charm, *Oth.*, 4.iii.20; token of someone's favour, *Rich.* 2, 5.iii.18; features, *Jul. Caes.*, 2.i.76.

feat, neat, becoming, *Tem.*, 2.i.264.

featly, with neatness and agility, *Tem.*, 1.ii.379.

feature, figure (not face), *Much Ado*, 3.i.60.

fedary, federary, accomplice, *Win. Tale*, 2.i.90.

fee, *sold in fee*, sold with absolute and perpetual possession, *Ham.*, 4.iv.22; *fee-grief*, grief possessed by some individual, *Mac.*, 4.iii.196; *fee-simple*, the most complete and absolute form of tenure or possession, *Rom. and Jul.*, 3.i.31.

feeder, servant, *Ant. and Cleo.*, 3.xiii.109.

felicitate, happy, *Lear*, 1.i.74.

fere, spouse, *Per.*, 1.*Prol*.21.

fern-seed, reputed to make the possessor invisible, 1 *Hen.* 4, 2.i.86.

festinate, speedy, *Lear*, 3.vii.10.

fetch, device, *Ham.*, 2.i.38.

fettle, make ready, *Rom. and Jul.*, 3.v.153.

fico, fig, figo, contemptuous expression, often accompanied by insulting gesture, 2 *Hen.* 4, 5.iii.117.

fights, protective screens used in fighting at sea, *Mer. Wives Win.*, 2.ii.123.

figure, appearance, real, imaginary, or assumed, *Much Ado*, 1.i.12; *Mer. Wives Win.*, 4.ii.193; writing, *Timon*, 5.i.152.

file, list, *Mac.*, 3.i.94.

fills, shafts, *Troil. and Cres.*, 3.ii.44.

film, gossamer, *Rom. and Jul.*, 1.iv.63.

fine, end, *All's Well*, 4.iv.35; conclusion of legal agreement as in *fine and recovery*, a process to break an entail and convert the tenure to fee-simple, *Mer. Wives Win.*, 4.ii.188.

fineless, without end, *Oth.*, 3.iii.177.

fire-drake, meteor, and so in slang a red nose, *Hen.* 8, 5.iv.41.

firk, beat, *Hen.* 5, 4.iv.28.

fit, spasm or attack of some illness, *Ham.*, 4.i.8; trick of grimacing, *Hen.* 8., 1.iii.7; perhaps punning on ' fit ' meaning canto or division of a poem, *Troil. and Cres.*, 3.i.54.

fitchew, polecat, applied to a courtezan, *Oth.*, 4.i.144.

fives, a disease of horses, *Tam. Shrew*, 3.ii.50.

flamen, priest in ancient Rome, *Cor.*, 2.i.203.

flap-dragon, something served in flaming spirits at Christmas parties, *L. Lab. Lost*, 5.i.38; *verb*, to gulp down, *Win. Tale*, 3.iii.95.

flapjack, pancake, *Per.*, 2.i.82.

flaw, gust of wind, or passion, *Cor.*, 5.iii.74.

fleckel'd, dappled, *Rom. and Jul.*, 2.iii.3.

fleer, sneering grimace, *Oth.*, 4.i.82.

flesh (to give a hound the flesh of the victim to rouse its keenness) so to introduce an untried soldier to bloodshed, *Lear*, 2.ii.44; *flesh his sword*, use it in his first fight, 1 *Hen.* 6, 4.vii.36.

fleshment, the satisfaction of a first success, *Lear*, 2.ii.118.

flew'd, with large chaps, *Mid. N. Dr.*, 4.i.117.

flirt-gill, loose woman, *Rom. and Jul.*, 2.iv.149.

flote, sea, *Tem.*, 1.ii.234.

flourish, embellishment, *L. Lab. Lost*, 2.i.14.

flower-de-luce, iris. *Win. Tale*, 4.iv.127; the lily of the French coat of arms, and so applied by Henry to Katherine, *Hen.* 5, 5.ii.208.

flux, secretion, *As You Like*, 3.ii.61.

fob, set aside by trickery, *Cor.*, 1.i.92.

foil (i) setting of a jewel, so something that shows up the value of an act or accomplishment, *Ham.*, 5.ii.247; (ii) *put to the foil*, deprive of commendation, *Tem.*, 3.i.46.

toin, thrust with rapier, *Mer. Wives Win.*, 2.iii.22.

toison, harvest, *Tem.*, 4.i.110.

fondly, foolishly, 2 *Hen. 4*, 4.ii.119.

foot-cloth, saddle-cloth hanging almost to ground, 2 *Hen. 6*, 4.i.54.

foppish, foolish, *Lear*, 1.iv.165.

force (*see* 'farce') stuff. *Troil. and Cres.*, 2.iii.217.

forehorse, leading horse as in a tandem, *All's Well*, 2.i.30.

forgetive (perhaps from 'forge' *cp. Mer. Wives Win.*, 4.ii.199) shaping, inventive, 2 *Hen. 4*, 4.iii.98.

fosset-seller, vendor of taps (faucets) for barrels, *Cor.*, 2.i.65.

fox, a sword (some makes were marked with a wolf's head), *Hen. 5*, 4.iv.9.

tracted, broken, *Hen. 5.* 2.i.121.

frampold, unpleasant, *Mer. Wives Win.*, 2.ii.82.

frank, sty, 2 *Hen. 4*, 2.ii.140.

franklin, freeholder but not numbered among the county families, *Cym.*, 3.ii.76.

frayed, frightened, *Troil. and Cres.*, 3.ii.31.

freshes, springs of fresh water, *Tem.*, 3.ii.64.

fret, to stop the string (with a pun on the normal meaning of 'fret'), *Ham.*, 3.ii.362.

frets, the points marked on the neck of a stringed instrument where the fingers may stop the string, *Lucrece*, 1140.

frieze, coarse cloth, *Oth.*, 2.i.126.

frippery, old clothes shop, *Tem.*, 4.i.225.

frontier, advanced fort, 1 *Hen. 4* 2.iii.49; frontier fortress, *Ham.*, 4.iv.16.

frontlet, band on forehead, so frown at *Lear*, i.iv.187.

frush, to batter, *Troil. and Cres.*, 5.vi.29.

fullam, kind of loaded dice, *Mer. Wives Win.*, 1.iii.82.

fustian (i) coarse cloth; (ii) ranting, 2 *Hen. 4*, 2.iv.179.

fustilarian, (comic formation) 2 *Hen. 4*, 2.i.58.

gaberdine, kind of cloak, *Mer. Ven.*, 1.iii.107.

gad, sharp metal point, *Titus*, 4.i.104; *upon the gad*, on the spur of the moment, *Lear*, 1.ii.26.

gage, pledge, as glove thrown down to pledge the owner to combat, *Rich. 2*, 4.i.25.

gainsay, to forbid, to prevent, *Troil. and Cres.*, 4.v.132.

Galen, Greek who became physician to the Emperor Marcus Aurelius; his voluminous writings on medical topics were authoritative in Shakespeare's day, *All's Well*, 2.iii.11.

gall, bile; as the liver was supposed to provide the capacity for resentment and courage it signifies manly spirit at *Ham.*, 2.ii.572.

Gallian, French, *Cym.*, 1.vi.65.

galliard, a lively dance usually in triple time, *Tw. Night*, 1.iii.125.

galliass, large type of galley, *Tam. Shrew*, 2.i.370.

gallimaufry, hotch potch, *Win. Tale*, 4.iv.321.

gallow, to terrify, *Lear*, 3.ii.44.

gallowglass, heavy-armed footman in army of Irish or from Scottish isles, *Mac.*, 1.ii.13.

gamut, musical scale, *Tam. Shrew*, 3.i.65.

garboil, disturbance, *Ant. and Cleo.*, 1.iii.61.

gaskins, wide breeches, *Tw. Night*, 1.v.23.

gasted, frightened, *Lear*, 2.i.55.

gastness, signs of fear, *Oth.*, 5.i.106.

gaudy night, feast, *Ant. and Cleo.*, 3.xiii.183.

gawds, gay trifles, *Mid. N. Dr.*, 1.i.33.

gaze, centre of attraction, *Mac.*, 5.viii.24.

geck, butt, *Tw. Night*, 5.i.330.

geminy, twin pair, *Mer. Wives Win.*, 2.ii.8.

generosity, the well born, *Cor.*, 1.i.209.

generous, well born, and so acting like a gentleman, *Ham.*, 4.vii.135.

genius, the spirit that is assigned to each individual as a guardian, *Mac.*, 3.i.55; so peculiar bent or nature, *Tw. Night*, 3.iv.123.

gennet, small horse, *Oth.*, 1.i.114.

gentility, gentlemanly conduct, *L. Lab. Lost*, 1.i.127.

gentle, of good birth, *Rich. 3*, 1.iii.73.

gentleness, courtesy, *Troil. and Cres.*, 4.i.22.

George, small figure of St. George slaying the dragon worn as a pendant by Knights of the Garter, *Rich. 3*, 4.iv.366.

german, germane, akin, *Oth.*, 1.i.114; cousin-german, first cousin, *Troil. and Cres.*, 4.v.121; related to the matter in hand, *Ham.*, 5.ii.155.

germen, germ, seed, *Lear*, 3.ii.8.

gest (i) warlike feat, *Ant. and Cleo.*, 4.viii.2; (ii) time limit, *Win. Tale*, 1.ii.41.

ghostly, concerned with spiritual welfare, *Rom. and Jul.*, 3.iii.49.

gib, male cat, *Ham.*, 3.iv.190.

gig, whipping-top, *L. Lab. Lost*, 4.iii.163.

giglet, -ot, a wanton, *M. Meas.*, 5.i.345.

gillyvor, gillyflower, *Win. Tale*, 4.iv.82.

gimmaled, jointed, *Hen. 5*, 4.ii.49.

gimmer, links in mechanism of clock, 1 *Hen. 6*, 1.ii.41.

glance, satirical comment, *As You Like*, 2.vii.57.

glass, hour glass, *Tem.*, 1.ii.240.

glass eyes, spectacles, *Lear*, 4.vi.170.

glaze, glare, *Jul. Caes.*, 1.iii.21.

gleek, to joke, gibe, *Mid. N. Dr.*, 3.i.134.

globe, head, *Ham.*, 1.v.97.

gloss, explanation, excuse, so fair outward show, *Timon*, 1.ii.16.

gloze, to explain, *Hen. 5*, 1.ii.40; to comment deceitfully, *Titus*, 4.iv.35.

gobbet, portions of flesh, 2 *Hen. 6*, 4.i.85.

God-den, God-i-goden (and similar forms) God give you good even! *Rom. and Jul.*, 1.ii.57 and 3.v.172.

God dild you, God yield, or repay, you! *Ham.* 4.v.40.

good year, a common exclamation, without any particular meaning, *Mer. Wives Win.*, 1.iv.110; used in an imprecation, *Lear*, 5.iii.24.

goose, tailor's iron, *Mac.*, 2.iii.15.

gorbellied, fat, overfed, 1 *Hen. 4*, 2.ii.85.

Gordian knot, an oracle foretold that the man who could unloose this intricate knot, in the acropolis of Gordium, would be ruler of the East; Alexander the Great cut it; so of solving a problem, *Hen. 5*, 1.i.46.

gorget, armour for throat, *Troil. and Cres.*, 1.iii.174.

Gorgon, a fabulous monster believed able to turn the beholder to stone, *Mac.*, 2.iii.70.

gospell'd, like good Christians, *Mac.*, 3.i.87.

goss, gorse, *Tem.*, 4.i.180.

gossip, one associated with parents at baptism of their child, a godparent, *Hen. 8*, 5.v.12; friend, woman fond of idle talk, *Titus*, 4.ii.151.

gossiping, enjoying the 'gossips' feast' at the 'rebirth' of the lost sons, *Com. Err.*, 5.i.418.

gourd, loaded dice, *Mer. Wives Win.*, 1.iii.82.

gout, drop, *Mac.*, 2.i.46.

government, self-control, conduct, *Oth.*, 3.iii.260; accordance with musical requirements, *Mid. N. Dr.*, 5.i.123.

graceful, blest with the grace of God, *Win. Tale*, 5.i.171.

graff, shoot, scion, *Per.*, 5.i.59.

graft, to insert shoots and so to incorporate, *Mac.*, 4.iii.51.

grafter, the tree from which the shoot for grafting has been taken, *Hen. 5*, 3.v.9.

grain, *in grain*, dyed in a colour that will not wash out, *Tw. Night*, 1.v.222; *against the grain*, contrary to inclination, *Cor.*, 2.iii.230.

gramercy, expression of thanks, *Mer. Ven.*, 2.ii.110.

grange, a lonely house in the country, *Oth.*, 1.i.107.

grate, to fret, annoy, *Ant. and Cleo.*, 1.i.18.

gratulate, gratifying. *M. Meas.*, 5.i.527.

greasily, indecently, *L. Lab. Lost*, 4.i.130.

great, *great morning*, broad day, *Troil. and Cres.*, 4.iii.1; *great belly doublet*, one stuffed

GLOSSARY

with lining; but Falstaff provided the stuffing himself, *Hen. 5*, 4.vii.46.

Greek, light fellow or wench, *Tw. Night*, 4.i.17.

Greensleeves, a ballad tune not tending to godliness, *Mer. Wives Win.*, 2.i.55.

grievance, inconvenience, affliction, *Two Gent. Ver.*, 1.i.17.

grieve, regret, *Lear*, 4.iii.53.

gripe, vulture, *Lucrece*, 543.

grize, step, *Tw. Night*, 3.i.121; *Oth.*, 1.iii.200.

groat, fourpenny piece, *Mer. Wives Win.*, 1.i.139.

ground, the theme in the bass over which the descant (q.v.) is constructed, so the subject to be elaborated, *Rich. 3*, 3.vii.49.

groundling, one who stood in the yard of the theatre, the cheapest part, *Ham.*, 3.ii.10.

guard, trimming to a garment, *M. Meas.*, 3.i.98; *guarded*, ornamented, *Hen. 8*, Prol. 16, *velvet-guards*, the women wearing them, 1 *Hen. 4*, 3.i.257.

guardant, protector, 1 *Hen. 6*, 4.vii.9.

guidon, pennant, *Hen. 5*, 4.ii.60.

guilder, Dutch coin, but for money generally, *Com. Err.*, 1.i.8.

guise, style, custom, 2 *Hen. 6*, 1.iii.40.

gules, heraldic name for ' red ', *Ham.*, 2.ii.451.

gurnet, fish with large head, 1 *Hen. 4*, 4.ii.12.

gust, taste, *Son.*, 114. 11.

gyves, fetters, *Ham.*, 4.vii.21.

h, *see* ache, *Much Ado*, 3.iv.48.

habiliments, costume, *Tam. Shrew*, 4.iii.166.

habit, costume, (sometimes combined with idea of corresponding) demeanour, *As You Like*, 3.ii.279.

habited, dressed, *Titus*, 2.iii.57.

habitude, nature, *Lov. Comp.*, 114.

hack, of doubtful meaning, *Mer. Wives Win.*, 2.i.45.

hackney, promiscuous wench, *L. Lab. Lost*, 3.i.29.

haggard, wild female hawk in training, *Tam. Shrew*, 4.i.177; so as *adj.*, of woman disobedient or unfaithful, *Oth.*, 3.iii.264.

haggled, with many wounds, *Hen. 5*, 4.vi.11.

hair, *against the hair*, contrary to nature, *Troil. and Cres.*, 1.ii.27; *courser's hair*, supposed to come to life in water, *Ant. and Cleo.*, 1.ii.187.

halberd, axe like weapon with long handle, *Rich. 3*, 1.ii.40.

halcyon (from Halcyone, changed with her husband Ceyx to a type of kingfisher; their breeding season in winter was supposed to be favoured with fine weather) calm, happy, 1 *Hen. 6*, 1.ii.131; a dead kingfisher if hung up was supposed to act as a weather-cock, *Lear*, 2.ii.73.

half-cheek'd, applied to inefficient or deficient bit, *Tam. Shrew*, 3.ii.53.

half-faced, thin faced (like the profile on the groat, a thin coin), *John*, 1.i.92; half seen, 2 *Hen. 6*, 4.i.98.

half sword, most closely engaged, 1 *Hen. 4*, 2.iv.157.

halidom, holidame, an oath (on holy relics) reduced by Shakespeare's time to a mere asseveration, *Two Gent. Ver.*, 4.ii.131.

Hallowmas, 1st Nov. (All Saints' Day), *Rich. 2*, 5.i.80.

hand fast, marriage contract, *Cym.*, 1.v.78.

handsaw (dialect form of ' heronshaw ') heron, *Ham.* 2.ii.375.

hangers, straps supporting scabbard, *Ham.*, 5.ii.154.

harbinger, forerunner, *Ham.*, 1.i.122.

Harry ten shillings, half-sovereign coined in reign of Henry VII, 2 *Hen. 4*, 3.ii.216.

hatchment, tablet showing the coat of arms of the deceased, *Ham.*, 4.v.210.

haught, haughty, 3 *Hen. 6*, 2.i.169.

haughty, ambitious, *Rich. 3*, 4.ii.37.

havoc, general slaughter, *Jul. Caes.*, 3.i.274;

Cor., 3.i.275; *cries on havoc*, the heap of slain speaks of an indiscriminate slaughter, *Ham.*, 5.ii.356.

hay (i) home thrust in fencing, *Rom. and Jul.*, 2.iv.26; (ii) country dance, *L. Lab. Lost*, 5.i.134.

hazard, game with dice, *Hen. 5*, 3.vii.83; risk, *Cor.*, 2.iii.253; term from tennis indicating a scoring stroke, *Hen. 5*, 1.ii.263.

head, muster of men, usually soldiers; rioters at *Ham.*, 4.v.98.

headland, part of field left, for convenience of working, unploughed till the very end, 2 *Hen. 4*, 5.i.13.

hebona (Folio reads *hebenon*) a poison (perhaps henbane, although there seems some reference to ebony), *Ham.*, 1.v.62.

Hecate, divinity of classical antiquity, associated with ghost world and worshipped in triform shape at cross-roads; *triple Hecate*, as Cynthia in heaven, Diana on earth, and Proserpine in hell, *Mid. N. Dr.*, 5.i.373.

hectic, continuous fever, *Ham.*, 4.iii.66.

hedge-pig, hedgehog, *Mac.*, 4.i.2.

heft, heaving, *Win. Tale*, 2.i.45.

hemp-seed, destined for the hangman's hempen rope, 2 *Hen. 4*, 2.i.56.

hent, grasp, or possibly occasion (hint), *Ham.*, 3.iii.88.

herbs of grace, rue, *Ham.*, 4.v.179.

Hercules, *and his load*, the sign hung outside the Globe Theatre showed Hercules carrying the world on his shoulders, *Ham.*, 2.ii.357.

Herod, *out-herods Herod*, to overact even more than the ranting character of Herod in the Miracle plays, *Ham.*, 3.ii.13.

hest, command, *L. Lab. Lost*, 5.ii.65.

hide fox, warning in game of hide-and-seek, *Ham.*, 4.ii.29.

high and low, dice loaded to throw high or low numbers, *Mer. Wives Win.*, 1.iii.83.

hight, named, *L. Lab. Lost*, 1.i.168.

hind, female deer, *As You Like*, 3.ii.91.

hint (sometimes spelt ' hent ' as at *Oth.* (Q1) 1.iii.142), occasion, *Tem.*, 1.ii.134.

hipped, lame, owing to injury to hip-bone, *Tam. Shrew*, 3.ii.48.

Hiren, pun on ' iron ' and Hyrin (Irene) a character in a play by Peele, 2 *Hen. 4*, 2.iv.165.

hive, straw hat, *Lov. Comp.*, 8.

hoar, whitish, *Ham.*, 4.vii.168.

Hobbididence (with Obidicut, Mahu, Modo, Flibberdigibbet), fiends, *Lear*, 4.i.61.

hoby-horse, ' the figure of a horse ' fastened round the waist of a morris dancer; the antics of this particular character in the dance were offensive to the Puritans, and the part came to be omitted, *Ham.*, 3.ii.130; a loose character, *L. Lab. Lost*, 3.i.27.

holding, consistency, *All's Well*, 4.ii.27; chorus of song, *Ant. and Cleo.*, 2.vii.109.

holidame, *see* halidom.

holy-ale (a coinage, by analogy with ' church-ale ', to rhyme with ' festival '; the text has ' holy dayes '), festivity, *Per.*, 1.Gower.6.

holy-rood day, 14th Sept., the feast of the Holy Cross, 1 *Hen. 4*, 1.i.52.

holy thistle, *see* Carduus Benedictus.

honey stalks, clover stalks, *Titus*, 4.iv.91.

honorificabilitudinitatibus, stock example of long word, *L. Lab. Lost*, 5.i.37.

hood, to blindfold hawk (when unhooded it bates), *Hen. 5*, 3.vii.108.

hoodman blind, blind-man's-buff, *Ham.*, 3.iv.77.

horn-book, sheet containing alphabet, etc. for children, protected with transparent covering of horn, *L. Lab. Lost*, 5.i.41.

horologe, clock, *Oth.*, 2.iii.122.

hose, includes various types of breeches and clothing (not stockings) for the lower limbs, 1 *Hen. 4*, 2.iv.208.

howlet, owl, *Mac.*, 4.i.17.

hox, hamstring, *Win. Tale*, 1.ii.244.

hoy, ferry, small vessel, *Com. Err.*, 4.iii.35.

hugger mugger, secretly and without due form, *Ham.*, 4.v.81.

hull, to furl sails and drift with the tide, *Tw. Night,* 1.v.191; so of the mind, *Hen.* 8, 2.iv.199.

humorous, humid, *Rom. and Jul.*, 2.i.31.

humour, corresponding to the four elements (earth, air, fire, water) were the four humours—black bile, blood, bile, phlegm. According as one or other predominated in a man's system so his temperament was choleric or phlegmatic or melancholy, and his complexion in keeping. The term was overworked, and parodied in Nym's use of it, e.g. *Mer. Wives Win.*, 1.i.120.

hunts-up, song to rouse hunters, warning of daybreak. *Rom. and Jul.*, 3.v.34.

hurricano, waterspout, *Lear*, 3.ii.2.

Hydra, many-headed monster, *Oth.*, 2.iii.295.

Hymen, whose presence was invoked at Greek marriages, so regarded as god of marriage; the torch was one of his symbols, *Tem.*, 4.i.23.

hyperbole, figure of speech characterised by exaggeration. *L. Lab. Lost*, 5.ii.407.

Hyperion, god of the sun, *Ham.*, 1.ii.140.

Hyrcania, south-east shore of Caspian sea; regarded as wild country and home of savage beasts; *th' Hyrcanian beast,* the tiger, *Ham.*, 2.ii.444. (Virgil mentions tigers of Hyrcania.)

hysterica passio, hysteria, *Lear*, 2.iv.56.

Icarus, son of Daedalus; father and son imprisoned by Minos of Crete escaped by using artificial wings; Icarus flew too near the sun, the wax of his wings melted and he fell into the Aegean Sea, 3 *Hen.* 6, 5.vi.21.

ice-brook, as giving the keenest temper to the sword-blade, *Oth.*, 5.ii.256.

Iceland dog, type of pet dog, used in derision at *Hen.* 5, 2.i.40.

idea, image, *Rich.* 3, 3.vii.13.

Ides, *of March*, 15th March, *Jul. Caes.*, 1.ii.18.

ignominy, ignomy, disgrace. *Troil. and Cres.*, 5.x.33.

illness, ruthlessness, *Mac.*, 1.v.17.

ill-temper'd, the humours being badly mixed, *Jul. Caes.*, 4.iii.114 (*see* humour).

illustrious, dim (not lustrous), *Cym.*, 1.vi.108.

imaginary, imaginative, *Hen.* 5, *Prol.*18.

imbar, to defend, *Hen.* 5, 1.ii.94.

imbrue, cover with blood, *Mid. N. Dr.*, 5.i.335.

immanity, inhumanity, 1 *Hen.* 6, 5.i.13.

immediately, for that particular case, *Mid. N. Dr.*, 1.i.45.

imminence, threaten'd evil, *Troil. and Cres.*, 5.x.13.

immoment, of no moment. *Ant. and Cleo.*, 5.ii.165.

immures, walled confine, *Troil. and Cres.*, Prol., 8.

impale, empale, encircle, *Troil. and Cres.*, 5.vii.5.

impasted, made into a crust, *Ham.*, 2.ii.453.

impeach, charge, ground of question, 3 *Hen.* 6, 1.iv.60.

impeachment, interference, *Hen.* 5, 3.vi.137; loss, *Two Gent. Ver.*, 1.iii.15.

impertinency, impertinent, what is beside the point, *Lear*, 4.vi.175; *Tem.*, 1.ii.138.

impeticos nonsense formation by fool, *Tw. Night,* 2.iii.25.

impitious, relentless and impetuous, *Ham.*, 4.v.97.

implorator, one who begs, *Ham.*, 1.iii.129.

impone (Q2 impawn) to stake, *Ham.*, 5.ii.146.

importance, importunity, *Tw. Night,* 5.i.350.

important, importunate, *Lear*, 4.vi.26.

importune, require, *M. Meas.*, 1.i.57.

imposition, charge, *M. Meas.*, 1.ii.82.

imposthume, septic swelling, so gathering of unhealthy features in body politic, *Ham.*, 4.iv.27.

imprese, device, family crest, *Rich.* 2, 3.i.25.

impress, call up or levy for war, *Mac.*, 4.i.95.

impugn, question the process, *Mer. Ven.*, 4.i.174.

imputation, prestige, *Troil. and Cres.*, 1.iii.339.

incapable, unable to realise, *Ham.*, 4.vii. 179; beyond the capacity, *Cor.*, 4.vi.121.

incarnadine, dye red, *Mac.*, 2.ii.62.

incarnate, in human form, *Hen.* 5, 2.iii.32.

incarnation and similar formations used of the devil are comic versions of 'incarnate', *Mer. Ven.*, 2.ii.23.

inch, islet, *Mac.*, 1.ii.63.

income, arrival, *Lucrece*, 334.

incomprehensible, beyond all bounds, 1 *Hen.* 4, 1.ii.179.

incontinent, at once (with pun on normal sense), *As You Like*, 5.ii.36.

incony, fine, *L.Lab. Lost*, 3.i.128.

incorporate, bound up together, *Cor.*, 1.i.128.

indent, to zigzag, *Ven. and Ad.*, 704; (from zigzag tear on matching halves of agreement) make a pact with, 1 *Hen.* 4, 1.iii.87.

index, catalogue of contents of work, so indication of what is to follow, *Ham.*, 3.iv.52.

indigested, unshaped, 3 *Hen.* 6, 5.vi.51.

indign, unworthy, *Oth.*, 1.iii.273.

indirect, treacherous, *As You Like*, 1.i.136.

indirection, roundabout process, *Ham.*, 2.i.66.

indirectly, casually, 1 *Hen.* 4, 1.iii.66.

indistinguish'd, boundless, *Lear*, 4.vi.271.

individable, *scene individable,* piece in which unity of place is observed, *Ham.*, 2.ii.395.

induction, first step, 1 *Hen.* 4, 3.i.2.

industrious, skilfully presented, *John*, 2.i.376.

industry, skill, 3 *Hen.* 6, 5.iv.11.

infection, *of a man,* unfinished specimen, *Rich.* 3, 1.ii.78.

infer, to produce evidence or reason for some conclusion or course, *Rich.* 3, 3.vii.12.

influence, what flows in from the stars and affects character or destiny, *M. Meas.*, 3.i.9.

inform, to assume material form, *Mac.*, 2.i.48.

informal, without reason, *M. Meas.*, 5.i.234.

ingenious, quick and sensitive, *Ham.*, 5.i.242; cleverly contrived, *Cym.*, 4.ii.187.

ingeniously, ingenuously, *Timon*, 2.ii.221.

inhabitable, uninhabitable, *Rich.* 2, 1.i.65.

initiate, of a beginner, *Mac.*, 3.iv.143.

inkle, tape, *Win. Tale*, 4.iv.204; thread, *Per.*, v.*Prol.*8.

inland, familiar with good society, *As You Like*, 3.ii.322 (inland, near centres of culture).

insane, causing madness, *Mac.*, 1.iii.84.

insinuate, to assume a cordial form of address, *Rich.* 2, 4.i.165.

insisture, of doubtful meaning. *Troil. and Cres.*, 1.iii.87.

instalment, stall, *Mer. Wives Win.*, 5.v.61.

instance, reason, *Ham.*, 3.ii.177; example, proof *Ham.*, 4.v.159; 2 *Hen.* 4, 3.i.103.

instruction, significance, *Oth.*, 4.i.41.

intelligent, informative, communicative, *Lear*, 3.vii.11.

intentively, with full attention to the whole story, *Oth.*, 1.iii.155.

interess'd, entitled, *Lear*, 1.i.84.

interest, right, title, 1 *Hen.* 4, 3.ii.98.

interlude, an early type of dramatic entertainment, so a bit of play-acting, *Lear*, 5.iii.90.

intituled, displayed (as in heraldry), *Lucrece*, 57.

intrinse, intrinsicate, intricate, *Lear*, 2.ii.70; *Ant. and Cleo.*, 5.ii.302.

investments, attire, *Ham.*, 1.iii.128.

iterance, repetition, *Oth.*, 5.ii.153.

iwis, assuredly, *Rich.* 3, 1.iii.102.

Jack, often used to indicate contempt, *Rich.* 3, 1.iii.53; with reference to knave at cards, *Tem.*, 4.i.197; figure on clock, *Rich.* 3, 4.ii.118; associated with ' Jill ' as common name and as measure of drink, *Tam. Shrew*, 4.i.43; the keys of the virginal (though the jacks were really only attached to the keys), *Son.*, 128, 5.

Jack-a-lent, dummy set up at Lent as a cock-shy. *Mer. Wives Win.*, 5.v.123.

Jack-an-apes, a monkey, *Hen.* 5, 5.ii.141; vain fellow, *All's Well*, 3.v.82.

jade, poor class of horse, *Tam. Shrew*, 1.ii.245.

jakes, privy, *Lear*, 2.ii.61.

jaunce, a going backwards and forwards on tiresome journey, *Rom. and Jul.*, 2.v.26.

jay, bedizzened wench, *Cym.*, 3.iv.47.

jealous, suspicious, *Oth.*, 3.iv.186; on guard against, *Lear*, 5.i.56.

jealous-hood, perhaps just jealous woman, *Rom. and Jul.*, 4.iv.13.

jealousy, fear, *Tw. Night*, 3.iii.8.

jennet, gennet, Spanish horse, *Oth.*, 1.i.114; *Ven. and Ad.*, 260.

jerk, sharp stroke of wit or whip, *L. Lab. Lost*, 4.ii.119.

jerkin, sleeveless jacket worn over doublet, for hard wear often made of leather, *2 Hen. 4*, 2.ii.165.

jesses, straps on the legs of hawk employed in sport, *Oth.*, 3.iii.265.

jet, strut, *Cym.*, 3.iii.5; (jut) intrude upon, *Titus*, 2.i.64.

jig, brisk dance, *Much Ado*, 2.i.62; customary after-piece with dancing to a play, *Ham.*, 2.ii.494.

Jill, see Jack.

Jockey, familiar form of Jack or John, *Rich. 3*, 5.iii.304.

joint-ring, gimmal-ring, in two or more parts, *Oth.*, 4.iii.71 (*see* gimmal-bit).

joint-stool (join-. join'd-) stool carefully carpenter'd, *Rom. and Jul.*, 1.v.5.

jordan, chamber-pot, *1 Hen. 4*, 2.i.18.

journal, daily, *Cym.*, 4.ii.10.

Jovial, *star*, Jupiter's planet which conferred on those who were born when it was in the ascendant a jovial nature, *Cym.*, 5.iv.105.

jowl, to dash, *Ham.*, 5.i.76.

Judas, tradition gave him red hair, *As You Like*, 3.iv.7.

Jug, shortened form of Joan, *Lear*, 1.iv.224.

jump, *noun*, hazard, *Ant. and Cleo.*, 3.viii.6; *verb*, to risk, *Mac.*, 1.vii.7; *adverb*, precisely, *Ham.*, 1.i.65.

jutty, projection, *Mac.*, 1.vi.6; *verb*, overhang, *Hen.* 5, 3.i.13.

juvenal, youth, *L. Lab. Lost*, 1.ii.8.

kam, contrary, *Cor.*, 3.i.304.

kecksy, hemlock-like weed, *Hen.* 5, 5.ii.52.

keech, roll of fat; of butcher's wife, *2 Hen. 4*, 2.i.90; of butcher's son, *Hen. 8*, 1.i.55.

keel, cool, keep pot from boiling over, *L. Lab. Lost*, 5.ii.907.

ken, range of vision, *2 Hen. 4*, 4.i.151.

Kendal green, coarse cloth made in Westmorland, *1 Hen. 4*, 2.iv.215.

kennel, channel, gutter, *2 Hen. 6*, 4.i.71.

kern, light armed Irish soldier, *Rich. 2*, 2.i.156.

kernel, seed, pip, *All's Well*, 2.iii.253.

kersey, coarse woollen cloth, *L. Lab. Lost*, 5.ii.413.

kettle, kettle-drum, *Ham.*, 5.ii.267.

kibe, chilblain on heel, *Ham.*, 5.i.137 (lack of ceremony and respect).

kickshaws, fancy trifle of food or deportment, *2 Hen. 4*, 5.i.27; *Tw. Night*, 1.iii.108.

kicky-wicky, wife, *All's Well*, 2.iii.273.

kiln-hole (doubtful), *Mer. Wives Win.*, 4.ii.48.

kindle (term used of the littering of rabbits) born, *As You Like*, 3.ii.317.

kindly, according to nature, *Much Ado*, 4.i.73; *adverb*, according to her kind (with ironic suggestion of kindness), *Lear*, 1.v.14.

kirtle, skirt, *2 Hen. 4*, 2.iv.264.

kiss, at bowls, balls just touching, *Cym.*, 2.i.2.

kissing-comfit, comfit for sweetening breath, *Mer. Wives Win.*, 5.v.19.

kite, term expressing abhorrence, *Lear*, 1.iv.262.

knap, knock sharply, *Lear*, 2.iv.121.

knot, plot in garden, *Rich. 2*, 3.iv.46.

knot-grass, a weed thought to check the growth of animals, so derisively at *Mid. N. Dr.*, 3.ii.329.

knotted, *curious-knotted*, elaborately laid out, *L. Lab. Lost*, i.1.236.

label, tag to a document to take the seal, *Rom. and Jul.*, 4.i.57.

labras, lips (labra), *Mer. Wives Win.*, 1.i.147.

lace, to trim a garment with, *Much Ado*, 3.iv.18; thread, streak, *Rom. and Jul.*, 3.v.8, *laced mutton*, courtesan, *Two Gent. Ver.*, 1.i.95.

lackey, to follow the movements of the tide as a footman his master, *Ant. and Cleo.*, 1.iv.46.

lade, empty by ladling, *3 Hen. 6*, 3.ii.139.

lady-smock, flower, *L. Lab. Lost*, 5.ii.882.

lag, suggested for 'legge' in Folio as meaning lowest class of people, *Timon*, 3.vi.80.

lag, late; *lag of*, later than, *Lear*, 1.ii.6.

Lammas-tide, 1st August, *Rom. and Jul.*, 1.iii.16; *Lammas Eve*, day before Lammas, *Rom. and Jul.*, 1.iii.18.

lampass, disease of horses, *Tam. Shrew*, 3.ii.48.

landrakers, thieves, *1 Hen. 4*, 2.i.71.

lank, to shrink, *Ant. and Cleo.*, 1.iv.71.

lantern, a vaulted chamber in a turret, *Rom. and Jul.*, 5.iii.84.

lap, to wrap, *Cym.*, 5.v.360; *lapp'd in proof*, clad as in impenetrable armour, *Mac.*, 1.ii.55.

Lapland, regarded as the haunt of witches and sorcerers, *Com. Err.*, 4.iii.11.

lapse, *lapsed*, arrested, *Tw. Night*, 3.iii.36; *laps'd in time and passion*, having allowed passion to fall off and time to pass idly, *Ham.*, 3.iv.107.

lard, to fatten, enrich, *Timon*, 4.iii.12; to cover, *Ham.*, 4.v.36.

latch, to catch, *Mac.*, 4.iii.195; to wound, *Lear*, 2.i.52; to touch, *Mid. N. Dr.*, 3.ii.36.

lath, *dagger of lath*, of wood, *Tw. Night*, 4.ii.122; so sarcastically of real weapon, *Titus*, 2.i.41.

latten, an alloy like brass, *Mer. Wives Win.*, 1.i.146.

lattice, *red lattice*, indicated ale-house, *2 Hen. 4*, 2.ii.76.

laud, hymn, *Ham.*, 4.vii.178.

laund, clearing in forest, *3 Hen. 6*, 3.i.2.

lavolt, lavolta, lively dance, *Hen.* 5, 3.v.33.

law-day, meeting of court *Oth.*, 3.iii.144.

lazar, a leper or an afflicted person, *Ham.*, 1.v.72.

leaguer, camp, *All's Well*, 3.vi.22.

leaping-house, brothel, *1 Hen. 4*, 1.ii.8.

learn, to teach, *Ham.* 5.ii.9.

leash, *leash of drawers*, three tapsters (for hounds were three to a leash), *1 Hen. 4*, 2.iv.6.

leasing, lying, *Tw. Night*, 1.v.91.

leather-coat, russet apple, *2 Hen. 4*, 5.iii.41.

leer, complexion, *Titus*, 4.ii.119; glance, *Mer. Wives Win.*, 1.iii.42.

lees, sediment in wine, *Troil. and Cres.*, 4.i.64.

leet, court under jurisdiction of lord of the manor, *Tam. Shrew*, Ind.ii.85.

Legion, name taken by unclean spirit in Mark, v.9, 'for we are many'; so host of fiends, *Tw. Night*, 3.iv.80.

legitimation, legitimacy, *John*, 1.i.248.

leiger, ambassador, representative, *M. Meas.*, 3.i.60; *Cym.* 1.v.80.

leman, sweetheart, *Tw. Night*, 2.iii.24.

lendings, *Off, off, you lendings*, clothes, as superfluities not given by nature, but lent by art, *Lear*, 3.iv.107.

Lent, forty days fast before Easter, when meat was supposed to be excluded from one's diet, *2 Hen. 4*, 2.iv.335.

lenten, *lenten entertainment*, m.agre like the restricted diet of Lent, *Ham.*, 2.ii.314.

l'envoy, conclusion of poem, marked off as such by form, *L. Lab. Lost*, 3.i.66.

less (sometimes used in negative or virtual negative expressions where meaning is 'more'), *Win. Tale*, 3.ii.54; *Cym.*, 1.iv.21; so *lesser, Troil. and Cres.*, 1.i.28.

GLOSSARY

let, *noun*, impediment, *Hen. 5*, 5.ii.65; *verb*, prevent, *Ham.*, 1.iv.85.

Lethe, 'the river of oblivion' in the underworld; *roots itself in ease on Lethe wharf*, as indifferent to the past, *Ham.*, 1.v.33.

letter, *affect the letter*, employ alliteration, *L. Lab. Lost*, 4.ii.52.

lettered, learned, *L. Lab. Lost*, 5.i.40.

level, *noun*, aim (from gunnery), *Hen. 8*, 1.ii.2; *verb*, aim at, *Ant. and Cleo.*, 5.ii.333.

lewd, of the baser sort, *Much Ado*, 5.i.316.

lewdster, lecherous person, *Mer. Wives Win.*, 5.iii.21.

liable, subject to, influenced by, *John*, 2.i.490.

libbard, leopard, *L. Lab. Lost*, 5.ii.544.

libel, lying publication, *Rich. 3*, 1.i.33.

liberal, becoming the free man or gentleman, *3 Hen. 6*, 1.ii.43; *liberal arts*, those suitable for a gentleman, *Tem.*, 1.ii.73; going beyond manners, gross, *Mer. Ven.*, 2.ii.170.

liberty, licence, *M. Meas.*, 1.iii.29; *liberties*, individual's rights, *Per.*, 1.ii.112; *the law of writ and the liberty*, classical rule and freedom from these canons of composition, *Ham.*, 2.ii.397.

lief, beloved, *2 Hen. 6*, 3.i.164; *had as lief*, would as willingly, *Ham.*, 3.ii.3.

lifter, pun on weight-lifter and thief, *Troil. and Cres.*, 1.ii.112.

lighten, enlighten, *2 Hen. 4*, 2.i.187.

lightning, lightening, a rally of the spirit, *Rom. and Jul.*, 5.iii.90.

light o' love, dance tune, light wench, *Much Ado*, 3.iv.38 and 40.

lily-liver'd, cowardly, *Lear*, 2.ii.15 (see liver).

limbeck, alembic for distilling, *Mac.*, 1.vii.67.

limber, not rigid, *Win. Tale*, 1.ii.47.

Limbo, Limbo patrum, the unbaptised and the virtuous pagans were received here after death; slang for prison, *Hen. 8*, 5.iv.61.

lime, limed, held, as a bird with birdlime, *Ham.*, 3.iii.68; to doctor wine or sack with lime, *Mer. Wives Win.*, 1.iii.14.

line-grove, grove of lime-trees, *Tem.*, 5.i.10.

link, torch, *1 Hen. 4*, 3.iii.42; material of, used as blacking, *Tam. Shrew*, 4.i.118.

linsey-woolsey, mixture of flax and wool; so unintelligible medley at *All's Well*, 4.i.11.

linstock, staff supporting the match with which the gunner touched off the cannon, *Hen. 5*, 3.Chor.33.

list, strip of cloth, *Tam. Shrew*, 3.ii.64; space enclosed for combat, *Mac.*, 3.i.70.

lither, yielding, *1 Hen. 6*, 4.vii.21.

little, *picture in little*, miniature, *Ham.*, 2.ii.362.

livelihood, life, animal vigour, *Ven. and Ad.*, 26.

lively, like life itself, *Timon*, 5.i.80.

liver, regarded as seat of more violent passions: love, courage, anger, *Tw. Night*, 1.i.37; *As You Like*, 3.ii.387; *livers white as milk*, of cowards, *Mer. Ver.*, 3.ii.86.

liver-vein, style of a lover, *L. Lab. Lost*, 4.iii.70.

livery, *sue my livery*, to take proceedings to regain inheritance, *Rich. 2*, 2.iii.129.

livery, to dress as with a livery, *Lov. Comp.*, 105.

lockram, coarse kind of linen, *Cor.*, 2.i.199.

lode-star, guiding-star, *Mid. N. Dr.*, 1.i.183.

lodge, *lodg'd*, flatten'd, *Mac.*, 4.i.55.

loggats, little logs of wood thrown at mark, *Ham.*, 5.i.90.

London-stone (the central milestone of Roman London from which distances were reckoned), ancient stone in Cannon Street, *2 Hen. 6*, 4.vi.2.

long purples, kind of orchis, *Ham.*, 4.vii.170.

long-staff, *sixpenny strikers*, those who would commit robbery with violence for petty sums, *1 Hen. 4*, 2.i.71.

loof, luff, *Ant. and Cleo.*, 3.x.18.

loon, lown, useless fellow, *Mac.*, 5.iii.11.

looped, full of holes, *Lear*, 3.iv.31.

loose, *at his very loose*, at the moment of discharge, *L. Lab. Lost*, 5.ii.730.

lop, smaller branches, *Hen. 8*, 1.ii.96.

Lord's sake, *for the Lord's sake*, the formula in which those imprisoned for debt begged alms of the passers-by, *M. Meas.*, 4.iii.17.

Love-in-idleness, pansy, *Mid. N. Dr.*, 2.i.168.

lozel, rascal, *Win. Tale*, 2.iii.108.

lubber, lout, *Lear*, 1.iv.89.

luce, pike, *Mer. Wives Win.*, 1.i.14.

Lucina, goddess presiding over birth, *Per.*, 3.i.10.

lucre, gain, *1 Hen. 6*, 5.iv.141.

Lud's town, London (the name of the mythical King Lud is preserved in Ludgate), *Cym.*, 3.i.32.

lune, mad fit, *Win. Tale*, 2.ii.30.

Lupercal, Roman festival on 15th February, connected with fertility rites, *Jul. Caes.*, 3.ii.95.

lurch, to deprive, *Cor.*, 2.ii.99.

lure, dummy bird to entice hawk to return, *Tam. Shrew*, 4.i.176.

luxurious, lascivious, *Mac.*, 4.iii.58.

lym, bloodhound, *Lear*, 3.vi.68.

Machiavel, regarded as the type of ruthless schemer, *3 Hen. 6*, 3.ii.193.

maculate, spotted, impure, *L. Lab. Lost*, 1.ii.88; *maculation*, impurity, *Troil. and Cres.*, 4.iv.63.

madrigal, song (though the 'madrigal' was a part-song of a very special type), *Mer. Wives Win.*, 3.i.16.

maggot-pie, magpie, *Mac.*, 3.iv.125.

magnanimous, great-hearted, *Troil. and Cres.*, 2.ii.200.

magnifico, Venetian magnate, *Mer. Ven.*, 3.ii.282.

Maid Marian, personage in the morris dance, *1 Hen. 4*, 3.iii.114.

mail, *mail'd up*, shrouded in, *2 Hen. 6*, 2.iv.31.

main, the number nominated before casting the dice at the game of hazard, *1 Hen. 4*, 4.i.47; so *main chance*, *2 Hen. 4*, 3.i.83.

main-course, mainsail, *Tem.*, 1.i.33.

mainly, violently, *1 Hen. 4*, 2.iv.193; strongly, *Ham.*, 4.vii.9.

major, *your major*, major premise in syllogism, *1 Hen. 4*, 2.iv.478.

make, *male and make*, husband and wife, *Lear*, 4.iii.34.

malapert, presumptuous, *Rich. 3*, 1.iii.255.

malcontent, disgruntled, *3 Hen. 6*, 4.i.10.

malignant, *malignant stars*, exerting evil influence, *1 Hen. 6*, 4.v.6.

malkin, slut, *Cor.*, 2.i.198.

mallard, a wild drake, *Ant. and Cleo.*, 3.x.20.

malmsey, sweet wine, *Rich. 3*, 1.iv.152.

malt-horse, brewer's dray-horse, *Tam. Shrew*, 4.i.113.

malt-worm, boozer, *2 Hen. 4*, 2.iv.322.

mammer, stammer, hesitate, *Oth.*, 3.iii.71.

mammet, doll, *Rom. and Jul.*, 3.v.185.

mammock, pull in pieces, *Cor.*, 1.iii.65.

man, (i) to provide a man-servant, *2 Hen. 4*, 1.ii.15; (ii) to tame a hawk, *Tam. Shrew*, 4.i.177.

manage, training or handling of a horse, *Hen. 8*, 5.iii.24; *L. Lab. Lost*, 5.ii.482.

mandragora, mandrake, a narcotic, *Oth.*, 3.iii.334; *Ant. and Cleo.*, 1.v.4; the root was thought to resemble the shape of a man and shriek when torn from the earth, *Rom. and Jul.*, 4.iii.47.

manner, the stolen article when found on the thief, so caught in the act, *1 Hen. 4*, 2.iv.306; *L. Lab. Lost*, 1.i.199 (where the company of a woman was the unlawful possession).

mansionry, abode, *Mac.*, 1.vi.5.

mantle, scum on stagnant water, *Lear*, 3.iv.131.

mappery, mere staff-work, *Troil. and Cres.*, 1.iii.205.

marches, the English districts adjacent to Scotland and Wales, *Hen. 5*, 1.ii.140.

marchpane, a sweetmeat like marzipan, *Rom. and Jul.*, 1.v.7.

margent, margin of book, *L. Lab. Lost*, 5.ii.8; commentary or explanation written in margin, *Ham.*, 5.ii.152.

mark, a sum of money (not a coin) value 13s. 4d., *Hen. 8*, 5.i.170.

marmoset, small monkey, *Tem.*, 2.ii.160.

Martin, *Saint Martin's summer*, supposed to run from about 23rd Oct. to 11th Nov., St. Martin's day, *1 Hen. 6*, 1.ii.131.

Martlemas, Martinmas, 11th Nov.; animals that could not be fed through the winter were killed at this season, *2 Hen. 4*, 2.ii.98.

martlet, house-martin, swallow, *Mac.*, 1.vi.4.

mary-bud, marigold bud, *Cym.*, 2.iii.23.

mast, acorns, food for swine, *Timon*, 4.iii.417.

mastic, meaning doubtful, perhaps censorious *Troil. and Cres.*, 1.iii.73.

mate, outwit, *2 Hen. 6*, 3.i.265; bewilder, *Mac.*, 5.i.76.

maugre, in spite of, *Tw. Night*, 3.i.148.

maund, basket, *Lov. Comp.*, 36.

mazard, head, *Ham.*, 5.i.87.

meacock, feeble, cowardly, *Tam. Shrew*, 2.i.305.

meal, stain, *M. Meas.*, 4.ii.79.

mean, middle part, tenor or alto, *L. Lab. Lost*, 5.ii.328; singer of such a part, *Win. Tale*, 4.iii.42.

mechanic, manual worker, *Cor.*, 5.iii.83.

medicine, of chemical preparations other than medicinal, *Oth.*, 1.iii.61; *that great med'cine*, the elixir of life or alchemist's stone that turned all to gold, so figuratively at *Ant. and Cleo.*, 1.v.36; the physician, *Mac.*, 5.ii.27.

meed, merit, *3 Hen. 6*, 2.i.36.

meetly, not bad, *Ant. and Cleo.*, 1.iii.81.

meiny, train, company, *Lear*, 2.iv.34.

melancholy, of various kinds, see *As You Like*, 4.i.10.

memorize, make memorable, *Mac.*, 1.ii.41.

mercatante, merchant, *Tam. Shrew*, 4.ii.63.

Mercury, messenger of the gods, so messenger, *Mer. Wives Win.*, 2.ii.72; patron of rogues and cheats, *Win. Tale*, 4.iii.25.

mere, complete, absolute, *Mer. Wives Win.*, 4.v.58.

mess, four, usual number in sub-divisions of company at banquet, *L. Lab. Lost*, 4.iii.203.

metaphysical, supernatural, *Mac.*, 1.v.26.

mete, measure, *2 Hen. 4*, 4.iv.77; *mete-yard*, measuring stick, *Tam. Shrew*, 4.iii.149; aim at, *L. Lab. Lost*, 4.i.125.

metheglin, spiced drink, *L. Lab. Lost*, 5.ii.233.

mew, shut up, *Mid. N. Dr.*, 1.i.71.

micher, truant, *1 Hen. 4*, 2.iv.396.

miching mallecho, skulking mischief ('mallecho' a Spanish word for 'evil deed'), *Ham.*, 3.ii.132.

might, *might not merit*, the intention not the performance, *Mid. N. Dr.*, 5.i.92.

milch, used of weeping, *Ham.*, 2.ii.511.

Mile-end, *Green*, where train-bands drilled, *2 Hen. 4*, 3.ii.271.

milk-liver'd, cowardly, *Lear*, 4.ii.50.

milliner, vendor of gloves, hats, etc., *1 Hen. 4*, 1.iii.36.

mill-sixpence, milled coin, not hammered as older pieces, *Mer. Wives Win.*, 1.i.139.

mineral, poison, *Oth.*, 2.i.291.

minikin, trim and feat, *Lear*, 3.vi.43.

minimus, of smallest size, *Mid. N. Dr.*, 3.ii.329.

minute-jacks, creatures of the minute, or busy about nothing, *Timon*, 3.vi.97.

minutely, every minute, *Mac.*, 5.ii.18.

mirable, wonderful, *Troil. and Cres.*, 4.v.142.

Misanthropos, the hater of mankind, *Timon*, 4.iii.52.

misgraffed, unsuitably mated, *Mid. N. Dr.*, 1.i.137.

misprision (i) undervaluing, scorning, *All's Well*, 2.iii.150; (ii) mistaking, *Mid. N. Dr.*, 3.ii.90.

missive, messenger, *Mac.*, 1.v.5.

mistress, at game of bowls, the jack, *Troil. and Cres.*, 3.ii.48.

mobled, muffled, *Ham.*, 2.ii.496.

model, plan, *2 Hen. 4*, 1.iii.42; copy, *Ham.*, 5.ii.50; imperfect manifestation of, *Hen. 5*, 2.Chor.16.

modern, ordinary, commonplace, *As You Like*, 2.vii.156; *modern grace*, common attractions, *All's Well*, 5.iii.214.

modest, reasonable, *Tw. Night*, 1.v.169.

module, copy, *All's Well*, 4.iii.94.

moldwarp, mole, *1 Hen. 4*, 3.i.149.

mome, dolt, *Com. Err.*, 3.i.32.

Monarcho, title assumed by mad Italian as emperor of the world, so of those with such notions, *L. Lab. Lost*, 4.i.92.

Monmouth cap, commonly worn by soldiers and sailors, *Hen. 5*, 4.vii.97.

monstruosity, the great 'snag', *Troil. and Cres.*, 3.ii.78.

montant, fencing term for particular thrust, *Mer. Wives Win.*, 2.iii.25.

monumental, *ring*, a momento from the possessor's ancestors, *All's Well*, 4.iii.16.

moonish, fickle, *As You Like*, 3.ii.376.

Moor Ditch, melancholy of Moor Ditch, occasioned by the smell of the ditch, especially when being cleaned out, *1 Hen. 4*, 1.ii.76.

mop, grimace, *Tem.*, 4.i.47.

mope, wander in body or mind, *Tem.*, 5.i.240; *Ham.*, 3.iv.81.

Morisco, a morris-dancer (supposed of Moorish origin), *2 Hen. 6*, 3.i.365.

morris, morris-dance, costume dance of fantastic kind; characters included Robin Hood, Maid Marian, *All's Well*, 2.ii.23; *Hen. 5*, 2.iv.25 (see hobby horse); *nine men's morris*, a game played on squares cut in the turf, *Mid. N. Dr.*, 2.i.98.

mort, the note on the horn that announces the death of the deer, *Win. Tale*, 1.ii.118.

mortise, hold the mortise, remain with timbers unloosened, *Oth.*, 2.i.9.

mose, *in the chine*, of horses, glanders, *Tam. Shrew*, 3.ii.48.

mot, motto, *Lucrece*, 830.

mother, hysteria, *Lear*, 2.iv.55.

motion, puppet-show, *Win. Tale*, 4.iii.91.

motley, fool's particoloured costume, *Lear*, 1.iv.145; one who plays the fool, *Son.*, 110, 2.

mould, earth, *Hen. 5*, 3.ii.21.

moulten, having moulted, *1 Hen. 4*, 3.i.152.

mountebank, to gain by false statements, *Cor.*, 3.ii.132.

mouse, to seize in the jaws and rend, *John*, 2.i.354.

mow, grimace, *Ham.*, 2.ii.360.

muniments, defences, implements, *Cor.*, 1.i.116.

murdering-piece, small cannon for grape-shot, *Ham.*, 4.v.92.

mure, wall, *2 Hen. 4*, 4.iv.119.

murrain, plague, *Troil. and Cres.*, 2.i.19.

muscadel, strong sweet wine, *Tam. Shrew*, 3.ii.168.

musit, gaps through which hare runs when hunted, *Ven. and Ad.*, 683.

musk, secretion from musk-deer, *Mer. Wives Win.*, 3.ii.60.

musk-cat, musk-deer, *All's Well*, 5.ii.19.

muss, a scramble, *Ant. and Cleo.*, 3.xiii.91.

mutine, *verb*, to rebel, *Ham.*, 3.iv.83; *noun*, mutineer, *Ham.*, 5.ii.6.

mutiny, *verb*, contend, *Ant. and Cleo.*, 3.xi.13; *noun*, dispute, *L. Lab. Lost*, 1.i.167.

mutual, common (as in ' Our Mutual Friend '), *Mer. Ven.*, 5.i.77.

mutuality, exchange (of intimacy), *Oth.*, 2.i.256.

mynheers (suggested for 'Anheires'), sirs, *Mer. Wives Win.*, 2.i.196.

Myrmidon, *the great Myrmidon*, Achilles whose followers were the Myrmidons, *Troil. and Cres.*, 1.iii.378.

mystery, craft, calling, *M. Meas.*, 4.ii.25; *Timon*, 4.iii.452.

nail, measure of length for cloth, one-sixteenth of a yard, *Tam. Shrew*, 4.iii.108.

naked, unarmed, *Oth.*, 5.ii.261; *naked bed*, naked, as was the habit, in bed, *Ven. and Ad.*, 397.

napless, threadbare, *Cor.*, 2.i.224 (the candidates really wore whitened garments to look as fine as possible; North's mistranslation here misled Shakespeare).

nave, hub of wheel, *Ham.*, 2.ii.490.

nayward, opposite belief, *Win. Tale*, 2.i.64.

nayword, byword *Tw. Night*, 2.iii.127; password, *Mer. Wives Win.*, 5.ii.5.

Nazarite, of Nazareth, *Mer. Ven.*, 1.iii.30 (the term 'Nazarene' was introduced by the Authorized Version of 1611).

neaf, fist, 2 *Hen. 4*, 2.iv.176.

Neapolitan, bone-ache, venereal disease, *Troil. and Cres.*, 2.iii.17.

near-legged, *before*, fore-legs close, *Tam. Shrew*, 3.ii.52.

neat, animal, ox, cow, calf, *Win. Tale*, 1.ii.125; *neat's leather*, shoe leather, *Jul. Caes.*, 1.i.26.

neb, mouth, *Win. Tale*, 1.ii.183.

neeze, sneeze, *Mid. N. Dr.*, 2.i.56.

nephew, a relation—cousin, etc., 1 *Hen. 6*, 2.v.64.

Nereides, sea-nymphs, fifty daughters of Nereus, *Ant. and Cleo.*, 2.ii.210.

nether-stocks, stockings, 1 *Hen. 4*, 2.iv.111; *wooden nether-stocks*, the stocks, *Lear*, 2.iv.10.

nice, coy, shy, mannerly, fastidious, *All's Well*, 5.i.15; *nice wenches*, those affecting shyness, wantons, *L. Lab. Lost*, 3.i.20.

nicely, subtly, ingeniously, *Rich. 2*, 2.i.84.

niceness, reserve, *Cym.*, 3.iv.154.

Nicholas, *Saint*, patron saint, of boys and scholars, *Two Gent. Ver.*, 3.i.292; *Saint Nicholas' clerks*, highway robbers, 1 *Hen. 4*, 2.i.60.

nick, *out of all nick*, beyond reckoning (nicks used on sticks to keep reckoning), *Two Gent. Ver.*, 4.ii.73; *in the nick*, at the appropriate time (to settle the bill), *Oth.*, 5.ii.320.

nightgown, dressing-gown, *Mac.*, 2.ii.70.

nimble-pinion'd, swift winged, *Rom. and Jul.*, 2.v.7.

noble, a gold coin worth 6s. 8d., *Rich. 2*, 1.i.88; the aristocratic party, *Cor.*, 3.i.29.

noise, often applied to musical sounds, *Ant. and Cleo.*, 4.iii.12; the men who make the noise, the band, 2 *Hen. 4*, 2.iv.11.

nole, head, *Mid. N. Dr.*, 3.ii.17.

nonce, for this particular purpose or occasion, *Ham.*, 4.vii.160.

non-come, Dogberry's term is of doubtful meaning, *Much Ado*, 3.v.57.

nonpareil, without an equal, *Tw. Night*, 1.v.238.

nook-shotten, all corners and angles, *Hen. 5*, 3.v.14.

nose-herb, scented plant, *All's Well*, 4.v.17.

novum, a game with dice, in which throws of nine and five were important, *L. Lab. Lost*, 5.ii.540 (the five characters were to enact the Nine Worthies).

nuncio, messenger, *Tw. Night*, 1.iv.27.

nut-hook, beadle, 2 *Hen. 4*, 5.iv.8.

o, *this wooden O*, the theatre (perhaps' The Globe), *Hen. 5*, 1.Chor.13; *this little O*, the globe itself, the earth, *Ant. and Cleo.*, 5.ii.81; *yon fiery oes and eyes of light*, the stars, *Mid. N. Dr.*, 3.ii.188.

oathable, that can be trusted to take an oath, *Timon*, 4.iii.135.

ob., abbreviation of 'obolus', a half-penny, 1 *Hen. 4*, 2.iv.521.

objection, accusation, 2 *Hen. 6*, 1.iii.153.

obliged, *obliged faith*, pledged, *Mer. Ven.*, 2.vi.7.

oblivious, causing forgetfulness, *Mac.*, 5.iii.43.

obloquy, shame, *All's Well*, 4.ii.44.

obscene, abominable, *Rich. 2*, 4.i.131.

obsequious, showing proper duty, *M. Meas.*. 2.iv.28; duty or love for the dead, *Ham.*, 1.ii.92.

observance, attention required by respect or love, *Troil. and Cres.*, 1.iii.31.

observant, one quick to attend to master's wishes, *Lear*, 2.ii.98.

observation, of a rite, *Mid. N. Dr.*, 4.i.101; of life itself and compliance with its requirements, *John*, 1.i.208.

observe, *Th' observ'd of all observers*, of all courtiers the most reverenced, *Ham.*, 3.i.154.

obstruct, obstacle, *Ant. and Cleo.*, 3.vi.61.

obstruction, *obstruction in the blood*, hindrance, *Tw. Night*, 3.iv.21; *cold obstruction*, death, where all that makes for life is shut off, *M. Meas.*, 3.i.120.

occasion, happenings, 2 *Hen. 4*, 4.i.72; so an opportunity or a reason for something, *he married but his occasion* (took the chance of marriage merely to further his interests), *Ant. and Cleo.*, 2.vi.127; *quarrelling with occasion*, deliberately misunderstanding the situation, *Mer. Ven.*, 3.v.48.

occulted, hidden, *Ham.*, 3.ii.78.

occupation, *voice of occupation*, vote of the manual worker, *Cor.*, 4.vi.98.

occupy, *as odious as the word 'occupy'*, because it was employed largely in an indecent sense (e.g. *Rom. and Jul.*, 2.iv.96), 2 *Hen. 4*, 2.iv.139.

Od's, Ud's, form of 'God' in oaths and exclamations. *As You Like*, 3.v.43; *Oth.*, 5.ii.72.

oeillades, inviting glances, *Mer. Wives Win.*, 1.iii.57; *Lear*, 4.v.25.

o'erflourish'd, decorated outwardly, *Tw. Night*, 3.iv.354.

o'erparted, given too difficult a part, *L. Lab. Lost*, 5.ii.578.

o'erpicturing, excelling in beauty what the imagination has pictured, *Ant. and Cleo.*, 2.ii.204.

o'er-sized, besmear'd, *Ham.*, 2.ii.456.

o'er-teemed, exhausted with child-bearing, *Ham.*, 2.ii.502.

o'er-wrested, *seeming*, exaggerated acting, *Troil. and Cres.*, 1.iii.157.

off-capp'd, stood bare-headed, *Oth.*, 1.i.10.

office, function, service, *Rich. 2*, 2.ii.137; the functionary, *Ham.*, 3.i.73.

'old, wold, *Lear*, 3.iv.118.

old, extreme (in some form), *Tam. Shrew*, 3.ii.31; *Mac.*, 2.iii.2.

oneyer, meaning doubtful, 1 *Hen. 4*, 2.i.74.

operant, active, *Ham.*, 3.ii.169.

opposite, adversary, *Tw. Night*, 3.iv.255.

opposition, *single oppositions*, single combats, *Cym.*, 4.i.13.

oppugnancy, discord, *Troil. and Cres.*, 1.iii.111.

orb, circle, *Mid. N. Dr.*, 2.i.9 (fairy rings); the circle or sphere in which the planets were supposed to move, *Rom. and Jul.*, 2.ii.110.

ordinance, what has been ordained in the past or is ordained for the future, *Jul. Caes.*, 1.iii.66; *Cym.*, 4.ii.146; rank, *Cor.*, 3.ii.12.

ordinant, provident, *Ham.*, 5.ii.48.

ordinary, meal (from name given to meal in a tavern), *Ant. and Cleo.*, 2.ii.229.

orgillous, proud, *Troil. and Cres.*, Prol. 2.

orifex, opening, *Troil. and Cres.*, 5.ii.149.

orison, prayer, *Ham.*, 3.i.89.

ort, fragment, *Timon*, 4.iii.397.

orthography, orthographer, pedantic in his use of words, *Much Ado*, 2.iii.18.

ostent, show, appearance, *Mer. Ven.*, 2.ii.181

ostentation, display, *Ham.*, 4.v.211.

othergates, in another and very different way *Tw. Night*, 5.i.186.

ouches, ornaments, 2 *Hen. 4*, 2.iv.48.

ought, owed, 1 *Hen. 4*, 3.iii.134.

ounce, lynx, *Mid. N. Dr.*, 2.ii.30.

ouphe, elf, goblin, *Mer. Wives Win.*, 5.v.55.

ousel, blackbird, *Mid. N. Dr.*, 3.i.114.

out-herod, *out-herods Herod*, to rant mor outrageously than Herod in the old Myster plays, *Ham.*, 3.ii.13.

out-peer, excel, *Cym.*, 3.vi.86.

out-vie, to outbid (as at cards), *Tam. Shrew*, 2.i.377.

overscutch'd, *huswifes*, well-whipped whores, so hardened to the trade, 2 *Hen.* 4, 3.ii.308.

overture, disclosure, declaration, *Tw. Night*, 1.v.196.

owe, to possess, *Lear*, 1.i.202.

oyes (Fr. oyez) the call of the public crier to secure attention, *Mer. Wives Win.*, 5.v.39.

pace, training (as of horses), discipline, *All's Well*, 4.v.60; *verb*, to train, *Per.*, 4.vi.62.

pack, to plot, *Titus*, 4.ii.156; *pack'd*, confederate, *Much Ado*, 5.i.285; *Com. Err.*, 5.i.219; to manipulate the cards dishonestly, to cheat, *Ant. and Cleo.*, 4.xiv.19.

packing, plotting, *Tam. Shrew*, 5.i.105.

paddock, toad, *Ham.*, 3.iv.190; *paddock calls* the witch's familiar spirit, *Mac.*, 1.i.9.

pageant (the wagon on which a scene in the Miracle plays was staged at the various stations appointed for performance) so of a ship, *Mer. Ven.*, 1.i.11; a show, sometimes with the notion of unreality or deception, *Tem.*, 4.i.155; *Oth.*, 1.iii.18.

pain, punishment, *Son.*, 141, 14; toil, *L. Lab. Lost*, 1.i.73.

painful, *painful warrior*, enduring toil and danger, *Son.*, 25.9.

painted, specious, false, *Ham.*, 3.i.53.

painted cloth, canvas hangings painted with figures and moral sentences were a cheap substitute for figured tapestries, 2 *Hen.* 4, 2.i.142; *right painted cloth*, the answer taken from the mottoes, etc. on the hangings, *As You Like*, 3.ii.258; *Lucrece*, 245.

paiock, possibly peacock, *Ham.*, 3.ii.278.

palabras, *paucas pallabris*, few words, *Tam. Shrew*, Ind.i.5; *Much Ado*, 3.v.16.

pale, palisade, so figuratively at *Ham.*, 1.iv.28; *Troil. and Cres.*, 2.iii.243; with idea of winter's whiteness at *Win. Tale*, 4.iii.4; *verb*, to encircle, 3 *Hen.* 6 1.iv.103 (with the crown).

palfrey, horse, *Titus*, 5.ii.50.

palisado, defence work of stakes, 1 *Hen.* 4, 2.iii.49.

pall (i) fail, *Ham.*, 5.ii.9; *pall'd fortunes*, ruined prospects, *Ant. and Cleo.*, 2.vii.81. (ii) to shroud, *Mac.*, 1.v.48.

pallet, bed, 2 *Hen.* 4, 3.i.10.

palliament, robe, *Titus*, 1.i.182.

palmy, lofty, flourishing, *Ham.*, 1.i.113.

palter, deal falsely, *Mac.*, 5.viii.20.

pantaloon, originally a stock character in Italian comedy; withered dotard—so figure of old age, *As You Like*, 2.vii.158.

Pantheon, temple at Rome (to all the Gods), *Titus*, 1.i.242.

paper, to serve with a writ or communication, *Hen.* 8, 1.i.80.

Paracelsus, Swiss alchemist of early 16th century; criticised academic medical opinion as represented in Galen; *Both of Galen and Paracelsus*, all schools of medical thought, *All's Well*, 2.iii.11.

paradox, contrary to general opinion, *Ham.*, 3.i.114; absurd statement, *Oth.*, 2.i.138.

paragon, *paragon'd*, regarded as perfect example of kind, *Hen.* 8, 2.iv.230; *paragons description*, surpasses attempts to describe ideal, *Oth.*, 2.i.62; compare, *Ant. and Cleo.*, 1.v.71.

parcel, part, *Oth.*, 1.iii.154; group, *Mer. Ven.*, 1.ii.97; *verb*, (perhaps) add to, *Ant. and Cleo.*, 5.ii.162; *parcell'd*, particular, *Rich.* 3, 2.ii.81.

pard, panther or leopard, *Tem.*, 4.i.260.

Paris balls, tennis balls, *Hen.* 5, 2.iv.131.

Paris garden, a bear-garden (for in this liberty on the Bankside was situated the ring for bear baiting), *Hen.* 8, 5.iv.2.

parish-top, kept to provide recreation in cold weather, *Tw. Night*, 1.iii.38.

paritor, summoner to the Bishop's court (the pranks inspired by Cupid giving him most work), *L. Lab. Lost*, 3.i.176.

parle, conversation (with pun on 'parle' = truce for discussion of terms), *Ham.*, 1.iii.123; *angry parle*, perhaps just a sharp encounter, *Ham.*, 1.i.62.

parlous, perilous, *As You Like*, 3.ii.40; shrewd, *Rich.* 3, 2.iv.35.

parmaceti, spermaceti, 1 *Hen.* 4, 1.iii.58.

partial, *a partial slander*, the accusation of partiality, *Rich.* 2, 1.iii.241.

partialize, affect with partiality, *Rich.* 2, 1.i.120.

partially, *affin'd*, bound by desire to favour a colleague, *Oth.*, 2.iii.210.

parti-coated, motley, the garb of the fool, *L. Lab. Lost*, 5.ii.754.

partisan, a blade mounted on a long pole, common weapon for guards, *Ham.*, 1.i.140.

Partlet, *Dame Partlet*, traditional name for the hen, *Win. Tale*, 2.iii.75.

party-verdict, individual's contribution to common decision, *Rich.* 2, 1.iii.234.

pash (i) *noun*, head, *Win. Tale*, 1.ii.128; (ii) *verb*, strike, *Troil. and Cres.*, 2.iii.198.

passado, a lunge in rapier fighting, *Rom. and Jul.*, 3.i.82.

passant (of heraldic figures), walking, *Mer. Wives Win.*, 1.i.17.

passion, Christ's sufferings (in oaths, etc.), *Mer. Wives Win.*, 3.i.57; physical or mental pain, 1 *Hen.* 4, 3.i.35; love, *Titus*, 2.i.36; a passionate speech, *Mid N. Dr.*, 5.i.307; *Ham.*, 3.ii.9; *verb*, feel sorrow, *Tem.*, 5.i.24.

passy, *measures pavin* (from Italian passamezzo pavana), a variety of pavan, which was slow and stately, *Tw. Night*, 5.i.192.

patch, fool, *Mid. N. Dr.*, 3.ii.9.

patchery, roguery, *Troil. and Cres.*, 2.iii.67.

patent, *virgin patent*, privilege of liberty as maid, *Mid. N. Dr.*, 1.i.80.

patine, circular metal plate (patine, plate used in the Eucharist), *Mer. Ven.*, 5.i.59.

patronage, maintain, 1 *Hen.* 6, 3.i.48.

Paul's, *known as well as Paul's*, as familiar as the old St. Paul's cathedral which was the 'Bond Street of London' till the days of the Commonwealth, the haunt of idlers and centre of commerce, 1 *Hen.* 4, 2.iv.508.

paunch, pierce his belly, *Tem.*, 3.ii.86.

pavin, *see* passy.

pax, representation of the Crucifixion, or reliquary, kissed by the celebrant and people at mass, *Hen.* 5, 3.vi.39.

peach, to give away one's confederates, 1 *Hen.* 4, 2.ii.43; proclaim, *M. Meas.*, 4.iii.10.

peak, to droop in spirit or strength, *Ham.*, 2.ii.561; *Mac.*, 1.iii.23.

pearl, cataract (with play on usual sense), *Two Gent. Ver.*, 5.ii.13.

peck, *you o'er the pales*, pitch you over the railings, *Hen.* 8, 5.iv.87.

peculiar, belonging to particular individual, personal, *M. Meas.*, 1.ii.86; *Troil. and Cres.*, 2.iii.161.

pedant, schoolmaster, *Tw. Night*, 3.ii.70; *pedascule* pedant, *Tam. Shrew*, 3.i.48.

peel'd, tonsured, 1 *Hen.* 6, 1.iii.30.

peise, *peised well*, well balanced, *John*, 2.i.575; *peize the time*, make it heavy and slow, *Mer. Ven.*, 3.ii.22.

pelican (the pelican was supposed to feed her young with her blood), *Ham.*, 4.v.143.

Pelion, the giants placed mount Ossa on mount Pelion in their attempt to scale the heavens, *Ham.*, 5.i.247.

pelting, *pelting wars*, poor fighting, *Troil. and Cres.*, 4.v.267; paltry, *Lear*, 2.iii.18.

pendulous, suspended overhead, *Lear*, 3.iv.66.

pensioners, royal body-guard, formed by Henry VIII, *Mer. Wives Win.*, 2.ii.70.

Pepin, father of Charlemagne, and so someone who lived long ago, *L. Lab. Lost*, 4.i.113.

perdu, a soldier on a post or task of special danger, so as good as lost, *Lear*, 4.vii.35.

perdurably, *fin'd,* eternally punished, *M. Meas.*, 3.i.116.

perdy (*French,* par dieu), *Tw. Night*, 4.ii.73; *Ham.*, 3.ii.288.

peregrinate, with the affectations of one who has seen the world, *L. Lab. Lost*, 5.i.12.

peremptory, determined, *Cor.*, 3.i.286.

perfect, certain, *Cym.*, 3.i.71; *perfect soul,* sound conscience, *Oth.*, 1.ii.31; *verb,* to instruct, *M. Meas.*, 4.iii.138.

perfection, performance, *Troil. and Cres.*, 3.ii.83.

perfumer, one who kept the rooms fresh with perfume, *Much Ado*, 1.iii.50.

periapt, a charm carried on the person, 1 *Hen.* 6, 5.iii.2.

perjure, *noun,* a perjurer, *L. Lab. Lost*, 4.iii.43; *perjur'd note,* the paper pinned to the perjurer setting out his guilt, *L. Lab. Lost*, 4.iii.121.

peroration, studied harangue, 2 *Hen.* 6, 1.i.100.

perpend, ponder, *As You Like*, 3.ii.60.

Persian, rich and ornate, *Lear*, 3.vi.79 (Edgar being in rags).

perspective, a picture that appeared coherent and intelligible only from one particular point of view, *Rich.* 2, 2.ii.18; illusion, *Tw. Night*, v.i.209.

pertaunt-like, ' pertaunt ' was perhaps a winning declaration at the card game of Post and Pair—perhaps a hand of four Queens (*see* Dr. Percy Simpson's letter, *T.L.S.*, 24 Feb. 45), *L. Lab. Lost*, 5.ii.67.

petar, a bomb or charge for blowing in gates, *Ham.*, 3.iv.207.

pew, *pew-fellow,* associate, *Rich.* 3, 4.iv.58.

phantasime, a fantastic fellow, *L. Lab. Lost*, 4.i.92.

phantasma, nightmare, *Jul. Caes.*, 2.i.65.

pheeze, castigate, *Tam. Shrew*, Ind.i.1; *Pheazar,* comic formation, *Mer. Wives Win.*, 1.iii.9.

Philip, name for sparrow, *John*, 1.i.231.

Philip and Jacob, 1st May, feast of Philip and James, *M. Meas.*, 3.ii.189.

Philip, Saint, *Saint Philip's daughters,* the daughters of Philip the Evangelist (Acts xxi, 8-9) had the gift of prophecy, 1 *Hen.* 6, 1.ii.143.

Philippan, *sword Philippan,* the sword he used in the victory at Philippi, *Ant. and Cleo.*, 2.v.23.

Philomel-a, the nightingale; according to the legend, Pandion, king of Attica, had two daughters. Philomel and Procne; Procne was married to Tereus who ravished Philomel and cut out her tongue to conceal his sin; she was changed to a nightingale, *Titus*, 4.i.48.

philosopher, *philosopher's two stones,* even better than the philosopher's stone that was supposed to turn base metals to gold, 2 *Hen.* 4, 3.ii.320.

Phoebe, Pheobus, the moon-goddess, the sun-god, *Mid. N. Dr.*, 1.i.209 and 1.ii.29 (Phibbus).

phoenix, a unique wonder, *Hen.* 8, 5.v.40.

phraseless, beyond description, *Lov. Comp.*, 225.

physical, good for the health, *Jul. Caes.*, 2.i.261.

pia mater, brain, *Tw. Night*, 1.v.108.

pick, pitch, *Cor.*, 1.i.198.

picked, finical, *L. Lab. Lost*, 5.i.11.

pickers and stealers, hands (' to keep my hand from picking and stealing ' *Catechism*), *Ham.*, 3.ii.327.

pick-thank, toady, 1 *Hen.* 4, 3.ii.25.

Pickt-hatch, a quarter of ill-repute in London, *Mer Wives Win.*, 2.ii.16.

pigeon-liver'd, spiritless, tame, *Ham.*, 2.ii.572.

pight, pitched, *Troil. and Cres.*, 5.x.24; fixed, *Lear*, 2.i.65.

pike, spike on buckler, *Much Ado*, 5.ii.19.

pilcher (i) pilchard, *Tw. Night*, 3.i.32; (ii) scabbard, *Rom. and Jul.*, 3.i.78.

pill, plunder, *Timon*, 4.i.12.

pin, peg in the centre of target, *L. Lab. Lost,*

4.i.129; *pin and web,* cataract, blindness, *Win. Tale*, 1.ii.291; *pin buttock,* narrow buttock, *All's Well*, 2.ii.17.

pinfold, pound for stray animals, *Lear*, 2.ii.8.

pink'd, *pink'd porringer,* a cap, *Hen.* 8, 5.iv.45.

pioned, *pioned and twilled brims,* meaning doubtful, *Tem.*, 4.i.64.

pip, *a pip out,* thirty-two when thirty-one (at card game) is needed, *Tam. Shrew*, 1.ii.32.

pipe-wine, wine from cask, *Mer. Wives Win.*, 3.ii.77.

pismire, ant, 1 *Hen.* 4, 1.iii.240.

pitch, height, *Ham.*, 3.i.86.

place, *pride of place,* the height from which hawk strikes, *Mac.*, 2.iv.12.

placket, slit in petticoat to allow it to slip on, so woman *Troil. and Cres.*, 2.iii.19.

plain-song, *the very plain-song of it,* the simple truth, *Hen.* 5, 3.ii.5.

planched, of boards, *M. Meas.*, 4.i.28.

plantage, vegetation (supposed to be affected by phases of moon), *Troil. and Cres.*, 3.ii.173.

plantain, plant with broad flat leaves, thought good for wounds, *L. Lab. Lost*, 3.i.68.

plantation, settlement, *Tem.*, 2.i.137.

plash, pool, *Tam. Shrew*, 1.i.23.

plate, silver coin, *Ant. and Cleo.*, 5.ii.92.

plate, to cover with armour, *Lear*, 4.vi.165 ; *plated Mars,* armed for battle, *Ant. and Cleo.*, 1.i.4.

plausive, pleasing, acceptable, *Ham.*, 1.iv.30; plausible, cunning, *All's Well*, 4.i.25.

pleached, thick-pleached, *Much Ado*, 1.ii.8; the boughs closely intertwined, *Much Ado*, 3.i.7; *pleach'd arms,* folded arms, *Ant. and Cleo.*, 4.xiv.73.

please-man, toady, *L. Lab. Lost*, 5.ii.463.

pleurisy, a plethora or excess, *Ham.*, 4.vii.117.

plighted, wrapped as in pleats, folded, *Lear*, 1.i.280.

plume, plumage, *Tem.*, 3.iii.65; *plume up,* dress up, express, *Oth.*, 1.iii.387. *plume-pluck'd,* dispossessed, *Rich.* 2, 4.i.108.

point, *point of war,* trumpet-call, 2 *Hen.* 4, 4.i.52; lace for keeping hose attached to doublet, 1 *Hen.* 4, 2.iv.207 (pun on ' point ' = sword-point); *armed at point exactly,* completely, *Ham.*, 1.ii.200; (in falconry) the height to which the hawk climbs before striking, 2 *Hen.* 6, 2.i.5; *point-devise,* in all particulars, precisely, *Tw. Night*, 2.v.145.

poise, weight, *Lear*, 2.i.120; momentum, *Troil. and Cres.*, 1.iii.207; *verb,* to weigh, estimate, *Troil. and Cres.*, 1.iii.339.

poke, pocket, *As You Like*, 2.vii.20.

poking-sticks, for ruffs, *Win. Tale*, 4.iv.223.

Polacks, Poles, *Ham.*, 1.i.63.

pole, pole-star, *Oth.*, 2.i.15.

pole-clipt, *vineyard,* the poles perhaps for the vines to climb on, *Tem.*, 4.i.68.

politic, *politic authors,* writers on state affairs, *Tw. Night*, 2.v.143.

politician, a political intriguer, *Lear*, 4.vi.171; *Ham.*, 5.i.78.

pomander, scent-ball, *Win. Tale*, 4.iv.590.

pomewater, kind of apple, *L. Lab. Lost*, 4.ii.4.

Pomgarnet, pomegranate, rooms in inns often having names, 1 *Hen.* 4, 2.iv.36.

Pontic sea, Black Sea, *Oth.*, 3.iii.457.

Poor-John, salted fish, *Tem.*, 2.ii.26.

pop'rin pear, kind of pear (from Poperinghe near Ypres), *Rom. and Jul.*, 2.i.38.

popularity, contact with the common people, 1 *Hen.* 4, 3.ii.69.

porpentine, porcupine, *Ham.*, 1.v.20.

porridge, pottage or soup, 1 *Hen.* 6, 1.ii.9.

port (i) gate, *Troil. and Cres.*, 4.iv.110; (ii) bearing, *Hen.* 5, 1.Chor.6; rank, wealth, *Mer. Ven.*, 3.ii.283.

portage (i) venture (what the sailor traded on his own), *Per.*, 3.i.35; (ii) port-holes, *Hen.* 5, 3.i.10.

portance, bearing, conduct, *Oth.*, 1.iii.139.

posied, *see* posy, *Lov. Comp.*, 45.

position, argument, assertion, *Troil. and Cres.*

3.iii.112; *in position*, in the statement, *Oth.*, 3.iii.238.

possession, possessed as by an evil spirit, *Com. Err.*, 5.i.44.

posset, *noun*, 'night-cap' of hot milk and spiced liquor, *Mac.*, 2.ii.6; *verb*, curdle, *Ham.*, 1.v.68.

post, *sheriff's post*, sheriff's notice-board, *Tw. Night*, 1.v.140; door-post of tavern, *Com. Err.*, 1.ii.64.

postern, side-door, *Win. Tale*, 1.ii.438.

post-haste, speeding-up, *Ham.*, 1.i.107; *haste-post-haste*, immediate, *Oth.*, 1.ii.37.

posy, inscription inside a ring (e.g. *Mer. Ven.*, 5.i.150), *Ham.*, 3.ii.147.

potch, stab, *Cor.*, 1.x.15.

potential, powerful, *Oth.*, 1.ii.13.

potents, potentates, *John*, 2.i.358.

pother, commotion, *Cor.*, 2.i.208.

potting, drinking, *Oth.*, 2.iii.72.

pottle, two-quart measure so tankard, *Oth.*, 2.iii.78.

pouncet-box, perforated scent-box, 1 *Hen. 4*, 1.iii.38.

powder, salt, 1 *Hen. 4*, 5.iv.112; *powdering-tub*, brine-tub (used of treatment for venereal disease), *Hen. 5*, 2.i.73.

practic, practical, *Hen. 5*, 1.i.51.

practice, intrigue, treachery, *Tw. Night*, 5.i.339; *Lear*, 1.ii.175.

practisant, performer of a stratagem, 1 *Hen. 6*, 3.ii.20.

practise, use some device, *Lear*, 3.ii.57; plot, *John*, 4.i.20.

praemunire, *compass of a praemunire*, open to a charge of maintaining papal authority in England, *Hen. 8*, 3.ii.340.

prætor, Roman magistrate, chiefly concerned with law, *Jul. Caes.*, 2.iv.34.

preambulate, to go before *L. Lab. Lost*, 5.i.68.

precedence, what is said before, *Ant. and Cleo.*, 2.v.51.

precedent, original, *Rich. 3*, 3.vi.7; token, *Ven. and Ad.*, 26; *adj.*, earlier, *Ham.*, 3.iv.98.

preceptial, *preceptial medicine*, suitable precepts or advice on conduct, *Much Ado*, 5.i.24.

precipitate, fall headlong, *Lear*, 4.vi.50.

precipitation, extent of the fall, *Cor.*, 3.ii.4.

precise, scrupulous, puritanical, *M. Meas.*, 1.iii.50 (also at 3.i.95 and 98, where the Folio reads 'prenzie').

precisian, puritan-like adviser, *Mer. Wives Win.*, 2.i.5.

pre-contract, engagement of marriage, *M. Meas.*, 4.i.70.

precurrer, forerunner, *Phoenix*, 6.

precurse, foreshadowing, *Ham.*, 1.i.121.

predominance, *spherical predominance*, compulsion of planetary influence, *Lear*, 1.ii.118.

predominant, in the ascendant or influential position, *All's Well* 1.i.185.

pregnancy, ingenuity, wit, 2 *Hen. 4*, 1.ii.160.

pregnant (i) clear, *Oth.*, 2.i.232; weighty, significant, *Ham.*, 2.ii.207; apt to respond or act, *Ham.*, 3.ii.59.

prejudicate, pass judgment on a matter before it is formally raised, *All's Well*, 1.ii.8.

premeditation, *cold premeditation*, discouraging consideration for any future scheme, 3 *Hen. 6*, 3.ii.133.

premised, sent before their time, 2 *Hen. 6*, 5.ii.41.

prenominate, name beforehand, *Troil. and Cres.*, 4.v.250; *prenominate crimes*, already mentioned, *Ham.*, 2.i.43.

pre-ordinance, decree already made, *Jul. Caes.*, 3.i.38.

preparations, accomplishments, *Mer. Wives Win.*, 2.ii.206.

prerogative, precedence, *Tam. Shrew*, 3.i.6; *All's Well*, 2.iv.39.

presage, prophecy, signs of future happenings, presentiment, *Son.*, 107, 6; *Rich. 2*, 2.ii.142.

prescript, *prescript praise*, praise as required by the subject of it, *Hen. 5*, 3.vii.45.

prescription, title founded on usage or antiquity, 3 *Hen. 6*, 3.iii.94.

present, immediate, *Ham.*, 4.iii.65; *present money*, ready money, *Mer. Ven.*, 3.ii.275.

presentation, show, disguise, *As You Like*, 5.iv.101.

presentment, dedication of book to patron, *Timon*, 1.i.29.

press, authority to impress soldiers, 1 *Hen. 4*, 4.ii.12.

press, *pressing to death*, refers to the pressing to death, with weights, of accused who would not plead, *M. Meas.*, 5.i.520.

pressure, impression, *Ham.*, 3.ii.24.

Prester John, a fabled and mysterious king of the East or Ethiopia, *Much Ado*, 2.i.238.

presuppos'd, *forms presuppos'd*, dressed as the false letter suggested, *Tw. Night*, 5.i.337.

pretence, purpose, *Cor.*, 1.ii.20; *pretence of danger*, malicious intention, *Lear*, 1.ii.84.

prevent, anticipate, *Ham.*, 2.ii.293.

prevention, interference, anticipatory counter-action, *Jul. Caes.*, 3.i.19.

prick, *noun*, mark on dial of clock, against hour, 3 *Hen. 6*, 1.iv.34; to mark centre of target, *L. Lab. Lost*, 4.i.125; *verb*, mark off on a list, *Jul. Caes.*, 4.i.1.

pricket, see buck.

prick-song, song set out in notation, *Rom. and Jul.*, 2.iv.21.

prig, thief, *Win. Tale*, 4.iii.96.

pr'mero, card-game, *Hen. 8*, 5.i.7.

primogenity, legal right of elder, *Troil. and Cres.*, 1.iii.106.

principality, Principalities, Archangels and Angels formed the third order of Heavenly beings, *Two Gent. Ver.*, 2.iv.148.

princox, forward fellow, *Rom. and Jul.*, 1.v.84.

Priscian, Roman grammarian, *a little scratch'd*, his rules violated somewhat, *L. Lab. Lost*, 5.i.25.

pristine, former, ancient, *Hen. 5*, 3.ii.77.

privilege, justification, explanation, *Mid. N. Dr.*, 2.i.220.

prize, contest, *play'd your prize*, played your game, *Titus*, 1.i.399.

prizer (i) prize-fighter, *As You Like*, 2.iii.8; (ii) valuer, *Troil. and Cres.*, 2.ii.56.

probation, examination, *Tw. Night*, 2.v.119; proof, *Ham.*, 1.i.156.

proceeder, *quick proceeders*, with play on idea of proceeding to a university degree in Arts, *Tam. Shrew*, 4.ii.11.

process, account, *Ham.*, 1.v.37; mandate, *Ham.*, 4.iii.63; by legal process, *Cor.*, 3.i.314.

proditor, traitor, 1 *Hen. 6*, 1.iii.31.

proface, may it do you good ! (formula before a meal), 2 *Hen. 4*, 5.iii.28.

progeny, race, *Cor.*, 1.viii.12; descent, 1 *Hen. 6*, 3.iii.61.

prognostication, according to the almanac's forecast, *Win. Tale*, 4.iv.778; *fruitful prognostication*, sign of future fertility, *Ant. and Cleo.*, 1.ii.49.

prolixious, time-wasting, *M. Meas.*, 2.iv.162.

Promethean, *heat*, life-giving fire, such as Prometheus took from Heaven, *Oth.*, 5.ii.12.

promulgate, announce, *Oth.*, 1.ii.21.

proof, of armour, fitness to be put to the proof, impenetrability, *Rich. 2*, 1.iii.73.

propend, incline, *Troil. and Cres.*, 2.ii.190.

propension, inclination, *Troil. and Cres.*, 2.ii.133.

proper-false, good-looking but deceitful at heart, *Tw. Night*, 2.ii.27.

property, a mere tool, *Jul. Caes.*, 4.i.40; *property of blood*, kinship, *Lear*, 1.i.113; *verb*, to treat as some inanimate object, *Tw. Night*, 4.ii.88.

Propontic, Sea of Marmora, *Oth.*, 3.iii.460.

propose, purpose, *Much Ado*, 3.i.12.

propugnation, protection, *Troil. and Cres.,* 2.ii.136.

prorogue, postpone, *Rom. and Jul.,* 2.ii.78.

Proteus, sea-god who assumed various forms, 3 *Hen.* 6, 3.ii.192.

proud-pied, with many fine colours, *Son.,* 98, 2.

provincial, of a particular province, *M. Meas.,* 5.i.314.

Provincial roses, rosettes covering the laces (Provencal roses), *Ham.,* 3.ii.270.

prune, preen, *Cym.,* 5.iv.118.

psaltery, stringed instrument, *Cor.,* 5.iv.48.

pudder, commotion, *Lear,* 3.ii.50.

pugging, thieving (doubtful), *Win. Tale,* 4.iii.7.

puissance, power, army, *John,* 3.i.339.

puke-stocking, cloth stocking, 1 *Hen.* 4, 2.iv.67.

punk, harlot, *Mer. Wives Win.,* 2.ii.122.

punto, thrust in fencing, *Mer. Wives Win.,* 2.iii.24; *punto reverso,* backhanded thrust, *Rom. and Jul.,* 2.iv.26.

purchas'd, acquired as opposed to possession by descent, e.g. *hereditary rather than purchas'd,* *Ant. and Cleo.,* 1.iv.14.

purgation, clearance of guilt, *Win. Tale,* 3.ii.7.

purl, flow, *Lucrece,* 1407.

purlieu, land bordering forest, *As You Like,* 4.iii.75.

purple-in-grain, see grain.

pursuivant, messenger, *Rich.* 3, 3.iv.90.

purveyor, officer who went ahead to see to lodging, etc., *Mac.,* 1.vi.22.

push, attack, 1 *Hen.* 4, 3.ii.66.

push-pin, children's game, *L. Lab. Lost,* 4.iii.165.

putter-out, *of five for one,* the voyager who put down a sum with a dealer on condition that he obtained on return five times the original, but forfeited the lot if he failed to return or keep the date fixed, *Tem.,* 3.iii.48.

puttock, bird of prey, kite, *Cym.,* 1.i.140.

puzzel, a drab, 1 *Hen.* 6, 1.iv.107.

quail, a loose woman, *Troil. and Cres.,* 5.i.50.

quaint, clever, 2 *Hen.* 6, 3.ii.274; charming, delicate, *Mid. N. Dr.,* 2.ii.7; *quaint mazes,* intricate paths, *Mid. N. Dr.,* 2.i.99.

quaintly, artfully, *Ham.,* 2.i.31; *Mer. Ven.,* 2.iv.6.

qualification, condition, *Oth.,* 2.i.269.

qualified, possessed, endowed, *Win. Tale,* 2.i.113; competent, *Lear,* 1.iv.34.

qualify, to moderate, *Lear,* 1.ii.153; dilute, *Oth.,* 2.iii.36; diminish, *Ham.,* 4.vii.113.

quality, natural parts, *Troil. and Cres.,* 4.iv.75; social position, *Lear,* 5.iii.120; acquired skill, profession (especially of actor), *Ham.,* 2.ii.426.

quarrel, cause for strife, *Ham.,* 4.iv.55.

quarry, heap of dead (from term used of deer killed in sport), *Ham.,* 5.ii.356.

quarter, area of camp or town assigned to a body of troops, 1 *Hen.* 6, 2.i.63 and 68; *keep good quarter,* watchful guard, *John,* 5.v.20; *have quarter,* have entrusted for protection, *Ant. and Cleo.,* 4.iii.24; on amicable terms, *Oth.,* 2.iii.172; *quarter'd fires,* camp fires, *Cym.,* 4.iv.18; dead, *Cor.,* 1.i.197.

quat, pimple, so contemptuously of a person, *Oth.,* 5.i.11.

quean, female, scold, 2 *Hen.* 4, 2.i.45.

queasy, *of a queasy question,* difficult nature, *Lear,* 2.i.17; upset, disgusted, *Ant. and Cleo.,* 3.vi.20.

quell, slaughter, *Mac.,* 1.vii.72.

quest, *crowner's quest law,* law as laid down at the coroner's inquest, *Ham.,* 5.i.22; party to make inquiry, *Oth.,* 1.ii.46.

questant, seeker for fame, *All's Well,* 2.i.16.

questrists, searchers, *Lear,* 3.vii.16.

quick, living, *Ham.,* 5.i.122; pregnant, *L. Lab. Lost,* 5.ii.665; sensitive part, *Ham.,* 2.ii.593; sharp, *Per.,* 4.i.28.

quicken, are born, *Oth.,* 3.iii.281; come to life again, *Ant. and Cleo.,* 4.xv.39.

quiddities, fine-spun arguments, *Ham.,* 5.i.96.

quietus, term signifying the discharge of a debt, *Son.,* 126, 12; release from the bondage of life, *Ham.,* 3.i.75.

quillet, legal quibble, *Ham.,* 5.i.97.

quintain, an object for tilting at, *As You Like,* 1.ii.230.

quintessence, the fifth essence, underlying the four elements (earth, air, fire, water), and forming the stars; so the most subtle extract or manifestation, *Ham.,* 2.ii.307.

quip, retort, sharp remark, *As You Like,* 5.iv.71.

quirk, clever stroke, *Oth.,* 2.i.63; shock, *All's Well,* 3.ii.47; turn of mind, *Tw. Night,* 3.iv.233.

quit, adj., quit with, of, even with, *Cor.,* 4.v.83.

quit, verb, release, *Tw. Night,* 5.i.308; release from, *Hen.* 8, 5.i.70; to remit, *Mer. Ven.,* 4.i.376; to requite, *Ham.,* 5.ii.68.

quittance, like for like, 2 *Hen.* 4, 1.i.108; recompense, *Hen.* 5, 2.ii.34.

quiver, agile, 2 *Hen.* 4, 3.ii.273.

quoif, close-fitting cap, *Win. Tale,* 4.iv.221.

quoit, cast, 2 *Hen.* 4, 2.iv.182.

quondam, former, *Troil. and Cres.,* 4.v.179.

quoniam, since, because, *L. Lab. Lost,* 5.ii.585.

quote, indicate (as a reference in a book), *L. Lab. Lost,* 2.i.245; mark out, *John,* 4.ii.222; observe, *Ham.,* 2.i.112; regard, *L. Lab. Lost,* 5.ii.774.

quotidian, *quotidian of love,* a fever that recurs daily, *As You Like,* 3.ii.339; *quotidian tertian,* Mistress Quickly's terminology (a tertian fever recurred every second day), *Hen.* 5, 2.i.116.

R, *the dog's name,* or letter, because 'arre' is like a dog's snarl, *Rom. and Jul.,* 2.iv.203.

rabato, kind of stiff collar, *Much Ado,* 3.iv.6.

rabbit-sucker, baby rabbit, 1 *Hen.* 4, 2.iv.422.

race, course, *John,* 3.iii.39.

race, herd, *Mer. Ven.,* 5.i.72; strain, e.g. *sensual race,* lust, *M. Meas.,* 2.iv.160; *race of heaven,* of heavenly descent, *Ant. and Cleo.,* 1.iii.37.

race, raze, *race of ginger,* root of ginger, *Win. Tale,* 4.iii.45.

rack, clouds drifting with the wind, *Ham.,* 2.ii.478; *leave not a rack behind,* no trace, even as unsubstantial as a cloud, *Tem.,* 4.i.156.

rack, verb, stretch, *Mer. Ven.,* 1.i.181; distort, misrepresent, *M. Meas.,* 4.i.63.

rackers, distorters, *L. Lab. Lost,* 5.i.17.

rage, madness, *Lear,* 4.vii.78; martial ardour, *John,* 2.i.265; *a poet's rage,* poet's enthusiasm, *Son.,* 17.11.

rage, verb, act madly, *Ant. and Cleo.,* 4.i.7.

raging-wood, raging mad, 1 *Hen.* 6, 4.vii.35.

raisins o' th' sun, sun-dried grapes, *Win. Tale,* 4.iii.46.

ramp, harlot, *Cym.,* 1.vi.133.

rampallian, of a woman, scoundrel, 2 *Hen.* 4, 2.i.57.

ramping, on hind legs in fighting attitude, 1 *Hen.* 4, 3.i.153.

rampir'd, fortified, *Timon,* 5.iv.47.

rangers, *Diana's rangers,* her virgin nymphs, *Cym.,* 2.iii.69.

rank, perhaps for 'rack' = easy pace, *As You Like,* 1.ii.88.

rank, adj., *rank Achilles,* overgrown in pride, *Troil. and Cres.,* 1.iii.318; *rank corruption,* uncheck'd, *Ham.,* 3.iv.148; *ranker rate,* greater price, *Ham.,* 4.iv.22; adv., completely, *Troil. and Cres.,* 1.iii.196.

rankle, inflict a wound that festers, *Rich.* 2, 1.iii.302.

ransack'd, queen, carried off, *Troil. and Cres.,* 2.ii.150.

rap, *thus raps you,* moves you to this strange fit, *Cym.,* 1.vi.50.

rapture, forcible seizure, *Per.,* 2.i.153; fit, *Cor.,* 2.i.197.

rascal, a lean and worthless deer, so term of contempt, *Cor.,* 1.i.157.

rash, sudden in operation, 2 *Hen.* 4, 4.iv.48;

hasty, demanding haste, *Troil. and Cres.*, 4.ii.60.

rash, *verb*, stick, *Lear*, 3.vii.57.

rate, price, *Ham.*, 4.iv.22; estimation, *Tem.*, 2.i.103; way of living, *Mer. Ven.*, 1.i.127.

rather, *the rather*, the sooner, *All's Well*, 3.v.39; *ratherest*, most of all, *L. Lab. Lost*, 4.ii.16.

ratify, *only numbers ratified*, correct in form only, *L. Lab. Lost*, 4.ii.116.

Ratolorum, corruption of Custos Rotulorum (Keeper of the Rolls), *Mer. Wives Win.*, 1.i.7.

ravel, *ravell'd sleave*, tangled skein (*see* sleid), *Mac.*, 2.ii.37; *Two Gent. Ver.*, 3.ii.52.

ravin, *adj.*, ravenous, *All's Well*, 3.ii.116; *verb*, devour, *M. Meas.*, 1.ii.123; *ravin'd shark*, devouring, *Mac.*, 4.i.24.

ravish, to infect, *Lucrece*, 778; tear out, *Lear*, 3.vii.37; *ravish'd queen*, carried off by force or guile, *Troil. and Cres.*, Prol. 8; *ravishing strides*, steps of the ravisher, *Mac.*, 2.i.55.

rawness, unprotected condition, *Mac.*, 4.iii.26.

ray'd, bemired, *Tam. Shrew*, 4.i.3.

raze, obliterate, *Mac.*, 5.iii.42; pluck off, *Rich. 3*, 3.iv.84; lay flat, *M. Meas.*, 2.ii.171.

raz'd, *raz'd shoes*, uppers cut pattern-wise, *Ham.*, 3.ii.271.

razure, obliteration, *M. Meas.*, 5.i.13.

reach, attainment, *Ham.*, 2.i.64.

reach, *verb*, *raught* (participle), taken hold of, *Ant. and Cleo.*, 4.ix.29; attain to in duration or numbers, *L. Lab. Lost*, 4.ii.38.

read, give learned instruction, *1 Hen. 4*, 3.i.46.

re-answer, give compensation, *Hen. 5*, 3.vi.124.

reason, *noun*, observation, *L. Lab. Lost*, 5.i.2; justice, *Titus*, 1.i.279; *verb*, discuss, *Lear*, 2.iv.263.

reave, reft (participle), taken away, *Ven. and Adon.*, 1174.

rebate, blunt, *M. Meas.*, 1.iv.60.

rebeck, fiddle with three strings, used as name of musician, *Rom. and Jul.*, 4.v.130.

recheat, call on horn for hounds, so of cuckold's horns, *Much Ado*, 1.i.208.

reck, *recks not his own rede*, heeds not his own advice, *Ham.*, 1.iii.51.

reckless, regardless of duty, *3 Hen. 6*, 5.vi.7.

reclaim, subdue, *1 Hen. 6*, 3.v.5.

recognizance, a legal bond, defining a debt, *Ham.*, 5.i.101; token, *Oth.*, 5.ii.217.

recoil, to degenerate, *Cym.*, 1.vi.127; to go back in thought, *Win. Tale*, 1.ii.154.

recollect, *recollected terms*, studied diction, *Tw. Night*, 2.iv.5.

recommend, deliver, *Tw. Night*, 5.i.85; inform, *Oth.*, 1.iii.41.

record, sing, *Two Gent. Ver.*, 5.iv.6; *recorded*, witness'd for, *Timon*, 4.iii.4.

recorder, kind of flageolet, *Ham.*, 3.ii.286.

recourse, flow, *Troil. and Cres.*, 5.iii.55; admittance, *Rich. 3*, 3.v.109.

recoverable, able to be repeated, *Timon*, 3.iv.13.

recovery, *see* fine.

recreation, taking food, *L. Lab. Lost*, 4.ii.156.

rector, ruler, *All's Well*, 4.iii.56; *rectorship*, rule, *Cor.*, 2.iii.202.

rede, counsel, *Ham.*, 1.iii.51.

red lattice, window of alehouse, *2 Hen. 4*, 2.ii.76; *red-lattice phrases*, language of alehouse, *Mer. Wives Win.*, 2.ii.23.

reduce, bring again, *Rich. 3*, 5.v.36.

reechy, smoky, unclean, *Cor.*, 2.i.199.

reed voice, piping voice, *Mer. Ven.*, 3.iv.67.

re-edify, rebuild, *Titus*, 1.i.351.

refel, refute, *M. Meas.*, 5.i.94.

refuge, hide away, *Rich. 2*, 5.v.26.

regard, object to the eye, *Oth.*, 2.i.40; observance of duty, *Lear*, 1.iv.265; estimation, *Troil. and Cres.*, 3.iii.128.

regiment, government, *Ant. and Cleo.*, 3.vi.95.

region, the heavens, *Ham.*, 2.ii.481; *region kites*, of the air, *Ham.*, 2.ii.574.

reguerdon, *noun*, reward, *1 Hen. 6*, 3.i.170; *verb*, to reward, *1 Hen. 6*, 3.iv.23.

reins, loins, *Mer. Wives Win.*, 3.v.20.

rejoindure, union, *Troil. and Cres.*, 4.iv.35.

rejourn, adjourn, *Cor.*, 2.i.65.

relation, application, *Mer. Ven.*, 4.i.243; *understood relations*, combinations rightly interpreted, *Mac.*, 3.iv.124.

religious, conscientious, *Tw. Night*, 3.iv.373.

relinquish, *relinquish'd of the artists*, given up by doctors, *All's Well*, 2.iii.10.

relish, *noun*, *grafted to your relish*, changed to your quality, *Cor.*, 2.i.180; characteristic mark or flavour, *Ham.*, 3.iii.92.

relish, sing, *Two Gent. Ver.*, 2.i.18.

relume, rekindle, *Oth.*, 5.ii.13.

remainder, *cut the entail from all remainders*, (legal terms) give away also anything that may remain after he has parted with his (inheritance) salvation, *All's Well*, 4.iii.261; *remainder viands*, food left over, *Troil. and Cres.*, 2.ii.70; *remainder biscuit*, *As You Like*, 2.vii.39.

remediate, remedial, *Lear*, 4.iv.17.

remission, *apt remission*, ready pardon, *M. Meas.*, 5.i.496.

remonstrance, *rash remonstrance*, sudden demonstration, *M. Meas.*, 5.i.390.

remorse, pity, *Lear*, 4.ii.73; *remorseful*, compassionate, *Two Gent. Ver.*, 4.iii.13; *remorseless*, without pity, *Ham.*, 2.ii.576.

remotion, flight, holding aloof, *Timon*, 4.iii.339; *Lear*, 2.iv.112.

render, *noun*, settlement of a debt or obligation, *Cym.*, 5.iv.17; confession, admission, *Timon*, 5.i.147; *verb*, give an account of, characterize, *As You Like*, 4.iii.121; *Cym.*, 2.iv.119.

rendez-vous, meeting place, *Ham.*, 4.iv.4.

renege, deny, *Lear*, 2.ii.73; resigns, *Ant. and Cleo.*, 1.i.3.

renew, repeat, *Hen. 5*, 1.ii.116.

repair, *noun*, resort, *Ham.*, 5.ii.210; *verb*, return, *Mid. N. Dr.*, 4.i.64.

repasture, food, *L. Lab. Lost*, 4.i.86.

repetition, reference to the past, *All's Well*, 5.iii.22.

repining, reluctant to praise, *Troil. and Cres.*, 1.iii.243.

replenished, full, complete, *Win. Tale*, 2.i.79.

replication, reply, *Ham.*, 4.ii.13; echo, reverberation, *Jul. Caes.*, 1.i.47.

reposure, placing, *Lear*, 2.i.68.

reprisal, prize, *1 Hen. 4*, 4.i.118.

reprobance, damnation, *Oth.*, 5.ii.212.

reprove, disprove, *2 Hen. 6*, 3.i.40.

repugn, resist, *1 Hen. 6*, 4.i.94.

repugnancy, resistance, *Timon*, 3.v.45.

repure, purify again, *Troil. and Cres.*, 3.ii.21.

repute, value, *2 Hen. 6*, 3.i.48.

require, to request, *Cor.*, 2.iii.1.

requiring, request, *M. Meas.*, 3.i.235.

requit, repaid, *Tem.*, 3.iii.71.

rere-mice, bats, *Mid. N. Dr.*, 2.ii.4.

resemblance, probability, *M. Meas.*, 4.ii.178.

resist, repel, *Per.*, 2.iii.29.

resolution, certainty, *Lear*, 1.ii.96.

resolve, dissolve, *Timon*, 4.iii.437; free from doubt, answer a question, *Jul. Caes.*, 3.i.132; *resolv'd correction*, purposed chastisement, *2 Hen. 4*, 4.i.213.

respect, *noun*, *without respect*, apart from its context, *Mer. Ven.*, 5.i.99; rank, estimation, *Jul. Caes.*, 1.ii.59; *base respects of thrift*, considerations of profit, *Ham.*, 3.i.178; deliberation, *Troil. and Cres.*, 2.ii.49; *upon respect*, deliberately, *Lear*, 2.iv.23; *verb*, consider, *Mid. N. Dr.*, 1.i.160; *respecting*, remembering, in comparison with, *Win. Tale*, 5.i.35.

respective, *respective lenity*, deliberate forbearance, *Rom. and Jul.*, 3.i.120; courteous, *John*, 1.i.188; to be admired, *Two Gent. Ver.*, 4.iv.191.

respectively, very warmly, *Timon*, 3.i.8.

respite, delay, *1 Hen. 6*, 4.i.170; *determin'd respite*, appointed end of the time (in which my crimes went unpunished), *Rich. 3*, 5.i.19.

rest, term from card game of primero signifying

the stake on which the game turned, the loss of which ended the game—so hazard everything, make an end of matter, *Rom. and Jul.*, 5.iii.110.

resting, immovable, *Jul. Caes.*, 3.i.61.

resty, sluggish, *Troil. and Cres.*, 1.iii.263; *Son.*, 100, 9.

retreat, withdrawal from pursuit, *2 Hen. 4*, 4.iii.71.

retrograde, with apparent backward motion in the heavens, *All's Well*, 1.i.186; contrary, *Ham.*, 1.ii.114.

return, *noun*, reply, *Hen. 5*, 2.iv.127; *verb*, to send back someone, *Timon*, 3.vi.37; to be handed over, *Ham.*, 1.i.91.

reverb, reverberate, *Lear*, 1.i.153.

reverberate, *hills*, re-echoing, *Tw. Night*, 1.v.256.

reverse, back-handed thrust in fencing, *Mer. Wives Win.*, 2.iii.24.

reversion, *in reversion*, in the future, *Troil. and Cres.*, 3.ii.89.

review, see again, *Win. Tale*, 4.iv.656.

revolution, change, as made by time or the turning of Fortune's wheel, *Ham.*, 5.i.88.

revolve, turn over in mind, *Tw. Night*, 2.v.128.

rhapsody, meaningless verbiage, *Ham.*, 3.iv.48.

Rhenish, Rhine wine, *Ham.*, 1.iv.10.

rheum, a flow of tears, saliva, etc., *bisson rheum*, blinding tears, *Ham.*, 2.ii.500; *Mer. Ven.*, 1.iii.112; a disease characterized by such an excessive flow, *Ant. and Cleo.*, 3.ii.57; *rheumatic diseases*, diseases brought on by an excessive flow, *Mid. N. Dr.*, 2.i.105; *rheumy*, causing the morbid condition, *Jul. Caes.*, 2.i.266.

ribaudred, *ribaudred nag of Egypt*, Egyptian harlot, *Ant. and Cleo.*, 3.x.10.

riggish, wantonly inclined, *Ant. and Cleo.*, 2.ii.244.

right, *adv.*, exactly, to the life, *Troil. and Cres.*, 1.iii.170.

right-hand, *right-hand file*, patricians, *Cor.*, 2.i.21.

rigol, circle, *golden rigol*, crown, *2 Hen. 4*, 4.v.36.

rim, lining of belly, *Hen. 5*, 4.iv.14.

ring, *crack'd within the ring*, coin rendered uncurrent by a crack extending inside the ring round the sovereign's effigy, *Ham.*, 2.ii.423.

ring-carrier, a go-between, *All's Well*, 3.v.89.

ripe, *sinking-ripe*, ready to sink, *Com. Err.*, 1.i.78; ready prepared, *Mid. N. Dr.*, 5.i.42.

rivage, shore, *Hen. 5*, 3.*Chor*.14.

rival, partner, *Ham.*, 1.i.13; *rivality*, partnership, *Ant. and Cleo.*, 3.v.8.

rivelled, wrinkled, *Troil. and Cres.*, 5.i.21.

rivo, a toper's exclamation, *1 Hen. 4*, 2.iv.107.

road, roadstead, *Mer. Ven.*, 1.i.19.

robustious, violent (in action or declamation), *Ham.*, 3.ii.9.

rogue, vagrant, *Lear*, 4.vii.39; *roguing*, wandering, *Per.*, 4.i.98.

roisting, rousing, *Troil. and Cres.*, 2.ii.208.

romage, turmoil, *Ham.*, 1.i.107.

Roman, *Roman hand*, the style of handwriting called Roman or Italian that replaced the English hand, *Tw. Night*, 3.iv.28.

rondure, sphere, *Son.*, 21, 8.

ronyon, scabby creature, *Mac.*, 1.iii.6.

rook, squat, *3 Hen. 6*, 5.vi.47.

ropery, knavery, *Rom. and Jul.*, 2.iv.142; *rope-tricks* (may be connected with 'ropery'), *Tam. Shrew*, 1.ii.109.

roted, learnt by rote, *Cor.*, 3.ii.55.

rother, ox, *Timon*, 4.iii.12.

round, *adj.*, *roundest manner*, plainest, *Lear*, 1.iv.53.

round, to whisper, *John*, 2.i.566.

roundel, a dance in a circle, *Mid. N. Dr.*, 2.ii.1.

roundly, unceremoniously, *Rich. 2*, 2.i.122.

roundure, circuit, *John*, 2.i.259.

rouse, a bumper, *Oth.*, 2.iii.60; carouse, *Ham.*, 2.i.58.

royal, gold coin, value 10 shillings, *1 Hen. 4*,

1.ii.136; (punning on royal = 10 shillings, noble = 6s. 8d., difference = 40 pence = ten groats), *Rich. 2*, 5.v.67.

roynish, scurvy, *As You Like*, 2.ii.8.

rub, *noun*, impediment (from game of bowls), *Cor.*, 3.i.60; *verb*, *rubb'd*, diverted from his course, *Lear*, 2.ii.149.

rubious, ruby-coloured, *Tw. Night*, 1.iv.31.

ruddock, robin, *Cym.*, 4.ii.225.

rudesby, rude fellow, *Tam. Shrew*, 3.ii.10.

rue, pity, *Titus*, 1.i.105.

ruffle, *noun*, ostentation, *Lov. Comp.*, 58; bluster, swagger, *Titus*, 1.i.313.

rug-headed, shaggy-hair'd, *Rich. 2*, 2.i.156.

rump-fed, fat-rumped, well-fed (but other suggestions put forward), *Mac.*, 1.iii.6.

runagate, deserter, fugitive, *Rom. and Jul.*, 3.v.89.

runaways (not satisfactorily explained), *Rom. and Jul.*, 3.ii.6 (*cp.* vagabonds, rascals, and runaways, *Rich.* 3, 5.iii.316).

russet, homespun cloth, so plain, genuine, *L. Lab. Lost*, 5.ii.413; *russet-pated*, greyheaded, *Mid. N. Dr.*, 3.ii.21.

ruth, pity, *ruthful*, pitiable, *Troil. and Cres.*, 5.iii.48.

Saba, Queen of Sheba; 'Saba' is the spelling used in the Bishops' Bible, *Hen.* 8, 5.v.23.

sable, black, *Ham.*, 2.ii.446.

sables, garment trimmed with a brown fur, for ceremonial or leisure, *Ham.*, 3.ii.125; 4.vii.80.

sack, a white wine of Sherry class from Spain or Canaries, *1 Hen. 4*, 1.ii.7.

sackbut, musical instrument of brass group, like trombone, *Cor.*, 5.iv.48.

Sackerson, a performing bear at Paris garden, *Mer. Wives Win.*, 1.i.269.

sacring bell, during Mass, the bell rung at elevation of Host; or bell calling to morning prayer, *Hen.* 8, 3.ii.295.

sad, serious, grave; *speak sad brow and true maid*, in all truth and sincerity, *As You Like*, 3.ii.200; *Jul. Caes.*, 1.ii.217; *sad-ey'd*, of serious countenance, *Hen. 5*, 1.ii.202; *sadness*, gravity, *3 Hen. 6*, 3.ii.77.

safe, sane, sound, *Oth.*, 4.i.266.

saffron, crocus-yellow (alluding to yellow starch'd ruffs, etc.), *All's Well*, 4.v.2.

Sagittary (i) the Centaur whom medieval romancers represent as fighting as an archer for the Trojans, *Troil. and Cres.*, 5.v.14 ; (ii) An inn with the sign of Sagittarius (but there are other explanations), *Oth.*, 1.i.159.

sail, ships, *armado of convicted sail*, defeated fleet, *John*, 3.iv.2.

sain, *tofore been sain*, said before, *L. Lab. Lost* 3.i.77.

salad days, youth, *Ant. and Cleo.*, 1.v.73.

salamander, thing to live in fire, so of toper's red face, *1 Hen. 4*, 3.iii.46.

sale-work, ordinary ready-made quality, *As You Like*, 3.v.43.

Salique, *Salique law*, law limiting succession to heirs male, *Hen. 5*, 1.ii.54.

sallet (i) salad, *2 Hen. 6*, 4.x.8; *sallets*, spicy or bawdy lines, *Ham.*, 2.ii.435; (ii) light helmet, *2 Hen. 6*, 4.x.10.

salt, *man of salt*, tearful, *Lear*, 4.vi.196; biting, *Troil. and Cres.*, 1.iii.371; wanton, *Ant. and Cleo.*, 2.i.21.

Saltiers, perhaps for 'Satyrs', *Win. Tale*, 4.iv.320.

salute, excite, please, *Hen.* 8, 2.iii.103.

sanctimonious, sacred, *Tem.*, 4.i.16.

sanctuarize, shelter, *Ham.*, 4.vii.127.

sandblind, almost blind, *Mer. Ven.*, 2.ii.31.

sanded, sand colour'd, *Mid. N. Dr.*, 4.i.117.

sandy, *sandy hour*, hour marked by the falling sand in hour-glass, *1 Hen. 6*, 4.ii.36.

sanguine, *sanguine coward*, full-blooded coward, *1 Hen. 4*, 2.iv.235; pink (and white) cheek'd, *Titus*, 4.ii.97.

sans, without, *As You Like*, 2.vii.166.

GLOSSARY

sarcenet, *adj.*, made of flimsy silk (Saracenic), *Troil. and Cres.*, 5.i.29; flimsy, 1 *Hen. 4*, 3.i.252.

Sarum, *Sarum plain*, Salisbury plain, *Lear*, 2.ii.78.

Saturn, planet under which saturnine characters were born, revengeful, *Much Ado*, 1.iii.10; *Titus*, 2.iii.31.

Savoy, palace in Strand, 2 *Hen. 6*, 4.vii.1.

say (i) serge, 2 *Hen. 6*, 4.vii.23; (ii) accent, quality, *Lear*, 5.iii.144.

'Sblood, by God's blood, *Ham.*, 2.ii.362.

scaffoldage, the boards of the stage, *Troil. and Cres.*, 1.iii.156.

scald, scurvy, *Ant. and Cleo.*, 5.ii.214.

scale, *scaled sculls*, scattered shoals, *Troil. and Cres.*, 5.v.22.

scamble, scramble, *John*, 4.iii.146.

scamels (various suggestions, e.g. seamells, seamews), *Tem.*, 2.ii.162.

scantling, sample, *Troil. and Cres.*, 1.iii.341.

scantly, depreciatingly, *Ant. and Cleo.*, 3.iv.6.

scarre (meaning doubtful), *All's Well*, 4.ii.38.

scathe, *noun*, injury, *John*, 2.i.75; *verb*, to injure, *Rom. and Jul.*, 1.v.82.

scatter, *scatter'd kingdom*, disunited realm, *Lear*, 3.i.31.

scene, *scene individable*, the locality of events unchanged, unity of place, *Ham.*, 2.ii.395.

schedule, document, *Jul. Caes.*, 3.i.3.

school, university, *Ham.*, 1.ii.113; the learned faculties, *All's Well*, 1.iii.231.

science, knowledge, *All's Well*, 5.iii.103.

scion, cutting for grafting, *Win. Tale*, 4.iv.93; bud, *Oth.*, 1.iii.331.

sconce, fort, *Hen. 5*, 3.vi.71; protection, *Com. Err.*, 2.ii.34; head, *Ham.*, 5.i.99.

scorch, cut, *Com. Err.*, 5.i.183.

score, *the score and the tally*, reckonings kept by notching a stick, 2 *Hen. 6*, 4.vii.32; *on the score*, in debt, *Tam. Shrew*, Ind.ii.21.

scot, *scot and lot*, in full, 1 *Hen. 4*, 5.iv.114.

scotch, *noun*, gash, wound, *Ant. and Cleo.*, 4.vii.10; *verb*, to cut, wound, *Cor.*, 4.v.186; *Mac.*, 3.ii.13 (where Folio reads scorch'd—*see* scorch).

scrimer, fencer, *Ham.*, 4.vii.100.

scrip, document, *Mid. N. Dr.*, 1.ii.3.

scrip, *scrip and scrippage*, shepherd's pouch (the second element being a nonce formation), *As You Like*, 3.ii.152.

scriptures, writings, letter (with reference to holy writ), *Cym.*, 3.iv.79.

scrowl, indicate roughly (as a scrawl may), *Titus*, 2.iv.5.

scroyle, rascal, *John*, 2.i.373.

scrubbed, undersized, *Mer. Ven.*, 5.i.162.

scrupulous, *scrupulous faction*, hesitating allegiance, *Ant. and Cleo.*, 1.iii.48.

sculls, shoals, *Troil. and Cres.*, 5.v.22.

scullion, kitchen drudge, *Ham.*, 2.ii.583.

scut, tail of a deer, *Mer. Wives Win.*, 5.v.17.

'Sdeath, by God's death, *Cor.*, 1.i.215.

sea-coal, pit coal (not charcoal), so called being brought to London by sea from Newcastle, 2 *Hen. 4*, 2.i.85.

seal, *seal'd quarts*, measures officially stamped as correct, *Tam. Shrew*, Ind.ii.86.

seam, fat, *Troil. and Cres.*, 2.iii.180.

sea-maid, mermaid, *Mid. N. Dr.*, 2.i.154.

sea-monster, that to which Hesione daughter of Laomedon King of Troy was exposed and from which she was delivered by Hercules, not for love but for a gift of horses, *Mer. Ven.*, 3.ii.57.

seamy, *seamy side*, worst side, *Oth.*, 4.ii.147.

sear, sere, sere or withered state, *Mac.*, 5.iii.23; *sear'd*, withered, *Lov. Comp.*, 14.

searcher, officer that reported on the cause of death and kept watch for cases of plague, *Rom. and Jul.*, 5.ii.8.

searching, *searching terms*, invective, 2 *Hen. 6*, 3.ii.311; *searching wine*, intoxicating, 2 *Hen. 4*, 2.iv.27.

second, supporter, *Lear*, 4.vi.195.

sect (i) a cutting, *Oth.*, 1.iii.331; (ii) a division, party, *Lear*, 5.iii.18; womankind, 2 *Hen. 4*, 2.iv.37.

sectary, *sectary astronomical*, an astrologer, *Lear*, 1.ii.143.

secure, *adj.*, free from all suspicion or care, *secure hour*, fearing no danger, *Ham.*, 1.v.61; *Oth.*, 3.iii.202; *verb*, to make careless, *Lear*, 4.i.21; *secure thy heart*, free it from anxiety, *Timon*, 2.ii.177.

security, *security is mortal's chiefest enemy*, lack of vigilance, *Mac.*, 3.v.32.

See, the See, Rome, *M. Meas.*, 3.ii.206.

seeded, come to a head, active, *Troil. and Cres.*, 1.iii.316.

seedness, sowing, *M. Meas.*, 1.iv.42.

seel, to close the eyes of a captured falcon by a thread through its eyelids, so to blind, *Oth.*, 3.iii.214; *Mac.*, 3.ii.46.

seeming, appearance, outward show true or false, *Win. Tale*, 4.iv.75; *Much Ado*, 4.i.55.

seld, *seld-shown flamens*, priests who seldom appear in public, *Cor.*, 2.i.203.

semblable, *adj.*, similar, 2 *Hen. 4*, 5.i.62; *noun*, *his semblable*, his like, *Timon*, 4.iii.22.

sennet (in stage directions) trumpet notes to mark entrance or exit of a procession, *Mac.*, 3.i.10 (S.D.).

se'nnight, week (from ancient custom of beginning day at sunset), *Oth.*, 2.i.77.

senseless, *senseless things*, objects without feeling, *Jul. Caes.*, 1.i.36; *senseless conjuration*, addressed to the inanimate earth, *Rich. 2*, 3.ii.23.

sensible, *the sensible avouch*, the evidence of one of the senses, *Ham.*, 1.i.57; capable of physical or spiritual feeling, *Mid. N. Dr.*, 5.i.180; *Mer. Ven.*, 2.viii.48; capable of being felt, *Mac.*, 2.i.36.

sensibly, *sensibly in grief*, affected by grief, *Ham.*, 4.v.147; *sensibly outdares*, in spite of being subject to pain, wounds, etc., *Cor.*, 1.iv.54.

sentence, moral saying, maxim, *Mer. Ven.*, 1.ii.9.

sententious, full of wise saws, *As You Like*, 5.iv.60.

septentrion, the north, 3 *Hen. 6*, 1.iv.136.

sequent, following, *Oth.*, 1.ii.41; consequent, *Lear*, 1.ii.102.

sequester, *noun*, separation, *Oth.*, 3.iv.37; *verb*, *sequest'red*, separated, *As You Like*, 2.i.33.

sequestration, separation, *Oth.*, 1.iii.343 (perhaps sequel).

sere, *tickle o' th' sere*, easily set off (like a gun with a low trigger pressure, the sere being part of the trigger mechanism), *Ham.*, 2.ii.322.

sergeant, bailiff, *Ham.*, 5.ii.328.

serpigo, skin disease, *Troil. and Cres.*, 2.iii.70.

servant, avowed lover, *Two Gent. Ver.*, 2.i.97.

set, *Who sets me else ?* Who puts down a stake (challenge) against me, *Rich. 2*, 4.i.57; (as in music), *Two Gent. Ver.*, 1.ii.81.

setter, spy for thieves, 1 *Hen. 4*, 2.ii.49.

several, *adj.*, *a several plot*, a private enclosure, *Son.*, 137.9; as opposed to common land, *L. Lab. Lost*, 2.i.222; *noun*, *severals*, particulars, *Hen. 5*, 1.i.86.

sewer, butler, servant responsible for service at table, *Mac.*, 1.vii.1 (S.D.).

'Sfoot, by God's foot, *Troil. and Cres.*, 2.iii.5.

shag, hairy, *shag-hair'd kern*, 2 *Hen. 6*, 3.i.367.

shale, shell, *Hen. 5*, 4.ii.18.

shamefac'd, modest, backward, *Rich. 3*, 1.iv.137.

shard, (i) broken bit of pottery, *Ham.*, 5.i.225; (ii) wing-case or wing of beetle, *Ant. and Cleo.*, 3.ii.20; *shard-borne*, *Mac.*, 3.ii.42; *sharded*, *Cym.*, 3.iii.20.

shark, *shark up*, gather as chance offers, *Ham.*, 1.i.98.

sheal'd, shell'd, *Lear*, 1.iv.198.

1371

shearman, cloth-cutter, *2 Hen.* 6, 4.ii.128.
sheav'd, *sheav'd hat,* straw hat, *Lov. Comp.,* 31.
sheep-biter, term of abuse, *Tw. Night,* 2.v.5.
sheer, pure, *Rich.* 2, 5.iii.61; *for sheer ale,* for ale alone, *Tam. Shrew,* Ind.ii.22.
shent, blamed, *Ham.,* 3.ii.388.
sherris, sack, from Xeres in Spain, *2 Hen.* 4, 4.iii.101.
shift, trick, *John,* 4.iii.7.
ship-tire, elaborate head-dress, *Mer. Wives Win.,* 3.iii.48.
shive, slice, *Titus,* 2.i.87.
shoal, shallow, *Mac.,* 1.vii.6 (Folio reads 'school'); *Hen.* 8, 3.ii.436.
shoon, shoes, *2 Hen.* 6, 4.ii.180.
shot, reckoning, *Cym.,* 5.iv.155; *shot-free,* without paying, *1 Hen.* 4, 5.iii.30.
shotten, *shotten herring,* herring that has shed its roe and is of little value, *1 Hen.* 4, 2.iv.122.
shough, shaggy dog, *Mac.,* 3.i.93.
shoulder-shotten, damaged in the shoulder, *Tam. Shrew,* 3.ii.52.
shove-groat, *shove-groat shilling* (same as an *Edward shovel-board, Mer.Wives Win.,* 1.i.139), smooth shilling for game of shove-halfpenny, *2 Hen.* 4, 2.iv.182.
shrewd, shrewish, *Mid. N. Dr.,* 3.ii.323; malicious, *All's Well,* 3.v.65; evil, *Ant. and Cleo.,* 4.ix.5.
shrieve, sheriff, *All's Well,* 4.iii.174.
shrift, confession and absolution, *Rom. and Jul.,* 2.iii.56.
shrill-gorged, shrill-throated, *Lear,* 4.vi.58.
shrine, image, *Rom. and Jul.,* 1.v.92.
shroud, shelter, *Ant. and Cleo.,* 3.xiii.71.
shrouds, ropes supporting mast, *John,* 5.vii.53.
shrow, shrew, *L. Lab. Lost,* 5.ii.46.
sicle, shekel, *M. Meas.,* 2.ii.149.
siege, seat, *M. Meas.,* 4.ii.94; *men of royal siege,* royal ancestors, *Oth.,* 1.ii.22.
silly, helpless, *Two Gent. Ver.,* 4.i.72.
simple, medicinal herbs were called simples because ingredients in medieval compounds, *Lear,* 4.iv.14; *Ham.,* 4.vii.144.
simplicity, folly, *Son.,* 66, 11.
simular, *simular man of virtue,* hypocrite, *Lear,* 3.ii.54; specious, *Cym.,* 5.v.200.
singule, to single out. *L. Lab. Lost,* 5.i.68.
sinister, left, *Troil. and Cres.,* 4.v.128; discourteous, *Tw. Night,* 1.v.165.
sir-reverence, corruption of 'save your reverence', *Rom. and Jul.,* 1.iv.42; *Com. Err.,* 3.ii.90.
sister, *Sisters Three,* the three Fates, *Mid. N. Dr.,* 5.i.327.
size, *sizes,* allowances, *Lear,* 2.iv.174; share, *Ant. and Cleo.,* 4.xv.4.
skains-mates, unexplained term of reproach, *Rom. and Jul.,* 2.iv.150.
skillet, kitchen pot, *Oth.,* 1.iii.272.
skipper, giddy youth, *Tam. Shrew,* 2.i.331.
skirr, scour, *Mac.,* 5.iii.35.
slab, sticky, *Mac.,* 4.i.32.
sleave, skein of silk, *Mac.,* 2.ii.37.
sledded, *sledded Polacks,* Poles on sledges, *Ham.,* 1.i.63.
sleeve-hand, wristband, *Win. Tale,* 4.iv.207.
sleid, *sleid silk,* untwisted silk, *Troil. and Cres.,* 5.i.29.
'Slid, By God's eyelid (*cp. Troil. and Cres.,* 1.ii.203); *Tw. Night,* 3.iv.374.
'Slight, By God's light, *Tw. Night,* 2.v.30.
slip, counterfeit coin, *Rom. and Jul.,* 2.iv.48 (with similar pun at *Troil. and Cres.,* 2.iii.24).
slipper, slippery, *Oth.,* 2.i.238.
slipshod, in slippers, *Lear,* 1.v.11.
sliver, *noun,* small branch, *Ham.,* 4.vii.174; *verb,* tear away, *Lear,* 4.ii.34.
slops, wide breeches, *2 Hen.* 4, 1.ii.28.
slubber, to scamp, *Mer. Ven.,* 2.viii.39.
smatch, taste, *Jul. Caes.,* 5.v.46.
smock, woman's undergarment, so a woman, *a shirt and a smock,* a man and woman, *Rom. and Jul.,* 2.iv.99.

smoke, drive from hiding with smoke, so show up faults, *All's Well,* 3.vi.93.
smooth, flatter, *Rich.* 3, 1.iii.48.
smug, spick and span, *Lear,* 4.vi.200.
sneap, snub, *2 Hen.* 4, 2.i.118.
sneck-up, expression of contempt, *Tw. Night,* 2.iii.90.
snipt-taffeta, *snipt-taffeta fellow,* over-dressed creature, *All's Well,* 4.v.2.
snuff, huff, *Lear,* 3.i.26; *to take in snuff,* to resent, *1 Hen.* 4, 1.iii.41.
sob, a rest during which a horse recovers its wind, so punningly at *Com. Err.,* 4.iii.22.
soiled, *soiled horse,* over-fed, *Lear,* 4.vi.122.
sole, unique, *John,* 4.iii.52.
solemnity, festivity, *Rom. and Jul.,* 1.v.61.
solidare, coin, *Timon,* 3.i.43.
sonties, saints, *Mer. Ven.,* 2.ii.39.
sooth, truth, *Mac.,* 1.ii.36; flattery, *Rich.* 2, 3.iii.136.
sop, cake or wafer in wine, *Tam. Shrew,* 3.ii.172.
sophister, one who makes wrong appear right, *2 Hen.* 6, 5.i.191.
sophisticated, disguised (by clothes), *Lear,* 3.iv.105.
Sophy, Shah of Persia, *Tw. Night,* 2.v.161.
sore, *see* buck.
sorel, *see* buck.
sort, *noun* (i) lot, *Troil. and Cres.,* 1.iii.376; (ii) rank, *M. Meas.,* 4.iv.15; collection, *Mid. N. Dr.,* 3.ii.13 ; *many in sort,* many together, *Mid. N. Dr.,* 3.ii.21; *verb,* ordain, *Rich.* 3, 2.iii.36; choose, *Two Gent. Ver.,* 3.ii.92; put among, *Ham.,* 2.ii.266; suit, *Ham.,* 1.i.109.
sortance, agreement, *2 Hen.* 4, 4.i.11.
souse, swoop down on, *John,* 5.ii.150.
sous'd, *sous'd gurnet,* fish treated in brine, *1 Hen.* 4, 4.ii.12.
South Sea, a *South Sea of Discovery,* a lengthy voyage in the unknown Pacific, *As You Like,* 3.ii.183.
sowl, pull, *Cor.,* 4.v.200.
Sowter, cobbler as name of hound, *Tw. Night,* 2.v.113.
span-counter, game in which a coin is thrown to hit or lie beside another, *2 Hen.* 6, 4.ii.152.
spavins, joint-disease of horse, *Tam. Shrew,* 3.ii.50.
spectacles, the eyes, *2 Hen.* 6, 3.ii.112.
speculation, vision, *Mac.,* 3.iv.95.
speculative, with power of seeing, *Oth.,* 1.iii.270.
sperr, *sperr up,* shut up, *Troil. and Cres.,* Prol. 19.
sphere, *the tuned spheres,* the Sun, Moon and Planets were considered as carried round the earth by transparent concentric spheres, whose motions produced a harmonious sound, *Ant. and Cleo.,* 5.ii.84.
spherical, *spherical predominance,* influence of planets, *Lear,* 1.ii.118.
spill, kill, *Lear,* 3.ii.8.
spital, hospital, *Hen.* 5, 5.i.75.
spleen, regarded as seat of anger, pugnacity, violent laughter, *M. Meas.,* 2.ii.122.
splinter, join (as with splints), *Oth.,* 2.iii.313.
spongy, soaked in drink, *Mac.,* 1.vii.71.
spot, pattern, *Oth.,* 3.iii.439.
sprag, quick, *Mer. Wives Win.,* 4.i.75.
springe, snare, *Ham.,* 1.iii.115.
springhalt, leg-disease in horse, *Hen.* 8, 1.iii.13.
square, to measure, *Troil. and Cres.,* 5.ii.130; to quarrel, *Mid. N. Dr.,* 2.i.30.
squarer, quarreller, *Much Ado,* 1.i.66.
squash, unripe peascod, *Mid. N. Dr.,* 3.i.172.
squene, squint, *Lear,* 3.iv.115.
squier, carpenter's rule, *L. Lab. Lost,* 5.ii.474.
squiny, squint, *Lear,* 4.vi.137.
staff, *staves,* lance shafts, *Rich.* 3, 5.iii.65.
staggers, disease in animals accompanied by giddiness, *Tam. Shrew,* 3.ii.51.
stale (i) bait, *Tem.,* 4.i.187; dupe, *Titus,* 1.i.304; (ii) urine, *Ant. and Cleo.,* 1.iv.62.

stamp, coin, medal, *Mac.*, 4.iii.153.

stanchless, insatiable, *Mac.*, 4.iii.78.

standing-bed, bed on legs, *Mer. Wives Win.*, 4.v.6.

staniel, poor type of hawk, *Tw. Night*, 2.v.105.

staple, wool before spinning into yarn, *L. Lab. Lost*, 5.i.15.

starting-hole, refuge, 1 *Hen. 4*, 2.iv.255.

state, *cons state*, get up matters of state, *Tw. Night*, 2.iii.139; chair of authority or dignity, *Tw. Night*, 2.v.42.

statist, statesman, *Ham.*, 5.ii.33.

statute-cap, to help the wool trade Parliament made the wearing of woollen caps compulsory on Sundays, *L. Lab. Lost*, 5.ii.281.

stickler-like, as an umpire, *Troil. and Cres.*, 5.viii.18.

stigmatic, marked out as wicked by some deformity, 2 *Hen. 6*, 5.i.215.

still, *adverb*, always, *still-vex'd Bermoothes*, always storm bound, *Tem.*, 1.ii.229.

stillitory, a still, *Ven. and Adon.*, 443.

stint, to cause to cease, *Troil. and Cres.*, 4.v.93; to cease, *Rom. and Jul.*, 1.iii.49.

stithy, smithy, *Ham.*, 3.ii.82.

stoccado, thrust, *Mer. Wives Win.*, 2.i.201; *alla stoccata*, at the thrust, *Rom. and Jul.*, 3.i.72.

stock, see **stoccado.**

stock-fish, dried cod, softened before cooking with beating, *Tem.*, 3.ii.67.

stole, garment, *Lov. Comp.*, 297.

stomach, *noun*, inclination, *As You Like*, 3.ii.20; courage, ambition, *Ham.*, 1.i.100.

stone-bow, cross-bow for discharging stones, *Tw. Night*, 2.v.43.

stoop, to descend upon prey, *Hen. 5*, 4.i.107.

store, increase, *Son.*, 11.9.

stoup, flagon, *Ham.*, 5.i.60.

stover, fodder, *Tem.*, 4.i.63.

straight-pight, erect, *Cym.*, 5.v.164.

strangeness, aloofness, *Troil. and Cres.*, 2.iii.122.

strappado, a punishment in which the victim is hoisted by a rope, let fall, and then brought up with a jerk, to dislocate his joints, 1 *Hen. 4*, 2.iv.230.

strike, shed evil influence, *Ham.*, 1.i.162; *strike the vessels*, tap the casks, *Ant. and Cleo.*, 2.vii.95.

strossers, *strait strossers*, narrow trousers, *Hen. 5*, 3.vii.53.

stuck, see **stoccado.** *Tw. Night*, 3.iv.263.

Stygian, of Styx, river of hell, *Troil. and Cres.*, 3.ii.9.

style, title, 1 *Hen. 6*, 4.vii.72.

subscribe, sign to, sign away, *Lear*, 1.ii.24; assess, characterize, *Rich. 2*, 1.iv.50; *Much Ado*, 5.ii.51; admit, *M. Meas.*, 2.iv.89; *all cruels else subscribe*, write off all other cruelties, *Lear*, 3.vii.64.

subscription, obedience, *Lear*, 3.ii.18.

succeed, follow as a natural or legal consequence, *Lear*, 1.ii.137; *bloody succeeding*, inevitable duel, *All's Well*, 2.iii.189.

success, *in whose success*, as their issue, *Win. Tale*, 1.ii.394; *success of mischief*, disastrous consequences, 2 *Hen. 4*, 4.i.47.

succession, those coming after in like condition, *All's Well*, 3.v.21; after condition, inheritance, *Ham.*, 2.ii.347.

sufferance, forbearance, *Hen. 5*, 3.vi.121.

suggest, persuade, instruct, *Son.*, 144, 2; *Cor.*, 2.i.235; seduce, *Oth.*, 2.iii.341.

suggestion, incitement, *Lear*, 2.i.73.

summoner, officer who cited persons before ecclesiastical courts, *Lear*, 3.ii.59.

sumpter, pack-horse, so drudge, *Lear*, 2.iv.215.

suppose, *counterfeit supposes*, deceptive substitutions, *Tam. Shrew*, 5.i.104.

surcease, *noun*, cessation, *Mac.*, 1.vii.4.

sur-rein'd, overridden, *Hen. 5*, 3.v.19.

suspiration, breathing, *Ham.*, 1.ii.79.

sutler, camp follower, *Hen. 5*, 2.i.108.

swabber, sailor who cleans up, *Tw. Night*, 1.v.191.

swaddling, *swaddling clouts*, wrappings for new-born infants, *Ham.*, 2.ii.379.

swarth, swath, *Tw. Night*, 2.iii.139.

swarth, *adj.*, dark, *Titus*, 2.iii.72.

swath, swathing, see **swaddling,** *Timon*, 4.iii.251.

sway'd, *sway'd in the back* (of horse), weakback'd, *Tam. Shrew*, 3.ii.52.

sweeting, apple, *Rom. and Jul.*, 2.iv.77.

swinge, *noun*, blow, *Troil. and Cres.*, 1.iii.207; *verb*, thrash, 2 *Hen. 4*, 5.iv.20.

swinge-bucklers, bold sparks, 2 *Hen. 4*, 3.ii.20.

Swithold, Saint Vitalis, invoked as protection against nightmare, *Lear*, 3.iv.118.

swoopstake, to take all, *Ham.*, 4.v.139.

sword-and-buckler, arms of lower ranks, so, as epithet, common, 1 *Hen. 4*, 1.iii.230.

'Swounds, by God's wounds, *Ham.*, 2.ii.571.

sympathise, share nature, *Hen. 5*, 3.vii.143; *sympathized error*, error shared in, *Com. Err.*, 5.i.396.

table (-s), *noun*, wood or canvas for painting on, *John*, 2.i.503; note-book (so, *table-book*), *Ham.*, 1.v.107; palm of hand, *Mer. Ven.*, 2.ii.145; backgammon, *L. Lab. Lost*, 5.ii.326; *verb*, listed, *Cym.*, 1.iv.5.

tabor, drum, *Tw. Night*, 3.i.9.

tabourine, soldier's side-drum, *Troil. and Cres.*, 4.v.275.

taffeta, changeable taffeta, shot silk, *Tw. Night*, 2.iv.73.

tag, rabble, *Cor.*, 3.i.248.

taint, *noun*, disgrace, *Troil. and Cres.*, 1.iii.374; *tainture*, evil state, 2 *Hen. 6*, 2.i.183; *verb*, discredit, *Oth.*, 2.i.262; to be affected, *Mac.*, 5.iii.3.

take, bewitch, *Ham.*, 1.i.163; *take out*, copy, *Oth.*, 3.iii.300.

tall, of a fine specimen of manhood or shipping, *Ant. and Cleo.*, 2.vi.7; *Mer. Ven.*, 3.i.5.

tame, *tamed piece*, broached cask of wine, *Troil. and Cres.*, 4.i.64.

tarre, to incite (as a dog), *Ham.*, 2.ii.349.

Tartar, Tartarus, hell, *Tw. Night*, 2.v.184.

task, to contract, *Cor.*, 1.iii.36; challenge, 1 *Hen. 4*, 5.i.51.

tassel-gentle, tercel male hawk, *Rom. and Jul.*, 2.ii.159.

tawdry-lace, necklace (originally from Saint Audrey's fair), *Win. Tale*, 4.iv.244.

tax, *noun*, censure, *All's Well*, 2.i.169; *verb*, to censure, *Ham.*, 1.iv.18.

taxation, censure, *As You Like*, 1.ii.76; demand, *Tw. Night*, 1.v.197.

teen, grief, *Tem.*, 1.ii.64.

tender (i) regard, *Lear*, 1.iv.209; (ii) offer, *Ham.*, 1.iii.99.

tent, *noun*, roll of linen for cleaning out a wound, *Troil. and Cres.*, 2.ii.16; *verb*, to probe, *Ham.*, 2.ii.593.

tercel, male goshawk, *Troil. and Cres.*, 3.ii.51.

Termagant, a ranting part in the Mystery cycles, thought to be a Mohammedan deity, *Ham.*, 3.ii.13.

termination, word, *Much Ado*, 2.i.221.

termless, beyond words, *Lov. Comp.*, 94.

tertian, occurring every other day, *Hen. 5*, 2.i.116.

tester, sixpence, *Mer. Wives Win.*, 1.iii.84.

testril, see **tester.**

tetchy, peevish, *Troil. and Cres.*, 1.i.95.

tetter, *noun*, scurf, *Ham.*, 1.v.71; *verb*, afflict as with the tetter, *Cor.*, 3.i.79.

thane, Scots title (the thanes become earls in last scene), *Mac.*, 5.viii.62.

Thessaly, *the boar of Thessaly*, the Calydonian boar that ravaged Thessaly, slain by Meleager, *Ant. and Cleo.*, 4.xiii.2.

Thetis, mother of Achilles, *Troil. and Cres.*, 1.iii.212.

thick, *thick-ey'd,* dim unheeding eyes, 1 Hen. 4, 2.iii.43; *thick-pleached,* with dense intertwining branches, *Much Ado,* 1.ii.8.

thin-belly, *thin-belly doublet,* unlined over belly, *L. Lab. Lost,* 3.i.17.

third, thread, *Tem.,* 4.i.3.

thirdborough, constable, *Tam. Shrew,* Ind.i.9.

Thracian, *Thracian singer,* Orpheus, *Mid. N. Dr.,* 5.i.49.

thrasonical, boastful (from Thraso, bragging soldier in *Eunuchus* of Terence), *As You Like,* 5.ii.29.

three-man song-men, singers of three-part catches, *Win. Tale,* 4.iii.40.

three-pile, rich velvet, *Win. Tale,* 4.iii.14; *three-pil'd hyperboles,* extravagant exaggerations, *L. Lab. Lost,* 5.ii.407.

threne, dirge (threnos), *Phoenix,* 49.

thrice-crowned, see Hecate.

thrift, profit, *Ham.,* 3.ii.60.

throe, pain, *Tem.,* 2.i.222.

thrum, *thread and thrum,* good and bad, *Mid. N. Dr.,* 5.i.278; *thrumm'd hat,* witch-cap of weaver's ends, *Mer. Wives Win.* 4.ii.66.

thwart, perverse, *Lear,* 1.iv.283; *adv.,* against intention, *Troil. and Cres.,* 1.iii.15.

tickle, so delicately adjusted as to be unsafe, 2 *Hen. 6,* 1.i.211.

tight (i) (of ship) sound, *Tem.,* 5.i.224; (ii) swift, *Ant. and Cleo.,* 4.iv.15.

tinct, colour, *Ham.,* 3.iv.91; the golden colour given by the alchemists' grand elixir to base metal, *Ant. and Cleo.,* 1.v.36; the elixir itself, *All's Well,* 5.iii.102.

tinctures, *tinctures, stains,* on handkerchiefs which would be dipped in the blood and kept as relics, *Jul. Caes.,* 2.ii.89.

tire, head-dress, *Mer. Wives Win.,* 3.iii.49 (so *tire-valiant* indicates a particular style).

tire, *tire on,* to devour (as a bird of prey), 3 *Hen. 6,* 1.i.269; *Cym.,* 3.iv.93.

tiring-house, dressing-room, *Mid. N. Dr.,* 3.i.4.

tisick, cough, *Troil. and Cres.,* 5.iii.101.

tissue, fabric woven of gold thread and silk, *Ant. and Cleo.,* 2.ii.203.

tithe, tenth, *Troil. and Cres.,* 2.ii.19.

tithing, locality (originally containing some ten families, or tenth of a hundred), *Lear,* 3.iv.132.

toast, toast in wine, *Mer. Wives Win.,* 3.v.3.

toaze, touze, draw, *Win. Tale,* 4.iv.724.

tod, *noun,* 28 lbs. of wool; *verb,* to make up a tod, *Win. Tale,* 4.iii.31.

toil, net, trap, *Ham.,* 3.ii.338.

token, *Lord's tokens,* marks of plague and so of death, of infection of love, *L. Lab. Lost,* 5.ii.423.

toll, pay the seller's due on a sale at market, *All's Well,* 5.iii.146.

tomboys, harlots, *Cym.,* 1.vi.121.

tongs, *the tongs and the bones,* a percussion instrument like the triangle, and clappers, *Mid. N. Dr.,* 4.i.27.

top-gallant, mast above top-mast, so the very height, *Rom. and Jul.,* 2.iv.184.

tortive, twisted, *Troil. and Cres.,* 1.iii.9.

touch, *noun,* inward sense or feeling, *Cym.,* 1.i.135; *one touch of nature,* a common characteristic, *Troil. and Cres.,* 3.iii.175; touchstone, *Timon,* 4.iii.387; *of noble touch,* of proved nobility, *Cor.,* 4.i.49; *verb,* to test, *Timon,* 3.iii.6; to infect, *John,* 5.vii.2.

touze, to tear, *M. Meas.,* 5.i.309.

train, *noun,* bait to trap, *Mac.,* 4.iii.118; *verb,* entice, *Com. Err.,* 3.ii.45.

trammel up, catch as in a net, so dispose of, *Mac.,* 1.vii.3.

translate, transform, *Mid. N. Dr.,* 3.i.108.

trash, to curb a hound's impetuosity by adding weight to the collar, so *Oth.,* 2.i.297.

traverse, soldier's drill order, *Oth.,* 1.iii.367; *adv., quite traverse,* missing aim with the lance at tilting and breaking it crosswise on the opponent, so *As You Like,* 3.iv.38.

tray-trip, game with dice in which three (trey) was the important throw, *Tw. Night,* 2.v.170.

treatise, recital, *Mac.,* 5.v.12.

treble-dated, with thrice man's span of life, *Phoenix,* 17.

trey, throw of three with dice, *L. Lab. Lost,* 5.ii.232.

tribunal, dais, *Ant. and Cleo.,* 3.vi.3.

tribune, officer elected by commons in Rome, *Cor.,* 1.i.213.

trick, *noun,* fashion, *M. Meas.,* 5.i.503; characteristic, *Lear,* 4.vi.106; gift, *Ham.,* 5.i.88; *verb,* cover (with reference to heralds' designs and their hatchings to indicate colours), *Ham.,* 2.ii.451.

tricking, furnishings, *Mer. Wives Win.,* 4.iv.78.

Trigon, the twelve signs of the Zodiac were grouped in threes (trigons) to correspond to earth, air, water, fire. 2 *Hen. 4,* 2.iv.255.

triple, the third, or one of three, *Ant. and Cleo.,* 1.i.12.

triumph, occasion of public rejoicing or recreation 3 *Hen. 6,* 5.vii.43; trump-card, *Ant. and Cleo.,* 4.xiv.20.

trophy, token, *Lov. Comp.,* 218; memorial, *Ham.,* 4.v.210.

tropically, metaphorically, *Ham.,* 3.ii.232.

truckle-bed, low bed that could be pushed under standing-bed, *Mer. Wives Win.,* 4.v.6.

truepenny, trusty fellow, *Ham.,* 1.v.150.

trundle-tail, long-tail'd dog, *Lear,* 3.vi.69.

trunk sleeve, wide sleeve, *Tam. Shrew,* 4.iii.138.

try, *bring her to try,* into the wind, *Tem.,* 1.i.33.

tucket, signal on trumpet, *Hen. 5,* 4.ii.35.

tuition, protection, *Much Ado,* 1.i.244.

Tully, *Tully's Orator,* Cicero's *De Oratore,* *Titus,* 4.i.14.

tun-dish, funnel, *M. Meas.,* 3.ii.161.

twiggen, wicker covering, *Oth.,* 2.iii.140.

twire, twinkle, *Son.,* 28.12.

umber, earthy brown colour, *As You Like,* 1.iii.108; *umber'd,* showing dark in the firelight, *Hen. 5,* 4.Chor.9.

umbrage, shadow, *Ham.,* 5.ii.119.

unable, weak, inadequate, *Lear,* 1.i.59.

unaccommodated, unprovided with what civilization gives, *Lear,* 3.iv.106.

unadvis'd, unconsidered, *Rom. and Jul.,* 2.ii.118.

unanel'd, without receiving extreme unction, *Ham.,* 1.v.77.

unattainted, impartial, *Rom. and Jul.,* 1.ii.85.

unavoided, not to be escaped, *Rich. 3,* 4.iv.217.

unbarb'd, unprotected, bare, *Cor.,* 3.ii.99.

unbated, unblunted, so of rapier without button on point, *Ham.,* 4.vii.138.

unbolt, explain, *Timon,* 1.i.54; *unbolted,* unsifted, so crude, *Lear,* 2.ii.61.

unbonneted, without removing the bonnet (cp. *Cor.,* 2.ii.25, where 'bonneted' means with cap in hand), *Oth.,* 1.ii.23.

unbookish, *unbookish jealousy,* uninstructed in ways of society, *Oth.,* 4.i.101.

unbraided, fresh and new, *Win. Tale,* 4.iv.201.

uncase, undress, *Tam. Shrew,* 1.i.202.

unclew, undo, *Timon,* 1.i.171.

uncoined, *uncoined constancy,* pure metal needing no formal stamp to give it worth, *Hen. 5,* 5.ii.153.

unconfirmed, uninstructed, *Much Ado,* 3.iii.107.

uncouth, unfamiliar and fearsome, *Titus,* 2.iii.211.

unction, ointment, *Ham.,* 3.iv.145.

underborne, lined, *Much Ado,* 3.iv.20.

undercrest, support worthily, *Cor.,* 1.ix.72.

under-skinker, tapster, 1 *Hen. 4,* 2.iv.22.

undertaker, venturer, *Tw. Night,* 3.iv.302.

undoubted, fearless, 3 *Hen. 6,* 5.vii.6.

unexpressive, beyond all praise, *As You Like,* 3.ii.10.

unhair'd, too young for a beard, *John,* 5.ii.133.

unhoused, without domestic responsibility, *Oth.,* 1.ii.26.

unhous'led, not have taken the sacrament, *Ham.*, 1.v.77.

unimproved, waiting to be given shape or purpose, *Ham.*, 1.i.96.

union, pearl, *Ham.*, 5.ii.264.

unkennel, disclose itself, *Ham.*, 3.ii.79.

unkind, unnatural, *Lear*, 3.iv.70; *Timon*, 2.ii.217.

unlimited, *poem unlimited*, drama not observing unities of time and place, *Ham.*, 2.ii.395.

unmann'd (of a hawk), still untrained by man, *Rom. and Jul.*, 3.ii.14.

unmoving, as if unmoving, *Oth.*, 4.ii.56.

unpaved, castrated, *Cym.*, 2.iii.31.

unpink'd, still lacking their pierced pattern. *Tam. Shrew*, 4.i.117.

unpregnant, barren of purpose, *Ham.*, 2.ii.562.

unprizable, beyond price, in value or worthlessness, *Cym.*, 1.iv.86; *Tw. Night*, 5.i.49.

unproper, not reserved for one man, *Oth.*, 4.i.68.

unrespective, thoughtless, *Rich. 3*, 4.ii.29; *unrespective sieve*, for what we no longer heed, *Troil. and Cres.*, 2.ii.71.

unseminar'd, castrated, *Ant. and Cleo.*, 1.v.11.

untented, incurable, too deep for the tent to clean and cure, *Lear*, 1.iv.300.

unvalued, priceless, *Rich. 3*, 1.iv.27; of no worth or rank, *Ham.*, 1.iii.19.

unyok'd, *unyok'd humour*, unrestrained mood, 1 *Hen. 4*, 1.ii.189.

upcast, throw at bowls, *Cym.*, 2.i.2.

upshoot, winning shot, *L. Lab. Lost*, 4.i.129.

up-spring, *up-spring reels*, a style of dance, *Ham.*, 1.iv.9.

urchin, hedgehog, *Titus*, 2.iii.101; hobgoblin *Mer. Wives Win.*, 4.iv.48.

urinal, doctor's glass for testing urine, *Two Gent. Ver.* 2.i.35.

usance, interest, *Mer. Ven.*, 1.iii.40.

use, custom, *Ham.*, 1.ii.134; *in use*, in trust, *Mer. Ven.*, 4.i.378; interest, *Son.*, 6.5.

usuring, profiteering, *Timon*, 3.v.110.

usurp'd, *usurp'd beard*, new-acquired beard, like a soldier's, *Oth.*, 1.iii.339.

utis, week beginning with a feast-day, so frolic, 2 *Hen. 4*, 2.iv.19.

utter, sell, *Rom. and Jul.*, 5.i.67.

utterance, *to th' utterance* (*à outrance*), in a fight to the death, *Mac.*, 3.i.71.

vade, fade, *Son.*, 54, 14.

vail, *noun*, sinking, *Troil. and Cres.*, 5.viii.7; *verb*, lower, *M. Meas.*, 5.i.20; lower in token of submission, *Cor.*, 3.i.98.

vails, dues, *Per.*, 2.i.148.

valanc'd, fringed (with a beard), *Ham.*, 2.ii.418.

validity, worth, *All's Well*, 5.iii.190; strength, *Ham.*, 3.ii.184.

value, *valued file*, the list giving the gift valued in each item, *Mac.*, 3.i.94.

Vanity, *Vanity the puppet*, Lady Vanity was a character in Morality plays, *Lear*, 2.ii.33.

vantbrace, armour for forearm, *Troil. and Cres.*, 1.iii.297.

varlet, squire, *Troil. and Cres.*, 1.i.1; but often used abusively: *varletry*, mob, *Ant. and Cleo.*, 5.ii.56.

vastidity, measureless space, *M. Meas.*, 3.i.70.

vaunt, first part, *Troil. and Cres.*, Prol.27.

vaunt-couriers, forerunners, *Lear*, 3.ii.5.

vaward, advance-guard, *Hen. 5*, 4.iii.130.

velure, velvet, *Tam. Shrew*, 3.ii.57.

velvet-guards, *see* guard.

vent (i) *vent of hearing*, ear, 2 *Hen. 4*, Ind. 2; (ii) *full of vent*, hot on the scent, *Cor.*, 4.v.223.

ventage, stops of wind-instrument, *Ham.*, 3.ii.348.

ventricle, one of the three divisions into which the brain was held to be divided, *L. Lab. Lost*, 4.ii.66.

venue, *veney*, thrust, *L. Lab. Lost*, 5.i.52; hit at fencing, *Mer. Wives Win.*, 1.i.259.

verbatim, orally, 1 *Hen. 6*, 3.i.13.

verge, circle, limit, 2 *Hen. 6*, 1.iv.22.

Veronesa, a ship charter'd from Verona, *Oth.*, 2.i.26.

via, *interjection*, go on, 3 *Hen. 6*, 2.i.182.

vice, The Vice was a character in the Morality plays, presented often as a buffoon, so *Ham.*, 3.iv.98.

vie, to call against or stake at cards, so to compete with, *Ant. and Cleo.*, 5.ii.98.

vigil, eve of a feast-day, *Hen. 5*, 4.iii.45.

Villiago, villain, slave, 2 *Hen. 6*, 4.viii.45.

viol-de-gamboys, *viol da gamba*, being held between the knees like the cello, *Tw. Night*, 1.iii.24.

virginalling, fingering, as if playing on the virginals, *Win. Tale*, 1.ii.125.

virtue, valour, *Lear*, 5.iii.104; the most excellent characteristic, *Timon*, 3.v.8.

virtuous, potent, *Mid. N. Dr.*, 3.ii.367.

visit, *strangely-visited*, terribly afflicted, *Mac.*, 4.iii. 150; punish, *John*, 2.i.179.

visitation (in two senses), affliction (of love) and visit, *Tem.*, 3.i.32.

visitor, like clergyman coming to console the afflicted, *Tem.*, 2.i.11.

visor, vizard, mask, *Rom. and Jul.*, 1.iv.30.

voiding-lobby, waiting-room, 2 *Hen. 6*, 4.i.61.

vouch, testimony, *Oth.*, 2.i.146.

waft, carry by sea, *John*, 2.i.73; beckon, *Mer. Ven.*, 5.i.11; move, *Win. Tale*, 1.ii.372.

waftage, transport (by ferry), *Troil. and Cres.*, 3.ii.10.

wafture, motion, *Jul. Caes.*, 2.i.246.

wag, to go about, *Titus*, 5.ii.87.

wage, *wag'd equal*, met on equal terms (like equal stakes), *Ant. and Cleo.*, 5.i.31.

waist, of ship, mid part, *Tem.*, 1.ii.197.

wake, *noun*, celebration on some holy day, beginning the evening before, *Lear*, 3.vi.73; *verb*, hold night revel, *Ham.*, 1.iv.8.

wall-ey'd, discolouration of eye, giving it threatening look, *John*, 4.iii.49.

wan, go pale, *Ham.*, 2.ii.547; *Ant. and Cleo.*, 2.i.21 (may mean, lost its youthful colour).

wappen'd, worn out, *Timon*, 4.iii.38.

ward, cell, *Ham.*, 2.ii.245; defence, *Mer. Wives Win.*, 2.ii.222.

warden, pear, *Win. Tale*, 4.iii.44.

warder, baton of rank, *Rich. 2*, 1.iii.118.

Ware, *bed of Ware*, at Ware in Hertfordshire, famous for its size (now in the Victoria and Albert museum), *Tw. Night*, 3.ii.44.

warp, distort, *All's Well*, 5.iii.49; change, *As You Like*, 2.vii.187; *warp'd*, distorted, *Lear*, 3.vi.52.

warrantise, authority, *Ham.*, 5.i.221.

warranty, permission, *Oth.*, 5.ii.63.

warren, game preserve, *Much Ado*, 2.i.191.

warrener, game-keeper, *Mer. Wives Win.*, 1.iv.25.

wassail (originally the salutation on drinking) carousing, *Ham.*, 1.iv.9.

waste, *waste blanks*, unused pages, *Son.*, 77, 10.

waste, *noun*, what is damaged (as in legal sense of damage to an estate by owner), *Rich. 2*, 2.i.103; desolation, *Ham.*, 1.ii.198; *verb*, *wasted time*, past time, *Son.*, 106, 1.

Wat, hare, *Ven. and Adon.*, 697.

watch, *a watch*, insomnia, *Ham.*, 2.ii.147; timepiece, *L. Lab. Lost*, 3.i.192; to tame hawk by denying it sleep, *Tam. Shrew*, 4.i.179.

water, brilliance of diamond, *Timon*, 1.i.20.

water-gall, secondary bow, *Lucrece*, 1588.

watering, drinking, 1 *Hen. 4*, 2.iv.15.

water-rug, hairy water-dog, *Mac.*, 3.i.93.

water-work, water-colours, 2 *Hen. 4*, 2.i.141.

weal, state, *Mac.*, 3.iv.76.

wealsmen, statesman, *Cor.*, 2.i.50.

weather, *keep the weather of*, control (as holding windward position at sea), *Troil. and Cres.*, 5.iii.26.

weather-fend, shelter, *Tem.*, 5.i.10.

weed, garment, *Mid. N. Dr.*, 2.i.256.

GLOSSARY

weet, to know, *Ant. and Cleo.*, 1.i.39.
weird, *Weird Sisters,* the Fates, *Mac.*, 1.iii.32.
welkin, sky, *Tem.*, 1.ii.4.
westward-ho, cry of boatmen going up Thames, *Tw. Night,* 3.i.131.
wezand, windpipe, *Tem.*, 3.ii.87.
wharf, river-bank, *Ham.*, 1.v.33.
Wheeson, Whitsun, 2 *Hen.* 4, 2.i.85.
whelk, pimple, *Hen.* 5, 3.vi.99.
whelk'd, in spirals, *Lear,* 4.vi.71.
whey-face, pale, *Mac.*, 5.iii.17.
whiffler, official who goes ahead of procession to clear the way, *Hen.* 5. 5.*Chor.*12.
whinid'st, very mouldy, *Troil. and Cres.*, 2.i.14.
whipping-cheer, served with the lash, 2 *Hen.* 4, 5.iv.5.
whipster, insignificant enough to be whipt, *Oth.*, 5.ii.247.
whirligig, like Fortune's wheel, *Tw. Night,* 5.i.362.
whist, hushed, *Tem.*, 1.ii.378.
white, *noun,* play on white on target and name of Bianca, *Tam. Shrew,* 5.ii.186; *adj.,* fresh (not cured), *Lear,* 3.vi.31.
white-lim'd, white-washed, *Titus,* 4.ii.98.
whiting-time, bleaching-time, *Mer. Wives Win..* 3.iii.115.
whitster, bleacher, *Mer. Wives Win.*, 3.iii.12.
whittle, small knife, *Timon,* 5.i.178.
whoreson, bastard, *Lear,* 1.i.22.
wild, weald, 1 *Hen.* 4, 2.i.54.
wild-goose chase, form of cross-country horse-racing, *Rom. and Jul.*, 2.iv.69.
wild mare, see-saw, 2 *Hen.* 4, 2.iv.237.
wilful-blame, deliberately culpable, 1 *Hen.* 4, 3.i.177.
wimpled, hooded, blind, *L. Lab. Lost,* 3.i.169.
Winchester, *goose* (the liberty of the Bankside, under the jurisdiction of the Bishop of Winchester, shelter'd many brothels; so the disease and its victims were named after him), *Troil. and Cres.*, 5.x.53.
Wincot, Wilmecot (home of Shakespeare's mother), *Tam. Shrew,* Ind.ii.20.
wind, *have the wind of,* have controlling position, *Titus,* 4.ii.133; *windy side of,* safe side of, *Tw. Night,* 3.iv.156.
windgalls, disease of horse's fetlock, *Tam. Shrew,* 3.ii.49.
windlass, means of winding, *Ham.*, 2.i.65.
wind'ring (perhaps wandering or winding), *Tem.*, 4.i.128.
winking, blind spell, *Ham.*, 2.ii.136.
winnowed, select, *Ham.*, 5.ii.187.
winter-ground, cover as against winter's frost, *Cym.*, 4.ii.230.
wise woman, witch, *Tw. Night,* 3.iv.97.
wittol, complacent cuckold, *Mer. Wives Win.*, 2.ii.267.
wood, mad, frantic, *Mid. N. Dr.*, 2.i.192.
woodcock, a fool (like the stupid bird), *Ham.*, 1.iii.115.

woodman, hunter, *Cym.*, 3.vi.28; so, of women, *M. Meas.*, 4.iii.158.
woollen, *lie in the woollen,* in blankets and no sheets, or in the grave (the shroud being by law of wool), *Much Ado,* 2.i.26.
woolward, with woollen inner garment, *L. Lab. Lost,* 5.ii.698.
working, causing a working of the feelings, *Hen.* 8, Prol. 3.
world, *go to the world,* marry, *Much Ado,* 2.i.287; *woman of the world,* married woman, *As You Like,* 5.iii.4.
worm, small snake, *Ant. and Cleo.*, 5.ii.242.
wort (i) vegetable, *Mer. Wives Win.*, 1.i.110; (ii) unfermented beer, *L. Lab. Lost,* 5.ii.233.
worthy, deserved, of praise or blame, *All's Well,* 4.iii.5.
wrangler, opponent, *Hen.* 5, 1.ii.264.
wrest, *noun,* key for tightening harp-strings, *Troil. and Cres.*, 3.iii.23; *verb,* draw out, *Titus,* 3.ii.44; misconstrue, *Much Ado,* 3.iv.30.
writ, document, *Ham.*, 5.ii.51.
writhled, wrinkled, 1 *Hen.* 6, 2.iii.23.
wroth, misfortune, *Mer. Ven.*, 2.ix.78.
wry, leaving path of virtue, *Cym.*, 5.i.5.
wry-neck'd, *fife,* played with the head turned away, *Mer. Ven.*, 2.v.29.

yare, quick and efficient, *Ant. and Cleo.*, 3.vii.38 (of ships); *M. Meas.*, 4.ii.53; *yarely, Ant. and Cleo.*, 2.ii.215.
yaw, (of ship) to steer unsteadily, *Ham.*, 5.ii.114.
yawn, gape in surmise, *Ham.*, 4.v.9.
yclad, clad, 2 *Hen.* 6, 1.i.33.
ycleped, called, *L. Lab. Lost,* 1.i.231.
Yead, Yedward, Edward, *Mer. Wives Win.*, 1.i.140; 1 *Hen.* 4, 1.ii.129.
yearn, grieve, *Hen.* 5, 4.iii.26.
yellowness, jealousy, *Mer. Wives Win.*, 1.iii.97.
yellows, jaundice (of horses), *Tam. Shrew,* 3.ii.50.
yeoman, *yeoman's service,* invaluable service (from the reputation the yeoman class had won in war), *Ham.*, 5.ii.36.
yerk, stab, *Oth.*, 1.ii.5.
yest, yeast, froth, *Win. Tale,* 3.iii.91; *yesty,* frothy, showy, *Ham.*, 5.ii.186.
yoke, *noun,* pair, *Mer. Wives Win.*, 2.i.156; *verb,* pair, *yok'd,* married, *Oth.*, 4.i.66.
younker, younger son, novice, *Mer. Ven.*, 2.vi.14.
yravish, ravish, *Per.*, 3.*Gower.*35.
yslaked, silenced, *Per.*, 3.*Gower.*1.

zany, a fool's 'stooge', *Tw. Night,* 1.v.84.
zenith, the culmination of his life, *Tem.*, 1.ii.181.
zodiac, year (in which sun completes its course through the Zodiac), *M. Meas.*, 1.ii.161.
Zounds, by God's wounds, *Oth.*, 1.i.87.